ENCYCLOPAEDIA OF SOCIOLOGY

Applied Sociology

Volume –1

Satish Mittal
Sushil Kumar Saxena

Commonwealth

Encyclopaedia of Sociology

Edition : 2026

ISBN 978-81-311-0377-7 (set)

Published by :
COMMONWEALTH PUBLISHERS (P) LTD.
4831/24, Govind Lane,
Ansari Road, Darya Ganj,
New Delhi - 110002
Ph. : 23242541, 23272541
e-mail : commonwealthpublishers2016@gmail.com

Distributed by :
ARJUN PUBLISHING HOUSE
4831/24, Govind Lane,
Ansari Road, Darya Ganj,
New Delhi - 110002
Ph. : 23242541, 23272541
e-mail : arjunbooks2001@gmail.com
arjunpubhouse@gmail.com

Laser Typesetting by :
Dimple Computers
Delhi

Printed at :
Milan Enterprises
Delhi

Preface

Sociology is often perceived as an academic profession, but there are many places outside of universities where sociology can be used to enhance personal and professional development. Applied sociology is a term that describes practitioners who use sociological theories and methods outside of academic settings with the aim to 'produce positive social change through active intervention'. More specifically, applied sociology might be seen as the translation of sociological theory into practice for specific clients.

Applied sociology is very resilient. The term has survived for more than a hundred years despite vague definitions and attempts to ignore or replace it. While sociology as a discipline and perspective may have increasing difficulties being appreciated in a culture of expanding individualism, personal liberty, and self-actualisation, people, and especially social organisations and government agencies, will need to choose wisely on the basis of evidence. The heart of applied sociology is social research, and as long as decision makers want to know the social facts and people are trained to provide them, applied sociology will flourish.

The book introduces students to sociology as an active and relevant way to understand human social interaction by offering a clear, direct linkage between sociology and its practical use. It will be an ideal supplement to traditional sociology texts to add an applied component to the course.

Authors

Contents

1

Introduction to Applied Sociology

Applied sociology is the oldest and most general term for what Lester F. Ward identified more than 100 years ago as:

> "The means and methods for the artificial improvement of social conditions on the part of man and society as conscious and intelligent agents,."

Applied sociology uses sociological knowledge and research skills to gain empirically based knowledge to inform decision makers, clients, and the general public about social problems, issues, processes, and conditions so that they might make informed choices and improve the quality of life. In its broadest sense applied sociology encompasses evaluation research, needs assessment, market research, social indicators, and demographics. It would also include directed sociological research in medicine, mental health, complex organisations, work, education, and the military to mention but a few.

Today, at the beginning of the twenty-first century, this concept of applied sociology fits nicely with the National Institutes of Health's and the National Institute of Mental Health's new funding initiatives in translational research, which require that scientists tie their research to practical applications. Translational research aims at converting basic biological and behavioural science research into forms that can address pressing issues in health care diagnosis, treatment, and delivery. By extension, this means that applied sociological research will produce descriptions, analyses, and findings that can be translated into ideas and lessons learned from previous activities or programs to be used by action organisations, including citizens groups, foundations, business, labour, and government. It is likely that in the near future, more public and private funding will continue to shift from basic to translational or applied research and from researcher-initiated grants to funder-defined contracts as universities become more engaged in community-based research and application. Early in the twentieth century, Ward separated applied sociology from civic and social reform. The relationship between applied sociology, on the one hand, and deliberate interventions based in sociological reasoning by social engineers and clinical sociologists, on the other, has been a source of contention ever since.

Origins of Applied Sociology

Auguste Comte (1798–1857), who created sociology, divided it into social statics, the study of the conditions and preconditions of social order, and social dynamics, the study of human progress and evolution. Comte wrote that the statical view of society is the basis of sociology but that the dynamical view is not only the more interesting of the two but more philosophical, since social dynamics would study the laws of the rise and fall of societies and furnish the true theory of progress for political practice. Comte envisioned a corps of positivist priests trained as sociologists, who would not possess any temporal power but rather would influence through teaching and provide informed direction to public opinion. They would impart useful scientific knowledge and social advice on all aspects of civil life. They would suggest action to the civil authorities but would never undertake such action on their own responsibility or initiative. It appears that Comte's applied sociologists would be neither basic researchers nor social activists/interventionists but rather occupy a translational role between the two.

In contrast, Herbert Spencer (1820–1903) argued against any form of artificial interference and that sociologists should convince the public that society must be free from the meddling of governments and reformers. He was very skeptical of the possibility of generating progress through legislation since such legislation is not based on the widest possible knowledge of the sociological principles involved.

Spencer was a strong advocate of *laissez faire* and coined the phrase "survival of the fittest" several years before Darwin wrote *Origin of the Species.* As a result, he is considered the founder of Social Darwinism. Spencer thought societies evolved from coercive militarism to peaceful industrialism in which individuals are free to move about and change their social relations without destroying social cohesion. The change from militarism to industrialism is an evolutionary process that depends on the rate of integration, and the slower the rate, the more complete and satisfactory the evolution. Therefore, evolution is a wholly spontaneous process that artificial human interference could in no way hasten but might fatally obstruct or divert.

Within academic circles, one of Spencer's early supporters was William Graham Sumner (1840–1910). Sumner introduced the first serious course in sociology in the United States at Yale University in 1875, adopting Spencer's *The Study of Sociology* as the text. Sumner promoted a sociology marked by conservative politics, descriptive accounts of societal evolution, and the nature of normative systems that define and control behaviour. In "The Absurd Effort to Make the World Over," Sumner strongly supported the idea that social evolution was almost entirely an automatic, spontaneous process that cannot be extensively altered by social effort. He favoured *laissez faire* policies and saw state activity as "ignorant social doctors" telling the Forgotten Man, that is, the hard working middle class, what to do for those who had failed in the struggle for existence.

Spencer was popularised in the United States through the efforts of Professor Edward Livingston Youmans, a chemist, educator, writer, and eventually an important agent and editor for D. Appleton and Company. In 1860, after reading the prospectus for *Principles of Psychology*, Youmans arranged for the first American publication of Spencer's works, and in 1872, became the founding editor of The Popular Science Monthly, which promoted science generally and evolution in particular. For Youmans, science was not limited to natural and biological phenomena but included the intelligent observation of the characters of people, the scrutiny of evidence in regard to political theories, the tracing of cause and effect in the sequences of human conduct, and the strict inductive inquiry as to how society has come to be what it is.

Spencer's ideas on evolution, antimilitarism, and peaceful industrialism became the focus of some adult education courses in the Second Unitarian Church in Brooklyn, New York. Youmans was acquainted with its minister, John White Chadwick. This group eventually formed the Brooklyn Ethical Association, and one of its objectives was "the scientific study of ethics, politics, economics, sociology, religion and philosophy, and also of physics and biology as related thereto". The Association devoted its 1881–82 sessions to Spencer's *The Study of Sociology. Within* 10 years, the Association created a class of Honorary Corresponding Members, which included Herbert Spencer himself; Thomas H. Huxley, President of the British Royal Society, who argued that humans created an ethical process that deviated from, and worked counter to, the natural course of evolution; Minot J. Savage, Unitarian minister in Chicago and Boston and author of *Social Problems;* Andrew Dickson White, historian and first president of Cornell University; Eliza A. Youmans, a pioneer in the field of botany and sister of Edward Youmans; and Joseph Le Conte, geologist, President of the American Association for the Advancement of Science in 1891, and author of "Race Problems in the South", published in the Association's *Man and the State.*

In 1892, the Brooklyn Ethical Association published Man and the State: Studies in Applied Sociology and in 1893, Factors in American Civilisation: Studies in Applied *Sociology.* This may be the first use of the term *applied sociology* in the title of a book. The association considered sociology to be the science of social evolution and sought to apply "evolutionary philosophy and ethics to the study and discussion of the pressing problems of politics and statesmanship to come before the people of the United States".

The preface to *Man and State* reaffirmed Spencer's views that societies grew in a regular and orderly way according to inherent laws that were not mechanically imposed. It noted that while a priori schemes of social reformers can stimulate thought, promote altruistic endeavour, and educate the individual, enacting these schemes into legislation would not abolish poverty or crime, or speed the renovation of society. The preface saw the role of sociology as a safer and wiser way of individual enlightenment and moral education. Sociology would subject the schemes of social reformers to the operations of the principle of natural selection, identify what is instructive and good in each, propose practical forward steps, and substitute the method of evolution for that of violent and spasmodic change, thereby, slowly promoting the permanent welfare of societies and individuals.

Lester F. Ward, who brought the term applied sociology into the discipline, spent most of his career as a paleontologist with the United States Geological Survey, joining the Sociology Department of Brown University in 1906 when he was 65. His early work focused on the relation of fossil plants to geological location in strata and this undoubtedly reflected an interest in evolution. In 1876, he published "The Local Distribution of Plants and the Theory of Adaptation" in *Popular Science Monthly,* which brought him to the attention of its editor, Edward Youmans. In addition, Ward's mentor, the noted geologist and explorer John Wesley Powell, wrote to Youmans in support of Dynamic Sociology or Applied Social Science, which was published in 1883.

Dynamic Sociology was the first major American work on sociology and although not intended as a text, was on the reading lists of early sociology courses. Ward differed sharply from Spencer and Sumner on laissez-faire individualism, and he argued for the efficacy of government as an agent of social reform, if it could be put on a scientific basis and purged of its corruption and stupidity. As a career government scientist with a legal background, Ward understandably took up Comte's idea of sociocrats, believing that government can directly improve the conditions of society in a conscious or "telic" manner if the legislators will only become social scientists or have gained knowledge of the nature and means of controlling the social forces and be willing to apply this knowledge. Scientific lawmaking would be based on a greater use of social statistics, with sociology as the chief source of information that is essential for any extensive development of scientific government.

On the other hand, Ward was very skeptical about the efforts of utopian social reform and socialist movements that favoured radical and abrupt changes in social structures. He was a "meliorist" who thought that much could be accomplished through education of both the public and government leaders. Ward wrote,

> Applied sociology is not government or politics, nor civic or social reform. It does not itself apply sociological principles; it only seeks to show how they might be. The most that it claims to do is to lay down certain general principles as guides to social and political action.

He added,

> "A sociologist, who takes sides on current events and the burning questions of the hour, abandons his science and becomes a politician."

Ward came to this mainly as a reaction to Spencer's writing, which Ward thought was prejudiced, not scientific, and not in harmony with Spencer's system as a whole and well before Max Weber called for value-free sociology.

Youmans was disappointed with the initial sales of Dynamic Sociology or Applied Social Science and suspected that the title, which was drawn directly from Comte's classification, was too close to Spencer's *Descriptive Sociology,* which in turn derived from Comte's social statics. Ward, who would become the first president of the American Sociological Society (later renamed American Sociological Association, or ASA), was a participant in many intellectual and scientific societies, including the Philosophical Society and Cosmos Club in Washington, D.C. and the Metaphysical Club. He may have come across the term applied sociology as a result of attending a meeting of the Ethical Association, at which Dr. Felix Adler, professor of Hebrew and Oriental Literature at Cornell University and founder of the ethical culture movement, among others, dealt with different methods of relieving human suffering and promoting human welfare. Ward wrote that this congress talked applied sociology from first to last. He was familiar with the new ethics that inquired into social conditions and sought to introduce modifications that would prevent existing evils and render their recurrence impossible.

This may have included the Brooklyn Ethical Association's two volumes of *Studies in Applied Sociology.* By the early 1890s, Ward also knew that several European sociologists were using the term *pure sociology.* He may have first used the terms pure and applied sociology in the titles of two summer school courses at the University of Chicago in 1897, which he repeated at the University of West Virginia in 1898 and then at Stanford University in 1899. He published *Pure* Sociology in 1903 and Applied Sociology in 1906. Ward himself did not do any sociological fieldwork or empirical research. Reformers at Hull House in Chicago did the earliest applied research in the United States. Despite his dislike for social reformers, Ward would probably have been pleased that it was done primarily by a group of women since he was a strong advocate of gender equality. Like Ward, Jane Addams was critical of socialism and abstract theories that impeded social learning by their inflexibility and tendency to divide people. She also thought that science could guide social reform through the patient accumulation of facts about the lives of the working poor. The key activist researcher was Florence Kelley (1859–1932), the daughter of a U.S. congressman, who studied at Cornell University and the University of Zurich and, in 1887, translated Engel's *The Conditions of the Working Class in England.* She came to Chicago in 1891 with her three children and became a resident of Hull House. Kelley, Addams and the other Hull House activists were convinced that once the overwhelming suffering of the poor was documented and publicised, meaningful reforms would be quickly put into place.

In 1892, the Illinois Bureau of Labour Statistics hired Kelley to investigate the "sweating" system in the Chicago garment industry. Then, in 1893, when the U.S. Congress commissioned a nationwide survey to investigate the slums of great cities and assess the extent of poverty in urban areas, she was selected to lead the survey effort in Chicago.

Kelley and others conducted a door-to-door survey in the Hull House district and, following the lead of Charles Booth's maps of poverty in London, created maps showing the nationality, wages, and employment history of each resident. Published in 1895, *The Hull-House Maps and Papers* offered no explanation for the causes of poverty and social disorder.

For Addams, practice was a priority over theory. In the preface, she claimed that this was not a sociological investigation to test or build theory but a constructive work that could help push the progressive agenda to address the injustices of poverty. As such, it simply recorded certain phases of neighbourhood life and presented detailed information that might prompt a humanitarian response from the government.

Kelley earned a law degree from Northwestern University and in 1899 moved to New York City to head the National Consumer's League (NCL) where she worked with Josephine Goldmark, director of research at NCL, to prepare the successful "Brandeis brief" defence of 10-hour workday legislation for women in *Muller v. Oregon* (1908), which like the *Brown v. Board of Education* (1954) school desegregation case almost 50 years later, used sociological evidence to support its case.

Jane Addams (1860–1935) followed her own applied and activist track in Chicago. Throughout her career, she maintained a tenuous relationship with academic sociology. In 1892, she taught a summer course on applied philanthropy and ethics with sociologist Franklin Giddings, and, in 1893, presided over a two-day conference at the Chicago World's Fair sponsored by the International Parliament of Sociology. She declined at least two offers to join the Sociology Department at Chicago, apparently over concerns about the limits on speech and political activism associated with university settings. Addams, however, did become a charter member of the American Sociological Society, was an invited speaker at several meetings, and published in the American Journal of Sociology (AJS) as well as other scholarly and popular journals. Two of her books received favourable reviews in the *AJS*.

But by 1920, a combination of backlash against social activism, the development of social theory to explain the causes as well as the effects of social problems, and gender discrimination marginalised Addams and other women sociologists from regular academic departments into what would become schools of social work.

If Addams and other social workers charted an independent course, Seba Eldridge (1885–1953) worked in social services before discovering sociology. Initially trained as a civil engineer, he came to New York City around 1907. He held a part-time position with the Bureau of Advice and Information of the New York Charity Organisation Society investigating and appraising civic and social agencies appealing for aid and occasionally resided at various East Side settlement houses, becoming familiar with the conditions of the people in the neighbourhoods. Eldridge knew of the work of Felix Adler and the Ethical Culture movement. In 1911, he began graduate study at Columbia University in social philosophy and finished his dissertation under John Dewey in 1925. But he also studied with both Franklin Giddings and William F. Ogburn and learned of their interests in scientific sociology, quantitative methods, and objectivity. From 1913 to 1915, he served as secretary of the Department of Social Betterment of the Brooklyn Bureau of Charities.

Eldridge wrote Problems of Community Life; an Outline of Applied Sociology in which he classified New York's social problems according to the attention given them by reformers and the general public along with the general plans that various philanthropies, social reform groups, and municipal agencies put forward for the better organisation of reform activities in the city. His suggestions for reform were few and emerged from the logic of the situations under analysis rather than from partisan interests (he was politically active on the side of anti- Tammany forces). In 1921, Eldridge joined the sociology faculty at the University of Kansas where he remained for the rest of his life. Much of his subsequent work focused on methods of improving the quality of citizenship, and he was well ahead of his time in advocating that social science departments should give students actual practice in the skills of citizenship through participation in community activities.

Not only was sociology being applied in social welfare and social policy, but it also gained an early toehold in industry. In January 1914, Henry Ford created a "profit sharing" plan that would pay workers up to $5 a day, when the average wage for an unskilled automobile worker was $2.40. The "profit sharing" was not a Taylorist scientific management bonus for additional quality work and was not directly tied to Ford Motor Company profits. Rather, it depended on workers maintaining good habits and taking care of their families and dependants. This was a radical concept and challenged the general belief that a sharp increase in the wages would have a bad effect because the workers would spend the additional money on drinking and gambling. Ford, however, wanted every worker to have a comfortable home and be able to own a Ford automobile. To select workers for the program and monitor their behaviour as well as test this "theory," he created a "Sociology Department" within Ford Motor Company.

The Department was headed by John R. Lee who was asked to identify which workers were qualified to participate in the "profit sharing" and then help the others to become qualified. This meant gathering information from the workers, and occasionally friends or neighbours, on their background, family situation, financial state, and personal habits through informal, semi-structured interviews. Recorded data included basic demographics; financial information, including life insurance and bank name, location and balance; and health information, including family doctor and habits such as smoking or drinking. In early 1914, investigators and interpreters, selected from among existing Ford employees, were highly visible as they drove Ford automobiles to the homes of the workers who were to be interviewed. The result was that 60 percent of the workers qualified for the "profit sharing".

However, the investigators were aggressive and some questions were intrusive. In addition, many non-English speaking workers did not qualify, possibly because of translation difficulties, and they and their families were angry. Lee then conducted a second phase, in the spring of 1914, to verify the initial findings and use better prepared translators. He told the investigators not to go into a home in a way that they would not want someone to come into theirs and cautioned them about delving into strictly personal matters. At the end of this phase, 69 percent of the workers were eligible. The company then began to Americanise its immigrant work force. In May 1914, it opened the Ford Language School, which taught English to workers after the first shift. Classes also stressed American ways and customs, encouraged thriftiness, and good personal and work habits. By the end of 1914, 87 percent of the workers qualified for the "profit sharing".

In 1916, Lee left Ford to develop the field of personnel management. Lee (1916) wrote a paper on the Ford profit-sharing system for the Annals of the American Academy of Political and Social Sciences. About 10 years later, Shenton noted in his *Practical Application of Sociology* that "certain businessmen have already made beginnings in sociological research and a number are conducting experiments under the observation of trained sociologists."

Academic Versus Applied Sociology

In 1916, sociology students at the University of Southern California started a journal, *Studies in Sociology,* but in October 1921, they changed its name to *Journal of Applied Sociology.* Alice Fesler explained that the name was taken from Ward's threefold classification of pure sociology, applied sociology, and social reform. The journal carried short pieces by students and well-known sociologists. A 1924 issue included "The Major Ills of the Social Survey" by Seba Eldridge, "A Race Relations Survey" by Robert E. Park, and "Social Psychology of Fads" by Emory Bogardus. But in 1927, the *JAS* was combined with the Bulletin of Social Research to become Sociology and *Social Research.* An editorial note explained that since productive research was the very basis of applied sociology, the journal would now publish significant pieces of research, although descriptions and analyses of social problems and the process, whereby they are reduced and solved, would still be printed. The journal would combine research and practice.

World War I marked the beginning of the end for the Progressive Era of social reforms to improve the lives of workers and immigrants, to conserve natural resources, and to make government more effective and less corrupt. In the social sciences, the acceptance of statistical thinking and quantification spurred the emergence of scientific methods, which in turn supported a growing dominance of the academic discipline over practical sociology and social activism. Social work was considered to be a technique and an art, not a science. In contrast, applied sociology was a science that could contribute to the development of an objective description of social problems and an understanding of their causes and could be used to guide social planning and social engineering. Applied sociology would attempt to keep an even keel of objective, value-free, social research amidst crosscurrents of political ideology and social activism.

In 1916, U.S. President Woodrow Wilson, a former Princeton professor of political science, supported a request by the National Academy of Sciences to create a National Research Council (NRC) to organise research and secure the cooperation of military and civilian agencies as a measure of national preparedness. In 1918, after the United States entered the war, Wilson issued an executive order under which the NRC was:

> to stimulate research in the mathematical, physical and biological sciences, and in the application of these sciences to engineering, agriculture, medicine and other useful arts, with the object of increasing knowledge, of strengthening the national defence, and of contributing in other ways to the public welfare.

In 1921, Congress passed the national origins immigration Quota Act that discouraged immigration from eastern and southern Europe. The next year, the NRC asked for social science representation on a study of human migration. The sociologist member of the Committee on the Scientific Problems of Human Migration was Mary Abby van Kleeck, the director of the Russell Sage Foundation's Department of Industrial Studies. Van Kleeck was a pioneer in industrial sociology, having conducted studies of unorganised workers and sweatshop labour. Other sociologists who attended a sponsored conference on migration, included Edith Abbott, Henry Fairchild, William Ogburn, and Robert Park.

On taking office in 1929, President Herbert Hoover established the President's Research Committee on Social Trends in the hope that social issues and problems could be scrutinised in the rational manner that had characterised his earlier efforts that reduced domestic consumption of food by 15 percent without rationing during World War I and his organisation of flood relief work and health improvement in 1927. The Rockefeller Foundation funded it for three years at $560,000, and William F. Ogburn (1886–1950), who coined the phrase "cultural lag," was named study director. He would also serve as director of the Consumers Advisory Board of the National Recovery Administration (NRA).

In his 1929 ASS Presidential address, Ogburn declared that "sociology as a science is not interested in making the world a better place in which to live." On the surface this appears to be a rejection of Ward's amelioration *and a revival of Sumner's* laissez-faire *position. But* Ogburn's main purpose was to ensure that scientific methods would be the basis for applied research and to distance it from ethics, religion, journalism, and propaganda. Like Ward, he did not believe that the sociologist as scientist should hold office or lead movements. Ogburn encouraged sociologists to be wherever data on significant social problems were to be found: on the staff of the courts, in factories, at political party headquarters, and in community centres. He wanted the sociologist to be there to discover new knowledge and relationships rather than as an executive, leader, or social worker who puts to use the information which the scientific sociologist furnishes. He even predicted that a great deal of research would be done outside of universities by government, trade unions, employers' associations, civic bodies, political parties, and social service organisations. Ogburn recognised that this research would be done for a specific purpose to prove a particular hypothesis or to gain a desired end. He asserted that to do this, the researchers should be free to follow the evidence and that they therefore must be sharply distinguished from the executives or policymakers.

This was already happening. The most well-known private sector applied research began in April 1927 at the Western Electric Plant in Hawthorne, Illinois. It would culminate with the publication of *Management and the Worker*, which described worker behaviours and interactions in the experimental Relay Assembly Test Room and the Bank Wiring Observation Room. A few years later in 1933, J. L. Moreno, in collaboration with Helen Hall Jennings, began consulting at the New York State Training School for Girls in Hudson, New York, where he developed his sociometric system and began the *Sociometric Review*, which was renamed Sociometry.

Ogburn also drew an interesting distinction between sociologists who are research scientists and social engineers who, like physicians, are not scientists but who apply reliable scientific procedures and relatively exact knowledge. The concept of social engineering was developed by William Tolman, who thought that industrialists should assume more social responsibility for their workers and should hire social engineers to be the primary intermediary between the industrialist and the employees.

Andrew Carnegie liked the idea and wrote an introduction to the book. Tolman also advocated that employers become involved with the workers and their families through programs for social insurance, profit sharing, and savings. These ideas may have led Henry Ford to set up the "Sociology Department" to support his "profit sharing" plan and John Lee to leave Ford and start personnel management. But the term *social engineering* was about to take on an ominous and decidedly negative connotation. In 1928, Stalin introduced the first Soviet five-year plan, and the Third Reich would soon adopt social engineering and use applied urban and rural sociology in their plans for the reorganisation of an expanded Germany and the expulsion and annihilation of the population of conquered territories. These developments were noted by several American sociologists, including Robert K. Merton, who advocated that scientists repudiate the application of utilitarian norms and quipped that:

> "an economy of social engineers is no more conceivable or practicable than an economy of laundrymen"

In 1934, *Social Forces* asked 23 prominent sociologists to contribute to a Round Table Symposium to address questions such as "What is the role of sociology in current social reconstruction?" Arthur E. Wood recounted that Charles Cooley said that in his early days he had the greatest difficulty in trying to tell his colleagues the difference between sociology and socialism. Borrowing terms from William James, Wood then identified three types of sociologists:

1. The tough minded who are all for objectivity but sit on the sidelines when it comes to the hard contests over practical issues;
2. The tender minded or welfare sociologists who come from a background of religion or social work and tinker around the edges without much knowledge or insight into the nature of the structure which they would change; and
3. The radicals, that is, those active in partisan or revolutionary movements, who have an analysis of the social order and a blue print of what should be done but whose strength lies in their dogmatism which does not qualify them as social scientists.

Without using the term applied sociology, Wood concluded that sociology could use descriptive analysis of social structures and processes involving critical evaluations to guide the tendencies of social change in the interest of reform.

The issue of the relationship between academic sociology and applied sociology in its various forms was part of a five-year struggle within the American Sociological Society over what Marklund calls the scientific detachment versus political involvement dilemma or as Stuart A. Queen, who worked for the American Red Cross and the Detroit Community Fund as well as teaching sociology at Kansas and Washington University, put it:

> "How to steer between the Scylla of academic isolation and the Charybdis of partisan activity."

At the 1931 annual meeting of the American Sociological Society, Maurice Parmelee, an early behaviourist and criminologist, Robert MacIver, and Pitirim Sorokin among others, distributed a memorandum in which they claimed that the programs and publications of the Society were devoted in considerable part to practical rather than to scientific problems, that as a result the public has the impression that the Society is a religious, moral, and social reform organisation rather than a scientific society, and that the Society has become in large part a society of applied sociology. To remedy this, they proposed that voting members have a higher university degree in sociology and be engaged in sociological research, writing, and teaching and that the Society assume control of the official journal, at the time the *American Journal of Sociology* controlled by the Chicago Sociology Department.

Martindale interpreted this as a conflict between the more populist and progressive Midwestern departments that were receptive to Ward's Comtean view of science as social reconstruction and the more academically conservative eastern departments linked to Sumner and Social Darwinism.

In 1934, the Society's Committee on Scope of Research reported that New Deal and other social welfare agencies were using sociological research for the solution of practical problems. It recommended a closer integration of sociologists with the sociological work of government, a more complete and discriminating canvass of research in progress and an emphasis on the region as the unit of research because of developments in social planning. Two years later, in 1936, the Committee on Opportunities for Trained Sociologists recommended the creation of a new permanent committee for the promotion of the professional (as opposed to the disciplinary) interests of sociologists.

The new committee would get sociological training and field experience recognised as a qualification or substitute qualification for certain Federal and state civil service positions, expand graduate training in sociology to meet the need for equipping students for technical positions, and involve sociology in state planning commissions and the reorganisation of state welfare systems, as well as publicise sociology. The Society, however, did not take up these recommendations. Applied sociology was set adrift in stormy seas as the academics opted for a narrower disciplinary and scientific learned society and the reformers moved into administrative positions in New Deal agencies.

Funding for Applied Sociology

Applied sociology received a substantial boost from World War II and then the War on Poverty. In both cases, research and observations collected in natural settings for applied purposes would generate new knowledge and contribute to sociological theories and concepts, as had been called for by Ogburn in his Society presidential address. Fifty years later, Peter Rossi in his ASA presidential address noted that many pieces of client-initiated applied work would, over time, be presented in the sociological literature as primarily basic research. In November 1941, the War Department established a Research Branch in the Information and Education Division to provide the army command quickly and accurately with facts about the attitudes of soldiers. Samuel Stouffer (1900–1960) became the director of the Troop Attitude Program and with the assistance of more than 100 sociologists, seven of whom would serve as presidents of the ASA, conducted more than 200 surveys during the war years with more than half a million soldiers. Topics covered included practices associated with trench foot, what articles were read in *Yank Magazine*, determining attitudes toward promotion and job assignments in the military, the attitudes of Negro soldiers, and the point system for personnel demobilisation after the war.

In December 1942, a compendium of troop-attitude studies was published for limited army staff distribution, but each succeeding issue was more widely distributed, eventually down to the company level. Stouffer saw the research branch as doing an engineering job, not a scientific one. The reports not only emphasised that problems could be treated at the local command level but also that they were of value in planning and policy activities, for example, estimates of the number of veterans who would go to college if federal aid were provided led to the GI Bill and accurately predicted the actual postwar experience. Nevertheless Stouffer noted that the channels of communication between the policymakers and the actual study directors in the Branch were often very unsatisfactory and the potential effectiveness in policy making of some of the research was lost.

Applied research was also conducted on the home front. In the fall of 1941, an Office of Facts and Figures was created in the Office of War Information (OWI) to collect survey data on public attitudes and behaviour concerning a broad range of war-related problems, including civilian morale and the effects of wartime regulations. The OWI needed a contractor and asked George Gallup who recommended Harry H. Field who had worked for him when they were both in the market research department of the advertising firm of Young and Rubicam. Through Gallup, Field was introduced to Hadley Cantril, Paul Lazarsfeld, and Samuel Stouffer who helped him establish the National Opinion Research Centre (NORC) at the University of Denver in the fall of 1941 (NORC would move to the University of Chicago in 1947). NORC got the contract for the civilian surveys and established a New York office in the building used by OWI. Early in 1942, Paul B.

Sheatsley, who was working for Gallup at the time, headed the survey research efforts. Many of the OWI surveys were simply fact-finding endeavours (how people disposed of their waste fats or how they were using their ration coupons), but others were pioneering efforts such as the first national measurement of racial attitudes.

The OWI employed Paul Lazarsfeld (1901–1976) among others. Lazarsfeld had come to the United States as a Fellow of the Rockefeller Foundation and served as director of the Foundation's Office of Radio Research, which moved to Columbia University in 1939 and became the Bureau of Applied Social Research in 1944. Over the years, Lazarsfeld and his students would conduct applied research for clients that would later contribute to modern market research, mathematical sociology, and mass communications research. His work on personal influence stemmed from applied work financed by a magazine publisher to convince would be advertisers that placing ads in the magazine would reach opinion leaders, and a BASR study for a pharmaceutical company on the adoption of a new drug revealed the roles played by professional and social ties among physicians. In 1983, three of Lazarsfeld's former students would be the directors of social research for the three major networks:

CBS, ABC, and NBC. Just before the war, the U.S. Department of Agriculture appointed Rensis Likert (1903–1981) director of the Division of Program Surveys in Bureau of Agricultural Economics. Likert had already developed his five-point scale and taught at New York University before becoming director of research for the Life Insurance Agency in Hartford, Connecticut, in 1935, where he conducted studies on the effectiveness of different styles of supervision. During the war, Likert and his colleagues conducted surveys of farmer's experiences and opinions. At the end of the war, Likert contacted Theodore M. Newcomb, who had worked with him during the war. Together they formed the Survey Research Centre (SRC) at the University of Michigan to conduct publishable studies for businesses, foundations, governmental and other agencies on all kinds of economic, social, and business problems.

To complement the survey focus, Likert suggested that the Research Centre for Group Dynamics (RCGD), then at the Massachusetts Institute of Technology, join SRC to form the Institute for Social Research (ISR) in 1948. The RCGD was founded by Kurt Lewin (1890–1947) and then headed by Dorwin Cartwright who had worked with Likert in the Division of Program Surveys. Likert had served on the Committee on Food Habits of the National Research Council, which funded Lewin's experiments demonstrating that food shoppers were more likely to change their buying habits as a result of a discussion followed by a public commitment than after a lecture by an expert. This led to his field theory involving food channels and the concept of gatekeepers. Lewin used the term *action research* and intended his research to result in guiding the actions needed to solve social problems, reducing the gap between social science knowledge and the use of that knowledge.

Early SRC research included an objective evaluation of a program to encourage acceptance of minority groups within the United Auto workers Union and a study of morale at a telephone company that led to improved productivity and job satisfaction. RCGD and the Tavistock Institute in London jointly published the journal *Human* Relations. In New Patterns of Management, Likert summarised the principles and practices used by highest producing managers and proposed a more effective system of management.

By 1960, these and other university-based social research centres were producing empirical findings that had a considerable impact on sociological theories, methods, and concepts. In 1961, the Society for the Study of Social Problems under the leadership of Alvin Gouldner focused its meeting on the topic of applied social science and major papers were published in *Applied Sociology: Opportunities and Problems*.

The papers explored practitioner-client relations and case studies in a variety of areas, including law, family, community, race relations, and delinquency. Years later, coeditor S. M. Miller revealed that he regretted the use of the term applied sociology because it was highly ambiguous—did it refer to sociologists employed outside academia, to academic sociologists who did studies for nonprofit and voluntary organisations whether paid for or not, to social activists or to public policy critics and intellectuals?—and because he saw little linkage between applied work and sociological study.

When Paul Lazarsfeld was elected ASA president, he proposed that the theme for the 1962 meetings be "Sociology in Action" or "Applied Sociology" to highlight the contribution of applied and case studies to theoretical and methodological advances. The ASA Executive Council, however, changed it to "Uses of Sociology," which also became the title of an edited volume of 31 invited papers. The term *uses* went beyond applied sociology to encompass where and to what extent sociological findings and perspectives were used by professionals, businesses, voluntary agencies, the military, schools, and public bodies. Authors were asked to address the difficulties of translating practical issues into research problems and to discuss the intellectual gaps between research findings and advice for action. According to Gollin, most authors had problems doing the latter—that is, identifying concrete applications of sociological ideas or findings.

In a provocative essay, Robert C. Angell raised some ethical issues concerning applied research. He worried that since such research is used to further the practical ends of business, voluntary associations, or government, it would take only a slight distortion in the sampling procedure or in the phrasing of questions to obtain findings desired by the client. Because they do not have the high calling of developing abstract scientific knowledge, he argued that the applied researcher cannot claim the special privileges that are sometimes enjoyed by those who do. For example, while it may be sometimes ethical to deceive subjects for the purpose of obtaining important new scientific knowledge, provided they are later debriefed, this justification cannot, in Angell's opinion, be used for applied research because the ends are not scientific ones.

These edited volumes on applied sociology written from the perspective of disciplinary sociology, however, failed to take the wind out of the sails. In fact, in his ASA presidential address, Rossi noted that from 1960 to 1980 applied social research enjoyed a boom period in which sociology, as a discipline, had not really shared. Essentially the War on Poverty generated large-scale applied research involving needs assessments for program planning, demonstration and pilot services, and program evaluations, which were risky, controversial, and could not easily be translated into academic publications. Dentler estimated that, from 1960 to 1975, approximately 100 social science research and development firms were established, a third of which were located in the Washington, D.C., suburbs. Finally several specialised applied social research centres were created, such as the Disaster Research Centre at the Ohio State University in 1963, now at the University of Delaware.

In 1964, the U.S. Office of Education commissioned James S. Coleman to determine how educational opportunity, defined as condition of school buildings, trained teachers, and curricula, were distributed by race and ethnicity. The Report, Equality of Educational Opportunity, which studied all 3rd, 6th, 9th, and 12th-grade students in 4,000 schools, not only documented the pervasiveness of segregation in the schools but went beyond the rather narrow Congressional mandate to explore how parental education and social status as well as peer pressures effected student achievement. If the findings were controversial, the subsequent implementation of mandated bussing and the flight of white families from city schools were even more so. Coleman, who originally supported school integration, changed his mind in the 1970s when he concluded that the policies that focused wholly on within-district bussing actually increased rather than reduced school segregation.

The Coleman Report belies the argument that doing applied research for government agencies substantially limits intellectual and political independence and that applied researchers are at the beck and call of decision makers and policy implementers. Rossi pointed out that the applied researcher could negotiate and in some cases broaden the scope of the study to include sociological variables and factors. On the other hand, it also illustrates Rossi's points that applied social research may be used in policy formation and become embroiled in rancorous controversy in which the work is attacked, misused, or misapplied, and that sociologists are ordinarily not directly involved in decision making, policy formation, or program implementation. Like Ward and Ogburn before him, Rossi warned that applied social research is not for would-be philosopher kings.

During this time, studies continued to bridge the gap between pure and applied research. For example, Benjamin Bloom's work on stability of IQ during early childhood later provided Head Start with data on where best to intervene with compensatory preschool educational programs, William Sewell's study on status attainment began as a state-sponsored survey of Wisconsin high school seniors, and Rosabeth Moss Kanter published her own research on corporations for a broader audience.

Professionalism In Applied Sociology

The late 1970s witnessed an increase in the production of M.A. and Ph.D., sociologists at a time when sociology departments were not hiring. A large number of new sociologists took positions outside academia in professional schools and in research units in government agencies, nonprofit organisations, and private consulting firms. Many wanted to present and publish their findings in sociological venues.

In the late 1960s, Alex Boros established what is believed to be the first graduate program in applied sociology at Kent State University. In 1978, a dinner conversation about the lack of applied sessions at the North Central Sociological Association (NCSA) meetings led to the formation of the Society for Applied Sociology. In 1979, SAS held sessions in conjunction with the NCSA. SAS was formally incorporated in 1984 with Boros as the first president, and it began publishing the Journal of Applied Sociology. In 1994, SAS approved a code of ethics for Applied Sociologists. Over the years, the presidency of SAS has been fairly evenly divided between applied sociologists who worked in academic institutions and those who either owned their own consulting firms or were employed by governmental, nonprofit, or business entities.

The late 1970s also saw the creation of the Clinical Sociological Association and the ASA Section on Sociological Practice. Then, in 1980, Peter Rossi became ASA president followed the next year by William Foote Whyte, both of whom considered themselves applied sociologists. An ASA Committee on Professional Opportunities in Applied Sociology, chaired by Howard Freeman, held a workshop in December 1981 titled "Directions in Applied Sociology." The papers presented were published in *Applied Sociology* and explored the then current status of applied sociology, the range of applied sociology roles in diverse settings, and the academic training of applied sociologists.

ASA also started a journal, the *Sociological Practice Review,* to provide a discipline sponsored publication for applied, clinical, and practising sociologists, and to disseminate knowledge on how sociology can be applied to practical problems. Reviewed in 1992 during its third year, it was found to have had difficulty attracting sufficient manuscripts along with falling subscriptions. Despite opposition by the majority of editors of other ASA journals, the publications committee, by one vote, recommended that it be supported for another three years. The Executive Office and Budget Committee, however, recommended discontinuance and the ASA Council agreed.

In 1991, ASA was awarded funds to establish the Sydney S. Spivak Program in Applied Social Research and Social Policy with the purpose of enhancing the visibility, prestige, and centrality of applied social research and the application of sociological knowledge to social policy. The Program supported a Congressional Fellowship and policy briefings by sociologists on topics such as HIV/AIDS, youth violence, immigrants, and reactions to terrorism. It also offered Community Action Fellowships of up to $2,500 to cover direct costs of sociologists working with community groups to conduct needs assessments, evaluation studies, and empirical research of community activities and planning, or to produce an analytical literature review to address the community group's goals.

The introduction to the *Uses of Sociology* noted that a Ph.D. in sociology did not really train students for employment outside academia. It asked what type of professional training would be needed, what role university research bureaus, centres and institutes would play, and whether sociologists should create programs within departments or separate schools of social research. Freeman and Rossi proposed that some departments having appropriately trained and motivated faculty, add applied training as an option for their graduate and undergraduate students. Such a program would provide a solid general grounding in the history, current trends, theories, and range of research methods in sociology, with additional practical and pragmatic skills of how to administer sample surveys and field research, how to select and work with a survey research organisation or train others to collect data, and how to write a response to a request for proposals as opposed to a journal article.

In her SAS Presidential address, Jeanne Ballantine reported on a study of where sociology majors were employed after graduation, what employers were seeking, and what undergraduate applied programs were providing. She found a variety of efforts ranging from one or two courses, to an internship or field experience, to a complete track or concentration. The demand for training generated a set of texts and supplements by Sullivan, Steele, Scarisbrick-Hauser, and Hauser, Du Bois and Wright, Dentler, Straus, Steele and Price, and Dukes, Petersen, and Van Valey.

SAS president Stephen Steele conducted a needs assessment survey of SAS members in 1992 and found an interest in strengthening training programs at the graduate and undergraduate levels. He appointed Harry Perlstadt to pursue this. In 1995, with the support of Joyce Iutcovich, SAS President and David Kallen, president of the Sociological Practice Association (SPA), they formed the Commission on Applied and Clinical Sociology. The commission created standards for undergraduate and graduate programs and, by 2005, had accredited three undergraduate programs and two masters level graduate programs. Accreditation standards help programs provide quality training with adequate resources and the Commission itself serves as a clearing-house for the programs.

In August 2000, SAS and SPA met together in Washington, D.C., with the theme Unity 2000. Both recognised they were small and could benefit from combining their resources and efforts. As the result of hard work by, among others, Ross Koppel and Joan Biddle of SPA and Augie Diana and Jay Weinstein of SAS, the two groups merged in 2005 to become the Association for Applied and Clinical Sociology (AACS), with a combined journal.

Since 1970, many Ph.D., sociologists have conducted applied research in a variety of settings. A 1995 National Science Foundation survey of Ph.D., sociologists found that less than half (45.8 percent) of all sociologists taught sociology at the postsecondary level and 27.1 percent of all Ph.D., sociologists were employed outside educational institutions. Unfortunately, only a few Ph.D., sociologists can be mentioned here. Michael Quinn Patton, one of the leading experts in evaluation research, wrote Utilisation-Focused Evaluation and was president of the American Evaluation Association. Terence C. Halliday is a Senior Research Fellow at the American Bar Foundation and

President of the National Institute for Social Science Information. He helped found and was chair of the ASA Sociology of Law section and served as editor of the interdisciplinary journal Law and Social Inquiry. Lola Jean Kozak, with the job title of health statistician/senior health researcher in the National Centre for Health Statistics, Centres of Disease Control, has done applied research on avoidable hospitalisation that has affected the Centres for Medicare and Medicaid Services. Sociologist William W. Darrow was the sole nonmedical scientist on the CDC Task Force in the early 1980s that did the initial investigations of what would be identified as the HIV/AIDS epidemic.

Applied Sociology in the 21st Century

Over the years, applied sociology has bridged sociological theory and sociological practice, bringing theory and ideas to professional practitioners and decision makers while, in return, contributing to the knowledge base of sociology as a science and discipline. To some extent, the history of applied sociology has been embroiled in what Andrew Abbott would identify as clarifications and disputes over jurisdictions between the academic discipline and the practice of the profession. Applied sociology has tried to steer clear of entanglements with social philosophy and ethics, on the one hand, and social engineering, reform, and activism on the other. But the very nature of applied sociology, and the interests of those who choose to do it, will mean that such jurisdictional tensions will continue well into the twenty-first century as they have for the past 150 years.

But the demand for applied sociology is not likely to slacken. The U.S. government has been commissioning social surveys and studies for over a century, and at the beginning of the twenty-first century, the NIH and NIMH roadmaps for research continue to look to and fund the applied side of the social and behavioural sciences. As Ogburn predicted, business, labour, community, and nonprofit service organisations all have a need for reliable and accurate data, needs assessments, and evaluations that applied sociology can provide. Evidence-based decision making and accountability will continue to be stressed as a rational necessity. Of course, decision makers and administrators will highlight those findings that meet their ends and ignore those that do not. In a few instances, applied findings will, unfortunately, be used for nefarious purposes as they were by the Soviets and Nazis. Although the primary focus of ASA will remain on basic research and academic positions, applied sociology will continue to be recognised as a specialty/derivative field. The newly formed Association for Applied and Clinical Sociology may professionalise sociology by bringing more practitioners into contact with disciplinary sociology, thereby following a pattern that already exists in economics, psychology, and political science. This may be strengthened as more departments develop applied research and sociological practice training programs at the undergraduate and graduate levels in response to societal demands.

Applied sociology is very resilient. The term has survived for more than a hundred years despite vague definitions and attempts to ignore or replace it. While sociology as a discipline and perspective may have increasing difficulties being appreciated in a culture of expanding individualism, personal liberty, and self-actualisation, people, and especially social organisations and government agencies, will need to choose wisely on the basis of evidence. The heart of applied sociology is social research, and as long as decision makers want to know the social facts and people are trained to provide them, applied sociology will flourish.

2

Clinical Sociology

Clinical sociology is as old as the field of sociology and its roots are found in many parts of the world. The clinical sociology specialisation, for instance, often is traced back to the fourteenth-century work of the Arab scholar and states person Abd-al-Rahman ibn Khaldun. Ibn Khaldun provided numerous clinical observations based on his varied work experiences such as Secretary of State to the ruler of Morocco and Chief Judge of Egypt.

Auguste Comte and Emile Durkheim are among those who frequently are mentioned as precursors to the field. Comte, the French scholar who coined the term sociology, believed that the scientific study of societies would provide the basis for social action. Emile Durkheim's work on the relation between levels of influence (e.g., social compared to individual factors) led Alvin Gouldner to write that "more than any other classical sociologist (he) used a clinical model." Albion Small, chair of the Department of Sociology at the University of Chicago and founding editor of *The American Journal of Sociology*, published "Scholarship and Social Agitation" in 1896. Small thought the primary reason for the existence of sociology was its "practical application to the improvement of social life". In Small's (1896:564) words:

> Let us go about our business with the understanding that within the scope of scholarship there is first science, and second something better than science. That something better is first prevision by means of science, and second intelligent direction of endeavour to realise visions. I would have American scholars, especially in the social sciences, declare their independence of do-nothing traditions. I would have them repeal the law of custom which bars marriage of thought with action. I would have them become more profoundly and sympathetically scholarly by enriching the wisdom which comes from knowing with the larger wisdom which comes from doing.

Clinical sociology, one of the fields that pairs science and action, is a humanistic, creative and multidisciplinary field that seeks to improve the quality of people's lives. Clinical sociologists assess situations and reduce problems through analysis and intervention. Clinical analysis is the critical assessment of beliefs, policies and/or practices with an interest in improving the situation. Intervention, the creation of new systems as well as the change of existing systems, is based on continuing analysis. Clinical sociologists have different areas of expertise such as health promotion, sustainable communities, social conflict or cultural competence and work in many capacities. They are, for example, community organisers, sociotherapists, mediators, focus group facilitators, social policy implementers, action researchers and administrators.

Many clinical sociologists are full-time or part-time university professors, and these clinical sociologists may undertake intervention work in addition to their teaching and research or they may focus on providing some combination of research and advice to those who do take actions (e.g., policymakers, the public, administrators, corporate boards, unions). If the focus of clinical sociologists is on advice/analysis for the public sector, this emphasis, in the last few years, has been referred to as public sociology.

The role of the clinical sociologist can be at one or more levels of focus from the individual to the inter-societal. Even though the clinical sociologist specialises in one or two levels of intervention (e.g., marriage counselling, community consulting, national policy development), the practitioner will move among a number of levels (e.g., individual, organisation and community or micro/meso/macro) in order to analyse and/or intervene.

Sociological practice is a general term that includes two areas, clinical sociology and applied sociology. Clinical sociology, as practised in the United States, emphasises hands-on intervention while applied sociology emphasises research for practical purposes. Both specialties require different kinds of specialised training. Some sociological practitioners only describe their work as "clinical" or "applied," while others say they work in both areas.

Those clinical sociologists who conduct research may do so before beginning an intervention project to assess the existing state of affairs; during an intervention and/or after the completion of the intervention to evaluate the outcome of that intervention. For some clinical sociologists, the research activity is an important part of their own clinical work. These sociologists have appropriate research training and look for opportunities to conduct research. Other clinical sociologists prefer to concentrate on the interventions and leave any research to other team members.

History of Clinical Sociology

American sociology emerged as a discipline in the 1890s at a time when the nation was struggling with issues of democracy, capitalism and social justice. Frustration led to public protests and the development of reform organisations. In this climate, it is not surprising that many of the early sociologists were scholar-practitioners interested in reducing or solving the pressing social problems that confronted their communities.

Clinical Sociology as a Concept

While many of the early sociologists were interested in practice, the earliest known proposal using the words "clinical sociology" was put forward by Milton C. Winternitz, a physician who was dean of the Yale School of Medicine from 1920 through 1935. At least as early as 1929, Winternitz began developing a plan to establish a department of clinical sociology within Yale's medical school. Winternitz wanted each medical student to have a chance to analyse cases based on a medical specialty as well as a specialty in clinical sociology.

Winternitz vigorously sought financial support for his proposal from the Rosenwald Fund, but was unable to obtain the necessary funds for a department of clinical sociology. He did note, however, the success of a course in the medical school's section on public health that was based on the clinical sociology plan. In 1929 Winternitz wrote about his effort to build a department in a report to the university president and the report was published in the Yale University *Bulletin*. Also published in 1930 was the speech Winternitz gave at the dedication of the University of Chicago's new social science building in which he mentioned clinical sociology.

Abraham Flexner, a prominent critic of medical education and director of the Institute for Advanced Study at Princeton, mentioned clinical sociology in 1930 in his *Universities: American, English, German*. Flexner did not approve of the Institute of Human Relations that Winternitz was establishing at Yale but did note that "Only one apparent novelty is proposed: a professor of clinical sociology."

Winternitz continued to write about the value of clinical sociology until 1936. One of his most forceful statements in support of the field appeared in his 1930-1931 annual report which stated, in part, "Not only in medicine and in law, but probably in many other fields of activity, the broad preparation of the clinical sociologist is essential..." The first discussion of clinical sociology by a sociologist was Louis Wirth's 1931 article, "Clinical Sociology," in *The American Journal of Sociology*. Wirth wrote at length about the possibility of sociologists working in child development clinics, though he did not specifically mention his own clinical work in New Orleans. Wirth wrote "it may not be an exaggeration of the facts to speak of the genesis of a new division of sociology in the form of clinical sociology."

In 1931, Wirth also wrote a career development pamphlet which stated:

> The various activities that have grown up around child-guidance clinics, penal and correctional institutions, the courts, police systems, and similar facilities designed to deal with problems of misconduct have increasingly turned to sociologists to become members of their professional staffs.

Wirth "urged (sociology students) to become specialists in one of the major divisions of sociology, such as social psychology, urban sociology... or clinical sociology."

In 1931, Saul Alinsky was a University of Chicago student who was enrolled in Burgess' clinical sociology course. Three years later, Alinsky's article, "A Sociological Technique in Clinical Criminology," appeared in the *Proceedings of the Sixty-Fourth Annual Congress of the American Prison Association*. Alinsky, best known now for his work in community organising, was, in 1934, a staff sociologist and member of the classification board of the Illinois State Penitentiary.

In 1944, the first formal definition of clinical sociology appeared in H.P. Fairchild's *Dictionary of Sociology*. Alfred McClung Lee, the author of that definition, later used the word clinical in the title of two articles – his 1945 "Analysis of Propaganda: A Clinical Summary" and the 1955 article "The Clinical Study of Society." Lee was one of the founders of the Society for the Study of Social Problems, the Association for Humanist Sociology and the Sociological Practice Association and also was, from 1976-77, president of the American Sociological Association.

Also appearing in 1944 was Edward McDonagh's "An Approach to Clinical Sociology." McDonagh proposed establishing social research clinics that would use groups to study and solve problems.

In 1946, George Edmund Haynes' "Clinical Methods in Interracial and Intercultural Relations" appeared in *The Journal of Educational Sociology*. Haynes was a co-founder of the National Urban League (1910) and the first African American to hold a U.S. government sub-cabinet post. His 1946 article, written while he was executive secretary of the Department of Race Relations at the Federal Council of the Churches of Christ in America, discussed the department's urban clinics. The clinics were designed to deal with interracial tensions and conflicts by developing limited, concrete programs of action.

First University Courses

The first clinical sociology course was taught by Ernest W. Burgess at the University of Chicago. In 1928 and 1929, the course was considered to be a "special" course and did not appear in the catalogue. The course was offered as a regular course from 1931 through 1933. The clinical sociology course continued to be listed in the catalogue for the next several years but was not taught after 1933.

The university catalogues did not include a description of the clinical sociology course, but it always was listed under the social pathology grouping. All courses in this section dealt with topics such as criminality, punishment, criminal law, organised crime, and personal disorganisation.

Many students enrolled in these first clinical sociology courses were placed in child guidance clinics. Clarence E. Glick, for instance, was the staff sociologist at the Lower North Side Child Guidance Clinic and Leonard Cottrell was the clinical sociologist at the South Side Child Guidance Clinic.

Two other universities offered clinical courses in the 1930s, namely Tulane University and New York University. The Tulane University (1929) course was designed to give students the opportunity to learn about behaviour problems and social therapy.

The New York University course, taught by Harvey Warren Zorbaugh, provided undergraduate and graduate preparation for visiting teachers, educational counsellors, clinicians, social workers and school guidance administrators. The major focus of the program was the solution of educational problems and other social dilemmas.

Zorbaugh, a faculty member in the School of Education, along with Agnes Conklin, offered a "Seminar in Clinical Practice" in 1930. The course was intended to qualify students as counsellors or advisers dealing with behavioural difficulties in schools. From 1931 through 1933 the clinical practice course, titled "Seminar in Clinical Sociology," was open to graduate students who were engaged in writing theses or conducting research projects in educational guidance and social work.

Harvey Zorbaugh, author of *The Gold Coast and the Slum: A Sociological Study of Chicago's Near North Side* (1929), had been involved with clinics at least since 1924, when Clifford Shaw and Zorbaugh organised two sociological clinics in Chicago. Zorbaugh was associate director of the Lower North Child Guidance Clinic in 1925 and also a founder, in 1928, of New York University's Clinic for the Social Adjustment of the Gifted. Zorbaugh was director of this clinic for intellectually gifted and talented preadolescent children at its inception and was actively involved in its work for over fifteen years. The clinic gave graduate students the opportunity to have supervised experiences in teaching, clinical diagnosis and treatment of children with behavioural problems.

Contemporary Contributions

While publications mentioning clinical sociology appeared at least every few years after the 1930s, the number of publications increased substantially after the founding of the Clinical Sociology Association in 1978. The Association, which later became the Sociological Practice Association, made publications a high priority, particularly in its early years. The *Clinical Sociology Review* and the theme journal, *Sociological Practice,* were published by the Association beginning in the early 1980s. These annual journals were eventually replaced by *Sociological Practice: A Journal of Clinical and Applied Sociology*, a quarterly publication.

The Clinical Sociology Association/Sociological Practice Association had a central role in the development of American clinical sociology. The Association helped make available the world's most extensive collection of teaching, research and intervention literature under the label of clinical sociology and it introduced the only clinical sociology certification process.

The Sociological Practice Association's certification process for clinical sociologists was available at the Ph.D. and M.A. levels. The Ph.D.-level process was adopted in 1983 and certification was first awarded in 1984. The Association began to offer M.A.-level certification in 1986. The Sociological Practice Association, along with the Society for Applied Sociology, also put in place the Commission on Applied and Clinical Sociology. The Commission has set standards for the accreditation of clinical and applied sociology programs at the undergraduate and graduate levels.The Sociological Practice Association and the Society for Applied Sociology merged in 2005. The name of the new association the Association of Applied and Clinical Sociology once again gives name recognition to clinical sociology.

Intervention and Interventionists

The basic intervention process with a client system, as outlined by Ronald Lippett and his colleagues), is divided into seven stages:

1. The client system discovers the need for help, sometimes with the assistance from the change agent;
2. The helping relationship is established and defined;
3. The change problem is identified and clarified;
4. Alternative possibilities for change are examined and the goals of the change are established;
5. Change efforts are actually attempted;
6. Change is generalised and stabilised and
7. The helping relationship ends or a different type of continuing relationship is defined.

Three points can be made about the stages:

1. Initial assessments of the situation may be conducted during the third stage, and process and outcome evaluations may be conducted during a number of the stages;
2. It is possible not only to progress through the stages but to cycle back through them as necessary; and
3. The length of time required for each stage will depend on a number of factors including the kind of change under consideration.

Clinical sociologists do differ in their areas of expertise and consultation models (e.g., control or influence, extent of citizen participation). A practitioner also may use a general consultation model in her/his practice to analyse, reduce or solve problems or she/he may use certain approaches depending on the particular areas of application and/or the specific set of circumstances. Bruhn and Rebach note that the "creative problem solver" can choose from a number of approaches including ones they describe as social systems, human ecology, life cycle and clinical.

It is useful to outline the principles, attitudes and tools needed by clinical sociologists in conducting interventions. While these may differ somewhat depending on the level of intervention (e.g., individual, community, nation), the following would be among those included: having an ethical framework; practising inclusiveness; working with the people's interests and opportunities; encouraging recognition of the viewpoints of others; demonstrating interdependence as a factor in the change process; encouraging capacity building; and having a long-term perspective. Change agents need to be open-minded, have courage and be able to work well with others.

The characteristics of the client system are particularly important during a period of change. The largest share of work in any change initiative generally must be undertaken by the client system. Therefore, the extent and quality of the change will depend, in large part, on the energy, capability (including available resources) and motivation of the client system.

The context in which change takes place is also very important. The change agent and the client system need to identify and review the internal and external forces that foster or resist change at the onset as well as throughout the process. These forces might be seen as biological, psychological, social/cultural, historical and/or environmental. This is a particularly creative part of the change agent's work, whether the interventionist is facilitative or directive, and is basic in the selection of intervention tools and techniques for effective, sustainable change.

Intervention for Socioeconomic Development

As an example, let's consider intervention in the area of socioeconomic development. Development is defined here as a planned and comprehensive economic, social, cultural and political process, in a defined geographic area, that is rights-based and ecologically oriented and aims to continually improve the wellbeing of the entire population and all of its individuals. Economic development is the process of raising the level of prosperity through increased production, distribution and consumption of goods and services. Social development, on the other hand, refers to the complexity of social dynamics (the interplay of social structures, processes and relationships) and focuses on:

1. The social concerns of the people as objects of development and
2. People-centred, participatory approaches to development. The individuals would be actively involved in open, meaningful participation in development and in the fair distribution of benefits.

The comprehensive definition of development (or socioeconomic development) has three components – social development, economic development and environmental protection.

According to James Midgley, it is not a new idea to link social interventions and economic activities. In the late 1800s, for example, the volunteer workers of the Charity Organisation Society in England helped impoverished individuals find employment and start small businesses. In 1954, the British authorities adopted the term "social development" to link social welfare and community development to the economic development efforts in their colonies. The development processes, however, were not smooth or effective for a number of reasons. For instance, post-colonial development efforts often were centralised, top down approaches and development strategies in the Global South frequently focused only on economic growth for the benefit of national elites and transnational corporations.

There has been a growing recognition that economic development is a source of dynamic changes and generates wealth, but it will not, by itself, create prosperity for all. Intervention is required for socioeconomic change. Four points about intervention, as outlined below, are specific to socioeconomic development intervention:

1. *Harmony between social and economic interventions*: Social interventions should contribute in a positive way to the economy, and economic interventions should improve the quality of people's lives. A review of this situation is particularly important when one or more parts of a client system assume that economic changes will inevitably lead to social progress.
2. *Rights-based development*: Rights-based development emphasises the primacy of human rights law and people's ability to determine or strongly influence state policies. Including "rights-based" in a definition of development is one way of underscoring the importance of human rights in the development process.
3. *Protection of vulnerable populations*: These groups could include refugees, immigrants, victims of war, racial/religious/ethnic minorities, children, elderly and women. Women, for instance, have been gaining formal rights but this progress has not been matched by an improvement in their quality of life. The hidden barriers and ceilings to women's participation are still in place and the shift to more responsibilities for

families and communities has been an increasing burden for women.

4. *Appropriate level of intervention*: Many countries have had, at some point, national social planning agencies but the planning approach has weakened or been abandoned over the years because of factors such as indebtedness, lack of resources or political pressure from groups that were politically conservative because they thought that planning should not be done at a national level as well as from advocates of community-based planning. These advocates thought that state agencies often had an inappropriate, top-down style of planning. Development requires a participatory approach to planning; because the levels are interconnected, it is necessary to involve, to some extent, most if not all intervention levels.

Clinical sociologists who work on socioeconomic development issues recognise the need to be able to have access to policymakers and/or work with those interest groups that can effectively lobby for change. Interventionists have to be knowledgeable about the substantive areas under discussion and be culturally competent, able to effectively work with teams and knowledgeable about how to encourage public participation and media coverage. They recognise the importance of working on all relevant intervention levels to help foster an effective, sustainable, rights-based development process.

Theories and Research Methods

Clinical sociologists frequently have training in more than one discipline and a great deal of experience in working with intervention teams whose members have a variety of backgrounds. Because of this, clinical sociologists integrate and use a broad range of theoretical approaches and, if they conduct research or collaborate with researchers, also have exposure to or use a range of research methods. Epistemology, theory and research methods are linked. The kind of research methods used and the ways in which they are used will generally reflect the epistemology and theories held by the interventionist or those responsible for the intervention.

Research Methods

Clinical sociologists who conduct research use a wide variety of research methods and techniques such as participatory action research, geographic information systems, evaluations, focus group analysis and surveys. But clinical sociologists probably are best known for their case studies. Case studies involve systematically assembling and analysing detailed, in-depth information about a person, place, event or group. This methodological approach involves many techniques such as document analysis, life histories, in-depth interviews and participant observation.

Sometimes the cases are directly related to intervention work (e.g., a critical evaluation of program outcomes) and sometimes they are analyses of situations (real or based on reality) that will be of assistance to policymakers and administrators who are considering interventions. An example of that kind of work would be the analysis of the tobacco control interventions in "Well City" which included a list of lessons/ intervention considerations.

Theories and Models

Clinical sociologists, in good part because of their interdisciplinary training and work experience, use a wide range of theories. Among the theories frequently used by clinical sociologists: grounded, standpoint, multicultural-liberationist, systems, conflict, interactionist, critical and social exchange. Theories, implicitly or explicitly, are a basis for the models that explain how practitioners should function. According to Lang and Taylor, "models represent appropriate, aspirational, or best practices; they include guidelines for implementing them."

Clinical sociologists use existing theory to formulate models that will be helpful in identifying and understanding problems and also to identify strategies to reduce or solve these problems. Clinical sociologists also have shown that practice can have an influence on existing theories and help in the development of new ones. Each of the areas of practice can have their own models. It might be useful to take one area of practice – mediation, for example - and briefly examine the theories and models used by practitioners coming from different disciplinary backgrounds.

Mediation

Mediation, an area of expertise for some clinical sociologists, is a semi-structured, creative process in which one or more impartial individuals assist disputants. Mediators usually "learn a particular model and approach to mediation that encompasses guidelines, rules, procedures, and ways of understanding mediation practice".

Stage models are frequently used for organisational and community disputes. One such model, according to Jennifer Beer, has seven stages: opening statement; uninterrupted time for each person to speak; exchange; setting the agenda; building the agreement; writing the agreement and closing. Beer notes that separate meetings (small caucuses of some participants and/or the mediator and one or more participants) can be held at any time during the mediation. Another model, developed by Jacqueline Morineau, has three stages: theory, crisis and catharsis. Lascoux discusses a six-stage model with the first stage (creation of context) being "the most delicate and the longest." Haynes describes a five-stage family mediation model in which the mediator continues to cycle through the stages as often as necessary. During the first stage of this model, the mediator gathers, verifies and shares the data.

The stages in the stage models are frequently not distinct and will differ depending on factors such as culture; mediator, sponsor or party preference; specialisation; type of mediation and complexity of case. Some models may be ones in which no or few stages are specified or expected while other models have many stages. A complicated community environmental dispute, for instance, might begin with a period in which possible participants are identified and discuss the likelihood that all will participate in some kind of conflict analysis. This group might then hold a series of facilitated sessions in which procedures are developed and approved that would be used in a mediation. All this preliminary work would take place before what one might think of as the actual mediation. Christopher Moore, in his 12-stage model of mediation, devotes the first five stages to the period *before* the meetings to discuss the problem/ situation actually takes place.

Even if there was one model that could be used in all or most situations, there can be differences, at times, in the order of the states or in the length of time devoted to certain stages. There also will be differences in the way mediators and organisations that hire mediators rely on the models. The models each provide a general flow for cases but there will be a range in their use by practitioners - from those who rigidly follow a prescribed model to those who would not think of doing so.

The model or models used by American mediators are related to their approaches to mediation (participant-centred, solution-oriented, transformative, narrative and humanist/ integrated process). The models and approaches are grounded in theory. The theories would include those that are biologically-based (e.g., social Darwinism, ethology, sociobiology), focused on the individual (e.g., social learning, social exchange, psychotherapy) and focused on social/political situations (e.g., sociotherapy, systems, conflict, multicultural/liberationist, land ethic, humanism).

The humanist/integrated process (HIP) approach, the preferred approach of some American clinical sociologists, emphasises humanism, cultural competency, empowerment, respect and creativity. The mediator is reflective in continually assessing the interaction between/among the parties and among the parties and the mediator. The HIP mediator is participant centred but flexible in terms of stages and approaches. Depending on the circumstances of the mediation, the mediator may integrate aspects of any of the other mediation approaches (e.g., transformational, solution-oriented).

Frequently the HIP approach is multicultural/liberationist and based on a particular view of humanist theory. This humanism, focusing on free and responsible individual choices, includes respectful consideration of the natural environment and fits very well with Aldo Leopold's land ethic theory. Leopold indicated that "a land ethic changes the role of Homo sapiens from conqueror of the land-community to plain member and citizen of it."

Mediation, like other areas of clinical practice, has a variety of theories and models that may be used as guideposts. Creative dispute intervention means that theories, models and intervention strategies may be adjusted as the work proceeds; new or refined models, theories and intervention strategies are seen as a normal part of the creative process.

Global Clinical Sociology

Interest in clinical sociology has been growing in a number of countries. For example, French is the predominant language of many, if not most, of the current international clinical sociology conferences and books and articles have appeared with clinical sociology in the title in France and French-speaking Canada. The French-language clinical sociologists emphasise clinical analysis although some also are involved in intervention. They have a solid international network and have done an excellent job of attracting non-sociologists to that network. Their literature is substantial. Particularly notable is the work of Jacques van Bockstaele and Maria van Bockstaele; Robert Sevigny; Eugene Enriquez; Vincent de Gaulejac and Shirley Roy and Jacques Rheaume. The van Bockstaeles, who have worked as organisational consultants for many years, have published a book on socio-analysis and Jacques Rheaume and his collegues in Montreal are completing a book on the development of clinical sociology in Quebec.

For many years, Italians have hosted clinical sociology conferences, published clinical sociology books and articles and hosted numerous clinical sociology training workshops. If one is interested in learning about clinical sociology in Italy, one would want to review the work of Michelina Tosi and Francesco Battisti and publications by Lucio Luison.

Clinical sociology also is found in other parts of the world such as Greece, Brazil, Mexico, Japan and Malaysia. According to Yuji Noguchi, clinical sociology was first noted in Japan in 1994 and the first textbooks were published in 2000 and 2001. Noguchi says there still is discussion of the definition and theoretical frameworks, but the Japanese also share with Americans "a practical concern with problem solving." Japanese clinical sociology focuses on health and illness. In Malaysia, Halim Wan has started a professional organisation of clinical sociologists and is writing two books about the field. One of the volumes focuses on the development of clinical sociology and the other is about his extensive experience as a practitioner.

The international development of clinical sociology has been supported primarily by three organisations. The clinical sociology division of the International Sociological Association (ISA) was organised in 1982 at the ISA world congress in Mexico City. Clinical sociologists also are members another ISA section the sociotechnics sociological practice division. The other major influence is the clinical sociology section of the Association internationale des sociologues de la langue francaise.

American scholar practitioners, with their focus on intervention, have had a strong role in the development of the field of clinical sociology, but now are only one of many national influences shaping the emerging global specialisation. Worldwide, clinical sociologists continue to be interested in health care, quality of life, national social policy, organisational development, conflict intervention and individual development. More recent clinical areas of analysis, research and intervention include public participation, environmental protection, tourism, globalisation, rights-based socioeconomic development, and security all major issues in an at-risk world.

3

Cyber Sociology

"Cybercultures" serves as a shorthand term to include the networked, electronic, and wired cultures of the last three decades of the twentieth century. Other terms used include Internet studies, new media studies, digital media studies, digital culture studies, networked culture studies, information society studies, and contemporary media studies. The number of terms available to choose from indicates the Tran disciplinary nature of the field.

Cyberspace is also often called "information space" or "technospace". It is defined as "new social spaces fostered by computerenabled automated information and communication technologies (AICTs)". Cyberculture, as defined by the Encyclopedia of New Media, refers to "cultures formed in or associated with online social spaces".

Technically, "ICTs" include the collection, processing, storage, retrieval, and transmission of information in the form of text, video, audio, and graphics for economic, social, cultural, scientific, and political applications among individuals, groups, institutions, and nations. Information is converted into digital form and transmitted through increasingly convergent technologies where the personal computer, the phone, the Internet, and multimedia provide an integrated form of communication.

Cyberspace is also produced by multimedia applications such as mobile phones, electronic surveillance, and video conferencing. As more people surf the Net via iPhones and the cell phone becomes ubiquitous across the world, "cyberspace" itself has to be redefined. While virtual reality (VR) environments are fashionable for academic studies of cyberculture, they do ***not***, as Lisa Nakamura rightly points out, constitute the bulk of the experience of users of digital technology. Blogs and games, the homepage and social networking, online shopping and chat are more central to the common and the everyday, and if cyberculture studies hopes to draw from the frameworks of cultural studies which is grounded in the everyday it must turn to the popular Internet rather than the exotic environments of VR labs. There is no *one* cyberculture: because it has been so normalised, appropriated, altered, and domesticated into our everyday lives, there are in fact many cybercultures, of which the Internet is perhaps the most common. With mobile telephony and 3G phones, we have cybercultures in the palm of our hands and access to a virtual world.

Cybercultures are a "formation" which is linked to and embedded in material contexts and conditions. These conditions generate, inform, and even govern the nature of cyberspace, its production, expansion, and application. This means that we need to see cybercultures as any other cultural process/ event/structure, positioning, representing, influencing, and affecting race, class, gender, sexuality, and identity in particular ways. Cyberculture studies extends the work of cultural criticism and cultural studies by locating cybercultures as affected by and affecting these actual identities of individuals.

As the Internet, digital media, and cybercultures become "normalised," domesticated, and integrated into the everyday life of individuals and organisations, we need to understand how they affect that everyday life. Do all sections of society acquire the same degree (or nature) of control over virtual worlds and representations in these worlds? Are cybercultures gendered in the everyday lives of individuals? These questions are important because they reveal cybercultures to be a set of social practices. Cybercultures are, like film or television or sport, cultural formations that have their own cultural politics (of race, economy, class, or gender).

In order to "read" cybercultures, we need to see them as techno*culture*. While cultures determine what forms of technologies develop, these technologies, in turn, shape cultures. Technology, in other words, is not merely an effect or cause of culture but is *both*: it determines and is determined by the culture in which it develops. There is a spirit and logic of a particular technology that feeds off and into the community and culture. In other words, one needs to locate any technology *within* its particular *material* contexts. All technology, in this reading, is context-bound. Technologies are not simply out there: they become a part of our lives, are incorporated into the everyday. They are "domesticated" and, in turn, inform the way we run our everyday lives *around* them. Technologies, in addition to possessing instrumental value, also possess cultural values of prestige, safety, and sociability values that increasingly inform the design and development of technological devices.

The mobile phone needs to be more than a phone – it now has to serve as a personal diary, a health indicator, an entertainment device, and a status symbol. Designers therefore need to account for those values that have become important and rendered desirable within a culture, and incorporate those into the "thing." The "thing" is therefore more than that: it represents aspirations, lifestyle choices, cultural values, sentiment, and functionality. A cell phone must be both efficient and attractive: one is the value of *productivity* and *instrumentality*, the other is *symbolic* and *cultural*. The ideology of individualism informs the design of the desktop and email. Hence Microsoft labels its software program MS *Office*, thereby suggesting that it serves a particular class of people (who work in offices rather than, say, at masonry or gardening). These are not technical details, they are social and cultural values. The name of the software program is rooted in real material contexts where, increasingly, office work and services or "knowledge work" are given more value than other forms of labour in the informational economy.

Similarly, technologies of databasing are governed by factors that are nontechnological such as transborder access of information, security concerns, questions of privacy, human capital, or conflicts. Finance, the market, and cooperative policies between nations are also factors in the operational mechanisms of databases. Where earlier the state or the archive controlled information (tax details, criminal records, population, birth and death records), digitisation opens up the possibilities of archivisation to various actors. The logic of technology is thus often a sociologic.

We also need to ask whether men and women use digital technology in the same way. Does digital culture significantly alter identities in the real world where race, ethnicity, class, and gender continue to remain key markers? Such questions are not about virtual worlds or electronic communication or digital gameworlds: they are about the lived experiences of humans around the world.

Cybercultures are driven by material considerations of profit and power, and affect people in their real lives. All this goes to show how technology must always be seen as contextual, and treated as technoculture where meanings, values, and functions are integrally associated with the object. Culture and technology are therefore not distinct but linked.

Cybercultures emerge in the context of large-scale movements of people, miscegenation of cultures leading to hybridised forms, dispersed forms of production, and, most importantly, the widespread "flows" of capital. Capital's increasing moves to control the production, circulation, and consumption of commodities demands greater connectivity but also increasing controls.

Nongovernmental organisations (NGOs) research and link up with dispersed locations in their bid to effect changes in societies across the world. Migrant workers (mainly from Asia) built Silicon Valley, which eventually headquartered the research and commercial aspects of the computer revolution. The Internet emerged out of a US Department of Defence project. The entertainment industry sought to spread as widely and as deeply as it could, and the demand for greater, continuous, and more varied entertainment fuelled Walkmans, mobile technologies of film, and entertainment on the move. Globalisation, arguably the most decisive social/political/cultural aspect of twentieth-century culture, would not be possible without ICTs.

The Information Society

The "information society" can be defined as an order where there is

1. Increasing convergence of telecommunications and computing in everyday life, production, consumption, and politics;
2. An increasing importance of knowledge production;
3. An ever-increasing number of people involved in information work;
4. Networking of cities and spaces via flows of information (through telecommunications networks); and

5. An increasing amount of information *exchange* in the form of text, images, and sound.

The world has moved on, according to Daniel Bell's famous thesis, to the state of a "post-industrial" society. This shift is characterised by a reduction in industrial labour and a concomitant expansion of the service industry and a "knowledge society." Instead of labourers and workers we have "professionals," a "new intelligentsia" who seek to fulfil the information needs of the post-industrial society. The information society is intimately linked to globalisation. Globalisation is marked by the following features:

1. The expansion of trade in terms of trading relationships and movement of capital.
2. The development of transnational and global communication networks.
3. The diminished role of the nation-state even within its territorial space.
4. The rise of transnational cultural, economic, and political networks (such as the International Monetary Fund, Greenpeace, and Amnesty International).
5. The increased presence of Western consumer products and cultural artifacts, or what is often called the "McDonaldisation" of the world.

A new international division of labour facilitated by the telecommunications networks is visible in the age of globalisation. Global and offshore finance, outsourced work, multiple and fractured sites of production and consumption, and cultural flows are all enabled by the new ICTs.

The increasing dependence on information collection, processing, and distribution in a globally connected world has led to what Manuel Castells characterises as an "informational order" where the "flows" of information are of paramount importance. Cash flows are in fact information flows.

Technocapitalism and Cybercultures

Globalisation has been enabled by the advent of highspeed communications. Capitalism is increasingly becoming *technocapitalism* because the distributed nature of production, marketing, and consumption demands technological linkages and synchronous, 24/7 communications. Manuel Castells's work, as noted above, has demonstrated how the flows of information assume prime importance in this context. It is the management of information and financial flows that becomes the key focus in globalised technocapitalism.

As an example of such flows in the age of informationalism, consider Amazon.com. Amazon.com is arguably the most successful.com company today. Having survived the.com bubble burst in 2000–2001, it has expanded astronomically since its founding to become the foremost example of the linkage between globalisation, technology, and commerce.

Amazon.com is a unique company because of the way it localises itself. While its name and web address are now a brand, the company uses a flexible screen geography as Martin Dodge points out, the screen is a micro-geography so that local cultural and even personal elements can be incorporated. This makes it a local "firm" for users, something like the old grocer down the street, because the Amazon.com website is designed for and by the individual user, to the extent that the entire website is in the local language. Amazon.com is a Seattle-based company, but it is a transnational one whose flows and networks of finance and product distribution are global. Finally, even if Amazon.com does not own a physical store, it possesses a massive material infrastructure "substrate" to its website.

In addition to the theme of commerce and globalising ICTs, other features draw our attention here. Increasingly, people, classes, and territories that are not significant for the informational society are excluded from the wired world. The old, African nations, the mentally ill, and inner-city ghettoes are all peripheral to the globalising ICT movement. Just as capitalism was driven by the logic of capital accumulation and production, the high-tech age is driven by the need to possess ever greater amounts of information, and those who lack this (the "information poor") are left out of the race. Human labour power is, however, central to this new condition as well. Automation, information gathering, and labour are, argues Douglas Kellner, analogous to mechanisation in the earlier age of capitalism. In such a new capitalist order, the information poor fall through the gap.

Globalisation has very clear material consequences from profits to poverty and these are the conditions in which cybercultural forms, the informational economy, and ICTs exist and function.

Materiality and Corporeality

Studies of cybercultures such as that by Howard Rheingold celebrate virtual worlds for enabling the user to transcend geography and the body. Disembodiment, it is argued, is the overcoming of the body's limitations in favour of pure rationality and thinking. When Hans Moravec describes the body as "mere jelly", the key assumption is that information, thinking, and the mind are more significant than the body (even though cyberpunk is often critical of such views of technologised bodies, which often represent cultural anxieties about "informatisation"). The theme of disembodiment and bodily transcendence also forms the basis of the work of cyber- and digital artists like Stelarc. The body's limitations disease, degeneration, aging can be overcome through technological prosthesis. What we have is an *augmented* body: the posthuman.

Subjectivity and identity are no longer rooted in the body. Subjectivity in the posthuman condition is "dispersed throughout the cybernetic circuit". The incorporation of data from the outside into the body and the extension of consciousness into other spaces through VR or cybernetic circuits suggests that consciousness need not be confined to the body. However, while the transcendence of the body's limits is attractive since in some respects it does away with degeneration and aging it poses its own problems. Since suffering, politics, and emancipation continue to be *embodied*, the transcendence of the body does not help. Besides, for women, minorities, and the socially marginalised, claims for justice must remain rooted in the *body* rather than in pure, disembodied, and abstract "consciousness."

It is also significant that any technology of corporeal transcendence can only be built through rigorous labour by very material bodies, often working in sweatshops and for low wages. On the more positive side, new developments in computer-driven prostheses and medicine can significantly improve the functions and therefore material life of differently abled, aging, and diseased bodies.

Digital Divide

It is a truism that resources and power are not evenly distributed among the people and nations of the world. The rise and rapid expansion of ICTs are subject to a similar condition of unequal access between, for example, Africa and Europe, leading to a "digital divide." Focusing primarily on Internet access as the focal point of networked culture, Pippa Norris suggests a three-layered digital divide: the *global divide*, referring to the divergence in Internet access between developed and developing nations; the *social divide*, referring to the divergence between Internet access and use between classes and sections within a particular society (termed "information rich" and "information poor"); and the *democratic divide*, referring to the difference in the nature/quality of use of the Internet and digital resources between users. An example of this digital divide, identified in September 2007, would be the rate of Internet use and population penetration:

1. Africa has 14.7 percent of the world's population and constitutes 3.5 percent of the world's total Internet use (though it shows the largest expansion of Internet use 874.6 percent between 2000 and 2007).
2. Europe has 12.3 percent of the world's population and constitutes 27.2 percent of world Internet use.
3. North America has 69 percent Internet penetration, even though it has only 5.1 percent of the world's population.
4. Within Asia, Afghanistan constitutes 0.1 percent of total users in Asia, and has 2.0 percent of its population wired. India constitutes 13.1 percent of total Internet users in Asia, and has 5.3 percent of its population wired. Hong Kong has 68.2 percent of its population wired, and Japan 68 percent.

The difference between users and Internet penetration is obvious from the statistics. However, the significance of this difference is not so obvious at first, and it is the nature of the digital divide that concerns us here in terms of agency, ability, and questions of power and identity.

The First World is increasingly "informatised," networked, and linked. The digital age in such cases might mean, for particular segments of society, *increased access* to health services (networks of healthcare workers, data, and expertise), education (distance learning, access to information), financial transactions (e-commerce), and civic engagement (online voting, public debates via the Internet). The personal computer and faster and cheaper connectivity alter the in dividual's or community's role in the public sphere, enabling individuals and communities to access information and therefore improve their lifestyles or conditions.

Within First World nations, however, racial and class inequalities exist in access to and use of digital resources: there is differential access for blacks and Chicano/ a populations, and there is a rural–urban divide. The digital divide therefore needs to be studied at the level of the nation, the institution, and the individual. White students without a PC at home might access the Internet in other places more than non-white students. Studies have shown that Caucasian children surf for humour and entertainment sites while African American children of the same age group often look up information, education, and race support activities, though the popular Internet seems not to show a racial divide among children.

However, the digital divide is not merely a question of access to a PC or the Internet. Other cultural factors such as language (the lack of English, for instance; among immigrants in the USA, who may need to find information about social welfare or laws) can determine the number of users. This brings us back to the question of *power* in debates about the digital era. The Internet arose as an elite, selective formation and expanded into a full-fledged technoelitism determined by capital. Differential access, infrastructure, and costs determine the power of individuals to spend time on the Internet or to form online communities. Questions of authority, including peer review, control of resources, respectability, and policymaking capability their *genealogy*, to be accurate continue to inform cybercultures. These are ultimately questions of power and are precisely the areas where subcultures like hackers make their *agency* known.

Cyberculture studies' emphasis on the political economy of ICTs pays attention to issues of power and justice, the social agenda, and the political consequences of ICTs. Cyberculture studies calls attention to the raced, gendered, and classed nature of the "information revolution," the effects of this revolution on different sectors of society, and the question of power that determines the course of the revolution.

E-Governance

A key element in the digital divide debate is that of e-governance. Enthusiasts of digital democracy argue that the expansion of the Internet and digital resources will enhance civic participation, communications between citizens and the state, and the state's responses to society. E-governance includes increased public services ranging from community health care to civil servants' responses to requests for local consultations. Where face-to-face meetings are difficult and expensive to arrange, networked cultures can fruitfully enable such interactions in cyberspace. Government and public service websites offer information about official processes, often for free. Research organisations have collated data from various countries and found that the UK and USA possess the highest number of government webbed operations.

The two key aims and principles in cases of e-governance are "informational transparency" and "communication interactivity". The first describes the amount of information offered by the government, while the second describes interactions between state agencies and citizens. Online publication and availability of official reports, administrative decisions, and policymaking processes could help citizens in voting, making representations to the state, understanding policies and regulations, and perhaps even making their own interventions. It could be argued that the process of e-governance seeks to increase transparency and enhance state–citizen communication. However, the mere availability of information does *not* ensure the quality or reliability of the information supplied.

Cyberculture studies is concerned with the role of ICTs in the formation of legislation and the impact of new technologies in the realm of political participation. Proceeding from its concern with the political economy of ICTs, cyberculture studies addresses issues of empowerment, control, political uses (and abuses) of new technologies, national identities, and new ways of citizenship participation in politics and governance.

Role of Civil Society

With their potential for greater connectivity both within the community and between the community and the state, digital technologies have been commonly understood to enhance civil society. NGOs, activists, experts, and the general public now have greater access to information and greater chances of linking together to lobby. In 1999 during the World Trade Organisation (WTO) meeting in Seattle, environmentalists, activists, anti-globalisation protesters, and labour unions came together to demonstrate. The International Civil Society website provided an hourly report on the demonstrations reports that were distributed/telecast to hundreds of NGOs worldwide. Such examples are taken to indicate a strengthening of grassroots activism.

Social movements increasingly use the Internet as a medium of communication, propaganda, and political mobilisation. Citizens' forums, state feedback mechanisms, and NGOs use the Internet and digital resources to strengthen their infrastructure, responses, and public interface.

Social movements with various focal points the environment, anti-racism, gay and lesbian rights, anti-globalisation, women's empowerment have turned to the Internet as a space where solidarities might be forged and reinforced. Listservs, online petitions, and emails have solicited funding and political support. People who might otherwise have refrained from street protests or similar expressions of political opinions swell the ranks of online petitioners. Political protests have gone online in other, more "damaging" ways blocking and defacing government websites, for instance in order to attract attention (an example of this is pro-Palestine hackers defacing American pro-Israel websites in 2000). More importantly, there is the possibility of globalising the movement itself because transnational linkages between organisations and groups are helped in their processes and public outreach programs by the medium. Protest and social movements are able to transmit their ideologies, beliefs, and values to a greater number of people and over larger territories than ever before. Manuel Castells suggests that the slow erosion of traditional political formations such as the political party and the trade union has enabled loose coalitions, ad hoc assemblages, and spontaneous mobilisation to "substitute" for permanent and more organised structures.

Citizen networks in towns and cities are now able to offer greater opportunities for the community and individuals to participate in debates about issues concerning them. University networks, local community networks for senior citizens, and help groups reach out to greater numbers through the medium of their websites, helplines, feedback mechanisms, and online discussion forums. Democratic processes of feedback, opinions, and debate are facilitated by the new ICTs, marking a whole new era for civil society and enhancing political, social, and cultural agency from opinion dissemination to political action.

However, it should also be kept in mind that such online political action might not have a *material* effect (the protests against the WTO or the Myanmar regime, for example, did not alter the course of events). There is a risk that cybercultural resistance or activism remains at the level of the virtual, with little or no impact upon the real world. A false sense of social commitment and empowerment emerges in online political activism – putting one's digital signature to an online petition is not the same as barricading a civil servant or blockading the road to obstruct traffic in order to articulate demands. We would also do well to recognise the irony that online petitioning could lead to a *withdrawal* from the material political demonstration that attracts attention and action.

With its interest in the political economy and material bases of information technology and digital cultures, cyberculture studies explores the ways in which organisations, individuals, campaigns, and civil society in general have appropriated or resisted ICTs.

Governing Cyberspace

While the digital era may herald improved citizen–state interaction through a democratising technology, at least in post-industrial societies, cyberculture and networks are themselves subject to governance and regulation. The "freedom" of cyberspace demands careful examination in the face of the hagiographers of "Internet culture."

Governance concerns not simply the hardware of wires, drives, terminals, and routers but also the consequence of modes of data transfer through codes, or protocols. Protocols (Transmission Control Protocol/Internet Protocol, TCP/IP, and the Domain Name System, DNS) are the material substrate of the Internet's distribution system and can be regulated. A protocol is defined as:

> "a language that regulates flow, directs netspace, codes relationships, and connects life-forms"

Protocols software rules are about power. With the Reston, Virginia, conference and the International Forum on the White Paper (IFWP) in 1998, mechanisms began to be put in place to regulate the "root." The Internet Corporation for Assigned Names and Numbers (ICANN) sought what it called "technical management," but it was in fact an organisational system that initiated "Internet governance." ICANN, Milton Mueller emphasises, is a new international regime formed around the Internet's use, where technical coordination is tied to the regulation of the industry.

Allocation of domain names and categories also involves issues of authority of the root administrator, as Mueller points out. Who decides whether the sites under the label kids really are appropriate for children? Address space allocation is influenced by *technical*, *economic*, and *policy* matters such as the uniqueness of identifiers, efficiency of consumption of the resources, and disputes among assignments of names.

Finally, the commercial interests of AOL or Microsoft drive and constitute the *institutional* governance of the Internet. Copyright laws, domain names, and national security concerns can result in regulation, via protocols, of the inherently uncontrollable, distributed Internet. Even search engines have their own politics and serve the interests of corporations like Microsoft or Yahoo! when they become transformed into advertising domains rather than "neutral" search mechanisms.

Identity in Cyberspace

Contemporary social and critical theory rejects the notion of a stable, unified, and coherent identity, instead seeing identity as the cumulative effect of a series of negotiations, differences, and discourses. In cyberspace identities are malleable as never before. Avatars (online identities), homepages, email IDs, and bodies are all inherently unstable. The disconnect between representation and the body (still a primary source of identity in the "real" world) is, by definition, infinite in cyberspace.

Cyberspace allows one to pick an identity, to masquerade, mimic, and transcend bodily identities and interact with the world as somebody else. In a world where race, class, gender, and sexuality can become obstacles in interactions with the world, cyberspace allows one to *choose* an identity that may have nothing to do with one's "real-life" gender or race. Critics see this as an enabling condition. It allows the closet gay to assert his identity, just as a woman can be involved in the "unfeminine" space of political discussion by masquerading as a man in relative safety. The ugly body can be (re)presented as beautiful and attractive in cyberspace because software allows individuals to choose the colour of their skin, hair, and eyes as well as change their shape. They can play any role they choose because it is difficult to authenticate the identity presented in cyberspace. The individual's subjectivity exists in a dispersed state, where the boundaries of the self are no longer the body or skin.

Identity in cyberspace can be *augmented* by making additions from a variety of choices. This shifting, malleable, and unstable identity in cyberspace is therefore often treated as "fluid." Once again, cyberculture studies' interest lies in the consequences and appropriation of new technologies.

Questions of identity must be further pared down to specific kinds of identity:

1. Racial,
2. Class, and
3. Gender.

Race

In February 2004, *Wired* magazine's cover showed a South Indian woman with her hand partly obscuring her face, dressed in what appeared to be bridal finery. The palm of her hand was inscribed with *mehndi*, a traditional form of bridal decoration in many parts of India. The *mehndi* were actually the text of computer code and instructions. The cover story by Daniel Pink, "The New Face of the Silicon Age," that complemented this visual image dealt with outsourcing and how high-tech jobs were being lost to India.

The visual was accurate insofar as the demographics go: South Indians constitute a sizeable chunk of programmers in the computer industry. The racial and gendered interpretation of the employment and technological scene by *Wired* is, of course, problematic. It not only racialises and genders the technological contexts of business process outsourcing, but also exoticises the "worker." The bridal finery suggests an identity that is full of promise and potential, even as the write-up expresses a definite antagonism and anxiety (Indian programmers are described by Pink as "the cause of fear and loathing," not only because Americans lose their jobs to them, but also, he adds, because they are forced to train these Indian software workers). This anxiety has visible cultural, social, and political consequences: organisations seeking to protect American jobs from the menace of outsourcing have sprung up and people stand for Congress on the anti-outsourcing ticket.

The Internet may facilitate the construction of pseudonymous and anonymous identities. However, this kind of "transcendence" of identity has two aspects that are more problematic than a simple question of "alternate" identities.

1. *Agency*: Do minorities, the disempowered, and the marginalised wish to transcend the crucial matrix of

race, community, and gender, and if they do, or are they capable of doing so?

2. *Representation*: How is race represented on the World Wide Web? This again links to issues both of power and agency. What ideologies inform the "coding" of race on the Internet? Since the Internet is a social process, cultural factors such as race are surely integral to the function, shape, and use of the technology.

There exists a fundamental paradox at the heart of cybercultures, one that fits right into the cultural studies paradigm where corporeality and materiality are central constituents of identity and power.

First, cyberspace is a "raced" medium where disembodiment, transcendence, and fluid identities are the privilege of the white race. When the entire cyberspace universe is made up of reconstituted, simulated, immaterial copies of the "real," where all identities are suspect, and where the difference between "original" and "copy" is blurred, there is a concomitant cultural anxiety about authenticity. That is, in times of uncertain identities, stereotypes of "authentic," unchanging, stable "natives" or the racial Other proliferate. It is in the context of the modified, unstable posthuman that there is a simultaneous search for the recognisable Other. This recognizable Other is often the woman or the black person. People who adopt different identities in cyberspace often have recourse to established stereotypes of gender and race, and thus essentialise and commodify the native, the woman, or the black person because they constitute the unchanging Other against which whites can conduct their posthuman alterations of identity. To adapt Donna Haraway's formulation, the cyborged human functions as the inappropriate/d posthuman only because there are suitably appropriate(d) stereotypes or what Nakamura terms *cybertypes*.

Second, and more worryingly in discourses of fluid identities, avatars, and disembodiment in hagiographies of the digital age, is the denial of embodiment. Real-life practices and experiences, issues of citizenship, the law, and medical science rooted in the body (the citizen is an individual *body*, the law categorizes/incarcerates individual *bodies* based on their actions, medicine treats diseased *bodies*) are very corporeal and material. Transcendence of the body is not an option for those who desperately need the body raced, classed, gendered, sexualised: a solid, recognizable, identified body for the sake of identity. Disembodiment becomes one more technocapitalist mode of *denying agency*. The discourses of multiple, shifting, fluid identities make absolutely no sense to people like minorities, women, or the differently abled because it is their embodiment that needs to be recognised and empowered. Online avatars, however glamorous or perfect they may be, do not erase or alleviate the problems of the offline body in an unequal society.

Finally, the matter of race does not end with the body but has a larger *material* context. It must be remembered that, genealogically speaking, the new ICTs grew out of the labour generated mostly by non-white workers in Silicon Valley. BPO works that enable global networking depend almost entirely on Asian labour. Bill Gates is reported to have stated that Microsoft's Beijing research centre is one of his company's most productive, before adding that when he met his company's ten best-performing employees:

> "nine of them had names I couldn't pronounce"

At this point it is important to see how power operates within technological development and innovation:

1. How does Microsoft control the research and harness the efforts of Asians in Silicon Valley and its offices worldwide?

2. How much of black or brown agency is "free" and how much of it is "owned" by Microsoft?

These questions are of *raced* power equations.

Companies regulate employees' lives, the acquisition of materials, the route taken by research and development, and the marketing of products. Their advertising arm also informs and influences consumer actions. Power here includes financial, social, and political power where the agency of the employee and the consumer is, at least invisibly, directed and controlled by the corporation or the state. In terms of race, the question of power is about the differentials that exist between cybertechnologies of categories such as white/non-white or First World/Third World.

Differential wages and work benefits, profit sharing, and institutional structures are *raced* structures. These are matters of power, identity, and "materials." Software programs written by Asians in Silicon Valley (by 1996 nearly half of the US government's temporary visas for high-tech workers were issued to Indians), BPO units in Indian cities, and the financial centres in First World nations, where decisions about software, copyrights, and company acquisitions are taken, constitute the *raced* social, cultural, and material contexts of cyberspace.

If the *augmentation* of the body is the *apparatgeist* – the spirit of the apparatus– of ICTs and the digital age, this augmentation is rooted in raced and classed structures that govern the design, research, circulation, and marketing of ICTs. Cyberculture studies is alert to this raced and classed nature of the informational economy.

Class

Questions of access, class, and technoelitism shift the focus on to more material matters such as cyberpower.

Cyberpower includes discussions about the freedom to access information (and therefore the politics of access), control over the Internet and the digital domain (hence the question of governance, domain name control, and the infrastructure that produces cyberspace), rights to privacy, and elitism. New York City has the largest concentration of fibber-optic wired buildings in the world, of which Harlem has one; South Central Los Angeles (the site of the 1990s race riots) has none. The difference in digital resources and connectivity in Sub-Saharan Africa and Singapore or Finland is very real and very worrying, especially since crucial areas such as health care and finance are increasingly worked through enhanced connectivity and rapid transmission of data and resources.

Even though these differences in infrastructure are being eroded, there is a considerable demographic, class, racial, and national distinction between the wired and unwired. The distribution, working, and structure of the Internet, mobile phone, router, and.com website that the ordinary person uses is controlled by a technoclass. The high-tech domain remains firmly in the hands of the techno-elite, who are predominantly white and male. In terms of social capital, the world's consumer societies privilege gadgets, connectivity, and speed, thus bestowing higher status upon those who possess all three. Status is also, in a sense, augmented through technoelitism.

Gender and Sexualities

If identities can be reinvented in cyberspace, what consequences does this facility have for gender? How do women use ICTs for their own empowerment? And how do the new environments of information technology portray women? How do women use mobile phones? Do they use them more to stay in touch with their family and homes than for pleasure and work? Do women surf for entertainment and pleasure rather than for information alone? Do women maintain separate, disguised identities in cyberspace that allow them to escape the constraints of their bodies and gender in the real world?

To begin with, there is the key problem of *access*. How many women have access to the wired world? This question needs to be further qualified and fine-tuned by paying attention to the class and racial profiles of women who do or do not have access.

A second problem is the *role of women* in the making of technology and as instruments of technical innovation and change. Feminist critics of technology have pointed out that not only do women *not* have equal rights of access to high tech, they are also rarely involved with the design and research that create the technology. Social constructionists argue that women may serve the purpose of (cheap) labour in the factory or laboratory, but they have little say in how the design is finalised and how the technology is adopted. The third key problem is that of *representation*. Since cybercultural terms such as "matrix" (derived from the Latin *mater*, meaning "mother"), motherboards, and "jacking in" are clearly coded in gender terms, it becomes important to ask how cyberspace becomes gendered. Representations of women as "techno-tards," sexualised beings, and passive users reinforce the gendered power equations from the real world. Feminist readings have found that stereotypes from the real world pervade even passing, camp, and drag on the Internet, thus suggesting that even cyberspace is as gendered as the real world.

Cyberfeminists therefore seek to feminise cyberspace by ensuring that the technology is appropriated for their use. Cyberfeminists seek to disturb power hierarchies by representing themselves in cyberspace, by seeking to control their online identities, and by being upfront with their sexualities. Their popular terminology contamination, virus, contagion suggests a disturbance within the cybercultural domain.

Space and Geography

Twentieth-century critical theory has been obsessed with space. Cybercultures that create alternate spaces and virtual universes, and alter our experience of spatiality and location, have, unsurprisingly, provided fertile ground for geographers and students of space. Numerous spatial metaphors have entered the discourse of cyberspace: information *highway*, electronic *neighbourhood*, virtual *travellers*, *surfing* the World Wide Web, and web*sites*.

Cyberspace's apparent lack of political boundaries lends it a certain glamour and exoticism. As such, our ideas of the nation-state, which are firmly tied to matters of territoriality, have altered. Transnational activities such as global markets, television, knowledge networks, and finance (and including, unfortunately, terrorism) have made it imperative that we modify what we understand as space.

Electronic space or cyberspace is different from the lived environment in significant ways. Where the lived environment, or social space, involves structures and artifacts such as schools, homes, factories, and hospitals that provide the location for social relations, electronic space consists of pictorial, aural, and textual artifacts that enable and mediate social relations. Cyberspace is a network of myriad electronic connections, linkages, interactions, and knowledge sharing. This is the *logic* of cyberspace a system of random or calculated linkages, which themselves are the result of social and cultural values, beliefs, and needs. It is also a space with its own contradictions. ICTs enable us to transcend borders and spaces we can be here and there at the same time while *simultaneously* providing us with precise information (via GPS) about our exact location. It is, clearly, difficult to privilege virtual spaces and virtual life when the real, material, and corporeal remains the centre of surveillance and possible threat. Cyberspace is a site of social relations, a process rather than a thing.

These networks could be of the market, of sociability, or of knowledge sharing, but they are basically *spaces of interaction*. Hence the term "digital formation", which gestures at this socioculturally informed/influenced dimension of interaction as the feature that generates spaces, seems appropriate to describe cyberspace. This means that cyberspace can be subject to the same stresses, strains, and manipulation as "real" social space, since it is embedded in the social.

It is possible, as Douglas Cowan has eloquently argued, that the experience of cyberspace as another place is basically the effect of its visual representation: we believe and imagine we are in the virtual shopping mall because it *looks* like a shopping mall. Indexicality by which we distinguish between places is based primarily on visual cues on webpages and images. Places are organised online for us around the experiences and expectations of/in that place, where the place is the site of possible action. This possible action could also be the platform for the formation of a community.

The Internet itself possesses a geography: its *technical geography* (the telecommunications infrastructure, routers, fibre optic cable networks, transmission hardware), its *user geography* (as manifest in the distribution of users in national/regional statistics), and finally the *economic geography* of Internet production. If the first is governed by corporate houses and business ventures, mergers, and acquisitions, the second is informed by the distribution of users and the third by the profits generated, e-commerce, and techno capitalism. AOL, Microsoft, Ericsson, Nokia, and IBM, with their control over the hardware, software, routers, and, more than anything else, the labour force, concentrate the ICTs in the hands (and coffers) of conglomerates and corporations. The economic geography of the Internet is precisely this selective, metropolitan, First World corporate control over large distances, manufacturing units, peoples, and media services through regulated and carefully plotted flows of capital.

Risks in Cyberspace

New and faster technologies seem to augment risk. Cybercultures generate their own forms of risk: computer crashes, cybersex addictions, privacy invasion, financial fraud, and stalking, among others. Building on Ulrich Beck's influential formulation of a "risk society," Joost Van Loon suggests that we live in a state of anticipating risk. Risk is always *potential*, always waiting-to-happen or " becoming-real", and technoscience is called upon to both conceal and reveal the risks involved.

In the digital age, the environment of "cybernetic space" is constituted and constructed through a process of flows and transcoding between commerce, law, media, and the military. The virtual becomes "real" only when all these elements add up. The system (hardware-software-wetware) and the environment (cybernetic space) constitute each other, where the boundaries between the two are increasingly difficult to find. This is the dialectic of the virtual and the real.

In the case of cybercultures, the risk-aversion ethos is more complicated than a mere outlining of the risk. The appearance of a computer virus poses a risk to systems. An indirect risk proceeds from this recognition: programmers, webmasters, and users send dozens of emails warning people of this potential risk, thereby adding to the load on the system. Thus, not only does the risk element – the virus –proliferate self-replicatingly through the medium, so does the process of risk warning and risk management.

Donald MacKenzie, exploring computer-related accidental deaths, has found that most of the catastrophic accidents may have involved faulty human–computer interaction rather than being "pure" computer failures. MacKenzie suggests that the risks involved cannot be based on past evidence (with computers or other forms of technology) because the incidence and complexity of computerisation are increasing. What is needed to assess risk, he suggests, is addressing not only the computer's technical aspects but also the cognitive and organisational aspects of their "real-world" operation. Developments in medical informatics and medical cybercultures have given rise to their own "brands" of risk. The debate over Nan technological particles in the USA and UK is an example of what is termed "stigmatisation," where popular science writing and fiction (the novels of Michael Crichton, especially his *Prey*, 2002, are a case in point) highlight the risks of nanotechnology. Nanotechnology represents both a highly advanced medical and engineering technology and an invisible risk because of the scale of the objects. Newspaper coverage in the UK, for instance, offered a mixture of hope at the new technology's potential and anxiety over its side effects. Wilkinson and colleagues prove how debates about risk are primarily about public policy and media coverage of the technology. This is the key moment in risk culture where the social implications of any technology occupy the foreground along with the scientific component.

Mediapolis and Space of the Other

The Internet is a medium through which we access distant parts of the world, strangers, and our immediate circle of friends and relatives. It serves an important social and political purpose. As Roger Silverstone envisages it, the mass media is a "space of appearance". The Other appears to us, is made known to us, only on our screens. It enables us to see difference. "Mediapolis" is the "mediated space of appearance in which the world appears and in which the world is constituted in its appearance, and through which we learn about those who are and who are not like us". The screen and the media construct the world for us, even as the medium is itself constructed *by* the world.

This means that we need to ask what "versions" of the Other or the world appear on our screens. How does the Internet orient the world to us and inform our orientation to the world? This set of questions takes us, Silverstone demonstrates, into the realm of ethics; it is:

> because the media provide ... the frameworks ... for the appearance of the other that they, de facto, define the moral space within which the other appears to us, and at the same time invite (claim, constrain) an equivalent moral response from us, the audience, as a potential or actual citizen.

This "moral response" turns the issue of representation into one of possible global citizenship where one is called upon to respond in certain ways to images of suffering, exploitation, and injustice.Minority and alternative voices that manage to find expression help constitute, in Silverstone's argument, a framework for the culture of globalisation, even when the media are governed by global capital. It might enable people to be cosmopolitan a "citizen of the world"with the increasing shareability and accessibility of the world. The stranger, the neighbour, and the Other all appear before us. The mediated space of appearance provides the setting where decisions and judgments are made. This marks the potential for a new civil society or a virtual one, to turn to its synonym where the Other is somebody we can recognize and hope to understand. Within cyberculture studies, the question of ethics, representations, and consumption of the Other on our screens and through information is a key one.

Aesthetics

Apple's Cube was the first computer in history to be displayed in the New York Museum of Modern Art's "Design" section. This transformed it from a machine into an art object with aesthetic appeal and values. Sean Cubitt, David Jay Bolter and Richard Grusin, and Bolter and Diane Gromala have focused on the design of the computer and specific art forms that have appropriated new media technologies.

In 2006, an anthology of essays exploring the possibilities of *aesthetic computing* appeared, marking the beginnings perhaps of a new "project" in the interface of computer technology, aesthetics, and art. Aesthetic computing is the "application of the theory and practice of art to the field of computing". It includes looking at the internal, mathematical structures of computing, the use of software to create art (often called "software art"), or the art of the interface. Aesthetic computing focuses on specific areas such as human–computer interaction (HCI), visualisation, or discrete structures. It also includes looking at the semiotics of the computer such as the location and design of the desktop or the arrangement of the hardware.

In terms of aesthetics and computers, computer art presents a different order of art. Computer-assisted art generates larger philosophical questions about the very *nature* of art. Since most computer artists use commercially developed software, what is the role of the individual "creator"? The computer is not simply an artist's tool because it performs a variety of functions and expands the artist's corporeal and mental abilities. It should therefore be treated as a creative partner of the artist.

While computer art seems to involve a more or less direct incorporation of computers and computing into the production of art forms, a less commonly noticed dimension is the art of the computer itself. The interface the most visible and immediate dimension of computing for the ordinary user can be regarded as a set of *signs*. Signs, as we know, are *cultural*. The interface consists of visible graphics that are the consequence of invisible software. This interface is also, as Nake and Grabowski emphasise, tied to our embodied existence. We perceive these objects that appear on our screen or emerge from our speakers. The interface often changes with a change in the way we operate, through our bodies, the mouse, or the pointer. That is, there is on the one hand the design and art of the "basic" interface that appears on the screen and, on the other, the changing "landscape" of the interface as we negotiate it via the cursor and clicks.

There is also the visualisation from cell biology to outer space we see in news reports and on our screens. Visualisation techniques involve a lot of computing and constitute what Stephen Wilson has termed the "information arts."

Finally, aesthetic computing includes looking at interaction digital design. Jonas Lowgren suggests that digital materials have to be shaped in such a way that users find them "good." Interaction design is the "shaping [of] the digital materials to create conditions for good use". Löwgren identifies 19 use qualities of digital designs, including playability, seductivity, usefulness, surprise, fluency control/ autonomy, elegance, and relevance. These are features to be accounted for and incorporated at the moment of design in order to enable and engage the user to use the interface and the program.

Clearly, cybercultures are a congeries of the economic, the technical, and the sociocultural. Cybercultures involve questions of labour and finance, of political control and power, of the individual and community. Any study of cybercultures must address all aspects of the information society. In order to do so, the approach must be eclectic and multi-sited, dealing with multiple aspects of cybercultures without sacrificing any. Most studies, including introductions such as this one, are a bricolage of approaches.

Thus, while it is tempting to reduce cybercultures to Internet cultures or digital cultures, the increasing convergence of technological forms invites a more broadbased perspective. Several innovative readings of and models for approaching cybercultures have been proposed, engaging the attention of scholars in media and communication studies, cultural studies, sociology, and the humanities.

Ethnographies of Cyberspace

If the Internet is a social formation or a social process, then it follows that, like social and cultural artifacts, it can be examined ethnographically. Following Christine Hine, three key areas for studying the Internet can be isolated ethnographically:

> travel and face-to-face interaction; text, technology, and reflexivity; and the making of ethnographic objects. The first calls for a redefining of what face-to-face interaction means. The Internet is a collection of texts, and the task of the ethnographer is to understand the meanings generated by these textual practices. Finally, the Internet must be treated as a cultural artifact that is linked to offline relationships and contexts, to situate it within larger contexts and see how the two complement each other.

Ethnographies of cyberculture, suggests Arturo Escobar, need to look at the ways in which software and applications are designed as well as used, the creation of online communities and networks, the popular cultural forms of such technologies (from cyberpunk to computer games), the cultural identities that emerge in the new technospaces, and the political economy of cyberculture (especially the relationship between capitalism, global economy, and power). An instance of such an ethnography would be the London School of Economics Young People New Media project studying the use of media by young people, the "individualisation" that results from this, and new forms of leisure, literacy, and sociability.

Apparatgeist Theory

James Katz and Mark Aakhus have developed a theory of *apparatgeist* to convey the logic and spirit of the new communications technology. "*Apparatgeist*," a neologism from "apparatus" (meaning "materials needed for a purpose" and "equipment") and the German *Geist* (meaning "spirit" or "mind"), gestures at the sense of movement, direction, and motive in any technology. It captures the individual and collective aspects of societal behaviour, even as it proposes the imbrication of the cultural situation with the extant technology. The *apparatgeist* of communication technology (Katz and Aakhus are working with mobile phones and personal communications technologies (PCTs), it must be noted) is that of "perpetual contact." Perpetual contact is its logic and its spirit, and governs the premises of design, development, and use of PCTs. It describes the logic of the very language of, say, MS Word.

Katz and Aakhus suggest that there is a sociologic of perpetual contact. People have explicit reasons (form, function, costs) and implicit ones (how others perceive them, beliefs about usefulness, appropriateness) for choosing particular models and designs. The *apparatgeist* of perpetual contact can be used productively to formulate an approach to cybercultures because it

1. Locates technology within the realm of social interaction;

2. Locates individual and cultural factors within technology;
3. Gestures at emotional/subjective and social/impersonal aspects of technologies of communication by foregrounding personal values, folk theories of contact, and even physical pleasure;
4. Emphasises the symbolic aspects of technology by paying attention to issues of class, and social roles and structures such as the family;
5. Links the individual, the material, and the social realms with the hardware–software elements of technology.

This last point takes us back to the social basis for technology by suggesting that the logic of perpetual contact is a sociologic that is rooted in social formations, structures, and therefore ideologies and politics. However, it must be noted that Katz and Aakhus suggest *one* "spirit" or logic here. As we know, "cybercultures" are a composite of many things. They are a world medium of communication and a storage and memory device. They mark the beginning, for some critics, of a global "mediapolis." Their key features include participation, collectivity, and connectivity. The Internet, perhaps the most significant component of popular cybercultures, is ageographical and supposedly democratic. It can also serve as a useful instrument of technocapitalism through surveillance and databanks.

The inherent complexity and myriad forms of cybercultures means that there cannot be any one spirit that informs and influences the domain. Thus, we propose, in addition to the *apparatgeist* of perpetual contact, a second one: that of *augmentation*.

Cybercultures constitute a significant condition of augmentation. This "spirit" applies to the design of cybercultural devices from iPhones that seek to *improve* reception to search engines that pursue *faster* and *more efficient* searches to *faster* computers. *Greater* storage, *enhanced* security, *more efficacious* medical technologies are the keywords in the *culture of augmentation* facilitated by the new technologies.

Greater participation and connectivity among a *larger* number of people more and more of the Other appears on screens today than ever before drive the Internet as a medium of communication, even as the state and the technocapitalist corporate body seek greater control over the medium (and this is the contradictory movement within the culture of augmentation: on the one hand the drive toward wider dissemination and greater freedom; on the other, the move for greater control and regulation). Wired and altered body states seek to *augment* the human in the move towards a posthuman condition. "Perpetual contact" and "augmentation" capture the spirit and logic of contemporary cybercultures.

Cultural Studies

Cyberculture is perhaps best "read" through the lens of cultural studies. The definition of cultural studies given by Cary Nelson and colleagues serves as a starting point here: cultural studies is "committed to the study of the entire range of a society's arts, beliefs, institutions, and communicative practices". A society's culture is taken to mean both a way of life and the set of practices, institutions, and structures of power that constantly negotiate meanings, where, through processes of inclusion and exclusion, some meanings, groups, and "texts" are valorised at the expense of others. Cultural studies involves a *political* reading of structures of power that influence, and often determine, meaning production in a culture, that harness the agency of others (including machines) for their ends, focusing on groups that are disempowered in cultural practices. Cultural studies, therefore, is interested in meanings (of poems, architecture, politics) and the structures in which meanings emerge (government, "literature," academia, industry). More importantly, it focuses on the way meanings are generated in everyday life through mass cultural forms (films, blogs, cookery shows) and social interaction rather than within high culture. Cultural studies foregrounds four basic themes: agency, genealogy, identity and power, and social space and corporeality.

Agency involves questions of the capability of individuals, communities, or objects to assert their will and effect changes.

Genealogy is the location of a particular technology or cultural artifact within specific histories, discourses, and power struggles. It involves questions of need, sentiment, power structures such as the law or medicine, financial profits, and symbolic power. As we have seen above, the new media and cybercultures have emerged within multiple contexts that provide their genealogy rather than a simple linearity of "progress." The Internet began life as a defence strategy planned and constructed by the US government in the eventuality of a nuclear war. Questions of control, therefore, continue to remain central to the so-called democratising technology of cybercultures, where protocols of data transfer, censorship, and surveillance seek to deploy the Internet as systems of control rather than freedom.

Identity is seen less as an essential or core "self" than as the product of social relations situated at the intersection of multiple discourses. Identities are seen as *constructs* rather than as immanent. They are negotiated rather than self-evident. In this view, technology is never neutral because it involves political questions about identity. Thus, questions about technoculture from a cultural studies perspective would be: How does the mobile phone or the Internet help construct an identity? Does technology influence communities' visibility and therefore validate identity?

Finally, a cultural studies approach to technology treats it as a contingent *social agent* that influences the use of space. This involves addressing three kinds of space: public "built" space, social space, and the body's space. The increasing surveillance of public space alters the experience of that space, and involves issues of rights of access and security. Social space includes the realm of politics; in cybercultures, this must be taken to include issues of electronic voting, opinion expression, and state feedback mechanisms, all of which contribute to the social and the political. NGOs and activists use ICTs to promote specific causes, often subversive to mainstream state politics, thus transforming cyberspace into a tool of political counterculture. The use of Internet technologies and digital devices radically alters the way humans use their bodies, augment them, and in specific ways transcend the body's problems and deficiencies. Devices that augment and enhance abilities enable users to exercise greater agency via the body. Penetrative scans, neurological implants, and surgical interventions that rely on transmission of data from and into the body, from the level of the skin to the DNA, are also factors that inform agency. Thus corporeal space is a crucial dimension in analysing the cultures of technology in the digital age.

Cybercultures which, it is worth emphasising, include mobile phone culture, Internet culture, biomedical cultures, digital networks of corporate bodies, the state and NGOs. financial flows, military appropriations and entertainment inform the identity of individuals or communities, determine profits and political responses from the state, and alter the body for a different or better lifestyle.

Thus cybercultures here are a *rhizome*, an *assemblage* of flows where multiple elements are connected, in contingent and dispersed ways, and all of which are embedded in the social and historical contexts of the technology. Cultural and material contexts influence telecommunications networks and cyberspace, and vice versa, in a kind of "recursive interaction". That is, one cannot treat cybercultures of the new ICTs as flows without locating these flows in actual material, cultural, and social conditions. In other words, digital formations are mixes of computer-centred network technologies and social contexts. We will come back to this nature of digital formation in our discussion of cybernetic space below. It is not the technology or a particular element that focuses our attention, but the *connections* of that technology or element with (and within) others. In short, it is not possible to see cybercultures as simply ICTs without reference to questions of:

1. Power (financial, political, cultural, agential);
2. Identity (gender, racial, individual/community, sexual);
3. Ideology (the politics of technocapitalism);
4. Culture (art, sport/games).

Cybercultures are recursively linked to, perpetually rooted in, return to, repeat, and reflect the material. Problems of agency, identity, and power from the domains of everyday material life are also reflected in, extended into, and inform cyberspace and cybercultures. We need to see computer games, online communities, electronic voting, or information databases of the body as always looping back into or connecting with the bodies that make and experience these "virtual," "immaterial" spaces. Dissociation of the virtual from the material runs the risk of depoliticising both its creation and its consequences. This means being alert not only to the cultural politics of the production, design, and dissemination of new media forms, but also to the ways in which people have used and subverted these forms. That is, while there is a politics (and profit) involved in the production of cybercultures, there is also a politics in their consumption. Protest movements that use ICTs, tactical media, feminist cyberpunk, and hacking patches in computer games are often unintentional appropriations of digital cultures. If power relations govern the production of cybercultures (in terms of design, funding for research, production, copyright, and monopolistic control), then power is also something the users possess and deploy in their appropriations of cybercultures.

4

Sociology of Poverty

Poverty has fallen rapidly over the past 40 years, but at different rates around the world. Asia has achieved the most rapid poverty reduction, particularly China, but also India and South East Asia. In contrast, little if any progress has been made in sub-Saharan Africa, where the number of people living on less than one dollar a day the internationally agreed definition of absolute poverty has doubled over the past 20 years.

Historically, rates of poverty reduction have been very closely related to agricultural performance particularly to the rate of growth of agricultural productivity. In simple terms, this indicates that the countries that have increased their agricultural productivity the most have also achieved the greatest reductions in poverty.

In Asia rapid productivity gains, achieved largely through the technological advances of the Green Revolution, provided a 'fast-track' route out of poverty by directly increasing producers' incomes and labourers' wages, by lowering the price of food and by generating new livelihood opportunities as success in agriculture provided the basis for economic diversification.

However, despite decades of investment in new agricultural technology and rural development, hunger and poverty continue to plague large areas of the developing world.

The problem is particularly acute where people depend on rain-fed agriculture, in particular sub-Saharan Africa, where the impact of new technologies has been less apparent and agricultural productivity has generally stagnated and even fallen in some areas.

Achieving the Millennium Development Goal (MDG) of halving the proportion of people living in absolute poverty by 2015 will depend largely on increasing agricultural productivity, which remains perhaps the single most important determinant of economic growth and poverty reduction. This fact is not lost on developing countries or their development agency partners, who are seeking ways to stimulate agricultural development. But serious doubts are emerging as to whether agricultural productivity can be increased where it is needed most, and what part, if any, small-scale farming will play in the future.

Underlying such doubts is a concern that the context in which small-scale agriculture could achieve productivity gains today is very different to that which prevailed in Asia during the halcyon days of the Green Revolution. Inherent differences in production capabilities and quite fundamental changes in the international agricultural context are combining to create a set of circumstances that are probably far less conducive to achieving the type of productivity transformation witnessed in Asia.

Development experts need greater understanding of the links between agricultural productivity and poverty. They also need to assess just how far they have changed and the extent to which small-scale agriculture can remain a ladder out of poverty for millions of poor people living in rural areas.

The State of World Poverty

Between 1981 and 2001, the percentage of the world's population living on less than a dollar a day fell from 40.4% to 21.1%. Even though world population grew by an estimated 1.5 billion over the same period, the numbers of people living in absolute poverty fell by almost 400 million to around 1.1 billion. These figures, while still presenting a picture of massive global poverty, represent probably the fastest rate of poverty reduction ever witnessed. However, the aggregate picture masks a story of variable progress (Table 1).

Table 1. Percentage and numbers of population living below the US $1 per day poverty line, 1981-2001

Region	% of population living below US $1 per day (1993 PPP)			Number of people living on less than US $1 per day (million)		
	1981	1990	2001	1981	1990	2001
East Asia and Pacific	57.7	29.6	14.9	795.6	472.2	271.3
China	63.8	33.0	16.6	633.7	374.8	211.6
Europe and Central Asia	0.7	0.5	3.7	3.1	2.3	17.6
Latin America and Caribbean	9.7	11.3	9.5	35.6	49.3	49.8
Middle East & North Africa	5.1	2.3	2.4	9.1	5.5	7.1
South Asia	51.5	41.3	31.3	474.8	462.3	428.4
India	54.4	42.1	34.7	382.4	357.4	358.6
Sub-Saharan Africa	41.6	44.6	46.9	163.6	226.8	315.8
Global figure	40.4	27.9	21.1	1481.8	1218.5	1092.7

In terms of the proportion of people in absolute poverty, significant reductions occurred in most regions between 1981 and 2001. Progress was most rapid in East Asia, primarily China, where the proportion of the population living in absolute poverty decreased from almost 64% to just 16.6%. Elsewhere progress was steady, with the stark exception of sub-Saharan Africa where the percentage of the population living on less than US $1 a day has increased from 41% to almost 47%.

In terms of the numbers of people living in absolute poverty, the picture is very different. Almost the entire reduction in numbers between 1981 and 2001 can be attributed to progress in China, along with generally small and disappointing reductions in other parts of East Asia, India (where over 350 million people still live in absolute poverty) and the Middle East. But in sub-Saharan Africa, the number of people in absolute poverty has effectively doubled.

Almost all of these changes (both positive and negative) can be explained by a variable performance in tackling persistent rural poverty. Changes in rural poverty figures tend to closely track changes in national poverty figures, primarily because poverty in the developing world is a largely rural problem. As an illustration, the national poverty headcount in India decreased from 36% to 29% between 1994 and 2000, while rural poverty decreased from 37% to 30%.

Moving away from the broad geographical distribution of poverty described above, the characteristics of poverty remain remarkably consistent:

1. Poverty remains a predominantly rural problem: 75% of the world's poor live in rural areas;
2. Poverty is concentrated amongst women, children and the elderly;
3. Poverty is most concentrated amongst vulnerable groups and castes, landless people and ethnic minorities), who often live in remote rural areas. In

Vietnam, for instance, the national poverty headcount fell from 58% to 29% during 1993–2002 for the whole country but remained at 68% in the northwestern hill areas, which are predominantly inhabited by ethnic minorities.

Gobal agricultural Production

Total agricultural production has increased rapidly during the past 40 years. Statistics from the Food and Agriculture Organisation of the United Nations indicate that between 1961 and 2001, global cereal production more than doubled (from 900 to 2,100 million tonnes), far outstripping the rate of growth of population. In the developing world as a whole, per capita food production rose by over 50% between 1961 and 2001. This has ensured that world food prices have declined progressively in real terms; Mitchell and Ingco (1993) report a 78% fall in food prices overall from 1950 to 1992.

Some of this increase reflects an expansion of the area under agriculture articularly in Africa but global yields have also increased over the same period, reflecting an increase in productivity through the introduction of new technologies and a major expansion of irrigation. (It is important to note the fundamental difference between increasing production and increasing productivity). The generally positive global picture masks large and quite fundamental regional variations. These are mapped out in Figures 1 and 2.

Agricultural performance in Asia over the past 40 years has been remarkable. Between 1961 and 2001, cereal production in the region's developing countries increased from 309 to 962 million tonnes, a rate of increase far in excess of population growth. In the same period, the expansion of agricultural land was comparatively modest (from 1.0 to 1.4 billion hectares). The growth in output came mostly from increasing agricultural productivity. For instance, cereals productivity nearly tripled from 1.2 to 3.3 tonnes/ha between 1961 and 2001 in developing Asia. This rate of productivity growth has had an enormous impact on economic development and poverty reduction.

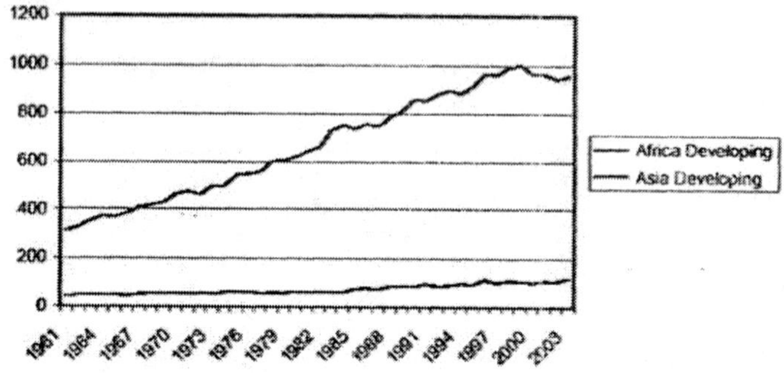

Figure 1. Cereals production 1961-2001, by developing regions (mln metric tonnes)

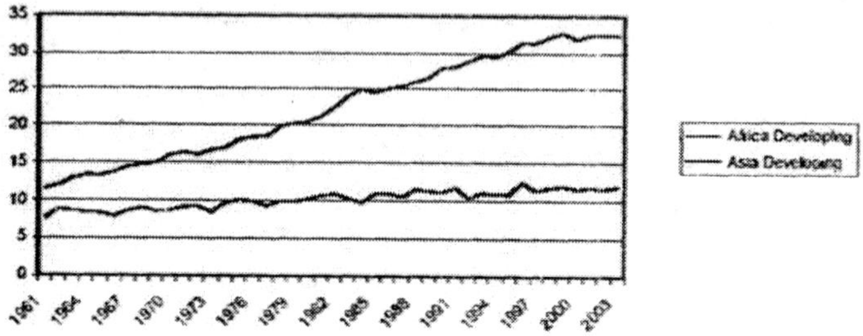

Figure 2. Cereals Yield 1961-2001, by developing regions (1,000 hg/ha)

In contrast, over the same period, the production of basic cereals in sub-Saharan Africa grew only fourfold, from 40 to 116 million tonnes, but the increase in production barely kept pace with population growth. Furthermore, productivity increases were very small.

Thus, while cereals productivity in Africa rose by a half (from 0.8 to 1.2 tonnes/ha), most of the output growth came from using more land and labour, not more productive use of those resources. The area of agricultural land in Africa expanded from one million to one billion hectares during 1961–2001. Weak productivity growth in agriculture had serious consequences for economic development and poverty reduction.

Agricultural Growth and Poverty Reduction

At the macroeconomic level, growth in agriculture has been consistently shown to be more beneficial to the poor than growth in other sectors. Furthermore, analysis reveals that increasing agricultural productivity has probably been the single most important factor in determining the speed and extent of poverty reduction during the past 40 years. Much of this evidence is derived from the Green Revolution in Asia – examples from Africa are noticeably fewer.

With respect to the pro-poor benefits of growth in agriculture, Datt and Ravallion showed that rural sector growth in India reduced poverty in both rural and urban areas, while economic growth in urban areas did little to reduce rural poverty. Warr provided evidence that growth in agriculture in a number of South East Asian countries significantly reduced poverty, but this was not matched by growth in manufacturing. Gallup et al. showed that every 1% growth in per capita agricultural Gross Domestic Product (GDP) led to 1.61% growth in the incomes of the poorest 20% of the population much greater than the impact of similar increases in the manufacturing or service sectors.

Numerous other studies reveal similar results, but emphasise the important qualification that the degree to which agricultural growth reduces poverty is usually conditional upon the initial distribution of assets (in particular land) and the initial level of inequality.

In terms of the role of agricultural productivity in reducing poverty, Thirtle et al., concluded from cross-country regression analysis that, on average, every 1% increase in labour productivity in agriculture reduced the number of people living on less than a dollar a day by between 0.6 and 1.2%. No other sector of the economy shows such a strong correlation between productivity gains and poverty reduction. The routes through which growth in agriculture achieve such a potent impact on poverty are considered below.

Four 'transmission mechanisms' critically link changes in agricultural performance, more especially productivity increases, to progress in reducing poverty:

1. Direct and relatively immediate impact of improved agricultural performance on rural incomes;
2. Impact of cheaper food for both urban and rural poor;
3. Agriculture's contribution to growth and the generation of economic opportunity in the non-farm sector; and
4. Agriculture's fundamental role in stimulating and sustaining economic transition, as countries (and poor people's livelihoods) shift away from being primarily agricultural towards a broader base of manufacturing and services.

Direct Impact on Rural Poverty

Poverty remains a predominantly rural problem and agriculture is generally central to rural livelihoods. Some 70% of the workforce in sub-Saharan Africa and 67% in South Asia are at least partly engaged in agriculture. Therefore, any improvement in rural incomes should if only by sheer weight of numbers have a major impact on poverty. The most useful assessments of the impact on poverty of changes in agriculture are those that follow farming communities' experiences over a long-term period. These studies showed that agricultural productivity gains have raised rural incomes in two ways: by directly increasing farmers' incomes and, of particular importance to the poorest, by increasing employment opportunities and wages.

Farmers' Incomes

De Janvry and Sadoulet estimate that in Asia, a 10% increase in total factor productivity in agriculture would raise the incomes of small-scale farmers by 5%. Acharya and Sophal report that in a 2001 sample of smallholder rice-producing farms in Cambodia, a 10% increase in yields resulted in an 8.8% increase in household incomes in dry season cultivation and a 4.4 % increase in wet season cultivation. Lipton and Longhurst and Hazell and Ramasamy provide similar evidence.

Two further observations on this issue deserve a mention. First, farm incomes have generally continued to rise despite declining market prices resulting from major output expansion. By adopting new technologies and expanding irrigation, farmers have been able to progressively reduce their unit costs of production and so remain profitable. Bangladesh provides an excellent example. Between 1980 and 2000, the real wholesale price of rice in Dhaka fell from 20 Taka to 11 Taka per kg, but over the same period, farmers increased yields from around 2 to 3.4 tonnes per hectare, effectively offsetting the impact of falling prices on their incomes. Second, there is no systematic evidence of smallholders being excluded from technology-led productivity gains. Lele and Agarwal cite evidence from Kenya, where small- and large-scale farmers exist alongside one another, grow the same crops and sell them in the same markets at similar prices. Rohrbach and Makhwaye report that in Botswana a high-yielding sorghum variety released in 1994 had been adopted by almost 50% of the nation's small-scale farmers, who had planted it within two years of its release. In some exemplary Green Revolution countries, the numerical importance of small farms in agriculture actually increased during the technological transformation of agriculture. The International Rice Research Institute (IRRI) reports that in India the proportion of land holdings of less than one hectare increased between 1960 and 1990 from 41% to 59% of the total number of holdings.

Employment

On-farm employment is critically important to poor people's livelihoods, and not just for the landless agricultural labouring is a key means for many farmers to supplement their incomes. Evidence on this subject is primarily drawn from the Green Revolution experience in Asia. In India increasing agricultural productivity associated with the adoption of new technologies clearly increased demand for labour. Furthermore, and of particular benefit to the poor, the majority of the additional labour used was hired rather than family labour. While intensification may involve some labour-economising innovations particularly mechanical threshing new varieties and irrigation have allowed farmers to double- and even triple-crop the land, which has consistently increased labour demand. Significant increases in agricultural wage rates have been recorded in many countries. Saxena and Farrington showed that agricultural labour wages in India rose at a rate of about 3% per annum during the 1970s and 1980s.

Impact of Reduced Food Prices

From the mid-1960s, when Green Revolution technologies

began to be adopted widely, increases in the production of staple foods in most developing countries have comfortably outstripped population growth. Only in sub-Saharan Africa have food supplies grown slower than the population during the past 40 years.

Given this significant increase in per capita supply, and the relatively low elasticity of demand for basic foods, the real world market prices of the major traded grains have been in near continuous decline since the early 1950s. At the individual country level, increased production of food grains has often had a dramatic effect on reducing prices. This is of great benefit to the poor, both in urban and rural areas where many people buy and grow their own food.

Once again, Bangladesh is a good example. Between 1980 and 2000, production of rice and wheat increased from less than 15 to over 25 million tones, increasing per capita availability from 425 to 510 grams per day, despite population increasing over the same period from 90 to 191 million. Real wholesale prices of rice and wheat in Dhaka have consequently fallen dramatically. Thus, poor people in urban areas (and net consumers of wheat and rice in rural areas) need a smaller proportion of their incomes to meet their basic food requirements.

Agriculture's Contribution to Growth

Agriculture remains the economic heart of most developing countries. In Africa it provides two thirds of employment, generates over one third of Gross National Income (GNI) and over half of export earnings. In Asia, where economic growth and diversification have been most rapid, agriculture still provides jobs for 60% of the working population and 27% of GNI. Given agriculture's relative dominance in the economy, it remains the most likely source of significant growth in most developing countries. More immediately, fluctuations in agricultural performance are felt quickly, not only in the agricultural sector, but also in the wider non-farm economy.

Empirical work clearly illustrates the importance of these links. Timmer's analysis of the Kenyan economy showed that between 1987 and 2001, the rate of growth of the non-agricultural sector depended strongly on growth in agriculture. Non-agricultural growth increased by 30% of the agricultural growth rate in the same year, and by 10% of the agricultural growth rate in the previous year. Stern found a similar and significant relationship between growth in the agricultural and non-agricultural sectors during 1965–1980 for a large number of developing countries.

The extent to which changes in agricultural performance influence the wider economy is determined by the size of the 'multiplier'. This is a measure of the extent to which a unit change in income earned in agriculture causes a change in income in the non-farm sector. The size of the multiplier will vary between places and over time, reflecting differences and changes in factors such as the amount of farm income spent on imported goods or saved. Thirtle et al., presents evidence from a number of studies and found multipliers ranging from 1.35 to 4.62.

These studies illustrate that agriculture given its size and the impact of multipliers is the most crucial sector for promoting broader economic growth and has greater 'knock-on' effects than any other sector. The case of Tamil Nadu is particularly interesting in this regard.

It has been argued that multiplier links in Africa are lower than in other parts of the world, and this has important consequences for wider economic development. However, Delgado et al., suggest a more optimistic estimate, with multipliers in excess of 1, indicating that the sector has considerable potential for stimulating broader economic growth.

Stimulating and Sustaining Economic Transition

The relative decline of agriculture's importance to the economy and people's livelihoods is an inevitable and desirable consequence of successful economic development. Rapid economic growth, sustained poverty reduction and substantial wealth creation have historically resulted from economic diversification, with less reliance on agriculture and more on manufacturing and services. However, history shows that most countries cannot successfully industrialise without with first achieving significant improvements in agricultural performance particularly increased agricultural productivity. This holds true for Europe, North America, Japan, and the emerging countries of Asia where industrialisation has been very clearly agriculturally led.

Understanding how growth in agriculture first stimulates and then sustains industrialisation has been the focus of much development thinking during the past 50 years. There is now a good theoretical understanding of how 'agricultural transformation' occurs, and a body of empirical evidence showing its effects. These are described in Lewis and Johnston and Mellor and summarised in Timmer. The studies emphasise a number of key functions provided only by growth in agriculture and that enable broader economic growth and development to occur:

1. Generation of additional demand for goods and services produced outside of the agricultural sector as agricultural-based incomes rise the size of agriculture and its multiplier effects is critically important here;
2. Generation of savings through increased farm incomes which can then be invested;
3. Provision of an available labour force;
4. Provision of affordable food which allows urban areas to develop and maintain wages rates at competitive levels; and

5. Provision of a raw material base to support manufacturing processing of agricultural commodities has often been the first activity to be industrialised in many countries.

Two factors are of central importance to understanding agricultural transformation. Increased productivity (as opposed to increased production) is one key. Broad-based growth and diversification do not happen when agricultural output increases simply by using additional land or labour. Instead, greater value must be added to the land and labour used, i.e. agricultural productivity increases. This is where the historical contrast between Asia and Africa is relevant.

The second factor is that there is a paradox at the heart of agricultural transformation. Investment and growth must begin in agriculture so that the wider economy can go on to outgrow it. There is nothing inherently wrong or undesirable in this transition quite the contrary but agriculture must grow rapidly before the transition can occur. Growth and poverty reduction strategies that aim to bypass agriculture will almost certainly fail and will probably leave the population and economy locked in low productivity agriculture and poverty.

Emerging Issues

Asia's progress in freeing millions from poverty over the past 40 years can be largely attributed to the region's success in increasing agricultural productivity. It was also important that wider circumstances, policies and measures allowed agricultural productivity to occur, and ensured its impact on the wider economy. However, the Asian experience stands in sharp contrast to Africa, where agricultural productivity has been stagnant, rates of economic growth disappointing and poverty is on the rise. Given the above, it is easy to reach the conclusion that without a significant improvement in agricultural performance specifically improving agricultural productivity the outlook for growth and poverty reduction in Africa remains poor. But Africa does not have a monopoly on poverty the largest numbers of poor people live in rural Asia. While many live in remote areas or those that are weakly integrated into the wider economy, many also live in places that have witnessed the full effect of the Green Revolution, but its impact on their poverty has been limited.

Few doubt that achieving the MDG of halving the number of people living in absolute poverty by 2015 will require a significant improvement in agricultural performance, particularly in Africa. But in looking at the future and the likelihood of this being achieved, differences of opinion emerge around two key questions:

1. Do the conditions exist for agricultural productivity to be increased where it is most needed and what part, if any, can small-scale agriculture play in achieving this?
2. Given quite fundamental differences in context between Asia in the Green Revolution and today's poorest countries, will the historical relationship between agricultural growth and poverty reduction continue to hold true?

The view taken on both these questions will have major policy implications.

Increasing the pace of poverty reduction most critically in Africa will depend upon the extent to which agricultural productivity can be increased through a step change in agricultural performance. Simply increasing output at current productivity levels and even this appears difficult in some places will have little long-term impact on growth or poverty. While agreement exists on the need to increase productivity, opinion is divided on whether rapid productivity gains, similar to those seen in Asia during the Green Revolution, can be achieved elsewhere.

Much of this debate focuses on whether the economic and physical preconditions that enabled the Green Revolution to happen exist in those regions as yet untouched by this kind of transformation. Inevitably this debate seeks to contrast Africa's failure with Asia's success, but such a stark characterisation of debate should be approached cautiously. There have been incidences of rapid productivity improvement in Africa and the lives of millions of poor people in Asia remain largely unchanged despite the Green Revolution. However, a qualified comparison of Asia in the 1960s–1970s and sub-Saharan Africa today provides a useful basis to explore these differences.

Differences in the Physical Resource Base

Africa's physical conditions are generally less conducive to improving agricultural productivity than those in Asia. Weather patterns are more unpredictable and soils generally less productive, making agriculture a risky venture. Farmers are often reluctant to adopt new and untried technologies because of the high cost of failure.

Availability of water resources is probably a major factor. Over the past 40 years, productivity gains achieved in irrigated areas have consistently outpaced those of rain-fed areas. For instance, maximum attainable land productivity in Indian rain-fed paddy rice production is 2,516 kg/ha compared to 8,161 kg/ha in irrigated paddy rice production. For wheat production, the respective numbers are 1,786 kg/ha and 4,352 kg/ha. Asia's success in realising the benefits of high-yielding varieties depended critically upon a massive expansion in irrigated area, from 40 million hectares in 1961–1963 to 71 million hectares in 1997–1999. In contrast, only 5 million hectares are currently irrigated in sub-Saharan Africa (most of it in South Africa), a small change from the figure of 3 million hectares irrigated in 1961–1963. While some further increase in irrigation in Africa could be achieved, it is questionable whether Africa's water resources could support expansion on the scale seen in Asia.

Differences in Population and Infrastructure Density

Here the argument is that Africa's population density has not yet reached the level that characterised Asia 40 years ago, and that allowed the efficient provision of rural infrastructure, such as roads and marketing facilities, in Green Revolution adopters. In the absence of such infrastructural support, the probability of small-scale farmers being able to move into semi-commercial production, which would give them the finance and incentive to purchase inputs, is much lower. Provision of rural infrastructure varies greatly in Africa, but even today it remains far below the level seen in Asia 30–40 years ago. Road density is crucial for agricultural intensification. Yet road density in Africa is only 34 miles per square kilometre, compared to 500 in India.

Declining Real Prices and Adverse Terms of Trade

The greatest advance of the Green Revolution took place during the 1960s, within a particular international price environment. Since then agricultural commodity prices have more than halved in real terms as global output has expanded. Although the rate of decline appears to have slowed down since the 1980s, the question remains are prices sufficiently remunerative to encourage farmers to innovate and take risks? Evidence has been found to support both sides.

Pessimists are particularly concerned over adverse movements in the maize fertiliser price ratio, and its implications for increasing fertiliser use, which is the key to raising yields and productivity. They note that while the real price of fertiliser has fallen, the decline in real food prices has been even greater. Optimists note that the link between international and These are all-India averages. Actual yields lie below these maximum values, with large variations in the gap between actual and maximum attainable yields over Indian states. Fan et al., calculate that in India, the increase in agricultural GDP of one rupee spent on road infrastructure is R3.17, compared to only R1.53 and R1.41 return to one rupee spent on education and irrigation, respectively. This high return also appears to hold true in Africa, as suggested by evidence from a 1998 project in Tanzania where the construction of 530 miles of rural roads in 23 districts reduced transportation costs by an average of 40%.

Local prices is often quite weak. Domestic markets, particularly in rural Africa, are poorly integrated into regional and international markets and high transport and distribution costs have, and may well continue to, offset at least some of the downward pressure on local prices caused by falling international prices. This is clearly illustrated in countries where the main staple is imported from neighbouring producers. Here domestic food prices are often more influenced by movements in fuel prices than changes in international commodity prices.

The impact of liberalisation on agricultural trade will have an uncertain bearing on the prices producers will realise. Accession to the World Trade Organisation (WTO) has required several countries to open up their domestic markets to competition. The impact has varied from country to country, from crop to crop and even within countries. Estimates by FAO and the United Nations Conference on Trade and Development (UNCTAD) on the impact of liberalisation on global prices have, in general, predicted an upward impact on world commodity prices, primarily as developed country production declines with the removal of farm subsidies.

Analyses of specific country experiences have shown more mixed outcomes. For example, a recent Oxfam study suggests that a 10% reduction in import tariffs on rice in Senegal resulted in a doubling of rice imports from Thailand. But even within developing countries, liberalisation will have mixed benefits tending to favour more outward-looking regions with better infrastructure and more competitive production systems. A study by Chen and Ravallion of the impact of China's accession to WTO shows that the richest rural regions benefited most, while less well developed regions suffered from falling prices due to increased openness. Predicting the producer price impact of liberalisation will be difficult, but it is unlikely to benefit the poorest agricultural producers and it seems likely that small-scale farmers will face more adverse terms of trade than their predecessors.

Impact of HIV/AIDS

A serious issue of growing importance is the impact of HIV/AIDS on agriculture. The epidemic is already having far-reaching effects on rural households and communities in sub-Saharan Africa. In Asia, although prevalence rates generally remain low, they are increasing rapidly. HIV/AIDS affects agricultural production through both labour and capital effects. Mortality and morbidity effects reduce the availability of labour, whilst the cost of treating and eventually burying those who develop AIDS diverts investments away from agriculture.

Since labour is one of the most important assets that poor people have, significant improvements in agricultural productivity will be compromised by HIV/AIDS. It will become more difficult to develop labour-intensive approaches as a strategy for reducing poverty. In certain regions and countries within Africa and Asia, it is possible that a combination of urban migration and HIV/AIDS may further exacerbate labour shortages, although this could drive up agricultural wage rates.

New Trade Standards

Globalisation, as characterised by the continued expansion in world trade, increasing interdependence of world markets and the internationalisation of world production, presents additional challenges to developing countries. One new aspect is the emergence of standards imposed by national and regional bodies (such as the European Union) for reasons such as food safety. Nationally and internationally imposed food safety and phytosanitary standards represent a new block to export markets for large numbers of developing country producers.

Impact of Changes in Domestic Supply Chains

The impact of globalisation also extends to domestic markets. Changes in supply chains, in particular the increasing presence of large supermarket chains in many developing countries, are creating new demands on quality, quantity and timeliness of products. To meet these new demands, agriculture is becoming increasingly industrialised and capital intensive, making it harder for individual family farmers to access markets. The most marked change has occurred in Latin America, but it is also increasingly evident in Africa. IFPRI estimates that supermarkets now account for up to 30% of food retailing in Kenya. The concern for many is that globalisation is offering opportunities to the rural poor, but as low-paid employees, rather than as farmers.

Changing Policy Context

A common characteristic of successful Green Revolution adopters was the primacy awarded to agriculture in national development efforts, and the role played by the state in supporting agriculture. From the 1950s onwards, Asian governments provided (and often subsidised) key inputs, constructed infrastructure (notably irrigation) and engaged in product markets to ensure stable, predictable and remunerative prices. Through such instruments, governments created a lower risk environment for agricultural innovation and increased its affordability for small-scale farmers with considerable success. In Africa, as Wiggins notes, occasional episodes of rapid agricultural development over the past 30 years have occurred when the state undertook a similar progressive role. In both instances, the approach was supported by the international development community.

Whether the provision of such public services is affordable or can be managed effectively by the state (and the evidence points to this being problematic), are matters for debate. First, it is clear that shifts in international views, particularly those of the international financial institutions, on which most of the poorest countries depend, now rule out many of the policy interventions that assisted innovation and rapid productivity growth in Asia. Just how far this has negatively influenced the diffusion of new technological innovation and slowed progress in increasing productivity is a moot point.

Second, whilst evidence about the precise impacts on agricultural production and agriculture-based livelihoods is very patchy, there may be policy implications associated with state involvement in driving production (in the face of reduced labour capacity) and people's access to food. Governments in Africa may be facing long-term welfare bills to support both food availability and access.

Agricultural Development Strategies

There is probably less of a consensus now particularly amongst development agencies on the best (in terms of impact on poverty and hunger) agricultural development strategy than at any time over the last half-century or longer. This is particularly true of Africa, where an unsuccessful model based on improving performance through technology supported by publicly owned development agencies has been replaced by the equally disappointing response of farmers to the liberalisation of markets. Key points in the debate are considered below.

Where should development efforts be focused to achieve the greatest return in terms of reducing poverty and hunger? Should they be focused on high-potential areas where development options are greatest, or in the poorest areas where there are fewer potentials and options, but where poverty is greatest?

Who should they be focused on? Here the debate sees at least three positions:

1. Accept the demise of the peasantry and work with large-scale farmers whose success will act as a catalyst to generate wealth and jobs for those whose farms are not viable. Proponents of this view identify changes in global supply chains as being major new obstacles to smallholders that will prove insuperable for many or most.
2. Work with smallholders, but accept that most innovation, investment and commercialisation will come from only that (possibly very small) portion with more land and capital than their neighbours. Some claim that these farmers will then create enough jobs locally, through hiring labour and spending on local goods and services, to boost the welfare of other farm households.
3. Focus on the poorest and most disadvantaged smallholders to beat poverty and hunger and reduce vulnerability directly.

Should they focus on less favoured areas? These include poor households in areas of low agricultural potential that are remote from markets and supplies of inputs. There are two positions on this question:

1. In remote areas, employment opportunities in the rural non-farm economy are often limited. Thus, in spite of poor prospects in farming, people are heavily dependent on crops and livestock for their livelihoods. The promotion of and investment in agriculture should therefore be viewed as a safety net provision in itself, irrespective of whether such agriculture is contributing to growth.
2. In many of these cases, food security will be assured more by the ability to buy in food, rather than by trying to produce more. The questions posed for such areas are those of jobs and incomes. The difficulty lies in trying to create jobs where resources and infrastructure are scarce and markets remote. The answer probably lies in a combination of marginal agriculture, forestry, fishing, tourism, public employment in provision of services and physical infrastructure (and its maintenance), public transfers for social protection and regional equity, and in migration to alternative opportunities. Agricultural development may not, in these areas, be a prime mover in reducing poverty and improving food security.

What is the role of technology? Should development efforts focus mainly on yield-raising technology or on less intensive approaches that minimise variation? Malawi is a good case in point which is the better option: high-yielding hybrid maize with fertiliser applications or lower-yielding open-pollinated varieties requiring less fertiliser? Which crops? Should the accent be on crops that will be largely consumed within the household or on income-generating cash crops?

Contrasting Views on Agricultural Strategies

Most analysts agree that the context for agricultural development has changed significantly over the last 40 or so years, and is probably now less conducive to the type of smallholderled agricultural development seen in Asia in the 1960s and 1970s. However, opinion is sharply divided on what these changes really mean for agriculture's role in poverty reduction and, in particular, what they imply for small-scale farming as a route out of poverty for millions of poor people. Two broad views exist: the smallholder optimists and the smallholder pessimists. Each offers a different interpretation of the impact of the changes outlined above on the role of agriculture in poverty reduction and suggests a very different development strategy for agriculture.

Smallholder Pessimists

Pessimists argue that with the changes described above, smallholder agriculture is becoming progressively less viable in many parts of the world. If these trends continue, the point will soon be reached where small-scale agriculture is so uncompetitive that it ceases to offer a direct route out of poverty for the rural poor.

This vision is consistent in many ways with the way agriculture has progressed in the developed world. It sees agriculture based around farmers who can operate within the framework of new conditions, with consolidation of small farms into larger commercial units being an inevitable consequence. While this process took generations to occur in the developed world, the pace of globalisation is such that it is occurring far more rapidly in the developing world today. Policy makers need to be aware of the possible outcomes.

As smallholder agriculture declines and rural areas become better connected to urban centres, offering new opportunities, the future for rural people may lie less in agriculture and more in other economic sectors. Pessimists note that this is already starting to happen in some places. Rural people are already diversifying their livelihoods away from agriculture and, for many, income from the non-farm rural economy, remittances, seasonal migration and even commuting are more important than that from agriculture. Pessimists argue that while agriculture was important to poverty reduction in the past and remains an activity conducted in rural areas, this does not mean that it will automatically remain the primary means of earning a livelihood for millions of rural poor, nor does it represent an effective route out of poverty.

Smallholder Optimists

This view, championed by Lipton and IFPRI, takes a totally different tack. It states that the basic Green Revolution recipe is as valid today as it was in the past. With the right policies and support, smallholders will innovate and increase productivity, which will directly reduce rural poverty and stimulate wider economic growth and development through the transmission mechanisms described above. Optimists argue that the classic links between agriculture and the wider economy that worked so well in Asia, can work elsewhere today and only the smallholder works at the scale required to have any meaningful impact upon poverty. Agriculture remains the most effective engine of growth and poverty reduction, and investing in the small-scale farm sector represents the most effective way of stimulating growth and reducing poverty. Optimists acknowledge the changes in context emphasised by the pessimists, but question the extent to which they represent terminal damage to the future of small-scale farmers, for example:

1. While global consolidation in food marketing has occurred, its impact on small-scale farmers, particularly

in Africa, may be relatively insignificant as the value of staple food consumption in Africa exceeds that of export commodities by a factor of three.

2. African farmers may face increasing difficulties operating in world markets, but abundant opportunities remain in domestic and regional markets for commodities such as maize, cassava and legumes, which are grown and consumed mainly by the poor.

Furthermore, the local price of these goods is generally less affected by global price trends, because of high transport costs relative to value.

1. Removal of state-provided input subsidies might have had less impact on the profitability of small-scale farming than would appear. A balanced assessment of the impact of liberalisation must take account of the frequent bias against output prices often implicit in state marketing systems, and the concealed taxation of farm sales through foreign exchange manipulation.
2. While the non-farm economy is of greater importance to livelihoods of the rural poor than has perhaps been recognised in the past, evidence consistently shows that it is itself largely driven by the performance of the agricultural sector.
3. For optimists, the bottom line is that 70% of the world's absolute poor are rural, and agriculture remains critical to their livelihoods, either directly through the on-farm economy or indirectly through agriculture's influence on the non-farm economy.

Different Sets of Policy Conclusions

The main difference between pessimists and optimists lies in their views about the timing of economic transition and whether it is possible to bypass the first stage in agricultural transformation, i.e. the stimulus provided by a major increase in agricultural productivity in staple food crops. Fundamentally:

1. Has the impact of globalisation spread so far and fast that small-scale farmers in Africa and Asia can no longer compete in their local markets against imported grains?
2. Have consumption patterns changed to such an extent, even amongst the poorest, that any increase in income will be spent largely on imported foodstuffs?
3. Is international penetration of local markets, and market integration at a national and regional level, developing at such a speed that opportunities in agricultural production no longer exist for poorer communities? And if this is happening, what are the options for the poorest?

The policy implications of the two perspectives are quite starkly different. For optimists the issue is not one of whether smallholders can succeed, but how to make sure they do. This perspective emphasises the need for increased direct investment in agriculture and rural development, with support focusing on creating institutions that will encourage and support smallholder-led agricultural development. This includes the public provision of input and output marketing services, infrastructure development and democratic processes of land reform. Price incentives will need to be in place, but optimists argue that incentives can largely be created by removing developed country policies that have artificially depressed international commodity prices.

Particular attention will need to be given to improving the productivity of staple food crops that are not internationally traded, but consumed by the poor and traded locally. As research into these crops attracts little private sector attention, there will be a need for public funding with international assistance. In addition, research must take greater account of differing natural resource environments, in particular water management and soil degradation, and become more focused and more region specific. In the future, labour intensive approaches may not be the most suitable as HIV/AIDS reduces labour availability in some African countries in particular.

For pessimists. the strategy is more or less the opposite. They emphasise the need to achieve the best outcome for the poor from current, rapidly changing trends. As far as agriculture is concerned, efforts should be focused on encouraging commercial production of non-staple cash crops, particularly those that result in robust links to the non-farm sector, as this will be the major provider of employment for the rural poor. Influencing international policy processes will be important, but primarily to ensure access to developed country markets for more processed and high quality products from developing countries. The rural poor will be best assisted by improving their access to health and education services to improve their human capital and through measures that increase their mobility so that they can move to take up opportunities in growth areas as they occur.

Social Power

The general thesis of this essay has been that man's particular relation to the environment is fundamentally similar to that of any other species, in that it is a continuing effort to exercise sufficient control to extract energy from the environment. Particularly typical of man, however, is his cultural mode of behaviour, which leads him to seek this security of control through the constant redefinition of himself and his environment, permitting him to develop his society into an ever-expanding system. The argument suggests that this constant expansion is inherent in man's energy-using role within the thermodynamic system, that he is not doing anything particularly "unnatural" by virtue of this behaviour.

This section has been concerned to relate man's society to energy. Our focus has not been on man's, particularly Western man's, headlong destruction of his environment; this is a matter of extraordinary importance, but it is outside the scope of our theoretical concern. It is probably the case that man as a species can live on earth for an indefinite period (indefinite in that it depends on the continuation of appropriate ecological conditions, and we cannot predict when these may eliminate man, quite apart from his abuse of them), but only if he:

1. Changes his choice of energy mix and
2. Reduces the amount of energy conversion he exercises, so as to achieve something approaching a steady-state system. Social power and control obviously play a major role in each of these choices.

"Energy mix" refers to the particular selection among the variety of energy forms available to man, that is, the kinds of resources that man exploits for his own continuance. Foremost in the public eye at the time of writing is the question of some specific resources, such as oil and increasingly rare minerals, and what the prospects may be for their availability in the future. Just as important as their availability is the problem of their residue after use. This is, in the broadest sense, the problem of waste, the remaining compounds and conditions that remain after conversion is accomplished, and for which there is no further technology. The problem of material and gaseous pollution is well before us; somewhat less attention has been paid to the problem of heat in the atmosphere, a consequence that is contingent on the use of almost all kinds of energy forms except direct solar conversion and that available from direct solar radiation, gravity, and the earth's movement (which includes winds and tides). In a recent review, William R. Frisken estimates that:

> On the longer term (say, more than 100 years) we have the more serious problem of beginning to warm the climate directly with our own energy conversion. This will be with us (in slightly different degree at any one time) whether we derive our energy from coal fires, nuclear reactors, or from fusion generators as yet only imagined.... if we continue to double our energy conversion rate every 17.5 years, in about 250 years it will equal the rate at which we absorb solar radiation at the earth's surface at the present time.

Of more immediate possible concern in atmospheric change is the greenhouse effect of carbon dioxide increase, which raises the temperature, although the nature of this process seems quite uncertain. Claude M. Summers argues that there are energy collectors, specifically those turning to solar and wind energy, that "would add no heat load to the earth's biosphere; they can be called invariant energy systems." However, Summers's estimate for the time at which we would be releasing heat at the absorption rate of the sun's radiation is only 99 years from now, not 250. If the problem of achieving the correct energy mix were merely a technical problem, the issue would be quite confounding in itself. It carries with it, however, an implicit and possibly even more difficult problem in the dimension of social power.

The relative mix of energy forms and sources available within any particular context will determine much about the amount and concentration of social power that we are likely to find there. The contemporary oil situation is as good an example as any. Oil has been contrived (with full intent by the industry) to be the major energetic resource of modern industrialism. From initial ownership of oil-bearing land to the ultimate consumer, oil engenders an incredibly complex power and control network that reaches deep into the government and economy of almost every nation in the world, as well as into a broad range of industries that are financially or technically dependent on the oil business. This is a vast coordinate operating unit that is bent both on retaining access to its own pluralistic resources and on utilising the power it gains there from to the continued benefit of the unit. The problem that confronts man, very realistically, is how the species can effect sufficient counter controls so as to exercise power over this complex coordinate system. If it were centralised, it might be somewhat easier, for then the centre could be captured. But the great survival advantage of coordinate units is that they have no single brain, no vulnerable single nervous system.

Clearly the question of social power and its basis in control is central to this issue. If it were possible to make oil less important in the energy mix, then the coordinate unit would be less powerful; but it is specifically trying to avoid that eventuality. But there is one thing that we ultimately cannot have, and that is a system based on the present energy mix, and this means specifically that we must reduce our dependence on oil and other nonrenewable energy resources.

The amount of energy being converted, if we accept the theory proposed earlier in the essay, cannot continue to accelerate and must in fact be reduced and level off. The complexity, and therefore much of the form, of social and political organisation is directly determined by the amount of energy that is being converted in the system. Since many of the particular forms of energy that we need are in terminal supply, we cannot indefinitely have an increase in the rate of conversion. This means that energy conversion and human society both have to level off into a steady-state condition. If the species does not devise some way to level off at its own rate, then it is quite simply the case that nature, of which it is a part, will level it off, if not all but eliminate it.

We might add here a point that was made earlier in the essay. At the maximal level of social organisation of the species it may be possible to have one operating unit that is ranked clearly above others in terms of the controls and power that it exercises, but it is quite impossible to have this operating unit constitute an additional level of integration above its lesser peers. The species will never achieve a monolithic power structure, simply because it will always be composed of parts that will be contending for control, and this inevitably means they will be exercising power over each other and contending for better positions from which to do this. Structurally, the top will always remain multiple. There will never be a single "supranational agency, a state above states," that will be able to indefinitely exercise independent power either for the benefit or to the detriment of man the species. Man can never be politically unified; he will ultimately find levels of living that will require less energy; and he will find that he has to change his energy mix. All these are safe, and not trivial, predictions; but they are also of very little immediate help. Can the theory of social power provide any clarification of the alternatives here?

Man is placing the environment out of control at a rate that is some function of the amount of energy converted. The more advanced the culture, the greater the consequent structuring of the environment. It is increasingly broadly recognised in scientific communities that man must reduce the amount of his energy conversion and that he must find away of achieving a steady-state economy and ecology. But there persists a nebulousness about the structure of this future. We tend to have dogmatic, but substantively indistinct, notions, such as Marx's "higher phase of communist society," or a kind of there-is-free-will-but-entropy-is-inevitable dualism. For example: "We could, for example, adopt as our cardinal philosophy the rule that no man or institution in our society may take any action that decreases the economic and social options of those who will live on the planet over the next 100 years. Perhaps only organised religion has the moral force to bring about acceptance of such a rule, but perhaps it could result also from an enlightened, widespread program of public education.'' In suggesting religion, Jorgen Randers and Donella Meadows have resorted to a device that worked in the chiefdom stage of evolution; they then suggest public education, the cure-all that has marked the modern era, without recognising that public education is a dependent variable of the system, not an independent variable that directs the system.

Harrison Brown foresees three future possibilities:

> The first and by far the most likely pattern is a reversion to agrarian existence. This is the pattern which will almost certainly emerge unless man is able to abolish war, unless he is able to make the transition involving the utilisation of new energy sources, and unless he is able to stabilise populations.

In spite of the difficulties that confront industrial civilisation, there is a possibility that stabilisation can be achieved, that war can be avoided, and that the resource transition can be successfully negotiated. In that event, mankind will be confronted with a pattern which looms on the horizon of events as the second most likely possibility the completely controlled, collectivised industrial society.

The third possibility confronting mankind is that of the worldwide free industrial society in which human beings can live in reasonable harmony with their environment. It is unlikely that such a pattern can ever exist for long. It certainly will be difficult to achieve, and it clearly will be difficult to maintain once it is established. Nevertheless, we have seen that man has it within his power to create such a society and to devise ways and means of perpetuating it on a stable basis. In view of the existence of this power, the possibility that the third pattern may eventually emerge cannot be ignored, although the probability of such an emergence, as judged by existing trends, may appear to be extremely low.

Brown then observes:

> Indeed, it is amply clear that, if man wills it, a world community can be created in which human beings can live comfortably and in peace with each other.

Like Randers and Meadows, Brown clearly sees the energy problems, but his first inclination is to be a little more realistic as to where this must ultimately lead. If nonrenewable resources cease to be available, then man must be reduced to an agrarian existence in which he can survive on renewable resources. But Brown, too, finds it hard to resist the culture in which he lives, and suggests that, if man could "abolish war," then this end might be avoided; and, further, that "if man wills it" a comfortable world community can be achieved. Perhaps Brown was not aware that war was a hallmark of neolithic societies, and that it has increased with the amount of power and energy in the system, not decreased. Man's will can have little to do with it unless expansion can be contained. Gregory Bateson also seeks a solution, and, like the others, he is acutely aware of the energy component. His concern, however, is that we maintain a "high civilisation." It is worthwhile to lay out his argument in some detail:

> It becomes then necessary to work toward a definition of "high."
>
> (a) It would not be wise even if possible to return to the innocence of the Australian aborigines, the Eskimo, and the Bushmen. Such a return would involve loss of the wisdom which prompted the return and would only start the whole process over.

This is an important and clever observation; and, as will be evident later, the possibility of starting "the whole process over" would seem likely. But Bateson's objection is phrased in terms of human mental specifically, memory capacity, and does not examine the inevitability even without that memory.

> (b) A "high" civilisation should therefore be presumed to have, on the technological side, whatever gadgets are necessary to promote, maintain (and even increase) wisdom of this general sort. This may well include computers and complex communication devices.
>
> (c) A "high" civilisation shall contain whatever is necessary (in education and religious institutions) to maintain the necessary wisdom in the human population and to give physical, aesthetic, and creative satisfaction to the people. There shall be a matching between the flexibility of people and that of the civilisation. There shall be diversity in the civilisation, not only to accommodate the genetic and experiential diversity of persons, but also to provide the flexibility and "preadaptation" necessary for unpredictable change.

Here Bateson proposes that "on the technological side" there will be available an establishment that is characteristic of a very high-energy civilisation, including computers and "complex communication devices." He also proposes a "diversity" that would require a high cost of upkeep.

> (d) A "high" civilisation shall be limited in its transactions with environment.

It shall consume unreplaceable natural resources only as a means to facilitate necessary change (as a chrysalis in metamorphosis must live on its fat). For the rest the metabolism of the civilisation must depend upon the energy income which Spaceship Earth derives from the sun. In this connection, great technical advance is necessary. With present technology it is probable that the world could only maintain a small fraction of its present human population, using as energy sources only photosynthesis, wind, tide, and water power.

Bateson evades some of the errors of the others. He does not directly invoke "will," education, or religion to solve the problem. He also realises that for man to obtain the immense amount of energy input necessary he will have to become ecologically extraterrestrial. Yet elsewhere Bateson seems to make clear that this would be unlikely: "The unit of survival is organism plus environment. We are learning by bitter experience that the organism which destroys its environment destroys itself." When Bateson argues that the organism can survive only in conjunction with its environment, but then holds that the future "high civilisation shall be limited in its transactions with environment," we are left a little uncertain of his meaning of the terms. Clearly the sun can be little more than an energy resource; everything else currently comes from the terrestrial system, one way or another.

Whereas Brown, Randers, and Meadows share the implicit dualism that Bateson observed was fundamental in the Book of Genesis, Bateson and Marx seem to argue that such a dualism may be avoided and that man can have the world and heaven too.

Anthropologists have often treated peasant or primitive societies as if they were in a steady state, only to find later that they were not. Nevertheless, there is some reason to assume that many societies have lived for extended periods in at least an oscillating or quasi-steady state. Certainly Australian hunting and collecting bands that survived into the last century must have achieved some kind of steady state, since they had been in approximately that state for a good many millennia.

If one looks to the total sociocultural systems within which people were working and on the basis of which they were surviving, there has been little let-up in population and cultural expansion since that time. Arguments that urban populations do not reproduce themselves and that birth rates decline with education are small backwashes in a picture that is otherwise flooded with growth. There have been many particular cases where population growth has declined for various reasons; but they have not been sufficient to change the overall expansion.

Besides the collectors, the only other type of society that might claim credit for establishing a steady state is the peasant. There is a literature in recent years that holds that these "part-societies" have devised a way to restrain advancement or expansion. Foster's theory of the "limited good" represents the ethic, while Wolf 's thesis concerning the "ceremonial fund" (that proved so useful in Schaedel's analysis of the organisation of pristine chief domships) and Ruben Reina's description of community pressure suggest some of the societal processes that may operate. While it is hard to argue that peasant populations characteristically are a steady state demographically, it probably is reasonable to argue that there are various devices that have been instituted over the centuries to restrict cultural expansion. Peasants, however, are necessarily subsectors (in Kroeber's terms, "half-societies"), and often fairly marginalised ones, of complex macrosocieties. They are subject to many kinds of pressures, not the least of which are rent, tax, tribute payments, and market disadvantages, which can only increase if the superordinates become aware that the peasants are finding their art lucrative. Even without a "ceremonial-fund" hypothesis, it is quite reasonable to anticipate a reticence on the part of peasants to display excessive success. But the question of peasants in the context of the steady-state issue is misleading, because the crucial issue is not whether the peasants expand, but whether the society as a whole is expanding. Where peasant society manifests a cultural homeostasis, it may simply be that upper sectors are expanding their cultural activities at the cost of peasant rents and taxes. If that is the case, then the society is, in fact, expanding.

The problem that confronts us is that human society has always been an expanding system, and there are implicit reasons for this in the nature of biology and culture. Yet it is clear that it cannot continue for much longer as an expanding system, that it will have to move to some other kind of state or states. Harrison Brown's suggested agrarian existence may be workable if it is principally the question of energy that concerns us. Most writers, however, Brown included, prefer to opt for a society with many of the advantages of a high-energy system, but to have it based on less use of energy. This poses a dilemma that is insoluble.

The question then boils down to whether Brown's agrarian proposal can stand up or whether even it faces serious problems. Since human society, like other societies, achieves survival at the ultimate cost of overproducing, it may be assumed that the continuing success of an agrarian adventure will also depend upon the society's constant push toward expansion, either cultural or demographic or both. Agrarian societies are already at such a high rate of energy expenditure that their rate of evolutionary change is relatively high, and they will necessarily manifest a tendency to move toward the limits of their environment, with the inevitable consequences in attempted cultural advance and demographic circumscription. Thus agrarian existence eventually implies an increased rate of conflict and an increased likelihood of again moving to chiefdomlike or kingdomlike levels of integration. Presumably the advance would be hindered or stopped at some point due to the absence of suitable energy forms, e.g., lack of adequate iron or other minerals. Thus man would presumably be contained at a steady state that would maximally be agrarian and empirically would probably consist of a rather wide variety of agrarian adaptations, contending and competing with each other depending upon the local circumstances. What would inevitably happen would be the repeated experiencing of adaptational catastrophe as the population grew beyond the limits of potential ecological production.

Catastrophe within living memory or some reminder within the environment that provides a signal of danger seems to be important. Bateson has observed that, "In principle, the homeostatic controls of biological systems must be activated by variables which are not themselves harmful." Within cultural systems too, it is not viable to wait until there is a series of catastrophes that make further signalling unnecessary. Rather, there must be some cultural meanings in the system that attach to variables to warn of impending danger so that the homeostatic mechanism may go into effect.

An additional feature of agrarian and higher-ordered societies is that their members are inevitably going to increasingly promote the exploitation of their fellow men for their own survival and benefit. Margalef, it will be remembered, argued this as a principle for ecosystems in general, and, as such, his argument is a detailing of the more general principle that Lotka set forth some years earlier. The dependency created by higher levels among the lower ones subordinate to them, with the inevitable marginalisation that follows, is inherent in agrarian cultures as well as others. (One must be careful here not to confuse rank peers with superordinate-subordinates at different levels.)

Although hunting and gathering societies did not appeal to Bateson as a potential way of life, given the ancestry of man, they have something to recommend them. The only approximately steady-state society that man has ever achieved is the hunting and gathering society. His tenure on earth has been principally in that condition, and the Australian aborigines and Bushmen of Africa give evidence that they have survived fairly successfully, at least until they were brought within the advantages of mercantilistic and industrial civilisation.

The nomadic aspect is important, since that serves to keep the birth rate down, and the collecting level is important, since the rate of energy use is so low that the rate of cultural advance would be equivalently low. This alternative has certain other features to recommend it. The mentalistic structures of man proved eminently qualified to handle the kinds of problems that were presented at that level. Also, the governing mechanisms of these societies are totally allocative; there simply is not enough environment controlled to permit a concentration of power. It would, incidentally, also fit the democratic idea and the Marxist ideals. All men would have equality before the law, a thing patently impossible in a complex system. "From each according to his ability, to each according to his needs" would be a reality. It would achieve what Marx described as that:

> "definitive resolution of the antagonism between man and Nature, and between man and man."

The problem of governance hinges on the fact that the kind of government we can anticipate depends upon the amount of energy in the system quite as much as do the kind of art, the kind of housing, the kind of recreation, and so forth. Just as a highly developed cinematography is impossible without the energy necessary for the diverse electrical, chemical, and developmental processes required, so it is difficult to have a centralised government without the available independent power that must come from reasonably well developed sources of food, shelter, and implements. The reason tribal organisations were prevalent during much of man's tenure and still visible widely during the past three hundred years was that it was not easy to get that extra power necessary to centralise.

By the same token, to assume that a "religion" or "widespread education" will produce an "ethic" can be meaningful only if the level of energy of the society and the level of power in the system are appropriate for those devices. Supernaturally oriented religions worked during chiefdoms, in lower-powered societies, because the governments were unable to support the bureaucracy and the number of nonproducers required. Proposals for utopian futures need to consider not only the energy sources but also the power structure that will necessarily come into being from any such energy base and the administration and communication systems that can be supported by that level of energy conversion. It is, perhaps, a little much to ask of man that, in order to survive, he cease to be human.

5

Social Impact of Globalisation

Since 1980s, the world economy has become increasingly "connected" and "integrated"; on the one hand the decreasing transportation costs and the diffusion of Information and Communication Technologies have implied a fast downgrading of the concept of "distance", while on the other hand gross trade, Foreign Direct Investment (FDI), capital flows and technology transfers have risen significantly. In most countries, the current wave of "globalisation" has been accompanied by increasing concern about its impact in terms of employment and income distribution.

The current debate is characterised by an acrimonious dispute between advocates and critics of globalisation. While this is true even as regards the employment and income distribution effects within the developed world, positions diverge even more sharply over the impact on Developing Countries (DCs). For instance, the optimists underline the link between increasing trade and economic growth and then they conclude that trade is good for growth and growth is good for the poor (both in terms of job creation and poverty alleviation). In contrast, the pessimists show that globalisation is quite uneven in its impact and gives rise to negative counter-effects on the previously protected sectors, the marginalisation of entire regions of the world economy and possible increases in within country income inequality (WCII). Another example of this kind of diversity of opinions is the debate about poverty indicators: supporters of globalisation underline the fact that worldwide absolute poverty has decreased over the last two decades, while critics of globalisation show that this result is almost entirely due to statistical artefacts and to the fast growth of China, while absolute poverty has increased in many DCs and relative poverty has increased in the majority of countries.

Globalisation and Employment

According to the theory of the relative comparative advantages, both trade and FDI should take advantage of the abundance of labour in DCs and so trigger a trend of specialisation in domestic labour-intensive activities and so involve an expansion in local employment.

However, contrary to this Heckscher-Ohlin (HO) prediction, the analysis of the recent literature supports the conclusion that the employment impact of increasing trade is not necessarily positive for a developing country. In particular, a relaxation of the hypothesis of homogeneous production functions across different countries allows for either the possibility of multiple equilibria, or for quite differentiated employment trends in the evolutionary "catching-up" models. In fact, when "total factor productivity" increases in the DCs as a consequence of globalisation, the employment enhancing competitive effect has to be compared with the direct labour-saving effect of the imported-technologies. In other words, in a developing country, the final employment impact of increasing trade depends on the interaction between productivity growth and output growth both in traded goods sectors and in non-traded sectors. The final outcome cannot be assessed *a priori* for different reasons. On the one hand, export may involve a demand-led economic and employment growth, but on the other hand–import may displace previously protected domestic firms, inducing labour redundancy.

Moreover, in the presence of supply constraints (lack of infrastructures, scarcity of skilled labour, under investment, inefficient labour market), even in the exporting sectors productivity growth may exceed output growth, to the detriment of job creation. Finally, domestic sheltered sectors (such as agriculture, public administration, construction, non-traded service) may act as labour sinks, often implying hidden unemployment and underemployment in the informal labour market.

Shifting our focus from trade to FDI inflows, when a developing country opens its borders to foreign capital, FDIs generate positive employment impacts both directly and indirectly through job creation within suppliers and retailers and also a tertiary employment effect through generating additional incomes and so increasing aggregate demand. Yet, all these positive employment effects of "greenfield" FDI have to be compared with the possible crowding-out of noncompetitive and previously sheltered domestic firms (implying bankruptcies and job losses); with the possible labour-saving effects of the new technologies brought about by multinational firms; and with the possible reduction in employment associated with FDI operating through Mergers and Acquisitions (M&A).

In fact, both imports and inward FDI may imply a "crowding out" of domestic production (especially formerly protected nascent industries; think, for instance, to the case of large urban state-owned firms in China).

This job displacement effect can be further amplified when FDI inflows are accompanied by financial liberalisation and consequent increases in the interest rate, in turn leading to shrinking domestic investments.

Since the overall employment impact of trade and FDI is uncertain from a theoretical point of view, it is important to collect data on these relationships and to empirically investigate the direct and indirect effects of globalisation on the domestic employment of a globalising DC.

Matusz and Tarr survey the studies carried out before 1995 on the impact of globalisation on employment in DCs. Comparing the level of employment before and after trade liberalisation the authors conclude that trade and FDI liberalisation has been beneficial for labour except in the transition countries of Eastern Europe. Ghose analyses the relationship between trade liberalisation and manufacturing employment. He highlights that although increasing trade and FDI have been relevant only in a small bunch of newly industrialised countries for those countries the growth of trade in manufactured products has implied a large positive effect on manufacturing employment. More evidence has been collected at the national level mostly for the manufacturing sector. It draws a contrasted picture of the effect of globalisation. In successfully integrating DCs, the employment effects of trade liberalisation has been mixed (mostly negative) in Latin America whereas they seem globally positive in Asian countries.

Indeed, the theoretical issues and the empirical evidence discussed in Lee and Vivarelli lead to the conclusion that the employment impact of trade and FDI is country and sector specific and that the HO theorem is actually rejected in most cases. For instance, Lall observes that – while there is a clear evidence that several DCs have exhibited export and employment growth as a consequence of opening to trade and FDI doubts can be cast about the belief that globalisation should always benefit employment growth within a DC; indeed, different "national absorptive capacities" in terms of institutional setting, labour skills, technological capabilities and competitiveness of domestic firms can amplify the positive employment impact of globalisation, while institutional mismatches between the market, the organisations and the government and lack of local capabilities can severely jeopardise the potential for economic and employment growth.

In this framework, Gros notes that opening to trade implies both an increase in value added and in labour productivity and so that the employment impact cannot be predicted a priori; empirically, the best results in terms of employment growth happen to be within the "non globalising" DCs (basically because of a lack of any improvement in labour productivity) and in the "slowly globalising" DCs which are characterised by a labour friendly balance between output and productivity trends.

Finally, Spiezia studies the employment impact of trade on the manufacturing sector. By comparing labour intensities of exported, imported and non-trade goods the author concludes that in 21 out of 39 sampled DCs an increase in the volume of trade resulted in an increase in employment; however, in the second group of 18 countries, increased integration produced a reduction in employment (in contrast with the HO theorem). As far as FDI is concerned, the author finds out that the impact of FDI on employment is increasing with per-capita income, resulting not significant for low income DCs.

Globalisation and Within-Country Income Inequality

On the one hand, the Stolper-Samuelson (SS) theorem predicts that both trade and FDI should take advantage of the abundance of low-skilled labour in DCs and so imply an increasing demand for domestic low skilled labour and hence decreasing within-country wage dispersion and income inequality.

Some important theoretical critiques can be addressed to the SS theorem. First, is the theorem valid in a global sense or in relation to the so-called "cones of diversification" (a cone of diversification being a group of countries characterised by similar endowment proportions, very similar production functions and supplying the same range of goods)? If SS theorem is valid not in relation to the world economy but in relation to a specific cone of diversification, it could be the case that countries abundant in unskilled labour in a global context are abundant in capital and skilled labour in comparison with some other country in the same cone: if such is the case, the SS theorem might have very different distributional consequences from those one would anticipate on the basis of a simplistic North-South interpretation of the theorem (for instance, in Mexico the equalising effect of trade and FDI with the USA may be more than compensated by the disequalising effect of competition by China and other newly industrialised Asian countries;).

Second, Feenstra-Hanson's model points out that what is unskillintensive in a developed country may be skill-intensive in terms of the labour market of the recipient DC; accordingly, shifting production from developed towards developing countries (both through FDI and import/export trade relationships) may imply increasing inequality both in the former and in the latter. For instance, outsourcing of production through FDI from the U.S. to Mexico implies that plants which were relatively intensive in unskilled labour in the U.S. would be relatively skill-intensive in Mexico (with a higher ratio of skilled/unskilled labour than domestic plants), thus raising relative wages and income inequality in both countries.

Third, the latter increasing inequality effect may be amplified by a possible "skillbiased" nature of technologies embodied both in FDIs and in importation of capital goods. Indeed, capital equipment and intermediate goods constitute the majority of increasing imports by DCs following liberalisation. For sake of clarity, we can look separately at FDI and importation.

If we think about FDI as a vehicle of new technologies, in addition to the direct effect, there are different channels through which skilled-biased innovation spill over from foreign to local firms: the demonstration effect (local firms adopt new technologies through imitation and reverse engineering); the vertical spillovers (backward and forward linkages lead to intra and inter-industry technology upgrading); labour turnover and spin-offs (workers trained in foreign owned firms may transfer important know-how to local firms by switching employers or by starting-up their own business); and the competition effect (technology upgrading in local firms becomes necessary because of competitive pressures from foreign firms).

More than other imports, imports of capital goods, embodying technological innovations are important both because of the role they play in contributing to capital upgrading and more generally to economic growth of DCs, and because they originate the so-called "skill-enhancing trade"). In fact, even without necessarily assuming that developed countries transfer their "best" technologies to the DCs, it is quite reasonable to expect that transferred technologies are relatively skill-intensive, i.e. more skill-intensive than those in use domestically before trade and FDI liberalisation. If such is the case, openness–via technology should imply a counter-effect to the SS theorem prediction, namely an increase in the demand for skilled labour, an increase in wage dispersion and so an increase in income inequality.

Finally, globalisation is often coupled with market-oriented policy reforms within the globalising DCs (such as the liberalisation of the domestic labour market or the privatisation of previously state-owned firms) which often imply possible increases in WCII. Hence, on the theoretical side, relaxing the HO hypothesis of technological homogeneity, and allowing for capital deepening and skill-biased technological change (SBTC), opens the way to an important possible counter-effect in terms of the distributional impact of globalisation, and so the theoretical prediction ceases to be univocal and becomes open to different outcomes depending on the relative importance of the determinants discussed so far.

On the empirical side and starting from simple correlation analyses, both Bowles and Dollar and Kraay do not find any significant correlation between changes in openness and changes in inequality. Turning the attention to more sophisticated econometric analyses, Edwards does not find any evidence linking trade liberalisation to increases in inequality; Higgins and Williamson–using a framework based on the unconditional Kuznets' curve fail to find any significant relationship between economic openness and inequality; Spilimbergo *et al.*, find that trade openness has a positive impact on income inequality in skill-abundant countries, but when they limit the analysis to DCs, they fail to find any significant relationship between trade and inequality; Ravallion finds no significant effect of exports as a share of GDP on Gini index changes across 50 countries (both developed and developing countries).

However, Birchenall concludes that, in the case of Colombia, liberalisation interpreted as a skill-biased technological change induced wage inequality, polarisation and higher labour mobility. Pavcnik *et al.*, show that trade reform in Brazil has contributed to the growing skill-premium through SBTC instigated by increased foreign competition (even though the overall effect on wage differentials is relatively small). Finally, Vivarelli does not find any significant distributional effect of trade openness and FDI inflows; however, in his study some evidence emerges that, in the early stages of openness to trade, importation may imply an increase in WCII (possibly via SBTC).

The main common conclusion of these empirical studies is that the popular idea that greater economic integration across countries is associated with an increase in inequality within DCs is not necessarily in contrast with theoretical considerations, but it cannot be significantly supported by available recent empirical evidence. As stated by Cornia globalisation *in se'* does not emerge as the main culprit of the current increase of WCII in DCs. Yet, recent evidence is consistent with the hypothesis that the diffusion of SBTC from richer to developing countries may imply at least temporarily an increase in within-country inequality.

Globalisation and Poverty Alleviation

As far as poverty reduction is concerned, trade and FDI are supposed to be beneficial to a DC's economic growth (for a much more critical point of view) and so given the expected overall neutrality in terms of their impact on income distribution globalisation should be a way to achieve poverty reduction.

Indeed, most DCs experienced a significant reduction in the proportion of their population living below the poverty line, including fast globalising countries like China, India, Vietnam. Conversely, many slow globalisers in the Sub-Saharan Africa registered an opposite trend.

While the apologists of globalisation support the view that current trends clearly indicate a decreasing global inequality, the critics show that this result mainly depend on the exceptional growth of China, while absolute poverty has increased in SSA and relative poverty (inequality) has increased in the majority of countries.

On the theoretical side, economic growth is not the only vehicle through which globalisation can affect poverty levels. In fact, globalisation deeply influences labour productivity (and this may imply higher wages on the one hand but job losses on the other hand); the demand for skills (with a possible redundancy of low skilled people concentrated below the poverty line); the need for macroeconomic stability (since stability implies low inflation, trade should affect the poor positively because the poor tend to be hardest hit by increasing inflation, however, liberalisation may also involve cautious and restrictive macroeconomic policies with an opposite effect); relative prices (with possible adverse or positive effects in terms of purchasing power of poor households depending on the basket of tariffs reductions and on the changes in the terms of trade); relative competitiveness of domestic firms (possibly crowded-out by more efficient multinationals), government revenues and expenditures, etc. On the whole, it is true that globalisation aids economic growth and that economic growth aids poverty reduction, but not unconditionally: the final outcome in terms of poverty reduction can be actually either amplified or diminished (even cancelled) by the complementary economic factors and policies which are part of the game.

To better understand the issue, it is also important to distinguish between trade and FDI on the one hand and financial liberalisation on the other hand. While increasing trade and FDIs seem to be associated with increasing economic growth and absolute poverty alleviation (although conditional on the occurrence of many complementary events), poverty can rise rapidly in the wake of increased vulnerability, occurrence of generalised economic crises and contagion of "innocent victims" which can all be related to fast financial liberalisation. Hence, the liberalisation of capital accounts may counterbalance the poverty alleviation effect of trade and FDI and surely be correlated with possible increases in income inequality (for an opposite view underlining the long-run welfare gains associated with financial liberalisation).

To conclude, nothing can assure that the relationship between globalisation and poverty alleviation has a 1 to 1 nature as implied for instance, by the optimistic slogan by Dollar and Kray when they state that "*trade is good for growth*, growth is good for the poor and so trade is good for the poor".

Focusing on the empirical studies, the above mentioned Dollar and Kraay classify countries into globalisers and non-globalisers according to their performance in raising their trade openness (export + import over GDP) and show that the former group has experienced higher growth rates during the period 1977-97. Then they show that the incomes of the poor rise proportionally with average incomes and that globalisation does not have any systematic effect on domestic income distribution. They therefore conclude that growth is good for the poor.

6

Globalisation and Global Culture

Globalisation involves expanding worldwide flows of material objects and symbols, and the proliferation of organisations and institutions of global reach that structure those flows. World culture refers to the cultural complex of foundational assumptions, forms of knowledge, and prescriptions for action that underlie globalised Flows, organisations, and institutions. It encompasses webs of significance that span the globe, conceptions of world society and world order, and models and methods of organising social life that are assumed to have worldwide significance or applicability.

While many types of global flows have been rising cyclically for centuries, it was only in the second half of the nineteenth century that a transnational cultural complex took a sufficiently organised form to constitute an emerging world culture. The primary locus of this nascent world culture was Europe, particularly the powerful Western European countries whose empires extended to most corners of the globe. Europeans promoted political and philosophical principles, societal and individual goals, modes of organising, and ways of conceiving and manipulating reality that they deemed universally applicable. Epitomised above all by technical and scientific principles and practical knowledge presumed to be invariant across time and space, emerging world culture also included more historically bound constructs and ideologies, such as nationalism, citizenship, and individualism. This early version of world culture, more properly called 'transeuropean' culture, was carried far and wide by missionaries, traders, military expeditions, colonialists, intellectuals, and travellers.

In this same period, transnational organisations and global structures emerged with increasing frequency, eventually to form a structural backbone or framework for world culture. The vast majority of these transnational organisations were products of international or global 'civil society'–voluntary associations founded and operated by individuals from many countries to pursue specific goals through democratically coordinated action. Typical early examples include the International Charity Association, the International Sugar Union, the Scandinavian Dental Association, the Permanent International Committee of Architects, and the International Meteorological Organisation. By the 1890s, such international nongovernmental organisations (INGOs) were appearing at the rate of more than 10 per year, across a wide range of social sectors, drawing participants mainly from Europe and North America but also from Latin American and some Asian countries, particularly India. These bodies defined themselves as global actors and sponsored periodic conferences at which universalistic issues, problems, methods, and solutions were proposed and debated. They came to constitute a formalised global public realm in which world culture was defined, documented, elaborated, and propagated to what the growing number of participants in this public realm were beginning to think of as a single world society.

The calamitous world wars of the twentieth century severely interrupted world-cultural structuration, but after each war the process rebounded quickly. States became increasingly engaged in transnational cooperative relationships through intergovernmental organisations (IGOs, which were rare before 1920). After World War II, the IGO population burgeoned to a total of several hundred organisations, while the number of INGOs soared into the thousands. This expanding complex of global organisations came to centre on the United Nations, whose agencies and programs became axes of global governance regimes in such major institutional areas as education, health, and development.

Until the 1970s, the content of world culture remained primarily Anglo-European, increasingly dominated by the USA. American popular culture and products proliferated throughout the globe–rock music, soap operas, blue jeans, Coca-Cola, fast foods, Hollywood movies. The globalisation of tastes in food, dress, and music also promoted a global identity model, that of the freely choosing, pleasure-seeking consumer. At a deeper level, the plethora of global organisations, both nongovernmental and intergovernmental, produced a range of standardised principles, models, and methods for the organisation of social life. For example, a basic world model of the modern nation-state crystallised, stipulating that the state was to be responsible not only for internal order and external defence but also for building a modern society and promoting citizen welfare and civic engagement. States were therefore expected to generate national educational systems, health care programs, retirement and unemployment insurance schemes, and cultural promotion programs, among many other duties. In particular sectors, globally legitimated models emerged to guide states in meeting these responsibilities, such as the standardised educational models that took shape under UNESCO's aegis in collaboration with a range of educational INGOs. Despite enormous variation in national circumstances and resources, states have implemented these models in remarkably uniform ways.

By the 1980s, world-cultural structuration had produced largely standardised global models for an enormous range of activities–in science, medicine, health, business, technology, even recreation and leisure (sports, tourism, entertainment). Pushed by the carriers of these models, including INGOs and IGOs but also business consultants, technical advisers, and academic consultants who explain and interpret the models, states, local governments, corporations, social movement organisations, and many other types of social units go to considerable lengths to keep up with the leading edges of world-cultural development. The net result is a tremendous force for the homogenisation of the world.

Globalisation and Cultural Differentiation

World culture is not only a homogenising force; it also engenders and supports diversity and differentiation. Recognition of this feature of world culture was slow in coming; through the 1970s, most analysts interpreted globalisation as essentially equivalent to homogenising Americanisation. Five factors are important for understanding world culture's promotion of heterogeneity; ironically, several of these are also important elements of world culture's homogenising capacity.

1. *Success of the nation-state political form*: Rapid decolonisation after 1945 produced a world organised almost entirely as independent states. Most new states have eagerly joined global governance organisations, debating and helping to shape agreements expressing world-culture principles and prescriptions. Citizens of the new countries became avid joiners of INGOs, expanding the range of their memberships much faster than citizens of older countries. Thus, the voices and views of the Third World are increasingly prominent in world-cultural development, and debates about proper social organisation and action are often less consensual

than in the past. Cultural controversy has been especially acute in such domains as women's rights, environmentalism, and human rights.

2. *Cultural relativism and the ideology of cultural authenticity*: Intellectual movements in the social sciences and humanities, coupled with the ideologies of nationalism and national self-determination, have made the principle of the fundamentally equal value of all human cultures a central assumption of world culture. Ethnocentrism has come to be seen as both trap and injustice; tolerance and, indeed, the championing of difference occupy the moral high ground. Of particular moral virtue in contemporary world culture are the poor, the excluded, the oppressed–marginal peoples whose right to their own cultures has been violated by the onslaught of globalisation (some see this as a return of 'noble savage' idealisation). This universalistic form of particularism impels peoples to emphasise or invent tradition and distinctiveness in counterpoint to universalistic world-cultural principles that are supposed to operate uniformly in all places. In Western societies, such particularism is stimulated by cosmopolitan connoisseurs seeking authentically exotic cuisine or ethnically distinct 'world' music, as the genre is known. At the same time, politically astute groups understand the power of purported cultural authenticity as a fulcrum for prying rewards from global systems, so distinction and difference have become strategic resources for collective mobilisation. In consequence, ethnonationalist movements of many sorts (Basques, Biafrans, Bretons, Croats, Eritreans, Quebecois, Scots, Tamils, etc.) and mulculturalist restructuring by states, churches, schools, and other organisations have become the order of the day.

3. *Regionalism*: Roughly half of the international organisations founded since 1950 have been regional in scope, activating European, Latin American, Asian, francophone, Islamic, Andean, and many other subglobal identities. Like ethno nationalism, regionalism has flourished in the wake of world-cultural intensification. Global structures, ideologies, principles, and models provide an overarching framework of commonality and shared meaning for disparate social units. With the framework well in place, diverse regional organisations and movements have expanded to implement, modify, and argue about the frameworks content and implications. We see the same process at work within international organisations and global corporations. For example, Cable News Network International (CNNI) began as a unitary organisation bringing a standardised English-language product to televisions around the world, but it eventually established numerous regional centres producing local-language broadcasting adapted to specific target audiences.
4. *Consumerism as adaptive interpretation*: While global popular culture contains products and symbols that penetrate most local markets, its accompanying ideology of economic freedom and consumer choice encourages varied uses and interpretations of standardised consumption patterns. For instance, consumers in Hong Kong might appreciate a McDonald's restaurant as much for its clean facilities as for its food. They expect fast, not smiling, service, and reserve the right to eat at their leisure. In a city pressed for space, the restaurant can become a gathering spot for youth or a favoured locale for birthday parties. By adapting marketing to local attitudes, McDonald's has lost its foreign aura,

blending into Hong Kong's diverse, cosmopolitan culinary scene. In Beijing, meanwhile, McDonald's American origins can be attractive to upwardly mobile Chinese as a symbol of participation in global society, but among many Koreans in Seoul those same origins evoke criticism. While not denying the power of multinational corporations to foster acceptance of their products and logos, recent research suggests that they must take into account the distinctive tastes of potentially fickle consumers. Popular culture increasingly creates global tastes, but it also creates critical consumers who keep this culture from becoming entirely uniform.

5. *Creolisation*: In many domains, the homogenising force of world culture encounters ingrained local tastes and traditions, which may in turn be the residue of earlier such encounters with neighbouring or colonisers. Due to creative interaction processes, common elements take different forms in different places. The spread of world culture therefore produces not homogeneity but new cultural melanges, each 'creolised' in its own way. A case in point is West-African popular music. Popular styles that themselves are blends of variegated traditions (Brazilian, blues, British rock) become the ingredients of new and distinctive styles. Adapting indigenous instruments or rhythms, African musicians participate in a global musical movement. Cultural Flows come from many directions, intersect in unpredictable ways, and continue on in new forms to yet other places. How they continue, and the publics they eventually reach, depend in part on the global commercial media system's marketing and genre promotion efforts, but that system is only one factor shaping local aesthetic orientations. Moreover, commercial interests have much to gain from

> promoting diversity. Thus, as new musical or other fads make their way across the globe, they produce new forms of localised diversity and unforeseen local reactions and interpretations. In the expressive realm, the varied forms of local-global interaction are not inexorably yielding to a standardised, stifling, hegemonic world culture.

Dimensions of Global Culture

Most discussions of world culture focus on its expressive or normative dimensions. Expressive (popular) culture includes media products, consumable goods that assume iconic status as symbols of modernity or avant-gardism, foods and clothing styles originating in particular cultures that become worldwide fads, and so on. Normative culture comprises the values and goals promoted by global corporations and organisations–fetishistic consumerism and capital accumulation, individualism and human rights, democracy and political participation, gender and racial equality. The expressive dimension has received the greatest attention, particularly with respect to the global popularity of American films, television shows, sports figures, and lifestyle elements. Some scholars decry the obliteration of local cultures; others argue in favour of creative interpretation and adaptation, as local cultures integrate new cultural elements while retaining their basic identities (hybridisation or creolisation). Similarly, analysts decry some aspects of normative cultural globalisation and praise others, often sharply disagreeing about the desirability of particular global norms and values and disagreeing as well about the extent to which a global normative consensus is emerging or even possible.

Less attention has been paid to the ontological and cognitive dimensions of world culture. At the ontological level, the reorganisation of social life in accordance with dominant world-cultural models engenders increasing individualism, the disenchantment of nature, reliance on rationalised images of society, and an action-oriented model of the individual. Put another way, world-cultural penetration changes prevailing views of 'the nature of things,' promoting the worldview that underlies such major modern institutions as formal education, experimental science, national accounting and statistical systems, and advanced- technology engineering. These and similar institutional complexes bring with them broad bodies of knowledge and distinctive cognitive styles, but the depth of cultural reconstruction they engender remains largely unexamined because few attempts have been made to come to grips with their cultural implications. Science, mathematics, bookkeeping, organisational structure, technology, tools, construction materials, land surveying–all these have achieved the status of almost unassailably universalistic activities, uninteresting because they are mundane, routine, matter-of-fact. Thus, these highly formalised arenas seldom become the focus of ideological debate, with the notable exceptions of such issues as nuclear power, genetically modified organisms, global warming, and large dams. The most highly institutionalised forms of cultural globalisation remain largely invisible.

Globalisation and Cultural Conflict

World culture engenders conflicts in world society through a process that has, as it were, turned the West against itself. By the 1970s, when scores of new states had formed in Africa and Asia, vociferous opposition to continued economic and cultural domination by Western countries (labelled neocolonialism and cultural imperialism, originally formulated in the West) began to penetrate global organisations, especially UN bodies. Various associations of less developed countries called for a restructuring of world society–a New World Economic Order and a New World Information Order that would put restraints on the operations of transnational corporations and shift resources to the poorer countries. Former colonies began assertively invoking world-cultural principles of equality and development as basic human rights. Further tensions arose as the global human rights sector (itself increasingly involving individuals and groups from outside the West) turned its scrutiny on the new states, decrying their selective championing of certain global universal while ignoring or severely violating others, especially those relating to the integrity and political participation of citizens. Thus, both the particularism of world culture (the moral legitimacy attributed to national or ethnic units) and its universalism (the insistence that all units abide by basic principles and values) yield forms of disagreement and conflict that would not emerge in a less globalised world.

As non-Western cultures and regions have become more prominent in the world polity, it makes increasing sense to speak of world cultures (in the plural) rather than a singular world culture. Dominant Western models have penetrated deeply in most places, but they have also evoked resistance as well as efforts to revivify and globalise alternative models. Most notable in this regard is the assertiveness of Islamic cultural carriers, particularly since the 1970s. Many Muslim leaders and organisations promote a societal model that infuses the state with religious precepts and recasts the relationship between state and citizen (codified in 1981 as the Universal Islamic Declaration of Human Rights). African and Asian models of social organisation and development have also emerged, and some observers argue that conflict in the twenty-first century will revolve primarily around grand civilisational axes rather than the nation-state clashes that have dominated in recent centuries.

By the same token, more fine-grained analyses of world culture(s) identify multiple models of central world-cultural constructs. For example, derived from the Western tradition are liberal, socialist, corporate, and welfare models of the state; from Asian sources, quasifamilial and state-led development models. Multiple models of the individual, the business enterprise, and the national polity are further examples. Worldcultural complexity has increased rapidly in recent decades, perhaps most sharply since the collapse of Communism and the end of the Cold War, as ever more cultural centres generate more alternative cultural constructions. Poorer and more peripheral societies are less able to bring their cultural models to the world-cultural table, but many participants in the global arena from richer societies have become strong advocates of the poor and peripheral, helping to ensure that world culture becomes yet more complex and incoherent but also more significant for national and local structuration and change.

Religion and World Culture

Since the early period of European expansion, many of the symbolic Flows, organising institutions, and foundational assumptions that constitute world culture have been religious in origin. Through conquest, evangelisation, and migration, Europeans made much of the world 'safe for Christianity,' giving emerging world culture a distinctively Christian cast even though most of the world did not become Christian. In the current phase of cultural globalisation, the overall role of religious institutions may have diminished but various religious actors on the global stage vitally affect world culture in new ways, notably by providing alternative worldviews. Religious globalisation has been important in constructing world culture, contributing to its heterogeneity, and producing new forms of conflict, as explained below.

Religion played a distinctive role in the construction of world culture, providing motivation for some globalisers and legitimating the actions of others. It also contributed to the foundations of contemporary world culture. The conception of societal progress that prevails almost everywhere stems in part from the Christian legitimation of rational world mastery; the global view of the individual as agent and citizen similarly has roots in Christian views of the person; the global script for organising society in a rational-legal manner and legitimating authority voluntaristically derives indirectly from Christian precedents. More concretely, missionaries not only spread their faith, they also provided education and health care in far-flung places, diffusing secular commitments that since have become globally entrenched. Their actions pre figured the efforts of later movements in global civil society referred to above. Today distinctly religious views are less obviously influential in world culture, yet they still shape its evolution. According to some, a vigorous Pentecostal movement, successfully expanding to Latin America, Asia, and Africa, carries with it the 'American' gospel of material success and individual wellbeing, thus supporting global corporate culture. The World Council of Churches, others argue, contributed centrally to global environmental concerns with its initiative on 'Justice, Peace, and the Integrity of Creation,' launched in 1983.

Religion's promotion of world-cultural heterogeneity reflects in part the increasing prominence of Third World voices in global religious organisations. Pope John Paul II has appointed a record number of non-Western bishops and cardinals. In the Anglican Church, non-Westerners significantly aid opposition to gay rights. Non-Western Pentecostals have not only grown dramatically in numbers, they have also devised their own spiritual practices to suit local circumstances. Cho Yong-Gi, pastor of the large Yoido Full Gospel Church in Seoul, initiated a world mission program that has sent hundreds of missionaries and established seminaries in several developed countries, including the USA.

Religion's relation to cultural relativism, another aspect of heterogeneity, varies greatly by tradition and is therefore more complex. In some cases, such as that of Hindu nationalism, religion becomes the primary vehicle for expressions of national distinctiveness. While few Christian churches accept the equal value of all cultures, many have in fact accommodated major cultural differences within loose doctrinal parameters. In Korea and Brazil, for instance, Pentecostal churches incorporate elements of traditional non-Christian spirituality. Islamic fundamentalism presents yet another variant, claiming global legitimacy for its defence of 'authentic' Islam while rejecting the value of other traditions. Finally, religion helps to promote heterogeneity through the creolisation process mentioned earlier. Pentecostalism is once again a case in point. An American-inspired movement with a core evangelical message and a secular commitment to material progress has become a mosaic of styles and practices as local congregations have adapted global models to their own needs without direct outside control. As new global movements make inroads in 'national' religious traditions, they produce new juxtapositions that creolise religious cultures. Of course, this process is not unprecedented. Many successful religious traditions have balanced universal ambition with local creativity to produce hybrid religiosity 'on the ground' in counterpoint to unification at the doctrinal level.

Religion also contributes to world-cultural pluralism and conflict. Religious traditions contain diverse views of the good society, leading to varying interpretations of seemingly shared global values. Some view the dominant form of world culture as a coercive, Christian-biased Western force that threatens the integrity of their own traditions. Islamic fundamentalists oppose what they perceive as a godless consumer culture that undermines people's faith and serves the political interests of the West. Pope John Paul II has critised an amoral, neoliberal world order that puts profits ahead of the needs of the poor.

Specific elements of world culture also provoke distinctly religious opposition. In recent decades, for example, the principle that women are citizens– individuals to be granted equal rights and opportunities has been institutionalised in world culture. Within many traditions, however, equality for women is problematic. The result is severe contestation of women's equality in some places, most notably by the Taliban in Afghanistan. These religiously inspired actors have helped generate a more general backlash against globalisation, even while they accept many basic elements of world culture. Religion becomes a vantage point from which to oppose the threat represented by globalisation as such. The struggle, as some groups see it, is between globalisation and their cultural survival.

In sum, religion is a central aspect of cultural globalisation, as traditions spread, transnational networks expand, national cultures become more mixed, and new ways of experiencing the world emerge. In many countries, religion mediates the pluralising effect of world culture. It plays an important role in the intense contest concerning global values and world order. Yet the construction of world culture has become a mainly secular process; it has no transcendent content in the conventional sense. Cultural heterogeneity and conflict themselves take many forms, only some of them religious. While world religion is intimately connected with globalisation and involved in the latter's dynamics, it is by no means a dominant force. Whether it can, or should, take on a greater role in defining the desirable world order is likely to be a central issue in future global cultural contestation.

Glocalisation as Globalisation

In social sciences it is often difficult to trace the origin of concepts. Concepts, theories and ideas are often products of collective endeavours. It would be extremely difficult to identify who used the term "globalisation" for the first time. According to Malcolm Waters whose book titled *Globalisation* is a fine primer, Roland Robertson was one of the early users of the term. More recently, Roland Robertson and Kathleen White edited *Globalisation: Critical Concepts* in 6 volumes is a tour de force which present some of the most important essays on this subject. No matter who coined it first, at the dawn of the 21st century globalisation as a concept, as a slogan, as a term is used more frequently than any other terms. In Singapore, from the inflow of foreign capital, technology, workers or "foreign talents", music, movies, popular culture, almost everything has resonance with globalisation. Globalisation is a heroic process, globalisation is a sinister process, depending on which side of the debate one stands. Some tend to see globalisation as a brakeless train crushing everything in its path, others see benefit in getting on board the train towards economic growth and modernisation.

Globalisation as a concept in social science has a short history. Even in the revised version of Raymond Williams', there is no entry on globalisation. The Harper Collins *Dictionary of Sociology* has an entry on "globalisation of production" but no entry on globalisation as such. The *Oxford Concise Dictionary of Sociology* has an entry on globalisation together with globalisation theory. It says:

> "Globalisation theory examines the emergence of a global cultural system. It suggests that global culture is brought about by a variety of social and cultural developments...".

The entry refers to the book edited by Martin Albrow and Elizabeth King *Globalisation, Knowledge and Society*. The term globalisation was probably first used as a book title in the Albrow and King edited book which was published drawing on the essays published in various issues of *International Sociology* the journal of International Sociological Association (1986-1990) Some of the journal articles contained globalisation as a phrase in the titles in the 1980s and even earlier. One could even claim that the first social science text that dealt with the subject of globalisation was *The Communist Manifesto*. One could even argue that Ibn Khaldun, the author of *Prolegomenon to the Universal History* was the real claimant of the credit. Globalisation as a social process is old and has a much longer history. Many writers have traced the early globalising processes in the dissemination of religion and culture, interactions of people, groups, communities through trade and commerce from the ancient times.

Sociology has been traditionally defined as the study of society. And as the boundaries of society have expanded from local community, through states to global society, sociology has become the study of the global society. This is a good illustration of how ideas, knowledge and (social) sciences expand with the changes and expansion of realities.

Sociology, it is often said, deals with the social life. In fact, all social sciences deal with social life or its various aspects. It is difficult to conceptualise *social* as a category. In sociology, there are two meanings of social. Social used in the sense of Wallerstein or for that matter Marx, encompasses technology, economy, politics and culture. Sociology is interested in the understanding of these broad processes, especially at their interrelatedness.

Globalisation, though it means many things to many people, is one of the master processes of our time. Globalisation as a field in sociology is a legatee of the macro-sociological interests and development. Globalisation study addresses itself to the connectivity of broad processes of technological, economic, political, cultural interrelationships. Whether one looks at the economic, cultural or media connectivity worldwide, one has to take a much broader understanding of society and social institutions. Sociology focuses its analytical lenses on the flows and processes in society whether at the local, national or global levels. In other words, sociology has a genuine claim over the field of globalisation.

Some contemporary writers accuse sociology, an archetypical social science, as a prisoner of nationstate. Anthony Giddens and Immanuel Wallertsien have both lamented that sociology has been the study of modern nation states. The definitions as well as the boundaries of society, which sociology seeks to study, often overlap with those of nation-state. Since the interest taken by sociologists such as Roland Robertson of Pittsburgh and others since the late 1970s, sociology has redefined its scope and field as the social scientific study of the global processes. Ulrich Beck has explicitly called for the development of new concepts to capture the new realities of interconnectedness, plurality multi-locality and multiplicity.

Sociology has established its claim over globalisation as a field of study historically. A return to national society centred focus would be a major regressive step towards objectivist, scientistic sociology and a return to what C Wright Mills called "abstracted empiricism". Or worse, sociology might become a residual discipline busy picking up areas left unattended by other social sciences. Sociology is not the only branch of social sciences that has a claim to study society because other branches of social sciences do study aspects of society. For example, institutional economists deal with social structure and cultural values to explain economic processes and market behaviours. Political scientists such as Robert Putnam have done important sociological studies of political processes. Such fields as political sociology illustrate the cross over of political science and sociology all the time. Social sciences are tasked to analyse society in all its various aspects and constellations.

The long-standing relationship between sociology and globalisation, gives sociology as a discipline a unique position to study all aspects of the field of globalisation, a master process in human society. This does not preclude the claims of other disciplines to the subject of globalisation and it reminds us the importance of each field's autonomy to venture out and explore using its own traditions and conceptual frames.

While globalisation as a framework is naturally biased in favour of macro-sociological issues, questions were raised to the viability of using this framework to study social realities on the ground. This led to a rethink of macro-macro relationship. Glocalisation as a concept arose to help alleviate the conceptual difficulties of macro-micro relationship.

Although it would be difficult to trace the first user of the term "glocalisation" in its original Japanese usage, the first time the term was used in English can be attributed to Professor Roland Robertson, a British/American sociologist, who migrated from United Kingdom to the United States where he spent most of his academic career at the University of Pittsburgh, Pennsylvania, USA. Robertson's original interests in sociology were in the areas of sociology of religion, sociological theories and cultural sociology. He also ventured into areas of comparative sociology and modernisation studies. His interest and knowledge of Japanese society led him to find out the use of the term "glocalisation" in Japan in Japanese language, a term the marketing experts were using by which they meant that products of Japanese origin should be localised that is, they should be suited to local taste and interests yet, the products are global in application and reach, hence a new term "glocalisation" was coined. Robertson and other sociologists interested in the subject of global processes could not help noticing that many of the social categories and practices assume a local flavour or character despite the fact that these products were invented elsewhere. Dutch sociologist Jan Nederveen Pieterse has for some time used terms such as mélange, hybridity, syncretism to capture similar processes with regard to culture. According to Nederveen Pieterse, there are three views on the issue of globalisation of cultures. The first view is the clash of cultures view expressed in terms of clash of the civilisations by writers like Samuel Huntington. The second notion is best expressed in the phrase of "McDonaldisation" of the world. This view obviously suggests a homogenised world, a world dominated by a single culture that erases differences of local cultures. The third view is that of hybridisation or synthesis. Much of human evolution of culture can be seen as exchanges, diffusion, etc. where crossbreeding, borrowing and adjusting to the local needs and so on were very common.

Evolution of the Concept Glocalisation

According to the dictionary meaning, the term "glocal" and the process noun "glocalisation" are "formed by telescoping global and local to make a blend". The term was modelled on Japanese word *dochakuka,* which originally meant adapting farming technique to one's own local condition. In the business world the idea was adopted to refer to global localisation. The word as well as the idea came from Japan. According to Wordspy, glocalisation means "the creation of products or services intended for the global market, but customised to suit the local cultures." Although the term glocalisation has come to frequent use since the late 1980s, there were several related terms that social scientists used and continue to use. One such related word, which has been in use in social sciences and related fields for quite some time is, indigenisation.

Some social scientists claimed that social sciences such as sociology and political science, even psychology were products of western social experiences therefore when these fields of inquiry were transported and transplanted to non-European or non-western contexts such as Latin America, Asia or Africa there was a need for indigenisation of these subjects. The idea of indigenisation has created quite a controversy among social scientists because it raises fundamental questions about the applicability of social scientific ideas and concepts. However, indigenisation can be seen as similar to localisation. In both these concepts, there is an assumption of an original or authentic "locality" or "indigenous system". One of the consequences of globalisation is that it opens up doubts about the originality and authenticity of cultures. If one takes a long-term view of globalisation, "locality" or "local" itself is a consequence of globalisation. There are hardly any sites or cultures that can be seen as isolated or unconnected from the global processes.

Robertson, one of the pioneers in the study of globalisation, did not view globalisation as a recent phenomenon nor did he see it as a consequence of modernisation. The theories of modernisation came under serious attack in sociology because of such assumptions as unilinearity and convergence. As our knowledge of the world increased, many writers pointed out that the cultural differences are not all that superficial and nonlinearity and mutiliniearity are better descriptions of global modernity. Besides divergence rather than convergence seems to have been the consequence of modernisation. Yet the divergent cultures and societies can be studied with the help of a globalised social science and there was no need for diverse, indigenised social sciences. Social sciences to claim scientific status could not afford to forfeit its claim to universality and universal knowledge. Social sciences must be context sensitive but not context dependent. It is in this context that Robertson conceptualised globalisation in the twentieth century as:

> *"the interpenetration of the universalisation of particularisation and the particularisation of universalism".*

Khondker building on Robertson's framework argued that globalisation or glocalisation should be seen as an interdependent process. "The problem of simultaneous globalisation of the local and the localisation of globality can be expressed as the twin processes of *macro-localisation* and *micro-globalisation*. Macro-localisation involves expanding the boundaries locality as well as making some local ideas, practices, institutions global. The rise of world wide religious or ethnic revivalist movements can be seen as examples of macro-localisation. Micro globalisation involves incorporating certain global processes into the local setting. Consider social movements such as the feminist movements or ecological movements or consider new production techniques or marketing strategies which emerge in a certain local context and over a period these practices spread far beyond that locality into a larger spatial and historical arena. Consider print industry or computer industry with a specific location of its emergence has now become a global phenomena. Overcoming space is globalisation. In this view of globalisation, globalisation is glocalisation. This view is somewhat different from the way Giddens conceptualises the relationship between the global and the local. Globalisation, for Giddens:

> "is the reason for the revival of local cultural identities in different parts of the world"

While in this view local is the provider of the response to the forces that are global, we argue that local itself is constituted globally. Ritzer in discussing glocalisation has added another should I say, redundant convoluted term "grobalisation" to refer to what he calls:

> "growth imperatives [pushing] organisations and nations to expand globally and to impose themselves on the local"

For Ritzer, globalisation is the sum total of glocalisation and "grobalisation". Wong argues, following Wind, that a global company does not mean that it has gone global all the way. There are companies that are part global, part regional or part local involving different domains such as portfolio, supply chain, research and development and business processes. In terms of mode of business practices, there could be independent operations, joint venture or alliances.

Key Propositions

The main propositions of gloclaisation are not too different from the main arguments of a sophisticated version of globalisation.

1. Diversity is the essence of social life;
2. Globalisation does not erase *all* differences;
3. Autonomy of history and culture give a sense of uniqueness to the experiences of groups of people whether we define them as cultures, societies or nations;
4. Glocalisation is the notion that removes the fear from many that globalisation is like a tidal wave erasing all the differences.

A number of books and articles on the subject of globalisation give the impression that it is a force that creates a uniform world, a world where barriers disappear and cultures become amalgamated into a global whole. The tensions and conflicts between cultures are nothing but the problems of a transitory phase. Ironically, the phase of transition has been around for a long period of time. And as we have entered the third millennia many of the age-old problems of differences of cultures and religion remain. Glocalisaton does not promise a world free from conflicts and tensions but a more historically grounded understanding of the complicated yet, pragmatic view of the world.

Globalisation is not Westernisation

Some writers view globalisation as the worldwide spread of "westernisation". This view is either erroneous or contains only partial truth. From a superficial point of view, various processes outwardly seem that the world is, indeed, becoming westernized. One could see the popularity of the western music, movies, and "McDonalds" as examples of westernisation. More and more countries are seeing the opening of McDonalds. More and more countries playing the top chart of the pop list of USA and Hollywood movies and US-made television serials (such as, *Friends* and *The Simpsons* are becoming ubiquitous to the extent that some writers even use the term "Americanisation" to describe these processes of cultural transmission. However, a closer look will reveal that these cultural goods have different meanings in different societal and cultural contexts with uneven impact on classes and age groups. Some of the products are consumed without any modification, others are modified and indigenised to suit the local contexts and there are exceptional situations where the intentions are completely inverted.

In the past, many writers found it necessary to distinguish modernisation from westernisation. Modernisation was believed to be a set of cultural practices and social institutional features that historically evolved in

Europe and North America, commonly referred to as the West. The need to separate westernisation from modernisation (in the past) was motivated more by nationalism than pure intellectual reasons, because historically speaking, most of the modern cultural traits began in the West, a historical fact which was difficult to accommodate in a nationalistic political culture. The Western scholars in the nineteenth century were also guilty of making exaggerated claims of western superiority. Max Weber, a German sociologist was correct to claim that the western rationality and science had become universal but his denigration of non-western cultures did not sit well among the larger intellectual community.

Many Indian sociologists took pains to delineate the differences between modernisation and westernisation. Similar discussions exist with regard to so-called westernisation of the Ottoman Empire, modernisation of Japan since the Meiji restoration of 1868 or modernisation of China in the early part of the 20th century such as the May 4th Movement of 1919. In the modernisation process, many of the late modernising societies were borrowing ideas and knowledge and technology most of which were generated in the early modernised societies in Europe. The geography of the West kept shifting. In the nineteenth century, when Germany was modernising, the idea of the West was limited to Western Europe only (mainly Britain and France). In some post-colonial situations the demarcation was based more on political expedience than logical or intellectual merits. Good westernisation came to be regarded as modernisation and bad modernisation was designated as westernisation. The distancing from westernisation can also be understood as a reaction to centuries of domination and exploitation of the colonies by the western (mainly European) powers. However, over time a more objective consideration of history indicate that many of the traits that spread worldwide originated in certain geographical regions yet as these traits were transplanted elsewhere, they became mutated and assumed different forms in different contexts. For example, parliamentary democracy evolved in England, with roots that go back to *Magna Carta* of 1215. However, as Westminster-style parliamentary democracy was institutionalised in India, Malaysia, and other former British colonies, they mutated in light of the local milieu.

Westernisation as a term is not equivalent to globalisation. Nevertheless, westernisation can be seen as an aspect of globalisation. Certain institutional features and cultural traits that originated in the west were put in place in many other geographical regions lock stock and barrel under the framework of global interconnections and diffusion or forced implantation under colonial age. Yet, over time these institutions and practices mutated and assumed new meanings. Therefore, westernisation can be seen as the beginning of the process. The cultural features borrowed or imitated themselves mutate in the source countries. Thus, westernisation as a category has limited conceptual value. One can associate certain literary forms, genres, and traits as part of the cultural zone we vaguely call "the west", yet these are mere influences as one can see in artistic, literary, architectural styles. For example, the great Indian film maker late Satyajit Ray was influenced by Hollywood films and the art of film making, but he did not want to replicate Hollywood movies in Calcutta. His movies were modern capturing local themes which he projected with a modern art form and technology. Hence it was truly global, or more appropriately, glocal. Presently, Singapore is establishing linkages with both Bollywood and Indian film industries as well seeking to play the role of an outsourced location for hi-tech Hollywood productions. Globalisation, like modernisation, is often a fusion. Westernisation as a concept has some value if used only as a descriptive rather than analytic category. As an analytic category it is rather limited.

Writers such as John Meyer have used the idea of isomorphism (a term borrowed from science, botany, in particular) which means replication of the same form yet separated from the main source. His research has shown that modern education not western education though it was perhaps modified and institutionalised in the west has spread worldwide and a similar set of values and practices have emerged in diverse settings. For example, college graduates command more social prestige and respect almost regardless of cultural contexts. Some cultures can give more rewards than others. Globalisation shows tendencies towards isomorphism, yet some people may continue to mistake this process for westernisation.

In the context of Singapore, the first generation leaders always emphasised the fact that although Singapore's economic development was dependent on western technology and capital, and it was reliant on multinational corporations to foster economic growth, the state maintained a certain degree of autonomy and formulated broad social development strategy.

Glocalisation and Hybridisation

In the discussion of glocalisation some writers tend to conflate it with hybridisation. This may be somewhat misleading. Glocalisation involves blending, mixing adapting of two or more processes one of which must be local. But one can accept a hybrid version that does not involve local In the context of higher education in Singapore a hybridised version comprising the original British model and the US model was accepted. One could find many such examples in matters of technology and business practices where two different systems or modes are combined for better results.

Glocalisation to be meaningful must include at least one component that addresses the local culture, system of values and practices and so on. One of the areas in Singapore where the evidence of glocalisation is quite visible is the area of mass communication and especially in the area of television programming. From televised drama, sitcoms, and even "reality shows" one finds attempts of glocalisation. Although some attempts are not always successful and there are instances when one can see unabashed imitation, by and large the idea of glocalisation and fusion remain appealing to many Singaporeans.

Technology and Glocalisation

Singapore, located in Southeast Asia, has attained the developed country status or High Income Economy according to the World Bank classification. Having experienced rapid state-led economic development under a favourable global economic climate, Singapore has been pursuing the goal of creating a knowledge-based economy since 1990s. Singapore's economic growth since her emergence in 1965 as an independent state entailed heavy investment in education and development of human resource in science and technology. Singapore's advancement in areas of knowledge and high technology is dependent to a large extent on international collaboration. Two aspects of Singapore's growth are striking: linkage with global market and a highly rational approach to governance, which is often evidenced by a near-absence of corruption. These two aspects have direct bearing on the issues of technological developments in Singapore. An additional factor that one has to take into account is the cultural diversity of Singapore's population. Singapore is both a multiethnic and multi-religious society, which provides an added dimension to the context of formulation of ethical standards. Its 4 million people (in 2004) comprise 76% Chinese, 14%

Malay, 7% Indian, and 3% others. As many as one quarter of Singapore's population is non-citizens which indicate Singapore's reliance on foreign human resources both at working class jobs as well as high end knowledge workers. Multicultural population-base and the varying sensitivity of various groups have influenced policies concerning biotechnology.

According to Stephen Haggard:

> "Singapore had already broken away from the typical policy pattern of a developing country as early as 1970. By the 1980s Singaporean policymakers were identifying the country with small European economies such as Switserland"

It has been noted by a number of writers that Singapore's economic development and social modernisation did not take place following a pure free market model. Singapore state was very much involved in guiding the market forces. On the one hand Singapore has relied heavily for multinational corporations to launch economic growth but it also built a high rate of savings through central Provident Fund. Singapore's development model showed certain mixed or hybrid quality. Soon after Singapore's independence, policymakers began to focus attention on development in sciences and technology. The strive for such development was aided in the process by close relationship with the Multinational Corporations who brought investments and employed technically qualified Singaporeans. Right from the early days of national development, Singapore was well integrated with not only the international economic system bit also with global knowledge systems. Singapore's export oriented economic development in the 1980s was dominated by IT and computer peripherals. In the 1990s emphasis on biotechnology followed an earlier emphasis on IT.

Singapore's development since her independence in 1965 can be described as a transformation from a Third

World society to a First World economy. Much of that development can be attributed to Singapore's adoption of modern technology. Choices of technology were not always preceded by controversies and debates. Both the government and the general public showed a great deal of pragmatism in the choice of technology. Although in most instances, technology was adopted without much modification, the mode of use, and so on there were imprints of adaptation and glocalisation. One such area is in the area of electronic road pricing system. The technology of monitoring cars from a scanner fitted in a gantry was not a Singaporean invention, but they way that technology was used was very Singaporean. Because of the drive to catch up, Singapore has always been ahead in adopting new technology. It is in recent years having achieved the developed status; some Singaporeans are showing concern with issues of privacy and so on because some of the new technology is intrusive. Singapore's love affairs with technology is evident in the fact that Singapore ranks among the top three countries in the world in terms usage of personal computers as well as hand phones. The only country ahead of Singapore in the number of Short Messaging Service (SMS) is Hong Kong. Whenever a new technology is invented, Singapore would be one of the first places where that technology would show up.

Singaporeans have a favourable attitude towards technology. Singapore International Airlines as well as Port Authority of Singapore (PSA) remain equipped with the state of the art technology. ATM machines in Singapore were introduced in the early 1980s. Singapore's public transport system is another place where one would find a great many applications of new technology. However, all cases of adaptation technology may not be seen as examples of glocalisation. In many instances, for example, computer technology in Singapore was implemented without any modifications. However as Singapore entered a new phase of research in the 1990s, namely in the area of biotechnology we fins evidence of glocalisation. Biotechnological research calls for a careful consideration of and orientation towards local cultural and ethical contexts. A good deal of attention has been given to these areas in Singapore. Another area where examples of glocalisation can be found in both Malaysia and Singapore is the area of architectural designs. In the post-socialist world, Singapore remains a unique society where 90% of the population lives in the houses built and then sold to the citizens. When Singapore was embarked on massive public housing program, it borrowed the so-called international style of very basic and practical designs, yet a new concept of public space though limited to the residents of the housing blocs evolved. These spaces known as void-decks were places for wedding, funeral or any such communal gatherings. New designs blending the western and local motifs emerged in Singapore.

Although the initial architectural thrust of Singapore can be viewed as "brutalism" driven by a sheer pragmatic consideration, over the years more attention has been given to the notions of fusion and hybridity, or in other words glocalisation.

7

Globalisation and Political Sociology

Over the past decade, the liberalisation of trade, finance, and investment across the world has opened vast new territories to dynamic economic actors. The rise of incomes in developing countries has created large new consumer markets. Producing across national boundaries has shifted research, development, and manufacturing activities involving higher and higher degrees of skill and value into other societies. At the same time, economic institutions are also changing. Corporations that were once vertically integrated are shrinking their boundaries and focusing on core specialisation. New partnerships, commodity chains, alliances, and mergers link producers, suppliers, and customers.

Before World War I, it was only the rare observer of the international economy who wondered about the effects on domestic politics of soaring levels of cross-border capital movements, migration, foreign direct investment, and the new transportation and communication technologies that accelerated movement of information and goods among countries. But the idea that globalisation undermines the autonomy and leverage of the nation-state appears in writings from this earlier period of internationalisation. Angell, reflecting on this theme on the eve of the war, had already identified the very same factors that today are imagined to be the motors of globalisation.

> This vital interdependence... cutting athwart frontiers is largely the work of the last forty years....[It is] the result of daily use of those contrivances of civilisation which date from yesterday—the rapid post, the instantaneous dissemination of financial and commercial information by means of telegraphy, and generally the incredible increase in the rapidity of communication which has put the half-dozen chief capitals of Christendom in closer contact financially, and has rendered them more dependent the one upon the other than were the chief cities of Great Britain less than a hundred years ago.

From this financial interdependence, Angell deduced the irrationality, indeed the unlikelihood, of war, for he thought it had become too costly to the fabric of international economic exchange to be a conceivable option. This line of theorising about the politics of open economies was cut off in its infancy by the disastrous failure of predictions such as Angell's and by the fact that national economies closed up at the time of the war. Between World War I and the 1980s, cross-border economic exchanges remained at far lower levels than they had reached at the turn of the century. As the magnitudes of trade, foreign direct investment, and short term capital flows across national boundaries have skyrocketed since the 1970s, social scientists have returned to Angell's questions.

In this new literature of the 1990s, there is a common understanding of globalisation as a set of changes in the international economy that tend to produce a single world market for goods, services, capital, and labour. In a formulation that recurs across the spectrum of views on globalisation, Glyn & Sutcliffe define it as:

> "The idea that the world is now really a single economy in the macroeconomic sense. That means that the main

> determinants of income and employment can now only be understood at a global and no longer a national level"

But beyond the definition, there is little agreement. Researchers disagree even on the basic characteristics of the globalisation process. This review lays out some of the issues that divide them, then focuses on unresolved debates over the political consequences of globalisation.

First if the rise in cross-border economic flows as a proportion of the world's economy is uncontestable, should this be interpreted as the advent of globalisation or as an extension and deepening of patterns of internationalisation and regionalisation? The case for globalisation as a new and irreversible phenomenon is made most strikingly in works written for a large public readership. The pioneer in this territory was Ohmae, who argued that the "interlinked economy" has wiped out national borders.

> "On a political map, the boundaries between countries are as clear as ever. But on a competitive map, a map showing the real flows of financial and industrial activity, those boundaries have largely disappeared"

Or, as a British commentator put:

> "[The state's] powers over the price of money... tax rates, industrial policy, the rate of unemployment, have been blown away"

Globalisation undermines the national state, these observers claim, not only by shrinking the resources under national control for shaping economic and social outcomes, but also by reducing government's legitimacy and authority in the eyes of the public. Across virtually all advanced industrial countries over the past two decades, there has been an erosion of public confidence in central governments. Even when analysts mention the role of specific national causes in this loss of trust, still they tend to emphasise the universality of the shifts—how everywhere globalisation destroys national control of information flows hence weakens a government's ability to influence its public. The effects of the internationalisation of the media, the marketing and export of American popular culture, and the deregulation of information all combine to weaken national values and traditions, and in so doing, they dry up the springs of support for national action. The effects of changes in the international economy are experienced through the national political leaders' diminished control both over the material determinants of a country's prosperity and over the vehicles for reaching common public understandings of national wellbeing. In this widely held view of the coming political order, the eclipse of the national state is the central fact.

This view of globalisation appears not only in the writings of those who are optimistic about the effects of these developments on societal wellbeing, like Ohmae and Friedman, but also in the analyses of those who find these changes threatening. *L'Horreur Economique*, which warns of the dire consequences of globalisation for employment and for national existence, became a best-seller in France.

In describing globalisation as a full-blown reality, these popular works accept as fact what many scholars more prudently identify as a strong and virtually irreversible trend. These analysts diverge in the weights they assign to various factors in explaining the breakdown of national controls over economies and the acceleration of trade and capital flows across borders. Some find that the key drivers of the process are new information technologies; others emphasise more heavily the role of financial liberalisation and deregulation, as well as the politics of interest and ideology that brought these policy shifts to fruition in all the major advanced countries. Yet others focus on a politics of interests set in motion by an "exogenous easing of trade"—changes in rules, technologies, or prices that reduce barriers to international exchange or increase the gains associated with such trade, thus creating new opportunities for some groups within society to gain from buying and selling across national boundaries. In this perspective, no matter what initiates liberalisation, the process gains momentum as some economic actors realise the possibilities for using their assets more profitably in more open markets.

Indeed, from this point of view, the effects of globalisation can be achieved without moving factors of production across borders. To lower wages in the United States, for example, the industrialist need not import labour from Mexico nor move his factories to Mexico. He simply needs to be able (to threaten) to do so. The potential of substituting foreign workers and production for domestic workers and production reduces labour's bargaining power by making the demand for domestic labour more elastic. In an opening international economy, then, increases in trade and foreign direct investment that are small relative to the size of the domestic economy may trigger large effects on factor and product prices, as Wood and Rodrik have argued. Globalisation may then come to have major effects on domestic economies and politics even where most investment is national and where goods and services made and sold in the domestic market dominate imports and exports. Despite their different weightings of the factors that produce the globalised economy, all of these accounts of globalisation share a common core, namely the declining relevance of national economic units.

In contrast to those who see evolution to a global economy as the determining process of economic life, there are scholars who interpret the changes of the past 20 years as internationalisation or as regionalisation. Hirst & Thompson distinguish between an international economy, in which the basic units remain national societies and actors, and a globalised economy, in which:

> "National economies are subsumed and rearticulated into the system by international processes and transactions"

In their view, the increases in capital mobility, trade, and foreign direct investment over the past two decades should be understood as intensified interaction among entities that remain distinctively national. Even the largest companies, free to invest their funds and develop their activities virtually anywhere in the world, in fact continue to concentrate a large proportion of their employment, investment, research and development, production, and sales in their own home countries, and thus are multinational rather than transnational corporations. Most economic activities are not traded across borders, and production for the domestic market and nontraded services dominate in all but a few small city-states, such as Singapore and Hong Kong.

Analysts who see change in the world economy as extension and deepening of older patterns of internationalisation, rather than as globalisation, also question whether any fundamentally new developments are occurring. If we consider the period from the mid-nineteenth century to the present, what can we learn about variations over time in the levels of mobility of goods, information, capital, and labour across national borders? If the levels of flow of resources across frontiers do have historical precedents, what can we learn from them about the ability of national states to regulate these economic transfers, and, more broadly, about the survival of national politics in an internationalising economy? Research on the international economy in the first two decades of the twentieth century has seriously challenged the new conventional wisdom about the globalised economy by pointing to internationalisation in the past. By 1913, in the most advanced countries, levels of capital and labour mobility across national boundaries were quite comparable to today's levels. Cable points out that it was only in the 1970s and 1980s that the share of trade in gross domestic product (GDP) for countries in the Organisation for Economic Cooperation and Development returned to levels that had already been reached in 1913. Foreign direct investment has been estimated at 9% of global GDP in 1913; subsequently it declined to less than half that amount, and by 1990 it had not yet returned to the 1913 level. An *Economist* survey on states and the international economy noted that capital flows were as mobile before World War I as they are today and that net capital transfers were significantly greater.

It would be a mistake, of course, to expect exact parallels between the situation obtaining in the international economic and political system linking the advanced countries of 1913 and today's international system. There have been real changes in global capital markets, relative even to the degree of integration achieved before the collapse during the two world wars and the Depression. The velocity and gross volume of capital movements today are on a scale that dwarfs those of the turn of the century. New financial instruments, new technologies of communication, and a greater concentration of asset holders with the growth of institutional investors have created a different environment.

Krugman points to several important differences between contemporary patterns of trade and those of the period of high internationalisation before World War I. Today's exchanges include significant proportions of intra-industry trade. The growing capabilities of developing countries have led to the rise in exports from low-wage to high-wage societies as well as to new possibilities for foreign direct investment and outsourcing from high-wage to low-wage economies. This fragmentation of production, enabled by new information and transportation technologies, is transforming industrial organisations in the advanced countries. Finally, in the contemporary global economy, in contrast to that of the earlier period, a number of trading states have emerged with very high ratios of trade to GDP. Despite the differences, the view from the longer perspective does not show an irreversible progression toward ever greater and unprecedented levels of internationalisation. Rather, the picture is of high levels of trade at the onset of World War I followed by a devastating shattering of the links of interdependence among the advanced countries, then by a gradual reweaving of the networks of the international economy, and finally a return (by the turn of the twenty-first century) to an international world with national constraints and opportunities that some of our more prescient great-grandparents had already glimpsed.

If there is something radically new in the world economy, some argue that it is not globalisation but regionalisation. The growth of trade and investment within each of the four major economic blocs—the European Union (EU), North America, Mercosur (Latin America), and East Asia—is far greater than the growth of exchanges among the blocs or between them and the rest of the world. If the phenomena to be explained are interpreted as regionalisation and not globalisation, then it makes sense to focus on the role of politics in building regional trade pacts (e.g. the EU and the North American Free Trade Agreement) rather than on changes in communication and transportation technologies or on economic theories of comparative advantage, whether in Heckscher-Ohlin or in Ricardo-Viner variants.

Others looking at the domestic economies of the major advanced countries argue that the most striking change over the past twenty years is not the increase in the proportion of the economy that is traded internationally (imports plus exports) but the rise of employment in services relative to manufacturing. Technological changes would explain far more of this transformation of domestic economic and social structures than would internationalisation.

In sum, although scholars have a common idea of what globalisation is or would be, they do not agree on whether the current changes in the international economic environment are caused by globalisation or by something else. Among the candidate theories for something else, internationalisation, regionalisation, and the rise of a service economy are the main alternatives.

Globalisation and Reshaping of Politics

Research on the impact of globalisation on domestic politics builds on a paradigm in political science that Gourevitch has aptly called "the second image reversed," a reference to Waltz's models of international relations theories. Waltz sought to identify studies that analyse how changes in international factors are transmitted into domestic life. How do changes in the international economy affect domestic actors? Do the same changes produce the same results in national politics everywhere?

According to Gourevitch's research on national responses to common international crises, the mechanism by which changes in the world market are brought into national politics is a process of transmission through changes in the prices domestic producer groups pay and receive. Gourevitch emphasises the possibilities of politicians' building different domestic coalitions of interests out of the groups mobilised by upheavals in their livelihood deriving from the international economy. In the countries Gourevitch discusses during the crises of 1873–1896, 1929–1949, and the 1970s, the basic "societal actors" or interests are the same: farmers, finance, labour, industrialists. Yet the patterns of accommodation these interests reached, under pressure from external events, and the economic policies these coalitions supported varied greatly from country to country. Party politics, state structures, intermediate associations, and politicians built different alliances among (the same) social groups.

If Gourevitch's map of societal interests reveals a determinacy in the presence and importance of groups in societies at the same level of economic development, his conception of their politics is far more open. Swedish and German farmers in the 1930s may have had similar preferences for protection from the market, but the Swedes ended up supporting a Social-Democratic alliance with workers, whereas the Germans ended up with Nazism. In the same research tradition, Katzenstein's work on neocorporatism in small open economies also focuses on variation in the responses of social groups under comparable pressures from the international economy, depending on political structures and policies. However similar the maps of social and economic interests in societies at comparable stages of economic advance, political reactions to shifts and shocks from the international economy are essentially indeterminate because they are mediated by political parties, ideologies, strategies, and contingent acts of leadership.

International Trade Theory

Whereas the "second image reversed" literature built on a proto-Marxist historical conception of social actors and a rather wide range of possible political outcomes under world economic pressures, the research inspired by international trade theory suggests both a simpler map of interests and a sharper set of predictions about groups' responses to change in the world economy. Standard theorems of international trade—Heckscher-Ohlin, Stolper-Samuelson, Ricardo-Viner—elaborate Ricardo's original insight about relative comparative advantage as the reason that nations find benefit in exchange. These theorems predict patterns of trade based on different national distributions of the factors of production, and they suggest that social groups, as defined by their stakes in the factors of production, will have their fortunes altered in predictable ways by trade opening or protectionism. If interests are distributed in patterns determined by the ownership of factors of production (land, labour, or capital), and these factors are mobile across borders, according to a Heckscher-Ohlin formulation, or as incorporated in traded goods and services, according to the Stolper-Samuelson model, then clear predictions follow about which groups will support and which groups will oppose economic openness. In societies that have relatively abundant capital, hence a comparative advantage in exporting capital or in exporting capital-intensive products, capitalists will support trade opening and labour will oppose it.

How to conceptualise factors of production, and hence social actors, is a major question for this research agenda. For example, should we think of labour as a single factor of production, and characterise societies as more or less endowed with it, or should we distinguish between more skilled and less skilled workers (as defined by education and training) and characterise the relative advantages of societies in terms of the abundance of skilled labour? If we conceive factors of production as scarce assets, should our analysis also include other assets that may create differential stakes in trade opening or closure? Scheve & Slaughter have tested the effects of home ownership in counties with trade-exposed industries on attitudes toward trade.

There is a clear division among scholars who ground politics in the responses of different interests to the international economy. On one side are the analysts, including Rogowski and Scheve & Slaughter, whose characterisation of factors is independent of the sector in which they are employed, and who assume relatively easy mobility of factors among industries. On the other side are those who see factors as specific to a particular industry and not so easily moved from one sector to another, as in Ricardo-Viner formulations of trade theory. For scholars in the latter camp, the critical variable for political responses to trade opening is the sector in which capitalists have invested or in which workers are employed, so that, for example, both shoe manufacturers and shoe-industry workers would oppose removing barriers to the entry of shoes from lower-cost producers. The shoe manufacturers could not quickly or profitably sell off their shoe factories and reinvest in new sectors; the workers have acquired particular skills in making shoes that may not be transferable to other jobs. If the Heckscher-Ohlin predictions based on factor type (labour, capital, or land) are too broad-gauge to capture the logic of economic interest, how much detail about the industry would we need to analyse the dynamic of political responses? Even in one industry, looking at one factor, there are multiple potentially important specificities. We might distinguish capitalists who held shares of footwear companies from those who owned physical plants, or we might distinguish shoe manufacturers in niche markets (high-fashion shoes, orthopedic shoes, work-protective shoes) from standard mass product makers (athletic shoes and the like).

These two approaches from trade theory lead to two distinct predictions about political preferences and behaviour. In a test of the two models, Scheve & Slaughter ask whether individual trade-policy preferences are better accounted for by factor type (which they define by worker skill levels) or by industry of employment (which they characterise by degrees of exposure to trade). They find that the skill level of workers is a better predictor of individual support for restrictions on trade than is employment in a trade-exposed industry. This result is consistent with a Heckscher-Ohlin factor-type model. Other empirical research, however, supports a Ricardo-Viner model. Frieden argues that in the short run, the specific-factors model better explains responses to trade, although over the long term Heckscher-Ohlin may prevail. Increasing integration of world markets would bring homogenisation of interests within factor types, so that eventually, political struggles over globalisation would become conflicts between labour and capital rather than between one industry's workers/ employers and another's.

Structural Constraints on Government in a Global Economy

If public policy is considered the result of the vector of interest group pressures, then the political models derived from trade theory suggest some simple predictions about the future of the state in a global economy. The growing mobility of capital and the relative immobility of labour would make governments increasingly responsive to the interests of capital. If taxes, industrial policy, environmental regulation, or industrial relations in any society are too costly or constraining, investors will pull up stakes and transfer them elsewhere; workers cannot move so easily. Therefore, the expected results of limiting taxation of capital are that labour will have to shoulder a greater part of the tax burden and that society's ability to fund social welfare expenditures will decline.

The shift in the domestic balance of power between capital and labour that globalisation promotes by rewarding mobile factors thus translates into a shift in domestic politics. Social democracy becomes less likely because capital's incentives for cross-class compromise are lowered by its growing power. Even when socialists win electoral majorities, as Mitterrand did in France in 1981, an open economy (in the case of France, the European economy) offers the holders of mobile assets the opportunity to enforce their preferences by threatening to exit. Although capital flight is hardly a new problem for the governments of the left, the range of policy instruments for dealing with it is far narrower than at any time since the beginning of the century.

Globalisation shrinks the state by reinforcing the political resources of those groups in society who desire limitation of the use of state powers to redress outcomes in the market. It also ties the hands of even those political forces whose ideological traditions support state intervention in production and redistribution. In this view, it hardly matters whether the left or the right wins elections; the constraints of the internationalised economy will oblige either party to follow the same monetary and fiscal policies or else face a loss of national competitiveness and investment.

Globalisation and Neoliberalism

One need not view the world through the lens of international trade theory to see links between globalisation and the shrinking of the nation-state. Whereas political economists who have developed political models out of theories of comparative advantage see openness linked to the power of the state by the dynamic of domestic interest struggles, others see globalisation as the result of ideological changes that have transformed national governments. The global spread of neoliberal doctrines has everywhere reduced the legitimacy of broad state involvement in the economy and reduced governments' ability to shape or to protect against market outcomes. The waves of deregulation that have swept away governmental powers virtually across the world over the past two decades have their origin in deep and complex value shifts. These changes first captured the parties of the right, but the Thatcher and Reagan "revolutions" were reenacted in even more far-reaching renunciations on the left.

At the same time, the end of the Cold War and the collapse of state socialism opened new terrain for economic liberalism. According to Wes, in 1978 one third of the world's work force lived in centrally planned economies. During the past decade, these economies became integrated into world markets. Even in China, the sole remaining major socialist country, capitalism and liberal market principles made major advances. Although it was possible to argue for more or less rapid "transition" to market economies, plausible alternatives to the market economy no longer seemed to exist. Both in liberal democracies and in the former state-socialist countries, the political appeal of socialist or left doctrines that would enlarge the state's mandate to regulate the economy evaporated. Where Communist parties have reemerged, they function mainly as vehicles of populist protest.

The spread of neoliberal norms was propelled not only by the failures of socialism but also by the advocacy of the United States. In a position of unchallenged dominance in global financial and trade institutions, the United States pushed for a rapid end to capital controls across the world and for making International Monetary Fund and World Bank assistance contingent on recipient countries' acceptance of sharp limitations on the role of government in the economy. From this perspective, globalisation, far from reflecting the spontaneous spread of world markets and the toppling of barriers by economic actors' eager for new opportunities, is a story driven by politics: ideological change, the contingencies of the collapse of the socialist economy, and US power in the world.

Evaluating the Constraints

Although important differences exist among scholars who

emphasise the role of US policy, new technologies, financial markets, or new political values in the irresistible rise of globalisation, most accounts advance some mixture of causes and feedbacks. The real divide in the literature lies between those who argue that globalisation, however it has come about, has eroded the autonomy and authority of national governments, and those who argue that however much globalisation may have occurred, national states still retain their basic powers. Empirical research intended to confirm or refute theory-driven predictions of the erosion of national government's capabilities has focused on four big questions. Has the state lost the levers that enabled it to make macroeconomic policy? Has the state lost the tools of industrial policy and other supply-side policies that played a major role in the postwar growth strategies of newly industrialising economies? Has the state lost the ability to raise the resources to finance extensive welfare and redistributional policies? More generally, have states lost the ability to sustain distinctive forms of capitalism within their societies—distinctive configurations of market and nonmarket institutions that reflect societal preferences and national traditions in the particular ways they build productive institutions and networks to connect economic organisations?

Macroeconomic Sovereignty

In the international economy of the post–World War II era, with capital controls and trade barriers, states were able to use interest rates, the exchange rate, and the supply of money as levers of control in their economies. When rapid economic growth was accompanied by inflation, governments could limit the consequences by obstructing the entry of foreign goods that might compete with more expensive domestic products and by blocking domestic capital from exiting in search of higher returns. When economic growth slowed, governments could devalue the currency to cheapen exports, lower interest rates to stimulate investment, and increase government spending to increase employment. When currencies came under speculative attack, countries responded with currency and investment controls.

In a world of free-moving financial capital, once policymakers renounce the use of capital and trade restrictions, the menu of macroeconomic options is shortened. At best, governments may choose between the value of the currency and the interest rate. The instruments of macroeconomic policy are even more limited in countries that have pegged their currency to the US dollar, as Hong Kong has, and in countries that link their currencies, as the Western Europeans have (first in the European Monetary System and then in a single currency, the euro). As demonstrated by the experience of the states that were hardest hit by the Asian financial crisis (e.g. Thailand), if a country is to stem the outflow of investors and keep the support of international financial institutions, then borders have to be kept open, even when interest rates soar and the currency collapses. Is this loss of manoeuvring room in monetary policy paralleled by a loss of autonomy in fiscal policy? Views divide widely on this point. Rodrik, among others, concludes that globalisation makes it hard to raise the tax burden in general. Globalisation reduces the taxation of capital, which is mobile, and shifts the tax burden onto labour, which is less mobile. Eichengreen explains that the:

> "Most basic principle of the theory of tax incidence is that elastically supplied inputs into production escape the burden of taxes; try to tax them and they vanish....It is not surprising that capital's share of taxes paid in the leading industrial countries that make up the Organisation for Economic Cooperation and Development (OECD) has shifted steadily downward in recent years."

Other research, however, contradicts these findings. Swank examines corporate tax burden in the 1990s for the 17 largest and richest OECD countries and finds little change since the 1970s. He analyses the impact of international capital mobility on corporate profits taxation for the period 1966–1993 and discovers that:

> "if anything, direct effects of globalisation of capital markets are associated with slightly higher business taxes and, to a degree, the diminution of tax policy responsiveness to the conditions that underpin investment"

With respect to trade, however, Swank reports a small positive effect of trade openness on the fall of business-profits taxation. Garrett, exploring the prospects for left-labour policies in the 1990s, concludes that trade openness and capital mobility do not diminish government's capacity to tax, nor even its options for increasing the progressivity of the tax system. Social democratic governments based on left-labour coalitions are associated with bigger government and higher corporate taxation than the Anglo-American liberal market systems, but the end of capital controls need not spell the end of redistributive politics. Garrett argues that business obtains many benefits from the state's role in economy and society, especially from public investments in human and physical resources and from redistributive expenditures that reduce social tensions arising from economic dislocation. Therefore, even mobile asset holders will remain in relatively high tax societies when these environments provide valuable public goods, such as a well-educated workforce, social stability, and proximity to cutting-edge research institutions.

Industrial Policy

How does globalisation affect the government's capacity to promote a particular set of economic activities within national territory? Both in advanced industrial countries and in developing countries, governments have used a variety of policies to encourage specific industries: preferential credit, export subsidies, research and development grants, military procurement, export subsidies, protection of the domestic market for domestic producers, and others. If government intervention was intended to attenuate a domestic shortage of capital for promising new activities, then globalisation should alleviate the problem, since domestic firms can now draw on world capital markets (not only on domestic savings) to finance new investments. But in most other respects, globalisation makes it more difficult or even impossible to use such policies as Japan, Korea, Singapore, and Taiwan developed in the postwar decades to build modern industries. Capital mobility makes it very difficult for governments to constrain local investors to provide funds for industry at lower rates of return than they would receive abroad. The extension across national borders of commodity chains that coordinate production functions distributed across multiple countries weakens the links of interdependence among domestic producers and retailers. The emergence of global suppliers capable of providing services and sub-assemblies for multinational corporations wherever they locate production may crowd out local suppliers and reduce the multinational corporations' need to cooperate with local producers and to transfer technology and know-how to them.

Most constraining, the rules of the new international trading order limit the kinds of help that governments can provide to domestic industries without violating the antidumping or ant competition provisions. The mutual charges of protectionism and hidden subsidy that the United States and the European Union have pressed against each other in the World Trade Organisation (WTO) over the past year regarding bananas, beef hormones, and the tax advantages that US corporations derive from offshore Foreign Sales Corporations are only the latest examples of the capacity of internationally accepted trade sanctions to restrain government support of particular industries. OECD debated an international treaty on the rights of foreign investors, the Multilateral Agreement on Investment, which is even more far-reaching in its implications for clipping the wings of governments. This accord would have obliged its signatories to treat foreign investment like domestic investment and would have constrained the regulatory options of governments at all levels. Negotiated in secret, the proposed treaty was stopped by a wave of attacks from nongovernmental organisations and social movements that orchestrated a campaign against the Multilateral Accord on Investment on the grounds that it protected the rights of capital but not labour and that it constrained democratic decision-making.

End of the Welfare State

Does globalisation destroy the welfare state? One of the deepest sources of anxiety about international openness is the fear that welfare-state institutions that have buffered the workings of market capitalism will no longer be sustainable. In part, the debate revolves around the issue of whether a race to the bottom in wages, social provision, and labour-market regulation is inevitable because of financial market liberalisation and because of capital's new opportunities of relocation in low-cost, low-regulation countries.

The empirical evidence suggests far greater resilience and capacity for adaptation within the format of universal social provision than these pessimistic readings of the new distribution of power within advanced societies suggest. First, as discussed above, corporate taxation as a share of tax revenues or as a share of gross domestic product has been quite stable, challenging the notion that states are engaged in a competitive downward spiral to reduce corporate taxes. Second, patterns of change in social expenditures vary significantly across countries. Pierson shows that these patterns do not correspond to the predictions that might be derived from assumptions about the vulnerability of social expenditure to pressures from mobile asset holders with increased openness. Swank analysed the impact of increasing capital mobility on total social spending in 15 advanced countries and concludes:

> Where institutions of collective interest representation—social corporatism and inclusive electoral institutions—are strong, where authority is concentrated and where the welfare state is based on the principle of universalism, the effects of international capital mobility are absent, or they are positive in the sense that they suggest economic and political interests opposed to neoliberal reforms, or adversely affected by globalisation, have been successful in defending the welfare state.

In contrast, where such institutions are weak, capital mobility has had a more dampening effect on social expenditure.

Is globalisation really the main explanation for the pressures on welfare state expenditure that are evident across developed countries? Domestic factors—e.g. the aging of the population, a productivity slowdown in service-based post-industrial economies, the maturation of welfare programs—may be at least as important as new developments in the international economy. The welfare state may be in for hard times, but globalisation matters only in conjunction with domestic variables that vary from state to state. Its effects on policy are not direct. Rather, where governments have been committed to preserving the basic features of the welfare state (as in the Netherlands), a range of reforms and accommodations have maintained the essential distributive elements of the old social compact.

National Varieties of Capitalism

Beyond the constraints that globalisation may exercise in economic policymaking, there remains the question of its impact on the institutional constellation of different national systems. Albert's *Capitalism vs. Capitalism* launched a debate over the societal foundations of economic performance.

Contributors to the varieties-of-capitalism literature, then, see more than one kind of industrial society and believe that the different institutional configurations, or production regimes, generate systematically different micro behaviours. From institutional configurations and differences in micro behaviours, these scholars deduce a theory of comparative institutional advantage. In this perspective, different production regimes, or different capitalisms, should be good at solving different kinds of coordination and production problems, and hence over time should come to specialise in and excel in those activities.

Are these varieties of capitalism, each with its distinctive assets and weaknesses, equally resilient in an open international economy? Within this question are two different issues. First, one may ask whether the characteristics of the new economy—however conceptualised—play to the strengths of some models of capitalism more than others. The American economy, with flexible labour markets, arms-length relations between investors and industry, research and development systems that favour radical change rather than incremental process improvements, well-developed financial markets, and so forth, might be better able to respond to global competition than, for example, German or Japanese capitalism. There are many claims made along these lines, but the evidence is far from clear. It is true that the German and Japanese economies have experienced major difficulties over the past few years, but if one compares the economic growth, employment, and productivity growth of these countries with that of the United States over a 10-year period that corresponds to the same phases of the business cycle, their performance is roughly equivalent. Although one variety of capitalism might do better at particular economic conjunctures, or at solving particular kinds of problems in innovation, production, or distribution, there is no compelling evidence that any of these constellations has a clear economic superiority across the board over time.

The second issue is as follows. If one believes that economic institutions depend on specific societal resources, then globalisation might differentially affect models of capitalism by undermining a society's ability to reproduce those resources. Capital mobility, for example, might have different effects in a country whose economic system relied heavily on labour-capital negotiation and cooperation in the workplace than in a country where skills are formed outside the workplace and acquired in markets.

New Agenda of Politics

The case for a decline of national power and sovereignty in an age of globalisation stands on two legs. One is the notion that the magnitude and velocity of international economic exchanges have eroded the state's capabilities. The other is the argument that the extension of market relations across national borders diminishes the citizen's attachment to national authority, leading to a decline in the legitimacy of central governments. Contemporary politics in advanced industrial countries provides much evidence of a growing distrust of elected politicians. But there are no signs that the electorate's disillusionment about their representatives reflects a deeper detachment from national loyalties, let alone a transfer of political allegiance and identification to regional or international bodies.

As pressures from the international economy intrude on domestic societies, citizens turn ever more urgently to their own governments for help. What many of them mean by help is protection from the unregulated flow of capital, labour, and information from outside national territory. In their view, domestic problems—e.g. unemployment, delocalisation of industry, immigrants, pornography on the internet—are carried into the community by this unregulated flow across unguarded national boundaries. Far from understanding the new relationships induced by internationalisation as the product of impersonal and inevitable market forces, many of these citizens see the new situation as one created by their own government's actions in opening the frontiers, in negotiating new trade treaties, and in legislating about immigration. Because the problems appear to have political origins, they appear reversible by government action. Thus, one paradoxical outcome of globalisation may be to refocus political attention on the role of the state on the boundaries of national territory. Citizens are mobilising along new lines of cleavage, and in many advanced countries, a new political camp has emerged, organised around a program of reinforcing national controls at the frontiers. Supporters of these views can be found across the political spectrum.

A twenty-first century of nation-states—an expansive, intrusive, and unregulated global economy—these are the future parameters of our opportunities and our dangers. Citizens increasingly understand the relative economic strengths and weaknesses of their societies as products of specific national political arrangements and of different national cultures, not as the result of diverse natural advantages. The combination of these elements makes it likely that the new age of globalisation will be one of international conflicts over the economy. We can already glimpse the character of these contests: a mix of conflicting visions of right and interest. The struggles between the United States and Japan in the Structural Impediments Initiative negotiations, between the United States and Europe over the "cultural exception" in the Uruguay Round, between the United States and Europe over beef hormones and genetically modified substances in foods, between Japan and China on the linkages between trade, aid, and nuclear weapons; in the conflicts heating up on internet content, on child labour, on "social clauses," environment, and trade—all reflect different national conceptions both of interest and of the basic norms of social life. Energised partly by interests, partly by ideals, these confrontations do not align one ideological camp against another nor one civilisation against another. They do not pit "Asian values" against "Anglo-American" values. Often they mobilise multiple and conflicting traditions within pluralistic national societies. In this way, the conflicts between societies that are induced by globalisation threaten to reopen old lines of domestic discord.

8

Technology and Social Change

We are in a new era of computerisation—one in which networked computer and communications systems are becoming part of the daily life of a significant percentage of the public. Allowing public access to the Internet was arguably the most pivotal public policy choice that stimulated this rise in networked computing.

Other behaviours that helped to popularise interest in the these new technologies include high levels of symbolic support from the Clinton–Gore White House, and the enthusiasm of business, entertainment, and technology journalists about "information super highways." The possibilities of widespread Internet use have also stimulated substantial developments in a variety of applications, such as electronic commerce, distance education, electronic publishing, digital libraries, and virtual communities.

The emergence of these new applications has excited considerable speculation about the social changes that could arise if these kinds of Internet uses were to become widespread. Would electronic commerce, as illustrated by Amazon.com and e-Bay, erode the markets of physical stores? Could distance education provide new opportunitie s for a sound, inexpensive, and convenient education at home? Would widespread distance education become commonplace and rapidly erode the demand for place-based colleges and universities? Would electronic journals develop rapidly as low-cost alternatives to increasingly expensive print journals? Would digital libraries erode the demand for "brick and mortar" libraries? In turn, if so much social activity shifted from face-to-face, place-based settings to these new online forums, would community life erode?

These are important kinds of questions to be asking now, especially while significant opportunities to shape these network-enabled activities still exist. Unfortunately, much of the writing about the social changes that these new information and communication technologies (ICTs) will or could catalyse has relied on oversimplified conceptions of the relationship between technologies and social change. There has been a substantial body of analytical and empirically grounded research about ICTs and social change that could better inform these kinds of discussions. Unfortunately, the research articles are scattered in the journals of several different fields, including communications, computer science, information systems, information science, and some social sciences. Each of these fields uses somewhat different nomenclature. This diversity of communication outlets and specialised terminologie s makes it difficult for many nonspecialists (and even specialists) to locate important studies. One impetus for coining a new term—*social informatics*—was to help make these ideas accessible to nonspecialists. The new appellation was also intended to strengthen communication between specialists, and to strengthen the dialogues between communities of designers and social analysts. *Social informatics* is the new working name for the interdisciplinary study of the design, uses, and consequences of information technologies that takes into account their interaction with institutional and cultural contexts.

Social informatics is a field that is defined by its topic (and fundamental questions about it) rather than by a family of methods, much like the fields of urban studies or gerontology. Social informatics has been a subject of systematic analytical and critical research for the last 25 years. This body of research has developed theories and finding that are pertinent to understanding the design, development, and operation of usable information systems, including computer networks, electronic forums, digital libraries, and electronic journals.

Research in Social Informatics

Throughout the 1970s and 1980s, much of the social informatics research focused on organisations because they were the major sites of computerisation. It is only in the last few years that many people who are not technical specialists have gotten computer systems for home use. The era of the Internet, or, specifically, public access to the Internet, raises issues about changes in areas such as working at home, communication, entertainment, and other personal uses.

In the 1970s and 1980s, often the questions about computerisation were phrased as deterministic impact questions, such as "What would be the impact of computers on organisational behaviour if we did X?"; "What would be the changes in social life if we did X?"; "Will computer systems improve or degrade the quality of work?" There are a number of studies in which people attempted to answer this last question, that of whether work life would improve for clerks, for engineers, for managers, and so on. The questions were often phrased in very simple, direct terms, namely, "Which will happen, X or Y?" And the answer was, "Sometimes X, and sometimes Y." There was no simple, direct effect. Much of the character of change depended on the relative power of the workers. For example, clerks fared less well, on average, than professionals. But secretaries, who are the aristocrats of the clerical class, sometimes experienced greater improvements in their work lives than did the workers, primarily women, who were processing transactions in the back rooms of banks and insurance companies. Occupational power played an important role in mediating and shaping the way computerisation restructured workplaces.

Other sets of questions were also examined, such as to what extent did organisations become centralised after computerisation? Strong arguments were made that computer systems would enable upper managers to have much more detailed information about the operations in workplaces (such as the shop floor, the editorial room, and the classroom) and that as a result, organisations would become more centralised. Others argued that they would become more decentralised. Many people wanted to know, "Well, which is it? Is it A or B?" Some studies found that information technology use led to some organisations' centralising, while other studies found that information technology use led to decentralisation. Many of the arguments that were framed in the form of "Is it A or B?" were based upon simple technological determinism, which has not been borne out in the reviews of the most methodologically sound studies. The analytical failure of technological determinism is one of the interesting and durable findings of social informatics research.

Today some analysts (and many pundits) frame claims about information technology in social life in deterministic ways, with claims such as "The Web means that the public will get better information than ever before" or "University courses on the Internet will soon eliminate most 'place based' colleges and universities." These are framings that people who study social informatics would be skeptical of. There is a large body of research about ICT impacts that reports that the consequences of computerisation depend upon the context in which systems are developed, implemented, and used.

As an alternative to the simple claim that the Internet provides better information, we ask contextual questions, such as "When will the Web enable the public to locate 'better information'? Under what conditions? For whom? For what?" For example, are people seeking information on the Internet to help them to better choose a doctor, and then placing more trust in that doctor? Or are people seeking alternatives to doctor-mediated medical care, such as information about health, herbal medicine, or postoperative care?

As alternatives to the claim that Internet courses will replace traditional college education, we ask about the conditions under which people will prefer one type of educational experience over the other. For example, online courses may be desirable to adults who don't live near an appropriate university, while a place-based education may be sought by teenagers who are looking for a social experience as well as formal education, or by people pursuing education in fields that require expensive specialised laboratory equipment. We ask about the roles courses and degrees play in many people's lives. We would ask about the life circumstances that could lead millions of people of the kind who now seek courses and degrees in in-place colleges to abandon them for online courses and degree programs.

These contingency questions don't lend themselves to snappy sound bites. But they do yield a very nuanced conceptual understanding. This kind of contextual inquiry illustrates the ways in which social informatics researchers frame questions in order to develop an analytical understanding of information technologies in social life.

Key Ideas of Social Informatics

The concept of computerised information systems as "sociotechnical networks" is one such idea that helps us understand the character of new electronic information spaces, such as discussion lists, groupware, electronic conferencing systems, and e-journals. The concept of sociotechnical networks helps analysts to overcome some key limitations of determinstic impact analyses. We introduce the concept and then develop it with several different examples.

Information Technologies as Sociotechnical Networks

To set the groundwork for sociotechnical networks, we start with a more general concept, that ICT, in practice, *is socially shaped.* In the standard (nonsocial informatics) accounts of ICT and social change, it is common to hear information technologies characterised as tools, and questions are asked about their social impacts. For example, in the 1970s, several people studied local governments to understand the impacts of computerised information systems on the nature of work, client relationships, and possible redistributions of power within organisations. However, were fined our views on the character of computerisation and how to conceptualise ICTs during the course of conducting the research. We found that local governments selectively adopted and developed different kinds of information systems, depending upon their form of internal organisation.

In some cities, a professional city manager's office or a central finance department exerted strong control over information systems developments. In these cities, the information systems development staff were often centralised and delegated projects to various departments. In contrast, other cities were much more decentralised and many departments, such as police or planning, controlled their own computer systems and their own information systems development staffs. In these cases, many more systems were tailored to help departmental managers better understand and control their functional areas. American local governments did not simply utilise computerised information systems. They organised their technical staffs in different arrangements and created different ICT pricing schemes for systems developments, reprogramming, and operations. They created different governance structures for regulating and directing their commitments to ICT. Professionals and managers who were seeking new information systems or changes in existing systems did not deal only with or even directly with computers; they had to mobilise an organisational system as well. We called this combination of equipment, people, governance structures, and ICT policies: "the local computing package" The local computing package is also an example of a sociotechnical network. A sociotechnical network brings together equipment, equipment vendors, technical specialists, upper-level managers, ICT policies, internal funding, and external grant funding with the people who will use information systems in the course of other work (such as policing, accounting, taxing, or planning). These elements are not simply a static list but are interrelated within a matrix of social and technical dependencies.

Table 1. Conceptions of ICT in organisations/society

Standard (tool) models	Sociotechnical models
ICT is a tool.	ICT is a sociotechnical network.
A business model is sufficient.	An ecological view is also needed.
One-shot ICT implementations are made.	ICT implementations are an ongoing social process.
Technological effects are direct and immediate.	Technological effects are indirect and involve different time scales.
Politics are bad or irrelevant.	Politics are central and even enabling.
Incentives to change are unproblematic.	Incentives may require restructuring (and may be in conflict).
Relationships are easily reformed.	Relationships are complex, negotiated, and multivalent (including trust).

Social effects of ICT are big but isolated and benign.	Potentially enormous social repercussions of ICT (not just quality of work life, but overall quality of life).
Contexts are simple (a few key terms or demographics).	Contexts are complex (matrixes of businesses, services, people, technology history, location, etc.).
Knowledge and expertise are easily made explicit.	Knowledge and expertise are inherently tacit/implicit.
ICT infrastructures are fully supportive.	Additional skill and work are needed to make ICT work.

Computing packages differed from one city to another. However, as the broad-brush sketch already drawn suggests, some were configured as rather centralised formations while others were more decentralised (and often more heterogeneous). The configurations of these local computing packages were influenced by the distribution of power within specificity governments—they were socially shaped. In turn, we found that the local computing configurations influenced both the mix of information systems in a city and the ways "similar information systems" were configured. We also found that the local mix of information systems and their uses in city decisions (such as annual budget hearings) tended to help reinforce the relative organisational power of the groups that exerted the most control over the local computing package. This pattern is an example of the concept of reinforcement politics.

During the course of conducting our research in the 1970s, we shifted from viewing ICT as having impacts to an appreciation that the impacts of ICT were socially shaped. We learned that complex equipment-in-use was necessarily embedded inextricably in a heterogeneous sociotechnical network. We also found that computerisation was a complex and often lengthy sociotechnical process.These sociotechnical concepts have been applied in subsequent research about the character of ICT in other kinds of organisations, including manufacturing; newer technologies, such as desktop computing in the 1980s and electronic journals in the 1990s; and larger-scale social settings, such as scientific communities and wired cities. Some of the ideas that developed from the sociotechnical networks approach are summarised in Table 1. These ideas derive from a much larger body of research.

Before we discuss some applications of the sociotechnical networks approach, we want to explain one kind of highly intertwined socio technical interaction network model. This model seems especially helpful in understanding electronic forums, including conferencing systems and electronic journals. In contrast, the characterisation of the computing package separated equipment (or technology) from social relationship s and resources. This analytical separation between artifacts and social worlds is very common, even in social shaping analyses. Some social informatics researchers have developed refined social shaping approaches. In these approaches, as in the concept of reinforcement politics, social relationships shape the kinds of artifacts selected, their configuration, and their typical modes of use. But artifacts are conceptualised as the products of engineering and as 100% separable from social relationships.

In the highly intertwined model, the technology in use and the social world are not seen as separate—they co-constitute each other. The model is highly (but not completely) intertwined because its adherents do not insist that this intertwining of technical and social elements is universal. Rather, it is commonplace, and a good heuristic for inquiry, especially with complex technologies. References to technologies and social entities and to the interactions between them are made largely for analytical convenience. For example, one might say, "Indiana University is using Web boards to support class discussions when the participants are not in class together." Indiana

University and its classes would be treated as social forms and Web boards would be viewed as material information technologies. In the highly intertwined model the Web boards could be examined to see how they are constituted as sociotechnical networks. For example, certain social relationships are inscribed into the Web boards when they are used (such as access controls that determine who can read and contribute to them). Other aspects of relationship s are shaped by supporting social protocols about legitimate content (to what extent are jokes or advertisements allowed in a specific class's Web board?).

Similarly, Indiana University in Bloomington can be seen as being co constitute d with diverse technologies. Its routine operations rest on a complex set of building technologies, heating/cooling technologies, food acquisition and preparation technologies, and information and communication technologies. Without these (and other technologies) we would have 35,000 students, 1500 faculty, and 2000 staff milling around in the forested hills of Bloomington, foraging for food and organising themselves just by face-to-face conversation, word of mouth, and rumour! In contrast, the Indiana University of 1880, with about 300 students and a few dosen faculty, functioned with much simpler technologies than those that are required for the much vaster contemporary university.

However, any means of recording information about enrolment, courses, requirements, and so on would require some kind of ICTs, however crude. In this sense, an organisation such as Indiana University is composed not just of people in social relationships, but also of diverse technologies. In fact, one can interpret many of the discussions of Internet-supported distance education as efforts to constitute new kinds of universities by changing their ICT infrastructures and pedagogies.

The highly intertwined sociotechnical model seems especially useful for understanding the social shaping and "consequences" of ICTs that form the primary communication media for groups. But even a more relaxed social shaping model raises concerns about simple claims concerning ICT's impacts (such as "The Internet is democratising politics").

Sociotechnical Interaction Networks

The use of the Internet to support scientific communication is one of the major shifts in the practice of science in this era, and it has generated much research and significant discussion. In the scientific communities, these communications include informal e-mail, the communication of conference programs as they gel, the sharing of preprints, access to electronic versions of journal articles, and the development of shared disciplinary corpuses. These communicative practices are becoming more important in many fields, although they are rarely the central communications media. However, only a few analyses take sufficient account of the ways in which the social dimensions of publications, such as the design of electronic journals, influence their use.

One common approach to conceptualising new forms, such as electronic journals, online newspapers, electronic forums, Web sites, and digital libraries, emphasises their technologically based information-processing features such as enabling authors and readers to communicate more directly, without the mediation of libraries or expensive publishers. The sociotechnical approach, explained next, views these new forms as mixing together technological elements and social relationships and creating an effectively inseparable ensemble.

From a technological information-processing perspective, new media such as electronic journals, databases, and preprint servers are said to reduce the costs of communication, expand the range of people and locations from which materials are accessible, and generally speed communications. According to this view, as scholars in all scientific fields work with data and communicate both formally and informally with other scholars, all of these electronic media forums should be adopted and used fairly uniformly.

Even the strongest proponents of electronic journals agree that technological design alone is not sufficient to ensure the quality of a journal. There is a strong consensus that the quality of a journal's scholarly content is important in making it viable, but there is substantial disagreement about the means of attracting high-caliber materials. All the proposals and counterproposal s for attracting high-quality authors rest on social analyses of a journal, rather than on purely technological analyses. For example, one aspect of electronic journals that is commonly discussed is the role of peer review. There are many ways of organising peer reviews, but all of the strategies for selecting reviewers and translating their assessments into feedback for authors and publication criteria for the journal are social processes. These social processes are supported by communication media, and the electronic media may facilitate or inhibit specific ways of organising reviewers, reviewing, and editing.

Intranets in Action

One way to illustrate a contextual inquiry of information technology and social behaviour is to examine case studies of organisations. A particular example comes from the studies of how some consulting firms have adopted and used computerised documentary systems. One major consulting firm, identified by the alias Alpha Consulting, bought specialised equipment and 10,000 copies of Lotus Notes for their staff in 1989. Lotus Notes, a documentary support system, is superficially similar to an Internet-like system, with bulletin boards, posting mechanisms, discussion groups, and electronic mail for organisations. Depending upon how Notes is used, it can act as an e-mail system, a discussion system, an electronic publishing system, and/or a set of digital libraries.

Alpha Consulting is an international consulting firm with tens of thousands of employees worldwide, about 10,000 of those employees located in the United States. Their director of information and technology believed that Lotus Notes was such a powerful technology that its usefulness would be patently evident, and that the main thing to do was to rapidly roll it out to the consulting staff and let them use it to find creative ways to share information. The director of information and technology felt that Lotus Notes was so revolutionarily valuable that people didn't even have to be shown illustrative business examples its use, and that providing examples would be counterproductive as it might stunt employees' imaginations. The consultants should simply be given an opportunity to use it, and they would learn how to use it in creative ways.

The director of information and technology was concerned that his firm was employing thousands of "line consultants" in different offices all over North America who were working on similar problems but rarely sharing their expertise. Sometimes a consulting team in Boston would be dealing with an issue very similar to one being handled by a consulting team in Toronto or San Francisco. The consultants had no easy way of sharing with consultants in other offices their solutions to the problems they were facing. Could the firm's line consultants use some kind of communication and computerised information system to store what they knew and then share it?

The first test of Lotus Notes involved the information technology staff. They tended to use Lotus Notes; they found it interesting and used it fairly aggressively for sharing information about their own projects. Alpha Consulting's tax consultants in Washington, DC, were another group that used Lotus Notes. These tax consultants studied the behaviour of the Internal Revenue Service and the U.S. Congress and disseminated tax advisories to Alpha Consulting offices around the country about changes in tax legislation that might affect their clients. These tax consultants made substantial use of Lotus Notes to broadcast their tax advisories.

The line consultants were intended to be Lotus Notes' primary users. However, organisational informatics researchers found that the senior line consultants, who were partners in the firm, tended to be modest users, while the more numerous junior line consultants, called associates, were actually low users. They often seemed uninterested in learning how to use Lotus Notes, readily gave up if they faced early frustrations with Notes, and as a group did not spend much time with it. Here we have a pattern of different groups within an organisation having different practices in working with Lotus Notes. How can we explain such differences?

One explanation focuses upon the incentive systems in the firm. A good place to start our analysis is with the associate consultants and the partners. Alpha Consulting—like many other large consulting firms in North America—reviews its consultants through a demanding promotion system. The associates receive an "up or out" performance review every 2 years. In the first few career reviews at major consulting firms, about half of the associates are fired. However, many of the associate consultants would prefer to be promoted to the status of partner. Consultants who are promoted to the status of partners can expect annual incomes of over $300,000 at these major firms. Partnerships are the golden ring that these firms use to motivate their associate consultants.

The associates are valued for their billable hours and are effectively required to bill almost all of their time. As they become more senior, their ability to attract new business becomes more critical. "Billable hours" means that they have an account that they can charge their time to. Lotus Notes, the revolutionary technology, was not provided to them with a training account to bill their time to. Consultants who wanted to use Lotus Notes had to have an account to charge their time against, and the initial learning time was on the order of 20 to 30 hours. In 1991, the consultants were billed at about $150 an hour, so they had to find a client who would be willing to pay $3000 to $4500 for them to learn a system whose value wasn't yet clear to them. Many had trouble justifying that amount of expenditure to any of their clients at the time when they were participating in the Lotus Notes rollout. There was also an important question as to what the consultants would actually do with Lotus Notes after they learned how to use it. Consequently, relatively few associates saw much value in Lotus Notes, and there were no exemplary demonstrations showing them how other successful line consultants used Lotus Notes.

On the other hand, the partners had substantial job security (which was similar to university tenure). They could afford to experiment with Lotus Notes. They were more willing to invest some time to explore, often using e-mail, occasionally developing and sending memos, and so on. Overall, this case study contradicts the popular "Nintendo generation" explanation: "In the future, we don't have to train people about computing, because the Nintendo kids (or the Net kids) will learn quickly." In this case, the younger consultants generally had less incentive to learn Lotus Notes than did the middle-aged and elderly partners.

But what about the information technology staff and the tax consultants? These groups also had an advantage in their forms of job security. Many of the information technology staff were technophiles who were willing to work with an interesting new application. Lotus Notes has been helpful for people who can invest time in learning how to use it, especially when they have joint projects and substantial motivations for communicating, for documenting work, for sharing memos, and so on.

The tax consultants, who were located in Washington, DC, had a significant incentive to show that they were visible and valuable in the firm. In their case, fixed salaries not based on billable hours allowed them more freedom to explore Lotus Notes' uses. Lotus Notes allowed them to broadcast for visibility: It gave them the ability, in effect, to electronically publish their advice and make it quickly available to many of the consultants around the firm who wanted to read the Lotus Notes database. They hoped it would enhance their visibility and thus show that the Washington, DC, office was not just overhead but an important contributing part of the firm.

In short, although they proved to be of considerable importance, organisational incentive systems were not part of the original marketing story of Lotus Notes. It was the interesting information-processing features enabled by Lotus Notes that were emphasised in numerous stories in the technical press.

Different organisations, or different organisational subunits with different incentive systems, might use Lotus Notes very differently. The way some consultants in Ernst and Young (E&Y), another major consulting firm, use Lotus Notes is instructive. In brief, E&Y created an organisation (Centre for Business Knowledge) whose charter was to organise E&Y's consultants ' know-how in specific high profile areas. The new organisation was staffed with consultants from other E&Y offices who were given 6-month assignments to play a special role as "knowledge networkers." By 1997, E&Y had developed 22 distinct cross-office networks of consultants with expertise in certain industries, organisational reforms, or technologies that were a focus of E&Y's business. Each consultant network was assigned a half-time person (the knowledge networker) to codify in Lotus Notes databases the insights from specific consulting projects, to prompt line consultants to add their own insights, and to edit and prune a project's discussion and document databases. In some cases, they developed topical "Power Packs" in Notes—a structured and filtered set of online materials, including sales presentations and proposal templates. Davenport observed that these knowledge networkers well understood their consultant network's topics, and that since these were short-term assignments for the consultants, they expected to utilise any newly gained expertise to advance their own careers when they returned to their consulting positions.

In this case, E&Y designed a human organisational "intelligence system" for sharing insights, ideas, and materials in specific topical areas. Lotus Notes served as an information support system—a medium for storing, organising, and communicating these materials.

Taken together, these cases illustrate varied consequences of Lotus Notes' use in large consulting firms, as opposed to one fixed effect. Finding such varied, conflicting consequences in different settings is common in this body of research. Our job as researchers is not simply to document the various consequences of computerisation, but also to theorise about them. For example, analysis of the different organisational incentive systems for different professionals increases our understanding of these disparate cases.

One key idea of social informatics research is that the social context of information technology development and use plays a significant role in influencing the ways in which people use information and technologies, and thus affects the consequences of the technology for work, organisations, and other social relationships. *Social context* does not refer to some abstract cloud that hovers above people and information technology; it refers to a specific matrix of social relationships. In the cases just described, social context is characterised by particular incentive systems for using, organising, and sharing information in different work groups and work roles. The different groups within Alpha Consulting and E&Y have different incentives to share information about the project know-how and thus the amount of use they make of Lotus Notes varies.

The cases of Alpha Consulting and E&Y also illustrate another important idea—that of conceptualising the design of computer and networked systems as a set of interrelated decisions about technology and the organisation of work. Unfortunately, thinking and talking about computerisation as a development of sociotechnical configurations rather than as simply installing and using a new technology is not commonplace. It is common for managers and technologists to discuss some social repercussions of new technologies, such as the sponsorship of projects, training people to use new systems, and controls over access to information. However, these discussions usually treat all or most social behaviour as separable from the technologies, whereas these two cases demonstrate that it is critical to take a more integrated sociotechnical view.

Public Access to Information via the Internet

There are innumerable examples of the use and value of the Internet in providing new kinds of communications to support a cornucopia of human activities in virtually every profession and kind of institution. In the United States, the professional and middle classes have found the Internet to be useful for communication with some government agencies, some forms of shopping, tracking investments, maintaining ties with friends and family via e-mail, and as a source of entertainment.

There are also many examples of ways in which the Internet enables the middle-class public to have better access to important information. In the United States, the public is beginning to turn to medical sources on the Web, finding answers and information on Web sites, in discussion groups, and so on. People may be seeking either alternative medical advice or information about issues that their doctors don't address well. Surgeons, for example, may be very skilled in surgery, but they may not be very good at giving people an understanding of what it takes to go through the recovery process. People sometimes find that certain Internet sources can be extremely helpful as alternative sources of information or as supplements to the information provided by their physicians. Anecdotal evidence suggests that the Internet may provide the means for many middle-class people to bypass the medical establishment. Anecdotal evidence also suggests that doctors' responses to their patients' feeling better informed and thus sometimes questioning or challenging their advice ranges from encouragement to annoyance. The changes in the patient–doctor relationship that may eventually result are as yet unclear.

In the United States, Vice-President Al Gore promotes networking for libraries, clinics, and schools by arguing that if they are wired together, their use will improve public education and enable substantially improved public services. How to actually transform such networks into meaningful social support systems is a question that remains unanswered.

While affordable telephone service and Internet service providers (ISPs) are usually available in more urban areas, access to ISPs, and even to basic telephone service, is more problematic in many rural areas. In 1995, about 28.8 million people in the United States 16 years of age and older had access to the Internet at work, school, or home, while 16.4 million people used the Internet, and 11.5 million used the Web. About 80% of these people used the Internet at least once a week. However, about 182 million people 16 years of age and older did not have access to the Internet. A 1997 nationwide household study found that computer ownership and e-mail access were rising rapidly: About 94% of households have telephones, 37% have personal computers, 26% have modems, and 19% have online access. The number of people with Internet access continues to rise rapidly.

It might appear that technological access is the primary roadblock to expanded Internet use. *Technological access* refers to the physical availability of suitable equipment, including computers that are of adequate speed and equipped with appropriate software for a given activity. Scenarios of "ordinary people" using the Internet often assume that computer support is easy to organise and that access to information and services is not problematic.

In contrast, *social access* refers to know-how—a mix of professional knowledge, economic resources, and technical skills—for using technologies in ways that enhance professional practices and social life. In practice, social access—the abilities of diverse organisations and people from many walks of life to actually use these services— will be critical if advanced technologies are to move from the laboratories and pilot projects into widespread use where they can vitalise the nation and the economy. Social access should not be viewed as an add-on to a technological structure. Many systems designers have learned, for example, that a well-designed system does not simply tack on a computer interface after its internal structure has been set in place. The design of human interfaces and internal structures is highly coupled for systems that effectively support people's work and communication. In a similar way, social access is integral to the design and development of systems and services that are to be widely used.

Some analysts do not view the provision of social access to the Internet for ordinary people as problematic, since they believe that access costs will rapidly decline and the public's computing skills will continue to rise. In this view, time and market developments will resolve most access issues. In contrast, we believe that getting good social access to the Internet is likely to prove troublesome for many people, based on the finding of careful studies of computer and Internet use.

Although 50% of U.S. households may have computers now, organisations have been the major adopters of networked information systems, especially as implementers of advanced technologies. There are few studies of computer use in households. In one careful study of ordinary households, researchers found that using the Internet is too hard for many ordinary people:

> Over 70% of the households called the help desk. Calls to the help desk represented the behaviour of some of the more sophisticated users. Less sophisticated users dropped out once they hit usability barriers. The kinds of problems logged by help-desk staff included problems in installing phone service, configuring the telecommunication software, busy signals (users often blamed themselves!), buggy software, inexperience with mice, keyboards, scroll bars, terminology, radio buttons, and menus. Yet, in our home interviews, we noted there were many more problems participants had not called about....
>
> We thought that as everyone learned how to use the computer and what the Internet could do for them, the

> influence of their initial computer skill would decline with time. We were wrong. Even after a year of experience with the Internet, participants' initial computer skill still constrained their Internet usage. This result held across different gender and age groups

These finding serve as a cautionary note about our expecting the North American public to rapidly form a network nation. One intriguing finding of the Home Net project is that families with adolescents made much more use of the Internet than those without. We suspect that many of these teenagers became critical on-site technical consultants for their parents.

In fact, a recent large-scale study reports a widening gap in Internet use within the U.S. population: The 1998 data reveal significant disparities, including the following:

1. Households with incomes of $75,000 and higher are more than 20 times more likely to have access to the Internet than those at the lowest income levels, and more than 9 times as likely to have a computer at home.
2. Whites are more likely to have access to the Internet from home than Blacks or Hispanics are to have access from any location.
3. Black and Hispanic households are approximately one-third as likely to have home Internet access as households of Asian/Pacific Islander descent, and roughly two-fifths as likely as White households.
4. Regardless of income level, Americans living in rural areas are lagging behind in Internet access.

Indeed, at the lowest income levels, those in urban areas are more than twice as likely to have Internet access as those earning the same income in rural areas. For many groups, the digital divide has widened as the information haves outpace the have-nots in gaining access to electronic resources. The following gaps with regard to home Internet access are representative:

1. The gaps between White and Hispanic households, and between White and Black households, are now more than 6 percentage points larger than they were in 1994.
2. The digital divides based on education and income level have also increased in the last year alone. Between 1997 and 1998, the divide between those at the highest and lowest education levels increased 25%, and the divide between those at the highest and lowest income levels grew 29%.

These are amazing finding, since the cost of purchasing an entry-level personal computer (PC) has declined considerably in the last few years. In addition, ISPs have become commonplace and connection costs have also declined. The costs of equipment alone cannot effectively explain these growing disparities.

Infrastructure for Computing Support Is Social As Well *As Technological.* PCs are much more complicated to install and use for a diverse array of tasks than are turnkey appliances such as televisions and videocassette recorders (VCRs). While it is a standing joke that most people don't know how to program their VCRs (and thus watch an LCD blinking 00:00), most people can reliably play a videotape and enjoy the resulting entertainment. In contrast, PCs that use networked services require much more complex configurations (including data rates and IP numbers) that can change with changes in network configurations and service providers.

Effective computer systems that use Internet services will require reliable complementary technological resources such as phone service and electricity, which, while generally available in urban settings, may be problematic after disasters or in remote regions. What is less well appreciated is how the infrastructure that makes computer systems workable also includes a variety of resources that are social in character. Skilled technical installers, trainers, and consultants are the most obvious social resources. In addition, people who use advanced networking applications need to be able to learn from others how to effectively integrate the applications into their working practices.

There is some debate about how much computer use has simplified in the last decade. It has probably become easier to use a stand-alone PC right out of the box. However, the dominant operating systems, such as Windows 95/98/NT or Unix (and Linux), can still stump even experts when applications or components interact badly.

System infrastructure is a sociotechnical system since technical capabilities depend upon skilled people, administrative procedures, and so forth, and social capabilities are enabled by simpler supporting technologies (e.g., word processors for creating technical documents, cellular telephones and pagers for contacting rapid-response consultants). Malfunctioning computer systems are not simply an opportunity loss such as a book that is bought but not read. When people organise their days around the expectations that key technologies will function correctly only to find that they don't, they then often spend considerable time attempting to get the systems to work, waiting for help to come, and so on.

Workable computer applications are usually supported by a strong sociotechnical infrastructure. The surface features of computer systems are the most visible and are the primary subject of debates and systems analyses. But they are only one part of computerisation projects. Many key parts of information systems are neither immediately visible nor interesting in their novelty. They include technical infrastructure such as reliable electricity. They also involve a range of skilled support—from people to document system features and train people to use them, to rapid-response consultants who can diagnose and repair system failures.

Much of the research about appropriate infrastructure comes from studies of systems that underperformed or failed. The social infrastructure of a given computer system is not homogeneous across social sites. For example, the Worm Community System was a collaboratory for molecular biologist s who worked in hundreds of university laboratories; key social infrastructure for network connectivity and (Unix) skills depended upon the laboratory's work organisation (and local university resources). Researchers found that the Worm Community System was technically well designed, but it was rather weak as an effective collaboratory because of the uneven and often limited support for its technical requirements in various university labs.

Social informatics research pertains to information technology developments and uses in any social setting, not just organisations. Social informatics researchers are especially interested in developing reliable knowledge about information technology and social change based on systematic empirical research in order to inform both public policy issues and professional practice. Our concepts and analyses provide increased understanding of the design, use, configuration, and/or consequences of ICTs so that they are actually workable for people and can fulfil their intended functions.

This careful contextual and empirically grounded analysis contrasts with high-spirite d but largely a priori promotions of technologies that may occasionally work well for some people and may occasionally be valuable but are sometimes abandoned or unusable and thus incur needless waste and inspire misplaced hopes.

The standard tool model tends to both underestimate the costs and complexities of computerisation and overestimate the generalisability of applications from one setting or group of individuals to another. The problems resulting from the use of this model may be likened to an invisible health problem such as migraine headaches. Those who suffer from migraine headaches experience severe pain and the resultant missed opportunities, decreased productivity, and generally reduced efficiency. Others who live or work with them can also be distressed or discommoded by the increased emotional volatility or unreliability caused by their ailment. However, many of us are almost completely oblivious to the chronic, but publicly invisible, suffering and loss being experienced by millions of people because of migraines.

In similar fashion, we may be ignorant of the needless waste and human distress that improperly conceived ICTs may cause. However, even if we do not work in an organisation that suffers from poorly realised ICTs, these wastes and stressors may affect us more directly and more frequently than we realise. Financial losses by private organisations will result in our paying more for their products and services (although we may be unaware of the reasons for the price increases). Similar losses in public organisations may raise our taxes or result in a diminution of services. New services that we might want to try may prove to be considerably more frustrating than we anticipate. For example, there is growing evidence that many students in Internet-based distance education courses have been extremely frustrated when key participants (instructors, administrators, students) approached this as simply a new way to present courses and thus overlooked important (mis)communication behaviours. To be most effective, computerised distance education requires the recognition that new conventions are needed, such as the development of new communication practices under conditions of asymmetrical power.

Social informatics researchers study specific ICTs in specific settings to develop concepts and theories that apply to many kinds of ICTs in many kinds of settings.Each ICT community, such as electronic publishing, digital libraries, distance education, and electronic commerce, has to learn expensive lessons anew. A major concern of social informatics researchers is to develop a cumulative body of research that will help many people effectively shape ICTs so that they can improve people's work and lives. Such research is trans-technologies and trans-institutional—that is, it develops concepts and theories that are applicable to understanding numerous kinds of ICTs and a wide variety of social settings.

9

Social Justices in Modern World

The Charter of the United Nations makes no explicit distinction between international justice, or justice among nations, and social justice, or justice among people. The Charter, of which the Statute of the International Court of Justice is an integral part, treats justice as a broad principle that ought to be applied in international relations. In the Preamble and Article 1 of the Charter, justice is associated with respect for international law. In Article 2, justice is linked to the sovereign equality of all Members and to the maintenance of peace and security. The references to peace and the equality of nations imply that each State should refrain from any use of force that may jeopardise or undermine the territorial integrity or political independence of another. Another implication is that the United Nations should not intervene in matters that are:

> "essentially within the domestic jurisdiction of any State"
>
> *(Article 2, para. 7)*

Except to enforce measures adopted by the Security Council in line with the provisions setout. The "one country, one vote" rule in the General Assembly is a visible manifestation of the Organisation's recognition of sovereign equality.

The concept of justice as defined above will be referred to in the present text as *international justice*, with the principles of sovereign equality, nonintervention, and equal voting rights constituting the *legal aspects of international justice*. By the mid-1960s another dimension of international justice had taken shape with the decolonisation of a number of countries. The United Nations assumed increasing responsibility for helping these newly independent Member States in their efforts to achieve economic and social progress. Gradually the concept of development was substituted for the early emphasis on progress and evolved into a core component of the Organisation's mandate. International cooperation for development was placed next to the maintenance of peace and security as a second pillar upon which the activities of the United Nations were based, the main objective being to narrow and ultimately close the gap between developed and developing countries. Efforts relating to this goal of bridging the distance separating poor and affluent nations are identified here as representing the *developmental aspects of international justice*.

Social Justice: Modern Concept

The concept of *social justice* and its relevance and application within the present context require a more detailed explanation. As mentioned previously, the notion of social justice is relatively new. None of history's great philosophers—not Plato or Aristotle, or Confucius or Averroes, or even Rousseau or Kant—saw the need to consider justice or the redress of injustices from a social perspective. The concept first surfaced in Western thought and political language in the wake of the industrial revolution and the parallel development of the socialist doctrine. It emerged as an expression of protest against what was perceived as the capitalist exploitation of labour and as a focal point for the development of measures to improve the human condition. It was born as a revolutionary slogan embodying the ideals of progress and fraternity. Following the revolutions that shook Europe in the mid-1800s, social justice became a rallying cry for progressive thinkers and political activists. Proudhon, notably, identified justice with social justice, and social justice with respect for human dignity.

By the mid-twentieth century, the concept of social justice had become central to the ideologies and programmes of virtually all the leftist and centrist political parties around the world, and few dared to oppose it directly. Social justice represented the essence and the raison deter of the social democrat doctrine and left its mark in the decades following the Second World War.

Of particular importance in the present context is the link between the growing legitimisation of the concept of social justice, on the one hand, and the emergence of the social sciences as distinct areas of activity and the creation of economics and sociology as disciplines separate from philosophy (notably moral philosophy), on the other hand. Social justice became more clearly defined when a distinction was drawn between the social sphere and the economic sphere, and grew into a mainstream preoccupation when a number of economists became convinced that it was their duty not only to describe phenomena but also to propose criteria for the distribution of the fruits of human activity.

The application of social justice requires a geographical, sociological, political and cultural framework within which relations between individuals and groups can be understood, assessed, and characterised as just or unjust. In modern times, this framework has been the nation-State. The country typically represents the context in which various aspects of social justice, such as the distribution of income in a population, are observed and measured; this benchmark is used not only by national Governments but also by international organisations and supranational entities such as the European Union.

At the same time, there is clearly a universal dimension to social justice, with humanity as the common factor. Slaves, exploited workers and oppressed women are above all victimised human beings whose location matters less than their circumstances. This universality has taken on added depth and relevance as the physical and cultural distance between the world's peoples has effectively shrunk.

In the contemporary context, social justice is typically taken to mean distributive justice. The terms are generally understood to be synonymous and interchangeable in both common parlance and the language of international relations. The concept of social/distributive justice is implied in various academic and theoretical works and in many international legal or quasi-legal texts (such as the Charter and Universal Declaration) that may only include broad references to "justice". In certain international instruments, including the Copenhagen Declaration and Programme of Action adopted by the World Summit for Social Development in 1995, references to social justice are more explicit.

Social justice is treated as synonymous with distributive justice, which again is often identified with unqualified references to justice, in the specific context of the activities of the United Nations, the precise reasons for which may only be conjectured. The United Nations has essentially from the beginning separated the human rights domain from the economic and social domains, with activities in the latter two having been almost exclusively focused on development. Issues relating to the distributive and redistributive effects of social and economic policies—issues of justice—have therefore been addressed separately from issues of rights, including those inscribed in the International Co-venant on Economic, Social and Cultural Rights. The unfortunate consequences of this dissociation must be acknowledged.

To support the concept of social justice is to argue for a reconciliation of these priorities within the context of a broader social perspective in which individuals endowed with rights and freedoms operate within the framework of the duties and responsibilities attached to living in society. Notwithstanding the implied associations between social justice, redistributive justice, and justice as a more general concept, the fact is that the explicit commitment to social justice has seriously deteriorated; over the past decade, the expression has practically disappeared from the international lexicon and likely from the official language of most countries. The position will be taken here that the United Nations must work to try to restore the integrity and appeal of social justice, interpreted in the contemporary context as distributive justice.

Returning to the Charter, it may be argued that while not explicitly stated, justice among people and for all the world's peoples is its fundamental rationale. As noted earlier, these priorities fall under the heading of international justice, whereby Governments are compelled to represent and serve their populations and act in their best interest, without discrimination, and the sovereign equality of all States is respected. In the Preamble to the Charter, the commitment to justice for people is expressed as a reaffirmation of "faith in fundamental human rights, in the dignity and worth of the human person, [and] in the equal rights of men and women". It requires the promotion of "social progress and better standards of life in larger freedom" and of "the economic and social advancement of all peoples". It underlies the third stated purpose of the

United Nations (after maintaining peace and friendly relations among nations), which is:

> "To achieve international cooperation in solving international problems of an economic, social, cultural or humanitarian character, and in promoting and encouraging respect for human rights and for fundamental freedoms for all without distinction as to race, sex, language, or religion"
>
> *(Article 1).*

This purpose is then reiterated in Article 13 as one of the functions of the General Assembly, and in Articles 60 and 62 in reference to the rôle of the Economic and Social Council in this regard. In short, justice derives from equality of rights for all peoples and the possibility for all human beings, without discrimination, to benefit from the economic and social progress disseminated and secured through international cooperation.

Economic Justice

Economic justice, defined as the existence of opportunities for meaningful work and employment and the dispensation of fair rewards for the productive activities of individuals, will be treated here as an aspect of social justice. The customary distinction between economic justice and social justice is intellectually unsatisfactory, as it serves to legitimise the dichotomisation of the economic and social spheres. This tendency can seriously limit the potential for the advancement of justice, particularly within organisations that exercise a normative function with regard to matters of development. In recent years there has been a discernable trend in international discourse towards the attenuation not only of the concept of social justice, but also of the related concepts of social development and social policy. The social sphere has in many respects been marginalised. One reason for the decline in "social" orientations is the failure to adopt a comprehensive perspective on what the concept encompasses. As asserted later, support for the idea of social justice has gradually diminished because its advocates and practitioners have neglected one of its essential dimensions, which is for individuals to have the opportunity to exercise their initiative and use their talents and to be fairly rewarded for their efforts. To acknowledge the necessity of viewing economic justice as an element of social justice is, again, to argue for a social perspective on human affairs. Economic justice is one among many interrelated dimensions of life in society. It is suggested here that the distributive and redistributive aspects of justice do not have to be separated or perceived as antagonistic.

Individuals, institutions, Governments and international organisations make judgments about what is just and what is unjust based on complex and generally unformulated frameworks of moral and political values. Such frameworks vary considerably across cultures and over time, but through the centuries prophets, philosophers and other intellectuals have repeatedly attempted to identify common ground that would allow all human beings in their own and in successive generations to agree on definitions of right and wrong, good and bad, just and unjust. It is often said that all great religions and philosophies embody the same core principles and values, and beyond the different metaphysics and institutional settings, reflect the same belief in the capacity of human beings to make moral judgments and to seek perfection in some form. Progress was originally a spiritual concept and was only later applied to the fruits of human technical ingenuity, and the same is true for the notion of justice, which has retained much of the timeless immanence deriving from its religious roots. The United Nations is an outgrowth and an expression of this quest for the universal, of this purposeful search for a common humanity. Notions such as human nature and natural law have found expression in the more modern concepts of the "social contract" and "social compact". To give justice among individuals and nations a more tangible character and contemporary relevance, the United Nations has used the language of rights, and of equality, equity and inequality, in reference to both positive objectives to be pursued and negative situations to be corrected.

Critical Domains of Equality and Equity

There are three areas of priority with regard to equality and equity highlighted in the Charter of the United Nations, the Universal Declaration of Human Rights, and the International Covenants on Human Rights, and in subsequent texts adopted by the General Assembly, notably the Copenhagen Declaration and Programme of Action and the United Nations Millennium Declaration. They include the following:

1. *Equality of rights:* primarily implying the elimination of all forms of discrimination and respect for the fundamental freedoms and civil and political rights of all individuals. This represents the most fundamental form of equality. As stated in article 1 of the Universal Declaration, "all human beings are born free and equal in dignity and rights", and article 2 is even more specific: "Everyone is entitled to all the rights and freedoms set forth in this Declaration, without distinction of any kind, such as race, colour, sex, language, religion, political or other opinion, national or social origin, property, birth or other status."
2. *Equality of opportunities:* which requires stable social, economic, cultural and political conditions that enable all individuals to fulfil their potential and contribute to the economy and to society. Interpreted restrictively, this form of equality is akin to equality of rights and means "simply" that societies and Governments refrain

from discrimination and allow individuals to freely pursue their aspirations and develop and apply their talents within the moral and legal limits imposed by respect for the freedom of others. Thus defined, it is often identified with justice and, in the sense described above, more precisely with economic justice. Support for this objective has been linked to the emergence of the laissez-faire doctrine, and from a philosophical perspective this aspect of equality is very close to liberalism and utilitarianism. Interpreted more broadly, equality of opportunities is linked to deliberate action, in particular the application of public policies, to correct and offset the many "unnatural" inequalities that separate individuals from different sociocultural backgrounds and milieus. With this levelling of the playing field, the financial and social success of individuals is largely determined by their natural talent, character, effort, and level of ambition, along with a certain measure of chance or fate. Meritocracy is the logical outcome. Policies focusing on health, education and housing are traditionally seen as particularly important for ensuring equality of opportunities, or *égalité des chances*. In political philosophy, this approach relates to the tradition of the social contract and is a critical aspect of social justice, as understood within socialist and social democratic conventions.

3. *Equity in living conditions:* for all individuals and households. This concept is understood to reflect a contextually determined "acceptable" range of inequalities in income, wealth and other aspects of life in society, with the presumption of general agreement with regard to what is just or fair (or "equitable") at any given time in any particular community, or in the world as a whole if universal norms are applied. This shift in terms, from equality to equity, derives from the

fact that equality in living conditions has never been achieved in practice (except on a very limited scale by small religious or secular communities), has never been seriously envisaged by political theorists or moralists (except in the context of describing attractive—or more often repulsive—utopias), and is today commonly perceived as incompatible with freedom. The pre-Marxist ideal—"from each according to his ability, to each according to his works"—would need to be applied, and for a very long time, within post-revolutionary societies. The truly egalitarian Marxist principle—"from each according to his capacities, to each according to his needs" —would only prevail (with any success) in the distant and quasi-utopian "end of history" referred to in communist theory. In short, equity is the most logical reference point in determining what is just and what is unjust with regard to living conditions and related matters within society. The lack of objective indicators makes this a daunting task, however. What constitutes the equitable distribution of income among social classes, occupations and age groups? From which perspective and on which basis are various manifestations of equity and inequity being assessed? What are the universal norms that allow the United Nations and other international organisations to make judgments and offer advice on the equitability of living conditions around the world? Equity is an inherently vague and controversial notion. Nonetheless, it is a pervasive preoccupation in all societies, both affluent and poor. Every society, even the laissez-faire variety, has engaged in the distribution and redistribution of income and wealth in some form, with policies generally favouring the poorest but sometimes benefiting the richest, and it is for this reason that issues of equity in living conditions remain central to the dialogue and debate on social justice.

Areas of Inequality in the Distribution of Goods, Opportunities and Rights

Going a step further in endeavouring to define the more concrete elements requiring consideration in relation to the idea of social justice, there are six areas of distributive inequality corresponding to situations that, from the perspective of those directly concerned and of the "impartial observer", require correction. Listed roughly in descending order in terms of their relative importance and in ascending order in terms of how difficult they are to measure, the highlighted areas of inequality are as follows:

1. *Inequalities in the distribution of income:* The distribution of income among individuals or households at the local or national level, based on classifications such as socioeconomic status, profession, gender, location, and income percentiles, is the most widely used measure of the degree of equality or inequality existing in a society. Though the statistical difficulties, particularly with regard to crosscountry comparisons, cannot be overemphasised, the distribution of income is relatively amenable to measurement, and if the resulting data are interpreted correctly and sufficient prudence is exercised, any problems that may arise are generally surmountable. With the availability of an income, individuals and households acquire the capacity to make choices and gain immediate access to a number of amenities. For most contemporary societies, income distribution remains the most legitimate indicator of the overall levels of equality and inequality.
2. *Inequalities in the distribution of assets:* including not only capital but also physical assets such as land and

buildings. There is normally a strong positive correlation between the distribution of income and the distribution of assets. Data from a variety of sources are generally available to Governments or independent statistical offices wishing to document what has traditionally been both a determinant of social status and political power and a source of political upheaval and revolution. As stated in article 17 of the Universal Declaration of Human Rights, "everyone has the right to own property alone as well as in association with others", and "no one shall be arbitrarily deprived of his property".

3. Inequalities in the distribution of opportunities for work and remunerated employment: In both developed and developing countries today, the distribution of work and employment opportunities is the main determinant of income distribution and a key to economic and social justice. The distinction between work and employment is important; "work" encompasses all independent economic activities and what is called the spirit of entrepreneurship (an element of which is the creation of small and medium-sized enterprises), and more generally the economic opportunities offered by society to all those who wish to seize them. Statistics on the distribution of employment opportunities and unemployment are more readily available than data on, for instance, the proportions of young people from different socioeconomic backgrounds who have managed to secure bank loans to start their own enterprises. As economies continue to diversify and become more and more service oriented, this sort of information will be increasingly useful. At the same time, the United Nations and its agencies, in particular the International Labour Organisation (ILO), cannot ignore the fact that the vast majority of people in the

world work in order to survive. Discrepancies in working conditions among those in different professions and social groups, including immigrants, constitute part of this item.

4. *Inequalities in the distribution of access to knowledge:* Considered in this context are issues relating to levels of enrolment in schools and universities among children from different socioeconomic groups, as well as issues linked to the quality of educational delivery in various institutions and regions. Education, including technical training and adult education, is critical for ensuring access to decent work and for social mobility, and in most societies is a strong determinant of social status and an important source of self-respect. Because schools and universities are no longer the only dispensers of knowledge, and in the light of the emergence of new learning modes and tools such as the Internet, access to various technologies is also considered in assessing education-related inequalities. Although the distinction between information and knowledge remains valid and relevant, a number of statistical publications now present certain types of data together, including, for example, gender-disaggregated statistics on the ownership of television sets, book acquisitions, and primary and secondary enrolment ratios.

5. *Inequalities in the distribution of health services, social security and the provision of a safe environment.* Traditional indicators of wellbeing such as life expectancy and child mortality rates, broken down by gender, socioeconomic status and area of residence, are typically used along with other data to identify and measure inequalities in the distribution of amenities all societies endeavour to provide for their members. As is the case with education, issues relating to the

availability, quality and accessibility of health and social services and facilities are critical but are difficult to analyse and measure. As stated in article 22 of the Universal Declaration of Human Rights:

> "everyone, as a member of society, has the right to social security and is entitled to realisation, through national effort and international cooperation ... of the economic, social and cultural rights indispensable for his dignity and the free development of his personality".

Social security, now often limited to social protection and safety nets, was a core component of the welfare state model adopted by countries around the globe after the Second World War. The sources of financing for social security benefits and the distribution of such benefits within a community remain pressing issues. Moving on to the last item, the right to a healthy and pleasant environment, not polluted by uncontrolled or predatory human activities, is considered by its proponents to constitute part of the third generation of human rights (the first generation having comprised civil and political rights and the second generation economic, social and cultural rights). Pollution, generated continuously by unregulated commercial activities and more dramatically and catastrophically through incidents such as the Chernobyl and Bhopal disasters, does not choose its victims. It is nevertheless true that rich and poor people have an unequal capacity to ensure a safe environment. Differentials in personal security and safety could also logically be placed under the heading of inequalities in the provision of a safe environment. Crime, in its many forms, is growing in most societies, and groups at the lower end of the socioeconomic scale continue to be disproportionately affected.

6. *Inequalities in the distribution of opportunities for civic and political participation:* This form of inequality is rarely discussed in international circles, perhaps because of its inherent complexity and sensitivity, and perhaps also because the practice of democracy is usually limited to the holding of elections; those who vote in presidential and parliamentary elections are implicitly considered participants in political life. Involvement in the electoral process notwithstanding, inequalities and inequities associated with political institutions and processes were key factors contributing to inequalities and inequities in society more generally. The way power is organised and distributed among society's various institutions and the manner in which political processes are carried out have a profound influence on how citizens see and find their place on the social ladder and within in the social fabric. This does not mean that the unequal distribution of political power is always the direct cause of other forms of inequality. Simple cause-effect relationships do not explain this highly complex phenomenon in which personal and social factors are intertwined. It is generally acknowledged, however, that the distribution of power and how it is exercised by those who have it are at the core of the different forms and manifestations of inequality and inequity.

Before moving on to an assessment of recent trends in the realm of social justice and international justice, brief consideration should be given to two complementary factors relating to the conceptual framework for social justice sketched.

First, the six types or areas of inequality reviewed above may be referred to as "vertical" inequalities. They derive from the division of an entire population—usually the inhabitants of a country but in some cases the members of a region, a city or an age group—along the lines of income or degree of political participation or other variables theoretically applicable to all. Using the earlier delineation of vertical inequalities as a guide, it would be important to establish some sort of typology of the forms of horizontal inequality that are generally considered and are deemed important from the perspective of social justice.

Second, further conceptual effort is required to examine the extent to which the three priority areas of equality/equity and the six areas of inequality that have been identified to lend operational content to the notion of social justice also apply to the developmental aspects of international justice. A number of the categories are clearly valid for both dimensions of justice, in particular the distribution of income, assets and access to knowledge, while others, such as the distribution of opportunities for political participation, would be applicable with some modifications in language—in this case a mention of the involvement of countries in the management of international organisations and other international arrangements such as the meetings of the Group of Eight industrialised countries. Other categories specifically relevant to issues of international justice in a fragmented and conflicted world also require consideration and could be addressed in the context of future discussion and debate.

Rising Inequalities among Countries

On two recent occasions, force had been used against States Members of the United Nations without the formal approval of the Security Council and outside the provisions of chapter VII of the Charter. Even prior to these events, the "right of intervention", legitimised by the overriding need to protect human rights and in particular to prevent genocide, had been openly and vigorously debated in international circles. Today, it is generally agreed that the principles of respect for national sovereignty and non-interference in the domestic affairs of a State can be legitimately suspended to address unchecked and unpunished violations of basic human rights and fundamental freedoms. Intolerance for such violations represents a heightening of the human consciousness and real progress, and is a necessary step in the building of a true world community. Vexing questions arise, however, with regard to the type of legal regime needed to govern this right of intervention. Assuming that satisfactory agreement could be reached on the nature and extent of the violations that would necessitate different degrees of condemnation and different modalities of intervention, and assuming that the role of a reformed Security Council in such matters was clearly defined, even-handedness and fairness would remain critical for the credibility and durability of such a system. Powerful countries would have to be subjected to the same rules as weak countries. The present state of affairs with regard to the use of the International Court of Justice and the International Criminal Court suggests that the world is not yet ready for an international legal regime subordinating national sovereignty to respect for fundamental human rights. Nonetheless, for all those who believe there are universal core values that define a common humanity and common standards of decency, the desirable direction of change in international law and international relations is clear.

Equality among Member States and Inequalities in Power

The sovereign equality of all countries is recognised within the United Nations, a fact perhaps best symbolised by the rule that each State—regardless of its sise, population, economic and financial status, military power, and level of cultural and political prestige and standing in the international arena—has one vote in the General Assembly. This rule gives the Organisation, with its near universal membership, its distinctiveness and legitimacy. However, international justice also requires recognition of the differences in power among States. Power implies influence and responsibility. An international organisation that ignored this fact and did not possess the characteristics of a world government would be reduced to impotence and irrelevance. Accordingly, the Charter established a balance between these two facets of international justice with the respective compositions and functions of the General Assembly and the Security Council.

This system is still in place 60 years later but is being subjected to increasing pressure and criticism. Concerns have prompted calls for reforming the composition of the Security Council, and questions have been raised regarding the role and effectiveness of the General Assembly. Voices urging the abandonment of the "one country, one vote" principle and its replacement with a weighted voting system have so far been rather muted, but the recalcitrance shown by those Member States impatient with international democracy has effectively stripped the General Assembly of its powers. Particularly since the call for a new international economic order by developing and non-aligned countries in the mid-1970s gave rise to complaints of "a tyranny of the majority", the General Assembly has largely been reduced to an annual forum without much influence in world affairs. In the mid-1980s, the major contributors to the United Nations budget demanded substantial organisational reforms. The main elements of the reform effort, initiated by General Assembly resolution 41/213 of 19 December 1986 on the review of the efficiency of the administrative and financial functioning of the United Nations, included a reduction in the number of international civil servants, a de facto freese in the regular budget (financed by assessed contributions), and the understanding that the pursuit of consensus would replace recourse to voting in deliberative bodies, notably the General Assembly. These elements remain in place. In exchange for such major concessions by Member States interested in facilitating the growth and dynamic functioning of the United Nations, the main powers promised to ensure the provision of adequate, secure and predictable financing for the Organisation's mandated activities.

Some 20 years later, the United Nations is facing serious financial and other difficulties, and the pursuit of consensus continues to prevail in the General Assembly as well as in the Economic and Social Council and its subsidiary bodies. Reliance on consensus, as employed within this unique context, nullifies the "one country, one vote" principle and means that the decisions, resolutions and declarations of the United Nations, notably in matters relating to development and globalisation, reflect the views and interests of a strong and influential minority. Obviously, powerful countries have a much greater capacity than weak countries to impose a consensus. In his report for the fifty-ninth session of the General Assembly, the Secretary-General states that "unfortunately, consensus (often interpreted as requiring unanimity) has become an end in itself. It is sought first within each regional group and then at the level of the whole. This has not proved an effective way of reconciling the interests of Member States. Rather, it prompts the Assembly to retreat into generalities, abandoning any serious effort to take action." One might assert that the previously alleged "tyranny of the majority" has been replaced by a "tyranny of the minority" in the age of globalisation.

Developmental aspect of International Justice

The various arguments advanced to support the legitimacy of an inquiry into the developmental aspect of international justice may be summarised as follows:

1. The State is no longer the main actor on the international scene, and its relevance will continue to

diminish as the process of globalisation gains momentum. Transnational actors—mainly corporations and banks but also international organisations and social and religious institutions and movements—are playing an increasingly important role. Modern information and communication technologies (ICT) ignore borders and national sovereignty. National policies, including those aimed at addressing inequalities that contribute to poverty and other social ills, are routinely bypassed and overridden by the decisions of global institutions regulating international finance and trade. The most powerful countries can still impose their views and exert their influence on others, but even they do not seem to be willing or able to control the transnational forces that have been unleashed on the world. Many States are economically, financially and politically weak and consequently have little or no say in international affairs affecting their development. As the Westphalian order is collapsing, there is no point in being concerned with the equality of its members. Those interested in the pursuit of international justice should work on developing processes and institutions that could regulate and balance the interplay of transnational forces rather than remaining preoccupied with inequalities among entities that are destined to be marginalised and ultimately disappear.

2. Along similar lines, it may be argued that there is an inherent futility in working to achieve greater equality between States in terms of development when there is no authority able to enforce measures that would ensure the realisation of such an objective. Demands for justice have traditionally been addressed to leaders, Governments and other entities with recognised authority and responsibility for the security and welfare of the groups concerned. The United Nations does not

possess such authority. International organisations with greater power and influence in economic and financial matters, in particular the World Trade Organisation (WTO), the World Bank and the International Monetary Fund (IMF), have different mandates. A world government with an enforceable mandate to ensure equality and justice between its constituents is not on the immediate horizon.

3. The objective of achieving greater equality between countries in terms of development presupposes that "development" is a clear concept agreed upon by all concerned and accepted as being in the common interest of humanity, including future generations. This might have been the case in the 1960s and 1970s, but many believe today that the dominant pattern of economic development is physically, politically and morally unsustainable. It encourages and actually feeds on acquisitiveness, consumerism and a predatory attitude towards nature. Others are convinced that development is a superfluous notion, as what matters most is a freeing of economic initiative—the pursuit of economic justice—and participation in the world economy through trade and openness to foreign investment. For both those committed to the search for a different meaning of economic and social progress and proponents of the laissez-faire political philosophy, ranking countries on a scale defined by a few economic aggregates and then trying to bring them all to the top of this scale is an artificial exercise.

4. Finally, even if inequality in development among countries is considered a legitimate issue, assigning it priority diverts attention from the pressing problem of growing inequalities among people and, within this context, the extreme poverty that persists in various parts of the world. The worst problems of inequality

and inequity exist within societies. Notwithstanding the trend towards globalisation and interdependence, States still have the capacity to alleviate or aggravate these problems. Inequality among countries, particularly inequality between developed and developing countries, is a long-term problem of growth and development. However, social injustice, inequalities and inequities within societies can be more immediately and effectively addressed by a wide range of policies and decisions at the local and national levels that might, for example, bring about changes in tax systems and in the institutions delivering public services. International organisations are in a position to at least influence these decisions.

Sensitive to these arguments, international justice, and particularly its developmental component, should remain high on the agenda of the United Nations for two compelling reasons:

1. First, States remain the indispensable building blocks of a viable international community. International organisations should be modified, expanded and created to address global problems and respond to global aspirations. In particular, global economic and financial powers need to be checked and balanced by global political institutions whose primary function is to represent the peoples of the world and endeavour to define and promote the common good. The viability and efficacy of such institutions, including the United Nations, hinges upon the active participation and informed consent of strong and responsible States genuinely seeking to act in the best interests of their citizens. A peaceful world community cannot emerge from the will of a few powerful countries or from the interplay of private interests and forces. States must assume more responsibility for the pursuit of peace and

justice. Greater equality in levels of development, measured traditionally or using indicators more sensitive to social and political conditions, would place more countries in a position to participate in the management of global affairs. This assertion is not based on naive optimism or the assumption of universal benevolence among peoples and their Governments. Simply put, countries and Governments less plagued by disorder and poverty and blessed with intangibles such as hope, respect from others, and a sense of their own worth and dignity have a greater capacity and are more likely to contribute to the building and maintenance of a harmonious world community. The various aspects of international justice are connected.

2. Second, links exist not only between the reduction in inequalities in levels of development and increased respect for the territorial and political integrity of each nation, but also between international justice, so understood, and social justice. Issues of inter-country and inter-country inequality are related first through the prevailing ideas on economic organisation and development. Policies and practices relating to market deregulation, free trade and domestic market protection, competition, labour costs and labour standards, systems of taxation, and tax exemptions and tax havens, for example, have a direct impact on various forms of equity and equality at both the national and international levels. Generally, the "rules of the game" established for international transactions strongly influence domestic conditions and the distribution of the fruits of economic activity. Currently, the freedom of action enjoyed by a few major public and corporate powers to set the rules of the game is paralleled by the relative impotence of a majority of lesser actors, including most of the Member States of the United

Nations. For a large number of countries, the reduction or prevention of inequalities and inequities at home would be greatly facilitated or even effected by a reduction in inequalities and inequities at the international and global levels. Certain features of the present world political economy, including those generally viewed as positive, such as the relatively free global movement of individuals with valued managerial or technical abilities, create or contribute to domestic imbalances and inequalities. In this example, the international-domestic link was established through the emergence of a transnational market for certain skills. This market affects national patterns of salary and income distribution owing not only to the crossborder movement of labour but also to the fact that there are talented individuals from developing countries who decide not to move abroad but are nevertheless in a better bargaining position because their skills are in demand elsewhere. This relatively new phenomenon of increased inequality among groups across national borders—characterised by a degree of homogeneity at both the top and bottom of the income and status ladder (among those with highly valued and little valued skills, respectively)—is an important development. Growing regional inequalities inside countries are also a product of the "entanglement" of various types of inequality and inequity within and between countries and derive in part from the characteristics of the global economy. International justice and social justice have advanced or regressed in parallel.

Decline in International Justice

Overall, the income gap between rich and poor countries and regions has been widening since the beginning of the

1980s. Per capita income in various world regions, expressed as a proportion of the average per capita income of the wealthier country members of the Organisation for Economic Cooperation and Development (OECD), evolved as follows between 1980 and the beginning of the twenty-first century: the relative share declined from 3.3 to 1.9 per cent in Africa, from 9.7 to 6.7 per cent in the Middle East and North Africa, and from 18 to 12.8 per cent in Latin America and the Caribbean, but rose from 1.2 to 1.6 per cent in South Asia and from 1.5 to 3.3 per cent in East Asia and the Pacific. Statistics on the world distribution of income indicate that in the 1990s a larger proportion of the African population moved into the lowest income quintile. The 2004 *World Bank Atlas* reveals that the 2.3 billion people living in low-income countries earn an average of US$ 450 per year, though in some economies the figure is as low as US$ 90; for the 3 billion people in middle income countries, the average is US$ 1,920, while the 971 million in high-income countries receive an average of US$ 28,550. In other words, the 1 billion people living in wealthier countries account for 80 per cent of the world's gross domestic product (GDP), while the 5 billion people in developing countries share the remaining 20 per cent. Within regions, income inequality among countries has also grown.

The rise in income inequality between countries has been accompanied by growing disparities in the ability of various countries and regions to reduce the extreme poverty affecting portions of their population. Statistics indicate that the share of people living on less than US$ 1 a day fell from 40 per cent in 1981 to 21 per cent in 2001, but this overall decline masks widely divergent regional trends. East Asia and the Pacific, led by China, reported the largest decline in extreme poverty, with the rate dropping from 58 to 16 per cent. Absolute poverty also declined in South Asia (from 52 to 31 per cent), but remained steady in Latin America (at around 20 per cent) and rose dramatically in the former Soviet Union and in Central Europe. In Africa, the number of people living in dire poverty nearly doubled.

In political terms, inequality between countries has certainly not declined in recent years. One country has gained hegemony, the Security Council has retained the same permanent members, and developing countries appear to have less leverage in world affairs than they did 20 years ago. Developing countries have made no significant progress in their quest for a greater say in the management of the world economy and for control over global private economic and financial forces. Financial and trade practices still favour the most powerful, and exceptions to general rules are granted more rarely and reluctantly than ever before. There are strong inequalities and imbalances in the global decision-making processes affecting all countries. The processes and operations associated with the formulation, implementation and evaluation of the rules and regulations governing the functioning of the world economy are still largely controlled by rich countries.

Financial dependency may be an important contributing factor; a number of Governments continue to rely on ODA for their daily operations. Personal security is another area of concern; countries at different levels of development remain extremely unequal in their degree of exposure to various risks and in their capacity to deal with the consequences of natural catastrophes or man-made conflicts and violence. Developing countries with low to moderate levels of power and influence have no more political autonomy now than they did several decades ago. For the countries of the world, the distance between the rich and the poor, the powerful and the weak, and the self-sufficient and the dependent is now often characterised as an abyss.

Issues Relating to the Reliability and Diversity of Sources of Information

It is necessary to outline the difficulties and considerations associated with conducting an analytical appraisal of the immensely complicated issue of equality and justice from a distributional perspective. First, there is the vastness of the issue, which in itself challenges the research capacity and analytical ability of an institution or group of people meeting periodically to share their knowledge and views, and a second important limiting factor is the paucity and poor quality of data. Justice, equity and equality can legitimately be explored from a philosophical, moral or political perspective, even by those who can only aspire to the breadth and depth of perspicacity shown by a John Rawls, John Stuart Mill or Jean-Jacques Rousseau. One could argue that in the United Nations itself more discussion and debate should be devoted to the philosophical, moral and religious foundations of the idea of justice and to the current understanding of the notion of universal human rights.

There are some significant problems relating to the availability, consistency and quality of data. For many developing countries, basic demographic, social and economic statistics do not come from national sources but are compiled by international organisations, with relevant data obtained through sample surveys, at best, but more often through comparisons, projections and extrapolations. These statistics often convey a partial and very superficial picture of living conditions among the people concerned. One unfortunate aspect of the bureaucratic or technocratic culture of international organisations is the general reluctance to complement and enrich limited statistical data with direct impressions, personal testimonies, anecdotal material, travelogues or works of fiction. A better balance will have to be sought at some point in the United Nations between different sources and forms of knowledge. In particular, empirical data will have to be complemented by the less measurable but richer knowledge of the human condition gained through real-world experience. Even when reliable statistics are available from national sources and the much used (and indeed indispensable) aggregates and averages for indicators such as per capita income and enrolment ratios are provided, data are generally not broken down enough to capture critical details relating the situation of specific population groups. In the present context, data on individuals in the top 5 per cent or 1 per cent in terms of income or assets could be further disaggregated in some countries to allow an examination of the situation of the very rich. Those at the other end of the socioeconomic scale would also benefit from a closer look; the extremely poor are rarely the focus of regular detailed analysis.

Data on social and economic conditions are often expressed in absolute numbers, percentages or ratios; indicators relying on other forms of measurement offer an added dimension to the analytical process. The use of the Gini coefficient, on which most analyses and comparisons of trends in income distribution are based, is a case in point. For example, an observed increase in income inequality in the United Kingdom of Great Britain and Northern Ireland since the beginning of the 1980s may be interpreted differently from a similar increase observed in the United States during the same period based on the countries' respective Gini scores; the United Kingdom currently has a Gini index of 32.5, which roughly corresponds to the levels in developing countries, whereas the index for the United States, at 41.4, is closer to the levels of most Latin American countries.

It should be noted that the qualitative aspects of inequality are often extremely difficult to measure; current statistics and indicators are glaringly inadequate in this respect. Only very specific and detailed enquiries could, for instance, reveal the extent of open and covert discrimination that in most societies affects people who are in any way different from the majority.

Major Areas of Inequality among People

Rising Inequality in the Distribution of Income

Inequalities in income distribution have worsened in most countries during the past 20 to 30 years. Typically, the share of total national income accruing to households in the top income decile has increased, while the share of the bottom 10 per cent has decreased. Between those at each end of the scale—the richest 1 per cent and the poorest 1 per cent—the gaps have grown even wider. In a number of countries, particularly in Asia, the rise in income inequality has been accompanied by a reduction in extreme poverty as measured by the threshold of US$ 1 per day or by national poverty lines. However, it appears that in the majority of countries around the world, both income inequality and extreme poverty have increased, affecting larger numbers and proportions of the population. The current situation in various regions and country groupings may be summarised as follows:

1. *In Africa*: poverty in the context of inadequate economic development is a dominant problem. Though data are scarce, income inequality appears to be significant and is becoming an issue of growing concern. Estimates put the Gini index at 44 per cent; the shares of total income for those in the highest and lowest income quintiles are 50 and 5 per cent respectively. Statistics indicate that about a quarter of Africa's residents are experiencing long-term poverty and that up to 60 per cent are extremely vulnerable and move in and out of extreme poverty. It should be noted

that the incidence of poverty and levels of inequality vary widely among countries, and there are indications that negative trends are being reversed in some parts of the continent.

2. *In Asia*: income inequality has grown very rapidly and dramatically in some countries, including China (whose Gini index is believed to have risen from 25 to 37.2 per cent between 1984 and 2000), and more slowly and steadily in other countries, notably Bangladesh, India, Indonesia, Malaysia, Pakistan, Sri Lanka and Thailand. At the same time, overall standards of living have improved as a result of fast economic growth, and extreme poverty affects a smaller proportion of the region's population today than it did 10 or 20 years ago. The trend towards a reduction in extreme poverty, initiated several decades ago, was interrupted by the financial crisis of 1996/97 but has resumed in recent years.

3. *Latin America:* has traditionally experienced high levels of income inequality, as evidenced by the region's current Gini index of around 44 per cent. Inequalities have increased during the past several decades, particularly in Brazil, Chile and Venezuela. The combined results of national household surveys indicate that 211 million people in the region were experiencing absolute poverty at the end of the 1990s, compared with 136 million in 1980 and 200 million in 1990.

4. *In Eurasia*: the region encompassing the former Soviet Union and Central and Eastern Europe, dramatic increases in both income inequality and extreme poverty occurred in the wake of the enormous political and social upheaval accompanying the shift from a planned economy to a market economy. In the Russian Federation, for example, the income share of the

poorest 20 per cent of the population fell from 11.9 per cent in 1991 to 5.9 per cent in 2001, while the share of the richest 20 per cent rose from 30.7 to 48.3 per cent. During this period, 80 per cent of the country's households experienced a drop in income. Absolute poverty affected 50 per cent of the population in the Russian Federation and around 80 per cent in most of the Central Asian republics at the end of the twentieth century. Over the past few years, with the resumption of a certain level of economic growth, levels of extreme poverty in the region have improved somewhat.

5. *Income inequality has increased markedly in a number of OECD countries*: towards the end of the 1990s, Gini indexes were 41.7 per cent for Australia, 41.4 per cent for the United States, 40.2 per cent for New Zealand, and 32.5 per cent for the United Kingdom. Levels of income inequality have remained stable in other OECD countries, including France, Germany, Japan, the Republic of Korea and Sweden, and have actually declined in Canada, Italy, Norway and Spain. A few other exceptions to the general trend of worsening income distribution are also worth noting; in Latin America, income inequality has improved in Honduras and Uruguay and has apparently remained relatively stable in Mexico.

Rising Inequality in the Distribution of Assets

Although asset distribution is not as well documented as income distribution, there is no question that both have been characterised by the same negative trend. During the past quarter of a century, the distribution of assets, especially capital, has become more skewed in favour of those at the top of the socioeconomic ladder. As labour has lost ground in relation to capital for the remuneration of the factors of production, the share of capital income in total income has increased, and this capital has been more heavily concentrated in fewer hands rather than more evenly distributed. The almost universal trend towards privatisation that swept the world during the last part of the twentieth century rarely, if ever, resulted in the spread of "popular capitalism". The main beneficiaries of the shift from a State-controlled, State-dominated, or even State-influenced economy to a more liberalised economy in various parts of the world have been those privileged few in positions of power or influence.

Nowhere have employees and small entrepreneurs succeeded in modifying the national distribution of assets to their advantage; few have been given the chance to try. The much freer circulation of capital and the opening up of investment opportunities across national borders, combined with the privatisation movement, have led to a global redistribution of assets characterised by the transfer of significant amounts of capital from national to foreign hands. In the mid-1990s, transnational corporations controlled half of the 100 largest companies in Latin America and accounted for 43 per cent of the sales of the region's top 500 companies.

Another factor contributing to the uneven distribution of assets is capital flight, which seriously hinders development in many countries. The highest incidence of capital flight occurs in Africa, Latin America and the Middle East; capital flight from severely indebted sub-Saharan African countries was recently estimated to have reached US$ 22 billion. The disappearance of land reform and land redistribution from the development agendas of most countries has further skewed the distribution of assets in the world. Almost everywhere, the position of the "haves" in society has been strengthened by the evolution of tax systems that benefit the owners of capital.

More Work Opportunities

Maintaining the distinction between opportunities for work—an important element of which is the capacity for initiative and entrepreneurship—and opportunities for employment, it is likely that the former have improved in a number of countries, particularly those that have abandoned or liberalised their rigid communist or socialist economic systems. Notwithstanding the well-publicised role of oligarchs and plutocrats in the Russian Federation, the opening of the country's economy is believed to have given many young men and women a chance to prove their worth and be rewarded accordingly. The same appears to be true for the former socialist countries of Central and Eastern Europe. In India, already a democracy, economic reforms and an overall policy more favourable to capitalist and free market ideals have led to more and better opportunities for young graduates and professionals both at home and abroad. Even in a number of well-established economies in which market-oriented reforms have been instituted in a very gradual and controlled manner, there are more economic opportunities available now than 20 years ago; the United Kingdom is a case in point.

Overall, these developments suggest that some progress has been made towards achieving economic justice. At the same time, however, the commitment made at the World Summit for Social Development to pursue the goal of full employment has largely been neglected. Globally, unemployment and underemployment have increased and now affect a much larger proportion of individuals on the lower rungs of the socioeconomic ladder—the poor, the uneducated, and those with skills not valued in the economy—than those with an education, social connections, and more highly valued skills. In both developed and developing countries, women and youth are disproportionately affected by unemployment and underemployment. Work and employment opportunities are generally more scarce in rural areas than in urban areas, even though rural residents make up the majority of the population in many developing countries, and the situation does not appear to be improving. In India, for instance, growth in rural employment stood at only 0.67 per cent at the end of the 1990s, the lowest rate registered in the country's post-independence history. In a significant number of countries, the gap between rural and urban salaries appears to have widened.

Around the world, new job opportunities have emerged predominantly in the services sector, and in developing countries in particular, most of these opportunities have been within the informal economy, where workers are poorly compensated and not provided with any kind of social security, and where labour laws and standards are seldom observed. Precarious working conditions are now the rule rather than the exception in many contexts, pointing to the treatment of labour as a "commodity", a practice denounced more than a century ago by Karl Marx and others. Seemingly everywhere, wages and other forms of remuneration have become increasingly unequal within and between sectors, communities, countries and regions, and between nationals and immigrants, the skilled and the less skilled, and urban and rural residents.

Even within the public services sector, which has generally been "downsised", differences in remuneration have widened as attempts have been made to reward initiative and competence rather than dedication and seniority. These trends suggest that while progress has been made in the realm of economic justice, with the rewarding of initiative and talent, levels of inequality have continued to increase. Employment and work opportunities have improved for a minority but have deteriorated, in both quantitative and qualitative terms, for the majority of people in the world.

Better Distribution of Information

Segments of the population that previously had little or no access to information now find it far more readily available. Radio, television and newspapers have touched the lives of people all along the socioeconomic spectrum in virtually every corner of every nation. Wired and wireless technologies have revolutionised the exchange and dissemination of information; Internet use has been characterised by exponential growth in every region of the world.

The ICT revolution is often considered one of the defining features of globalisation; its social, economic, cultural and political implications are enormous but have yet to be fully understood. Knowledge is also transferred through these new technologies; distance learning and other non-traditional options have made education more accessible to many. In a more traditional context, there has been consistent improvement in school and university enrolment ratios.

Even in Africa, which continues to face serious challenges in many areas of development, estimates indicate that between the early 1980s and 2000, primary enrolment ratios increased from 78 to 89 per cent for girls and from 85 to 95 per cent for boys, and rates of illiteracy declined from 61 to 46 per cent for women and from 40 to 29 per cent for men. In China, primary enrolment reached 98.6 per cent in 2000, and 97 per cent of those completing primary school were continuing on to the secondary level. Latin America is believed to have achieved full primary enrolment. In India, overall literacy rose from 52 per cent in 1991 to 65 per cent in 2000.

Globally, a higher proportion of young people from poor and modest households now have the opportunity to acquire knowledge. The quality and depth of educational provision has been the subject of intense controversy, however. Mention is often made of the poor quality of education provided in primary schools in both developed and developing countries, and at the tertiary level gaps in educational quality appear to be widening. Children of wealthy and well-connected families have a much better chance of attending prestigious (or simply good) universities either at home or abroad than do children of families with limited means. The inter-generational transfer of inequalities in education remains a persistent problem. In Latin America, for example, around 75 per cent of young people in urban areas are from households in which the parents received less than 10 years of education, and on average, more than 45 per cent of them fail to complete the 12 years of schooling considered necessary to secure a decent and stable job and income. Just over 30 per cent of young people whose parents did not complete their primary education manage to finish the secondary cycle, compared with 75 per cent of those whose parents had at least 10 years of schooling.

There appears to be a strong link between rising inequalities in the distribution of opportunities for a quality education and the recent tendency to commercialise education and treat it as a commodity subject to the rules of an open and competitive market economy. For years, international financial institutions overseeing the implementation of structural adjustment programmes encouraged the Governments of developing countries to charge fees for the delivery of primary education. This reform component was discarded following widespread protests, but there are many other indications that, within the general context of the weakened commitment to public service and reduced support for universal social programmes, education is increasingly being treated as merchandise and pupils as customers. If nothing is done to address this issue, schools and universities of quality will be accessible only to the privileged classes, while the masses will have to be satisfied with lower-priced and often mediocre institutions.

Growing Inequalities in Healthcare and Social Security

In health, as in education, traditional indicators suggest overall progress. In Latin America, life expectancy at birth has increased from 67 to 70 years, which reflects overall health gains for the majority of the population and not only for the 5 or 10 per cent at the top of the income ladder. Similarly, the decline in infant mortality in Africa, from 96 to 85 deaths per 1,000 live births, has not benefited the small, affluent urban elite exclusively.

The optimism generated by such data must be tempered, however, as a number of critical health challenges and inequalities remain. Perhaps most serious is the HIV/AIDS pandemic, a tragedy of immense magnitude that is in many ways comparable to the great plagues of the past in that it has caused enormous suffering and has seriously undermined social, economic, cultural and political stability and development in a number of settings. Poor people living in developing countries have been especially hard hit, as they tend to be more vulnerable to HIV infection, generally receive less assistance and support from society and the medical establishment, and often lack access to life-saving medications. It should be recalled that one of the Millennium Development Goals is to ensure that, through cooperation with the pharmaceutical industry, individuals in developing countries are provided with access to affordable essential medications.

Some countries and regions have experienced a regression during the past few decades, even in terms of broad indicators such as life expectancy and infant mortality. This has been especially true in Eurasia. At least until recently—and the evidence of a reversal is far from overwhelming—health conditions were deteriorating dramatically in much of the region, particularly in the Russian Federation in the context of general neglect, the under-financing of public services, and the breakdown of a wide range of social institutions. An actual decline in life expectancy was registered—a rather exceptional development in these modern times.

This overall decline in health conditions was accompanied by increased inequalities, as the affluent minority had access to higher-quality private health care and facilities at home or abroad. The health sector, perhaps to an even greater degree than the education sector, is becoming highly commercialised in many parts of the world. It is fast becoming an industry driven by supply and demand, with producers and consumers, and those with means have a distinct advantage over the poor in terms of their ability to secure a wide array of quality services. Social security systems are under severe stress, as the demand for services far exceeds available resources in many settings, and private insurance is increasingly seen as an alternative to publicly financed systems of protection. Those living in more affluent countries typically have greater access to health information and are theoretically in a better position to understand their health and nutritional needs and the workings of the healthcare system.

Nonetheless, the residents of richer countries tend to be prone to obesity, while poor people in developing countries are undernourished, and many are starving. Those higher on the social ladder, particularly in developed countries, are also more aware of environmental challenges and are better able to protect themselves from pollution and other hazards. Affluent countries and social groups consume more energy and are therefore the biggest polluters, but they are also the ones with the greatest capacity to mobilise resources to ensure a clean environment.

Opportunities for Participation in Civic and Political Life

Apart from the intense focus on issues of violence and security in recent years, the international discourse has concentrated on the progress of democracy. Since the collapse of the Soviet Union, a great many countries have shifted from dictatorial or authoritarian regimes to political systems or structures that incorporate at least some aspects of democracy, including the holding of elections. In and around the Russian Federation, in Latin America, in Africa, and to some extent in Asia, the practice of democracy—even in limited form—is now the rule rather than the exception. The remaining authoritarian and single-party regimes seem to be increasingly on the defensive, as the isolation and strict control of more informed citizens are allegedly more difficult to achieve and sustain.

Political participation is presumably less hampered now than in the past by inequalities in social status, as privileges and opportunities for advancement are no longer reserved exclusively for those in the more elevated social classes, positions and professions, and the subservience and passivity of the masses, once resigned to their unalterable circumstances, are largely a thing of the past. In rigid, hierarchical social systems in which roles, duties and responsibilities are clearly defined, those in the lower and larger part of the pyramid must either accept or revolt against the status quo. During the time of Adam Smith and Voltaire this stratification was called social inequality and was considered the main obstacle to political and social progress. When money becomes the main determinant of social status and stratification, social mobility increases significantly, which theoretically makes political participation easier as it is more directly linked to individual choice. In such circumstances, individuals and communities tend to become more aware of their rights and options; logically, they should have a better understanding of the legitimate and illegitimate use of power, of what constitutes an abuse of their human rights, and of how they can seek protection from and redress for such abuse.

Opportunities for political participation have unquestionably increased on the whole, but for very many people around the globe involvement in the political process remains an impossibility. Oppressive political regimes, structures and institutions still exist in all parts of the world. In many countries, democratic principles and practices constitute a facade that does little to conceal authoritarian, plutocratic or, at best, elitist and technocratic political structures, institutions and processes. Those experiencing poverty or other forms of extreme hardship are engaged in a constant struggle for survival and do not have the time, energy or resources to participate in a res publica that is often distant and abstract, sometimes personalised and revered, and sometimes hated, but rarely understandable or accessible—even for citizens that are economically and socially integrated.

The old debate centring around the Marxist and liberal perspectives on society—between those arguing for the primacy of "real" rights and freedoms and those committed to the protection of "formal" liberties—has not lost its relevance, as the official doctrine of the United Nations founded on the inseparability of the two "sets" of human rights (civil/political and economic/social/cultural) has yet to find general acceptance and to be translated into effective policies. Few political regimes seriously attempt to reach the poor and disenfranchised. Periodic opportunities to vote in presidential or parliamentary elections are often enough to maintain the veneer of democracy and generally allow political elites to reinforce their positions of power and influence; at times constituents are treated to alternate political views in the exercise of power. Such scenarios reflect very little actual political participation; good citizenship involves the exercise of other privileges, duties and responsibilities. During much of the last century, political parties and unions often served as vehicles for political participation and the expression of views on the organisation of society; however, their role has weakened considerably over the past several decades.

Many members of the national and international political and financial elite assert that it is important to reach a consensus on how societies should be organised and on which objectives they should pursue, and contend that resistance to such consensus could only be attributable to a lack of information, ignorance or obscurantism. The majority of established political parties seem to share this view, or to be unable to challenge it effectively; however, there are other organisations and movements that are questioning the wisdom of such an approach. The emergence of non-governmental organisations (NGOs) and other civil society institutions as a collective political force represents a concrete manifestation of political participation on the part of responsible citizens. However, for these organisations to operate effectively as political entities, similar to political parties and unions in recent history, new forms of political representation must be developed that incorporate structures and processes conducive to the expression of views and concerns and meaningful political activity. At present, there are a number of factors discouraging or even preventing organised and effective political participation, including the weakening of the public sphere (whose primary function appears to be maintaining law and order), the increasing power and influence of the corporate sector, and the escalating violence in many areas of the world.

With violence comes the overt or insidious militarisation of societies; mobilisation should not be confused with participation. The latter is an expression of an individual's informed free will. It implies choice and the use of critical thinking and judgment. It requires a peaceful environment and cannot be motivated by fear. A great many people in today's world have experienced the traumas of war, ethnic conflict, terrorism or torture, or the devastating effects of natural disasters. Like the HIV/AIDS epidemic, these phenomena are intrinsically negative and ought to be prevented by all possible means. They affect mainly those who are economically, socially and politically weak. Individuals and families with money, social connections, and an elevated social position are usually better able to protect themselves from the effects of man-made and natural threats and disasters than are poor people.

Progress in Critical aspects of "Horizontal" Equality

While progress is often slow and uneven and subject to local reversals, the equality of rights, opportunities and conditions for women and men constitutes a fundamental dimension of justice that is steadily improving. In terms of gender equality, particularly as it relates to the status and treatment of girls and women in society, significant advances have been made with regard to the adoption and enforcement of legislation (and particularly in the application of corrective measures addressing long-standing male biases and outright discrimination against women), the provision of educational opportunities, access to participation in political processes and institutions, and the availability of work and employment opportunities; respect for the principle of equal pay for equal work is growing but has not yet been fully achieved. Biases, prejudice and discrimination still exist in many contexts, often to an extreme degree; very few societies can be said to have achieved true equality between women and men. One disturbing development has been the recent surge in various forms of religious fundamentalism and secular obscurantism, which threaten the idea that all human beings have equal rights and fundamental freedoms. On the whole, however, it seems reasonable to assert that the trend towards greater equality between men and women has not been halted or reversed during the current period of social, political and intellectual upheaval.

Various other forms of horizontal inequality, particularly as experienced by ethnic and other minority groups, were being given a certain amount of priority on national and international agendas. Within the United Nations, for example, a forum for indigenous peoples has recently been created. In a number of countries and regions, the political debate on poverty and inequality has increasingly focused on the relative wealth and social position of groups defined by their ethnicity or race rather than on the growing income gap between the rich and the poor. In another domain, greater overall equality is currently being sought, and to some extent achieved, for persons with disabilities; the United Nations has been at the forefront of developments in this area. These trends suggest that in today's world, inequalities associated with various forms of discrimination have a much better chance of being addressed, if not redressed, than do inequalities deriving from the functioning of the economy.

Social Injustice: Current state of Affairs

Growing disparities in the distribution of income and assets, the direct link between socioeconomic class and access to quality health care and education, and the decline in the participation of average citizens in public affairs are only a few of the many indications that social justice is receding, both as an objective of Governments and as a feature of societies. If one also takes into account the worsening of absolute poverty, particularly in affluent countries, it becomes readily apparent that the world is experiencing overall social regression, at least as measured by the traditional yardsticks of the founding texts of the United Nations. The spread of a global culture of consumption, competition and greed, the weakening of traditional forms of social inequality deriving from the uneven distribution of privileges based on birth and status, and the right of citizens to vote in elections give many societies the appearance of being more democratic when it truth they remain plutocratic and elitist.

Development and International Cooperation

By the end of the 1960s, international cooperation for development had become the most visible endeavour of the United Nations. As the cold war was effectively "freezing" the Security Council and its peacemaking and peacekeeping activities and seriously constraining the potentially immense role of the Organisation with regard to human rights and fundamental freedoms, development, seen as the progressive reduction and eventual closing of the gap between developed and underdeveloped countries, rose to the top of the international agenda. Close to half of the regular budget and an equivalent proportion of the staff of the United Nations were mobilised in support of economic and social development. In contrast, "political" matters (including Security Council activities), legal issues, and the development of international law and human rights together were allocated less than 10 per cent of the Organisation's human and financial resources. New programmes and funds were created, including the United Nations Development Programme (UNDP), the United Nations Conference on Trade and Development (UNCTAD) and the United Nations Population Fund (UNFPA). Extrabudgetary resources, obtained through voluntary contributions provided by affluent countries in addition to their assessed contributions to the regular budget and to the then-small peacekeeping budget, gave the Organisation more flexibility in its development-oriented activities.

These additional resources were used to address major issues of international concern, including refugees and later the environment and human habitat, but they were also earmarked for research, analyses and publications by the Secretariat on conceptual and political problems of development and economic and social progress. Governments providing these voluntary contributions clearly had a political agenda, which is just as true today, but this agenda included a number of items of benefit to the Organisation, such as strengthening the capacity of the Secretariat to devise or further elaborate economic models and forecasts and to assess social and environmental indicators that could complement economic indicators and provide a comprehensive measure of the progress or regression of societies. In a context of steady growth in the Organisation's regular budget, such loosely "tied" financial aid—representing about 35 per cent of the total annual expenditure of the United Nations by the beginning of the 1980s—gave the Secretary-General and the Secretariat the capacity to establish a strong and respected voice in the debate on development and to play a significant role in concrete development activities. Third world development constituted the most dynamic part of the United Nations and its most recognised face in rich and poor countries alike.

At the beginning, the growth model offered by the regimes of the countries that emerged victorious from the Second World War and, very soon after, the example offered by the rapid reconstruction and economic recovery of defeated countries, particularly Germany and Japan, were accepted without question. Economic growth, through judicious investments, the establishment of a modern infrastructure, employment creation, education and training, and a mix of public and private initiatives, constituted the key to development. Outside the Soviet Union and its sphere of domination in Central and Eastern Europe, the influence of communism on development theory and practice was relatively limited. After all, the concept of organising investments and other public activities for economic development within the framework of an annual or medium-term plan had been conceived by France and the United Kingdom and applied in some of their colonies since the end of the nineteenth century. Communism and the power of the Soviet Union were, for the countries of the third world, more a source of political leverage in their efforts to gain independence from colonial and neocolonial powers than an inspiration for their development strategies.

The nonaligned movement was, as its name suggests, a political effort to avoid dependence on either of the superpowers of the time. It proposed ideas and strategies for establishing effective relations with these superpowers, for defining the global position and status of formerly colonised countries, and for combating neocolonialism. It did not, however, furnish a new theory of economic growth or a new vision of social progress. Western countries were all more or less applying Keynesian principles and implementing policies that represented a rather happy mix of liberalism and socialism. Ideological controversies essentially reflected an East-West divide. It was in this context that Western countries were able to agree, in 1969, to earmark between 0.7 and 1 per cent of their gross national income for ODA to help the developing countries of the world. A series of 10-year International Development Strategies were adopted by the General Assembly, and monitoring results showed that they not only shaped international cooperation for development but also influenced the national policies of both developing and developed countries.

Seeking a New Distribution of Power in the World

The pursuit of international cooperation for development through the United Nations was characterised by enormous difficulties and controversies. In progressive quarters, the development model itself was seen as flawed. Widespread reliance on exports of primary commodities and imports of manufactured goods within the developing world meant that countries along the "periphery" were largely dependent on those at the "centre". Strategies were devised for import substitution and, more ambitiously, for economic and political self-reliance. Rural development programmes were adopted to address the rural-urban migration associated with traditional industrial development and the consequent spread of urban slums. Different approaches to development were formulated by social scientists, particularly in Latin America. The almost exclusive reliance on economic development among experts and politicians was seen as excessive and gave rise to calls for institutional, social and cultural development.

The articulation of social and economic priorities and policies entailed extensive debate. A unified approach to economic and social development was devised; social and economic analyses and indicators would be given equal consideration in assessing societal wellbeing and formulating comprehensive development plans. Social planning found a niche in the institutional structure of the United Nations. The development of trade relations prompted the Secretariat to sponsor a number of initiatives. The adoption of the Generalised System of Preferences allowed developing countries to participate in world trade without full exposure to the competition of advanced economic powers, and the rise of transnational corporations to global prominence led to the establishment of the United Nations Centre on Transnational Corporations and the United Nations Centre for Science and Technology for Development; intergovernmental commissions focusing on these areas were also set up. These and other such initiatives were not welcomed by the most powerful Western countries, but on the whole, through successes and failures, international cooperation for development through the United Nations and its specialised agencies continued along its established course. It was generally acknowledged that the United Nations system deserved some credit not only for the decolonisation process but also for contributing significantly to the betterment of the human condition in a number of developing countries.

The "oil crisis" at the beginning of the 1970s and the adoption by the General Assembly of resolutions incorporating the Declaration and the Programme of Action on the Establishment of a New International Economic Order and of another resolution that included the Charter of Economic Rights and Duties of States collectively marked a turning point in the brief history of the United Nations as a global forum and an agent for development and international justice. These events brought about a shift in the attitude of the major industrialised countries, in particular the United States, vis-a-vis the treatment of the question of development in the United Nations. The oil crisis served to underline the dependence of many countries and regions, particularly Europe and Japan, on oil-producing developing countries that, through the establishment of cartels, had acquired the capacity to control the prices of their products. Ultimately the crisis led to an extended slowdown in economic growth—again, chiefly in Europe and Japan. Perhaps most importantly, there was evidence that developing countries were using this opportunity to try to modify the balance of economic power in the world in their favour and to practice a form of economic nationalism that could seriously hinder the development of global capitalism.

The above-mentioned documents on the establishment of a new world economic order emphasise the right of every State to regulate and control foreign investment and the activities of transnational corporations within its borders.

Recognition is also given to the right of each State to choose its political, social and economic systems; nationalisation and expropriations are considered permissible within this context. Other controversial provisions of these texts relate to science and technology transfer and research cooperation. Full disarmament is also envisaged, as is cooperation in environmental protection. The Charter of Economic Rights and Duties of States was adopted by the General Assembly in December 1974 by 120 votes to 6, with 10 abstentions.

In March 1975, the Second General Conference of the United Nations Industrial Development Organisation adopted the Lima Declaration and Plan of Action on Industrial Development and Cooperation. In this Declaration, it was stated that the share of developing countries in total world industrial production "should be increased to the maximum possible extent and as far as possible to at least 25 per cent of total world industrial production by the year 2000, while making every endeavour to ensure that the industrial growth so achieved is distributed among developing countries as evenly as possible." Irrespective of its substantive merits, this target was immediately taken by commentators of the Western world as clear evidence of the irresponsibility of activist developing countries and of their supporters in the secretariats of international organisations. It was both ridiculed as an unattainable objective and denounced as an attempt to place the world economy and its market forces within the straight jacket of world planners and technocrats.

Millennium Declaration and Millennium Development Goals

It was arguably at this point that the most powerful developed countries decided to effectively neutralise the role of the United Nations and its specialised agencies as forums for debate and for important decisions regarding the functioning of the world economy. From the mid-1970s onward, these countries relied increasingly on the better-controlled Bretton Woods institutions, strengthening their role and influence in global economic development, and pressed for the reform of the United Nations, which was formally initiated at the end of 1986 and is still very much on the international agenda. With the collapse of the Soviet bloc at the end of the 1980s, the United States and its allies no longer had any major obstacles to the dissemination of their views on the organisation of the world economy and on the meaning of international justice.

Developing countries, partly out of conviction and partly because they sense the probable futility of resistance and understand the need to adapt to the new global political configuration, have abandoned their demands for revolutionary changes in the world economic and political order and are now pursuing an incremental approach in defence of their interests. Rather than controlling the activities of transnational corporations in their territories, they are offering fiscal and other incentives to attract private foreign investment. Nationalisation and expropriation have disappeared from their political vocabulary. They pursue arrangements and agreements through the WTO to promote their exports and gain access to the markets of affluent countries. Global trade and participation in the world economy are the order of the day; self-reliance and self-sufficiency are perceived as antiquated concepts. Developing countries continue to press for concessions in traditional areas of negotiation between the North and the South, requesting further debt reduction or increased ODA, but their efforts are essentially focused on gaining a foothold in the dynamic sectors of the world economy. Justice is sought through efforts to ensure the elimination of measures and practices (such as domestic agricultural subsidies) that allow some countries to maintain an unfair advantage over others. The leaders of developing countries contend that if the guiding principle of the world market economy is competition on an open and even playing field, obstacles to fair competition should be removed.

The most important text adopted by the United Nations in recent decades is the Millennium Declaration, which reflects a consensus on what constitutes just relations between countries with unequal power and affluence. First, it is a text centred on people rather than nations. In section I of the Declaration, entitled "Values and principles", mention is made of "the sovereign equality of all States, respect for their territorial integrity and political independence, [and the] resolution of disputes by peaceful means and in conformity with the principles of justice and international law". However, among the six fundamental values considered "essential to international relations in the twenty-first century"—namely, freedom, equality, solidarity, tolerance, respect for nature, and shared responsibility—the first three clearly apply to people rather than countries. Tolerance may also be included in this group, as it implies acceptance of the differences and richness within and between societies and "a culture of peace and dialogue among all civilisations". Respect for nature is a value that transcends national boundaries. The last of these values, shared responsibility, necessitates the multilateral management of "worldwide economic and social development", in which the United Nations has played and will continue to play a central role.

Second, consistent with the emphasis on people, section III of the Declaration focuses on development and poverty eradication. The right to development is mentioned, but its application for "everyone" and to "the entire human race" suggests that it is regarded more as an individual and collective right than a right of nations.

Reference is made to the "abject and dehumanising conditions" endured by billions of "our fellow men, women and children" in extreme poverty. There is no mention of the distribution of income and wealth among countries or of the various gaps that separate developed from developing countries. It is stressed that development will depend first on "good governance within each country" but also on "good governance at the international level and on transparency in the financial, monetary and trading systems". The multilateral trading and financial system must be "open, equitable, rule-based, predictable and nondiscriminatory". The special needs of least developed countries are addressed in this section, and industrialised developed countries are called upon to undertake various measures for their benefit, including:

1. The cancellation of bilateral debt "in return for their making demonstrable commitments to poverty reduction" and
2. The granting of "more generous development assistance", again, "especially to countries that are genuinely making an effort to apply their resources to poverty reduction".

Third, and most importantly, the eighth Millennium Development Goal—to "develop a global partnership for development"—is perfectly representative of the "new deal" or "new global contract" between developed and developing countries. Within the framework of this Goal, which is the only one directly pertaining to international development cooperation, specific attention is to be given to the creation of an open, rule-based, predictable, and nondiscriminatory trading and financial system; the special needs of least developed, landlocked and small island developing States; the debt issue; and cooperation with the private sector to provide access to affordable essential drugs and information and communication technologies.

In addition, strategies aimed at providing youth with opportunities for decent and productive work are to be developed and implemented in cooperation with developing countries. Associated with the various dimensions of Goal 8 are 16 indicators for monitoring progress that relate to ODA provision, market access, debt sustainability, youth unemployment, and access to essential drugs, telephone lines, personal computers and the Internet.

These texts, especially the Millennium Development Goals, have become very much a part of the international discourse and have even found their way into the national political debates of both developed and developing countries, and into the board discussions and policies of the World Bank, the regional development banks and the IMF.

Even the WTO, notorious for its lack of interest in the development activities and pronouncements of the United Nations, has expressed its commitment to the realisation of the Goals. This interest and approval has not been limited to official circles and the political establishment; civil society organisations have expressed their strong support and are working in the field to achieve the objectives and targets established at the beginning of the new millennium. This is truly exceptional for an initiative of the United Nations.

A resolution of the General Assembly rarely enjoys such wide exposure or what amounts to virtually universal acceptance; clearly, the Millennium Declaration and the associated Millennium Development Goals reflect the spirit of these times and are consistent with popular sensibilities.

International Justice through Cooperation and Partnership

The conception of international justice embodied in the Millennium Declaration and the Millennium Development Goals is in tune with the dominant political culture of the modern era. Countries are cognizant of the need to engage in a global partnership for development. True partnership derives from mature, pragmatic and effective interaction. Partners are not necessarily equal but must respect each other and draw comparable benefits from their relationship. Trade constitutes the basis of this relationship and is theoretically beneficial for everyone, at least in the long run. All societies participate in the exchange of goods and services, and as globalisation is extended to all parts of the world, it will be trade that unites all countries and all peoples. The old functionalist idea that trade brings development and prosperity and that prosperity brings peace—one of the intellectual and political pillars of the United Nations—still has wide appeal. Countries forming partnerships in the quest for material prosperity are no longer identified as being from the "North" or the "South".

The division of the world into poles, with the accompanying connotations of superiority and obligation and the established cycle of demands and concessions, is avoided in the Millennium texts; all countries meet in the global market. If the rules prevailing in this market are transparent, predictable and fair, the rich will get richer and the poor will get rich, and one of those much-heralded win-win situations will occur. It is not envisaged, in this culture of partnership for development, that the rich and powerful countries will have to sacrifice part of their wealth to help the less affluent. The words "distribution", "redistribution", "taxation" and "transfer" are carefully avoided, and the notion of solidarity—one of the six values listed at the beginning of the Millennium Declaration—is absent from the body of the Declaration and from the Goals. While least developed countries are to be treated with some sort of positive discrimination with regard to trade, debt and development assistance, this does not represent a moral obligation or the pursuit of global justice but rather an exchange that entails fair compensation for their dedication to poverty reduction.

Under the terms of this global partnership, developed countries and international organisations, notably the WTO, are to promote the development of a world economy with open, rule-based and predictable arrangements in trade and finance, ensuring an even terrain for competition. Affluent countries and international agencies are also to provide development assistance, but an increasing proportion of this support is to be given to least developed countries. Developing countries, for their part, have to improve levels of organisation and efficiency in their domestic affairs. Good governance is an essential condition for development. It is normally associated with the practice of democracy and with respect for human rights. Unless otherwise indicated, good governance is understood as the authority exercised by institutions that operate according to the rule of law, that are not corrupt, and that facilitate the free exercise of private initiative by both domestic and foreign sources. The central role of private initiative and of the private sector is emphasised in the eighth Millennium Development Goal. The private sector is a partner in development on par with States.

This conception of international justice, which essentially amounts to fair competition and an element of solidarity with, or even charity for, the poorest and weakest countries, not only reflects the dominant political culture, but is also consistent with a deeply ingrained current of thought among the intellectual and political elites of developing countries. This current of thought reflects long-standing concerns that centre around the issue of national pride. Countries compelled to accept aid may experience humiliation and a sense of obligation to donors. Moreover, assistance always comes with conditions. It does not really matter that these conditions have changed from requiring that the financial aid be used for importing material and goods from the donor to stipulating that recipients must hold elections or guarantee human rights. In some respects, the latter are even more intolerable than the former. They represent an interference in domestic affairs that is more intrusive than the traditional mercantile arrangements of former coloniser. Frequently, they reflect a double standard and a certain amount of hypocrisy. From a pragmatic perspective, external aid in all its forms is ultimately ineffective and detrimental to the fabric of society. It prevents the emergence of responsibility, initiative, entrepreneurship, and other values and practices that are indispensable to the development of any society. What developing countries really need is access to international markets for their products and global freedom of movement for their people. It would be difficult to attribute even part of the success of those countries that are making great economic strides and gaining respect in the international arena to the provision of traditional bilateral or multilateral aid and assistance. From this perspective, the eighth Millennium Development Goal represents a step in the right direction, which is expunging all traces of paternalistic assistance from the notions of international justice and international cooperation.

Bibliography

Acemoglu, D. 1998, Why do New Technologies Complement Skills? Directed Technical Change and Wage Inequality, *Quarterly Journal of Economics*, vol. 113, pp. 1055-89.

Albert M. 1993. *Capitalism vs. Capitalism*. New York: Four Walls Eight Windows

Albrow, Martin and Elizabeth King (Ed) 1990. *Globalization, Knowledge, and Society*. London: Sage

Alinsky, Saul. 1934. "A Sociological Technique in Clinical Criminology." Pp. 167-78 in Proceedings of the Sixty-Fourth Annual Congress of the American Prison Association

Bruhn, John G. and Howard M. Rebach. 1996. *Clinical Sociology: An Agenda for Action*. New York: Plenum.

Burawoy, Michael. 2004. "The Critical Turn to Public Sociology." Pp. 309-326 in

Carmel, Erran, Whitaker, Randall D., and George, Joey F. 1993. PD and joint application design: A transatlantic comparison. *Communications of the ACM* 36(6):40–48.

Cimoli, M. and G. Dosi, 1995. *Technological Paradigms, Patterns of Learning and Development: An Introductory Roadmap*, in "Journal of Evolutionary Economics", vol 5, pp.243-268.

Davis, Donald R. 1996, Trade Liberalization and Income Distribution, *NBER Working Paper no. 5693*, National Bureau of Economic Research, Cambridge (Mass.).

Dollar D. and Kraay, A. 2001. Growth is Good for the Poor, *mimeo*, Development Research Group, The World Bank, Washington, March.

Dutton, William. 1999. The web of technology and people: Challenges for economic and social research. *Prometheus* 17(1):5–20.

Easterly, W. 2001. "The Lost Decades: Developing Countries' Stagnation in Spite of Policy Reforms 1980-1998", *Journal of Economic Growth*, vol.6, pp.135-157.

Garrett G. 1996. "Trade, capital mobility and the domestic politics of economic policy". In *Internationalization and Domestic Politics*, ed. R Keohane, H Milner, pp. 79–107. New York: Cambridge Univ. Press

Ghose, A. K. 2000, Trade Liberalization and Manufacturing Employment, *ILO Employment Paper* 2000/3, International Labour Office, Geneva.

Giddens, Anthony. 2000. *Runaway World*. New York: Routledge

Harding, Sandra., ed. 2004. *The Feminist Standpoint Theory Reader*. New York: Routledge.

Hirst P, Thompson G. 1996. *Globalization in Question*. Cambridge, MA: Blackwell

Katzenstein P. 1985. *Small States inWorld Markets:Industrial Policy in Europe*. Ithaca,NY: Cornell Univ. Press

Khondker, Habibul (1994) "Globalization Theory: A Critical Analysis" Department of Sociology Working Paper, National University of Singapore.

Kiesler, Sara, ed. 1997. *The culture of the Internet*. Mahwah, NJ: Lawrence Erlbaum Associates..

MacIntyre A, ed. 1994. *Business and Government in Industrialising Asia*. Ithaca, NY: Cornell Univ. Press

Midgley, James. 1994. "Defining Social Development: Historical Trends and Conceptual Formulations." *Social Development Issues* 16/3:3-19.

Moore, W.E. (1966) "Global Sociology: The World as a Singular System" *American Journal of Sociology*, 71 (5)

Nederveen Pieterse, Jan, (2004) *Globalization and Culture*, Rowman and Littlefield, Lanham, Maryland.

Ohmae K. 1990. *The Borderless World*. New York: Harper Collins

Perez, C. (1983), "Structural Change and the Assimilation of New Technologies in the Economic and Social System", *Futures*, vol.15, pp.357-375.

Ritzer, G (2000). *The McDonaldization of Society*, Thousand Oaks, California: Pine Forge,

Rosenberg, Rosalind. 1982. *Beyond Separate Spheres: The Intellectual Roots of Modern Feminism*. New Haven: Yale University Press.

Timasheff, Nicholas S. and George A. Theodorson. 1976. *Sociological Theory, Its Nature and Growth*. New York: Random House.

Vandenbroucke F. 1998. *Globalisation, Inequality,and Social Democracy*. London: Inst. Public Policy Res.

Waters, Malcolm (1995) *Globalization*. London: Routledge

World Bank. 1993. *The East Asian Miracle: Economic Growth and Public Policy*. New York: Oxford Univ. Press

Index

ENCYCLOPAEDIA OF SOCIOLOGY

Social Research Survey and Statistics

Volume –2

Satish Mittal
Sushil Kumar Saxena

Commonwealth

Encyclopaedia of Sociology

Edition : 2026

ISBN 978-81-311-0377-7 (set)

Published by :
COMMONWEALTH PUBLISHERS (P) LTD.
4831/24, Govind Lane,
Ansari Road, Darya Ganj,
New Delhi - 110002
Ph. : 23242541, 23272541
e-mail : commonwealthpublishers2016@gmail.com

Distributed by :
ARJUN PUBLISHING HOUSE
4831/24, Govind Lane,
Ansari Road, Darya Ganj,
New Delhi - 110002
Ph. : 23242541, 23272541
e-mail : arjunbooks2001@gmail.com
arjunpubhouse@gmail.com

Laser Typesetting by :
Dimple Computers
Delhi

Printed at :
Milan Enterprises
Delhi

Preface

Social research refers to research conducted by social scientists. Social research methods may be divided into two broad categories—quantitative and qualitative. Quantitative designs approach social phenomena through quantifiable evidence, and often rely on statistical analysis of many cases to create valid and reliable general claims, while qualitative designs emphasise understanding of social phenomena through direct observation, communication with participants, or analysis of texts, and may stress contextual and subjective accuracy over generality.

Social scientists employ a range of methods in order to analyse a vast breadth of social phenomena: from census survey data derived from millions of individuals, to the in-depth analysis of a single agents' social experiences; from monitoring what is happening on contemporary streets, to the investigation of ancient historical documents. The methods rooted in classical sociology and statistics have formed the basis for research in other disciplines, such as political science, media studies, and market research.

This book offers a comprehensive introduction to the field of research methods as practised by sociologists and other social scientists. Emphasising the importance of the research process, the book shows how social scientists design research studies, introduces variety of observation modes and covers the prons and cons of social research. The use of examples is excellent and aids very much in conveying difficult concepts and ideas.

Authors

Contents

1

Introduction to Social Research

Social research refers to research conducted by social scientists. Social research methods may be divided into two broad categories:

1. *Quantitative designs* approach social phenomena through quantifiable evidence, and often rely on statistical analysis of many cases (or across intentionally designed treatments in an experiment) to create valid and reliable general claims
2. *Qualitative designs* emphasize understanding of social phenomena through direct observation, communication with participants, or analysis of texts, and may stress contextual and subjective accuracy over generality

Social scientists employ a range of methods in order to analyse a vast breadth of social phenomena; from census survey data derived from millions of individuals, to the in-depth analysis of a single agents' social experiences; from monitoring what is happening on contemporary streets, to the investigation of ancient historical documents. The methods rooted in classical sociology and statistics have formed the basis for research in other disciplines, such as political science, media studies, and market research.

Social research is the scientific study of society. More specifically, social research examines a society's attitudes, assumptions, beliefs, trends, stratification and rules. The scope of social research can be small or large, ranging from the self or a single individual to spanning an entire race or country. Popular topics of social research include poverty, racism, class issues, sexuality, voting behaviour, gender constructs, policing and criminal behaviour.

Social research determines the relationship between one or more variables. For example, sex and income level are variables. Social scientists will look for underlying concepts and cause-and-effect relationships of a social issue. Before even beginning research, scientists must formulate a research question. For example, a researcher might ask if there is a relationship between a person's sex and his or her income level. Do men have higher incomes than women? Are women most likely to be poor?

A third variable, race, can be added to the question. Then the social scientist can pose a research question: Does race and sex affect a person's income level? Social scientists will then collect data, organize and analyse information and create a report of their findings. People conducting social research must also consider ethics, biases and the reliability and validity of the research they're conducting. They must decide which form of sampling to use, how to measure information, how to analyse data and present their findings.

Research can be conducted using surveys, reports, observation, questionnaires, focus groups, historical accounts, personal diaries and census statistics. There are two types of research: qualitative research and quantitative research. Qualitative research is inductive, meaning the researcher creates hypotheses and abstractions from collected data. Most data is collected via words or pictures and mostly from people. Researchers are interested in how people make sense of their lives and in the research process itself.

Quantitative research is the complete opposite and most often involves numbers and set data. Quantitative data is efficient but focuses only on the end result, not the process itself, as qualitative research does. Quantitative data is precise and is often the result of surveys or questionnaires.

METHODOLOGY

Social scientists are divided into camps of support for particular research techniques. These disputes relate to the historical core of social theory (positivism and antipositivism; structure and agency). While very different in many aspects, both qualitative and quantitative approaches involve a systematic interaction between theory and data. The choice of method often depends largely on what the researcher intends to investigate. For example, a researcher concerned with drawing a statistical generalization across an entire population may administer a survey questionnaire to a representitive sample population. By contrast, a researcher who seeks full contextual understanding of an individuals' social actions may choose ethnographic participant observation or open-ended interviews. Studies will commonly combine, or 'triangulate', quantitative *and* qualitative methods as part of a 'multi-strategy' design. For instance, a quantitative study may be performed to gain statistical patterns or a target sample, and then combined with a qualitative interview to determine the play of agency.

An extreme form of ethnographic participant observation is practised when a group of social scientists:

1. Build and occupy an experimental community,
2. Observe and record their own behaviours,
3. Experimentally test possible solutions to their personal and social problems,
4. Deliberately adopt experimentally validated solutions, and

5. Publish reports about the evolution of their culture. A fictional experimental community, and Los Horcones, a *real* experimental community.

Sampling

Typically a population is very large, making a census or a complete enumeration of all the values in that population infeasible. A 'sample' thus forms a manageable subset of a population. In positivist research, statistics derived from a sample are analysed in order to draw inferences regarding the population as a whole. The process of collecting information from a sample is referred to as 'sampling'. Sampling methods may be either 'random' (random sampling, systematic sampling, stratified sampling, cluster sampling) or non-random/nonprobability (convenience sampling, purposive sampling, snowball sampling). The most common reason for sampling is to obtain information about a population. Sampling is quicker and cheaper than a complete census of a population.

Types of Method

The following list of research methods is neither exclusive nor exhaustive:

Quantitative Methods

1. Chi-square test
2. Cluster analysis
3. Regression analysis
4. Spearman's rank correlation coefficient
5. Statistical surveys and questionnaires
6. Student's t-test
7. Survey research
8. Quantitative marketing research

Qualitative Methods

1. Analytic induction
2. Archival research
3. Content analysis
4. Ethnography
5. Focus group
6. Historical method
7. Life history
8. Longitudinal study
9. Morphological analysis
10. Participant observation
11. Semi-structured interview
12. Structured interview
13. Textual analysis
14. Unstructured interview

Foundations of Social Research

Sociological Positivism

The origin of the survey can be traced back at least early as the Domesday Book in 1086, whilst some scholars pinpoint the origin of demography to 1663 with the publication of John Graunt's *Natural and Political Observations upon the Bills of Mortality*. Social research began most intentionally, however, with the positivist philosophy of science in the early 19th century.

Auguste Comte (1798–1857) first described the epistemological perspective of positivism in *The Course in Positive Philosophy*, a series of texts published between 1830 and 1842. These texts were followed by the 1844 work, *A General View of Positivism* (published in English in

1865). The first three volumes of the *Course* dealt chiefly with the physical sciences already in existence (mathematics, astronomy, physics, chemistry, biology), whereas the latter two emphasized the inevitable coming of social science. Observing the circular dependence of theory and observation in science, and classifying the sciences in this way, Comte may be regarded as the first philosopher of science in the modern sense of the term. For him, the physical sciences had necessarily to arrive first, before humanity could adequately channel its efforts into the most challenging and complex "Queen science" of human society itself.

Modern social research, and indeed the formal academic discipline of sociology, began with the work of Émile Durkheim (1858–1917). While Durkheim rejected much of the detail of Comte's philosophy, he retained and refined its method, maintaining that the social sciences are a logical continuation of the natural ones into the realm of human activity, and insisting that they may retain the same objectivity, rationalism, and approach to causality. Durkheim set up the first European department of sociology at the University of Bordeaux in 1895, publishing his Rules of the Sociological Method (1895). In this text he argued:

> "[o]ur main goal is to extend scientific rationalism to human conduct... What has been called our positivism is but a consequence of this rationalism."

Durkheim's seminal monograph, *Suicide* (1897), a case study of suicide rates amongst Catholic and Protestant populations, distinguished sociological analysis from psychology or philosophy. By carefully examining suicide statistics in different police districts, he attempted to demonstrate that Catholic communities have a lower suicide rate than that of Protestants, something he attributed to social (as opposed to individual or psychological) causes. He developed the notion of objective *suis generis* "social facts" to delineate a unique empirical object for the science of sociology to study. Through such studies he posited that sociology would be able to determine whether any given society is 'healthy' or 'pathological', and seek social reform to negate organic breakdown or "social anomie". For Durkheim, sociology could be described as the "science of institutions, their genesis and their functioning".

Methodological Assumptions

Social research is based on logic and empirical observations. Charles C. Ragin writes in his *Constructing Social Research* book that "Social research involved the interaction between ideas and evidence. Ideas help social researchers make sense of evidence, and researchers use evidence to extend, revise and test ideas". Social research thus attempts to create or validate theories through data collection and data analysis, and its goal is exploration, description and explanation. It should never lead or be mistaken with philosophy or belief. Social research aims to find social patterns of regularity in social life and usually deals with social groups (aggregates of individuals), not individuals themselves (although science of psychology is an exception here). Research can also be divided into pure research and applied research. Pure research has no application on real life, whereas applied research attempts to influence the real world.

There are no laws in social science that parallel the laws in the natural science. A law in social science is a universal generalization about a class of facts. A fact is an observed phenomenon, and observation means it has been seen, heard or otherwise experienced by researcher. A theory is a systematic explanation for the observations that relate to a particular aspect of social life. Concepts are the basic building blocks of theory and are abstract elements representing classes of phenomena. Axioms or postulates are basic assertions assumed to be true. **Propositions are** conclusions drawn about the relationships among concepts, based on analysis of axioms. Hypotheses are specified expectations about empirical reality which are derived from propositions. Social research involves testing these hypotheses to see if they are true.

Social research involves creating a theory, operationalisation (measurement of variables) and observation (actual collection of data to test hypothesized relationship). Social theories are written in the language of variables, in other words, theories describe logical relationships between variables. Variables are logical sets of attributes, with people being the 'carriers' of those variables (for example, gender can be a variable with two attributes: male and female). Variables are also divided into independent variables (data) that influences the dependent variables (which scientists are trying to explain). For example, in a study of how different dosages of a drug are related to the severity of symptoms of a disease, a measure of the severity of the symptoms of the disease is a dependent variable and the administration of the drug in specified doses is the independent variable. Researchers will compare the different values of the dependent variable (severity of the symptoms) and attempt to draw conclusions.

Rules for Social Research

Although there are no laws in social science that parallel laws in the natural sciences, there is consensus about fundamental rules or principles about how to do social research. When social scientists speak of "good research" the focus is on how the research is done whether the research is methodologically sound rather than on whether the results of the research are consistent with personal biases or preconceptions. Glenn Firebaugh summarizes the principles for good research in his book *Seven Rules for*

Social Research. The first rule is that "*There should be the* possibility of surprise in social research." As Firebaugh elaborates: "Rule 1 is intended to warn that you don't want to be blinded by preconceived ideas so that you fail to look for contrary evidence, or you fail to recognize contrary evidence when you do encounter it, or you recognize contrary evidence but suppress it and refuse to accept your findings for what they appear to say." In addition, good research will "look for differences that make a difference" (Rule 2) and "build in reality checks" (Rule 3). Rule 4 advises researchers to replicate, that is, "to see if identical analyses yield similar results for different samples of people" The next two rules urge researchers to "compare like with like" (Rule 5) and to "study change" (Rule 6); these two rules are especially important when researchers want to estimate the effect of one variable on another. The final rule, "Let method be the servant, not the master," reminds researchers that methods are the means, not the end, of social research; it is critical from the outset to fit the research design to the research issue, rather than the other way around.

Types of Explanations

Explanations in social theories can be idiographic or nomothetic. An idiographic approach to an explanation is one where the scientists seek to exhaust the idiosyncratic causes of a particular condition or event, i.e. by trying to provide all possible explanations of a particular case. Nomothetic explanations tend to be more general with scientists trying to identify a few causal factors that impact a wide class of conditions or events. For example, when dealing with the problem of how people choose a job, idiographic explanation would be to list all possible reasons why a given person (or group) chooses a given job, while nomothetic explanation would try to find factors that determine why job applicants in general choose a given job.

2

Quantitative Research Methods

Quantitative research refers to the systematic empirical investigation of quantitative properties and phenomena and their relationships. The objective of quantitative research is to develop and employ mathematical models, theories and/or hypotheses pertaining to phenomena. The process of measurement is central to quantitative research because it provides the fundamental connection between empirical observation and mathematical expression of quantitative relationships.

Quantitative research is used widely in social sciences such as psychology, sociology, anthropology, and political science. Research in mathematical sciences such as physics is also 'quantitative' by definition, though this use of the term differs in context. In the social sciences, the term relates to empirical methods, originating in both philosophical positivism and the history of statistics, which contrast qualitative research methods.

Qualitative methods produce information only on the particular cases studied, and any more general conclusions are only hypotheses. Quantitative methods can be used to verify, which of such hypotheses are true.

A comprehensive analysis of 1274 articles published in the top two American sociology journals between 1935 and

2005 found that roughly two thirds of these articles used quantitative methods.

Quantitative research is generally made using scientific methods, which can include:

1. The generation of models, theories and hypotheses
2. The development of instruments and methods for measurement
3. Experimental control and manipulation of variables
4. Collection of empirical data
5. Modelling and analysis of data
6. Evaluation of results

In the social sciences particularly, quantitative research is often contrasted with qualitative research which is the examination, analysis and interpretation of observations for the purpose of discovering underlying meanings and patterns of relationships, including classifications of types of phenomena and entities, in a manner that does not involve mathematical models. Approaches to quantitative psychology were first modelled on quantitative approaches in the physical sciences by Gustav Fechner in his work on psychophysics, which built on the work of Ernst Heinrich Weber. Although a distinction is commonly drawn between qualitative and quantitative aspects of scientific investigation, it has been argued that the two go hand in hand. For example, based on analysis of the history of science, Kuhn concludes that "large amounts of qualitative work have usually been prerequisite to fruitful quantification in the physical sciences". Qualitative research is often used to gain a general sense of phenomena and to form theories that can be tested using further quantitative research. For instance, in the social sciences qualitative research methods are often used to gain better understanding of such things as intentionality (from the speech response of the researcher) and meaning (why did this person/group say something and what did it mean to them?).

Although quantitative investigation of the world has existed since people first began to record events or objects that had been counted, the modern idea of quantitative processes have their roots in Auguste Comte's positivist framework.

Quantitative Methods are research techniques that are used to gather quantitative data-information dealing with numbers and anything that is measurable. Statistics, tables and graphs, are often used to present the results of these methods. They are therefore to be distinguished from qualitative methods.

In most physical and biological sciences, the use of either quantitative or qualitative methods is uncontroversial, and each is used when appropriate. In the social sciences, particularly in sociology, social anthropology and psychology, the use of one or other type of method has become a matter of controversy and even ideology, with particular schools of thought within each discipline favouring one type of method and pouring scorn on to the other.

Advocates of quantitative methods argue that only by using such methods can the social sciences become truly scientific; advocates of qualitative methods argue that quantitative methods tend to obscure the reality of the social phenomena under study because they underestimate or neglect the non-measurable factors, which may be the most important. The modern tendency (and in reality the majority tendency throughout the history of social science) is to use eclectic approaches.

Quantitative methods might be used with a global qualitative frame. Qualitative methods might be used to understand the meaning of the numbers produced by quantitative methods. Using quantitative methods, it is possible to give precise and testable expression to qualitative ideas. This combination of quantitative and qualitative data gathering is often referred to as mixed-methods research.

Use of Statistics

Statistics is the most widely used branch of mathematics in quantitative research outside of the physical sciences, and also finds applications within the physical sciences, such as in statistical mechanics. Statistical methods are used extensively within fields such as economics, social sciences and biology. Quantitative research using statistical methods starts with the collection of data, based on the hypothesis or theory. Usually a big sample of data is collected this would require verification, validation and recording before the analysis can take place. Software packages such as SPSS and R are typically used for this purpose. Causal relationships are studied by manipulating factors thought to influence the phenomena of interest while controlling other variables relevant to the experimental outcomes. In the field of health, for example, researchers might measure and study the relationship between dietary intake and measurable physiological effects such as weight loss, controlling for other key variables such as exercise. Quantitatively based opinion surveys are widely used in the media, with statistics such as the proportion of respondents in favour of a position commonly reported. In opinion surveys, respondents are asked a set of structured questions and their responses are tabulated. In the field of climate science, researchers compile and compare statistics such as temperature or atmospheric concentrations of carbon dioxide.

Empirical relationships and associations are also frequently studied by using some form of General linear model, non-linear model, or by using factor analysis. A fundamental principle in quantitative research is that correlation does not imply causation. This principle follows from the fact that it is always possible a spurious relationship exists for variables between which covariance is found in some degree. Associations may be examined between any combination of continuous and categorical variables using methods of statistics.

Measurement

Views regarding the role of measurement in quantitative research are somewhat divergent. Measurement is often regarded as being only a means by which observations are expressed numerically in order to investigate causal relations or associations. However, it has been argued that measurement often plays a more important role in quantitative research. For example, Kuhn argued that within quantitative research, the results that are shown can prove to be strange. This is because accepting ,a theory based on results of quantitative data. could prove to be a natural phenomenon. He argued that such abnormalities are interesting when done during the process of obtaining data, as seen below:

> When measurement the parts from theory, it is likely to yield mere numbers, and their very neutrality makes them particularly sterile as a source of remedial suggestions. But numbers register the departure from theory with an authority and finesse that no qualitative technique can duplicate, and that departure is often enough to start a search .

In classical physics, the theory and definitions which underpin measurement are generally deterministic in nature. In contrast, probabilistic measurement models known as the Rasch model and Item response theory models are generally employed in the social sciences. Psychometrics is the field of study concerned with the theory and technique for measuring social and psychological attributes and phenomena. This field is central to much quantitative research that is undertaken within the social sciences.

Quantitative research may involve the use of *proxies* as stand-ins for other quantities that cannot be directly measured. Tree-ring width, for example, is considered a reliable proxy of ambient environmental conditions such as the warmth of growing seasons or amount of rainfall. Although scientists cannot directly measure the temperature of past years, tree-ring width and other climate proxies have been used to provide a semi-quantitative record of average temperature in the Northern Hemisphere back to 1000 A.D. When used in this way, the proxy record (tree ring width, say) only reconstructs a certain amount of the variance of the original record. The proxy may be calibrated (for example, during the period of the instrumental record) to determine how much variation is captured, including whether both short and long term variation is revealed. In the case of tree-ring width, different species in different places may show more or less sensitivity to, say, rainfall or temperature: when reconstructing a temperature record there is considerable skill in selecting proxies that are well correlated with the desired variable.

Chi-square Test

A chi-square test (also chi-squared or χ^2 test) is any statistical hypothesis test in which the sampling distribution of the test statistic is a chi-square distribution when the null hypothesis is true, or any in which this is *asymptotically* true, meaning that the sampling distribution (if the null hypothesis is true) can be made to approximate a chi-square distribution as closely as desired by making the sample size large enough.

Some examples of chi-squared tests where the chi-square distribution is only approximately valid:

1. Pearson's chi-square test, also known as the chi-square goodness-of-fit test or chi-square test for independence. When mentioned without any modifiers or without other precluding context, this test is usually understood (for an exact test used in place of χ^2).
2. Yates' chi-square test, also known as Yates' correction for continuity.
3. Mantel–Haenszel chi-square test.
4. Linear-by-linear association chi-square test.
5. The portmanteau test in time-series analysis, testing for the presence of autocorrelation
6. Likelihood-ratio tests in general statistical modelling, for testing whether there is evidence of the need to move from a simple model to a more complicated one (where the simple model is nested within the complicated one).

One case where the distribution of the test statistic is an exact chi-square distribution is the test that the variance of a normally-distributed population has a given value based on a sample variance. Such a test is uncommon in practice because values of variances to test against are seldom known exactly.

If a sample of size n is taken from a population having a normal distribution, then there is a well-known result which allows a test to be made of whether the variance of the population has a predetermined value. For example, a manufacturing process might have been in stable condition for a long period, allowing a value for the variance to be determined essentially without error. Suppose that a variant of the process is being tested, giving rise to a small sample of product items whose variation is to be tested. The test statistic T in this instance could be set to be the sum of squares about the sample mean, divided by the nominal value for the variance (i.e. the value to be tested as holding).

Then T has a chi-square distribution with $n-1$ degrees of freedom. For example if the sample size is 21, the acceptance region for T for a significance level of 5% is the interval 9.59 to 34.17.

Cluster Analysis

Cluster analysis or clustering is the assignment of a set of observations into subsets (called *clusters*) so that observations in the same cluster are similar in some sense. Clustering is a method of unsupervised learning, and a common technique for statistical data analysis used in many fields, including machine learning, data mining, pattern recognition, image analysis and bioinformatics.

Types of Clustering

Hierarchical algorithms find successive clusters using previously established clusters. These algorithms usually are either agglomerative ("bottom-up") or divisive ("top-down"). Agglomerative algorithms begin with each element as a separate cluster and merge them into successively larger clusters. Divisive algorithms begin with the whole set and proceed to divide it into successively smaller clusters.

Partitional algorithms typically determine all clusters at once, but can also be used as divisive algorithms in the hierarchical clustering. Density-based clustering algorithms are devised to discover arbitrary-shaped clusters. In this approach, a cluster is regarded as a region in which the density of data objects exceeds a threshold. DBSCAN and OPTICS are two typical algorithms of this kind.

Subspace clustering methods look for clusters that can only be seen in a particular projection (subspace, manifold) of the data. These methods thus can ignore irrelevant attributes. The general problem is also known as Correlation clustering while the special case of axis-parallel subspaces is also known as *Two-way clustering*, *co-clustering* or biclustering: in these methods not only the objects are clustered but also the features of the objects, i.e., if the data is represented in a data matrix, the rows and columns are clustered simultaneously. They usually do not however work with arbitrary feature combinations as in general subspace methods. But this special case deserves attention due to its applications in bioinformatics. Many clustering algorithms require the specification of the number of clusters to produce in the input data set, prior to execution of the algorithm. Barring knowledge of the proper value beforehand, the appropriate value must be determined, a problem on its own for which a number of techniques have been developed.

Distance Measure

An important step in most clustering is to select a distance measure, which will determine how the *similarity* of two elements is calculated. This will influence the shape of the clusters, as some elements may be close to one another according to one distance and farther away according to another. For example, in a 2-dimensional space, the distance between the point ($x = 1, y = 0$) and the origin ($x = 0, y = 0$) is always 1 according to the usual norms, but the distance between the point ($x = 1, y = 1$) and the origin can be 2, $\sqrt{2}$ or 1 if you take respectively the 1-norm, 2-norm or infinity-norm distance.

Common distance functions:

1. The Euclidean distance. A review of cluster analysis in health psychology research found that the most common distance measure in published studies in that research area is the Euclidean distance or the squared Euclidean distance.
2. The Manhattan distance (aka taxicab norm or 1-norm)
3. The maximum norm (aka infinity norm)

4. The Mahalanobis distance corrects data for different scales and correlations in the variables
5. The angle between two vectors can be used as a distance measure when clustering high dimensional data.
6. The Hamming distance measures the minimum number of substitutions required to change one member into another.

Another important distinction is whether the clustering uses symmetric or asymmetric distances. Many of the distance functions listed above have the property that distances are symmetric (the distance from object *A* to *B* is the same as the distance from *B* to *A*). In other applications, this is not the case.

Hierarchical Clustering

Hierarchical clustering creates a hierarchy of clusters which may be represented in a tree structure called a *dendrogram.* The root of the tree consists of a single cluster containing all observations, and the leaves correspond to individual observations.

Algorithms for hierarchical clustering are generally either *agglomerative*, in which one starts at the leaves and successively merges clusters together; or *divisive*, in which one starts at the root and recursively splits the clusters.

Any valid metric may be used as a measure of similarity between pairs of observations. The choice of which clusters to merge or split is determined by a linkage criterion, which is a function of the pairwise distances between observations. Cutting the tree at a given height will give a clustering at a selected precision. In the following example, cutting after the second row will yield clusters {a} {b c} {d e} {f}. Cutting after the third row will yield clusters {a} {b c} {d e f}, which is a coarser clustering, with a smaller number of larger clusters. For example, suppose this data is to be clustered, and the euclidean distance is the distance metric.

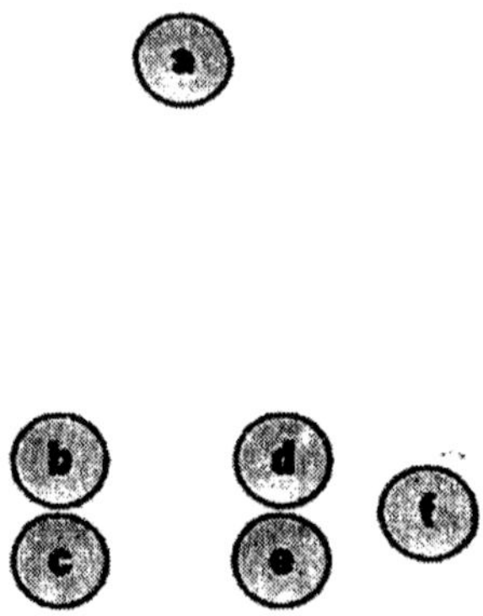

Figure 1. Raw Data

The hierarchical clustering dendrogram would be as such:

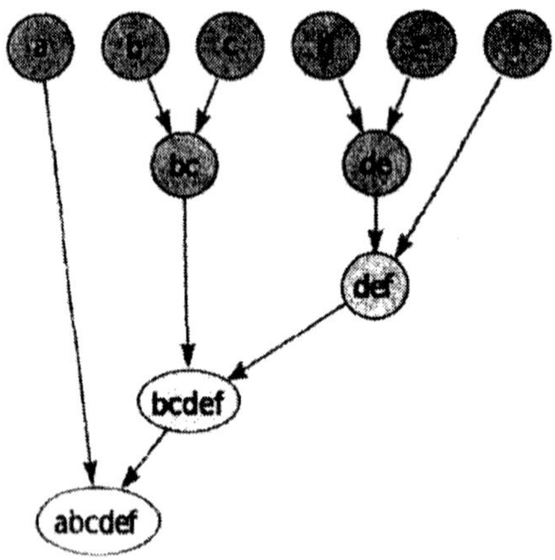

Figure 2. Traditional Representation

This method builds the hierarchy from the individual elements by progressively merging clusters. In our example, we have six elements {a} {b} {c} {d} {e} and {f}. The first step is to determine which elements to merge in a cluster. Usually, we want to take the two closest elements, according to the chosen distance.

Optionally, one can also construct a distance matrix at this stage, where the number in the *i*-th row *j*-th column is the distance between the *i*-th and *j*-th elements. Then, as clustering progresses, rows and columns are merged as the clusters are merged and the distances updated. This is a common way to implement this type of clustering, and has the benefit of caching distances between clusters. A simple agglomerative clustering algorithm is described in the single-linkage clustering page; it can easily be adapted to different types of linkage.

Applications

Market Research

Cluster analysis is widely used in market research when working with multivariate data from surveys and test panels. Market researchers use cluster analysis to partition the general population of consumers into market segments and to better understand the relationships between different groups of consumers/potential customers.

1. Segmenting the market and determining target markets
2. Product positioning
3. New product development
4. Selecting test markets

Educational Research

In educational research analysis, data for clustering can be **students, parents,** sex or test score. Clustering is an important method for understanding and utility of cluster in educational research. Cluster analysis in educational research can be used to find out data exploration, cluster confirmation and hypothesis testing

1. *Data exploration*: is used when there is little information about which schools or students will be grouped together. It aims at discovering any meaningful clusters of units based on measures on a set of response variables.
2. *Cluster confirmation*: is used for confirming the previously reported cluster results
3. *Hypothesis testing*: is used for arranging cluster structure.

In 2002, Hattie used cluster analysis in the project 'School Like Mine' to compare students' achievement in literacy and numeracy by the type of school they attended. 2707 majority and minority students in New Zealand are classified into different clusters according to school size, student ethnicity, region, size of civil jurisdiction and socioeconomic status for comparison. The cluster in this research is calculated across five dimensions, decile, region, size, minority and rurality. All schools are placed into one of twenty clusters that are used in the asTTle software as a basis of student achievement comparison. The result shows that using the power of socioeconomic status to describe schools is analysed and found inadequate. Euclidean distance was used as the clustering method in this research. Schools that are alike were clustered together. In addition, dendrogram. By clustering schools, Hattie suggested that school types had no significant relation with performance of schools.

Common Cluster techniques in Educational Research

All cluster techniques have two basic concerns: firstly, the measurement of similarity between individual profiles; and secondly, the use of that measure to form the groups or clusters. Brennan described Iterative Relocation as the most important cluster technique in behavioural and educational research. It has been adopted at Lancaster to create typologies of pupils based on personality and behavioural items to identify types of students and to isolate the skills considered to be important for certain grades of technologist in industry. Other similarity coefficients are available and the one chosen will depend upon the type of data gained.

As described by Bennett, Iterative Relocation can better be understood in its procedures described below: Number of groups should be decided. This is often an arbitrary decision and the groupings are random. The analysis then proceeds by computing the group profile (or group centroid) of each group, which is the cumulative frequencies of all variables measured. Each individual should be compared with each of the group centroids. A number of formulae are available for measuring this similarity. Among others, Wishart has found error sum of squares, a measure of dissimilarity, to be one of the most successful coefficients for continuous data. When relocate or alters the composition of groups and recalculate the group centroids are completed, a new iteration cycle commences. This sequence of comparison and relocation continues until all individuals are in the group whose central profile is most similar to their own. The solution is then said to be stable. The analysis is then continued by reducing the number of groups by one (N-1). This is achieved by a fushion process whereby a measure of dissimilarity (error sum of squares) between all pairs of group centroids is calculated again. The two most similar groups are then combined to reduce one group. Recalculate the group centroids and repeat steps 2 and 3 until the solution is stable for the N-1 group level. This process can continue until the two level group is reached, at which point the analysis is complete.

Advantages of Cluster Analysis

Frisvad of BioCentrum-DTU said that cluster analysis is a good way for quick review of data, especially if the objects are classified into many groups. In the above example, 'Schools Like Mine' 23 clusters of school with different properties were clearly clustered. Cluster Analysis is easy for user to assign or nominate themselves in to a cluster they would most like to compare with in exist school cluster database because each cluster is clearly named with understandable terms.

Cluster Analysis provides a simple profile of individuals. Given a number of analysis units, for example school size, student ethnicity, region, size of civil jurisdiction and social economic status in this example, each of which is described by a set of characteristics and attributes. Cluster Analysis also suggests how groups of units are determined such that units within groups are similar in some respect and unlike those from other groups.

Disadvantages of Cluster Analysis

Object can be assigned in one cluster only For example in 'Schools Like Mine', schools are automatically assigned into the first twenty-two clusters. However, if schools want to compare themselves with integrated schools, they will have to manually assign themselves into cluster twenty-three. Data-driven clustering may not represent the reality because once a school is assignted to a cluster, it cannot be assigned to another one. Some schools may have more than one significant property or fall on the edge of two clusters

Clustering may have detrimental effects to teachers who work in low-decile schools, students who are educated in them, and parents who support them, by telling them the schools are classified as ineffective, when in fact many are doing well in some unique aspects that are not sufficiently illustrated by the clusters formed.In k-means clustering methods, it is often requires several analysis before the number of clusters can be determined. It can be very sensitive to the choice of initial cluster centres.

Regression Analysis

Regression analysis includes any techniques for modelling and analysing several variables, when the focus is on the relationship between a dependent variable and one or more independent variables. More specifically, regression analysis helps us understand how the typical value of the dependent variable changes when any one of the independent variables is varied, while the other independent variables are held fixed. Most commonly, regression analysis estimates the conditional expectation of the dependent variable given the independent variables that is, the average value of the dependent variable when the independent variables are held fixed. Less commonly, the focus is on a quantile, or other location parameter of the conditional distribution of the dependent variable given the independent variables. In all cases, the estimation target is a function of the independent variables called the regression function. In regression analysis, it is also of interest to characterize the variation of the dependent variable around the regression function, which can be described by a probability distribution.

Regression analysis is widely used for prediction and forecasting, where its use has substantial overlap with the field of machine learning. Regression analysis is also used to understand which among the independent variables are related to the dependent variable, and to explore the forms of these relationships. In restricted circumstances, regression analysis can be used to infer causal relationships between the independent and dependent variables.

A large body of techniques for carrying out regression analysis has been developed. Familiar methods such as linear regression and ordinary least squares regression are parametric, in that the regression function is defined in terms of a finite number of unknown parameters that are estimated from the data. Nonparametric regression refers to techniques that allow the regression function to lie in a specified set of functions, which may be infinite-dimensional.

The performance of regression analysis methods in practice depends on the form of the data-generating process, and how it relates to the regression approach being used. Since the true form of the data-generating process is not known, regression analysis depends to some extent on making assumptions about this process. These assumptions are sometimes (but not always) testable if a large amount of data is available. Regression models for prediction are often useful even when the assumptions are moderately violated, although they may not perform optimally. However, in many applications, especially with small effects or questions of causality based on observational data, regression methods give misleading results

The earliest form of regression was the method of least squares, which was published by Legendre in 1805, and by Gauss in 1809. Legendre and Gauss both applied the method to the problem of determining, from astronomical observations, the orbits of bodies about the Sun. Gauss published a further development of the theory of least squares in 1821, including a version of the Gauss–Markov theorem.

The term "regression" was coined by Francis Galton in the nineteenth century to describe a biological phenomenon. The phenomenon was that the heights of descendants of tall ancestors tend to regress down towards a normal average (a phenomenon also known as regression toward the mean). For Galton, regression had only this biological meaning but his work was later extended by Udny Yule and Karl Pearson to a more general statistical context. In the work of Yule and Pearson, the joint distribution of the response and explanatory variables is assumed to be Gaussian. This assumption was weakened by R.A. Fisher in his works of 1922 and 1925. Fisher assumed that the conditional distribution of the response variable is Gaussian, but the joint distribution need not be. In this respect, Fisher's assumption is closer to Gauss's formulation of 1821.

Regression methods continue to be an area of active research. In recent decades, new methods have been developed for robust regression, regression involving correlated responses such as time series and growth curves, regression in which the predictor or response variables are curves, images, graphs, or other complex data objects, regression methods accommodating various types of missing data, nonparametric regression, Bayesian methods for regression, regression in which the predictor variables are measured with error, regression with more predictor variables than observations, and causal inference with regression.

Classical assumptions for regression analysis include:

1. The sample must be representative of the population for the inference prediction.
2. The error is assumed to be a random variable with a mean of zero conditional on the explanatory variables.
3. The variables are error-free. If this is not so, modelling may be done using errors-in-variables model techniques.
4. The predictors must be linearly independent, i.e. it must not be possible to express any predictor as a linear combination of the others.
5. The errors are uncorrelated, that is, the variance-covariance matrix of the errors is diagonal and each non-zero element is the variance of the error.

6. The variance of the error is constant across observations (homoscedasticity). If not, weighted least squares or other methods might be used.

These are sufficient (but not all necessary) conditions for the least-squares estimator to possess desirable properties, in particular, these assumptions imply that the parameter estimates will be unbiased, consistent, and efficient in the class of linear unbiased estimators. Many of these assumptions may be relaxed in more advanced treatments.

Assumptions include the geometrical support of the variables. Independent and dependent variables often refer to values measured at point locations. There may be spatial trends and spatial autocorrelation in the variables that violates statistical assumptions of regression. Geographic weighted regression is one technique to deal with such data. Also, variables may include values aggregated by areas. With aggregated data the Modifiable Areal Unit Problem can cause extreme variation in regression parameters. When analysing data aggregated by political boundaries, postal codes or census areas results may be very different with a different choice of units.

Regression Diagnostics

Once a regression model has been constructed, it may be important to confirm the goodness of fit of the model and the statistical significance of the estimated parameters. Commonly used checks of goodness of fit include the R-squared, analyses of the pattern of residuals and hypothesis testing. Statistical significance can be checked by an F-test of the overall fit, followed by t-tests of individual parameters.

Interpretations of these diagnostic tests rest heavily on the model assumptions. Although examination of the residuals can be used to invalidate a model, the results of a t-test or F-test are sometimes more difficult to interpret if the model's assumptions are violated. For example, if the error term does not have a normal distribution, in small samples the estimated parameters will not follow normal distributions and complicate inference. With relatively large samples, however, a central limit theorem can be invoked such that hypothesis testing may proceed using asymptotic approximations.

Regression with "limited dependent" variables

The phrase "limited dependent" is used in econometric statistics for categorical and constrained variables. The response variable may be non-continuous ("limited" to lie on some subset of the real line). For binary (zero or one) variables, if analysis proceeds with least-squares linear regression, the model is called the linear probability model. Nonlinear models for binary dependent variables include the probit and logit model. The multivariate probit model is a standard method of estimating a joint relationship between several binary dependent variables and some independent variables. For categorical variables with more than two values there is the multinomial logit. For ordinal variables with more than two values, there are the ordered logit and ordered probit models. Censored regression models may be used when the dependent variable is only sometimes observed, and Heckman correction type models may be used when the sample is not randomly selected from the population of interest. An alternative to such procedures is linear regression based on polychoric correlation (or polyserial correlations) between the categorical variables. Such procedures differ in the assumptions made about the distribution of the variables in the population. If the variable is positive with low values and represents the repetition of the occurrence of an event, then count models like the Poisson regression or the negative binomial model may be used.

Interpolation and Extrapolation

Regression models predict a value of the *Y* variable given known values of the *X* variables. Prediction within the range of values in the dataset used for model-fitting is known informally as interpolation. Prediction outside this range of the data is known as extrapolation. Performing extrapolation relies strongly on the regression assumptions. The further the extrapolation goes outside the data, the more room there is for the model to fail due to wrong assumptions. For example, regression model failing the homoscedasticity assumption will make bigger mistakes the further out the extrapolation is.

It is generally advised that when performing extrapolation, one should accompany the estimated value of the dependent variable with a prediction interval that represents the uncertainty. Such intervals tend to expand rapidly as the values of the independent variable(s) moved outside the range covered by the observed data. For such reasons and others, some tend to say that it might be unwise to undertake extrapolation.

However, this does not cover the full set of modelling errors that may be being made: in particular, the assumption of a particular form for the relation between *Y* and *X*. A properly conducted regression analysis will include an assessment of how well the assumed form is matched by the observed data, but it can only do so within the range of values of the independent variables actually available. This means that any extrapolation is particularly reliant on the assumptions being made about the structural form of the regression relationship. Best-practice advice here is that a linear-in-variables and linear-in-parameters relationship should not be chosen simply for computational convenience, but that all available knowledge should be deployed in constructing a regression model. If this knowledge includes the fact that the dependent variable cannot go outside a certain range of values, this can be made use of in selecting the model — even if the observed dataset has no values particularly near such bounds. The implications of this step of choosing an appropriate functional form for the regression can be great when extrapolation is considered. At a minimum, it can ensure that any extrapolation arising from a fitted model is "realistic" (or in accord with what is known).

Other Methods

Although the parameters of a regression model are usually estimated using the method of least squares, other methods which have been used include:

1. Bayesian methods, e.g. Bayesian linear regression
2. Least absolute deviations, which is more robust in the presence of outliers, leading to quantile regression
3. Nonparametric regression, requires a large number of observations and is computationally intensive
4. Distance metric learning, which is learned by the search of a meaningful distance metric in a given input space.

Software

All major statistical software packages perform least squares regression analysis and inference. Simple linear regression and multiple regression using least squares can be done in some spreadsheet applications and on some calculators. While many statistical software packages can perform various types of nonparametric and robust regression, these methods are less standardized; different software packages implement different methods, and a method with a given name may be implemented differently in different packages. Specialized regression software has been developed for use in fields such as survey analysis and neuroimaging

SPEARMAN'S RANK CORRELATION COEFFICIENT

Spearman's rank correlation coefficient or Spearman's rho, named after Charles Spearman and often denoted by the Greek letter ρ (rho) or as r_s, is a non-parametric measure of statistical dependence between two variables. It assesses how well the relationship between two variables can be described using a monotonic function. If there are no repeated data values, a perfect Spearman correlation of +1 or "1 occurs when each of the variables is a perfect monotone function of the other.

The Spearman correlation coefficient is often thought of as being the Pearson correlation coefficient between the ranked variables. In practice, however, a simpler procedure is normally used to calculate ρ. The n raw scores X_i, Y_i are converted to ranks x_i, y_i, and the differences $d_i = x_i$ " y_i between the ranks of each observation on the two variables are calculated.

If there are no tied ranks, then ñ is given by:

$$\rho = 1 - \frac{6\sum d_i^2}{n(n^2 - 1)}$$

If tied ranks exist, Pearson's correlation coefficient between ranks should be used for the calculation:

$$\rho = \frac{\sum_i (x_i - \bar{x})(y_i - \bar{y})}{\sqrt{\sum_i (x_i - \bar{x})^2 \sum_i (y_i - \bar{y})^2}}$$

One has to assign the same rank to each of the equal values. It is an average of their positions in the ascending order of the values.

There are several other numerical measures that quantitify the extent of statistical dependence between pairs of observations: these are discussed at correlation and dependence. The most common of these is the Pearson product moment correlation coefficient.

An alternative name for the Spearman rank correlation is the "grade correlation"; in this, the "rank" of an observation is replaced by the "grade". In continuous distributions, the grade of an observation is, by convention, always one half less than the rank, and hence the grade and rank correlations are the same in this case. More generally, the "grade" of an observation is proportional to an estimate of the fraction of a population less than a given value, with the half-observation adjustment at observed values. Thus this corresponds to one possible treatment of tied ranks. While unusual, the term "grade correlation" is still in use.

Interpretation

The sign of the Spearman correlation indicates the direction of association between *X* (the independent variable) and *Y* (the dependent variable). If *Y* tends to increase when *X* increases, the Spearman correlation coefficient is positive. If *Y* tends to decrease when *X* increases, the Spearman correlation coefficient is negative. A Spearman correlation of zero indicates that there is no tendency for *Y* to either increase or decrease when *X* increases. The Spearman correlation increases in magnitude as *X* and *Y* become closer to being perfect monotone functions of each other. When *X* and *Y* are perfectly monotonically related, the Spearman correlation coefficient becomes 1. A perfect monotone increasing relationship implies that for any two pairs of data values X_i, Y_i and X_j, Y_j that X_i " X_j and Y_i " Y_j always have the same sign. A perfect monotone decreasing relationship implies that these differences always have opposite signs.

The Spearman correlation coefficient is often described as being "nonparametric." This can have two meanings. First, the fact that a perfect Spearman correlation results when *X* and *Y* are related by any monotonic function can be contrasted with the Pearson correlation, which only gives a perfect value when X and Y are related by a linear function. The other sense in which the Spearman correlation is non-parametric is that its exact sampling distribution can be obtained without requiring knowledge of the joint probability distribution of X and Y.

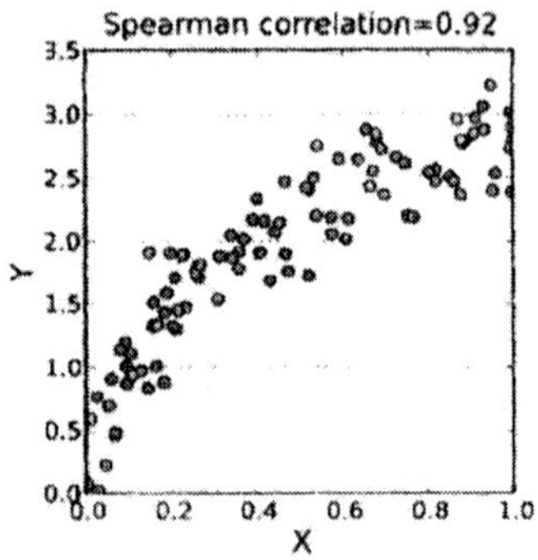

Figure 3. A positive Spearman correlation coefficient corresponds to an increasing monotonic trend between X and Y.

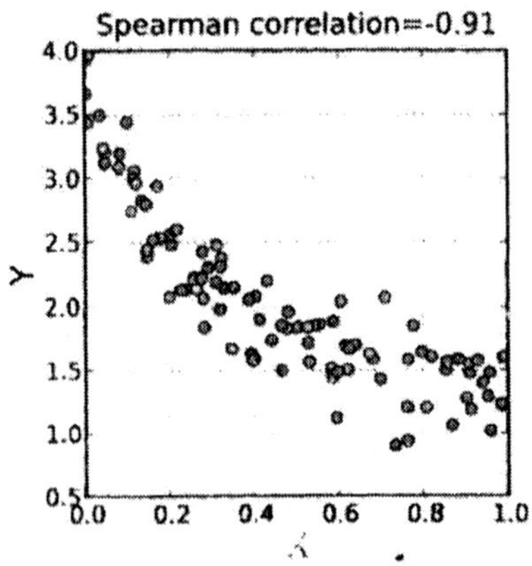

Figure 4. A negative Spearman correlation coefficient corresponds to a decreasing monotonic trend between X and Y.

Statistical Surveys and Questionnaires

Statistical surveys are used to collect quantitative information about items in a population. Surveys of human populations and institutions are common in political polling and government, health, social science and marketing research. A survey may focus on opinions or factual information depending on its purpose, and many surveys involve administering questions to individuals. When the questions are administered by a researcher, the survey is called a structured interview or a researcher-administered survey. When the questions are administered by the respondent, the survey is referred to as a questionnaire or a self-administered survey.

Structure and Standardization

The questions are usually structured and standardized. The structure is intended to reduce bias. For example, questions should be ordered in such a way that a question does not influence the response to subsequent questions. Surveys are standardized to ensure reliability, generalisability, and validity. Every respondent should be presented with the same questions and in the same order as other respondents.

In organizational development (OD), carefully constructed survey instruments are often used as the basis for data gathering, organizational diagnosis, and subsequent action planning. Some OD practitioners (e.g. Fred Nickols) even consider survey guided development as the *sine qua non* of OD.

Serial Surveys

Serial surveys repeat the same questions at different points in time, producing repeated measures of data. There are three basic designs for a study with more than one measurement occasion: cross-sectional design, longitudinal design, and time-series design.

1. Cross-sectional surveys use different units (respondents) at each of the measurement occasions, by drawing a new sample each time. The time intervals may be different between measurement occasions, but they are the same for all units (respondents). A study that administers a survey once is also considered cross-sectional.
2. Longitudinal surveys use the same units (respondents) at each of the measurement occasions, by recontacting the same sample from the initial survey for the following measurement occasion(s), and asking the same questions at every occasion. The time intervals may be different between measurement occasions, but they are the same for all units (respondents).
3. Time-series surveys also use the same units (respondents) at each of the measurement occasions, but the difference with longitudinal study designs is that in time-series designs both the number of measurement occasions and the time intervals between occasions may be different between units (respondents).

Advantages and Disadvantages of Surveys

Advantages

1. It is an efficient way of collecting information from a large number of respondents. Very large samples are possible. Statistical techniques can be used to determine validity, reliability, and statistical significance.
2. Surveys are flexible in the sense that a wide range of information can be collected. They can be used to study attitudes, values, beliefs, and past behaviours.

3. Because they are standardized, they are relatively free from several types of errors.
4. They are relatively easy to administer.
5. There is an economy in data collection due to the focus provided by standardized questions. Only questions of interest to the researcher are asked, recorded, codified, and analysed. Time and money is not spent on tangential questions.
6. Sample surveys are usually cheaper to conduct than a full census.

Disadvantages

1. They depend on subjects' motivation, honesty, memory, and ability to respond. Subjects may not be aware of their reasons for any given action. They may have forgotten their reasons. They may not be motivated to give accurate answers; in fact, they may be motivated to give answers that present themselves in a favourable light.
2. Structured surveys, particularly those with closed ended questions, may have low validity when researching affective variables.
3. Although the individuals chosen to participate in surveys are often randomly sampled, errors due to nonresponse may exist. That is, people who choose to respond on the survey may be different from those who do not respond, thus biasing the estimates. For example, polls or surveys that are conducted by calling a random sample of publicly available telephone numbers will not include the responses of people with unlisted telephone numbers, mobile (cell) phone numbers, people who are unable to answer the phone (e.g., because they normally sleep during the time of day the survey is conducted, because they are at work,

etc.), people who do not answer calls from unknown or unfamiliar telephone numbers. Likewise, such a survey will include a disproportionate number of respondents who have traditional, land-line telephone service with listed phone numbers, and people who stay home much of the day and are much more likely to be available to participate in the survey (e.g., people who are unemployed, disabled, elderly, etc.).

4. Survey question answer-choices could lead to vague data sets because at times they are relative only to a personal abstract notion concerning "strength of choice". For instance the choice "moderately agree" may mean different things to different subjects, and to anyone interpreting the data for correlation. Even yes or no answers are problematic because subjects may for instance put "no" if the choice "only once" is not available.

Characteristics of Researcher-administered Surveys

1. Fewer misunderstood questions and inappropriate responses.
2. Fewer incomplete responses.
3. Generally higher response rates and better information on nonresponse, but...
4. Respondents may be unwilling to discuss sensitive topics with a stranger.
5. Greater control over the environment that the survey is administered in.
6. Additional information can be collected from respondent.
7. Subject to interviewer bias (e.g. answers influenced by desire to impress interviewer).
8. Generally expensive/time-consuming to run.

Characteristics of Self-administered Surveys

1. Respondents are more likely to stop participating midway through the survey (drop-offs).
2. Respondents cannot ask for clarification.
3. Low response rate in some modes.
4. Often respondents returning survey represent extremes of the population-skewed responses (consequence of low response rates).
5. Allows shy respondents to answer sensitive questions in private.
6. No interviewer intervention available for probing or explanation.
7. Respondents can read the whole questionnaire before answering any questions.
8. Free of interviewer bias.

Questions and Response Formats

Usually, a survey consists of a number of questions that the respondent has to answer in a set format. A distinction is made between open-ended and closed-ended questions. An open-ended question asks the respondent to formulate his own answer, whereas a closed-ended question has the respondent pick an answer from a given number of options. The response options for a closed-ended question should be exhaustive and mutually exclusive. Four types of response scales for closed-ended questions are distinguished:

1. Dichotomous, where the respondent has two options
2. Nominal-polytomous, where the respondent has more than two unordered options
3. Ordinal-polytomous, where the respondent has more than two ordered options

4. (bounded) Continuous, where the respondent is presented with a continuous scale

A respondent's answer to an open-ended question is coded into a response scale afterwards.

Modes of Data Collection

There are several ways of administering a survey, including:

Telephone

1. Use of interviewers encourages sample persons to respond, leading to higher response rates.
2. Interviewers can increase comprehension of questions by answering respondents' questions.
3. Fairly cost efficient, depending on local call charge structure
4. Good for large national (or international) sampling frames
5. Some potential for interviewer bias
6. Cannot be used for non-audio information (graphics, demonstrations, taste/smell samples)
7. Unreliable for consumer surveys in rural areas where telephone penetration is low
8. Three types:
   a. Traditional telephone interviews
   b. Computer assisted telephone dialling
   c. Computer assisted telephone interviewing (CATI)

Mail

1. The questionnaire may be handed to the respondents or mailed to them, but in all cases they are returned to the researcher via mail.

2. Cost is very low, since bulk postage is cheap in most countries
3. Long time delays, often several months, before the surveys are returned and statistical analysis can begin
4. Not suitable for issues that may require clarification
5. Respondents can answer at their own convenience (allowing them to break up long surveys; also useful if they need to check records to answer a question)
6. No interviewer bias introduced
7. Large amount of information can be obtained: some mail surveys are as long as 50 pages
8. Response rates can be improved by using mail panels
    a. Members of the panel have agreed to participate
    b. Panels can be used in longitudinal designs where the same respondents are surveyed several times

Online Surveys

1. Can use web or e-mail
2. Web is preferred over e-mail because interactive HTML forms can be used
3. Often inexpensive to administer
4. Very fast results
5. Easy to modify
6. Response rates can be improved by using Online panels members of the panel have agreed to participate
7. If not password-protected, easy to manipulate by completing multiple times to skew results
8. Data creation, manipulation and reporting can be automated and/or easily exported into a format that can be read by PSPP, DAP or other statistical analysis software

9. Data sets created in real time
10. Some are incentive based (such as Survey Vault or YouGov)
11. May skew sample towards a younger demographic compared with CATI
12. Often difficult to determine/control selection probabilities, hindering quantitative analysis of data
13. Used in large scale industries.

Personal In-home Survey

1. Respondents are interviewed in person, in their homes (or at the front door)
2. Very high cost
3. Suitable when graphic representations, smells, or demonstrations are involved
4. Often suitable for long surveys (but some respondents object to allowing strangers into their home for extended periods)
5. Suitable for locations where telephone or mail are not developed
6. Skilled interviewers can persuade respondents to cooperate, improving response rates
7. Potential for interviewer bias

Personal Mall Intercept Survey

1. Shoppers at malls are intercepted - they are either interviewed on the spot, taken to a room and interviewed, or taken to a room and given a self-administered questionnaire
2. Socially acceptable people feel that a mall is a more appropriate place to do research than their home

3. Potential for interviewer bias
4. Fast
5. Easy to manipulate by completing multiple times to skew results

Methods Used to Increase Response Rates

1. *Brevity*: single page if possible
2. Financial incentives
    a. Paid in advance
    b. Paid at completion
3. Nonmonetary incentives
    a. Commodity giveaways (pens, notepads)
    b. Entry into a lottery, draw or contest
    c. Discount coupons
    d. Promise of contribution to charity
4. Preliminary notification
5. *Foot-in-the-door techniques:* start with a small inconsequential request
6. *Personalization of the request*: address specific individuals
7. *Follow-up requests*: multiple requests
8. Claimed affiliation with universities, research institutions, or charities
9. Emotional appeals
10. Bids for sympathy
11. Convince respondent that they can make a difference
12. Guarantee anonymity
13. Legal compulsion (certain government-run surveys)

Sampling

Sample selection is critical to the validity of the information that represents the populations that are being studied. The approach of the sampling helps to determine the focus of the study and allows better acceptance of the generalizations that are being made. Careful use of biased sampling can be used if it is justified and as long as it is noted that the resulting sample may not be a true representation of the population of the study. There are two different approaches to sampling in survey research:

1. There is nonprobability sampling approach. In this approach the researcher does not know each element's probability of selection in the sample. The most commonly used nonprobability sampling method is the convenience sampling approach. With this method, it only samples those who are available and willing to participate in the survey. The use of this approach allows for convenience for the researcher while possibly losing data validity due to the lack of representation.
2. The probability sampling approach for research methods gives each element a known chance of being included in the sample. This method is closer to a true representation of the population. It can be difficult to use due to cost of a rigorous sampling method, and difficulty in obtaining full coverage of the target population, but the generalizations that come from it are more likely to be closer to a true representation of the population. Different forms of probability sampling are designed to achieve various benefits - e.g. theoretical simplicity, operational simplicity, detailed information on subpopulations, or minimal cost. Some common forms:

3. *Equal probability of selection designs (EPS)*: in which each element of the population has an equal chance of being included in the sample. This uniformity makes EPS surveys relatively simple to interpret. Forms of EPS include Simple random sampling (SRS) and systematic sampling.
4. *Probability-proportional-to-size designs (PPS)*: in which 'larger' elements (according to some known measure of size) have a higher chance of selection. This approach is common in business surveys where the object is to determine sector totals (e.g. "total employment in manufacturing sectors"); compared to EPS, concentrating on larger elements may produce better accuracy for the same cost/sample size.
5. *Stratified random sampling approach*: in which the population is divided into subpopulations (called strata) and random samples are then drawn separately from each of these strata, using any probability sampling method (sometimes including further sub-stratification). This may be done to provide better control over the sample size (and hence, accuracy) within each subpopulation; when the variable/s of interest are correlated with subpopulation, it can also improve overall accuracy. Another use for stratification is when different subpopulations require different sampling methods for instance, a business survey might use EPS for businesses whose 'size' is not known and PPS elsewhere.

Student's t-test

A *t*-test is any statistical hypothesis test in which the test statistic follows a Student's *t* distribution if the null hypothesis is supported. It is most commonly applied when the test statistic would follow a normal distribution if the value of a scaling term in the test statistic were known. When the scaling term is unknown and is replaced by an estimate based on the data, the test statistic (under certain conditions) follows a Student's *t* distribution.

The t-statistic was introduced in 1908 by William Sealy Gosset, a chemist working for the Guinness brewery in Dublin, Ireland ("Student" was his pen name). Gosset had been hired due to Claude Guinness's innovative policy of recruiting the best graduates from Oxford and Cambridge to apply biochemistry and statistics to Guinness' industrial processes. Gosset devised the *t*-test as a way to cheaply monitor the quality of stout. He published the test in Biometrika in 1908, but was forced to use a pen name by his employer, who regarded the fact that they were using statistics as a trade secret. In fact, Gosset's identity was unknown to fellow statisticians.

Uses

Among the most frequently used *t*-tests are:

1. A one-sample location test of whether the mean of a normally distributed population has a value specified in a null hypothesis.
2. A two sample location test of the null hypothesis that the means of two normally distributed populations are equal. All such tests are usually called Student's *t*-tests, though strictly speaking that name should only be used if the variances of the two populations are also assumed to be equal; the form of the test used when this assumption is dropped is sometimes called Welch's *t*-test. These tests are often referred to as "unpaired" or "independent samples" *t*-tests, as they are typically applied when the statistical units underlying the two samples being compared are non-overlapping.

3. A test of the null hypothesis that the difference between two responses measured on the same statistical unit has a mean value of zero. For example, suppose we measure the size of a cancer patient's tumour before and after a treatment. If the treatment is effective, we expect the tumour size for many of the patients to be smaller following the treatment. This is often referred to as the "paired" or "repeated measures" *t*-test: see paired difference test.
4. A test of whether the slope of a regression line differs significantly from 0.

Most *t*-test statistics have the form $T = Z/s$, where Z and s are functions of the data. Typically, Z is designed to be sensitive to the alternative hypothesis (i.e. its magnitude tends to be larger when the alternative hypothesis is true), whereas s is a scaling parameter that allows the distribution of T to be determined.

The assumptions underlying a *t*-test are that:

1. Z follows a standard normal distribution under the null hypothesis
2. ps^2 follows a χ^2 distribution with p degrees of freedom under the null hypothesis, where p is a positive constant
3. Z and s are independent.

In a specific type of *t*-test, these conditions are consequences of the population being studied, and of the way in which the data are sampled. For example, in the *t*-test comparing the means of two independent samples, the following assumptions should be met:

1. Each of the two populations being compared should follow a normal distribution (which can be tested using a normality test, such as the Shapiro-Wilk and Kolmogorov–Smirnov tests, or which can be assessed graphically using a normal quantile plot).

2. If using Student's original definition of the *t*-test, the two populations being compared should have the same variance (testable using Levene's test Bartlett's test, or the Brown–Forsythe test; or assessable graphically using a normal quantile plot). If the sample sizes in the two groups being compared are roughly equal, Student's original *t*-test is highly robust to the presence of unequal variances. Welch's t-test is insensitive to equality of the variances regardless of whether the sample sizes are similar.
3. The data used to carry out the test should be sampled independently from the two populations being compared. This is in general not testable from the data, but if the data are known to be dependently sampled (i.e. if they were sampled in clusters), then the classical *t*-tests discussed here may give misleading results.

Unpaired and Paired Two-Sample T-Tests

Two sample *t-tests* for a difference in mean can be either unpaired or paired. Paired t-tests are a form of blocking, and have greater power than unpaired tests when the paired units are similar with respect to "noise factors" that are independent of membership in the two groups being compared. In a different context, paired t-tests can be used to reduce the effects of confounding factors in an observational study.

The unpaired, or "independent samples" *t*-test is used when two separate sets of independent and identically distributed samples are obtained, one from each of the two populations being compared. For example, suppose we are evaluating the effect of a medical treatment, and we enrol 100 subjects into our study, then randomise 50 subjects to the treatment group and 50 subjects to the control group. In this case, we have two independent samples and would use the unpaired form of the *t*-test. The randomisation is not essential here—if we contacted 100 people by phone and obtained each person's age and gender, and then used a two-sample *t*-test to see whether the mean ages differ by gender, this would also be an independent samples *t*-test, even though the data are observational.

Dependent samples (or "paired") *t-tests* typically consist of a sample of matched pairs of similar units, or one group of units that has been tested twice (a "repeated measures" *t*-test). A typical example of the repeated measures *t*-test would be where subjects are tested prior to a treatment, say for high blood pressure, and the same subjects are tested again after treatment with a blood-pressure lowering medication.

A dependent *t*-test based on a "matched-pairs sample" results from an unpaired sample that is subsequently used to form a paired sample, by using additional variables that were measured along with the variable of interest. The matching is carried out by identifying pairs of values consisting of one observation from each of the two samples, where the pair is similar in terms of other measured variables. This approach is often used in observational studies to reduce or eliminate the effects of confounding factors.

Alternatives to the *T*-Test for Location Problems

The *t*-test provides an exact test for the equality of the means of two normal populations with unknown, but equal, variances. (The Welch's *t*-test is a nearly-exact test for the case where the data are normal but the variances may differ.) For moderately large samples and a one tailed test, the *t* is relatively robust to moderate violations of the normality assumption.

For exactness, the *t*-test and Z-test require normality of the sample means, and the *t*-test additionally requires that the sample variance follows a scaled χ^2 distribution, and that the sample mean and sample variance be statistically independent. Normality of the individual data values is not required if these conditions are met. By the central limit theorem, sample means of moderately large samples are often well-approximated by a normal distribution even if the data are not normally distributed. For non-normal data, the distribution of the sample variance may deviate substantially from a χ^2 distribution. However, if the sample size is large, Slutsky's theorem implies that the distribution of the sample variance has little effect on the distribution of the test statistic. If the data are substantially non-normal and the sample size is small, the *t*-test can give misleading results.

When the normality assumption does not hold, a non-parametric alternative to the *t*-test can often have better statistical power. For example, for two independent samples when the data distributions are asymmetric (that is, the distributions are skewed) or the distributions have large tails, then the Wilcoxon Rank Sum test (also known as the Mann-Whitney U test) can have three to four times higher power than the *t*-test. The nonparametric counterpart to the paired samples t test is the Wilcoxon signed-rank test for paired samples. For a discussion on choosing between the t and nonparametric alternatives.

One-way analysis of variance generalizes the two-sample *t*-test when the data belong to more than two groups.

Survey Research

Survey research a research method involving the use of questionnaires and/or statistical surveys to gather data about people and their thoughts and behaviours. This method was pioneered in the 1930s and 1940s by sociologist Paul Lazarsfeld. The initial use of the method was to examine the effects of the radio on political opinion formation of the United States. One of its early successes was the development of the theory of two-step flow of communication. The method was foundational for the inception of the Quantitative research tradition in sociology.

Quantitative Marketing Research

Quantitative marketing research is the application of quantitative research techniques to the field of marketing. It has roots in both the positivist view of the world, and the modern marketing viewpoint that marketing is an interactive process in which both the buyer and seller reach a satisfying agreement on the "four Ps" of marketing: Product, Price, Place (location) and Promotion.

As a social research method, it typically involves the construction of questionnaires and scales. People who respond (respondents) are asked to complete the survey. Marketers use the information so obtained to understand the needs of individuals in the marketplace, and to create strategies and marketing plans.

Typical General Procedure

Simply, there are five major and important steps involved in the research process:

1. Defining the Problem.
2. Research Design.
3. Data Collection.
4. Analysis.
5. Report Writing & presentation.

A brief discussion on these steps is:

1. *Problem audit and problem definition*: What is the problem? What are the various aspects of the problem? What information is needed?
2. *Conceptualisation and operationalisation*: How exactly do we define the concepts involved? How do we

translate these concepts into observable and measurable behaviours?

3. *Hypothesis specification:* What claim(s) do we want to test?
4. *Research design specification*: What type of methodology to use? examples: questionnaire, survey
5. *Question specification*: What questions to ask? In what order?
6. *Scale specification*: How will preferences be rated?
7. *Sampling design specification:* What is the total population? What sample size is necessary for this population? What sampling method to use? examples:
   a. *Probability Sampling*: (cluster sampling, stratified sampling, simple random sampling, multistage sampling, systematic sampling) &
   b. *Nonprobability sampling*: (Convenience Sampling, Judgement Sampling, Purposive Sampling, Quota Sampling, Snowball Sampling, etc.)
8. *Data collection*: Use mail, telephone, internet, mall intercepts
9. *Codification and re-specification*: Make adjustments to the raw data so it is compatible with statistical techniques and with the objectives of the research - examples: assigning numbers, consistency checks, substitutions, deletions, weighting, dummy variables, scale transformations, scale standardization
10. *Statistical analysis*: Perform various descriptive and inferential techniques on the raw data. Make inferences from the sample to the whole population. Test the results for statistical significance.
11. *Interpret and integrate findings*: What do the results mean? What conclusions can be drawn? How do these findings relate to similar research?

12. *Write the research report*: Report usually has headings such as:
    a. Executive summary;
    b. Objectives;
    c. Methodology;
    d. main findings;
    e. Detailed charts and diagrams.

The design step may involve a pilot study to in order to discover any hidden issues. The codification and analysis steps are typically performed by computer, using software such as DAP or PSPP. The data collection steps, can in some instances be automated, but often require significant manpower to undertake. Interpretation is a skill mastered only by experience.

Statistical Analysis

The data acquired for quantitative marketing research can be analysed by almost any of the range of techniques of stătistical analysis. which can be broadly divided into descriptive statistics and statistical inference. An important set of techniques is that related to statistical surveys. In any instance, an appropriate type of statistical analysis should take account of the various types of error that may arise, as outlined below.

Reliability and Validity

Research should be tested for reliability, generalisability, and validity. Generalisability is the ability to make inferences from a sample to the population.

Reliability is the extent to which a measure will produce consistent results. Test-retest reliability checks how similar the results are if the research is repeated under similar circumstances. Stability over repeated measures is assessed with the Pearson coefficient. Alternative forms reliability checks how similar the results are if the research is repeated using different forms. Internal consistency reliability checks how well the individual measures included in the research are converted into a composite measure. Internal consistency may be assessed by correlating performance on two halves of a test (split-half reliability). The value of the Pearson product-moment correlation coefficient is adjusted with the Spearman-Brown prediction formula to correspond to the correlation between two full-length tests. A commonly used measure is Cronbach's a, which is equivalent to the mean of all possible split-half coefficients. Reliability may be improved by increasing the sample size.

Validity asks whether the research measured what it intended to. Content validation (also called face validity) checks how well the content of the research are related to the variables to be studied. Are the research questions representative of the variables being researched. It is a demonstration that the items of a test are drawn from the domain being measured. Criterion validation checks how meaningful the research criteria are relative to other possible criteria. When the criterion is collected later the goal is to establish predictive validity. Construct validation checks what underlying construct is being measured. There are three variants of construct validity. They are convergent validity (how well the research relates to other measures of the same construct), discriminant validity (how poorly the research relates to measures of opposing constructs), and nomological validity (how well the research relates to other variables as required by theory).

3

Qualitative Research Methods

Qualitative research is a method of inquiry appropriated in many different academic disciplines, traditionally in the social sciences, but also in market research and further contexts. Qualitative researchers aim to gather an in-depth understanding of human behaviour and the reasons that govern such behaviour. The qualitative method investigates the why and how of decision making, not just what, where, when. Hence, smaller but focused samples are more often needed, rather than large samples.

Qualitative methods produce information only on the particular cases studied, and any more general conclusions are only hypotheses. Quantitative methods can be used to verify which of such hypotheses are true. Until the 1970s, the phrase 'qualitative research' was used only to refer to a discipline of anthropology or sociology. During the 1970s and 1980s qualitative research began to be used in other disciplines, and became a significant type of research in the fields of education studies, social work studies, women's studies, disability studies, information studies, management studies, nursing service studies, political science, psychology, communication studies, and many other fields. Qualitative research occurred in the consumer products industry during this period, with researchers investigating new consumer products and product positioning/advertising opportunities. The earliest consumer research pioneers including Gene Reilly of The Gene Reilly Group in Darien, CT, Jerry Schoenfeld of Gerald Schoenfeld & Partners in Tarrytown, NY and Martin Calle of Calle & Company, Greenwich, CT, also Peter Cooper in London, England, and Hugh Mackay in Mission, Australia. There continued to be disagreement about the proper place of qualitative versus quantitative research. In the late 1980s and 1990s after a spate of criticisms from the quantitative side, new methods of qualitative research evolved, to address the perceived problems with reliability and imprecise modes of data analysis. During this same decade, there was a slowdown in traditional media advertising spending, so there was heightened interest in making research related to advertising more effective.

In the last thirty years the acceptance of qualitative research by journal publishers and editors has been growing. Prior to that time many mainstream journals were prone to publish research articles based upon the natural sciences and which featured quantitative analysis.

In simplified terms- Qualitative means a non-numerical data collection or explanation based on the attributes of the graph or source of data. For example, if you are asked to explain in qualitative terms a thermal image displayed in multiple colours, then you would explain the colour differences rather than the heat's numerical value.

First, in qualitative research, cases can be selected purposefully, according to whether or not they typify certain characteristics or contextual locations.

Second, the researcher's role receives greater critical attention. This is because in qualitative research the possibility of the researcher taking a 'neutral' or transcendental position is seen as more problematic in practical and/or philosophical terms. Hence qualitative researchers are often exhorted to reflect on their role in the research process and make this clear in the analysis.

Third, while qualitative data analysis can take a wide variety of forms, it differs from quantitative research in its focus on language, signs and meaning. In addition, qualitative research approaches analysis holistically and contextually, rather than being reductionistic and isolationist. Nevertheless, systematic and transparent approaches to analysis are almost always regarded as essential for rigor. For example, many qualitative methods require researchers to carefully code data and discern and document themes consistently and reliably.

Perhaps the most traditional division between the uses of qualitative and quantitative research in the social sciences is that qualitative methods are used for exploration or for explaining puzzling quantitative results. Quantitative methods, by contrast, are used to test hypotheses. This is because establishing content validity - do measures measure what a researcher thinks they measure? - is seen as one of the strengths of qualitative research. Some consider quantitative methods to provide more representative, reliable and precise measures through focused hypotheses, measurement tools and applied mathematics. By contrast, qualitative data is usually difficult to graph or display in mathematical terms.

Qualitative research is often used for policy and program evaluation research since it can answer certain important questions more efficiently and effectively than quantitative approaches. This is particularly the case for understanding how and why certain outcomes were achieved but also for answering important questions about relevance, unintended effects and impact of programs such as: Were expectations reasonable? Did processes operate as expected? Were key players able to carry out their duties? Did the program cause any unintended effects?

Qualitative approaches have the advantage of allowing for more diversity in responses as well as the capacity to adapt to new developments or issues during the research process itself. While qualitative research can be expensive and time-consuming to conduct, many fields of research employ qualitative techniques that have been specifically developed to provide more succinct, cost-efficient and timely results. Rapid Rural Appraisal is one formalised example of these adaptations but there are many others.

Data Collection

Qualitative researchers may use different approaches in collecting data, such as the grounded theory practice, narratology, storytelling, classical ethnography, or shadowing. Qualitative methods are also loosely present in other methodological approaches, such as action research or actor-network theory. Forms of the data collected can include interviews and group discussions, observation and reflection field notes, various texts, pictures, and other materials.

Qualitative research often categorizes data into patterns as the primary basis for organizing and reporting results. Qualitative researchers typically rely on the following methods for gathering information: *Participant Observation, Non-participant Observation, Field Notes, Reflexive Journals, Structured Interview, Semi-structured Interview, Unstructured Interview, and Analysis of documents and materials.*

The ways of participating and observing can vary widely from setting to setting. Participant observation is a strategy of reflexive learning, not a single method of observing. In participant observation researchers typically become members of a culture, group, or setting, and adopt roles to conform to that setting. In doing so, the aim is for the researcher to gain a closer insight into the culture's practices, motivations and emotions. It is argued that the researchers' ability to understand the experiences of the culture may be inhibited if they observe without participating.

Some distinctive qualitative methods are the use of focus groups and key informant interviews. The focus group technique involves a moderator facilitating a small group discussion between selected individuals on a particular topic. This is a particularly popular method in market research and testing new initiatives with users/workers.

One traditional and specialized form of qualitative research is called cognitive testing or pilot testing which is used in the development of quantitative survey items. Survey items are piloted on study participants to test the reliability and validity of the items.

In the academic social sciences the most frequently used qualitative research approaches include the following:

1. *Ethnographic*: Research, used for investigating cultures by collecting and describing data that is intended to help in the development of a theory. This method is also called "ethnomethodology" or "methodology of the people". An example of applied ethnographic research, is the study of a particular culture and their understanding of the role of a particular disease in their cultural framework.
2. *Critical Social Research*: used by a researcher to understand how people communicate and develop symbolic meanings.
3. *Ethical Inquiry*: an intellectual analysis of ethical problems. It includes the study of ethics as related to obligation, rights, duty, right and wrong, choice etc.
4. *Foundational Research*: examines the foundations for a science, analyses the beliefs and develops ways to

specify how a knowledge base should change in light of new information.

5. *Historical Research*: allows one to discuss past and present events in the context of the present condition, and allows one to reflect and provide possible answers to current issues and problems.
6. *Grounded Theory*: is an inductive type of research, based or "grounded" in the observations or data from which it was developed; it uses a variety of data sources, including quantitative data, review of records, interviews, observation and surveys.
7. *Phenomenology*: describes the "subjective reality" of an event, as perceived by the study population; it is the study of a phenomenon.
8. *Philosophical Research*: is conducted by field experts within the boundaries of a specific field of study or profession, the best qualified individual in any field of study to use an intellectual analyses, in order to clarify definitions, identify ethics, or make a value judgment concerning an issue in their field of study.

Data Analysis

Interpretive Techniques

The most common analysis of qualitative data is observer impression. That is, expert or bystander observers examine the data, interpret it via forming an impression and report their impression in a structured and sometimes quantitative form.

Coding

Coding is an interpretive technique that both organizes the data and provides a means to introduce the interpretations of it into certain quantitative methods. Most coding requires the analyst to read the data and demarcate segments within it. Each segment is labelled with a "code" – usually a word or short phrase that suggests how the associated data segments inform the research objectives. When coding is complete, the analyst prepares reports via a mix of: summarizing the prevalence of codes, discussing similarities and differences in related codes across distinct original sources/contexts, or comparing the relationship between one or more codes.

Some qualitative data that is highly structured (e.g., open-end responses from surveys or tightly defined interview questions) is typically coded without additional segmenting of the content. In these cases, codes are often applied as a layer on top of the data. Quantitative analysis of these codes is typically the capstone analytical step for this type of qualitative data.

Contemporary qualitative data analyses are sometimes supported by computer programs. These programs do not supplant the interpretive nature of coding but rather are aimed at enhancing the analyst's efficiency at data storage/retrieval and at applying the codes to the data. Many programs offer efficiencies in editing and revising coding, which allow for work sharing, peer review, and recursive examination of data.

A frequent criticism of coding method is that it seeks to transform qualitative data into quantitative data, thereby draining the data of its variety, richness, and individual character. Analysts respond to this criticism by thoroughly expositing their definitions of codes and linking those codes soundly to the underlying data, therein bringing back some of the richness that might be absent from a mere list of codes.

Recursive Abstraction

Some qualitative datasets are analysed without coding. A

common method here is recursive abstraction, where datasets are summarized, those summaries are then further summarized, and so on. The end result is a more compact summary that would have been difficult to accurately discern without the preceding steps of distillation.

A frequent criticism of recursive abstraction is that the final conclusions are several times removed from the underlying data. While it is true that poor initial summaries will certainly yield an inaccurate final report, qualitative analysts can respond to this criticism. They do so, like those using coding method, by documenting the reasoning behind each summary step, citing examples from the data where statements were included and where statements were excluded from the intermediate summary.

Mechanical Techniques

Some techniques rely on leveraging computers to scan and sort large sets of qualitative data. At their most basic level, mechanical techniques rely on counting words, phrases, or coincidences of tokens within the data. Often referred to as content analysis, the output from these techniques is amenable to many advanced statistical analyses.

Mechanical techniques are particularly well-suited for a few scenarios. One such scenario is for datasets that are simply too large for a human to effectively analyse, or where analysis of them would be cost prohibitive relative to the value of information they contain. Another scenario is when the chief value of a dataset is the extent to which it contains "red flags" (e.g., searching for reports of certain adverse events within a lengthy journal dataset from patients in a clinical trial) or "green flags" (e.g., searching for mentions of your brand in positive reviews of marketplace products).

A frequent criticism of mechanical techniques is the absence of a human interpreter. And while masters of these methods are able to write sophisticated software to mimic some human decisions, the bulk of the "analysis" is nonhuman. Analysts respond by proving the value of their methods relative to either a) hiring and training a human team to analyse the data or b) letting the data go untouched, leaving any actionable nuggets undiscovered.

Paradigmatic Differences

Contemporary qualitative research has been conducted from a large number of various paradigms that influence conceptual and metatheoretical concerns of legitimacy, control, data analysis, ontology, and epistemology, among others. Research conducted in the last 10 years has been characterized by a distinct turn toward more interpretive, postmodern, and critical practices.

Guba and Lincoln identify five main paradigms of contemporary qualitative research: positivism, postpositivism, critical theories, constructivism, and participatory/cooperative paradigms. Each of the paradigms listed by Guba and Lincoln are characterized by axiomatic differences in axiology, intended action of research, control of research process/outcomes, relationship to foundations of truth and knowledge, validity, textual representation and voice of the researcher/participants, and commensurability with other paradigms.

In particular, commensurability involves the extent to which paradigmatic concerns "can be retrofitted to each other in ways that make the simultaneous practice of both possible". Positivist and postpositivist paradigms share commensurable assumptions but are largely incommensurable with critical, constructivist, and participatory paradigms. Likewise, critical, constructivist, and participatory paradigms are commensurable on certain issues (e.g., intended action and textual representation).

Analytic Induction

Analytic induction refers to a systematic examination of similarities between various social phenomena in order to develop concepts or ideas. Social scientists doing social research use analytic induction to search for those similarities in broad categories and then develop subcategories. For example, social scientist may examine the category of 'marijuana users' and then develop subcategories for 'uses marijuana for pleasure' and 'uses marijuana for health reasons'. If no relevant similarities can be identified, then either the data needs to be re-evaluated and the definition of similarities changed, or the category is too wide and heterogeneous and should be narrowed down.

In the earlier sociological papers (from 1940s and 1950s) this term could also be used to mean the search for "universals" in social life, where "universal" meant an invariant, complete, positivistic propriety (i.e. "all black males between 35 and 40 vote for Democrats").

This principle was formulated in 1934 by Florian Znaniecki in order to identify universal propositions and causal laws. It is contrasted with enumerative research, which can only identify correlations and cannot explain outliers in statistical relationships. The principle was further refined by Alfred Lindesmith, Donald Cressey and Howard S. Becker. Eventually it became one of the classic research methods in ethnography.

According to Znaniecki analytic induction involves "inducing laws from a deep analysis of experimentally isolated instances", and is more advanced them simply defining and using terms in advance of research. It involves inductive rather than deductive reasoning) and allows modification of social concepts throughout research. This allows an accurate reflection of the studied phenomena

Archival Research

An archive is a collection of historical records, as well as the place they are located. Archives contain primary source documents that have accumulated over the course of an individual or organization's lifetime.

In general, archives consist of records that have been selected for permanent or long-term preservation on grounds of their enduring cultural, historical, or evidentiary value. Archival records are normally unpublished and almost always unique, unlike books or magazines for which many identical copies exist. This means that archives (the places) are quite distinct from libraries with regard to their functions and organization, although archival collections can often be found within library buildings.

A person who works in archives is called an archivist. The study and practice of organizing, preserving, and providing access to information and materials in archives is called archival science.

Archivists tend to prefer the term "archives" (with an S) as the correct terminology to serve as both the singular and plural, since "archive," as a noun or a verb, has acquired meanings related to computer science.

Users and Institutions

Historians, genealogists, lawyers, demographers, filmmakers, and others conduct research at archives. The research process at each archive is unique, and depends upon the institution in which the archive is housed. While there are many different kinds of archives, the most recent census of archivists in the United States identified five major types: academic, business (for profit), government, non-profit, and other. There are also four main areas of inquiry involved with archives: material technologies, organizing principles, geographic locations, and tangled embodiments of humans and non-humans. These areas help to further categorize what kind of archive is being created.

Academic

Archives in colleges, universities, and other educational facilities are typically housed within a library, and duties may be carried out by an archivist or a librarian. Occasionally, history professors may also run a smaller archive. Academic archives exist to preserve and celebrate the history of their school and academic community. An academic archive may contain items such as papers of former professors and presidents, memorabilia related to school organizations and activities, and items the academic library wishes to remain in a closed-stack setting, such as rare books or thesis copies. Access to the majority of these archives is by appointment only. Users of academic archives are often graduate students and those wishing to view rare or historical documents for research purposes. Many academic archives work closely with alumni relations departments to help raise funds for their library or school. Because of their library setting, a degree certified by the American Library Association is preferred for employment in an academic archive in the United States.

Business (for profit)

Archives located in for-profit institutions are usually those owned by a private business. Examples of prominent business archives in the United States include Coca-Cola (which also owns the separate museum World of Coca-Cola), Procter and Gamble, Motorola Heritage Services and Archives, and Levi Strauss & Co. These corporate archives maintain historic documents and items related to the history of their companies. Business archives serve the purpose of helping their corporations maintain control over their brand by retaining memories of the company's past. Especially in business archives, records management is separate from the historic aspect of archives. Workers in these types of archives may have any combination of training and degrees, from either a history or library background. These archives are typically not open to the public and only used by workers of the owner company, although some will allow approved visitors by appointment. Business archives are concerned with maintaining the integrity of their company, and therefore selective of how their materials may be used.

Government

Government archives include those run on a local and state level as well as those run by the national (or federal) government. Anyone may use a government archive, and frequent users include reporters, genealogists, writers, historians, students, and people wanting information on the history of their home or region. Many government archives are open to the public and no appointment is required to visit.

In the United States, National Archives and Records Administration (NARA) maintains central archival facilities in the District of Columbia and College Park, Maryland, with regional facilities distributed throughout the United States. Some city or local governments may have repositories, but their organization and accessibility varies widely. State or province archives typically require at least a bachelor's degree in history for employment, although some ask for certification by test (government or association) as well.

In the UK the National Archives, formerly known as the Public Record Office, is the government archive for England and Wales. The National Monuments Record [15] is the public archive of English Heritage. The National Archives of Scotland, located in Edinburgh, serve that country while the Public Record Office of Northern Ireland in Belfast is the government archive for Northern Ireland.

A network of local authority-run record offices and archives exists throughout England, Wales and Scotland and holds many important collections, including local government, landed estates, church and business records. Many archives have contributed catalogues to the national Access 2 Archives programme and online searching across collections is possible.

In France, the Directorate of the Archives of France (*Direction des Archives de France*) in the Ministry of Culture manages the National Archives (*Archives nationales*) which possess 364 km. (226 miles) of archives as of 2004 (the total length of occupied shelves put next to each other), with original records going as far back as A.D. 625, as well as the departmental archives (*archives départementales*), located in the *préfectures* of each of the 100 *départements* of France, which possess 1,901 km. (1,181 miles) of archives (as of 2004), and also the local city archives, about 600 in total, which possess 449 km. (279 miles) of archives (as of 2004). Put together, the total volume of archives under the supervision of the Directorate of the Archives of France is the largest in the world.

Most intergovernmental organisations keep their own historical archives. However, a number of European organisations, including the European Commission, choose to deposit their archives with the European University Institute in Florence.

Church

The most famous Church Archives is the Vatican Secret Archive. The collections of the Church Archives include Archdioceses, dioceses and parishes archives in the Roman Catholic and Episcopalian Churches and another kinds of archives in the different denominations of the Christian Churches, manuscripts, Church records, local Church records, photographs, oral histories, audiovisual materials, and architectural drawings.

Non-profit

Non-profit archives include those in historical societies, not-for-profit businesses such as hospitals, and the repositories within foundations. Non-profit archives are typically set up with private funds from donors to preserve the papers and history of specific persons or places. Often these institutions rely on grant funding from the government as well as the private funds. Depending on the funds available, non-profit archives may be as small as the historical society in a rural town to as big as a state historical society that rivals a government archives. Users of this type of archive may vary as much as the institutions that hold them. Employees of non-profit archives may be professional archivists, para-professionals, or volunteers, as the education required for a position at a non-profit archive varies with the demands of the collection's user base.

Electronic Archiving

Archives can take many forms. However when pertaining to specifically databases there are three main forms, described by new media artist Bill Viola; branching, matrix, and schizo.

Branching

In the branching format one option can potentially lead to numerous other options. Imagine a tree diagram, where multiple branches branch off of one branch. The same rule applies here.

Matrix

The matrix form is not as linear as the branching form. The matrix structure is like a grid where there is no direct path to follow. An individual has the ability to view any archival information regardless of their previous selection. Thus, it is a non-linear archival structure. The user is only restrained by the amount of content there is to view.

Schizo

Also referred to as the spaghetti style by Bill Viola, schizo is a form of archives that is completely random. The user has no control over what they are capable of experiencing. Information is presented to them without any preordained trend. There is no restriction due to topics but in return the user has no control over the information being presented to them.

Web Aarchiving

The process of collecting data from the World Wide Web and preserving it in an archive, such as an archive site. Examples of web archives

1. Side bars
2. Blogs
3. Calendar
4. Tag cloud
5. News websites

Other

Some archives defy categorisation. There are tribal archives within the Native American nations in North America, and there are archives that exist within the papers of private individuals. Many museums keep archives in order to prove the provenance of their pieces. Any institution or persons wishing to keep their significant papers in an organized fashion that employs the most basic principles of archival science may have an archive. In the 2004 census of archivists taken in the United States, 2.7% of archivists were employed in institutions that defied categorization. This was a separate figure from the 1.3% that identified themselves as self-employed.

Another type of archive is public secrets. This is an interactive testimonial in which women incarcerated in the California State Prison System reveal their stories about what happened to them. The function of the archive is to unfold the stories of the women who want to express themselves and want their stories to be heard. This collection of stories includes the women's direct speeches and also a recording of the women saying their speech.

The archives of an individual may include letters, papers, photographs, computer files, scrapbooks, financial records or diaries created or collected by the individual regardless of media or format. The archives of an organization (such as a corporation or government) tend to contain other types of records, such as administrative files, business records, memos, official correspondence and meeting minutes.

Content Analysis

Content analysis is a methodology in the social sciences for studying the content of communication. Earl Babbie defines it as:

> "the study of recorded human communications, such as books, websites, paintings and laws."

It is most commonly used by researchers in the social sciences to analyse recorded transcripts of interviews with participants.

Content analysis is also considered a scholarly methodology in the humanities by which texts are studied as to authorship, authenticity, or meaning. This latter subject include philology, hermeneutics, and semiotics.

Harold Lasswell formulated the core questions of content analysis:

> "Who says what, to whom, why, to what extent and with what effect?." Ole Holsti offers a broad definition of content analysis as "any technique for making inferences by objectively and systematically identifying specified characteristics of messages."

Offers a six-part definition of content analysis:

> "Content analysis is a summarizing, quantitative analysis of messages that relies on the scientific method (including attention to objectivity, intersubjectivity, a priori design, reliability, validity, generalisability, replicability, and hypothesis testing) and is not limited as to the types of variables that may be measured or the context in which the messages are created or presented."

In 1931, Alfred R Lindesmith developed a methodology to refute existing hypotheses, which became known as a content analysis technique, and it gained popularity in the 1960s by Glaser and is referred to as "The Constant Comparative Method of Qualitative Analysis" in an article published in 1964-65. Glaser and Strauss referred to their adaptation of it as "Grounded Theory." The method of *content analysis* enables the researcher to include large amounts of textual information and systematically identify its properties, e.g. the frequencies of most used keywords by locating the more important structures of its communication content. Yet such amounts of textual information must be categorised analysis, providing at the end a meaningful reading of content under scrutiny. David Robertson for example created a coding frame for a comparison of modes of party competition between British and American parties. It was developed further in 1979 by the *Manifesto Research Group* aiming at a comparative content-analytic approach on the policy positions of political parties.

Since the 1980s, content analysis has become an increasingly important tool in the measurement of success in public relations (notably media relations) programs and the assessment of media profiles. In these circumstances, content analysis is an element of media evaluation or media analysis. In analyses of this type, data from content analysis is usually combined with media data (circulation, readership, number of viewers and listeners, frequency of publication). It has also been used by futurists to identify trends. In 1982, John Naisbitt published his popular *Megatrends*, based on content analysis in the US media.

The creation of coding frames is intrinsically related to a creative approach to variables that exert an influence over textual content. In political analysis, these variables could be political scandals, the impact of public opinion polls, sudden events in external politics, inflation etc. *Mimetic Convergence*, created by F. Lampreia Carvalho for the comparative analysis of electoral proclamations on free-to-air television is an example of creative articulation of variables in content analysis. The methodology describes the construction of party identities during long-term party competitions on TV, from a dynamic perspective, governed by the logic of the contingent. This method aims to capture the contingent logic observed in electoral campaigns by focusing on the repetition and innovation of themes sustained in party broadcasts. According to such post-structuralist perspective from which electoral competition is analysed, the party identities, 'the real' cannot speak without mediations because there is not a natural centre fixing the meaning of a party structure, it rather depends on ad-hoc articulations. There is no empirical reality outside articulations of meaning. Reality is an outcome of power struggles that unify ideas of social structure as a result of contingent interventions. In Brazil, these contingent interventions have proven to be mimetic and convergent rather than divergent and polarised, being integral to the repetition of dichotomised worldviews.

Mimetic Convergence thus aims to show the process of fixation of meaning through discursive articulations that repeat, alter and subvert political issues that come into play. For this reason, parties are not taken as the pure expression of conflicts for the representation of interests (of different classes, religions, ethnic groups but attempts to recompose and re-articulate ideas of an absent totality around *signifiers* gaining positivity.

Every content analysis should depart from a hypothesis. The hypothesis of *Mimetic Convergence* supports the Downsian interpretation that in general, rational voters converge in the direction of uniform positions in most thematic dimensions. The hypothesis guiding the analysis of *Mimetic Convergence* between political parties' broadcasts is: 'public opinion polls on vote intention, published throughout campaigns on TV will contribute to successive revisions of candidates' discourses. Candidates re-orient their arguments and thematic selections in part by the signals sent by voters. One must also consider the interference of other kinds of input on electoral propaganda such as internal and external political crises and the arbitrary interference of private interests on the dispute. Moments of internal crisis in disputes between candidates might result from the *exhaustion* of a certain strategy. The moments of *exhaustion* might consequently precipitate an inversion in the thematic flux.

As an evaluation approach, content analysis is considered by some to be quasi-evaluation because content analysis judgments need not be based on value statements if the research objective is aimed at presenting subjective experiences. Thus, they can be based on knowledge of everyday lived experiences. Such content analyses are not evaluations. On the other hand, when content analysis judgments are based on values, such studies are evaluations.

As demonstrated above, only a good scientific hypothesis can lead to the development of a methodology that will allow the empirical description, be it dynamic or static.

The Process of a Content Analysis

According to Dr. Klaus Krippendorff, six questions must be addressed in every content analysis:

1. Which data are analysed?
2. How are they defined?
3. What is the population from which they are drawn?
4. What is the context relative to which the data are analysed?
5. What are the boundaries of the analysis?
6. What is the target of the inferences?

The assumption is that words and phrases mentioned most often are those reflecting important concerns in every communication. Therefore, quantitative content analysis starts with word frequencies, space measurements (column centimeters/inches in the case of newspapers), time counts (for radio and television time) and keyword frequencies. However, content analysis extends far beyond plain word counts, e.g. with Keyword In Context routines words can be analysed in their specific context to be disambiguated. Synonyms and homonyms can be isolated in accordance to linguistic properties of a language.

Qualitatively, content analysis can involve any kind of analysis where communication content (speech, written text, interviews, images...) is categorized and classified. In its beginnings, using the first newspapers at the end of 19th century, analysis was done manually by measuring the number of lines and amount of space given a subject. With the rise of common computing facilities like PCs, computer-based methods of analysis are growing in popularity. Answers to open ended questions, newspaper articles, *political party manifestoes, medical records or systematic* observations in experiments can all be subject to systematic analysis of textual data. By having contents of communication available in form of machine readable texts, the input is analysed for frequencies and coded into categories for building up inferences. Robert Philip Weber notes:

> "To make valid inferences from the text, it is important that the classification procedure be reliable in the sense of being consistent: Different people should code the same text in the same way"

The validity, inter-coder reliability and intra-coder reliability are subject to intense methodological research efforts over long years.

One more distinction is between the manifest contents (of communication) and its latent meaning. "Manifest" describes what (an author or speaker) definitely has written, while latent meaning describes what an author intended to say/write. Normally, content analysis can only be applied on manifest content; that is, the words, sentences, or texts themselves, rather than their meanings.

Dermot McKeone has highlighted the difference between prescriptive analysis and open analysis. In prescriptive analysis, the context is a closely-defined set of communication parameters (e.g. specific messages, subject matter); open analysis identifies the dominant messages and subject matter within the text.

A further step in analysis is the distinction between dictionary-based (quantitative) approaches and qualitative approaches. Dictionary-based approaches set up a list of categories derived from the frequency list of words and control the distribution of words and their respective categories over the texts. While methods in quantitative content analysis in this way transform observations of found categories into quantitative statistical data, the qualitative content analysis focuses more on the intentionality and its implications.

ETHNOGRAPHY

Ethnography is a research strategy often used in the social sciences, particularly in anthropology and in some branches of sociology. It is often employed for gathering empirical data on human societies/cultures. Data collection is often done through participant observation, interviews, questionnaires, etc. Ethnography aims to describe the nature of those who are studied through writing. In the biological sciences, this type of study might be called a "field study" or a "case report," both of which are used as common synonyms for "ethnography".

Ethnographic studies are usually holistic, founded on the idea that humans are best understood in the fullest possible context, including: the place where they live, the improvements they've made to that place, how they are making a living and providing food, housing, energy and water for themselves, what their marriage customs are, what language(s) they speak and so on. Ethnography has connections to genres as diverse as travel writing, colonial office reports, the play and the novel. Many cultural anthropologists consider ethnography the essence of the discipline. It would be a rare program in graduate cultural anthropology that didn't require an ethnography as part of the doctoral process.

Ethnographic methodology is not usually evaluated in terms of philosophical standpoint (such as positivism and emotionalism). Ethnographic studies nonetheless need to be evaluated in some manner. While there is no consensus on evaluation standards, Richardson provides 5 criteria that ethnographers might find helpful.

1. *Substantive Contribution*: "Does the piece contribute to our understanding of social-life?"
2. *Aesthetic Merit*: "Does this piece succeed aesthetically?"
3. *Reflexivity*: "How did the author come to write this text...Is there adequate self-awareness and self-exposure for the reader to make judgments about the point of view?"
4. *Impact*: "Does this affect me? Emotionally? Intellectually?" Does it move me?
5. *Expresses a Reality*: "Does it seem 'true'—a credible account of a cultural, social, individual, or communal sense of the 'real'?"

Data Collection Methods

One of the most common methods for collecting data in an ethnographic study is direct, first-hand observation of daily participation. This can include participant observation. Another common method is interviewing, which may include conversation with different levels of form and can involve small talk to long interviews. A particular approach to transcribing interview data might be genealogical method. This is a set of procedures by which ethnographers discover and record connections of kinship, descent and marriage using diagrams and symbols. Questionnaires can be used to aid the discovery of local beliefs and perceptions and in the case of longitudinal research, where there is continuous long-term study of an area or site, they can act as valid instrument for measuring changes in the individuals or groups studied. Traditionally, the ethnographer focuses attention on a community, selecting knowledgeable informants who know well the activities of the community. These informants are typically asked to identify other informants who represent the community, often using chain sampling. This process is often effective in revealing common cultural common denominators connected to the topic being studied. Ethnography relies greatly on up-close, personal experience. Participation, rather than just observation, is one of the keys to this process.

Differences Across Disciplines

The ethnographical method is used across a range of different disciples, primarily by anthropologists but also frequently by sociologists. Cultural studies, economics, social work, education, ethnomusicology, folklore, geography, history, linguistics, communication studies, performance studies, psychology, usability and criminology are other fields which have made use of ethnography.

Cultural and Social Anthropology

Cultural anthropology and social anthropology were developed around ethnographic research and their canonical texts which are mostly ethnographies: e.g. *Argonauts of the Western Pacific* by Bronisaw Malinowski, *Coming of Age in Samoa* by Margaret Mead, *The Nuer* by E. E. Evans-Pritchard, *Naven* by Gregory Bateson or "The Lele of the Kasai" by Mary Douglas. Cultural and social anthropologists today place such a high value on actually doing ethnographic research that ethnology—the comparative synthesis of ethnographic information—is rarely the foundation for a career. The typical ethnography is a document written about a particular people, almost always based at least in part on emic views of where the culture begins and ends. Using language or community boundaries to bound the ethnography is common. Ethnographies are also sometimes called "case studies." Ethnographers study and interpret culture, its universalities and its variations through ethnographic study based on fieldwork. An ethnography is a specific kind of written observational science which provides an account of a particular culture, society, or community. The fieldwork usually involves spending a year or more in another society, living with the local people and learning about their ways of life. Ethnographers are participant observers. They take part in events they study because it helps with understanding local behaviour and thought. Classic examples are Carol Stack's *All Our Kin*, Jean Briggs' "Never in Anger", Richard Lee's "Kalahari Hunter-Gatherers," Victor Turner's "Forest of Symbols," David Maybry-Lewis' "Akew-Shavante Society," E.E. Evans-Pritchard's "The Nuer" and Claude Lévi-Strauss' "Tristes Tropiques". Iterations of ethnographic representations in the classic, modernist camp include Bartholomew Dean's recent contribution, *Urarina Society, Cosmology, and History in Peruvian Amazonia.*

A typical ethnography attempts to be holistic and typically follows an outline to include a brief history of the culture in question, an analysis of the physical geography or terrain inhabited by the people under study, including climate, and often including what biological anthropologists call habitat. Folk notions of botany and zoology are presented as ethnobotany and ethnozoology alongside references from the formal sciences. Material culture, technology and means of subsistence are usually treated next, as they are typically bound up in physical geography and include descriptions of infrastructure. Kinship and social structure (including age grading, peer groups, gender, voluntary associations, clans, moieties, and so forth, if they exist) are typically included. Languages spoken, dialects and the history of language change are another group of standard topics. Practices of childrearing, acculturation and emic views on personality and values usually follow after sections on social structure. Rites, rituals, and other evidence of religion have long been an interest and are sometimes central to ethnographies, especially when conducted in public where visiting anthropologists can see them.

As ethnography developed, anthropologists grew more interested in less tangible aspects of culture, such as values, worldview and what Clifford Geertz termed the "ethos" of the culture. Clifford Geertz's own fieldwork used elements of a phenomenological approach to fieldwork, tracing not just the doings of people, but the cultural elements themselves. For example, if within a group of people, winking was a communicative gesture, he sought to first determine what kinds of things a wink might mean (it might mean several things). Then, he sought to determine in what contexts winks were used, and whether, as one moved about a region, winks remained meaningful in the same way. In this way, cultural boundaries of communication could be explored, as opposed to using linguistic boundaries or notions about residence. Geertz, while still following something of a traditional ethnographic outline, moved outside that outline to talk about "webs" instead of "outlines" of culture.

Within cultural anthropology, there are several sub-genres of ethnography. Beginning in the 1950s and early 1960s, anthropologists began writing "bio-confessional" ethnographies that intentionally exposed the nature of ethnographic research. Famous examples include *Tristes Tropiques* by Claude Lévi-Strauss, *The High Valley* by Kenneth Read, and *The Savage and the Innocent* by David Maybury-Lewis, as well as the mildly fictionalized *Return to Laughter* by Elenore Smith Bowen (Laura Bohannan). Later "reflexive" ethnographies refined the technique to translate cultural differences by representing their effects on the ethnographer. Famous examples include "Deep Play: Notes on a Balinese Cockfight" by Clifford Geertz, *Reflections on Fieldwork in Morocco* by Paul Rabinow, *The Headman and I* by Jean-Paul Dumont, and *Tuhami* by Vincent Crapanzano. In the 1980s, the rhetoric of ethnography was subjected to intense scrutiny within the discipline, under the general influence of literary theory and post-colonial/post-structuralist thought. "Experimental" ethnographies that reveal the ferment of the discipline include *Shamanism, Colonialism, and the Wild Man* by Michael Taussig, *Debating Muslims* by Michael F. J. Fischer and Mehdi Abedi, *A Space on the Side of the Road* by Kathleen Stewart, and *Advocacy after Bhopal* by Kim Fortun.

Sociology

Sociology is another field which prominently features ethnographies. Urban sociology and the Chicago School in particular are associated with ethnographic research, with some well-known early examples being *Street Corner Society* by William Foote Whyte and *Black Metropolis* by St. Clair Drake and Horace R. Cayton, Jr.. Some of the influence for this can be traced to the anthropologist Lloyd Warner who was on the Chicago sociology faculty, and to Robert Park's experience as a journalist. Symbolic interactionism developed from the same tradition and yielded several excellent sociological ethnographies, including *Shared Fantasy* by Gary Alan Fine, which documents the early history of fantasy role-playing games. Other important ethnographies in the discipline of sociology include Pierre Bourdieu's work on Algeria and France, Paul Willis's *Learning To Labour* on working class youth, and the work of Elijah Anderson, Mitchell Duneier, Loic Wacquant on black America and Glimpses of Madrasa From Africa, 2010 Lai Olurode. But even though many sub-fields and theoretical perspectives within sociology use ethnographic methods, ethnography is not the *sine qua non* of the discipline, as it is in cultural anthropology.

Communication Studies

Beginning in the 1960s and 70s, ethnographic research methods began to be widely employed by communication scholars. Studies such as Gerry Philipsen's analysis of cultural communication strategies in a blue-collar, working class neighbourhood on the south side of Chicago, *Speaking 'Like a Man' in Teamsterville,* paved the way for the expansion of ethnographic research in the study of communication.

Scholars of communication studies use ethnographic research methods to analyse communication behaviours, seeking to answer the "why" and "how come" questions of human communication. Often this type of research results in a case study or field study such as an analysis of speech patterns at a protest rally or the way firemen communicate during "down time" at a fire station. Like anthropology scholars, communication scholars often immerse themselves, participate in and/or directly observe the particular wikt: social group being studied.

Other fields

The American anthropologist George Spindler was a pioneer in applying ethnographic methodology to the classroom.

Anthropologists like Daniel Miller and Mary Douglas have used ethnographic data to answer academic questions about consumers and consumption. In this sense, Tony Salvador, Genevieve Bell, and Ken Anderson describe design ethnography as being "a way of understanding the particulars of daily life in such a way as to increase the success probability of a new product or service or, more appropriately, to reduce the probability of failure specifically due to a lack of understanding of the basic behaviours and frameworks of consumers."

Businesses, too, have found ethnographers helpful for understanding how people use products and services, as indicated in the increasing use of ethnographic methods to understand consumers and consumption, or for new product development (such as video ethnography). The recent Ethnographic Praxis in Industry (EPIC) conference is evidence of this. Ethnographers' systematic and holistic approach to real-life experience is valued by product developers, who use the method to understand unstated desires or cultural practices that surround products. Where focus groups fail to inform marketers about what people really do, ethnography links what people say to what they actually do—avoiding the pitfalls that come from relying only on self-reported, focus-group data.

Ethics

Gary Alan Fine argues that the nature of ethnographic inquiry demands that researchers deviate from formal and idealistic rules or ethics that have come to be widely accepted in qualitative and quantitative approaches in research. Many of these ethical assumptions are rooted in positivist and post-positivist epistemologies that have adapted over time, but nonetheless are apparent and must be accounted for in all research paradigms. These ethical dilemmas are evident throughout the entire process of conducting ethnographies, including the design, implementation, and reporting of an ethnographic study. Essentially, Fine maintains that researchers are typically not as ethical as they claim or assume to be — and that "each job includes ways of doing things that would be inappropriate for others to know".

Fine is not necessarily casting blame or pointing his finger at ethnographic researchers, but rather is attempting to show that researchers often make idealized ethical claims and standards which in actuality are inherently based on partial truths and self-deceptions. Fine also acknowledges that many of these partial truths and self-deceptions are unavoidable. He maintains that "illusions" are essential to maintain an occupational reputation and avoid potentially more caustic consequences. He claims, "Ethnographers cannot help but lie, but in lying, we reveal truths that escape those who are not so bold". Based on these assertions, Fine establishes three conceptual clusters in which ethnographic ethical dilemmas can be situated: "Classic Virtues," "Technical Skills," and "Ethnographic Self."

Much debate surrounding the issue of ethics arose after the ethnographer Napoleon Chagnon conducted his ethnographic fieldwork with the Yanomamo people of South America.

Focus Group

A focus group is a form of qualitative research in which a group of people are asked about their perceptions, opinions, beliefs and attitudes towards a product, service, concept, advertisement, idea, or packaging. Questions are asked in an interactive group setting where participants are free to talk with other group members. The first focus groups were created at the Bureau of Applied Social Research by associate director, sociologist Robert K. Merton. The term itself was coined by psychologist and marketing expert Ernest Dichter.

In the world of marketing, focus groups are seen as an important tool for acquiring feedback regarding new products, as well as various topics. In particular, focus groups allow companies wishing to develop, package, name, or test market a new product, to discuss, view, and/or test the new product before it is made available to the public. This can provide invaluable information about the potential market acceptance of the product.

In the social sciences and urban planning, focus groups allow interviewers to study people in a more natural setting than a one-to-one interview. In combination with participant observation, they can be used for gaining access to various cultural and social groups, selecting sites to study, sampling of such sites, and raising unexpected issues for exploration. Focus groups have a high apparent validity - since the idea is easy to understand, the results are believable. Also, they are low in cost, one can get results relatively quickly, and they can increase the sample size of a report by talking with several people at once.

Types of Focus Groups

Variants of focus groups include:

1. *Two-way focus group*: one focus group watches another focus group and discusses the observed interactions and conclusion
2. *Dual moderator focus group*: one moderator ensures the session progresses smoothly, while another ensures that all the topics are covered
3. *Dueling moderator focus group*: two moderators deliberately take opposite sides on the issue under discussion
4. *Respondent moderator focus group*: one and only one of the respondents are asked to act as the moderator temporarily
5. *Client participant focus groups*: one or more client representatives participate in the discussion, either covertly or overtly

6. *Mini focus groups*: groups are composed of four or five members rather than 6 to 12
7. *Teleconference focus groups*: telephone network is used
8. *Online focus groups*: computers connected via the internet are used

Traditional focus groups can provide accurate information, and are less expensive than other forms of traditional marketing research. There can be significant costs however : if a product is to be marketed on a nationwide basis, it would be critical to gather respondents from various locales throughout the country since attitudes about a new product may vary due to geographical considerations. This would require a considerable expenditure in travel and lodging expenses. Additionally, the site of a traditional focus group may or may not be in a locale convenient to a specific client, so client representatives may have to incur travel and lodging expenses as well.

The use of focus groups has steadily evolved over time and is becoming increasingly widespread.

Benefits/strengths of Focus Group Discussions

1. Group discussion produces data and insights that would be less accessible without interaction found in a group setting—listening to others' verbalized experiences stimulates memories, ideas, and experiences in participants. This is also known as the group effect where group members engage in "a kind of 'chaining' or 'cascading' effect; talk links to, or tumbles out of, the topics and expressions preceding it"
2. Group members discover a common language to describe similar experiences. This enables the capture of a form of "native language" or "vernacular speech" to understand the situation

3. Focus groups also provide an opportunity for disclosure among similar others in a setting where participants are validated. For example, in the context of workplace bullying, targeted employees often find themselves in situations where they experience lack of voice and feelings of isolation. Use of focus groups to study workplace bullying therefore serve as both an efficacious and ethical venue for collecting data

Problems and Criticism

However, focus groups also have disadvantages: The researcher has less control over a group than a one-on-one interview, and thus time can be lost on issues irrelevant to the topic; the data is tough to analyse because the talking is in reaction to the comments of other group members; observers/ moderators need to be highly trained, and groups are quite variable and can be tough to get together. Moreover, the number of members of a focus group is not large enough to be a representative sample of a population; thus, the data obtained from the groups is not necessarily representative of the whole population, unlike the data of opinion polls.

Focus groups are "One shot case studies" especially if they are measuring a property-disposition relationship within the social sciences, unless they are repeated. Focus groups can create severe issues of external validity, especially the reactive effects of the testing arrangement. A fundamental difficulty with focus groups (and other forms of qualitative research) is the issue of *observer dependency*: the results obtained are influenced by the researcher, raising questions of validity. The issue evokes associations with Heisenberg's famous Uncertainty Principle. As Heisenberg said, "What we observe is not nature itself, but nature exposed to our method of questioning." Indeed, the design of the focus group study (e.g. respondent selection, the questions asked, how they are phrased, how they are posed, in what setting, by whom, and so on) affects the answers obtained from respondents. In focus groups, researchers (and the moderators and observers of the focus group, if the researcher is not there) are not detached observers but always participants. Researchers must take this into account when making their analysis.

Another issue is with the setting itself. If the focus groups are held in a laboratory setting with a moderator who is a professor and the recording instrument is obtrusive, the participants may either hold back on their responses and/or try to answer the moderator's questions with answers the participants feel that the moderator wants to hear. Another issue with the focus group setting is the lack of anonymity. With all of the other participants, there can not be any guarantee of confidentiality. Again we have to deal with the issues of the reactive effects of the testing arrangement.

Douglas Rushkoff argues that focus groups are often useless, and frequently cause more trouble than they are intended to solve, with focus groups often aiming to please rather than offering their own opinions or evaluations, and with data often cherry picked to support a foregone conclusion. Rushkoff cites the disastrous introduction of New Coke in the 1980s as a vivid example of focus group analysis gone bad. In addition there is anecdotal evidence of focus groups rebelling, for instance the name for the Ford Focus, was created by a focus group which had grown bored and impatient and the irony of this was not picked up by the marketing team.

Jonathan Ive, Apple's senior vice president of industrial design, also said that Apple had found a good reason not to do focus groups:

> "They just ensure that you don't offend anyone, and produce bland inoffensive products."

Historical Method

The historical method comprises the techniques and guidelines by which historians use primary sources and other evidence to research and then to write histories in form of accounts of the past. The question of the nature, and indeed the possibility, of sound historical method is raised in the philosophy of history, as a question of epistemology.

Principles

The following core principles of source criticism were formulated by two Scandinavian historians, Olden-Jorgensen and Thurén:

1. Human sources may be relics (e.g. a fingerprint) or narratives (e.g. a statement or a letter). Relics are more credible sources than narratives.
2. A given source may be forged or corrupted; strong indications of the originality of the source increases its reliability.
3. The closer a source is to the event which it purports to describe, the more one can trust it to give an accurate description of what really happened.
4. A primary source is more reliable than a secondary source, that is more reliable than a tertiary source and so on.
5. If a number of *independent* sources contain the same message, the credibility of the message is strongly increased.
6. The tendency of a source is its motivation for providing some kind of bias. Tendencies should be minimized or supplemented with opposite motivations.
7. If it can be demonstrated that the witness (or source) has no direct interest in creating bias, the credibility of the message is increased.

Procedures

Bernheim and Langlois & Seignobos proposed a seven-step procedure for source criticism in history:

1. If the sources all agree about an event, historians can consider the event proved.
2. However, majority does not rule; even if most sources relate events in one way, that version will not prevail unless it passes the test of critical textual analysis.
3. The source whose account can be confirmed by reference to outside authorities in some of its parts can be trusted in its entirety if it is impossible similarly to confirm the entire text.
4. When two sources disagree on a particular point, the historian will prefer the source with most "authority" - i.e., the source created by the expert or by the eyewitness.
5. Eyewitnesses are, in general, to be preferred, especially in circumstances where the ordinary observer could have accurately reported what transpired and, more specifically, when they deal with facts known by most contemporaries.
6. If two independently created sources agree on a matter, the reliability of each is measureably enhanced.
7. When two sources disagree (and there is no other means of evaluation), then historians take the source which seems to accord best with common sense.

Historical Reliability

Noting that few documents are accepted as completely reliable, Louis Gottschalk sets down the general rule, "for each particular of a document the process of establishing credibility should be separately undertaken regardless of the general credibility of the author." An author's trustworthiness in the main may establish a background probability for the consideration of each statement, but each piece of evidence extracted must be weighed individually.

R. J. Shafer offers this checklist for **evaluating** eyewitness testimony:

1. Is the real meaning of the statement different from its literal meaning? Are words used in senses not employed today? Is the statement meant to be ironic (i.e., mean other than it says)?
2. How well could the author *observe* the thing he reports? Were his senses equal to the observation? Was his physical location suitable to sight, hearing, touch? Did he have the proper social ability to observe: did he understand the language, have other expertise required (e.g., law, military); was he not being intimidated by his wife or the secret police?
3. *How* did the author report?, and what was his *ability* to do so?
   a. Regarding his *ability* to report, was he biased? Did he have proper time for reporting? Proper place for reporting? Adequate recording instruments?
   b. *When* did he report in relation to his observation? Soon? Much later? Fifty years is much later as most eyewitnesses are dead and those who remain may have forgotten relevant material.
   c. What was the author's *intention* in reporting? For *whom* did he report? Would that audience be likely to require or suggest distortion to the author?
   d. Are there additional clues to intended veracity? Was he indifferent on the subject reported, thus probably not intending distortion? Did he make statements damaging to himself, thus probably not seeking to distort? Did he give incidental or casual

information, almost certainly not intended to mislead?

4. Do his statements seem inherently improbable: e.g., contrary to human nature, or in conflict with what we know?
5. Remember that some types of information are easier to observe and report on than others.
6. Are there inner contradictions in the document?

Louis Gottschalk adds an additional consideration:

> "Even when the fact in question may not be well-known, certain kinds of statements are *both incidental and probable* to such a degree that error or falsehood seems unlikely. If an ancient inscription on a road tells us that a certain proconsul built that road while Augustus was princeps, it may be doubted without further corroboration that proconsul really built the road, but would be harder to doubt that the road was built during the principate of Augusutus. If an advertisement informs readers that 'A and B Coffee may be bought at any reliable grocer's at the unusual price of fifty cents a pound,' all the inferences of the advertisement may well be doubted without corroboration except that there is a brand of coffee on the market called 'A and B Coffee.'"

LIFE HISTORY METHOD

In sociological and anthropological research, a life history refers to the overall picture of the informant's or interviewee's life. The purpose of the interview is to be able to describe what it is like to be this particular person, that is, the one being interviewed.

The method was first used when interviewing indigenous peoples of the Americas. The subjects were native American leaders. One interviewed them, and the subjects were asked to describe their lives as such, what it was like to be that particular person. The purpose of the interview was to capture a living picture of a disappearing (as such) people/way of life.

Later the method was used to interview criminals and prostitutes in Chicago. The subjects were asked to tell about their lives. The interviewers also looked at social- and police-records, and the society in general in which the subject lived. The result was a report in which one could read about:

1. Chicago at that particular time;
2. How the subject viewed his own life (i.e. 'how it was like to be this particular person') and
3. How society looked upon the subject what the consequence of this was for that particular person—i.e. 'social work'/-help, incarceration etc.

The most famous use of life history in connection of the Chicago school, was in connection with the Polish Peasant study by W.I Thomas and Florian Znaniecki. They employed a Polish emigrant to write his own life story, which they then interpreted and analysed. The approach fell later in disrepute, as quantitative methods gained the upper hand in sociology. Only in the 1970s was the method revived, mainly through the efforts of Daniel Bertaux and Paul Thompson who started doing life history research in such professions as bakers or fishermen. The revival of the life history method spread rapidly through Europe, with major research initiatives in Germany, Italy, Finland.

In both cases, the one doing the interview should be careful not to ask "yes or no"-questions, but to get the subject to tell "the story of his or her life", in his or her own words. This is called the "narrative" method. It is common practice to begin the interview with the subject's early childhood and to proceed chronologically to the present. Another approach, dating from the Polish Peasant, is to ask participants to write their own life stories. This can be done either through competitions (as in Poland, Finland or Italy) or by collecting written life stories written spontaneously. In these countries, there are already large collections of life stories, which can be used by researchers.

Longitudinal Study

A longitudinal study is a correlational research study that involves repeated observations of the same items over long periods of time often many decades. It is a type of observational study. Longitudinal studies are often used in psychology to study developmental trends across the life span, and in sociology to study life events throughout lifetimes or generations. The reason for this is that unlike cross-sectional studies, longitudinal studies track the same people, and therefore the differences observed in those people are less likely to be the result of cultural differences across generations. Because of this benefit, longitudinal studies make observing changes more accurate and they are applied in various other fields. In medicine, the design is used to uncover predictors of certain diseases. In advertising, the Communicus System, the design is used to identify the changes that advertising has produced in the attitudes and behaviours of those within the target audience who have seen the advertising campaign.

Because most longitudinal studies are observational, in the sense that they observe the state of the world without manipulating it, it has been argued that they may have less power to detect causal relationships than do experiments. But because of the repeated observation at the individual level, they have more power than cross-sectional observational studies, by virtue of being able to exclude time-invariant unobserved individual differences, and by virtue of observing the temporal order of events.

Longitudinal studies allow social scientists to distinguish short from long-term phenomena, such as poverty. If the poverty rate is 10% at a point in time, this may mean that 10% of the population are always poor, or that the whole population experiences poverty for 10% of the time. It is not possible to conclude which of these possibilities is the case using one-off cross-sectional studies.

Types of longitudinal studies include cohort studies and panel studies. Cohort studies sample a cohort, defined as a group experiencing some event (typically birth) in a selected time period, and studying them at intervals through time. Panel studies sample a cross-section, and survey it at (usually regular) intervals.

A retrospective study is a longitudinal study that looks back in time. For instance a researcher may look up the medical records of previous years to look for a trend.

Participant Observation

Participant observation is a type of research strategy. It is a widely used methodology in many disciplines, particularly, cultural anthropology, but also sociology, communication studies, and social psychology. Its aim is to gain a close and intimate familiarity with a given group of individuals (such as a religious, occupational, or sub cultural group, or a particular community) and their practices through an intensive involvement with people in their natural environment, usually over an extended period of time. The method originated in field work of social anthropologists, especially the students of Franz Boas in the United States, and in the urban research of the Chicago School of sociology.

In anthropology, participant-observation is organized so as to produce a kind of writing called ethnography. It can be applied or academic in nature. A key principle of the method is that one may not merely observe, but must find a role within the group observed from which to participate in some manner, even if only as "outside observer." Overt participant-observation, therefore, is limited to contexts where the community under study understands and permits it. Critics of overt participant observation argue that study is subsequently restricted to the public fronts socially constructed by actors. Gatekeepers ensure that known research never goes backstage, making covert strategies necessary especially when conducting studies on government entities or criminal organisations.

Such research usually involves a range of methods: informal interviews, direct observation, participation in the life of the group, collective discussions, analyses of personal documents produced within the group, self-analysis, and life-histories. Although the method is generally characterized as qualitative research, it can (and often does) include quantitative dimensions. Participant observation is usually undertaken over an extended period of time, ranging from several months to many years. An extended research time period means that the researcher will be able to obtain more detailed and accurate information about the people he/she is studying. Observable details (like daily time allotment) and more hidden details (like taboo behaviour) are more easily observed and understandable over a longer period of time. A strength of observation and interaction over long periods of time is that researchers can discover discrepancies between what participants say—and often believe—should happen (the formal system) and what actually does happen, or between different aspects of the formal system; in contrast, a one-time survey of people's answers to a set of questions might be quite consistent, but is less likely to show conflicts between different aspects of the social system or between conscious representations and behaviour.

Participant observation has its roots in anthropology and its use as a methodology can be attributed to Abû Rayhân Bîrûnî (973-1048), a Persian anthropologist who carried out extensive, personal investigations of the peoples, customs and religions of the Indian subcontinent. Like modern anthropologists, he engaged in extensive participant observation with a given group of people, learnt their language and studied their primary texts, and presented his findings with objectivity and neutrality using cross-cultural comparisons.

Participant observation was used extensively by Frank Hamilton Cushing in his study of the Zuni Indians in the later part of the nineteenth century, followed by the studies of non-Western societies by people such as Bronisaw Malinowski, Edward Evans-Pritchard, and Margaret Mead in the first half of the twentieth century. It emerged as the principal approach to ethnographic research by anthropologists and relied on the cultivation of personal relationships with local informants as a way of learning about a culture, involving both observing and participating in the social life of a group. By living with the cultures they studied, these researchers were able tc formulate first hand accounts of their lives and gain novel insights. This same method of study has also been applied to groups within Western society, and is especially successful in the study of subcultures or groups sharing a strong sense of identity, where only by taking part might the observer truly get access to the lives of those being studied. Since the 1980s, some anthropologists and other social scientists have questioned the degree to which participant observation can give veridical insight into the minds of other people. At the same time, a more formalized qualitative research program known as grounded theory, initiated by Glaser and Strauss, began gaining currency within American sociology and related fields such as public health. In response to these challenges, some ethnographers have refined their methods, either making them more amenable to formal hypothesis-testing and replicability, or framing their interpretations within a more carefully considered epistemology.

The development of participant-observation as a research tool has therefore not been a haphazard process, but instead has practised a great deal of self-criticism and review. It has as a result become specialized. Visual anthropology can be viewed as a subset of methods of participant-observation, as the central questions in that field have to do with how to take a camera into the field, while dealing with such issues as the observer effect. Issues with entry into the field have evolved into a separate subfield. Clifford Geertz's famous essay on how to approach the multifaceted arena of human action from an observational point of view, in *Interpretation of Cultures* uses the simple example of a human wink, perceived in a cultural context far from home.

A variant of participant observation is observing participation, described by Marek M. Kaminski, who explored prison subculture being a political prisoner in communist Poland in 1985. "Observing" or "observant" participation has also been used to describe fieldwork in sexual minority subcultures by anthropologists and sociologists who are themselves lesbian, gay, bisexual, or transgender; the different phrasing is meant to highlight the way in which their partial or full membership in the community/subculture that they are researching both allows a different sort of access to the community and also shapes their perceptions in ways different from a full outsider. This is similar to considerations by anthropologists such as Lila Abu-Lughod on "halfie anthropology", or fieldwork by bicultural anthropologists on a culture to which they partially belong. The sociological methods known as grounded theory (Glaser and Strauss). overlap significantly with the more formalized versions of participant observation.

Semi-Structured Interview

A semi-structured interview is a method of research used in

the social sciences. While a structured interview has a formalized, limited set questions, a semi-structured interview is flexible, allowing new questions to be brought up during the interview as a result of what the interviewee says. The interviewer in a semi-structured interview generally has a framework of themes to be explored.

However, the specific topic or topics that the interviewer wants to explore during the interview should usually be thought about well in advance (especially during interviews for research projects). It is generally beneficial for interviewers to have an interview guide prepared, which is an informal "grouping of topics and questions that the interviewer can ask in different ways for different participants". Interview guides help researchers to focus an interview on the topics at hand without constraining them to a particular format. This freedom can help interviewers to tailor their questions to the interview context/situation, and to the people they are interviewing.

Structured Interview

A structured interview (also known as a standardised interview or a researcher-administered survey) is a quantitative research method commonly employed in survey research. The aim of this approach is to ensure that each interview is presented with exactly the same questions in the same order. This ensures that answers can be reliably aggregated and that comparisons can be made with confidence between sample subgroups or between different survey periods.

Structured interviews are a means of collecting data for a statistical survey. In this case, the data is collected by an interviewer rather than through a self-administered questionnaire. Interviewers read the questions exactly as they appear on the survey questionnaire. The choice of answers to the questions is often fixed (close-ended) in advance, though open-ended questions can also be included within a structured interview.

A structured interview also standardises the order in which questions are asked of survey respondents, so the questions are always answered within the same context. This is important for minimising the impact of context effects, where the answers given to a survey question can depend on the nature of preceding questions. Though context effects can never be avoided, it is often desirable to hold them constant across all respondents.

Structured interviews can also be used as a qualitative research methodology. These types of interviews are best suited for engaging in respondent or focus group studies in which it would be beneficial to compare/contrast participant responses in order to answer a research question. For structured qualitative interviews, it is usually necessary for researchers to develop an interview schedule which lists the wording and sequencing of questions. Interview schedules are sometimes considered a means by which researchers can increase the reliability and credibility of research data.

Unstructured Interview

Unstructured Interviews are a method of interviews where questions can be changed or adapted to meet the respondent's intelligence, understanding or belief. Unlike a structured interview they do not offer a limited, preset range of answers for a respondent to choose, but instead advocate listening to how each individual person responds to the question.

The method to gather information using this technique is fairly limited, for example most surveys that are carried out via telephone or even in person tend to follow a structured method. Outside of sociology the use of such interviews is very limited.

Aaron Cicourel and John Kitsuse used the method in 1963 for their interviews. It enabled them to ask further questions beyond what they already had planned, in addition, it enabled them to clarify meaning of the responses they received. There are both advantages and disadvantages of unstructured interviews. The advantages are that the data collected is said to be valid as it is an exact account of what the interviewee has said. The researcher can also find out important information which did not seem relevant before the interview and ask the interviewee to go further into the new topic. Unstructured interviews are also more suitable for sensitive subjects such as "domestic violence" as many people would lie in a more formal interview and also their response may not be on the preset question list. The disadvantages of interviews in general is the "interviewer effect". This is when the interviewee response is affected by the presence of the researcher due to either his/her race, ethnicity, colour, or response to certain answers. Unstructured interviews can also be very time consuming as the conversation can go on and on. The data collected is prone to digression and much of the data collected could be worthless. The data is also not reliable as it can not be done again with the same results due to a number of factors. Unstructured interviews are usually small scale so it is hard to generalise with the results as only a small number of the population can be interviewed. Also Data collection is hard to categorise as there is likely to be a variety of different answers. Coding will require more work when choosing categories for the respondents.

4

Statistical Survey

Statistical surveys are used to collect quantitative information about items in a population. Surveys of human populations and institutions are common in political polling and government, health, social science and marketing research. A survey may focus on opinions or factual information depending on its purpose, and many surveys involve administering questions to individuals. When the questions are administered by a researcher, the survey is called a structured interview or a researcher-administered survey. When the questions are administered by the respondent, the survey is referred to as a questionnaire or a self-administered survey.

Structure and Standardisation

The questions are usually structured and standardized. The structure is intended to reduce bias. For example, questions should be ordered in such a way that a question does not influence the response to subsequent questions. Surveys are standardized to ensure reliability, generalisability, and validity. Every respondent should be presented with the same questions and in the same order as other respondents.

In organizational development (OD), carefully constructed survey instruments are often used as the basis for data gathering, organizational diagnosis, and subsequent action planning. Some OD practitioners even consider survey guided development as the *sine qua non* of OD.

Serial Surveys

Serial surveys repeat the same questions at different points in time, producing repeated measures of data. There are three basic designs for a study with more than one measurement occasion: cross-sectional design, longitudinal design, and time-series design.

1. *Cross-sectional surveys:* use different units (respondents) at each of the measurement occasions, by drawing a new sample each time. The time intervals may be different between measurement occasions, but they are the same for all units (respondents). A study that administers a survey once is also considered cross-sectional.
2. *Longitudinal surveys:* use the same units (respondents) at each of the measurement occasions, by recontacting the same sample from the initial survey for the following measurement occasion(s), and asking the same questions at every occasion. The time intervals may be different between measurement occasions, but they are the same for all units (respondents).
3. *Time-series:* surveys also use the same units (respondents) at each of the measurement occasions, but the difference with longitudinal study designs is that in time-series designs both the number of measurement occasions and the time intervals between occasions may be different between units (respondents).

Advantages and Disadvantages of Surveys

Advantages

1. It is an efficient way of collecting information from a

large number of respondents. Very large samples are possible. Statistical techniques can be used to determine validity, reliability, and statistical significance.

2. Surveys are flexible in the sense that a wide range of information can be collected. They can be used to study attitudes, values, beliefs, and past behaviours.
3. Because they are standardized, they are relatively free from several types of errors.
4. They are relatively easy to administer.
5. There is an economy in data collection due to the focus provided by standardized questions. Only questions of interest to the researcher are asked, recorded, codified, and analysed. Time and money is not spent on tangential questions.
6. Sample surveys are usually cheaper to conduct than a full census.

Disadvantages

1. They depend on subjects' motivation, honesty, memory, and ability to respond. Subjects may not be aware of their reasons for any given action. They may have forgotten their reasons. They may not be motivated to give accurate answers; in fact, they may be motivated to give answers that present themselves in a favourable light.
2. Structured surveys, particularly those with closed ended questions, may have low validity when researching affective variables.
3. Although the individuals chosen to participate in surveys are often randomly sampled, errors due to nonresponse may exist. That is, people who choose to respond on the survey may be different from those who

do not respond, thus biasing the estimates. For example, polls or surveys that are conducted by calling a random sample of publicly available telephone numbers will not include the responses of people with unlisted telephone numbers, mobile (cell) phone numbers, people who are unable to answer the phone (e.g., because they normally sleep during the time of day the survey is conducted, because they are at work, etc.), people who do not answer calls from unknown or unfamiliar telephone numbers. Likewise, such a survey will include a disproportionate number of respondents who have traditional, land-line telephone service with listed phone numbers, and people who stay home much of the day and are much more likely to be available to participate in the survey (e.g., people who are unemployed, disabled, elderly, etc.).

4. Survey question answer-choices could lead to vague data sets because at times they are relative only to a personal abstract notion concerning "strength of choice". For instance the choice "moderately agree" may mean different things to different subjects, and to anyone interpreting the data for correlation. Even yes or no answers are problematic because subjects may for instance put "no" if the choice "only once" is not available.

Characteristics of Researcher-administered Surveys

1. Fewer misunderstood questions and inappropriate responses.
2. Fewer incomplete responses.
3. Generally higher response rates and better information on nonresponse, but...
4. Respondents may be unwilling to discuss sensitive topics with a stranger.

5. Greater control over the environment that the survey is administered in.
6. Additional information can be collected from respondent.
7. Subject to interviewer bias (e.g. answers influenced by desire to impress interviewer).
8. Generally expensive/time-consuming to run.

Characteristics of Self-administered Surveys

1. Respondents are more likely to stop participating midway through the survey (drop-offs).
2. Respondents cannot ask for clarification.
3. Low response rate in some modes.
4. Often respondents returning survey represent extremes of the population - skewed responses (consequence of low response rates).
5. Allows shy respondents to answer sensitive questions in private.
6. No interviewer intervention available for probing or explanation.
7. Respondents can read the whole questionnaire before answering any questions.
8. Free of interviewer bias.

Questions and Response Formats

Usually, a survey consists of a number of questions that the respondent has to answer in a set format. A distinction is made between open-ended and closed-ended questions. An open-ended question asks the respondent to formulate his own answer, whereas a closed-ended question has the respondent pick an answer from a given number of options. The response options for a closed-ended question should be exhaustive and mutually exclusive. Four types of response scales for closed-ended questions are distinguished:

1. Dichotomous, where the respondent has two options
2. Nominal-polytomous, where the respondent has more than two unordered options
3. Ordinal-polytomous, where the respondent has more than two ordered options
4. (Bounded)Continuous, where the respondent is presented with a continuous scale

A respondent's answer to an open-ended question is coded into a response scale afterwards.

Modes of Data Collection

There are several ways of administering a survey, including:

Telephone

1. Use of interviewers encourages sample persons to respond, leading to higher response rates.
2. Interviewers can increase comprehension of questions by answering respondents' questions.
3. Fairly cost efficient, depending on local call charge structure
4. Good for large national (or international) sampling frames
5. Some potential for interviewer bias (e.g. some people may be more willing to discuss a sensitive issue with a female interviewer than with a male one)
6. Cannot be used for non-audio information (graphics, demonstrations, taste/smell samples)
7. Unreliable for consumer surveys in rural areas where telephone penetration is low

8. Three types:
   a. Traditional telephone interviews
   b. Computer assisted telephone dialling
   c. Computer assisted telephone interviewing (CATI)

Mail

1. The questionnaire may be handed to the respondents or mailed to them, but in all cases they are returned to the researcher via mail.
2. Cost is very low, since bulk postage is cheap in most countries
3. Long time delays, often several months, before the surveys are returned and statistical analysis can begin
4. Not suitable for issues that may require clarification
5. Respondents can answer at their own convenience (allowing them to break up long surveys; also useful if they need to check records to answer a question)
6. No interviewer bias introduced
7. Large amount of information can be obtained: some mail surveys are as long as 50 pages
8. Response rates can be improved by using mail panels
   a. Members of the panel have agreed to participate
   b. Panels can be used in longitudinal designs where the same respondents are surveyed several times

Online Surveys

1. Can use web or e-mail
2. Web is preferred over e-mail because interactive HTML forms can be used
3. Often inexpensive to administer

4. Very fast results
5. Easy to modify
6. Response rates can be improved by using Online panels-members of the panel have agreed to participate
7. If not password-protected, easy to manipulate by completing multiple times to skew results
8. Data creation, manipulation and reporting can be automated and/or easily exported into a format that can be read by PSPP, DAP or other statistical analysis software
9. Data sets created in real time
10. Some are incentive based (such as Survey Vault or YouGov)
11. May skew sample towards a younger demographic compared with CATI
12. Often difficult to determine/control selection probabilities, hindering quantitative analysis of data
13. Used in large scale industries.

Personal in-home Survey

1. Respondents are interviewed in person, in their homes (or at the front door)
2. Very high cost
3. Suitable when graphic representations, smells, or demonstrations are involved
4. Often suitable for long surveys (but some respondents object to allowing strangers into their home for extended periods)
5. Suitable for locations where telephone or mail are not developed

6. Skilled interviewers can persuade respondents to cooperate, improving response rates
7. Potential for interviewer bias

Personal Mall Intercept Survey

1. Shoppers at malls are intercepted: they are either interviewed on the spot, taken to a room and interviewed, or taken to a room and given a self-administered questionnaire
2. Socially acceptable: people feel that a mall is a more appropriate place to do research than their home
3. Potential for interviewer bias
4. Fast
5. Easy to manipulate by completing multiple times to skew results

Methods Used to Increase Response Rates

1. *Brevity*:- single page if possible
2. Financial incentives
   a. Paid in advance
   b. Paid at completion
3. Nonmonetary incentives
   a. Commodity giveaways (pens, notepads)
   b. Entry into a lottery, draw or contest
   c. Discount coupons
   d. promise of contribution to charity
4. Preliminary notification
5. *Foot-in-the-door techniques*: start with a small inconsequential request

6. *Personalization of the request*: address specific individuals
7. *Follow-up requests*: multiple requests
8. Claimed affiliation with universities, research institutions, or charities
9. Emotional appeals
10. Bids for sympathy
11. Convince respondent that they can make a difference
12. Guarantee anonymity
13. Legal compulsion (certain government-run surveys)

SAMPLING

Sampling is that part of statistical practice concerned with the selection of an unbiased or random subset of individual observations within a population of individuals intended to yield some knowledge about the population of concern, especially for the purposes of making predictions based on statistical inference. Sampling is an important aspect of data collection.

Researchers rarely survey the entire population for two reasons: the cost is too high, and the population is dynamic in that the individuals making up the population may change over time. The three main advantages of sampling are that the cost is lower, data collection is faster, and since the data set is smaller it is possible to ensure homogeneity and to improve the accuracy and quality of the data.

Each observation measures one or more properties (such as weight, location, colour) of observable bodies distinguished as independent objects or individuals. In survey sampling, survey weights can be applied to the data to adjust for the sample design. Results from probability theory and statistical theory are employed to guide practice.

In business and medical research, sampling is widely used for gathering information about a population.

Process

The sampling process comprises several stages:

1. Defining the population of concern
2. Specifying a sampling frame, a set of items or events possible to measure
3. Specifying a sampling method for selecting items or events from the frame
4. Determining the sample size
5. Implementing the sampling plan
6. Sampling and data collecting

Population Definition

Successful statistical practice is based on focused problem definition. In sampling, this includes defining the population from which our sample is drawn. A population can be defined as including all people or items with the characteristic one wishes to understand. Because there is very rarely enough time or money to gather information from everyone or everything in a population, the goal becomes finding a representative sample (or subset) of that population.

Sometimes that which defines a population is obvious. For example, a manufacturer needs to decide whether a batch of material from production is of high enough quality to be released to the customer, or should be sentenced for scrap or rework due to poor quality. In this case, the batch is the population.

Although the population of interest often consists of physical objects, sometimes we need to sample over time, space. or some combination of these dimensions. For instance, an investigation of supermarket staffing could examine check-out line length at various times, or a study on endangered penguins might aim to understand their usage of various hunting grounds over time. For the time dimension, the focus may be on periods or discrete occasions.

In other cases, our 'population' may be even less tangible. For example, Joseph Jagger studied the behaviour of roulette wheels at a casino in Monte Carlo, and used this to identify a biased wheel. In this case, the 'population' Jagger wanted to investigate was the overall behaviour of the wheel (i.e. the probability distribution of its results over infinitely many trials), while his 'sample' was formed from observed results from that wheel. Similar considerations arise when taking repeated measurements of some physical characteristic such as the electrical conductivity of copper.

This situation often arises when we seek knowledge about the cause system of which the *observed* population is an outcome. In such cases, sampling theory may treat the observed population as a sample from a larger 'super population'. For example, a researcher might study the success rate of a new 'quit smoking' program on a test group of 100 patients, in order to predict the effects of the program if it were made available nationwide. Here the super population is "everybody in the country, given access to this treatment", a group which does not yet exist, since the program isn't yet available to all.

Note also that the population from which the sample is drawn may not be the same as the population about which we actually want information. Often there is large but not complete overlap between these two groups due to frame issues etc. Sometimes they may be entirely separate - for instance, we might study rats in order to get a better understanding of human health, or we might study records from people born in 2008 in order to make predictions about people born in 2009. Time spent in making the sampled population and population of concern precise is often well spent, because it raises many issues, ambiguities and questions that would otherwise have been overlooked at this stage.

Sampling Frame

In the most straightforward case, such as the sentencing of a batch of material from production (acceptance sampling by lots), it is possible to identify and measure every single item in the population and to include any one of them in our sample. However, in the more general case this is not possible. There is no way to identify all rats in the set of all rats. Where voting is not compulsory, there is no way to identify which people will actually vote at a forthcoming election (in advance of the election).

These imprecise populations are not amenable to sampling in any of the ways below and to which we could apply statistical theory.

As a remedy, we seek a *sampling frame* which has the property that we can identify every single element and include any in our sample. The most straightforward type of frame is a list of elements of the population (preferably the entire population) with appropriate contact information. For example, in an opinion poll, possible sampling frames include:

1. Electoral register
2. Telephone directory

Not all frames explicitly list population elements. For example, a street map can be used as a frame for a door-to-door survey; although it doesn't show individual houses, we can select streets from the map and then visit all houses on those streets.

The sampling frame must be representative of the population and this is a question outside the scope of statistical theory demanding the judgment of experts in the particular subject matter being studied. All the above frames omit some people who will vote at the next election and contain some people who will not; some frames will contain multiple records for the same person. People not in the frame have no prospect of being sampled. Statistical theory tells us about the uncertainties in extrapolating from a sample to the frame. In extrapolating from frame to population, its role is motivational and suggestive.

> To the scientist, however, representative sampling is the only justified procedure for choosing individual objects for use as the basis of generalization, and is therefore usually the only acceptable basis for ascertaining truth.
>
> —Andrew A. Marino

It is important to understand this difference to steer clear of confusing prescriptions found in many web pages.

In defining the frame, practical, economic, ethical, and technical issues need to be addressed. The need to obtain timely results may prevent extending the frame far into the future.

The difficulties can be extreme when the population and frame are disjoint. This is a particular problem in forecasting where inferences about the future are made from historical data. In fact, in 1703, when Jacob Bernoulli proposed to Gottfried Leibniz the possibility of using historical mortality data to predict the probability of early death of a living man, Gottfried Leibniz recognized the problem in replying:

> Nature has established patterns originating in the return of events but only for the most part. New illnesses flood the human race, so that no matter how many experiments you

> have done on corpses, you have not thereby imposed a limit on the nature of events so that in the future they could not vary.

Kish posited four basic problems of sampling frames:

1. *Missing elements*: Some members of the population are not included in the frame.
2. *Foreign elements*: The nonmembers of the population are included in the frame.
3. *Duplicate entries*: A member of the population is surveyed more than once.
4. *Groups or clusters*: The frame lists clusters instead of individuals.

A frame may also provide additional 'auxiliary information' about its elements; when this information is related to variables or groups of interest, it may be used to improve survey design. For instance, an electoral register might include name and sex; this information can be used to ensure that a sample taken from that frame covers all demographic categories of interest. (Sometimes the auxiliary information is less explicit; for instance, a telephone number may provide some information about location.)

Having established the frame, there are a number of ways for organizing it to improve efficiency and effectiveness.

It's at this stage that the researcher should decide whether the sample is in fact to be the whole population and would therefore be a census.

Probability and Nonprobability Sampling

A probility sampling scheme is one in which every unit in the population has a chance (greater than zero) of being selected in the sample, and this probability can be accurately determined. The combination of these traits makes it possible to produce unbiased estimates of population totals, by weighting sampled units according to their probability of selection.

Example: We want to estimate the total income of adults living in a given street. We visit each household in that street, identify all adults living there, and randomly select one adult from each household. (For example, we can allocate each person a random number, generated from a uniform distribution between 0 and 1, and select the person with the highest number in each household). We then interview the selected person and find their income. People living on their own are certain to be selected, so we simply add their income to our estimate of the total. But a person living in a household of two adults has only a one-in-two chance of selection. To reflect this, when we come to such a household, we would count the selected person's income twice towards the total. (In effect, the person who is selected from that household is taken as representing the person who isn't selected.)

In the above example, not everybody has the same probability of selection; what makes it a probability sample is the fact that each person's probability is known. When every element in the population *does* have the same probability of selection, this is known as an 'equal probability of selection' (EPS) design. Such designs are also referred to as 'self-weighting' because all sampled units are given the same weight.

Probability sampling includes: Simple Random Sampling, Systematic Sampling, Stratified Sampling, Probability Proportional to Size Sampling, and Cluster or Multistage Sampling. These various ways of probability sampling have two things in common:

1. Every element has a known non-zero probability of being sampled and

2. Involves random selection at some point.

Nonprobability sampling is any sampling method where some elements of the population have *no* chance of selection (these are sometimes referred to as 'out of coverage'/ 'undercovered'), or where the probability of selection can't be accurately determined. It involves the selection of elements based on assumptions regarding the population of interest, which forms the criteria for selection. Hence. because the selection of elements is non-random, nonprobability sampling does not allow the estimation of sampling errors. These conditions give rise to exclusion bias, placing limits on how much information a sample can provide about the population. Information about the relationship between sample and population is limited, making it difficult to extrapolate from the sample to the population.

Example: We visit every household in a given street, and interview the first person to answer the door. In any household with more than one occupant, this is a nonprobability sample, because some people are more likely to answer the door and it's not practical to calculate these probabilities.

Nonprobability Sampling includes: Accidental Sampling, Quota Sampling and Purposive Sampling. In addition, nonresponse effects may turn *any* probability design into a nonprobability design if the characteristics of nonresponse are not well understood, since nonresponse effectively modifies each element's probability of being sampled.

Sampling Methods

Within any of the types of frame identified above, a variety of sampling methods can be employed, individually or in combination. Factors commonly influencing the choice between these designs include:

1. Nature and quality of the frame
2. Availability of auxiliary information about units on the frame
3. Accuracy requirements, and the need to measure accuracy
4. Whether detailed analysis of the sample is expected
5. Cost/operational concerns

Simple Random Sampling

In a simple random sample ('SRS') of a given size, all such subsets of the frame are given an equal probability. Each element of the frame thus has an equal probability of selection: the frame is not subdivided or partitioned. Furthermore, any given *pair* of elements has the same chance of selection as any other such pair (and similarly for triples, and so on). This minimises bias and simplifies analysis of results. In particular, the variance between individual results within the sample is a good indicator of variance in the overall population, which makes it relatively easy to estimate the accuracy of results.

However, SRS can be vulnerable to sampling error because the randomness of the selection may result in a sample that doesn't reflect the make-up of the population. For instance, a simple random sample of ten people from a given country will *on average* produce five men and five women, but any given trial is likely to overrepresent one sex and underrepresent the other. Systematic and stratified techniques, discussed below, attempt to overcome this problem by using information about the population to choose a more representative sample.

SRS may also be cumbersome and tedious when sampling from an unusually large target population. In some cases, investigators are interested in research questions specific to subgroups of the population. For example, researchers might be interested in examining whether cognitive ability as a predictor of job performance is equally applicable across racial groups. SRS cannot accommodate the needs of researchers in this situation because it does not provide subsamples of the population. Stratified sampling, which is discussed below, addresses this weakness of SRS.

Simple random sampling is always an EPS design, but not all EPS designs are simple random sampling.

Systematic Sampling

Systematic sampling relies on arranging the target population according to some ordering scheme and then selecting elements at regular intervals through that ordered list. Systematic sampling involves a random start and then proceeds with the selection of every *k*th element from then onwards. In this case, *k*=(population size/sample size). It is important that the starting point is not automatically the first in the list, but is instead randomly chosen from within the first to the *k*th element in the list. A simple example would be to select every 10th name from the telephone directory (an 'every 10th' sample, also referred to as 'sampling with a skip of 10').

As long as the starting point is randomised, systematic sampling is a type of probability sampling. It is easy to implement and the stratification induced can make it efficient, *if* the variable by which the list is ordered is correlated with the variable of interest. 'Every 10th' sampling is especially useful for efficient sampling from databases.

Example: Suppose we wish to sample people from a long street that starts in a poor district (house #1) and ends in an expensive district (house #1000). A simple random selection of addresses from this street could easily end up with too many from the high end and too few from the low end (or vice versa), leading to an unrepresentative sample. Selecting (e.g.) every 10th street number along the street ensures that the sample is spread evenly along the length of the street, representing all of these districts. (Note that if we always start at house #1 and end at #991, the sample is slightly biased towards the low end; by randomly selecting the start between #1 and #10, this bias is eliminated.)

However, systematic sampling is especially vulnerable to periodicities in the list. If periodicity is present and the period is a multiple or factor of the interval used, the sample is especially likely to be *un*representative of the overall population, making the scheme less accurate than simple random sampling.

Example: Consider a street where the odd-numbered houses are all on the north (expensive) side of the road, and the even-numbered houses are all on the south (cheap) side. Under the sampling scheme given above, it is impossible' to get a representative sample; either the houses sampled will all be from the odd-numbered, expensive side, or they will all be from the even-numbered, cheap side.

Another drawback of systematic sampling is that even in scenarios where it is more accurate than SRS, its theoretical properties make it difficult to *quantify* that accuracy. (In the two examples of systematic sampling that are given above, much of the potential sampling error is due to variation between neighbouring houses - but because this method never selects two neighbouring houses, the sample will not give us any information on that variation.)

Systematic sampling is an EPS method, because all elements have the same probability of selection (in the example given, one in ten). It is *not* 'simple random sampling' because different subsets of the same size have different selection probabilities e.g. the set {4,14,24,...,994} has a one-in-ten probability of selection, but the set {4,13,24,34,...} has zero probability of selection.

Stratified Sampling

Where the population embraces a number of distinct categories, the frame can be organized by these categories into separate "strata." Each stratum is then sampled as an independent sub-population, out of which individual elements can be randomly selected. There are many several potential benefits to stratified sampling.

First, dividing the population into distinct, independent strata can enable researchers to draw inferences about specific subgroups that may be lost in a more generalized random sample.

Second, utilizing a stratified sampling method can lead to more efficient statistical estimates (provided that strata are selected based upon relevance to the criterion in question, instead of availability of the samples). Even if a stratified sampling approach does not lead to increased statistical efficiency, such a tactic will not result in less efficiency than would simple random sampling, provided that each stratum is proportional to the group's size in the population.

Third, it is sometimes the case that data are more readily available for individual, preexisting strata within a population than for the overall population; in such cases, using a stratified sampling approach may be more convenient than aggregating data across groups (though this may potentially be at odds with the previously noted importance of utilizing criterion-relevant strata).

Finally, since each stratum is treated as an independent population, different sampling approaches can be applied to different strata, potentially enabling researchers to use the approach best suited (or most cost-effective) for each identified subgroup within the population.

There are, however, some potential drawbacks to using stratified sampling. First, identifying strata and implementing such an approach can increase the cost and complexity of sample selection, as well as leading to increased complexity of population estimates. Second, when examining multiple criteria, stratifying variables may be related to some, but not to others, further complicating the design, and potentially reducing the utility of the strata. Finally, in some cases (such as designs with a large number of strata, or those with a specified minimum sample size per group), stratified sampling can potentially require a larger sample than would other methods (although in most cases, the required sample size would be no larger than would be required for simple random sampling.

A stratified sampling approach is most effective when three conditions are met

1. Variability within strata are minimized
2. Variability between strata are maximized
3. The variables upon which the population is stratified are strongly correlated with the desired dependent variable.

Advantages over other Sampling Methods

1. Focuses on important subpopulations and ignores irrelevant ones.
2. Allows use of different sampling techniques for different subpopulations.
3. Improves the accuracy/efficiency of estimation.
4. Permits greater balancing of statistical power of tests of differences between strata by sampling equal numbers from strata varying widely in size.

Disadvantages

1. Requires selection of relevant stratification variables which can be difficult.

2. Is not useful when there are no homogeneous subgroups.
3. Can be expensive to implement.

Poststratification

Stratification is sometimes introduced after the sampling phase in a process called "poststratification". This approach is typically implemented due to a lack of prior knowledge of an appropriate stratifying variable or when the experimenter lacks the necessary information to create a stratifying variable during the sampling phase. Although the method is susceptible to the pitfalls of post hoc approaches, it can provide several benefits in the right situation. Implementation usually follows a simple random sample. In addition to allowing for stratification on an ancillary variable, poststratification can be used to implement weighting, which can improve the precision of a sample's estimates.

Oversampling

Choice-based sampling is one of the stratified sampling strategies. In choice-based sampling, the data are stratified on the target and a sample is taken from each strata so that the rare target class will be more represented in the sample. The model is then built on this biased sample. The effects of the input variables on the target are often estimated with more precision with the choice-based sample even when a smaller overall sample size is taken, compared to a random sample. The results usually must be adjusted to correct for the oversampling.

Probability Proportional to Size Sampling

In some cases the sample designer has access to an "auxiliary variable" or "size measure", believed to be correlated to the variable of interest, for each element in the population. This data can be used to improve accuracy in sample design. One option is to use the auxiliary variable as a basis for stratification, as discussed above.

Another option is probability-proportional-to-size ('PPS') sampling, in which the selection probability for each element is set to be proportional to its size measure, up to a maximum of 1. In a simple PPS design, these selection probabilities can then be used as the basis for Poisson sampling. However, this has the drawbacks of variable sample size, and different portions of the population may still be over- or under-represented due to chance variation in selections. To address this problem, PPS may be combined with a systematic approach.

Example: Suppose we have six schools with populations of 150, 180, 200, 220, 260, and 490 students respectively (total 1500 students), and we want to use student population as the basis for a PPS sample of size three. To do this, we could allocate the first school numbers 1 to 150, the second school 151 to 330 (= 150 + 180), the third school 331 to 530, and so on to the last school (1011 to 1500). We then generate a random start between 1 and 500 (equal to 1500/3) and count through the school populations by multiples of 500. If our random start was 137, we would select the schools which have been allocated numbers 137, 637, and 1137, i.e. the first, fourth, and sixth schools.

The PPS approach can improve accuracy for a given sample size by concentrating sample on large elements that have the greatest impact on population estimates. PPS sampling is commonly used for surveys of businesses, where element size varies greatly and auxiliary information is often available for instance, a survey attempting to measure the number of guest-nights spent in hotels might use each hotel's number of rooms as an auxiliary variable. In some cases, an older measurement of the variable of interest can be used as an auxiliary variable when attempting to produce more current estimates.

Cluster Sampling

Sometimes it is cheaper to 'cluster' the sample in some way e.g. by selecting respondents from certain areas only, or certain time-periods only.

Cluster sampling is an example of 'two-stage sampling' or 'multistage sampling': in the first stage a sample of areas is chosen; in the second stage a sample of respondents *within* those areas is selected.

This can reduce travel and other administrative costs. It also means that one does not need a sampling frame listing all elements in the target population. Instead, clusters can be chosen from a cluster-level frame, with an element-level frame created only for the selected clusters. Cluster sampling generally increases the variability of sample estimates above that of simple random sampling, depending on how the clusters differ between themselves, as compared with the within-cluster variation.

Nevertheless, some of the disadvantages of cluster sampling are the reliance of sample estimate precision on the actual clusters chosen. If clusters chosen are biased in a certain way, inferences drawn about population parameters from these sample estimates will be far off from being accurate.

Multistage sampling Multistage sampling is a complex form of cluster sampling in which two or more levels of units are embedded one in the other. The first stage consists of constructing the clusters that will be used to sample from. In the second stage, a sample of primary units is randomly selected from each cluster (rather than using all units contained in all selected clusters). In following stages, in each of those selected clusters, additional samples of units are selected, and so on. All ultimate units (individuals, for instance) selected at the last step of this procedure are then surveyed.

This technique, thus, is essentially the process of taking random samples of preceding random samples. It is not as effective as true random sampling, but it probably solves more of the problems inherent to random sampling. Moreover, It is an effective strategy because it banks on multiple randomisations. As such, it is extremely useful.

Multistage sampling is used frequently when a complete list of all members of the population does not exist and is inappropriate. Moreover, by avoiding the use of all sample units in all selected clusters, multistage sampling avoids the large, and perhaps unnecessary, costs associated traditional cluster sampling.

Matched Random Sampling

A method of assigning participants to groups in which pairs of participants are first matched on some characteristic and then individually assigned randomly to groups.

The procedure for matched random sampling can be briefed with the following contexts:

1. Two samples in which the members are clearly paired, or are matched explicitly by the researcher. For example, IQ measurements or pairs of identical twins.
2. Those samples in which the same attribute, or variable, is measured twice on each subject, under different circumstances. Commonly called repeated measures. Examples include the times of a group of athletes for 1500m before and after a week of special training; the milk yields of cows before and after being fed a particular diet.

Quota Sampling

In quota sampling, the population is first segmented into mutually exclusive subgroups, just as in stratified sampling. Then judgment is used to select the subjects or units from each segment based on a specified proportion. For example, an interviewer may be told to sample 200 females and 300 males between the age of 45 and 60.

It is this second step which makes the technique one of nonprobability sampling. In quota sampling the selection of the sample is non-random. For example interviewers might be tempted to interview those who look most helpful. The problem is that these samples may be biased because not everyone gets a chance of selection. This random element is its greatest weakness and quota versus probability has been a matter of controversy for many years

Convenience Sampling

Convenience sampling (sometimes known as grab or opportunity sampling) is a type of nonprobability sampling which involves the sample being drawn from that part of the population which is close to hand. That is, a sample population selected because it is readily available and convenient. The researcher using such a sample cannot scientifically make generalizations about the total population from this sample because it would not be representative enough. For example, if the interviewer was to conduct such a survey at a shopping centre early in the morning on a given day, the people that he/she could interview would be limited to those given there at that given time, which would not represent the views of other members of society in such an area, if the survey was to be conducted at different times of day and several times per week. This type of sampling is most useful for pilot testing. Several important considerations for researchers using convenience samples include:

1. Are there controls within the research design or experiment which can serve to lessen the impact of a non-random, convenience sample whereby ensuring the results will be more representative of the population?
2. Is there good reason to believe that a particular convenience sample would or should respond or behave differently than a random sample from the same population?
3. Is the question being asked by the research one that can adequately be answered using a convenience sample?

In social science research, snowball sampling is a similar technique, where existing study subjects are used to recruit more subjects into the sample.

Line-intercept Sampling

Line-intercept sampling is a method of sampling elements in a region whereby an element is sampled if a chosen line segment, called a "transect", intersects the element.

Panel Sampling

Panel sampling is the method of first selecting a group of participants through a random sampling method and then asking that group for the same information again several times over a period of time. Therefore, each participant is given the same survey or interview at two or more time points; each period of data collection is called a "wave". This sampling methodology is often chosen for large scale or nationwide studies in order to gauge changes in the population with regard to any number of variables from chronic illness to job stress to weekly food expenditures. Panel sampling can also be used to inform researchers about within-person health changes due to age or help explain changes in continuous dependent variables such as spousal interaction. There have been several proposed methods of analysing panel sample data, including MANOVA, growth curves, and structural equation modelling with lagged effects. For a more thorough look at analytical techniques for panel data.

Event Sampling Methodology

Event sampling methodology (ESM) is a new form of sampling method that allows researchers to study ongoing experiences and events that vary across and within days in its naturally-occurring environment. Because of the frequent sampling of events inherent in ESM, it enables researchers to measure the typology of activity and detect the temporal and dynamic fluctuations of work experiences. Popularity of ESM as a new form of research design increased over the recent years because it addresses the shortcomings of cross-sectional research, where once unable to, researchers can now detect intra-individual variances across time. In ESM, participants are asked to record their experiences and perceptions in a paper or electronic diary.

There are three types of ESM:

1. *Signal contingent*: random beeping notifies participants to record data. The advantage of this type of ESM is minimization of recall bias.
2. *Event contingent*: records data when certain events occur
3. *Interval contingent*: records data according to the passing of a certain period of time

ESM has several disadvantages. One of the disadvantages of ESM is it can sometimes be perceived as invasive and intrusive by participants. ESM also leads to possible self-selection bias. It may be that only certain types of individuals are willing to participate in this type of study creating a non-random sample. Another concern is related to participant cooperation. Participants may not be actually fill out their diaries at the specified times. Furthermore, ESM may substantively change the phenomenon being studied. Reactivity or priming effects may occur, such that repeated measurement may cause changes in the participants' experiences. This method of sampling data is also highly vulnerable to common method variance.

Further, it is important to think about whether or not an appropriate dependent variable is being used in an ESM design. For example, it might be logical to use ESM in order to answer research questions which involve dependent variables with a great deal of variation throughout the day. Thus, variables such as change in mood, change in stress level, or the immediate impact of particular events may be best studied using ESM methodology. However, it is not likely that utilizing ESM will yield meaningful predictions when measuring someone performing a repetitive task throughout the day or when dependent variables are long-term in nature.

Replacement of Selected Units

Sampling schemes may be *without replacement* (WOR—no element can be selected more than once in the same sample) or *with replacement* (WR—an element may appear multiple times in the one sample). For example, if we catch fish, measure them, and immediately return them to the water before continuing with the sample, this is a WR design, because we might end up catching and measuring the same fish more than once. However, if we do not return the fish to the water (e.g. if we eat the fish), this becomes a WOR design.

Sample Size

Formulas, tables, and power function charts are well known approaches to determine sample size.

Formulas

Where the frame and population are identical, statistical theory yields exact recommendations on sample size. However, where it is not straightforward to define a frame representative of the population, it is more important to understand the cause system of which the population are outcomes and to ensure that all sources of variation are embraced in the frame. Large number of observations are of no value if major sources of variation are neglected in the study. In other words, it is taking a sample group that matches the survey category and is easy to survey. Bartlett, Kotrlik, and Higgins published a paper titled *Organizational Research: Determining Appropriate Sample Size* in Survey Research Information Technology, Learning, and Performance Journal that provides an explanation of Cochran's formulas. A discussion and illustration of sample size formulas, including the formula for adjusting the sample size for smaller populations, is included. A table is provided that can be used to select the sample size for a research problem based on three alpha levels and a set error rate.

Steps for Using Sample Size Tables

1. Postulate the effect size of interest, a, and a.
2. Check sample size table
   a. Select the table corresponding to the selected á
   b. Locate the row corresponding to the desired power
   c. Locate the column corresponding to the estimated effect size.
   d. The intersection of the column and row is the minimum sample size required.

Sampling and Data Collection

Good data collection involves:

1. Following the defined sampling process
2. Keeping the data in time order
3. Noting comments and other contextual events
4. Recording non-responses

Most sampling books and papers written by non-statisticians focus only in the data collection aspect, which is just a small though important part of the sampling process.

Errors in Sample Surveys

Survey results are typically subject to some error. Total errors can be classified into sampling errors and non-sampling errors. The term "error" here includes systematic biases as well as random errors.

Sampling Errors and Biases

Sampling errors and biases are induced by the sample design. They include:

1. *Selection bias*: When the true selection probabilities differ from those assumed in calculating the results.
2. *Random sampling error*: Random variation in the results due to the elements in the sample being selected at random.

Non-sampling Error

Non-sampling errors are caused by other problems in data collection and processing. They include:

1. *Overcoverage*: Inclusion of data from outside of the population.
2. *Undercoverage*: Sampling frame does not include elements in the population.
3. *Measurement error*: E.g. when respondents misunderstand a question, or find it difficult to answer.

4. *Processing error*: Mistakes in data coding.
5. *Non-response*: Failure to obtain complete data from all selected individuals.

After sampling, a review should be held of the exact process followed in sampling, rather than that intended, in order to study any effects that any divergences might have on subsequent analysis. A particular problem is that of *non-response*. Two major types of nonresponse exist: unit nonresponse (referring to lack of completion of any part of the survey) and item nonresponse (submission or participation in survey but failing to complete one or more components/questions of the survey). In survey sampling, many of the individuals identified as part of the sample may be unwilling to participate, not have the time to participate (opportunity cost), or survey administrators may not have been able to contact them. In this case, there is a risk of differences, between respondents and nonrespondents, leading to biased estimates of population parameters. This is often addressed by improving survey design, offering incentives, and conducting follow-up studies which make a repeated attempt to contact the unresponsive and to characterize their similarities and differences with the rest of the frame. The effects can also be mitigated by weighting the data when population benchmarks are available or by imputing data based on answers to other questions.

Nonresponse is particularly a problem in internet sampling. Reasons for this problem include improperly designed surveys, over-surveying (or survey fatigue), and the fact that potential participants hold multiple e-mail addresses, which they don't use anymore or don't check regularly. Web-based surveys also tend to demonstrate nonresponse bias; for example, studies have shown that females and those from a white/Caucasian background are more likely to respond than their counterparts.

Survey Weights

In many situations the sample fraction may be varied by stratum and data will have to be weighted to correctly represent the population. Thus for example, a simple random sample of individuals in the United Kingdom might include some in remote Scottish islands who would be inordinately expensive to sample. A cheaper method would be to use a stratified sample with urban and rural strata. The rural sample could be under-represented in the sample, but weighted up appropriately in the analysis to compensate.

More generally, data should usually be weighted if the sample design does not give each individual an equal chance of being selected. For instance, when households have equal selection probabilities but one person is interviewed from within each household, this gives people from large households a smaller chance of being interviewed. This can be accounted for using survey weights. Similarly, households with more than one telephone line have a greater chance of being selected in a random digit dialling sample, and weights can adjust for this.

Weights can also serve other purposes, such as helping to correct for non-response.

History

Random sampling by using lots is an old idea, mentioned several times in the Bible. In 1786 Pierre Simon Laplace estimated the population of France by using a sample, along with ratio estimator. He also computed probabilistic estimates of the error. These were not expressed as modern confidence intervals but as the sample size that would be needed to achieve a particular upper bound on the sampling error with probability 1000/1001. His estimates used Bayes' theorem with a uniform prior probability and it assumed his sample was random. The theory of small-sample statistics developed by William Sealy Gossett put the subject on a more rigorous basis in the 20th century. However, the importance of random sampling was not universally appreciated and in the USA the 1936 *Literary Digest* prediction of a Republican win in the presidential election went badly awry, due to severe bias. More than two million people responded to the study with their names obtained through magazine subscription lists and telephone directories. It was not appreciated that these lists were heavily biased towards Republicans and the resulting sample, though very large, was deeply flawed.

5

Significance of Statistics in Social Research

As with any domain, the ease with which anomalous phenomena can be studied using traditional scientific methods depends on the type of purported evidence for the phenomena. The evidence tends to fall into two categories. In one category, including areas such as alien abductions and reincarnation, evidence is completely anecdotal and it is not possible to design situations that invite these phenomena to occur on demand. The second category includes topics that can be invited to occur on demand. This category includes purported abilities such as telepathy, clairvoyance or precognition, the possibility of distant healing through prayer, and so on. The common theme is that the phenomena can be requested in randomised controlled experiments, and the results can be measured and compared to what would be expected by chance alone. It is this type of situation for which statistical methods are generally applicable.

Throughout this chapter the terms "statistics" and "statistical methods" are used in the broad context of an academic subject area including the design, data collection, and analysis of studies involving randomisation or natural variability. A standard definition is:

> Statistics is a collection of procedures and principles for gaining and processing information in order to make decisions when faced with uncertainty.

The scientific process is generally considered to occur in two phases, one of discovery and one of justification. Statistical methods most often play an important role in the discovery phase. These methods are an intermediate step between the anecdotal evidence or theoretical speculations that lead to discovery research, and the justification phase of the research process in which elaborated theories and comprehensive understanding are established.

Whether in medicine, parapsychology or some other field, most discovery research is initiated because anecdotal evidence, theory based on previous research, or analogies from other domains suggest a possible relationship or effect. For instance, there have been reports of precognitive visions and dreams throughout recorded history, so researchers are attempting to reproduce the precognitive effect in the laboratory. In medicine, theory would suggest that aspirin and similar drugs might help reduce the chances of a heart attack because they tend to thin the blood. So researchers have designed randomised controlled experiments to compare the use of aspirin-type drugs to placebos for reducing the occurrence of vascular disease. Prior research on cortical pathways in the brain led psychologists to predict that listening to classical music might enhance spatial-temporal reasoning. So they designed a randomised experiment to test that hypothesis, and indeed found better spatial abilities in participants after listening to Mozart than after silence or listening to a relaxation tape. The "cause" of the effect is not clear. Scientists are continuing the discovery phase by investigating the impact of different types of musical experience on spatial reasoning in order to formulate more specific theories.

In each case, the justification phase of research would follow only after reasonable theories had been formulated based on the statistical results of the discovery phase. For example, the discovery phase for the reduction in heart attacks after taking aspirin has included a variety of studies using different drug formulations and doses, various vascular diseases and levels of health, and so on. The justification phase will come after enough evidence has been accumulated to speculate about physiological causes, and will be based mainly on biochemical knowledge rather than statistical methods. The discovery phase of research in precognition might lead to modified theories, which could then be solidified in the justification phase. This distinction illustrates an important point about statistical methods, which is that they cannot be used to prove anything definitively. There is always an element of uncertainty in results based on statistical methods. These results can suggest causal pathways, but cannot verify them conclusively.

Use of Statistics

There seems to be a misconception among some scientists about the role of statistical methods in science, and specifically about the situations for which statistical methods are most useful. That misconception has sometimes been used in an attempt to negate the evidence for anomalous phenomena. For example, Hyman, in his review of the U.S. government's remote viewing program, wrote:

> Only parapsychology claims to be a science on the basis of phenomena whose presence can be detected only by rejecting a null hypothesis

It is the role of statistics to identify and quantify important effects and relationships before any explanation has been found, and one of the most common means for doing so is to use empirical data to reject a "null hypothesis" that there is no relationship or no effect. There are countless scientific advances that would not have been possible without the use of such statistical methods. Typically, these advances are made in the discovery phase when anecdotal evidence or scientific theory suggests that a relationship or effect might exist, and studies are designed to test the extent to which that can be verified statistically. Only after such studies have indicated that there is almost certainly a relationship do scientists begin to search for a cause or justification. For instance, the link between smoking and lung cancer was first explored when an astute physician noticed that his lung cancer patients tended to be smokers. Numerous studies were then done to explore the link between smoking behaviour and subsequent lung cancer, and a statistical relationship was established long before a causal mechanism was determined.

Statistical methods are only useful in situations for which exact replication is not possible. Unlike some experimental domains in the physical sciences, studies relying on statistical methods involve natural variability in the system, and thus the results cannot be precisely predicted or repeated from one experiment to the next. Even if there is a physiological explanation for the results, natural variability in humans or other systems create natural variability in outcomes. For instance, a particular drug may lower blood pressure for known reasons, but it will not lower everyone's blood pressure by the same amount, or even have the exact same effect every day on any given individual. Statistical methods are designed to measure and incorporate natural variability among individuals to determine what relationships or trends hold for the aggregate or on average. Here are some of the kinds of situations for which statistical methods are or are not useful:

1. They are clearly not needed to determine a relationship that holds every time, such as the blinking response to a wisp of air in the eye, or the fact that a book will drop if you release it in midair.

2. They are not needed once a causal mechanism is understood even if a relationship does not hold every time, such as trying to determine whether or not pollen causes hay fever or sex causes pregnancy.
3. They are useful to indicate the *existence* of a relationship or effect that does not occur every time or in every individual and that does not already have a causal explanation. For instance, the use of aspirin to reduce the risk of heart attacks was established statistically over ten years ago, but it is only recently that causal explanations have been explored.
4. They are useful to establish the average *magnitude* of effects and relationships that do not occur every time. One simple example is the batting average for a baseball player. Finding the probability of hitting a ball or a home run is akin to finding the probability of a "hit" in a remote viewing experiment. In each case "hits" happen a certain proportion of the time, but no one can predict in advance when they will occur.

In summary, whereas sometimes scientific research starts with a causal theory and proceeds to verify it with data, statistical methods are most useful in situations where the process happens in reverse. There may be speculation about possible relationships stemming from observations or theories, but the focus is on learning from data. Quite commonly, a relationship is established with near certainty based on large amounts of data (such as the relationship between smoking and lung cancer) before a causal mechanism is determined or even explored.

Statistical Evidence

There are a number of statistical methods that are used to infer the existence of relationships and estimate their strength. The two most commonly used methods for single studies are hypothesis testing and confidence intervals.

These two inferential methods for single studies have been standard practice for many decades. In recent years there has been a trend towards using statistical methods to examine the accumulated evidence across many studies on the same topic. In the past, reviews of a collection of studies were subjective and qualitative but the recent trend is towards quantitative methods, which collectively are called "meta-analysis." There is some debate about whether or not meta-analysis provides better evidence than one large well-implemented study on a topic but there is no doubt that meta-analysis can provide a more complete picture than individual small studies.

Replication is at the heart of any science relying on experimental evidence because any single study potentially could have unrecognized flaws that produce spurious results. (Consider, for example, attempted replications of cold fusion.) However, the meaning of replication is different for studies on living systems, requiring inferential statistical methods, than it is for studies that are supposed to have fixed and predictable outcomes. Variability among individuals can mask real differences or relationships that hold for the aggregate, and will result in somewhat different outcomes even when a study is replicated under similar conditions. If the natural variability is small and the relationship or difference is strong then similar results should emerge from each study. But when the variability is large, the relationship is weak or the effect is rare, the variability may mask the relationship in all but very large studies. For instance, because lung cancer rates are low for both smokers and nonsmokers, we would not expect to see smokers develop more lung cancer than nonsmokers in every small group of both, even though lung cancer rates for smokers are at least nine times what they are for nonsmokers. It is only when examining the trend across studies (or conducting one very large study) that the higher lung cancer rates in smokers would become obvious. Before considering some simple methods used to examine evidence through combining studies, a brief overview of standard inferential statistics is provided. It is important to understand these methods in order to understand the extensions of them used in meta-analysis.

Hypothesis Testing

For many decades hypothesis testing was the core of statistical methodology. If the results of the hypothesis test used in a study were "statistically significant" the study was determined to be a success. Unfortunately, if the results were not statistically significant the study was often deemed a failure, and the effect under consideration was thought not to exist. Before explaining why that reasoning is flawed, a brief review of hypothesis testing is required. The procedure follows four basic steps:

1. Establish two competing hypotheses about one or more factors:
    a. *Null Hypothesis:* There is no relationship, no difference, no effect, nothing of interest, only chance results.
    b. *Alternative Hypothesis:* There is a relationship, difference or effect of interest. It is obviously the goal of most research studies to conclude that the alternative hypothesis is true, since the null hypothesis represents the status quo that would be accepted without any new knowledge or data.
2. Collect data from a sample of individuals, representative of the larger population about which the hypotheses have been proposed.
3. Use the data to calculate a "test statistic" and resulting "*p*-value." The *p*value is one of the most misunderstood concepts in statistics. It is calculated by *assuming* that

the null hypothesis is true, then finding the probability of observing data as contrary to it as that which has just been observed, or more so. It does *not* represent the probability that the null hypothesis is actually true given the observed data, something it is commonly misinterpreted to mean. It only represents how unlikely the observed data or something more contrary to the null hypothesis would be if the null hypothesis were actually true.

4. Use the *p*-value to make a conclusion. Though perhaps not wise in all cases, it is standard practice to conclude that the null hypothesis is false ("reject the null hypothesis") and the alternative is true ("accept the alternative hypothesis") if the *p*-value is 0.05 or less. The notation for this cutoff value in general is a so the standard practice is to reject the null hypothesis if the *p*-value is less than a. Otherwise, the proper conclusion is simply that the null hypothesis cannot be rejected based on the evidence presented.

It is rarely prudent to actually "accept" the null hypothesis. The reasoning behind this imbalance between the two hypotheses is based on the types of erroneous conclusions that could be made. The selected value a by definition, provides control over the probability of erroneously rejecting the null hypothesis when it is true (called a type 1 error) and thus declaring an effect exists when it does not. As mentioned, this probability is usually set at 0.05. There is no similar control over the probability of making the mistake of accepting the null hypothesis when it is false, and thus declaring that there is no effect when in fact there is. This mistake is called a type 2 error. It is denoted by b, which is an unknowable value because it depends on the unknown magnitude of the real effect. (If we knew that magnitude we would not be testing it.)

The probability that the null hypothesis is rejected and thus the alternative hypothesis is accepted is called the *power* of a test. When the null hypothesis is true, the power of the test is the probability of a type 1 error (a), and is designated by the researcher (usually at 0.05). The more interesting situation is when the alternative hypothesis is true, in which case the power is the probability of correctly detecting that fact and concluding that there is an effect or relationship. Numerically in this case the power is 1- b because b represents the probability of *not* detecting a real effect when it exists. There is a trade-off between making the two types of errors that is reflected by the choice of a. Larger values of a make it easier to reject the null hypothesis, thus increasing the power to detect a real relationship. But the trade-off is that larger a values mean it is easier to conclude a relationship exists in situations where it does not.

The power of a test is also closely tied to the sample size. A very large sample provides a test powerful enough to reject the null hypothesis even when the effect is very small. In contrast, a small sample has very little power to reject the null hypothesis even if the effect is moderately large. Thus, the way to enhance the power of a test without having to increase the probability of a type 1 error is to increase the amount of data collected.

For example, a very large study conducted by the Steering Committee of the Physicians' Health Study Research Group compared heart attack rates for 22,071 male physicians who were randomly assigned to take either aspirin or a placebo tablet every other day for five years. The null hypothesis was that taking aspirin has no more effect on heart attack rates than taking a placebo. The alternative hypothesis was that taking aspirin does have an impact on heart attack rates.

There were 17.13 heart attacks per 1000 men in the group taking the placebo, but only 9.42 heart attacks per 1000 men in the group taking aspirin. The *p*value for this study was extremely small, indicating that if there really is no impact from taking aspirin, a difference as large as the one observed in this study (or larger) would be extremely unlikely to occur in a study with 22,071 participants. In fact the study was terminated earlier than planned because the results were so striking. (Note that stopping a study early is *statistically not justified because it could be stopped* at a time favourable to the alternative hypothesis. This "optional stopping" was one basis for criticism of early parapsychological experiments. However, ethical issues sometimes outweigh statistical issues in medical trials.)

The estimated "odds ratio" from the study, giving the odds of having a heart attack when taking a placebo compared with when taking aspirin, is 17.13/9.42 = 1.8. (Technically, this is the "relative risk" and the odds ratio is slightly more complicated. However, they are numerically very similar for events with low probability like that of having a heart attack.) At 1.8, the odds of having a heart attack were almost double when taking a placebo compared with when taking aspirin. This is obviously a striking effect with important medical applications. However, suppose that only one-tenth as many physicians, or about 2200, had participated in the study but that the heart attack rates per 1000 had still been about 17 for the placebo group and 9 for the aspirin group. Although the odds ratio from the data would still indicate that almost twice as many men had heart attacks when taking a placebo compared with when taking aspirin, the evidence would not have been convincing at all using traditional reasoning. The *p*-value would have been about 0.09, which is generally not considered small enough to reject the null hypothesis. Notice that it would not be reasonable to conclude that there is *no* impact from taking aspirin. The justifiable conclusion would be that there is not enough evidence in this study to conclude whether or not aspirin has an impact on heart attack rates, even though the numbers are suggestive. The *p*-value demonstrates that chance alone would result in differences this large or larger about 9% of the time based on samples of 2200.

This example illustrates one of the problems associated with methods commonly used to do qualitative reviews of groups of studies. Often, those reviews simply count how many studies achieved statistically significant results (rejected the null hypothesis), and discount any study that did not do so. Or, worse, often such reviews count these "unsuccessful" studies as evidence that no relationship or effect exists. This technique, called "vote counting" will lead to erroneous conclusions particularly when a series of small studies have been conducted, each of which had very low power to detect a real effect. At the very least, such reviews should consider the role of power when interpreting the results.

Confidence Intervals

One of the disadvantages of hypothesis testing is that the results do not provide a measure of the magnitude of the relationship or effect. For instance, in the example of the impact of aspirin on heart attack rates, the results of the hypothesis test would only provide information that the *p*-value is almost zero. The heart attack rates for the two groups and the odds ratio would not be provided as part of the standard information accompanying the test. The other major method of statistical inference is to construct a "confidence interval." The interval is computed from sample data that are supposed to be representative of a larger population. There is a numerical measure in the population about which information is desired, such as the odds ratio for heart attack rates if men were to take a placebo *vs.* if they were to take aspirin. The measure has been computed for the sample, but the sample value will obviously not equal the desired population value exactly. The confidence interval provides a range of numbers that almost certainly does cover the unknown population value. As would be expected, the larger the number of participants in the sample, the shorter the resulting interval will be. A "confidence level," typically 95% or 99% accompanies the interval, indicating how likely it is that it actually covers the unknown population value.

For example, in the study measuring heart attack rates, there was an observed odds ratio of about 1.8, meaning that the rate of heart attacks for those taking a placebo was about 1.8 times what it was for those taking aspirin. A 95% confidence interval for the odds ratio ranges from 1.63 to 2.59, indicating that if all men similar to these were to take a placebo, the heart attack rate could be as little as 1.63 times what it would be if they had taken aspirin instead, or it could be as high as 2.59. The likelihood that the interval covers the true, unknowable odds ratio is about 95%. The interval could also be presented in the other direction, giving a 95% confidence interval for the reduced odds of getting a heart attack after taking aspirin, ranging from 0.39 to 0.61.

Notice that the information provided by the confidence interval is more interesting than the results of the hypothesis test, because the interval provides a numerical assessment of *how much* the risk of heart attack is reduced by taking aspirin. Individuals can then decide if the reduced risk is worth the effort, expense and possible side effects of taking aspirin. Further, because the range of values is completely above one, the confidence interval provides evidence that there really is a beneficial impact of taking aspirin. In other words, the confidence interval can be used to reject the null hypothesis that there is no difference in heart attack rates after taking aspirin *vs.* a placebo. In general, in situations involving a single population parameter, this simple method can be used for determining whether or not the result is "statistically significant" based on the confidence interval. If the value given in the null hypothesis is covered by the computed 95% confidence interval, then the null hypothesis would not be rejected using the standard criterion of 0.05. If the null value is not in the interval, the null hypothesis is rejected.

As with hypothesis testing, if the sample had been much smaller, the confidence interval results would have been less precise. For instance, if there had been one-tenth as many men in this study, but similar heart attack rates, the 95% confidence interval for the difference would have ranged from a *reverse* difference in which the odds of a heart attack after placebo were only 0.9 times what they were with aspirin, to a beneficial odds of 3.9 times the rate after placebo than after aspirin. The impact of taking aspirin would have been inconclusive, just as it was in this hypothetical situation using hypothesis testing. Even though most of the interval is in the direction indicating that aspirin reduces the heart attack rate, the interval includes values indicating no effect or a negative effect, and those possibilities cannot be ruled out.

In summary, the results of a single study can sometimes be used to conclude that a relationship or effect is "statistically significant" and to estimate its magnitude. However, if the results of one study are not "statistically significant," it does not mean that there is no relationship or effect in the population, especially if the sample size for the study was small. Further, no single study can provide conclusive evidence for a relationship or effect. It is only through replication of the direction and magnitude of an effect across studies that we can determine whether a relationship or effect has been statistically demonstrated.

Combining Evidence

It has already been noted that studies in which statistical methods are most useful are those involving measurements with natural variability and lack of perfect replication. It is also the case that most studies that use statistical methods involve relationships or effects that are not obvious to the naked eye, and thus that are not strong enough to be confirmed without large amounts of data. Strong relationships that are clearly visible have generally been tested and confirmed by now. For instance, long ago humans determined what substances were poisonous, but only recently have we begun to identify and confirm that eating certain foods can alter our chances of getting various diseases. Since most studies currently conducted involve these smaller effects, the power of these studies to detect real relationships is low unless they amass large amounts of data. Therefore, in many cases it is only by combining data across studies that enough evidence can be accumulated to make conclusions.

Meta-Analysis

Meta-analysis is a collection of techniques for quantitatively combining similar studies. Often the subject of controversy, but two are most relevant. First, by combining a large number of small studies all designed to measure the same thing, there begins to be enough data to reach a conclusion that the individual studies were not large enough to justify. Second, by combining studies that use slightly different procedures, treatments, participants, and so on, conclusions can be made about how results are the same or different when these factors are changed.

Almost all meta-analyses have a common fundamental plan. The first step is to identify an effect or relationship of interest and summarize it in the form of a population parameter. A number of studies designed to measure this effect are then identified, for which the outcome of each study can be quantified as the sample version of the parameter of interest. These sample statistics are then evaluated by comparing them to what would be expected by chance if there were no effect or relationship, and by determining whether or not they remain consistent when other factors change.

For instance, in studies of remote viewing, the population effect of interest is whether or not remote viewing works better than would be expected by chance. This effect is quantified as the probability that a judge would be able to pick the correct target from a set of four (or five) possibilities, based on the response of the remote viewer. Studies in which judges were actually given this task are collected, and the actual proportion of sessions for which the judge picked the correct target is recorded for each study, as the sample statistic of interest. These can then be compared to the chance probability of ¼ (if there were four choices), and can also be grouped and compared based on whether targets were pictures *vs.* actual locations or events, and so on. Thus, from a number of small inconclusive studies, conclusions can be reached by weighing the contribution of each study appropriately. Sometimes studies are weighted according to how large they were, and sometimes they are weighted based on how well they were conducted.

There are many decisions to be made when conducting a meta-analysis, such as whether to include only peer-reviewed studies, whether to combine data across conditions, and so on. Thus two meta-analyses of the same subject area could easily reach different conclusions. The more similar are the studies being combined, and the more careful one is to identify all appropriate studies, the more reliable are the results of a meta-analysis. Like most statistical procedures, meta-analyses can be done well or poorly, and the results must be interpreted accordingly. One of the simplest and most informative tools that can be used in meta analysis is to construct a graph depicting confidence intervals for the specified parameter for each of the studies. If the studies are similar, the results can be combined into a single confidence interval as well. We illustrate this procedure for a medical example and then for an example from parapsychology.

A Classic Example: Antiplatelets and Vascular Disease

A good example of the graphical display of confidence intervals is provided by Mann in a news story about meta-analysis in *Science* magazine. The original meta-analysis appeared in the *British Medical Journal*. The analysis combines the results of 25 clinical studies to determine whether or not there is a relationship between vascular disease (such as heart attacks and strokes) and antiplatelet agents such as aspirin for people who had already had an incident. The relationship was measured using the odds ratio for having a heart attack or stroke given that one is taking an antiplatelet agent compared with taking a placebo. If the antiplatelet drugs have no effect, the odds ratio should be about 1.0. An odds ratio below 1.0 indicates that the drugs have a beneficial effect, while an odds ratio above 1.0 indicates a detrimental effect.

The studies are divided into three types depending on whether they were treating stroke patients (cerebrovascular), heart attack patients (myocardial infarction), or patients with angina pain. After each set of studies a 95% confidence interval is presented for the combined results of that type. Finally, at the bottom of the graph, a 95% confidence interval is shown for the combined results of all 25 studies. If the results of the three types of studies had been very different, it would not have been advisable to combine them.

Notice that very few of the individual studies were "statistically significant" as illustrated by the fact that their confidence intervals cover the chance odds ratio of 1.0. A naive "vote-count" of the number of studies for which the null hypothesis (that antiplatelets have no effect) could be rejected, would appear as if there was little or no use for these drugs in preventing vascular disease reoccurrence. In contrast, the graphical analysis, originally presented by the Antiplatelet Trialists' Collaboration, makes it strikingly obvious that these drugs do work to reduce the odds of a second attack. For the combined data the results indicate that the odds of a second occurrence are reduced by about 25% as a result of taking antiplatelets. In fact the conclusion from the abstract of the original article was clear:

Ganzfeld Studies

Meta-analysis has been used in a number of areas in parapsychology, but was first applied to ganzfeld studies, and an overview and history of this work serves as a good example of the use of meta-analysis in parapsychology. Ganzfeld studies were introduced to parapsychology in the early 1970s and were the subject of a debate in the early 1980s between parapsychologist Charles Honorton and skeptic Ray Hyman. The debate focused on meta-analysis of the ganzfeld studies that had been done up until that time. Much of the disagreement between Honorton and Hyman followed from their impressions of whether the studies contained too many flaws to allow conclusions to be drawn.

In a paper written shortly after the Hyman-Honorton exchange, Akers criticized the use of meta-analysis as a retrospective method in parapsychology. He noted that as long as there is disagreement about the quality of individual studies, there will be disagreement about meta-analyses of them. He suggested that agreement for protocols be reached *before* conducting future experiments:

> It is time for parapsychologists and their critics to shift attention away from past research and to focus on designs for future research. If experimental standards can be agreed upon before this research begins, much of the methodological controversy can be avoided

As a result of the debate Hyman and Honorton did just that. They agreed to a set of experimental conditions that would alleviate flaws identified in the original collection of studies. Honorton constructed a laboratory that met those conditions, called the Psychophysical Research Laboratories (PRL) and a new series of studies were conducted.

Detailed descriptions of ganzfeld studies are given elsewhere, and only a short description leading to the relevant statistics is given here. A typical study proceeds by asking a receiver to describe a target, usually being simultaneously viewed by a sender isolated from the receiver. The targets in the studies considered here were either photographs or short video segments. For each session the target is randomly selected from a larger set. Three "decoys," that could equally well have been randomly selected to be the target, are bundled with the target for judging purposes. The receiver completes the description and then is shown the four choices (actual target and three decoys), and is asked to identify the one most likely to have been the target based on the receiver's statements during the session. Of course the receivers and everyone in contact with them are blind as to the actual target at this stage.

By chance the receiver has a one in four chance of getting the correct answer, called a "direct hit." This probability is based on the random selection of the target, so it does not depend on what the receiver said. The population parameter of interest is thus the probability that the target selected during judging will be the correct target. The null hypothesis being tested is that this probability is indeed one in four. Presumably, if some sort of psychic functioning is operating, that probability is greater than the chance value of ¼. The sample statistic used to test this hypothesis is the percentage of direct hits over a series of sessions in a study. The number of sessions in these studies tends to be relatively small, so that it is common, as with the studies of antiplatelets and vascular disease, to find wide confidence intervals and inconclusive results.

Table 1 lists the original ganzfeld studies considered in the Hyman-Honorton debate, with a few caveats. First, studies with fewer than 20 sessions were combined, because the statistical method used to construct the confidence intervals is not appropriate with fewer than 20 sessions.

Table 1. Original Ganzfeld Studies

Study #	# of Sessions	# of Direct Hits	Proportion Hits	95% Confidence Interval
1	32	14	0.44	0.27 to 0.61
8	30	13	0.43	0.26 to 0.61
11	30	7	0.23	0.08 to 0.38
12	20	2	0.10	0.00 to 0.23
18	28	8	0.29	0.12 to 0.45
21	20	7	0.35	0.14 to 0.56
31	20	12	0.60	0.39 to 0.81
33	100	41	0.41	0.31 to 0.51
34	40	13	0.33	0.18 to 0.47
38	27	11	0.41	0.22 to 0.59
39	60	27	0.45	0.32 to 0.58
41	48	10	0.21	0.09 to 0.32
7,16,17,19	37	23	0.62	0.47 to 0.78
ALL	492	188	0.38	0.34 to 0.43

Second, studies by one experimenter were removed because they have been criticized as possibly being fraudulent. Inclusion of those studies would increase rather than decrease the strength of the results, so their removal makes it more difficult rather than easier to reject the null hypothesis. Finally, only studies that provided the number of direct hits based on four choices were included.

Table 1 includes the study number as assigned by Honorton, the number of sessions, number of direct hits, proportion of direct hits, and a 95% confidence interval for the estimated probability of a direct hit for the larger population the sessions in the study represent. Notice that five of the individual studies and the combined data from the small studies have confidence intervals entirely above chance, since the lower ends are still above 0.25. In other words, five of the studies were statistically significant and the remaining seven were not. However, the data from the combined studies clearly indicate that the probability of a direct hit is different from the chance value of 0.25. In fact, a 95% confidence interval extends from 0.34 to 0.43.

As mentioned, in the debate between Hyman and Honorton a number of potential flaws were identified that could have inflated the success rates in these studies for reasons other than the intended explanation that psychic functioning is possible. Further studies conducted by Honorton and others at PRL were supposed to have eliminated those flaws. Therefore, the results of those studies probably represent a more realistic assessment of the probability of achieving a hit in this ganzfeld procedure. There is a statistical paradigm that allows the preconceived biases of different assessors of information to be taken into account, called Bayesian statistical methods. Matthews has recently argued that this is a more appropriate way to assess results in parapsychology.

Repeatability Problem

Throughout the literature in parapsychology there is concern expressed about the "repeatability" of psi effects. For example, an entire conference was held in 1983 entitled

"The Repeatability Problem in Parapsychology". But much of the concern is unwarranted when the problem is considered from a correct statistical perspective. "Repeatability" has often been misinterpreted to mean that a statistically significant effect should be able to be produced in every experiment, and that psi has not occurred in an experiment unless the results are statistically significant. This interpretation ignores the issue of power. For example, suppose the true probability of a hit in each ganzfeld session is about 0.33, when 0.25 is expected by chance, and the usual criterion of 0.05 is used to define statistical significance. Then in an experiment with ten trials the power will be only 0.073, with 50 trials the power will be 0.27, and even with 100 trials the power will only be 0.54. In other words, ganzfeld experiments of the size typically conducted should not be "successful" very often, even if the true effect is that the target can be correctly guessed about a third of the time.

Table 2. PRL Ganzfeld Studies

Study #	# of Sessions	# of Direct Hits	Proportion Hits	95% Confidence Interval
1	22	8	0.36	0.16 to 0.56
2	9	3	0.33	0.03 to 0.63
3	35	10	0.29	0.14 to 0.44
101	50	12	0.24	0.13 to 0.35
102	50	18	0.36	0.23 to 0.49
103	50	15	0.30	0.17 to 0.43
104	50	18	0.36	0.23 to 0.49
105	6	4	0.67	0.29 to 1.00
201	7	3	0.43	0.06 to 0.80
301	50	15	0.30	0.17 to 0.43
302	25	16	0.64	0.45 to 0.83
ALL	355	122	0.34	0.29 to 0.39

A more appropriate definition of repeatability of an effect is that the estimated magnitude of the effect (odds ratio, hit rate, and so on) falls within the same range from one repetition of an experiment to the next. This definition leads to a different kind of problem that has been discussed in parapsychology, called the "decline effect". It is based on the observation that the magnitude of psi effects sometimes declines over time, possibly even reaching chance levels. One possible statistical explanation for this effect is "regression toward the mean," a common occurrence in statistical studies. If numerous research studies are done, then by chance some of them will have results that are much stronger than the true effect in the population. Those studies will be published and receive attention. When additional replications are done, chance dictates that the results will be unlikely to again reach those unusual extremes. Thus, the results that are initially higher than their population equivalent will both receive initial attention and fail to replicate in subsequent attempts. Other possible explanations include the fact that replications may be conducted by different researchers and they may introduce subtle or overt changes that dampen the effect. The decline is more commonly observed across researchers than within a single lab.

It may be that there is some other, more interesting explanation for the observed decline effect. In fact, it is not just in parapsychology that the decline effect has appeared. For instance, LeLorier *et al.*, compared 40 different medical treatments for which both a meta-analysis and a large, controlled randomised experiment were available. They found that the agreement between the results of the meta-analysis and the subsequent clinical trial was only moderate, although the results were usually at least in the same direction. For certain medical treatments, the effect in the large clinical trial represented a decline from what would be expected based on the meta-analysis. Further investigation of this phenomenon may provide interesting clues for mind-matter research.

Making Conclusions Based on Data

The use of statistical methods cannot provide conclusive proof of the physical reasons causing a relationship or an effect. For example, the antiplatelet and vascular disease studies were based on randomised controlled trials, which means that all factors other than the blind, random assignment of the antiplatelet or placebo should have been similar across groups. Because of this, we can reasonably infer that the reduction in the occurrence of vascular disease was actually *caused* by taking the antiplatelet. But that still tells us nothing about the physical process in the human body causing that relationship. The answer to that question is not going to be found in statistics. Similarly, meta-analyses of ganzfeld and other parapsychological experiments can lead to convincing evidence that the null hypothesis is not true, but cannot provide answers about the mechanism causing the non-chance results. That leads to an unresolvable debate about whether or not psi exists because the conclusion that psychic functioning is at work rests on ruling out all other possible explanations for the non-chance results. Skeptics are often convinced that an alternative explanation is more probable, even if they cannot identify what it is.

There are, however, some steps that can be taken to strengthen the evidence for one explanation over another. One technique is to look at studies that are similar in concept but have procedural differences, and see if the results are similar. Another is to look for consistent magnitude of effects when other factors are changed. For example, in establishing the causal relationship between smoking and lung cancer, researchers noted that a few decades after men started smoking in large numbers during World War I, they started having higher lung cancer rates. But women started smoking in large numbers during World War II, and indeed it was a few decades after that time that women started having higher lung cancer rates.

Acceptance of Statistical Results

The intent of this section was to show the extent to which statistical methods and meta-analysis can be used to establish relationships and effects as a precursor to finding causal explanations. Utilizing an example from the medical literature and an example from parapsychology illustrates the parallels across subject areas. In general, the steps used to establish relationships and effects can be summarized as follows:

1. A strong non-chance effect or relationship exists in the accumulated data, based on hypothesis testing, confidence intervals, or some other method.
2. The magnitude of the effect is similar across laboratories, or to the extent that it differs, reasonable explanations are found.
3. Consistent patterns are found when other factors are changed or manipulated, such as the observed reduction in lung cancer rates when number of cigarettes smoked is reduced.
4. Alternative explanations for the results are ruled out.

6

Social Research: Variables and Measurement

RESEARCH QUESTION

A research question states the aim of a research project in terms of cases of interest and the variables upon which these cases are thought to differ.

A few examples of research questions are:

1. 'What is the age distribution of the students in my statistics class?'
2. 'Is there a relationship between the health status of my statistics students and their sex?'
3. 'Is any relationship between the health status and the sex of students in my statistics class affected by the age of the students?'

We begin with very clear, precisely stated research questions such as these that will guide the way we conduct research and ensure that we do not end up with a jumble of information that does not create any real knowledge. We need a clear research question (or questions) in mind before undertaking statistical analysis to avoid the situation where huge amounts of data are gathered unnecessarily, and which do not lead to any meaningful results.A great deal of the confusion associated with statistical analysis actually arises from imprecision in the research questions that are meant to guide it. It is very difficult to select the *relevant* type of analysis to undertake, given the many *possible* analyses we could employ on a given set of data, if we are uncertain of our objectives. If we don't know why we are undertaking research in the first place, then it follows we will not know what to do with research data once we have gathered them. Conversely, if we are clear about the research question(s) we are addressing the statistical techniques to apply follow almost as a matter of course.

In this example, as in many others, the cases are individual people. It is important to bear in mind, however, that this is not always so. For example, if I am interested in retention rates for high schools in a particular area, the cases will be high schools. It is individual high schools that are 'stamped' with a label indicating their respective retention rate. In the research questions listed above, *all* the students in my statistics class constitute my target population (sometimes called a universe).

A population is the set of all possible cases of interest.

In determining our population of interest, we usually specify the *point in time* that defines the population – am I interested in my currently enrolled statistics students, or those who completed my course last year as well? We also specify, where relevant, the *geographic region* over which the population spreads.

For reasons we will investigate later, we may not be able to, or not want to, investigate the entire population of interest. Instead we may select only a subset of the population, and this subset is called a sample.

A sample is a set of cases that does not include every member of the population.

A variable is a condition or quality that can differ from one case to another. The opposite notion to a variable is a constant, which is simply a condition or quality that *does not* vary between cases. The number of cents in a United States dollar is a constant: every dollar note will always exchange for 100 cents. Most research, however, is devoted to understanding variables – whether (and why) a variable takes on certain traits for some cases and different traits for other cases.

Operationalisation of Variables

Where do variables come from? Why do we choose to study particular variables and not others? The choice of variables to investigate is affected by a number of complex factors, three of which we will emphasize here.

1. *Theoretical framework*: Theories are ways of interpreting the world and reconciling ourselves to it, and even though we may take for granted that a variable is worthy of research, it is in fact often a highly charged selection process that directs one's attention to it. We may be working within an established theoretical tradition that considers certain variables to be central to its worldview. For example, Marxists consider 'economic class' to be a variable worthy of research, whereas another theoretical perspective might consider this variable to be uninteresting. Analysing the world in terms of economic class means not analysing it in other ways, such as social groups. This is neither good nor bad: without a theory to order our perception of the world, research will often become a jumble of observations that do not tie together in a meaningful way. We should, though, acknowledge the theoretical preconceptions upon which our choice of variables is based.

2. *Pre-specified research agenda*: Sometimes the research question and the variables to be investigated are not determined by the researchers themselves. For example, a consultant may contract to undertake research that has terms of reference set in advance by the contracting body. In such a situation the person or people actually doing the research might have little scope to choose the variables to be investigated and how they are to be defined, since they are doing work for someone else.
3. *Curiosity-driven research*: Sometimes we might not have a clearly defined theoretical framework to operate in, nor clear directives from another person or body as to the key concepts to be investigated. Instead we want to investigate a variable purely on the basis of a hunch, a loosely conceived feeling that something useful or important might be revealed if we study a particular variable. This can be as important a reason for undertaking research as theoretical imperatives. Indeed, when moving into a whole new area of research, into which existing theories have not ventured, simple hunches can be fruitful motivations.

These three motivations are obviously not mutually exclusive. For example, even if the research agenda is specified by another person, that person will almost certainly be operating within some theoretical framework. Whatever the motivation, though, social inquiry will initially direct us to particular variables to be investigated. At this initial stage a variable is given a conceptual definition.

The conceptual definition (or nominal definition) of a variable uses literal terms to specify the qualities of a variable. A conceptual definition is much like a dictionary definition; it provides a working definition of the variable so that we have a general sense of what it 'means'.

The operational definition of a variable specifies the procedures and criteria for taking a measurement of that variable for individual cases. A statement such as 'a student's health status is measured by how far in meters they can walk without assistance in 15 minutes' provides one operational definition of health status.

The determination of an operational definition for a variable is a major, if not *the* major, source of disagreement in research. Any variable can usually be operationalised in many different ways, and no one of these definitions may be perfect. For example, operationalising health status by observing a student's ability to complete a walking task leaves out an individual's own subjective perception of how healthy they feel.

What criteria should be used in deciding whether a particular operational definition is adequate? In the technical literature this is known as the problem of construct validity. Ideally, we look for an operationalisation that will vary when the underlying variable we think it 'shadows' varies. A mercury thermometer is a good instrument for measuring changes in daily temperature because when the underlying variable (temperature) changes the means of measuring it (the height of the bar of mercury) also changes. If the thermometer is instead full of water rather than mercury, variations in daily temperature will not be matched by changes in the thermometer reading. Two days might actually be different in temperature, without this variation being 'picked up' by the instrument. Coming back to our example of health status, and relying on an operational definition that just measures walking distance covered in a certain time, we might record two people as being equally healthy, when in fact they differ. Imagine two people who each walk 2200 meters in 15 minutes, but one of these people cannot bend over to tie their shoelace because of a bad back. Clearly there is variation between the two people in terms of their health their state of wellbeing. But this variation will not be recorded if we rely solely on a measure of walking ability.

To illustrate further the 'slippage' that can occur in moving from a conceptual to an operational definition, consider the following example. A study is interested in people's 'criminality'. We may define criminality conceptually as 'non-sanctioned acts of violence against other members of society or their property'. How can a researcher identify the pattern of variation in this variable? A number of operational definitions could be employed:

1. Counting a person's number of criminal arrests from official records;
2. Calculating the amount of time a person has spent in jail;
3. Asking people whether they have committed crimes;
4. Recording a person's hair colour.

Clearly, it would be very hard to justify the last operationalisation as a valid one: it is not possible to say that if someone's level of criminality changed so too will their hair colour! The other operational definitions seem closer to the general concept of criminality, but each has its own problems: asking people if they have committed a crime may not be a perfect measure because people might not be truthful about such a touchy subject. Counting the number of times a person has been arrested is not perfect – two people may actually have the same level of criminality, yet one might have more recorded arrests because they are a member of a minority group that the police target for arrest. This operationalisation may thereby actually be measuring a different variable from the one intended: the biases of police rather than 'criminality'. Using any of these operational definitions to measure a person's criminality may not perfectly mirror the result we would get if we could 'know' their criminality. A number of factors affect the extent to which we can arrive at an operational definition of a variable that has high construct validity.

1. *The complexity of the concept*: Some variables are not very complex: a person's sex, for example, is determined by generally accepted physical attributes. However, most variables are rarely so straightforward. Health status, for example, has a number of dimensions. At a broad level we can differentiate between physical, mental, and emotional health; two people might be physically well, but one is an emotional wreck while the other is happy and contented. If we operationalise health status by looking solely at the *physical* dimension of its expression, important differences in this variable may not be observed. Indeed each of these broad dimensions of health status physical, mental, and emotional are conceptual variables in themselves, and raise problems of operationalisation of their own. If we take physical health as our focus, we still need to think about all of its particular forms of expression, such as the ability to walk, carry weight, percentage of body fat, etc.
2. *Availability of data*: We might have an operationalisation that seems to capture perfectly the underlying variable of interest. For example, we might think that number of arrests is a flawless way of 'observing' criminality. The researchers, though, may not be allowed, for privacy reasons, to review police records to compile the information. Clearly, a less than perfect operationalisation will have to be employed, simply because we cannot get our hands on the 'ideal' data.
3. *Cost and difficulty of obtaining data*: Say we were able to review police records and tally up the number of arrests. The cost in doing so, though, might be prohibitive, in terms of both time and money. Similarly, we might feel that a certain measure of water pollution is ideal for assessing river degradation, but

the need to employ an expert with sophisticated measuring equipment might bar this as an option, and instead a subjective judgment of water 'murkiness' might be preferred as a quick and easy measure.

4. *Ethics*: Is it right to go looking at the details of an individual's arrest record, simply to satisfy one's own research objectives? The police might permit it, and there might be plenty of time and money available, but does this justify looking at a document that was not intended to be part of a research project?

For these (and other) reasons a great deal of debate about the validity of research centres around this problem of operationalisation. In fact, many debates surrounding quantitative research are not actually about the methods of analysis or results of the research, but rather whether the variables have been 'correctly' defined and measured in the first place. Unless the operational criteria used to measure a variable are sensitive to the way the variable actually changes, they will generate misleading results.

Scales of Measurement

We have, in the course of discussing the operationalisation of variables, used the word 'measurement', since the purpose of deriving an operational definition is to allow us to take measurements of a variable.

Measurement (or observation) is the process of determining and recording which of the possible traits of a variable an individual case exhibits or possesses. The variable 'sex' has two **possible traits**, female and male, and measurement involves deciding into which of these two categories a given person falls. This set of categories that can possibly be assigned to individual cases makes up a scale of measurement. A scale of measurement specifies a range of scores (also called points on the scale) that can be assigned to cases during the process of measurement.

A discrete variable has a finite number of values. A continuous variable can vary in quantity by infinitesimally small degrees. For example, the sex of students is a discrete variable with only two possible categories (male or female). Discrete variables often have a unit of measurement that cannot be subdivided, such as the number of children per household. Other examples of discrete variables are the number of prisoners per jail cell, the number of welfare agencies in a district, and the number of industrial accidents in a given year.

The age of students, on the other hand, is a continuous variable. Age can conceivably change in a *gradual* way from person to person or for the same person over time. Because of this, continuous variables are measured by units that can be infinitely subdivided. Age, for example, does not have a basic unit with which it is measured. We may begin by measuring age in terms of years. But a year can be divided into months, and months into weeks, weeks into days, and so on. The only limit is exactly how precise we want to be: years capture less variation than months, and months less than weeks. *Theoretically*, with a continuous variable we can move gradually and smoothly from one value of the variable to the next without having to jump. *Practically*, though, we will always have to 'round off' the measurement and treat a continuous variable *as if* it is discrete, and this causes the scale of measurement to 'jump' from one point on the scale to the next. The *scale* is by necessity discrete, even though the underlying variable is continuous.

The use of a discrete measurement scale to measure age, whether we do it in years or months, causes us to cluster cases together into groups. The points on the scale act like centres of gravity pulling in all the slight variations around them that we do not want to worry about. We may say that two people are each 18 years old, but they will in fact be different in terms of age, unless they are born precisely at the same moment. But the slight difference that exists between someone whose age is 18 years, 2 months, 5 days, 2 hours, 12 seconds... and someone whose age is 18 years, 3 months, 14 days, 7 hours, 1 second... might be irrelevant for the research problem we are investigating and we treat them the same in terms of the variable, even though they are truly different. No measurement scale can ever hope to capture the full variation expressed by a continuous variable. The practical problem we face is whether the scale captures *enough* variation to help us answer our research question. The second rule of measurement is that *a scale must allow us to assign each case into one, and only one, of the points on the scale*. This statement actually embodies two separate principles of measurement. The first is the principle of exclusiveness, which states that no case should have more than one value for the same variable. For example, someone cannot be both 18 years of age and 64 years of age. Measurement must also follow the principle of exhaustiveness, which states that every case can be classified into a category. A scale for health status that only had 'healthy' and 'very healthy' as the points on the scale is obviously insufficient; anyone who is less than healthy cannot be measured on this scale.

Levels of Measurement

A scale of measurement allows us to collect data that give us information about the variable we are trying to measure.

Data are the measurements taken for a given variable for each case in a study. Scales of measurement, however, do not provide the same amount of information about the variables they try to measure. In fact, we generally talk about measurement scales having one of four distinct levels of measurement: nominal, ordinal, interval, and ratio. We speak of *levels* of measurement because *the higher the level of measurement the more information we have about a variable.* These levels of measurement are a fundamental distinction in statistics, since they determine much of what we can do with the data we gather. In fact, when considering which of the myriad of statistical techniques we can use to analyse data, usually the first question to ask is the level at which a variable has been measured.

Nominal Scales

The lowest level of measurement is a nominal scale. A nominal scale of measurement classifies cases into categories that have no quantitative ordering. Notice that to ensure the scale is exhaustive this nominal scale, like most nominal scales, has a catch-all category of 'Other'. Such a catch-all category, sometimes labelled 'miscellaneous' or 'not elsewhere counted', at the end of the scale often provides a quick way of identifying a nominal scale of measurement.

Another easy way to detect a nominal scale is to rearrange the order in which the categories are listed and see if the scale still 'makes sense'. For example, either of the following orders for listing religious denomination is valid:

Christian Muslim Jewish Hindu Other

or

Muslim Jewish Hindu Christian Other

Obviously, the order in which the categories appear does not matter, provided the rules of exclusivity and exhaustiveness are followed. This is because there is no sense of rank or order of magnitude: one cannot say that a person in the 'Christian' category has more or less religion than someone in the 'Hindu' category. In other words, *a variable measured at the nominal level varies qualitatively but not quantitatively*: someone in the Christian category is qualitatively different to someone in the Hindu category, with respect to the variable 'Religion', but they do not have more or less Religion.

It is important to keep this in mind, because *for convenience* we can assign numbers to each category as a form of shorthand (a process that will be very useful when we later have to enter data into SPSS). Thus we may code – assign numbers to – the categories of religion in the following way:

1	2	3	4	5
Muslim	Jewish	Hindu	Christian	Other

These numbers, however, are simply category labels that have no quantitative meaning. The numbers simply identify different categories, but do not express a mathematical relationship between those categories. They are used for convenience to enter and analyse data. We could just as easily have used the following coding scheme to assign numerical values to each category:

1	5	6	8	9
Muslim	Jewish	Hindu	Christian	Other

Ordinal Scales

An ordinal scale of measurement also categorizes cases. Thus nominal and ordinal scales are sometimes collectively called categorical scales. However, an ordinal scale provides additional information.

An ordinal scale of measurement, in addition to the function of classification, allows cases to be ordered by degree according to measurements of the variable. Ordinal scales, that is, enable us to rank cases. Ranking involves ordering cases in a quantitative sense, such as from 'lowest' to 'highest', from 'less' to 'more', or from 'weakest' to 'strongest', and are particularly common when measuring attitude or satisfaction in opinion surveys. For example, assume that in trying to measure age we settle on the following scale:

18 years or less	19 to 65 years	Over 65 years

This scale clearly does the task of a nominal scale, which is to assign cases into categories. In addition to this it also allows me to say that someone who is in the '19 to 65 years' category *is older* than someone in the '18 years or less' category. Put another way, the '19 to 65 year-old' is ranked above someone who is '18 years or less'. Unlike nominal data, a case in one category is not only different to a case in another, it is 'higher', or 'stronger', or 'bigger', or more 'intense': *there is directional change.*

Unlike nominal scales, we *cannot rearrange the categories* without the ordinal scale becoming senseless. If we construct the scale in the following way, the orderly increase in age as we move across the page from left to right is lost:

19 to 65 years	Over 65 years	18 years or less

As with nominal data, numerical values can be assigned to the points on the scale as a form of shorthand, but with ordinal scales *these numbers also need to preserve the sense of ranking.* Thus either of the following sets of numbers can be used:

1 = 18 years or less		23 =18 years or less
2 = 19 to 65 years	or	88 =19 to 65 years
3 = Over 65 years		99 =Over 65 years

Either coding system allows the categories to be identified and ordered with respect to each other, but the numbers themselves do not have any quantitative significance beyond this function of ranking.

One common mistake in statistical analysis is to treat scales that allow either a 'No' or 'Yes' response as only nominal, when they are almost invariably ordinal. Consider a question that asks participants in a study 'Do you feel healthy?' We can say that someone who responds 'Yes' is not only different in their (perceived) health level, but they also have a higher health level than someone who responds 'No'. Practically any question that offers a Yes/No response option can be interpreted in this way as being an ordinal scale.

Interval/ratio Scales

Ordinal scales permit us to rank cases in terms of a variable; we can, for example, say that one case is 'better' or 'stronger' than another. But an ordinal scale does not allow us to say *by how much* a case is better or stronger when compared with another.

A ratio scale has a value of zero indicating cases where no quantity of the variable is present. In other words, not only can we say that one case has more (or less) of the variable in question than another, but we can also say how much more (or less). Thus someone who is 25 years old has 7 years more age than someone who is 18 years old; we can measure the interval between them. Moreover, *the intervals between points on the scale are of equal value over its whole range*, so that the difference in age between 18 and 25 years is the same as the difference in age between 65 and 72 years.

Clearly the numbers on an interval scale do have quantitative significance. Hence these numbers are termed the values for the variable.

Notice that an observation of 0 years represents a case which possesses no quantity of the variable 'age'. Such a condition is known as a true zero point and is the defining characteristic of a ratio scale, as opposed to an interval scale. For example, heat measured in degrees Celsius does not have a 'true' zero. There is a zero point, but 0°C does not indicate a case where no heat is present – it is cold but not that cold! Instead, 0°C indicates something else: the point at which water freezes. However, this fine distinction between interval and ratio scales of measurement is not important for what is to follow. We can generally perform the same statistical analyses on data collected on an interval scale that we can on data collected on a ratio scale, and thus we speak of one interval/ratio level of measurement. The importance of the distinction between nominal, ordinal, and interval/ratio scales is the amount of information about a variable that each level provides.

A specific scale can provide different levels of measurement depending on the *particular variable we believe it is measuring*; it can be, to some degree, a matter of interpretation. For example, we may have a scale of job types broken down into clerical, supervisory, and management. If we interpret this scale as simply signifying different jobs, then it is measuring job *classification* and is nominal. If we see this scale as measuring job *status*, however, then we can hierarchically order these categories into an ordinal scale.

Univariate, Bivariate, and Multivariate Analysis

We have just spent some time discussing the notion of levels of measurement, since the nature of the scales we use to measure a variable affects the kinds of statistical analysis we can perform. The other major factor involved in determining the analysis we perform is the *number* of variables we want to analyse.

The next two questions are more complex; they are not interested in the way in which students vary in terms of age alone. The second links differences in age with health status, and the third throws the sex of students into the mix. A question that addresses the possible relationship between two variables leads to bivariate statistical analysis, while a question looking at the interaction among more than two variables requires multivariate statistical analysis. This distinction between univariate, bivariate, and multivariate analyses replicates the way in which statistical analysis is often undertaken. In the process of doing research we usually collect data on many variables. We may collect data on people's weekly income, their age, health levels, how much TV they watch, and a myriad number of other variables that may be of interest. We then analyse each of these variables individually. Once we have described the distribution of each variable, we usually then build up a more complex picture by linking variables together to see if there is a relationship among them. Everyone probably has a common-sense notion of what it means for two variables to be 'related to', or 'dependent on', each other. We know that as children grow older they also get taller: age and height are related. We also know that as our income increases the amount we spend also increases: income and consumption are related. These examples express a general concept for which we have an intuitive feel: as the value of one variable changes the value of the other variable also changes.

To further illustrate the concept of related variables, assume, for example, that we believe a person's income is somehow related to where they live. To investigate this we collect data from a sample of people and find that people living in one town tend to have a low income, people in a different town have a higher level of income, and people in a third town tend to have an even higher income. These results suggest that 'place of residence' and 'income level' are somehow related. If these two variables are indeed related, then when we compare two people and find that they live in different towns, they are also likely to have different income levels. As a result we do not treat income as a wholly distinct variable, but as somehow 'connected' to a person's place of residence. To draw out such a relationship in the data we collect, we use bivariate descriptive statistics that do not just summarize the distribution of each variable separately, but rather describe the way in which changes in the value of one variable are related to changes in the value of the other variable.

If we do believe two variables are related we need to express this relationship in the form of a theoretical model. A theoretical model is an abstract depiction of the possible relationships among variables. Determining the model that characterizes any possible relationship between the variables specified by our research question is not always so easy. Consider again the example of income and place of residence. We can model the possible relationship between these two variables in many different ways.

One-way Direct Relationship with Income as Dependent

This models the relationship as a one-way street running from place of residence to income (Figure 1). We may have a theory that argues job and career opportunities vary across towns and this affects the income levels of people living in those towns. In this case we argue that there is a pattern of dependence with income as the dependent variable and place of residence as the independent variable.

Place of residence *dependent*	⟶	Income *independent*

Figure 1. One-way direct relationship with income as dependent

One-way Direct Relationship with Place of Residence as Dependent

Another group of social researchers may disagree with the previous model; they come from another theoretical perspective that agrees there is a pattern of dependence between the two variables, but it runs in the other direction. People with high incomes can choose where they live and will move to the town with the most desirable environment. Thus place of residence is the dependent variable and income is the independent variable (Figure 2).

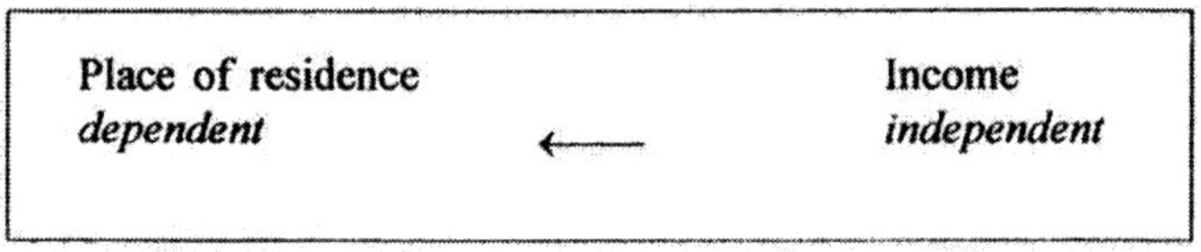

Figure 2. One-way direct relationship with place of residence as dependent

Two-way Direct Relationship with Place of Residence and Income Mutually Dependent

A third group of researchers may agree that the two variables are related, but believe that both types of causality are operating so that the two variables affect each other. In this model, it is not appropriate to characterize one variable as the independent and the other as the dependent. Instead they are mutually dependent (Figure 3).

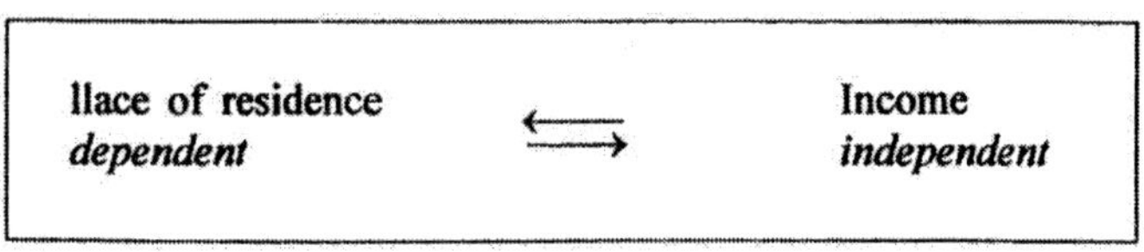

Figure 3. Two-way direct relationship with place of residence and income mutually dependent

The important point to remember is that we choose a model based on particular theoretical views about the nature of the world and people's behaviour. These models may or may not be correct. Statistical analysis cannot prove any of the types of causality illustrated above. All it can show is some statistical relationship between observed variables based on the data collected. The way we organize data and the interpretation we place on the results are contingent upon these theoretical presuppositions. The same data can tell many different stories depending on the theoretical preconceptions of the storyteller. For instance, we have presented the three simplest models for characterizing a relationship between two variables. There are more complex models that involve the relationship between three or more variables.

Descriptive Statistics

We have discussed some conceptual issues that arise when we plan to gather information about variables. Usually the first task of data analysis is the calculation of descriptive statistics.

Tolstoy's *War and Peace* is a very long book. It would not be possible to do such a book justice in any way other than to read it from cover to cover. However, this takes a lot of time and concentration, each of which may not be readily available. If we want simply to get a gist of the story, a shorter summary is adequate. A summary reduces the thousands of words that make up the original book down to a few hundred, while (hopefully) retaining some of the essence of the story. Of course, the summary will leave out a great deal of detail, and the way the book is summarized for one purpose will be different from the way it is summarized for another. Nevertheless, although much is lost, something is also gained when a book so large is summarized effectively.

The same holds true with research. Most research projects will generate a wealth of information. Presenting the results of such research in their complete form may be too overwhelming for the reader so that an 'abridged version' is needed; descriptive statistics provide this abridged version.

Descriptive statistics are the numerical, graphical, and tabular techniques for organizing, analysing, and presenting data.

The great advantage of descriptive statistics is that they make a mass of research material easier to 'read'. By *reducing* a large set of data into a few statistics, or into some picture such as a graph or table, the results of research can be clearly and concisely presented. Assume we conduct a survey that gathers the data for the age of 20 students in my statistics class, and obtain the following results:

18, 21, 20, 18, 19, 18, 22, 19, 20, 18, 19, 22, 19, 20, 18, 21, 19, 18, 20, 21

This arrangement of the measurements of a variable is called a distribution.Descriptive statistics tease out some important feature of the distribution that is not evident if we just present the raw scores. For example, we might calculate a single figure for the 'average' age and present this single number as part of the results of the research. The measure of 'average' chosen will certainly not capture all the information contained in the primary data – no description ever does that – but hopefully it will give a general notion of what the 20 cases 'look like' and allow some meaningful interpretation. We have just introduced the notion of 'average' as an important feature of a distribution of scores in which we might be interested. In more technical terms this is one of many numerical techniques for describing data since it involves the use of mathematical formulas for making calculations from the raw data. There are also a variety of graphs and tables in which data can be represented visually to make the information easier to read.

Table 1. Types of descriptive statistics

Type	*Function*
Graphs	Provide a visual representation of the distribution of a variable or variables
Tables	Provide a frequency distribution for a variable or variables
Numerical measures	Mathematical operations used to quantify, in a single number, particular features of distributions

Given the array of descriptive statistics available, how do we decide which to use in a specific research context? The considerations involved in choosing the appropriate descriptive statistics are like those involved in drawing a map. Obviously, a map on the scale of 1 to 1 is of no use (and difficult to fold). A good map will be on a different scale, and identify only those landmarks that the person wanting to cover that piece of terrain needs to know. When driving we do not want a roadmap that describes every pothole and change of grade on the road. We instead desire something that will indicate only the major curves, turn-offs, and distances that will affect our driving. Alternatively a map designed for walkers will concentrate on summarizing different terrain than one designed for automobile drivers, since certain ways of describing information may be ideal for one task but useless for another. Similarly, the amount of detail to capture through the generation of descriptive statistics cannot be decided independently of the purpose and audience for the research. Descriptive statistics are meant to *simplify* to capture the essential features of the terrain but in so doing they also leave out information contained in the original data. In this respect, descriptive statistics might hide as much as they reveal. Reducing a set of 20 numbers that represent the age for each of 20 students down to one number that reflects the average obviously misrepresents cases that are very different from the average.

In other words, just as a map loses some information when summarizing a piece of geography, some information is lost in describing data using a small set of descriptive statistics: it is a question of whether the information lost would help to address the research problem at hand. In other words, the choice of descriptive statistics used to summarize research data depends on the research question we are investigating.

7

New Trends in Survey Methodology

For years. survey mythologists as well as the public have focused on response rates as quality indicators. This focus has changed in recent years. For one, even surveys with traditionally high response rates have fallen below expectations. In addition to empirical evidence over the last decade has increasingly demonstrated that non-response rates are poor indicators of non-response bias for single survey estimates.

The shift in focus, away from non-response rates towards bias is visible in several ways. It is visible for example in the requirement of a detailed plan to evaluate non-response bias before the U.S. Office of Management and Budget approves data collections sponsored by federal statistical agencies. It is also visible in research initiatives to develop alternative indicators for survey quality. Those alternative indicators can be grouped into two sets– single indicators at the survey level (which is similar to the current use of the response rate), and individual indicators at the estimate level.

Among the set of single indicators are variance functions of non-response weights (e.g., coefficients of variation of non-response weights), variance functions of post-stratification weights (e.g., coefficients of variation of post stratification weights), variance functions of response rates on subgroups defined for all sample cases (both respondents and non-respondents), goodness of fit statistics on propensity models, and R-indexes, which are model-based equivalents of the above. Researchers from the Netherlands, UK, Belgium, Norway and Slovenia formed a joint project (RISQ) to develop and study such R-indexes.

The second set of indicators is produced on a survey estimate level. It is evident that non-response bias is item specific and thus estimate-level indicators would have the soundest theoretical basis. Examples of estimate specific indicators are:

> comparisons of respondents and non-respondents on auxiliary variables; correlation between post-survey non-response adjustment weights and the analysis variable of interest (y) measured on the respondent cases; variation of means of a survey variable y within decides of the survey weights; and fraction of missing information on y. The latter is based on the ratio of between-imputation variance of an estimate and the total variance of an estimate based on imputing values for all the non-respondent cases in a sample.

All data collection conducted or sponsored by the U.S. Federal statistical agencies has to be approved by the Office of Management and Budget (OMB), which ensures that performance standards developed by the Interagency Council on Statistical Policy (ICSP) are met. Conducting or sponsoring is defined here as any information that the agency collects using its own staff and resources, another agency or entity through a contract or cooperative agreement.

The approval by OMB is not just an attempt to reduce burden on the respondents but to ensure "that the concepts that are being measured be well known and understood, and shown to be reliable and valid". OMB applications require information from the data collection agency on questionnaire design procedures, field tests of alternative versions of their measures, re-interviews with sub-samples of respondents, and the like. Pretests and pilot studies are encouraged, and the OMB guidelines spell out how those can be conducted.

No criteria are specified to quantify potential measurement error. The development of a plan to evaluate non-response bias is required only in cases where projected unit response rate falls below 80 percent. survey variables of interest. Thus we cannot revise our survey quality indicators without also changing survey operations.

Survey operations, the procedures of data collection, are themselves subject to quality assessment and quality indicators. Oh 'Muircheartaigh and Heeringa presented a set of criteria at the MC conference in Berlin, another example for quality assessment of survey operations are the OMB guidelines. Independent of those guidelines, there are a couple of recent developments in survey operations that are informative for the German data collection context.

Survey Operations

While survey mythologists and statisticians are aware of the fact that response rates are a poor indicator of non-response error and are even less suitable as indicator of the overall survey quality, the drop in response rates has nevertheless engaged survey researchers in rethinking current practices. The increasing difficulty to gain cooperation has heightened the awareness of potential biases in surveys and created a need to evaluate survey procedures given the threat of losing precision through decreasing sample sizes. Changes in field work procedures require cost-quality trade-off decisions.

Surveys conducted with a responsive design use paradata to carry out those cost-quality trade-off decisions during the field work period. Such paradata are not only used to inform decision making during field operations but are increasingly seen as tools to evaluate measurement error or conduct post-survey bias adjustments. Multiple-mode surveys are often a response to cost-quality trade-off analyses prior to the start of the survey, but they are also a reaction to coverage problems that arise when mode-specific frames do not cover the entire population. An extreme form of multiple-mode surveys are those where the respondent recruitment is separated from the actual data capture. The most prominent examples are access panels or opt-in polls.

Responsive Design

Survey organisations have used sub-sampling and two-phase designs for a long time. However, such design decisions were often only informed by estimates of a current response rate and qualitative information from field supervisors. Those efforts were also hampered by the inability to reach every sample unit in the sub-sample, and with that the statistical properties in the two-phase design are not necessarily unbiased. The second-phase response rates are related to the efforts used in the second phase, as well as first-phase design characteristics such as non-response, mode of data collection, and incentive structure.

During the last decade survey organisations within the U.S. And some European countries started to systematically base design decisions on quantitative information gathered during early phases of the fieldwork period. The most prominent and detailed published example is given by the Social Research Centre at Institute for Social Research of the University of Michigan and is labelled as responsive design. These responsive designs are characterised by four features. First, a set of design characteristics is identified that potentially effect cost and errors of survey estimates. Second, this set of indicators is monitored through the initial stages of the data collection. Third, in subsequent phases of the data collection the features of the survey are altered based on cost-error trade-off decision rules.

Finally, data from the separate phases are combined into a single estimator. An example of data collected are interviewer hours that are spent calling on sample households, driving to sample areas, conversing with household members and interviewing sample people. One key element of such a responsive design is the ability to track key estimates as a function of estimated response propensities (conditioned on a design protocol). If survey variables can be identified that are highly correlated with the response propensity, and it can be seen that point estimates of such key variables are no longer affected by extending the field period, then one can conclude that the first phase of a survey (with a given protocol) has reached its phase capacity and a switch in recruitment protocol is advisable.

Using non-contact error as an example, one can expect that a given recruitment protocol has reached its capacity if the percentage of households with access impediments stabilises over repeated application of the recruitment protocol (e.g. repeated call-backs). Applying this method, Groves and Heeringa concluded for the National Survey of Family Growth cycle field period that 10–14 calls produced stable cumulative estimates on the vast majority of the key estimates. A necessary condition for tracking key survey estimates concurrently is the possibility and willingness of interviewers not only to record respondent data and paradata electronically but also to submit the data in a timely manner to the survey managers. In the case of NSFG, the submissions occurred every evening.

Paradata

Paradata (data about the process of data collection) were already mentioned in the previous section as an important tool to guide fieldwork decisions. Increasingly paradata are also used as tools for survey non-response adjustment, and for detection and modelling of measurement error. The latter is already more common in Web surveys, where keystroke files are readily available due to the nature of the task. Even face-to-face surveys now include the capability for electronically capturing survey-process data. Examples are keystroke files obtained from computer-assisted personal interview (CAPI) or audio computer-assisted self interview (Audio-CASI) surveys, or through digital recordings of the (partial) interviews.

Paradata of potential use for non-response adjustments are collected in conjunction with household listings and when contact attempts are made to sample units. Recently, the U.S. Census Bureau implemented an automated system for collecting contact histories for CAPI surveys. Other governments have started using similar procedures. For example, the Research Centre of the Flemish Government (Belgium) began to use contact forms in their surveys based on the work of Compelling et al. The time of contact (day and time), the data collection method (in-person or by telephone), and other information is recorded for each contact attempt with each sample unit.

A standard contact form has also been implemented since 2002 (round one) of the European Social Survey, and contact data were recently released publicly by the U.S. National Centre for Health Statistics (NCHS) for the 2006 National Health Interview Survey. Thus contact protocol data increasingly are available for each sample unit which makes those data an attractive source for non-response-adjustment variables. Other large survey projects collecting observations of neighbourhoods and housing unit characteristics include the 2006 Health and Retirement Study (HRS), Phase IV of the Study of Early Child Care (SECC), the Survey of Consumer Finances (SCF), the National Survey on Drug Use and Health, the British Election Study (BES), the British Crime Survey (BCS), the

British Social Attitudes Survey (BSA), and the Survey of Health, Ageing and Retirement in Europe (SHARE).

Inspired by Groves and Cooper, some researchers linked interviewer observations to the likelihood of response. Copes and Fare wall successfully used the interviewer assessed interest of sample members about participating in the British National Survey of Sexual Attitudes and Lifestyle as a predictor for the likelihood of response. Lyon demonstrated how observations on multi-unit structures and door intercoms predict the amount of effort that is required to contact sample households in the British Crime Survey.

Bates et al. used contact information from the 2005 National Health Interview Survey (NHIS) to predict survey participation. They examined the effect of various respondent questions, concerns, and reasons for reluctance recorded by interviewers on the survey response. For the U.S. National Survey of Family Growth where Groves and Heeringa used a series of process and auxiliary variables to predict a screening and interview propensity for each active case. Those variables can be groups into observations on each interviewer, observations on segments made by people listing, observations about each listed housing unit made by people listing addresses, observations on each call to the, observations on each call yielding a contact with a household member, observations for each interviewer day (the number of hours spent travelling to the segment, the number of hours spent on administrative activities, the number of hours spent attempting screening interviews, the number of hours spent attempting main interviews).

The expected screening and interview propensities were summed over all cases within a sample segment and grouped into propensity strata. The propensity strata were used by supervisors to direct the work of interviewers. Propensity models using call-record paradata were also estimated for the Wisconsin Divorce Study and the U.S.

Current Population Survey. Both, Olson and Fricker then examined measurement error as a function of response propensity. Lately, more studies have tried to establish a relationship between paradata collected during the contact process (or as interviewer observations) and key survey variables. A systematic evaluation of the quality of such paradata, however, is very limited. For example, measurement error properties of these data, collected either through interviewer observation or through digital recordings of timing or speech are currently being studied by Casas-Cordero and Jans.

Auxiliary variables and alternative frames

Next to paradata there is a second set of data sources that is now increasingly of interest to survey designers, that of commercial mass mailing vendors. These lists are of interest in the creation of sampling frames, to enhance survey information and to evaluate non-response bias. In face-to-face surveys in the U.S. Two methods of infield housing unit listing are most common. Traditional listing in which listers are provided with maps showing the selected area and an estimate of the number of housing units they will find. Dependent listing in which listers are given sheets pre-printed with addresses believed to lie inside the selected area.

Those addresses come either from a previous listing or from a commercial vendor. Listers travel around the segment and make corrections to the list to match what they see in the field. The latter appears to be less expensive. There is a third method of creating a housing unit frame, which involves procuring lists of residential addresses from a commercial vendor and identifying those that fall inside the selected areas, geo-coding will be used instead of actual listings. The coverage properties of such frames still under study. Survey research organisations are currently exploring the U.S. Postal-Service delivery sequence files to replace traditionally used PSUs (Census blocks) with Zip-Codes. While this last development is U.S. Specific, it is nevertheless of interest as it provides the possibility to stratify with rich datasets, or to pre-inform interviewers about potential residents and their characteristics. This information can be used for tailored designs. In Germany, dependent listing and enhanced stratification was already used for the IAB-PASS study.

Multiple-modes

Several U.S. Federal statistical agencies have explored the use of mixed-mode surveys. The two main reasons mixed-mode studies are usually considered are cost and response rates. There are three prominent types of multiple-mode studies: modes are administered in sequence, modes are implemented simultaneously, and a primary mode is supplemented with a secondary mode.

The American Community Survey (ACS), which replaced the Census long form, is an example of a sequential application of modes. Respondents are first contacted by mail, non-respondents to the mail survey are contacted on the phone (if telephone numbers can be obtained) and finally in-person follow-ups are made to a sample of addresses that remain un-Interviewed. Parallel to the primary data collection a method sample is available to examine various error sources. The Bureau of Labour Statistics (BLS) is currently using multiple modes for the Current Employment Statistics (CES) program.

Firms are initiated into the survey via computer-assisted telephone interview (CATI), kept on CATI for several month, and are then rolled over to touchline data entry, the internet, fax etc. Experiments are undertaken to evaluate measurement error separately from non-response error for each of these modes. The National Survey of Family Growth has as its primary mode CAPI, but sensitive information (e.g., number of abortions) is collected through Audio-CASI.

With the attraction of responsive design and the acknowledgement of imperfect sampling frames, mixed-mode surveys are attractive. Research is underway to explore the interaction between non-response and measurement error for these designs. The European Social Survey program just launched a special mixed-mode design in four countries to examine appropriate ways of tailoring data collection strategies, and to disentangle mode effects into elements arising from measurement, coverage, and sample selection.

Another large scale study within Europe that experiments with mixed modes is the UK Household Longitudinal Study (UKHLS) under supervision of the Institute for Social and Economic Research. On the administrative side, the Social Research Centre at the University of Michigan is currently constructing a new sample management system that will allow more efficient ways to carry out mixed-mode surveys. The new system will manage sample across data collection modes (F2F, Telephone, Web and supplementary data modes such as bio-markers, soil samples etc.) and will allow easy transfer of sample between modes and interviewers (e.g., between CAPI and centralised CATI).

Reduction of Response Burden

Another development related to measurement error can be seen most recently in large scale surveys. Researchers at the Bureau of Labour Statistics (BLS) are investigating survey redesign approaches to reduce respondent burden in the Consumer Expenditure Survey. One proposed method is multiple matrix sampling, a technique for dividing a questionnaire into subsets of questions and then administering them to random sub-samples of the initial sample. Matrix sampling has, for a long time, been used in large-scale educational testing. This method is growing in popularity for other types of surveys where respondent burden is an increasing concern. Another method from educational testing that is currently under exploration is adaptive testing. Most applications of this method are currently tested in health surveys but survey issues regarding context effects arise.

Interviewer

All of the above mentioned developments have one feature in common. They alter and extend the task interviewers have to perform. In the past there was already a tension between the dual role of interviewers, as they are adaptive and flexible when recruiting respondents into the sample and on the other hand neutral question delivery entities with ideally as little individuality as possible to reduce interviewer effects. Now, the number of tasks required from one interviewer is even higher, as they span observations, bookkeeping, handling technology, explaining technology, switching between different questionnaire flows, and the like. With this increased burden/expectations on the interviewer, a more careful look at interviewer performance seems necessary. Survey organisations (NORC in the U.S., Nat Cent and ONES in the U.K.) have already started to analyse interviewer performance across various surveys combined with Census data or questionnaires to the interviewer; others investigate alternatives to conventional interviewers.

Compared to Germany it seems to be more common for U.S. Data collection firms to have interviewers that only work for one particular survey organisation (and with that are used to a particular survey house culture), or if they work with others those would be social survey research organisations as well. More importantly it is common for interviewers to be trained centrally from the survey agency at the beginning of their employment and at the beginning of new large scale assignments. Unlike in Germany, face-to-face survey interviewers tend to be paid by the hour no by complete cases. This results in a different incentive structure and also opens the possibility for interviewers to spend time on the aforementioned additional tasks. It goes without saying that the costs of face-to-face surveys are often 10-fold of what is common in Germany.

In summary survey mythologists are conducting new and exciting research into the trade-offs between cost and response rates. As part of these efforts research is done on how best to use non-survey data, either to inform about non-response bias or measurement error, but also to supplement data collection and reduce respondent burden. Research is under way to understand error properties of mixed-mode and multiple-frame surveys, but conclusive results are lacking. The German data infrastructure initiative has the possibility to contribute to this research.

An overarching theme in all of the above mentioned developments is the increased interest in a relationship between various error sources. In Germany there are several good opportunities to engage in research related to the intersection of error sources, especially given the exceptional data linkage efforts that have taken; here Germany is clearly taking the lead compared to the U.S. However, what could be improved in Germany is the collaboration between survey organisations and researchers, the amount of data shared between those organisations and the willingness to systematically allow for randomness experiments in data collection protocol.

8

Unobtrusive Research Methods

One justification for the use of unobtrusive methods lies in the methodological weaknesses of interviews and questionnaires. As Web et al. put it:

> Interviews and questionnaires intrude as a foreign element into the social setting they would describe, they create as well as measure attitudes, they elicit atypical role and response, they are limited to those who are accessible and who will cooperate, and the responses obtained are produced in part by dimensions of individual differences irrelevant to the topic at hand.

Interviews and questionnaires create attitudes in part because respondents commonly try to manage impressions of themselves in order to maintain their standing in the eyes of an interviewer. A fairly consistent finding on surveys, for example, is that respondents will claim to have an opinion about fictitious or obscure matters. Looking at voting behaviour, Presser and Target found that some of those who claim in surveys to have voted have not done so. According to Presser and Target, misreporting of voting behaviour correlates with factors such as education and interest in politics.

Perhaps because they regard themselves as the kind of people who should vote, the better educated and politically aware feel under pressure to report having voted even when they had not done so. Bradburn et al. found a tendency for survey respondents to over report socially desirable behaviours when interviewed using less anonymous. Broadly, the more anonymous the method, that is, the less it involved face-to-face contact, the more likely respondents were to admit to socially undesirable behaviour.

More recently, Tourganeau and Smith have also found evidence that more private methods of data collection yield gains in the reporting of sensitive behaviours. The characteristics of interviewers can under some circumstances affect the answers respondents give to particular kinds of question. In a study using both black and white interviewers, Schuman and Converse found little evidence that the race of the interviewer influenced responses to questions relating to racial discrimination, poor living conditions, or personal background. They did find, however, that black respondents were less likely to agree with statements expressing hostile attitudes towards whites when the interviewer was white than when the interviewer was black.

How one asks a question in an interview or on a questionnaire can have, sometimes subtle, sometimes substantial, effects on the responses received. Variations in wording, for example, can affect how people respond. Smith found across a variety of surveys that the word 'welfare' in questions about financial support for the disadvantaged produces lower levels of positive response than the word 'poor'.

There is some evidence that respondents use the response categories attached to questionnaire items on surveys as cues to researchers' expectations about the range of particular behaviours. In one experiment, respondents, when asked if they suffered from headaches 'frequently', reported three times as many headaches a week as those asked whether they suffered headaches 'occasionally'. It seems, moreover, that respondents dislike giving responses that seem extreme relative to the scale of responses presented to them.

As Schuman and Presser point out, survey questions are never asked in isolation but as part of a flow of questions. Thus, the context or order in which questions appear can have consequences for the responses to them. Respondents, for example, sometimes adjust their response to a later question in order to make it consistent with an answer they have given previously. In various ways, responses to specific questions on a particular topic can be affected by responses to a general question on the same topic. Juxtaposing questions having an alternate form sometimes induces, it seems, a norm of reciprocity which can distort responses. Schuman and Presser argue that, although question order effects are not pervasive, neither are they rare.

The extent to which interviewing might intrude as a foreign and reactive element in the research situation can be seen in Veroff et al.'s longitudinal study of couples in first marriages. Compared with a control group, couples who were frequently interviewed showed more variability in reported levels of marital satisfaction during the second year of the study. By the fourth year, however, those who had been interviewed more frequently had generally more positive perceptions of their marriage than those interviewed less frequently. Veroff et al. speculate that the interviews might have caused couples at various points to reflect on their marriage in ways that affected the quality of the relationship.

Participation in a study, in other words, can change the attitudes and behaviour of those being studied. Depth interviewing might be less subject to reactive effects than survey interviewing. Yet, even here problems can arise, at least when sensitive topics are involved. The threatening character of interviews on relatively intimate matters can be gauged, for example, from reports of interviewees lapsing into embarrassed silence or needing to use alcohol as a prop while being interviewed. In Maureen Padfield and Ian Proctor's qualitative study of young adult women, the gender of the interviewer seemed to make little difference to what was disclosed in the interview, except in relation to one particular issue.

Women volunteered information about having had an abortion to Padfield, the female interviewer, but not to Proctor. In addition, some of Proctor's respondents revealed on re-interview by Padfield that they had an abortion. It is not clear what accounts for this pattern, but an implication might be that interviewer effects are not entirely absent in qualitative research. As Web et al. point out, respondents have to be accessible and to be willing to answer a researcher's questions for interview and questionnaire methods to be effective. There is, however, a fairly widespread perception that survey response rates have fallen in the United States, the United Kingdom and, perhaps, in some other countries as well.

Steeh examined non-response to two long-running US surveys associated with the Survey Research Centre at the University of Michigan. In both, refusal rates rose steadily between 1952 and 1979. According to Groves, a long-term increase in refusal rates has also been seen for a number of large-scale government surveys in the United States. Over a rather long time period, Goyder found declining response rates in both the United States and Canada for interview studies, though not for postal surveys. Those who do not respond to surveys are, of course, different in their social characteristics from those who do. Goyder suggests in a careful synthesis that, although many of the commonly assumed demographic correlates of non-response do not survive statistical controls for other factors, 'socioeconomic status and age are key components of socio-demographic refusal bias in surveys'.

Concern over reactivity extends beyond interview-based methods. In the 1930s, a series of experiments on the relationship between work place conditions and levels of production attained classic status. During experiments at the Hawthorn works of the Western Electric Company into the effects of changing lighting levels, it was noticed that production went up whether levels of illumination were increased or decreased.

The explanation suggested for this phenomenon was that the workers had responded not to the experimental variable– the level of lighting intensity – but to being singled out for study. Dubbed the 'Hawthorn Effect', these experiments were an early intimation that social science measurement could be artefacts. In other words, simply by their presence researchers could unwittingly but systematically distort their own findings.

Research on the role of artefacts in social science experiments crystallised in the 1960s and early 1970s. Broadly speaking, attention was directed to three areas:

— The role of 'demand characteristics'.

— The effects of 'experimenter expectancies'.

— The possible over-reliance on volunteer subjects.

One suggested that the experimental situation is one that motivates participants to be 'good subjects'. Research subjects therefore try to act in ways they presume will make the experiment successful. In order to do this they look for clues to the true purpose of the experiment in the experimental situation, in their own wider knowledge and, in the case of students, in campus gossip. The sum total of such clues Orne refers to as the 'demand characteristics' of the experiment.

Rosenthal presented evidence that researchers who were encouraged to believe that an experiment would yield results within a particular range produced findings in line with their expectation. Subsequently, Rosenthal and Rubin reported on a meta-analysis of a large number of studies dealing with experimenter expectancies. The pooled results from these studies suggested that expectancy effects are to be found in a wide range of research areas. Rosenthal and Rostow have also presented evidence to suggest that a variety of background and attitudinal variables distinguish those willing to participate in social-psychological experiments from those who are not.

According to Rosenthal and Rostow, volunteering is also associated with a variety of situations factors to do with the investigation itself, the characteristics of the researcher and the incentives offered for participation. As Campbell concedes, one can argue that an assessment of this kind is overly pessimistic. Arguments that direct elucidation methods are incorrigibly reactive have been vigorously contested, and have provoked revisionist claims. In a careful study using hierarchical multi-level modelling, Hox et al. point out that interviewer effects found in earlier studies might not have survived appropriate statistical controls.

Alternatively, they suggest, effects found in previous studies might have come about through the cumulation of small differences between interviewers. Smith has argued that the image of free-falling survey response rates is an exaggeration. Examining non-response rates for a range of different surveys over relatively long time periods, he found varying trends in response rates, although he does concede that, 'In both the United States and elsewhere increases in both overall non-response and refusals do outnumber declines...'

Even the celebrated Hawthorn Effect has not escaped critical scrutiny. According to Parsons, the workers, who were paid according to output, could see records of their output, and worked harder to increase their earnings. Kruglanski suggests that experimental studies showing the presence of demand characteristics (or subject artefacts to use his preferred term) do not stand up well to critical scrutiny since researchers have not always been clear about what produces artefacts or how exactly they affect experimental variables.

Kruglanski also argues that Rosenthal and Rosnow's research on volunteer subjects shows volunteering to be associated with such a heterogeneous range of factors that it is difficult to see how volunteer bias could operate in particular studies. Reviewing a large number of studies, Barber concludes that there is some evidence for the biasing effects of experimenter expectancies.

However, he also argues that, in many cases, other explanations, such as failure to follow precisely experimental protocol, can account for the results found in particular experiments. Nevertheless, one can still argue that social researchers are over-reliant on direct elucidation methods. Despite the United States and Britain's very different methodological cultures, one heavily quantitative, the other qualitative, social research in both countries still relies heavily on the direct elucidation of data from respondents.

Only a little more than one-quarter (29.5 per cent) of articles appearing in major sociology journals in 1995 (N. = 220) in the United States (American Journal of Sociology, American Sociological Review and Social Forces) and in the United Kingdom (British Journal of Sociology, Sociological Review and Sociology) used data sources, mainly documents, that were not collected by questionnaire or interview.

A justification for the use of unobtrusive methods sees them less as alternatives to direct elucidation methods, and rather more as complementary to those methods. In fact, having stressed the reactivity of interviews and questionnaires Web et al. reserve their greatest scorn for studies using only a single method of data collection. For them, the principal objection to traditional data collection methods is typically 'that they are used alone'.

Web et al. argue that data collection methods used singly are inferior to the use of multiple methods. They use a metaphor from geology, the idea of an 'out cropping', to point to how theory might guide the selection of data points. Any given theory has innumerable implications and makes innumerable predictions. The testing of theory can be done only at available out cropping, those points where theoretical predictions and available instrumentation meet. Any one such out cropping is equivocal, but the more remote or independent such checks, the more confirmatory their agreement.

The idea that data and theory meet at available out cropping is clearly a justification for the use of multiple sources of data. The argument is that the results one gets from one's research are always to some degree an artefact of the method used to collect the data. In other, any finding is potentially subject to a 'plausible rival hypothesis' that the findings reflect availabilities inherent in the data collection method. However, these availabilities are not the same across methods. In particular, the problems of reactivity that afflict direct elucidation methods are absent when data are collected unobtrusively. From this point of view, configuration different methods, each of which is fallible in a different way, gives greater purchase on the problem to hand than an over-reliance on a single method.

An added attraction of unobtrusive methods over directly elicited data in conflict situations is that they reduce the potential physical hazards associated with having to venture into dangerous locales in order to carry out interviews. Another way to see this is to recognise that researching sensitive or dangerous topics encourages researchers to innovate in order to find pathways around the obstacles certain topics put in their way. Methodological innovation has its drawbacks, notably in an absorption with the technical fix, but it also requires an imaginative cast of mind.

As C. Wright Mills argued, imagination forms a counter to trained incapacity. Technical competence in research skills, even of the highest quality, is leavened by imagination. Kellehear points out that Web et al.'s work predates the advent of 'post-structuralist' approaches in the social sciences. Kellehear uses the term loosely to refer to a variety of contemporary theoretical stances such as de-constructions, discourse analysis, narrative analysis, phenomenology and semiotics, many of which can be collected together, Alasuutari suggests, under the rubric of 'cultural studies'.

As Atkinson observes, these approaches have 'roots in diverse philosophical, theoretical and methodological inspirations'. They share, however, a hostility to the notion that the task of social science is measurement, whether unobtrusive or not, as opposed to interpretive or critical understanding of social reality. The somewhat surprising intersection of those approaches with that of Web et al. lies in a rather sideways glance at traditional sources of data in social research. In the post-structuralist vision, everything in and of the world is irredeemably cultural, and therefore open to study, no matter how seemingly peripheral, insignificant or taken for granted.

In addition, shaped by literary or humanistic study, such approaches have usually been less wedded to elicited data than traditional social science disciplines. Instead, they focus on the cultural meaning of products, artefacts and objects, in a sense revalorising soutces marginalised by dominant social science. In particular, textual materials, from the very grand to the very humble, products of popular culture and material culture find themselves falling under the post-structuralist gaze.

Origin of Unobtrusive Measures

Although the term is Bouchard's, Web et al. might easily have described Unobtrusive Measures as an inventory. Indeed, with only some injustice, can be read simply as an extended list of instances held together by little more than the non-reactivity they have in common. Formal sociologists such as Simmel and Goffman were fond of 'astrictive instantiation', the piling on of examples, as a way of demonstrating the ubiquity, significance and interpenetration of social forms.

The many and varied examples Web and colleagues deploy urge the reader to recognise that the use of unobtrusive measures is both possible and desirable. Inventories have been used as a method for collecting data. Although the term 'inventory' is still sometimes used to refer to the set of items making up a psychometric scale, methods of this kind are rare today. If they survive at all, it is in the form of time budgets. Used to collect data, inventories are unwieldy and often reflect a rather theoretical tendency towards factual accumulation. The more common use of the inventory is to list in a readily retrievable form resources of various kinds. Survey researchers, for example, can turn to published inventories to locate well validated attitude scales for inclusion in their questionnaires. The advent of the Internet, for example, produced a blizzard of inventories, in print and on line, of list serves, news groups and websites.

Creating an inventory of measures provides a database of retrievable examples. Since inventories are inclusions in character, an inventory makes visible the range, scope and relevance of the measures contained within it. As a result, it becomes easy to identify gaps or miscellaneous elements within the overall framework. Inclusion also ensures that the reader is very likely to find something that catches the interest. Inventorial organisation encourages browsing. Browsing in its turn encourages the 'discovery of accidents'.

This is because the salience of each browsed item, and the basis on which it is 8 Unobtrusive methods in social research deemed salient, tend to be assessed independently for each item. To put this another way, relevance, rather than being imposed, emerges out of browsing. The problem is that although browsing is useful, it is also quite limited. As Dabs points out, there can be 'too many measures, some of which, quite frankly, are worthless. If one included a measure of every sign or effect of a phenomenon, the number would be endless. There are more measures than phenomena, and one must carve out a domain of measures likely to be useful and to the point'.

Just as inventories are unwieldy as data collection tools without some means of data reduction, resource inventories are similarly unwieldy unless the user has a mechanism or a methodology that allows retrieval of relevant items in the database. In the original incarnation of Unobtrusive Measures such a methodology was conspicuous by its absence. In other words, there is little explicitly to guide a researcher seeking un elicited data relevant to a particular research problem. Two different approaches to dealing with this problem have been taken in subsequent writing.

On the one hand, some writers have adopted what might be called an orientational approach. This stresses the importance of the stance the researcher brings to possible and actual sources of data. The orientational approach can be contrasted with a taxonomic strategy, the basic aim of which is to identify particular properties of measures. From these properties, it is argued, one might be able to produce a generative taxonomy that could be used to produce on demand unobtrusive measures fitted to specific research purposes.

Although implicit in much of Web et al.'s writing, the most clear-cut expression of the orientational approach can be found in Web and Wick's discussion of the principles governing the use of unobtrusive measures. The first principle is that investigators should 'construct and impose multiple indices that converge'. The preference here is for capturing the complexities of social situations through the use of multiple theories, which provide potentially competing explanations needing adjudication, multiple methods of research and multiple sources of data. Second, enthusiasts for unobtrusive methods 'assume noise is rare'.

In other words, much of what we see around us can be considered as a potential source of data. Such data should not be discarded out of hand even when at first sight they seem to be trivial, perplexing or out of the ordinary. A third principle is that 'investigators believe in amortisation'. The assumption is that data, no matter how they are generated, can have more than one purpose and can be put to more than one use. Data obtained opportunistically should not be seen as inherently inferior to data designed for a particular purpose. Fourth, those committed to the use of unobtrusive methods 'find foolishness functional'.

What Web and Wick have in mind here is the importance of being able to reflect on problems in an imaginative, playful, even fanciful, way. Such reflection serves, as they put it, to 'generate novel inputs and permit people to recognise and break the singular focus toward a problem in which they had persisted'. Fifth, unobtrusive measures require the researcher to 'ponder the variance rather than the mean'. If one measures some phenomenon, a focus on how it is distributed can be as useful as an inspection of a typical case.

Web and Wick add that the absence of variance can in some cases be theoretically significant. For example, power in an organisation can be indexed by the degree to which some within it have less discretion than others. Finally, 'investigators use expectancy as a control', that is 'sophisticated and successful use of unobtrusive measures requires that investigators lay out in advance what they expect to find so that the surprise when they don't find it is visible and documented'. There is in this a strand of what Gouldner calls 'methodological romanticism'.

It is impossible here to do justice to Gouldner's complex argument about the multifaceted influence of Romanticism on the social sciences. For present purposes, what is important are his observations on how Romanticism affected the way in which social scientists think about data. First, Romanticism encouraged an 'open' conception of data. Faced with the disappearance of peasant culture under the impact of industrialisation, writers in the German Romantic tradition undertook direct observation of rural life. In doing so, they extended the scope of social research to encompass those previously thought of as 'low, indecorously deviant, and worthy only either of contempt or neglect'.

The idea that nothing social escapes the purview of the social scientist was fostered in this way. There are, of course, other less Romantic influences that have also encouraged an open conception of data; the application of random sampling methods to the selection of respondents is an obvious example. Romanticism, however, did not simply widen the scope of what might be studied. In true Romantic manner it encouraged a particular sensibility towards data. Gouldner identifies three aspects of this sensibility.

First, the Romantics blessed 'the ordinary, everyday world with the pathos of the extraordinary'. Ordinary, mundane things, Gouldner goes on, 'were to be rescued by viewing them from a perspective that endowed them with new and enhanced value, rather than being routinised, ignored or thing afield'. Web and Wick's assumption that 'noise is rare' invokes a concept–signal-to-noise ratio– from modern electronics. Nevertheless, the contention that data can be found anywhere and everywhere, even in dustbins, has a Romantic cast to it. A second aspect of methodological Romanticism is a preference for solutions to research problems which rely on imagination, insight or vision rather than standardised procedures. The slogan 'foolishness is functional' trades on just such a preference.

Foolishness helps, for example, to spark and maintain interest in a research topic. More significantly, it aids the development of novel analytic 10 Unobtrusive methods in social research perspectives and counters what Web and Wick regard as a 'preoccupation with rational models' on the part of researchers. Notice how the slogan 'foolishness is functional' is premised on an incongruity. A third strand of methodological Romanticism is a fondness for the grotesque.

We tend today to associate ideas of the grotesque with monstrosity., for example, points to how popular tradition surrounding the monster in Marry Shelley's Frankincense increasingly focused on his size and physically.) More properly, the term refers to the juxtaposition of incongruous elements. As Gouldner notes, imagination in the social sciences is often taken to arise out of incongruity, from the analyst's ability to shift from one perspective to another or to juxtapose in a meaningful way seemingly incompatible elements.

Many of Web et al.'s examples provide an ingenious bridging of the commonplace and the significant. On the one hand, the population and settings that figure in these examples are immediately recognisable. (Even those of us who have not bought jade or played baseball can identify the situations described as instances of more prototypical encounters.) On the other hand, although the measurements and instruments used have a rather humble quality, they are heavily consequential for the analytic purposes of the investigator.

Moreover, to the extent that they encourage the reader to respond with 'Why didn't I think of that?', the various examples celebrate the ingenuity and imagination of those investigators. It would be a mistake to overemphasise the Romantic elements in Web and Wick's account. There seems to be some contradiction between an opportunistic, data are where you find them, stance and the principle of using expectancy as control, setting out what you expect so that your surprise registers when you don't find it. Moreover, although Web and Wick stress that expectancy comes from eclecticism, they tend to restrict their examples to variability in distributions.

Might not a more systematic, taxonomic strategy be a better approach to generating unobtrusive measures? The generative taxonomy proposed by Web et al. takes the form of a large matrix. Specific unobtrusive measures are located in relation to the two dimensions of the matrix. One of these dimensions is the characteristic the researcher wishes to investigate. Web et al. suggest the following categorisation. In relation to a particular characteristic a researcher is likely to want to know:

— The probability of its occurrence.
— Its capacity to perform some task or role.
— Its social value.
— The sentiment attached to it.
— The affective states surrounding it.
— Its degree of category membership.
— Its standing on some trait or dispositions dimension.

The second dimension of the taxonomy refers to features of unobtrusive measures that provide a basis for making inferences about the characteristic of interest. Web et al. suggest that 13 features of a characteristic can be measured:

— Frequency, how often something occurs.

— Its magnitude or size.

— The degree of latency, or time taken for some subsequent action, event or consequence to take place.

— The degree of resistance to change associated with the characteristic.

— The degree of functional smoothness or ability to perform skilfully associated with the characteristic.

— The level of association those who possess the characteristic have with socially similar or dissimilar others.

— The acquisition of things of value (a measure of interest):

— The consumption of valued goods (a measure of liking).

— The willingness to expend effort (a measure of interest).

— The inappropriateness of responses (a measure of hidden characteristics).

— Bias or the degree of divergence from expected standards.

— Cognitive articulation, the ability to make more or less fine discrimination between different objects.

— The revolter, the extent to which traces divulge information about characteristics.

There are some immediately obvious problems here. Although Web et al. stress the importance of multiple methods, most of the categories they describe seem to involve only single measures. Web et al. acknowledge that the generative taxonomy is hardly elegant; some of the categories overlap, and the dimensions they present do not have a clear logical structure. In addition, it is not clear what relationship there is, if any, between the generative taxonomy and the typology of data sources Web et al. originally set forward.

The characteristics Web et al. list are primarily concerned with the analysis of performances, dispositions, affective states and (marginally) social relationships. It is not obvious whether these categories are relevant only to certain areas of social psychology or are meant to have general applicability. Presumably those with other disciplinary, or even sub-disciplinary interests, might produce a different set of features. Sociologists, for example, might prefer to focus on acts, activities, meanings, participation, relationships and settings. It would also seem appropriate to distinguish characteristics in relation to some level of scale. Is the characteristic to be assessed, in other words, at the individual, group, organisational, socialite or some other level?

While it is relatively easy to fit examples from Web et al.'s work into the taxonomy, it is not clear how much independent generative power the taxonomy has. In fact, the idea of a generative taxonomy sits uneasily with other aspects of Web et al.'s work. It is difficult, for example, to reconcile a taxonomic approach with Web et al.'s emphasis on the imaginative and opportunistic use of data.

Some of the examples (including the famous hatching chicks) derive from anecdotal reports and, as is common in published work, authors usually dwell more on their findings than on how the data were generated. In other cases, however, it is hard to avoid the conclusion that often the measures used simply reflect expedience and/or what was available to hand. It seems, then, that suitable sources of data cannot simply be 'read off' from theoretical concerns; they have to be found by means of a directed search.

Another way to put this is to say that the generation of unobtrusive measures involves the use of heuristics. Heuristics are rules of thumb that help to increase the probability of solving a problem, typically by providing methods for 'eliminating unfavourable solutions, narrowing down the search space, [and] breaking complex problems into sub-problems'. A close reading of Web et al.'s work suggests that underpinning their discussion of various data sources are a set of implicit heuristic strategies for finding data sources relevant to a particular research problem.

This is perhaps seen more clearly if their (passive) typology of data sources is recast into a (more active) classification of modes of data acquisition. This means that, instead of focusing on physical traces, observation and documents, one should ask for a given social context what data can be captured, what can be found and what can be retrieved. According to Dabs, proponents of unobtrusive measures tend to assume that 'entities move through time and space and through social and physical encounters, all the while shedding signs that, taken cumulatively, reveal their true nature'.

One important set of signs are 'ephemeral traces', as Dabs calls them. Such traces 'make up much of the ordinary behaviour of people and organisations'. However, 'unless someone or something is there to make a record, the ephemeral trace is lost'. Ephemeral traces need to be captured, in other words, if they are to be of use to the social scientist. (Used in this sense, the term 'capture' need not imply a preexisting, external 'objective' reality; merely that if some things are not 'frozen', they disappear.) Identifying ephemeral traces relevant to a particular research problem is highly dependent on theoretical and cultural knowledge.

In many cases researchers will draw directly on this knowledge. In other cases, the overwhelming 'naturalness' of such knowledge is precisely the problem. Human beings have a well-developed cultural sense. They also have a perceptual apparatus highly sensitive to interaction cues. As a result they often apprehend and understand the activity of others in ways they find difficult to articulate. The basic heuristic is therefore to ask:

What features of some setting or situation can be made perceptually, normative or culturally problematic and how? In the social sciences three strategies have generally been used to problematic social situations. These might conveniently be labelled 'perceptual shift', 'decentring' and 'disruption'. Perceptual shift involves altering the normal way in which we perceive human activity, perhaps by changing the time base for observation or the depth of focus through which some setting is viewed.

This strategy often depends on shifting the capabilities of normal human perception. Decentring involves explicitly attending to those interaction or communicative features of settings or situations that are normally only implicitly apprehended. A conscious shift from focusing on the content of speech to paralinguistic features, such as pauses, pitch, intonation and the like, is an obvious example. Disruption involves altering a social situation in some way so that its underlying features are revealed.

Ephemeral traces, which need to be captured, can be distinguished from physical traces that are normally found in situ. The basic question in considering the generation of physical traces is as follows:

> 'How are the physical properties of objects inadvertently implicated in their social use?'

In part, the answer Web et al. give to this question is a quasi-economic one. They tend implicitly to see research problems where the use of physical traces is appropriate in terms of production, consumption, demand and supply. More specifically, a basic heuristic they employ is to ask in effect, 'What production is implicated in consumption?' It is this that triggers their interest in garbage, litter and so on. They also ask the converse question, 'What consumption is implicated in production?' However, in practice they resolve this by asking the somewhat different question of how demand is naturally calibrated. Doing so leads them to consider the frequencies to which car radios are tuned, the size of suits of armour, the abrasion of surfaces and so on.

Related to all of this is a somewhat different heuristic: 'What performative opportunities do objects offer?' This allows one to consider graffiti, inscriptions and the like. Web et al. distinguish between running records, on the one hand, and what they refer to as episodic and private records on the other. A heuristic for identifying data from running records relevant to a given research question is to ask: 'At what points and in what ways in society is information logged about social behaviour?' The same heuristic can be applied to identifying at least some kinds of episodic records, given their largely bureaucratic character.

More generally, however, although Web et al. recommend that greater effort be put into identifying and locating potential caches of data, to use Glazer and Strauss's term, they do not suggest ways of doing so. Relevant heuristics, in other words, must be found elsewhere. In information science the growth of the World Wide Web in particular has encouraged renewed interest in how researchers 'forage' for sources of documentary data. If one takes this metaphor seriously, an appropriate heuristic might be to treat repositories as field sites, and to adapt to documentary work the sampling strategies typical of field research. Drawing on procedures advocated by Hallmarks et al., documentary sources might be regarded as research 'sites', and their producers as 'informants'. Using personal knowledge, knowledgeable others and published guides, procedures analogous to snowball sampling can then be put in train. When no more likely sites are generated, sampling stops.

9

Documentary Methods in Social Research

Social research is an activity that is undertaken to find an answer or explanation regarding a particular social phenomenon. It involves systematic collection of data about such a social phenomenon for the purpose of finding and or understanding patterns and regularities in it. Social science departments in most universities require some of their final year students to undertake a small piece of social research, commonly referred to as a 'research project' in partial fulfilment of the requirements for the award of a degree.

A social research project is normally small in scale and is intended to gauge the student's ability to convert social research knowledge (acquired in class) into social research skills. Depending on how the student performs in the research project, the department will know whether the student is competent to undertake independent research in the future or to work with little supervision as a research assistant. To the majority of social scientists the idea of a research project is that it is something that is 'original' and for which 'new data' must be collected. To this end the social survey method, sometimes supplemented by in-depth interviews and participant observation, is selected as the method of choice, and very few social scientists ever think of re-analysing existing data sets.

Although social surveys, in-depth interviews and participant observation have been tried and tested, they are not the only ones available nor are they always useful. There is another research method that is often marginalised or when used, it is only as a supplement to the conventional social surveys. This is the documentary research method or the use of documentary sources in social research. This method is just as good and sometimes even more cost effective than social surveys, in-depth interviews or participant observation. The use of documentary methods refers to the analysis of documents that contain information about the phenomenon we wish to study. Pane and Pane describe the documentary method as the techniques used to categorise, investigate, interpret and identify the limitations of physical sources, most commonly written documents whether in the private or public domain.

Unfortunately, documentary research methods have often been incorrectly considered a monopoly of professional historians, librarians and information science specialists, whilst social scientists rely on surveys and in-depth interview methods, the professional sociologist in particular. In the event that social scientists use documentary research methods, it is only to supplement information collected through social surveys and in-depth interviews, but *seldom as the main or principal* research method. No wonder that in order to undertake a research project, most students (following this poor example by their academic advisors) tend almost instinctively to think of questionnaires as the tools of data collection. Although social surveys are a respected research method, they are not always appropriate or cost effective.

Documentary Sources

A document is an artefact which has as its central feature an inscribed text. Simply put, a document is a written text.

Documents are produced by individuals and groups in the course of their everyday practices and are geared exclusively for their own immediate practical needs. They have been written with a purpose and are based on particular assumptions and presented in a certain way or style and to this extent, the researcher must be fully aware of the origins, purpose and the original audience of the documents. It must be noted that documents are not deliberately produced for the purpose of research, but naturally occurring objects with a concrete or semipermanent existence which tell us indirectly about the social world of the people who created them. A document, unlike a speech, can have an independent existence beyond the writer and beyond the context of its production.

There are two types of documents that are used in documentary study, namely primary documents and secondary documents. Primary documents refer to eyewitness accounts produced by people who experienced the particular event or the behaviour we want to study. On the other hand secondary documents are documents produced by people who were not present at the scene but who received eyewitness accounts to compile the documents, or have read eyewitness accounts.

Documentary sources provide what Scoot characterises as mediate access as opposed to proximate access. Mediate or indirect access becomes necessary if past behaviour must be inferred from its material traces, and documents are the visible signs of what happened at some previous time. This is in contradistinction to proximate or direct access whereby the researcher and his sources are contemporaneous or co-present and the researcher is a direct witness of the occurrences or activities.

Documents range from public through private to personal documents. The list of public document sources include government publications such as Acts of Parliament, policy statements, census reports, statistical bulletins, reports of commissions of inquiry, ministerial or departmental annual reports, consultancy reports, etc. Private documents often emanate from civil society organisations such as private sector businesses, trade unions and non-governmental organisations, as well of course from private individuals. They include minutes of meetings, board resolutions, advertisements, invoices, personnel records, training manuals, interdepartmental memos and other annual reports, etc. The list of personal documents include household account books, photo albums, address books, medical records, suicides notes, diaries, personal letters, etc.

Sources of Documents

Most countries regularly produce crucial documents that can be easily accessed relatively cheaply. Documents can be found in ministry and departmental libraries, office shelves of officials, newspapers 'morgues' and even store rooms! The Central Statistics Offices in many countries produce statistical bulletins on various topics such as health, economics, employment, the cost of living, economic growth, housing and the population census reports and other topics.

Handling Documentary Sources

The general principles of handling documentary sources are no different from those applied to other areas of social research. In all cases data must be handled scientifically, though each source requires a different approach. Scott has formulated quality control criteria for handling documentary sources. These are authenticity, credibility, representativeness and meaning. Authenticity refers to whether the evidence is genuine and from impeccable sources; credibility refers to whether the evidence is typical of its kind, representativeness refers to whether the documents consulted are representative of the totality of the relevant documents, and meaning refers to whether the evidence is clear and comprehensible.

Authenticity

Authenticity refers to whether the evidence is genuine and of reliable and dependable origin. Authenticity of the evidence for analysis is the fundamental criterion in any research. The researcher therefore has a duty and a responsibility to ensure that the document consulted is genuine and has integrity. This is in the same way that an interviewer must be sure of the identity of the interviewee or the participant observer must be sure of being in the right place and that the activities observed are not stage-managed for onlookers, but the 'normal' activity of the people involved.

There are, however, many instances where documents may not be what they purport to be. For example wills, legal documents, diaries and letters can be forged or falsified, and even literary works may be attributed to authors who did not write them. This places an enormous responsibility on researchers to satisfy themselves that the documents being analysed are not forgeries and are indeed what they purport to be. Documents should therefore not be taken for granted. According to Platt, circumstances may arise that necessitate a close scrutiny of a document.

Such circumstances include the following:

- When the document does not make sense or has obvious errors.
- When there are internal inconsistencies in terms of style, content and so on.
- When there are different versions of the same document.

- — When the version available is derived from a dubious, suspicious or unreliable secondary source.
- — When the document has been in the hands of a person or persons with vested interest in a particular reading of the text.

Having established the authenticity of a document, the researcher must also authenticate the authorship, that is, verify that the name inscribed on the document is that of the author. Instances exist where authors have been incorrectly named, or where documents were falsely presented as being the work of certain well-known personalities, such as the so-called 'Hitler Diaries' in the 1980s.

But what does the researcher do when confronted with a government document signed by a minister or a company's annual report signed by the board chairman? In all probability the government document would have been written by civil servants whilst the annual report will have been written by the chief executive officer with the help of his staff. Under these circumstances it is better to take for granted the names of the authors inscribed on the documents.

Credibility

Credibility refers to whether the evidence is free from error and distortion. According to Scott the question of credibility should concern the extent to which an observer is sincere in the choice of a point of view and in the attempt to record an accurate account from that chosen standpoint.

Representativeness

The question of representativeness applies more to some documents than to others. Representativeness refers to whether the evidence is typical of its kind, or if it is not, whether the extent of its untypical is known. Documents such as the Household Income and Expenditure Surveys were prepared by professional statisticians using generally accepted sampling frames and random selection procedures. This is clear from the methodology section of these reports. The fact that some of the findings are actually embarrassing to the government testifies to their representativeness and authenticity.

Meaning

Meaning refers to whether the evidence is clear and comprehensible. The ultimate purpose of examining documents is to arrive at an understanding of the meaning and significance of what the document contains. However, what documents contain can have either a literal or face value meaning, and an interpretative meaning. According to Scott, the literal meaning of a document gives only its face value meaning, from which its real significance must be reconstructed. On the other hand, in an interpretative understanding, the researcher relates the literal meaning to the contexts in which the documents were produced in order to assess the meaning of the text as a whole. Another important point to be considered in the use of documentary sources is how to decide which inference to make from a document about matters other than the truth of its factual assertions.

For example,. information on the growth of both gross domestic product and per capital income is given in factual quantitative terms. On its own, this type of information may lead people to expect more equitable distribution of income and a higher standard of living. But when this information is read together with information on sectorial and structural changes in the economy, ownership and control of the means of production, employment patterns and income distribution, the picture is more complex.

This is because statistics only give face value meaning. Statistics are only 'raw materials' which must be interrogated and their real meaning reconstructed. One can only make sense of this welter of apparently disparate bits and pieces of information, by situating it within a theoretical context. It is the theory that reorders the data, and inferences come as a matter of interpretation of the raw material informed by theory.

10

Ethics in Social Research

Ethical discussions usually remain detached or marginalised from discussions of research projects. In fact, some researchers consider this aspect of research an afterthought. Yet, the moral integrity of the researcher is a critically important aspect of insuring that the research process and a researcher's findings are "trustworthy" and valid.

The term ethics derives from the Greek word ethos which means character. To engage with the ethical dimension of your research requires asking yourself several important questions:

— What moral principles guide your research?

— How do ethical issues enter into your selection of a research problem?

— How do ethical issues affect how you conduct your research—the design of your study, your sampling procedure, etc.?

— What responsibility do you have toward your research subjects?

— For example, do you have their informed consent to participate in your project?

— What ethical issues/dilemmas might come into play in deciding what research findings you publish?

— Will your research directly benefit those who participated in the study?

History of Research Ethics

Formal consideration of the rights of research subjects grew out of the revelations of the terrible atrocities that were performed in the guise of scientific on Jews and other racial and ethnic minority groups in Nazi concentration camps during World War II. One result of the revelations of these appalling medical experiments perpetrated in the name of science resulted in the creation, in 1949, of the Nuremberg Code, a code of ethics, which starts off with the stipulation that all research participation must be voluntary.

Other codes of ethics soon followed, including the Declaration of Helsinki. This code was specifically developed "in part as an alternative to the Nuremberg Code, which dealt exclusively with non-therapeutic [research promising no direct benefit to the subject] research". This code protects research subjects in both therapeutic and non-therapeutic contexts. The Declaration of Helsinki notes several central procedures that should be applied in biomedical research:

Every biomedical research project involving human subjects should be preceded by careful assessment of predictable risks in comparison with foreseeable benefits to the subject or to others... The right of the research subject to safeguard his or her integrity must always be respected. Every precaution should be taken to respect the privacy of the subject and to minimise the impact of the study on the subject's physical and mental integrity and on the personality of the subject.

The Council for International Organisation of Medical Sciences (CIOMS) was also created for those researching in developing nations. Throughout the history of scientific research, ethical issues have captured the attention of scientists and the media alike. While extreme cases of unethical behaviour are the exception not the rule in the scientific community, an accounting of these projects can provide important lessons for understanding what can happen when the ethical dimension of research is not considered holistically within the research process.

Laws Governing Research Process

Unfortunately, when the Tuskegee experiment began, there was no institutional review board (IRB) to oversee the goals of the project. It was not until the mid 1960s that the federal government began the process of developing a set of "official, which ultimately led to the passage by Congress in 1974 of the National Research Act. This act set up an Office for the Protection of Risks (OPRR) and was housed in the National Institutes of Health (NIH). The act called for the establishment of a "Commission on Protection of Human Subjects of Biomedical and Behavioural Research".

These ethical principles were released by the Commission in 1978 in a report known as the "Belmont Report," which was later revised to incorporate additional protections for young children who participate in the research process. In 1991, these revised guidelines, known as the Common Rule, received widespread adoption by federal agencies. The Common Rule mandated, among other things, that any institution receiving federal funds for research must establish an institutional review committee.

These committees, known as Institutional Review Boards (IRBs), have the job of watching over all research proposals that involve working with human subjects and animals. Universities and colleges, for example, that receive federal funding for research on human subjects are required by federal law to have review boards or forfeit their federal funding. IRBs are responsible for carrying out U.S.

Government regulations for human research. They must determine whether the benefits of a study outweigh its risks; that consent procedures have been carefully carried out and that no one group of individuals has been unfairly treated or left out of the potential positive outcomes of a given study. This is, of course, important in a hierarchically structured society where we can't simply assume racism, sexism, homophobia, and classicism won't make their way into research. Certain types of research, for example, educational research dealing with "instructional strategies," may have an "exempt status" and a full review by an IRB may not be required.

It is noteworthy that, over the course of more than four decades, even after the USPHS had finally set up a Code of Research Ethics for the treatment of research subjects, the Tuskegee experiment was still allowed to continue. This raises questions about how effective and accountable research projects are to IRBs as well as about the effectiveness of the range of professional ethics codes that are part of most professional associations and currently serve as guidelines for conducting research.

Protection of Research Subjects

It has been over thirty years since the government issued its regulations for protecting human subjects in research studies receiving federal funding, there continue to be cases involving human subjects that have resulted in harm and death. As one researcher notes: "The history of research involving human subjects has been described by ethicists as one of 'progress propelled by scandal'". Concerning the current scandals in the field of biomedical research, Alvino says:

> ... The highly publicised death of Jesse Gelsinger, a research subject who died as a result of his participation in a gene therapy trial at the University of Pennsylvania, aroused

> significant media attention and public concern regarding the safety of clinical trials. His story is far from unique... Medical research suffered another blow... When it was discovered that researchers and pharmaceutical companies involved in research at Cornell and Tufts had failed to notify the National Institutes of Health that six gene therapy research subjects had died during experiments over a nineteen-month period.

At the centre of many of the debates regarding the protection of human subjects is the question of whether informed consent procedures are sufficient to protect human subjects, and the ability of IRBs to oversee the research process in their home institutions. Why didn't the IRBs report the deaths of research subjects to the federal agencies involved in funding these projects? Were the research subjects given proper information regarding the side effects of the study? In the case of Jesse Gelsinger, he was an 18-year-old college student at the time he participated in the University of Pennsylvania study in 1999. An investigation of his death showed that

— He in fact was not a good candidate for the study in the first place.

— He was not provided with adequate information concerning the extreme adverse side effects that other participants in the study had experienced. Jesse's father notes:

"It looked safe. It was presented as being safe... I was misled". This has too often been the case. Professional associations such as the American Educational Research Association (AERA), the American Sociological Association (ASA), and the American Psychological Association (APA) also outline general ethical guidelines for their members.

The American Psychological Association's website for example, outlines specific ethical categories of conduct, from general principles of professional conduct that deal with issues such as integrity and justice to more practice-specific concerns such as privacy and confidentiality of patients and research subjects. There are also ethical guidelines on record keeping and fees as well as ethical guidance on issues that may come up in a therapeutic situation, such as those especially pertaining to sexual intimacy with clients and therapy with former sexual partners. There are also guidelines for resolving ethical issues, such as how to handle complaints and discrimination.

Thus far we have been focusing on biomedical research. To what extent do the ethical issues in the sciences carry over into the behavioural and social sciences? Researchers conducting biomedical studies often present a "protocol" that outlines the specific steps they will follow in conducting research on human subjects. Qualitative research is, by its very nature, open to discovery and change in research goals. It may be nearly impossible for the qualitative researcher to account for all of the happenings in the research setting, and it may be hard to go back and forth to a Human Subjects Committee (like an IRB) for approval each time a project takes an unexpected turn. Adler and Adler argue that obtaining informed consent hits those researchers practising participant observation the hardest:

Participant observation has a fuzziness about what is research and what is not, as ethnographers are observers of everyday life and may be generating insights and gathering data from people in all kinds of situations (a waitress at a restaurant, a fellow passenger on an aeroplane, a person whose child is the same age as one's own). They may not know in advance what information will drift their way and that may prove explicitly useful, either currently or in the future.

In addition, there is often a very personal engagement with research subjects that is often not found to the same extent in biomedical research, raising even more prominently the possibility of undue power, influence, and authority being wielded in the research process.

There are some "classic" examples of extreme violations of ethics in the annals of behavioural and social scientific research as well. Perhaps one of the most egregious comes from a 1963 research project on "obedience to authority," conducted by psychologist Stanley Milgram. Milgram wanted to understand the conditions under which individuals obey authority figures. His research protocol called for deceiving volunteer subjects into thinking they were involved in an experiment on the impact of punishment on memory. Volunteers first read a series of word associations to the individuals (confederates) under a variety of experimental conditions:

— Where they could not see or hear the confederate.

— They could hear the confederate protest but not see the confederate.

— They could hear and see the confederate.

— Same conditions as (3) except the subject was required to place the confederate's hand on a shock plate.

If confederates were unable to repeat the words, volunteers were asked to administer an "electric shock" to them, increasing the voltage for each wrong answer in order to enhance learning. Subjects had a fake voltage meter in front of them with readings "from slight to severe shock," with a sign warning of the danger in using the equipment posted next to the meter. Some subjects protested upon hearing confederates complain about pain and other medical problems. Even though some volunteers wanted to quit the experiment, the researcher in charge insisted that they continue, saying that he (the researcher) would take responsibility. Some subjects, however, did not protest and even went on to administer what they considered the "highest," most lethal, shock to a confederate, even when they had received no feedback that the person was even alive.

Stanley Milgram's experiment deceived his volunteer subjects and failed to obtain their informed consent. The protocol of this experiment did not allow subjects to quit even when some protested and asked that it be stopped. In addition, some subjects experienced psychological distress knowing they actually could administer what would be considered a lethal shock to another human being.

Ethical Dilemma of Covert Research

Some researchers argue that their research must be conducted in a "covert" manner in order to obtain the information they need to understand certain social phenomena. For example, researchers have gone undercover to study such underground cultures as the drug culture and used deception in order to find out about the inner workings of the social life of drug dealers and drug takers, often observing individuals engaging in illegal activities and sometimes finding themselves asked to engage in these same activities. There would be no point in asking for the informed consent of the members of this closed society, since they would most likely not want their organisation studied. Williams, who did participant observation on a subculture of cocaine users and dealers in the after-hours clubs in an inner city, notes the following concerning his undercover activities:

I was in a Brokenly club where I was already conspicuous as a non-user of cocaine. It seems that I was also overzealous. In the sense that I was staring too much and asking too many questions. One of the club's owners came over to me and said "Listen, my man, if you're undercover, I got people that' ll take care of that." I was not sure whether he meant force or bribery, but in any case I stopped going to that club... As a researcher, I knew what data I needed: information on cocaine users and the associated nightlife, street myths about use... But as most researchers know there is a quid pro quo in every research situation... I was asked to do a variety of favours, such as lending money and finding social workers... On many occasions I was asked to engage in illegal acts.... This and similar requests put me in an awkward position.

— Is it ethical to go undercover?

— Is it ethical to engage in illegal activities under the guise of research?

One can imagine those social scientists studying deviant behaviours, such as life in the underground drug trafficking world, and how difficult it might be to obtain the informed consent of everyone involved in order to study the inner workings of the illicit drug trade.

— What does the researcher do when he or she confronts information or situations where individuals are observed to engage in major violations of the law?

— Is the researcher ethically obligated to report such activity?

— What about the risks the researcher is taking in terms of his or her own life if they do so?

Deception in research doesn't have to occur by going "undercover" in carrying out research projects. The Milgram experiment was a study in deception. From the start, Milgram did not truthfully explain the nature of the experiment, and he deceived subjects into thinking they were in fact applying electrical shocks to another human being. Some qualitative social science research methods, like fieldwork, also require some type of deception between the researcher and the researched. Sociologist Herbert Gans, conducting fieldwork in Park Forest, a suburb near Chicago, in Boston's West End, and in Levit town, a New Jersey suburb, relates his personal reflections on the anxiety he experienced in what he finds is "the deception inherent in participant observation":

Once the field worker has gained entry, people tend to forget he is there and let down their guard, but he does not; however much he seems to participate, he is really there to observe and even to watch what happens when people let down their guard. He is involved in personal situations in which he is, emotionally speaking, always taking and never giving, for he is there to learn and, thus, to take from the people he studies, whereas they are always giving information, and are rarely being given anything. Of course they derive some satisfaction from being studied, but when they ask the participant observer to give—for example, help or advice must usually refuse in order to maintain his neutrality.

Moreover, even though he seems to give of himself when he participates, he is not really doing so and, thus, deceives the people he studies. He pretends to participate emotionally when he does not; he observes even when he does not appear to be doing so and like the formal interviewer, he asks questions with covert purposes of which his respondents are likely to be unaware. In short, psychologically, the participant observer is acting dishonestly; he is deceiving people about his feelings and in observing when they do not know it, he is spying on them. Herbert Gans represents a particular point of view on the role of the researcher as participant in the fieldwork experience.

The idea that the researcher should remain neutral and "detached" from the research subject tells us that he or she aspires to the goal of "objectivity" in the research process. This objectivity then is enhanced by deception. Yet, as we have seen, this frame on the research process is one of many paradigms one can bring to the fieldwork experience. There are those who believe the researcher does not need to maintain distance between the researcher and the researched. Ann Oakley, in fact, critiques this model of neutrality and instead argues for bridging this divide through empathy and affinity. Other ethnographers feel that this form of closeness between researcher and researched also has its problems and that one can become too close to respondents. This in turn can create a series of conflicts and deceptions. Ethnographer Judith Stacey comments:

> ... The irony I now perceive is that the ethnographic method exposes subjects to far greater danger and exploitation than do more positivist, abstract, and "masculinity" research methods. And the greater the intimacy—the greater the apparent mutuality of the researcher/researched relationship—the greater is the danger. Stacey notes that the further involved she became with her respondents the further exposed she became to situations within the field that left her open to the possibility of manipulating and betraying her respondents. So we can see that issues of disclosure and trust are actually very complex. Some might argue that a certain amount of "strategic" deception is needed when researchers are especially interested in "studying up".

The study of elates is not a common practice within the social sciences. The elite and semi-elite population hold key positions within society, yet their activities and power remain invisible to the average citizen. Elates often protect their privacy through a myriad of self-imposed barriers, ranging from unlisted phones and mail accounts to the hiring of staff to screen their calls and contacts and security personnel to prevent unwanted contact with those outside their elite culture. Adler and Adler note that current IRB and professional associations who fear lawsuits have developed codes of ethics that now ban all aspects of covert research, using the argument that it is almost impossible to obtain informed consent. In addition, these boards cannot protect the researcher from revealing the identity of their respondents if they are asked to do so by officials investigating their research findings.

Adler and Adler note:

> Clearly, if we are being told that we cannot protect our own subjects from official investigation short of our or their going to jail, which not everyone is willing to do, some changes are necessary. Is the new system the best way? If you fundamentally shut down research there is no risk to subjects because researchers will not know anything. Johnson and Athlete reflect on professional ethics, given their 65 years of combined experience as university scholars.

They note the lack of legal protection of social scientists regarding the confidentiality of their sources as a "political" and not a moral issue:

In the United States, the first amendment of the constitution protects journalists by guaranteeing free speech and a free press. Social scientists lack such protection regarding confidentiality of sources, however, and we surmise that this is best seen as a political, rather than a moral one. If social scientists had such protection, we speculate that we might be addressing a different set of ethical issues—perhaps ones such as how social scientists abuse their constitutional protection.

Adler and Adler argue that ethics boards have overstepped their function, which has resulted in the unanticipated outcome of favouring the dominant classes over the weaker: "Powerful, elite groups can now better hide their mechanisms of control, while weak and powerless groups have lost the ability to tell their stories from their own perspective". These researchers lament the fact that covert research, such as that done by Serving Goffman in his classic work, Asylums, which provides readers with a bird's eye view of the treatment of the mentally ill by those who care for them, and that carried out by Gary Marx on the activities of control agencies such as the police, will no longer be possible under the new ethics guidelines.

Haggerty has identified what he terms an "ethics creep" that has taken over social science research "in the name of ethics." He defines this term as follows: "This is characterised by a dual process whereby the regulatory system is expanding outward to incorporate a host of new activities and institutions, while at the same time intensifying the regulation of activities deemed to fall within its gambit".

Conflicts of Interest

Academics are under financial pressures from their universities to obtain grants for research. More and more of these grants are coming from commercial institutions such as drug companies:

> The sharp increase in privately funded (i.e., industry sponsored) research has created an atmosphere that breeds conflicts arising from compelling financial incentives. These conflicts may arise from researchers' financial relationships with companies whose products they are studying, whether the research is sponsored by the government or by the company itself.

In some cases, universities are becoming enmeshed with industrial research interests. Angell points out the problem of academic medicine being "for sale." She notes:

> Academic medical institutions are... Increasingly beholden to industry... Some academic institutions have entered into partnerships with drug companies to set up research centres and teaching programs in which students and faculty members essentially carry out industry research. Both sides see great benefit in this arrangement. For financially struggling medical centres, it means cash. For the companies that make the drugs and devices, it means access to research talent, as well as affiliation with a prestigious brand.

It is possible that in some cases members of a university's own IRB boards can have a vested interest in the very studies they have oversight on. Alvino notes:

> Although IRB members are supposedly foreclosed from participating in review of any project or study in which they

> have a conflicting interest... There is no way to ensure that the research facility or individual researchers are not operating under such conflicts. An article in the L. A. Times cited a Yale University study which remarked that "one quarter of the biomedical researchers at universities had commercial ties serious enough to raise questions of financial conflict".

— What are the ethical implications of accepting funding for research?

— How can academics and IRBs work together most effectively?

— How can funding sources, such as the National Science Foundation (NSF) or The National Institute of Mental Health (NIMH), help alleviate the tensions between funding research and ethics?

Divided Loyalties

Bell and Nutt talk about their "divided loyalties" in terms of how their professional and occupational commitments pull them in many different directions, creating ethical dilemmas arising from the multiple roles they bring to a research setting. Linda Nutt describes how her professional role as a social work practitioner who is "bound by general social work codes of practice" conflicted with her role as researcher:

> As she was leaving the home of a new career following the research interview Linda Nutt noticed an unambiguously sexually explicit picture in the hallway. For most researchers this would not be an issue; art is a matter of personal taste. But Linda Nutt wasn't just a researcher she was also a practitioner. Frequently when children are placed in foster homes little is know about their life experiences so new careers are instructed to assume that all children have been sexually abused unless specifically told otherwise... There is a statutory responsibility to disregard confidentiality where children are at risk. Nonetheless, because she wanted to keep the roles clear and separate—to act as a researcher (and be in

> receipt of information) and not as an employee... (Who could give then information), Linda Nutt chose not to tackle this issue with these new careers but spent several days considering this ethical dilemma. In the end the social worker practitioner identity overcame that of the researcher identity and Linda Nutt informed the local authority of her unease regarding the picture and its potential impact upon the foster children.

Some researchers employ research techniques that raise ethical issues regarding how human subjects are treated. Human notes what he calls the "softening up" techniques to get at more personal information from respondents who may be unwilling to talk:

The insidiousness of softening-up techniques is demonstrated by some impertinent questions reserved for the latter and more compliant stages of the interviews and questionnaires: having scrupulously sought and obtained a general consent from respondents and their parents.

By its very nature, qualitative research often requires emotional engagement with those with whom we build knowledge. Jean Duncombe and Julie Jessop discuss how some researchers can lack sympathy for their respondents and "fake" their interest and concern for those they research. Jean Duncombe describes how she wound up treating some of her respondents in a research project she was conducting:

> ... We found it more difficult to achieve rapport where we did not spontaneously feel empathy with our interviewees. For example in an early study of Youth Training Schemes (YTS), Jean felt she established a "genuine," if shallow rapport with the YTS trainees and with the more conscientious employers who took training seriously, because she was "on their side." But with the more exploitative employers and trainers (who provided neither jobs nor training), she knew she was faking rapport to "betray" them into revealing their double standards, and sometimes whilst smiling at them she almost smiled to herself, thinking: "What a revealing quote"... Julie felt uncomfortable and personally

> compromised when she found that, in order to obtain a "good" interview, it seemed necessary to smile, nod and appear to collude with views she strongly opposed.

Researchers are human just like everyone else. Accordingly, we all bring our own likes, dislikes, emotions, values, and motivation to our research projects. It is unrealistic to expect that you will always like those you research, or that you will always naturally feel 100% engaged. This being said, bear in mind that it is you, the researcher, who has initiated this process and involved others (your subjects). Consider this carefully as you contemplate your ethical obligations to your research participants, but as you think through these issues, do so with your own "humanness" in mind—be realistic and fair to all involved.

Solution for Ethical Abuses

A major principle underlying many of the ethical policies which have historically grown up around the issue of how to treat research subjects has been the use of "informed consent," the right of subjects to decide anonymously whether they will be involved in a research endeavour. Some ethicists question the extent to which informed consent has lived up to the promise of anonymity for research subjects. Research has pointed out that subjects do not always understand the medical aspects of the clinical project they are participating in, and some do not even know that they may in fact be participating in a research trial.

There are many instances in which there is failure to fully disclose to research subjects the full extent of the risks and benefits of participating in a study, and this has led to some disastrous research outcomes for some of those who participated in clinical trials and biomedical research. There is, then, a practice and a reality to providing informed consent. There exists a wide variation in how well researchers carry out the policy of informed consent in their ongoing research projects. For example, we present two types of letters on informed consent a researcher might write to parents regarding their child's participation in a research project on body image. Wee observe that "Letter A" contains a much more detailed account of the research problem, including several research goals and an explanation of how the research will be carried out.

This research project will study pre-teen and adolescent attitudes about body image and self-esteem. Some of the questions that we will explore are:

— From whom and where do pre-teens learn perceptions of body image and self-esteem? For example, what role do peers and the mass media play in influencing pre-teens' and adolescents' attitudes about their weight and body image?

— What factors (if any) appear to "protect" pre-teen and adolescent girls against feelings of low self-esteem, and what factors (if any) contribute to a depressed sense of body esteem?

Attached you will find a consent form which, upon agreement, is to be signed by your daughter and yourself and brought to the Health Centre the day of the interview. Explain the research project as a "cover story," and this may be built into the original design of the research project:

> The selection or invention of details to constitute the cover story and convince intended respondents is an element in the design of a research project. That requires skills of persuasion. Investigators develop a sense of what details allay fears and what prompt suspicions. As in other types of negotiation, such as bargaining over salaries, the initiating party uses a gambit declaring a position which it may concede and which supposes an opposition of interests between the negotiating parties.

The investigator will reveal further information if required but in many cases subjects will not be briefed to ask pertinent questions and the project will move on quickly from negotiation to interview. If respondents initially refuse to participate in a research project, rather than accepting the right of the researched to act autonomously, this is often viewed as a failure on the part of the researcher, and there is a tendency of the researcher to break down "the defences of respondents" through a variety of means, from group pressure to exploitation of friendships. To this issue, Human says:

> In various ways research projects trade upon a relationship with agencies in power or authority. Sutherland was able to research the secretive and exclusive Rom community, which was normally hostile to representatives of the world outside it by exploiting her role as teacher of its children.

There are even times when following ethical guidelines may not always be in the best interests of your research respondents. Baez points out the ethical conundrum he experienced in maintaining the confidentiality of his respondents. Baez interviewed 16 minority faculty members regarding their personal experiences with the tenure and promotion process at one private university. He notes that maintaining confidentially can be a double-edged sword.

Keeping the interviews confidential, especially for untenured faculty, allowed him to obtain candid data regarding racism and sexism within this university. On the other hand, confidentiality prevented him from reporting "... Serious contradictions within an institution that, through institutional documents and public comments by key administrators, purported to be supportive of racial and cultural diversity... I could not do so without feeling that I would be identifying my respondents to others in the institution". Bear in mind that you often don't know what your research will teach you, and it can be very difficult not to try and effect social change in some situations.

Patton notes that respondents are now maintaining their right to "tell their stories" without hiding their identities, especially when they see the project as an opportunity to gain empowerment through telling their stories and perhaps becoming a catalyst for social change. Patton suggests a number of important ethical dilemmas that flow from this new viewpoint on confidentiality:

- Should the researcher "impose confidentiality against the wishes of those involved?"
- Are human subjects committees "patronising and disempowering" if they turn down those respondents who wish to reveal their identities?
- Does the research subject make the choice independent of others in their social context?
- What about the privacy of significant others in their lives, such as children, spouse, and extended family members?

Beyond all of these considerations, some researchers are very cognisant of ethics in practice, attempt to use informed consent, and still experience challenges. Sarah Maddison is a feminist sociologist at the University of New South Wales in Australia where she focuses on gender and social policy. Maddison encountered several problems when trying to use informed consent in her ethnographic work with a feminist student group. Let's join Maddison behind the scenes.

Practice of Ethics in Social Research

Ethics exist within a social context. Ethical rules cannot possibly apply to all events that can happen in a given project. Rubin and Rubin note that ethical guidelines do not begin to cover all of the ethical dilemmas you may face in the practice of social research:

> You cannot achieve ethical research by following a set of preestablished procedures that will always be correct. Yet,

> the requirement to behave ethically is just as strong in qualitative interviewing as in other types of research on humans—maybe even stronger. You must build ethical routines into your work. You should carefully study codes of ethics and cases of unethical behaviour to sensitise yourself to situations in which ethical commitments become particularly salient. Throughout your research, keep thinking and judging what are your ethical obligations. A useful distinction we might keep in mind here is the difference between what Human terms ethical codes and ethical values.

Agreeing to comply with ethical codes as outlined in an informed consent proposal does not absolve the researcher from adhering to the underlying ethical values contained in these codes, yet very often "they invite observance in the letter rather than in the principle". Human reminds us that the danger is that many researchers think their moral obligation begins and ends with the signing of the letter of consent. In some cases an informed consent letter is seen as one protecting the researcher more than the researched. Iinformed consent, when mechanically applied using a form or some verbal formula, becomes more of a protection for the researcher than the researched. Informed consent obtained in this way is unilateral rather than bilateral and protects the researcher against charges from participants that they did not understand fully the intent or outcome of the research. Ethics does not exist in a vacuum. As King, Henderson, and Stein note:

> ... The ethics of human subjects research may be universal but is at the same time deeply particularised, so that what autonomy or informed consent or confidentiality or even benefit and harm means depends on the circumstances. The circumstances do not determine whether any of these "Western" moral concepts applies, but how.

Emergent Issues in Ethics Research

King, Henderson, and Stein's observations on ethical behaviour point to a shift in thinking about how ethics is incorporated into the research process. They discuss a paradigmatic shift in thinking of ethics as a based on moral principles (principality paradigm) largely independent of specific circumstances, to one based on a view of ethics embedded in contextual relationships (relationship paradigm). A principality might be concerned about the inherent "relativistic" point of view contained within a relational ethics perspective, while a rationalist might charge a principality with "moral imperialism, paternalism and absolutism.

Ethics viewed through each of these paradigmatic lenses asks different types of questions, and it weighs in differently on what priorities should be stressed in a discussion of the ethics of human subjects research. Up to now, a principality paradigm has guided the development of the ethics guidelines for IRBs and professional associations. What is needed to move the discussion of ethics forward is a more concerted dialogue between these two perspectives, and perhaps, some say, even a synthesis.

11

Mixed Methods in Social Research

After a period in the paradigmatic wilderness, mixed methods research has regained not just acceptability, but popularity, with a significant number of studies arguing its virtues in terms of greater understanding and/or validation of results. But all is not "plain sailing"—working with mixed methods raises a range of issues above and beyond those encountered within a particular methodology. Not the least of these is that there is no one mixed methods methodology, and the term can be applied to widely divergent approaches to research.

Tashakkori and Teddlie argued that the term "mixed model" is more appropriate than "mixed method" for research in which different approaches are applied at any or all of a number of stages through the research, their point being that mixing often extends beyond just the methods used in the research. Indeed, mixing of methodologies within a broad quantitative or qualitative approach may raise almost as many issues as when working across approaches; mixing may also occur across different disciplinary traditions, for example, in social history, or when scientists engage in social research to evaluate the impact of their work. It becomes necessary, therefore, to clarify just what is being mixed—and how it is being mixed. The "mixing" may be nothing more than a side-by-side or sequential use of different methods, or it may be that different methods are being fully integrated in a single analysis.

Defining Qualitative and Quantitative

Qualitative and quantitative approaches have been distinguished (and thereby defined) on the basis of the type of data used (textual or numeric; structured or unstructured), the logic employed (inductive or deductive), the type of investigation (exploratory or confirmatory), the method of analysis (interpretive or statistical), the approach to explanation (variance theory or process theory), and for some, on the basis of the presumed underlying paradigm (positivist or interpretive/critical; rationalistic or naturalistic).

Perhaps our inability to clearly specify what all of us have a general sense of is indicative of the lack of a clear distinction—that what we are talking about is a continuum with a number of independent dimensions along which any particular research may be placed. If one uses numbers, interpretation is still involved. If one's data are texts, counting may still be appropriate. Variables do not necessarily have clear-cut meanings; processes can be revealed through numeric analysis as well as through narrative, and so on.

This inability to definitively distinguish one approach from another has implications for the acceptability of mixing methods in that "lines of conflict" cannot be clearly drawn. Because there is no necessary congruence between the different dimensions of the quantitative, qualitative distinction, the terms themselves are most useful either for giving a sense of overall direction in a study, or simply as descriptors of the type of data being used (textual or numeric). Even the latter is problematic (suggesting that approach and data type are necessarily linked), but it at least avoids the problems associated with suggesting there are such things as quantitative or qualitative **paradigms** or methodologies.

Paradigms

Approaches taken to defining "qualitative" and "quantitative" have long been associated with different paradigmatic approaches to research—different assumptions about the nature of knowledge (ontology) and the means of generating it (epistemology). The idea that one's paradigmatic view of the world might be related to the way one went about researching the world was prompted by Kuhn, while Guba and Lincoln's work on naturalistic inquiry contributed significantly to the "paradigm wars" of the '80s.

Their concerns about the paradigmatic assumptions underlying research were taken up by many writing about approaches to social research and social research methodology in that period. Much of the concern arose as a reaction to the earlier dominance of the "positivist" world view that privileged objective observation and precise measurement over interpretation of subjective experience and constructed social realities. Researchers holding the belief that there were strong associations between paradigm, methodology and methods consequently considered different methodologies and methods to be philosophically incompatible, making their combination logically impossible.

During this period, therefore, mixed **methods research** was strongly attacked and fell from favour amongst mythologists. The positivist approach to social and behavioural science, adopted at the urging of John Stuart Mill and others in order to build respectability among scientists, has, How and Eisenhardt have suggested, not only served social science badly, but also has largely been ignored as a basis for natural science. They argue that all scientific observation, analysis and theorising involves acts of interpretation, and all investigation is theory laden.

It may be too simplistic to suggest, however, that if all research is interpretive, there is no problem. Following their review of 56 mixed methods studies, Greene, Caracelli and Graham concluded: "Our own thinking to date suggests that the notion of mixing paradigms is problematic for designs with triangulation or complementary purposes, acceptable but still problematic for designs with a development or expansion intent, and actively encouraged for designs with an initiation intent".

It could be said that paradigmatic issues raised by mixed methods research remain unresolved. Indeed, one can't research or prove paradigms, and paradigmatic debates can never be resolved. The early 1990s saw a series of rejoinders to those who had given paradigms so much attention (particularly evident in the Educational Researcher) and a shift in emphasis to the more tractable issues of design and methods and features of the knowledge claims that could be generated.

Pragmatism increasingly overruled purity as the perceived benefits of mixing methods in "getting research done" came to be seen as outweighing the importance of the philosophical difficulties in their use. Thus, according to Miles and Huberman :

> "The question, then, is not whether the two sorts of data and associated methods can be linked during study design, but whether it should be done, how it will be done, and for what purposes."

Purpose and Design

Often the purpose for choosing a mixed methods design is not made clear by the researcher, potentially leading to confusion in the design phase of the study. Some studies may not be considered to have employed mixed methods at all in so far as they do not give recognition to the full contribution of each method. Purposes necessitating mixed methods may be corroboration, expansion or initiation. Initiation, in the form of an iterative, nested, holistic or transformation design, requires an integration of methods in contrast to the simpler component designs typically used for corroboration or expansion. Where the purpose of the research is made clear, and is theory-driven (i.e. presented through a logical chain of evidence) then that substantive focus becomes a super-ordinate goal which limits tensions in mixing of methods.

Much of the writing about mixed methods designs has focused on the use of component (parallel or sequential) designs in which the different elements are kept separate, thus allowing each element to be true to its own paradigmatic and design requirements (but raising the issue of whether, in such cases, these really do constitute a mixed methods study or rather, are two separate studies which happen to be about the same topic).

Likewise, most reports of mixed methods studies report either parallel or sequential component designs. Few studies report truly integrated designs—perhaps because the technology for managing integrated analyses is still in development. Triangulation is a term which has been greatly misused in relation to both purpose and design since Denzin's popularisation of it. It was initially conceived as the conduct of parallel (or otherwise duplicated) studies using different methods to achieve the same purpose, with a view to providing corroborating evidence for the conclusions drawn, i.e. as a technique of validation (drawn from the concept of triangulation in surveying).

It has, in more recent years, often been used loosely as a synonym for mixed methods without regard to either of the conditions inherent in the original concept and has as a consequence lost the power of its original meaning. It has been argued that, in any case, triangulation does not assist validation as each source must be understood on its own terms. The original model of triangulation assumes a single reality and ignores the symbolic interactions foundation of much qualitative work which proposes that different methods (or researchers or participants) will necessarily view or construe the object of the research in different ways.

And as researchers use different methods, they play different roles and have different relationships with the researched—the latter, for example, being variously labelled as respondents, subjects, participants or informants. Alternative methods may also "tap different domains of knowing" or encourage or allow expression of different facets of knowledge or experience. For example, people responding to interviews or open ended questions will often raise quite different issues to those provided for in a structured questionnaire asking essentially the same question. Interviews and focus groups generate different information, reflecting public versus private views and a preparedness to deal with more sensitive issues in interviews.

While the use of parallel methods may not, therefore, provide corroborative evidence, they may well add depth or breadth to a study and perhaps even hold the key to understanding the processes which are occurring. In the third edition of his work, Denzin himself abandons the idea of triangulation as a tool of validity, suggesting rather that it overcomes personal biases from single methodologies. "The goal of multiple triangulation is a fully grounded interpretive research approach. Objective reality will never be captured. In-depth understanding, not validity, is sought in any interpretive study". (This statement implies that objective reality and validity are the same thing, and that each is unrelated to in-depth understanding. It seems that it is difficult not to tie oneself in knots, whichever way one turns!)

Despite its being one of the more common reasons given for engaging in a mixed methods study, it would appear that corroboration of findings is not only a dubious intention but one that is almost doomed to failure.

Methods

Although they may be implied, when it comes to reporting studies, paradigms are rarely mentioned. The focus is much more on the actual methods used and results obtained. Despite the tendency for some to write about quantitative and qualitative paradigms, or to assume that someone working with numbers and statistics has a positivist perspective, it is generally recognised that there are no direct or exclusive correspondences between paradigms, methodology and methods. Indeed, "...research methodologies are merely tools, instruments to be used to facilitate understanding". With debate on the value of quantitative versus qualitative methods moderating to a recognition that both have a place, the "real issues", according to Patton, have become "methodological flexibility and appropriateness".

When methods are mixed without careful consideration of the particular assumptions or rules and expectations regarding their conduct, corruption of those methods can occur such that results obtained by them become subject to question. Assumptions regarding sampling, which will be discussed separately, provide the most blatant but not the only example of this problem. Mixed method studies in which just a few observations or interviews are conducted to supplement quantitative data collection "cheapen" qualitative methods in a way which Patton likened to a comparison between loving intimacy and a one-night stand.

The corruption may be out of ignorance, or because those using multiple strategies for investigation take short-cut in order to cope with the greater time commitment required. The term "Blitzkrieg ethnography", for example, has been applied to work conducted in a number of multi-site-multi-method studies claiming an ethnographic component, where there has not been proper immersion in the site.

"Ethnography is a methodological approach with specific procedures, techniques, and methods of analysis", and for the method to be valid one needs to adopt its values as well as its techniques. Conflicts of this type might be alternatively interpreted as disciplinary purists being precious about the traditional approaches to research of their discipline, or at least, the labelling of those approaches. The balance needs to be struck, then, between adherence to a total package of techniques, perspectives and values associated with a traditional method, and the ability to draw useful strategies from those traditions—recognising the ways in which they have been modified and the implications of doing so.

Mixed methods often combine nomothetic and idiographic approaches in an attempt to serve the dual purposes of generalisation and in-depth understanding—to gain an overview of social regularities from a larger sample while understanding the other through detailed study of a smaller sample. Full integration of these approaches is difficult, hence the predominance of component studies. Case-oriented quantification has been proposed as a way of bringing these together by providing understanding of the individual while also supporting typification. Kuckartz' software program, winMAX, was specifically written to support such a goal.

Similarly, Reagin's method of qualitative comparative analysis (QCA), also translated into software, is an attempt to develop typologic and related understanding while retaining the richness of the qualitative case.

In each case, the qualitative database is necessary to provide understanding of the meaning of the concepts and variables used, and of how the statistically derived models work out for "real people", but the statistical analysis provides also access to patterns, trends and underlying dimensions in the data not readily evident in the detail of the qualitative analyses. Such methods as these, in which the same data are treated both hermeneutical and statistically, along with those proposed by Kuckartz and Reagin, provide integrated (holistic) techniques for viewing data both nomothetically and geographically.

In the final analysis, methodology must be judged by how well it informs research purposes, more than how well it matches a set of conventions. What counts for good research will not necessarily match what counts as orthodox methodology. The standards How and Eisenhardt suggest should be applied include:

— Do the methods chosen provide data which can answer the question?

— Are the background assumptions coherent?

— Are the methods applied well enough that the results are credible?

Sampling

Typically one expects quantitative research to rely on a large, randomly drawn sample, while qualitative studies are associated with smaller, purposes (non-random) samples. But there are no statistics for generalising from small purposes samples and it is not possible to do fine hermeneutical analysis on data from large random sample. Cases for detailed study can be identified from within larger samples, while computerisation can facilitate testing, across a larger selection of texts, of the generality of ideas developed through fine-grained interpretive analysis of a subset of those texts. With computerisation of qualitative analysis and the increasing use of qualitative analysis software by those trained only in quantitative approaches to research, there is a tendency for those researchers to attempt to include much larger volumes of unstructured data than have traditionally been used in qualitative approaches. Stratified random sampling or quota sampling replaces purposes sampling so as to meet expectations for generalisation of results as understood in statistical terms—and the inappropriate application of rules of one method distorts, and potentially invalidates, the assumptions of another.

When qualitative programs can provide statistical summaries, there is a temptation to over interpret numbers (frequency or cross-tabulated data) generated through coding texts from a small, purposively drawn sample. Where the total is less than 20, it is inappropriate to report percentages, and few inferential statistical procedures can be applied to such small samples. The chi-square statistic cannot be validly used to test a relationship between variables where there are small expected frequencies (nor where categories are not mutually exclusive), and samples in the range of 10 to 20 cases per variable are required for multi-variety analyses.

At the same time, there is nothing to be gained from substituting vague terms (more, most) for actual numbers, where those numbers are available. The researcher's view of the generic and specific properties of a single case provides a basis for sampling decisions. The opportunity for detailed study while maintaining balance and variety may be more important than satisfying selection criteria based on a sampling of attributes. Symbolic interactionists argue that every case is a sample of its broader population, that similarities across a population are greater than differences between population, and therefore that it is appropriate to treat each case as being, in general terms, representative of their population. These approaches are unacceptable, however, to statisticians.

It is with integrated methods that apply both hermeneutical and statistical analyses to the same data that difficulties are most likely to arise, however, generating a need to "trade off" between the intensiveness of detailed hermeneutical analysis and the extensiveness of statistical inference to larger population. Sampling issues must be resolved with respect to the purpose of the research, and in particular how the results are to be generalised to a population beyond the sample. It matters, for example, whether it is descriptive information or understanding of a process that is to be learned and generalised from the sample.

Without computerisation, the researcher's capacity to integrate different data types in an analysis is limited. Typically, statistical data have been analysed using a computer, "in-depth" text data have been analysed without. Recent developments in computer software for qualitative data analysis (QDA) have brought about a revolution in textual analysis. Even more recent developments in QDA software—specifically the ability to export coding information in tabular form—herald a revolution for integrated mixed methods analysis. It is in the conversion of qualitative data to quantitative code for statistical analysis (often referred to as the quantities of qualitative data) that most issues arise.

The Use of Codes

Coding or categorising of data is undertaken to facilitate understanding and retrieval of information in almost any approach to analysis. Whether they are called variables, themes, concepts, categories or values, responses are "coded". And codes are the means by which data are transferred from one format into another, or between QDA and statistical software. The kinds of things codes can stand for are similar in the different software, but the way they are generated and the way they are used are often quite different, making for potential complication of interpretation when they are read in a different context.

While categories developed through a qualitative analysis may be defined a priori, QDA software allows for generation of new codes as analysis is progressing, for rearrangement of codes without loss of data, and for some software, for coding on from existing codes into new categories. Researchers using a statistical program, in contrast, need to define their variables before coding, and changing them involves re-categorising already coded data. These differences may become an issue if a researcher is determined to have a common coding system across data types in order to force comparability of conclusions from the different data sources.

Both statistical and QDA programs use codes for demographic and project related information as well as to capture topic themes and concepts. Representational/ descriptive categories (e.g. does research), instrumental/ interpretive categories (e.g. being stimulated by or passionate about research) and analytic concepts (identification as a researcher, addiction to research) are each able to be represented by codes or scores in the various software. But it is at this point that the similarity ends. A code in a statistical data set has to totally represent the category or concept it stands for. Unlike a qualitative data set, there is no recourse to the original source to check what was meant by it or to review different interpretations of it.

Because codes are the only medium for communicating information in a quantitative data set, they are necessarily precise in what they are conveying, they are single-dimensional and directional. With qualitative data the text supporting a code is always available for review, and dimensions within it (which may not have been initially apparent to the coder) may become obvious through that review, or may be revealed through pattern or comparative analyses.

Thus qualitative coding has singularity rather than single dimensional, in that in all text about a particular issue or idea or experience may be assigned the same code, regardless of the way it is expressed. Often, as well, such coding is multidirectional, as for example when all text about competence is coded together, simply because it is about that concept and regardless of whether it is about high or low levels of competence. (It is possible that analysis will reveal different dimensions for—or types of—competence, other than its quantity.)

When a qualitative theme code is quantities, its meaning becomes fixed and single-dimensional. Where directional was not embodied in the qualitative coding, then statistical analysis involving these variables must be carefully interpreted. The exported variable may simply have been a record of whether an issue was raised or a feeling discussed, without indication of how it was dealt with or perceived. If direction is needed for interpretation in the statistical analysis, it will be necessary to code on the qualitative data to provide that directional before exporting the coding information. This is perhaps the most critical issue in interpretation of quantities data.

The Counting of Codes

The way in which (qualitative) texts are segmented within QDA software, whether data are being exported for each coded segment or whole documents, the way overlapping codes are dealt with, and the method of scaling all have implications for the generation, processing and interpretation of numeric data from coding of qualitative text.

Depending on the program being used, the researcher may have a choice of exporting dichotomous (0/1) codes indicating presence or absence of a concept, counts giving the frequency of mention, or a measure indicating the relative volume of text coded a particular way in a document. Counts (other than 0/1) are influenced by the way data are segmented as a basis for counting, and frequency counts are affected by the overall length of the source documents. Counts and proportions are also problematic from the point of view that they assume a level of (ratio) scaling that ignores the meaning of missing data (scored as 0) in a qualitative data set and the potential disjuncture between 0 and 1 in a continuous scale derived from such data.

In practical terms, QDA software packages differ in whether information relating to each coded segment is the basis for exported data or whether data for each document or case as a whole is being exported. This has implications for data handling (e.g. the need to aggregate data in order to obtain patterns for respondents), as well as for the recognition of intersections in coding. Researchers using exported coding information therefore need to test out and become familiar with the transfer syntax used by their selected software.

Issues for Statistical Analysis

Inferential statistics are based on an assumption of random or representative selection of cases, and error rates in derived estimates of population characteristics are proportional to sample size. Sample selection and sample sizes therefore limit the kind of statistical procedures that might legitimately be used and the capacity to generalise to a larger population.

Each statistical technique carries particular assumptions which must be met for appropriate use of that technique. For data derived from qualitative coding, most measures (including scaled measures) will be nominal or ordinal rather than interval, distributions may be unknown and normality cannot be 8 assumed. For descriptive reporting, medians are likely to be more appropriate than means. Lack of independence in observations for some types of data can create a problem of multi-cholinergic.

Similarly, chi-square analysis carries an assumption that categories on the same axis are mutually exclusive. While classic multi-variety techniques based on the general linear model are strict in their assumptions, exploratory multi-variety techniques such as cluster and correspondence analysis can generally be applied to quantities data where conditions of normality and randomness are not necessary met—although even these techniques are not appropriate if all variables are not equally relevant to all cases.

Different approaches to data analysis treat variations and exceptions differently. Statisticians will often simply dismiss "outliers" from their analysis, and rely on probability estimates to deal with variation across the sample. Variation is "error" where the goal is to describe the typical. In a qualitative approach the researcher uses variation to illuminate developing theories and modifies theory to take account of exceptions.

A Pragmatist's Approach to Analysis

When evidence from different sources is conflicting, one has to determine how to weight the different components—or, preferably, seek reasons for the discrepancy. Ultimately, mixed methods analysis (like almost any other!) Is a process of piecing together bits of a puzzle to find answers to questions. Numbers should be used where they help to answer questions, verbal comments should never be ignored. "From data in the form of numbers, one makes inferences in the same way as with data in the form of words, not by virtue of probabilities algorithms.

Statistics are not privileged. Inference is not mechanised. With this way of viewing knowledge, 'mixed' methods may even be a misnomer, as both surveys and participant observation yield equivalent data. Inferences are based on the inquirer's coordinating multiple lines of evidence to gain an overall understanding of the phenomenon... Yet, because the inquirer is the instrument, all information flows through a single perspective".Rules are often broken: the wise mixed methods researcher knows what assumptions underlie the methods of analysis being used, understands the implications of not fully meeting those assumptions, and takes that into account in drawing and presenting conclusions.

Pragmatics

Quite apart from arguments about paradigms, methods and analysis, there are a number of quite practical issues that impact on mixed methods research. Most obviously, use of multiple methods increases the amount of time required to complete a study and the cost of conducting the study, particularly if a component design is being used.

The more critical practical problem relates to the level of researcher skills and knowledge available. Good mixed methods research requires a good working knowledge of the multiple methods being used, their assumptions, analysis procedures and tools, and an ability to understand and interpret results derived from those different methods. While they might be able to adapt to and learn new methods, researchers brought up in the traditions of a particular discipline often do not have knowledge of other methodologies, particularly the tacit knowledge that comes from years of immersion in the literature and research associated with those methodologies.

But years of disciplinary training can also create a methodological prejudice which can result in a tendency to choose methods that are within one's expertise rather than because they are the best way of answering the questions set. The level of understanding of the audience, similarly, can be a problem. The mixed methods researcher needs to convey methods which may be unfamiliar to readers from one side or the other. Stockholders, granting bodies, thesis examiners, journal editors and readers all may struggle with particular (but different!) Elements of a presentation; each has their own biases and methodological preferences and tends to understand terms used from the perspective of their own framework, even where an alternative framework is spelt out.

Writing Up

Writing mixed methods is rather like writing qualitative analysis in that it is unlikely to follow a traditional format. In determining how best to present the ideas and evidence generated through the completed study, the issue becomes one of the degree to which quantitative and qualitative components can or should be integrated. While this may be influenced by the degree to which they were integrated throughout the study, it is not necessarily determined by that.

All too often, the results and conclusions from one type of data or analysis are presented and then the results and conclusions for the other before an attempt is made to draw them together in a general conclusion (if at all). If the different approaches were designed to contribute together to a common understanding then, even where they were used side-by-side or in sequence, separation of the different components in reporting and interpreting those results is likely to lead to a report which is disjointed and potentially repetitive. Better to progressively unveil relevant evidence on a path to a common conclusion, than to organise on the basis of method used.

Mixed methods are used to enrich understanding of an experience or issue through confirmation of conclusions, extension of knowledge or by initiating new ways of thinking about the subject of the research. Mixed methods are inherently neither more nor less valid than specific approaches to research. As with any research, validity stems more from the appropriateness, thoroughness and effectiveness with which those methods are applied and the care given to thoughtful weighing of the evidence than from the application of a particular set of rules or adherence to an established tradition.

12

Reliability and Validity in Social Research

The use of reliability and validity are common in quantitative research and now it is reconsidered in the qualitative research paradigm. Since reliability and validity are rooted in positivist perspective then they should be redefined for their use in a naturalistic approach. Like reliability and validity as used in quantitative research are providing springboard to examine what these two terms mean in the qualitative research paradigm, triangulation as used in quantitative research to test the reliability and validity can also illuminate some ways to test or maximise the validity and reliability of a qualitative study.

Researchers who use logical positivism or quantitative research employ experimental methods and quantitative measures to test hypothetical generalisations, and they also emphasise the measurement and analysis of causal relationships between variables. To illustrate the meaning of quantitative research for its use of explaining social problems, Bogdan and Biklen note:

> Charts and graphs illustrate the results of the research, and commentators employ words such as 'variables', 'population' and 'result' as part of their daily vocabulary... even if we do not always know just what all of the terms mean... but we know that this is part of the process of doing research. Research, then as it comes to be known publicly, is a synonym for quantitative research.

Quantitative research allows the researcher to familiarise him/herself with the problem or concept to be studied, and perhaps generate hypotheses to be tested. In this paradigm:

— The emphasis is on facts and causes of behaviour.

— The information is in the form of numbers that can be quantified and summarised.

— The mathematical process is the norm for analysing the numeric data.

— The final result is expressed in statistical terminological.

Generally, quantitative research "...supported by the positivist or scientific paradigm, leads us to regard the world as made up of observable, measurable facts" though their assumption that "social facts have an objective reality" and "variables can... be identified and relationships measured" is problematic. The notion of 'measuring' means to understand, say, educational issues by performing an operation called 'measurement' on the physical world by the observer. Stiffens defines measurement as the assignment of numerals to objects or events according to rules. From these definitions, one may perceive measurement as necessarily objective, quantitative and statistically relevant. Simply put, measurement can be about numbers, objective hard data.

A quantitative researcher attempts to fragment and delimit phenomena into measurable or common categories that can be applied to all of the subjects or wider and similar situations. In his/her attempts, the researcher's methods involve the "use of standardised measures so that the varying perspectives and experiences of people can be fit into a limited number of predetermined response categories to which number are assigned".

For example, a quantitative researcher may prepare a list of behaviour to be checked or rated by an observer using a predetermined schedule or numbers (scales) as an instrument in his/her method of research. Thus, a quantitative researcher needs to construct an instrument to be administered in standardised manner according to predetermined procedures. But the question is if the measuring instrument measures what it is supposed to measure. In the broadest sense, devising a test or the validity of an instrument is on focus. The significance of this test is to ensure replicability or repeatability of the result.

Reliability and Validity

Reliability and validity are tools of an essentially positivist epistemology.

Reliability

Joppe defines reliability as:

> ...The extent to which results are consistent over time and an accurate representation of the total population under study is referred to as reliability and if the results of a study can be reproduced under a similar methodology, then the research instrument is considered to be reliable. Embodied in this citation is the idea of replicability or repeatability of results or observations.

Kirk and Miller identify three types of reliability referred to in quantitative research, which relate to:

— The degree to which a measurement, given repeatedly, remains the same.

— The stability of a measurement over time.

— The similarity of measurements within a given time period.

Charles adheres to the notions that consistency with which questionnaire test items are answered or individual's scores remain relatively the same can be determined through the test-re-test method at two different times. This attribute of the instrument is actually referred to as stability. If we are dealing with a stable measure, then the results should be similar. A high degree of stability indicates a high degree of reliability, which means the results are repeatable. Joppe, detects a problem with the test-re-test method which can make the instrument, to a certain degree, unreliable.

She explains that test-re-test method may sensitise the respondent to the subject matter, and hence influence the responses given. We cannot be sure that there was no change in extraneous influences such as an attitude change that has occurred. This could lead to a difference in the responses provided. Similarly, Crocker and Algina note that when a respondent answer a set of test items, the score obtained represents only a limited sample of behaviour.

As a result, the scores may change due to some characteristic of the respondent, which may lead to errors of measurement. These kinds of errors will reduce the accuracy and consistency of the instrument and the test scores. Hence, it is the researchers' responsibility to assure high consistency and accuracy of the tests and scores. Thus, Crocker and Algina say, "Test developers have a responsibility of demonstrating the reliability of scores from their tests". Although the researcher may be able to prove the research instrument repeatability and internal consistency, and, therefore reliability, the instrument itself may not be valid.

Validity

The traditional criteria for validity find their roots in a positivist tradition, and to an extent, positivism has been defined by a systematic theory of validity. Within the positivist terminology, validity resided amongst, and was the result and culmination of other empirical conceptions: universal laws, evidence, objectivity, truth, actuality, deduction, reason, fact and mathematical data to name just a few.

Joppe provides the following explanation of what validity is in quantitative research:

> Validity determines whether the research truly measures that which it was intended to measure or how truthful the research results are. In other words, does the research instrument allow you to hit "the bull's eye" of your research object? Researchers generally determine validity by asking a series of questions, and will often look for the answers in the research of others.

Wainer and Braun describe the validity in quantitative research as "construct validity". The construct is the initial concept, notion, question or hypothesis that determines which data is to be gathered and how it is to be gathered. They also assert that quantitative researchers actively cause or affect the interplay between construct and data in order to validate their investigation, usually by the application of a test or other process. In this sense, the involvement of the researchers in the research process would greatly reduce the validity of a test.

Insofar as the definitions of reliability and validity in quantitative research reveal two strands: Firstly, with regards to reliability, whether the result is replicable. Secondly, with regards to validity, whether the means of measurement are accurate and whether they are actually measuring what they are intended to measure. However, the concepts of reliability and validity are viewed differently by qualitative researchers who strongly consider these concepts defined in quantitative terms as inadequate. In other words, these terms as defined in quantitative terms may not apply to the qualitative research paradigm. The question of replicability in the results does not concern them, but precision, credibility, and transferability provide the lenses of evaluating the findings of a qualitative research. In this context, the two research approaches or perspectives are essentially different paradigms.

Reliability and Validity in Qualitative Research

Qualitative research uses a naturalistic approach that seeks to understand phenomena in context-specific settings, such as "real world setting [where] the researcher does not attempt to manipulate the phenomenon of interest". Qualitative research, broadly defined, means "any kind of research that produces findings not arrived at by means of statistical procedures or other means of quantification" and instead, the kind of research that produces findings arrived from real-world settings where the "phenomenon of interest unfold naturally". Unlike quantitative researchers who seek causal determination, prediction, and generalisation of findings, qualitative researchers seek instead illumination, understanding, and extrapolation to similar situations.

Qualitative analysis results in a different type of knowledge than does quantitative inquiry because one party argues from the underlying philosophical nature of each paradigm, enjoying detailed interviewing and the other focuses on the apparent compatibility of the research methods, "enjoying the rewards of both numbers and words". This means such methods like interviews and observations are dominant in the naturalist (interpretive) paradigm and supplementary in the positive paradigm, where the use of survey serves in opposite order.

Although it has been claimed that quantitative researchers attempt to disassociate themselves as much as possible from the research process, qualitative researchers have come to embrace their involvement and role within the research. Patton supports the notion of researcher's involvement and immersion into the research by discussing that the real world are subject to change and therefore, a qualitative researcher should be present during the changes to record an event after and before the change occurs. However, both qualitative and quantitative researchers need to test and demonstrate that their studies are credible. While the credibility in quantitative research depends on instrument construction, in qualitative research, "the researcher is the instrument". Thus, it seems when quantitative researchers speak of research validity and reliability, they are usually referring to a research that is credible while the credibility of a qualitative research depends on the ability and effort of the researcher. Although reliability and validity are treated separately in quantitative studies, these terms are not viewed separately in qualitative research. Instead, terminology that encompasses both, such as credibility, transferability, and trustworthiness is used.

To understand the meaning of reliability and validity, it is necessary to present the various definitions of reliability and validity given by many qualitative researchers from different perspectives.

Although the term 'Reliability' is a concept used for testing or evaluating quantitative research, the idea is most often used in all kinds of research. If we see the idea of testing as a way of information elucidation then the most important test of any qualitative study is its quality. A good qualitative study can help us "understand a situation that would otherwise be enigmatic or confusing".

This relates to the concept of a good quality research when reliability is a concept to evaluate quality in quantitative study with a "purpose of explaining" while quality concept in qualitative study has the purpose of "generating understanding". The difference in purposes of evaluating the quality of studies in quantitative and quantitative research is one of the reasons that the concept of reliability is irrelevant in qualitative research. According to Stenbacka, "the concept of reliability is even misleading in qualitative research. If a qualitative study is discussed with reliability as a criterion, the consequence is rather that the study is no good".

On the other hand, Patton states that validity and reliability are two factors which any qualitative researcher should be concerned about while designing a study, analysing results and judging the quality of the study. This corresponds to the question that "How can an inquirer persuade his or her audiences that the research findings of an inquiry are worth paying attention to?". To answer to the question, Healy and Perry assert that the quality of a study in each paradigm should be judged by its own paradigm's terms.

For example, while the terms Reliability and Validity are essential criterion for quality in quantitative paradigms, in qualitative paradigms the terms Credibility, Neutrality or Conformability, Consistency or Dependability and Applicability or Transferability are to be the essential criteria for quality. To be more specific with the term of reliability in qualitative research, Lincoln and Guba use "dependability", in qualitative research which closely corresponds to the notion of "reliability" in quantitative research.

They further emphasise "inquiry audit" as one measure which might enhance the dependability of qualitative research. This can be used to examine both the process and the product of the research for consistency. In the same vein, Clont and Seale endorse the concept of dependability with the concept of consistency or reliability in qualitative research. The consistency of data will be achieved when the steps of the research are verified through examination of such items as raw data, reduction products, and process notes.

To ensure reliability in qualitative research, examination of trustworthiness is crucial. Seale, while establishing good quality studies through reliability and validity in qualitative research, states that the "trustworthiness of a research report lies at the heart of issues conventionally discussed as validity and reliability". When judging (testing) qualitative work, Strauss and Corbin suggest that the "usual canons of 'good science'... require redefinition in order to fit the realities of qualitative research"

In contrast, Stenbacka argues that since reliability issue concerns measurements then it has no relevance in qualitative research. She adds the issue of reliability is an irrelevant matter in the judgement of quality of qualitative research. Therefore, if it is used then the "consequence is rather that the study is no good".

To widen the spectrum of conceptualising of reliability and revealing the congruence of reliability and validity in qualitative research, Lincoln and Guba states that: "Since there can be no validity without reliability, a demonstration of the former validity is sufficient to establish the latter reliability;". Patton with regards to the researcher's ability and skill in any qualitative research also states that reliability is a consequence of the validity in a study.

The concept of validity is described by a wide range of terms in qualitative studies. This concept is not a single, fixed or universal concept, but "rather a contingent construct, inescapably grounded in the processes and intentions of particular research methodologies and projects". Although some qualitative researchers have argued that the term validity is not applicable to qualitative research, but at the same time, they have realised the need for some kind of qualifying check or measure for their research.

For example, Creswell & Miller suggest that the validity is affected by the researcher's perception of validity in the study and his/her choice of paradigm assumption. As a result, many researchers have developed their own concepts of validity and have often generated or adopted what they consider to be more appropriate terms, such as, quality, rigor and trustworthiness.

The discussion of quality in qualitative research initiated from the concerns about validity and reliability in quantitative tradition which "involved substituting new term for words such as validity and reliability to reflect inter pretivist qualitative conceptions".

The issue of validity in qualitative research has not been disregarded by Stenbacka as she has for the issue of reliability in qualitative research. Instead, she argues that the concept of validity should be redefined for qualitative researches. Stenbacka describes the notion of reliability as one of the quality concepts in qualitative research which "to be solved in order to claim a study as part of proper research".

In searching for the meaning of rigor in research, Davies and Dodd find that the term rigor in research appears in reference to the discussion about reliability and validity. Davies and Dodd argue that the application of the notion rigor in qualitative research should differ from those in quantitative research by "accepting that there is a quantitative bias in the concept of rigor, we now move on to develop our re-conception of rigor by exploring subjectivity, reflexivity, and the social interaction of interviewing".

Lincoln and Guba argue that sustaining the trustworthiness of a research report depends on the issues, quantitatively, discussed as validity and reliability. The idea of discovering truth through measures of reliability and validity is replaced by the idea of trustworthiness, which is "defensible" and establishing confidence in the findings.

If the issues of reliability, validity, trustworthiness, quality and rigor are meant differentiating a 'good' from 'bad' research then testing and increasing the reliability, validity, trustworthiness, quality and rigor will be important to the research in any paradigm.

Testing Validity and Reliability

So far, the concepts of reliability and validity as they have been redefined for their usefulness in qualitative research have been presented. Now, the question which remains to be answered is 'How to test or maximise the validity and as a result the reliability of a qualitative study?'

If the validity or trustworthiness can be maximised or tested then more "credible and defensible result" may lead to generalisability which is one of the concepts suggested by Stenbacka as the structure for both doing and documenting high quality qualitative research. Therefore, the quality of a research is related to generalisability of the result and thereby to the testing and increasing the validity or trustworthiness of the research.

In contrast, Maxwell observes that the degree to which an account is believed to be generalisable is a factor that clearly distinguishes quantitative and qualitative research approaches. Although the ability to generalise findings to wider groups and circumstances is one of the most common tests of validity for quantitative research, but Patton states generalisability as one of the criteria for quality case studies depending on the case selected and studied. In this sense the validity in quantitative research is very specific to the test to which it is applied – where triangulation methods are used in qualitative research. Triangulation is typically a strategy (test) for improving the validity and reliability of research or evaluation of findings. Mathison elaborates this by saying:

Triangulation has risen an important methodological issue in naturalistic and qualitative approaches to evaluation in order to control bias and establishing valid propositions because traditional scientific techniques are incompatible with this alternate epistemology.

Patton advocates the use of triangulation by stating "triangulation strengthens a study by combining methods.

This can mean using several kinds of methods or data, including using both quantitative and qualitative approaches". However, the idea of combining methods has been challenged by Barber. She argues while mixing paradigms can be possible but mixing methods within one paradigm, such as qualitative research, is problematic since each method within the qualitative paradigm has its own assumption in "terms of theoretical frameworks we bring to bear on our research".

Even though triangulation is used in quantitative paradigm for confirmation and generalisation of a research, Barber does not disregard the notion of triangulation in qualitative paradigm and she states the need to define triangulation from a qualitative research's perspective in each paradigm. For example, in using triangulation of several data sources in quantitative research, any exception may lead to a disconfirmation of the hypothesis where exceptions in qualitative research are dealt to modify the theories and are fruitful.

In this view, Healy and Perry explicate on the judging validity and reliability within the realism paradigm which relies on multiple perceptions about a single reality. They argue the involvement of triangulation of several data sources and their interpretations with those multiple perceptions in the realism paradigm.

Another paradigm in qualitative research is constructiveness which views knowledge as socially constructed and may change depending on the circumstances. Crotty defined constructions from the social perspectives as "the view that all knowledge, and therefore all meaningful reality as such, is contingent upon human practices, being constructed in and out of interaction between human beings and their world, and developed and transmitted within an essentially social context".

In any qualitative research, the aim is to "engage in research that probes for deeper understanding rather than examining surface features" and constructions may facilitate toward that aim. The constructions notion, that reality is changing whether the observer wishes it or not, is an indication of multiple or possibly diverse constructions of reality. Constructions values multiple realities that people have in their minds. Therefore, to acquire valid and reliable multiple and diverse realities, multiple methods of searching or gathering data are in order. If this calls for the use of triangulation in the constructions paradigm, then the use of investigators, method and data triangulations to record the construction of reality is appropriate.

An open-ended perspective in constructions adheres with the notion of data triangulation by allowing participants in a research to assist the researcher in the research question as well as with the data collection. Engaging multiple methods, such as, observation, interviews and recordings will lead to more valid, reliable and diverse construction of realities. To improve the analysis and understanding of construction of others, triangulation is a step taken by researchers to involve several investigators or peer researchers' interpretation of the data at different time or location. In a related way, a qualitative researcher can "use investigator triangulation and consider the ideas and explanations generated by additional researchers studying the research participants".

Triangulation may include multiple methods of data collection and data analysis, but does not suggest a fix method for all the researches. The methods chosen in triangulation to test the validity and reliability of a study depend on the criterion of the research.

Bibliography

Abramson, J.J. and Abramson, Z.H. (1999). *Survey Methods in Community Medicine: Epidemiological Research, Programme Evaluation, Clincal Trials* (5th edition). London: Churchill Livingstone/Elsevier Health Sciences.

Adler, P. A. & Adler, P. (1987). *Membership roles in field research.* Newbury Park, CA: Sage. ISBN 978-0803927605

Becker, Howard S., *The epistemology of qualitative research.* University of Chicago Press, 1996. 53-71. [from Ethnography and human development : context and meaning in social inquiry / edited by Richard Jessor, Anne Colby, and Richard A. Shweder] OCLC 46597302

Boas, Franz (1943). Recent anthropology. *Science*, 98, 311-314, 334-337.

Charles C. Ragin, (1994). *Constructing Social Research: The Unity and Diversity of Method*, Pine Forge Press.

Creswell, J. W. (2003). *Research design: Qualitative, quantitative, and mixed method approaches.* Thousand Oaks, CA: Sage Publications.

Denzin, N. K., & Lincoln, Y. S. (2000). *Handbook of qualitative research 2nd ed.).* Thousand Oaks, CA; Sage Publications.

DeWalt, K. M. & DeWalt, B. R. (2002). *Participant observation.* Walnut Creek, CA: AltaMira Press.

Durkheim, Émile (1895). *The Rules of Sociological Method.* 8th edition, trans.

Fischer, C.T. (Ed.) (2005). *Qualitative research methods for psychologists: Introduction through empirical studies.* Academic Press. ISBN 0-12-088470-4.

Flyvbjerg, B. (2006). "Five Misunderstandings About Case Study Research." Qualitative Inquiry, vol. 12, no. 2, April 2006, pp. 219-245.

Gianfranco Poggi (2000). *Durkheim.* Oxford: Oxford University Press.

Giddens, A. (1990). *The consequences of modernity.* Stanford, CA: Stanford University Press.

Glenn Firebaugh, (2008). *Seven Rules for Social Research*, Princeton University Press,

Groves, R.M. (1989). *Survey Errors and Survey Costs* Wiley.

Haralambos & Holborn. (2004). *Sociology: Themes and perspectives.* 6th ed, Collins Educational.

Holliday, A. R. (2007). *Doing and Writing Qualitative Research. 2nd Edition.* London: Sage Publications

Jerald Greenberg & Robert Folger (1988), *Controversial Issues in Social Research Methods*, New York: Springer-Verlag.

Kaminski, Marek M. (2004). *Games Prisoners Play.* Princeton University Press. ISBN 0-691-11721-7.

Lawrence Neuman, W. (2006). *Social Research Methods: Qualitative and Quantitative Approaches*, 6th edition, Allyn & Bacon.

Mahoney, J & Goertz, G. (2006) A Tale of Two Cultures: Contrasting Quantitative and Qualitative Research, *Political Analysis, 14*, 227–249. doi:10.1093/pan/mpj017

Malinowski, B. (1922/1961). *Argonauts of the Western Pacific.* New York: E. P. Dutton.

Miles, M. B. & Huberman, A. M. (1994). *Qualitative Data Analysis.* Thousand Oaks, CA: Sage.

Ornstein, M.D. (1998). "Survey Research." *Current Sociology* 46(4): iii-136.

Pamela Maykut, Richard Morehouse. 1994 Beginning Qualitative Research. Falmer Press.

Patton, M. Q. (2002). *Qualitative research & evaluation methods (3rd ed.).* Thousand Oaks, CA: Sage Publications.

Pawluch D. & Shaffir W. & Miall C. (2005). *Doing Ethnography: Studying Everyday Life.* Toronto, ON Canada: Canadian Scholars' Press.

Shaughnessy, J. J., Zechmeister, E. B., & Zechmeister, J. S. (2006). *Research Methods in Psychology.* McGraw-Hill Higher Education.

Stebbins, Robert A. (2001) *Exploratory Research in the Social Sciences.* Thousand Oaks, CA: Sage.

Taylor, Steven J., Bogdan, Robert, *Introduction to Qualitative Research Methods*, Wiley, 1998, ISBN 0-471-16868-8

Van Maanen, J. (1988) Tales of the field: on writing ethnography, Chicago: University of Chicago Press.

Wacquant, Loic. 1992. "Positivism." In Bottomore, Tom and William Outhwaite, ed., *The Blackwell Dictionary of Twentieth-Century Social Thought*

Wolcott, H. F. (1999). *Ethnography: A way of seeing.* Walnut Creek, CA: AltaMira Press.

Ziman, John (2000). *Real Science: what it is, and what it means.* Cambridge, Uk: Cambridge University Press.

Index

Encyclopaedia of Sociology

Social Problems

Volume –3

Satish Mittal
Sushil Kumar Saxena

Commonwealth

Encyclopaedia of Sociology

Edition : 2026

ISBN 978-81-311-0377-7 (set)

Published by :
COMMONWEALTH PUBLISHERS (P) LTD.
4831/24, Govind Lane,
Ansari Road, Darya Ganj,
New Delhi - 110002
Ph. : 23242541, 23272541
e-mail : commonwealthpublishers2016@gmail.com

Distributed by :
ARJUN PUBLISHING HOUSE
4831/24, Govind Lane,
Ansari Road, Darya Ganj,
New Delhi - 110002
Ph. : 23242541, 23272541
e-mail : arjunbooks2001@gmail.com
arjunpubhouse@gmail.com

Laser Typesetting by :
Dimple Computers
Delhi

Printed at :
Milan Enterprises
Delhi

Preface

Social issues are matters which directly or indirectly affect a person or many members of a society and are considered to be problems, controversies related to moral values, or both. Our society consists of people from different religious, linguistic and ethnic backgrounds and we are currently experiencing social tensions of various kinds. They are related to the pattern of social change. In particular the rise of middle class migration of people from villages to cities, increase in the degree of economic inequality, spread of education and media are playing key role. The tensions in the lives of people at individual, family and community level is clearly visible. Most of the conflicts and tensions revolve around the issue of identity.

In this modern world, it is inevitable that many of the social problems which have so far been seen as national in character will assume a global character. Global social problems are those which cannot be confined within national boundaries and which need both national and international attention if they are to be ameliorated.

This book provides an original and much-needed introduction to global social problems. The most important global social issues are explored and suggestions to recover from each problems are also described. It will be essential reading for undergraduate students in the social science, particularly those studying social policy, sociology and politics.

Contents

1

Introduction to Social Problems

India is one of the developing nations of the modern world. It has become an independent country, a republic, more than a half century ago. During this period the country has been engaged in efforts to attain development and growth in various areas such as building infrastructure, production of food grains, science and technology and spread of education. The life expectancy has increased and many diseases have been controlled. However, there are many areas in which Indian society is experiencing a variety of problems. Some of these problems have their roots in our colonial past while others are related to demographic changes, sociopolitical conditions and cultural processes.

POVERTY

A large section of the Indian society is suffering from poverty. Poverty is a phenomenon which is objective as well a subjective. Objectively poverty implies a dehumanising condition in which people are unable to look after the basic needs. Subjectively poverty stands for perceived deprivation. As such it is relative and any body can feel poor by comparing himself as herself with a rich person. Poor people lack the necessary resources and capacity to satisfy basic needs like food, shelter, health and education. They live under difficult conditions which are not conducive for development of their human potential. Poverty interferes with development in many ways. For instance lack of or inadequate nutrition arrests mental development during early childhood. The unavailability of stimulating environment and absence of effective role models decreases the motivation level.

A large section of poor children do not go to school. Even if they go they become drop out and fail to complete education. In this context it may be pointed out that poverty is also related to the social structure. A number of low caste, scheduled tribe and backward communities have been put to discrimination for many centuries. They are socially disadvantaged and are deprived from the experiences necessary for development on account of their membership of specific groups. In this sense they are doubly deprived.

Studies have shown that the children from the background of poverty and social disadvantage flag behind their counterparts from the enriched background. Their cognitive development and performance is found to be at a lower level. Studies of perception, memory an intelligence have demonstrated it several times. The studies have also shown that the performance between the advantaged and disadvantaged children increases with advancing age. It has also been found that the poverty condition is de-motivating and makes a person more vulnerable. Low level of achievement motivation and greater need for dependence in these people make them less effective in coping with the problems of every day life. As a result the poor become marginalised and can not contribute to the mainstream of the society.

The question why some people are poor has been answered in many ways. The search for causes of poverty has lead to many answers. It has been located in the individual, in the social structure, or the culture of the people. For instance many people blame the victim and consider the poor as responsible for the characteristics or dispositions of the people. A detailed analysis of the problem of poverty shows that poverty is caused by multiple factors. The social and economic structure in India promotes inequality, and social disadvantages. The life in the poverty condition reinforces certain behaviour pattern, values and coping styles which, reduce the chances of upward social mobility.

SOCIAL TENSIONS

The Indian society consists of people from different religious, linguistic and ethnic backgrounds. Since long there has been cultural give and take between the people from India and other countries. Since 1947 when India gained political independence the country has been engaged in the gigantic task of nation building. Efforts have been made to put nation on the path of socioeconomic development.

The transformation of nation as a self sufficient and cohesive political entity has proved to be a difficult challenge. The colonial past, socioeconomic disparities in the society and raised aspirations have culminated in a complex situation. Traditionally the Indian society was hierarchically arranged and the different communities and caste groups showed a pattern of social distance in which low caste, tribes and minority groups were discriminated against and looked down upon. Many of the communities were considered as untouchable.

The Indian constitution prohibits against such discrimination and has abolished untouchability. However, it is still practised in certain ways. All these condition have created a situation in which various kinds of social tensions have become very frequent events are as follows:

— If we look at the historical trends we notice that the partition of India led to considerable degree of violence and the harmonious relations between Hindus and Muslims were disturbed. As a result suspicion and mistrust has developed between Muslims and Hindus. This has led to a number of clashes and conflicts which have been violent and have generated hatred.

— Various parts of the country are experiencing separatist movements. You must have read about political movements in North East part of India (Assam, Nagaland, Tripura) where demands for separate political identities have been raised from time to time. The Kashmir region is experiencing the negative impact of cross-border terrorism and people are suffering. The Nuxalite movement in certain parts (Andhra Pradesh, Bihar, Madhya Pradesh) is also creating political instability and problems of governance.

— Caste-related prejudice and discrimination has also been on rise in certain parts of the country. In the course of socialisation people acquire negative attitudes and stereotypes. Many times these are not founded in our real life experiences. Instead, they are based on false information, personal impressions and hearsay. However, they are very powerful and shape our behaviour in important ways. Thus if we have prejudice against some one it may lead to aggression, hostility and harm doing towards the target groups. In recent years inter group conflicts related to caste have moved from the social to the political arena of life. In fact caste based alliances, groups and organisation are growing fast. They utilise caste-related identity for political gains. Today caste-affiliations are not so important in social or religious matters as they are in political matters. In this context the rise of low caste groups who often call them selves Dalits is becoming a prominent feature of modern India. The presence of this group has changed the complexion of Indian political scene.

On the whole the Indian society is currently experiencing social tensions of various kinds. They are related to the pattern of social change. In particular the rise of middle class migration of people from villages to cities, increase in the degree of economic inequality, spread of education and media are playing key role. The tensions in the lives of people at individual, family and community level is clearly visible.

Most of the conflicts and tensions revolve around the issue of identity. Assertion of separate identity and promoting the same with different tactics is becoming a central problem. People use identities in an emotionally charged way to create a group structure for promoting certain goals. Thus associations, committees and organisations are created to serve these purposes. The creation of identity involves strategies which enhance similarity within the group and difference between the groups. In this way a diversion of "in group" or "own group and "out group" or other group is created. This kind of differentiation is present in almost all societies. This also implies that the differences across groups cannot be totally eliminated.

Some psychological intervention for enhancing group behaviour Since groups are inevitable and constitute an important part of our social reality what we need is to recognise the essence and value of pluralism. All groups are important and play distinct role. We need to appreciate this diversity in our social life in a positive manner. The approach should be to evolve a strategy in which diverse groups and communities are able to live distinct patterns of life the way they want. The various groups or communities should compliment each other and help in achieving their goals. Super ordinate goals may be created that may be shared by all the groups. To this end the following steps may prove very helpful.

— Increasing dialogue amongst the diverse groups existing in the society.

— Building an atmosphere of mutual trust and harmony.

— Equity and equality of opportunity for different groups needs to be ensured.

— Greater opportunities for mutual care, respect and complementary need to be created.

Gender Discrimination

Women and men are equally important for the growth and development of individual and social lives. The women play the important role as mother and the same makes it unique. However, careful analysis of Indian society indicates that the situation is not good for women folk. The sex ratio of male and female in the India population has been changing and becoming unfavourable towards women. In the Indian society women are considered major contributors to family and society.

We have gods and goddesses both and one of the incarnation of lord Shiva is Ardhanareeshwar, which is made of half male and half female in its constitution. Unfortunately this equality and prominence tells an incomplete fact. The women are also subjected to discrimination in learning, dowry deaths and expatiations of various kinds which are very common. In fact the women are becoming targets of atrocities of many types. The same is manifested in discrimination against them from very early period. The incident of infanticide, early marriage, emphasis on domestic activities and lessor emphasis on education and career have made women's lives full of problems.

They are discriminated against from early childhood. The Indian dependence on others (e.g. parents, husbands) becomes fate of the majority of the women folk. The pattern of discrimination against women varies across rural, urban and tribal areas. They are assigned diverse responsibilities and treated as relatively weaker and less competent. This image is still prevailing in various sections of the society. It is reflected in the discriminatory practices in the family such as distribution of work, food and social activities. The girl child is usually burdened with responsibilities that are beyond her capacity. Such exploitation function as obstacles in the process of development and growth of the girl child.

When a girl child matures and becomes an adult she is often found to be physically weak and mentally constrained. They are neither able to realise their potential nor able to contribute to the mainstream of society. Their contributions are often limited to family and that too are ignored.

However, some Indian women have been able to overcome the barriers in their path and became successful in many walks of life. In this connection one can mention the names of Pandita Rama Bai, Sarojini Naidu, Indira Gandhi who emerged as leaders at national level. The provision for education, legal provisions about the age of marriage and reservation for women in various walks of life has contributed to change in their situation. Today the presence of women in various occupations and public offices is much more prominent than what it used to be during earlier periods. However, the Indian society has still to go a long way as for as gender equality is concerned.

Corruption, Illiteracy and Urbanisation

As a developing country India is facing a number of problems which need careful analysis and demands steps for their solution. These problems are many in number. The salient ones include corruption, illiteracy and urbanisation. Let us briefly discuss these problems. Corruption refers to those transactions which involve unduc benefits to some people who don't deserve or are not entitled for them.

Such transactions make some people recipients of financial benefits, physical and social resources that make these people capable of exhorting power over others and controlling the rewards and punishments for others. This is often reflected in the formation of a nexus between politicians and criminals. Use of money to bribe and drawing benefits that are not feasible under the law of the land. Misuse and misappropriation of resources for personal benefits is creating a gulf between "haves" and "have not". The use of black money and scans of various types that have been discovered in recent years clearly tell that corruption is adversely influencing the growth and development of Indian society.

Illiteracy is another major problem before the society. It's a sad state of affairs that a country which had higher level of literacy (than British) at a time when British came two centuries ago is now facing the challenge of a huge number of people who are illiterate and cannot read or write. The lack of these skills renders them deprived of the opportunities for upward social mobility. Such people have to depend on others for various things and are exploited in various ways. For example the poor rural people are asked to put their thumb impression of various legal documents and are subjected to exploitation and legal hassles.

Keeping these negative consequences in view the government is trying to universes primary education. The lack of reading and writing skills makes a person incapable of availing the various opportunities to help themselves. Each and every educated person, therefore, is expected to contribute to the literacy mission and making it a success. Urbanisation is another problem that deserves serious attention. There is increasingly greater migration from villages to cities. This situation is generating pressures on cities which were meant for a definite size of population.

The limited civic facilities, civilian organisations and structures are facing difficulties in meeting the demands of the people. The mega cities like Mumbai, Kolkata Chennai and Delhi have crossed the limits for which they are capable of. This situation creates a number of problems such as unauthorised and illegal activities, emergence of slums, problem of waste disposal creation of floes, crime and health related problems. The social organisation, economy and environmental planning in many cities are becoming unmanageable.

Also, urbanisation is linked with certain kinds of attitude like consumerism and individualism. Consumerism emphasises on exploitation of resources for personal consumption without any concern for society and environment. This attitude is responsible for the ecological imbalance that is widely experienced in today's world. Similarly the individualistic attitude favours the view that the individual is the ultimate reality and all processes need to be explained at individual level. The individual is free and responsible to his or her self only.

The social problems described above deal with different domains of life. You can see that the solutions for these problems require inputs from different disciplines. The role of psychology is prominent as it deals with behaviour. Modification of attitudes, feelings and pattern of behaviour are significant. Psychologists can contribute by providing strategies for achieving these goals.

2

Issue of Poverty

Poverty is the lack of basic human needs, such as clean water, nutrition, health care, education, clothing and shelter, because of the inability to afford them. This is also referred to as absolute poverty or destitution. Relative poverty is the condition of having fewer resources or less income than others within a society or country, or compared to worldwide averages. About 1.7 billion people live in absolute poverty; before the industrial revolution, poverty had mostly been the norm.

Poverty reduction has historically been a result of economic growth as increased levels of production, such as modern industrial technology, made more wealth available for those who were otherwise too poor to afford them. Also, investments in modernising agriculture and increasing yields is considered the core of the anti-poverty effort, given three-quarters of the world's poor are rural farmers.

Today, continued economic development is constrained by the lack of economic freedom. Economic liberalisation includes extending property rights, especially to land, to the poor, and making financial services, notably savings, accessible. Inefficient institutions, corruption and political instability can also discourage investment. Aid and government support in health, education and infrastructure helps growth by increasing human and physical capital.

Causes

Scarcity of Basic Needs

Before the industrial revolution, poverty had been mostly accepted as inevitable as economies produced little, making wealth scarce. In Antwerp and Lyon, two of the largest cities in western Europe, by 1600 three-quarters of the total population were too poor to pay taxes. In 18th century England, half the population was at least occasionally dependent on charity for subsistence. In modern times, food shortages have been reduced dramatically in the developed world, thanks to agricultural technologies such as nitrogen fertilisers, pesticides and new irrigation methods. Also, mass production of goods in places such as China has made what were once considered luxuries, such as vehicles or computers, inexpensive and thus accessible to many who were otherwise too poor to afford them.

Rises in the costs of living make poor people less able to afford items. Poor people spend a greater portion of their budgets on food than richer people. As a result poor households, and those near the poverty threshold can be particularly vulnerable to increases in food prices. For example in late 2007 increases in the price of grains led to food riots in some countries. The World Bank warned that 100 million people were at risk of sinking deeper into poverty. Threats to the supply of food may also be caused by drought and the water crisis. Intensive farming often leads to a vicious cycle of exhaustion of soil fertility and decline of agricultural yields. Approximately 40% of the world's agricultural land is seriously degraded. In Africa, if current trends of soil degradation continue, the continent might be able to feed just 25% of its population by 2025, according to UNU's Ghana-based Institute for Natural Resources in Africa.

Health care can be widely unavailable to the poor. The loss of health care workers emigrating from impoverished countries has a damaging effect. For example, an estimated 100,000 Philippine nurses emigrated between 1994 and 2006. There are more Ethiopian doctors in Chicago than in Ethiopia.

Overpopulation and lack of access to birth control methods drive poverty The world's population is expected to reach nearly 9 billion in 2040. However, the reverse is also true, that poverty causes overpopulation as it gives women little power to plan childhood, have educational attainment, or a career.

Barriers to Opportunities

The unwillingness of governments and feudal elates to give full-fledged property rights of land to their tenants is cited as the chief obstacle to development. This lack of economic freedom inhibits entrepreneurship among the poor. New enterprises and foreign investment can be driven away by the results of inefficient institutions, notably corruption, weak rule of law and excessive bureaucratic burdens. Lack of financial services, as a result of restrictive regulations, such as the requirements for banking licenses, makes it hard for even smaller micro-savings programs to reach the poor.

It takes two days, two bureaucratic procedures, and $280 to open a business in Canada while an entrepreneur in Bolivia must pay $2,696 in fees, wait 82 business days, and go through 20 procedures to do the same. Such costly barriers favour big firms at the expense of small enterprises, where most jobs are created. In India before economic reforms, businesses had to bribe government officials even for routine activities, which was a tax on business in effect.

Corruption, for example, in Nigeria, led to an estimated $400 billion of the country's oil revenue to be stolen by

Nigeria's leaders between 1960 and 1999. Lack of opportunities can further be caused by the failure of governments to provide essential infrastructure.

Opportunities in richer countries drives talent away, leading to brain drains. This is mainly caused by richer countries' restrictions on Freedom of Movement of the poor, uneducated class. Entry visas are granted with much higher probability to the rich and educated of developing countries. Brain drain has cost the African continent over $4 billion in the employment of 150,000 expatriate professionals annually. Indian students going abroad for their higher studies costs India a foreign exchange outflow of $10 billion annually.

Poor health and education severely affects productivity. Inadequate nutrition in childhood undermines the ability of individuals to develop their full capabilities. Lack of essential minerals such as iodine and iron can impair brain development. Two billion people (one-third of the total global population) are affected by iodine deficiency. In developing countries, it is estimated that 40% of children aged 4 and younger suffer from anaemia because of insufficient iron in their diets.

Similarly substance abuse, including for example alcoholism and drug abuse can consign people to vicious poverty cycles. Infectious diseases such as Malaria and tuberculosis can perpetuate poverty by diverting health and economic resources from investment and productivity; malaria decreases GDP growth by up to 1.3% in some developing nations and AIDS decreases African growth by 0.3-1.5% annually.

War, political instability and crime, including violent gangs and drug cartels, also discourage investment. Civil wars and conflicts in Africa cost the continent some $300 billion between 1990 and 2005. Arteria and Ethiopia spent hundreds of millions of dollars on the war that resulted in minor border changes. Shocks in the business cycle affect poverty rates, increasing in recessions and declining in booms. Cultural factors, such as discrimination of various kinds, can negatively affect productivity such as age discrimination, stereotyping, gender discrimination, racial discrimination, and caste discrimination.

Max Weber and the modernisation theory suggest that cultural values could affect economic success. However, researchers have gathered evidence that suggest that values are not as deeply ingrained and that changing economic opportunities explain most of the movement into and out of poverty, as opposed to shifts in values.

Effects of Poverty

The effects of poverty may also be causes, as listed above, thus creating a "poverty cycle" operating across multiple levels, individual, local, national and global.

Health Problems

Hunger, disease, and less education describe a person in poverty. One third of deaths-some 18 million people a year or 50,000 per day-are due to poverty-related causes: in total 270 million people, most of them women and children, have died as a result of poverty since 1990. Those living in poverty suffer disproportionately from hunger or even starvation and disease. Those living in poverty suffer lower life expectancy. According to the World Health Organisation, hunger and malnutrition are the single gravest threats to the world's public health and malnutrition is by far the biggest contributor to child mortality, present in half of all cases.

Every year nearly 11 million children living in poverty die before their fifth birthday. 1.02 billion people go to bed hungry every night. Poverty increases the risk of homelessness. There are over 100 million street children worldwide. Increased risk of drug abuse may also be associated with poverty.

According to the Global Hunger Index, South Asia has the highest child malnutrition rate of the world's regions. Nearly half of all Indian children are undernourished, one of the highest rates in the world and nearly double the rate of Sub-Saharan Africa. Every year, more than half a million women die in pregnancy or childbirth. Almost 90% of maternal deaths occur in Asia and sub-Saharan Africa, compared to less than 1% in the developed world.

Women who have children born in poverty cannot nourish the children efficiently with the right prenatal care. They may also suffer from disease that may be passed down to the child through birth. Asthma is a common problem children acquire when born into poverty.

Education

Research has found that there is a high risk of educational underachievement for children who are from low-income housing circumstances. This often is a process that begins in primary school for some less fortunate children. In the US educational system, these children are at a higher risk than other children for retention in their grade, special placements during the school's hours and even not completing their high school education. There are indeed many explanations for why students tend to drop out of school. For children with low resources, the risk factors are similar to excuses such as juvenile delinquency rates, higher levels of teenage pregnancy, and the economic dependency upon their low income parent or parents.

Families and society who submit low levels of investment in the education and development of less fortunate children end up with less favourable results for the children who see a life of parental employment reduction and low wages. Higher rates of early childbearing with all the connected risks to family, health and well-being are maturely important issues to address since education from preschool to high school are both identifiably meaningful in a life.

Poverty often drastically affects children's success in school. A child's "home activities, preferences, mannerisms" must align with the world and in the cases that they do not these students are at a disadvantage in the school and most importantly the classroom. Therefore, it is safe to state that children who live at or below the poverty level will have far less success educationally than children who live above the poverty line. Poor children have a great deal less health care and this ultimately results in many absences from the academic year. Additionally, poor children are much more likely to suffer from hunger, fatigue, irritability, headaches, ear infections, flu, and colds. These illnesses could potentially restrict a child or student's focus and concentration.

Housing

Slum-dwellers, who make up a third of the world's urban population, live in a poverty no better, if not worse, than rural people, who are the traditional focus of the poverty in the developing world, according to a report by the United Nations.

Most of the children living in institutions around the world have a surviving parent or close relative, and they most commonly entered orphanages because of poverty. Experts and child advocates maintain that orphanages are expensive and often harm children's development by separating them from their families. It is speculated that, flush with money, orphanages are increasing and push for children to join even though demographic data show that even the poorest extended families usually take in children whose parents have died.

Violence

According to a UN report on modern slavery, the most common form of human trafficking is for prostitution, which is largely fuelled by poverty. In Zimbabwe, a number of girls are turning to prostitution for food to survive because of the increasing poverty. In one survey, 67% of children from disadvantaged inner cities said they had witnessed a serious assault, and 33% reported witnessing a homicide. 51% of fifth graders from New Orleans have been found to be victims of violence, compared to 32% in Washington, DC.

Drug Abuse

Unemployment and distance from rural areas are where most drug abuse occurs. Drug abuse can result in a community shouldering the impact of many nefarious acts such as stealing, killing, theft, sexual assault, and prostitution. Drug abuse is synonymous with poor performance in school & work, and a general malaise of intra-personal intelligence. People who have abused drugs and have spent all of their money buying substances—i.e. heroin, alcohol, methamphetamine etc.—become addicts. This induces a downward spiral in the functionality of most addicts, as the drugs and poverty can be cyclical. When an addict has no other way to support their addiction they result to illegal measures to obtain income. This is where a community becomes affected by drug abuse.

Absolute Poverty

Poverty is usually measured as either absolute or relative poverty (the latter being actually an index of income inequality). Absolute poverty refers to a set standard which is consistent over time and between countries. The World Bank defines extreme poverty as living on less than US $1.25 (PPP) per day, and moderate poverty as less than $2 a day. It estimates that "in 2001, 1.1 billion people had consumption levels below $1 a day and 2.7 billion lived on less than $2 a day."

Six million children die of hunger every year - 17,000 every day. Selective Primary Health Care has been shown to be one of the most efficient ways in which absolute poverty can be eradicated in comparison to Primary Health Care which has a target of treating diseases. Disease prevention is the focus of Selective Primary Health Care which puts this system on higher grounds in terms of preventing malnutrition and illness, thus putting an end to Absolute Poverty.

The proportion of the developing world's population living in extreme economic poverty fell from 28 percent in 1990 to 21 percent in 2001. Most of this improvement has occurred in East and South Asia. In East Asia the World Bank reported that "The poverty headcount rate at the $2-a-day level is estimated to have fallen to about 27 percent, down from 29.5 percent in 2006 and 69 percent in 1990." In Sub-Saharan Africa extreme poverty went up from 41 percent in 1981 to 46 percent in 2001, which combined with growing population increased the number of people living in extreme poverty from 231 million to 318 million.

In the early 1990s some of the transition economies of Eastern Europe and Central Asia experienced a sharp drop in income. The collapse of the Soviet Union resulted in large declines in GDP per capita, of about 30 to 35% between 1990 and the trough year of 1998 (when it was at its minimum). As a result poverty rates also increased although in subsequent years as per capita incomes recovered the poverty rate dropped from 31.4% of the population to 19.6%· The World Bank issued a report predicting that between 2007 and 2027 the population of Georgia and Ukraine will decrease by 17% and 24% respectively.

World Bank data shows that the percentage of the population living in households with consumption or income per person below the poverty line has decreased in each region of the world since 1990:

Region	1990	2002	2004
East Asia and Pacific	15.40%	12.33%	9.07%
Europe and Central Asia	3.60%	1.28%	0.95%
Latin America and the Caribbean	9.62%	9.08%	8.64%
Middle East and North Africa	2.08%	1.69%	1.47%
South Asia	35.04%	33.44%	30.84%
Sub-Saharan Africa	46.07%	42.63%	41.09%

Other human development indicators have also been improving. Life expectancy has greatly increased in the developing world since WWII and is starting to close the gap to the developed world. Child mortality has decreased in every developing region of the world. The proportion of the world's population living in countries where per-capita food supplies are less than 2,200 calories per day decreased from 56% in the mid-1960s to below 10% by the 1990s. Similar trends can be observed for literacy, access to clean water and electricity and basic consumer items.

There are various criticisms of these measurements. Shaohua Chen and Martin Ravallion note that although "a clear trend decline in the percentage of people who are absolutely poor is evident... with uneven progress across regions... The developing world outside China and India has seen little or no sustained progress in reducing the number of poor".

Since the world's population is increasing, a constant number living in poverty would be associated with a diminishing proportion. Looking at the percentage living on less than $1/day, and if excluding China and India, then this percentage has decreased from 31.35% to 20.70% between 1981 and 2004.

The 2007 World Bank report "Global Economic Prospects" predicts that in 2030 the number living on less than the equivalent of $1 a day will fall by half, to about 550 million. An average resident of what we used to call the Third World will live about as well as do residents of the Czech or Solvate republics today. Much of Africa will have difficulty keeping pace with the rest of the developing world and even if conditions there improve in absolute terms, the report warns, Africa in 2030 will be home to a larger proportion of the world's poorest people than it is today.

The reason for the faster economic growth in East Asia and South Asia is a result of their relative backwardness, in a phenomenon called the convergence hypothesis or the conditional convergence hypothesis. Because these economies began modernising later than richer nations, they could benefit from simply adapting technological advances which enable higher levels of productivity that had been invented over centuries in richer nations.

Relative Poverty

Relative poverty views poverty as socially defined and dependent on social context, hence relative poverty is a measure of income inequality. Usually, relative poverty is measured as the percentage of population with income less than some fixed proportion of median income. There are several other different income inequality matrix, for example the Gini coefficient or the Theil -Index. Relative poverty measures are used as official poverty rates in several developed countries. As such these poverty statistics measure inequality rather than material deprivation or hardship. The measurements are usually based on a person's yearly income and frequently take no account of total wealth. The main poverty line used in the OECD and the European Union is based on "economic distance", a level of income set at 60% of the median household income.

Economic Aspects of Poverty

Economic aspects of poverty focus on material needs, typically including the necessities of daily living, such as food, clothing, shelter, or safe drinking water. Poverty in this sense may be understood as a condition in which a person or community is lacking in the basic needs for a minimum standard of well-being and life, particularly as a result of a persistent lack of income.

Analysis of social aspects of poverty links conditions of scarcity to aspects of the distribution of resources and power in a society and recognises that poverty may be a function of the diminished "capability" of people to live the kinds of lives they value. The social aspects of poverty may include lack of access to information, education, health care, or political power.

Poverty may also be understood as an aspect of unequal social status and inequitable social relationships, experienced as social exclusion, dependency, and diminished capacity to participate, or to develop meaningful connections with other people in society. Such social exclusion can be minimised through strengthened connections with the mainstream, such as through the provision of relational care to those who are experiencing poverty.

The World Bank's "Voices of the Poor," based on research with over 20,000 poor people in 23 countries, identifies a range of factors which poor people identify as part of poverty. These include:

- Precarious livelihoods.
- Excluded locations.
- Physical limitations.
- Gender relationships.
- Problems in social relationships.
- Lack of security.
- Abuse by those in power.
- Dis-empowering institutions.
- Limited capabilities.
- Weak community organisations.

David Moore, in his book The World Bank, argues that some analysis of poverty reflect pejorative, sometimes racial, stereotypes of impoverished people as powerless victims and passive recipients of aid programs.

Ultra-poverty, a term apparently coined by Michael Lipton, connotes being amongst poorest of the poor in low-income countries. Lipton defined ultra-poverty as receiving less than 80 percent of minimum caloric intake whilst spending more than 80% of income on food. Alternatively a 2007 report issued by International Food Policy Research Institute defined ultra-poverty as living on less than 54 cents per day. BRAC (NGO) has pioneered a program called Targeting the Ultra-Poor to redress ultra-poverty by working with individual ultra-poor women.

Voluntary Poverty

Among some individuals, such as ascetics, poverty is considered a necessary or desirable condition, which must be embraced in order to reach certain spiritual, moral, or intellectual states. Poverty is often understood to be an essential element of renunciation in religions such as Buddhism (only for monks, not for lay persons) and Jainism, whilst in Roman Catholicism it is one of the evangelical counsels.

Certain religious orders also take a vow of extreme poverty. For example, the Franciscan orders have traditionally foregone all individual and corporate forms of ownership. While individual ownership of goods and wealth is forbidden for Benedictines, following the Rule of St. Benedict, the monastery itself may possess both goods and money, and throughout history some monasteries have become very rich.

In this context of religious vows, poverty may be understood as a means of self-denial in order to place oneself at the service of others; Pope Honorius III wrote in 1217 that the Dominicans "lived a life of voluntary poverty, exposing themselves to innumerable dangers and suffering, for the salvation of others". Following Jesus' warning that riches can be like thorns that choke up the good seed of the word, voluntary poverty is often understood by Christians as of benefit to the individual–a form of self-discipline by which one distances oneself from distractions from God.

Poverty Reduction

Poverty has historically been accepted as inevitable as non-industrialised economies produced very little while population grew almost as fast making wealth scarce. Poverty reduction, or poverty alleviation, has been largely as a result of overall economic growth. Food shortages were common before modern agricultural technology and in places that lack them today, such as nitrogen fertilisers, pesticides and irrigation methods. The dawn of industrial revolution led to high economic growth, eliminating mass poverty in what is now considered the developed world. World GDP per person quintupled during the 20th century. In 1820, 75% of humanity lived on less than a dollar a day, while in 2001, only about 20% do. Today, continued economic development is constrained by the lack of economic freedom. Economic liberalisation requires extending property rights to the poor, especially to land. Financial services, notably savings, can be made accessible to the poor through technology, such as mobile banking. Inefficient institutions, corruption and political instability can also discourage investment. Aid and government support in health, education and infrastructure helps growth by increasing human and physical capital.

Poverty alleviation also involves improving the living conditions of people who are already poor. Aid, particularly in medical and scientific areas, is essential in providing better lives, such as the green revolution and the eradication of smallpox. Problems with today's development aid include the high proportion of tied aid, which mandates receiving nations to buy products, often more expensive, originating only from donor countries. Nevertheless, some believe that small changes in the way each of us in affluent nations lives our lives could solve world poverty.

Economic Liberalisation

Extending property rights protection to the poor is one of the most important poverty reduction strategy a nation could take. Securing property rights to land, the largest asset for most societies, is vital to their economic freedom. The World Bank concludes increasing land rights is 'the key to reducing poverty' citing that land rights greatly increase poor people's wealth, in some cases doubling it. It is estimated that state recognition of the property of the poor would give them assets worth 40 times all the foreign aid since 1945. Although approaches varied, the World Bank said the key issues were security of tenure and ensuring land transactions were low cost. In China and India, noted reductions in poverty in recent decades have occurred mostly as a result of the abandonment of collective farming in China and the cutting of government red tape in India.

New enterprises and foreign investment can be driven away by the results of inefficient institutions, notably corruption, weak rule of law and excessive bureaucratic burdens. It takes two days, two bureaucratic procedures, and $280 to open a business in Canada while an entrepreneur in Bolivia must pay $2,696 in fees, wait 82 business days, and go through 20 procedures to do the same. Such costly barriers favour big firms at the expense of small enterprises, where most jobs are created. In India before economic reforms, businesses had to bribe government officials even for routine activities, which was a tax on business in effect.

However, ending government sponsorship of social programs is sometimes advocated as a free market principle with tragic consequences. For example, the World Bank presses poor nations to eliminate subsidies for fertiliser even while many farmers cannot afford them at market prices. The re-configuration of public financing in former Soviet states during their transition to a market economy called for reduced spending on health and education, sharply increasing poverty.

Trade liberalisation increases total surplus of trading nations. Remittances sent to poor countries, such as India, are sometimes larger than foreign direct investment and total remittances are more than double aid flows from OECD countries. Foreign investment and export industries helped fuel the economic expansion of fast growing Asian nations. However, trade rules are often unfair as they block access to richer nations' markets and ban poorer nations from supporting their industries. Processed products from poorer nations, in contrast to raw materials, get vastly higher tariffs at richer nations' ports.

A University of Toronto study found the dropping of duty charges on thousands of products from African nations because of the African Growth and Opportunity Act was directly responsible for a "surprisingly large" increase in imports from Africa. Deals can sometimes be negotiated to favour the developing country such as in China, where laws compel foreign multinationals to train their future Chinese competitors in strategic industries and render themselves redundant in the long term. In Thailand, the 51 percent rule compels multinational corporations starting operations in Thailand give 51 percent control to a Thai company in a joint venture.

Capital, Infrastructure and Technology

Long run economic growth per person is achieved through increases in capital (factors that increase productivity), both human and physical, and technology. Improving human capital, in the form of health, is needed for economic growth. Nations do not necessarily need wealth to gain health. For example, Sri Lanka had a maternal mortality rate of 2% in the 1930s, higher than any nation today. It reduced it to.5-.6% in the 1950s and to.06% today. However, it was spending less each year on maternal health because it learned what worked and what did not. Knowledge on the cost effectiveness of health care interventions can be elusive but educational measures to disseminate what works are available, such as the disease control priorities project. Promoting hand washing is one of the most cost effective health intervention and can cut deaths from the major childhood diseases of diarrhoea and pneumonia by half.

Human capital, in the form of education, is an even more important determinant of economic growth than physical capital. De-worming children costs about 50 cents per child per year and reduces non-attendance from anaemia, illness and malnutrition and is only a twenty-fifth as expensive to increase school attendance as by constructing schools.

UN economists argue that good infrastructure, such as roads and information networks, helps market reforms to work. China claims it is investing in railways, roads, ports and rural telephones in African countries as part of its formula for economic development. It was the technology of the steam engine that originally began the dramatic decreases in poverty levels. Cell phone technology brings the market to poor or rural sections. With necessary information, remote farmers can produce specific crops to sell to the buyers that brings the best price.

Such technology also helps bring economic freedom by making financial services accessible to the poor. Those in poverty place overwhelming importance on having a safe place to save money, much more so than receiving loans. Also, a large part of micro-finance loans are spent on products that would usually be paid by a checking or savings account. Mobile banking addresses the problem of the heavy regulation and costly maintenance of saving accounts. Mobile financial services in the developing world, ahead of the developed world in this respect, could be worth $5 billion by 2012. Safaricom's M-Pesa launched one of the first systems where a network of agents of mostly shopkeepers, instead of bank branches, would take deposits in cash and translate these onto a virtual account on customers' phones. Cash transfers can be done between phones and issued back in cash with a small commission, making remittances safer.

Aids

Welfare Aids

Aid in its simplest form is a basic income grant, a form of social security periodically providing citizens with money. In pilot projects in Nàmibia, where such a program pays just $13 a month, people were able to pay tuition fees, raising the proportion of children going to school by 92%, child malnutrition rates fell from 42% to 10% and economic activity grew 10%. Aid could also be rewarded based on doing certain requirements.

Conditional Cash Transfers, widely credited as a successful anti-poverty program, is based on actions such as enrolling children in school or receiving vaccinations. In Mexico, for example, the country with the largest such program, dropout rates of 16-19 year old in rural area dropped by 20% and children gained half an inch in height. Initial fears that the program would encourage families to stay at home rather than work to collect benefits have proven to be unfounded. Instead, there is less excuse for neglectful behaviour as, for example, children are prevented from begging on the streets instead of going to school because it could result in suspension from the program.

Welfare states have an effect on poverty reduction. Currently modern, expansive welfare states that ensure economic opportunity, independence and security in a near universal manner are still the exclusive domain of the developed nations. Commonly constituting at least 20% of GDP, with the largest Scandinavia welfare states constituting over 40% of GDP. These modern welfare states, which largely arose in the late 19th and early 20th centuries, seeing their greatest expansion in the mid 20th century, and have proven themselves highly effective in reducing relative as well as absolute poverty in all analysed high-income OECD countries.

Development Aid

A major proportion of aid from donor nations is 'tied', mandating that a receiving nation buy products originating only from the donor country. This can be harmful economically. For example, Arteria is forced to spend aid money on foreign goods and services to build a network of railways even though it is cheaper to use local expertise and resources. Money from the United States to fight AIDS requires it be spent on U.S brand name drugs that can cost up to $15,000 a year compared to $350 a year for generics from other countries. Only Norway, Denmark, Netherlands and Britain have stopped tying their aid.

Some think tanks and NGOs have argued that Western monetary aid often only serves to increase poverty and social inequality, either because it is conditioned with the implementation of harmful economic policies in the recipient countries, or because it's tied with the importing of products from the donor country over cheaper alternatives, or because foreign aid is seen to be serving the interests of the donor more than the recipient. Critics also argue that some of the foreign aid is stolen by corrupt governments and officials, and that higher aid levels erode the quality of governance.

Policy becomes much more oriented toward what will get more aid money than it does towards meeting the needs of the people. Problems with the aid system and not aid itself are that the aid is excessively directed towards the salaries of consultants from donor countries, the aid is not spread properly, neglecting vital, less publicised area such as agriculture, and the aid is not properly coordinated among donors, leading to a plethora of disconnected projects rather than unified strategies.

Supporters of aid argue that these problems may be solved with better auditing of how the aid is used. Immunisation campaigns for children, such as against polio, diphtheria and measles have save millions of lives. Aid from non-governmental organisations may be more effective than governmental aid; this may be because it is better at reaching the poor and better controlled at the grassroots level. As a point of comparison, the annual world military spending is over $1 trillion.

Debt Relief

One of the proposed ways to help poor countries that emerged during the 1980's has been debt relief. Given that many less developed nations have gotten themselves into extensive debt to banks and governments from the rich nations, and given that the interest payments on these debts are often more than a country can generate per year in profits from exports, cancelling part or all of these debts may allow poor nations "to get out of the hole". If poor countries do not have to spend so much on debt payments, they can use the money instead for priorities which help reduce poverty such as basic health-care and education. Many nations began offering services, such as free health care even while overwhelming the health care infrastructure, because of savings that resulted from the rounds of debt relief in 2005.

Role of Education and Skill-building

Universal public education has some role in preparing youth for basic academic skills and perhaps many trade skills, as well. Apprenticeships clearly build needed trade skills. If modest amounts of cash and land can be combined with a modicum of agricultural skills in a temperate climate, subsistence can give way toward modest socialite wealth. As has been mentioned, education for women will allow for reduced family size—an important poverty reduction event in its own right.

While all components mentioned above are necessary, the portion of education pertaining to the variety of skills needed to build and maintain the infrastructure of a developing (moving out of poverty) society: building trades; plumbing; electrician; well-drilling; farm and transport mechanical skills (and others) are clearly needed in large numbers of individuals, if the society is to move out of poverty or subsistence. Yet, many well-developed western economies are moving strongly away from the essential apprenticeships and skill training which affords a clear vocational path out of modern urban poverty.

Micro-loans

One of the most popular of the new technical tools for economic development and poverty reduction are Micro-loans made famous in 1976 by the Grameen Bank in Bangladesh. The idea is to loan small amounts of money to farmers or villages so these people can obtain the things they need to increase their economic rewards. A small pump costing only $50 could make a very big difference in a village without the means of irrigation, for example. A couple of hundred dollars for a small bridge linking a village to a city where it can market farm products is another example. A specific example is the Thai government's People's Bank which is making loans of $100 to $300 to help farmers buy equipment or seeds, help street vendors acquire an inventory to sell, or help others set up small shops.

Micro-enterprise Development adds teaching of basic financial principles and general business training before providing loan capital, thus is very practical and sound approach to fighting poverty. This approach is advocated by Five Talents as the way to ensure that entrepreneurs and their communities benefit now and in the future with documented success stories

Good Institutions

Efficient institutions that are not corrupt and obey the rule of law make and enforce good laws that provide security to property and businesses. Efficient and fair governments would work to invest in the long-term interests of the nation rather than plunder resources through corruption.

Researchers at UC Berkely developed what they called a "Weberianness scale" which measures aspects of bureaucracies and governments Max Weber described as most important for rational-legal and efficient government over 100 years ago. Comparative research has found that the scale is correlated with higher rates of economic development. With their related concept of good governance World Bank researchers have found much the same: Data from 150 nations have shown several measures of good governance (such as accountability, effectiveness, rule of law, low corruption) to be related to higher rates of economic development.

Funds from aid and natural resources are often diverted into private hands and then sent to banks overseas as a result of graft. If Western banks rejected stolen money, says a report by Global Witness, ordinary people would benefit "in a way that aid flows will never achieve". The report asked for more regulation of banks as they have proved capable of stanching the flow of funds linked to terrorism, money-laundering or tax evasion.

Examples of good governance leading to economic development and poverty reduction include Thailand, Taiwan, Malaysia, South Korea, and Vietnam, which tend to have a strong government, called a hard state or development state. These "hard states" have the will and authority to create and maintain policies that lead to long-term development that helps all their citizens, not just the wealthy. Multinational corporations are regulated so that they follow reasonable standards for pay and labour conditions, pay reasonable taxes to help develop the country, and keep some of the profits in the country, reinvesting them to provide further development.

The United Nations Development Program published a report in April 2000 which focused on good governance in poor countries as a key to economic development and overcoming the selfish interests of wealthy elates often behind state actions in developing nations. The report concludes that "Without good governance, reliance on trickle-down economic development and a host of other strategies will not work." Despite the promise of such research several questions remain, such as where good governance comes from and how it can be achieved. The comparative analysis of one sociologist suggests that broad historical forces have shaped the likelihood of good governance.

Ancient civilisations with more developed government organisation before colonialism, as well as elite responsibility, have helped create strong states with the means and efficiency to carry out development policies today. On the other hand strong states are not always the form of political organisation most conducive to economic development. Other historical factors, especially the experiences of colonialism for each country, have intervened to make a strong state and/or good governance less likely for some countries, especially in Africa. Another important factor that has been found to affect the quality of institutions and governance was the pattern of colonisation (how it took place) and even the identity of colonising power. International agencies may be able to promote good governance through various policies of intervention in developing nations as indicated in a few African countries, but comparative analysis suggests it may be much more difficult to achieve in most poor nations around the world.

Other Approaches

The role of women in poverty have also contributed to the cause of household survival. Thus, poverty reduction can only be actively done by understanding the level of gender role and gender differences within households. This will help reduce factors of poverty aside from the obvious income disparities. When given more rights and opportunities women begin to receive more education, thus increasing the overall human capital of the country; when given more influence women seem to act more responsibly in helping people in the family or village; and when better educated and more in control of their lives, women are more successful in bringing down rapid population growth because they have more say in family planning.

Another approach that has been proposed for alleviating poverty is Fair Trade which advocates the payment of an above market price as well as social and environmental standards in areas related to the production of goods. The efficacy of this approach to poverty reduction is controversial.

Community and monetary economist Thomas H. Greco, Jr. has argued that the mainstream global economy with its debt-based currency has built-in structural incentives that create poverty through keeping money scarce. Greco points to the success of modern barter clubs and historical local currencies such as the Wörgl Experiment at revitalising stagnant local economies, and calls for the creation of community currency as a means to reduce or eliminate poverty.

The Toronto Dollar is an example of a local currency oriented towards reducing poverty. Toronto Dollars are sold and redeemed in such a way that raise funds which are then given as grants to local charities, primarily ones oriented towards reducing poverty. Toronto Dollars also provide a means to create an incentive for welfare recipients to work: Toronto dollars can be given as gifts to welfare recipients who perform volunteer work for charitable and non-profit organisations, and these gifts do not affect welfare benefits.

Some have argued for radical economic change in the system. There are several fundamental proposals for restructuring existing economic relations, and many of their supporters argue that their ideas would reduce or even eliminate poverty entirely if they were implemented. Such proposals have been put forward by both left-wing and right-wing groups: socialism, communism, anarchism, libertarianism, binary economics and participatory economics, among others.

Inequality can be reduced by progressive taxation, wealth tax, and inheritance tax. In law, there has been a move to establish the absence of poverty as a human right. The IMF and member countries have produced Poverty Reduction Strategy papers or PRSPs. In his book" The End of Poverty", a prominent economist named Jeffrey Sacks laid out a plan to eradicate global poverty by the year 2025. Following his recommendations, international organisations such as the Global Solidarity Network are working to help eradicate poverty worldwide with intervention in the areas of housing, food, education, basic health, agricultural inputs, safe drinking water, transportation and communications.

The Poor People's Economic Human Rights Campaign is an organisation in the United States working to secure freedom from poverty for all by organising the poor themselves. The Campaign believes that a human rights framework, based on the value of inherent dignity and worth of all persons, offers the best means by which to organise for a political solution to poverty.

3

Inequality and Social Conflicts

The links between inequality and violent conflict is one of the oldest concerns of political economy. "We maintain that if a state is to avoid the greatest plague of all—I mean civil war, though civil disintegration would be a better term—extreme poverty and wealth must not be allowed to arise in any section of the citizen-body, because both lead to both these disasters". It is almost a universal assumption that an inequitable distribution of resources and wealth will provoke violent rebellion.

For example, in 1562 Montaigne met a small group of Indians from Brazil (the subject of his essay, On Cannibals) and asked them what they found most remarkable about their visit to France. One of the answers was that they had noticed among us some men gorged to the full with things of every sort while their other halves were beggars at their doors, emaciated with hunger and poverty. They found it strange that these poverty-stricken halves [sic] should suffer such injustice, and that they did not take the others by the throat or set fire to their houses

And yet it is just as obvious and historically established that sharply skewed income and wealth distribution does not always or even usually lead to rebellion. This is generally taken to mean that the inequality is legitimised in one way or another; that the inequality comes with a degree of power and repression that are simply too great to overcome; or that there are various obstacles preventing collective action.

Inequality in some form or other is a constant of all hierarchical social order. Violence too is prevalent in human society. However, while organised violent political conflict ebbs and flows: it is interspersed with periods of peace. Thus:

— Inequality may not be a cause of conflict and may not perhaps be necessary or sufficient for violent conflict;

— Some characteristics of this inequality, rather than inequality itself, may be more relevant; and

— Perhaps something in the intensity of inequality, measured in various ways (including but not limited to the Gini coefficient may be relevant to the outbreak of violent conflict (implying a threshold that itself may vary with social, political and cultural conditions as well as with the average level of income).

Studying inequality usually involves the study of symptoms and outcomes. This is especially true of large sample quantitative studies of the links between inequality and political conflict. However, to understand the links from inequality to conflict (if they exist), rather than just trying to identify statistical patterns of event regularity, we need to study what produces and underpins inequality and how this might relate to conflict. This is all the more necessary if large sample quantitative studies do not generate unequivocal results.

Yet the long history of interest in the links between inequality and violent conflict has not been matched by an evolving progression in theory or empirical certainty. Lichbach frets over the lack of theoretical progress. And Cramer argues that empirically there remains huge indeterminacy in this discussion of linkages between economic inequality and violent political conflict. One of the more recent trends in thinking about violent conflict has been the ascendancy of neoclassical economic analysis and modelling. Much of this eschews reference to earlier studies, as though work in other disciplines were a territory without history. However, there is really little, if anything, new in this neoclassical economic explanation of violent conflict. Most of the explanations have been put forward in earlier rational choice, methodologically individualist work.

Research on Conflict and Inequality

There are various ways of distinguishing among theories of violent conflict at a general theoretical level: that is, distinguishing what kind of theoretical tradition they spring from. This section briefly characterises a few of these schema and general forms of theoretical framework for explaining violent political conflict. The set of approaches highlighted might not be exhaustive but does capture most of the range as well as illustrating a dynamic aspect of the question, such as how various theoretical approaches have fared during the past 20 or 30 years.

The discussion makes one broad illustrative point. A comparison of these frameworks shows that claims about the link from inequality to violent political conflict may reflect more than one analytical approach. Overlapping claims about an inequality-conflict relationship may contain contrasting theories of the mechanisms by which inequality "translates" into violent conflict. This review partly hopes to disentangle these claims. It also hopes to highlight the enduring imprecision in most discussions of what Lichbach called the "economic inequality–political conflict (EI-PC) nexus".

Since the literature on inequality and conflict is generally located within the political economy of development, the discussion is restricted to conflict theories that have an obvious bearing on or source in this development field, including development economics, new growth theory, historical political economy and political science. Among various possible ways of organising and classifying theories of conflict (particularly "internal war", "intrastate conflict" or "civil war"), three are particularly useful.

One of these divides all such theories at a "branch point" where a fundamental choice of perspective is made: between contingency and inherence. A second distinguishes between "deprived-actor" theories and "rational-actor" theories. A third cuts the pack three ways: into theories, or stories, emphasising behaviour, ideas or relations. However, this section also briefly highlights neoclassical economic theories of violent conflict. These theories have become increasingly popular and, in some circles, influential since the mid-1990s. Although representing one strand of rational-actor theory, orthodox economic theories or models themselves are somewhat inconsistent and allow for varying distributional arguments.

The image of a territorial encounter, between disciplines, is appropriate for a field in which some claim argued that all theories of conflict priorities at a fundamental level either the significance of contingency in unleashing collective violence or that of inherent propensities to violence. Collective violence driven by contingency is, according to this framework, largely affective, though this does not rule out some purposive, rational influence. By contrast, theories stressing an inherent disposition toward collective violence emphasise rational calculation over "irrational", affective outbursts.

From the perspective of contingency, war and other forms of collective violence are rarities or abnormal; and they are produced by extraordinary circumstances that work, typically, through what has been called the "frustration-aggression" nexus. Processes of development are responsible for eruptions of collective violence since they cut people loose from their "traditional" moorings (and mores), producing extreme frustrations, while the formation of new political institutions, which might manage the consequences of frustration, often flag behind. A range of mediating factors, secondary but still significant, and the locus of contingency, are necessary prompters of violence: cultures of violence, perhaps; ideological provocations; and/or the balance of coercive powers.

The most renowned, and still influential, example of this kind of theory about collective violence was Gurr's relative deprivation theory. Relative deprivation captured people's "perceptions of discrepancy between their value expectations (the goods and conditions of the life to which they believe they are justifiably entitled) and their value capabilities (the amounts of those goods and conditions that they think they are able to get and keep)". Note that this is a tension akin to Gerschenkron's in late industrialising nations between the promise of the benefits of industrialisation and the obstacles blocking the way to reaping those benefits. Thus, for Gurr, relative deprivation was likely to increase during the early stages of development, producing frustration and a socially unusual proclivity to aggression that might materialise into actual collective violence, given the specific constellation of (contingent) mediating factors. Gurr and Duvall formulated the link to political violence thus:

Magnitude of political violence = RD + (RD x JUST x BALANCE) + e where RD is relative deprivation, JUST is justification (beliefs, traditions), BALANCE captures the distribution of coercive and institution resources of dissidents versus the state, and e is an error term. This formulation neatly captured the mediating role of balance and justification. "Justification" has been sustained in the literature, for example, the recent emphasis on "perception" of grievance, inequality and so on, rather than on their objective presence only as an important determinant of conflict.

So-called inherency theories do not presume that collective violence is produced by aberrant conditions or rare combinations of extraordinary forces. Rather, they rest on an assumption that violence is an ever-present, entirely normal disposition in political life: violence is just one stretch of a continuum of collective action encompassing a range of forms of political competition. And violence, or nonviolence, is picked out from this continuum of options on the basis of rational calculation.

Processes of development may or may not present cost-benefit judgements that favour collective violence. Eckstein pictured this kind of analysis in terms of collective action theory. Thus, political life is dominated by interest groups vying for power. Nonmembers of some core ruling alliance of interests would make claims, demanding entry or recompense for claims made upon them. Depending on the reaction of the core group, this conflict of interests might lead to violence, for example, around "multiple sovereignty" claims.

Especially important in this model is the balance of coercive power and resources between groups. For it is precisely on the basis of this balance that groups will calculate the utility of war. Given that tactical choice based on objective indicators matters more than "virulent affect" in inherency theories, cultural traditions and social memory matter far less than in contingency theories. Nonetheless, it is still unclear why collective violence is not more common, from this perspective; and the answer will to some extent be driven by contingencies, accidents of history affecting facilitating factors and the coercive balance.

Another review of the inequality-conflict linkage argues for a fundamental division between analytical frameworks or "scientific research programmes" (SRPs) in terms of the deprived-actor/rational-actor distinction. Deprived-actor explanations stress the role of preferences, beliefs, values, hearts and minds. People form expectations, but in deprived-actor stories these are formed relative to other people's attributes, experience or performance. Rational-actor stories, on the other hand, assume that expectations and objectives are identified not relative to others but in self-referential processes. And decisions are taken largely in calculating terms: choices are made, based on cost-benefit judgements, and the keys lie in resources and opportunities more than beliefs.

Eckstein associates inherency theory especially with the work of Tilly on state formation and war, particularly in early modern Europe; and Lichbach identifies Tilly as a particular critic of the deprived-actor theory. In Tilly's work, with its focus on the politics of resource mobilisation, challengers make claims that are incompatible with the survival of the state in its existing form. These claims gather legitimacy when the state alienates significant groups of people by its failure to meet obligations or make reciprocal transfers to balance its own claims (taxes, levies) upon the population. If the central power cannot or will not effectively block the scope for extreme action, there is then a moment of multiple sovereignty in which mutually exclusive claims generate violence. Collective violence, in this kind of scenario, is a function of a lack of power, that is, where constraints on an inherent disposition toward violence are not effectively blocked.

Tilly himself has produced an alternative schema for distinguishing between theories of violent conflict. Thus, there are ideas theories, behaviour theories and relations theories of violence. For the purposes of this chapter, it is important only to note the following. First, Tilly observes that many explanations of social and political violence involve combinations of at least two of these underlying theoretical perspectives. Second, this analytical schema suggests a further distinction. For while Tilly is viewed as a member of the rational-actor, inherency-theory camp, this camp itself is not harmonious.

Tilly's work is clearly "relational" compared, for example, to neoclassical economic theories of conflict that are also very much rational-actor stories. Third, and related to this, there are different versions of what constitutes rationality. Neoclassical economic theory is based on methodological individualism and rational choice, in which rationality is basically non-relational and is tied to specific maximising utilitarian goals. However, there are other theories of rationality that priorities relational rationality and a wider range of goals influencing rational calculation. Further, an analysis may be influenced strongly by rational-actor assumptions but not be methodologically individualist.

In recent years, neoclassical economics has escaped its own confines and addressed a far wider range of social phenomena than before, including collective violence and war. According to some, there has been a period of "economics imperialism", as both its detractors and champions call it, and the analytical tools and fundamental axioms of neoclassical economics have come to dominate the social sciences in general. Certainly, neoclassical economics has had increasing influence on the study of violent conflict in developing countries in recent years. This has been driven especially by the theoretical work of Hirshleifer among others, and by the empirical models and policy work of Collier and his colleagues. Cramer provides a critique of this literature.

One apparent inconsistency in Collier—or, alternatively, one source of overlap between contingency and inherency theories—is that he claims to look for the rare but his assumptions, which, given his models, really derive theoretically from Hirshleifer, are that violence is a constant possibility, an option available to choice-making individuals. Arguably, the root of this ambiguity lies in an assumption that normality contains market perfection, since this is, after all, the benchmark against which he judges opportunities for violence to spring from market "distortion", suggesting that capitalism itself is naturally pacific. Keynes too assumed that economic activity and capitalism would overcome a fundamental disposition to violence, turning interests against passions.

Recent work by neoclassical economists has also created an analytical distinction between greed and grievance as alternative sources of civil war. This distinction also affects judgements of the role of inequality in the origins of wars. The greed and grievance distinction has achieved a fairly widespread influence. Although proponents of this distinction do not couch their analysis explicitly in these terms, grievance echoes "affective" outbursts of violence generated from the frustration-aggression nexus, while greed reflects cool calculating rationality associated with the inherency theory.

Inequality may have a role in more than one of these analytical perspectives. At first sight, though, inequality fits most neatly into a tradition of Eckstein's contingency theories, or Collier's (rejected) "grievance-based war. Inequality as a source of conflict is not precisely equivalent to relative deprivation. For relative deprivation focuses on the frustration engendered by current deprivation relative not necessarily to others within a polity but to what people perceive as justifiable.

A society could have a fairly even distribution of goods, assets and even opportunities but still fail to live up to people's perceptions, which no doubt would cause widespread frustration. Nonetheless, various indicators of inequality within a society may be a fair proxy for relative deprivation, since it would seem to justify grounds for frustration relative to those doing well in that society. Inequality, in other words, is likely to reveal or provoke a sense of relative deprivation. Nafziger and Auvinen make the link explicit, arguing that relative deprivation "often results from vertical (class) or horizontal (regional or communal) inequality".

The important implication of relative deprivation theory, however, is that inequality itself, and even perceived relative deprivation, will not cause violence without other mediating factors, notably "justification". That justification may come from "culture". However, another possibility, more awkward to contain within Eckstein's schema, is that justification may come from political and economic process and social relations. At one extreme, it is argued by Grinner that inequality, relative deprivation and grievous social conditions are a constant in most societies and that, therefore, the significance of "ideological moments" is more than just a secondary factor. Grinner argues that the incidence of collective violence in Central America ebbs and flows with the influence of particular ideologies of various times such as, for example, at one stage the communist revolutionary ideas affecting Central American intellectuals in the aftermath of the Cuban Revolution and, at another stage, the influence of liberal democratic ideology. In this kind of story, the contingency of external ideological influence is elevated to a central role, fitting nicely in Tilly's "ideas" category of theories of violent conflict. For Stewart), relative deprivation, to cause violent conflict, must have an objective and subjective base in horizontal inequality, that is, unequal distribution along regional, religious or ethnic lines. The point here is that violence will emerge from collective action among competitive groups, mobilising people around collective identity. Again, in this kind of story the brick wall dividing collective action from relative deprivation theories, or inherency from contingency theories, disintegrates.

Indeed, a priori there is nothing in most assumptions that inequality causes conflict that forces a fundamental choice between whether human society has an inherent, ever-present disposition toward collective violence and whether society is fundamentally peaceable. Nor is there a predetermined choice of whether—in violence potentially caused by inequality—violence is rational or affective. Inequality, therefore, may play a role both in theories that stress one or the other, or a combination of the two.

What Claims Have Been Made About the Relationship Between Inequality and Conflict?

It is perhaps not surprising that the politically most unstable nations are often characterised by market inequities. One approach to the problem has been to look for observable event regularities on the basis of multi-country samples, usually testing cross-sectional distributional data against the incidence of various forms of collective violence, including civil wars, protests, political murders and unconstitutional regime changes, and the one more recently in vogue, complex humanitarian emergencies (CHEs).

Distribution in these studies tends to be captured through either the income or the land Gini coefficients. A number of such studies did claim earlier to find some correlation but differed according to whether the data and their testing supported either a linear or a curvilinear relationship between distribution and collective violence. Thus Russett (found evidence of a linear relationship in a study relating the Gini coefficient of land distribution to a cumulative score of violent political deaths per million between 1950 and 1962. On the other hand, Nagel argued for a curvilinear relationship, in this case starting from data from different provinces in Vietnam but also looking at a wider sample of cases.

The curvilinear relationship takes the form of an inverted U shape: discontent begins at zero in an egalitarian society and increases up to some threshold level, beyond which discontent then tails off again as extreme inequality is approached. The argument would be that comparison is more odious where the difference between one person and a chosen comparator is fairly small, but that as this difference increases the tendency to compare oneself enviously, and hence to be locked into the frustration-aggression nexus, diminishes. Zimmerman summarising his own review of the literature on inequality, among other macro-statistical variables, argues:

> "Altogether, the limited empirical evidence available suggests a linear positive relationship between socioeconomic inequality and political violence".

He cautions, nonetheless, that the data and selection methods in sampling undermine confidence in most such studies and highlights the weaknesses in relying on cross-sectional rather than longitudinal datasets.

Recent proponents of the argument that economic inequality brings about violent political conflict and instability include Muller and Nafziger and Auvinen. Muller puts the argument in the context of debates over the relationship between development and democratisation. While a rising level of income per capita might well be a nurturing source of democratisation, largely because of the changes in the class composition and balance of society, Muller argues, there is typically a counter-vailing tendency insofar as rising levels of income usually imply increasing inequality in the distribution of income.

This is because "a high level of income inequality radicalism the working class, enhances class polarisation, and reduces the tolerance of the bourgeoisie for political participation by the lower classes". Muller cites his own cross-national study of 33 countries that showed a correlation between income inequality and the binary variable of stability versus instability of democracy between 1960 and 1980. Nafziger and Auvinen list high-income inequality along with stagnation and decline in real gross domestic product (GDP), a high ratio of military expenditures to national income, and a tradition of violent conflict as the main sources of humanitarian emergencies.

Large income inequality exacerbates the vulnerability of population to humanitarian emergencies. Nafziger and Auvinen use a Gini coefficient measure of inequality, applied to data from Deininger and Squire widely seen as the most reliable available data on inequality. This analysis explicitly claims that the evidence supports "objective grievances" contributing to war and humanitarian emergencies. The analysis also moves from a Gini coefficient measure of inequality to case study evidence of regional and ethnic, or "horizontal" inequalities arising from government discrimination.

There is also an argument from an orthodox economic perspective, stating that one of the reasons why inequality is bad for growth is that it provokes political instability and conflict. Nafziger and Auvinen cite in support the work of Alesina and Perotic whose cross-section study of 71 developing countries found that income inequality was associated with social discontent and sociopolitical instability (measured, for example, by the incidence of political assassinations), which in turn are correlated with lower investment.

Thus, inequality has of late been folded into the endogenous growth literature. In this literature, there are three main mechanisms by which inequality harms growth. First, inequality perpetuates a distorted human capital market, mis-allocating resources over time so that the wealthy over invest in the education of their offspring and the poor under invest. Suboptimal human capital investment then feeds into lower growth. Second, income inequality works on growth rates through a democratic political mechanism.

Thus, where inequality is high, the "median voter" may be expected to vote for redistributed taxes which, in turn, will reduce the return to investment and therefore act as a disincentive to capital. Third, inequality may reduce growth rates by deterring investment through political instability or war. Such claims are backed up by the literature on income inequality, human and "social" capital, and violent crime. Fajnzylber et al. Hsieh and Pugh all find in cross-sectional studies that increasing income inequality raises violent crime rates, while Wilson and Daly argue that life expectancy itself may be a psychosocial determinant of risk-taking behaviour, but that including in the model a measure of economic inequality adds significant extra predictive power. If Alesina and Perotti, Muller, Nafziger and Auvinen, and others subscribe implicitly to the linear relationship thesis, other work, mainly in the form of case studies, takes forward the idea of a curvilinear relationship.

However, curvilinear relationships come in two basic varieties, each mirroring the other exactly—one taking a U shape and the other an inverted U shape. A U-shaped relationship, in which (possibly for each level of income) there is some optimal distribution that minimises conflict, holds that either an increase or a decrease from this middle range of inequality will disturb the social peace. It might be in this middle range of inequality that Hirschman's "tolerance for inequality" dominates), according to which some people, observing the incomes of others pulling away from their own, interpret this as a signal of social mobility and patiently await a turn for the better in their own fortunes.

However, at higher degrees of inequality this effect would break down, as many people severed their own expectations from those of the beneficiaries of a higher Gini coefficient. And lower levels of inequality might reflect stagnant hopes and a free-for-all. By contrast, an inverted U curve would trace a pattern in which rising inequality (across or within societies) is associated first with increasing violent conflict and then, when inequality has reached extreme levels, with a decline in the incidence of violent conflict.

Higher degrees of inequality would, perhaps, be associated with extremes in the repressive capabilities of the state and elates. Nagel's version of the curvilinear relationship mapped differences in the intensity of violent conflict across societies marked along a range of degrees of inequality. However, it might be necessary to break down the relationship within particular societies. Thus, within a given society there might be both a sharp total range of inequality and also a series of smaller, more localised gaps in wealth, income, opportunity and so on.

Potentially, these smaller but more localised gaps might be more relevant in the origin of violent conflicts than the full social spread captured, for example, in a single Gini coefficient. Formally, this might represent a curvilinear relationship between inequality and violence where inequality is increasing in localised areas, while national distributional extremes are less relevant to conflict. In other words, a curvilinear relationship might hold at local levels irrespective of whether total social inequality is high or low by comparison with other societies.

Alternatively, local distributional conflicts over a relatively short range of inequality may combine with the dynamics of conflict related to grander national inequality (or, indeed, to other causes). André and Platteau, for example, argue that inequality nationally was not the prime source of the paroxysm of violence in Rwanda in 1994, but that, nonetheless, the increasing local level intensity of distributional tension contributed to the speed with which political violence spread through Rwandan society. Their own evidence shows an increasing intensity of local social conflict and disputes as a consequence of demographic pressure plus extensive rather than intensive agricultural development policies. The productivity constraint arising from this policy led to a shrinkage of average farm sizes and the emergence of a (formally illegal) land market, thanks to distress sales. Thus, some people were able to accumulate larger land holdings, generating inequality and tension. Other evidence suggests that while the overall Gini coefficient for Rwanda may not be extremely high by international standards, it is both an underestimate and on the increase.

A related example is Kriger's work on peasant involvement in the liberation war in Zimbabwe. According to this argument, the liberation war did not succeed on the basis of the mobilisation of the rural masses around a national redistribution project but because of the combination of nationalist ideologies with a patchwork of localised agendas of change, most involving one or another form of control over allocation decisions—for example, young men's interest in overturning gerontocratic village order, or women's struggles with men.

Within studies of the linkages of inequality to conflict, there is a distinction between arguments favouring the central role of land inequality and those stressing the significance of national and principally urban income inequality. André and Platteau's argument takes an intermediate and subtle position in this debate: claiming that rising land and economic inequality in rural Rwanda (driven by population increase and agricultural policies that failed to encourage intensification) was a secondary causal factor in the genocide, helping to determine the intensity of violence but not its basic origin. Others are more direct in their claims.

For example, Bains-marie et al. reduce a range of very different examples of principally rural violent conflict into a set of outcomes produced by unequal land distribution. Cases as divergent as El Salvador and post-independence Mozambique come to support the claim that as well as static and dynamic efficiency costs, large farms and the land inequality that goes with them entail social costs including unrest and civil war.Russett presented evidence of a linear relationship between the land tenure Gini coefficient and a cumulated score of violent political deaths (per million population) from 1950–1962, for 47 countries. And Huntington's argued that "Where the conditions of landownership... are inequitable and where the peasant lives in poverty and suffering, revolution is likely, if not inevitable, unless the government takes prompt measures to remedy these conditions".

Midlarsky and Roberts argue that El Salvador and Nicaragua bear out the "land mal-distribution" hypothesis, since compared to other middle-income developing countries, they experienced above average population growth in the 1950s and 1960s, their land Gini scores (around 0.8) were well above the global mean of 0.6, and landless households represented a high proportion of the total labour force. Muller and Seligson, however, argue that this case is weakened by a closer comparison within the Central American region. Both Costa Rica and Panama, during the same period, were characterised by remarkably similar preconditions (presumed often to be the "objective conditions of grievance and conflict") and yet remained peaceful. Costa Rica's population growth rate from 1960 to 1970 was, at 3.4 per cent annually, higher than Nicaragua's or El Salvador's and among the highest in the world. Land concentration as captured in the land Gini coefficient was about the same in Costa Rica and Panama as it was in El Salvador and Nicaragua; and the first two countries also had substantial shares of landless households in the total labour force.

Against these arguments—proposing linear or curvilinear relationships between inequality and violent political conflict or contrasting land with national income inequality, and from a variety of analytical perspectives—there are other claims that inequality simply is not a significant causal variable in the origins of conflict. Collier states: "Inequality does not seem to affect the risk of conflict. Rebellion does not seem to be the rage of the poor. ... Conflict is not caused by divisions, rather it actively needs to create them." Using the same Deininger and Squire dataset mined by Nafziger and Auvinen with some of their own interpolations, Fearon and Laitin find contrary results: notably, that, whether in a bivariate model or part of a multivariate equation, the Gini coefficient estimates "do not come close to either statistical or substantive significance.

The poor quality of the inequality data, available for only 108 countries, does not allow us to go beyond the claim that there appears to be no powerful cross-national relationship between inequality and civil war onset". Mitchell and Parvin also offered evidence that, if anything, equality was more disturbing of social peace than higher inequality, which—through a combination of encouraging expectations of mobility and an increase in the repressive powers of elates—would contain conflict.

An early version of Collier's models of civil war also set out the hypothesis that higher degrees of inequality would be a disincentive to rebellion, since under these conditions it would be expected that elates would allow the state to raise taxation on their wealth in order to fund a military response sufficient to protect the status quo. Weed, among others, gives evidence in support of this argument that basically there is no meaningful relationship, and thus that violent political conflict is typically caused by factors other than inequality. A final point here is to note that, historically, inequality varies very little and very slowly, and yet violent conflict and political violence appear to fluctuate more widely. Hence, at the very least, inequality must be insufficient to explain conflict, whether or not it is necessary.

Such an array of hypotheses and claims is bewildering. One explanation might be, as Lichbach argues, that the authors of different studies do not read one another; and that there is a babble of monologues rather than any constructive dialogue. "For example, students of black protest in the United States and of conflict cross-nationally have both been concerned with the EI-PC nexus, yet both have neglected each other's work". There have been some efforts to overcome this; for example, the World Bank's Web guide to inequality and its linkages to economic performance and social phenomena includes literature on violent crime as well as on civil war.

Nonetheless, to some extent there is still a problem of insufficient engagement across studies and, indeed, methodologies. However, this can only help explain part of the problem. As we have seen, even studies using the same dataset (for example, Deininger and Squire's inequality dataset) come to different conclusions about the relationship between income inequality and violent political conflict, civil war or complex humanitarian emergencies. This suggests that estimations of the relationship in statistical studies are sensitive to model specification and/or sampling variations. However, there are two larger issues that probably help to account for the cacophony of claims about inequality and its sociopolitical consequences.

Empirical Problems

Some of those who have recently argued that inequality is not a cause of political violence acknowledge that inequality data are highly imperfect and that this clouds our assessment of the relevance of inequality in conflict models. Thus Collier and Hoeffler note that "there is insufficient data to introduce distributional considerations into the empirical analysis". Meanwhile, as mentioned earlier, Fearon and Laitin state that because of the poor quality of the inequality data, it is difficult to go beyond the claim that there is no cross-national relationship between inequality and the onset of civil war. Therefore, rather than using this problem as a basis for rejecting the political significance of inequality in its entirety and substituting some other claim, the role of inequality might simply evade this kind of quantitative analysis.

This empirical problem is in fact extreme. It extends beyond the quality of Gini coefficient data, though it certainly encompasses this issue. There are great difficulties in the measurements of both dependent and independent variables in trying to assess the role of inequality in the origin of violent political conflict. Data on income inequality are often insufficient, especially as a basis of inter-country comparison. Measuring land inequality is far from straightforward. And there are problems with available data (as well as categorical bases of datasets) for violence and conflict.

Recent research into economic inequality in Latin America confirms the dangers of building causal arguments on inequality data. Székely and Hilgert), analysing household survey data from 18 Latin American countries, find that ranking among these countries in terms of conventional inequality indicators are illusory. Scores are driven by variations in the characteristics of the data and their treatment. Hence our "ideas about the effect of inequality on economic growth are also driven by quality and coverage differences in household surveys and by the way in which the data is [sic] treated".

This research only confirms the criticisms that have long been made of distributional data and the inferences that can be drawn from them. These criticisms arguably amount to more than modest qualifications: rather, they suggest that—even if it were methodologically supportable—it is not possible to draw credible inferences from the available data on inter-country comparison about patterns of event regularity involving inequality in wealth and income. The problem with inequality data is not exclusive to poor countries. Atkinson and Brandolini, for example, show the dramatic impact of adopting different datasets on inequality on rankings among countries of the Organisation for Economic Co-operation and Development (OECD).

If the focus is on "land inequality" rather than national income inequality (or the land Gini coefficient versus the national income Gini coefficient), there are still difficulties in measuring effectively for comparative purposes. For Central America up to the late 1970s, for example, the land Gini scores are virtually identical. Yet, historically, the structure of rural society in Central America has varied considerably. One may, for example, get more sense of variation from measures of "mini-fundisación", that is, of the extent of impoverished smallholders in the presence of large farms.

Thus Midlarsky's "patterned inequality" captures the concentration of land holdings between smallholders and large farm-holders across different countries; while Muller et al. propose an index of "bifurcated inequality" derived from the proportion of small farms and from the average sizes of small farms relative to large farms. Or one may focus on the share of total agricultural land dominated by the largest farms, to capture their control of land supply. Further, rural inequality involves tenancy, and tenancy arrangements vary widely in security and the income-generating potential of the land they farm. Beyond this it is necessary to examine also the characteristics of rural labour markets and how these mediate conditions of life and political organisation.

Meanwhile, there are considerable complications with the empirical analysis of "violent political conflict". These complications take two main forms: the reliability of evidence for instances and degrees of intensity of conflict; and the choice of categorisation systems. The first problems arise with the reporting of violence. In wartime, health information systems and, particularly, civil registration systems that would record deaths and their causes, often break down).

Moreover, there are complications of interest as well as practical constraints that undermine reliable data collection involving political violence, armed conflict or even some forms of interpersonal or "social" violence. Research from the Medical Research Council in South Africa, for example, uses the analytical device of an "iceberg of sexual violence and coercion": rapes reported to and recorded by the police represent only the tip protruding above the social surface. In northeast Africa, there have been claims of a trend of rising violent conflict between herders and farmers; however, it is difficult to confirm or reject such claims when there are only occasional and variable exercises in recording such conflict and, thus, there is no reliable time-series data.

As Murray et al. point out, most published analyses of deaths from conflict have relied on press reports of eyewitness accounts and of official pronouncements from conflict contestants. Both sources are clearly subject to error and political manipulation. Brockett argues that it is difficult to assess the relative merits of competing arguments concerning the political consequences of land inequality when they rely on "the grossly inaccurate data set provided by the World Handbook of Political and Social Indicators". It is not just that this dataset underestimates the incidence of political violence in various countries, but, more significantly, that "a more accurate reporting would alter both the rankings between countries and the magnitude of the intervals between country scores, thereby substantially altering quantitative analyses utilising this data set".

Thus, "the Handbook reports deaths in Honduras during the mid-1970s as twice as numerous as in either El Salvador or Guatemala! In reality, Honduras would rank fourth with Guatemala far ahead for all five". Remote rural deaths are less likely to attract news coverage than urban assassinations. Brockett also gives an example of variation in news coverage tied to particular interests. In 1975 a "bananagate" scandal involving a US multinational's allegedly corrupt ties to the president of Honduras led to unprecedented coverage of Honduran affairs in the New York Times, including a mention of six people killed at a peasant training centre in June of that year. Similar incidents prior to the scandal had gone unremarkable the next person one meets is from a different ethnic group in a given country—the "ethno-linguistic fragmentation index". However, measuring diversity is not entirely straightforward. One clear example is Schetter's observation that for Afghanistan one estimate puts the number of ethnic groups in the country at 200, while another study estimates 50 different groups.

A further problem is the counting of indirect and non-battlefield deaths. Kaldor, among others, claims that the ratio of civilian to military deaths in war had swung from 1:8 in the early twentieth century to roughly 8:1 by the end of the century. The ratio of indirect to direct conflict deaths has been quoted in recent years as 9:1. However, these claims have slightly shaky foundations that are not always acknowledged. Murray et al. cite one cross-sectional study indicating that "the total disability adjusted life years lost in 1999 due to the indirect effects of military conflicts occurring between 1991 and 1997 was about the same as the number lost due to the direct effects of all wars in 1999".

A different kind of empirical problem arises in establishing classification systems as the basis of datasets for statistical studies. At one level, this is a matter of selecting the coding rules to adopt: which rules determine whether a particular conflict, for example, is included in a dataset on "civil wars". At another level it is a matter of whether the civil war category itself, or any other, is a valid one. Zambians discusses in detail the problems of different rules applied to the inclusion or exclusion of events from civil war datasets—a variation that holds in some cases even for researchers claiming to use the same coding system. The main obstacles include the setting of a threshold for inclusion of a conflict as a "proper" civil war and deciding whether or not to include non-battlefield, civilian deaths. Variations in coding civil wars lead to substantial differences in the results of regressions of the most typical variables used in civil war models on the incidence of such conflicts. However, one can question why a specific dataset of civil wars makes sense. From the perspective of research on inequality and

Brazil is characterised by an extraordinary array of forms of social and political violence—from the "everyday violence" suffered by the poor (both actual physical violence and "structural violence"), through the violent conflicts surrounding the institutionalisation of private property rights on the northern Amazonian frontier and the conflict between large landowners (in some cases with police connivance) and the landless movement, the Movement Sem Terras (MST), to the urban violence of "funk balls", drug-related violence, against street children, and the institutionalised incentives encouraging police violence). The distribution of income and wealth in Brazil is widely accepted to be one of the most unequal in the world. For example, Deininger and Squire give a Gini observation (with an "OK" quality assurance) of 63.42 for 1989. Sutc life shows, in one illustration of Brazilian inequality, that average wages of Brazilian white males are some three times greater than those of their black male compatriots.

Studies of the relationship between economic inequality and violent political conflict have looked at a range of categories of violence and conflict, from homicide rates to civil wars. Sometimes claims are made that shorten the results of different studies without fully acknowledging these differences. For example, Nafziger and Auvinen draw on the claims of Alesina and Perotti for their argument that inequality does matter in the origins of CHEs. Yet Alesina and Perotti claimed to find a pattern linking inequality with political instability measured through the incidence of political assassinations, which is a very different category from the CHEs.

There is possibly a need for more direct research on the whole range of manifestations of social violence and violent political (collective) conflict. Alternatively, there is a need to focus on a greater range of more specifically defined categories. For the analytical challenge is to establish constructive categorisation systems that help to reveal more than they obscure, given that virtually all classification systems impose artificial discontinuities on reality. The problems are especially intense where variation within a given category is as great as that between categories. This is almost certainly the case, for example, with the distinction between "civil wars" and other political conflicts.

The upshot is that there are no grounds for accepting any "event regularity" holding across countries when it comes to inequality and its consequences for violent conflict. There is a baffling array of empirical claims. The data on which statistical studies of the problem are based are massively unreliable. And the literature has paid too little attention to the pitfalls of commonly used classification systems and their implications for the enquiry into the consequences of inequality. Faced with this predicament, some take the view that one can quietly discard the problem and push an alternative claim about the causes of violent political conflict. However, the real implication of such uncertainty is the nagging possibility that inequality might still be significant, at least sometimes and to the origins or "epidemiology" of some conflicts.

Processes, Mechanisms and Relations

All the statistical studies reviewed above are focused on outcomes. They relate the observable, specifically quantifiable (arguably, at any rate), facts and signs of inequality. They are propelled by a widespread belief in the possibility of finding event regularities of a probabilities kind, captured by econometric, polimetrics and in historical studies by climacteric analysis. At least for the study of inequality-conflict linkages, they have not been very successful. This should encourage an exploration into what lies behind this quantifiable surface, and into the causes of the inequality that various techniques try to measure.

Since it is not likely to be just the fact of inequality or even a given degree of measurable intensity of inequality that provokes a certain class of political or social outcomes such as civil war, it is worth looking deeper into the processes, mechanisms and relations that generate and sustain inequality. Hirschman's notion of the varying "tolerance for inequality" is one route to this enquiry. More recently, Stewart's analysis of "horizontal inequality" is another. And Tilly's concept of "categorical inequality" sustained by particular mechanisms is, arguably, the most fruitful recent contribution.

Hirschman's reflections of the proposed workings of a "tunnel effect" were prompted specifically by two episodes of violent political conflict in the late 1960s and early 1970s: the Biafra war in Nigeria and the civil war in Pakistan leading to the independence of Bangladesh. Observing that both these "development disasters" followed periods of developmental surges rather than the protracted stagnation so commonly associated nowadays with civil wars, Hirschman argued for the existence of a social mechanism that could suppress relative deprivation, the frustration-aggression nexus, or, more plainly, envy. As development proceeded, some people's fortunes improved while others were left behind, and thus inequality typically increased.

But the expectations of those left behind might be raised rather than overwhelmed by bitterness. Greater inequality effectively gave information about social and economic change that could be interpreted as a signal of hope even for those not immediately benefiting from development. However, this tunnel effect must be qualified. First, it would not last indefinitely and would at some stage stop functioning. Second, the suspension of envy would be unlikely to operate where the opportunities provided by economic development were, or were seen to be, monopolised by certain groups, while excluding others. Third, beneficiaries of change are not always politically quiet or supportive of inequality: a plausible overlapping of the end of the tunnel effect with the continued politicisation of educated middle-class urbanites around redistributed objectives would provide the classic conditions of revolutionary coalition building.

There are elements in Hirschman's analysis of the changing tolerance for inequality of an interest in what has come to be known recently as "horizontal inequality". Thus, Stewart argues that most studies of the relationship between economic inequality and political conflict have understood it only in terms of "vertical inequality", that is, the distribution of income across the whole population of individuals from richest to poorest and as captured by the Gini coefficient. However, she argues, horizontal inequality is far more significant, reflecting as it does differential standards of living and access to public sector employment, political rights, education opportunities, and so on among collective groups within a society.

These groups might fall into various classification kinds, for example, religious, regional, class or ethnic. On this basis, Stewart constructs a matrix of possibilities, while acknowledging the difficulty in pinning down precisely (by quantitative scores, for example) the comparative role of horizontal inequality across a sample of countries. On one hand, this scheme of horizontal inequality is simply another form of outcome description, a 90-degree rotation of vertical inequality, as it were.

On the other hand, however, the conception in terms of exclusion from certain rights and opportunities, as well as a focus on average income levels, shifts attention to discriminatory social relationships. Stewart's matrix of horizontal inequality raises many questions and qualifications, some of which she herself addresses. For example, why is it that a situation of high intragroup inequality in Kenya (among the Kikuyu) seemed to work against collection action to redress exclusion from the chief political opportunities, while high intragroup inequality in Rwanda (among the Hutus) did not stop mass murder through a deflective, scapegoating mechanism?

The politics of inequality and the significance of varying degrees of institutionalisation of group inequality are issues tackled in Tilly's framework of "categorical inequality". Like Hirschman, Tilly effectively discusses the tolerance for inequality, addressing the question of the extraordinary durability of social inequality and highlighting the mechanisms that account for this durability.

However, perhaps in a similar vein to the horizontal inequality analysis and dovetailing to some extent with Hirschman's note on heterogeneous societies, Tilly's framework highlights inequality between social pairings—citizens versus non-citizens, men and women, black and white, Anglican and Catholic in pre-emancipation England, the differential property rights of large landowners and peasants, and so on. Categorical inequality is distinguished sharply from the continuous distributions of income captured by, say, the Gini coefficient and in some cases tying inequality in income to returns to the purported distributions of individual attributes.

In this organisational (rather than principally individual or ideological) analysis, inequality between categorical pairings is sustained by social mechanisms: exploitation is at its core; where there is exploitation there is, typically, opportunity hoarding by one group (of access to jobs, control of certain markets, political position and so on); emulation spreads categorical inequality through various branches of a society and internationally; and adaptation ensures that even the disadvantaged develop footholds of survival and acquiescence in the system.

In this approach, exclusion is not simply a negative, an absence, but a directly relational factor that is at the same time a form of inclusion in a given social system. Where the state takes a direct interest in creating and supporting categorical inequality, as is common, it adds the coercive element that further fixes the paired inequality. According to this perspective, redressing this kind of inequality is only possible through sustained political action and in circumstances where the benefits accruing to the beneficiaries from exploitation and/or opportunity hoarding fade and the costs of maintaining the system rise.

Examples would include the rising cost of discrimination against English Roman Catholics during international wars, when legal restrictions prevented the army from recruiting Irish Catholic soldiers; and the rising cost to South African capitalists of that most extreme form of institutionalised categorical inequality, apartheid. For the most part, the "histories of landlord-tenant relations, religious inequalities, and social movements indicate... that organisers generally have a difficult time stimulating shared awareness of oppression and determination to resist, that even with intense organising efforts they fail except in special structural circumstances".

It is true that there is little to distinguish, in Tilly's analysis, between various types of inequality. Some might argue, as does Wood, that the difference that constitutes class identity "is, by definition, a relationship of inequality and power, in a way that sexual or cultural 'difference' need not be". This might lead one to look for varied types of political conflict over inequality—where, for example, the intensity of conflict might be greater where the fundamental form of exploitation and the character of direct relationships of power and inequality defining society are at stake. In such conditions—essentially those of that protracted, disruptive, uneven moment of transition commonly known as development—it is also worth noting the relations among relations, or the relations between identity sources.

Thus, the fundamental institutional arrangements of power and exploitation may be in flux and at stake, and may be seen in class terms (such as landlords, peasants, wage labourers and capitalists), but political mobilisation in reaction to the social crisis often takes other identity terms. Hobsbawm for example, stresses how ethnic nationalism is typically a defensive reaction to modern, transitional crises. This fundamental developmental perspective is not always stressed even in the process-related or relational accounts of inequality and conflict, or indeed the outcome-based statistical explorations of the problem. And yet the fundamental upheaval of capitalist development must be central to most modern violent political conflict.

Capitalist development, or industrialisation, is the modern form of a more general phenomenon of transition—or socialite metamorphosis. In transition, as Gellner argued "tomorrow is not just another day; it is an other day, altogether". From this perspective, illiberal politics and violent conflict are unsurprising features of what might be called—re-inventing Gramsci's use of the phrase—a "war of position". Retreating from class analysis, even formal economic theorists have engaged with this predicament. Pagano, for example, draws on Fred Hirsch's concept of "position goods" to argue that the fact that consumption by some people of certain "goods" necessarily implies their "negative consumption" by others and that, consequently, the existence of such goods makes conflict likely.

4

Alcoholism

Alcoholism, also known as alcohol dependence, is a disabling addictive disorder. It is characterized by compulsive and uncontrolled consumption of alcohol despite its negative effects on the drinker's health, relationships, and social standing. Like other drug addictions, alcoholism is medically defined as a treatable disease. The term "alcoholism" is a widely used term first coined in 1849 by Magnus Huss, but in medicine the term was replaced by "alcohol abuse" and "alcohol dependence" in the 1980s DSM III. Similarly in 1979 an expert World Health Organisation committee disfavoured the use of "alcoholism" as a diagnostic entity, preferring the category of "alcohol dependence syndrome". In the 19th and early 20th centuries, alcohol dependence was called dipsomania before the term "alcoholism" replaced it.

The biological mechanisms underpinning alcoholism are uncertain, however, risk factors include social environment, stress, mental health, genetic predisposition, age, ethnic group, and sex. Long-term alcohol abuse produces physiological changes in the brain such as tolerance and physical dependence. Such brain chemistry changes maintain the alcoholic's compulsive inability to stop drinking and result in alcohol withdrawal syndrome upon discontinuation of alcohol consumption. Alcohol damages almost every organ in the body, including the brain; because of the cumulative toxic effects of chronic alcohol abuse, the alcoholic risks suffering a range of medical and psychiatric disorders. Alcoholism has profound social consequences for alcoholics and the people of their lives.

Alcoholism is the cyclic presence of tolerance, withdrawal, and excessive alcohol use; the drinker's inability to control such compulsive drinking, despite awareness of its harm to his or her health, indicate that the person might be an alcoholic.

Questionnaire-based screening is a method of detecting harmful drinking patterns, including alcoholism. Alcohol detoxification is conducted to withdraw the alcoholic person from drinking alcohol, usually with cross-tolerance drugs, e.g. benzodiazepines to manage withdrawal symptoms. Post-medical care, such as group therapy, or self-help groups, usually is required to maintain alcoholic abstention.

Often, alcoholics also are addicted to other drugs, most often benzodiazepines, which might require additional medical treatment. The alcoholic woman is more sensitive to alcohol's deleterious physical, cerebral, and mental effects, and increased social stigma, in relation to a man, for being an alcoholic. The World Health Organisation estimates that there are 140 million alcoholics worldwide.

Alcohol Misuse

Alcoholism is characterised by an increased tolerance of and physical dependence on alcohol, affecting an individual's ability to control alcohol consumption safely. These characteristics are believed to play a role in impeding an alcoholic's ability to stop drinking. Alcoholism can have adverse effects on mental health, causing psychiatric disorders to develop and an increased risk of suicide.

Physical Symptoms

Long term alcohol abuse can cause a number of physical symptoms, including cirrhosis of the liver, pancreatitis, epilepsy, polyneuropathy, alcoholic dementia, heart disease, nutritional deficiencies, and sexual dysfunction, and can eventually be fatal. Other physical effects include an increased risk of developing cardiovascular disease, malabsorption, alcoholic liver disease, and cancer. Damage to the central nervous system and peripheral nervous system can occur from sustained alcohol consumption.

Women develop long-term complications of alcohol dependence more rapidly than do men. Additionally, women have a higher mortality rate from alcoholism than men. Examples of long term complications include brain, heart, and liver damage and an increased risk of breast cancer. Additionally, heavy drinking over time has been found to have a negative effect on reproductive functioning in women. This results in reproductive dysfunction such as anovulation, decreased ovarian mass, problems or irregularity of the menstrual cycle, and early menopause. Alcoholic ketoacidosis can occur in individuals who chronically abuse alcohol and have a recent history of binge drinking.

Psychiatric Symptoms

Long term misuse of alcohol can cause a wide range of mental health problems. Severe cognitive problems are not uncommon; approximately 10 percent of all dementia cases are related to alcohol consumption, making it the second leading cause of dementia. Excessive alcohol use causes damage to brain function, and psychological health can be increasingly affected over time.

Psychiatric disorders are common in alcoholics, with as many as 25 percent suffering severe psychiatric disturbances.

The most prevalent psychiatric symptoms are anxiety and depression disorders. Psychiatric symptoms usually initially worsen during alcohol withdrawal, but typically improve or disappear with continued abstinence. Psychosis, confusion, and organic brain syndrome may be caused by alcohol misuse, which can lead to a misdiagnosis such as schizophrenia. Panic disorder can develop or worsen as a direct result of long term alcohol misuse.

The co-occurrence of major depressive disorder and alcoholism is well documented. Among those with comorbid occurrences, a distinction is commonly made between depressive episodes that remit with alcohol abstinence ("substance-induced"), and depressive episodes that are primary and do not remit with abstinence ("independent" episodes). Additional use of other drugs may increase the risk of depression.

Psychiatric disorders differ depending on gender. Women who have alcohol-use disorders often have a co-occurring psychiatric diagnosis such as major depression, anxiety, panic disorder, bulimia, post-traumatic stress disorder (PTSD), or borderline personality disorder. Men with alcohol-use disorders more often have a co-occurring diagnosis of narcissistic or antisocial personality disorder, bipolar disorder, schizophrenia, impulse disorders or attention deficit/hyperactivity disorder. Women with alcoholism are more likely to have a history of physical or sexual assault, abuse and domestic violence than those in the general population, which can lead to higher instances of psychiatric disorders and greater dependence on alcohol.

Social Effects

The social problems arising from alcoholism are serious, caused by the pathological changes in the brain and the intoxicating effects of alcohol. Alcohol abuse is associated with an increased risk of committing criminal offences, including child abuse, domestic violence, rape, burglary and assault. Alcoholism is associated with loss of employment, which can lead to financial problems. Drinking at inappropriate times, and behavior caused by reduced judgment, can lead to legal consequences, such as criminal charges for drunk driving or public disorder, or civil penalties for tortious behavior, and may lead to a criminal sentence.

An alcoholic's behavior and mental impairment, while drunk, can profoundly impact those surrounding them and lead to isolation from family and friends. This isolation can lead to marital conflict and divorce, or contribute to domestic violence. Alcoholism can also lead to child neglect, with subsequent lasting damage to the emotional development of the alcoholic's children.

Alcohol Withdrawal

As with similar substances with a sedative-hypnotic mechanism, such as barbiturates and benzodiazepines, withdrawal from alcohol dependence can be fatal if it is not properly managed. Alcohol's primary effect is the increase in stimulation of the GABAA receptor, promoting central nervous system depression. With repeated heavy consumption of alcohol, these receptors are desensitized and reduced in number, resulting in tolerance and physical dependence. When alcohol consumption is stopped too abruptly, the person's nervous system suffers from uncontrolled synapse firing. This can result in symptoms that include anxiety, life threatening seizures, delirium tremens, hallucinations, shakes and possible heart failure. Other neurotransmitter systems are also involved, especially dopamine and NMDA.

Acute withdrawal symptoms tend to subside after one to three weeks. Less severe symptoms (e.g. insomnia and anxiety, anhedonia) may continue as part of a post withdrawal syndrome gradually improving with abstinence for a year or more. Withdrawal symptoms begin to subside as the body and central nervous system restore alcohol tolerance and GABA functioning towards normal.

Causes of Alcoholism

A complex mixture of genetic and environmental factors influence the risk of the development of alcoholism. Genes which influence the metabolism of alcohol also influence the risk of alcoholism, and may be indicated by a family history of alcoholism. One paper has found that alcohol use at an early age may influence the expression of genes which increase the risk of alcohol dependence. Individuals who have a genetic disposition to alcoholism are also more likely to begin drinking at an earlier age than average. Also, a younger age of onset of drinking is associated with an increased risk of the development of alcoholism, and about 40 percent of alcoholics will drink excessively by their late adolescence. It is not entirely clear whether this association is causal, and some researchers have been known to disagree with this view.

Severe childhood trauma is also associated with an general increase in the risk of drug dependency. Lack of peer and family support is associated with a increased risk of alcoholism developing. Genetics and adolescence are associated with an increased sensitivity to the neurotoxic effects of chronic alcohol abuse. Cortical degeneration due to the neurotoxic effects increases impulsive behaviour, which may contribute to the development, persistence and severity of alcohol use disorders. There is evidence that with abstinence, there is a reversal of at least some of the alcohol induced central nervous system damage.

Alcohol's primary effect is the increase in stimulation of the GABAA receptor, promoting central nervous system depression. With repeated heavy consumption of alcohol, these receptors are desensitized and reduced in number, resulting in tolerance and physical dependence. The amount of alcohol that can be biologically processed and its effects differ between sexes. Equal dosages of alcohol consumed by men and women generally result in women having higher blood alcohol concentrations (BACs). This can be attributed to many reasons, the main being that women have less body water than men. A given amount of alcohol, therefore becomes more highly concentrated in a woman's body. A given amount of alcohol causes greater intoxication for women due to different hormone release compared to men.

Prevention of Alcoholism

The World Health Organization, the European Union and other regional bodies, national governments and parliaments have formed alcohol policies in order to reduce the harm of alcoholism. Targeting adolescents and young adults is regarded as an important step to reduce the harm of alcohol abuse. Increasing the age at which licit drugs of abuse such as alcohol can be purchased, the banning or restricting advertising of alcohol has been recommended as additional ways of reducing the harm of alcohol dependence and abuse. Credible, evidence based educational campaigns in the mass media about the consequences of alcohol abuse have been recommended. Guidelines for parents to prevent alcohol abuse amongst adolescents, and for helping young people with mental health problems have also been suggested.

Management

Treatments are varied because there are multiple perspectives of alcoholism. Those who approach alcoholism as a medical condition or disease recommend differing treatments than, for instance, those who approach the condition as one of social choice. Most treatments focus on helping people discontinue their alcohol intake, followed up with life training and/or social support in order to help them resist a return to alcohol use. Since alcoholism involves multiple factors which encourage a person to continue drinking, they must all be addressed in order to successfully prevent a relapse. An example of this kind of treatment is detoxification followed by a combination of supportive therapy, attendance at self-help groups, and ongoing development of coping mechanisms. The treatment community for alcoholism typically supports an abstinence-based zero tolerance approach; however, there are some who promote a harm-reduction approach as well.

Detoxification

Alcohol detoxification or 'detox' for alcoholics is an abrupt stop of alcohol drinking coupled with the substitution of drugs, such as benzodiazepines, that have similar effects to prevent alcohol withdrawal. Individuals who are only at risk of mild to moderate withdrawal symptoms can be detoxified as outpatients. Individuals at risk of a severe withdrawal syndrome as well as those who have significant or acute comorbid conditions are generally treated as inpatients. Detoxification does not actually treat alcoholism, and it is necessary to follow-up detoxification with an appropriate treatment program for alcohol dependence or abuse in order to reduce the risk of relapse.

Group Therapy

Various forms of group therapy or psychotherapy can be used to deal with underlying psychological issues that are related to alcohol addiction, as well as provide relapse prevention skills. The mutual-help group-counseling approach is one of the most common ways of helping alcoholics maintain sobriety. Alcoholics Anonymous was one of the first organizations formed to provide mutual, nonprofessional counseling, and it is still the largest. Others include LifeRing Secular Recovery, SMART Recovery, and Women For Sobriety.

Rationing and Moderation

Rationing and moderation programs such as Moderation Management and DrinkWise do not mandate complete abstinence. While most alcoholics are unable to limit their drinking in this way, some return to moderate drinking. A 2002 U.S. study by the National Institute on Alcohol Abuse and Alcoholism (NIAAA) showed that 17.7 percent of individuals diagnosed as alcohol dependent more than one year prior returned to low-risk drinking. This group, however, showed fewer initial symptoms of dependency. A follow-up study, using the same subjects that were judged to be in remission in 2001–2002, examined the rates of return to problem drinking in 2004–2005. The study found abstinence from alcohol was the most stable form of remission for recovering alcoholics. A long-term (60 year) follow-up of two groups of alcoholic men concluded that "return to controlled drinking rarely persisted for much more than a decade without relapse or evolution into abstinence."

Medications

A variety of medications may be prescribed as part of treatment for alcoholism. Some of the medications currently in use are:

— *Antabuse* (disulfiram) prevents the elimination of acetaldehyde, a chemical the body produces when breaking down ethanol. Acetaldehyde itself is the cause of many hangover symptoms from alcohol use. The overall effect is severe discomfort when alcohol is ingested: an extremely fast-acting and long-lasting uncomfortable hangover. This discourages an alcoholic from drinking in significant amounts while they take the medicine. A recent 9-year study found that incorporation of supervised disulfiram and the related compound carbamide into a comprehensive treatment program resulted in an abstinence rate of over 50 percent.

— *Temposil* (calcium carbimide) works in the same way as Antabuse; it has an advantage in that the occasional adverse effects of disulfiram, hepatotoxicity and drowsiness, do not occur with calcium carbimide.

— *Naltrexone* is a competitive antagonist for opioid receptors, effectively blocking the effects of endorphins and opiates. Naltrexone is used to decrease cravings for alcohol and encourage abstinence. Alcohol causes the body to release endorphins, which in turn release dopamine and activate the reward pathways; hence when naltrexone is in the body there is a reduction in the pleasurable effects from consuming alcohol. Naltrexone is also used in an alcoholism treatment method called the Sinclair Method, which treats patients through a combination of Naltrexone and continued drinking.

— *Campral* (acamprosate) stabilises the brain chemistry that is altered due to alcohol dependence via antagonising the actions of glutamate, a neurotransmitter which is hyperactive in the post-withdrawal phase.

Epidemiology

Substance use disorders are a major public health problem facing many countries. "The most common substance of abuse/dependence in patients presenting for treatment is alcohol." In the United Kingdom, the number of 'dependent drinkers' was calculated as over 2.8 million in 2001. About 12% of American adults have had an alcohol dependence problem at some time in their life. The World Health

Organization estimates that about 140 million people throughout the world suffer from alcohol dependence. In the United States and western Europe 10 to 20 percent of men and 5 to 10 percent of women at some point in their lives will meet criteria for alcoholism.

Within the medical and scientific communities, there is broad consensus regarding alcoholism as a disease state. For example, the American Medical Association considers alcohol a drug and states that "drug addiction is a chronic, relapsing brain disease characterized by compulsive drug seeking and use despite often devastating consequences. It results from a complex interplay of biological vulnerability, environmental exposure, and developmental factors (e.g., stage of brain maturity)."

Alcoholism has a higher prevalence among men, though in recent decades, the proportion of female alcoholics has increased. Current evidence indicates that in both men and women, alcoholism is 50–60 percent genetically determined, leaving 40–50 percent for environmental influences. Most alcoholics develop alcoholism during adolescence or young adulthood.

A 2002 study by the National Institute on Alcohol Abuse and Alcoholism surveyed a group of 4,422 adults meeting the criteria for alcohol dependence and found that after one year, some met the authors' criteria for low-risk drinking, even though only 25.5 percent of the group received any treatment, with the breakdown as follows: 25 percent were found to be still dependent, 27.3 percent were in partial remission (some symptoms persist), 11.8 percent asymptomatic drinkers (consumption increases chances of relapse) and 35.9 percent were fully recovered — made up of 17.7 percent low-risk drinkers plus 18.2 percent abstainers.

In contrast, however, the results of a long term (60 year) follow-up of two groups of alcoholic men by George

Vaillant at Harvard Medical School indicated that "return to controlled drinking rarely persisted for much more than a decade without relapse or evolution into abstinence." Vaillant also noted that "return-to-controlled drinking, as reported in short-term studies, is often a mirage."

The most common cause of death in alcoholics is from cardiovascular complications. There is a high rate of suicide in chronic alcoholics, which increases the longer a person drinks. This is believed to be due to alcohol causing physiological distortion of brain chemistry, as well as social isolation. Suicide is also very common in adolescent alcohol abusers, with 25 percent of suicides in adolescents being related to alcohol abuse. Approximately 18 percent of alcoholics commit suicide, and research has found that over 50 percent of all suicides are associated with alcohol or drug dependence. The figure is higher for adolescents, with alcohol or drug misuse playing a role in up to 70 percent of suicides.

Alcohol has a long history of use and misuse throughout recorded human history. Biblical, Egyptian and Babylonian sources record history of abuse and dependence on alcohol. In some ancient cultures alcohol was worshiped and others its abuse was condemned. Excessive alcohol misuse and drunkenness were recognised as causing problems thousand of years ago. However, the defining of habitual drunkenness as it was then known as and its adverse consequences were not well established medically until the 18th century. In 1647 a Greek monk was the first to document that chronic alcohol misuse was associated with toxicity to the nervous system and body which resulted in a range of medical disorders such as seizures, paralysis and internal bleeding. In 1920 the effects of alcohol abuse and chronic drunkenness led to the failed prohibition of alcohol being considered and eventually enforced briefly in America. In 2005 the cost of alcohol dependence and abuse was estimated to cost the USA economy approximately 220 billion dollars per year, more than cancer and obesity.

Social and Cultural Problems

The various health problems associated with long-term alcohol consumption are generally perceived as detrimental to society, for example, money due to lost labor-hours, medical costs, and secondary treatment costs. Alcohol use is a major contributing factor for head injuries, motor vehicle accidents, violence, and assaults. Beyond money, there are also significant social costs to both the alcoholic and their family and friends. For instance, alcohol consumption by a pregnant woman can lead to fetal alcohol syndrome, an incurable and damaging condition.

Estimates of the economic costs of alcohol abuse, collected by the World Health Organization, vary from one to six percent of a country's GDP. One Australian estimate pegged alcohol's social costs at 24 percent of all drug abuse costs; a similar Canadian study concluded alcohol's share was 41 percent. One study quantified the cost to the UK of *all* forms of alcohol misuse in 2001 as £18.5–20 billion.

Stereotypes of alcoholics are often found in fiction and popular culture. The 'town drunk' is a stock character in Western popular culture. Stereotypes of drunkenness may be based on racism or xenophobia, as in the depiction of the Irish as heavy drinkers. Studies by social psychologists Stivers and Greeley attempt to document the perceived prevalence of high alcohol consumption amongst the Irish in America.

Alcoholism in Family Systems

Alcoholism in family systems refers to the conditions in families that enable alcoholism, and the effects of alcoholic behavior by one or more family members on the rest of the family. Mental health professionals are increasingly considering alcoholism and addiction as diseases that flourish in and are enabled by family systems. Family members react to the alcoholic with particular behavioral patterns. They may enable the addiction to continue by shielding the addict from the negative consequences of his actions. Such behaviors are referred to as codependence. In this way, the alcoholic is said to suffer from the disease of addiction, whereas the family members suffer from the disease of codependence.

Alcoholism is one of the leading causes of a dysfunctional family. As of 2001, there were an estimated 26.8 million children of alcoholics (COAs) in the United States, with as many as 11 million of them under than age of 18. Children of addicts have an increased suicide rate and on average have total health care costs 32 percent greater than children of nonalcoholic families.

Adults from alcoholic families experience higher levels of state and trait anxiety and lower levels of differentiation of self than adults raised in non-alcoholic families. Additionally adult children of alcoholics have lower self-esteem, excessive feelings of responsibility, difficulties reaching out, higher incidence of depression, and increased likelihood of becoming alcoholics.

Alcoholism does not have uniform effects on all families. The levels of dysfunction and resiliency of the non-alcoholic adults are important factors in effects on children in the family. Children of untreated alcoholics score lower on measures of family cohesion, intellectual-cultural orientation, active-recreational orientation, and independence. They have higher levels of conflict within the family, and many experience other family members as distant and non-communicative. The cumulative effect of the family dysfunction may affect the children in families with untreated alcoholics' ability to grow in developmentally healthy ways.

5

Drug Abuse

Since the 1960s, and in a context of rapid and deep socioeconomic changes throughout the world, the international drug control system has succeeded in containing the spread of annual illicit drug use to around 200 million people, or 5% of the world population aged 15-64. This compares very favourably with the much higher prevalence of tobacco use, which causes 5.4 million deaths per year. The system was set up to restrict the use of controlled drugs to medical and scientific purposes and, while containment of illicit use to relatively low levels is already a remarkable achievement, Member States have always had a more ambitious goal in mind.

In 1998, 37 years after the 1961 Single Convention, a special session of the UN General Assembly (UNGASS) decided to work towards the "elimination or significant reduction" of illicit drug production and abuse by 2008, and adopted a series of sectorial plans to reach that objective.

Gathered at the end of the 10-year period, Member States were not satisfied with the results and declared that they were still "gravely concerned about the growing threat posed by the world drug problem." There is no single measure of the year-on-year evolution of the world drug problem. There is not even a clear definition of what is meant by the expression the 'world drug problem'. Since public health is at the heart of the international drug control system, the prevalence of illicit drug use is generally considered a central, though imperfect, indicator of the status of the problem. Illicit drug use is a multifaceted issue, however.

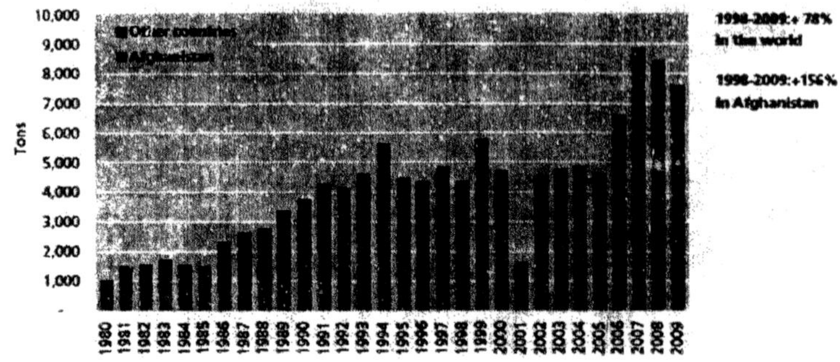

Figure 1. Global potential opium production, 1980-2009

In particular, different drugs produce different effects and present different risks to users. At the international level, annual prevalence of drug use, by drug category, has thus become the most standardised indicator to monitor the evolution of illicit drug use. Unfortunately, only a minority of countries have adequate national prevalence monitoring systems in place. Producing a precise, reliable and sensitive measure of the evolution of the world drug problem over the last decade on that basis is therefore very difficult.

Data on illicit drug supply can help fill the information gap, at least for some drugs. The bulk of cocaine and opium production is concentrated in a few locations and successful efforts to develop annual surveys in the context of the 1998 Plan of Action have provided a coverage that is systematic enough to closely follow the evolution of the global opiate and cocaine markets from the supply side.

Data on illicit opiates supply, arguably the most problematic drug category and always a core preoccupation of the international drug control regime, show that global opium production increased by close to 80% between 1998 and 2009. Increases in Afghanistan more than offset remarkable declines in South-East Asia during that period. There were encouraging declines in the last three years, but Afghan production was still more than 150% higher in 2009 than in 1998. With strong increases after 2005, production seems to have well exceeded world demand and led to the creation of large stockpiles, but it is clear that the global opiate market has not been eliminated, or significantly reduced, since 1998.

Figure 2. Global potential cocaine production (Mt.), 1990-2008

The evolution of cocaine production has not been as dramatic as in the case of opium during the same decade. Contrasting trends were recorded in various locations, including a long-term decline of use in North America but an increase in Europe, reductions in production in Colombia and increases in Peru or the Plurinational State of Bolivia. At the global level, these changes essentially amounted to geographical shifts and displacements in supply and demand. As a whole, the market has not been eliminated or significantly reduced over the last decade.

Figure 3. Estimated annual value of some global criminal markets in the 2000s

Data on cannabis and amphetamine-type stimulants are too patchy to allow year-on-year monitoring of the global market, but there were no indications of large reductions at the global level for these substances either. Member States have decided to continue their efforts to achieve the initial UNGASS objective. Accordingly, illicit drug supply and demand should be "eliminated or significantly reduced" by 2019. Their decision was made in a context of renewed criticism from some parts of civil society against the international drug control system and its perceived inefficacy, but governments were remarkably unanimous in their perception of the world drug problem, in the renewal of their political commitment to the international policy framework, and in their resolve to address shortcomings and obtain better results.

Can overall drug supply and demand be "eliminated or significantly reduced" by 2019, as called for by the Member States? At the national level, one can hope that many countries will be able to significantly improve their drug control situation within a decade. There are a number of encouraging developments in this respect. Will these local successes translate into an overall improvement at the global level?

The increase in world population alone (by some 0.8 billion people, or 11%) during the next decade should automatically increase the size of world drug markets, even if drug use prevalence rates remain constant. The potential impact of other risk factors such as urbanisation (+20% during the next decade) and the growth of megacities in the developing world could make matters worse, as drug use is typically higher in urban than in rural areas.

As regards cannabis, there is no global market per se to control and monitor. The global picture is made up of a patchwork of multiple and distinct submarkets, typically national or regional in nature. Monitoring their evolution and addressing them as a whole may thus neither be the easiest, nor necessarily the most useful, thing to do. Monitoring systems are largely missing, and current methods used to estimate the size and evolution of the global cannabis problems are not sensitive. That creates a serious technical problem for any attempt to closely monitor, guide and measure a global elimination approach. There are additional obstacles.

Cannabis production and consumption are found everywhere and there is no longer a clear consensus among national authorities on how to tackle the issue. Under these conditions, a significant reduction of the aggregate cannabis problem at the global level by 2019 would more likely be a matter of coincidence than the result of internationally concerted action. Even if such a reduction were to occur, it would be difficult to detect and reliably measure it, given the lack of a clear baseline and persistent data gaps.

Unlike for cannabis, there is a clear political consensus **on heroin, cocaine** and, to a large extent, amphetamines stimulants (ATS). In the case of ATS, because of the existence of independent, mostly regional or even national, supply and demand markets, às well as the ease, discretion and changing nature of synthetic drugs manufacture, the problem also tends to defy a global approach and overall predictions over the period considered.

Nevertheless, ATS have gained a large share of the global drug market over the last two decades and have come to represent a major and evolving threat for present and future drug control efforts. Since 1990, ATS manufacture has spread, with more than a third of Member States reporting this activity on their territory. Moreover, the global number of ATS users is likely to exceed the number of opiate and cocaine users combined.

These drugs require international vigilance, the adoption or strengthening of specific regulations and control measures at the global level, and the development of strong regional strategies is-by far-the most widely produced, seized and consumed drug worldwide, causing increased health problems in many countries, linked to its spread and rising potency in several (mostly developed) countries over the last decade. Deaths related to cannabis use are rare, however, and dependency tends to emerge only after long periods of use.

As cannabis production is widespread, most of its production is intended for local or regional consumption. Overseas trafficking in cannabis is less frequent and appears to have further lost importance with the development of high-potency cannabis production in greenhouses in the industrialised countries. The role of trans-national organised crime groups in the cannabis market is thus more limited than for other drugs, and so are the security threats related to its production, trafficking and consumption.

The global illicit opiate and cocaine markets represent two of the biggest trans-national drugs and crime threats of our time. Tens of thousands of the millions of opiate users worldwide die every year. Opiates are at the origin of two thirds of all drug treatment demand in Europe and Asia. The opiate market generates an annual turnover of up to US$65 billion, of which some US$ 55 billion for heroin alone.

Moreover, the opiate market is inter-linked with severe national and international security problems, particularly in Afghanistan and Pakistan. In terms of health impact, cocaine comes next, and represents as big a trans-national organised crime threat as heroin. Estimates suggest that the global retail sales figure (some US$88 billion) is even higher than for opiates, and the impact of the cocaine trade on stability can also be severe in some places.

The global heroin and cocaine markets appear simultaneously as persistent problems from a previous era of drug control, priorities for interventions due to the severity of their impacts on affected societies and good candidates for a global solution within a reasonable time-frame. Since they are both source from relatively concentrated production areas, most of their components are directly or indirectly linked. The resulting trans-national drug economies they form, from production to trafficking and consumption, can thus be addressed as a whole and be affected by shocks and ripple effects.

Not only are holistic market control approaches possible in these two cases, but, as shown by history, they are also a necessity. Local successes against illicit cultivation in the past–there were many– have always been offset by displacements to other locations, and closed trafficking routes replaced by new ones. Illicit production is presently largely entrenched in rural areas that are difficult to control. On the demand side, increases in cocaine consumption in Europe have tended to compensate reductions in North America, and the stabilisation of heroin use in West Europe has been offset by a deterioration of the situation in the Russian Federation. Meanwhile, **the size and** concentration of the trafficking flows to these main destination markets have often created havoc in vulnerable production and transit areas by overwhelming local law enforcement capacities, generating corruption, fuelling violence and instability, and spreading addiction. A clear lesson from the history of cocaine and heroin control is that the mere sum of uncoordinated national and sectorial efforts, even successful ones, cannot result in global success. Another lesson is that countries with limited means cannot resist, and counter the impact of, powerful trans-national trafficking flows on their own.

With the benefit of experience, success against these two markets appears to be within reach and would result in the removal of a large chunk of the world drug problem and many of its associated ills. As regards the availability of tools and data to guide interventions and monitor their impact, the situation is much better than in the case of other drugs. Production is already measured on a yearly basis and national data on trafficking is well reported by Member States. There is relatively good demand data from OECD countries, and gaps in other important consuming countries, particularly for heroin, could relatively easily be remedied by prevalence surveys for cocaine or by indirect measures, such as treatment multiplier methods, for heroin.

Global opium production and global coca production have grown by a factor of 6 (cocaine) and 7 (opium) during the last three decades. Eliminating or significantly reducing the world heroin and cocaine markets will thus require more effective approaches than in the past. What can be done? The first thing is to remedy the biggest shortcomings of previous approaches. Member States have recognised an essential one: a lack of integration. In the 2009 Political Declaration, Member States acknowledged "the importance of promoting, in order to enhance the effectiveness of drug control measures, an integrated approach in drug policies". This call is echoed in the new Plan of Action, notably in its Art. 27, under the title "Addressing supply and demand reduction together":

> "While drug trafficking is a multifaceted issue than can be effectively tackled only by reducing both supply and demand, this inter-linkage is often not taken into account."

To achieve the 2019 objectives, the international community needs to interweave drug supply and demand reduction interventions and integrate national efforts into the framework of renewed international strategies on the scale of the cocaine, heroin and ATS markets. To do so, it is urgent to improve our understanding of how these illicit trans-national drug economies operate.

Nature and Extent of Drug Use

Globally, UNODC estimates that between 155 and 250 million people, or 3.5% to 5.7% of the population aged 15-64, had used illicit substances at least once in the previous year. Cannabis users comprise the largest number of illicit drug users. Amphetamine-type stimulants are the second most commonly used illicit drugs, followed by opiates and cocaine.

However, in terms of harm associated with use, opiates would be ranked at the top. A comprehensive understanding of the extent of the drug use problem requires a review of several indicators the magnitude of drug use measured by prevalence (lifetime, annual, past 30 days) in the general population, the potential of problem drug use as measured by drug use among young people, and costs and consequences of drug use measured by treatment demand, drug-related morbidity and mortality. Additionally, to understand the dynamics of drug use in a country or region, it is important to look at the overall drug situation rather than merely the trends for individual drugs.

To illustrate, long-term trends in use of different drugs and overall drug use are presented for the United States of America, the United Kingdom, Australia and Spain where trend data over a longer period of time is available. Although short-term changes and trends might be observed in the use of different drugs, long-term trends suggest that the magnitude of the core of the problem does not change considerably in a few years. Indeed, to impact the drug use situation, long-term interventions for prevention of drug use and drug dependence treatment and care, along with supply reduction efforts, are required.

Problem Drug Use

At the core of drug use lie the problem drug users; those that might be regular or frequent users of the substances, considered dependent or injecting and who would have faced social and health consequences as a result of their drug use. Information on problem drug users from a policy and programme planning perspective is important as this drives the need and nature of the services required to address the diverse needs for treatment and care of drug dependent persons.

Lack of a global standard definition of a problem drug user One of the main challenges for UNODC remains the compilation of data reported by Member States and their comparability across countries and regions. The Commission on Narcotics Drugs in its forty-third session in 2000 endorsed the paper on 'Drug information systems: principles, structures and indicators' –also known as the 'Lisbon Consensus Document'. The document outlines the set of core epidemiological indicators to monitor the drug abuse situation, against which

Member States could report their respective situations through the Annual Reports Questionnaire (ARQ). One of the core indicators in the paper was 'high-risk drug consumption'. The assumption was that some drug information systems: principles, structures and indicators. Taking behaviours were particularly associated with severe problems and as such merit the attention of policymakers.

The document further elaborated that high-risk consumption included information on the number of drug injectors, estimates of daily users and those who are dependent. One challenge in measuring problem drug users or high-risk drug consumption is that most of these behaviours are hidden and have low prevalence. Therefore, they are poorly covered by general population estimates. Specific methods are required to gather information on such behaviours.

Out of the 110 Member States who responded to the 2008 ARQ on the extent and pattern of drug use, only 24 reported information on problem drug use. The definitions and methods of calculation differ from country to country. One country in Africa defines problem drug use as "drug users who constitute social harm and insecurity and drug users who relapse after rehabilitation." In North America, the DSM-IV3 defines the criteria for illicit drug dependence or abuse, while one country in Asia only considers heroin injectors as problem drug users.

The European Monitoring Centre for Drugs and Drug Addiction (EMCDDA), in its efforts to compile comparable information on problem drug use, defines it as "injecting drug use or long duration/regular use of ploidies, cocaine and/or amphetamines." The broad scope and differences in defining and understanding problem drug use in different regions signifies the need for setting common parameters, based on an already acceptable definition or criterion, for example, DSM-IV or ICD – 10, for determining, reporting and comparing the extent of harmful or high risk drug use at global level.

Number of Problem Drug Users is Stable

Based on the global estimates of cannabis, opiate, cocaine and amphetamine-type stimulant users, and using the relative risk coefficient, it is estimated that in 2008, there were between 16 and 38 million problem drug users (between 10%-15% of estimated drug users) in the world. The broad range of the estimate reflects the uncertainties in the available data globally.

In Europe, the prevalence rate of problem drug users varies between 2.7 in Greece and 9.0 in UK as rate per 1,000 population aged 15-64. The United Kingdom, Italy and Spain are on the higher end of the range, whereas Greece, Germany and Hungary are countries with low rates of problem drug use.

In the United States, million people-or 2.8% of the population aged 12 and older-were considered substance dependent, abusing illicit substances in 2008. Cannabis was the illicit substance with the highest rate of past year dependence, followed by pain relievers (ploidies) and cocaine. In Canada, 2.7% of the population aged 15 and older were reported to have experienced at least one type of harm in the past year due to illicit drug use. 'Harm' in the Canadian reports is classified as harm to physical health, or in the social, employment and legal spheres.

Injecting Drug Users (IDU)

Among the most problematic drug users are those who inject drugs. The last available estimate of the global number of IDU remains the one developed by the UNODC/UN AIDS reference group in 2008, which estimated that there are 15.9 million people who inject drugs (between 11 – 21.2

million). Of these, 3 million may be living with HIV (range 0.5-5.5 million). East Europe (1.5%) and Australia and New Zealand (1.03%) have a high prevalence of injecting drug use. In absolute numbers, East Europe has one of the highest numbers of injecting drug users. In East Europe most of the injectors are using opiates, while in Australia and New Zealand, methamphetamine is the main substance being injected.

Gap in Provision of Services to Problem Drug Users

The estimate of the global number of problem drug users provides the range of the number of people who need assistance to address their drug problems, including treatment of drug dependence and care. Comparing this with the number of people who are in treatment provides the magnitude of the unmet need for treatment of illicit drug use. Notwithstanding the gap in reporting and coverage of services, Member States reported that between 42% (in South America) and 5% (in Africa) of problem drug users were treated in the previous year. It can be estimated that globally, between 12% and 30% of problem drug users had received treatment in the past year, which means that between 11 million and 33.5 million problem drug users in the world have an unmet need for treatment interventions.

During the High-level Segment of the Commission on Narcotic Drugs in 2009, Member States adopted a Political Declaration and Plan of Action. The Plan of Action called for Member States to ensure that access to drug treatment is affordable, culturally appropriate and based on scientific evidence, and that drug dependence care services are included in the health care systems. It also called for the need to develop a comprehensive treatment system offering a wide range of integrated pharmacological (such as detoxification and opioid agonist and antagonist maintenance) and psychosocial (such as counselling, cognitive behavioural therapy and social support) interventions based on scientific evidence and focused on the process of rehabilitation, recovery and social reintegration.

The costs for the delivery of evidence-based treatment is seen to be much lower than the indirect costs caused by untreated drug dependence (prisons, unemployment, law enforcement and health consequences). Research indicates that spending on treatment produces savings in terms of a reduction in the number of crime victims, as well as reduced expenditures for the criminal justice system. At a minimum there was a 3:1 savings rate, and when a broader calculation of costs associated with crime, health and social productivity was taken into account, the rate of savings to investment rose to 13:1.

These savings can improve disadvantaged situations where opportunities for education, employment and social welfare are undermined, and increase possibilities for families to recover battered economies, thus facilitating social and economic development. Trends in the main drugs of concern in problem drug users as indicated by treatment demand. An analysis of the number of treatment services provided in a country according to the main drug for admission can provide information on the drugs that are most problematic in terms of health and social consequences and need for intervention.

The treatment demand data presented here cover the 10-year period from the late 1990s to 2008. Data for all but 2008 were published in the World Drug Report 2000 and WDR 2005 through 2009. The data show that there is generally, in each region, a clear, and over the past 10 years consistent, drug type that dominates treatment. This suggests marked regional differences in the drugs that affect problem drug users. Indeed, in the last decade, the primary drug for treatment has remained cannabis in Africa, cocaine in South

America and opiates in Asia and Europe. The two notable exceptions are:

— North America, where a dominant drug for treatment demand does not emerge, and rather, the percentage breakdown of drugs has become more uniform over time.

— Oceania, which has experienced over time one of the biggest changes in the primary treatment drug from opiates to cannabis.

The changes observed over the last decade in the contribution that each drug has made to treatment admissions suggest an ongoing diversification of problem drug users in some regions. The contribution of cannabis to treatment demand is increasing in Europe, South America and Oceania, while admissions for synthetic opiates in North America sharply increased in the last few years, compensating for decreased admissions for heroin. In Europe, the admissions for stimulants (cocaine and amphetamine-type stimulants) and cannabis have also increased over time, in parallel with a decline in admissions for opiates.

Interpreting trends in treatment demand data is challenging as patterns and trends over time can reflect a mixture of factors, such as:

— The development and improved coverage of drug treatment reporting systems.

— Statistical artefacts, for example, resulting from different countries reporting in a region in different time periods (notably in Africa).

— Changing patterns of consumption including prevalence, frequency of drug use and the typical amounts used on each occasion.

— Prevention measures and the availability, accessibility and utilisation of treatment services;

— Response of the criminal justice system to drug offenders, such as compulsory treatment as an alternative to imprisonment.

Opiates

Opiates are clearly the main problem drug as indicated by treatment demand over the past 10 years in Europe (with at least 55% of demand) and Asia.

Opiates have also increased their contribution in Africa from 8% to 20%. While there has been an increase in opiate-related treatment in Africa over the last decade, the strong increase is, however, to some extent, a statistical artefact as previous treatment data (dating back more than 10 years) were removed and could not be replaced as no new data were forthcoming. Therefore, data from smaller island countries - such as Mauritius or the Seychelles, where the proportion of opiate treatment has historically been very high - contribute more to the treatment demand for opiates in Africa.

Opiate-related treatment has recently exhibited a large increase in North America, from 10% to 23%, reflecting the rising abuse of synthetic ploidies, and are possibly starting to emerge in South America. Oceania has experienced a striking decline in the contribution of opiates to treatment demand from 66% to 26%, in line with the severe heroin shortage of 2001 in Australia which convinced many heroin addicts to give up their habit.

Synthetic Opioids

Treatment demand data from the United States of America and Canada both show an increase of problem drug users linked to the use of synthetic opioids/ prescription medicine and a decline in the heroin-related problem users. In the United States, admissions where opiates were the primary drug of concern increased by 34% between 1997 and 2007 (typically representing 29-32% of demand for treatment, excluding alcohol). Heroin is still the major contributor to the treatment demand for opioids, but this has become less marked with the steady increase in demand for treatment for synthetic opioids.

The contribution of heroin to opioid admissions has continually declined from 94% to 73%, with the number of admissions for heroin starting to decline in 2002. In contrast, the number of admissions for other opiates/synthetic opioids has increased from, 274 to 90,516 between 1997 and 2007, from contributing just 6% of opioid admissions in 1997 to 27% in 2007. A similar situation is found in Canada. Treatment demand for prescription opioids has been greater than for heroin/ opium over the past few years, and it is still increasing.

Treatment demand data from Ontario show that the number of admissions for opioids increased 55% between 2004/2005 and 2008/2009, or from 14.7% to 18.5% of all drug treatment demand (excluding alcohol and tobacco). This increase is attributable to the 68% rise in admissions for prescription opioids/codeine. The contribution of prescription opioids/codeine to all admissions (excluding alcohol and tobacco) has increased from 12.1% to 16.5%, while the heroin/opium contribution has declined from 2.6% to 2.0%.

Cannabis

Although it is the world's most widely used drug, cannabis is often thought to be the least harmful and of little interest to public health, in spite of the fact that evidence in recent years has shown that the use of cannabis can create remarkable levels of harm. Data on treatment demand for cannabis and medical research have pointed to the potentially severe health consequences of cannabis use.

The most probable adverse effects of cannabis use include dependency, increased risk of motor vehicle accidents, impaired respiratory function, cardiovascular disease and adverse effects of regular use on adolescent psychosocial development and mental health. The rising number of cannabis-related problem drug users is often not correlated with a similar rise in the overall number of cannabis users, suggesting that the risks associated with the use of cannabis have been increasingly recognised and diagnosed in recent years. Rising levels in cannabis potency in many parts of the world have also contributed to the increased risk of cannabis use.

Cannabis is clearly the dominant drug for treatment in Africa with consistently over 60% of demand. Over the past 10 years, cannabis has been making an increasing contribution to treatment demand in Europe, South America and Oceania. Only North America has seen a reduction in the contribution of cannabis to treatment demand compared to other drugs.

Treatment episodes where cannabis was the primary drug of concern increased in Australia by 34%, from 23,826 to 31,864 between 2002 and 2008 alone, despite a sharp decline in cannabis use among the general population. Possible explanations for the increasing trend in the problematic use of cannabis and cannabis-related harm include:

> increased consumption among older users reflecting dependence among those who have had a long history of use that was initiated at a relatively young age; and the increased availability of cheaper and possibly higher potency cannabis. Referrals from the criminal justice system do not seem to have had an influence on the increase in the numbers entering treatment in Australia.

Contributing factors for increasing treatment demand for cannabis in Europe remain uncertain Cannabis ranks second for treatment demand at the European level and its contribution to drug treatment demand has been steadily increasing. The EMCDDA has been documenting rising levels of demand for treatment from cannabis-related problems since 1996, but there are wide discrepancies between countries. In 2006, 21% of all European clients and 28% of new clients entered treatment with cannabis as the primary drug of concern. In Denmark, Germany, France, Hungary and Turkey the percentage of new clients seeking treatment for cannabis as the primary drug was greater than 50%.

However, reasons for the increase in demand have proved difficult to identify and EMCDDA recommends further research to tackle this issue. The effect of poly-drug use in the treatment statistics should not be disregarded. While drug treatment seekers in the past may have been registered almost automatically for heroin, they may now be more accurately registered as having cannabis as the primary problem drug while consuming other drugs as well. Moreover, the increasing complexity of drug use makes it difficult to have a simple characterisation of problem drug users according to a single drug type. In the context of drug users combining the use of different drugs to get the effect they want to achieve, the use of cannabis becomes potentially more harmful because its effect combined with other drugs can be very different from when it is used alone.

Cocaine is the main problem drug in the Americas, but its contribution is declining in North America Treatment demand for cocaine is most dominant in the Americas, where coca cultivation is concentrated. Cocaine is the main problem drug according to treatment demand for South America, and where once it appeared to be on the decline, over the last few years, the situation has stabilised.

Although cocaine was the main drug for treatment in North America in the late 1990s, the cocaine-related treatment demand has been declining over the last decade, and was responsible for just 31% of total treatment demand in 2008. In Europe, the treatment demand, in contrast, increased from 3% to 10% over the same period. Cocaine-related treatment demand in Africa accounts for less than 10% of the total, and in Asia and Oceania demand is negligible.

Asia has the highest percentage of admissions for amphetamine-type stimulants (ATS), where it ranks as the second most important drug. In Oceania and North America, treatment demand for ATS has increased to some 20% since the late 1990s. Otherwise, demand for treatment has remained below approximately 10% in other regions, with a possible recent emergence in South America. It should be noted that treatment for ATS is often administered differently than for other drugs, and can be easily under-reported.

6

Problem of Mental Illness

Mental disorder or mental illness is a psychological or behavioral pattern associated with distress or disability that occurs in an individual and is not a part of normal development or culture. The recognition and understanding of mental health conditions has changed over time and across cultures, and there are still variations in the definition, assessment, and classification of mental disorders, although standard guideline criteria are widely accepted.

Currently, mental disorders are conceptualized as disorders of brain circuits likely caused by developmental processes shaped by a complex interplay of genetics and experience. In other words, the genetics of mental illness may really be the genetics of brain development, with different outcomes possible, depending on the biological and environmental context.

Over a third of people in most countries report meeting criteria for the major categories at some point in their life. The causes are often explained in terms of a diathesis-stress model and biopsychosocial model. Services are based in psychiatric hospitals or in the community. Diagnoses are made by psychiatrists or clinical psychologists using various methods, often relying on observation and questioning in interviews. Treatments are provided by various mental health professionals.

Psychotherapy and psychiatric medication are two major treatment options as are social interventions, peer support and self-help. In some cases there may be involuntary detention and involuntary treatment where legislation allows. Stigma and discrimination add to the suffering associated with the disorders, and have led to various social movements campaign for change.

Problems associated with people with mental illness pose a significant challenge for modern policing. This guide begins by describing the problem and reviewing factors that increase the challenges that police face in relation to the mentally ill. It then identifies a series of questions that might help you analyse your local policing problems associated with people with mental illness. Finally, it reviews responses to the problems and what we know about these from evaluative research and police practice.

Over the last decade, many police agencies have sought to improve their response to incidents involving people with mental illness, especially emergency mental health situations. These new developments, however, have been targeted almost exclusively at improved handling of individual incidents. Little attention has been devoted to developing or implementing a comprehensive and preventive approach to the issue.

Classifications

The definition and classification of mental disorders is a key issue for mental health and for users and providers of mental health services. Most international clinical documents use the term "mental disorder". There are currently two widely established systems that classify mental disorders—*ICD-10 Chapter V: Mental and behavioural disorders*, part of the International Classification of Diseases produced by the World Health Organization (WHO), and the *Diagnostic and*

Statistical Manual of Mental Disorders (DSM-IV) produced by the American Psychiatric Association (APA). Both list categories of disorder and provide standardized criteria for diagnosis. They have deliberately converged their codes in recent revisions so that the manuals are often broadly comparable, although significant differences remain. Other classification schemes may be used in non-western cultures (see, for example, the *Chinese Classification of Mental Disorders*), and other manuals may be used by those of alternative theoretical persuasions, for example the *Psychodynamic Diagnostic Manual*. In general, mental disorders are classified separately to neurological disorders, learning disabilities or mental retardation.

Unlike most of the above systems, some approaches to classification do not employ distinct categories of disorder or dichotomous cut-offs intended to separate the abnormal from the normal. There is significant scientific debate about the different kinds of categorization and the relative merits of categorical versus non-categorical (or hybrid) schemes, with the latter including spectrum, continuum or dimensional systems.

There are many different categories of mental disorder, and many different facets of human behavior and personality that can become disordered.

Anxiety or fear that interferes with normal functioning may be classified as an anxiety disorder. Commonly recognized categories include specific phobias, generalized anxiety disorder, social anxiety disorder, panic disorder, agoraphobia, obsessive-compulsive disorder and post-traumatic stress disorder.

Other affective (emotion/mood) processes can also become disordered. Mood disorder involving unusually intense and sustained sadness, melancholia or despair is known as Major depression or Clinical depression (milder but still prolonged depression can be diagnosed as dysthymia). Bipolar disorder (also known as manic depression) involves abnormally "high" or pressured mood states, known as mania or hypomania, alternating with normal or depressed mood. Whether unipolar and bipolar mood phenomena represent distinct categories of disorder, or whether they usually mix and merge together along a dimension or spectrum of mood, is under debate in the scientific literature.

Patterns of belief, language use and perception can become disordered (e.g. delusions, thought disorder, hallucinations). Psychotic disorders in this domain include schizophrenia, and delusional disorder. Schizoaffective disorder is a category used for individuals showing aspects of both schizophrenia and affective disorders. Schizotypy is a category used for individuals showing some of the characteristics associated with schizophrenia but without meeting cut-off criteria.

Personality—the fundamental characteristics of a person that influence his or her thoughts and behaviors across situations and time—may be considered disordered if judged to be abnormally rigid and maladaptive. Categorical schemes list a number of different such personality disorders, including those sometimes classed as eccentric (e.g. paranoid, schizoid and schizotypal personality disorders), to those sometimes classed as dramatic or emotional (antisocial, borderline, histrionic or narcissistic personality disorders) or those seen as fear-related (avoidant, dependent, or obsessive-compulsive personality disorders). If an inability to sufficiently adjust to life circumstances begins within three months of a particular event or situation, and ends within six months after the stressor stops or is eliminated, it may instead be classed as an adjustment disorder. There is an emerging consensus that so-called "personality disorders", like personality traits in general, actually incorporate a mixture of acute dysfunctional behaviors that resolve in short periods, and maladaptive temperamental traits that are more stable. Furthermore, there are also non-categorical schemes that rate all individuals via a profile of different dimensions of personality rather than using a cut-off from normal personality variation, for example through schemes based on the Big Five personality traits.

Eating disorders involve disproportionate concern in matters of food and weight. Categories of disorder in this area include anorexia nervosa, bulimia nervosa, exercise bulimia or binge eating disorder.

Sleep disorders such as insomnia involve disruption to normal sleep patterns, or a feeling of tiredness despite sleep appearing normal.

Sexual and gender identity disorders may be diagnosed, including dyspareunia, gender identity disorder and ego-dystonic homosexuality. Various kinds of paraphilia are considered mental disorders (sexual arousal to objects, situations, or individuals that are considered abnormal or harmful to the person or others).

People who are abnormally unable to resist certain urges or impulses that could be harmful to themselves or others, may be classed as having an impulse control disorder, including various kinds of tic disorders such as Tourette's syndrome, and disorders such as kleptomania (stealing) or pyromania (fire-setting). Various behavioral addictions, such as gambling addiction, may be classed as a disorder. Obsessive-compulsive disorder can sometimes involve an inability to resist certain acts but is classed separately as being primarily an anxiety disorder.

The use of drugs (legal or illegal), when it persists despite significant problems related to the use, may be defined as a mental disorder termed substance dependence or substance abuse (a broader category than drug abuse). The DSM does not currently use the common term drug addiction and the ICD simply talks about "harmful use". Disordered substance use may be due to a pattern of compulsive and repetitive use of the drug that results in tolerance to its effects and withdrawal symptoms when use is reduced or stopped.

People who suffer severe disturbances of their self-identity, memory and general awareness of themselves and their surroundings may be classed as having a dissociative identity disorder, such as depersonalization disorder or Dissociative Identity Disorder itself (which has also been called multiple personality disorder, or "split personality"). Other memory or cognitive disorders include amnesia or various kinds of old age dementia.

A range of developmental disorders that initially occur in childhood may be diagnosed, for example autism spectrum disorders, oppositional defiant disorder and conduct disorder, and attention deficit hyperactivity disorder (ADHD), which may continue into adulthood.

Conduct disorder, if continuing into adulthood, may be diagnosed as antisocial personality disorder (dissocial personality disorder in the ICD). Popularist labels such as psychopath (or sociopath) do not appear in the DSM or ICD but are linked by some to these diagnoses.

Disorders appearing to originate in the body, but thought to be mental, are known as somatoform disorders, including somatization disorder and conversion disorder. There are also disorders of the perception of the body, including body dysmorphic disorder. Neurasthenia is an old diagnosis involving somatic complaints as well as fatigue and low spirits/depression, which is officially recognized by the ICD-10 but no longer by the DSM-IV.

Factitious disorders, such as Munchausen syndrome, are diagnosed where symptoms are thought to be experienced (deliberately produced) and/or reported (feigned) for personal gain.

There are attempts to introduce a category of relational disorder, where the diagnosis is of a relationship rather than on any one individual in that relationship. The relationship may be between children and their parents, between couples, or others. There already exists, under the category of psychosis, a diagnosis of shared psychotic disorder where two or more individuals share a particular delusion because of their close relationship with each other.

Various new types of mental disorder diagnosis are occasionally proposed. Among those controversially considered by the official committees of the diagnostic manuals include self-defeating personality disorder, sadistic personality disorder, passive-aggressive personality disorder and premenstrual dysphoric disorder.

Two recent unique isolated proposals are solastalgia by Glenn Albrecht and hubris syndrome by David Owen. The application of the concept of mental illness to the phenomena described by these authors has in turn been critiqued by Seamus Mac Suibhne.

Dangerousness

Police officers encounter people with mental illness in many different types of situations, in roles that include criminal offenders, disorderly persons, missing persons, complainants, victims, and persons in need of care. According to one Texas study, the five most frequent scenarios are as follows:

- A family member, friend, or other concerned person calls the police for help during a psychiatric emergency.
- A person with mental illness feels suicidal and calls the police as a cry for help.
- Police officers encounter a person with mental illness behaving inappropriately in public.
- Citizens call the police because they feel threatened by the unusual behaviour or the mere presence of a person with mental illness.
- A person with mental illness calls the police for help because of imagined threats.

Of these typical situations, ones involving the threat of suicide were rated as the most difficult to handle. Each of the others listed above was rated as somewhat difficult to handle. The two behaviours that were rated as most problematic overall were threatening suicide and nuisance behaviours.

These are the most common situations in which police encounter people with mental illness. It is important to realise, though, that when police officers handle some of these situations they do not always realise that mental illness is involved (such as a shoplifting or a disorderly person). Officers may try to handle the situation as usual (by giving directions, issuing commands, or making an arrest, for example) but not get the cooperation or compliance expected, sometimes leading to escalating tension. This highlights the importance of training in mental illness recognition as well as crisis management techniques.

A fairly common perception is that people with mental illness are disproportionately involved in violent crime. This is true in one respect but not in another. A small subset of people with mental illness, those who are actively experiencing serious psychotic symptoms, are more violent than the general population. Research suggests several factors associated with this group's violent behaviour, including drug and alcohol abuse, noncompliance with medication requirements, and biological or biochemical disorders. In general, however, "violent and criminal acts directly attributable to mental illness account for a very small proportion of all such acts in the United States.

Most persons with mental illness are not criminals, and of those who are, most are not violent." Police interactions with people with mental illness can be dangerous, but usually are not. In the United States, 982 of 58,066 police officers assaulted in 2002, and 15 of 636 police officers feloniously killed from 1993 to 2002, had "mentally deranged" assailants. These represent one out of every 59 assaults on officers and one out of every 42 The Problem of People with Mental Illness officers feloniously killed—relatively small portions of all officers assaulted and killed.

Encounters with police are more likely to be dangerous for people with mental illness than for the police. An early study found that an average of nine New York City police shootings per year between 1971 and 1975 involved emotionally disturbed people. Between 1994 and 1999, Los Angeles officers shot 37 people during encounters with people with mental illness, killing 25. A review of shootings by the police from 1998 to 2001 in the United Kingdom indicated that almost half involved someone with a known history of mental health problems. It is estimated that people with severe mental illness are four times more likely to be killed by police. Serious injury and death of people with mental illness at the hands of the police are especially tragic, for obvious reasons. Reduction of such injuries and deaths should be a high-priority objective for every police agency.

The harms associated with the police handling of people with mental illness are implicit in the situations and examples the table provides, but deserve some discussion. A person with mental illness may harm other citizens by committing personal or property crimes or engaging in disorderly and disruptive behaviour. Alternatively, a person with mental illness may be harmed as a crime victim, as an abused family member or patient, as a person who suffers through self-neglect, or as a person whose mental health problem has left him or her erroneously subjected to criminal charges and jail confinement. Society in general may be harmed if excessive police, criminal justice, and/or medical resources are consumed by problems associated with people with mental illness.

It is important to keep the concept of harm in mind when addressing this particular problem, because there is a tendency to simply define people with mental illness as the problem, and getting them out of sight as the solution. In contrast to most police problems, however, this is not one that involves wholly voluntary behaviour—rather, it involves behaviour that medical conditions cause or compound. Consequently, police have to be careful not to blame people with mental illness, but instead focus on behaviour that causes harm to self or others.

The police problem of people with mental illness is closely connected to three other problems noted below. This guide does not specifically address these problems, but addressing people with mental illness in your jurisdiction may require that you take on these problems, as well:

— Homelessness.

— Drug abuse.

— Alcohol abuse.

The people the police encounter who have mental health problems or emergencies are also frequently homeless. For example, a Honolulu study found that 74 percent of law violators who the police believed to have a mental disorder were also homeless. In London, about 30 percent of minor offenders referred for admission to a station-house diversion program for the "mentally disordered" were living on the streets.

Similarly, the people with mental illness the police encounter are likely to have substance abuse problems. About three-quarters of jail and prison inmates with mental illness also have a substance abuse problem. Current substance abuse was identified for about half of psychiatric emergency room referrals in New York State, and nearly two-thirds of psychiatric emergency patients evaluated by a police-mental health out reach team in Los Angeles were known to be serious substance abusers.

Causes of Mental Ddisorders

Mental disorders can arise from a combination of sources. In many cases there is no single accepted or consistent cause currently established. A common belief even to this day is that disorders result from genetic vulnerabilities exposed by environmental stressors. However, it is clear enough from a simple statistical analysis across the whole spectrum of mental health disorders at least in western cultures that there is a strong relationship between the various forms of severe and complex mental disorder in adulthood and the abuse (physical, sexual or emotional) or neglect of children during the developmental years. Child sexual abuse alone plays a significant role in the causation of a significant percentage of all mental disorders in adult females, most notable examples being eating disorders and borderline personality disorder.

An eclectic or pluralistic mix of models may be used to explain particular disorders, and the primary paradigm of contemporary mainstream Western psychiatry is said to be the biopsychosocial (BPS) model, incorporating biological, psychological and social factors, although this may not always be applied in practice. Biopsychiatry has tended to follow a biomedical model, focusing on "organic" or "hardware" pathology of the brain. Psychoanalytic theories have continued to evolve alongside congitive-behavioural and systemic-family approaches been popular but are now less so. Evolutionary psychology may be used as an overall explanatory theory, and attachment theory is another kind of evolutionary-psychological approach sometimes applied in the context of mental disorders. A distinction is sometimes made between a "medical model" or a "social model" of disorder and disability.

Studies have indicated that genes often play an important role in the development of mental disorders, although the reliable identification of connections between specific genes and specific categories of disorder has proven more difficult. Environmental events surrounding pregnancy and birth have also been implicated. Traumatic brain injury may increase the risk of developing certain mental disorders. There have been some tentative inconsistent links found to certain viral infections, to substance misuse, and to general physical health.

Abnormal functioning of neurotransmitter systems has been implicated, including serotonin, norepinephrine, dopamine and glutamate systems. Differences have also been found in the size or activity of certain brain regions in some cases. Psychological mechanisms have also been implicated, such as cognitive (e.g. reason), emotional processes, personality, temperament and coping style.

Social influences have been found to be important, including abuse, bullying and other negative or stressful life experiences. The specific risks and pathways to particular disorders are less clear, however. Aspects of the wider community have also been implicated, including employment problems, socioeconomic inequality, lack of social cohesion, problems linked to migration, and features of particular societies and cultures.

Gender-specific indicators of mental illness incorporate physical or sexual abuse, stress, loss of social network, rape and domestic violence, high progesterone oral contraceptives, and mood disorders during early reproductive years . It is important to note that the intersection of biological, social, and behavioral health problems may result in exacerbated mental health issues. The disproportionate effects of these issues on women's lives limit their coping skills, leading to negative behaviors such as substance abuse. Finally, these circumstances improve the risk of poor physical health, anxiety, and depression.

Management and Treatment

Treatment and support for mental disorders is provided in psychiatric hospitals, clinics or any of a diverse range of community mental health services. In many countries services are increasingly based on a recovery model that is meant to support each individual's independence, choice and personal journey to regain a meaningful life, although individuals may be treated against their will in a minority of cases. There are a range of different types of treatment and what is most suitable depends on the disorder and on the individual. Many things have been found to help at least some people, and a placebo effect may play a role in any intervention or medication.

A major option for many mental disorders is psychotherapy. There are several main types. Cognitive behavioral therapy (CBT) is widely used and is based on modifying the patterns of thought and behavior associated with a particular disorder. Psychoanalysis, addressing underlying psychic conflicts and defenses, has been a dominant school of psychotherapy and is still in use. Systemic therapy or family therapy is sometimes used, addressing a network of significant others as well as an individual. Some psychotherapies are based on a humanistic approach. There are a number of specific therapies used for particular disorders, which may be offshoots or hybrids of the above types. Mental health professionals often employ an eclectic or integrative approach. Much may depend on the therapeutic relationship, and there may be problems with trust, confidentiality and engagement.

A major option for many mental disorders is psychiatric medication and there are several main groups. Antidepressants are used for the treatment of clinical depression as well as often for anxiety and other disorders. Anxiolytics are used for anxiety disorders and related problems such as insomnia. Mood stabilizers are used primarily in bipolar disorder. Antipsychotics are mainly used for psychotic disorders, notably for positive symptoms in schizophrenia. Stimulants are commonly used, notably for ADHD.

Despite the different conventional names of the drug groups, there may be considerable overlap in the disorders for which they are actually indicated, and there may also be off-label use of medications. There can be problems with adverse effects of medication and adherence to them, and there is also criticism of pharmaceutical marketing and professional conflicts of interest.

Electroconvulsive therapy (ECT) is sometimes used in severe cases when other interventions for severe intractable depression have failed. Psychosurgery is considered experimental but is advocated by certain neurologists in certain rare cases.

Counseling (professional) and co-counseling (between peers) may be used. Psychoeducation programs may provide people with the information to understand and manage their problems. Creative therapies are sometimes used, including music therapy, art therapy or drama therapy. Lifestyle adjustments and supportive measures are often used, including peer support, self-help groups for mental health and supported housing or supported employment (including social firms). Some advocate dietary supplements.

Prognosis depends on the disorder, the individual and numerous related factors. Some disorders are transient, while others may last a lifetime. Some disorders may be very limited in their functional effects, while others may involve substantial disability and support needs. The degree of ability or disability may vary across different life domains. Continued disability has been linked to institutionalization, discrimination and social exclusion as well as to the inherent properties of disorders.

Even those disorders often considered the most serious and intractable have varied courses. Long-term international studies of schizophrenia have found that over a half of individuals recover in terms of symptoms, and around a fifth to a third in terms of symptoms and functioning, with some requiring no medication. At the same time, many have serious difficulties and support needs for many years, although "late" recovery is still possible. The World Health Organization concluded that the long-term studies' findings converged with others in "relieving patients, carers and clinicians of the chronicity paradigm which dominated thinking throughout much of the 20th century." Around half of people initially diagnosed with bipolar disorder achieve syndromal recovery (no longer meeting criteria for the diagnosis) within six weeks, and nearly all achieve it within two years, with nearly half regaining their prior occupational and residential status in that period. However, nearly half go on to experience a new episode of mania or major depression within the next two years. Functioning has been found to vary, being poor during periods of major depression or mania but otherwise fair to good, and possibly superior during periods of hypomania in Bipolar II.

Despite often being characterized in purely negative terms, some mental states labeled as disorders can also involve above-average creativity, non-conformity, goal-striving, meticulousness, or empathy. In addition, the public perception of the level of disability associated with mental disorders can change.

PREVALENCE OF MENTAL DISORDERS

Mental disorders are common. World wide more than one in three people in most countries report sufficient criteria for at least one at some point in their life. In the United States 46% qualifies for a mental illness at some point. An ongoing survey indicates that anxiety disorders are the most common in all but one country, followed by mood disorders in all but two countries, while substance disorders and impulse-control disorders were consistently less prevalent. Rates varied by region. Such statistics are widely believed to be underestimates, due to poor diagnosis (especially in countries without affordable access to mental health services) and low reporting rates, in part because of the predominant use of self-report data rather than semi-structured instruments. Actual lifetime prevalence rates for mental disorders are estimated to be between 65% and 85%.

A review of anxiety disorder surveys in different countries found average lifetime prevalence estimates of 16.6%, with women having higher rates on average. A review of mood disorder surveys in different countries found lifetime rates of 6.7% for major depressive disorder (higher in some studies, and in women) and 0.8% for Bipolar I disorder.

In the United States the frequency of disorder is: anxiety disorder (28.8%), mood disorder (20.8%), impulse-control disorder (24.8%) or substance use disorder (14.6%).

A 2004 cross-Europe study found that approximately one in four people reported meeting criteria at some point in their life for at least one of the DSM-IV disorders assessed, which included mood disorders (13.9%), anxiety disorders (13.6%) or alcohol disorder (5.2%). Approximately one in ten met criteria within a 12-month period. Women and younger people of either gender showed more cases of disorder. A 2005 review of surveys in 16 European countries found that 27% of adult Europeans are affected by at least one mental disorder in a 12 month period.

An international review of studies on the prevalence of schizophrenia found an average (median) figure of 0.4% for lifetime prevalence; it was consistently lower in poorer countries.

Studies of the prevalence of personality disorders (PDs) have been fewer and smaller-scale, but one broad Norwegian survey found a five-year prevalence of almost 1 in 7 (13.4%). Rates for specific disorders ranged from 0.8% to 2.8%, differing across countries, and by gender, educational level and other factors. A US survey that incidentally screened for personality disorder found a rate of 14.79%.

Approximately 7% of a preschool pediatric sample were given a psychiatric diagnosis in one clinical study, and approximately 10% of 1- and 2-year-olds receiving developmental screening have been assessed as having significant emotional/behavioral problems based on parent and pediatrician reports.

While rates of psychological disorders are the same for men and women, women have twice the rate of depression than men . Each year 73 million women are afflicted with **major depression**, and suicide is ranked 7th as the cause of death for women between the ages of 20-59. Depressive disorders account for close to 41.9% of the disability from neuropsychiatric disorders among women compared to 29.3% among men. .

Imapcts on Society and Culture

Different societies or cultures and even different individuals in a culture can disagree as to what constitutes optimal versus pathological biological and psychological functioning. Research has demonstrated that cultures vary in the relative importance placed on, for example, happiness, autonomy, or social relationships for pleasure. Likewise, the fact that a behavior pattern is valued, accepted, encouraged, or even statistically normative in a culture does not necessarily mean that it is conducive to optimal psychological functioning.

People in all cultures find some behaviors bizarre or even incomprehensible. But just what they feel is bizarre or incomprehensible is ambiguous and subjective. These differences in determination can become highly contentious.

The process by which conditions and difficulties come to be defined and treated as medical conditions and problems, and thus come under the authority of doctors and other health professionals, is known as medicalization or pathologization.

In the scientific and academic literature on the definition or classification of mental disorder, one extreme argues that it is entirely a matter of value judgements (including of what is normal) while another proposes that it is or could be entirely objective and scientific (including by reference to statistical norms). Common hybrid views argue that the concept of mental disorder is objective but a "fuzzy prototype" that can never be precisely defined, or alternatively that it inevitably involves a mix of scientific facts and subjective value judgments.

A number of professions have developed that specialize in the treatment of mental disorders, including the medical speciality of psychiatry (including psychiatric nursing), a subset of psychology known as clinical psychology, social work, as well as mental health counselors, marriage and family therapists, psychotherapists, counselors and public health professionals. Those with personal experience of using mental health services are also increasingly involved in researching and delivering mental health services and working as mental health professionals. The different clinical and scientific perspectives draw on diverse fields of research and theory, and different disciplines may favor differing models, explanations and goals.

Religious, spiritual, or transpersonal experiences and beliefs are typically not defined as disordered, especially if widely shared, despite meeting many criteria of delusional or psychotic disorders. Even when a belief or experience can be shown to produce distress or disability—the ordinary standard for judging mental disorders—the presence of a strong cultural basis for that belief, experience, or interpretation of experience, generally disqualifies it from counting as evidence of mental disorder.

Current diagnostic guidelines have been criticized as having a fundamentally Euro-American outlook. They have been widely implemented, but opponents argue that even when diagnostic criteria are accepted across different cultures, it does not mean that the underlying constructs have any validity within those cultures; even reliable application can prove only consistency, not legitimacy.

Advocating a more culturally sensitive approach, critics such as Carl Bell and Marcello Maviglia contend that the cultural and ethnic diversity of individuals is often discounted by researchers and service providers.

Cross-cultural psychiatrist Arthur Kleinman contends that the Western bias is ironically illustrated in the introduction of cultural factors to the DSM-IV: that disorders or concepts from non-Western or non-mainstream cultures are described as "culture-bound", whereas standard psychiatric diagnoses are given no cultural qualification whatsoever, reveals to Kleinman an underlying assumption that Western cultural phenomena are universal. Kleinman's negative view towards the culture-bound syndrome is largely shared by other cross-cultural critics, common responses included both disappointment over the large number of documented non-Western mental disorders still left out and frustration that even those included were often misinterpreted or misrepresented.

Many mainstream psychiatrists are dissatisfied with the new culture-bound diagnoses, although for different reasons. Robert Spitzer, a lead architect of the DSM-III, has hypothesized that adding cultural formulations was an attempt to appease cultural critics and stated that the formulations lack any scientific motivation or support. Spitzer also posits that the new culture-bound diagnoses are rarely used, maintaining that the standard diagnoses apply regardless of the culture involved. In general, mainstream psychiatric opinion remains that if a diagnostic category is valid, cross-cultural factors are either irrelevant or are significant only to specific symptom presentations.

Clinical conceptions of mental illness also overlap with personal and cultural values in the domain of morality, so much so that it is sometimes argued that separating the two is impossible without fundamentally redefining the essence of being a particular person in a society. In clinical psychiatry, persistent distress and disability indicate an internal disorder requiring treatment; but in another context, that same distress and disability can be seen as an indicator of emotional struggle and the need to address social and structural problems. This dichotomy has lead some academics and clinicians to advocate a postmodernist conceptualization of mental distress and well-being.

Such approaches, along with cross-cultural and "heretical" psychologies centered on alternative cultural and ethnic and race-based identities and experiences, stand in contrast to the mainstream psychiatric community's active avoidance of any involvement with either morality or culture. In many countries there are attempts to challenge perceived prejudice against minority groups, including alleged institutional racism within psychiatric services.

Three quarters of countries around the world have mental health legislation. Compulsory admission to mental health facilities (also known as involuntary commitment or sectioning), is a controversial topic. From some points of view it can impinge on personal liberty and the right to choose, and carry the risk of abuse for political, social and other reasons; from other points of view, it can potentially prevent harm to self and others, and assist some people in attaining their right to healthcare when unable to decide in their own interests.

All human-rights oriented mental health laws require proof of the presence of a mental disorder as defined by internationally accepted standards, but the type and severity of disorder that counts can vary in different jurisdictions. The two most often utilized grounds for involuntary admission are said to be serious likelihood of immediate or imminent danger to self or others, and the need for treatment. Applications for someone to be involuntarily admitted may usually come from a mental health practitioner, a family member, a close relative, or a guardian. Human-rights-oriented laws usually stipulate that independent medical practitioners or other accredited mental health practitioners must examine the patient separately and that there should be regular, time-bound review by an independent review body. An individual must be shown to lack the capacity to give or withhold informed consent (i.e. to understand treatment information and its implications). Legal challenges in some areas have resulted in supreme court decisions that a person does *not* have to agree with a psychiatrist's characterization of their issues as an "illness", nor with a psychiatrist's conviction in medication, but only recognize the issues and the information about treatment options.

Proxy consent (also known as substituted decision-making) may be given to a personal representative, a family member or a legally appointed guardian, or patients may have been able to enact an advance directive as to how they wish to be treated. The right to supported decision-making may also be included in legislation. Involuntary treatment laws are increasingly extended to those living in the community, for example outpatient commitment laws (known by different names) are used in New Zealand, Australia, the United Kingdom and most of the United States.

The World Health Organization reports that in many instances national mental health legislation takes away the rights of persons with mental disorders rather than protecting rights, and is often outdated. In 1991, the United Nations adopted the Principles for the Protection of Persons with Mental Illness and the Improvement of Mental Health Care, which established minimum human rights standards of practice in the mental health field. In 2006, the UN formally agreed the Convention on the Rights of Persons with Disabilities to protect and enhance the rights and opportunities of disabled people, including those with psychosocial disabilities.

The term insanity, sometimes used colloquially as a synonym for mental illness, is often used technically as a legal term. The insanity defense may be used in a legal trial (known as the mental disorder defence in some countries).

The social stigma associated with mental disorders is a widespread problem. Some people believe those with serious mental illnesses cannot recover, or are to blame for problems. The US Surgeon General stated in 1999 that: "Powerful and pervasive, stigma prevents people from acknowledging their own mental health problems, much less disclosing them to others." Employment discrimination is reported to play a significant part in the high rate of unemployment among those with a diagnosis of mental illness. Efforts are being undertaken worldwide to eliminate the stigma of mental illness, although their methods and outcomes have sometimes been criticized.

A 2008 study by Baylor University researchers found that clergy in the US often deny or dismiss the existence of a mental illness. Of 293 Christian church members, more than 32 percent were told by their church pastor that they or their loved one did not really have a mental illness, and that the cause of their problem was solely spiritual in nature, such as a personal sin, lack of faith or demonic involvement. The researchers also found that women were more likely than men to get this response. All participants in both studies were previously diagnosed by a licensed mental health provider as having a serious mental illness. However, there is also research suggesting that people are often helped by extended families and supportive religious leaders who listen with kindness and respect, which can often contrast with usual practice in psychiatric diagnosis and medication.

Media coverage of mental illness comprises predominantly negative depictions, for example, of incompetence, violence or criminality, with far less coverage of positive issues such as accomplishments or human rights issues. Such negative depictions, including in children's cartoons, are thought to contribute to stigma and negative attitudes in the public and in those with mental health problems themselves, although more sensitive or serious cinematic portrayals have increased in prevalence.

In the United States, the Carter Center has created fellowships for journalists in South Africa, the U.S., and Romania, to enable reporters to research and write stories on mental health topics. Former US First Lady Rosalynn Carter began the fellowships not only to train reporters in how to sensitively and accurately discuss mental health and mental illness, but also to increase the number of stories on these topics in the news media. There is a World Mental Health Day, which the US and Canada subsume under a Mental Illness Awareness Week.

The general public have been found to hold a strong stereotype of dangerousness and desire for social distance from individuals described as mentally ill. A US national survey found that a higher percentage of people rate individuals described as displaying the characteristics of a mental disorder as "likely to do something violent to others", compared to the percentage of people who are rating individuals described as being "troubled".

Despite public or media opinion, national studies have indicated that severe mental illness does not independently predict future violent behavior, on average, and is not a leading cause of violence in society. There is a statistical association with various factors that do relate to violence (in anyone), such as substance abuse and various personal, social and economic factors.

In fact, findings consistently indicate that it is many times more likely that people diagnosed with a serious mental illness living in the community will be the victims rather than the perpetrators of violence. In a study of individuals diagnosed with "severe mental illness" living in a US inner-city area, a quarter were found to have been victims of at least one violent crime over the course of a year, a proportion eleven times higher than the inner-city average, and higher in every category of crime including violent assaults and theft. People with a diagnosis may find it more difficult to secure prosecutions, however, due in part to prejudice and being seen as less credible.

However, there are some specific diagnoses, such as childhood conduct disorder or adult antisocial personality disorder or psychopathy, which are defined by or inherently associated with conduct problems and violence. There are conflicting findings about the extent to which certain specific symptoms, notably some kinds of psychosis (hallucinations or delusions) that can occur in disorders such as schizophrenia, delusional disorder or mood disorder, are linked to an increased risk of serious violence on average. The mediating factors of violent acts, however, are most consistently found to be mainly socio-demographic and socio-economic factors such as being young, male, of lower socioeconomic status and, in particular, substance abuse (including alcoholism) to which some people may be particularly vulnerable.

High-profile cases have led to fears that serious crimes, such as homicide, have increased due to deinstitutionalization, but the evidence does not support this conclusion. Violence that does occur in relation to mental disorder (against the mentally ill or by the mentally ill) typically occurs in the context of complex social interactions, often in a family setting rather than between strangers. It is also an issue in health care settings and the wider community.

7

Trafficking in Persons and Smuggling of Migrants

It is important to distinguish between trafficking in persons and smuggling of migrants for two reasons:

— The constituent elements of the respective offences are different.

— The response required of your authorities will vary, depending on the offence. The definitions for trafficking in persons and migrant smuggling are found in the Protocol to Prevent, Suppress and Punish Trafficking in Persons, especially women and children (Trafficking Protocol) and the Protocol against the Smuggling of Migrants by Land, Sea and Air (Smuggling Protocol) respectively.

Trafficking in Persons

Article 3 of the Trafficking Protocol clarifies that trafficking in persons has three constituent elements:

— An act (what is done).

— The means (how it is done).

— Exploitative purpose (why it is done).

Article 5 further requires countries to ensure that the conduct contained in article 3 is criminalised in their domestic legislation. It is important to remember that the definition contained in the Trafficking Protocol is meant to provide a level of consistency and consensus around the world on the phenomenon of trafficking in persons; domestic legislation, however, need not follow the precise language of the Trafficking Protocol. Rather, domestic legislation should be adapted in accordance with domestic legal systems and give effect to the meaning and concepts contained in the Trafficking Protocol.

The Trafficking Protocol requires that the crime of trafficking be defined through a combination of the three constituent elements and not the individual components, though in some cases these individual elements will constitute criminal offences independently. For example, the act of abduction or the non-consensual application of force (assault) will likely constitute separate criminal offences under domestic criminal legislation. In criminal law terms, these three constituent elements can also be identified as the actus reus—the material or physical element(s)—and the men rea—the mental element. No conviction may be rendered in the absence of these two criminal law concepts, fundamental to criminal systems around the world.

Actus Reus Requirements

The actus reus or material elements of trafficking in persons vary depending on the legislation of your country. In the case of the crime of trafficking as defined in the Trafficking Protocol, the actus reus requirement is split into two parts.

1. The offence must include any one of the following:
   - Recruiting.
   - Transporting.
   - Transferring.
   - Harbouring.

— Receiving a person.

Some or all of these terms are likely to have a clearly defined meaning in your domestic legal system.

2. It must also contain at least one of the following means:

   — Use of force.

   — Threat of force.

   — Coercion.

   — Abduction.

   — Fraud.

   — Deception.

   — Abuse of power or of a position of vulnerability.

   — Giving or receiving of benefits.

Men Rea Requirement

The men rea requirement reflects the state of mind of the person charged with an offence. Only those with a sufficient "guilty mind" can be found liable for a criminal offence. In certain jurisdictions and in certain cases, criminal liability may be "strict" ("strict liability" offences).

The requisite mental element required in a trafficking in persons case is that the person committed the material act(s) with the intention that the victim be "exploited" (as defined by a country's domestic anti-trafficking legislation).

The Trafficking Protocol does not define exploitation but gives a non-exhaustive list of forms of exploitation:

> "shall include, at a minimum, the exploitation of the prostitution of others or other forms of sexual exploitation, forced labour or services, slavery, or practices similar to slavery, servitude or the removal of organs."

Again, it is important to remember that the Trafficking Protocol obligation to criminalise trafficking in persons does not require that domestic legislation use the precise language by the perpetrator when committing the material acts of the offence. It is the purpose that matters, not the practical result attained by the perpetrator. Thus, the fulfilment of the dolus specialist element does not require that the aim be actually achieved.

In other words, the "acts" and "means" of the perpetrator must aim to exploit the victim. It is not therefore necessary that the perpetrator actually exploits the victim contained in the definition of trafficking in persons. Rather, domestic legislation should be drafted in a way that is consistent with your domestic legal framework, provided it contains a combination of the constituent elements contained in the definition. An offence of trafficking in persons should not require that actual exploitation take place.

As is clear from the Trafficking Protocol, actual exploitation need not occur provided there is a manifestation of intention to exploit the individual. All that is required is that the accused committed one of the constituent acts, employing one of the listed means for the purpose or, put another way, with the intention that the individual be exploited. The mental element can be proven in a number of ways. It should be noted that the Trafficking Protocol requires that countries only criminalise trafficking in persons when conducted intentionally as per Article 5(1). This speaks to the mental element. However, countries are not precluded from allowing the men rea requirement to be established on a lesser standard, i.e. via recklessness, wilful blindness or even criminal negligence, subject to the requirements of the domestic legal system.

Other examples of trafficking in persons, as contemplated by the Trafficking Protocol Forced marriages may involve an act, means and purpose that fit the definition of trafficking as defined in the Protocol. The act may be transfer or receipt of a person; the means will include force, threats, coercion or abduction; the purpose may be sexual exploitation and/or servitude.

In some societies where a member of a family commits a crime, a young female from the offenders' family may be sent to live in servitude with a priest or with the victim's family to "repay" the crime. The act may be receipt or harbouring; the means may be coercion, abuse of power or of a position of vulnerability; the purpose may be sexual or labour exploitation, servitude or slavery.

Diplomatic staff frequently employ servants. In a number of cases around the world some of these servants have been recruited and forced to provide labour within the households. Forcible abduction and conscription of children and adults into armed forces during times of conflict can also be prosecuted as a trafficking crime. Children are especially vulnerable to military recruitment due to their emotional and physical immaturity. The act may be recruitment, transporting, or receiving a child or adult, the means (in the case of adults) may be the use or threat of use of force, or the abuse of a position of vulnerability and the purpose may be servitude, forced labour, or sexual exploitation.

In some countries, particularly those with an already established adoption market, illicit adoption practices are becoming more common and can be prosecuted under the umbrella of trafficking crimes. Children may be forcibly separated from their mothers who were coerced into signing blank documents that were later made into illegal contracts. The act may be transporting or receiving a child and the purpose may be slavery or sexual exploitation. It is unnecessary to establish a means when the trafficking victim is under 18 years of age, however coercion, fraud and deception are commonly used on the mother to provide signatures, blood samples and birth certificates.

Peacekeeping and post-conflict operations create circumstances in which trafficking in persons, mainly women for sexual exploitation, has flourished in the past. The act may be recruiting, transferring or receiving, the means may be coercion, deception or abuse of power or of a position of vulnerability and the purpose may be sexual exploitation, servitude, or forced labour.

The Issue of Consent

Article 3(b) of the Trafficking Protocol states that the consent of a victim of trafficking in persons to the intended exploitation is irrelevant once it is demonstrated that deception, coercion, force or other prohibited means have been used. Consent, therefore, cannot be used as a defence to absolve a person from criminal responsibility. In trafficking cases involving children, the Trafficking Protocol states that trafficking in persons is made out regardless of the use of prohibited means.

Both of these instances reflect the simple fact that no person can consent to being exploited, because in the case of adults, consent has been negated through the use of improper means and, in the case of children, their vulnerable position makes it impossible for them to provide consent in the first place. The issue of consent is complex since consent can take many forms. The following examples illustrate the question of consent.

Example of Negated Consent

Twenty-three-year-old Anita lives in Central Asia. She wants to live and work abroad and one day answers a newspaper advertisement for waitressing work abroad that specifically requires the ability to speak her native language. Anna answers the ad and when her plane lands, a man takes her to an apartment where she meets a dozen other women.

She asks them if they all work at the restaurant as waitresses. They laugh at her and one says:

> "Restaurant? You're not going to work at a restaurant! You'll find out tonight where you are working!" Anna is held for six months and prostituted by her traffickers, who claim to have purchased her for several hundred dollars. They say she owes them money for her plane ticket, accommodation and food. They beat her when she refuses a client.

Example of Deceit Regarding the Conditions of Work

Bela lives in a South American country and works as a prostitute. One day, a regular client who visits her periodically when conducting business in her city, tells her that she could make much more money in the North American city where he lives. This client, called Nick, tells her that the prostitutes in his city go out to the clubs all the time, make a lot of money, and have a lot of fun. Nick tells her he will buy her plane ticket, so Bela agrees and gets a visa to travel to the new city.

Nick meets Bela at the airport and she stays at his house for a few days. One day, a group of men come to the house to take her to her new place of work. The men give Nick $US 10,000 and take Bela to a town outside the city. There she is put to work in three brothels and has to have sex with up to nine customers a day. If she refuses, her debt is increased. All of the money paid for her services goes either to the brothel owners or to the men who bought her. She is told that she cannot leave before her debt is reimbursed. She sees violence used against some of her friends.

Migrant Smuggling

Article 3 of the Smuggling Protocol establishes that migrant smuggling is comprised of the following elements:

— Procuring the illegal entry of another person.

— Into another state.

— For the purpose of financial or material gain.

Article 3(b) further defines "illegal entry" as the crossing of (international) borders without complying with the necessary requirements for legal entry into the receiving State. Article 6 of the Smuggling Protocol requires, amongst other things, the criminalisation of the offence of migrant smuggling.

Examples of Criminal Legislation

Belgium

Article 77 of the Immigration Law criminalises smuggling in persons, and article ibis penalises involvement in the entry into Belgium of a foreigner if violence, intimidation, coercion or deception were used, or abusing the vulnerability of a foreigner in terms of his or her illegal status, precarious situation, pregnancy, disease or disability. Both laws are used to prosecute smuggling in persons, with the difference that violations of Ibis carry a harsher sentence. Aggravating circumstances include violations conducted on a "regular" basis or carried out by an organised association (consisting of two or more persons) and the penalties increase to 10 to 15 years and a fine.

Colombia

Colombia's broad trafficking law includes smuggling offences and states that "anyone who promotes, induces, constrains, enables, finances, cooperates or participates in a person's transfer within the national territory or abroad by resorting to any form of violence, ruse or deception, for exploitation purposes, to lead such person to work in prostitution, pornography, debt bondage, begging, forced labour, servile marriage, slavery for purposes of obtaining financial profit or any other benefit either for himself or for another person, shall incur 10 to 15 years' imprisonment and a fine..." The law criminalises facilitation of illegal migration for the purpose of profit and has provisions regarding obtaining profit or property from smuggling punishable by six to eight years' imprisonment.

Elements of a Case of Migrant Smuggling

The actus reus or material elements of migrant smuggling vary depending on the legislation of your country. In the case of the crime of smuggling, as defined in the Smuggling Protocol, the actus reus requirement includes the following:

— Procurement of an illegal entry of another person.

— Entry into another country by the other person, a smuggled migrant who is neither a national nor permanent resident of that country.

— Agreement to receive a financial or other material benefit.

The Smuggling Protocol does not define "procurement". Generally speaking, this refers to the act of bringing about a specific thing; in the case of migrant smuggling, the illegal entry of another person into a country.

The men rea requirement reflects the state of mind of the person charged with an offence. Only those with a sufficient "guilty mind" can be found liable for a criminal offence. In certain jurisdictions and in certain cases, criminal liability may be imposed in "strict liability" offences even in the absence of men rea.

The requisite mental element required in a smuggling of migrants case is that the person committed the material act(s) intentionally and in order to obtain a financial or other material benefit, directly or indirectly. Hence, smuggling for non-profit purposes does not fall under the scope of the Smuggling Protocol.

The mental element can be proven in a number of ways. It should be noted that the Smuggling Protocol requires that countries only criminalise smuggling of migrants when conducted intentionally as per article 6(1). This speaks to the mental element. However, countries are not precluded from allowing the men rea requirement to be established on a lesser standard, i.e. via recklessness, wilful blindness or even criminal negligence, subject to the requirements of the domestic legal system.

Again, it is important to remember that the Smuggling Protocol obligation to criminalise smuggling of migrants does not require that domestic legislation use the precise language contained in the definition of smuggling of migrants. Rather, domestic legislation should be drafted in a way that is consistent with your domestic legal framework, provided it contains a combination of the constituent elements contained in the definition. It is also important to note that migrants are not to be made liable to criminal prosecution under the Smuggling Protocol for the fact of having been the object of smuggling as per article 6 of the Smuggling Protocol.

Differences between Trafficking in Persons and Migrant Smuggling

In practice, it may be difficult to distinguish between these two crimes in the first instance. In many cases, victims of trafficking may first start out as smuggled migrants. Consequently, in investigating trafficking in persons cases, it may sometimes be necessary to rely on measures against smuggling. It is critical, however, that those investigating smuggling cases be familiar with the crime of trafficking in persons as the consequences of treating a trafficking case as one of migrant smuggling can be severe for the victim.

Identifying the Differences

In some cases it may be difficult to quickly ascertain whether a case is one of human smuggling or trafficking. The distinctions between smuggling and trafficking are often very subtle and there are overlaps. Identifying whether a case is one of trafficking in persons or people smuggling can be very difficult for a number of reasons:

— Some trafficked persons might start their journey by agreeing to be smuggled into a country illegally, but find themselves deceived, coerced or forced into an exploitative situation later in the process.

— Traffickers may present an opportunity that sounds more like smuggling to potential victims. They could be asked to pay a fee in common with other people who are smuggled. However, the intention of the trafficker from the outset is the exploitation of the victim. The fee was part of the fraud and deception and a way to make a bit more money.

— Smuggling may be the planned intention at the outset but a too-good-to-miss opportunity to traffic people presents itself to the smugglers/traffickers at some point in the process.

— Criminals may both smuggle and traffic people, employing the same routes.

— Conditions for a smuggled person along the journey may be so bad it is difficult to believe a person could have consented to this.

Having said this, there are a number of key differences between migrant smuggling and trafficking in persons:

Consent

Migrant smuggling generally involves the consent of those being smuggled. Victims of trafficking, on the other hand, have either never consented or, if they initially consented, that consent has been rendered meaningless by the improper means of the traffickers.

Trans-nationality

To smuggle a person means to facilitate the person's illegal border crossing and entry into another country. Trafficking in persons, on the other hand, need not involve the crossing of any border. Where it does, the legality or illegality of the border crossing is irrelevant. Thus, while migrant smuggling is always, by definition, trans-national, trafficking in persons need not be.

Exploitation

The relationship between smuggler and smuggled migrant usually ends after the facilitation of the border crossing. Smuggling fees are paid up front or upon arrival. The smuggler has no intention to exploit the smuggled person after arrival. Smuggler and migrant are partners, albeit disparate, in a commercial operation that the migrant enters willingly. Trafficking involves the ongoing exploitation of the victims in some manner to generate illicit profits for the traffickers. It is the intention of the trafficker that the relationship with the exploited victims will be a continuous one and extend beyond the crossing of the border in the final destination. Smuggling can become trafficking, e.g. when the smuggler sells the person and the accumulated debt, or deceives/coerces/forces the person to work off transportation costs under exploitative conditions.

Source of the Profit

One important indicator of whether a case is one of smuggling or of trafficking in persons is how the offenders generate their income. Smugglers generate their income from fees to move people. The trafficker in contrast continues to exert control over the trafficked victim in order to achieve additional profits through the ongoing exploitation of the victim.

Appropriate Charges

As explained above, the offence of trafficking in persons may involve many different acts and many different actors. The offence is committed by acts of recruitment, transportation, transfer, harbouring or receipt of persons, by means of the threat or use of force or other forms of coercion, of abduction, of fraud, of deception, of the abuse of power or of a position of vulnerability or of the giving or receiving of payments or benefits to achieve the consent of a person having control over another person, for the purpose of exploitation.

Trafficking cases, by their nature, are very likely to involve other offences. These offences may be an integral part of the trafficking process, and can be used to prove that an element of the trafficking in persons offence has been committed. They can also be charged separately or utilised as alternative charges, depending on the legal system. They can also be called underlying offences to trafficking.

Other offences may be committed against the trafficking victim or others, but would not be an integral part of the trafficking offence. These should be charged separately.

EXAMPLES

Identifying whether trafficking in persons or smuggling of migrants has taken place can be difficult in practice. Please look at these examples which illustrate the basic differences between the two. Please note that cases have to be seen in the context of domestic law and local circumstances. In this module we examine cases in light of the Trafficking in Persons and Smuggling of Migrants Protocol.

Appropriate Charges

As explained above, the offence of trafficking in persons may involve many different acts and many different actors. The offence is committed by acts of recruitment, transportation, transfer, harbouring or receipt of persons, by means of the threat or use of force or other forms of coercion, of abduction, of fraud, of deception, of the abuse of power or of a position of vulnerability or of the giving or receiving of payments or benefits to achieve the consent of a person having control over another person, for the purpose of exploitation.

Trafficking cases, by their nature, are very likely to involve other offences. These offences may be an integral part of the trafficking process, and can be used to prove that an element of the trafficking in persons offence has been committed. They can also be charged separately or utilised as alternative charges, depending on the legal system. They can also be called underlying offences to trafficking.

Other offences may be committed against the trafficking victim or others, but would not be an integral part of the trafficking offence. These should be charged separately. Underlying offences to trafficking may include but are not limited to:

— Slavery.

— Slavery-like practices.

— Servitude.

— Forced or compulsory labour.

— Debt bondage.

— Forced marriage.

— Forced abortion.

— Extortion.

— Torture.

- Cruel, inhumane or degrading treatment.
- Rape.
- Sexual assault.
- Assault.
- Bodily injury.
- Murder.
- Kidnapping.
- Abduction.
- Unlawful confinement.
- Labour exploitation.
- Withholding identity papers.
- Violations of immigration law.
- Money-laundering.
- Corruption.
- Abuse of office.
- Smuggling of migrants.

Investigation and prosecution of the individual acts mentioned above can be particularly useful in situations and in countries where:

- A distinct criminal offence of trafficking does not yet exist.
- The penalties for trafficking do not sufficiently reflect the nature of the crime and do not have any deterrent effects.

In cases where the existing evidence is not sufficient in order to prosecute for trafficking but may be sufficient to prosecute for such underlying offences. In systems that allow plea bargains, in general it would be recommended to charge for all possible offences, so that in the case of a plea bargain, some charges may be crossed out. Where the evidence is there, for a number of reasons, you should aim at prosecuting perpetrators under the offence of trafficking in persons. If possible in your legal system, utilise underlying offences as alternative charges to increase chances for a conviction.

If the criminal offence of trafficking exists in your jurisdiction, the underlying offences are particularly useful in situations where you do not find sufficient evidence for the prosecution of trafficking. The evidence may still be sufficient for prosecution of the individual criminal acts, the underlying offences to trafficking such as unlawful confinement, sexual assault, bodily injury, withholding of identity documents, etc. In these situations your only option may be to prosecute for the individual criminal acts.

Even if you initially choose to prosecute traffickers under the offence of trafficking in persons but the evidence does not support your case beyond reasonable doubt, the evidence may suffice for conviction for the underlying offences. Hence, the underlying offences can also be invoked in addition to prosecuting under the offence of trafficking in persons. The provisions can also be invoked as additional or overlapping offences to demonstrate the seriousness of a particular trafficking operation.

As a practitioner you know that investigating suspects and prosecuting defendants with trafficking offences can be very complex, time consuming and costly. It is therefore not surprising that there are a number of examples of cases where trafficking in persons is present, indeed is the driving force—may be the reason deter of a case—but the only charges laid are for the underlying offences such as unlawful confinement, sexual assault, bodily injury, withholding of identity documents, etc.

Failing to prosecute for trafficking offences may be appealing in the short term, but has a number of potentially significant long term consequences. In many occasions a trafficking charge may give a victim access to victim support services, protection, and assistance that would not otherwise be available. These victim support services can include the possibility of a reflection period, temporary or even permanent residence status in the destination country, and support services at various levels, including accommodation, health care, legal and psychological counselling and access to resettlement packages. This is of importance to you for a number of reasons.

Trauma can affect the quality of the testimony of trafficking victims. Providing support, protection and assistance to victims of trafficking helps the victim overcome the most severe consequences of trauma and helps you to build the trust of a trafficking victim. You are not likely to get that trust if you cannot provide proper support for victims. Without trust you are unlikely to get the quality of testimony you require.

In many jurisdictions the laying of a charge for trafficking in persons will trigger various protection and assistance measures for victims. It may also mean that the victim is not prosecuted for offences he or she may have committed in the process of trafficking. Prosecuting the victim for offences he or she may have committed as a direct consequence of being trafficking may destroy the relationship that you have to build in order to gain the best possible witness testimony for your case. It may directly significantly weaken the witness testimony and contribute to the victim's decision not to cooperate with the criminal justice system. Failing to prosecute for trafficking in persons offences may also mean that the wider trafficking networks are left to operate without any disruptions.

Jurisdiction

Trafficking in persons cases may involve a number of jurisdictions. Where this is the case a decision has to be taken about which jurisdiction the prosecution should take place in. There are a number of principles that should guide this decision. It is very important to identify as soon as you can that it is possible a case can be prosecuted in more than one jurisdiction.

Once this possibility is identified the next consideration is where it is most feasible to prosecute. Any decision made on which jurisdiction is best placed to prosecute should be made on a case-by-case basis taking into account all the relevant factors. The basic principle underlying any decision is that a person should not be prosecuted more than once for the same criminal conduct. This applies even where a person has been acquitted of a charge relating to that conduct in another jurisdiction. This is known as the principle of in idem or double jeopardy.

Prosecutions should take place in the jurisdiction where the majority of criminalist took place or where the majority of the loss took place. In trafficking cases, this is often, but not automatically, the destination location where exploitation took place.

8

Global Menace of HIV/AIDS

HIV kills by weakening the body's immune system until it can no longer fight infection. Opportunistic infections are illnesses such as pneumonia, meningitis, some cancers, tuberculosis (TB), or other parasitic, viral, and fungal infections that occur when the immune system is weakened.

HIV generally progresses over a decade before developing into AIDS, but there is a long delay after infection before symptoms become evident. Early HIV-related symptoms include chronic fatigue, diarrhoea, fever, weight loss, persistent cough, skin rashes, herpes and other oral infections, swelling of the lymph nodes, and memory loss or other mental changes. AIDS is almost always fatal without treatment, although a few individuals have survived with AIDS untreated for up to 20 years. Current drug regimen, such as highly active nitrate rivalry therapy (HAART), slow the virus' replication in the body. Slower replication rates lessen the burden on the immune system, thereby reducing HIV-related illnesses and allowing patients to live longer, higher-quality lives. There is no cure for AIDS: The disease resurrects if HAART is halted.

Risk and Vulnerability

When AIDS was first identified in the 1980s, public health

officials assumed its spread could be halted by informing people how to protect themselves from infection and by safeguarding blood supplies. This approach has been successful in politically organised communities with access to information and resources:

It reduced incidence among white gay men in North America, Australia, and Western Europe, for example. But population in less developed and socially fragmented countries had little access to accurate information or effective prevention programs, and the virus continued to spread. In the late 1980s, as the epidemic surged and shifted from people with high-risk behaviour to the general population, especially in developing countries, public health professionals realised they needed to better understand the causes of individual infection and the forces driving the pandemic.

They knew HIV transmission was linked to specific behaviour such as having multiple sex partners, commercial sex, and injecting drug use, but they also realised that these behaviours were influenced by political, economic, social, cultural, and environmental factors—including poverty, military conflict, powerlessness, and gender inequality. Understanding the factors High-Risk Behaviour High-risk behaviour—unprotected sex with multiple partners, injecting drug use, and commercial sex—can increase vulnerability to HIV infection. While heterosexual sex between multiple partners has been the driving force behind the epidemics in sub-Saharan Africa, injecting drug use and commercial sex have been the main drivers of epidemics in Asia.

Injecting drug users are more susceptible to HIV infection because they sometimes use contaminated needles and syringes, which are an efficient mode of transmission. Sex workers face increased risk of infection because they engage in sex with multiple partners, often with no protection. The interaction between commercial sex and injecting drug use heightens vulnerability, as many injecting drug users engage in commercial sex to finance their drug habits and a considerable proportion of sex workers also inject drugs.

Many countries have seen high levels of HIV for injecting drug users and sex workers, but they have yet to experience epidemics within the general population. However, once HIV is established in high-risk groups, it can easily spread to the general public via bridge groups, such as clients of sex workers. These bridge population can infect their own spouses and partners with HIV. Risk and Vulnerability of Women Whereas men were most affected at the beginning of the epidemic, women's rates of new infection now surpass men's, especially in countries where women live in poverty and have relatively low status. In sub-Saharan Africa, women make up 57 percent of adults living with HIV. The gender gap is especially pronounced among Africans younger than age 25.

In sub-Saharan Africa, women ages 15 to 24 are three times more likely to be infected than young men their age. Biological, cultural, and socioeconomic conditions contribute to women's greater vulnerability to HIV. During unprotected vaginal intercourse, a woman's risk of becoming infected is up to four times higher than that of a man. The vagina has a greater area of susceptible tissue compared with the male urethra and often sustains microcornea during intercourse. In addition, HIV-infected semen typically contains a higher viral concentration than do vaginal secretions.

The risk of HIV infection increases for people who have other sexually transmitted infections (STIs). Research shows that some untreated STIs in either partner can increase the risk of HIV transmission as much as tenfold. This is especially significant for women because many STI cases in women go untreated. Women's symptoms are often latent or difficult to see, and many women who have been diagnosed with STIs do not receive medical treatment.

Socioeconomic factors, including women's lack of access to education or personal income, and unequal property rights perpetuate women's greater vulnerability to HIV infection. Many women fear their husbands or partners will abandon them if they try to control how and when they have sex and whether their partner uses a condom. Moreover, poverty drives some women into the sex industry, where sexual trafficking and commercial sex promote continued exposure to HIV. Furthermore, men control the main tool for reducing the risk of sexual transmission of HIV:

> the male condom. Even though the female condom has improved prevention options for women, men's involvement is still crucial. Cultural traditions such as male dominance and older men's preference for young women contribute to women's vulnerability. Throughout the world, prevailing views about masculinity encourage men to undertake risky sexual behaviours—multiple sex partners, alcohol consumption prior to intercourse, and sexual violence—that make women more vulnerable to HIV and other STIs.

In many cases, a wife's marriage and fidelity do not protect her from HIV because her husband's sexual behaviour before or during marriage puts her at risk. For example, in India, many new infections occur among married women whose husbands have frequented sex workers and, according to one study, married women in Nicaragua are twice as likely to be HIV-positive as are sex workers. Violence against women, including sexual violence, is most often inflicted by a husband or partner and can also be a factor in HIV infection.

According to one South African study, women who experienced violence from their partners were 48 percent more likely to be HIV-positive than those who had not. Young girls are at even greater risk of infection because of their social vulnerability both before and during marriage. Most infections in young women are a result of unprotected sex and reflect a power imbalance that limits women's ability to negotiate or control sexual interactions, especially with older men. Additionally, young girls face heightened biological risks because their reproductive tracts are not yet fully developed.

High-Risk Situations

Military conflicts and natural disasters bring together populations with different levels of HIV infection, thereby increasing the potential for new infections. During such times, socioeconomic and health structures begin to break down as populations are displaced from their homes and communities. The massive population dislocations during the 1994 genocide in Rwanda, for example, mixed urban populations with high levels of HIV with rural populations with low levels of HIV, helping expand the epidemic into rural areas. In recent years, more than 50 million people in over 70 countries have been affected by emergencies stemming from armed conflict and natural disasters. While all population groups in emergency situations may face increased risks of HIV, women and children are the most vulnerable and least able to protect themselves.

Some engage in risky behaviours, such as sex work, in an effort to survive. Children may be separated from their parents, recruited as child soldiers, or placed in situations that may make them more vulnerable to infection. Additionally, as security situations deteriorate, women and girls are often subjected to sexual violence and rape. Military personnel also face heightened risks of contracting or spreading HIV through risky sex during long deployment away from home.

Given the immediate needs of health care, shelter, food, and water, the threat of HIV infection has not historically been a priority in emergency situations. But humanitarian and relief efforts are now beginning to integrate HIV programs into emergency responses. In some cases, especially when conflicts limit the freedom of movement, the greatest threat of HIV transmission can occur during the period of peace following a time of conflict. For example, the civil war in Angola probably slowed the spread of HIV because trade and travel were halted for almost three decades. However, the threat of HIV in Angola has risen since the end of the war in 2002 because of the return of refugees, the opening of borders, increased trade, and more travel.

Labour migration—which involves millions of people every year—also leads to increased vulnerability and spread of HIV. Some of the factors that contribute to migrant and mobile workers' increased vulnerability include frequent travel, long separations from spouses or partners, limited access to health services, and minimal social contact or recreational opportunities. Without family and community support systems, migrants are more likely to engage in risky behaviours and potentially pass those risks on to their own family and community members.

Orphans and Vulnerable Children

The rising HIV infection rates among women, particularly in sub-Saharan Africa, expose children to increased HIV risk even before they are born. In 16 sub-Saharan African countries, at least 5 percent of pregnant women ages 15 to 24 attending prenatal clinics between 2001 and 2003 were HIV-positive. However, fewer than 10 percent of pregnant women were offered services to prevent mother-to-child transmission. In the absence of preventive measures, approximately one-third of children born to HIV-positive mothers will contract HIV. UN AIDS estimates that 2.3 million children were living with HIV at the end of 2005.

Fewer than 5 percent of children who need podiatric AIDS treatment are receiving it. Many HIV-infected children bear a double impact: Not only are they living with the disease themselves, but they have also lost one or both parents to AIDS. At the end of 2003, 15 million children had lost at least one parent to AIDS.

The number of children orphaned by AIDS is increasing at an unprecedented rate. Without AIDS, the percentage of children who are orphans would be expected to decline because of general improvements in health, but AIDS is dramatically increasing the percentage and number of orphans, especially in countries hard hit by the epidemic. As more parents develop AIDS and die, the number of orphans will continue to rise over the next 10 years. In sub-Saharan Africa, AIDS had orphaned 12 million children by 2003; by 2010, 18 million children are expected to be orphaned by AIDS. In South Africa alone, the number of orphans is expected to increase from 2.2 million in 2003 to 3.1 million in 2010.

Children in resource-poor environments are exceedingly vulnerable to a variety of adverse conditions even before the AIDS-related death of a parent or guardian. Basic needs like schooling, food, shelter, and health care are jeopardised, while children face an increased risk of abuse, exploitation, and social isolation. Psychosocial needs are significant as children deal with the trauma of impending or actual parental loss as well as possible disclosure issues about their parent's or their own HIV status, adjustment to new living and family circumstances, and real or perceived increases in economic and family responsibilities.

Children may serve as the primary caretaker of ailing parents, assume responsibility for younger siblings, or assume additional duties in the household. If the primary wage earner falls ill, children may leave school to find work to help support the family. Illnesses in the family may also divert funds that were previously available for school fees. Families of people living with HIV and AIDS often encounter stigma and discrimination that may deny children access to education and even health care.

Children orphaned by AIDS are at an increased risk of exploitation and abuse. Weak or poorly enforced laws can result in orphans being cheated out of their inheritance. Economic demands may force children, girls in particular, into commercial sex work or relationships with older men to obtain food, shelter, or money. Without the protection of a parent or loving guardian, children may become victims of trafficking, exploitive labour conditions, or violence. These risky conditions increase the orphaned child's vulnerability to HIV.

Health and Demographic Effects

AIDS has exacted a devastating toll on population and health over the last 25 years. The number of people living with HIV has surged from a few thousand in the 1980s to 40 million by 2005, and has spread to all world regions. The epidemic has triggered an upsurge in previously rare infections and malignancies and is contributing to an explosive TB epidemic around the world. HIV has reversed hard-won gains in child survival and life expectancy in sub-Saharan Africa and in a growing number of countries and communities worldwide. Because AIDS tends to strike the young and sexually active, AIDS deaths have also distorted the age and sex profiles of the populations in heavily affected communities and countries. The unbalanced ratios affect population growth as well as the social and economic health of these areas.

HIV and Tuberculosis

Tuberculosis is re-emerging in many parts of the world and

now infects about one-third of the world's population. Some countries now face HIV and TB epidemics simultaneously. In sub-Saharan Africa, up to 70 percent of TB patients are infected with HIV. AIDS and TB interact destructively, each hastening the progression of the other. TB is a leading cause of death among people with HIV and is responsible for an estimated 13 percent of AIDS deaths. Most people infected with TB, but not HIV, remain healthy: Only 5 percent to 10 percent will develop an active case of TB. HIV, however, triggers the active--and thus infectious—form of TB. A person with an active case of pulmonary TB can infect an average of 10 to 15 people every year with TB if he or she does not receive treatment.

HIV infection also makes TB more difficult to diagnose. People with HIV or AIDS often develop multi-drug-resistant TB, detectable only through special laboratory tests often not available in low-income countries. TB is curable in HIV-infected individuals, but treatment is much more expensive and typically requires a strict regimen of drugs for approximately six months. Strict adherence to treatment often is difficult for residents in developing countries, where access to health care is limited.

HIV and Malaria

Malaria and HIV are the most common infections and the most important causes of death and illness in sub-Saharan Africa. An estimated 30 million Africans are infected with HIV, and between 300 million and 500 million people suffer from malaria each year. There is increasing evidence that malaria and HIV interact such that HIV infection reduces the effectiveness of antimalarial drugs. HIV is associated with increased risk of malaria infection; more severe disease and death; and in pregnant women, more episodes of malaria and fever, and more adverse birth outcomes.

Lower Life Expectancy

AIDS is the fourth leading cause of death worldwide. In 2005, UN AIDS estimated that 3.1 million adults and children died of AIDS, of whom 2.4 million were in sub-Saharan Africa. Conversely, AIDS-associated deaths in some countries have decreased dramatically, because of effective new medications. In Brazil, government policies to provide universal treatment of AIDS patients reduced AIDS deaths as much as 70 percent between 1996 and 2002 one-third of children infected with HIV through mother-to-child transmission die before they reach age 1, and approximately 60 percent die by age 5.

The UN estimated that child mortality increased in South Africa from 62 to 74 deaths per 1,000 children under age 5 between the late 1990s and early 2000s. If not for AIDS mortality, under mortality would have been 43 deaths per 1,000 children. During the same period in Swaziland, under mortality rose from 109 to 143 deaths per 1,000 children; it would have been 73 in 2003 without the AIDS epidemic.

Improvements in public health and living standards throughout the world boosted average life expectancy in the mid- to late 1980s, but the surge of AIDS deaths has halted progress in many countries and caused a precipitous decline in several countries in sub-Saharan Africa. Lesotho's life expectancy is projected at 39 years in 2015–2020, but would have risen to 69 years without the AIDS epidemic. Some countries outside of sub-Saharan Africa are also experiencing AIDS-related reductions in life expectancy.

AIDS shortened projected life expectancy for 2015–2020 by four years in Cambodia and by seven years in Haiti. In sub-Saharan Africa, where women are infected with HIV at younger ages and in larger numbers than men, some countries are seeing even lower life expectancies among women. Between 2000 and 2005, female life expectancy dropped below male life expectancy because of AIDS in Kenya, Malawi, Zambia, and Zimbabwe. Kenya posted the largest difference—46 years for women and 48 years for men. Slower Population Growth Populations continue to grow in many heavily affected countries, although the growth is less than it would be in the absence of AIDS.

In Uganda, for example, the UN projects the population at 51 million by 2020, up from 29 million in 2005. If the country had not experienced an AIDS epidemic, the 2020 total would be about 5 million higher. The effect is much greater in South Africa, where AIDS mortality will nearly halt population growth in the next 15 years despite high fertility. South Africa is projected to add fewer than 1 million people to its 2005 population of 47.4 million in 15 years. If the country had escaped the AIDS epidemic, the UN estimates South Africa's 2020 population would be 63.1 million.

AIDS-related deaths are altering the age structure in severely affected countries. In southern Africa between 1985 and 1990, most deaths occurred among children under age 5 and adults over age 60, while only one-fifth of all deaths were among adults ages 20 to 49. Between 2000 and 2005, high AIDS mortality among young and middle-age adults meant that people ages 20 to 49 accounted for almost 60 percent of all deaths. South Africa embodies many of the changes projected for populations severely affected by AIDS. By 2020, fewer children will be born because of deaths and lower fertility among HIV-positive women. Many children will die of AIDS-related causes during childhood.

Social and Economic Impact

In heavily affected countries, HIV has overwhelmed public health systems and has stretched health care providers, infrastructure, and budgets beyond capacity. However, AIDS is much more than a health crisis. Its effects extend to nearly every dimension of social and economic life, especially in the worst-affected countries. Although the magnitude of the epidemic varies, in every country, AIDS primarily strikes adults between ages 25 and 45—people who were infected in their adolescent and young adult years. HIV and AIDS rob employees from the labour force, providers and caretakers from families, and teachers from communities. Public Health Burden Health sectors feel the impact of HIV through such direct costs as the expense of medical treatment, supplies, and personnel, and through such indirect costs as falling numbers of trained medical providers and increasing stress on health systems struggling to respond to the epidemic.

Global Challenges

HIV and AIDS continue to overwhelm the health systems in many countries. People living with HIV generally have a range of health care needs, spanning primary care and basic treatment for infections to hospitalisation and psychosocial counselling. Where antiretroviral drugs are available, health systems need to monitor patients and manage the complex treatment regimens.

The increased need for care is especially problematic in countries that already find it hard to meet the most basic health care needs of their populations. WHO has reported that nations need between US$35 and US$40 per capita each year to finance minimum general health services packages, including antiretroviral therapy for people living with AIDS. However, the average amount spent in 2001 was US$23, and only US$6 of this came from public spending.

Many countries, including some of the poorest, are increasing their domestic spending on HIV and AIDS. South Africa increased HIV/AIDS spending in its 2003/2004 national budget by 86 percent from the previous fiscal year. AIDS is usurping health sector resources needed to treat other health problems. In many hospitals in sub-Saharan Africa, for example, AIDS patients are crowding out other patients:

> AIDS patients frequently occupy more than half of hospital beds in some sub-Saharan Africa countries. In Cote devoir and Uganda, between 50 percent and 80 percent of adult hospital beds are occupied by patients with HIV-related conditions. The loss of health care staff to AIDS is another blow to the health care sector in heavily affected countries. Their loss is particularly painful given the escalating need for their professional skills as more people fall ill with AIDS. According to the health service in South Africa, 14 percent of staff (mostly nurses) died from AIDS between 1997 and 2001. AIDS also undermines health workers' morale as their workload and stress increase and they witness high mortality among children, young adults, and colleagues.

Impacts on Business, Agriculture, and Labour

Because AIDS affects people in their prime working ages, businesses are suffering severe effects from the epidemic. This is especially true in some sub-Saharan African countries, where as much as one-third of the work-engage population is infected with HIV. In high-prevalence countries, AIDS is consuming business profits because of three primary factors: increased operating costs, decreased productivity, and declining markets.

AIDS was initially believed to be primarily an urban phenomenon, but it now clearly threatens the lives and livelihoods of rural communities throughout the less developed world. AIDS-related deaths among farm workers threaten agricultural production and food security, most notably in sub-Saharan Africa where a large segment of society relies on agriculture. The Food and Agriculture Organisation (FAO) estimates that 7 million agricultural workers died of AIDS between 1985 and 2000 in the 25 hardest-hit countries in sub-Saharan Africa. FAO projects that 16 million more agricultural workers could die because of AIDS by 2020. In the worst-affected countries, losses in the agricultural labour force will range from 13 percent in Tanzania to 26 percent in Namibia by 2020. The loss of agricultural labourers in southern Africa will cause an estimated 3 percent loss in grain output. By disrupting agricultural production, AIDS can undermine countries' export capacity and thus their ability to earn foreign exchange. In Africa, agriculture accounts for 70 percent of employment, 24 percent of the gross domestic product, and 40 percent of the foreign exchange earnings. The International Labour Organisation (ILO) reports that subsistence agriculture employs 80 percent of the population of Swaziland, and export farming is responsible for 10 percent of the gross domestic product.

Farm households coping with AIDS may sell assets such as livestock, equipment, or land to support ill family members and pay for funeral expenses. Time devoted to care, funerals, and mourning of family members with AIDS reduces productivity and jeopardises households' ability to produce and purchase food. Moreover, important knowledge and skills are lost as deaths mount among the agricultural population. Women in agricultural households are particularly hard hit since they often provide the labour for farming, but must increasingly spend their time caring for sick family members.

Without the necessary labour and resources for planting and harvesting, some families leave their land. A survey in Zambia showed that chronically ill heads of households in rural areas reduced the area of land they cultivated by more than half, reducing crop production and food availability.

As incomes decline and more money is spent on health care, less money is available to spend on food, which can lead to malnutrition. Nutritional deficiencies can speed up the progression from HIV to AIDS and increase susceptibility to opportunistic infections. People living with AIDS need more calories than other people, especially if they have suffered significant weight loss. Individuals on antiretroviral drugs also have specific nutritional needs, and inadequate nutrition can affect their tolerance to the drugs and adherence to drug regimens.

Imapcts on Governance and Public Service

In countries heavily affected by HIV, the epidemic affects governance and public service in three main ways: The country loses hard-to-replace political leaders and civil servants; revenues decline and costs rise; and demand for social services increases. Taken together, these factors exert significant pressure on the governments of less developed countries.

At the highest levels, AIDS is taking the lives of national leaders—including ministers, parliamentarians, and cabinet members—although most of these are not classified as AIDS deaths because the families fear stigmatisation. Nations are losing their leaders and their years of political experience, undermining future national stability and security. Zambia held 14 special elections between 1964 and 1984 because of the death of an incumbent. From 1985, when the first case of HIV was recorded in the country, to 2003, Zambia held 59 by-elections due to incumbent deaths, of which occurred when the epidemic was in full force. The ranks of civil servants are also being depleted, Deaths among skilled civil servants are especially difficult to absorb in countries with low levels of literacy and education.

Many of these countries rely on a small pool of staff members to develop and administer services. Declining revenues and rising costs compound the loss of civil servants. In heavily affected countries, AIDS is reducing productivity and earnings. In 33 countries in sub-Saharan

Africa, the annual growth rate for the gross domestic product per capita declined by 0.7 percent between 1992 and 2002 because of the AIDS epidemic. Meanwhile, domestic government spending on AIDS has increased considerably. Between 1999 and 2002, low- and middle-income countries doubled their expenditures on AIDS programs to US$995 million. At the same time that costs rise and revenues decline, the demands on public services increase.

HIV generally affects the poorest households disproportionately, contributing to rising poverty and greater social welfare needs. Furthermore, millions of orphaned children will require new or expanded public services. Funding or investments in some public services are reduced because of increased expenditures on health care and social welfare. Prevention, Care, and Treatment In this third decade of the epidemic, there is still neither a cure nor vaccine for AIDS. Life-prolonging drugs have become more affordable and accessible, yet treatment is still largely unavailable to most people who need it in developing countries.

As of June 2005, out of the 6.5 million people needing treatment in these countries, only an estimated 1 million were receiving it. While antiretroviral treatment prolongs the lives of many AIDS patients, it does not cure AIDS. More than 50 HIV vaccine candidates have undergone clinical trials since 1987 and researchers continue to develop strategies for improving defences against the virus. Despite this progress, a safe and effective vaccine is years away. As HIV continues to spread, prevention remains the backbone of programs to curb the epidemic for the foreseeable future. However, there is a need for more comprehensive programs that encompass prevention, care, treatment, and support interventions. Comprehensive prevention programs for people living with HIV include:

- — General education about the risk of sexual transmission.
- — Support for low-risk behaviour, including condom use.
- — Diagnosis and treatment of STIs.
- — Counselling and testing for HIV.
- — Preventing mother-to-child transmission.
- — Ensuring the safety of blood and blood products.
- — Needle exchange programs.
- — Reducing the stigma attached to HIV and AIDS.

Comprehensive care and treatment programs include antiretroviral therapy, prevention and treatment of opportunistic infections, palliative and home-based care, psychosocial support, post exposure prophylaxis (primarily for exposure to HIV as a result of rape or needle stick), and support for orphans and children of people living with AIDS.

Prevention and Care

The various components of the prevention and care continuum are mutually reinforcing. The availability of HIV care and treatment services can be a powerful incentive for people to seek counselling and testing. Without such services, people have little incentive to learn their HIV status. Counselling provides an opportunity to educate infected people about the importance of and methods for preventing the infection of others.

Experts often cite counselling and testing for HIV—at AIDS clinics or as routinely offered by health providers—as a crucial entry point for effective prevention, treatment, and care. Access to care and treatment also helps reduce the stigma associated with HIV infection, encourages more people to get tested for HIV, and may promote behaviour change. But convincing people to change their behaviour is difficult, especially if they believe that they are not personally at risk or that they can be successfully treated for AIDS. Studies in more developed countries have shown that some people practice high-risk sexual behaviour when they know that effective AIDS therapies are available.

Prevention programs are much more likely to be successful if they involve policymakers and community lead-12. Public policies that support HIV-prevention programs enable people to protect themselves. Successful prevention programs also address the factors that put individuals, families, and communities at risk of HIV infection and that increase their vulnerability to infection. Prevention programs are effective only if they can reach the majority of people most at risk, especially young adults and marginalised groups such as sex workers, men who have sex with men, injecting drug users, and the sexual partners of those infected. Successful programs are tailored to focus on the main modes of transmission in any given community.

Sexual transmission is the primary mode of transmission in most countries, especially in less developed regions, but transfusions of contaminated blood, injecting drug use, and mother-to-child transmission are responsible for up to 30 percent of all global HIV infections. If prevention activities are focused on these groups when an epidemic is localised, the prevalence of HIV in the general population can remain low. However, even when the epidemic is localised, there is still a need for prevention programs for the general population.

In sub-Saharan Africa, successful prevention programs focus on preventing transmission through heterosexual intercourse, from mothers-to-children, and through contaminated blood. In Southeast Asia, the primary focus is preventing transmission through sex and injecting drug use. In Eastern Europe, the emphasis is on transmission via injecting drug use. In Latin America and in high-income countries, prevention efforts need to encompass homosexual and heterosexual transmission, as well as transmission through injecting drug use.

Preventing Sexual Transmission

The most common mode of HIV transmission is sexual contact. Men and women with multiple sexual partners, including sex workers and their clients, men who have sex with men, and youth are the groups at highest risk of sexual transmission.

The most effective prevention programs promote or include interventions such as abstinence, delay in sexual debut and mutual fidelity, as well as limiting the number of sexual partners; consistent and correct condom use; STI treatment; counselling and testing, and a supportive social and policy environment. A program that focuses only on a few components may not serve the entire population and will have minimal national impact. The most effective mix of these components depends on cultural context as well as specific prevention needs and characteristics of key groups. Effective programs also consider the economic, social, and cultural factors that may affect individual's behaviour.

Sexual debut at a young age, multiple partners, inter-generation sex, STI infection, and unprotected sex are HIV risk factors that can be mediated through behaviour change. These changes require education about modes of HIV transmission, education on how to delay onset of sexual debut, strategies to eliminate high-risk sex or adopt safer behaviours or seek services, and access to supplies or services needed for protection.

Male circumcision is expected to become an important additional tool in reducing the risk of acquiring HIV. Negotiation skills and empowerment are also important so people, especially women and girls, can protect themselves.

Abstinence is the prevention method emphasised in programming directed at youth, the demographic with the highest rate of new infections. Strategies to promote abstinence include changing social norms, sex education, and peer education. "Secondary abstinence" among people who have had sex can also reduce risk of HIV. Abstinence-only programs have been criticised for being unresponsive to the needs of people who are raped, economically dependent on sex work, or are in unions with an HIV-infected spouse or partner.

While abstinence and mutual monogamy with an un infected partner are effective preventive behaviours, they may be difficult to maintain. Consistent condom use has been very effective in protecting against the transmission of HIV and other STIs in people who are sexually active. In married or monogamous couples, one common barrier to condom use is a concern that it implies infidelity. Teaching strategies to negotiate condom use can increase acceptability to sexual partners while addressing these concerns. In Thailand and Cambodia, commercial sex establishments with condom-use policies reduced HIV transmission among sex workers and their clients, as well as in the general population. Consistent condom use reduces HIV transmission in zero discordant couples (in which only one partner is HIV positive) approximately sixfold.

Condoms also prevent STIs, which may contribute up to a tenfold increase in susceptibility to HIV. STIs such as syphilis or gonorrhoea can be treated with antibiotics to reduce this risk, while infections that cannot be cured—genital herpes, for example—may be controlled by cyclophoria or other antiviral medications. Even without medication, people with incurable STIs benefit from medical attention by receiving counselling on safer sex, partner notification strategies, and general health information. STI services can address both biological and behaviour risk factors in sexually active people through treatment and counselling.

The Brazil HIV/AIDS program has demonstrated that education about and access to condom use among young people are effective. Condom use at first sexual intercourse among young Brazilians increased from less than 5 percent in 1986 to 63 percent in 2003. Ongoing research has demonstrated that male circumcision can protect against HIV infection. Circumcision is not practised in many areas of eastern and southern Africa, which may be one reason for the high HIV prevalence in those regions. A clinical trial in South Africa found that circumcised men were 61 percent less likely to become infected with HIV than men who were not circumcised. In Rakai, Uganda, a recent study has demonstrated that male circumcision reduced HIV infection in female partners by 30 percent. If subsequent studies confirm these findings, male circumcision could become an important tool for the control of HIV.

There are several factors that may reduce the risk of HIV infection in circumcised men. The absence of foreskin can shorten drying time following sexual contact, which reduces the life expectancy of HIV and the amount of time the skin is in direct contact with the virus. The total surface area of the penis and the number of target cells, abundant on the foreskin, are reduced through circumcision.

Several studies have indicated that most adult men would undergo circumcision if they believed it protected them against HIV infection. Male circumcision may prove effective in reducing HIV infection, but it is not a panacea for prevention. Circumcision does not The Global Challenge of HIV and AIDS offer complete protection from HIV. A comprehensive prevention approach including education about abstinence, being faithful, and condom use should be available to all men, circumcised or not, to prevent the spread of the virus.

A UN Work Plan on Male Circumcision is developing technical guidance on programmatic, social, and clinical issues concerning the expansion of male circumcision services. These guidelines will assist country program managers to ensure that male circumcisions are being performed appropriately while minimising the risk of clinical complications, the stigma and discrimination against circumcised and uncircumcised men, and to avoid undermining other HIV-prevention strategies.

Preventing HIV Transmission via and Injecting Drug

There are an estimated 13 million injecting drug users worldwide, and as many as 3.3 million are infected with HIV. Between 5 percent and 11 percent of all AIDS cases are related to injecting drug use, which is a major mode of HIV transmission in southern and Eastern Europe, most of Asia and North America, and parts of South America. Injecting drug use is also an important source of infection in North Africa and the Middle East. Transmission in injecting drug users is primarily a result of sharing contaminated needles. However, all drug users, injecting or non-injecting, can play a role in spreading HIV to the general population through sexual transmission, especially users who trade sex for drugs or money, or who engage in risky sexual behaviours when impaired by drugs.

The spread of HIV in people using drugs is often rapid and difficult to control. The underground culture and social stigma attached to drug use and HIV make this population difficult to reach. Studies show, however, that given the appropriate information and opportunity, many injecting drug users will change their drug-using and sexual behaviours to protect themselves and their partners from HIV. Education programs have succeeded in reducing HIV transmission among people who inject drugs in several developed countries, including Australia, Canada, and the

United States. Harm reduction models, such as needle exchange programs, can minimise the use of contaminated needles. Concerns that needle exchange programs increase the frequency of drug use have not been realised. Methadone and buprenorphine treatment can reduce dependency on illegal drugs, thereby reducing high-risk behaviours. Ensuring condom availability and teaching correct condom use can curb unprotected sex. STI and other health care services reduce risk while creating opportunities for counselling or referrals to drug treatment programs. For drug users living with HIV or AIDS, care, treatment, and support services can be integrated into drug treatment programs.

Preventing Transmission via HIV-Infected Blood

Some of the first people identified with HIV acquired the infection from infected blood products in high-income countries. Thousands of people were infected through blood products in the 1980s, but the number of such infections plummeted when tests to screen blood and blood donors became widely used. In more developed countries, the dramatic reduction of HIV transmission from blood is one of the greatest success stories in the battle against the epidemic. However, contaminated blood continues to cause between 5 percent and 10 percent of new HIV infections worldwide and is especially problematic in low-income countries that have inadequate health infrastructures.

Unsanitary blood collection practices infected thousands of villagers in rural China in the 1990s. Preventing the transmission of HIV through blood and blood products involves establishing a well-organised blood transfusion service; exercising universal precautions during blood collection and handling; recruiting safe blood donors; using effective blood tests for HIV and other infectious diseases; ensuring appropriate use of blood and blood products, including avoiding unnecessary transfusions; and preventing health problems, such as anaemia, that require blood transfusions.

Preventing Iatrogenic Transmission

Unsafe medical practices contribute to iatrogenic transmission—the unintentional transmission of HIV by medical personnel. Health care workers, particularly in rural areas, may not receive adequate training in universal safety precautions. Ineffective sterilisation techniques and poor sanitation practices in medical facilities can expose health workers and patients to blood and other body fluids containing HIV. Improper disposal of used syringes, needles, and other medical equipment is another potential hazard.

Cultural expectations of medical care may increase the risk of iatrogenic HIV transmission. In some areas, a medical visit is considered incomplete without an injection—often unnecessary injections of antibiotics, vitamins, analgesics, or chloroquine. HIV can survive in needles that are used for intramuscular and subcutaneous injections and pose a risk for HIV transmission if reused. In 2000, the reuse of injection equipment accounted for an estimated 5 percent of new HIV infections. Transmission between provider and patient is also a risk in health care settings. Health care workers are commonly exposed to blood or infectious products in the course of routine work. Practising universal precautions, such as wearing gloves and masks, consistently allows for non-stigmatising care for all people, regardless of patient or provider's HIV status.

Traditional healers are a significant source of care in many regions of the world, and many engage in activities that could expose them or their patients to HIV. Some practitioners believe the source of HIV is not biologically rooted, making precautions seem unnecessary. Contact with contaminated equipment may occur through common cultural practices including scarification, male and female circumcision, and tattooing.

Preventing Mother-to-Child Transmission

The great majority (90 percent) of HIV-positive children acquired the virus from their mother. The risk of a mother transmitting the virus to her baby is around 15 percent to 30 percent—a risk that increases to as high as 45 percent with prolonged breast-feeding.. Approximately 800,000 infants are newly infected with HIV annually, nearly all in developing countries; 90 percent of infected children live in sub-Saharan Africa. Risk of transmission is affected by factors related to the virus, the mother, the delivery process, the baby, and how the infant is fed.

During pregnancy and delivery, the mother's health, disruption of the placental barrier, pre-term delivery, and haemorrhage are significant predictors of the child's infection. After delivery, breast-feeding is the most important risk factor. Without treatment, an estimated one in every seven infants breast-fed by an HIV-positive mother becomes infected through breast milk.

Current strategies for preventing mother-to-child transmission include primary prevention of HIV in girls and women; counselling and testing in pregnant women; family planning services to reduce pregnancy in infected mothers; preventive antiretroviral drug therapy; follow-up care and treatment for mother and infant; and nutritional counselling and breast-milk substitutes, if appropriate. The most effective drug therapy tested so far is long-course HAART, which can reduce transmission to 2 percent. HAART's complexity and cost have limited its use in resource-poor settings. Shorter, simpler, and less costly regimens are available.

The most practical and least expensive (US$4 per dose) of these options is nevirapine. Single doses can be given at birth to both the mother and infant. Boehringer-Ingelheim, the company that manufactures nevirapine, has made the drug available for free in less developed countries to prevent mother-to-child transmission. But many women are developing a resistance to nevirapine and similar drugs, making them less useful in the future. A recent study reported that up to 69 percent of women may have resistance to this class of drugs one to four months after nevirapine prophylactic treatment is discontinued. WHO is currently reviewing the policy implications of this finding and is likely to recommend a combination of HAART for the prevention of mother-to-child transmission.

Based on trial data from Zambia, WHO, UNICEF, and UN AIDS recommend the use of cotrimoxizole to reduce mother-to-child transmission. In regions where children under 18 months of age cannot be reliably tested, cotrimoxizole prophylaxis is recommended for all children born to HIV-infected mothers. Cotrimoxizole can also prevent and treat Pneumocystis pneumonia, as well as other opportunistic infections, in children infected with HIV.

Helping Orphans and Vulnerable Children Because HIV is infectious, there is a high risk that a child who loses one parent to AIDS will lose the other one as well. While the increasing availability of treatment will slow the rate of increase in children orphaned by AIDS, the number of orphans and vulnerable children will continue to rise for the foreseeable future. When children are left without parents, communities must respond to their needs to avoid their exploitation, ensure their welfare, and promote healthy development.

Most of the children orphaned by AIDS in sub-Saharan Africa are cared for by extended family members. Some of these caretakers are HIV-infected or are responsible for other family members living with HIV and AIDS, which can create both financial and emotional burdens. Many extended families are unable to provide the school fees, food, and health care costs of additional children. In many high-HIV-prevalence regions, community-based organisations help families meet the needs of the orphan households through material, financial, emotional, or psychosocial support to the children and the caretaker.

Community support for families is more cost-effective than other options that countries are trying, including building or expanding orphanages. While orphanages can meet the immediate, urgent needs of an orphaned child, they are not the best long-term situation. Orphanages are expensive to operate, often fail to meet the developmental needs of the child, and can isolate children from community support systems.

Managing HIV and AIDS

In 2005, an estimated 6.5 million people needed antiretroviral treatment; only about 15 percent—1 million people—had access to it. In sub-Saharan Africa, around 11 percent of those in need of treatment were receiving it. The main reasons for this shortfall include the high cost of treatment; procurement challenges; inadequate health infrastructure, including a lack of health care providers; insufficient political commitment at the national level; inadequate or uncertain financial resources; and the persistent stigma that often prevents people from seeking care.

The clinical objectives of antiretroviral therapy are to suppress the replication of the virus and restore immune function of the body; limit the likelihood of viral resistance to antiretroviral drugs; and reduce HIV-related morbidity and mortality.

Since the introduction of entire travellers in 1996, drug therapy has transformed HIV from a progressive terminal illness to a manageable chronic disease. Drugs, although they cannot cure it. The current antiretroviral drugs—which fall into three main classes—work by blocking enzymes that are important for the replication and functioning of HIV in the body. A newer class of entire travellers—entry inhibitors—works differently: It fights HIV after it has infected the immune system. Entry inhibitors offer hope to people who have developed resistance to current HIV medications. Combining drugs from different classes is the most effective therapy for thwarting AIDS, because the virus can develop resistance to drugs used individually. A similar multi-drug approach is used to treat cancer and TB.

Recent studies have shown that low-cost regimens can prevent some of the opportunistic infections that commonly occur with HIV, including TB and Pneumomycosis carinae pneumonia (PCP), and other major causes of illness, such as non-typhoid salmonella infections and cerebral toxoplasmosis. Preventive therapy for TB would be especially effective in sub-Saharan Africa, where TB is a major cause of death in HIV-positive individuals. Using cotrimoxazole to treat PCP patients who have HIV can significantly reduce hospitalisation and mortality from other bacterial opportunistic infections. Fungal infections, a major cause of illness and death in HIV-positive individuals, respond to preventive therapy with fluconazole. These simple preventive therapies could reduce illness in people living with HIV. Their relatively low cost means they could reach a much wider population than more expensive antiretroviral drugs. However, further research is needed on who should receive them for how long and how the therapies affect drug resistance in the long term.

The broad goal of clinical care (including drug therapy) is to improve the quality of life of people living with HIV by improving access to comprehensive prevention and care programs. Evidence from both developed and developing countries has shown that antiretroviral therapy can dramatically prolong the lives of persons living with HIV, enabling them to remain productive members of their community, support their families, and raise their children.

Clinical care programs can also help reduce the number of orphans and vulnerable children by prolonging the lives of parents; reduce mother-to-child transmission; and lessen the risk of sexual transmission because of lower viral load in body fluids. Care programs also combat stigma and discrimination associated with HIV and AIDS.

Palliative care is an important component of comprehensive care for people living with HIV. Many people experience pain, diarrhoea, nausea, cough, shortness of breath, fatigue, fever, and confusion, as well as damaging psychosocial stress associated with illness, stigma, and end-of-life issues. Preventing these symptoms through palliative care prevents pain and unnecessary visits to health care facilities and allows people with AIDS to remain as active as possible in their community. Traditional healing, local remedies, and a mix of support services can also play a significant role. Training home-based care providers, community volunteers, or family members in palliative care can enhance the quality of life of people living with AIDS.

Home-based care offers a variety of benefits to people living with HIV and AIDS, as well as their families, especially to people with uncertain access to health care facilities. Home-based care providers have a unique opportunity to identify vulnerable children in the household who may need services.

Access to Treatment

A recent and dramatic rise in global funding, aggressive international initiatives, and lower costs of entire travellers have increased access to treatment in several countries. The most successful national treatment programs in developing countries are in Brazil and Botswana. Brazil's treatment program demonstrates the importance of political commitment, adequate national resources, the close involvement of civil society, and comprehensive prevention and treatment programs. Brazil's program also shows the considerable level of resources needed to provide universal access and comprehensive prevention and treatment services.

The Brazilian government provided nearly 90 percent of these resources. The commitment of huge resources has certainly worked for Brazil—a middle-income country—but most developing countries may not be able to afford to provide free treatment for everyone in need. The African Comprehensive HIV/AIDS Partnerships (ACHAP) in Botswana program is a joint effort between the government of Botswana, the Bill & Melinda Gates Foundation, and the Merck Company Foundation/Merck Company Inc. that has dramatically improved national access to treatment. The program was launched in 2000 and reached 42,000 with antiretroviral drug therapy (56 percent of those in need) by December 2004.

The antiretroviral drugs used most often to treat AIDS belong to three major classes: nucleoside reverse transcriptase inhibitors (NRTIs), non-nucleoside reverse transcriptase inhibitors (NNRTIs), and protease inhibitors. A fourth class of drugs called entry inhibitors (including fusion inhibitors) is now available. Entry inhibitors work by preventing HIV from entering T-cells. Healthy Tcells are crucial for the body's defense against pathogens like HIV.

Treatment coverage continues to improve in several countries as a result of increased resources from the U.S. President's Emergency Plan for AIDS Relief and the Global Fund to Fight AIDS, Tuberculosis, and Malaria. The President's Emergency Plan expects to reach 2 million people in 15 focus countries by 2008. The Global Fund has committed nearly US$2.5 billion to HIV/AIDS and estimates that more than 1.8 million people will be on entire travellers through grants.

Despite these efforts, the vast majority of people living with HIV will go without effective treatment for several years to come. Many people living with HIV lack access to health facilities and cannot afford to pay reduced, but still substantial, co-payments for treatment. Many developing countries do not have the financial resources and infrastructure to support a large-scale HIV treatment program. The most neglected populations for treatment are often children, women, rural important initiatives expanded the arsenal of weapons in the battle against HIV and AIDS.

Fund to Fight against AIDS

In 2001, the UN created the Global Fund to Fight AIDS, Tuberculosis and Malaria, with a target of US$9 billion to support integrated approaches to prevention, care, support, and treatment. The establishment of the fund helped refocus attention not only on HIV, but also on two other important threats to international health: tuberculosis (TB) and malaria. The Global Fund disburses funds to implementing agencies, a diverse group representing multiple sectors of society. Donors to the Global Fund include the governments of more than 50 countries, as well as foundations, corporations, and private donors. The Global Fund also finances programs for malaria and TB, diseases that are rampant in many high-HIV-prevalence countries.

The Global Fund has committed US$2.5 billion to HIV prevention, care, and treatment programs in countries around the world. Between 2001 and 2005, the Global Fund provided treatment for 220,000 people with HIV, more than 1.1 million people with malaria, and 600,000 people with TB. If fully funded, the Global Fund aims to provide 1.8 million people with antiretroviral therapy (ART) and 62 million people with voluntary counselling and testing, and to support more than 1 million orphans with medical services, education, and community care.

In 2003, the U.S. President's Emergency Plan for AIDS Relief was initiated as a five-year, US$15 billion global initiative to fight HIV and AIDS outside the United States. The Emergency Plan has a strong emphasis on care and treatment, with 55 percent of funds devoted to treatment, 15 percent for palliative care, 20 percent for HIV/AIDS prevention (with at least 33 percent for promoting abstinence until marriage), and 10 percent for helping orphans and vulnerable children. Fifteen focus countries (Botswana, Cote devour, Ethiopia, Guyana, Haiti, Kenya, Mozambique, Namibia, Nigeria, Rwanda, South Africa, Tanzania, Uganda, Zambia, and Vietnam) receive Emergency Plan funds. ART has been provided to more than 235,000 people living with HIV; more than 1.1 million have been reached with essential care services. Treatment may increase at a faster rate since funds can now be spent on much less expensive generic antiretroviral drugs (ARVs), following a ruling by the U.S. Food and Drug Administration in 2005.

The 3 by 5 Initiative was launched by the World Health Organisation (WHO) and UN AIDS in September 2003. Its goal: To provide antiretroviral drugs to 3 million people living with AIDS in developing countries by the end of 2005, and to reach at least half of the people in need. The UN AIDS/WHO initiative relied on partnerships with the Global Fund, the Emergency Plan, the World Bank, national governments, and non-governmental organisations (NGOs). By mid-2005, approximately 1 million people in the developing world had access to ARVs, 2 million below the target number. Fourteen low- to middle-income countries surpassed the 3 by 5 goal of providing ARVs to more than 50 percent of those in need. However, ART reached only about 15 percent of all those in need, well below the target of 50 percent.

The 3 by 5 goals proved too ambitious, given the many barriers to rapidly scaling up ART, especially in poor countries. Some countries lacked the political commitment needed for rapidly increasing access to ART. Bottlenecks in supply, limited human capacity, high drug prices, and poor infrastructure within many developing countries were also major obstacles.

Funding from donors was often unpredictable and insufficient, and technical assistance from WHO and other agencies could not overcome the weak infrastructure in many countries. Although the 3 by 5 goals were not met, the plan did help many countries deliver ART to more people, improve health infrastructure, and, most important, demonstrate the feasibility of treating large numbers of people living with AIDS in the developing world.

The Global Challenge of HIV and AIDS residents, and marginalised populations such as injecting drug users and sex workers. Drug therapy programs need to closely involve civil society, especially community-based organisations of people living with HIV, and ensure equal access to clinical care for women, children, and other vulnerable and marginalised populations. Treatment for children with HIV poses special challenges. Without treatment, at least one-half of infected infants will die before their second birthday; yet even determining the HIV status of infants is difficult. The antibody tests used in developing countries cannot detect HIV infection in children less than 18 months of age. The more costly antigen tests that can measure infection in very young children are rarely available. Children are also vulnerable because they usually cannot advocate for their own health care and depend on parents or guardians to initiate medical visits. Children also have limited treatment options—most AIDS drugs formulations are not appropriate for children—and treatment regimens must be constantly monitored because effective doses change as children grow.

Only about 5 percent of an estimated 700,000 children in need of antiretroviral therapy received it in 2005.

Expanding Counselling and Testing

Counselling and testing services for HIV have long been a component of HIV prevention and care programs in more developed countries and are proving to be a cost-effective way of reducing risky behaviours and of leading patients to other services. A study of data from Kenya, Tanzania, and Trinidad documented a 43 percent reduction in unprotected sex among people who received voluntary counselling and testing (VCT) for HIV. Counselling and testing programs involve raising community awareness, pre- and post-test counselling, psychological support, and referral to relevant services. HIV counselling helps people cope with personal stress and make decisions related to HIV.

It enables an individual or couple to evaluate their risk of contracting or transmitting HIV and helps them avoid it. Counselling helps people deal with the stigma and discrimination associated with HIV. The very act of being tested, for example, may have negative consequences in communities where HIV-positive people are stigmatised.

Despite their importance, counselling and testing services tend to be of limited quality and coverage in less developed countries. A lack of trained staff, concerns about confidentiality, stigma and discrimination, clients' lack of knowledge about services, and limited resources are some of the reasons why VCT programs are inadequate or under used.

Many countries are increasing the availability and use of testing and counselling services by shifting from voluntary counselling and testing, in which a person goes to a health facility for the primary purpose of receiving an HIV test, to routine testing, in which all patients arriving at a facility are routinely offered an HIV test. Tests with same-day results also increase use, because they eliminate the need for patients to return to a health clinic to receive their results—and more patients will actually learn their HIV status.

Several countries have successfully increased counselling and testing services. Botswana, one of the highest prevalence countries, was the first in Africa to routinely offer HIV testing in both public and private clinics. A growing body of evidence suggests that making HIV testing part of standard care reduces the stigma associated with the disease and increases the number choosing to be tested. Routine testing, mass media campaigns promoting the value of knowing HIV status, and learning the benefits and the wide availability of treatment, have dramatically increased the use of counselling and testing services in Botswana.

In Kenya, the introduction of routine testing (with the option of refusal) in antenatal care clinics doubled the use of testing and counselling from 37 percent to 75 percent in one month. Lesotho has taken the concept of routine testing one step further to community-based door-to-door testing in their KYS (Know Your Status) campaign. This is an attempt to significantly boost the number of people who know their HIV status. Currently, only 9 percent of men and 13 percent of women are aware of their status in a country with an adult HIV prevalence of 30 percent. The program includes training community leaders as prevention and treatment supporters, involving people living with HIV in adherence and prevention activities, and recruiting 7,500 health workers for counselling and testing.

Challenges in HIV Control

Despite major medical and technological breakthroughs and advances, the AIDS epidemic continues its relentless spread in many resource-poor settings. AIDS continues to be one of the most devastating and important global public health and developmental problems. However, HIV and AIDS control must compete with other emergencies, including civil strife, natural disasters, and continuing threats of emerging infectious diseases such as Ebola, SARS, and avian influenza. Three key challenges for the future are controlling further spread of the epidemic in infants and young adults; treating, caring for, and supporting the neglected millions of people living with HIV; and mitigating the epidemic's impact on the millions of people affected by AIDS in resource-constrained countries. To meet these challenges, the international community and national governments and civil society need to take a number of steps, including:

— Increasing resources available for comprehensive prevention, care, treatment, and support services.

— Ensuring that prevention remains the backbone of AIDS control programs, even with expanded treatment access.

— Improving the health infrastructure and capacity for delivery of services.

— Improving technologies for the treatment and prevention of AIDS.

— Reducing poverty, illiteracy, and other social, economic, and political actors that increase vulnerability to infection.

— Reducing the stigma and discrimination against those living with HIV.

Improving Resources for HIV Programs

Resources available for HIV and AIDS have increased from US$300 million in 1996 to US$10 billion in 2006. Despite this increase, UN AIDS estimates that US$22 billion is needed by 2008 to ensure an adequate response to the expanding AIDS epidemic. The response would include low-cost HAART, treatment of opportunistic infections, and support for orphans and vulnerable children. Providing such support will likely require major increases in national government allocations; greater support from the private sector; and substantial increases in international assistance.

Prevention and treatment programs for the AIDS pandemic have been inadequate, small-scale, and fragmented in most countries, particularly in less developed regions. With few exceptions, the efforts have failed to slow the spread of the virus or to reduce the damaging effects of the pandemic. However, public health and policy experts cite a number of strategies that could help meet the need for an expanded and comprehensive response. An effective response should include strategic planning, a multi-sectorial approach, and the active involvement of non-governmental organisations (NGOs).

Ideally, HIV programs should also include state-of-the-art technical strategies; adequate distribution of resources at the community level; development of human capacity as well as technical and operational competence; and better management and supply of drugs and commodities. Program planners also need to anticipate the costs of expanded coverage, program evaluation, and future technological developments. An expanded and comprehensive response also requires improving public- and private-sector capacity to expand care and treatment services, including new technologies such as HAART and vaccines. But the most critical challenge is the effective application of current technologies on a large enough scale to curb the epidemic, improve access to care and treatment, reduce stigma and discrimination for persons living with HIV, and support and protect orphans and vulnerable children.

Integrating Prevention and Treatment

Programs to prevent HIV transmission often compete with programs to treat people suffering from AIDS for scarce resources and political support. But new mathematical models confirm there is a asynergy between prevention and treatment efforts, and that both are crucial for controlling the AIDS epidemic. Successful prevention programs help reduce the number of new infections and ultimately the number of people who need treatment. Successful treatment programs not only prolong the lives of people living with HIV but will also slow the spread of HIV by lowering the viral load of people with the virus.

Effective care and treatment programs can reduce AIDS deaths, but a long-term decline will be driven by preventing new infections. Treatment programs can also enhance prevention efforts by reducing stigma. Scaling up both treatment and prevention efforts could avert about one-half of new HIV infections and prevent more than one-fourth of AIDS-related deaths over the next two decades.

Search for a Vaccine

A safe, stable, efficacious, affordable, and accessible HIV vaccine would significantly enhance HIV prevention and help control the global epidemic. HIV vaccine development and testing has greatly accelerated over the last few years, notably with the Global HIV Vaccine Initiative, an alliance of independent organisations trying to accelerate the development of a vaccine by sharing information and working cooperatively.

HIV researchers say that an ideal vaccine is at least seven to 10 years away because of many scientific, ethical, legal, and financial stumbling blocks. HIV infection and the human immune response are highly complex, and research and development are costly and time-consuming. In addition, there are no appropriate animal tests or alternate models for investigating possible vaccines. Human clinical trials always raise ethical and legal issues, especially when trials involve a fatal infectious agent like HIV. More than 30 HIV vaccine candidates were in clinical trials as of mid-2005.

One large-scale efficacy trial completed in 2003 demonstrated that people are willing to participate in vaccine trials. The search for a vaccine is not limited to people living in high-income countries; nine developing countries are currently conducting or preparing to conduct HIV vaccine trials. The full participation of people living in the hardest-hit areas is important to ensure that a vaccine is effective against different sub-types of the virus. One of the greatest barriers to an effective vaccine is the lack of financial incentive to produce it. Current investment in HIV vaccine development is around US$682 million per year, less than 1 percent of spending on all health product development. Private-sector involvement in vaccine development has been limited and only four pharmaceutical companies currently have vaccines in clinical trials. Governments, small biotechnology companies, and NGOs have broadened ongoing research, but more resources are needed to hasten the process.

If an effective HIV vaccine becomes available, the international community will need to address new challenges, including determining who will benefit the most from the vaccine and ensuring equitable access; understanding behavioural issues raised by a vaccine; developing new tests to differentiate between vaccine-induced and active HIV infection; and raising sufficient resources to deliver the vaccine.

Developing Microbicide

Millions of women around the world are not able to protect

themselves from HIV infection. Most prevention strategies rely on abstinence, monogamy, condom use, fewer sexual partners, and treatment of STIs. However, many women are powerless to demand condom use or refuse sex. A woman may risk HIV infection through other sexual partners her husband may have had. Microbicide would give women much more control over their risk of infection. A microbicide is a substance—usually a gel, cream, or suppository—that can be applied to the vagina or rectum to prevent or substantially reduce the transmission of STIs or HIV. Microbicide can kill or immobilise the pathogen by creating a barrier between the pathogen and the vagina or rectum or by preventing the pathogen from replicating once it has entered the cells.

A woman could use a microbicide if her partner does not use a condom, as an adjunct to condom use, and as backup protection in the event of condom failure. Microbicide could be applied before sexual intercourse and without the knowledge of the sexual partner. The search for a microbicide suffered a major setback when a study in Cameroun showed that nonoxynol-9 (N-9), a widely used spermicide, did not protect users against HIV. It may even increase the risk slightly when used frequently.

About 30 microbicide are in various stages of development in 2006. Five of these are in or about to enter large-scale clinical trials. The development of an effective and affordable microbicide would place HIV prevention in the hands of women and has the potential to avert between 2.5 million and 3.7 million infections over three years. The antiretroviral drug ten favour may also be an effective pre-exposure prophylactic agent. Ten favour can be taken once daily by mouth and has few side effects in people living with HIV.

Research in un infected animals has shown that ten favour may reduce the risk of HIV infection if taken prior to exposure to the virus. Clinical trials in Cambodia, Nigeria, and Cameroun to evaluate the effectiveness of ten favour in preventing human infection were halted in 2004 and 2005 because of pressure from activist groups about ethical concerns. Despite these setbacks, new trials have begun to determine if ten favour can effectively protect people from HIV infection.

Protecting Human Rights

Human rights protections are critical for reducing vulnerability to HIV, protecting the dignity of persons affected by the virus, and sharing medical advances with less developed countries. Women's rights are especially relevant to the fight against HIV. Combating gender inequality tackles one of the root causes of the epidemic: women's inability to protect themselves from HIV. AIDS experts have outlined several ways to enhance women's rights to reduce their vulnerability and exposure to HIV, including promoting sexual responsibility among boys and men, developing female-controlled prevention methods such as microbicide, and increasing women's economic opportunities.

Violations of the rights of those living with HIV have been documented worldwide and have included denial of medical care, breaches of the right to privacy, restriction of HIV information for certain populations, and discrimination in employment and housing. Under international law, governments are obligated to respect, protect, and fulfil the human rights of people vulnerable to HIV, those living with HIV/AIDS, and those affected by the disease.

The right of people in less developed countries to have access to life-saving drugs is a crucial human rights issue in the context of HIV. AIDS activists argue that lack of resources at the individual and national levels, inadequate health infrastructure, and protecting pharmaceutical companies' investments and patents are no longer acceptable reasons for denying treatment access to AIDS patients in less developed countries. Human rights groups, people living with HIV, and civil and political leaders have joined in the call to make HIV related treatments available and affordable to less developed countries. As a result, prices of antiretroviral drugs have dropped dramatically, therapies have been offered at cost or free to less developed countries, resources are becoming available to provide treatment and care, and pharmaceutical patent rights are being challenged. Despite these changes, the vast majority of people living with HIV in less developed countries will not have access to treatment in the foreseeable future.

9

Population Problems

The present is unexpectedly a critical time for population change and policy. We are little more than half way through the great population growth spurt that began in the middle of the twentieth century, but developed-country governments seem to be losing interest in the issue. This loss of interest may have a significant demographic impact. The probable reasons for the declining interest are a vague belief that the present demographic change has a momentum of its own, a reaction to the International Conference on Population and Development (ICPD) in Cairo in 1994 which may misinterpret the complex document that came out of that meeting, and a preoccupation with below-replacement-level fertility in the developed world.

Huge population growth is not now past history. United Nations estimates and medium projections show a world population numbering 2.5 billion in 1950, 6.1 billion in 2000 and 9.3 billion in 2050. The next half-century will see almost as many people added to the world's population as the last half-century, and thereafter there may be one or two billion more people before growth comes to a halt. Global fertility decline is believed to have traversed over four-fifths of the journey from a total fertility rate of 5.0 in 1950 to 2.1 in 2050.

But because of population growth momentum and an ever-expanding base population, the additions to world population did not peak until the 1990s at around 80 million per year, and are only a little below that now. There are two main messages for future-glazers and policy makers. The first is that projections are far from certain. The second is that projections are necessarily based on past experience–including past policy experience–and, if this changes, then the projections must do so too. The lack of certainty is shown by the fact that for 2050 the United Nations provides, in addition to the Medium Projection of 9.322 billion, a Low Projection of 7.866 billion and a High Projection of 10.934 billion.

The High Projection is over three billion or almost 40 per cent above the Low Projection. Another recent projection, by Lutz and others, provides a 2050 median figure of 8.797 billion, with an 80 per cent probability of it falling between 7.347 and 10.443 billion. The latter projection's "most likely" figure for 2050 is about half a billion below that of the United Nations but still implies huge growth and great uncertainty about its magnitude.

Most analysts have preferred during recent years to employ the United Nations Medium Projection because it has proved in these years to be remarkably accurate. This period of near-certainty may be passing. Two years after its release in 1999 of the 1998 projections, the United Nations produced revised figures raising the 2050 Medium estimate by 413 million people, 96 per cent of the difference being attributable to new figures for Africa and Asia, mostly in sub-Saharan Africa and South Asia. The United Nations Population Division said that 59 per cent of the upward adjustment was explained by countries (mostly in sub-Saharan Africa) failing to begin fertility declines as early as expected, and 32 per cent was because of greater sluggishness than anticipated in fertility decline in such large countries as Bangladesh, India and Nigeria.

Twentieth-century projections were based on twentieth-century experience, and that was propelled by a near-consensus among powerful donor countries and their citizens about the need to give population control high policy priority and adequate funding. This played a role in developing-country governments adopting population policies that brought down levels of fertility and population growth faster than socioeconomic change alone would have done. It also played a role in the development of contraception suited to large-scale family planning programmes in poor, under educated countries. That consensus is now held with less fervour and this is reflected in funding and First World leadership. The result will almost certainly be slower fertility decline and greater population growth which must be reflected in adequate population projections.

The reasons for the loss of fervour are several. One is the initial success in reducing fertility, and its reflection in United Nations and other statistics. The world is less homogeneous than the reaction to these changes suggested. Fertility decline was persistent in relatively well-off and educated Latin America and in rapidly economically developing parts of East and Southeast Asia. However, there was the potential for problems elsewhere which was often not noted, but which can be observed in the three large countries pinpointed in the most recent United Nations projections as being unexpectedly sluggish. There are many reasons why the fertility transition may be slow in some parts of sub-Saharan Africa.

Among the people there are cultural resistance and among governments a lack of enthusiasm for leadership in the area: for these reasons national family planning programmes are unlikely to be like those of Asia or to have the same effect. There is also a very low level of development, with a high proportion of the population practising subsistence farming. Here extra hands produce extra food, and there will be extra hands where few children go to school. There are 20 countries in sub-Saharan Africa where women still have six or more children and there is little sign of fertility decline. These 20 countries average an infant mortality rate over 150 per thousand, a life expectancy of 45 years, and a per capita gross national income in purchasing power parity of a little over US$850.

Perhaps more significantly, only half their girls of primary school age are in school as are one-third of those of secondary school age (net enrolment ratios). Compared with African countries like Ghana, Kenya and South Africa where there have been marked falls in fertility, their infant mortality rates are two to three times higher, their income levels lower, and their girls' secondary school enrolment level half. Ghana and Kenya laid the foundation of their fertility decline before the African economic crisis which began in the mid-1980s.

Their populations already assumed that children's health could be guarded by modern medicine and that both boys and girls would normally go to school. The subsequent economic crisis and the family financial outlays associated with cost recovery in structural adjustment programmes did not reverse these assumptions but rather convinced many parents that their educational and health expectations could be maintained only if they had children more widely spaced. The poorer countries did not participate in this two-step process but are still beset by few and fee-charging schools and health facilities. They are also facing the beginning of demographic transition in an era of AIDS.

Except in a few, mostly Southern African countries, the African fertility decline is largely an urban phenomenon, since the nature of families, the occupations of adults and the roles of children and expectations for them are very different in the towns from those in the countryside. The slow movers tend to be less urbanised than the countries where fertility decline is taking place, and especially tend to lack big cities. Finally, the higher-fertility countries have often had more immediate concerns than demographic ones, for they include most of sub-Saharan Africa's war-torn countries: Liberia, Sierra Leone, Arteria, Somalia, Uganda, Angola and the Congo Democratic Republic.

Threshold explanations are not now popular, but some explanation of this kind is probably relevant to the situation in the large sluggish countries of South Asia. Bangladesh is probably the prime example, a country where a comparatively expensive and efficient family planning programme, assisted by a marked degree of socioeconomic change, halved its birth rate during the late 1970s and 1980s, only to find that the total fertility rate stagnated around 3.3 through the 1990s. As a consequence, the 2000 74 United Nations Population Projections show it reaching replacement fertility 30 years later than did the 1998 projections.

What had not been previously taken into account is that Bangladesh is the poorest country in the world to have reduced the total fertility rate to 3.3, and it has done so with an infant mortality rate around 70, more than twice the level found in East and Southeast Asia. Bangladesh achieved such low fertility partly by overcoming the problems of purdah by having family planning workers call at every house with the hormonal contraceptive methods favoured in Muslim societies, but ironically donors, with less funding for family planning programmes, are now calling for a greater resort to centralised services and the use of permanent or long-term methods.

India, which has largely funded its own programme, has long sought cheapness with its concentration on sterilisation. It has achieved extraordinary success in its South but to a much lesser extent in its Hindi belt of large northern states (where child mortality is also relatively high). There are similarities in Nigeria where the southern half of the country has paralleled the fertility decline of Ghana and Kenya, but where the poorer, higher-mortality and solidly Muslim north, like neighbouring Niger and Chad, maintains high fertility. ICPD produced a Programme of Action, which, like the product of other international consensuses, was complex, not entirely internally consistent, and easily misunderstood.

It proclaimed that the population movement was no longer to be driven by demographic fears, while at the same time devoting a good deal of space to population growth and its implications. It placed its main emphasis on improving the female situation, especially in the areas of education and reproductive health, while partly justifying or at least noting that this would mean demographic gains in terms of lower child mortality and declining fertility. It sought to achieve reproductive health programmes of a type that the best family planning programmes had always hoped for.

Nevertheless, it discouraged many involved in existing family planning programmes by seeming to condemn what they had hitherto regarded as past successes and by appearing to ask for more than their countries' health services could provide in the foreseeable future. It has almost certainly also confused donors who had not previously considered that the much more expensive national educational and health services warranted the same proportional support as did the family planning programmes.

But Western donor support for family planning programmes has also been weakened by the realisation that the end of demographic transition may not take the form of equal birth and death rates but of below-replacement fertility. This appears to have been achieved already in countries where 44 per cent of the population of the world lives, and began to manifest itself in sustained fertility declines in developed countries from the 1970s. It is partly a product of more girls going to school and more women being in the work force, but it is also the product of forces released by the global effort to limit population growth, namely the invention of better contraception, and the moral support for young couples or young women having few children.

Many policy-makers have now heard the argument that the move to limit population growth in developing countries was either never necessary or no longer necessary. Indeed, the impression has been given that ultimately fertility decline would be a disaster for all countries in that they would move towards a situation where over 30 per cent of the population would be aged, in the sense that they were over 65 years of age, and that this would place an unbearable burden on the working population in supporting old-age pensions and health services by means of high taxes.

The demographic situation is, in fact, much more complex than this, although these complexities have been insufficiently, or unconvincing, spelled out to governments. First, not everyone is convinced that China is below or far below replacement-level fertility, and without its inclusion the proportion of the world's population in this category is halved to 22 per cent. Secondly, very low fertility, with little chance that completed cohort fertility will eventually come close to replacement level as older women continue to have births deferred from their younger years, is largely confined to Central, Eastern and Southern Europe, Japan and South Korea, and possibly Canada, around 750 million or one-eighth of the human race.

Thirdly, population momentum ensures that crisis even in 75 these countries is not imminent. If the present situation continues, it will be one-third of a century before Italy, Spain and Japan experience population decline of half of one per cent per annum and 30 per cent or more of their populations over 65 years, and half a century before Germany does. My point here is that the rich nations should still be primarily concerned with world population growth. By 2050 global population could be 8.9 billion, as the 1998 United Nations Revision Medium Projection calculated, or 9.3 billion as calculated in the 2000 Medium Projection. It could also be the 10.9 billion of the 2000 High Projections or, increasingly unlikely, the 7.9 billion of the 2000 Low Projection.

The peak global populations could range between 9 and 12 billion; or, according to the Lots and others 80 per cent probability projections, between 8 and 12 billion. With regard to the long-term stability of the world's ecosystems and our ability to feed everyone adequately and to give them a reasonably good life, that margin of 3 or 4 billion extra people may be critical. We may well be able to achieve these aims with 12 billion people but we are much more certain of being able to do so with 9 billion, and risking the additional 3 billion does not seem to be a worthwhile experiment.

Just what is likely to happen in the rich countries? The simple answer is that low fertility will continue to characterise these societies. But the situation is far from simple. Because total fertility rates are at present depressed by a continuing deferment of the age of women at marriage and childbearing, most overstate the threat to population replacement. In Europe, Scandinavia, France, Britain, Ireland and perhaps even the Netherlands will probably come close to replacing themselves, as will the United States. In any case, the traditional countries of immigration, the United States, Canada, Australia and New Zealand are unlikely to experience declining population.

On the other hand, much of Southern, Eastern and Central Europe, as well as Japan and South Korea, will face declining population if present trends continue. But two points are important: first, even with present trends, substantial declines are in most cases decades away; second, fertility rates may not remain so low. The reason that fertility may not remain so low is that nationalism is not dead. When real decline is experienced, policies and popular sentiments are likely to turn towards espousing motherhood in a way that may make similar efforts in the 1930s or in Eastern Europe between the 1950s and 1970s look puny.

The post-1960s fertility declines were the result not merely of economic change, but also of a changing attitude to small families and even childlessness, partly arising from the "population explosion" debate. My guess is that in the coming decades we will see the opposite occurring, with popular and governmental lauding of two- and even three-child families, and quite dramatic policy changes to make them possible. The present very low fertility is less the realisation of parental family building aims than the product of the financial difficulties experienced by families in high-consumption societies not having two breadwinners, and by the massive problems faced by mothers in continuing with their education or work or maintaining their position and rate of promotion in employment.

These difficulties arise from insufficient support from governments, employers and husbands. We know that, when Sweden poured money into free preschool support in the 1980s and early 1990s (for gender-equity, not demographic reasons), fertility rose to replacement levels, only to fall again by one-third when these expenditures were cut back as Sweden met the criteria for joining the European Union. The time may come when it is the achievement of motherhood that is linked to getting university scholarships, paying house mortgages and remaining on the fast promotion track.

Such policy and social changes may not be promoted merely by demographic nationalism but also by a variant of the women's movement and by powerful forces aiming at greater gender equity. Italy is already becoming introspective about the causes of its very low fertility as social scientists link it to husbands' failure to share domestic duties and child care, and relate this in turn to men marrying late after years of living as young adults in their parents' homes with mothers teaching them to expect to do nothing in the way of domestic tasks. What is to be hoped is that governments in developed countries can 76 become sufficiently sophisticated to deal with a bipolar world, so that their domestic population policies are separated from their technical aid attitudes to high-fertility countries.

Low fertility is rapidly changing the age structures of developed countries and demographers will continue to monitor this. Whether this portends economic disaster is open to question. The main employed age group, 20-64 years, a more sensible definition for rich countries than 15-64 years, remains a constant proportion of the population at around 56 per cent. The only change is that the burden of dependency shifts from supporting the young to doing the same for the old. This is an important emotional issue in the West where the young tend to be a family responsibility involving direct family expenditure while the old are a state responsibility paid for by family taxation.

This picture is not universal, and, in any case, the changed effect on the national economy is probably not as great as most of the debate has suggested. Moreover, there is a tendency to underrate the efficiency of the modern economy and to overrate its potential for employment. It has shown itself quite capable of producing rising standards of living while up to 10 per cent of the work force is unemployed and another 5-10 per cent prematurely retired. Thus, although the tax base for supporting the aged could be adequately broadened by increasing the retirement age to 70 years, this may not be necessary. In fact, the economy may be at its healthiest if we do not do this, carrying with it, as the policy would, the need to provide unemployment relief for 65-69-year-olds.

INTERMEDIATE FERTILITY LEVEL COUNTRIES

hese are defined by the United Nations Population Division as countries with total fertility rates in the range 2.2-4.9. For this analysis, we have defined "large" as being characterised in 2000 by a population of 30 million or more. This group constitutes 18 countries (Algeria, Egypt, Morocco, Sudan, Kenya, South Africa, Mexico, Argentina, Brazil, Columbia, Turkey, Bangladesh, India, Iran, Indonesia, Myanmar, Philippines and Vietnam) with a total population of 2.260 billion or 46 per cent of that of the developing world, 63 per cent without China. India alone constitutes 45 per cent of their population. For analytical purposes we will add three more large high-fertility-level countries to form an "extended" group:

Nigeria, Tanzania and Pakistan. Thus extended, the 21 countries constitute 53 per cent of the population of the developing world, and India forms 39 per cent of the total. The United Nations Population Division has been right to be cautious about overstating the speed of fertility decline. In comparison to other sources (DHS, INED, PRB), however, it seems now to be overstating the Bangladesh TFR, given as 3.6 in World Population 2000 and 3.7 by averaging the 1995-2000 estimate and 2000-2005 medium projection in the 2000 Review of Population Prospects.

A more probable estimate would seem to be around 3.3. Conversely, the TFRs of North Africa (Algeria, Egypt, Morocco, Sudan) appear to be understated, although less so in the averaged projections than in the World Population 2000 sheet. It might also be noted that some countries are difficult to treat as a single unit. In Nigeria the TFR in the relatively poor Muslim north is still around 7.0 while in the richer, more educated and predominately Christian south it is in the 4-5 range, comparable with Ghana and Kenya. Conversely, in Sudan it is the richer Muslim north that is characterised by lower fertility.

There no longer seem to be any barriers to most countries reaching replacement-level fertility and subsequently falling below that level; certainly not an income barrier, for Moldova and Armenia, with per capita purchasing power parity incomes (pci ppp) similar to that of India, exhibit TFRs of 1.4 and 1.1 respectively. Similarly, religious barriers are not insuperable, with fertility in Catholic Italy and Spain being little more than half replacement level, and in Muslim North Africa declining persistently. Threshold analysis has fallen into some disrepute, but low fertility levels are significantly correlated with high per capita incomes, low child mortality, high female educational and employment levels, and 77 urbanisation.

Employing such measures (pci ppp over US$2,000; under-five mortality below 75 per 1000 births; over 30 per cent of girls in secondary school; and over 40% urbanisation), 13 of the 21 countries examined here seem likely to exhibit below-replacement-level fertility well before 2050: a group in South America (Argentina, Brazil, Colombia and Mexico), another group in North Africa (Algeria, Egypt, Morocco), five Asian countries (Indonesia, Iran, Philippines, Turkey, Vietnam) and one in sub-Saharan Africa (South Africa).

Those less likely to do so by these criteria are Sudan, Nigeria, Kenya, Tanzania, Bangladesh, India, Pakistan and Myanmar. If another factor is added, government resolve in the form of an efficient family planning programme likely to be kept in place as fertility declines, then India, and possibly Bangladesh, could be transferred to the first group. Latin American fertility decline may have been retarded by the Catholic Church, as is evidenced by Argentina, which has a pci ppp around that of Hungary or the Czech Republic, but has been characterised by a TFR which over half a century from 1950 to 2000 fell only from 3.2 to 2.6.

Nevertheless, there may be a delayed parallel with the experience of Italy, Spain and Portugal, where TFRs were in the range 2.5-2.9 in 1965-1970, above those of Northern and Central Europe, but where now, at 1.1-1.5, they are below those of Northern Europe. Very low fertility may not even require employment for all women. Ever-higher levels of children's education, enforced by the principle of keeping up with the Joneses, may be enough. The foundation for fertility decline in Africa was laid by economic development, but subsequently the major force in reducing fertility seems to have been the costs of providing education and health care for children as African economies found themselves in trouble, and ensuing structural adjustment programmes imposed user pays fees for these services. Among the Indian urban elite single -child families are no longer rare.

Other factors may be more important, particularly the globalisation of markets and the consumer society, the aim of giving all girls a good education, and the belief that educated women should be employed outside the home. This has been given a new twist by the analysis of the factors determining Italy's very low fertility. It has been argued that many women cannot manage to stay successfully in the work force in a patriarchal society where husbands give little help with child care and other domestic work, and where the state does not intervene to help with preschool child care or employment provisions that do not penalise women for dropping out of the work force while they have young children.

It has also been argued that men are conditioned not to help in the household by their mothers during the long period of being in the parental house until marriage at, on average, almost 30 years of age. This has been compared with supposedly more helpful husbands in Northern Europe and the United States and more helpful governments in Northern and Central Europe. The irony of this comparison is that the Mediterranean patriarchal model is far more common in the world than the Northern European model and characterises Latin America, North Africa, sub-Saharan Africa, Western Asia, South Asia and East Asia. If the analyses of the Italian situation are correct, then below-replacement fertility may characterise most of the world by 2050.

My hunch about the 2000 Revision is that it is largely on the right track except for the medium projection bottoming so widely at a total fertility rate of 2.1 which is unlikely to prove the lower limit for the majority of countries. My interpretation of the evidence is that the caution about Bangladesh was justified but that it has now been somewhat overdone in terms of when replacement fertility will be reached.

Population Growth: Challenges And Opportunities

Human beings evolved under conditions of high mortality due to famines, accidents, illnesses, infections and war and therefore the relatively high fertility rates were essential for species survival. In spite of the relatively high fertility rates it took all the time from evolution of mankind to the middle of the 19th century for the global population to reach one billion. The twentieth century witnessed an unprecedented rapid improvement in health care technologies and access to health care all over the world; as a result there was a steep fall in the mortality and steep increase in longevity. The population realised these changes and took steps to reduce their fertility but the decline in fertility was not so steep. As a result the global population has undergone a fourfold increase in a hundred years and has reached 6 billion.

Demographic Transition

Demographers refer to these changes from stable population with high fertility and mortality to a new stability in population due to low fertility and mortality patterns as demographic transition. Demographic transition occurs in four phases; of these the first three phases are characterised by population growth. In the first phase there is a fall in death rate and improvement in longevity; this leads to population growth. In the second phase there is a fall in birth rate but fall is less steep than fall in death rates and consequently there is population growth.

In the third phase death rates plateau and replacement level of fertility is attained but the population growth continues because of the large size of population in reproductive age group. The fourth phase is characterised by fall in birth rate to below replacement level and reduction in the proportion of the population in reproductive age group; as a result of these changes population growth ceases and population stabilises. Experience in some of the developed countries suggest that in some societies even after attainment of stable population there may be a further decline in fertility so that there is a further reduction in the population- so called negative population growth phase of the demographic transition.

Different countries in the world have entered the demographic transition at different periods of time; there are also substantial differences in the rate of demographic transition and time taken to achieve population stabilisation.

Global Population Scenario

In 1901 the world population was 1.6 billion. By 1960, it became 3 billion, and by 1987, 5 billion and in 1999, 6 billion. Currently, one billion people are added every 12 - 13 years. During the last decade there has been substantial decline in birth rate. The reasons for decline vary from society to society; urbanisation, rising educational attainment, increasing employment among women, lower infant mortality are some major factors responsible for growing desire for smaller families; increasing awareness and improved access to contraception have made it possible for the majority of the couple to achieve the desired family size. In some countries slowing of the population growth has been due to an increase in mortality (e.g. HIV related mortality in sub-Saharan Africa).

As a result of all these the decline in the global population growth during the nineties is steeper than the earlier predictions. Currently, the annual increment is about 80 million. It is expected to decrease to about 64 million by 2020 -25 and to 33 million by 2045 -50; 95 % of the growth of population occurs in developing countries. Most demographers believe that the current accelerated decline in population growth will continue for the next few decades and the medium projections of Population Division of United Nations, that the global population will grow to 8.9 billion by 2050 is likely to be achieved.

Changing Age Structure of the Population

During demographic transition along with the growth in number there are changes in the population age structure. While the importance of the population growth as a determinant of quality of life is universally understood, the profoundly serious consequences of changing age structure especially if it occurs too rapidly is not understood by many. Population pyramids graphically represent complex changes in age structure of the population so that it can be readily understood and interpreted.

Currently nearly half of the global population is below 25 years of age and one sixth are in the age group 15-24. Their choices, efforts and lifestyles will determine not only the population growth but also future improvement in the quality of life in harmony with global ecology. In developed countries the reproductive age group population is relatively small; their fertility is low and the longevity at birth is high. Population profiles of these countries resemble a cylinder and not a pyramid.

These countries have the advantages of having achieved a stable population but have to face the problems of having a relatively small productive work force to support the large aged population with substantial non-communicable disease burden. Some of the developing countries have undergone a very rapid decline in the birth rates within a short period. This enabled them to quickly achieve population stabilisation but they do face the problems of rapid changes in the age structure and work force which may be inadequate to meet their manpower requirements.

In contrast the population in most of the developing countries (including India) consist of a very large proportion of children and persons in reproductive age. Because of the large reproductive age group (Population momentum) the population will continue to grow even when replacement level of fertility is reached (couples having only two children). It is imperative that these countries should generate enough employment opportunities for this work force and utilise the human resources and accelerate their economic growth. Planners and policy makers in developing countries like India have to take into account the ongoing demographic changes (number and age structure of the population) so that available human resources are optimal utilised as agents of change and development to achieve improvement in quality of life.

Demographic Transition in India

Over the last four decades there has been rapid fall in Crude

Death Rate (CDR) from 25.1 in 1951 to 9.8 in 1991 and less steep decline in the Crude Birth Rate (CBR) from 40.8 in 1951 to 29.5 in 1991. The annual exponential population growth rate has been over 2% in the period 1961-90. During the nineties the decline in CBR has been steeper than that in the (CDR) and consequently, the annual population growth rate has fallen below 2%.

The rate of decline in population growth is likely to be further accelerated during the next decade. The changes in the population growth rates have been relatively slow, steady and sustained. As a result the country was able to achieve a relatively gradual change in the population numbers and age structure. The short and long term adverse consequences of too rapid decline in birth rates and change in age structure on the social and economic development were avoided and the country was able to adapt to these changes without massive disruptions of developmental efforts. In spite of the uniform national norms set under the 100% Centrally Funded and Centrally Sponsored Scheme (CSS) of Family Welfare, there are substantial differences in the performance between States as assessed by IMR and CBR. Though the decline in CBR and IMR has occurred in all States, the rate of decline is slower in some States.

At one end of the spectrum is Kerala with mortality and fertility rates nearly similar to those in some of the developed countries. At the other end, there are four large northern States (Uttar Pradesh, Bihar, Madhya Pradesh and Rajasthan) with high Infant Mortality Rate and Fertility Rates. Though the decline in CBR, IMR and CDR has occurred in all States, the rate of decline was slower in some States like U.P. And Bihar. There are substantial differences in CBR and IMR not only between States but also between the districts in the same state.

In view of these findings, the NDC Committee on Population recommended that efforts should be made to provide reproductive and child health services at district level and undertake decentralised area-specific micro planning and implementation of appropriate interventions. In response to this recommendation Dept. of Family Welfare has abolished the practice of fixing targets for individual contraceptives by the Central Government from April 1996 and had initiated decentralised district based, planning (based on community need assessment), implementation, monitoring and mid-course corrections of FW programme. The experience of states with district based planning, implementation and the impact are being closely monitored.

Consequences of Population Growth

Environmental Consequences

In many developing countries continued population growth has resulted in pressure on land, fragmentation of land holding, collapsing fisheries, shrinking forests, rising temperatures, loss of plant and animal species. Global warming due to increasing use of fossil fuels (mainly by the developed countries) could have serious effects on the populous coastal regions in developing countries, their food production and essential water supplies. The Intergovernmental Panel on Climate Change has projected that, if current greenhouse gas emission trends continue, the mean global surface temperature will rise from 1 to 3.5 degrees Celsius in the next century.

The panel's best estimate scenario projects a sea-level rise of 15 to 95 centimetres by 2100. The ecological impact of rising oceans would include increased flooding, coastal erosion, salination of aquifers and coastal crop land and displacement of millions of people living near the coast. Patterns of precipitation are also likely to change, which combined with increased average temperatures, could substantially alter the relative agricultural productivity of different regions. Greenhouse gas emissions are closely linked to both population growth and development.

Slower population growth in developing countries and ecologically sustainable lifestyles in developed countries would make reduction in green house gas emission easier to achieve and provide more time and options for adaptation to climate change. Rapid population growth, developmental activities either to meet the growing population or the growing needs of the population as well as changing lifestyles and consumption patterns pose major challenge to preservation and promotion of ecological balance in India. Some of the major ecological adverse effects reported in India include:

— Severe pressure on the forests due to both the rate of resource use and the nature of use. The per capita forest bio-mass in the country is only about 6 tons as against the global average of 82 tons.

— Adverse effect on species diversity:

    — Conversion of habitat to some other land use such as agriculture, urban development, forestry operation. Some 70-80 % of fresh water marshes and lakes in the Gangetic flood plains has been lost in the last 50 years.

    — Tropical deforestation and destruction of mangroves for commercial needs and fuel wood. The country's mangrove areas have reduced from 700,000 ha to 453,000 ha in the last 50 years.

    — Intense grazing by domestic livestock

    — Poaching and illegal harvesting of wildlife.

    — Increase in agricultural area, high use of chemical fertilisers pesticides and we decides; water stagnation, soil erosion, soil salinity and low productivity.

— High level of bio-mass burning causing large-scale indoor pollution.

— Encroachment on habitat for rail and road construction thereby fragmenting the habitat. Increase in commercial activities such as mining and unsustainable resource extraction.

— Degradation of coastal and other aquatic ecosystems from domestic sewage, pesticides, fertilisers and industrial effluents.

— Over fishing in water bodies and introduction of weeds and exotic species.

— Diversion of water for domestic, industrial and agricultural uses leading to increased river pollution and decrease in self-cleaning properties of rivers.

— Increasing water requirement leading to tapping deeper aquifers which have high content of arsenic or fluoride resulting health problems.

— Disturbance from increased recreational activity and tourism causing pollution of natural ecosystems with wastes left behind by people.

The United Nations Conference on Environment and Development acknowledged population growth, rising income levels, changing technologies, increasing consumption pattern will all have adverse impact on environment. Ensuring that there is no further deterioration depends on choices made by the population about family size, life styles, environmental protection and equity. Availability of appropriate technology and commitment towards ensuring sustainable development is increasing throughout the world. Because of these, it might be possible to initiate steps to see that the natural carrying capacity of the environment is not damaged beyond recovery and ecological balance is to a large extent maintained. It is imperative that the environmental sustainability of all developmental projects is taken care of by appropriate inputs at the planning, implementation, monitoring and evaluation stages.

Urbanisation

The proportion of people in developing countries who live in cities has almost doubled since 1960 (from less than 22 per cent to more than 40 per cent), while in more developed regions the urban share has grown from 61 per cent to 76 per cent. Urbanisation is projected to continue well into the next century. By 2030, it is expected that nearly 5 billion (61 per cent) of the world's 8.1 billion people will live in cities. India shares this global trend toward urbanisation.

Globally, the number of cities with 10 million or more inhabitants is increasing rapidly, and most of these new "megacities" are in developing regions. In 1960, only New York and Tokyo had more than 10 million people. By 1999, the number of megacities had grown to 17(13 in developing countries). It is projected that there will be 26 megacities by 2015, (18 in Asia; of these five in India); more than 10 per cent of the world's population will live in these cities. India's urban population has doubled from 109 million to 218 million during the last two decades and is estimated to reach 300 million by 2000 AD. As a consequence cities are facing the problem of expanding urban slums.

Like many other demographic changes, urbanisation has both positive and negative effects. Cities and towns have become the engines of social change and rapid economic development. Urbanisation is associated with improved access to education, employment, health care; these result in increase in age at marriage, reduction in family size and improvement in health indices. As people have moved towards and into cities, information has flowed outward.

Better communication and transportation now link urban and rural areas both economically and socially creating an urban-rural continuum of communities with improvement in some aspects of lifestyle of both.

The ever increasing reach of mass media communicate new ideas, points of reference, and available options are becoming more widely recognised, appreciated and sought. This phenomenon has affected health care, including reproductive health, in many ways. For instance, radio and television programmes that discuss gender equity, family size preference and family planning options are now reaching formerly isolated rural populations. This can create demand for services for mothers and children, higher contraceptive use, and fewer unwanted pregnancies, smaller healthier families and lead to more rapid population stabilisation.

But the rapid growth of urban population also poses some serious challenges. Urban population growth has outpost the development of basic minimum services; housing, water supply, sewerage and solid waste disposal are far from adequate; increasing waste generation at home, offices and industries, coupled with poor waste disposal facilities result in rapid environmental deterioration. Increasing automobiles add to air pollution. All these have adverse effect on ecology and health. Poverty persists in urban and peri-urban areas; awareness about the glaring inequities in close urban setting may lead to social unrest.

Rural Population and their Development

Over seventy per cent of India's population still lives in rural areas. There are substantial differences between the states in the proportion of rural and urban population (varying from almost 90 per cent in Assam and Bihar to 61 per cent in Maharashtra). Agriculture is the largest and one of the most important sector of the rural economy and contributes both to economic growth and employment. Its contribution to the Gross Domestic Product has declined over the last five decades but agriculture still remains the source of livelihood for over 70 per cent of the country's population. A large proportion of the rural work force is small and consists of marginal farmers and landless agricultural labourers. There is substantial under employment among these people; both wages and productivity are low. These in turn result in poverty; it is estimated that 320 million people are still living below the poverty line in rural India.

Though poverty has declined over the last three decades, the number of rural poor has in fact increased due to the population growth. Poor tend to have larger families which puts enormous burden on their meagre resources, and prevent them from breaking out of the shackles of poverty. In States like Tamil Nadu where replacement level of fertility has been attained, population growth rates are much lower than in many other States; but the population density is high and so there is a pressure on land. In States like Rajasthan, Uttar Pradesh, Bihar and Madhya Pradesh population is growing rapidly, resulting in increasing pressure on land and resulting land fragmentation.

Low productivity of small land holders leads to poverty, low energy intake and under nutrition, and this, in turn, prevents the development thus creating a vicious circle. In most of the states non-farm employment in rural areas has not grown very much and cannot absorb the growing labour force. Those who are getting educated specially beyond the primary level, may not wish to do manual agricultural work. They would like better opportunities and more remunerative employment. In this context, it is imperative that programmes for skill development, vocational training and technical education are taken up on a large scale in order to generate productive employment in rural areas. The entire gamut of existing poverty alleviation and employment generation programmes may have to be restructured to meet the newly emerging types of demand for employment.

Rural poor have inadequate access to basic minimum services, because of poor connectivity, lack of awareness, inadequate and poorly functional infrastructure. There are ongoing efforts to improve these, but with the growing aspirations of the younger, educated population these efforts may prove to be inadequate to meet the increasing needs both in terms of type and quality of services.

Greater education, awareness and better standard of living among the growing younger age group population would create the required consciousness among them that smaller families are desirable; if all the felt needs for health and family welfare services are fully met, it will be possible to enable them to attain their reproductive goals, achieve substantial decline in the family size and improve quality of life.

Water Supply

In many parts of developed and developing world, water demand substantially exceeds sustainable water supply. It is estimated that currently 430 millions (8% of the global population) are living in countries affected by water stress; by 2020 about one fourth of the global population may be facing chronic and recurring shortage of fresh water. In India, water withdrawal is estimated to be twice the rate of aquifer recharge; as a result water tables are falling by one to three meters every year; tapping deeper aquifers have resulted in larger population groups being exposed to newer health hazards such as high fluoride or arsenic content in drinking water.

At the other end of the spectrum, excessive use of water has led to water logging and increasing salinity in some parts of the country. Eventually, both lack of water and water logging could have adverse impact on India's food production. There is very little arable agricultural land which remains un exploited and in many areas, agricultural technology improvement may not be able to ensure further increase in yield per hectare. It is, therefore, imperative that research in biotechnology for improving development of food grains strains that would tolerate salinity and those which would require less water gets high priority. Simultaneously, a movement towards making water harvesting, storage and its need based use part of every citizens life should be taken up.

Food Security

Technological innovations in agriculture and increase in area under cultivation have ensured that so far, food production has kept pace with the population growth. Evolution of global and national food security systems have improved access to food. It is estimated that the global population will grow to 9 billion by 2050 and the food production will double; improvement in purchasing power and changing dietary habits (shift to animal products) may further add to the requirement of food grains. Thus, in the next five decades, the food and nutrition security could become critical in many parts of the world especially in the developing countries and pockets of poverty in the developed countries.

In India one of the major achievements in the last fifty years has been the green revolution and self-sufficiency in food production. Food grain production has increased from 50.82 in 1950-51 to 200.88 million tons in 1998-99.

It is a matter of concern that while the cereal production has been growing steadily at a rate higher than the population growth rates, the coarse grain and pulse production has not shown a similar increase. Consequently there has been a reduction in the per capita availability of pulses and coarse grains.

Over the last five decades there has been a decline in the per capita availability of pulses. During the last few years the country has imported pulses to meet the requirement. There has been a sharp and sustained increase in cost of pulses, so there is substantial decline in per capita pulses consumption among poorer segment of population. This in turn could have an adverse impact on their protein intake. The pulse component of the "Pulses and Oil Seeds Mission" need to receive a major thrust in terms of R&D and other inputs, so that essential pulse requirement of growing population is fully met. Rising cost of pulses had a beneficial effect also. Till eighties in central India wages of landless labourers were given in the form Kesari Dal which was cheaper than cereals or coarse grains. Consumption of staple diet of Kesari Dal led to crippling disease of neuro lathyrism. Over the last three decades the rising cost of pulses has made Kesari Dal more expensive than wheat or rice and hence it is no longer given to labourers as wages for work done; as a result the disease has virtually disappeared from Central India.

Over years the coarse grain production has remained stagnant and per capita availability of coarse grain has under gone substantial reduction; there has been a shift away from coarse grains to rice and wheat consumption even among poorer segment of population. One of the benefits of this change is virtual elimination of pellagra which was widely prevalent among low income group population in Deacon Plateau whose staple food was sorghum.

Coarse grains are less expensive than rice and wheat; they can thus provide higher calories for the same cost as compared to rice and wheat. Coarse grains which are locally produced and procured if made available through TPDS at subsidised rate, may not only substantially bring down the subsidy cost without any reduction in calories provided but also improve "targeting"—as only the most needy are likely to access these coarse grains.

Another area of concern is the lack of sufficient focus and thrust in horticulture; because of this, availability of vegetables especially green leafy vegetables and yellow/red vegetables throughout the year at affordable cost both in urban and rural areas has remained an unfulfilled dream. Health and nutrition education emphasising the importance of consuming these inexpensive rich sources of micro-nutrients will not result in any change in food habits unless there is harnessing and effective management of horticultural resources in the country to meet the growing needs of the people at affordable cost. States like Tamil Nadu and Himachal Pradesh have initiated some efforts in this direction; similar efforts need be taken up in other states also.

Nutrition

At the time of independence the country faced two major nutritional problems; one was the threat of famine and acute starvation due to low agricultural production and lack of appropriate food distribution system. The other was chronic energy deficiency due to poverty, low-literacy, poor access to safe-drinking water, sanitation and health care; these factors led to wide spread prevalence of infections and ill health in children and adults. Kwashiorkor, marasmus, goitre, berry, blindness due to Vitamin-A deficiency and anaemia were major public health problems.

The country adopted multi-sectorial, multi-pronged strategy to combat the major nutritional problems and to improve nutritional status of the population. During the last 50 years considerable progress has been achieved. Famines no longer stalk the country. There has been substantial reduction in moderate and severe undernutrition in children and some improvement in nutritional status of all segments of population. Kwashiorkor, marasmus, pellagra, lathyrism, berry and blindness due to severe Vitamin-A deficiency have become rare.

However, it is a matter of concern that milder forms of Chronic Energy Deficiency (CED) and micronutrient deficiencies continue to be widely prevalent in adults and children. In view of the fact that population growth in India will continue for the next few decades, it is essential that appropriate strategies are devised to improve food and nutrition security of families, identify individuals/families with severe forms of CED and provide them assistance to over come these problem. Operational strategy to improve the dietary intake of the family and improve nutritional status of the rapidly growing adult population would include:

— Ensuring adequate agricultural production of cereals, pulses, vegetables and other foodstuffs needed to fully meet the requirement of growing population.

— Improving in purchasing power through employment generation and employment assurance schemes.

— Providing subsidised food grains through TPDS to the families below poverty line.

— Exploring feasibility of providing subsidised coarse grains to families Below Poverty Line (BPL).

Operational strategies to improve health and nutritional status of the growing numbers of women and children include:

— *Pregnant and lactating women*: screening to identify women with weight below 40 Kg and ensuring that they/ their preschool children receive food supplements through Integrated Child Development Services Scheme (ICDS); adequate antenatal intrapartum and neonatal care.

- *0-6 months infants:* Nutrition education for:
  - Early initiation of lactation.
  - Protection and promotion of universal breast feeding.
  - Exclusive breast feeding for the first six months; unless there is specific reason supplementation should not be introduced before 6 months.
  - Immunisation, growth monitoring and health care.
- Well planned nutrition education to ensure that the infants and children do:
  - Continue to get breasted.
  - *Get appropriate cereal pulse:* vegetable based supplement fed to them at least 3 - 4 times a day – appropriate help in ensuring this through family/ community/work place support.
  - Immunisation and health care.
- *Children in the 0:* 5 age group:
  - Screen by weighment to identify children with moderate and severe undernutrition.
  - Provide double quantity supplements through ICDS.
  - Screening for nutrition and health problems and appropriate intervention.
- *Primary school children:*
  - Weigh and identify those with moderate and severe chronic energy deficiency.
  - Improve dietary intake to these children through the midday meal.
- Monitor for improvement in the identified undernourished infants, children and mothers; if no improvement after 2 months refer to physician for

identification and treatment of factors that might be responsible for lack of improvement.

— Nutrition education on varying dietary needs of different members of the family and how they can be met by minor modifications from the family meals. Intensive health education for improving the life style of the population coupled with active screening and management of the health problems associated with obesity.

Population Projections and their Implications

Right from 1958 the Planning Commission has been constituting an Expert Group on Population Projections prior to the preparation of each of the Five Year Plans so that the information on the population status at the time of initiation of the Plan and population projections for future are available during the preparation of the Plan. Population projections have been utilised not only for planning to ensure provision of essentials necessities such as food, shelter and clothing but also prerequisites for human development such as education, employment and health care. Over the years there has been considerable refinement in the methodology used for population projections and substantial improvement in the accuracy of predictions. The projections made by the Standing Committee on Population Projection in 1988 for the year 1991 was 843.6 million; this figure was within 0.3% of the 846.3 million reported in the Census 1991. In 1996, Technical Group on Population Projections, had work out the population projections for the country and the states for the period 1996 to 2016 on the basis of census 1991 and other available demographic data.

Economic Implications

Population growth and its relation to economic growth has been a matter of debate for over a century. The early

Malthusian view was that population growth is likely to impede economic growth because it will put pressure on the available resources, result in reduction in per capita income and resources; this, in turn, will result in deterioration in quality of life. Contrary to the Malthusian predictions, several of the East Asian countries have been able to achieve economic prosperity and improvement in quality of life inspite of population growth. This has been attributed to the increase in productivity due to development and utilisation of innovative technologies by the young educated population who formed the majority of the growing population. These countries have been able to exploit the dynamics of demographic transition to achieve economic growth by using the human resources as the engine driving the economic development; improved employment with adequate emoluments has promoted saving and investment which in turn stimulated economic growth.

However, not all countries, which have undergone demographic transition, have been able to transform their economies. Sri Lanka in South Asia underwent demographic transition at the same time as South East Asian countries but has not achieved the economic transition. It is now realised that population growth or demographic transition can have favourable impact on economic growth only when there are optimal interventions aimed at human resource development (HRD) and appropriate utilisation of available human resources.

For India the current phase of demographic transition with low dependency ratio and high working age group population, represents both a challenge and an opportunity. The challenge is to develop these human resources through appropriate education and skill development and utilise them fully by giving them appropriate jobs with adequate emoluments; if this challenge is met through well planned schemes for HRD and employment generation which are implemented effectively, there will be improved national productivity and personal savings rates; appropriate investment of these savings will help the country to achieve the economic transition from low economic growth - low per capita income to high economic growth - high per capita income. It is imperative to make the best use of this opportunity so as to enable the country and its citizens to vault to the high income- high economic growth status and stabilise at that level.

Interstate Differences

There are marked differences between States in size of the population and population growth rates, the time by which replacement level of fertility is to be achieved and age structure of the population. If the present trend continues, most of the Southern and the Western States are likely to achieve TFR of 2.1 by 2010. Urgent energetic steps to assess and fully meet the unmet needs for maternal and child health (MCH) care and contraception through improvement in availability and access to family welfare services are needed in the States of UP, MP, Rajasthan and Bihar in order to achieve a faster decline in their mortality and fertility rates.

The five states of Bihar, Uttar Pradesh, Madhya Pradesh, Rajasthan and Orissa, which constitute 44% of the total population of India in 1996, will constitute 48% of the total population of India in 2016. These states will contribute 55% of the total increase in population of the country during the period 1996-2016. In all the states performance in the social and economic sector has been poor. The poor performance is the outcome of poverty, illiteracy and poor development which coexist and reinforce each other.

The quality and coverage under health services is poor and the unmet need for FW services is about 30%. Urgent energetic steps are required to be initiated to assess and fully meet the unmet needs for maternal and child health (MCH) care and contraception through improvement in availability and access to family welfare services in the states of UP, MP, Rajasthan and Bihar in order to achieve a faster decline in their mortality and fertility rates. The performance of these states would determine the year and size of the population at which the country achieves population stabilisation.

There are also marked differences between States in socioeconomic development. Increasing investments and rapid economic development are likely to occur in the States where literacy rates are high; there is ready availability of skilled work force and adequate infrastructure. In these States, population growth rates are low. If equitable distribution of the income and benefits generated by development is ensured, substantial increase in per capita income and improvement in quality of life could occur in these States in a relatively short time.

In majority of States with high population growth rates, the performance in the social and economic sector has been poor. The poor performance could be the outcome of a variety of factors including paucity of natural, financial or human resources. Poverty, illiteracy and poor development coexist and aggravate each other. In order to promote equity and reduce disparity between States, special assistance has been provided to the poorly performing States. The benefits accrued from such assistance has to a large extent depended upon:

— The States' ability to utilise the available funds; improve quality & coverage of services and facilities, increase efficiency and improve performance.

— Community awareness and ability to utilise the available services.

— In spite of the additional assistance provided, improvement in infrastructure, agriculture and industry have been suboptimal and the per capita income continues to be low in most of the poorly performing States.

— These States also have high birth rates and relatively low literacy rates. It is imperative that special efforts are made during the next two decades to break this vicious self perpetuating cycle of poor performance, poor per capita income, poverty, low literacy and high birth rate so that the further widening of disparities between States in terms of per capita income and quality of life is prevented.

The higher population growth rates and low per capita income in poorly performing States are likely to have a major impact on several social sector programmes. The health status of the population in these States is poor; the health sector programme will require inputs not only for improving infrastructure and manpower, but also increasing efficiency and improving performance. The Family Welfare Programme has to address the massive task of meeting all the unmet needs for MCH and contraception so that there is a rapid decline in mortality and fertility rates. Due to high birth rate, the number of children requiring schooling will be large.

The emphasis in the education sector on primary education is essential to ensure that the resource constraints do not result in an increase in either proportion or number of illiterates. Emphasis on pre-vocational and vocational training in schools will enable these children to acquire skills through which they will find gainful employment later.

Migration

The available data from census shows that until 1991 both

internal and international migration has been negligible. The Technical Group while computing the population projection up to 2016, has assumed that the component of migration between major States and from India will be negligible. This assumption may not be valid if there is further widening of the disparity between States in terms of economic growth and employment opportunity.

Given the combination of high population growth, low literacy and lack of employment opportunities in the poorly performing States, there may be increasing rural to urban migration as well as interstate migration especially of unskilled workers. Such migration may in the short run assist the migrants in overcoming economic problems associated with unemployment. However, the migrant workers and their families may face problems in securing shelter, education and health care. It is essential to build up a mechanism for monitoring these changes. Steps will have to be taken to provide for the minimum essential needs of the vulnerable migrant population.

Labour, Employment and Manpower

Population, which is engaged in any economic activity (employed persons) and population seeking work (unemployed) constitute Labour Force. India has the second largest labour force in the world. Projection of labour force is prerequisite ensuring optimal utilisation of available human resources. Manpower development is then taken up to provide adequate labour force, of appropriate skills and quality to different sectors so that there is rapid socioeconomic development and there is no mismatch between skills required and skills available. Planning also attempts to provide enabling environment for employment generation (both self employment and wage employment) in public, private and voluntary sectors in urban and rural areas.

Labour force in India will be increasing by more than 10 million per annum during 1997-2012. It will be imperative to plan for and achieve adequate agricultural and industrial growth to absorb this work force. Most of the persons entering the labour force will be educated and have some skills. Increasing literacy and decreasing birth rates may result in more women seeking economically productive work outside home. It will be important to generate appropriate and re-numerative employment at places where labour force are available so as to reduce interstate and urban migration in search of employment. Attempts should be made to eliminate bonded labour, employment of children and women in hazardous industries and minimising occupational health hazards.

Planners face the challenge to have sustained high economic growth rate in sectors that are labour-intensive to ensure adequate employment generation for productively utilising this massive work force. If the massive work force of literate, skilled, aware men and women in age-group 20-60 years get fully employed and adequately paid they could trigger off a period of rapid economic development. As they have very few dependant children and elders there will be increased savings and investments at household level; this in turn will improve the availability of resources for accelerating economic growth. The current stage of demographic transition thus provides the country with the opportunity window for using human resources as the engine to power economic development and improving the quality of life of all the citizens.

Sex Ratio

The reported decline in the sex ratio during the current century has been a cause for concern. The factors responsible for this continued decline are as yet not clearly identified. However, it is well recognised that the adverse sex ratio is a reflection of the gender disparity. Higher childhood mortality in girl children is yet another facet of the existing gender disparities and consequent adverse effect on survival.

In the reproductive age group the mortality rates among women are higher than those among men. The continued high maternal mortality is one of the major factors responsible for this. Effective implementation of the Reproductive and Child Health Programme is expected to result in a substantial reduction in maternal mortality. At the moment, the longevity at birth among women is only marginally higher than that among men. However over the next decade life expectancy among women will progressively increase. Once the reproductive age group is crossed, the mortality rates among women are lower as women outlive and outnumber men in the age group 65 and above. The needs especially of the widowed women have to be met so that quality of life does not deteriorate.

The census 2001 will collect and report vital data on sex disaggregated basis; this will be of help in identifying and taking up appropriate interventions in correcting gender disparity; continued collection, collation, analysis and reporting of sex disaggregated data from all social sectors will also provide a mechanism to monitor whether girls and women have equal access to services.

Increasing Longevity

Over the coming decades the country will be facing a progressive increase both in the proportion and number of persons beyond 60 years of age. Over the next 20 years the population of more than 60 years will grow form 62.3 million to 112.9 million; the subsequent decades will witness massive increase in this age group. Increasing longevity will inevitably bring in its wake increase in the prevalence of non-communicable diseases.

The growing number of senior citizens in the country poses a major challenge and the cost of providing socioeconomic security and health care to this population has to be met. Currently several region and culture specific innovative interventions to provide needed care to this population are underway; among these are efforts to reverse the trend of break up of joint families. If these efforts succeed, it will be possible to provide necessary care for rapidly increasing population of senior citizens in the subsequent two decades within the resources of the family and the country.

Majority of the people in their sixties will be physically and psychologically fit and would like to participate both in economic and social activities. They should be encouraged and supported to lead a productive life and contribute to the national development. Senior citizens in their seventies and beyond and those with health problems would require assistance. So far, the families have borne major share in caring for the elderly. This will remain the ideal method; however, there are growing number of elderly without family support; for them, alternate modes for caring may have to be evolved and implemented. Improved health care has "added years to life". The social sectors have to make the necessary provisions for improving the quality of life of these senior citizens so that they truly " add life to years."

Health Implication of Demographic Transition

It was earlier assumed that population growth during demographic transition will lead to overcrowding, poverty, undernutrition, environmental deterioration, poor quality of life and increase in disease burden. Experience in the last few decades have shown that this may not always be correct. India is currently in the phase of demographic transition when the increase in population is mainly among younger, better educated and healthy population with low morbidity and mortality rate. The challenge for the health sector is to promote healthy life styles, improve access to and utilisation of health care so that the country can achieve substantial reduction in mortality and morbidity.

Occupational health and environmental health programme need be augmented to ensure that working population remain healthy and productive. If these challenges are fully met, it is possible to accelerate reduction in morbidity and mortality rate in this age group and improve health indices of the country.

With growing number of senior citizens there may be substantial increase in health care needs especially for management of non-communicable diseases. Increasing availability and awareness about technological advances for management of these problems, rising expectations of the population and the ever escalating cost of health care are some of the problems that the health care system has to cope with. Health care delivery systems will have to gear up to taking up necessary preventive, promotive, curative and rehabilitative care for growing population of senior citizens.

Implications on FW Programme

There will be a marginal decline in the population less than 15 years of age (352.7 million to 350.4 million). The health care infrastructure will therefore be not grappling with ever increasing number of children for providing care and they will be able to concentrate on: a. Improving quality of care; b. focus on antenatal, intranatal and neonatal care aimed at reducing neonatal morbidity and mortality; c. Improve coverage and quality of health care to vulnerable and under served adolescents; d. promote inter sectorial coordination especially with ICDS programme so that there is improvement in health and nutritional status; e. Improve coverage for immunisation against vaccine preventable diseases. The economic challenge is to provide needed funds so that these children have access to nutrition, education and skill development. The challenge faced by the health sector is to achieve reduction in morbidity and mortality rate in infancy and childhood, to improve nutritional status and eliminate ill-effects of gender bias.

There will be a massive increase of population in the 15-59 age group (from 519 million to 800 million). The persons in this age group will be more literate and have greater access to information; they will therefore have greater awareness and expectation regarding both the access to a wide spectrum of health care related services and the quality of these services. Under the Reproductive and child health care programme efforts are underway to provide:

— Needed services for this rapid growing population

— To broaden the spectrum of services available and

— To improve quality and coverage of health care to women, children and adolescents, so that their felt needs for health care are fully met.

— To improve the participation of men in the planned parenthood movement.

While providing the package of services, efforts will have to be made to improve the quality of services, make services more responsive to users' needs, ensure that health workers and health care providers have the necessary skills and supplies they need and there is a strong and effective referral system to manage all the risk cases. Family welfare Programme is attempting to improve the logistics of supply of drugs and vaccine to make sure good quality drugs are available at appropriate time.

Simultaneously the IEC efforts are being directed to:

— Ensure responsible reproductive /sexual behaviour.

— Improve awareness about reproductive health needs.

— Promote community participation and optimal utilisation of available services.

— Essential Reproductive and Child Health Services.

Though it is desirable that the entire package of services indicated under comprehensive RCH care is made available to all those who need it, will not be possible to immediately implement such a comprehensive package at primary health care level on a nationwide basis. After consultation with experts a package of essential reproductive health services for nationwide implementation at primary health care settings has been identified. Essential components recommended for nationwide implementation include:

— Prevention and management of unwanted pregnancy.

— Services to provide antenatal, intranatal and postnatal, and neonatal care.

— Services to promote child health and survival.

— Prevention and treatment of RTI/STD.

Most of these services are already being delivered under the Family Welfare Programme. However, there are wide variations in the quality and coverage of services not only between states but also between districts in the same state. The focus under RCH Programme is therefore on the improvement in the quality and coverage of the services over and above the existing level in all districts/states in an incremental manner so that there is over all improvement maternal and child health indices.

10

Threats of Terrorism

The subject of "terrorism" seized the world's attention in late as a result of one fairly brief, yet highly dramatic and destructive, attack on two of the core symbols of the world's most powerful political actor, the United States of America. The targeting of the World Trade Center in New York City, the symbol of the United States' enormous global economic power, and the Pentagon Building in Washington, DC, the symbol of the United States' overarching military superiority, was well planned, coordinated, and executed. The attack itself attained symbolic stature as an affront to the established global order, a challenge to the world's dominant power, and an announcement that the prevailing US-led global order was not viewed, or valued, equally by all those whose daily lives are increasingly caught in the vortex of post-Cold War change.

Of course, the problem of terrorism was already well-known when the planes struck their targets in full view of a vast, global, tele-connected audience and created their indelible psychic images of sophisticated savagery. The politics of terror, and the overpowering fear that terror produces in its wake, lay at the very foundation of the evolution of social order. And it is the ultimate irony of societal development that modern acts of savagery have attained such high levels of sophistication. In its most simple terms, terror has stood as the stark alternative to civility in social relations from the time of humankind's earliest recorded reflections.

Analysing the Problem of Terrorism

Contemporary analyses of the problem of terrorism have usually foundered between the perceptual extremes that are inherent in the amorphous ideas of terror: conceptualizations of terrorism are either too broad to be analytically useful, too narrow to be analytically meaningful, or too complex to be applied systematically. The conceptualizations themselves are all too often politically motivated as the analyst attempts to rationalize a distinction between civil and uncivil applications of violence: (useless) terror and (useful) enforcement, (undisciplined) terrorism and (disciplined) war, and (dishonorable) terrorists and (honorable) "freedom fighters." Conceptual confusion is further exacerbated by the often cavalier usage of the pejorative term "terrorist" to refer to any political opponent, much as "communist" was used for political effect in the West during the Cold War.

Hoffman offers an example of a broad definition, "[Terrorism is] the deliberate creation and exploitation of fear through violence or the threat of violence in the pursuit of political change." Hoffman attempts to differentiate his definition of terrorism from criminal and lunatic violence by emphasizing the "altruistic" and "intellectual" qualities of terrorist motivation. However, it seems clear that all acts of terrorism are criminalized acts that are made particularly effective because they are unconventional (extralegal or non-rational) applications of violent or coercive behavior.

The parallels between terrorism, state repression, organized crime, and war are too great to be discounted. The use of arbitrary and indiscriminate violence in wartime has become increasingly criminalized since the establishment of the Nuremberg trials at the end of the Second World War in . State repression, or "state terror," which finds its most extreme form in totalitarianism has become increasingly scrutinized and criminalized by the international community. In a similarly broad definition, Carr goes so far as to equate terrorism with conventional warfare, with one very important distinction: "Terrorism is warfare deliberately waged against civilians with the purpose of destroying their will to support either leaders or policies that the agents of such violence find objectionable."

For Carr, terror is established through the unrestrained demonstration of violence; it is an induced emotional state intended to disable the will in individuals to resist, or seek rectification for, a perceived injustice through the credible threat (fear) of unspecified, unbearable consequences. While both Hoffman and Carr concentrate on the serious psycho-social affects of terror, their perspectives are separated widely by the perquisites of power: Hoffman's low-power, non-state terrorists using terror to challenge authority and facilitate change, Carr's high-power, state terrorists using terror to establish authority and facilitate conquest.

Schmid and Jongman provide an example of a definition of terrorism which, due ironically to their attempt to increase definitional specificity, is far too complex (and, at once, too broad) to be applied systematically in research. For them, terrorism is

> [a]n anxiety-inspiring method of repeated violent action, employed by (semi-) clandestine individual, group, or state actors, for idiosyncratic, criminal or political reasons, whereby – in contrast to assassination – the direct targets of violence are not the main targets. The immediate human victims of violence are generally chosen randomly (targets of opportunity) or selectively (representative or symbolic targets) from a target population, and serve as message generators. Threat- and violence-based communication processes between terrorist (organizations), (imperilled)

> victims, and main targets are used to manipulate the main target (audience(s)), turning it into a target of terror, a target of demands, or a target of attention, depending on whether intimidation, coercion, or propaganda is primarily used

The core qualities of Schmid and Jongman's definition are its inclusion of state actors, as well as non-state actors, as potential agents; its inclusion of wide ranges of power and political intent, and its recognition that acts of violence must be reiterative and somewhat arbitrary in order to induce widespread terror (rather than the more immediate response of revulsion to acts of brutality). Pillar emphasizes this later point in his definition of terrorism, that terror gains its greatest strength from its focus on the possible future rather than the knowable present.

A variant of the "narrow" approach to defining the problem of terrorism has been to identify a special class of terrorist activity, that is, "international," or "transnational," terrorism.8 This conceptualization has gained currency among policy-makers, particularly in "global powers" of the West, as it appears, on surface, to focus on a particular subset of terrorist actions with "global scope," thereby inferring that this subset of terrorism stands as a direct threat to the "global social order.

The concept is based on two important, implicit, a priori assumptions: first, the West, and particularly the US, is the recognized authority leading the establishment of an emerging global order and, second, the actions taken by the leading authorities in establishing and maintaining the emerging global order are either legitimate by definition (an extended form of the classic raison d'état) or that the interests of populations affected by the global order are adequately represented within the emerging global political system. This narrow form of terrorism, then, is conducted by those, usually non-state actors who may or may not receive support from dissident states or populations, who are intent on challenging, and changing, the terms of the prevailing social order. The essential qualities of this conceptualization relate to issues of distance and jurisdiction.

The first quality, distance or "reach," may be best viewed as simply a spatial artifact, often made salient by asymmetries of power between contending groups and established authorities. That is, challengers to a particular form of social order take advantage of available technologies and the prevailing vulnerabilities associated with distance by using, or seeking to exploit, available advantages in communication, information, and mobility to identify and attack relatively distant (and comparatively weak) outposts of authority. This spatial component of international terrorism is not unique, however. Opposition always operates near the boundaries of the collective consciousness as it is shaped by central authorities. Most acts of non-international terrorism have similar qualities of combining local, proximate, and distant action. In a strategic interaction between distanced groups, what is considered local to one is necessarily considered distant by the other. Agents of violence find it logistically easier to conduct local attacks but strategically important to demonstrate their capability to mount attacks on relationally distant targets located in their opponent's heartland. The perceived value, and therefore the terror potential, of targets increase with proximity to the heartland (and breach of the security perimeter).

Two contending groups rarely occupy the exact same political space and, even when they do share competing claims to authority over the same political space, their "heartlands" remain spatially distinct and separated even when their territorial or jurisdictional interests contend and overlap. So, for instance, the Irish Republican Army has operated mainly in the British province of Northern Ireland but has conducted operations in London at the center of the British heartland; the Tamils of Sri Lanka have struck targets both in Colombo (the Sinhalese heartland) and in India, including the May assassination of Indian Prime Minister Rajiv Gandhi; and Chechen militants have allegedly struck targets as "remote" as Moscow.

The relatively recent "internationalization" of anti-authority terrorism may be simply a function of increased popular access to distance or technological reach. Friedman has referred to this phenomenon as the "super-empowered individual." Such strategic behavior is not confined to asymmetric power relationships or non-state actors. The US air raids against Tokyo in April and NATO air raids against Belgrade during the Kosovo war are similar demonstrations of the capability to mount "distant" attacks in the opposition's heartland.

The second essential quality of international terrorism, jurisdiction, is particularly important in defining potential remedies to a contestation between groups or individuals. Operating outside of, or across, an established juridical boundary complicates remedial action (ameliorative or coercive) and limits the range and/or effectiveness of institutional options. With the lack of definitive and effective instruments for addressing the problem of terrorist action in international law and institutions, ambiguities and uncertainties of juridical responsibility provide special opportunities and vulnerabilities for exploitation both by terrorist agents and affected authorities.

In the absence of established institutional mechanisms, it can be expected that those entities that are most greatly affected and who enjoy the greatest capacity for direct action will act within such a "political vacuum" in terms of their own perspectives and according to their own interests, that is, unilaterally. The unregulated strategic interactions of the most directly affected parties played out in the greater communal space will undoubtedly serve to terrorize the entire system, creating a global imperative to act. But the ability to respond rationally and effectively will be limited by selection biases inherent in our understandings of the problem.

Again, selection biases often reflect asymmetries of power. Powerful actors have recourse to a wide array of instrumentalities to promote their parochial interests, whereas weak actors may feel they have very few options to demonstrate their position and the strength of their resolve other than violence. Diffuse and indirect actions often have very direct consequences, as Galtung has argued with his concept of "structural violence." Such structural violence, that is, violence embedded in the underlying structures of social relationships, is necessarily biased toward power and established authority and, thus, makes it particularly difficult to identify the interactive, reciprocal, and alternating qualities of "terrorist" and "terrorized."

The problems of distance and jurisdiction act within a context of immediacy and imperative created by the violent attack and, as such, treatments of the problem of international terrorism tend to favor emotive and reactive responses, focusing on the symptoms and rarely considering the nature of the problems that might have stimulated such extreme or radical actions. While studies of international terrorism usually contain the recognition of the political intent of terrorist acts, the convention of non-negotiation with terrorists often obviates the identification of possible motives and, thus, stifles our ability to avoid or preclude the resort to terrorism (which would, of course, obviate the need to negotiate with terrorists).

In addition to ignoring the structural foundations of terrorism, the literature on international terrorism does not usually include reference to comparable attacks on agents and institutions of international organizations such as the UN, international NGOs, and international journalists, thus confounding that concept with "anti-internationalist" or "anti-US" resistance. This is especially confusing in a global environment where the vestiges of "anti-colonialism" often intertwine with emerging strands of "anti-globalism." In systematic studies of international terrorism, the US, Israel, and the former colonial powers of Western Europe account for the vast majority of the targets of international terrorist acts.

The fact that the US, especially, enjoys an unprecedented extent of "international reach" in global affairs and, therefore, runs an unprecedented level of risk from engendered international contention should not be conflated with, and used as, a measure of the general security of the global system. In this sense, both the United States' proactive policies and reactions to those policies must be included in any objective measure of the affects of such strategic interaction on global security.

Perhaps the most difficult aspect to reconcile in our various attempts to define terrorism has been the almost universal claim that terrorism is necessarily political. Beyond the broadest sense of what is political, that is, the sense in which all actions taken in a social context are inherently political, the idea that an action is political implies that the action is instrumental in pursuing or achieving some commonly understood goal. On surface, action in pursuit of a goal must be considered rational, however, when the evidence strongly suggests that such action is largely ineffective in attaining the desired goals, the action, or strategy, must be considered irrational in practice. This is the "lesson" that Carr argues in The Lessons of Terror, that is, that terror is not rational; it is, rather, counter-productive to the general pursuit of political goals.

This is the central argument in my earlier examination of the problem of violence in the context of societal and systemic development. This rationality conundrum presents terrorism as an unsolvable problem. The conundrum can only be reconciled by examining the emotive qualities of terrorism: that terrorism is borne of an emotive or psychic impulse in search of a political expression. Perhaps the most powerful emotive impulse is vengeance, whether as a result of a perceived injustice or indignity or an act of humiliation.

Such powerful emotive impulses are often individuated, internalized, and personalized by affected individuals leading to acts of self-destruction where the unworthy self becomes the target for retribution of perceived wrongs. The act of externalizing these emotive impulses may be facilitated by political rhetoric that emphasizes the commonality of the aggrieved and a common source of grievances. In this politicization of vengeance and other, lesser forms grievance, the rationalization of externalization and the identification of targets for retribution find expression in a common political perspective and agenda for action.

Common emotional impulses provide the impetus for overcoming collective action problems among politically disempowered individuals. The immediate and direct goal of such emotive action is to establish the capacity to "strike back." Although the impetus to "strike back" implies grievance and, thus, a desire for political change, the immediate and realizable goal is to inflict hurt, not to effect change. The politics of terror, in this instance, are imposed from the outside, recast on the inside, and redirected toward an external target. This emotive, relational quality makes (non-repressive) terrorist action less amenable to rational deterrent strategies. Deterrent actions can be viewed as consistent with, and therefore validation of, the structures of perceived injustice and very often widen the scope of persons directly affected by the actions of authorities and, so, can actually stimulate rather than deter further acts of terrorism.

It can be seen that it is the political quality of common experience, the common attribution of causal agent or target, and the collective coordination, or mobilization, of emotive response that differentiates (non-repressive) organized terrorist action from lesser forms of terror, such as psychotic, sociopathic, or criminal violence. Even these lesser (less-politicized) forms of terror can create a climate of terrorism that has serious effects on social relations, especially when those ostensibly random non-organized acts of disturbed individuals attain a sense of regularity and arbitrariness.

For example, psychotic and sociopathic terror have become more extreme and regularized in US society such that hardly a week goes by without news of another attack on a school or a multiple murder-suicide. This form of terror is much closer to most Americans and is likely to have produced more diffuse effects than the more dramatic but far less frequent form of political terrorism that has culminated in the September , , events and the subsequent "war on terrorism" in Afghanistan. Similarly, terror does not need to be premeditated as is evidenced in the regularity of "spontaneous" Hindu-Muslim riots in India.

Such communal pogroms are not unique to this context but have been, and continue to be, a fairly common method used to maintain power asymmetries in situations of communal competition. Purely sociopathic terrorism, such as the anarchist groups that have operated in Western democracies, are particularly difficult to sustain as they lack sufficient emotive strength (they are steeped mainly in malaise, disaffection, and indignation) and, by nature of their ideological perspective, can not define a common political agenda other than the destruction of the existing order.

Organized terror, while it can be orchestrated to a certain extent among "violence sycophants" (i.e., those individuals who are predisposed to value and commit violence), is most problematic when it achieves a broad network of popular support. Even the "super-empowered individual" who ultimately "pulls the trigger" requires a relatively broad base of support in order to ensure secrecy long enough to realize their full capacity for technological empowerment. Although greater and more accessible technologies of destruction make possible greater power to the individual actor, the preparation of such technologies for actual implementation draw greater aversion, publicity, and attention. Terror requires secrecy and secrecy demands silence not only by those who are integral to the conspiracy but, also, all potential witnesses (i.e., the "sea" in which the "fish" must swim).

Silence is sometimes a function of ignorance (particularly in the first instance of a new form of terrorist action) but is most often achieved through popular, supportive, and cooperative behavior. As such, most terrorist cells operate in close association with larger, more conventional political associations that are sympathetic with the terrorists' political rhetoric and agenda but uncomfortable with the terrorists' methods.

Equally important to the instrumental and operational aspects of broad, popular support is the creation of a supportive rhetorical environment in which extremist rhetoric may reverberate, amplify, and escalate over time. Terrorism, as a political act, stands at once at the nexus between individual and collective action, the emotional and rational, the conventional and the unconventional. It is can be the strongest form of protest or the weakest form of rebellion or a specialized tactic in warfare. Above all else, it is the most personal form of violence.

The nature and quality of the association between the tactical terrorist organization and the larger support network are crucial in defining the scope, efficacy, resilience, and persistence of terrorist activity. Carr makes a particularly strong argument regarding the "galvanizing" effects of terrorist tactics on the strategic interactions between contending groups. Rather than undermining, intimidating, or disabling the will to support contention, the intentional targeting of noncombatant populations, that is the actual, potential, or imagined oppositional support base, further polarizes the contending groups and strengthens and fortifies the affected group's collective resolve to resist and/or strike back.

Carr claims this as compelling evidence of the inevitable failure of terror. Like the myth of the Hydra, terrorist organization tends to recreate and regenerate itself in direct response to the strength of coercive attempts to thwart its activities and remove its leaders or operatives: as one head is removed, several others appear to take its place. Even when the organizational structure is broken completely in a mass sweep of operatives, if there is no attendant change in the underlying conditions that gave rise to the original terrorist psyche, the organization of affected individuals will most likely be recreated over a period of time and such activity will reemerge.

This is surely the general experience of brutal dictatorships and a large part of the reason why these forms of governance are inherently unstable, giving way eventually to more open and less coercive forms of governance. This is also the lesson of the use of "right-wing death squads" in places such as El Salvador, Colombia, and Algeria that create great death, injury, and mayhem but are ineffective in quelling dissent, even when great care is taken to identify and target the leadership cadres of the opposition. It is surely the lesson of the Israeli-Palestinian terrorist conflict which has continued in various forms for seventy years or more.

The strong emotive quality of terrorism is at once a powerful motivating and an inherently limiting factor. Terror is a dynamic, transitional quality that rarely exists for long periods of time without transforming to or integrating with more complex forms of instrumental conflict behavior. The strength of our emotional responses tends to wane over time unless transferred to hate. More often, strong emotional responses stimulate the search for rationality; in this application repeated, or re-stimulated, emotional responses can be very important in sustaining levels of activity.

The greatest threat of terrorism lay not in its capacity to threaten, and deliver, personalized violence but, rather, in its relation to the more institutionalized forms of violence. Terrorist activity is commonly associated, as Carr argues, with all forms of warfare. It is a common instrument in separatist violence, used both by government authorities and separatist agents. Terrorism's greatest strategic value may lay in its demonstration effects, that is, its capacity for signaling both the group's strength and resolve and the target's complicities and vulnerabilities.

Terrorism—Goals and Motivations

Terrorism may not be successful in achieving tangible political goals, but, through its capacity to galvanize public opinion, it may be instrumental in polarizing contending groups and stimulating group members to increase their support for more conventional tactics such as protest or the transformation of protest to open, armed rebellion. These conventional conflict strategies are generally more acceptable alternatives to terrorist activities.

Where terrorism exists without ties to these more collective forms of conflict, it is generally due to one of two reasons: terrorism, as a limited form of engagement, more quickly and effectively overcomes collective action problems that may retard or thwart the mobilization of mass conventional action or state repression may prevent the formation of mass movements, in which case terrorism may be the only available avenue for demonstrations of dissent. Terrorist activity is often the prelude to the transformation of non-violent protest movements to armed rebellion. The transformation of protest to armed conflict provides a tactical niche for acts of terrorism.

The emotive content of terrorist motivation makes it compatible with both political, as argued above, and spiritual rationalizations or justifications. Terrorist activity can be doubly emotive as the moral and ethical dimensions of terrorist action have to be reconciled in the mind of the terrorist.

The sole redeeming quality, so to speak, of the theocratic rationalization is that it is at once empowering and restraining. The appeal to cosmic authorization implies recognition that the contemplated deed is wrong and regretted and that the course of remedial action must be "fit" within the theological parameters of spiritual beliefs in divine benevolence. Purely secular (political) rationalizations of terror may not provide either of these inhibiting qualities: the recognition of transgression and the need for redemption. The recent examples of Nazism and Communism verify this apprehension regarding the qualities of purely human rationalizations of "social engineering".

The contemporary predominance of secular government also contributes to the utility of sectarian rationalizations of dissent as accentuating the moral divide between an unjust temporal authority and aspirations for an ideal and just society in its place. This separation of "state and church" may also help to explain the recent claims of analysts, like Hoffman, that "terrorist incidents perpetrated for religious motives result in so many more deaths [than those with purely political motives]."Such claims are based on statistical artifacts generated by selection biases in data collection.

From this brief discussion of the various conceptualizations of terrorism, a common thread seems to emerge from which the core elements of an operational definition of the terrorist action may be identified. The essential defining quality of terrorism is that it is a direct and intentional violation of the intrinsic vulnerability of the human condition; in the context of the modern state and its structures of collective security this translates into the intentional targeting of civilian, non-combatant populations.

As McKeogh explains, "It is because it is a breach of the principle of non-combatant immunity that terrorism is forthrightly condemned: its wrongness consists primarily in the fact that it targets, not military installations and personnel, but civilian ones." This essential quality has two fundamental political forms which derive from the prevailing structures of authority in societal systems and are part of the same strategic interaction process: repressive (state) and expressive (non-state) terrorism. The underlying assumption of terrorism is that it is a primarily emotive, rather than rational, action in direct pursuit of psychic, rather than, material goals.

Factors that contribute to determining the strength and persistence of the "terror" produced by violence against non-combatant populations include the dramatic, shocking (i.e., extraordinary) impact of the attack(s); the intensity of media coverage; the frequency, lethality, and arbitrariness of the attacks; the perceived potential for future attacks, and the recognized connections between individualized acts of contention and collective action.

The historical record of terrorism seems to indicate that it is becoming less ordinary, that there is a strong negative relationship between the scope and frequency of terrorism and the pace of societal development in specific locations and that the general trend has been a gradual decrease in the scope and frequency of terrorism over the course of evolution of human societies. An important caveat is the positive relationship between the destructive capabilities of terrorism and the general extent and pace of technological development: the "super-empowered terrorist." Think, for example, of the very powerful, subliminal terrorism produced by the growing availability of the technologies of mass destruction and the fear that these weapons may fall into the hands of ill intent.

Types of Terrorism

In early 1975, the Law Enforcement Assistant Administration in the United States formed the National Advisory Committee on Criminal Justice Standards and Goals. One of the five volumes that the committee wrote was entitled *Disorders and Terrorism*, produced by the Task Force on Disorders and Terrorism under the direction of H.H.A. Cooper, Director of the Task Force staff. The Task Force classified terrorism into six categories.

— *Civil disorder*—A form of collective violence interfering with the peace, security, and normal functioning of the community.

— *Political terrorism*—Violent criminal behaviour designed primarily to generate fear in the community, or substantial segment of it, for political purposes.

— *Non-Political terrorism*—Terrorism that is not aimed at political purposes but which exhibits "conscious design to create and maintain a high degree of fear for coercive purposes, but the end is individual or collective gain rather than the achievement of a political objective."

— *Quasi-terrorism*—The activities incidental to the commission of crimes of violence that are similar in form and method to genuine terrorism but which nevertheless lack its essential ingredient. It is not the main purpose of the quasi-terrorists to induce terror in the immediate victim as in the case of genuine terrorism, but the quasi-terrorist uses the modalities and techniques of the genuine terrorist and produces similar consequences and reaction. For example, the fleeing felon who takes hostages is a quasi-terrorist, whose methods are similar to those of the genuine terrorist but whose purposes are quite different.

— *Limited political terrorism*—Genuine political terrorism is characterized by a revolutionary approach; limited political terrorism refers to "acts of terrorism which are committed for ideological or political motives but which are not part of a concerted campaign to capture control of the state.

— *Official or state terrorism*–"referring to nations whose rule is based upon fear and oppression that reach similar to terrorism or such proportions." It may also be referred to as Structural Terrorism defined broadly as terrorist acts carried out by governments in pursuit of political objectives, often as part of their foreign policy.

Several sources have further defined the typology of terrorism:

— Political terrorism

— Sub-state terrorism

— Social revolutionary terrorism

— Nationalist-separatist terrorism

— Religious extremist terrorism

— Religious fundamentalist Terrorism

— New religions terrorism

— Right-wing terrorism

— Left-wing terrorism

— Single-issue terrorism
— State-sponsored terrorism
— Regime or state terrorism
— Criminal terrorism
— Pathological terrorism

Domestic Terrorism

The relationship between domestic terrorism and democracy is very complex. Terrorism is most common in nations with intermediate political freedom, and is least common in the most democratic nations. However, one study suggests that suicide terrorism may be an exception to this general rule. Evidence regarding this particular method of terrorism reveals that every modern suicide campaign has targeted a democracy–a state with a considerable degree of political freedom. The study suggests that concessions awarded to terrorists during the 1980s and 1990s for suicide attacks increased their frequency.

Some examples of "terrorism" in non-democracies include ETA in Spain under Francisco Franco, the Shining Path in Peru under Alberto Fujimori, the Kurdistan Workers Party when Turkey was ruled by military leaders and the ANC in South Africa. Democracies, such as the United Kingdom, United States, Israel, Indonesia, India, Spain and the Philippines, have also experienced domestic terrorism.

While a democratic nation espousing civil liberties may claim a sense of higher moral ground than other regimes, an act of terrorism within such a state may cause a dilemma: whether to maintain its civil liberties and thus risk being perceived as ineffective in dealing with the problem; or alternatively to restrict its civil liberties and thus risk delegitimizing its claim of supporting civil liberties. This dilemma, some social theorists would conclude, may very well play into the initial plans of the acting terrorist(s); namely, to delegitimize the state.

Religious Terrorism

R..ligious terrorism is terrorism performed by groups or individuals, the motivation of which is typically rooted in the faith based tenets. Terrorist acts throughout the centuries have been performed on religious grounds with the hope to either spread or enforce a system of belief, viewpoint or opinion. Religious terrorism does not in itself necessarily define a specific religious standpoint or view, but instead usually defines an individual or a group view or interpretation of that belief system's teachings.

Perpetrators of Terrorism

The perpetrators of acts of terrorism can be individuals, groups, or states. According to some definitions, clandestine or semi-clandestine state actors may also carry out terrorist acts outside the framework of a state of war. However, the most common image of terrorism is that it is carried out by small and secretive cells, highly motivated to serve a particular cause and many of the most deadly operations in recent times, such as the September 11 attacks, the London underground bombing, and the 2002 Bali bombing were planned and carried out by a close clique, composed of close friends, family members and other strong social networks. These groups benefited from the free flow of information and efficient telecommunications to succeed where others had failed.

Over the years, many people have attempted to come up with a terrorist profile to attempt to explain these individuals' actions through their psychology and social circumstances. Others, like Roderick Hindery, have sought to discern profiles in the propaganda tactics used by terrorists. Some security organizations designate these groups as *violent non-state actors*. A 2007 study by economist Alan B. Krueger found that terrorists were less likely to come from an impoverished background (28% vs. 33%) and more likely to have at least a high-school education (47% vs. 38%). Another analysis found only 16% of terrorists came from impoverished families, vs. 30% of male Palestinians, and over 60% had gone beyond high school, vs. 15% of the populace.

To avoid detection, a terrorist will look, dress, and behave normally until executing the assigned mission. Some claim that attempts to profile terrorists based on personality, physical, or sociological traits are not useful. The physical and behavioral description of the terrorist could describe almost any normal person. However, the majority of terrorist attacks are carried out by military age men, aged 16–40.

State Sponsors

A state can sponsor terrorism by funding or harboring a terrorist organization. Opinions as to which acts of violence by states consist of state-sponsored terrorism vary widely. When states provide funding for groups considered by some to be terrorist, they rarely acknowledge them as such.

State Terrorism

As with "terrorism" the concept of "state terrorism" is controversial. The Chairman of the United Nations Counter-Terrorism Committee has stated that the Committee was conscious of 12 international Conventions on the subject, and none of them referred to State terrorism, which was not an international legal concept. If States abused their power, they should be judged against international conventions dealing with war crimes, international human rights and international humanitarian law. Former United Nations Secretary-General Kofi Annan has said that it is "time to set aside debates on so-called 'state terrorism'. The use of force by states is already thoroughly regulated under international law" However, he also made clear that, "regardless of the differences between governments on the question of definition of terrorism, what is clear and what we can all agree on is any deliberate attack on innocent civilians, regardless of one's cause, is unacceptable and fits into the definition of terrorism."

State terrorism has been used to refer to terrorist acts by governmental agents or forces. This involves the use of state resources employed by a state's foreign policies, such as using its military to directly perform acts of terrorism. Professor of Political Science Michael Stohl cites the examples that include Germany's bombing of London and the U.S. atomic destruction of Hiroshima during World War II. He argues that "the use of terror tactics is common in international relations and the state has been and remains a more likely employer of terrorism within the international system than insurgents." They also cite the First strike option as an example of the "terror of coercive diplomacy" as a form of this, which holds the world hostage with the implied threat of using nuclear weapons in "crisis management." They argue that the institutionalized form of terrorism has occurred as a result of changes that took place following World War II. In this analysis, state terrorism exhibited as a form of foreign policy was shaped by the presence and use of weapons of mass destruction, and that the legitimizing of such violent behavior led to an increasingly accepted form of this state behavior.

State terrorism has also been used to describe peacetime actions by governmental agents such as the bombing of Pan Am Flight 103. Charles Stewart Parnell described William Ewart Gladstone's Irish Coercion Act as terrorism in his "no-Rent manifesto" in 1881, during the Irish Land War. The concept is also used to describe political repressions by governments against their own civilian population with the purpose to incite fear. For example, taking and executing civilian hostages or extrajudicial elimination campaigns are commonly considered "terror" or terrorism, for example during the Red Terror or Great Terror. Such actions are often also described as democide or genocide which has been argued to be equivalent to state terrorism. Empirical studies on this have found that democracies have little democide.

Funding

State sponsors have constituted a major form of funding; for example, PLO, DFLP and some other terrorist groups were funded by the Soviet Union.

"Revolutionary tax" is another major form of funding, and essentially a euphemism for "protection money". Revolutionary taxes are typically extorted from businesses, and they also "play a secondary role as one other means of intimidating the target population".

Other major sources of funding include kidnapping for ransoms, smuggling, fraud and robbery.

Tactics of Terrorism

While terrorists act according to different motivations and goals, all such groups have one tactic in common: intimidation or coercion of the public or the government in order to effect social or political change. Terrorism uses violence, or threat of violence, against one portion of a society to compel the greater body of that society or their leaders to make a change out of fear. Terrorism often exploits propaganda techniques to ensure the public receives the intended message. The term Propaganda of the Deed, coined by Malatesta, Cafiero, and Covelli, states that the message is most strongly conveyed through violence.

In the media, terrorist violence is most commonly portrayed as being carried out via an improvised explosive device, although chemical weapons have been used on occasion. Vehicles from pick-up trucks to planes, like in the September 11, 2001 attacks, have been used as guided incendiary device. In the failed 2002 airliner attack shoulder-launched surface-to-air missiles were fired at an airliner while taking off. Concerns have also been raised regarding attacks involving nuclear weapons or biological weapons.

However, despite the popular image of terrorism as bombings alone, and the large number of casualties and higher media impact associated with bombings, conventional firearms are as much if not more pervasive in their use. In 2004, the European Council recognized the "need to ensure terrorist organisations and groups are starved of the components of their trade," including "the need to ensure greater security of firearms, explosives, bomb-making equipment and technologies that contribute to the perpetration of terrorist outrages."

Terrorist groups may arrange for secondary devices to detonate at a slightly later time in order to kill emergency-response personnel attempting to attend to the dead and wounded. Repeated or suspected use of secondary devices can also delay emergency response out of concern that such devices may exist. Examples include a (failed) device that was meant to release cyanide-gas during the February 26, 1993 World Trade Center bombing; and a second car bomb that detonated 20 minutes after the December 1, 2001 Ben Yehuda Street Bombing by Hamas in Jerusalem.

Training

There are and have been training camps for terrorists. The range of training depends greatly on the level of support the terrorist organization receives from various organizations and states. In nearly every case the training incorporates the philosophy and agenda of the groups leadership as justification for the training as well as the potential acts of terrorism which may be committed. State sanctioned training is by far the most extensive and thorough, often employing professional soldiers and covert operatives of the supporting state.

Preparation

Preparation of a major attack such as the September 11, 2001 attacks may take years, whereas a simpler attack, depending on the availability of arms,resources,and more it may be almost spontaneous.

Cover

Where terrorism occurs in the context of open warfare or insurgency, its perpetrators may shelter behind a section of the local population. Examples include the intifada on Israeli-occupied territory, and insurgency in Iraq. This population, which may be ethnically distinct from the counter-terrorist forces, is either sympathetic to their cause, indifferent, or acts under duress.

Terrorists preparing for the September 11, 2001 attacks changed their appearance to avoid looking radical.

Funding

Funding can be raised in both legal and illegal ways. Some of the most common ways to raise funds are through front groups, charitable organizations, or NGOs with similar ideologies. In the absence of state funding, terrorists may rely on organized crime to fund their activities. This has included kidnapping, drug trafficking, or robbery. Additionally, terrorists have also found many more sources of revenue.

Communication

Even though old-school communication methods like radio are still used, the revolution in communication technology over the past 10-15 years has dramatically changed how terrorist organizations communicate. E-mails, fax transmissions, websites, cell phones, and satellite telephones have made it possible for organizations to contemplate a global strategy. However, too great a reliance on this new technology leaves organizations vulnerable to sophisticated monitoring of communication and triangulation of its source.

Terrorism and Human Rights

The issue of terrorism and human rights has long been a concern of the United Nations human rights program, but it has become more urgent following the attack of 11 September 2001 on the United States of America and the worldwide surge in acts of terrorism. OHCHR condemns terrorism unequivocally and recognises the duty of States to protect those living within their jurisdictions from terrorism. The Office of the High Commissioner for Human Rights has placed a priority on protection of human rights, notably the right to life, and the question of protecting human rights in the context of counter-terrorism measures.

The Secretary-General, the High Commissioner for Human Rights, and others in the UN system have emphasised that human rights norms must be rigorously respected by all, including in states of emergency. As Secretary-General Kofi Annan stated at a special meeting of the Security Council's Counter-Terrorism Committee with International, Regional, and Sub-Regional Organisations, on 6 March 2003, "Our responses to terrorism, as well as our efforts to thwart it and prevent it, should uphold the human rights that terrorists aim to destroy. Respect for human rights, fundamental freedoms and the rule of law are essential tools in the effort to combat terrorism—not privileges to be sacrificed at a time of tension."

On 28 September 2001, the Security Council adopted Resolution 1373 under Chapter VII of the UN Charter, obligating States to implement more effective counter-terrorism measures at the national level and to increase international cooperation in the struggle against terrorism. The resolution created the Counter-Terrorism Committee (CTC) to monitor action on this issue and to receive reports from States on measures taken.

Former High Commissioner Mary Robinson and the late High Commissioner Sergio Vieira de Mello both addressed the CTC, urging it to take account of human rights in its review of counter-terrorism measures. Mr. Vieira de Mello, speaking to the CTC in October 2002, stated his conviction that "the best - the only - strategy to isolate and defeat terrorism is by respecting human rights, fostering social justice, enhancing democracy and upholding the primacy of the rule of law." Since then, the CTC and the UN Human Rights Committee have exchanged briefings on their working methods and areas of concern.

In resolution 1456, the Security Council declared that "States must ensure that any measure taken to combat terrorism comply with all their obligations under international law, and should adopt such measures in accordance with international law, in particular international human rights, refugee, and humanitarian law." Human rights law has sought to strike a fair balance between legitimate national security concerns and the protection of fundamental freedoms. It acknowledges that States must address serious and genuine security concerns, such as terrorism. The balance is reflected in the International Covenant on Civil and Political Rights (ICCPR) as well as in regional instruments.

Threats to national security may, under very specific conditions, lead to a state of emergency under which certain rights are subject to derogation (suspension). However, certain rights are never subject to derogation. The question of states of emergency and derogation is addressed in article 4 of the ICCPR. In July 2001, the UN Human Rights Committee adopted General Comment No. 29, concerning ICCPR article 4, in which it clarified the scope of non-derogable rights and identified elements which cannot be subject to lawful derogation. Despite the importance of the fight against terrorism, some UN human rights bodies have expressed concern that counter-terrorism measures may infringe on human rights. For example, UN special rapporteurs and independent experts, at their annual meeting in Geneva in June 2003, adopted the following joint statement .

The special rapporteurs and independent experts express alarm at the growing threats against human rights, threats that necessitate a renewed resolve to defend and promote these rights. They also note the impact of this environment on the effectiveness and independence of special procedures.

Although they share in the unequivocal condemnation of terrorism, they voice profound concern at the multiplication of policies, legislation and practices increasingly being adopted by many countries in the name of the fight against terrorism which affect negatively the enjoyment of virtually all human rights - civil, cultural, economic, political and social.

They draw attention to the dangers inherent in the indiscriminate use of the term "terrorism", and the resulting new categories of discrimination. They recall that, in accordance with the International Covenant on Civil and Political Rights and pursuant to the Convention against Torture and Other Cruel, Inhuman or Degrading Treatment or Punishment, certain rights are non-derogable and that any measures of derogation from the other rights guaranteed by the Covenant must be made in strict conformity with the provisions of its article 4.

The special rapporteurs and independent experts deplore the fact that, under the pretext of combating terrorism, human rights defenders are threatened and vulnerable groups are targeted and discriminated against on the basis of origin and socio-economic status, in particular migrants, refugees and asylum-seekers, indigenous peoples and people fighting for their land rights or against the negative effects of economic globalisation policies.

They strongly affirm that any measures taken by States to combat terrorism must be in accordance with States' obligations under the international human rights instruments. They are determined, in the framework of their respective mandates, to monitor and investigate developments in this area and call upon all those committed to respect for human rights, including the United Nations, to be vigilant to prevent any abuse of counter-terrorism measures.

OHCHR action on the issue of human rights and terrorism is guided in part by General Assembly resolution 58/187 (2003) and Commission on Human Rights resolution 2003/68 ("Protection of human rights and fundamental freedoms while countering terrorism"). These resolutions call on the High Commissioner's office to:

a) examine the question of the protection of human rights and fundamental freedoms while countering terrorism, taking into account reliable information from all sources;

b) make general recommendations concerning the obligation of States to promote and protect human rights and fundamental freedoms while taking actions to counter terrorism; and

c) provide assistance and advice to States, upon their request, on the protection of human rights and fundamental freedoms while countering terrorism, as well as to relevant United Nations bodies.

The issue of human rights and terrorism is also addressed in General Assembly resolution 58/174 (2003) and Commission on Human Rights resolution 2003/37 ("Human rights and terrorism").

The Office also implements the findings of the Secretary-General's Policy Working Group on Terrorism, in particular its sub-group on human rights and terrorism. Based on a Policy Working Group recommendation, the Office published in 2003 the Digest of Jurisprudence of the UN and Regional Organisations on the Protection of Human Rights while Countering Terrorism. The Digest, which is available as an OHCHR publication, makes several important contributions, for example by clarifying the concept of non-derogable rights under both the United Nations and regional human rights systems.

It addresses the core principles of necessity and proportionality, which are fundamental to lawful counter-terrorism measures. Through excerpts from findings of the UN and regional human rights bodies, the Digest shows concerns that have been expressed over practices which are in use or under consideration by States today, such as the use of military tribunals to try civilians, and detention practices which disregard recognised international standards.

In 1997, the Sub-Commission on the Promotion and Protection of Human Rights recommended the appointment of a Special Rapporteur to conduct a comprehensive study on human rights and terrorism. The Special Rapporteur has submitted a series of reports to the Sub-Commission since then. International attention became focused on terrorism with the attack on World Trade Centre twin towers and

Pentagon on September11, 2001. Since it was the first time that such attacks were experienced by the USA on its surface, it shook up the entire country from the President downwards. And for the first time terrorism became a four letter word in the USA. The citizen on the street and the entire power structure of the USA felt humiliated at the gall of the attackers.

A similar incident, back home, was the attack on Indian Parliament on December 13, 2001.Here the situation was different in the sense that for the first time such a serious attack was mounted on the symbol of Indian Republic in the capital of the country. It gave the government a powerful argument in favour of 'streamlining' and 'providing more teeth' to the existing anti-terror laws. The power structure of our country did not react qualitatively very different from the power structure of the United States except that the latter was in a position to take independent decisions in its interest unhindered by any other limitations. The power structure of our country felt strengthened in its pleadings in the court of the USA against Pakistan.

The international bulwark of joint action concerning any development that impinges on the international law rightfully belongs to the United Nations. The new situation created by the attack on the twin towers exposed the impotence of the world body and underlined the position of the USA as an undeclared rival of the United Nations. On the home turf, the government received widespread popular support in favour of the existing laws designated as 'anti terror laws' and a fillip to adopt more such measures with the result that in the general atmosphere created by this attack in favour of license to curtail liberties, the attempts to browbeat and suppress the media, Indian and foreign, did not evoke much protest.

Even when those elected representatives who had supported such 'anti-terrorism' laws in the Parliament were themselves detained under these laws there was not much hue and cry against it. While in the USA the brunt of anti-terrorism steps was borne by the foreigners, mainly the foreigners from Asian countries, in India it fell on the common citizen. It had happened in the past also when the TADA was in operation. It was widely applied on trade union workers, political activists, and defenders of Human Rights.

One fallout of the United States campaign against terrorism was destruction of Afghanistan and conversion of Pakistan into one of the bases for mounting attacks on Afghanistan, compelling the country to completely reverse its policy vis-à-vis Taliban Afghanistan. There are strong possibilities at present (which may turn into a reality by the time these lines appear in print) that the USA may start a second war against Iraq. How far is the USA concerned with containing Iraq in its 'criminal' intentions and how far is it concerned with its oil is an important question. It is also important to note that it has been made clear that while the USA has the right to pre-emptive strikes, India (or for that matter Pakistan) does not.

The point to be noted here is that while all anti-terrorism fortifications, technological and armament based, in countries in the Asian sub-continent and the limited wars as anti-terrorism steps, prove a tremendous strain on the economy of such countries, they result in a huge surplus creation for the American armament industry. Such situations, therefore, receive solid backing of the American politico-economic structure. As other under developed countries step up the process of equipping for 'containing and facing terrorist acts' the American economy, and also the economics of its European allies, net increased demand in these fields. Limited wars between two under developed countries or against such a country by the U.S. creates increased demands in Defence Industries of the U.S. and its allies.

The Armament industry thrives during such wars. Armaments are produced for destruction and are needed again and again as the war goes on. The relationship of the development of capitalist countries and the resources and markets of the underdeveloped countries has been forcefully laid bare by political and economic thinkers like A.A. Berle, John Kenneth Galbraith, Paul A Baran, Paul A Sweezy, and others. The above may appear a disjointed narration but there is a binding string running right through. In today's unipolar world scene anti-terrorism campaigns, especially those emanating from the U.S.A., cannot be separated from globalisation and the end aim turns out to be service of American economy.

Some laws restrict even human rights as defined by the United Nations. True, some restrictions may be inevitable because society in the real world is not Utopia as visualised by Sir Thomas More wherein everything is perfect or idealistic and all the citizens are selfless. The spirit of capitalism, today's reigning philosophy, derives from selfishness of human beings. In a society of self-less citizens Capitalism will fail. Capitalism has to have laws to safeguard the selfish spirit of the individual. It is not called individualism for nothing.

One person's rights ends where the other person's rights begin. We have to be clear and conscious, therefore, that when we make a law and restrict the freedoms of the citizens, the restrictions have to be minimum, well defined, and open to justiciability. There have to be clear and strong safe guards and the restrictions have to be, the especially in the case of human rights, temporary.

In today's scenario we have also to see whether our laws serve our interests. The interests of an under developed country may clash with the interest of developed countries, though their will always be grey areas. Such a situation needs fearless and honest leadership. We have to beware that compelled by globalisation or 'need to curb terrorism' we may not be surviving the interest of the developed world. Just as terrorism is temporary, curbs on human rights also have to be temporary as human rights are permanent.

In short, the argument, we have to understand that every act of terrorism infringes on the human rights of the people. We also have to accept that laws restrict rights of the people, necessarily or unnecessarily. But we have to be clear that we have to define terrorism in the context of our country and have to devise temporary limitations on the rights of the people.

Counter-terrorism

Counter-terrorism is the practices, tactics, techniques, and strategies that governments, militaries, police departments and corporations adopt to prevent or in response to terrorist threats and/or acts, both real and imputed.

The tactic of terrorism is available to insurgents and governments. Not all insurgents use terror as a tactic, and some choose not to use it because other tactics work better for them in a particular context. Individuals, such as Timothy McVeigh, may also engage in terrorist acts such as the Oklahoma City bombing.

If the terrorism is part of a broader insurgency, counter-terrorism may also form a part of a counter-insurgency doctrine, but political, economic, and other measures may focus more on the insurgency than the specific acts of terror. Foreign internal defense (FID) is a term used by several countries for programs either to suppress insurgency, or reduce the conditions under which insurgency could develop.

Counter-terrorism includes both the detection of potential acts and the response to related events.

The concept of anti-terrorism emerges from a thorough examining of the concept of terrorism as well as an attempt to understand and articulate what constitutes terrorism in Western terms. In military contexts, terrorism is a tactic, not an ideology. Terrorism may be a tactic in a war between nation-states, in a civil war, or in an insurgency.

Counter-terrorism refers to offensive strategies intended to prevent a belligerent, in a broader conflict, from successfully using the tactic of terrorism. The US military definition, compatible with the definitions used by NATO and many other militaries, is "Operations that include the offensive measures taken to prevent, deter, preempt, and respond to terrorism." In other words, counter-terrorism is a set of techniques for denying an opponent the use of terrorism-based tactics, just as counter-air is a set of techniques for denying the opponent the use of attack aircraft.

Anti-terrorism is defensive, intended to reduce the chance of an attack using terrorist tactics at specific points, or to reduce the vulnerability of possible targets to such tactics. *"Defensive measures used to reduce the vulnerability of individuals and property to terrorist acts, to include limited response and containment by local military and civilian forces."*

To continue the analogy between air and terrorist capability, offensive counter-air missions attack the airfields of the opponent, while defensive counter-air uses antiaircraft missiles to protect a point on one's own territory. The ongoing Israeli-Palestinian conflict, Sri Lankan Civil War, and Colombian Civil War are examples of conflicts where terrorism is present, along with other tactics, so that participants use counter- and anti-terrorism to limit the opponent's use of terror tactics

Building a counter-terrorism plan involves all segments of a society or many government agencies. In dealing with foreign terrorists, the lead responsibility is usually at the national level. Because propaganda and indoctrination lie at the core of terrorism, understanding their profile and functions increases the ability to counter terrorism more effectively.

Most counter-terrorism strategies involve an increase in standard police and domestic intelligence. The central activities are traditional: interception of communications, and the tracing of persons. New technology has, however, expanded the range of military and law enforcement operations.

Domestic intelligence is often directed at specific groups, defined on the basis of origin or religion, which is a source of political controversy. Mass surveillance of an entire population raises objections on civil liberties grounds.

To select the effective action when terrorism appears to be more of an isolated event, the appropriate government organizations need to understand the source, motivation, methods of preparation, and tactics of terrorist groups. Good intelligence is at the heart of such preparation, as well as political and social understanding of any grievances that might be solved. Ideally, one gets information from inside the group, a very difficult challenge for HUMINT because operational terrorist cells are often small, with all members known to one another, perhaps even related.

Counterintelligence is a great challenge with the security of cell-based systems, since the ideal, but nearly impossible, goal is to obtain a clandestine source within the cell. Financial tracking can play a role, as can communications intercept, but both of these approaches need to be balanced against legitimate expectations of privacy.

Today, many countries have special units designated to handle terrorist threats. Besides various security agencies, there are elite tactical units, also known as special mission units, whose role is to directly engage terrorists and prevent terrorist attacks.

Such units perform both in preventive actions, hostage rescue and responding to on-going attacks. Countries of all sizes can have highly trained counter-terrorist teams. Tactics, techniques and procedures for manhunting are under constant development.

Most of these measures deal with terrorist attacks that affect an area, or threaten to do so. It is far harder to deal with assassination, or even reprisals on individuals, due to the short (if any) warning time and the quick exfiltration of the assassins. Of course, if the assassination is done by a suicide bomber, exfiltration becomes moot.

These units are specially trained in tactics and are very well equipped for CQB with emphasis on stealth and performing the mission with minimal casualties. The units include take-over force (assault teams), snipers, EOD experts, dog handlers and intelligence officers.

The majority of counter-terrorism operations at the tactical level, are conducted by state, federal and national law enforcement agencies or intelligence agencies. In some countries, the military may be called in as a last resort. Obviously, for countries whose military are legally permitted to conduct police operations, this is a non-issue, and such counter-terrorism operations are conducted by their military.

Bibliography

Atkinson, J. (2006) *Private and Public Protection: Civil Mental Health Legislation*, Edinburgh, Dunedin Academic Press.

Babb, Sarah (2009). *Behind the Development Banks: Washington Politics, World Poverty, and the Wealth of Nations*. University of Chicago Press.

Caldwell, John C. and Pat Caldwell (1986). *Limiting Population Growth, and the Ford Foundation Contribution*. London: Frances Pinter.

Chaliand, Gerard. (2007).*The History of Terrorism: From Antiquity to al Qaeda*. Berkeley: University of California Press.

Frank, Ellen, (2006). *Dr. Dollar: How Is Poverty Defined in Government Statistics?* Dollars & Sense, January/February 2006

Fried, Yehuda and Joseph Agassi, (1976). *Paranoia: A Study in Diagnosis*. Boston Studies in the Philosophy of Science, 50.

Galanter, Marc (2005). *Alcohol Problems in Adolescents and Young Adults: Epidemiology, Neurobiology, Prevention, Treatment*. New York, NY: Kluwer Academic/Plenum.

Giddens, A (1996). *The Constitution of Society*. California: University of California Press. pp. 14–19.

Giddens, Anthony. (2006). *Sociology* (5th edition), Polity, Cambridge.

Greener R (2002). "AIDS and macroeconomic impact". in S, Forsyth (ed.). *State of The Art: AIDS and Economics*. IAEN. pp. 49–55.

Hedblom; Jack H. (2007). *Last Call: Alcoholism and Recovery*. Baltimore, MD: Johns Hopkins University Press.

Hirst P, Thompson G. 1996. *Globalization in Question*. Cambridge, MA: Blackwell.

Hockenbury, Don and Sandy (2004). *Discovering Psychology*. Worth Publishers.

Hoffman, Bruce. (1988). *Inside Terrorism*. New York: Columbia University Press.

Hooper E (1999). *The River : A Journey to the Source of HIV and AIDS* (1st ed.). Boston, MA: Little Brown & Co. pp. 1–1070

Khantzian, E.J. (1985). The Self-medication hypothesis of addictive disorders: Focus on heroin and cocaine dependence. In: *Am. L. Psychiatry* 142: (pp. 1259-1264).

Lutz, Wolfgang, Warren Sanderson, and Sergei Scherbov (2001). The end of world population growth. *Nature*, vol. 412, No. 2 (August), pp. 543-546.

Neugarten & Datan, (1973); Elder, (1975). In: *Journal of Health and Social Behavior* 37 (pp.75-91) The effects of role socialization on the initiation of cocaine use: An event history analysis from adolescence into middle adulthood. Burton, R., (1996).

O'Farrell, Timothy J. and William Fals-Stewart (2006). *Behavioral Couples Therapy for Alcoholism and Drug Abuse*. New York, NY: Guilford Press.

Over M (1992) (PDF). *The macroeconomic impact of AIDS in Sub-Saharan Africa, Population and Human Resources Department*. The World Bank. http://www.worldbank.org/aidsecon/macro.pdf. Retrieved 2008-05-03.

Porter, Roy (2002). *Madness: a brief history*. Oxford [Oxfordshire]: Oxford University Press.

Post, F.; Holt, S. (2009). "Recent developments in HIV and the kidney". *Current opinion in infectious diseases* **22** (1): 43–48.

Smart, Lesley (2007). *Alcohol and Human Health*. Oxford, UK: Oxford University Press.

Smeeding, Timothy M., Michael O'Higgins, and Lee Rainwater. (1990). *Poverty, Inequality and Income Distribution in Comparative Perspective*. Urban Institute Press.

Stephen C. Smith, (2005). *Ending Global Poverty: A Guide to What Works*, New York: Palgrave Macmillan.

Triest, Robert K. (1998). "Has Poverty Gotten Worse?" *Journal of Economic Perspectives*.

United Nations (2001). *World Population Prospects: The 2000 Revision*, vol. I, *Comprehensive Tables* United Nations.

Vandenbroucke F. 1998. *Globalisation, Inequality,and Social Democracy*. London: Inst. Public Policy Res.

Wallace, Ruth A. & Alison Wolf. (1995). *Contemporary Sociological Theory: Continuing the Classical Tradition*, 4th ed., Prentice-Hall.

Waters, Malcolm (1995) *Globalization*. London: Routledge.

Willis, Evan. (1996). *The Sociological Quest: An introduction to the study of social life*, New Brunswick, New Jersey, Rutgers University Press.

World Bank, (2004). "World Development Report 2004: Making Services Work For Poor People".

Index

ENCYCLOPAEDIA OF SOCIOLOGY

Indian Social Organisation

Volume –4

Satish Mittal
Sushil Kumar Saxena

Commonwealth

Encyclopaedia of Sociology

Edition : 2026

ISBN 978-81-311-0377-7 (set)

Published by :
COMMONWEALTH PUBLISHERS (P) LTD.
4831/24, Govind Lane,
Ansari Road, Darya Ganj,
New Delhi - 110002
Ph. : 23242541, 23272541
e-mail : commonwealthpublishers2016@gmail.com

Distributed by :
ARJUN PUBLISHING HOUSE
4831/24, Govind Lane,
Ansari Road, Darya Ganj,
New Delhi - 110002
Ph. : 23242541, 23272541
e-mail : arjunbooks2001@gmail.com
arjunpubhouse@gmail.com

Laser Typesetting by :
Dimple Computers
Delhi

Printed at :
Milan Enterprises
Delhi

Preface

The term "social organisation" means the systematic ordering of social relations. It implies the interdependence of parts, which is an essential and important feature of all enduring collectivities such as, groups, communities, and societies. These interdependent parts consist of a set of roles and social positions, values, norms and beliefs found in society. The social values of a society are usually based on religious beliefs. Behaviour is based on values, and hence religious beliefs play an important role in determining social behaviour. There are many religious groups in India and the country has declared itself to be secular. This means that all religions are to be treated equally by the state.

When we speak of social organisation, we talk about the arrangement of actions which conform with the norms and values of society. Thus, to understand the social organisation of a particular society, we need to study the systematic ordering of social relations, including changes that have taken place over time in them. In any description of social organisation of a people we need to refer to the ideological basis of the way the people act.

This book is intended to provide a detailed description of the social organisation of different religious groups living in India. Written in a lively and accessible style, it would be of great value for the students, teachers, researchers, anthropologists and the general public alike.

Authors

Contents

1

Indian Social System

Indian society is multifaceted to an extent perhaps unknown in any other of the world's great civilisations. Virtually no generalisation made about Indian society is valid for all of the nation's multifarious groups. Comprehending the complexities of Indian social structure has challenged scholars and other observers over many decades. The ethnic and linguistic diversity of Indian civilisation is more like the diversity of an area as variable as Europe than like that of any other single nation-state. Living within the embrace of the Indian nation are vast numbers of different regional, social, and economic groups, each with different cultural practices. Particularly noteworthy are differences between social structures in the north and the south, especially in the realm of kinship systems. Throughout the country, religious differences can be significant, especially between the Hindu majority and the large Muslim minority; and other Indian groups—Buddhists, Christians, Jains, Jews, Parsis, Sikhs, and practitioners of tribal religions—all pride themselves on being unlike members of other faiths.

Access to wealth and power varies considerably, and vast differences in socioeconomic status are evident everywhere. The poor and the wealthy live side by side in urban and rural areas. It is common in city life to see a prosperous, well-fed man or woman chauffeured in a fine car pass gaunt street dwellers huddled beneath burlap shelters along the roadway. In many villages, solid cement houses of landowners rise not far from the flimsy thatched shacks of landless labourers. Even when not so obvious, distinctions of class are found in almost every settlement in India.

Urban-rural differences can be immense in the Indian Society. Nearly 74 percent of India's population dwells in villages, with agriculture providing support for most of these rural residents. In villages, mud-plastered walls ornamented with traditional designs, dusty lanes, herds of grazing cattle, and the songs of birds at sunset provide typical settings for the social lives of most Indians. In India's great cities, however, millions of people live amidst cacophony—roaring vehicles, surging crowds, jammed apartment buildings, busy commercial establishments, loudspeakers blaring movie tunes—while breathing the poisons of industrial and automotive pollution. Gender distinctions are pronounced. The behaviour expected of men and women can be quite different, especially in villages, but also in urban centers. Prescribed ideal gender roles help shape the actions of both sexes as they move between family and the world outside the home.

Crosscutting and pervading all of these differences of region, language, wealth, status, religion, urbanity, and gender is the special feature of Indian society that has received most attention from observers: caste. The people of India belong to thousands of castes and castelike groups—hierarchically ordered, named groups into which members are born. Caste members are expected to marry within the group and follow caste rules pertaining to diet, avoidance of ritual pollution, and many other aspects of life.

The study of Indian society necessitates that we try to understand the basic elements which provide the blueprint for thought and action. How are relationships organised through the history and in the contemporary times? What the rules and norms for individual and social conduct and from where they derive legitimacy are some of the issues which need to be understood. Indian society is extremely diverse in terms of societies, cultures and social behaviour. Sociologists, however, point to caste system as an organising principle of Indian society. It is seen to be providing the basic frame around which relationships across groups are organised. Legitimacy for the caste divisions is derived from Hinduism the great religion of the Indian continent. Sociologists, however, also point out that earlier social science understandings were derived from great Hindu texts that these act as the *guiding principles* for social behaviour. The contextual realities vary a great deal.

Social Hierarchy in Indian Society

India is a hierarchical society. Within Indian culture, whether in the north or the south, Hindu or Muslim, *urban* or village, virtually all things, people, and groups of people are ranked according to various essential qualities. If one is attuned to the theme of hierarchy in India, one can discern it everywhere. Although India is a political democracy, in daily life there is little advocacy of or adherence to notions of equality.

Castes and castelike groups—those quintessential groups with which almost all Indians are associated—are ranked. Within most villages or towns, everyone knows the relative rankings of each locally represented caste, and people's behaviour toward one another is constantly shaped by this knowledge. Between the extremes of the very high and very low castes, however, there is sometimes disagreement on the exact relative ranking of castes clustered in the middle.

Castes are primarily associated with Hinduism but also exist among other Indian religious groups. Muslims sometimes expressly deny that they have castes—they state that all Muslims are brothers under God—but observation of Muslim life in various parts of India reveals the existence of castelike groups and clear concern with social hierarchy. Among Indian Christians, too, differences in caste are acknowledged and maintained.

Throughout India, individuals are also ranked according to their wealth and power. For example, there are "big men" (*bare admi*) and "little men" (*chhote admi*) everywhere. "Big men" sit confidently on chairs, while "little men" come before them to make requests, either standing or crouching down on their haunches, certainly not presuming to sit beside a man of high status as an equal. Even men of nearly equal status who might share a string cot to sit on take their places carefully—the higher-ranking man at the head of the cot, the lower-ranking man at the foot.

Within families and kinship groupings, there are many distinctions of hierarchy. Men outrank women of the same or similar age, and senior relatives outrank junior relatives. Several other kinship relations involve formal respect. For example, in northern India, a daughter-in-law of a household shows deference to a daughter of a household. Even among young siblings in a household, there is constant acknowledgment of age differences: younger siblings never address an older sibling by name, but rather by respectful terms for elder brother or elder sister. However, an older sibling may address the younger by name.

Even in a business or academic setting, where colleagues may not openly espouse traditional observance of caste or class ranking behaviour, they may set up fictive kinship relations, addressing one another by kinship terms reflecting family or village-style hierarchy. For example, a younger colleague might respectfully address an older colleague as *chachaji* (respected father's younger brother), gracefully acknowledging the superior position of the older colleague.

Varna System

In the Indian social system, Varna is only a reference category and not a functioning unit of social structure, and only refers broadly to the ascribed status of different jatis. It is also a classificatory device. In it, several jatis with similar ascribed ritual status are clustered together and are hierarchically graded. The three upper levels—the Brahman, the Kshatriya, and the Vaishya—are considered twice-born, as in addition to biological birth they are born a second time after initiation rites. The Sudra, the fourth level, includes a multiplicity of artisans and occupationally-specialised jatis who pursue clean, i.e. non-polluting occupations. Though the Varna hierarchy ends here, but there is a fifth level which accommodates those following supposedly unclean occupations that are believed to be polluting. They are *Antyaja,* i.e., outside the Varna system. They constitute what are known as the Dalit.

Origin of the Varna

There are several passages in the oldest Vedic literature dealing with the origin of the varnas. The four orders of society are believed to have originated from the self-sacrifice of *Purusha*—the creator, the primeval being. *Purusha* is said to have destroyed himelf so that an appropriate social order could emerge. The oldest is the hymn in the *purusha-sakta* of the Rig-Veda which says that the Brahmana Varna represented the mouth of the purusha,-which word may be translated as the "the Universal Man", referring perhaps to mankind as a whole,—the Rajanya (i.e. Kshatriya) his arms, the Vaisya his thighs and the Sudra his feet.

But it has been shown that there are other passages, apart from the Purusha-Sukta, in which the division of society in to Varnas, though not in the rigid form of later times, is mentioned. Thus, in Rig-Veda, the three varnas, the Brahma, Kshatam, and Visah are mentioned; while in Rig-Veda, the four varnas are referred to thus: "One to high sway (i.e. Brahmana), one to exalted glory (i.e. the Kshatriya), one to pursue his gain (i.e. the Valsya) and one to his labour (i.e. the Sudra),- all to regard their different vocations, all moving creatures hath the Dawn awakened. Haug's opinion on the origin of the institution of caste seems to be correct. "It has been of late asserted" he observes, "that the original parts of the Vedas do not know the system of caste. But this conclusion was prematurely arrived at without sufficiently weighing the evidence. It is true that caste system is not to be found in such a developed state; the duties assigned to the several castes are not so clearly defined as in the law books and Puranas. But nevertheless the system is already known in the earlier parts of the Vedas, or rather presupposes. The barriers only were not as insurmountable as in later times.

S.C.Dube gives the Triguna theory of the origin of the Varna system i.e. the philosophic speculation of ancient India identified three *gunas*—inherent qualities—in human beings, animate and inanimate objects, and in human actions: *sattva, rajas,* and *tamas. Sattva* consisted of noble thoughts and deeds, goodness and virtue, truth and wisdom. *Rajas,* on the other hand, were characterised by high-living and luxury, passion and some indulgence, pride, and valour. At the bottom was *tamas,* with the attributes of coarseness and dullness, overindulgence without taste, the capacity to carry out heavy work without much imagination. Those with *sattvic* qualities were classified as Brahman, those with *rajasic* as Kshatriya and Vaishya, and those with *tamsic* qualities as Sudra. Another third theory takes account of ethnic admixture, culture contact, and functional specialisation. Any of these three components cannot singly explain the origin of the Varna. In the initial stage of the evolution of Hindu society-the Vedic stage-race and complexion were important factors, but in its fully evolved form it was only a make-believe phenomenon, not a biological reality. Aryanisation was the result of culture contact, but it was not a one-way process involving donor-recipient relations. The Vratya pre-Aryan traditions asserted themselves and in the process modified the Aryan scheme of social organisation, rituals, beliefs, world-view, and its ethos. Groups were incorporated *en masse* into the emerging social order, adopting some new features, retaining some old characteristics, and imparting their imprint on the wider society.

Reverting to the *Purusha-Sakta*, an allegorical meaning is by the whole *sakta* with reference to the *Purusha* and the creation of varnas from his limbs. The *Purusha* is described as being himself "this whole universe, whatever has been and whatever shall be" Further, we are also told that the moon sprang from his mind (*manas*), the Sun from his eyes, Indra and Agni were created out of his mouth, and air or wind from his breath. Again, from his navel arose the atmosphere (*antariksham*), from his head the sky, from his feet the earth (*bhumi*), and from his ear the four quarters (*disah)*; in this manner, the worlds were created.

There is a great deal of theorising in the Epic and the Dharma-Sastra literature on the problem of the origin and development of varnas; There were no distinct castes or classes of men in the *Krita* Yuga, according to the Mahabharata At another place, the sage Bhrigu says that only a few Brahmanas were first created by the great Brahman. But later on, the four divisions of mankind Brahmana, Kshatriya, Vaisya and Sudra developed. The complexion (*varnah*) of the Brahmanas was white (*sita*) that of Kshatriyas red (*lohitah*), that of the Viasyas yellow (*pitakah)*, and that of the Sudras black (*asitah)*—thus does the rishi Bhrigu explain his theory of the origin of the varnas to Bharadwaja.

At first the whole world consisted of **Brahmanas.** Created equally by Brahman, men have, on account of their acts, been divided into various varnas. The theory goes on to explain how the four varnas and other castes (*jatayah*) arose out of the one original class of Dvijas (twice-born). Those who found excessive pleasure in enjoyment became possessed of the attributes of harshness and anger; endowed with courage, and unmindful of their own dharma, (*tyakta-sva-dharmah*), those Dvijas possessing the quality of redness (*raktangah*), became Kshatriyas. Those again, who, unmindful of the duties laid down for them, became endued with both the qualities of Redness and Darkness *(pitah)* and followed the occupations of cattle breeding and agriculture, became Vaisyas. Those Dvijas, again, who were given to untruth and injuring other creatures, possessed of cupidity (*lubdhah*), who indiscriminately followed all sorts of occupations for their maintenance (*sarva-karmo'pa-jivinah*), who had no purity of behaviour (*saucha-paribhrashtah*), and who thus, nursed within them the quality of Darkness (*krishnah*) Became sudras. Thus "divided by there occupations, the Dvijas, (who were, in the first instance, all Brahmanas) due to falling away from the duties of their own order, became members of the other three varnas. None of them, therefore, is prohibited from carrying out all the activities of dharmas and yajnas. Further, those who, through their ignorance, fell away from their prescribed duties and led a loose life (svachchandacharacheshtitah), endied in reducing themselves to the various lower castes (jatayah), viz. the Pisaçhas (feinds), the Raksasas (globilins), the Pretas (the evil-spirited), and the various mlechchha (barbarian or outcast)jatis (castes).

The theory that the four varnas proceeded from the limbs of the creator is also held by Manu-Smriti. And, in order to protect this whole universe (*sarvasya)*, differential duties and occupations have been assigned to the different varnas (prithak-karmani) by him. Manu then goes on to eulogise the Brahmana varna as the supreme creation of God. He further positively asserts that the Brahmana, Kshatriya, Vaisya and sudra are the only varnas in existence; there is no fifth varna; and with this, Yajnavalkya, Baudhayana and Vasishtha also agree.

Manu's theory of the origin of mixed castes is, in certain respects, different from that of the Mahabharata. Sons begotten by twice-born men (dvijas, i.e. Brahmanas, Kshatriyas and Vaisyas) of wives from the immediate lower class belong no doubt to the varna of their fathers respectively but they are censured on account of the fauly inherent in their mothers (*matri-dosha*). Such is the traditional (*sanatana*) law (*vidhih)* applicable to children of a wife from a varna only one degree lower than her husband's. The real mixture of varnas (varnas-samkarah) therefore arises with offsprings born of a woman two or three degrees lower. Thus the son born of a Brahmana father and a Vaisya mother would be called an Ambashtha; that born of a Brahmana father and a sudra mother would be called Nishada, and so on. The mixture of varnas takes place in other ways also. Of a Kshatriya father and Brahmana mother spring issues belonging to the Suta caste; children born of a Vaisya father and Kshatriya mother or a Brahmana mother belong to Magadha and Videha castes respectively; and so on And, inter-marriages between these new castes give rise to newer and newer castes, so that the process goes on multiplying.

Duties of the Varna

The division into four Varnas is here correlated to the duties of each Varna. Their origin is a symbolic representation of the rank and functions of the four Varnas. In the cultural body-image the head, the arms, the thighs, and the feet are ranked in descending order, so are the traditional functions.

The *Purusha-Sukta* has been interpreted as having an allegorical significance behind it from another point of view. Thus, the mouth of the *Purusha* from which the Brahmanas are created is the seat of speech; the Brahmanas therefore are created to be teachers and instructors of mankind.

According to Manu, a Brahman should always and assiduously study the Veda alone and teach the Vedas. It is also the privilege of a Brahman to officiate as a priest and as a means of livelihood permitted to receive gifts from a worthy person of the three higher varnas. This is known as *pratigraha.*

The arms are symbol of valour and strength; the Kshatriya's mission in this world is to carry weapons and protect people. Thus, defence and war, administration and government were the functions assigned to the Kshatriya. It is difficult to interpret that portion of the hymn which deals with the creation of the Vaisyas from the thighs of the Purusha. But the thigh may have been intended to represent the lower portion of the body, the portion which consumes food, and therefore the Vaisya may be said to be created to provide food to the people. Trade, commerce and agriculture were the work of the Vaishya. The creation of the Sudra from the foot symbolises the fact that the Sudra is to be the "footman", the servant of other varnas. The Sudra ranked the lowest by serving others though crafts and labour.

The whole social organisation is here conceived symbolically as one human being-the "Body Social", we may say—with its limbs representing the social classes based on the principle of division of labour. The Mahabharata states the same thing thus: Our obeisance to That (*Purusha*) who consists of Brahmanas in the mouth, Kashtras in the arms, Vaishya in the entire regions, stomach and thighs, and Sudras in the feet.

Responsibilities and Status

In the above mentioned fourfold classification of duties according to Dharmashastras, there was an ascending order of responsibilities. While Brahmin was given the highest position he was also entrusted with maximum responsibilities. The entire task of preserving Dharma was mainly the responsibility of the Brahmin. The next social status in Varna hierarchy was given to the Kshatriya as he had the responsibility of defending the nation in times of war and administering law and order in the society. He provided social justice with the help of the Brahmin scholar. The Vaishyas and Sudras had lesser responsibilities and therefore were assigned lower status. The Sudra gradually came to be so much looked down upon that he could not touch a Brahmin. The Sudra could not be initiated into the Vedic study and the only ashram out of the four that he was entitled to, was that of the householder.

Characteristics of Caste System

Caste may be defined as a hereditary endogamous group which decides the individual's status in the social stratification and his profession. Caste is also defined as an aggregate of persons whose share of obligations and privileges is fixed by birth, sanctioned and supported by magic and or religion. Ketkar defines caste as a social group having two characteristics-memberships confirmed to those who are born of members and includes all persons so born and the members are forbidden by an inexorable social law to marry outside the group. According to Cooley when a class is somewhat strictly hereditary, we may call it caste. When status is wholly predetermined, so that men are born to their lot in life without any hope of changing it, then class takes the form of caste.

According to G.S. Ghurye, caste in India is a Brahminic child of the Indo-Aryan culture, cradled in the land of the Ganges country. Abbe Dubbois first propounded the political theory of the origin of Caste in India. However, the complex social structure based upon castes appears impossible that the aim of caste system would have been to maintain the dominance of the Brahmin priests over Hindu society according to Majumdar.

The traditional theory attributes the origin of the caste system to the creator Brahma who created the four varnas. According to Hutton, the caste system originated in the religious customs and rituals of the non-Aryan group particularly the theory of Manu. The traditions of endogamy, untouchability etc. has their roots in Manu. According to Majumdar, caste system was developed to save Aryan Race and culture from intermixing with other races.

There are various characteristics which determine the caste of a person. These are given below:

1. *Determination by birth*: The membership of a caste is determined by birth. A person remains the member of a caste unto which they are born and this does not undergo change even if change takes place in his status, occupation, education, wealth, etc.

2. *Rules and regulations concerning food:* Each individual caste has its own laws which govern the food habits of its members. Generally, there are no restrictions against fruit, milk, butter, dry fruit, etc. but kachcha food (bread, etc.) can be accepted only from a member of one's own or of a higher caste.

3. *Definite occupation*: In the Hindu scriptures there are mention of the occupations of all varnas. According to Manu, the functions of the Brahmins, Kshatriyas, Vaishyas and the Sudras are definite. The function of the Brahmins is to study the Vedas, teach, guide and perform religious rituals, to give and receive alms. Sudras have to do menial work for all the other varnas.

Having developed from the varna system, the occupations in caste system are definite.

4. *Endogamous group*: The majority of persons marry only within their own caste. Brahmins, Kshatriyas, Sudras and Vaishyas all marry within their respective castes. Westermarck has considered this to be a chief characteristic of the caste system. Hindu community does not sanctify inter-caste marriage even now.

5. *Rules concerning status and touchability*: The various castes in the Hindu social organisation are divided into a hierarchy of ascent and descent one above the other. In this hierarchy the Brahmins have the highest and the untouchables the lowest place. This sense of superiority is much exaggerated and manifests in the south. The very touch and sometimes even the shadow of a member of the lower caste is enough to defile an individual of a high caste. In Kerala, a Namboodari Brahmin is defiled by the touch of a Nayar, but in the case of a member of a Tiyyar caste a distance of 36 feet must be kept to avoid being defiled and in the case of a member of the Pulayana caste the distance must be ninety six feet. The stringent observation of the system of untouchability has resulted in some low castes of the Hindu society being called 'untouchables' who were, consequently, forbidden to make use of places of worship, cremation grounds, educational institutions, public roads and hotels etc., and were disallowed from living in the cities.

Mobility of the Varnas

There seems to be a constant upward and downward social mobility between the different Varnas. Yajnavalkya speaks of two kinds of such mobility. When a lower Varna changed into a higher varna, it was known as *jatyutkarsa* or uplift of the caste. On the other hand, if a person belonging to a higher varna gradually descended into a lower Varna, it was known as *jatyapakarsa* or the degeneration of the caste. Provisions for both these processes of social mobility in stratification were laid by different Dharmasastras with minor distinctions about the conditions. It was particularly based upon two conditions, firstly, upon the following of the vocation of some other Varna for five to six generations and secondly, marrying into different Varnas for as much period. It may be easily guessed that in practice such mobility happened only in exception, since the process had to be covered for several generations, but it is clear that the Dharmasastras did prescribe change of Varnas by means of interaction between the Varnas both upwards and downwards. This can be through marriage and education.

While varna dharma had to be followed in normal circumstances, in abnormal circumstances the Dharmasastras prescribe what is known as *Apad* Dharma or that which is worthy of following in exceptional circumstances. Manu enumerate ten means of maintaining oneself in *apad* (distress) *viz*, learning, arts and crafts, work for wages, service i.e., carrying out another's orders, rearing cattle, sale of commodities, agriculture, contentment, alms, money-lending. Out of these some cannot be followed by Brahmin or a Kshatriya when there is no distress.

The Dharmasastras maintained that Brahmins doing certain things are to be treated as Sudras. Without studying the Veda but works hard to master something else is quickly reduced to the status of a Sudra together with his family. Thus, *Apad* Dharma does not mean the license to do whatever one likes to do in the times of trouble. There are numerous cases of so many notable persons who refused to change their allotted duties even in the face of extremely adverse circumstance. Again, even when such a change was permitted, it was always looked down and never appreciated.

Caste Structure and Kinship

Caste structure is intimately related to the kinship system amongst the Hindus in India. The sole reason for this relationship lies in the endogamous nature of caste system. Caste is basically a closed system of stratification, since members are recruited on the criteria of ascribed status. In other words, an individual becomes a member of a caste in which he or she is born. Thus it is an ascribed status. Even if there is social mobility in the caste system through the process of Sankritisation, urbanisations, etc it is only a positional change rather than a structural change.

A person remains the member of his/her caste irrespective of his/her individual status. Any movement in the structure occurs in the social mobility of the caste group in the local hierarchy of the society, which is only a shifting of its position from one level to another.

Kinship is a method or a system by which individuals as members of society relate themselves with other individuals of that society. There are two types of kinship bonds. One is consanguinal and the other is affinal. Consanguinal ties are ties of blood such as, between mother-daughter, mother-son, father-daughter, etc. Affinal ties are ties through marriage, such as, between husband-wife, husband-wife's brother, etc.

Kinship in India is largely an analysis of the internal structure of the sub-caste. Sub-caste is the largest segment of a caste and it performs nearly all the functions of caste like endogamy, social control, etc. For example, the Brahmin caste has several sub-castes like endogamy, social control, etc. For example, the Brahmin caste has several sub-castes like the Gaur Brahmins, the Kanyakubjis, the Saraswat Brahmins, etc. It is these segments of the main caste of Brahmins which form the effective functioning group within which social interaction, marriage etc. takes place. However, these segments are also subdivided and have a regional connotation too, like the Sarjupari Brahmins of North India are those who originally lived beyond the river Saryu or Ghaghara.

The effective caste group is the caste population of a single village while the effective sub caste group within which marriage and kinship takes place is composed of the people belonging to the region around the village having several scores of settlements. Due to the practice of endogamy and restriction in social intercourse a person marries within the sub-caste group, or at the most caste group in India; which extends generally, beyond the village to a larger region.

Kinship system found in various parts of India differs from each other in many respects. However, generally speaking, we can distinguish between the kinship system in the Northern region, the Central region and the southern region.

North India is in it self a very large region, having innumerable types of kinship systems. This region includes the region between the Himalayas in the North and the Vindhyas in the South. In this region a person marries outside the village since all the members of one's caste in a village are considered to be brothers and sisters, or uncles and aunts. Marriage with a person inside the village is forbidden. In fact, an exogamous circle with a radius of four miles can be drawn round a man's village.

Hypergamy is practiced in this region according to which a man takes a wife from a clan, which is lower in status to his own clan. That is, a girl goes in marriage from a lower status group to a higher status group within a sub-caste. The effect of the hypergamy and village exogamy is that it spatially widens the range of ties. Several villages become linked to each other through affinal and matrilateral links. In his study of the Ramkheri village in Madhya Pradesh, Adrian Mayer not only described the Rajput caste and other sub-castes of the village but also the regions around it as well.

The clans, lineages, and kutumbs are all part of the internal structure of the caste at the same time being part of the kinship organisation. These groups are all the time increasing and branching off with time.

The organisation of family in the northern region is mainly patriarchal patrilineal and patrilocal. The lineage is traced through the male, i.e., patrilineal system is followed in this region. It is patriarchal because authority lies with the male head of the family and it is patrilocal because after marriage the bride is brought to reside in the father's house of the bride-groom.

Generally, in most of the castes in the north such as the Jats, an agricultural caste of South Punjab, Delhi and Haryana the "four-clan" rule of marriage is followed. According to this rule,

1. A man cannot marry in the clan to which his father (and he himself) belongs:
2. To which his mother belongs;
3. To which his father's mother belongs; and
4. To which his mother's mother belongs

In the northern region, therefore, marriage with cousins, removed even by two or three degrees is viewed as an incestuous union. In most parts of the region, as mentioned earlier, village exogamy is practiced by most of the castes, especially the Brahmin, kshatriya and Vaishya castes. This rule is known in Delhi, Haryana and Punjab, as the rule of Sassan.

In Central India which includes Rajputana the Vindhyas, Gujrat, Maharashr and Orrissa we find the general practice of caste endogamy. Hypergmy is most characteristic of the Rajputs of this region and village exogamy is also found in this region. However, in this region especially in Gujarat and Maharashtra amongst some caste communities we find cross-cousin marriages being practised. Here there is a tendency for a man to marry his mother's brother's daughter. But marriage with the father's sister's daughter is taboo. The preference for a single type of cross-cousin marriage seems to move away from the taboo of marrying cousins of any class in the northern region. Thus, in many ways this preference suggests a closer contact with the practices of the southern region.

The southern region comprises states like Karnatak, Andhra Pradesh, Tamil Nadu and Kerala where the Dravidian languages are spoken. This region is distinct from the northern and central regions of India in the sense that here we find basically preferential rules of marriage. Here a man knows whom he has to marry while in most areas in the north a man knows whom he cannot marry.

Most of the parts of the Southern region except some, like the Malabar, follow the patrilineal family system. Here also we find exogamous social groups called *gotras*. The difference between the exogamous clans in the north is that a caste in a village is held to be of one patriclan and therefore, no marriage is allowed within a village.

Sometimes even a group of villages are supposed to be settled by one patrilineage and marriage between them is prohibited.

In the South, there is no identification of a *gotra* with one village or territory. More than one inter-marrying clans may live in one village territory and practice inter-marriage for generations. Thus the social groups; which are formed due to this kind of marriage pattern in the South shows a centripetal tendency (of moving towards a centre) as against the centrifugal (of moving away from the centre) tendency of social groups found in north Indian villages. In the South, a caste is divided in to a number of *gotras*. The first marriage creates obligations about giving and receiving daughters. Hence, within exogamous clans, small endogamous circles are found to meet inter-family obligations and a number of reciprocal alliances are found in South Indian villages.

Apart from castes, which are patrilineal in the southern region, we also find some castes, such as the Nayars of Malabar district who follow matrilineal system of kinship. Their household is made up of a woman, her sisters and brothers, her daughters and sons and her daughter's daughters and sons. Amongst them, property passes from the mother to the daughter. But the authority even in this system lies with the brother, who manages the property and takes care of his sister's children; Husbands only visit their-wives in this system. The Nayar matrilineal house is called a *Tharavad*. Nayar is a broad category of castes of which not all of them follow the same kinship system.

The relationship between the caste structure and the kinship system is so inter-twined that we cannot understand one without understanding the details of the other. In this section we have explained the regional variations found in the relationship between the caste structure and related kinship pattern.

Sub-Caste

A sub-caste is considered a smaller unit within a caste. In the village setting usually we find that there is only one sub-caste living there. A larger number of sub-castes indicate the late arrivals to a village. Thus for all practical purposes a sub-caste represents the caste in the village. In the wider setting of a region, however, we find many sub-castes. One example from Maharastra is of Kumbhar (potters). The subcaste is the smallest endogamous groups and it has some mechanisms like *panchayats* to regulate the behaviour of members in the traditional setting. In a village, the difference between caste and sub-caste does not come to the surface but in a region, the difference is visible.

Four Stages of Life

It is the *dharma* of a Hindu to pass through four different *ashram* (stages) in their life. The first Ashram is called *brahmacharya ashram* (the educational stage) from which the fourth Varna, Sudra and women of the first three varna are barred. It ends at marriage. The second stage of life is called the *grihasthashram*. During this a man rears a family, earns a living and performs his daily personal and social duties. After this a man gradually enters the third stage of life called the *vanaprashthashram*. During this stage the householder relinquishes his duties in the household, and devotes his time to religious pursuits. His links with his family are weakened. During this ashram a man retires into the forest with or without his wife leaving behind the householder's cares and duties. The final phase of Hindu's life begins with the stage known as the *sanyasashram*. In this stage one attempt to totally withdraw oneself from the world and its cares by going to the forest and spending the rest of life in pursuit of *moksha*. Like the Varna system, the *varnashram* is a model that is not compulsory but recommended.

Purushartha

The Hindu scriptures declare four goals in human life and they are called the *purushartha*. The term *purushartha* not only denotes what the objectives of life should be but it also means what the objectives of life are as the result of the psychological tendencies of the individual. The *purushartha* consists of dharma, *Artha, Kama* and *Moksha* in the same order.

First, every human being needs to obey the law of nature by strictly following dharma. Dharma is the stability of the society, the maintenance of social order, and the general welfare of mankind. And whatever conduces to the fulfilment of this purpose is called 'dharma'.

Artha is the acquisition of wealth, is regarded as the primary purpose of life, as without it, human existence is impossible. One has to live before one can live well. *Artha* is the foundation upon which the whole structure of life has been built and all the other purushrthas can be achieved only by the fulfilment of this primary purpose in life. The acquisition of wealth is through dharmic actions and wealth needs to be used in the preservation of dharma.

Kama means desires, desires of varying degrees. It is from dharma that artha and kama result. Man recognises here that *artha* and *kama* satisfy the psychological tendencies of man and they form essentially the two fundamental aspirations of every individual. It is implied what one desires need to be within the threshold of one's wealth and within dharmic values!

Now the word *moksha* means the ultimate freedom from birth and death or the deliverance of the soul from bondage. From the *advaitic* point of view, *moksha* results from the extinction of false knowledge (ignorance). The self-knowledge is the aim and end of man's misery and bondage.

In support of the realisation of self, the Upanishads outline several additional explanations. The universe has the natural tendency to guide the realisation by the human soul. The natural forces of the universe maintain the balance between the material objects, living plants, conscious animals, and intelligent human beings. The transition from human consciousness into divine (transcendental) consciousness is a long and laborious process. Ordinarily, within the span of a single lifetime, it is not feasible to transit from human to divine. Life is a continuous journey, carried over and continued through the succeeding lives till the attainment of SELF realisation.

According to Hindu *sastra-karas* (i,e,. those who have written the *sastrasm* the scientific treatises) have taken man into influence his life and its conduct: He is considered in relation to : (i) *dela,* (place, region) which may be said to be the regional approach to the study of society; (ii) *kala* (time) which, we may say, constitutes the historical approach to the study of society, (iii) *srama* (effort) which takes in to account man with reference to his nurture and development in the contemporary environment; and (iv) *guna* (natural traits), which refers to the natural inherent psycho-biological equipment of man.

In sharp contrast with such attitude, the Hindu, in his *sastric* discussions of social life and practices, first raises the fundamental question of the significance of man's existence on earth, gives consideration to basic questions of the relation between man and the possible ultimate purpose and fulfilment of his existence, and, upon such bases, seeks to define and formulate his relations with every other thing, person, event and circumstance in the world.

Thus, for the Hindu, the individual's relations with the ultimate principle of the Universal or Primal Cause defines his relations with other men, with his family, with the group or society in which he lives or with which he comes in contact, with his village and his country; and, indeed, with the entire animate and inanimate creation. The whole of the life of an individual is, for the Hindu, a kind of schooling and self-discipline. Now, during the course of this schooling and self discipline, he has to pass through four stages, four grades of training, as it were called the *Ashrams.* And, in regard to the *Ashrams*, too, every item and stage and phase has to be defined in terms of the already defined relations between man and God. Here, therefore, practically we start with supernatural basis; upon this we erect the superstructure of man's earthly career. The earthly existence has thus to be defined primarily in terms of dharma; and dharma has to be interpreted in the concrete in terms of karma. The *ashram* scheme, therefore, defines our dharma in and through a life of worldliness, of *samsara,* before it, and beyond its pale; and, in practice it seeks to delineate the implications of dharma in terms of karma. This scheme of transition from one stage to another is prescribed for men of upper castes only, women are supposed to help and support their husbands in proper fulfillment of these goals.

In order to understand the psycho-moral basis of the *ashrams* proper, it is advisable that we should look in to the theory of the *purushartha* which concern themselves with the understanding, justification, management and conduct of affairs of the individual's *purushartha* are four, viz, *dharma, artha, kama* and *moksa*. We speak of this life in relation to the group, in and through the *asramas*. The *purushartha* as the 'psycho-moral' bases of the *asrama* theory, because, on the one hand, the individual receives a psychological training through the *asramas* in terms of lessons in the use and management of the *purushartha;* while, on the other hand, in actual practice, he has to deal with the society in accordance with these lessons. It is in the light of the understanding of the meaning and place of the *purushartha* in the asrama scheme that we shall be able to comprehend the right method, way and outlook for the management of each of the asramas.

It is usual to translate these terms dharma, artha, kama and moksa in English by such words as morality, wealth, desires or passion, and salvation respectively. But the Sanskrit terms are potent with deeper meanings than these English words singly convey. Thus, the word dharma is derived from the Sanskrit root *dhri* meaning 'to hold together, to preserve.' The social implications and meaning of dharma as a principle for maintaining the stability of society is brought out by God Sri Krishna in three verses in the Mahabharata: In advising Arjuna as to what is dharma he explains that " dharma is created for the well-being of all creation", and further that "all that is free from doing harm to any created being is certainly dharma; for, indeed, dharma is created to keep all creation free from any harm" Sri Krisna proceeds, next, to give a still more comprehensive view of dharma: " Dharma is so called because it protects (dharanat) all; dharma preserves all that is created. Dharma, then, is surely that principle which is capable of preserving the universe". *Artha,* on the other hand, is to be understood as referring to all the means necessary for acquiring worldly properity, such as wealth or power. And k*ama* refers to all the desires in man for enjoyment and satisfaction of the life of the senses, including the sex drive to which the word *kama* more prominently refers. The term refers to the native impulses, instincts and desires of man, his natural mental tendencies, and finds its equivalent, we may say, in the use of the English terms "desires", "needs", "basic or primary motives", "urges", or "drives" and the collective use of the term *kama* would refer to the totality of the innate desires and drives of man. The term is also often used in a broader sense to include socially acquired motivation too. Dharma, *artha* and *kama,* therefore, refer respectively to the moral, material and mental resourees, accessories and energies available to man.

Of these three, *artha* and *kama* refer to two of man's earthly belongings, while dharma stands on a higher level. At its lowest level of manifestation, *kama* is understood in the sense of pure sex drive, and is said to be one of the six "enemies" of human being.

But it is equally true that a human being cannot conduct his life without *artha* which constitutes the material means of living, and *kama* which helps the propagation of the species. Therefore, it is needed that the correct quality and quantity, the place, and the time of *artha* and *kama*, have to be determined and laid down by the wise sages. This is done in terms of dharma, which defines, for man, the proper quantum, place and season, for the right functioning of *artha* and *kama.* By attending to his dharma, therefore, a person is able to live a proper life even though it may be lived in terms of artha and kama.

In the opinion of Manu, the good of humanity lies in a harmonious management or co-ordination of the three (*trivarga*), viz, *dharma, artha* and *kama.* Says he: "some declare that the good of man consists in dharma, and *artha*; others opine that it is to be found in *kama* and *artha;* some say that dharma alone will give it; while the rest assert that *artha* alone is the chief good of man here below (on earth). But the correct position is that the good of man consists in the harmonious co-ordination of the three".

Now, *artha* and *kama* have to be practised by the individual with reference to one or more other individuals. So also, the practice of dharma cannot be possibly conceived as existing apart from the relation between he individual and the group, except when the dharma directed is entirely in the interest of the *moksha* of the individual, as in the case of the *samnyasin* (the recluse), in whose case *artha* and *kama* become transformed and get merged in to *moksha.* Thus, on the whole, the *purusharthas* are concerned both with the individual as well as the group. They enunciate and justify the kinds of relation between the individual and the group; they define the just relations between activities of the individual and those of the group; they also state explicitly and by implication, the improper relations between the individual and the group with a view to enabling the individual to avoid them. Thus, the *purushartha* control both the individual and the group, and also their-relations.

Here, it is to be remembered that when we refer to *artha* and *kama* as *purusharthas*, we refer to them in their proper proportions, that is to say, only in the best sense of these words. *Artha* refers to the problem and activities connected with the finding, making, gathering, conserving and organising of the material necessities of life and all that accompanies the same. Similarly, *kama* refers to the sex and the reproductive aspect, its understanding, its right functions, its functioning, its organisation and management both with reference to the individual and the group. As we have pointed out above, *Kama* in the wider sense refers to all the innate desires and urges of man. Dharma seems to be the arbiter, the conscience keeper, the director, the interpreter, of the properties that govern the right functioning and management of the relations between the inner man and the outer man and between the individual anJ the group. Dharma is, therefore, the holder of the balance in terms of which *artha* and *kama* have to be dealt with weighed, practiced and apportioned. *Moksha,* on the other hand, seems to be concerned mainly with the individual. It refers, perhaps, to the appeal of the inner man to the individual, unaffected by the group. It is perhaps too personal an outlook that defines the struggle and hope and justification within the individual for *moksha*. But, from the Hindu's point of view, we must also remember, that the inner personality of the individual, at its best, is identified by him not only with the group, nor only with the society, nor with the nation, nor the race, nor even with he entire human race, but with the whole creation, animate and inanimate, seen and unseen, which includes all these and is still much more than all these. In the light of these considerations, the goal of *moksha* does not possess the narrow individual outlook, for the Hindu nor is it to be pursued exclusively and directly by an individual unless and until he has duly satisfied all his social debts (*rinah*) or obligations.

Purity and Pollution

Many status differences in Indian society are expressed in terms of ritual purity and pollution. Notions of purity and pollution are extremely complex and vary greatly among different castes, religious groups, and regions. However, broadly speaking, high status is associated with purity and low status with pollution. Some kinds of purity are inherent, or inborn; for example, gold is purer than copper by its very nature, and, similarly, a member of a high-ranking Brahman, or priestly, caste is born with more inherent purity than a member of a low-ranking Sweeper caste. Unless the Brahman defiles himself in some extraordinary way, throughout his life he will always be purer than a Sweeper. Other kinds of purity are more transitory—a Brahman who has just taken a bath is more ritually pure than a Brahman who has not bathed for a day. This situation could easily reverse itself temporarily, depending on bath schedules, participation in polluting activities, or contact with temporarily polluting substances.

Purity is associated with ritual cleanliness—daily bathing in flowing water, dressing in properly laundered clothes of approved materials, eating only the foods appropriate for one's caste, refraining from physical contact with people of lower rank, and avoiding involvement with ritually impure substances. The latter include body wastes and excretions, most especially those of another adult person. Contact with the products of death or violence are typically polluting and threatening to ritual purity.

During her menstrual period, a woman is considered polluted and refrains from cooking, worshiping, or touching anyone older than an infant. In much of the south, a woman spends this time "sitting outside," resting in an isolated room or shed. During her period, a Muslim woman does not touch the Quran. At the end of the period, purity is restored with a complete bath. Pollution also attaches to birth, both for the mother and the infant's close kin, and to death, for close relatives of the deceased.

Members of the highest priestly castes, the Brahmans, are generally vegetarians (although some Bengali and Maharashtrian Brahmans eat fish) and avoid eating meat, the product of violence and death. High-ranking Warrior castes (Kshatriyas), however, typically consume nonvegetarian diets, considered appropriate for their traditions of valour and physical strength.

A Brahman born of proper Brahman parents retains his inherent purity if he bathes and dresses himself properly, adheres to a vegetarian diet, eats meals prepared only by persons of appropriate rank, and keeps his person away from the bodily exuviae of others (except for necessary contact with the secretions of family infants and small children).

If a Brahman happens to come into bodily contact with a polluting substance, he can remove this pollution by bathing and changing his clothing. However, if he were to eat meat or commit other transgressions of the rigid dietary codes of his particular caste, he would be considered more deeply polluted and would have to undergo various purifying rites and payment of fines imposed by his caste council in order to restore his inherent purity.

In sharp contrast to the purity of a Brahman, a Sweeper born of Sweeper parents is considered to be born inherently polluted. The touch of his body is polluting to those higher on the caste hierarchy than he, and they will shrink from his touch, whether or not he has bathed recently. Sweepers are associated with the traditional occupation of cleaning human faeces from latrines and sweeping public lanes of all kinds of dirt. Traditionally, Sweepers remove these polluting materials in baskets carried atop the head and dumped out in a garbage pile at the edge of the village or neighbourhood. The involvement of Sweepers with such filth accords with their low-status position at the bottom of the Hindu caste hierarchy, even as their services allow high-status people, such as Brahmans, to maintain their ritual purity.

Members of the Leather-worker (Chamar) caste are ascribed a very low status consonant with their association with the caste occupation of skinning dead animals and tanning the leather. Butchers (Khatiks, in Hindi), who kill and cut up the bodies of animals, also rank low on the caste hierarchy because of their association with violence and death.

However, castes associated with ruling and warfare—and the killing and deaths of human beings—are typically accorded high rank on the caste hierarchy. In these instances, political power and wealth outrank association with violence as the key determinant of caste rank.

Maintenance of purity is associated with the intake of food and drink, not only in terms of the nature of the food itself, but also in terms of who has prepared it or touched it. This requirement is especially true for Hindus, but other religious groups hold to these principles to varying degrees. Generally, a person risks pollution—and lowering his own status—if he accepts beverages or cooked foods from the hands of people of lower caste status than his own. His status will remain intact if he accepts food or beverages from people of higher caste rank. Usually, for an observant Hindu of any but the very lowest castes to accept cooked food from a Muslim or Christian is regarded as highly polluting.

In a clear example of pollution associated with dining, a Brahman who consumed a drink of water and a meal of wheat bread with boiled vegetables from the hands of a Sweeper would immediately become polluted and could expect social rejection by his caste fellows. From that moment, fellow Brahmans following traditional pollution rules would refuse food touched by him and would abstain from the usual social interaction with him. He would not be welcome inside Brahman homes—most especially in the ritually pure kitchens—nor would he or his close relatives be considered eligible marriage partners for other Brahmans.

Generally, the acceptance of water and ordinary foods cooked in water from members of lower-ranking castes incurs the greatest pollution. In North India, such foods are known as *kaccha khana*, as contrasted with fine foods cooked in butter or oils, which are known as *pakka khana*. Fine foods can be accepted from members of a few castes slightly lower than one's own. Local hierarchies differ on the specific details of these rules.

Completely raw foods, such as uncooked grains, fresh unpeeled bananas, mangoes, and uncooked vegetables can be accepted by anyone from anyone else, regardless of relative status. Toasted or parched foods, such as roasted peanuts, can also be accepted from anyone without ritual or social repercussions. Thus, a Brahman may accept gifts of grain from lower-caste patrons for eventual preparation by members of his own caste, or he may purchase and consume roasted peanuts or tangerines from street vendors of unknown caste without worry.

Water served from an earthen pot may be accepted only from the hands of someone of higher or equal caste ranking, but water served from a brass pot may be accepted even from someone slightly lower on the caste scale. Exceptions to this rule are members of the Waterbearer (Bhoi, in Hindi) caste, who are employed to carry water from wells to the homes of the prosperous and from whose hands members of all castes may drink water without becoming polluted, even though Waterbearers are not ranked high on the caste scale.

These and a great many other traditional rules pertaining to purity and pollution constantly impinge upon interaction between people of different castes and ranks in

India. Although to the non-Indian these rules may seem irrational and bizarre, to most of the people of India they are a ubiquitous and accepted part of life. Thinking about and following purity and pollution rules make it necessary for people to be constantly aware of differences in status. With every drink of water, with every meal, and with every contact with another person, people must ratify the social hierarchy of which they are a part and within which their every act is carried out. The fact that expressions of social status are intricately bound up with events that happen to everyone every day—eating, drinking, bathing, touching, talking—and that transgressions of these rules, whether deliberate or accidental, are seen as having immediately polluting effects on the person of the transgressor, means that every ordinary act of human life serves as a constant reminder of the importance of hierarchy in Indian society.

There are many Indians, particularly among the educated urban elite, who do not follow traditional purity and pollution practices. Dining in each others' homes and in restaurants is common among well-educated people of diverse backgrounds, particularly when they belong to the same economic class. For these people, guarding the family's earthen water pot from inadvertent touch by a low-ranking servant is not the concern it is for a more traditional villager. However, even among those people whose words and actions denigrate traditional purity rules, there is often a reluctance to completely abolish consciousness of purity and pollution from their thinking. It is surely rare for a Sweeper, however well-educated, to invite a Brahman to dinner in his home and have his invitation unself-consciously accepted. It is less rare, however, for educated urban colleagues of vastly different caste and religious heritage to enjoy a cup of tea together. Some high-caste liberals pride themselves on being free of "casteism" and seek to accept food from the hands of very low-caste people, or even deliberately set out to marry someone from a significantly lower caste or a different religion. Thus, even as they deny it, these progressives affirm the continuing significance of tràditional rules of purity, pollution, and hierarchy in Indian society.

Social Interdependence

One of the great themes pervading Indian life is social interdependence. People are born into groups—families, clans, subcastes, castes, and religious communities—and live with a constant sense of being part of and inseparable from these groups. A corollary is the notion that everything a person does properly involves interaction with other people. A person's greatest dread, perhaps, is the possibility of being left alone, without social support, to face the necessary challenges of life. This sense of interdependence is extended into the theological realm: the very shape of a person's life is seen as being greatly influenced by divine beings with whom an ongoing relationship must be maintained.

Social interaction is regarded as being of the highest priority, and social bonds are expected to be long lasting. Even economic activities that might in Western culture involve impersonal interactions are in India deeply imbedded in a social nexus. All social interaction involves constant attention to hierarchy,. respect, honor, the feelings of others, rights and obligations, hospitality, and gifts of food, clothing, and other desirable items. Finely tuned rules of etiquette help facilitate each individual's many social relationships.

Western visitors to India are sometimes startled to find that important government and business officials have left their posts—often for many days at a time—to attend a cousin's wedding or participate in religious activities in a distant part of the country. "He is out of station and will be back in a week or two," the absent official's office-mates blandly explain to the frustrated visitor. What is going on is not laziness or hedonistic recreation, but is the official's proper recognition of his need to continually maintain his social ties with relatives, caste fellows, other associates, and God. Without being enmeshed in such ties throughout life, a person cannot hope to maintain long-term efficacy in either economic or social endeavour. Social bonds with relatives must be reinforced at family events or at rites crucial to the religious community. If this is not done, people who could offer vital support in many phases of life would be alienated.

In every activity, there is an assumption that social ties can help a person and that their absence can bring failure. Seldom do people carry out even the simplest task on their own. From birth onward, a child learns that his "fate" has been "written" by divine forces and that his life will be shaped by a plan decided by more powerful beings. When a small child eats, his mother puts the mouthfuls of food into his mouth with her own hand. When a boy climbs a tree to pluck mangoes, another stands below with a basket to receive them. When a girl fetches water from the well in pots on her head, someone at her home helps her unload the pots. When a farmer stacks sheaves of grain onto his bullock cart, he stands atop the cart, catching the sheaves tossed up to him by his son.

A student applying to a college hopes that he has an influential relative or family friend who can put in a good word for him with the director of admissions. At the age of marriage, a young person expects that parents will take care of finding the appropriate bride or groom and arranging all the formalities. At the birth of a child, the new mother is assured that the child's kin will help her attend to the infant's needs. A businessman seeking to arrange a contract relies not only on his own abilities but also on the assistance of well-connected friends and relatives to help finalise the deal. And finally, when facing death, a person is confident that offspring and other relatives will carry out the appropriate funeral rites, including a commemorative feast when, through gifts of clothing and food, continuing social ties are reaffirmed by all in attendance.

2

Religious Communities in India

It is impossible to kno4w India without understanding its religious beliefs and practices, which have a large impact on the personal lives of most Indians and influence public life on a daily basis. Indian religions have deep historical roots that are recollected by contemporary Indians. The ancient culture of South Asia, going back at least 4,500 years, has come down to India primarily in the form of religious texts. The artistic heritage, as well as intellectual and philosophical contributions, has always owed much to religious thought and symbolism. Contacts between India and other cultures have led to the spread of Indian religions throughout the world, resulting in the extensive influence of Indian thought and practice on Southeast and East Asia in ancient times and, more recently, in the diffusion of Indian religions to Europe and North America. Within India, on a day-to-day basis, the vast majority of people engage in ritual actions that are motivated by religious systems that owe much to the past but are continuously evolving. Religion, then, is one of the most important facets of Indian history and contemporary life.

A number of world religions originated in India, and others that started elsewhere found fertile ground for growth there. Devotees of Hinduism, a varied grouping of philosophical and devotional traditions, officially numbered

687.6 million people, or 82 percent of the population in the 1991 census. Buddhism and Jainism, ancient monastic traditions, have had a major influence on Indian art, philosophy, and society and remain important minority religions in the late twentieth century. Buddhists represented 0.8 percent of the total population while Jains represented 0.4 percent in 1991.

Islam spread from the West throughout South Asia, from the early eighth century, to become the largest minority religion in India. In fact, with 101.5 million Muslims (12.1 percent of the population), India has at least the fourth largest Muslim population in the world (after Indonesia with 174.3 million, Pakistan with 124 million, and Bangladesh with 103 million; some analysts put the number of Indian Muslims even higher—128 million in 1994, which would give India the second largest Muslim population in the world).

Sikhism, which started in Punjab in the sixteenth century, has spread throughout India and the world since the mid-nineteenth century. With nearly 16.3 million adherents, Sikhs represent 1.9 percent of India's population.

Christianity, represented by almost all denominations, traces its history in India back to the time of the apostles and counted 19.6 million members in India in 1991. Judaism and Zoroastrianism, arriving originally with traders and exiles from the West, are represented by small populations, mostly concentrated on India's west coast. A variety of independent tribal religious groups also are lively carriers of unique ethnic traditions.

The listing of the major belief systems only scratches the surface of the remarkable diversity in Indian religious life. The complex doctrines and institutions of the great traditions, preserved through written documents, are divided into numerous schools of thought, sects, and paths of devotion. In many cases, these divisions stem from the teachings of great masters, who arise continually to lead bands of followers with a new revelation or path to salvation. In contemporary India, the migration of large numbers of people to urban centers and the impact of modernisation have led to the emergence of new religions, revivals, and reforms within the great traditions that create original bodies of teaching and kinds of practice. In other cases, diversity appears through the integration or acculturation of entire social groups—each with its own vision of the divine—within the world of village farming communities that base their culture on literary and ritual traditions preserved in Sanskrit or in regional languages. The local interaction between great traditions and local forms of worship and belief, based on village, caste, tribal, and linguistic differences, creates a range of ritual forms and mythology that varies widely throughout the country. Within this range of differences, Indian religions have demonstrated for many centuries a considerable degree of tolerance for alternate visions of the divine and of salvation.

Religious tolerance in India finds expression in the definition of the nation as a secular state, within which the government since independence has officially remained separate from any one religion, allowing all forms of belief equal status before the law. In practice it has proven difficult to divide religious affiliation from public life. In states where the majority of the population embrace one religion, the boundary between government and religion becomes permeable; in Tamil Nadu, for example, the state government manages Hindu temples, while in Punjab an avowedly Sikh political party usually controls the state assembly. One of the most notable features of Indian politics, particularly since the 1960s, has been the steady growth of militant ideologies that see in only one religious tradition the way toward salvation and demand that public institutions conform to their interpretations of scripture. The vitality of religious fundamentalism and its impact on public life in the form of riots and religion-based political parties have been among the greatest challenges to Indian political institutions in the 1990s.

India is a land of several religious communities. As hordes of people came to India in search of fertile lands, better resources and opportunities, and to escape from cruel regimes, they also brought with them their cultures, a component of which is religion. Broadly speaking. Indian religions may be divided into two categories: first, those which are of local origin, and second, those which were introduced from other parts of the world. Under the first category, we may place Hinduism, and those religious movements that emerged on the Indian soil and later became independent religions, such as Buddhism, Jainism, and Sikhism. Placed under the second category are Zoroastrianism. Judaism, Christianity, and Islam. In India, none of them could remain isolated. Rather, continuous interactions took place (and are taking place even now) between the local religious communities and those which came from outside. From these interactions there came up composite culture of India.

We shall study the characteristics of each of the religions found in India in a time sequence, i.e., beginning with the oldest religion and moving to those that are relatively younger.

Hinduism

About eighty-three per cent of India's population is Hindu. Besides India, Hindus are found in other countries of Asia, Africa, the Caribbean Islands, Fiji, and the United Kingdom.

Hinduism is one of the most ancient religions of the world. Its roots can be traced^ back to the Indus Valley

Civilisation, around 3000 B.C. Archaeologists point out that the worship of Shiva and the mother goddess *(shakti)* came into existence in the pre-Aryan period (3000-2000 B.C.). Having such a long history, it is obvious that Hinduism has developed over a period of time and is bound to show a far greater diversity in its thoughts and practices than any other religion.

The doctrines of Hinduism are not contained in any one sacred book. Hinduism does not have a single historical founder. Hindus worship innumerable gods and goddesses. But at the same time, they also have the concept of one God, from whom everything emerges and in whom everything dissolves. At one end, if Hinduism is polytheistic (consists of many gods and goddesses), at the other, it is monotheistic (the concept of one God). It is interesting that one need not believe in the existence of god in order to be a Hindu. Contradictory beliefs are contained in Hinduism. There are no particular beliefs or practices that are common to all Hindus. Hinduism comprises a vast body of sacred literature such as the Vedas, Upanishads, Dharmashastra, Puranas, Darsanas, Agamas and Tantras, etc. These texts deal with the philosophical issues; some of them deal with the performance of rituals in temples and households. As is true of the philosophical matters, in rituals also, there is a great deal of variation.

Hinduism is intimately connected with Hindu society with the result that it is difficult to say where one ends and the other begins. Because of this, some authors say that Hinduism may be understood as a way of life. The social basis of Hinduism is found in caste system, which according to Rig Veda has a divine origin. The four social categories, called *varna*, emerged from the body *of the purusa*, the first being who was sacrificed in a ritual. Social categories that at one time were regarded as untouchable were not part of this scheme. This model of caste with four varnas known as the *chaturvarna* system.

However, in reality, there are not four but innumerable castes that are endogamous, i.e., marry within. They are known *asjatis*. Each of them has a monopoly over an occupation and claims to fall in one or the other *varna*. When Hindu sacred and legal texts speak of caste, it is mostly *varna* that they have in view and very rarely *jati*. The concepts of purity and pollution are central to Hinduism, and thus caste system, although the strictness with which they are observed differs from one caste society to another.

Certain concepts central to Hinduism are *dharma*, *karma*, and *moksa*. The word *dharma* means 'duty', and each individual is advised to live according to the duty laid down for one's caste, sex, and age. The net balance of good and bad deeds in previous births is called *karma*. It determines whether one will be born a human or animal, or will be released forever from the cycle of birth and death. The permanent release from the world is called *moksa* (salvation'), which should be the aim of every Hindu. But one should think of one's salvation after having accomplished one's household duties as successfully as possible.

In the course of its history, Hinduism has undergone many changes. Certain Hindu institutions, such as untouchability, *sati* (i.e., a woman following her husband to death), human sacrifice, female infanticide (i.e., killing of female children), were severely criticised by the British. One of the great reformers of the nineteenth century was Raja Ram Mohan Roy, who founded a religious society called Brahmo Samaj in 1828. Dayananda Saraswati, who founded Arya Samaj in 1875, also worked for a revival of Vedic Hinduism.

Vedas and Polytheism

Hinduism in India traces its source to the Vedas, ancient

hymns composed and recited in Punjab as early as 1500 B.C. Three main collections of the Vedas—the Rig, Sama, and Yajur—consist of chants that were originally recited by priests while offering plant and animal sacrifices in sacred fires. A fourth collection, the Atharva Veda, contains a number of formulas for requirements as varied as medical cures and love magic. The majority of modern Hindus revere these hymns as sacred sounds passed down to humanity from the greatest antiquity and as the source of Hindu tradition.

The vast majority of Vedic hymns are addressed to a pantheon of deities who are attracted, generated, and nourished by the offerings into the sacred flames and the precisely chanted mantras (mystical formulas of invocation) based on the hymns. Each of these deities may appear to be the supreme god in his or her own hymns, but some gods stand out as most significant. Indra, god of the firmament and lord of the weather, is the supreme deity of the Vedas. Indra also is a god of war who, accompanied by a host of storm gods, uses thunderbolts as weapons to slay the serpent demon Vritra (the name means storm cloud), thus releasing the rains for the earth. Agni, the god of fire, accepts the sacrificial offerings and transmits them to all the gods. Varuna passes judgment, lays down the law, and protects the cosmic order. Yama, the god of death, sends earthly dwellers signs of old age, sickness, and approaching mortality as exhortations to lead a moral life. Surya is the sun god, Chandra the moon god, Vayu the wind god, and Usha the dawn goddess.

Some of the later hymns of the Rig Veda contain speculations that form the basis for much of Indian religious and philosophical thought. From one perspective, the universe originates through the evolution of an impersonal force manifested as male and female principles. Other hymns describe a personal creator, Prajapati, the Lord of creatures, from whom came the heavens and the earth and all the other gods. One hymn describes the universe as emerging from the sacrifice of a cosmic man (*purusha*) who was the source of all things but who was in turn offered into the fire by gods. Within the Vedic accounts of the origin of things, there is a tension between visions of the highest reality as an impersonal force, or as a creator god, or as a group of gods with different jobs to do in the universe. Much of Hinduism tends to accept all these visions simultaneously, claiming that they are all valid as different facets of a single truth, or ranks them as explanations with different levels of sophistication. It is possible, however, to follow only one of these explanations, such as believing in a single personal god while rejecting all others, and still claim to be following the Vedas. In sum, Hinduism does not exist as a single belief system with one textual explanation of the origin of the universe or the nature of God, and a wide range of philosophies and practices can trace their beginnings somewhere in the hymns of the Vedas.

By the sixth century B.C., the Vedic gods were in decline among the people, and few people care much for Indra, Agni, or Varuna in contemporary India. These gods might appear as background characters in myths and stories about more important deities, such as Shiva or Vishnu; in some Hindu temples, there also are small statues of Vedic deities. Sacrificial fire, which once accompanied major political activities, such as the crowning of kings or the conquest of territory, still forms the heart of household rituals for many Hindus, and some Brahman families pass down the skill of memorising the hymns and make a living as professional reciters of the Vedas. One of the main legacies of Brahmanical sacrifice, seen even among traditions that later denied its usefulness, was a concentration on precise ritual actions and a belief in sacred sound as a powerful tool for manifesting the sacred in daily life

Karma and Liberation

The Upanishads, originating as commentaries on the Vedas between about 800 and 200 B.C., contain speculations on the meaning of existence that have greatly influenced Indian religious traditions. Most important is the concept of *atman* (the human soul), which is an individual manifestation of *brahman*. *Atman* is of the same nature as *brahman*, characterised either as an impersonal force or as God, and has as its goal the recognition of identity with *brahman*. This fusion is not possible, however, as long as the individual remains bound to the world of the flesh and desires. In fact, the deathless *atman* that is so bound will not join with *brahman* after the death of the body but will experience continuous rebirth. This fundamental concept of the transmigration of *atman*, or reincarnation after death, lies at the heart of the religions emerging from India.

Indian religious tradition sees karma as the source of the problem of transmigration. While associated with physical form, for example, in a human body, beings experience the universe through their senses and their minds and attach themselves to the people and things around them and constantly lose sight of their true existence as *atman*, which is of the same nature as *brahman*. As the time comes for the dropping of the body, the fruits of good and evil actions in the past remain with *atman*, clinging to it, causing a tendency to continue experience in other existences after death. Good deeds in this life may lead to a happy rebirth in a better life, and evil deeds may lead to a lower existence, but eventually the consequences of past deeds will be worked out, and the individual will seek more experiences in a physical world. In this manner, the bound or ignorant *atman* wanders from life to life, in heavens and hells and in many different bodies. The universe may expand and be destroyed numerous times, but the bound *atman* will not achieve release.

The true goal of *atman* is liberation, or release (*moksha*), from the limited world of experience and realisation of oneness with God or the cosmos. In order to achieve release, the individual must pursue a kind of discipline (yoga, a "tying," related to the English word yoke) that is appropriate to one's abilities and station in life. For most people, this goal means a course of action that keeps them rather closely tied to the world and its ways, including the enjoyment of love (*kama*), the attainment of wealth and power (*artha*), and the following of socially acceptable ethical principles. From this perspective, even manuals on sexual love, such as the *Kama Sutra* (Book of Love), or collections of ideas on politics and governance, such as the *Arthashastra* (Science of Material Gain), are part of a religious tradition that values action in the world as long as it is performed with understanding, a *karma-yoga* or selfless discipline of action in which every action is offered as a sacrifice to God. Some people, however, may be interested in breaking the cycle of rebirth in this life or soon thereafter. For them, a wide range of techniques has evolved over the thousands of years that gives Indian religion its great diversity. The discipline that involves physical positioning of the body (hatha-yoga), which is most commonly equated with yoga outside of India, sees the human body as a series of spiritual centers that can be awakened through meditation and exercise, leading eventually to a oneness with the universe. Tantrism is the belief in the Tantra (from the Sanskrit, context or continuum), a collection of texts that stress the usefulness of rituals, carried out with a strict discipline, as a means for attaining understanding and spiritual awakening. These rituals include chanting powerful mantras; meditating on complicated or auspicious diagrams (mandalas); and, for one school of advanced practitioners, deliberately violating social norms on food, drink, and sexual relations.

A central aspect of all religious discipline, regardless of its emphasis, is the importance of the guru, or teacher. Indian religion may accept the sacredness of specific texts and rituals but stresses interpretation by a living practitioner who has personal experience of liberation and can pass down successful techniques to devoted followers. In fact, since Vedic times, it has never been possible, and has rarely been desired, to unite all people in India under one concept of orthodoxy with a single authority that could be presented to everyone. Instead, there has been a tendency to accept religious innovation and diversity as the natural result of personal experience by successive generations of gurus, who have tailored their messages to particular times, places, and peoples, and then passed down their knowledge to lines of disciples and social groups. As a result, Indian religion is a mass of ancient and modern traditions, some always preserved and some constantly changing, and the individual is relatively free to stress in his or her life the beliefs and religious behaviours that seem most effective on the path to deliverance.

Buddhism

Buddhism began with the life of Siddhartha Gautama, a prince from the small Shakya Kingdom located in the foothills of the Himālayas in Nepal. Brought up in luxury, the prince abandoned his home and wandered forth as a religious beggar, searching for the meaning of existence. The stories of his search presuppose the Jain tradition, as Gautama was for a time a practitioner of intense austerity, at one point almost starving himself to death. He decided, however, that self-torture weakened his mind while failing to advance him to enlightenment and therefore turned to a milder style of renunciation and concentrated on advanced meditation techniques. Eventually, under a tree in the forests of Gaya (in modern Bihar), he resolved to stir no farther until he had solved the mystery of existence. Breaking through the final barriers, he achieved the knowledge that he later expressed as the Four Noble Truths: all of life is suffering; the cause of suffering is desire; the end of desire leads to the end of suffering; and the means to end desire is a path of discipline and meditation. Gautama was now the Buddha, or the awakened one, and he spent the remainder of his life traveling about northeast India converting large numbers of disciples. At the age of eighty, the Buddha achieved his final passing away (*parinirvana*) and died, leaving a thriving monastic order and a dedicated lay community to continue his work.

By the third century B.C., the still-young religion based on the Buddha's teachings was being spread throughout South Asia through the agency of the Mauryan Empire. By the seventh century A.D., having spread throughout East Asia and Southeast Asia, Buddhism probably had the largest religious following in the world.

For centuries Indian royalty and merchants patronised Buddhist monasteries and raised beautiful, hemispherical stone structures called stupas over the relics of the Buddha in reverence to his memory. Since the 1840s, archaeology has revealed the huge impact of Buddhist art, iconography, and architecture in India. The monastery complex at Nalanda in Bihar, in ruins in 1993, was a world center for Buddhist philosophy and religion until the thirteenth century. But by the thirteenth century, when Turkic invaders destroyed the remaining monasteries on the plains, Buddhism as an organised religion had practically disappeared from India. It survived only in Bhutan and Sikkim, both of which were then independent Himalayan kingdoms; among tribal groups in the mountains of northeast India; and in Sri Lanka. The reasons for this disappearance are unclear, and they are many: shifts in royal patronage from Buddhist to Hindu religious institutions; a constant intellectual struggle with dynamic Hindu intellectual schools, which eventually triumphed; and slow adoption of popular religious forms by Buddhists while Hindu monastic communities grew up with the same style of discipline as the Buddhists, leading to the slow but steady amalgamation of ideas and trends in the two religions.

Buddhism began a steady and dramatic comeback in India during the early twentieth century, spurred on originally by a combination of European antiquarian and philosophical interest and the dedicated activities of a few Indian devotees. The foundation of the Mahabodhi Society (Society of Great Enlightenment) in 1891, originally as a force to wrest control of the Buddhist shrine at Gaya from the hands of Hindu managers, gave a large stimulus to the popularisation of Buddhist philosophy and the importance of the religion in India's past.

A major breakthrough occurred in 1956 after some thirty years of Untouchable, or Dalit, agitation when Bhimrao Ramji Ambedkar, leader of the Untouchable wing within the Congress, announced that he was converting to Buddhism as a way to escape from the impediments of the Hindu caste system. He brought with him masses of Untouchables—also known as Harijansor Dalits—and members of Scheduled Castes, who mostly came from Maharashtra and border areas of neighboring states and from the Agra area in Uttar Pradesh. By the early 1990s, there were more than 5 million Buddhists in Maharashtra, or 79 percent of the entire Buddhist community in India, almost all recent converts from low castes. When added to longtime Buddhist populations in hill areas of northeast India (West Bengal, Assam, Sikkim, Mizoram, and Tripura) and high Himalayan valleys (Ladakh District in Jammu and Kashmir, Himachal Pradesh, and northern Uttar Pradesh), and to the influx of Tibetan Buddhist refugees who fled from Tibet with the Dalai Lama in 1959 and thereafter, the recent converts raised the number of Buddhists in India to 6.4 million by 1991. This was a 35.9 percent increase since 1981 and made Buddhism the fifth largest religious group in the country.

The forms of Buddhism practiced by Himalayan communities and Tibetan refugees are part of the Vajrayana, or "Way of the Lightning Bolt," that developed after the seventh century A.D. as part of Mahayana (Great Path) Buddhism. Although retaining the fundamental importance of individual spiritual advancement, the Vajrayana stresses the intercession of bodhisattvas, or enlightened beings, who remain in this world to aid others on the path.

Most other Buddhists in India follow Theravada Buddhism, the "Doctrine of the Elders," which traces its origin through Sri Lankan and Burmese traditions to scriptures in the Pali language, a Sanskritic dialect in eastern India. Although replete with miraculous events and legends, these scriptures stress a more human Buddha and a democratic path toward enlightenment for everyone. Ambedkar's plan for the expanding Buddhist congregation in India visualised Buddhist monks and nuns developing themselves through service to others. Convert communities, by embracing Buddhism, have embarked on social transformations, including a decline in alcoholism, a simplification of marriage ceremonies and abolition of ruinous marriage expenses, a greater emphasis on education, and a heightened sense of identity and self-worth.

Traditions of Enlightened Masters

A number of avowedly Hindu monastic communities have grown up over time and adopted some of the characteristics associated with early Buddhism and Jainism, while remaining dedicated to the Hindu philosophical traditions. One of the oldest and most respected of the Hindu orders traces its origin to the teacher Shankara (788-820), believed by many devotees to have lived hundreds of years earlier. Shankara's philosophy is a primary source of Vedanta, or the "End of the Veda," the final commentary on revealed truth, which is one of the most influential trends in modern Hinduism.

His interpretation of the Upanishads portrays *brahman* as absolutely one and without qualities. The phenomenal world is illusion (*maya*), which the embodied soul must transcend in order to achieve oneness with *brahman*. As a wandering monk, Shankara traveled throughout India, combating Buddhist atheism and founding five seats of learning at Badrinath (Uttar Pradesh), Dwaraka (Gujarat), Puri (Orissa), Sringeri (Karnataka), and Kanchipuram (Tamil Nadu). In the 1990s, those seats are still held by successors to Shankara's philosophy (Shankara Acharyas), who head an order of orange-clad monks that is highly respected by the Hindu community throughout India. Activities of the *acharyas*, including their periodic trips away from their home monasteries to visit and preach to devotees, receive exposure in regional and national media. Their conservative viewpoints and pronouncements on a variety of topics, although not binding on most believers, attract considerable public attention.

The initiation of a renunciant usually depends on the judgment of an *acharya* who determines whether a candidate is dedicated and prepared or not; he then gives to the disciple training and instructions including the initiate's own secret formula or mantra. After initiation, the disciple may remain with his teacher or in a monastery for an indefinite period or may wander forth in a variety of careers. The Ramanandi order in North India, for example, includes holy men (sadhus) who practice ascetic disciplines, militant members of fortified temples, and priests in charge of temple administration and ritual.

There are other orders of renunciants who lead still more austere existences, including naked ascetics who wander begging for their food and assemble for spectacular parades at major festivals. A few dedicated seekers still withdraw to the fastness of the Himalayas or other remote spots and work on their meditation and yoga in total obscurity. Others beg in populated areas, sometimes engaging in fierce austerities such as piercing their bodies with pins and knives. They are a reminder to all people that the path of renunciation waits for anyone who has the dedication and the courage to leave the world behind.

Another kind of renunciation appears in the cult of Shridi Sai Baba, who achieved national and international fame in the twentieth century. He wasa holy man (died 1918)—who appeared in 1872 in Maharashtra and lived a humble life that blended meditation and devotional techniques from a variety of sources. This saint has a small but dedicated following throughout India.

A later saint was Satya Narayana Raju, who renamed himself as Satya Sai Baba, born in 1926 in Andhra Pradesh. At age thirteen, he experienced the first of several seizures that resulted in a changed personality and intense devotional activity, leading to his statement that he is the second incarnation of Sai Baba. By 1950 he had set up a retreat at Puttaparti in what later became Andhra Pradesh and was accepting disciples. His fame spread along with numerous apocryphal stories of his ability to perform miracles. The cult has expanded to include publishing, social service, and education institutions and includes an international association of thousands of believers.

JAINISM

The oldest continuous monastic tradition in India is Jainism, the path of the Jinas, or victors. This tradition is traced to Vardhamana Mahavira (599-527 B.C.), the twenty-fourth and last of the Tirthankaras (Sanskrit for fordmakers). According to legend, Mahavira was born to a ruling family in the town of Vaishali, located in the modern state of Bihar. At the age of thirty, he renounced his wealthy life and devoted himself to fasting and self-mortification in order to purify his consciousness and discover the meaning of existence. He never again dwelt in a house, owned property, or wore clothing of any sort. Following the example of the teacher Parshvanatha (ninth century B.C.), he attained enlightenment and spent the rest of his life meditating and teaching a dedicated group of disciples who formed a monastic order following rules he laid down. His life's work complete, he entered a final fast and deliberately died of starvation.

The ancient belief system of the Jains rests on a concrete, understanding of the working of karma, its effects on the living soul (*jiva*), and the conditions for extinguishing action and the soul's release. According to the Jain view, the soul is a living substance that combines with various kinds of nonliving matter and through action accumulates particles of matter that adhere to it and determine its fate. Most of the matter perceptible to human senses, including all animals and plants, is attached in various degrees to living souls and is in this sense alive. Any action has consequences that necessarily follow the embodied soul, but the worst accumulations of matter come from violence against other living beings. The ultimate Jain discipline, therefore, rests on complete inactivity and absolute nonviolence (ahimsa) against any living beings. Some Jain monks and nuns wear face masks to avoid accidently inhaling small organisms, and all practicing believers try to remain vegetarians. Extreme renunciation, including the refusal of all food, lies at the heart of a discipline that purges the mind and body of all desires and actions and, in the process, burns off the consequences of actions performed in the past. In this sense,

Jain renunciants may recognise or revere deities, but they do not view the Vedas as sacred texts and instead concentrate on the atheistic, individual quest for purification and removal of karma. The final goal is the extinguishing of self, a "blowing out" (nirvana) of the individual self.

By the first century A.D., the Jain community evolved into two main divisions based on monastic discipline: the Digambara or "sky-clad" monks who wear no clothes, own nothing, and collect donated food in their hands; and the Svetambara or "white-clad" monks and nuns who wear white robes and carry bowls for donated food. The Digambara do not accept the possibility of women achieving liberation, while the Svetambara do. Western and southern India have been Jain strongholds for many centuries; laypersons have typically formed minority communities concentrated primarily in urban areas and in mercantile occupations. In the mid-1990s, there were about 7 million Jains, the majority of whom live in the states of Maharashtra (mostly the city of Bombay, or Mumbai in Marathi), Rajasthan, and Gujarat. Karnataka, traditionally a stronghold of Digambaras, has a sizable Jain community.

The Jain laity engage in a number of ritual activities that resemble those of the Hindus around them. Special shrines in residences or in public temples include images of the Tirthankaras, who are not worshiped but remembered and revered; other shrines house the gods who are more properly invoked to intercede with worldly problems. Daily rituals may include meditation and bathing; bathing the images; offering food, flowers, and lighted lamps for the images; and reciting mantras in Ardhamagadhi, an ancient language of northeast India related to Sanskrit. Many Jain laity engage in sacramental ceremonies during life-cycle rituals, such as the first taking of solid food, marriage, and death, resembling those enacted by Hindus. Jains may also worship local gods and participate in local Hindu or Muslim celebrations without compromising their fundamental devotion to the path of the Jinas. The most important festivals of Jainism celebrate the five major events in the life of Mahavira: conception, birth, renunciation, enlightenment, and final release at death.

At a number of pilgrimage sites associated with great teachers of Jainism, the gifts of wealthy donors made possible the building of architectural wonders. Shatrunjaya Hills (Siddhagiri) in Gujarat is a major Svetambara site, an entire city of about 3,500 temples. Mount Abu in Rajasthan, with one Digambara and five Svetambara temples, is the site of some of India's greatest architecture, dating from the eleventh through thirteenth centuries A.D. In Karnataka, on the hill of Sravana Belgola, stands the monolithic seventeen-meter-high statue of the naked Bhagwan Bahubali (Gomateshvara), the first person in the world believed by the faithful to have attained enlightenment, so deep in meditation that vines are growing around his legs. At this site every twelve years, a major concourse of Jain ascetics and laity participate in a purification ceremony in which the statue is anointed from head to toe. Carved in 981, the statue is considered the holiest Jain shrine. In addition to its lavish patronage of shrines, the Jain community, with its long scriptural tradition and wealth gained from trade, has always been known for its philanthropy and especially for its support of education and learning. Prestigious Jain schools are located in most major cities. The largest concentrations of Jains are in Maharashtra (more than 965,000) and Rajasthan (nearly 563,000), with sizable numbers also in Gujarat and Madhya Pradesh.

Sikhism

Sikhism has about 20 million believers worldwide but has an importance far beyond those numbers because Sikhs have played a disproportionately large role in the armed forces and public affairs in India for the last 400 years. Although most Indian Sikhs (79 percent) remain concentrated in the state of Punjab, nearly 3.5 million Sikhs live outside the state, while about 4 million live abroad. This Sikh diaspora, driven by ambition and economic success, has made Sikhism a world religion as well as a significant minority force within the country.

Early History

Sikhism began with Guru Nanak (1469-1539), a member of a trading caste in Punjab who seems to have been employed for some time as a government servant, was married and had two sons, and at age forty-five became a religious teacher. At the heart of his message was a philosophy of universal love, devotion to God, and the equality of all men and women before God. He set up congregations of believers who ate together in free communal kitchens in an overt attempt to break down caste boundaries based on food prohibitions. As a poet, musician, and enlightened master, Nanak's reputation spread, and by the time he died he had founded a new religion of "disciples" (*shiksha* or sikh) that followed his example.

Nanak's son, Baba Sri Chand, founded the Udasi sect of celibate ascetics, which continued in the 1990s. However, Nanak chose as his successor not his son but Angad (1504-52), his chief disciple, to carry on the work as the second guru. Thus began a lineage of teachers that lasted until 1708 and amounted to ten gurus in the Sikh tradition, each of whom is viewed as an enlightened master who propounded directly the word of God. The third guru, Amar Das (1479-1574), established missionary centers to spread the message and was so well respected that the Mughal emperor Akbar visited him. Amar Das appointed his son-in-law Ram Das (1534-81) to succeed him, establishing a hereditary succession for the position of guru. He also built a tank for water at Amritsar in Punjab, which, after his death, became the holiest center of Sikhism.

By the late sixteenth century, the influence of the Sikh religion on Punjabi society was coming to the notice of political authorities. The fifth guru, Arjun Das (1563-1606), was executed in Lahore by the Mughal emperor Jahangir (1605-27) for alleged complicity in a rebellion. In response, the next guru, Hargobind (d. 1644), militarised and politicised his position and fought three battles with Mughal forces. Hargobind established a militant tradition of resistance to persecution by the central government in Delhi that remains an important motif in Sikh consciousness. Hargobind also established at Amritsar, in front of the Golden Temple, the central shrine devoted to Sikhism, the Throne of the Eternal God (Akal Takht) from which the guru dispensed justice and administered the secular affairs of the community, clearly establishing the tradition of a religious state that remains a major issue. The ninth guru, Tegh Bahadur (1621-75), because he refused Mughal emperor Aurangzeb's order to convert to Islam, was brought to Delhi and beheaded on a site that later became an important *gurdwara* (abode of the guru, a Sikh temple) on Chandni Chauk, one of the old city's main thoroughfares.

These events led the tenth guru, Gobind Singh (1666-1708), to transform the Sikhs into a militant brotherhood dedicated to defense of their faith at all times. He instituted a baptism ceremony involving the immersion of a sword in sugared water that initiates Sikhs into the Khalsa (*khalsa*, from the Persian term for "the king's own," often taken to mean army of the pure) of dedicated devotion. The outward signs of this new order were the "Five Ks" to be observed at all times: uncut hair (*kesh*), a long knife (*kirpan*), a comb (*kangha*), a steel bangle (*kara*), and a special kind of breeches not reaching below the knee (*kachha*). Male Sikhs took on the surname Singh (meaning lion), and women took the surname Kaur (princess). All made vows to purity their personal behaviour by avoiding intoxicants, including alcohol and tobacco. In modern India, male Sikhs who have dedicated themselves to the Khalsa do not cut their beards and keep their long hair tied up under turbans, preserving a distinctive personal appearance recognised throughout the world.

Much of Guru Gobind Singh's later life was spent on the move, in guerrilla campaigns against the Mughal Empire, which was entering the last days of its effective authority under Aurangzeb (1658-1707). After Gobind Singh's death, the line of gurus ended, and their message continued through the *Adi Granth* (Original Book), which dates from 1604 and later became known as the *Guru Granth Sahib* (Holy Book of the Gurus). The *Guru Granth Sahib* is revered as a continuation of the line of gurus and as the living word of God by all Sikhs and stands at the heart of all ceremonies.

Most of the Sikh gurus were excellent musicians, who composed songs that conveyed their message to the masses in the saints' own language, which combined variants of Punjabi with Hindi and Braj and also contained Arabic and Persian vocabulary. Written in Gurmukhi script, these songs are one of the main sources of early Punjabi language and literature. There are 5,894 hymns in all, arranged according to the musical measure in which they are sung. An interesting feature of this literature is that 937 songs and poems are by well-known *bhakti* saints who were not members of the lineage of Sikh gurus, including the North Indian saint Kabir and five Muslim devotees. In the *Guru Granth Sahib*, God is called by all the Hindu names and by Allah as well. From its beginnings, then, Sikhism was an inclusive faith that attempted to encompass and enrich other Indian religious traditions.

The belief system propounded by the gurus has its origins in the philosophy and devotions of Hinduism and Islam, but the formulation of Sikhism is unique. God is the creator of the universe and is without qualities or differentiation in himself. The universe (*samsar*) is not sinful in its origin but is covered with impurities; it is not suffering, but a transitory opportunity for the soul to recognise its true nature and break the cycle of rebirth. The unregenerate person is dominated by self-interest and remains immersed in illusion (*maya*), leading to bad karma. Meanwhile, God desires that his creatures escape and achieve enlightenment (nirvana) by recognising his order in the universe. He does this by manifesting his grace as a holy word, attainable through recognition and recitation of God's holy name (*nam*). The role of the guru, who is the manifestation of God in the world, is to teach the means for prayer through the *Guru Granth Sahib* and the community of believers. The guru in this system, and by extension the *Guru Granth Sahib*, are coexistent with the divine and play a decisive role in saving the world.

Where the *Guru Granth Sahib* is present, that place becomes a *gurdwara*. Many Sikh homes contain separate rooms or designated areas where a copy of the book stands as the center of devotional ceremonies. Throughout Punjab, or anywhere there is a substantial body of believers, there are special shrines where the *Guru Granth Sahib* is displayed permanently or is installed daily in a ceremonial manner. These public *gurdwaras* are the centers of Sikh community life and the scene of periodic assemblies for worship. The typical assembly involves group singing from the *Guru Granth Sahib*, led by distinguished believers or professional singers attached to the shrine, distribution of holy food, and perhaps a sermon delivered by the custodian of the shrine.

As for domestic and life-cycle rituals, well into the twentieth century many Sikhs followed Hindu customs for birth, marriage, and death ceremonies, including readings from Hindu scriptures and the employment of Brahmans as officiants. Reform movements within the Sikh community have purged many of these customs, substituting instead readings from the *Guru Granth Sahib* as the focus for rituals and the employment of Sikh ritual specialists. At major public events—weddings, funerals, or opening a new business—patrons may fund a reading of the entire *Guru Granth Sahib* by special reciters.

Twentieth-Century Developments

The existence of the Khalsa creates a potential division within the Sikh community between those who have undergone the baptism ceremony and those who practice the system laid down in the *Guru Granth Sahib* but who do not adopt the distinctive life-style of the Khalsa. Among the latter is a sect of believers founded by Baba Dayal named the Nirankaris, who concentrate on the formless quality of God and his revèlation purely through the guru and the *Guru Granth Sahib*, and who accept the existence of a living, enlightened teacher as essential for spiritual development. The dominant tendency among the Sikhs since the late nineteenth century has been to stress the importance of the Khalsa and its outward signs.

Revivalist movements of the late nineteenth century centered on the activities of the Singh Sabha (Assembly of Lions), who successfully moved much of the Sikh community toward their own ritual systems and away from Hindu customs, and culminated in the Akali (eternal) mass movement in the 1920s to take control of *gurdwaras* away from Hindu managers and invest it in an organisation representing the Sikhs. The result was passage of the Sikh Gurdwara Act of 1925, which established the Central

Gurdwara Management Committee to manage all Sikh shrines in Punjab, Haryana, and Himachal Pradesh through an assembly of elected Sikhs. The combined revenues of hundreds of shrines, which collected regular contributions and income from endowments, gave the committee a large operating budget and considerable authority over the religious life of the community. A simultaneous process led to the Akali Dal (Eternal Party), a political organisation that originally coordinated nonviolent agitations to gain control over *gurdwaras*, then participated in the independence struggle, and since 1947 has competed for control over the Punjab state government. The ideology of the Akali Dal is simple—single-minded devotion to the Guru and preservation of the Sikh faith through political power—and the party has served to mobilise a majority of Sikhs in Punjab around issues that stress Sikh separatism.

There is no official priesthood within Sikhism or any widely accepted institutional mechanism for policy making for the entire faith. Instead, decisions are made by communities of believers (*sangat*) based on the *Guru Granth Sahib* —a tradition dating back to the eighteenth century when scattered bodies of believers had to fight against persecution and manage their own affairs. Anyone may study the scriptures intensively and become a "knower" (*giani*) who is recognised by fellow believers, and there is a variety of training institutes with full-time students and teachers.

Leaders of sects and sectarian training institutions may feel free to issue their own orders. When these orders are combined with the prestige and power of the Central Gurdwara Management Committee and the Akali Dal, which have explicitly narrow administrative goals and are often faction-ridden, a mixture of images and authority emerges that often leaves the religion as a whole without clear leadership. Thus it became possible for Sant Jarnail Singh

Bhindranwale, head of a training institution, to stand forth as a leading authority on the direction of Sikhism; initiate reforms of personal morality; participate in the persecution of Nirankaris; and take effective control of the holiest Sikh shrine, the Golden Temple in Amritsar, Punjab, in the early 1980s. His takeover of the Golden Temple led to a violent siege and culminated in the devastation of the shrine by the army in 1984. Later terrorist activities in Punjab, carried out in the name of Sikhism, were performed by a wide range of organisations claiming to represent an authoritative vision of the nature and direction of the community as a whole.

ISLAM

Islam is India's largest minority religion, with Muslims officially comprising 12.1 percent of the country's population, or 101.6 million people as of the 1991 census. The largest concentrations—about 52 percent of all Muslims in India—live in the states of Bihar (12 million), West Bengal (16 million), and Uttar Pradesh (24 million), according to the 1991 census. Muslims represent a majority of the local populations only in Jammu and Kashmir (not tabulated in 1991 but 65 percent in 1981) and Lakshadweep (94 percent). As a faith with its roots outside South Asia, Islam also offers some striking contrasts to those religions that originated in India.

Origins and Tenets

Islam began with the ministry of the Prophet Muhammad (570-632), who belonged to a merchant family in the trading town of Mecca in Arabia. In his middle age, Muhammad received visions in which the Archangel Gabriel revealed the word of God to him. After 620 he publicly preached the message of these visions, stressing the oneness of God (Allah), denouncing the polytheism of his fellow Arabs, and calling for moral uplift of the population. He attracted a dedicated band of followers, but there was intense opposition from the leaders of the city, who profited from pilgrimage trade to the shrine called the Kaaba. In 622 Muhammad and his closest supporters migrated to the town of Yathrib (now renamed Medina) to the north and set up a new center of preaching and opposition to the leadership of Mecca. This move, the hijrah or hegira, marks the beginning of the Islamic calendar and the origin of the new religion of Islam. After a series of military engagements, Muhammad and his followers were able to defeat the authorities in Mecca and return to take control of the city. Before his death in 632, Muhammad was able to bring most of the tribes of Arabia into the fold of Islam. Soon after his death, the united Arabs conquered present-day Syria, Iraq, Egypt, and Iran, making Islam into a world religion by the end of the seventh century.

Islam means submission to God, and a Muslim is one who has submitted to the will of God. At the center of the religion is an intense concentration on the unity of God and the separation between God and his creatures. No physical representation of God is allowed. There are no other gods. The duty of humanity is to profess the simple testimony: "There is no god but God (Allah), and Muhammad is his Prophet." Obedience to God's will rests on following the example of the Prophet in one's own life and faithfulness to the revelations collected into the most sacred text, the Quran. The Five Pillars of Islam are reciting the profession of faith; praying five times a day; almsgiving to the poor; fasting (abstaining from dawn to dusk from food, drink, sexual relations, and smoking) during the month of Ramazan (the ninth month of the Islamic calendar, known as Ramadan in Arab countries), the holy month when God's revelations were received by Muhammad; and making the pilgrimage (hajj) to Mecca at least once during one's life if possible. People who obey God's commandments and live a good life will go to heaven after death; those who disobey will go to hell. All souls will be resurrected for a last judgment at the end of the world. Muslims view themselves as followers of the same tradition preserved in the Judaic and Christian scriptures, accept the prophetic roles of Ibrahim (Abraham), Musa (Moses), and Isa (Jesus), and view Islam as the final statement of revealed truth for the entire world.

Regulation of the Muslim community rests primarily on rules in the Quran, then on authenticated tales of the conduct (*sunna*) of the Prophet Muhammad, then on reasoning, and finally on the consensus of opinion. By the end of the eighth century, four main schools of Muslim jurisprudence had emerged in Sunni Islam to interpret the sharia (Islamic law). Prominent among these groups was the Hanafi school, which dominated most of India, and the Shafii school, which was more prevalent in South India. Because Islam has no ordained priesthood, direction of the Muslim community rests on the learning of religious scholars (ulama) who are expert in understanding the Quran and its appended body of commentaries.

Early leadership controversies within the Muslim community led to divisions that still have an impact on the body of believers. When Muhammad died, leadership fell to his father-in-law, Abu Bakr, who became the first caliph (*khalifa*, or successor), a position that combined spiritual and secular power. A separate group advocated the leadership of Ali, the cousin and son-in-law of the Prophet, who had married his daughter Fatima. Leadership could have fallen to Ali's son Husayn, but, in the power struggle that followed, in 680 Husayn and seventy-two followers were murdered at Karbala (now in modern Iraq).

This leadership dispute formed the most crucial dividing point in Islamic history: the victorious party went on to found the Umayyad Dynasty (661-750), which had its headquarters at Damascus, leading the majority of Muslims in the Sunni path. The disaffected Shiat Ali (or Party of Ali) viewed only his line as legitimate and continued to follow descendants of Husayn as their leader. Among the followers of this Shiapath, there is a party of "Seveners" who trace the lineage of imams down to Ismail, the Seventh Imam and eldest son of the Sixth Imam. The Ismailis are the largest Shia group in India, and are concentrated in Maharashtra and Gujarat. A second group, the "Twelvers" (the most numerous Shia group worldwide), traces the lineage of imams through twelve generations, believing that the last or Twelfth Imam became "hidden" and will reappear in the world as a saviour, or Mahdi, at some time in the future.

The division between Sunni and Shia dates back to purely political struggles in the seventh century, but over time between the two major communities many divisive differences in ritual and legal interpretations have evolved. The vast majority of Muslims are Sunni, and in contemporary India 90 percent of Muslims follow this path. Sunnis have recognised no legitimate caliph after the position was abolished in Turkey in 1924, placing the direction of the community clearly with the ulama.

Public worship for the average Muslim consists of going to a mosque (*masjid*)—normally on Fridays, although mosques are well attended throughout the week—for congregational prayers led by a local imam, following the public call to prayer, which may be intoned from the top of a minaret (*minar*) at the mosque. After leaving their footwear at the door, men and women separate; men usually sit in front, women in back, either inside the mosque or in an open courtyard. The prayer leader gives a sermon in the local regional language, perhaps interspersed with Arabic or Farsi (sometimes called Persian or Parsi) quotations, depending on his learning and the sophistication of the audience. Announcements of events of interest that may include political commentary are often included. Then follow common prayers that involve responses from the worshipers who stand, bow, and kneel in unison during devotions.

Islamic Traditions in India

Muslims practice a series of life-cycle rituals that differ from those of Hindus, Jains, or Buddhists. The newborn baby has the call to prayer whispered into the left ear, the profession of faith whispered into the right ear, honey or date paste placed in the mouth, and a name selected. On the sixth day after birth, the first bath occurs. On the seventh day or a multiple of the seventh, the head is shaved, and alms are distributed, ideally in silver weighing as much as the hair; a sacrifice of animals imitates the sheep sacrificed instead of Ishmael (Ismail) in biblical times. Religious instruction starts at age four years, four months, and four days, beginning with the standard phrase: "In the name of God, the Beneficent, the Merciful." Male circumcision takes place between the ages of seven and twelve. Marriage requires a payment by the husband to the wife and the solemnisation of a marital contract in a social gathering. Marriage ceremonies include the donning of a nose ring by the bride, or in South India a wedding necklace, and the procession of the bridegroom. In a traditional wedding, males and females attend ceremonies in different rooms, in keeping with the segregation of sexes in most social settings. After death the family members wash and enshroud the body, after which it is buried as prayers from the Quran are recited. On the third day, friends and relatives come to console the bereaved, read the Quran, and pray for the soul of the deceased. The family observe a mourning period of up to forty days.

The annual festivals of Islam are based on a lunar calendar of 354 days, which makes the Islamic holy year independent of the Gregorian calendar. Muslim festivals make a complete circuit of the solar year every thirty-three years.

The beginning of the Islamic calendar is the month of Muharram, the tenth day of which is Ashura, the anniversary of the death of Husayn, the son of Ali. Ashura, a major holiday, is of supreme importance for the Shia. Devotees engage in ritualised mourning that may include processions of colorful replicas of Husayn's tomb at Karbala and standards with palms on top, which are carried by barefoot mourners and buried at an imitation Karbala. In many areas of India, these parades provide a dramatic spectacle that draws large numbers of non-Muslim onlookers. Demonstrations of grief may include bouts of self-flagellation that can draw blood and may take place in public streets, although many families retain personal mourning houses. Sunni Muslims may also commemorate Husayn's death but in a less demonstrative manner, concentrating instead on the redemptive aspect of his martyrdom.

The last day of Ramazan is Id al Fitr (Feast of Breaking the Fast), another national holiday, which ends the month of fasting with almsgiving, services in mosques, and visits to friends and neighbors. Bakr Id, or Id al Zuha (Feast of Sacrifice), begins on the tenth day of the Islamic month of Dhul Hijjah and is a major holiday. Prescribed in the Quran, Id al Zuha commemorates Ibrahim's willingness to sacrifice Ishmael (rather than Ishaq—Isaac—as in the Judeo-Christian tradition) according to God's command, but it is also the high point of the pilgrim's ritual cycle while on the hajj in Mecca. All of these festivals involve large feasts, gifts given to family and neighbors, and the distribution of food for charitable purposes.

A significant aspect of Islam in India is the importance of shrines attached to the memory of great Sufi saints.

Sufism is a mystical path (*tariqat*) as distinct from the path of the sharia. A Sufi attains a direct vision of oneness with God, often on the edges of orthodox behaviour, and can thus become a *pir* (living saint) who may take on disciples (*murids*) and set up a spiritual lineage that can last for generations. Orders of Sufis became important in India during the thirteenth century following the ministry of Muinuddin Chishti (1142-1236), who settled in Ajmer, Rajasthan, and attracted large numbers of converts to Islam because of his holiness. His Chishtiyya order went on to become the most influential Sufi lineage in India, although other orders from Central Asia and Southwest Asia also reached to India and played a large role in the spread of Islam. Many Sufis were well known for weaving music, dance, intoxicants, and local folktales into their songs and lectures. In this way, they created a large literature in regional languages that embedded Islamic culture deeply into older South Asian traditions.

In the case of many great teachers, the memory of their holiness has been so intense that they are still viewed as active intercessors with God, and their tombs have become the site of rites and prayers by disciples and lay people alike. Tales of miraculous deeds associated with the tombs of great saints have attracted large numbers of pilgrims attempting to gain cures for physical maladies or solutions to personal problems. The tomb of the *pir* thus becomes a *dargah* (gateway) to God and the focus for a wide range of rituals, such as daily washing and decoration by professional attendants, touching or kissing the tomb or contact with the water that has washed it, hanging petitions on the walls of the shrine surrounding the tomb, lighting incense, and giving money.

The descendants of the original *pir* are sometimes seen as inheritors of his spiritual energy, and, as *pirs* in their own right, they might dispense amulets sanctified by contact with them or with the tomb. The annual celebration of the *pir* 's death is a major event at important shrines, attracting hundreds of thousands of devotees for celebrations that may last for days. Free communal kitchens and distribution of sweets are also big attractions of these festivals, at which Muslim fakirs, or wandering ascetics, sometimes appear and where public demonstrations of self-mortification, such as miraculous piercing of the body and spiritual possession of devotees, sometimes occur. Every region of India can boast of at least one major Sufi shrine that attracts expressive devotion, which remains important, especially for Muslim women.

The leadership of the Muslim community has pursued various directions in the evolution of Indian Islam during the twentieth century. The most conservative wing has typically rested on the education system provided by the hundreds of religious training institutes (*madrasa*) throughout the country, which have tended to stress the study of the Quran and Islamic texts in Arabic and Persian, and have focused little on modern managerial and technical skills. Several national movements have emerged from this sector of the Muslim community. The Jamaati Islami (Islamic Party), founded in 1941, advocates the establishment of an overtly Islamic government through peaceful, democratic, and nonmissionary activities. It had about 3,000 active members and 40,000 sympathisers in the mid-1980s. The Tablighi Jamaat (Outreach Society) became active after the 1940s as a movement, primarily among the ulama, stressing personal renewal, prayer, a missionary and cooperative spirit, and attention to orthodoxy. It has been highly critical of the kind of activities that occur in and around Sufi shrines and remains a minor if respected force in the training of the ulama. Other ulama have upheld the legitimacy of mass religion, including exaltation of *pirs* and the memory of the Prophet. A powerful secularising drive led to the founding of Aligarh Muslim University (founded in 1875 as the

Muhammadan Anglo-Oriental College)—with its modern curriculum—and other major Muslim universities. This educational drive has remained the most dominant force in guiding the Muslim community.

Zoroastrianism

According to the 1991 census, there were 79,382 members of the Zoroastrian faith. Some 79 percent lived in Maharashtra (primarily in Bombay) and most of the rest in Gujarat. Zoroastrians are primarily descendants of tenth-century immigrants from Persia who preserved the religion of Zoroaster, a prophet of Iran who taught probably in the sixth century B.C. Although the number of Parsis steadily declined during the twentieth century as a result of emigration and low birth rates, their religion is significant because of the financial influence wielded by this mostly trading community and because they represent the world's largest surviving group of believers in this ancient faith.

Originally, the Parsis were shipbuilders and traders located in the ports and towns of Gujarat. Their freedom from food or occupational restrictions based on caste affiliation enabled them to take advantage of the numerous commercial opportunities that accompanied the colonial expansion of trade and control. Substantial numbers moved to Bombay, which served as a base for expanding their business activities throughout India and abroad. A combination of Western commercial contacts and English-language education during the colonial period made the Parsis arguably the most cosmopolitan community in India. Socially, they were equally at home with Indians and Westerners; Parsi women enjoyed freedom of movement earlier than most high-caste Hindu or upper-class Muslim women. In contemporary India, Parsis are the most urban, elite, and wealthy of any of the nation's religious groups. Their role in the development of trade, industry, finance, and philanthropy has earned them an important place in the country's social and economic life, and several have achieved high rank in government.

The source of Parsi religion is a body of texts called the *Avesta*, which includes a number of sections in archaic language attributed to Zoroaster himself, and which preserve the cult of the fire sacrifice as the focus of ritual life. The supreme spirit is Ahura Mazda (or Ohrmazd), whose will is manifest in the world through the actions of bountiful immortals or good spiritual attributes that support life and love. Opposing the supreme spirit is the force of evil, Angra Mainyu (or Ahriman), which is the cause of all destruction and corruption in the world. Equipped with free will, humans can choose sides in this struggle and after death will appear at the bridge of judgment. People who choose to do good deeds go to heaven, those who commit evil go to hell. The opposed cosmic forces battle through the history of the universe, until at the end of time there will be a final judgment and a resurrection of the dead to a perfect world.

The extensive ritual life of devout Parsis revolves around sacred fires, of which there are three grades dependent on extensive ceremonial preparation. The highest two grades can only be maintained in fire temples by hereditary priests, who undergo extensive purificatory rites and wear special face masks to prevent polluting the flames with breath or saliva, while the third grade of fire can exist in the household. The most important rite for most lay people is the Navjote, which occurs between the seventh and fifteenth year of life, and initiates the young person into the adult community. The ceremony involves purifying bathing, reciting *Avesta*-based scriptures, and being invested with a sacred shirt (*sudrah*) and waist thread (*kusti*) that should always be worn thereafter. Marriage is also an important rite, complete with scriptural recitations. At death, great care is taken to avoid pollution from the body, and funeral services usually take place within twenty-four hours. The dead are then disposed of by exposure to vultures on large, circular "towers of silence" (*dakhma*). Most rituals take place in the home or in special pavilions; congregational worship at fire temples is limited to spring and autumn festivals.

The towns of Sanjan, Nausari, and Udvada in Gujarat are of prime importance to Parsis, having long served as community centers before mass migration to Bombay in the nineteenth century. Bombay is home to 70 percent of India's Parsis, where the management of Parsi affairs rests in the hands of a *panchayat*, the assembly that serves as a charitable and educational organisation providing a comprehensive social welfare system at the local level.

JUDAISM

Trade contacts between the Mediterranean region and the west coast of India probably led to the presence of small Jewish settlements in India as long ago as the early first millennium B.C. In Kerala a community of Jews tracing its origin to the fall of Jerusalem in A.D. 70 has remained associated with the cities of Cranganore and Kochi (formerly known as Cochin) for at least 1,000 years. The Pardesi Synagogue in Kochi, rebuilt in 1568, is in the architectural style of Kerala but preserves the archaic ritual style of the Sephardic rite, with Babylonian and Yemenite influence as well. The Jews of Kochi, concentrated mostly in the old "Jew Town," were completely integrated into local culture, speaking Malayalam and taking local names while preserving their knowledge of Hebrew and contacts with Southwest Asia. A separate community of Jews, called the Bene Israel, had lived along the Konkan Coast in and around Bombay, Pune, and Ahmadabad for almost 2,000 years. Unlike the Kochi Jews, they became a village-based society and maintained little contact with other Jewish communities. They always remained within the orthodox Jewish fold, practicing the Sephardic rite without rabbis, with the synagogue as the center of religious and cultural life. A third group of Jews immigrated to India, beginning at the end of the eighteenth century, following the trade contacts established by the British Empire. These Baghdad Jews came mostly from the area of modern Iraq and settled in Bombay and Calcutta, where many of them became wealthy and participated in the economic leadership of these growing cities.

The population of the Kochi Jews, always small, had decreased from 5,000 in 1951 to about fifty in the early 1990s. During the same period, the Bene Israel decreased from about 20,000 to 5,000, while the Baghdad Jews declined from 5,000 to 250. Emigration to Australia, Israel, Britain, and North America accounts for most of this decline. According to the 1981 Indian census, there were 5,618 Jews in India, down from 5,825 in 1971. The 1991 census showed a further decline to 5,271, most of whom lived in Maharashtra and Mizoram

CHRISTIANITY

The first Christians in India, according to tradition and legend, were converted by Saint Thomas the Apostle, who arrived on the Malabar Coast of India in A.D. 52. After evangelising and performing miracles in Kerala and Tamil Nadu, he is believed to have been martyred in Madras and buried on the site of San Thómé Cathedral. Members of the Syro-Malabar Church, an eastern rite of the Roman Catholic Church, adopted the Syriac liturgy dating from fourth century Antioch. They practiced what is also known as the Malabar rite until the arrival of the Portuguese in the late fifteenth century. Soon thereafter, the Portuguese attempted to latinise the Malabar rite, an action which, by the mid-sixteenth century, led to charges of heresy against the Syro-

Malabar Church and a lengthy round of political machinations. By the middle of the next century, a schism occurred when the adherents of the Malankar rite (or Syro-Malankara Church) broke away from the Syro-Malabar Church. Fragmentation continued within the Syro-Malabar Church up through the early twentieth century when a large contingent left to join the Nestorian Church, which had had its own roots in India since the sixth or seventh century. By 1887, however, the leaders of the Syro-Malabar Church had reconciled with Rome, which formally recognised the legitimacy of the Malabar rite. The Syro-Malankara Church was reconciled with Rome in 1930 and, while retaining the Syriac liturgy, adopted the Malayalam language instead of the ancient Syriac language.

Throughout this period, foreign missionaries made numerous converts to Christianity. Early Roman Catholic missionaries, particularly the Portuguese, led by the Jesuit Saint Francis Xavier (1506-52), expanded from their bases on the west coast making many converts, especially among lower castes and outcastes. The miraculously undecayed body of Saint Francis Xavier is still on public view in a glass coffin at the Basilica of Bom Jesus in Goa. Beginning in the eighteenth century, Protestant missionaries began to work throughout India, leading to the growth of Christian communities of many varieties.

The total number of Christians in India according to the 1991 census was 19.6 million, or 2.3 percent of the population. About 13.8 million of these Christians were Roman Catholics, including 300,000 members of the Syro-Malankara Church. The remainder of Roman Catholics were under the Catholic Bishops' Conference of India. In January 1993, after centuries of self-government, the 3.5-million-strong Latin-rite Syro-Malabar Church was raised to archepiscopate status as part of the Roman Catholic Church. In total, there were nineteen archbishops, 103 bishops, and about 15,000 priests in India in 1995.

Most Protestant denominations are represented in India, the result of missionary activities throughout the country, starting with the onset of British rule. Most denominations, however, are almost exclusively staffed by Indians, and the role of foreign missionaries is limited. The largest Protestant denomination in the country is the Church of South India, since 1947 a union of Presbyterian, Reformed, Congregational, Methodist, and Anglican congregations with approximately 2.2 million members. A similar Church of North India has 1 million members. There are 473,000 Methodists, 425,000 Baptists, and about 1.3 million Lutherans. Orthodox churches of the Malankara and Malabar rites total 2 million and 700,000 members, respectively.

All Christian churches have found the most fertile ground for expansion among Dalits, Scheduled Castes, and Scheduled Tribe groups. During the twentieth century, the fastest growing Christian communities have been located in the northeast, among the Khasis, Mizos, Nagas, and other hill tribes. Christianity offers a non-Hindu mode of acculturation during a period when the state and modern economy have been radically transforming the life-styles of the hill peoples. Missionaries have led the way in the development of written languages and literature for many tribal groups. Christian churches have provided a focus for unity among different ethnic groups and have brought with them a variety of charitable services.

Tribal Religions

Among the 68 million citizens of India who are members of tribal groups, the religious concepts, terminologies, and practices are as varied as the hundreds of tribes, but members of these groups have one thing in common: they are under constant pressure from the major organised religions. Some of this pressure is intentional, as outside missionaries work among tribal groups to gain converts.

Most of the pressure, however, comes from the process of integration within a national political and economic system that brings tribes into increasing contact with other groups and different, prestigious belief systems. In general, those tribes that remain geographically isolated in desert, hill, and forest regions or on islands are able to retain their traditional cultures and religions longer. Those tribes that make the transition away from hunting and gathering and toward sedentary agriculture, usually as low-status labourers, find their ancient religious forms in decay and their place filled by practices of Hinduism, Islam, Christianity, or Buddhism.

One of the most studied tribal religions is that of the Santal of Orissa, Bihar, and West Bengal, one of the largest tribes in India, having a population estimated at 4.2 million. According to the 1991 census, however, only 23,645 people listed Santal as their religious belief.

According to the Santal religion, the supreme deity, who ultimately controls the entire universe, is Thakurji. The weight of belief, however, falls on a court of spirits (*bonga*), who handle different aspects of the world and who must be placated with prayers and offerings in order to ward off evil influences. These spirits operate at the village, household, ancestor, and subclan level, along with evil spirits that cause disease, and can inhabit village boundaries, mountains, water, tigers, and the forest. A characteristic feature of the Santal village is a sacred grove on the edge of the settlement where many spirits live and where a series of annual festivals take place.

The most important spirit is Maran Buru (Great Mountain), who is invoked whenever offerings are made and who instructed the first Santals in sex and brewing of rice beer. Maran Buru's consort is the benevolent Jaher Era (Lady of the Grove).

A yearly round of rituals connected with the agricultural cycle, along with life-cycle rituals for birth, marriage and burial at death, involves petitions to the spirits and offerings that include the sacrifice of animals, usually birds. Religious leaders are male specialists in medical cures who practice divination and witchcraft. Similar beliefs are common among other tribes of northeast and central India such as the Kharia, Munda, and Oraon.

Smaller and more isolated tribes often demonstrate less articulated classification systems of the spiritual hierarchy, described as animism or a generalised worship of spiritual energies connected with locations, activities, and social groups. Religious concepts are intricately entwined with ideas about nature and interaction with local ecological systems. As in Santal religion, religious specialists are drawn from the village or family and serve a wide range of spiritual functions that focus on placating potentially dangerous spirits and coordinating rituals.

Unlike the Santal, who have a large population long accustomed to agriculture and a distinguished history of resistance to outsiders, many smaller tribal groups are quite sensitive to ecological degradation caused by modernisation, and their unique religious beliefs are under constant threat. Even among the Santal, there are 300,000 Christians who are alienated from traditional festivals, although even among converts the belief in the spirits remains strong. Among the Munda and Oraon in Bihar, about 25 percent of the population are Christians. Among the Kharia of Bihar (population about 130,000), about 60 percent are Christians, but all are heavily influenced by Hindu concepts of major deities and the annual Hindu cycle of festivals. Tribal groups in the Himalayas were similarly affected by both Hinduism and Buddhism in the late twentieth century. Even the small hunting-and-gathering groups in the union territory of Andaman and Nicobar Islands have been under severe pressure because of immigration to this area and the resulting reduction of their hunting area.

Modern Changes in Religions

The process of modernisation in India, well under way during the British colonial period (1757-1947), has brought with it major changes in the organisational forms of all religions. The missionary societies that came with the British in the early nineteenth century imported, along with modern concepts of print media and propaganda, an ideology of intellectual competition and religious conversion. Instead of the customary interpretation of rituals and texts along received sectarian lines, Indian religious leaders began devising intellectual syntheses that could encompass the varied beliefs and practices of their traditions within a framework that could withstand Christian arguments.

One of the most important reactions was the Arya Samaj (Arya Society), founded in 1875 by Swami Dayananda (1824-83), which went back to the Vedas as the ultimate revealed source of truth and attempted to purge Hinduism of more recent accretions that had no basis in the scriptures. Originally active in Punjab, this small society still works to purify Hindu rituals, converts tribal people, and runs centers throughout India. Other responses include the Ramakrishna order of renunciants established by Swami Vivekananda (1863-1902), which set forth a unifying philosophy that followed the Vedanta teacher Shankara and other teachers by accepting all paths as ultimately leading toward union with the undifferentiated *brahman*. One of the primary goals of the Ramakrishna movement has been to educate Hindus about their own scriptures; the movement also runs book stores and study centers in all major cities. Both of these paths are directly modeled on the institutional and intellectual forms used by European missionaries and religious leaders.

During the 1930s and 1940s, again responding to institutional models from Europe, the more activist

Rashtriya Swayamsevak Sangh (RSS—National Volunteer Organisation) emerged to protect Hinduism. The RSS had been founded in 1925 by Keshav Baliram Hedgewar (1889-1944), a native of Maharashtra who was concerned that Hinduism was in danger of extinction from its external foes and needed a strong, militant force of devotees to protect it. Members believe that the Indian nation is the divine mother to whom the citizen devotes mind and body through *karma-yoga*, or disciplined service. Training consists of daily early morning meetings at which the saffron, white, and green Indian flag and the swallow-tailed, red-ocher RSS banner are raised as rows of members salute silently. There are then group drills in gymnastic exercises, sports, discussions of patriotic themes from a primarily Hindu viewpoint, group singing of nationalist songs, and a final assembly with saluting. Throughout India in the early 1990s, there were cells (*shakha*) of fifty to 100 members from all walks of life (the RSS rejects class differences) who were devoted to the nation. Although it has attracted hundreds of thousands of members from all over India, the RSS has never projected itself as a political party, always remaining a national club that is ready to send its members to trouble spots for the defense of the nation and the national culture, embodied in Hinduism. The Jana Sangh, established in 1951, was the RSS's political arm until it joined the Janata Party in 1977 and its membership split away in 1980 to form the BJP.

Another activist organisation is the Vishwa Hindu Parishad (VHP—World Hindu Council), founded in 1964. The VHP runs schools, medical centers, hostels, orphanages, and mass movements to support Hinduism wherever it is perceived as threatened. This ultraconservative organisation played a role in the extensive agitation for the demolition of a mosque in Ayodhya, leading to the destruction of the structure during a huge demonstration in 1992. As a result of the VHP's complicity in the affair, the Ministry of Home

Affairs imposed a two-year ban on the Vishwa Hindu Parishad under the Unlawful Activities Act. When the ban expired in December 1994, the government reimposed it for two additional years.

The spread of Hindu "communal" (that is, religious) sentiment parallels a similar rise in religious chauvinism and "fundamentalist" ideologies among religious minorities, including Muslims and Sikhs. Against this background of agitation, the periodic outbreak of communal riots in urban areas throughout India contributes to an atmosphere of religious tension that has been a hallmark of the national political scene during the twentieth century. Hindu-Muslim riots, especially in North India, reached a peak during the partition of India in 1947 and periodically escalated in urban areas in the early 1990s. This strife typically involves low-income groups from both communities in struggles over land, jobs, or local resources that coalesced around a religious focus after seemingly trivial incidents polarised the two communities. In practice, although members of other religious communities are the victims of violence, rioters are rarely motivated by religious instructors, although fundamentalist agitators are often implicated. The situation in North India became complicated during the 1980s by Sikh terrorism connected with the crisis in Punjab, the widespread anti-Sikh riots after Prime Minister Indira Gandhi's assassination in November 1984 by her Sikh bodyguards, and a series of terrorist or counterterrorist actions lasting into the 1990s. In all of these cases, many observers believe that religion has appeared as a cover for political and economic struggles.

The perception that one's religion is in danger receives periodic reinforcement from the phenomenon of public mass religious conversion that receives coverage from the news media. Many of these events feature groups of Scheduled Caste members who attempt to escape social disabilities through conversion to alternative religions, usually Islam, Buddhism, or Christianity. These occasions attract the attention of fundamentalist organisations from all sides and heighten public consciousness of religious divisions. The most conspicuous movement of this sort occurred during the 1950s during the mass conversions of Mahars to Buddhism. In the early 1980s, the primary example was the conversion of Dalits to Islam in Meenakshipuram, Tamil Nadu, an event that resulted in considerable discussion in the media and an escalation of agitation in South India. Meanwhile, conversions to Christianity among tribal groups continue, with growing opposition from Hindu revivalist organisations.

Alongside the more publicised violent outbreaks, there have been major nonviolent changes, as new sectarian movements continue to grow and as established movements change. For example, the Radhasoami Satsang movement of North India, which includes adherents in Punjab and Uttar Pradesh, encompasses yogic ideas on the relationship between humans and the universe, the *bhakti* saint tradition including select Sikh influences, and the veneration of the enlightened guru. The dominant tendency of these new religions, following the example of the great teachers of the past that was reiterated by Mahatma Gandhi and most modern gurus, remains nonviolence to all living beings and acceptance of the remarkable diversity of Indian religion.

3

Social Organisation among Hindus

Religion is a system of beliefs, emotional attitudes and practices, by means of which a group of people attempt to cope with the ultimate problems of life. Religion and social life are interrelated and it plays an important role in social control. Religious values impose a certain type of behaviour. The rituals of religion make one to have respect for the sacred. Religion also has a bearing on other social institutions. It lays down norms and values, which should guide the relationships within a family and other social groups. The sacred texts often indicate how a people should be governed. Religious beliefs also have an effect on economic behaviour, e.g. the concept of *artha* and the protestant ethic. Religion has acted both as hindrance and help in social change. Where religion has tended to be traditional, it has resisted change. However, where it has moved with the time it has often advocated change.

Generally speaking, the process of doing things in an orderly fashion is called organisation. When we speak of social organisation, we talk about the arrangement of actions which conform with the norms and values of society. Thus, to understand the social organisation of a particular society, in this case Hindu society, we need to study the systematic ordering of social relations, including changes that have taken place over time in them.

Religious Concepts

Hinduism is one of the oldest religions in the world. It is a religion followed by several racial and ethnic groups. The Hindu sacred texts deal with the ethical behaviour of an individual of a family and of society in general. They also discuss and prescribe rules of administration, politics, statesmanship, legal principles and statecraft. The rules of conduct apply to personal and social life. Here, we will discuss only some religious concepts, which provide an understanding of the ways in which Hindu society is organised.

A life of righteousness for a Hindu is possible through the fourfold scheme of practical endeavour. It comprises the concepts of *dharma, artha, kama* and *moksha.*

i) *Dharma* is honest and upright conduct or righteous action.

ii) *Artha* means a righteous and honest pursuit of economic activities.

iii) *Kama* is the fulfillment of one's normal desires.

iv) *Moksha* is liberation, that is absorption of the self into eternal bliss.

Related to these four concepts are the concepts of *karma* and *samsara.*

Depending upon one's deeds *(karma)* one is able to reach the stage of *moksha* or liberation. The stage of *moksha* or liberation is a term for describing the end of the cycle of birth and rebirth. The cycle of birth and rebirth is known as *samsara.* The Hindus believe that each human being has a soul and that this soul is immortal. It does not perish at the time of death. The process of birth and rebirth goes on until *moksha* is attained. This cycle of transmigration is also known as *samsara,* which is the arena where the cycle of birth and rebirth operates. One's birth and rebirth in a particular state of existence is believed by the Hindus to be dependent on the quality of one's deeds *(karma)*.

For a Hindu, the issue of liberation is of paramount significance. Let us discuss a little more about these two concepts, i.e., *Karma* and *Samsara*.

The concepts of *dharma, artha, kama* and *moksha* are related to tenets of *karma* and *samsara*. *Karma* is a word used for all activity or work. *Samsara* is the term used for the arena where the cycle of birth and rebirth continues to operate until one attains liberation. This is also called the theory of reincarnation or *punarjanma*. Actions are divided into good or bad on the basis of their intrinsic worth. Good deeds bring fame, merit and are the path to heaven. Bad deeds bring notoriety and lead to punishment and life in hell. It is recognised that an individual's overall position in a future life depends on the way he or she lives the present one. This belief, which gave a positive or negative value to certain actions, developed into a general theory of actions and is called the *karma* theory. The concept of karma is fully developed and woven into the belief in re-birth, which in turn is related to the belief concerning heaven, hell, and *moksha*. An individual's fate after death is determined by the sum total of grades and attributes of his or her actions or deeds *(karma)* during his or her life. Better birth and status is obtained if there is a surplus of many good deeds in a person's life. Otherwise one's status falls in the next life. Another related belief-is that the world moves in a cyclical process (birth and death follow one another). By following one's *karma* prescribed within the fourfold scheme of *dharma, artha, kama, moksha* an individual strives to get out of this otherwise infinite cyclical process of birth and death. Depending on one's previous and present *karma*, one prospers or suffers in this world. Later after death he either gains heaven or is punished with life in hell. Thus a human being after death may become a denizen or inhabitant of heaven or hell, may be reborn as an animal, or even be reborn as a tree. All this depends on one's *karma*. An individual usually wanders through many births till he or she finds final release or *moksha*.

Relevance to Hindu Social Structure

The belief in *karma* and *dharma* has direct relevance to Hindu social organisation, which is based on an arrangement of castes into a graded order. This hierarchy, in turn, is linked with the quality of one's *karma*. One can say that if one's actions are good, one will be born in a higher caste in the next birth. Hindu society is supposed to be governed by rather strict rules of caste behaviour. There are, on the other hand, some general rules governing the behaviour of all members irrespective of caste. Castes coexist with different norms of behaviour and a continuity with the past in terms of one's actions in the previous birth. Whatever position one may be born into, one must fulfil the functions, without attachment, without hatred and resentment. Whatever may be one's *dharma*, its performance through one's *karma* brings blessings.

Each person has a duty *(dharma)* appropriate to one's caste and one's station in life. As mentioned before, the term *dharma* refers to honest and upright conduct or righteous action. *Dharma* has two aspects; one normative and the other naturalistic. The normative aspect refers to duty or path to be followed. The naturalistic meaning implies the essential attributes or nature, for example, the dharma or nature of water is to flow. The Hindus believe that one must follow one's *dharma* to achieve ultimate liberation from the cycle of births and deaths in this world. An individual belongs to a family and a caste group and has to perform his or her *dharma* (in the sense of its naturalistic aspect) accordingly. The main aim of following one's *dharma* is to eventually achieve *moksha* or liberation.

Dharma relates not only to the caste but also to the different stages in one's life. As part of following one's *dharma* a Hindu goes through the life cycle rituals which are carried out in the context of marriage, family and caste. Let us now look at the size and spread of the Hindu community in India.

The Hindu Community

Hinduism is one of the most ancient religions of the world. Its earliest literary productions were the four Vedas. These comprise hymns and ritual ceremonies of the early Aryan settlers, who were a pastoral and agricultural people. The Vedic period covers about 2500 B.C. to 600 B.C. The Upanishadic teachings, also of this period, contain philosophical reflection of human life. The period of the Epics succeeded that of the Upanishads. In the *Ramayana* and *Mahabharata* philosophical doctrines were often presented in the form of stories and parables. Many other doctrines followed including the *Bhakti* movement of Ramanuja, Vaishnavism, Saktism, Brahmo and Arya Samaj, Ramakrishna, and Aurobindo. Thus, Hindu doctrine developed in several stages.

Demographically the Hindus are the largest percentage of the population of India comprising 82.64 percent in 1981. Even though the absolute number of people who follow Hinduism increased from 549 million in 1981 to 672 million (82.4 percent) in 1991, there was a marginal decrease in terms of percentage points (Census of India 1991). We find that in some states of India the percentage of Hindus is somewhat higher or much lower than the national average. In 1981, those above it included Himachal Pradesh (95.4), Orissa (95.4) and Madhya Pradesh (92.9). In 1991, in ten States the percentage of Hindus was above the national average. Himachal Pradesh (95.8 percent) has the highest concentration of Hindus. In 1981 those below the national average included the States of West Bengal (76.9), Sikkim (67.2), Manipur (60.0), Kerala (58.1), Punjab (36.9), Jammu and Kashmir (32.2), Meghalaya (18.0) and Nagaland (14.4). In comparison, a total of four States had Hindu population less than 50 percent in 1991 with the lowest being in Meghalaya (5.04 percent). The low figures are due to other religious denominations being higher. The percentage increase for 1971-81 among Hindus was highest in Nagaland (88.4) followed by Sikkim (47.2). Total population rose by 24.69 per cent during 1971-81 and for Hindus the rise was 24.15 per cent. This was in keeping with high fertility and low mortality rates found in this community.

MARRIAGE SYSTEM

Before we discuss specific institutions of the Hindus in India, let us emphasise how widely spread this community is. Consequently, in the areas of marriage or family, there are regional variations. What you will read in these pages is a generalisation covering the common elements and mentioning in passing about the variations. By and large, to marry and raise a family is a sacramental activity for the Hindus. Let us first look at the institution of marriage and then at the family in the Hindu community.

Marriage is a sacred duty for all Hindus. It is an obligatory sacrament because the birth of a son is considered by many Hindus as necessary for obtaining ***moksha***. In order to perform important rituals towards gods and ancestors, the sacred texts decree that it is obligatory for a Hindu to be married and have male descendants. Today, a large number of Hindus may, however, not believe in and practice these traditional ideas and associated customs.

Marriage is considered to be one of the sacraments sanctifying the body, mind and soul of the groom and bride. Therefore at the proper age and time, every Hindu woman and man is expected to get married. A wife is considered to be instrumental in helping her husband fulfil the four kinds of *purushartha*, namely, *dharma, artha, kama* and *moksha*. According to this view of marriage, a man is thought to be incomplete without wife and children.

When we discuss Hindu marriage, we should also speak of the eight forms of marriage, which describe the ways marriages are traditionally consecrated among the Hindus.

Eight Forms of Hindu Marriage

Before enumerating these eight forms, let us make it clear that here we are not talking about the usual usage in sociology regarding the forms of marriage. In sociology we discuss monogamy, polygamy and group marriage etc. under the topic of forms of marriage. In that respect, it will suffice to note here that monogamy (i.e., a man is married to one woman at a time) is the usual form of marriage among the Hindus. But various forms of polygamy are also found in the Hindu community. A widow is allowed to remarry among lower castes.

Higher castes usually prohibit widow marriage. The Hindu Marriage Act of 1955 permits divorce on the grounds of insanity, leprosy, adultery, etc. Coming back to the forms of marriage among the Hindus, only the first four of the following eight forms bring purification to ancestors on the sides of father and mother, the remaining four forms produce no such value. The eight forms are given below.

1. *The Brahma form*: It comprises the gift or giving away of the daughter by the father to a man, who has learnt the Veda.

2. *The Daiva form*: It involves the giving away of the daughter by the father to a priest, who duly officiates at a sacrifice, during the course of

3. *The Arsha form*: It consists of the daughter being given away by the father to a man after receiving a cow and a bull from the bridegroom, not with an intention of selling the child, but in accordance with the requirement of the *dharma*.

4. *The Prajapatya form*: In this form of marriage, the father gives away his daughter to the bridegroom and addresses the couple to perform their *dharma* together.

5. *The Asura form*: It involves a payment by the bridegroom to the bride's father for obtaining a wife.

6. *The Gandharva form*: Here the bride and the bridegroom agree to marry at their own consent. Such a decision to marry is consequently consecrated by going through the sacred rites of marriage.

7 *The Rakshasa form*: This is described as a marriage, through force.

8. *The Paishacha form:* In this form, a man first seduces a woman (who may be intoxicated or mentally retarded) and subsequently marries her.

Of these eight forms of marriage, the giving away the daughter by her father described in the first four is considered as the ideal form. The right to give a maiden in marriage is held by the father, the grandfather, the brothers, the kinspersons and the mother, in that order.

The Hindus lay stress on pre-marital chastity on the part of both the male and the female. The marital bond is also to be respected through mutual fidelity. There are also forms of endogamy (marriage within a certain group) and exogamy (marriage outside the group) for which rules are laid down. These rules are designed to regulate the Hindu marriage in the sense of specifying the choice of spouses within specific groups.

Endogamy

The widest category of endogamy for a Hindu is his or her *varna*. Within each *varna* are several castes and sub-castes which are considered to be the categories for endogamy in the region. We do also come across some inter-caste/ inter-subcaste marriages in contemporary times. Yet, these are few and far between. The rule of caste/ subcaste endogamy is the prescribed mode followed by most of the Hindus all over India.

Exogamy

As regards the rule of exogamy, a Hindu is enjoined not to marry within his own gotra. The word *'gotra'* in this context denotes one's extended family or the clan. The *gotra* of a family is usually named after the ancestor who founded the family. People with a common ancestor are not allowed to marry each other. At present, the rule of exogamy is usually defined in terms of prohibition of marriage within five generations on the mother's side and seven generations on the father's side. However this rule can be circumvented by letting someone of a different *gotra* do the *kanyadaan*, that is the rite of giving the daughter away in marriage. There is a clearly defined limit upto which persons are considered to be related in such a way that their marriage cannot be permitted.

There are marked differences in north India and south India in this regard. In north India, a marriage between both the cross and parallel cousins is prohibited while in south India, cross-cousins are allowed to marry. Thus, the *gotra* rule, as understood in north India, does not apply to the Hindus of south India.

The most common form of marriage is that the bridegroom and his group goes to the bride's home. There the bride is given away by the father or her guardian with due rituals and ceremonies. Variations, of course, occur according to the region and caste.

THE HINDU FAMILY

For a Hindu, the event of marriage signifies the completion of the *brahmacharya ashrama* i.e., the stage of a celibate-life. Marriage heralds the beginning of the householder stage *(grihastha)*. Now, begins the process of the preservation and continuity of the *kula* or the family. A Hindu home symbolises the continuity of its living members, past members that are no more and future members that are yet to come. The living members are considered to be the trustees of the home. It is supposed to belong to the ancestors and includes the interests of the male descendants of the family. The individual as such does not belong to the home. One only performs one's *dharma*. The home is the place where *dharma* and *karma* are practised by the people who are enjoined to remain detached yet conduct the affairs of the world. For a Hindu, his or her life in the stage of a householder is lived and regulated in terms of *dharma* and *karma*. In performing these two activities, one also performs one's *artha* and *kama*. This process leads one towards the final goal, *moksha*.

Form of Hindu Family

The most striking feature of a Hindu family is its jointness. That is to say the unit of residence is often not confined to the parents and their children only. It usually includes three generations living under the same roof and sharing the family property in common.

Whether living in a nuclear or a joint family most Hindu families prefer that each member goes through some basic life-cycle rituals. These sacraments have been prescribed by the sacred texts and are meant for purifying body and mind. The sacraments are supposed to help make the human being into a social being. Some of them purify a human being in the present life and others help in the life-after-death. From birth to death, the sacraments (rituals) help in organising and disciplining the life of the Hindus, and enabling them to perform the *dharma* in accordance with their status. There is diversity in the observance of the sacrament. Depending on the region and caste, different numbers of sacraments are observed. There are rituals from which women are excluded.

Yet other rituals have special significance for them. Thus for a female the nuptial ceremony is regarded as being of equal significance to the sacrament of *upanayan* (the stage when a male child is initiated into the study of the Veda).

Relations among Family Members

As the concepts of *dharma* and *karma* are so much a part of the Hindu way of life both at normative and behavioural levels, we find that each member in the family has his or her prescribed *sacred duty.* General principles of differentiation on the basis of age and sex regulate the relations within the Hindu family, in terms of precedence, obedience and subservience.

Males are more respected than females, and members senior in age command more respect than the younger members. For example, the father is respected more than the mother and has greater authority. The father's mother by virtue of her age, is respected by all members who are younger to her. It is considered ideal for a man and wife to live with all their married sons in a joint family. They are to be respected and cared for by the sons and their wives and children. It is expected that the sons and their wives will perform their duties to the satisfaction of the parents, and thereby earn their blessings and religious merit.

The sons have a right in their fathers' ancestral property. The age old rules of inheritance which are still customary gave ownership and inheritance rights to males, while they give only maintenance rights to females. These customary rules continue to prevail even today. The Hindu Succession Act and the Hindu Adoptions and Maintenance Act, 1956, however, introduced some changes. The Act makes the husband legally responsible for the maintenance of his wife and children. According to this Act (which is also applicable to Jains, Buddhists and Sikhs), the property of a Hindu comes down to his sons, daughters, widow and mother. Daughters legally have a share equal to that of sons in their father's property. In actual practice customs and tradition continue to be so powerful that very few women are able to take advantage of their rights. From being a member of the primary group, such as the family, one goes on to being a part of one's lineage and subcaste/caste. The largest category of this belongingness for a Hindu can be expressed in terms of the idea of *varna*. Let us now understand the *varna* system among the Hindus.

Stages of Life

The Life of a Hindu is considered to be divisible into four stages, namely

i) *brahmacharya ashram*

ii) *grihastha ashram*

iii) *vanaprastha ashram*

iv) *sanyasa ashram*

It is the *dharma* of a Hindu to pass through these stages in one's life. The male members of Brahman, Kshatriya and Vaishya *varna* pass through four different *ashram* (stages) in their life. The first *ashram* .. called *brahmacharya ashram* (the educational stage) from which the fourth *varna,* viz., *Sudra* and women of the first three *varna* are barred

Brahmacharyashram ends (after studentship) at marriage. Celibacy is prescribed till marriage.

The second stage of life is called the *grihasthashram*. During this a man rears a family, earns a living and performs his daily personal and social duties. Following this a man gradually enters the third stage of life called the *vanaprashthashram*. During this stage the householder relinquishes his duties in the household, and devotes his time to religious pursuits. His links with his family are weakened. During this *ashram* a man retires into the forest with or without his wife leaving behind the householder's cares and duties. The final phase of a Hindu's life begins with the stage known as the *sanyasashram*. In this stage one attempts to totally withdraw oneself from the world and its cares by going to the forest and spending the rest of life in pursuit of *moksha*. The four stages of a Hindu's life just described are together called the *varnashrama* system. There is an ideal scheme, which correlates the *vamashrama* phases to ages at which a particular *ashram* begins. However, it is the endeavour that is important and not the age at which this begins. Thus Hinduism permits young unmarried sanyasi, as well as those who never go beyond *grihasthashrama*. Thus there is nothing compulsory about living life in the *varnashram* scheme. It is, however, highly recommended.

At present most Hindus do not systematically go through the *varnashrama*. They do, however, accept these stages to be the ideal ways in which a Hindu should spend his life. Like the four *varna*, the four stages of life are models. In real life, we find that occupations associated with each *varna* are not followed precisely in accordance with what is written in the sacred texts. Today a Brahman may be employed in a shoe company, selling shoes to all the customers irrespective of their *varna* or caste. As we said before, the Hindus are divided into castes or *jati* which are hereditary groups.

Jati System

Jati or castes are hereditary groups in *hierarchical* relation to one another, similar to the hierarchy among *varna*. Brahman castes are the highest while untouchable castes are the lowest. Those between these two extremes are placed according to regional hierarchies.

A caste group can be seen as an extended kin group because members of a caste marry among themselves. Caste endogamy is also explained by the term *beti vyavahar* as against *roti vyavahar*. *Beti vyavahar* refers to the practice of giving and taking of the daughters *(beti)* of different families within a caste. *Roti vyavahar* means only the giving and taking of food *(roti)* with certain categories of people. It is possible to have *roti vyavahar* with people of castes other than one's own. Lower castes accept cooked food and water from higher castes but the opposite is traditionally not permitted. There are certain rules and conditions which regulate the type of food which is accepted when offered to a person of higher caste. The caste groups claim their superior status by showing the evidence of their dietary practices in terms of acceptance/non-acceptance of food and water from particular castes. Besides food, there are also customary discriminatory practices related to different caste groups. For example, the untouchable castes were not permitted to enter certain parts of upper caste streets or houses and temples. This is a typical example of the idea of purity and pollution on which the ideology of caste is supposed to be based. When we consider a caste to be high or low on the basis of its purity or pollution level, we refer to it as a ritual hierarchy of castes. The level of purity/pollution is judged by the prevalent practices relating to acceptance/non-acceptance of food, entry to sacred places and widow-remarriage. In all these hierarchically arranged caste-groups, the scheme of *dharma, artha, kama* and *moksha* is followed without hatred or resentment towards the lower or the higher group. In other words, people born into a caste accept the sacred duty *(dharma)* of their caste and do not question the right to the higher caste-people to social privileges. Within their own caste they organise themselves for fulfilling several purposes. Let us say a few words about caste councils, which have specific functions in regulating the behaviour of their caste members.

Caste Councils and Caste Associations

Generally each caste has its council. The leaders in the council are usually the elderly members of the caste. Caste councils act as a judiciary for caste groups and help settle disputes related to marriage, separation, divorce or any other untoward behaviour of their caste members. The caste councils are localised covering many villages.

Caste associations are recent phenomena. They are engaged in various activities. For example, they run educational institutions, cooperatives, hospitals, old age homes and orphanages. From time to time they print and distribute among their members pamphlets containing information about new rules of behaviour regarding marriage ceremonies, gifts, widow remarriage, etc. They also publicise the nature of punishment to be meted out to defaulters. These associations are generally regional. They also act as political pressure groups. The caste councils and caste associations regulate the behaviour of caste members.

Interdependence

There is interdependence among caste groups. A member of a caste not only interacts within his own caste but also with other castes. Both aspects are very important for the socio-economic and political organisation of the Hindus. We shall now discuss a little about the inter-caste relationships. For the Hindus, the caste system is a coherent and comprehensive system with rituals and occupational hierarchy. The occupational division of castes also helps to maintain equilibrium in the economic sphere. Being religiously oriented, members of different castes accept their rituals and occupational position. Within the framework of caste ideology, they perform their *dharma* and *karma* and endeavour to improve their present and future life. In both the ritual and economic spheres, members of different castes are dependent on one another. Members of different castes are vertically organised which is more manifest in the rural society. The context of Hindu social organisation is to be seen as a system of interdependence among the members of different caste groups. The *jajmani* system is an important aspect of this interdependence.

JAJMANI SYSTEM

In rural areas of India, it was found that a village generally comprises several Hindu castes, each living in different clusters. These castes have relationships of giving and taking of services among one another. Usually the peasant castes are numerically preponderant. Due to their numerical majority and also their economic power they have been called dominant castes by sociologists. The dominant caste needs services of the carpenters, blacksmith, potter, barber, washerman for various farming and ritual activities. The peasants pay in cash and kind for these services from other castes. The castes providing these services depend for their livelihood on the patronage of the dominant caste. In turn, the servicing castes also give support to their patrons in matters of political group formation. The relationship of patron and client among these interacting caste groups usually continue from generation to generation. Thus, the villagers are bound in a system of the exchange of services. Without this exchange the normal day-to-day life may not run smoothly. This is why this aspect is a very important part of Hindu social organisation.

The interdependence among caste groups is also evident in the ritual sphere apart from politico-economic activities. Pilgrimage, worship, recitation of holy texts, life cycle ritual ceremonies, fairs and festivals are rituals which bring together members of different castes. Without a whole series of interaction among them, these activities are just not possible. The instance of a Hindu wedding (one of the life cycle ritual ceremonies) is a case which illustrates this point. Here, a Brahman priest is needed to perform the sacred rites, the barber is required for the shaving and bathing, the drummer beats the drums, the washerman brings freshly laundered clothes, the untouchable takes the charge of sweeping the floor, the gardeners bring flowers and so on.

We can also look at the temple activities as an example of interdependence among castes. Members of different castes perform their respective sacred duties (*sva-dharma*) for the up-keep of the temple. The priestly castes perform the worship, the goldsmith caste provides ornaments for the idols, other castes provide services like cooking, tailoring, filling water, playing drums and so on. Among the Hindus, temples do not figure as prominently in terms of organised systems, as such institutions as the Mosque and Church of the Muslims and Christians respectively. People belonging to different castes organise and perform their duties to earn religious merit and improve their life after death. Each person considers his or her contribution to the temple as one's duty and improves his or her *karma*. No task is less or more important when performed in the context of one's caste membership and one's *ashram* in life. This shows that the ritual aspect of social activities of caste groups forms an important part of social organisation. This aspect is most reflected in collective behaviour at festivals, fairs and pilgrimages. This is the reason why we are now going to discuss here the festivals, fairs and pilgrimages among the Hindus.

Festivals and Pilgrimages

Festivals, pilgrimages and other ceremonial occasions are usually linked with religion. As such they show how both personal identity of the individuals as well as collective identity of the groups are highlighted by the patterns of interaction during these events. Festivals manifest the social cohesion and solidarity of the community. We begin our discussion of this aspect of social organisation by describing festivals, fairs and pilgrimages among the Hindus.

Festivals

Most of the Hindu festivals are linked to the arrival of particular seasons. For example, the festival of *Diwali* marks the arrival of winter season while that of *Holi* signifies the beginning of summer season. Some festivals are associated with eclipses and movements of the heavenly bodies such as the moon and other planets. Many festivals are held in the honour of the deities like Krishna, Siva, Durga, Lakshmi and Rama, e.g., *Dussehra, Durgapuja, Janmashtami,* etc. Local festivals have their roots in the ecology of the region, celebrating myths associated with plants like coconuts, *tulsi (basil),* the sacred tree, or with animals, like elephants, snakes and monkeys. There are regional festivals connected with the agricultural cycle such as the occasion of first ploughing, sowing or harvest. Among the artisans, carpenter, blacksmith and brass-workers, people worship the deity called Vishwakarma.

We shall not go into the ritualistic aspect of these festivals. The emphasis here is on the role these festivals play in social life of the people. During festivals, people in a locality get together and their participation in a common activity enhances their feeling of belonging to a community. These occasions also provide the chance to people for buying and selling special commodities. By preparing special food and wearing special clothes, people bring about the feelings of freshness and change in their day-to-day life. This regenerates them for carrying the routine activities. Recurrence of festivals and associated rituals strengthens their faith in the stability and integrity of their social order.

Festivals like *Holi, Diwali* and *Dussehra* are celebrated on a scale, which includes participation of Hindus as well as non-Hindus. They provide occasions for a meeting across religions.

Associated with festivals are fairs, which are held at prescribed times on a holy spot. Sometimes, fairs assume independent significance and attract the participation of cross-section of society. Some famous fairs such as the fair of Sonepur or Pushkar draw people from all over the country. In these fairs, craftsmen bring their special artware, artists come to present their shows, agricultural surplus is brought for selling, brisk trading summer season|n cattle, horses, elephants. Each fair is both and movements a secular occasion and people participate in both with equal enthusiasm.

Pilgrimage

Not very different from a fair is a pilgrimage. The cultural unity of the Hindus is expressed in the institution of pilgrimage. When a pilgrim goes to the southern pilgrim centre at Rameshwaram, he or she also aspires to reach the northern end of the country, at Badrinath. Most pilgrims also aspire to go to Puri in the east and to Dwarikanath in the west.

In these places of pilgrimage, there is often a fair being held during the periods pilgrims arrive in large numbers. Generally, people go to these places in large groups. Such groups are mostly formed on the basis of kin relationships. They may also include neighbours, friends and business partners.

Different sects of Hinduism have acquired pilgrim centres around the whole country over time. Besides the four centres in the four directions, the Sakta sect has more than fifty centres of pilgrimage. There are seven places of pilgrimage, dedicated to the Sun god, Surya. One of them is in Multan, in West Pakistan. Despite linguistic, racial, and cultural differences, most Hindus undertake long and arduous journeys to the many varied pilgrim places. This adds an important dimension to their social life.

4

Muslim Social Organisation

The word 'Islam' means submission to the will of Allah. The followers of Islam called Muslims believe that Quran is the true word of Allah. They believe the Quran was revealed to mankind through the medium of his Prophet and messenger, Muhammed. Islam came into being in the early seventh century in west central Arabia but its systematic formulation and establishment took place only 622 AD, when Muhammed emigrated from the city of Mecca to Medina. Thus Muslim calendar records events from the first lunar month of that year July 16th 622 AD.

Prior to the emergence of Islam in Western Central Arabia, there were only clusters of warring tribes. Prophet Muhammed brought in a number of social reforms and established a well ordered set of beliefs and practices. Islam, as a religion, became established in this region and began to spread as a political community or "ummah" with its own laws and socio-political institutions. Today Muslims form about one seventh of the world's population. They are highly concentrated in Asia and Africa. Their tiniest concentration is in Oceania (includes Polynesia, Micronesia and Melanesia).

With regard to the emergence of Islam in India, it was introduced into India by Arab traders, who gradually established settlements on the western and eastern coasts of south India. They obtained permission to practice their religion. Sind was conquered by the Arabs early in the eighth century and north west Punjab by the Turks in the eleventh century. The Delhi Sultanate was established by 1206 AD. It was about the sixteenth century that Mughals built up an extensive empire. The establishment of Muslim government at any place was usually followed by the construction of a mosque and other related socio-religious activities. As the Muslim rule strengthened in India, their numbers also increased. The large numbers of Muslims in India are mainly due to conversion.

Today numerically the Muslims comprise the largest minority community in India. According to the 1981 census Muslims constituted around twelve percent of the total population in India. In 1991 also their strength remained same as in the previous decade, around twelve percent of the total population. In 1981 Jammu and Kashmir had the highest percentage of Muslims (64.19 percent). In 1991, the Muslim population was highest in Assam. In Punjab, Himachal Pradesh and Orissa the Muslim population is low. In Kerala and in West Bengal Muslims formed nearly 21 percent of the total population of those states in 1981. Assam (28.43), Kerala (23.3), Uttar Pradesh and West Bengal were the States, which had Muslim population in 1991 above national average. Some States such as Sikkim and Meghalaya had Muslim population less than 1 per cent.

TENETS OF ISLAM

Islam means submission to or acceptance of the will of God. Its perfect form is found in the teachings of the Quran and the Sunnah (acts and sayings of Prophet Muhammed). Islam is a monotheistic religion, i.e. it believes in one God who is considered the Creator of the universe, of time and space whose law governs everything that exists. The Quran is the word of God, revealed to his messenger, Prophet

Muhammed, in order to lead mankind on a righteous path. The Muslims believe that there will be a 'Last Day' when God will judge all mankind. The belief is that on the judgement day, those who have led a good life will be rewarded and those who have led a bad life will be punished.

The important commands of Islam are prayer, fasting, pilgrimage to Mecca, performance of all that is enjoined and abstinence from what is forbidden and *Jihad* or striving in the way set by God with all the resources at one's disposal. The social rules of behaviour include among other things the observation of the principles of equality and brotherhood among Muslims and of earning one's livelihood through personal labour. The totality of beliefs and practices is called the *Shariah* (path) of Islam. Now let us examine the Islamic view of social equality in order to understand the link between what is believed and what is practised in relation to their social organisation.

Islam is claimed by its believers to be a religion of equality. There are a number of Quranic verses that instruct the Muslims that in evaluating an individual they should not accord much importance to such factors as race, nationality, or ancestry. What matters is the extent to which a Muslim practices the teachings of the Quran. Muslims insist that the principle of equality be upheld in day-to-day living. All Muslims irrespective of their group affiliation could say namaz together and that they need not observe restrictions on eating and drinking together whenever an occasion arises. It is also held that there are no formal restrictions on inter-group (caste) marriages, and that, in fact, Islam encourages it. The existence of an inter-group hierarchy is also denied.

Social Divisions Among Muslims

The most popularly known division among the Muslims, all over the world, is the division between Shias and Sunnis.

They hold the divergent views of and interpretations over Islamic texts and tradition. In India, a vast majority of Muslims are Sunnis. Apart from these kind of divisions there are also other kinds of social groupings among Muslims in India, which reflect the influence of Hindu beliefs and practices specially those relating to caste system.

Muslims in India are divided into two major sections, (i) those who claim to be the descendants of early Muslim immigrants and (ii) those of indigenous origin whose ancestors were converted to Islam. The former section has often been called *Ashraf* or *Shurafa* (singular *sharif*, Arabic words, meaning honourable), while the latter section does not have a specific name. In Bengal, according to Risley, it was designated as *Ajlaf* (for clean occupational castes) and *Arzal* (for unclean castes).

Here, we will first discuss the *Ashraf* category of Muslims and then Muslim converts of Indian origin.

Ashraf

In the Muslim social hierarchy, the descendants of immigrants from Persia, Afghanistan, Arabia and Turkistan are recognised as the highest category of Muslims in India. The Indian Muslim castes, known as Sayyed, Shaikh, Mughal and Pathan comprise this category.

Sayyed are considered to be descended from Fatima's line. She was the daughter of the Prophet Muhammed. As direct descendants of the Prophet, Sayyed are accorded highest social status among the Muslims. They are subdivided into two lineage sections, Hasani and Husaini. After the names of the descendants of Hasan and Husain. Further subdivisions of Sayyed are called Jafari from Jafar as Sadiq, Rizvi from Ali ibr Muras ar-Raza and so on. Some Sayyed subdivisions are named after the disciples of Sayyed saints such as Chishti, Jalali and Oadiriya.

In the second rank of social hierarchy of the Muslims come the Shaikh. They are considered to be the descendants of early Muslims migrants of Mecca and Medina. They trace their descent from either (i) The Ansar or Ansari (the helpers), meaning those who provided shelter to the Prophet and his followers, or (ii) the Muhajirum the immigrants, meaning those who were citizens of Mecca and migrated to Medina as the followers of the Prophet.

The Mughal and Pathan subdivisions of the *Ashraf* rank third in the social hierarchy of the Muslims. Both are almost equal in social status. Those who came to India with the Mughal (concept form of the word Mongol) armies and subsequently settled here were known as the Mughal. Their main subdivisions, based on different ethnic and tribal origins, are Chagtai, Uzbek, Tajik, Turkmans and Qizilbarh.

The Pathan are descendants of those who migrated to India from Afghanistan or from the Pashto-speakers of the North Western Frontier Province of Pakistan. At present, regional subdivisions of Pathan Muslims are based on their prolonged residence in one or the other parts of India, e.g., Rohila Pathan are the inhabitants of Rohilkhand region. Mostly, the Pathan have four major sub-sections namely, Yusufzai, Lodhi, Ghani and Vakar. These sub-sections are further divided into sub-sub-sections, such as, Ghilzai, Mohammed, Mohammedzai, Tarin, Durrangi.

Among the *Ashraf* groups, are also included those pseudo-*Ashraf* who claim descent from one of the Ashraf caste. Ansari has given several examples of attempts by some groups for raising their social status through their claims to Ashraf descent. Ansari has given a long list of certain castes, mentioned in the 1931 census report of Uttar Pradesh. These Muslim castes have tried to raise their social status by claiming new surnames and also corresponding high social status.

Muslim Converts

The Muslim converts of Indian origin are generally called by their caste names. In this group are placed three distinct groups, namely, converts from high caste of the Hindus, converts from clean occupational castes and converts from unclean occupational castes (Bhangi or sweeper, Chamar or tanner). We will briefly speak about each of the three groups.

Converts from High Castes

In the social hierarchy of the Muslims in India, converts from high castes of the Hindus are placed below the rank of *Ashraf*. Many of the Rajput branches of a family in north India have Muslim branches, e.g., the Bais, Bhatti, Bisen, Chandel, Bargujar, Chauhan, Pawar, Rathore, Tomar. At times some of these groups try to mix with higher-ranking groups of Muslims. By and large these converts still follow some of the Hindu practices, e.g., they do not marry first cousins, either cross or parallel. Islamic law allows the marriage of near-kin whereas among the Hindus in north India, prohibition regarding marriage extends to distant degrees of kinship relations on both father's and mother's sides.

Clean Occupational Castes

Clean castes are those, which are permitted contact with higher castes under certain rules. These are opposed to unclean castes which are not permitted any contact with higher castes. The matter of cleanliness is considered in terms of the nature of one's traditional occupation. Some occupations involve necessary contact with the persons of higher castes. People who perform such occupations belong to clean castes. For example, a barber has to necessarily come in close contact with his client. A barber belongs to a clean caste.

The castes, belonging to clean occupations rank below the *Ashraf* and Muslim Raiputs, comprise the bulk of Muslim population in India. The descendants of the converts from Hindu clean castes belong to this category. The process of conversion often involved either groups in different castes of the whole caste group. Many castes of this kind have both Hindu and Muslim sections. For example, it is common to find a carpenter, tailor, laundryman, potter, barber, and goldsmith in both the Hindu and Muslim communities.

These sections operate exclusively in matters of family, marriage and kinship while they also act as one in trade union activities. We can divide these castes in three groups, namely, (a) castes without a Hindu counterpart in existence at present, (b) castes with a larger Muslim section and a smaller Hindu section, (c) castes which are opposite of (b), i. e., with a smaller Muslim section and a larger Hindu section. Let us briefly discuss each of these groups.

Ansari (1959-60: 41-42) includes the following castes of Uttar Pradesh in this group.

a) Atishbaz (firework maker), Bhand (jester), Bhatiyara (innkeeper), Bhishti (water carrier), Gaddi (grazier), Momin Julaha (Muslim weaver), Mirasi (Musician), Qassab (butcher), and Faqir (beggar). According to Ansari, all these castes have exclusive Muslim following. Only in some cases there are Hindu castes with similar occupations. But these groups are known by different caste-labels. For example, a Bhishti (water carrier) in Hindu community is known as Kahar.

b) Castes with larger Muslim and smaller Hindu section in Uttar Pradesh, according to Ansari are known by the following names.

   Darji (tailor), Dhuniya (cotton carder), Kunjra or Kabariya (green grocer), Manihar (bangle maker),

Saigalgar (metal sharpener), and Rangrez (cloth printer).

Ansari's account of these castes is based mainly on his study of the 1931 census reports. It is possible that this situation has now changed. In fact, we need fresh data on this aspect to say something with certainty.

c) Castes with larger Hindu than Muslim sections have obviously provided few followers to Islam. Speaking about Uttar Pradesh, Ansari includes Dhobi (Laundry man), Kumhar (potter), Nai or Hajjam (Barber) and Teli (oil presser) in this group.

Muslim sections of these castes are identified on account of their separate caste councils (Panchayat). These are endogamous castes, practising their own ceremonies and customs.

Unclean Castes

Lastly, we have the Muslim untouchables, occupying bottom place in the Muslim social hierarchy. These people do the menial tasks, including scavenging and sweeping. They are descendants of converts who retained their low social status along with their caste name, occupation and poverty. For example, a Bhangi (scavenger), either a Muslim or a non-Muslim, is not permitted to enter a mosque. In theory, it is possible for a Muslim Bhangi to pray in a mosque, but in practice his entry into a mosque is disapproved. On the other hand, an untouchable Muslim is permitted to learn Quran while an untouchable Hindu is not supposed to learn religious texts.

Kin Relationships

Having discussed social divisions among the Muslims, let us now see how these divisions reflect the operation of caste and kin relationships in Muslim social organisation. Cultural characteristics constituting caste among the Hindus may in turn be used to evaluate the situation of Muslims in India. Such a discussion will help us to follow the interrelation between caste and kinship systems. We can see how caste relationships also act as kin groups. These cultural characteristics may be put as follows.

i) caste is endogamous

ii) it involves occupational specialisation

iii) castes are hierarchically ordered

iv) there are restrictions on social intercourse and commensality.

Endogamy: Zat & Biradari

Muslims use the term *zat* (equivalent of caste) to express the purity of descent. The *zat* is, therefore, primarily an endogamous unit of society. The households belonging to each *zat* in the village conceive of themselves as a collectivity and designate themselves as *bhai-band or biradari* (literally caste-brotherhood). This solidarity among the members is not merely a fictional notion, but rests on demonstrable kinship linkages. Since all the households belonging to each caste are descendants of one common ancestor, or a few related common ancestors, who had settled in the village at the time it was established or subsequently related by ties of common descent. On account of the custom of preferential cousin marriage prevalent among some *bhai-band* or *biradaris,* there always exists a tie of descent among them.

The *biradari* resembles caste in the features of its inner structure, e.g. membership is determined only by birth and the group boundaries are maintained through endogamy. However, violations of the rules of endogamy are not dealt with in an identical manner; they range from mere disapproval to outright excommunication. Among the

Ashraf, the caste brotherhoods are subdivided again into *Biadharis* (marriage circles) to provide a restricted circle in which to choose a wife. Sometimes the endogamous circle becomes so narrow that it includes only the extended kinship group of the person's parents. Such a limited kinship group is generally termed a *kuf.* Whereas the Biradari generally functions for all ceremonial intercourse, the *biadhari* (marriage circles) within the *Biradari* is restricted to the choosing of wives. The Muslim Rajputs are very endogamous, but do not marry first cousins as the Ashrafs do.

Some of the occupational castes such as the Qasab (butcher), Manihar (bracelet maker) are almost strictly endogamous and they generally do not marry outside their castes. Certain other occupational castes, such as Julaha (weaver), Nai (barber), Kumhar (potter) may even practice isogamy (marrying equals). Finally the Bhangi (scavanger) caste is confined to itself for marriage purposes. A clean caste person would not and does not like to establish marriage relations with Bhangis.

Occupational Specialisation

The second attribute of caste or *Biradari,* which resembles the Hindu caste, is their association with a traditional occupation. An exception to this is the various *Ashraf* groups whose names are indicative of their origin or descent. But in the case of many others groups the various names are indicative of the respective traditional occupations.

Since the division of castes entails a degree of occupational specialisation amongst them, the relationship among the different castes tends toward economic interdependence. The different castes participate in this system in different capacities according to their place in the productive organisation revolving around land. The *Ashraf* groups, who are predominantly landowners and whose principal occupation in the village is cultivation, form the nucleus of the system of economic interdependence among the castes. They are referred to as the *jajmans*. Muslim castes, whose names imply a traditional occupation, render specialised and traditional economic and ritual services for their *jajmans*. Some of the Muslim castes in this respect are Barhai (carpenter), Darzi (tailor), Dhobi (laundryman) Kumhar (potter), Lohar (blacksmith), Nai or Hajjam (barber), Sunar (goldsmith) Teli (oil presser) Bhishti (water carrier), Gaddi (grazier), Julaha (weaver), Qasab (butcher) etc. Each of these occupational castes, with both Hindu and Muslim section, is sometimes united for trade-union purposes. But for social and ceremonial purposes each section is generally limited to itself.

Hierarchical Ordering

The third important attribute of caste is the hierarchical ordering of various Muslim groups. Every Muslim caste has its definite place within the total social organisation. Each caste is considered to be either high or low in relation to other castes. The *Ashraf* castes top the social ranking when compared to the other Muslim castes. Further, every Muslim belongs to a certain caste, his/her social status is, therefore, defined and often fixed according to the status of the caste to which he/she belongs. All the Muslim castes, like Hindu castes, are graded into a hierarchical scheme. The *Ashrafs*, almost by common consensus, are assigned the highest position in the ranking strata by virtue of their supposed descent from Prophet Mohammad. The Bhangis and Chamars are assigned the lowest rank. The Muslim Rajputs are ranked lower than *Ashraf* but are considered higher than the various clean occupational castes. The latter are superior to the Muslim untouchables but inferior to Muslim Rajputs.

Restrictions on Social Intercourse

Finally, one observes the presence of restrictions on social intercourse and commensalism (i.e. eating together) among the various Muslim castes. The various *Ashraf* groups observe no restriction in inter-group commensality among themselves. There are, however, several restrictions on commensal relations with the rest of the caste groupings who are considered inferior to

The various *Ashraf* groups assign low status to the non-Ashraf groups because it is maintained that the latter do not observe certain ritual cleanliness *(paki)*.

Social Control

Having described how Muslim social organisation is internally differentiated and hierarchically ranked, we shall now turn to other organisational aspects of Muslim society, specially those which restrict and control individuals and groups within the prescribed normative framework. Such an organisation takes two forms: direct control through a governing body, such as a council, and indirect control through public opinion. The Hindu social organisation operates and maintains itself through an operation of both these forms. Let us look at both of them in a little more detail. When particular acts of individuals are not approved by their caste fellows they become the victim of severe criticism. If a violation is serious, the criticism takes the form of action and the offender faces a social boycott the extent of which varies according to the nature of the offence. The other mode of control, through an authoritative body, is generally paractised among the occupational castes where such a body is known as the panchayat. membership in the caste panchayat generally includes all the adult males of the caste; the caste headman, known as *Sarpanch* is usually elected. In a situation of emergency, generally when a member of the caste has committed an offence, the whole panchayat is summoned to hear the case. The caste panchayat then gives its judgement. The most frequent punishment among them is a strict social boycott which is termed as *hugga pani band* (i.e. such a person is not welcomed or entertained by fellow caste members) or *zat biradari bahar* (expulsion from the caste brotherhood).

Among *Ashraf* and some of the higher occupational castes like higher Hindu castes, no authoritative caste council functions. Instead, the general caste opinion of approval and disapproval passes through the communicative network among caste members. Among the *Ashrafs*, joint family functions as the basic unit which controls its members in almost all social and personal matters; in the case of most occupationally related castes which have well organised caste Panchayats, the joint family remains comparatively less significant in social affairs. Among Muslims, Bhangi (Scavenger), Dhobi (washerman), Teli (oil presser), Julaha (weaver) etc. have well organised panchayats which function both as trade unions and as social organisations.

Family, Marriage and Inheritance

The regulation of the Shariah along with the traditions of the Prophet provides us with a framework for identifying practices relating to Muslim marriage, family and inheritance. The Shariah consists of regulations pertaining to marriage, family and inheritance. The traditions of the Prophet include records of the Prophet's own manner of living and pronouncements on various matters of daily life. These traditions have become a source of normative guidance for Muslim social life. Let us discuss these traditions relating to family, marriage and inheritance in Muslim society in greater detail.

Family

Muslims, like other communities in India, live in small and large households. Both types of families, i.e., joint family and nuclear family, are found among the Muslims. The size of the family varies from four to eight members or as large as twenty five in number. Vast majority of the joint families are located in the rural areas and more nuclear families are located in urban areas.

Patrilineal and Matrilineal Family: Muslim family is usually patrilocal and patrilineal. After marriage the couple establishes the family at the place of the husband. Exceptions to patrilineal family are rare but not altogether absent. For instance, with the absence of a male heir, the head of the family may invite his daughter and her conjugal family to establish residence in his house. In such a situation, son of the daughter is adopted and becomes the legal heir to property. Another example of departure from the normative type of patrilocal and patrilineal family is the matrilineal families found in Lakshadweep Islands, Malabar district (Kerala) and Ratnagiri districts (Maharashtra) in India.

Family Break-up: In Islam, celibacy is discouraged and Muslims are enjoined to marry and multiply. Although divorce is a common phenomenon among Muslims, Islam does not permit divorce to be taken lightly. This is indicated in the Prophet's words, "of all things Allah has made lawful for his servants, the most hateful to him is divorce,". Thus Islam wanted to provide both for family stability as well as divorce in situations where marital maladjustments render healthy family life impossible.

Husband and Wife: Among Muslims, it is the duty of the husband or head of the family to provide for the maintenance of the family. In Islam, the wife has a legal right to be maintained by the husband. The social life of the majority of the Muslim women is confined within the family. She spends a major portion of her time in taking care of household matters and in the upbringing of children. Her social and emotional needs are fulfilled by her family. In fact her role and function in the family determines her social position in the family.

Sons and Daughters: Within the Muslim family sons and daughters generally do not enjoy equal social position. In the past even the birth of a girl was considered as an unfortunate and unpleasant event in the Muslim family). However, these days children are given equal treatment in routine general matters. But in important matters such as education, choice of career,. choice of partner in marriage, the daughters are sometimes discriminated and sons are favoured.

Segregation of Women: Another notable practice among the Muslim families is *'purdah'* or seclusion of women. Majority of Muslims still live in joint families, where women reside in separate part of the house called *'Zanana'* . The seclusion of women from participation in certain spheres of life is enforced through the custom of *'purdah'*. In the past, this custom was considered as a symbol of higher social position of the family. Social change and education has made some dent in this custom. Yet even today this custom remains an important aspect of the Muslim family.

Marriage

Let us examine here the essential features of Muslim marriage in the context of Islamic religion, which has provided the ideological foundation for social behaviour.

Nikah: Marriage among Muslims is known by the Arabic word *'Nikah'*. It takes place in the form of contract and is not considered as sacrosanct (exceedingly sacred). It is obligatory in character. Muslim law maintains that the main objective of *'Nikah'* is procreation and legalisation of children. The essential elements of Muslim marriage are: a) marriage proposal is made by or on behalf of the concerned parties; b) acceptance of the proposal in the presence of one or two male and two female witnesses; c) settlement of Dower or *Mehr*.

The arrangement of marriage is largely the responsibility of the parents, particularly that of the father. In the past, bride or bridegroom had no say in the selection of his or her partner. This disadvantage was even more glaring in the case of female. With the passage of time male members of Muslim community have acquired some freedom in the choice of their spouse. In case of woman the situation has not much changed

Age at Marriage: Islamic law does not specify any particular age limit for marriage. The only condition is that a minor girl cannot join the husband after marriage. Although young girls may be married but the girl should join the husband only after attaining maturity. This interpretation is not related to age but to attainment of puberty. According to the latest amendment of 'Child Marriage Restraint Act' of 1929 the minimum marriageable age of male and female is 21 years and 18 years respectively. Nevertheless early marriage is still widely prevalent in the Muslim community.

Marriage Ceremony: The ceremony of Muslim marriage, i.e. *'Nikah'* is conducted by 'kazi'. It is customary to recite verses from Quran so as to seek Allah's blessings for the couple. Consent is sought from both the individuals. In order to complete the marriage ceremony, a formal document *'Nikahnama'* is prepared. Notwithstanding other aspects, *'Nikahnama'* specifies the nature of Dower or *Mehr*. *Mehr* is a particular sum of money or property, which the bride is entitled to receive from bridegroom in consideration of marriage. It's a sort of guarantee for the security of the woman. *Mehr* is an indispensable custom without which no Muslim marriage can acquire social or legal legitimacy. *Mehr* is not a fixed amount of money or property. It varies according to the social and economic status of the concerned families. The mode of payment is also flexible. It can be paid either immediately after the marriage or postponed till some mutually agreeable future date.

Mehr and Dowry: Islamic Law never mentioned about dowry. But in reality it has become a common practice. Broadly speaking, the amount of *Mehr* has been reduced to a mere symbolic value. Usually it is several times smaller than the dowry, which the parents of many girls pay at the time of marriage. Thus the ritualisation of *Mehr* and the increasing practice of dowry have adversely affected the status of Muslim women and their marriage prospects.

Polygamy: A notable practice associated with Muslim marriage is polygamy or plurality of wives. In Islam, a Muslim male may have four wives at a time. However, he must be able to treat them on equal and just bases. In India, this practice of plurality of wives became popular during the Muslim Rule. These days it is becoming less prevalent. It has considerably decreased among the urban and educated sections of Muslim population.

Islam permits marriage between both parallel and cross cousins. A notable preferential choice is whereby a male marries his father's brother's daughter. Mohammedan Law also provides for certain restrictions in marriage so far as other communities are concerned. A Muslim woman cannot marry a '*Kithabian*' or non-Muslim. But a male can marry a '*Kithabia*'. Let us make it clear that '*Kithabia*'*(n)* is an individual who believes in a religion revealed through a book {other than Quran) but does not engages in the practice of 'idol' or 'fire' worship, etc.

Divorce and Remarriage: Under Muslim Personal Law, husband enjoys unlimited freedom in matters of divorce. He is permitted to divorce his wife according to his own pleasure or without assigning any reason or cause. On the other hand, a woman does not enjoy such a freedom. This custom has resulted in man's domination arid power over the woman. Although the Prophet gave to the women, the right of obtaining separation on reasonable grounds but in practice this is not so. In general there are two types of divorce, i.e *'talaq'* and *'khol'*. *Talaq* is exjudicial divorce and it becomes effective when the husband unilaterally pronounces the word *'Talaq'* thrice. In *'Khol'*, divorce takes place by mutual consent.

After divorce a woman is not free to remarry immediately. She is supposed to wait for a specified period before seeking remarriage. This period is called *'iddat'*. On the whole *'talaq'* is considered the most detestable custom in Islam. In India, with the 'Dissolution of Muslim Marriage Act', 1939, Muslim woman got the right to divorce her husband on certain specified grounds but men still enjoy much greater freedom as compared to women in matters of divorce. The Quran and Islamic tradition favour widow marriage. The responsibility for marrying a widow lies with her parents. Although the provision for widow marriage is clearly stated yet until recent times such marriages were presented because of socio-cultural considerations.

Inheritance: Though Islamic society is patrilineal, women in Islam enjoy the right to inherit property. Islamic jurisprudence defines not only the scope of the property a woman may own-by inheritance, by gift and by the fruits of her own labour but also recognises the absolute ownership of it. Both daughters and widows inherit property, including land and houses, from their parents and husbands. Islamic law grants women, even if childless, remarried or divorced complete rights over their inherited property. However, women inherit smaller shares of wealth than men do, a son's share is twice that of a daughter.

Life Cycle Rituals and Festivals

Life cycle rituals and festivals constitute important elements of every religious community. They serve, apart from other things, the purpose of reaffirming one's faith in one's religion. Some of the (important Muslim ceremonies include life-cycle rituals around birth, marriage and death. A few important ones are (i) the naming of the child (ii) circumcision which is done by a barber or in a hospital (iii) the *Bismillah* ceremony, which initiates a child into reading Quran. Feasts and celebrations associated with these ceremonies and festivals not only make for social solidarity among the believers but also allow people from different socio-religious backgrounds to meet and know each other. Let us now look at some important festivals among Muslims. They have two main festivals, namely, *Id-ul-Fitr and Id-ul-Azha.*

On the last day of *Ramzan* and on the sighting of the moon, we have *Id-ul-Fitr*. A prayer service is held. Muslims exchange embraces and greetings after prayers and participate in feasting and merriment. As is clear, these major religious activities and festivals make for social solidarity among Muslims and strengthen their social organisation

Ramzan occurs in the ninth month of the calendar. It is the month of self-purification, and commiseration with the poor. Quran is recited regularly.

Another important festival is *Id-Ul-Adha* or *Bakr-Id.* It is celebrated on the tenth day of the month *Dhul Hijja*. This involves a sacrifice made by pilgrims and performed as part of the ceremonies of *Hajj* in Arabia. The ceremony is observed simultaneously by all Muslims the world over. The Muslims offer food among household members, friends and relatives and the poor. The celebration of the Prophet's birthday, *Idi-Milad* and death anniversaries of famous saints have also been added to the list of Muslim festivals. Besides these festivals, many Muslims celebrate several Hindu festivals. For example, the Moghul converts gave official status to celebration of *Diwali* and *Holi.*

Mubartam, is the first month of the Muslim calendar, commemorates the martyrdom of Imam Husain. Ta'zia processions of the Imams grave are carried out on this day. *Muharram* is not a festival in the usual sense of the term but a commemoration and a period of mourning. On the appearance of the new moon the *fatiha* (opening chapter of the Quran) is recited in the *imam bara* and some refreshment *(sherbet)* taken. The observance lasts ten to twelve days.

5

Sikh Social Organisation

The Sikhs are those who follow the teachings of ten leaders, whom they call *Guru*. All these Gurus lived between 1469 A.D. and 1708 A.D. in Punjab. This State is the Northern part of India. Over the centuries, guided by the Gurus, the Sikh religion expanded and increased its strength in India. However, in 1947 Punjab was divided between India and Pakistan. Many Sikhs who had lived in what became Pakistan were made homeless. They had to migrate to different countries. Sikhs have settled in many parts of the world including the United Kingdom, Canada, the United States of America, Germany and Kenya. There are not more than 12 million Sikhs in the world. Most of these are settled in Punjab. They comprised a little less than 2 per cent of India's 800 million population in 1981. In 1991 their strength was 1.99 percent of the total population. The Sikhs are spread all over India. They are also in many professions including business, academics, civil service, medicine and defence of India.

The Sikh population by head of household is 1.95 per cent of the total population of India. However, there were differences in state-wise percentages. Thus in Haryana they constituted 6.21 percent, while in Punjab they constituted 60.75 percent of the population of the two states respectively. These were the two states where Sikh percentage was higher than the national average. However, there were states where this average was much lower. These states included Andhra Pradesh (0.03), Bihar (0.11), Gujarat (0.07), Rajasthan(1.44) and so on. In terms of percentage increase over 1971-81 this had been most in Sikkim (242.5) which had 0.10 percentage of Sikhs. In Orissa (39.85) and in M. P. (44.5) the percentage increase in Sikh population over 1971-81 had been 26.15. In 1991, Punjab (63 per cent) and Haryana (5.81 per cent) were the only two states, which had Sikh population higher than the national average. There were only a handful of people who follow Sikkism in States such as Nagaland, Sikkim, Tripura etc.

Over 80 percentage of the Sikhs are farmers. Next to this profession, army career is the next most popular vocation. They form ten per cent of the armed forces. The Sikh farmers played the leading role in the Green Revolution in the Sixties raising the wheat yield per acre by three hundred per cent! Again three of the nine Indians who climbed Mount Everest were Sikhs. They are eminent in many areas of life in India.

Ideological Basis Of Sikhism

The Sikh religion clearly represents a case of fission and fusion in the religious ideology of Indian society. Around five hundred years ago, it had its origins in the wider religious revolt, called *bhakti* movement which was primarily directed against the bigotry and caste-based narrowism in which the then Hindu religion in a specific region was steeped. In this variant of Hinduism, the caste system which was founded upon the notion of ritual purity and pollution and accorded top position to the Brahmin and lowest to the Shudra was particularly isolated for its inhuman bias. The same *Bhakti* movement also tended to define the relationship between man and the God in simple terms of 'devotion', 'supplication' and purity of conduct.

The movement thus tended to build a fraternity of the devoted ones, bound together in their common love of God. It came down with a heavy hand upon the iniquitous caste system, which imposed upon the lowly 'untouchables' a variety of indignities and restrictions. These included those concerning *commensality*, interdining, marriage and even of physical contact. It is worth mentioning here that the untouchables under the caste system were denied any social status or identity. The status they were accorded was that which accrues to a slave and one, which reduces a human being to the level of a 'commodity'.

Sikhism strongly denounced this caste-sanctioned inequity and declared a fraternity of God's beings. In this there were neither any barriers nor any caste-based system of inequality. Thus a spirited affirmation of the principle of religious egalitarianism and a contemptuous rejection of the purity-pollution barrier by Sikhism became a point of fission which tore away this newly-born religion from the then practised brand of Hinduism.

Simultaneously, Sikhism also declared an open revolt against an endless array of 'inhuman' practices carried on in the name of religion, most of which were simply repugnant to human sensibility and sensitivity. But, sanctioned as they were by the Brahmans themselves, who were the ritual leaders of the Hindu society, they were hardly challenged with any degree of effectiveness. Thus, the cycle of mental and moral domination by Brahmans continued, oppressing all the castes—but most of all, the lowly untouchables. Sikhism emerged and evolved as a revolt against all this religious bigotry and irrationality.

Guru Nanak

Sikhism was founded by Guru Nanak who was born in the year 1469 in a place called Talwandi-Nankana Sahib, now in Pakistan. His father, a high caste Hindu called Kalyan

Chand (also fondly addressed as 'Kalu') of the Bedi Kshatriya clan, was a village accountant in the service of the local Muslim landlord. Nanak received an education in traditional Hindu lore and the ruiments of Islam. Early in life he began associating with holy men. For a time he worked as the accountant of the Afghan chieftain at Sultanpur. There, a Muslim family servant, Mardana who was also a musician, joined him. Nanak began to compose hymns. Mardana put them to music and together they organised community hymn singing. From the offerings made, they organised a free canteen. Even now, no payment is required to be made for eating in such a place which is maintained from voluntary donations by 'devotees' and is fondly called *guru-ka-langar*, or the free kitchen of the spiritual master.

Here Muslims, as well as Hindus of all castes eat together. It is not just the question of different castes having the facility of eating together; rather they had to eat together in order to show c nformity to Sikhism, since denial of caste-barriers was the basic characteristic of Sikhism.

At Sultanpur, Nanak had his first vision of God, in which he was ordered to preach to mankind. One day he disappeared into the water while bathing in a stream. Reappearing from it on the third day, he proclaimed: "There is no Hindu, there is no *Mussalman*".

Many miracles and marvels are associated with the life of Guru Nanak. It is important to remember that many incidents of his life as passed down historically sharply highlight some fundamental features of Sikhism. In other words, principles of religious morality in Sikhism are not taught or preached as abstractions. Rather, they are illustrated and affirmed in the way the Sikh gurus lived their lives. This character of the Sikh norms and morals adds a touch of immediate familiarity to the religion and its fundamental precepts. It removes from them the mystique, which often shrouds principles of religious morality.

For example, Guru Nanak, in one of his spiritual sojourns to Haridwar, demonstrated the futility of propitiating the far-off and unknown gods. Nanak saw some high caste pilgrims throw water in the direction of the sun by way of propitiating their ancestors. On seeing this he began to throw water in the opposite direction. When asked to account for this 'odd' behaviour of his, he explained that he was trying to water his fields. He said that these were only a few hundred miles away while the sun and the ancestors were in any case located much further.

In another incident, Nanak demonstrated the sanctity of honestly earned bread, another central canon of Sikh faith. While stopping over in a town during one of his spiritual wanderings, he deliberately chose to dine at the house of a poor carpenter, rejecting an invitation from a rich money-lender. There he demonstrated that he was correct. He squeezed the bread of the money-lender. Drops of blood came out of it. He then squeezed the bread of the carpenter. Drops of milk came out of it. He said that the money-lender earned his livelihood by exploiting the poor while the carpenter earned his livelihood through honest means. Hence he preferred to dine with the carpenter.

The purpose here is not to lend unqualified credulity to this 'folk' version of the incident. Instead the idea is to emphasise the popular perception held of both the Gurus and Sikhism. These incidents also illustrate popular beliefs in the pragmatic and livable character of Sikh faith.

Another central canon of Sikh faith has a direct relevance on the connection between religious precept and the practical day-to-day morality. This is a positive injunction by the Gurus for a virtuous engagement in the duties of a householder rather than withdrawai from the world as idealised in Hinduism or in Buddhism. The withdrawal from the affairs of this illusion-ridden world is idealised in Hinduism. It prescribes the eventual superiority of *sanyasa*, total withdrawal from the world, as something that everyone should try to approximate in the last stage of life. In Buddhism it is idealised via the formal injunction of Buddha that eventually, one should totally cut oneself off from both the urge to act and the fruits of one's actions (*karma*).

This message is brought home by the founder of Sikhism in the way he lived his life. He interspersed his spiritual sojourns or wanderings with the life of a peasant-householder Consequently, asceticism, penance, celibacy and so on have hardly any place in Sikhism.

Nanak's Concept of God

Theologically, Nanak's concept of God is proximate to the concept of *shudha-advaita* (pure or unqualified monism) which is an important school of Hindu *vedantic* philosophy. Accordingly, Nanak holds that the only entity, which exists in the world, is that of God and what everything else, in one way or the other, partakes of that entity. So much so that even *maya* or 'illusion', which mystifies this supreme reality, is created by God.

God, according to Nanak, is a 'formless', timeless, all powerful master-creator who is not influenced by feelings of jealousy and discrimination. As such he fears none and favours none. Nanak also addresses God by some 'personal' names such as Rab, Rahim, Govinda, Murari and Hari. As it can be easily seen, these invocations of God are derived both from Muslim as well as Hindu pantheons. But, perhaps the most important reason for choosing these invocations lies in the creed that Nanak was evolving. He wanted to emphasise the centrality of one-and-the-same-God apart from his diverse manifestations, as visualised by different religions. As such, he chose them from amongst the most popular usages then current among both Hindus and Muslims.

Nanak chose *Wahi-guru* as the specific way of addressing God by the members of Sikh faith. The term literally means 'hail O Guru'. Thus, an invocative or exclamatory expression has, by way of usage, turned into a proper noun.

Sacred Scripture

Every religion or religious system centres around a sacred text or set of texts having a governing or a regulating effect upon its followers and their life. Varying from religion to religion, the sacred text or texts contain, among other things, a set of instructions to be obeyed by the followers. These instructions regulate a certain range of their temporal activities.

For example, certain religions like Islam give detailed instructions to be followed. These cover virtually all the major situations that one may encounter in one's life. These may range from the minute method of worship and prayer to the death rites. They also provide rules for distributing the property of deceased parents between the heirs. On the other hand, there are religions like Hinduism which do not go into all those details about the way temporal life should be led. Hinduism stresses all the same many do's and dont's which should be strictly pursued. These include rules regarding purity and pollution or rules regarding choice of the marriage mate. Sikh scripture represents almost an extreme case of emphasising only the central canons or ethical morals which should be followed bv the Sikhs in their day-to-day life.

The sacred scripture of Sikhs-The *Adi-Granth* or as reverentially called, the *Granthsahib*, was compiled by the

5th Sikh Guru, Guru Arjan Dev. It is in the script known as *Gurumukhi*, currently recognised as Punjabi. However, the hymns included in the Granth are in several languages, such as Persian, old Punjabi, medieval Prakrit, Hindi, Marathi, Multani and several local dialects, with an abundant treasure of Sanskrit and Arabic vocabulary. The Granth is the life-blood of Sikhs and is worshipped by them as respectfully as they would respect and worship their living guru. That is why, the *Granth* is normally addressed by Sikhs as Guru *Granth Sahib*, as if it is a living guide, master or a guru.

The *Granth* is handled by the devotees more like a person than a book. It is placed on a comfortable seat, flanked by colourful silken cloth sheets, which are regularly changed. It is impossible to find these clothings unclean or unkempt. The *Granth* is opened with a fine and graceful mannerism to the chanting of specific hymns in the small hours of the day. It is put to rest once again with a punctilious religious routine. After the *Granth* is closed for the night it is draped in fine colourful sheets and placed in a secluded 'room' specifically made for the purpose. All such rituals are maintained at all religious functions or at such functions as marriage or death where the presence of the *Granth* is considered necessary. The *Granth* is placed in all places of Sikh worship-called Gurudwara (the guru's bode).

Some Sikh devotees also place it in their homes and look to its upkeep with all the prescribed rituals and religious solemnity. This characteristic sanctity accorded by the Sikhs to their religious scripture, the *Granth*, is incomparable with any other known religion.

A unique feature of Sikh scripture, which is not shared by any other religious scripture, lies in that it includes religious hymns not merely of the Sikh gurus, but also of several Hindu as well as Muslim saints who were contemporaries of the Sikh gurus. Most of these Hindu saints whose hymns have been included were drawn from the lowly castes, such as cobbler, butcher, barber, etc. who normally occupy bottom rungs of the Hindu caste ladder. The daily readings and recitations from the *Granth* make no distinction whatsoever between hymns of the Sikh guru and those of other. This aspect of the Sikh scripture, even though normally viewed as a 'good' and humanistic feature, still remains a puzzle. This is because no religion makes it a part of its daily worship to recite instructions or hymns not belonging to their own founders.

This can be understood only when we appreciate the central emphasis underlying the Sikh theology, philosophy and ethics. Sikhism emerged, as emphasised above, as a critique and refinement of the then existing ideas of religion and religious morality. As such, it tended to emphasise the relevance of some of the universal human values such as brotherhood and equality. It also emphasises the irrelevance of status whether economic or caste, in one's quest for God. It explains why 'saints' and devotees from across the religious and caste boundaries found their honoured place in the *Adi Granth*. They upheld these values.

What is the spiritual status of 'gurus' vis-a-vis God? It is important to re-affirm that Sikhism is a strongly monistic religion. That is why the ten Sikh gurus, even though held in utmost reverence, are not equated with God. There is only one God or *Akalpurush* (or the 'timeless being') who alone 'deserves' to be worshipped. The injunction of the much-honoured tenth guru of Sikhs, Guru Gobindsingh to his followers is noteworthy: Anyone, who calls me "God", shall perish in the fire of hell. This, however, does not imply that in terms of their religious sentiment, the Sikhs always find it possible to keep to a clear distinction between the two. Despite this, it needs to be stated that the *Granth* emphasises the 'inevitable' and instrumental role of the 'guru' in realising God. Let us also mention how the sacred book *Granth* came to be equated with a guru.

The Granthsahib and the Guru

The line of Sikh gurus, starting from their founder-Guru Nanak, went as far as the tenth Guru, Guru Gobind Singh. He enjoined upon Sikhs to regard the sacred *Granth* as their 'Guru' and turn to it for all advice and instruction for seeking direction of life. We find that today it is worshipped and read with regard and reverence.

Another historical circumstance, which nurtured this attitude of Sikhs for their sacred scripture, is the long period of persecution and suffering undergone by them at the hands of the Muslim rulers, starting from the time of their fifth guru, Guru Arjan Dev (1581-1606), to much after the tenth guru, Guru Gobind Singh (1675-1709), in fact, till the execution of Banda Singh Bahadur (in 1716) who took over the military leadership of the Sikh community after assassination of the tenth guru. Of the ten Sikh gurus, fifth Guru, Guru Arjan Dev ('guru' between 1581-1606) and the ninth Guru, Guru TeghBahadur ('guru' between 1664-1675) were executed by the Muslim rulers, whereas the last and the tenth Guru, Guru Gobind Singh ('guru' between 1675-1708), was assassinated by British hired assassins. Banda Bahadur took over the military command of the Sikh community after the tenth guru and for eight years defied the Mughals and devastated large tracts of eastern central Punjab. He was eventually captured along with seven hundred of his followers, and was executed in Delhi in the summer of 1716. During all these long years of struggle when they were hunted for their creed and at times even pushed into the remote forests, the *Granth* continued to be the centre of their day-to-day existence and chief source of inspiration.

Institution of Khalsa and Five Emblems

The pacifist religion of Guru Nanak took to arms by the time of Guru Hargobind. Less than hundred years after Guru

Nanak's passing away in 1539, Sikhism accepted use of arms for self-defence. The fifth Guru, Guru Arjan Dev, the father of Guru Hargobind, had earlier been executed by the Muslim rulers. Fifty years later, in 1699, taking to arms was formally incorporated into the main corpus of Sikhisim by Guru Gobind Singh via the institution of *Khalsa*. This had taken place as a result of severe repression and persecution let loose by the Muslim rulers against the Sikhs. Let us discuss the institution of *Khalsa*, which restructured the religious ethos among the Sikhs.

Khalsa literally means "the pure" (from the Persian *Khales*, also meaning 'pure'). On April 13,1699, Guru Gobind Singh baptised the first batch of five Sikhs and gave them the common surname, Singh (lion). Kaur 'lioness' is the corresponding surname given to all Sikh women.

The Sikhs were baptised by Guru Gobind Singh in the famous five emblems. All start with a 'k'. All believers are to maintain these in order to keep the status of a 'sikh'.

First of the Ks is *Kesa* (hair). A *Khalsa* must keep the hair unshorn. A *Khalsa* who cuts off his hair is a renegade (*patit*). The holiness of unshorn hair is older than Guru Gobind Singh, the founder of Khalsa. Many of the earlier Gurus followed the tradition of letting the hair and beards grow. The other four are *Kangha* (comb); *Kacch* (drawers) worn by the soliders; *Kirpan* (sabre); and *Kara* (bracelet) of steel, commonly worn on the right wrist.

The baptism of Sikhs into the material qualities of valour and fearlessness meant a departure from the earlier pacifist tradition. Yet it inherited an essential continuity with the past tradition in more than one way. The first of the baptised Sikhs were drawn from five different caste groups. This underscored the essential equality between men of all castes and creeds as emphasised by the founding Guru Nanak. Yet another continuity with the past lay in the concept of *Sant Sipahi* (saint-solider). This implied that a Sikh would not wield a sword for the sake of doing so. Instead, it was to be done for a right cause and for the defence of one's just rights. In addition, a Sikh was supposed to lead a noble, virtuous and pure life.

As already mentioned above, Sikhs made a strong impact upon the Mughal rulers via Banda Bahadur but did not have a strong political organisation to displace them by their own rule. The subsequent course of the evolution of *Khalsa* political power was simple. For some years the *Khalsa* vanished into the hills. However, when Mughal power waned due to the invasion in 1738-1739 of the Persian Nader Shah, they re-emerged into the plains.

The Sikhs formed into *misls* (from Persian *mesals*, meaning both "example" and "equal"). They began to demand protection money from towns and villages. The series of invasions by Ahmad Shah Durrani, 1747-1769, completely destroyed Mughal administration. In the battle of Panipat in 1761 the Afghans crushed the rising Maratha power in the north. In the gap thus created, the Sikhs moved in as rulers of the Punjab.

This situation of political instability in Punjab eventually culminated in Ranjit Singh (1780-1839) establishing the first and the last kingdom of Sikhs in Punjab, stretching right upto the Khyber pass in the north. Ranjit Singh was an enlightened and secular king and ruled till 1839.

He respected all religions and gave liberal benefices to sacred places of all religions. This was followed by ten years of internecine warfare and palace stratagems plus clever political machinations by the British which ended finally in the annexation of Punjab by them in 1849. The annexation was followed by a period of an inexplicable intimacy between the Sikhs and the British. The Sikhs strongly sided with the British administration in quelling the mutiny of 1857 and also enlisted in large numbers in the British army at the time of First World War.

Some writers, for example, Khushwant Singh, maintain that this expression of loyalty on the part of Sikhs reflected a longing for peace and order after long years of bloodshed and disorder in Punjab.

The unprovoked massacre of four hundred innocent people by the British at the Jalianwala Bagh, Amritsar, on April 13, 1919, set the Sikh against the British. Secondly, despite the popular Sikh protest the British sided with the *mahants*, the hereditary priests controlling the *gurudwaras*. Thus Sikhs turned completely against them. These factors as well as the rising temper of the independence movement pushed the Sikhs into the national movement, now led by Mahatma Gandhi. Independence in 1947 was accompanied by partition of the country and the Sikh community suffered enormously through pillage and manslaughter. At present, there are problems of compatibility between the perceived interests and political aspirations of the Sikhs on the one hand and the national policy on the other. From this description of political history of the Sikhs, we now turn to their social institutions.

Sikh Institutions

Sikh institutions seem to emanate from the centrality of ethos, philosophy and theology of Sikhism. Quite a few of the institutions like marriage, kinship, property are, on the other hand, common between the Hindus and Sikhs. Almost all the important festivals of Hindus are celebrated by Sikhs as well.

Social ties between the Hindus and Sikhs including the marital ties continue to thrive. Many sub-caste groupings among the Punjabis underlying the main caste categories like Aroras, Khatris continue to be common between them. Even though Sikhism came up primarily as a revolt against the Hindu legacy of caste, it continues to use caste titles as a principle of social location and departure. These are, however, shorn of the purity-pollution barrier. We discuss here those institutions, which are peculiar to the Sikh community. Around these institutions can be observed much of the collective behaviour of the community.

The Gurudwara

Literally meaning the guru's abode this is the Sikh name or nomenclature for a place of worship. This is the seat of the holy *Granth* and of regular recitations from it, interspersed by singing of religious hymns. There are some *gurudwaras* associated with important happenings in the lives of the gurus. *Gurudwara* Sisganj in the Chandni Chowk of Delhi is associated with the martyrdom of the ninth Guru Tegh Bahadur. *Gurudwara Bangla Sahib* is associated with the 8th Guru Harkishan. There are over 200 historical *gurudwaras* associated with the Gurus. These are controlled by the *Shiromani Gurudwara Prabhandak* Committee (S.G.P.C.) set up by the Sikh *Gurudwara* Act of 1925- offerings are made at *gurudwara* and are used for their upkeep as well as the Khalsa schools and colleges. Golden Temple of Harmandar *Sahib gurudwara* at Amritsar is the most sacred *gurudwara* of Sikhs. It has the same sanctity for Sikhs as Kashi for Hindus, Mecca for the Muslims, Vatican for the Catholics or Jerusalem for the Jews.

It was built by the fifth guru of the Sikhs, Guru Arjan Dev (1563-1606 AD). The foundation of the temple was laid down by Sayyid Main Mir—a Muslim saint of Lahore. This fact in itself highlights religious catholicity of Sikhism. There are certain other features of this temple, which dramatise, symbolically, certain essential features of Sikhism and its philosophy.

First of all, the temple was made at the ground level lower than the rest of the city—a fact which, according to some underscores the humility of the founding gurus. Second, the temple has four main gates, which open in four different directions, which is taken to mean that the temple was thrown open equally to all the four castes. Some others, however, interpret this feature thus: the Golden

Temple has four doors in the four natural directions in order to instruct people of other religions who believe the abode of God to be in a certain direction or at a certain place. However, God is not confined to a certain direction. So, according to them, *Harmandar* means *'mandar' or temple for 'har'. This means it is for every one. In this phrase, the word 'mandar'* is a Sanskritik expression, whereas *'har'* is a Persian expression.

There is yet another feature of Golden Temple, which takes us right to the centre of the Sikh religious ethos. The complex of the Golden Temple is made up of two parts. First is the main part, called *harmandar*. It is set in the centre of a tank. The tank itself is located by a wide corridor for the pilgrims to go around as an act of religious supplication. *Gurbani* or the religious hymns from the *Granth* are sung or recited in this part of the temple for most part of day and night.

The second part of the sacred complex, which lies outside and ahead of the main gate of the *Harmandar*, is called *Akaltakht* or God's court. Since the very inception of the *Harmandar* the *Akaltakht* has been the seat of temporal authority of the Sikh gurus. They sat there, as if on the 'throne' vis-a-vis their followers and considered issues of temporal import including political issues. These two seats of 'spiritual' and 'temporal' authority were and are regarded as integral parts of the basic ethos of the Sikh community. Thus, the idea of separating 'religion' from 'polities' does not appeal to the Sikhs.

Sadh Sangat

No act of Sikh worship is complete without the holy gathering or *Sadh Sangat* which is virtually equated with God's presence. Such a gathering or *'sangat'* is supreme. It can take any decision, whether of religious or temporal import, which is binding upon the rest of the community. It can even censure reprimand, or punish a person for any impropriety committed by him. Maharaja Ranjit Singh is on record having received punishment in the form of cuts of cane upon his skin from a religious gathering at Golden Temple, Amritsar, for an act of moral impropriety committed by him. Gurus, particularly Guru Gobind Singh, have in several hymns recognised the superiority of *Sadh Sangat* over their own commands.

Guru ka Langar

The secular and equalitarian character of Sikhism was manifested through the institution of *langar* community kitchen. Here everyone, without any discrimination of caste and creed, sat together and ate in company. This is also sometimes called the principle of *pangat* or the queue. This again indicates the equal status of everyone in the presence of the Guru.

Even though initiated by the founding Guru Nanak, the institution of *langar* was formalised by the Guru Angad at a place called Goindwal. This was approximately 20 miles away from the city of Amritsar. Every *gurudwara*, big oil small, has a *langar* attached to it and is maintained from offerings made at that gurudwara.

As indicated above, there has been an inflow of a certain caste bias from Hinduism into the social life of Sikhs. This is reflected especially in the area of marital selection. But the said caste bias stayed far short of its traditional rigour and severity with which it is encountered in the Hindu social life. This has been made possible by repeatedly de-emphasising the caste inequality through the institutions of *sangat* and *langar* in the day-to-day life of the Sikhs.

These institutions, therefore, prove functional for maintaining equality, so essential for the very survival of Sikh religious ethos.

Economic Orientation

The basic orientation to engage in economic activity flows, at least partly, from one's religious norms and values. This is what has been a major idea in Max Weber's analysis of the origin and development of the spirit of capitalism in contemporary Europe. The argument presupposes that the individuals in question are religious enough to let religious values hold away over them.

Thus, it has often been argued that a majority of the Sikh families, even after they were completely uprooted at the time of the partition of the country in 1947, built themselves to both 'fame' and 'prosperity'. Sikhs have been proverbially projected as compulsive do-gooders even in the teeth of most adverse circumstances. Their long-standing history of sufferings and persecution imparted the kind of fortitude that lies tacit under a highly resilient attitude. Second, a highly 'secular' and equalitarian attitude, which is reinforced by their institutions of *langar* and *sangat*. A part of their daily religious routine also seems to import the kind of pragmatism and realism which is required in the pursuit of business.

Still another mental attribute, which is conducive towards the same and is that of demystifying reality. This is apparently encouraged by the simple way some of the basic canons of their religion have been stated and repeated. The high 'achievement' orientation of their personality is evidenced by the fact that Sikhs today are found in virtually all the western countries, specifically in large numbers in Canada, the United States of America and United Kingdom where economic opportunities are relatively greater.

6

Social Organisation among Christians

In India there is no one homogeneous Christian community, but there are many different ones, organised around regional, language and sectarian bases. There are Kerala, Goan Tamil, Anglo-Indians in North India, Naga and North East Indian Christians, who are different in their language, socio-cultural practices and economic status. It is difficult to speak about a general Christian way of life in India for these very reasons. There are many churches, many denominations or groups, many sects or brotherhoods among them.

According to the 1981 Census there were 18 million Christians in India and the percentage of Christians in India's population accounted to 2.43 per cent. The total Christian population had almost kept up with the national increase of 24.69 per cent over 1971-81. In 1991 their population was 2.32 percent of the total population. However, the distribution of Christian population has been very uneven in India. There are dense settlements of Christians in some parts of the country while in other regions there are small and scattered Christian communities. In Andhra Pradesh, in the year 1981, the Christians represented 2.68 percent of the total population. In Kerala the percentage of Christians was 20.6. So also Manipur had a 29.7 per cent Christian population.

In fact, Meghalaya with 52.6 percent and Nagaland with 80.2 percent registered the highest concentration of Christian populations. Tamil Nadu had 5.78 percent Christian which was over twice the national average. Very low percentages of the Christian population had been recorded in some central and northern states of the community. For example, Jammu and Kashmir 0.14 percent, Madhya Pradesh 0.7 percent, Rajasthan 0.12 percent and Uttar Pradesh 0.15 percent. In 1991, the highest concentration of Christians was found in Nagaland (87.46 percent) and Meghalaya (85.73 percent). In some States such as Himachal Pradesh, Rajasthan, Haryana etc. the Christian population was very low.

Christianity in India

Christianity came to Kerala through the work of St. Thomas, a disciple of Jesus in the first century and in the fourth century through the influence of traders from Syria. Accounts show that St. Thomas, a follower of Jesus, converted several Nambuthiri Brahmans to Christianity. Thomas is said to have landed in the ancient port of Muziris in 52 A.D.

The Christians of St. Thomas were very prosperous, and historians write that the local kings were very pleased with them and gave them several privileges. In 345 A.D. a Christian, Thomas of Cana set out with permission from the Bishop of his land, and came to Kerala with a number of Christians from Jerusalem, Baghdad and Nineveh.

The Indian Church of St. Thomas came into a close relationship with the Persian Church from the time of the arrival of this immigrant group. However, in the sixteenth century, Persia lost control over the Indian church for the St. Thomas Christians came under the ritual domination of the Portuguese who had arrived in India for purposes of trade. When the Portuguese arrived in India they found a well established Christian Church, where the believers spoke of themselves as being "the Christians of St. Thomas". They are also called the Syrian Christians.

This period began with the 'discovery' of a sea route to India by Vasco de Gama in 1498. Trade was not their only concern. The priests who followed the first Portuguese travellers and discoverers began the establishment of Portuguese rituals in the Churches of Kerala. The Christians of St. Thomas loved their ancient ceremonies, and they did not want to transfer their loyalty from the Patriarch of the East (who was like their Pope) to the Pope of Rome.

It was only in 1653 that the St. Thomas Christians were able to free themselves from Portuguese domination. At this time a division was created in the community of St. Thomas Christians, between those who followed the Pope, and those who followed the Patriarch of the Eastern churches. Historical events, such as the coming of the English divided the community into several more groups. Some of these are called the Anglican (now a part of the church of South India) Mar Thoma, Evangelical and the Yakoba. The Yakoba are themselves divided into two parties because of a church quarrel. Yet, all these groups or denominations share a similar culture. The church practices of each of the group is somewhat different.

In 1509 Alfonso de Albuquerque saw that if the Portuguese were to consolidate their commercial interests they must have a permanent residential interest in India. Goa became central in this interest, and along with administrators the ships of the Portuguese also carried priests. Evangelical work among the native people of Goa began with the work of Franciscan friar Antony de Loueo in 1517. In 1542, Francis Xavier arrived in Goa, and soon after he began his work amongst the Paravas, the fisher-folk in the Coromandel Coast.

The Dutch followed the Portuguese in the colonisation of India and consequently, its commercial exploitation. However, they were not zealous in spreading the Christian faith, and they did not arouse the deep hostility that the Portuguese did. The English followed the Dutch, and they spread the Gospel through missionaries.

In 1793, Carey and Thomas of the Baptist Missionary society arrived in Kolkata, where they proceeded to translate and print the Bible in the vernacular. In 1806, Rev. Cahudius Buchanan was already writing about the importance of the dissemination of the Bible in Malabar, and he was aided in his plans by the British Resident in Travancore. Benjamin Bailey spent decades in the translation of the Bible in Kottayam, Kerala.

In the North East hills of India the first attempt to preach Christianity was made by William Carey, the founder of Serampore College near Calcutta. He sent one of his early converts named Krishna Chandra Pal to the Khasi hills in 1813.

Christian Missions were from a very early period interested in education. Western ideas were introduced through the schools and colleges set up by Christian missionaries, and in turn had its impact in the growth of the National movement. We know how close Mahatma Gandhi was to C.F. Andrews and how the gentleness of Jesus' life made a profound impact on the ideas on non-violence that Gandhi evolved, for liberating the country from its colonial fetters.

TENETS OF CHRISTIAN FAITH

However, in spite of regional variations as described above there are certain tenets, which unite Christian life and experience all over the country. The first of these is that all Christians believe that Jesus Christ of Nazareth is their saviour. They believe that Jesus was born to Mary, a virgin, and that God, the Father, sent him to redeem people of their sins. The concept of virgin birth, is accepted alike by Catholic, Protestant and Orthodox Christians in India. Christianity asserts that Jesus was the Son of God. However, Jesus' father on earth was Joseph. He was a carpenter who protected Mary and took her away to Bethlehem where the baby Jesus was born in a stable. The story of the poverty surrounding Jesus' birth is a very important one for Christians. It establishes the background of much of what Jesus taught, and the manner in which his teachings celebrated poverty, meekness and humility.

The Life of Jesus

The life of Jesus is the central principle around which Christians in India organise their ritual life. The two most important religious festivals of the Christians are Christmas and Easter. Christmas marks the anniversary of Jesus' birth, and is celebrated by attending the Church, eating festival food, wearing new clothes and greeting friends and neighbours. In India, there would be differences among Christians in the kind of festive food that is served, or the kind of clothes that are worn. These are, however, regional differences of custom. The belief that Jesus' birth must be celebrated and this celebration unites Bengali, Punjabi, Tamil, Goan, Malayali, Konkan or Naga Christians. Similarly, all Christians mourn the crucifixion of Jesus on Good Friday, and celebrate his Resurrection, or victory over death on Easter Sunday. All Christians believe that Jesus was killed by his enemies who hated what he taught; but on the third day, he arose from the tomb and convinced his followers of his divinity, for soon after he ascended to heaven. The Christian church then came into existence with the belief in the Resurrection of Jesus. The Eucharist service, which is the central part of Christian rituals, enacts the life of Jesus. It is like a sacred drama, which is performed so that the Christians may continually remember the life of Jesus, hear again his teachings, and try to live their lives in the way that he taught his disciples. Let us now briefly discuss the various elements of Christian faith.

Various Elements of Christian Faith

Christianity is a historical religion, and all Indian Christians accept that their Master, born in the Middle East, was Jesus of Nazareth. The Bible is the sacred book of the Christians. It provides the basis for Christian beliefs and the norms for Christian behaviour. The Four Gospels (a part of the Bible) of Matthew, Mark, Luke and John to be found in the Bible are often read by all Christians in the country. These are memories of Jesus' life; they affirm that Jesus is authentically human, as well as Lord, Messiah (Christos, the Son of God).

For all Christians in India as elsewhere, the reality of God is affirmed in Jesus' life on earth. All Christians accept the propriety of speaking of God in a three-fold manner, as Father, Son and Holy Spirit. This is a problem of great theological complexity, and among Christians there can be differences in the interpretation of the relationship between Father, Son and Holy Spirit. Let us, for our purposes merely say that all Christians believe in the Trinity. They believe also that the Universe has been divinely created, that people are sinful, and that Jesus was sent to earth so that people and God could become reconciled. The Christian Church was founded by Jesus and his spirit is constantly present and sustains all the Church and all believers. Finally, all Christians believe that all human life (human history) must one day close, and then will follow the day of judgement when people will either be rewarded or punished according to the kinds of life they have led.

Social Organisation in India

Christianity, like any other religion, is a way of life. Differences in the social organisation of Christianity will arise from the historical, cultural, political and geographical environment in which the community is founded. Thus the social organisation of Christians in Goa, Delhi, Punjab, Nagaland or Tamil Nadu will differ from one another depending upon the region and its culture and/or sectarian differences. The social organisation of Christians of St.

Thomas, called the Syrian Christians, has been described in order to show you the specific nature of organisation of a particular Christian community in India. It is only one example of Christian life in our country, but it may help you to understand what Christianity is about. The following sections describe Christian social organisation in terms of family, the role of Priest, Church and Christmas among Syrian Christians of Kerala. The interaction between and some common rituals of the Christians and Hindus have also been referred. In the earlier sections, the origins of Christians in India and some of their basic beliefs have been given. All this should give you some ideas regarding the social life and organisation of the Christians in India.

The Christian Family

The Syrian Christian family is a very close knit one. Let us look at Christian family relationships, and see what they say about this particular Indian Christian community.

The Husband's Mother

When a Christian bride enters her husband's home, her husband's mother would have a very important role to play in her new life. Close relations between a Syrian Christian husband and wife, specially in the early years, are thought to be unseemly. When they move into an independent household with the birth of children, that husband and wife complement each other, but a certain reserve always marks their relationship.

The closeness of family bonds, which characterises the Syrian Christian family, is a tribute in fact to the relationship between a woman and her son's wives. It is not merely cooking and the organisation of the household that a bride learns from her husband's mother. She learns the Christian virtues of charity and piety as well. However, there are often tensions between the two women, since the relationship is an unequal one.

The Husband's Father

The relation of a Syrian Christian woman to her husband's father is one of respect. He is the head of the household till the time of his death. However, by the time he is about sixty years of age, he may retire from active social life. While actual control of property may be in the hands of the sons, the father is treated with great respect, and his advice is always sought. It is he who leads the family at prayer when after dinner the family kneels together on the carefully laid out reed mats. Further, it is the father who gives formal permission, necessary economic assistance and the blessings when a couple want to set up house separately. The relationship between sons and fathers is one marked by devotion, affection, obedience and respect on the one side, and by patronage and authoritarianism on the other. This relation, full of tensions, is also reflected in the relation of the bride to her husband's father.

For many Christians, while they live in *nuclear households* (consisting of parents and their unmarried children) the ideal family that they generally desire are *three generations*, in which all the sons bring their brides into the paternal households, and live all together with their children.

However, in practice, amongst the Syrian Christians, the sons set up separate households with the birth of children.

The Grandparents

For these Christians, grandparents play a very important role because they live close by. The paternal grandmother is an important person in the life of the child, particularly as the child grows up. A teasing relationship is often evident. Even before they go to formal school, they accompany their grandmother every day to the parish church. It is to her that they recount the events of the day. She teaches them stories from the bible and songs about Jesus.

On the other hand, with the grandfather the relationship is one of great formality. This is the consequence of authoritarianism and patrilineality. The grandfather in the Christian household is the *griha nayakan* (head of the house) and this idea of domestic authority is pervasive, he leads in family prayers, gets priority in being served the best at meal times, makes all important decisions regarding property, money and the arrangement of marriages.

The Mother's Brother

The mother's brother is of great importance to the children. Gifts from the mother's brother are received on occasions of marriage and birth. The mother's brother always brings abundant quantities of fruit and sweet foods called *palaharam* when he comes to visit. Many Christmas vacations are spent at the mother's brother's house with the maternal grandparents. Here the children are honoured and beloved guests.

As they grow up, however, their father's house becomes more important. It now becomes the centre of their life, particularly when they are sons. It is to this house and property that they will be heirs. This is "their own house" as opposed to their "mother's brother's house".

Patrilocal Residence

Patrilocal residence (staying in the same locality as the father) is of great importance to these Christians. Brothers always live in neighbouring houses, food and garden products are often shared. They visit each other, celebrate rituals and ceremonies in each other's houses, share sorrows and difficulties. The link between them is that they are of the same blood and the same name.

Patrilineage

For the Syrian Christian, the patrilineage is important, and the significance of house names must be understood in this respect. A man is better known as Vazhapallil Paul or Pallivadikal Thomas, for the house name carries the ideas of property, privileges and lineage. It expresses the idea of patrilineal descent or of membership in a lineage organised around the male descendants of an ancestor.

In contrast to descent is filiation, which relates an individual to both parents, not merely to the father and his male relatives. The relation of children to their mother is in striking contrast to their relation with their father. It is to the mother that the young child turns to for every need, and she mediates between the child and the father, the latter being a distant figure. In fact, among these Christians all women should be like Mary, the mother of Jesus. They must be gentle, soft and humble like the *matav* (mother).

Women are never formally included in the affairs of the outside world, those relating to the domain of property and income for instance. Even in the question of marriage it is the fathers who meet, discuss financial and practical matters and fix the alliance. Women cook, clean, take care of children and are devoted to the religious life, spending much time in prayer and attending devotions at the Church.

Inheritance

Till 1986, women were given *stridhanam* by their fathers, which was seen to be their share in father's wealth. It was controlled not by women, but by the husband's father. After a Supreme Court ruling in 1986, a woman may inherit equally with her brothers should her father die without writing a will. Written wills, however, ensure even today that it is sons who inherit property, while daughters are given away in marriage with *stridhanam,* which is never really hers to use, since her husband's father or her husband will control it.

Inheritance customs express the dominant place of the father in the Syrian Christian household. Traditionally the concept of equal share was never of importance to the Syrians. Property was divided according to the whim of the father, or according to the need of his children. The question of manipulation and favouritism arose frequently. The writing of wills has always been very popular amongst these Christians, and the father has absolute control over his sons.

What does this brief discussion of the Christian family show? It describes patriarchal authority which is in fact the basis of Christian social organisation. The next section will discuss the church in the context of Christian social organisation.

The Church

Here we will look at the priest, the church and the celebration of a Christian festival, i.e. Christians, in order to understand more aspects of Christian social organisation.

The construction of the traditional Syrian church in Kerala follows the principles laid down by the Hindu *Shastras* on architecture. It is surrounded by a courtyard on all sides. The walls are similar to Hindu temple walls in height, width and design. Inside, the Church is whitewashed;

sometimes there are religious paintings on the wall or ceilings. These pictures tell the story of Jesus, and often have pictures of St. Thomas, who is said to have brought Christianity to Kerala. The altar is placed on a higher platform, and no one may climb the steps upto this sanctuary. It's a holy place. Only the priests and his assistants are allowed access to the altar, the holy vessels, the cross and candles that are kept there. There are no chairs or pews in the traditional Syrian Church. The floor is covered with reed mats, and on these the people kneel and pray. The men stand on the left side facing the altar; the women stand on the right side. There is an aisle between them, down which the priest's assistants will walk swinging the container of burning incense, which purifies the air. Many churches have silver or bronze oil lamps that have wicks burning in them. The devotees come and pour oil into these lamps and each will light a wick in honour of Jesus. In each of these churches there will usually be a large stone cross in the outer courtyard, which can be seen from very far away.

The church is the heart of Christian social life. People in the villages visit the church every evening for *Sandhya Namaskaram* and in the morning for *Vishudha Qurbana*, the Holy Sacrifice. The Holy Sacrifice is a symbol of the life of Jesus. The priest, through the rituals of the church, acts out of the great mystery of the life of Jesus. The mystery of religious belief lies in that moment and practical reality is kept away, while the sacred world is for that moment brought closer. Everyday, the people participate in the great mystery of the Sacrifice, and specially on Sundays the churches are full. The two greatest festivals are Christmas and Easter, which are celebrated with great joy. In fact, for many traditional Christians, the perception of time is not according to the Western calendar year, but centres around the life of Jesus. It begins with the birth of Christ.

The Priest

The Christian priest is greatly respected by his parishioners. When he conducts prayers and offers the sacrifice (as the central rite of Christianity is called) he stands in place of Jesus Christ. He has the power to reveal the sacred world to those who believe. The Christian priest is a man of God. Amongst the Yakobas, the priest is expected to grow a long beard, and wear a round black cap, loose trousers and a flowing black or white gown. These are the signs by which a priest is known. He must be always calm and disciplined.

When he goes to the Church he must not talk to anyone, all of his being must be directed to God. When people are in trouble, ill, suffering or dying he must be with them. At times of joy, feasting, marriages, births, entering a new house, he must be present to bless the occasion. No one will start a celebratory meal without the priest. If the village is having an exhibition of fire-crackers on a feast day or a function, the priest must be present. He is given the best place to sit in, the best food, and the greatest respect.

The prelates or Bishops of the Church are treated with even greater respect. It is only on festivals and other important occasions that the people meet them. At other times they live in the monastery in meditation and prayer. The Bishops are the leaders of the community. Every Christian knows them by sight and by name. To be related to a Bishop in anyway is of great value. As soon as the Christians see a Bishop, all conversation stops, every one stands at attention. Even if the Bishop is younger than many of his parishioners, they express great respect, almost awe. Those who come to him must bow their heads and receive a blessing with his handcross.

Christmas

Twenty five days before Christmas are days of Lent or

abstinence, to mark the coming of great Joy. The days before Christmas are days of hectic activity. The house is cleaned and made ready for guests. On Christmas Eve all the churches are open, decorated with green leaves and plants. The houses on the roadside look bright with lights. The streets are full of children. Each Christian house is marked by a big star, because when Jesus was born, a bright star was seen in the sky. There is usually among these Christians of Kerala, no practice of decorating a tree, buying new clothes or sending greeting cards. What is given great importance is going to Church, eating an elabourately cooked meal and spending the day together with relations and friends. Those who are wealthy have their houses white washed, while others clean, polish and wash their houses for a week.

The first part of the Christmas service begins on the twenty-four evening. The main service takes place in the early hours (3 a.m.) of the twenty-fifth of December. In the evening prayers, the priest tells the people about the birth of Christ to Virgin Mary. He tells them of the wise men who came from the East and gave Jesus gifts, and how shepherds came to see the child who was born in Bethlehem. The priest tells the people again how poor Jesus was born in a manger, wrapped in rags amongst animals. After these hymns and prayers of the evening, the people go home.

At 3 a.m. on Christmas morning all the Christians will be walking to their church. They bring with them oil, candles and incense as gifts for the church. In the Church, the priest wears very beautiful golden and green robes, the candles are all lit, and the Church is filled with the fragrance of incense. In the Christmas songs and prayers that follow an important place is given to Mary. She is *deva mata* (mother of God) *rajmakal,* a princess and David *putri* (a daughter of King David).

After the celebration of Qurbana (Holy Sacrifice) the people kiss the Cross and leave their gifts of incense and oil. They are like the shepherds and the wise men who came to Jesus at his birth and left offerings for him.

Dawn breaks as people leave the Church. The narrow roads and bylanes are full of early morning worshippers each greeting the other. No one is dressed in his or her newest or best, all come to Church in simple ordinary clothes, usually white cotton. It is enough that they have woken up at 2.30 a.m. to express their devotion and belief in the birth of Jesus.

Having described one of their rituals, we shall now try to show in the next section, how Christianity in India is to be understood in relation to its regional cultural dimensions. Here we have described the relation of Christianity to Hinduism in Kerala.

Relation with Hinduism

The Christians of Kerala are in a specific cultural relationship to their Hindu neighbours. We will take some examples here in order to understand how the Christian and the Hindu share many aspects of their social life together. Let us first look at calendar and time.

Calendar and Time

The Malayalam era follows the Christian era by 825 years. It is still used in everyday speech when referring to the past, for marking the dates of the establishment of churches, houses and gravestones. If you wish to know which year 2005 is in the Malayalam era, you only have to subtract 825 years.

The months have names different from the Western calendar months. Each month has a certain attribute or character. Thus *Karkadam* (July-August) is considered to be the worst, a time of rain and hunger. *Kanni* (September-October) is thought to be a bad and inauspicious month, and during this period house construction will not begin, nor will marriages take place. *Dhanu* is the best season, and it is the time of Christmas, which the Christians celebrate with great joy.

The calculation of time according to moments is still done by the *nazhika*. The day is divided into 60 *nazhikas,* and each *nazhika* is 60 vinazhikas (24 seconds). This precise way of calculating time is used by people in making traditional (Ayurvedic) medicines, which follow given rules, held by both Hindus and Christians to be life laws of nature.

Days have special significance in terms of auspicious and inauspicious. Wednesdays are considered so dangerous that there is a saying that even a leopard cub will not emerge from its mother's womb. Fridays and Tuesdays were considered auspicious by both Hindus and Christians for oil baths and washing the head in the most elaborate fashion. On these days men would avoid travel, as this would cause extra work on a day which belonged to the women. Let us look at another example, that of house building, now.

Building of Houses

The Hindu *asari* (craftsman) who builds for the Christian, follows the customs and rules that he would for a Hindu client. The Christian places wholehearted trust in the *thachan* or carpenter who follows the rules laid down by the *Thatchu Shastra.* These are rules of measurement, location and construction. The Christian house is in architectural style essentially like any Hindu house of similar status, A traditional house-builder said, "In this matter the Christians have full faith in the Hindu *Shastras*. They know that if we do not do as the books say then some misfortune will befall the house or the occupants."

Elements of Caste in Christianity

The Syrian Christians of Kerala believe that their ancestors were Brahmans who were converted to Christianity by St. Thomas, a follower and friend of Jesus who came to Kerala in 52 A. D. The Christians believe that when they converted from Hinduism to Christianity, they were forced to break away from their original caste group.

However, their caste status is maintained by them because they are careful to behave in certain ways, which are in keeping with caste defined behaviour. They maintain the traditional boundaries and distances between high and low castes, even though this is against the moral laws of Christian life. It was the only way in which they could survive, and survive they did for almost two thousand years. Adaptation and compromise were the two laws by which this Christian community lived for many centuries. Even today, in spite of the many changes brought about by modernisation, they sustain their daily life, many of the traditional customs of the past. Let us look at some of these.

Like the Hindus, they have faith in horoscopes; like their Hindu neighbours they too tie the *tali* or marriage locket; they observe death pollution often to fifteen days, and the rituals of bathing to remove death pollution called *pula kuli*. Like the Hindus, they celebrate *onam* and *vishu* (harvest and new year festivals). They also celebrate *annaprasanam* (first feeding of a child with rice).

7

Zoroastrian Social Organisation

Zoroastrianism is one of the oldest religions of the world. It takes its name from "Zarasthustra" (Zoroaster) who probably lived around the beginning of the first millennium B.C. His life period is dated diversely by historians as being anywhere between the fourth to ninth century B.C. Another name for Zoroastrianism is "*Mazdaism*" and is derived from the name of the religion's supreme God "Mazda" (meaning wise) or *Ahura Mazda* (meaning wise Lord). Fire is worshipped as a symbol of *'Ahura Mazda'* since it has the characteristics of purity and brightness.

The roots of Zoroastrianism can be located in an Iranian tribal and basically pastoral society. Research suggests that historically this religion originated in the eastern and south central regions of the Iranian world. It began between the great mountain ranges of the Hindukush and Seistan, an area that today is divided between Iran and Afganisthan. By 500 B.C. Zoroastrianism had become the leading faith in Persia and Medea (now modern Iran). The Iranian-Zoroaster influence faced a serious challenge with the conquest of Iran by the Islamic Arabians in the seventh century A.D. The exodus or mass migration of Zoroastrians into other regions of the world can be seen to be a direct result of the forced Islamisation of Iran.

The Zoroastrian religion was introduced in India about eighth century A.D. It is said that the first batch of Zoroastrians or Parsis reached Diu about 766 A.D. However, they abandoned it and set out for another place of residence. They took refuge in Gujarat. During their voyage to Gujarat from Diu their ship was overtaken by a storm. The voyaging Parsis took a vow that if they reached the shore in Gujarat safely they would establish the most sacred fire temple (called Atash Behram) there. The vow was duly fulfilled and a fire temple was consecrated in Sanjan (in Gujarat) where the Parsis landed safely. They took to agriculture and horticulture in and around Sanjan. As their numbers increased they spread to other parts of Gujarat. When the Muslims conquered Sanjan in the fifteenth century, the sacred fire was moved frequently and finally established at Udvada. The fire temple in Udvada is looked upon as the most sacred temple of the Parsis. Zoroastrian immigrants to India are said to have come from Pars. This is why they are known as Parsee. (Parsi also sometimes spelt as Parsee). The Parsi community has adopted Gujarati as their official language. Let us now look at their numbers.

Zoroastrian Population

The Zoroastrian population around the world is estimated to be roughly 1,30,000 of which 82,000 are believed to be in India. Of this 82,000, more than 78.5 percent are reported to be living in Bombay. The strength of the Parsi population in India has varied between 80,000 and 82,000 as is evident from the recorded population censuses between 1881-1981. Their strength decreased to 76,382 by the year 1991. The Parsi community in India is found mainly in Maharashtra and specially in Bombay, Gujarat and Deccan. In 1991 a majority of 79.2 percent of Zorastrians lived in Maharashtra, followed by Gujarat (16.92 percent).

Socio-Economic Life

Migrating to India over 1300 years ago, the Parsis have been an important part of the economic, political, educational and social life of India. Prior to and during the Muslim rule they lent their support to Hindu princes whenever it was needed. They played an important role in the Mughal administration. Following the arrival of the British they were among the first people to adopt to the western style of life and to English education. The Parsis began in India as a small mercantile community. They excelled themselves in trade and commerce. Two of the leading areas of economic activity in the nineteenth century, shipbuilding and the textile industry, owe their rapid growth mainly to the investment and trading initiative of the Parsis. Thus, early growth of the modern shipping industry in India is associated with the name of a Parsi family the Wadias. They were commissioned by the British for the management of the biggest shipyard in Bombay continuously for 150 years from 1735-1885. Another Parsi, D.R. Bannaji owned a personal fleet of thirty trading vessels (i.e. ships). Between 1915 and 1925, nearly 20 percent to 30 percent of the cotton mills in Bombay were owned by Parsis.

Parsis have also been contributing greatly to the steel, chemical, cement, and other heavy industries. This has been so both during the British India and post Independent India. We have all heard about the Tata family. They were pioneers of the steel industry in India. Today they also run a host of other industries such as jute, chemical, tea, textile, printing, insurance, and so on. The Tata family is not only associated with industry but also with education and social work.

Parsis eminent in the political, economic, educational and social work in India during the nineteenth and early twentieth centuries included B.M. Malabari, S.S. Bengali, N.

Fardoonji, P.M. Mazban, Sir P. Mehta, Sir D. Wacha, Maneckji, D. Petit, J. Tata, C.J. Readyymony and so many others.

The Parsis began in India as a small mercantile community. Gradually, a number of their families became successful industrial entrepreneurs, merchants, educationalists, social reformers, lawyers and pioneers in many other fields.

Proof of their open attitude with regard to occupational selection lies in that many of the Parsis derive their family names from the occupations their ancestors pursued in India. Many of their descendents still do so. Interesting family titles thus include: Unwala (wool dealer), Kapadia (cloth dealer), Jhaveri (jeweller), Motiwala (pearl dealer), Biscuitwala (biscuit dealer), Batliwala (bottle dealer), Ginwala (wine dealer), Sodawaterwala (Soda dealer), Mondalwala (wine dealer), etc.

In general, Parsis are represented in different jobs. There is evidence to indicate that they have held many types of posts. Supportive data for this is available as early as the middle of the nineteenth century.

Currently more and more Parsis are establishing themselves in the scientific and other professions. Homi J. Bhabha was the pioneer of nuclear research in India and General S.H.F.J. Manekshaw is the first Field Marshall of the Indian Army. Modern education is widely shared by all the various communities in India and the entrepreneurial skills of communities like Sindhis, Punjabis and Marwaris have come to the fore in modern India. However, Parsis continue to do well in most fields of endeavour. Socio-economic life of this community is influenced by the tenets of Zoroastrianism. We shall now describe the main features of this religion.

Tenets Of Zoroastrianism

Zoroaster, the founder of Zoroastrianism preached monotheism (belief in one supreme God and a deep moral life. He was against idol worship and over emphasis of ritual sacrifice. The basic tenets of Zoroastrianism are outlined mainly in two texts. The first of these is the *Avesta* or the *Zend Avesta*—it is a collection of texts gathered in writing roughly between the fourth and sixth century A.D. The second is the *Gatha* which comprises texts which are attributed to Zarathustra. These belonged initially to the oral tradition. The *Gathas* are five in number. The first four are ethical and philosophical. They describe and emphasise the omnipotence of or all pervading nature of *"Ahura Mazda"*. They also deal with the problem of evil due to the activities of the evil spirit. The fifth *Gatha*, is a hymn on the occasion of Zoroaster's daughter's marriage. The *Gathas* are written in *Avesta* which closely resembles Vedic Sanskrit. *Ahura Mazda* is considered to be the supreme God. He is the creator of heaven and earth, day and night, light and darkness. Life is seen as a struggle between the forces of good and evil.

The evil spirit is *"Angra Mainyu"*. One has to choose between good and evil. The ethical dualism (dualism indicated in the existence of good spirits and evil spirits) that Zoroaster preached, emphasised that there are differences between

human actions motivated by goodness and those that are motivated by evil. Purity in thoughts, words and deeds implies the will to do good. Anything that is not guided by this motive is apt to turn into evil. Therefore the primary task of man is to live a righteous life. He must fight against the evil spirits along with his creator *Ahura Mazda*. They will be helped by a host of good spirits. One who lives a righteous life attains paradise. This is described as a state of immortal holiness in thought, word and deed. If one leads an impious life that person is condemned to an eternal hell of evil thoughts, deeds, and physical torment. The Parsis believe that the soul lives on after death. It meets its fate on the day of judgement, under the supervision of *Ahura Mazda*.

An important feature of Zoroastrianism is that it does not preach celibacy, asceticism, renunciation or self denial in life. It demands strict purity in thought, word and deed. This consists of abstinence from acts like adultery, rape, and the like.

Purity is essentially associated with fire. For the Parsis fire is worshipped as a symbol of purity, energy, force, light and radiance. And fire is a symbol of *Ahura Mazda*. Zoroastrian temples take the form of fire temples and are of three grades—*Atash Behrams*, *Agiaris* and *Dadgahs*, in that order of sacredness. Once the sacred fire is installed in a fire temple it must always be kept alive (always kept burning).

Many fire temples are places of pilgrimage for the Parsis. The oldest fire is known as the ''Iranshah" which is supposed to have been burning for more than 1300 years. This is in Udvada. All Parsis have sacred flames burning in their houses also. These flames are kept burning constantly. In the fire temple the priest reads portions of the sacred scripture—the *Avesta*, five times a day. In each household, a Parsi is also expected to say prayers five times each day.

The translation of the sacred texts, including the Avesta was completed in 1820, from Pahalvi (ancient language) to Gujarati. The average Parsi is thus able to have access to the sacred texts for daily use in prayers. Zoroastrianism does not advocate fasting for religious merit.

The *Gathas* of Zoroaster is another source of information about Zoroastrian belief. They present the picture of a society in which agriculture and herds of domestic animals had come to be looked upon with affection. In the sacred prayer "Behram Yesht" the reverence that is shown to the cow is evident. This aspect of Zoroastrian faith (respect to the cow) reflects the interaction with Hinduism as Hindus also look upon the cow as a sacred animal. We will now discuss some of the rites, rituals and customs observed by the Parsis relating to birth, initiation, death, marriage and family. These reflect the belief systems discussed above. They also indicate the adaptations the Parsis have made as a result of the interaction with local dominant population and their rulers at different points in time.

Zoroastrian beliefs are closely linked with the way day-to-day life is carried on by the members of Parsi community. In the next section, we will see how basic rites and religious ceremonies form an important part of Parsi social life.

Aspects Oof Social Organisation

In this section we describe important life cycle rituals relating to birth and death. The social institutions of marriage and family are also discussed here. The Parsi system of inheritance and succession, the Panchayat and Festivals also figure in our discussion of the social organisation.

Rites of Initiation and Death

Even though Zoroastianism does not emphasise ritualism especially rituals sacrifices, there are some basic rites and religious ceremonies which form an integral part of the organisation of Parsi social life.

Rites of Initiation

Initiation rites mark the birth of a child into the Parsi family. On this occasion the child's lips are steeped in *haoma* (the sacred liquor). Full membership into the community is granted only when the child (both to a boy and a girl) attains the age between seven and fifteen. He or she then receives the girdle or cord called the *Kushti* or *Kusti*. This ceremony usually takes place before a child attains puberty. This initiation rite is called *Navjot* or *Naojote* (meaning new birth) and marks the admission of a Parsi boy or a girl into Zoroastrian faith. In addition, there is a host of other purificatory rites, which are often performed by many Parsis. They include the *padyab* (meaning ablution) *nahn* (meaning bath) or washing of one's body. The *bareshnum* is a complicated ritual performed at special places with the participation of a dog. The left ear of the dog is touched by the person concerned. The gaze of this animal is believed to put the evil spirit to flight. The purification rites for the initiation of priests and corpse-bearers, involve, apart from other things *gomez* (consecrated urine), originally cow's urine following Indo-Iranian practices and ideas.

Death Rites

The Parsi custom of disposing the dead is indeed unique. Death rites are probably the most elaborate of the Parsi rites. These reflect, among other things, their attitude to life and life after death. Parsis do not burn or bury their dead lest this should pollute fire or earth and make them liable to a strict punishment. They carry the dead body, amidst elaborate rituals, to a place built high up for this purpose. This is called a dokhma or 'Tower of Silence'. The body is left there to be eaten up by vultures.

The removal of the dead body (for its final disposal) must only be done during the daytime. As for the Tower of Silence, its interior consists of three concentric circles, one each for men, women and children. The corpses are exposed without any dress. The vultures do not take long (an hour or two at the most) to remove the flesh off the bones. The bones are dried by the sun, and later swept into a central well. Formerly, the bones were kept in an ossuary, (the place where bones of the dead are deposited) or what they called *astodan,* to preserve them from rain and animals. The morning of the fourth day is marked as the most solemn observance in the death ritual. It is believed that the departed soul reaches the next world and appears before the deities who are to pass judgement over it. The souls, they believe would be judged in the presence of *Ahura Mazda* and his helping spirits.

Marriage and Family

Marriage is solemnised and sanctified by a religious ceremony but it is a contract. The prayers are recited from the Avesta. As a result of Hindu influence, prayers are recited in Sanskrit too. Marriage is, by and large monogamous. Consent of both the boy and girl is essential for finalising marriage. Zoroastrianism prescribes strict monogamy. Religious tradition does not approve of child marriage. Dissolution of marriage (divorce or separation) is allowed under certain conditions. In fact in 1936, The Parsi Marriage and Divorce Act outlined clearly conditions under which divorce can be allowed. It also stated that both parties in marriage (husband and wife) could initiate 78 divorce proceedings. This law has been based on the liberal principles of Zoroastrianism, which grants rights to both men and women.

A Zoroastrian woman is considered as an equal partner in marriage and family. Both men and women are entitled to religious and secular education. Parents of the bride and the groom contribute to the expenses involved in setting up of their new household. A woman enjoys inheritance rights both in her capacity as a daughter and as a wife. Remarriage is allowed and a widow does not have to forego inheritance rights over her husband's property if she remarries.

Thus Zoroastrianism has sanctioned liberal attitudes and practices regarding marriage and family. However, some of the less liberal attitudes and customs of the local population with which the Parsis came into contact have also made their impact on the institutions of marriage. Research has pointed out that by the seventeenth century A.D. Parsis settled in Gujarat had begun to pattern their social relationships after the Hindu society. Thus child marriage became common, some males practised bigamy or polygyny and widow remarriage was not easy. The evil practice of dowry also became prevalent. Horoscopes (birth charts) came to be prepared for Parsi children by Hindu priests.

These customs, especially dowry, bigamy, polygyny, child marriages, ban on widow remarriage, and divorce, came to be challenged by the enlightened sections of the Hindu and Parsi community including the members of Parsi Panchayat. Many members of Parsi community pointed out that these customs were not sanctioned by Zoroaster and therefore had to be stopped. Their concerted efforts indeed led to the removal of many of these practices. For instance, as a result of the vigorous campaigning by the social reformers of the nineteenth and early twentieth century, the 1929 Sarda Act was passed. This act penalised marriages of girls below 14 years of age and boys below 18 years. However, by this time there were hardly any child marriages among the Parsis. In fact, since then, the age of marriage has been rising, and since the 1960's the average age at marriage for Parsi men have been between 25-28 years. For Parsi women this is between 23-25 years.

One important aspect regarding marriage and family, in which women suffer a disability even today, has been the aspect of inter-religious marriage. The child of a Parsi father and non-Parsi mother, whether in wedlock or out of it, can be initiated into the Zoroastrian faith by the Navjote or

Naojote ceremony. However, neither by religion nor by law can a child of a Parsi mother and a non-Parsi father be admitted into Zoroastrianism. The steady decline in the size of the Parsi population can be traced, (to some extent) to the increasing number of marriages between Parsi women and non-Parsi men. Children born of such marriages are not recognised as Zoroastrians. Hence the decline in the number of members enumerated as Parsis. The Parsi community has not been able to stop such inter-religious marriages since Parsi girls enjoy the right to choose their spouses. Conservative members have their reservations and resentment against marriage between a Parsi and a non-Parsi. A Parsi boy's marriage with a non-Parsi girl is accepted with greater grace than the marriage of a Parsi girl with a non-Parsi boy. Since Zoroastrianism is not a proselytising religion (it does not preach or practise conversion) it does not easily accept non-Parsi members into its fold.

Parsi girls marrying a non-Parsi boy by the 1954 Special Marriage Act have made a claim to the Parsi Panchayat that they must be given the right to visit the fire temple and remain a Parsi. It must be pointed out that these girls (those marrying non-Parsis) do not lose their rights of inheritance or intestate succession.

Inheritance and Succession

A feature of the rules governing the Parsi intestate (without making a will) is that the share of male heir is double that of a female heir of the same degree. For example, if a male Parsi dies leaving a widow and children, the property will be divided so that the share of each son and widow will be double the share of each daughter. Further if a male Parsi dies leaving one or both parents in addition to his wife and children, the property will be divided so that the father will receive a share equal to half the share of a son. The mother will receive a share equal to half the share of the daughter. On the other hand if a female Parsi dies intestate her husband and her children, will receive an equal share of her property.

Among Parsis adoption is not recognised by custom or law for purposes of inheritance and succession. A Parsi widow without any children, can adopt a son on the 4th day of her husband's death. This is for the temporary purpose of performing certain religious rites for the dead man. This adoption is for a limited purpose and does not grant any property rights on the adopted *"palak"*.

What is clear, from these Parsi rules of inheritance and succession. is that while they recognise the woman's right to inheritance and succession, the Parsi daughter's share of her father's property remains half of that of a son. It must be pointed out that most of these provisions were enacted in 1939. At that time these rules conferred more rights to women than the then existing Hindu and Muslim laws.

Parsi Panchayat

Earlier we had mentioned that the Parsi Panchayat (also called *Anjuman*) played a role in reforming certain practices which reflected the infiltration of non-Zoroastrian elements into Parsi institutions (eg. child marriage, ban of remarriage, polygyny etc). In this section we will briefly examine the role of the Parsi Panchayat in India.

From the time Parsis landed in India, there were some members among them who negotiated with the rulers and traders on behalf of their community. Gradually the Parsi Panchayat or Council of Elders came into being. This was established in Surat and Navsari around the middle of the seventeenth century.

It consisted of both priests and laypersons. In this context, it is important to talk of the divisions, which have existed, in Parsi society in India. In India, the Parsis are divided into two sections: namely the *Mobeds* (or priests) and Behdin (or laity). Priests for a long time were exclusive and intermarriage was seldom permitted. Only the son of a priest could become a priest. In terms of the Parsi Panchayat, in the seventeenth century though priests were members of the Panchayat, the laity members played a greater role in the economic role of the Parsis in India. Towards the last quarter of the seventeenth century the British started developing Bombay into their main trading centre. The Parsi community began to make full use of this trading venture in Bombay. The Parsi Panchayat played an active role in promoting the economic interests of the community. It also provided some inner stability and order to the Parsi community.

The Bombay Panchayat was formally recognised to punish members of the community who went against the traditionally accepted Parsi norms (religious and social). Punishable acts included committing bigamy or insulting members of the priestly class. A person requiring divorce and permission to marry a second wife had to represent his case in writing to the Panchayat. When the bad conduct of a wife was established the Panchayat used to punish the guilty woman by taking her securities before granting the husband permission to remarry. Those who were given permission to marry a second time had to get their marriage ceremony performed only by the priest named by the Panchayat. This would vary depending on whether the applicant belonged to the *Shehenshah* sect or the *Kadmi* sect.

Here we need to mention another social division. The Parsis are divided into two sections on the question of pronunciation of the *Avestan* prayers and the intercalation (this word means, to insert as a day on the calendar) in the Iranian-Zoroastrian calendar. In ancient Iran the length of the year was known to be 365 days and 6 hours. This difference of 6 hours was made up once in **120 years** by adding one month known as *Kabisa*. Those who followed this method called themselves *Kadmis* or *Kadims*, meaning the ancient. While the Parsis who did not follow this calendar came to be known as *Shehenshahis*. Fire temples are open to both these sections. Intermarriage among these sects is quite common. For the *Shehenshahi* Parsis the New Year falls at the end of August, while for the *Kadmis* it falls a month ahead at the beginning of August. The Parsi Panchayat kept these divisions in mind when it tried to arrive at any decision. Those who violated the rules were to be turned out of the community and punished, as the Panchayat thought proper. Besides obtaining permission from the Panchayat to marry a second time (when the first wife is alive) a man had to very often pay the Panchayat some amount of money as charity. Among the punishments which could be imposed by the Panchayat were forbidding: (i) priests to enter the house of the person punished; (ii) the person to visit the Parsi temple; and (iii) the person to go to the Tower of Silence.

Other punishments included beating the offender with a shoe, shaving a woman's head, and excommunicating the deviants from the community and so on. The Panchayat continued to wield a strong influence over the religious-social life of the community till 1830. After this the sons of the old members took over and began considering their positions in the Panchayat as personal possessions. They behaved high handedly and in a biased manner. Henceforth, the Panchayat became an institution of class discrimination. Thus serious breaches like bigamy were now glossed over by the Panchayat, so far as the richer members of the community were concerned. This made some of the 'elderly' members resign their positions on the Panchayat. It had virtually become a powerless institution. The British Government also withdrew its recognition from the Panchayat. In 1865, a Parsi Law Reform Association and later in 1961 a Government Commission worked on drafting a bill which gave the Parsi community, a written law of their own. It was entitled the Parsi Marriage and Divorce Act of 1865 and Parsi Succession Act of 1865. These Acts have been amended in subsequent years to liberalise and facilitate legal proceedings relating to marriage and succession.

Festivals

So far we have discussed the emergence of Parsi community in India, their basic tenets, some of the important rites and customs of the Parsis and the role of the Parsi Panchayat. There is another area of Zoroastrian social organisation that reflects the collective entity of the Parsis. The area which rejuvenates the Zoroastrian way of life are the Parsi Festivals.

Feasting is a necessary component of Parsi worship. In other words it is not just a 'desirable' or an expected mode of behaviour but one that is religiously enjoined upon Parsis. It follows directly from their fountainhead, Zoroaster, who enjoins every Parsi to lead a happy and joyous life. The principal festivals in the Parsi year are the six seasonal festivals, *Gahnbars* and the days in the memory of the dead at the Parsi year's end. Also, each day of the month and each of the twelve months of the year is dedicated to the deity. The day named after that month is when the great feast day of that particular deity is held. The new year festival, Noruz or Navroz is the most joyous and beautiful of Zoroastrian feasts. It is a spring festival in the honour or *Rapithwin,* who is the personification (i.e. considered as person) of noonday and summer. The festival to *Mithra or Mehragan* (noble spirits) was traditionally an autumn festival. This festival was as honoured as the spring feast of *Norus*.

8

The Institution of Family

Broadly speaking, "family" refers to the group comprising parents and children. It may also refer, in some places, to a patri-or matrilineage or to a group of cognates, that is, persons descended from the same ancestor. In some other cases, it may refer to a group of relatives and their dependants forming one household. All this refers to the compositional aspect of this institution. Another aspect is that of the residence of its members. They usually share a common residence, at least for some part of their lives. Thirdly, we can also speak of the relational aspect of the family. Members have reciprocal rights and duties towards each other. Finally, the family is also an agent of socialisation. All these aspects make this institution different from other units of social structure.

Family is one of the most important social institutions. Most of the world's population lives in family units. The specific form and behaviour patterns found within a family have shown variations through time across countries of the world and even within a country. A sociologist looks at the institution both in terms of an ideal type and a reality. He/she ascertains the ideals of the family system partly because they are a guide to behaviour and also because these ideals act as values, a set of norms which are passed from one generation to another. A sociologist also studies the actual way in which a family is patterned and re-patterned within a society, in a particular group through time. She will also try to identify the forces, which have been responsible for changing certain aspects of the family units in a particular manner.

Types of Family

Normally the basic unit of social structure contains the two primary links of kinship. These are of parenthood and siblingship. In simple terms, a family usually comprises various combinations and permutations of these relationships. In the Indian context, we generally speak of the contrast between nuclear and joint family types.

A classification of families into joint and nuclear types is usually based on the way in which families are organised. For instance, the most popular definition of a nuclear family is to refer to it as a group consisting of a man, his wife and their unmarried, children. The joint family is commonly defined as the nuclear family plus all kin belonging to the side of husband, and/or wife living in one homestead.

Frequently, the term 'extended' family is used instead of the term joint family to indicate that the combination of two or more nuclear families is based on an extension of the parent-child relationship. Thus, the patrilineally extended family is based on an extension of the father-son relationship, while the matrilineally extended family is based on the mother-daughter relationship. The extended family may also be extended horizontally to include a group consisting of two or more brothers, their wives and children. This horizontally extended family is called as the fraternal or collateral family.

We say that the nuclear and the joint family systems have to be viewed as a continuum. This means that these two types of family systems have to be looked at as something interrelated in a developmental cycle. The structure of a family changes over a time period in terms of size, composition, role and status of persons, the family and societal norms and sanctions. There probably is rarely a family in India, which remains perpetually nuclear in composition. Often additional members like an aged parent or unmarried brothers and sisters may come to live with a man, his wife and unmarried children. The nuclear family then, is a stage in a cycle with other structural types of families. Even when certain forces have enjoined the establishment of nuclear household, for a relatively long period of time, the ritual, economic and sentimental link with relatives who compose a joint family are often maintained.

While discussing the nature of nuclear family in India, Pauline Kolenda has discussed additions/modifications in nuclear family structure. She gives the following compositional categories.

1. *Nuclear family* refers to a couple with or without children.
2. *Supplemented nuclear family* indicates a nuclear family plus one or more unmarried, separated, or widowed relatives of the parents, other than their unmarried children.
3. *Subnuclear family* is identified as a fragment of a former nuclear family for instance a widow/widower with her/his unmarried children or siblings (unmarried or widowed or separated or divorced) living together.
4. *Single person household*
5. *Supplemented subnuclear family* refers to a group of relatives, members of a formerly complete nuclear family along with some other unmarried, divorced or widowed relative who was not a member of the nuclear family. For instance, a widow and her unmarried

children may be living together with her widowed mother-in-law. In the Indian context, it is easy to find all these types of family. However, in terms of societal norms and values, these types relate to the joint family system.

The Hindu Joint Family

Much has been written about the joint family system, especially the Hindu joint family system. The patrilineal, patrivirilocal (residence of the couple after marriage in the husband's father's home), property owning, co-residential and commensal joint family, comprising three or more generations has been depicted as the ideal family unit of Hindu society.

M.S. Gore points out that ideally, the joint family consists of a man and his wife and their adult sons, their wives and children, and younger children of the paternal couple. In this ideal type the oldest male is the head of the family. The rights and duties in this type of family are laid down to a great extent by the hierarchical order of power and authority. Age and sex are the main ordering principles of family hierarchy.

The frequency and the nature of contact/communication between members vary on the basis of sex. A married woman, for instance works in the kitchen with her mother-in-law and sisters-in-law. Younger members are required to show respect to the older members and can hardly question the authority or decision taken by elders even when it directly concerns them. Children of the joint family are children of all the male members in the parental generation.

Emphasis on conjugal ties (i.e. between husband and wife) is supposed to weaken the stability of the joint family. The father-son relationship (filial relationship) and the relationship between brothers (fraternal relationship) are more crucial for the joint family system than the husband-wife or conjugal relationship.

In a nuclear family the husband and wife relationship is important for the survival of the system. Hence, in M.S. Gore's view, it would be inappropriate to look at the joint family system as a collection of nuclear families. Having said that joint families are not merely a collection of nuclear families we must examine what constitutes jointness.

Nature of Joint Family

There are two aspects of joint family system in India based on

1. What constitutes jointness?
2. Who constitutes a joint family?

Both the sub-sections will show us how the seemingly nuclear families in India are actually parts of larger family groups, which share the idea of 'jointness'.

Let us look at what is jointly shared by the members of a joint family. Their jointness is reflected in the factors of commensality, common residence, joint ownership of property, cooperation and sentiment of jointness, ritual bonds like worship of common deity. We shall discuss them one by one.

1. *Commensality:* Most of the studies of joint family use commensality (eating together) as a defining criterion. The joint family is the hearth group; members cook and eat food from the same kitchen.
2. *Common Residence*: In some studies the joint family as the residential family group is stressed. Though it is possible to find a joint family having the same hearth but not sharing the same dwelling or vice versa, by and large commensality and common residence are taken as essential ingredients of jointness.

3. *Joint Ownership of Property*: Some scholars have regarded joint ownership of property or *coparcenary* as the essence of jointness, irrespective of the type of residence and commensality. In legal terms, this is the most crucial factor used for defining a joint family.

4. *Cooperation and Sentiment*: Scholars like I.P. Desai and K. M. Kapadia point out that jointness should be looked in functional terms. A functionally joint family lays stress on fulfilment of obligations towards kin.

   A patrilineal joint family may consist of a number of households headed by males related through the father. They may be located even at distant places and may not even have property in common. But what is common is that they identify themselves as members of a particular 'family', cooperate in rituals and ceremonies, render financial and other kinds of help; and they cherish a common family sentiment and abide by the norms of joint living.

5. *Ritual Bonds:* The ritual bonds of a joint family are considered to be an important component of jointness. A joint family, thus, is bound together by periodic propitiation of the dead ancestors. The members perform a *'shraddha'* ceremony in which the senior male member of the joint family propitiates his dead father's or mother's spirit, offering it the *'pinda'* (balls of cooked rice) on behalf of all the members.

Another ritual bond among joint family members can be a common deity worship. In many parts of South India, each joint family has a tradition of worshipping a particular clan or village deity. Vows are made to these deities in times of joy and trouble. The first tonsure, donning of the sacred thread, marriages etc. are celebrated in or near the deity's temple. Srinivasa of Tirupathi and Subramanya of Palani are two well-known Hindu deities who have a large number of South Indian families attached to them.

Still another important bond is pollution. Birth and death results in pollution and the group observing pollution consists of the members of the joint family, patrilineal or *matrilineal*. The bonds created by ancestor worship, family deities and observation of pollution persist even after the joint family has split into separate or smaller residential and commensal units.

From the above discussion of joint family it becomes clear that common kitchen or hearth, common residence, joint rights to property and the fulfillment of obligation towards kin and ritual bonds have been outlined as the main criteria for defining what constitutes jointness. Many scholars have pointed out that of these dimensions, co-residence and commensality, are the immediately identifiable characteristics of a joint family. Such a consideration, they feel, would also accommodate family patterns found in non-Hindu communities like the Muslims, Christians, etc. It would also accommodate families, which hardly have anything by way of ancestral or immovable property.

Kin Relationship between the Members

We can say that a joint family may consist of members related lineally or collaterally or both. There is more or less an unanimous agreement that a family is essentially defined as "joint" only if it includes two or more related married couples. Also it has been observed that these couples may be related (i) lineally (usually in a father-son relationship or occasionally in a father-daughter relationship), or, (ii) collaterally (usually in a brother-brother relationship/or/ occasionally in a brother-sister relationship). Both these types refer to the compositional aspect of the patrilineal joint family. In matrilineal systems, found in South-west and North-east India, the family is usually composed of a woman, her mother and her married and unmarried daughters. The mother's brother is also an important member of the family; he is the manager of the matrilineal joint family affairs. The husbands of the female members live with them. In Kerala, a husband used to be a frequent visitor to the wife's household and he lived in his mother's household.

Pauline Kolenda presents the following types of joint family on the basis of the relatives who are its members.

a) *Collateral joint family*: It comprises two or more married couples between whom there is a sibling bond. In this type, usually a brother and his wife and another brother and his wife live together with unmarried children.

b) *Supplemented collateral joint family:* It is a collateral joint family along with unmarried, divorced or widowed relatives. The supplemented relatives are generally the widowed mother of the married brothers or the widower father, or an unmarried sibling.

c) *Lineal joint family:* Two couples, between whom there is a lineal link, like between a parent and his married son or some times between a parent and his married daughter, live together.

d) *Supplemented lineal joint family:* It is a lineal joint family together with unmarried, divorced or widowed relatives who do not belong to either of the lineally linked nuclear families; for example, the father's widower brother or the son's wife's unmarried brother or sister.

e) *Lineal collateral joint family:* In this type three or more couples are linked lineally and collaterally. For instance we can have a family consisting of parents and their two or more married sons together with the unmarried children of the couples.

f) *Supplemented lineal—collateral joint family:* In this type are found a lineal collateral joint family plus unmarried, widowed, separated relatives who belong to one of the nuclear families (lineally and collaterally linked), for example, the father's widowed sister or brother or an unmarried nephew of the father.

Number of Generations in One Unit

A joint family is also seen in terms of generations present in it. Some researchers, like I.P. Desai and T.N. Madan emphasise that the number of generations present in a family is important for identifying a joint family. A joint family is commonly defined as a three generational family. For instance a man, his married son and his grand children constitute a joint family.

Sharing of Common Property

Researchers, like F.G. Bailey, T.N. Madan, have advocated the limitation of the term joint family to a group of relatives who form a property owning group, the coparcenary family. M.S. Gore, for instance, defines a joint family as a group consisting of adult male coparceners and their dependants. The wives and young children of these male members are the dependents.

The female members have not been included in the category of the coparcenary. They have rights of residence and maintenance only as dependents. In 1937 an attempt was made to confer the same right, i.e., the right of inheritance of property on a Hindu widow as her son would have in the estate of her deceased husband. The Act enabled her to enjoy the income only from the immovable property of her husband during her lifetime.

Until the passing of the Hindu Succession Act, 1956, two systems of inheritance dominated among patrilineal

Hindus. In one system (called the Mitakshara school, adopted in most regions) a son has a vested interest in his father's ancestral property from the moment of his birth. The father cannot give away any part of this property to the detriment of his son's interest. Under the other system (the Dayabaga school, adopted in Bengal and Assam) the father is the absolute owner of his share and has a right to alienate his property the way he wants.

Among the patrilineal Hindus, some movable property is given to the daughters at the time of marriage as *stridhana.* With the passing of the Hindu Succession Act of 1956, a uniform system of inheritance has been established. The individual property of a male Hindu, dying intestate (having made no will), passes in equal shares between his son, daughter, widow and mother. Male and female heirs have come to be treated as equal in matters of inheritance and succession. Another important feature of the Act is that any property possessed by a female Hindu is held by her as her absolute property and she has full power to deal with it the way she likes. This Act has also given a woman the right to inherit from the father as well as from the husband. However the benefit conferred on a woman is limited when compared to the rights of the male members who still have rights to coparcenary ancestral property by birth. Daughters are not part of the coparcenary and have no birthrights.

The difficulty of looking at joint family as a coparcenary family unit is that it does not take into account those joint families, which possess little in the form of immovable or moveable property.

Variability in and Prevalence of Joint Family

Variability: We identified a joint family in terms of what is shared and who shares it. We went through this exercise in this manner so that we can identify and analyse the multitude of factors that make a joint family. But we must remember that a joint family is a composite whole of both the "who and what" components. The exact composition or members and what is actually shared by these members in a particular family will vary through time and will also vary between families.

The following factors relating to the compositional aspect explain these variations within a family and between families.

a) *The culturally patterned time of break-up:* It differs across caste, community and region. The time, when a married son or brother breaks away to form a separate residential and commensal unit, may vary within a family and between families.

b) *Demographic profiles:* Based on such factors like average life expectancy, average age at marriage, average number of children born per couple, age of father at the birth of various children etc., we will again find variation in the pattern of joint family living.

c) *The influence of education, spatial mobility and diversification of occupation* also bring about variation.

ii) *Prevalence:* By comparing seventy six studies which included family types across villages, caste communities and other population, Pauline Kolenda outlined the pattern of prevalence of joint family in India. She observed that (a) joint family both lineal and collateral was more characteristic of higher twice-born castes and least characteristic among the economically poor and the untouchables, (b) there are regional differences in the proportion of joint families. For instance, the Gangetic plains showed higher incidence of joint families than Central India, i.e., in Madhya Pradesh, Western Rajasthan, parts of Maharashtra, and (c) there seem to be differences in the customary time of break-up of the joint family in various groups and places in India.

In conclusion, we can say that there is something like a patterned cycle of rearrangement of family living through time. As mentioned before, the family in India has to be viewed as a process, in terms of a developmental cycle. Some studies have described the Indian family types as stages in a family cycle.

Developmental Process Of The Family

What is means by the developmental process? It denotes a movement, which occurs in a particular pattern. Developmental process of the family denotes that elements of family life take shape in a particular manner and direction. It relates essentially to the process of fission and/ or fusion occurring in the residential and compositional aspects of family living. We now look at the ideal of joint family living and elaborate the processual view of family life.

The Ideal of Joint Family Living

The Indian patrivirilocal family can be viewed in terms of a cycle. A nuclear family develops into a joint family after the marriage of a son and coming of a daughter-in-law. After the death of the father, brothers often separate. In some places, like Andhra Pradesh, sons are expected to stay together with the parents till all the children in the family are married. After this they tend to separate. Thus, the process of fission takes place and the joint family is broken into relatively smaller family units. The parents may then choose to live with one of the sons. Some parents live alternately with all the sons. There may be other kin members who come to live with members of a nuclear family. For example a widow may come to live with her brother, his wife and children if she has no children of her own. In spite of the alterations that occur in the compositional and/or the residential aspect of family living, what holds a family together is the recognition of oneness between the father and the son's households or between the brothers' households. A son's family is in a sense an extension of the father's family. In fact they are considered as 'one family'. It is in this family that the incoming wife has to be incorporated. Formal obligations towards relations by marriage and towards the daughters of the house are expected to be shared by the members of this 'one family'. In the developmental cycle of this 'one family', the emergence of fission in the form of nuclear households can be related to many factors.

One important factor is the high bargaining power of the wife. It has been pointed out that nuclear families develop out of joint families where the wife has high bargaining power. This means that in groups where the wife has a right to legal divorce, where bride price is given and where there is economic and social support to a woman from her natal family, there are considerable possibilities for the formation of nuclear households or fission in the 'one family'.

Those who have studied the family as a process point out that a particular type of composition of a household should be looked at as a stage in the developmental cycle. The presence of nuclear households should not be taken as indicative of change in the institution of joint family. Such families should be viewed as units, which will grow up into joint families when the sons grow up and marry. This may or may not happen in reality. Rather at the level of norms and expectations, most families try to achieve this ideal. We should also look at the other side of the coin. That is the side in which the concept of joint family living is not found for several reasons.

The idea of the developmental cycle of the family does not apply universally to all groups. For instance, among artisans any kind of joint family living may be more advantageous than among very poor agricultural groups where organisation of labour or pooling of labour offers little advantage. An illustration of this point can be given from the study by Cohn of the Chamars of Senapur, who are landless labourers. Among them the achievement of a joint family is difficult because of demographic, economic factors as well as due to the role of women and mobility. Let us look at these factors.

a) *Demographic factor*: With low life expectancy there is much less chance of three generations existing at the same time.

b) *Economic factors:* With no property, contribution to the income of the family is the major asset for this group. Since old people may not have the capacity to work and contribute to the family resources, they are not considered as essential and important persons in the family.

c) *Role of women:* Due to the poor financial position of the family, women are required to take up paid employment outside the home. So the traditional division of labour in a joint family where women look after the home and children and men go out to work cannot operate. Women's economic activities make the continuity of the joint family difficult

d) *Mobility*: Movement of individuals from one place to another, in search of better economic opportunity, also makes joint family living difficult.

Having discussed the factor of non-occurrence of joint family in certain groups, now we shall also look at the areas of changes in the family,

Changes in Family Structure

In order to measure the overall changes taking place in the family as an institution in India, we need to identify the major forces or factors that have brought about changes in the family structure. A host of interrelated factors, economic, educational, legal, demographic, have affected the family in India. The impact has been differentially felt by different groups through time. Let us look at each factor separately keeping in mind that all these factors had a cumulative effect on different aspects of family living.

Factors of Change

Generally the factors leading to changes in the family are discussed in the context of the issue of disintegration of the joint family. In addition, we will discuss these factors also in the context of social changes occurring since the British rule in India.

Economic Factors

Monetisation (introduction of cash transactions), diversification of occupational opportunities for employment in varied spheres, technological advancements (in communication and transport) are some of the major economic factors, which have affected the joint family system in India.

The economic system established by the British encouraged monetisation i.e., cash payment for services rendered and goods sold. The British also threw open opportunities for employment in government service. Those who were attracted by the employment opportunities and facilities provided by the British, often left their traditional occupations and moved to cities or towns where these occupations were available. This meant residential separation from their ancestral home. If they were married, they sometimes took their wives and children (and even one or two relatives) along with them. Since Independence, opportunities for and diversification of occupations have increased. With a constitutional commitment to promote equality between the sexes and to integrate women into the development process, a further impetus has emerged to draw women into varied kinds of occupations. In families where both the men and women go out to work, role relationships between different members of the family are affected.

Educational Factors

Again it was during the British rule that opportunities for higher education emerged in a significant way. All castes and communities had access to the facilities provided by the British with regard to education. Some of those who were able to gain access and exposure to English-medium education (exposure specially to the individualistic, liberal and humanitarian ideas) began to question some of the Hindu customs and practices relating to child marriage, denial of rights of education to women, property rights of women and ill-treatment of widows. Educated young men not only desired to postpone their marriage to a much later age than what was prescribed by family tradition, but also wanted to marry women with some educational background. Educated women (especially college educated) were expected to have a different kind of influence on family matters than uneducated or less educated women.

Legal Factors

Legislations regarding employment, education, marriage, and property, have affected the family system in many ways. Labour laws passed for the benefit of employees like the Indian Workmen Compensation Act (1923), the Minimum Wages Act 1948, helped to reduce the economic reliance of members on the joint family for economic support. In 1930 the Hindu Gains of Learning Act was passed whereby it was declared that the property acquired by a Hindu out of his education was his personal property though his education was paid for by the joint family. The distinction between self-acquired property and joint family property was drawn. In 1937, during the British rule a law was passed by which a woman acquired a limited right to her husband's property. She could hold the property of her husband after his death as a limited owner during her lifetime. But after she died the property devolved to the heirs (usually the sons) of the husband.

With regard to marriage, the Child Marriage Restraint Act was passed in 1929, to curb infant marriages. It prescribed the minimum age (18 and 14 years respectively) at marriage for boys and girls. This Act also aimed to give women an opportunity for education. Now in India the prescribed minimum age at marriage is 21 for boys and 18 for girls.

After Independence the Hindu Succession Act (1956) was passed which gave a daughter and a son equal rights to the father's property. These legislations challenged the inheritance patterns that prevailed in joint families prior to the passing of this Act and the dependent position of women within the family.

Urbanisation

The process of urbanisation has also affected the pattern of family life in India. It denotes the movement of people from rural to urban areas and a shift from agricultural to non-agricultural occupations. It also implies the adoption of an urban way of life. Urban life reflects increased density of population, heterogeneity of population, diversification and increased specialisation of occupations, complex division of labour. It also includes increased availability of educational and health facilities. Limited availability of living space, impersonality and anonymity also characterise urban life.

Partly as a result of population pressure on land, there has been a continuous influx of people into cities seeking education, jobs, medical care etc. What impact does migration to cities have on the families in villages? Residential separation due to mobility of members from one place to another affects the size and composition of the family. A man may take his wife and children along with him to establish a nuclear family in the city. There have been many studies, which show that migration to cities from villages and small towns has contributed to the rapid disintegration of large size family units. These observations have been mainly based on census data, which show a high percentage of nuclear families in cities. In the city, with problems of finding accommodation and limited space available for living, it becomes difficult for an average urbanite to maintain and support a large family.

The other factors which have been held responsible for encouraging smaller units are i) opportunities for higher education ii) heightened ambitions iii) increased occupational mobility iv) growing sense of individuality (i.e., thinking in terms of individual needs and ambitions rather than in terms of kinship needs and larger familial requirements).

Factors Leading to Reinforcement of Joint Family

So far we have talked about the forces that were seen to negatively affect the joint family functioning as commensal, co-residential and large size unit. Sociologists while trying to measure the changes taking place in family life observe that urbanisation and industrialisation have, in fact, served to strengthen some aspects of joint family system. Here we will discuss three important studies to illustrate our point.

1. K.M. Kapadia, for instance, has drawn our attention to the fact that families, which have migrated to cities, still retain their bonds with their joint family in the village or town. Even after they residentially separate themselves from a joint family and form a nuclear family, they do not function as an isolated or completely independent unit in the city. These, families retain their kinship orientation and joint family ethic. This is evident from the physical presence of relatives at the time of certain events like birth, marriage, death, illness and so on. Sometimes members from the families living in a city go to the village to participate in such events or sometimes members from the rural family come to the city to involve themselves in functions or ceremonies or activities of their kin members.

   The joint family ethic is very much evident in the performance of certain role obligations. These may include physical and financial assistance to kin members. A family in the city has the duty to give shelter and sustenance to all subsequent immigrants from the rural family, mostly young men in pursuit of education and work or relations seeking medical treatment in urban centres. So it can happen that in the course of time, a kind of joint family is formed in the city, which is linked to the family in the village by close family ties, by a system of mutual rights, duties and obligations and also by the undivided family property.

ii) Again the thesis that the joint family is dysfunctional to the process of industrialisation has been challenged by those who point out that some of the successful industrial establishments in the country are managed by the individuals who strictly live by joint family rules. They maintain coresidence, common hearth, contribute and share economic resources. In his study *The Indian Joint Family in Modern Industry*, Milton Singer points out that the joint family continues to be the norm among industrial entrepreneurs, despite changes in their material conditions of living. He observes that changes have taken place, within three generations, in residential, occupational and educational spheres. Social mobility has increased and ritual observations have been reduced in number and/or in importance. However, these alterations, he points out, have not transformed the joint family into isolated nuclear families. On the contrary, a modified joint family organisation has emerged in the urban industrial setting where even members from the ancestral home or village move into the urban setting. Thus, according to Singer, the industrial centre has simply become a new area for the working of the joint family system.

iii) Kolenda in her study *Regional Differences in Family Structure in India* observes that industrialisation serves to strengthen the joint family because an economic base has been provided to support it or because more hands are needed in a renewed family enterprise or because kin can help one another in striving for upward mobility.

No doubt the joint family that functions today in urban settings is different in many ways from the joint family which functioned in pre-independent and non-industrial India. For instance many of the coresidential, commensal joint families in urban areas remain joint because it is the norm or due to some advantages, or because of shortage of accommodation. Yet, there may be considerable separation in the management of household expenses on entertainment, education of children etc. Certain expenses may be regarded individual, like those on clothes, education, and vacation. These internal arrangements are different not only between urban and rural families but also between families in an urban area.

Among many families, across caste, class, region and communities, it is possible to find that sons along with the members of their nuclear family unit define the household of the parents as the 'main home' or 'common home'. This distinction may be given to a) the household of the eldest brother or to b) that of the brother with whom the parents live or, to c) that of the brother who lives on the ancestral or parental property. Also presence of a parental home (where one son and a parent live) or of a joint household of two brothers helps to keep the households (of parents and sons and of brothers) closer to each other, for it provides a kind of common meeting ground for all. Married daughters or sisters also come to this home. There may also be a greater sense of economic obligation between members of this "family" distributed in more than one household, residence and hearth.

Emerging Patterns of Family Life

Today there are varied patterns of family living. In urban areas both male and female members of the family may go for gainful employment outside the home. In some families the parents of the husband may live with his wife and children. While in some others, members of the wife's family may be living with the couple and their children. With both the husband and the wife going outside the home for gainful employment and with the absence or limited availability of child care facilities, presence of kin members to look after the home and children comes handy for the smooth functioning of the household. Those working couples who prefer to live in nuclear families and who fear or resist interference from kin members, try to organise their household with professional help from outside the family (like cooks, maid servants, crèches). Aged parents, who formerly used to look towards their eldest son or other sons for support in old age, are now adjusting themselves to the new demands of family life by making economic provisions for their old age. Even within a city parents and married sons may reside separately. Another trend in family life in India is that girls are prepared to support their parent or parents in old age, and it is not impossible to find a widowed mother or parents staying with a married daughter (mainly, in the absence of sons) to help her to manage the household. Measures have been provided at the legal level to ensure that dependant old parents are looked after by a daughter if she is self-reliant even after her marriage. Bilateral kinship relations are more and more recognised and accepted today in many nuclear households in the cities.

9

Systems of Kinship

Since India is a land of immense diversity, its different regions reflect different systems of kinship. In the limited scope of two units, it is not possible to even outline all the various types of kinship systems found in India. As the country's two major geographical divisions, the north and the south, present two distinct forms and have been described in sociological literature as such, we introduce you to the North Indian and South Indian systems of kinship. You must remember that this does not mean that there are no further varieties of kinship systems in certain pockets of both North and South India. Indeed. India's north eastern parts, as well as, other regions in its west and south provide many other types.

The kinship system refers to a set of persons recognised as relatives either by virtue of a blood relationship or by virtue of a marriage relationship. In sociology, all blood relationships are known by a technical term, consanguinity. Similarly, all relationships through marriage are given the term affinity. For example, the relationships between mother and son/daughter, sister and brother/sister, father and son/daughter are consanguinal, while relationships between father/mother-in-law and daughter-/son-in-law are affinal.

Mostly, it is the social recognition of these relationships that is more important than the actual biological ties. Networks built around kin relationships play a significant role in both rural and urban social life in India.

Approaches to Study Kinship System

Sociological studies of kinship in India cover descriptions, comparisons and analytical problems based on the findings from various regions. Approaches to the study of kinship can be broadly classified under two headings (i) the Indological approach and (ii) the Anthropological approach. Here, we will discuss these approaches one by one.

Indological Approach

As the social institutions of Indian society are rooted in literary and learned traditions, many sociological studies have made use of textual sources for explaining the ideological and jural bases of our institutions. For example, K.M. Kapadia has used classical texts to describe Hindu kinship. *Hindu Social Organisation* by P.H. Prabhu is also based on Sanskrit texts. Similarly, Irawati Karve and G.S. Ghurye have extensively worked on Indian kinship system. Both have used textual sources to explain kinship pattern in different regions of India from a socio-historical perspective. We can, therefore, say that Indological approach to the study of kinship has provided a framework to understand the elements of continuity and change in the system.

Anthropological Approach

Anthropologists have looked at kinship systems from the point of view of descent and alliance.

Descent Approach

Kinship in our society is used for establishing clear-cut

corporate social units. Each one of us is a member of such a cooperating and closely bound group of people. One can depend upon the help and support given by such people. Such cooperating local groups are always larger than elementary families of spouses and their children. When these groups are recognised or defined on the basis of shared descent, anthropologists call them descent groups. Formally speaking there are six possible avenues for the transmission of descent group membership, from parents to children. These are:

1. *patrilineal*—where descent is traced in the male line from father to son,
2. *matrilineal*—where descent is traced in the female line from mother to daughter,
3. *double (duolineal or bilineal)*—where descent is traced in both the father's line as well as mother's line for different attributes such as movable property in one line and immovable in another,
4. *cognatic (bilateral)*—where attributes are transmitted equally through both parents. Here no unilineal groups can be formed but group structure can be cognatic, that is, the group of kinpersons on the father's and mother's side. Membership can be acquired through either the father or the mother,
5. *parallel descent*—a very rare form of descent where descent lines are sex specific. Men transmit to their sons while women to their daughters, and finally
6. *cross or alternative type descent*—this is also very rare. Here men transmit to their daughters and women to their sons.

In India, we generally find the patrilineal and matrilineal descent systems. Of the two, patrilineal system is more common. The description and analysis of kin relationships in a descent group have given us a fairly comprehensive sociological understanding of certain types of kinship systems in India. For example, E.K. Gough has discussed the unity of the lineage with corporate rights on land. She has focused on roles and inter-personal relationships in the wider kinship. T.N. Madan has studied the role of kinship as an organising principle in the Kashmiri Brahmin society. He has brought out the strong patrilineal ideology that characterises kinship system of the Kashmiri Pandits.

In sociological studies the terms 'line', 'lineal', 'lineage' etc. with or without the prefix 'patri' or 'matri' have in the past been used in at least four different ways.

2. they have been used to denote corporate descent groups, i.e., lineage proper,

2. often employed to denote the chosen line of inheritance, succession etc. in a given society,

3. in the study of relationship terminologies the expression "two line prescription" has sometimes been used to refer to terminological structures which are consistent with "bilateral cross-cousin marriage",

4. regardless of which lines (matriline or patriline or both) are chosen for the above three purposes, lineal relatives refer to one's ascendants or descendants. Lineal relatives are those who belong to the same ancestral stock in a direct line of descent. Opposed to lineal relatives are collaterals who belong to the same ancestral stock but not in a direct line of descent.

All of these usages, except the fourth, are context specific. i.e., they refer to particular situations. Here, social relations and groups are emphasised and sociologists study them in terms of interaction, norms and values of a particular society. For example, some scholars, following the theory of lineages or descent groups, have discussed the relation between mother's brother and sister's son in patrilineal societies. They use the idea of 'complementary filiation', i.e., the relationship ego has with the relatives on the mother's side in a patrilineal society. In a matrilineal society it refers to the relationship ego has with the relatives on his father's side. In a patrilineal society a person's maternal group is the affinal group of that person's father. This is the group, from which the person's father has taken a wife. For this reason some sociologists like to consider the question of affinity in its own right, rather than as a complementary set of relationships. We may say that in descent approach, the emphasis is laid on social organisation of descent groups. As a result, there is little focus on the 'affinity' aspect of *relationships.*

Alliance Approach

Another concept that figured prominently in the study of kinship systems in India is that of alliance. Kinship includes the consideration of the patterns and rules of marriage. When a sociologist pays special attention to these aspects of kinship, we say that he/she is following the alliance approach to understand the patterns of kinship. Many studies of kinship in India have focused on marriage as an alliance between two groups and on kinship terminology, as a reflection of the nature of alliance. Because of their concentration on relationships arising out of marriage, we say that these studies follow the alliance approach. The main exponent of this approach is Louis Dumont. He has emphasised the role played by marriage in the field of kinship in South India. By showing the opposition between consanguines and affines as reflected in the Dravidian kinship terminology, Dumont has made an important contribution to our understanding of kinship system in India in general and of South India in particular. He has applied to South India a structural theory of kinship. It brings out the repetition of intermarriage through the course of generations.

This pattern highlights the classification of kinsmen into two categories of parallel and cross relatives.

The alliance approach to the study of kinship has helped sociologists to discuss and explain the distinction between bride-givers and bride-takers. In addition, it has also included the discussion on the notion of *hypergamy* (i.e., the bride-45 takers are always superior to bride-givers), practice of dowry in relation to hypergamy and ideas of exchange in marriage.

Dimensions Of Kinship System

In order to describe the features of kinship systems found in North and South India, we need to focus on certain aspects. Here, we are going to identify four aspects.

1. *Kinship Groups:* Kin relationships provide both a method of passing on status and property from one generation to the next effective social groups for purposes of cooperation and conflict. So we need to identify the form of descent or of tracing one's relationships. In other words, we speak of the social groups within which relatives cooperate and conflict. That is why, we need to describe kinship groups.
2. *Kinship Terminology:* The list of terms used by the people to refer to their kin relationships expresses the nature of kinship system. This is why by describing kinship terminology, we are able to throw light on the kinship system. Most features of the kinship system of any society are usually reflected in the way kinship terms are used in that society. Generally a person would apply the same term to those relatives who belong to the same category of kin relationships. In this case, these relatives would also occupy similar kinship roles.

3. *Marriage Rules:* Just as kinship groups describe the form of kinship system found in a society, so also rules for marriage, categories of people who may/ may not marry each other, relationships between bride-takers and bride-givers provide the context within which kin relationships operate. Talking about these issues gives us an understanding of the content of kin relationships. It is therefore necessary to speak of marriage rules for understanding any kinship system.

4. *Exchange of Gifts:* Sociologists like to describe social relationships between various categories of relatives. As there are always two terms to any relationship, kinship behaviour is described in terms of pairs. For example, the parent-child relationship would describe kinship behaviour between two generations.

In this way, we feel that by describing the above four dimensions of the kinship system in relation to North and South India, we will be able to give you a fairly general picture of the patterns of kinship in the two regions.

Kinship Diagrams

Before ending this section on dimensions of kinship systems, let us also mention that the depiction of different types of kinship groups, marriage rules and their implications is made much easier by the help of kinship diagrams. Sociologists and anthropologists invariably use them for explaining various kinship structures. For following a kinship diagram you need to simply remember the following ways of drawing kinship diagrams.

1. The symbol D refers to a male and the symbol O refers to a female. When these symbols are shown in black, i.e., ▲ or, ● it means that the particular male or female is dead.

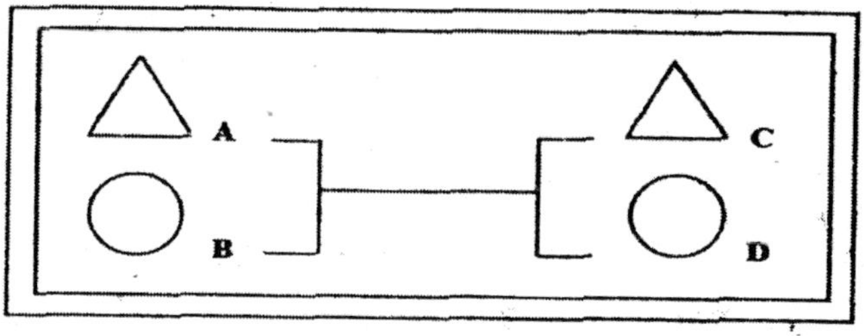

Figure 1. Basic kinship diagram

2. The symbol [refers to sibling relationship. It expresses brother/brother, sister/sister or brother/sister relationships. The symbol], on the other hand, expresses the husband-wife or the marriage relationship.

3. Thirdly, a horizontal line—connecting the symbols [and], denotes filiation or the relationship between the parent/s and child/children. Thus, with the use of above symbols, kin relationships are expressed to denote genealogical connections and to depict the structure of kinship groups. Let us take an example and see what the following diagram shows.

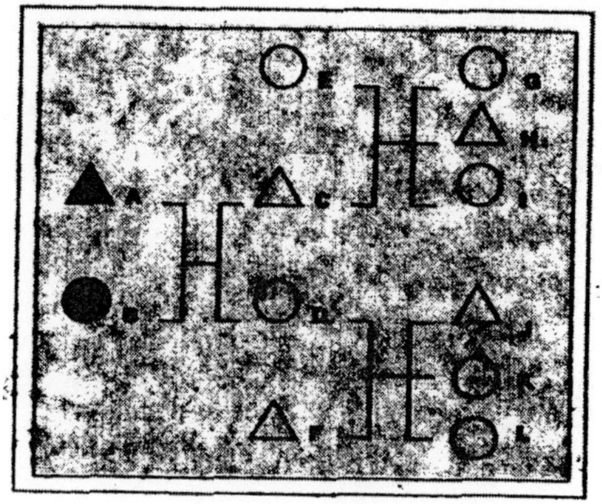

Figure 2. Elaboration of basic kinship diagram

This diagram shows that A is married to B, and C and D are the children of A and B. This simple diagram can be extended endlessly with the help of the same symbols. In this example you can further show that both C and D have their spouses and children. We can show that C is married to E, and G, H and I are the children of C and E. Similarly, D is married to F, and J, K and L are the children of D and F. This diagram will also show that GHI are the cross-cousins of JKL and that A and B are grandparents of G, H, I, J, K and L and they are now dead. Similarly, you can also locate mother's brother of J, K and L and father's sister of G, H and I. This diagram is drawn in the following manner.

Kinship System In North India

Let us first define what we mean by North India. For purposes of describing the kinship systems found in India, Irawati Karve identified four cultural zones the Northern, the Central, the Southern and the Eastern zones. The northern zone, according to Karve, lies between the Himalayas to the north and the Vindhya ranges to the south. In this region, the majority of the people speak languages derived from Sanskrit.

Some of these languages are Hindi, Bihari, Sindhi, Punjabi, Assamese and Bengali. In such a large region, we cannot say that there is one kinship system. The differences of language, history and culture bring about a high degree of variation within the region. We may, however, try to look at the pattern of kinship organisations of the communities in this region on the basis of broad and general features. We can describe the basic structure and process of kinship system in this area in terms of four features that is i) kinship groups, ii) kinship terminology iii) marriage rules, and iv) ceremonial exchange of gifts among kin. Now, we take up each of these features to discuss the kinship system in North India.

Kinship Groups

Sociological studies in various parts of North India show that social groups, such as patrilineage, caste, subcaste provide the basis for cooperation or conflict among the people. We now discuss these groups.

Patrilineage

We can say that broadly speaking kinship organisation in North India is based on unilineal descent groups. When the lineage membership group is traced on the basis of shared descent in one line, we call it a unilineal descent group. In North India, we have mostly patrilineal descent groups. This means that the descent is traced in the male line from father to son. Members of patrilineages cooperate as well as show antagonism in various situations. Let us see how this takes place in terms of a) cooperation, b) conflict and c) inheritance of status and property.

Cooperation. Members of a patrilineage cooperate in ritual and economic activities. They participate together in life cycle rituals. In settlement of disputes, the senior men of the lineage try to sort out the matter within the lineage. Cooperation among lineage members is strengthened because they live close together in the same village. As the farm-lands of lineage members are normally located in the same village, they set up their houses almost next to each other. In this situation, there is constant exchange of material resources from the household of one member to another. This pattern of cooperation is amply described in the studies of kinship patterns in North India by Lewis, Minturn and Hitchcock, Beremen, Nicholas. In terms of theoretical approach to the study of kinship we can say that these studies follow the descent approach because they examine the pattern of cooperation and conflict in descent groups.

Conflict. Lineage members help each other, but conflict also characterises kinship relations among them. For example, T.N. Madan shows how in a Kashmir village, rivalry among brothers leads to partition of the joint family. Later, this rivalry takes more intense form in the relationships between the children of brothers.

Inheritance of Status and Property. From one generation to the next, transmission of status and property takes place according to certain rules. In North India, these generally pass in the male line. In other words, we have a predominantly patrilineal mode of inheritance in North India. For this reason, composition of patrilineage becomes very important. Thus, the lineage fellows cooperate for economic and jural reasons. They share jural rights and therefore they cooperate in order to keep the rights. However, they also fight among themselves about who is to get more benefits from those rights. Pradhan has described how the Jats and other landowners of Meerut and other districts around Delhi have a certain portion of the village lands and how it cannot be transferred out of the lineage. To keep the land within the lineage, its male members have to remain united. Thus, it becomes a main principle of their social organisation. Let us now discuss the second kinship group.

Clan

A lineage is an exogamous unit, i.e., a boy and a girl of the same lineage cannot marry. A larger exogamous category is called the clan. Among the Hindus, this category is known as *gotra*. Each person belongs to the clan of his/her father and cannot marry within the clan or *gotra*. One usually knows about the common ancestor of lineage members as an actual person. But the common ancestor of a clan is generally a mythical figure. The members of a lineage live in close proximity and therefore have greater occasions for cooperation or conflict. Common interests or action do not characterise the relationships among clan members because they are usually scattered over a larger territory and their relationships are often quite remote. These relationships do become significant only in the context of marriage.

Caste and Subcaste

Besides lineages and clans, the kinship system operates within the families of the caste groups, living in one village or a nearby cluster of villages. As castes are endogamous, i.e., one marries within one's caste, people belonging to one caste group are kinspersons in the sense that they are already related or can be potentially related to each other. Caste-fellows generally come forward to help each other when others challenge their honour and status. They may also hold rituals together and help each other economically.

Subcaste is the largest segment of caste and it performs nearly all the functions of caste, such as endogamy and social control. In this respect, we can say that the internal structure of the subcaste would provide us the framework within which we can see the operation of kinship system. The members of a subcaste cooperate as kinspersons. They, depending on the context, work together as equals in the sphere of ritual activities and political allies in socio-economic activities.

As Vidyarthi has shown in the case of a very small subcaste, one may trace one's relationship with most members of the subcaste. On the other hand, in the case of a subcaste spreading over many villages, one may be limited to maintaining relations with only a part of the total number of kin. Klass in his study of marriage rules in Bengal calls this part of the total as one's 'effective jati' i.e., those people of the sub-caste with whom one actually has relationships of cooperation or conflict.

Among the subcaste kin, we should also include those related to a person through marriage. Here, generally a person's kin through mother are called uterine kin and those through spouse are known as affinal kin. These relatives are not members of one's family or lineage or clan. They are expected to help and support each other and, actually do so when an occasion arises for such an action. While a person belongs to only one lineage, one clan or one subcaste, he would always have a string of relatives who do not belong to his lineage/clan/subcaste.

Here we should mention how sociologists, following the descent approach to study kinship systems, try to explain the fact of special place of the relationship between a person and his/her mother's brother. For example, A.R. Radcliffe-Brown went to the extent of coining a new term to express this relationship. Following the principle of filiation (i.e., the relationship between a father and son in the case of a patrilineal society), a person's relationship with his mother's brother is to be understood by the idea of filiation on mother's side or the principle of 'complementary filiation'. Without going into further details about this theoretical issue, we would like to tell you that those following the alliance approach like to explain the same fact in terms of repetition of intermarriage through generations.

Fictive Kin

We should also mention, in passing, the recognition of fictive kinship among villagers. Often, people, who are not related either by descent or marriage, form the bonds of fictive kinship with each other. We find the evidence of such a practice in many tribal and village studies.

Mahapatra points out that fictive kinship is a mechanism to provide even such kin who are not ordinarily found in a particular situation. For example, in North India where village exogamy is a normal practice, it is rare to find a brother to a daughter-in-law living in the same locality. She can get a brother only through a fictive relationship. In urban context, you must have frequently come across small children who call any older man 'uncle' and an older woman 'aunty'. This shows how easily we make use of kinship idiom in our day-to-day behaviour towards total strangers. These transitory relationships do not however assume much importance in terms of actual kin ties and behaviour associated with them.

Kinship Terms

A comparison and analysis of the various kinship terms helps us to understand the kinship structure, its make-up and the behaviour associated with each term. In other words, kinship terms provide the context and the idiom for our social relationships. In this sense, kinship terms do not just tell us about biological and social relationship. They help us to look at the whole way of social life. Only after studying the language, values and behaviour of the particular people can we fully appreciate the significance of their kinship terms. Many times the same kinship term is used to denote different meanings in different contexts. This is the reason why the study of kinship terms is closely associated with the study of language and culture. Here, we discuss how this is the case in relation to the kinship terms used in the linguistic regions of the northern zone.

The kinship terminology is the expression of kinship relations in linguistic terms. In the case of North India, we can call the system of terminology as descriptive. This is because the kinship terms generally describe the relationship from the point of view of the speaker. In a few words, even the most distant kin relationships can be accurately described. Unlike the English terms, uncle, aunty, cousin, which do not reveal age, patrilateral/matrilateral ties, the North Indian kinship terms are very clear. For example, when we say *chachera bhai,* it can be easily translated as father's younger brother's *(chacha's)* son, who stands in the relationship of a brother *(bhai)* to the speaker. Similarly, *mamera bhai* means mother's brother's *(mama's)* son. According to L. Dumont, the North Indian kinship terminology is descriptive in the sense that it describes elementary relationships starting from Ego. The elementary relationships of filiation upwards and downwards, siblingship (sister/brother) and marriage comprise the first set of terms. Then we have the relationships of the second order. These are formed by combining two elementary relationships, i.e., filiation + filiation, filiation + siblingship, siblingship + filiation, marriage + filiation, marriage + siblingship. The third order of relationships is represented by filiation + marriage + filiation. Further, for Dumont, the North Indian kinship terminology is not a classificatory type of terminology because it does not classify the kinship terms according to the number of principles of opposition. However, to emphasise the patrilineal descent, we find a clear-cut distinctionmade between parallel and cross-cousins. The children of one's brother are *bhatija* (for male child) and *bhatiji* (for female child). The children of one's sister are *bhanja* (for male child) and *bhanji* (for female child). A person's parallel relatives are members of his/her descent group and therefore they also live nearby in the same village. In contrast, a person's sister's children or cross relatives are members of a different descent group. They are also residents of a different place.

Social Behaviour

Irawati Karve has given a list of kinship terms in North Indian languages. She makes use of kinship terminologies to describe and compare kinship systems in various parts of India. She studies the terms and also uses the findings for understanding the influences which have played a part in shaping them. Besides Iravati Karve, we can also give another example of the analysis of Indo-Aryan kinship terms, made by G.S. Ghurye. He has highlighted the jural and ideological aspects of kinship systems through a comparison of kinship terms in North Indian languages. For example, among the Sarjupari Brahmins the term *'maan'* refers to the bride-taker. In ideological terms, *'maan'* reflects the high status of the bride-taker as compared to the bride-giver. In jural terms it denotes the fact that bride-takers do not share property with the bride-givers.

The very usage of kinship term also makes clear the kind of behaviour expected from a kin. For example, Oscar Lewis , in his study of a North Indian village, has described the pattern and relationship between a person and his elder brother's wife. This is popularly known as *Devar-Bhabhi* relationship, which is characteristically a joking relationship.

As a contrast to the joking relationship is the behaviour of avoidance between a woman and her husband's father. Similarly, she has to avoid her husband's elder brother. The term for husband's father is *shvasur* and for husband's elder brother is *bhasur. Bhasur* is a combination of the Sanskrit word *bhratr* (brother) and *shvasur* (father-in-law), and is, therefore, like father-in-law.

Marriage Rules

Because every time a marriage is contracted, new kinship bonds come into being, we can clearly see the relevance of marriage rules for discussing the patterns of kinship organisation. In the context of North India, we find that people know whom not to marry. In sociological terms, the same thing can be expressed by saying that there are negative rules of marriage in North India. We can also say that marriage is allowed only outside a defined limit. Let us see what this limit or the rule of exogamy is in North India.

Clan Exogamy

Belonging to one's natal descent line is best expressed in matters of marriage. No man is allowed to marry a daughter of his patriline. In North India lineage ties upto five or six generations are generally remembered and marriage alliances are not allowed within this range. In such a situation the lineage turns into the clan and we speak of *gotra* (clan) and *gotra bhai* (clan mates). Widely used Sanskrit term *gotra* is an exogamous category within a subcaste. Its main use is to regulate marriages within a subcaste.

The Four Clan Rule

In this connection, you may refer to the four-*gotra* or four-clan rule. In Irawati Karve's words, according to this rule, a man must not marry a woman from (i) his father's *gotra,* (ii) his mother's *gotra,* (iii) his father's mother's *gotra,* and (iv) his mother's mother's *gotra.* In other words, this rule prohibits marriage between two persons who share any two of their eight *gotra* links. This means that the rule of exogamy goes beyond one's own lineage. Another related kind of exogamy, which exists in North India, is village exogamy. A village usually has members of one or two lineages living in it. Members belonging to the same lineage are not permitted to intermarry. This principle extends even to the villages, which have more than two lineages. In other words, a boy and a girl in a village in North India are like a brother and sister and hence cannot intermarry.

It is important here to give you a word of caution. We have spoken about lineage, clan and subcaste in relation to organisation of kinship patterns. But we have not mentioned terms like *kutumb, biradari, khandan, bhai bandh* etc. These denote various colloquial meanings of the general terms (lineage, clan and subcaste) in local languages. The local terms are used in various contexts to signify different levels of kinship arrangements. In our discussion, we have limited ourselves to social structure and function in broad terms and avoided conflicting usages of local terms. Now we look at the groups within which marriage is preferred/ prescribed, in the context of North India.

Marriages within the Subcaste

Associated with local terms is the idea of the status of various units within the subcaste. Taking the example of the Sarjupari Brahmin of Mirzapur district in Uttar Pradesh, studied by Louis Dumont, we find that each of the three subcastes of Sarjupari Brahmins of this area is divided into three houses (kin groups or lineages) which range hierarchically in status. The marriages are always arranged from lower to higher house. This means that women are always given to the family, which is placed in the house above her own. In this context, we can also refer to the popular saying in North India that 'the creeper must not go back'. The same idea is reflected by another North Indian saying that *'pao pujke, ladki nahin le jainge'* (i.e., once we have washed the feet of the bridegroom during the wedding ceremony, we cannot accept a girl from his family, because this will mean that we allow that side to wash our feet or allow the reversal of relationships). This shows clearly that marriage rules in North India maintain a hierarchic relationship between the bride-givers and bride-takers. In terms of negative rules of marriage in North India, the above description reflects the rule that a man cannot marry his father's sister's daughter or his patrilateral cross-cousin. This is called the rule of no reversal.

As shown in Figure 3, Lineage B has given the woman (M) in marriage to the man (P) of lineage A. P is given the high ritual status of 'pao puj' in marriage ceremonies. If P's daughter is married to the man of lineage B, then P will have to give the same high ritual status to the man of lineage B. But lineage B is, according to the rule of hypergamy, lower to lineage A and therefore, this marriage will be a reversal of roles. In North India, such a reversal is not allowed and thus, we find the rule of prohibition on marriage with patrilateral cross-cousins.

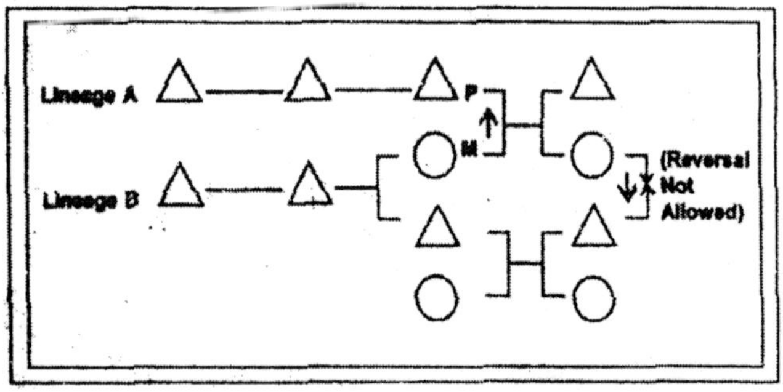

Figure 3. The rule of no reversal

Another principle should also be mentioned here. It is rule of no repetition. This means that if the father's sister has been married in a family *(khandan)*, one's own sister cannot be given in marriage to that same family . The term family or *khandan* is used here as a smaller unit of a lineage. This rule of no repetition implies the negative rule of prohibition on the marriage with matrilateral cross-cousins. In other words, a man cannot marry his mother's brother's daughter. This can be depicted in a simple kinship diagram.

As depicted in Figure 4, lineage B has given women D in marriage to the man E of lineage A. In the next generation, if a woman is again given in marriage to a man of lineage A, then a repetition will occur. A prohibition on repetition shows that matrilateral cross-cousin marriage is barred in North India. Thus, we find that both patrilateral and matrilateral cross-cousin marriages are not allowed in North India. In other words, the two rules, the rule of no reversal and the rule of no repetition, put together define the negative rules of marriage in North India.

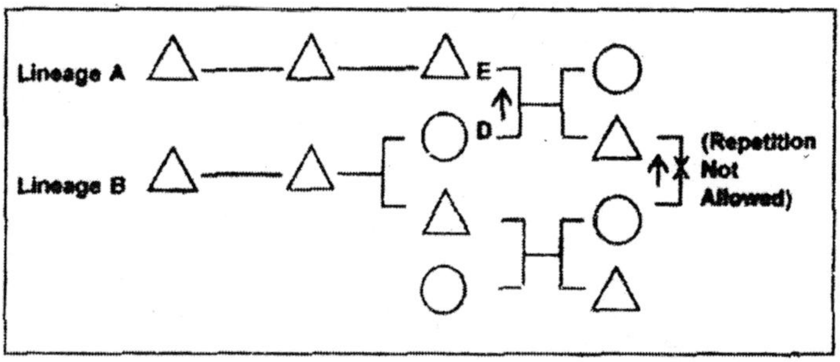

Figure 4. The rule of no repetition

Highlighting the structural implications of marriage rules in North India, T.N. Madan in his study of the Kashmiri Pandits distinguishes three classes of wife-givers and wife-takers from the perspective of the household (i) those who give it wives and those who take wives from it, (ii) those who give wives to those in class (i) and (iii) those who take wives from class (i). These three classes have unequal relationships. However honour and prestige go in the opposite direction to women in marriage. This means that wife-takers are superior to wife-givers and by the fact of giving a wife to a group, one receives honour and prestige within one's own group. Figure 5 shows how the rule of hypergamy in North India acts as a form of exchange between women and dowry on the one hand and prestige and honour on the other.

In figure 5, A, B and C are patrilineages which are ranked by high to low status. The upward arrows indicate that lineage C has given the woman and dowry to the man of lineage B. As bride-givers, the lineage C is lower to B and the lineage B is lower to A. The rule of hypergamy accords lower status to bride-givers. At the same time by giving the women and dowry to high-status lineages, the lower status lineages gain prestige and power within their groups. Thus, the downward arrows indicate the movement of prestige and honour in the direction opposite to women and dowry. In other words, women and dowry are exchanged for prestige and honour among the hierarchically arranged lineages of a subcaste/caste in North India.

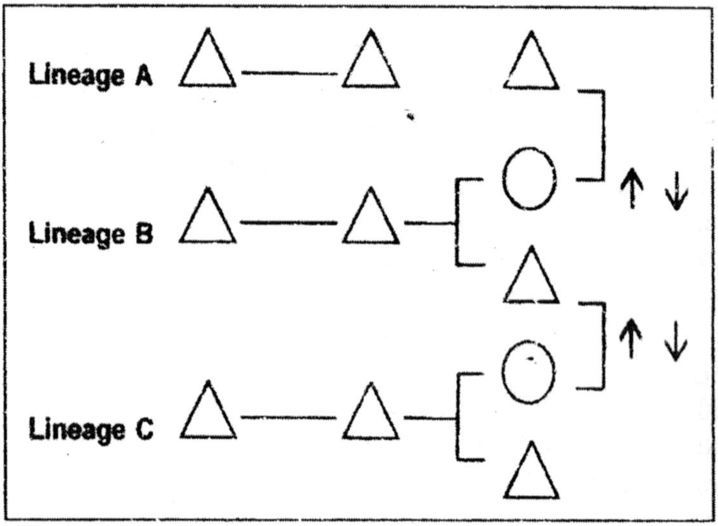

Figure 5. Hypergamy in north India as an exchange

Ceremonial Exchange of Gifts among Kin

Ceremonial exchange of gifts on the occasions of life cycle rituals provides us with the understanding of a patterned behaviour among various categories of kin. Generally, the bride-givers, in correspondence with their inferior status vis-a-vis bride-takers, initiate the process of gift-giving during marriage and continue to give greater amounts of gifts. In other words, you can say that gift-giving and receiving is a well-defined social activity. Let us take two examples of this behaviour.

L. Dumont has pointed out that mother's brother (uterine kin) and wife's brother (affinal kin) have similar ceremonial functions. Not only this, as wife's brother becomes, after a few years, mother's brother to the children, there is little difference between the two. A.C. Mayer has described in his study of kinship in a village in Malwa that all gifts given by one's mother's brother are called *mamere*. In contrast to the gifts given by the mother's brother, there are gifts known as *ban,* given by one's agnates. *Ban* is the term used also for the gift, which is given by other relatives such as the groom's sister's husband to the groom's wife's brother. This shows that the groom's sister's husband (or father's sister's husband in the context of the ascending generation) is viewed to be a part of agnatic kin vis-a-vis the *groom's wife's brother (or mother's brother for the* ascending generation).

In sociological vocabulary we can put the same thing in this way. We look at the groom's sister's husband (zh) or father's sister's husband (fzh) as a wife-taker. Similarly, we look at the groom's wife's brother (wb) or his mother's brother (mb) as a wife-giver. Now if the gift to A's wife-givers (i.e., mother's brother or wife's brother) by A's wife-taker (sister's husband or father's sister's husband) and by A's agnates are known by the same term *'ban'* then we can say that in opposition to A's wife-givers, his agnates and wife-takers have been merged into one category. This is so because for the groom's wife's brother (or mother's brother) the groom is a wife-taker and groom's wife-taker is his sister's husband or father's sister's husband. These two sets of wife-takers are on one side and the wife-givers are on the other.

To this example of ceremonial gift-giving at wedding we can add one more, given by L. Dumont. He has shown a similar distinction being made between wife-givers and wife-takers (the terms used by L. Dumont) in the context of gift-giving at the end of mourning in a village of Gorakhpur district in Eastern Uttar Pradesh. Here, the main mourner is generally a son or an agnate of the deceased. The ceremony of tying a turban on the head of the main mourner is done by an affine who has taken a wife. In other words, the turban is preferably tied by sister's husband (zh) or father's sister's husband (fzh). Then again for the ceremony of *shaiyyadan* (gift of a bed), a sister's husband (zh) or father's sister's husband (fzh) is asked prohibition the gift. This ceremony emphasises their status within takers. The priest clearly asks for those who have rother and daughters to come forward for receiving the *shaiyya* (bed). Thus, of the two kinds of affines (the wife's-taker and wife-giver) the affines of the wife-taking type are preferred over the affines of wife-giving type. In the hypergamous situation wife-takers are higher than the wife-givers and therefore in ceremonial gift-giving they remain at the receiving end while the wife-givers remain at the giving end.

Flow of gifts from affinal kin (wife's relatives) and uterine kin (mother's relatives) have also been recorded in the studies made by F.G. Bailey in Orissa and Oscar Lewis in Rampur. According to A.C. Mayer, the function of the gifts made by uterine and affinal kin is similar, i.e. to enhance the status of wife-takers. In sociological terms, we say that this type of exchange of gifts shows the hypergamous nature of marriage in North India. In other words, the woman is always given into the group, which is higher in status, and the flow of gifts from the family maintains this distinction forever. This, in turn, explains the nature of kin relationships in North India.

10

Marriage: Changing Patterns

Marriage is an important social institution. It is a relationship, which is socially approved. The relationship is defined and sanctioned by custom and law. The definition of the relationship includes not only guidelines for behaviour relating to sex but also regarding things like the particular way labour is to be divided and other duties and privileges. Children born of marriage are considered the legitimate offspring of the married couple. This legitimacy is important in the matter of inheritance and succession. Thus marriage is not only a means of sexual gratification but also a set of cultural mechanisms to ensure the continuation of the family. It is more or less a universal social institution in India.

The religious texts of many communities in India have outlined the purpose, rights and duties involved in marriage. Among the Hindus, for instance, marriage is regarded as a socio-religious duty. Ancient Hindu texts point out three main aims of marriage. These are *dharma* (duty), *praja* (progeny) and *rati* (sensual pleasure). That is to say that marriage is significant from both the societal as well as the individual's point of view. Marriage is significant in that it provides children especially sons who would not only carry on the family name but also perform periodic rituals including the annual *"shraddha"* to propitiate the dead ancestors. Majority of the Hindus look upon son(s) as a support in old age to parents and as the most important source of economic enrichment to the family. Marriage, in the Hindu system, enables a man to enter into the stage of a householder. Both a man and a woman are regarded incomplete without marriage.

Even among other communities in India, marriage is regarded as an essential obligation. Islam looks upon marriage as "*sunnah*" (an obligation) which must be fulfilled by every Muslim. Christianity holds marriage as crucial to life and lays emphasis on the establishment of a mutual relationship between husband and wife and on their duty to each other.

The significance attached to marriage is reflected in the fact that only a very small percentage of men and women remain unmarried. The Report of the Committee on the Status of Women in India has indicated that only 0.5 percent of women never marry in India. By and large girls are brought up to believe that marriage is a woman's destiny; married state is desirable and motherhood is a cherished achievement. Only a very small percentage of men and women remain unmarried by choice. Today, marriage is still considered important and necessary, and only few individuals remain unmarried by choice. Goals of marriage are, however, undergoing changes especially for the urban and educated sections of the population. The older notions regarding large size family, (i.e., large number of children especially sons being the source of status for parents) are being replaced by preference for small size family. Marriage for self-fulfillment rather than primarily for procreation or societal welfare is also becoming prevalent.

Age of Marriage

Apart from marriage being universal, early marriage is also common in India. Though there are differences between various religious groups, classes and castes in the matter of age at marriage, the median age at marriage is low in India. As early as the 18th and nineteenth century, efforts have been made to curb infant or child marriage. Reformers like Raja Rammohun Roy, Ishwar Chandra Vidyasagar, Jyotiba Phule and others in the nineteenth and early twentieth century opposed child marriage. In 1929, the Child Marriage Restraint Act was passed (popularly known as the Sarda Act) and the minimum age for marriage for girls and boys was fixed at 14 years and 17 years respectively. The Act was made applicable to all Indians. The latest amendment has raised the minimum age for marriage for boys and girls to 18 years and 21 years, respectively. Though the age at marriage of females in India has been rising slowly since around the middle of the twentieth century; the level at the end of the twentieth century was low in comparison to the most of the low fertility countries.

Low Age at Marriage

In spite of legislations, and governmental and non-governmental efforts to educate the people about the dangers of early marriage, age at marriage is low in India. The 1971 Census data on marital status of women indicate that the average age of marriage for girls in more than one-third of the total number of districts in our country was below 15 years. The mean age at marriage for females for the year 1991 was 18.3. The female age at marriage was lowest in Rajasthan (17.5) followed by states of Madhya Pradesh and Bihar (17.6 and 17.8 respectively) and it was highest in Kerala (22.3) followed by Assam and Punjab (21.1 and 21.0 respectively. In newspapers and journals we read about marriage melas, specially in rural areas, in which the average age of the bride is reported to be below fifteen years. In some states like Orissa, Madhya Pradesh, Uttar Pradesh and Rajasthan, child marriages continue.

Low age at marriage is related with the near universality of marriage in India. Marriage is regarded essential and thought of a girl's marriage is entertained right from her childhood. In some regions, the existence of clear-cut expectations, preferences, and rules regarding choice of a marriage partner also lead to early marriage. The desire and concern to preserve the chastity or purity of women is yet another factor. In fact, till the 1920's among certain upper castes, pre-puberty marriages were not only popular but also mandatory. There is the belief that the onset of puberty is the right age for marriage for a girl as she is then ready for maternity. This is also another important factor leading to early marriage .

Rise in the Age at Marriage

Female age at marriage rose from 16.1 years in 1961 to 19.3 in 1991. The rural urban gap in female age at marriage for 1991 is 2 years and this indicates that in spite of rise in age at marriage a wide gap persists between the rural and urban areas of the country. It is important to point out on the basis of growing evidence that age at marriage has not been low for all communities in India. For instance, among many of the hill tribes in India the average age at marriage has been above 15 years for girls. Also among the Christians, Parsis and some educated sections living in urban areas, the age at marriage has been above the minimum age prescribed by law.

You may ask what have been some of the factors that have helped in raising the age at marriage among certain sections of the population. Research suggests that in urban areas and for the well to do in rural areas education and the need for employment of boys have raised the age of marriage. In states where the literacy rate is high, age at marriage is also much higher than in those states where literacy level is low.

While, it is encouraging to note that education has helped in raising the age at marriage, it has however led to some unintended consequences. Education combined with increasing demands for dowry have led to a rise in the age at marriage. Educated girls seek educated boys and the price (dowry) of an educated groom in the 'marriage market' is high. Since most marriages in India are arranged, parents arrange a marriage only when they meet the dowry demands. Thus, necessarily the marriages of the girls are postponed and age at marriage increases.

Forms Of Marriage

All the commonly listed forms of marriage, namely, *monogamy* (marriage of a man to a woman at a time), and polygamy (marriage of a man or woman to more than one spouse) are found in India. The latter, that is polygamy, has two forms, namely, polygyny (marriage of a man to several women at a time) and polyandry (marriage of a woman to several men at a time). In ancient texts of the Hindus we find references to eight forms of marriage.

Monogamy, Polygyny, Polyandry

In this section, we shall focus only on monogamy, and both forms of polygamy. With regard to the prevalence of these three forms, one has to distinguish between what is permitted and what is practised by different sections of the population through time.

Monogamy

Among the Hindus, until the passing of the Hindu Marriage Act of 1955, a Hindu man was permitted to marry more than one woman at a time. Although permitted, polygyny has not been common among the Hindus. Only limited sections of the population like kings, chieftains, headmen of villages, members of the landed aristocracy actually practised polygyny.

We may say that those who had the means and the power to acquire more than one wife at a time were polygynous. The other important reasons for polygyny were the barrenness of the wife and or her prolonged sickness. Among some occupational groups like the agriculturists and artisans, polygyny prevailed because of an economic gain involved in it. Where women are self-supporting and contribute substantially to the productive activity a man can gain by having more than one wife.

Concerted efforts to remove this practice were made in the nineteenth century and early twentieth century by social reformers like Raja Rammohun Roy, Ishwar Chandra Vidyasagar, Dayanand Saraswati and others. After Independence, the Hindu Marriage Act of 1955 established monogamy for all Hindus and others who came to be governed by this Act. Some of the 'other' communities covered by this Act are the Sikhs, Jains and Buddhists. Strict monogamy is prescribed in Christian and Parsi communities.

Polygyny

Islam, on the other hand, has allowed polygyny. A Muslim man can have as many as four wives at a time, provided all are treated as equals. However, it seems that polygynous unions have been restricted to a small percentage of Muslims, namely the rich and the powerful.With regard to the tribal population, we find that the customary law of the tribals in general has not forbidden polygyny. Polygyny is more widespread among the tribes of north and central India.

Polyandry

Polyandry is even less common than polygyny. A few

Kerala castes practised polyandry until recently. The Toda of the Nilgiris in Tamilnadu, the Khasa of Jaunsar Bawar in Dehradun district of Uttaranchal and some North Indian castes practise polyandry. In the fraternal form of polyandry, the husbands are brothers. In 1958, C.M. Abraham has reported that in Central Travancore fraternal polyandry was practised by large number of groups like the Irava, Kaniyan, the Vellan and the Asari.

The factors that are related to the prevalence of polyandry are

a) desire to prevent division of property within a family (especially in fraternal polyandry)

b) desire to preserve the unity and solidarity of the sibling group (in fraternal polyandry)

c) the need for more than one husband in a society where men are away on a commercial or military journey

d a difficult economy, especially an unfertile soil, which does not favour division of land and belongings (Peter 1968).

Prevailing Patterns

Monogamy is the most prevalent form of marriage in India. However, bigamous (having two spouses at a time) marriages have been reported among the Hindus in many parts of India. It is the man who very often commits bigamy and escapes punishment by turning the loopholes of the law to his advantage. It is the wife who is often unaware of his second marriage, and even if she is aware of it, is unaware of her legal rights and accepts her fate. Social and economic dependence on husband and inadequate social condemnation of the man's actions are some of the reasons for the wife's acceptance of the husband's second marriage.

Among the Muslims it is the man who is allowed to have four wives. Among them men enjoy greater privileges than women. A Muslim woman cannot marry a second time when her first husband is alive or if she has not been divorced by him.

Selection Of Spouse

There are three striking features regarding selection of spouse in India. Firstly the rules of endogamy, including those of hypergamy, indicate the groups into which a person is expected to find a spouse. Secondly, rules of exogamy, on the other hand, prohibit a person form marrying into certain groups. Both the rules of endogamy and exogamy are linked mainly to the caste and kinship structure. Thirdly, marriages in India are mostly arranged by the parents or elders.

Rule of Endogamy

The rule of endogamy requires an individual to marry within a specified or defined group of which he or she is a member. The group may be a caste, clan, racial, ethnic or religious group.

Religious and caste endogamy are two of the most pervasive forms of endogamy in India. Though legally permitted, inter-religious marriages are not commonly arranged or popular. In India there are innumerable castes which are divided into innumerable sub-castes which are further divided into subsections and each one of them is endogamous. The endogamous unit, for many Hindu sub-castes, consists of a series of kin clusters living in a fairly restricted geographical area. The operation of the rule of endogamy shows interesting variation by region and religion.

In South India, for instance, among many castes marriage with some relatives is preferred. In the Marathi, Telugu, Tamil and Kannada speaking areas, marriages with the cross-cousins (children of father's sisters or mother's brothers) are preferred. In North India, neither the parallel nor the cross-cousins can intermarry. In North India, on the other hand, there is a tendency to marry into villages that are not farther than twelve or thirteen kilometres from one's village. Social and economic links are restricted to a few kin groups residing in certain areas. There are spatial as well as social boundaries which limit the field of marriage and these boundaries vary from region to region.

Endogamous rules are operative in non-Hindu sections of the population too. Among the Muslims, the 'Syeds', recognised as an aristocratic class, are divided into various endogamous groups. Sometimes the endogamous group is so small that it includes only the extended families of a man's parents.

Muslims permit marriages between both cross (mother's brother's children and father's sister's children) and parallel (mother's sister's children and father's brother's children) cousins. In fact, the father's brother's daughter is a preferred mate. Among Muslims the concept of purity of blood seems to be mainly responsible for preference of marriage between close relatives particularly between children of siblings. Many Muslim groups in North and Western India consider marriage between children of two brothers as most desirable. It is held that the desire to keep the family property within the family has been another important reason for close kin marriages. It is generally believed that marriage of the near kin helps to mitigate the conflict between a mother-in-law and daughter-in-law and this helps to strengthen the intra-as well as inter-familial ties.

Rule of Hypergamy

According to the rule of hypergamy, the status of the husband is always higher than that of the wife. Those who follow this rule always seek for their daughters those men who have social status higher than their own. It is a rule whereby marriage takes place or is generally arranged within a sub caste between a girl of a lower social status and a boy of a higher social status. This practice has occurred mainly among different subsections of a caste or sub caste rather than between castes. It is found that the tendency towards hypergamous stratification is available among all castes. Each caste is divided into several sub-castes, which are again divided into hierarchically ordered groups. It is quite clear that the rule of hypergamy operates within the confines of each endogamous group.

In ancient scriptures, it is given that *anuloma* marriages, based on the rule of hypergamy whereby a girl is married to a boy from upper caste sub-caste, were permitted. It is also given that *pratiloma* marriages, based on the rule of hypogamy, whereby a girl is married to a boy from a lower caste sub-caste, were not permitted. It would seem that in ancient times hypergamy *(anuloma)* across the four fold *varna* order was acceptable while hypogamy *(pratiloma)* was not permitted.

Practice of hypergamy has been found among such groups as the Rajput and the Jat of North India, Anavil Brahmin and Patidar of Gujarat, Maithil Brahmin of Bihar, Rarhi Brahmin of Bengal and among the Kanyakubja and Saryupari Brahmin of Uttar Pradesh to some extent. It has also been found among the Nayar, Kshatriya and Ambalavasi of Kerala.

The practice has shown a regional pattern. For instance, among the Rajput of Uttar Pradesh, traditionally girls were given in marriage from east to the west direction within a sub-caste. This is so because the Rajput clans were associated with a geographic region and a corresponding rating by region. Prestige of regions increased towards the westerly direction.

In the areas where hypergamy is practised, clans and lineages are of unequal status. Research has indicated that female infanticide among the Jat and Rajput was mainly a consequence of hypergamy. This was so because the girls of the highest groups had very little choice for marriage. Boys of their group could marry lower down while they had only the boys in groups which were at least equal to their own. Dowry has been generally high in hypergamous communities. Men from the Kulin subcaste of Bengal (belonging to the Rarhi Brahmin caste) often married many women at a time and demanded huge dowries.

This is so because they are ranked as the highest subcaste and women of this group have to be married within the group.

Exogamy

Exogamous rules are complementary to endogamous rules. These rules prohibit marriage between members of certain groups. The prohibition may be so narrow as to include those members within the elementary family (i.e. marriage between a brother and sister or parent and child) or so wide to include all those with whom genealogical kinship can be traced. The prohibition placed, on sexual intercourse between persons related in certain prohibited degrees of kinship is called incest, e.g., sexual relations or marriage between a brother and sister are defined as incestuous in most groups. The definitions of these groups, however, show variations mainly by region and religion. In North India, a girl born within a village is considered the daughter of the village and hence cannot marry a boy from her own village. Thus, the village becomes the exogamous unit here. In South India, the exogamous unit in one's own generation is defined by one's own sisters/brothers and real and classificatory parallel cousins.

Two other kinds of exogamy, which have been prevalent among several Hindu communities in North and South India, are sagotra and *sapinda* exogamy.

Sagotra exogamy: In the context of the 'twice born' castes (belonging to the Brahmin, Kshatriya and Vaishya *varna* across) India *sagotra* exogamy applies to those who trace descent from a common ancestor, usually a *rishi* or a sage. All these people cannot intermarry. The term *gotra* is commonly used to mean an exogamous category within a *jati.* One of its principal uses is to regulate marriage alliance. All members of a *gotra* are supposed to be descendants of or associated with the same ancestral figure.

A four-clan rule or four *gotra* exogamous rule prevails among Hindu castes in North India. In accordance with this four clan *(gotra)* rule, a man cannot marry a girl from (i) his father's *gotra* or clan, (ii) his mother's *gotra* or clan, (iii) his *dadi's*, i.e. his father's mother's *gotra* or clan, and (iv) his *nani's*, i.e., his mother's mother's gotra or clan. In almost all castes in the northern zone, according to Karve , the marriage between cousins is prohibited.

Sapinda: Sapinda exogamy indicates the prohibition placed on the inter-marriage between certain sets of relatives. *Sapinda* represents the relationship between the living member and their dead ancestors. The term *sapinda* means (i) those who share the particles of the same body (ii) people who are united by offering *'pinda'* or balls of cooked rice to the same dead ancestor. Hindu lawgivers do not give a uniform definition regarding the kinship groups within which marriage cannot take place. Some prohibit marriage of members within seven generations on the father's side and five generations of members from Mother —' the mother's side. Some others have restricted the prohibited generations to five on the father' and three on the mother's side. Several others have permitted the marriage of cross-cousins (marriage of a person with his father's sister's children or mother's brother's children).

The Hindu Marriage Act of 1955 does not allow marriage within five generations on the father's side and three on the mother's side. However, it permits the marriage of cross- cousins where this is customary. The patrilineal joint family is an important exogamous unit among Hindus. This much is quite clear from the fact that marriage is prohibited within five generations on the father's side.

Among Christians and Muslims, the elementary or nuclear family is the exogamous unit. Moplah Muslims of North Malabar in Kerala live in matrilineal units and among them matrilineage is the exogamous unit. Lineage exogamy also exists among the Muslim Gujjars of Jammu and Kashmir. Among the Nayars, who are a matrilineal group, a girl can never marry her mother's brother.

Arranged Marriages

Majority of the marriages in India are fixed or arranged by parents or elders on behalf of and/or with the consent of the boy or the girl involved in marriage. When marriage is fixed by parents or elders it is called an arranged marriage. This is in contrast to marriage by self choice (popular example of marriage by self choice is the so called "love marriage"). In some instances both these types of selection of one's spouse can be found together.

The prevalence of arranged marriages in India can be traced in relation to what has been said before, that is (i) existence of the rules of endogamy which limit marriage alliance within certain groups, (ii) the rules of exogamy which disallow marriage within *gotra*, (iii) regulations about prescriptive (allowing) and proscriptive (prohibiting) rules about marriage with parallel and cross-cousins and (iv) customs which indicate a specific preference for marriage between certain types of relatives or groups. All these factors make arranged marriages the most desirable form of selection of spouse. Choice of spouse cannot be left to the decision of the young if these restrictions and preferences are to be effectively carried out. The restrictions placed on free interaction between a boy and a girl in India is yet another factor which does not allow marriage by self choice. Though the measure of participation in choosing one's life partner has shown

variations between different groups, by and large, marriage arranged by parents/ elders is the most prevalent form of selection of spouse. For majority of the high caste Hindus, matching of horoscope (charts relating to one's birth under certain astrological calculations) constitutes an important element in the final choice of the marriage partner. Today apart from astrologers matching the horoscopes of a boy and a girl, computers are also used to match horoscopes. Among the Muslims, the parents, elders or *wali* (guardian) arrange a marriage.

Recent Trends

To what extent are the rules of endogamy, hypergamy, exogamy and arranged marriages operative today? Intercaste marriages are now recognised by law and take place on a larger scale than before. These intercaste marriages constitute only a very small proportion of the total number of marriages taking place. They are increasing at a slow rate. Caste endogamy is still highly relevant in the context of the patterns of selection of spouse. Many caste organisations devise all kinds of strategies to confine marriages within their castes and subcastes. There are even marriage *"melas"* (fairs) to ensure that the choice of the spouse is made within the particular subcaste.

Though majority of marriages continue to be arranged by parents/elders/*wali*, the pattern of choosing one's spouse has undergone some modifications today. We find the following patterns i) marriage by parents'/elders' choice without consulting either the boy or girl, ii) marriage by self-choice, iii) marriage by self-choice but with parents' consent, iv) marriage by parents' choice but with the consent of both the boy and the girl involved in the marriage, v) marriage by parents' choice but with the consent of only one of the two partners involved. Very often, the boy is consulted and his consent is taken. Parents/elders do not think it is important to ask the girl whether she approves the match. Among urban educated classes arranged marriage with the consent of the boy and the girl is often the most preferred pattern. Marriages are even arranged through newspaper advertisement for both the boy and the girl.

Marriage Rites

Rites constitute an important part of marriage in India. We find variations in rites not only in terms of religion but also in terms of caste, sect and rural or urban residence. Let us look at some of the basic rites in a few communities in India.

Basic Rites of Marriage in Different Communities

For the Hindus, marriage is a sacrament. This means that a Hindu marriage cannot be dissolved. It is a union for life. This is also reflected in the marital rites. Some of the essential rites are *kanyadan* (the giving off of the bride to the groom by the father), *panigrahana* (the clasping of the bride's hand by the groom), *agniparinaya* (going around the sacred fire by the bride and the groom), *lajahoma* (offering of the parched grain to the sacrificial fire) and *saptapadi* (walking seven steps by the bride and the groom). These basic rituals are not confined to the twice born castes (the Brahmin, Kshatriya and Vaishya) only, but these are also performed with some variations among other castes too. Some invite a Brahmin priest to recite the *mantra* which are religious invocations. The ritual of *kanyadan* is the most popular of all the basic rituals.

If we analyse the significance of the rituals of Hindu marriage we find that they stress male primacy and superiority and reflect the notion of transfer of the bride from her father's side to her husband's side. While emphasising life partnership for the two people involved in marriage, the basic rituals exhort the bride to follow the husband, to act according to his wishes and to remain steadfast in loyalty and love. In fact, marriage is the first major *samskara* (life cycle ritual) for a Hindu woman.

In some regions, among certain castes, the pre-marriage ritual is more elaborate than the actual wedding ceremony. For instance, among certain sections of the Nayar castes in Kerala, the actual marriage constitutes only the exchange of cloth between the bride and the groom, mutual garlanding and going around the lighted lamps. The pre-marital ritual of "*talikettu kalyanam*" is more elaborate than the actual marriage ceremony.

Certain sections of the Jain community (like the Digambara and Svetambara) and the Sikh community have marriage customs and rituals which are similar to those of the Hindus. The core ceremony of the Sikhs however is different. It is called "*anand karaj*" and is solemnised in the presence of the Guru Granth Sahib, the holy book of the Sikhs. The main ceremony consists of the bridal couple going four times around the holy book. Appropriate verses, known as '*shabad*' are recited by the officiating priest. Unlike Hindus, Sikhs do not have any particular period or season for marriages.

Muslim marriage is not a sacrament. Rather, it is a contract, which can be terminated. Among the Muslims, the marriage rituals show variation by sect and region. Some rites of the Shia sect of the Muslims differ from the Sunni, a sect among the Muslims. However, the essential ceremony of Muslim marriage is known as the *nikah.* The ceremony is performed by the priest or the *kazi.* The *nikah* is considered to be complete only when the consent of both the groom and the bride has been obtained. A formal document known as *nikahnama* bears the signatures of the couple. Among certain sections, the signatures of two witnesses are also included in the document and the document may also contain details of the payment to be made to the bride by the groom. This payment is called the *mehr* which is a stipulated sum of money or other assets paid to the wife either immediately after the wedding or postponed till some future date.

Many of the marriage customs and rituals of the Muslims are similar to those of the Hindus. Thus, customs like smearing of turmeric, applying *mehndi,* mock testing of the bride's proficiency at domestic work are as much a part of the Muslim marriage as Hindu marriage. In fact, among the Moplah Muslims of Kerala, the *nikah* ceremony is performed as laid down by Islam but their marriage is not regarded complete without the Hindu function *'kalyanam'*.

What is most significant to note in the rituals of Muslim marriage is that the custom of paying a *mehr* to the wife provides some sort of guarantee of security to the woman.

Among the Christians, the wedding takes place in a church. The exchange of the ring is an important ritual among them. Some sections of the Christians, like the Syrian Christians of Kerala, have the Hindu rite of the groom tying a *'tali'* on the bride's neck. *Tali* is a symbol of the married state of Hindu women in South India.

Among Christians, the following pronouncement, which forms a part of the marriage rites, reflects the importance assigned to the relationship of the husband and wife, rather than the relationship between the families of the husband and the wife. "Man shall leave his father and mother and shall cleave to his wife and they shall be one flesh." This outlook emphasises the fact that marriage is a bond between two individuals and not between two families. It does not focus on the transfer of the girl from one family to another. As a part of marriage celebrations all communities hold wedding processions and feasts. Their scale may vary according to the socio-economic status of the bride and bridegroom's families.

Customary Marriages

While rites constitute an important component of marriage among many communities, there are sections or groups of people who do not have religious rites in marriage. Marriages with no rites are referred as customary marriages. These marriages are based on simple practices. For instance, in some groups living in the Himalayan tract, putting a ring in the bride's nose is a customary form of marriage. Customary forms of marriage are generally found among those groups where divorce and secondary marriages are permitted and practised. Secondary marriage of a widow or a separated or divorced woman is usually celebrated in a simple way, which indicates essentially the renewal of her married state.

Today marriage rites have been condensed to a great extent. The Special Marriage Act of 1954 provides for secular and civil marriage before a registrar. This Act applies to all Indian citizens who chose to make use of its provisions, irrespective of religious affiliations. Civil marriage enables persons to avoid the expense of traditional weddings. However, weddings continue to be an expensive affair for a large majority of people. Large sums of money, gifts of jewellery, furniture, vessels, clothes have to be bought and generally the expenses are more for the bride's side than the groom's side.

Transfer Of Wealth in Marriage

Marriage, in most cases, involves material as well as non-material transactions between the bride-giver and the bride-taker. It involves, with a few exceptions, the transfer of the wife to the husband's family. Two major types of transfers of material wealth accompany marriage. In one, wealth travels in the opposite direction of the bride and in another it travels along with the bride in the same direction. The former is identified as bride price while the latter as dowry.

Bride-Price

The tradition of bride-price is found among certain patrilineal tribes and some castes in the middle and lower rung of the caste ladder. The form and amount of bride-price vary from region to region, from tribe to tribe and within a tribe from time to time. Some pay only cash, some others only in kind while some pay both in kind and cash. Payment in kind includes a wide variety of things like clothes, ornaments, tools and implements, liquor, grain, cattle, goats and other forms of livestock. For instance, among the Uraon tribe of Chotanagpur a man takes sets of clothes for the bride's relatives. Bhumias of Orissa give cash, five or six sarees and three goats as bride-price. Bargaining for bride-price is also common. In some tribes, the groom offers his services to the bride's father as a form of bride-price.

Under the local influence of high caste values and practices, some groups have given up their custom of bride-price and have adopted the custom of dowry. For example, the peasants of the villages of Karnataka and the Godia (or the cowherds) caste in Andhra Pradesh have given up their custom of bride-price and adopted the custom of dowry.

Bride-price or the payment in cash and/or kind to the bride's father by the groom's father reflects the transfer of authority over the bride from her father to the groom and his family. The idea of compensation for the loss of a productive worker is also implicit in it. The bride's family loses a productive worker when the girl gets married and leaves her parental home. So, the bride's family is paid a compensation for this loss. The girl is a source of wealth and prestige to her natal family, that is the family in which she is born. In this sense, the transaction implies the transfer of all that the girl stands for.

Practice of Dowry

Broadly speaking, dowry refers to a specific category of gifts given by the bride's side to the groom's side. This set of gifts symbolises the transfer of wealth from the bride's side to the groom's side. This act confers prestige and honour to both the sides. The bride-giver gains prestige within his community by giving dowry while the bride-taker receives both wealth and prestige in his own and other communities. Of late it has become groom-price.

Today, in legal terms, dowry constitutes what is given to the son-in-law and or to his parents on demand either in cash or in kind by the bride's side. There are, of course, regional variations in the practice and people's understanding of the term 'dowry'. Some view it mainly as 'groom-price' and often the price paid to the groom depends on the groom's qualifications, job, social status regardless of the bride's parents' ability to pay the price demanded by the groom's side. Some include in the custom of dowry i) what is given to the bride during and after the wedding, during occasions like festivals, child birth, initiation etc. in the first few years of marriage ii) what is given to the bridegroom before or after marriage and iii) what is presented to the in-laws of the girl.

Here, we need to note that (a) dowry constitutes an array of gifts given to the groom's side over time and (b) what is given at the time of the wedding is substantial and conspicuous. Goods that constitute dowry are i) movable property like sarees, jewels, silver vessels, cash, vehicles like car, tractor and ii) immovable property such as land, house, factories, jobs etc.

The form and amount of dowry and purpose to which dowry is put have shown variations based on caste, class, region and socio-economic status. Among the landowning castes of Andhra Pradesh (like Reddy, Kamma) a father may give to his daughter land and jewellery. The cash may be handed over to the groom or his parents but the land is registered in the name of the daughter. Money also is deposited in the name of the bride or put in trust for her. In North India, where there has been a tradition of giving large utensils to the girl, the utensils generally come under the use and control of the in-laws. The amount of cash involved in dowry varies mainly according to the socio-economic status and expectations of the groom's community as well as the socio-economic status of the bride's family. Again, the gift in cash or in kind involved in dowry may be put to productive purposes or just hoarded as wealth by the bride, the groom and/or his family.

The practice of giving gift to the girl at the time of and after the wedding has been viewed as *streedhana.* This means that the gifts given to the daughter are a kind of property given to the daughter of the house who has to leave her natal home to join her husband. *Streedhana* reflects the notion of female right to property. It is looked as a source of wealth for the married daughter to fall back in times of crisis and need. In many regions of South India, the gifts (ornaments, vessels) given to the daughter belong to her exclusively and she has the right to use them the way she wants. Her in-laws generally do not claim possession over them.

Today, the practice of dowry has taken a very ugly turn. In many instances, the practice of dowry has worsened. Educated girls look out for boys who are more qualified than them. Highly qualified boys demand a high dowry. As a result of increase in dowry demand, parents often are unable to get their daughters married. If they do, they get them married beyond their means and are subject to different kinds of continuing pressures in the form of dowry demands from the groom's side. We often hear of dowry deaths or the girl being sent back to her parents' home for not fulfilling the dowry demands. Today, we even hear cases of unmarried girls committing suicide in order to ease the burden of their anxious, guilt-ridden parents, who have not been able to settle a marriage for them.

In 1961, the Government of India passed the Dowry Prohibition Act. In 1984 and again in 1986, the Act was amended to make the law more stringent and effective. For instance, today, the husband and his family can be penalised for demanding dowry if his bride dies within seven years of the marriage in other than normal circumstance. We even have a Dowry Prohibition Cell to look into complaints about dowry.

All this does not mean that there are no marriages taking place without dowry. There are progressive young people who voice their strong opinion against dowry and marry without it. There are at the same time, young, educated people who accept this practice and say they see no harm in it. Some get away by saying that it is their parents (whose wishes they never want to disobey) who perpetuate this practice. Even among other communities, like the Muslim and Christian, some people demand dowry. Often, discord in family is caused because of the continuous demand for dowry even after marriage. This may lead to divorce.

Divorce And Widow Remarriage

No discussion of marriage is complete without considering the issues of divorce and remarriage. Here, we look first at the possibilities and mechanism of dissolving a marriage and then discuss briefly the question of widow remarriage in India.

Divorce

The possibilities and mechanisms of dissolving a marital union have varied through time, between and within communities. Hindu marriage is in theory a sacrament and irrevocable. However, among many *non-dwija* (or non-twice born) castes, divorce is customarily allowed. When we say non-twice born castes, we mean those castes, which do not observe the practice of performing the life-cycle rituals or Hindu *Samskara.* Their performance symbolises the second birth or social birth of a biological person and hence the term twice-born for the first three categories of Hindu castes—the Brahmin, Kshatriya and Vaishya, which must and do perform these rituals. The notion that marriage is indissoluble has gradually been eroded and through legislation, the right of divorce has been introduced in all legal systems in India.

The grounds for divorce have been spelt out both by custom and by law in different communities. During 1940-48, several provinces and states passed laws permitting divorce for Hindus. The Special Marriage Act of 1954 introduced and 'clarified the grounds for divorce'. It has been available to all Indians who have chosen to register their marriages under this Act. The Hindu Marriage Act of 1955 was amended several times since 1955 (the next one being in 1976) to incorporate a wide range of grounds for divorce available to both men and women coming under the purview of this Act. Some of the important grounds for divorce outlined by law are i) impotency, ii) lunacy (for a specified time period), iii) disappearance for seven years, iv) contagious disease, v) rape, vi) homo-sexuality, and vii) bestiality (sexual relationship between a human being and a lower animal). Now adultery and cruelty have also become the grounds on which divorce may be sought. The condition that one can apply for divorce after three years of marriage has been reduced to one year. The waiting period of divorce by mutual consent is now only 6 months.

Among the Muslims, marriage is a contract and divorce is allowed. Muslim law provides for different types of divorce of which *talaq* and *khol* need special mention. *Talaq* is an exjudicial divorce. It becomes effective if pronounced thrice unilaterally by the husband. It signifies the power the husband has to divorce his wife at will. The other form of divorce *khol* takes place by mutual consent.

Public attitude to divorce in a Hindu dominated culture is not yet very liberal in spite of the legal permission for divorce. In many communities of the Indian population, divorce even when it is required is not sought, despite legal provisions. Even in cases where women have turned to the legal system for help, law is not very clear about the rights of a woman in her marriage. For instance, the respective judgments of Andhra Pradesh High Court and Punjab High Court in two cases relating to the Hindu woman's right in the matter of being a wife or a mother reflect the ambiguity. In one case in Andhra Pradesh the judgment favoured the woman. Her right to decide whether she wanted to bear the child of the husband whom she did not find compatible was upheld. In the other case in Punjab, the wife was held guilty for refusing to bear a child by her spouse whom she did not find compatible. Women activists point out that though our constitution supports the notion of equality between sexes, the laws passed to promote such a notion have not been able to end the discrimination shown toward women. Even among the Muslims, where divorce has been permitted for a long time, laws favour men more than the women.

Widow Remarriage

Certain sections of the Indian population have a tradition of widow remarriage. Levirate alliances have been reported among the Ahirs of Haryana, some Jats and Girjans and several castes in U.P. and among the Kodagu of Mysore. In a levirate marriage, a man is obliged to marry the widow of a brother.

In many castes of the Hindu fold, widow remarriage has been customarily sanctioned and practised. Only those castes which imitate the life-style and values of the high castes adopt the practice of banning widow remarriage. Widow remarriage is permitted among the Muslims, Christians and Parsis. Among the Jains local and caste customs determine the issue.

Generally, everywhere the widower has the right to remarry. The 1971 census of India showed that there were 8 million widowers as against 23 million widows. In the year 1991, among the elderly (60+ age group) the percentage of widows was 60.7 and that of widowers was 19 (Census of India 1991). It is often said that the problem of widow remarriage is the problem only of a section of society because only the high castes put a strict ban on widow remarriage. Not only this, in the past, widows of some priestly castes, royal families were also expected to commit the practice of sati orwidow burning. The practice of widow burning comprises self-immolation of the widow on the funeral pyre of her husband. Respect is paid to such women who end their lives as a mark of devotion to their husbands.

As early as in the nineteenth century, reformers like Vidyasagar, fought against the practice of sati and exploitation of widows. In 1856, the Hindu Widows Remarriage Act legalised the marriage of widows of all castes. Traditional notions about widow remarriage and the treatment of widows still seem to be prevalent. Widows are still regarded as inauspicious; they are not expected or permitted to participate in certain religious and social functions. It is shocking to hear that widows are still burnt alive on their husband's pyre and there is a section of the population, which glorifies such act. The most recent case of law being enacted to protect the woman victim is the law against the practice of widow burning or sati. This was passed by the Parliament in response to a national demand

and reaction following the burning of a young educated woman, Roop Kanwar, on the funeral pyre of her husband in Deorala, a village in Rajasthan. The Act is called Commission of Sati (Prevention) Act, 1987.

11

Language, Ethnicity, and Regionalism in Indian Society

India's ethnic, linguistic, and regional complexity sets it apart from other nations. To gain even a superficial understanding of the relationships governing the huge number of ethnic, linguistic, and regional groups, the country should be visualised not as a nation-state but as the seat of a major world civilisation on the scale of Europe. The population—estimated at 936.5 million in 1995—is not only immense but also has been highly varied throughout recorded history; its systems of values have always encouraged diversity. The linguistic requirements of numerous former empires, an independent nation, and modern communication are superimposed on a heterogeneous sociocultural base. Almost 8 percent of the population, approaching 65 million people at the time of the 1991 census, belongs to social groups recognised by the government as Scheduled Tribes, with social structures somewhat different from the mainstream of society. Powerful trends of "regionalism"—both in the sense of an increasing attachment to the states as opposed to the central government, and in the sense of movements for separation from the present states or greater autonomy for regions within them—threaten the current distribution of power and delineation of political divisions of territory.

Linguistic Relations

The languages of India belong to four major families: Indo-Aryan (a branch of the Indo-European family), Dravidian, Austroasiatic (Austric), and Sino-Tibetan, with the overwhelming majority of the population speaking languages belonging to the first two families. (A fifth family, Andamanese, is spoken by at most a few hundred among the indigenous tribal peoples in the Andaman Islands, and has no agreed upon connections with families outside them.) The four major families are as different in their form and construction as are, for example, the Indo-European and Semitic families. A variety of scripts are employed in writing the different languages. Furthermore, most of the more widely used Indian languages exist in a number of different forms or dialects influenced by complex geographic and social patterns.

Sir George Grierson's twelve-volume *Linguistic Survey of India*, published between 1903 and 1923, identified 179 languages and 544 dialects. The 1921 census listed 188 languages and forty-nine dialects. The 1961 census listed 184 "mother tongues," including those with fewer than 10,000 speakers. This census also gave a list of all the names of mother tongues provided by the respondents themselves; the list totals 1,652 names. The 1981 census—the last census to tabulate languages—reported 112 mother tongues with more than 10,000 speakers and almost 1 million people speaking other languages. The encyclopedic *People of India* series, published by the government's Anthropological Survey of India in the 1980s and early 1990s, identified seventy-five "major languages" within a total of 325 languages used in Indian households. In the early 1990s, there were thirty-two languages with 1 million or more speakers.

The Indian constitution recognizes official languages. Articles 343 through 351 address the use of Hindi, English, and regional languages for official purposes, with the aim of a nationwide use of Hindi while guaranteeing the use of minority languages at the state and local levels. Hindi has been designated India's official language, although many impediments to its official use exist.

The constitution's Eighth Schedule, as amended by Parliament in 1992, lists eighteen official or Scheduled Languages. They are Assamese, Bengali, Gujarati, Hindi, Kannada, Kashmiri, Konkani, Malayalam, Manipuri, Marathi, Nepali, Oriya, Punjabi, Sanskrit, Sindhi, Tamil, Telugu, and Urdu. (Precise numbers of speakers of these languages are not known. They were not reported in the 1991 census, and estimates are subject to considerable variation because of the use of multiple languages by individual speakers.) Of the official languages, approximately 403 million people, or about 43 percent of the estimated total 1995 population, speak Hindi as their mother tongue. Telugu, Bengali, Marathi, and Tamil rank next, each the mother tongue of about 4 to 5 percent (about 37 million to 47 million people); Urdu, Gujarati, Malayalam, Kannada, and Oriya are claimed by between 2 and 3 percent (roughly 19 million to 28 million people); Bhojpuri, Punjabi, and Assamese by 1 to 2 percent (9 million to 19 million people); and all other languages by less than 1 percent (less than 9 million speakers) each.

Since independence in 1947, linguistic affinity has served as a basis for organising interest groups; the "language question" itself has become an increasingly sensitive political issue. Efforts to reach a consensus on a single national language that transcends the myriad linguistic regions and is acceptable to diverse language communities have been largely unsuccessful.

Many Indian nationalists originally intended that Hindi would replace English—the language of British rule (1757-1947)—as a medium of common communication. Both

Hindi and English are extensively used, and each has its own supporters. Native speakers of Hindi, who are concentrated in North India, contend that English, as a relic from the colonial past and spoken by only a small fraction of the population, is hopelessly elitist and unsuitable as the nation's official language. Proponents of English argue, in contrast, that the use of Hindi is unfair because it is a liability for those Indians who do not speak it as their native tongue. English, they say, at least represents an equal handicap for Indians of every region.

English continues to serve as the language of prestige. Efforts to switch to Hindi or other regional tongues encounter stiff opposition both from those who know English well and whose privileged position requires proficiency in that tongue and from those who see it as a means of upward mobility. Partisans of English also maintain it is useful and indeed necessary as a link to the rest of the world, that India is lucky that the colonial period left a language that is now the world's predominant international language in the fields of culture, science, technology, and commerce. They hold, too, that widespread knowledge of English is necessary for technological and economic progress and that reducing its role would leave India a backwater in world affairs.

Linguistic diversity is apparent on a variety of levels. Major regional languages have stylised literary forms, often with an extensive body of literature, which may date back from a few centuries to two millennia ago. These literary languages differ markedly from the spoken forms and village dialects that coexist with a plethora of caste idioms and regional lingua francas. Part of the reason for such linguistic diversity lies in the complex social realities of South Asia. India's languages reflect the intricate levels of social hierarchy and caste. Individuals have in their speech repertoire a variety of styles and dialects appropriate to various social situations. In general, the higher the speaker's status, the more speech forms there are at his or her disposal. Speech is adapted in countless ways to reflect the specific social context and the relative standing of the speakers.

Determining what should be called a language or a dialect is more a political than a linguistic question. Sometimes the word *language* is applied to a standardised and prestigious form, recognised as such over a large geographic area, whereas the word *dialect* is used for the various forms of speech that lack prestige or that are restricted to certain regions or castes but are still regarded as forms of the same language. Sometimes mutual intelligibility is the criterion: if the speakers can understand each other, even though with some difficulty, they are speaking the same language, although they may speak different dialects. However, speakers of Hindi, Urdu, and Punjabi can often understand each other, yet they are regarded as speakers of different languages. Whether or not one thinks Konkani—spoken in Goa, Karnataka, and the Konkan region of Maharashtra—is a distinct language or a dialect of Marathi has tended to be linked with whether or not one thinks Goa ought to be merged with Maharashtra. The question has been settled from the central government's point of view by making Goa a state and Konkani a Scheduled Language. Moreover, the fact that the Latin script is predominantly used for Konkani separates it further from Marathi, which uses the Devanagariscript. However, Konkani is also sometimes written in Devanagari and Kannada scripts.

Regional languages are an issue in the politically charged atmosphere surrounding language policy. Throughout the 1950s and 1960s, attempts were made to redraw state boundaries to coincide with linguistic usage. Such efforts have had mixed results. Linguistic affinity has often failed to overcome other social and economic differences. In addition, most states have linguistic minorities, and questions surrounding the definition and use of the official language in those regions are fraught with controversy.

States have been accused of failure to fulfill their obligations under the national constitution to provide for the education of linguistic minorities in their mother tongues, even when the minority language is a Scheduled Language. Although the constitution requires that legal documents and petitions may be submitted in any of the Scheduled Languages to any government authority, this right is rarely exercised. Under such circumstances, members of linguistic minorities may feel they and their language are oppressed by the majority, while people who are among linguistic majorities may feel threatened by what some might consider minor concessions. Thus, attempts to make seemingly minor accommodations for social diversity may have extensive and volatile ramifications. For example, in 1994 a proposal in Bangalore to introduce an Urdu-language television news segment (aimed primarily at Muslim viewers) led to a week of urban riots that left dozens dead and millions of dollars in property damage.

Languages of India

About 80 percent of all Indians—nearly 750 million people based on 1995 population estimates—speak one of the Indo-Aryan group of languages. Persian and the languages of Afghanistan are close relatives, belonging, like the Indo-Aryan languages, to the Indo-Iranian branch of the Indo-European family. Brought into India from the northwest during the second millennium B.C., the Indo-Aryan tongues spread throughout the north, gradually displacing the earlier languages of the area.

Modern linguistic knowledge of this process of assimilation comes through the Sanskrit language employed in the sacred literature known as the Vedas. Over a period of centuries, Indo-Aryan languages came to predominate in the northern and central portions of South Asia.

As Indo-Aryan speakers spread across northern and central India, their languages experienced constant change and development. By about 500 B.C., Prakrits, or "common" forms of speech, were widespread throughout the north. By about the same time, the "sacred," "polished," or "pure" tongue—Sanskrit—used in religious rites had also developed along independent lines, changing significantly from the form used in the Vedas. However, its use in ritual settings encouraged the retention of archaic forms lost in the Prakrits. Concerns for the purity and correctness of Sanskrit gave rise to an elaborate science of grammar and phonetics and an alphabetical system seen by some scholars as superior to the Roman system. By the fourth century B.C., these trends had culminated in the work of Panini, whose Sanskrit grammar, the *Ashtadhyayi* (Eight Chapters), set the basic form of Sanskrit for subsequent generations. Panini's work is often compared to Euclid's as an intellectual feat of systematisation.

The Prakrits continued to evolve through everyday use. One of these dialects was Pali, which was spoken in the western portion of peninsular India. Pali became the language of Theravada Buddhism; eventually it came to be identified exclusively with religious contexts. By around A.D. 500, the Prakrits had changed further into Apabhramshas, or the "decayed" speech; it is from these dialects that the contemporary Indo-Aryan languages of South Asia developed. The rudiments of modern Indo-Aryan vernaculars were in place by about A.D. 1000 to 1300.

It would be misleading, however, to call Sanskrit a dead language because for many centuries huge numbers of works in all genres and on all subjects continued to be written in Sanskrit. Original works are still written in it, although in much smaller numbers than formerly. Many students still learn Sanskrit as a second or third language, classical music concerts regularly feature Sanskrit vocal compositions, and there are even television programs conducted entirely in Sanskrit.

Around 18 percent of the Indian populace (about 169 million people in 1995) speak Dravidian languages. Most Dravidian speakers reside in South India, where Indo-Aryan influence was less extensive than in the north. Only a few isolated groups of Dravidian speakers, such as the Gonds in Madhya Pradesh and Orissa, and the Kurukhs in Madhya Pradesh and Bihar, remain in the north as representatives of the Dravidian speakers who presumably once dominated much more of South Asia.

The oldest documented Dravidian language is Tamil, with a substantial body of literature, particularly the Cankam poetry, going back to the first century A.D. Kannada and Telugu developed extensive bodies of literature after the sixth century, while Malayalam split from Tamil as a literary language by the twelfth century. In spite of the profound influence of the Sanskrit language and Sanskritic culture on the Dravidian languages, a strong consciousness of the distinctness of Dravidian languages from Sanskrit remained. All four major Dravidian languages had consciously differentiated styles varying in the amount of Sanskrit they contained. In the twentieth century, as part of an anti-Brahman movement in Tamil Nadu, a strong movement arose to "purify" Tamil of its Sanskrit elements, with mixed success. The other three Dravidian languages were not much affected by this trend.

There are smaller groups, mostly tribal peoples, who speak Sino-Tibetan and Austroasiatic languages. Sino-Tibetan speakers live along the Himalayan fringe from Jammu and Kashmir to eastern Assam. They comprise about 1.3 percent, or 12 million, of India's 1995 population. The

Austroasiatic languages, composed of the Munda tongues and others thought to be related to them, are spoken by groups of tribal peoples from West Bengal through Bihar and Orissa and into Madhya Pradesh. These groups make up approximately 0.7 percent (about 6.5 million people) of the population.

Despite the extensive linguistic diversity in India, many scholars treat South Asia as a single linguistic area because the various language families share a number of features not found together outside South Asia. Languages entering South Asia were "Indianised." Scholars cite the presence of retroflex consonants, characteristic structures in verb formations, and a significant amount of vocabulary in Sanskrit with Dravidian or Austroasiatic origin as indications of mutual borrowing, influences, and counterinfluences. Retroflex consonants, for example, which are formed with the tongue curled back to the hard palate, appear to have been incorporated into Sanskrit and other Indo-Aryan languages through the medium of borrowed Dravidian words

Hindi and English

For the speakers of the country's myriad tongues to function within a single administrative unit requires some medium of common communication. The choice of this tongue, known in India as the "link" language, has been a point of significant controversy since independence. Central government policy on the question has been necessarily equivocal. The vested interests proposing a number of language policies have made a decisive resolution of the "language question" all but impossible.

The central issue in the link-language controversy has been and remains whether Hindi should replace English. Proponents of Hindi as the link language assert that English is a foreign tongue left over from the British Raj. English is used fluently only by a small, privileged segment of the population; the role of English in public life and governmental affairs constitutes an effective bar to social mobility and further democratisation. Hindi, in this view, is not only already spoken by a sizable minority of all Indians but also would be easier to spread because it would be more congenial to the cultural habits of the people. On the other hand, Dravidian-speaking southerners in particular feel that a switch to Hindi in the well-paid, nationwide bureaucracies, such as the Indian Administrative Service, the military, and other forms of national service would give northerners an unfair advantage in gov-ernment examinations. If the learning of English is burdensome, they argue, at least the burden weighs equally on Indians from all parts of the country. In the meantime, an increasing percentage of Indians send their children to private English-medium schools, to help assure their offspring a chance at high-privilege positions in business, education, the professions, and government.

Linguistic States

The constitution and various other government documents are purposely vague in defining such terms as national languages and official languages and in distinguishing either one from officially adopted regional languages. States are free to adopt their own language of administration and educational instruction from among the country's officially recognised languages, the Scheduled Languages. Further, all citizens have the right to primary education in their native tongue, although the constitution does not stipulate how this objective is to be accomplished.

As drafted, the constitution provided that Hindi and English were to be the languages of communication for the central government until 1965, when the switch to Hindi was mandated. The Official Languages Act of 1963, pursuing this mandate, said that Hindi would become the sole official national language in 1965. English, however, would continue as an "associate additional official language." After ten years, a parlia-mentary committee was to consider the situation and whether the status of English should continue if the knowledge of Hindi among peoples of other native languages had not progressed sufficiently. The act, however, was ambiguous about whether Hindi could be imposed on unwilling states by 1975. In 1964 the Ministry of Home Affairs requested all central ministries to state their progress on the switch to Hindi and their plans for the period after the transition date in 1965. The news of this directive led to massive riots and self-immolations in Tamil Nadu in late 1964 and early 1965, leading the central government, then run by the Congress, to back away from its stand. A conference of Congress leaders, cabinet ministers, and chief ministers of all the states was held in New Delhi in June 1965. Non-Hindi-speaking states were assured that Hindi would not be imposed as the sole language of communication between the central government and the states as long as even one state objected. In addition any of the Scheduled Languages could be used in taking examinations for entry into the central government services.

Before independence in 1947, the Congress was committed to redrawing state boundaries to correspond with linguistics. The States Reorganisation Commission, which was formed in 1953 to study the problems involved in redrawing state boundaries, viewed language as an important, although by no means the sole, factor. Other factors, such as economic viability and geographic realities, had to be taken into account. The commission issued its report in 1955; the government's request for comments from the populace generated a flood of petitions and letters. The final bill, passed in 1956 and amended several times in the 1960s, by no means resolved even the individual states' linguistic problems.

Even regions with a long history of agitation for a linguistic state sometimes have found the actual transition less than smooth. For example, proponents began lobbying for a Te-lugu-speaking state in the early twentieth century. In 1956 the central government formed a single state, Andhra Pradesh, composed of the predominantly Telugu-speaking parts of what in British India had been the Madras Presidency and the large polyglot princely state of Hyderabad. Although more than 80 percent of the residents (some 53 million people as of 1991) of Andhra Pradesh speak Telugu, like most linguistic states it has a sizable linguistic minority. In this case, the minority consists of Urdu speakers centered in the state's capital, Hyderabad, where nearly 40 percent (some 1.7 million people in 1991) of the population speak that language. Linguistic affinity did not form a firm basis for unity between the two regions from which the state had been formed because they were separated by cultural and economic differences. Although there were riots in the late 1960s and early 1970s in support of the formation of two separate states, the separation did not occur.

The violence that broke out in the state of Assam in the early 1980s reflected the complexities of linguistic and ethnic politics in South Asia. The state has a significant number of Bengali-speaking Muslims—immigrants and their descendants who began settling the region in the late nineteenth and early twentieth centuries. The Muslims came in response to a British-initiated colonisation plan to bring under cultivation land left fallow by the Assamese. By the 1931 census, the Assamese not only had lost a hefty portion of their land but also had become a disadvantaged minority in their traditional homeland. They represented less than 33 percent of the total population of Assam, and the Muslim immigrants (who accounted for roughly 25 percent of the population) dominated commerce and the government bureaucracy.

Assamese-Bengali rioting started in 1950, and in the 1951 census many Bengalis listed Assamese as their native tongue in an effort to placate the Assamese. Further immigration of Bengali speakers after the formation of Bangladesh in 1971 and a resurgence of pro-Bengali feeling among earlier immigrants and their descendants reawakened Assamese fears of being outnumbered. Renewed violence in the early and mid-1980s was sufficiently serious for the central government to avoid holding general elections in Assam during December 1984.

Social Context of Language

Contemporary languages and dialects, as they figure in the lives of most Indians, are a far cry from the stylised literary forms of Indo-Aryan or Dravidian languages. North India especially can be viewed as a continuum of village dialects. As a proverb has it, "Every two miles the water changes, every four miles the speech." Spoken dialects of more distant villages will be less and less mutually understandable and finally become simply mutually unintelligible outside the immediate region. In some cases, a variety of caste dialects coexist in the same village or region. In addition, there are numerous regional dialects that villagers use when doing business in nearby towns or bazaars.

Since the late eighteenth and early nineteenth centuries, regional languages, such as Bengali, Punjabi, and Marathi, have become relatively standardised and are now used throughout their respective states for most levels of administration, business, and social intercourse. Each is associated with a body of literature. British rule was an impetus for the official codification of these regional tongues. British colonial administrators and missionaries learned regional languages and often studied their literatures, and their translations of English-language materials and the Bible encouraged the development of written, standard languages. To provide teaching materials, prose compositions, grammars, and textbooks were often commissioned and, in some cases, were closer to everyday speech than was the standard literary language. Industrialisation, modernisation, and printing gave a major boost to the vocabulary and standardisation of regional tongues, especially by making possible the wide dissemination of dictionaries.

Such written forms still often differ widely from spoken vernaculars and village dialects. Diglossia—the coexistence of a highly elaborate, formal language alongside a more colloquial form of the same tongue—occurs in many instances. For example, spoken Bengali is so divergent from written Bengali as to be nearly another tongue. Similarly, Telugu scholars waged a bitter battle in the early twentieth century over proper language style. Reformers favored a simplified prose format for written Telugu, while traditional classicists wished to continue using a classical literary poetic form. In the end, the classicists won, although a more colloquial written form eventually began to appear in the mass media. Diglossia reinforces social barriers because only a fraction of the populace is sufficiently educated to master the more literary form of the language.

The standard regional language may be the household tongue of only a small group of educated inhabitants of the region's major urban center that has long exercised politico-economic hegemony in a region. Even literate villagers may have difficulty understanding it. The more socially isolated—women and Dalits —tend to be more parochial in their speech than people of higher caste, who are often able to use a colloquial form of the regional dialect, the caste patois, and the regional standard dialect. An educated person may master several different speech forms that are often so different as to be considered separate languages. Western-educated scholars may well use the regional standard language mixed with English vocabulary with their colleagues at work. At home, a man may switch to a more colloquial vernacular, particularly if his wife is uneducated. Even the highly educated frequently communicate in their village dialects at home.

Only around 3 percent of the population (about 28 million people in 1995) is truly fluent in both English and an Indian language. By necessity, a substantial minority are able to speak two Indian languages; even in the so-called linguistic states, there are minorities who do not speak the official language as their native tongue and must therefore learn it as a second language. Many tribal people are bilingual. Rural-urban migrants are frequently bilingual in the regional standard language as well as in their village dialect. In Bombay, for example, many migrants speak Hindi or Marathi in addition to their native tongue. Religious celebrations, popular festivals, and political meetings are typically carried on in the regional language, which may be unintelligible to many attendees. Bilingualism in India, however, is inextricably linked to social context. South Asia's long history of foreign rule has fostered what Clarence Maloney terms "the linguistic flight of the elite." Language—either Sanskrit, Persian, or English—has formed a barrier to advancement that only a few have been fortunate enough to overcome.

Throughout the twentieth century, radio, television, and the print media have fostered standardisation of regional dialects, if only to facilitate communication. Linguistic standardisation has contributed to ethnic or regional differentiation insofar as language has served as a cultural marker. Mass communication forces the adoption of a single standard regional tongue; typically, the choice is the dialect of the majority in the region or of the region's preeminent business or cultural center. The use of less standard forms clearly labels speakers outside their immediate home base.

To fulfill its purposes, the regional language must be standardised and taught to an increasing percentage of the population, thereby encroaching both on its own dialects and the minority languages of the region. The language of instruction and administration affects the economic and career interests and the self-respect of an ever-greater proportion of the population.

Ethnicity

Tribes

Tribal peoples constitute roughly 8 percent of the nation's total population, nearly 68 million people according to the 1991 census. One concentration lives in a belt along the Himalayas stretching through Jammu and Kashmir, Himachal Pradesh, and Uttar Pradesh in the west, to Assam, Meghalaya, Tripura, Arunachal Pradesh, Mizoram, Manipur, and Nagaland in the northeast. Another concentration lives in the hilly areas of central India (Madhya Pradesh, Orissa, and, to a lesser extent, Andhra Pradesh); in this belt, which is bounded by the Narmada River to the north and the Godavari River to the southeast, tribal peoples occupy the slopes of the region's mountains. Other tribals, the Santals, live in Bihar and West Bengal. There are smaller numbers of tribal people in Karnataka, Tamil Nadu, and Kerala, in western India in Gujarat and Rajasthan, and in the union territories of Lakshadweep and the Andaman and Nicobar Islands.

The extent to which a state's population is tribal varies considerably. In the northeastern states of Arunachal Pradesh, Meghalaya, Mizoram, and Nagaland, upward of 90 percent of the population is tribal. However, in the remaining northeast states of Assam, Manipur, Sikkim, and Tripura, tribal peoples form between 20 and 30 percent of the population. The largest tribes are found in central India, although the tribal population there accounts for only around 10 percent of the region's total population. Major concentrations of tribal people live in Maharashtra, Orissa, and West Bengal. In the south, about 1 percent of the populations of Kerala and Tamil Nadu are tribal, whereas about 6 percent in Andhra Pradesh and Karnataka are members of tribes.

There are some 573 communities recognised by the government as Scheduled Tribes and therefore eligible to receive special benefits and to compete for reserved seats in legislatures and schools. They range in size from the Gonds (roughly 7.4 million) and the Santals (approximately 4.2 million) to only eighteen Chaimals in the Andaman Islands. Central Indian states have the country's largest tribes, and, taken as a whole, roughly 75 percent of the total tribal population live there.

Apart from the use of strictly legal criteria, however, the problem of determining which groups and individuals are tribal is both subtle and complex. Because it concerns economic interests and the size and location of voting blocs, the question of who are members of Scheduled Tribes rather than Backward Classesor Scheduled Castesis often controversial. The apparently wide fluctuation in estimates of South Asia's tribal population through the twentieth century gives a sense of how unclear the distinction between tribal and nontribal can be. India's 1931 census enumerated 22 million tribal people, in 1941 only 10 million were counted, but by 1961 some 30 million and in 1991 nearly 68 million tribal members were included. The differences among the figures reflect changing census criteria and the economic incentives individuals have to maintain or reject classification as a tribal member.

These gyrations of census data serve to underline the complex relationship between caste and tribe. Although, in theory, these terms represent different ways of life and ideal types, in reality they stand for a continuum of social groups. In areas of substantial contact between tribes and castes, social and cultural pressures have often tended to move tribes in the direction of becoming castes over a period of years. Tribal peoples with ambitions for social advancement in Indian society at large have tried to gain the classification of caste for their tribes; such efforts conform to the ancient Indian traditions of caste mobility. Where tribal leaders prospered, they could hire Brahman priests to construct credible pedigrees and thereby join reasonably high-status castes. On occasion, an entire tribe or part of a tribe joined a Hindu sect and thus entered the caste system en masse. If a specific tribe engaged in practices that Hindus deemed polluting, the tribe's status when it was assimilated into the caste hierarchy would be affected.

Since independence, however, the special benefits available to Scheduled Tribes have convinced many groups, even Hindus and Muslims, that they will enjoy greater advantages if so designated. The schedule gives tribal people incentives to maintain their identity. By the same token, the schedule also includes a number of groups whose "tribal" status, in cultural terms, is dubious at best; in various districts, the list includes Muslims and a congeries of Hindu castes whose main claim seems to be their ability to deliver votes to the party that arranges their listing among the Scheduled Tribes.

A number of traits have customarily been seen as establishing tribal rather than caste identity. These include language, social organisation, religious affiliation, economic patterns, geographic location, and self-identification. Recognised tribes typically live in hilly regions somewhat remote from caste settlements; they generally speak a language recognised as tribal.

Unlike castes, which are part of a complex and interrelated local economic exchange system, tribes tend to form self-sufficient economic units. Often they practice swidden farming—clearing a field by slash-and-burn methods, planting it for a number of seasons, and then abandoning it for a lengthy fallow period—rather than the intensive farming typical of most of rural India. For most tribal people, land-use rights traditionally derive simply from tribal membership. Tribal society tends to be egalitarian, its leadership being based on ties of kinship and personality rather than on hereditary status. Tribes typically consist of segmentary lineages whose extended families provide the basis for social organisation and control. Unlike caste religion, which recognises the hegemony of Brahman priests, tribal religion recognises no authority outside the tribe.

Any of these criteria can be called into question in specific instances. Language is not always an accurate indicator of tribal or caste status. Especially in regions of mixed population, many tribal groups have lost their mother tongues and simply speak local or regional languages. Linguistic assimilation is an ongoing process of considerable complexity. In the highlands of Orissa, for example, the Bondos—a Munda-language-speaking tribe—use their own tongue among themselves. Oriya, however, serves as a lingua franca in dealings with Hindu neighbors. Oriya as a prestige language (in the Bondo view), however, has also supplanted the native tongue as the language of ritual. In parts of Assam, historically divided into warring tribes and villages, increased contact among villagers began during the colonial period and has accelerated since independence. A pidgin Assamese developed while educated tribal members learned Hindi and, in the late twentieth century, English.

Self-identification and group loyalty are not unfailing markers of tribal identity either. In the case of stratified tribes, the loyalties of clan, kin, and family may well predominate over those of tribe. In addition, tribes cannot always be viewed as people living apart; the degree of isolation of various tribes has varied tremendously. The Gonds, Santals, and Bhils traditionally have dominated the regions in which they have lived. Moreover, tribal society is not always more egalitarian than the rest of the rural populace; some of the larger tribes, such as the Gonds, are highly stratified.

Economic and Political Conditions

Most tribes are concentrated in heavily forested areas that combine inaccessibility with limited political or economic significance. Historically, the economy of most tribes was subsistence agriculture or hunting and gathering. Tribal members traded with outsiders for the few necessities they lacked, such as salt and iron. A few local Hindu craftsmen might provide such items as cooking utensils. The twentieth century, however, has seen far-reaching changes in the relationship between tribals and the larger society and, by extension, traditional tribal economies. Improved transportation and communications have brought ever deeper intrusions into tribal lands; merchants and a variety of government policies have involved tribal peoples more thoroughly in the cash economy, although by no means on the most favorable of terms. Large areas fell into the hands of nontribals around 1900, when many regions were opened by the government to homestead-style settlement. Immigrants received free land in return for cultivating it. Tribal people, too, could apply for land titles, although even title to the portion of land they happened to be planting that season could not guarantee their ability to continue swidden cultivation. More important, the notion of permanent, individual ownership of land was foreign to most tribals. Land, if seen in terms of ownership at all, was viewed as a communal resource, free to whoever needed it. By the time tribals accepted the necessity of obtaining formal land titles, they had lost the opportunity to lay claim to lands that might rightfully have been considered theirs. Generally, tribals were severely disadvantaged in dealing with government officials who granted land titles. Albeit belatedly, the colonial regime realised the necessity of protecting tribals from the predations of outsiders and prohibited the sale of tribal lands. Although an important loophole in the form of land leases was left open, tribes made some gains in the mid-twentieth century. Despite considerable obstruction by local police and land officials, who were slow to delineate tribal holdings and slower still to offer police protection, some land was returned to tribal peoples.

In the 1970s, the gains tribal peoples had made in earlier decades were eroded in many regions, especially in central India. Migration into tribal lands increased dramatically, and the deadly combination of constabulary and revenue officers uninterested in tribal welfare and sophisticated nontribals willing and able to bribe local officials was sufficient to deprive many tribals of their landholdings. The means of subverting protective legislation were legion: local officials could be persuaded to ignore land acquisition by nontribal people, alter land registry records, lease plots of land for short periods and then simply refuse to relinquish them, or induce tribal members to become indebted and attach their lands. Whatever the means, the result was that many tribal members became landless labourers in the 1960s and 1970s, and regions that a few years earlier had been the exclusive domain of tribes had an increasingly heterogeneous population. Unlike previous eras in which tribal people were shunted into more remote forests, by the 1960s relatively little unoccupied land was available. Government efforts to evict nontribal members from illegal occupation have proceeded slowly; when evictions occur at all, those ejected are usually members of poor, lower castes. In a 1985 publication, anthropologist Christoph von Fürer-Haimendorf describes this process in Andhra Pradesh: on average only 25 to 33 percent of the tribal families in such villages had managed to keep even a portion of their holdings. Outsiders had paid about 5 percent of the market value of the lands they took.

Improved communications, roads with motorised traffic, and more frequent government intervention figured in the increased contact that tribal peoples had with outsiders. Tribes fared best where there was little to induce nontribals to settle; cash crops and commercial highways frequently signaled the dismemberment of the tribes. Merchants have long been a link to the outside world, but in the past they were generally petty traders, and the contact they had with tribal people was transient. By the 1960s and 1970s, the resident nontribal shopkeeper was a permanent feature of many villages. Shopkeepers often sold liquor on credit, enticing tribal members into debt and into mortgaging their land. In the past, tribes made up shortages before harvest by foraging from the surrounding forest. More recently shopkeepers have offered ready credit—with the proviso that loans be repaid in kind with 50 to 100 percent interest after harvest. Repaying one bag of millet with two bags has set up a cycle of indebtedness from which many have been unable to break loose.

The possibility of cultivators growing a profitable cash crop, such as cotton or castor-oil plants, continues to draw merchants into tribal areas. Nontribal traders frequently establish an extensive network of relatives and associates as shopkeepers to serve as agents in a number of villages. Cultivators who grow a cash crop often sell to the same merchants, who provide consumption credit throughout the year. The credit carries a high-interest price tag, whereas the tribal peoples' crops are bought at a fraction of the market rate. Cash crops offer a further disadvantage in that they decrease the supply of available foodstuffs and increase tribal dependence on economic forces beyond their control.

This transformation has meant a decline in both the tribes' security and their standard of living.

In previous generations, families might have purchased silver jewelry as a form of security; contemporary tribal people are more likely to buy minor consumer goods. Whereas jewelry could serve as collateral in critical emergencies, current purchases simply increase indebtedness. In areas where gathering forest products is remunerative, merchants exchange their products for tribal labour. Indebtedness is so extensive that although such transactions are illegal, traders sometimes "sell" their debtors to other merchants, much like indentured servants.

In some instances, tribes have managed to hold their own in contacts with outsiders. Some Chenchus, a hunting and gathering tribe of the central hill regions of Andhra Pradesh, have continued to specialise in collecting forest products for sale. Caste Hindus living among them rent land from the Chenchus and pay a portion of the harvest. The Chenchus themselves have responded unenthusiastically to government efforts to induce them to take up farming. Their relationship to nontribal people has been one of symbiosis, although there were indications in the early 1980s that other groups were beginning to compete with the Chenchus in gathering forest products. A large paper mill was cutting bamboo in their territory in a manner that did not allow regeneration, and two groups had begun to collect for sale the same products the Chenchus sell. Dalits settled among them with the help of the Chenchus and learned agriculture from them. The nomadic Banjara herders who grase their cattle in the forest also have been allotted land there. The Chenchus have a certain advantage in dealing with caste Hindus; because of their long association with Hindu hermits and their refusal to eat beef, they are considered an unpolluted caste. Other tribes, particularly in South India, have cultural practices that are offensive to Hindus and, when they are assimilated, are often considered Dalits.

The final blow for some tribes has come when nontribals, through political jockeying, have managed to gain legal tribal status, that is, to be listed as a Scheduled Tribe. The Gonds of Andhra Pradesh effectively lost their only advantage in trying to protect their lands when the Banjaras, a group that had been settling in Gond territory, were classified as a Scheduled Tribe in 1977. Their newly acquired tribal status made the Banjaras eligible to acquire Gond land "legally" and to compete with Gonds for reserved political seats, places in education institutions, and other benefits. Because the Banjaras are not scheduled in neighboring Maharashtra, there has been an influx of Banjara emigrants from that state into Andhra Pradesh in search of better opportunities.

Tribes in the Himalayan foothills have not been as hard-pressed by the intrusions of nontribals. Historically, their political status was always distinct from the rest of India. Until the British colonial period, there was little effective control by any of the empires centered in peninsular India; the region was populated by autonomous feuding tribes. The British, in efforts to protect the sensitive northeast frontier, followed a policy dubbed the "Inner Line"; nontribal people were allowed into the areas only with special permission. Postindependence governments have continued the policy, protecting the Himalayan tribes as part of the strategy to secure the border with China.

This policy has generally saved the northern tribes from the kind of exploitation that those elsewhere in South Asia have suffered. In Arunachal Pradesh (formerly part of the North-East Frontier Agency), for example, tribal members control commerce and most lower-level administrative posts. Government construction projects in the region have provided tribes with a significant source of cash—both for setting up businesses and for providing paying customers.

Some tribes have made rapid progress through the education system. Instruction was begun in Assamese but was eventually changed to Hindi; by the early 1980s, English was taught at most levels. Both education and the increase in ready cash from government spending have permitted tribal people a significant measure of social mobility. The role of early missionaries in providing education was also crucial in Assam.

Government policies on forest reserves have affected tribal peoples profoundly. Wherever the state has chosen to exploit forests, it has seriously undermined the tribes' way of life. Government efforts to reserve forests have precipitated armed (if futile) resistance on the part of the tribal peoples involved. Intensive exploitation of forests has often meant allowing outsiders to cut large areas of trees (while the original tribal inhabitants were restricted from cutting), and ultimately replacing mixed forests capable of sustaining tribal life with single-product plantations. Where forests are reserved, nontribals have proved far more sophisticated than their forest counterparts at bribing the necessary local officials to secure effective (if extralegal) use of forestlands. The system of bribing local officials charged with enforcing the reserves is so well established that the rates of bribery are reasonably fixed (by the number of plows a farmer uses or the amount of grain harvested). Tribal people often end up doing unpaid work for Hindus simply because a caste Hindu, who has paid the requisite bribe, can at least ensure a tribal member that he or she will not be evicted from forestlands. The final irony, notes von Fürer-Haimendorf, is that the swidden cultivation many tribes practiced had maintained South Asia's forests, whereas the intensive cultivating and commercial interests that replaced the tribal way of life have destroyed the forests.

Extending the system of primary education into tribal areas and reserving places for tribal children in middle and high schools and higher education institutions are central to government policy, but efforts to improve a tribe's educational status have had mixed results. Recruitment of qualified teachers and determination of the appropriate language of instruction also remain troublesome. Commission after commission on the "language question" has called for instruction, at least at the primary level, in the students' native tongue. In some regions, tribal children entering school must begin by learning the official regional language, often one completely unrelated to their tribal tongue. The experiences of the Gonds of Andhra Pradesh provide an example. Primary schooling began there in the 1940s and 1950s. The government selected a group of Gonds who had managed to become semiliterate in Telugu and taught them the basics of written script. These individuals became teachers who taught in Gondi, and their efforts enjoyed a measure of success until the 1970s, when state policy demanded instruction in Telugu. The switch in the language of instruction both made the Gond teachers superfluous because they could not teach in Telugu and also presented the government with the problem of finding reasonably qualified teachers willing to teach in outlying tribal schools.

The commitment of tribes to acquiring a formal education for their children varies considerably. Tribes differ in the extent to which they view education positively. Gonds and Pardhans, two groups in the central hill region, are a case in point. The Gonds are cultivators, and they frequently are reluctant to send their children to school, needing them, they say, to work in the fields. The Pardhans were traditionally bards and ritual specialists, and they have taken to education with enthusiasm. The effectiveness of educational policy likewise varies by region. In those parts of the northeast where tribes have generally been spared the wholesale onslaught of outsiders, schooling has helped tribal people to secure political and economic benefits. The education system there has provided a corps of highly trained tribal members in the professions and high-ranking administrative posts.

Many tribal schools are plagued by high dropout rates. Children attend for the first three to four years of primary school and gain a smattering of knowledge, only to lapse into illiteracy later. Few who enter continue up to the tenth grade; of those who do, few manage to finish high school. Therefore, very few are eligible to attend institutions of higher education, where the high rate of attrition continues.

Practices

The influx of newcomers disinclined to follow tribal ways has had a massive impact on social relations and tribal belief systems. In many communities, the immigrants have brought on nothing less than the total disintegration of the communities they entered. Even where outsiders are not residents in villages, traditional forms of social control and authority are less effective because tribal people are patently dependent on politico-economic forces beyond their control. In general, traditional headmen no longer have official backing for their role in village affairs, although many continue to exercise considerable influence. Headmen can no longer control the allocation of land or decide who has the right to settle in the village, a loss of power that has had an insidious effect on village solidarity.

Some headmen have taken to leasing village land to outsiders, thus enriching themselves at the expense of the rest of the tribes. Conflict over land rights has introduced a point of cleavage into village social relations; increased factional conflict has seriously eroded the ability of tribes to ward off the intrusion of outsiders. In some villages, tribal schoolteachers have emerged as a new political force, a counterbalance to the traditional headman. Changes in landholding patterns have also altered the role of the joint family. More and more couples set up separate households as soon as they marry. Because land is no longer held and farmed in common and has grown more scarce, inheritance disputes have increased.

Hunters and gatherers are particularly vulnerable to these far-reaching changes. The lack of strong authority figures in most hunting and gathering groups handicaps these tribes in organising to negotiate with the government. In addition, these tribes are too small to have much political leverage.

Forced settlement schemes also have had a deleterious impact on the tribes and their environment. Government-organised villages are typically larger than traditional hunting and gathering settlements. Forest reserves limit the amount of territory over which tribes can range freely. Larger villages and smaller territories have led, in some instances, to an increase in crime and violence. Traditionally, hunters and gatherers "settled" their disputes by arranging for the antagonists simply to avoid one another; new, more circumscribed villages preclude this arrangement.

Tribal beliefs and rituals have altered in the face of increased contact with Hindus and missionaries of a variety of persuasions. Among groups in more intense contact with the Hindu majority, there have been various transformations. The Gonds, for example, traditionally worshiped clan gods through elaborate rites, with Pardhans organising and performing the necessary rituals.

The increasing impoverishment of large sections of the Gond tribe has made it difficult, if not impossible, to support the Pardhans as a class of ritual specialists. At the same time, many Gonds have concluded that the tribal gods were losing their power and efficacy. Gonds have tended to seek the assistance of other deities, and thus there has been widespread Hinduisation of Gondi belief and practice. Some tribes have adopted the Hindu practice of having costly elaborate weddings—a custom that contributes to indebtedness (as it has in many rural Indian families) and subjects them to the cash economy on the most deleterious of terms. Some families have adapted a traditional marriage pattern—that of capturing a bride—to modern conditions, using the custom to avoid the costly outlays associated with a formal wedding.

Christian missionaries have been active among sundry tribes since the mid-nineteenth century. Conversion to Christianity offers a number of advantages, not the least of which is education. It was through the efforts of various Christian sects to translate the Bible into tribal languages that those tongues acquired a written script. Christian proselytising has served to preserve tribal lore and language in written form at the same time that it has tended to change drastically the tribe's cultural heritage and belief systems. In some instances, the introduction of Christianity has driven a wedge between converts and their fellow tribal members who continue to adhere to traditional beliefs and practices

Jews and Parsis

There are several groups descended from ancient settlers in India. These groups include the Jews, the first group of whom are said to have migrated from West Asia and to have settled in Cranganore (also the traditional first site where Muslims later arrived in India) on the Malabar Coast of Kerala in the first century A.D., a second group of Jews who fled the Arabian Peninsula in the face of Muslim ascendancy in the seventh century, and the Parsis, who came to India in the eighth century A.D. to escape Muslim persecution in Persia.

Portuguese

The European powers left a small ethnic imprint on India. The Portuguese came first and left last, but at no time had they extensive dominions such as the Indian kingdoms and empires or the lands of the British in India. The Austrians, Danish, Dutch, and French had yet smaller territories for shorter periods. By the time truly large numbers of Europeans came to spend their working lives in India as part of the British Raj, racist prejudices that were largely absent in earlier centuries had developed in the Europeans. Improvements in transportation (the steamship and the Suez Canal) also had made travel swifter and safer so at least the more prosperous classes could return to Europe on leave to marry or choose brides coming on the so-called "fishing fleets" for tourism and husband-hunting.

There are around 730,000 Portuguese Indians, commonly known as Goans or Goanese, about half of whom live in the state of Goa and the others elsewhere in India. They are descended from Indians in the former Portuguese colony who assimilated to Portuguese culture and in many cases are the descendants of Indo-Portuguese marriages, which the Portuguese civil and religious authorities encouraged.

Anglo-Indians

The largest group of European Indians, however, are descendants of British men, generally from the colonial service and the military, and lower-caste Hindu or Muslim women. From some time in the nineteenth century, both the British and the Indian societies rejected the offspring of these unions, and so the Anglo-Indians, as they became known, sought marriage partners among other Anglo-Indians. Over time this group developed a number of caste-like features and acquired a special occupational niche in the railroad, postal, and customs services. A number of factors fostered a strong sense of commu-nity among Anglo-Indians. The school system focused on English language and culture and was virtually segregated, as were Anglo-Indian social clubs; the group's adherence to Christianity also set members apart from most other Indians; and distinctive manners, diet, dress, and speech contributed to their segregation.

During the independence movement, many Anglo-Indians identified (or were assumed to identify) with British rule, and, therefore, incurred the distrust and hostility of Indian nationalists. Their position at independence was difficult. They felt a loyalty to a British "home" that most had never seen and where they would gain little social acceptance. They felt insecure in an India that put a premium on participation in the independence movement as a prerequisite for important government positions. Some Anglo-Indians left the country in 1947, hoping to make a new life in Britain or elsewhere in the Commonwealth of Nations, such as Australia or Canada. Many of these people returned to India after unsuccessful attempts to find a place in "alien" societies. Most Anglo-Indians, however, opted to stay in India and made whatever adjustments they deemed necessary.

Like the Parsis, the Anglo-Indians are essentially urban dwellers. Unlike the Parsis, relatively few have attained high levels of education, amassed great wealth, or achieved more than subordinate government positions. In the 1990s, Anglo-Indians remained scattered throughout the country in the larger cities and those smaller towns serving as railroad junctions and communications centers.

Constitutional guarantees of the rights of communities and religious and linguistic minorities permit Anglo-Indians to maintain their own schools and to use English as the medium of instruction. In order to encourage the integration of the community into the larger society, the government stipulates that a certain percentage of the student body come from other Indian communities. There is no evident official discrimination against Anglo-Indians in terms of current government employment. A few have risen to high posts; some are high-ranking officers in the military, and a few are judges. In occupational terms, at least, the assimilation of Anglo-Indians into the mainstream of Indian life was well under way by the 1990s. Nevertheless, the group will probably remain socially distinct as long as its members marry only other Anglo-Indians and its European descent continues to be noted.

Africans

Still another foreign-origin group, usually known collectively as Siddhis, are the descendants of Africans brought to India as slaves. Although most African-origin Indians are descendants of the large influx of slaves brought to western India in the seventeenth century, the first Africans reportedly arrived on the Konkani Coast in the first century A.D. as a result of the Arab slave trade, and there was an important African presence, including several short-term rulers, in Bengal in the fifteenth century. Siddhis (the name means lord or prince in African usage) sometimes rose to prominent—even ruling—governmental and military positions during the Mughal and British periods. Most modern-day Siddhis are Muslims and are engaged in agricultural pursuits. They are found in Gujarat, Daman and Diu, Maharashtra, Karnataka, Andhra Pradesh, and other states and union territories, where they are designated as Scheduled Tribe members.

Regionalism

The formation of states along linguistic and ethnic lines has occurred in India in numerous instances since independence in 1947. There have been demands, however, to form units within states based not only along linguistic, ethnic, and religious lines but also, in some cases, on a feeling of the distinctness of a geographical region and its culture and economic interests. The most volatile movements are those ongoing in Jammu and Kashmir and Punjab. How the central government responds to these demands will be an area of scrutiny through the late 1990s and beyond. It is believed by some officials that conceding regional autonomy is less arduous and takes less time and fewer resources than does meeting agitation, violence, and demands for concessions.

Telangana Movement

An early manifestation of regionalism was the Telangana movement in what became the state of Andhra Pradesh. The princely ruler of Hyderabad, the nizam, had attempted unsuccessfully to maintain Hyderabad as an independent state separate from India in 1947. His efforts were simultaneous with the largest agrarian armed rebellion in modern Indian history. Starting in July 1946, communist-led guerrilla squads began overthrowing local feudal village regimes and organising land reform in Telugu-speaking areas of Hyderabad, collectively known as Telangana (an ancient name for the region dating from the Vijayanagar period). In time, about 3,000 villages and some 41,000 square kilometers of territory were involved in the revolt. Faced with the refusal of the nizam of Hyderabad to accede his territory to India and the violence of the communist-led rebellion, the central government sent in the army in September 1948. By November 1949, Hyderabad had been forced to accede to the Indian union, and, by October 1951, the violent phase of the Telangana movement had been suppressed. The effect of the 1946-51 rebellion and communist electoral victories in 1952 had led to the destruction of Hyderabad and set the scene for the establishment of a new state along linguistic lines. In 1953, based on the recommendation of the States Reorganisation Commission, Telugu-speaking areas were separated from the former Madras States to form Andhra, India's first state established along linguistic lines. The commission also contemplated establishing Telangana as a separate state, but instead Telangana was merged with Andhra to form the new state of Andhra Pradesh in 1956.

The concerns about Telangana were manifold. The region had a less developed economy than Andhra, but a larger revenue base (mostly because it taxed rather than prohibited alcoholic beverages), which Telanganas feared might be diverted for use in Andhra. They also feared that planned dam projects on the Krishna and Godavari rivers would not benefit Telangana proportionately even though Telanganas controlled the headwaters of the rivers. Telanganas feared too that the people of Andhra would have the advantage in jobs, particularly in government and education.

The central government decided to ignore the recommendation to establish a separate Telangana state and, instead, merged the two regions into a unified Andhra Pradesh. However, a "gentlemen's agreement" provided reassurances to the Telangana people. For at least five years, revenue was to be spent in the regions proportionately to the amount they contributed. Education institutions in Telangana were to be expanded and reserved for local students. Recruitment to the civil service and other areas of government employment such as education and medicine was to be proportional. The use of Urdu was to continue in the administration and the judiciary for five years. The state cabinet was to have proportional membership from both regions and a deputy chief minister from Telangana if the chief minister was from Andhra and vice versa. Finally, the Regional Council for Telangana was to be responsible for economic development, and its members were to be elected by the members of the state legislative assembly from the region.

In the following years, however, the Telangana people had a number of complaints about how the agreements and guarantees were implemented. The deputy chief minister position was never filled. Education institutions in the region were greatly expanded, but Telanganas felt that their enrollment was not proportionate to their numbers. The selection of the city of Hyderabad as the state capital led to massive migration of people from Andhra into Telangana. Telanganas felt discriminated against in education employment but were told by the state government that most non-Telanganas had been hired on the grounds that qualified local people were unavailable. In addition, the unification of pay scales between the two regions appeared to disadvantage Telangana civil servants. In the atmosphere of discontent, professional associations that earlier had amalgamated broke apart by region.

Discontent with the 1956 gentlemen's agreement intensified in January 1969 when the guarantees that had been agreed on were supposed to lapse. Student agitation for the continuation of the agreement began at Osmania University in Hyderabad and spread to other parts of the region. Government employees and opposition members of the state legislative assembly swiftly threatened "direct action" in support of the students. The Congress-controlled state and central governments offered assurances that non-Telangana civil servants in the region would be replaced by Mulkis, disadvantaged local people, and that revenue surpluses from Telangana would be returned to the region. The protestors, however, were dissatisfied, and severe violence, including mob attacks on railroads, road transport, and government facilities, spread over the region. In addition, seventy-nine police firings resulted in twenty-three deaths according to official figures, the education system was shut down, and examinations were cancelled. Calls for a separate Telangana state came in the midst of counter violence in Andhra areas bordering Telangana. In the meantime, the Andhra Pradesh High Court decreed that a central government law mandating replacement of non-Telangana government employees with Mulkis was beyond Parliament's constitutional powers.

Although the Congress faced dissension within its ranks, its leadership stood against additional linguistic states, which were regarded as "antinational." As a result, defectors from the Congress, led by M. Chenna Reddy, founded the Telangana People's Association (Telangana Praja Samithi). Despite electoral successes, however, some of the new party leaders gave up their agitation in September 1971 and, much to the disgust of many separatists, rejoined the safer political haven of the Congress ranks.

In 1972 the Supreme Court reversed the Andhra Pradesh High Court's ruling that the Mulki rules were unconstitutional. This decision triggered agitation in the Andhra region that produced six months of violence.

Throughout the 1970s, Andhra Pradesh settled into a pattern of continuous domination by Congress (R) and later Congress (I), with much instability and dissidence within the state party and constant interference from Indira Gandhi and the national party. Chenna Reddy, the erstwhile opposition leader, was for a time the Congress (I) state chief minister. Congress domination was only ended by the founding of the Telugu National Party by N.T. Rama Rao in 1982 and its overwhelming victory in the state elections in 1983.

Polls taken after the end of the Telangana movement showed a certain lack of enthusiasm for it, and for the idea of a separate state. Although urban groups (students and civil servants) had been most active in the movement, its support was stronger in rural areas. Its supporters were mixed: low and middle castes, the young and the not so young, women, illiterates and the poorly educated, and rural gentry. Speakers of several other languages than Telugu were heavily involved. The movement had no element of religious communalism, but some observers thought Muslims were particularly involved in the movement. Other researchers found the Muslims were unenthusiastic about the movement and noted a feeling that migration from Andhra to Telangana was creating opportunities that were helping non-Telanganas. On the other hand, of the two locally prominent Muslim political groups, only one supported a separate state; the other opposed the idea while demanding full implementation of the regional safeguards. Although Urdu speakers were appealed to in the agitation (e.g., speeches were given in Urdu as well as Telugu), in the aftermath Urdu disappeared from the schools and the administration.

The Telangana movement grew out of a sense of regional identity as such, rather than out of a sense of ethnic identity, language, religion, or caste. The movement demanded redress for economic grievances, the writing of a separate history, and establishment of a sense of cultural distinctness. The emotions and forces generated by the movement were not strong enough, however, for a continuing drive for a separate state. In the late 1980s and early 1990s, the People's War Group, an element of the Communist Party of India (Marxist-Leninist), renewed violence in Andhra Pradesh but was dealt with by state police forces.

Gorkhaland

The Gorkhaland movement grew from the demand of Nepalis living in Darjiling District of West Bengal for a separate state for themselves. The Gorkhaland National Liberation Front led the movement, which disrupted the district with massive violence between 1986 and 1988. The issue was resolved, at least temporarily, in 1988 with the establishment of the Darjiling Gorkha Hill Council within West Bengal.

Historically, Darjiling belonged to the kingdom of Sikkim, which had lost it several times since the eighteenth century. The ethnic identity "Gorkha" comes from the kingdom with that name that united Nepal in the late eighteenth century and was the focal point of Nepalese in the British army.

Immigration from Nepal expanded with British rule in India, and some 34 percent of the population of Darjiling in 1876 was of Gorkha (also seen as Gurkha) ethnicity. By the start of the twentieth century, Nepalese immigrants made a modest socioeconomic advance through government service, and a small anglicised elite developed among them. In 1917 the Hillmen's Association came into being and petitioned for the administrative separation of Darjiling in 1917 and again in 1928 and 1942. In 1928 the Akhil Bharatiya Gorkha League (All India Gorkha League) was formed. It gained additional support after World War II with the influx of ex-soldiers from the Gurkha regiments who had been exposed to nationalist movements in Southeast Asia during service there.

During the 1940s, the CPI organised Gorkha tea workers. In presentations to the States Reorganisation Commission in 1954, the CPI favored regional autonomy for Darjiling within West Bengal, with recognition of Nepali as a Scheduled Language. The All India Gorkha League preferred making the area a union territory under the national government.

The state of West Bengal nominally has been supportive of the use of the Nepali language. The West Bengal Official Language Act of 1961 made Nepali the official language of the hill subdivisions of Darjiling,

Kalimpong, and Kurseong, where Nepalese are a majority. The state legislative assembly passed a resolution in 1977 that led Parliament to amend the national constitution to include Nepali as a Scheduled Language. However, the Gorkhaland National Liberation Front has accused the state government of failure to actually implement use of the language.

The Gorkhaland movement distinguished Darjiling Gorkhas from nationals of Nepal legally resident in India, from Nepali-speaking Indian citizens from other parts of the country, and even from the majority in neighboring Sikkim, where Nepali is the official language. The movement was emphatic that it had no desire to separate from India, only from the state of West Bengal. Gorkhaland supporters therefore preferred to call the Gorkhas' language Gorkhali rather than Nepali, although they did not attempt to claim there is any linguistic difference from what other people call Nepali. The 1981 census of India, whether in deference to this sentiment or for some other reason, called the language *Gorkhali/Nepali*. However, when the Eighth Schedule of the constitution was amended in 1992 to make it a Scheduled Language, the term *Nepali* alone was used.

In 1986 the Gorkhaland National Liberation Front, having failed to obtain a separate regional administrative identity from Parliament, again demanded a separate state of Gorkhaland. The party's leader, Subhash Ghising, headed a demonstration that turned violent and was severely repressed by the state government. The disturbances almost totally shut down the districts' economic mainstays of tea, tourism, and timber. The Left Front government of West Bengal, which earlier had supported some form of autonomy, now opposed it as "antinational." The state government claimed that Darjiling was no worse off than the state in general and was richer than many districts. Ghising made lavish promises to his followers, including the recruitment of

40,000 Indian Gorkhas into the army and paying Rs100,000 for every Gorkha writer. After two years of fighting and the loss of at least 200 lives, the government of West Bengal and the central government finally agreed on an autonomous hill district. In July 1988, the Gorkhaland National Liberation Front gave up the demand for a separate state, and in August the Darjiling Gorkha Hill Council came into being with Ghising as chairman. The council had authority over economic development programs, education, and culture.

However, difficulties soon arose over the *panchayat*elections. Ghising wanted the hill council excluded from the national law on *panchayat* elections. Rajiv Gandhi's government was initially favorable to his request and introduced a constitutional amendment in 1989 to exclude the Darjiling Gorkha Hill Council, along with several other northeast hill states and regions (Nagaland, Meghalaya, Mizoram, and the hill regions of Manipur), but it did not pass. However, in 1992 Parliament passed the Seventy-third Amendment, which seemed to show a newly serious commitment to the idea of local self-government by *panchayats*. The amendment excluded all the hill areas just mentioned except Darjiling. Ghising insisted this omission was a machination of West Bengal and threatened to revive militant agitation for a Gorkhaland state. He also said the Gorkhaland National Liberation Front would boycott the village *panchayat* elections mandated by the amendment. A large portion of his party, however, refused to accept the boycott and split off under the leadership of Chiten Sherpa to form the All India Gorkha League, which won a sizable number of *panchayat* seats.

In 1995 it was unclear whether the region would remain content with autonomy rather than statehood. In August 1995, Sherpa complained to the state government that Ghising's government had misused hill council funds, and West Bengal chief minister Jyoti Basu promised to investigate. Both Gorkha parties showed willingness to use general shutdowns to forward their ends. The fact that so many people were willing to follow Sherpa instead of the hitherto unchallenged Ghising may indicate that they will be satisfied with regional autonomy.

Ladakh

The region of Ladakh is isolated in the Himalayas next to Tibet and differs radically from the rest of the state in that the majority of the population is culturally, ethnically, religiously, and linguistically close to Tibet. There also is a Muslim minority. The region has no interest in the separatist and Islamicist sentiments of the Vale of Kashmir.

Following several years of discontent and agitation about the position of Ladakh District in the state of Jammu and Kashmir, the central government passed the Ladakh Autonomous Hill Development Councils Act in May 1995. The 1995 act established councils for the Leh and Kargil subdistricts and allotted them powers for economic development, land use, and taxation. Elections for the Leh council were held in August 1995. Congress (I) won all twenty-two elective seats unopposed; the governor of Jammu and Kashmir was authorised to appoint four members from among minorities and women.

The Northeast

Northeastern India is made up of the states of Assam, Meghalaya, Tripura, Arunachal Pradesh, Mizoram, Manipur, and Nagaland. Certain tensions exist between these states and a relatively distant central government and between the tribal peoples, who are natives of these states, and migrant peoples from other parts of India. These tensions have led the natives of these states to seek a greater participation in their own governance, control of their states' economies, and their role in society. Emerging from these desires for greater self-governance are new regional political parties and continued insurgent movements. In addition to the more frequently analysed regional movements in Jammu and Kashmir, Punjab, and states such as Assam and Nagaland in the northeast, there are other regional movements, such as those in the Tripura and Miso tribal areas.

In May 1995, the state government of Tripura extended the area covered by the Tripura Tribal Areas Autonomous District Council, a result of the tripartite accord among the central government, the state government, and the Tripura National Volunteers movement concluded in 1988. In the elections in July 1995, the Left Front, led by the Communist Party of India (Marxist), defeated the alliance of the Congress (I) and the local Tripura Tribal Youth Association, which had controlled the council since 1990. The new council proceeded to dissolve the more than 400 development committees at various levels under its jurisdiction for corruption and inaction and promised to constitute new ones swiftly.

In June 1995, the Assam government signed an agreement with two organisations of the Mising tribe, the Mising Autonomous Demand Committee and the Mising Greater Council, to set up an autonomous council for the Misings. The council will include villages with majority tribal populations in four districts of Assam, with a total population expected to be about 315,000. However, villages in so-called Reserve Forest Areas will be included only with the approval of the central minister of state with independent charge of environment and forests. This decision is a possible source of discontent because tribals frequently feel themselves hampered by restrictions on the use of forests by the government. However, in July 1995 the Mising Bane Kebang boycotted the swearing in of the interim council because it said the Mising Autonomous Demand Committee had kept it out of its formation.

Bibliography

Ahmad, Imitiaz (ed.) 1976. *Family, Kinship and Marriage Among Muslims in India.* Manohar: New Delhi.

Ansari, Ghaus. 1959-60. Muslim Caste in Uttar Pradesh. A Study of culture contact. *The Eastern Anthropologist*, 13 (2): 1-83.

Augustine. J.S. (ed.) 1982. *The Indian Family in Transition.* Vikas Publishing House: New Delhi

Banerjee, A.C. 1983. *The Sikh Gurus and the Sikh Religion.* Munshiram Manoharlal Pvt. Ltd.: Delhi

CSWI (Committee on the Status of Women in India) 1974. *Towards Equality.* Department of Social Welfare, Government of India: New Delhi

Desai, A.R., 1984. *Rural Sociology in India.* Bombay: Popular Prakashan

Dhillon, D.S. 1988. *Sikhism: Origin and Development.* Atlantic Publishers: Delhi

Dube, Leela 1974. *Sociology of Kinship.* Popular Prakashan: Bombay

Dube, S.C. 1990.*Indian Society* New Delhi: National Book Trust, India.

Dubois, Abbe J.A. 1906. *Hindu manners, customs and ceremonies,* Oxford: Clarendon Press.

Dumont, Louis, 1980. *Homo Hierarchicus: The caste system & its implications.* Delhi: Oxford University Press.

Dutt, N.K.1986. *Origin and Growth of Caste in India,* Calcutta: Firma KLM.

Eliade M. (Ed.) 1987. *Zoroastrianism. In The Encyclopedia of Religion.* Volume 15, Macmillan Publishing: New York.

Ghurye, G.S.1961. *Caste, Class and Occupation.* Bombay: Popular Book Depot.

Gore, M.S. 1968. *Urbanization and Family Change in India.* Popular Prakashaa: Bombay

Gould, H.A. 1987. *The Hindu Caste System.* Chanakya Publications: Delhi.

Gupta, A.R., 1984. *Caste hierarchy and social change: a study of myth and reality.* New Delhi: Jyotsna.

Haugh, M. 1987. *The Parsis: Essays on their Sacred Language Writings and Religion.* Cosmo Publications: New Delhi.

Hutton, J.H., 1946. *Caste in India: Its Nature. Functions and Origins.* Cambridge: Cambridge University Press.

Jackson, Paul S.J. (ed.) 1988. *The Muslims of India: Beliefs and Practices.* Theological Publications: Bangalore, Chapter I, II & III.

Jain, Shobhita 1996. *Bharat mein Parivar. Vivah aur Natedari.* Rawat Publishers: Jaipur

Kapadia, K.M. 1972. *Industrialization and rural society: A study of Atul-Bulsar,* Bombay: Popular Books.

Karve, I. 1953. *Kinship organization in India,* Poona Deccan College.

Kolenda, Pauline 1987. *Regional Differences in Family Structure in India.* Rawat Publication: Jaipur

Madan, T.N. 1965. *Family and Kinship A Study of the Pandits of Rural Kashmir.* Asia Publishing House: New Delhi

Mayer, A.C., 1960, *Caste and kinship in central India: A village and its region.* London: Routledge & Keagan Paul

Prabhu, P.H. 1979. *Hindu Social Organisation: A Study in Socio-Psychological and Ideological Foundations.* Popular Prakashan Pvt. Ltd.: Bombay.

Radhakrishnan, S. 1979. *The Hindu View of Life.* Blackie and Son Pvt. Ltd.: Bombay.

Risley, Herbert. 1969. *The People of India,* Delhi: Oriental Book Reprint Corporation.

Saiyyed. V.V. and Mohammad, Talib 1995. *Religion and Ethnicity among Muslim.* Rawat: Jaipur

Sharma, J.B. and Sharma, S.R. 1999. *Parsis in India.* Popular Prakasan: Bombay

Singer, Milton & B.S. Cohn (eds.). 1968. *Structure and Change in Indian Society.* Philadelphia

Singh, Yogendra.1999. *Social Stratification and Change in India.* New Delhi: Manohar publications.

Singh,Gopal 1987. *The Religion of the Sikhs.* Allied Publishers Private Limited: Delhi

Srinivas, M.N. 1964. *Caste in modern India & other essays.* Bombay: Asia Publishing House,

Thapar, Romesh, (ed.). 1977. *Tribe, Caste and Religion.* New Delhi: Macmillan.

Uberoi, Patricia (ed.) 1994. *Family, Kinship and Marriage in India.* Oxford University Press: New Delhi.

Index

ENCYCLOPAEDIA OF SOCIOLOGY

Sociology of Family

Volume – 5

Satish Mittal
Sushil Kumar Saxena

Commonwealth

Encyclopaedia of Sociology

Edition : 2026

ISBN 978-81-311-0377-7 (set)

Published by :
COMMONWEALTH PUBLISHERS (P) LTD.
4831/24, Govind Lane,
Ansari Road, Darya Ganj,
New Delhi - 110002
Ph. : 23242541, 23272541
e-mail : commonwealthpublishers2016@gmail.com

Distributed by :
ARJUN PUBLISHING HOUSE
4831/24, Govind Lane,
Ansari Road, Darya Ganj,
New Delhi - 110002
Ph. : 23242541, 23272541
e-mail : arjunbooks2001@gmail.com
arjunpubhouse@gmail.com

Laser Typesetting by :
Dimple Computers
Delhi

Printed at :
Milan Enterprises
Delhi

Preface

Sociology of the family examines the family, as an institution and a unit of socialisation, through various sociological perspectives, particularly with regard to the relationship between the nuclear family and industrial capitalism, and the distinct gender roles and concepts of childhood which arose with it. The topic is a common component on introductory and pre-university academic curricula, as it is perhaps the most simple institution to which one may apply many fundamental sociological approaches.

This book presents sociological analysis of the system of family and marriage, and focuses on family as an institution in society. It uniquely encompasses many facets of society and students are able to learn about family seen through a cultural and historical perspective. The book sets a high conceptual standard, but uses informal writing and minimal jargon. It presents the perspectives of critical and questioning academics within a scholarly, well-researched text. It addresses a host of real world issues and practical concerns. The book strikes the right balance between covering the core theoretical and conceptual issues associated with the subject while adopting a central thesis that gives structure to the field and stimulates further enquiry. An extremely well-written and engaging book, it takes an upbeat and argumentative style that brings the subject matter to life.

Authors

Contents

1

Introduction to Family Sociology

The sociology of the family examines the family, as an institution and a unit of socialisation, through various sociological perspectives, particularly with regard to the relationship between the nuclear family and industrial capitalism, and the distinct gender roles and concepts of childhood which arose with it. The sociology of the family is a common component on introductory and pre-university academic curricula, as it is perhaps the most simple institution to which one may apply many fundamental sociological approaches.

Sociological studies of the family look at:

1. Demographic characteristic of the family members: family size, age, ethnicity and gender of its members
2. Social class of the family, the economic level and mobility of the family, professions of its members, the education levels of the family members
3. What spheres of life are important in and to the family unit
4. The effect of social change on the family
5. The interactions of the family with other social organizations.

6. Diversity of family forms in contemporary societies in relation to ideology, gender differences, and state policies such as those concerned with marriage

Examples of specific issues looked at include:

1. Changing roles of family members. Each member is restricted by the sex roles of the traditional family, these roles such as the father as the worker and the mother as the homemaker are declining, the mother is becoming the supplementary provider and she retains the responsibilities of child rearing. Therefore the females' role in the labour force is "compatible with the demands of the traditional family". Sociology studies the adaptation of the males role to caregiver as well as provider. The gender roles are increasingly interwoven.
2. Increase in sole occupancy dwellings and smaller family sizes
3. Average age of marriage being older
4. Average number of children decreasing and first birth at later age
5. The historical pattern of fertility. From baby boom to baby bust (instability)
6. The ageing population. The trend towards greater life expectancy.
7. Rising divorce rates and people who will never marry.

Research methods in the sociology of the family can be broken down to three major approaches, each with its own strengths and weaknesses; which need be employed in a study, then, relies largely on the subject of, and questions posed by, the research.

One approach is survey research of contemporary families. This holds the benefit of leaving statistical data and large and hopefully random samples from which a researcher can interpolate the general traits of a society. However, survey respondents tend to answer as would feel regular or ideal rather than as things might actually be. It also gives a very one-sided explanation view of a larger group which does not sufficiently allow for contention.

Another method is ethnographic research of families. Where surveys allow for broad but shallow analyses, observation allows sociologists to obtain rich information on a source of a much more limited size. It allows the research an "insider" perspective, and through this closer look a better idea of the actual social framework of families. Where surveys are strong, however, ethnographic research is weak. By reducing the size of a sample size, it may be no longer evident how representative the family being researched is to families at large within a society, and then also does not allow much room in linking the specific traits of the families being observed to a society more generally.

Finally, a researcher can use documented studies of families from the past as a source of information. These sources may include very personal items (such as diaries), legal records (census data, wills, court records), and matters of public record (such as sermons).

Sociology of Motherhood

In many cultures, especially traditional western, a mother is usually the wife in a married couple. Her role in the family is celebrated on Mother's Day. Anna Reeves Jarvis was a woman who originally organized Mother's Work Day's protesting the lack of cleanliness and sanitation in the work place. Anna died in 1905 and her daughter created a National Mother's Day to honour her mother. Mothers frequently have a very important role in raising offspring and the title can be given to a non-biological mother that fills this role. This is common in stepmothers (female married to biological father). In most family structures the mother is both a biological parent and a primary caregiver. In East Asian and Western traditional families, fathers were the heads of the families, which meant that his duties included providing financial support and making critical decisions, some of which must have been obeyed without question by the rest of the family members." Some Asian American men are brought up under stringent gender role expectations such as a focus on group harmony and filial piety, carrying on their family name and conforming to the expectations of the parents"

As with cultural concepts of family, the specifics of a mother's role vary according to cultural mores. In what some sociologists term the "bourgeois family", which arose out of typical 16th- and 17th-century European households and is often considered the "traditional Western" structure, the father's role has been somewhat limited. In this family model the father acts as the economic support and sometimes disciplinarian of the family, while the mother or other female relative oversees most of the childrearing. This structure is reflected, for example, in societies which legislate "maternity leave" but do not have corresponding "paternity leave."

However, this limited role has increasingly been called into question. Both feminist and masculist authors have decried such predetermined roles as unjust. A nascent father's rights movement seeks to increase the legal standing of fathers in everything from child-custody cases to the institution of paid paternity leave or family leave.

Sociology of Fatherhood

According to anthropologist Maurice Godelier, a critical novelty in human society, compared to humans' closest biological relatives (chimpanzees and bonobos), is the parental role assumed by the males, which were unaware of their "father" connection.

In many cultures, especially traditional western, a father is usually the husband in a married couple. Many times fathers have a very important role in raising offspring and the title can be given to a non-biological father that fills this role. This is common in stepfathers (males married to biological mothers). In most family structures the father is both a biological parent and a primary caregiver.

In East Asian and Western traditional families, fathers are the heads of the families, which means that their duties include providing financial support and making critical decisions, some of which must be obeyed without question by the rest of the family members.

As with cultural concepts of family, the specifics of a father's role vary according to cultural folkways. In what some sociologists term the "bourgeois family", which arose out of typical 16th- and 17th-century European households and is considered by some the "traditional Western" structure, the father's role has been somewhat limited. In this family model the father acts as the economic support and sometimes disciplinarian of the family, while the mother or other female relative oversees most of the childrearing. This structure is enforced, for example, in societies which legislate "maternity leave" but do not have a corresponding "paternity leave."

However, this limited role has increasingly been called into question. Both feminist and masculist authors have decried such predetermined roles as unjust. A nascent father's rights movement seeks to increase the legal standing of fathers in everything from child-custody cases to the institution of paid paternity leave or family leave.

Sociology of Childhood

In the last two or three decades the sociology of childhood has gained increasing attention and triggered numerous empirical studies as well as intensive theoretical disputes, starting in the Scandinavian and the English-speaking countries. Up to this time, sociology had approached children and childhood mainly from a socialisation perspective, and the emergence of the new childhood sociological paradigm ran parallel to the feminist critique of sociological traditions. Childhood sociologists attacked the "adultocentric" approach and the "separative view" of sociology towards children. Not surprisingly, then, the key works in the sociology of childhood are quite interdisciplinary, linking history, cultural studies, ethnomethodology, and pedagogy.

The current Sociology of childhood is organized around two central discussions:

> *The child as a social actor:* This approach derives from youth sociology as well as ethnography. Focusing on everyday life and the ways children orientate themselves in society, it engages with the cultural performances and the social worlds they construct and take part in. Theory and research methodology approach children as active participants and members of society right from the beginning. Thus they are neither analysed as outsiders to society nor as merely 'emergent' members of society. Therefore, the sociology of childhood distinguishes itself from the established concepts of socialisation research and developmental psychology of the last decades.

> *The generational order*: The second approach centres on socio-structural and socio-theoretical questions concerning social equality and social order in a society, which categorizes their members by age and segregates them in many respects (rights, deeds, economical participation, ascribed needs etc.). These issues can be summarized under the overall concept of the "generational order". Thus the categorization of societal members by age is far from being an innocent representation of natural distinctions, but rather a social construction of such a "natural truth". It is, therefore, a relevant component of social order and deeply connected to other dimensions of social inequality. Social and economic

> changes and sociopolitical interventions thus become central topics in childhood sociology. The analysis of these issues has increased awareness of the generational inequality of societies.

Questions about socialisation practices and institutions remain central in childhood research. But, they are being dealt with in a new, more sociological way. To analyse socialisation processes means, therefore, to reconstruct the historically and culturally varying conceptions, processes and institutions of disciplining and civilization of the offspring. In addition, the strategies of habitus formation and the practices of status (re-)production are considered. The sociology of social inequality and the sociology of the family and private life are, therefore, important fields for childhood sociologists.

Children's own action, their resistance, cooperation, and collective action among peers has to be taken into account. Meanwhile widespread anthropological assumptions concerning a universal human nature, based on a view of individual and society as opposed to each other, should be omitted from the conceptual repertoire of sociological childhood research. They are the legacy of the older socialisation approach and they legitimate some forms of childhood and education practices as indispensable and even as a "natural" requirement of society, while devaluing others. In this way they generally legitimate western middle class childhood and mask inequality and the interests of social order.

Family System

In human context, a *family* is a group of people affiliated by consanguinity, affinity, or co-residence. In most societies it is the principal institution for the socialisation of children. Extended from the human "family unit" by affinity, economy, culture, tradition, honour, and friendship are concepts of family that are metaphorical, or that grow increasingly inclusive extending to nationhood and humanism. There are also concepts of family that break with tradition within particular societies, or those that are transplanted via migration to flourish or else cease within their new societies. As a unit of socialisation and a basic institution key to the structure of society, the family is the object of analysis for sociologists of the family. Genealogy is a field which aims to trace family lineages through history. In science, the term "family" has come to be used as a means to classify groups of objects as being closely and exclusively related. In the study of animals it has been found that many species form groups that have similarities to human "family"—often called "packs."

One of the primary functions of the family is to produce and reproduce persons, biologically and socially. Thus, one's experience of one's family shifts over time. From the perspective of children, the family is a *family of orientation:* the family serves to locate children socially and plays a major role in their enculturation and socialisation. From the point of view of the parent(s), the family is a *family of procreation,* the goal of which is to produce and enculturate and socialize children. However, producing children is not the only function of the family; in societies with a sexual division of labour, marriage, and the resulting relationship between two people, it is necessary for the formation of an economically productive household. A *conjugal* family includes only the husband, the wife, and unmarried children who are not of age. The most common form of this family is regularly referred to in sociology as a nuclear family. A *consanguineal* family consists of a parent and his or her children, and other people. Although the concept of consanguinity originally referred to relations by "blood", Cultural anthropologists have argued that one must understand the idea of "blood" metaphorically and that many societies understand family through other concepts rather than through genetic distance. A *matrilocal* family consists of a mother and her children. Generally, these children are her biological offspring, although adoption of children is a practice in nearly every society. This kind of family is common where women have the resources to rear their children by themselves, or where men are more mobile than women.

The diverse data coming from ethnography, history, law and social statistics, establish that the human family is an institution and not a biological fact founded on the natural relationship of consanguinity. Early scholars of family history applied Darwin's biological theory of evolution in their theory of evolution of family systems. American anthropologist Lewis H. Morgan published *Ancient Society* in 1877 based on his theory of the three stages of human progress from Savagery through Barbarism to Civilization. Morgan's book was the "inspiration for Friedrich Engels' book" *The Origin of the Family, Private Property and the State* published in 1884. Engels expanded Morgan's hypothesis that economical factors caused the transformation of primitive community into a class-divided society. Engels' theory of resource control, and later that of Karl Marx, was used to explain the cause and effect of change in family structure and function. The popularity of this theory was largely unmatched until the 1980s, when other sociological theories, most notably structural functionalism, gained acceptance.

Hunting and Gathering Families

At an early stage of development societies may practice hunting and gathering. Ideal type characteristics for these societies include.

a) Small groups (30–100 people)

b) Open, elliptical camps

c) Simplistic technology

d) Children spaced apart 4–5 years in age (due to low fat diet and regular lactation)

Ideal type characteristics for labour division is as follows:

1. Women
   (i) Gather 80% of food supply
   (ii) Plant
   (iii) Manage distribution of food
   (iv) Care for children
   (v) Build/repair shelters
2. Men
   (i) Hunt
   (ii) Prepare the fields
   (iii) Care for children
   (iv) Build structures
3. Children
   (a) Help to gather food
   (b) Discipline is passive
   (c) Cared for by siblings, parents, and other adults

The general ideology of these groups is typically:

1. Egalitarian (no hierarchy of power; men, women, children cooperate)
2. Monogamus and bilineal
   (a) Trial marriage
   (b) Divorce not common, nor traumatic
      (i) No wealth to divide
      (ii) Children continue to be cared for by multiple adults

Industrialized Families

Industrialisation dramatically changed the role of the family as an institution and unit of socialisation. With the development of capitalism, the "nuclear family" and contemporary notions of "childhood" arose:

1. Physical context
   - (i) Solid permanent structures; doors close off families from one another
   - (ii) Small scale agriculture and flocks
   - (iii) Private property
   - (iv) Wider political and social contact for boys
2. Division of labour
   - (a) Women and girls
     - (i) Preserve and prepare foods
     - (ii) Begin to be seen as domestic
   - (b) Men and boys
     - (i) Care for flocks
     - (ii) Broader social knowledge and ties
     - (iii) Begin to be seen as public leaders
3. Ideology
   - (a) Hierarchy
     - (i) Stratification by gender
     - (ii) Stratification by class
   - (b) Marriage and divorce
     - (i) Become more formalized (parents take control)
     - (ii) Reinforces class privilege
     - (iii) Divorce becomes more problematic
     - (iv) Divorce becomes more problematic

Kinship

Archaeologist Lewis Henry Morgan (1818–1881) performed the first survey of kinship terminologies in use around the world. Although much of his work is now considered dated, he argued that kinship terminologies reflect different sets of distinctions. For example, most kinship terminologies distinguish between sexes (the difference between a brother and a sister) and between generations (the difference between a child and a parent). Moreover, he argued, kinship terminologies distinguish between relatives by blood and marriage (although recently some anthropologists have argued that many societies define kinship in terms other than "blood"). Morgan made a distinction between kinship systems that use *classificatory* terminology and those that use *descriptive* terminology.

Morgan's distinction is widely misunderstood, even by contemporary anthropologists. Classificatory systems are generally and erroneously understood to be those that "class together" with a single term relatives who actually do not have the same type of relationship to ego. (What defines "same type of relationship" under such definitions seems to be genealogical relationship. This is problematic given that any genealogical description, no matter how standardized, employs words originating in a folk understanding of kinship.)

What Morgan's terminology actually differentiates are those (classificatory) kinship systems that do not distinguish lineal and collateral relationships and those (descriptive) kinship systems that do. Morgan, a lawyer, came to make this distinction in an effort to understand Seneca inheritance practices. A Seneca man's effects were inherited by his sisters' children rather than by his own children. Morgan identified six basic patterns of kinship terminologies:

1. *Hawaiian:* only distinguishes relatives based upon sex and generation.
2. *Sudanese*: no two relatives share the same term.
3. *Eskimo*: in addition to distinguishing relatives based upon sex and generation, also distinguishes between lineal relatives and collateral relatives.
4. *Iroquois:* in addition to sex and generation, also distinguishes between siblings of opposite sexes in the parental generation.
5. *Crow:* a matrilineal system with some features of an Iroquois system, but with a "skewing" feature in which generation is "frozen" for some relatives.
6. *Omaha*: like a Crow system but patrilineal.

Western Kinship

Most Western societies employ Eskimo kinship terminology. This kinship terminology commonly occurs in societies based on conjugal (or nuclear) families, where nuclear families have a degree of relative mobility. Members of the nuclear use descriptive kinship terms:

1. *Mother*: a female parent
2. *Father*: a male parent
3. *Son*: a male child of the parent(s)
4. *Daughter*: a female child of the parent(s)
5. *Brother*: a male child of the same parent(s)
6. *Sister*: a female child of the same parent(s)
7. *Grandfather*: father of a father or mother
8. *Grandmother*: mother of a mother or father
9. *Cousin*: two people that share the same Grandparent(s)

Such systems generally assume that the mother's husband has also served as the biological father. In some families, a woman may have children with more than one man or a man may have children with more than one woman. The system refers to a child who shares only one parent with another child as a "half-brother" or "half-sister." For children who do not share biological or adoptive parents in common, English-speakers use the term "stepbrother" or "stepsister" to refer to their new relationship with each other when one of their biological parents marries one of the other child's biological parents.

Any person who marries the parent of that child becomes the "step-parent" of the child, either the "stepmother" or "stepfather." The same terms generally apply to children adopted into a family as to children born into the family. Typically, societies with conjugal families also favour neolocal residence; thus upon marriage a person separates from the nuclear family of their childhood (family of orientation) and forms a new nuclear family (family of procreation). However, in the western society the single parent family has been growing more accepted and has begun to truly make an impact on culture.

The majority of single parent families are more commonly single mother families than single father. These families face many difficult issues besides the fact that they have to rear their children on their own, but also have to deal with issues related to low income. Many single parents struggle with low incomes and must cope with other issues, including rent, child care, and other necessities required in maintaining a healthy and safe home. Members of the nuclear families of members of one's own (former) nuclear family may class as lineal or as collateral. Kin who regard them as lineal refer to them in terms that build on the terms used within the nuclear family:

1. Grandparent
   (a) *Grandfather*: a parent's father
   (b) *Grandmother*: a parent's mother

2. *Grandson:* a child's son
3. *Granddaughter:* a child's daughter

For collateral relatives, more classificatory terms come into play, terms that do not build on the terms used within the nuclear family:

1. *Uncle:* father's brother, mother's brother, father's/ mother's sister's husband
2. *Aunt*: father's sister, mother's sister, father's/mother's brother's wife
3. *Nephew*: sister's son, brother's son, wife's brother's son, wife's sister's son, husband's brother's son, husband's sister's son
4. *Niece*: sister's daughter, brother's daughter, wife's brother's daughter, wife's sister's daughter, husband's brother's daughter, husband's sister's daughter

When additional generations intervene (in other words, when one's collateral relatives belong to the same generation as one's grandparents or grandchildren), the prefixes "great-" or "grand-" modifies these terms. Also, as with grandparents and grandchildren, as more generations intervene the prefix becomes "great grand-", adding an additional "great-" for each additional generation. Most collateral relatives have never had membership of the nuclear family of the members of one's own nuclear family.

1. *Cousin*: the most classificatory term; the children of aunts or uncles. One can further distinguish cousins by degrees of collaterality and by generation. Two persons of the same generation who share a grandparent count as "first cousins" (one degree of collaterality); if they share a great-grandparent they count as "second cousins" (two degrees of collaterality) and so on. If two persons share an ancestor, one as a grandchild and the other as a great-grandchild of that individual, then the

two descendants class as "first cousins once removed" (removed by one generation); if they shared ancestor figures as the grandparent of one individual and the great-great-grandparent of the other, the individuals class as "first cousins twice removed" (removed by two generations), and so on. Similarly, if they shared ancestor figures as the great-grandparent of one person and the great-great-grandparent of the other, the individuals class as "second cousins once removed". Hence one can refer to a "third cousin once removed upwards".

Cousins of an older generation (in other words, one's parents' first cousins), although technically first cousins once removed, are often classified with "aunts" and "uncles". Similarly, a person may refer to close friends of one's parents as "aunt" or "uncle", or may refer to close friends as "brother" or "sister", using the practice of *fictive kinship*. English-speakers mark relationships by marriage (except for wife/husband) with the tag "-in-law". The mother and father of one's spouse become one's mother-in-law and father-in-law; the female spouse of one's child becomes one's daughter-in-law and the male spouse of one's child becomes one's son-in-law. The term "sister-in-law" refers to three essentially different relationships, either the wife of one's sibling, or the sister of one's spouse, or, in some uses, the wife of one's spouse's sibling. "Brother-in-law" expresses a similar ambiguity. No special terms exist for the rest of one's spouse's family. The terms "half-brother" and "half-sister" indicate siblings who share only one biological or adoptive parent.

Economic Functions

Anthropologists have often supposed that the family in a traditional society forms the primary economic unit. This economic role has gradually diminished in modern times, and in societies like the United States it has become much smaller, except in certain sectors such as agriculture and in a few upper class families. In China the family as an economic unit still plays a strong role in the countryside. However, the relations between the economic role of the family, its socioeconomic mode of production and cultural values remain highly complex

Political Functions

On the other hand family structures or its internal relationships may affect both state and religious institutions. J.F. del Giorgio in *The Oldest Europeans* points out that the high status of women among the descendants of the post-glacial Paleolithic European population was coherent with the fierce love of freedom of pre-Indo-European tribes. He believes that the extraordinary respect for women in those families meant that children reared in such atmospheres tended to distrust strong, authoritarian leaders. According to del Giorgio, European democracies have their roots in those ancient ancestors.

Sociological Views on Modern Families

The different types of families occur in a wide variety of settings, and their specific functions and meanings depend largely on their relationship to other social institutions. Sociologists have a special interest in the function and status of these forms in stratified (especially capitalist) societies. The term "nuclear family" is commonly used, especially in the United States and Europe, to refer to conjugal families. Sociologists distinguish between conjugal families (relatively independent of the kindred of the parents and of other families in general) and nuclear families (which maintain relatively close ties with their kindred). The term "extended family" is also common, especially in the United States and Europe. This term has two distinct meanings. First, it serves as a synonym of "consanguinal family". Second, in societies dominated by the conjugal family, it refers to *kindred* (an egocentric network of relatives that extends beyond the domestic group) who do not belong to the conjugal family. These types refer to ideal or normative structures found in particular societies.

Any society will exhibit some variation in the actual composition and conception of families. Much sociological, historical and anthropological research dedicates itself to the understanding of this variation, and of changes in the family form over time. Thus, some speak of the *bourgeois family*, a family structure arising out of 16th-century and 17th-century European households, in which the family centres on a marriage between a man and woman, with strictly defined gender-roles. The man typically has responsibility for income and support, the woman for home and family matters.

According to the work of scholars Max Weber, Alan Macfarlane, Steven Ozment, Jack Goody and Peter Laslett, the huge transformation that led to modern marriage in Western democracies was "fuelled by the religio-cultural value system provided by elements of Judaism, early Christianity, Roman Catholic canon law and the Protestant Reformation". In contemporary Europe and the United States, people in academic, political and civil sectors have called attention to single-father-headed households, and families headed by same-sex couples, although academics point out that these forms exist in other societies. Also the term *blended family* or *stepfamily* describes families with mixed parents: one or both parents remarried, bringing children of the former family into the new family.

Contemporary society generally views family as a haven from the world, supplying absolute fulfilment. The family is considered to encourage "intimacy, love and trust where individuals may escape the competition of dehumanizing forces in modern society." During industrialization, "[t]he family as a repository of warmth and tenderness (embodied by the mother) stands in opposition to the competitive and aggressive world of commerce (embodied by the father). The family's task was to protect against the outside world." However, Zinn and Eizen note, "The protective image of the family has waned in recent years as the ideals of family fulfilment have taken shape. Today, the family is more compensatory than protective. It supplies what is vitally needed but missing in other social arrangements". "The popular wisdom," Zinn and Eitzen say, is that the family structures of the past were superior to those today and families were more stable and happier at a time when they did not have to contend with problems such as illegitimate children and divorce. They respond to this, saying, "there is no golden age of the family gleaming at us in the far back historical past". "Desertion by spouses, illegitimate children, and other conditions that are considered characteristics of modern times existed in the past as well." Still others argue that whether or not we view the family as "declining" depends on our definition of "family." The high rates of divorce and out-of-wedlock births indicate a decline in the institution of the family. No longer are marriages arranged for political or economic gain, and children are not expected to contribute to family income. Instead, people choose mates based on love. This increased role of love indicates a societal shift toward favouring emotional fulfilment and relationships within a family, and this shift necessarily weakens the institution of the family.

Oedipal Family Model and Fascism

The model, common in the western societies, of the family triangle, husband-wife-children isolated from the outside, is also called *oedipal model of the family*, and it is a form of patriarchal family. Many philosophers and psychiatrists analysed such a model. One of the most prominent of such studies is *Anti-Œdipus* by Deleuze and Guattari. In the family, they argue, the young develop in a perverse relationship, wherein they learn to love the same person who beats and oppresses them. The family therefore constitutes the first cell of the fascist society, as they will carry this attitude of love for oppressive figures in their adult life. Kindship and family forms have often been thought to impact the social relations in the society as a whole, and therefore been described as the *first cell* or the *building social unit* of the structure of a society. Fathers torment their sons.

Deleuze and Guattari, in their analysis of the dynamics at work within a family, "track down all varieties of fascism, from the enormous ones that surround and crush us to the petty ones that constitute the tyrannical bitterness of our everyday lives". As it has been explained by Deleuze, Guattari and Foucault, as well as other philosophers and psychiatrists such as Laing and Reich, the patriarchal-family conceived in the West tradition serves the purpose of perpetuating a propertarian and authoritarian society. The child grows according to the oedipal model, which is typical of the structure of capitalist societies, and he becomes in turn owner of submissive children and protector of the woman. Some argue that the family institution conflicts with human nature and human primitive desires and that one of its core functions is performing a suppression of instincts, a repression of desire commencing with the earliest age of the child.

As the young undergoes physical and psychological repression from someone for whom they develop love, they develop a loving attitude towards authority figures. They will bring such attitude in their adult life, when they will desire social repression and will form docile subjects for society. Michel Foucault, in his systematic study of sexuality, argued that rather than being merely repressed, the desires of the individual are efficiently mobilized and used, to control the individual, alter interpersonal relationships and control the masses. Foucault believed organized religion, through moral prohibitions, and economic powers, through advertising, make use of unconscious sex drives. Dominating desire, they dominate individuals. According to the analysis of Michel Foucault, in the west:

> "the [conjugal] family organization, precisely to the extent that it was insular and heteromorphous with respect to the other power mechanisms, was used to support the great "maneuvers" employed for the Malthusian control of the birthrate, for the populationist incitements, for the medicalisation of sex and the psychiatrization of its nongenital forms."
>
> —Michel Foucault, *The History of Sexuality* vol I, chap. IV, sect. *Method*, rule 3, p.99

The Family Equality Council envisions a future in which all families, regardless of creation or composition, will be able to live in communities that recognize, respect, protect, and celebrate individuals for supporting one another and sustaining loving families.

A study performed by scientists from Iceland found that mating with a relative can significantly increase the number of children in a family. Many societies consider inbreeding unacceptable. Scientists warn that inbreeding may raise the chances of a child inheriting two copies of disease-causing recessive genes, leading to genetic disorders and higher infant mortality. Scientists found that couples formed of relatives had more children and grandchildren than unrelated couples. The study revealed that when a husband and wife were third cousins, they had an average of 4.0 children and 9.2 grandchildren. If a woman was in relationship with her eighth cousin, then the number of children declined, showing an average of 3.3 children and 7.3 grandchildren.

Natalism is the belief that human reproduction is the basis for individual existence, and therefore promotes having large families. Many religions, e.g., Islam, Catholicism and Judaism, encourage their followers to procreate and have many children. In recent times, however, there has been an increasing amount of family planning and a following decrease in total fertility rate in many parts of the world, in part due to concerns of overpopulation. Many countries with population decline offer incentives for people to have large families as a means of national efforts to reverse declining populations.

2

Paradoxes of Family Sociology

Sociological theories are developed around the identification and resolution of paradoxes. This has proved to be an effective technique with which diverse arguments are presented to a variety of audiences. It has been employed by sociologists and other social scientists from a range of theoretical perspectives and methodological affiliations. Family sociology is no exception to these observations, and paradoxes can be identified in both classic and contemporary contributions to the field. It has been pointed out, for example, that Talcott Parsons went against mid-twentieth century common sense by arguing that 'higher divorce rates do not necessarily indicate a flight from the institution of marriage but may, paradoxically, reflect the high expectations that individuals have of marital relations', and Brigitte and Peter Berger and Ceridwen Roberts suggest that such reasoning applies also to later decades.

More recently Arlie Hochschild has written about the 'curious outcome' whereby a gap has emerged between the high status accorded to care in political rhetoric and the less attractive situation in which careers find themselves: 'Ideologically, "care" went to heaven. Practically, it's gone to hell'. The paradoxical character of care is at the heart of many of family sociology's paradoxes, and care also provides a good example of the way in which the resolution of these paradoxes often has policy-related implications.

Paradoxes are used not only to puzzle an audience but also to engage and to instruct. They can be considered to have contributed to the revitalisation of family sociology that Morgan has identified, as paradoxical discrepancies between popular beliefs about families and actual family practices have attracted much attention. Such discrepancies require analysis and explanation, and this has been an important spur to the re-engagement of family sociologists with theoretical concerns. It has also helped to prompt the re-engagement of family sociologists with policy-related concerns, such as those linked to the distribution of resources within families. In addition, these are issues in which wider audiences have an interest, and it is instructive that several of the sociologists who can be considered public intellectuals have engaged with paradoxical aspects of family issues. Paradoxes are powerful tools and, as Castells has observed in another context, there is no shortage of them in the contemporary world.

The Paradoxes

The first paradox emerges from Hilary Graham's study of lone mothers and poverty. One of her respondents expressed the view that 'even though I have less money I think actually I feel better off but I think that is because I'm in control of the money'. The women in her study 'were poor and economically dependent yet at the same time had a degree of control over their poverty and dependency denied to many married women'. In consequence, 'single parenthood can represent not only a different but a preferable kind of poverty for lone mothers'. This account of lone mothers being 'better off poorer' is a classic example of paradoxes that take the form *less is more*. The household may have less money coming in to it, but the exposure of the fallacy of assuming that households pool resources explains how women in poorer households may be better off financially and in terms of being in control of their finances than their married counterparts.

A second paradox is that identified by Nick Buck and Jacqueline Scott who observe that the evidence does not support the expectation that divorce rates would be lower among couples who cohabit prior to marriage. Thus although 'it might seem that the growth in cohabitation would reduce the divorce rate and that couples who cohabit before they marry would have more stable marriages', the evidence suggests the opposite, that 'marriages preceded by cohabitation are more, rather than less, likely to end in divorce'. This finding has been reproduced by some other studies, and Joanne Paetsch and Nicholas Bala suggest that there are two reasons for this paradoxical correlation: 'that people who choose to cohabit are different from people who choose to marry first', and 'that the act of living together itself changes the relationship and encourages instability'. Cohabitors may be more reluctant to marry and may also be 'less likely to engage in the activities that encourage commitment and longevity in the relationship'. The expectation that cohabitation serves as a trial marriage from which only compatible couples go on to marry is not borne out, and the paradox of having experience of living together not translating into more marital stability is explained by the argument that the comparison between married couples who cohabit first and those who do not is not a comparison of two groups who are equivalent in all other respects. In such circumstances *more is less*.

A third paradox relates to the impact of developments in domestic technology. The widely-held assumption that 'domestic technology liberates housewives' is at odds with research findings that indicate that 'housework hours have actually risen with the invention of new household appliances'. As Ann Oakley noted, this presents a paradox that directs attention to 'the standards housewives set for themselves' in the context of 'the "glorification" of women's domestic role'. Jonathan Gershuny's more recent analysis of time budgets for the second half of the twentieth century indicates that hours spent by women on housework have declined as their involvement in paid work has increased, but he notes that his research relating to earlier decades supports the paradoxical contention that 'domestic labour-saving devices may mean more domestic work'. The 'perfectly straightforward explanation' for this outcome is that 'though labour per task declines as new technologies spread to more and more households, more tasks are carried out clothes are changed more often, standards of cleanliness or cooking are raised'. In addition, as Michael Bittman and Jocelyn Pixley observe, 'the aggregate time spent by *full-time* housewives has not significantly altered'. In short, domestic technology may mean 'more work for mother', or at least not less, and the paradox is that 'the more things change, the more they stay the same'.

A fourth paradox is related to the third in that it concerns perceptions of the continuing inequality in the domestic division of labour that studies consistently report. Ken Dempsey's research found that 'wives who declared the division of housework and childcare or leisure arrangements were fair frequently compared their situation with that of other women, such as their mothers, sisters, friends and neighbours, or their husbands with their fathers, friends' husbands and so forth. They said that they were doing as well or better than other women or that their husbands were no worse or in some instances better than the men with whom they compared them. A typical comment was: "Can't complain. Look how hard my mother had it"'. There are echoes here of an earlier generation of researchers' findings about the definition of 'good husbands' emerging out of favourable comparison with the stereotype traditional figure who was 'mean with his money, ...callous in sex, harsh to his children and violent when drunk'. Wives' sense of injustice can be further tempered if their husbands are apparently generous with gifts that, as Colin Bell and Howard Newby noted, can be effective as 'a means of social control'. Arrangements judged unfair according to the standards of equality can nevertheless be perceived as fair where other points of comparison are brought into play, explaining how worse (than the ideal) can be better.

Points of comparison also figure in a fifth paradox relating to the diversification of family and household patterns whereby the past continues to exercise an unexpectedly powerful influence. Judith Stacey has described recent developments in terms of a movement 'backward toward the postmodern family', and has elaborated on this theme by highlighting the discrepancies between many people's backward looking idealization of family life and the more prosaic character of their life histories: 'Many who contributed actively to such postmodern family statistics as divorce, remarriage, blended families, single parenthood, joint custody, abortion, domestic partnership, two-career households, and the like still yearned nostalgically for the "Father knows best" world they had lost'. Jacqueline Burgoyne and David Clark's study of step-families highlighted the 'pervasiveness of the nuclear family norm' among their respondents. Their desire for 'ordinariness' suggests that, to the extent that these step-family members were pioneers at all, they were 'reluctant pioneers'. Jeffrey Weeks and his colleagues have also noted the appeal of 'the comforting envelopment of "the family"' to people in non-heterosexual relationships who live in 'families of choice' and among whom 'friendship circles are spoken about as equivalent to the idealised family (and infinitely preferable to the real one)'. In a similar fashion, Elisabeth Beck-Gernsheim's notion of 'post-familial families' is the product of paradoxical reasoning whereby

'The answer to the question "What next after the family?" is thus quite simple: the family! Only different, more, better'. Another way of expressing this idea is that found in David Cheal's discussion of Batja Boh's work which he summarises as '*convergence to diversity*'. This '*destandardisation* of the family' is the predictable outcome of the paradox identified by Beck and Beck-Gernsheim's which involves people in contemporary societies being 'under pressure simultaneously to become individuals and adopt standardized strategies'. The trajectory may thus be understood as one of a paradoxical movement backwards into the future.

A sixth paradox is that family relationships are characterised by both intimacy and distance, closeness and exclusion. John Gillis has written of how we may find ourselves 'at home with families of strangers', and both Gérard Vincent's and Leonore Davidoff and her colleagues' discussions of 'family secrets' highlight that these involve family members withholding knowledge from each other as well as from outsiders.

Diane Vaughan's study of the process of Uncoupling begins with a chapter on secrets in which it is noted not only that 'We all are secret-keepers in our intimate relationships' but also that 'It may be, in fact, that keeping these secrets makes all relationships possible'. Conversely, as Lynn Jamieson notes, a couple may have 'close association and privileged knowledge' without any 'sense of closeness' since 'they may feel trapped together as strangers who know nothing of each other's inner worlds'. The description of the typical mining husband in the classic community study Coal Is Our Life as 'a comparative stranger' to his wife and family is an example of how things used to be in traditional working-class marriages, but more recent studies suggest that Intimate Strangers continues to be an apposite term to employ.

What Chiara Saraceno refers to as the 'paradoxes of privacy' include the observation that private life may under certain circumstances be 'more possible outside the family' despite its designation as the private sphere par excellence. In addition, the role of the state in 'the social construction of the family as the space of relationships at once private, intimate and regulated' leads on to a seventh paradox, that policy-makers have a long history of intervention in a sphere constructed as 'natural'. In her recent survey of family policy in the European Union, Linda Hantrais notes that 'Governments in EU15 member states and candidate countries have long intervened with repressive, coercive, permissive and proactive policies to stem the decline in the birth rate and encourage family formation' but that such interventions have at best a mixed record. The pattern of policies prompting unexpected reactions can be explained (in part at least) by pointing out 'that family events are not always the result of rational choices, reached after careful reflection and negotiation'; put another way, there exists 'a paradox between objective situations and subjective perceptions'. Simon Duncan and Rosalind Edwards's analysis of lone mothers not taking up job opportunities made available to them because of their 'gendered moral rationalities' is just one of many examples that could be cited to illustrate the point that people's behaviour that appears paradoxical to policy-makers can make perfect sense to those people themselves, while the policy-preferred course of action is perceived by them as anything but natural. Family sociology has its own parallels to well-intentioned policy interventions in other fields that have been shown to be Fatal Remedie.

Family Relationships

This is by no means an exhaustive list of paradoxes that are to be found in the field of family sociology. Several studies of family relationships, for example those in the field of migration which demonstrate the value of distant kin relations for migrants , confirm the veracity of Mark Granovetter's classic paradoxical argument concerning 'the strength of weak ties'. Mention could be made in addition of the argument advanced by Bill Jordan and his colleagues that 'putting the family first' may involve altruism between relatives but can have quite the opposite effect in terms of damaging wider sets of social relationships through excessive and ultimately self-defeating competition between families for positional goods. This is a theme in family sociology that finds many echoes.

Put bluntly, the family can be considered an institution geared to socialization that is nevertheless 'anti-social' in its effects, an inversion of the classic 18th-century paradox (found in the writings of Bernard Mandeville and Adam Smith) of private vices being public virtues. Another paradox of family sociology is Michael Young and Jean Stogdon's reference to growing involvement of grandparents in bringing up children as 'the new old age', one effect of which is to 'keep them young'. There are further paradoxes where roles typically understood as parental are taken on by children, as in Tim and Wendy Booth's study of children whose parents have learning difficulties, or Carol Smart and her colleagues' exploration of families and divorce in which children engage in 'monitoring and managing the relationship between parents', or Julia Brannen and her colleagues' analysis of children 'taking responsibility' within families. Nor is the theme of paradox restricted to analyses of recent family relationships, as is indicated by Elizabeth Roberts's conclusion to her oral history research that 'many of the changes in the lives of women and their families are full of paradox and ambiguities', with many of the gains qualified by accompanying losses.

One of the remarkable things about the pervasiveness of references to paradoxes in family sociology is that they are to be found in diverse analyses that draw on a variety of different methodological and theoretical traditions and that consider a range of facets of family relationships. One aspect of paradoxes that helps to explain their popularity is their attention-grabbing character, most obviously when the paradox can be captured in a title such as Viviana Zelizer's Pricing the Priceless Child or Peggy Levitt's The Transnational Villagers.

David Riesman's best-selling The Lonely Crowd could also be mentioned in this context, bearing in mind the importance it attaches to parents in promoting the shift from 'tradition-direction' to 'inner-direction', as could Lillian Rubin's Intimate Strangers . Paradoxes clearly have the capacity to puzzle an audience, but this is only a part of their function since they also serve to engage and to instruct. It is one thing to present to people the idea that less is more, or that more is less, that worse is better, that irrational behaviour is rational, that unfair is fair, that the more things change, the more they stay the same, that intimacy is compatible with secrecy, and that the death of the family will result in its survival, but things cannot satisfactorily be left there.

Only by showing how these paradoxes are resolved can their potential to engage an audience be fully exploited. Irving Horowitz has commented that sociological writing in this vein works best when it reveals 'the forces at work in moving a specific paradox to resolution or dissolution', not least because of the engagement with ordinary people's everyday lives that this allows. His view that 'everyday life is the location of the social-scientific vocation'suggests the intriguing notion that family sociology's resurgence from its 'marginalization' may have some connection to the engagement by family sociologists with paradoxes, because these paradoxes frequently involve the inversion of everyday common sense.

Mark Granovetter's observation that 'paradoxes are an antidote to theories which explain everything all too neatly' certainly applies very nicely to family sociology. Paradoxes embody the sort of challenges to conventional theoretical understandings that were necessary to make family sociology 'interesting again'; the resolution of paradoxes frequently calls upon approaches that 'provide members of families/ relationships with agency and identify "the family" as a site of change without assuming that "the family" merely responds to important changes elsewhere'.

The conventional idea of relationships between family members as a dependent variable to be explained by reference to some external factor such as industrialization failed because of its inability 'to provide any way of analysing the variety of family types empirically found in industrial society'. Other general approaches that anticipated a broad movement towards the death of the family, of which there have been many, also fall down because of the discrepancy between their neatness and the 'patterned mess' that characterises contemporary family arrangements.

As Cheal rightly notes, 'diversity of family composition.... does not mean that the cultural ideal of family has disappeared, or even that the family has declined'. Rather, the resolution of the paradox of family robustness at the same time as family types proliferate lies in the recognition that it is less useful to think about 'the family' as a uniform entity than it is to think about 'family practices', and that family practices can take many forms. Put another way, 'families "are" what families "do"'. A parallel can be drawn between family sociology and community sociology, about which Philip Abrams observed a quarter of a century ago: 'the paradox of community is the coexistence of a body of theory which constantly predicts a the collapse of community and a body of empirical studies which finds community alive and well'. Community sociology was revitalised by recognition that community relationships can take many forms, and family and community sociology frequently go hand-in-hand.

An illustration of the potential of paradoxes to lead to productive re-thinking of theoretical positions can be found in the work of Beck and Beck-Gernsheim. Their starting point was to argue that the logic of the process of individualization is to produce a society 'without families and children', made up of single individuals 'unhindered by a relationship, marriage or family'. Their acknowledgement of the existence of 'post-marital marriage' and the 'post-familial family' highlights the unsustainability of the initial position when confronted by phenomena that from that standpoint appear paradoxical. The resolution lies in recognition that the experience of individualized lifestyles prompts 'a longing for the opposite world of intimacy, security and closeness'. What appears from the point of individualization theory to be puzzling becomes much less so when people's broader agendas are considered.

Analyses framed in terms of the resolution of paradoxes do not have to be complex. Indeed, part of their attraction lies in their simplicity. For example, Ann Oakley's exposition of women's economic disadvantage is remarkably straightforward: 'The paradox of working more and earning less than men derives from the double meaning of work for women: working inside the home for love and outside it for money; maintaining the health of families through housework and by earning a wage'. Thus women work more and earn less than men because not all work is paid, and because their performance of unpaid work has adverse effects on women's involvement in paid work. Another simple yet effective resolution of a paradox is Arlie Hochschild's analysis of how an employer may introduce family-friendly policies that lead to more not less time being spent at work: 'In this new model of family and work life, a tired parent flees a world of unresolved quarrels and unwashed laundry for the reliable orderliness, harmony and managed cheer of work.... Some people find in work a respite from the emotional tangles at home' Likewise, Brigitte and Peter Berger's explanation of divorce statistics is readily graspable, even though it is 'the opposite of what conventional wisdom holds: People divorce in such numbers not because they are turned off marriage but, rather, because their expectations of marriage are so high that they will not settle for unsatisfactory approximations'. And the same could be said about the other paradoxes outlined above, that they are puzzles that have solutions: the explanation of how lone mothers are 'better off poorer', the reasons why cohabitation prior to marriage is associated with higher not lower divorce rates, the way in which developments in domestic technology may not reduce time spent on housework, the perceived fairness of unequal domestic workloads, the way that family continues to be a reference point in an age of growing household diversity, the notion of family secrets and the public influences on the private sphere. All of these involve some challenge to common sense yet are accessible to popular and policy-making audiences as well as to professional sociologists.

This is not to argue that sociological analyses are always best presented as paradoxes. There are many other presentational devices available with which to engage an audience, including metaphor and analogy, shock, irony, and autobiography. Talcott Parsons and Robert Bales were tentative in their suggestion that an analogy be drawn between 'the family in a highly differentiated society and the germ plasm of the higher organisms' but it is an idea that was influential. Accounts of certain aspects of family relationships such as domestic violence and abuse are necessarily shocking, and it is instructive that Sara Scott's study of ritual abuse is subtitled 'beyond disbelief'. There is also something shocking about Arlie Hochschild's stark presentation of the situation of women 'forced to choose between equality and marriage'. There is irony in the title of Christine Delphy and Diana Leonard's Familiar Exploitation, while autobiography is drawn upon in the analysis of domestic and personal relationships developed by Ann Oakley, whose acknowledgements in Housewife include thanks to her family 'for the experience of my own oppression as a housewife' that prompted her to write the book.

Family sociology might be considered particularly suited to the exposure of paradox. Leonore Davidoff and her colleagues' description of the sphere of family relationships as a 'dense tangle of love, hate, pity, care, duty, loyalty, calculation, self-interest, patronage, power, [and] dependency' comes in a section headed 'Family Paradoxes' and it would be surprising indeed to find that the relations between these diverse elements were not paradoxical. This theme has been drawn upon extensively, and the receptiveness of academic, popular and policy-related audiences to arguments presented in this way suggests that it continues to have a contribution to make to the revitalization of family sociology.

3

Social Trends Affecting Families

By the year 2000, the world population stood at 6100 million. Geographical distribution of the world population show that 2 per cent, amounting to 127 million persons, lived in Central Asia, and another 22 percent amounting to 1353 million persons, lived in South Asian countries.

The population size in almost all of the countries in the South and Central Asian region shows a significant increase in the last few decades. Nevertheless, during 1980-1990 and 1990-2000 decades, countries in South Asia experienced a significant decline in the average annual rate of population growth. Afghanistan is the only exception showing an increase in the growth rate and its population. India, the most populous country in the region, with a population of over thousand million, showed a decline in its population growth rate amounting to 1.77 per cent per annum during the last decade. During the same period, Sri Lanka experienced the lowest growth rate in the region with a growth rate amounting to 1.05 per cent per annum.

Central Asian countries in general, compared to South Asian countries, have reported a relatively low rate of population growth during the last couple of decades. Except for Turkmenistan, the rest of the Central Asian countries during the period 1990-2000 declined to a level of 2.0 percent of annual growth.

Determinants of Change in Family Structure

Fertility Change

The reduction in average annual rate of population growth, which is a global phenomenon, primarily occurred due to reductions in fertility levels. An inevitable outcome of declining fertility rates and increasing age at first birth in most of the countries in the world is a reduction in family size. Although the fertility rates in the rest of the Asian countries have declined significantly, in South Asia, the decline has been much slower. The Total Fertility Rate (TFR) of Bhutan, Maldives and Pakistan was well over five live births per woman, even during the period of 1995-2000. India still reports a TFR of over three children. Sri Lanka is the only country in South Asia to have reached the replacement level fertility with a TFR of 2.1. It is especially noteworthy that major fertility declines in Asia have occurred in populations that are poor, with large rural proportions.

Since 1970s all the Central Asian countries have moved from high to low fertility, indicating a much faster fertility transition than that achieved by the South Asian countries. For instance, none of the Central Asian countries reported a TFR of over 4.0 during the period of 1995-2000. The highest fertility was reported by Tajikistan (TFR of 3.7) and the lowest, that is the replacement level, by Kazakhstan.

Fertility decline is due to the combined effect of substantial socioeconomic development achieved during in the last two decades and the effective implementation of family planning programmes. The contribution of socioeconomic development to fertility decline was mainly by increasing the cost of children. It became irrational for many people to have large families. A main, emerging feature in the modern family system is the changing attitude towards the value of children. In traditional societies, where human labour was a source of strength to the family, more children were preferred to fewer. But as the economic contribution from the children in a family decreased, because of a move away from agriculture, the need for large numbers of children decreased. Improvements in health care and child survival also contributed. The emphasis was on the quality of life rather than the quantity of children, a new concept added to family values.

Experience of some South and Central Asian countries indicates that achievement of low fertility levels does not require a collapse of traditional familial values and behaviours. Nevertheless in most of these countries, the recent movement towards replacement level fertility or below has at first partly, and then wholly, been a result of delayed marriage and, to a lesser degree, increased single hood, both linked to the rising status of women.

Change in Age at Marriage

In many countries in Asia where significant declines in fertility are being experienced, reductions in the proportion of people married have often coincided with or preceded declines in marital fertility. A substantial increase of the proportions never married, among both males and females, at young ages, has been noted in many countries. For instance, in Bangladesh, the proportion of females never married in the age group 20-24 increased from 4.6 per cent to 18.5 during the period of 1970 and 2000. Corresponding estimates for Sri Lanka do not show a marked increase in the proportions of never married, but they remain at a significantly high level of 61-63 per cent. The same is noted in Kazakhstan where an increase from 32 per cent to 40 per cent is shown. In the year 2000 Turkmenistan reported a significantly higher proportion of never married females in the age group 20-24.

A consequence of the increase in the proportion of never married young adults is the gradual upward trend of the average age at marriage. In the 1970s the singulate mean age at marriage of females was lowest in Bangladesh and highest in Sri Lanka. The highest increase in average age at marriage of females during the period 1970 to 1990 was observed in India and the least in Sri Lanka. In the Central Asian countries, too, similar trends in females postponing their age at entry to marriage can be observed.

A higher median age at first birth is an indicator of lower fertility. Postponement of marriage among females in South and Central Asian countries resulted generally in postponement of childbearing. The age at which women start childbearing is an important demographic determinant of fertility.

Change in Mortality

Mortality declines, particularly infant mortality, everywhere preceded fertility declines. Improved survival rates of children mean that when women reached the age of 30 they increasingly had achieved the completed family size they desired. Earlier, much larger numbers of births were required to achieve the desired completed family size. The countries in South and Central Asia that have achieved a low level of fertility also have a low level of infant mortality.

During the period 1970-1975 in all the South Asian countries except Sri Lanka, the infant mortality rates exceeded 100 infant deaths per every 1000 live births. In the last three decades infant mortality has declined significantly in every country and this trend undoubtedly influenced the fertility decline. Sri Lanka, which initiated its mortality transition much earlier than any other country in South Asia, reached an infant mortality rate of 23 by 1995-2000. Afghanistan and Pakistan, where the decline of infant mortality is significantly lower, over the last three decades have reported a relatively high fertility. Diverse situations can be seen in infant mortality at present among the South Asian countries, where Sri Lanka reported an IMR of only 23 compared to 165 in Afghanistan.

Over the last three decades all the Central Asian countries, were able to maintain the declining trend, even though Kazakhstan and Kyrgyzstan indicate a slight upward movement in IMR in the last decade. However, in comparison with South Asian countries, excluding Sri Lanka and Maldives, all the countries in Central Asia are well ahead in their mortality transition and reported of lower infant mortality, which is a prerequisite for fertility decline. Mortality decline, followed by fertility decline, alters the age structure of the population and also the structure within individual families.

Change in Size and Structure of the Households

A family may be defined as a group of persons related to a specific degree, through blood, adoption, or marriage. The difficulty is that comparative data on the family in the broad definition of the term is not available. The available statistics relate to households, defined by location, community or living arrangements. A household is defined in many surveys as a person or a group of persons that usually live and eat together. It is important to distinguish between a family, where members are related either by blood or by marriage, and a household, which involves the sharing of a housing unit, facilities and food.

A comparison of average household size over the period of 1970s/1980s to 1990s for South Asian countries in general indicate a declining trend. The largest country in the region, India indicated a marginal decline in average household size from 5.5 to 5.4 persons during the 1980s and 1990s. Over the period of 1970s/1980s to 1990s an increase in average household size is noted for Afghanistan and Pakistan where fertility had not declined significantly. In these countries, the nuclear family is not the norm. High fertility and social and cultural factors favour co-residence of the extended family where non-relatives also may live. Over the past three decades Sri Lanka has demonstrated a clear decline in the average household size and reported the lowest figure for the region. The Sri Lankan trend is believed to be strongly associated with the nucleation of the household unit along with a significant reduction in fertility. Average household size of Central Asian countries, in general, is smaller than that of South Asian countries, as the fertility transition, which was initiated earlier in Central Asia.

Due to many demographic, socioeconomic and political reasons family members may disperse. Consequently, the size of the household could be reduced but not the size of the family. In Asian countries, most young people after their marriage live jointly with their parents and later move to another place whenever custom imposes or economic conditions permit the new couple to do so. Lloyd and Duffy believe that, beyond this natural ebb and flow of family members, families are becoming more dispersed. Young and older adults, spouses, and other relatives who might otherwise have shared a home are now more likely to live apart.

Families with a large number of persons are still the norm in South Asian countries. In the 1990s Pakistan reported the highest percentage of households (74.2 per cent) with 5 or more members. Bangladesh, India and Nepal all indicate a marginal decline in prevalence of large households, Sri Lanka indicated the strongest decline. In Central Asian countries the prevalence of large households is lower than in South Asia, but the region has further potential for reduction. For example households with 5 or more members in Kazakhstan have declined from 31.2 per cent during the 1990s to 27.9 in 2000.

The reduction of the family size could be attributed partly to economic difficulties, low levels of income, the high cost of living, the costs of education of children and the desire to maintain a better standard of living, which is best achieved within the more affordable smaller size family. Consequently, the nuclear family with its parents and children, became the model of society and soon ruled out the traditional, extended family usually constituting three generations.

A few decades ago in South Asian countries single person households were virtually not existent. As a result of population ageing, migration, and other social and economic changes occurring in the region, there is an emerging trend of single person households. For example, over the last few years in Nepal the proportion of single person households increased from 3.2 to 4.0 per cent. There is a more significant increase of such households in the countries of Central Asia. In Kazakhstan the figure has increased from 11.6 per cent to 13.1 per cent over the last few years.

Female Headed Households

In many societies in Asia, the oldest male is designated as the head of household regardless of whether he is the primary source of economic support, the authority figure, or fulfils other tasks purportedly performed by household heads. In the mean time female headed households have become a steadily growing phenomenon.

The increase in female headed households could be due to variety of reasons including widowhood, migration, non-marital fertility and marital instability. In recent decades an increasing number of women, particularly rural women, have become heads of households because men, the traditional heads of households, had left for work or other reasons. Moreover due to civil unrest, and displacement, a refugee situation exists in a number of countries in the region, often resulting in females taking over the task of running the household.

The highest proportion of female-headed households in South Asia can be observed in Sri Lanka where the figure increased from 19 per cent in the 1990s to 20 percent in 2000. In Sri Lanka the increase is mainly due to the existing political unrest. Consequently a significant number of young widows have emerged as female heads of households.

A note worthy feature of female headed households is that the majority are widowed women, and the average size of their households are comparatively small. As noted in the 1994 Demographic Survey of Sri Lanka, 56 per cent of the female heads were found to be widowed while only 37 per cent were married. In contrast a mere 2 per cent of the male heads were reported to be widowed while 95 per cent were currently married. In Nepal and India, the proportions of female headed households are increasing. Central Asian countries contain a significantly higher proportion of female headed households. In Kazakhstan and Uzbekistan 32 and 22 per cent of total households respectively, are headed by females.

A new social issue in many developing countries is seen in context of these female headed households because they have mostly one adult who is solely responsible for earnings. A typical feature is that these households are smaller than male headed households. The 1993 National Household Survey of Sri Lanka, show that 66 per cent of households in the country comprised of 1-4 members, while male headed are estimated to be 44 per cent only. Thus in many instances male headed households are comprised with more than one member for economic participation consequent to this female headed households are poorer than the male headed ones.

Marriage Dissolution

It is no longer the case that all marital unions, whether formal or informal reach the final dissolution through death. A considerable proportion of unions are disrupted suddenly for reasons such as desertion, separation or divorce. An obvious failure in family relationship is where husband and wife cease to live together.

Divorce is the final dissolution, leaving both spouses legally free to enter another marriage contract. A variety of grounds for divorce is recognized across the countries in the Asian region, and of those the two broad categories are cruelty and desertion. The law has not only initiated legal changes to enhance the status of women and their children within the family, but also it contributes largely to dissolution of unsatisfactory marriages. Separation or divorce may stigmatize a woman in Asian countries, reducing her social status and shrinking her support network, causing sometimes community members or her ex-partner's kin to reject her.

In many countries, the incidence of divorce is increasing and this phenomenon is no exception to the South and Central Asia. In the last decade, Bangladesh, India and Sri Lanka reported an increase in the proportion of divorced women in the age group 45-49. Incidence of divorce is more prevalent and increasing among, women in Central Asia than in South Asia. For instance almost one out of ten women in Kazakhstan in age 45-49 was divorced while in Nepal divorce is virtually nonexistent. It is worth noting that at young ages risk of divorce is higher. This is supported by evidence from a number of Demographic and Health Surveys. Nevertheless most divorced women tend to remarry subsequently. Those women who are divorced at latter ages are more likely to remain single for the rest of their lives and live with their dependents.

Divorce is sometimes thought to be the only solution to an unbearable relationship. It frees the spouse and children from a situation which may be damaging to the entire family. The idea that when a couple has children it will be less likely to divorce is widely accepted in most societies. Even in Western societies a significantly large proportion of divorced couples does not have any living children. In South Asian culture, too, childlessness exerts a strong effect on the divorce rate. However it is believed that in the last couple of years even in most of the Asian cultures a growing proportion of divorces involve couples with young children. Religion acts as a damping factor to the divorce process in many South Asian countries. Marriage among Muslims is civil and contractual, whereas it is sacramental and eternal for Hindus.

While divorce may mean a prolonged period of discontent, the death of a partner may come suddenly and interrupt a happy or an unhappy union. Widowhood is most likely to strike older persons and therefore worsen the economic problems of ageing. Death of a spouse can result in single parenthood for women for two main reasons: First is that women have longer life expectancy and second is that at the time of marriage of almost all couples, the husband is significantly older than his wife. Since marital fertility continues even in advanced ages of reproductive span, widows are often left with dependent children to support.

Bangladesh reported the highest proportion of widowed women in the age group 45-49 in the 1990s and has shown further increases. At present approximately one out of every five women in that age group is already widowed. The lowest proportion is reported in Nepal. Bangladesh and India indicate an increase in the incidence of widowhood, while in Nepal and Sri Lanka the opposite is true. Presumably in Sri Lanka the decline in widowhood is expected with the decrease in age difference between husband and wife. For instance the difference between male and female age at marriage in Sri Lanka in 1963 was about 6 years, while by 1981 the figure has dropped to 3.5 years. This trend would have made a reduction in the percentage of women widowed in the age 45-49. Widowhood percentages of the Central Asian countries show no difference.

Women's Economic Participation

The commercialization process which opened markets in many developing countries has succeeded in replacing the traditional co-operation in economic relationship, with that of competition. In this process, the social institutions in these countries found themselves in conflict with the key aspects of the new economic systems.

The economics of the family and the sexual division of labour within the family are very much determined by opportunities in the labour market. The economic system has facilitated the freeing of women from household chores and their entrance to the labour market. The market has invented a number of new labour-saving methods to enable women to supply their labour in the market; consequently women's share of the labour force has increased in almost all the countries in the world with no exception to South and Central Asia.

Furthermore, deregulation of labour markets has resulted in weakening income and employment securing and the 'feminisation' of many jobs traditionally held by men. The declining ability of men to earn a 'family wage' along with the growing need for cash for family maintenance has resulted in an increasing number of female members (particularly the wife) in the family engaging in economic activities. The highest female share of the labour force in 1970 was noted in Bangladesh while the lowest one was in Pakistan. In almost all the countries in the region an increase in the women's share in the labour force is shown in 1995. The increase of divorce and separation, female headed households and single parent households all indicate the pressure on females, to engage in economic activities to maintain the family unit. However the income that she receives in many instances is not sufficient to maintain her family. At the same time, mothers throughout the region are still expected to carry out significant domestic workload which are vital forms of economic production, though often not remunerated in cash. When both wage-earning and non-wage-earning forms of economic activity are accounted for it becomes evident that women provide a substantial or sole economic support to a larger proportion of families in the region.

Migration

Population movements beyond country boundaries have increased, particularly during the last two to three decades. Some of the major causes of such migratory trends are increasing globalization, economic interdependence, rapid population growth, ecological deterioration, civil war, ethnic and religious conflicts and increased poverty.

International Migration

The out migration of professionally and technically qualified persons in search of employment overseas, particularly to the United Kingdom, North America and Australia, dates back to the late 1960's. In recent decades labour migrants, refugees and asylum seekers have also migrated from this region. Since 1995 Canada, Australia and New Zealand have opened new avenues for all types of migrants and paved the way for thousands of professionally and technically qualified persons to migrate.

Labour Migration

Economic development in the Middle East countries since

the 1970's, which paved the way for a massive technological development and an expanded construction industry, opened up new employment opportunities in overseas employment for skilled, semiskilled and unskilled labour from South and Eastern Asia. This market expanded in the 1980s and 1990s. Contract migration, where migration was defined to be for a short period only, mostly one to two years, with a facility for renewal was a popular form by which migration was organized. The impetus of contract migration for families in the region, was large and varied. An economic impact was seen at the family, community and village level of the out-migrants and a sociocultural impact was experienced at the point of destination and also among return migrants at the point of origin.

Contract labour migration involves most countries of South Asia, particularly Bangladesh, India, Pakistan and Sri Lanka. The statistics are not available in Central Asian countries. In 1992 Pakistan had the major proportion of migrants, with Bangladesh in second place. The situation for Sri Lanka is more difficult to read because two sets of figures are provided; workers deployed by licensed agencies (approximately 50,000 in 1993) and workers who went abroad irrespective of the recruitment process (129,000 in 1993). The difference tells of the relative smaller percentage of labour outflow captured by the recruiting industry (approximately 40 percent).

Female Labour Migration

In Bangladesh and Pakistan where deep rooted social and religious values limited the participation of women in employment outside the home, migration appears to be negligible. Among half a million Pakistani workers who were reported to have left during 1984- 1989 only a couple of hundred were women, mostly nurses and domestic workers. The number of women originating in Bangladesh has probably been higher but still insignificant compared to the number of male migrants from that country. Women predominate among labour migrants from Sri Lanka during the 1990s. India, which has traditionally been a major source of female workers, lacks adequate data relative to female migration.

Impact of International Migration on the Family

A large proportion of short term migrant labour of both males and females came from poverty stricken families. The intention of these migrants was purely to achieve a better livelihood for the families. A majority of the migrants were migrating for the first time, which indicated that they were inexperienced and had only an average level of education. A large percentage of such persons, especially females, were either semi skilled or unskilled. Unskilled labour was provided largely by females who migrated as housemaids.

Contract migration requires a temporary separation from the family, and living in a culturally, ethnically and religiously different environment in the host country. Neither male nor female migrants to the Middle East are usually accompanied by their families. Training for migrants and an adequate comprehension of cultural differences at the point of destination for the migrants, and training for adjustment and coping during the period of absence for the family are required. Mechanisms for such training were not in place at the point of origin or at the point of destination, during the initial phase of the process of contract migration. Some of the countries have attempted to put in place some administrative mechanisms to impart the necessary training and adjustment.

Temporary migration impacts on the families of female migrants and on the migrants themselves. In most of the host countries female migrants are housemaids and the status of females is lower than that of males. The decision to migrate is usually purely economic, to earn some money for the household.

Within Sri Lanka, in the last quarter of 1995, various reports in the news media throw light on the dimension of the social impact of the family of the migrant. During the observed period of three months, forty-nine migration related adverse incidents had been reported, including thirteen suicides and deaths of migrants or members of the family. Others, such as clandestine love affairs (migrant or spouse) and instances of abandoning the family, were observed. Evidence available at the Foreign Employment Bureau of Sri Lanka supports some of these contentions. These are aspects which are often overlooked by policy which makers promoting migration for employment as one answer for high levels of prevailing unemployment in some of the countries of origin. The magnitude and dimension of the social consequences demand a serious in depth investigation of the issue from the socio cultural perspective. The negative consequences of labour exports, particularly of female migration, have led to vocal lobbies urging a ban or regulation of such movement from time to time.

Evidence of stress and strain is becoming increasingly manifest in marital and family relationships. Successive empirical investigations have demonstrated that the price paid by families was in the form of disruption of family life and disorientation of matrimonial and social relationships. Incidents of family break-up due to migration are reported to be increasing. Sociologists have found a high potential towards bigamy or polygamy as a result of separation of married couples through migration. The past experiences in Sri Lanka show that the divorce rate is higher among migrant families. Another survey, conducted in Sri Lanka indicated that wasteful consumption, increased alcoholism and gambling, devaluation of the moral values of migrant women -particularly the unmarried - and the problem of social reintegration upon return are among negative effects highlighted. These are "symptomatic' of the emigrant social order". The consequences of male out migration have also been observed. Cases of men gambling and wasting money, obliging their wives to repeat migration as a mode of survival, were also noted in this survey.

The migration of married persons in substantial proportions and delayed marriage of women have had an impact on patterns of growth of the population. This dimension of demographic phenomena affecting population growth patterns has not been quantitatively assessed yet. Nevertheless one reason for the observed rise in the age of marriage of women, estimated to be 25 years. Would be the out flow of unmarried women, whose inclinations may be to postpone marriage until they earned a substantial amount of money through foreign employment. The expected outcome is a sound economic foundation for the couple to settle down to family life. Such arrangements tend to reduce the expected family size because of delayed active fertility.

Transfer of the dependency burden of the family from the younger to older generations in the short run is an immediate outcome of the migration of prime working age members of the family. Changes in the age composition of the family occur, with a skewed effect in the direction of a larger proportion of older persons in the family.

Transference of decision making in the family from traditional male heads of household to female members who are earning substantial incomes for the family from foreign employment is observed. Emergence of a new phenomenon in the form of female dominated household planning has emerged as a significant feature among some of the migrant families. Women's contribution to the household economy in the poor South Asian countries is not well documented and mostly unrecognized in the national accounts. In recent years, because of their contribution of foreign remittances, a new socioeconomic scenario has been created which significantly increased the accounted and recognized economic role of women in the community and family structure of the region.

The majority of migrants for temporary employment abroad is married and has left their spouses and children behind. The duration of stay by migrants in Middle East countries is approximately 2 -3 years, with the opportunity for home leave on completion of one year's work. The workers long absences from their households - especially in the case of married persons with young children - make it necessary for them to seek the assistance of parents or other siblings to attend to the needs of the young children and to assist the spouse left behind. When an immediate family member is not available, the assistance of distant relatives is sought.

A parallel development is the more active participation of the male spouse in multiple family roles hitherto performed by females only, particularly in families where married women have migrated (child care, marketing). As the circumstances require, a relocation of a part of the chores performed by the migrant member of the family among other members within the family, to an elder child or to a close family relative (e.g. grandparent, aunt) is observed. In some instances, such redistribution of family responsibilities within the family had a negative effect. For example the elder child may be discouraged from schooling to look after the younger siblings left behind or to attend to other household chores. Such instances are a matter of concern and have caused breakdowns of family ties and family disruption.

One outcome of short term overseas migration for employment is that grandparents are called upon to play a significant role as members of the extended family. The sharing of responsibilities have also contributed to the sharing of income of the migrants outside the nuclear family unit. The extended family system, which was virtually collapsing due to lifestyle changes brought in by various urbanization and westernization processes, has risen again. Where available, members of the extended family step in to fill the family role void left by the migrant member, activating a positive reaction. Such a process signifies increased interdependence among family members and a strengthening of the family network

The consequences of parental out-migration for extended periods have to be seen in their manifold dimensions. In Sri Lanka for example, based on a rough estimate for 1996, the stock of contract workers currently abroad amounts to 550,000. A survey of 224 children left behind by their mothers revealed that 80% of them were less than 15 years of age. Such separations had lasting repercussion on the child's personality development, conduct, performance in studies and even attitudes to society and life. Experiences of socioeconomic, cultural and psychological impacts of contract migration on the immediate family system in Sri Lanka is also high lighted in several surveys. Hettige refers to psychological and behavioural problems of children and deterioration of parent child relationships. Interviews with doctors and counsellors reported in the same study in Sri Lanka bring out the concern expressed by health, nutritional and education experts over these negative aspects of migration. The extent to which surrogate parents can make up for deprivation of maternal care is a controversial issue. In urban areas, where the extended family system is more diluted, adverse impacts on children would be stronger.

The social impact of return migration is mainly related to reintegration and social adjustment of returnees. Problems of readjustment/reintegration of the returnee migrant to the family and community have visible manifestations, because of prolonged exposure of the family member to work and living away from the family. For example a higher incidence of divorce is reported among migrants. The incidence of divorce and separation was found to be higher in the first year after return. One conclusion can be that migration has a negative effect on marital stability.

Another adverse social consequence of overseas migration, particularly, among poorer migrants, is the impact of the sometimes incompatible sociocultural experience of the returnee migrant' member on the traditional family life. The long absence from home, and exposure to a totally different economic and social situation and cultural milieu - while increasing the levels of income of the migrating partner and the family have contributed to upsetting traditional family relationships.

The importance of the family as a component part of the migratory process has not received the policy attention it deserves. Migration of family members can have favourable or adverse effects depending on the circumstances. Provisions made by households to cope with the void created by the migration of a family member are a dimension which has a far reaching social impact.

Internally Displaced Persons and Refugees

Nearly all the South Asian and Central Asian countries are afflicted by refugee problems. The refugee issues may affect more than the two directly involved countries. Bhutanese refugees, for instance, are an issue both in India and Nepal. Afghanistan is the major refugee producing country in the region. There is no scope for complacency as many areas are not free from regional and ethnic problems and sectarian activities which cut across national boundaries

Internal Migration

Rural to urban migration enhances the process of

urbanization and is inevitably linked to the process of economic development. The flow of people from rural to urban areas occurs largely for economic reasons. There are other reasons, such as the better educational or health services available in urban areas, that function as pull factors to draw people from rural to urban areas.

Social and economic disparities and lack of job opportunities in rural areas have resulted in increased rural to urban migration in many South Asian countries. The process of urbanization may be described as irreversible. Emergence of "the big city" phenomenon in Asian countries is linked to large scale rural to urban migration. Such a migration pattern occurs within the framework of high population growth in which the agriculture sector is unable to absorb the additional labour supply of the growing rural population. Syed notes "population mobility whether between or within the rural and urban sectors, is related to sustainable development. People who moved out of unsustainable systems in rural areas to rapidly growing urban centres often move into urban poverty. Thus development planners are faced with problems of growing demands on inadequate urban infrastructure. The vicious circle of poverty moves from rural to urban areas.

Another major internal migration process is rural to rural migration. The predominance of the agriculture sector and the opening up of new agricultural land have been the major reasons for rural to rural migration. This is especially true of South Asian countries where population mobility is still dominated by rural to rural migration. In absolute numbers an increase in the rural to rural type of mobility can be observed in Bangladesh, India, Nepal, Pakistan Sri Lanka and Afghanistan.

Impact of Internal Migration on Family

As much as there is a substantial impact of international

migration on the family, internal migration also affects the structure and the functions of the family. For married women the chances to break out from a confined role appear to be greater in urban than in rural areas. They can more easily evade the direct control of their family, causing traditional family structures to collapse and paving the way for development of new ones. Such outcomes are particularly important in patrilineal and patrilocal societies, when migration results in living away from the woman's in-laws which in turn encourages the development of more intimate and egalitarian relationships between the husband and wife. Thus a study of urban neighbourhoods in a city in northern India found that the trend towards the incorporation of married women into their husband's kin network was weak; nevertheless stronger ties were observed between the women concerned and the family of origin than was typical in traditional rural India.

Married women migrating from rural to urban areas of South Asian countries often experience not only a transition from an extended to a nuclear family but also an important change in the nature of their economic activity. From being unpaid family workers, they become wage earners. Such change is likely to enhance the independence of women and to strengthen their role in decision making within the family. In general the higher a women's income as a proportion of total family income is, the more power she holds in the family

Urbanization and the Effects on Family

The increased proportions of population residing in urban areas of South Asian countries, observed during last the two decades and with the potential for faster growth in the immediate future, is a major development trend affecting families. Urbanization processes tend to stabilize the nucleation of the family system because urban congestion and housing patterns, particularly of the low income groups, discourage large households. The demographic transition occurring in some of the South Asian countries reached a stage of low mortality and low fertility (tending towards replacement level fertility) which also tended to enhance the process of family nucleation. A gradual collapse of the extended family system in these countries tended to create new problems of family support for the young dependents and older persons in the family. Time series data showing the age structure of urban areas of South Asian countries indicate that the proportion of older persons increased and the proportion of working age population and the proportion of working parents is high. Moreover, consequent to rural to urban migration and rapid urbanization processes, a small average household size is observed for urban areas, compared to rural, in most of the South and Central Asian countries.

Adoption of urban life styles tended to influence health profiles in the family. Changes in the quality of food consumed, including adoption of a "fast food culture" for convenience, and increased preferences for such food types particularly among the younger generations, are beginning to show negative results. Stress caused by conflict between work and family life also has negative effects. The result is a change in the epidemiological profile of the urban population in the region by increasing the mortality and morbidity due to diseases originating from life style changes.

Various types of unhealthy housing exist in urban areas. Living with congestion and pollution has more or less become a way of life for families living in slum and shanty dwellings. Unplanned industrial development in urban areas, and the resultant over urbanization seen in most of the major cities and other urban centres of South Asia have caused massive environmental degradation and pollution problems. Provision of necessary services, safe water supply, sewerage and other services and facilities for families living in urban areas, has become major problems for urban planners.

Ageing and Retirement

Demographic Ageing

Demographic ageing is defined as an increase in the share of the aged population in relation to other segments in the age structure of a population. Manifold changes occurring in developing countries, together with the rising living standards and adoption of advanced medical technology have caused significant changes in the levels of fertility and mortality. The changing demographic scenario in the South and Central Asian countries has led to a significant increase in the proportion of older persons. Thus, as much as in developed regions, population ageing is emerging as a serious problem in many South and Central Asian counties. These trends have interacted with major changes in patterns of individual and family life. In combination with economic development and social change, increases in the average lifetime of the individual allow for greater time spent in family roles.

The demographic ageing process and the resultant issues are an outcome of irreversible changes. Among the observed effects of mortality decline are changes that occurred in fertility. In addition to the impact of social change, which reduced the desirability of large families, the success of family planning programmes contributed to a decline in fertility. Lower fertility meant that the proportion of older persons to the total population began to rise. International migration of younger persons further aggravated the situation. The age selectivity of migration skewing towards younger ages contributed to the ageing of societies.

The highest proportion of older persons (age 60 years and more) is reported in Sri Lanka. The medium variant projection shows that this proportion would increase to 18 per cent by 2025. The country least affected by ageing is Afghanistan, where at present less than 5 per cent of the population is enumerated as elderly. In general, Central Asian countries demonstrate a relatively higher tendency towards ageing than South Asian countries with Kazakhstan having the highest proportion of older persons.

Among South Asian countries, Sri Lanka has achieved the steepest fertility decline along with the highest levels of life expectancy at birth. The projected female life expectancy at birth of Sri Lanka, for the period 2000-05, is 75.9 years, while for Afghanistan, the projected level is 43.5 years. In Maldives, Nepal and Pakistan the life expectancy at birth of males is higher than that of females. By 2025-30 it is projected that in all countries of South Asia females will enjoy longer life spans than males. Life expectancy patterns of mature age groups in the region show that, currently, females at age of 60 in all countries have a higher remaining life expectancy than males. For instance in Sri Lanka males at age 60 are expected to live a further 17 years while females of the same age are expected to live for approximately 20 years. It is also expected that this gap will further widen in the coming years. The Central Asian countries in general report higher life expectancy than South Asia.

In South and Central Asian countries the growth rate of the population aged 60 and above exceeds the growth rate of the total population. More significant is the progressive upward trend in the growth rate of older persons and declining trends in national growth rates. Projections indicate a pronounced increase in the elderly population in the decades to come, leading to changes in the dependency ratios. The result is that increasingly large proportions of older persons will be dependent on a gradually declining proportion of people of working age (those who are 15 to 59 years). Associated with these trends affecting the economy are implications related to family support of older persons.

Support ratios, which measure the number of persons in the working ages per every older person, have declined in most countries in South Asia. The support ratio will decline significantly in the next two decades and Sri Lanka could experience the lowest level. Among most of the Central Asian countries, an increase was observed in the potential support ratio during the period 1975-2000. However, in the coming decades, the ratio is expected to decline significantly, which could erode the well being of older persons.

Older persons in South and Central Asian countries face many problems such as insolvency, loss of authority, social insecurity, inadequate health care services, insufficient recreational facilities, lack of overall physical and mental care problems associated with living arrangements etc. Ultimately these problems affect the family.

Impact of Ageing on Family

Caring for older persons seems to have other implications that are an outcome of changing societal norms and the resultant changes that had taken effect within families. The traditional obligations towards parents and the duty, to provide them with the love and care that they deserve, are now difficult to fulfil. The prospect of the younger people living with their parents is becoming increasingly difficult if not impractical, as the search for employment opportunities takes them more to locations away from their homes and to distant lands.

The process of ageing ultimately leads to loss of formal occupation, resulting in loss of income in most cases, causing economic hardship in old age. When the sole means of survival is the income from occupation, as is usually the case, this would undoubtedly be a hard blow. Not only will self sufficiency and economic independence be lost, but overall standards of living will decline.

The bulk of employment in South and Central Asian Countries is in the agricultural sector. A large majority of persons are employed as casual and regular labourers, farmers, part-time workers and other types of wage labourers, self employed persons, domestic labour and other minor employees. These types of traditional occupations bring only a marginal income, sufficient for one to lead a hand-to-mouth existence. They do not come with pensions. Hence at retirement, low income earning segments of the labour force become more vulnerable to economic hazards.

In the South Asian countries a substantial proportion of the non-agricultural working age population who are in the non-formal sector are left without any definite source of income in their old age. This category represents primarily those who have been employed in the non permanent subsidiary industries. They have little job security, and chronic levels of unemployment prevailing in the region mean that most older persons are not working in recent times.

After retirement a major proportion of people and their families feel additional economic hardship. In the rural sector, the proportion engaged in agricultural self-employment is observed to be highest in Sri Lanka with 42 percent, followed by Bangladesh and Pakistan with 21 percent and 10 percent respectively. Only the civil servants and employees in the private sector are assured of a pension or a superannuation benefit. The degree of benefits at retirement is directly linked to the type of employment of persons.

In South and Central Asian countries, there has been a long tradition of supporting the older members of the family, a feature which is still prevalent, and provides economic security for the majority of older persons, particularly in the rural areas. Nevertheless, changing family patterns and size, have weakened this security system of older persons. One of the important side effects of population ageing is the increase in the number of generations in families and the emergence of a sizeable generation of older persons with (and potentially dependent upon) elderly children.

There is a long standing tradition of mutual support between older persons and other family members in Asian countries. It is therefore important to be aware of the demographic, social and economic facets of such mutual support, which are interrelated with the continuous concern, ability and participation of older persons to play an active role through support given to the family, including the family budget. Such support given by the elderly reflects not only their concern for the wellbeing of the family, but also their ability to contribute.

Past experience in Pakistan shows that older persons provided monetary assistance to the family budget from their savings. In such instances, the economic status of older persons is positively associated with their ability to be self-sufficient in basic needs. Data from the same country show that the financial contribution of older persons to the family budget is related to their good health and other variables such as age, educational level, ability to continue working past retirement age and having a higher income at age 50. To achieve security, it is assumed that older persons drew at least some money from their savings accumulated over their working lives. Those who worked as employees may also have had some money from employment but the pensions paid in Pakistan are generally small.

Ageing has caused changes in the structure of the population in the region. In this respect the age pyramid of population provides a visual insight to the relative sizes of older and younger cohorts. The dramatic shift in the age pyramid of a population towards more mature age groups occurs with population ageing and could also be understood as a shift in the relationships within a family between the younger and the older generations. With high fertility, the middle segment of the population pyramid whc constitute, the "productive" generation had to accept the responsibility of supporting many young dependents and few old dependants. With a low fertility regime, at least after the passage of few generations, the size of older and young cohorts become more similar.

A large majority of older Sri Lankans are cared for by their families, in most cases by co-residing children. More than 80 per cent of older persons live with their children and two thirds live in households with at least four other people.

In traditional peasant agrarian societies, production tends to be family- based and unspecialised. Successive generations tend to have the same occupation, typically farming. Parental authority over children is reinforced by parent's longer experiences and expertise, and co residence of parents and adult children makes both economic and social sense. With modernization production shifts to more specialized processes, modern market economies are dependent on an inherent division of labour. Increasing individualism in the labour market eventually diffuses in to other areas of life, including the legal system, family relations and social values. Parental authority of elderly parents over adult children weakens, and generally loses most of its economic and legal basis. Changing out looks, and the need for adult children to move in search of employment result in declines in coexistence of multi generational members of the family. This is particularly the case in the event of rapid urbanization, where the members of the extended family living in rural areas are left behind in rural areas, as children move to the cities. This is an important process affecting the family structure.

Increased schooling may break down traditional values and norms, including family values, which entails a specific obligation for the children to support and care for their elderly parents. Although the evidence for such effects remains incomplete, such situations may occur due to two reasons: increased schooling results in children spending less time receiving care and guidance from their parents, and hence the feeling of debt towards the parents is reduced and secondly because of the content in formal schooling which in some developing countries is heavily westernized and the system tends to inculcate western values of individualism and self realization. Both processes make the younger generation less willing to sacrifice time to provide physical care for elderly parents. This may be a major problem in the family in relation to care giving aspects of support for older persons.

With further development, are older persons in South Asia, less likely to receive care and support from their children? The answer given by most experts on ageing in South Asia is a qualified "yes". Norms about the care of older persons by their children were traditional and strong in most of South Asia and appeared to remain strong. Despite this, traditional patterns of co-residence are eroding in many countries. There are also isolated reports of physical separations between elderly parents and their children contributing to the neglect of older persons. Intergenerational co-residence and support of older persons by their children also appear to be less common in the more "modernized" sectors of the population suggesting that as societies modernize, traditional intergenerational relationship will tend to break down. Thus although family support and care of the elderly are unlikely to disappear in the near future, family care of older persons seems to decrease as the countries and areas of South Asian region indicates.

Impact of Ageing on Health Care Costs

Population ageing leads to increased health care costs. These have an impact on both government health expenditures and household expenditures.

After the age of 65 years or so, the probability of disability or of impairment in general functioning increases dramatically. While people are increasingly living beyond seventy years of age, the increased life expectancy is not necessarily additional years of life free of disability. As the number of disabled older persons increases, these individuals will need additional support in order to maintain themselves. Current levels and patterns of the prevalence of disability among older persons needs appropriate assessment. Mobility is one of the first things to be affected by disability. In old age the usual weaknesses are worsened by disabilities. With increasing numbers of older persons, the number of persons with disabilities is likely to grow. This poses a major economic hardship for many South Asian families, the majority of whom are poor or very poor.

Within the domain of extended family relationships, the concern expressed and help given by the family members to older persons during sickness or disability is usually more conspicuous. In fact the main social security comprising physical, emotional and monetary support for older persons is provided by the family or close relations.

The traditional solidarity between generations helps to ensure a sufficient level of social security. Such mutual help has not only been prevalent for the sustenance of family social and economic ties but has also extended beyond the domains of the family to the community level. Especially at the time of marriages, sickness, old age disability and in emergencies.

The problem of care for older persons is likely to be especially acute for older women, who constitute the majority of older persons in virtually all low mortality populations. Because of greater longevity among women in most countries in Asia, and the tendency for men to marry women younger than themselves, women are more likely than men to end their lives as widows. The implication of this is a serious gender asymmetry in the support and care of older persons. The economic and social problems for older women are in many cases worse than for men. Older women are often economically dependent on others, especially in populations where female economic activity in general is low. The prolonged care of such women (because of longer life span) necessitate that those on whom they depend for livelihood, should have sufficient financial resources.

Impact of Hiv/Aids Pandemic on the Family

Few HIV infections and AIDS cases were detected in Asia before the mid 1980's. Since then, the number of HIV infection has continued to rise markedly in several Asian countries. During the year 2000, 5.3 million persons were newly infected with HIV. More than 700.000 of these new infections are in South and South East Asia. More than 173,000 AIDS cases have been reported from many countries of this region. Of these 90 per cent were reported from the Tamil region and 7 per cent from India.

UNAIDS estimated that the most rapid growth of HIV/AIDS infections in South Asia was occurring in India. There is a serious threat of a major generalized epidemic. In 2001, India had a population of 1,025,096,000 and out of this population 3,800,000 adults were infected with HIV/AIDS. The number cases had increased by 300,000, from 1999 to

2001. In India approximately 9 per cent of people infected by HIV died in 1999. The Indian epidemic is fueled by both married and unmarried men visiting sex workers.

The 3.86 million Indians living with HIV/AIDS shows the magnitude of the spread of the disease and that the Indian case is strikingly diverse. The spread of the disease in other countries of the sub continent is slower. In 1999, only 73 thousand were infected with HIV/AIDS in Pakistan, 33 thousand in Nepal, thirteen thousand in Bangladesh, and 7 thousand in Sri Lanka. In Afghanistan, Bhutan, and Maldives the number of people infected with HIV AIDS was less than a thousand.

In Kazakhstan, in 2001, 6 thousand adults were living with HIV infection. Evidence indicates that a small number people are infected with HIV in Central Asian countries but that the epidemic is growing. In 2001, Iran had 2 thousand adults with HIV/AIDS, Kyrgystan, Tajikistan, Uzbekistan and Turkmenistan had less than thousand each.

Impact on the Family

AIDS strips the family of assets and income earners. The costs for a family of a prolonged illness include additional expenditures particularly on health, lost income, and reallocation of work and domestic responsibilities. The illness or deaths of parents because of HIV can deplete family structures. Children don't get parental love, protection and care. Often children are sent to relatives for upbringing or grandparents have to stand in as parents for their grandchildren. Family incomes usually decline because sickness makes adults unable to work. Children often have to take on adult roles in the family and they have to take on responsibilities, including earning money, for the survival of the family in the absence of capable adults caretakers.

Mukiza–Gapere and Ntozi note that AIDS also affects on the traditional way of managing the household when the head dies. As a consequence new patterns are emerging. There are now quite a number of households headed by widows, single women who never married, widowers and children under 18 years of age who are orphans.

Because children lose their parents to HIV/AIDS, they have to drop out of school. Among the orphaned children, boys drop out of school to earn money to offset the loss of income when parents die. Girls drop out of school because they assume the responsibility for caring for parents who are ill or to care for younger siblings. Orphans may run away from home to escape stigma and poverty or they may be sent to live with relatives or neighbours. When parents die families must reduce cash expenditures and school fees can represent a major expense that families can no longer afford. Many children who lose parents must work to try to replace the income that was lost. Children become decision makers responsible for the social and economic future of the family. Lyons (undated) notes that younger children are taking on roles as parent, nurse and provider in the family. The AIDS epidemic is unusual in that its chief targets are not the old and the weak. It kills people of any age, but particularly those who are most productive and who are the breadwinners, leaving large numbers of vulnerable survivors with no means of support.

HIV/AIDS increases the number of orphans in the world. An estimated 14 million children have lost one or both parents due to AIDS. In South and South East Asia there were estimated to be 1,800,000 orphans and in Central Asia and Eastern Europe there were fewer than 5000 in 2001. As the number of adults dying of AIDS rises over the next decade increasing number of orphans will grow up without parental love and be deprived of their basic rights to house foods health and education.

AIDS patients are cared for by their families with most of the burden borne by women including wives, mothers, sisters, daughters, aunts and grandmothers. Especially because of the very different roles played by women and men death is a gendered experience. The death of women will also impact home and family, as fathers have to accept the mother's role in the home.

Globalization

Currently the subject, "globalization" might be the theme given highest priority in the world development debates. The word globalization is comprehended and defined differently by different people. Concisely and simply, the term globalization can be comprehended as a mass process in which or by which, various, geographical regions, economies and states and the people belonging to different cultures of the globe are linked together in an efficient and meaningful way. Actually it is a combination of various administrative, economic and political processes paving the way for increased global interdependence. According to the 1997 report of the Asia Pacific Commission, globalization is a process in which capital, goods and services, technology, information, and various cultural items flow freely beyond national boundaries.

The process of globalization is continuing on a daily basis at unprecedented levels. Substantial changes in consumption and investment sphere have occurred due to huge increases in foreign direct investments and the large amounts of international bank lending. In the sphere of work and pleasure the effect of globalization is shown by the increasing numbers of migrant workers and tourists. The changes in communications are reflected in the rapid increase of telephone and Internet usage. Globalization of the privatization process is reflected in the massive growth of the number of multinational companies. There are about 53000 multinationals and 450000 affiliates in the world now.

There are differing views on the impact of globalization. While some view it as an engine of development and transfer of technologies, others see it as a new version of neo-colonialism operating at the expenses of poor countries. "Globalization is proceeding at a breakneck speed, but the process is uneven and unbalanced with uneven participation of countries and people in the expanding opportunities of the process".

Impacts on Central and South Asian Family

The positive impact of economic globalization on the institution of family in South and Central Asian regions cannot be taken for granted. The new era of globalization has caused most of the governments of the region to restrict and curtail the welfare oriented policies that they implemented for a long period in the past in an effort to increase competitiveness. Budgetary cuts in health and education sectors have the greatest impact on the family domain and its functioning. Most of the population in the region are poor and are highly dependent upon the welfare provisions of the government, while in some of the countries governments have reduced welfare provisions for the needy.

In countries where increases are shown in the total government expenditure the increase is actually in the capital expenditure of the educational sector. The general budgetary reductions in the welfare public expenditure have had serious effects on family functions and structures of these countries. For example, the Public Investment Programme of the Ministry of Finance and Planning (1981) show, that in Sri Lanka during the 1981-1985 period allocation of resources for health amounted to one per cent of GDP and constituted 4.1 per cent of the total government expenditure. This allocation increased marginally to 1.6 per cent of the GDP during the second half of 1980s. But in the previous 1978-82 period, the allocation amounted to an average of 19 per cent total government expenditure. Such recurrent expenditure reductions have resulted in substantial declines in the use of diagnostic equipment, over crowding in hospitals, inefficiencies in provision of health care services and overall decline in the quality of the services rendered.

These changes in welfare policies will directly affect the health and the nutrition level of the new born members of the family. It has the potential to affect the desire to have more children in view of the related economic and health care burden and thereby cause reductions in the fertility level and make way for reductions in overall population growth.

Sociocultural globalization agents like information technology, mass media including television and tourism industries also take part in creating the necessary attitudes and the background for such demographic changes. The effect of globalization can be observed among the traditional extended families who mostly depend on traditional agriculture based economic activities. Shortage of a sufficient number of healthy members would affect the productivity of such farming families and the newly emerging burden of providing for physical and mental health care needs of older persons in the face of challenges of globalization on the welfare sector, have become great problems. The issue of caring for and treating the growing numbers of people infected with HIV/AIDS as a result of developments of migration and tourism, is also badly affected by these cut backs.

In the education sector similar trends are visible. Although slight increments in government expenditure, in terms of GNP, for education have been continued, recurrent expenditures have been relatively reduced, which means either families will have to earn more to keep their children educated to the levels and types that global markets demand or just give up and let the children be absorbed in to a lower level of available jobs, in the same markets, when they grow up.

Most families, especially urban families are influenced by the sociocultural agents of globalization such as television, movies, and radios which drive them in the direction of consumerism. The new trend is marked by the emergence of a new urban middle class (NUMC), stimulated by the trends in globalization and information technology. The new middle class families live in modern houses and apartments; own luxury vehicles and other status symbols; engage in overseas travelling; educate their children in international colleges; shop at modern supermarkets with credit cards; seek private hospitals and services for maintaining health care.

At first, the new life style had been restricted to NUMC only, but with the expansion of liberalized media technologies NUMC consumerism patterns seems to be invading rather rural families and wider social strata rapidly. Hettige and Mayor, assert that a study conducted by them in 1992 revealed that the impact of television on intra family relations had been quite considerable, irrespective of the class position of the respondents. This situation could be generalized for the countries of the region to a greater or lesser extent.

Struggle for Survival and Implications

Alternative ways and means have been found by families to balance increasing expenses due to welfare reductions and ever growing high inflation levels. The newly embraced global life styles require more and more income. The dual forces of globalization, namely economic and sociocultural, have not only put pressure on the families living in this region but also have introduced almost new, alternative, methods of income generation for the house hold units for their benefit. Foreign employment opportunities, free trade zones and huge expansion of tourism are some of the areas offering employment due to globalization, a process that has intensified in recent decades.

A significant characteristic of these new employment avenues is the increased demand for female labour. The employment patterns in garment factories and assembly industries are largely labour intensive with a high demand for unskilled cheap labour. Countries like Sri Lanka and India have facilitated foreign investment through economic policy, legislation and provision of infrastructure and establishments such as free trade zones with attractive incentives for the investors. There are three such zones situated in Sri Lanka, while India has two such sites. Most of the South Asian countries currently gain a major part of their foreign earnings through the overseas labour force, a majority of whom are women. The tourism industry has become a major income generator, and one of the most influential agents of change in the process of sociocultural globalization taking place in South Asian societies particularly, in India, Maldives and Sri Lanka.

The situation of Sri Lanka confirms to a large extent these contentions. Currently, approximately 80 to 95 per cent of the labour force in all three FTZs consists of women and approximately 75 per cent of the migrant labour is female. The increased number of females participating in foreign employment and the increase of unskilled female labour in overseas employment, exceeding that of male participation, is one aspect of globalization that profoundly affects families. In the tourism industry, the total employment cumulative of both direct and indirect jobs, had risen to 87,360 by 1995 although it showed a slight decline by 1996. The number of tourist arrivals showed a sharp increase in resent years.

The new trends of globalization have presented certain challenges for the traditional family institution. These are the effects of increasing employment, especially for female members of the families. When those employed women are married, and for those who are working away from home, problems may arise in the smooth functioning of the family. The traditional roles may be subject to new pressures.

Changes in the division of roles within the family is marked by the fact that in most cases migrant and garment factory women have become the main providers for their house holds. In such households remittances earned by migrant women and the monthly wages from garment factory work has become the main sources of family income. "Migrant women generally earn about Rs. 4000-6000 per month. The "breadwinner" status of the migrant women has been documented in many studies. On the other hand working daughters in families are no longer dependents in those family units but they actively participate in fulfilling the material needs of that unit. Most of their income is essential for the unit as a means for getting better care for the sick members, educating younger members and getting access to the material items such as television and Hi-Fi sets which have become day to day needs for a global life style.

Implications of Income Generation on Family

When the institution of family attempts to adjust to the globalization process, a related set of problems in family roles, structure and norms is encountered. Defects that have emerged in the smooth functioning of the family-based socialisation process are: the problems of nutritional status of children and disorders in adult and child sexual behaviour and degradation of overall intra family relationships. These are now becoming more and more common in countries of South Asia.

Dazinger points out that, the children of working class families with working mothers show a low level of achievement in their educational performance, relative to their middle class mates. The level and pattern of the socialisation process is in fact defined by the social class affected; the changes in the globalization process have paved the way for mothers as well as fathers to be employed, resulting in stagnating socialisation occurring within the family sphere and resulting in poor performances of children in later phases of their development. Furthermore as Dias points out, the issue of child nutrition is highly correlated with the mother's employment status.

Two contrary outcomes are seen affecting the family socialisation process. Mothers' income from employment supports the family to maintain sufficient nutritional levels for the children. Yet malnutrition problems persist among children of working mothers, due to the quantity and the quality of food that they consume. Among mothers who are working away from home, breast feeding of infants is ignored, and incorrect timing of feedings prevail, due to tight working conditions and routines enforced by the work ethics. Thus there is positive and negative interaction on the quality of life of the children of employed mothers. According to a study by Hettige, husbands of migrant wives do not provide adequate care to the children left behind by the employed migrant mothers; most of these husbands tend to engage in sexual relationships outside of wedlock.

An important sociocultural change agent due to globalization is the tourist industry which provides direct and indirect employment and good income to a substantial number of families who subsequently experience various disruptions in family life. Most of the families in tourist areas adopt new social values and life styles. According to media reports over 30,000 child prostitutes are located in tourist areas of Sri Lanka. The number of drug addicts, including heroin and marijuana addicts is ever increasing. In some families, the husbands motivate their own spouses to provide sexual services for the foreigners. Such changes in the behavioural patterns lead to complex types of family disorders and life style changes in the region as globalization takes place.

Phase of Transition Towards Nuclear Concept

In recent decades, globalization has tended to promote the nucleation of family units. Difficulties of child bearing and rearing due to formal sector employment, lack of government incentives, global cultural influences, and rural to urban migration have diminished the importance of the extended family. The nuclear family has a high capacity for mobility. This capability is advantageous as families move from one place to another within short periods of time due to the instability and working routines involved with new kinds of jobs.

Another adaptive method of coping with new trends is for families to consume services they no longer provide directly to their members. Moving towards substitutes for familial functions and services is marked by a growing number of day care centres, super markets and takeaway restaurants, homes for the aged, and paid hospitals for health care.

So as we try to understand how families in this region respond to the process of globalization, we are left with only one general conclusion which implies that the future outcome will be nothing but complete nucleation of families and westernization of family norms and structure with emerging family types such as single parent families. But it is not wise to generalize findings among the countries belonging to one geographical region but with sharply varying sociocultural backgrounds. A country-by-country assessment is needed before recommending any regional policies.

Effects of Major Trends on Functions of Families

Families the world over have undergone rapid changes in their structure, functions and responsibilities during the last two decades and this is no less true in South Asia, where predominately traditional value systems with patriarchal customs and beliefs prevailed. Some of the major causes for change are universal, while there are other country and culture specific changes.

Poverty, privatization, promotion of open market economies, advances in technology and science, effects of advances in health and epidemiological transition, changes caused by demographic transition, modernization and industrialization, urbanization, globalization, are common trends affecting families. Internal and international migration, armed conflicts, and the global pandemic of HIV/AIDS have contributed to changes in value systems affecting families in South and Central Asian countries.

The family has acclaimed universal importance and acceptance as the basic unit of society. It has been attributed with biological functions such as reproduction, social functions pertaining to nurturing and socialisation of children, caring and support for older persons, the sick, and those with disabilities. It is the institution responsible for maintaining and building relationships among family members as well as with the community. Some of the community functions rendered by a family are helping the family members and those outside the immediate family circle in many instances by becoming members of community based organizations. In Sri Lanka the Death Donation Societies and Mutual Aid Societies are examples that illustrate the inter and intra family support systems, that exist in the community. Inculcation of values and spiritual development, performed by the family essential for the sustainability of the society fulfilled through socialisation. Providing bread and butter to its members i.e. provision of a regular supply of food is the most important economic function of a family.

A well functioning family is an asset to the society while the malfunctioning family is a burden. Therefore it is the obligation and the duty of the society to strengthen and maintain families for their optimal functioning. The institution of the family in South Asian countries is still strong in its fulfilment of functions and obligations. Nevertheless, policy interventions for the well being of families are lacking in South Asian countries.

Poverty

Poverty is common in South Asian countries. It is a dehumanizing condition which leads to marginalisation and alienation of families, making family members vulnerable to social ills. Poverty has, in a way, determined the family structure. Many poor families are large in size. One explanation for the perseverance of high fertility in Bangladesh is that economic insecurity leads parents to desire a large number of children, who are considered assets in the patriarchal production structure and an insurance against old age destitution and poverty. The conceptualisation is that when parents become aged, the children will look after them

In Sri Lanka an affluent family has only one or two children; the tendency in the middle class is generally to have a smaller family. In a poor family usually, 4–8 children are found, especially in the dry zone areas. Agricultural communities need more labour and in that context, a large family is a resource base and acts as insurance for old age support. In the long run large families create problems especially about inheritance of land and property. In an agricultural society this is very crucial as fragmentation of land occurs with every generation.In Bangladesh some parents prefer sons to daughters because they have higher earning potential and are expected to assist in times of crisis or when parents are aged and no longer able to support themselves.

Poverty can cause people to take part in antisocial activities such as the production and sale of illicit liquor, drugs, theft, robberies and prostitution. Drinking, drug abuse and gambling have a high prevalence in poor families compared to well to do families. Most of them are unskilled casual labourers, venders or serving in the informal sector. They are unable to fulfil the familial roles and functions satisfactorily. This causes future generations to be uneducated, and inadequately socialized. Therefore, any poverty related policy should be a comprehensive social policy, which would address various aspects of poverty and its impact on the family. One such intervention is the in-home service and out-of-home services provided by the state through social welfare programmes. In home services are those provided to a family in order to help it live together more safely, more comfortably or more harmoniously in its own home. The family's ability to live together in its own home is enhanced by giving support. In-home services for South Asian countries could be financial aid, protective services for children, daycare for children, older people and persons with disabilities and counselling. Out-of-home services are mainly for children and would be provided through adoption, foster care institutional care and intervention by the judicial system.

Modernization, Industrialization and Westernization

In South Asian countries where predominantly a traditional society existed for generations especially with an extended family system, a vacuum is created between the traditional society and the modern society, when modernization, industrialization and urbanization take place. This leads to adjustment problems and feelings of insecurity and alienation from traditional land and family. Extended family no longer exists due to physical, social and economic environments, particularly in the urban settings, creating the problems of caring for children, older persons and the sick. Other social problems such as housing, sanitation, and crime are on the increase. Family disruptions take place specifically due to adjustment problems and collapse of family values. The association of modernization, industrialization and urbanization processes and the declines in fertility rate is a positive sign for development.

The Institution of Family and Effects of Globalization

Globalisation accelerates the free flow of labour across continents. Further it decreases the bargaining power of labour, making it increasingly powerless. It is the developing countries that are at a greater disadvantage. Globalization and open economies have created opportunities for migration and this has influenced the family to change its structure. Specifically unskilled men and woman in large numbers are migrating to middle-east countries seeking employment. The traditional decision making responsibility of the male head of the family, in a patriarchal society started collapsing with foreign employment and improved economic status of women. In most of the families, with overseas employed women, the husband become "house husband" as opposed to the "bread winner" of the family; he in fact was dependent on the wife and it has affected changes in traditionally defined familial relationships, roles and duties of the house hold. In the Export Processing Zones of Sri Lanka a majority of the work force is female. Therefore internal migrations as well as international migration has been able to shift male dominance allowing females also to make decisions or participate in family decision making in Sri Lanka.

The availability of advanced communication systems to international migrants is an advantage because they can have regular contact with their family members which helps to maintain family relationships. The workers who are employed abroad, with a higher level of education, can afford such a facility. In Sri Lanka many migrants to the Middle East are unskilled and uneducated who do not have regular contacts with family members. This tends to break down the family relationships. Therefore, the introduction of policies to facilitate advanced communication technology to enable family dialogue at all income levels of the society is necessary.

Another area of needed intervention is managing earnings. The evidence from Sri Lanka shows that many families of middle-east migrants are leading a marginal life because of their ignorance in spending, though they earned much from overseas employment. Therefore policy interventions should be directed towards budget counselling.

Social welfare is mostly a non-profit service delivery system. However due to budget deficits and structural adjustments governments are forced to cut down expenses on social welfare. Privatization of non-profit earning delivery services have converted such services to profit earning business enterprises and the marginal low income families cannot afford such services.

By the end of the second millennium, almost all South and Central Asian countries spent a substantial proportion of the Gross Domestic Product on military expenditure. Sri Lanka, India and Nepal have experienced internal conflicts causing much money to be spent to curb such internal conflicts. Bangladesh is experiencing constant strikes and work stoppages. As a result industrial peace is at stake. All these factors contribute to inflation and low economic outputs. It is necessary to have a safety net to prevent hardship for families. A suggested policy intervention could be targeted social welfare programmes. These programmes could be implemented to embrace marginalised families.

Population ageing in South Asian countries is a common feature which increases the dependency ratio and puts pressure on families. The traditional values that prevailed in the extended family system ensured economic and social support for aged parents, to be supplied by the children. The emergence of the nuclear family in place of the extended family, and international migration has made older persons more prone to destitution. Thus governments are compelled to take remedial measures to uplift the living standards of older persons. Government policy intervention and increased budgetary allocations are necessary to provide welfare programmes for older persons. Voluntary other private sector organizations can also play a major role in this regard.

Social functions of families in South Asia are care and socialisation of children, care for sick and older family members and maintaining relationships within the family and outside. Outside intervention is often necessary to assist families in these tasks. This intervention could be provided through subject specific social policy legislation. When family disputes occur, families could be counselled instead of taking disputes to courts. Police social work could be introduced. Social work is a profession concerned with the relationships between people and their environments that affect the ability of people to accomplish life tasks and realize aspirations and values and alleviate distress. Adequate policy intervention had not been achieved in the region in building up the profession of social work to achieve a satisfactory level of service delivery at the grassroots level.

4

Sociological Study of Marriage

The current institution of marriage serves several functions. In the traditional marriage, a young man and woman fall in love, and pledge to be sexually faithful to each other, live together, be intimate friends, pool financial assets, and cooperate as a team that develops and executes a common plan of life that is an important element in each individual's separate life plan. This common plan of life includes bearing and raising children together. The mutual pledge that establishes a marriage is a lifelong vow, "for better or for worse, in sickness and in health, until death do us part." As the quoted words indicate, there is an insurance aspect to marriage. Good and bad fortune is shared, and if one suffers disaster, the spouse is expected to lend a steady helping hand. In infirmity and in old age, spouses assume caretaker roles. To some extent, the insurance aspect of marriage extends across generations.

Ideologies of Marriage

Lockean Libertarianism

What business does the government have in sticking its nose into people's private affairs? What affairs could be more legitimately private than relationships involving sex and love? These questions resonate with many individuals across a wide range of ideologies and beliefs. For many of us these questions will strike us as rhetorical questions to which the obvious answers are "none" and "none." These responses reflect a Lockean libertarian strain in the social thinking of many intelligent and thoughtful people.

But of course matters are more complex, even as viewed from a Lockean libertarian perspective. Sex and love tend to bring about new children, and causing a child to exist is a social act with wide consequences for other people who could not be supposed to consent to bear these consequences. Libertarians will regard with equanimity the showering of externalities in the form of benefits that typically accompany the creation and upbringing of a responsible competent person who becomes a useful member of society. The libertarian will insist that the receipt of such benefits does not generate any reciprocal obligations to benefit those who benefit us in these unconsented to ways.—at least, not obligations that are legitimately enforceable and that justify forcible imposition on people's liberty to lead their lives as they choose. But bringing children into the world can and often does impose net costs on people who do not consent to bear these costs. The introduction of one extra person may strain scarce resources. A Lockean Proviso may be triggered, affecting everyone's property rights. (Left-wing and right-wing Lockean will disagree about the details of these matters.) Bringing a child into the world and failing to see to it that the child is properly socialized may be the moral equivalent of tossing into a crowd an inexpertly wired bomb that might or might not explode and injure one person or many. In these and perhaps other ways causing a child to exist might be violating the rights of others.

Even if two individuals brought a child into existence in an isolated world in which no one would be affected in any way except the two parents and the child, the Lockean will surely hold that by bringing a child into the world one incurs obligations to that child to sustain its wellbeing and prepare it for adult life. It is not clear what a Lockean libertarian view entails concerning the shape and strength of the child's rights to aid from its parents. Whatever minimal acceptable threshold level of parental care is set by those rights, it would seem that these rights are legitimately enforceable. For example, if one parent significantly violates obligations of care toward his child, it would be morally legitimate for the other parent to compel compliance.

From the fact that an activity violates Lockean rights it does not automatically follow that there is a legitimate regulatory role for the state to play. Perhaps Lockeanism rightly understood implies anarchism, so there are no legitimate functions for the state to fulfil. But if Lockeanism does allow that a minimal night watchman state could be morally legitimate, the legitimate functions that such a state would serve would surely include enforcement of children's rights to adequate care from their parents.

Activities that bring children into the world may violate the Lockean rights of non-contentious other people by wrongfully bringing it about that a newborn person has rights to a share of what used to be other people's resources or by creating undue risk via neglectful parenting that the newborn child will eventually commit antisocial acts. These possibilities aside, activities that bring children into the world may wrongfully threaten to establish a state of affairs in which a child's right to care from its parents is not fulfilled. These considerations provide grounds for legitimate Lockean restriction of family life. These considerations are exhaustive. In particular, a social scientific finding that (for example) restricting people's legal opportunity to exit from marital arrangements would increase the expected wellbeing of the adults who enter these arrangements by contract would provide no reason at all for any state or private use of coercion to restrict people's legal opportunity in this way. Lockean adults are perfectly at liberty to enter into less than optimal or even self-destructive marital arrangements if they choose. Moreover, a social scientific finding that restricting adult individuals' freedom to cohabit on whatever terms they find mutually agreeable would increase children's average wellbeing appreciably (though no child would fail to get the minimal level of parental care to which she is strictly entitled according to Lockean rights theory if the restriction is not enforced) would provide no legitimate reason for enforcing such a restriction. Rights are trumps, according to the Lockean.

Prioritarian Consequentialism

Mutually pleasureable casual sex is a significant human good. Whether the sexual desire that motivates this activity is directed at a member of the human species of the opposite sex or of the same sex is morally inconsequential so far as we can see. If humans were psychologically capable only of sustaining casual sexual encounters, the state as the agent of a decent society should seek to promote casual sex, both the frequency and the quality of such encounters. A complication is that humans are typically capable of a greater good, the building and sustaining of long-term sexual partnerships in which mutual sexual sharing is combined with intimate friendship and cooperation in shared life projects, the complex relationship being cemented by assurances (or the confident mutual expectation) of mutual commitment and fidelity. Call this a committed sexual friendship (CSF). Moreover, casual sex sometimes facilitates and sometimes obstructs CSF in a host of familiar and complex ways. Casual sex is the usual experimental prelude to a CSF between two people, and in a wide variety of situations, having casual sex with a person will tend to trigger strong desires either to sustain a casual sexual relationship with that person or to develop a CSF with that person. Casual sexual encounters thus become an arena in which deceit, fraud, exploitation, and wasted investment are common. Despite its intrinsic desirability, promiscuity justifiably has a bad reputation. For many people in many situations, the pursuit of promiscuity tends to lead to the wrongful imposition of harms on one's associates and to inhibit the development of otherwise feasible CSF for self and others.

At this point a legitimate state interest in the character of people's romantic and sexual relationships becomes discernible, an interest that is distinct and separate from the interest in promoting childrearing practices that are conducive to increased lifelong wellbeing of the individuals formed by these practices. The state should promote CSF and seek to enhance the quality of people's CSF relationships, on the ground that on the whole and on the average, people will be better off forming and sustaining such relationships than not doing so.

The prioritarian pursues this concern with a twist. She assigns greater moral value to obtaining wellbeing gains for people, the worse of they would be without those gains. Regarding romance and CSF, she gives extra weight, not to securing gains for those who are disadvantaged specifically with regard to those goods, but to those who are worse off in well being prospects generally.

Whether or not one accepts the prioritarian placement of a thumb on the scale in favour of the badly off, everyone should agree that the issue of how to treat conflicts of interest between those with poor life prospects and those with good life prospects has a large influence on people's views on appropriate state policy. Many policies that work just fine for competent choosers, who tend to fill the ranks of the better off, will work to the disadvantage of less competent choosers, who tend to be less well off overall. A difficult issue of distributive fairness arises here, and reappears in many social policy choices.

In principle there is no limit to the sorts of considerations that could legitimately figure in the moral cost-benefit calculation that would determine morally right social policy concerning romance, sex, and childrearing according to prioritarian principle. Anything that affects people's wellbeing now or in future can tilt the scale. Three considerations loom large in determining appropriate state policy in this domain. Two have been mentioned:

1. The state has a legitimate interest in promoting good childrearing to boost people's lifetime expected wellbeing, and
2. The state has a legitimate interest in promoting CSF to boost people's lifetime expected wellbeing. A third is equality between men and women
3. The state has a legitimate interest in promoting social arrangements that bring us closer to a world in which being born a woman is not per se disadvantageous, that is, a world in which the average wellbeing level of men and women is roughly the same.

Traditional Marriage

What we have called the "traditional" model of marriage is roughly the main conception of it in twentieth-century America lightly modified by concerns for equality between men and women. The light modification is that role expectations for husband and wife are left unspecified. The more traditional ideal of marriage would stipulate that the wife is to be homemaker and the husband the breadwinner and would urge the wife to obey and the husband to command wisely. Here the husband is understood to be male, the wife female.

The traditional ideal of marriage receives some legal protection. By law in most jurisdictions, marriage is between one man and one woman. Property that accrues to either spouse is jointly owned by the couple. If a marriage lasts for several years, there is a presumption that both spouses have contributed to the income potential of the spouse with higher income potential, so there is income sharing required by law if the marriage dissolves. The state also sets the terms of divorce, and in contemporary practice, this generally means that each marriage contract must contain an easy exit clause via the option of no-fault divorce. Some states offer no-fault divorce but fault-based determination of terms of alimony. Except in states that now allow the option of more restrictive covenant marriage, no person may sign a legally binding marriage contract that provides for no exit via divorce or includes clauses that render divorce difficult.

The traditional ideal of marriage is sustained by social norms and by dominant trends in most people's desires. Even in the contemporary world, in which marriage and family life is buffeted by social forces awareness of which is now widely shared, most of us grow up wanting and expecting to become married. Although there is greater social acceptance than in the past of living as an adult without marrying, and of living as a married adult without having and raising children, most people still want marriage, and a childless couple is an object of pity. For that matter, men mostly probably hanker after the days in which the traditional division of marital roles between husband and wife was regarded as unproblematic, and some women have not freed themselves from similar hankerings.

Traditional marriage is a package deal bundling together several distinct functions. The question immediately arises, whether or not these various functions are better fulfilled by being bundled in this way than they would be if they were assigned separately. Of course to some extent legal and social marriage arrangements are a shell that can be moulded to different shapes and filled with different content as times change and people's needs with them. The household economy of the family is no longer so important as it was, say, at the beginning of the twentieth century. Goods and services that used to be produced in the home are now purchased in the marketplace and brought to the home for consumption. Still, the marriage form is a significant determiner of marital substance—what sorts of lives people will live within the institution or alongside it.

The traditional marriage ideal presumes that the lover of your life will also be the person with whom you share childrearing joys and responsibilities if you have children. Why this presumption? The qualities that make one a good lover and intimate friend are not the same as the qualities that make one a good cooperative partner in the enterprise of childrearing, and it is a commonplace that the two sets of qualities do not always cohere in the same person. Imagine that Maria, a heterosexual woman, has a long-term exclusive sexual friendship with Igor, but lives with her long-term friend Frances. The two women friends pool their finances and jointly share parenting responsibilities for the children they bear. In effect, Maria is married, but the marital status roles are split across two persons. Perhaps this arrangement is a bad idea, perhaps not. One wonders why the state should put its stamp of approval behind one particular bundling of social roles, the ones constitutive of traditional marriage.

In discussing alternatives to traditional marriage the discussion can easily veer off into irrelevant silliness. Some forms of family life that might look attractive from some normative theoretical armchair perspective might be ways of living that no actual persons will ever come to desire or desire strongly enough to make the way of living a socially recognized and viable option for people. In the absence of tyrannical uses of state power that no sensible normative principles would condone, the imaginary alternatives are just that, imaginary alternatives. The discussion of such alternatives is no more fruitful than reflections on what life would be like if humans had wings to fly.

Consider as a starting point what we will call the Lockean baseline option: The state should simply enforce whatever voluntary contracts individuals make with one another concerning romantic, sexual, family, and marital arrangements—provided these arrangements:

1. do not wrongfully impose costs on unconsenting third parties and
2. do not run afoul of the state's legitimate interest in ensuring that every child has an adequate level of nurturance, education, and socialisation.

One complication is what to do about risky contracts. Suppose some types of romantic contracts individuals might be prone to make do not necessarily issue in harm to children, but are associated with greater risks of unacceptable harms to children than other sorts of arrangements.

The prioritarian approach veers off from the Lockean regulatory regime for another reason already noted. Suppose that romantic arrangements of types A and B both lead to outcomes for children above the Lockean baseline set by children's rights, but that the A type arrangements issue in significantly better above-baseline outcomes for children and do not incur any other significant moral costs, compared to the B type arrangements. Prioritarianism will then favour regulation by state policy that tends to induce people to opt for A rather than B (provided some feasible regulation passes a prioritarian cost-benefit assessment), but the Lockean prohibits any coercive restriction of people's liberty with respect to their activities that violate no one's rights.

The same opposition of principle emerges for the desiderata of promoting CSF and promoting equality in men's and women's life prospects. But insofar as there is uncertainty, perhaps in-principle ineliminable uncertainty, in the normative and empirical measurement that enables us to judge what the weighted wellbeing consequences would be of adopting one or another mariutal regulatory regime, prioritarianism in practice might disagree with Lockeanism mainly in being more permissive: in allowing that any of several different and opposed regulatory regimes might be equally good, so far as we can know, from the standpoint of achieving best outcomes.

Two assumptions are stated below. If accepted, they do not suffice to show that society should depart from enforcing the Lockean baseline all the way to giving legal privileges to traditional marriage. But they do suggest that the state ought to be fostering some cousin or other close relative of traditional marriage. Exactly what type of regulatory regime might be best, is a question that remains open, for all that this chapter argues or asserts.

1. On the whole and on the average, a child is better off if raised under the steady supervision of a small number (larger than one) of parent or guardian individuals who have primary direct responsibility for meeting the child's needs and carry out this function without interruption until the child is full-grown.
2. On the whole and on the average, an adult is better off if he or she lives with at least one other adult who is both a long-term friend and a long-term sexual partner.

Given 1 and 2, there is some reason for the state, acting as the agent of a decent society, to promote steady parenting and CSF cohabitation. This does not yet yield a rationale for promoting arrangements that combine these roles, but perhaps reasons are not far to seek. Given that time is a scarce resource, if one is going to rear children and cohabit in a CSF relationship, it is convenient if both activities occur under the same roof with the same partners. Moreover, the shared project of parenting is for many people an important and valued dimension of CSF. Also, having a successful long-term friendship and sexual relationship with the same person(s) with whom one is carrying out a long-term childrearing project gives one extra incentive to stay the course and continue cooperatively participating in the parenting role. Successfully cooperating in the childrearing endeavour could also induce one to persist in a CSF with that person that was encountering troubles that would spell doom for the relationship were it not for the shared parenting. (Of course, in a culture that prizes and glorifies romantic fulfilment, when individuals are raising children and engaged in CSF together and the romance goes sour, there is pressure to split apart even if the parenting enterprise regarded separately is proceeding in a satisfactory way. The bundling of roles can foster instability of parenting partnerships.)

The bundling of roles in marriage as we currently understand it creates a certain oddity, in current campaigns for legal recognition of same-sex marriage. In our culture, society promotes and celebrates CSF by assigning legal and social privilege to marriage, so unsurprisingly those of us who press for an end to discrimination and prejudice against same-sex sexual activity and same-sex CSF campaign for same-sex marriage. The legal recognition of same-sex message expresses the correct idea that the important goods that are achieved in sexual activity, sexual friendship, and CSF are equally available in homosexual and in heterosexual relationships. But this concern is somewhat orthogonal to the concerns of people who think of marriage primarily as a device for facilitating healthy childrearing and for disciplining adult humans' obsessive quest for romantic fulfilment in the service of healthy childrearing. The point emerges clearly if one imagines that over the long haul in a society that does not impose any stigma on homosexuality or discriminate against nonheterosexuals in any way, it turns out that lesbian couples choose to have children and engage in childrearing as often or more often than heterosexual couples do, whereas gay male couples virtually never do so. In such a society, imagined to be free of sexual orientation prejudice, society might take various steps to promote CSF but reserve certain legal constraints and privileges deemed constitutive of "marriage" and intended to enhance the quality of childrearing to lesbian and heterosexual couples which are presumed to be uniquely likely to be part of this enterprise.

Polygyny

One's natural moral rights include this right of alienation and waiver, and the right is morally important. Each individual has her own life to live, and the judgment as to how best to live it is hers. Nonwaivable and inalienable rights would be a grievous affront to this expansive ideal of personal sovereignty.

But this ideal of personal sovereignty is too expansive. We humans tend to be very imperfectly reasonable and rational guardians of our own best interests. So even if one is striving to be reasonably prudent, one may fail, and fail in such a drastic way that duties of beneficence are triggered, so that another person who can stop one from stepping off the cliff may be morally required to give one a coercive helpful protective shove. And a bad marital choice can be the equivalent of inadvertently jumping off a cliff. But suppose one is not ill-informed at all, but simply wants to make a ruin of one's life, either by self-abnegating sacrifice of one's own large interests to get small benefits for others, or just as a perverse expression of one's autonomy. Only a hard paternalism, which critics say has an acrid moral smell, would countenance forcible restriction of someone's liberty to prevent her from self-harming conduct that results from fully informed and voluntary choice. But here the metaphor of self-ownership seems to be helpful in charting the moral limits to personal sovereignty. The idea of self-ownership is that each adult person should be regarded as having over herself the same full rights to use and abuse that a person who has full private property rights in an object has over that object. But private ownership rights are always limited by an element of stewardship. As Locke says of the initial acquisition of unowned land, if one lets the property one acquires go to waste, one's property right is eroded and at the limit, forfeited. To carry through the metaphor of self-ownership, we should acknowledge that each person, the rightful owner of herself, has a duty of stewardship toward herself, a duty to make something worthwhile of her life for herself and for others. Grievously viciously imprudent conduct voluntarily chosen violates this no waste requirement and hence opens the individual to morally permitted restriction of her liberty against her will for her own good.

Setting aside the Lockean libertarian doctrine as, in this context, too extreme, we are left with the harder issue, whether a sensible paternalism or some related moral position would endorse legal disfavouring of polygynous marriage. A related moral principle might be a moral constraint against exploitation. One might hold that morality forbids a person, contemplating interaction with another on terms that give the first person the lion's share of the benefits, to profit in this exploitive way. One might then hold that the law should follow the track of morality and stand against the interaction, not in order to prevent loss to the one would get the short end of the stick in this arrangement, but to prevent the wrongful gains of the willing exploiter.

NONWELFARIST IDEALS

Permitting polygamy is morally right if it is part of a package of policies that maximizes weighted wellbeing and wrong otherwise. Proposed policies are righter or wronger, depending on how far they diverge from what would produce the best outcome for people. Such an approach is controversial in familiar ways. In the context of assessing the meaning of marriage, a consequentialism of wellbeing might fail to register people's belief that some modes of conduct are morally wrong, in and of themselves, whatever the consequences.

The prioritarian's relentless sifting to find the impact on human wellbeing might seem crass from some ideal-based perspectives. Broadly, one might hold that there are impersonal values worth respect that are not reducible to the wellbeing of humans (and other animals). In this spirit one might hold that such strivings as the search for scientific understanding and the creation of ideal community in marriage are morally valuable for themselves, as worthy ends, quite apart from any contribution they might make to human wellbeing. The advocate of such nonwelfarist ideals might add that we misunderstand human wellbeing if we do not see it as properly subordinated to other moral goals. In some cases one pays proper attention to the wellbeing of people by helping them gain the proper relationship and orientation to nonwelfarist goals. Here gaining the good for people partly consists in assisting them successfully to pursue excellent goods that are not at all goods for people. Some values are not for us; rather, we should be for them. Some debates about the meaning of marriage centre on such values, to which the welfarist consequentialist is blind.

DIVORCE

An element of the meaning of any contemporary marriage is

the likelihood of its collapse. Roughly one-half of first marriages commencing in recent years down to the present in the U.S. are likely to end in divorce. The level of divorce has stabilized slightly below its peak level reached in 1980, but this tailing off of the divorce rate is not especially good news to fans of stable marriage, because it has been accompanied by a decreased tendency for people to engage in marriage rather than cohabit without formal ties.

Presumably there is an optimal level of divorce as well as an optimal distribution of marriages into those that endure and those that break apart. The optimal level and distribution would ideally balance the interests of children, adult married partners, and affected other people. The prioritarian doctrine supplies a schema for determining a proper weighting of interests and hence a morally right determination of optimal level and distribution Presumably the optimal level and distribution of divorce are determined in tandem with the determination of the optimal level and distribution of undertakings of marriage commitments. Some who get divorced should never have taken the vow, but surely not all; for some, marriage is a reasonable gamble that turns out badly. The idea of the optimum here is the optimum that feasible alterations in state policy could achieve. But it is hard to get any clear idea as to what these optima might be.

The ideal of romantic love is that a couple should stay intact just so long as mutual love endures between the romantic partners, so there is some presumption that if mutual love between husband and wife ceases, so should the marriage. Even if mutual love endures, its persistence may not be enough to enable the couple to avoid inflicting unhappiness on each other that is remediable only by means of separation and divorce.

These obvious considerations evidently do not by themselves amount to a case for easy divorce. Individuals may tend systematically to underestimate their own vices that might be causing their marriage to be foundering and to overstate the likely causal contribution of what they perceive to be their spouse's vices toward marital discord. Hence their belief that divorce will improve the quality of their lives may systematically tend to be illusory. Making divorce difficult rather than easy to obtain may alter the incentives potentially divorcing people face in a way that encourages them to expend more energy on fixing their broken marriage instead of abandoning it, to their mutual benefit.

At the level of abstract speculation, one might just as well surmise that people will systematically tend to stick with the devil they know, the unhappy marriage they are presently enduring, rather than risk the devil they don't know, the uncertainties of life after divorce. Or people may adhere too strenuously to misguided ideals of unconditional love and commitment—stand by your man, no matter what sort of undesirable he turns out to be. The more prevalent these scenarios are, the more counterproductive it would be to seek to erect new hurdles to divorce with an eye to discouraging people from taking this course.

In other words, the prioritarian willingness in principle to endorse paternalistic restriction of marriage relationships for the good of the adult marital partners does not carry any direct implications for policy. People can be foolish and imprudent both by exiting too quickly from marriages that should endure and from failing to exit quickly enough from marriages that should be terminated. Simply providing multiple options of less restrictive and more restrictive forms of marriage—from marriage lite to non-dissolvable union—is not a solution, because people may choose the wrong form that does not suit their particular propensities and traits.

There is also the possibility that prudent marital partners will find themselves with opposed interests concerning whether or not their marriage should end. One partner may be better off if the marriage ends, the other partner worse off. Making divorce difficult and costly favours those whose interests are aligned with the survival of their marriage; making divorce easy and cheap favours those whose interested are aligned with its termination.

Here the issue of no-fault versus fault-based divorce and divorce settlement arises. If one marriage partner is better off if the marriage continues and the other is better off if the marriage is dissolved, how one balances the interests of the opposed parties surely varies depending on whether or not one thinks one of the parties has been abusive or in other ways vicious in behaviour toward the spouse. But even if one favours fault-based divorce settlements in principle, in practice one might suppose fault finding efforts by courts will not be sufficiently reliable and sensitive to sustain the integrity of the procedures. However, even if it is assumed that fault-finding procedures will work badly, one might still favour them, on the ground that they might help foster a cultural shift toward greater social disapproval of those who fail to sustain marriage until death do us part. But would such increased public censoriousness be a good thing or a bad thing on balance?

Childbirth

A crucial factor in determining appropriate state policy toward family life is normative population policy. Should we seek population increase or decrease? At what rate? Since potential parents in given circumstances are variously capable of raising children effectively, society will seek not simply population increase, decrease, or steady state, but will differentially favour reproduction by the more able or alternatively work to change the circumstances of the less able to boost their parenting prospects. At some lower level of parenting ability, society actively should discourage individuals whose childrearing capacities are at that level or below from giving birth and raising their own children. If there is no morally acceptable way to discourage childbirth, society needs mechanisms of separating incompetent parents from their children, either by encouraging adoption or installing children in orphanages or less drastically by channelling resources to children in ways that neither depend on the intelligent cooperation nor reinforce the authority of the incompetent parents. These draconian-sounding types of policies are double-edged swords, which can harm more than they help, if poorly designed and operated. But a state that has administrative competence at its disposal has the responsibility to be a nanny state, and in some respects an aggressive nanny state.

Differences

Any regulatory regime for marriage faces the daunting task of balancing many sets of potentially conflicting interests—between children seeking nurturance and adults seeking adult fulfilment, between individuals with different romantic propensities who would benefit differentially under different types of regulatory regime, and between men and women. How it is reasonable to cope with the last-mentioned conflict depends crucially on the extent to which men and women are different in traits and needs in ways that either cannot be eliminated or should not be eliminated.

Many years ago the economist Victor Fuchs commented that "many types of evidence of different sorts suggests that on the whole and on the average women want to have children more than men and care more for their welfare." The evidence to which Fuchs alludes might be misleading or not; suppose it is not. The differences between men and women that Fuchs cites might be for all practical purposes fixed or alterable; suppose they are fixed. There might be other significant differences as well—for example, a different propensity to violence. What then?If we seek equality of life prospects between men and women, in a world of difference, the task for social policy would be to arrange institutions and practices so that the differences between men and women do not work to the disadvantage of either group. The aim would not be equal treatment of men and women but treatment that so far as is feasible given other moral goals, leads to equal life prospects on the average between men and women.

Notice that the prioritarian's commitment to such equality is shallow. Equality of any sort is desirable, for the prioritarian, only in so far as equality in the circumstances serves the goal of maximizing weighted wellbeing. The prioritarian is a calculating feminist, not a committed feminist.

In broad terms one might regard contemporary advanced industrial democracies including Europe and the U.S. as undergoing a long transformation toward societies in which men and women participate equally and on equal terms in the labour market and in market entrepreneurial activity. This transformation puts pressure on many institutions, notably the family. It is simply not yet clear what forms of romantic and marital practices will best suit such sexually egalitarian societies. The marriage forms we have inherited limp along, and the ailments we now bemoan may prove temporary or may ultimately require prosthetic or more radical therapy. Should traditional marriage give way to a regime of Lockean contract? Should fluid cohabitation arrangements replace the traditional family arrangement or should we engineer a new puritanism if we can? Since we don't yet have good answers to these and related questions, perhaps we should regulate with a light hand, letting a hundred flowers (and doubtless thousands of weeds) bloom, experiments in living that might provide bright ideas for future improvement.

Reassessing Marriage

In 1675, Grace Allenson, reflectingon her unhappy marriage, told her servant 'that if she might have but bread and water to live on she were happy if she could but be quiet with it'. Charles Pearson, a merchant tailor, also echoed *The Book of Homilies*' sentiment that quiet in marriage should be prized above houses, servants, money, land and possessions. In the advert that he placed in 1756 in the *York Courant*, announcing his and his wife's mutually agreed separation, he mused 'What is all the World without Quietness?' More than tranquillity, quiet evoked peace of mind and body, undisturbed by rage or passion.

It is vital to understand married life in the past. Marriage mattered in much the same ways as it matters today. Governments attempted to control it, the church tried to retain some hold on it, pundits bemoaned its state, and most proclaimed it the key to social order. Matrimony has always been at once a public and a private institution. The pre-modern household, a social and economic institution, linked to other households in a chain of credit, often had the conjugal couple at its centre. Marriage shaped the lives of most adults, whether they entered informal or formal versions of it, or did not marry through choice or circumstance. It marked physical, emotional and economic maturity and depending upon sex wealth, status and participation in civic and social duties and rights. It is hardly surprising that historians have used it to explain demographic shifts and to explore kinship, parenting, economics, work, law, property ownership, violence, sexuality and reputation. Though matrimony is frequently discussed by historians, few historical studies are entirely devoted to it. The formal rules and informal customs associated with its making and, to a lesser extent, its breaking have received some attention.

Information about the experience of late medieval marriage is limited. In this period matrimonial cases that came before the church courts were mostly about the formation of marriage rather than its breakdown, providing little detailed information about married life. Even elite experience of marriage is less accessible than in later centuries, given the scarcity of personal records like letters, memoirs and diaries. The most useful surviving sources relate to work. Inevitably this shapes the questions that are asked about marriage, centring on a debate about what wives' contributions to the domestic economy and household meant in terms of relative power between spouses. The consensus among historians is that late medieval spouses worked equally hard to ensure the efficient functioning of their households. Elite wives hired and fired domestic servants, and in their husbands' absence managed estates and acted unilaterally to protect their land or goods. Rural and urban couples of lower social status formed economic partnerships and their work is described by historians as complementary. Thus while wives' productive labour varied according to locality, was less specialised than their husbands' and adapted to their reproductive life-course, it contributed to a successful household. Where historians disagree is about how far this translated into any type of power within marriage. Alice Clark, writing in the early twentieth century, personifies the traditional approach with her argument that wives' contributions to their husbands' enterprises rendered them mistresses of the business as well as domestic sphere. Their work was so important that young unmarried people did the 'menial' domestic tasks usually associated with married women. Not only did wives gain public value from this 'family enterprise', husbands could be fruitfully involved in parenting.

The view that joint labour caused some practical equality between spouses still has its supporters, but on the whole the idea that the pre-industrialised world was a 'golden-age' for women has been adapted or rejected. The revised version demonstrates that women's overall status fluctuated. For example, following the Black Death they enjoyed increased work opportunities and improved wages. Pertinently, it is proposed that this allowed them to defer matrimony or exercise a wider choice of marriage partner. In turn, the economic recession and increase in labour supply by the late fifteenth century reduced women's opportunities, making marriage their only economic option. It is inferred that the former state granted wives more independence and value, while the latter caused a hardening of gender divisions, relegating women to a more passive role in marriage formation, and, one imagines, within married life itself. The theory is rejected, on the other hand, by historians who insist that there was continuity in women's status in both marriage and work and who question the link between the two. They point out that female subordination was unaffected by changes in the availability and remuneration of labour because both failed to improve women's social power or legal rights. Thus, whatever work wives did, husbands controlled material resources, the work that was done and the profits that labour brought.

Historians of early modern marriage do not resolve the debate. Having found little evidence that wives achieved formal power as a result of their contributions to the domestic economy, the question has in some sense become less urgent and its serious analysis is left to medievalists. Historians who investigate early modern marriage continue to be interested in questions of relative power and authority, but their approach is framed by the nature of the sources, which shift the basis of the debate from work to emotion. In the first place, personal records are more widely available. The way historians have used these sources has varied. Thus Lawrence Stone's controversial account of an emotional transition from cold distant marital relationships in the sixteenth century to initially more patriarchal, but ultimately closer relations between spouses in the seventeenth century has been replaced by case studies which reveal the affectionate, dynamic nature of specific marriages from several social ranks.

Secondly, the increase in advice literature for married couples after the Reformation helps structure the debate about marriage around patriarchy. Thus, it often turns on how far this ordering principle of the household, with men as heads of household exercising authority over their subordinate wives, children and servants, was mitigated by love, personal character or, occasionally, wives' material contributions. There was a tendency to propose that these factors rendered most early modern marriages companionate. Recently, a rather less cosy image of wedlock has been offered. Laura Gowing's reconstruction of sixteenth- and seventeenth-century London marriage is very different. These couples shared few activities, goals or expectations because their social and cultural lives were gendered to such an extent that they were entirely oppositional. In spite of the female agency that she demonstrates, the conjugal power relationship was depressingly skewed in favour of men.

Thirdly, litigation concerned with conjugal breakdown, which replaced disputes in the church courts about marriage contracts from the sixteenth century, also shapes analysis of marriage. The most detailed suits were separation from bed and board, which was sought by couples on the grounds of adultery and cruelty, and it is noticeable that most work about married life actually considers wife-beating and extramarital sex. Male violence can provide evidence about the exercise of male power within the early modern household. Detailed information about wife-beating in matrimonial litigation, its legal status, the advice supplied to husbands about correcting their wives, and references to domestic violence in popular literature have all inspired studies of wife-beating. The evidence is ambiguous, however, and has resulted in two positions. In one view, male violence was an accepted, or at least, expected, feature of married life, and considered a rational response to female disobedience. There is, nevertheless, evidence that husbands' potential to beat their wives was legally, socially and culturally controlled. Wife-beating paralleled public violence in that it was tolerated when it corrected inappropriate actions, was exercised in a limited way and monitored by neighbours, friends and family. In the light of these restrictions on male tyranny, therefore, other historians argue that contemporaries viewed wife-beating as abnormal, irrational behaviour, which represented unmanliness. Bothviews about wife-beating infer an unchanging male desire to use violence against women. Similarly, work on the sexual double standard prevalent in literary, prescriptive and legal writings, and studies of the numerous defamation cases in the church courts relating to sexual slander, privilege chastity as the key to single, married and widowed women's reputations. For example, defamation cases imply that wives needed to avoid any behaviour that raised suspicion, because it would lead to marital conflict and damage their standing in the local community. In this context, the fact that most adultery separation cases were brought against wives leads to the conclusion that men's extramarital sexual behaviour was unlikely to be punished within or outside marriage, and consequently had little effect on their reputation.

The influence of the source material is striking when we consider the marriages of wage labourers. The lack of personal records means that discussion about their unions is often restricted to the mechanics of the making and breaking of matrimony. Stone speculated, for example, that the poor's lack of property permitted freedom of choice regarding who and when to marry, and made it easy for poorer men to abandon unsatisfactory marriages. Similarly, sources such as parish poor-relief records, settlement papers and prosecutions of vagrants, all of which reveal evidence of desertion, highlight the instability of the maniages of those vulnerable to poverty and form a bleak picture of callous male deserters and their pitiful starving wives. This approach has been counter-balanced recently by more perceptive work that shows that the lower ranks were subject to constraint in making marriage. For example, in periods of social, economic or demographic stress, parish authorities frequently prevented the marriages of the poor. Even more significant is Diane O'Hara's reassessment of the making of marriage in the sixteenth century, which reveals the extent to which poorer people themselves exercised caution on entering marriage. Her conclusions that men's and women's choice of marriage partner was influenced by material calculation, rather than personal attraction, raise many questions about married life itself.

It is not easy to characterise marriage between 1660 and 1800 because the secondary literature is so fragmentary and the same sources as those in studies of earlier periods tend to be used, in spite of a wider range of available evidence, like newspapers, better surviving quarter sessions records, and the plethora of related cases in the equity courts and civil suits. Stone's *Road to Divorce* and LeahLeneman's account of separation and divorce in Scotland are useful, but catalogue the formal methods of leaving marriage rather than exploring the nature of married life itself.

It is also problematic that people writing about nineteenth-century married life have preconceptions about the eighteenth century. One claim that needs to be tested, for example, is that working conditions in the pre-industrial household fostered conjugal friendship and harmony. This hypothesis is linked to escalating industrialization, which reopens the question of the relationship between the economic role of wives and their power status within marriage. Anna Clark, for instance, proposes that shifts in employment patterns and different working conditions influenced the quality of relationships between spouses. This approach recalls that of Alice Clark, by centring on whether women's employment opportunities were declining, forcing them to depend on their husbands, or increasing, creating independence, and how husbands reacted in terms of violence. Issues about gender, class and shifts in working conditions coalesced in literature about separate spheres for men and women and a new emphasis on the ideology of domesticity. Both inform another problematic claim, which is that men's role as husbands only came under sustained criticism in the Victorian era. It is an argument that is surely shaped by the proliferation in legislation pertaining to divorce, wife-beating and married women's rights to property and children, which places much emphasis on male cruelty, the class aspects of wife-beating, and the sexual double-standard.

This overview of work on marriage across five centuries reveals that, regardless of the period under consideration, historians seem to be divided into two views about marriage, which can be described as pessimistic or optimistic. For example, pessimistic medievalists concede that married women might have contributed equally to their household, but insist that their work was different, controlled by their men folk and rated secondary to men's. Since it never altered the dominant ideology about women or their legal, economic or political standing, their state in marriage remained one of dependence. In public terms, the lives of married men and women were particularly divergent with few common experiences. For pessimistic early-modernists, the sexual double-standard ensured that wives' lives were shadowed by their sexual reputation, which restricted their personal and public activities. Husbands, in contrast, bathed in the sunshine of permissiveness, for their wives turned a blind eye to infidelity, and their personal sexual behaviour had little impact on their reputation. All are sure that wife-beating was common and not abnormal. In sum, pessimists tend to see spouses' experiences as oppositional. Optimists propose that marriage was more mutual and complementary, whether they define it as a partnership or companionate, depending on the period in which they specialise. They argue that the pre-industrial household encouraged harmony between spouses because they often worked together in the same trade, craft or occupation.

Such economic partnerships caused wives' contributions to be socially valued and led to shared goals and less likelihood of domestic violence. Optimists invoke the formal and informal restrictions on male tyranny, the recommendations in most advice literature that husbands be affectionate, and the cultural demands that men employ self-control, along with wifely 'non-confrontational' tactics, to emphasise the extent to which the potential in marriage for men's oppression was tempered. Furthermore, spouses' complementary social interests and joint economic endeavours led to some shared components of reputation, which softened the blow of the sexual double-standard.

The two views are partly explicable because contemporary culture itself, whether sermon, pamphlet, ballad or newspaper, promoted an idealised view of harmonious relations between spouses while simultaneously demanding female subjection. Historians have offered a range of explanations for this contradictory state of affairs. Some differentiate between a restrictive ideal and a permissive reality. Keith Wrightson concludes that patriarchal and companionate marriage were 'poles in an enduring continuum in marital relations', but that most were the latter form because the potential for very authoritarian relationships was mitigated by the demands of daily life. Tim Stretton observes that it was the gap between reality and prescription that facilitated patriarchy's success, by ensuring that if women could not live up to the positive images that were promoted, they tried not to live down to the negative ones. Another view is that early modern people saw no inconsistency between male authority and affectionate partnership. Anthony Fletcher, for example, argues that protestant conduct-book writers and their male audience saw little discrepancy in their twin values. While they were eager to experience the strong bonds of mutual marital love, they wanted to maintain social and gender order in uncertain times. Sara Mendelson and Patricia Crawford nonetheless note that male writers stressed subjection, while female writers emphasised companionship. Other historians have argued that the inconsistency in the advice about marital relations was recognised. Thus Linda Pollock comments that the sexes were reared and socialised to deal effectively with the dual demands made on them of subordination and competence. What is clear is that one of the reasons for the patriarchal system's longevity was that it allowed flexible behaviour. Fletcher has shown how it was adapted, as a gender system, in order to ensure its success. Pollock has concluded more recently that patriarchal power was not simply mitigated, but that the structural conditions of the system limited its fullest expression. She critiques any simplistic categorisation of family relations as either affectionate or oppressive, observing that they could be many things at different times because relationships changed over a lifetime according to circumstances and priorities.

Nonetheless, the pessimistic and optimistic models are problematic for several reasons. The discrepancies between them cannot be explained by variations in regional economics and industries, or the couples' rank, wealth and life-course. Marriages from a similar period, social status and local environment, whether rural or urban, have been characterised by both approaches. Both views of marriage are largely from a male perspective and, given the sources, even that perspective is restricted to an educated elite male opinion. Optimists and pessimists alike tend to take it for granted that husbands either implemented their power over their wives to its full extent, or benevolently lessened it at their own whim. Yet this fails to take account of recent findings about manhood, reputation, patriarchy and the experience of the common law doctrine of coverture. Men did achieve status from their position in their household and domestic economy. Nonetheless, many had difficulties in achieving economic mastery, occupational independence, and full or unquestioned authority within the household and family, and their credit status was contingent upon many factors. Equally, it ignores evidence that women's reputations rested upon a broader foundation than just chastity, drawing on their position as housewives, as well as their occupational status and charitable works. It is also becoming clear that married women were less restricted in their daily lives than their status under coverture would indicate. Amongst other limitations, this left married women unable to own or manage personal and real property and prevented them from entering contracts. Yet numerous ordinary married women have been discovered organising their own property and participating in the commercial

5

Modern Trends in Marriage and Divorce

There is tension within sociology between discussing the nature and success of a relationship within marriages and marriage as a social institution responding to wider social forces. Perhaps it is an institution where the private trouble and public issue come to sharp realisation (as in C. Wright Mills). The notion of an empty shell marriage is a comment on the success or otherwise of marriage, and it would be expected that if divorce is difficult then there are bound to be many empty shell marriages. The same sociological issue is expressed in an era of easier divorce. For Anthony Giddens, late modernity is a period where the flux of individualism takes place, and this is reflected in the emotional content of marriages. The stress is on enjoying a special relationship, and this is bound to be temporary as the relationship fades. He calls this confluent love, and it is the love that determines the rapidity of the process of marriage and divorce, rather than external conditions affecting the institution of marriage and the rapidity of love. He contrasts this with romantic love, which meant each person in the marriage getting the right partner in a form of mutual projection and wholeness one with the other. This uniting and aiming for a successful marriage despite its equalitarian aims hid the reality of the sexual division of labour. Romantic love, focussing on the person, will try to extend a marriage longer, unless the other person becomes someone other than seemed to be the case at the time of marriage. The other basis of marriage is duty and obligation, which will extend a marriage too so long as they exist (for example, obligation to be parents to growing children until they leave home). So considering a successful or happy marriage has to mean a marriage of a positive relationship and substance, although this is a difficult broad definition to achieve, given that a marriage may have as its purpose a kinship function especially if familial and effectively arranged or constrained by social parameters.

The contrast made between divorce statistics and the success or happiness of marriage is to compare the increase in divorce and the condition of marriage itself at the same time. A number of long term trends have shown divorce increase. As divorce has increased, does it show that marriage has become more unsuccessful and in decline over the long term? Perhaps a higher divorce rate shows a stronger state of marriage, so that those marriages which continue are at least successful marriages. In the short term, in the 1990s, when people were more able to divorce, the divorce rate falling might have its own message.

Long terms trends include changes in the law. Before 1857 divorce was only possible by Act of Parliament. It meant it was restricted to the people who had access to Parliament: the wealthy and powerful. Therefore many unsuccessful marriages had to continue. There would be very many empty shell marriages, when the love had gone but the formal marriage continued. Perhaps some marriages could be annulled, meaning always void, but any visible relationship or consummation of the marriage would make annulment impossible. Over time the divorce law has liberalised, so that reasons for divorce were expanded and access to legal funds to get a divorce became easier. In 1969 the Divorce Reform Act allowed for the first time guiltless irretrievable breakdown to be a reason for divorce, and in 1996 the Family Law Act did not even require evidence of breakdown.

Therefore, although divorce rose, marriages were not becoming more unsuccessful, but rather marriages that continued to exist would be, in general, evidence of bieng the opposite of empty shells - though the existence of a marriage cannot itself indicate its relationship.

Before 1857 marriage was very definitely for life, and reflected the life-long nature of its sacrament. The sacred marriage could not be undone. Once consummated, it was fixed. However, a second reason for more divorce over the long term has been the secularisation of marriage, and a breaking down of the Christian belief for staying married. Rather than stay in an unsuccessful sacred marriage, as was the social obligation, marriage has become more of a contract. Of course some people maintain Christian and other religious beliefs against divorce.

Over the long term women have become more economically independent and this means they no longer have to stay in a marriage that does not serve their emotional and practical needs. Economic independence has allowed women the potential of happier marriages. Even the welfare state has allowed a greater possibility of ending an unsuccessful marriage.

With few economic options, women have in the past put up with abusive marriages, being in arenas of physical and mental oppression. With more options available women can escape.

However, in the 1990s divorce fell. The reason was the decline in first marriages, which has happened for some 40 years. First marriages are more vulnerable to divorce. In the 1990s, when people could divorce easily, fewer first marriages meant fewer divorces. People cohabit and test their relationship more, although these relationships do break up readily. Even if they do, and even if they are in effect a first marriage without being married, they do not impact on the divorce statistics. It means marriages that do happen are more robust. Second marriages happen by those who have road-tested marriage, who have experience of the pitfalls and know the limitations of marriage better. These marriages, with perhaps a stronger sense of companionship, last longer.

Some examples give insight into marriage and success. Most women divorce men for unreasonable behaviour. This gives practical evidence for the latter two long-term trends quoted above. It shows women getting out of violent or situations or those of neglect, where there is negative emotion.

The biggest reason men divorce is for women having an adulterous relationship. This does not necessarily mean that more women than men commit adultery. It may well mean that women still reluctantly tolerate a man having an affair whereas a woman is not tolerated by her husband when she has an affair. The importance of such reasoning is that success and statistics cannot be equated, as statistics do not easily reveal gender imbalances around negative events in marriage. Perhaps women continue to tolerate unsuccess in marriage as they have done in the past, whereas men have been freer to remove their offending partner.

Modern society may be more stressful, and perhaps the increase in the nuclear family has taken away support structures for marriages. Nevertheless divorce means if anything a continuation in the position of marriage, that the marriage is working, whereas this cannot be said so confidently about the existence of marriages in the past.

Every marriage is individual and represents a series of private troubles that couples tolerate or deal with through divorce. The children are their children, the loss of love is theirs. At a higher level, however, the easing of divorce law has allowed marriages that do last to be the successful ones. Stigmas against divorce (such as religious) that kept marriages going have now eased, and economic circumstances have allowed women more freedom. So the public issue is not one that more divorce has indicated more unsuccessful relationships, but that unsuccessful relationships can be released from marriage.

In the end, families continue after divorce, because there are many structures to functioning families. Marriage also continues, given the popularity of remarriage. A remarriage suggests development in the expectations of marriage, that knowing the pitfalls of failure a further marriage is more likely to be successful and even happy (as statistics show a lower proportion of second marriages end in divorce).

Trends in Marriage and Divorce

The family is not a static institution. In recent decades, marriage rates have fallen, divorce rates have risen, and the defining characteristics of marriage have changed. The economic approach to the family seeks to explain these trends by reference to models that can also explain how and why families form. Gary Becker's 1981 *Treatise on the Family* proposed a theory based on "production complementarities", in which husband and wife specialize in the market and domestic spheres, respectively, and hence are more productive together than apart. Production complementarities also arise in the production and rearing of one's own children. However, production complementarities—at least as initially described—are decreasingly central to modern family life. Increased longevity and declining fertility mean that most of one's adult life is spent without one's own children in the household, and the rise in marital formation at older ages, including remarriage, means that many families form with no intention of producing children. Moreover, increases in female labour force participation suggest that household specialization has either declined or taken on a different meaning.

These changes have come about as what is produced in the home has been dramatically altered both by the emergence of labour-saving technology in the home and by the development of service industries that allow much of what was once provided by specialized homemakers to be purchased in the market. The availability of birth control and abortion has affected the potential consequences of sex both in and out of marriage, while changes in divorce laws have altered the terms of the marital bargain. These forces also have important feedback effects, changing the pool of marriageable singles across the age distribution, thereby affecting search, marriage, remarriage, and the extent of "churning" in the marriage market.

To remain relevant to the 21st century, the theory of the family will need to push beyond the production of own children and traditional notions of specialization, and must seek to uncover the forces that yield the modern family form. This may mean re-conceiving the notion of household production or, as we argue, extending models of the family beyond the notion of a household-based firm, and toward emphasizing motivations such as consumption, complementarities, and insurance as central to marriage. Furthermore, the theory of the family as originally developed was a theory of household formation rather than a theory of legal marriage. Couples have become increasingly likely to form households without entering into a marriage, adding a new dimension for considering decisions surrounding family formation.

Some facts about marriage and divorce in the United States over the last 150 years: the divorce rate—measured as the number of new divorces each year, on a per capita basis—has risen, while the marriage rate has fluctuated around a relatively stable mean. The timing of these changes suggests that social and economic factors strongly influence the marriage market. Marriage rates rose during, and in the wake of, the two World Wars and fell during the Great Depression. The divorce rate fell during the Depression and spiked following World War II.

Developments since the 1960s appear to reflect more subtle influences, and have been the focus of heated political debate as the heyday of marriage gave way to rapid social change. Divorce rates rose sharply, doubling between the mid-1960s and the mid-1970s. During this period, family life was potentially altered by many factors: the rise of the women's liberation movement, the sexual revolution, the Supreme Court's granting of marriage as a "fundamental" right under the U.S.

Constitution and thus the abolition of laws restricting marriage between races, the elimination in many states of fault-based divorce, and a sharp rise in women's labour force participation. Yet when viewed over the longer time period, we see that while the 1970s had exceptionally high divorce rates, the low divorce rates in previous decades were also somewhat exceptional. Fitting a simple trend line to the divorce rate between 1860 and 1945 (excluding the post-World War II surge in divorce), suggests that some of the runup in divorce in the latter third of the 20th century reflects the divorce rate reverting to levels consistent with earlier trends, following unusually low divorce in the 1950s and early 1960s. Indeed, based on extrapolation, family scholars as early as the turn of the last century had predicted future divorce rates like those actually witnessed in the 1980s. While the 1970s overshot the trend, the subsequent fall in divorce has put the divorce rate back on the trend-line and by 2005 the annual divorce rate projected by the pre-1946 trend is quite close to actual divorce rates.

Also points to a remarkable and often overlooked fact: the divorce rate per thousand people actually peaked in 1981, and has been declining over the ensuing quarter century. The divorce rate in 2005—3.6 divorces per thousand people—is at its lowest level since 1970. The number of people entering marriage, as a proportion of the population, in the U.S. has also been falling for the past 25 years, and the marriage rate is currently at its lowest point in recorded history. Marriage rates rose as the divorce rate rose, but reached an earlier peak in 1972. Yet even when measuring the number of divorces relative to the "at-risk population" (that is, those who are currently married), we see a similar decline in the divorce rate over the last 25 years falling from a peak of 22.8 divorces per 1,000 married couples in 1979 to 16.7 divorces in 2005. The sustained decline in divorce over the past quarter century provides an ideal testing ground for assessing the validity of alternative theories of why the divorce rate rose in the late 1960s and into the 1970s; unfortunately, such tests are mostly absent from the existing literature.

Impact of Divorce on Children

There exists substantial controversy—and uncertainty—about the impact of divorce on children. While children from divorced households fare worse along a range of outcomes than those from intact households, this observation does not speak to the policy-relevant question of whether those children would have been better off if their parents had not divorced. The conflict in these households may be such that children are actually better served by their parents divorcing. Thus, comparisons of the "happily married" with the "unhappily divorced" are likely irrelevant for those choosing between an unhappy marriage and an unhappy divorce. Moreover, the difficulty in establishing a causal link between divorce decisions and children's outcomes is compounded by the possibility that the type of parents and households that end up divorced are likely different from those who do not. These differences may themselves lead to worse outcomes for children even if the parents were to remain married. Additionally, unobserved negative shocks to the family may both lead to divorce and negative outcomes for children, further confounding attempts at causal inference.

The shrinking gap between the ages of husbands and wives helps explain the fourth striking fact: those over 65 are now much more likely to be married than at any other time in the past. In fact, those over 65 are now as likely to be married as are those aged 16 to 65. The larger proportion of people married at older ages reflects greater life expectancy for both men and women and a decreasing gap in the difference between men's and women's life expectancy.

Additionally, some of this increase in the proportion of those over 65 who are married stems from an increase in the proportion marrying at older ages, with these later age marriages potentially being facilitated by a thicker remarriage market in recent decades that allowed greater remarriage following either divorce or the death of a spouse.

This changing age profile of marriage also points to the declining role of fertility and childrearing in married life. In 1880, 75% of married people lived in a household in which their own children were present. That proportion has fallen steadily over the past 125 years, and by 2005 only 41% of married people had their own children present in their household. This dramatic shift reflects the confluence of many factors, including declining fertility, increased longevity, increasing rates of marriage at later, post-childbearing ages, rising non-marital births, and rising divorce.

COHABITATION

So far we have discussed patterns in formal marriage. Yet the decision to form a household with another is increasingly becoming decoupled from the decision to marry. Indeed, in recent decades, cohabitation has emerged as an important institution, as both a precursor to, and sometimes a substitute to, marriage. This decoupling of domestic arrangements from the legal (and social) status of relationships raises important new questions for economic analysis of the family, as early models treated marriage and household formation almost identically. Yet these labels also have substantive economic content, determining the default allocation of property rights following separation, tax treatment of the couple, and eligibility for both social programs and employment-related family benefits. Growing social acceptance of non-marital relationships and the changing legal institutions surrounding marriage, leads one to ask: what distinguishes marital relationships from cohabiting relationships, and how has this distinction changed?

However empirical analysis related to these questions is beset by a simple difficulty: until recently, few available data collections contain information on non-marital cohabiting relationships.

The available data documenting the rise of cohabitation suggests that levels of cohabitation were low prior to 1970 and that they have grown at a roughly constant rate since then, with perhaps faster growth in the past decade. This assessment comes from three sources. First, in 1995 the Current Population Survey started allowing people to identify themselves as an "unmarried partner" of the householder (rather than just "partner/roommate"). These data suggest that cohabitation rates among adults have risen from 2.9 percent in March 1995 to 4.7 percent in March

2005. Second, a similar change was made for the Census, which recorded a 3.5 percent cohabitation rate among adults in 1990 and 5 percent in 2000, one-in-nine of whom were same-sex couples (with roughly equal numbers involving male and female same-sex couples). Finally, for earlier periods, Fitch et al. analyse Census data and calculate a proxy measure of cohabitation, the number of persons of the opposite sex sharing living quarters ("POSSLQ"), documenting that there was virtually no rise in cohabitation between 1880 and 1970, followed by roughly constant growth in the years hence.

The 2002 National Survey of Family Growth found that 50 percent of women aged 15 to 44 had cohabited at some point and 9 percent were currently cohabiting. In the United States, cohabitation has thus far largely been a stepping stone toward marriage, with most people who cohabit either ending their relationship or marrying within a few years. Among those currently cohabiting, the vast majority expect their cohabitation to lead to marriage. Indeed, 34 percent enter cohabitation having announced a plan to marry. Even among the remaining two-thirds who enter cohabitation without being engaged, 36 percent were "almost certain" that they would marry their current partner, and another 46 percent thought that there was either "a pretty good chance" or "a 50-50 chance" of marrying their partner. Contrary to stereotypes, men and women express similar expectations about their likelihood of marrying their cohabiting partners. Such beliefs regarding their future likelihood of marriage, however, are not always warranted. Among those couples who were cohabiting in January 1997, slightly more than half were no longer together 5 years later, and only a quarter had married.

While most cohabitation do not end in marriage, most marriages are preceded by cohabitation. Among those entering first marriages in the early 2000s, 59 percent had cohabited with their future spouse prior to marriage. Premarital cohabitation with one's future spouse is even more common among those who have previously divorced, with 75 percent of those remarrying in the early 2000s preceding their wedding with a period of cohabitation. (Moreover, this differential is robust to controlling for the higher age of most remarriages.) This trend to premarital household formation may also explain some of the rise in measured age at first marriage. Cohabiting couples represent a bit more than half of all first marriages, and these couples typically entered into domesticity about two years prior to marriage, thus high recent rates of premarital cohabitation may explain up to a year of the rise in mean age at first marriage.

While it might seem that cohabiting before marriage should reduce uncertainty about the quality of a couple's match, U.S. couples who cohabit before marriage have been historically more likely to divorce than those who do not. This pattern may reflect differential selection into cohabitation, as those who live together prior to marriage may be doing so because they are less certain of the quality of their match, or because they stand to gain less from marriage. In other words, those who choose to cohabit may have been more likely to divorce even if they had not lived together first. Cohabitation may also be responsible for some of the reduction in divorce rates witnessed over the past 25 years as separations that previously occurred while legally married may now occur during premarital cohabitation. The difficulty in making any of these attributions convincingly lies in constructing a counterfactual: Would the cohabitating couple still have separated if they had married earlier?

Cohabitation is clearly evolving, and some couples are currently entering cohabitation as a permanent or semipermanent state. Among those cohabiting in 2002, a little over one-fifth had been doing so for five years or more, indicating that some couples are treating cohabitation as a more permanent state. While for some the decision to cohabit may reflect a lower commitment to one's partnership, for others this choice may reflect a lower value of the institutional structure of marriage rather than a lower commitment. For instance, an increasing number of dual-career couples, combined with high marginal tax rates on secondary earners may face a "marriage penalty", while increasing social acceptance of cohabitation may have diminished social stigma. Additionally, the incremental value of formal marriage in enforcing intertemporal commitments is smaller when divorce laws allow one partner to unilaterally dissolve the relationship. Similarly, prenuptial contracts have reduced the role of family law as an important default for allocating property at divorce.

International Comparisons

Family life varies widely across industrialized nations. Americans marry, divorce, and remarry at rates higher than in most other countries with comparable income levels. This greater "churning" in marriage is reminiscent of the cross country labour market literature, in which the United States is known for its greater labour market entry and exit.

Marriage appears to be more central and cherished in the United States than in many other countries. Italy is similar to the U.S. in many respects—both countries have low cohabitation rates and few consider marriage to be an outdated institution, although the United States is by far the greatest outlier in the low proportion agreeing with that sentiment. Yet a major difference arises when examining divorce rates. In Italy divorce rates are extremely low and those who divorce in Italy remain divorced (which accounts for why the proportion of the population "currently divorced" remains at levels similar to the United States). While Americans reveal their willingness to exit bad marriages in their high rates of divorce, only 43 percent agree that "divorce is usually the best solution when a couple can't seem to work out their marriage options," compared with an overwhelming majority in every other country including Italy.

Sweden provides a particularly stark counterpoint to the United States and Italy, and is an interesting example of the "Nordic model" of the family. Swedish marriage rates are low and cohabitation rates are high. Yet fertility—and particularly non-marital fertility—remains quite high, consistent with an emerging social norm in Sweden that childbirth and formal marriage need not be linked. Other high-income countries may be moving toward the Nordic model, albeit slowly. For instance, France, Canada, and the United Kingdom have cohabitation rates similar to Sweden and high rates of out-of-wedlock childbirth.

Another point in which the United States seems exceptional is the relatively young age at which women are giving birth. The age at which women have children has been rising in all the countries, and in 2002, the average age at child birth was over 30 in Italy and Sweden, and 29 or higher everywhere, save the United States where the average age was 27.

Earlier, we documented the declining importance of children to married life—at least for the United States, where today only a minority of married households include own children. This may be even more evident in other industrialized nations, where the trend toward out-of-wedlock childbirth is also paired with a greater proportion of women marrying at older (post-fertility) ages. For instance, in the U.S., Canada, the U.K., France, and Sweden, between a quarter and a third of marriages involved women at least 35 years old. In Italy the proportion was only 15%, partially reflecting the country's very low rate of remarriage. Moreover, aggregate fertility— whether married or not—is currently quite low in many European nations, a fact that beyond portending changes in the family, points to a looming "demographic crisis" in many countries.

Driving Forces of Family Change

The economic approach to the family seeks to explain how and why families form, and in so doing, this approach highlights the potential forces that change family formation. Couples marry, and stay married, when the gains from marriage exceed the gains from being single. These gains come from production complementarities (such as household specialization and the raising of one's children), the benefits of risk pooling, and from consumption complementarities (such as from the joint consumption of public goods and from shared leisure activities). Thus, reduced market discrimination against women and technological advances that allow much of what was once produced by skilled-labour in the home to be purchased or produced with little skill reduce the benefits from specialization of spouses in the home and market spheres, thereby decreasing the gains from marriage. Simultaneously, increasing leisure time and wealth along with the changing landscape defining sexual relations potentially raises the gains from consumption complementarities. These changes in tastes, technology, and the institutional or legal environment have altered gains from marriage.

Technology of Birth Control

The Economist cited the birth control pill as the invention that "defined the 20th century." In 1960, the first birth control pill was approved by the FDA and diffused rapidly to married woman; by 1965, 41 percent of married women under 30 who used contraceptives were on "the pill". However, laws limiting the distribution to unmarried women slowed broader diffusion of the pill until the early 1970s, when such laws were finally overturned by the Supreme Court in *Eisenstadt v. Baird.* This ruling quickly facilitated distribution of the pill to unmarried women and by 1976, three-quarters of ever contracepting single 18 and 19 year olds had used the pill.

The birth control pill was an important innovation in two respects: it was far more effective than other forms of birth control and, unlike other forms of contraception, the pill allowed contraceptive decisions to be made privately by a woman, rather than jointly with her partner. In the early 1970s, women also gained greater access to abortion through the legalization of abortion by five states in 1970 and nationwide through the Supreme Court's decision in *Roe v. Wade* three years later. Both the birth control pill and abortion decreased the probability of an unwanted pregnancy. This improved control over fertility changed the timing of marriage and births, and also facilitated the increase in women's accumulation of human capital by reducing the risk of disruption to women's education or labour market plans.

The pill also reduced the cost of waiting to marry, by allowing sex outside of marriage with little fear of an unwanted pregnancy. The lower cost of delaying marriage led to longer courtships, and courtship was also more informative (due to greater sexual contact). Thus, those entering marriage did so with less uncertainty about their compatibility, thereby reducing the number of bad matches. One effect of this change was to lower the probability of divorce; another effect was to encourage others to wait longer to marry, as fears receded that those left unmarried by their mid-twenties would confront an adversely-selected set of potential spouses. Examining college-educated women, Goldin and Katz demonstrate that differential access to the pill across states and cohorts robustly predicts subsequently higher age at first marriage, lower divorce, and lower marriage rates. They also demonstrate qualitatively similar, albeit smaller, effects from the legalization of abortion.

While greater access to birth control and abortion did reduce unplanned pregnancies, out-of-wedlock births increased following these technological innovations. Akerlof, Yellen, and Katz address this puzzle by arguing that women's new found control over pregnancy increased pressure on them to engage in premarital sexual relations and reduced their ability to extract a commitment to marry in the event of a pregnancy. Thus, those who did not adopt the pill, or who suffered contraceptive failure, gained the option of choosing between abortion instead of pregnancy, but if choosing pregnancy, typically lost the offer of a subsequent "shotgun marriage."

Akerlof, Yellen, and Katz document a decline between the late 1960s and late 1980s in the percentage of parents marrying when faced with an out-of-wedlock pregnancy and argue that—at least in an accounting sense—this failure to marry subsequent to pregnancy explains much of the growth in out-of-wedlock births seen over this period.

While birth control has made sex safer in terms of an unwanted pregnancy, the emergence of AIDS has made sex riskier. Specifically, AIDS changes the benefit of sex within a monogamous relationship relative to that from casual sexual encounters, which may involve greater health risks, or costs of prevention through safe sex practices.

Differences in infection and transmission rates across subgroups also changes the costs of some pairings, and Francis provides intriguing evidence that greater knowledge of the risk of AIDS reduces the probability of men choosing same-sex partners, while increasing prevalence of same-sex partnerships among women.

Household Technology

The spread of indoor plumbing and electricity in the first half of the twentieth century, along with the myriad of household appliances that diffused throughout the last century (particularly in the 1950s and 1960s), led to vast increases in the productivity of housework. Homemakers suddenly had freezers, washing machines, dryers, steam iron, and a lucky few, dishwashers, at their disposal. Greenwood, Seshadri, and Yorukoglu document this rise in household appliances over the last century and cite evidence that the time required to clean a load of laundry fell from four hours using manual methods to only 41 minutes when aided by a 1940s era electric washing machine and dryer. These breakthroughs in the invention of household appliances heralded a new age of freedom for housewives, freeing them of the drudgery of household production and turning them into "household managers" of an electric army.

Electricity and household appliances are "labour-saving" in that one can now produce the same bundle of home-produced goods in less time. While substitution effects may lead to some increased consumption of home-produced goods, income effects from these timesaving advances may also be important, increasing the household's consumption of both home- and market-produced goods. Greenwood, Seshadri, and Yorukoglu suggest that the timesaving effects of these new technologies dominated, leading women to spend less time working in the home and more time in the market, thereby increasing female labour force participation.

Moreover, this technical change is unlikely to have been skill-neutral. Even basic tasks like laundry take much less skill with a modern washer and dryer. (Anyone who has tried to do laundry on a scrub board or rock knows that it is quite difficult!) In turn, this lower skill requirement has reduced the returns to specialization in home production. Indeed, this skill-substituting technical change parallels the decline in the field of home economics, the historically female-dominated subject devoted to developing skills such as sewing and cooking.

Additionally, a growing service sector and increasing commoditisation have created ready market substitutes for products that were previously the exclusive domain of home producers. Perhaps most significantly, technological improvements in the mass production of food led to the increased availability of factory-prepared food. Cutler, Glaeser, and Shapiro credit these innovations with the 50 percent reduction in food preparation and cleanup times for both working and non-working women between 1965 and 1990.

These changes in household technology have implications for family formation. If the returns to specialization *within* a household fall, then the opportunity cost of remaining single rather than marrying falls. Moreover, in a time when men were specialized in market production, and household production required specialized labour inputs, it was not surprising that women with specialized market skills had less to gain from marriage, and were therefore less likely to marry. It is only as women have entered the labour market *en masse* that the education gap in marriage rates among women has closed.

Consider a further implication of these changes. Greenwood and Vandenbroucke credit technological progress with reducing the workweek from 70 hours in 1830 to 41 hours in 2002, and Aguiar and Hurst document a rise in leisure over the past 40 years that corresponds roughly to an additional 5-10 weeks of vacation per year. As the mix of household activities has shifted, optimal matching in the marriage market has likely changed. Thus, one might expect these changes to have made leisure and consumption complementarities more important drivers of matching than the production complementarities emphasized by Becker.

For instance, while Becker had predicted that those with high wage rates will tend to marry those with lower wage rates ("negative assortative mating") because the benefits from the division of labour within a household can make the earning abilities of the man and the woman substitutes, this argument loses force in two-career couples. Thus, as marriage comes to be built more around consumption complementarities we might expect it to increasingly involve the pairing of those with similar income and interests.

An alternative complementarity arises from thinking about households as insurance units. While the increase in female labour force participation has reduced specialization in the home, it may have increased the benefit from household risk-sharing. As such, we may see a different form of negative assortative matching, as people seek spouses whose labour income risk is negatively correlated with their own.

Changes in Wage Structures

A large literature in labour economics has documented increasing wage inequality since the 1970s. These changes reflect several factors, including: skill-biased technical change, a declining real value of the minimum wage, and the deunionisation of the American workforce. Gould and Paserman argue that this change directly impacts marriage markets, raising the importance of "searching for Mr. Right." That is, rising wage inequality has increased the returns to further search and thus increased the option value of remaining unmarried. Gould and Paserman test this effect of inequality on marriages rates by examining the consequences of differences across cities in the rates at which inequality grew through the 1970s and 1980s. They find that in cities in which wage inequality rose fastest, the proportion of young women who were married fell quite dramatically. Indeed, their estimates suggest that this rising wage inequality may account for up to one-third of the decline in the marriage rate of 21 to 30 year old women.

Another important change in the wage structure derives from the decline in the gender wage gap. Blau and Kahn describe these changes as emanating from a decline in explicitly sexist personnel policies (partly driven by the increasing reach of anti-discrimination law), increased labour market experience among women (and increased returns to this experience), declining occupational segregation, and de-unionization. In the face of these trends, the comparative advantage of wives in home rather than market production has declined, driving an increasing share of men into home production, or reducing the value of specialization within marriage.

Beyond possibly reducing the attractiveness of marriage, the reduction in the wage gap may have other, subtle effects. For instance, Becker, Landes, and Michael explain the historically younger age at which women marry by noting that the specialized investments made by women in home economics were much less useful to singles. Indeed, as women have come to invest more in market skills, so too the age at which they choose to marry has drawn closer to parity with men. Caucutt, Guner, and Knowles argue that rising returns to labour market experience may also have important dynamic effects, raising the incentive for highly educated women to delay the timing of fertility in favour of developing stronger prospects in both labour and marriage markets.

The difficulty in empirically assessing the effects of changes in labour markets on family outcomes is that a strong reverse channel likely confounds any easy inference. For instance, women who forecast later or more fragile marriages may choose to invest more in their careers, leading to better labour force outcomes for women. As one example of such a dynamic, Johnson and Skinner find that women who anticipate a future divorce are more likely to participate in the labour market. Similarly, Stevenson finds that unilateral divorce laws led to an increase in labour force participation for both married and unmarried women.

Changes in the Legal Structure of Marriage

Governments set the parameters which define the family as a legal institution. These parameters define who is to be granted marriages, divorces, and parental rights, and articulate subsequent obligations. The law also provides a set of default property rights in case of separation or death, and defines families for the purposes of taxation and government programs.

In the U.S., the 1960s ushered in a wave of large-scale deregulation of the family. Consequently, the role that the government plays in deciding both who can marry and divorce has steadily diminished. In the 1950s some state legislatures began to repeal laws restricting marriage between racial groups. These anti-miscegenation laws were eliminated nationwide in 1967 by the Supreme Court ruling in *Loving v. Virginia*. Which argued that marriage was "one of the 'basic civil rights of man'" (in this issue, Fryer discusses patterns of interracial marriage over time). This ruling set the stage for further deregulation of marriage, including providing a legal challenge to state marriage bars for those deemed "unsuitable", such as felons, the disabled, those with a low IQ, and "deadbeat dads".

Supreme Court rulings in the 1960s and 1970s also changed the nature of family relationships by eliminating many of the legal distinctions stemming from the marital status of a child's parents. In 1968 the Supreme Court ruling in *Levy v. Louisiana* (391 U.S. 68) granted equal protection under the Fourteenth Amendment to illegitimate children. Five years later, the 1973 ruling in *Gomez v. Perez* overturned state laws exempting men from financial responsibility for illegitimate children. These rulings reduced both the social and economic cost of bearing a child out-of-wedlock, and thus may help to explain the decline in shotgun marriages. This remains an under researched topic in need of further scrutiny.

During this period, states also began to consider reducing their role in divorce proceedings. In the 1950s, most states required evidence of marital fault before allowing a marriage to be dissolved. Beginning in the late 1960s, many states introduced "irreconcilable differences" as grounds for divorce; effectively ushering in a period of unilateral divorce—divorce upon the request of either spouse, regardless of the wishes of his or her partner. In addition to the passage of unilateral divorce laws during this period, many states removed fault as a consideration in property division and some states changed laws governing property division subsequent to divorce. Currently all but five states have some form of unilateral divorce and two-thirds allow unrestricted unilateral divorce.

These legal changes fundamentally alter the basis of the marriage contract. They remove the ability to make intertemporal contracts within marriage—one spouse cannot promise not to leave his or her spouse in the future. They shift the right to divorce (and hence bargaining power) from the party most interested in preserving the marriage to the person who most wants out of the marriage. While the old laws had allowed divorce only if there was sufficient evidence of fault, many divorces involved couples where there was mutual consent to divorce. These couples used private bargaining to determine uncontested (and often manufactured) claims of fault to present to the courts. Thus, the fault-based system essentially allowed mutual consent divorce, but not unilateral divorce.

Becker, Landes, and Michael argued that the divorce rate would be unaffected by a shift from consent to unilateral divorce laws. They argued that this shift simply represents the reallocation of an existing property right from one spouse to the other—namely the right of oneself or one's spouse to remarry. Invoking the Coase theorem, they suggested that "the allocation of property rights or legal liability does not influence resource allocation when the parties involved can bargain with each other at little cost." Yet the assumptions required for Coasian bargaining, including symmetric information, transferable utility, and the absence of important transaction costs, may be unrealistic for the marginal divorce.

Many empirical papers have investigated whether unilateral divorce laws have led to a rise in the divorce rate with several reaching conflicting findings. Most recently, Wolfers tests these competing views by analysing divorce rates and divorce laws across U.S. states from 1956-1998. He finds that divorce rates rose sharply in the two years following the adoption of unilateral divorce laws, as the courts catered to pent-up demand for divorce. Subsequently, the divorce rate reverted back toward earlier levels, and a decade after these reforms there is no discernable effect on the divorce rate. Despite apparent conflict in this literature, it is worth emphasizing the point of substantial agreement: each of these authors finds that liberalised divorce laws had at most a small effect on divorce rates, and these reforms explain very little of the rise in divorce over the past half century.

While Coasian bargaining predicts little change in divorce rates, it does predict changes in intra-household distribution, as these changes affect each spouse's options outside marriage, and hence their bargaining position. Stevenson and Wolfers find that female suicide and domestic violence fell in states that adopted unilateral divorce laws. They interpret these findings as suggesting that unilateral divorce laws shift bargaining power to women.

These laws may also affect both the likelihood of marriage and intertemporal decision making within marriage. Rasul finds that the reduced gains from marriage under unilateral divorce led to a decrease in marriage rates. Research by Stevenson focuses on the difficulty in intertemporally contracting when marriages can be unilaterally dissolved. Analysing a sample of newlyweds (so as to minimize selection due to changes in divorce), she finds that the adoption of unilateral divorce laws led to a decrease or delay in several forms of investment whose returns are at least partly marriage-specific, including having children, household specialization, and the financial support of a spouse's education.

Shocks to Marriage Market Matching Function

A key insight of "search" models of the labour market is that the ease with which workers can locate relevant job openings determines equilibrium employment, unemployment duration, and bargained wages. So too, in the marriage market, the ease with which potential partners can meet and decide whether to date affects if, when, and to whom marriage occurs. Moreover, changes in the marriage market "matching function" have effects beyond the dating phase, as an important factor shaping behaviour within marriage is the threat that a spouse may file for divorce—a threat whose impact is shaped by an assessment of one's likely chances on the remarriage market.

McKinnish provides intriguing evidence of a shock to matching: increasingly sexually-integrated workplaces now create greater opportunities for men and women to meet. Analysing data from the 1990 census, she shows that working in an industry or occupation comprised of a greater share of members of the opposite sex is more likely to lead a marriage to end in divorce, a phenomenon she labels "another form of on-the-job search." While she does not analyse effects on marriage, these effects could plausibly go in either direction: the increased likelihood (and speed) with which one meets an acceptable spouse could increase marriage, while greater current, and future, exposure to potential mates raises the option value of remaining single. A related shock to future marital patterns—and surely a useful focus for future research—comes from sharply changing gender ratios on college campuses: women were a distinct minority of undergraduates in 1960, they are now a clear majority.

The potential of the Internet to increase the efficiency of matching provides another important shock. Indeed, it inspired a bold claim in *Wired*: "Twenty years from now, the idea that someone looking for love without looking for it online will be silly, akin to skipping the card catalogue to instead wander the stacks because 'the right books are found only by accident'... serendipity is the hallmark of inefficient markets, and the marketplace of love, like it or not, is becoming more efficient." Data from Forrester Research suggests that in 2004, 16 percent of singles are using online personals, and a September 2005 Internet Tracking Poll suggests that 3 percent of internet users who are currently coupled first met online. Online search differs from offline search in two important ways: it expands the set of potential partners and it affords a degree of anonymity. Each of these characteristics shapes the contours of online dating. For instance, Forrester data suggest that over one-third of those using online personals are currently married.

The Internet's potential to change matching is perhaps greatest for those facing thin markets or difficulty in meeting potential mates. Indeed, the Forrester data reveals that those who perceive themselves as facing such markets are more likely to use online personals: blacks and Asians are three times as likely as whites, those with physical disabilities are twice as likely as those without, and gays are four times as likely as straights. Not surprisingly then, several large dating sites exist to serve these niche matching markets, including various ethnic groups, gays, lesbians, the elderly, farmers, persons living with specific disabilities, and those who are HIV-positive.

The larger mainstream dating sites also allow for narrowly-tailored searches, reversing the typical temporal pattern of courtship from assessing attraction before suitability, to one in which couples can ensure that they are appropriately matched on information about religion, fertility and marriage aspirations, income or other important factors, before ever meeting. While this may hark back to the days of parents selecting suitable mates for their children, these matches may be importantly different in the characteristics desired for matching than those selected by parents or other matchmakers. The targeted search offered by the Internet might lead one to forecast greater endogamy (within-group matching). Hitsch, Hortaçsu, and Ariely examine the characteristics of couples whose dates were arranged through an online dating service, and find, however, that the correlations of characteristics such as age, height, weight, beauty, income, and education were qualitatively similar to those observed among married couples. Yet even within these groups, Internet search allows for the selection of mates with similar consumption and leisure preferences.

While the Internet may yet transform marriage markets, it is too early to assess whether those matched on the Internet are better matched than they would have been without the Internet, whether marriage rates will subsequently rise, and what impact this will have on divorce. The tremendous amount of search being done online by those already married is potentially a harbinger of rising divorce rates, yet this affect may be ameliorated by improved match quality in new marriages.

Finally, search and matching can have an important role in amplifying shocks to the marriage market. For instance, Chiappori and Weiss note that if the divorce rate rises, then—assuming undirected search—one might meet more divorcees in the course of a day. Thus, were one to divorce, the probability of remarrying is higher, making divorce a more attractive option; this thick market externality creates a self-reinforcing rise in divorce.

Interpreting the Evidence

Our analysis of the family has pointed to trends in family life and possible driving forces, but we have provided little interpretation of the welfare implications of these trends. Without some discussion of welfare, drawing conclusions about desirable family policies is impossible. A common argument for a policy response to recent trends notes that, on average, divorced people are worse off—and married people better off—financially, physically, and emotionally. These associations often lead to the recommendation that policymakers should focus on reducing the rate of marital dissolution, or on promoting marriage. Yet, there is little hard evidence that these policies would be welfare-enhancing. Instead, these policy prescriptions are founded on an assumption that divorce *causes* people to be worse off, rather than that people who are worse off face a greater risk of divorce. Furthermore, it is important to differentiate between the average marriage—which is likely a happy one—and the marginal marriage that may be created or spared by government policy, which may be quite different.

Indeed, the economic theory of the family points precisely in this direction. Becker, Landes, and Michael argue that "the majority of divorces results from uncertainty and unfavourable outcomes." Thus, we would expect to see those who suffer adverse shocks to be more likely to both divorce and remain unmarried following a divorce, thereby contributing disproportionately to the stock of the currently divorced. Empirical research has found evidence for such a pattern: Charles and Stephens find that the divorce hazard rises following a spouse's layoff and they suggest that this increased probability of divorce stems from the information conveyed about the person's suitability as a spouse, rather than stemming directly from financial losses. The theory of the family also suggests that marriage is most likely to occur when the potential gains from marriage are large. Individuals with high earning potential have more to gain from domestic arrangements that allow them to specialize in market production; those with a "love of fun" have more to gain from shared leisure and consumption; and those with good health have more to gain due to the greater potential longevity of their marriage. Thus, we should expect that the wealthy, healthy, and happy are more likely to marry.

Ultimately, purely observational studies cannot convincingly establish whether people are better or worse off as a result of marriage or divorce. The problem is that a number of factors linking wellbeing and marital status are unobservable to the researcher. One response is to seek natural experiments that may lead to a sort of random variation across marital status. A small number of quite promising studies have taken this tack and found quite surprising results. For instance, an earlier literature had shown that the economic status of divorced women was lower than that for married women, a fact that had led to concern that divorce impoverishes women. Bedard and Deschênes exploit the fact that divorce is more likely to follow if the first child born is a girl than a boy to assess the effects of those "random" divorces caused by child gender. They find that divorced women have *higher* household income and annual earnings than never-divorced women, a fact that is attributable to divorced women working more intensively and the potential for divorced women to join higher income households (such as their parents').

6

Economic Inequality in Family

Throughout history, male/female has defined an enduring binary embodied in access to jobs, income, and wealth. Women's economic history shows how for centuries sex has inscribed a durable inequality into the structure of American labour markets that civil and political rights have moderated but not removed. This economic experience of women reflects the paradox of inequality in America: the coexistence of structural inequality with individual and group mobility. Women, like African Americans, have gained what T.H. Marshall labelled civil and political citizenship. No longer are they legally disenfranchised, and discrimination on account of race and gender is against the law. They have also increased their social citizenship, as represented by access to jobs and education, and women, in particular, benefit from many programs of the welfare state. Yet, they remain unequal. On the whole, they earn less than men, end up in occupational ghettos, bump up against glass ceilings, and find themselves, in relation to men, as poor as ever.

The process of internal differentiation characteristic of the history of groups defined by sex, race, or ethnicity provides the key to understanding how the paradox of inequality works. As a group, women, like blacks, experienced mobility that disrupted the processes which had systematically excluded them from access to jobs and income. But their assaults on durable categorical inequalities had their limits. Men/whites redrew category boundaries, retaining their hold on economic advantage while women/ blacks assimilated into and reproduced existing economic and occupational hierarchies among themselves. In the United States, group mobility did not challenge structural inequality—instead, it rein-forced it. This process of differentiation—the key to the paradox of inequality— is very important to understand. It is one of the primary ways that inequality works in America, and it poses serious issues and dilemmas for public policy.

Many kinds of inequality—in domestic, social, and political spheres—have shaped women's experiences. Crucial as these are, they are not, with a few exceptions, which concentrates on labour market inequality and women's market work. Market work is crucial because exclusion from the market has been the first source of women's economic inequality. Occupation, after all, has been the principal gateway to income. Because only a tiny percentage of people have had investments or other sources of capital with which to support themselves, most people without market work have been dependent on family and friends or on charity or the state.

Even within the universe of market work, inequality is an idea with multiple dimensions. Its relations with sex, or for that matter, with race, ethnicity, or age, require examination from different vantage points—a point not appreciated or observed in most analyses of inequality. Here, then, we add a note to the methodological or conceptual study of inequality as well as to its substance. That is, we proceed by analysing the relations among sex and inequality through four lenses: (1) *participation*—the share of women who worked; (2) *distribution*— the kind of jobs women held; (3) *rewards*—the relative income they received; and

(4) *differentiation*—the distance among women on scales of occupation and earnings.

Participation

The first question is, how many women worked? As simple as it sounds, the question is fraught with ambiguity and controversy. There is, first, the problem of defining "work" for women. Limiting work to employment for pay in the labour market excludes many of women's historic economic activities, such as labour on family farms, taking in boarders and lodgers, or domestic manufacture. It is clear that the addition of domestic work alters trends in women's labour force participation derived only from the census's occupational statistics. With keeping boarders considered as work, married women's labour force participation did not change very much between the beginning of the twentieth century and World War II. But measured by occupation alone, it nearly tripled. There is no right answer to the question these numbers pose: what is the correct way to calculate the labour force rates for women? Rather, the answer depends on the purpose.

Participation in market work is not an unambiguous measure. Wo-men may have entered the wage labour market not because they wanted to but be-cause they had to—only through wage-labour could the wives or widows of many workers assure their families adequate food, shelter, and clothing. Whether women have worked on account of necessity or choice, they have found themselves excluded from the labour market, either entirely or from its best opportunities. Throughout the twentieth century, the history of women's relation to market work has been characterized by their segregation into a small fraction of jobs and by the prohibition of most married women from any labour force participation at all. Women have attempted to reconstitute labour markets along less gendered lines by attempting to break through these exclusionary practices and dismantle barriers, and their assault on labour market inequalities composes a major strand in their modern history. From whichever perspective one views women's relation to the wage-labour market, however, the theme remains inequality— whether the inequality of women forced by necessity into low-wage, dead-end jobs or excluded from participation in the labour market and access to its best rewards.

The increased participation of married women in market work constitutes the most important and dramatic development in the history of women's employment in the twentieth century. In 1900, about 6 percent of married women were in the paid labour force; by 1990, the figure had multiplied nearly 10 times to 59 percent, where it remained in 2000. The first great burst of women into market work happened in the two decades after 1940. In those years a great barrier to married women's market work—the prohibition against employing married women in many white-collar industries and in teaching— began to crumble in the face of labour shortages and the demands of educated women. Nonetheless, in 1960 paid work was still a minority experience for married women—3 of 10 were in the workforce. By 1980, the proportion had nearly reached a majority; by 1990 it was the norm. Single women, of course, always were in the workforce more often than those who had married, but the difference between single and married women narrowed over the century.

The intersection of history and experience becomes even more vivid with women's labour force participation considered by age cohorts. Only a relatively small fraction of married women born before the start of the 20th century—in terms of the data here the pre-World War I cohorts—participated in market work at any age. Among women born in 1915 and 1925—mothers of the baby boom—the situation had changed markedly. Many more of them worked, and their labour force participation increased until their late 40s or early 50s. At age 25, 20 percent of married women born in 1925 had entered market work—a fraction that swelled to 42 percent when they were 35 years old and 60 percent at age 45, when for the most part their children had left school. It was among these women born between the cusp of World War I and the middle of the Great Depression—women with more formal education than any previous cohorts— that the combination of marriage with market work *at some point* became an expected practice. Among married women born later in the century, market work started at younger ages, or, more accurately, did not end with marriage and childbirth. It was, in fact, nearly universal. Among the post World War II cohort, 38 percent of 25 year old married women born in 1945, 59 percent born in 1955, and 70 percent born in 1965 worked. These were the first cohorts of women to combine motherhood of young children with paid employment.

Education played a key part in the surge of married women into the work-force partly because of the increased number of jobs that demanded advanced education—health care, which, below the level of physician, women dominate, is one example—and partly because educated women sought work outside the home commensurate with their training and skills. Throughout the twentieth century, in fact, women in the labour force had stayed in school longer than men. More than half the working women born in the 1910s had at least a high school education (12 years of schooling), a fraction only reached by men born in later decades. These distinctions persisted: women workers born in the 1960s, for instance, had attended college more often than men. Clearly, the supply of educated women demanding employment had become a powerful force driving women's increased participation in market work. Demographic shifts also impelled women into the workforce. Later marriages, more divorces, and rising numbers of single-parents gave women new reasons to sup-port themselves both before and during marriage. Important, too, was consumption. Women of the baby boom cohorts, raised in the prosperous 1960s and early 1970s, expected a rising standard of living. But with male wages stagnating, few men could provide it, and women's earnings became the only road to increased family prosperity—indeed, in many cases the only road to family economic survival.

As a result, the American labour force looked very different at the beginning, middle, and end of the century. In 1940, only about one-quarter of the labour force consisted of women. By 2000, the proportion had reached 46 percent. In 1940, 48 percent of the female labour force consisted of women who had never been married; in 2000, that fraction had dropped to about one-quarter.

Generalizations about labour force participation rates gloss over the differences among women divided by race, ethnicity, and geography. Here, however, one of them cannot be entirely put aside: the different experiences of black and white married women. Married black women, as is well known, always engaged in market work more than married white women. But, in the course of the twentieth century, the differences among cohorts of white and black married women narrowed sharply as married white women entered the labour force. Among women born in 1895, 25 year old married black women were about 5 times more likely than their white counterparts to work. Among those born in 1935, the difference had dropped to 13 percent and for those born in 1975 it was 7 percent.

In one way, however, the labour market participation of white and black women went in opposite directions. This was the experience of women-on-their-own (women with an absent spouse, formerly married women, or those who had never married). In 1950 and 1960, young white women-on-their-own began to work more than black women. In fact, the labour force participation of black women-on-their-own began to fall until 1970 when it turned upward. In 2000, though, it still remained below the rate for white women. Why did this happen? It did not result from the shift of black women out of agriculture. For it happened among women regardless of whether they lived on farms. Nor was it because the availability of welfare allowed some unmarried black mothers to withdraw from the labour force. Rather, job opportunities for black women declined when domestic labour nearly disappeared as a mass occupation.

At the same time, black women more often than white lacked *educational qualifications for jobs that required* advanced skills, and they may have met discrimination in hiring. The problem with the discrimination argument is that racism should have been a more powerful influence earlier in the century. However, when most of the jobs open to black women were in domestic service or agriculture, race worked in their favour: these were the jobs for which they were preferred. Conversely, limited education left a large number of them less ready for the clerical and, after 1980, managerial and professional jobs, into which women were moving with astonishing speed. Indeed, black working women born before the 1940s had received much less education than their white counterparts. The great majority of black women in the labour force born in the 1890s—82 percent—had spent 8 years or less in school compared to 50 percent of white working women. (After mid-century, educational attainment soared among both white and black women, with black women making spectacular gains that greatly reduced the difference between them and white women. But until late in the century, most adult black women had far less education than white women.) Instead of moving into newly opened clerical and managerial jobs, many black women found employment in contingent work, or in jobs with poor working conditions. As a consequence, they left jobs more often or were laid off more frequently than white women. Adding to their problems, a great many of the rising number of unmarried black mothers lacked child care and other supports necessary to hold a job. In fact, one researcher estimates that the proportion of unmarried mothers among African American women explains from 53 percent to 68 percent of the employment gap between black and white women.

Distribution

With exclusion from market work an index of inequality, the situation of women—notably married women—improved dramatically during the twentieth century. But all work is not equal. Thus, the question is, what kinds of jobs did women hold? Here the picture is mixed. One can view the glass as half empty or half full. Women's occupational history, in short, reflected the paradox of inequality—mobility coupled with persistent inequalities that resulted in differentiated experiences among women divided by race, ethnicity, and class.

Consider the major trends. First, work as a domestic servant—women's major occupation outside of agriculture early in the twentieth century—dwindled to insignificance by the end of the twentieth century. Indeed, in the late 19th and early 20th centuries, the rise of clerical work dominated the story of women's entrance into new kinds of work. It was for a very long time the only new female occupation that did not represent an extension of women's traditional work— taking care of children, tending the sick, or minding the home. The proportion of working women engaged in clerical work rose from 9 percent in 1910 to 35 percent in 1970 before falling back to 31 percent in 1990 and 30 percent in 2000 as women entered other forms of work.

The increased importance of clerical employment highlights two trends in white-collar office work: first was its feminisation. In 1910, 66 percent of clerical workers were men. By 1950, the proportion had dropped to 37 percent and in 2000, it was 24 percent. Three occupational categories—bookkeepers; stenographers, typists, and secretaries; and clerks—composed the bulk of most clerical jobs, and they feminised at different rates. In 1910, 38 percent of bookkeepers, 85 percent of stenographers and typists, and 18 percent of clerks were women. Women became a majority of bookkeepers between 1910 and 1920 and of clerks in the 1950s. By 2000, 96 percent of stenographers, 89 percent of bookkeepers, and 72 percent of clerks were women. One other branch of clerical work was feminised from the start: in 1910, 90 percent of telephone operators were women—a fraction that persisted throughout the century. In part, but only in part, the shift of women into clerical work responded to changes in occupational structure—the growing prominence of office work in the economy. But women's clerical employment grew at nearly twice the rate of clerical work itself. And it outstripped overall job growth among women. The important point is that the feminisation of the office represented a "real" shift in women's work, not simply a response to compositional changes in workforce demography or occupational structure.

Second, clerical work no longer served as the first step on the ladder into management. It became, instead, a largely permanent status identified not by decision-making but, rather, by the exercise of routinised skills. In the 1880s, technological change—the widespread adoption of the typewriter which had been patented in 1868—transformed clerical work. Other new technologies, however, soon followed: "The cash register was patented in 1879, dictating machines and stereotypes in the 1880s, the mimeograph machine in 1890, the Hollerith machine which was used to tabulate the 1890 census, a full-listing adding machine... in 1892, and the first front strike typewriter in 1895." In the 1910s, "a second great wave of office machine invention took place." A list of the machines commonly found in American offices in 1919 included 30 items, none of which had been available before the 1880s. Machines facilitated the standardization of tasks. "By the early years of the twentieth century clerical work, which had been described in 1871 as requiring 'knowledge of languages, skills in accounts, familiarity with even minute details of business, energy, promptitude, tact, delicacy of perception' had become, for the majority of office workers, routine and mechanical."

However, for many office workers clerical work prior to the introduction of machines also was dull and routine, and most of the men who worked as clerks spent the bulk of their time copying correspondence and other documents. The main skill they needed was good penmanship. In the long run, office machines may have routinised clerical work, but in their early years, the skills demanded by the typewriter and adding machines were new and challenging. Thus, women did not take over clerical work because it became less skilled. More to the point was the conjunction of rising demand—the sheer increase in the number of office jobs to be filled in the late nineteenth and early twentieth century—with the availability of young women who wanted work. Young women, increasingly high school graduates, wanted work commensurate with their educations. Clerical wages were good compared to other available jobs; unemployment was low; working conditions usually were clean and safe, and the status was relatively high. At the same time, young men educationally qualified for clerical jobs increasingly went on to college or sought jobs in management while employers, who could absorb only a fraction of male clerks into managerial positions, worried about what to do with them in the long run and looked for workers whose tenure on the job would be temporary. Young women, therefore, were ideal: they were cheap, available, and educated, and they understood that they would leave when they married. However, argues sociologist Samuel Cohn, they did not make equal inroads into the offices of all industries. Industries where the cost of labour was low compared to the cost of capital—where clerical workers composed a small proportion of the workforce—felt less pressure to feminise their office staffs than did industries where the cost of clerical work ate into profits.

Throughout the twentieth century, relatively few women worked in skilled manual crafts or as unskilled labourers. Semiskilled factory work as operatives was, however, increasingly important through mid-century. Self-employment also remained a minor theme in women's work experience. In 1920, 12 percent of working women were self-employed. After an increase in 1940 and 1950—probably the result of unusual conditions during the Great Depression and War—self-employment settled back to around 4 percent until the 1980s: it rose to 6 percent in 1990 and then increased to 7 percent by 2000. The stability in the fraction of self-employed women, however, masks changes in the kinds of work they performed. The first theme is differentiation: self-employed women entered a much broader array of occupations throughout the century. The second theme is the changing nature of work. In 1910, two-thirds of self-employed women were domestics of one sort or another. By mid-century, domestic proprietor-ship had nearly disappeared, its place taken by other forms of business—for the most part, small retail concerns (46 percent) and beauty parlours (10 percent). By the last decades of the century, women who supplied independent business services and temporary workers (defined as independent contractors) had risen to prominence among self-employed women. Owners of other businesses joined by independently-employed teachers of one sort or another also remained important components.

Unlike self-employment, jobs in management became much more common. Between 1970 and 1990, women finally made inroads into managerial positions. "The increasing representation of women among the ranks of managers," writes sociologist Jerry Jacobs, represents "the most dramatic shift in the sex composition of an occupation since clerical work became a female-dominated field in the late 19th century." Unlike the feminisation of clerical work, the movement of women into managerial and professional work was facilitated by the state: the Equal Pay Act of 1963, Title VII of the 1964 Civil Rights Act and the formation of the Equal Employment Opportunities Commission, and other measures mandating affirmative action. Equal Employment measures and Affirmative Action proved especially important in increasing the proportion of black women in public jobs.

The proportion of women working as managers multiplied roughly 3 times, from 3 percent to 9 percent across these decades. As a result, women began to close the gap with men. The share of managers who were men declined from 86 percent in 1950 to 61 percent in 2000. Between 1960 and 2000, the share of women among professionals (excluding teachers) increased as well—from 35 per cent to 51 percent. (Women always dominated teaching: throughout the century their fraction of teachers fluctuated between 72 and 84 percent.) Thus, the share of women who were either managers or professionals more than doubled from 12 percent in 1970 to 28 percent in 2000. Together with women in teaching, clerical, and sales jobs, they made up about 72 percent of the female labour force compared to about 40 per cent in 1920.

Among managers and professionals, however, jobs were not divided evenly by sex. Men still dominated the best work. After a study of jobs, authority, and earnings among managers, Reskin and Roos conclude:

> Women managers were concentrated near the bottom of chains of command; they tended to supervise workers of their own sex, consistent with conventions that women should not supervise men; they were substantially less likely than men to exercise decision-making authority; and their involvement in decision making was largely confined to offering input into decisions that men made.

Even with teachers excluded, stratification by sex among professionals remains strong. Since early in the century, women have dominated the human services professions (nurses, librarians, social workers, and so on). In 1910, they composed 81 percent and in 2000, 78 percent. At the same time, while their share of the most prestigious professions rose, they remained a minority, and they also remained a minority among scientific and technical professionals, increasing their share from 1 percent in 1910 to 20 percent in 2000. They did better, however, in some other categories, although, again, ones that offered less prestige, pay, and authority. Women remained close to parity with men among arts and entertainment professionals; they increased their representation in business service professions from 0 in 1910 to 58 percent in 2000 and among technicians from 27 percent in 1920 (the first year with data on the category available) to 57 percent in 2000.

Two other points about the distribution of women in jobs are important. First, sharp as these figures for occupational segregation are, they underestimate the concentration of women in various kinds of work. The reason is that they rest on broad occupational categories rather than on specific jobs. Broken down by jobs, occupational segregation appears even more intense. A study by Tomaskovic-Devey illustrates the point. Using a large sample from North Carolina, he found that "the average man in North Carolina is in an *occupation* that is nationally 27% female, but he holds a job that is only 8% female. The average woman is in an occupation 65% female, but a job that is 88% female." These figures have huge consequences, he shows, because of their impact on earnings. Two processes—the allocation of women to segregated jobs and the devaluation of jobs dominated by women—account for 75 percent of the gap between the earnings of men and women in his sample. The other point about this history of occupational segregation is more optimistic: the movement of women into new kinds of work represents real change, not just a response to structural shifts in the economy. Sociologist Suzanne M. Bianchi calculated indexes of occupational dissimilarity between men and women for 1970, 1980, and 1990 and decomposed changes into those accounted for by desegregation and by structural shifts. She found that 75 percent of the growing similarity in the work of women and men resulted from occupational desegregation and 25 percent from structural shifts.

Given the persistence of occupational segregation, it is not surprising that a number of major industries remained highly segregated by sex. Others under went striking change. Thus, mining, construction, logging, and work in steel mills and blast furnaces remained 80 percent to 90 percent male throughout the century as did employment in the railroad industry, trucking, taxi, water, and garbage industries and automobile repairing. Women, by contrast, remained at least 40 percent of conventionally female industries, mainly in apparel and textile manufacturing, personal and household service of one form of another, some varieties of retailing, education, and hospitals (as nurses). The largest list of industries, however, consists of the ones in which women gained a substantial presence during the century, increasing at least 20 percentage points as a share of the workforce.

These included some forms of manufacturing, many forms of retailing, commerce, the professions, leisure and recreation, and public administration: in short, all types of industries except those requiring heavy labour or a few, such as truck driving, where men by one means or another managed to retain a strong hold or where employers felt less compelled to replace them with women.

Women made especially large inroads into the world of commerce, a result reflected in the number of them in clerical and, after 1970, managerial occupations. In banking and credit, the fraction rose from 10 percent to 48 percent at mid-century to 69 percent in 2000; in insurance from 25 percent to 44 percent to 65 percent. There were similar spikes in security and brokerage services and in real estate, advertising, and accounting, auditing, and bookkeeping. These trends should be interpreted cautiously. To be sure, women held many more managerial jobs in these industries, but they also made up the foot soldiers—the secretaries and clerks who performed routinised work in the new white collar factories. In 2000, for instance, 63 percent of women in the banking and credit industries held clerical jobs.

What explains the inroads made by women into so many occupations after 1970? The answer, Reskin and Roos argue, lies in the intersection of changes in labour queues—the attractiveness of women as workers to employers—and job queues—the attractiveness of jobs to women. "The fundamental reason for women's disproportionate entry into new occupations," they stress, was "a short age of male workers." In some occupations, men were unavailable because the service sector had expanded so rapidly that demand had exceeded the supply of men with the right qualifications. At the same time, often a combination of automation and reduced pay had rendered many jobs unattractive to men who looked elsewhere for work. Thus, the movement of women into new forms of work did not take jobs away from men. Women entered occupations that were expanding—where the number of openings was increasing—and/or ones that "were no longer worth preserving as male territory."

In this situation, employers turned to women for a variety of reasons. Anti-discrimination legislation and law suits filed by women against employers coupled with government affirmative action regulation made discrimination costly. In some occupations, too, newly automated tasks seemed extensions of "women's work"—as in the introduction of keyboards that resembled typewriters or the emphasis on communications skills in dealing with clients. Women were sought, too, in occupations where the clients were, increasingly, other women. And, with the pressure of competition from deregulation at home and globalized industry abroad, many employers looked for ways to cut costs. Because they would work for less pay, women suddenly became much more attractive. Women responded readily to increased employer demand. Anticipating opportunities, confident of the impact of affirmative action and public opposition to discrimination, many enrolled in M.B.A. programs and other varieties of professional training hitherto dominated by men. As women entered new forms of work, their presence created a virtuous circle that led to the employment of still more women. Employers less often preferred men, the sex-typing of many forms of work eroded, women used their informal networks to get jobs for other women, and some men "fled... feminising jobs... "

Rewards

How should we assess women's occupational and industrial changes during the twentieth-century? On the one hand, these patterns point to continued occupational segregation and to women's disproportionately low representation in the better jobs. On the other hand, they show immense change.

In other words, they highlight the paradox of inequality. Women moved into a great array of occupations and industries. In large numbers, they did jobs almost never done by women before. They made special progress in the best categories of work—clerical early in the century, managerial at its close—and in attractive industries like real estate, advertising, and investment. One way to assess these changes is to follow the money. How, overall, did women's earnings compare to men's? Within occupations, did their pay approach parity with men's? Here, unfortunately, we can only provide data since 1940, the first year when the census asked for information on income. For the years since 1940, however, amid all the complex data, one finding stands out: the durability of women's inequality.

Between 1940 and 1980 the main story is the stability in women's earnings as a share of men's: among full-time nonagricultural workers, 58 percent in 1940 and 55 percent in 1980. Then, in the 1980s, women's earnings moved upward. Women's median earnings as a fraction of men's rose to 67 percent. However, black women's wages, which increased in the 1960s and 1970s, showed signs of reversal in the 1980s. Part of the reason was the cutback in publicly-funded jobs in which they had developed a relatively well-paying niche. The gap between the earnings of men and women did not result from their occupational distribution. That is, it did not reflect women clustering in low paying jobs. In fact, in all major categories of non-agricultural work women consistently earned less than men, even though in most occupations women improved their economic position. In the same years, the fraction of women in poverty dropped sharply. But women composed a larger fraction of the poverty population, and the ratio of their poverty to men's widened.

While women in managerial jobs did earn considerably more than women operatives, they still earned less than male managers—a point that highlights the limits of occupational titles for gauging economic progress. Job titles inflated to show progress toward ending sex discrimination often masked the real content of work, the relegation of women to less remunerative positions, and the glass ceilings against which they bumped. Women often did not earn as much as men in less desirable or prestigious jobs. Male clerical workers often earned more than female managers and male operatives more than female crafts workers while predominantly female occupations paid less to begin with.

Women's lower earnings did not result from less education. At every educational level, women earned less than men. In 1940, for instance, among individuals with 12 years of schooling, women earned 59 percent as much as men. In 1970, among workers with four or more years of college, women earned 58 percent of men's median income. In 2000, the ratio had improved, but, still, for women with four or more years of college was only 68 percent. However, for both men and women, returns to higher education increased sharply in the last half of the 20th century. Between 1940 and 2000, the ratio of high school graduates' to college graduates' median earnings decreased from 59 to 50 for women and 60 to 52 for men.

The relative earnings of younger women, however, have improved. By 2000, the ratio of women's earnings to men's had risen from 62 for women born 1946– 55 to 68 and 82 for the next two cohorts. If young women continue on this trajectory—if the gain toward income parity with men persists over time—the result will herald a revolution in one of the nation's most historically durable inequalities. That is one way to interpret these numbers. But there is another side to the story. Young men and women started with similar earnings, but men advanced further and faster. Take women born in 1956–65 as an example. In 1980, the ratio of their earning's to men's was 82; in 1990, it had declined to 75, and in 2000 to 68. For women born in 1966–75, the ratio went down from 92 in 1990 to 82 in 2000—still higher than for women of any other age, but lower than a decade earlier. Over time, men capitalized a relatively small initial advantage into a commanding lead.

DIFFERENTIATION

By 2000, women were arrayed in a much wider variety of jobs and industries than earlier in the century, and their earnings ranged from the top to the bottom of the income scale. Differentiation had emerged as a key theme in their economic history. As they improved their occupations and incomes, women stratified, replicating among themselves the nation's durable structure of inequality. Here, too, women's experience exemplified the paradox of inequality. For instance, in 1940, women with 4 or more years of higher education earned 33 percent more than those with only a high school education; by 2000, the difference had skyrocketed to 200 percent.

Women were much less concentrated in a small number of occupations at the close of the twentieth century than at its start. The number of occupational titles needed to account for about three-quarters of the female labour force rose from only 11 in 1910 to 18 in 2000. Together, the occupations that employed at least 1 percent of women workers accounted for 94 percent of all women workers in 1910, 87 percent in 1940 and 80 percent in 2000. The two largest female occupations in 1910—private household service and farm labourers—together accounted for nearly a third of women in the labour force. In 1940, the largest occupations, operative and private household worker together accounted for 28 percent; by 2000, clerical related white-collar work, the major category, contained 14 percent of women workers. Thus, as women moved into different kinds of work, they also entered a wider array of jobs.

By the end of the twentieth century, working women were arrayed more evenly along the income scale than ever before. Consider women who worked full time divided into earnings quintiles by gender for 1940 and 2000. The enduring disparity between men and women is, again, the first pattern to stand out. In each year women were found more often at the bottom, less often at the top. But in 2000, the disparities, sharp as they were, were much less than those a half century earlier. An index which measures the degree to which each of the sexes is under or over represented in an occupational quintile for a given year shows the same trend. Women's over-representation in the lowest quintiles declined while women's presence in the highest two quintiles increased. Differentiation, it is clear, characterized the economic as well as the occupational profile of twentieth century women.[50] Economic differentiation also emerges from statistics that measure income inequality.

BANKING

The contradictory trends in women's occupational and economic history— evidence of both progress and continued inequality—emerge clearly by looking at banking and credit, an industry that feminised during the twentieth-century. In 1910, 95 percent of its employees were men; in 2000, 69 percent were women. The share of women increased steadily after 1910, reaching a majority during the 1960s. Until 1990, most of the women in banking—80 percent to 90 percent—worked in clerical jobs. And, as banking feminised, most of the industry's clerical jobs went to women, jumping from 14 percent in 1910 to 43 percent in 1920—a reflection of the second wave of feminisation in clerical work. By 1950, women were nearly two-thirds and, in 1980, 85 percent. As women moved into clerical work, taking over the position of teller, men moved into management and professional positions. Men were 93 percent of managerial workers in 1920, 80 percent in 1970, and 61 percent in 1980.

Banking had been a traditional man's domain for two reasons: sex stereotypes about women's interests and mental capacities and the physical demands of the job:

> Men handled financial matters because it was assumed that women were not interested in such activities and furthermore women's minds were incapable of and unaccustomed to what was referred to as, 'doing figuring' and making financial transactions. Since [the] early medium of exchanges included heavy gold and silver commodities as well as currency, women were presumably unable to handle such heavy items. Moreover, large posting and accounting books used in banking were presumed difficult for women to lift.

Bank jobs opened to women in the twentieth-century when the increased volume of work required many more clerks to file paperwork and record transactions. Their numbers swelled briefly during World War I and then fell back again until World War II caused another labour shortage, which brought many more women into banks as tellers, bookkeepers, and minor officers—positions previously held by men. As bankers developed new services, expanded their customer base, and introduced "sophisticated accounting and financial policies," they needed to increase both the overall size of their staffs and the number with advanced training. For the latter, they turned increasingly to college-educated men who began their banking careers in managerial-training positions, rather than, as in earlier time, as clerks and tellers. Thus, "the teller's position diminished in prestige, responsibility, skill, and advancement opportunities. And in keeping with tradition, the teller's salary remained low." Few men applied for jobs as tellers, and, "by default rather than by design," women were hired in their place. "Teller" was now "redefined as a typical 'woman's job.' "

Nonetheless, after 1970, women made striking inroads into both management and professional and technical positions in banking and credit. Until the late 1960s, in fact, women generally were not allowed in banks' managerial training programs. In the 1970s, however, deregulation put more competitive pressure on the industry, and banks consolidated and opened many more branches. Branch managers, often, were women. During the 1970s, bank employment grew 50 percent while the number of bank managers jumped 86 percent. At the same time, the earnings and prestige of bank managers deteriorated, and young men began to look elsewhere for white-collar careers. Banks also hired more women because of the pressure of federal regulations and anti-discrimination laws and because women launched successful and highly publicized suits against them for employment discrimination. Although many women were hired or promoted into managerial positions, they were shunted primarily into the less prestigious, powerful, and remunerative managerial specialities, which included retail banking; men still filled most of the managerial jobs in commercial banking, the most attractive branch of the industry.

In 1970, women composed 21 per cent of bank managers. In a decade, this fraction had almost doubled to 39 per cent; in the next decade it rose again to 53 per cent. In 2000, it was 55 percent. In the same three decades, the share of women among professional and technical employees also increased dramatically, from 34 per cent to 52 per cent. By 2000, 33 per cent of women in banking, compared to 63 per cent of men, held managerial or professional positions. Women remained under-represented in the best work, but they had made genuine inroads into the better jobs. In this, their experience in banking and credit encapsulated the wider economic history of women, the paradox of inequality: an increase in participation, a shift upward in occupational distribution, and a differentiation that brought their social structure closer to the overall structure of inequality.

But occupational improvement did not erase disparities in earning. Within the major occupational categories in banking and credit, women continually earned less than men. Women in managerial and professional positions earned a lot more than clerical workers: in 2000; the median annual earnings (in 1990 dollars) for women managers were $25,869 compared to $13,536 for women in clerical jobs. Movement up the occupational ladder, therefore, brought substantial increases in pay for women and boosted the number of women in banking and credit earning higher salaries. But in 2000, male managers' median annual earnings were $39,856—much higher than women's in the same category of work, and as late as 1970, the median earnings of male clerical workers were only slightly less than those of women managers. In fact, between 1940 and 2000, there was little change in the ratio of women's to men's earnings: for managerial employees it hovered between 50 and 65 percent, for professionals and technicians from 56 percent to 75 percent, and for clerical workers, from 39 percent to 87 percent (a sharp increase from 73 percent in 1980).

Nonetheless, younger women in banking were closing the economic distance between them-selves and men. In 2000, among managers, 50–59 year old women earned 57 percent as much as men; 40–49 year olds earned 53 percent; 30–39 year olds 63 percent; and 20–29 year olds, 76 percent. Among clerical workers, the ratio jumped from 56 for 50–59 year olds to 89 among 20–29 year olds. But, over time, as elsewhere in the economy, men outpaced women in economic gains. Consider, for example, the managers born between 1956 and 1965. In 1980, the ratio of women's income to men's was 88. By 1990, it had fallen to 71 and by 2000 to 54. For managers born between 1966 and 1975, the decline was similar. The pattern even held with clerical workers. There are two ways to interpret these ratios. One is as progress; young women had finally moved toward income equality with men. The other is less hopeful: young men and women started out at similar salaries, but, over time, men moved up the economic ladder faster, leaving women increasingly behind. Perhaps women's prospects had improved, but, then again, perhaps they hadn't.

The history of gender relations traces what Charles Tilly calls a "durable inequality"—a persistent inequality among paired categories over time. These inequalities—black/white is another—retain their power through four mechanisms that Tilly terms "exploitation," "opportunity hoarding," "emulation," and "adaptation." By exploitation, he means that the more powerful member of a category uses its resources to appropriate a disproportionate share of what the less powerful member produces and perpetuates its power through any one of a number of means—legislation, work rules, or outright repression.

With opportunity hoarding, the less powerful member of the category makes its peace, more or less, by finding ways to promote its own interests; it looks for ways to advance within a category rather than to break down the distinctions between them. The development of ethnic niches—where ethnic groups take hold of an occupation and pass it on to their members—is one historically very important example; another is labour union practices that favour relatives or friends for membership. The third and fourth mechanisms—emulation and adaptation—are general social processes; they can be seen at work outside of as well as within relations of inequality. Emulation is simply the tendency for individuals and groups to reproduce the organizational models with which they are familiar; adaptation refers to the ways in which members of each category build routines and social relation-ships that facilitate daily interaction and reinforce their interest in maintaining category boundaries.

The historical record is clearer about how exploitation and opportunity hoarding shaped women's inequality in the twentieth century than it is about the role of emulation and adaptation. Exploitation took various forms: rules that prohibited the employment of married women, actions by labour unions concerned with preserving male family wages, and hegemonic cultural ideas that assigned married women to domestic labour while devaluing the kinds of market work they performed, to name three that were particularly important.

Opportunity hoarding refers to the creation of occupational niches by and for women, which is another way to describe the feminisation of occupations. Excluded from most occupations, women seized what openings there were, making them their own, and filling vacancies with other women trained in new educational programs— from commercial courses in high schools to social work schools in universities— that channelled women into the expanding slots in a limited number of occupations. It took powerful exogenous forces to interrupt these processes. Actions by the state; demand induced by labour shortages, structural shifts, and technological change; supply created by higher education; economic pressures from inflation and rising standards of consumption; changes in patterns of marriage and divorce; and the militancy of women striving for equity: all these came together in the last decades of the twentieth century to mount a powerful assault on the enduring inequalities that separated the experience of women and men.

And young women could count some major gains. But the structures they at-tacked were so powerful that victories were only partial. At the beginning of the twenty-first century, whether women would continue to modify this ancient form of categorical inequality, whether young women had finally begun to dismantle the durable walls that have limited women's economic achievements, or whether they had reached the limit of their power, remained to be seen.

In Tilly's account, the mechanisms that perpetuate durable inequalities are relentless rather than paradoxical. They do not account for the mobility of groups and individuals within the disadvantaged categories that compose social structures. They account for only one side of the paradox of inequality. They do not show why groups, such as women, remain unequal despite great individual gains in occupation, education, and income. The answer, a crucial supplement to the theory of durable inequality, lies in the process of internal differentiation—in American history, characteristic of women, African Americans, and most ethnic groups. The grooves etched deeply into hegemonic social structures provide the routes along which advancement takes place. Women assimilated into and reproduced existing economic hierarchies among themselves. For this reason, their mobility did not challenge the structure of inequality; instead it reinforced it.

There are powerful lessons in this history of the paradox of inequality. The most obvious is that access—political and civil citizenship—is not enough. Access promotes individual and group interests but does little to diminish the structures of inequality. What, then, erodes inequality itself? What would promote mobility without extreme differentiation? How can mobility be accomplished without replicating and reinforcing existing economic inequalities? The history of women—like the history of African Americans—is rich in examples of how not to meet these goals, and it poses a standard against which to analyse and evaluate "progress." But how to intervene—how to turn the history of inequality into a wholly positive story rather than a paradox—remains an excruciatingly difficult, but crucial, question for theory and policy.

7

Gender Roles in Family

It is important to examine traditional gender roles and family systems in different populations to understand their impact on couple dynamics. These roles and expectations play a significant part in the way couples interact, family decision-making, and even how one might define marital satisfaction. Hispanic culture is traditionally associated with distinct gender roles for men and women, known as "machismo" and "marianismo," which dictate certain behavioural expectations for members of that community. In addition, there is a strong emphasis on family and community ("familismo") that interacts with the couple's expectations and decision-making while reinforcing the importance of cultural and societal norms.

These cultural values differ significantly from European/Caucasian norms, which have influenced U.S. culture, and can serve as both a protective factor and as a challenge to successful couple relationships. Curriculum developers and program operators need to consider what parts of these traditional roles marriage education programs should try to preserve and what parts might be an obstacle to healthy couple relationships.

Traditional and idealized cultural expectations of appropriate male and female behaviour are often referred to as machismo or marianismo. Machismo is described as being dominant, virile, and independent whereas marianismo emphasizes being submissive, chaste, and dependent. Although some research argues that these traditional gender roles are outdated and inapplicable, other studies show that they do influence behaviour and interaction in Hispanic couples.

For men, the cultural emphasis on machismo can translate into a positive outcome where the man serves as provider and sacrifices for the family or a negative one that emphasizes dominance and control. The positive side of this gender expectation is that it encourages men to work hard to provide for and protect their family. Some research also shows that the negative interpretations of machismo are less common than the stereotype would indicate. This research argues that Hispanic fathers are much more nurturing and egalitarian than one might expect, perhaps due to the traditional emphasis on familial obligations.

Unfortunately, the other side of these traditional behaviours is that Hispanic men are often seen as cold and domineering, due to the cultural emphasis on their economic role in the family and not on caretaking. Dr. Roberto Reyes, professor of Human Development and Family Science at Messiah College discussed this issue further. Dr. Reyes indicated that some research has shown that when men face difficulties finding employment and are unable to "live up to" their perceived role in the family they have increased self doubt which manifests as withdrawal from the family unit. Some research claims that when Latino men cannot define themselves in a positive, productive way in society they will define themselves in more negative, possibly stereotypical gender identity (drinking, aggression, etc.). What's more, men may feel justified in engaging in destructive behaviours such as infidelity or substance abuse as long as they are fulfilling their cultural obligations to provide for their family economically.

The primary role emphasized for women in Hispanic tradition is that of mother instead of wife. The cultural construct of "familismo" is defined as "an emphasis on family relationships and a strong value placed on childbearing as an integral part of family life and the feminine gender role". This leads women to define themselves through their family and children instead of independently or as part of a couple. The role of martyr is also idealized, with women expected to be submissive and sacrifice themselves for their families. For marriage education providers, this stereotype provides both an opportunity and a challenge. It means that women will be extremely dedicated to their families and the good of their children, which can be a powerful motivator for participating in marriage education workshops. However, women may see themselves as a mother first and place the couple relationship at a lower priority. In many cases, the idea of "parenthood" is valued over "partnerhood." In addition, the emphasis on the wife's quiet submission and the husband's dominance and independence may make it more difficult for Hispanic women to communicate directly and assertively with their husbands.

Although Hispanic couples immigrating to the United States may acculturate away from traditional behaviours, it is important to recognize that these cultural expectations can still hold. Furthermore, the definition of a "good" relationship can vary dramatically across culture, country of origin, and level of acculturation. For example, some couples that are less acculturated may not view egalitarianism as an important part of a healthy relationship. It is also necessary to remember that different members of a couple may acculturate at different rates, particularly with regards to these traditional gender roles. For example, men often tend to acculturate more quickly than their wives because they often arrive in the United States before the rest of the family and have more exposure to mainstream culture through the workplace. However, shifting gender roles may have a more pronounced effect for Hispanic women than for men due to the greater difference between expectations for their behaviour in the Hispanic community and mainstream culture. Marriage educators should be aware that different levels of acculturation are correlated with increased marital conflict as expectations and behaviours change.

Lastly, a stereotype does exist that more conservative gender roles such as those described above can lead to increased domestic violence in the Hispanic community. In fact, traditional Hispanic gender roles can be both oppressive and protective when it comes to domestic violence. The woman's role as sacrificing and subservient can lead to greater tolerance of domestic violence, as can the strong commitment to the family and the institution of marriage. The view of men as the dominant decision -makers can also encourage controlling behaviours. Lastly, because of their role in the home, Hispanic women are often economically dependent on men, making it more difficult to leave the relationship. However, although these more dangerous facets of traditional gender roles can encourage domestic violence, Hispanic men who embrace the positive side of machismo might be less likely to be violent. These values instruct men to protect their families, including their wives, which is incompatible with a domestic violence scenario.

Gender Roles in Extended Family

Another strong cultural value in the Hispanic community is that of familismo, which was defined above as "an emphasis on family relationships and a strong value placed on childbearing as an integral part of family life and the feminine gender role." This includes a strong emphasis on family obligation, the value of children and community and the importance of past and future generations. These values often play out in couples' priorities and decision-making. The boundaries between what are couple issues and what is a family or community issue is often blurred. As with the cultural expectations described above with respect to gender roles, the traditional emphasis on familismo can be protective or it can pose a challenge to the couples themselves and to marriage educators.

Familismo can strengthen a couple's relationship with some of the positive associations it brings. The importance of extended family provides couples with an extensive social support network that can assist them in times of emotional or economic difficulty. In addition, the emphasis on stability and community means that the importance of the couple's relationship is validated and supported by the extended family. Dr. Rolando Díaz-Loving, head of the Psychosocial Research Unit at the National Autonomous University of Mexico, explained that this support network need not come exclusively from blood relatives. In many instances, the process of migration and immigration may leave couples isolated from extended family, and support networks are created with others in the community. "Compadres" and "godparents" may be viewed as part of the family, and their influence on the couple's relationship is seen as just as important.

A strong sense of familismo may actually encourage a couple to participate in a given program. If a couple is convinced that marriage education is the best thing to do for their family, this obligation can be used to motivate their attendance and engagement in the program. For example, couples may choose to attend a marriage education program if they're convinced that it's the best thing they can do for their children.

While the involvement of extended family in the lives of Hispanic couples can help support and validate their relationships and families, this also means that marriage educators must deal with the challenge of extended family being involved in decision-making. The extended family and generational differences associated with length of time in the United States can be a stressor in Hispanic families. Childrearing, for example, may be considered the couple's domain in mainstream culture but is considered a family affair in the Hispanic community. This can cause conflict particularly when the couple is more or less acculturated than older generations. In addition, children can be exposed to differing values and behaviours than those of their parents because of time spent with extended family.

Some couples may be dealing with a recent separation from their extended family and social network, particularly those who are recent immigrants. Technology can help mitigate this separation by keeping immigrants informed of what is happening in their countries of origin, but the elimination of a valuable support network can be extremely difficult for couples to deal with. Other factors, such as substance abuse and incarceration, can also sever extended family ties. Regardless of the cause for separation from extended family members, marriage educators should be aware of the impact this may have on the couple relationship.

Traditional Gender Roles

Traditional gender roles in the Hispanic community are well-defined, and there is some research on how closely they reflect actual behaviour. However, there is much that is unknown about how these expectations play out for couples, particularly immigrants to the United States. There is little conclusive information about how closely traditional gender roles apply, particularly when some literature emphasizes the importance of machismo and marianismo whereas others, such as the parenting literature, seem to contradict these expectations. There are even some who question whether machismo and the patriarchal system even exist in Hispanic families. Dr. Luis Zayas, professor of Social Work and Psychiatry at the Washington University School of Medicine illustrated this point by stating that many view the mother as being the most significant member of the family and offending or disappointing her is most influential in determining behaviour.

Furthermore, it is unclear how gender roles are affected by immigration to the United States and acculturation to mainstream norms and expectations. There is a contradiction between the hypothesis that acculturation would deconstruct traditional gender norms and the assertion in some literature that even highly acculturated couples can still exhibit very traditional roles and behaviours. In addition, it would be helpful to investigate what behaviours and norms expressed as part of traditional cultural gender roles help protect couples. Marriage education programs would do well to preserve these behaviours.

Lastly, as was emphasized throughout the discussion, although there are some commonalities among the Hispanic community, there are also a range of differences based on country of origin, class, and degree of acculturation. More detailed research is needed to determine what these similarities and differences are.

Two particular questions were raised with regards to the interaction of extended family networks with couple dynamics. First, what effect might intervening at the couple level have on other parts of the family system? It is possible that a marriage education intervention, for example, that questions certain cultural norms might cause conflict between generations. A better understanding of generational differences and family systems can help curriculum developers create culturally appropriate tools for couples.

Second, what is the effect of immigration and acculturation on social support? One hypothesis is that couples are forced into social isolation after immigrating because they have less access to traditional family support networks. However, another possibility is that couples replace traditional social supports with new friends and jobs as they assimilate into the mainstream culture. If this transition does occur, it may not happen equally for both members of the couple. For example, a husband might replace lost social supports more quickly because of his integration into the workplace. This may leave his wife feeling disconnected from her partner in addition to losing her traditional support system. How does this aspect of differential acculturation affect couple dynamics?

Role of Men and Boys in Achieving Gender Equality

This chapter is intended as a broad guide to issues involving men and boys in the promotion of gender equality. It cites recent international research on masculinities, men and boys, and also cites useful discussions of the policy questions involved.

Equality between women and men is recognized as a principle in international law, articulated in many United Nations documents from the 1948 Universal Declaration of Human Rights onwards. The idea that men and boys might have a specific role in realizing this principle has only been articulated recently.

Issues about gender equality were placed on the public agenda by women mainly. The reason is clear – it is women who are disadvantaged by the main patterns of gender inequality, therefore it is women who should have a claim for redress. This logic is so strong that gender issues have been widely regarded as "women's business" and of no concern to men and boys. But this belief can no longer be held.

Men and boys are unavoidably involved in gender issues. There are pragmatic reasons for this. Any reform agenda requires resources. The existing pattern of gender inequality men's predominant control of economic assets, political power, cultural authority, and armed force means that men (often, specific groups of men) control most of the resources required to implement women's claims for justice.

There are also broader reasons to do with the nature of gender. Contemporary research has shown gender inequalities to be embedded in a complex system of relationships, which can be detected at every level of human experience from individual emotion and interpersonal relationships to economic organization, culture and the state. The key points about gender systems include:

1. Gender relations are an interactive system of connections and distinctions among people (and groups of people) what happens to one group in this system affects the others, and is affected by them;
2. Gender relations are not superficial, but are deeply embedded in organizational routines, in religious and legal concepts, and in the taken- for-granted arrangements of people's lives (such as the distinction between "home" and "work");
3. Gender relations are multidimensional, interweaving relationships of power, economic arrangements, emotional relationships, systems of communication and meaning, etc.;
4. Gender systems are diverse and changing – they arise from different cultural histories in different parts of the world, have changed in the past and are undergoing change now.

Moving towards a gender-equal society is therefore a complex task, involving profourd institutional change as well as the small details of everyday life. Gender change brings to light issues that are normally unnoticed, and may be difficult to deal with such as the way public policies (e.g. industrial regulation, police practices, development policies) often impact specifically on men without actually naming men or acknowledging the gendered character of their impact. It is not possible to move gender systems far towards equality without broad social consensus in favour of gender equality and that consensus must include men and boys.

Men and boys are thus, in several ways, gatekeepers for gender equality. Whether they are willing gatekeepers who will support practical reforms, is an important question. The answer varies from one situation to another, and has to do with the ways men's beliefs and practices are shaped by the gender system just described. Research has repeatedly shown that patterns of gender inequality are interwoven with social definitions of masculinity and men's gender identities. To move towards a gender-equal society often requires men and boys to think and act in new ways, to reconsider traditional images of manhood, and to reshape their relationships with women and girls. Changes of this kind are already happening in many parts of the world, but not in all situations or with all men and boys.

Men and boys are most likely to support change towards gender equality when they can see positive benefits for themselves and the people in their lives. Even when they cannot see personal benefits, however, men and boys have a responsibility in this area. As long as any systematic gender inequalities persist, delivering advantage to men over women and promising future advantage to boys, the advantaged have an ethical responsibility to use their resources to change the system.

Emergence of Issues about Men and Boys

The role of men and boys in relation to gender equality has recently emerged as an issue in international discussions.

This development crystallized at the Fourth World Conference on Women, held at Beijing in 1995. Paragraph 25 of the *Beijing Declaration* committed participating Governments to "encourage men to participate fully in all actions towards equality." The detailed *Platform for Action* that accompanied the *Declaration* prominently restated the principle of shared power and responsibility between men and women, and argued that women's concerns could only be addressed "in partnership with men" towards gender equality. The *Platform for Action* went on to specify areas where action involving men and boys was needed and was possible: in education and the socialisation of children, childcare and housework, sexual health, gender-based violence, and the balancing of work and family responsibilities.

A similar approach was followed in the twenty-third special session of the United Nations General Assembly held in the year 2000. The *Political Declaration* of this session made an even stronger statement on men's responsibility, [Governments] "Emphasize that men must involve themselves and take joint responsibility with women for the promotion of gender equality". The accompanying *Outcome Document* reaffirmed statements in the *Platform for Action* about specific areas of action. The *Outcome Document* spelled out at some length the "obstacles" to the achievement of the strategic objectives of the *Platform*, and parts of this discussion identify problems about men, in relation to sex practices, violence, and men's participation in family life.

The role of men and boys has also been addressed in other recent international meetings. These include the 1995 World Summit on Social Development and its review session in 2000, and the Twenty-sixth special session of the General Assembly on HIV/AIDS in 2001. UNESCO convened an expert group meeting in 1997 on "Male roles and masculinities in the perspective of a culture of peace." In 1997 the Nordic Council of Ministers adopted an "Action Plan for Men and Gender Equality." In the same year the Council of Europe conducted a seminar on equality as a common issue for men and women, and chose the role of men in promoting equality as a theme at a ministerial conference. The European Commission has recently funded a research network on men and masculinities. In 1998 the Latin American Federation of Social Science (FLACSO) initiated a series of conferences about masculinities, boys and men across Latin America and the Caribbean. The first conference in this series had the specific theme of gender equality.

These policy discussions have occurred against the background of an upsurge of societal concern with issues about men and boys, much broader than the policy focus on gender equality.

There are diverse social movements attempting either to reform or restore traditional masculinity. There have been extensive media debates about the "new fatherhood" and supposed changes in men's involvement in families. In education there has been talk of boys' gender-specific "failure" in school and there are many proposals for special programmes for boys. Men's violence against women has been the subject of practical interventions, research, and extensive debate. There has been increasing debate about men's health and illness from a gender perspective. In developed countries, there is a popular therapeutic movement that addresses men's problems in relationships, sexuality and identity.

Accompanying these debates has been a remarkable growth of research about men's gender identities and practices, masculinities, boys' education, images of men, and related matters. Academic journals have been founded for specialized research on men and masculinities; there have been many research conferences; and there is a rapidly growing international literature on the area. Now there is a far more sophisticated and detailed scientific understanding of issues about men, masculinities and gender than ever before. This is an important resource for policy thinking on gender equality.

These concerns are worldwide. Debates on violence, patriarchy and ways of changing men's conduct have occurred in countries as diverse as Canada, Germany and South Africa. Issues about men, boys, sexuality and fatherhood have been debated and researched in Brazil, Mexico, and many other countries. A men's centre with a reform agenda has been established in Japan, where conferences have been held and media debates about traditional patterns of masculinity and family life continue. A "travelling seminar" discussing issues about men, masculinities and gender equality has been touring India. Debates about boys' education, men's identities and gender change are active from Denmark to New Zealand.

Gender equality policy implications : The task for gender equality policy is to take account of these societal concerns, and to use the growth of knowledge, in developing strategies concerning men and boys.

Men's and Boys' Capacity for Equality

The public debates about men and boys have often been inconclusive. But they have gone a long way, together with the research, to shatter a widespread belief that has hindered gender reform. ["Gender reform" in this context refers to any systematic attempt to change gender relations in pursuit of a specific goal, e.g. gender equality.] This obstacle is the belief that men cannot change their ways, that "boys will be boys", that rape, war, sexism, domestic violence, aggression or self-centredness are "natural" to men. This belief (often expressed in pseudo-biological language) justifies gender inequality on the grounds of the fixed nature of the human male.

On the contrary, there are now many documented examples of the diversity of masculinities and of men's and boys' capacity for equality. Examples from the research literature include:

1. Life-history research in Chile has shown that there is no unitary Chilean masculinity, despite the cultural homogeneity of the country. While a hegemonic model is widely diffused across social strata, there are many men who depart from it, and there is significant discontent with traditional roles.
2. Though groups of boys in schools often have a dominant or hegemonic pattern of masculinity, there are usually also other patterns present, some of which involve more equal and respectful relations with girls. Research in British schools, for instance, shows how boys encounter alternative models of masculinity as they grow up.
3. Changes have occurred in men's practices within certain families, where there has been a conscious shift towards more equal sharing of housework and childcare. The sociologist Risman, who has documented such cases in one region of the United States, calls them "fair families." It is clear from her research that the change has required a challenge to traditional models of masculinity. It is not a simple change of schedule.
4. In the Shanghai region of China there is a local cultural tradition of relative gender equality, and specifically of willingness by men to be involved in domestic work. Research by Da shows this tradition persisting among Shanghainese men even in circumstances of migration to another country.

5. In the early stages of the HIV/AIDS epidemic, the need for new patterns of care giving became apparent. A strong response emerged in gay communities which ranged from domestic services and counselling to home nursing and hospice care – extensively involving men, as well as women, as caregivers.

Gender equality policy implications : The task for gender equality policy is to recognize and build on the known capacities of men and boys for developing a gender equal way of life.

Patterns of Men's Support

Intellectual and public advocacy. There is a long tradition of advocacy for gender equality by male intellectuals as well as by women. In Europe, for instance, well before modern gender equality documents were written, the great British philosopher Mill published "The Subjection of Women", which established the presumption of equal rights, and the great Norwegian dramatist Ibsen made gender oppression an important cultural theme. In the following generation the pioneering Austrian psychoanalyst Adler established a powerful psychological argument for gender equality. A similar tradition of men's advocacy exists in the USA.

Organizational and political alliance: Many of the historic gains by women's advocates have been won in alliance with men who held organizational or political authority at the time. For instance, the introduction of Equal Employment Opportunity measures in NSW, Australia, occurred with the strong support of the Premier of the day and the head of a reforming enquiry into the public sector, though support from other men was variable. The Australian union movement, confronting a long history of sexism, has produced some senior men with a commitment to gender equality. For the first time in its history, this union confederation has now twice in succession elected women as its national president.

Campaigns among men. Sometimes men's support for gender equality takes the form of campaigning and organizing among men. The most prominent example is the US National Organization of Men Against Sexism (NOMAS), which now has a continuous history of more than 20 years. Men's groups concerned with reforming masculinity, publications advocating change, and campaigns among men in support of gender equality (for instance on violence against women), are found widely, for instance in Mexico, South Africa and the UK. These initiatives have usually been on a relatively small scale or for a limited period.

Youth work and "menswork." Men have been active in creating educational programmes for boys and young men intended to combat sexism and allow youth to explore new ways of being men. Similar strategies have been developed for adult men, sometimes in a religious context and sometimes in a health or therapeutic context. There is a strong tradition of such work in Germany, with programmes that combine the search for self-knowledge with the learning of anti-sexist behaviour. Work of the same general kind has developed in Brazil, the USA and other countries.

Research on Men's Attitudes to Gender Equality.

Though there are many problems with measuring attitudes on gender issues, survey research can give useful indications of broad patterns. European research in particular has shown no consensus among men either for or against gender equality – rather, there exist substantial divisions of opinion. Sometimes a three-way pattern appears, with about one-third of men supporting change towards equality, about one-third opposing it, and one-third undecided or flexible. Broad examinations of the survey evidence from Germany, Japan and the United States have shown a long-term trend of growing support for change, i.e. a movement away from traditional gender roles, especially among the younger generation.

The research literature provides many analysed cases of men's and boys' involvement in changing gender relations and changing understandings of masculinity. Some examples:

1. Historical research shows changing cultural definitions of masculinity. A pioneering study showed the interweaving of national identity with re-definitions of manhood over a century of New Zealand history. Similar research has traced the collapse of traditional "men's culture" with the rise of consumer culture in Japan, and the displacement of a conservative and patriarchal manhood by a more secular and globalized ideal of manhood in Ireland.

2. Psychological and educational research shows personal flexibility in the face of cultural images of masculinity. Men and boys can negotiate, or strategically use, conventional definitions of masculinity rather than be controlled by them. It is even possible to teach boys (and girls) how to do this in school classrooms.

3. Sociological research shows adolescents and young men responding creatively to changing socioeconomic circumstances. These responses include the valorization of more egalitarian and less aggressive forms of masculinity, and attempts to create more involved models of young fatherhood.

4. Industrial research shows men's involvement in changing workplace relations. For instance an ethnography from Canada shows male steelworkers first resisting, then (with union endorsement) supporting, the arrival of women in heavy industrial employment.

Perhaps the most extensive social action on these issues, combining government and non-government initiatives, has occurred in Scandinavia. This includes provisions for paternity leave which have had high rates of take-up, among the most dramatic of all demonstrations of men's willingness to change gender practices. Holter sums up the research and practical experience: "The Nordic 'experiment' has shown that a majority of men can change their practice when circumstances are favorable...When reforms or support policies are well-designed and targeted towards an ongoing cultural process of change, men's active support for gender equal status increases."

Men's and Boys' Resistance to Gender Equality

There is some explicit opposition to gender equality measures. Campaigns have been mounted by certain groups who believe that men and boys are disadvantaged by existing institutions or policies. An example is "father's rights" groups, which combat a perceived bias towards women in divorce cases. These groups believe that judges in family courts are systematically biased against men, so men generally lose custody of children, bear unequal financial burdens, etc. Another example is the "What About the Boys?" campaign, mounted by people who believe boys, not girls, are the disadvantaged group in education, and that special programmes for boys are needed. These arguments have now been widely circulated in mass media and have gained the attention of politicians and policymakers in some of the developed countries.

Another type of opposition, more common among men in business and government, rejects gender equality measures because it rejects all government action in support of equality, in favour of the unfettered action of the market. In principle, gender equality is consistent with market ideologies under the rubric of the "level playing field." In practice, neo- liberalism has often weakened gender equality measures, de-funded women's groups, and removed social protection machinery that was particularly important to women. Men collectively are better positioned in the market economy than women are, so a shift of social resources into the market is likely to result in redistribution towards men.

There are varying reasons for men's resistance to gender equality:

1. *Material benefits*–the "patriarchal dividend" to men from gender inequalities. Men may have an expectation of informal benefits, such as receiving care and domestic service from women in the family. Godenzi has emphasized material inequalities of income and time: "Men's violence against women is both a means and an expression of the conditions of inequality between men and women."
2. *Identity problems about change*–if social definitions of masculinity include being the breadwinner and being "strong", then men may be offended by women's professional progress because it makes men seem less worthy of respect. Similarly, caring for children, the elderly, or the sick may seem unmanly or feminising. If fear of femininity is combined with homophobia, anxieties about change may be severe.
3. Resentment against gender equality programmes, especially from those men who get little or none of the patriarchal dividend–programmes to benefit women and girls are seen by some angry men as undeserved advantages which are unavailable to men.
4. *Ideological defence of male supremacy*–research on domestic violence suggests that male batterers often hold very conservative views of women's role in the family. In many parts of the world there exist ideologies that justify men's supremacy on grounds of

religion, biology, cultural tradition or organizational mission (e.g. in the military). It is a mistake to regard these ideas as simply outmoded, because they may be actively modernized and renewed.

Structure of Gender Equality Policy

In almost all current policy discussions, adopting a "gender perspective" *substantially* means addressing women's concerns. This is understandable, given the main pattern of gender inequality, and was the only way by which gender issues could come onto the public agenda. But it has some consequences which create challenges now.

In both national and international gender equality policy documents, women are constituted as the subjects of the policy discourse. The agencies or meetings which formulate, implement or monitor the policies usually have names referring to women, actual examples being "Department for Women", "Ministry of Women's Equality ", "Prefectural Women's Centre", "Commission on the Status of Women." Such bodies have a clear mandate to act for women; they do not have equally clearly a mandate to act *in respect of men.*

Consequently, in documents such as the *Beijing Platform for Action* and the Beijing *Outcome Document*, men are rarely explicitly named or concretely discussed. Men are implicitly present as background throughout these documents. In every statement about women and inequality there is an implied comparison with men as the privileged group; in the discussions of violence against women, men are implicitly present as the "perpetrators"; in discussions of gender and HIV/AIDS men were construed as "the problem"; in discussions of women's exclusion from power and decision-making men are implicitly present as the power holders.

When men are present only as a background category in a policy discourse about women, it is difficult to raise issues about men's and boys' interests, problems or differences except by falling into a backlash posture and affirming "men's rights", or by moving outside the gender framework altogether. It is difficult to attract men to partnership in such a policy realm.

If large numbers of men are to support and implement gender equality policy, it will be necessary for that policy to speak, in concrete and positive ways, to their concerns, interests, hopes and problems. The political task is to do this *without weakening the drive for justice for women and girls* that animates current gender equality policy.

Some policymakers have approached this problem by restructuring gender equality policy in the form *of parallel policies* for women and men. For instance, some recent health policy initiatives in Australia have added a "men's health" document to a "women's health" document. Similarly, in some school systems a "boy's education" strategy has been added to a "girls' education" strategy.

This acknowledges the wider scope of gender issues, but this approach risks weakening the "equality" rationale of the original policy. It may redefine women and men, or girls and boys, simply as different market segments for some service, and forget about the relations between them. Ironically, the result may be to promote more gender segregation, not less. This has certainly happened in education, where some privileged segregated boys' schools have jumped on the "gender equality" bandwagon and now market themselves as experts in catering for the special needs of boys.

On the other hand, bringing men's problems within an existing framework of policies for women may weaken the authority that women have so far gathered in that policy area. In the field of gender and development, for instance, it is argued by some that "bringing men in" – given the larger context where men still control most of the wealth and institutional authority – may undermine, not help, the drive for gender equality. In broad terms, the solution to the dilemma is to focus gender equality policy on the *relations between groups rather than on the groups themselves*. But in practice, this is hard to do.

Reasons for Change from the Perspective of Men and Boys

Early statements often assumed that men had the same interest as women in escaping from restrictive sex roles. Experience has shown that this picture is inadequate. Yet it contains an important truth, that men and boys often have substantial reasons to support change. These reasons fall into four main groups.

Relational interests. When "men" are considered statistically as an aggregate of individuals, they appear to have an unshakeable interest in defending inequality. But in reality, men are not isolated individuals. As the poet Donne said, "No man is an island, entire of itself." Men and boys live in social relationships, many with women and girls: wives, partners, mothers, aunts, daughters, nieces, friends, classmates, workmates, professional colleagues, neighbours, and so on. The quality of every man's life depends to a large extent on the quality of those relationships. Living in a system of gender inequality which limits or damages the lives of the women and girls concerned, inevitably degrades the lives of the men and boys too.

For instance, very large numbers of men are fathers, and about half of their children are girls. Some men are sole parents, and are then deeply involved in caregiving – an important demonstration of men's capacity for care. Even in intact partnerships with women, many men have close relationships with their children, and psychological research shows the importance of these relationships. Many men make sacrifices for their children, and desire a more active fatherhood. To make sure that daughters grow up in a world that offers young women security, freedom, and opportunities to fulfil their talents, is a powerful reason for many men to support gender equality.

Personal wellbeing. Current unequal gender systems have damaging effects on the wellbeing of men as well as women, though the pattern of effects is different. A quarter-century ago, a classic paper argued "Warning: the male sex role may be dangerous to your health." Since then, health research has documented specific problems for men and boys, among them: premature death from accident, homicide and suicide; foci of occupational injury in industries such as mining, transport and heavy manufacturing (closely related to gender segregation in the workforce); higher levels of drug abuse, especially alcohol and tobacco; and in some countries at least, a relative unwillingness by men to seek medical help when it is needed. Some of these patterns arise from, or are sustained by, attempts by boys and men to assert a tough and dominant masculinity. A striking example is competitive sport, where the use of bodies as weapons and the denial of pain is associated with masculine prestige on the one hand, and injury and illness on the other.

The relative exclusion of women from paid employment is associated with a widespread model of the man as "breadwinner." Social and economic pressures on men to compete in the workplace, to increase their hours of paid work, and sometimes to take second jobs, are among the most powerful constraints on gender reform. Desire for a better work/life balance is widespread among employed men. On the other hand, where unemployment is high, the lack of a paid job can be a damaging pressure on men who have grown up in the expectation of being a breadwinner. This is, for instance, an important gender issue in post-apartheid South Africa. Opening alternative economic paths and moving towards what German discussions have called "multioptional masculinities", may do much to improve men's wellbeing.

Collective interests. Men may also support gender equality because they see its relevance to the wellbeing of the community they live in. In situations of mass poverty and under-employment, for instance in cities in developing countries, flexibility in the gender division of labour may be crucial to a household which requires women's earnings as well as men's. In village communities, maximizing the total labour resources may be vital to prosperity or even survival. Men may recognize that they benefit in the long run from the growth in collective wellbeing that flows from the better education of women, from improvements in women's health, etc.

Men are likely to benefit from broad social and cultural changes associated with gender equality. Less rigidity and stereotyping of masculinity will increase options for men and is likely to yield benefits in mental health and psychological wellbeing. By removing an important source of prejudice and hostility, a move towards gender equality is likely to improve social inclusion generally.

It will also yield benefits in security. Civil and international violence is strongly associated with dominating patterns of masculinity and with marked gender inequality in the state. Movement towards gender equality makes it more possible for men to adopt historically "feminine" styles of nonviolent negotiation and conflict resolution, as illustrated by women's recent role in negotiating to overcome intractable civil conflicts. More moves towards the achievement of gender equality, and a reduction in violence and in pressures on men, is also likely to mitigate the social effects of coercive systems of social control, such as prisons. Many more men than women are currently imprisoned, with damaging consequences. Rates of imprisonment are especially high among the men of marginalised ethnic groups.

Principle. Many of the men who become active in gender reform do so because gender equality follows from political or ethical principles that are important to them. These include religious, socialist, or broad democratic beliefs.

In the past, many men who believed in a principle of social equality did not see it as applying to the relations between women and men. They supposed gender relations to be governed by natural difference, or assumed they would be reformed some time in the future after another principle of equality (e.g. class equality, national independence) was achieved. For men to act now for gender equality has often required a specific stimulus, such as living or working with women who have a consciousness of gender issues. There is, it seems, a broad awareness among young men of old patterns of manhood being under challenge. This awareness, as shown in research with young men in Germany and Japan, leads in varied directions, sometimes to support for equality.

Impacts of Major Contemporary Issues

Globalization and Development

The vast economic changes of recent generations have impacted on the lives of men as well as women, though in varying ways. It is only recently however that there has been a focused discussion of globalization's impact on men and masculinities.

There is evidence from many parts of the world of upheaval in the lives of men and in cultural images of manhood. To give an example, a recent examination of popular culture in Arab countries by Ghoussoub finds many signs of rapid change. Those men whose identities are still grounded in traditional gender concepts face dilemmas because of the increased status of women in Arab societies, while other men are engaged in a search that the author calls "a chaotic quest for a definition of modern masculinity." The same point could be made of most other regions of the world.

The transformation of subsistence economies, the spread of the market economy and the introduction of agricultural machinery and new crops, have destabilised traditional gender divisions of labour in rural society. Those men who enter the cash economy from village society must create new gender arrangements; if they become migrant labourers, for instance, they may be separated from wives and children for long periods. Generally, men more than women have been the beneficiaries of rural development – but not all men. Poverty has developed on a mass scale, one of its effects being migration to cities, often pioneered by men in search of jobs.

In the course of global development, new polarisations have opened among men, with some becoming rich and powerful to an unprecedented degree while many remain poor and marginalised. Many families have become dependent on women's earnings and men have to adjust to changed power balances within their families. For young men growing up in dislocated rural or urban- fringe communities there are few economic prospects, and violence against women may develop as a means of masculine assertion.

However gender relations in poor communities are not necessarily oppressive or even antagonistic; there is enormous diversity in situations around the world. Indigenous knowledge, the subject of considerable recent discussion in Africa, may see gender differently from

Western models, and this may be an asset in resisting globalization pressures and sustaining egalitarian alternatives. As research in Latin America shows, men in urban working-class communities are very much aware of the impact of economic crisis and restructuring, engage in ongoing political debate and are often sharply critical of antidemocratic trends. This continuing community discussion provides an important context for gender equality politics. There are features of men's lives in urban settings that may motivate a concern with gender equality issues, for instance a tension between a definition of masculinity focused on family relations, and a definition around freedom and independence.

Work/Life Balances

In many parts of the world men have been defined as "breadwinners", responsible for paid work, while women have been defined as "housewives" but many people now see this sharp division as untenable. The question of work/life balance arises in many forms, because of the diversity of workplaces and economic situations, as well as different cultural traditions and processes of change. Labour migration provides extreme examples of work/life imbalances resulting from economic change. For instance, South African men recruited to provide the labour force for gold mining were often separated from their families for months or years at a time, housed in bare barracks at the mines, where practically a new way of life had to be constructed in an all male environment.

It is not only working-class men who experience imbalances. Economic development in Japan, for instance, created life paths for middle-class men that required long hours in the workplace and resulted in a very high level of gender segregation in the family as well as the office. Sharp debate has now arisen about this "salaryman" model, with criticism of gender dichotomies and attempts to define other life patterns for men – though gender division remains common.

Where masculinity is centrally defined through paid work, and femininity is strongly associated with childcare and domestic work, the result can be a marginalisation of men from family life. Norwegian family research has shown the profound emotional and cultural consequences of this peripheral position for men. It is not easy to overcome, even though in the same country, there have been very progressive policies to encourage fathers' participation in infant care and women's integration into paid workplaces.

The emergence of "family friendly" or "flexible" employment policies and practices marks the recognition by employers and governments of the importance of work/home relationships. This recognition is important, but these policies are immediately paradoxical. Flexibility in employment conditions has mainly been applied to women. In some cases parental leave is only available to women (and is called "maternal leave").

In some countries, Australia for instance, employment statistics show that it is mainly women who have part-time and casual employment, while time-budget studies show most men have done little to increase their contribution to domestic labour. Thus "family friendly" policies may actually reinforce the gender division of labour. This can only be changed by men decreasing their hours in the workplace and increasing their domestic commitments and their use of part-time work, parental leave, etc. Yet the current trend in developed economies – given growing economic insecurity is for a rise, not a fall, in employed men's average hours of work. Public policy may redress this, for instance by making overtime work more expensive for employers, or by linking promotion to caregiving.

The growth of the global economy creates new issues. The careers of business executives involve frequent international travel and relocations to different countries. The transnational corporation the dominant economic institution of our time thus becomes the site of an extreme work/home division in the lives of its most influential employees, who are, overwhelmingly, men. New technologies such as e-mail have become a way of extending work hours, not reducing them. Though research on this issue is still at an early stage, a global, business masculinity seems to be emerging, in forms which do not offer good solutions to work/life imbalances.

HIV/AIDS, Sexuality and Reproductive Health

Sexual and reproductive health is another field where issues about men have been difficult to formulate. Population policies and demographic research have often had a focus on women as the unit of reproduction and as the target of contraception and sexual health interventions, leaving men aside. Early discussions of HIV/AIDS did focus on one group of men, the gay men of developed countries, but ignored other men. Initial discussions of gender in the world epidemic focused on women's vulnerability and treated men abstractly as the problem. Gradually, however, a more differentiated and practice-oriented approach to men has emerged. This was signalled by the 2000-01 World AIDS Campaign which proclaimed "Men Make a Difference." An understanding of masculinities is now informing discussions of AIDS prevention strategies.

The spread of HIV and progression to AIDS are significantly related to the position of men in gender relations. In most gender systems men have predominant control, or predominant initiative, in sexuality. Men who hold gender ideologies which priorities men's pleasure over women's, or assume men have rights to women's bodies, increase women's vulnerability, and so do specific sexual practices that custom may allow or encourage. Yet men's safety may also be compromised by the same forces. The position of power is often associated with a hegemonic masculinity that values risk-taking, or sees "virility" as the measure of a man's worth. Models of masculinity that emphasize toughness and an appearance of competence and control may make youth believe in their own invulnerability, be deceived by social myths and misinformation, fail to get necessary knowledge (especially in absence of adequate/ appropriate sex education). Masculine ideologies also seem to be involved in some men's and youth's failure to get medical care even when it is available.

The social impact of AIDS is also related to the different positioning of men and women in gender relations. The gender division of labour not only shapes the spread of the virus, but also the economic survival consequences when specific groups of people fall ill or die for instance, younger men as an agricultural workforce. If gender ideology makes men unused to caregiving, or even defines caregiving as unmanly, there may be a social deficit in needed support. Gender ideologies that include homophobic contempt for men and misogynist contempt for sexually active women, reinforce the stigmatization of people living with AIDS.

Economic changes that disrupt established patterns of men's employment may provoke reactions of anger and despair that increase infection risks for both men and women. In sexuality research responding to the HIV/AIDS pandemic, the diversity of men's sexual behaviour and identities is apparent, including fluidity and change within the categories of "heterosexual" and "homosexual." In a context of Western-dominated globalization, certain sexual/ gender identities for men have been given worldwide circulation. These identities interact with local sexual and gender cultures, creating complex mixtures, hybrids, and systems of alternatives. New possibilities for men's self-understanding and behaviour are constantly being created.

Among these changes are positive responses by groups of men to the HIV/AIDS epidemic and to issues of reproductive health. They include caregiving in AIDS-affected communities education programmes directed to youth, community leadership directed to both prevention and care, and many of the responses to the pandemic by professional men as well as professional women.

Gender-Based Violence

Violence is an important means by which gender inequalities are maintained. A culture of violence subordinates and injures women, and also subordinates and injures many men. Violence against women, homophobic violence, and racist violence have common roots in violent men's beliefs in hierarchy, narrow conceptions of masculinity, and anxie ties about their own status.

A good deal is now known about the conditions of men's domestic violence particularly. It may be instrumental, a way of maintaining control over a woman, or it may be intended as punishment, when a woman's claim for autonomy is seen as a violation of the man's (husband's) entitlements. These attitudes may now be gaining a global dimension through the international sex trade and Internet "mail order bride" business. Men's movements to end men's violence against women, using information from research on violent men, have now arisen in many countries.

In recent discussions the gendered character of violence in civil conflict, terrorism and military interventions have come into focus, especially as an issue in the prevention of war. Research and policy discussions have begun to concern themselves closely with the masculine character of crime, international relations, armed conflict and political violence.

Important insights have emerged from criminological research. Criminal violence is not just the consequence of a preexisting "masculinity", i.e. an expression of the gendered character of men. In many situations, crime is a resource for *constructing masculinity* it is a way by which men can achieve status, acquire resources and assert their dominance. Public violence can arise from situations of masculine challenge, where a conflict has arisen and each participant feels manhood is at stake in not backing down. In some cultural settings the possession of weapons is an important symbol of masculinity, and where guns are easily available this contributes to a high level of violence within the community.

Modern states do not rely on individual motivation to sustain their military capabilities. Research on armed forces has repeatedly shown *institutionalized masculinities* of a particular kind, embedded in training, organizational culture, specific organizational practices, etc. These institutionalized gender patterns have the function of sustaining group loyalty and willingness to participate in the organizational violence which is the raison d'être of armed forces. They may have severe consequences for women recruited into the armed forces but treated as outsiders, or for civilian women who come within the scope of military operations and suffer collateral damage.

These points also seem to apply to the irregular forces involved in insurrections and civil violence. They are mainly composed of men (often very young men), and as research on the Palestinian *intifada* and the South African anti-apartheid struggle shows, may put these young men through a vehement if informal training that emphasizes aggressiveness, physical bravery, distrust of authority, and loyalty to the immediate group. At the same time, civil conflict severely disrupts regular education and many of the ties that would have given young men a secure place in families and communities. The result may be a continuing problem in the aftermath of civil conflict, with men who were once regarded as heroes now marginalised and impoverished, possibly very angry, and well trained in violence.

Whether current world struggles involving "terrorism" involve significantly new gender patterns has yet to be established. The groups involved in the best-known attacks resemble regular armed forces and insurrectionary forces in being mainly composed of men, and it seems likely that they are groups with little concern for gender equality. Something new is more strongly suggested by the responses of powerful states to these events. Action by professional military forces using high levels of technology (e.g. intensive aerial bombing) produces conflicts with very lopsided casualty figures in which the risk to the intervening forces is low while damage to the targets of intervention is severe. Stiehm observes that "if one uses force on others from a position in which one is unassailable, one is, in essence, an executioner." If this perception becomes widespread, it could change the cultural meaning of military masculinity profoundly.

Educational Strategy for Gender Equality

The "education and training of women" the *Beijing Platform for Action* mentioned several points about boys, such as the need to provide adequate sexual and reproductive health education, the importance of nondiscriminatory curriculum content, and the need to give boys the skills for housework and care work. These points, however, are only beginnings for an educational strategy.

The education of boys and young men is certainly an important issue for gender equality. It is rightly regarded as a key to stopping the HIV pandemic; it is important to the prevention of violence against women; it is important in breaking down gender segregation in the workforce; and it is crucial to improving the health and wellbeing of boys and men themselves. Long-term changes in the gender order, if not to be achieved by compulsion, must to a large extent be achieved through education. Yet education is not a panacaea for gender problems. Gender equality advocates sometimes assume that if boys were socialized differently, they would automatically behave better towards women when they are men and this is far too simple a view of how education works.

To be realistic, it must be acknowledged that there are considerable difficulties in formulating a gender equality strategy for the education of boys. Many boys have troubled relationships with schools. In the developed countries (though not always in developing countries) boys learn to read later than girls, on average; have more conflict with schools; have a higher rate of dropout from secondary schooling, and proceed to higher education in smaller numbers. In public debates about gender and education, girls and young women have increasingly been perceived as the "winners" in education and boys as the "losers." Gender equality measures intended to benefit girls are now often polemically represented, in public debates, as being attacks on boys. Attempts are being made to make schools and curricula more "boy-friendly", in opposition to a supposed feminisation of education, and to recruit more men into elementary school teaching to provide "role models" for boys.

There is some value in these ideas but also much misunderstanding. A better gender balance in teaching would help, though this should apply to all levels of the teaching workforce. Changing rates of progression are complex products of social expectations, changing labour market conditions, changing technologies, etc. Boys from privileged social backgrounds, who benefit from class and ethnic advantage, do extremely well in schools and universities. Boys' difficulties in schools are markedly concentrated among boys from social backgrounds marked by poverty, ethnic or racial inequality, or social disruption.

Gender equality measures in relation to boys will only have credibility, in contemporary education systems, if they form part of a wider approach that addresses educational problems concerning boys. The problems of boys' alienation and disrupted education will only be solved by strategies that address the general problem of social justice in education, strategies that move education systems from a focus on competition and exclusion to a focus on inclusion and common learnings. In turn, a social justice approach in education requires a "gender-oriented pedagogy" that will speak to the concerns and needs of boys as well as girls. It is essential, then, to place gender equality goals in education in the context of an understanding of boys' gender development, and in the context of the practical methods available in education systems.

Boys' Gender Development

Polemical positions on boys' education often rest on oversimplified models of boys' gender development. The "backlash" position usually rests on some version of biological essentialism, i.e. the model where masculine aggressiveness, dominance and other characteristics are supposed to be fixed by the genes, emerging "naturally" in the course of growth. Biological essentialism is very unsatisfactory as an account of gender. It is based on speculation, it lacks credible mechanisms of development, and it is contradicted by evidence of social diversity in gender systems. "Socialisation" is often seen as the only alternative. But this too is unsatisfactory as a theory of gender development. The socialisation model generally assumes that the learner is passive, that learning of social norms is a linear process, and that the norms themselves are unitary. All these assumptions are wrong, in the light of what is known about both human learning and gender systems. There is now extensive research on gender in child development and education, especially in schools. While more is known about the gender development of girls, enough research on boys has been done to provide a broad picture of the process, at least in developed countries. Key conclusions are:

1. Gender learning is a highly active process, in which both boys and girls search out cultural material about gender and process it. They do not wait to have gender norms imposed on them. When they do learn gender images, they incorporate them actively into their fantasy, games and interactions. Boys as well as girls practice, use and reflect on gender, sometimes dividing along gender lines and sometimes crossing gender boundaries. An active negotiation about gender, its meanings, and hierarchies of masculinity, begins early and continues through adolescence. This activity and interest can be used in gender equality education, as a strong motive for exploring new possibilities.

2. Gender development passes through different stages, given the changing intellectual and social capacities of the child, and the changing social setting. The gender issues in early childhood, for instance, are different from those in adolescence though there is an active process of gender construction going on at both times. There does not seem to be any one "critical period" in which the direction of development is decisively fixed. All periods of growth are appropriate for gender education; while patterns of gender identity and conduct established at one period are subject to revision and change later on. It follows that gender equality initiatives for boys must be age-appropriate and must be continuing.

3. Gender development is multidimensional. It involves cognitive and emotional learning, physical development, the learning of social skills, and the development of personal identities. An imbalance often develops in secondary and tertiary education, when boys and young men emphasize technical and intellectual training, or sports, and are under-represented in humanities courses that explore issues of emotion and relationship. This may reflect boys' own stereotyped views of gender difference; it is a major problem about the curriculum in boys' education. Gender equality strategy for boys must address curriculum issues and consider the spectrum of development.

4. Bodily activities such as sport, fighting and sexuality are very important in young people's thinking about masculinities, especially in defining hierarchies between hegemonic and subordinated masculinities. Nevertheless, the specific meanings of bodily activities such as football vary from one culture to another. Gendered training of the body begins as early as preschool. Physical events such as puberty may change self-perceptions and trigger changed responses from other people. Difficulties in this area may be crucial in the turn to violence by young male offenders. Gender equality initiatives for boys must address issues about male bodies and their meanings.

5. Gender learning occurs in multiple sites, from the family to schools, peer groups, and workplaces. These settings have different gender regimes. Because men in most societies are relatively absent from early childcare, boys' development often begins in a setting controlled by women; some theories suggest this creates emotional pressure, later, for boys to mark themselves off sharply from women and the feminine.

Some institutions designed for boys, such as sporting clubs and boys' schools, define a strongly-marked, even exaggerated, masculinity in their organizational culture. But there is considerable diversity in the gender regimes of schools. Most boys will experience a range of gender relations in the course of growing up. Gender equality initiatives can make good use of this diversity of experience. Gender equality policy should discourage segregated education and encourage inclusiveness.

6. Boys' gender learning is affected by the wider social context. The ethnic composition of a school, or the social class background of its students, may strongly affect hierarchies among boys, and the definition of the most honoured or hegemonic form of masculinity. Gender equality curricula for boys should not reflect only one culture or social background, but should explore difference and plurality.

7. In the course of gender development, boys encounter many conflicts and contradictory demands, and they meet conflicting responses from adults and other children. Over time, most successfully resolve the conflicts and develop a trajectory through life as a gendered person, create a specific identity, and develop their characteristic style of conduct. The resolutions and the trajectories are varied. This important fact is already visible in elementary school and secondary school contexts, leading on to the multiple masculinities in adult groups. The complexities of growth also produce internal complexities of character. Adult masculinities often involve compromises between contradictory emotions, or allow flexibility where the same person can produce different gender practices at different times. Gender equality initiatives can make an important contribution by allowing boys and youth to explore the complexity of identities and relationships.

Most research on boys' gender development and education has been done in developed countries. Though many of the principles outlined above will apply more widely, there is every reason to expect that the cultural and economic circumstances of developing countries will shape gender learning for boys in specific ways.

Models of Educational Action

Education systems have strong organizational constraints, which tend to cast gender equality initiatives in specific practical forms. There is, nevertheless, a range of models to draw on, involving different methods and different groups of men and boys.

Specific-purpose programmes for boys. Within a school or college, a targeted programme concerned with gender issues may be set up. Many such programmes exist, with titles such as "Boys Talk", covering issues of masculine identity, personal problems, friendship, relationships with girls, families, sexuality, and violence. The quality of these programmes varies greatly, and there has been little evaluation of their effectiveness. They are popular with school adminstrators and with parents, as a way for schools to "do something for boys." Specific purpose programmes can transcend institutional formality to make effective informal links between adults and youth. Such programmes can address difficult issues. One of the most sophisticated is the "Step by Step" programme created by Denborough, which addresses the problem of male violence, and uses ideas from research on multiple masculinities to introduce participants to alternative narratives for their lives.

Whole-school agendas. Research on schools has shown that gender inequalities are embedded in the whole organizational pattern of a school, the gender regime which includes the division of labour among its staff, the hierarchies in its curriculum, its physical education programme, its dress codes, its library, etc. To change the gender education of boys (and girls) a school may need to reassess, and change, its gender regime as a whole; and some schools have undertaken this task. If a school fails to consider whole-school issues, a smaller specific purpose programme within it may be ineffective.

Mainstream curriculum and pedagogy. Some gender effects are little noticed because they are embedded in the routine curriculum (what is taught) and pedagogy (how it is taught) of a school or college. For instance, strong gender divisions are often embedded in the way technical education courses are arranged. Youth in schools are highly sensitive to the opportunities that schools offer to address gender issues, and mainstream classes provide the main opportunities for doing so. What is required is a "gender-oriented pedagogy" within the existing structures.

Youth work and informal education. Programmes outside schools and colleges are familiar venues for educational work with boys (e.g. sports teams and youth clubs). They often highlight the role of men as gender educators, not just as targets of gender education. These venues can be used for reconsideration of masculinity, providing an attractive setting for boys and youth to discuss bodies, careers, relationships, sexuality, etc. Motives for participating include the desire for exchange with other youth, personal growth, need for expressing non-traditional masculinities, and commitment to reform gender relations. Informal educational possibilities exist in peer group networks (an important strategy for community-based HIV/AIDS education), and also in families, where a great deal of gender education actually occurs.

Mass marketing. Gender equality issues including domestic violence, rape, and HIV/AIDS prevention have been addressed by mass media campaigns. Such campaigns generally resemble advertising more than education, and tend to simplify and stereotype issues. In HIV/AIDS education they have not achieved a good response from men. Media campaigns often try to appeal to boys and male youth by the use of "role models" such as celebrity sporting figures. The paradox of using footballers in an attempt to reduce violence, or to get boys to rethink masculinity, is evident. Since commercial mass media are also a major source of sexism and images of violence, other types of media for youth may be more fruitful.

Government and Public Policy

Government has a powerful influence on the gender practices of men. The state constitutes gender relations in a variety of ways, from the laws defining marriage to the symbolic meanings attached to nationhood. The state deals with the gender relations in society through many policies and interventions, from employment and development policy to the whole apparatus of the "welfare state" including social security, health and education. Though named gender policies mainly address women, in virtually every policy area where government action affects women, it also affects men. Further, "mainstream" policies (e.g. in economic affairs, security) are often substantially about men without acknowledging the fact, and may also have important effects on gender relations. Governments therefore have many opportunities for action in relation to men in pursuing gender equality.

One of the most important arenas of action concerns government as employer. Public sector agencies employ very large numbers of men and women, and put them to work in organizations that have internal gender divisions of labour, and organizational cultures that define gender in specific ways. These internal gender arrangements affect the way public organizations work and the way they change. In many parts of the world, governments have moved strongly towards equal opportunity principles and practices, often ahead of the private sector. One result is that the public sector has a relatively high proportion of women, and women are more likely to be promoted to very senior positions than in the corporate sector. Government can thus provide a socially important model of fair employment. How this should be done is still under discussion, with an active debate about "mainstreaming" equal opportunity policy in recent years.

Still, the great majority of public sector policy-making positions, worldwide, are held by men. Therefore the way men act in government is vital for gender equality outcomes. Research on gender in bureaucracies shows considerable diversity in outlooks and practices among men. There are some traditionalist men who use their organizational power to maintain the status quo and hinder the advancement of women. There are also men in bureaucracies with strong commitments to fairness and gender equality, who support the necessary reforms. Their experience is the best source of "best practice" models fo. men in organizational life. Indeed some men work alongside women in gender equality units. Often it is the younger men in bureaucracies who more readily accept gender equality.

For good gender equality outcomes, it is vital to have support from men in the top organizational levels of government. This seems to be true both in central and local government. Having a proactive CEO leads to support for gender equality from other men in the organization. It is important not only that men in powei support equality measures, but also that they support the women involved in gender equality processes.

Two background features of public sector organizations affect men's orientation to gender equality processes. One is the commitment of many public sector workers to an ideology of public service. Many believe that the state exists to serve the common good, and see their work as defined by the public interest. These beliefs may be a powerful support for men to act in the cause of gender equality. There is, however, a strong contemporary trend towards restructuring public sector agencies on the corporate model, often involving privatization and outsourcing, and emphasizing market mechanisms in place of bureaucracy. This trend is changing the character of public sector employment and may replace conceptions of the public interest with market ideas. The consequences for gender equality are mixed; they need careful scrutiny.

Businesses, Non- governmental Organizations and Unions

Organizations in civil society and the private sector have their own internal gender regimes that affect the social positions of women and men. Corporations may function as exemplary employers in terms of gender equality, introducing fair employment practices, anti-discrimination measures and gender inclusive decision-making. Regrettably they often do not function this way. Here, as in the public sector, the men who hold predominant organizational power are vital in the process of change.

Non-governmental organizations (NGOs) have played a pioneering role in some issues about men and gender. They have also played a pioneering role in the field of men's health. This has resulted in a degree of credibility that may be important in gender equality issues. Among the problems of NGO action are small-scale and uncertain funding. This creates the problem of promising initiatives, for instance in the education of boys, not being followed up. The relative vulnerability of NGOs may make it difficult for them to risk initiatives which might alienate powerful community groups and gender reform is a risky area.

Unions have a capacity to affect consciousness as well as practice; they have wide credibility in working-class communities, though their reach does not extend into the informal economy. They have often, in the past, defended male workers' interests exclusively, and it has taken long and difficult struggles to change the masculinised culture of old-style unionism. Change is occurring, as more unionists see that solidarity extends across genders (as it extends across races and nationalities); indeed, the survival of unionism in the modern workforce depends on the participation of women. Women workers, in turn, are generally benefited by being unionized. Men in the union movement now commonly accept the principle of gender equality. Some men turn this into positive action, such as programmes against sexual harassment in the workplace, and against domestic violence in workers' homes. Shortage of resources among unions hampers follow-up of initiatives among male workers.

Union action is likely to be crucial in extending "equal opportunity" benefits from the professional and managerial class to the working class. Union meetings and processes may also be a particularly important venue for debating and resolving the practical problems of men's support for gender equality.

Alliances with Women

Many people find it hard to imagine an alliance of men and women for gender equality, and there are real difficulties in the way of such alliances. Since the growth of an autonomous women's movement, the main impetus for reform has been located in women's groups, not mixed groups. Some currents in the women's movement, especially those concerned with men's violence, are reluctant to work with men, and many women are sceptical of men's willingness to change. On their side, many men regard women's groups with disdain, or consider that gender reform is only a "women's issue" and not the business of men. Men who interest themselves in gender issues are often regarded with suspicion.

Nevertheless, some feminists argue that alliances for change between women and men are possible, even crucial for achieving gender equality. In some social movements, for instance environmentalism, there is a strong ideology of gender equality. The men in these movements encounter women's strength and often make conscious attempts to overcome sexism and reorganize their lives as men. Masculinity politics is a complex field, and though some men are hostile to gender equality, some men's movements are pro-equality and are oriented towards cooperation with wo men.

In local government, practical alliances between women concerned with gender equality, and men from anti-racist and working-class movements, have been effective in a variety of countries. The same is true in the arena of state policy-making. Alliances within government between gender equality activists, mostly women, and reform-minded bureaucrats and politicians, mostly men, have underpinned many advances in gender equality policy. Even in the field of men's violence against women, there has been cooperation between women's groups and men's groups, for instance in prevention work. This cooperation can be an inspiration to grassroots workers, and a powerful demonstration of women's and men's common interest in a peaceful and equal society.

The concept of "alliance" is itself important, in preserving autonomy for women's groups, in pre-empting a tendency for any one group to speak for others, and in defining a credible role for men. In some early attempts to formulate a gender equality strategy for men, the role defined was that of dependent auxiliaries to the women's movement. This was not a position that attracted many men as supporters, while it downplayed the distinctive experiences and resources that men might bring to the struggle for gender equality. An "alliance" approach allows these resources to be used, and helps in defining a position of dignity for the men as well as the women involved in gender reform.

Men's Movements

The diversity of masculinities documented in recent research is reflected in the diversity of "men's movements." A study in the United States found at least eight different tendencies, each with a different agenda for the making or remaking of masculinity. Similar diversity can be found in other countries. It follows that there is no unified political position for men in relation to gender equality, and no authoritative representative of "men's interests."

Men's movements have generally had a marginal position in public policy-making concerned with gender equality. Those men's movements that seek to enter the policy-making process are not necessarily pursuing gender equality indeed, this has sometimes been a vehicle of "backlash" politics.

The experience of men's movements specifically concerned with gender equality therefore needs to be examined closely. A well-known example is the "White Ribbon Campaign" which mobilized public opinion and educated men and boys for the prevention of men's violence against women. Originating in Canada, in response to the massacre of women in Montreal in 1989, the White Ribbon Campaign achieved very high visibility in that country, with support from political and community leaders and considerable outreach in schools and mass media. More recently it has spread to other countries. Groups concerned with violence prevention have appeared in other countries, such as Men Against Sexual Assault in Australia and MOVE in the United States. While they have not achieved the visibility of the White Ribbon Campaign they have built up a valuable body of knowledge about the successes and difficulties of organizing among men.

The most extensive experience of men organizing around issues of gender and sexual politics is that of homosexual men in anti-discrimination campaigns, the gay liberation movement, and community responses to the HIV/AIDS pandemic. Many heterosexual men see no lessons here for themselves but homosexual masculinities and heterosexual masculinities are not so different as stereotypes would suggest. Gay men have pioneered in areas such as community care for the sick, community education for responsible sexual practices, representation in the public sector, and overcoming social exclusion, which are important for all groups of men concerned with gender equality.

The struggle for gender equality must engage the energy and passion of men, as it already has with women. Men have specific obstacles to overcome, especially the fact that for many, a move towards gender equality is against their short-term interests. These obstacles can be overcome by a passion for equality or a vision of the general benefits to humanity. At this point, when a historic change in consciousness is required of men, men's movements are important in articulating the issues, engaging men and youth in the process, and providing support for people working for change.

All social movements experience human wear and tear, sometimes "burnout" among those committed to the work. The women's movement has been in the forefront of social change movements in recognizing the need for personal support for their activists. The same need arises among men (though conventional masculinity encourages men to deny such needs). Engaging men more deeply in gender equality struggles will create a need for support which women's groups can hardly be expected to meet! Pro-equality men's movements are therefore an important resource in sustaining the human capacity to continue gender change in the long run.

The Way Forward

Inviting men to end men's privileges and remaking masculinities to sustain gender equality, will strike many people as a strange or utopian project. Yet it is already under way. The diversity of masculinities, of men's identities and practices, complicates the process but is also an important asset. As this diversity becomes better known, men and boys can more easily see a range of possibilities for their own lives, and both men and women are less likely to think of gender inequality as unchangeable. It becomes possible to identify specific groups of men who might engage in alliances for change.

There is a spectrum of masculinity politics in the contemporary world some groups and movements supporting gender equality and some opposing it. It is not reasonable to expect a worldwide consensus for gender equality. What is possible is that those forms of masculinity politics which support gender equality might become hegemonic among men. It is possible that groups supporting equality provide the agenda for public discussion about men's lives and patterns of masculinity. There is already a broad cultural shift in masculinity politics towards a historical consciousness about gender, an awareness that gender customs came into existence at specific moments in time and can always be transformed by social action. What is needed now is a widespread sense of agency among men, a sense that this transformation is something they can share in, as a practical proposition. This is, indeed, no more than the cultural presupposition of the "joint responsibility" of men invoked by the General Assembly declaration of the year 2000.

For gender equality politics to become hegemonic among men does not require that other political views should vanish. It does require effective responses to the resistance that comes from men still committed to gender privilege, or from men who accept gender equality in principle but do little about it in practice. An active process of debate, persuasion, and contestation is required. Masculinity politics should be thought of as a dialectic, not an expression of fixed identities or positions. There are many forums in which this dialectic can occur, from family homes to mass media, workplaces and voluntary organizations as well as parliaments and international bodies.

Is a revolution in masculinity required, before gender equality can be achieved? Some men have already undertaken profound transformations of personal character and relationships in pursuit of a vision of equality. This is a difficult undertaking, sometimes with high human costs, and its outcome is by no means certain. All honour and respect to those who attempt it. However it is not practical to ask all men to engage in revolutionary personal change. Nor is it necessary, before a dynamic of social change can begin. The core of gender reform is setting up processes of change that will transform unequal gender relations. Men can become partners in such processes by taking specific steps in workplaces and families to equalize resources, share power, end violence and harassment, share childcare, etc. "Step by step", as Denborough put it in his work on violence with male youth, can achieve major change, provided the change process keeps going. Given the diversity of masculinities, and the diversity of social situations, change will happen at different paces in different men's lives.

Since men are collectively the beneficiaries of most gender inequalities, and are the agents of most gender-based violence, it is not surprising that men are for the most part defined negatively in gender policy discourse. It is therefore very important to see gender equality as a positive project for men. Gender equality is an undertaking for men that can be creative and joyful. It realizes high principles of social justice, it produces better lives for the women that men care about, and it will produce better lives for the majority of men in the long run. This can and should be a project that generates energy, that finds expression in creative arts as well as formal politics, and that can illuminate all aspects of men's lives.

The international dimension of this issue is important. As noted above, issues concerning men and boys are now debated and researched worldwide. This research has documented great diversity in constructions of masculinity and in men's situations. It should not be assumed that methods suitable for one context will work in all others. Women involved in gender equality work have come to recognize the importance of cultural difference and diversity; the same lesson should be applied with men.

At the same time, it is one world, and cultures inevitably interact with each other. The creation of world society, and contemporary globalisation, are real processes. Global level forums with their own gender regimes have been created. A world politics of gender equality now exists and men must find places in it. At the very least, it is important to learn from each other, and to pool ideas and experiences. More positively, international exchanges can be important in providing support, stimulating creativity and imagination about men's lives, and sustaining the vision of a gender-equal world.

8

Changing Family Planning Scenario

The Family Welfare Programme in India has experienced significant growth and adaptation over the past half century since its inception in 1951. During this period, financial investments in the programme have substantially increased and service delivery points have significantly expanded. Services administered through the programme have been broadened to include immunisation, pregnancy, delivery and postpartum care, and preventive and curative health care. The range of contraceptive products delivered through the programme has widened. Multiple stakeholders, including the private sector and non-governmental sector, have been engaged in providing contraceptive services. Of late, the programme has been integrated with the broader Reproductive and Child Health Programme. The couple protection rate has quadrupled from 10 per cent in 1971 to 44 per cent in 1999. Notwithstanding these achievements, several issues continue to daunt the programme and many goals remain underachieved: a significant proportion of pregnancies continue to be unplanned; the contraceptive needs of millions of women remainunmet; several sub-population groups including adolescents and men continue to be neglected and under-served; and contraceptive choice remains conspicuous by its absence, as is quality of care within the programme.

Recognition of the changes worldwide and the challenges that are faced by the programme has led to the development of several new policy initiatives. Recently, the programme focus has shifted away from vertical family planning services towards the provision of comprehensive integrated reproductive health care at all levels of the health sector.

Changing Policy and Programme Environment

The Family Welfare Programme in India was launched with the objective of reducing birth rates to the extent necessary to stabilise population at a level consistent with the requirements of the national economy. The programme has since evolved through a number of stages, and has changed direction, emphasis and strategies. During the first decade of its existence, family planning was considered more a mechanism to improve the health of mothers and children than a method of population control. Clinic-centred family planning service delivery, along with health education activities, were promoted during this period. Over time however, the primary focus of the programme became the achievement of demographic goals.

With growing concerns about the rate of population growth and its adverse effect on the pace of social and economic development, the Third Five-year Plan period (1961–66) marked a subtle shift in the emphasis of the programme from the welfare of women and children to the macro objective of population stabilisation. At the same time, an extension-education approach replaced the original clinic centred approach, and the programme was integrated with health services. During 1965–75, the programme was further integrated with the maternal and child health programme. This period also witnessed the introduction of time-bound method specific targets within the programme.

As is well known, the target-oriented approach became highly coercive during the Emergency period (1975–77). The National Population Policy 1976 called for a "frontal attack on the problems of population" and inspired state governments to "pass suitable legislation to make family planning compulsory for citizens" and to stop childbearing after three children, if the "state so desires". The backlash of the coercive approach compelled subsequent governments to stress the voluntary nature of family planning acceptance. The Population Policy 1977 clearly underscored that "compulsion in the area of family welfare must be ruled out for all times to come," and emphasised the need for an educational and motivational approach to make acceptance of family planning completely voluntary. However, in the 1980s, the time-bound, target-oriented approach was revived and efforts to encourage the use of reversible methods were initiated. Incentive payments were vigorously promoted during this period, leading to the violation of women's rights in some cases.

The 1990s witnessed dramatic changes in the family welfare policy and programme in the country. The passing of the 72nd and 73rd Constitutional Amendments and the Panchayati Raj and Nagar Palika Acts in 1992 set in motion the process of democratic decentralisation, and brought the Family Welfare Programme, legally, in the domain of panchayati raj institutions. In addition, several factors including stagnation in the Family Welfare Programme, organised pressure from multiple constituencies to bring issues of quality and choice into the programme, and the recognition of inherent constraints in the programme contributed to changes in policy approach. The International Conference on Population and Development in 1994 and the Beijing Women's Conference in 1995 further catalysed the process of policy change. In 1996, the government took the radical decision of abolishing method-specific contraceptive targets that had been used to guide, monitor and evaluate the programme for decades, replacing it with what was initially called the Target-free Approach, where health workers' case loads would be determined by needs identified at the community level, rather than centrally-assigned. In 1997, to avoid misconceptions and to direct the programme more towards addressing clients' needs, the Target-free Approach was renamed as the Community Needs Assessment Approach, and decentralised participatory planning was initiated. The government has provided broad guidelines for conducting community needs assessment and has given states the responsibility for working out the practical details of implementation.

The Reproductive and Child Health Programme, which was launched in 1997, espouses the principles of client satisfaction and high quality comprehensive and integrated health services. It seeks to integrate services for the prevention and management of unwanted pregnancy, the promotion of safe motherhood and child survival, and the prevention and management of reproductive tract infections and sexually transmitted infections. The programme aims to expand services to meet the needs of hitherto under served and neglected population groups, including adolescents, and economically and socially disadvantaged groups, such as urban slum and tribal populations. It envisages utilising and upgrading the existing health infrastructure to deliver these services. To make the programme a people's programme, the new approach champions local needs-based, decentralised, participatory planning and monitoring, and seeks to involve several stakeholders, including non-governmental organisations (NGOs), the private sector, panchayati raj institutions and civil society in more meaningful ways to move the new agenda forward.

The new approach represents a dramatic change in the culture of the Family Welfare Programme, and for the first time in the history of the programme in India, attention has been focused on gender concerns. The Reproductive and Child Health Programme seeks to address gender issues impinging on women's health by improving quality of care, including promoting better interaction between providers and clients; increasing the availability of female health care providers at the primary health care level; addressing neglected concerns of women such as reproductive tract infections; addressing the needs of neglected population subgroups such as adolescents; organising gender sensitisation training for stakeholders; encouraging male involvement in reproductive health; and facilitating women's and men's participation in programme monitoring through client feedback.

The Reproductive and Child Health Programme has been carried out with varying intensity and clarity in different parts of the country. Preparations for launching the second phase of the Reproductive and Child Health Programme are currently under way.

The National Population Policy, adopted in February 2000, further legitimised the paradigm shift to client-based services. The National Population Commission was set up in May 2000 to guide the translation of policy rhetoric into programmes. In March 2001, an Empowered Action Group was set up by the Government of India to facilitate focused efforts to promote the Reproductive and Child Health Programme in the states of Uttar Pradesh, Bihar, Madhya Pradesh, Rajasthan, Orissa, Chhattisgarh, Jharkhand and Uttaranchal which have been lagging behind in a number of socio-demographic indices. Several state governments have also framed state-specific population policies thereby broadening the policy discourse within the states.

The National Population Policy provides a policy framework for achieving the twin objectives of population stabilisation and promoting reproductive health within the wider context of sustainable development. The immediate objectives of the National Population Policy are to address the unmet need for contraception, the limitations in health care infrastructure and the shortages in health personnel, and to provide integrated service delivery for basic reproductive and child health care. In the medium term, the National Population Policy aims to achieve the goal of bringing the total fertility rate to replacement level by 2010. The National Population Policy has delineated twelve strategic themes to achieve these objectives, including decentralised planning and implementation, convergence of service delivery at the grassroots, empowering women and encouraging male involvement, meeting the unmet need for family welfare services, addressing the needs of disadvantaged and under-served population groups, and forging public–private partnerships.

The National Population Policy affirms the government's commitment to the provision of quality services, information and counselling, and expanding contraceptive method choices in order to enable people to make voluntary and informed choices. Disincentives have not been included in the Policy, though several promotional and motivational measures are to be implemented at the community and individual level. Unlike in the past, these incentives are not just for sterilisation but have been linked to poverty, delayed marriage, antenatal and delivery care, birth registration, birth of a girl child and immunisation. These include, to list a few, rewarding and honouring Panchayats and Zilla Parishads for exemplary performance in universalising the small family norm, achieving reductions in infant mortality and birth rates, and promoting literacy with completion of primary schooling; providing cash incentives to mothers who have their first child after 19 years of age; and rewarding couples below the poverty line who marry after the legal age of marriage, register the marriage, have their first child after the mother reaches the age of 21, accept the small family norm, and adopt a terminal method after the birth of the second child. However, it is a cause of great concern that some of the policies adopted by the states espouse strategies and mechanisms that are diametrically opposed to the principles of equity and equality that the new National Population Policy entails. In their urgency to reduce population numbers, some states, including Andhra Pradesh, Madhya Pradesh, Maharashtra and Rajasthan, have articulated several open or "veiled" disincentives. The population policy of Madhya Pradesh, for example, advocates debarring individuals marrying before the legal age at marriage from seeking jobs, getting admission in educational institutions and applying for loans. The policy also calls for debarring individuals with more than two children from contesting local body elections. These policies will negatively affect women who hardly play a role in deciding the age at which they are married or the number of children they bear.

These new policy and programme initiatives articulate laudable principles and goals. The challenge lies in translating these principles into reality.

The Contraceptive Scenario

Over the decades, contraceptive use has been increasing in India. At the same time, there is a substantial unmet need for contraception. The contraceptive scenario is also characterised by the predominance of non-reversible methods, limited use of male/couple-dependent methods, substantial levels of discontinuation, and negligible use of contraceptives among both married and unmarried adolescents. As will be seen in the following discussion, there are wide regional variations in all these aspects.

Contraceptive Use

Official statistics report that 87 million eligible couples, out of an estimated total of 171 million eligible couples, were effectively protected against conception by various contraceptive methods in the year 2000. Data from National Family Health Survey (NFHS)–2 indicate that nearly one-half of currently married women were using some method of contraception in 1998–99. Contraceptive prevalence increased with age except at the older ages (8 per cent among adolescent girls vs. 67 per cent among women aged 35–39 years), with education (43 per cent among illiterate women vs. 57 per cent among women with a high school education), with standard of living (40 per cent among women from households with a low standard of living index vs. 61 per cent among women from households with a high standard of living index), and with number of living children (5 per cent among women with no living children vs. 68 per cent among women with three living children. Similarly, at each parity, current use was lower among women with no sons than among women with one or more sons, with a maximum differential at parity three, indicating that strong son preference prevails in India (at parity three, 38 per cent of women with no sons vs. 62 per cent with one son and 75 per cent with two sons). Most of these differentials have persisted over time. Contraceptive prevalence varied widely among the states, from less than 30 per cent in Meghalaya, Bihar and Uttar Pradesh to more than 60 per cent in Delhi, Haryana, Himachal Pradesh, Punjab, West Bengal, Maharashtra and Kerala.

A comparison with data from NFHS–1 reveals an 18 per cent increase in contraceptive prevalence during the six-and-a-half years between the two surveys. Although contraceptive prevalence differs among the states, there has been an overall increase in contraceptive use in almost all states during the 1990s. The exceptions are Goa, Jammu and Kashmir, and Meghalaya. The northeastern states of Nagaland and Arunachal Pradesh recorded the maximum increase (by 133 per cent and 50 per cent, respectively). Among the four large northern states of Bihar, Madhya Pradesh, Rajasthan and Uttar Pradesh, all except Bihar recorded increases ranging between 21 per cent and 42 per cent during this period. A preliminary comparison of data from the Reproductive and Child Health Survey–1 (1998–99) and the first phase of the Reproductive and Child Health Survey–2 (2002), reflecting changes after the introduction of the Community Needs Assessment Approach and the Reproductive and Child Health Programme, also indicate an increase in contraceptive use in all the major states, particularly Uttar Pradesh, Madhya Pradesh and Himachal Pradesh.

Method-Mix

A "cafeteria approach," whereby clients are provided with a choice of contraceptive methods, has been adopted by the Family Welfare Programme since the 1960s. However, it is well documented that, until recently, the emphasis of the programme remained skewed towards promoting non-reversible methods, particularly female sterilisation. Hence, not surprisingly, female sterilisation continues to be used by the majority of contraceptive users in India. Nationally, data from NFHS–2 show that sterilisation accounted for 84 per cent of the contraceptive prevalence rate due to modern methods and 75 per cent of overall current contraceptive prevalence. Although reported by only a negligible minority, sterilisation was the most commonly adopted method even among married adolescents in India. A review of data on contraceptive behaviour of adolescents in Asian countries shows that India is the only country where such a pattern prevails.

The predominance of sterilisation is observed in almost all states. For example more than 90 per cent of modern contraceptive method users are sterilised in all the southern states and Bihar, and the situation is most skewed in Andhra Pradesh, where 97 per cent of all modern method users are sterilised. The exceptions include Delhi, Punjab and a few northeastern states where fewer than three in five users of modern methods are sterilised. A comparison with data from NFHS–1 indicates that the same pattern prevailed throughout the 1990s. At the state level, the percentage share of non-reversible methods in current prevalence increased in Delhi and Arunachal Pradesh, declined in Punjab, West Bengal, Assam and Meghalaya, and remained almost the same in the other states.

Nationally, the use of natural family planning methods was reportedly low, accounting for just 10 per cent of current contraceptive use. Among the states, the use of natural methods was relatively common in West Bengal, Assam, Manipur, Punjab, Sikkim and Goa. In West Bengal, more than one in four current users were using a natural family planning method.

Use of Male/Couple- Dependent Methods

In India, gender inequalities favour men and sexual and reproductive health decisions are usually made by them. Therefore, there is a growing realisation that unless men are reached, the Reproductive and Child Health Programme, including family welfare efforts, will have limited impact. Direct evidence on the use of male methods is scarce as men have been excluded from most of the national surveys, and small-scale studies exploring the contraceptive behaviour of men are limited. Data from NFHS–2, based on the responses of currently married women, show that one in ten currently married "couples" were using male/couple-dependent contraceptive methods (condoms, vasectomy, withdrawal and periodic abstinence) in 1998–99, which translates into 21 per cent of total current contraceptive prevalence. The use of male/couple-dependent methods was as low as 2–3 per cent of currently married couples in Mizoram, Bihar and Karnataka, and as high as 23–28 per cent of currently married couples in West Bengal, Delhi and Punjab.

Small-scale studies of women and men also reflect the limited use of male/couple-dependent methods. For example, in a study of women in the slums and villages in Maharashtra, male-dependent methods accounted for less than 10 per cent of total contraceptive prevalence. In a study of married men in the tribal areas of Maharashtra, male/couple-dependent methods accounted for 16 per cent of overall contraceptive use. However, another study of married men in Uttar Pradesh reports that one in three current users were using either condoms or male sterilisation.

During the six-year period between NFHS–1 and NFHS–2, the use of male/couple-dependent methods remained the same. At the state level, all the southern states recorded a decline, ranging from 21 per cent to 46 per cent in the proportion of currently married couples using male/couple-dependent methods during the 1990s. Among the four major northern states, while Madhya Pradesh and Bihar recorded a decline, the proportion of couples using male methods increased in Uttar Pradesh and Rajasthan. Data specifically on the use of condoms reveal that only a small minority (3.1 per cent) of currently married couples were using condoms. Condom use was typically low in almost all states, except Delhi and Punjab, where 18 per cent and 14 per cent, respectively, of currently married couples were using condoms. During the 1990s, according to survey data, condom use increased marginally from 2.4 per cent in 1992–93 to 3.1 per cent in 1998–99. Despite the introduction of "no-scalpel" vasectomy and campaigns to promote male involvement in family planning and reproductive health, the acceptance of vasectomy remained negligible—2 per cent of currently married couples nationally. In fact, during the

1990s, the acceptance of vasectomy declined substantially (by 44 per cent) nationally, a pattern established during the post-Emergency period.

Contraceptive Practice Among the Unmarried

Available evidence suggests that a substantial proportion of unmarried adolescent boys and girls are sexually active, placing them at risk of unintended pregnancy and sexually transmitted infections. 15–30 per cent of adolescent boys and up to 10 per cent of girls in India were sexually active before marriage. Little is known about the contraceptive behaviours of unmarried adolescents. Demographic and Health Surveys and other national surveys have largely excluded this group and only a few small-scale studies have explored the contraceptive behaviours of unmarried adolescents. Because relatively few unmarried adolescents report being sexually active, data on contraceptive use from these studies may not accurately reflect their contraceptive behaviours. These studies indicate, however, that a large majority of unmarried, sexually active adolescents do not use any contraceptive method. Those who report practising contraception often use natural methods, which are more difficult for adolescents to use consistently and effectively because they require accurate knowledge of the reproductive cycle and active cooperation of the partner.

According to a review of studies on premarital sexual behaviour among adolescent boys in India, the vast majority had engaged in unprotected sex, even with commercial sex workers. A study of male students in Mumbai reveals that 43 per cent of sexually experienced students never used a condom, and 45 per cent had used a condom only occasionally. Yet another study of adolescent males in a slum setting in Uttar Pradesh shows that 58 per cent of sexually experienced males reported ever having used a condom during any act of intercourse, 32 per cent reported condom use in relations with sex workers, and 56 per cent in relations with a friend or relative. Protection against pregnancy appears to motivate most condom use. Similarly, in a study of unmarried and married men in Orissa, 19 per cent of sexually active unmarried men reported condom use during the last sexual act. Among those who reported condom use, 61 per cent mentioned prevention of pregnancy as the main reason for use, indicating that condom promotion efforts aimed at young men should stress the dual protection properties of condoms. These findings highlight the need for innovative strategies to reach out to unmarried young people with better information and services.

Contraceptive Discontinuation and Switching

As contraceptive use increases and becomes a more established behaviour, prevalence is no longer a sufficient marker of programme success. Contraceptive continuation may become more important than acceptance in increasing contraceptive prevalence. An analysis of contraceptive continuation rates and the reasons why women discontinue using contraceptive methods could provide important information about the adequacy of services provided. As the Family Welfare Programme in the country is currently making vigorous efforts to shift its emphasis from non-reversible methods to reversible methods, and expand service delivery beyond the bounds of the public sector, information on contraceptive discontinuation and switching assumes greater significance. Data on contraceptive continuation/discontinuation, switching and failure are, however, limited.

In India, as the vast majority (66 per cent) of ever users are sterilised, only a small proportion of ever users have the option of discontinuing use. Nationally, data from NFHS–2 show that one in ten currently married women who have ever used a contraceptive method (which translates into about one in three [29 per cent] ever users of reversible methods) had discontinued use at the time of the survey. Though the desire for a child was cited as the main reason for discontinuation (30 per cent), the fact that more than one-third reported method-related reasons such as method failure, side effects and inconvenience highlights the need for improved quality of services.

The data also show that younger women (15–24-year-olds) were more likely to discontinue using contraceptives compared to older women. Younger women were also more likely to mention desire for a child, but less likely to mention side effects, as their main reason for discontinuation. However, younger women were no more likely than older women to discontinue use due to method failure or difficulty in accessing a suitable method. Notably, contraceptive discontinuation was comparatively higher in the northern and northeastern states, particularly the latter, than in the southern states. Moreover, women who discontinued using contraceptives in the northern and northeastern states more frequently reported difficulty in accessing a method or inconvenience in using a method as reasons for discontinuation, compared with women in the southern states.

Information on method-specific discontinuation rates from small-scale surveys shows, not unexpectedly, higher discontinuation rates for pills and condoms than intrauterine devices (IUDs). Estimates derived from data on contraceptive history over a three-year period in Uttar Pradesh show that four-fifths of the IUD users continued use for up to 20 months and only 50 per cent of pill users continued for up to 10 months. A prospective study of women using IUDs and oral pills in Gujarat reveals that 43 and 62 per cent respectively discontinued the method by the end of the twelfth month, and after eighteen months, the proportion discontinuing the method increased to 62 and 73 per cent respectively. The tendency to discontinue use appears to be more common in rural areas than in urban areas. For example, in a study of IUD users in Karnataka, 50 per cent of the rural users, compared to 30 per cent of the urban users, discontinued use within one year of acceptance.

It is important to assess whether women using a contraceptive method switch to an alternative method immediately after discontinuing the method they have been using. However, information on patterns of contraceptive switching in India is sparse. As with contraceptive discontinuation, the option of contraceptive switching is limited as many ever users had never used any other method before sterilisation.

An analysis of data on future use of contraception available from NFHS–2 sheds light on the intended pattern of switching among current discontinuers and indicates that one-third intend to use another method within 12 months from the time of the survey, another one-third intend to use a method sometime later, and the rest do not intend to use any method at all. While nearly one-half (46 per cent) of the potential contraceptive switchers plan to use female sterilisation, one-fifth plan to switch to pills, one-tenth to condoms, and another one-tenth to natural family planning. Among discontinuers who intend to switch to a method within 12 months, the choice tends to be more in favour of reversible methods (48 per cent for modern reversible methods, 10 per cent for natural family planning methods and 33 per cent for non-reversible methods).

A prospective follow-up study of IUD and oral pill users in Gujarat shows that about one-third of those who discontinued IUD use after 12–18 months did not switch to any other method, one in ten switched to female sterilisation, one in twenty to natural methods, 3 per cent to oral pills and 3 per cent to condoms. Among oral pill discontinuers, while over one in four did not switch to any method, the tendency was to switch to other spacing methods like IUDs or natural methods, followed by a terminal method.

Unmet Need for Contraception

Despite improved availability and access to contraceptive services, a substantial proportion of pregnancies in India are unplanned (mistimed or unwanted). It is estimated that if all unwanted births could be eliminated, the total fertility rate would drop to the replacement level of fertility. Data from NFHS–2, for example, show that 21 per cent of all pregnancies that resulted in live births in the three years preceding the survey (including current pregnancies) were unplanned—12 per cent mistimed and 9 per cent definitely unwanted. In all likelihood, this is an underestimate of unintended pregnancies because longitudinal survey data reveal women's tendency for ex post revision of their preferences in favour of the wantedness of existing children. Moreover, a substantial proportion of unintended pregnancies may be terminated through induced abortion. Estimates show that about 6.7 million induced abortions take place annually in India. Several studies report that the desire to limit family size and to space the next birth are the main reasons for abortion mentioned by the majority of abortion seekers. These findings provide clear evidence of the substantial unmet need for contraception among women in India.

The concept of unmet need for contraception, originally coined to reflect the discrepancy between fertility preferences and contraceptive use has evolved over time. Conventionally, currently married women who are not using any contraceptive method but who do not want any more children, or who want to wait two or more years before having another child, are defined as having an unmet need for family planning. It has been suggested that the concept of unmet need be expanded to include women's future fertility preferences; potential clients other than married women, including unmarried women and men (whether married or unmarried), and women who are dissatisfied with their current method or are using an inappropriate method; and qualitative as well as quantitative dimensions of care. Following the recent shift in the reproductive health paradigm, in India too, researchers have called for an expansion of the concept to reflect "the extent to which women are achieving their reproductive intentions in good health". The conventional concept, however, continues to guide programme design in the country.

Magnitude

By the conventional definition, NFHS–2 reports that 16 per cent of currently married women have an unmet contraceptive need—8.3 per cent for spacing and 7.5 per cent for limiting—which translates into one-fourth of women who wish to space or limit births. It is estimated that if all women who say they want to space or limit their births were to use family planning, the contraceptive prevalence rate would increase from 48 per cent to 64 per cent of currently married women. Based on the current population of 1,027 million married women, this implies that approximately 40 million married women have an unmet need. While the needs of the vast majority of women who wish to stop childbearing are being satisfied, the needs of women who wish to delay or space childbearing remain largely unsatisfied. For example, it is estimated that the needs of 86 per cent of women who wish to stop childbearing are addressed by the existing services, compared to the needs of 30 per cent of women who wish to delay their next pregnancy.

What is disturbing is the finding that the current programme is addressing only a small part of the contraceptive demand of young women, particularly those who are yet to begin or are still in the process of forming their families. Young women are more likely to have an unmet need for contraception. Data from NFHS–2 indicate that 25 per cent of young women, compared to 17 per cent of women aged 25–34 years and 7 per cent of women 35 years and above, had an unmet need for contraception. When translated in terms of young women who wish to space or limit births, this implies that the existing service delivery system is addressing the contraceptive needs of only 44 per cent of young women. Among women who have not given birth, the contraceptive needs of only 25 per cent of women are satisfied. In addition to the strong programme emphasis on sterilisation until recently, this may be partly due to the neglect of young women by the programme that perceives a contraceptive need among young people only after they have completed their family formation. Evidence is emerging, however, that young couples, despite community norms that favour a first child soon after marriage, would prefer delaying the first birth until they have spent more time together to know each other better.

There are pronounced regional differences in the proportion of women with an unmet need for contraception. NFHS–2 data show that the level of unmet need was higher in the northern and northeastern states than in the southern states — 19 per cent vs. 11 per cent. There are substantial differences in unmet need within each region as well. In the southern states, for example, 8 per cent of married women in Andhra Pradesh had an unmet need for contraception, compared to 17 per cent in Goa. Similarly, the level of unmet need in the northern states ranged from 7 per cent in Punjab to 25 per cent in Bihar and Uttar Pradesh. In the northeastern states, unmet need ranged from 16 per cent in Mizoram to 36 per cent in Meghalaya.

National and Regional Trends

Nationally, the proportion of women with an unmet need declined marginally (by 19 per cent) during the six years between NFHS–1 and NFHS–2. The decline was more pronounced in the case of unmet need for spacing (25 per cent) than for limiting (12 per cent). The trends in unmet need for spacing and limiting for different age groups, indicate that the decline was concentrated in the group of women 35 years and above and the least decline was reflected in the younger age group.

A comparison of state-level estimates of unmet need for contraceptives in 1992–93 and 1998–99 shows that the level of unmet need declined in the majority of the states, ranging from as low as 2 per cent in Bihar to 54 per cent in Haryana. However, the northeastern states, except Assam, recorded an increase in the level of unmet need during this period. While the level of unmet need increased marginally (by 9 per cent) in Manipur, it increased substantially (by 41 per cent) in Meghalaya.

It is important to bear in mind that individuals move rapidly in and out of the unmet need state, making the subgroups with an unmet need a moving target. Moreover, unmet need is determined by a combination of factors including the extent of exposure to the risk of pregnancy, the efficacy of contraceptive practice and intentions about childbearing.

Barriers to Meeting Contraceptive Needs

The Family Welfare Programme has been successful in spreading the message of the small family norm, improving contraceptive acceptance and reducing fertility rates but its achievements have been modest. While contextual and structural factors (high levels of illiteracy, poor access to sources of knowledge, poverty, and gender- and non-gender-based disparities) are partly responsible, the direction, emphasis and strategies followed hitherto in the Family Welfare Programme have largely contributed to the limited success of the programme. There is an increasing recognition of various barriers to promoting contraceptive choice and meeting contraceptive needs in the country. Several measures to address these have been launched in recent years.

Limited Knowledge

As is known, the small family norm is widely accepted (the mean ideal family size reported by young people is currently 2.5 children) and general awareness of contraception is universal (99 per cent of currently married women in the reproductive age group were aware of at least one contraceptive method). However, awareness of reversible (modern or natural) methods is relatively limited among both women and men. Nationally, for example, only 71 per cent of currently married women were aware of condoms. In some major states including Andhra Pradesh, Karnataka, Madhya Pradesh and Orissa, fewer than three in five currently married women were aware of condoms. What is more disturbing is the finding that awareness of specific reversible methods, which are more suitable for young women, is even more limited among younger women compared to older women. For example, only three-fifths of married adolescents were aware of condoms, compared to nearly three-fourths of women aged 20–34 years. Also disturbing, particularly in the context of increasing premarital sexual experience among unmarried boys and girls, is the evidence from small-scale studies that a substantial proportion of unmarried boys and girls lack contraceptive knowledge.

Knowledge of contraception, as usually measured in national surveys, is unlikely to reflect a familiarity with and understanding of contraceptives adequate to lead to use. Of equal importance as awareness of contraceptive methods is knowledge of where these methods can be obtained, what the main side effects are and how to use the selected method correctly. Evidence from a number of small-scale studies in various parts of the country indicates that inadequate knowledge of contraceptive methods is a reason for not accepting family planning. Incomplete or erroneous information on where to obtain methods and how to use them is strongly associated with unmet need. Studies assessing correct, adequate and timely knowledge of contraceptive methods among women and men are limited, but suggest that a small proportion have complete and timely knowledge of various contraceptive methods. For example, a study of married men in Gujarat reports that knowledge about the correct use of condoms was low; only a small minority knew about when to put on a condom, how to use it properly and that it should not be reused. In a study of men in rural Maharashtra, while 92 per cent were aware of condoms, only 29 per cent knew about its correct use. A small-scale study conducted in Karnataka reports that while 56 per cent of women and 61 per cent of men interviewed were aware of reversible methods, a much smaller proportion—31 per cent of women and 52 per cent of men—was aware of at least one service outlet for reversible methods.

Information, education and communication (IEC) efforts need to be strengthened, and integrated within the training of all health providers. The Reproductive and Child Health Programme recognises the importance of IEC efforts in promoting a demand for services, including family planning services, but the lack of adequate collaboration between the health sector and IEC units is reportedly rendering these efforts ineffective. Similarly, the experience of a scheme to involve Zilla Saksharata Samitis in IEC activities pertaining to the Reproductive and Child Health Programme shows that operationalisation at the ground level is a huge challenge. Under this scheme, these samitis are encouraged to utilise local resource persons and institutions from the district to design and deliver IEC programmes on reproductive and child health in the local language. This scheme is currently in different phases of implementation in 227 districts in the country and 22 Zilla Saksharata Samitis have completed these activities. An evaluation of the scheme in a number of districts in Gujarat shows that the involvement of Zilla Saksharata Samitis and IEC functionaries, who are to play a vital role in this venture, is completely missing. These educational activities are mainly organised by the staff of the primary health centres with some support from the local Panchayat.

Gender Inequalities and Limited Male Involvement

Within the patriarchal setup in India, women have relatively little power. Young women are particularly powerless, secluded and voiceless in matters relating to their own lives, and are constrained from exercising choice in sexual and reproductive matters. Nationally, data from NFHS– 2 shows that only one in two ever-married women participated in decisions about their own health care. The role of the husband has been noted in several studies of decision-making related to the use of contraception, especially during the early years of marriage. Most couples do not discuss with each other when to have their first child, birth spacing or contraception. Nationally, for example, fewer than one in five currently married women reported discussing family planning with their husbands. Studies also show that most men approve of contraception only after having a second or third child, and that husbands' approval of a particular method is critical.

Given that men dominate in reproductive health matters, promoting shared responsibility and the active involvement of men in safe and responsible sexual relationships, family planning, safe motherhood and responsible parenthood is critical. The National Population Policy and the Reproductive and Child Health Programme recognise this synergy, but men's roles have not been properly defined in government programmes. There have been some efforts to promote the use of male methods such as vasectomy and condoms, and initiatives to re-popularise vasectomy, including IEC campaigns and training of surgeons in "no-scalpel" vasectomy, have been launched in several states. Though these efforts have proved successful in some districts in Andhra Pradesh, a similar change has not occurred in most other states.

Male health workers could play an important role in promoting male involvement in reproductive and child health. However, two-thirds of primary health centres in India do not have a male health worker. Moreover, the Reproductive and Child Health Programme document offers no clear guidelines on the role and responsibilities of male health workers. Karnataka's experience shows that involving male health workers in the community needs assessment process can be problematic. Male workers in the state, who traditionally focus on malaria and tuberculosis screening and follow-up, viewed reproductive and child health as the domain of the female worker. The Reproductive and Child Health Programme must take cognisance of this fact and redefine the role of male health workers and impart suitable training to them.

Limited efforts to involve men in reproductive health matters have been carried out by a few NGOs. These NGO experiences have demonstrated that men are potentially interested in becoming more supportive and involved in reproductive health programmes. The challenge is how to encourage more such efforts while, at the same time, finding the means to incorporate what NGOs have learned in the design and implementation of public programmes. It is encouraging that such collaborations are emerging. For example, in Maharashtra, Foundation for Research in Health Systems has been working with the state government to develop interventions to include men in reproductive health services and provide education to adolescent boys within a government programme.

Many studies report that reproductive decision-making often is beyond the control of young women and their husbands, and it is the extended family's decision on what is permissible that influences the husband/couple's decision. Access to appropriate contraception is frequently thwarted by the family and peer pressure. Hence, it is also important to engage other gatekeepers, including senior men and women in the family and influential people in the community, in reproductive health programmes.

Limited Informed Choice

The public sector essentially provides five contraceptive methods—two forms of tubectomy (laproscopy and minilap), vasectomy (including "no-scalpel" vasectomy), IUDs, oral pills (combined) and condoms. Efforts to broaden the basket of choices have been under way, including clinical trials to assess the safety and efficacy of available methods such as estrogen-progestogen combination injectable, vaginal rings and long-acting IUDs, and the development of new methods of male and female fertility regulation. As part of expanding contraceptive choice, the government has introduced emergency contraceptive pills in the Reproductive and Child Health Programme. However, most women and men, particularly those who rely on the public sector—indeed 76 per cent of current users of modern methods relied on this sector—do not have access to a wide range of contraceptives. Methods that are perceived as less effective, including pessaries, spermicides and diaphragms, or that are controversial, including injectable and implants, are either dropped or not introduced in the public programme or are given low priority by health workers. The recently introduced emergency contraceptive pills are currently available through medical officers only at the district and subdistrict level.

Not only is access to a wider choice of methods limited, but providers also often do not assist women and men to exercise their right to contraceptive choice by offering them complete and accurate information about the variety of methods available. Nationally, for example, data from NFHS–2 show that only 15 per cent of users of modern contraceptive methods who were motivated by providers, friends or others were informed about at least one alternative method. Private and NGO sector health workers were more likely to inform clients about alternative methods than were public sector health workers (28 per cent vs. 19 per cent). Providers have a distinct bias towards sterilisation. Several small-scale studies of clients and providers conducted in the early 1990s report that most women were informed about female sterilisation and only a minority were told about reversible methods. In a qualitative study in rural Karnataka, medical officers were reported to have asked investigators why couples should be told to use reversible methods if they voluntarily accept sterilisation. This bias seems to have been carried over to the clients. For example, a large majority (65 per cent) of women who intend to use contraception reported that they intend to use female sterilisation.

Evidence from a growing number of studies suggests that pre-acceptance counselling of clients on how the method works, what the expected side effects are and how to manage the side effects is typically lacking or limited in the Family Welfare Programme across the country. Nationally, data from NFHS–2 indicate that only 22 per cent of users of any modern method were informed of its possible side effects at the time of accepting the method. Similarly, data from the Reproductive and Child Health Survey–1 report that only one-third of sterilisation users (35 per cent), fewer than one-half of IUD users (46 per cent) and fewer than one-fourth of pill users (23 per cent) were informed of the side effects before accepting the method. The provision of pre-acceptance counselling was lacking or limited even in those states where contraceptive prevalence was relatively high such as Kerala and Tamil Nadu. Hence, not surprisingly, data from NFHS–2 show that among those who discontinued use at the time of the survey, more than one-fourth (29 per cent) reported side effects and other method-related concerns as reasons for discontinuing use. Small-scale studies on reasons for contraceptive discontinuation conducted in various parts of the country, including Gujarat, Karnataka, Madhya Pradesh, Maharashtra, Orissa and Uttar Pradesh, also reiterate these findings. In most of these studies, more than half of women discontinuing use of IUDs and oral pills reported side effects as the reason. There is, however, evidence that if women are informed earlier about the side effects that they might experience in the first few months of method use, continuation rates will improve significantly.

Available evidence on users' perspectives/client acceptability of various methods, though limited, suggests that many of the reversible methods that are not currently being promoted are acceptable to women in rural and urban areas. For example, in a feasibility study of user perspectives on the desirability of including the diaphragm among other contraceptive methods, 8 per cent of study participants accepted the diaphragm, and all users, irrespective of their educational level, reported that they thought the method was appropriate and easy to use. Twice as many married adolescents accepted the diaphragm as compared to older women. Similarly, evidence is emerging that if provided with complete information on all available contraceptive methods, women do make an informed choice overriding provider bias. For example, in a study where 8,077 potential clients were provided with detailed information on various methods, including IUDs, oral pills, condoms, sterilisation and Norplant, the majority (80 per cent) opted for reversible methods irrespective of their literacy status and only 17 per cent accepted sterilisation. While Norplant was the first choice of the provider for 35 per cent of the women, only 5 per cent of women preferred and accepted Norplant.

The Government of India's radical decision to remove Centre-driven targets for family planning has been perceived by many as a small but right step towards furthering informed choice, and thereby reproductive rights. Facilitating informed choice is envisaged as a strategic measure in the Reproductive and Child Health Programme and the National Population Policy 2000. Though the new policy formulations are path-breaking in bringing the language of choice and rights into national discourse, the mechanisms to translate the rhetoric into action are not clearly defined, and the strategies delineated contravene the ethos of choice and rights. In the revised target-free manual, for example, a system called "client segmentation" is used to guide a client's method choice.

Limited Access to and Availability of Services

Over the decades, there has been considerable expansion and strengthening of the health care infrastructure, and family welfare services are now an integral part of services provided by primary, secondary and tertiary care institutions across the country. Currently, about 137,271 subcentres (1/4579 population) and 22,975 primary health centres (1/

27364 population) in rural areas, and 871 health posts and 1,083 family welfare centres in urban areas provide family planning services at the grassroot level. Access to contraceptive methods has increased significantly, and only a negligible minority of women (4 per cent as per NFHS–2 data) perceived availability, accessibility or cost as major impediments to using contraception. Yet, in practice, access to and availability of services are critical issues of concern. Gaps in infrastructure, manpower, equipment and supplies at the primary health centre level remain. A recent survey of health facilities across the country reports that most primary health centres were not adequately staffed: almost one in ten was functioning without any doctor and 80 per cent did not have a female medical officer. The situation was particularly grim in Orissa, Rajasthan and Uttar Pradesh where 95 per cent or more primary health centres did not have a female medical officer. Nearly one-half of primary health centres did not have an auxiliary nurse-midwife; in states such as Orissa, Uttar Pradesh and Bihar, 87-94 per cent did not have an auxiliary nurse-midwife.

Where workers are available, they are generally poorly trained and have little knowledge of the methods they are to provide. The facility survey referred to earlier reveals that only 16 per cent of primary health centres had physicians trained in conducting sterilisation, and only two-third had at least one paramedical staff trained in IUD insertion. While female health workers in many studies reported that they had received training in IUD insertion, the majority did not feel confident about actually inserting an IUD in field settings or showed little awareness of the precautions to be taken. A survey in Maharashtra observes that only one-third of the 80 health workers had correct knowledge of oral pills and only 43 per cent could give adequate advice on a method convincingly. It is encouraging that the Reproductive and Child Health Programme has laid greater emphasis on skill upgradation and gender sensitisation training, and a nationwide reproductive and child health training programme has been launched to upgrade the skills of health providers and managers to deliver the reproductive and child health package of services. However, it is a matter of concern that a mid term review of the training component of the Reproductive and Child Health Programme notes that the modules and training focus more on the technical areas of service delivery and give little importance to the newer focus areas, such as gender sensitivity, life-cycle approach, client focus and quality of services, which are the pillars underlying the paradigm shift. It has also been pointed out that lack of state ownership of training programmes, and inadequate technical support by the collaborating centres, have significantly affected the quality and pace of training. The draft Programme Implementation Plan of the Reproductive and Child Health Programme–2 also recognises the limitations of the existing training programme.

Health or family planning workers are required to regularly visit each household in their assigned areas to provide information related to health and family planning, counsel and motivate women to adopt appropriate health and family planning practices, and deliver other related services. However, data from NFHS–2 indicate that only 13 per cent of women had received a home visit from a health or family planning worker during the 12 months preceding the survey, and women without any children were least likely to receive a home visit. Only 11 per cent of women who were visited at home reported that they received family planning services. State-level data show that fewer than 2 per cent of women in several states, including Punjab, Haryana, Delhi, Arunachal Pradesh, Nagaland, and Jammu and Kashmir, received a home visit from a health or family planning worker in the 12 months preceding the survey. Only in four states— Gujarat, Mizoram, Tamil Nadu and Maharashtra— had at least a quarter of women received such a visit. Several small-scale studies also reveal significant shortcomings in the frequency and regularity of outreach services, the time devoted by workers to such activities and the length of time spent with clients. Additionally, outreach services are reported to be almost non-existent in remote and tribal areas. Moreover, health workers at the community level are often looked upon with distrust, and identified as interested only in recruiting "cases" for family planning.

The Reproductive and Child Health Programme recommends that women who do not deliver in institutions receive three postpartum visits, during which they are to be given an abdominal examination, and provided advice on family planning, breast feeding and baby care. Data from NFHS–2 show not only that postpartum checkups are almost nonexistent but also that family planning is given the lowest priority among the various components of postpartum care. Nationally, fewer than one in five noninstitutional births was followed by a postpartum checkup. Among those who received a postpartum checkup, only 27 per cent of mothers received family planning advice, compared to 43 per cent receiving advice on breast-feeding and 46 per cent receiving advice on baby care. Adolescent mothers and women delivering for the first time were less likely than older women to receive advice on family planning. Notably, mothers received advice about family planning during postpartum checkups for only 14 per cent of first births, although these women are more likely to need advice on birth spacing and contraception. Clearly, health workers and other providers tend to overlook adolescents and young women until they are further advanced in their reproductive careers.

Stockouts and erratic supplies of reversible contraceptives make it unrealistic to expect providers to offer clients a choice of methods. The survey of health facilities referred to earlier reports that only 56–61 per cent of primary health centres had some stocks of condoms, IUDs and oral pills on the day of the survey. The situation was worse in states like Bihar, Orissa and Uttar Pradesh where fewer than one-fifth of primary health centres had some stocks of these methods.

Though the overall situation is far from satisfactory, many new initiatives and the restructuring of existing measures have been successful in improving access to and availability of contraceptive and other reproductive health services. Of particular interest are initiatives by NGOs and experiments with public–private partnerships. The social marketing and social franchising of selected reproductive health services by Janani, a registered society in Bihar, is one such example.

Combining a strong market-based approach with a community-based distribution system, Janani has been able to provide quality family planning services at an affordable price in rural areas. Janani's experiences have clearly shown that couples are willing to adopt family planning methods and pay for quality services that are easy to access. An evaluation conducted in 2001 reports that the system has been successful in attracting illiterate and nulliparous women, population groups often overlooked by public sector providers. The Innovations in Family Planning Services project in Uttar Pradesh is yet another example of successful delivery in areas with little or no access to reproductive and child health services. The project has contributed to increased regular contact with clients, improvements in contraceptive method-mix and use of temporary methods. A survey of married women in the reproductive age group in five project districts reports that about two-fifths of women had met with a community health worker in the six months prior to the survey. In comparison, NFHS–2 data for Uttar

Pradesh show that only 3 per cent of women received at least one home visit by a health worker in the 12 months prior to the survey.

Poor Quality of Services

It is now widely acknowledged that the quality of family planning services is generally poor. Several studies report that little consideration is given to interpersonal interactions. Women are often treated as ignorant and incapable of intelligent action. Service providers tend to disregard women's need for privacy, and are uncaring about women's dignity. Pre-acceptance counselling and check-up are conspicuous by their absence. Post-acceptance follow-up services are also limited, especially in the case of reversible methods. Nationally, for example, data from NFHS–2 show that three in four sterilisation users and two in five users of other modern methods received follow-up services. Data from the Reproductive and Child Health Survey–1, however, indicate that a much smaller percentage of women (only one in four) received a follow-up visit from a health worker after accepting the method—27 per cent in the case of sterilisation, 13 per cent for IUD and 7 per cent for pills. In many states, fewer than one in ten women reported receiving a follow-up visit. It is commonly observed that auxiliary nurse-midwives do not maintain their registers adequately to follow up users, and lack a clear idea of how many have continued/discontinued the method.

Though long ignored as an issue within reproductive health care in India, there is a current programmatic shift towards incorporating quality of care within public sector services. To improve the quality of services, the Reproductive and Child Health Programme emphasises the need to assess client needs and perceptions, sensitise and orient health workers about the new ethos, involve the community including panchayati raj institutions in setting priorities and monitoring the quality of services, setting quality assurance guidelines and conducting refresher training for skill upgradation. However, moving beyond rhetoric to actually implementing change has not yet been noticeably achieved in many parts of the country. Assessments in various states in the early days of the implementation of the Reproductive and Child Health Programme show that not all programme managers and policy makers are convinced about the new emphasis on quality and choice. For example, an assessment in Karnataka reports that all officials believed that targets were the only way to ensure efficient functioning of auxiliary nurse-midwives and better implementation of the programme: "Monitoring is always in terms of figures and numbers, we first look at the numerical targets and then we look at the quality of work". This clearly highlights that the concept of quality orientation is alien to health care providers at all levels.

To date, limited progress has been made in involving panchayats in the Reproductive and Child Health Programme and profound interstate differences prevail. States like Kerala have embarked on decentralised planning and monitoring programmes utilising panchayati raj institutions, and have devolved powers and finances to these institutions. In some other states, panchayati raj institutions are mainly involved in planning and monitoring without devolution of powers and finances, and in others, panchayati raj institutions have not started participating in the programme.

Similarly, early assessments show that the Community Needs Assessment Approach is yet to become fully operational in many parts of the country and its implementation varies across districts within each state, as well as across states. Many states continue to impose targets, setting local goals based on the previous year's centrally-assigned targets. Incidents where NGOs, under government–NGO partnership, were forced to set targets, use district/state-level indicators and not permitted to follow the Community Needs Assessment Approach have been reported. In many states, the involvement of women and other stakeholders in community needs assessment was reported to be minimal. Moreover, the data generated using community needs assessment have not yet been properly used for setting local goals, nor have they been used for making midcourse corrections.

The Way Forward

Though the Family Welfare Programme has experienced significant growth and modification over the past half century, pregnancies continue to be unplanned and the unmet need for contraception remains substantially high. Important subgroups, such as adolescents, are neglected or under-served, the vast majority of contraceptive users are sterilised, contraceptive choice is conspicuous by its absence and the quality of care is limited within the programme.

The 1990s witnessed a growing recognition of the challenges faced by the programme, which led to the development of several new policy initiatives. These initiatives mark seminal changes in the way that health and family welfare issues are viewed in the country. The language of gender equality, equity, women's empowerment, choice, client satisfaction and quality of services has been brought into discussions around women's health. Several programmatic initiatives in moving forward the policy agenda have been taken up.

Early assessments of the impact of the new policy and programme initiatives suggest some improvement in overall indicators such as contraceptive prevalence rate and the magnitude of unmet need for contraception. However, underlying issues including limited contraceptive choice, poor quality of services, restricted access, gender inequalities and lack of male involvement continue to plague the programme. Mechanisms to address these issues remain elusive and the strategies outlined in policies remain poorly implemented. A review of the Reproductive and Child Health Programme–1 highlights inter-district and interstate variations in its implementation. Several lacunae, including low level of ownership of and commitment to reproductive and child health at the state level, weak programme management at the district level, particularly in the Empowered Action Group states, and inadequate decentralisation of processes, remain.

A beginning has been made to promote expanded and informed contraceptive choice, but considerable efforts have to be made by various stakeholders before contraceptive choice can become a reality in India. There is clearly a need for improving programme implementation and directing programme focus to hitherto under-served population groups and poorly served areas.

9

Changing Families and Role of State

According to the 2001 census, India consists of 192.7 million households spread over 0.59 million villages and about 5,000 towns. The Indian society exhibits considerable variations between regions, between rural and urban areas, between classes, and finally, between different religious, ethnic and caste groups. The Indian society is, in fact, a congeries of micro-regions and subcultures and differences between which are quite crucial from sociological angles. Furthermore, the differences are also discernible with respect to the level of female literacy, sex ratio, age at marriage of girls, incidence of dissolution of marriage, household size, female workforce participation rate, marital practices, gender relations and authority structure within the family. Diversities inherent in Indian society are also reflected in the plurality of family types.

It would be noticed from the subsequent discussion that the magnitude of changes that the Indian family has experienced over a period of a centaury appears to be far greater than the expectations of Indian sociologists and anthropologists. The virtual disappearance of traditional joint family from the urban scene, increase in the life expectancy of women from 23 years in 1901-10 to 65 years (it is higher than that of men by three years) in 2009, rise in the proportion of female headed households, decrease in the average age of household heads, increase in the incidence of separation and divorce, greater tension and conflicts between wife and husband, parents and sons and between brothers, increased freedom of marital choice, passing of child marriages, shrinking of kinship ties, continuous consultations between sons and parents on familial matters, greater involvement of females in decision making process, increase in the mean age at marriage of female from 13 years in 1901 to 18.3 years in 2001, rise in the level of female education, decline in total fertility rate from 4.9 in 1971 to 2.76 in 2009 are concrete and clinching evidence to suggest a whole range of changes in the family system— its structure, functions, core values and regulative norms. In course of these changes many new problems have surfaced, while some of the old ones, such as dowry, divorce, lack of intergenerational solidarity, discord between siblings and gender violence have got further intensified.

IN JOINT FAMILY SYSTEM

Since time immemorial the joint family has been one of the salient features of the Indian society. But the twentieth century brought enormous changes in the family system. Changes in the traditional family system have been so enormous that it is steadily on the wane from the urban scene. There is absolutely no chance of reversal of this trend. In villages the size of joint family has been substantially reduced or is found in its fragmented form. Some have split into several nuclear families, while others have taken the form of extended or stem families. Extended family is in fact a transitory phase between joint and nuclear family system. The available data suggest that the joint family is on its way out in rural areas too.

The joint family or extended family in rural areas is surviving in its skeleton or nominal form as a kinship group. The adults have migrated to cities either to pursue higher education or to secure more lucrative jobs or to eke out their living outside their traditional callings, ensuing from the availability of better opportunities elsewhere as well as the rising pressure of population on the limited land base. Many of the urban households are really offshoots of rural extended or joint families. A joint family in the native village is the fountainhead of nuclear families in towns. These days in most cases two brothers tend to form two independent households even within the same city owing to the rising spirit of individualism, regardless of similarity in occupation, even when the ancestral property is not formally partitioned at their native place.

The nuclear family, same as elsewhere, is now the characteristic feature of the Indian society. According to the census of India data, of all the households nuclear family constituted 70 percent and single member or more than one member households without spouse (or eroded families) comprised about 11 percent. The extended and joint family or households together claim merely 20 percent of all households. This is the overall picture about the entire country, whereas in the case of urban areas the proportion of nuclear family is somewhat higher still. The available data from the National Family and Health Survey-1 of 1992-93 (henceforth NFHS) suggest that joint family does not make up more than five percent of all families in urban areas. An extended family, which includes a couple with married sons or daughters and their spouses as well as household head without spouse but with at least two married sons, daughters and their spouses, constitute a little less than one fifth of the total households.

With further industrial development, rural to urban migration, nuclearisation of families and rise of divorce rate and the proportion of single member household is likely to increase steadily on the line of industrial West. This is believed to be so because the states, which have got a higher level of urbanization, tend to have a higher proportion of single member households. Similarly, about a couple of decades ago almost 20 percent households contained only one person in the USA. More or less, a similar situation exists in other developed countries as well, and above all, not a single country has recorded decline in the proportion of single member household during the last three decades. In fact, the tendency is more towards increase in the proportion of single member households.

As the process of family formation and dissolution has become relatively faster now than before, households are progressively more headed by relatively younger people. Census data from 1971 onward have clearly borne out that at the national level over three-fifths of the households are headed by persons aged less than 50. There is every reason to believe that proportion of households headed by younger persons is likely to constitute a larger proportion than this in urban areas where the proportion of extended family, not to speak of joint family, is much smaller than that of rural areas.

The emergence of financially independent, career-oriented men and women, who are confident of taking their own decisions and crave to have a sense of individual achievement, has greatly contributed to the disintegration of joint family. Disintegration of joint family has led to closer bonds between spouses, but the reverse is also true in certain cases. For many, nuclear family is a safer matrimonial home to a woman. In bygone days people generally lived in joint families, yet familial discord never escalated into extreme physical violence or death, as we so often come across such instances in our day-to-day life and also know through national dailies, both electronic and print media..

Changes in Authority Structure

Once the authority within the family was primarily in the

hands of family elders commonly known as *Karta* in Hindi. The general attitude of members of the family towards the traditional patriarch was mostly one of respect. Loyalty, submissiveness, respect and deference over the household were bestowed on him. These attributes also encompassed other relationships in the family, such as children to their parents, a wife to her husband, and younger brothers to their older brothers. Within a household no one was supposed to flout the will of his elders. The father, or in his absence the eldest brother, was consulted on all important family matters like pursuing litigation in courts of law, building a house, buying and selling of property and arranging marriages, etc. The joint family did not allow the neglect or disregard of elders. The age-grade hierarchy was quite strong. Now the people of younger generation, particularly those with modern tertiary education, do not seem to show the same reverence which their fathers had for their parents or elders.

Among women, patriarch's wife was the paramount authority. In fact, women's position depended on the position of their husbands in the household. The wife of the household head or mother-in-law was in charge of the household. Her word was law or at least had the same force. Her decisions were made for the entire family and not for the welfare of the individuals in it. Young women in the family were expected to be dutiful and obedient. Self-assertion, even in bringing up their own children, was blasphemy. Widows and those spurned by their husbands were assured of the family roof, though mostly as voiceless members.

With a view to absolving themselves of responsibility now parents cleverly encourage their educated sons and daughters-in-law to take independent decision in a joint and extended family situation, leave aside urban areas, the similar situation has started to emerge in rural areas too. This is not unusual when sons and daughters tend to possess a higher level of education and a greater degree of exposure of the world outside the family than ever before. Now boys and girls, contrary to the old practice, are beginning to assert their wishes in mate selection. Parental decisions are no more supreme. Changes concerning erosion of authority of old guards, particularly in matters of mate selection, are on gradual decline in rural areas too.

Yet another interesting fact about the change in authority structure within the family is that about nine percent of all the households are headed by women, while the NFH Survey-1 gives a slightly higher figure (about 10 percent). Most of the female household heads are usually independent and gainfully employed. In the absence of their husbands, either because of death, separation, transfer in job or business engagement, women are themselves able to run the affairs of their family. Long distance migration of men for employment is also an important reason for the emergence of such households. The phenomenon of female-headed household assumes significance in the Indian society because in the past when the joint family system was so preponderant that the female-headed household was quite an uncommon phenomenon.

Changes in Marital Practices

The traditional system of values of the Indian society, especially that of Hindus, has been such that it stood for the practice of early as well as universal marriage for females. Child marriage or prepuberty marriage all through has been an archetypal institution of India. The mean age at marriage was reported to be quite low in the 19th century and so also in earlier days. The mean age at marriage for females was about 13 years between 1901 and 1931 censuses and it did not differ much between different communities. Of all the legal measures the Child Marriages Restraint Act 1929 (and its further amendments in 1949, 1955 and 1978) happened to be quite effective one. Rise in the age at marriage really became conspicuous during the post independence era, that is, during the period onward 1950. The act was further amended in 1978 wherein boys' marriage age was raised to 21 and girls' age to 18 years. On the whole, the state level census information for the last one hundred years has revealed a clear rise in the age at marriage for girls. During 1891-1991 the age at marriage increased by 4 to 7 years in different parts of the country. Data from NFHS-2 (1998-99) have shown further increase in the age at marriage of females from 18.5 years to 21.5 years at the national level which greatly destabilised the persistence of high fertility regime in the country (the Census of India, 2001 has estimated a somewhat lower age at marriage). Out-of-wedlock birth is highly unacceptable and hence extremely rare in India.

A new law banning child marriage was passed in December, 2006. The law provides certain positive initiatives for the intervention of courts to prevent child marriages through stay orders. In India, the National Family Health Survey-2 found that 65 percent of girls are married by the time they are eighteen. Child marriages are solemnized during times of festivals such as *Akshaya Tritiya, Akha Teej, Ram Navami, Basant Panchami and Karma Jayanti*. According to UNICEF's 'State of the World's Children-2009' report, 47 percent of India's women aged 20-24 were married before the legal age of 18, with 56 percent in rural areas.

Child marriages have been prevalent in many cultures throughout human history, but have gradually diminished since some countries started to urbanize and experience changes in the ways of life for the people of these countries. An increase in the advocacy of human rights, whether as women's rights or as children's rights, has caused the traditions of child marriage to decrease greatly as it was considered unfair and dangerous for the children. Today, child marriage is usually practised in countries where cultural practices and traditions of child marriage still have a strong influence. Although child marriages have been outlawed a long time ago, South Asia has currently the highest prevalence of child marriage of any region in the world. India, as noted above, happens to be a forerunner in this regard.

Yet another important marital practice is consanguineous marriage which has been the notable feature of a large segment of the Indian society since long. Through the ages the system of cross-cousin and cross-uncle niece marriages has been the most favoured kind of marriage in South India. The most desirable mate for a man has been his own sister's daughter or mother's brother's daughter. In the face of rising dowry practices across the country consanguineous marriages have appreciably declined in South India in recent years. However, such marriages have remained tabooed among the vast majority of Hindus of North India. The Hindu Marriage and Divorce Act 1955 prohibits marriage among close relatives— called *sapinda* marriage. The *sapinda* relationship extends as far as the third generation in the line of mother and the fifth in the line of father. In North India only Muslims, certain scheduled castes and scheduled tribes tend to practise consanguineous marriages. Singh has reported that most of the tribal groups practise consanguinity of both types such as marriages with the father's sister's daughter, the mother's brother's daughter and the elder sister's daughter.

The Indian society has been a highly endogamous. Marriage within the same sub-caste has been followed very strictly. The scheduled tribes are also endogamous, but most of the tribal communities practise clan exogamy. Polygamy, more particularly polygyny, has been one of salient features of Indian family. It has been more popular among Muslims than Hindus. Here it is not suggested that the incidence of polygyny is more common than monogamy. The polygamous males often derived support from age-old scriptures and mythological stories. But mainly those who had no issue from the first wife practised such marriages. With the rise in the level of literacy the incidence of polygyny has receded even among the Muslims despite the fact that such marriages have got full cultural and legal sanction. While monogamy is the predominant form of marriage, there are a large number of tribes practising sororal polygyny and non-sororal polygyny.

Dissolution of Marriage

The dissolution of marriage has been quite uncommon and rare in India for a long time. In case of any crisis or threat to stability of marriage, caste, community, kinsmen, tended to have played a dominant say. People had both respect for and fear of social values and public opinion. Authority of community, though implicit, has been supreme. The system of religious belief has provided enough sustenance to the institution of marriage and family. Individual choice has always been subservient to the communal sentiment or public opinion. Hindu marriage is taken as a lifelong union for the couple, as it is a sacrament, rather than a contract between the couple to live in a social union so long as it is cordially feasible. Even in the event of frequent mental and physical torture, most Indian women persist in marriage, since remarriage of divorced or separated women is quite difficult. Morality relating to sex is so highly valued that every male wants to marry a virgin girl only. In the past Hindus demanded prenuptial chastity on the part of both, but now it is by and large limited to females. Virginity is regarded as the girls' greatest virtue and a symbol of respectability. Under the circumstances remarriage of women is so difficult that annulment of marriage is a very hard choice or option.

Despite all these there has been a significant change in the views and attitudes towards sanctity of marriage in the recent past, especially in cities. Marriage is no longer held to be a 'divine match' or a 'sacred union'. Now it is more like a transfer of a female from one family to another, or from one kinship group to another. The marriage is no longer sanctified as it was believed in the past, and is viewed only as a bonding and nurturing lifelong relationship and friendship. The rather flippant and superficial reasons given by many women and men to break a marriage may not portend well for the future. Indian marriages are still largely resilient and lasting, whereas in many developed countries they seem to break up for seemingly trivial reasons. Marriages are very vulnerable or fragile there. One in every four or five marriages breaks up despite more space and freedom in the West. The longevity of marriage in most developed countries ranges on an average from five to seven years. While in India divorce rates are among the lowest in the world. Only one out of 100 marriages ends up in divorce here. These days divorce rates in India's urban sphere are, however, slowly mounting.

Marriage counsellors, formerly pooh-poohed at, have today assumed a lot of importance in guiding couples through stormy seas and averting the imminent pain of divorce. Today in cities there is disenchantment with the system of arranged marriages in a large number of cases. The Indian family is faced with a new kind of social and psychological constraints. The women, however, tend to be more concerned about their marriage than men and in case of a problem they are expected to go for counselling. They are expected to take the lead to resolve conflicts and when they give up the effort, the marriage is generally over. In today's shifting values and changing times, there is less reliance on marriage as a definer of sex and living arrangements throughout life. Today in cities there is disenchantment with the system of arranged marriages. There is a greater incidence of extramarital relationships, including open gay and lesbian relationships, a delay in the age at marriage, higher rates of marital disruption and more egalitarian gender-role attitudes among men and women. It is reported that in big metropolises a new system of 'live-in-arrangements' between pairs, particularly in upper stratum of society, is steadily emerging as a new kind of family life. Anyway, a relatively higher divorce rate in cities, *inter alia*, connote that marriage is an institution in trouble, or else expectations are so high that people are no longer willing to put up with the kinds of dissatisfactions and empty-shell marriages that the previous generations tolerated.

Problems of Dowry

Now, let us come to the rising problem of dowry which has become one of the serious social evils of the Indian society in the recent years. Dowry, or the bridegroom price, refers to a lump sum of money with or without some tangible assets constituting an essential part of the wedding settlement, which is transferred by the bride's household to that of her prospective spouse before the actual solemnization of marriage. Sometimes dowry also accompanies or follows the marriage of a daughter. The dowry and its cognate problems have become so serious that the marriage of daughters tends to bring in nightmarish experiences for scores of parents these days. The menace of dowry has become so severe over the years that the Government of India had to enact the Dowry Prohibition Act in 1961, which was further amended in 1986. But the legislative measures to do away with this practice have so far proved an ineffective exercise.

The dowry has gained social legitimacy across all communities and regions. Marriage negotiations tend to break down if there is no consensus between the bride's and bridegroom's families regarding the mode or amount of payment of dowry. Dowry, as said before, has become such an essential consideration for marriage that rarely any marriage can take place without it. It may be regarded as a functional imperative for family formation in contemporary India. In very rare cases demands for dowry are eschewed. If the groom's parents, for instance, sense that they can reap greater economic or personal benefits in modes other than the dowry in a lump cash from bride's parents, dowry is not demanded under the pretext that it is an evil of Indian society.

When the dowry amount is not considered sufficient or the expected demands are not met easily, the bride is often harassed, abused and tortured. The dissatisfied husband takes recourse to violence to show his displeasure with the marriage in order to extract additional transfers from the wife's family by threatening her with separation if new demands are not complied with. The dowry related harassment most likely arises from complete lack of respect for the woman and rapacious avarice for money. The woman, as a bride, is subjected to humiliation and brutal behaviour, because she is the softest and the surest means of extracting maximum amount of money or wealth from her parents to enhance one's economic position in society. Since the bride is helpless in her new home and physically so powerless that she cannot retaliate against the coercive tactics or actions of others. Not many women have enough guts to divorce their husbands on the ground of frequent mental or physical torture, since they have nothing to fall back upon in a traditional and poorly developed country like India.

The disturbing fact about dowry related violence is that it is not confined to any particular group, social stratum, geographical region or even religion. Rather, it is regarded as a universal phenomenon, cutting across all sorts of boundaries, as it has already been stressed before. It is claimed to be on continuous increase in the country. It has been often reported that like clockwork every 12th hour a dowry related death claimed to have taken the lives of over 20,000 women across the country between 1990 and 1993. It has also been reported that at least three girls are burnt for dowry related demands every day in the State of Karnataka. This may be taken as a matter of grave concern, for the incidence of dowry death is one of the typical problems of the Indian society. In view of continuing failure of the state through legal means, the civil societies should come forward to fight the menace of dowry. The crux of the matter is that those who have got sons or more sons than daughters tend to have developed vested interests in the persistence of this practice.

Domestic Violence

Violence within family settings is primarily a male activity. The prime targets are women and children. The women have been victims of humiliation and torture for as long as we have written records of the Indian society. Despite several legislative measures adopted in favour of women during the last 150 years, continuing spread of modern education and women's gradual economic independence, countless women have continued to be victims of discrimination and violence in the country. Increasing family violence in modern times has compelled many social scientists to be apologists for the traditional joint family- as happy and harmonious, a high-voltage emotional setting, imbued with love, affection and tenderness. India's past has been so romanticized by certain scholars that they have regarded the joint family as the best form of family.

There are data showing that in India 40 percent of women have experienced violence by an intimate partner. These stark figures underline the fact that, although the home and community are places where women provide care for others, they are also places where millions of women experience coercion and abuse. A study of five districts of the State of Uttar Pradesh has revealed that 30 percent of currently married men acknowledge physically abusing their wives. Similarly, the multi-sectoral survey done by the International Clinical Epidemiologists Network (INCLEN) has reported that two out of every five married women reported being hit, kicked, beaten or slapped by their husbands. About fifty percent of the women experiencing physical violence also reported physical abuse during pregnancy.

With the rise in the level of education and exposure to mass media, women tend to have greater awareness of the notion of gender equality, faith in the effectiveness of legal action to protect their rights, and confidence in such institutions as family courts and certain voluntary organizations working for women. Yet there is no sign of abatement in gender related violence. Cases of domestic violence, like wife-battering and forced incest with the women of the household, are so personal and delicate that they are seldom reported to the police or law courts. The recent legislation of anti-domestic violence act of 2005 would certainly take care of the problem of gender-based violence of the Indian woman to a very large extent.

There is another side of the story of domestic violence as well which has remained uncovered, particularly by feminist writers. It is roughly estimated that every year more than 58000 educated women are making the life of their husbands hell by misusing anti-dowry law and domestic violence act and under these laws legal terrorism is continuing openly to extort money from the husbands and their families. More than 52000 married men are ending their life due to various type of harassment and domestic violence faced form their beloved wives in the form of verbal abuse, financial abuse, mental abuse, sexual abuse, relationship cheating, etc.

Problems of Children

Children constitute a little over 30 percent of the total population of the country according to the 2001 Census of India. Evidence suggests that they are quite vulnerable and their exposure to violations of their protection rights remains widespread and multiple in nature. The manifestations of these violations are very varied, ranging from child labour and child trafficking to commercial sexual exploitation and many other forms of violence and abuse. With an estimated 12.6 million children engaged in hazardous occupations, for instance, India has the largest number of child labourers under the age of 14 in the world. Although poverty is often cited as the cause underlying child labour, other factors such as discrimination, social exclusion, as well as the lack of quality education or existing parents' attitudes and perceptions about child labour and the role and value of education need also to be considered.

While systematic data and information on child protection issues are still not always available, evidence suggests that children in need of special protection belong to communities suffering disadvantages and social exclusion such as scheduled castes and scheduled tribes, and the poor. It has been estimated that 46 percent children from scheduled tribes and 38 percent from scheduled castes are out of school. The lack of available services as well as the gaps persisting in law enforcement and in rehabilitation schemes also constitute a major cause of concern. The children of poor families, especially those of artists, craftsmen, and other professions are trained by their parents and elders of the family in their vocations such as weaving, tanning, sweeping dyeing, hairdressing, painting, carpentry and agriculture. A vast number of children grow up lending a helping hand to elders in their home-industries. The practice or intergenerational transfer of traditional callings more or less is still continuing. Such kids who lack formal schooling, but working and specializing in some craft or their traditional callings help them build a career.

Indeed, the poverty in India forces many parents to send their children to earn extra money. The employers who hire such children pay them paltry wages. One can see boys of poor families act as vegetable vendors throughout India. Children of construction workers help in bringing water, cleaning vessels or collecting twigs for fuel. Their parents are compelled to come to cities when monsoon fails and they cannot cultivate their lands.

Children are also subjected to gender based discrimination. Discrimination against women in fact starts the day she is born. Sometimes it also starts when she is in her mother's womb as a foetus. The practice of female foeticide, despite being illegal, is vigorously practised in urban India. The girl child's right to survival, health care and nutrition, education, social opportunities and protection has to be recognized and made a social and economic priority. Along with this the basic structural inequalities that cause poverty, malnutrition and the low status of women have to be addressed, if these rights are to be ensured. Within family parents are first to practise gender based discrimination and it is the first school of learning where girls are inculcated the values of their being inferior to their brothers.

Although India loves their children, still thousands of children roam the streets of major cities around the country and receive neither education, proper food, clothing, or a bed to sleep in at night. Why are these children roaming and begging in the streets? What should be done and who is willing to do something to help these poor children? A mind and heart that cares, awareness presentations through multimedia, contributions, talking and sharing information among friends, education, self-help initiatives and good old fashion kindness are all that is needed to get these kids off the streets. Basically they need five things for their living: food, clothing, shelter, medical assistance and education.

Contrary to the above, there are children who belong to the well-off sections of society, but they are also not free from problems. They are facing a different kind of problem either due to lack of adequate care or attention from their working parents or due to heavy expectation from them by their parents in a fiercely competitive modern world full of uncertainties in life. In cases of working mothers, children are placed in an entirely different situation. The demands of city life are such that both wife and husband tend to remain outside their home for work even at the cost of interests of their children. Working couples are unable to give proper care and affection to their children. Obviously, latchkey children of working couples are strangers to the sense of security enjoyed by their own parents. The system of surrogate mothers or the Montessori and Kindergarten systems of schooling has proved to be a very poor substitute for family as an agent of socialisation. With the diminished role of family as an agent of socialisation juvenile delinquency is on the increase. In the past children enjoyed security of a kind unknown today. Growing up under the joint care of adults made them feel responsible for all the extended members of the family, besides their own parents. Now children are at greater strain than ever before because in general parents intend to accomplish those things in their life through their children what they themselves could not be able to achieve, no matter how difficult they are. Children are put under great stress and stain to score high marks at schools to be able to meet the ever-increasing challenges of fiercely competitive world of education and employment. In addition to helping their children achieve higher goals of life, women, sometimes both the parents, have to work harder with a view to attaining economic independence and maintaining a higher standard of living of their family.

As stated above, there has been appreciable decline in fertility over the years. This has not been possible without recording drastic changes in the attitude of people towards the size of family and the value system of patriarchy and patriliny. Based on studies on fertility behaviour and contraceptive practices one can conclusively contend that perhaps no element of the Indian social system has experienced greater changes than the system of family during the post-independent period. This is clearly borne out by various empirical investigations. Despite considerable decline in fertility or lesser burden of children on the family, there is no improvement in the quality of care of children especially in rural areas.

There hardly exists any preschool or community centre in villages. There also does not exist even a basic facility of play ground for children. The older children have to mind the younger children at home and sometimes they are also expected to lend helping hands to their parents in the household chores as and when required. The poor children learn the expected roles of life of their own with the passage of time, while the well-off peasantry send their children to private schools (also called public schools in the Western world) in towns and cities for better schooling.

Problems of Elderly

The family has started facing a new kind of problem emanating from a relatively faster pace of demographic transition. The incredible increase in life expectancy may be a big triumph of the 20th century, but it has posed one of the toughest problems before the 21st century India. Census reports have revealed that the Indian population approximately tripled during the last 50 years, but the number of elderly people had in fact increased more than fourfold. Based on the continuation of the trend, the United Nations has predicted in one of its report that the Indian population would again grow by 50 percent by the middle of this century, whereas the elderly population is likely to have another fourfold increase in its size.

Table 1. Projected Age Composition of India's Population in Million, 2010-2050

Age groups	*2010*	*2020*	*2030*	*2040*	*2050*
0-14	374	364	338	309	294
	(30.8)	(26.7)	(22.8)	(19.7)	(18.2)
15-59	749	868	962	1011	1004
	(61.6)	(63.5)	(64.8)	(64.7)	(62.2)
>60	92	135	185	245	316
	(7.4)	(9.8)	(12.4)	(15.6)	(19.6)
Total population	1,215	1,367	1,485	1,565	1,614
Median age (Yrs.)	25.0	28.1	31.7	35.3	38.4
Dependency ratio-Total	56	49	45	44	47
Dependency ratio-Child	48	40	33	28	27
Dependency ratio-Old	8	9	12	15	20
Life expectancy at birth	64.0	67.0	70.0	72.0	73.0

It is estimated the that during the next five decades the size of the population would grow by about 50 percent, but the number of older people would increase fourfold. The proportion of older people in the population would grow at a higher pace than the other groups. It is estimated that the elderly people (60+) would constitute 20 percent of the total population which would be quite huge in terms of absolute number—316 million. The Indian policymakers must take a critical note of the rising trends of incoming age wave of older people and the declining trend of the proportion of younger people. Such developments would cause strain on the resources due to increase in more inactive people.

It is apparent from Table 1 that the Indian population would be gradually swinging to a greyer one by the next few decades. It is estimated that the median age of the population would increase gradually from 25 years in 2010 to 31.7 years in 2030 and, finally, to 38.4 years in 2050. Similarly, the old age dependency ratio will climb up from 8 percent in 2010 to 20 percent in 2050, while the child dependency ratio is expected to come down from 56 percent to 27 percent during this period. Hence, every three working Indians may have to take care of one elderly person by 2050 as compared to about eight working persons at present. It has been estimated that an Indian of age 63 today is likely to survive about a decade more in 2050.

Longer life expectancy and incremental dependency ratio will possibly strain the family and the state support system for the older people. Increase in individuals' age is usually followed by increased prevalence of chronic diseases and disability and hence the elderly population is taken as a big burden for the family, community and ultimately the entire nation. Many young people consider the old member of their family as an obstacle to the advancement of their career as well as an economic burden for their family life, as the older parents become frail due to greater incidence of diseases and disability, eventually becoming bedridden in the family and later forced to stay in nursing homes during the terminal stages of their life. This scenario causes young people to have a negative image of the older people and early in their life they adopt a ageistic outlook towards the older people.

In the past the joint family system not only provided a suitable umbrella to manage personal risks, such as risks of premature death and excessive longevity, but also laid down the norms of intergenerational relationships as well as the role of each member. The elderly played a significant role in decision making regarding household matters, while the younger people were entrusted with the responsibility of ensuring wellbeing of their ageing parents. But these days in smaller families, they are gradually marginalised in the decision-making process. Hence, the family that traditionally took care of the elderly or sick, widows and orphans is beginning to rely on society as a whole. As the number of old persons is rising and the social environment is changing, the proportion of the destitute among them may also be increasing. These factors are also leading to the need for a large number of old-age homes where the old people may enjoy the remaining part of their life in a group of their own.

As a consequence of the breakdown of traditional joint and extended families the elderly people are being steadily marginalised in society generally. Moreover, due to some habits and unhealthy lifestyles, the elderly people tend to suffer from tuberculosis, asthma, cancer, cardiovascular problems, etc., apart from the other gerontological problems. But the healthcare facilities for the aged people are not satisfactory. A well-equipped, separate division in Indian hospitals is increasingly required for the comprehensive care of elderly people. Such a facility will not only cure the old physically, but will also ensure their mental wellbeing. It will simultaneously arrange medical treatment as well as improve their quality of life. The government as well as the private healthcare providers have to build up the necessary infrastructure to meet the healthcare requirements of the increasingly ageing population. It may be further aggravated due to the exponentially increasing healthcare expenses, though neglecting those expenses may worsen their quality of life.

Under the prevailing situation, the non-governmental organizations and civil societies are expected to play a central role to help out those ageing people who are destined to lead an uncared and solitary life. At the same time, there may be some amount of solace as well because the kind of problem relating to intergenerational solidarity the Indian society is facing is relatively much less serious compared to the developed world, since a vast majority of the elderly people tend to live with their sons or if not with them for some reasons, their sons or other close kinsmen often remain in constant touch with them to attend any exigency which may arise in their life. It is clearly evident from the NFHS-2 data that over 80 percent of the elderly people live with their sons, daughters or other kinsmen. An elderly person living alone does not constitute more than five percent, while the elderly couples living independently of any young person in the household is not more than 10 percent of the total households at any ages between 60 and 80 years.

An aged person has the right to decide about personal needs and aspirations, depending upon capacity. Only a sound social security system can protect such rights by assuring regular income during the post-retirement years. But developing such a system for the Indian population is a quite difficult task, as a majority of them do not currently enjoy any type of old-age income security. Neither the government nor the public sector alone can formulate it; the private sector cannot develop it in isolation either. Joint approaches and strategies will be required to design and build up a robust old-age income security system.

A little over 40 percent (19.18 million) of salaried employees and 289.59 million are engaged in the unorganized sector (including self-employed professionals, farmers, shopkeepers, taxi drivers, casual labourers, etc.) are deprived of being covered by any compulsory retirement benefit plans. In other words, about 92 percent of working Indians are not covered under any old-age income security plan. Despite the absence of any regular income, a significant proportion of these people stay well above the poverty line during their working life. But they are likely to sink below the poverty line in their old age, simply because they could not accumulate adequate amounts of savings while they were in the workforce. The reason behind this trend is because of the non-availability of any suitable framework for savings and investments.

The Planning Commission of India has assessed that about 92 percent of working Indians do not enjoy any formal old-age income. Consequently, the Project Old Age Social and Income Security (OASIS) Committee projected that these people might sink below the poverty line as a result of the non-availability of adequate post-retirement income. On the other hand, framing suitable policies regarding the availability of the pension plans, allowing the participation of the private players in the pension sector, ensuring the availability of need-based pension products, and increasing the level of consumer awareness about old-age income requirements will help to mobilize a large amount (about Rs.4,065 billion) of very long-term funds by the year 2025.

The importance of this sector in the Indian economy cannot be overlooked. This informal sector of the Indian economy offers employment opportunities to about 92 percent of the working people and contributes 59 percent of the GDP, including reasonable export earnings. Considering the existence of this void, Project OASIS Report warned that the demographic transition coupled with poor coverage by existing provisions suggests that we are inexorably moving towards an India with a gigantic number of destitute elderly. Faced with such huge numbers, a social safety net for the retired workers or a poverty alleviation programme, which aims to pay even a modest subsidy, would require a staggering expenditure— much beyond the capacity of the government. Moreover, the Indian constitution has entrusted some responsibility to the state in relation to the social security of the people. But the obligation of the state regarding old-age income security of the people is primarily limited to the organized workforce. However, due to irregular incomes, retirement is considered a luxury for people of the unorganized sector. This may be observed from the high level of their participation in the workforce, even beyond the generally accepted age of retirement.

It is high time that the Indian policy makers assess the impact of the forthcoming age wave. The process of pension sector reforms should be accelerated, suitable steps should be undertaken to build the required healthcare facilities and a suitable social security system should also be designed. If change is not effected, the family support system as well as the state-sponsored facilities may crash in the near future, thereby jeopardizing the wellbeing of elderly people. It may cause the emergence of a gigantic number of penniless, sick and elderly people in the streets and public places.

State, Law and Family

Considerable changes have taken place in the traditional role of women. Once the priority for the young women was the husband, but now it has shifted to their career and in addition deep resentments tend to surface when the husbands are reluctant to take part in the household chores. The urban women are seen in many different roles. With 54 percent of the level of female literacy rate in India at the 2001 census, though much lower by the standard of developed countries, it is not unusual to see women working as clerks, typists, receptionists, nurses, doctors, school and college teachers, lawyers, police, social workers and social activists. Women can assume still greater public roles in society than what we see today. They tend to show lower workforce participation rate because not many suitable jobs are available for them outside their home. But on the contrary countless people often believe that women inherently tend to have stronger attachments with family and household responsibilities. On the whole, with the rise in education, urbanization and opportunity to proper employment, women are much freer now to come out of their homes with a view to meeting their family expenses. With the rise in education and economic development, the women would steadily move towards greater economic independence in course of time.

The urban woman is in a position to exercise much greater authority than before. Despite her increased duties, the urban woman seems to have emerged as the stronger partner. It is she who monitors children's homework, tutors them in areas of weakness or laziness. Mothers dropping and picking up children— from school or coaching classes in computer and cricket or tennis— by bus, moped, scooter or car, is a common sight today in Indian cities. Mother has become the primary agent of socialisation. But all mothers are not equally free to mind their children.

With the rise in modern education, gainful engagement, quality of health condition and a fewer number of children, family life may not be always well. The State of Kerala can be cited as one of the examples. Those who are unhappy with current state of family life are on the gradual increase in the state. It is all the more acute in urban areas where the hold of traditional norms and values has largely dissipated. The consumer culture sweeping the urban society and the breakdown of the extended or joint family system have contributed to this. Reports show that the number of cases pending in the family courts is on the increase. The number of children running away from homes has also gone up.

Consumption of alcohol has touched an all time high. Modernization has created dilemmas for family life. Under the new socioeconomic urban milieu there has been a tremendous increase in the family violence. With a view to tackling increasing violence in the family, the Government of India introduced a very useful Domestic Violence Act in 2005. This would certainly go a long way in restraining the incidence of domestic violence in the country.

Legislations

India, as said before, does not have any systematic coherent family policy, but the government has always been sensitive to the problems concerning family formation and dissolution, rights of women and children, the practice of child marriages, dowry, domestic violence and so forth. This is apparent from various legislations enacted, amended and implemented by the Government of India as well as the state governments as and when necessitated. They are together called family laws. Family law is that area of law which deals with family-related issues and domestic relations including the nature of marriage, civil unions, and domestic partnerships; issues arising during marriage, including spousal abuse, dowry, legitimacy, adoption, surrogacy, child abuse, and child abduction, the termination of the relationship and ancillary matters including divorce, annulment, property settlements, alimony and parental responsibility orders.

The following legislations are an important part of the Indian family laws: Hindu Widows Remarriage Act, 1856 and 1956; The Converts' Marriage Dissolution Act, 1866; The Indian Christian Marriage Act, 1872; The Kazis Act, 1880; The Anand Marriage Act, 1909; The Child Marriage Restraint Act, 1929 and 1978; The Parsi Marriage and Divorce Act, 1936; The Foreign Marriage Act, 1969; The Hindu Women's Right to Property Act, 1937; The Special

Marriage Act, 1954; The Hindu Marriage and Divorce Act, 1955; The Hindu Succession Act, 1956; The Hindu Minority and Guardianship Act, 1956; The Hindu Adoptions and Maintenance Act, 1956; The Suppression of Immoral Traffic in Women and Girls Act, 1956, 1978 and 1886; The Dowry Prohibition Act,1961 and 1986; The Muslim Women (Protection of Rights on Divorce) Act, 1986; The Child Labour Prohibition and Regulation Act, 1986; and The Domestic Violence Act, 2005. In addition to these, most states of the Indian Union have got their own family laws more or less on the line of these legislations, considering the significance of local practices and the system of belief.

Remarriage of Widows

For long Hindus believed that Hindu widows once married were incapable of contracting a second valid marriage, and the offspring of such widows by any second marriage were held to be illegitimate and incapable of inheriting property. The Widow Remarriage Act was passed in 1856, prohibiting enforced widowhood practised mainly among Brahmins and a few other castes such as Rajputs, Banias and Kayasthas. The law was also designed as a relief for child widows whose husbands died before consummation. The Act was further amended in 1956 to incorporate certain provisions in favour of second marriage. This was done with a view to promoting good morals and to ensure the public welfare. All rights and interests which any widow may have in her deceased husband's property by way of maintenance, or by inheritance to her husband or to his lineal successors would cease on her remarriage. Yet the problem of young widows in India has not vanished. Currently widows account for nine percent of the female population and only 40 percent of them are over 50 years of age. This suggests that despite laws 60 percent of widows do not contract second marriage for one reason or the other. Dreze, has contended that the overall incidence of widow remarriage is as low as 1 in 5 or 6. Chen, has reported that only few widows remarry in India. Within her sample of 562 widows, she has argued that the widow remarriage rate is about nine percent. The census data, however, have revealed that widow remarriage rate has been on the gradual rise, especially in towns and cities.

Child Marriages

Both during ancient and medieval periods, child marriages were widely prevalent in India. The young girls lived with their parents till they reached puberty. Early marriage led to the problem of early widowhood because of high death rates. Since widow remarriage was not possible among caste Hindus, the child widows were condemned to a life of great agony, shaving heads, living in isolation, and shunned by the society. Hence, the child marriage was outlawed in 1869 through the Indian Penal Code. The first law addressing child marriage was the Native Marriage Act, 1872, which was promulgated by the British colonial regime and fixed 14 as the age of consent to marriage. The Child Marriage Restraint Act, 1929 was passed during the tenure of British rule and in order to incorporate some necessary changes and also to raise the age at marriage to 18 for girls and 21 for boys and it was amended in 1949,1955 and 1978. The object of the Child Marriage Restraint Law of 1929 was to eliminate a practice which was potentially detrimental to the life and health of a girl child. Yet the child marriages, as said before, are still widely practised in India. According to the 2001 census, out of 593 districts in the country there are 190 districts where the mean age at marriage of females is less than 18 years. The persistence of child marriages implies that laws prohibiting such marriages are not so effective. The state machinery is not so efficient or successful in tackling such a serious social evil because of poor regard for law generally. According to the 'National

Plan of Action for Children 2005', a goal has been set to eliminate child marriage completely by 2010. This plan is proving to be successful, though it is still difficult to monitor every child marriage due to the sheer size of India's population.

Dowry

What began as a gift of land to a woman as her inheritance in an essentially agricultural economy today has degenerated into gifts of gold, clothes, consumer durables and large sums of cash, which sometimes entails the impoverishment and heavy indebtedness of poor families. In the course of time dowry has become a widespread evil and it has now assumed menacing proportions. Surprisingly it has spread to different communities across the country, which were traditionally non-dowry taking communities. With the increasing greed for the easy inflow of money on account of a bride the chilling stories of bride burning started coming to light.

With a view to eradicating the rampant social evil of dowry from the Indian society, the Parliament passed the Dowry Prohibition Act in 1961 which applies not merely to Hindus but to all communities like— Muslims, Sikhs, Christians and others. Giving, taking and demanding dowry is a criminal offence under the Dowry Protection Act and the Indian Penal Code. Under the Dowry Prohibition Act only Metropolitan Magistrate or the Magistrate of the first class is competent to try these offences. Where any person is prosecuted for taking or abetting the taking of any dowry or the demanding of dowry, the burden of proving that he has not committed an offence shall be on him. The giving, taking or even abetting to give or take dowry amounts to an offence punishable with imprisonment for not less than 5 years and with fine which shall not be less than Rs. 15,000/- or the amount of value of the dowry, which ever is more.

If any person demands directly or indirectly, from the parents or other relatives of a bride or bridegroom, as the case may be, any dowry, he shall be punishable with an imprisonment for a term which shall not be less than six months but which may extend to two years and with fine which may extend to Rs. 10,000/-.

The Indian Penal Code provides that where any women dies an unnatural death within seven years of her marriage and it is shown that she was harassed or subjected to cruelty by her husband or his relative for dowry, such death shall be called a dowry death. The husband or the relative shall be deemed to have caused the death of the women. The offence is punishable with imprisonment of not less than seven years. Whoever, being a husband or relative of the husband subjects such women to cruelty shall be punished with imprisonment for a term of three years. Despite such stringent laws dowry is being increasingly practised throughout the country. It has assumed such an alarming proportion that the number of cases of bride-burning and bride-torture, both mental and physical, in law courts is rising, and the media are agog with ever-increasing number of such instances. This is a reflection of a very serious kind of lapse on the part of the state machinery.

Divorce

As per the ancient Hindu laws there was no place for divorce and it was with the codification of Hindu law that the first grounds for the new age laws were laid down. All major religions have their own laws which govern divorces within their own community, and separate regulations exist regarding divorce in inter-faith marriages. Hindus, including Buddhists, Sikhs and Jains, are governed by the Hindu Marriage Act, 1955; Christians by the Indian Divorce Act, 1869; Parsis by the Parsi Marriage and Divorce Act, 1936; and Muslims by the Dissolution of Muslim Marriages Act,

1939, which provides the grounds on which women can obtain a divorce, and the uncodified civil law. Civil marriages and inter-community marriages and divorces are governed by the Special Marriage Act, 1956. Other community specific legislation includes the Native Converts' Marriage Dissolution Act, 1866 that allows a Hindu to appeal for a divorce if a spouse converts to Christianity.

In most Western nations, there are approximately 16 distinct reasons for which divorces are granted. In India, however, only five main reasons are generally accepted as sufficient grounds for divorce: (1) Adultery, (2) Desertion, (3) Cruelty, (4) Impotency, and (5) Chronic Disease.

The women, having being given in marriage by her father or other guardian before she attained the age of 15 years, repudiated the marriage before attaining the age of 18. The Muslim Marriage Act, 1939 restricts Muslim women's right to seek divorce by placing conditions that did not exist in Islamic law and are difficult to prove, such as cruelty and impotency. But a Muslim man has the right to unilateral divorce of triple *talaq*. Polygamy among Muslims continues to remain an issue. While under the Hindu Marriage Act, 1955, polygamy has been declared illegal. Muslim personal law makes the man the sole guardian of a child.

While the Indian intelligentsia often feel that one should have the right to divorce, it is still a highly stigmatizing action. Women are looked upon more harshly than men in this regard. There continue to be segments of Indian society that feel divorce is never a right option, regardless of how abusive or adulterous the husband may be which adds to the greater disapproval for women. A divorced woman often can return to her family, but may not be wholeheartedly welcomed. There is also the risk that a divorced woman's presence would ward off possible marriages for other daughters within the household. Unavoidably, the overall status of the family and household are lowered by having a divorcee living with amongst them. A woman's class and caste are a major factor in her acceptance back into society. Women from higher classes tend to have an easier time than middle or lower class women in returning to the social order after a divorce. An exception to this model is the extreme bottom of the society who have experienced little rebuff from peers after a divorce. This results from their already atypical status in society. For these reasons, among some other factors, the divorce rate is less than one percent here according to the 2001 Census of India.

Succession and Right to Property

As India has been a highly patriarchal and patrilineal society since ancient days, the Indian women, same as men, never enjoyed the right to be a coparcener in the property of an undivided family or had no right to succession. In order to enhance the position of women in society and extend a sense of dignity in their life, the necessity for laws relating to succession was realised, though the realisation was quite late. Under the Indian Succession Act, 1925, everyone was entitled to equal inheritance, except Hindus, Sikhs, Jains, Buddhists and Muslims. For these communities, excluding the Muslims, a separate legislation known as the Hindu Succession Act, 1925 was introduced. In view of certain shortcomings or limitations it was amended in 1956 and 1991. Under this Act the Hindu women, along with women of some other communities, had an equal right to parental property in the absence of a will; but the women tended to forgo their right at the time of marriage possibly accepting dowry as a compensation for a share.

The Hindu Succession Act, however, makes provision for a Hindu undivided family to ensure that property remains with the male line of descent. A son gets a share equal to that of his father; a daughter gets only a share in her father's share. She cannot reside in the family home unless she is single or divorced, and cannot claim her share of property as long as the men of the family continue to live in it. And a Hindu woman has no right to her matrimonial home, unless she can prove that it was purchased with her earnings. However, this law could not do the needful as there was another law, the Mitakshara coparcenaries (Hindu Law) that had an overriding effect on entitlement of women. According to Mitakshara coparcenaries, in a joint family, a daughter had a much smaller share of property compared to the son. If the family owned a dwelling house, then the daughter's right was confined only to the right of residence and not possession or ownership.

Some Muslim laws have been nominally codified in the Shariat Act, 1937, the Dissolution of Muslim Marriages Act, 1939 and the Muslim Women (Protection of Rights on Divorce) Act, 1986. The Shariat Act states that Muslim Personal Law will govern Muslims and that law has priority over custom. In practice, personal law is based mostly on the interpretations of the Quran. There are four schools of jurisprudence and many more legal traditions, which produce different interpretations. Women's right to property under Muslim law does have Quranic sanctions but is limited to half of what their brothers get. However, the 1937 Act categorically denies women any right to agricultural land.

The Parliament of India passed the Hindu Succession (Amendment) Act, 2005 wherein daughters and sons have been equal rights to property. According to this law, any woman, irrespective of the marital status, has full right to inherit ancestral property just like a son of the family. This law has completely abolished the Hindu Succession Act 1956 by giving equal rights to daughters in the 'Hindu Mitakshara Coparcenary property', as sons have.

But the theoretical reforms so far have not been adequate to give all Indian women a right to property on the same footing and terms as men. It varies with region and religion. Even where law has given a right, conventions and practices do not recognize them. Women themselves relinquish their rights. Women, as daughters, wives, daughters-in-law, mothers or sisters tend to lose out and often suffer deprivation. There are numerous laws that forbid discrimination between the sexes, but in reality none are effective enough to actually bring about a revolution; a change in society. There is a need for legislation in Muslim Law to give equal share of property to the widow and daughter along with sons as done in Turkey.

Right to Maintenance

Maintenance is a right to livelihood when one is incapable of sustaining oneself. Right to maintenance forms a part of the personal law. Obligation of a husband to maintain his wife arises out of the status of the marriage. Hindu law, one of the most ancient systems of law, recognises right of any dependent person including wife, children, aged parents and widowed daughter or daughter-in-law to maintenance.

The Hindu Adoptions and Maintenance Act, 1956, provides for this right. Under the Hindu law, the wife has an absolute right to claim maintenance from her husband. But she loses her right if she deviates from the path of chastity. In assessing the amount of maintenance, the court takes into account various factors like position and liabilities of the husband. It also judges whether the wife is justified in living apart from husband. Maintenance is a right to get necessities which are reasonable from another. Maintenance includes not only food, clothes and residence, but also the things necessary for the comfort and status in which the person entitled is reasonably expected to live. Right to maintenance is not a transferable right.

Apart from the relationship of husband and wife other relations in which there is economic dependency are also considered to be entitled to maintenance under the Hindu Adoptions and Maintenance Act, 1956. Accordingly a widowed daughter-in-law is entitled maintenance from her father-in-law to the extent of the share of her diseased husband in the said property. The minor children of a Hindu, whether legitimate or illegitimate, are entitled to claim maintenance from their parents. Similarly, the aged and infirm parents of a Hindu are entitled to claim maintenance from their children. The term parent here also includes an issueless stepmother.

Under the Muslim law, the Muslim Women (Protection of Rights on Divorce) Act, 1986 spells out objective of the Act as 'the protection of the rights of Muslim women who have been divorced by, or have obtained divorce from, their husbands.' The Act says that divorced woman is entitled to have a reasonable and fair provision and maintenance from her former husband, and the husband must do so within the period of idda and his obligation is not confined to the period of idda. This Act *inter alia* provides that a divorced Muslim woman is entitled to (a) reasonable and fair provision and maintenance to be made and paid to her within the iddat period by her former husband; (b) where she herself maintains children born to her, a reasonable and fair provision and maintenance to be made and paid by her former husband for a period of two years from the respective dates of birth of such children; (c) an amount equal to the sum of mehr or dower agreed to be paid to her at the time of her marriage or at any time thereafter according to the Muslim law and (d) all property given to her before or at the time of marriage or after her marriage by her relatives or friends or by husband or any relatives of the husband or his friends.

Under the Christian law a woman can claim maintenance from her spouse through criminal proceeding or/and civil proceeding. Interested parties may pursue both criminal and civil proceedings, simultaneously, as there is no legal bar to it. In criminal proceedings, the religion of the parties does not matter at all, unlike in civil proceedings. If a divorced Christian wife cannot support her in the post divorce period, she need not worry as a remedy is in store for her in law. Under the Indian Divorce Act, 1869, she can apply for alimony/maintenance in a civil court or High Court and, husband is liable to pay her alimony such sum, as the court may order, till her lifetime. The Indian Divorce Act, 1869 which is only applicable to those persons who practise Christian religion *inter alia* governs maintenance rights of a Christian wife.

Laws of maintenance are of course in place, but they are not very effective and efficient in this part of the world. Laws do not always work for the poor or helpless. The state is often found indifferent to such people. The legal process is very tortuous and torturous here. Illiterate, semiliterate and the poor woman can seldom dare to take recourse to the court of law. People often fail in their legal obligations to provide maintenance regularly and adequately to the divorced or separated wife, widows and other dependents. It is often seen that women in difficult situations are usually helped or rescued by their parents rather than by the state. Sometimes certain parents are also either not inclined or in a position to help out such needy women. Since the single women have very little to fall back upon, marriages are relatively more durable here despite all odds.

Gender Inequality

Gender inequalities refer to the obvious or hidden disparities among individuals based on sex. This problem in simple term is known as 'gender bias' which means gender stratification or drawing differences between a girl and a boy, i.e., a male or a female. In India, women were considered as an oppressed section of the society and they were neglected for centuries. Hence the Constitution of India has incorporated provisions to guarantee equality before law and equal protection of laws for all. Similarly, there shall be no discrimination against any citizen on the ground of sex. In addition, since independence, a number of laws have been enacted in order to provide protection to women. For instance, The Dowry Prohibition Act 1961, The Equal Remuneration Act 1986, The Hindu Marriage Act 1956, The Hindu Succession Act 1956, The Muslim Women (Protection of Rights on Divorce) Act, 1986, The Commission of Sati (Prevention) Act 1987, the Protection of the Women from Domestic Violence Act 2005, etc. But the laws are hardly implemented in letters and spirit. There is a massive and clinching evidence of gender bias in different walks of life. With respect to degree of prevalence of gender bias India ranks 10th out of 128 countries of the world.

The sense of insecurity, humiliation and helplessness always keep a women mum. Our whole socialisation is such that for any unsuccessful marriage which results in such violence or divorce, it is always the woman, who is held responsible. Cultural beliefs and traditions that discriminate against women may be officially discredited, but they continue to flourish at the grassroots levels. Family relations in India are governed by personal laws. The three major religious communities are– Hindu, Muslim and Christian each have their separate personal laws. They, as said before, are governed by their respective personal laws in matters of marriage, divorce, succession, adoption, guardianship and maintenance. In the laws of all the communities, women have fewer rights than that of men in corresponding situations. It is really sad that women of the minority communities in India continue to have unequal legal rights and even the women of the majority community have yet to gain complete formal equality in all aspects of family life. This is basically the problem of gender inequality. However, inequality between men and women can take many different forms. Indeed, gender inequality is not one homogeneous phenomenon, but a collection of disparate and interlinked problems. The issue of gender inequality is one which has been publicly reverberating through society for decades. The problem of inequality in employment being one of the most pressing issues today.

The most significant factor in continued use of law to enforce patriarchal privilege is that men still control not only the legal process and the interpretation of laws, but also the subject matter and vantage point of law. It is well known that law is strictly restricted in its capacity to deliver gender justice, which in itself is contingent on the nature of law and its functioning. In this connection it is worthwhile to recall that the law itself is not a monolithic entity, which simply progresses or regresses. Historically, the development of law has been an uneven one. That is to say, more than not, what law promises on paper cannot carry through in reality. That is why law-as-legislation and law-in-practice are most of the time in contradiction with each other. To cite an example, the Indian constitution explicitly enshrines formal equality for women, but the lives and experiences of India women relentlessly continue to be characterized by substantive inequality, inequity and discrimination.

Several legal reforms have taken place since independence in India, including on equal share of daughters to property. Yet gender equality with respect to succession or right to property remains illusive. Establishment of laws and bringing practices in conformity thereto is necessarily a long drawn out process. The government, the legislature, the judiciary, the media and civil society have to perform their roles, each in their own areas of competence and in a concerted manner for the process to be speedy and effective.

Domestic Violence

The Domestic Violence Act, 2005 has concretely dealt with the problem of domestic violence taking into consideration all the related laws and has attempted to reduce the numerous ancillary problems generally faced by such legislations. This legislation is well placed in the Indian context and social scenario, clearly reflective of the mindset of the Indian men. The Act is thus a very vital piece of legislation from the feminist point of view. The occurrence of domestic violence against women arises out of the patriarchal setup, the stereotyping of gender roles, and the distribution of power, real or perceived, in society. Following such ideology, men are believed to be stronger and more powerful than women. They control women and their lives and as a result of this power play, they may hurt women with impunity. The Domestic Violence Act was passed in furtherance of the recommendations of the United Nations Committee on the CEDAW (Convention of the Elimination of all forms of Discrimination Against Women). The Domestic Violence Act promotes the rights of women guaranteed under Articles 14 and 15 of the Constitution of India. Domestic violence is one among several factors that hinder women in their progress, and this Act seeks to protect them from this evil. The Act deals with various forms of abuse that were either not addressed earlier, or that were addressed in ways not as broad as done here.

This piece of legislation has been long over due. It is a comprehensive law and addresses all issues related to women. It is for the first time that an Act has been passed to address women's issues in such detail. The Act is an extremely progressive one not only because it recognizes women who are in a live-in-relationships but also extends protection to other women in the household, including sister and mother thus the Act includes relations of consanguinity, marriage, or through relationships in the nature of marriage, adoption, or joint family thus, 'domestic relationships' are not restricted to the marital context alone. In addition to physical violence of beating, slapping, hitting, kicking and pushing, the Act also covers sexual violence like forced intercourse, forcing his wife or mate to look at pornography or any other obscene pictures or material and child sexual abuse. Another good thing about the Act is the fact that it deals with domestic violence regardless of the religion of the parties, as many a time wrongs are perpetrated (ab)using the protection afforded by personal laws. It is thus secular in outlook in protecting women's rights. The new law also addresses sexual abuse of children and forcing girls to marry against their wishes. This certainly proves that the new Act has been formed keeping the current relationship culture in India and the irregularities in the previous domestic violence laws in mind. It is, however, too early to predict the usefulness of this legislations to its target beneficiaries and the society as a whole.

Uniform Civil Code

In India this term refers to the concept of an overarching Civil Law Code. A uniform civil code administers a common set of secular civil laws to govern all people, irrespective of differences in community, religion and region. This supersedes the right of citizens to be governed by different personal laws based on their religious or ethnic identity. The common areas covered by a civil code include: Personal status, rights related to acquisition and administration of property and marriage, divorce and adoption. Such codes are in place in most modern nations, but not so far in India. Here most family law is determined by the religion of the parties concerned. Hindus, Sikhs, Jains and Buddhists come under Hindu law, whereas Muslims and Christians have their own laws. Muslim law is based on the Shariat.

The passage of the Hindu Code Bills in the 1950s marked a turning point in the history of the Muslim Personal Law. Until this time, Muslim Personal Law had existed side by side with similar religious laws for Hindus and other communities. The Hindu Code Bills were a series of laws aimed at thoroughly secularising the Hindu community and bringing its laws up to modern times. The affect of the Hindu Marriage Act was to prohibit polygamy and to increase the right of the divorced wife to maintenance or alimony. The act applied to everyone in India except Muslims, Christians, Parsees, and Jews. Since Jews and Parsees were a very small minority, and since Christians were governed under an already modern or progressive law, Muslims remained the only large community with a distinct religious law that had not been amended to reflect modern concepts.

When the Indian government ratified the CEDAW (Convention of the Elimination of all forms of Discrimination Against Women) in 1993, it modified laws that were created under the colonial administration. This brought the secular-Muslim divide created after independence into sharp focus. As a matter of fact, the Constitution of India contains in it a series of contradictions that have made it difficult for the government of India to reform or dismantle Islamic personal law. India's leaders at the time of framing of constitution for republic India wanted a secular constitution on the model of a Western democracy. But surprisingly what resulted was not secularism in the Western sense of the term, but rather a 'secular' state with religious laws for its religious groups. In India 'secular' means 'non-intervening in the matter of Islamic religion.

Those wishing to reform the Muslim Personal Law have often cited Muslim countries as examples that such reform is possible. In this regard a question is often raised that if Muslim countries can reform Muslim Personal Law, and if Western democracies have fully secular systems, then why are Indian Muslims living under laws passed in the 1930s? There are Muslims who are in favour of either doing away with the Personal Law or reforming it. Enumerable liberal Muslim intelligentsia have opined through the media that polygamy should be banned outright, women should have an easier time petitioning for a divorce, the husbands should not be able to use the triple talaq method of divorce and the maintenance be granted as it is with the non-Muslims. Yet the old system continues to perpetuate.

In India, the experiment of personal laws for various groups has been a failure in achieving equal treatment for all citizens. The country legislated away all of the personal laws, with the exception of laws applying to Muslims who are regarded as minority. Other minorities have been brought into line along Western standards of secular and equal rights. However, out of fears of creating widespread rioting and rebellion, the government has shelved any reforms for the Muslim community. It has refused to find a legal route that would enforce equal rights for over 70 million of its Muslim female citizens. The vast majority of Muslims led by the Jumiat-al-Ulama and other orthodox Muslim groups have fought tooth and nail against any change in their Personal Law. The Muslim community stubbornly rejects reform, and in essence its rejection may ensure that its privileged position is intact. Most Muslims are resistant to change because they believe that any change in their personal law would result in the destruction of Muslim culture in India.

Family Court

With a view to protecting possible threats to marriage, dignity of women and interests of other members in society, the Government of India introduced the system of family courts in 1984 through enactment of a legislation. The

Family Courts Act 1984 was adopted as a part of the trends of legal reforms concerning women. The Act is expected to facilitate satisfactory resolution of disputes concerning the family through a forum expected to work expeditiously in a just manner and with an approach ensuring maximum welfare of society and dignity of women. Family courts are expected to deal with marriage, matrimonial dissolution, maintenance and alimony, custody, education and support of children, settlement of spousal property and guardianship and custody of child's person and property. Matters relating to will, however, are as usual dealt with by civil courts.

The Family Courts Act was set up to promote conciliation and secure speedy settlement of disputes relating to marriage and family affairs, based on non-adversarial and multi-disciplinary approach. The Family Courts are expected to (i) adopt a radically different approach than that adopted in ordinary civil proceedings, and (ii) make reasonable efforts for conciliated settlement before the trial commenced, and during this stage the proceedings are to be informal. Gender sensitized personnel, including judges, social workers and other trained staff are expected to hear and resolve family related issues by eliminating the rigid rules of procedure. To preserve the informality of procedures, it was specifically laid down that the parties to a dispute were not entitled, as a matter of right, to be represented by legal practitioners. The FCs are supposed to follow simplified rules of evidence and procedure so as to effectively deal with the family disputes, and for achieving this purpose the Code of Civil Procedure was amended. Judges responsible for bringing about conciliation are supposedly committed to the need to protect and preserve the institution of marriage and to promote the welfare of children. Till April 2009 there were 153 FCs in existence in India.

Bibliography

Aguiar, Mark and Erik Hurst (2007) "Measuring Trends in Leisure: The Allocation of Time over Five Decades" *Quarterly Journal of Economics*, 122(3), forthcoming.

Alanen, L. and Mayall, B. (eds.) (2001): *Conceptualizing Child-adult Relations*, London.

Allen, Douglas W. (1992) "Marriage and Divorce: Comment", *American Economic Review*, 82(3).

Bass, L. (Ed.) (2005): *Sociological Studies of Children and Youth*. Vol. 10, Amsterdam

Becker, Gary S. (1981) *A Treatise on the Family*, Harvard University Press: Cambridge.

Bedard, Kelly and Olivier Deschenes (2005) "Sex Preferences, Marital Dissolution, and the Economic Status of Women" *Journal of Human Resources*, 40 (2): 411-434.

Bittman, M. and Pixley, J. (1997) *The Double Life of the Family, Myth, Hope and Experience*. Allen and Unwin, Sydney.

Blau, Francine D. and Lawrence M. Kahn (2000) "Gender Differences in Pay", *Journal of Economic Perspectives*, 14 (4): 75-99.

Buehler-Niederberger, D. (1998): The Separative View. Is there any Scientific Approach to Children. in D.K. Behera (Ed.), Children and Childhood in our Contemporary Societies. Delhi: Kamla-Raj Enterprises, pp. 51–66.

Caucutt, Elizabeth, Nezih Guner, and John Knowles (2002) "Why Do Women Wait? Matching, Wage, Inequality, and the Incentives for Fertility Delay" *Review of Economic Dynamics*, 5 (4): 815-855.

Charles, Kerwin and Melvin Stephens (2004) "Disability, Job Displacement and Divorce", *Journal of Labor Economics*, 22 (2): 489-523.

Cherlin, Andrew (1981) *Marriage, Divorce, Remarriage*, Harvard University Press: Cambridge, MA.

Coontz, Stephanie (2005) *Marriage, a History: From Obedience to Intimacy, or How Love Conquered Marriage*. New York: Viking.

Corsaro, William (2005). *The Sociology of Childhood*. Thousand Oaks, CA: Pine Forge Press.

Cutler, David, Edward Glaeser, and Jesse Shapiro (2003) "Why Have Americans Become More Obese"*Journal of Economic Perspectives*, 17 (3): 93-118.

Dahl, Gordon (200) "Myopic Matrimony and Dropout Decisions? Evidence Using State Laws for Marriage, Schooling and Work", *National Bureau of Economic Research Working Paper #* 11328, Cambridge, MA.

Edgar, Don & Patricia (2008), *The New Child: in search of smarter grown-ups*, Wilkinson Publishing, Melbourne, Australia

Jenks, Chris (2005): *Childhood* (2nd edition), New York

Parsons, Talcot. (1955). *Family, Socialization and Interaction Process*. Robert F. Bales and James Olds. Free press.

Prout, A. (2004): *The Future of Childhood. Towards the Interdisciplinary Study of Children*, London.

Qvortrup, J. *et al.* (Eds.) (1994): *Childhood Matters. Social Theory, Practice and Politics*. Wien, Avebury.

Rasul, Imran (2006) "The Impact of Divorce Laws on Marriage", *mimeo*, University College, London.

Stevenson, Betsey (2006) "Divorce-Law Changes, Household Bargaining, and Married Women's Labor Supply Revisited", *mimeo*, University of Pennsylvania.

Waite, Linda J. and Maggie Gallagher (2000) *The Case for Marriage*, New York: Random House.

West Virginia State Archives."Ann Maria Reeves Jarvis."WVA&H West Virginia Archives& History.West Virginia Division of Culture and History,2009.Web.9-25-2009.http://www.wvculture.org/hiSTory/jarvis.html

Wolfers, Justin (2006) "Did Unilateral Divorce Raise Divorce Rates? A Reconciliation and New Results", *American Economic Review*, 96(5) 1802-1820.

Zelizer, Vivianne A. (1985): *Pricing the Priceless Child. The Changing Social Value of Children*. New York.

Index

ENCYCLOPAEDIA OF SOCIOLOGY

Criminology and Penology

Volume – 6

Satish Mittal
Sushil Kumar Saxena

Commonwealth

Encyclopaedia of Sociology

Edition : 2026

ISBN 978-81-311-0377-7 (set)

Published by :
COMMONWEALTH PUBLISHERS (P) LTD.
4831/24, Govind Lane,
Ansari Road, Darya Ganj,
New Delhi - 110002
Ph. : 23242541, 23272541
e-mail : commonwealthpublishers2016@gmail.com

Distributed by :
ARJUN PUBLISHING HOUSE
4831/24, Govind Lane,
Ansari Road, Darya Ganj,
New Delhi - 110002
Ph. : 23242541, 23272541
e-mail : arjunbooks2001@gmail.com
arjunpubhouse@gmail.com

Laser Typesetting by :
Dimple Computers
Delhi

Printed at :
Milan Enterprises
Delhi

Preface

Criminology is the scientific study of the nature, extent, causes, and control of criminal behaviour in both the individual and in society. It is an interdisciplinary field in the behavioural sciences, drawing especially upon the research of sociologists, social anthropologists and psychologists, as well as on writings in law. Areas of research in criminology include the incidence, forms, causes and consequences of crime, as well as social and governmental regulations and reaction to crime.

Penology is a section of criminology that deals with the philosophy and practice of various societies in their attempts to repress criminal activities, and satisfy public opinion via an appropriate treatment regime for persons convicted of criminal offences. Penology is concerned with the effectiveness of those social processes devised and adopted for the prevention of crime, via the repression or inhibition of criminal intent via the fear of punishment. The study of penology therefore deals with the treatment of prisoners and the subsequent rehabilitation of convicted criminals.

This book introduces the key conceptual debates and approaches in criminology and penology. Analytic in presentation, holistic in interpretation, with examples and narration in simple language, this book has been planned as a textbook for students and a reference tool for researchers.

Authors

Contents

1

Introduction to Criminology

Criminology is the scientific study of the nature, extent, causes, and control of criminal behavior in both the individual and in society. Criminology is an interdisciplinary field in the behavioral sciences, drawing especially upon the research of sociologists, social anthropologists and psychologists, as well as on writings in law.

Areas of research in criminology include the incidence, forms, causes and consequences of crime, as well as social and governmental regulations and reaction to crime. For studying the distribution and causes of crime, criminology mainly relies upon quantitative methods. The term *criminology* was coined in 1885 by Italian law professor Raffaele Garofalo as *criminologia*. Around the same time, but later, French anthropologist Paul Topinard used the analogous French term *criminologie*.

CRIMINOLOGY—SCHOOLS OF THOUGHT

In the mid-18th century, criminology arose as social philosophers gave thought to crime and concepts of law. Over time, several schools of thought have developed. It is important to note, that while there have been numerous schools of criminological thought throughout history, for the most part, the newer schools were a revitalization of the former and not a competing point of view. The current school most criminologists belong to is the Chicago School; however, there are still a great many who feel that a sub-cultural theory of deviance is the better explanation of criminogenesis.

Classical School

The Classical School, which developed in the mid 17th century, was based on utilitarian philosophy. Cesare Beccaria, author of *On Crimes and Punishments* (1763–64), Jeremy Bentham, inventor of the *panopticon*, and other classical school philosophers argued that:

(1) People have free will to choose how to act.

(2) Deterrence is based upon the notion of the human being as a 'hedonist' who seeks pleasure and avoids pain, and a 'rational calculator' weighing up the costs and benefits of the consequences of each action. Thus, it ignores the possibility of irrationality and unconscious drives as motivational factors

(3) Punishment (of sufficient severity) can deter people from crime, as the costs (penalties) outweigh benefits, and that severity of punishment should be proportionate to the crime.

(4) The more swift and certain the punishment, the more effective it is in deterring criminal behavior.

The Classical school of thought came about at a time when major reform in penology occurred, with prisons developed as a form of punishment. Also, this time period saw many legal reforms, the French Revolution, and the development of the legal system in the United States.

Positivist School

The Positivist school presumes that criminal behavior is caused by internal and external factors outside of the individual's control. The scientific method was introduced and applied to study human behavior. Positivism can be broken up into three segments which include biological, psychological and social positivism.

Italian School

Cesare Lombroso, an Italian prison doctor working in the late 19th century and sometimes regarded as the "father" of criminology, was one of the largest contributors to biological positivism and founder of the Italian school of criminology. Lombroso took a scientific approach, insisting on empirical evidence, for studying crime. Considered as the founder of criminal anthropology, he suggested that physiological traits such as the measurements of one's cheek bones or hairline, or a cleft palate, considered to be throwbacks to Neanderthal man, were indicative of "atavistic" criminal tendencies. This approach, influenced by the earlier theory of phrenology and by Charles Darwin and his theory of evolution, has been superseded. Enrico Ferri, a student of Lombroso, believed that social as well as biological factors played a role, and held the view that criminals should not be held responsible when factors causing their criminality were beyond their control. Criminologists have since rejected Lombroso's biological theories, with control groups not used in his studies.

Lacassagne School

Lombroso's Italian school was rivaled, in France, by Alexandre Lacassagne and his school of thought, based in Lyon and influential from 1885 to 1914. The Lacassagne School rejected Lombroso's theory of "criminal type" and of "born criminals", and strained the importance of social factors. However, contrary to criminological tendencies influenced by Durkheim's social determinism, it did not reject biological factors. Indeed, Lacassagne created an original synthesis of both tendencies, influenced by positivism, phrenology and hygienism, which alleged a direct influence of the social environment on the brain and compared the social itself to a brain, upholding an organicist position. Furthermore, Lacassagne criticized the lack of efficiency of prison, insisted on social responsibilities toward crime and on political voluntarism as a solution to crime, and thus advocated harsh penalties for those criminals thought to be unredeemable ("recidivists") for example by supporting the 1895 law on penal colonies or opposing the abolition of the death penalty in 1906.

Hans Eysenck, a British psychologist, claimed that psychological factors such as extraversion and neuroticism made a person more likely to commit criminal acts. He also includes a psychoticism dimension that includes traits similar to the psychopathic profile, developed by Hervey M. Cleckley and later Robert Hare. He also based his model on early parental socialization of the child; his approach bridges the gap between biological explanations and environmental or social learning based approaches.

Sociological Positivism

Sociological positivism postulates that societal factors such as poverty, membership of subcultures, or low levels of education can predispose people to crime. Adolphe Quetelet made use of data and statistical analysis to gain insight into relationship between crime and sociological factors. He found that age, gender, poverty, education, and alcohol consumption were important factors related to crime. Rawson W. Rawson utilized crime statistics to suggest a link between population density and crime rates, with crowded cities creating an environment conducive for crime. Joseph Fletcher and John Glyde also presented papers to the Statistical Society of London on their studies of crime and its distribution. Henry Mayhew used empirical methods and an ethnographic approach to address social questions and poverty, and presented his studies in *London Labour and the London Poor*. Émile Durkheim viewed crime as an inevitable aspect of society, with uneven distribution of wealth and other differences among people.

Chicago School

It is the concept in which individuals learn to recover from the effects of criminal behaviour and bring about justice in the work of criminology.

The Chicago school arose in the early twentieth century, through the work of Robert E. Park, Ernest Burgess, and other urban sociologists at the University of Chicago. In the 1920s, Park and Burgess identified five concentric zones that often exist as cities grow, including the "zone in transition" which was identified as most volatile and subject to disorder. In the 1940s, Henry McKay and Clifford R. Shaw focused on juvenile delinquents, finding that they were concentrated in the zone of transition.

Chicago School sociologists adopted a social ecology approach to studying cities, and postulated that urban neighborhoods with high levels of poverty often experience breakdown in the social structure and institutions such as family and schools. This results in social disorganization, which reduces the ability of these institutions to control behavior and creates an environment ripe for deviant behavior.

Other researchers suggested an added social-psychological link. Edwin Sutherland suggested that people learn criminal behavior from older, more experienced criminals that they may associate with.

Theories of Crime

Theoretical perspectives used in criminology include

psychoanalysis, functionalism, interactionism, Marxism, econometrics, systems theory, postmodernism, etc.

Social structure theories

This theory is applied to a variety of approaches within criminology in particular and in sociology more generally as a conflict theory or structural conflict perspective in sociology and sociology of crime. As this perspective is itself broad enough, embracing as it does a diversity of positions.

Social Disorganization

Social disorganization theory is based on the work of Henry McKay and Clifford R. Shaw of the Chicago School. Social disorganization theory postulates that neighborhoods plagued with poverty and economic deprivation tend to experience high rates of population turnover. These neighborhoods also tend to have high population heterogeneity. With high turnover, informal social structure often fails to develop, which in turn makes it difficult to maintain social order in a community.

Social Ecology

Since the 1950s, social ecology studies have built on the social disorganization theories. Many studies have found that crime rates are associated with poverty, disorder, high numbers of abandoned buildings, and other signs of community deterioration. As working and middle class people leave deteriorating neighborhoods, the most disadvantaged portions of the population may remain. William Julius Wilson suggested a poverty "concentration effect", which may cause neighborhoods to be isolated from the mainstream of society and become prone to violence.

Strain Theory

Strain theory, (also known as Mertonian Anomie), advanced by American sociologist Robert Merton, suggests that mainstream culture, especially in the United States, is saturated with dreams of opportunity, freedom and prosperity; as Merton put it, the *American Dream*. Most people buy into this dream and it becomes a powerful cultural and psychological motivation. Merton also used the term *anomie*, but it meant something slightly different for him than it did for Durkheim. Merton saw the term as meaning a dichotomy between what society expected of its citizens, and what those citizens could actually achieve. Therefore, if the social structure of opportunities is unequal and prevents the majority from realizing the dream, some of them will turn to illegitimate means (crime) in order to realize it. Others will retreat or drop out into deviant subcultures.

Subcultural Theory

Following on from the Chicago school and Strain Theory, and also drawing on Edwin Sutherland's idea of differential association, subcultural theorists focused on small cultural groups fragmenting away from the mainstream to form their own values and meanings about life.

Albert K. Cohen tied anomie theory with Freud's reaction formation idea, suggesting that delinquency among lower class youths is a reaction against the social norms of the middle class. Some youth, especially from poorer areas where opportunities are scarce, might adopt social norms specific to those places which may include "toughness" and disrespect for authority. Criminal acts may result when youths conform to norms of the deviant subculture.

Richard Cloward and Lloyd Ohlin suggested that delinquency can result from differential opportunity for lower class youth. Such youths may be tempted to take up criminal activities, choosing an illegitimate path that provides them more lucrative economic benefits than conventional, over legal options such as minimum wage-paying jobs available to them.

British subcultural theorists focused more heavily on the issue of class, where some criminal activities were seen as 'imaginary solutions' to the problem of belonging to a subordinate class. A further study by the Chicago school looked at gangs and the influence of the interaction of gang leaders under the observation of adults.

Sociologists such as Raymond D. Gastil, have explored the impact of a Southern culture of honor on violent crime rates.

Trait theories

At the other side of the spectrum, criminologist Lonnie Athens developed a theory about how a process of brutalization by parents or peers that usually occurs in childhood results in violent crimes in adulthood. Richard Rhodes' *Why They Kill* describes Athens' observations about domestic and societal violence in the criminals' backgrounds. Both Athens and Rhodes reject the genetic inheritance theories.

Control Theories

Another approach is made by the social bond or social control theory. Instead of looking for factors that make people become criminal, those theories try to explain why people do *not* become criminal. Travis Hirschi identified four main characteristics: "attachment to others", "belief in moral validity of rules", "commitment to achievement" and "involvement in conventional activities". The more a person features those characteristics, the less are the chances that he or she becomes deviant (or criminal). On the other hand, if those factors are not present in a person, it is more likely that he or she might become criminal. Hirschi expanded on this theory, with the idea that a person with low self control is more likely to become criminal.

A simple example: someone wants to have a big yacht, but does not have the means to buy one. If the person cannot exert self-control, he or she might try to get the yacht (or the means for it) in an illegal way; whereas someone with high self-control will (more likely) either wait or deny themselves that need. Social bonds, through peers, parents, and others, can have a countering effect on one's low self-control. For families of low socio-economic status, a factor that distinguishes families with delinquent children from those who are not delinquent is the control exerted by parents or chaperonage.. In addition, theorists such as Matza and Sykes argued that criminals are able to temporarily neutralize internal moral and social behavioral constraints through techniques of neutralization.

Symbolic Interactionism

Symbolic interactionism draws on the phenomenology of Edmund Husserl and George Herbert Mead, as well as subcultural theory and conflict theory. This school of thought focused on the relationship between the powerful state, media and conservative ruling elite on the one hand, and the less powerful groups on the other. The powerful groups had the ability to become the 'significant other' in the less powerful groups' processes of generating meaning. The former could to some extent impose their meanings on the latter, and therefore they were able to 'label' minor delinquent youngsters as criminal. These youngsters would often take on board the label, indulge in crime more readily and become actors in the 'self-fulfilling prophecy' of the powerful groups. Later developments in this set of theories were by Howard Becker and Edwin Lemert, in the mid 20th century. Stanley Cohen who developed the concept of "moral panic"

Rational Choice Theory

Rational choice theory is based on the utilitarian, classical school philosophies of Cesare Beccaria, which were popularized by Jeremy Bentham. They argued that punishment, if certain, swift, and proportionate to the crime, was a deterrent for crime, with risks outweighing possible benefits to the offender. In *Dei delitti e delle pene* (On Crimes and Punishments, 1763–1764), Beccaria advocated a rational penology. Beccaria conceived of punishment as the necessary application of the law for a crime: thus, the judge was simply to conform his sentence to the law. Beccaria also distinguished between crime and sin, and advocated against the death penalty, as well as torture and inhumane treatments, as he did not consider them as rational deterrents.

This philosophy was replaced by the Positivist and Chicago Schools, and not revived until the 1970s with the writings of James Q. Wilson, Gary Becker's 1965 article titled "Crime and Punishment" and George Stigler's 1970 article "The Optimum Enforcement of Laws." Rational choice theory argues that criminals, like other people, weigh costs/risks and benefits when deciding whether or not to commit crime and think in economic terms. They will also try to minimize risks of crime by considering the time, place, and other situational factors.

Gary Becker, for example, acknowledged that many people operate under a high moral and ethical constraint, but considered that criminals rationally see that the benefits of their crime outweigh the cost such as the probability of apprehension, conviction, punishment, as well as their current set of opportunities. From the public policy perspective, since the cost of increasing the fine is marginal to that of the cost of increasing surveillance, one can conclude that the best policy is to maximize the fine and minimize surveillance.

With this perspective, crime prevention or reduction measures can be devised that increase effort required to commit the crime, such as target hardening. Rational choice theories also suggest that increasing risk of offending and likelihood of being caught, through added surveillance, police or security guard presence, added street lighting, and other measures, are effective in reducing crime.

One of the main differences between this theory and Jeremy Bentham's rational choice theory, which had been abandoned in criminology, is that if Bentham considered it possible to completely annihilate crime (through the panopticon), Becker's theory acknowledged that a society could not eradicate crime beneath a certain level. For example, if 25% of a supermarket's products were stolen, it would be very easy to reduce this rate to 15%, quite easy to reduce it until 5%, difficult to reduce it under 3% and nearly impossible to reduce it to zero (a feat which would cost the supermarket so much in surveillance, etc., that it would outweight the benefits). This reveals that the goals of utilitarianism and classical liberalism have to be tempered and reduced to more modest proposals to be practically applicable.

Such rational choice theories, linked to neoliberalism, have been at the basics of crime prevention through environmental design and underpin the Market Reduction Approach to theft by Mike Sutton (criminologist) which is a systematic toolkit for those seeking to focus attention on "crime facilitators" by tackling the markets for stolen goods that provide motivation for thieves to supply them by theft.

Routine Activity Theory

Routine activity theory, developed by Marcus Felson and Lawrence Cohen, draws upon control theories and explains crime in terms of crime opportunities that occur in everyday life. A crime opportunity requires that elements converge in time and place including (1) a motivated offender (2) suitable target or victim (3) lack of a capable guardian. A guardian at a place, such as a street, could include security guards or even ordinary pedestrians who would witness the criminal act and possibly intervene or report it to police. Routine activity theory was expanded by John Eck, who added a fourth element of "place manager" such as rental property managers who can take nuisance abatement measures.

Conflict Criminology

Largely based on the writings of Karl Marx, conflict criminology claims that crime is inevitable in capitalist societies, as invariably certain groups will become marginalised and unequal. In seeking equality, members of these groups may often turn to crime in order to gain the material wealth that apparently brings equality in capitalist economic states. Conflict criminology derives its name from the fact that theorists within the area believe that there is no consensual social contract between state and citizen.

The conflict theory assumes that every society is subjected to a process of continuous change and that this process creates social conflicts. Hence, social change and social conflict are ubiquitous. Individuals and social classes, each with distinctive interests, represent the constituent elements of a society. As such, they are individually and collectively participants in this process but there is no guarantee that the interests of each class will coincide. Indeed, the lack of common ground is likely to bring them into conflict with each other. From time to time, each element's contribution may be positive or negative, constructive or destructive. To that extent, therefore, the progress made by each society as a whole is limited by the acts and omissions of some of its members by others. This limitation may promote a struggle for greater progress but, if the less progressive group has access to the coercive power of law, it may entrench inequality and oppress those deemed less equal. In turn, this inequality will become a significant source of conflict. The theory identifies the state and the law as instruments of oppression used by the ruling class for their own benefit.

There are various strands of conflict theory, with many heavily critiquing the others. Structural Marxist criminology, which is essentially the most 'pure' version of the above, has been frequently accused of idealism, and many critics point to the fact that the Soviet Union and such states had as high crime rates as the capitalist West. Furthermore, some highly capitalist states such as Switzerland have very low crime rates, thus making structural theory seem improbable.

Instrumental Marxism partly holds to the above, but claims that capitalism in itself cannot be blamed for all crimes. A seminal book on the subject, *The New Criminology* (by Taylor, Walton and Young) was considered groundbreaking and ahead of its time at the point of its publication in 1973. However, 11 years later, co-author Jock Young turned against the work, claiming it too was overly idealistic, and began to form yet another line of criminological thought, now commonly known as Left realism

Sellin was a sociologist at the University of Pennsylvania and one of the pioneers of scientific criminology. His method involved a comprehensive view of the subject incorporating historical, sociological, psychological, and legal factors into the analysis. He applied both Marxism and Conflict Theory to an examination of the cultural diversity of modern industrial society. In a homogenous society, norms or codes of behaviour will emerge and become laws where enforcement is necessary to preserve the unitary culture. But where separate cultures diverge from the mainstream, those minority groups will establish their own norms. Socialisation will therefore be to the subgroup and to the mainstream norms. When laws are enacted, they will represent the norms, values and interests of the dominant cultural or ethnic group which may produce Border Culture Conflict.

When the two cultures interact and one seeks to extend its influence into the other, each side is likely to react protectively. If the balance of power is relatively equal, an accommodation will usually be reached. But if the distribution of power is unequal, the everyday behaviour of the minority group may be defined as deviant. The more diversified and heterogeneous a society becomes, the greater the probability of more frequent conflict as subgroups who live by their own rules break the rules of other groups.

Vold suggests, in theoretical criminology which contains inaccurate dates for references, approaching an understanding of the social nature of crime as a product of the conflict between groups within the same culture. Humans are naturally social beings, forming groups out of shared interests and needs. The interests and needs of groups interact and produce competition in an increasingly political arena over maintaining and/or expanding one group's position relative to others in the control of necessary resources (money, education, employment, etc.). The challenge for all groups is to control the state for their own sectional interests. Hence, the group which proves most efficient in the control of political processes, obtains the mandate to enact laws that limit the behaviour of other groups and, in some cases, prevent the fulfilment of minority group needs. Although the theory has some interest, it is limited in its application to the criminal law because it is not so much the law that represents sectional interests, but the way in which it is enforced. For example, the definition of theft might remain constant but the allocation of resources to investigate and prosecute theft may be unequally distributed between blue-collar and white-collar versions of the behaviour.

Austin Turk draws on the work of Ralf Dahrendorf who expanded on Marxism's emphasis on the social relations of production as a key to understanding power and focused on the struggle in a modern industrial society for institutional authority. This is power exercised by the social institutions that dominate everyday life; the authority vested in groups which control key positions in religious, educational, governmental, and even family relations. This authority can be linked to economic position, but it is not necessarily dependent upon it.

Turk argues that some conflict is beneficial to society because it encourages society to consider whether the current consensus is justified, i.e. there is a balance between stasis and evolution. In this debate, there is a distinction between cultural norms which set out what behaviour is expected, and social norms which represent the reality of what happens. Those who have the power transform their cultural norms into law. The mechanisms for enforcement determine the social norms and so affect the beliefs and actions of the majority of citizens. If those who are subject to the laws agree with the law's cultural values, there will be co-operative enforcement by the community and the policing agencies.

Conflict emerges when the subjects do not support the cultural norms in particular laws and the policing agencies attempt their rigorous enforcement, e.g. the policing of soft drugs. There may also be conflict within the enforcement system. Whereas the police may set of policy of tolerance, judges may wish to enforce the law with more severe penalties. If fewer offenders are brought before the courts, the judges may increase the severity of the sentences in an attempt to offer a general deterrent.

Contemporary Criminological Studies

Today's cultural and critical criminologists define themselves through the opposition to rational choice-inspired theories, which they perceive to rest on an ontologically simplistic conception of human beings as hedonistic opportunists whose behaviour can be manipulated by adjustments of costs, benefits, opportunities and technologies of control.

Early romantic accounts of crime/delinquency as a form of seduction or proto-political resistance to the powerlessness and dull monotony of working life are now being challenged by late-modern hybrid theories. These theories examine the ways in which criminals are incorporated into consumerism's value-system and fantasies, as argued by Robert Reiner in his book *Law and Order*, yet initially excluded in their economic and social lives. Combining elements of strain theory with cultural theory and symbolic interactionism, Jock Young, in *The Exclusive Society*, uses the metaphor of *bulimia* to depict the tense opposition between inclusion and exclusion. Simon Hallsworth and Keith Hayward adopt a similar approach in their respective works *Street Crime* and *City Limits*, and in further work

Hayward reintroduces the Freudian term 'narcissism' to explain the insecure yet aggressive, acquisitive sentiments and motivations behind criminality. In *Criminal Identities and Consumer Culture*, Steve Hall, Simon Winlow and Craig Ancrum draw upon Continental philosophy and Lacanian psychoanalysis to take late-modern hybrid theories to a new level of sophistication as they explain how the dynamic tension between inclusion and exclusion prolongs the narcissistic subject throughout the life-course in an aggressive struggle for identities of social distinction expressed by the acquisition and display of consumer culture's status-symbols.

Both the Positivist and Classical Schools take a consensus view of crime — that a crime is an act that violates the basic values and beliefs of society. Those values and beliefs are manifested as laws that society agrees upon. However, there are two types of laws:

— Natural laws are rooted in core values shared by many cultures. Natural laws protect against harm to persons (e.g. murder, rape, assault) or property (theft, larceny, robbery), and form the basis of common law systems.

— Statutes are enacted by legislatures and reflect current cultural mores, albeit that some laws may be controversial, e.g. laws that prohibit cannabis use and gambling. Marxist criminology, Conflict criminology and Critical Criminology claim that most relationships between state and citizen are non-consensual and, as such, criminal law is not necessarily representative of public beliefs and wishes: it is exercised in the interests of the ruling or dominant class. The more right wing criminologies tend to posit that there is a consensual social contract between State and citizen.

Therefore, definitions of crimes will vary from place to place, in accordance to the cultural norms and mores, but may be broadly classified as blue-collar crime, corporate crime, organized crime, political crime, public order crime, state crime, state-corporate crime, and white-collar crime.

2

Criminological Theory

Criminology is the body of knowledge which regards crime as a social phenomenon. It includes the processes of making laws, breaking laws, and the reacting toward the breaking of laws. Together, these three processes form a unified sequence of events. Criminologists have adopted methods of study from varying social and behavioural sciences. Like other scientists, criminologists measure and assess crime over time and place. They also measure the characteristics of criminals, crimes, and victims using various methods. Certain acts, regarded as "undesirable" by political society are defined as such. Society reacts by punishment, treatment, or prevention. These sequences of events come together to comprise the object matter of criminology.

While many people are intimidated at their very first encounter with theory, it is used almost on a daily basis. You may be one who believes that theory is abstract and has no fundamental basis in the real world. However, whether you realise it or not, you use theory almost all the time. We all make assumptions and generalisations about certain things we are in contact with daily; thus we theorise. Theories are logical constructions that explain natural phenomena. They are not in themselves always directly observable, but can be supported or refuted by empirical findings. Theory and empirical research are connected by means of hypotheses, which are testable propositions that are logically derived from theories. The testable part is very important because scientific hypotheses must be capable of being accepted or rejected.

Theories can be simple or complex, it depends on how relationships are made in formulating them. Theory can be fun, depending on how it is applied. If you spend the day in a shopping mall you can see how much fun theory can be. So why study theory? The truth of the matter is, we need theory in order to function, in order to better understand the world around us. Life would be pretty dull if we couldn't generalise or make assumptions about people and things. Most of our daily theories tend to be illogical and are a product of our own selective observation. Often we perceive what we want to perceive. Human behaviour tends to be very complex, almost abstract. Theories on crime causation are complex, too. Most theories introduced here are from research, both past and present, on criminal behaviour which reflects both systematic observation and very careful logic. Theories not only provide a framework for us to interpret the meanings of observed patterns but they help us to determine when these patterns are meaningful and when they are not.

Classical School

Classical criminology grew out of a reaction against the barbaric system of law, justice and punishment that was in existence before 1789. It sought an emphasis on free will and human rationality. The Classical School was not interested in studying criminals, but rather lawmaking and legal processing. Crime, they believed, was activity engaged in out of total free will and that individuals weighed the consequences of their actions. Punishment is made in order to deter people from committing crime and it should be greater than the pleasure of criminal gains. Classical theory emphasised a legal definition of crime rather than what defined criminal behaviour.

The Declaration of Independence and the US Constitution reflect the Classical movement, thus the law of today is classical in nature. Two famous writers during this classical period were Cesare Beccaria and Germy Bentham, both led the movement to human rights and free will. Becceria thought that crime could be traced to bad laws, not to bad people. A new modern criminal justice system would be needed to guarantee equal treatment of all people before the law. His famous book, *On Crimes and Punishment* presented a new design for the criminal justice system that served all people. His book dubbed him the "father of modern criminology."

Bentham's concern was upon utilitarianism which assumed the greatest happiness for the greatest number. He believed that individuals weigh the probabilities of present and future pleasures against those of present and future pain. Thus people acted as human calculators, he believed, and that they put all factors into a sort of mathematical equation to decide whether or not to commit an illegal act. He believed then that punishment should be just a bit in excess of the pleasures derived from an act and not any higher than that. The law exists to create happiness for all, thus since punishment creates unhappiness it can be justified if it prevents greater evil than it produces. Classical School Positive

Positive School

Positivists, unlike the classical reformers, sought to explain the world around them. They saw behaviour as determined by biological, psychological, and social traits. They focused on a deterministic view of the world, on criminal behaviour instead of legal issues, and the prevention of crime through the treatment (or reformation) of offenders. The use of scientific techniques was important to the positivists. Data was collected in order to explain different types of individuals and social phenomena. Naturalists and anthropologists formed the theory of evolution which was a very critical component to the study of human criminal behaviour by the positivists. Humans were responsible for their own destinies.

The focus on positivism then is on systematic observations and the accumulation of evidence and objective fact within a deductive frame work, thus moving from a general statement to a more specific one.

Cesare Limbers replaced the notion of free will and rationality with the notion of determinism. Together with his followers, Enrico Ferri and Raffaele Garofalo, he developed the positivist school of criminology which sought explanations for criminal behaviour through scientific research and experimentation. Limbers believed in the "criminal born" man and woman. He believed they had physical features of ape like creatures that were not fully developed as humans were. Lombroso measured thousands of live and dead prisoners to prove his theory. He noted that criminals lacked moral sense, had an absence of remorse and used much slang. Lombroso later added social and economic factors to his list of crime causation but said they were second in nature to biological, predetermined factors. His theory however has been kept alive, not by agreement but by much criticism.

Chicago School

The theme of the Chicago school focused upon human behaviour as determined by social and physical environmental factors, rather than genetic, personal characteristics. The school believed the community to be a major factor on human behaviour and that the city functioned as a microcosm. Researchers from this school developed empirical sociology, that is, studying humans in their natural environment rather than an armchair look at the social environment. Chicago theorists combined data, such as individual cases with population statistics which constructed an important foundation that has since been the basis for many criminological theories of today.

Members of this school focused upon the city of Chicago (hence the name) as a source for many answers to its probing questions. Many scholars of this time believed that urbanisation and mobility into the city was a cause for many of the problems experienced at the time.

Crime was fostered mainly in the slums. Many unemployed people, male, female, young and old, became transients. A plethora of social problems emerged, ranging from poor sanitation, inadequate housing, juvenile gangs, vice, to name a few. People were no longer closely-knit, nor were communities familiar.

Many had no one to turn to during these troubled times. Crime was mainly fostered in the slum areas, where many of the immigrants lived. People began to form their own support groups and gangs, which emphasised deviant values. All of this served as a laboratory for the new sociologists at the University of Chicago.

The school contributed two methods of study. The first was the usage of official data, such as census reports, housing/welfare records and crime figures. High areas of crime, truancy and poverty were applied to different geographical areas of the city. The second method was the life history, as first studied by early Chicago school theorist, W.I. Thomas. This contributed a shift away from theoretical abstracts to more concrete approaches of the real world and real world related phenomena. The process of becoming deviant or criminal was explained by psychosocial phenomena. They wanted to present human behaviour in its natural environment, and this is why the Chicago School is often referred to as the Ecological School. Further observations by researchers provided a clear analysis that the city was a place where life is superficial, where people are anonymous, where relationships are transitory and friendship and family bonds are weak. They saw the weakening of primary social relationships as leading to a process of social disorganisation.

Chicago criminologists clearly saw pathology in the city which led to criminality. Much of the research conducted by Shaw and McKay illustrated this point. The Chicago School clearly stressed humans as social creatures and their behaviour as a product of their social environment. The social environment provides values and definitions that govern behaviour. Urbanisation and industrialisation break down older and more cohesive patterns of values, thus creating communities with competing norms and value systems.

The breakdown of urban life results in basic institutions such as the family, friendships and other social groups to become so impersonal, almost anonymous. As values became fragmented, opposing definitions about proper behaviour arise and come into conflict with other behaviour. Chicago School.Disorganisation is more prevalent in the centre of the urbanised city, and decreases with distance. Thus, crime developed through frequent contact with criminal traditions, goals and values that have developed over a period of time in disorganised areas of the city.

Cohen & Felson's Routine Activities

Larry Cohen and Marcus Felson proposed their Routine Activities theory in 1979. It remained very popular in the 1980s. Their theory is closely linked with the Rational Choice perspective in that it focuses on the characteristics of crime rather than on the characteristics of the offender. Cohen and Felson argue that there will always be a vast supply of crime motivation and that such motivation and supply of offenders remains constant. They state that three crucial components are necessary for a predatory criminal act, that is, violent crimes against the person and crimes which an offender attempts to stale a direct object. These three elements include motivated offenders, suitable targets, (something worth taking), and the absence of capable guardians, in order to prevent would be criminal acts. If one such component is missing, crime is not likely to occur. If all three elements are present, then the chances for crime increase.

Cohen and Felson argue that the rate in which crime rises is equal to the number of suitable targets and the absence of individuals to protect those targets. The routine patterns of work, play, and leisure affect the convergence in time and place of the would be offenders, suitable targets, and absence of guardians, they argue. The number of caretakers, acting as guardians, who are at home during the day has decreased because of an increase participation of women into the work force. Homes are often left unguarded while both parents are at work and children are either in day care or at school.

Also, the growth of suburban living and the decline rate of traditional neighbourhoods has decreased the number of familiar guardians, such as family, neighbours, or friends. Finally, the baby boom generation coming of age during the years 1960 to 1980 resulted in an excess number of motivated offenders. Routine Activities states that criminal offences are related to the nature of everyday patterns of social interaction. Cohen and Felson used their approach to explain the rise in crime between the years 1960 to 1980.

They were concerned with the changes occurring in society, which they believed led to social disorganisation, which further led to crime opportunity. Their perspective shows that crime is not sole related to biological and psychological characteristics, nor to social or economic conditions, but that it is just as important to concentrate on situations factors which give rise to criminal opportunity. Routine Activities approach is important to crime prevention and to the changing of conditions and circumstances in which crime is committed.

One measure of situation crime prevention is target hardening. Target hardening makes it more difficult for offenders to carry out crimes on specific targets. The use of locked doors, windows, alarm systems, watch dogs, and community crime watch programs are all examples of target hardening—making it harder to become a victim of crime.

Social Disorganisation

The growth of cultural relativity, that is, the view that cultures are not better or worse than one another, but simply different, in sociology led to a questioning of the existence of a universal set of values. The pronounced social changes following World War I and the Great Depression, included immigration, urbanisation, and industrialisation into the U.S. The crowding of large cities and the cultural diversity within them led to a huge urban development, which was conducive to deviance.

An explanation was needed to sort out and understand this new phenomena. The concept of Social Disorganisation is largely associated with the "Chicago School" of sociology and was based on the work of W.I. Thomas and Florian Znaniecki as well as Clifford Shaw and Henry McKay, to name a few. Thus, the term social disorganisation refers to both an explanation of deviance and a state of society that produces it. It was the result of intellectual development that had taken place since 1910 in Sociology. It rooted its explanation of deviance in social norms and community activities. Crime was seen as a product of uneven development in society, with change and conflict which affects the behaviour of those within it. This theory emphasised that society was organised when people are presumed to have developed agreement about fundamental values and norms, with behavioural regularity. Social organisation, or social order, exists when there is a high degree of internal bonding to individuals and institutions in a conventional society. This cohesion consists largely of agreement about goals that are worth striving for and how to behave and how to not behave. Simply put, social disorganisation is social disorder.

It was believed that social organisation involved an integration of customs, teamwork, high morale, and bonding. This led to harmonious social relationships. Such a group showed solidarity and homogeneous and traditional behaviour. Social disorganisation theorists believe social disorganisation existed in much of city life. They made such a relationship almost unmistakable. They used the city as their laboratory in which they studied deviance and crime. They concentrated their research on disorganised local areas, slums or inner-city areas of high crime, prostitution, suicide and other deviant forms of behaviour. Thus, in their theoretical framework, social patterns of the urban environment produced social disorganisation, which led to crime and deviance.

Thomas and Znaniecki compared the conditions immigrants had left in Poland with those they found in Chicago. They also studied the assimilation of Polish immigrants. They found that older immigrants were not very much affected by the move, due to managing to continue living as peasants, even in the urban slums. The younger generation did not grow up on these Polish farms and thus were city dwellers. They had very little traditions of the Old World and were not assimilated into the new ones. The rates of crime and delinquency started to rise and Thomas and Znaniecki attributed this to social disorganisation, which they defined as the breakdown of effective social bonds, family and neighbourhoods associations, as well as social controls in the community. Their study influenced others to come.

Robert Park and Ernest Burgess introduced an ecological analysis of crime causation. Ecology is the study of animals and plants and how they relate to one another in their natural habitat. Park and Burgess then examined area characteristics instead of criminals for their explanations of high crime. They developed the idea of natural urban areas, which consisted of concentric zones which extended out from downtown central business district to the commuter zone at the fringes of the city. Each zone had its own

Social Disorganisation Concentric Zone Theory

Clifford Shaw and Henry McKay were researchers at the Chicago's Institute for Juvenile Research and maintained a close relationship with Chicago's Sociology department. They were interested in Park and Burgess's conception of the "natural urban area" of Chicago and used this model to investigate the relationship between crime rates—mainly delinquency—and the various zones of Chicago.

They found that the crime rate was distributed throughout the city, delinquency occurred in the areas nearest to the business district, that some areas suffered from high consistent delinquency rates no matter the make-up of the population, that high delinquency areas were characterised by a high percentage of immigrants, non-whites, lower income famines, and finally, and that high-delinquency areas had an acceptance of non-conventional norms, which competed with conventional ones. They collected their data from over 56,000 juvenile court records with covered a period of time from 1900-1933. However, there were problems with the concept of social disorganisation and these problems are what contributed to its decline. First, it confused cause and effect. That is, it described community factors related to crime and deviance, but it must be able to distinguish the consequences of crime from disorganisation itself; it didn't.

Many early social disorganisation theorists were not careful in clarifying the concept of disorganisation. Second, social disorganisation was rather subjective and judgmental, all the while pretending to be objective. Observers failed to free themselves from biases and placed their own value judgments on behaviours.

Third, it tried to explain crime as an almost entirely lower-class phenomena, and in no way included middle and upper-class deviance and crime rates. Thus, it was biased, in that it favoured middle-class standards. Those in the lower strata were assumed to have higher levels of crime rates because their members lived in the most socially disorganised areas of the city.

Fourth, social change was often confused with social disorganisation, and little attention was paid to explain why some social changes were disorganised and why others were organised. Finally, what is disorganised? At some times, things may seem like disorganisation but at other times, they may be highly organised systems of competing norms and values. The concept produces a bit of ambiguity.

Durkheim's Anomie

Emile Durkheim, a French sociologist, introduced the concept of anomie in his book The Division of Labour in Society, published in 1893. He used anomie to describe a condition of deregulation that was occurring in society. This meant that rules on how people ought to behave with each other were breaking down and thus people did not know what to expect from one another. Anomie, simply defined, is a state where norms (expectations on behaviours) are confused, unclear or not present. It is normlessness, Durkheim felt, that led to deviant behaviour.

In 1897, Durkheim used the term again in his study on Suicide, referring to a morally de-regulated condition. Durkheim was preoccupied with the effects of social change. He best illustrated his concept of anomie not in a discussion of crime but of suicide. In The Division of Labour in Society, Durkheim proposed two concepts. First, that societies evolved from a simple, non-specialised form, called mechanical, toward a highly complex, specialised form, called organic. In the former society people behave and think alike and more or less perform the same work tasks and have the same group-oriented goals. When societies become more complex, or organic, work also becomes more complex. In this society, people are no longer tied to one another and social bonds are impersonal.

Anomie thus refers to a breakdown of social norms and it a condition where norms no longer control the activities of members in society. Individuals cannot find their place in society without clear rules to help guide them. Changing conditions as well as adjustment of life leads to dissatisfaction, conflict, and deviance. He observed that social periods of disruption (economic depression, for instance) brought about greater anomie and higher rates of crime, suicide, and deviance. Durkheim felt that sudden change caused a state of anomie. The system breaks down, either during a great prosperity or a great depression, anomie is the same result.

Merton's Strain Theory

Robert K. Merton, an American sociologist, borrowed Durkheim's concept of anomie to form his own theory, called Strain Theory. It differs somewhat from Durkheim's in that Merton argued that the real problem is not created by a sudden social change, as Durkheim proposed, but rather by a social structure that holds out the same goals to all its members without giving them equal means to achieve them. It is this lack of integration between what the culture calls for and what the structure permits that causes deviant behaviour.

Deviance then is a symptom of the social structure. Merton borrowed Durkheim's notion of anomie to describe the breakdown of the normative system. Merton's theory does not focus upon crime persay, but rather upon various acts of deviance, which may be understood to lead to criminal behaviour. Merton notes that there are certain goals which are strongly emphasised by society. Society emphasises certain means to reach those goals (such as education, hard work, etc.,) However, not everyone has the equal access to the legitimate means to attain those goals. The stage then is set for anomie/strain.

Merton presents five modes of adapting to strain caused by the restricted access to socially approved goals and means. He did not mean that everyone who was denied access to society's goals became deviant. Rather the response, or modes of adaptation, depend on the individual's attitudes toward cultural goals and the institutional means to attain them. The conformist is the most common mode of adaptation.

Such individuals accept both the goals as well as the prescribed means for achieving the goal. Conformists will accept, though not always achieve, the goals of society and the means approved for achieving them. Innovators accept socialite goals but have few legitimate means to achieve those goals, thus they innovate (design) their own means to get ahead. The means to get ahead may be through robbery, embezzlement or other such criminal acts. Ritualists, the third adaptation, abandon the goals they once believed to be within their reach and thus dedicate themselves to their current lifestyle. They play by the rules and have a daily, safe routine. Re-treatists, the fourth fifth adaptation is given to those who give up not only the goals but also the means. They often retreat into the world of alcoholism and drug addiction. These individuals escape into a nonproductive, non-striving lifestyle. The final adaptation, that of rebel, occurs when the cultural goals and the legitimate means are rejected. Individuals create their own goals and their own means, by protest or revolutionary activity.

Agnew's General Strain Theory

In the mid 70s, strain theory came under heavy attack after having dominated deviance research in the decade of the 60s, prompting that it become abandoned. However, since that time, strain theory has survived such attacks, but has left behind a diminished influence. In 1992, Robert Agnew proposed a general strain theory that focuses on at least three measures of strain. He argues that actual or anticipated failure to achieve positively valued goals, actual or anticipated removal of positively valued stimuli, and actual or anticipated presentation of negative stimuli all result in strain.

Agnew's strain theory focuses primarily on negative relationships with others, in that a person is not treated in a way that he or she expects or wants to be treated. He argues that people are pressured into criminal or deviant acts by negative affective states, such as anger, which results in negative relationships. Such a negative affect leads to pressure which then leads to illegitimate ways to attain a goal.

Other strain theories explain strain in a way that relationships with others prevent one from reaching positively valued goals. They focus primarily on goal blockage, that which is often experienced by the middle or lower classes.

Agnew argues that strain theory is central in explaining crime and deviance, but that it needs more revision to play such a central role in sociology. His theory is written at a social-psychological level so that it focuses on an individual's immediate social environment. Much of the theory is focused toward adolescent criminality—delinquency, because so much of the data available for testing involves surveys of adolescents. He argues that his theory is capable of overcoming empirical and theoretical criticisms associated with previous versions of strain theory.

Agnew suggests that criminologists pay special attention to the magnitude, recency, duration, and clustering of such strainful events. He spells out that several cognitive, emotional, and behavioural adoptions to strain receive little or not attention. He proposes a series of factors that determine whether a person will cope with strain in a criminal or conforming manner, including temperament, intelligence, interpersonal skills, self-efficacy, association with criminal peers, and conventional social support.

Subculture Theories

In criminology, subcultures theories emerged as a way to account for delinquency rates among lower-class males, of these the infamous teenage gang. Subculture theories believe that the delinquent subcultures emerged in response to the special problems that the members of mainstream society do not face.

The strain theorists explained crime as a result of frustrations suffered by lower-class individuals deprived of legitimate means to reach their goals. Cultural deviance theories assumed that people became deviant by learning the criminal values of the group to which they belonged to. This laid down the foundation for subculture theories during the 1950s.

A subculture is defined as a subdivision within the dominant culture that has its own norms, values and belief system. These subcultures emerge when individuals in similar circumstances find themselves virtually isolated or neglected by mainstream society. Thus they group together for mutual support. Subcultures exist within the larger society, not apart from it. The members of the subculture are different from the dominant culture.

The subculture theories we will look at are extensions of strain, social disorganisation and differential association theories. Subculture theories help to explain why subcultures emerge (extension of strain), why they take a particular shape (extension of social disorganisation), and why they continue from one generation to another (extension of differential association).

For instance, Marvin Wolfgang and Franco Ferracuti's Subculture of Violence thesis argues that the value system of some subcultures not only demands but also expects violence in certain social situations. It is this norm which affects daily behaviour that is in conflict with the conventional society. Here we will explain the subculture theories proposed by Albert Cohen, (Subculture of Delinquency), Richard Cloward & Lloyd Ohlin (Differential Opportunity), Walter Miller (Lower-Class Focal Concerns) and Marvin Wolfgang & Franco Ferracuti (Subculture of Violence). To better understand and appreciate subculture theories one must first probe into the historical time period of the 1950s. The values of the middle class were dominant and anything else was not considered normal.

Peaking urbanisation produced more and more deteriorated cities in America. The suburbs of the middle class were emerging. Delinquency was mainly perceived as a problem of the lower class. The middle class "we-they" separation led to seeing itself as the far superior class.

Cohen's Subculture of Delinquency Theory

In 1955 Albert K. Cohen wrote Delinquent Boys. He attempted to look at how such a subculture began. Cohen found that delinquency among youths was more prevalent among lower class males and the most common form of this was the juvenile gang. Cohen, a student of Sutherland and Merton, learned from Sutherland that differential association and cultural transmission of criminal norms led to criminal behaviour, while Merton taught him about structurally induced strain.

Delinquent subcultures, according to Cohen, have values that are in opposition to those of the dominant culture. These subcultures emerge in the slums of some of the nation's largest cities. Often, they are rooted in class differentials, parental aspirations and school standards. Cohen notes that the position of one's family in the social structure determines the problems the child will later face in life. Thus, they will experience status frustration and strain and adapt into either a corner boy, college boy, or a delinquent boy.

Corner boys lead a conventional lifestyle, making the best of a bad situation. They spend most of their time with peers and receive peer support in group activities. These boys are far and few between. Their chances for success are limited. Cohen argues that their academic and social handicaps prevent them from living up to middle-class standards.

Delinquent boys, on the other hand, band together to define status. Their delinquent acts serve no real purpose. They often discard or destroy what they have stolen. Their acts are random and are directed at people and property. They are a short-run hedonistic subculture with no planning. They often act on impulse, often without consideration for the future. Members are loyal to one another and allow no one to restrain their behaviour.

Stealing, in the delinquent gang, serves as a form of achieving peer status within the group, with no other motive. Cohen declared that all children seek social status, but not everyone can compete for it in the same way. Reaction-formation, a Freudian defence mechanism, serves to overcome anxiety, as a hostile overreaction to middle class values can occur. A delinquent subculture is created to resolve problems of lower-class status.

Much of Cohen's work has been both praised and criticised. It helps to answer questions that remain unresolved by strain and cultural deviance theories. His notion of status deprivation and the middle-class measuring rod has been very useful to researchers. His theory, however, fails to explain why some delinquent subcultures eventually become law-abiding, even when this social class position is fixed. Later, he expanded his theory to include not only lower-class delinquents but also variants of middle-class delinquents and female delinquent subcultures. Cohen's theory stimulated later formations of new theories.

Cloward & Ohlin's Differential Opportunity Theory

In 1959, Richard Cloward noted that Merton's anomie theory specified only one structure of opportunity. He, however, argued for two and not one. He thus proposed that there are also illegitimate avenues of structure, in addition to legitimate ones.

In 1960 he and Lloyd Ohlin worked together and proposed a theory of delinquent gngs known as Differential Opportunity Theory. This theory, like Cohen's theory, combines the strain, differential association as well as the social disorganisation perspectives. Delinquent subcultures, according to Cloward and Ohlin, flourish in the lower-classes and take particular forms so that the means for illegitimate success are no more equally distributed than the means for legitimate success.

They argue that the types of criminal subcultures that flourish depend on the area in which they develop. They propose three types of delinquent gangs. The first, the criminal gang, emerge in areas where conventional as well as non conventional values of behaviour are integrated by a close connection of illegitimate and legitimate businesses. This type of gang is stable than the ones to follow. Older criminals serve as role models and they teach necessary criminal skills to the youngsters.

The second type, the conflict or violent gang, is non stable and non integrated, where there is an absence of criminal organisation resulting in instability. This gang aims to find a reputation for toughness and destructive violence. The third and final type, the re-treatist gang, is equally unsuccessful in legitimate as well as illegitimate means. They are known as double failures, thus retreating into a world of sex, drugs, and alcohol. Cloward and Ohlin further state that the varying form of delinquent subcultures depended upon the degree of integration that was present in the community.

Miller's Lower-Class Focal Concerns

Walter Miller didn't see juvenile delinquency as being rooted in the rejection of the middle-class value system, as did other subculture theorists, but in the value system of the lower class. It is this value system that generates delinquent acts. This value system emerged as a response to living in the slums.

Miller was an anthropologist who was familiar with enthnography. Having closely studied the lower class areas in Boston, in 1955, he came up with his own conclusions, and thus his Lower-Class Focal Concerns theory. He saw society as composed of different social groups. Each group had its own subculture. He used the concept of focal concerns, and not value, to further describe things that were important to the subculture. These "focal concerns" are important aspects in the subculture and require constant attention and care.

Miller identified six focal concerns to which the lower class give attention to. The concern over trouble is a major feature of the lower class. Getting into trouble and staying out of trouble are very important daily preoccupations. Trouble can either mean prestige or landing in jail.

Toughness, another concern, further represents a commitment to law-violation and being a problem to others. Machismo and being daring is stressed. The third focal concern is that of smartness. It is the ability to gain something by outsmarting or conning another. Prestige is often the reward for those demonstrating such skills. Another focal concern is excitement. Living on the edge for thrills and doing dangerous things as well as taking risks is a crucial concern. Another focal concern is that of fate. It is a crucial concern to the lower class. Many believe that their lives are subject to forces outside of their control. The last focal concern focuses upon autonomy.

This signifies being independent, not relying on others and rejecting authority. Miller further observed that an absence of a father in a young boy's life posed a problem for learning appropriate male behaviour. This served as a device for gangs to accommodate the problem faced by young males who had no presence of a father figure. Miller's theory has however received mixed reviews. Many say that he disregarded the fact that many lower class people actually do conform to socialite norms.

Labelling Theories

A group of labelling theorists began exploring how and why certain acts were defined as criminal or deviant and why other such acts were not. They questioned how and why certain people thus became defined as criminal or deviant.

Such theorists viewed criminals not as evil persons who engaged in wrong acts but as individuals who had a criminal status placed upon them by both the criminal justice system and the community at large.

From this point of view, criminal acts thus themselves are not significant, it is the social reaction to them that are. Deviance and its control then involves a process of social definition which involves the response from others to an individual's behaviour which is key to how an individual views himself. To make this point, let's briefly examine a crucial point made by sociologist Howard S. Becker, in 1963.

> "Deviance is not a quality of the act the person commits, but rather a consequence of the application by others of rules and sanctions to an offender. The deviant is one to whom that label has successfully been applied; deviant behaviour is behaviour that people so label."

Labelling theory focuses on the reaction of other people and the subsequent effects of those reactions which create deviance. When it becomes known that a person has engaged in deviant acts, she or he is then segregated from society and thus labelled, "whore," theif," "abuser," "junkie," and the like. Becker noted that this process of segregation creates "outsiders", who are outcast from society, and then begin to associate with other individuals who have also been cast out. When more and more people begin to think of these individuals as deviants, they respond to them as such; thus the deviant reacts to such a response by continuing to engage in the behaviour society now expects from them.

Howard Becker's Developmental Career Model

Howard Becker's developmental career model is a social-process approach. Becker argues that deviance exists in the eye of the beholder, much like beauty. He stresses that no act is intrinsically deviant, but must be defined as such. Becker's notion of a developmental process is that it precedes the attainment of a deviant identity or career. He uses the process of becoming a marijuana user as an unfolding sequence of steps that lead one to a commitment and participation in a deviant career. He argues that such an identity occurs over time, having both a historical and longitudinal course. In his example, for instance, the person must have access to the drug; must experiment with the drug; the person must continue to use the drug. Each of these steps involves some subtle changes in the person's attitude and perspective, as well as their behaviour, he argues. "The circumstances that determine movement along a particular path includes properties of both the person and of the situation," he states.

Social Control Theories

Theories of social control focus on the strategies and techniques which help regulate human behaviour and thus lead to conformity and compliance of the rules of society, including the influences of family, school, morals, values, beliefs, etc., Does existence of rules guarantee peaceful existence of the group? Who is to ensure compliance with such rules? Social control theorists are out to study such questions. They are interested in learning why people conform to norms, they ask why people conform in the face of so much temptation, peer pressure, and inducement. Juveniles and adults conform to the law in response to certain controlling forces which are present in their lives. Thus, they are likely to become criminal when the controlling forces in their lives are defective or absent.

Social control theorists argue that the more involved and committed a person is to conventional activities, the greater the attachment to others (such as family and friends), the less likely that a person is to violate the rules of society.

Social control has its roots in the early part of this century in the work of sociologist E.A. Rose. Rose believed that belief systems, not specific laws, guide what individuals do and this serves to control behaviour, no matter the forms that beliefs may take.

Social control is often seen as all-encompassing, practically representing any phenomenon leading to conformity, which leads to norms. Others see social control as a broad representation of regulated mechanisms placed upon society's members. In other words, social control regards what is to be considered deviant, violations of the law, right or wrong.

Social control mechanisms can be adopted as laws, norms, mores, ethics, etiquette, and customs, which all control and thus define behaviour. Social control theory is viewed from two perspectives. The macro-social perspective explores formal control systems for the control of groups, including the legal system such as laws, law enforcement, powerful groups in society (who can help influence laws and norms) and economic and social directives of government or private organisations. Such controls can serve to be either positive or negative. On the other hand, the micro-social perspective focuses on informal control systems, which help to explain why individuals conform. It also considers the source of control to be external, that is, outside of the person.

Walter Reckless' Containment Theory

In 1961 sociologist Walter C. Reckless proposed Containment Theory, which explains delinquency as the interplay between two forms of control known as inner (internal) and outer (external) containments. Containment theory assumes that for every individual a containing external structure as well as a protective internal structure exist. Both buffer, protect, and insulate an individual against delinquency. Reckless wanted his theory to explain not only delinquency, but also conformity. Containment theory shows that society produces a series of pulls and pushes toward the phenomenon of delinquency. It suggests that these inner and outer containments help to buffer against one's potential deviation from legal and social norms and work to insulate a youth from the pressures, pulls, and pushes of deviant influences.

Of the two, Reckless suggested that inner containments are more important. It is these inner containments, he argued, that form one's support system. The stronger one's inner containments, the least likely one would commit crime; the weaker one's inner containments, the more prone to crime one would become.

Inner containments, simply put, are "self" components. They are the inner strength of one's personality. These include a good self-concept, strong ego, well developed conscience, high sense of responsibility, and high frustration tolerance. Outer containments refer to one's social environment. These are normative constraints in which society and groups use to control its members. Outer containments include belonging (identification with the group), effective supervision, cohesion among group members (togetherness), opportunities for achievement, reasonable limits and responsibilities, alternative ways and means of satisfaction (if one more ways are closed), reinforcement of goals, norms values, and discipline.

Internal pushes are personal factors which include restlessness, discontent, rebellion, anxiety, and hostility. External pulls include deviant peers, membership in a deviant/criminal gang, and pornography. Finally, external pressures refer to the adverse living conditions which give rise to crime. These include relative deprivation, poverty, unemployment, insecurity, and inequality.

2.21. Travis Hirschi's Social Bond Theory

Travis Hirschi took his theory to a different approach. He didn't attempt to explain why individuals engage in criminal acts, but rather why individuals choose to conform to conventional norms. It is, in a strict sense, not a theory of crime causation, but rather a theory of pro-social behaviour used so often by sociologists and criminologists to better explain deviance and criminality.

In 1969 Travis Hirschi presented four social bonds which promote socialisation and conformity. These include attachment, commitment, involvement and belief. He claimed that the stronger these four bonds, the least likely one would become delinquent. Hirschi first assumes that everyone has potential to become delinquent and criminal and it is social controls, not moral values, that maintain law and order. Without controls, he argues, one is free to commit criminal acts. Hirschi further assumes that a consistent value system exists and all of society is thus exposed to such a system. Moral codes are then defied by delinquents because their attachment to society is weak. While Sykes and Matza believe that delinquents share the same values and attitudes as non delinquents, Hirschi views delinquents as rejecting such social norms and beliefs.

The first bond, attachment, refers to one's interest in others. One's acceptance of social norms and the development of social conscious depend on attachment for other human beings. Hirschi views parents, schools, and peers as important social institutions for a person. Attachment takes three forms—attachment to parents, to school, and to peers. While examining attachment to parents Hirschi found that juveniles refrain from delinquency due to the consequences that the act would most likely produce, therefore putting such a relationship between parent and child in jeopardy.

In some respect, can argue that this acts as a primary deterrent to engaging in delinquency. Strength, however, in such a deterrent would largely depend on the depth and quality of the parent-child interaction. The amount of time child and parent spend together are equally important, including intimacy in conversation and identification that may exist between parent and child.

While examining the bond with school, Hirschi found that an inability to do well in school is linked with delinquency, through a series of chain events. He argued that academic incompetence leads to poor school performance, which leads to a dislike of school, which leads to rejection of teachers and authority, which results in acts of delinquency. He argued that one's attachment to school depends on how one appreciates the institution and how he/she is received by fellow peers and teachers. Hirschi also noted that he found that one's attachment to parents and school overshadows the bond formed with one's peers.

The second bond is that of commitment and it involves time, energy, and effort placed on conventional lines of action. In other words, the support of and equal partaking in social activities tie an individual to the moral and ethical code of society. Hirschi's control theory holds that people who build an investment in life, property, and reputation are less likely to engage in criminal acts which will jeopardise their social position. A lack of commitment to such conventional values will cause an individual to partake in delinquent or criminal acts.

The third bond is involvement. The is addresses a preoccupation in activities which stress the conventional interests of society. Hirschi argues that an individual's heavy involvement in conventional activities doesn't leave time to engage in delinquent or criminal acts. He believes that involvement in school, Travis Hirschi's Social Bond family, recreation etc., insulates a juvenile from potential delinquent behaviour that may be a result of idleness.

The final bond is that of belief and it deals with assents to society's value system—which entails respect for laws, and the people and institutions which enforce such laws. Hirschi argued that people who live in common social settings share similar human values. If such beliefs are weakened, or absent, one is more likely to engage in antisocial acts.

Also, if people believe that laws are unfair, this bond to society weakens and the likelihood of committing delinquent acts rises. Even with its weaknesses, Hirschi's theory held a position of importance in criminology for several decades. More than anything, social control theorists want to explain delinquency, not adult crime persay.

However, since the characteristics of the theory are found present in adolescents, they are also present in post-adolescent behaviour, argues one critic. Hirschi's theory remains silent on this analysis. Many other critics have faulted Hirschi's work because he used too few questionnaire items to measure social bonds. He failed to describe the chain of events that result in inadequate social bonds.

There was also a creation of an artificial division of socialised verses un-socialised youths. Finally, Hirschi's theory explains no more than 50 percent of delinquent behaviour and only a 1-2 percent difference in future delinquency, while it is supposed to explain why delinquency occurs.

Sykes and Matza's Techniques of Neutralisation

In the 1960s David Matza, and his associate Gresham Sykes, developed a different perspective on social control which explains why some delinquents drift in and out of delinquency. Neutralisation Theory, or Drift theory as it is often called, proposed that juveniles sense a moral obligation to be bound by the law. Such a bind between a person and the law remains in place most of the time, they argue. When it is not in place, delinquents will drift.

According to Sykes and Matza, delinquents hold values, beliefs, and attitudes very similar to those of law-abiding citizens. In fact, they feel obligated to be bound by law. Then, if bound by law, how can they justify their delinquent activities? The answer is that they learn "techniques" which enable them to "neutralise" such values and attitudes temporarily and thus drift back and forth between legitimate and illegitimate behaviours.

They maintain that at times delinquents participate in conventional activities and shun such activity while engaging in criminal acts. Such a theory proposes that delinquents disregard controlling influences of rules and values and use these techniques of neutralisation to "weaken" the hold society places over them. In other words, these techniques act as defence mechanisms that release the delinquent from the constraints associated with moral order.

In Delinquency and Drift, David Matza suggested that people live their lives on a continuum somewhere between total freedom and total restraint. The process by which a person moves from one extreme of behaviour to another extreme is called drift, and this is the very foundation of his theory.

Along with Sykes, Matza rejected the notion that subcultures of delinquency maintain an independent set of values than the dominant culture. They hold that delinquents actually do appreciate culturally held goals and expectations of the middle-class, but feel that engaging in such behaviour would be frowned upon by their peers. Such beliefs remain almost unconscious, or subterranean, because delinquents fear expressing such beliefs to peers.

Techniques of Neutralisation suggest that delinquents develop a special set of justifications for their behaviour when such behaviour violates social norms. Such techniques allow delinquents to neutralise and temporarily suspend their commitment to socialite values, providing them with the freedom to commit delinquent acts.

Sykes and Matza's theoretical model is based on the following four observations:

— Delinquents express guilt over their illegal acts.

— Delinquents frequently respect and admire honest, law-abiding individuals.

— A line is drawn between those whom they can victimise and those they cannot.

— Delinquents are not immune to the demands of conformity.

Thus, Sykes and Matza propose the five Techniques of Neutralisation. *Denial of responsibility.* Delinquent will propose that he/she is a victim of circumstance and that he/she is pushed or pulled into situations beyond his/her control. ("It wasn't my fault!") Sykes and Matza's Techniques of Neutralisation (Drift Theory) Denial of injury.

Delinquent supposes that his/her acts really do not cause any harm, or that the victim can afford the loss or damage. ("Why is everyone making a big deal about it; they have money!") Denial of the victim. Delinquent views the act as not being wrong, that the victim deserves the injury, or that there is no real victim. ("They had it coming to them!") Condemnation of the condemners. Condemners are seen as hypocrites, or are reacting out of personal spite, thus they shift the blame to others, being able to repress the *feeling that their acts are wrong.*

Appeal to higher loyalties. The rules of society often take a back seat to the demands and loyalty to important others. ("My friends depended on me, what was I going to do?!") Sykes and Matza further argued that these neutralisation are available not just to delinquents but they can be found throughout society. Attempts have been made over the years to verify the assumptions made by Neutralisation Theory, and the results have, thus far, been inconclusive. Studies have indicated that delinquents approve of social values, while others do not. Other studies indicate that delinquents approve of criminal behaviour, while others seem to oppose it.

Neutralisation Theory, however, remains an important contribution to the field of crime and delinquency. Social bond theorist, Travis Hirschi, asked an important question: do delinquents neutralise law-violating behaviour before or after they commit an act? Neutralisation theory loses its credibility as a theory which explains the cause of delinquency if juveniles use techniques of neutralisation before the commission of a delinquent deed and therefore becomes a theory which simply describes reactions that juveniles incur due to their misdeeds. The theory does fail on the account that it doesn't clearly distinguish why some youths drift into delinquency and others do not. The theory remains too abstract and vague to be of any practical use unless we understand why drift occurs, critics have argued.

3

Crime Trends in India

Crime is present in various forms in India. Organized crime include drug trafficking, gunrunning, money laundering, extortion, murder for hire, fraud, human trafficking and poaching. Many criminal operations engage in black marketeering, political violence, religiously motivated violence, terrorism, and abduction. Other crimes are homicide, robbery, assault etc. Property crimes include burglary, theft, motor vehicle theft, and arson. Corruption is a significant problem.

Organised Crime

In India, organised crime is at its worst in the commercial capital of India, the city of Mumbai. The first well-known organised gang to emerge was that of Varadharaj Mudaliar in the early sixties. His illegal activities included illicit liquor, gold smuggling, gambling, extortion and contract murders. Three other gangs emerged shortly thereafter namely, Haji Mastan, Yusuf Patel and Karim Lala. Haji Mastan and Yusuf Patel resorted to gold smuggling whereas Karim Lala operated in drugs.

During Emergency in 1975 when there was crackdown on the Mafia, new gangs emerged. Dawood Ibrahim, the most successful, came in conflict with the Pathan gangs of Alamzeb and Amirzada which led to bitter internecine gang warfare. The Pathan gangs were liquidated to leave the field free for Dawood Ibrahim. In 1985, there was increased police pressure which made Dawood Ibrahim to flee. In March 1993, Dawood Ibrahim was behind the serial bomb blasts in Mumbai in which 257 persons died and 713 were maimed.

Public and private property worth several millions of rupees was destroyed. Investigation revealed trans-national character of the conspiracy the objective of which was to cripple the economy, create communal divide and spread terror in the commercial capital of India. Dawood Ibrahim, Tiger Memon and Mohammed Dosa are operating from Dubai.

Their field of activity is to extort money from builders and film producers, mediate in monetary disputes, and undertake contract (Supari) killings. There have been instances of investment of the dirty money in business with the result that unsuspecting businessmen have fallen prey to the Mafia warfare. The killings of Thaquiuddin Wahid of East West Airlines in 1996, Sunil Khatau of Khatau Mills in 1994, Om Prakash Kukreja of Kukreja Builders in 1995 and Ramnath Payyade, a prominent hotelier in 1995 are grim reminders of Mafia in Mumbai.

The other gangs of Mumbai indulging in organised crime are those of Chhota Rajan (Drug Trafficking and Contract Killings), Arun Gawli (Contract Killings and Protection Money), Late Amar Naik (Protection Money) and Chhota Shakeel.

State of Maharashtra has enacted Maharashtra Control of Organised Crime Act, 1999. Other forms of organised crime in India are kidnapping for ransom, un-running, illicit trafficking in women and children, money laundering etc.

Organised crime exists in other cities too, though not to the same extent as in Mumbai. Ahmedabad city has been the hotbed of liquor mafia because of Prohibition policy (Banning of liquor). The Mafia became synonymous with the name of Latif who started in mid seventies as a small time bootlegger and grew up to set up a 200 strong gang after eliminating rivals with intimidation, extortion, kidnapping and murders. He won municipal elections from five different constituencies with strong political patronage. He was killed by police in an encounter in 1997.

There are several gangs operating in Delhi from neighbouring State of Uttar Pradesh indulging in kidnapping for ransom. The going rate was around Rupees 10-50 millions. Land Mafia has political connections and indulges in land grabbing, intimidation, forcible vacation etc. Of late, the gang-lords of Mumbai have started using Delhi as a place for hiding and transit. Chhota Rajan group is strengthening its base in Delhi.

Boom in construction activities in Bangalore city has provided fertile breeding for the underworld. Builders are used for laundering black money. Forcible vacation of old disputed buildings is a popular side business for the underworld. The local gangsters in the State of Karnataka have connections with the underworld of Mumbai. One of the Mumbai gang operating here is the Chhota Rajan gang.

Illicit Drug Trafficking

India is geographically situated between the countries of Golden Triangle and Golden Crescent and is a transit point for narcotic drugs produced in these regions to the West. In India opium is grown under official control of Narcotics Commissioner in three states namely Uttar Pradesh, Rajasthan and Madhya Pradesh. It is exported to foreign countries for medicinal purposes. Indian opium is considered best in world. Turkey & Australia are the other licit opium growing countries in the world.

A part of the licit opium enters the illicit market in different forms. Besides, there is illicit cultivation of opium in the hill tracks of some states. There is a moderately sized chemical industry producing precursor materials for lawful purposes. The illicit cultivation of opium as well as the precursor chemicals can be used for manufacture of heroin. However, there is a great price differential between India and the West.

A Kilogram of Heroin that goes for a hundred thousand Rupees in India may fetch Rupees ten million in the international market. Illicit drug trade in India has centered around five major substances, namely heroin, hashish, opium, herbal cannabis and methaqualone. The Indo-Pak border has traditionally been most vulnerable to drug trafficking.

Drugs trafficking through India consists of Hashish and Heroin from Pakistan, Hashish from Nepal, White Heroin from Myanmar and Heroin from Bangladesh. In the early eighties, the Border State of Punjab became affected with narco-terrorism with the smuggling of narcotic drugs and arms from across the border.

This was also the time when drug Mafia emerged in Golden Crescent countries. There were a number of seizures of a mixed consignment of narcotic drugs and arms in Punjab. In 1996, 64 % of the heroin seized was from the Golden Crescent. Although opium production is strictly under Government control in India, illicit poppy plantations have been reported in some places.

Drug addiction in India has not assumed such a serious magnitude as in some of the western countries, but there are no grounds for complacency. There have been reports 199 of drug use among the students of universities in Delhi, Mumbai, Calcutta and Chandigarh. The society does not agitate too much with consumption of Bhang, crushed leaves of the cannabis plant. It is customary in some places to consume Bhang on the popular festival of Holi. There is no such tolerance for charas or ganja which are derived from the same cannabis plant.

Prevention of Illicit Traffic in Drugs and Psychotropic

Substances Act, 1988 provides for detention of persons connected with illicit drug trafficking up to two years. An officer of the rank of Joint Secretary to the Government, specially empowered under the Act, can issue orders for detention of the any person (including a foreigner) with a view to preventing him from engaging in illicit traffic of narcotic drugs and psychotropic substances. On an average about 50 persons are detained under the Act every year.

There were 18273 cases registered under the NDPS Act in 1998 which was an increase of 31.8 % over 1988, but a decrease of 4.2 % over the quinquennial average of 1993-1997. 21386 persons were arrested under the NDPS Act of which major work was done by Narcotics Control Bureau, a central agency for dealing with cases of drug trafficking. It has registered 11330 cases in 1998 of which 5809 cases were for Ganja, 2713 were for Heroin and 1771 cases were for Hashish. 62591 kgs of Ganja, 8478 kgs of Hashish and 597 kgs of Heroin were seized. During 1998, 12601 persons were arrested by Narcotics Control Bureau, which included 95 foreigners.

11612 persons were prosecuted in a court of law, 2782 persons were convicted and 5712 persons were acquitted. 16.9 % of drug cases pending in trial were disposed by the courts during 1998. Property worth Rupees 23.85 million was forfeited and worth Rupees 30.64 million was frozen. In a recent case, the Government of Orissa (State Government) confiscated property worth over Rupees thirty million of drug lord Mohammed Azad Parvez of Balasore, Orissa which included an ice factory, a saw mill, a market complex, a cloth store, three residential buildings and three acres of land.

The accused was apprehended by Narcotics Control Bureau in 1998 on charge of heroin trafficking along with his wife and associates. Financial investigation was conducted by the agency into the movable and immovable properties under Chapter V-A of the NDPS Act, which led to confiscation.

India is signatory to three UN Conventions on Narcotics Drugs and Psychotropic Substances held in 1961, 1971 and 1988. India is a party to the United Nations Convention against Illicit Traffic in Narcotic Drugs and Psychotropic Substances Act, 1988. Government of India has entered into bilateral agreement and Memorandum of Understanding with a number of countries. The countries with which India has signed bilateral agreement for drug control are USA, UK, Afghanistan, Mauritius, Russian Federation, Myanmar, Zambia, UAE, Iran, Egypt, Bulgaria, Romania, Mauritius. India has also signed a special bilateral agreement with 200 Pakistan in this regard.

Illeagal Firearms

Trafficking

Small arms used in guerilla warfare in some parts of the world are now available at cheap cost in other parts of the world. According to an estimate, there could be 750 million small weapons for such arms trafficking. India has a long coastline of about 7500 kms. And a long border with Pakistan, Nepal, Bhutan, China, Myanmar and Bangladesh. Border Security Force guards the borders, but it is not possible to have presence across each and every inch of the border. Customs Department has also seized illicit arms in significant quantities.

In India, states of Punjab and Jammu & Kashmir have been particularly vulnerable to arms trafficking across the border. More than 7500 pistols and revolvers, 2500 magazines and 28000 rounds of ammunition have been seized from the state of Jammu and Kashmir. During 1997, the Border Security Force seized several AK series rifles, 7 heavy machine guns, 204 pistols/revolvers, 18 rocket launchers, 54 other type of rifles and ammunition from Punjab and Jammu & Kashmir.

On 17th February 1996, Delhi police recovered 361 pistols of 0.30 calibre with the inscription "Made in China by Norinco", 728 magazines and 3738 live rounds in a cavity in the undercarriage of a caravan bus. A Swiss national and an Iranian living in Pakistan since 1981 were detained. Investigation disclosed that this in fact was the second consignment, the first one having been successfully transported in 1995. 22 persons including five foreign nationals have been prosecuted in the court of law in this case.

Delhi Police caught five fugitive members of the Chhota Rajan gang including an Assam Rifles jawan and two Nepali nationals who were planning to set up a major arms and money distribution base in Delhi.

In 1993, a consignment of AK-56 rifles, magazines, live rounds and hand grenades were sent from a Gulf country to land at the coast of Dighi Jetti in the State of Gujarat. Subsequently huge quantity of arms, ammunition and explosives (RDX) were smuggled by sea route at Shekhadi in District Raigad. These were used for Bomb blasts in Mumbai on 12th March 1993, which caused terror, widespread damage, and loss of 257 lives and maiming of 713 persons. During investigation, some of the arms recovered included 62 AK-56 rifles with 280 magazines and 38,888 rounds, 479 hand grenades, 12 pistols of 9 mm make with ammunition, 1100 electric detonators, 2313 kgs. Of

RDX and many other weapons. In the state of Madhya Pradesh in central India, 24 AK-56 rifles, 5250 cartridges, 81 magazines and 27 hand grenades were recovered by police on 4th November 1995.

Hijacking of an Indian Airlines flight on the 24th December 1999 in Kandahar was the latest incident of the use of illegal weapons in the hands of terrorists. After investigation, the CBI filed a charge-sheet in the court of law against five hijackers and their accomplices.

A sensational case called Purulia arms drop case was an example of illicit arms trafficking by air. On 17th December 1996, an Antonov 26 aircraft dropped over 300 AK 47/56 rifles and 20,545 rounds of ammunition, dragons sniper weapons, rocket launchers and night vision devices in Purulia village in West Bengal. The aircraft was bought from Latvia for US$2 million and chartered by a Hong Kong 201 registered company Carol Airlines.

Payments were made mostly from foreign bank accounts. The aircraft picked up consignment of arms from Bulgaria using end-users certificate issued by a neighbouring country. The arms were airdropped over Purulia in the state of West Bengal.

This case was investigated by the Central Bureau of Investigation and charge-sheeted in the City Sessions Court, Calcutta. After trial, the court found the accused persons guilty of offences under Indian Penal Code, Explosive Substances Act, Arms Act, Explosives Act, and the Aircraft Act and sentenced Mr. Peter James Gifran Van Kalkstein Bleach (British National), Mr. Alexander Klichine, Mr. Eiger Moskvitine, Oleg Gaidash, Evgueni Antimenko, Mr. Eiger Timmerman (all Latvian nationals) and Vinay Kumar Singh (Indian national) to various terms of rigorous imprisonment on 2nd February 2000.

The five Latvians were released on 22nd uly 2000 when their sentences were commuted by the President of India. Illicit trafficking in arms is punishable under Arms Act, 1959. The incidence of the Arms Act cases showed an increase of 20.8 % over the decade 1988-1998. In 1998, 63518 cases were reported which showed a decrease of 4.2% over the quinquennial average of 1993-1997 and 14.3 % over 1997. 66868 persons were arrested for violation of the Arms Act. 19.3 % of cases pending trial were disposed by the courts in 1998.

WOMEN AND CHILDREN TRAFFICKING

Commercial sex in India is a 400000 million Rupees annual business. *Thirty percent of the sex workers are children* who earn about Rupees 110000 million every year.

There could be about 0.3 million child sex workers in India of which 0.1 million could be less than 18 years of age. 15% of the sex workers are in the six metropolitan cities of Mumbai, Calcutta, Delhi, Chennai, Bangalore and Hyderabad. Delhi receives sex workers from 70 districts, Mumbai from 40, Bangalore from 10 and Calcutta from 11 districts. Some sex workers have also come from Nepal and Bangladesh.

Mumbai and Goa have had incidence of paedophilic offences too. These places draw a number of foreign tourists. Fear of AIDS has contributed to the involvement of minor girls in the business because demand for virgins has increased exponential with the fear of infection. There is also a myth that young girls in their prepuberty can not be infested with AIDS. A number of young girls from southern India have been sent to the Arab countries. There have also been reports that India has served as a transit point for trafficking of young virgins from Nepal, Myanmar and Bangladesh to the Middle East, mostly Dubai.

Suppression of Immoral Traffic in

Women and Girls Act, 1956 was the main Act to deal with these offences. This Act was amended in 1978 and was re-enacted under the name of 'Immoral Traffic (Prevention) Act in 1986' to rectify some lacunae in the older Act. Punishment could be imprisonment for a period of 7-10 years or for life. Indian Penal Code stipulates that sexual intercourse with or without her consent with a girl less than 16 years of age amounts to rape punishable with imprisonment for life.

National Commission for Women is a body that reviews laws, conducts inquiries for re-dressal of complaints, undertakes promotional research for policies, advises the Government and ensures custodial justice for women.

Section 10 (4) of National Commission for Women Act, 1992 gives the Commission powers of a Civil Court. The National Commission for women has formed an Expert Committee and has formulated a ten year National Plan of Action to co-ordinate with the ninth and tenth Indian Five Year Plans. There were 8695 cases reported under the Immoral Traffic (Prevention) Act in 1998.

The number of cases showed a steadily declining trend up to 1996 but increased by 4.5 % over 1997. 15363 cases of kidnapping of women and girls were reported in 1998, which were up by 4.8 % over the previous year. 146 cases of importation of girls were reported in 1998 compared to 78 cases in the previous year showing an increase of 87.2 %. 171 cases of procuration of minor girls were reported in 1998 as against 87 in 1997 but 206 in 1994. 11 cases of selling of minor girls for prostitution, 13 cases of buying minor girls for prostitution and 699 cases of kidnapping of minor girls were reported. 17247 male and 1217 female offenders were arrested for kidnapping and abduction of women and girls. 12879 persons were arrested under the Immoral Traffic (Prevention) Act.

MONEY LAUNDERING

In India, money laundering is indulged in mainly by corporate houses to evade taxes unlike in some other countries where it is mostly related to illicit drug trafficking. Nonresident Indians have been given some special banking facilities.

These facilities are misused to bring back the money as white money. For example, a portfolio account is opened in a foreign country and the money is laundered back to be invested in the stock markets. Another modus operandi is to launder the money through bogus exports.

The conversion of black money is done by over-invoicing of the products to countries like Russia and the former Soviet Republic countries. Some shell companies are set up to issue bill or invoices accompanied by bogus transport receipts in order to obtain funds against these documents from bank/ financial institutions and then divert major' part of such proceeds by issue of cheques in the names of nonexistent front companies of cheque discounters. The cheque discounters then hand-over cash immediately to the party after deduction of their commission.

The cheque discounters are generally associated with commodities market where fake transactions in commodities can largely go unnoticed. The cheque discounters also issue fake Letters of Credit and false bills. The cheque discounters file income tax returns in which the commission is shown as taxable income.

In India, tackling problem of laundered money is correlated with the problem of tackling black money. There is a wide gap between the number of persons with taxable income and the numbers who actually pay income tax. This is despite the requirement of compulsory filing of income tax returns by any one having taxable income. Benami Transactions (Prohibition) Act makes the pseudo owner the real owner of the benami property. Tax raids and seizures, penalties and prosecution have been some of the measures to check black money.

However, success has not been satisfactory. Certain special measures such as Voluntary Disclosure Scheme under which the evader discloses income on promise of concession rates and immunity from penalties and prosecution. There have been other schemes like issue of Special Bearer Bonds, Special Levy on deposits in the National Housing Bank, waiver of penalty and interest, Foreign Remittance Scheme in 1991-92, India Development Bonds, and Gold Bond Scheme of 1992.

Money laundering had so far been dealt with under the Foreign Exchange Regulation Act, 1973, but with effect from June, 2000, FERA has been replaced by Foreign Exchange Maintenance Act and a Bill to enact money laundering law to be named The Prevention of Money Laundering Bill has been introduced in the Parliament by the Government of India.

Money laundering has been proposed to be a cognisable crime punishable with rigorous imprisonment of 3-7 years which could be extended to 10 years and a fine up to Rupees 0.5 million. The acquisition, possession or owning of money, movable and immovable assets, from crime, especially drugs and narcotics crimes, would tantamount to money laundering. Concealment of information on proceeds or gains from crime made within India or abroad is an offence too. An adjudicating authority is proposed which would have powers to confiscate properties of money launderers. An administrator may be appointed to manage the confiscated assets. An appellate tribunal is proposed to be set up with three members to hear appeals from the orders of the adjudicating authority. The rulings of the adjudicating authority are thus not contestable in the local courts. Financial institutions are expected to maintain transaction records and furnish these to the adjudicating authority. Failure to do so is punishable too.

The alternative remittance system through non-banking channels is called Hawala in India. It is based on trust in which the remitter pays the Hawala dealer in foreign country and the associate of the Hawala dealer pays the receiver in the home country. Since Hawala dealings are illegal, the transactions take place through word of mouth or other non-conventional means of communication. Since there is no audit, no control and no check, anonymity of the customers is maintained.

There are hawala dealers in India and wherever people from Indian subcontinent are settled. Hawala routes are used both by ordinary people as well as drug traffickers, terrorists and unscrupulous businessmen.

In one of the cases of money laundering dealt with by the Central Bureau of Investigation, an organised group of the Hawala dealers operating from London and Dubai used to receive remittances from foreign banks for transferring to India. A telephonic message in coded words would be passed to agents in India to pay money in Indian rupees.

The remittances so received by the above mentioned persons in dollars or Pound Sterling at London and Dubai were used for purchase of gold, drugs, arms, ammunition and explosives through the underworld. The arms, ammunition and explosives were used to be smuggled into India and sold to various criminal/terrorist groups while the drug used to be distributed to the traffickers. Electronic Payment Technologies are coming to India and these are going to pose new challenges to Law Enforcement Agencies. The anonymity in transactions is bound to promote money laundering and other offences. The money launderer finds the electronic money easy to convert and transfer, and safe to store. The format of legal framework, code of conduct of business and self-regulation regarding commerce is under examination.

Trans-national Organised Criminal Groups

Dawood Ibrahim Gang

Dawood Ibrahim group is the most dreaded mafia gang with country-wide network and foreign connections. He has stationed himself in Dubai since 1985 and has indulged in drug and arms trafficking, smuggling, extortion and contract killings.

His brother Anees Ibrahim looks after smuggling, drugs and contract killings; Noora looks after film financing and extortion; and Iqbal is in charge of the legitimate business which includes stock broking in Hong Kong. Anees is in legitimate business too managing Mohd. Anees Trading Company in Dubai. His business interests in India are shopping centres, hotels, airlines and travel agencies in Mumbai with an annual turnover of about Rupees 20000 million. Extradition of offenders from Dubai has not been possible since there is no extradition treaty with Dubai. Moreover, some of these offenders have strong social links with politicians and other top personalities in Dubai.

Chhota Rajan Gang

Chhota Rajan was a member of Dawood gang but parted company after the 1993 serial bomb blasts in Mumbai. He raised his own gang in 1994-95 which is reported to have a membership of 800 persons today. Chhota Rajan himself is in a foreign country to avoid elimination from Dawood gang. His gang indulges in drug trafficking and contract killings. In collaboration with another local gang, he organised killing of a trusted leader of Dawood Ibrahim gang, Mr. Sunil Samant, in Dubai in 1995.

Babloo Shrivastava Gang

"Om Prakash Shrivastava Babloo Shrivastava" is facing 41 cases of murder, kidnapping for ransom etc. He was arrested in Singapore in April 1995 on the basis of a Red Corner Notice issued by INTERPOL and extradited to India in August 1995. He has since been in jail but his gang has continued to indulge in organised kidnapping and killings. The ransom amount is received by them in foreign countries through hawala (alternative non-banking remittance channel). The power of this gang has dwindled after his arrest.

Electronic Surveillance

The Government of India has made a legal provision in the licensing conditions formulated along with the cellular operators to make it mandatory on the part of the cellular companies to provide parallel monitoring facilities for all communications being received and emanating from a particular mobile set. Cellular operators operating in four metropolitan cities of Mumabi, Calcutta, Delhi and Chennai have made this facility available whereas others are bound to provide this facility within three years of the initiation of the mobile network.

Interception of messages, transmitted or received by any telegraph is covered under subsection 2 of section 5 of the Indian Telegraphic Act-1885 which states:

> "On occurrence of any public-emergency, or in the interest of the public safety, the Central Government or a State Government or any officer specially authorised in this behalf by the Central Government or a State Government may, if

> satisfied that it is necessary or expedient so to do in the interests of the sovereignty and integrity of India, the security of the State, friendly relations with foreign States of public order or for preventing incitement to commission of an offence, for reasons to be recorded in writing, by order, direct that any message or class of messages to or from any person or class of persons, or relating to any particular subject, brought for transmission by or transmitted or received buy any telegraph, shall not be transmitted, or shall be intercepted or detained, or shall be disclosed to the Government making the order or an officer thereof mentioned in the order."

The issue of the constitutional validity of this section came under scrutiny of the Supreme Court of India in a writ petition filed by the People's Union for Civil Liberties. The Supreme Court passed a judgement on 18th December, 1996, upholding the constitutional validity of the Act but laid down certain guidelines prescribing that the order will be issued by the Home Secretaries at the Centre and in the States. A copy of the order should be sent to the Review Committee within a week. The order will cease to have an effect after two months unless renewed. The Review Committee will review the order passed by the authority concerned within two months of the passing of the order. The total period shall not exceed six months.

IMMUNITY

There is provision in Section 306 of the Criminal Procedure Code to obtain evidence of an accomplice by tender of pardon subject to his making full and true disclosure of facts and circumstances concerning an offence. This provision is applicable in offences punishable with imprisonment of seven years or more.

Witness and Victim Protection Programme

There is no legislation at present for protection of witnesses and the members of their families. Section 171 of the Criminal Procedure Code prohibits the police officers to carry the complainant or witness to court. The intention of such legislation appears to be to ensure independence of evidence given by the witnesses without any influence of police. In cases where it is important to keep the trial proceedings away from public gaze, resort could be made to the provisions of in-camera trial at the desire of the parties concerned or the court itself. In camera trial is permitted under section 237(2) of Criminal Procedure Code. Its validity has been upheld by the Supreme Court of India in the so-called Carter Singh case.

Asset Forfeiture System

The following provisions for forfeiture of proceeds of crime exist:

— Criminal Law Amendment Ordinance.

— Sections 111 and 112 of Customs Act.

— Foreign Exchange Maintenance Act.

— Smugglers and Foreign Exchange.

Manipulators (Forfeiture of Property) Act: "This Act applies to persons convicted under the Sea Customs Act 1878, Custom Act 1962 or detained under Conservation of Foreign Exchange and Prevention of Smuggling Act.

The main purpose of the Act is to forfeit the illegally acquired properties of such smugglers and foreign exchange manipulators in whosoever's name these may have been kept. It shall not be lawful for any person to whom the Act applies to hold any illegally acquired property either by himself or through any other person on his behalf. Any property so held is liable to be forfeited to the Central

Government. Section 6 provides for issuance of show cause notice of forfeiture and section 7 provides for passing of final orders of forfeiture.

Under section 8, burden of proving that any property specified in the notice is not illegally acquired property shall be on the person affected and under section 11, transfer of properties specified in the notice can be declared null and void."

— Section 68 of Narcotic Drugs and Psychotropic Substances Act.

— Sections 102 and 452 of Criminal Procedure Code.

International Co-operation in Criminal Matters

India has entered into Mutual Legal Assistance Agreements / Treaties in criminal matters with United Kingdom (Agreement concerning the investigation and prosecution of crime and the tracing, restraint and confiscation of the proceeds and instrument of crime, including currency transfers and terrorist funds), Canada, France, Russia, Kyrgyzstan, Kazakhstan (all Mutual Legal Assistance Agreements in Criminal Matters), Egypt, China, Romania, Bulgaria and Oman.

Mutual Legal Assistance Treaty has been negotiated with United Arab Emirates but is yet to be ratified. Negotiations are going on for signing of treaty on Mutual Legal Assistance in Criminal Matters with countries such as Australia, Norway, Mongolia, Turkmenistan, Bulgaria, Hong Ling, Ukraine, Uzbekistan and Azerbaijan. India has extradition treaty with Nepal, Belgium, Canada, Netherlands, United Kingdom, United States of America, Switzerland, Bhutan and Hong Kong.

Extradition Treaty is in various stages with Russia, Germany, UAE, Bulgaria, Thailand, France, Ukraine, Romania, Oman, Spain, Kazhakastan, Greece, Egypt,

Malaysia and Mauritius. India has extradition arrangements with Sweden, Tanzania, Australia, Singapore, Sri Lanka, Papua New Guinea, Fiji and Thailand. Section 166 Criminal Procedure Code deals with reciprocal arrangements regarding processes. A court in India can send summons or warrants in duplicate to a court in a foreign country for service or execution and the said foreign court will cause the service or execution. Section 166-A of Criminal Procedure Code deals with letter of request to the competent authority for investigation in foreign country.

A criminal court in India may issue a letter of request to a court or a competent authority to examine orally any person supposed to be acquainted with facts and circumstances of the case, to record his statement made in the course of such examination and also to require such person or any other person to produce any document or thing. Section 166-B deals with letter of request from a country or place outside India to a court or an authority for investigation in India. Under its provision, the Central Government may forward a letter of request received from a foreign country to a magistrate who may summon such person and record his statement. The Central Government can also send the letter to a police officer who will investigate into the offence.

Extradition Act, 1962 deals with extradition of fugitive criminals. Extradition can be made if the offence is an extradition offence i.e. an offence provided for in the extradition treaty with a State which is a treaty state and for other countries, an offence which is specified under the Second Schedule.

Under this schedule, there are 18 types of offences. India is a signatory to the South Asia Association for Regional Cooperation (SAARC) Convention for Suppression of Terrorism. SAARC countries consist of India, Pakistan, Bangladesh, Nepal, Sri Lanka, Maldives and Bhutan.

Pursuant to the SAARC Convention, India enacted the SAARC Convention (Suppression of Terrorism) Act. Extraditable crimes include unlawful seizure of aircraft; unlawful acts against the safety of civil aviation; crimes against internationally protected persons; common law offences like murder, kidnapping, hostage taking; and offences relating to firearms, weapons, explosives and dangerous substances etc. when used as a means to perpetrate indiscriminate violence involving death or serious injury, or serious damage to property.

4

White Collar Crime

Criminologist and sociologist Edwin Sutherland first popularised the term "white collar crime" in 1939, defining such a crime as one "committed by a person of respectability and high social status in the course of his occupation." Sutherland also included crimes committed by corporations and other legal entities within his definition. Sutherland's study of white collar crime was prompted by the view that criminology had incorrectly focused on social and economic determinants of crime, such as family background and level of wealth.

According to Sutherland's view, crime is committed at all levels of society and by persons of widely divergent socioeconomic backgrounds. In particular, according to Sutherland, crime is often committed by persons operating through large and powerful organisations. White collar crime, Sutherland concluded, has a greatly-underestimated impact upon our society.

Sutherland's definition is now somewhat outdated for students of the criminal law. As white collar crime began to capture the attention of prosecutors and the public in the mid-1970s, the term came to have definitions quite different from the one Sutherland used. Indeed, studies have shown that crimes we generally consider "white collar," such as securities fraud and tax fraud, are committed not just by persons of "high social status" but by people of divergent backgrounds. Thus, although the term "white collar crime" is a misnomer, it continues in widespread use. This is probably so because "white collar crime" provides a convenient moniker for distinguishing such crime in the public mind from "common" or "street" crime.

As an alternative to the socioeconomic definition, many define "white collar crime" based instead upon the manner in which the crime is committed. In 1981, the United States Department of Justice described white collar crime as nonviolent crime for financial gain committed by means of deception by persons whose occupational status is entrepreneurial, professional or semiprofessional and utilising their special occupational skills and opportunities; also, nonviolent crime for financial gain utilising deception and committed by anyone having special technical and professional knowledge of business and government, irrespective of the person's occupation.

This definition focuses on the use of deception as the criminal means. The defendant, however, still must be at least "semiprofessional" or have "special technical and professional knowledge." Thus, in some ways, this definition is still too narrow. Not all defendants in white collar cases have professional or semiprofessional status, nor do they necessarily possess special skills. A defendant in a tax fraud or false claims case, for example, might have neither of these characteristics.

Perhaps a better way to look at white collar crime is to focus on the ways that practitioners and judges distinguish white collar crime from common or street crime. A "white collar" prosecutor or defence attorney, for example, would more likely define "white collar crime" as crime that does not:

— Necessarily involve force against a person or property.

— Directly relate to the possession, sale, or distribution of narcotics.

— Directly relate to organised crime activities.

— Directly relate to such national policies as immigration, civil rights, and national security.

— Directly involve "vice crimes" or the common theft of property.

Sometimes the criminal statute itself will render almost all crimes charged under that statute "white collar" by definition. For example, charges brought under the securities fraud and antitrust criminal statutes are generally "white collar" crimes under the above definition. On the other hand, under some criminal statutes charges can be brought for both white collar and non-white collar offences depending on the nature of the defendant's conduct. For example, conspiracy, extortion, and obstruction of justice are charges often brought in both white collar and non-white collar cases.

The most common and notable white collar crimes include crimes committed both in the corporate and governmental settings, and crimes committed by individuals. It is important to note that not all court cases relating to white collar crime are criminal cases. As discussed more fully below, some statutes, such as the securities laws, the environmental laws, and the federal racketeering ("RICO") statute, provide for both civil and criminal liability. In most instances, the statutory interpretations that courts provide in the civil cases will also control in criminal cases brought under those statutes. Therefore, an understanding of the leading civil cases interpreting those statutes is important in determining potential criminal liability.

White collar criminal offences are, of course, defined by both state and federal law. This text will focus on federal law, and make comparisons to state law where helpful. This coverage is representative of the range of federal—and equivalent state—white collar criminal statutes, but cannot be comprehensive given the hundreds of such statutes in existence.

Enforcement of White Collar Crime Statutes

Harm Caused by White Collar Crime

Prosecutors have powerful reasons to target white collar criminals. Most important, white collar crime causes huge financial losses to federal, state, and local governments, to private organisations, and to individuals. In fact, in 1988 the United States Supreme Court acknowledged the severity of the white collar crime problem, stating that white collar crime "is one of the most serious problems confronting law enforcement authorities."

A few examples tell the story. First, during the 1980s, the country was rocked by insider trading scandals. Subsequent investigations revealed that corporate insiders made huge profits by trading on secret information, to the detriment of ordinary investors who did not have that information when trading.

Further, such fraud threatened to undermine public confidence in the securities markets themselves. Second, in the late 1980s and early 1990s, the savings and loan industry collapsed. This occurred in some substantial part because executives of those institutions engaged in wide-scale fraudulent practices. Thousands of persons lost their life savings as a result. Finally, in 2002, Wall Street was rocked by corporate accounting scandals. Allegations have been made that this occurred at least in part because of wrongdoing by corporate executives and their accountants.

Difficulties in Enforcing White Collar Statutes

One reason white collar crime remains widespread is that it

is often very difficult to detect. Unlike street and common property crimes, white collar crimes are usually committed in the privacy of an office or home; usually there is no eyewitness, and only occasionally is there a "smoking gun." Instead, the government's proof is more likely to depend upon circumstantial evidence culled from a complex paper trail.

Moreover, the government's ability to identify white collar crimes is sometimes hampered by lack of resources and expertise. Particularly with respect to financial crimes such as tax fraud and money laundering, prosecutors may require technical assistance from government entities other that the Department of Justice. Finally, the sheer scope of many white collar crimes taxes many United States Attorneys' offices. Apart from investigations that often last years, trials in complex white collar cases can easily last weeks or months. This is particularly true as the federal government has expanded its white collar efforts in recent decades to areas previously covered primarily by state and local law enforcement.

Federalism in White Collar Prosecutions

Federal and State Overlap

Criminal law in the United States is primarily adopted and enforced at the state level; fewer than one in twenty criminal cases is brought at the federal level. Although most state cases involve street crimes, a large number are white collar cases. Indeed, most states have adopted a wide range of white collar criminal statutes, many of which parallel their federal counterparts.

In many instances, then, white collar criminal activity can be prosecuted at the state level, the federal level, or both. Under the doctrine of dual sovereignty, the state government and the federal government may prosecute the same conduct, assuming that state or federal law provisions do not bar successive prosecutions in the particular instance. As a matter of policy, the Department of Justice will bring a federal action after a state Largely in response to these scandals, Congress enacted the Serbians-Oxely Act, which was signed into law in July 2002. Provisions of the Act relevant to white collar crime are discussed in the materials below.

The largest and most complex white collar cases, however, are usually brought at the federal level. This occurs for at least two reasons. First, many such cases involve wide-ranging activities that spread across state lines and that are, therefore, appropriate for federal prosecution. Second, many of the cases involve highly complex criminal schemes the investigation and prosecution of which require resources that most state law enforcement agencies simply do not possess.

Complementing the federal government's ability to fight white collar crime are the many specialised administrative divisions that investigate, and sometimes bring, the cases. For example, the Securities and Exchange Commission ("SEC"), which cannot itself bring a criminal case, possesses highly sophisticated resources for identifying and investigating instances of securities fraud. Where the fraud is believed to be criminal, the SEC can refer the matter to the United States Department of Justice for prosecution. Otherwise, the SEC can initiate a civil action, as can a private party. Similarly, the Internal Revenue Service and Customs Agency provide expertise and resources for investigating sophisticated money laundering schemes and other financial crimes.

Federal Jurisdiction

Of course, a federal case cannot be brought in the absence of a constitutional basis for federal jurisdiction. Jurisdiction for most federal white collar crimes is based upon the Commerce Clause, which provides that Congress may "regulate Commerce with Foreign Nations, and among the several states, and with the Indian Tribes."

The United States Supreme Court recently voided a non-white collar federal statute for lack of a jurisdictional basis. The Court found that the activity did not meet the requisite requirement of "substantially affecting interstate commerce." White collar statutes and cases brought under those statutes, however, generally

This policy precludes the initiation or continuation of a federal prosecution, following a prior state or federal prosecution based on substantially the same acts or transactions unless three substantive prerequisites are satisfied: first, the matter must involve a substantial federal interest; second, the prior prosecution must have left that interest demonstrably un-vindicated; and third, applying the same test that is applicable to all federal prosecutions, the government must believe that the defendant's conduct constitutes a federal offence, and that the admissible evidence probably will be sufficient to obtain and sustain a conviction by an unbiased trier of fact..... In that case, the Court said that Commerce Clause jurisdiction is met even when the activity is purely intrastate, so long as an effect on interstate commerce can be proven meet the interstate commerce requirement.

Other sources of federal jurisdiction include the postal power,15 and the taxing power.

Debate Concerning the Federalisation of Crimes

Nonetheless, in the 1970s and 1980s Congress began to adopt laws, such as the RICO and money-laundering statutes, criminalising a broad range of activities that have traditionally been the subject of state law. For example, a federal RICO case can be based not only upon such crimes as mail fraud, securities fraud, and bank fraud, but also upon the commission of state law crimes such as bribery and extortion. Arguably, some federal statutes used in white collar cases reach activities that would more appropriately be handled at the state level. As discussed below, federal prosecutors have, for example, used the mail and wire fraud statutes used in both ordinary fraud and local political corruption cases.

Parallel Civil and Administrative Proceedings

Under statutes that provide for both civil and criminal penalties, the white collar defendant may face successive or concurrent proceedings. For many reasons, including the increased criminalisation of regulatory matters, multiple proceedings in white collar cases have become even more common in recent years.

In Robertson, the Supreme Court overturned an appeals court decision that had invalidated a RICO conviction on the ground that the criminal acts had not substantially affected interstate commerce, and reinstated the conviction.

Parallel proceedings may be brought in a number of areas, including health care fraud, environmental crime, and securities fraud. In some areas, such as securities fraud, the government (in this instance, the Securities and Exchange Commission) or a private plaintiff may bring a civil action. As a general matter, the substantive legal rules in criminal cases also apply to civil cases; the reverse is also true.

The government has many reasons to institute civil or administrative proceedings in addition to or instead of criminal proceedings. These reasons include the ability to recoup money, to obtain injunctive relief, or to protect the public from further harm. The United States Attorneys' Manual now sets forth methods for coordinating criminal, civil, and administrative proceedings.

The possibility of such proceedings raises important issues in two areas. First, prosecutors have much discretion in deciding whether to leave matters to civil and/or administrative proceedings, or to bring criminal charges. Second, multiple proceedings raise important tactical issues for both sides.

A prosecutor, for example, may be unfavourably disposed to a civil proceeding that occurs prior to or concurrently with a criminal case. During the civil case, defence counsel may be able to learn the identity and gain the testimony of government witnesses. Pre-trial and trial examination of government witnesses by defence counsel provides the defence with the prosecution's evidence well in advance of the criminal trial, evidence that would not otherwise be available to the defence. Further, that testimony could be used to impeach the government witnesses at the criminal trial should the testimony be inconsistent.

Parallel proceedings also raise difficult issues for the defendant. For example, a defendant in a civil case will face the difficult choice of deciding to testify, thereby waiving the Fifth Amendment privilege against self-incrimination, or not to testify, and thereby allowing that failure to be used in favour of the government in the civil case.

Pro-secutorial Discretion in White Collar Crime

Perhaps in more than any other area of the criminal law, prosecutors in white collar matters have enormous discretion in deciding whether to bring a criminal case, and in deciding what charges to bring if they do decide to indict. This is true for several reasons. First, as noted above, in some circumstances civil penalties may be available. In that instance, the criminal prosecutor must decide whether civil remedies are sufficient in the context of the particular defendant's actions. If so, then the prosecutor might decide that criminal charges are unwarranted. Second, where parallel state and federal criminal proceedings can be brought, a prosecutor must decide whether additional criminal punishment for the same conduct is appropriate.

A state prosecutor may decide to bring a parallel proceeding if there is no statutory or case law prohibiting such a proceeding. In addition, some federal statutes prohibit a prosecution where the defendant has been tried to a verdict in state court. Also, the Pro-secutorial agency may have policies governing the issue. For example, the United States Department of Justice has a policy against a successive federal prosecution unless the latter is necessary to vindicate a substantial federal interest.

Finally, and most importantly, the nature of white collar statutes often cedes vast discretion to prosecutors. Many of these statutes are at once broad and vague. This problem sometimes arises because many white collar crimes encompass economic regulations that some believe are best left to civil enforcement. Indeed, the United States Supreme Court has noted the difficulty in distinguishing criminal acts from those that fall within the "gray zone of socially acceptable and economically justifiable business conduct."

The phenomenon of extending the criminal law to areas for which it may not be suited is referred to as "over-criminalisation." Because many white collar statutes are broad and vague, the task of defining the particular crime falls in the first instance to prosecutors, and ultimately to the courts. Particularly during the 1980s, prosecutors began to read white collar statutes quite broadly, and the courts were required to attempt to set the boundaries of criminal liability. As discussed more fully below in connection with the particular white collar crimes, students of white collar crime must remain aware of the often uncertain boundary of criminal liability under these statutes.

General Criminal Law Principles to White Collar Crime

Of course, white collar crimes are governed by the general principles of criminal law. Thus, with some exceptions, to gain a white collar conviction the government must prove:

- The required mental state, or mens rea.
- The required physical component, or actus reus (generally either the defendant's conduct, such as entering into a conspiracy, or a result of the defendant's actions, such as causing damage to a federal computer).
- Where the crime requires a result, that the defendant's acts *caused* the result. Further, general principles of liability for the acts of others ("vicarious liability") apply in white collar cases, as do principles relating to attempts and other "inchoate," or incomplete, crimes.

Mens Rea Issues in White Collar Cases

With the narrow exception of strict liability crimes, there is a presumption that the elements of any federal crime will include a mens rea requirement. Determining both the level of mens rea required, and whether that level of mens rea has been proven, are difficult issues in many white collar cases.

"Knowledge" requires a finding that the defendant knew the act or result would almost certainly occur. "Recklessness" requires a finding that the defendant was aware of a substantial and unjustifiable risk that the act or result would occur. Each of these types of mens rea is subjective, requiring that the fact finder conclude that the defendant personally possessed the required state of mind. The fourth level of mens rea—"negligence" is an objective test judged by the reasonable person standard. "Negligence" requires a finding that the defendant should have known that the act or result would occur.

Finally, in some limited areas generally known as public welfare offences, the particular statute may eliminate the general requirement that mens. In this case, the Court used the term "intent" as a synonym for mens rea. This use of the word "intent" can be confusing because "intent"—particularly in the case of "specific intent"—is also used to describe a particular level of mens rea. Indeed, courts in general are notoriously imprecise when using mens rea terminology. In many cases, it may be easier to determine the required level of mens rea by looking at the substantive definition the court uses rather than the label it employs.

Purpose and Knowledge

The most litigated levels of mens rea in white collar criminal cases involve the concepts of "purpose" and "knowledge." For example, in Gypsum, the Court held that mens rea is an element that must be proven in a criminal antitrust case. The Court further found that the required level of mens rea, in cases where anti-competitive effects have been shown, is knowledge that the defendant's actions would have such effects.

In a footnote, the Court also implied that purpose to engage in actions with an anti-competitive effect would suffice in cases where such an effect cannot be proven. Another issue arises in connection with the meaning of the term "knowledge." In some limited areas, the Supreme Court has held that the government must prove that the defendant knew that the alleged acts violated the law. This issue also arises under the terms "will-fullness" and "specific intent," discussed below.

Will-fullness

Another mens rea issue that often arises in white collar cases concerns the definition of the word "will-fully." Many white collar statutes require proof that the defendant acted "will-fully." As discussed in various contexts below, the term is interpreted to mean many different things, including recklessness, knowledge, and purpose.

Indeed, the United States Supreme Court has found that "will-fullness" sometimes requires that the government show that the defendant actually intended to violate the law. Sometimes termed "specific intent," this high proof requirement is limited to particular areas of the law, such as tax fraud. In Cheek v. United States, for example, the Court abandoned the traditional doctrine that "ignorance of the law is no excuse" in connection with tax fraud offences, and imposed an intent to violate the law requirement. As the Court explained, "this special treatment of criminal tax offences is largely due to the complexity of the tax laws."

Recklessness and Negligence

Either by statutory authority or case law, some white collar convictions may be based upon recklessness. This means that the government need not show that the defendant intended or even knew that the harm would occur, but merely was aware of the risk. In some limited areas such as certain environmental crimes, a conviction may be based upon mere negligence.

Strict Liability

In "public welfare offences," a defendant may be liable for a white collar crime absent any showing of mens rea. The Supreme Court has rejected constitutional challenges to these laws. The Court's decisions are largely based upon a policy determination that it is within Congress's powers to dispense with the mens rea requirement where laws (such as food and drug laws) seek to prevent significant physical harm to the public.

Vicarious Liability

As in other areas of criminal law, a white collar defendant may be liable for someone else's crime. For example, under the law of conspiracy, co-conspirator may be liable for each other's criminal acts under special rules relating to conspiracies. Aiding and abetting liability generally requires the government to prove both the act of aiding and abetting, and mens rea as to:

— The act of aiding and abetting,

— The goal that the object crime be achieved.

Inchoate Crimes

Many white collar offences are "inchoate," that is, the defendant may be criminally liable even though the criminal objective is never achieved. Classic inchoate crimes include both conspiracy and attempts to commit crimes.

There are many examples of white collar statutes that provide for inchoate liability. For instance, an "endeavour" to obstruct justice is sufficient under the primary federal obstruction of justice statute. The crime of tax evasion reaches "any person who will-fully attempts in any manner to evade or defeat any tax imposed by this title or the payment thereof...." Finally, Note that fraud offences, including those under the mail and wire fraud statutes, and the various securities fraud statutes, are complete irrespective of whether the defendant succeeds in defrauding the victim.

Application of Criminal Procedure Principles to White Collar Crime

Federal constitutional criminal procedure principles apply to all the crimes discussed below. Principally, the cases raise issues under the Fifth Amendment's Self-Incrimination Clause and under the Fourth Amendment's prohibition against unreasonable government searches and seizures. As to the Fifth Amendment, chapter (The Right Against Compelled Self-Incrimination) supplements discussions of the various Fifth Amendment issues that arise in the other chapters below. In particular, Self-Incrimination Clause issues arise in connection with environmental crime, securities fraud, obstruction of justice, perjury, and false statements.

As to the Fourth Amendment, the United States Constitution prohibits the government from conducting "unreasonable searches and seizures." Most of the evidence in white collar cases is not obtained by searches and seizures, but rather by voluntary responses to grand jury subpoenas. Occasionally, however, a search and seizure issue may arise in a white collar case. On occasions when search warrants are used, they are subject to objection on reasonableness grounds. These issues are discussed below in connection with environmental crimes, computer crimes, and grand jury subpoenas. Fourth Amendment doctrine is both vast and complex, and readers should refer to criminal procedure sources for a more in-depth discussion.

5

Drug Addiction and Alcoholism

In medical terms, a drug is any substance that when taken into a living organism may modify one or more of its functions. Drugs can provide temporary relief from unhealthy symptoms and/or permanently supply the body with necessary substances the body can no longer make. Some drugs produce unwanted side affects. Some drugs lead to an unhealthy dependency that has both physiological and behavioural roots.

The mind is our most important tool. With our mind, we solve the problems we face in life. Drugs do several things that harm ones ability to think or to be fully aware of the present surroundings. These effects continue long after the effects of the drug appear to have worn off. Addictive drugs activate the brains reward systems.

The promise of reward is very intense, causing the individual to crave the drug and to focus his/her activities on getting and taking the drug. The ability of addictive drugs to strongly activate brain reward mechanisms and their ability to chemically alter the normal functioning of these systems can produce an addiction. Drugs also reduce a person's level of consciousness, impairing the ability to think or be fully aware present surroundings.

The drug taker is not moving in the same series of events as others. This can be slight, wherein the person is seen to make occasional mistakes, or it can be as serious as total insanity-where the events apparent to him are completely different from those apparent to anyone else. And it can be all grades in between. It isn't that the drug user doesn't know what's going on. It is that he perceives something else going on instead of the actual series of events that are happening around him.

Drug Addiction

The life cycle of addiction begins with a problem, discomfort or some form of emotional or physical pain a person is experiencing. They find this very difficult to deal with. We start off with an individual who, like most people in our society, is basically good. This person encounters a problem or discomfort that they do not know how to resolve or cannot confront. This could include problems such as difficulty "fitting in" as a child or teenager, anxiety due to peer pressure or work expectations, identity problems or divorce as an adult. It can also include physical discomfort, such as injury or chronic pain.

The person experiencing the discomfort has a real problem. He feels his present situation is un-endurable, yet sees no good solution to the problem. Everyone has experienced this in their life to a greater or lesser degree. The difference between an addict and the non-addict is that the addict chooses drugs or alcohol as a solution to the unwanted problem or discomfort.

Drugs and Problems

This person tries drugs or alcohol. The drugs appear to solve the problem. He feels better. Because he now seems better able to deal with life, the drugs become valuable to him. The person looks on drugs or alcohol as a cure for unwanted feelings. The painkilling effects of drugs or alcohol become a solution to his discomfort. Inadvertently the drug or alcohol now becomes valuable because it helped him feel better. This release is the main reason a person uses drugs or drinks a second or third time. It is just a matter of time before he becomes fully addicted and loses the ability to control his drug use. Drug addiction, then, results from excessive or continued use of habit-forming drugs in an attempt to resolve the underlying symptoms of discomfort or unhappiness.

Addiction Progresses

Analogous to an adolescent child in his first love affair, the use of drugs or alcohol becomes obsessive. The addicted person is trapped. Whatever problem he was initially trying to solve by using drugs or alcohol fades from memory. At this point, all he can think about is getting and using drugs. He loses the ability to control his usage and ignores the horrible consequences of his actions.

How Drugs Affect Behaviour

The addict will now attempt to withhold the fact of his drug use from friends and family members. He will begin to suffer the effects of his own dishonesty and guilt. He may become withdrawn and difficult to reason with. He may behave strangely. The more he uses drugs and alcohol, the guiltier he will feel, and the more depressed he will become. He will sacrifice his personal integrity, his relationships with friends and family, his job, his savings, and anything else he may have in an attempt to get more drugs. The drugs are now the most important things in his life. His relationships and job performance will go dramatically downhill.

Alcohol and Drug Tolerance

In addition to the mental stress created by his unethical

behaviour, the addict's body has also adapted to the presence of the drugs. He will experience an overwhelming obsession with getting and using his drugs, and will do anything to avoid the pain of withdrawing from them. This is when the newly-created addict begins to experience drug carvings. He now seeks drugs both for the reward of the "pleasure" they give him, and also to avoid the mental and physical horrors of withdrawal. Ironically, the addict's ability to get "high" from the alcohol or drug gradually decreases as his body adapts to the presence of foreign chemicals. He must take more and more, not just to get an effect but often just to function at all. At this point, the addict is stuck in a vicious descending spiral. The drugs he abuses have changed him both physically and mentally. He has crossed an invisible and intangible line. He is now a drug addict or alcoholic.

Drugs and Personality Change

There is such a thing as a "drug personality". It is artificial and is created by drugs. Drugs can change the behaviour of a person from his original personality to one secretly harbouring hostilities and hatreds he does not permit to show on the surface. This establishes a link between drugs and increasing difficulties with crime, production and the modern breakdown of social and industrial culture. The drug personality includes such characteristics as:

— Mood swings

— *Unreliable*: Unable to finish projects.

— Unexpressed resentment and secret hatreds.

— *Dishonesty*: Lies to family, friends, employers.

— Withdraws from those who love him. Isolates self.

— May appear chronically depressed.

— May begin stealing from family and friends.

Biochemical Aspects of Addiction

Drugs are broken down in the liver into resides (chemical compounds which are closely related to the original substance). Most of these resides are eliminated rapidly from the bloodstream, but some can become trapped in the fatty tissues of the body. Although there are various types of tissues that are high in fat content, the one thing in common-and the problem that needs to be addressed-is that these drug resides remain for years.

Tissues in our bodies that are high in fats are turned over very slowly. When they are turned over, the stored drug resides are released into the bloodstream and reactivate the same brain centres just as if the person actually took the drug. The former addict now experiences a drug re-stimulation (or "flashback") and drug carvings. This is common in the months after an addict quits and can continue to occur for years, even decades.

Cycle of Quitting, Withdrawal, Craving and Relapse

When the addict initially tries to quit, cells in the brain that have become used to large amounts of these resides are now forced to deal with much decreased amounts. Even as the withdrawal symptoms subside, the brain "demands" that the addict give it more of the drug. This is called drug craving. Craving is an extremely powerful urge and can cause a person to create all kinds of "reasons" they should begin using drugs or drinking again. He is now trapped in an endless cycle of trying to quit, craving, relapse and fear of withdrawal. Eventually, the brain cells will again become used to having lowered drug resides. But, because deposits of drug or alcohol resides release back into the bloodstream from fatty tissues for years, cravings and relapse remain a cause of concern. The presence of resides, even in microscopic amounts, can make the brain react as if the addict had actually taken the drug again and can set up cravings and cause relapse even after years of sobriety.

Drug Addiction and Alcoholism

No one wants to be a drug addict or alcoholic, but this doesn't stop people from getting addicted. The most commonly asked question is simply-how? How could my son, daughter, father, sister, or brother become a liar, a thief, someone who cannot be trusted? How could this happen? And why won't they stop? The first thing you must understand about addiction is that alcohol and addictive drugs are basically painkillers.

They chemically kill physical or emotional pain and alter the mind's perception of reality. They make people numb. For drugs to be attractive to a person there must first be some underlying unhappiness, sense of hopelessness, or physical pain. Whether a person is genetically or biochemically predisposed to addiction or alcoholism is a controversy that has been debated for years within the scientific community. One school of thought advocates the "disease concept", embracing the notion that addiction is an inherited disease, and that the individual is permanently ill at a genetic level, even for those experiencing long periods of sobriety.

Another philosophy argues that addiction is a dual problem consisting of a physical and mental dependency on chemicals, compounded by a preexisting mental disorder that physicians categorise into diagnoses such as clinical depression, bipolar disorder, etc. It is true that addictive drugs stimulate the brain's pleasure centres causing either a reduction of pain or a heightening of mood.

A third philosophy subscribes to the idea that chemical dependency stems from chemical imbalances in the neurological system. The truth in this theory is that repeated use of addictive drugs results in a physical dependency or tolerance where increased amounts of the drug must be taken to achieve the same results. Tolerance occurs when the person no longer responds to the drug in the way that he/she initially responded. So for example, in the case of heroin or morphine, tolerance develops rapidly to analgesic (painkilling) effects of the drug. While the development of tolerance is not addiction, many drugs that produce tolerance also have addictive potential. The fact remains that there is scientific research to support all of these concepts. The question of whether addiction is genetic, behavioural or biochemical does not have an absolute answer. The one distinguishing feature that is present in every theory or philosophy of the causes of, and cures for, addiction is the ability of the drug to dominate the individuals behaviour, regardless of whether physical dependence is also produced by the drug or not.

There is a wide variety of treatment methods being used today, their administration being based on whatever school of thought the treatment provider believes in. With a 16 % to 20 % recovery rate based on statistical analyses of national averages, the message is clear that we have a lot more to learn if we are to bring the national recovery rate to a more desirable level. There is a fourth school of thought that has proven to be more accurate. It has to do with the life cycle of addiction. This data is universally applicable to addiction no matter which hypothesis is used to explain the phenomenon of drug dependency.

Ending Drug Addiction the Narconon Way

The NARCONON programme, first established in 1966, is unique. It is a proven get off and stay off drugs programme. The key to the successes of the NARCONON programme is the Drug Rehabilitation Technology. This methodology has been used successfully by hundreds of thousands of people around the world to rid themselves of the need for drugs and regain control of their lives.

The NARCONON programme, unlike more traditional treatment, deals with both the physical and mental problems brought about by drug use. We restore the addict, both mentally and physically, to the person he was before he began using drugs or alcohol. The end result is a success rate that is 3 to 4 times that of other programmes.

While drugs and their metabolised quickly become undetectable in blood and urine, some as rapidly as 3 days after last usage, drug metabolised remain stored in fatty tissues for years. That accumulated drug resides continue to cause adverse symptoms led to the development a programme aimed at reducing levels of toxins in the body to assist in recovery.

6

Sex Crime

To understand sex crime, it is important to understand the varieties of human sexual behavior, the processes by which certain types of sexual behaviors are deemed deviant and criminal, and the multiple perspectives from which the behavior is defined and controlled. Sexual behavior has been defined and explored in terms of normal sexuality, sexual deviance, sexual disorder, and sexual crime. Sex offenses are crimes of violence. However, the sexual nature of such acts requires understanding of the overlapping concepts of sexual deviance, sexual disorder, and sexual crime. It is important to keep in mind three key points in thinking about sexual deviance, sexual disorders, and sexual crimes:

- Overlap occurs between informal, formal, and medical definitions and control of sexual deviance.
- The designation of a variety of sexual practices as a disease or an objectively abnormal condition is inconsistent with cross-cultural evidence suggesting that sexuality norms are relative across time and place.
- There is disparity between the reality of sexual practices in American society and the formal and informal social control of sexual deviations.

In other words, there are a wide range of sexually deviant behaviors.What is defined as deviant or not is rooted in religion, culture, law, and science. Sexual behavior is controlled informally through stigmatisation, formally through the criminal law, and medically through clinical diagnosis. Sexual disorders identified as criminal (by the legal system) or pathological (by psychology and psychiatry) are socially constructed as such despite differences in sexual norms across time and place. As a result of informal, formal, and medical definitions and control of sexual deviance, most sexual behavior is conducted behind closed doors and sexual behavior is rarely discussed openly despite major commercial and Internet markets for deviant, pathological, and criminal sexual services.

The designation of the parameters of "normal sexuality" are subjective, time and culture bound, and dependent on an array of sociopolitical forces. In fact, understanding sex crime may require more of an understanding of normal sexuality than of abnormal psychology. The finding that 65% of college-age men have engaged in some form of sexual misconduct, including sexual contact with children, coercive sex with women, frottage, and obscene phone calls, suggests that the divide between people most consider "normal" and those viewed as sexually deviant or criminal may be smaller than we think.

Normal Sexuality

Definitions of sexual deviance and the social control of sexual behavior through law are based on cultural views of acceptable "normal" sexual behaviour. Normal sexuality is rooted in Judeo-Christian doctrine and the criminal law. Normal sex is monogamous, procreative, heterosexual intercourse between married persons.

Much more research attention has been given to sexual deviance than to the subject of normal sexuality. The dearth of research on normal sexuality may be, at least in part, the result of the difficulties in obtaining a sample of individuals willing to openly discuss their sexual behavior and sexual fantasies. What is "normal" in the statistical sense (the behavior that most people actually engage in behind closed doors) does not necessarily coincide with social prescriptions for normal sexual behavior, and what's normal in one culture, time, or place may be deviant or criminal in another.

Human sexuality is a complex concept that has to be understood through multiple lenses and disciplinary perspectives. Sex researchers Masters and Johnson noted that human sexual behavior is both learned and instinctive and impacted by a range of biological, psychological, and sociocultural influences. Alfred Kinsey, a zoologist who conducted one of the first systematic studies of human sexuality, states:

To each individual, the significance of any particular type of sexual activity depends very largely upon his previous experience. Ultimately, certain activities may seem to him to be the only things that have value, that are right, that are socially acceptable; and all departures from his own particular pattern may seem to him to be enormous abnormalities. But the scientific data which are accumulating make it appear that, if circumstances had been propitious, most individuals might have become conditioned in any direction, even into activities which they now consider quite unacceptable.

There is little evidence of the existence of such a thing as innate perversity, even among those individuals whose sexual activities society has been least inclined to accept. There is an abundance of evidence that most human sexual activities would become comprehensible to most individuals, if they could know the background of each other individual's behavior. To understand human sexuality and all of its forms requires suspension of judgment and attention to the conditioning processes, social forces, and environmental events that shape the biological (and more innate) aspects of human sexual behavior.

Research on and theories of sexuality come from a range of intersecting perspectives. Human sexuality is studied within the disciplines of psychology, sociology, socio-biology, criminology, cultural anthropology, biology, medicine, theology, history, and law. The psychological perspective focuses on the ways in which sexuality and sexual arousal are shaped by emotions, personality dynamics, motivation, attitudes, beliefs, and interpersonal behaviors.

The sociological perspective looks at the ways in which sexuality and its definition and social control are shaped by the society in which a person lives. The socio-biological perspective views sexuality as a genetic adaptation to the environment with the belief that sex differences in males and females are functional and adaptive in an evolutionary sense. The criminological perspective focuses on sexual offenses, the causes and consequences of such behavior, and its control.

The cultural anthropology perspective looks at cross-cultural variations in sexual behavior and the meaning that behavior holds for individuals in particular cultures and communities. The biological perspective focuses on the physical aspects of sexuality—anatomy, physiology, development, and maturity of the body's sexual systems.

The medical perspective emphasises sexual health—the maintenance of sexual wellbeing and the conditions associated with disease and individual and social distress. From historical and theological perspectives, sexuality is shaped by historical forces—the term sexuality evolves in connection with the past as well as biblical views of sexuality and sexual behavior. Finally, from a legal perspective, certain sexual behaviors are identified as a social threat. Laws regarding criminal sexual behavior differ across time, place, and across federal, state, and local systems.

Sexual Deviance

The types of behaviors viewed as sexually deviant are, from sociological, criminological, and anthropological perspectives, socially constructed and change across time and place. For example, homosexual and bisexual behaviors have historically been included in texts on sexual deviance and sex crimes. However, with changing conceptions of homosexuality in society, many no longer view such behaviour as "deviant."

This shift in thinking about homosexuality is reflected in the repeal of sodomy laws in most states across the United States as well as the removal of homosexuality from the Diagnostic and Statistical Manual of Mental Disorders. Furthermore, laws against adultery and fornication have existed throughout history based on the notion that adultery is a threat to the sanctity of marriage.

The amount of force with which sexually deviant behaviors are socially controlled and officially targeted is also dictated by social forces and factors such as politics and demographic shifts. For example, in his book Moral Panic, Jenkins argues that panics over sex crimes have historically occurred during periods in which the majority population is aging.

Concern about sex crimes was at its lowest in the United States during periods of high tolerance for sexual experimentation and highest in 1915, 1950, 1985, and post-1995. Following the sexual revolution of the 1960s, the increasing conservative stance on a range of issues during the 1980s Reagan era was associated with the aging of the baby boomers who supported get-tough campaigns on drugs, crime, and child abuse as a way to control their own children. According to Jenkins, "Preventing sexual acts against the young can be a way of regulating sexual acts by that population", and the post-1995 furore over sex predators and cyber-stalkers is the result of a changing cultural landscape in which American culture is becoming increasingly feminist, with heightened sensitivity and concern over issues of sexual exploitation and violence.

Thus, the types of behaviors viewed as "normal" versus "deviant" change across time and place as do the formal and informal mechanisms of social control that target deviant sexual behavior. What's deviant and who we are willing to put in prison and for how long depend to a large extent on sociocultural and political forces. Sociology, specifically deviance theory, offers a lens through which to view the historical changes in definitions of normal and deviant sexual behaviors and the cultural dynamics of legislative changes such as sexual predator laws, three-strikes laws, sex offender registration, and civil commitment regarding sex crimes.

Sexual Disorders

From medical and psychological perspectives, sexual pathologist have long been recognised. A century ago, Krafft-Ebing published Psychopathia Sexualise documenting case studies of sexual disorders including fetishism, sadism, masochism, transsexualism, transvestism, nymphomania, sexual bondage, and lust murder. Today, sexual disorders are identified in the Diagnostic and Statistical Manual of Mental Disorders, Fourth Edition, Text Revision (DSM-IV-TR), including behaviors that are sexually deviant in the sense that they are associated with some form of individual or interpersonal distress. Some, but not all of the DSM sexual disorders are crimes. The DSM-IV-TR classifies sexual disorders under the heading, Sexual and Gender Identity Disorders. This category includes gender identity disorders, sexual dysfunctions, and paraphysial.

Sexual Dysfunctions

Sexual dysfunctions involve a disturbance in sexual desire that causes distress and interpersonal difficulty. Gender identity disorders, a type of sexual dysfunction, are characterised by cross-gender identification and persistent discomfort with one's assigned sex. Other sexual dysfunctions include:

— *Sexual desire disorders:* absent or markedly diminished sexual appetite

— *Sexual arousal disorders*: inability to achieve or maintain "lubrication-swelling response to sexual excitement" (in women) or "adequate erection" (in men)

— *Orgasmic disorders*: delay in or absence of orgasm (in men or women) or premature ejaculation (in men)

— *Sexual pain disorders*: genital pain before, during, or after intercourse.

The behavioural symptoms of sexual dysfunctions and gender identity disorders are not crimes. These are sexual disorders associated with particular psychological, emotional, or behavioural symptoms that result in distress and interpersonal difficulty.

Paraphilias

Paraphilia literally means "abnormal love." In contrast with the sexual dysfunctions and gender identity disorder, symptoms of many paraphilias are criminal behaviors. Paraphilias are a group of persistent sexual behavioural patterns characterised by sexual fantasies, urges, or behaviors involving non-human objects (fetishism, trans-vestic fetishism), suffering or humiliation (sexual sadism, masochism), children (pedophilia), or other non-consenting person (voyeurism, frotteurism, exhibitionism). All of the paraphilias involve a particular behavior associated with sexual arousal, urges, and fantasies:

— *Exhibitionism: exposure* of one's genitals.

— *Fetishism: the* use of non-living objects such as women's underwear, bras, etc.

— *Frotteurism: touching* and rubbing against non-consenting persons

— *Pedophilia: sexual* activity with a prepubescent child

— *Sexual masochism: being* beaten, bound, humiliated, and/or made to suffer

— *Sexual sadism: deriving* sexual excitement from psychological or physical suffering of the victim

— *Transvestite fetishism: cross*-dressing by a male in women's attire

— *Voyeurism: observing* unsuspecting individuals who are in the process of undressing, naked, and/or engaged in sexual activity, sometimes referred to as scoptophilia, the "sexualisation of the sensation of looking".

— *Paraphilia not otherwise specified: paraphilias* that do not meet the criteria for specific categories The DSM-IV-TR category paraphilias not otherwise specified includes behaviors that are sometimes considered nuisance sex behaviors, but may also be associated with extreme sex crimes such as sexual homicide.

Many paraphilias that would be classified in this category have been found in sexual homicide cases. Paraphilias exist on a continuum varying in degree of severity and dangerousness, and multiple paraphilias are often found in one person with one being dominant. The following is a non-comprehensive list of sexual behaviors that may be classified as a paraphilia not otherwise specified or are sexual behaviors engaged in by actual sexual homicide offenders at some point in their lives:

— *Animal torture: torture*, mutilation, and killing of animals for sexual gratification and experimentation (Physical cruelty to animals is one of the criteria for conduct disorder, which, in some cases, is the childhood precursor to antisocial personality disorder and psychopathy).

— *Anthropophagy: eating* flesh and/or slicing parts of the body (i.e., cannibalism).

— *Auto-eroticism: sexual* arousal through self-stimulation (e.g., masturbation to pornography, sexual asphyxia, or aquaerotic asphyxiation).

— *Coprophilia: sexual* interest in and gratification from touching faeces.

— *Coprophagia: sexual* arousal through eating faeces (a variant of coprophilia).

— *Erotophonophilia: sexual* arousal from killing.

— *Gerontophilia: sexual* interest in elderly persons.

— *Infibulation: engaging* in self-torture such as piercing genitals with sharp objects (e.g., needles, pins).

— *Klismaphilia: sexual* arousal through receiving or administration of enemas.

— *Mixoscopia or triolism: sexual* arousal from seeing oneself in sexual scenes or sharing a sexual partner with another person and watching.

— *Necrophilia: engaging* in sexual acts with dead bodies.

— *Necrofetishism: fetish* for dead bodies that may involve keeping bodies or body parts in one's home.

— *Partialism: exclusive* sexual focus on particular parts of the body.

— *Piquerism: sexual* arousal through stabbing, wounding, or cutting.

— *Pygmalionism: sexual* involvement with dolls or mannequins.

— *Pyromania: sexual* arousal by fire setting.

— *Urophilia: sexual* interest in drinking or touching urine.

— *Zoophilia or bestiality: sexual* activity with animals.

It is important to underscore that sexual dysfunctions and gender identity disorder are mental disorders, not crimes. Paraphilias (i.e., sexual sadism, sexual masochism, fetishism, transvestic fetishism) are not criminal unless the behavioural symptoms of these disorders cross over into acts that are harmful to non-consenting second or third parties. For example, as the Meiwes-Brandes case illustrates, sexual masochism and sexual sadism may involve consenting or non-consenting persons.

Sadism and masochism (S&M) is widely practised between consenting adults. Such behavior is generally seen by the larger society as sexually deviant, but engaging in S&M activities is not a crime, and in many cases, may not be a diagnosable paraphilia. An individual can be diagnosed with a paraphilia if the behavior causes marked distress or interpersonal difficulty. Individuals who consensually engage in S&M who are not distressed by the behavior are not likely to be diagnosed with sexual masochism or sexual sadism.

To illustrate further, a person with a fetish for women's underwear who purchases the underwear for his own use or obtains undergarments from friends or acquaintances has not committed a crime. But, someone who steals women's underwear can be charged with burglary or theft. For example, 30-year-old Sung Koo Kim, a Brigham Young University student, was arrested in Portland in June 2004, charged with burglary and theft for stealing at least 3,000 pairs of women's underwear from college dorms, and sentenced to six years in prison. In Kim's case (as in the case of Armin Meiwes's sexually motivated manslaughter), his fetishism (a paraphilia) led to theft and burglary (criminal behavior), but the paraphilia itself was not a crime. Police also found 40,000 pictures of women being tortured and raped on Kim's computer. But this, and even paedophiliac or sexual homicide fantasies (provided the pornography does not involve children), does not constitute a crime.

Sex Crimes

Sex crimes are differentiated from sexual disorders and sexual deviance in that they are behavioural acts that violate the law. As is true with all types of crimes, the legal terminology and laws regarding what is and is not a sex crime vary across states and the federal system. The lines between normal, deviant, and disordered sexuality and sex crimes are sometimes hazy. The same or similar acts may be designated as a sex crime or not depending on the law in particular times and places or whether the act has been reported/identified or not.

Legal Definitions of Sex Offenses

From a legal perspective, sex offenses are acts deemed both sexually deviant and a threat to individuals and public safety. Behaviors that generally fall into the category of sex crimes are those in which the offender engages in a sexual act with a non-consenting victim. Sexual assault and rape, child molestation, child rape, sexual misconduct with a minor, indecent liberties, voyeurism, sexual violation of human remains, and custodial sexual misconduct are examples of sexual behaviors legally defined as 'sex offenses. In Washington State, sex offence is defined as:

— Any offence defined as a sex offence by RCW 9.94A. 030 (listed in above paragraph).

— Any violation under RCW 9A.44.096 (sexual misconduct with a minor in the second degree).

— Any violation under RCW 9.68A.090 (communication *with a minor for immoral purposes*).

— Any federal or out-of-state conviction for an offence that under the laws of this state would be classified as a sex offence under this subsection.

— Any gross misdemeanour that is, under chapter 9A. RCW, a criminal attempt, criminal solicitations, or criminal conspiracy to commit an offence that is classified as a sex offence under RCW 9.94A.030 or this subsection.

The U.S. Criminal Code lists sex offenses under Sexual Abuse and Sexual Exploitation of Children. Offenders convicted of a federal sex crime are those who cross state lines, kidnap their victims, or commit their offence within the jurisdictional boundaries of federal law. As in state laws, federal sex offenses involve sex acts or sexual contact with a non-consenting person or sexual exploitation of children such as cases involving children in "sexually explicit behaviors" for pornographic enterprises.

The U.S. Criminal Code defines sexual contact as "the intentional touching, either directly or through the clothing, of the genitalia, anus, groin, breast, inner thigh, or buttocks of any person with an intent to abuse, humiliate, harass, degrade, or arouse or gratify the sexual desire of any person." Sex act is defined as:

— Contact between the penis and the vulva or the penis and the anus, and for purposes of this sub-paragraph contact involving the penis occurs upon penetration, however slight;

— Contact between the mouth and the penis, the mouth and the vulva, or the mouth and the anus.

— The penetration, however slight, of the anal or genital opening of another by a hand or finger or by any object, with an intent to abuse, humiliate, harass, degrade, or arouse or gratify the sexual desire of any person.

— The intentional touching, not through the clothing, of the genitalia of another person who has not attained the age of 16 years with an intent to abuse, humiliate, harass, degrade, or arouse or gratify the sexual desire of any person.

Sexually explicit conduct refers to actual or simulated:

— Sexual intercourse, including genital-genital, oral-genital, anal-genital, or oral-anal, whether between persons of the same or opposite sex.

— Bestiality.

— Masturbation.

— Sadistic or masochistic abuse.

— Lascivious exhibition of the genitals or pubic area of any person.

Of the crime categories, sex crimes, especially those committed against children, are the most publicly abhorred and socially controlled. Sexual predators, pedophiliac priests, serial rapists, and child molesters are the targets of an enormous amount of news media attention and punitive measures. Public fear of sex crime and anger toward sex offenders has driven legislation such as sexual psychopath and sexual predator laws, two- and one-strike laws, and sex offender registration. Even in prison, sex offenders are the lowest on the offender hierarchy and, as a result, are victimised and aggressively targeted by other offenders.

Catholic priest John Geoghan preyed on young boys in Boston parishes for 30 years before his crimes were uncovered in 1998. He was defrocked by the church after

150 victims came forward to say they had been raped or fondled by Geoghan. Geoghan was sentenced in 2002 to 9 to 10 years in prison for sexually molesting a 10-year-old boy, and the Boston Archdiocese paid $10 million in civil settlements to other victims.

While in prison, Geoghan's attorneys \said he was harassed by corrections officers and received numerous infractions for insolence. Geoghan was moved from a medium security prison to the new maximum security prison, Souza-Baranowski Correctional Centre. A year later, while in the protective custody unit, Geoghan was brutally murdered by Joseph Druse, a convicted killer serving life without parole and with a known hatred of pedophiles, who got into Geoghan's cell, beat him, and used a bed-sheet to bind and strangle him to death.

Sexual Psychopathy and Sexual Predator Laws

The terms sexual predator and sexual psychopath are legal terms used to impose civil commitment of dangerous sex offenders whose behavior is associated with mental illness and pathological tendency to re-offend. Sexual deviance and psychopathy have been associated in the literature since the 1800s. Early writers used the term sexual psychopath to refer to sex offenders whose behaviors were rooted in psychopathology.

Individuals referred to as sexual psychopaths in the literature over the last two centuries would not necessarily be those considered psychopaths today (i.e., based on a high score on the Psychopathy Checklist-Revised). Although a subset of sexual offenders are psychopathic, most sex offenders are not psychopaths, most psychopaths are not sex offenders, and the legal definitions of sexual psychopathy and sexual predator in the past and today are not synonymous with traditional or contemporary psychological definitions of psychopathy. Of the civilly committed sexually violent predators housed in the Special Commitment Centre in Washington State, only 27.5% exceed the PCL-R cutoff score of 30 to be classified as psychopathic and 41.1% have been diagnosed with antisocial personality disorder.

The intertwining of the terms sexual deviance and psychopathy in the research literature made its way into law in the 1930s with the psychopathic personality and sexual psychopath laws. These laws were designed to civilly commit sex offenders whose behavior can be attributed to mental illness, with the idea that sexual psychopaths, unlike other types of offenders, were sick and could be treated. The sexual psychopath laws were based on six assumptions:

- A mental disability exists called sexual psychopathy.
- Persons suffering from sexual psychopathy are at higher risk of dangerously re-offending than are other types of offenders.
- Sexual psychopaths can be identified by mental health experts.
- The dangerousness of sexual psychopaths can be predicted.
- Treatment is available for the sexual psychopath.
- Large numbers of persons so diagnosed can be cured.

Even though virtually none of the six assumptions was supported empirically or otherwise, 25 states had enacted sexual psychopath laws by the 1960s. By the 1980s, most of these laws were repealed because treatment was ineffective, and it was determined that sexual psychopathy did not describe a homogeneous group of offenders whose behavior could be treated, predicted, or "cured." In urging the repeal of the sexual psychopath laws, the Group for the Advancement of Psychiatry (GAP) declared that:

First and foremost, the sex psychopath and sexual offender statutes can best be described as approaches that have failed. The discrepancy between the promises in sex statutes and performances have rarely been resolved.... The notion is native and confusing that a hybrid amalgam of law and psychiatry can validly label a person a "sex psychopath" or "sex offender" and then treat him in a manner consistent with a guarantee of community safety. The mere assumption that such a heterogeneous legal classification could define treatability and make people amenable to treatment is not only fallacious; it is startling.

The sexual psychopath laws illustrate the difficulties in using a clinical concept (psychopathy) to define a criminal behavior (sex offending) in such a way as to identify and predict dangerousness for the purpose of public safety.

Despite the troublesome history of the sexual psychopath laws, these laws were resurrected in the 1990s. The new laws replaced the term sexual psychopath with sexual predator. Washington State was the first to enact the sexual predator law under the Community Protection Act of 1990, which extended post-release supervision for certain sex offenders, required sex offender registration, and established a new law for the civil commitment of "sexually violent predators."

The law was revived in the aftermath of and public outcry in response to a number of high-profile cases including the 1989 rape of a 7-year-old boy by Earl Shrines, an offender who had previously served a 10-year sentence for kidnapping and assaulting two teenage girls. The case was particularly horrific because Shrines had cut off the boy's penis and because he had a lengthy previous history of sexual violence toward children. The sexual predator law differs from the old sexual psychopath laws by subjecting the offenders to civil commitment after they serve a full prison term, based on a process involving petition by the prosecuting attorney or attorney general, a finding of probable cause, a forensic evaluation, and trial. The broad definition of sexually violent predators under Washington's law may do no better than previous sexual psychopath laws in terms of designating a homogeneous group of offenders who are predictably dangerous with an identifiable (and treatable) mental illness.

The law has been challenged since its inception for committing offenders deemed "un-treatable" to in determinant civil confinement for treatment. In recent years a series of state and U.S. Supreme Court rulings have pressured states that have sexual predator laws to prove they are working to treat and release civilly committed sex predators rather than indefinitely confine them.

Understanding the history behind the sexual psychopath and sexual predator laws illustrates the need for meaningful offender topologies (in science and law) that identify homogeneous groups of offenders. It is crucial that legal concepts reflect and are consistent with clinical concepts that have an empirical basis and direct implications for treatment and management of offenders. It could be argued that sexual psychopath and predator laws represent clinical concepts sloppily applied by legislatures in the name of public safety.

Jenkins notes that the term sexual predator was a media construction created, in part, by the Westley Dodd and Earl Shriner cases and Jack Olsen's 1991 book *Predator* (about a Washington State serial rapist) and the local appeal and familiarity with legislators and media. These laws, historically and at present, are an attempt to link personality and mental disorders with a criminal behavior and treatment with punishment—a long-standing and unresolved dilemma in criminal justice.

Washington State was the first state in the United States to enact legislation specifically directed at sex offenders. Washington State enacted the Community Protection Act of 1990, which required sex offender registration and civil commitment of sexually violent predators. The Washington legislation coincided with and was driven by public dissatisfaction over violent crime and an awareness of predatory crime.

Under the law, sex offenders released to the community are required to register their address with law enforcement and those deemed sexually violent predators, on completion of their prison sentence, are civilly committed. The Washington State legislation, considered by some at the time and still today to be a draconian revival of the old habitual offender laws of the early 1900s, was fuelled in part by anger, fear, and panic over high-profile offenders including (Continued).

The exact number of Bundy's victims is unknown. Bundy's earliest victims were college students from the University of Washington and other universities in Washington State who he lured by wearing a fake cast or sling to get sympathy, asking for help, or posing as an authority figure. Bundy murdered most of his victims by hitting them in the head with a blunt object, and then took their bodies to remote locations where he had sex with their corpses and applied make-up to them. He confessed that he had decapitated some of his victims with a hacksaw. Eleven of Bundy's victims were from Washington State.

— *Kevin Coe:* Fredrick "Kevin" Coe committed rapes in Spokane, Washington's South Hill area in 1981. Coe served a 25-year sentence for one of the rapes but was said to have committed over 40 rapes that terrorised the city. Coe's case was the subject of *Jack Olsen's book Son:* A Psychopath and His Victims and a made-for-TV movie. Coe was released in 2006 and the state immediately filed a violent sexual predator action to detain Coe for a probable cause hearing to determine his status as a sexually violent predator. At the time of this writing he is housed at the Washington State Special Commitment Centre on McNeil Island awaiting a civil commitment trial.

— *Charles Campbell:* In 1982 Campbell murdered Renae Wicklund, her 8-year-old daughter Shannah, and a neighbour, Barbara Hendrickson. Wicklund had testified in a rape case years earlier that Campbell had attacked and sodomised her and held a knife to her baby's throat. Campbell committed the murders while on work release after doing time for the rape. Campbell was executed by hanging in 1994.

— *Gene Raymond Kane:* In 1988 Diane Ballasiotes was raped and murdered in Pioneer Square in Seattle by a convicted sex offender, Gene Kane. Kane had served a 13-year sentence for attacking two women and was placed on work release in downtown Seattle. Ballasiotes's mother, Ida Ballasiotes, became a powerful force in Washington State as a state legislator.

— *Earl Shriner:* In 1989 Shriner raped and mutilated 7-year-old Ryan Alan Hade. Shriner had a 24-year history of sexual assaults against children and had served a sentence for murdering a 15-year-old classmate when he was 16. After his release from prison, he committed more crimes and was sent to prison for 10 years.

He was released in 1989, when he committed the heinous offence against Hade. He lured Hade out of sight with a doughnut when the boy was riding his bike in the woods near his home. Shriner was sentenced to life without the possibility of parole. Tragically, Hade later died in 2005 at age 23 in a motorcycle crash.

— Westley Allan Dodd: In 1989 Dodd murdered 10- and 11-year-old brothers William and Cole Neer and 4-year-old Lee Iseli in Vancouver, Washington. Dodd sexually assaulted and stabbed the Cole brothers to death and weeks later abducted Iseli from a park and sexually assaulted him in his home for 2 days and then hanged him with a rope in his closet. Dodd kept a journal of the assault and murders and took Polaroid pictures of Iseli before and after his death, including a photo of the boy hanging in the closet. Dodd was executed by hanging in 1993.

— *Gary Ridgway:* Although Gary Ridgway, the Green River Killer, was not caught and convicted until 13 years after the Community Protection Act of 1990 was enacted, bodies of the Green River Killer victims first began to be discovered in 1982, and the years of frustration and speculation surrounding the case likely influenced the enactment of the sex offender law.

In November 2004 Gary Ridgway pled guilty to the sexual homicides of 48 women, including prostitutes and teen runaways. Ridgway strangled his victims after having sex with them and engaged in necrophilia with at least some of his victims' bodies.

He was sentenced to life without parole after reaching a plea agreement with prosecutors. Frustration over the legal inability to detain offenders that criminal justice officials had deemed too dangerous for release and the succession of horrific offenses committed by offenders with sexually violent criminal histories culminated in the Washington State 1990 sex offender registration and civil commitment legislation. Parents of murdered children, citizens, criminal justice officials, and legislators called for legal action that would enhance public safety by making the public aware of sex offenders in their midst and providing legal means to indeterminately incarcerate.

The civil commitment component of the Washington Community Protection Act involves end of-sentence review petitioned by the prosecuting attorney or attorney general, consisting of a probable cause hearing to determine whether or not the offender meets the legal definition of "sexually violent predator." If probable cause exists, then a court will hold a full hearing to determine if civil commitment should be ordered. The legal definition of sexually violent predator in Washington State is "any person who has been convicted of or charged with a crime of sexual violence and who suffers from a mental abnormality or personality disorder which makes the person likely to engage in predatory acts of sexual violence if not confined in a secure facility."

Sex Offender Topologies

Sex crimes are committed by a heterogeneous group of offenders whose behaviour reflects diverse offending patterns. According to Nicholas Groth, author of Men Who Rape: The Psychology of the Offender, One of the most basic observations one can make regarding men who rape is that not all such offenders are alike. They do not do the very same thing in the very same way or for the very same reasons. In some cases, similar acts occur for different reasons, and in other cases, different acts serve similar purposes.

The heterogeneity of sex offenders has made it difficult to draw conclusions necessary to deal with the population in the criminal justice system. Investigative practices, sentencing, correctional supervision, and treatment depend on clear understanding of who sex offenders are, the nature of their offending, the factors and developmental pathways that shape their behavior, and propensity for future offending.

Researchers have long attempted to develop meaningful topologies of sex offenders. Sex crimes and sex offenders have been classified based on factors such as motivation, victim type, modus operandi, nature of offence, and association with other criminal offenses. The most common sex offender typology is the distinction between the rapist and the child molester, based on age of victim. Many researchers have used this distinction as a starting point, developing more sophisticated sub-types of the two general categories including aspects of offender motivation and nature of offence.

The length of civil commitment is indefinite, but an offender may be released from confinement to the community or to less restrictive community custody. Such release is based on a further finding that the offender participated in treatment and mental health staff determine that the offender has made treatment gains that reduce the likelihood of re-offense and risk to public safety.

The Washington State Community Protection Act set the stage for sexual violent predator legislation in another 20 states, driven by similar stories around the country including the murder of Polly Klaas by Richard Allen Davis, the 1990 abduction and disappearance of Jacob Wetterling in Minnesota, and the 1994 rape and murder of Megan Kanka in New Jersey by a convicted sex offender who lived across the street.

Their typology assimilates a vast body of theory and research on sex offender typologic and modes of aggression, and has been replicated within and outside the Massachusetts Treatment Centre. The Massachusetts Treatment Centre typologic illustrate the crucial factors associated with sex offending behavior and the features that differentiate types and sub-types.

For example, a Type 1 rapist (opportunistic, high social competence) commits rape for very different reasons than the Type 5 rapist (sexual, sadistic, high social competence), requiring a different law enforcement strategy in terms of investigative direction. The Type 1 rapist is likely to be psychologically "normal," engaging in rape behavior if the opportunity arises (e.g., during the course of a felony for profit, in a date-rape or group/gang rape situation). A Type 5 rapist is likely to be psychopathological disordered, possess highly developed fantasies, and engage in elaborate planning and predatory stalking of victims.

The offense committed by the Type 5 rapist is more likely to involve signature aspects, with the rape leading to murder. Similarly, the Axis I/Type 2–Axis II/Type 3 child molester (low fixation, low social competence; low contact, low physical injury, non-sadistic) differs considerably from the Axis I/Type 0–Axis II/Type 1 offender (high fixation, low social competence; high contact, interpersonal meaning). These differences have important implications for mental health treatment and criminal justice policy and practice regarding sex offenders.

General Categories of Sex Crimes

For the purpose of understanding the similarities and differences between three major categories of sex crime, rape and sexual assault, child molesting, and sexual homicide are discussed here with attention to the heterogeneity of offenders and typologic developed within each category. Offenders in each group differ in motivation, victim selection, nature of sexual acts, and other characteristics. Understanding of the types of offenses as well as the sub-types within each general category is important in identifying the origins and development of sexual offending and in sorting through the varieties of sex offense behaviors.

Rape

Rape is commonly defined as non-consensual vaginal, oral, or anal penetration by force, or threat of force. The National Violence Against Women Survey conducted in 1996 by the National Institute of Justice and Centres for Disease Control and Prevention found that 17.6% of the 8,000 women and 3% of the 8,005 men surveyed have been victims of a completed or attempted rape. In 2005, there were 93,934 forcible rapes in the United States, a 3.4% increase from 2001. However, since 1996, rape arrests have decreased 2.4%, with a rape rate for 2005 estimated at 62.5 per 100,000. (Rape data have been generally collected for female victims only; the UCR rape rate is based on estimates of the U.S. Female population from census data.) Prior to the 1990s, the U.S. Rape rate vacillated with increases in the 1940s, mid-1960s to early 1980s, and from 1985 to 1992.

The following are a number of key findings regarding rape:

— Forcible rape comprises 91.4% of all reported rape offenses.

— An estimated 91% of rape and sexual assault victims are female and 99% of offenders are male.

— Three out of every four rape incidents are committed by offenders with whom the victim had a prior relationship.

— Women report being raped or sexually assaulted by a friend or acquaintance in 38% of rape/sexual assault victimisation.

— On college campuses, during any given academic year, 2.8% of all women will experience a completed or attempted rape.

— Most rapes occur between 6 pm and 6 am, in the victim's own home, by a single offender who is an acquaintance or a family member of the victim.

— Stranger rapes account for 20% of single offender victimisations, but 76% of victimisations involving multiple offenders. Multiple offender rapes account for approximately 7% of all rapes.

— Of all rapes committed from 1992 to 2000, 39% of attempted rapes and 17% of sexual assaults against females resulted in injury and most injured rape victims do not receive medical treatment for their injuries.
— Most rapes (approximately 65%) are not reported to police.
— Adolescents are responsible for 50% of sexual assaults on children and 30% of rapes of adolescent and adult women.

One of the most central issues in the literature on rape is the absence of the behavior from the list of paraphilias in the DSM. Rape is a crime, not a sexual disorder is not listed as a paraphilia in the DSM-IV-TR, in part, because it is a culturally reinforced behavior that is not fundamentally distinguished by psychopathology.

In 1975, Brown miller wrote Against Our Will: Men, Women, and Rape, which argued that rape is a culturally supported crime of violence used by men as a tactic of terror against women. In Brown miller's view, rape is "nothing more or less than a conscious process of intimidation by which all men keep all women in a state of fear".

Brown miller and other feminist writers have argued that social and cultural forces (e.g., patriarchal ideology, hyper-masculine values, rape myths, pornography, media depictions of women and the linking of sex and violence) work together to foster a rape-conducive climate, and the fear of rape that girls and women have to live with restricts their movement and their choices and serves the function of female subjugation. In her landmark work, Intercourse, Dworkin argued, The men as a body politic have power over women and decide how women will suffer:

> which sadistic acts against the bodies of women will be construed to be normal.

In the United States, incest is increasingly the sadism of choice, the intercourse itself wounding the female child and socialising her to female status—early; perhaps a sexual response to the political rebellion of adult women; a tyranny to destroy the potential for rebellion. "I felt like I was being ripped up the middle of my legs all the way to my throat," one incest victim said. "I was sure that if I looked down, I would be on two parts of the bed."... Incestuous rape is becoming the central paradigm for intercourse in our time.

Women are supposed to be small and childlike, in looks, in rights; child prostitution keeps increasing in mass and in legitimacy, the children sexually used by a long chain of men—fathers, uncles, grandfathers, brothers, pimps, pornographers, and the good citizens who are the consumers; and men, who are, after all, just family, are supposed to slice us up the middle, leaving us in parts on the bed.

Women see themselves as prey and men as predators, and are afraid to jog at night or take a walk to the corner store after dark, while men don't give such behaviors a second thought, attesting to the gender disparity that exists regarding fear of rape and sexual assault. Accepting rape as a paraphilia links rape behavior with psychopathology, negating the extent to which the behavior is culturally supported. Sexual stereotypes about women (and men) fuel and facilitate rape behavior.

Cultural norms about what is and is not humiliating for whom are expressed and reflected in particular acts committed by rapists. Rapists' thinking errors, neutralisation techniques, excuses, and justifications are founded in and shaped by cultural stereotypes, rape myths, images in media and pop culture, and subcultural norms and values. On the other hand, clinical interviews with rapists provide some support for the classification of rape as a paraphilia. Many rapists have recurrent and repetitive urges and fantasies to commit rape and a history of other paraphilias associated with their rape behavior, and extreme forms of rape behavior such as sadistic rape and sexual homicide are associated with personality disorder and mental illness. Thus, there appears to be a continuum of rape proneness within the general male population.

Rape is a culturally reinforced behavior committed by individuals with Axis I mental illnesses and Axis II personality disorders, and by "normal rapists" who cannot be diagnosed with either. Those at the middle to higher end of the continuum hold more rape-prone attitudes and beliefs, which interact with other factors to produce rape behavior. Questions remain regarding what the critical interactive factors are and how they shape behavior in different types of rapists.

The issue of whether or not rape is an uncontrollable paraphilia versus a consciously chosen crime is intertwined with perspectives on rape as a sexual crime or a crime of violence. The argument that rape is a crime of violence, not sex, has been challenged on a number of levels. Feminist writers of the 1970s and 1980s such as Brown miller, MacKinnon, and Dworkin argued that rape is an act of violence against women and that heterosexual sex itself is an act of violence and female subjugation.

Others suggest that this sort of equating of sex and violence is a narrow and empirically baseless redefinition of the term sexual. Naffine offers an alternative feminist perspective on rape, suggesting that the notion that men can harm women through rape (and sex) must be de-constructed—"rape is a language, a particular expression of sexuality", a "masculine cultural construct" that pits male violence against female vulnerability. In other words, the cultural notion that any woman can be destroyed and terrorised by the male penis actually reinforces rape behavior, causing women (and men) to equate rape with death, providing the cultural framework within which rapists can use (and come to understand) sex as a means of violence. Research suggests that sexual and aggressive processes interact in sexual assault, that sexual arousal is crucial to sex offender behavior, and that rape is "neither an act of violence nor an act of sexual passion—it is a crime of sexual violence".

The extent to which rapists and rape events are similar or differ has been the subject of much research attention. Rape is often classified, based on the victim-offender relationship, into four types—stranger rape, acquaintance rape, date rape, and partner/marital rape. Other rapist types noted by Groth and others include gang rape, male rape, and child rape. Regardless of the victim-offender relationship, rape is a learned behavior that involves the use of cognitive distortions and neutralisation that all allow offenders to psychologically validate their behaviors. This is true for all types of rapists:

Most rapists share the same belief system, regardless of whether they are convicted offenders or college students, whether they are raping a stranger or their wives, and whether they define themselves as rapists or believe they are "normal." These belief systems include beliefs that rape is justified and that women and men are sexual enemies.

The culturally supported hyper-masculine cognition of rapists play a central role in instigating, sustaining, and defending rape. These cognition include excessive sexual preoccupation, rape and seduction fantasies and scripts, rape-supportive belief systems, rape myth acceptance, and hyper-masculine self-definition. Rape cultures and hyper-masculine subcultures such as some fraternities and athletic teams create a context within which rape behavior is validated and reinforced.

The relationship context appears to be associated with differences in the dynamics of rape and attributions of who is to blame. Studies suggest that the closer the relationship between the offender and victim, the less power tactics are used by the offender as a method of force and coercion and that alcohol and drug tactics are more likely to be used in date and acquaintance rape contexts.

Perceptions of the cause of rape (male pathology, male hostility, victim precipitation) and who is to blame (offender, society, victim) also differ depending on type of rape, with the perception that female precipitation (blaming the victim) is most closely associated with partner and date rape whereas male pathology/hostility (blaming the offender) is least associated with rapes that involve known offenders. Mc Cabe and Wauchope found that rapists who attack strangers most commonly engaged in vaginal penetration and kissing/fondling, suggesting that even rapists who do not know their victims may be trying to convince themselves that their assaults are consensual and mutually enjoyable.

Types of rape behavior have also been classified based on motivational factors. Groth's work represents one of the first attempts to develop an empirical rape typology. Groth identified three motivational rape patterns: power, anger, and sadistic rape. Power rapists commit rape for the sexual conquest. Sexual desire is not the primary aim of the power rapist. Rather, the assertion of masculinity, power, control, strength, domination, and intimidation are the primary goals, and the behavior is associated with feelings of omnipotence and entitlement.

Anger rapists commit rape as an expression of rage and retaliation. The anger rape is characterised by physical brutality and a surprise or blitz (sudden, immediate) attack. Sex is used as a weapon and rape an expression of anger, and the offender often engages in humiliating sexual acts to degrade the victim. Like the power rapist, the anger rapist does not commit rape for sexual arousal or satisfaction. For the anger rapist, satisfaction and relief come from the expression of anger, not sexual gratification. Sadistic rapists commit rape for pleasure and arousal. For the sadistic rapist, sexuality and aggression are linked and pleasure is achieved through bondage, torture, and ritualistic behaviors such as forcing the victim to behave in a particular way or through focus on and mutilation of particular parts of the victim's body. The sadistic rape is premeditated and instrumental and many sadistic rapists commit sexual homicide.

Groth's power-anger-sadistic typology has been expanded by a number of authors. The power assertive, power reassurance, anger retaliatory, and anger excitation typology is the expansion of Groth's original work and has become one of the best-known rape (and sexual homicide) typologic. The typology can be practically applied to law enforcement to provide information regarding the offender's behavioural parameters that offers informed direction for investigative practices.

Other researchers have noted differences with respect to the particular types of attack. For example, anger retaliatory rapists are noted for their blitz-style attacks whereas power assertive rapists are more likely to use the con approach. A study by Silverman et al. involving the analysis of 1,000 rape cases found that blitz and confidence styles of attacks are important categories of rape that have implications for victim services.

Blitz rape victims are more likely to have been confronted with a weapon and to have been threatened with murder whereas confidence victims are more likely to have consumed alcohol or drugs and been subjected to a prolonged rape incident. Victims of confidence rapes are more likely to experience guilt and self-blame in the aftermath of the attack. These findings suggest that victim out-reach strategies may need to be directed and modified to fit the type of attack a victim has experienced. Returning to the Massachusetts Treatment Centre rapist typology (which can be seen as a more complex empirically based extension of Groth's original anger-power-sadistic typology that assimilates multiple rape typologic in the academic literature), rape is classified into nine motivational types: opportunist–high social competence, opportunist–low social competence, pervasive anger, overt sadism, muted sadism, sexual–high social competence, sexual–low social competence, vindictive–high social competence, vindictive–low social competence.

Child Sexual Assault

Sexual assaults against children are a major social concern that has influenced criminal justice legislation and policy and practice in social and health services. Results from meta-analyses of studies of the prevalence of child sexual abuse suggest that somewhere between 22 and 40% of women and 8 and 13% of men have been sexually abused at some point during their childhood.

Others cite findings suggesting the numbers are higher—7 to 53% of girls and 3 to 37% of boys. Data from the UCR National Incident-Based Reporting System (NIBRS) shows that 67% of all victims of sexual assault reported to law enforcement agencies between 1991 and 1996 were juveniles, with more than half of the juvenile victims under the age of 12, and one of every seven (14% of all sexual assault victims) under age 6. The sexual crimes committed against juveniles include forcible fondling (84%), forcible sodomy (79%), assault with an object (75%), and forcible rape (46%). The perpetrators of sexual abuse of children tend to be male adolescents or adults known to the child and members of the same household.

Substantiated cases of child sexual abuse decreased 30% nationwide from a high of 149,800 in 1992 to 103,600 in 1998. Possible explanations for the decrease include actual decline in incidence due to public awareness, prevention programs, and increased sentence length and monitoring of sex offenders or changes in policies, practices, and attitudes that have reduced the amount of child sexual abuse reported and substantiated. A survey sponsored by the Centre for Missing and Exploited Children found that one in five youths received a sexual solicitation over the Internet in the past year, and one in 33 received an aggressive sexual solicitation. Only a fraction of these incidents were reported to parents or authorities. Additional data from the NIBRS shows that:

- The single age with the greatest number of sexual assault victims is age 14, and there are more sexual assault victims at age 2 than there are in any age group above 40.
- Juvenile victims of sexual assault were more likely to be male (18%) than adult victims (4%), and 27% of those under age 12 are male.
- Young juveniles are more likely to be sexually assaulted in the hours when meals are served and after school.
- Weapons other than the offender's hands and feet are rarely used in the sexual assault of young juveniles.
- Only 3% of sexual assaults of children under age 6 involved strangers, and such assaults are the least likely of all crimes to result in arrest or some form of clearance.

Child sexual assault can take many forms beyond the image that many conjure when they think of the typical child molester. Most child sex offenders do not fit the stereotype of the lurking dirty old man. This is one of the reasons why many sex offenders who harm children continue their behavior for long periods of time without being detected. The following are case examples of sexual assaults against children reflecting a range of behaviors and victim-offender relationships:

— Mary Kay Letourneau, a 35-year-old high school teacher and married mother of four, pled guilty in 1998 to two counts of second-degree child rape for having sex with a 13-year-old student and giving birth to a daughter conceived in the relationship. Letourneau was sentenced to 6 months behind bars followed by sex-offender treatment. She was also ordered to disclose her "sexual deviancy" to any potential partners, avoid places where minors are known to congregate, and not initiate or prolong contact with children. Following the sentence, Letourneau quickly violated the terms of her supervision by again having sex with her victim, Vili Fualaau, and was sent back to prison to serve the full 7½ year sentence. In prison, it was learned she had become pregnant by Fualaau again, and she gave birth to a second daughter. In June 2004, her release date was postponed until she found a suitable address where neighbors were informed of her status as a sex offender. In May 2005, 9 months after she was released from prison, Letourneau and Fualaau married in a lavish media wedding for which the couple was reportedly paid $750,000.

— Sixty-one-year-old Wilburn Vernon Biggers of Charleston, South Carolina, was sentenced in 2004 to 5 years in federal prison after pleading guilty to using the Internet to entice a minor for sex. Biggers contacted someone in an Internet chat room he thought was a 15-year-old female and persuaded "her" to meet him for a sexual encounter. He rented a motel room and went to a restaurant for his meeting with the supposed teen. The person Biggers had chatted with was a law officer with the South Carolina Computer Crime Center. He was arrested on federal charges that led to his guilty plea.

- John Geoghan, a Boston Catholic priest, was found guilty in January 2002 of molesting a boy in a swimming pool a decade earlier and sentenced to 9 to 10 years in prison. More than 130 people accused Geoghan of sexual abuse during his 30-year career in six parishes. Geoghan was defrocked in 1998 and sent to prison in 2002. In 2003 he was murdered in prison.
- A Connecticut man, Donald Bailey, 52, was arrested in 2003 and charged with firstdegree sexual assault and risk of injury to a minor.After receiving a complaint about the sexual abuse of a child, state police served a search-and-seizure warrant at his home seizing VHS tapes, 8-mm video-tapes, a personal computer, and photographs. Police said one of the video tapes showed Bailey directing minors in compromising positions. Bailey was charged with first-degree sexual assault, three counts of risk of injury to a minor, employing a minor in an obscene performance, promoting a minor in an obscene performance, and possession of child pornography.
- A 41-year-old man was charged with statutory rape in San Francisco for paying to have sex with a 14-year-old. He pleaded guilty and was sentenced to 3 years' probation in exchange for testifying against the girl's pimp.
- A 60-year-old Wisconsin man, previously convicted of incest in 1990 and placed on probation, pleaded guilty in 2004 to two counts of first-degree sexual assault of his two granddaughters. The girls, now age 6 and 9, were sexually assaulted between 1998 and 2003.
- A 20-year-old woman was convicted of sexually assaulting her 3-year-old niece after she gave the child a bath and inserted her finger into the child's vagina. When questioned, the woman said she didn't know

why she did it and didn't get any sexual feelings from the act.

As this list indicates, child sexual assaults take many forms and involve very different types of offenders and victims including incest, pedophilia, child rape, sexual exploitation of minors, and Internet child luring. Sexual acts involved in sex crimes against children range from fondling to sexual homicide.

Typologic of child sex offenders tend to group offenders into two general types:

> situations offenders, who sexually abuse children when the opportunity arises, and preferential offenders, who are sexually attracted to children. Researchers have also classified child sex offenders in terms of high and low deviancy, passive and active offense pathways, fixated and regressed types, and secure and insecure adult attachment with the primary distinction between types being severity of behavior and level of sexual preference for children. The Knight and Prentky child molester typology is, like their rape typology, one of the more sophisticated and empirically based classification systems for child sex offenders.

Common sub-types found in most child molester typologic include a type of offender with a long-standing sexual interest in/preference for children, a type that sexually offends under stress, and a type that sexually offends because they can (because children are easy targets for exploitation). These types are generally defined as follows:

— Fixated type: Long-standing, exclusive sexual preference for children. Few are married and there is minimal history of dating and peer interaction. Victim is generally known to the offender before sexual contact occurs. Sexual offense involves minimal force or aggression, including acts that are typically non-genital (kissing, caressing, sucking, fondling).

— Regressed type: Offender generally has established adult relationships and is likely to be married and have achieved a high level of social and sexual adaptation. At times of stress, the offender regresses, turning to an inappropriate sex object (a child) who is seen as a love object. The offense is likely to include genital sex. This type of offender may experience remorse. guilt, and shame in the aftermath of the offense.

— Exploitative type: Offender exploits weaknesses of the child to gratify his own sexual needs and will use aggression if necessary to get the child to comply. The offender is most likely to assault a stranger victim and does not care about the child's emotional or physical well being.

The Massachusetts Treatment Center Child Molester Typology is grounded, in part, on this more general typology. However, the researchers have identified additional features that more accurately differentiate homogeneous sub-types of offenders. Danni and Hampe note that the Massachusetts Treatment Center typology is "the best example of research today in viewing sex offenders from a multidimensional perspective" but that it may be too complex and difficult to apply in practice for the average criminal justice professional.

The Massachusetts Treatment Center typology draws on information regarding sexual acts committed. injury to victim, victim-offender relationship, and degree of premeditation and planning gleaned from diagnoses and information obtained by trained clinical professionals. This information may not be readily available to criminal justice agencies dealing with offenders.

Danni and Hampe suggest that correctional supervision can be enhanced by more simply differentiating between pedophiles, hebophiles, and incest offenders. Analysis of pre-sentence investigation report data from a sample of 168 child sex offenders under community supervision in Wyoming yielded the following types:

— Pedophiles: Engage in sexual activity with a prepubescent child. Pedophiles try to seduce their victims with gifts, trips, and so on. Many pedophiles have a history of being sexually victimised themselves in childhood. Motivation is sexual arousal/seduction. Their behavior is less likely to be discovered, and offenders are most difficult to supervise and treat. Treatment needs are lifelong and must be confrontative and probing.

— Hebophiles: Have sexual preference for children who have reached puberty and interpret sexual involvement with their victim as reciprocal. Their behavior is episodic and impulsive. Motivation is a reciprocal sexual relationship. Behavior is more likely to be discovered because victims are older and may be more inclined to/capable of disclosure. They are able to recognise wrongdoing and more amenable to treatment.

— Incest offenders: Engage in sexual activity with their own children for their own selfish pleasure. Usually have successful sexual relationships with adults, and are motivated by anger. Behavior is less likely to be discovered because sexual abuse is within family unit and less likely to be disclosed. Supervision requires extensive collateral contacts. The many typologic developed to explain and understand sexual offenders who assault children illustrate the complexity of the issue and the difficulties in merging research and practice to deal with sex offenders. If there are truly 24 possible types of sex offenders, the critical task for mental health and criminal justice is to employ appropriate investigative, treatment, and management practices that specifically address the risks, needs, and responsively of each type.

Sexual Homicide

Sexual homicide is the most severe form of sexual offending and the most complex in terms of offender psychopathology and developmental history. Sex offenders as a group have a higher likelihood to commit murder than non-sex offenders. The homicide rate among sex offenders is one per 400 sex offenders compared to one per 3,000 of the general population of non-sex offenders.

Sex offenders who commit homicide are a subset of offenders who show histories of sadism, fetishism, voyeurism, early-onset criminal careers, fire setting, animal cruelty, antisocial personality disorder, pornography collection, learning disabilities, and alcohol and drug abuse. The following are key findings in Meloy's review of the literature on sexual homicide:

— Most sexual homicide offenders are male and kill their first victim (usually a female stranger or casual acquaintance) prior to age 30.

— Sexual murderers usually have more than one paraphilia.

— Fantasy plays a central role in sexual homicide and can be inferred from offender productions (e.g., crime scene evidence, narratives, drawings).

— Sexual homicides usually evidence M.O. And signature.

— Sexual homicides are opportunistic rather than impulsive acts.

— Adolescents commit sexual homicide at the same rate as adults.

— Victim-offender relationships in sexual homicide are unusual in that they are similar to paraphilias in the selection of primarily stranger victims, but dissimilar to other crimes of violence that tend to involve known or related victims.
— Most sexual killers are not psychotic.
— All sexual killers evidence narcissistic and psychopathic personality traits.
— Not all serial killers may meet the criteria for antisocial personality disorder.
— Sexual murderers are less adaptive, more dysfunctional, and more schizoid and use more primitive defences than other psychopaths.
— There is no evidence of biological anomalies, psychological factors, or social deviancies that predict sexual homicide.

In Psychopathia Sexualise, Krafft-Ebing wrote of lust murder, a special category of sexual behavior whereby sexual arousal is achieved through murder. Krafft-Ebing suggested that rape can be followed by three types of murder—unintentional murder, to destroy the witness, and murder out of lust.

According to Krafft-Ebing, who published his work around the time of Jack the Ripper, only the latter should be considered lust murder, presumed when "injuries of the genitals are found, the character and extent of which are such as could not be explained by merely a brutal attempt at coitus; and, still more, when the body has been opened, or parts (intestines, genitals) torn out and are wanting". Contemporary researchers define sexual homicide more broadly as the "intentional killing of a person during which there is sexual behavior by the perpetrator" and the "killing of a person in the context of power, sexuality, and brutality".

These definitions include rape-murders as well as murders in which sexual acts were committed after death involving overt and symbolic sexual behavior. Sexual motivation is inferred through victim attire/lack of attire, exposure of the sexual parts or sexual positioning of the victim's body, insertion of foreign objects into the victim's body cavities; evidence of sexual intercourse (oral, anal, vaginal); and substitute sexual activity, interest, or sadistic fantasy. Sexual homicide is a statistically rare phenomenon. The UCR does not collect data on sexual homicide, and the actual base rate of the crime is unknown. It is estimated that fewer than 1% of all murders are sexual homicides, most committed by males who kill their first victim before age 30. Victims of sexual homicide are most often children, adolescent girls, and women who are strangers or acquaintances of the offender. The following are case examples of sexual homicide offenses against children:

— Marc Dutroux, a 47-year-old Belgian electrician, raped and murdered several young girls with accomplices including his wife, Michelle Martin. Dutroux raped, drugged, and buried alive two teenage girls and kidnapped and left two 8-year-olds to starve in an underground cell while he was serving a 4-month sentence for car theft. Martin fed the couple's dogs upstairs while the girls starved to death. In 2004, Dutroux received a life sentence while Martin and another male accomplice received sentences of 30 and 25 years, respectively.

— Westley Allan Dodd, executed in 1993 at age 28, four years after he murdered three young boys. Dodd murdered 10- and 11-year-old brothers William and Cole Neer, whom he sexually assaulted and stabbed to death, and Lee Iseli, a 4-year-old whom he abducted and sexually assaulted in his home for two days and then hung with a rope in his closet. He kept a journal of the assault and murder and took Polaroid pictures of Iseli before and after his death, including one of the boy hanging in the closet.

— Jeremy Sagastegui, executed in 1998, stabbed, sexually assaulted, and drowned Kievan Sarbacher, a 3-year-old boy under his care. He then waited for Kievan's mother, Melissa Sarbacher, to return home. When she returned, he shot her and her friend, Lisa Vera-Acevado, who had accompanied Sarbacher home. Sagastegui confessed to detectives, telling them it "was a thrill" to watch the mother die, that he "annually raped the boy using a jar of Vaseline" and then wrapped him in a towel "so his guts wouldn't spill out all over the place."

He told police the boy "was probably going to grow up to be a murderer." Notorious serial killers such as Gary Ridgway, Ted Bundy, Jeffrey Dahmer, John Gacy, and Arthur Shaw-cross are examples of serial sexual homicide offenders. While all serials are not sexual homicide offenders, most sexual homicide offenders do not stop with one offense if they are successful at avoiding getting caught. There are few, if any, documented cases of sexual homicide committed by females, particularly involving male victims. However, some sexual homicide offenders use their consensual sex partners to assist them in the murder of female stranger victims.

Cultural factors (such as pornography and gender stereotypes) play a strong role in the development of the sexual homicide offender. Most offenders who go to this behavioural extreme have complicated developmental histories of psychopathology, escalating paraphilias, highly developed fantasies, and experimentation.

Many rapists, lust murderers, and sexually motivated murderers have histories of sexual behavior reflecting multiple nuisance paraphilias that have escalated through fantasy to experimentation (with dolls, animals, people), and finally to the commission of acts of sexual homicide that often involve further experimentation and escalation in the nature and severity of wound infliction. Serial sexual homicide offenders have significantly higher rates of paraphilias (particularly fetishism and cross-dressing); antisocial behaviors as youths, sexual sadism, psychopathy, personality disorders (primarily antisocial, borderline, and narcissistic personality disorders.

Two of the best-known models explaining sexual homicide (and serial murder) are Hickey's trauma control model and the motivational model developed by Ressler, Burgess, and Douglas, based on FBI Behavioural Science Unit interviews with 36 serial killers in the late 1970s and early 1980s. Arrigo and Parcel offer a model that integrates the two theories, with attention to the development and escalation of paraphilic behaviors. This integrative model suggests that sexual homicide is part of a paraphilic process, a cyclical system of behaviors. The authors suggest that sexual homicide is rooted in and maintained by the following features:

— *Formative development: Predispositions* factors interact with early childhood trauma to set the stage for paraphilic behaviors.

— *Low self-esteem: Feelings* of inadequacy and self-doubt, the outgrowth of predisposition factors and early childhood trauma, fuel patterned responses that take the form of fantasy. Fantasy operates as a stand-in for interpersonal relationships that the person is incapable of forming as a result of feelings of rejection and failure.

— *Early fantasy and paraphilic development: Social* isolation mobilises paraphilic involvement.

Fantasy, masturbation. facilitation, and paraphilic stimuli (fetishes, rituals) become part of a cyclical process. The particular paraphilic involvement is directly related to early childhood trauma (e.g., a fetish for a particular item is associated with some aspect of the offender's childhood or person the offender was closely involved with in childhood).

— *Paraphilic process: The* paraphilic process is cyclical, involving interacting elements including paraphilic stimuli and fantasy, orgasmic conditioning, and facilitation.

— *Stressors: Feelings* associated with early childhood trauma act as triggering mechanisms.

Environmental, situational, or interpersonal events that generate strong feelings and reinforce early trauma are stressors that trigger a momentary loss of control that "feeds back" to the need to engage in paraphilic behavior. Response to stressors can include extreme behavior such as sexual homicide.

— *Behavioural manifestations: The* paraphilic behavior functions as a reinforcer, sequences back to the fantasy, and escalating into more extreme behaviors.

— *Increasingly violent fantasies: As* fantasies become increasingly violent, paraphilic stimuli progress in intensity, duration, and frequency. Each time the individual engages in fantasy and paraphilic behavior, the need for increased stimulation and violent sexual arousal ensues, becoming part of the cycle or feedback loop.

The identification of an offense theme is particularly important in understanding sexual homicide. Because such offenses are so extreme, the behaviors committed within such acts reflect the psychopathology of the offender. The behavioural evidence found in sexual homicide reflects a continuum of organised-disorganised behaviors and related psychopathology. In sexual homicide, the offense themes and signature aspects of the offense are often strikingly salient and unusual. Behaviors such as evidence of planning, style of attack, type of weapon used, severity of wounds to victim's body, selection of victim, disposition or positioning of body, evidence of severe cruelty and torture offer insights into who the offender is. The unique sexual fantasy of the offender is acted out in sexual homicide. The offender's fantasy contains demographic, relational, paraphilic, situational, and self-perception components that are revealed through the offender's behavior. Meloy offers the following example:

> ... The perpetrator may imagine that a 15-year-old female (demographic) becomes his sex slave (relational), and he is able to annually and orally rape her at his whim (paraphilic) in his isolated mountain cabin (situational), thus enhancing his sense of omnipotence and gratifying himself sadistically (self-perception).

Thus, the victim's age, victim-offender interaction, nature of sex acts, location of offense, and evidence of offender self-perception (inferred through evidence of antemortem wounds and other crime scene evidence) contain key information regarding the offender's fantasy, way of relating, and psychopathology and the overall theme of the offense.

There are a number of well-known typologic of sexual homicide. Although not all serial murders are sexual homicide offenders, many serial murder typologic have been applied to sexual homicide with the belief that most serial killers are sexually motivated and most sexual homicide offenders will not stop their behavior if given the chance to continue. Typologic most often noted in discussions of sexual homicide include Holmes and De Burger's motivational serial murder typology and Keppel and Walter's sexual homicide typology. The Holmes and De Burger typology includes four types, each similar to one of the types in the Keppel and Walter power-anger typology:

— *Visionary killer: Motivated* by psychosis; auditory and visual hallucinations tell the offender to kill and engage in particular acts (Ed Gein is an example of a visionary killer). Similar to Keppel and Walter's power reassurance type.

— *Mission serial killer: Motivated* by revenge/retaliation against a particular group of people. Offender is in touch with reality and acts on a conscious, self-imposed duty to rid the world of a particular group of people (Gary Ridgway is an example of a mission killer). Similar to Keppel and Walter's anger retaliatory type.

— *Hedonistic serial killer: Motivated* by lust and thrill. Killing is an eroticism experience fuelled by the linking of sex and violence in the developmental history of the offender (Jerry Brudos is an example of a hedonistic killer). Similar to Keppel and Walter's anger excitation type.

— *Power-control serial killer: Motivated* by power, omnipotence, entitlement, with sexual gratification from domination of the victim. Similar to Keppel and Walter's power assertive type.

Many sexual homicide offenders have a history of cruelty to animals involving sadistic experimentation. Merz-Perez and Hide suggest that three types of offenders can be explained by three motivational theories illustrating the links between animal cruelty and human violence. The first theory, displaced aggression theory, states that individuals hurt animals and people to control and express displaced anger.

The authors suggest that Jeffrey Dahmer is an example of this type of offender because he experienced intense self-hatred and anger toward his parents. As a child, Dahmer dissected and mutilated animals, practising techniques he would later use on victims including severing the head of a dog and impaling it on a stick. The second theory, sadistic theory, explains animal and human violence in terms of pleasure.

Sadistic offenders, such as Leonard Lake, enjoy the process of killing and the shock and terror expressed by victims. The third theory, the sexually polymorphous theory, states that individuals harm animals and people for sexual pleasure. For these offenders, sexual homicide is necessary for sexual arousal. Henry Lee Lucas is an example of a sexually polymorphous type. Dahmer, Lake, and Lucas all had histories of animal cruelty in childhood, fantasy, and escalating propensity for violence. Their motivation differ, but all are sexual homicide offenders. Merz-Perez and Heide's typology suggests that, even within the small group of identified sexual homicide offenders, motives are heterogeneous.

Meloy's typology of sexual homicide offenders distinguishes between two types of offenders based on an integrative model of offense behavior. The model is particularly useful in that it integrates existing literature, taking into account biological, psychological, and developmental contributions to sexual homicide and behavioural manifestations reflected in crime scene evidence.

Offenders are distinguished based on nature of offense (organised or disorganised), clinical diagnosis (DSM Axis I and Axis II), level of psychopathy (severe or mild/moderate), attachment pathology (chronically detached or attachment hunger), autonomic nervous system arousal (hypo-reactive or hyper-reactive), and presence or absence of early trauma. Based on this model, there are two types of sexual homicide offenders:

— Compulsive: characterised by organised offense characteristics, sexual sadism, antisocial or narcissistic personality, severe psychopathy, chronic detachment, and hypo-reactivity (need high level of stimulation for arousal), early trauma often absent.

— Catathymic: characterised by disorganised offense characteristics, mood disorder, various personality traits and disorders, mild-moderate psychopathy, attachment hunger, and hyper-reactivity (need low level of stimulation for arousal); early trauma often present This model is an important contribution to the literature on sexual homicide. The bimodal classification scheme is both practical (for use in the criminal justice system). And theoretically and empirically rich.

Sex Offending and Gender

Sexual assault data are difficult to collect because many victims do not report the offense. Policies, practices, and public perception can influence reporting practices, and official statistics tend to underestimate the extent of sexual offenses. This is especially problematic in determining the extent of rape and sexual assault committed against males because masculinity norms make it difficult for many men to report rape.

Furthermore, when females are the perpetrators of sexual assault and rape, the problem is compounded by legal definitions of rape, which define rape behavior in terms of male penetration of a female. However, many jurisdictions have made their legal definitions of rape and "sexual intercourse" gender neutral. For example, a person is guilty of rape in the first degree in Washington State when such person engages in sexual intercourse with another person by forcible compulsion by which the perpetrator or an accessory:

— Uses or threatens to use a deadly weapon or what appears to be a deadly weapon.

— Kidnaps the victim.

— Inflicts serious physical injury, including but not limited to physical injury, which renders the victim unconscious.

— Feloniously enters into the building or vehicle where the victim is situated.

Sexual intercourse is defined as follows:

— Has its ordinary meaning and occurs upon any penetration, however slight.

— Also means any penetration of the vagina or anus however slight, by an object, when committed on one person by another, whether such persons are of the same or opposite sex, except when such penetration is accomplished for medically recognised treatment or diagnostic purposes.

— Also means any act of sexual contact between persons involving the sex organs of one person and the mouth or anus of another whether such persons are of the same or opposite sex.

Female Sex Offenders

Sex offending has been viewed as a predominantly male behavior. And, in fact, female sex offending is rare in comparison with similar offenses committed by men. However, female sexual offenders have been identified in increasing numbers in recent years and it is likely that this number will continue to grow with changing perceptions of the gendered nature of crime.

Cultural views of women as non-aggressive, nurturing caretakers have historically masked sexual abuse committed by females. The widely held belief that women are not capable of sex crimes has allowed many female sex offenders to go unnoticed, but there are documented cases of a heterogeneous group of female sex offenders who abuse children, other women, and men. Victims of female sex offenders tend to be child relatives or acquaintances. Female offenders account for 5% of female child molestation and 20% of male child molestation.

Female sexual offenders report a higher incidence of sexual abuse in childhood than do male sexual offenders and a history of drug and alcohol abuse, poor coping skills, and depression and personality disorders. Female sex offenders engage in many forms of sexual offending including sexual contact disguised as caretaking, sexual acts committed with a co-offender (usually a male), indirect participation in sexual assault by allowing victims to be assaulted with their knowledge and assistance, and indirect sexual acts (e.g., walking around nude in front of children for the purpose of sexual arousal, masturbating in front of children), ritual/group sexual abuse, and (in rare cases) rape of men.

In many respects, acts of female sexual violence and assault resemble sexual behavior committed by men, with the exception that women do not force their penises into victims in the process of assault. Hislop asks the question on many people's minds regarding the notion of female sex offenders:

> "What harm can be done without a penis?"

This question gets to the heart of the gendered nature of sexual offending and Naffine's call for the de-construction of the harm associated with rape discussed previously. As long as sex offending and rape are viewed as exclusively male behaviors involving the use of the penis as a weapon, female sex offenders will remain undetected, male victims will be overlooked, and male offenders will use the social construction of the penis-as-weapon in the cognitive schemes that fuel and neutralise their rape behaviors.

Research on female sex offenders is in its infancy. No psychological instruments currently available are specific to female sexual offending, and much of what's known about female sexual offenders is based on case studies and small samples. The studies that have been conducted suggest that females commonly engage in the same sex acts with children as do male child molesters (including fondling, oral stimulation, and intercourse). Sexual penetration with objects may be more commonly engaged in by female sexual offenders and some studies suggest that the abuse committed by female offenders may be more severe than that committed by men. Female sexual abusers have been reported to use fingers or objects to penetrate their victims' vaginas and rectums including bizarre objects such as sticks, lit matches or candles, knives, metal toys, bottles, knitting needles, lit cigarettes, coat hangers, thorny rose stems, vacuum cleaner parts, goldfish, light bulbs, dildos, and vibrators. There are also documented cases in which females are penetrated by their male and female victims.

Little is known regarding the existence of female sexual sadists, lust murderers, or sexual homicide offenders. Cases of sexual sadism, sexual homicide, and serial murder committed by women have been documented, but again, much of what is known has been gleaned from case studies rather than empirical investigation.

The problem with the lack of knowledge regarding female sexual offenders is twofold. First, many researchers apply theories and research developed from male offender samples to females. This "add women and stir" approach has hindered understanding of the nature and dynamics of female sexual offending. Much of what we know about female offenders in general, and female sexual offenders in particular, is shredded in stereotypes and researcher bias. Second, even though there are documented cases of female sexual offending and the available statistics under-report the incidence and prevalence of female sexual offending, sexual offending is still predominantly a male offense. Because female sexual offending is such a rare phenomenon, it is difficult to conduct empirical research on such a low-base-rate behavior.

One question of interest is whether or not the definition of sexual homicide should be expanded to include female sexual homicide offenders, or if the motives of female serial murders have historically been misinformed. Despite documented cases to the contrary, some researchers and law enforcement professionals continue to proclaim that there is no such thing as a female serial killer let alone a female

sexual homicide offender. Aileen Wuornos is often (incorrectly) referred to as the "first female serial killer" by the popular press and some academics and members of law enforcement. Some authors suggest that though her murders were not sexually sadistic, they do meet the general definition of sexual homicide found in the forensic literature—"an intentional killing during which there is sexual activity by the perpetrator", and that her behavior may represent a variant of serial sexual homicide by a female offender. With the virtual absence of research and theory on female sexual homicide, examination of the possibility of a female variant of this behavior through analysis of the Wuornos and other cases is an important area for future research.

Male Rape and Sexual Assault Victims

An area that is perhaps just as under-researched as female sexual homicide is the rape and sexual assault of adult men. It would appear from the literature and statistics on sex offending that rape and sexual assault are rarely committed against men, except in prison settings. However, researchers have acknowledged that even though rape and sexual assault are predominantly crimes committed by men against women, there may be many more male victims than research and statistics reflect.

Male rape victims experience shame, stigmatisation, and unique pressures to keep quiet about their victimisation. Accounts of male rape victims also suggest that many do not report such crimes because they believe males can't be raped or they feel responsible in some way for their victimisation. Greater attention is beginning to be paid to the phenomenon of male rape committed by male offenders, but the phenomenon of male rape and sexual assault committed by female offenders (in particular cases in which women force adult males to engage in sexual intercourse) is barely mentioned in the literature beyond an occasionally anecdotal account in passing.

The popular perception of rape as a male crime of violence against women has resulted in the lack of attention to the phenomenon of male rape. As with the focus on female sex offenders, attention to male rape raises criticism that such focus distracts from the larger problem of sexual violence by men against women. However, the feminist writings of the 1970s and the attention to the power-violence elements of rape drew research attention to male rape, particularly in prisons and other correctional facilities.

Early writings on male rape include an essay by Brown miller on the power dynamics of male-on-male rape in prison, and a section on male rape in Groth's work, which included accounts of rapes committed by heterosexual-, homosexual-, and bisexual-identified offenders who committed rapes outside of the prison setting (involving predominantly stranger or acquaintance rapes in cases where the victim was a hitchhiker picked up by the offender or assaulted in an outdoor setting).

It is estimated that approximately 5 to 10% of reported rapes in the United States and the United Kingdom (where the bulk of the research has been conducted) involve male victims. Because male victims are much less likely to report having been raped, the prevalence of male rape is largely unknown. Male rape occurs in diverse contexts such as military organisations, in warfare, and in psychiatric institutions, prisons, and community settings.

The typical male rapist is a young. Fualaau was 21. The two have been together ever since, were married in 2005 in a ceremony that aired on Entertainment Tonight, and live with their two daughters in the Seattle area.

Virtually every study conducted on the subject suggests the motivation for male rape is anger or attempt to overpower, humiliate, and degrade victims rather than lust, passion, or sexual desire. Homosexual men are victims at a much higher rate than heterosexual men, and Black victims are over-represented in relation to their percentage in the communities in which studies have been conducted. Beauregard and Proulx conducted a case study analysis of 10 sexual murderers of adult male victims and proposed a typology of sexual homicide murderers of men (the authors avoid the term homosexual homicide because sexual murderers of men encompass those who kill both heterosexual and homosexual men), which yielded three distinct types: the avenger (motivated by anger and revenge), the sexual predator (motivated by sexual fantasies), and the nonsexual predator (instrumental motivated robbery that turned into murder on victim resistance).

Beauregard and Proulx's typology suggests that sexual murderers of men are more likely motivated by revenge and profit, which has not been found to be a primary motivation of sexual homicide murderers of women. In his important and pioneering work, Male on Male Rape, Scarce notes that the reality of male rape "invokes a recognition of self vulnerability and homophobia". Whereas girls and women grow up learning about the possibility of rape and the normalisation of sexual violence against women, male rape is rarely discussed, and when the images of male rape appear (in media, TV, film), the reaction is often mockery or malicious humour (e.g., "drop the soap jokes"). Male rape victims experience many of the traumatic effects of rape that female victims experience (e.g., post-traumatic stress, anger, stigma, shame, body image and self-esteem issues), but appear to experience other effects to a greater degree than female victims such as surprise, conflicting sense of sexual orientation (interpreting the experience as an act of sex), and heightened sense of vulnerability. Male rape victims also have difficulty seeking support and resources in the aftermath of rape. According to a male rape survivor,

Development of Sex Offending Behaviour

The question How does a person become a sex offender? Is of primary interest to those in the mental health and criminal justice systems who hope to understand these offenders in order to treat and manage their behaviors. Although most criminal behavior is understandable or at least imaginable, sex crimes, particularly the sexual homicide of children, are incomprehensible to the average person.

For those who are not personally or professionally involved in the treatment or management of sex offenders, the question is often a matter of curiosity regarding what exactly would compel a person to engage in the most socially stigmatised and unconscionable of all criminal behaviors. For others, perhaps those who have been victims of sexual assault or who have a family member accused or convicted of a sex crime, answers may bring hope, understanding, or alleviation of anxiety and guilt. Some victims of sex crimes, both children and adults, blame themselves for many years in the aftermath of the offense. Family members of sex offenders often wonder what they could have done to prevent the behavior. Understanding what it takes to create a person who thinks he is entitled to rape any woman he sees on the street, who sexually preys on children, or who is sexually aroused by domination, torture, and mutilation offers hope that a social problem of such magnitude can be managed, dealt with, or controlled.

The complexity and ambiguity of the answers academics and clinicians are able to provide is far from satisfactory. Researchers have made gains in identifying developmental themes and risk factors for sex offending behavior, but as is true with most human behavior, the answers do not come in a convenient magic potion.

In thinking about what makes a person a sex offender, the first step is to separate remote or developmental influences that contribute to deviant sexual preference, fantasy, urges, and aggression from factors that contribute to the behavioural act of committing a sexual offense. In other words, some people are diagnosed with pedophilia because they have a sexual preference for children involving urges and fantasies and do not act on these thoughts and feelings. Such a person is a paedophile, but not a sex offender, until the fantasies are acted on. So the question "How does a person become a sex offender?" Involves asking two sub-questions:

— How does a person develop deviant sexual preferences, urges, and fantasies?

— What is it that sends people with these fantasies, preferences, and urges over the edge? Some types of sex offenders such as rapists and situational child molesters have developed "normal" sexual preferences. So the first sub-question applies differently depending on the type of offender. However, even rapists who have no history of mental disorder, paraphilia, or deviant sexual arousal patterns generally have urges and fantasies before they commit their crimes. So if we speak of urges rather than sexual preference, both questions can be asked of all types of sex offenders.

The literature on the development of sex offending consists of two distinct avenues of theory and research—aetiological theories and risk assessment. Aetiological theories attempt to explain the developmental processes that set the stage for sex offending behavior. The risk assessment explains sex offending behavior in terms of risk and protective factors that make a person more or less inclined to commit sex offending behavior. Beech and Ward integrate both approaches, offering an integrative model of sex offending behavior that explains sex offending in terms of:

— *Developmental factors: abuse*, rejection, attachment problems

— *Static factors: persistence* and range of offending, psychosocial problems (antisocial history), historical risk factors not subject to change (e.g., never married, number of past offenses, etc.).

— Stable dynamic factors: offense-supportive cognition, level of interpersonal functioning, self-regulation problems

— *Acute dynamic factors: physiological* arousal, deviant thoughts and fantasies, need for intimacy, affective states

— Triggering events/*Contextual risk factors: victim* access, social dislocation, substance abuse, relationship conflict, antisocial peers, noncooperation with supervision

Deviant Sexual Preferences

No one decides what their sexual orientation will be—whether they will be attracted to males, females, adults, or children. Similarly, people have little say in whether they will develop a mental illness or personality disorder, or the sorts of environmental conditions in which they will be raised as children. Although "heterogeneity of developmental background and offense behavior is the rule with sexual offenders" factors such as sexual abuse in childhood, attachment disruptions in infancy, dysfunctional family environment, conditioning processes, social learning, biological predisposition to mental disorder, or particular personality traits appear to shape sex (and other) offending behavior.

Studies of sex offenders reveal a long list of remote risk factors for sex offending behavior, many of which are also seen in violent offenders.Explaining any criminal behavior requires attention to biological, sociological, cultural, psychological, routine activity/opportunity, and phenomenology factors. The sex offender develops the urge, fantasy, and/or sexual preference associated with the offense through cumulative misfortune. Biologically based sexual drive, misdirected through conditioning processes and reinforced by early childhood sexual victimisation, is all it takes to create the urge or inclination to sexually offend. But it takes more than this to actually act on such urges.

Particular childhood risk factors appear to be associated with sex offending later in life including maternal neglect, lack of supervision, sexual abuse by a female, witnessing intrafamilial violence, and cruelty to animals. Being a male and a victim of sexual abuse in childhood are the most frequently cited risk factors for becoming a sex offender later in life. Factors that contribute to the development and expression of human sexuality also influence sex offending behavior. Genetic factors such as aggressiveness and impulsiveness, sex drive, neurotransmitter, and hormones play a role as do attachment processes and sociocultural factors. Childhood stressors such as poor child-parent bonds, low self-esteem, poor quality of relationships, inadequate emotional coping skills, and prior sexual abuse lead to reliance on sexualise coping (masturbation, sex acts) as an escape from difficult issues. Frequent pairing of sexual arousal through masturbation with inappropriate fantasy (particularly involving violence and control) leads to increased likelihood of using sex offense behavior as a coping mechanism.

In recent years, research on the development of sex offending behavior has focused a great deal on early childhood attachment. Attachment theory is based on the universality of attachment processes in humans and primates.

Bonding and attachment between infants and primary care-givers are universal needs in humans and primates. When primary care-givers are inaccessible, inconsistent, and fail to nurture or there is disruption in the bonding process, infants will fail to attach and may detach permanently. This theory has been applied to sex offenders, psychopaths and predatory offenders, and serial killers. Sex offenders have insecure/ disorganised attachment styles that interfere with their ability to form close interpersonal relationships.

Disorganised attachment refers to the lack or collapse of a strategy for dealing with the need for security and comfort under stress. Disorganised attachment styles are seen in children who have experienced neglectful, chaotic, abusive circumstances and perceive their parent simultaneously as a source of both comfort and distress. Sex offending is a distorted attempt by individuals who do not have the ability to form appropriate relationships to seek closeness, "one of several available external-interpersonally based self-regulatory strategies".

Individuals with insecure attachment styles have a particular vulnerability to sex offending when they are exposed to particular biological, sociocultural, and situational factors that reinforce or facilitate such behavior. Sex offenders experience more loneliness, interpersonal anxiety, external locus of control, and avoidance and engage in coercive sexual behavior to satisfy their emotional needs.

Sex offending behavior is reinforced through a chain of conditioning and cognitive processes that set the stage for an ongoing cycle of offending behaviour:

Once a sexual offense has been perpetrated, memories are established that may be elaborated into inappropriate sexual fantasies, thus leading to urges to re-offend. In addition, offenders employ a number of cognitive distortions such as minimisation or victim blaming, to reduce feelings of guilt and fear of being caught, thus allowing the cycle of sexual offending to repeat.

Deviant Fantasies

The development of the urge to sexually offend is determined by biological, psychological, and sociological/ environmental forces beyond the offender's control, but for those who do not have a clinically diagnosable psychosis (who have the potential to be declared legally insane), the decision to act on the urge to commit a sex crime falls more clearly within the bounds of free will and conscious choice. It is at this stage of the offending process that psychological, routine activity/opportunity, and phenomenology factors play a greater role. For example, proximate risk factors found to be associated with the behavioural expression of pedophilia include psychiatric disorders, substance abuse disorders, and psychosocial stress involving the loss of a relationship. Sex offending occurs when vulnerable individuals experience stress, proximate risk factors (such as mental illness, substance use, exposure to pornography) and, from a routine activities perspective, are in close proximity to an available victim in the absence of guardians and social controls.

Cultural facilitation, though not the source of the desire to offend, are powerful situational/contextual factors that fuel fantasy development and facilitate sex offending behavior. Facilitation include alcohol and drug use, social climate, pornography, books, media, Internet chat rooms, computer images, films, and aspects of pop culture that validate (or are interpreted to validate) sex offending behavior.

For example, Michael Briere pleaded guilty in June 2004 to the murder of Holly Johne's, a 10-year-old Toronto girl. After his arrest, he told police that on the evening of the offense he had viewed child pornography on the Internet on his home computer and was overwhelmed by a desire for sex with a little girl. He then stepped outside his apartment, abducted Holly Johne's, dragged her into his bedroom, sexually assaulted her, and then killed her. Her body, which Briere admitted dismembering, was found in parts in various places in Toronto. The behaviour of all types of sex offenders, from rapists to child molesters to sexual homicide offenders, is influenced by cultural facilitation in some way. Pornography appears to play a key role in the fantasy development that precipitates sex offending and sexual homicide.

The role of the Internet in facilitating sex offending behavior has only begun to be empirically explored. Recent research by Quayle and Tailor suggests that viewing pornography on the Internet normalises sex offending behavior in the minds of potential offenders and provides a social network for production and trade of child pornography and Internet seduction of children.

When potential sex offenders use pornographic magazines or videos, they tend to do so in isolation. The Internet offers a virtual community where deviant sexual interests and distorted cognition are justified and validated within an on-line subculture. This "community" facilitates sexual offending by coaching users and justifying their behavior in isolation from the "real world" in which cognitive distortions and sex offending behaviors would be challenged.

For potential sex offenders who are already socially and emotionally isolated, the Internet decreases social engagement with mainstream society while reinforcing sexually deviant fantasy. There is some evidence in this initial research to suggest that the particular experience of using Internet pornography may empower some potential sex offenders, facilitating an increase in actual contact offenses, but for others, it may promote a move to sexually exciting, but legal behaviors (e.g., sexual activity with adults).

Other facilitation such as use of drugs and alcohol (by the offender and/or the victim in the case of date and acquaintance rapes), media images linking sex and violence and depicting gendered cultural stereotypes, mental illness, involvement in hyper-masculine subcultures, and stress such as the loss of a job or the dissolution of a relationship can be the "straw that broke the camel's back" for edge-sitters who have the urges and inclination to sexually offend, but haven't yet acted on them. For example, Gary Ridgway, the Green River Killer, began his career as a sexual homicide offender after his first divorce, and his offending behavior increased during problematic periods in his relationships with women.

Sex offending behavior is associated with static and dynamic risk factors and a particular developmental history. The urge to sexually offend is rooted in biological forces and early childhood experiences that lead to sex offending as a coping strategy. This strategy is more likely and more often employed when particular stressors or dis-inhibiting facilitation are present. Burk and Burkhart offer a rich synopsis of biological, sociocultural, and attachment processes that explain how a person becomes a sex offender:

Every person is equipped with a drive to survive, and so, even violent acts with socially devastating consequences can come to serve as a means for self preservation.... Any behavior, adaptive or maladaptive, can come to serve a self-regulatory purpose and assist the individual in reestablishing internal control. Empirical observations regarding the background of sexual offenders suggest that maladaptive strategies (substance use, interpersonal violence, sexual deviance, property crimes, impulsive behavior) are readily modelled in the environment and consequently, may be more likely to be adopted.

Thus, this complex attachment system may serve as a diathesis which interacts with particular stressors (previous sexual victimisation, exposure to misogynists cultural/media stimuli, peer deviance) to potentiate controlling/abusive behavior.... Processes other than attachment continue to influence the individual throughout their development, and factors such as conditioned sexual arousal, opportunity and chance likely play equal or greater parts in the maintenance of continued sexual offenses.

Thus, the ways in which particular biological, sociological/environmental, psychological, and cultural factors and forces play out in a person's life as well as the meanings attached to particular events and opportunities one encounters steer a person in one direction or the other. Sex offending becomes a deeply rooted and conditioned coping strategy, a deviant and socially destructive variant of the more benign strategies individuals with more fortunate life histories and developmental circumstances use.

7

Basics of Penology

Penology is a section of criminology that deals with the philosophy and practice of various societies in their attempts to repress criminal activities, and satisfy public opinion via an appropriate treatment regime for persons convicted of criminal offenses. Penology is concerned with the effectiveness of those social processes devised and adopted for the prevention of crime, via the repression or inhibition of criminal intent via the fear of punishment.

The study of penology therefore deals with the treatment of prisoners and the subsequent rehabilitation of convicted criminals. It also encompasses aspects of probation (rehabilitation of offenders in the community) as well as penitentiary science relating to the secure detention and retraining of offenders committed to secure institutions.

Penology concerns many topics and theories, including those concerning prisons (Prison reform, Prisoner abuse, Prisoners' rights, and Recidivism), as well as theories of the purposes of punishment (such as Deterrence, Rehabilitation, Retribution, and Utilitarianism). Contemporary penology concerns itself mainly with criminal rehabilitation and prison management. The word seldom applies to theories and practices of punishment in less formal environments such as parenting, school and work-place correctional measures.

History

Historical theories of punishment were based on the notion that fearful consequences would discourage potential offenders. Example of this principle can be found in the Draconian law of ancient Greece and the Bloody Code which persisted in Renaissance England, when (at various times) capital punishment was prescribed for over 200 offenses. Similarly, certain headed offenses under Sharia hadith tradition may incur fearful penalties.

Modern theories of the punishment and rehabilitation of offenders are broadly based on ancient scriptural texts of the Christian Bible and the Moslem Qur'an, which principles only reappeared in Europe some time after the publication of a seminal pamphlet "On Crimes and Punishments" published by Cesare, Marquis of Beccaria in 1764. It is based on the notion of proportionality. Previously, (for example, under England's Bloody Code) the penalty of theft had been the same regardless of the value stolen, giving rise to the English expression "It is as well to be hanged for a sheep or a lamb"

Subsequent development of the ideas of Beccaria made non-lethal punishment more socially acceptable. Consequently convicted prisoners had to be reintegrated into society when their punishment was complete.

Western Approach

In Europe, and many westernized legal systems, criminal punishments now tend to be in accordance with a popular theory once expressed by Martin Luther King around 1958: "Hate be gets hate; violence be gets violence; toughness be gets a greater toughness. We must meet the forces of hate with the power of love... Our aim must never be to defeat or humiliate the white man (i.e. our enemies), but to win his friendship and understanding."

Penologists have consequently evolved occupational and psychological education programs for offenders detained in prison, and a range of community service and probation orders which entail guidance and aftercare of the offender within the community.

The importance of inflicting some measure of punishment on those persons who breach the law is however maintained in order to maintain social order and to moderate public outrage which might provoke appeals for cruel vengeance. European penalties can only be imposed by a criminal court and include fines, damages, unpaid compensatory work, and mandatory training as well as physical detention.

Denunciation

Denunciation in the context of sentencing philosophy refers to the disapproval of an act by society that is expressed by the imposition of a sentence. This can be considered as one of the purposes of sentencing, as well as being a possible justification for the imposition of a sentence.

Denunciation arguments can be used to justify more serious sentences than are required by the principles of retribution and deterrence. Denunciation arguments can also be used to justify the existence of laws which are never in practice enforced; they stand as statements of a society's values rather than working parts of a criminal justice system.

Incapacitation

Incapacitation in the context of sentencing philosophy refers to the effect of a sentence in terms of positively preventing (rather than merely deterring) future offending. Imprisonment incapacitates the prisoner by physically removing them from the society against which they are deemed to have offended. Long term imprisonment with the intention to incapacitate is often used by criminal justice systems against habitual criminals who recidivate.

Examples of incapacitation include back-to-back life sentences, three-strikes sentencing, and other habitual offender laws. Cutting off a hand of a thief is also an example; this acts to prevent further thefts in a drastic manner, in addition to it having a perceived deterrent effect on others.

Rehabilitation

The assumption of rehabilitation is that people are not permanently criminal and that it is possible to restore a criminal to a useful life, to a life in which they contribute to themselves and to society. A goal of rehabilitation is to prevent habitual offending, also known as criminal recidivism. Rather than punishing the harm out of a criminal, rehabilitation would seek, by means of education or therapy, to bring a criminal into a more normal state of mind, or into an attitude which would be helpful to society, rather than be harmful to society.

This theory of punishment is based on the notion that punishment is to be inflicted on an offender so as to reform him/her, or rehabilitate them so as to make their reintegration into society easier. Punishments that are in accordance with this theory are community service, probation orders, and any form of punishment which entails any form of guidance and aftercare towards the offender.

This theory is founded on the belief that one cannot inflict a severe punishment of imprisonment and expect the offender to be reformed and to be able to reintegrate into society upon his release. Indeed, the United States Code states that sentencing judges shall make imprisonment decisions "recognising that imprisonment is not an appropriate means of promoting correction and rehabilitation". Although the importance of inflicting punishment on those persons who breach the law, so as to maintain social order, is retained, the importance of rehabilitation is also given priority. Humanitarians have, over the years, supported rehabilitation as an alternative, even for capital punishment.

Practical Difficulties

Rehabilitation theories present however the following deficiencies:

First, there are no sound scientific research to determine how different individuals react to the same rehabilitating methods.

Second, rehabilitation may depend more decisively on the individual psychological background, hence on his particular motives to commit crimes, than on the rehabilitating methods or philosophy.

Third, a rehabilitation program may prove to be too costly and complex to be successfully implemented in most countries.

Finally, rehabilitation must refer to the sociological findings on the socialisation and re-socialisation processes, as change in lifelong socially acquired patterns of behavior and values entails a much more complex–and sometime traumatic–change on the individual's structure of character.

Psychopathy and Recidivism

Criminal recidivism is highly correlated with psychopathy. The psychopath is defined by an uninhibited gratification in criminal, sexual, or aggressive impulses and the inability to learn from past mistakes. Individuals with this disorder gain satisfaction through their antisocial behavior and lack remorse for their actions.

Findings indicate psychopathic prisoners have a 2.5 time higher probability of being released from jail than undiagnosed ones, even though they are more likely to recidivate.

It has been shown that punishment and behavior modification techniques do not improve the behavior of a psychopath. Psychopathic individuals have been regularly observed to become more cunning and better able to hide their behaviour. It has been suggested by them traditional therapeutic approaches actually make psychopaths if not worse, then far more adept at manipulating others and concealing their behavior. They are generally considered to be not only incurable but also un-treatable.

Psychopaths also have a markedly distorted sense of the potential consequences of their actions, not only for others, but also for themselves. They do not, for example, deeply recognise the risk of being caught, disbelieved or injured as a result of their behaviour.

8

Nature and Types of Punishment

Punishment is the authoritative imposition of something negative or unpleasant on a person or animal in response to behavior deemed wrong by an individual or group. Inflicted unpleasantness without authority is not punishment, but is characterised as something else. Punishment may be administered following a formal decision process, or informally within any organised group, for example, a family. Punishment does not automatically cause deterrence, prevention, or reform, and hence, is not a guarantee these outcomes will occur. Furthermore, punishment can be part of a process of disciplining. Punishment also has justifications. For example, in the western societies there are four fundamental justifications: retribution, deterrence, rehabilitation, and incapacitation.

The word is the abstract sub-stantivation of the verb to punish, which has been recorded in English since 1340, deriving from Old French punish-, an extended form of the stem of pannier "to punish", from Latin punier "inflict a penalty on, cause pain for some offense", earlier pioneer, from poena "penalty, punishment of great loss". Latin punier possibly was inspired by the Phoenician method of execution by means of crucifixion. Therefore the Carragheenin crosses were called signal poenae "signs of the Phoenicians".

Colloquial use of "punish" for "inflict heavy damage or loss" is first recorded in 1801, originally in boxing; the meaning "hard-hitting" is from 1811. Just deserts no doubt reflects this in modern theories of punishment.

The concept of matching fair consequences to crimes is called justice. The concept of punishments being abusively employed is called abuse of justice, a form of injustice, or (more generally) abuse of power. For example false imprisonment and political imprisonment are examples of where the authority has misused their power to impose punishments.

In common usage, the word "punishment" might be described as "an authorised imposition of deprivations—of freedom or privacy or other goods to which the person otherwise has a right, or the imposition of special burdens—because the person has been found guilty of some criminal violation, typically (though not invariably) involving harm to the innocent."

Introduced by B.F. Skinner, punishment has a more restrictive and technical definition. Along with reinforcement it belongs under the Operant Conditioning category. Operant Conditioning refers to learning with either punishment or reinforcement. It is also referred to as response-stimulus conditioning. In psychology, punishment is the reduction of a behavior via application of an adverse stimulus ("positive punishment") or removal of a pleasant stimulus ("negative punishment").

Extra chores or spanking are examples of positive punishment, while making an offending student lose recess or play privileges are examples of negative punishment. The definition requires that punishment is only determined after the fact by the reduction in behavior; if the offending behavior of the subject does not decrease then it is not considered punishment. There is some conflation of punishment and aversive, though an aversive that does not decrease behavior is not considered punishment.

Scope of Application

Punishments are applied for various purposes, most generally, to encourage and enforce proper behavior as defined by society or family. Criminals are punished judicially, by fines, corporal punishment or custodial sentences such as prison; detainees risk further punishments for breaches of internal rules. Children, pupils and other trainees may be punished by their educators or instructors (mainly parents, guardians, or teachers, tutors and coaches).

Slaves, domestic and other servants used to be punishable by their masters. Employees can still be subject to a contractual form of fine or demotion. Most hierarchical organisations, such as military and police forces, or even churches, still apply quite rigid internal discipline, even with a judicial system of their own (court martial, canonical courts).

Punishment may also be applied on moral, especially religious, grounds, as in penance (which is voluntary) or imposed in a theocracy with a religious police (as in a strict Islamic state like Iran or under the Taliban) or (though not a true theocracy) by Inquisition.

History and Rationale

The progress of civilisation has resulted in a change alike in the theory and in the method of punishment. In primitive society punishment was left to the individuals wronged or their families, and was vindictive or retributive: in quantity and quality it would bear no special relation to the character or gravity of the offense.

Gradually there would arise the idea of proportionate punishment, of which the characteristic type is an eye for an eye. The second stage was punishment by individuals under the control of the state, or community, in the third stage, with the growth of law, the state took over the primitive function and provided itself with the machinery of justice for the maintenance of public order. Henceforward crimes are against the state, and the exaction of punishment by the wronged individual is illegal (compare Lynch Law).

Even at this stage the vindictive or retributive character of punishment remains, but gradually, and specially after the humanist movement under thinkers like Beccaria and Jeremy Bentham, new theories begin to emerge. Two chief trains of thought have combined in the condemnation of primitive theory and practice.

On the one hand the retributive principle itself has been very largely superseded by the protective and the reformative; on the other punishments involving bodily pain have become objectionable to the general sense of society. Consequently corporal and even capital punishment occupy a far less prominent position, and tend everywhere to disappear.

It began to be recognised also that stereotyped punishments, such as belong to penal codes, fail to take due account of the particular condition of an offence and the character and circumstances of the offender. A fixed fine, for example, operates very unequally on rich and poor.

Modern theories date from the 18th century, when the humanitarian movement began to teach the dignity of the individual and to emphasise his rationality and responsibility. The result was the reduction of punishment both in quantity and in severity, the appearance of the prison system, and the first attempts to study the psychology of crime and to distinguish between classes of criminals with a view to their improvement.

These latter problems are the province of criminal anthropology and criminal sociology, sciences so called because they view crime as the outcome of anthropological viz. Social conditions. The law breaker is himself a product of social evolution and cannot be regarded as solely responsible for his disposition to transgress. Habitual crime is thus to be treated as a disease. Punishment can, therefore, be justified only insofar as it either protects society by removing temporarily or permanently one who has injured it, or acting as a deterrent, or aims at the moral regeneration of the criminal. Thus the retributive theory of punishment with its criterion of justice as an end in itself gives place to a theory which regards punishment solely as a means to an end, utilitarian or moral, according as the common advantage or the good of the criminal is sought.

In his 1975 book *Discipline and Punish,* Michel Foucault describes in detail the evolution of punishment from hanging, drawing and quartering of medieval times to the modern systems of fines and prisons. He sees a trend in criminal punishment from vengeance by the King to a more practical, utilitarian concern for deterrence and rehabilitation.

A particularly harsh punishment is sometimes said to be draconian, after Draco, the lawgiver of the classical polish of Athens. But as the adjective Spartan still testifies, its wholly militarised rival Sparta was the harshest a state of law can be on its own citizens, e.g. crypteia (including flogging for being caught when stealing as ordered).

In operant conditioning, punishment is the presentation of a stimulus contingent on a response which results in a decrease in response strength (as evidenced by a decrease in the frequency of response). The effectiveness of punishment in suppressing the response depends on many factors, including the intensity of the stimulus and the consistency with which the stimulus is presented when the response occurs. In parenting, additional factors that increase the effectiveness of punishment include a verbal explanation of the reason for the punishment and a good relationship between the parent and the child. There are also parent/child relations that never acquire punishment, cause nothing wrong has been done.

Reasons for Punishment

There are many possible reasons that might be given to justify or explain why someone ought to be punished; here follows a broad outline of typical, possibly contradictory, justifications.

Rehabilitation

Some punishment includes work to reform and rehabilitate the wrongdoer so that they will not commit the offence again. This is distinguished from deterrence, in that the goal here is to change the offender's attitude to what they have done, and make them come to see that their behavior was wrong.

Incapacitation / Socialite Protection

Incapacitation is a justification of punishment that refers to when the offender's ability to commit further offenses is removed. This is a forward-looking justification of punishment that views the future reductions in re-offending as sufficient justification for the punishment. This can occur in one of two ways; the offender's ability to commit crime can be physically removed, or the offender can be geographically removed.

The offender's ability to commit crime can be physically removed in several ways. This can include cutting the hands off a thief, as well as other crude punishments. The castration of offenders is another punishment that can be justified by incapacitation, furthered by recent media coverage in Britain of the proposed chemical castration of sexual offenders. Incapacitation, in this sense, can include any number of punishments including taking away the driving license of a dangerous driver but can also include capital punishment.

Despite this, incapacitation is predominately thought of as incarceration. Imprisonment has the effect of confining prisoners, physically preventing them from committing crimes against those outside, i.e. protecting the community. Before the widespread use of imprisonment, banishment was used as a form of incapacitation. Nowadays courts have a flexible array of sentence options available to them that can restrict offender's movements, and subsequently their ability to commit crime. Football hooligans can, for example, be required to attend centres during football matches.

Selective incapacitation is a modified form of incapacitation that rationalises the practice of giving only dangerous and persistent offenders long, and in some case indefinite, prison sentences. The approach adopts a utilitarian viewpoint that regards the protection, and subsequent happiness, of the majority as justification of giving excessive and indefinite prison sentences. There is, however, strong moral opposition to this concept.

Deterrence/Prevention

To act as a measure of prevention to those who are contemplating criminal activity. This deterrence is intended to prevent a re-offence by the offender by imposing a punishment that he/she wouldn't want to experience again. The aim is also to deter others in the community from committing the same or a similar offence by making an example of the offender. If this is the chief reason for punishment, the sentence may appear over-harsh when assessed against some of the other reasons.

Restoration

For minor offences, punishment may take the form of the offender "righting the wrong"; for example, a vandal might be made to clean up the mess he/she has made. In more serious cases, punishment in the form of fines and compensation payments may also be considered a sort of "restoration". Some libertarians argue that full restoration or restitution on an individualistic basis is all that is ever just, and that this is compatible with both re-tribulations and a utilitarian degree of deterrence.

Retribution

Retribution is the practice of "getting even" with a wrongdoer—the suffering of the wrongdoer is seen as good in itself, even if it has no other benefits. One reason for modern centrally-organised societies to include this judicial element is to diminish the perceived need for "street justice", blood feud and vigilantism. However, some argue that this is a "zero-sum game", that such acts of street justice and blood revenge are not removed from society, but responsibility for carrying them out is merely transferred to the state.

Retribution sets an important standard on punishment —the transgressor must get what he deserves, but no more. Therefore, a thief put to death is not retribution; a murderer put to death is. Adam Smith, who is credited as the father of Capitalism, wrote extensively about punishment. In his view, an important reason for punishment is not only deterrence, but also satisfying the resentment of the victim. Moreover, in the case of the death penalty, the retribution goes to the dead victim, not his family. (So, to extend Smith's views, a murderer can be spared the death penalty only by the victim's express wish, made when he was alive.) One great difficulty of this approach is that of judging exactly what it is that the transgressor "deserves". For instance, it may be retribution to put a thief to death if he steals a family's only means of livelihood; conversely, mitigating circumstances may lead to the conclusion that the execution of a murderer is not retribution.

Education

From German Criminal·Law, Punishment can be explained by positive prevention theory to use criminal justice system to teach people what are the social norms for what is correct and acts as a reinforcement. It teaches people to obey the law and eliminates the free-rider principle of people not obeying the law getting away with it.

Denunciation/Condemnation

Punishment can serve as a means for society to publicly express condemnation of a crime. This serves the dual function of curbing public anger away from vigilante justice, while concurrently stigmatising the condemned in an effort to deter future criminal activity. This is also known as the "Expressive Theory." Punishment, viewed in this way, helps to give society a sense of moral uprightness, tending to confirm its moral right to have a justice system that exacts punishment on those who do not confirm to society's norms. Such a purpose can be readily accused of being hypocritical.

TYPES OF PUNISHMENT

There are punishments that can be inflicted by the commandment of court; and are either corporal, or pecuniary, or ignominy, or imprisonment, or exile, or mixed of these.

Corporal Punishment

Corporal punishment is the deliberate infliction of pain as retribution for an offence, or for the purpose of disciplining or reforming a wrongdoer, or to deter attitudes or behaviour deemed unacceptable. The term usually refers to methodically striking the offender with an implement, whether in judicial, domestic, or educational settings. Corporal punishment may be divided into three main types:

— Parental or domestic corporal punishment: within the family—typically, children punished by parents or guardians;

— School corporal punishment: within schools, when students are punished by teachers or school administrators;

— Judicial corporal punishment: as part of a criminal sentence ordered by a court of law. Closely related is prison corporal punishment, ordered either directly by the prison authorities or by a visiting court.

Corporal punishment of minors within domestic settings is lawful in all 50 of the United States and, according to a 2000 survey, is widely approved by parents. It has been officially outlawed in 26 countries.

Corporal punishment in school is still legal in some parts of the world, including 20 of the States of the USA, but has been outlawed in other places, including Canada, Kenya, Japan, South Africa, New Zealand, and nearly all of Europe except the Czech Republic and France. Judicial corporal punishment has virtually disappeared from the western world but remains in force in many parts of Africa and Asia.

Corporal Punishment in the Home

Domestic corporal punishment, i.e. of children and adolescents by their parents, is usually referred to colloquially as "spanking", "whipping", "smacking," or "slapping."

In an increasing number of countries it has been outlawed, starting with Sweden in 1979. In some other countries, corporal punishment is legal, but restricted (e.g. blows to the head are outlawed and implements may not be used, and/or only children within a certain age range may be spanked).

In the United States and all African and most Asian nations, "spanking," "whipping," "smacking," or "slapping" by parents is currently legal; it is also legal to use certain implements such as a belt or paddle.

In Canada, spanking by parents or legal guardians (but nobody else) is legal, as long as the child is not under 2 years or over 12 years of age, and no implement other than an open, bare hand is used (belts, paddles, etc. are strictly prohibited). Provinces can legally impose tighter restrictions than the aforementioned national restrictions, but none currently does so.

In the UK, spanking or smacking is legal, but it may not leave a mark on the body and in Scotland since October 2003 it has been illegal to use any implements when disciplining a child.

Corporal Punishment in Schools

Legal corporal punishment of school students for misbehaviour involves striking the student on the buttocks or the palm of the hand in a premeditated ceremony with an implement specially kept for the purpose such as a rattan cane or spanking paddle, or with the open hand. It is not to be confused with cases where a teacher lashes out on the spur of the moment, which is not "corporal punishment" but violence or brutality, and is illegal almost everywhere.

Corporal punishment used to be prevalent in schools in many parts of the world, but in recent decades it has been outlawed in nearly all of Europe, and in Japan, Canada,

South Africa, New Zealand and other countries. It remains commonplace and lawful in many Asian, African and Caribbean countries.

In the United States, the Supreme Court ruled in graham v. Wright that school corporal punishment does not constitute cruel and unusual punishment under the Eighth Amendment. Paddling is used in schools in a number of Southern states, though it is on the decline. However, 30 states ban corporal punishment in public schools, and two states, New Jersey and Iowa, additionally prohibit it in private schools.

In Canada, corporal punishment has been banned in public and private schools since 2004. Every province but Alberta, Saskatchewan, and Ontario already had provincial bans prior to 2004. The first province to ban school corporal punishment was British Columbia, in 1973.

In the UK, corporal punishment was outlawed in state schools in 1987 and in all private schools by 2003.

Corporal punishment of male students has, in most cultures, generally been more prevalent and more severe than that of female students. In Queensland, Australia, school corporal punishment of girls was banned in 1934, but for boys in private schools it is still legal as of 2010. In Singapore and Malaysia, schoolboys are routinely caned for misbehaviour while the caning of girls at school is forbidden by law.

Judicial or Quasi-Judicial Punishment

Some countries retain judicial corporal punishment, including a number of former British territories such as Botswana, Malaysia, Singapore and Tanzania. In Malaysia and Singapore, for certain specified offences, males are routinely sentenced to caning in addition to a prison term. The Singapore practice of caning became much discussed around the world in 1994 when American teenager Michael P. Fay was caned for vandalism.

A number of countries with an Islamic legal system, such as Saudi Arabia, Iran, Sudan and northern Nigeria, employ judicial whipping for a range of offences. As of 2009, some regions of Pakistan are experiencing a breakdown of law and government, leading to a reintroduction of corporal punishment by ad hoc Islamists courts. As well as floggings, Saudi Arabia uses amputations or mutilation as a method of punishment. Such penalties are highly controversial. However, the term "corporal punishment" has since the 19th century usually meant caning, flogging or whipping rather than other kinds of physical penalties such as amputation.

Pros and Cons of Corporal Punishment

According to its proponents, corporal punishment offers several advantages over other kinds of punishment, such as that it is quicker to implement, costs nothing, and deters unruliness.

The American Psychological Association opposes the use of corporal punishment in schools, juvenile facilities, child care nurseries, and all other institutions, public or private, where children are cared for or educated. It claims that corporal punishment is violent and unnecessary, may lower self-esteem, and is liable to instil hostility and rage without reducing the undesired behaviour. The APA also states that corporal punishment is likely to train children to use physical violence.

A proponent of corporal punishment, David Benatar points out that using this last argument, fining people also teaches that forcing others to give up some of their property is an acceptable response to unwanted behaviour in others. According to Benetar, the key difference lies in the legitimacy of the authority administering the punishment: "There is all the difference in the world between legitimate authorities—the judiciary, parents, or teachers—using punitive powers responsibly to punish wrongdoing, and children or private citizens going around beating each other, locking each other up, and extracting financial tributes (such as lunch money). There is a vast moral difference here and there is no reason why children should not learn about it. Punishing children when they do wrong seems to be one important way of doing this."

Incarceration

Incarceration is the detention of a person in jail, typically as punishment for a crime. People are most commonly incarcerated upon suspicion or conviction of committing a crime, and different jurisdictions have differing laws governing the function of incarceration within an larger system of justice. Incarceration serves four essential purposes with regard to criminals:

- To punish criminals for committing crimes.
- To isolate criminals to prevent them from committing more crimes.
- To deter others from committing crimes.
- To rehabilitate criminals.

Incarceration rates, when measured by the United Nations, are considered distinct and separate from the imprisonment of political prisoners and others not charged with a specific crime. Historically, the frequency of imprisonment, its duration, and severity have varied considerably. There has also been much debate about the motives for incarceration, its effectiveness and fairness, as well as debate regarding the related questions about the nature and aetiology of criminal behavior.

Wilkenson notes that overall heterogeneity of a society may provide a meta-explanation for the variance in incarceration rates:

> There may be a multidirectional causality where close-knit societies are least likely to offend against one another. Knowing ones' neighbors may hence bridge econometric explanations across communities. Or put another way, except perhaps for crimes of passion, people do not offend against people they know well.

Penology and justice studies emphasise description and analysis of antecedents of criminal behavior and outcomes of consequences imposed by criminal justice on the criminal behavior. An example of a modern quantitative study of factors influencing the criminal behavior is the study by Krus and Hoehl.

In the study by Krus and Hoehl, variables that might explain differences in incarceration rates among population were located by a computer-aided search of the compendium of world ranking, compiled by the Facts on File Corporation and the World Model Group, containing over 50,000 records on more than 200 countries.

They argued that predictor variables explained about 69% of variance in the international incarceration rates. Cited as especially important were unequal distribution of wealth (the explanation perhaps favoured by liberals) and family disintegration. According to Krus and Hoehl, these variables act in concert: the presence of one variable does not always precipitate crime, but the presence of both variables often does precipitate crime. In many countries, it is common for prisoners to be paroled after serving as little as one third of their sentences.

China

In 2001 the incarceration rate in China was 111 per 100,000

in 2001 (sentenced prisoners only), although this figure is highly disputed in the West. Chinese human rights activist Harry Wu, now an American citizen, who spent 19 years in forced-labour camps for criticising the government, alleging that 16 to 20 million of his countrymen are incarcerated, including common criminals, political prisoners, and people in involuntary job placements. Even ten million prisoners would mean a rate of 793 per 100,000. Involuntary job placement is where the education system decides what vocational training or college major you will get, according to your aptitudes and availability of classroom seats. This was standard practice at least until 1978.

Denmark

Denmark also has a low incarceration rate with a total of 3774 inmates in the country. Denmark has 59 people in prison for every 100,000 citizens. 62 violent crimes such as rape, murder, robbery, and aggravated assault were reported. There were 322 Property Crimes reported.

England and Wales

In 2006 the incarceration rate in England and Wales is 139 persons imprisoned per 100,000 residents, while in Norway it is 59 inmates per 100,000, whilst the Australian imprisonment rate is 163 prisoners per 100,000 residents, and the rate of imprisonment in New Zealand last year was 179 per 100,000.

India

India has one of the lowest incarceration rates with only 281,000 prisoners in their jails. This is just a fraction of their total population, 1,129,866,154. India reported 1,764,630 crimes in 2007. There were 236,313 assaults and 111,296 burglaries.

United States

The United States' incarceration rate is, according to official reports, the highest in the world, at 737 persons imprisoned per 100,000. A report released in 2008 indicates that in the United States more than 1 in 100 adults is now confined in an American jail or prison. The United States has 4% of the world's population and 25% of the world's incarcerated population.

In the U.S., most states strictly limit parole, requiring that at least half of a sentence be served. For certain heinous crimes, there is no parole and the full sentence must be served.

Conditions of Incarceration

Severe punishments (such as beatings, prolonged sleep deprivation, sensory deprivation, chaining) have been often inflicted on prisoners. There are many reasons given for justification of such punishment. In the 16th century, the Bishop of Trier, Binsfeld, in his Tractatus de Confessionals Malefactors claimed that since the sinfulness of the world increases, God also allows increasing the severity of punishments.

A movement to abolish cruel treatment of prisoners began during the Age of Enlightenment and continued throughout the 19th and 20th centuries. However, there have been continual arguments for severe punishments, perhaps increasing somewhat in the early years of the 21st century. Contemporary justifications for such punishment often revolve around the "rights of the victims". Often underlying these perspectives are opinions that stress the vindictive eye-for-the-eye notions of the Old Testament and Qur'an, over the notion that the primary goal of incarceration should be the reform and re-education of prisoners to facilitate their reintegrating into society.

Within the framework of penology, the trend toward increasing the severity of punishments is reflected in publications such as Block's advocacy of policy initiatives aimed at increasing the unpleasantness of prison life that would likely be "a cost-effective method of fighting crime" and Arpaio and Sherman's 1996 book claiming that the increase in the severity of treatment of prisoners will result in decrease in recidivism.

Arpaio and Sherman proposed to increase the severity of imprisonment by the construction of tent prison camps in the Mojave Desert where summer temperatures reach 120 degrees Fahrenheit, by serving prisoners foul-tasting food, by humiliating prisoners by cross-dressing, and by reinstatement of the chain gangs. Mauer documents some other the measures used to implement the increasing the unpleasantness of prison life policies that include shooting around prisoners to keep them moving, forced consumption of milk of magnesia, placing naked inmates in strip cells, and handcuffing inmates for long periods of time.

Incarceration and Torture

As noted above, cruel treatment has long been a feature of incarceration. Taken to extremes, such treatment might be described as torture. Torture has, for much of history, been seen as a tolerable or even necessary component of imprisonment, whether performed as punishment or as part of interrogation. Recent controversial cases described by critics as torture of incarcerated people include the Abu Ghraib military prison in Iraq and the Guantanamo Bay, Cuba scandal.

Capital Punishment

Capital punishment, the death penalty, or execution is the killing of a person by judicial process as a punishment for an offense. Crimes that can result in a death penalty are known as capital crimes or capital offences. The term capital originates from Latin capitals, literally "regarding the head" (Latin caput). Hence, a capital crime was originally one punished by the severing of the head.

Capital punishment has in the past been practised in virtually every society, although currently only 58 nations actively practice it, with 95 countries abolishing it (the remainder having not used it for 10 years or allowing it only in exceptional circumstances such as wartime). It is a matter of active controversy in various countries and states, and positions can vary within a single political ideology or cultural region. In the European Union member states, Article 2 of the Charter of Fundamental Rights of the European Union prohibits the use of capital punishment.

Today, most countries are considered by Amnesty International as abolitionist, which allowed a vote on a nonbinding resolution to the UN to promote the abolition of the death penalty. However, over 60% of the world's population live in countries where executions take place insofar as the four most populous countries in the world (the People's Republic of China, India, United States and Indonesia) apply the death penalty and are unlikely to abolish it in the near future

Execution of criminals and political opponents has been used by nearly all societies—both to punish crime and to suppress political dissent. In most places that practice capital punishment it is reserved for murder, espionage, treason, or as part of military justice. In some countries sexual crimes, such as rape, adultery, incest and sodomy, carry the death penalty, as do religious crimes such as apostasy in Islamic nations (the formal renunciation of the state religion). In many countries that use the death penalty, drug trafficking is also a capital offense. In China, human trafficking and serious cases of corruption are punished by the death penalty. In millilitres around the world courts-martial have imposed death sentences for offenses such as cowardice, desertion, insubordination, and mutiny.

The use of formal execution extends to the beginning of recorded history. Most historical records and various primitive tribal practices indicate that the death penalty was a part of their justice system. Communal punishment for wrongdoing generally included compensation by the wrongdoer, corporal punishment, shunning, banishment and execution. Usually, compensation and shunning were enough as a form of justice. The response to crime committed by neighbouring tribes or communities included formal apology, compensation or blood feuds.

A blood feud or vendetta occurs when arbitration between families or tribes fails or an arbitration system is nonexistent. This form of justice was common before the emergence of an arbitration system based on state or organised religion. It may result from crime, land disputes or a code of honour. "Acts of retaliation underscore the ability of the social collective to defend itself and demonstrate to enemies (as well as potential allies) that injury to property, rights, or the person will not go unpunished." However, in practice, it is often difficult to distinguish between a war of vendetta and one of conquest.

Severe historical penalties include breaking wheel, boiling to death, flaying, slow slicing, disembowelment, crucifixion, impalement, crushing (including crushing by elephant), stoning, execution by burning, dismemberment, sawing, decapitation, scaphism, or neck-lacing.

Elaboration of tribal arbitration of feuds included peace settlements often done in a religious context and compensation system. Compensation was based on the principle of substitution which might include material (e.g. cattle, slave) compensation, exchange of brides or grooms, or payment of the blood debt. Settlement rules could allow for animal blood to replace human blood, or transfers of property or blood money or in some case an offer of a person for execution. The person offered for execution did not have to be an original perpetrator of the crime because the system was based on tribes, not individuals. Blood feuds could be regulated at meetings, such as the Viking things. Systems deriving from blood feuds may survive alongside more advanced legal systems or be given recognition by courts (e.g. trial by combat). One of the more modern refinements of the blood feud is the duel.

In certain parts of the world, nations in the form of ancient republics, monarchies or tribal oligarchies emerged. These nations were often united by common linguistic, religious or family ties. Moreover, expansion of these nations often occurred by conquest of neighbouring tribes or nations. Consequently, various classes of royalty, nobility, various commoners and slave emerged.

Accordingly, the systems of tribal arbitration were submerged into a more unified system of justice which formalised the relation between the different "classes" rather than "tribes". The earliest and most famous example is Code of Hammurabi which set the different punishment and compensation according to the different class/group of victims and perpetrators.

The Torah (Jewish Law), also known as the Pentateuch (the first five books of the Christian Old Testament), lays down the death penalty for murder, kidnapping, magic, violation of the Sabbath, blasphemy, and a wide range of sexual crimes, although evidence suggests that actual executions were rare. A further example comes from Ancient Greece, where the Athenian legal system was first written down by Draco in about 621 BC: the death penalty was applied for a particularly wide range of crimes, though Solon later repealed Draco's code and published new laws, retaining only Draco's homicide statutes. The word draconian derives from Draco's laws. The Romans also used death penalty for a wide range of offenses.

Islam on the whole accepts capital punishment. The Abashed Caliphs in Baghdad, such as Al-Mu'tadid, were often cruel in their punishments. In the One Thousand and One Nights, also known as the Arabian Nights, the fictional storyteller Sheherazade is portrayed as being the "voice of sanity and mercy", with her philosophical position being generally opposed to punishment by death. She expresses this though several of her tales, including "The Merchant and the Jinni", "The Fisherman and the Jinni", "The Three Apples", and "The Hunchback".

Similarly, in medieval and early modern Europe, before the development of modern prison systems, the death penalty was also used as a generalised form of punishment. During the reign of Henry VIII, as many as 72,000 people are estimated to have been executed. In 18th century Britain there were 222 crimes which were punishable by death, including crimes such as cutting down a tree or stealing an animal. Thanks to the notorious Bloody Code, 18th century (and early 19th century) Britain was a hazardous place to live. For example, Michael Hammond and his sister, Ann, whose ages were given as 7 and 11, were reportedly hanged at King's Lynn on Wednesday, September 28, 1708 for theft. The local press did not, however, consider the executions of two children newsworthy.

Although many are executed in China each year in the present day, there was a time in Tang Dynasty China when the death penalty was abolished. This was in the year 747, enacted by Emperor Xuanzong of Tang. When abolishing the death penalty Xuanzong ordered his officials to refer to the nearest regulation by analogy when sentencing those found guilty of crimes for which the prescribed punishment was execution. Thus depending on the severity of the crime a punishment of severe scourging with the thick rod or of exile to the remote Lingnan region might take the place of capital punishment. However the death penalty was restored only twelve years later in 759 in response to the An Lushan Rebellion. At this time in China only the emperor had the authority to sentence criminals to execution. Under Xuanzong capital punishment was relatively infrequent, with only 24 executions in the year 730 and 58 executions in the year 736.

The two most common forms of execution in China in the Tang period were strangulation and decapitation, which were the prescribed methods of execution for 144 and 89 offenses respectively. Strangulation was the prescribed sentence for lodging an accusation against one's parents or grandparents with a magistrate, scheming to kidnap a person and sell them into slavery and opening a coffin while desecrating a tomb.

Decapitation was the method of execution prescribed for more serious crimes such as treason and sedition. Interestingly, and despite the great discomfort involved, most Chinese during the Tang preferred strangulation to decapitation, as a result of the traditional Chinese belief that the body is a gift from the parents and that it is therefore disrespectful to one's ancestors to die without returning one's body to the grave intact.

Some further forms of capital punishment were practised in Tang China, of which the first two that follow at least were extra-legal. The first of these was scourging to death with the thick rod which was common throughout the Tang especially in cases of gross corruption. The second was truncation, in which the convicted person was cut in two at the waist with a fodder knife and then left to bleed to death. A further form of execution called Ling Chi (slow slicing), or death by/of a thousand cuts, was used in China from the close of the Tang dynasty in roughly 900 CE to its abolition in 1905.

When a minister of the fifth grade or above received a death sentence the emperor might grant him a special dispensation allowing him to commit suicide in lieu of execution. Even when this privilege was not granted, the law required that the condemned minister be provided with food and ale by his keepers and transported to the execution ground in a cart rather than having to walk there.

Nearly all executions under the Tang took place in public as a warning to the population. The heads of the executed were displayed on poles or spears. When local authorities decapitated a convicted criminal, the head was boxed and sent to the capital as proof of identity and that the execution had taken place.

It is also important to note that in Tang China, when a person was sentenced to decapitation for rebellion or sedition, punishment was also imposed on their relatives by reason of association. This was the case whether or not the relatives were actually guilty of participation in the crime. In such cases fathers of the convicted under 79 years of age and sons aged over 15 were strangled. Sons under 15, daughters, mothers, wives, concubines, grandfathers, grandsons, brothers and sisters were enslaved and uncles and nephews were banished to the remotest reaches of the empire. Sometimes the tombs of the family's ancestors were levelled, the ancestors' coffins were destroyed and their bones scattered.

Despite its wide use, calls for reform were not unknown. The 12th century Sephardic legal scholar, Moses Maimonides, wrote, "It is better and more satisfactory to acquit a thousand guilty persons than to put a single innocent man to death." He argued that executing an accused criminal on anything less than absolute certainty would lead to a slippery slope of decreasing burdens of proof, until we would be convicting merely "according to the judge's caprice." His concern was maintaining popular respect for law, and he saw errors of commission as much more threatening than errors of omission.

The last several centuries have seen the emergence of modern nation-states. Almost fundamental to the concept of nation state is the idea of citizenship. This caused justice to be increasingly associated with equality and universality, which in Europe saw an emergence of the concept of natural rights.

Another important aspect is that emergence of standing police forces and permanent penitential institutions. The death penalty became an increasingly unnecessary deterrent in prevention of minor crimes such as theft. The argument that deterrence, rather than retribution, is the main justification for punishment is a hallmark of the rational choice theory and can be traced to Cesare Beccaria whose well-known treatise

On Crimes and Punishments, condemned torture and the death penalty and Jeremy Bentham who twice critiqued the death penalty. Additionally, in countries like Britain, law enforcement officials became alarmed when juries tended to acquit nonviolent felons rather than risk a conviction that could result in execution. Moving executions there inside prisons and away from public view was prompted by official recognition of the phenomenon reported first by Beccaria in Italy and later by Charles Dickens and Karl Marx of increased violent criminality at the times and places of executions

The 20th century was one of the bloodiest of the human history. Massive killing occurred as the resolution of war between nation-states. A large part of execution was summary execution of enemy combatants. Also, modern military organisations employed capital punishment as a means of maintaining military discipline. The Soviets, for example, executed 158,000 soldiers for desertion during World War II. In the past, cowardice, absence without leave, desertion, insubordination, looting, shirking under enemy fire and disobeying orders were often crimes punishable by death. One method of execution since firearms came into common use has almost invariably been firing squad. Moreover, various authoritarian states—for example those with fascist or communist governments—employed the death penalty as a potent means of political oppression. According to the declassified Soviet archives, 681,692 people were shot in 1937 and 1938 alone–an average of 1,000 executions a day. Partly as a response to such excessive punishment, civil organisations have started to place increasing emphasis on the concept of human rights and abolition of the death penalty.

Among countries around the world, almost all European and many Pacific Area states (including Australia, New Zealand and Timer Leste), and Canada have abolished capital punishment. In Latin America, most states have completely abolished the use of capital punishment, while some countries, such as Brazil, allow for capital punishment only in exceptional situations, such as treason committed during wartime.

The United States (the federal government and 35 of the states), Guatemala, most of the Caribbean and the majority of democracies in Asia (e.g. Japan and India) and Africa (e.g. Botswana and Zambia) retain it. South Africa, which is probably the most developed African nation, and which has been a democracy since 1994, does not have the death penalty. This fact is currently quite controversial in that country, due to the high levels of violent crime, including murder and rape.

Advocates of the death penalty argue that it deters crime, is a good tool for police and prosecutors (in plea bargaining for example), improves the community by making sure that convicted criminals do not offend again, provides closure to surviving victims or loved ones, and is a just penalty for their crime. Opponents of capital punishment argue that it has led to the execution of wrongfully convicted, that it discriminates against minorities and the poor, that it does not deter criminals more than life imprisonment, that it encourages a "culture of violence", that it is more expensive than life imprisonment, and that it violates human rights.

Global Distribution

Since World War II there has been a trend toward abolishing the death penalty. In 1977, 16 countries were abolitionist. According to information published by Amnesty International in 2010, 95 countries had abolished capital punishment altogether, 9 had done so for all offences except under special circumstances, and 35 had not used it for at least 10 years or were under a moratorium. The other 58 retained the death penalty in active use.

According to Amnesty International, at least 714 executions were known to have been carried out in 18 countries in 2009. In addition, there are countries which do not publish information on the use of capital punishment, most significantly China, which is estimated to execute hundreds of people each year. At least 17,000 people worldwide were under sentence of death at the beginning of 2010.

The use of the death penalty is becoming increasingly restrained in retentionist countries. Singapore, Japan, Taiwan, South Korea and the U.S. Are the only developed countries that have retained the death penalty. The death penalty was overwhelmingly practised in poor and authoritarian states, which often employed the death penalty as a tool of political oppression. During the 1980s, the democratisation of Latin America swelled the rank of abolitionist countries. This was soon followed by the fall of communism in Central and Eastern Europe, which then aspired to enter the EU. In these countries, the public support for the death penalty varies but it is decreasing. The European Union and the Council of Europe both strictly require member states not to practice the death penalty. On the other hand, rapid industrialisation in Asia has been increasing the number of developed retentionist countries. In these countries, the death penalty enjoys strong public support, and the matter receives little attention from the government or the media. This trend has been followed by some African and Middle Eastern countries where support for the death penalty is high.

Some countries have resumed practising the death penalty after having suspended executions for long periods. The United States suspended executions in 1967 but resumed them in 1977, then again on 25 September 2007 to 16 April 2008; there was no execution in India between 1995 and 2004; and Sri Lanka declared an end to its moratorium on the death penalty on 20 Nov. 2004, although it has not yet performed any executions. The Philippines reintroduced the death penalty in 1993 after abolishing it in 1987, but abolished it again in 2006.

9

Theoretical Approaches to Punishment

In order to better understand the nature of punishment, it is first necessary to examine its conceptual basis, and then consider the various theories that have been developed to morally justify society's infliction of punishment. These theories are deterrence, retribution, just deserts, rehabilitation, incapacitation, and more recently, restorative justice.

We use the word punishment to describe anything we think is painful; for example, we refer to a "punishing work schedule" or a "punishing exercise program." We also talk of punishment in the context of parents or teachers disciplining children. However, in this discussion we will consider punishment in a particular sense. Flew argues that punishment, in the sense of a sanction imposed for a criminal offense, consists of five elements:

— It must involve an unpleasantness to the victim.
— It must be for an offense, actual or supposed.
— It must be of an offender, actual or supposed.
— It must be the work of personal agencies; in other words, it must not be the natural consequence of an action.
— It must be imposed by an authority or an institution against whose rules the offense has been committed. If

this is not the case, then the act is not one of punishment but is simply a hostile act.

Similarly, direct action by a person who has no special authority is not properly called punishment, and is more likely to be revenge or an act of hostility. In addition to these five elements, Benn and Peters add that the unpleasantness should be an essential part of what is intended.

The value of this definition of punishment resides in its presentation of punishment in terms of a system of rules, and that it distinguishes punishment from other kinds of unpleasantness. Another definition of punishment proposed by Garland is "the legal process whereby violators of criminal law are condemned and sanctioned in accordance with specified legal categories and procedures".

Thinking about the issue of punishment gives rise to a number of questions, the most fundamental of which is, why should offenders be punished? This question might produce the following responses:

- They deserve to be punished.
- Punishment will stop them from committing further crimes.
- Punishment tells the victim that society disapproves of the harm that he or she has suffered.
- Punishment discourages others from doing the same thing.
- Punishment protects society from dangerous or dishonest people.
- Punishment allows an offender to make amends for the harm he or she has caused.
- Punishment ensures that people understand that laws are there to be obeyed.

Some of the possible answers to the question of why offenders should be punished may conflict with each other. This is because some answers are based on reasons having to do with preventing crime whereas others are concerned with punishment being deserved by an offender. When a court imposes a punishment on an offender, it often tries to balance the sorts of reasons for punishment noted earlier, but sometimes certain purposes of punishment dominate other purposes. Over time there have been shifts in penal theory, and therefore in the purpose of punishment due to a complex set of reasons including politics, public policy, and social movements.

Consequently, in a cyclical process, an early focus on deterrence as the rationale for punishment gave way to a focus on reform and rehabilitation. This, in turn, has led to a return to punishment based on the notion of retribution and just deserts.

As Garland argues, punishment is a complex concept, and an approach to punishment that is limited to a reading of moral philosophy fails to represent the full dimension and complexity of the subject. For moral philosophers, the "ought" of punishment is of great importance and leads to a set of questions including:

— What should be the goals of punishment.

— What should be the values contained in and promoted by the criminal law.

— What is the purpose of punishment?

In contrast to the philosophical view of punishment, the sociological perspective is concerned with the "is" of punishment; that is, what punishment is actually intended for, and the nature of penal systems. The third perspective on punishment is offered by criminologists and policy makers, who focus on penalties for offenses and policy concerns relevant to the punishment of offenders.

Some critics, such as Bean, argue that criminology has tended to ignore the moral and sociological implications of punishment in favour of the social and personal characteristics of offenders, as well as the nature of penal institutions and methods of social control.

In the same vein, Nigel Walker points out that the practical ends of penal action, particularly with the aims of sentencing and the administration of prisons and probation, are concerns that pay little attention to the philosophy or sociology of punishment.

PHILOSOPHICAL APPROACH

In the philosophical debate about punishment, two main types of theories of punishment dominate: utilitarian theory and retributive theory. These philosophical theories have in turn generated further theoretical discussions about punishment concerned with deterrence, retribution, incapacitation, rehabilitation, and more recently, restorative justice. Theories that set the goal of punishment as the *prevention of future crime* (deterrence) are usually referred to as utilitarian because they are derived from utilitarian philosophy.

Past oriented theories (theories that focus on the past-actions of the offender) are referred to as re-tributaries because they seek-retribution from offenders for their crimes. The re-tributaries conception of punishment includes *the notion that the purpose of punishment* is to allocate moral blame to the offender for the crime and that his or her future conduct is not a proper concern for deciding punishment.

Deterrence

People are deterred from actions when they refrain from carrying them out because they have an aversion to the possible consequences of those actions. Walker suggests that although penologists believe that penalties do, in fact, deter, it is hard to determine whether the kind of penalty or its severity has any effect on whether a particular penalty is successful. Some question whether deterrence is morally acceptable.

Corporal Punishment

On May 4, 1994, Michael Fay, a U.S. Teenager who had pleaded guilty to several acts of vandalism in Singapore, was caned by Singapore's authorities. He was stripped, bent at the hip over a padded trestle, tied down at his ankles and wrists, and his buttocks were lashed by a martial arts specialist four times with a four-foot long, half-inch wide stick of rattan soaked in antiseptic. Fay, 18, had lived in Singapore since 1992, and was sentenced to four months in prison, a fine of $2,230, and the caning after his guilty plea.

The sentence of corporal punishment secured great media attention in the United States, with many people expressing their views. President Clinton, in a personal letter to the Singapore president, urged him to spare the rod and revoke the punishment, which Clinton described as "extreme." Also, 24 U.S. Senators appealed to the president of Singapore that clemency would be "an enlightened decision." However, U.S. Public opinion expressed support for the punishment, some even writing to the Singapore Embassy in Washington expressing their approval. In Day ton, Ohio, where Fay's father lived, citizens supported the punishment by a 2 to 1 margin. The Singapore courts and government rejected the various appeals for clemency, except for reducing the number of lashes. A Home Affairs Ministry official stated that Singapore was able to keep its society orderly and crime free because of its tough laws against antisocial crimes and that Singapore did not have a situation where acts of vandalism were commonplace like

New York where even police cars were vandalised. To utilitarian philosophers like Bentham, punishment can be justified only if the harm that it prevents is greater than the harm inflicted on the offender through punishing him or her. In this view, therefore, unless punishment deters further crime, it simply adds to the totality of human suffering.

In other words, utilitarians justify punishment by referring to its beneficial effects or consequences. In this sense, utilitarian theory is a consequentiality theory that considers only the good and bad consequences produced by an act as morally significant. Bentham is considered the main proponent of punishment as deterrence, and he expressed his early conception of the notion as follows:

> Pain and pleasure are the great springs of human action. When a man perceives or supposes pain to be the consequence of an act he is acted on in such manner as tends with a certain force to withdraw him as it were from the commission of that act. If the apparent magnitude be greater than the magnitude of the pleasure expected he will be absolutely prevented from performing it.

Becarria took a similar position to Bentham, arguing that "the aim of punishment can only be to prevent the criminal committing new crimes against his countrymen and to keep others from doing likewise". Utilitarians understand punishment only as a means to an end, and not as an end in itself. They perceive punishment in terms of its ability to reduce crime and do not focus on the punishment that "ought" to be imposed on offenders.

To utilitarians, a "right" punishment (or one with the greatest utility) is one that is beneficial to the general welfare of all those affected by the criminal act. Critics of utilitarianism argue that because utilitarians see the aim of punishment as promoting public welfare and maximising the happiness of all, this means that utilitarians are willing to punish the innocent in order to achieve that objective. Those supporting the theory of punishment as deterrence distinguish between individual deterrence and general deterrence. Individual deterrence involves deterring someone who has already offended from re-offending; general deterrence involves dissuading potential offenders from offending at all by way of the punishment administered for a particular offense.

Individual deterrence relies on offenders receiving a taste of the punishment they will receive if they re-offend, and can be seen operationally in the "short, sharp, shock punishments" such as boot camps, which are used as an alternative to imprisonment and are clearly aimed at subjecting offenders to a regime that will shock them out of any further criminal conduct. General deterrence takes the form of legislation imposing penalties for specific offenses in the belief that those penalties will deter or prevent persons from committing those offenses. An example of an attempt at general deterrence would be significantly increasing the penalties for driving under the influence (DUI) in an effort to deter citizens from drunk driving.

Bey levelled after carrying out a comprehensive review of studies that have considered the deterrent effects of punishment concluded that,... There exists no scientific basis for expecting that a general deterrence policy, which does not involve an unacceptable interference with human rights, will do anything to control the crime rate. The sort of information needed to base a morally acceptable general policy is lacking. There is some convincing evidence in some areas that some legal sanctions have exerted deterrent effects. These findings are not, however, generalises beyond the conditions that were investigated. Given the present state of knowledge, implementing an official deterrence policy can be no more than a shot in the dark, or a political decision to pacify "public sentiment."

The empirical evidence suggests that, generally, punishment has no individual deterrent effect. Walker argues that evidence from research studies has established that capital punishment has no greater effect than life imprisonment. Nagin comments on the difficulty in distinguishing between individual deterrence and rehabilitation. In another overview of research on deterrence, Nagin identifies three sets of studies, which he refers to as interrupted time-series studies, ecological studies, and perceptual studies.The first set, time-series studies, explores the effect of specific policy initiatives such as police crackdowns on open-air drug markets.

Nagin finds that such policy targeting has only a temporary effect, and is therefore not a successful deterrent. Ecological studies look for a negative association between crime rates and punishment levels that can be interpreted as having a deterrent effect. Nagin points out that a number of such studies have been able to isolate a deterrent effect.

In perceptual studies, the data comes from surveys. Such surveys have found that self-reported criminality is lower among those who see sanctions, risks, and costs as higher. Nagin therefore concludes that, collectively, the operations of the criminal justice system exert a substantial deterrent effect.

In discussing whether the threat of punishment has a deterrent effect, Andenaes explains that two positions are usually debated. Bentham's position is that man is a rational being who chooses between courses of action having first calculated the risks of pain and pleasure. If, therefore, we regard the risk of punishment as sufficient to outweigh a likely gain, a potential criminal applying a rational approach will choose not to break the law.

The alternative position considers this model unrealistic, arguing that people remain law-abiding, not because they fear the criminal law, but as a result of moral inhibitions and norms of conduct.

Criminals, they argue, do not make rational choices but act out of emotional instability, through lack of self-control, or as a result of having acquired the values of a criminal subculture.

Andenaes points out the dangers of generalisation; that is, he suggests it is necessary to distinguish between various offenses such as murder or drunk driving. Offenses vary immensely in terms of an offender's motivation, and any realistic discussion of general deterrence ought to take into account the particular norms and circumstances of each particular type of offense. He also notes that the threat of punishment, although directed to all persons, affects individuals in different ways.

For example, in his view, the law-abiding citizen does not need the threat of the law to remain law-abiding. On the other hand, the criminal group may well fear the law but still break it, and the potential criminal might have broken the law if it had not been for the threat of punishment.

It follows that the threat of punishment seems relevant only to the potential criminal. In some cases, however, there is evidence that punishment has a deterrent effect on individuals. Andenaes refers to a study of department store shoplifting where amateur shoplifters were treated as thieves by the store management and reacted by changing their attitudes and experiencing great emotional disturbance. This contrasts with the professional shoplifter who does not register any shock at getting caught and accepts jail as a normal hazard of the trade.

Tullock, after surveying the economic and sociological models of deterrence, concludes that multiple regression studies show empirically that increasing the frequency or severity of punishment does reduce the likelihood of a given crime being committed. However, Blumstein, Cohen, and Nagin contend that although the evidence does establish a negative association between crime rates and sanctions, this does not necessarily establish the general deterrent effect of sanctions. This is because, in their view, the negative association can be explained by lower sanctions being the effect, and not the cause, of higher crime rates.

Implementation of Punishment

For the utilitarian who regards punishment as bad in itself, a particular punishment will be justified only if the suffering it inflicts is less than the harm caused by the criminal act that would have taken place had there been no punishment. If various forms of punishment would achieve the same result, a utilitarian will opt for the most lenient punishment that minimises the potential suffering. It follows that if a sentence of capital punishment or the lesser punishment of a term of imprisonment are both equally effective in deterring murder, the utilitarian will choose the lesser punishment and regard capital punishment as unjustified. However, utilitarian approaches can result in the infliction of excessive punishment.

Ten gives the example of petty thefts being widespread in society with hundreds of cases occurring, frequently perpetrated by efficient thieves who are difficult to catch. The harm caused by each individual theft is minor, but the total harm, according to utilitarian approaches, is great and may, therefore, be greater than the harm caused by severely punishing one minor criminal. If a newly enacted law were to impose a punishment of 10 years imprisonment on a petty thief, and no less a penalty would have a deterrent effect, it is arguable that a utilitarian would have to accept what would be considered an excessive sentence for the one petty thief unlucky enough to be arrested and convicted.

Retribution

Retribution is the theory that punishment is justified because it is deserved. Systems of retribution for crime have long existed, with the best known being the lex talionis of Biblical times, calling for "an eye for an eye, a tooth for a tooth, and a life for a life". Re-tributionists claim a moral link between punishment and guilt, and see punishment as a question of responsibility or accountability.

Once society has decided upon a set of legal rules, the re-tributaries sees those rules as representing and reflecting the moral order. Society's acceptance of legal rules means that the re-tributaries accepts the rules, whatever they may be; accepts that the rule makers are justified in their rule making; and claims that those who make the rules provide the moral climate under which others must live.

Accordingly, re-tributivists cannot question the legitimacy of rules. They argue that retribution operates on a consensus model of society where the community, acting through a legal system of rules, acts "rightly," and the criminal acts "wrongly". It follows that the re-tributaries position makes no allowance for social change or social conditions, looking instead only to crime.

Raising the issue of the social causes of crime or questioning the effectiveness of punishment are irrelevant considerations to a re-tributaries. It has been suggested by van den Haag and Kleinig that in historical terms, the lex talionis did not operate as a demand for retribution. Instead, it set a limit on the nature of that retribution, and therefore prevented the imposition of excessive penalties in the course of acts of vengeance. Capital punishment may be the only form of punishment still supported by appeals to the lex talionis.

The basic principle of lex talionis is that punishment should inflict the same on the offender as the offender has inflicted on his or her victim. It can, therefore, be seen as a crude formula because there are many crimes to which it cannot be applied. For instance, what punishment ought to be inflicted on a rapist under lex talionis? Should the state arrange for the rape of the offender as his due punishment?

In addition, the lex talionis can be objected to because its formula to determine the correct punishment considers solely the harm caused by the crime and makes no allowance for the mental state of the offender or for any mitigating or aggravating circumstances associated with the crime. Thus, even though a person's death may have been brought about accidentally or negligently, the lex talionis, strictly applied, would still call for the imposition of the death penalty.

A further objection is found in the view that in a civilised society, certain forms of punishment are considered too cruel to be defended as valid and appropriate. For example, a sadistic murderer may horribly torture his or her victim, but society would condemn the imposition of that same form of punishment on the offender.

It can also be said that although the death penalty may constitute a just punishment according to the rule of lex talionis, it should nevertheless be abolished as part of "the civilising mission of modern states".

Retributivists believe that wrongdoers deserve to be punished and that the punishment imposed should be in proportion to the wrongdoing the offender committed. In contrast to utilitarians, retributivists focus their line of reasoning on the offender's just desert (a proportionate punishment) and not on the beneficial consequences of punishment.

Retributivists ask questions such as "Why do offenders deserve to be punished?" And "How are their just deserts to be calculated and translated into actual sentences?"

A number of explanations have been suggested to justify retribution, including the notion that retribution is a payment of what is owed; that is, offenders who are punished are "paying their debt to society".

Walker notes that this seems to confuse the "victim" with "society" because we generally do not perceive offenders as liable to pay compensation or make restitution to their victims; furthermore, if society is compensated for anything at all, it is for a breach of its peace.

Censure is also an important component in retributaries thinking. For example, Andrew von Hirsch, the leading theorist on just deserts sentencing, writes:

> ... Desert and punishment can rest on a much simpler idea, used in everyday discourse: the idea of censure... Punishment connotes censure. Penalties should comport with the seriousness of crimes so that the reprobation on the offender through his penalty fairly reflects the blameworthiness of his conduct.

For von Hirsch, censure is simply holding someone accountable for his or her conduct and involves conveying the message to the perpetrator that he or she has will-fully injured someone and faces the disapproval of society for that reason. On the part of the offender, an expression of concern or remorse is expected. As well, the censure expressed through criminal law has the role of providing third parties with reasons for not committing acts defined as criminal. In other words, censure can have a deterrent effect.

Some theorists of desert argue that notions of censure cannot be adequately expressed verbally or symbolically, and that hard treatment is needed to properly express socialite disapproval.

The notion of the expressive or communicative character of punishment is closely associated with the idea of "punishment as censure." This conception recognises punishment as comprising not merely harsh treatment, but also elements of condemnation, denunciation, and censure.

Thus, for example, punishment in the form of a fine is quite different from the payment of a tax, although both involve payment to the state. In the same vein, imprisonment contrasts with other forms of detention such as quarantine or detention for psychiatric disorders. Imprisonment, it is argued, carries with it an expressive function of censure, whereas detention for reasons of quarantine or for mental disorder does not. Feinberg explains the expressive function of punishment in the following terms:

> Punishment is a conventional device for the expression of attitudes of resentment and indignation, and of judgments of disapproval and reprobation, on the part either of the punishing authority himself or of those "in whose name" the punishment is inflicted. Punishment, in short, has a symbolic significance largely missing from other kinds of penalties.

Feinberg further argues that punishment expresses more than disapproval; it amounts to a symbolic method of hitting back at the criminal and of expressing "vindictive resentment." In similar fashion, H. Morris contends that punishment serves to teach offenders a moral lesson so that in the process of being punished and being made aware that a crime violated communal values, they will come to see what is good and choose it in the future. According to this account, the aim of punishment is to persuade and not to manipulate or coerce.

However, as Morris himself points out, this approach does not account for the punishment of those who are already repentant, nor is it able to cope with those who understand the values of society but are indifferent or opposed to them.

Over the last two decades, the notion of punishment as a communicative practice has developed. This notion asserts that punishment communicates to the criminal a response appropriate to the crime committed. Communication requires that the person to whom the communication is directed must be an active participant in the process and must receive and respond to the communication. Additionally, the communication should appeal to the person's rational understanding.

The communication must be focused primarily on the offender being punished as a response to him or her, and must be justified by his or her offense. The message communicated by punishment must focus on and be justified by the offender's past offense and must be appropriate to that offense. Duff argues that the message communicated should be the degree of censure or condemnation the crime deserves.

In the context of criminal law, censure might be communicated in a formal conviction of guilt or through a system of harsh punishments such as imprisonment, fines, or community service. Duff argues that the aim of hard treatment is ideally to cause the offender to understand and repent the crime committed. It should attempt to direct his or her attention to the crime, and give him or her an understanding of crime as a "wrong." It should also cause the offender to accept the censure that punishment communicates as deserved. By undergoing hard punishment, the offender can become reconciled with the community and restored back into the community from which the offense caused him or her to be excluded.

Philosophers such as Duff see the main benefit of punishment as the effect on the offender. They argue that punishment has the effect of restoring the offender to the community in the same way that penance restores a penitent to the communion of the church. Nozick sees retributive punishment as a message from those whose values are assumed to be correct and normative to someone whose act or omission has displayed incorrect and non-normative values.

Walker explains that "man is a rule making animal," and that rules and notions of rules are acquired during childhood. Rules, in the form of transactions involving promises, establish codes of normative conduct including "penalising rules" that specify action to be taken against those who infringe the rules. It follows that failing to penalise an offender for infringing the rules would itself be an infringement of those rules; thus, an unpunished infringement would create two infringements.

Another theory that attempts to justify punishment as a retributive act is that an offender should be viewed as a person who has taken an unfair advantage of others in society by committing a crime, and that imposing punishment restores fairness.

Philosophers such as Herbert Morris, John Finis, and Jeffrie Murphy subscribe to the unfair advantage theory. For example, Morris argues that the effect of criminal law is to confer benefits on society, because others are not permitted to interfere with areas of an individual's life since certain acts are proscribed and prohibited. In order to gain the benefits of non-interference, individuals must exercise self-restraint and not engage in acts that infringe the protected areas of the lives of others. It follows that when a person violates the law but continues to enjoy its benefits, he or she takes an unfair advantage of others who follow the law.

Punishment, it is argued, is therefore justified because it removes this unfair advantage and restores the balance of benefits and burdens disturbed by the criminal activity.

The unfair advantage argument has been challenged by those who argue that it distorts the nature of crime itself.

For example, the wrongfulness of rape does not merely consist of taking unfair advantage of those who obey the law. Also, it is difficult to show that offenders have in any real sense "willed" their own punishment.

Additionally, although unfair advantage might constitute an ideal theory for the justification of punishment, the question arises about whether it can be applied to an actual society. In other words, do those who commit criminal acts actually take an unfair advantage for themselves? Finally, some retributivists argue that punishment is morally justified because it gives satisfaction. James Fitzjames Stephen, an English Victorian judge, is often cited as an advocate of this theory.

Retributive theories of punishment argue that punishment should be imposed for past crimes and that it should be appropriate to the nature of the crime committed; that is, the severity of the punishment should be commensurate with the seriousness of the crime. Sometimes, retributive punishment is confused with notions of revenge. Critics of re-tributionist theories of punishment argue that retribution is basically nothing more than vengeance. However, Nozick argues that there is a clear distinction between the two because "retribution is done for a wrong, while revenge may be done for an injury or harm or slight and need not be a wrong". He also points out that whereas retribution sets a limit for the amount of punishment according to the seriousness of the wrong, no limit need be set for revenge.

In this sense, therefore, revenge is personal whereas the person dispensing retributive punishment may well have no personal tie to the victim. As Nozick points out, "revenge involves a particular emotional tone, pleasure in the suffering of another". A further distinction between the two is that retribution in the form of punishment is inflicted only on the offender, but revenge may be carried out on an innocent person, perhaps a relative of the perpetrator.

Just Deserts

Up until about 1970, criminologists generally thought of retribution as vengeance. During the 1970s, criminologists reconsidered the idea of retribution and advanced new formulations.

By the 1980s, the new re-tributionist theory of just deserts had become influential. Importantly, the new thinking indicated that although there should continue to be treatment programs, a defendant would not ordinarily be incarcerated in order to receive treatment. Influential writings such as Struggle for Justice and Doing Justice, which were written in the aftermath of the riot at Attica Prison in 1971, elaborated on the new re-tribulations in philosophical and civil libertarian terms.

This theory gained support as a reaction against the perceived unfairness of systems that favoured treatment that had developed over the first half of the 20th century, especially the use of the indeterminate sentence. This form of sentence vested the power of determining the date of release to a parole board, and signifies the practice of individualised sentencing. The latter attempted to sentence according to the treatment needs of the offender, rather than the seriousness of the offense.

One of the criticisms of indeterminate sentencing was the fact that the sentencing courts had a wide discretion in choosing a sentence, and although they tended to adopt tariffs for classes of crime, individual judges could depart from them without providing reasons.

Along with the just deserts movement, many states and federal sentencing authorities repealed indeterminate sentencing laws with the aim of reducing judicial discretion in sentencing and promoting consistency and certainty, as well as a set of standards that would help in the process of deciding the sentence.

Among the retributivists, Kant argued that the aim of penalties must be to inflict desert, and that this was a "categorical imperative." By this he meant that inflicting what was deserved rendered all other considerations irrelevant. Just deserts proponents emphasise the notion that punishment should be proportionate; that is, there should be a scale of punishments with the most serious being reserved for the most serious offenses, and that penalties should be assessed according to the seriousness of the offense.

This is often called tariff sentencing. In this method of punishing, the offender's potential to commit future offenses does not come into consideration, but his or her previous convictions are taken into account because most proponents of just deserts support reductions in sentence for first offenders.

Desert theorists contend that punishment should convey blame for wrongdoing, and that blame is attached to offenders because they have done wrong. Consequently, the blameworthiness of the offender is reflected in the punishment imposed. Thus, advocates of desert focus on two dimensions only—the harm involved in the offense and the offender's culpability.

Von Hirsch enlarges on these two main elements, stating that, in looking at the degree of harm, a broad notion of the quality of life is useful because "invasions of different interests can be compared according to the extent to which they typically affect a person's standard of living". As to culpability, he suggests that the substantive criminal law, which already distinguishes intentional from reckless or negligent conduct, would be useful in sentencing law.

Von Hirsch argues that a focus on the censuring aspect of punishment has coincided with a change in criminological thinking. Criminologists had previously regarded the blaming aspects of punishment as stigma that might create obstacles to the reintegration of the offender into the community and might also cause the offender to reinforce his or her own deviance, making him or her more likely to continue offending.

Desert theorists now emphasise that responding to criminal acts with a process of blaming encourages the individual to recognise the wrongfulness of the action, to feel remorse, and to make efforts to refrain from such conduct in the future. In contrast, a deterrent punishment requires the individual to simply comply or face the consequences.

The difference between the two approaches is that a moral judgment is required from the offender under just deserts that is not required under a purely deterrent punishment. During the 1980s, many states, as well as the Federal Sentencing Commission, introduced desert-based sentencing schemes.

In considering questions of proportionality and seriousness, the issue arises as to how offenses are to be ranked in terms of their seriousness. Who is to determine the degrees of seriousness? In some jurisdictions, the judge's views determine the issue; other approaches include the use of sentencing commissions and legislating sentencing schedules.

In California, the Determinant Sentencing Laws allow politicians and others to raise the tariffs for offenses in response to public or media pressure in order to give effect to "get tough on crime" policies.

Some critics argue that just deserts theory leads to harsher penalties, but von Hirsch contends that the theory itself does not call for harsher penalties, and that sentencing schemes relying specifically on just deserts theory tend not to be severe. He draws attention to sentencing guidelines in Minnesota and Oregon that provide for modest penalties by U.S. Standards.

The Minnesota Sentencing Guidelines provide a grid with a horizontal axis showing previous convictions and a vertical axis showing offense type. The sentencing judge is required to locate the appropriate cell on the grid for the offender being sentenced, where the severity of the offense and the number of previous convictions intersect. Each cell stipulates a presumptive prison term that represents the normal period of incarceration for a standard case of that offense. In addition to the presumptive sentence, there is a band indicating the range that should apply in the actual case. For example, in the case of an aggravated burglary, where the offender has three previous convictions, there is a presumptive term of 49 months and a range of 45 to 53 months. The actual sentence depends on aggravating and mitigating factors.

According to Hudson, sentencing guidelines have had the effect of reinforcing relatively lenient punishments in states with that tradition, although states with a history of imposing severe punishments, such as New Mexico and Indiana, have produced severe schedules and guidelines. The fundamental difficulty with deserts theory is that it lacks any principle that determines a properly commensurate sentence. Deserts are determined by a scale of punishment that fixes the most severe penalty. This might be imprisonment or death. It then determines ordinal proportionate penalties for lesser offenses. It follows that if imprisonment is the most severe penalty, then proportionality will provide shorter terms of imprisonment and noncustodial penalties for lesser offenses.

If the term of imprisonment for severe offenses is moderate, then short sentences and penalties such as probation will soon be reached on the scale of seriousness. If the penalty for the most serious offenses is death, it follows that long terms of imprisonment will be proportionate penalties for less serious offenses.

This is the situation that prevails in many states. Many argue that retribution based on just deserts fails to account for the problem of just deserts in an unjust world. Just deserts theory ignores social factors like poverty, disadvantage, and discrimination, and presumes equal opportunity for all.

Tonry notes that most sentencing commissions in the United States will not allow judges to bring personal circumstances into account in their sentencing decisions, despite the fact that the average offender has a background that is likely to be either deeply disadvantaged or deprived. Zimring suggests that desert sentencing fails to take account of the fact that there are multiple desecrations involved in the sentencing power.

He points to the legislature that sets the range of sentences, the prosecutor who has the legal authority to select a charge, the judge as the sentencing authority, and the correctional authority, which is able to modify sentences after incarceration, as constituting a multiplicity of decisions and desecrations that make the task of achieving just and proportionate sentences extremely problematic.

Since prosecutors and legislators act under political influence and attempt to implement policies that reflect public opinion, the sentencing process is not the monopoly of the trial judge, but is all too often an expression of varying perspectives based on periodic concerns about whether current philosophies reflect notions of being "tough on crime."

Reconciling Utilitarian and Retributive Theories

Is it possible to reconcile utilitarian and retributive theories of punishment? For utilitarians, desert is not seen as necessary to justify punishment nor as a reason for punishment because desert does not look to the consequences of punishment—it simply punishes. For the utilitarian, the only good reasons for punishment relate to the consequences of that punishment.

The contrast between the two theories lies in the fact that for utilitarians, the aim of punishment is to control future action, whereas the retributivists see the aim in terms of desert. The strength of the utilitarian argument is that rules can be changed according to changes in society, but that no such change is built into theories of retribution.

Can a re-tributaries ever be forgiving or merciful? During the sentencing process, offenders often say they are remorseful for their actions, and in this sense remorse represents regret and self-blame. Those charged with the task of determining the sentence are urged to accept statements of remorse as mitigating factors.

The issue, therefore, is whether genuine remorse should lead a sentence towards leniency. If the sentence is a utilitarian, he or she will be concerned only about whether a remorseful offender will be less likely to re-offend. However, for the re-tributaries, the question is whether remorse should mitigate culpability.

According to Walker, forgiveness has no degrees but may take the form of "interested" or "disinterested" forgiveness, with the victim being interested and the sentencing authority disinterested.

He suggests that whether from a utilitarian or re-tributaries viewpoint, the sentencing authority must choose the sentence that is most appropriate, and that a re-tributaries may take extenuating circumstances into account. He considers, however, that forgiveness, being an act of absolution, should not be considered an extenuating circumstance.

Thus, according to Bean, "forgiveness is a moral sentiment where ill-will is no longer retained. It may occur before or after punishment but does not affect it". Mercy must be distinguished from forgiveness because granting mercy is an act, but forgiveness is an attitude of mind. Mercy may be prompted by expressions of remorse or by a statement that the victim has forgiven the offender. Walker argues that mercy is not equivalent to "reasoned leniency" and that mercy, in effect, suggests other considerations such as proportionality and any suffering experienced by the offender, and mitigation generally.

Fundamentally, therefore, mercy is a synonym for various kinds of leniency and has no force or effect of its own.

Rehabilitation

Retribution and deterrence involve a process of thinking that proceeds from the crime to the punishment. However, rehabilitation is a more complex notion involving an examination of the offense and the criminal, and a concern for the criminal's social background and punishment. Further, those in favour of rehabilitation theories acknowledge the possibility of additional problems developing during the offender's sentence or treatment that may be unconnected with the offense and which may require an offender to spend additional periods in treatment or confinement.

Utilitarian theory argues that punishment should have reformative or rehabilitative effects on the offender. The offender is considered reformed because the result of punishment is a change in the offender's values so that he or she will refrain from committing further offenses, now believing such conduct to be wrong. This change can be distinguished from simply abstaining from criminal acts due to the fear of being caught and punished again; this amounts to deterrence, not reformation or rehabilitation by punishment. Proponents of rehabilitation in punishment argue that punishment should be tailored to fit the offender and his or her needs, rather than fitting the offense.

Underpinning this notion is the view that offenders ought to be rehabilitated or reformed so they will not re-offend, and that society ought to provide treatment to an offender. Rehabilitationist theory regards crime as the symptom of a social disease and sees the aim of rehabilitation as curing that disease through treatment.

In essence, the rehabilitative philosophy denies any connection between guilt and punishment. Bean outlines the strengths of the rehabilitation position as being its emphasis on the personal lives of offenders, its treatment of people as individuals, and its capacity to produce new thinking in an otherwise rigid penal system. He suggests its weaknesses include an unwarranted assumption that crime is related to disease and that social experts can diagnose that condition; treatment programs are open-ended and do not relate to the offense or to other defined criteria; and the fact that the offender, not being seen as fully responsible for his or her actions, is capable of manipulating the treatment to serve his or her own interests.

In addition, rehabilitation theory tends to see crime as predetermined by social circumstances rather than as a matter of choice by the offender. This, it is said, denies the agency of the offender and arguably treats an offender in a patronising, infantilism way. Indeterminate sentences gave effect to the rehabilitative perspective because terms of imprisonment were not fixed at trial, but rather the release decision was given to institutions and persons operating within the criminal justice system, including parole boards, probation officers, and social workers.

The notion of rehabilitation enjoyed considerable political and public support in the first half of the 20th century, but modern rehabilitationists now argue that fixed rather than determinant sentences should be the context for rehabilitation. They argue that with indeterminate sentences, offenders become preoccupied with their likely release date, and this leads to their pretending to have made more progress in treatment than is really the case.

The demise of rehabilitation as a theory of punishment began in the 1970s and was the result of a complex set of factors, one of which was a much quoted article by Martinson who argued that "nothing works"; that is, that no treatment program works very successfully in preventing re-offending, and that no program works better than any other. Martinson later attempted to rectify this pessimistic view of rehabilitation and treatment by acknowledging that some programs work, sometimes, for some types of offenders.

Nevertheless, from that point on, policy makers and legislators abandoned rehabilitation as an objective of punishment. Other the issue of indeterminate sentencing, the publication of Criminal Sentences:

> Law without Order by Marvin Frankel, then a federal judge, which argued that judges exercised "almost wholly unchecked and sweeping authority" in sentencing, provided substantial support to the proponents of determinate sentencing. By the 1980s, the re-tributionist theory of just deserts had become the most influential theory of punishment.

Nowadays, rehabilitationists contend that their rationale for punishment is the only one that combines crime reduction with respect for an offender's rights. According to this view, although capital punishment and long terms of imprisonment may deter and will certainly incapacitate, rehabilitation can be accomplished only if criminals re-enter society; consequently extreme punishments should be ruled out.

Rotman for example, argues in favour of a "right's oriented rehabilitation," which accepts the offender's liability to receive punishment but claims a corresponding right on his or her part to "return to society with a better chance of being a useful citizen and staying out of prison."

This perspective is often termed "state-obligated rehabilitation," and contends that if the state assumes the right to punish, it should ensure that no more harm is inflicted than was intended when the sentence was pronounced. That is, the intent of the prison sentence is deprivation of liberty and not loss of family ties or employability. Rotman, for one, argues that a failure to provide rehabilitation amounts to cruel and unusual punishment. Carlen and Matthews argue that states are entitled to punish offenders because offenders act out of choice.

However, they suggest that the offenders' choices are often limited because of circumstances and social conditions like poverty and inequality, which might lead people into crime. Therefore, Hudson claims, the state should recognise that it plays a part in causing crime and should recognise its role toward crime prevention by providing rehabilitation to assist the offender in not committing further crime.

The offender, on his or her part, has a corresponding obligation to take part in rehabilitation programs offered by the state. In this view, rehabilitation may be seen as an alternative to punishment rather than as something to be achieved through the means of punishment.

As Carlen contends, a purely punitive approach to sentencing does little to decrease crime and serves only to increase the prison population.

Incapacitation

Penal practice has always tried to estimate the risk that individual offenders might commit crimes in the future and has tried to shape penal controls to prevent such crimes from happening. Through the in capacitative approach, offenders are placed in custody, usually for long periods of time, to protect the public from the chance of future offending.

In utilitarian theory, incapacitation is seen as a good consequence of punishment because, when serving his or her sentence, the offender is removed from society and is therefore unable to commit further offenses. This applies regardless of whether the offender is deterred, reformed, or rehabilitated through the punishment he or she is given. Incapacity may also be present in other forms of punishment such as parole, in the sense that although the offender is free from incarceration, he or she is placed under supervision, which may restrict his or her opportunity to commit crime.

Some criminologists claim that certain offenders commit crimes at very high rates, and that applying a policy of selective incapacitation aimed at these "career criminals" will assist with the aims of crime prevention.

There are two basic objections to following a policy of incapacitation based on selecting offenders for this kind of punishment. The first is that predicting criminal dangerousness is problematic and will inevitably mean that a number of persons will suffer incapacitation who would not have committed further crimes if left free, because, given the inaccuracies of prediction, it is necessary to lock up or incapacitate large numbers of non-dangerous offenders so we can ensure we incapacitate dangerous offenders.

Second, there is the moral objection that it is wrong in principle to punish offenders based on a prediction of their future conduct; that is, they ought to be punished for what they have done and not for what they might do in the future.

Morris argues that sentences intended to incapacitate an offender ought to be permitted only where there exists reliable information showing a high probability of future offending. Morris suggests that taking account of dangerousness in the future should be considered to be statements about an offender's present condition and not as a prediction of future conduct.

Some of the problems inherent in capacitative sentencing include the following:

— It works only if we lock up those who would have committed further offenses if they had been left free.

— If those we lock up are not immediately replaced by new recruits.

— If the crimes committed after release are not so frequent or serious so as to negate the effects of the crimes prevented through in capacitative sentencing.

Ethical questions that arise from the sentencing rationale of incapacitation include:

— Is it ethical to punish persons for crimes not yet committed?

— Is it ethical to base punishment on inaccurate predictions?

— Is it ethical to punish a repeat offender for a past crime he or she committed and has already been punished for?

The notion of incapacitation is reflected in such punishment policies as three-strikes legislation, mandatory minimum sentences, and truth in sentencing.

Restorative Justice

Braith waite argues that restorative justice has been "the dominant model of criminal justice throughout most of human history for all the world's peoples," and that it is grounded in traditions from ancient Greek, Arab, and Roman civilisations and in Hindu, Buddhist, and Confucian traditions.

Braith waite emphasises that restorative justice means restoring victims as well as offenders and the community. In addition to restoring lost property or personal injury, restoration means bringing back a sense of security. He points to the shame and dis-empowerment suffered by victims of crime. He observes that Western legal systems generally fail to incorporate victims' voices because the justice system often excludes their participation.

Restoring harmony based on an acceptance that justice has been done is, in his view, inadequate. Essentially, restorative justice proponents emphasise the need to support both victims and offenders, and see social relationships as a rehabilitative vehicle aimed at providing formal and informal social support and control for offenders.

Rather than separating out the offender as a subject for rehabilitation, restorative justice sees social support and social control of offenders as the means to rehabilitation. The origins of restorative justice in the United States lie in part in court orders for reparation taking the form of restitution and community service.

Since the 1970s, restitution and community service have been employed as sentencing tools in criminal and juvenile courts, and during the 1980s an expansion occurred in victim–offender mediation programs resulting partly from interest in restitution and community service programs.

Along with the increased interest in these alternative sanctions, attention to the interests of victims increased during the 1990s, focusing on repair and healing influenced by the "faith community" and feminists. Today, numerous programs can be brought under the rubric of restorative justice, but they often remain small-scale experiments and tend to be associated with community approaches to crime control. In considering the nature of a restorative justice approach to offenders, it is useful to note the three core principles suggested by Van Ness and Strong.

— Justice requires the healing of victims, offenders, and communities injured by crime.

— Victims, offenders, and communities should be permitted to actively involve themselves in the justice process in a timely and substantial manner.

— Roles and responsibilities of the government should be rethought and in its promotion of justice, government should be responsible for preserving a just order and the community should be responsible for establishing peace.

Restorative justice may be considered unique in its emphasis on not just one component of the criminal justice system such as punishment, but as incorporating victims, offenders, and the community in its strategies and designs.

In relation to offenders, Bazemore and Dooley state that there is a normative focus on harm and repair. Repair, in the context of restorative justice, implies a particular form of rehabilitation. However, Bazemore and Dooley concede that there is an absence of theory to explain how the operation of restorative justice is supposed to bring about a change in the offender.

Some restorative justice proponents argue that repair in relation to offenders involves a focus on restoring, strengthening, and building relationships between offenders, victims, and communities, and therefore intervention intended to prevent future crime must focus not only on the offender's obligation to repair harm done to victims and the community, but also on the need to repair broken relationships between the offender and the community, the victim and the community, and the victim and the offender.

Critics of restorative justice point to its too ready assumption that it will be possible to secure agreement between offenders, victims, and communities. Garland notes that one of the functions of punishment is to relieve the feelings of victims and communities where crimes are committed, and that restorative justice avoids the ceremonies and rituals of criminal law that recognise these emotions.

In addition, it can be argued that a greater reliance on restorative justice and a consequent restriction on the operation and expression of criminal law might lead to a situation in which those victims processed through restorative justice might come to believe or feel that the harm they have suffered is of less importance than "real crime."

Feminists, who have argued for severe sentencing for domestic violence, have adopted this argument. Criminalisation and punishment show the limits of tolerance, and depenalising through restorative justice processes tends to suggest that society has a different attitude towards certain kinds of behaviour.

Von Hirsch, in his investigation into the basis for restorative justice, contends that no clear principles have been formulated for restoring the harm done by offenders to community standards, and unlike victim restitution, which involves a task of mediation between the victim and the offender, there are no disputed claims involved in crime because, for example, a robber appropriates something that is clearly the property of the victim. Volpe has warned of the propensity of restorative justice to widen the net of social control.

Sociological Approach

In sociological terms, punishment raises questions such as why particular punishments were used and why they are no longer used; why a punishment like capital punishment has been abandoned to a great extent in the West; and why imprisonment has become the major form of punishment for criminal activity.

In social terms, research has concluded that punishments depend less on philosophical arguments and more on the currents and movements in social thinking and in climates of tolerance and intolerance. A focus on history and changes in social conditions has illuminated the relationship between punishment and society, which in turn has broadened the investigation of the notion of punishment into questions concerned with how order and authority are maintained in society.

Garland summarises social theory about punishment as: "that body of thought which explores the relations between punishment and society, its purpose being to understand punishment as a social phenomenon and thus trace its role in social life." Garland has argued that punishment is the product of social structure and cultural values. Thus, whom we choose to punish, how we punish, and when we punish are determined by the role we give to punishment in society. If we construe criminal punishment as a wrong for a wrong, then we must conclude that society is, in a sense, wronging the offender.

We must therefore ask, "can the infliction of pain or a wrong upon an offender be justified ethically?" To answer this question, one must first look at the purpose of criminal punishment and question the various rationalise put forward for punishment, such as deterrence, incapacitation, rehabilitation, just deserts, retribution, and restorative justice.

Sociological perspectives on punishment include the thinking of Durkheim, Weber, the Marxist tradition, and post-Marxist sociologies of punishment, particularly that propounded by Foucault. Sociologists expand the notion of punishment to "penalty," which they explore in various societies at various times. Hudson defines penalty as... The complex of ideas (about proper punishment, about effective punishment), institutions (laws, policies and practices, agencies and buildings) and relationships (who has the power to say who is punished, whose ideas count, what is the relationship of those who punish and are punished to the rest of society) involved in the punishment of offenders.

Only a broad outline of the various perspectives on penalty will be provided here. According to Durkheim, society has an objective reality apart from the individuals who comprise it, and he argues that people behave according to social rules that, together with customs and traditions, form a culture for a particular society. Durkheim took a functionalist approach; that is, he examined aspects of social life in terms of the functions they performed in society.

He applied this approach to punishment by looking at the functions that punishment fulfils in maintaining social order. Durkheim identified beliefs and sentiments held by members of society, which he called the "conscience collective," and argued that crimes are those acts which violate that conscience collective and produce a punitive reaction. He developed two laws of penal evolution. The first is that punishment is more intense the less developed a society is and the more the central power within that society is of an absolute nature.

Thus, in industrial societies, collective sentiments are embodied in law rather than in religion, so crimes are seen as wrongs against individuals. He tried to demonstrate that penalties changed from ancient societies to his time, from aggravated penalties such as death with torture and mutilation to reduced forms of punishment. In his second law, he develops the notion of punishments having lesser intensity, arguing that imprisonment will become the main punishment replacing death and torture.

Overall, Durkheim sees the function of punishment as promoting social solidarity through the affirmation of values, and argues that punishment's importance lies in its expression of outrage upon the commission of an offense. He believed punishment to be a "passionate reaction" to crime, and this expressive view of punishment can be seen in modern-day notions of censure in re-tribulations.

His focus was not, therefore, on whether punishment was effective in controlling crime, but in its function as a means of maintaining social solidarity through expressions of outrage and through the affirmation of socialite values. Among critics of Durkheim, Garland suggests that Durkheim's analysis of punishment is focused too strongly on punishment's expressive function, causing all other explanations to be discarded.

Nevertheless, Garland points out that Durkheim's insight into the role of punishment—as one of expressing community outrage against criminal acts—does single out one aspect of punishment that seems to resonate in the context of today's debates about "getting tough on crime." In similar fashion, Mead in The Psychology of Punitive Justice contends that the indignation that members of society feel towards the criminal amounts to a cultural sublimation of the instincts and hostilities that the individual has tamed in the interest of social cooperation with others.

Weber's ideas on punishment are implied rather than made explicit in his notions about authority and power in modern society. Having identified three types of authority, the traditional, the charismatic, and the legal, Weber promoted legal authority—the process of making rules by those given the right to rule—as being the most appropriate form of rule for modern societies. For Weber, legal authority carries with it a duty to obey laws.

He argued that systems of laws might be rational or irrational; in a rational system of criminal law, crimes would be defined and rules put forward for adjudicating those crimes. He favoured formal rationality, which he termed "bureaucratic rationality," and saw this as an essential feature of a modern state. His notion of bureaucratic rationality appears in certain features of modern society, such as our processes for making judgments according to rules and the way in which office holders exercise authority.

Developments such as a professional police force and a judiciary as well as due process can be traced to the bureaucratisation of society. Marxist perspectives on punishment evolve out of Marx's concern for the place of capitalism and the relations between production and society. In his view, institutions like law are shaped to parallel the relations of production and the maintenance of the capitalist system. Marxist penologists have argued that punishment regulates the supply of labour; this view was put forward in 1939 by Rusche and Kirchheimer in Punishment and Social Structure.

In discussing the history of punishment in Europe from the 13th century until the development of capitalism, the authors perceive the severity of punishment as being tied directly to the value of labour. Thus, the severity of punishment, they argue, is relatively lenient when labour is scarce and its value high, whereas when labour is abundant, punishments become more intense.

Another key aspect of their view is the principle of less eligibility. The argument is that the conditions the offender will experience in prison must be worse than anything he or she is likely to endure outside the prison in order to restrain the "reserve army of labour" from crime; that is, to serve as a deterrent to the lowest social classes. The idea of less eligibility encompasses matters like discipline, diet, accommodation, and general living conditions in prisons.

Rusche argued that this principle limited penal reform because punishments and prison conditions could not be improved beyond a point that would bring the offender into line with the standard of life of the least advantaged non-offender. This analysis has been criticised for its economic reductions (it only offers an economic argument to explain changes in punishment).

Nevertheless, it has led to a series of studies that have tested the basic framework and found some correlation between punishment and the labour market in the United States over time. The important point is that the authors, together with other Marxists, have provided the insight that all punishment cannot be understood simply as a response to crime. In other words, when changes in the use of imprisonment and other punishments are examined in historical contexts, other factors appear to have influenced their development.

Other Marxist theorists like Melossi and Pashuknis have asked why imprisonment persists, as opposed to other forms of punishment. One answer from Pashuknis is that there is a correspondence between the development of wage labour, which puts a price on time, and paying for crime by "doing time." In this sense, Marxist theory concerning the relations of production is found mirrored in the punishment of imprisonment, and Marxists therefore argue that a crucial principle in society is the exchange of equivalence.

Punishment, therefore, becomes an exchange transaction in which the offender pays his debt, an expression commonly used today both in that form and in the notion of "paying a debt to society". Marxist analysis of society generally has been heavily criticised by feminists for ignoring gender and for outmoded interpretative frameworks.

In 1977, Michel Foucault published Discipline and Punish: The Birth of the Prison, revolutionising the study of penalty and punishment by presenting the notion of penalty and highlighting discipline as the key element in modern forms of punishment. In his complex exploration of penalty, Foucault follows an approach that examines the issue from the ground up through a detailed examination of penal practices. His central focus is the exercise of power in modern society and its linkages with knowledge to exercise power of and over the body.

Describing first the effect and content of the public execution, Foucault shows how the infliction of pain on the body gave way to an exercise of power through the new practice of disciplining the individual through institutions such as the factory and the modern prison, and how this led to the development of a class of "delinquents."

Foucault claims that disciplinary regulation is the fundamental principle of social control in modern society and is most fully realised in the form of the prison. Foucault emphasises the role of punishment in producing the "right-thinking citizen"; that is, the trained and disciplined individual. Foucault draws on both Weber (in his emphasis on bureaucratisation) and Durkheim (in his description of punishment as an expressive force) in his account of penalty. However, he adopts a much broader analytic framework that links punishment and penalty and connects them directly to changes in society and to the exercise of power over the individual. Foucault's ideas have inspired many followers including.

10

Prison Reforms

A prison is a place in which people are physically confined and, usually, deprived of a range of personal freedom. Other terms are penitentiary, correctional facility, and jail (or gaol), although in the United States "jail" and "prison" usually refer to different sub-types of correctional facility. Jails are conventionally institutions which form part of the criminal justice system of a county and house both inmates awaiting trial and convicted mis-dominants. Prisons form part of the criminal justice system of a state and only house convicted felons, usually for longer periods of time than jails. Imprisonment or incarceration is a legal penalty that may be imposed by the state for the commission of a crime.

A criminal suspect who has been charged with or is likely to be charged with criminal offense may be held on remand in prison if he is denied or unable to meet conditions of bail, or is unable or unwilling to post bail. A criminal defendant may also be held in prison while awaiting trial or a trial verdict. If found guilty, a defendant will be convicted and may receive a custodial sentence requiring imprisonment.

As well as convicted or suspected criminals, prisons may be used for internment of those not charged with a crime. Prisons may also be used as a tool of political repression to detain political prisoners, of conscience, and "enemies of the state", particularly by authoritarian regimes. In times of war or conflict, prisoners of war may also be detained in prisons. A prison system is the organisational arrangement of the provision and operation of prisons, and depending on their nature, may invoke a corrections system. Although people have been imprisoned throughout history, they have also regularly been able to perform prison escapes.

For most of history, imprisoning has not been a punishment in itself, but rather a way to confine criminals until corporal or capital punishment was administered. There were prisons used for detention in Jerusalem in Old Testament times. Dungeons were used to hold prisoners; those who were not killed or left to die there often became galley slaves or faced penal transportations. In other cases debtors were often thrown into debtor's prisons, until they paid their jailers enough money in exchange for a limited degree of freedom.

Only in the 19th century, beginning in Britain, did prisons as we know them today become commonplace. The modern prisons system was born in London, as a result of the views of Jeremy Bentham. The notion of prisoners being incarcerated as part of their punishment and not simply as a holding state until trial or hanging, was at the time revolutionary.

Britain practised penal transportation of convicted criminals to penal colony in the British colonies in the Americas, from the 1610s through the American Revolution in the 1770s and to penal colonies in Australia between 1788 and 1868. France sent criminals to tropical penal colonies including Louisiana in the early eighteenth century. Penal colonies in French Guiana operated until 1951 (in particular, infamous Lie du Diable (Devil's Island)). Katorga prisons were established in the 17th century in Tsardom of Russia in under populated areas of Siberia and the Russian

Far East that had few towns or food sources. Since these times, Siberia gained its fearful connotation of punishment.

The first "modern" prisons of the early 19th Century were sometimes known by the term "penitentiary" (a term still used by some prisons in the USA today or the Dutch "Penitentiare Inrichting/Institution): as the name suggests, the goal of these facilities was that of penance by the prisoners, through a regimen of strict disciplines, silent reflections and perhaps forced and deliberately pointless labour on tread wheels and the like. This "Auburn system" of prisoner management was often reinforced by elaborate prison architecture, such as the separate system and the panopticon. It was not until the late 19th Century that rehabilitation through education and skilled labour became the standard goal of prisons.

Design and Facilities

Male and female prisoners are typically kept in separate locations or separate prisons altogether. Prison accommodation, especially modern prisons in the developed world, are often divided into wings. A building holding more than one wing is known as a "hall". Many prisons are divided into two sections, one containing prisoners before trial and the other containing convicted prisoners. Amongst the facilities that prisons may have are:

— A main entrance, which may be known as the 'gate lodge' or 'sally port'.

— A religious facility, which will often house chaplaincy offices and facilities for counselling of individuals or groups.

— An 'education facility', often including a library, providing adult education or continuing education opportunities.

— A gym or an exercise yard, a fenced, usually open-air-area which prisoners may use for recreational and exercise purposes.

— A health care facility or hospital.

— A segregation unit (also called a 'block' or 'isolation cell'), used to separate unruly, dangerous, or vulnerable prisoners from the general population, also sometimes used as punishment.

— A section of vulnerable prisoners (VPs), or protective custody (PC) units, used to accommodate prisoners classified as vulnerable, such as sex offenders, former police officers, informants and those that have gotten into debt or trouble with other prisoners.

— A section of safe cells, used to keep prisoners under constant visual observation, for example when considered at risk of suicide.

— A visiting area, where prisoners may be allowed restricted contact with relatives, friends, lawyers, or other people.

— A death row in some prisons, a section for criminals awaiting execution.

— A staff accommodation area, where staff and corrections officers live in the prison, typical of historical prisons.

— A service/facilities area housing support facilities like kitchens.

— Industrial or agricultural plants operated with convict labour.

— A recreational area containing a TV and pool table.

Prisons are normally surrounded by fencing, walls, earth works, geographical features, or other barriers to prevent escape. Multiple barriers, concerting wire, electrified fencing, secured and defensible main gates, armed guard towers, lighting, motion sensors, dogs and roving patrols may all also be present depending on the level of security. Remotely controlled doors, CCTV monitoring, alarms, cages, restraints, non-lethal and lethal weapons, riot-control gear and physical segregation of units and prisoners may all also be present within a prison to monitor and control the movement and activity of prisoners within the facility.

Modern prison designs have sought to increasingly restrict and control the movement of prisoners throughout the facility while permitting a maximal degree of direct monitoring by a smaller corrections staff. As compared to traditional large landing-cellblock designs which were inherited from the 19th century and which permitted only intermittent observation of prisoners, many newer prisons are designed in a decentralised "popular" layout.

Smaller, separate and self-contained housing units known as "pods" or "modules" are designed to hold between sixteen and fifty prisoners each and are arranged around exercise yards or support facilities in a decentralised "campus" pattern. A small number of corrections officers, sometimes a single officer, is assigned to supervise each pod.

The pods contain tiers of cells arranged around a central control station or desk from which a single officer can monitor all of the cells and the entire pod, control cell doors and communicate with the rest of the prison. Pods may be designed for high-security "indirect-supervision", in which officers in segregated and sealed control booths monitor smaller numbers of prisoners confined to their cells. An alternative is "direct-supervision", in which officers work within the pod and directly interact with and supervise prisoners, who may spend the day outside their cells in a central "day room" on the floor of the pod. Movement in or out of the pod to and from exercise yards, work assignments or medical appointments can be restricted to individual pods at designated times and is generally centrally controlled.

Goods and services, such as meals, laundry, commissary, educational materials, religious services and medical care can increasingly be brought to individual pods or cells as well. Despite these design innovations, overcrowding at many prisons, particularly in the U.S., has resulted in a contrary trend, as many prisons are forced to house large numbers of prisoners, often hundreds at a time, in gymnasiums or other large buildings that have been converted into massive open dormitories.

Lower-security prisons are often designed with less restrictive features, confining prisoners at night in smaller locked dormitories or even cottage or cabin-like housing while permitting them freer movement around the grounds to work or activities during the day.

Security Levels

The levels of security within a prison system are categorised differently around the world, but tend to follow a distinct pattern. Most developed countries divide prisons into separate security classes depending on the inmate population and the security needed to keep them under control.

Accordingly, most developed countries have classes ranging from the most secure, which typically hold violent prisoners and those judged most likely to escape, to the least, which are most often used to house nonviolent offenders or those for whom more stringent security is deemed unnecessary. Below are some different examples of prison classifications from around the world.

United States

— *Supermax:* As the name implies, the custody level goes beyond Maximum by segregating the "worst of the worst" criminals and terrorists who pose a threat to national security. These inmates have individual cells and are kept in lock down for 23 hours per day. Meals are served through "chuck holes" in the cell door, and each inmate is permitted out of their cell for one hour of exercise per day, alone. They are permitted no contact with other inmates and are under constant surveillance via closed-circuit television cameras.

— *Administrative:* Administrative security is a classification of prisons or detention centres that are for a specific purpose, such as housing mentally ill offenders. These range in levels of security From Minimum to Administrative Maximum Security (ADMAX). As in the case of ADX Florence in Colorado.

— *Maximum:* A custody level in which both design and construction as well as inmate classification reflect the need to provide maximum external and internal control and supervision of inmates primarily through the use of high security perimeters and extensive use of internal physical barriers and check points. Inmates accorded this status present serious escape risks or pose serious threats to themselves, to other inmates, to staff, or the orderly running of the institution. Supervision of inmates is direct and constant.

— *High:* The "Middle Ground" for violent crimes, High security institutions have highly-secured perimeters (featuring walls or reinforced fences), multiple- and single-occupant cell housing, the highest staff-to-inmate ratio, and close control of inmate movement.

— *Medium:* A custody level in which design and construction as well as inmate classification reflect the need to provide secure external and internal control and supervision of inmates. Inmates accorded to this status may present a moderate escape risk or may pose a threat to other inmates, staff, or the orderly running of the institution. Supervision remains constant and direct. Through an inmate's willingness to comply with institutional rules and regulations, increased job and program opportunities exist.

— *Close Security:* Close Security prisons are institutions which house inmates too dangerous for Low Security, but who did not commit a crime worthy of incarceration in a Medium Security Facility. These prisons are rare, as most inmates fall into either "Medium", or "Low" Security Classifications. These facilities are often located in separate areas of a Low or Medium security Prison.

— *Low:* A custody level in which both the design and construction as well as inmate classification reflect the goal of returning to the inmate a greater sense of personal responsibility and autonomy while still providing for supervision and monitoring of behavior and activity. Inmates within this security level are not considered a serious risk to the safety of staff, inmates or to the public. Program participation is mandated and geared toward their potential reintegration into the community. Additional access to the community is limited and under constant direct staff supervision.

— *Minimum:* The Lowest Level of Security to which an inmate can be assigned directly. This type of Prison is typically a "Prison Farm", or other work-oriented facility, and most often houses petty or "White collar" criminals.

— *Pre-release:* A custody level in which both design and construction as well as inmate classification reflect the goal of restoring to the inmate maximum responsibility and control of their own behavior and actions prior to their release. Direct supervision of these inmates is not required, but intermittent observation may be appropriate under certain conditions. Inmates within this level may be permitted to access the community un-escorted to participate in programming to include, but not limited to, work release or educational release.

England and Wales

In England and Wales, prisoners are assigned security classes when they are sentenced. Thus prisons are given security classifications depending on the prisoners it is designed to hold. Therefore, prisons classified as "A" would typically house prisoners assigned the "A" category during sentencing, and be designed with the level of security necessary for that class. The categories of prisoners in descending order are:

— *Category A:* prisoners are those whose escape would be highly dangerous to the public or national security.

— *Category B:* prisoners are those who do not require maximum security, but for whom escape needs to be made very difficult.

— *Category C:* prisoners are those who cannot be trusted in open conditions but who are unlikely to try to escape.

— *Category D:* prisoners are those who can be reasonably trusted not to try to escape, and are given the privilege of an open prison.

Prisoners at 'D Cat' (as it is commonly known) prisons, are, subject to approval, given ROTL (Release On Temporary License) to work in the community or to go on 'home leave' once they have passed their FLED (Full License Eligibility Dates), which is usually a quarter of the way through the sentence. The British prison system is also divided into "Open" and "Closed" prisons. Categories A-C are considered "Closed" prisons as prisoners cannot be trusted to interact with society, while category D prisons are generally "Open", meaning that prisoners with a good record and who are approved can be allowed limited function in society such as home-leave or a nominal employment.

Types of Prisons

Prisons for juveniles are known as young offender institutes or similar designation and hold minors who have been remanded into custody or serving sentence. Many countries have their own age of criminal responsibility in which children are deemed legally responsible for their actions for a crime. Countries such as Canada may try and sentence a juvenile as an adult, but have them serve their sentence in a juvenile facility until they reach the age of majority, at which time they would be transferred to an adult facility.

Military Military Prison

Prisons form part of military systems, and are used variously to house prisoners of war, unlawful combatants, those whose freedom is deemed a national security risk by military or civilian authorities, and members of the military found guilty of a serious crime.

Political Political Prisoner

Certain countries maintain or have in the past had a system of political prisons; arguably the gulags associated with Stalinism are best known, although contemporary Guantanamo Bay detention camp run by the US held (again arguably) primarily political prisoners.

Psychiatric Psychiatric Hospital

Some psychiatric facilities have characteristics of prisons, particularly when confining patients who have committed a crime and are considered dangerous. In addition, many prisons have psychiatric units dedicated to housing offenders diagnosed with a wide variety of mental disorders.

Rehabilitation

Meta-analysis of previous studies shows that prison sentences do not reduce future offenses, when compared to nonresidential sanctions. This meta-analysis of one hundred separate studies found that post-release offenses were around 7% higher after imprisonment compared with nonresidential sanctions, at statistically significant levels. Another meta-analysis of 101 separate tests of the impact of prison on crime found a 3% increase in offending after imprisonment. Longer periods of time in prison make outcomes worse, not better; offending increases by around 3% as prison sentences increase in length.

Effective rehabilitation programs reduce the likelihood of re-offense and recidivism. Effective programs are characterised by three things: first, they provide more hours for people with known offense risk factors (the Risk Principle); secondly, they address problems and needs that have a proven causal link to offending (the Needs Principle); and thirdly, they use cognitive-behavioural approaches to behaviour modification (the Responsibility Principle).

Providing rehabilitation to people at lower risk of re-offending results in a 3% reduction in re-offending, while providing rehabilitation to people with a high risk of re-offending is three times as effective, resulting in a 10% reduction in subsequent offending. Risk factors for re-offending are: age at first offense, number of prior offenses, level of family and personal problems in childhood and other historical factors, along with level of current needs related to offending. Those individuals who had many personal and family problems in childhood, started offending before puberty, and have committed multiple priors are more likely to re-offend in future, according to longitudinal studies internationally.

In support of the Needs Principle, programs that specifically target crinogenic needs (causal needs and problems), see a 19% reduction in re-offending. In support of the Responsibility Principle, there is a 23% reduction in re-offending after participating in programs that use cognitive-behavioural methods to bring about changes in behaviour, thinking, and relationships. When all three principles are effectively applied, the impact on offending is a 26–32% reduction, compared to a 3–7% increase in offending found with imprisonment alone.

Residential approaches—whether in prison or some other live-in option—tend to be less effective than nonresidential approaches. These researchers found that effective programs delivered in the community were followed by a 35% reduction in re-offending, whereas effective programs delivered in residential settings (such as prisons and halfway houses) were followed by a 17% reduction in re-offending. One very likely reason for this is that for teens and adults, mixing with antisocial peers increases the risk of offending. In prison or residences inmates spend a great deal of time with other people immersed in criminal pursuits and beliefs, whereas in community-based programs there is more opportunity to mix with people involved in constructive, law-abiding activities. Antisocial peers in prisons and residences can form a very powerful pressure group, subtly and not so subtly influencing the behavior of other inmates.

Resocialisation

Resocialisation is a sociological concept dealing with the process of mentally and emotionally "retraining" a person so that he or she can operate in an environment other than that which he or she is accustomed to. Resocialisation into a total institution involves a complete change of personality. Key examples include the process of re-socialising new recruits into the military so that they can operate as soldiers (or, in other words, as members of a cohesive unit) and the reverse process, in which those who have become accustomed to such roles return to society after military.

Population Statistics

As of 2006, it is estimated that at least 9.25 million people are currently imprisoned worldwide. It is probable that this number is likely to be much higher, in view of general under-reporting and a lack of data from various countries, especially authoritarian regimes.

In absolute terms, the United States currently has the largest inmate population in the world, with more than 2½ million or more than one in a hundred adults in prison and jails. Although the United States represents less than 5% of the world's population, over 25% of the people incarcerated around the world are housed in the American prison system. Pulitser Prize winning author Joseph T. Hallinan wrote in his book Going Up the River: Travels in a Prison Nation, "so common is the prison experience that the federal government predicts one in eleven men will be incarcerated in his lifetime, one in four if he is black." In 2002, both Russia and China also had prison populations in excess of 1 million. By October 2006, the Russian prison population declined to 869,814 which translated into 611 prisoners per 100,000 population.

As a percentage of total population, the United States also has the largest imprisoned population, with 739 people per 100,000 serving time, awaiting trial or otherwise detained.

In March 2007, the United Kingdom had 80,000 inmates in its facilities, one of the highest rates among the western members of the European Union (EU) (a record formerly held by Portugal). The highest imprisonment rates among the larger EU members include that of Poland, which in August 2007 had about 90,000 inmates, i.e. 234 prisoners per 100,000 inhabitants, while the highest rates are in the Baltic states Estonia, Latvia and Lithuania with estimated rates of 240, 292 and 333 respectively in 2006.

The high proportion of prisoners in some developed countries is from various causes, but the attitude toward drug-taking plays a considerable part. In undeveloped countries, rates of incarceration are often lower. In general, such societies have fewer goods to steal and a more community based social system, with less judicial law-enforcement. Also their economies may not support the high cost of incarceration.

Asia and Oceania

Many prisons in Australia were built by convict labour in the 1800s. During the 1990s, various state governments in Australia engaged private sector correctional corporations to build and operate prisons whilst several older government run institutions were de-commissioned. Operation of Federal detention centres was also privatised at a time when a large influx of illegal immigrants began to arrive in Australia.

New Zealand

New Zealand currently maintains 19 prisons around the country. The Department of Corrections has an annual budget of NZD$748 million and assets worth over NZD$1.7 billion. Official statistics show that there are currently 7,605 prisoners within the New Zealand correctional system. + 5,795 staff. Break-outs are only at 0.15 per 100 prisoners and there is a rate of only 15% positive drug results during random drug testing in NZ prisons.

France

The French Ministry of Justice's French Prison Service division has 194 prisons in mainland and the overseas territories. As of 1 January 2009, statistics showed approximately 52,000 available places, with around 58,000 "hosted" prisoners. France is home to Fleury-Mérogis Prison, Europe's largest correctional facility.

Germany

Germany has 194 prisons (of which 19 are open institutions). Official statistics showed 80,214 places on March 31, 2007. On the same day, there were 75,719 prisoners. This is less than the highest value of 81,176 prisoners on March 31, 2003.

Ireland

Most jails in the Republic of Ireland were built in the 19th century, including Kilmainham Gaol (no longer in use), Mount joy Prison and Portlaoise Prison. A new €30m prison is planned at Thornton Hall to replace Mount joy.

Poland

As of the end of August 2007, Poland officially declared 90,199 prisoners, giving an imprisonment rate per 100,000 inhabitants of about 234. The overpopulation rate (number of prisoners held compared to number of places for prisoners) was estimated by the official prison service as 119%.

The growth rate of imprisonment in Poland during 2006–2007 was approximately 4% annually, based on the August 2007 estimate of 90,199 prisoners and the June 2005 estimate of 82,572 prisoners.

Turkey

Prisons in Turkey are classified as closed, semi-open and open prisons. Closed prisons are separated into different kinds according to its structure and the number of prisoners held. Examples are A type, B type, E type and F type. F types are high security prisons, known in the USA as Supermax.

North America

In the United States penal system, a jail is a correctional institution used to detain persons who are in the lawful custody of the state, including accused persons awaiting trial and those who have been convicted of a crime and are serving a sentence of less than one year. Jails are generally small penitentiaries run by individual counties and cities, though some jails in larger communities may be as large and hold as many inmates as regular prisons. As with prisons, some jails have different wings for certain types of offenders, and have work programs for inmates who demonstrate good behavior.

Jails are typically operated by city or county governments, and house prisoners who are being detained before trial or serving sentences less than one year. Approximately half of the U.S. Jail population consists of pre-trial detainees who have not been convicted or sentenced. Prisoners serving terms longer than one year are typically housed in correctional facilities operated by state governments. Unlike most state prisons, a jail usually houses both men and women in separate portions of the same facility. Some jails lease space to house inmates from the federal government, state prisons or from other counties for profit.

In 2005, a report by the Bureau of Justice Statistics found that 62 percent of people in jails have not been convicted, meaning many of them are awaiting trial. As of 2005, local jails held or supervised 819,434 individuals. Nine percent of these individuals were in programs such as community service, work release, weekend reporting, electronic monitoring, and other alternative programs.

In the United States, as compared to regular 'main line' state and federal prisons, in which prisoners have already been investigated and classified by corrections personnel before being assigned to a level of security, in which many of the prisoners are committed for longer periods of time, and in which the population is on average older, jails usually house prisoners who are on average younger and have varying or unknown histories and propensities for violence or disciplinary problems. As a result, many jails operate their booking and receiving units at a relatively high level of correctional security, and also witness a disproportionately large amount of violence and disciplinary problems as compared to main line facilities.

There are three main management styles common in most U. S. Jails. The first and oldest style is Intermittent Surveillance. Intermittent Surveillance involves rows of cells along security corridors. These corridors are patrolled by staff providing periodic observation. Most problems occur between these intermittent patrols. The second supervisory style is Remote Surveillance. Remote Surveillance involves cells and their corresponding day rooms divided into "pods" which are under constant supervision by jail staff from a central control room.

Staff in the central control room commonly observe three to four "pods" at one time. The third and most recently conceived supervisory style is Direct Supervision. Direct Supervision involves a day room with numerous cells under constant and direct supervision by staff who are stationed inside the housing unit. Staff are constantly interacting with inmates and controlling inmate behavior. The success of

Direct Supervision relies on the staff's ability to control this behavior and for facility management to create detention environments that facilitate the staff's effectiveness. This style is also the most cost effective of the three.

The 52 penitentiaries in Canada are operated by the federal government, and are for those who have been sentenced to serve more than 2 years of custody. The boundary of two years separating provincial and federal custody underlies the sentencing of some offenders to "two years less a day", so they can serve their sentences in provincial correctional institutions.

Reforms in Prison Systems

All men are born equal and are endowed by their creator with some basic rights. These rights are mainly right to life and liberty, but if any person doesn't comply with ethics of the society then that person is deprived of these rights with proper punishment. Many experts believe that the main objective of prisons is to bring the offenders back to the mainstream of the society. Various workshops had been organised by the State Government in collaboration with NGO's to bring reforms in the current prison systems.

Many reforms can be made in jail administration, which are mainly: A- Class prisoners can meet their own expenditure by depositing certain amount fixed by the Government for enjoying special services like tea, newspapers, pillow, and 3 times non vegetarian food in a week and if they are vegetarian they will be served ghee, dhal and buttermilk. Many inmates usually complain about inadequate quality and quantity of food, which is required to be improved. The food is required to be prepared in better hygienic conditions.

Rehabilitation of inmates will be meaningful only if they are employed after release and for that purpose educational facilities should be introduced or upgraded. In many jails, inmates including hard-core criminals and women had joined various courses offered by IGNOU and their respective State Universities. Courses mainly offered by then are BA, MA, MBA & other post graduation courses. The inmates can also join the classes of 10th and +2 for basic guidance. In many jails with a view of imparting vocational training a fully fledged computer training centres has been established.

The inmates are also provided training in carpentry and fabric painting. Many jails have also initiated programs for women empowerment by training then in weaving, making toys, stitching and making embroidery items. Wage earning and gratuity schemes and incentives are also used to reduce the psychological burden on the convicts. Recently, the Government of Himachal Pradesh had lifted ban on wearing Gandhi cap in jails. Various seminars are organised by jail authorities to enlighten the prisoners on their legal rights, health and sanitation problems, HIV/AIDS and issues of mental health, juveniles, minorities and steps to reduce the violence in prisons.

The open prison system has come as a very modern and effective alternative to the system of closed imprisonment. The establishment of open prisons on a large scale as a substitute for the closed prisons, the latter being reserved for hard-core criminals shall be one of the greatest prison reforms in the penal system.

Yet several steps have been taken to improve the conditions of prisons, but much more is required to be done. Central Government along with NGO's and prison administration should take adequate steps for effective centralisation of prisons and a uniform jail manual should be drafted throughout the country. The uniformity of standards can be maintained throughout all the States. Thus such practices will help in changing the traditional and colonial outlook of the Indian Prison System and also help the prisoners to become more responsible, creative and potential citizen.

Indian jails in recent times have witnessed unprecedented happenings.Sometimes back the prisoners at Agra jail posed lots of problems for the jail authorities in order to create better standards of existence within four walls of jail. The Article 21 in crystal clear terms states that prisoners claim right over free legal service. However, the reality is otherwise. They rot in jail for years, being devoid of legal representation, which leads to development of sadistic traits within them. The prison authorities seem intent on converting them into hard core criminals with little realisation of the fact that prison term is meant to readjust the attitude of offenders to the requirements of life.

Needless to say, there is urgent need to introduce better atmosphere within jails via prison reforms. On the one hand 'high profile' prisoners have access to quality facilities and, on the other, the ordinary prisoners, including the under trials, are forced to live hellish life, leading to violent clashes and suicides or even jailbreaks. A creation of better world within jails is the only mean to stop the occurrence of such grim episodes.

In India Jails are generally no better than dungeons. Thousands of under trials (men and women) have been waiting for years for the courts to decide their fate, one way or the other. Many of them have been languishing because of the mulish judicial process. The arrears in the courts are so huge that even petty crimes cannot be disposed of quickly-the result is that hundreds are spending their years in cells in the company of hardened criminals because there is none to bail them out, even if the bail amount is a paltry Rs 500; the pile-up of pending cases in courts is matched only by the pile-up of prisoners in jails. A telling, if not chilling example is that of an unfortunate man in Assam who was thrown behind bars when he was a young man and remained there for decades without his case ever coming up before a court until he was released, courtesy media glare. When he was released, he had become old and feeble and a bit unhinged!

For a few influential men, finally nabbed by the long arm of the law, jail sentence is not all that distressing, though. The recent elections brought to light many such characters:

— Take the case of Mitrasen Yadav who lent a helping hand to his party and is a co-accused in a murder case. He benefited from presidential pardon after being awarded life imprisonment but later was accused of cheating, dacoity and rioting. He is no stranger to jail. He is one of the VIPs of Indian jails.

— Amarmani Tripathi, the prime-accused in poetess Madhumita Shukla murder case, addressed a public meeting in the Lakshmipur assembly segment over a mobile phone from inside the Dehradun jail.

— Another politician, Abhay Singh, with a known criminal background, conducted a meeting of his supporters inside the jail to work out a strategy for the election campaign of his wife. He was also accused of issuing threatening calls to voters from inside the prison. That he is an accused in several murder cases seems to have made him even more influential.

— Yet another don, who found virtue in politician's clothes, was reported to have been constantly sending "messages" to voters to vote for him.

A report prepared at the instance of the Allahabad High Court showed a long list of criminal cases pending against politicians, the longest dating back to 22 years! What is more alarming is the status of a number of criminal cases is not known and the State government submitted to the court that the case files concerning some members of parliament and legislative assemblies were missing. The cases relate to rioting and murder, including the killing of Manjunath, the officer who sought to expose the petrol adulterator-politician nexus.

Jail does not come in the way of influential politicians and others leading their normal lives. A raid in a Meerut jail recently led to recovery of cell phones and other prohibited items. The recovery led to a fight between the police and the inmates of the high-security prison. The inmates injured several policemen and snatched back the cell phones and other articles seized from them. Selling unauthorised and contraband items inside the jail, for a prohibitive price, is common. Cigarettes could cost Rs 20 a stick, a meal of the inmate's choice, Rs 500, a local call Rs 20 and so on.

The former U.P. Minister, Amarmani Tripathi, jailed for murdering his mistress, is reported to have hosted a wedding anniversary bash inside the jail for a co-accused in the murder case. A U.P minister's reaction to the bash was typically nonchalant:

> "you cannot stop anyone from celebrating an occasion concerning him, his family or near and dear ones-within the premises of the jail. As per my knowledge, there was no violation of the Jail Manual-these are the pearls of wisdom that flowed out of the minister!

Three men, who have been recently sentenced to death for the murder of former Punjab Chief Minister, Beant Singh, escaped from jail three years ago. Subsequent inspection of the jail revealed that they not only led a luxurious life but had also enclosed their cells in such a way that their activities inside the cell could not be noticed. Thus they tunnelled their way out of the jail!

As the former director of Central Bureau of Investigation, Mr. Joginder Singh, points out, the escape of

Phoolan Devi's killers from the high security Tihar Jail and other similar escapes of prisoners highlight the ineptitude and complicity of jail staff. Tihar jail is a complex of seven prisons that can hold 4,000 prisoners. But more than 12,000 prisoners are lodged there. So crowded has it become that there have been some avoidable deaths owing to intense humidity; it prompted the High Court to order the release of under trials lodged there for petty crimes.

Jails in India continue to be governed by a law enacted by the British in 1894, with the clear objective of giving the natives the treatment they deserved. All major efforts at reforms have been superficial and do not effectively tackle the basic problems of Indian jails. Indira Gandhi's incarceration after the emergency apparently gave her an insight into the conditions of jails. It led her to appoint, as soon as she regained power, the Mullah Committee, to suggest changes in the system after a national review.

The committee recommended that the Constitution be amended to shift the subject of prisons from the State to the Concurrent List. This did not happen since States were determined not to part with any of the power given to them by the Constitution. The result is that the Centre cannot deal directly with prisons-so much so that according to the Bihar Jail Manual, foreign nationals lodged in prison are entitled to better treatment than Indians.

11

Situational Crime Prevention

Situational crime prevention departs radically from most criminology in its orientation. Proceeding from an analysis of the circumstances giving rise to specific kinds of crime, it introduces discrete managerial and environmental change to reduce the opportunity for those crimes to occur. Thus it is focused on the settings for crime, rather than upon those committing criminal acts. It seeks to forestall the occurrence of crime, rather than to detect and sanction offenders. It seeks not to eliminate criminal or delinquent tendencies through improvement of society or its institutions, but merely to make criminal action less attractive to offenders.

Central to this enterprise is not the criminal justice system, but a host of public and private organisations and agencies—schools, hospitals, transit systems, shops and malls, manufacturing businesses and phone companies, local parks and entertainment facilities, pubs and parking lots—whose products, services and operations spawn opportunities for a vast range of different crimes.

Dozens of documented examples now exist of successful situational prevention involving such measures as surveillance cameras for subway systems and parking facilities, defensible space architecture in public housing, target hardening of apartment blocks and individual residences, electronic access for cars and for telephone systems, street closures and traffic schemes for residential neighbourhoods, alcohol controls at festivals and sporting fixtures, training in conflict management for publicans and bouncers, and improved stocktaking and record keeping procedures in warehouse and retail outlets.

Many of these successes were obtained by hard-pressed managers seeking practical ways to solve troublesome crime problems confronting their businesses or agencies. Only rarely were they assisted by criminologists, who, excepting a small handful of government researchers overseas, have generally shown little interest in situational prevention. In addition, situational prevention has rarely been accorded attention in policy debates about crime control, especially those in the United States.

This neglect stems from two mistakes of modern criminology. First, the problem of explaining crime has been confused with the problem of explaining the criminal. Most criminological theories have been concerned with explaining why certain individuals or groups, exposed to particular psychological or social influences, or with particular inherited traits, are more likely to become involved in delinquency or crime. But this is not the same as explaining why crime occurs.

The commission of a crime requires not merely the existence of a motivated offender, but, as every detective story reader knows, it also requires the opportunity for crime. In Cohen and Felson's terminology, it also requires the availability of a suitable target and the absence of a capable guardian. Thus, crime cannot be explained simply by explaining criminal dispositions. It also has to be shown how such dispositions interact with situational factors favouring crime to produce a criminal act.

The second related mistake of modern criminology has been to confuse the problem of controlling crime with that of dealing with the criminal. The surest route to reducing crime, it has been assumed, is to focus on the offender or potential offender.

Most textbook discussions of crime control have therefore distinguished only between two broad kinds of measures, formal and informal social control. Formal control refers to society's formally constituted legal institutions of the Law and the criminal justice system designed to sanction offenders, to confine or rehabilitate them, and to deter crime among the population at large. Informal social control refers to society's attempts to induce conformity through the socialisation of young people into the norms of society, and through people's supervision of each other's behavior, reinforced by rule making, admonition and censure. Whether formal or informal, these controls are exclusively focused upon offenders, actual or potential.

It has been argued that one important consequence of failing to separate the problems of dealing with offenders and controlling crime has been to divert the criminal justice system from its essential purpose of dispensing justice. More germane to the present discussion, however, is that this failure has also resulted in the criminological and policy neglect of a third important group of crime control measures, additional to formal and informal social controls, but intertwined with and dependent on them. These are the extensive "routine precautions" taken by individuals and organisations.

Every day, we all do such things as lock our doors, secure our valuables, counsel our children, and guard our purses to reduce the risk of crime. To this end, we also buy houses in safe neighbourhoods, we invest in burglar alarms and we avoid dangerous places and people. Similarly, schools, factories, offices, shops and many other organisations and agencies routinely take a host of precautions to safeguard themselves, their employees and their clients from crime. It is into this group of crime control measures that situational crime prevention fits. Indeed, it can be regarded as the scientific arm of routine, precautions, designed to make them more efficient and beneficial to society as a whole.

Criminologists and policy analysts have assumed that the principal value of these precautions is not in reducing overall crime rates, but in protecting individual people and agencies from victimisation. This is partly because situational measures focused on particular places or highly specific categories of crime cannot make much impression on the overall crime statistics. It has also been assumed, however, that faced with impediments offenders will merely displace their attention elsewhere, with no net reduction in crime.

This assumption flows directly from the dispositions error of modern criminology and, as shown below, is not supported by empirical research which has generally found rather little displacement. Reducing opportunities for crime can indeed bring substantial net reductions in crime. As this evidence becomes more widely known, and situational prevention is taken more seriously by policy makers, the debate will move on to the ethical and ideological implications of situational measures. This is already apparent in countries such as Britain and the Netherlands where situational prevention is becoming an integral, though still small, component of government crime policy.

These countries have seen a shift in the discourse of crime control, which is no longer seen to be the exclusive province of the government, but something that must be shared with all sectors of society. Consequently, a multitude of public and private actors are now finding that their routine precautions are becoming a matter of public duty. More significantly, governments now seem to be promoting a range of precautionary measures that many people find objectionable. When video surveillance of public places and street closures in residential areas become part of official policy, fears of Orwellian methods of social control are unleashed. These concerns are reinforced by developments in technology that make people believe government control is becoming too pervasive, intrusive and powerful. These worries about the application of situational controls are widespread, and have become entangled with diverse ideological objections from across the political spectrum.

Definition of Situational Prevention

Situational prevention comprises opportunity-reducing measures that:

— Are directed at highly specific forms of crime.

— Involve the management, design or manipulation of the immediate environment in as systematic and permanent way as possible.

— Make crime more difficult and risky, or less rewarding and excusable as judged by a wide range of offenders.

Several features of the definition relevant to the more extended discussion of situational crime prevention below should be noted. First, it makes clear that situational measures must be tailored to highly specific categories of crime, which means that distinctions must be made, not between broad categories such as burglary and robbery, but rather between the different kinds of offenses falling under each of these categories.

Thus, Poyner and Web have recently argued that preventing domestic burglaries targeted on electronic goods may require different measures from those needed to prevent domestic burglaries targeted on cash or jewellery. This is because of the many differences that existed between the two kinds of burglary in the British city they studied. When the targets were cash or jewellery, burglaries occurred mostly in older homes near to the çity center and apparently were committed by offenders operating on foot. When the targets were electronic goods such as TVs and VCRs, the burglaries generally took place in newer, more distant suburbs and were committed by offenders with cars. The cars were needed to transport the stolen goods and had to be parked near to the house but not so close as to attract attention. The layout of housing in the newer suburbs allowed these conditions to be met and Poyner and Web's preventive suggestions consisted principally of means to counter the lack of natural surveillance of parking places and road ways in new housing developments. These suggestions were quite different from those they made to prevent burglary in the inner city, which focused more on improving security and surveillance at the burglar's point of entry.

The need to tailor measures to particular offenses should not be taken to imply that offenders are specialists—only that the commission of specific kinds of crime depends crucially on a constellation of particular environmental opportunities and that these opportunities may need to be blocked in highly specific ways. Indeed, the second important feature of the definition of situational prevention is the implicit recognition that a wide range of offenders, attempting to satisfy a variety of motives and employing a variety of methods, may be involved in even highly specific offenses. It is further recognised that all people have some probability of committing crime depending on the circumstances in which they find themselves. Thus situational prevention does not draw hard distinctions between criminals and others.

The third point deriving from the definition is that changing the environment is designed to affect assessments made by potential offenders about the costs and benefits associated with committing particular crimes. These judgments are dependent on specific features of the objective situation and determine the likelihood of the offense occurring. This implies some rationality and a considerable degree of adaptability on the part of offenders.

The definition recognises, fourth, that the judgments made by potential offenders include some evaluation of the moral costs of offending. We may all be prepared to steal small items from our employers, but few of us would be willing to mug old ladies in the street. Not all offenses are equally reprehensible, even in the eyes of the most hardened offenders. This means that making it harder to find excuses for criminal action may be sometimes be an effective opportunity-reduction technique. It also means that differences in the moral acceptability of various offenses will impose limits on the scope of displacement. Finally, the definition of situational prevention is deliberately general in that it makes no mention of any particular category of crime.

Rather, situational prevention is assumed to be applicable to every kind of crime, not just to "opportunistic" or acquisitive property offenses, but also to more calculated or deeply-motivated offenses. Whether offenses are carefully planned or fuelled by hate and rage, they are all heavily affected by situational contingencies. Thus, rates of homicide are importantly influenced by the availability of handguns. All offenders, however emotionally aroused or determined, take some account of the risks and difficulties of particular situations. With respect to crimes thought to be the province of "hardened" offenders, evidence is now accumulating of successes achieved by situational measures, including the virtual elimination of aircraft hi jackings by baggage screening and substantial reductions in robbery achieved by target hardening measures in post offices, convenience stores and banks.

Crimes of sex and violence have been regarded as less amenable to situational controls because they are less common and less likely to cluster in time and space.

However, some examples will be provided below of the successful control of violence through deflecting offenders (for example, by preventing the congregation of large groups of drunken youths at pub-closing time) or through situational controls on alcohol and weapons.

One particularly instructive example of controls on a "crime facilitated" is provided by the introduction of Caller-ID in New Jersey, which, by threatening the anonymity of callers, seems to have produced a substantial reduction in obscene phone calling. Without this evidence, many people might have argued that obscene phone calling, a sexual crime that seems to strike at random, is precisely the kind of offense that would be unamendable to situational controls. A similar argument might have been made about domestic violence, but encouraging evidence is beginning to emerge from an experimental program in England that providing personal alarms to repeat victims may inhibit the aggressor. The lesson is that the limits of situational prevention should be established by closely analysing the circumstances of highly specific kinds of offense, rather than by theoretical arguments about the presumed nature of motives for broad categories of crime such as sexual or violent offenses.

Components of Situational Crime Prevention

Much existing activity falling under the definition of situational crime prevention represents problem-solving undertaken by managers in a variety of public and private agencies. In some instances, mistakes might have been avoided and less time taken to develop solutions had those involved been familiar with the elements of situational prevention.

The development of situational prevention was stimulated by the results of work on correctional treatments undertaken in the 1960s and 1970s by the Home Office Research Unit, the British government's criminological research department. This work contributed to the demise of the rehabilitative ideal and forced researchers in the Unit, charged with making a practical contribution to criminal policy, to review the scope and effectiveness of other forms of crime control. The review concluded that there was little scope for reducing crime through the essentially marginal adjustments that were practically and ethically feasible in relation to policies of incapacitation, deterrent sentencing, preventive policing or "social" prevention.

But it did identify opportunity-reduction as a worthwhile topic for further research, largely on the basis of some findings about mis behavior in institutions. It had been discovered in the course of the work on rehabilitation that the probability of a youth's absconding or re-offending while resident in a probation hostel or training school seemed to depend more upon the nature of the institutional regime to which he was exposed than on his personality or background. Particularly important appeared to be the opportunities for mis behavior provided by the institutional regime—opportunities that could be "designed out."

If institutional misconduct could in theory be controlled by manipulating situational factors, it was reasoned that the same might be true of other, everyday forms of crime. Though not consistent with most current theory, support for the Home Office position was found in criminological research that had found immediate situational influences to be playing an important role in crime, including:

— Burt's studies of delinquency in London, showing that higher rates of property offending in the winter were promoted by longer hours of darkness.

— Harts horn and May's experimental studies of deceit, showing that the likelihood of dishonest behavior by children was dependent on the level of supervision afforded.

— Geographical studies showing that the distribution of particular crimes is related to the presence of particular targets and locations such as business premises, drinking clubs, and parking lots.

— Demonstrations that fluctuations in auto theft reflect the number of opportunities as measured by the numbers of registered vehicles.

The Home Office position was also consistent with psychological research on personality traits and behavior that was finding a greater than expected role for situational influences, and with an emerging body of work on the sociology of deviance, including studies by: Matza who argued against deep motivational commitment to deviance in favour of a "drift" into misconduct; Briar and Piliavin who stressed situational inducements and lack of commitment to conformity; and Yablonsky and Short and Strode beck who evidenced the pressures to deviance conferred by working class gang membership.

Taken together, this body of work suggested that criminal conduct was much more susceptible to variations in opportunity and to transitory pressures and inducements than conventional "dispositions" theories allowed. It was also becoming clear from interviews with residential burglars that the avoidance of risk and effort plays a large part in target selection decisions. This dynamic view of crime provided a more satisfactory basis for situational prevention and led to the formulation of a simple "choice" model. This required information not only about the offender's background and current circumstances, but also about the offender's

— Immediate motives and intentions.

— Moods and feelings.

— Moral judgments regarding the act in question.

— Perception of criminal opportunities and ability to take advantage of them or create them.

— Assessment of the risks of being caught as well as of the likely consequences.

This model, dubbed "situational control theory" by Down's and Rock, was subsequently developed into the rational choice perspective on crime, but it served initially to deflect criminological criticism of the theoretical nature of situational prevention and, more importantly, to guide thinking about practical ways of reducing opportunities for crime.

Defensible Space and Problem-Oriented Policing

While the concept of situational prevention was British in origin, its development was soon influenced by two independent, but nonetheless related, strands of policy research in the United States. These involved the concepts of "defensible space" and "crime prevention through environmental design" or CPTED, both of which had preceded situational prevention, but, because of the trans-Atlantic delay in the dissemination of ideas, had not been the stimulus to its development.

Oscar Newman's "defensible space" ideas represented a brilliant attempt to use architectural form to rescue public housing in the United States from the depredations of crime. Newman, an architect, believed that the design of public housing developments discouraged residents from taking responsibility for public areas and from exercising their normal "territorial" instincts to exclude predatory offenders. In particular, he criticised the large scale of the buildings which made it impossible for residents to recognise strangers, the multitude of unsupervised access points that made it easy for offenders to enter projects and to escape after committing crime, the location of projects in high crime areas, and their stark appearance which contributed to the stigma attaching to them.

Newman supported these criticisms with statistical analyses of crime in public housing. He also provided a wealth of detailed design suggestions for creating "defensible space" through reducing anonymity, increasing surveillance and reducing escape routes for offenders. "Defensible space" has sometimes been described as merely an extension of Jane Jacobs' ideas about the relationship between crime and the layout of streets and land use in American cities. As noted by Coleman, however, this fails to do justice to Newman's unique contribution.

He was focused upon buildings and architecture rather than urban planning, he moved beyond description to undertake quantitative analyses of the relation between specific design features and crime, and he was deeply involved in implementing change through the introduction of design modifications in housing developments. Despite the theoretical and methodological criticisms made of his work, Newman's ideas have greatly influenced the design of public housing all over the world. In particular, they have helped to rid many cities of high rise public housing blocks. With regard to the present discussion, they also stimulated efforts by the Home Office researchers engaged on situational prevention to undertake some early tests of "defensible space" notions in a British context.

In addition to Jane Jacobs, other influences on Newman included architectural ideas about the relation between environment and behavior and ethological writings on "territoriality" by authors such as Ardrey. This mix of ideas was rather different from that giving rise to C. Ray Jeffery's concept of "crime prevention through environmental design." Jeffery claimed that the failures of the criminal justice system (in terms of limited reformative capacity, cruelty and inequity) stemmed from a flawed model of crime, in which "... the genetic basis of behavior is denied and... The environments in which crimes occur are ignored". Drawing upon a "bio-social theory of learning," he argued that punishment and treatment philosophies had to be abandoned in favour of a preventive approach which took due account of both genetic predisposition and the physical environment.

American criminology has been unreceptive to genetic explanations of behavior and Jeffery's general theory of criminal behavior has enjoyed less success than his concept of CPTED. Encompassing a broader set of techniques than "defensible space" and extending beyond the residential context, CPTED was adopted by the Westing house Corporation as the more suitable designation for its ambitious program of research to extend the defensible space concept to school and commercial sites.

"Problem-oriented policing" constituted a somewhat later influence on the development of situational prevention. Goldstein argued that the route to greater operational effectiveness for the police was not through improvements in organisation and management, but through the detailed analysis of the everyday problems they handle and the devising of tailor-made solutions.

This process requires "identifying these problems in more precise terms, researching each problem, documenting the nature of the current police response, assessing its adequacy and the adequacy of existing authority and resources, engaging in a broad exploration of alternatives to present responses, weighing the merits of these alternatives, and choosing from among them". This formulation of problem-oriented policing—captured in the four-stage SARA model, Scanning, Analysis, Response and Assessment—reflects the same action research paradigm underpinning situational prevention. Nevertheless, some important differences exist between the concepts.

In particular, problem-oriented policing is not exclusively focused on crime and is primarily a police management approach; situational prevention, on the other hand, is a crime control approach that can be utilised within any organisational or management structure and is open, not just to the police, but to whoever can muster the resources to tackle the problem in hand.

With respect to crime control, therefore, situational prevention represents a broader approach than problem-oriented policing. Because it encompasses the entire range of environments (and objects) involved in crime and because it encompasses legal and management as well as design solutions, situational prevention is also broader than CPTED (which tends to be focused on design of the built environment). For example, server intervention programs to control drunken driving and the provision of "call trace" facilities to private telephone subscribers as a deterrent to obscene phone calling would more readily fall under the definition of situational, than CPTED measures.

Rational Choice Perspective

The earlier "choice" model formulated to guide situational prevention efforts has more recently been developed into a "rational choice" perspective on crime. This borrows concepts from economic theories of crime, but seeks to avoid some of the criticisms made of these theories, including that:

— Economic models mostly ignore rewards of crime that cannot easily be translated into cash equivalents.

— Economic theories have not been sensitive to the great variety of behaviors falling under the general label of crime, with their variety of costs and benefits, and instead have tended to lump them together as a single variable in their equations.

— The formal mathematical modelling of criminal choices in economic theories often demands data that are unavailable or can only be pressed into service by making unrealistic assumptions about what they represent.

— The image in economic theory of the self-maximising decision maker, carefully calculating his or her advantage, does not fit the opportunistic and reckless nature of much crime.

Under the new formulation, relationships between concepts were expressed, not in mathematical terms as was the case in Becker's normative model, but in the form of "decision" diagrams. Concepts were adapted from the other disciplines involved in the analysis of criminal decision making, as well as economics, to give greater weight to non-instrumental motives for crime and the "limited" or "bounded" nature of the rational processes involved. It was assumed, in other words, that crime is purposes behavior designed to meet the offender's commonplace needs for such things as money, status, sex and excitement, and that meeting these needs involves the making of (sometimes quite rudimentary) decisions and choices, constrained as these are by limits of time and ability and the availability of relevant information.

A second important new premise was that a decision-making approach to crime requires that a fundamental distinction be made between criminal involvement and criminal events (a distinction paralleling that between criminality and crime). Criminal involvement refers to the processes through which individuals choose

— To become initially involved in particular forms of crime.

— To continue.

— To desist.

The decision process at each of these stages is influenced by a different set of factors and needs to be separately modelled. In the same way, the decision processes involved in the commission of a particular crime (i.e. the criminal event) are dependent upon their own special categories of information. Involvement decisions are characteristically multi-stage and extend over substantial periods of time. Event decisions, on the other hand, are frequently shorter processes, utilising more circumscribed information largely relating to immediate circumstances and situations.

Finally, and this is of special importance for situational prevention, it was recognised that the decision processes and information utilised could vary greatly among offenses. To ignore these differences, and the situational contingencies associated with them, may be to reduce significantly the scope for intervention.

Cornish and Clarke's formulation of the rational choice perspective has been characterised by Opp as a "wide" model compared with the "narrow" economic formulation. This wide model was primarily developed to assist thinking about situational prevention, but it was not intended to be limited to this role. Indeed, Cornish has argued that many features of the rational choice perspective make it particularly suitable to serve as a criminological "meta-theory" with a broad role in the explanation of a variety of criminological phenomena.

Environmental Criminology

Rational choice premises have generally been supported by recent studies in which offenders have been interviewed about motives, methods and target choices. The offenders concerned have included burglars, shoplifters, car thieves, muggers bank and commercial robbers and offenders using violence.

These studies of offender decision making constitute one of two major analytic paths followed in the past decade by "environmental criminology". The other path has involved "objective analysis of the spatial and temporal variation in crime patterns in order to discover aggregate factors influencing the patterns". When such analyses involve aggregate crime rates or "macro" level data for countries or states, they rarely produce findings with preventive implications. "Micro" level analyses, on the other hand, of specific categories of crime occurring in specific kinds of buildings or sites are generally the most productive Introduction 11 in preventive terms.

Analyses at an intermediary "meso" level can also lead to useful preventive suggestions as shown by Poyner and Web's study mentioned above of domestic burglary in two British communities. This study is also illustrative of research on the criminal's "journey to work" undertaken, among others, by Brantingham and Brantingham, Maguire and Rengert and Weasel chick. Among the findings of these studies are that the risks of commercial robbery may be increased by being located close to a main road and those of domestic burglary by being located on the outskirts of an affluent area. In both cases, the explanation is that the offender's target search time is thereby reduced.

Research on the criminal's journey to work is conceptually related to another body of criminological work—routine activity theory—which has also contributed to the theoretical base of situational prevention. The routine activity approach stated three minimal elements for direct-contact predatory crime: a likely offender, a suitable target, and the absence of a capable guardian against crime. It avoids speculation about the source of the offender's motivation, which distinguishes it immediately from most other criminological theories. Instead, it focuses upon the convergence in space and time of the three elements of crime, that is to say upon the conditions favouring the occurrence of a criminal event, rather than the development of a criminal disposition.

This reflects its intellectual roots in the human ecology of Amos Hawley, who recognised that the timing of different activities by hour of day and day of week are important for the understanding of human society. These points are also central to the routine activity approach, which is focused upon changes from moment to moment and hour to hour in where people are, what they are doing, and what happens to them as a result. In support of their approach, Cohen and Felson sought to demonstrate that increases in residential burglary in the United States between 1960 and 1970 could largely be explained by changes in "routine activities" such as the increasing proportion of empty homes in the day (due to more single person households and greater female participation in the labour force) and the increased portables of televisions and other electrical goods.

Cohen and Felson's analysis also illustrates the relationship between routine activity theory and the victimological work on "lifestyles," stimulated by the flood of National Crime Survey data first released in the 1970s. One of the tenets of "lifestyle" theory is that the differential risks of victimisation are partly a function of differential exposure to offenders. This exposure varies not only with the socio-demographic characteristics of the victim (age, race, place of residence, etc.), but also with the victim's lifestyle. A person's work and leisure activities that increase exposure to potential offenders (such as alcohol consumption in public places or late-night use of public transport) increase the risks of victimisation.

The implication of this is that risks might be reduced by modifying patterns of activity. A further important finding of victimological research, the implications of which are being explored in a series of recent studies by Ken Pease and colleagues, is that some people and targets are repeatedly subject to victimisation and might therefore be prime candidates for preventive attention. A similar point has been made by Sherman et al. in relation to the "hot spots" of crime, places that are the source of repeated calls for assistance to the police.

Lifestyle and routine activity theories have both made opportunity a respectable topic of research in criminology and have helped attract serious scholarly interest to situational prevention. Both theories are still evolving and Felson himself has made some attempts to expand the scope of routine activity theory. He has defined minimal elements for some categories of crime other than direct-contact predatory offenses and, in order to accommodate social control theory, has proposed a fourth minimal element for predatory crimes, "the intimate handler", or someone who knows the likely offender well-enough to afford a substantial brake on the latter's activities. Clerk has argued that the contribution of routine activity theory to crime prevention could be enhanced by adding a fifth element which he refers to as "crime facilitation," These are such things as automobiles, credit cards and weapons that comprise the essential tools for particular forms of crime.

Opportunity Structure for Crime

Environmental criminology, the rational choice perspective and routine activity and lifestyle theories have all helped to strengthen situational prevention in different ways, reflecting their different origins and the purposes for which they were developed. By interviews with offenders and analysis of crime patterns, environmental criminology has provided rich information about the motives and methods of offenders, which has been valuable in thinking about counter measures.

The rational choice perspective has provided a framework under which to organise such information so that individual studies produce more general benefits. As will be seen below, it has also assisted analysis of displacement.

Lifestyle theory has focused attention on what victims might do to reduce their risks of crime. And routine activity theory has served to extend preventive options by directing attention to features of the three essential elements of crime and their convergence.

For example, the idea of convergence has led to the suggestion that "deflecting offenders" be recognised as a distinct technique of situational prevention. Cushion has argued that the differences among the various theoretical approaches may turn out to be mainly of historical interest and that a synthesis is inevitable and desirable.

There are three components of the criminal opportunity structure. These are targets (cars, convenience stores, ATM machines, etc.), victims (e.g. women alone, drunks, strangers) and crime facilitation. These latter include tools, such as guns and cars, as well as dis-inhibitors such as alcohol or other drugs. The supply of targets and their nature is a function of

— The physical environment, including the layout of cities, the kinds of housing, technology and communications, transportation and retailing systems, the numbers of vehicles and the supply of drugs and alcohol.

— The lifestyles and routine activities of the population, including patterns of leisure, work, residence and shopping; these patterns either hinder or facilitate guardianship.

The physical environment also determines the supply of facilitation, while lifestyles and routine activities play a large part in supplying the victims of personal and sexual attacks. Physical environment and lifestyles and routine activities are themselves determined by the broader socioeconomic structure of society, including demography, geography, urbanisation and industrialisation, health and educational policy, and legal and Introduction 13 Source: Clerk political institutions.

The numbers of potential offenders and their motives is also partly determined by the socioeconomic structure of society through many of the mechanisms (alienation, subcultural influence, neglect and lack of love, etc.) identified by traditional criminology, and partly by lifestyle and routine activities which impact upon the nature of social control afforded by "intimate handlers" and in other ways. The opportunity structure is not simply a physical entity, defined at any one point in time by the nature of the physical environment and the routine activities of the population.

Rather, a complex interplay between potential offenders and the supply of victims, targets and facilitation determines the scale and nature of opportunities for crime. Potential offenders learn about criminal opportunities from their peers, the media and their own observation, but they are differentially sensitised to this information as well as being differentially motivated to seek out and create opportunities. Thus, offender perceptions and judgments about risks, effort and rewards play an important part in defining the opportunity structure.

Before moving from the theoretical background of situational crime prevention to its other components, some questions about the scope and reach of situational prevention arising from the model of the opportunity structure should be addressed. The first is that, if everything seems to flow from the socioeconomic structure, should not preventive effort be focused at that level? Could not large scale reductions in a wide range of crimes be achieved by tackling the disposition to offend through improved welfare and educational programs? Would this not be more efficient than undertaking the vast number of small-scale efforts to address highly specific crime problems implied by the situational focus? One answer to these questions is that "social" crime prevention is already focused at the socioeconomic level and that the opportunity structure requires attention in its own right.

However, Morris and Hawkins and Wilson have noted that we do not know how to bring about some of the needed social changes, such as making parents love their children more. As for better welfare and education, these may be seen as desirable but often as demanding resources that society cannot afford. Finally, when Sweden and some other European countries enhanced welfare and achieved more equitable income distribution, this was followed not by reductions in crime but by increases.

A second question concerns deterrence and is as follows: Rather than attempting to manipulate the opportunity structure (with the attendant costs and inconvenience of this strategy), might it not be more efficient simply to raise the stakes of offending through heavier punishments? In fact, interviews with offenders have shown that they pay much closer attention to the immediate chances of getting caught than to the nature of the punishment they might receive later. Rather than increasing punishment, it is therefore more efficient to make the offender more fearful of being caught, and one component of situational prevention does indeed consist of increasing the risks of being caught through a process that Cushion refers to as "situational deterrence."

A final set of questions concerns the interplay between the objective reality of the opportunity structure and the way this is perceived by potential offenders. How do offenders learn about criminal opportunities and what factors come into play when they make decisions about which ones to pursue? What proportion of crimes are the result of opportunities seized, and what proportion of ones that are sought or created. At issue here is the question of whether opportunities for crime really are in infinite supply as some have argued. If so, this has serious implications for a strategy advocating their reduction. What matter the few reductions that can be achieved in criminal opportunities if these are infinite?

Consideration of the realities of crime helps provide an answer. While it may be true in theory that every dwelling and automobile provides not just one opportunity for crime, but, if considered over time, a set of almost endless opportunities, this ignores the fact that households and automobiles are afforded substantial guardianship for much of the time. Even when unguarded, they may in actuality provide few rewards for crime.

The average household contains only a few portable goods that can be converted into cash and there are limits to the number of stolen VCRs and television sets that the offender can store. It is also unclear how many such "hot" items can be off-loaded onto the market without provoking a determined response from law enforcement. Clarification of these issues needs to be sought in more research of the kind recently published by Cromwell et al., in which they undertook detailed interviews with residential burglars about their working methods.

Action Research Methodology

The standard methodology for a situational project, situational prevention's second component, is a version of the action research model in which researchers and practitioners work together to analyse and define the problem, to identify and try out possible solutions, to evaluate the results and, if necessary, to repeat the cycle until success is achieved. The influence of the action research paradigm can be seen in the following specification of the five stages of a situational prevention project :

— Collection of data about the nature and dimensions of the specific crime problem.

— Analysis of the situational conditions that permit or facilitate the commission of the crimes in question.

— Systematic study of possible means of blocking opportunities for these particular crimes, including analysis of costs.

— Implementation of the most promising, feasible and economic measures.

— Monitoring of results and dissemination of experience.

As mentioned, this is essentially the same problem-solving methodology used in problem-oriented policing as well as in many other forms of social intervention, and because of its extensive pedigree has required little modification for use in situational crime prevention. However, it represents an ideal not always followed in practice.

Opportunity-Reducing Techniques

Unlike the action research methodology which has seen little modification, the classification of opportunity-reducing techniques, the third component of situational prevention, is constantly undergoing change. This is made necessary by developments:

— In theory which suggest new ways of reducing opportunities.

— In practice as new forms of crime are addressed by situational prevention.

— In technology which opens up new vistas for prevention, just as it does for crime.

The fact that the classification of techniques is constantly being refined is evidence of the vitality of the situational approach and, indeed, these re-classifications help further to stimulate its development by calling attention to new forms of opportunity-reduction.

So long as the measures to induce guilt or shame are focused on highly specific categories of offending and are delivered at the point when criminal decisions are being made, they believe that the danger can be avoided of confusing the nature of situational prevention. For example, the message "Shoplifting is stealing" is much more likely to affect the situational calculus, and would thus qualify as a situational measure, when displayed in high risk stores than when displayed on school notice boards where it is intended to reduce the disposition to theft. Before describing the sixteen techniques, and presenting examples of each, it should be noted that there is some unavoidable overlap among categories. For example, measures that increase the effort demanded for crime and delay the offender will also increase the risks of apprehension. This means that there is sometimes difficulty in deciding where a particular measure best fits into the classification indeed some measures can serve more than one purpose:

— *Target hardening:* An obvious, often highly effective way of reducing criminal opportunities is to obstruct the vandal or the thief by physical barriers through the use of locks, safe, screens or reinforced materials. Changes in design, including a slug rejecter device substantially reduced the use of slugs in New York parking meters and, more recently, in the ticket machines of the London Underground. Transparent screens to shield the bus driver significantly reduced assaults on one transit system; anti-bandit screens on post office counters in London in the 1980s was conservatively estimated by Ekblom to have cut robberies by 40 percent; and the installation of fixed and "pop-up" screens is believed to have been an important element in reducing over-the-counter robberies in Australian banks.

— *Access control:* Access control refers to measures intended to exclude potential offenders from places such as offices, factories and apartment blocks. The portcullises, moats and drawbridges of medieval castles suggest its preventive pedigree may be as lengthy as that of target hardening. It is also a central component of defensible space, arguably the start of scientific interest in situational prevention. A sophisticated form of access control lies in the use of electronic personal identification numbers (PINs) that are needed to gain access to computer systems and bank accounts. Poyner and Web found that a combination of access controls introduced on a South London public housing estate, including entry phones, fencing around apartment blocks and electronic access to the parking garage, achieved a significant reduction in vandalism and theft. They also found that the introduction of a reception desk on the ground floor of a tower block led to a marked reduction in vandalism, graffiti and other incivility.

— *Deflecting offenders:* At soccer matches in Britain, rival groups of fans have been segregated in the stadium to reduce fighting and their arrival and departure has been scheduled to avoid the periods of waiting around that promote trouble. Scheduling the last bus to leave immediately after pub closing time, is intended to interfere with another of Britain's less admirable traditions, the closing time brawl. Hope has suggested that crowds of drunken young people on the streets at closing time could also be reduced by avoiding the concentration of licensed premises in particular parts of the city. Bell and Burke show that the leasing of a downtown parking lot in Arlington, Texas, relieved severe congestion on weekend nights in nearby streets, and associated crime problems, by providing a venue for teenage cruising. These are all examples of "deflecting offenders" away from crime targets, a situational technique suggested by routine activity theory.

— *Controlling facilitation:* Saloons in the Wild West routinely required customers to surrender their weapons on entry because of the risk of drunken gun fights. In more recent times, the manufacture of "less lethal weapons" in the form of guns that shoot wax bullets, electricity or tranquillisers has been advocated. The Scottish Council on Crime suggested that in some pubs beer should be served in plastic mugs to prevent their use as weapons, and recent studies in Britain of the injury potential of different kinds of broken glass have led to the recommendation that toughened glass be used for beer glasses. Controls on a range of other crime facilitation have been proposed including checks and credit cards (which facilitate fraud) and telephones (which may facilitate drug dealing, frauds and sexual harassment). To reduce drug dealing, pay phones have been removed from places where drug dealers congregate or have been altered to make them more difficult to use for dealing. A new computerised phone system in Rikers Island jails substantially reduced illicit phone calls by inmates and also had the unexpected benefit of reducing fights over access to the phones.

— *Entry/exit screening:* Entry screening differs from access control in that the purpose is less to exclude potential offenders than to increase the likelihood of detecting those not in conformity with entry requirements. These requirements may relate to prohibited goods and objects or, alternatively, to possession of tickets and documents. Exit screens, on the other hand, serve primarily to deter theft by detecting objects that should not be removed from the protected area, such as items not paid for at a shop. Developments in electronics have resulted in the increasing use of these situational techniques in retailing, as evidenced by the spread of merchandise tagging, bar-coding and "electronic point of sales" systems.

— *Formal surveillance:* Formal surveillance is provided by police, security guards and store detectives, whose main function is to furnish a deterrent threat to potential offenders.

— *Surveillance by employees:* In addition to their primary function, some employees, particularly those dealing with the public, also perform a surveillance role by virtue of their position. These include a variety of "place managers" such as shop assistants, hotel doormen, park keepers, parking lot attendants and train conductors. All these employees assume some responsibility for monitoring conduct in their work places. Canadian research has shown that apartment blocks with doormen are less vulnerable to burglary. In Britain, less vandalism has been found on buses with conductors and on public housing estates with resident caretakers. Public telephones in Britain which get some surveillance by employees, such as those in pubs or railway stations, also suffer fewer attacks. A two-thirds reduction in offenses at a parking lot in England followed the employment of attendants to cover high risks periods of the day. Rewarding cashiers for detection of forged or stolen credit cards helped to reduce annual losses from credit card frauds by nearly $1 million dollars at an electronics retailer in New Jersey. Once again, CCTV surveillance has been found effective when these cameras are provided for employee use. Cameras installed for use of station staff produced substantial reductions in muggings and thefts at four high risk stations on the London Underground. Vandalism of seats on a fleet of 80 double-deck buses in England was substantially reduced through the provision of CCTV for drivers, though only a few buses were equipped with the cameras.

— *Natural surveillance*: Householders may trim bushes at the front of their homes and banks may light the interior of their premises at night in attempting to capitalise upon the "natural" surveillance provided by people going about their everyday business.

— *Target removal:* A church in Northern Spain has recently installed a machine at its entrance that allows people to use their bank or credit cards to make donations. (In reporting this development, a local Spanish newspaper could not resist the headline "Through Visa. The person making the donation has a receipt for tax purposes and the church may receive larger gifts. Since money is not being deposited, the church has also reduced its theft risk through "target removal." An earlier application of this same situational technique, quoted by Pease, comes from the days of the Californian Gold Rush. Plagued by robberies of stage coaches, one mine started casting its silver into 400-pound cubes, about one foot on each side. These were simply too heavy for a robber, or even a gang of them, to carry off on horseback. Other examples of target removal come from attempts to deal with attacks on public telephones in Great Britain and Australia. Because the kiosk itself (specially the glass) is more frequently vandalised than the phone, kiosks in high risk locations have been replaced by booths. In addition, the smaller, highly vulnerable, glass panes in earlier kiosks have been replaced by larger panes in more recent designs. A third pay phone example is provided by the introduction of the Phone card, which by dispensing with the need for pay phones to store large sums of cash, has removed an important target for theft. A variety of cash reduction measures, including the use of safe with time locks, substantially reduced robberies of betting shops in Australia. 'Pease has shown that a package of measures to prevent repeat victimisation of houses on a public housing estate in Britain, including the removal of gas and electric coin meters which were frequent targets for theft, reduced burglaries on the estate from 526 in the year before intervention to 132 three years later.

— *Identifying property:* Writing one's name in a book is a simple form of property marking. The most developed programs of identifying property relate to vehicles. Registration of motor vehicles was required in some U.S. States from almost the beginning of the century and, subsequently, all vehicles sold in the United States were required to carry a unique Vehicle Identification Number (or VIN). More recently, the Motor Vehicle Theft Law Enforcement Act 1984 has mandated the marking of all major body parts of "high risk" automobiles with the VINs.

— *Reducing temptation:* In certain city streets it is unwise to wear gold chains or leave cars parked which are attractive to joyriders. Some temptations are less obvious. For example, phone directories which are not gender-neutral might promote obscene phone-calls to women. It has also been found in extensive experimental research that the mere presence of a weapon, such as a gun, can induce aggressive responses in some people. Known as the "weapons effect", this gives further support to gun control. The weapons effect barely enters the subjective world of potential offenders and James Wise has argued that this is also true of many inducements to vandalism, for example when the surface characteristics of a wall almost invite graffiti. Many of his suggestions for a "gentle deterrent" to vandalism consist of reducing such temptations. For example, he has suggested that the glass covering fire alarm handles should be mirrored because bad luck would follow its breaking. Another example of reducing temptation is "rapid repair" on the grounds that leaving damaged items un-repaired invites further attacks. Samdahi and Christensen provided support for this policy by demonstrating that picnic tables that had been scratched and carved were more than twice as likely to be damaged further than other tables. Zimbardo showed that a car left parked in poor condition in an inner city area rapidly attracted further depredation. Smith found that school boys in England who admitted recent similar vandalism acts, reported they would be more likely to damage fences or write on them when these already showed signs of vandalism and graffiti. Substantially reduced rates of crime and vandalism on the metropolitan railways of Victoria, Australia, were reported by Carry and Spring following the introduction of "Travel Safe," a program consisting of rapid repair of vandalism and graffiti as well as of more generally enhanced security. This advocacy of rapid repair and good maintenance has been taken a step further by Wilson and Kelling who have argued in their famous "broken windows" article that the failure to deal promptly with minor signs of decay in a community, such as pan-handling or soliciting by prostitutes, can result in a quickly deteriorating situation as hardened offenders move into the area to exploit the breakdown in control.

— *Denying benefits:* Related to reducing temptation, but conceptually distinct, is denying the benefits of crime to offenders. The recent development of security-coded car radios that require a thief to know the radio's PIN before it can be used in another vehicle constitutes an excellent example of this principle. Cars fitted with these radios have been found to have lower theft rates in studies in Australia and in Germany and the United States. These successes suggest that this principle might usefully be extended to VCR's and TV's so as to reduce the rewards of burglary. A further example of the principle in action is provided by "ink tags," which are designed to deny shoplifters the benefits of stealing. If tampered with, these tags release ink and indelibly stain garments to which they are attached, and these tags may be even more effective than the familiar electronic merchandise tags.

— *Rule setting:* All organisations find it necessary to have rules about conduct in their fields of governance. For example, most businesses regulate employees' telephone use and all retail establishments require their employees to follow strict cash handling and stock control procedures. Organisations such as hospitals, schools, parks, transportation systems, hotels and restaurants must, in addition, regulate the conduct of the clienteles they serve. Any ambiguity in these regulations will be exploited where it is to the advantage of the individual. One important strand of situational prevention, therefore, is rule setting—the introduction of new rules or procedures (and the clarification of those in place), which are intended to remove any ambiguity concerning the acceptability of conduct. For example, in attempting to reduce "no-shows," many restaurants will only accept reservations if callers leave a telephone number where they can be contacted if they do not appear. Some popular restaurants are now also requiring that reservations be accompanied by a credit card number against which a charge can be made for no-shows. A Manhattan restaurant reports that the scheme reduced no-shows at Thanksgiving from a total of 65 in the year before the scheme was introduced to zero in the two subsequent years. The same edition of the New York Times reports that taxicab fares from Kennedy airport to Manhattan have been fixed at a standard $30 to prevent visitors being cheated. Fisherman in California have also recently been required to wear their fishing licenses, rather than merely to carry them, in a successful effort to get more anglers to comply with license purchase requirements. Not all such rules require the backing of the law.

— *Stimulating conscience:* This situational technique can be distinguished from society's more general informal social control by its focus on specific forms of crime occurring in discrete, highly limited settings. Rather than attempting to bring about lasting changes in generalised attitudes to law breaking, these measures serve simply to stimulate feelings of conscience at the point of contemplating the commission of a specific kind of offense. For example, signs at store entrances announce that "shoplifting is stealing" and in the Port Authority Bus Terminal in Manhattan they proclaim that "Smoking here is illegal, selfish and rude." Mobile roadside speed monitors have been used to give immediate feedback (without issuing fines) to individual cars travelling above the speed limit. An example of a more intensive and coordinated attempt to increase such informal sanctions is provided by recent advertising campaigns mounted in Australia to reinforce the powerful deterrent impact of random breath testing. These made use of the slogan, "Good mates don't let mates drink and drive." Finally, in Britain, government television campaigns that accompany crackdowns on those who evade purchasing licenses required to own a television (the license fees help to finance the British Broadcasting Corporation) show those detected being treated by the police and courts as "common criminals." The British government has been repeating its advertising campaigns for more than two decades and claims (though without producing evidence) that applications for television licenses sharply increase whenever the campaigns are mounted.

Controlling Dis-inhibitors

Crime is not only facilitated by tools such as weapons, but also by psychological Dis-inhibitors, which include:

— Alcohol and drugs, which undermine the usual social or moral inhibitions, or impair perception and cognition so that offenders are less aware of breaking the law.

— Propaganda, which can be directed at the dehumanisation of target groups and can provide the moral certainties and justifications that ordinary people need to commit atrocities and war crimes.

— Television violence, which like propaganda, might "reduce or break down those inhibitions against being violent that parents and other socialising agencies have been building up in boys".

The "V-chip," which under the Telecommunications Act of 1996 will become a feature of every new television set sold in America, allows parents to block reception of violent television programs. This is a situational response to the problem and constitutes an example of "controlling Dis-inhibitors," though most examples of this technique relate to controls on drinking. Access to cars by intoxicated drivers can be restricted by Breathalysers built into the ignition, a measure that is sometimes mandated for recidivist drunk drivers. A faculty-student committee at Rutgers University decided that beer should be served from kegs rather than cases at dormitory parties on grounds that

— Cases are easier to conceal.

— In the words of a student:

> "If you have one keg and a line of 20 people behind it, people will get less alcohol than if you had a refrigerator and people were throwing out beer".

The value of controls on drinking have been demonstrated in a variety of studies. Bjor et al. argue that "rationing" the amount of alcohol that individuals could bring into a Swedish resort town on Midsummer Eve helped to reduce drunkenness and disorderly conduct. Olsson and Wikstrom concluded that permanent closing of liquor stores on Saturdays in Sweden had reduced crimes of public drunkenness, assault and vandalism, and domestic disturbances in the summer months, and perhaps also for the remainder of the year. Introduction of a widely supported local ordinance banning the consumption of alcohol in public in central Coventry in England was followed by large reductions in complaints of insulting behavior and in numbers of people who regarded public drinking as a problem in the city.

Effectiveness of Situational Prevention

The examples of successful interventions mentioned in the course of describing the sixteen opportunity-reducing techniques, belong to its fourth component, the body of evaluated practice. This component also includes the evidence on displacement, but before moving to this topic it should be noted, in case a different message has been communicated through the cataloguing of successes, that situational prevention is not one hundred percent effective. Though reductions in crime may be considerable (often more than 50 percent), situational measures usually ameliorate, not eliminate a problem. In addition, situational measures do not always work as intended for a variety of reasons, including the following:

— Measures have sometimes failed due to technical or administrative ineptitude, as when anti-climb paint to deter school break-ins was too thinly applied, or when a scheme to defeat vandalism by replacing broken windows with toughened glass proved too complicated for school maintenance staff to administer.

— Some measures have been too easily defeated by offenders, as in the case of the early steering locks in the U.S. And Britain which proved vulnerable to slide hammers, and that of the "smart" credit cards in France which could be disabled by stamping on the chip.

— Too much vigilance has sometimes been assumed on the part of guards or ordinary citizens: Security guards rarely monitor CCTV systems as closely as designers expect; people pay far less attention to the street outside their homes than is sometimes assumed by neighbourhood watch schemes and defensible space designs; and people rarely respond to car alarms so that the main result of their increasing use has been to reduce further the quality of life in cities.

— Measures have occasionally provoked offenders to unacceptable escalation as in the case of the bullet-proofing of token booths on the New York subway which resulted in some attacks on booths with gasoline-fuelled fires.

— Some measures have facilitated rather than frustrated crime: Ekblom cites the example of pickpockets on the London Underground who stationed themselves near signs warning of theft to see which pockets were checked by passengers on reading the signs; and one result of introducing traffic bollards in Vancouver to frustrate cruising "Johns" was to give prostitutes somewhere to sit when propositioning clients who had slowed down.

— In other cases, measures have been defeated by the carelessness or idleness of potential victims. Residents routinely frustrate entry control systems on apartment buildings by propping open doors to save themselves from answering the door bell. The preventive value of the early security-coded radios was reduced because car owners failed to enter their private codes, thus allowing the radios to revert to a standard code known to thieves.

— The preventive value of these radios was further reduced because thieves did not always know which were security-coded and continued to steal ones they could not use; this flaw was remedied by a continuously blinking light fitted to indicate that the radio was security-coded.

— Some inappropriate measures have been introduced because no proper analysis of the problem was undertaken. For example, Harris and Clerk argued that the parts marking provisions of the federal Motor Vehicle Theft Law Enforcement Act of 1984 were bound to fail because parts marking was restricted only to "high risk" automobiles; leaving aside the resultant scope for displacement, most of the defined "high risk" models are taken not for dismantling and sale of their constituent parts, but for joy-riding which will not be deterred by parts marking.

— Other measures have proved unsuitable because insufficient thought has been given to users' needs. For example, one security innovation left senior citizens "trapped inside a fortress of heavy doors and electronic card-key devices which they found difficult to understand and to operate, while neighbors were no longer able to keep a friendly eye on them".

— Finally, some measures have had a detrimental effect on the environment. Weidner argues that floor-to-ceiling turnstile railings installed at one New York City subway station did reduce fare evasion, but only at the cost of creating what was in many people's view "a draconian, prison-like environment." This could have been avoided had other, possibly equally effective measures, been taken instead.

These examples make clear that situational measures do not always work in intended ways. In addition, measures that work in one setting may not do so in another. An example is provided by helmet-wearing laws that dramatically (but fortuitously) reduced motorcycle theft in Germany, but which had little effect in the United States. This was because the laws were not universally applied as in Germany, but were introduced in a piecemeal and inconsistent fashion.

None of the failures of situational prevention seriously call into question the basic validity of the concept, but they suggest that matters may be more complex than those implementing measures sometimes appreciate. Measures must be carefully tailored to the settings in which they are applied, with due regard to the motives and methods of the offenders involved. Where the stakes are high, offenders must be expected to test the limits of the new defences and to be successful sometimes in identifying vulnerability. This process may be assisted by the arrival on the scene of more resourceful or determined criminals than was previously the case. And this again may sometimes result in the greater use of violence. For the less serious forms of crime, measures that depend upon natural surveillance or the vigilance of employees may be expected to lose their value as people become more complacent.

That preventive measures may have a limited life is not a counsel of despair; rather, it is a fact that must influence the choice among preventive options of varying difficulty and cost. The challenge for research is to help practitioners avoid the pitfalls by providing a sounder base of knowledge upon which to act. All we know at present is that some measures work well in certain conditions. What we need to know is which measures work best, in which combination, deployed against what kinds of crime and under what conditions. We also need to have much better information about the financial costs of particular crime prevention measures. As discussed below, this will require a greatly increased investment in evaluative research. It also means that the commitment to situational prevention has to be long term, which for many organisations and agencies will mean developing a permanent in-house capability.

Bibliography

Barak-Glantz, I.L., E.H. Johnson (1983). *Comparative criminology*. Sage.

Beccaria, Cesare (1764). Richard Davies, translator. ed. *On Crimes and Punishments, and Other Writings*. Cambridge University Press. pp. 64.

Beirne, Piers (March 1987). "Adolphe Quetelet and the Origins of Positivist Criminology". *American Journal of Sociology* 92(5): pp. 1140–1169.

Bursik Jr., Robert J. (1988). "Social Disorganization and Theories of Crime and Delinquency: Problems and Prospects". *Criminology* 26: p. 519–539.

Chambliss, W. & Seidman, R. (1971). *Law, Order, and Power*. Reading, Mass.: Addison-Wesley.

Clarke, Ronald V. (1992). *Situational Crime Prevention*. Harrow and Heston.

Cloward, Richard, Lloyd Ohlin (1960). *Delinquency and Opportunity*. Free Press.

Cohen, Lawrence, and Marcus Felson (1979). "Social Change and Crime Rate Trends". *American Sociological Review* 44 (4): 588.

Cornish, Derek, and Ronald V. Clarke (1986). *The Reasoning Criminal*. Springer-Verlag.

Dahrendorf, Ralf. (1959). *Class and Class Conflict in Industrial Society*. Stanford, CA: Stanford University Press.

Deflem, Mathieu (2006). *Sociological Theory and Criminological Research: Views from Europe and the United States*. Elsevier. pp. 279.

Eck, John, and Julie Wartell (1997). *Reducing Crime and Drug Dealing by Improving Place Management: A Randomized Experiment*. National Institute of Justice.

Felson, Marcus (1994). *Crime and Everyday Life*. Pine Forge.

Ferrell, J., Hayward, K., Morrison, W. and Presdee, M. (2004) *Cultural Criminology Unleashed*, London: Glasshouse Press

Garland, David (2002). "Of Crimes and Criminals". in Maguire, Mike, Rod Morgan, Robert Reiner. *The Oxford Handbook of Criminology, 3rd edition*. Oxford University Press. pp. 21.

Gary Becker, "Crime and Punishment", in *Journal of Political Economy*, vol. 76 (2), March-April 1968, p.196-217

George Stigler, "The Optimum Enforcement of Laws", in *Journal of Political Economy*, vol.78 (3), May-June 1970, p.526-536

Gottfredson, M., T. Hirschi (1990). *A General Theory of Crime*. Stanford University Press.

Hall, S., Winlow, S. and Ancrum, C. (2008) *Criminal Identities and Consumer Culture*, Cullompton: Willan

Hayward, K. and Yar, M. (2006), 'The 'Chav' Phenomenon: Consumption, Media and the Construction of a New Underclass', in *Crime, Media, Culture*, Vol. 2, 1: 9-28

Hayward, Keith J. (2004). *City Limits: Crime, Consumerism and the Urban Experience*. Routledge. pp. 89.

Hester, S., Eglin, P. 1992, *A Sociology of Crime*, London, Routledge.

Hirschi, Travis (1969). *Causes of Delinquency*. Transaction Publishers.

Katz, J. (1988), *The Seductions of Crime*, New York: Basic Books

Kornhauser, R. (1978). *Social Sources of Delinquency*. Uni. of Chicago Press.

McLennan, Gregor, Jennie Pawson, Mike Fitzgerald (1980). *Crime and Society: Readings in History and Theory*. Routledge. pp. 311.

Mead, George Herbert (1934). *Mind Self and Society*. University of Chicago Press.

Merton, Robert (1957). *Social Theory and Social Structure*. Free Press.

Presdee, M. (2000), *Cultural Criminology and the Carnival of Crime*, London: Routledge

Raymond D. Gastil, "Homocide and a Regional Culture of Violence," American Sociological Review 36 (1971): 412-427.

Rhodes, Richard (2000). *Why They Kill: The Discoveries of a Maverick Criminologist*. Vintage.

Shaw, Clifford R. and McKay, Henry D. (1942). *Juvenile Delinquency and Urban Areas*. The University of Chicago Press.

Siegel, Larry J. (2003). *Criminology*. Thomson-Wadsworth. pp. 139.

Taylor, Ian R., Walton, Paul & Young, Jock. (1988) *The New Criminology: For a Social Theory of Deviance (International Library of Sociology)*, Routledge.

Thorsten. (1938) *Culture Conflict and Crime*. New Jersey: Social Science Research Council.

Turk, Austin. (1969). *Criminality and Legal Order*. Chicago: Rand McNally.

Vold, George. (1958). *Theoretical Criminology*. New Jersey: University of Delaware Press.

Wilson, Harriet (1980). "Parental Supervision: A Neglected Aspect of Delinquency". *British Journal of Criminology* 20.

Index

ENCYCLOPAEDIA OF SOCIOLOGY

Rural Sociology

Volume –7

Satish Mittal
Sushil Kumar Saxena

Commonwealth

Encyclopaedia of Sociology

Edition : 2026

ISBN 978-81-311-0377-7 (set)

Published by :
COMMONWEALTH PUBLISHERS (P) LTD.
4831/24, Govind Lane,
Ansari Road, Darya Ganj,
New Delhi - 110002
Ph. : 23242541, 23272541
e-mail : commonwealthpublishers2016@gmail.com

Distributed by :
ARJUN PUBLISHING HOUSE
4831/24, Govind Lane,
Ansari Road, Darya Ganj,
New Delhi - 110002
Ph. : 23242541, 23272541
e-mail : arjunbooks2001@gmail.com
arjunpubhouse@gmail.com

Laser Typesetting by :
Dimple Computers
Delhi

Printed at :
Milan Enterprises
Delhi

Preface

Rural life is the principal pivot around which the social life revolves. Human society through-out its history has been so largely under the pressure of agricultural and rural forces that up to the present sociology as a science of society has virtually been the sociology of rural life. A world view of the sociology of rural life is important for the development of the science. In order to balance the vogue of agricultural economics as an educational discipline and a guide to public action in India, major emphasis is now required upon a sound rural sociology.

Rural sociology is the scientific study of rural society. It involves a systematic study of rural society, its institutions, activities, interactions and social change. It not only deals with the social relationships of man in a rural environment but also takes urban surroundings into consideration for a comparative study. It provides us with valuable knowledge about the rural social phenomena and social problems which helps us in understanding rural society and making prescriptions for its all round progress and prosperity.

This book presents the key concepts of rural sociology in the form of evaluation and analysis made by eminent sociologists. It would be of great value for the students, teachers, trainees, agriculturists, social workers, planners, politicians and general public.

Authors

Contents

1

Rural Social Organisation

India is home to largest number of poor people in the world. Of 1.13 billion people, 27.8 per cent live below poverty line (below the accepted income levels of consumption requirements as per the conservative standards of Indian government). The face of this deep and persistent poverty is observable in poor spending on health, undignified ageing, poor educational standards, malnourished bodies, inferior housing, poor infrastructure resulting in deterioration in the quality of life, child labour, poor service delivery, less importance attached with safety measures etc. All of them have severe implications for interpersonal relationships within the household, village, work place, and in the larger community. At the same time, in recent times, wealth accumulation through businesses in India is reported, indicating increasing economic inequality. On the other hand, India is also marked by another interesting dynamics. It is the origin home for largest number of religions. Buddhism, Jainism, Hinduism, Sikhism all were born here.

It is also important to note the peculiar institution of caste, i.e., dividing human beings into social hierarchies according to their occupation, is peculiar to Indian culture. Thus, while the economic view of India may be depicting a weak face of the interpersonal relations, institutions of religion and society present a view of strong bonding.

Interestingly, in many measures of happiness, south Asian countries have performed much better than the Western countries.

The proximity defines relationship to great extent, and therefore the way human settlements are laid out is important significance for the way relationships are fostered in the human communities. India has some of the highest dense cities in the world, such as New Delhi, and Mumbai. However, majority of the Indian population lives in rural areas. Currently, 28.3 per cent of Indian population live in urban areas. Moving to urban areas and settling there is seen as a part of livelihood—getting educated and gaining jobs. The facilities and structure of interaction are substantially different in both urban and rural areas. The rural areas are marked with face-to-face interaction, while urban areas are, generally, thought to have secluded living with one's own family in a room in a building. However, this is not wholly correct in the Indian context.

About 50% of urban population lives in slums or shanties, with minimal facilities. Most of the facilities (e.g. toilet, water taps) for the people in the slums are to be shared as common facilities. Such a housing situation forces people to come in regular touch with other persons in the settlement. Thus, it could be safely concluded that only about 10-15% of Indians lead a life in which primary interaction is restricted to the immediate members of his/her family.

The wide spread face-to-face interaction in the day-to-day living has important implications for the kind of relationships that is possible. The relationships becomes multilayered, and it takes a multiplex dimension, which means a strain of relation that has happened in one dimension would easily spill into other dimension. For instance, since the people live in close proximity, their culture, eating habits, pattern of conversation etc are easily visible to others. If the eating habit of one household is not socially approved by the values of other, it is likely that a rumour could be easily spread around and such a household could be socially excluded by others in the settlement. The excluded household may be prevented to draw water from a common well, or even prevented from accessing to public schools etc. This multilayered structure of existence in India is succinctly put by Rath et al as follows:

> "The basic and primary unit of the society is the elementary or joint family. Every family belongs to an exogamous division of a caste and several such divisions constitute an endogamous caste or an endogamous section of a large caste. On the other hand, every family belongs to the community with whom it shares a settlement site, be it a village or a hamlet attached to a village. In socio-religious affairs control of the individual is threefold – that of his family, his village and his
>
> caste".

In the Indian context, Beteille has shown that caste is to be considered as an important analytical category, besides class, to understand power structure. Anthropologists consider certain castes to be dominant, according to the numerical factor and the political and economic power that one caste is able to wield over other castes. Often, numerically, the majority of the population of a village are from a single caste. This single caste could be the 'dominant caste' of the particular village. In addition to the numerical strength, economic power too contributes to decide whether a caste is dominant. People from other castes too live in the same village. But, they would not able to exert dominance in the village. In addition to this caste factor, religion plays significant role in determining the social structure of rural India.

Urban-rural coexistence is another major challenge that modern India is facing. Education and upbringing in upper middle class contexts provides English medium education to a few elite minorities, while the vernacular medium education shapes the psyche of the large majority. The way their identity is formulated is through different pathways since the type of education shapes their views on country, history, self-perception and value system. These identities clash where they may be competing on resources or even working together.

The intermix of geographical and social settlement is also visible from the general division of Aryan and Dravidian cultures. Though the historical debate, that Aryan invasion pushed the Dravidians into the southern India, is not completely settled, the crux of the social settlement and the divide into North Indian population and South Indian population is clear and loud.

The language deepens this divide. The south Indians who speak languages of Dravidian origin, and north Indians who speak languages of Sanskrit (or Aryan) origin is an important divide. However, these distinct identities, when working in a national framework of single constitution, and institutions such as parliament, courts, bureaucracy, corporate houses, living in the same neighbourhood etc, creates important dynamics.

Even beyond the Dravidian-Aryan divide, between the states of India too there are important variations. For instance, since 1970s, there are important clashes between locals and migrants from other states in the cities of Mumbai, Kolkata and Madras. The local people are averse to migrants from other states coming and occupying the jobs, and availing public services. These conflicts are rooted in the limited available resources and social identities of people. The ethnic violence for autonomy in Kashmir and Sri Lanka are also manifestations of conflict mediated through social identity.

Dissecting this identity from Indian philosophical perspective is essential to understand how relations are important in Indian context.

Anthropology of Rural India

The anthropology of rural India has been dominated by an emphasis on caste that has inhibited an integrated approach to understanding Class. Using an ethnographic approach that takes into account the symbolic and material aspects of caste and class, this chapter focuses on the attempts to form a "community" of potters among a large group of potter-artisans in central India. It is problematic, however, to view this community as a federation of potter castes or as simply a bloc of c lasses. Katznelso n's insights into different aspects of class formation help to understand how caste and class get constructed in the formation of a community. Here the apparently caste-based dispositions of potters reveals a class consciousness that is culturally organised by a custom that men work the potter's wheel and women do the marketing.

In the 1980s and 1990s, the anthropology of caste in India underwent a radical revision in reaction to the revolution in caste studies that Louis Dumont's structuralist approach heralded in the 1960s and 1970s. The critiques highlighted three debilitating effects of Dumont's approach:

1) that it thwarts the comparative aim of sociology and anthropology, since Indians are represented as being so different as to preclude comparison,
2) that it makes the reality of caste stand for India, which is far more complex, and
3) that it explains caste in idealist ways as a cultural construct devoid of material content, resulting in the mythology of a single hierarchy based on purity and pollution, along which all castes in India can purportedly be arranged.

The last critique has also been extended to show how Dumont mistakenly makes secular power appear as subordinate to ritual status. But, despite the critical import of these critiques, they do not bring class into the study of caste in any systematic manner. Anthropological studies of India seem to remain removed from developing an integrated approach to caste and class.

Fuller and Spencer note that the decline in the 1970s of the "village studies model" of Indian anthropology enabled a shift of focus from caste and the caste system towards other and larger structures such as class, religion, and violence. But it is noteworthy that debates on class formation in India have long been dominated by economists, historians, Marxists, development sociologists, and some political scientists. There is, however, a small body of classic anthropological works that have dealt with caste and class and some more recent works. The anthropology of India arguably is still weak on discussing political and economic issues, especially those that integrate the traditional strengths of studying caste with attention to issues of class.

The Caste System

Conventional anthropological understanding of caste are not totally devoid of material content. For example, Srinivas advanced the concept of "dominant caste" as the most useful way to understand caste on the ground. A dominant caste has six attributes; namely, a sizeable amount of the arable land locally available, strength of numbers, a high place in the local hierarchy, Western education, jobs in government administration, and urban sources of income. But the historian and sociologist, Mukherjee, points out that

> all these attributes are secondary or tertiary expressions of the formation of the top stratum of the *class* structure in rural society. But the pro collimation of class relations was an anathema to these conservative scholars. So, class was forcibly funnelled into an amorphous identity of the "Dominant Caste" because, as later admitted by its progenitor, all its six attributes need not be present in one caste entity. In other words, the "Dominant Caste" could be identified in (2^6-1=) 63 ways!

Mukherjee argues that the concept of dominant caste is actually an attempt at speaking of the ways in which the caste structure has increasingly articulated itself within a class structure, and that social reality today is neither caste in itself nor caste and class, but actually caste in class where the "class structure has cut across the caste hierarchy, forming new alliances and antagonism".

Indeed it is in the process of withering away with the march of history or otherwise remains atavistic, such as the distinction between the Jews and Gentiles, the Hindus and the Muslims. Yet, it is propped up, for their own sake, by the politicians and a brand of social scientists.

Mukherjee is too quick to announce the death of caste in India. Moreover, it does injustice to the large body of critical work on the social production of identities, forms of social distinction, and formation of group interests other than class that exist in ideological space and competition with class, all of which show that phenomena such as caste are not simply imagined and propped up by scholars and politicians. Finally, one wonders how atavistic institutions such as caste or religious identities continue to exist if they are but conjured up by scholars and politicians.

An earlier attempt to integrate an analysis of caste, class, and capitalism in today's India used statistical evidence of occupational categories and caste identities to show that whereas Indian feudalism was shaped closely by caste, colonial transformations, especially in land, gave a severe blow to the association of caste and class. It was only with the development of capitalist agricultural relations in India after independence that this correlation was broken. Thus Omvedt writes, "class and caste are no longer absolutely correlated: economic differentiation has affected almost every caste." This internal differentiation of castes has meant that virtually all castes, regardless of their rank in the ritual hierarchy, have members in different class positions (agricultural labour, small and middle peasantry, capitalist farmers). It has also meant that whereas capitalist farmers are the least differentiated in terms of caste (being mostly from the upper castes), it is the rural proletarians who are the most differentiated in terms of caste. In other words, upper castes are diverse in class terms and lower classes are diverse in caste terms.

The above works locate caste within larger processes of capitalism and class, but do not explore the notions of dominance and differentiation in any significant manner. These remain abstract theoretical constructs (rather than concrete historical social processes) that allude to the existence of structures within which people make their histories, but stop short of showing how histories are made. Despite these shortcomings, the insistence on caste as having a material basis shaped by capitalism can be extended to include the work of symbols in its concrete existence, since dominance and authority are legitimised through symbols. Ethnographic approaches, as exemplified by the works of Meillassoux, Gupta, and Mencher, are needed to take analysis of caste in this direction.

Reacting against Dumont's idealist theories of caste and also seeking to make a case for the existence of caste outside India (in parts of Africa), Meillassoux drew attention to relations of production within what appear to be caste relations or relations of kinship, reproduction, and status. He tried to show how the relations of *jajmani* were actually relations of clientship that depended on exploitation of the labouring classes, and argued that a strong case exists to view caste in the form of *varna* as class, at least in its genesis in ancient India. The subsequent development of classes accompanied by frequent conquests paved the way for increased fragmentation of society and the rise of endogamous communities or castes in their new form of *jati*. The move from varna to jati corresponded with a change from the generalised exploitation of the Asiatic mode of production to the localised exploitation of the feudal mode of production. Since jati is a pre-capitalist mode of production (i.e., Indian feudal effect), "... It would be too much to ask for a casteless system in modern India where the introduction of capitalism was not accompanied by an industrial revolution... And where, as a result, pre-capitalist remnants are still prevalent". In sum, a key reason advanced by these scholars for why caste exists in contemporary India, is that capitalist relations require caste relations to reproduce itself in a post-colonial setting. Yet another reason is that caste processes disorganised class formation. Social reproduction of capitalism and disorganisation of class formation are why caste is not simply an atavism in today's India.

There remains the need to demonstrate the processes whereby capitalism in India gives rise to the peculiar configuration of class-caste relations. Such a task requires a focus on relations between castes that simultaneously comprehends the dynamics within a caste, since it is at this level of group formation that the following questions can be posed: How do castes originate as groups that represent themselves to others and to their own membership? How do class and other differences emerge within a caste? Most important, how does the claim of a community become the key mode of accommodation and contradictions within today's caste groups in India? These questions have not been commonly posed since most studies assume existing caste-groups and tend to focus on inter-caste dynamics. As a result, they do not address processes of class formation that take place only within the space of caste and community in India.

Class Analysis

A useful heuristic device for studying class is Katznelson's view to analyse it at four "levels" (which are perhaps better understood as aspects), each of which takes a different perspective: first, class as part of the structure of capitalist economic development; second, class as life patterns within particular social formations (class as an experience dealing with patterns of life and social relations with respect to work and residence); third, class as shared dispositions resulting from subjectively lived experiences of "objective" positions and limits to action; and fourth, class as conscious collective action to affect society and the position of the class within it. With their customary focus on human interaction, culture, power, and community, anthropologists could contribute to the latter two aspects, while historians, sociologists, and economists usually centre analyses at the first two levels. Interestingly many of the latter specialists have turned to anthropological insights in their efforts to understand class and capitalism. The question of class formation is best understood as "concerned with the conditional (but not random) process of connection between the four levels of class".

One anthropologist's approach to social reproduction and economic anthropology could be read as emphasising exactly such a connection between these aspects of class analysis. "Cultural particularities are part of the class structure because they are crucial to the structure of exploitation and they might or might not be pertinent to class consciousness and the meaningful organisation of class identity". Culture is not merely part of a superstructure that is independent of or determined by the infrastructure. Rather, culture is part of the structure of society since it structures the crucial social process of exploitation. Most interesting here is that culture as structure goes into the making of class in the sense that Marxists have repeatedly emphasised, that "classes should be defined in terms of what people (in some sense) have to do, not by what they actually do".Finally, it is possible that these aspects of class could be viewed as mutually dependent or even as constituting each other. Not all forms of class action are possible, given the class structure of a society, and not all class dispositions can be compatible with particular forms of class action. Such considerations are appropriate for studying a place like India, a country that has much in common with less advanced capitalist countries, but which is also unmatched for its class formations and the role of the still relatively autonomous state, even in the age of privatisation and liberalisation. One would thus not assume a priori that the trajectory of class formation in India would follow a model based on England, or that class-consciousness of Indian workers would be signalled in ways similar to English workers.

The Case of Chhattisgarh Potter Caste

The late 1960s saw the birth of an organisation called the Chhattisgarh Potter Caste Community (referred henceforth as CPCC) in three districts of the central Indian state of Chhattisgarh. This organisation claims to represent about 40,000 people, all of whom belong to the *Jhariya* Potters caste and the overwhelming majority of whom are traditional potters. Almost all potters produce utilitarian items such as pots and pans, roof tiles made on the potter's wheel, and ritual items linked to the local agricultural and Hindu festival cycle. In this region, men work the potter's wheel while women gather firewood and do the marketing. Children may help with preparing the clay and firing items in the kiln.

The leaders who formed the CPCC are not potters, although all of them come from families who were potters a generation or more ago. Numbering no more than 100, these Potters are employed as (or retired) factory or clerical workers in industry or government, teachers, lawyers, or are small businessmen in retailing or restaurants. There also are other, smaller Potter castes in this region that have either migrated from other states such as Rajasthan and Madhya Pradesh or reside in those districts within Chhattisgarh and are not represented by the CPCC. While a few of these Potter castes are potters, most of them are entirely divorced from pottery and engage in petty trade and businesses like those from Rajasthan, while others are brick-makers.

In 1971, the leaders of the CPCC tried to unite all castes of Potters as the Chhattisgarh Potter Organisation (CPO) to represent all Potters in the region. But only the leaders of the various caste organisations currently belong to the CPO. The CPO in turn operates as a branch of the All India Potters Organisation (AIPO), a national organisation head-quartered in Delhi that is the ideological inspiration for Potter organisations in various states. The conventional characterisation of groups that attempt to form collectives of endogamous caste-groups by establishing horizontal and vertical links in modern India is that they are a federation of castes.But why should artisans like potters in today's India choose to politically represent themselves in the form of a Potter Organisation rather than a potter trade union? Related to the question of the form of collective action of group workers is that of the class character of the CPCC, the CPO, and the AIPO. The easy answer to both questions would take the form of arguing that the CPO and AIPO are examples of class alliances or blocs, since one class (potters, who are petty commodity producers in household economies) is part of a coalition with other classes (a mix of factory workers and petty bourgeoisie, such as clerical workers, teachers, and petty merchants, with the caveat that they all claim to be Potters) in which the latter classes take the lead for the Potter organisation on the basis of caste unity. Yet, such a conclusion does not illuminate the process of class formation in India. It cannot shed light on how, for example, class takes root as a lived category of experience, if it does so at all in India. For it cannot be simply assumed that potters consider themselves as a different class than their leaders who are Potters but not potters. Pursuing this line of thinking will eventually lead to what Mitra has called the "sterile debate" of studying class and caste "as if caste had no economy, and class no culture."

The various classes within the caste of Potters identify only what Wright calls the class locations of individuals, but fail to determine whether the leaders and the potters in the Potter organisations are linked to each other as two classes in a class relation; i.e., a social relation of production in which there is an unequal distribution of rights and powers over productive resources, control over the labour process, and the products of labour. It is only when such locations are placed within class relations that it is possible to view a class structure of society as the sum total of class relations. This requires taking into account the fact that potter-artisans have a diversity of work experiences and relations with capital. While all potters subsist on making utilitarian and ritual pottery for the market, many potter households depend on one or more members working in agriculture during the agricultural season, as wage labour making bricks, in construction, or as contract workers making roof tiles. Some have their most direct contact with capital working part of the year for a government financed co-operative while others, having joined the chronically unemployed, have lost faith in their traditional occupation.

Both class and caste in India articulate with a process that has increasingly become a key form of collective action for groups seeking to shape relations with the state and the market in their own perceived interests. This is the process of forming communities, and it provides an important lesson: that politics can produce a particular consciousness, rather than the other way around. Questioning the basis of community is critical because it challenges prevalent assumptions of culture as shared, rather than as used by and on behalf of capital to disorganise classes. As Narotzky emphasises, the task is to use the terms "culture" and "community" seriously and go past the fragmentation that pervades new narratives of capitalist society. What follows here is an ethnographic example that brings out the connections between aspects of class: structure, conditions, dispositions, and action in the context of community-making.

This case study, as it is about artisans, is focused on how capitalism has affected artisans formations. In pre-colonial India, artisans were intimately connected to the peasantry through the village economy and the demurrable and jajmani relations of production. In the urban settings they were the industrial class of the future, but very dependent upon royal patronage. British colonialism shattered these relations. The artisans created by colonialism remained independent petty commodity producers but without the status of village employees that was ensured by the caste system through closed labour markets. They were hence deprived of land guarantees and denied protected markets for their goods. Thus, an important axis of change for artisans in India was in the realm of social relations of production. In comparison, changes in the forces of production or technology have been far less important for the history of modern Indian artisans even after independence. As mentioned earlier, the CPCC was formed by those Potters who no longer were potters. Its genesis was explained by a high-ranking official of the CPCC:

> Before the Chhattisgarh Kumbhkar Samaj [CPCC] became an official organisation, the elder potters of every village in the region used to meet and make someone unofficially the *Ra ja* (King), the *Divan* (Chief Court Minister) and the *Mantri* (Court Minister). The object of such an arrangement was to exclusively resolve the problems within the particular samaj of potters such as someone's wife running away with

> someone else, a married woman going back to her mother's place and staying there, any man taking on more than one wife, etc. That time there was no problem of clay and firewood and hence it was never talked about in the meetings. Then slowly some educated and younger members of the samaj were invited to take part in the meetings. They were of the view that discussions restricted to resolving marital conflicts alone would not be useful to the samaj. It was then that the Chhattisgarh Kumbhkar Samaj [CPCC] became more organised leading to its official status.

The rise of the CPCC was aided by some recent developments in capitalism in India and state policies towards small-scale industry and artisans, including the rapidly shrinking market for clay products due to the increasing popularity of plastic and aluminium substitutes, the competing powerful interests of brick makers and paper industries for clay and wood respectively, the political changes that required traditional industries such as potters to dialogue more closely with the local state representatives rather than village councils for ensuring "protection" and "development," and the higher educational status of the CPCC leaders which made them more suitable representatives than practising potters. Significantly, to underscore their modernity, the leaders changed their official titles, substituting President for King, Vice-President for Court Minister, and Prime Minister for Chief Court Minister.

Social reproduction is attempted through control over what Potters call *roti-beti-len-den* (lit., exchange of bread and daughters, but referring to endogamy and patrimony). This case of a caste-based disposition conceals a more complex class consciousness that is historically contingent on a particular condition of production relations that is culturally organised; i.e., male potters at the wheel and female potters doing the marketing.

Social Hierarchy

A fine-graded social hierarchy dominates all types of interpersonal relationships in Indian context. The identity of other person (caste, religion, region, occupation etc) is recognisable from a few minutes of conversation and by knowing the surname. The interaction pattern changes even in formal contexts based on this (such as a claimant approaching a government official). Hierarchical interaction prevents scientific temper to prevail, and to give credit to the quality of the argument. Rather, it is the power structure and persons in higher hierarchies, whose opinions are valued and respected. Such an interaction becoming the dominant mode, in the patriarchal society, a woman's life has been often pictured as determined by man's choices: The oft-quoted verse reads:

> 'Her father protects her in childhood, her husband protects her in youth and her sons protect her in old age'. Hierarchical relations are meant to 'protect'.

However, when this protection slips into exploitation is unclear, but loud. For instance, a girl who may break caste solidarity and fall in love with a boy from another caste may be subjected to serious violence such as rape or parading her naked in the community. Such extreme violence is termed as communicator justice. In similar way, teacher-student relationship is supposed to be sacred. With huge amount of respect given from student to the teacher, memorisation by the student, of what teacher imparts, is an integral part of learning. Questioning and critical comments by the students are supposed to be questioning the hierarchy. Such a hierarchical relationship even justifies violence by the teacher on students.

In all the hierarchical relations, the tone of voice, body language, the way clothes are worn, all matters. The way by which such subtle differences are meticulously maintained indicate how the maintenance of hierarchy is done and subordination of some to others is systematically prevailed. Thus, relationships are patterned in such as way to maintain inequalities in the society. However, an important factor that breaks this hierarchy is education. Various corners of India it has been pointed out those who are educated question the value of hierarchy. Sometimes, acquisition of education by the young persons and their questioning of the elders are perceived as inter-generations differences. However, in Indian context, it must also be viewed as tendency to transcend hierarchy based on age.

Tolerance has been proclaimed as one of the hallmark of Indian culture. This is another mechanism of relationship to maintain the diversity. At the same time, this facet reveals another ambiguous nature of relationships in India. Recent communal violence in India (between Hindu-Muslim; Hindu-Christian) have shown that tolerance between communities existed as long as both communities were equally in poor economic conditions. Once a community progressed in economic realm or few members of one community converted to other community for economic gains, the tolerance broke down. Kakar has pointed out such origin of intolerance due to 'identity-threat' to the communities.

IDENTITY

In the Western theories (of law, state and morality) a person, who could make choices is the key building block of society. This person hood is without any relation to others in the society. Here the individual exists relational and "each needs the other antithetically". Indian conception of human being had a different orientation from this person-individual divide. While a conscious process of de-individualisation was considered as necessary for salvation, exercise of personal will was considered to be folly and thus was viewed with mistrust. "India seeks for the combining and unifying factor within diversity and individuality. Her series and types are based on the dogma of an underlying unity beyond the accidental appearances of individuals and specific instances". Thus, the original meaning of persona (in Latin) indicating the mask through which the actor portrays a character (svabhava) comes closer to Indian understanding of human being.

In the West, two traditions played seminal role for its emergence: First, through American social psychology Mead and Goffman used identity as a principle of social organisation. Second, in the psychoanalytic tradition Erikson used identity as the key principle around which personality is organised. Both these traditions dealt with the way identity of the individual was shaped through socialisation process. The political aspect of identity formation, and dialogical relationship between individual and collective identity came to the academic discourse through anthropological discourse in 1980s and 1990s. Rather than ascribed identity, identifies six sources of identity: sociological, occupational, geo-basic, national, co-cultural and ethnic). For examples, in India, 4693 communities derive identity on the basis of environment, religion, language, places of settlement and occupations. Apart from these there are identities such as illiterate, poor etc.

Although quite a lot of insights on identity formation are from Western Psychological tradition like Erikson, the life-cycle development in Indian tradition may not be neglected while explaining 'identity' in India. The works of Kakar, Paranjpe and Roland provide insights into identity formation in traditional Indian culture. The development of 'we-self' (Roland, 1988) for children in traditional Hindu joint families make them a member of the family and help them to identify with the joint family system, where the muffling of the personal interests for the sake of family interest takes place. Thus traditional families in India provide a foundation stone for the later social identification process and the collective behaviour/group behaviour among the citizens. The Indian understanding of divine through– advaita or non-divisiveness of reality – is the basis of this type of nurturing the relationship with others in great importance. With the attainment of Brahma-jnana (divine knowledge), which gives a sense of equality distinction of any kind disappears, and rather than individuals and persons, types emerge as social units. This sense of type as social unit is the key foundation for the collective identity. The implication of the collective identity is de-emphasising individual dignity and differentiation. Thus, the strain of relationship may easily be experienced. For instance, if loan is not given for the business of brother, it will not be morally approved since individual progress by accumulation may not be encouraged. Thus, being forced to think like the group and the danger for entrepreneurship could be observed.

Economic Inequalities

Indian economy is characterised by its informality. About 90% of the population make their livelihood in the informal sectors. This is also primarily because about 60% of the population make their living based on agriculture. The exchange relations in the agrarian activities–labour, loans, irrigation arrangements, marketing of products–are all informalised and these are mostly carried out through kinship or geographical neighbours. Formal markets and credits are limited, and failure of agriculture (due to lack of rain or any other) may result in strain of relationships since lack of repayment of loan is a breach of trust. Thus, series of suicides that took place in India due to agrarian distress has also to be viewed as misplaced trust and shame leading to human calamity.

Even in the urban context, informal economy dominates. Most of the Indian businesses are owned and managed by families. Banias, Aggarwals, Guptas, the Chettiars, Parses, Gujarati Jains, Muslim Khojas, Kutchi Memons, Marwaris, Maheshwaris, Oswals, Porwals and Khandelwals are well-known groups of family businesses. Some of the well-known names in the Indian corporate world, such as Ambanis, Tatas, Birlas, Bajaj, Singhanias, Modis are also rooted in the family businesses. Most of these businesses have not come to an established scenario as to how to distinguish between what is in the interest of a family and what in the interest of a company. The internal family feud has affected the businesses and shareholders. Some of such family businesses have been split up and formed into different ventures. However, the high trust with which the operations are possible in this framework has shown that there is great saving on the transaction cost.

Informal economy is also visible in the small-scale business operations. As many as seven types of relationships are woven together to make the business of street vending in the Southern states of India. Taking this view, both from rural and urban areas, what is important to be observed is that commodification of labour (dis-embedding of labour from the individuals) has not yet taken place in Indian context. As a result, labour relations are mediated through traditional power equations in the society.

In the informal economy, getting a job is a matter of relationship. The qualifications of the candidate and the requirements of the employer all could be compromised as long as relationship could be maintained. Since trust is an important element in such occasions of gaining job, corruption around gaining jobs remain a close secret. As a result, the bureaucracies, military forces, universities all of them get a colour of the social since the recruitment itself has been coloured through relationships.

The informal economy also has important implications for the social security or the arrangement of living after work life. Informal economy forces a care economy, since the social security arrangements are informal and family-based. There are few *institutional arrangements* to take care of the infirm and the weak. As a result, home care is the predominant mode of social security. However, households are not homogeneous. Understanding the heterogeneity is essential to understand the power distribution and thus the social security available based on the relationships. In most of the Indian languages the term for 'house' also stands for 'home'. For example, the term ghar can be translated "equally well as 'house', meaning the habitation; as 'household', meaning the socioeconomic living arrangements; and as 'family' meaning the network of power and emotional attachment". There are variety of arrangements for habitation, socioeconomic living and power relations. For example, it has also been pointed out that adult sons, after their marriage, often live apart in adjacent premises as a separate household for privacy, and all such separate households together are also referred as 'home'. Therefore, interpretations of availability of informal care could differ by which meaning the household is referred to.

An average Indian household size is 5.3. But, often, households are differentiated depending on how many generations live together. It is assumed that old parents in traditional societies live in three-generation joint families. This assumption is often not realistic, and in the context of younger generation migrating to cities, it is likely that older parents may be left alone in a house in the villages. Reliance on such informal supports for social security brings gendered dimensions to relationships. Thus, where the men lived on to old age, they had the support from their wife in the household dynamics. Culturally too Indian men depended on the women for maintenance than some one else. But, women in their old age find there is no one to depend on.

This interrelationship between economy and relationships show that livelihoods are based on relations, rather than commodities or resources. Even the risk is mitigated through relations. For instance, in Bangladesh the collective credit groups or self-help groups thrived in which loan repayment was done on group insurance, and the mutual trust forced the individual members to pay up the loans in time. Such a pattern spread to most of the South Asian countries in a successful fashion. In similar way, many of the farmers resorted to cooperative farming and cooperative dairying to address the risk of multinational corporate houses in the business. These instances raise the question as to whether deprivation and inequality foster relationships in positive way or not.

Relations Determine Well-being

Gift giving is a typical expression for solidarity in Indian culture. Most of the life events such as birth ceremonies, marriage, death all of them have elaborate set of gifts those are to be given to each other among relatives, neighbours and friends. As Marcel has put such gifts bring moral obligations, and reciprocity is implied. Gift giving among equals is often reciprocated through gifts. However, in the country like India, gift giving between higher and lower classes are reciprocated through pre-understood obligations (often in a work based relationship). For instance, a landowner would provide huge gift for the tenant during a marriage of tenant's daughter. The tenant would need to spend longer hours in the farm to express increased loyalty or reciprocate in similar way. Inability to 'measure' the implications of such gifts often gives way for strain of relationships and quarrels. Some of the gifting systems are institutionalised to benefit the poor people. For instance, during the month of Ramadan, Muslim community provides monetary gifts, such as grains, money or clothes, (Zakat) for the poorest Muslim household in the community, and that household is able to gain sustenance through this.

In 1980s there was an interesting debate among sociologists as to whether poverty induce collective action. Obviously, there were arguments from both sides and consensus was not possible. The debate, however, documented evidences from various parts of the world as to how poor people came together to fight oppression and structural injustices. India is one of the finest examples in this scenario, where social capital has been used to circumvent the economic inequalities. The social mobilisation, particularly the Gandhian model of protest through mass mobilisation has created relationships around social issues. This is evidenced through movements such as Naxalism, soft-terrorists, environment group activism and protest against displacements. In all the cases, the group that comes together experience injustice from the state or wider market forces. People come together, often being coordinated through a charismatic figure, to fight against a force, which they would not have been able to do as immobilised individuals.

Another important development that has taken place in recent times in the Indian politics is the mobilisation of the social groups, and lower castes into vote banks. Near the time of elections, the social groups organise public meetings in common spaces, which are often attended by the political leaders. Often, the fixing of a candidate for election is by taking into consideration the social composition of a particular constituency. In some of the Indian states, chief ministers have come to such positions through caste politics. As a matter of fact, such mobilisations have been part of Indian history. Sikhism was mobilised among the lower caste as a protest against injustices within Hinduism. Amedkar movement was aimed to bring emancipation for the lower castes to correct social and economic inequalities.

What is much more prominent is the formation of civil society institutions in the form of Non-Governmental Organisations in structured manner to work for development organisations. Often they are also called non-profit organisations. It is estimated that there are 1.18 million such organisations existing in India alone. The sheer existence of such a large number or organisations indicate how easily people come together to agree on some plan of action. What is important to be noted about such civil society activities is also that, these are not exceptions to the social identities. For instance, in small towns of north India, there may be a group of people migrated from the southern state of Kerala. Their population in a small town may be about 200 households. These households may come together to celebrate a region specific festival. At the same time, this small migrant group may be further divided into different religions or castes (e.g. Kerala Christian Association, Ayyapa Samaj, SNDP etc). Multiplicity of such civil society organisations makes social exclusion almost impossible. Thus, even if poverty may be deeply persisting, even poor people are included in some form of organisation or another.

2

Changing Rural Life

In recent years the Indian government has made huge investments in development of infrastructure like roads, telecommunication, etc. It has also passed legislation to benefit rural citizens. For example, under universal service obligation, each village should have a village public telephone installed and maintained by the service providers. Also, the "Right To Information Act" passed recently was to make the government system accountable to the citizens. However, civil society organisations are often unaware of such legislation and they fail to leverage the benefits. Corporate houses, private business houses and largely urban citizens are making effective use of the provisions. Thus, the benefits are inequitably distributed between the rural and urban areas. This rural-urban divide in accessing infrastructure services coupled with inability of civil society organisations to utilise the existing provisions has contributed to the slow growth of livelihood opportunities in rural areas.

Initial poverty eradication efforts in India concentrated on supply of agricultural technologies, inputs and services that were often 'production' orientated. However, they were not targeted towards the poor or were largely inappropriate to the needs of the poor and the benefits were mostly captured by the wealthy. Later, the approach changed towards 'capacity building' in sector organisations to equip people and organisations with the skills and resources to do a better job but, overall little has changed since the new skills are not used. All these approaches tended to be sect oral and supply-driven and the results were not very encouraging. The concept of livelihoods and livelihoods analysis emerged in the mid nineties closely associated with poverty reduction strategies.

Understanding the livelihood systems of the poor is crucial to effective poverty reduction. Livelihoods of the poor can never be understood in any one-track logic be it economic, social, technical, cultural or political. The livelihood systems are made up of very diverse elements which taken together constitute the physical, economic, social and cultural universe wherein the families live.

Thus, the livelihood system is more than just a set of physico-economic preconditions for continued existence. It also encompasses psychosocial dimensions of experience of living. The livelihoods approach puts households of the poor as its central focus. It takes holistic consideration of things that the poor might be vulnerable to, assets and resources that help them thrive and survive, policies and institutions that impact their livelihoods, how the poor respond to threats and opportunities and what sort of outcomes the poor aspire to.

Agriculture and allied activities support livelihoods of nearly 70 percent of India's rural population. In recent years, land based livelihoods of small and marginal farmers are increasingly becoming unsustainable, since their land has not been able to support the family's food requirements and fodder for their cattle. As a result, rural households are forced to look at alternative means for supplementing their livelihoods.

Changing Trends in Agriculture

Majority of the India farmers derive their livelihood from agriculture. During the Tenth Five Year Plan, gross domestic product (GDP) originating from agriculture and allied activities was 2.3 percent compared to 8.0 percent in the industrial sector and 9.5 percent services sector. During this plan period, the growth in the agriculture and allied activities averaged 2.3 percent which is lower than that of 3.2 percent during the 1990s and 4.4 percent during the 1980s. Also, there is a shift from staples to cash crops which is the major reason for food insecurity. From 1960-61 to 1998-99 the area under grain crops has gone down from 45 million hectares to 29.5 million hectares, area under cotton has increased from 7.6 to 9.3 million hectares and area under sugarcane has increased from 2.4 to 4.1 million hectares. Since 199091, due to the new economic policies, the area under food grains and coarse grains have declined by 2 and 18 percent respectively while area under non-food cash crops such as cotton and sugarcane have increased by 25 and 10 percent respectively.

However, production of milk has increased from 84.4 m tonnes to 97.1 m tonnes. Production of eggs has increased from 38729 millions to 46231 millions. Notwithstanding increased availability of milk, fruits, vegetables, fish and other produce, the agricultural sector is facing the new challenges of diminishing land resources, factor productivity decline, threatened loss of bio-diversity, natural resource degradation, widening economic inequality, etc that have serious implications on the livelihoods of the poor. Indian agriculture has also come under significant adjustment pressure from market liberalisation and globalisation.

The changing consumer preferences have added to the complexities of adjustment. The food consumption pattern in India is diversifying towards high value commodities. The decline in per capita consumption of cereals, in particular coarse cereals, has worsened the nutritional status of the rural poor. In the case of the poor, total consumption of high value cereals like rice has declined by 10 percent due to rise in prices of cereals in real terms during the 1990s and dietary diversification towards non-food grains. Similarly, average daily intake of protein by the Indian population decreased from 60.2 grams to 57 grams in the rural area between 1993-94 and 2004-05.Recent studies indicate that household level food security for the poor households is changing for the worst.

Household Level Food Security Its Importance

As P Sainath, puts it: "Seldom has policy been so forcefully implemented as in the 1990s. For ten years, governments have assaulted the livelihoods and food security of the poor. That security does not lie in mountains of grain but in millions of jobs and workdays for people". Food security at the national, state or district level does not automatically ensure food security at the household level. Today, commercial crops are being recommended by Agriculture Departments to improve the economic status of farmers without explicit consideration of their household level food security. What most small and marginal farmers often need is food crops such as short duration cereals, millets and fodder crops to meet their family's food and fodder needs.

For scientists, modernising agricultural production through technological alternatives seems to emerge as a natural path to food security. Development and dissemination of green revolution technologies are classic examples of the approach for attaining national food sufficiency when hunger and starvation were widespread. Farmers in resource rich regions of India successfully adopted these technologies that account for about 35 percent of the cultivated area. But, in the ramified areas (65 percent), technology adoption varied considerably. In semi-arid areas, the record is even miserable despite improved technologies being available.

Our observations in the semi-arid areas indicate that some small and marginal farmers sought modern agricultural technologies on their own, without any assistance from the extension network; and there is a majority who, despite all extension efforts, refuse to change from their traditional way of farming. Households that face difficulties in ensuring their own food supply, first try to reach this threshold by intensifying production of subsistence crops (maize and pigeon pea). Households that have crossed food security threshold then invest more in commercial crops like tomatoes and brinjal, etc. Evidently, it suggests that neither the technologies seem inappropriate nor it appears to be a failure of the extension network. The security of the family's livelihood system as a whole plays the determining role in technology adoption or non-adoption.

It is important to realise that livelihood security has to be understood from the farmers' perspective. *Food security is a subjective concept defined as an individual farmer's own perception as to whether S/he has been able to support the family's food and fodder requirements adequately round the year using all resources under his control.* Food security is only one (although extremely important) element of livelihood security. But since farmers never make their decisions in a one-track logic, it seems possible that the one-track security based on food alone would have to be enlarged to the more holistic notion of security of livelihood, or speaking even more simply life-security. Livelihood security encompasses food security, social security and psychic security. Each one of them has some basic minimum threshold level to achieve and maintain and also must be pursued in a balanced way.

There are evidences to suggest that many of the household decisions (e.g. sending children to school, participation in community organisations, etc.) Are directly related to whether the households are below or above the food security threshold.

In the absence of food security off-farm income from migration becomes a stabilising component in the over all livelihood security. Many development agencies seek to reduce distress migration by providing opportunities to farmers to increase their income from land based activities through commercialisation of agriculture. Often the approaches taken are sectorial and fragmented.

Migration and Livelihoods

Every year millions of poor families migrate in search of work. They are forced to migrate due to a livelihoods collapse in the villages. These distress migrants often lock their homes, take a few meager belongings and move across long distances. The children accompanying their parents are forced to drop out of school. The numbers of such children under the age of 14 years is estimated to be around 9 million.

Being away from their village, they do not belong to the places where they go and increasingly lose acceptance in their own villages. They are disconnected from their community, culture and traditions, unable to take part in festivals, fairs, religious and social functions, which are an integral part of their lives thus losing their sense of identity. The vulnerability of people who cross state boundaries is even greater as they find themselves increasingly at the mercy of their contractors. The family members or children left behind in villages do not know where the family has gone, or how to contact them. Dealing with emergencies, particularly back home is difficult, especially for those who go long distance.

Distress migrants find themselves with hardly any skills, assets or education. Earnings from migration are survival level and not enough to build assets. On the contrary, medical or other personal emergencies and the unsteady nature of work often push them further into debt. Those who own a few animals have to arrange that they are cared for or just end up selling them off at low prices – thus depleting their assets.

The work sites largely have no basic facilities like water, marketplace, schools, health centres, etc. Migrants are at the mercy of their employers for all their needs. Contractors retain control of labourers not only financially but also physically, forcing them to work even when they are sick or injured. If there resident communities nearby, migrants are usually shunned by local people, and regarded as bad elements or thieves.

Given the difficulties encountered by illiterate and under-informed migrants in accessing provisions that have been made for them by the State, there appears to be a need for support from elsewhere. A number of civil society organisations have taken up the cause of building the capacity of migrants to demand their rights from contractors and government officials.

A particularly striking example of a successful migrant support programme is the one initiated by the Grameen Vikas Trust (GVT). It has worked closely with the panchayats of source villages and has developed an informal system of identity cards for migrants. With these cards, migrants have something to show the authorities at railway stations and bus stands, common points in their journey when they are open to harassment. GVT has liaised with NGOs in the neighbouring state of Rajasthan to set up migrant resource centres that provide them with information on job availability, wage rates and rights.

By all accounts such migrant support programmes have achieved more success than official programmes in ensuring fair pay and better working conditions. The widespread system of subcontracting that operates in non-farm sector employment especially in construction projects fudges responsibility and accountability so that it becomes very difficult for government officials to implement protective legislation.

Given the problems associated with agriculture and distress migration, occupational diversification is a means to make livelihoods sustainable as agriculture alone cannot sustain the growing population in villages, it is imperative that the RNFS (RNFS) is strengthened. The RNFS plays a crucial role in providing livelihood security to the poor.

Trends in Rural Non-Farm Sectors

The rural non-farm economy is the backbone of numerous towns scattered throughout India as well as the primary source of income and employment for many of India's poor. The sector therefore plays a key role in determining future prospects for employment growth and poverty alleviation in the country. The RNFS is closely linked to agriculture. A large share of rural manufacturing involves agro-processing and the production and supply of farm inputs. Agricultural performance therefore tends to influence growth in the non-farm economy. A growing agriculture demands production inputs in addition to supplying raw materials to transport, processing and marketing firms. Moreover, agriculture provides the livelihood of more than 70 per cent of the rural labour force and as such, increases in farm income tend to stimulate demand for consumer goods.

Interestingly, development of the RNFS in the 1980s resulted in a remarkable reduction in poverty. However, this is an area which has received casual treatment from the policy makers, economists, politicians, social activists, entrepreneurs and more importantly, the communities themselves. Despite this neglect, it is said that 90 percent of the additional employment during the reform period was due to the non-farm sector. According to the National Sample Survey, the percentage of employment in the RNFS in total rural employment increased from 18.4 per cent in 1983, to 21.6 per cent in 1993-94 and 23.8 per cent in 1999-2000.

The additional employment created in the RNFS during the reform period was 8.54 millions. Out of these, 36 percent of the additional employment in RNFE during the reform period was due to construction, 27 percent was due to manufacturing and repair services and 25.5 percent was due to transport, storage and communication. The contribution of retail trade was 13 percent while that of hotels and restaurants was only 4 percent. In the case of community and personal services, there was a decline in employment while the employment of social services (education and health) increased. The shares show that around 63 percent of the additional employment was due to construction and transport, storage and communications. It is not clear whether the creation of additional employment in these activities led to improvements in the well being of the poor.

Although the RNFS has tremendous potential of removing unemployment in villages, the government has not been serious to address the basic problems plaguing this sector. Major bottlenecks in the holistic development of the RNFS are poor quality of employment and incomes, shortage of skilled manpower, unavailability of credit facilities, absence of marketing networks, poor transportation facilities, low public investment in villages, lack of basic amenities in rural areas, poor law and order scenario, erratic power supply, etc. Besides, not much has been done to develop technologies relevant for the sector. Entrepreneurs are by and large reluctant to invest in the rural non-farm sector. Not many NGOs and political groups are engaged in empowering the rural communities to be pro-active and develop RNFS enterprises on their own.

GLOBALISATION AND VULNERABILITY

Rural livelihoods are affected by the process of Globalisation.Special Economic Zones (SEZ) are created across India to promotion exports. Commerce and Industries Minister Kamal Nath claims that exports will ultimately grow five times, GDP will increase by 2 percent, and 30 lakh jobs will be generated by SEZs across India. The government also claims that SEZs will attract global manufacturing through Foreign Direct Investment (FDI), enable the transfer of modern technology and create incentives for infrastructure.

To date, the central government has approves 237 SEZs in 19 states (occupying 86,107 hectares) out of which 63 of these SEZs have already been notified. Around 23 SEZs are operational, 18 in the IT sector. Total amount of land to be acquired across India is estimated to be around 150,000 hectares. This land – predominantly agricultural and *typically multi-cropped is capable of producing close to 1 m* tonnes of food grain. If SEZs are seen to be successful in the future and more cultivated land is acquired, they will they will endanger the country's food security.

Reliance Industries has sought permission to build India's biggest Special Economic Zone near Mumbai comprising more than 14,000 hectares of land. Similarly, Some 400 SEZ projects, offering incentives to big *businesses had been approved (formally and in-principle)* amounting to 1,25,000 hectares. Some estimates show that close to 114,000 farming households and an additional 82,000 farm worker families that are dependent on these farms for their livelihoods will be displaced. The total loss of income to farming and farm worker families is at least Rs 212 crore a year not include other income lost due to the demise of local rural economies. Such developments by the MNCs and Corporate Sector are playing with the emotional, economical and cultural interests of farmers, fisherfolk, scalepan workers and agriculturalists in the area. Their entire livelihood is dependent on the farmland. It is an amazing feature of this exclusive area of India where people have farmlands and they also do inland fishing. India's Special Economic Zones have drawn sharp criticism from a wide range of environmental and human rights groups, as well as farmers, villagers, fishing and agricultural workers who face losing their land, homes and livelihoods. Critics point to a lack of transparency and unwillingness to hold open public consultations on the SEZ issue.

Correspondingly, the entry of corporate retail into India is nothing but a hijack of India's vibrant, well organised retail service economy. Corporate retail will not create two million jobs; but it will destroy 38 million livelihoods of people involved in running small shops and street markets. The growth being projected as a new contribution to the economy hides the destruction of the contribution of the 40 million people involved in small retail to the Indian economy.

Corporate retail is being described as organised retail. And small scale decentralised and highly networked indigenous retail is being falsely referred to as unorganised. However Indian trade is highly organised and has existed for centuries on the basis of low cost and high efficiency. India needs the self organised skills of our traders, shopkeeper, hawkers and vendors both to provide employment to millions and affordable friendly community service for basic needs to society.

India is a land of retail democracy. Hundreds of thousands of weekly haats and bazaars are located across the length and breadth of our country by people's own self-organisational capacities. India's streets are bazaars – lively, vibrant, safe and the source of livelihood for millions. India has the highest shop density in the world, with 11 outlets per 1000 people not including the village hats.

Our retail democracy is characterised by high levels of livelihoods in retail with nearly 40 million employed accounting for 8 percent of the employment and 4 percent of the entire population. It is predominantly self organised with low capital input and highly decentralised. In a country with large population and high levels of poverty, this model of retail democracy is the most appropriate in terms of ecological sustainability and economic viability. By 2011, more than 6600 mega stores are planned with investment of Rs. 40,000 crore. Reliance plans to invest $5 billion over next four years to open thousands of retail stores. Walmart's partner Bharti also plans to invest up to $2.5 billion in new stores in the next eight years. The entry of the giant corporate retail in India's food market will have direct impact on India's 650 million farmers and 40 million people employed in tiny retail.

Coping Strategy of the Poor

A review of coping mechanisms reveals that a very small group of medium farmers is able to cope with adverse climatic conditions merely through the sale of available stocks. On the other end of the spectrum, landless labourers can only resort to seasonal migration due to lack of any productive assets or availability of alternative employment options in the village. Small/marginal farmers use a variety of adaptation options such as sale of cattle, shifts to other subsistence crops, wage labour, as well as seasonal migration. This range of options, however, constitutes only temporary coping measures. During adverse periods, farmers have implemented a range of livelihood and coping strategies to reduce their vulnerability ranging from appeasing the Lord Indra (the god of rain) to some social support system reduction of food consumption and change in the pattern of food consumption changing their occupation to households either sold or mortgaged their lands and household assets. Options that enhance longer-term adaptive capacity (such as institutional credit, crop insurance, and use of drought-resistant varieties) are not used by farmers due to procedural complexities and stringent eligibility criteria, compounded by lack of awareness.

Social Protection

Poverty alleviation has been one of the guiding principles of the planning process in India. The role of economic growth in providing more employment avenues to the population has been clearly recognised. The growth-oriented approach has been reinforced by focusing on specific sectors which provide greater opportunities to the people to participate in the growth process. The various dimensions of poverty relating to health, education and other basic services have been progressively internalised in the planning process. Central and state governments have considerably enhanced allocations for the provision of education, health, sanitation and other facilities which promote capacity building and well-being of the poor. Investments in agriculture, area development programmes and afforestation provide avenues for employment and income. Special programmes have been taken up for the welfare of scheduled castes (SCs) and scheduled tribes (STs), the disabled and other vulnerable groups. Antipoverty programmes that seek to transfer assets and skills to people for self-employment, coupled with public works programmes that enable people to cope with transient poverty, are the third strand of the larger antipoverty strategy. The targeted public distribution system (TPDS) protects the poor from the adverse effects of a rise in prices and ensures food and nutrition security at affordable prices.

Poverty rates in India have declined over the last decade, but the incidence of poverty remains high at 28 percent. India's surge in growth and rapid expansion in public spending in the past decade has created new possibilities for its social protection system. Basic subsistence needs and services remain the priority in some areas but with the need to re-examine delivery mechanisms for traditional safety nets in the changing economy. Other areas face second generation challenges of expanding social protection instruments to deal with economic modernisation, and the new risks and vulnerability it brings. Some of the programmes the government has implemented/implementing are Pradhan Mantri Gram Sadak Yojana, Swarnjayanti Gram Swarozgar Yojana, Sampoorna Grameen Rozgar Yojana (SGRY), Indira Awaas Yojana, National Rural Employment Guarantee Act-2005, National Social Assistance Programme, National Food for Work Programme, among others.

The Government spending remains focused on social protection programs to alleviate chronic poverty. Spending on food programs remains high, and is mostly focused on rural areas. A safety net for the urban poor is very limited. In 2004 the Government spent around 4.3 percent of GDP on core social protection programs, 2.2 percent was spent on safety nets and the remainder on formal sector pensions. However, these social protection programs have not reduced poverty as India had hoped they would. Many of the programs have been subject to frequent adjustments, through re-branding rather than significant change. In addition, these programmes lack cross-program coherence. Poor implementation and limited flexibility in responding to the variations in the priority needs of poor households are serious governance have made limited impact on poverty reduction.

However, the importance of social protection is growing as it is reflected in the Government's Common Minimum Program. Increased resources and political priority given to social protection stem from social concerns that India's high growth has not been sufficiently inclusive.

Information Systems for Sustainable Rural Livelihood

Development projects need relevant and good quality information. By definition, development interventions are oriented to changing people's lives. They attempt to target those who are marginalised and vulnerable to disruptions. Until recently top down methods were dominant in which most essential decisions about what issues will be addressed and how the information will be used were made by "specialists" (as opposed to community members). Projects are designed based on information that they have about the people in question, their needs, conditions, and concerns. When organisations base their actions on insufficient or faulty information, the result is a misplaced intervention that has little correspondence to the needs the poor. Such projects may actually have a negative effect on poor as they undermine traditional practices or cause local communities to invest their scarce resources in unviable activities. Vulnerable population may actually become more destitute as a result of such poorly informed interventions.

There are many successful information and communication technology (ICT) initiatives in India oriented towards rural development. Now this has received due attention of policy makers, implementers for success of government projects through National governance plan (NeGP). The objective of NeGP is to provide a portfolio of services to the citizens through common services centres (CSC) integrated with e-government backbone to not only set up a good e-governance system but also to establish a support structure for sustainable livelihood opportunities. In order to support the rural households, the Government of India is planning to set up 100,000 common service centres (CSC) for 600,000 latest by September 2008. The financial outlay is around Rs. 23,000 Crores. These centres are expected to provide 80 common services with active support from district, state and central administration as well as business sector. The CSCs are meant for optimising transaction cost and time. It is also envisaged that these CSCs will support online transactions for government services. This is primarily aimed to reduce the distance that a villager normally travels to transact. A villager usually would prefer a better transaction cycle to happen in the village itself to support their livelihood prospects.

These CSCs are conceptualised on supply-driven model and are expected to provide pre-determined services. Experience of such supply driven projects have more failures than successes. This is primarily due to poor sustainability attributed to gap in supply and demand of the services needed by the rural citizens. Therefore there is a need to develop models to capture local demand on participatory mode with a suitable interface with supply-driven government systems.

The rapid changes at the macro level that India witnessed since the early nineties has contributed to the instability of the livelihood systems of the poorer section of both rural and urban households. While the benefits of globalisation process have largely accrued to the urban sector growth the rural sector has been left behind. Slowdown in agricultural growth and productivity, changing cropping patterns, increase in distress migration, changing consumption patterns, government policies favouring industrial houses, among others have seriously undermined the food and livelihood security of the poorer households. An integrated, multidimensional and holistic approach to poverty eradication efforts is crucial to preserve and enhance the livelihoods of the poor.

3

Rural Sociology: Modern Views

Views of Chicago School

The Chicago School of urban sociology attempted to explain the social structure of the city in terms of what they called the 'biotic' and 'cultural' levels. Robert Park was the key theorist. On the one hand, he well knew that city life is a product of conscious activity. Thus economics, politics and the law are all examples of the 'social' or 'cultural' level; a result of conscious and purposeful activity. On the other hand, Park and other Chicago sociologists placed particular emphasis on the largely unconscious processes which go into making city life and the spatial structure of the city. These constituted the 'biotic' level. This emphasis thus focused on the biological or psychological processes underlying conscious human activity. Such processes, Park believed, are largely responsible for 'natural areas', for the sorting of the physical structure of cities into areas of, for example, housing for different classes and nationalities. This process is analogous to the structuring of space in the natural world, the making of relatively separate natural 'communities' in the context of the struggle for survival by different species.

Park's emphasis was in part on the Darwinian struggle for survival in human societies, whether in the form of mutualist support or outright competition. But it was also on the struggle for social recognition, the making of personality in the process of interaction with other people.' Men invade one another's lives', he argued, 'in their efforts to direct, control and give expression to their own conflicting impulses'. But all this was taking place in the context of massive social disruption. Chicago was of course the home of many immigrants who had lost their traditions, values and older, often more collective, ways of life.

The insights of the human ecologists of the Chicago School have now been largely abandoned. This is partly due to serious flaws in this line of thinking. Critique has centred on, for example, their neglect of the cultural level, their confusion over whether 'community' was a sociological concept or a concrete thing and, more specifically, their failure (despite their inclusion of the 'cultural' level) to see cities in the context of capitalist societies. Nevertheless, there remains a strong case for restoring some of the Chicago School's basic insights in the light of modern research. Such a strategy offers an improved understanding of the processes underlying the structure of the modern city and the forms of cultural politics associated with city life.

Writing around the turn of the last century, Kropotk in argued that the globe was being carved up as a result of the massive extension of capitalist industry. On the one hand, each nation was becoming increasingly specialised. A new spatial division of labour was developing, one which attributed a specialised role to each nation. The result was the division of humanity into 'national workshops having each of them its own speciality'. On the other hand, such spatial divisions pre-supposed and depended on an ever-extending globalisation, on the active development of trade between nations. Such divisions were good for capitalist profits, but they meant an increasing separation between people and the land. The new divisions meant little contact between people and the physical and social characteristics of their landscapes. The relationship between people and their environment was being severed.

Kropotk in saw the emergent spatial division of labour as closely associated with fast-emerging social divisions. Capitalism was bringing increased fragmentation between producers and consumers, manual and intellectual workers and, amongst the labourers, a mass of further fragmented relations. People were therefore being increasingly estranged not only from nature but from one another. Importantly, these processes were also acting against an inborn human nature; social division was closely linked to de-skilling, to the misuse of human beings' natural endowments. According to Kropotk in :

> 'Skilled artisanship is being swept away as a survival of a past condemned to disappear. The artist who formerly found aesthetic enjoyment in the work of his hands is substituted by the human slave of an iron slave'.

Kropotk in's anarchist politics led him to argue for a reintegration:

> 'Have the factory and the workshop at the gates of your fields and gardens, and work in them'.

This would permit the kind of the mutualism which Kropotk in felt was a characteristic of the evolved human species but which, he argued in Mutual Aid, had gone un-realised since the days of the mediaeval city. People would be integrated not only with nature and with other people but with their essential nature.

Such a vision can of course be criticised. Kropotk in romanticised the past of the agricultural worker and of the mediaeval city in particular. His treatment of gender relations is nonexistent. His particular approach to a biotic level of explanation (one assuming an essentially mutualist human species) is at least open to question. Nevertheless, Kropotkin's analysis (and especially his emphasis on estranged relations between people and nature, between towns and nature, and between social and spatial divisions of labour) is essential if we wish to understand current tensions and contradictions surrounding urban and rural life.

Today's global division of labour is clearly quite different from that outlined by Kropotkin. De-industrialisation is now deeply affecting the developing countries. Manual work is increasingly concentrated in 'the Third World'. As Clark puts it: 'low-cost workers in developing countries undertake labour-intensive tasks of manufacture and assembly *under the direction of*, and specifications drawn up by, technicians and managers based in the developed world'. If Kropotkin's emphasis on the global market was right it is now difficult to consider countries as 'national workshops'. The specialisation of nations is eroded as footloose industries are now able to settle in almost any part of the globe. To an increasing extent the globe is now one massive 'workshop ' for a global capitalism; social, political as well as economic life being thoroughly stretched across national frontiers.

The fortunes of today's cities and rural areas in societies such as Britain are indeed closely linked to the emergence and practices of global capital and trans-national corporations. Rural sociology now points, for example, to the role of multinational corporations in the restructuring of old agricultural economies and their replacement by new forms of intensive production. Central to this process of control is the penetration of capitalist control into virtually all aspects of agricultural production, often with very serious repercussions for humans, animals and the rest of the environment. Perhaps the most spectacular example is the sequences of the genetic code and its manipulation for food production. Given such developments, it seems likely that rural sociology will increasingly focus on struggles surrounding food production. On the one hand, transnational corporations backed by national and international organisations such as the World Trade Organisation will continue to attempt the domination of the food chain. Biotechnology will be given an ever-increasing role as will other forms of intervention, such as drugs, to stimulate animal growth and resist disease. On the other hand, such technologies will generate resistance. This will come from organisations and networks attempting to revive the older forms of production, rural re-population and more local and democratic forms of management. The 'biotic level' again becomes apparent. Struggles against capital-intensive farming are only partly about eating more healthiiy. They are also about recovering a sense of human identity and control in the context of powerful economic and political forces.

The spatial division of labour in Britain and other societies is likely to remain one in which the research and management functions of trans-national companies remain distant from the manufacturing processes for which they are responsible. This social-cum-spatial distancing poses continuing problems of control by high-level executives over subordinate social groups, but it is likely to be a continuing trend into the twenty-first century. Headquarters will typically remain located in cities and regions offering a high quality of life, good links with research universities and a continuing supply of well-qualified graduates. Examples are Boston (Massachusetts) and California's 'Silicon Valley'. In Britain they include the Cambridge region ('Silicon Fen') and spread south and west down the 'M4 corridor' towards Bristol.

At one level, Kropotkin's utopia may seem finally realised in some of these regions. 'Counter urbanisation' will continue, though perhaps on a declining scale. This will ensure that increasing numbers of relatively affluent households in owner-occupied homes will be able to enjoy a form of rural idyll in small cities and settlements. This may look like the fusion between fields, factories and workshops for which Kropotkin pleaded. But any such merger between fields, human society and nature will be of a mainly aesthetic kind. The computer executives living in Silicon Fen have little or no link with, or understanding of, the land owned and run by the 'barley barons' of East Anglia. The bio-tech scientists living in the West of England have precious little meaningful link with the regions they share with farmers and livestock. Meanwhile, counter urbanisation and the continued 'hollowing-out' of the city will result in increased spatial as well as social polarisation. It will leave behind in the city large numbers of people on low or minimal incomes, single-parent house-holds and elderly people. Their contact with the more affluent members of their own species may be very limited. But they will share at least one thing with the middle classes; a continuing estrangement from nature and the causal processes of the natural world.

Since Kropotkin's day a new system of international finance has been developed. This too has immense significance for the spatial development of society over the next twenty-five years. London, New York and Tokyo have become and (despite competition from other centres such as Frankfurt) are likely to remain key global financial centres. These are amongst the 'world cities'. They contain not only the headquarters of financial and corporate institutions but the key central government institutions. At the same time such cities will remain wholly dependent on the mass of relatively unskilled, low-paid, workers living in the cities to keep them in business.

Global economic, social and political change and their links to the spatial division of labour are now an established feature of social theory, especially that stemming from geographical writers such as Harvey and Massey. Harvey's analysis also stresses the impacts of 'flexible accumulation': systems of production which are partly displacing the Fordist mass production of standard products with flexible, under-unionised labour processes and 'just-in-time' forms of production. These relatively recent social innovations, with their heavy dependence on temporary labour, subcontracting and self-employment are leading, Harvey argues, to further disorientation for the human subject, adding to the uncertainties generated by a financial capitalism which has few long-term loyalties to particular places.

However, Harvey – and indeed Massey also – touch on newer and still emergent forms of sociology, especially those focusing on culture and human identity. These authors have made important contributions to an understanding of the role of place in the context of such globalisation. Harvey, for example, argues that home and community are made into places of security and retreat in a world which has become largely unknowable and uncontrollable. Heritage and tradition become central to this largely defensive role for place or locality:

> The assertion of any place-bound identity has to rest at some point on the motivational power of tradition... The irony is that tradition is now often preserved by being commodified and marketed as such. The search for roots ends up at worst being produced and marketed as an image, as a simulator or pastiche (imitation communities constructed to evoke images of some folksy past, the fabric of traditional working-class communities being taken over by an urban gentry).

Similarly, Harvey argues that qualitative meanings and concerns surrounding place have become especially important. Localities are occupied on the grounds that they feel simply better as places in which to live and work. The aesthetics of place (the room and the home, as well as the community and region) assumes a central role in a society which is fluid and extremely difficult to predict.

Massey, however, takes issue with such a conceptualisation. Harvey's view, she believes, offers an over-defensive view of the culture of place in contemporary capitalism. The notion of place as simply a haven, a retreat or home is also, she suggests, a gendered claim. It is one which tacitly assumes the fixed entity of the mother, the wife who remains there as solace and pick-me-up for the harassed and insecure male. Similarly, it is a picture which denies that places are themselves subject to change. 'You may leave and dream of the places you once knew, but meanwhile they have themselves moved on'. Massey argues in terms of an open sense of place, one in which boundaries are 'essentially open and porous'. Globalisation is linked to local diversity. In the small villages around Silicon Fen, for example, Massey notes:

> There are high-tech scientists, mainly men, whose work is based in Cambridge, though they often have computers with modem links at home as well. The companies they work for operate in a highly internationalised part of the economy, and these employees spend their time in constant contact with, and physically travelling between, colleagues and customers all round the world. Their activity spaces, and those of the companies where they work, are thoroughly multinational. At the other extreme are people who have never been to London and only rarely have made it as far as Cambridge.

Cultural View

The second, and now rapidly-developing form of sociology in urban and rural studies is concerned with the culture, or cultures, of cities and landscapes. They are returning to themes which were once central to the Chicago School. Savage and Warde write that 'the study of urban culture has returned to the agenda'. It has 'returned' in the sense that developments since the Chicago School have largely dismissed the idea of an 'urban culture' or indeed of a number of 'urban cultures'.

Such a notion is, according to the early work of Castles, 'ideological' in the sense that it ascribed to urbanity, to living in cities, processes (such as the separation of individuals from one another) which are best ascribed to capitalism; to, say, the alienation of people in the labour process.

Nevertheless, despite the best efforts of earlier forms of political economy, urban culture, or cultures, are indeed now back on the agenda. The key concerns here are with the constructions (or, perhaps more accurately, the 'construals') of rural as well as urban life. Urban and rural sociology now emphasise people's many and often contested construals. Indeed, the prime theme here is contestation. No one construal has preference in terms of its explanatory power. Many construals are made and these are often in conflict.

The rise of the cultural turn in rural as well as urban sociology is connected to developments within the wider sphere of social and political theory. Theories of new social movements, for example, argue that emergent forms of politics and political resistance maintain culture at their core. Such movements are seen as, perhaps above all else, carving out new ways of life and new forms of personal and collective identity. Furthermore, people are making diverse ways of life. And they are doing so for themselves–writing their own biographies in a globalising society subject to constant upheaval. All this, it is argued, is in contrast to the older forms of social movement which were organised around social inequalities and dominant and unchallenged forms of science.

How, according to this newer literature, do the new social movements relate to city life? The urban context emerges as central. As Hetherington puts it, 'identity politics is distinctly spatial politics'. The making of identity is socially-cum-physically embodied. Clubs, social networks and the '24 hour city' phenomenon are all good indicative examples. Environmental questions are as likely to figure as much in these urban settings as in rural areas, not least because of the rising levels of pollution generated by contemporary cities. Urban sites are created 'turfs', places marginalised or neglected by capitalism and mainstream lifestyles where people make themselves, carving out new ways of life in relation to one another and their environment. Nevertheless, precisely because of their concentration and resistance to dominant cultural forms, they are also potential sites for repression and sometimes outright violence.

Identity-making by alternative cultures in the city are paralleled by counter-cultures using the countryside. 'Place' is again made centrally important. Ecologically-based movements, for example, attribute a mystical, aesthetic and sacred significance to the natural environment. Borrowing from Buddhist, indigenous and even Celtic literature, these movements stress the interconnections of humans with nature and (as with the theory of Gaia) attribute a spiritual and moral significance to nature as a self-realising system. The earth becomes personified as living organism; a goddess or mother figure. Places which are economically and politically marginal are again the settings for such politics of place, but the picture in the countryside is again one of potential and real contestation as the 'tribes' seeking harmony with nature run up against authority in the shape of, for example, property-owners, the National Trust and the law.

In a modern society such as Britain, however, the position is highly diverse and complex. Recent research shows there is no one overarching construal of nature. As Mac Naghten and Urry have shown, nature is indeed construed by many people as possessing intense spiritual or symbolic value, 'a source of goodness'. But, they write, 'there is no such thing as nature, only natures'. What 'nature' actually is remains a matter of intense contest and debate. It is also seen as, for example, animals or endangered species under threat. Such varied constructions are important in terms of providing intellectual resources for political movements. 'There is no nature simply waiting to be conserved,' Mac Naghten and Urry argue, 'but rather all forms of its conservation entail judgements as to what indeed is nature'.

Extreme diversity of people's constructions of city-existence is also the recurrent issue when we turn to current urban sociology. As is now well rehearsed, some early urban analysts argued that there is one distinctive urban way of life. With is well known for arguing that the size, density and heterogeneity of cities led to isolation and social disorganisation. The strong sense of community, identity and association found in rural areas has, he believed, been fragmented. People feel isolated and social disorder ensues. There were, of course, strong links here with Tonneaus on Gemeinschaft and Gesellschaft.

But as is also well known, With's highly influential hypothesis has come under sustained attack. As Savage and Warde and others have outlined, empirical studies showed community still being actively made in cities and ample alienation and social breakdown in the countryside. Furthermore, it is not clear that a single urban culture every existed. Cities, it has long been argued, are actually composed of a mosaic of different cultures and lifestyles. The newer types of cultural theory again stress the multiplicity of coexisting urban cultures and indeed the early Chicago School itself insisted that such proliferation was a central feature of urban life. As Savage and Warde put it: 'Birth's view that there was an urban culture always sat somewhat uncomfortably with the Chicago School's recognition of the existence of varied practical cultures in the Western city'.

George Simmel's work remains centrally important to urban sociology. His emphasis, like that of Birth, was on the fragmentation and diversity of urban experience but, most importantly, he alludes to an underlying human nature. And in pointing to the attempted restoration by the individual of a sense of self in the chaos and confusion of modernity he is referring, albeit in a somewhat elusive way, to the kind of 'biotic' level of explanation used by the Chicago School. Simmel's work has been inaccurately conflicted with the work of Birth and indeed his understanding of the city and city life does at first seem similar to that author, particularly in terms of his focus on the supposed alienation and isolation of city life. Simmel was not, however, contrasting 'urban' and 'rural' ways of life. Rather, and this is why he remains so relevant today, the metropolis is seen as the epicentre of modernity. It is the place in which modern life was experienced most acutely and where humans attempt to adapt themselves (more accurately, their selves) in relation to their experience. City life is where the culture of modernity, the active separation of persons from persons and the reconstruction of social and personal identity is found in its most extreme form.

The diversity of urban cultures and of constructions of the city, therefore, remain the hallmark of much contemporary sociological work on the city. On the one hand, the focus is on difference, specificality, meaning, values and signification. On the other hand, the new work is simultaneously about power, about cities as settings within which power is both exercised and resisted. Sexual identity and the city are now a core theme. Writers such as Castles have shown, for example, how in a city such as San Francisco gay men used parts of the city as a way of asserting and celebrating 'difference'. Examples in the British case are the 'gay villages' in towns such as Brighton and Manchester. At the same time, celebration of sexual difference is no longer limited to the creation of self-contained communities.

The large contemporary city can also be seen as a site of challenge to the patriarchal and oppressive forms of family life characteristic of suburbs and small towns. 'The city offers women freedom,' she writes, 'after all, the city normalises the carnival esque aspects of life'. In a parallel way, West wood and Williams point to the role in making and even reproducing racial difference. They refer to 'the racialisation of city spaces'. But here the tone is less celebratory, more defensive. Such racialisation of the contemporary large city can again open people up to further harassment. West wood and Williams adopt a Foucauldian line of analysis in arguing that:

> The visibility of ethnicity 'others' produces the global cities with which we are familiar but it also allows racism to operate as a disciplinary mode in which the fact of being seen provides optimum conditions for surveillance and for identification as an alien and threatening existence.

In turning from the relation between dominant and subordinate cultures to the ways in which these are articulated in a spatial context, it comes as no surprise to find the aesthetic, visual and architectural component of urban living again looming especially large. These physical elements of city life generate personal recollections and memories, as well as associations and expressions of past societies. Precisely how these processes actually operate is very difficult to uncover, but the work of Benjamin will surely remain central to a future urban and rural sociology in this respect. His work can be seen as an aesthetic and psychic version of Marx and Angels's view that each society contains within it the seeds of a new society. Forms of architecture, for example, are based on older precedents. Buildings therefore act as 'collective memories' of older societies and forms of social oppression. But at the same time they can be emancipatory; offering glimpses of new, non-hierarchical and classless ways of life. These are difficult to see, however; the commodities on which a modern city and economy is organised acts like a dream world, lulling the senses. Ending alienation depends on awakening from the dream, or at least realising its revolutionary potential.

Manchester's 'gay village'–towards which this Lesbian and Gay March is progressing–can be seen as a product of what Fark and his colleagues in the Chicago School called 'the biotic level'. The Chicago group believed that subconscious, biologically-based, processes (in particular the struggle for space and the making of identity) do much to explain the formation of distinct spatial districts. Park et al. Nevertheless recognised that the biotic level is linked to, and is often expressed by, the 'cultural' level; more conscious and purposeful activities expressed through, for example, the market, politics and the law. Note that Manchester's gay village is now very popular amongst hetero-Sexually. It is also being marketed worldwide by the British Tourist Authority. Photo: Geoff Stafford.

Architectural historians have long attempted to 'read' city-forms as simple expressions of the society in which they were constructed. However, there are severe difficulties here. Understanding a society solely through interrogating the particular 'text' of a city ignores the context in which that city was created. A more promising strategy has again been to recognise contestation, this time over urban meaning. One of the earliest and best-known examples of this alternative is Harvey's study of the basilica of the Sacred Cower in Paris. The significance of this site was hotly contested between political left and right after it was constructed by the Catholic Church following the defeat of the revolutionary communard. No doubt its meaning for many people has again changed as it has been made into a prominent tourist site. But such meanings are always in flux and different social groups will associate different meanings to the same monument. It is instructive to note how professional architects and designers are now taking different sides in these contestations. Whereas they may earlier have attempted to design a built form which was assumed to be read in the same way by everyone, now some of them are recognising a diversity of meanings. Some architects are now working more closely with the individuals for whom they are designing.

In both urban and rural sociology, a strong form of social constructions prevails, one which focuses on meaning and social identity and the aesthetic. This is clearly helpful for understanding the diverse ways in which people interpret their environments (including some abandoned parts of the 'hollowed out' city) and how such interpretations are linked to resistance to dominant world-views. The difficulties start if we assume that an understanding of people's construals is all that is needed for an understanding of human beings and their relations with their environment. The problem becomes most evident if we consider human society's relations with the non-human environment. It is one thing to understand the vastly varying ways in which 'nature' or city life are construed. It is quite another thing if this should lead to a denial of underlying causal mechanisms. Sopor makes the point concisely with reference to 'nature' when she argues that the hole in the ozone layer is not a hole in language. It is a hole in the ozone layer.

Physical, biological, social, economic and political relations, processes and causal mechanisms which are real, 'out there' and independent of discourse need to be recognised by both urban and rural sociology. Further-more, such processes and mechanisms are 'in here' in the sense that psychology, biology and other disciplines representing what the Chicago School called 'the biotic level' clearly indicate that humans are themselves composed of mechanisms which are instinctive or in complex ways a product of our genetic inheritance. Strong social constrictions is, at worst, sociology's form of disciplinary reductions: an ultimately doomed attempt to contain all understanding (including those of the sciences) within strict sociological limits. Another way of making the same point is to say that, while all knowledge is socially constructed, some knowledge is better than others: referring to an objective reality.

Biotic Level

Sociology has not allowed the above two forms of urban analysis to remain entirely separate. Drawing partly from Bourdieu, for example, Zukin shows brilliantly how capitalism actively invests in forms of culture and urban ways of life. Cities have become sites of consumption, with people buying into ways of life, visual experience and forms of entertainment providing a sense of personal and collective identity. At the same time capital uses consumption in cities as a means of accumulation, cities made into booster-regions through making themselves into 'fantasy cities'. Simultaneously, urban lifestyles and forms of consumption are a means of identity-making, especially amongst the better-off middle classes.

Such understanding remains confined, however, to the sphere of the economy and culture. Mainstream sociology has remained largely averse to the Chicago School's 'biotic level'. This is partly due to the reductions and essentialism still often associated with biological and psychological thought. But such problems are no excuse for sociologists engaging in a similar practice; sociologists every aspect of human affairs. Furthermore, a recognition of an embodied human being does not necessarily entail an essentialist view of the human subject. Some of the theories touched on above implicitly or otherwise recognise a biotic level. Kropotkin's vision of an essentially mutualist human nature (one remaining un-realised by contemporary society) is an example. Simmel's suggestion of human identity being made in the midst of the complexity of modern life clearly relies on some notion of the human psyche. Similarly, Benjamin's notion of the city was a complex combination of surrealist thought and historical materialism.Clearly, the precise ways in which the biotic level is developed and characterised in a future urban and rural sociology (and indeed in sociology at large) will be a matter of considerable debate. Indeed, such debate has already begun. On the one hand, there are those such as Pinker who argue that much of human beings' behaviour (for example, altruism and an instinctive liking for savannah-type landscapes) can be attributed to our evolutionary inheritance, to our attempt to survive during the time we evolved as humans. On the other hand, authors such as Benton argue that this is making far too many claims regarding our biologically inbuilt 'species-being'. Humans, they would say, are characterised by their immense flexibility, one which enables them to adapt to changed historical circumstances. Furthermore, evolution happens at a number of levels and in a number of spheres. Humans have co-evolved in ecosystems and with other species and an understanding of human nature as 'essentially' based on our hunter-gatherer inheritance again does not allow humans to be seen as coevolving, changed by (as well as changing) their environment.

Nevertheless, the application of biological and evolutionary thought to human behaviour has already been started by some sociologists. One of the clearest recent applications comes from Saunders. Saunders suggests that socio-biology lends support to some of sociology's dominant themes. As is now well-known, the theory of 'the selfish gene' implies that as humans we are programmed to seek out those with whom we are genetically close or those with whom we are familiar. Those predisposed to favour self over others and their genetic stock will therefore have been less likely to survive into subsequent generations. Ethologists and others have taken the socio-biological view even further and suggested that religion, ethnicity and territory act as forms of genetic marker. While we may not be genetically linked to the people with whom we share the same territory or ethnic group, such categories and concepts are said to be realising genetically inbuilt and therefore still powerful predispositions to support kin. Tonneaus in the 1880s wrote of 'the natural will' and of the 'inborn and inherited' feelings which underpinned *Gemeinschaft*. The way in which that natural will is most commonly articulated, he argued, is through blood-ties (and in particular the tie between mother and child), shared territory and common religious beliefs. Saunders, and the ethologists and others on whom he draws, are therefore suggesting that the Chicago School's 'biotic level' (interpreted in 'selfish gene' terms) is still alive and well and deeply influencing human affairs. And as regards specifically urban questions, such an explanation helps explain patterns of residential segregation. Again, these are partly a product of markets and politics and culture, but Saunders asks the rhetorical question: 'Is there some fourth factor also operating, some sort of "natural" or "instinctive" process which leads us to seek out others like ourselves?'

Saunders's representation of 'the biotic level' makes very strong claims for the role of biology and 'the selfish gene'. But popular though this kind of biology still is, an active rejection of the kind of reductions thinking suggested by 'selfish gene' thinking is now occurring. This will probably lead to a corresponding decline in explanations based on this understanding of 'biotic' processes. A more productive alternative is to start recovering the kind of perspective on human nature advanced by Kropotkin. But Marx, despite giving little attention to 'urban' and 'rural' matters, is probably even more helpful as a starting point for understanding 'the biotic level'.

Marx's theory of alienation (of people from one another, of people from nature, of people from the products they make and of people from their own nature) clearly depended on a notion of an underlying human essence. The full aesthetic and spiritual capacity of human beings, he argued, is realised through relations both with their own species and with nature more widely. Human beings also need to have control over what they make. Furthermore, and unlike other species, they have the capacity to link general ideas to knowledge based on practical experience. And yet contemporary capitalism, Marx argued, depends on a systematic separation of people from one another, from nature and from their inborn capacities. This latter includes their aesthetic capacities and spiritual needs. Items are assessed solely for their monetary worth.

As Marx put it: 'The dealer in minerals sees only the commercial value, and not the beauty and peculiar nature of the minerals'. Marx's notion of the human species-being was a set of assertions about 'the biotic level', about humans as a biological sort. But, bearing in mind more recent research, there are reasons for accepting at least some of his account. Piaget, for example, showed how human beings develop during their lifetimes as social and identity-making animals.

As a result of their practical engagement with the world, children eventually emerge as language-making animals with a strong capacity for abstract thought and for linking concrete experience with abstract ideas. They also develop a strong sense of self in relation to the rest of the social world. Recent research on autism in humans (in which people have little awareness of themselves or of others) is showing up those parts of the brain necessary for the emergence of this sense of self. In all, there is now a great deal of new work available on what Marx called 'man's species being' and on what the Chicago School called the 'biotic level' of human behaviour.

So how, then, might an incorporation of the 'biotic level' actually help urban and rural sociology in particular and sociology more generally? How does it help link the two forms of urban and rural sociology outlined earlier: political economy and culture? Well-established forms of urban and rural sociology emphasise globalisation, the stretching of social life across time and space, a growing global interconnections, a speeding up of interactions of all kinds. At the same time, they point to a separation of people from one another on one hand and from their environments on the other. They point to the growing social and spatial division of labour and underline how the de-skilling process remains a central feature of modern industry. Furthermore, the commodification of aesthetics and the aestheticisation of the contemporary economy continue apace. The key point is that if this analysis is broadly correct, then the newer forms of urban and rural sociology with their cultural, creative and local emphasis, are showing how people (as a species with distinct biological-cum-psychological predispositions) are simultaneously attempting to reassert their own human nature, their 'species-being' in the context of the continuing maelstrom of social, economic, political and environmental change. Centrally, these needs include a spiritual and aesthetic dimension, a need to relate to one another and to their environment. But, as Harvey points out, oppositions cultures can be all too easily incorporated and marketed by capitalism itself. It is at this point that we begin to see some of the complex links between 'biotic' and 'cultural' levels.

In Britain and in many other societies, there is now a vast and rapidly growing range of 'third sector' economic activities such as local exchange and trading schemes, community banks, self-build schemes, micro credit systems and organic food producers. Many of these are organised along co-operative lines. Such experiments or mini-utopias are often attempting to establish new, locally controlled and (even more important) less autocratic ways of working together and with their physical and ecological environments. Furthermore, if the Marxian understanding of 'the biotic level' sketched out above is broadly correct, these too are attempting to realise the biologically-based need of people for a sense of association, security and social identity. There is no reason why the search for stability in the home or in the community should be envisaged as regressive. These experiments or 'escape attempts' are not only finding ways of realising basic human needs. They are also asserting or prefiguring new, potentially more progressive, ways (males, for example, doing as much of the caring and restorative work as females) of fulfilling these needs.

Raymond Williams's book, *The Country and the City*, offers an excellent indication of how the two kinds of urban and rural sociology outlined here can be combined to understand the complex links between economic and political processes on the one hand and people's construals of urban and rural life on the other. Williams argued strongly that everyday life and human consciousness in cities and in the countryside is a product of power relations and, in the current day, massive and globalised flows of capital. Relations between town and countryside, he argued are 'the product, however mediated, of a set of decisions about capital investment made by the minority which controls capital and which deter-mines its use by calculations of profit'. But his analysis of English literature and social thought also showed so well how people have continually made sense of themselves and their lives through the active interpretation and reinterpretation of powerful images.

Notions of 'country' and 'city' have long had central roles to play in this process. They are the ideological battlegrounds over which power relations are often fought. The dominant and recurring image of the country has been that of a timeless and wholly natural social and environmental order. It is an idyll now deployed by, amongst others, powerful interests within the Countryside Coalition. By contrast, the city is still consistently portrayed as a place of the future, a site of both threat and opportunity.

Note, however, that these images are disembodied. They are all about mythological past and futures which are not based on real; material, relationships between people and their environment. One way to start countering such reveries is to develop an understanding of the relations between capitalism and people as a natural sort. Such an understanding could provide the basis of alternative urban and rural utopias. These would not only be environmentally sustainable. The would also aim to realise and extend the capacities of the human species.

4

Social Issues in Rural India

India. Rural India presents a baffling dichotomy of images: poverty and growing potential of rural markets. Relative productivity ratios of 1:3.4:4.2 per unit of labour in agriculture, industry and services, respectively seem in conducive to equitable society and economic development. Clearly economic reforms have succeeded in transferring capital from inefficient to efficient sectors, but yet to achieve a corresponding transfer of labour.

We have seen in India, the economic impact of innovation in agriculture in '70s through the Green Revolution. Though it caused some environmental problems, there is little doubt about the stimulus it provided to the national economy. Rural India is in deep and continuing distress, and is crying out for food and work. Economic and political empowerment of Dalits continue to be resisted by non-Dalit castes across the country. This reflects the failure of public institutions and political parties to make the polity democratic and egalitarian.

The industrial slowdown of the late 1990s was largely a fallout of indifferent agricultural growth and the drop in non-farm income generation activities in Rural India. Can India achieve 7-8% growth merely on the strength of Services and Export sectors? Overlooking rural-urban linkages amounts to feeble economics and suicidal politics.

Enhanced access to quality roads, power and water supplies remains a pipedreams, despite all the promises made by successive governments. Living conditions (from kutcha houses to semi-public and pucca structures, from bio-mass to LPG for cooking, etc) in rural India seem to have been improving in recent years, as highlighted by the recent NSSO Survey (59th Round). The Common Minimum programme (CMP) should be seen as a package that promises to make growth more sustainable by addressing a key variable – rural demand. After a decade and a half of reform, we seem close to arriving at the right growth-welfare mix.

India's increasing urban-rural divide can be effectively dealt with only through the provision of urban facilities in rural areas (PURA), as stressed by the President Dr. Abdul Kalam. The UNCTAD's World Investment Report (WIR), 2005 says developing countries are emerging as favoured locations for the conduct of R&D by MNCs so as to tailor, and dovetail, products and processes that would integrate local production into the MNC's global value-added systems.

India is sitting on the blitzkrieg of becoming a super power and it is the Indian rural sector that is going to drive that super growth. The Government of India has made rural economic development in general, and rural infrastructure development in particular, is a key priority. India has launched the "Bharat Nirman" (Building India) program, which entails investing over US $ 40 Billion, equivalent to 5 per cent of FY2005 GDP, in six critical areas of rural infrastructure over four years starting from 2005.

Rural Education

A firm beginning has been made, complete with a detailed proposal with an outlay of Rs. 81,327 Crore during the 11th Plan, by the HRD Ministry to the Planning Commission, for universalising the Secondary Education in the country, as it has been done in primary education (Sarva Shiksha Abhiyan).

Water Crisis

Integrated Water Resources Management is based on the perception of water as an integral part of the ecosystem, a natural resource, and a social and economic good. India is heavily dependent upon ground-water sources for freshwater (e.g. for 80 – 90% of domestic water supply in rural areas); much less upon the other sources–rain and surface water (lakes, tanks and rivers). Failure of governance in managing water resources has led to extensive, unsustainable dependence on ground-water. Ground-water accounts for 50% of irrigation and 80% of water supply. India faces a turbulent water future. The only solution is effective management. Demand will have to brought down to match supply, and the focus will have to swing back to surface water supply system. Part of the solution, John Briscoe said, lies in demarcating clearly water entitlements, de-monopolising public irrigation departments, and developing transparent water information systems, apart from building public infrastructure.

India needs dams, a fact borne by two simple statistics: we get 50% of our rain in 15 days and over 90% of river flows take place in just four months. Irrigation goes a long way in improving the lot of a village. Studies show correlation between the percentages of irrigated cropped area and the percentage of population below poverty line (More irrigated area, Less People below poverty line in villages). Augmentation on the supply side may indeed be necessary through: large projects, ground-water drilling and rainwater harvesting (and micro watershed development).

The question of access, equity, and equality in Water Resources gets directly to the use of irrigation water. Has the expansion of irrigation benefited small farmers? Have the interclass differences in irrigation widened or narrowed? What is the regional (State) distribution of irrigation by farm size? Deshpande et al point out that the growth rate of all major sources of irrigation was found to be inversely related with the farm size in majority of the states between 1970-71 and 1990-91. Complex issues of equity and social justice in regard to water distribution are required to be addressed.

Rural water supply in India, both the Central and State Governments have achieved, is the largest of its kind in the world and significant progress due to sustained efforts. The country is facing now, three major challenges in the water sector:

a. Lippage of covered habitations.

b. Water quality problems.

c. Sustainability of sources and systems. Study Reports also reveal that Ground Water (GW) depletion has aggravated water quality problem (like excess fluoride, arsenic and brackishness), which has resulted in diseases like fluorosis and arsenical dermatitis.

Prior to the green revolution, sustainable use of water resources was commonplace. Water is also necessary for better sanitation, and improved hygiene. Patients from middle class family are suffering from water-borne diseases. India can't uncage its 'tiger' economy or claim to have enter J into the 21st century sans better water, sanitation and hygiene. Moni makes a powerful plea for an informalities blueprint for integrated water resources planning and management at grass roots level in relation to climate change and sustaina' gricultural development.

Public Governance

Over the last decade and a half since India has embraced the path of reforms, there have been several dramatic changes in the economic landscape. Reforms have been largely focused on areas like foreign trade, industrial investments and financial services, with the hope that the trickle-down effect will ensure that prosperity reaches all sections of society.

Despite the notable success of these initiatives in several sectors of the economy, in almost every election the Government that has accelerated reforms has been voted out of power. The clear absence of a substantial enough audience among the electorate supporting reforms has something to do with the nature of the reforms that have been implemented.

Though the effective implementation of the 1991 economic reforms has made the economy and the corporate sector more robust, the reforms have not really impacted the everyday lives of a substantial part of the electorate. These are areas like education, health, child nutrition, drinking water, women's welfare, village autonomy, etc. That are the primary concerns of the common man.

Moreover, the interface between the citizen and the instrumentalist of the government–the police force, the judiciary, the ration inspector, he RTO, the sub-registrar, the tehsildar, the tax-man, the municipal inspector et al–has been largely unaffected by the forces of reform.

Successive governments continue to allocate increasingly larger resources to antipoverty programmes that account for a large part of the federal and state budgets. There is, however, no evidence to suggest any improvement on the old benchmark of 15 paisa / rupee of welfare allocation finally reaches the intended beneficiary. The day may not be far off when policy makers are held squarely responsible for the continuing endemic poverty, given that the means to eradicate it are very much at hand.

The best way to improve the quality of public services is to provide access to more information so that the citizens are aware of the basis of decision-making in government. The work culture has degenerated into one of survival without decision-making since this is the sure path to not being found guilty of wrong doing and hence the clear route to career progression. Scientific and Technical Departments are not exceptional too. It is expected that the Right To Information (RTI) Act 2005 will provide necessary scope and hope to reverse the trend, and usher in "SMART" Government.

Health Issues

India has 5,03,900 doctors, 7,37,000 nurses, 162 medical colleges, 143 pharmacy colleges, 3,50,000 chemists, 15097 hospitals accounting for 8,70,161 beds, 23,000 PHCs, 1,37,000 Sub-centres serving semi-urban and rural areas, and 3000 Community Health Centres. Non-availability of doctors in PHCs and CHCs is a huge problem in rural India. In addition, PHCs are woefully lacking in basic medicines and other facilities. Mass health and education cannot be out source to NGOs.

There exists a sharp disconnect between urban and rural healthcare in India, and if we continue to ignore this deepening divide, we run the risk of establishing our socioeconomic fabric. India has 30% of World's TB Population and no new drug during the last 40 years. The Rural–Urban Divide is apparent with a higher elderly population reported in rural households.

For many people in the remote regions of India, medical help is inaccessible and beyond means. The rural resident has no cash for healthcare, a lack of paying capacity. In fact, the cost of staying alive pushes one-quarter Indians below poverty line. Those who require hospitalisation are perennially repaying debts. In fact, rural indebtedness caused by illness is far greater than that caused by crop failure. Developing and maintaining sustainable healthcare delivery for people in the poorest countries is indeed a challenge. There is an urgent need to provide access to affordable healthcare in a sustainable manner.

The only viable proportion is an insurance model that will support millions across India's rural hinterland through a network of hospitals and clinics. Yeshasvini, Karnataka's Health Insurance Plan (premium is Rs. 120 per annum) and Arogya Raksha Yojana–a private initiative for the rural population could be a path-breaking model. According to Dr. Devi Prasad Shetty, Founder of Narayana Hrudayalaya (Bangalore), this scheme worked primarily because of the Government. Dr. Shetty says that we underestimate the power of government and how much trust the poor have in it. Yeshasvini has tapped the power of the cooperative sector. A PPP model is also being developed based on the existing but ineffective Primary Health Centres (PHCs). As Winston Churchill once said:

> "Insurance brings the miracles of mathematical probability to the rescue of the masses".

The time has come to provide basic healthcare to our billion people. India is currently way off the track from achieving the UN's MDG targets. There is no dearth of information on what is actually happening on the ground. India may be a major IT Power and a Nuclear weapons State, but when it comes to looking after its children, especially girls, it lies the bottom of the heap at 127th on the Human Development. The UN HD Report 2005 makes sorry reading. The statistics are stark: over 2.5 million children of "Mother India" die every year, accounting for one in children deaths across the world. Of these, 50 per cent are girls.

The Human development Index (HDI) is a summary measure that incorporates into one index:

(i) Life expectancy.

(ii) Adult literacy and gross enrolment in primary, secondary and tertiary education.

(iii) Per capital income.

The UN's HD Report 2005 places India at 127th out of 177 countries. It's doubly ironic that India, attempting to a global healthcare hub, has got it so terribly wrong inside its hearth. The downward spiral that the index showcases this year must be addressed immediately, and tackled on a war footing. The Report concludes that "but, overall, the evidence suggests that the pick-up in growth has not translated into a commensurate decline in poverty" and "it will take India until 2106 to catch up with high-income countries".

Fundamentally, India can wipe out disease by attacking the root cause – poverty and malnutrition. According to the Micronutrient Imitative Report:

> "Controlling Vitamin and Mineral Deficiencies", "the Country needs to invest less than Rs. 5 per child every year to tackle the problem of micronutrient deficiencies'.

We in India have the necessary infrastructure but the services are not operative and not effective. Technical knowledge and an effective public health system also may not be always the answer. Sometimes, understanding the social determinants of disease can help in its prevention. Awareness and "partnership" with the civil society can check disease. The ambitious National Rural Health Mission (NRHM) of the Union Health Ministry has envisaged ASHAs (Accredited Social health Activists) as the central component of the Mission, who would be the first port of call for health related demands including basic curative needs. In addition, the NRHM also seeks to introduce systematic changes in the health acre delivery systems by improving the quality, access and demand aspects of health services. The NRHM has been set up with an allocation of about Rs. 6,700 Crore, consistent with its NCMP to step up public expenditure in the healthcare from 0.9% to 2–3 % of GDP. The success of NRHM depends upon the motivation levels of the Activated Social Health Activist (ASHA).

Success in the long-term battle against diseases is increasingly becoming dependent on education and efficient infrastructure by leverage IT. Telecom and IT have a major role in healthcare management. The importance of tele-medicine and electronic data capture in providing enhanced medical information for diagnosis and treatment is key to building an efficient model. Additionally, building data bases and disease registries will enable such insurance programmes to evaluate the incidence and diversity of diseases at an epidemiological level. E-Health System is an essential requirement at Panchayati level.

ENERGY PROBLEMS

Rural electrification is a vital programme for socioeconomic development and for bridging the urban-rural divide. Apart from improving the quality of life and aiding activities like education, it is an essential input for rural economic activities such as agriculture and rural industries.

Over 86 Million Indian Housewives, covering nearly 40% of our population, use liquefied petroleum Gas (LPG) for cooking. To add to their comfort, the Government-owned Oil marketing companies, at heavily subsidised rates, is distributing domestic LPG, thus insulting to a very large extent from the steep rise in international prices. Moreover, most of the burden of subsidy, running to over Rs. 10,000 Crore a year, is borne by the Public Sector Oil Companies. What will be ratio of Rural-Urban divide in LPG subsidy?

As the energy crunch looms large, fossil fuel stocks are falling. Many countries are switching to bio-fuels. India is importing crude oil worth of Rs. 1,17,000 **Crore and bio**-diesel production will help in saving foreign ex-change. The power of wind is free, no expensive drilling for oil, no bruising the countryside to displace thousands of people for building a dam. Only wind turbine is required to spin power out of thin air. It can be in our backyard or hilltop. While wind blows, power can be generated. It is essential to harness the potential of wind into an energy source for homes and industries.

India has started with a 5% ethanol blend with petrol, which can be increased to 10 & 20 % progressively. The fact is that Indian sugar mills make ethanol from molasses, a by-product. This circuitous route can never generate the high volumes required, at the right price. Instead, what is required is that the industry produces ethanol directly from cane, as it is done in Brazil. One tonne of sugar produces 100 kg of sugar and 50 kg of ethanol. But the entire one tonne of sugarcane, if fed directly into a distillery, can produce 500 kg of ethanol.

It, therefore, makes good commercial sense to produce ethanol as a main product in an independent distillery, rather than as a by-product in a sugar factory. Such distilleries can pay double the price of a sugar factory to farmers.

But sugarcane is an irrigated, water intensive crop. What about a dry land farmer who depends on rainfed crops?. Fortunately, new technology is available to produce ethanol from grain and stem juice of crops like sweet sorghum (meethi jowar), barley and maize, which are starchy. A distillery can extract 380 litres of ethanol from one tonne of such crops. The distillery would be willing to pay double the price to a dry land farmer compared to what he gets from his crops today. In this way, ethanol can usher in rural prosperity.

In the first place, cane needs to be grown mainly in Bihar and Eastern U P, along the Gangetic Plains, for sound agro-climatic reasons. It is plain wrong to have water-intensive cane in drier Maharashtra. The sugarcane crop would provide valuable flood-resistance in flood-prone eastern UP and northern Bihar, apart from boosting incomes in the region.

The day may not be far when the world starts importing ethanol from India, just as it imports crude oil from the middle east. The Central Government is likely to come up with a clear-cut Bio-Diesel Policy by early 2006, after the Energy Policy Committee submits its report to the Government by November 30, 2005. The Central Government is also likely to set up a committee to promote the cultivation of jatropha and other tress, which can be used for the production of bio-diesel, by involving Panchayats. There were about 2.5 Lakh Panchayats in the country and if each of them cultivated Jatropha in 50 acres, the production would meet the growing demand for oil in the country.

Rural Poverty

In recent years, there appears to have been a resurgence of interest in what may be called "Gandhian Economics". Gandhi advocated the percept of limitations of wants to take care of one's need and not greed. This is relevant in the era of long-term sustainability of ecosystem. The basic problem is not solved because it was not taken up at all. Gopinathan Nair quotes "Mahatma Gandhi had said that the lowest stratum of society had to be uplifted first. But until now, this has not been done". Gandhiji was emphatic in placing the needs and concerns of the Poor at the heart of any economic development, and also advocated that wealth beyond the needs of self should be carefully used to benefit the weaker sections. His approach was opposite of the 'trickle-down" thinking, which says that if economic growth is fast enough, its benefits will sooner or later percolate to the poor as well.

Joan Martinez-Alier postulates that the negative environmental impact of economic growth is felt much more by the Poor and Powerless than by the rich and powerful within nations as also across nations. Poverty Alleviation Programmes (PAPs) are seen as in developing countries as means of overcoming the imperfection of factor markets. An individual is poor due to factors such as: lack of skill lack of assets, lack of credit and information, obsolete skill nonexistence of market, and other infrastructure.

In developing countries, one can observe two categories of people in rural areas – the farms and non-farms. The non-farms are again subdivided into skilled and non-skilled. On an average, the non-farms constitute about 40-50% of the total rural population. The SITRA Evaluation Report of the Union Ministry of Rural Development reveals that:

a. Targeting the more disadvantaged could achieve greater reduction of poverty.

b. Poor rural artisans from backward social groups readily use improved toolkits to raise their income from craftsmanship.

c. The strongest impetus to poverty alleviation comes from economic growth and human capital development.

The rural poor can be a giant profit centre if tapped correctly and ethically. Prahlad discusses about how the future will develop from the serving the Poor as the innovations developed will be superior – top quality, low price, high volume and world-scale.

Rural Employment Issue

The demand for extending policy of reservations to the private sector has created confrontation between a section of political class and captains of industry represented by FICCI and CII. Unemployment is on the rise. While job opportunities are expanding in high technology sectors, the manufacturing sector is not able to absorb new entrants in the job market. Moreover, decrease in capital investment in agriculture in the '90s has hit job opportunities in rural India. The supply of unskilled and unemployable is very high and so the wage they can command is very low. We have to train our labour so as to enable them earn higher wages, through greater productivity. Can the existing ITIs be used to under-take training in rural areas?

The National Rural Employment Guarantee (NREG) Act 2005 provides enhancement of livelihood security, giving at least 100 days of guaranteed wage employment in every financial year to every household, whose adult members volunteer to do unskilled manual work. Panchayats at districts, intermediate and village levels will be the principal authorities for planning and implementation of the scheme. Improved communication technologies and the proposed ICT kiosks in every village can be used to better inform people about the NREGS.

The NREG Act 2005 can provide the basis of a permanent social security system and even act as an instrument for planned and equitable rural development. Right To Information (RTI) Act 2005 can be used for transparent and effective implementation of the NREG Act 2005. While the NREGS aims at generating employment for the poor, Bharat Nirman has at its core the idea of improving infrastructure in the rural areas. It is highly unlikely that Convergence of NREGS and Bharat Nirman will take place. A Universal EGS offer a chance for rural reconstruction and for establishing a society that respects the dignity of life. The National Advisory Council (NAC) has suggested to the Central Government to consider growing trees on private wastelands to enhance income of farmers and produce bio-mass, and also include wasteland development under the NREG Scheme.

ITC's partnership with the Khadi and Village Industries Commission (KVIC) to source and distribute KVIC's agabattis signifies a lot more than the lofty ideal of a private corporation supporting a predominantly rural enterprise. To boost manufacturing, organised retail must grow. Lessons from ITC's Khadi tie-up are that ITC shall become Wal-Marts and the Tescos, epitome of modern retailing, in India.

Foreign Direct Investment (FDI) in retail is welcome and the benefits of organised retail far outweigh the costs: millions of jobs, lower prices and greater tax compliance that the organised retail would create. Modern retailing sharply reduces the intermediation costs of connecting the producer to the consumer. This saving, even if shared by many, means that the consumer pays less while the producer gets more. At present, developing a retail distribution network is an expensive, risky business in India.

Land Reforms

The Planning Commission Review has recommended strong land re-forms measures–conferring of ownership of forest land and distribution of surplus land–to improve the lot of Dalits and Tribals in the poverty stricken Koraput–Bolangir–Kalakhandi (KBK) Region of Orissa. It has suggested a national authority be set up to acquire land as a state pool and distribute it to the SC/STs on the lines of the Malaysian Model for Malay people or Bhumiputras. The case for priorities land distribution is based on the fact that 80% of the SC/STs in the region are dependent on agriculture.

Farming and Food Processing Industries

India is an agricultural country and its economy is predominantly dependent on the food industry. Typically, for a farmer, farm expenses are around 70-75% of the cash receipts. A sizable fraction of this expenditure is expended on the production process–about 5–8 months prior to marketing of the farm produce. As there is considerable time gap between the time of initial spending and receipts from the final farm produce, a farmer is highly vulnerable to price fluctuations farm produces and farm inputs as planning is done at the time of sowing based on the prevailing such relationships. One possibility is that the Futures Market could provide a perfect collateral for the lenders to advance larger loans on easier terms to farmers and ensuring a minimum risk business for both the lender and the farmer.

A recent study by the Union Ministry of Agriculture had demonstrated that farm incomes have fallen in the past five years. Farmers are producing more only to find no buyers. And when they eventually get buyers, they are paid half of what they deserve. While the rich and industrialised countries made up for the loss in farm incomes by providing direct payments first linked to production and now linked to the farm area (de-coupled payments), farmers in the developing countries continued to suffer silently. Much of the agrarian stress that has engulfed the countryside therefore is being misconstrued as the outcome of non-availability of credit. The crying need of the hour is to come up the strategies that provide a stable and assured income to the farm sector.

How will the integration of the rural markets with the global value chain eventually rescue Indian farmers from the prevailing agrarian crisis? The emphasis on allowing FDI in retail sector is aimed at taking advantage of the farmers. Will they have to wait endlessly for buyers to purchase their pro-duces? As of now, the profits are being shared among the traders, processors, wholesalers, and retailers.

With economic growth and a rise in disposable incomes, the consumption basket has changed (from once dominant Cereals to Milk, Fruits, Vegetables and Poultry products). Rising incomes, urbanisation and globalisation have opened new vistas for agriculture diversification, which will succeed only if non-traditional farm produce find acceptance. Shortening the supply chain between the farmer and the consumer is necessary.

The Central Ministry of Food Processing Industries, is all geared up for developing a strong and vibrant food processing sector; with a view to add value to the farm produce, increase shelf life, create increased job opportunities and income in rural areas, and create surplus for exports and stimulating demand for processed food. Several Infrastructure Development Programmes Viz., Food Park, packaging centre, integrated cold chain facilities, value added centres, irradiation facility, modernised abattoir, are being undertaken.

The Food Safety and Standards Bill 2005, a new integrated food law, called for abolition of nine acts, modification of seven central Acts, and innumerable state laws in relation to food, in order to harmonise legislation, rule, and regulation under a harmonised structure. This FS&S Bill is the latest in a series of recent initiatives that seek to diversify agriculture and encourage one of its vital complements, the food processing industry, which is an important link in the food value chain. The FS&S Bill 2005 will be in the interest of farmers, as most raw materials will come within its ambit, the consumers will stand to benefit with quality food, and the export market of packaged Indian food will vastly grow in view of adherence to strict quality measures (GMP, GHP, HACCP). According to Roopa Vajpeyi (Editor, Consumer Voice) and reported in the Economic Times, the FS&S Bill 2005 do not put consumers centre stage but leans towards industry.

Till recently all Small and Micro Enterprises (SMEs) managed all their business process manually. It is strongly believed that intense deployment of Information and Communication Technologies (ICT) will help small organisations grow business and become mid-sized organisations. A CRM designed for SMEs must incorporate all features that would automate their existing functions. CIM is a very important part of CRM and a key enabler in delivering the 360-degree customer view. While SMEs are mostly B2B-centric with three-quarters of their revenues derived from customers in other business sectors (small, medium and large), more than half of the revenues of India's SMEs are generated from customers indicating a B2C focus. There is a clear indication that CRM is here to stay and the focus will be more on SMEs.

The present thrust of the economic agenda for agriculture does not go beyond linking the producer with the markets, and in the process providing an escape route for the Government to withdraw from operations such as procurement and administered prices. The Planning Commission is likely to set a target of 8% for the 11th Plan, with a special focus on agriculture. Agricultural growth has been well below target since 1996 and something dramatic is needed to double agricultural growth. Montek Singh Ahluwalia said the farm sector has turned into a "critical weakness" as the 9th Plan banked heavily on an agricultural growth target of 4% but could achieve only half of it, as did the 10th Plan.

Rural Credit

When Maharashtra embarked upon stimulating its rural economy, it opted for the cooperative route. It gave jobs and fair prices to the farmers, and also provided political platforms for promoters. The Amul Model of cooperatives, backed by sophisticated processing technologies ushered in the white revolution, taking India to the top of the milk-production ladder even as it galvanised the rural economy. Bhupinder Singh Hooda informed that dairy cooperatives would be set up in every village of the Haryana State for procurement of milk to enable the farmers to enhance their income.

Cooperative Societies provide working capital of over Rs. 2,27,111 Crore to the rural masses and there are about 5.03 Lakh cooperative societies with the membership of more than 20.9 Crore. The increased target for rural credit disbursals at Rs. 1,05,000 Crore is far from being achieved. The rural poor did not ruin the cooperative sector. The Independent Commission on Banking and Financial Policy 2005 states that the most urgent need is to increase credit provision to the rural areas for both agricultural credit and non-agricultural areas. Doubling the flow of agricultural credit in the next few years is not the answer. Farmers have committed suicide because of their inability to repay loans. Credit is therefore a part of the problem.

Rural India is fast emerging as a prospect for the bankers. Bankers have stepped out from narrow confines of their branches to nurture Self Help Groups (SHGs), which ultimately give cushion to the survival and growth of banking business. The banking activities in rural India will grow when the big industrial houses (viz. PEPSI, ITC, Mahindra & Mahindra, TATA, RELIANCE, SHRIRAM, GODREJ and BHARTI) firmly put their footprints in rural India. This is a good opportunity for the public sector banks to boost the SHG movement to enable the villages to absorb the benefits of globalisation. India's SHG movement is the world's largest-ever social movement, which has targeted one third of the India's poor. The recovery from SHGs all over India is always above 90%. The SHGs play an important role in providing timely credit to the rural people.

A vision document on technology and the financial sector, placed on the RBI's website, enumerates opportunities available to individual banks and institutions through continuous technological upgradations. As the RBI has pointed out, the big challenge is to ensure that the benefits of technology percolate to every type of banks and to all sections of customers, especially those living in rural areas.

COPING WITH MONSOON

Fifty years ago, our economy was described as being gamble on the monsoon. Even today, after decades of post-independence development, the monsoon continues to govern the very pulse of life in our country. Al-though Rural India is still dependent on monsoons, non-farm incomes account for a significant proportion of household income and the non-farm was about 34% of the total household income in 1993-94, fairly distributed evenly spread across consumption expenditure categories.

Green revolution bypassed the rainfed regions, whose productivity has not increased significantly in the last five decades. Simulation and prediction of the Indian monsoon remains a tough challenge. Yet, we possess a wealth of data that can be used to derive farming strategies tailored to local rainfall variability. Such strategies are especially vital for rainfed areas.

ECONOMIES OF CLUSTERS

Locational proximity has tremendous advantages for sourcing supplies, pooling resources, and learning by interacting. In today's world of heightened import competition, knowledge workers on site need a more conductive ambiance. If Special Economic Zones (SEZs) are to become engines of productivity and export as in China, India need to convert entire Tehsils into SEZs so as to provide the required scale economies and the required mind-set. A full tehsil will have the land and scale to make possible an independent power station, independent water supply facility, and may be an independent port and airport. But let us make a start at tehsil level.

Disaster Management

The time has come for "green building technology" to benefit middle and lower classes, besides Rural India, in order to achieve goals of energy independence and "housing for all". Every year, the Government is losing 2 per cent of its GDP in disaster management in the form of relief and rehabilitation package, which in fact is a waste. According to Pranab Mukherjee, the proposed "Disaster Management Policy" should lay stress as to how the future disasters could be prevented from happening through proper warning systems.

Kyoto Protocol & Employment Opportunities

India, which signed the Kyoto protocol in 2002, may soon become the nerve centre of a booming global carbon trading market. A fraction of trillion-dollar market is coming to India and can easily create thousands of employment opportunities. However, as in many other countries, structured programmes to train manpower in this area are still nonexistent.

Corruption and Liberalisation

Famines, Natural Calamities, and Political Corruption scandals are acute events that evoke strong responses in democracies such as India. However, as Nobel Laureate Professor Amartya Sen pointed out many years ago, such societies seem to be less sensitive to endemic malnutrition and other severe deprivations. India ranks at 88 among 159 countries [in a Corruption Perceptions Index score of 2.9 on a scale of 0 (highly corrupt) to 10 (highly clean)] with respect to the rating of Transparency International Report. This is dispiriting news, coming soon after the Human Development Report of the UNDP, which has placed India at a dismal 127 in a list of 177 countries. This shows that liberalisation has not fared any better in this respect than decades of the license-permit Raj.

Right To Information

The Right To Information Act 2005 comes into force all over the country on October 12. Citizens should make use of it to ensure transparency and good governance triumph. This Act is derived from our fundamental right of expression under Article 19. If we do not have information on how our Government and Public Institutions function, we cannot express any in-formed opinion on it. Various Supreme Court Judgments have accepted this, since 1977. Democracy revolves around the basic idea of citizens being at the centre of governance. This RTI provides for a time bound and de-fined process for citizens to access information about all actions taken by public authorities.

ICT for Development

India has knowledge and natural resources. India has many states, which are minerals-rich, income-poor. Sustaining economy of the country, extraction of natural wealth from the earth's crust is essential. As there is science to explore wealth, there is also technology to exploit the natural resources with modern technique, and there is legislation also to control the degradation of the environment.

Science and Technology (Viz., Biotechnology, CARTOSAT, EDUSAT, Broad-band Network, Mobile computing, AGMARKNET, governance, etc) offers tremendous opportunities for improving rural livelihoods. Digital opportunities have emerged as a "power tool" for fostering agricultural growth, poverty reduction and sustainable resource use in developing countries. Rural India should be given a chance through digital networks for farmers, e-Cooperatives, and digital SMEs to usher in a "digital inclusion" for fostering rural prosperity and grassroots level development. Grassroots level access to information will hopefully help "bridge theory and reality at grassroots". National e-Governance Programme (NeGP), State-wide Area Network (SWAN) and NICNET Programme facilitate Grassroots level access to Information as well as Grassroots level information to access.

As technologies and services over the Network start talking to each other, they enjoy efficiency never seen before. Service Oriented Architecture (SOA) is a design philosophy usually implemented using web services. The benefits of SOA are with respect to "efficiency", "responsiveness", and "adapt-ability". This will facilitate a consistent architectural framework, unconstrained by technologies, within which applications can be rapidly developed, integrated and reused.

The Rajiv Internet Village Initiative (Rajiv) comprises providing broad-band connectivity to every village at affordable prices, delivery of services online and imparting computer literacy training to at least one member of each family. These centres provide G2C and B2C services through PPP model. According to Rajasekara Reddy, even urban people realise that rural transformation is very much necessary for them.

India has a vast knowledge in social sectors. Grassroots democracy has firmly taken root since the 73rd and 74th Amendments to the Constituent in 1992 making elections to the Local Government Bodies mandatory. An ICT-triggered rural knowledge revolution can help to break the barriers that stand between localised rural economies and the globalised market. Using technology, an area in which India has expertise, rural India can be accorded its place in the world economy, while still maintaining its predominantly agrarian economy. Mission 2007 is intended to be a nationwide movement providing a New Deal for Rural India.

Meeting the Millennium Development Goals (MDGs)

The Millennium development Goals (MDGs) are a set of time bound and measurable goals and targets for combating poverty, hunger, diseases, illiteracy, environmental degradation and discrimination against women. It consists of 8 goals, 18 targets and 48 indicators, covering the period 1990 to 2015. India is on track to achieving the Goal of halving income poverty by 2015, but on most other counts of education, gender empowerment, infant & maternal mortality, it is lagging behind and expected to achieve targets sometime between 2015 and 2040. Governments have the tendency to work "for" the poor and not "with" the poor. Governments do not know how to be participatory, gender sensitive and consultative with the affected community. Appropriate governance programme may facilitate to overcome this problem. Erna Witoelar advocates that governments should balance pro-poor policies with economic growth to achieve MDGs. There are enough resources, technology, information, and knowledge to achieve the MDGs by 2015.

The key to meeting the Millennium Development Goals (MDGs) is an increase in investment in people (health, education, nutrition, and family planning), environment (water and sanitation, soils, forests, and bio-diversity) and infrastructure (road, power, and ports). The UN Report tilted "Investing in Development: A Practical Plan to Achieve the Millennium Development Goals" shows that the MDGs can be achieved by 2015. The reason that the MDGs are feasible is that powerful existing technologies give us the tools to make rapid advances in the quality of life and economic productivity of the World's Poor. Investments in soil nutrients and water harvesting could help farmers double or triple their food yields. Rural roads, truck transport, and electricity could bring new economic opportunities to remote villages.

On the Millennium Development Goals, Economist Jaffrey Sachs, who is Director, UN Millennium Project, said that "the Indian Government needs to do more in terms of health coverage, water resources, maternal mortality and AIDS", while addressing the TERI's Sustainable Development Summit 2005 at Delhi.

Suggested Action Plan:

1. Reaching the Unreached through Public services.
2. From digital divide to digital opportunities for sustainable development and economic growth at grassroots level.
3. Sustainable development of SMEs – Reducing spatial disparities and enhancing opportunities for employment and development.
4. Fostering agricultural growth, poverty reduction and sustainable resources use.
5. Sustainable Development and Earth care Policies in the areas of : water, Energy, Education, Health, Agriculture and Rural development, and Bio-diversity.
6. Village cluster Development through Sustainable societies in a Viable Rural Space.
7. Grassroots level Governance.
8. Moving towards "ONE INDIA" to usher in a remarkable change in the life of the common man.
9. Poor to be the real target of secular public policies.
10. Why not give a choice to the potential NREG Candidate – to go for the employment guarantee or sign up for the skill initiative?
11. Promote Yeshasvini under the NREG Scheme.
12. Improve governance, education and healthcare through ICT.

13. Broad-band services over a technology neutral platform in rural and re-mote areas.
14. Dairy Cooperatives in every village for procurement of milk to enable the farmers to enhance their income.
15. Rural electrification through renewable sources.
16. Creating the right Human resources to reach heights in food processing.
17. Digital Network Farmers (AGRISNET, AGMARKNET, AgRIS, co-operatives, Digital SMEs, etc).
18. Mainstream ICT for Grassroots level Planning for economic and social Development (DISNIC).

5

Rural Food Systems and Environment

There has been a growing separation of people from the production of their food since the industrial revolution, when machines began to replace human labour on farms and people moved into cities that grew around the factories and became industrial centres. With an increase in food production labour efficiency, fewer people were needed to supply enough food for the entire population. The population of urban areas, defined as cities with over 2,500 people, increased from 200 million to over 2.5 billion during the period from 1950 to 1996. Urban migration also moved people away from rural and natural landscapes on which they had been dependent for food and other amenities for centuries.

Trade and delocalisation of food have generally had positive effects on food availability in industrialised countries while having negative consequences in many developing countries. There are notable exceptions to this situation in India, and South and East Asia. The trade of food raw materials from developing countries to industrialised countries, a trade between countries with different currencies of extremely different "buying-powers," will also act as a drain of natural resources from South to North. Most people today live in places that are distant from production fields, an emerging trend that is a result of our transformation from urban to rural societies in all countries. As an urbanised species, humans have created a distinct division between agriculture and city life. While we recognise that this boundary is often a blurred one, it may be more conceptual than physical, since there are obviously many areas of transition between farming and subdivisions, such as rural acreages.

Physical separation of people from food production has resulted in a degree of indifference about where and how food is produced, especially where food is plentiful and inexpensive as in most industrialised countries. The global system could be said to provide "unprecedented and unparalleled choice—any food, any time, anywhere... from a global vending machine". The food becomes a de-contextualised industry product on the market, without any clear connections to either life support functions in ecosystems or social functions in the socio-economical production system—a "thing" without a history with ethical aspects to bother with. Furthermore, this food system is for the people who can afford it, and most undernutrition is a result of economic inequities that result in lack of buying power for the poor. The majority of people likewise are un-aware of the environmental consequences of an industrial food system, both regarding its supply side and its waste production side. But at the same time, there is growing concern about food safety, diet, and health.

One consequence of physical separation is a psychological distance of most citizens from production agriculture, as described by Kloppenburg et al. In a testimony on the U.S. Food system, "What is eaten by the great majority of North Americans comes from a global everywhere, yet from nowhere that they know in particular." A brief walk through a supermarket in any large city in the North, if the packing cases are visible, reveals fresh and processed products from northern and southern Europe,

North and southern Africa, Latin America and the U.S., and often New Zealand. Most people select their purchases without concern about the source. When unconcerned about the source of food, people do not consider the consequences of the system for others who produce food nor for the environment.

Another consequence of specialisation and fewer people in farming is the creation of border areas, or city limits, between urban housing and agricultural production areas. People on opposite sides of this boundary have very different goals and needs for land use, and there are emerging conflicts between groups that may not easily understand each other.

One approach to better understanding of linkages between people and their food supply is the study of agro-ecology, a growing field that encompasses both education and research in all the steps in the food system. When we study resource use, efficiency, cycling of materials, global and local distribution of production and benefits in the food system, it is possible to more rigorously compare and contrast different alternatives. Such analysis can help lead to design of more efficient and equitable systems that can be valuable into the future, and thus can contribute to sustainable development in society.

When everyone was involved with hunting and gathering there was obviously no separation of people from their food supply nor any rural/urban divide. With the gradual advent of agriculture starting about 10,000 years ago, there was the be-ginning of settlements in most desirable areas for food production. Non-mobile tribes could encourage greater attention to food production by those who were more skilled in agriculture, and these people could grow more than was needed for their families. This allowed for the specialisation in communities with some people focusing on tools and crafts, some on support services for fledgling societies, and some on local government. For millennia people remained relatively close to agriculture and food, and only in the past two centuries have grown away more rapidly from this vital part of their existence.

Accelerating urbanisation has accentuated this separation of people from food production. We have a situation today that was well summarised by Kloppenburg et al., as they described the growing separation of people from most knowledge about how their food was produced and who produced it. When distant from production fields, consumers are often completely unfamiliar with the impacts of production practices on the land and the overall ecology of that unknown place where others till the soil. It is unlikely that they could have much more than an abstract concept of farming, and certainly no in-depth understanding of the environmental and social implications of the types of systems where their food is grown. When the role of the consumer is confined to purchase of food from an unknown source, and a small fraction of their income is spent for this essential need, it is not surprising that most people are uninterested in any change in the food system, or even questioning why change might be needed.

In addition, the globalised, agro-industrial complex works to conceal production practices and environmental degradation from distant consumers. Although there is more information available today about food and nutrition—through the internet, local, national and international publications, health and nutrition classes in schools, and books and libraries—than in any period in history, this information is embedded in the industrial world with its standardised quality conventions and logic of mass commodity production. In industrial countries, consumers have become increasingly dependent on intermediary systems of information. Confidence is to a lesser extent attributed directly to the farmer or the butcher or the baker, because we do not know them. Instead we must trust in abstract systems to provide us with relevant information.

Although we have vast amounts of information about the components and nutritional value of food, this information is scattered, and *lacks context and linkages to both its site specific ecosystem supports and its human individual experiences.* The information is based on the same de-contextualised perspective as the market system that delivers the commodities: a thing is a thing and should be evaluated in terms of its component properties that are measured in SI-units (eg. kg, m, Nm), or be evaluated in monetary units without a history of connection, relations, and dependency. As consumers, we are expected to process a lot of abstract information about food, to take expert knowledge into consideration, and to conduct risk analyses as part of modern living.

In today's global food system, it is no surprise that people who pull food off the supermarket shelf in Oslo or Chica-go have little knowledge or concern about where their bananas were produced and what the effects of insecticides (perhaps banned in their own countries) had on the people at the other end of the supply line, or on their families who may have used the chemical containers for storage of food or water. They are unaware that their instant coffee was produced by small farmers in Viet Nam as a result of massive support from the World Bank, which promotes global political and economic decisions driving similar coffee farmers in Kenya and Costa Rica from the market, while helping international food companies to assure cheap supplies and higher profits. Furthermore, there is little concern about the potato farmer or apple grower several kilometres away from their homes who must compete with large farms in Germany or New Zealand for space on the supermarket shelves.

If there is awareness of a rural/urban linkage, it is likely in the annoyance that comes from field cultivator dust or odours from hog confinement operations as city people drive by on a nearby highway. For instance, a survey in Norway showed that among 12 criteria, 63% of the consumers considered "Avail-ability of high quality food" as very important when making purchases. "Availability of organically produced foods" and "locally produced foods" were considered very important criteria by only 13% and 8% of consumers, respectively, and were ranked number nine and 11 after other criteria mostly related to convenience in shopping and price. Nevertheless, the increasing number of people who buy ecological food are, in fact, more concerned about its origins than the average customer, perhaps indicating an increasing interest in this matter. There is also a growing movement for "fair trade" products where the source and methods of production are known.

Challenges at the Interface

At the boundary between rural and urban areas there may be more than indifference or lack of communication— there can often be outright hostility. To understand the types of problems and challenges that people face while living near the boundary between rural and urban areas, it is useful to explore briefly the different objectives, activities, and lifestyles of city folks and farm families.

People who grow up on farms are accustomed to the odours and dust that are generated by producing crops and animals, while this may be foreign to people in cities. The need for early and late hours during peak times of planting and harvest are an accepted part of farming, yet these activities may interrupt urban people in their daily lives, as they try to sleep or have a party in their yard in the evening. The expectations of people who move to the edge of the city for quiet, pastoral scenes filled with wildlife may give way to shock at the sight of a modern mono-culture industrial farm with its hundreds of hectares of one or two crops. Slow tractors and large equipment moving down the county road are part of farming, yet may be an unexpected annoyance to someone from the city who is late driving to work. Farm people are accustomed to livestock, and know how to open and close gates; this may be foreign to people in the city.

Ecological Principles

One approach to conceptualising and planning an urban/rural linkage is to consider the organisation of natural systems and how they function. Ecological principles of structure and function can be useful because they represent centuries of evolution in survival and efficient resource use in natural systems, even though our human objectives as system managers differ from those of a natural system. How ecology relates to current and future farming alternatives has been discussed in several creative books. As these sources point out, farms can be made more ecologically friendly and less dependent on chemical fertilisers and pesticides, two of the major objections of urban neighbouring. If we envision the interface between rural and urban activities as a vibrant and living zone of connection rather than a place that requires an inert barrier of separation, it is possible to apply some principles of ecology to the planning process. These can include both the biophysical components of the system as well as those that involve the human participants.

Natural systems are open and interactive, and they function in a holistic way. As we learn more about their complexity and organisation, it becomes clear that the unique combination of plants and animals in each place leads to resilience and dynamic permanence. The structure and functions of natural systems have evolved to fit the natural resources of a given location. Agro-ecology explores how these same functions can be incorporated into farming systems and food systems. Some of the changes to agro-ecosystem management can help us address the broad challenge of creating a positive interface with solutions that will address the multiple questions from each side of the boundary. A systems approach is different from our frequent reductionist and mechanistic perspective of isolating and solving one issue at a time, just as we would in repairing an isolated machine. For example, a well-designed perennial and woody area between urban and rural activities could have multiple functions that meet multiple goals, such as cleaning air, reducing sound and visual distraction, and producing economic plants that would benefit people on both sides.

Because natural systems are bio-diverse, they have component plants and animals that play different roles in maintaining the ecosystem. Nutrients are taken up, used, and returned to the soil complex, and water is likewise cycled through the system. There is minimal extraction of bio-mass from the system, thus it can run on its own resources rather than requiring expensive inputs and imports of materials from elsewhere. An area that connects with other natural forests or fields can serve as valuable habitat for wildlife, a key part of integrated natural systems and a boon to those people who want to observe this aspect of the system. If a system is well designed using native species, it may be able to propagate new plants and attract animals from nearby, thus maintaining itself with minimal cost of upkeep, which would be desirable for everyone. A natural boundary could serve as an effective buffer area or separation between rural and urban people and activities, and could do so at minimal cost. Such an area could also host recreational activities that provide another "output" from the place.

Alternative Food Networks

There is strong evidence that all over Europe new food

networks are emerging. They represent a turn from the industrial world to the domestic world where food is embedded in face-to-face-interactions, trust, traditions and each unique place. There are more local and ecological products that support local economies. Renting et al. Call them short food supply chains (SFSC) because they cut short the long, anonymous supply chains that characterise an industrial food system. In addition, they bring producers and consumers closer and construct more transparency where common information may be shared. Renting et al. Differentiate between *face-to-face SFSCs*, such as farm shops, farmers' markets, roadside sales, pick your own, box schemes, home deliveries, and mail order, and *proximate SFSCs*, such as farm shop groups, regional sales clubs, consumer cooperatives, community supported agriculture, restaurants, dedicated retailers, and catering for institutions such as business canteens, schools, and public institutions.

Close proximity of urban people to farms provides numerous opportunities for exchange of goods and services that build economic linkages as well as communication and rap-port. The farm shop is a growing type of enterprise in the Nordic Region and in North America, where vegetables, meats, and crafts can be marketed directly to shoppers who are interested in buying food and other products made close to home. Those who are successful in this type of direct marketing find that a range of products, assured high quality and fresh produce, and prices that are competitive with local commercial stores can help build a consistent market. An essential factor is the sincere desire to work directly with customers and to build personal relationships. A real advantage of direct sales is that the farmer collects all of the value of the product, rather than having value added to raw products by processors, wholesalers, and retailers down the food chain. Most farm shops can move a wide range of products, but relatively limited amounts of each. They often require a person to be on duty for long hours, but have the advantage of building rapport with customers and neighbours. In Madison, Wisconsin the REAP Food Group recently published a "Farm Fresh Atlas" that shows where to find farmers, markets, cheese makers, cooperatives, and restaurants offering locally grown and locally produced food in the capital region.

Since many vegetable crops are labour intensive, and a change from producing cereals or other extensive crops in-creases the farm labour demand, the proximity of a farm to a town can enhance the potential for using urban labour for farm work. There may be limited opportunities for jobs in town, especially for young people, while a part-time job on the farm can be a valuable point of entry into the working world through a productive and satisfying work experience. Having city children working on the farm further builds relationships between rural and urban families, and may in fact create new markets for produce.

Consumer or community-supported agriculture (CSA) started in Germany and Switzerland, and was imported to the U.S. In the mid 1980s. In CSA, organic or environmentally safe farming is combined with bringing the consumer closer to the farmer and the farm. In a CSA organisation, the farmer(s) and a group of consumers share both the risks of farm production and the harvest. A study by Cooley and Lass (1998) shows that CSA potentially can bring economic benefits to both farmers and consumers. Creative farmers in many areas have enlarged and assured their markets for vegetables by recruiting customers willing to sign a contract for one growing season. CSA initiatives usually include a payment of one lump sum for a season of vegetables, delivered to a central pick-up point or retrieved each week from the farm by the customers. In the case of Ames, Iowa, the consumers organised the CSA and went out to find and contract with farmers to supply their needs. The

CSAs have been called "partnerships of mutual commitment between farmers and consumers" by Van En and Roth. With this arrangement, the customer shares with the farmer both the risks and the bounty of a given year. This relationship is rarely found in a supermarket culture where even the price of local produce is so conditioned by the glob-al food system that it usually appears unconnected to any changes in weather or markets on the local scene. Kloppenburg et al. Describe the CSA as a useful model of how we can sell food while nurturing many other types of human relationships that include building friendships, finding plea-sure in the process of shopping, sharing the aesthetics in food, developing loyalty to farmers, and all of these in addition to the consumer buying high-quality food from someone they know. The CSA is an example of positive rural/urban linkages that are growing in many parts of the world.

Less formal but equally important consumer commitments are established in the farmers' markets that are found in many cities on Saturdays and at other times during the week. Here there is a similar loyalty to farmers who consistently supply a quality product, and customers seek out growers with whom they have established rapport and who have good produce at a fair price. The new farmers' markets concept has been described as a success from the perspective of the producers, the customers, and the local community. At an international scale it is probably the most influential alternative outlet for food in terms of impact on production, customers reached, geographical spread and economic importance. In the U.S. The number of markets, the number of producers and consumers at-tending markets, and even the proportion of farmers relying on farmers' markets as their main channel has grown steadily for more than 30 years. Farmers' markets have recently spread to Europe, for example in Sweden in 1999 and beginning in

Norway only in 2004, and can be seen as part of a "quality turn" among consumers. Because of a short growing season in northern latitudes, most farmers' markets are seasonal in these areas, often May through October, but some in places such as California run through the entire year. Cities such as Lincoln, Nebraska block off streets in whole city blocks, while Madison, Wisconsin dedicates the entire street system around capital square each Saturday morning through the growing season. Markets may be found in large parking lots of malls or even supermarkets, and the latter report increased sales on the days when customers are drawn to the farmers' markets even though these would appear to be in direct competition.

Some farmers establish longer-term relationships with customers at these markets, leading to sales direct from the farm through more of the year. Such arrangements for direct sale of produce seem to violate the principle of economy of scale found in the global system, but they certainly reduce the length of supply lines and transportation costs, and bring most of the value of produce directly to the one who grows and prepares it for the market.

Another innovative approach to bringing urban citizens in contact with farms and farmers is the *Selbsternte* (self-harvest) practice. This practice was developed in the 1990s in Austria by ecologically oriented consumers and organic farmers. On agricultural land with-in the urban area, the farmers prepare the land and sow rows of different vegetables, one long row of each. Subplots are then constructed, perpendicular to the direction of the rows, so that each subplot will contain about 20 different vegetables. After the initial preparation and planting, the subplots are handed over to the consumers for further management and harvest. This practice was later taken up in Germany, and in 2002 was also tried in Norway. Such a system initiates a powerful way of bringing consumers in close contact with agriculture and farmers, and builds an awareness and appreciation of the complexity of growing food.

A major challenge in developing alternatives to the dominant, de-localised food system is creating alternatives that become larger and more efficient. The different methods of direct sale offer interesting options, but only for a small pro-portion of all consumers. Most consumers are not willing to travel to farms, or to visit markets. Therefore, the alternatives become marginal in the overall system.

The challenge for the growth of alternative approaches is related to the difficulty in competing with the dominant system. In the current growth phase, there is a need for some protected space for the alternatives. Institutional buying represents one such protected space. Most institutions have common goals, beyond profit maximisation, and can therefore protect initiatives that provide services other than cheap food. What comes from local producers will often be organically grown, fresh, and high quality. In the Nordic Region, there has been a rapid growth over the past ten years of institutional buying of organic food from local sources. Hospitals, kindergartens, schools, homes for elderly, and public canteens are the most common participants.

The direct sale of food from farmer to consumer need not be limited to weekend farmers' markets or CSAs of limited scope in small communities. A national initiative in Finland about localising food was written by the stockholders including the ministry of environment, farmers' association, consumers' association, and representatives of research and education. One outcome from this work was that especially in public catering, local food has good growth potential. The public caterers emphasise freshness of raw materials in local delivery, knowledge of food origin, lack of food additives, and good taste. Information about the origins and processors were considered by the caterers as adding to food safety. One-to-one marketing is seen as a good opportunity for producers who aim at adding value through high quality, and many suppliers are organic farmers. One of the challenges is to balance the demand and supply, as some public caterers operate relatively large kitchens and serve thousands of meals daily. It is obvious that seasonably needs to be accepted by the consumers. Seasonal food may become more appreciated as a quality by both caterers and by customers, depending on their values: some appreciate strawberries during the local season, while others demand this delicacy every morning.

Such examples of localising food systems represent a growing trend in Finland, and especially among those who provide food for communal kitchens in schools, day care centres, and hospitals. All the participants of the food chain have been challenged to view the system as a whole, and the process has awakened a need for emphasising cooperation. One of several research proposals in this area aims at identifying changes needed in the activity system at a county (municipality) level, in order to direct an increasing share of the county's budget for food to local purchases (Laura Seppänen et al. Unpublished). Implementing a large scale local food system, such as one for a county, town or city, will require a number of elements to function well. Close collaboration between farmer organisations and those who currently market food in the city is essential, since it would be difficult and expensive to duplicate a food distribution and sales infrastructure that already is in place.

There must be willingness to participate by a substantial number of people in the food system as well as motivation among consumers to give this new local system an opportunity to succeed. With a location at 60 degrees N. Lat., the growing season is relatively short, even with the moderating influence of the nearby Baltic Sea. Although a limited number of vegetable products can be grown successfully and profitably, maximum use must be made of low-cost energy such as passive solar heating or renewable wood burning to heat green-house structures. High-quality storage facilities will enhance the availability of local produce for a longer part of the year. There will be need for careful and targeted research on growing and processing vegetables and fruits, as well as small animals and their products, and the results of this work must be available to farmers interested in the program.

Both farmers and consumers would benefit from this system of food import substitution. The major benefits would be the availability of fresh and locally grown food at a price competitive with that which is imported; stimulating the local economy by substituting local food products for imports; and establishing closer links between farmers and consumers through the contacts in markets, field tours, and other activities used to publicise the program. Many see the importance of reconnecting people with their food supply, and programs are being implemented on a small scale.

Models for Food Systems

Danish Model

In Denmark there is a type of conceptual city-wall separation between the open landscape and the more continental city and village conglomerations. The separation is mainly based on the wish to develop something urban, and there are tools to develop already existing urban structures and to pre-serve them. The border for the built land in urban areas will become like a ring around historically urbanised areas. On the other side of the "wall," nature conservation laws for agri-culture and open space are very strong. For example, if someone starts to build in this open space or agricultural land, even if there is consent from the local authorities, a non-government agency or individual can take them to court.

An example of innovative thinking and futuristic planning for Denmark was presented in the conference on *Multi-functional Landscapes* in Roskilde in 2000. Tress and Tress presented a series of scenarios for the next 20 years in an urban/rural boundary area north of Copenhagen. The four options included business as usual and urban development, near-total conservation of natural areas and little development, and two intermediate scenarios that maintained most land in farming and natural conditions while including limited development within the landscape. They included active participation of stockholders in planning for integrated activities, among them industrial agriculture, tourism, and recreation as well as places for housing. The authors used advanced visualising techniques to illustrate the alternative options for the future. This was a powerful method of showing how the future could look as a way of helping communities make decisions.

Swedish Model

The rural/urban boundary in Swedish development has focused more on the built-up or urban side of the border, and true to national tradition this is a functional approach. The concentrated living area concept was and is central to planning. This was used in the Swedish "million project," a conscious effort to move one million citizens from rural areas to ready-built urban housing near industry. The focus has always been for efficiency and cost-saving on infrastructure and transport, as well as the physical concentration of services and cultural activities. Optimum size of the suburban cities around Stockholm was determined by the population size necessary to fill a five-star restaurant, which was also built in the middle of each housing development. A public transportation system was also integrated in the planning and implementation of those suburban cities.

The Swedish border for urbanisation is not necessarily set around old city centres as in Denmark, nor is the location necessarily determined for saving soils and farmlands. The focus has been on conscious modernisation that concentrates population along main roads and rail-roads at suitable distances from industrial areas. One result has been leaving large, non-cultivated open spaces that were formerly agricultural lands between these housing concentrations.

Norwegian Model

In Norway the divide between urban and rural has always been motivated by resource conservation, both soil and land. The focus has been on preserving both cultivated crop land and recreation areas (such as the *friluftsområde* or "open air surroundings" of the Marka area north of Oslo with about 6000 km of ski trails), and to some degree cultivated forests. Rather than sprawl, there has been a concentration of housing and other structures in satellite areas located on forest land of low productivity. These developments have often come first, and then the infrastructure such as roads and rail-roads are built to them.

The motivation is currently shifting toward greater efficiency, with a national model that coordinates land and transportation planning. This is similar to the Swedish model described above. Since the great settlement period following World War II is ebbing, focus is turning more to the current built environment, with established urban areas and qualities, similar to the Danish model. A growing number of people recognise the value of the model for open space, especially forest open to the public established around Oslo, where un-limited sprawl could have occurred if there had not been such a border. Some details of Norwegian law are provided.

Eco-belt Concept in North America and Europe

Agriculture and city living are generally separated in most of the Nordic Region and North America. In the U.S., rapid growth of cities and an accelerating takeover of productive lands near cities with what is called "urban sprawl" are serious problems. Along with growth of the human population at a rate of about 1.2% per year (due to births plus immigration) each new citizen is using land at a rate that is 40 to 60% greater than was the case a mere two decades ago. Although these figures appear to be small when compared to the total land area of the continental U.S. (Excluding Alaska), a continuation of this trend for two generations will result in a reduction from the current 0.8 ha of productive farmland per person to about 0.3 ha per person by the year 2050. If this trend is not altered, it means that food production per unit of land will have to triple to maintain current levels of food for domestic consumption as well as for export. There is a serious need to contain urban growth, to seek more intensive models of land use, and to plan effectively for a future when this resource will become even more scarce.

Most countries in northern Europe have a long history of maintaining a relatively fixed and stable boundary between urban housing and development and the agricultural production lands surrounding the towns, although the tradition is changing in some places. Green belts are put in place and respected by these cultures, and thus there is little purchase of lands adjoining towns and cities in speculation that this land will soon be used for more intensive building of houses or expansion of industry. These permanent boundaries are respected as part of the current land use pattern, and there is a high level of public involvement and debate about any proposed change. Such a situation is quite different from the sprawl that occurs in countries such as the U.S. Where individual land ownership is connected to a series of property rights and cultural libertarian norms. Focus is on the rights of each person to make decisions that are best for them as individuals, often connected to how much personal economic advantage can be gleaned from the situation, without regard for the public good or the wrongs that this may cause in the long term. One proposal that would solve this land conversion problem is the establishment of eco-belts or green corridors surrounding towns and cities. This concept would guide the development of woody and mixed planting in a strip that surrounds the city and establishes a permanent boundary between urban housing and development and rural land used for agriculture. An Eco-belt would be wide enough to provide for buffering of most of the undesirable problems that arise from close proximity of houses and farming activities. It could be a multiple use area that includes bicycle and walking trails, habitat for wildlife, and pleasing view-scapes for adjoining urban and rural residents.

With agreement on how to use the common resources, there could be production of Christmas trees and other foliage plants for harvest, edible mushrooms and berries, and firewood, creating some economic or nonmonetary value-added advantages to such an area. The ownership of the eco-belts could be public, in private land trusts, or in organisations of those who live on both sides of the area. This positive rural/urban linkage could promote education and communication about agriculture for the neighbours, and serve as a means of finding labour for intensive agricultural production and a connection for sale of products from the farms. This type of win-win situation would not only solve the challenges that arise at an interface between two different lifestyles, it would preserve a permanent boundary and protect farmland from encroachment for other economically vi-able but less desirable types of growth.

Education for Agro-ecology and Food Systems

The NOVA University Network in the Nordic Region has recently offered a course in *Agro-ecology and Food Systems* through the Norwegian University of Life Sciences (UMB). This grew out of a farming and food systems course previously offered by NLH and NOVA University. In this 8-week course, students study the food system as a whole, including energy and materials flows, transportation, distribution, values and attitudes of stockholders, and resource cycling in the current food system. They apply knowledge and experience from prior courses in Agro-ecology and production into a study of the entire food system and its ecology. Local food systems are found to contain elements of regional and global food sources. Yet it is useful to compare them to the current global food chain, in terms of resources used for production and transportation, the freshness and nutritional quality of products, economics, and the social impacts of alternative food systems.

During the course, a comprehensive field project is completed that involves a food inventory of one county by each student team. Students interview farmers, food processors, marketers, government officials, and consumers to better understand how they perceive the food system, how food moves through the system, and how much of the food is produced locally. They make use of recent surveys such as the consumer opinion research conducted in Hedmark County in Norway, one of the project areas. At the request of local government officials, students have calculated what percentage of the food consumed is locally produced, and have provided guidelines on the potential for converting a certain percentage of the total local food system to an ecological food base.

Innovation plays a key role in this course, based on the recognition that past experiences will not bring us the necessary ideas for creating alternative and sustainable food systems. "You can not solve a problem with the same thoughts that created it," is a statement attributed to Albert Einstein. It is the combination of ecological literacy and creativity that can provide us the link to a sustainable future. Therefore, based on a comprehensive overview of the present system, the students launch into a three-day session where they use visionary thinking to clarify the desired future situation for that food system. The session on visionary thinking is followed up with sessions on dialogue and creative problem solving.

The boundary between urban areas with concentrated houses, industry, commerce, and other intensive land uses and rural areas dedicated to agriculture and natural resource conservation has become less defined as cities expand. The place where cities end and farms begin is more uniquely identified in many European cities with a long tradition of separate uses of land and well defined borders.

To separate urban living and rural farming activities we have focused on physical barriers to mitigate some of the most immediate problems. These take the form of fences, walls, roads, or planted buffer strips that screen off or filter out problems from farms that can be prevented from reaching a nearby subdivision, or can keep out the dogs and snow mobiles that often trespass on farm and pasture land. Rather than creating barriers that only have costs and no apparent eco-nomic returns, we propose using eco-belts or other constructed planting that will physically separate the two property uses in a permanent way, provide some products and services, and at the same time enhance positive linkages between people living on either side of the interface. Permanent areas or green belts around cities are more common in Europe, where centuries of conflict in land use have been resolved through consensus, common law, and most recently by statute. There is much to be learned from these patterns.

More concrete economic and social linkages between urban and rural can be established through local food systems that take several forms: direct sale by farmers to urban consumers, farmers' markets, community supported agriculture, and shared ownership or leasing of agricultural production activities by consumers. All involve an interaction of producer with consumer, and can result in education and better relationships between the two groups. Local food systems can also lend a degree of security to the food supply in times of political and economic uncertainty. Although it is unrealistic to advocate complete food self sufficiency in today's complex global context, a degree of self-reliance would be highly desirable to reconnect people with their food supply. It is this physical and psychological connection that is the focus of local food system initiatives in cities from Santa Cruz to Helsinki. It is the same connection that we are attempting in university courses on Agro-ecology and food systems, where students work with farmers, processors, marketers, consumers, and government officials to first understand the cur-rent system and then design rational alternatives for the future. It is this innovative approach to education that will open our minds and equip the next generation of graduates to deal with complex challenges in the food system in very unique ways. Examples have been described from North America and the Nordic Region that are providing some useful models for this improvement in rural-urban linkages.

In spite of the success in these several model activities, as well as the growing awareness of the importance of healthy nutrition and a livable environment, we are continually impressed by the level of disinterest in the general population. One ongoing challenge is finding ways to motivate skeptical and complacent consumers to vote with their food budget to encourage local production. Another is to encourage people's decisions to improve their current housing and surroundings and discourage city dwellers from moving out and converting farmland to acreages. Lastly we envision education as the best hope for people to learn about ecosystem services and the need to understand where and how food is produced, how this impacts the ecosystem, and how urban and rural people can work together across the boundaries that currently divide them.

6

Rural Health Infrastructure

The healthcare services are divided under State list and Concurrent list in India. While some items such as public health and hospitals fall in the State list, others such as population control and family welfare, medical education, and quality control of drugs are included in the Concurrent list. The Union Ministry of Health and Family Welfare (UMHFW) is the central authority responsible for implementation of various programmes and schemes in areas of family welfare, prevention, and control of major diseases. In the case of health the term infrastructure takes on a wider role than mere physical infrastructure. Healthcare centres, dispensaries, or hospitals need to be manned by well trained staff with a service perspective.

The current conditions of physical infrastructure, staff, access, and usage are laid out here before identifying critical gaps and requirements in infrastructure and services. Issues related to institutions, financing, and policy are discussed in the context of these critical need gaps and the potential role of the private sector in healthcare provisional in villages is explored.

Physical Infrastructure

The healthcare in rural areas has been developed as a three-tier structure based on predetermined population norms. The sub centre is the most peripheral institution and the first contact point between the primary healthcare system and the community. Each sub centre is manned by one Auxiliary Nurse Midwife (ANM) and one male Multipurpose Worker [MPW(M)]. A Lady Health Worker (LHV) is in charge of six sub-centres each of which are provided with basic drugs for minor ailments and are expected to provide services in relation to maternal and child health, family welfare, nutrition, immunisation, diarrhoea control, and control of communicable diseases. Sub-centres are also expected to use various mediums of interpersonal communication in order to bring about behavioural change in reproductive and hygiene practices. The Sub-centres are needed for taking care of basic health, needs of men, women and children. As per the figures provided by the UMHFW there were 146,026 sub centres functioning in September 2005—about 12 per cent lower than the prescribed number as per government norms.

Primary Health Centres (PHCs) comprise the second tier in rural healthcare structure envisaged to provide integrated curative and preventive healthcare to the rural population with emphasis on preventive and promotive aspects. (Promotive activities include promotion of better health and hygiene practices, tetanus inoculation of pregnant women, intake of IFA tablets and institutional deliveries.) PHCs are established and maintained by State Governments under the Minimum Needs Programme (MNP)/ Basic Minimum Services Programme (BMS). A medical officer is in charge of the PHC supported by fourteen paramedical and other staff. It acts as a referral unit for six Sub-centres. It has four to six beds for inpatients. The activities of PHC involve curative, preventive, and Family Welfare Services. There were 23,236 PHCs functioning in September 2005 compared to 23,109 a year earlier, according to the Ministry of Health. Though the numbers appear to be increasing there is still a shortfall of about 16 per cent when compared to the required norms for PHCs.

Community Health Centres (CHC) forming the uppermost tier are established and maintained by the State Government under the MNP/BMS programme. Four medical specialists including Surgeon, Physician, Gynaecologist, and Paediatrician supported by twenty-one paramedical and other staff are supposed to staff each CHC. Norms require a typical CHC to have thirty indoor beds with OT, X-ray, Labour Room, and Laboratory facilities. A CHC is a referral centre for four PHCs within its jurisdiction, providing facilities for obstetric care and specialist expertise. There were 3346 CHCs in the country, almost a 50 per cent shortfall.

About 49.7 per cent of the sub-centres, 78.0 per cent of the PHCs and 91.5 per cent of CHCs are located in the government buildings. The rest are located either in rented buildings or rent free Panchayat/Voluntary Society buildings. As on September 2005, overall 60,762 buildings are required to be constructed to house Sub-centres. Similarly, for PHCs 2948 and for CHCs 205 additional buildings are still required.

Data on facilities within these centres are not available. Most reports and evaluation studies point to the lack of equipment, poor or absence of repairs, improper functioning, or lack of complementary facilities such as 24-hour running water, electricity backups, and so on. But conditions being what they are, unreliable electricity and water supplies also take their toll on the performance of these centres.

Human Resource

Generally rural public health facilities across the country are having a difficult time attracting, retaining, and ensuring regular presence of highly trained medical professionals. The higher the level of training required for the position, the greater is this need gap.

There exists shortfall across all cadres in the posts of MPW(F)/ANM, MPW(M), Health Assistant (Female)/LHV, and that of Health Assistant (Male). The large shortfall in Male Health Workers, has resulted in poor male participation in Family Welfare and other health programmes and overburdening of the ANMs. This shortage is despite government efforts to train health workers through various training programmes throughout the country for more effective and systematic service delivery.

PHC is the first contact point between the village community and the Medical Officer. The dearth of trained doctors, lab technicians and pharmacists is acutely felt. What these data do not reveal is that even if the personnel are present, their level of participation in providing health services is lower than desired due to lack of supplies, inadequately functioning equipment, poor monitoring of the staff, and so on.

Overall about 49.9 per cent of the sanctioned posts of specialists at CHCs were vacant in September 2005 which translates to a shortfall of 6110 specialists at the CHCs as compared to the requirement for existing infrastructure on the basis of existing norms. Even though the government prescribes norms for health care infrastructure, it clearly lacks the capacity to implement them on the ground.

The paucity of skilled health workers is corroborated by results of a household survey based data. The round two of Reproductive Child Health Survey (RCHS), conducted by IIPS for Ministry of Health and Family Welfare sampled 15,794 villages from all states of the country in the period 2002-4. The results are quite revealing and in fact reinforce the administrative data available. Around 95 per cent of the villages have a health provider of some type. However, the majority are Anganwadi workers and can be categorised as health workers only under a very liberal definition of health care. The percentage of villages with trained birth attendants is alarmingly low (37 per cent) and almost 64 per cent of the villages do not have any doctor.

Table 1. Status of Health Infrastructure in Villages

Infrastructure/Services	*% Villages*
Connected with Roads	73.9
Having any Health Provider	95.3
Having Trained Birth Attendant	37.5
Having Anganwadi Worker	74.2
Having a Doctor (Private & Visiting)	43.5
Having a Private Doctor	30.5
Having a Visiting Doctor	25.0

Absenteeism

In addition to the shortage of service providers, the system is plagued by poor involvement and participation of those who are employed. There is a great degree of absenteeism among education and health providers that has been the focus of research in recent times.

Choudhury et al. Measured teacher and health workers' absence in nearly nationally representative samples in several countries using a common methodology based on direct observations during unannounced visits. The survey data reveals that absenteeism among the primary health providers, in India, is the highest (40 per cent) among the surveyed countries. Their survey findings reveal that absence is fairly widespread, rather than being concentrated in some areas. High ranked and more powerful providers, such as doctors are absent more often than lower-ranking ones as are men more than women. The primary reason for absenteeism appears to be the quality of infrastructure at the facility. The findings did not unambiguously support the notion that 'government service providers' choose to absent themselves because they are unlikely to be fired for this but the clear conclusion was that their decision to go to work was strongly influenced by the working conditions they faced. It was also found that health workers (mostly the doctors) who were found to be absent from the public clinics during the survey were mostly engaged in private medical practice.

Table 2. Provider Absence Rates by Country and Sector

	Absence rates (%) in	
Country	*Primary Schools*	*Primary Health Centre*
India	25	40
Bangladesh	16	35
Ecuador	14	–
Indonesia	19	40
Peru	11	25
Uganda	27	37
Unweighted Average	19	35

A study on health care delivery in rural Rajasthan by Banerjee et al. carried out a continuous facility survey in which each of 143 public facilities were visited weekly during regular hours for an entire year. Around 45 per cent of the doctors were found absent from primary health centres. It was also found that at sub centre and aid posts the doors were closed 56 per cent of the time. Moreover, the patterns of absence from duty as well as closure of facility were found to be unpredictable, so people could not even count on facilities being open on certain days or certain times.

This rate of absenteeism can be attributed to the fact that there is certainly a serious lack of zealous administrative action towards effective service provisions. The government has failed to provide the basic infrastructure and incentive structure (not necessarily monetary but in terms of job environment and recognition) for doctors and other health workers to be motivated enough to do their job.

Access to Infrastructure

Even if a healthcare provider is not present in a village, he/she can be reached easily, some basic access issues would be taken care of. However, we find many limitations especially in the context of road connectivity and adequate transport services. Many of the healthcare facilities, public or private, are not accessible throughout the year to about a third of the villages. Private and government hospitals are relatively more accessible as they are typically located in areas well connected by metalled roads.

Table 3. Percentage Villages with Access to various Health Care Facilities round the Year (access by type of facility)

Infrastructure/Services	*% Villages*
PHC	68.3
Sub centre	43.2
Govt. Dispensary	67.9
Govt. Hospital	79.0
Private Clinic	62.7
Private Hospital	76.7

Administrative data above showed that (1) a well defined system of public healthcare provision exists, (2) there is some shortfall in infrastructure, (3) there is a significant problem with the adequacy of working facilities (supplies and equipment) within these centres, (4) there is a significant lack of adequately trained staff, and (5) there continues to be a lack of adequate access to the facilities that exist.

IT for Accessible Healthcare Provisional

It is well known that many doctors are not willing to serve in the rural areas due to lack of facilities even if they are paid high salaries. However, as telecom network is spreading swiftly and the government is keen to provide

Broad-band connectivity to all parts of the country, information technology can be effectively harnessed to improve the delivery of health services.

ROLE OF PRIVATE HEALTHCARE SERVICES

Rural population have been observed to typically report *fewer* ailments than those in urban areas. This could be due to many reasons including those related to perception, age, lack of appreciation of health care requirements and so on. It is important to note however, that the awareness level about ailments or health problems has increased both in rural and urban areas between 1995–6 and 2004 as revealed by the NSS 60th round 2004. While 52 per cent of rural untreated patients in 1995–6 did not consider their ailments as serious, this figure stood at only 32 per cent in 2004.

On the average, almost 9 per cent of the rural population in 2004 report some ailment within the past fifteen days from the day of survey during NSS 60th Round. This figure was much lower in 1995–6 (only about 5.5 per cent). It is not clear why this may have increased so dramatically, especially since NSS survey methodologies have not changed significantly between the two surveys. The incidence of treatment, however, does not appear to have changed significantly over the years and hovers around 82 per cent for rural areas and 90 per cent for urban in both 2004 and 1995–6.

If an ailment is treated it could be institutional (hospitalisation) or noninstitutional (outpatient). These services could be availed of in public or private facilities. The private sector has become the dominant source of health care services, both institutional or noninstitutional for patients in rural and urban areas. Of those seeking treatment, 78 per cent rural and 81 per cent urban patients are availing private noninstitutional facilities and 58 per cent rural and

62 per cent urban patients are going to private hospitals. W e also find that the dependence on the private sector is significant across all income ranges from the poorest to the richest, and utilisation for public facilities is only very marginally higher among the poorest segments.

The role of the government health services has diminished despite higher costs of private sector services. Why is this so?

One reason is lack of adequate infrastructure and personnel at public health care facilities. The second has to do with an orientation towards delivery of quality services—this is integral to health care provision. The third has to do with accessibility, timing, and availability of services at the place and time required. There is another issue related to quality. It is not clear whether private sector providers necessarily provide better quality health care or is this merely the perception of the user group.

Unlike other markets for goods and services, the health care provider is also the main supplier of information on treatment requirements to the user. Since a large section of the rural user group is illiterate and unaware, the motivation to over-treat is but natural in the private sector. Hence even in villages where geographical accessibility is not a constraint, villagers tend to fall victims of this phenomenon in case they choose to seek the services of private practitioners. That, unfortunately, is not all. A very large proportion of the rural health care providers in the private sector are not qualified. They are often illegal medical practitioners or under-qualified for the task at hand. The quality of treatment is, therefore, suspect. In other services such a situation may not have allowed a market to develop at all. However, the necessity of availing some relief from the ailment forces many to go to providers despite knowing that the quality of advice/care is suspect.

Finding Quality Healthcare Solutions

Ideally the presence of public health care should take care of both the ability to pay and ability to process information on the quality of health care. But it so happens that especially for those residing in the smaller and far off villages, many public services are out of reach geographically and often such consumers are left with their needs un met. The private sector cannot emerge in such areas because of lack of adequate scales. In other words, more important than the price is the issue of geographical accessibility for many rural residents. Lack of physical infrastructure and staff both contribute to this problem of access.

While economic history is full of examples of how in such situations some market solutions emerge that are in the interests of both providers as well as consumers, we do not have to wait for such solutions to emerge by themselves, where there are broadly three areas where pro-active policy-making can make a difference.

The first is to expand the public provision and find ways around the staff and infrastructure constraints. Issues of regulation and pricing then are subsumed within the system. The problem at the policy level would be to find a way to finance it. At the administrative level, however, we have another serious problem, as it is difficult to imagine the government maintaining and sustaining quality health care service provision for all.

An important policy innovation could be to enable greater private sector involvement in the sector, while directly subsidising the poor through health care stamps etc to transfer resources to the poorest segments. Since the private sector is already the dominant force, the critical issue here would be to find a viable and sustainable system of monetary transfers to the identified poorest target group.

The call for public-private partnerships in the infrastructure sector is an urgent one and the health care sector has not been left out. A public-private partnership of sorts has been prevalent in the health care sector from the pre-independence period where land is allocated and credit provided at sub-market rates to private players to build healthcare facilities in return for making a few services available to the poor free or at nominal prices. Other types of public-private partnerships such as government financing and private provision are still largely absent in India.

Any institutionalised expansion of the role of the private sector will entail some form of least intrusive regulation, along medical practitioners in poorer neighbourhoods. In general, the performance of healthcare providers both private and public was much worse in poorer clusters than in rich neighbourhoods. Since the private sector doctors are directly accountable to the patient, they were found to be making greater effort, although they did tend to over-prescribe medicines that were ineffective simply to please the client. With a strong consumer re-dressal mechanism.

While it is difficult enough to foresee large-scale competent governmental administration of an expanded healthcare mechanism, it is even more difficult to foresee effective regulation of private sector activities. We draw a strong conclusion, that others may disagree with and that is, there is little the state can do to *effectively* regulate the practices of private practitioners, whether legal and illegal, in rural areas. Regulation costs money and manpower resources which are already in short supply where availability of quality care for the poor is concerned. In other words, mechanisms that involve a greater role of the private sector typically do not guarantee either (i) assured geographical access in the hinter-lands, or (ii) effective regulation to ensure quality health care provision.

In the view of the authors, the answer to both the problems lies in technology. First consider geographical access. Technologies exist today which make it possible to fit in a wide range of testing and basic operating equipment into medical vans the size of a bus. The spread of the rural road network will also now make almost all villages accessible by road. Private or the public players can operate these services for those locations that are most remote.

Instead of focusing on regulation of the private sector players, policy should focus on consumer information and consumer re-dressal mechanisms. This would require a well spread IT network, backed by (i) a system of providing free basic information on health and health care, and (ii) a mechanism whereby, consumer complaints are investigated and followed up at the block level. As long as consumers do not have significant complaints against a practitioner (whether legal or illegal, qualified or untrained) there is no need to prevent him from providing his services. But if significant and repeated complaints are received then the practitioner should be investigated upon and punished or prevented from practising further. Of course, many checks and balances would be required in this system as well.

Financing Healthcare

When we look at the profile of diseases we can see that rural– urban differential in the proportion of hospitalisation within each ailment is negligible, except for the heart diseases, where the proportion of hospitalisation cases in the urban areas was almost double that in the rural areas.

The average medical expenditure on health for both hospitalisation and non-hospitalisation cases in rural areas is lower than in urban areas. However, household income lost per treated person is much higher in the rural areas than urban for non-hospitalisation cases. In either scenario, private players play a dominant role.

There are demonstrated differences between the payment patterns of the rich and the poor in both inpatient and outpatient care. Those from poorer sections depend more on income and less on savings (as they are likely to have minimal savings). Similarly, in the event of a negative health occurrence, the poorest sections are most propendent to sell their assets. It is also not surprising that friends and relatives are significant contributors to health care costs.

What is however surprising is that although clearly identifiable differences exist between the financing sources of the poorest and richest segments, the differences are not dramatic. What is also interesting is that the differences in hospitalisation cost between public and private facilities have a magnitude of 2. In other words, the private sector does not appear to be charging much more than public facilities.

While significant user charges are being paid by all economic segments for availing of health care services, the question remains as to who will pay for the expansion and rationalisation of health care facilities to augment physical, technical as well as human resource infrastructure to cater better to the needs of the economically challenged sections of the society. Clearly it is not the user but the state or the central government budget that must bear the load of this expense.

While dearth of financial resources at the state-level cannot be denied, studies can prove that states that spend the least on health care on per capita basis also tend to be the ones that are the least distressed financially—as in states with low per capita state budget deficit are surprisingly spending less per capita on healthcare than states with higher per capita budget deficits.

States such as Bihar and UP have among the lowest budgetary deficit on a per capita basis. These states also tend to have poor health indicators. And they also spend among the lowest in health care on a per capita basis. For these states, spending more on health care is possible. Though it would, in all likelihood, worsen their budgetary deficit, it would be no worse than many of the better performing states such as Himachal, Delhi or Kerala.

This provides us some hope. Those states that currently spend the least on health care, can at some cost to their deficit, increase health care expenditures. Thus Bihar, Uttar Pradesh, Chhattisgarh, Madhya Pradesh, Jharkhand, Orissa, and Assam, that spend the least on health care on a per capita basis are also among the states that have the lowest per capita budgetary deficit. Whether states can or should do so, is of course a political-economic question. One potential source of funds could be the private sector backed by rural health insurance.

Way Forward

Rural Health care services suffer from a shortage in public sector infrastructure. The failure of the public delivery system today is an outcome of systemic breakdown of accountability relationships within the institutional framework. There is a shortfall not only in terms of physical infrastructure but also human resource, measured even against the minimal norms prescribed by the government. Even though the posts of health workers at various levels are sanctioned, many of them are lying vacant. The existing facilities are underutilised. Most health workers especially the 'doctors' do not want to serve in the rural areas due to overall infrastructure inadequacy and lack of incentives. This leads to widespread absenteeism from service and closure of facility. Moreover, there is no accountability in the public sector service. The public doctors quite often provide private services instead of going to their designated centres.

Even though a well-structured public health care system exists, the infrastructure as well as **the staff that are** required to provide the health care services is inadequate from many different perspectives. Many rural residents are not able to obtain treatment for basic ailments either due to the non-presence of health care services in the vicinity, or due to lack of funds to access the same. Even for basic health care services such as reproductive and child health, we find that significant proportions continue to remain untreated. Immunisation, antenatal care, deliveries in the presence of professionally trained personnel, and so on all show large un met needs figures.

The private sector is filling in the un met need to an extent and this role is rapidly expanding. Today private sector health care provision in rural areas is *greater* than that by the public sector. But despite the presence of a large, dynamic, and what appears to be a well spread out private health care provision network, access issues remain important because in remote and far flung habitations, the private sector does not have the incentive to set up shop and in the absence of adequate penetration by public sector health centres, these areas remain unserved. But, there is little consensus on the possible answer. Under the new scenario, regulatory mechanisms and the role of new information technologies have come under the scanner as possible solution baskets in providing accessible and effective quality healthcare to the vast Indian rural population.

A question which is begging an answer is what should be the role of the current public health care system. Though public–private partnerships are growing, there are still financial as well as logistical constraints to starting large scale ventures under such arrangements.

Thus, ineffective and inadequate public service has paved way for the growth of the private sector health care in the country. The private sector is not only filling up the gaps left by the public sector but is also emerging as the key player in terms of service provision. But in terms of quality of service both the public and the private sector have failed. The two most important issues which emerge with regard to rural health infrastructure in the country are *lack of access* for many and *poor quality* of service.

Any systemic problem requires a phase-wise systematic solution. Nothing can be changed at once but a systematic approach guided by pilot studies should be a part of larger vision reforms and strategies for systemic reform. Introducing mobile medical vans in the rural areas can solve the problem of accessibility. Mobile vans equipped with basic medical facilities could supplement a primary health centre and travel to those areas where the primary health centres do not exist or have failed to meet the requirements of the people. These vans could have a schedule of visits in particular areas and could also be called in times of emergency. The introduction of adequate mobile vans could solve the problem of accessibility to a great extent and more efficient and quality services could reach at the grassroots level.

The quality of service can be improved by increasing the awareness level of the users. Though the government runs many Information, Education, and Communication activities, it has failed to raise the awareness levels. Government along with private providers should try to establish the consumer information and re-dressal cells more effectively. Dissemination of information should be computerised and there should be an online grievance re-dressal forum. The users should have access to any information on health and other issues and similarly be empowered to post their grievances online to the designated authority. This will not only improve the quality of service but also increase the accountability of the service provider. It is expected that if the Common Service Centre programme (rural computerisation) of the government is functional within the stipulated time period then many of these problems could be minimised if not solved completely. Regulations will require an overseeing mechanism that is not feasible or practical in the current scenario. Over all, the private sector is here and will be the dominant force in all sectors including rural health care. This should not be ignored, rather it should be considered as a starting point for all future thoughts on health care policy formulation. The best way to control poor practices is through greater consumer awareness, consumer re-dressal mechanisms, and through community action. These are now increasingly possible due to changes in information and medical technologies.

7

Gender and Rural Microfinance

A concern with gender issues in financial services is not new. Nor can it be dismissed as a Western or donor-imposed agenda. From the early 1970s, women's movements in a number of countries, notably India, became increasingly interested in the degree to which women were able to gain access to and benefit from poverty-focused credit programmes and credit cooperatives.

The problem of women's access to credit was highlighted at the first International Women's Conference in Mexico in 1975, leading to the setting up of the Women's World Banking network. In the wake of the second International Women's Conference in Nairobi in 1985, there was a mushrooming of government and NGO-sponsored income-generating programmes for women, many of which included savings and credit. Then, in the 1990s, micro-finance programmes such as the Grameen Bank and some affiliates of the Foundation for International Community Assistance (FINCA) and ACCION International increasingly began to target women, not only as part of their poverty mandate, but also because they found women's repayment rates to be significantly higher than men's.

The expansion of Micro-finance since the 1990s has significantly increased women's access to facilities for small loans and savings. This increased access to Micro-finance has been seen as contributing not only to poverty reduction and financial sustainability, but also to a series of 'virtuous spirals' of economic empowerment, increased well-being and social and political empowerment for women themselves, thereby addressing goals of gender equality and empowerment. Some of the dimensions of and inter-linkages among the various virtuous impact spirals identified in the literature are decribed below.

First, increasing women's access to Micro-finance services can lead to their *economic empowerment.* Women's roles in household financial management may improve, in some cases enabling them to access significant amounts of money in their own right for the first time. This might enable women to start their own economic activities, invest more in existing activities, acquire assets or raise their status in household economic activities through their visible capital contribution. Increased participation in economic activities may raise women's incomes or their control of their own and household income. This, in turn, may enable them to increase longer-term investment in and productivity of their economic activities, as well as their engagement in the market.

Second, increasing women's access to Micro-finance can increase *household well-being.* This is partly the result of economic empowerment, but may occur even where women use Micro-finance services for the activities of other household members, for example husbands or children. Even where women are not directly engaged in income-earning activities, channelling credit or savings options to households *through women* may enable them to play a more active role in intra-household decision-making, decrease their own and household vulnerability, and increase investment in family welfare. This situation may benefit children through increasing expenditure on their nutrition and education, particularly for girls. It can also lead to improved well-being for women and enable them to bring about changes in gender inequalities in the household. It is also likely to benefit men as a result of the increased household income.

Third, a combination of women's increased economic activity and increased decision-making in the household can lead to wider *social and political empowerment.* Women, themselves, often value the opportunity to make a greater contribution to household well-being – giving them greater confidence and sense of self-worth. The positive effects on women's confidence and skills, their expanded knowledge and the formation of support networks through group activity and market access can lead to enhanced status for all women in a community. In some societies where women's mobility has been very circumscribed and women previously had little opportunity to meet women outside their immediate family, there have been very significant changes. Individual women who gain respect in their households may then act as role models for others, leading to a wider process of change in community perceptions and men's increased willingness to accept change.

Most Micro-finance providers can cite case studies of women who have benefited substantially from their services both economically and socially. Some women who were very poor before entering the programme have started an economic activity with a loan and have built up savings, thereby improving their own and household well-being, as well as relationships in the household, and becoming more involved in local community activities. Some women, and many women in some contexts, show enormous resourcefulness and initiative when provided with a loan or given the chance to save without interference from family members. Impact studies that differentiate by poverty level generally find benefits to be particularly significant for the 'better-off poor', who have some education and contacts on which to build in conducting a successful enterprise.

Finally, women's *economic empowerment at the individual level* can make potentially significant contributions at the macro level through increasing women's visibility as agents of economic growth and their voices as economic actors in policy decisions. This, together with their greater ability to meet the needs of household well-being, in turn increases their effectiveness as agents of poverty reduction. Micro-finance groups may take collective action to address gender inequalities within the community, including such issues as gender violence and access to resources and local decision-making. Higher-level organisation may further reinforce these local changes, leading to wider movements for social and political change and promotion of women's human rights at the macro level. Some NGOs have used Micro-finance strategically as an entry point for wider social and political mobilisation of women around gender issues. Savings-and-credit groups have at times become the basis for mobilising women's political participation.

Moreover, these three dimensions of economic empowerment, well-being and social and political empowerment are potentially mutually reinforcing 'virtuous spirals', both for individual women and at the household, community and macro level.

Importance of Gender Mainstreaming

Despite the potential contribution of Micro-finance to women's empowerment and well-being, there is a long way to go before women have equal access to financial services in rural areas or are able to fully benefit from them. This is partly because of contextual differences in the gender division of labour. Although there are significant differences among and within regions in the types of crops and other economic activities in which they are involved, women tend to be restricted to subsistence food crops and the marketing of lower-profit goods. Although there are significant differences in household, family and kinship structures, women are also almost universally disadvantaged in access to and control of incomes (from their own or household economic activities) and assets (particularly land). These differences and inequalities affect the types of financial services they need and also the ways in which they are able to use and benefit from them.

This does not mean that Micro-finance should cease attempting to target women – they have a right to access all types of financial services and to the removal of all forms of gender discrimination among financial service providers. The right of women to equality is enshrined in agreements and conventions on women's human rights signed by most governments.

Rather, these gender differences and inequalities mean that gender-blind product design and service delivery are not enough, and that gender dimensions must be as integral to financial service provision as are poverty and financial sustainability concerns.

Despite some advances, women's access to Micro-finance is still unequal. Statistics on client or membership numbers, even when gender desegregated, say very little about the quality of the services accessed by women compared with those for men. Women generally receive lower loan amounts, and this cannot be completely accounted for by demand factors. Some women have extremely good business ideas requiring larger loans, but they face discrimination in accessing such loans, with the result that their businesses collapse because they are forced to purchase inferior equipment or materials. Most programmes to which women have access do not give them sufficiently large loans to purchase assets such as land and housing. Many require assets as collateral or the signature of a 'male guardian'. In many rural village banks and credit-

and-savings cooperatives, women are the majority of savers, but men receive the majority of loans. The exceptions are women-only organisations or those having an effective gender policy. Because men form the majority in decision-making bodies, the interest rates are fixed in favour of borrowers, leading to lower levels of financial sustainability.

In some cases, and particularly for poor women, Micro-finance may undermine existing informal systems, such as crisis funds in rotating savings-and-credit associations (ROSCAs), if better-off women divert ROSCA funds as loan-interest payments to MFIs (Mayoux 2001a). Availability of credit may also reduce the willingness of patrons and relatives to give interest-free loans or access to more charitable forms of credit from traders.

Moreover, a recent study has found that women's access to loans decreases compared with that of men as NGOs transform into formal institutions and become more profitable and 'mature'.

The degree to which women are able to benefit from minimalist financial services that do not take gender explicitly into account depends largely on context and individual situation, and may also change over time. However, none of the expected linkages between women's access to financial services and empowerment can be assumed to occur automatically.

First, women's programme membership, numbers and size of loans and repayment data cannot be used as indicators of actual access or proxy indicators of empowerment. Registration of loans in women's names does not necessarily mean participation even in decisions about loan applications. Men may take the loans from women or directly negotiate loans in women's names with male credit officers, as an easier way of getting access to credit. Loans may be repaid from men's earnings, through women forgoing their own consumption, or from income or borrowing from other sources. High demand for loans by women may be more a sign of social pressure to access outside resources for in-laws or husbands than of empowerment.

Second, the contribution of financial services to increased income varies widely. Evidence suggests that, particularly in South Asia and parts of Latin America, most women use loans for their husband's activities. Even where they use loans for their own activities, women's choice of activity and the ability to increase their incomes are seriously constrained by gender inequalities in access to other, supplementary resources for investment; responsibility for household subsistence expenditure; lack of time due to unpaid domestic work; low levels of mobility; and vulnerability –all of which limit women's access to profitable markets in many cultures. The rapid expansion of loans for poor women may saturate the market for 'female' activities or products and cause profits to plummet, affecting even more those poorer women with no access to credit.

The degree to which credit contributes to increased incomes for women (as well as for men) also depends largely on how well the delivery of credit is adapted to the economic activities being financed. Agricultural loans that arrive late or are not large enough to pay for inputs may simply burden a woman with debt that she cannot repay from the proceeds of the activity she wished to finance. Compulsory savings and insurance premiums may constitute a further drain on resources for investment, unless they are designed in the interests of the borrower and not just to limit risk and increase financial sustainability for the financial institution.

Third, women's increased contribution to household income does not ensure that women necessarily benefit or that there is any change in gender relations within the household. Although women do, indeed, often feel more in control and have a greater sense of self-worth, these subjective perceptions are not necessarily translated into actual changes in well-being, benefits or gender relations in the household. Although in some contexts women may seek to increase their influence within joint decision-making processes, rather than seek independent control of income, neither of these outcomes can be assumed to occur. Evidence indicates that, in response to women's increased (but still low) incomes, men may withhold more of their contribution to the household budget for their own luxury expenditure. Men are often very enthusiastic about women's savings-and-credit programmes because their wives no longer 'nag' them for money.

Small increases in access to income may come at the cost of heavier workloads, increased stress and diminished health. Women's expenditure patterns may replicate rather than counter gender inequalities, and may continue to disadvantage girls. Without substitute care for small children, the elderly and the disabled, and services to reduce domestic work, many organisations report that women's outside work adversely affects children and the elderly. Daughters, in particular, may be withdrawn from school to assist their mothers. Although, in many cases, women's increased contribution to household well-being has considerably improved domestic relations, in others it has intensified tensions. This problem affects not only poor women, but women from all economic backgrounds, indicating that the empowerment process must have effective strategies to work with men on changing attitudes and behaviours.

Fourth, the economic empowerment of individual women and their participation in group-based Micro-finance programmes are not necessarily linked to social and political empowerment. Earning an income and finding time to attend group meetings for savings-and-credit transactions may take women away from other social and political activities – and experience suggests that where meetings focus only on such transactions, women commonly want to decrease the length and frequency of group meetings over time. Women's existing networks may come under serious strain if their own or others' loan-repayment or savings contributions become a problem. The contribution of financial services to women's social and political empowerment depends very much on other factors, such as staff attitudes in interacting with women and men, the types and effectiveness of core training (for savings, credit and group formation) and other capacitybuilding, the types of non-financial support services or collaboration with other organisations.

Where women are not able to significantly increase incomes under their control or negotiate changes in intra-household and community gender inequalities, they mav become dependent on loans to continue in very low-paid occupations with heavier workloads while enjoying little benefit. For some women, Micro-finance has been positively dis-empowering:

1. *Credit is also debt.* If credit is badly designed and used, the consequences for individuals and programmes can be serious. Debt may lead to severe impoverishment or abandonment and put serious strains on networks with other women.
2. *Savings and pension instalments are forgone consumption and investment.* In many contexts, particularly where inflation is high, depositing cash with financial institutions may not be the best use of poor peoples' resources, compared with investing in other assets or directly in livelihoods.
3. *Insurance premiums*, in addition to representing forgone consumption and investment, may be lost when

a crisis prevents poor people from continuing payments.

4. *Remittance transfers reduce the funds available to migrants* in the host country, and may distort local markets and consumption patterns in the recipient country without leading to local economic development.

The contribution of Micro-finance alone appears to be most limited for the poorest and most disadvantaged women. Where repayment is the prime consideration or where the main emphasis of programmes is on existing micro-entrepreneurs, all the evidence suggests that these women are the most likely to be explicitly excluded by programmes and peer groups.

Finally, very little research has been done on the gender impact of financial services for men. Any financial intervention available to any household member has the potential to reinforce or challenge existing inequalities in ways that may contribute to or undermine the poverty and potential of other household members. As noted earlier, research suggests that financial services targeted at men contribute less to household well-being and food security. When financial services automatically treat men as heads of household, they may reinforce what are often only informal rights that men have over household assets, labour and income. In other words, they may seriously undermine women's informal rights. As in other areas of development, such outcomes may have consequences not only for the women and households involved, but for the effectiveness of the intervention and the sustainability of the institutions.

There is a need for much greater understanding of the ways in which different types of products and services affect women and men from different backgrounds and in various contexts. The generic question 'Does Micro-finance empower women?' Is not very useful or meaningful. The identification and weighting of standardised SMART indicators (specific, measurable, attainable, realistic, timely) can be controversial because of the complexity of empowerment itself and the frequent trade-off between its various dimensions, e.g. between levels of income earned and time available for other activities, and between women's autonomy and the effort they have to put into changing abusive relationships. Women's own goals and preferences vary significantly with context and between women even within the same context.

The main justification for in-depth impact assessment is to improve practice, and this requires careful attention to the high degree of variation in financial services and the institutions delivering them. Which particular aspects of the products and services or institution delivering them can contribute to which dimension of empowerment? In many contexts, information is likely to be unreliable because of the clients' incentives to alter their responses depending on the actual or perceived consequences of those responses for their future access to credit. The gender of both the respondent and interviewer affect responses even from members of the same household. Given the costs of credible research and impact assessment, it is the view of the author that more systematic market research that includes information on impact is the most useful approach, though current methodologies need to be more effectively designed in terms of their ability to collect qualitative and quantitative information on empowerment, particularly the dimensions important to clients.

Equality and Empowerment: Institutional Implications

Achieving gender equality and empowerment goals depends not on expanding financial services, per se, but on the specific types of financial services that are delivered in various contexts to women from different backgrounds and by different types of institutions or programmes. Given the contextual and institutional constraints, gender mainstream in rural finance entails more than increasing women's access to small savings, loan and micro-insurance programmes or to a few products designed specifically for women. It calls for effective methodologies for product design, structural and cultural changes in organisations providing financial services at all levels, appropriate linkage with non-financial services of various types and mainstream gender in policies at the macro level.

Addressing gender issues will thus require not only a strategy to mainstream gender equality of access, but also strategies to ensure that this access then translates into empowerment and improved well-being, rather than merely feminisation of debt or capturing women's savings for programme financial sustainability. Even in minimalist Micro-finance institutions, there are other measures that can be taken to increase the contribution of Micro-finance services to gender equality and women's empowerment.

At the core is a mainstream of women's needs, concerns and language: not as a marginal concern, but as a central and resource element in planning and implementation at all levels. This methodology implies looking beyond the purely economic and market concerns to issues of non-market work and activities, power relations and underlying forms of social, cultural and political gender discrimination.

Organisational Gender Mainstream

A range of different types of institutions currently provide rural financial services. Some target women mainly or exclusively, or have a written or informal gender policy. The variations among organisational models can significantly influence gender outcomes and have implications for the most effective ways in which gender can be mainstream.

In all types of institutions, the most cost-effective means of maximising contributions to gender equality and empowerment is to develop an institutional structure and culture that is woman-friendly and empowering, and that manifests these traits in all interactions with clients. A full discussion of frameworks and methodologies for institutional gender mainstream is outside the scope of this guide.

It is possible for these changes in institutional culture and structure to be integrated into *all forms* of rural financial services *in some way*, including commercial and state banks as well as MFIs, membership-based financial organisations and integrated development programmes. The changes are consistent with financial sustainability. Many of these strategies cost little, for example recruitment, promotion and sexual harassment policies. In fact, mainstream banks are sometimes way ahead of NGOs in implementing staff gender policies (examples include Barclays in Kenya – dating back to the 1980s – and Khushali Bank in Pakistan). Commercial banks increasingly have gender or equal opportunity policies to encourage and retain skilled women staff. Some offer child care facilities and have implemented pro-active promotion policies for women to attain greater diversity in the organisation and better develop new market niches.

The promotion of diversity, of which gender is one dimension, is a key element of best business practice in the West. In many social settings, increasing the number of women on the staff is essential if the number of women clients is to be increased. Although a gender policy may entail some costs (for example, parental leave and better transport for women staff members to increase security), they are likely to be compensated by higher levels of staff commitment, efficiency and retention. Unhappy and harassed staff members are inefficient and change jobs frequently, and training new staff is costly.

This is not to say that there are no serious challenges, potential tensions or costs. Mere formal change is not enough. Real change requires

1. A change in organisational culture and systems. This requirement raises the issue of staff participation in decision-making – a key tenet of best business practice;
2. A shift in the norms of behaviour for women and men;
3. Willingness and support for change at all levels, among field staff, mid-level staff, senior management and donors.

It is also important to incorporate gender indicators into information systems, so that institutions are aware of the status of gender equality in access and benefits. The extent and type of gender-based information will obviously differ from institution to institution, depending on the nature of the information systems. The recent advances in 'social performance management' (SPM) offer a particularly important opening in relation to gender.

From Access to Empowerment

The outcomes of programmes to provide financial services depend greatly on whether products are designed for particular client groups and contexts, on how products are delivered, and on the organisation responsible for delivery. Product design is rarely gender neutral, and inevitably affects household and community relations – for good or ill. It may either reinforce or challenge the prevailing gender inequalities that shape women's needs and priorities, their access to different types of services, and the degree to which they benefit.

Women have fewer and different resources for accessing financial products. Their different balance of opportunities and constraints affects how and how much they benefit from various products. Women's gender role and gendered expectations affect their expressed short-term practical needs, as well as their longer-term strategic needs to build assets, access markets, decrease vulnerability, and increase information and organisation. Finally, as discussed previously, products accessed mainly by men may reinforce or challenge gender inequalities through the implicit or explicit assumptions made about male and female roles and power relations within households and communities. This affects the products' potential contributions to poverty reduction and local economic growth.

Research on women's access to finance in the 1970s and 1980s focused mainly on lack of credit as a constraint to economic activity. In the 1990s, with the rise of Micro-finance, most debates on product design focused on issues of financial sustainability: interest rates on loans, the desirability of mobilising savings, and the need for insurance products to reduce the risk to organisations of default. A widespread consensus developed about how to increase women's access to financial services, based on poor women's access to resources and power and the particular physical and social assets they could contribute to programmes. Products were very limited to simplify management for field staff, generate predictable cash flows for programme managers, and be comprehensible to clients. Many programmes had only one loan product, with compulsory savings as a condition for accessing loans and, in some cases, compulsory insurance for the assets.

These measures increased women's access to financial services, but often had limited impact on incomes. Loans were too small, and repayment schedules inappropriate, for activities that had a time flag between investment and returns. Although suited to trade in urban areas and small-livestock enterprises, the loans were ill adapted to agriculture, large-livestock enterprises, or new and more risky economic activities. Where savings and insurance payments were compulsory, these not only often failed to benefit clients, but also created problems with household financial management.

Poor women, like the rest of society, have a variety of financial needs, which they seek to address through diverse types of financial provision. Rural Micro-finance now covers a range of different products including the following:

1 loans of varying amounts, time frames and conditions for a range of livelihood activities (including both agricultural and off-farm activities), asset-building and consumption;

2 leasing arrangements for assets;

3 savings services of different types to meet different needs, from day-to-day household cash-flow management to long-term asset-building;

4 pensions to reduce long-term vulnerability;

5. Insurance to reduce risk and vulnerability to crises;

6. Remittance transfer services to enable migrants to send more of their earnings home for investment in livelihoods and asset-building, as well as for consumption and to reduce the vulnerability of family members left behind.

7. External interventions to increase access to financial services must first understand existing financial systems, including

8. Informal financial mechanisms: ROSCAs and accumulating savings-and-credit associations (ASCAs); burial societies for death insurance; cash or kind advances or savings arrangements with relatives and patrons; retail stores offering consumer goods on credit or hire purchase; moneylenders, pawnbrokers and informal deposit collectors;

9. Private-sector linkages: large-scale farmers, traders, processors and employers providing credit as part of sharecropping or leasing agreements; subcontracting and outsourcing systems; market transactions or employment arrangements; shopkeepers and traders offering credit for purchases.

Many of these may be extremely expensive options for clients. They may also exclude and discriminate against women, particularly poor women. It is crucial that financial service providers understand these systems and complement them, increasing the range of financial choices that can benefit people, rather than undermining existing systems.

The financial products available in rural areas are likely to change significantly over the next few years, owing to technological advances, innovations in information and delivery technologies, and the increasing entry of commercial banks into Micro-finance. Improved financial information and planning systems permit greater product diversification and client-centred product development. This is particularly the case where clients also have some experience of financial services, and an increasingly sophisticated understanding of their financial needs and of financial management.

Technological advances such as computerised services, automated teller machines (ATMs) and mobile banking through phones, mobile phones and mobile units make service delivery less dependent on expensive infrastructure, able to reach into increasingly remote areas, and promise increasingly accessible and accountable services in rural areas. Banks such as ICICI Bank in India currently aim to give universal access to loan products and other services. This strategy would consist of a number of elements: rolling out credit cards and ATMs in villages to give everyone individual access; building and maintaining individual credit histories through credit bureaux; basing credit decisions on scoring models (risk-based lending); moving from group-based to individual lending; and tracking clients through their life cycle to offer customised products for life cycle needs. These developments could significantly increase the scale of out reach. They promise credit and other services on terms far better than any currently offered by MFIs, owing to economies of scale arising from their large investment in technology.

The extent to which women will have equitable access to and benefits from these services remains to be seen. Technological advances have considerable potential to make financial services accessible to women even in remote and conservative areas. Women's groups can manage mobile banking; communications enterprises can be set up in villages (for example, Grameen's mobile phone initiatives); computer programmes and material can be made accessible to people who cannot read or write. There are, however, also developments that may make women's access more difficult:

1. Women enjoy less ownership of and access to technology, including mobile phones.
2. It may be harder for women to build up credit histories, because either they do not have the sort of financial history required (e.g. they may not pay domestic bills) or their credit history may be linked to that of other family members, particularly husbands.
3. ATMs may be set up in public areas for men, rather than in places easily accessed by women.

In this new climate of rapid expansion and commercialisation, it will be particularly important to ensure that products both are accessible to women and benefit them. This will require consideration of collateral requirements and ways in which credit histories can be built up. It is also important to locate the machines strategically –

e.g. near the beer house (men's space) or near a grocery shop (women's space) – and to determine who gets access to mobile phones and to ensure that they are of a suitable design. Otherwise, the rapid expansion of rural Micro-finance may further entrench existing gender inequalities within households and communities, either through leaving women behind or offering products that make them further indebted and overburdened.

Credit

As indicated by research on patterns of credit use among poor women and men, and by the experience of numerous clients after many loan cycles, women's credit needs are very varied:

1. Women need longer-term credit or leasing arrangements to build assets – to construct houses, buy land, and lease land, either under their own names or at least jointly. They also need credit to purchase 'female assets' such as jewellery, or redeem them from pawnbrokers and moneylenders, thereby transferring general household wealth into assets they can easily access and control, and which grow in value and provide some security.
2. Women need access to credit for investment in a variety of viable, profitable activities, including off-farm activities. Women often require larger amounts than are usually offered to them in order to diversify out of 'female' activities or to expand their range of products, especially where local markets are saturated with such products and skills.
3. Households that sell their agricultural labour, as well as farming households, need consumption loans to avoid resorting to moneylenders in slack and 'hungry' seasons. Other than being needed in themselves, these loans may free up significant amounts of money spent

on high-interest payments to moneylenders for investment in production at other times of the year. Providing such loans to men as well as women would reduce the worrying trend of men taking less responsibility for household well-being when they perceive that women have access to additional cash.

4 Households need loans to pay for children's education and to meet social obligations that are essential in maintaining social capital and the well-being of children, particularly daughters after marriage. Again, giving men as well as women access to such loans would strengthen men's responsibility for children and not place the entire burden on women.

Until recently, debates about credit have focused mainly on issues of interest rates. However, designing loan products that benefit clients also involves many other decisions, which can significantly affect the degree to which clients are able to use and benefit from loans. These include:

1. Eligibility and collateral requirements (who is eligible and the risks involved);
2. Application procedures (complexity), repayment schedules (grace periods and whether interest calculation is fixed rate or declining balance);
3. Loan size and appropriateness to the levels of investment needed;
4. Design of loan products for specific purposes or activities.

Each of these decisions has gender dimensions relating to women's gender-specific activities and power relations within the household.

Some very interesting innovations in loan products have been introduced recently, but given the variety in women's preferences and requirements, the particular product that should be offered in a given context should be decided on the basis of market research.

The loan products available in rural areas are likely to change significantly over the next few years, with advances in technology and the increasing entry of commercial banks into Micro-finance. It is important to ensure that gender issues are mainstream in the current debates about larger-scale rural finance and leasing arrangements for agricultural development and value-chain upgrading.

Savings

Debates on extending the reach of Micro-finance to the very poorest people increasingly focus on savings facilities. For many women, including very poor women, savings facilities are essential in increasing the amount of income under their control and in building assets. In remote areas, mobilisation and intermediation of member savings may be crucial first steps before accessing external loan funds. A number of studies have observed that savings led groups perform better than credit-led ones.

Women may already have effective ways of saving, and women's lack of interest in saving with any one particular institution may be less a sign of 'lack of thrift or savings culture' and more a rational response to bad savings products or a wish to diversify where they entrust their resources. Common modes of saving include ROSCAs and other mutual savings arrangements, burial societies and also investment in assets such as livestock that can be sold in times of need. Savings schemes offered by financial service providers may be less efficient for women, particularly if savings are a condition of loans. Savings programmes may also divert resources from indigenous savings groups, which often provide a safety net for very poor women. In Cameroon and other parts of Africa, for instance, some revolving savings associations maintain a 'trouble fund' for times of crisis.

Savings also have to come from *somewhere* – often from forgone investment or consumption. Badly designed savings products, particularly compulsory savings, may thus harm women's ability to increase profits and, among very poor women, their nutrition and health. Savings facilities may increase women's control of household income, but, as mentioned, when savings are regarded as 'a women's affair', men's sense of responsibility for the household may decline.

In designing savings facilities, a number of key issues must be considered, including whether savings are compulsory or voluntary, the level of initial deposit required, ease of withdrawal, confidentiality, accessibility of the provider, and interest rates. All of these have gender dimensions, and it is likely that many women will require a range of different types of savings provision. For example, compulsory savings systems are one of the few ways for some women to protect income against the demands of husbands and other family members. If savings are only voluntary, women may be less able to oppose the demands of other family members to withdraw them. At the same time, they are likely to need some access to liquid cash for emergencies from a provider who is easily accessible. In many parts of Africa, for example, where in-laws are likely to take the wife's as well as the husband's property when he dies, women's ability to have confidential savings accounts may be a crucial and necessary means of security for the future. Confidentiality may also be important to avoid witchcraft or the jealousy of other women. On the other hand, public knowledge of savings may in some circumstances increase social status and access to credit.

Several recent innovations in savings products can make a significant contribution to women's empowerment. Pensions – which are essentially a long-term savings product – have received far less attention than other instruments such as insurance. However, pensions are potentially a key component of empowerment, because they offer women security for their old age and have many other implications (for example, reducing women's vulnerability in the household or influencing family-size decisions). Some pension products for women exist in India, but pensions are an area in which much more needs to be done. In Bangladesh, the Income Generation for Vulnerable Groups Development Programme (Bangladesh Rural Advancement Committee [BRAC]) and the Tangail Infrastructure Development Project (German Agency for Technical Cooperation [GTZ]) are examples of how grant-based or employment-based approaches and financial services can be complementary.

Insurance

Although savings-and-loan products from financial service providers can reduce vulnerability to crises and shocks, they generally do not enable people to accumulate sufficient funds to cope with major crises. Over the last decade, an increasing number of MFIs have developed micro-insurance products to address various sources of vulnerability. These products include compulsory insurance against loan defaults, and health, life, livestock, property and index-based weather insurance. Micro-insurance is one of the most rapidly moving areas of innovation.

Despite the clear need for insurance products and their great potential to contribute to the development of the rural sector, the viability and desirability of specialised Micro-insurance institutions for poor people have been questioned. Most people engage in various forms of 'self-insurance', such as diversifying their livelihood strategies, savings of different types, building of assets, and investing in social capital that can be called on in times of hardship. Some communities have collective forms of informal insurance such as burial societies. As with savings, it is crucial that Micro-insurance products from financial institutions complement rather than undermine such systems.

Much concern has been expressed over badly designed Micro-insurance products that are being foisted on vulnerable people, particularly as a condition of loans in order to reduce risk for the institution. In some cases, Micro-insurance providers have collapsed, taking all the premiums with them. Several private insurers, particularly in parts of Africa, have become profitable by selling a substantial volume of policies to poor households. In many cases, the new policyholders did not understand what they were purchasing or how to make a claim, and they did not benefit. Wider questions emerge over whether poor people can or should be expected to spend scarce resources insuring themselves against all the risks of poverty caused by bad governance, poor state health systems, and environmental disasters arising from climate change and global warming. There is an inevitable mismatch between the range of hazards against which poor people need insurance and the level of premiums they are able to pay, which undermines the potential of insurance provision.

Debates about insurance also have specific gender dimensions: women are vulnerable in different ways. Gender inequality affects how women relate to institutions of all types, and women also face specific risks because of gender discrimination or cultural norms:

1. Unequal control of property makes women extremely vulnerable in cases of divorce or widowhood.
2. Gender differences in crops grown make women's crop and weather insurance needs different from those of men.
3. Women's lower incomes make them less able to invest in risk-reducing technology or services, such as disease-resistant strains of livestock, reliable equipment or veterinary care.

4. Women's responsibility to care for the sick means that the ill health of their children and partners affects their own ability to earn.
5. Women are more susceptible to certain diseases, including AIDS, and to the complications of pregnancy and childbirth.
6. Women's physical vulnerability makes their property particularly vulnerable to theft and crime.
7. Women's prevalence in informal-sector enterprises makes them particularly vulnerable to harassment by the authorities (for example, their property may be confiscated and market stalls destroyed).

All these risks point to the need for insurance products that decrease the vulnerability women face.

At the same time, they also face gender-specific constraints that present particular challenges for providers:

1. Women's lower incomes make them less able to afford insurance payments. While it may be very important for women to contribute to life and health insurance schemes for themselves and their husbands, insurance may not be the best solution where marriages are unstable. Women pay premiums, maybe out of heir own consumption and investment funds, maybe to insure loans that men use, and they risk forfeiting these premiums if they cannot maintain payments following divorce, or if they make unsuccessful claims following the death of their former partners.
2. In many cultures, women are less literate and physically less mobile than men. Unless these factors are taken into consideration, they may be less able to understand policy conditions and pursue claims. They may be deceived into taking up schemes that are not to their advantage and may be less able to take advantage

even of good insurance schemes without considerable follow-up by providers.

3. Insurance policies often explicitly exclude health concerns that apply to large numbers of women (pregnancy is one example), because they present too great a risk for insurers.
4. There are also gender challenges in insurance for men. For example, in polygamous households, which of the spouses should receive or pay for a husband's life insurance, and which spouse would benefit from his health insurance, or other types of insurance husbands may take out on household property.

These gender challenges point to the need for detailed market research to develop products that both respond to women's needs and are available at a price they can pay. Insurance should not be seen as a panacea, but part of a broader programme to address the underlying causes of risk and vulnerability facing poor women and men. While insurance is in high demand and some programmes have been successful among the better-off poor, it is doubtful that insurance can focus only on the needs of very poor people and remain financially sustainable. There is an inevitable trade-off between comprehensiveness of coverage and levels of premiums. The keys to success are the scale of out reach and attention to the diversity of clients and risks across the rural population. Some programmes, rather than attempting to provide insurance themselves, have linked with state insurance providers and the private sector, and have lobbied within the larger system for provision for poor people. Others are looking to group funds that provide emergency loans, linked to specific agreements with health care services. Depending on the context, these may provide a better option for very poor women, or part of a basket of options, in addressing some of the vulnerability they face.

Remittances

Remittance transfer services can contribute very significantly to poverty reduction and livelihood development. Remittances from migrant labourers between regions within countries and internationally have become a force for wealth creation, particularly in poorer regions. In 2006 it was estimated that at least US$300 billion would be sent home globally by some 200 million international migrants, both men and women. This sum is three times the amount of official development assistance (ODA) and superior to foreign direct investment. Even these high figures understate the importance of remittances, because they do not estimate such remittances sent through informal channels–which may be at least twice or three times the stated figures for some remittance corridors – and disregard domestic remittances. Nor are they an accurate predictor of what potential remittances might be if safe and cost-effective remittance services were available.

It is very important to develop cost-effective, formal services to transfer remittances through secure channels such as banks and other financial intermediaries. The remittance industry consists of formal and informal fund transfer agents. These range from a few global players, such as large money transfer operators (Western Union, MoneyGram) and commercial banks (Bank of America and ICICI Bank in India), to credit unions (including the World Council of Credit Unions) and hundreds of smaller agencies serving niche markets in specific geographic remittance corridors. Costs per transfer vary widely and often greatly surpass actual transfer costs in markets with little competition.

Various measures have been proposed or implemented to improve remittance services by money transfer operators, banks and others. Micro-finance and other smaller institutions generally have to enter into relationships with commercial banks because of regulatory constraints–for example, on transactions involving foreign exchange and access to national payment systems. However, no such constraints exist for remittances among areas in the same country. In India, for example, MFIs and NGOs have developed a number of remittance arrangements. Technological advances such as mobile phones also make cost-effective remittance services for poor people more possible.

Remittance flows are not gender neutral. Women are an increasing proportion of migrants, and in specific destination countries their numbers are growing faster than those of men. A recent study by the United Nations International Research and Training Institute for the Advancement of Women (INSTRAW) found that women represented almost half of the international migrant population. Women constitute 70–80 per cent of all migrants from some countries, notably the Philippines. The amount of money sent to households by migrant women and men, how it is sent and, specifically, how it is used are determined not only by the market, but also by the gendered power relations within households and economies.

Migration by women may bring about positive changes in gender inequalities. In some countries, women have better chances than men for good jobs in such sectors as service and health care. When women migrants send remittances home, they may significantly improve their individual standing in their families and communities, and men in the families left behind may be forced to take on women's care and work roles. When migration in a community is predominantly by women, this may also lead to community wide changes in perceptions of women's roles.

There are also gender differences in the effects of migration, and under other aspects women may benefit less than men. Women often have fewer employment options in the host country, are often limited to badly paid 'female' jobs, and thus are likely to earn lower incomes than men and have lower levels of remittances to send home. Some families place considerable pressure on women to migrate to support them, which, coupled with limited employment opportunities, can lead to abuses like sex trafficking and domestic slavery. Even where spouses both migrate, they frequently send remittances independently and for different purposes. Although this is not universally the case, women migrants (particularly independent ones) direct most of their remittances to their families' basic needs, while men spend more on personal expenditures.

Migration by men may increase women's decision-making power in the families and communities left behind. Women may become acting heads of households, with greatly increased control of household resources and decisions, and, in most cases, assume productive roles previously carried out by men. However, some women left behind may be highly dependent on male earnings and face high levels of material and emotional insecurity, as well as an increased workload. Women may have a very limited voice in, or be completely excluded from, decisions about how to invest community migrant funds. Negotiations between remitting and recipient wives and husbands may place a major strain on relationships. Security may also be a particular issue for women trying to access remittance payments if this involves travelling alone with large amounts of cash.

These gender differences for both migrants and recipients need to be taken into account in the design of remittance services that enable women to send money specifically to the people they wish to send it to (e.g. directly to children) or to safely access remittances sent to them. Development agencies working with migrants may set up Micro-finance services in the recipient communities to enable women to better use remittances for productive and economic activities, rather than for consumption. It will always be important for migrant associations to ensure that they do not discriminate against women and fully consult with them, as well as with men, in the design of services.

Demand-driven Product Development

There have been useful innovations in product design that promise to make products that are both more adapted to needs and more likely to benefit clients–and in a way that is financially sustainable. Recently, in recognition of some of the risks and benefits of the rapid expansion of financial services, there has been increasing emphasis on participatory market research to develop appropriate products. It is now generally accepted that such research and 'knowing your clients' is good business practice. The Self-Employed Women's Association (SEWA) in India has always consulted members on product development. Indeed, it originated in a participatory survey of women workers in the informal sector. The Grameen Bank has just undergone a four-year reassessment and redesign based on extensive client research, which has significantly increased its out reach and sustainability. ICICI Bank conducts participatory market research and also funds in-depth research on the needs of micro-finance clients through the Centre for Micro-finance Research in Chennai.

Of particular note has been the development of participatory market research tools by the capacity-building organisation Micro-save. Many Micro-finance organisations have been trained in and use variants of these tools. However, although they can be adapted to address gender issues and identify differences between women and men, this has not so far been done. For gender analysis, outcomes obviously must be disaggregated by gender. Disaggregation by other dimensions such as poverty level, ethnic background, age and marital status would render an even better idea of differences among women and among men. In many cultures, it is likely that women facilitators would be needed to work with women. Moreover, there is insufficient emphasis on the need to differentiate between designing products that vulnerable clients can be persuaded to buy and those that would really benefit them.

A critical part of ensuring that good product design and consumer protection principles become a reality is to promote financial literacy, so that clients are able to make an informed input into product development, know their rights, and understand the information provided. A number of financial literacy courses and methodologies have been developed. So far, financial literacy programmes have been developed mostly for women. However, financial literacy training for men could contribute significantly to changing men's attitudes and behaviour. If such training were a condition of access to loans, it is more likely that men would attend such courses rather than generic gender training.

Oxfam Novib – with partners LEAP, in the Sudan, and Green Home and Bukonzo Joint Savings, in Uganda – is developing an innovative, combined market research and financial literacy methodology.

Based on experience with the Gender Action Learning System (GALS) for working with people who cannot read and write, the underlying idea is that these tools can be used both as part of any organisation's market research process or on an ongoing basis by Micro-finance groups, themselves, as a continual process of participatory product development. At the same time, the tools are designed to increase participants' understanding of their situation and financial literacy and hence are an empowerment process in itself.

The 'livelihood road journeys' and 'trees' can be used as business plans and loan contracts with MFIs or even banks. In India, the Sudan and Uganda, groups now use some of these tools – with very little external supervision – to increase the poverty inclusion of their groups and develop their own livelihood plans. Individuals are also teaching the individual planning tools to others in their households and communities. Thus the methodology has the potential to be self-replicating and, once established, instead of being a cost to the organisation, could be an effective means of recruiting reliable new clients able to credibly communicate their own financial needs.

Participation and Macro-level Strategies

For some women, well-designed financial products delivered by a gender-aware organisation may be sufficient to significantly improve their livelihoods and help them change the gender inequalities that constrain achievement of their aspirations for themselves and their families. Evidence suggests that this is particularly the case for 'better-off' poor women and those in reasonably dynamic market contexts, where access to capital or safe savings facilities is the main constraint on economic activity, and where the political context is supportive of gender equality.

For many others, particularly poorer women, and even for women exporters and large-scale entrepreneurs, this is not the case. Even if rural finance increases women's access to financial services on a large scale, markets may become distorted or saturated with a narrow range of economic activities, and indebtedness may be high. Unless women's incomes increase, they are unlikely to find sufficient money for savings, insurance or other financial services. Unless there are investment opportunities in the local economy, women will probably not use remittance transfers to invest in local economic activities.

This means that rural Micro-finance services need to look beyond product design to find ways of increasing women's livelihood skills and empowerment. This does not necessarily mean adding on 'empowerment components' such as non-financial services and organisational development, although these also have their place. Even in minimalist organisations, there are ways of mainstream a gender equality and empowerment vision into existing core activities– again, at minimal cost beyond those of the initial design and an inception phase.

There has recently been renewed interest in the provision of other complementary services ('credit-plus', as it is often called). Rural Micro-finance is a cost-efficient means of delivering, or at least linking, a wide range of development interventions, as well as enhancing client–and hence organisational– financial sustainability. Apart from their savings-and-credit initiatives, many NGOs and an increasing number of MFIs provide a range of other, separately funded interventions for women and men.

There are a number of ways in which cost-efficient complementary services could be offered more effectively and sustainably:

1. Mutual learning and information exchange within groups could meet many basic training needs if systems are properly set up and funded initially. This training does not substitute for professional (and expensive) training, but it enables such training to be targeted to those areas where it is really needed, and it builds peoples' capacities to absorb, benefit from, and disseminate such training.

2 Implement a cross-subsidy: charge better-off clients (including men) for some services, such as business services and business registration, or charge clients for more advanced training after they have taken subsidised basic courses. GALS is made sustainable in Uganda through funding from cooperative funds.

3 Encourage loans for service provision by Micro-finance clients or larger private firms. Examples include loans to midwives and health practitioners to buy equipment to provide better service, or loans to set up child care facilities or waste management services on a commercial basis.

Financial institutions lacking the scope to introduce non-financial services themselves can collaborate with other service providers. By developing formal or informal links with providers of other services, Micro-finance programmes can increase their contribution at minimal cost and give providers of other services ready access to a sizeable, organised constituency of poor women, which would in turn contribute to the sustainability of their own services.

Inter-organisational collaboration between Micro-finance programmes and specialist providers of other types of services could take several forms. A Micro-finance programme could advertise complementary services available from other organisations, such as advice and information on legal rights offered by local women's movements. This could be done simply through putting leaflets on the counter for clients to read, or could take a more direct form of collaboration in promotion. A Micro-finance programme could refer clients to other organisations or make special arrangements for programmes, groups or individuals to pay for particular services. Collaboration could also take the form of sharing the costs of developing training programmes and innovations or conducting research. Any or all of these means could be combined to increase cost-effectiveness over time. For example, after an initial focus on identifying mutual learning possibilities, collaborating organisations could apply for donor funds to develop them. They could then introduce service charges for their better-off members or nonmembers at a later date. In other cases, although the Micro-finance services or programmes themselves may be financially sustainable, complementary services may need to be treated as ongoing commitments to be met through donor funding – especially when services are seeking to reach very poor women.

In many rural areas, particularly more remote areas with inadequate infrastructure, separating the delivery of financial services from other types of complementary support is not necessarily the most cost-efficient strategy, because it entails parallel sets of staff, high transport costs and duplication of other costs. The desirability or undesirability of separating functions needs to be judged on the basis of the particular context, the level of expertise required for the types of financial and non-financial services needed, and the capacity of particular organisations and staff. It is also possible to separate the costs of delivering different services without separating their operational delivery.

In all the above, it is vital to stress that gender equality of access and women's empowerment are not 'complementary' or 'credit-plus' as are literacy or business training. They are crosscutting strategies that must be mainstream through the delivery of financial services themselves and other complementary interventions. At the same time, gender mainstream measures must complement rather than substitute for gender-specific services, particularly women's rights training for women (and men), as well as legal and other support for women with very difficult household situations.

Participation and Collective Action

In Micro-finance programmes targeted at reducing poverty, group-based savings and credit have been seen as key innovations, combining efficiency with empowerment. Many types of group-based delivery have evolved, with varying degrees of control and function. For example, groups may be responsible for client identification, savings collection and loan dispersal, loan follow-up and repayment, mutual guarantees for loans, product design, more cost-effective service delivery, and pressuring peers to establish and maintain credit discipline. Most group-based Micro-finance programmes focus on women – or, conversely, most rural finance services directed at women are group-based MFIs. Rural cooperatives are an exception since membership is based on the assumption that households are headed by men. Rural financial institutions targeting men are much more likely to give loans to individuals, because experience suggests that men are generally less likely to favour group loans and group activities in general.

Although MFIs clearly benefit from providing savings and credit services to women's groups, the benefits for women are not so obvious. Groups can be a powerful force for change at the local level and for lobbying and advocacy at the national level, yet participation does not necessarily guarantee empowerment. Many rural finance programmes provide group-based services offering small loans, mostly to women, concurrently with services offering larger, individual loans, mostly to men. Men have other options and may not be interested in group-based finance. It is crucial to track gender differences in applications and subsequent approval for the whole range of financial services–and to take appropriate steps to ensure equal access for men and women if inequalities are found.

The benefits of economic collaboration should not be assumed. Collaboration needs to be based on a sound economic rationale, supported by appropriate management and technical training and assistance. Nor can it be assumed that groups add to women's networks or increase their access to information. For example, landless Arab women, often very constrained in the types of activity they can undertake outside the home, may nevertheless have extensive information networks of friends and kin. The pressures of saving and of repaying loans can strain existing friendship networks and exclude more disadvantaged women. Experience suggests that savings and credit groups frequently exclude the poorest people or women with household problems because they are seen as too great a financial risk. Exclusion may increase when MFIs channel funds through existing groups.

The issue of group liability (i.e. when members guarantee each other's loans) has been the subject of much debate. Mutual liability groups, particularly the Grameen model, were once widely promoted as a good mechanism for encouraging repayment and providing social collateral. In practice this strategy often proved counterproductive: if one member defaults and some others are unable or unwilling to cover the default, there is less incentive for any of the others to repay, because they will still not get a loan.

A programme that punishes poor people for unavoidable debt contradicts its broader development mission. It faces potentially costly social consequences, as well, in terms of negative brand image and reduced ability to attract new borrowers, particularly in competitive environments. Group liability also strengthens tendencies to exclude the poorest women. It is now widely accepted that it is better to build incentives for individuals into the design of the loan product (for example, the prospect of another loan or declining-balance interest rates) and to rely on general, social peer pressure rather than legal collective liability. Grameen itself has abandoned its original model, though it still promotes groups for other purposes.

When procedures to obtain and manage savings and credit are time-consuming, there may be little time left for the group to discuss other matters. Over time, women commonly reduce the length and frequency of group meetings to get on with other things. Groups do not automatically question gender roles and may simply replicate prevailing social hierarchies among women and between men and women.

Promoting strong, equitable and socially inclusive groups and federations requires time, energy and commitment from group members and programme staff. It requires specific skills and a careful balancing of member responsibilities with leadership. Participation and management become more difficult and complex as organisations grow in size. Women often need support, particularly in the form of information, organisational and leadership skills, and in the actual strategies they decide to employ. If all of this energy is focused on accessing financial services, little time remains for other activities and collective action.

Sometimes women are keen to develop their own financial associations, because they lack alternatives or they receive better, cheaper services than when they resort to distant, male staffed banks. In other contexts, it may be more empowering to link women (individually or in groups) with professional, woman-friendly financial services, and free women to focus on other issues, such as women's marketing associations or women's rights organisations. In some situations, gender relations may be challenged and changed more effectively by promoting mixed-sex organisations in which women's participation and authority are high. This cautionary message does not mean that savings and credit groups cannot make very valuable contributions to women's empowerment.

Savings and credit groups can provide an acceptable forum for women to come together to discuss gender issues and organise for change. For example, the women's groups of Zambuko Trust in Zimbabwe spontaneously invited a woman to give talks on "how to manage your husband and mother-in-law". In South Asia and Africa, Micro-finance groups have demonstrated their potential to promote change with respect to domestic violence, male alcohol abuse, and dowries.

A number of rural Micro-finance programmes have laid the basis for increasing women's ownership of land and their property rights, which are fundamental to women's ability to access and benefit from rural finance. In the financial sustainability literature, women's equal property rights are explicitly regarded as an essential part of the enabling environment for gender and Micro-finance. In addition to the development of specific products, such as Grameen Bank's housing loan and land leasing products, Micro-finance programmes have employed a number of strategies to support improvements in women's property ownership and rights through Micro-finance initiatives.

Thus rural finance programmes can provide a potentially large and organised grassroots base for developing advocacy and lobbying strategies around gender issues and for political mobilisation. Women's political participation is essential in making their collective voice heard in policy formation. Women's participation in group-based rural finance programmes can increase their awareness of wider political processes and their leadership capacities for participating in politics. By increasing the participation of half the population, rural finance programmes can significantly contribute to improving local governance and developing democratic systems.

In India, many organisations are involved in promoting women's leadership in local council bodies. SEWA, for example, promotes women's unions and organisations. Grameen Bank and other MFIs in Bangladesh disseminated voter education material to women through their organisation before the last elections. In Africa, CARE-Niger has been very effective in developing women's leadership to compete in local elections.

A number of Micro-finance programmes have developed other innovations to put women's groups at the forefront of citizenship development in rural areas. In India, Hand in Hand, Swayam Shikshan Prayog and ANANDI developed rural information centres to help women obtain information from the Internet and as a resource for the groups or clusters to generate income. Illiteracy no longer needs to be a barrier to using such facilities: software and technology can now make much information accessible through voice transmission, video and other formats. Despite support from numerous donors, however, many information centres remain under used for lack of community organisation and training, or they are dominated by male youth (in some places for down loading pornography). When managed by women's SHGs or cluster organisations, the centres often provide effective services to the community.

More careful consideration should be given to the levels and types of decisions for which women's participation is needed in order to strengthen their empowerment, to decide who should participate, and the types of participation that can be most empowering. It is important to be clear about the potential costs and benefits for women and to have a participatory process for identifying the actual costs and benefits and the best ways forward.

Groups and programmes do not need to be women-only to help bring about change. Involving men can avoid unnecessary gender conflict and enable women to be more open about their needs and aspirations in the wider community. Male support can be encouraged by developing new male role models and men's networks for change. There are significant opportunities for change in mixed programmes in which men staff work on gender issues with men, and women leaders bring women's concerns before a male organisation. Some mixed programmes have very effectively organised men alongside women to address domestic violence and abandonment of women. In women-only programmes, men can be invited to some women's meetings, provided they do not dominate. Mixed programmes also require a participatory process to establish internal norms for promoting gender equality in leadership positions.

Participation does not need to be group-based. Many rural finance programmes use participatory tools for consulting clients and members – for example, for market research, programme design and participatory monitoring and evaluation. Especially in cooperatives and self-managed programmes, there are well-established systems for participatory decision-making. Many MFIs originally started as NGOs that saw themselves at the cutting edge of participatory methodologies. Banks and the private sector now view participation as good management practice for responding to clients in a competitive marketplace.

Contemporary management literature liberally refers to 'empowering' staff to enable them to contribute their knowledge and expertise to improve products and the organisation itself. An organisation that possesses strong structures enabling everyone to contribute ideas can become an efficient learning organisation, capable of responding rapidly to changing market realities. A common strategy to facilitate such learning is participatory market research. As the supply of rural finance increases, flexibility and learning will be crucial if programmes are to survive and contribute to development.

Promoting Gender-equitable Rural Micro-finance

There are a range of potential measures that organisations such as IFAD can take at the meso and macro levels to promote an enabling environment for rural Micro-finance that also makes a significant contribution to gender equality and women's empowerment. A particularly important role is the collation of information and exchange of experience on gender innovations. Many of the more costly non-financial services, for example financial literacy, might be better offered through a network of providers, and there is a need to collect comparative information on gender access and impact from various types of providers in order to assess the best strategies. It is also important that these good practices, and women's own strategies and perspectives, move from being marginal gender 'specialists' to being an integral part of mainstream training for bankers and other staff–essential as they are to ensuring that over half the potential Micro-finance clients benefit from their services. The implication for donors such as IFAD of all these institutional possibilities is that they will most likely need to draw on gender expertise in organisational gender audit and training if they are to help the organisation identify the most efficient and effective ways of implementing strategies such as those outlined above. Ideally, this would involve a set of agreed organisational gender indicators and the introduction of a gender rating system capable of differentiating;

1. Partners and projects at the forefront on innovation on gender, which could provide examples to others;
2. Those open to change but that do not yet have capacity and thus require capacity-building;
3. And those not interested in change.

Over time, a decision would need to be made as to whether to continue to fund the last, as their development contribution is likely to be far less than the other two.

Development agencies such as IFAD operate not only by promoting and supporting rural financial institutions and stockholder participation, but also by promoting a conducive policy and regulatory environment. Enabling and promoting the above gender strategies requires gender equity to be mainstream at this macro level – in regulatory frameworks, the advocacy strategies of Micro-finance networks, and other supporting interventions.

First, if all Micro-finance institutions promoted by development agencies were required, or at least encouraged, to mainstream gender equity in some of the ways discussed above, this would go a long way not only towards increasing gender equality of access, but also towards facilitating a conducive environment for women's empowerment. If members of Micro-finance networks and banks promoted a vision of women's empowerment in promotional materials, *advertising and interactions with their millions of clients*, this would be a significant contribution not only to the empowerment of their clients, but also to changing attitudes towards women's economic activities and social roles in the community and internationally.

Second, as products and competitors proliferate in the Micro-finance market, a recent concern has been consumer protection: do people know what it is they are signing, and how can they be protected from abuse? A number of prominent Micro-finance networks have now agreed on consumer protection guidelines.

Third, rural finance institutions and banks are increasingly concerned with their impact on local and national economies, both in terms of market distortion and environmental sustainability. There has been increasing interest in value chain finance from donors and institutions in order to better target credit to those parts of the value chain that can best promote increased production, incomes and employment. Most value chain analysis and development has so far been gender blind, with the likely outcome of further marginalising women. Thus it is crucial that gender issues are fully mainstream in this new development. However, there *are* ways of doing so.

Finally, many Micro-finance networks are involved in advocacy on issues affecting the sector. Gender issues are rarely part of this advocacy–despite early recognition of the importance of changing property legislation to enable women to take real advantage of sustainable financial services. There is a need for these networks to include lobbying and advocacy on issues such as women's property rights, informal-sector protection, and violence, which affect their clients and thus sustainability, as well as the whole development process.

8

Decentralised Rural Governance

Panchayat is a nomenclature associated with rural life in India from time immemorial. It continued to survive with bureaucratic support in the colonial period, but with very little power, authority and activity. The several efforts to bring it back to the democratic process of the country after the inauguration the Indian republic in 1950 did not take firm root. However, since 1992, following the 73rd constitutional amendment Panchayats have acquired a new meaning as "institutions of local self-government" with the specific task to prepare and implement "plans for economic development and social justice". Many have perceived this *new constitutional change as heralding a third stratum of* government in Indian federal polity.

Local governments have no relevance if they are not responsive, transparent, participatory and accountable to the people and in the Indian context, the most deprived sections of society such as the dalits, tribals, fisher folk and women. Quite often, it is said that 'politics is about power'. Yes, but democratic politics is and should be about bringing power down to the people or empowering them. Decentralisation therefore may be defined as the empowerment of the local population through the empowerment of local governments, (LGs). It is here that the politics of democratic decentralisation assumes relevance. Kerala has been widely acknowledged as a state that has progressed in promoting local democracy and decentralised planning far outdistancing all other Indian states.

Panchayat Amendment

This section seeks to review the 73rd Constitutional Amendment, which we may call Panchayat amendment under three sub-heads: (a) Salient features of the 73rd Constitutional Amendment (CA); (b) A critical review of the state conformity acts passed by all the State Assemblies and which seek to implement the constitutional mandate; and (c) A brief evaluation of decentralised planning and local democracy in Kerala. In all these reviews, interalia answering the following questions are given importance. How far can the Panchayats succeed in institutionalising local democracy? Are the LGs empowered, responsive, participatory, transparent and accountable? How far has decentralisation helped to reduce poverty understood in the broad sense of "capability deprivation"?

Some important features of the Panchayat amendment are given below:

1. A key role is assigned to the gram sabha, 'the assembly of the citizen voters' as a deliberative and deciding body. In this manner an element of direct democracy is introduced at the lowest level. That is one way to broaden downward accountability as well.
2. An uniform three-tier structure across the country with the Village, Block (intermediate) and District as appropriate levels.
3. Direct election at all levels is made regular and mandatory. An independent State Election Commission is established for superintendence, direction and control of the electoral process and preparation of electoral rolls as well as to conduct five yearly elections.

4. In all the *Panchayats*, seats are to be reserved for SCs and STs (Scheduled Castes or Dalits and Scheduled Tribes) in proportion to their population. One third of the total seats is to be reserved for women. One-third positions of presidents of Panchayats at all levels also will be reserved for women. Obviously these are ways to empower the under privileged.

5 For assigning expenditure responsibilities to the Panchayati Raj Institutions (PRIs) an illustrative list of 29 subjects are mentioned in the XIth schedule of the constitution. This list of functional assignments is prepared to identify the areas for planning for economic development and social justice. Each state legislature is required to make, not only functional devolutions keeping the list as illustrative guidelines, but also to provide adequate power and authority to the PRIs to enable them to function as 'institutions of local self-government'.

6. Setting up of a State Finance Commission once in five years to review the financial position of the local governments and to make suitable recommendations to the state on the distribution of funds among Panchayats.

These and several other features derived from the Panchayat amendment have the potential to alter the character of the two-tier federal polity of India significantly. The constitution defines Panchayats as "institutions of self-government" [Article 243 (d)] and requires the state legislature to create such institutions. Tremendous political opportunities emerge from the extension of participatory democracy through the institutions of village Panchayat, Gram sabha, affirmative provisions for dalits, advises (tribals), women and so on. Real improvement in the self-esteem of the vulnerable sections of society can come only through a process of meaningful participation. The nature of the accountability arrangements is also expected to move downward to the people rather than to the bureaucratic superior officers. The efficient use of local resources through decentralised spatial planning mandated in the constitution is an important means to promote economic development. Enhancing the quality of public service delivery, be it primary school, primary health care, drinking water supply, sanitation and so on can be ensured only through citizen's involvement and participation. This is an important means to promote horizontal equity in a country known for its widespread disparities in the level of endowment and development.

The potential for democratising development and governance in rural India depends not only on the historical background of the state, the political will and approach towards decentralisation, but also on the details of the conformity legislation enacted and the manner in which it is sought to be implemented by each state. One of the serious mistakes of the 73rd and 74th Amendments has been the wide discretion given in the Constitution to each state legislature in shaping the conformity act and rules thereof. Considerable latitude has been given in regard to the revenue and expenditure assignments of local governments. The most prominent is the discretion given to the states to "endow the *Panchayats* with such powers and authority as may be necessary to enable them to function as institutions of self-government". On this and several other vital aspects regarding planning, maintenance of accounts, and their audit, and so on, 'may' predominates in the constitution. The diversity and weakness in the content and character of the conformity legislation in the country could be traced to this 'original sin' committed in the two Amendments. Moving the 73rd Amendment in the Lok Sabha on December 1, 1992, the then Minister of State for Rural Development said: "The Constitution Amendment Bill casts a duty on the Centre as well as the states to establish and nourish the village Panchayats so as to make them effective self governing institutions". Indeed, the public discourse on democratic decentralisation in India today after over a decade of this Act should keep posing the question whether the village Panchayats in India are self-governing institutions or not? Have the Centre and States worked sincerely "to establish and nourish the village Panchayats"? This is what we try to answer in what follows.

Conformity Acts and their Working

Democratic decentralisation is neither deconcentration nor delegation. It is *devolution.* A Task Force on Decentralisation of the government of India (GOI) defines devolution thus:

> *"Devolution in the context of the Panchayats, means that when the authority in respect of a specific activity is transferred from the state to the local governments, the latter should have the prerogative of taking decisions in respect of planning and implementation of such activity. In fact functions, funds and functionaries are complementary to one another in the process of devolution of responsibilities and powers upon the Panchayats".*

Here local governance is seen as an integral element of the federal system and involves devolution of functions, funds and functionaries to Panchayats. A perusal of the Conformity Acts of the major states in India leads one to the firm conclusion that no state except Kerala has devolved powers and resources. Actually several state conformity acts use languages such as the 'state may by notification' or 'subject to such rules as may be made from time to time', 'the government may alter' and the like. These undoubtedly are overriding powers that will render ineffective the process of building self-governing democratic institutions at the sub-state level. A few specific comments based on the conformity Acts are noted below.

One, for devolution to happen the three F's functions, funds and functionaries should be transferred simultaneously as explicitly noted in the Government of India definition cited above. With the exception of Kerala, the progress made has been halting, piecemeal and in several cases retrograde. Even in Kerala, the progress in regard to administrative autonomy leaves many things to be desired. Creating an efficient bureaucracy or administrative set up responsive to the rural society is an issue that is side-lined by all states.

There is very little autonomy statutory because functional assignments are permissive. Andhra Pradesh, Assam, Bihar, Gujarat, Haryana, Orissa, Punjab and Uttar Pradesh are prominent examples. Even in West Bengal widely hailed as a good case of decentralisation, the PRIs (Panchayati Raj Institutions) function more as agents of the state government than as autonomous institutions. Although Bihar's Panchayat Act, 1993 is generous in assigning several functions to the PRIs, it is "subject to such conditions as may be prescribed from time to time". Moreover the Bihar Act defines the Zilla Parishad as a superior body over the Gram Panchayats (GPs) endowed with power to suspend the executive orders of GPs. Even Gujarat with a long tradition of PR system "has not been very successful in providing to its village level institutions, the functional and financial autonomy which is integral to self governance". While erosion of autonomy is bad enough, the worst cases are those states where the PRIs continue to be dominated by MPs (Members of Parliament) and MLAs (members of legislative assembly).

Two, the GPs in several states are not adequately strengthened financially and technically to deliver even some of the basic services not to speak of the developmental responsibilities under the new dispensation. In some states civic services which traditionally belonged to the Panchayats like street lighting, provision of drinking water supply, sanitation and drainage, primary health care and the like have not been entrusted to them. Instead, some of these services are provided by the state departments. In Haryana, GPs practically deal with only drinking water and construction and maintenance of roads to the exclusion of all others.

Three, because almost all the 29 subjects assigned to PRIs are state-concurrent, there is need for role clarity to avoid duplication and overlapping. While any effort to strengthen the reach and quality of basic services through GPs is to be welcomed, unless there is clear role clarity as between the state on the one hand and the three-tiers on the other in regard to functional assignments, decentralisation can only result in more confusion, delay in implementation and add to the difficulties in evolving an efficient transfer system. Several states have repeated the 29 subjects *mentioned in the Panchayat amendment* as functions of all the three tiers. Only a few states like Andhra Pradesh, Kerala, Gujarat and Madhya Pradesh (MP) have broken the 29 subjects into activities and sub-activities. Clear functional mapping is a necessary condition to ensure efficient decentralisation.

Four, PRIs in most states have ignored the constitutional mandate to plan for 'economic development and social justice'. Kerala, Himachal Pradesh, Madhya Pradesh, Bihar and West Bengal have statutory recognised this. But in no state except in Kerala this important mandate has been made into a detailed bottom up planning process. In Madhya Pradesh, the task of planning and implementation of schemes for economic development and social justice has been given to 'district governments' created by delegating various powers and responsibilities of the state to District Planning Committees (DPCs) and calling them subordinate agencies of the government for this purpose. It is difficult to consider this process as bottom up planning. In Bihar, the statute gives powers to the Zilla Parishad to plan for economic development and social justice. But this power remains only in the statute books. West Bengal assigns the Gram Sansad the responsibility to guide GP in regard to planning for economic development and social justice. But in reality, West Bengal too has very little bottom up planning. In Karnataka, PRI planning continues to be "essentially a top down process".

Five, there are multiple channels of transferring resources to PRIs. Some of them work as parallel agencies (e.g. District. Rural Development Agency) transgressing the functional domain of PRIs. According to the Planning Commission, the share of Centrally Sponsored Schemes (CSSs) in the plan budget of Central Ministries has currently increased to 70 percent against 30 percent in the early 1980s. In addition to the CSSs, there are 26 sectoral programmes falling under the 29 subjects of the XIth schedule which the Central Ministries handle. The state governments are also equally guilty of this transgression game. The Janmabhoomi, the Village Education Committee, Economic Restructuring Project and the like handled by the Andhra Pradesh Government, have virtually marginalised the PR regime of the state. The Gram Vikas Samitis of Haryana, the Joint Forest Management Committees of Gujarat, Rajasthan's Watershed Programme, the Water Use Groups and Site Implementation Committees of Uttar Pradesh and the District Government in Madhya Pradesh are other cases to be specially mentioned in this context. Multiple channels of resource flow can only lead to inefficient planning, duplication, corruption and waste of resources, besides undermining the effectiveness of democratic decentralisation.

Six, turning to tax assignments, the pattern of pre 73rd Amendment regime has been repeated in a large number of states. No state seems to have anticipated the expanding needs of decentralised governance and made appropriate changes in the revenue assignments to local bodies. The intermediate and district Panchayats are not given substantial taxing powers. Only GPs are endowed with taxing powers. The number of taxes assigned to GPs ranges from two in Tamil Nadu to twelve in Andhra Pradesh and Gujarat. By and large, the tax base covers property, persons and business. The taxes assigned to GPs generally are not elastic or productive. Even where several taxes are assigned, the autonomy of the PRIs in exercising them is considerably restricted by rules, restrictions and conditions.

Seven, probably the most important aspect in deepening local democracy relates to strengthening the Gram Sabha. Most legalisation authorise the Gram Sabha only to "consider" "examine" "discuss" the budgets, audited reports etc. States like Andhra Pradesh, Karnataka and Madhya Pradesh authorise gram sabha to review programmes of work current or new. The Kerala Panchayat (Amendment) Act, 1999 has empowered Gram Sabhas (every ward has a gram sabha) in regard to planning, selection of schemes and beneficiaries and so on, besides giving authority to "scrutinise" budget, accounts and the like. Quarterly meetings of gram sabhas are mandatory in Kerala. The gram sabhas are not made the kingpin of local democracy in most other states.

In brief, the statutory framework created for local democracy in India leaves many things to be desired. Kerala stands head and shoulders above all other states in creating a proper legal framework with enabling provisions for local democracy and decentralisation to function. The above criticisms, however should not make us to ignore the fact that the 73rd Amendment has endeavoured to fill a major institutional vacuum in rural governance in India. How the opportunities provided are made use of is a matter of democratic practice as well. In the country as a whole, there are 231,630 gram Panchayats, with over 2.4 million elected representatives. In 77,210 Gram Panchayats women are presidents. At the intermediate level, there are 5912 Block Panchayats with 1970 women heads. Of the 594 Zilla Parasites or district level Panchayats, about 200 have women presidents. Including the urban local bodies, there are about three million elected representatives out of which one million women occupy positions as members or heads – a unique world record. The SC/ST functionaries are over 6,60,000. It is important to note that several micro studies conducted in different parts of India show that women representatives belong to the lower socioeconomic strata. Although the number of local level representatives is large, the women and SC/ST representatives face formidable objections from the upper castes and vested interests throughout the country. The pages of the *Panchayati Raj Update* of the Institute of Social Sciences which has been reporting monthly the progress in every state during the last decade are replete with stories of atrocities against and killings of dalits, advises and women who got elected in the two Panchayat elections.

According to one study "Illiteracy, poverty, the hostility of caste Hindus and above all noncooperative and extremely unsympathetic government officials counter effective dalit participation in Panchayati raj institutions". It is also important to note that re-distributive land reforms which is a necessary condition for social equity and meaningful participation has failed in India except in Kerala and West Bengal. Despite the innumerable constraints, the situation is not definitely hopeless. While there are 'proxy' Panchayat women presidents, there are all women Panchayats as well. There are innumerable cases where the traditionally disadvantaged groups assume the responsibility for supervising as well as implementing the programmes relating to health, education, shelter, antipoverty programmes etc, besides fighting evils like alcoholism, violence against women and local crimes, Baviskar, Mohanty *et al*, Poornima and Vinod Vyasalu among others.

As regards the linkage between decentralised government and poverty reduction, the correlation is not automatic. Several studies point out that there has been rapid decline in rural poverty in West Bengal due to the PRIs which have created a production-friendly environment in agriculture and cooperation in implementing the antipoverty programmes of the Central and State government and so on. Providing security of tenure to 4 million assets-poor households through land reforms is something to write home about. Even so, it is important to point out that the performance of West Bengal in building the capabilities of rural people leave many things to be desired especially in the matter of elementary education and primary health care. West Bengal also failed to provide autonomous space to Panchayats via clear functional mapping, untied funds and independent tax assignments. In short, we can say from the West Bengal's experience that PRIs bear potential for poverty reduction but the linkage is not automatic. The nature and magnitude of this depends a great deal on the empowering process and policy initiatives of the state government concerned. Indian democracy can succeed only by removing the powerlessness of the common people through bottom up participatory planning. Support guidelines and policy initiatives by the higher level of governments should be complementary to help this process.

Features of Decentralised Democracy in Kerala

The real watershed in Kerala's decentralisation process and planning begins from mid-1996 when the Left Democratic Front Government that came to power in May 1996 took several landmark initiatives and measures to transform the relations between local government and society. They took to a campaign mode called the People's Plan Campaign (PPC) for the ninth Five-Year Plan. The United Democratic Front (UDF) government which came to power in May 2001 abandoned the campaign mode. We may outline the salient features of the decentralisation planning framework that has evolved since mid-1996 in the state.

The Left Democratic Front Government which came to power in May 1996, took the momentous decision to devolve 35-40 percent of the State Plan funds to the local bodies as against 2.35 percent during the Eighth Plan. This massive fiscal decentralisation is characterised as a 'big bang' approach. Each local body was required to prepare a comprehensive area plan before it could lay claim to this plan fund. The underlying objective of the people's plan initiative was to rally behind the local governments, the bureaucracy, the technocracy and the people.

The decision to devolve a big plan share of plan funds to LSGs was followed up by a series of legislative amendments to the Kerala Panchayat Act, 1994 and Kerala Municipal Act 1994 and institutional reforms (most of them recommended by the Committee on Decentralisation of Powers, popularly called Sen Committee) that virtually sought to provide functions, finance and functionaries – along with autonomy and powers to the local government. In the words of the Sen Committee:

> *"Local self-government is essentially the empowerment of the people by giving them not only the voice, but the power of choice as well, in order to shape the development they feel is appropriate to their situation. It implies maximum decentralisation of powers to the elected bodies to function as autonomous units with adequate power, authority and resources to discharge the basic responsibility of bringing about 'economic development and social justice".*

Based on the principle of subsidiarity, Kerala has divided the functions of the various tiers of the rural and urban local governments into activities and sub activities. Compared to other states this is an important milestone in the progress of decentralisation process in the country in ensuring role clarity and functional autonomy.

All the expenditure responsibilities dealing with poverty alleviation and all state-sponsored and centrally sponsored schemes for poverty alleviation are transferred to the newly created three-tiered PRIs, notably to the village Panchayats. The state government's role is now limited to monitoring and capacity building. This is not the case in the other states in India.

Planning was used as an "instrument of social mobilisation" during the People's Plan Campaign. This is very much in the public action tradition of Kerala.

The plan entitlement of each local government is decided according to a formula with sixty percentage weight age on population, and a one third weight age to backwardness to bring in an equalisation element besides some incentive for tax efforts.

A detailed methodology of decentralised planning, from needs identification by the Gram Sabha to final approval by the District Planning Committee needed for administrative sanction in implementing projects, had been drawn up by the State Planning Board. Local planning in Kerala involves a multi-stage process that has broadened the avenues of people's participation. Obviously, the intent in creating a multi-stage process is to provide participatory spaces for the citizens, local elected representatives and officials to discuss the development projects. The key institutions involved in local planning besides the local government are the gram sabhas, development seminars, and the task forces. The process begins in the gram sabhas – specially called for the purpose – which deliberate and determine local development needs and priorities. Based on the priorities of the gram sabhas and based on the analysis of the primary and secondary data collected, a detailed development report is prepared for each gram Panchayat. A development seminar is organised at the Panchayat level in which experts, elected members, representatives of gram sabha, and wider public participate. The development seminar helps to concretes further the problems and needs of the Panchayat. On the basis of this, duly constituted Task Forces prepare projects with the help of experts and the bureaucracy. The local plan is prepared incorporating these projects. The size of the plan depends on the local resources which the local body can raise (own source revenue, beneficiary contribution, voluntary contribution etc) and the plan grants from the state and the Centre (by way of Centrally Sponsored Schemes). The plans thus formulated are consolidated with the higher-level plans (block and district level) during which all projects are vetted for technical and financial viability.

For purposes of implementing projects without leakages and corruption, committees of beneficiaries with representation for women and scheduled castes are sought to be created. The process is important not only because of the wide opportunities provided for people's participation, but also for reducing the power and domination of an entrenched bureaucracy which generally support the rent-seeking interests rather than improving the community's welfare. It may be noted that all other institutional innovations created such as the right to information, citizen's charter, transparency guarantees, Ombudsman, Appellate Tribunal, Performance Audit and so on are also designed to deepen democracy and accountability to the people. Right to information is made a statutory right. This is a powerful step against corruption. Every Panchayat has to draw up as per the statutes a citizen's charter specifying the quality of services a citizen is entitled to from the Panchayat. This is another important measure to ensure downward accountability. The Ombudsman created to hear complaints from panchayts and people and without whose approval no action against a Panchayat by the state government is possible helps to promote local democracy.

Besides strengthening the traditional audit system through Local Fund Audit Department, a special concurrent audit system called Performance Audit system has been instituted to serve as a mid-course corrective and guiding mechanism to put the fledging systems of local governments in proper place. As part of PPC, considerable attention was given to what has come to be called social audit. Basically, social audit as it came to be experimented in Kerala refers to the evaluation of the quality, fund utilisation, punctuality in observing time schedule and general performance of the project works of local governments through beneficiary committees and further by the Gram Sabha.

Criteria-based selection of beneficiaries is another significant feature of Kerala's decentralisation. This is ensured through clear enunciation of eligibility and prioritisation criteria, application in writing, awarding of marks to each criterion, reading out of marks in Gram Sabha/Ward Sabha meetings and so on.

The devolution of over one-third of state plan funds to local governments as untied grant gives them considerable autonomy. But it is subject to the condition that 40 percent of the Plan allocation is spent on productive sectors, 10 percent for women-related projects called Women Component Plan (WCP) and that no more than 30 percent be spent on infrastructure. The emphasis on building the production base especially of the agricultural sector is particularly important, given the long-standing stagnation the agricultural sector of Kerala. The plan allocation specially earmarked for scheduled castes and tribes [called Special Component Plan (SCP) and Tribal Sub Plan (TSP)] administered by bureaucracy are now passed on to the local self-governments and involve SC/ST representatives.

The village Panchayats which interact with the Gram Sabha and which alone have revenue-raising powers among the rural local bodies are given more functions and resources (70%of rural share of plan as against 15% each to the block and district Panchayats). The gram sabha is strengthened and empowered legally. It is mandated that the GS meets at least four times a year. Every ward has a gram sabha whose functions range from expressing the local needs and fixing plan priorities to supervising projects. For the first time in India, the Gram Panchayats have started to make their own plans and that too with considerable involvement of the people.

A massive capacity building exercise in a cascading fashion (involving 600 Key Resources Persons (KRP's) at the state level, 10,000 District Resource Persons (DRPs) at the district/block level and 100,000 resources persons at the local level (LRPs)) has been launched under the Kerala Institute of Local Administration (KILA). With the abolition of the campaign process, this corps also disappeared.

Availability of internal resources is one of the basic conditions for successful decentralised governance and autonomy. Relatively speaking, Kerala has a strong own resource base. That Kerala Panchayats on an average raise a per capita own revenue (taxes and non-tax revenue) of Rs.57 compared to less than one rupee in Uttar Pradesh and Rs.16 in Karnataka where decentralisation ostensibly made headway.

This shows that Kerala has considerable local choice. Given the fact that only 40 percent of the tax potential of Kerala is tapped, there is immense scope for local choice in Kerala and expanding the plan size.

The active association of local governments with Kudumbasree, the State Poverty Eradication Mission, which is a poor women-oriented self-help group initiative against poverty has taken the antipoverty efforts from a project approach to a holistic process approach. Apart from the women-oriented Community Based Organisations (CBOs) associated with the Kudumbashree, as part of the People's Plan initiative, CBOs including all households (poor as well as non-poor) have been started in some GPs as part of its social mobilisation and social auditing effort. They were formed in order to get involved in the selection of beneficiaries, cultural activities, projects like education, health, drinking water and promotion of village level unity and so on.

Decentralised Planning: A Critical Evaluation

It is çlear from the above discussion that Kerala's decentralised planning and decentralisation initiatives have features that foster democracy definitely way ahead of the other Indian states. But what has been the progress on the ground? We adduce below certain macro and micro level evidences that help to answer this question.

One of the reasons for the larger devolution of plan funds to the PRIs and the insistence by the State Planning Board to devote a minimum of 40 percent of them to productive sectors was largely to remove the stagnation in agriculture and help to build the material base of the economy.

A larger devolution to the local governments, especially to the Gram Panchayats (70 percent of rural share) should increase the output of the agricultural and allied sectors more than the others. John and Chathukulam examine how far the productive sector in the local areas have triggered economic growth. Empirical evidences adduced by the authors show that the Panchayats they studied followed more a redistributes strategy than a productivity-based intervention. Several other field studies also corroborated this.

K.N Jayan's study which covers 18 agricultural projects implemented during the period from 1998-99 through 200001 in the Vaikkom Gram Panchayat (Kottayam district) is important because it examines each project proposal, the process of decision-making, implementation and the final outcome. Categorising the productive sector projects as (a) individual – based (target beneficiaries are individuals), (b) institution based (target beneficiaries are a group of persons) and (c) common property resource-based (target is improvement /maintenance of a common property resource), the author brings out the great chasm between the objectives (quite often unduly exaggerated) and final outcome. The Task Force on Agriculture formulating ambitious or ill-conceived projects, the voluntary technical personnel making indifferent scrutiny, the direct beneficiaries turning inactive, the officialdom which is supposed to provide quality inputs and timely advice becoming unresponsive and the people's representatives not monitoring, a wide gap between objectives and outcome was observed. What the author concludes about the project on equipment for fishermen groups is relevant for several others as well. "The objective of the project was vaguely written 'to increase fish production' and 'to reduce poverty among fishermen'. Panchayat took no initiative in detecting whether the objectives are fulfilled or not".

Another evaluative study on selected agricultural projects in 1998-99 by Prema (undated) in three Panchayats in the Malappuram district (Amarambalam in Nilambur Block, Thirurangadi in Thirurangadi block and Kottakkal in Malappuram block) reports that most of the agricultural projects related to paddy cultivation, vegetable gardening, coconut improvement, banana cultivation and soil conservation. 83 percent of the beneficiaries interviewed by the author reports that due to the implementation of the projects under people's plan, they could bring more area under cultivation and could take to double cropping (e.g. the vegetable production schemes of the Panchayats utilised the paddy summer fallows; irrigation and drainage projects indirectly helped in bringing hitherto uncultivated / abandoned land under cultivation). While the farmers in Amarambalam were unanimous in saying that the area under paddy has not increased in their Panchayat, they all agreed that productivity has increased. The farmers in all the three GPs reported that the lack of technical services and timely supply of inputs have affected the farming operations significantly. After examining all the crop sector projects from 1997-2000 the author concludes that the majority of the projects were individual beneficiary centred. One of the important lacunae reported is that most of the projects had no forward and backward linkages. [A. Prema]. Even though there were several projects under the People's Plan, 75 percent of the sample farmers have rated them as 'good' and 17 percent 'very good' with none reporting them 'bad'. The social rate of participation defined as those who have attended all the gram sabha meetings ranges from 45.9 percent in Amarambalam to 67.7 percent in Kottakkal.

The study of Nalini Nayak *et al* on the wetland resources of Madayi, Mattool, Cherukunnu, Ezhome and Kunhimangalam Panchayats of Northern Kerala shows that PRIs were not involved in the innumerable problems faced by those engaged in farming, fishing and matmaking. Construction of ponds and reclamation of wetlands for establishing modern farms have not only encroached the common property resources but have created havoc through bringing about massive land use changes as well. Introduction of modern shrimp farms raises the question of local land use priorities which alter the land use patterns in the long run, apart from alienating the local population from the life support system of the area. The decline in the extent of mangroves and the changes of shoreline environments have not attracted the attention of the Panchayats in the area despite "the people's participation" in local planning.

Nair and Kumar hypothesise that beneficiaries' participation is a crucial determinant in the sustainability of the development projects implemented under the PPC and verifies this hypothesis by selecting 20 projects from a sample frame of 45 projects implemented in 15 GPs and 5 BPs (Block Panchayats) in the Thiruvananthapuram district. The sample frame was fixed after eliminating all minor projects costing less than Rs. 200,000 in GPs and Rs.300,000 in BPs and construction projects like roads, bridges, school building etc as well as unfinished projects. Only 15 out of the 20 sample projects had "some participation by the beneficiaries at some activity stage or other". Beneficiary participation in none of the 15 projects fulfilled the threefold criteria of genuine participation measurement used by the authors viz. Exercising some decision-making authority, realising some empowerment and enjoying a limited sense of ownership. Of the 15 participatory projects, beneficiaries' participation was genuine and active only in six. In seven other projects participation was mostly passive and mobilised by the Panchayats after formulating the projects. In two other cases participation was only notional. Not only that there were serious lapses in some of the sample projects, the productive outcome too was equally unsatisfactory. Based on "unrealistic and highly exaggerated" estimates, a project costing Rs.1.3 million ended with no outcome at all. Besides corruption and indifferent cooperation by the beneficiaries, outright thefts were also reported. Out of five irrigation projects, only two succeeded in producing concrete results. As the authors conclude:

> *"Faulty formation of projects, dependency syndrome, interference on political or parochial interests, and Panchayat's decision to blindly follow the governmental*

> *guidelines without proper investigation about its appropriateness and feasibility are among the major causes for this sad state of affairs. We conclude that in a majority of the social development projects taken up under the people's planning in Kerala, there was no genuine or effective participation by the beneficiaries. The sustainability of the projects would have improved with genuine or effective participation".*

The field reports cited above relate to the productive sectors and people's participation. As regards the impact of decentralisation on poverty, there are some reported evidence which affirms that the overall impact of decentralisation on poverty has been positive. S.M Vijayanad a former Local Administration secretary and currently planning secretary is highly positive about the linkage between decentralisation and poverty when he says:

> *"The experience of the first few years of decentralisation has proved that in providing basic minimum needs, infrastructure like housing, water supply, sanitation and connectivity, the local governments have performed creditably. The speed and extent of coverage as well as efficiency in providing minimum needs has been superior to that of the state government. It is pertinent to note that funds spent on poverty reduction programmes by local governments significantly exceed earlier investments. This is suggestive of the higher priority given to antipoverty programmes by local governments. The spread of this investment is also much broader and generally more equitable".*

Although this is an official view, the observation that the local governments have been more efficient than the state government in poverty alleviation is something to be taken note of. By and large, official statistics suggest that the infrastructure facilities of government schools, Anganwadis, hospitals, rural libraries etc. Have improved. In places where the beneficiary committees worked well, they have effectively helped to conserve resources and improve the quality of services to the people. Another major area of achievement is in regard to housing. The official records show that nearly 4,98,000 new houses were constructed (this does not include 1,88,000 houses repaired) and that over 31 percent of these had gone to SC and ST categories. The projects relating to women (women component plan) according to several observers leave many things to be desired. A KSSP publication notes: "most of the projects coming under the women component plan were silly and make a mockery of the concept behind it". Actually the best part of the people's campaign is that it promoted a development culture where the scheduled castes, scheduled tribes and women have turned from being recipients of beneficiaries to people engaged in the shaping of their lives. The claim that the People's Plan Campaign has led to a development culture above partisan consideration however, has been strongly contested. According to Rene Veron, "Local development reports and plans may make the prioritisation process more transparent, but are no guarantee against favouritism and nepotism".

As regards the question of social mobilisation, given the sociopolitical situations relating to associational civil life in contemporary Kerala, "decentralistion with mass involvement" of the campaigners was bound to fail as a sustainable democratic alternative. Clientelism has enveloped civil life and all political parties, left as well as right. Under such a regime, rationality suffers because people take to partisan rhetoric and positions. Purposive collective choice becomes very difficult. An average Keralite is a member of several organisations, social, cultural, religious, political, economic and so on. More than half the population can be said to be actively involved in organised civic life. But the moot question is how far this social fragmentation has hampered Kerala's decentralised development? To quote Tharakan (who was the Director of Kerala Institute of Local Administration under the PPC regime): "It is evident that Kerala society has deep fissures created by clientelistic party affiliations while there are also reports that caste and community interests are reappearing in manifold ways. In Kerala society, polarised by clientelistic party coalitions, it is difficult for local level organisations by themselves to rise above divisive interests". Tornquist who notes a great political deficit in the substantial decentralisation of Kerala recommends, even a 'repoliticisation' of the democratic politics of the state. Indeed, there are serious problems in meaningfully embedding decentralisation in Kerala in the emerging social setting of the state.

Lessons from Kerala

What lessons do the democratic decentralisation and bottom up planning offer for other states in India or for other countries in the world? Some general observations are given below.

One, *devolution* is the keyword in creating 'institutions of local self-government'. The review of the conformity legalisation shows how the various state Panchayat acts have failed to provide effective devolution of functions, funds and authority to the PRIs. Kerala's amendment to its Panchayat act in 1999 provides the statutory framework for creating functional, financial and administrative autonomy at the level of the third stratum of government. Without creating such a necessary condition, no state in India can move forward on the road to decentralised governance.

Two, democratic decentralisation should not be a partisan or narrow political agenda. For it to succeed, both the ruling and opposition parties should own it. Despite the rhetoric of support which the UDF government which came to power in 2001 gave to decentralisation, some of their actions were not giving the right signals to democratic decentralisation. The increase in the cabinet strength from 14 to 20, the creation of separate ministries for local administration and rural development, the introduction of the MLA's local area development fund, several executive orders which virtually killed the beneficiary committee system (which was an innovative way to fight corruption and improve the quality of public works) the abandonment of the voluntary expert scrutiny system and so on have given a wrong signal to the officials and the public. The gram sabha meetings have been considerably weakened. When the meetings are routinised or not held as required and the preparation of minutes are stereotyped and attendance register fudged, one feels frustrated at the manner in which local democracy unfolds in Kerala. Several other institutional arrangements have been weakened and in some cases even vulgarised. The real question is what a political scientist (Olle Tornquist) has raised: how to overcome the political deficit of substantial democratisation? Not only Kerala, the country as a whole will have to take this question for reflection and action.

Three, Kerala, banking on its public action tradition took to a 'big bang' approach. It was actually a 'learning by doing' programme. While several arguments can be said in favour of this, it is a fact that Kerala's administrative and technical capabilities also have been severely strained due to the sudden and swift actions and arrangements involved. The multi-stage process involving transect walk, data collection, preparation of development projects with the help of sectoral Task Force teams associating technical and non technical volunteers and so on did not become a sustained operation. If it failed in Kerala, it can never be easier in the other parts of the country. Making exaggerated estimates of costs, setting unrealistic targets, indifferent monitoring by the Panchayat committee members, holding development seminars in a routine fashion and above the author has verified minute books and gram sabha records in several gram panchayats. All deliberately neglecting or vulgarising the vital organ of gram sabhas – all these provide the need for better participation of people and modifying the existing institutional arrangements.

Four, clientelist politics can deeply undermine the possibility of building participatory democracy. Kerala has all the ingredient for enhancing democratic values and democratic practice such as right to information, citizen's charter, quarterly gram sabha, Ombudsman and so on. But none of this can work effectively in an atmosphere of partisan and patronage politics. The way the beneficiary committee system is allowed to die without any protest from any quarters (The evaluation of A.R.V Pillai et al of 500 beneficiary committees during the people's plan campaign found that 25 percent of them worked well despite the heavy odds they had to fight against the rentier class lobby) does not speak highly of the emerging democratic practice in Kerala.

Five, given the development tasks mandated by the constitution PRIs have an important role in improving agricultural production and productivity. PRIs of Kerala did pay attention to this. The outcomes reported show a mixed result. There is tremendous scope for improvement. But the state and the local sector should try to pull together in a spirit of meaningful division of labour.

Six, the nature of fiscal decentralisation determines the extent of freedom and autonomy of a local government significantly. The operational autonomy of a local government that does not have taxing powers, and spending powers will be very limited. Kerala's local choice is considerably enhanced because of the higher proportion of own source revenue of the gram Panchayats. Even in Kerala

60 percent of the potential remains untapped. A citizen who pays tax will be more interested in scrutinising and evaluating the working of the Panchayat than one who has no such obligations.

In this context the nature of the transfer system assumes great significance. In India horizontal equity can be considerably enhanced through an appropriate system of intergovernmental transfers. Untied grants, matching grants, specific grants and other transfer arrangements can be made purposive through meaningfully designing the transfer system for the promotion of democratic decentralisation. The State Finance Commission has a critical role in ensuring equity, efficiency and democracy at the local level. But most of them have failed in this mission.

Seven, the constitutional mandate to create participatory democracy, through creating 'institutions of self-government' and preparing and implementing plans for "economic development and social justice" need an altogether different paradigm of politics, development and culture. The few success stories of social audit that happened in Kerala show that given the right leadership and institutions, the nature and character of democracy and local development can be significantly changed for the better. Actually, there is a "lack of a scholarly public discourse on the politics of popular democratisation" in Kerala and probably much more in India.

Eight, the proven outcome of the effective linkage between the Kudumbashree, the local governments and the community-based organisations of the poor women show that, unless the poor are fostered as the agents of their development, the linkage between decentralisation and poverty reduction could not be firmly established. In this pattern, the local government acts as the facilitator of the self-help initiatives of the poor. Being located nearest to the people, the local government has a comparative advantage in developing a synergist relationship between the government and the community-based organisations for strengthening poverty alleviation efforts. The conventional poverty approach perceiving the poor as the object of development should not be the dominant approach in seeking to establish a viable linkage between poverty reduction and decentralisation.

9

IT and Rural Development

Modern information technology (IT), associated in our minds with developed country markets and capital-intensive methods of production, has any relevance for a country where many millions still lack basic needs. Nevertheless, there are many efforts underway in India and other developing countries to demonstrate the concrete benefits of IT for rural population, and to do so in a manner that makes economic sense.

There are two types of potential economic gains from the use of IT. First, there are both static and dynamic efficiency gains. Static gains are one-time, and come from more efficient use of scarce resources, allowing higher consumption in the present. It is useful to distinguish two kinds of static efficiency gains. One kind pertains to increases in operating efficiency, while the other comes from reduced transaction costs. In both cases, the channel for gains is through more effective and lower cost information storage, processing and communication. Dynamic gains come from higher growth, potentially raising the entire future stream of consumption. The second type of potential benefit comes .from reductions in economic inequality, to the extent that such reductions are an agreed-upon social goal, and therefore a social benefit. The two types of gains may conflict, if growth requires increased inequality, or they may be mutually reinforcing, where broad sharing of the benefits of growth enhances the rate of growth. We can discuss the role of IT in achieving greater economic gains along both dimensions, without having to commit to a particular position on the relationship between inequality and growth. However, a focus on using IT for rural development is, at least on the surface, supportive of reduced inequality along with increased efficiency and growth.

Of course, benefits that are measurable as increased market-based economic activity, and hence show up in national accounts statistics, are not the only component of development. Development can also include improvements in the capabilities of the population, such as education, health and nutrition, independently of any direct or indirect economic impact. The ability to participate in democratic decision-making also falls into this category. Broad-based improvements in capabilities can also have positive impacts on long-run economic well being, but this is not a necessary condition for desiring such improvements.

Turning to specific impacts, note that IT involves the electronic processing, storage and communication of information, where anything that can be represented in digital form is included in the term 'information'. Thus news, entertainment, personal communications, educational material, blank and filled-out forms, announcements, schedules, and so on are all information. Software programs that process data (searching, tabulating, and calculating, for example) are also information in this sense, representing a particular kind of intermediate good. We can use standard economic characterisations to classify the different kinds of information. For example, entertainment, personal communications, and sometimes news, are final goods. Educational material, job announcements, or some kinds of news (weather news for farmers, for example) are intermediate goods, typically used for improving income-earning opportunities.

Information goods typically have the characteristic that one person's use does not reduce their availability for another person. Thus, a message or weather news can be viewed by many people, simultaneously or sequential. Depending on the content of the news or message, different people may place different evaluations on the information. Only friends and relatives may be interested in a personal message, all farmers in a district may be interested in local weather news, and so on. The ability to share information among users can impact the feasibility of providing it on a commercial basis. IT dramatically increases shareability of information, and this affects the economics of private provision of information goods and services.

The government may provide information goods because they are shareable and non-excludable (pure public goods). The classic example of a pure public good is national defence, but such goods may also be local in nature, such as public parks or law and order. Of course many local share able goods can be provided exclusively, in which case private provision is a feasible alternative, in a club-like arrangement. Here, government provision may be justified more on equity grounds than on the basis of failure of private provision. In some cases, government financing through taxes or statutory user charges can be combined with out sourcing of delivery to private providers to achieve both equity and efficiency goals.

Often, private provision is feasible, but neglects the spill over benefits that it creates, in which case government subsidisation may be socially beneficial. For example, primary education has private economic benefits that people are willing to pay for, but it can also have substantial non-economic benefits to the individual and to others in the society (improved understanding, ability to make sound judgments, political decision-making capacity, and so on). Additional roles of government that are important to bring out are in redistribution to achieve equity objectives, and in regulation of private activities through licensing and certification. In both cases, the government also uses economic resources, and IT has a potential role in increasing the efficiency of government.

For both government and private provision, one of IT's main direct benefits is in increasing efficiency by economising on resource use in the operations of firms as well as in market transactions. Information that would otherwise be conveyed through face-to-face contact, post, courier, print delivery, telegraph or telephone may instead be communicated in digital electronic form via the Internet. Efficiency gains from Internet use are not automatic: the telephone, in particular, is an efficient means of communication for many types of information. IT also requires new investment, so the benefits of trips, time and paper saved must be weighed against the costs of installing and maintaining the new infrastructure. Efficiency benefits of IT are not restricted to the communication itself. IT can improve the efficiency of the telephone network, and it can make it possible to track and analyse communications. Word processing, maintaining accounts, inventory management, and other such activities that may not require long-distance communications are also made more efficient by IT.

Experience with Internet use in developed countries suggests that information exchange related to the completion of market transactions is especially valuable. The ability of IT-based communications (combined with storage and processing) to bring together buyers and sellers more effectively represents major potential gains. These gains can come about through lower search costs, better matching of buyers and sellers, and even the creation of new markets. The successes of auction and employment websites in the

US illustrate these gains. In the rural Indian context, farmers selling their crops and buying inputs, parents seeking matrimonial alliances for their children, and job seekers are all potential users of Internet-based matching services.

Efficiency gains of IT can also come about through the enabling of new goods and services. In many cases, the new good is related to something available earlier, but is presented in a form that reduces costs and expands the size of the market. For example, recorded music is a mass-consumption item, whereas only a small minority of the population could afford or have access to live performances by the highest quality musicians. Educational material is another example where recording and duplication can replace more expensive, skilled-labour-intensive alternatives for delivery. The possibilities for inter-activity with IT-based educational materials illustrate the advantages of IT over older technologies based only on recording and duplication. Inter-activity also implies personalisation, in that an individual can select the precise content that he or she wishes to see. This feature also distinguishes IT-based content from what was available through previous technologies. Finally, the sheer volume of information that is accessible through IT is much greater than before: this also allows new kinds of services to be provided at a cost that is affordable to larger segments of the population.

We have outlined the potential static efficiency benefits of IT, but the direct dynamic benefits in terms of higher growth are harder to identify. Of course, if IT economises on current resources, more is available for investment, which can increase growth. If IT increases the efficiency of education delivery to the broader population, this investment in people (human capital acquisition) is also likely to lead to higher growth. IT may also have positive impacts through impacts on the innovation process. For example, IT can make innovation easier by allowing simulation and low-cost testing of new designs or searching through possible chemical compounds for beneficial drugs. Finally, IT may speed the diffusion of innovations through better communications, which may stimulate further innovation – though this last channel is speculative.

An important barrier to realising the economic benefits of IT is the often-substantial up-front cost of investment in new infrastructure – both hardware and software. In developed countries such as the US, large potential customer bases and efficient capital markets help overcome this barrier. Hardware and software designed for developed country markets can easily be adapted to serve higher income consumers in developing countries, but this leaves out the majority of the population in developing countries. Thus, one potential consequence of IT is an exacerbation of inequality, as only higher income groups enjoy its benefits – this is the so-called 'digital divide'.

On the other hand, because government-provided goods and services, including redistributed transfer payments, are often aimed at lower income groups, to the extent that IT can increase the efficiency and effectiveness of government, the benefits of IT will be more widely spread, partly reducing 'digital divide' concerns. However, achieving these benefits requires more than just internal use of IT: beneficiaries of government services (particularly the economically disadvantaged) must be able to access IT resources also. While governments may invest in such front-end interfaces with citizens (and have done so in developed countries), the cost of doing so for governments in developing countries may be prohibitive. Such governments typically already have difficulties in raising sufficient resources through taxes and user charges.

While successful examples of implementation of 'e-governance' initiatives exist, there is a conceptual alternative. This comes from recognising the fact that citizens typically incur private costs (often substantial) in availing of government-provided services. If the use of IT can reduce such costs, even low-income individuals may be willing to pay at least some fraction of the cost savings, and there is scope for private provision of intermediate services that reduce the cost of access to government. Of course, this idea is not specific to IT: private intermediaries already help in filling out forms, getting access, and so on. One difference that IT can make is in reducing costs even further, often by an order of magnitude. In broad terms (as is also the case with electronic marketplaces and job-matching boards), IT changes the scope and nature of intermediation.

Private providers may therefore have a role in delivering IT-based information services that are complementary to government services, as well as in providing conventional private goods and services. However, the private individual benefits that determine the prices charged by private providers may not reflect the overall social benefits of provision. As discussed earlier, these may include benefits such as greater awareness and participation in the political process. In such cases, there may be a role for government subsidisation of private provision. This assumes that government provision is likely to be less efficient than private provision, which seems to be true in some cases in developing as well as developed countries. In either case, richer information flows increase the transparency with which the government operates, thereby promoting better monitoring, and potentially – depending on whether electoral and legal institutions are effective – greater accountability. The ultimate payoff is more efficient delivery of government services.

Looking at the case of India, in cities and larger towns, cyber kiosks have already begun to proliferate. Urban population densities, income levels, cultural attitudes and telecom infrastructure all seem to be sufficient for the commercial success of these enterprises. The falling cost of hardware and the availability of a variety of English language software have also supported this trend. Finally, the government's belated opening up of Internet service provision to competitive entrants has been a crucial supporting development. In non-Internet IT-related services, IT education has clearly taken off in cities as well, inspired by India's success in software exports.

In rural areas and smaller towns, however, the various demographic and socioeconomic factors such as income levels, cultural attitudes, and geographic and social fragmentation may not be present in configurations that would easily enable the diffusion of commercial access to various IT-enabled services. Furthermore, the market power of traditional rural intermediaries may act as a barrier to partial innovations in how matching of buyers and sellers is conducted. Finally, vernacular language requirements and different demand patterns imply the need for software that is tailored for fragmented rural markets.

Rural IT: Issues and Conceptual Framework

We examine the potential for rural IT use, both from supply and demand perspectives. On the supply side, we examine the technical and organisational issues that arise for delivering IT-based services to rural population in India. On the demand side, we examine the potential benefits that IT can bring to these population, if the implementation is successful. We begin with the demand side, as a way of motivating the supply side issues.

Potential sources of demand for IT-based services can be framed in terms of a simple flow diagram representing the decisions of rural households. We will treat a typical household as engaged in farming, though this will not be true for all of them.

Non-production decisions of households can be roughly divided into pure consumption activities, as well as human capital investment in education and health. The boundary is fuzzy, since even basic food consumption has nutritional impacts and therefore a human capital component. These activities generate impacts on operations, since they affect the quality of decision-making, as well as household labour inputs: we indicate this with the vertical arrows. While poorer households may be severely limited in their consumption, a significant proportion of rural households in India have incomes sufficient to support some discretionary consumption. In some cases, consumption may be only superficially discretionary – social norms may dictate spending on activities relating to marriage and other life cycle events.

Finally, the right most box captures household saving, again something that is not feasible for all rural households, but is an activity of growing importance. Saving may be for consumption smoothing, investment, or precautionary reasons.

Even this simplified and summary picture of rural households' economic activity illustrates that they engage in a broad range of transactions and decisions with economic impacts. What is noteworthy besides this complexity is that many decisions are made with very limited information, and that market interactions are often subject to high transaction costs, due to imperfections in information, as well as high transportation costs, inefficient intermediation and time delays. High transaction costs will always prevent marginal transactions from being undertaken; in extreme cases, the market may fail to function at all. Given this scenario, the role of IT can be understood in terms of reducing transaction costs, as well as improving the efficiency of decision making within households (both as producers and as consumers).

Reductions in communication and transaction costs are particularly beneficial where they can allow new markets to develop, in the sense that existing goods and services, otherwise restricted to urban areas, or to a very limited segment of rural population, now can be offered to broad cross-sections of the rural population. Examples include financial services, particular types of education, health services, long distance communications, and expertise on a range of production-related decisions. Whether this can be done in a sustainable manner depends on the supply conditions for IT-based rural services.

The organisational structure typically requires commercial goals of profitability to be built in. This is easily done through a standard corporate structure. It is clear that, for scalability, some minimum size of the organisation is required. In addition, there are fixed costs of innovation that can be spread more effectively across a larger organisation. Social goals can be incorporated in two ways. For organisations that are dedicated specifically to rural IT-based services delivery, controlling ownership of the corporation by a non-profit entity provides the social focus. For existing corporations with broader businesses, social goals may enhance reputation, meet corporate social responsibility guidelines, or otherwise be consistent with the mission and values of the organisation. In other words, including social goals may make good bottom-line business sense.

For both types of organisations, building the right capabilities requires some effort. Creating what amounts to a brand new infrastructure for rural IT service delivery requires a broad mix of skills, and finding talented and trained people who can be effective in a role that mixes entrepreneurial tasks with corporate line responsibilities, all in an unfamiliar rural environment, can be a challenge. One solution to the potentially insurmountable problem of collecting the necessary talent and skills is to enter into partnerships with other organisations that may provide specific pieces of the overall package that is needed: application software, content, maintenance services, technology, marketing, and so on. These partnerships can pose their own problems, particularly in goal alignment and consequent performance monitoring requirements. Of course all these organisational issues are well recognised in management writing and experience: what is important is to recognise their critically in a setting that has more typically been the arena of pure 'social service' entities such as governments and NGOs. It is also critical to recognise that the organisational innovation required in this case is an order of magnitude greater than the task of selling consumer goods in rural areas, something that is now accepted as a given in India. The greater complexity and variety of the services being delivered through IT is the root cause of this difference.

The second stage of the supply chain in concerns access to electric power and Internet connectivity. In both cases, a major constraint is the failure of the public sector to deliver adequate power and telecommunications to rural India. Privatisation has helped in the case of telecommunications, as has technological change. In fact, innovation in digital communications technologies is the foundation of all rural IT-based service delivery. While conventional telephone connectivity has often proved inadequate for Internet access in rural areas, because the quality of existing voice lines is too poor to sustain data transmission, several innovations provide alternatives that are likely to be cost effective. These include wireless in local loop (WLL), fibre optic cables, and high-powered versions of Wi-Fi. The Internet boom in the United States clearly played a role in pushing down costs and speeding innovation in fibre optics and wireless transmission. In some cases, VSAT satellite connectivity has been used for Internet access, but it is not very cost effective. The major challenges for connectivity are likely to be regulatory, having to do with interconnection to the main network, and with maintenance, rather than with the fundamental technological choices and implementation.

Electric power is more of a problem, and this is true throughout India. Battery backups are a very partial solution to the lack of reliable power supplies, and solar technologies may be more promising in the near future: they are already in use in existing rural IT efforts. The difficulty is that having to rely on these alternatives and backups unnecessarily raises costs of operation. Of course this is true for all of India's economy. It is well recognised that the power sector is the major bottleneck, with capacity well short of demand, and the quality of transmission and distribution remaining poor.

The third stage of the supply chain is the most straightforward, because of the standardisation of components of desktop computing and peripherals, rapid technological improvements, falling costs of production, and, most recently, price reductions resulting from changes in tariffs on imported hardware. It is now possible to fully equip a single-computer rural Internet kiosk for less than Rs. 50,000, including CD drive, printer, scanner, power backup, and web cam. Potentially, the highest cost component is the operating system, since Windows enjoys a virtual monopoly on the desktop. However, Microsoft seems to have concession pricing for socially oriented developing country initiatives, and this helps to reduce costs. The operating system is still typically in English, but as long as simple drills can take kiosk operators to local language applications and content, this is not a substantial usage barrier. One can conclude that this stage of the supply chain is easiest to implement, with a highly standardised, almost cookie-cutter approach – although ongoing maintenance can be a challenge. The major business decision is whether to have more than one computer per kiosk, but experience suggests that one is sufficient for almost all situations, at least in the beginning.

The next stage of the supply chain, namely applications, presents more challenges. The range of possible applications is vast. Many IT-based services require non-IT logistics or processes as complements. Availability of local language software becomes more of a constraint. There is much more variation across localities, not just regions. Delivery of services or development of content often stretch the resources and expertise of the primary provider, and require varied partnerships or other contractual relationships. Deciding the sequences, scope and sophistication of various applications can be a major challenge, since many of the services are being offered for the first time, or are being delivered in novel ways that challenge existing institutional frameworks and relationships. Pricing for low income markets, where market penetration is limited in any case, and where some services may be perceived as public goods that are traditionally unpriced, presents another major challenge. In the case of financial services or government records or services, substantial government cooperation may be required, raising political and bureaucratic hurdles. In some ways, of course, the essence of the success of the rural IT-based-service business model depends on the selection, quality and pricing of the services being offered. What is interesting is that a substantial amount of learning has occurred in this arena, in just a few years.

Implementation: Cases, Impacts and Lessons

The discussion of several rural-IT initiatives is based on field visits conducted over a two-year period, from December 2001 to December 2003, as well as discussions with various members of each organisation. It is useful to describe each initiative separately, rather than organise the discussion according to value chain components or demand-side factors, as this provides a better sense of each overall effort.

Drishtee

Drishtee. Com had its origins in Gyandoot, a government project in Dhar district of Madhya Pradesh, in central India. Gyandoot provided an intranet for 33 village information kiosks, offering a range of mainly e-governance-related services. The most prominent of these is land record certificates, which are needed by landowners for transactions such as sale or leasing of land. While Gyandoot was a specific local initiative, involving heavy support from the District Collector, Drishtee has attempted to take that model and rapidly replicate it across the country. Currently, Drishtee has over 100 rural Internet kiosks in several states, run by franchises according to a revenue sharing arrangement. In Drishtee's case, a kiosk has, at least initially, just one computer. The setup cost is in the range of Rs. 50,000.

Drishtee is a commercial organisation, with specific social objectives of targeting benefits to the rural poor built into its vision and strategy. Drishtee has developed some software on its own, but also relies on various partners for software development, as well as, in some cases, other partners for management of district hubs, from which kiosks in a district are managed. Thus Drishtee's model involves not only franchising individual kiosks, but also potentially franchising district hubs. Partnering with local district hub 'channel partners' allows Drishtee to expand faster without creating a bulky organisation, spreads risks, and also insulates Drishtee from some of the commercial pressures that might conflict with social objectives. At the same time, it reduces Drishtee's ability to monitor and implement the achievement of social objectives. This tension between commercial success and meeting social objectives is a general challenge for all the rural IT initiatives examined here. Despite some challenges, Drishtee appears to have built a capable but lean organisation, with learning having been systematised in a manner that makes it transferable across locations, permitting more effective scaling up.

Electric power and telecom connectivity have posed challenges for Drishtee, since it is a pure start-up, without resources for heavy investments in infrastructure. It uses standard battery backup for power interruptions, and has relied mainly on dial-up Internet access, though it is experimenting with Wi-Fi for district-level intranets. In some cases, it has set up kiosks even without phone connectivity, relying on physical delivery of information. Software has also been developed that economises on bandwidth for information exchange, making the constraint of dial-up access less severe.

The software and hardware for basic kiosk operations are quite standardised, and their cost has been falling. Drishtee was able to get concession terms for using the Windows operating system. Various local language software applications have been developed, for e-governance, market price information, buying and selling, and so on.

With the origins in Gyandoot playing a role, simple e-governance, such as making government forms available and allowing a variety of complaints to be relayed to the district level government, has typically been the lead service in setting up operations in a new district. In this context, informal partnerships with district level government officials (both state and local) have been very significant. For example, in Sirsa and Jaipur districts, Drishtee has been able to act as a significant intermediary for information exchange between the district government and constituents. It obviously remains limited in its ability to improve the internal functioning of government. Nevertheless, Drishtee's approach can be viewed as achieving the right kind of 'embedded autonomy' at the local level, to use Peter Evans' term, meaning a socialite structure with coherent institutions that are autonomous, but nevertheless connected through institutionalised channels for continual negotiation of goals and policies.

Expanding the range of services has meant tying up with content partners, particularly organisations such as Agri-watch, which provides a substantial quantity and range of agricultural information to farmers. Agri-watch is essentially developing into a large-scale Internet portal for farmers, and Drishtee's role can be seen as providing last-mile access to this rich information, through its kiosks. It is difficult to quantify the benefits of this service, but its popularity with farmers suggests that it is valuable. Related examples from the cases of ITC and n-Logue will provide a more definite assessment of these benefits.

Drishtee's pricing scheme for e-governance services follows a set model. The full cost of a transaction such as obtaining, filling out and submitting a government form is estimated, including imputing the value of time spent in travel. The kiosk owner's fee for this is then set at about 10 percent of the estimated transaction cost, also taking into account possible willingness-to-pay considerations in choosing "pricing points" such as Rs. 5, 10 or 20. Assuming that these fees can cover the full cost of the kiosk owner and Drishtee (which depends largely on generating sufficient volume) the saving in transaction costs is substantial. The savings in such cases are generated by reductions in travel and time costs. There may also be benefits in terms of improving the effectiveness of transactions (e.g., if a complaint through this channel more likely to be addressed), but these are harder to quantify.

In the case of other services, such as matching buyers and sellers, or providing horoscopes or matrimonial advertising, additional services require partners who can provide software, maintenance, content or other components of the complete service. Education has played a limited role in Drishtee's offerings, though kiosk owners have often used the presence of a computer and peripherals to offer computer training, as well as other off-line services such as printing and games. The benefits in these examples are reductions in transaction costs for existing transactions, improved quality of successful matches, and potentially most significant, completion of activities (e.g., training, entertainment, communications) that would otherwise not take place because of high transaction costs.

Finally, Drishtee has appeared to learn rapidly with respect to the selection and training of kiosk owners, and eliciting the preferences of rural Internet kiosk users. This partly reflects the organisation's own structure and character. As a lean start-up, it seems to have attracted people who are relatively in tune with rural market environments. The process has not been painless, and there are still challenges in managing operations that are spread across several states, but Drishtee's ability to manage its own human resources and the end users of its services has grown over time.

In sum, Drishtee has emerged as a typical start-up. Without very substantial financial resources, it has still managed to expand, and it has built an organisation with strong competencies in what may be broadly termed 'rural IT-based service delivery.' This judgment holds despite Drishtee's lack of any clear strength in technology, applications, partnerships or ability to scale. In all these dimensions, it is 'good enough,' but it appears to have built a strong, low-cost organisation from scratch, one that may be well suited to delivering at least some components of the overall service. This competence is discussed further in the context of Aksh, a former Drishtee partner.

Aksh

Aksh is essentially a fibre optic cable company, with its core competence in laying and maintaining cable. Its revenue model is driven by the content and data that can be delivered over this cable. Therefore it has an interest in increasing such content delivery. While urban areas in India have seen substantial penetration of cable TV, through a model (now in transition) of largely unregulated local operators, the rural market remains largely unserved. The bottleneck has been the lack of last mile infrastructure, since there is a significant percentage of rural households (especially in richer districts) that can afford cable TV. Aksh, along with other companies such as Reliance, has received licenses for laying a new fibre optic network in rural areas.

In the case in point, Aksh rapidly laid a large fibre optic network in rural Jaipur district (excluding the city itself). It initially partnered with Drishtee for the development and maintenance of kiosks that would act as distribution points for cable TV access, as well as Internet kiosks. The Drishtee franchise model, interface and services were adopted, but with the brand name of "Gramdoot."

There are several reasons for this shift in the business relationship. Most obviously, Aksh's far greater size, resources and hardware capabilities give it an advantage in setting up and maintaining the hardware aspects of the kiosks. The rapid expansion of kiosks in Jaipur, with over 100 being set up within six months, stretched Drishtee's human resources beyond their limits. It was also not feasible to hire and train large numbers of people for servicing the kiosks. Second, the needs of the cable TV business, and some degree of competition that emerged with another cable TV provider in the same district created additional problems of maintenance (e.g., Aksh's cables were cut by the competitor) and conflicts in terms of priorities for bringing

Internet-based services online – essentially, Internet services were the tail of the cable TV dog. Finally, Aksh's incentive was to control and brand the effort to score points for corporate social responsibility.

In any case, the model of rural IT-kiosks managed by a large company with incentives to provide access to large numbers of rural households appears to be scalable and sustainable. Cable TV over fibre optic networks provides a strong revenue base, and a range of Internet-based services and content can be provided through partnerships. As companies such as Drishtee also scale up, they may be more effective in providing the necessary scale for ongoing management of the kiosks, including training services and customer relationship management. For now, providing software is easier for start-ups in such cases.

The history of Aksh's initiative means that the range of services provided in their kiosks, the revenue model, and pricing structures currently follow the Drishtee model. Hence the earlier discussion of benefits transfers over to this case. The importance of cable TV revenues, however, suggests that these kiosks may emphasise a range of entertainment services more than utility services such as agriculture-related information or e-governance. It is conceivable, however, that kiosk operators will be able to span the entire range of services. The bandwidth available will certainly support a full range of offerings, and the issues will be managerial attention and the perceptions of rural users. One important implication of greater bandwidth is that video interactions are possible, and Drishtee and Aksh have been able to test several communication services based on this. The power of video over text is in increasing the richness of information exchange, as well as greatly increasing the attractiveness and acceptance of all the services offered by the kiosks.

N-Logue

While Aksh and Drishtee are mostly active in north India, n-Logue has its origin and chief presence in the south. It is a for-profit corporation, with majority ownership residing with a non-profit organisation. The main impetus for n-Logue came from the IIT Chennai research group headed by professor Ashok Jhunjhunwala. This group has been responsible for a stream of hardware and software innovations that enable rural IT-based service delivery, through connectivity and applications.

The core innovation at the heart of n-Logue's operations is a WLL technology, Cordect, which provides joint wireless Internet and voice connectivity. The kiosk-level hardware is relatively inexpensive, and adds only marginally to the overall cost of a kiosk. However, the construction of WLL towers and maintenance of the WLL hub is relatively costly, and this fixed cost requires a substantial density of kiosks within a particular radius of the tower. The n-Logue model is designed to achieve this density, with kiosks generating returns from fairly small user population (somewhat smaller than in the case of Drishtee and Aksh). Another constraint on this connectivity model is the requirement of clear lines of sight, and therefore relatively flat topography. Nevertheless, large parts of India are still suitable for this implementation. Furthermore, n-Logue has progressed well beyond being simply a connectivity provider, to delivering a range of services – these can be adapted to different connectivity technologies. N-Logue is the second largest organisation in this field, supporting over 500 rural-IT kiosks.

The WLL technology does provide several strengths. It overcomes lack of dial-up connectivity, and provides an extra revenue stream for kiosk operators, through voice calls. Furthermore, it has greater bandwidth than traditional fixed line dial-up, which allows a wide range of applications to be delivered. In particular, the IIT Chennai group has been able to develop video applications that are sufficiently compressed to work within the constraints of the WLL.

In general, the close links with the IIT Chennai group have given n-Logue access to a range of software innovations for delivery and implementation of various applications in the fields of education, health and agriculture. For example, web cams have been used for remote diagnostics for diseases of people, animals and plants. A considerable amount of local language software has been created quite rapidly and effectively. The university connection is important, and stands out as a model for other providers to emulate.

N-Logue has also been able to leverage its university connections to build strong partnerships across the board. The Tamil Nadu government has been strongly supportive of n-Logue's operations in Madurai district, where numerous innovations have been piloted and show cased. MIT's Media Lab has also been involved in the initial stages, and ICICI Bank is piloting various financial services products in kiosks in Madurai. IN Nellikuppam district, n-Logue has partnered with EID-Parry to improve sugar farmers' access to information, and reduce their transactions costs in dealing with Parry's large sugar factory in the district, through improved tracking and settlements of payments. In this case, the factory chimney has also served as a base for the tower, and the control hub is housed in the factory, substantially reducing fixed costs. Parry plans to use those kiosks that are under its own brand (several dozen in total) to offer processed foods to farmers.

N-Logue also appears to have developed a very capable organisation, and has expanded beyond Tamil Nadu into other southern states, as well as the west and north of India. One advantage that emerged in discussions was the relative ease of establishing organisational capabilities, training kiosk operators, and serving rural communities in the south relative to the north of India. This reflects higher proportions of the population with basic education, greater population densities, and, in general, a more structured and stable civil society. A factor that seemed to emerge in all cases was the greater average success of women kiosk operators, possibly reflecting the fact that there is greater untapped potential for rural women, given their otherwise more restricted employment opportunities.

Overall, n-Logue has several strengths compared to Drishtee, in terms of access technology, software applications and partnerships. Nevertheless, the two organisations are quite similar in terms of the range of services offered, and their ability to deliver close to an 'end-to-end' solution. Their social goals are more salient than those of Aksh, and each has achieved a substantial geographic reach and partnership capability. There are some differences in emphasis in terms of applications, services, and revenue models (Drishtee relies more on overall revenue sharing, whereas n-Logue charges mainly for connectivity). In each case, however, there has been a demonstration that rural IT-based services are commercially feasible, and as a corollary, provide quantifiable economic benefits. Since estimates of the overall market size suggest that it can support at least 50,000 kiosks, and these two organisations, plus Aksh, have less than 1,000 kiosks, there appears to be substantial room for further growth.

ITC

ITC stands out as a large Indian corporation serving global markets. Its kiosks are called e-choupals, and they have several differentiating features. The key distinguishing factor is that the e-choupals are totally designed to support ITC's agricultural products supply chain. This gives them a focus that is not present even in EID-Parry's kiosks in

Nellikuppam. In addition, the e-choupals are totally owned and set up by ITC, with the operators not having any investment or risk of their own. Furthermore, e-choupal operators are, because of the focus, always substantial farmers, and therefore always male. All these features make the e-choupals different from the previous three initiatives.

The e-choupal initiative has involved a clear focus and strong direction from the head of ITC's International Business Division. ITC has been able to turn its substantial organisational and managerial capabilities toward this initiative. Management trainees are heavily immersed in the e-choupal model as part of their inculcation into ITC's workings. There are four kinds of e-choupals, tailored very specifically for four different products: shrimp, coffee, wheat and soyabeans. The first two of these involve large commercial farmers, and the focus is on creating Internet access to global market information to guide production and supply decisions. There are a few dozen of these e-choupals. In the case of wheat and soyabeans, there are many small farmers, and over 2,000 e-choupals have been set up, in several states of India.

The description here is based on soychoupals. Wheat choupals are somewhat similar, with the final market and products being somewhat different. Soybeans are pressed to extract oil, which is sold domestically, while the remainder is exported as animal feed. Thus they are a cash crop, without the regulated market conditions or subsistence consumption associated with a food grain such as wheat. Soychoupals are used as registry points for procurement of soybeans. Actual procurement is done at factories and warehouse hubs, but the initial logging in is done through the e-choupal, which provides price information and therefore price certainty. In fact, the e-choupal price acts as a floor price for procurement – the factory or warehouse price can be higher. E-choupals also provide access to local market (*mandi*) prices and global market price information on soybeans and derivative products, to allow farmers to compare prices. They give access to operational information, developed by ITC experts, pertaining to cropping, seeds, fertiliser, and so on.

E-choupals are set up by ITC, with solar power backup and VSAT connectivity. The equipment cost for the e-choupal is borne by ITC, with the selected farmer providing the location. In addition to the adoption advantages that come from using a farmer with high social status as the operator, the house should be spacious and sturdy enough to house all the required equipment, including the VSAT and solar panel on the roof. E-choupal farmers take an oath to serve the village, and they are trained by ITC. While there is an important element of social pressure and pride of work, the operators also receive commissions on soyabean shipments booked through the E-choupals. This provides substantial revenue to the e-choupal operator.

The narrow (at least initial) focus of the E-choupals and the substantial commitment of financial and human resources by ITC has made rapid expansion possible, as well as quick acceptance by farmers. The narrow range of applications has limited software requirements, and operators bear no risk in the ITC model. The longer-term goal is, however, to use E-choupals and warehouse hubs as sales points for soyabean oil, tractor rental, and eventually a range of ITC produced consumer goods.

The initial benefits of the ITC effort include a substantial reduction in transaction costs, from 8 percent of a transaction, down to 2 percent, approximately. It is estimated that these gains are shared roughly equally between ITC and individual farmers. Some of this gain may be at the expense of traditional intermediaries, who operate in *mandis*, but much of it comes from genuine efficiency gains, including clearer quality guidelines and measurement, greater timeliness and reduced waits, quicker payments, and reduced uncertainties. To some extent, traditional intermediaries are co-opted in the new process, by being hired to perform tasks such as handling payments at ITC's receiving points.

Clearly the use of information technology is just a part of ITC's overhaul of its supply chain, but speedy delivery of complex information pertaining to market conditions makes IT essential. It might be asked what acts as a check on ITC's market power in this process. Clearly, the traditional *mandi* system, with its accompanying government regulation and oversight, acts as continuing competition. More significantly, ITC's concern with its reputation acts as a disciplining device. Finally, the long term goal of selling back to farmers as customers also gives ITC an incentive to cultivate relationships with individual farmers. In fact, farmers view ITC as treating with greater respect and dignity than is the case in traditional *mandi* interactions.

It is quite conceivable that the ITC model will not broaden significantly beyond the two-way flow of agricultural produce from farmers to ITC, and processed foods, consumer goods and inputs from ITC to farmers, without extending to e-governance, entertainment, health or education-related services. Instead, other firms may provide these services in similar locations to ITC E-choupals.

TARAhaat

TARAhaat has evolved in a somewhat unusual manner. It achieved well-publicised success with Internet kiosks in Bundelk hand in Uttar Pradesh. These kiosks were very much along the lines of those implemented by Drishtee and n-Logue, with a mix of e-governance services, market price information, and so on. TARAhaat's long-range plans include a comprehensive portal for rural information services and an extended vision of its 'TARAkendras' as community centres. However, in its expansion into Punjab, at the invitation of the administrator of Bathinda district, its model evolved quite differently.

While the Bundelk hand model had used VSAT connectivity, this was not economical for a commercially sustainable expansion. While Punjab is a high-income state with relatively good infrastructure, the level of telephone connectivity turned out to be too poor for practical Internet use. Other issues arose with the substantially greater investment required by TARAkendra operators, since the model assumed that each kiosk with have three or four computers. Perhaps the greatest problem was in building an organisation for implementation. While TARAhaat is a subsidiary of Development Alternatives, an established NGO, it is set up as a corporation, with social goals meant to be enforced through ownership by the non-profit parent. The expansion of TARAhaat required building an organisation from scratch, and this turned out to be a slow process. There were also problems with establishing effective partnerships with local and state government, and TARAhaat has mostly gone it alone.

TARAhaat does have an educational content partner, called TARAgyan. In association with various partners, TARAgyan is developing local language content and software for use in TARAkendras. Basic IT education is an important part of TARAgyan's actual and potential offerings, but it is not the exclusive focus. In fact, there has been a substantial diversification into developing materials for English language instruction, rural marketing, personality development, and so on. This development was initially very slow, though it may be picking up steam.

10

Rural Poverty and Agrarian Crisis

Recent years have seen the development of an extensive and disquieting literature on trends in rural poverty in India and their relationship to agricultural growth. A recurring theme in much of this literature is that agricultural growth has been accompanied by a steady deterioration in distributional terms, involving not only an increase in relative inequality but also an increase in absolute impoverishment Indeed, it is argued that these trends are the natural consequence of the type of agricultural growth which can be expected within the existing institutional structure in Indian agriculture. This latter proposition has important implications for policy. It raises doubts about the scope for achieving even the fairly minimal welfare objective of alleviating absolute poverty in the future, at least through the kind of agricultural development that is currently deemed feasible, i.e. growth without radical institutional change.

Ideally, the observed changes in the incidence of poverty over different sub-periods should be explained in terms of some explicit model of the determinants of rural poverty and the behaviour of these determinants over the sub-periods In this context, it is obviously relevant to consider the rate of agricultural growth, the factors determining its distribution across farm sizes, its impact on tenancy conditions, its effect on the demand for labour, etc.

A popular peasant saying that "abundance of water destroys life; paucity of water destroys life" signifies agriculture's link with monsoon. The vagaries of nature have been associated with ups and downs in cultivation. In addition, disease and pests can also affect crops. When the produce is good, a glut in the market can through low prices lead to poor returns from cultivation. Increasing cost can also adversely affect returns. Spurious inputs could also leave the farmer in a quandary. The increasing dependence on inputs from the market has also brought about greater demand for credit, which adds another important dimension to the difficulties. There are multiple risks in agriculture – income, yield, price, input, technology and credit among others.

In recent years, one observes an increasing incidence of farmers' suicides. Suicide being a multifaceted and complex phenomenon, the risks are identified either in the neurobiological or socioeconomic domain. The former are predisposing in nature and are internal to the individual whereas the latter are the precipitating ones and are external to the individual. A relatively higher suicide among a particular subgroup is indicative of a larger socioeconomic malaise.

The features of the current agrarian crisis are briefly elaborated as follows. First, there has been a decline in the trend growth rate of production as well as productivity for almost all crops from the mid-nineties. Further, the value of output from agriculture has been declining from late nineties. Second, there is an excessive dependence of a large section of the population on agriculture (in 2004-05 nearly 64 per cent of the rural persons were from households whose members major activity status was either self-employed in agriculture or agricultural labour). This also indicates that rural non-farm employment opportunities are limited. Third, with declining size-class of holding and an increasing preponderance of marginal holdings (63 per cent as per 2000-01 agricultural census) along with poor returns from cultivation indicates that income for farm households is very low. Fourth, the much talked about green revolution had a greater focus on rice and wheat under irrigated condition bypassing crops and regions under rainfed or dry land conditions (which is three-fifths of the 141 million hectares of net sown area in the country during 2003-04). There has been a failure to capitalise on the vast network of institutes to provide and regulate new technology (including the usage of biotechnology), and a virtual absence of extension service. Fifth, the neglect of agriculture in plan resource allocation has led to a decline of public investments in irrigation and other related infrastructure. Sixth, supply of credit from formal sources to the agricultural sector is inadequate leading to greater reliance on informal sources at higher interest burden. Last, but not the least, with changing technology and market conditions the farmer is increasingly being exposed to the uncertainties of the product as well as factor markets.

Poor Returns to Cultivation

On an average, returns to cultivation per farmer household is Rs.11,259/ in 2002-03. To account for the drought in the said year even if one increases the returns by one-third then also it would be less than Rs.15,000/, which given a family size of 5.5 turns out to be less than eight rupees per capita per day. This means that other sources of income would become necessary if the farmer household has to stay above the poverty line. About 60 per cent and 10 per cent of farmer households obtain some returns from farm animals and non-farm business respectively and per farmer household monthly returns from these are Rs.85/-and Rs.236/ respectively. In addition, farmer households will also get income from wages and salaries. As expected, returns per household increases with land size. Average family size also increases with land size indicating that the increase in per capita returns would not be as large. Across caste groups, scheduled castes (SCs, who generally own the marginal lands) have the least returns and above them are scheduled tribes (STs) and from both these groups, the other backward classes (OBCs) fare better, but the returns for all these three groups is lower than the total average. Almost two-fifths of the farmers indicated that they do not like farming as a profession. This group, on an average, fares worse than those who like farming as a profession.

Overall, there is not much diversification and the income of an average farmer household from cultivation would hardly suffice to meet some basic day-to-day requirements. The *Situation Assessment Survey of Farmers, 2003* (SAS) indicates that the monthly per capita income to a farmer household is much lower than the monthly per capita consumption expenditure. This holds for near landless, lower marginal, upper marginal, small and semi-medium farmers. Only medium and large farmers have income higher than their consumption expenditure. The nominal farm business income per hectare of gross cropped area deflated by Consumer Price Index for Agricultural Labour (CPIAL) seems to be slowly declining with wide fluctuation during 1993-94 to 1999-2000.

At a time, when the Indian economy is growing at about eight to nine per cent per annum and edging towards the double-digit figure the rural/agrarian scenario is not doing well. At 1999-2000 prices, share of agriculture in gross domestic product is at 20 per cent in 2004-05, down from 41 per cent in 1972-73; whereas during the same period the share of employment in agriculture using usual principal and subsidiary status declined at a much slower pace from 74 per cent to 57 per cent only. Ratio of worker productivity in agriculture to worker productivity in non-agriculture is about one-fifth. The agrarian/rural sector is lagging behind but it continues to employ a large proportion of the Work-force.

Farmers' Suicides

Poor agricultural income and absence of non-farm avenues of income is indicative of the larger malaise in the rural economy of India. One manifestation of this has been the increasing incidence of farmers' suicides. The suicide mortality rate (SMR, suicide death for 100,000 persons) for male farmers in India increased from 12.3 in 1996 to 19.2 in 2004 and then reduced to 18.2 in 2005 whereas SMR for male non-farmers increased from 11.9 in 1996 to a peak of 14.2 in 2000 and thereafter declined to 13.4 in 2005. During 2001-05, there were 86,922 farmers' suicides, of which, 86 per cent were males. Across major states, the states where SMR for male farmers is higher that of the national average of 17.5 and SMR for male non-farmers in that state are Kerala, Maharashtra, Chhattishgarh, Karnataka, Tamil Nadu and Andhra Pradesh. Among smaller states/union territories the incidence are high in Pondicherry, Dadra & Nagar Haveli, Delhi, Goa and Sikkim.

Public policy and media attention have already highlighted the farmers' suicides in parts of Kerala, Maharashtra, Karnataka and Andhra Pradesh. In selected districts of these states, the central government and the respective state governments have announced measures to deal with distress. What is intriguing is that the relatively higher incidence of farmers' suicides in Chhattishgarh and Tamil Nadu seems to have gone unnoticed. Chattishgarh scenario is worrying because cultivators form nearly 45 per cent of its workers, as per 2001 census. Tamil Nadu situation is serious because some recent studies based on verbal autopsies point out that suicides as per police records are underestimates. Further probing is required in these states. Studies in the other four states have **identified** multiple risk factors that coexist and reinforce each other. The distribution of the risk factors based on a study in Western Vidarbha, Maharashtra.

The most common thing was indebtedness (96 out of 111 cases, 87 per cent). From all those indebted, 44 per cent were harassed for repayment of loan and in 33 per cent of cases the creditor insisted on immediate repayment. Next in importance is fall in economic position (74 per cent). Indebtedness per se need not lead to economic downfall, but when repayment is difficult and the household may resort to sale of assets. Similarly, a fall in economic position can also lead greater reliance on credit, and thereby increasing the debt burden. Not discussing one's problem with others (55 per cent) leads to closing an avenue for letting out ones pent up feelings and frustration.

Crop failure is mentioned in 40 per cent of the cases and most of these also mentioned about loss in second or third sowing due to delay in rainfall. There were a few cases which mention fire or theft. Crop loss can also happen due to excessive untimely rain, say, during the time of harvest. Crop failure can lead to economic downfall and make it difficult to repay existing loans. This will also increase the need for additional credit. Crop failure leading to fall in economic position is quite straight forward, but the causal links can also be the other way round. A house that had some fall in economic position or was heavily indebted could not take additional loans for investing in agriculture (say, during a pest attack) and this can lead to a reduction in yield or total crop failure. Incidentally, the year of survey when pockets witnessed crop loss, the overall scenario was a glut in the market and as a result many individuals faced yield and price shock simultaneously.

Change in social status was identified in 36 per cent of the cases. This can be associated with a fall in economic, position. Harassment by creditors or their agents due to nonpayment of loans can also lead to a loss of face in the community. Crop failure due to unsuccessful experimentation by a farmer who was recognised as successful entrepreneur may find a change in his social status – people who earlier came for advice are now providing solace.

A socially important role of a brother/father is to get one's sister/daughter married. Communities have norms in terms of age and expenditure. A farmer is largely dependent on a good return from his produce to fulfil this obligation. Thus, crop failure, greater credit burden or a fall in his economic position can come in his way of fulfilling this obligation. Inability to conduct sister's/daughter's marriage can be socially humiliating. It can also increase intra-household conflicts. To complete this social obligation a farmer may also take loans thinking that he can repay the amount after the harvest. Recent marriage of a sister/ daughter or inability to get one's sister/daughter married has been identified as a risk factor in 34 per cent of the cases.

Recent suicides in a nearby village are identified as an additional risk factor (32 per cent). There could be an imitation effect because an individual who is facing some similar socioeconomic problem can relate to the earlier incident and contemplate suicide. Under addiction (28 per cent – mostly alcohol) an individual may indulge in an act of self-harm without being aware of the consequences. Alternatively, getting intoxicated could be a reaction to get out of depression that can be associated with some socioeconomic problem. Change in the individual's behaviour (26 per cent) including disputes with neighbours/ others (24 per cent) could be indicating the need for some psychosocial help.

Personal health problem of the deceased was identified in 21 per cent of the cases. From these, 26 per cent (6 cases) were those with some mental health problem. Illness gets aggravated due to poor economic condition because it makes care seeking difficult. Similarly, ill health can lead to a loan to meet medical expenses and also reduce the ability to work aggravating the economic condition. If the sick person is some other member (3 per cent of the cases) then the breadwinner has the added frustration and helplessness in not being able to provide appropriate care for an ailing parent/spouse/child.

Death of another member in the family before the incident was identified in 10 per cent of the cases. The near ones death could have been because of not receiving appropriate health care. Inability to provide care is largely because of the poor economic condition rooted in the larger agrarian crisis. Suicide history in the family could be identified in 6 per cent of the cases. This could be indicative of a genetic factor. However, as mentioned earlier such individual factors are predisposing in nature and they can be intensified with some additional risk factors. On average, 4.8 risk factors were identified.

Suicide is a rare event. Under duress, some farmers end up committing suicide. Closer probing does point to some idiosyncratic factors. However, they do not occur in isolation. Systemic factors also have their role. For every farmer who commits suicide, there are many in distress. The larger agrarian crisis is much more widespread and just not only confined to regions witnessing farmers' suicides.

Agrarian Crisis

In addition to the weather related uncertainties, the farmer is also faced with market, spurious inputs, technology and credit related vulnerability among others. Some of these are summarised. Production or yield loss is an important risk. Weather, pests and disease of plants, spurious quality of inputs could be the possible reasons. The risk is real because even today crop loss can adversely affect the consumption requirements of many farmer households. Price shocks are also matter of concern. The conventional argument was that such incidents happened during a good year and the increase in production should compensate the farmer. An implicit assumption in this is that prices are based on local supply and demand. Integration with the global market has led to greater price volatility.

The farmers are preceptors in the product as well as in the input markets. Such a situation could lead to increase in input costs and decrease in output prices, and hence, decline in profitability and returns from cultivation. As indicated earlier, returns from cultivation per farmer household in 2002-03, as per SAS, was Rs.11,259/ only and the paid out expenses was more than two-fifths of the total value of output. With such low levels of income, it would be difficult to meet day-to-day consumption requirements. The farmer cannot use his own resources for carrying out next year's cultivation or be in a position to use saved resources to tide over any crisis. Saving from these for bad years is impossible. What is more, normal social obligations such as education, marriage and healthcare expenses on account of family members turn out to be burdensome.

Another critical factor is credit. Availability of timely and adequate credit does help the farmer by reducing transaction costs, particularly so when input related expenditure are rising. In 2003, SAS estimates indicate that 58 per cent of the outstanding debt was for agricultural purposes. Further, more than two-fifths of the total outstanding debt is from informal sources. Such debts from moneylenders and input dealers would carry greater interest burden and thereby increasing the cost further. The recent All India Debt and Investment Survey (AIDIS) indicates that from the total noninstitutional outstanding debt for cultivator households on end June 2002, nearly three-fourths carried interest rate of 20 per cent or more per annum and more than half of these carried interest rate of 30 per cent or more per annum. A crop failure leading to nonpayment would further escalate the interest burden. Thus, inability to repay would further increase the risks.

Other matters of concern are the dominance of the informal credit provider and the possible inter-linked nature of contracts that may be extended to the input and output markets. Livelihood opportunities are constrained by the absence of adequate non-farm avenues. Poor public facilities on health and education would further add to the woes.

Risk management in agriculture should address yield, price, credit, income or weather related uncertainties among others. Improving water availability will facilitate diversification of cropping pattern, but this should go hand in hand with policies that increase non-farm employment. Improving agricultural extension that addresses de-skilling because of technological changes and also facilitates appropriate technical know-how for alternative forms of cultivation such as organic farming will be of help. Availability of affordable credit requires revitalisation of the rural credit market. There is also a strong case for regulating private credit and input markets. A challenge for the technological and financial gurus is to provide innovative products that reduce costs while increasing returns. Organising farmers through a federation of self-help groups (SHGs) with government, banks and other stockholders playing a pro-active role would be welcome. Besides, public institutions, there is need for a greater involvement from the civil society.

Assessment of Rural Poverty

In India, poverty is defined on the basis of a minimum per capita daily nutritional requirement of 2,100 calories in urban areas and 2,400 calories in rural areas. These figures are based on the recommendations submitted in 1979 by the Government of India Task Force on Minimum Needs and Effective Consumption Demand. According to the report of the Task Force, the poverty line was defined as per capita monthly expenditure of Rs 49.09 in rural areas and Rs 56.64 in urban areas at 1973/74 prices, corresponding to per capita daily calorie requirements in rural and urban areas. The definition covers expenditures on food and non-food items (such as fuel, clothing, housing, health, education and social services) and ensures adequacy of calorie consumption. That works out at an annual family income of Rs. 11,000 at 1991/92 prices.

For the estimation of persons living below the poverty line, National Sample Survey (NSS) data on household consumption are utilised and are applicable to the national level as well as at State and Union Territories levels. The poverty estimates are made separately for rural and urban areas at the national and State levels. The poverty line defined by the Task Force at 1973/74 prices has been updated for the reference year. The estimates of persons living below the poverty line for the years 1983/84, 1987/88 and 1993/94, based on the methodology used at present by the Planning Commission (i.e., Task Force methodology).

The Planning Commission methodology for estimating the proportion and number of poor, which has been in use since 1979, has previously been regarded by some analysts as giving an inadequately representative picture of the incidence of poverty in India. Scholars and academicians have raised conceptual and methodological issues in that regard.

An expert group, constituted to look into the methodology for the estimation of poverty at the national and State levels as well as re-examine the question of definition of the poverty line, recommended a modified methodology. The estimates of poverty based on the expert group methodology. The expert group provided estimates of poverty until 1987/88. Attempts to estimate the incidence of poverty for 1993/94 by using the expert group methodology have been constrained by the availability of data.

Table 1. Persons living below the poverty line in India, 1983/84, 1987/88 and 1993/94 (Million)

Year	*Rural*	*Urban*	*Combined*
1983/84	180.66	37.7	218.37
	(37.73%)	1 (21.68%)	(30.08%)
1987/88	168.30	33.11	201.41
	(28.37%)	(16.82%)	(25.49%)
1993/94	141.05	27.52	168.57
	(21.68%	(11.55%)	(18.96%)

Criticism has been voiced of the poverty estimates by the Planning Commission. Some analysts have attempted independent estimations of the poverty line. Other studies have estimated that there was a sharp decline in poverty between 1973/74 and 1986/87. After 1986/87 the decline continued at a slower pace until 1989/ 90. However, between 1989/90 and 1992/93 poverty increased sharply. Thereafter it declined again in 1993/ 94 but was still higher than that in 1987/88. These analyses would suggest that poverty increased sharply in the first 18 months of the economic reform period. However, in 1993/94, trends were reversed.

The independent analyses also showed that there was no uniformity regarding the trends in the various States. The trends in poverty also need to be viewed in the general context of the structural reforms initiated in early 1991 which involved a fairly sharp contraction in fiscal and monetary policy from 1990/91 to 1992/93, followed by high fiscal deficits from 1993/94 onwards.

Table 3. Estimates of poverty in India, 1983 and 1987/88 (Millions)

Year	*Rural*	*Urban*	*Combined*
1983	271.515	75.293	327.008
	(45.61%)	(42.15%)	(44.76%)
1987/88	229.396	83.352	312.748
	(39.06%)	(40.12%)	(39.34%)

It must also be noted that the decade of 1980s saw the Indian economy undergoing a consumptionled boom which was spurred mainly by the increase in the government revenue deficit. During that decade increased access to external debt continued. The same period also saw comparatively high agricultural growth. With massive growth in government expenditure the quantum of flow of public resources to rural areas was definitely more significant It must also be remembered that the period saw an increased expansion of rural development programmes aimed at strengthening the redistributed growth concept. There were, admittedly, leaks in the programmes but nevertheless there was a resultant massive transfer of resources into the rural areas. In addition, the development of better infrastructure and mobility in the rural areas contributed to a growing flow of funds in the rural sector.

Development Strategies of Past Decades

During the first three five-year plans, the main emphasis was on achieving higher growth rates. The plans were influenced by the "growth model" of capital accumulation and saving/ investment. There was a common belief that as capital was accumulated and growth stimulated. Poverty would be alleviated through the "trickle down" effect of growth. The strategy emphasised investment in heavy and capital goods industries to achieve rapid industrialisation and economic development. The development of heavy industries was synonymous with industrialisation. Development along socialist lines was presumed to expedite economic growth, expand employment opportunities and reduce disparities and concentration of economic power.

The government announced its first industrial policy in 1956, accepting the creation of a socialistic pattern of society as the goal of economic planning. Accordingly, the second five-year plan emphasised development of basic and heavy industries. The plan laid special emphasis on the production of iron and steel, heavy chemicals, textiles and development of heavy engineering and machine building industry. The industrial policy of 1956 accepted the establishment of a socialistic pattern of society as a goal. That necessitated the development of industries which produced machines for manufacturing goods. The stress on industries continued during the third five-year plan as well with stronger emphasis on achieving self-sufficiency in food grains and establishing progressively greater equality of opportunity.

During the above period, no specific attempts were made to remove poverty among individuals. Some rural development projects with a bearing on rural poverty alleviation were implemented, such as the Intensive Agriculture District Programme (IADP) in 1960 and the Intensive Agriculture Area Programme (IAAP) in 1964, which covered 1,596 blocks in 150 districts. Later on high yielding varieties (HYV) were introduced increasing agricultural production.

By the beginning of the third five-year plan, Indian planners felt that the Indian economy had entered the "takeoff stage" and that the first two plans had created an institutional structure upon which further progress could be made. Consequently, the third plan aimed at the establishment of self-reliant and self-generating economy. The experience of the earlier plans suggested that agriculture should be assigned top priority. The third plan accordingly gave top priority to agriculture together with emphasis on the development of basic industries.

The overambitious plans from 1951 to 1966 met with a number of problems and failures. The Plans were unable fulfil the expectations of the common people; several difficulties and bottlenecks, especially during the third plan, such as inflation, wars, droughts during 1963/ 64 and 1965/ 66, and non-achievement of targets etc. Seriously disturbed the economy as well as society. In spite of massive investment during the three plans, the living standard of the masses was not improved. Poverty and inequalities in the distribution of income and wealth remained as acute as before. Unemployment increased from 5.3 million in 1956 to about 9.6 million in 1966.

The period of 1966-1969 in Indian planning may be categorised as transitional from a "growth approach" to a "distribution from growth approach". During that period, three annual plans were implemented: the fourth plan, which was due in 1966, and a draft outline of what had been prepared was postponed until 1969 for the revision of objectives and priorities.

Distribution from Growth from 1969 Onwards

The fourth plan was aimed at accelerating the tempo of development in conditions of stability and at reducing fluctuations in agricultural production as well as the impact of uncertainties in foreign aid. Its objectives were to raise the standard of living through programmes which were, at the same time, designed to promote equality and social justice. The plan laid particular emphasis on improving the conditions of the less privileged and weaker sections of society, especially through the provisions of employment and education. Efforts were also directed towards reducing the concentration, and bringing about a wider diffusion, of wealth, income and economic power. The average annual growth rate envisaged was 5.7 per cent.

The special programmes introduced for the poor during the fourth plan may be categorised as "area development programmes" and "family beneficiary programmes". The basic objectives of those special programmes were the transfer and creation of assets, skills development and creation of infrastructure as well as directly taking up developmental works in the backward areas. The major area development programmes launched during that period were DPAP, DDP, ITDP, together with the Small Farmers Development Agency (SFDA) family beneficiary programme.

The fifth five-year plan faced a major economic crisis which arose from inflation fuelled by the hike in crude oil prices. The final draft of the fifth plan proposed the achievement of two main objectives: (a) the removal of poverty; and (b) the attainment of self-reliance through a higher rate of economic growth, better distribution of income and a significant stepup in the domestic savings rate. The fifth plan was, however, terminated in 1978 and the concept of rolling plans was introduced. The first of the new plans sought to reconcile the objectives of higher production with those of greater employment. The focus was the enlargement of the employment potential in agriculture and allied activities, encouragement to the household sector and small industries producing goods for mass consumption, and the raising of the incomes of the poor through a minimum needs programme.

The sixth plan had the removal of poverty as its foremost objective even though it was recognised that the task could be accomplished only in the long term. The strategy adopted for the sixth and the seventh plans essentially comprised: (a) moving simultaneously towards strengthening the infrastructure for agriculture and industry, in order to create conditions for an accelerated growth in investments, output and exports; and (b) through special programmes designed for the purpose, providing increased opportunities for employment, especially in the rural areas and the unorganised sector, and meeting the minimum basic needs of the people.

The eighth plan recognised human development as the ultimate goal of planning. Employment generation, population control, literacy, education, health, the supply of drinking water and adequate food, and basic infrastructure were listed as priorities.

POVERTY ALLEVIATION PROGRAMMES

Initially, India adopted a development strategy which was based on the trickle-down concept. When that development strategy failed to meet the basic needs of millions of rural poor, the need for direct intervention in favour of the poor was recognised. Consequently, the government embarked on the preparation and implementation of comprehensive and coherent antipoverty programmes. Some of them are briefly discussed below.

Wage Employment Programme

In 1961, the Rural Manpower Programme was initiated as a wage employment programme to provide seasonal employment for 100 days to the needy target groups. Another scheme of a similar nature but offering wider coverage, the Crash Scheme for Rural Employment was launched in 1971. The Food for Work Programme, which was later renamed as the National Rural Employment Programme (NREP), was started in 1977 by utilising available surplus stocks of food-grains to create rural infrastructure. It became an integral part of the sixth five-year plan and remained operational until March 1989 as a centrally sponsored programme. Later, in 1983, a new scheme called the Rural Landless Employment Guarantee Programme (RLEGP) was launched. Financed by the central government and implemented by the different States, it remained in operation until March 1989. In 1989/90 NREP and RLEGP were merged to create the new national wage employment programme, Jawahar Rozgar Yojana (JRY). A salient feature of JRY was that the financing as well as planning and implementation functions were devolved to the elected village *panchayats*. That provision was expected to ensure better utilisation of funds. In addition, the cost of administering the programme was expected to decline.

The main features of the wage employment programmes in India have been:

(a) The creation of gainful employment in the rural areas;

(b) The creation of community assets for direct and continuing benefits to the poverty groups;

(c) Supporting and giving boost to the economic activity in rural areas leading to rapid growth of rural economy;

(d) Improvement in the overall quality of life in the rural areas.

Since 1993/94, JRY has been implemented in three streams. Under the first stream, 75 per cent of the total programme funds were allocated among the States/ Union Territories according to their share of the rural poor. Further, the allocations to the districts within each State/ Union Territory were made on the basis of an index of backwardness; the index took into account the proportion of rural scheduled caste/tribe population in the district and inverse of agricultural production per agricultural worker, with equal weights.

The second stream of JRY, introduced in 120 backward districts of 12 States which had a concentration of unemployment and underemployment, provided a substantial increase in the flow of funds to those districts. The district authorities could take up any works including construction, water harvesting, farm forestry, primary school buildings, *anganwadis*, public health centres, markets and the creation of other infrastructure facilities which were required for more sustained employment and social development. The second stream of JRY was merged with Employment Assurance Scheme as at the end of 1995.

Under the third stream, special and innovative projects such as those aimed at the prevention of labour migration, the enhancement of women's employment, special programmes through voluntary organisations for drought-proofing and watershed development etc. Were taken up.

The Employment Assurance Scheme (EAS) was launched in 1993/94 in 1,752 identified backward blocks situated in drought prone, desert, tribal and hill areas, and in which the revamped public distribution system was in operation. EAS has since been extended to all the blocks of the country. Under EAS assured employment for 100 days of unskilled manual work is provided to those who seek it during the lean agricultural season. The secondary objective is the creation of rural infrastructure and community assets. Water and soil conservation works, minor irrigation works, rural roads, the construction of primary school buildings and *anganwadis* are permissible works under the scheme.

Self Employment Programmes

Another component of the antipoverty programmes in India was the self-employment programme, the most extensive of which was the Integrated Rural Development Programme (IRDP), launched in 1978. The basic aim of IRDP has been to provide assets to the asset-less target groups (such as small and marginal farmers, agricultural labourers and rural artisans) through income-generating activities that would enable them to break the poverty cycle. The programme has been financed partly by government subsidies and partly by bank credit. The programme has been implemented by an autonomous agency, the District Rural Development Agency set up especially for the purpose. The management of the programme has been coordinated at the State level under the guidance of a High Power Coordination Committee. The responsibility for providing the policy frame and general guidelines for implementation has rested with the Ministry of Rural Areas and Employment at the national level..

While the main objectives of IRDP remain unchanged, there have been some important modifications in the scheme as a result of feedback from the field as well as findings of the concurrent evaluations. There has been a shift in the programme strategy towards achieving qualitative results and investment in infrastructure. Furthermore, a new category of beneficiaries has been identified for assistance under the programme. That category comprises educated unemployed rural youth living below the poverty line, who are eligible for subsidies of up to 50 per cent of project costs, subject to a ceiling of Rs 7,500. In addition, a group of five or more beneficiaries engaged in a group venture can now receive a subsidy of up to 50 per cent of the project cost, subject to a maximum of Rs 125,000. IRDP has been successful in providing incremental income to poor families; however, it has not been adequate in enabling the beneficiaries to cross the poverty line on a sustained basis, mainly because of low per family investment.

The fourth round of the concurrent evaluation of IRDP was completed in September 1993. The results revealed certain significant trends concerning the efficacy of the programme and its impact on poverty during the 1990s. Of the total beneficiaries assisted under the programme, 14.81 per cent of the earlier beneficiary families had been able cross the revised poverty line of Rs 11,000 per annum, while 50.4 per cent of the families had been able to cross the earlier poverty line of Rs 6,400 per annum compared to 28 per cent during 1989. An analysis of family income at the national level revealed that total family income had increased by between 51 and 100 per cent in 22.85 per cent of the cases and by more than 100 per cent in 25.83 per cent of the cases, after assistance under the programme.

The average level of per family investment has been rising gradually in monetary terms but in real terms the increase has been inadequate and, in some cases, sub-critical as a result of inflationary trends and increase in cost index. The per family investment, which had averaged Rs 2,797 in the sixth Plan, rose to an average of Rs 4,626 in the seventh Plan and further to Rs 10,244 in 1994/95; however, the latter figure was below the normative level of Rs 12,000 for 1994/95. In 1995/96 the per family investment was approximately Rs 12,361 which was below the targeted level of Rs 13,500 fixed for that year. The sub-critical levels of financing of IRDP beneficiaries in the initial years of the programme had resulted in the suboptimal utilisation of assets and inadequate income generation adversely impacting on the quality of lending in general and the recovery position in particular.

Recovery of loans under IRDP has been poor; the rate declined from 41.34 per cent to 30.78 per cent. The low rate led to a decline in the credit made available to the programme by the banking sector.

Inadequate development of infrastructure, forward and backward linkages and market facilities has been another area of concern under IRDP. In an attempt to fill critical infrastructure gaps and strengthen linkages and marketing facilities, the allocation under IRDP for the development of programme infrastructure was increased from 10 to 20 per cent in all States, and to 25 per cent in the northeastern States.

In its initial years, IRDP was implemented along similar lines as SFDA and the Marginal Farmers and

Agricultural Labourers Agency, under which enhanced productivity of small and marginal farmers was sought through crop loans for the promotion of HYV, multiple cropping, horticulture, soil conservation, land development, minor irrigation, use of improved seeds; it was instrumental in spreading new technology in agriculture to small and marginal farms through the provision of credit at subsidised rates.

The major achievement of IRDP was the promotion of on farm activities in the animal husbandry sector, such as dairy, poultry, fishery etc. For the benefit of small and marginal farmers. Land assets being limited, provision of non-land assets to the poor was an alternative way of achieving income generation. Given their labour-intensive and land-saving nature, the poorer households were better suited for those activities. The growth of the dairy sector during the 1980s was much helped by the Operation Flood Project, an integrated dairy development programme started in 1970. Wherever dairy projects were promoted under IRDP along milk routes, the small and marginal farmers making use of infrastructure facilities were able to bring about sustained increase in their income levels.

The third major area of IRDP assistance to the rural poor was in the small business and services sector. Since a large segment of the rural poor are landless, around 50 per cent of IRDP activities have now been concentrated in the secondary and tertiary sectors. Assistance has been offered to those rural poor with no access to land by introducing suitable projects based on local resources and local requirements. Those projects include processing industries, handloom production and handicraft etc. The success of IRDP activities in that sector has been dependent on the development of a skill base among the poor, the upgrading of technology, the establishment of forward and backward linkages, and the availability of infrastructure and marketing tieups. In view of the diversification of the rural economy and the growth potential of the non-farm sector, the need remains to further strengthen ISB sector activities under IRDP.

During the past 15 years IRDP has covered more than 50 million families and the government has disbursed more than Rs 9 billion in subsidies. Of the total families covered, 45 per cent have been from scheduled castes and tribes; 33 per cent of the beneficiaries in the programme have been women. Over the years there has been considerable diversification of the activities under IRDP. At the beginning of the programme the primary sector accounted for 94 per cent of the beneficiaries. That percentage has come down to about 50 per cent with the share of secondary and tertiary sectors rising to roughly 20 and 30 per cent respectively.

Three IRDP sub-programmes have been implemented during the past few years to supplement the efforts on self-employment. Launched in 1979, the Training of Rural Youth for Self-Employment (TRYSEM) was aimed at providing basic technical and managerial skills to the rural youth from families below the poverty line to enable them to take up self- employment in the broad fields of agriculture and allied sectors, industries, services and business activities. That objective was subsequently enlarged in 1983 to include wage employment for trained youth. TRYSEM played an important role in facilitating the diversification of activities taken up under IRDP. In 1992, a sub-programme was launched to enable rural artisans to enhance the quality of their products, increase their production and income, and to ensure a better quality of life with the use of improved tools. Under the scheme, artisans from different crafts and who were living below the poverty line were to be given improved tools to enable them to enhance the quality/ quantity/market potential of their products; the aim was also to prevent migration to the urban areas. The third sub-programme, Development of Women and Children in Rural Areas, was launched in 1982. Initially, it was implemented in only 50 districts as a pilot scheme; later, it was extended to all districts of the country. The basic objective was to provide income-generating skills and activities to poor women in rural areas, thereby improving their social and economic status.

Agricultural Growth and Credit

India's development efforts in the past have led to the emergence of a very diversified and robust agricultural sector. The sector provides a livelihood for about 66 per cent of the labour force, contributes nearly 31 per cent in national income and accounts for a sizable share of the total value of Indian exports. The production of food-grains increased significantly from 54.2 million tons in 1949/50 to more than 190 million tons in 1995/ 96. Animal husbandry and dairy farming is estimated to account for 26 per cent of the total value of agricultural output. According to NSS estimates, the animal husbandry sub-sector has registered a higher average long-term growth rate of employment relative to agriculture (crop husbandry).

Landless, marginal and small farmers engage in this activity either on a full-time basis for gainful employment or as a way to supplement their income. Livestock development programmes are suitable for the weaker sections of the rural population. Apart from offering substantial direct employment the livestock segment also has *a large built-in potential for generating indirect employment* in several ancillary activities such as manufacturing livestock feed and the production of dairy and poultry equipment; in addition, a large number of animal-based industries use hides, skins, bones wool, bristles etc.

Providing access to institutional credit for small and marginal farmers and other weaker sections, to enable them to adopt modern technology and improved agricultural practices, has been the major objective of the credit policy. Loans are disbursed through a multi-agency network comprising commercial banks, regional rural banks and cooperatives.

Although there has been an overall increase in agricultural credit, there remains a grave problem concerning overdue payments which has inhibited credit expansion and the economic viability of the lending institutions, especially cooperatives and rural banks. In 1994, the Reserve Bank of India de-regulated the interest rate structure for cooperatives both for lending (subject to a minimum of 12 per cent) and for raising deposits. The move was expected to improve the viability of the cooperative banks. The Reserve Bank of India has taken steps towards setting up a Rural Infrastructure Development Fund at the National Bank for Agriculture and Rural Development.

Rural Industrialisation

The promotion of cottage and village industries has been an integral part of Indian planning. The Industrial Policy Resolution, recognised the importance of decentralised centres and their close linkages with the large industries. All the five-year plans gave attention to improving productivity skills and opportunities in the rural industrial sector. To encourage industry in the backward areas, schemes for a transport subsidy and an investment subsidy were designed. Small and village industries were recognised as a major avenue of employment in rural and semi-urban areas. The strategy of the plans has been one of encouraging research and innovation in traditional occupations, upgrading of technology, the dispersal of industries through the growth centre approach and the setting up of infrastructure development centres for tiny units in rural areas. In the new economic order rural, industries will have to focus special attention on technological upgrading and modernisation, in order to compete efficiently and increase productivity. Their product planning strategy must be re-oriented to enhance their share in the domestic and international markets.

Approximately 7 per cent of rural households are engaged in industrial activities. With the increase in agricultural production and with more availability of local resources and skills, the rural areas will provide better scope for setting up of agro-based industries. State intervention, particularly in the areas of strengthening basic infrastructure facilities in rural areas, will help in creating a favourable investment climate. The central government has also been vigorously pursuing self-employment opportunities through the development of rural industry. The scheme of the Prime Minister's Rojgar Yojana (PMRY) is aimed at helping youths to set up micro-enterprises in urban as well as rural areas. Similarly, the Khadi and Village Industry Commission has taken up a number of self-employment schemes aimed at promoting village and cottage industries and, at the same time, opening large avenues of employment.

Rural Roads

The importance of rural roads to rural development was recognised in a major way for the first time in the fifth five-year plan when they were included as a part of the Minimum Needs Programme (MNP). It was recognised that roads play a significant role in opening up backward areas and accelerating socioeconomic development. The programme envisaged the connection, via all-weather roads, of those villages with a population of 1,500 and above. In hilly, tribal, desert and coastal areas, the objective was to connect a cluster of villages of matching population. India has about 600,000 villages of various population sizes. The improvement of the economic conditions among the rural population, a good percentage of which is below the poverty line, hinges crucially on the provision of accessibility by means of such roads. In addition, the construction of rural roads is highly labour-intensive, generating gainful employment for millions of unemployed and underemployed rural people.

Since habitats in the hilly, tribal, coastal and desert areas are sparse, the norms for rural roads in those areas under MNP were revised during the seventh five-year plan. The purpose of the revision was to speed up the linkage of those areas.

Marketing of Farm Products

The marketing of farm products in India, by and large, operates under the normal forces of supply and demand. Private trade is the centrepiece of the Indian market mechanism. Government intervention is limited through mainly farm support policies and the promotion of organised marketing of agricultural commodities. To achieve that objective, most of the State governments have enacted the legislation necessary for the regulation of agricultural produce markets.

A number of organisations and institutions currently function to deal with product and area-specific problems that have a bearing on production, pricing and marketing of agricultural products. The most important of those institutions are the Food Corporation of India, the Cotton Corporation of India, the Jute Corporation of India and the Commodity Boards.

Agricultural marketing is also closely linked to a network of cooperatives at the primary, State and national levels. Marketing cooperatives are operating in almost all mandis. Cooperative societies are functioning in the area of fruit and vegetable processing, sugarcane crushing, cotton ginning and pressing etc. The marketing of agriculture produce through cooperatives has registered a remarkable growth

At the national level, NCDC plans and promotes programmes for the production, processing, marketing, storage, export and import of agricultural produce through cooperatives. The National Agricultural Cooperative Marketing Federation of India Ltd (NAFED) is an apex cooperative organisation dealing in the procurement, distribution, export and import of selected agricultural commodities. NAFED is a central nodal agency for undertaking price support operations for pulses and oil-seeds and market intervention operations for horticultural items such as onions, potatoes, grapes, black pepper and red chillies etc. A few other organisations in the cooperative sector are the National Cooperative Tobacco Growers' Federation as well as the Tribal Cooperative Marketing Development Federation of India Ltd which attends specifically to the marketing problems of the tribal areas.

Specialised commodity boards continue to operate for rubber, coffee, tea, tobacco, spices, coconut, oil-seeds and vegetable oils, horticulture etc. The National Dairy Development Board (NDDB) is also engaged in the marketing of agricultural commodities, Separate Directorates have been functioning for the development of raw agricultural materials like sugarcane, jute, tobacco, oil-seeds, rice, millet, cotton, pulses, cashew nuts, cocoa, spices etc. Various organisations are active in the field of agricultural commodity exports, such as the State Trading Corporation, the Cashew Nuts Export Promotion Council, the Shellac Export Promotion Council and the Agricultural and Processed Feed Export Development Authority, all of which also promote/boost agriculture exports. The role of cooperatives in the total marketing of agricultural produce, although relatively small, has been progressively expanding.

Success in raising the level of milk production and marketing is ascribed to the Operation Flood Project. Started by NDDB, the project is basically designed to link rural milk producers with urban consumers and is currently in its third phase of implementation. About 70,000 Dairy Cooperative Societies have been organised in 170 milk sheds, involving about 9 million farmer members so far. The export earnings from the livestock sector and related products rose from Rs 7,920 million in 1988/89 to Rs 16,720 million in 1994/95.

Impact of Reforms on Rural Poverty

The central government has taken a number of initiatives aimed at basic economic restructuring and reforms, with the objective of putting the Indian economy on the path of sustainable economic growth. The new policy aims at macroeconomic adjustments and structural reforms in the areas of industrial policy, trade and exchange rate policies, foreign investment policy, tax reforms, financial sector and public sector reforms.

However, those reforms involve social costs. In the first place, fiscal discipline has forced limits on Government spending which could affect investment in the social sectors. Economic restructuring may also involve temporary job losses. While total employment may increase in the process, it is necessary to ensure that the hardship imposed on any section of labour as a result of such restructuring is minimised. Recognising the need to create a social safety net, the government has taken several major steps.

From the beginning, the economic reform programme has been guided by the twin goals of accelerated and sustained growth and social equity. The goals have been pursued through the promotion of broad based, employment-generating growth, enhanced Five-Year Plan outlays for poverty alleviation and social sectors such as health and education and the building of social safety nets to cushion the possible adverse effects of reforms on vulnerable sections during the stage of transition. Therefore the importance of the special employment programmes of IRDP and JRY that are targeted on the poorest segments of Indian society have been considered as important elements.

The lower incidence of poverty in 1993/94, despite the intervening crisis of 1991/92, suggests that the various policies and programmes adopted in the process of economic reforms have helped the poor in the country. Other available evidence also supports this view. Average real wages of unskilled agricultural labour which reflect the economic conditions of agricultural labourers, declined by 6.2 per cent in the crisis year of 1991/92 for the country as a whole. But in subsequent years they increased steadily, showing an average growth of 5.1 per cent per annum from 1992/93 to 1994/95 for the country as a whole. The all India infant mortality rate was virtually unchanged in the crisis years of 1991 and 1992, before resuming its pattern of decline in 1993 and 1994. Similarly, the death rate rose slightly in 1991 and 1992 before reverting to its declining trend in 1993 and 1994. Those trends were consistent with the view that while general living standards were adversely affected by the economic crisis of 1991/92, the reform-induced recovery led to the improvements in general living standards in 1993 and 1994.

Expenditure on the social sectors, including rural development, health and education, had to be restrained in the first year of the reform because of the severity of the fiscal crisis. However, it was subsequently stepped up substantially, reflecting the improvement in the fiscal situation that had taken place over the previous years. Despite stringent resource constraints the government had steadily increased expenditure on the social sectors and on programmes for poverty alleviation. The allocation for rural development, which encompasses the major programmes for poverty alleviation, was increased from Rs 31 billion in 1992/93 to Rs 77 billion in 1995/96 and to Rs 86 billion in 1996/97. Correspondingly, the share of the social sectors and antipoverty plan rose from 35 per cent in 1992/93 to 47 per cent in 1995/96.

The government also accorded high priority to poverty alleviation programmes. The Central Plan allocations for social sectors and poverty alleviation prcgrammes were considerably increased in 1996/97. The outlay for elementary education rose considerably, mainly because of the programme of nutritional support to primary school students. The allocations for health and rural development, which encompasses the major poverty alleviation programmes, increased by 21.6 and 12 per cent respectively in 1996/97, compared with the allocations in 1995/96.

Several important new schemes for social uplift and poverty alleviation have been launched in India during recent reform years, including EAS for providing 100 days of unskilled manual labour to the rural poor, PMRY which is aimed at providing work for unemployed youth through the creation of micro-enterprises, NSAP which encompasses old age pensions, family benefits in case of death of the family breadwinner and maternity benefits, the Rural Group Life Insurance Scheme with a subsidised premium, the National Programme of Nutritional Support to Primary Education (also known as the Midday Meal Scheme) aimed at providing nutritious meals to children in primary school, the Mahila Samridhi Yojana to promote the savings habit among rural women. The weaker sections, especially scheduled castes/ scheduled tribes and women, have been given importance in special programmes on poverty alleviation and employment as well as in several other programmes. The Public Distribution System (PDS) was recently streamlined in order to target the poorer sections of the population.

The above discussion have underlined that despite the progress of economic reforms in India since 1991 the emphasis on poverty alleviation programmes has not diminished. Government intervention has continued in all rural development and welfare programmes. The revised development strategy lays greater emphasis on providing employment opportunities to the rural poor. EAS is now being extended all over the country. The other antipoverty programmes has also been restructured to equip them to achieve their objective of poverty alleviation. Several government programmes are aimed at strengthening the rural markets to make agricultural produce more economic for the benefit of the rural poor.

The government has also continued to provide institutional security for the rural poor. Investment in agro-forestry and export orientation of agriculture produce will also lead to improvement in the rural areas. The rural credit institutions have continued to receive support and have been further strengthened. Efforts have also been intensified to strengthen the grassroots level democratic institutions. The seventy-third amendment of the Constitution has now received constitutional sanction for the village *panchayat* institutions. *Panchayats* are being formed in all States and powers are being delegated to them. These institutions will now have control of all rural development programmes. The policies of the Government of India are to encourage the growth of non-governmental organisations (NGOs). Their participation is generally encouraged as a matter of strategy in all rural development programmes. The government has taken several steps to strengthen the safety net for the rural poor. JRY, PMRY, NSAP, the Midday Meal Programme, the Indira Was Yojana, PDS and a number of other programmes now provide a reasonable safety net for the weakest sections of Indian society. The basic minimum services identified for priority are steps in that direction.

Social Funds and Institutions

Social funds (SFs) have expanded rapidly in recent years. By May 2001, total World Bank investment in SFs was $3.5 billion for more than 98 projects in 58 countries. Although the reviews have been mixed or highly critical, SFs may continue to expand rapidly.

Although SFs differ in design and content, they have some common features. Characterised as 'demand driven " and decentralised initiatives, their salient features are: (i) they make grant funds available to communities or municipalities to choose from a menu of projects (e.g. a well, health centre, school, road repair); (ii) project design and construction are decentralised to local actors comprising private firms, NGOs, local governments and community groups; (iii) community groups contract the design or construction firms or equipment suppliers, monitor project execution and/or take responsibility for operations and maintenance; and (iv) a local contribution of 10-15 percent of project costs is often required.

SFs started in Latin America primarily to mitigate the hardships of structural adjustment. They were meant to provide employment through public works and emergency social services in rural areas, and to compensate for layoffs as a result of downsizing of the public sector in urban areas. By the mid-1990s, several SFs were elevated to more permanent status, in view of their potential as an alternative mode of delivery of public services.

District Poverty Initiative Projects (DPIPs)

The broad objectives of DPIPs are: (i) to create income earning opportunities for the rural poor; (ii) to empower disadvantaged groups; and (iii) to promote more effective, accountable and inclusive *Panchayats* (village councils) and other local support and service organisations.

The need for DPIPs arose from the unsatisfactory performance of existing antipoverty programmes such as *Swaranjayanti Gram Swarozgar Yojana* (SGSY) and Employment Assurance Scheme (EAS), sponsored by the Government of India. The reasons cited are (i) high administrative costs, (ii) their supply driven nature, and (iii) limited focus on organisations and the skills of the poor.

The design of DPIPs is guided by various considerations, reflecting World Bank's experience of rural development projects in India and elsewhere. These include:

1. Empowerment of disadvantaged groups by giving them control over funds;
2. Ensuring that group investments are demand driven;
3. Fostering group formation of the most disadvantaged around common interests;
4. Ensuring local ownership by requiring cash contributions for group subprojects and creation of village funds;
5. Strengthening of local governments at the district and village levels;
6. Ensuring transparency of the project's performance;
7. Facilitating attitudinal and behavioural changes among various stockholders; and
8. Strengthening infrastructures support and expansion of income opportunities in 2000 villages in Madhya Pradesh..

Institutions, and Implementation

To ensure that the benefits accrue mostly to the poor, two mechanisms are proposed: one is geographic targeting and the other is group targeting. The first will involve selection of the poorest blocks and villages/habitations in 14 districts; and the second will require actively promoting collective action, organisation, information and the skills of the poorest first, so that they can negotiate better with formal organisations and demand project and other forms of assistance.

Primary stockholders are beneficiary organisations (i.e. Common Interest Groups (CIG)), facilitation organisations (Project Facilitation Team (PFT), NGOs), project management and support units (State Project Unit (SPU), and District Project Unit (DPU)), and government. Human resource development would be the responsibility of District Capacity Building Organisations (either NGOs or government agencies).

With a view to ensuring that the poorest are aware of funding possibilities under the project and the procedures to be followed, there is considerable emphasis on dissemination of information and communication. A communication specialist at the State level would support the district units, and PFTs would carry out communication activities at the village level.

To be eligible for subproject financing, villagers would organise themselves into Common Interests Groups (CIGs), with the majority being poor. PFTs would help ensure inclusion of the disadvantaged by building their capacity and assisting them in accessing DPIP funds.

At the village level, the CIGs would identify and submit proposals to the Village Development Committee-composed of all elected *Panchayat* members, and representatives of all CIGs for appraisal. The VDC would appraise them in consultation with the PFTs, and priorities them for the given budget. The VDC would submit them to the District Sub-Committee for approval and disbursement. CIGs would be responsible for implementation and operation, and would get assistance from government, NGOs or private sources. All subprojects would require a community cash contribution of 5 percent, and an additional contribution of 10 percent to be deposited in a Village Fund.

At the state level, the overall budgetary allocation would be the responsibility of the Board of the Society for Poverty Alleviation Initiatives (MPSPAI), chaired by the Chief Minister. Budgetary allocations in the first year would be on the basis of the target population, and in the second on the basis of performance.

Monitoring would ensure that project stockholders understand better the reasons for a project's success or failure, as well as learn from the experience in other DPIP states.

Innovations

The DPIP has several innovative features. Creation of a Board with the Chief Minister as the Chairman is designed to ensure that the project has the full backing of the state government, and considerable autonomy. The emphasis on quick and flexible disbursals through streamlining of procedures at the district and village levels (disbursals by the DPU into CIG bank accounts, for example, would cut bureaucratic delays) seeks to remedy bunching of expenditure in the last two or three months of a financial year and large un-spent balances. The shift of emphasis from supply driven to demand driven allocations with considerable attention to ensuring that the poorest (e.g. Scheduled Castes and Tribes) have access to them and are enabled to improve their well-being is appealing. In this context, the priority assigned to dissemination of information and communication at different stages of decision-making – in particular, to making the poorest aware of opportunities for enhancing their incomes and for capacity building is noteworthy. Moreover, the focus on not just economic betterment but also on empowerment of the disadvantaged through their more effective participation in decisions that are crucial to their well-being is a significant departure. Ownership of assets created (e.g. a school, an irrigation canal) through mandatory community contributions would contribute to their sustainability. Finally, without periodic and systematic monitoring and evaluation, the flexibility in the design and implementation of the project would be of limited value. So to avoid distortions considerable emphasis is placed on monitoring and cross-learning from DPIPs in different states.

Assessment

Whether the DPIPs live up to their promise would of course depend on how they are implemented.

Aberrations

Although the composition of decision-making bodies at the state, district and village level varies, with different mixes of bureaucrats, elected representatives, NGOs and CIGs, there is an interplay of vested interests. At the state level, senior bureaucrats often have the upper hand with their easier access to project information, allocation procedures, and donor's priorities and concerns. On the other hand, often pitted against them are politicians who are more amenable to locally powerful interests. At lower levels, a mixed pattern is sometimes observed with elements of collusion and conflict. While line agencies placed under elected bodies seldom cooperate, some lower level functionaries that work closely with elected bodies collude to secure rents. The point therefore is that whatever the organisational form and the composition, there will be vested interests that are not likely to promote the interests of the poor. The evidence cited below illustrates.

A similar structure was established for Mewat Area Development Project (MADP), a collaborative project of the Haryana government and IFAD. The Mewat Area

Development Board functioned as an extension of Haryana government in which key decisions were taken by senior civil servants and duly approved by the Chairman. Occasionally there were political demands (e.g. a political rally in support of the Chief Minister was classified as 'Development Support Communications' for funding under the MADP) that were accommodated without any fuss as long as these did not interfere with bureaucratic control over financial allocations and disbursals. As there were frequent and large shortfalls in expenditure relative to outlays the expenditure was barely 36 per cent of the outlay in the first five years of this project with a seven year span the Mewat Development Agency had more or less a free hand in allocating funds in a piecemeal and *ad hoc* manne. It was not so much the local needs and priorities that dictated the allocations but the political clout of local politicians.

> A particularly serious aberration came to light that the MDA was tight-lipped about.

Briefly, a wasteland management scheme was prepared by the Panchayat of Agon. The proposal envisaged the reclamation of 400 acres of land in this village, through levelling, installation of tube-wells, field-bunding and plantations. Half the reclaimed area (about 200 acres) was to be leased out to the chronically poor for a period of 3-5 years, and the remaining half was to be auctioned to the non-poor. Given the un reliability of the below the poverty line (BPL) lists, it was proposed to identify the poor during a meeting of the village assembly. Costs of the first year's *rabi* (winter) and *kharif* (summer) crops for the poor were to be covered by the MDA. After the expiry of the first lease, it was projected that about 50 per cent of the initial beneficiaries would have accumulated enough savings to buy their own plots of land or to engage in other remunerative activities. The remaining 50 per cent were expected to be in a position to compete for land leases at an auction along with others. Even though this scheme was not included in the original version of MADP, its participatory orientation (since the proposal was worked out by the Panchayat with the support of the local community) and poverty alleviating potential had considerable appeal. As a result, it was included in the MADP and a special budgetary provision was made. Soon after the levelling work started. However, after levelling of 13 acres, there was no progress. A general impression was that tardiness of release of funds was the main reason. When we started making discreet enquiries, hardly any clues emerged. As the officials were tight lipped and there was in fighting among Panchayat members, we had no leads whatsoever until we ran into a local politician. He revealed how an influential *Jat* MLA (a member of the legislative assembly) had manipulated the transfer of funds to a similar project in a predominantly *Jat* area (while the scheme was meant for the betterment of the backward *Meos*). We followed up this lead and found corroborative evidence. What was surprising was that this manipulation was not detected in any of the supervision missions.

Collusion, Capture and Rents

The subproject proposals prepared by CIGs would be submitted to the VDC, consisting of Panchayat members, representatives of CIGs and other people selected by the *Gram Sabha*. In consultation with the PFT, the VDC would appraise these proposals and submit the approved list to the Gram Sabha which in turn would forward it to the ZP DPIS. Although CIGs would be responsible for the implementation and operation of subprojects, the VDC would have overall responsibility for implementation at the village level. Thus local institutions especially the VDC and to some extent the Gram Sabha would have a pivotal role.

Although the Appraisal Reports emphatically reject relying on *Panchayat Raj* Institutions (PRIs), it is difficult to understand how the dominance of *Panchayats* and through them of locally powerful individuals can be avoided especially since all *Panchayat* members are included in the VDC.Bribes, commissions, and embezzlement of funds were common. Given the quasi-monopoly power of the *Panchayats* in land allotment, public employment and other services, there were ample opportunities for earning rents. Even under the revamped system, our survey revealed that transparency in decision-making of the *Panchayats* was lacking. Information relating to outlays, eligibility requirements, selection of activities and muster rolls of participants was tightly controlled by a small group of *Panchayat* members and a few key functionaries. Local elates benefited in several ways either as participants or through contracts for supplies or through assets built that favoured them more than the community (e.g contour bunding). Acts of corruption remained undetected, or unpunished, if detected, largely because of the ineffectiveness of the *Gram Sabha*. The *Gram Sabha* meetings seldom took place. Even when they did, they were no more than rituals. They were not publicised, their frequency was disputed, the agenda were manipulated, caste and other important factors influenced decisions, and intimidation and violence were frequently employed to force compliance. On the other hand, higher authorities were powerless under the new legislation (i.e. the 73rd Constitutional Amendment) because the Chairpersons of the *Panchayats* can only be dismissed if there is a no-confidence motion against them.

In any case, going by field-evidence from Maharashtra villages, the experience of working with parallel organisations such as the VDCs that draw largely upon the Panchayats has been unsatisfactory. This is largely because the VDCs reproduced many of the shortcomings of the Panchayats in particular, locally powerful individuals manipulated decisions of the former to serve their own interests better, and the poorest were excluded.

Briefly, two parallel organisations (viz. The Village Development Assembly and Village Development Council, the VDA and VDC, respectively) were created to target the rural poor under the Maharashtra Rural Credit Project (MRCP). The motivation underlying these new institutions was similar i.e. to avoid heavy dependence on the Panchayats.

In principle, the VDAs/VDCs had an important role in identifying beneficiaries, arranging for loans and in their follow-up. Their formation, representativeness and functioning were thus crucial to the targeting of the MRCP. However, the picture that emerged from our survey of three villages in Pune District was not encouraging.

The VDCs were constituted by the participating banks somewhat hastily and in an ad hoc manner to launch the MRCP. Locally influential persons/groups along with a few SC/ST representatives were inducted. A few *Panchayat* members – including the *Sarpanch* – were also included. The relationship between the VDAs and VDCs was somewhat vague. Although bank officers and NGOs were supposed to participate in the VDC meetings, it was usually a ritual.

Since there were no elections and usually the bank nominated SC/ST and other members, the VDC was not a representative body. Moreover, the nominated SC/ST members were unaware of the objectives, procedures and decisions.

The VDC met once a month. The agenda were not announced. The venue was a *Gram Panchayat* office or a temple. As there was no quorum, the meeting was held even if there were several absentees. Selection of MRCP beneficiaries was seldom discussed. Either the *Sarpanch* or the *Gram Sevak* nominated the beneficiaries. The list of poor households (i.e. those below the poverty line) was in the custody of the *Gram Sevak*. Although the list was faulty (sometimes 80-90% of the households in a village were included), no questions were asked about its reliability. Even self-nomination of influential persons (a Vice-President of a VDC, for example, nominated himself) was seldom challenged. If the poorest got included in the list of potential beneficiaries, it was either through the initiative of NGOs and *Sahyoginis* (field-workers of NGOs) or through their own determined efforts. Attention was also drawn to the nexus between bank staff and VDC, resulting in substantially higher loans to relatively affluent persons. The minutes (including the list of beneficiaries) were usually in the custody of the Chairperson or the Secretary of the VDC. That the exclusion of the poorest was to some extent deliberate cannot therefore be ruled out.

To sum up, the functioning of the VDCs was neither participatory nor transparent. Given the weak accountability mechanisms, arbitrary selection of beneficiaries remained uncontested. So the replacement of the *Gram Panchayat* and *Gram Sabha* by the VDC and VDA, respectively, hardly made a difference.

Incentive Compatibility

As noted earlier, in the organisational set up, there will be different mixes of officials, elected representatives, NGOs and others. There is a strong presumption that these stockholders – officials and elected representatives on the one hand, and elected representatives of the *Panchayats* at different levels on the other can be induced to work together towards the betterment of the lives of the rural poor, through sensitisation to some basic values and appropriate performance based rewards. More generally, some recent work has drawn attention to asynergy between public and civil society organisations, driven presumably not so much by economic rewards as by a desire for civic engagement, a sense of collective identity and social responsibility. A special case of asynergy is embeddedness in which the public–civic relations are mutually reinforcing. It must, however, be emphasised that the criteria for determining successful cases differ and the range of activities and contexts covered is large. More often than not, the public – civic relationships are *adversary*, or *displacing*, or *competitive*. The Indian evidence is mixed.

In the initial phase of reorganisation of the *Panchayats* in Uttar Pradesh (UP), following the 73rd Constitutional Amendment, there was an arbitrary reassignment of responsibilities. All areas except village hygiene and sanitation remained under the overall control and supervision of state and district agencies in blatant violation of the constitutional provisions. Effectively, the District Magistrate retained overall responsibility for some of the most important antipoverty programmes (such as the JRY and IRDP). That the bureaucracry (or, more generally) official agencies could overextend its (their) domains had a lot to do with an unstable party coalition (between the Samajwadi Janta Party and Bhartiya Janta Party) and unsettled conditions in the hill areas. In a striking contrast, the Karnataka case points to another source of aberrations: relative bargaining strength and skills of the Panchayats at different levels. Given a relatively stable political environment and a well carved out role for the bureaucracy, the battlefield shifted to the *Panchayats*. As it turned out, most of the major schemes were monopolised either by the *Zilla Panchayats* or *Taluk Panchayats*, especially the latter, with a minimal role for the *Gram Panchayats*.

More pertinent in the present context is the "People's Planning Campaign " launched by the State Planning Board in Kerala in 1996. Not only were community choices similar to those of line agencies earlier but there was also a general neglect of ecological considerations.

As part of this Campaign, 100,000 volunteers were trained to assist local bodies. In *Gram Sabha* (village assembly/ward) meetings, more than two million people expressed their felt needs; voluntary experts and ward representatives identified the main problems and drafted development reports; based on these reports, sectoral task forces—comprising local officials, voluntary experts and resource persons—drafted project proposals; Village *Panchayats* then priorities these proposals within a broad set of guidelines for sectoral allocations; the local plans of 991 Village *Panchayats* were integrated in 152 block *Panchayat* plans and 14 district *Panchayat* plans; in consultation with district-level officers, block and district-level *Panchayat* representatives approved the plans in seminars; and, finally, district and block-level expert committees gave the required technical sanctions.

The local plans in 1997-98 produced nearly 68,000 projects, from repairing irrigation ponds, to developing cooperative vegetable gardens, to establishing women's enterprises, building houses for squatter families and reviving ritual traditions. Delays were avoided through informal rules developed between different stockholders. The adoption of productive and sustainability goals in the local plans, however, shows a mixed record. Compliance with prescribed sectoral allocations was weak since the majority of projects were consumption-oriented, individual beneficiary schemes were more common than group-based activities, and subsidy rates were high. The bulk of beneficiary contributions were mandatory contributions for receiving subsidised goods. Furthermore, the projects were partial interventions such as single-crop schemes that neglected ecology and marketing. In sum, most projects were qualitatively similar to those implemented by line agencies earlier.

Among the few exceptions to this record, however, was the establishment of a "labour bank" through the initiative of an agricultural officer of a south Keralan village *Panchayat*, designed to ensure assured supply of labour at short notice, a crucial requirement for paddy cultivation. A new body, the "Farmers' Helping Group", composed of *Panchayat* representatives, of farmers and labourers, and government officers, was constituted. This Group negotiated a fixed wage rate, provided training and subsidised farm inputs. As a result, within a short period, there was agricultural intensification and employment generation, and reversal of environmentally unsound conversion of wet land. Both the participating labourers and farmers benefited.

Another exception relates to the integration of environmental concerns in some sectoral projects. For housing projects, for example, an NGO produced environment-friendly building materials. In a few cases committed government officers and scientists were instrumental in promoting the use of environment-friendly technology. In general, however, this was not the case (e.g. soil and water conservation projects failed as they were not part of an overall watershed management plan).

While decentralised planning thus expanded the scope for civil society, *Panchayats*, NGOs and officials to implement sustainable-development projects, community participation alone did not lead to environmental projects. To some extent, the neglect of environmental impact assessment and monitoring of environmental standards by state institutions also contributed to the unimpressive record of decentralised planning in sustainable development.

Although it was notable for its financial devolution and the involvement of communities in identifying, designing and implementing projects, the new Kerala model failed to produce the desired results for several reasons.

Despite the greater transparency in decision-making, the network among locally influential persons led to an arbitrary selection of projects. One of the reasons was that, confronted with the often harsh trade-offs between immediate livelihood needs and long-term environmental protection, the former apparently became a stronger consideration. As a lesson borne out by decentralised planning in sustainable development, it bears repeating that sensitivity to environmental concerns cannot be taken for granted even in communities that depend heavily on natural resources. The immediate concerns expressed in village development plans need to be counterbalanced by the spatial and temporal externalities that would be articulated in higher-level planning. This is easier said than done, considering the difficulty of reconciling conflicting interests between popular participation and top-level planning.

A crucial requirement for community-based development is to clearly identify and strengthen areas of asynergies between the state government, the local bodies and the civil society. The Kerala model has tried to induct local civil servants into the process of decentralised planning. In addition, the transparency of financial allocations has also increased. Yet much depends on the commitment and dynamism of a few officials and development volunteers.

Common Interests Groups (CIGs)

CIGs are central to the DPIP as a mechanism for targeting the rural poor. These groups would also be responsible for implementation of approved subprojects. As the most disadvantaged groups or the poorest lack information and organisational skills, the DPIPs seek to overcome these constraints through awareness-building and training.

Self-help groups (SHGs) were formed in Mewat for channelling credit to women. Although composed entirely of women from (relatively) affluent households, already a significant shortcoming, SHG formation and their linkage to banks has tended to be slow. The main reasons were male resistance, a generally helpful attitude of bank staff and limited interaction with NGO field-staff. Nevertheless, benefits to SHG members and to the community at large were not negligible. By contrast, the majority of members of SHGs in Pune District (about 80 percent) were poor. In most cases, the formation of SHGs and their interface with a bank took about two years or more. They functioned satisfactorily and contributed substantially to both household and community welfare. The evidence, however, also points to exclusion of the poorest, due to lack of information, social resistance, and biases of implementing agencies. In fact, the training imparted by the NGOs was much too brief (2-3 days) while that given through more specialised agencies largely irrelevant. Besides, training modules specifically for the poorest/most disadvantaged groups did not exist.

That the exclusion of the poorest was widespread was confirmed in other cases as well. This is of course not surprising, given the nature of 'the common interests'. But there were other problems too that affected their functioning and limited their welfare enhancing impact.

As dairying is an important source of supplementary income for both poor and non-poor households in Mewat, its development was assigned considerable importance in the MADP. Given a large number of small suppliers of milk and colluding private buyers, usually the former were at the mercy of the latter. The entire output of milk net of self-consumption requirements was pre-committed to a buyer at a low price. Milk Producers' Cooperatives as part of a three-tier Federation were promoted under the MADP with a view to ensuring that small suppliers of milk obtained remunerative prices and substantially larger supplementary incomes. As part of this promotional strategy, 177 dairy marketing cooperatives and 36 mini dairy units and milk collection centres were set up; and the milk chilling centre in Nuh was revived.

The cooperatives comprised mostly (relatively) affluent households, with average incomes almost two and a half times the poverty cutoff point. The average landholding was 10.5 acres; each household had cattle (buffaloes, cows, calves); and all but one also owned other assets in the form of agricultural equipment (hand pump, tractor) and consumer durables (TV, radio, bicycle, motor cycle).

Whether milk producers' cooperatives had the desired effect on the well-being of milk suppliers seems doubtful primarily because the latter continued to depend heavily on private buyers despite the fact that the price offered by them was lower. Private buyers compensated partly for the lower price by offering advance cash payment and/ or credit for buying buffaloes and contingencies. Given the acute need for credit, some members switched back to private buyers when family circumstances changed or it became imperative to borrow. Mismanagement of Village Cooperatives and lack of transparency in their functioning, and inefficient milk testing procedures contributed to a growing disillusionment among the milk suppliers. As a result, in some cooperatives there was a sharp reduction in membership, a marked reduction in milk collection and the viability of the Federation was threatened.

Another CIG comprised farmers involved in horticulture. The soil and climatic conditions of Mewat favour horticulture. Several kinds of vegetables and fruits are grown easily. Two strategic options were relevant: expand the area under agriculture by expanding irrigation and/or intensify horticulture in the irrigated areas by introducing better quality inputs and improved pre-harvest and post-harvest management practices. For various reasons, the MDA chose the latter option.

The beneficiaries were highly affluent farmers, with an average income nine times higher than the poverty cutoff point. Besides, the participants reaped substantial benefits in the form of higher yields and revenues. Full potential benefits were, however, not realised due to marketing, credit and input supply constraints. Nor was technical support adequate.

The selection of beneficiaries was largely ad hoc in nature, resulting in the exclusion of marginal and small farmers in violation of eligibility criteria. Rationing worked against the participation of the poor. Being less informed, they were less likely to present themselves at places where they could register with the scheme. They were also excluded because assistance was restricted to those favoured by the *Panchayats*.

Mewat is mostly semi-arid and subject to frequent droughts. Two-thirds of the area has brackish water, restricting its use for irrigation. As a result of excessive pumping, the water table has fallen steadily. Since the Aravali Hills are devoid of vegetative cover, the heavy runoff during the monsoon season causes acute soil erosion. Excessive grazing of animals has aggravated the drought-proneness of the region. Under these conditions, considerable importance was attached to soil and water conservation under the MADP. The objective of this component was to increase rainfed cultivation over 16000 ha. With better watershed management practices. In principle, the strategy was to use state-of-art techniques with active community involvement. It was proposed to form watershed associations or committees around the work-sites.

Most of the beneficiaries of watershed development were quite well-off. While the benefits in the form of prevention of heavy runoff were non-negligible, changes in cropping patterns and increases in yields were well below the potential. Consequently, employment and wages also rose slightly. An important reason was deficient rainfall during the three years preceding the survey. The design and execution of watershed projects were also unsatisfactory in some respects. Specifically, in the absence of a master plan for watershed development, it is doubtful whether the sites selected reflected regional priorities; there were some design defects and the quality of compaction in some of the structures was unsatisfactory; and the communities' involvement in the design and execution of these projects was minimal. As a consequence, the communities did not 'own' these assets, raising serious concerns about their maintenance and durability.

Reluctance to contribute towards the maintenance of watershed structures had little to do with lack of ability to contribute since most of the beneficiaries were well above the poverty threshold. Rather, it reflected an attitude of dependence on an outside agency (i.e. MDA) and absence of a sense of ownership. Besides, another major contributory factor was the cynical attitude of Soil and Water Conservation staff towards the community and local institutions-especially the Panchayats. Inactivity of and factionalism within the *Panchayats* tended to reinforce this cynicism.

An analysis of determinants of cooperation in irrigation communities, based on a large survey in Tamil Nadu, yields additional insights. Cooperation is low when inequality in landholding is high, and when there are strong urban or market connections. On the other hand, cooperation is positively linked to duration of access to water, social homogeneity, small group size, and proportional cost sharing. Besides, when the water allocation rules are crafted by the village elite, there are fewer violations by them. But when the rules are jointly crafted, as opposed to by the elite or by the government, there is greater compliance.

Dynamic Group Network Externalities

There is often a presumption that formation of CIGs especially SHGs is costly because it involves lengthy involvement of an external agency (usually an NGO). In the context of the DPIP, the PFT performs this function. This presumption does not take into account the dynamic effects of the SHGs (or, for that matter, of any other CIG). A successful SHG, for example, stimulates the formation at a much lower cost-of other groups in the same or neighbouring villages. The cost of delivering credit to the poor through SHGs may therefore be substantially lower. Some other externalities on the benefit side are likely to be equally, if not more important. If participation in an SHG imparts greater self-confidence to women, adds to their social awareness and broadens their spheres of activities, the valuation of such benefits of SHGs could enhance substantially the cost-effectiveness of credit through them.

There was general confirmation of a few successful SHGs inducing the formation of other SHGs in the same and neighbouring villages over time in the Mewat study. A mechanism cited by several respondents referred to SHG members inviting their friends/relatives from different villages to attend training/orientation camps. Many of these returned to their villages to motivate others to form SHGs. NGOs also contributed significantly to the transmission of group network externalities by drawing attention to success stories when addressing male resistance. The formation of "knock-on" SHGs was reportedly much quicker. Many of them were mixed and functioning (at the time of the survey). More significant, however, was the transformation of women's role in the community sphere where SHG members (as well as other women) became more assertive about larger social concerns (e.g. prohibition).

Bibliography

Aby, Stephen H. (2005). *Sociology: A Guide to Reference and Information Sources,* Littleton, Colorado, Libraries Unlimited Inc.

Alatas, S. H. (2006). "The Autonomous, the Universal and the Future of Sociology". *Current Sociology* 54: 7–23 [15].

Ashley D, Orenstein DM (2005). *Sociological theory: Classical statements (6th ed.).* Boston, Massachusetts, USA: Pearson Education. pp. 3–5, 32–36.

Babbie, Earl R. (2003). *The Practice of Social Research, 10th edition.* Wadsworth, Thomson Learning Inc.

Ben-David, Joseph; Teresa A. Sullivan (1975). "Sociology of Science". *Annual Review of Sociology* 1: 203–222.

Berger, Peter L. *The Sacred Canopy: Elements of a Sociological Theory of Religion* (1967). Anchor Books 1990 paperback.

Boudon, Raymond. (1991). "Review: What Middle-Range Theories are". *Contemporary Sociology,* Vol. 20 Num. 4 pp 519–522.

Collins, Randall. (1994). *Four Sociological Traditions.* Oxford, Oxford University Press.

Coser, Lewis A. (1971). *Masters of Sociological Thought : Ideas in Historical and Social Context,* New York, Harcourt Brace Jovanovich.

Dahrendorf, Ralf. (1959). *Class and Class Conflict in Industrial Society.* Stanford: Stanford University Press.

Durkheim, Émile. (1895). *The Rules of the Sociological Method.* Cited in Wacquant (1992).

Giddens, A (1996). *The Constitution of Society.* California: University of California Press. pp. 14–19.

Giddens, Anthony. (2006). *Sociology* (5th edition), Polity, Cambridge.

Kaern, Phillips & Cohen. (1990) *Georg Simmel and Contemporary Sociology.* Springer Publishing.

Kevin J. Christiano, et al., (2008). *Sociology of Religion: Contemporary Developments,* Lanham, Maryland: Rowman & Littlefield Publishers.

Landis, Judson R (1989). *Sociology: Concepts and Characteristics* (7th ed.). Belmont, California: Wadsworth.

Macionis, John J (1991). *Sociology* (3rd ed.). Englewood Cliffs, New Jersey: Prentice Hall.

Macy, Michael; Willer, Robb (2002). "From Factors to Actors: Computational Sociology and Agent-Based Modeling". *Annual Review of Sociology* 28: 143–66.

Merton, Robert K. (1959). *Social Theory and Social Structure. Toward the codification of theory and research*, Glencoe: Ill.

Nash, Kate (2000). *Contemporary Political Sociology*. United Kingdom: Wiley-Blackwell. pp. 1–3.

Nisbet, Robert A. (1967). *The Sociological Tradition*, London, Heinemann Educational Books.

Piven, F. (1988) *Why Americans Don't Vote: And Why Politicians Want it That Way* Pantheon.

Randall Collins, Cited in Horowitz, Irving (1994) *The Decomposition of Sociology* Oxford University Press.

Rickman, H. P. (1960) *The Reaction against Positivism and Dilthey's Concept of Understanding*, The London School of Economics and Political Science.

Ritzer, George and Douglas J. Goodman. (2004). *Sociological Theory, Sixth Edition.* McGraw Hill.

Saunders, Peter (1990). *Social Class and Stratification*. Routledge.

Slattery, Martin. (1993). *Key Ideas in Sociology*. Cheltenham: Nelson Thornes, Ltd.

Wallace, Ruth A. & Alison Wolf. (1995). *Contemporary Sociological Theory: Continuing the Classical Tradition*, 4th ed., Prentice-Hall.

Watson, Tony J. (2008). *Sociology, Work, and Industry*. Routledge.

Weber, Max *The Nature of Social Action* in Runciman, W.G. 'Weber: Selections in Translation' Cambridge University Press, 1991. p7.

White, Harrison C (2008). *Identity and Control. How Social Formations Emerge.* Princeton, Princeton University Press.

Willis, Evan. (1996). *The Sociological Quest: An introduction to the study of social life*, New Brunswick, New Jersey, Rutgers University Press.

Index

ENCYCLOPAEDIA OF SOCIOLOGY

Urban Sociology

Volume –8

Satish Mittal
Sushil Kumar Saxena

Commonwealth

Encyclopaedia of Sociology

Edition : 2026

ISBN 978-81-311-0377-7 (set)

Published by :
COMMONWEALTH PUBLISHERS (P) LTD.
4831/24, Govind Lane,
Ansari Road, Darya Ganj,
New Delhi - 110002
Ph. : 23242541, 23272541
e-mail : commonwealthpublishers2016@gmail.com

Distributed by :
ARJUN PUBLISHING HOUSE
4831/24, Govind Lane,
Ansari Road, Darya Ganj,
New Delhi - 110002
Ph. : 23242541, 23272541
e-mail : arjunbooks2001@gmail.com
arjunpubhouse@gmail.com

Laser Typesetting by :
Dimple Computers
Delhi

Printed at :
Milan Enterprises
Delhi

Preface

Urban sociology is the sociological study of social life and human interaction in metropolitan areas. It is a normative discipline of sociology seeking to study the structures, processes, changes and problems of an urban area and by doing so providing inputs for planning and policy making. Urban sociologists use statistical analysis, observation, social theory, interviews, and other methods to study a range of topics, including migration and demographic trends, economics, poverty, race relations, economic trends, etc.

After the industrial revolution, sociologists such as Max Weber, and particularly Georg Simmel in works such as *The Metropolis and Mental Life,* focused on the increasing process of urbanization and the effects it had on feelings of social alienation and anonymity. The Chicago School is a major influence in the study of urban sociology. Many of their findings have been refined or rejected, but the lasting impact of the Chicago School can still be found in today's teachings.

The present book provides an indispensable introduction to urban sociology. It not only includes clear explanations of theories and evidence, but also covers the most cutting-edge research, data, and debates. Written in a lively and accessible style, the book has been specially designed to support students' understanding, and to develop their critical responses to the literature.

Authors

Contents

1

Urbanisation and Urban Development

Urbanisation is an integral part of the process of economic growth. As in most countries, India's towns and cities make a major contribution to the country's economy. With less than 1/3 of India's people, its urban areas generate over 2/3 of the country's GDP and account for 90% of government revenues.

Urbanisation in India has expanded rapidly as increasing numbers of people migrate to towns and cities in search of economic opportunity. Slums now account for 1/4 of all urban housing. In Mumbai, for instance, more than half the population lives in slums, many of which are situated near employment centers in the heart of town, unlike in most other developing countries.

At present approximately 307 million Indians lives in nearly 3700 towns and cities spread across the country. This is 30.5% of its population, in sharp contrast to only 60 millions (15%) who lived in urban areas in 1947 when the country became Independent. During the last fifty years the population of India has grown two and half times, but Urban India has grown by nearly five times. In numerical terms, India's urban population is second largest in the world after China, and is higher than the total urban population of all countries put together barring China, USA and Russia.

Table 1. India: Urban Population 1901 – 2001

	Urban population (million)	Percentage of Urban to total population	Decadal growth rate (percent)
1901	29.9	10.8	—
1911	25.9	10.3	0.4
1921	28.1	11.2	18.3
1931	33.5	12.0	19.1
1941	44.2	13.9	32.0
1951	62.4	17.3	41.4
1961	78.9	18.0	26.4
1971	109.1	19.9	38.2
1981	159.5	23.3	46.1
1991	217.6	25.7	36.4
2001	306.9	30.5	41.0

At the 1991 census, two-third of the country's urban population lived in Class-I cities with more than 1,00,000 population.

Table 2. Distribution of urban population by size class of towns

Class	Population Range	No. of Towns	Share of urban Population
I	1,00,000 & above	300	65.20%
II	50,000 to 99,999	345	10.95%
III	20,000 to 49,999	947	13.19%
IV	10,000 to 19,999	1,167	7.77%
V	5,000 to 9,999	740	2.60%
VI	Less than 5,000	197	0.29%
	All Classes	3,696	100%

About one-third of Urban India (71 million) lives in metropolitan cities (million plus). The number of such cities in India has increased from 1 in 1901 to 5 in 1951 to 23 in 1991 to 40 in 2001. Out of the total increase in the country's urban population of 58 million between 1981 and

1991, 44 million were added to Class I cities alone. 28 million persons were added in metropolitan cities.

Urban areas are the engines of productivity and growth in the country. This is manifest in the increasing contribution of urban sector to national income.

Table 3. Urban contribution to national income

Year	Percentage of Urban to total population	Estimated contribution to national income
1951	17.3	29%
1981	23.3	47%
1991	25.7	55%
2001	30.5	60%

Growth of employment (main workers) in urban India during 1981-91 was recorded at 38% against 16% in rural areas and 26.1% in the country as a whole.

Environmental Impacts of Urbanisation

Some of the chief forces driving urbanisation today are shifting of jobs from agriculture to industry and the concentration of economic opportunities in the urban areas. Urbanisation is associated with higher incomes, improved health, higher literacy, improved quality of life and other benefits. Yet along with the benefits of urbanisation come environmental and social ills. Since with urbanisation the concentration of people is increasing in cities so is the demand for basic necessities like food, energy, drinking water and shelter. The result is in terms of poor quality housing, lack of water supply and sanitation facility and lack of proper waste disposal facility leading to spread of communicable diseases.

Urbanisation affects the environment in three major ways: implications due to urban poverty which is a result of migration, stressed infrastructure and management systems and finally incresing consumerism. These problems warrant major concerns on three accounts. Firstly the prevailing pattern and trend of Urbanisation is more material and energy intensive. Secondly the discharge of pollutants and generation of solid waste in cities is particularly harmful because it is uncontrollable and thirdly the financial, institutional, technological and infrastructure systems available for help to control these problems in the region at present are inadequate.

Urban Waste

Increasing urbanisation is resulting in the generation of increasing amounts of solid waste. It is estimated that 20-50 percent of the solid waste generated remains uncollected. In New Delhi, 3,880 tons of garbage is produced per day, yet only 2,420 tons is collected for disposal. Even if collected, municipal solid waste remains a problem in many cities.

As the living standards are rising the organic content in the waste is reducing and non-biodegradable wastes like metal, plastic and glass are on a rise. Urbanisation and increasing trend of consumerism in cities are the main factors leading to generation of more waste.

Urban Water Quality

Ever increasing urbanisation and their growing amounts of waste have over taxed the natural recycling capabilities of local rivers and lakes. Of the many problems associated with urban effluents, nutrient loading or eutrophication of local waters is one of the most serious problems. Poor water resource management too contributes to water problems.

Urban Transportation

Transportation systems are a major contributor to the decay of urban environment and reduced quality of life in the metropolitan areas due to their contribution to atmospheric emissions, noise and risk of accidents. Increasing vehicular pollution in major urban centers is becoming an area of growing concern. Poor maintenance of vehicles, degraded condition of roads and use of un-pure fuels primarily precipitate the problems of air and noise pollution arising from operation of motorised vehicles.

Urban Air Quality

Urban air quality has deteriorated largely on account of growth in industrial activity, transportation needs and energy production. In India, ambient air quality status derived from a network of 290 stations covering 90 towns and cities in recent years indicates that while suspended particulate matter (SPM) is consistently critical in many cities, the concentration of nitrogen oxides and sulphur dioxide is also increasing and is already transiting from moderate to high to critical levels. As estimated, 2000 metric tones of air pollutants are emitted into the atmosphere everyday, vehicular sources contributing the maximum.

Energy demand: Urbanisation has profound effect on the amount and type of energy consumed. Along with population growth, economic development and industrialisation, urbanisation is one of the principal forces driving the increase in energy demand. Although the traditional rural societies rely heavily upon the human and animal energy and on nearby wood or fuel, today urban societies are characterised by their reliance on fossil fuels and electricity. These patterns of energy use lead to different environmental impacts.

Water Demand

India although has enormous reserve of water, but it still suffers from urban water supply problems. The growing demand of water, along with poor water resource management and mounting pollution levels contributes to water supply problems in and around cities. Urbanisation is leading to change in lifestyle and consumption pattern, which is leading to increased demand for water. As number of people in urban area increases, so does the demand for food and hence for irrigation in agricultural areas close to cities. These pressures can quickly result in demand for water that surpass local water supply.

Poor water management practices exacerbate local water shortages. Inefficient water distribution system is another major source of water loss. Water scarcity is closely linked with water quality. Freshwater lakes and rivers provide affordable and easy accessible water, but uncontrolled discharge of domestic sewage and industrial effluents has left many urban rivers heavily polluted and their water is unsafe for use. Already struggling with uneven distribution of water resources and local water scarcity, the total water demand is projected to double by 2025 in India.

Responses

Rapid urbanisation accounts for most of the renewable and non-renewable resource consumption and waste generation. These long-term ecological concerns are relevant to urbanisation as they grow and prosper, their consumption of resources and generation of wastes will rise accordingly, unless action is taken now to promote the efficient use of resources and minimisation of waste. The challenge is to seek new management approaches that provide both for the needs of urban residents and protect environmental resources on which human life depends. Environmental Management Systems (EMS) is a new management approach for urban local bodies that can lead cities towards eco-cities.

India has entered the new century with a whopping 300 million urban population. Urbanisation continues to increase steadily bringing with it both the benefits of infrastructure growth and the environmental ills. The administrative units of small towns/cities, municipal towns and industrial townships are expected to satisfy a broad spectrum of citizens' needs to provide various facilities and services. It has been observed that within their levels of jurisdiction they are unprepared to address the complex environmental challenges that are confronting them.

Operation and development of urban areas involves:

— Infrastructure development

— Resource utilisation

— Availability of support systems to sustain ever growing population

Therefore, to achieve sustainable development, each operational unit in an urban area needs to manage the environmental aspects arising from its activities and services in a systematic procedure. The EMS framework integrates the environment into everyday business operations, and environmental stewardship becomes part of the daily responsibility of employees and citizens across. At different levels of townships, the relevance of EMS is:

— *At the township administration level:* To integrate environment management and promote the use of a systematic standard procedure in township administration.

— *At the facility level:* To establish a management system in their day to day operation of the facility to minimise the environmental impacts, optimise resource utilisation and manage the waste in a standarised and continual procedure.

— *At the residents level:* To involve all residents in a participatory manner for minimising the environmental impacts arising out of their use of the facilities and in the process of designing, establishing, implementing and maintaining the management system in a continual manner.

Till date, EMS as per ISO 14001 was widely accepted by industries. Realising the requirements of the management and the residents of the municipalities/towns/townships, Development Alternatives initiated facilitation of EMS in three Industrial townships of India and all the three has been certified for their ISO 14001 implementation. Implementation of EMS in townships is a good role model for other urban local bodies to replicate.

Implementation of EMS for township is much different from implementing EMS for the factory; primarily because the processes in factory are known and the same have controllable parameters measurable on certain yardstick. The processes in township are only partially controllable as the inputs having environmental impacts are generated at individual level (at household level) and the commitment to a cause is unlikely to be uniform. Organisational structure can modulate the output through methodologies adopted, but unless inputs have regulated performance which, could be otherwise inconsistent.

Sustainable Urban Development

Sustainable development means attaining a balance between environmental protection and human economic development and between the present and future needs. It means equity in development and sectorial actions across space and time. It requires an integration of economic, social and environmental approaches towards development. Sustainable urban development refers to attaining social equity and environmental protection in urbanisation while minimising the costs of urbanisation.

UN General Assembly convened a conference on the "human environment" at Stockholm in June 1972, which came out with guiding principles on "human environment". It emphasised that man has the fundamental right to environment of quality and also that he has a responsibility towards protecting the environment for present and future generations. It also maintained that natural resources of the earth must be safeguarded for the benefit of present and future generations.

About a decade later, to address the issues concerning continuing depletion of natural resources and unsustainable development, the World Commission on Environment and Development was created in 1983. Popularly known as Brundt land Commission, it described sustainable development as *"development that meets the needs of the present without compromising the ability of future generations to meet their own needs"*. After twenty years of Stockholm Declaration, the UN Conference on 'Environment and Development' (also known as 'Earth Summit') was held at Rio-de Janeiro in 1992 that adopted an action plan, popularly known as 'Agenda 21'. The agenda 21 promised to reduce poverty, provide clean water and health care, and protect the natural resources and so on.

Also to be noted that some of the Millennium Development Goals have urged for ensuring environmental sustainability and reduction of the percentage of the population under extreme poverty. Similarly, explaining implications of climate change for sustainable development the Intergovernmental Panel on Climate Change notes (IPCC) the importance of social and environmental equity in development. Thus all the major world conferences and initiatives taken so far on environment and development have stressed on economically viable development, socially equitable development and protection of the environment for attaining sustainable development. Sustainable *urban* development specifically means achieving a balance between the development of the urban areas and protection of the environment with an eye to equity in employment, shelter, basic services, social infrastructure and transportation in the urban areas. With rapid expansion of urban population around the world there has arisen a wide awareness about minimising the environmental costs of urbanisation. Concerns are raised at environmental damages and depletion of non-renewable resources and rising levels of pollution in urban areas. In recent times cities have become places of urban environmental degradation and wasteful use of resources, which is proving to be costly to generations present and future. In order to mitigate the problem we require to minimising the depletion of non-renewable resources and resort to environmentally sustainable economic development. But this has to be done in ways that are socially, economically and politically acceptable. While planning for sustainable development of the towns, we should also take into account the factor of climate change. According to this, ensuring environmental sustainability means taking steps, which include

a) integration of the principles of sustainable development in the policies and programmes of the country,

b) reversal of loss of environmental resources,

c) reduction of the proportion of people without sustainable access to safe drinking water,

d) improving the lives of slum dwellers.

Role of Environment and Climate Change in Sustainable Urban Development

While planning for sustainable development of the towns, we should also take into account the factor of climate change. Explaining implications of climate change for sustainable development the Intergovernmental Panel on Climate Change notes "*Sustainable development represents a balance between the goals of environmental protection and human economic development and between the present and future needs. It implies equity in meeting the needs of people and integration of sect oral actions across space and time.*" One of the greatest challenges that the world is facing today is climate change.

Climate change is the variation in the earth's global climates over time. It involves changes in the variability or average state of the atmosphere over durations ranging from decades to millions of years. These changes can be caused by dynamic process on earth, external forces including variations in sunlight intensity and more recently by human activities. Human influences can be by increase in CO_2 levels due to combustion of fossil fuels, aerosols, cement manufacture etc. Other factors like ozone depletion, animal agriculture and deforestation also change climate. The effect of climate change can be found on among other things, on rising sea level that may accelerate coastal erosion, on increasing temperature, on increase in intensity of natural disaster, and very importantly on vector borne diseases. There has been an increasing trend in the annual mean temperature in India. In recent decades the east coast has been experiencing fewer rainy days while the northwest has been experiencing heavy summer monsoon. There have also been some extreme climatic events like heat wave, intense rain, floods and droughts in India.

Researchers have documented the increase in frequency of hot days and multiple-day heat waves in the past century. There has been record rainfall in Mumbai, India on 26 to 27 July 2005, which led to loss of large numbers of lives. Consecutive droughts between 2000 and 2002 caused crop failures, mass starvation and affected millions of people in Orissa. Also, increased water stress poses to be a major problem for India. Accelerated glacier melt is likely to cause increase in the number and severity of glacial melt-related floods, slope destabilisation and a decrease in river flows as glaciers recede. The researchers have predicted that with the current trend in the melt of glaciers, the Ganga, Indus, Brahmaputra and other rivers could likely become seasonal rivers in the near future and affect the lives of people residing around them.

Thus, it is likely that climate change will hamper sustainable development of India as it increases the pressures on natural resources and the environment associated with rapid urbanisation, industrialisation and economic development. In order to reduce the effect of climate change, we need to include climate-proofing concepts in national development initiatives. Urban areas mostly face problems of air quality pollution, green house gases, unsustainable consumption and of inadequate sanitation and water supply.

Thus translated into policy initiatives, environmental sustainability of urban form should aim at energy efficiency in transport and buildings, optimal planning solutions in terms of locations, distances and spaces, which will reduce air and noise pollution. It should also aim at sustainable management of sanitation and water supply, promote equity in provision of services and of course reduce deforestation. The recently announced National Action Plan on Climate Change by the Prime Minister in June 2008 visualises to make economic development of India energy efficient.

All these concerns, questions and initiatives about sustainable environment and climate change have resulted in experiments and debates over city forms that are sustainable. Before discussing the relevant city forms it would be pertinent to discuss the sustainable management of urban basic services and the inefficiency in the land policy in India and its implications for sustainable city form and development in India, which is done in the next part.

Deficiency and Options for Sustainable Management

Deficiencies

Sustainable city planning should aim at achieving social and environmental equity while improving the lives of the people. For that to happen we need to have a sustainable city form as well as provision and proper management of the services. Thus, in order for a city or urban area to be sustainable it needs to produce and manage basic services like water, waste, energy, and transportation in a way that it conforms to the principles of sustainable development. In other words, the city should be able to produce and distribute the services in an economic, environment friendly and equitable way.

Cities in the developing countries are deficient in the provision of basic services that pollute the environment. It is to be noted that though there are some differences between cities and between rich and poor nations, in general urban infrastructure systems are designed without much attention to environmental and social impacts. Mostly the delivery of the services like water, energy, waste, transportation, are based on non-renewable energy sources. Moreover, the inequality in the provision of these services is very high. Indian cities are characterised by high density of population, deficiency in services and air pollution.

Let us see the status regarding these in India. In urban India in 2001, 69 per cent of the households had safe drinking water, 61 per cent of the households had their latrine facilities within their houses and only 35 per cent of the households had closed drainage facilities. Eighty eight per cent (88%) of the urban households had electricity and only 0.2 per cent had solar energy in 2001. In Delhi, the capital city of India, 77 per cent of the urban households had tap as source of drinking water, 63 per cent had their latrine facilities within their premises and 52 per cent of the households had closed drainage facilities. Delhi generated 5922 tonnes of solid waste per day in 2004-05. Air pollution has become a major problem in Indian cities. Taking the case of Delhi, we find that there are around 54 lakh vehicles in Delhi. Around 70 per cent of the air pollution in Delhi happens to be due to vehicles. It has been found in a World Bank study based on 1994-95 air quality data that around 10,000 people die every year prematurely due to air pollution in Delhi alone.

According to Delhi Medical Association the incidence of asthma in Delhi is ten times the national average (Centre for Science and Environment). Densities of Indian cities are very high. Management of the basic services should be done keeping in mind the deficiency in the services, the environmental impacts and the inequality in the provision of the services. Thus we have two issues here, the first one is covering the deficiencies in services and the second one involves how to provide the services in an environment friendly way.

Sustainable Management of Urban Basic Services

Management of Water Supply

The effect of climate change on water supply will be negative in almost all the countries. Thus care should be taken that energy efficient alternative systems are innovated. As for efficient practices, water consumption can be limited by using raw water, recycled water for gardening and landscaping. In the state of Vermont, U.S.A., a waste-water treatment system uses a series of tanks containing plants and other organisms to naturally clean waste-water that serves 500,000 people per year. There have been other scattered evidences of use of waste-water but the example of a city doing it on large scale is rare. In India the water from Sewage Treatment Plants (STP) in factories are used for landscaping and gardening. However, in developing countries the main challenge is to provide clean drinking water to all the urban residents adopting sustainable water management practices. Rainwater harvesting has its possibilities for partially managing water supply. Conservation of old water bodies like lakes, ponds can be made for increased and sustainable water supply. It has been considered as an optional reform under Jawaharlal Nehru National Urban Renewal Mission (JNNURM) in India. In Delhi itself, one after another marsh lands and water bodies are being converted in residential areas, garbage dumps, petrol pumps and so on, the latest victim being the Jahangirpuri marsh land. Marsh lands recharge ground water substantially. Much is yet to be done regarding this in India. Other environmentally sustainable methods can be explored.

Management of Waste

Waste management practices should be started from the production and distribution stages of economic activities through reuse and recycling. Reuse of things like metals, glass, paper, plastic, textiles, organic waste and water will reduce demand for energy, raw materials, fertilisers and fresh water sources. However, care should be taken that hazardous wastes do not go for recycling. Plastic should be used less. In Delhi more than 5000 tonnes of municipal solid waste is generated everyday, which is disposed of in landfills. Too much land is being consumed for disposal and is creating danger of ground water contamination. As such the department of environment of the government of India recommended that other 'best practices' in waste management should be adopted in a large scale. The practices include, vermi-culture, pelletisation, aerobic composting and so on. A research study by NEERI has recommended mechanical composting as the viable option for such a huge amount of waste. The Supreme Court of

India, hearing public interest litigation on solid waste management of Delhi directed the Municipal Corporation of Delhi to improve the system.

Management of Energy

Energy management practices should be encouraged in the planning of buildings and the city form. Buildings and city forms that are energy efficient and use sustainable energies like solar and wind energies should be considered. There are fragments of evidences in India of settlements using solar power, water recycling techniques and waste management practices. But in general the environment friendly techniques are yet to be practised in urban areas, especially in large cities where the differences would be felt. City forms should be such that it uses energy efficient transport. Coming to the financing part, it can be said that the policies should help energy efficient practices. The loans should be easily available and tax benefits provided for such practices.

Reduction in Inequality

Management of basic services in the cities should reduce inequality in services between rich and poor. The concept of commercial viability does not hold for social services always. City form should take into account social conditions also. The ability of urban poor to pay for the full cost of water supply would remain low in India. Thus reduction in grant of the government and introduction of private sector in this sector is likely to make the situation worse. It is also well known that much of the subsidised schemes in the past have gone to the middle and high-income areas. Apart from deficient, non-environment friendly and unequal basic services, the other major problem in developing a sustainable city form in India is inefficient land policy of the country, which we discuss next.

Inefficiency In Land Policy Of India

Land is an important input for producing goods and services for urban development. Under the conventional analysis, factors of production i.e. land, labour and capital flow to make goods and services but the social and environmental consequences are not reflected in such analysis. Sustainable urban development does take account of social and environmental effects and means balance between the development of the areas and protection of the environment with an eye to equity in employment, shelter, basic services, social infrastructure and transportation in the urban areas. For this to happen, one has to ensure that land is properly used to meet these objectives. Urban India is plagued by shortage of housing facilities and scarcity of land for social overheads like roads, footpaths, parks, schools and so on. The roots of these problems can be found in the inadequate, inefficient, iniquitous land policy of the country. This is why it is important to have an effective and appropriate land policy that would promote sustainable development.

National Commission on Urbanisation of India recognised the need for adequate supply of land, efficiency and equity in allocation of land and promotion of flexibility in land use. Thus it mentioned that the objectives of urban land policy should be:

a) to achieve an optimum social use of urban land,

b) to make land available in adequate quantity to both public authorities and individuals at reasonable prices

c) to encourage cooperative community effort as well as individual builders to develop land and construct houses,

d) to prevent concentration of land in few hands,

e) to use land to finance urban development,

f) to encourage socially and economically efficient allocation of land so that land development conserves resources and land utilisation is optimal,

g) to promote flexibility in land use in response to a growing city.

Also, the Eleventh Five Year Plan of India emphasises, "governments at appropriate levels including local authorities, have to strive to remove all possible obstacles that may hamper equitable access to land". It identifies failure to adopt appropriate urban land policies and land management practices as the primary cause of inequity and poverty. Thus the Eleventh Five year Plan calls for a flexible land policy which will make conversion from one use to another, cost efficient and promote equity. It judges that urban planning tools like master planning, zoning and regulations are not enough for the requirement of land supply for rapid urbanisation. The problem has also been addressed somewhat by Jawaharlal Nehru Urban Renewal Mission in India.

Sustainable City Form

Thus one side of the problem is inefficient land policy, which blocks supply of land for efficient and equitable housing, social infrastructure, basic services and transportation. The other side of the problem is how best or optimal the urban areas can be planned so that the *urban form* can be sustainable. In recent times cities have been found to pollute the environment and deplete the natural resources. This has prompted the need for finding an urban form that will be sustainable. Various ideas have come up with solutions. One such idea for sustainable urban form is compact city. This necessarily means a high density, mixed land use and efficient public transport planning, which encourages pedestrian oriented habitation. It may be high-rise like Hong Kong or low rise as suggested by National

Commission on Urbanisation (NCU) of India and so on. It should be remembered that "high density" is a relative term depending on the culture and the environment of the country.

The two important issues about high-density cities are the costs and benefits of the form and how dense should it be and "higher than what"? The two main benefits of compact city are reduced dependency on private cars and preservation of greenery while the main costs are more air pollution, noise, crime and overcrowding. A literature review of the various studies finds social and environmental benefits of compactness of a city. The benefits can be summarised as

a) protection of the countryside, green space and bio-diversity;

b) reduction of travel distance, emission, greenhouse gases and thus global warming;

c) reduction of materials for construction of infrastructure;

d) have economies of scale in providing social institutional services like hospitals, banks and

e) in having a better interactive community life.

The various costs have been found as

a) exploiting open and green urban spaces;

b) overcrowding;

c) traffic congestion;

d) ill health;

e) crime and

f) high-energy demand in compact high-rise buildings.

But the relationship is not so simple. The concept has been developed in relation to developed economies with sprawling areas but it has not been tested adequately on high-density developing countries. However, a study conducted in China measures the urban compactness of the city. This study may be somewhat relevant for Indian cities because both have high population densities and both are developing countries.

The study measures compactness by the non-agricultural population density in built-up area of the city. It tests the argument that urban compactness exploits the economies of scale for public services (e.g. schools, public buses, public utilities) and environmental resources (e.g. land, petrol and water). It also examines that too much compactness may cause negative environmental externalities. To examine the arguments in Chinese context 16 representative variables on environmental aspects were taken.

To implement compact city form policy, it is necessary to maximise the advantage and minimise the disadvantage. It finds that urban compactness of the 45 core Chinese cities will improve accessibility of services, reduce per capita domestic energy consumption and more or less promote infrastructure efficiency and use of public transport. But compactness i.e. high population density aggravates negative externalities, like, air pollution, noise and loss of green space. It also finds that environment efficiency is positive up to a level of approximately 168 persons per hectare. National Commission on Urbanisation (NCU) of India recommended low-rise high density (LRHD) built-form for Indian cities. It explains that such form is less expensive to maintain and has the advantages of security of neighbourhood protection.

Most important of all is that it satisfies the criteria of *equity*. It says "income profile and afford ability considerations suggest that a range of small and medium plot sizes, between 25 sq m to 100 sq m (with some plots perhaps up to 200 sq m) can satisfy the needs of over 95 per cent of the urban population". The Commission explains that this typology is more economical than apartments because no space is required for public circulation and lifts and also it provides much better living conditions. It would also reduce the disparities in our urban areas.

According to this form, a 50 sq m plot per family with five members will generate a net density of 1000 persons per hectare (i.e. a gross residential density of 500 persons per hectare). Similarly, a 100 sq m plot would generate a gross residential density of 250 persons per hectare. It also states that high gross densities found in inner city can be tackled by interventions in city structure and by adjusting land use allocation in within the city itself to create spaces for social overheads. Its recommendations for built form specifies that residential sites should be provided so that 1) 50 per cent of the lands are in plots between 25 to 100 sq m, 2) 25 per cent of the land are in the plots between 100 to 200 sq m and 3) 25 per cent of the land are in these or any other sizes. The Commission also recommended that, "these plots should be leased out not to individuals buyers, but to co-operative societies. Should the members of a cooperative society decide to pool their land and build group housing or apartments, they should be free to do so, provided the total number of dwelling units remains the same. This maintains the principle of urban equity and, at the same time, allows the construction of apartment buildings at higher FARs." The report also says that, "as long as our cities remain within density thresholds (i.e. neighbourhood densities of 250 to 1,000 persons /ha) there are efficient and cost effective solutions within our resources."

Talking about densities, it points out that the densification can be increased at selected nodal points depending on the holding capacity of the area. It should be related to the mass transport network. Though the net densities recommended by NCU seems to be on higher side, it would be worth mentioning that cities in India are rather densely populated. The cities of India are already compact if seen by the standard of densities. As concluded in the case of Chinese cities the negative externalities of high population density may be relevant for the cities of India as well. For example, high population density aggravates negative externalities, like, air pollution, noise and loss of green space. But like the high density Chinese cities high population density may improve accessibility of services, reduce per capita domestic energy consumption and more or less promote infrastructure efficiency and use of public transport. However, there is dearth of study to support this in the Indian context. Other options like *multi-modal urban region* may provide some solution with the help of transport, which can be environmentally sustainable. This will be discussed next.

Multi-modal Urban Region

Transport has an important role in meeting the goals of urban sustainability. One of the challenges of a sustainable urban form is to meet the economic performance objectives and environmental sustainability of a city at the same time. It may be useful to build multi modal urban region and supply transport to take care of the different urban and economic activities. For this to happen the land use and transport policies will have to match the demand of different activities. The idea is to create a city that performs well economically and conforms to the objectives of environmental sustainability. In order to be economically efficient a city needs to reduce production costs, e.g. costs of receiving inputs and distributing outputs. It also needs to reduce travel time between the different related companies, between the company and the workers' homes. At the same time the enlargement of the space of the urban labour market enables the companies to choose from a large pool of workers and also gives the workers a variety of jobs to choose from. An economically efficient city also creates economies of scale for services and housing markets. It has been argued by Prud'homme and Lee that actual extent of the spatial markets engaged in economic functioning rather than the city size is what matters. Also the jobs those are accessible rather than those showed in statistics that are significant. Two more factors namely, the speed of its transport system and the geographical spread of activities affect economic performance.

The combination of speed, size and spread determines the effective labour market according to Prud'homme and Lee. Ken worthy and Lobe comparing the data on speed and spread of 46 cities of the world found that, American cities use cars, have higher speed and travel distance and low land use density. On the other extreme, rich Asian cities like Hong Kong, Tokyo and Singapore use slow speed public transport, travel less distances and have concentrated land use density. European cities use public transport as well as cars and have moderate densities of land use. Thus the challenge is to find an urban form, which gives an effective size of urban market by combining land use policies and transport alternatives.

Two factors are important in this regard which are accessibility i.e. acceptable time and environmental sustainability i.e. reducing costs like CO_2 emissions, air pollution, traffic noise. One solution that has been offered in the literature is multi modal urban region. The idea is to create an environment friendly transport system and create activity places that are reachable within acceptable time limits. For this to happen, activity locations should be created which can be reached:

a) without moving, by walking, by cycling,

b) by public transport,

c) by energy efficient cars.

Land-use and transportation implications of this is to create:

a) multi-functional homes/work-places which does not need travel,

b) develop multi-functional neighbourhoods, which can be accesses by walking, cycling,

c) develop nodes having functional concentrations that can be reached by public transport and

d) develop multi-functional urban regions which can be reached by energy efficient cars.

In Randstad, the highly urbanised west of the Netherlands, modal specialisation are found to hold for relationships between different areas. In 1997, it was found that within the large city bicycle dominates the mode, the train is used considerably between the large cities while car is the dominant mode for other middle and long destinations. This also gives an indication of the possibility of polycentric developments in sustainable city form. However, much needs to be researched on to get an optimal solution and may be for different conditions.

National transport policy of India, 2006, advocated public transport and recommended to promote road transport, which are energy efficient, conserves environment and meets social demand. It noted that it is needed to promote public transport to reduce negative externalities, like air pollution and congestion. It also advised to promote Non-Motorised transport. The national policy recommended, "Transit Oriented Development" with high-density areas and urged for developing new satellite towns along major transport corridors. It also discourages sprawl through taxes and fees.

Like most of the developing countries, in India a large percentage of people travel by cycling and walking by compulsion as they are poor and cannot afford motorised transport. Walking and cycling has an inverse relation with city size in India. But then it varies among the large cities. For example, in Delhi walking and cycling is more common than in Mumbai and Kolkata. Perhaps Mumbai and Kolkata's better public transport explains the difference. Lack of good public transport in Delhi has resulted in use of private cars. It may be mentioned here that Delhi Transport Corporation (DTC) has recently introduced air conditioned bus services in some routes and is making profits. More such options in other routes may reduce use of private cars. One should keep in mind that low density sprawled development makes it difficult for public transport system to survive. This makes a case for high-density polycentric development with multi modal region.

2

Human Settlements in Peri-urban Areas

Third World cities are divided into two distinct sectors: formal and informal, or urban and peri-urban. Peri-urban and informal sector settlements are also commonly referred to as squatter settlements, marginal settlements, shanty towns, urban slums, or illegal settlements. A consensus definition of peri-urban areas or urban informal sectors has been difficult to achieve among practitioners and researchers; however, there is general agreement to include settlements that are marginal to the physical and regulatory boundaries of the formal city. In other words, local and national governments consider the urban formal sector legitimate, but do not approve of peri-urban/informal sector settlements.

Peri-urban settlements largely develop outside of government control and do not follow strictly formal and traditional urban planning and development processes. It is important to note, though, that the peri-urban sector is not monolithic and, more often than not, informal settlement development is a hybrid of formal and informal systems.

Peri-urban areas are characterised by uncertain or illegal land tenure, minimal or no infrastructure, low incomes, and lack of recognition by formal governments. Families who live in informal settlements build on the cheaper land outside city limits, on land within city limits that is not zoned for housing, on land that has not been urbanised with infrastructure, or on land considered dangerous or environmentally fragile. Many informal settlements begin as land invasions with families illegally squatting on the land.

Other informal settlements begin with the legal landowner illegally subdividing and selling the land without formal land registration or basic service provisions. Families often pay the former owner or occupant the full purchase price, but receive in return no registered title to the land. They generally do not participate in local government and are unconnected to the municipal service network. Finally, they tend to be ignored by municipal authorities, who find themselves overwhelmed by the informal sector sheer numbers and needs, which far outstrip the capacity of the local planners and government.

The peri-urban population should, therefore, be a focus of concern. Spatially, peri-urban areas are growing much more rapidly than formal urban districts; in many cities, the peri-urban sections are already bigger than the formal areas. Their rapid growth and informal status have resulted in low levels of sanitation services. The lack of these services in particular, inadequate excreta (human waste) management threatens the public health and environment of the peri-urban settlement, as well as the urban area as a whole. But even the few institutions that recognise the problem and want to do something about it find that little knowledge or experience exists about how to address this problem constructively.

Characteristics of Peri-urban Areas

This section identifies the common characteristics of peri-urban areas, especially those that distinguish them from rural and formal urban areas. It also identifies common sanitation practices in peri-urban settlements.

An estimated 600 million people in urban areas of the Third World now live in life and health threatening homes and neighbourhoods, primarily in peri-urban settlements. These homes and neighbourhoods share two characteristics that bear serious potential health effects:

1. The presence of pathogenic microorganisms (especially those in human excreta), caused by lack of infrastructure and related inadequate water supply to remove them
2. Crowded, cramped housing conditions The removal and safe disposal of excreta and waste water from washing, bathing, and other domestic uses in peri-urban settlements are critical health and environmental needs. Many rivers in Third World cities are literally large open sewers. Surface and ground-water contamination is widespread in many developing countries, and the resulting environmental degradation is more and more apparent along rivers and sea coastal areas.

Impact on Health and the Environment

Most urban areas (both informal and formal) in Africa and Asia, including many cities with one million or more inhabitants, have no effective means of off-site disposal of excreta (for example, water-borne sewage systems or collection and treatment systems for latrine contents). Rivers, streams, canals, gullies, and ditches are the destinations of most untreated human excrement and household waste. Such waste accumulates on streets, in open spaces between houses, in stagnant pools of water, and on wasteland.

Latin American cities are a little better off. The formal urban areas in most of these cities have some collection and distribution systems; however, most existing systems are in disrepair. The recent cholera epidemic in Latin America, for example, has been partly attributed to the contamination of water distribution systems by adjacent leaky sewage pipes. In addition, most water-borne sewage collected is disposed untreated into rivers that also serve as sources of water for drinking, bathing for families living in peri-urban settlements, and irrigation for farmers living downstream. Moreover, as in Africa and Asia, the growing peri-urban areas throughout Latin America, which often make up more than 50 percent of a cites population, lack sewerage or latrine collection systems (Table 1).

Table 1. Estimated Percentage of Third World Urban Population Without Sanitation Services (1987)

City	*Country*	*Present urban population without sanitation services*
Luanda	Angola	71
Lusaka	Zambia	66
Karachi	Pakistan	51
Bogotá	Colombia	45
Manila	Philippines	35
Nairobi	Kenya	35
Lima	Peru	33
Caracas	Venezuela	30
Mexico City	Mexico	30
Tunis	Tunisia	30
Ankara	Turkey	24
São Paulo	Brazil	22

The crowding of large numbers of people in peri-urban areas creates conditions very favourable to the rapid spread of a variety of infectious diseases, often in the form of disastrous epidemics such as the previously cited cholera outbreak in Latin America. Indeed, an increasing volume of literature suggests that health problems resulting from a lack of sanitation facilities (among other factors) are greater among the urban poor living in overcrowded peri-urban settlements than they are either in the rest of the urban areas or in rural areas. A recent World Bank study suggests that, in contrast to higher-income urban dwellers and some rural population, the urban poor have a lower life expectancy at birth and a higher infant mortality rate . A variety of intestinal parasites is usually present in poor urban population, with roundworms and whipworm often observed at higher levels of incidence than in corresponding rural population. Likewise, the accumulation of waste water as a result of the limited soil area to absorb it in densely settled urban areas has led to increased transmission of filariasis in many cities.

The fundamental reason for undertaking urban sanitation improvement programs is to improve health, but in general it has been difficult to demonstrate a causal relationship between the two, although a recent WASH study concluded at least that sanitation interventions in urban areas had a higher health impact than do water supply interventions.

In addition to threatening health, the lack of excreta management systems in Third World cities is having a tremendous negative effect on the environment contaminating surface and ground-water with organics, nutrients, and solids. Because of their current and growing size and density, and their lack of adequate infrastructure, peri-urban areas are the largest source of focal contamination in cities. Men, women, and children often defecate on open ground. Their faces wash down the hillsides through various neighbourhoods or through low-lying flood plains to a river or other water source. Many cities are literally awash in excreta.

Even in communities where widespread use of pit latrines has been achieved, human waste can still harm the environment. Unlike sparsely settled rural areas, peri-urban settlements have high population densities, and the sheer numbers of closely spaced latrines can overwhelm the carrying capacity of soils and pollute underground aquifers.

The lack of adequate sanitation systems for families living in these growing peri-urban areas is a major contributor to water pollution in the city. Removing and disposing of excreta in ways that prevent human contact are central to reducing the burden of disease and environmental degradation. This degradation uncontrolled and far reaching is in itself as compelling a justification for action as the impact of inadequate sanitation on health.

Population Growth in Peri-Urban Areas

The world is becoming increasingly urban. Urban areas of developing countries are growing faster than either the urban areas of developed countries or the rural areas of the developing world. The population of some urban areas doubled during the International Drinking Water Supply and Sanitation Decade (1981-90). Between 1980 and the year 2000, 85 percent of the worlds urban growth is expected to take place in developing countries. According to United Nations data, 1.3 billion people, or approximately 25 percent of the Third World population, now live in urban centres; by the year 2020, it is anticipated that more than 50 percent of the population in the developing world will be living in cities. The estimated annual growth rate of the developing worlds urban areas will range from 1.5 percent in Latin American cities to 4.8 percent in African cities. Between 75 and 90 percent of this growth will take place in the peri-urban or informal sector. By the year 2000, the exploding growth in Third World settlements that do not benefit from formal urban infrastructure could result in as many as one billion people living without adequate excreta disposal.

Characteristics That Set Peri-Urban Areas Apart

Peri-urban settlements have a number of unique characteristics that distinguish them from formal urban and rural areas; these characteristics are outlined below.

Poor Physical Site Conditions and Complicated Site Layouts

Poor urban families searching for a plot of land on which to build a home are strongly influenced by the existing market prices for urban land; inevitably the land that is most desirable for residential construction is the most expensive. The more affordable sites are areas that are undesirable for formal development, such as those located on steep slopes, along gullies and ravines, on soil that is too rocky to excavate easily, in desert lands, or in areas prone to flooding. Poor families move on to these lands because they are relatively cheap to purchase or because illegal occupation of such sites is less likely to be challenged.

Since informal urban settlers lack technical know-how and assistance, they often develop their areas haphazardly, without allowing adequate space for installing infrastructure lines. Urban settlers in parts of Africa and Asia build their houses according to village traditions that is, patterned according to family formation, with houses directly abutting their neighbours on all sides, with no room left for service right-of-ways.

Limited Water Availability

Most peri-urban settlements do not generally have piped water; instead, increasingly they have water vendors who sell water at market cost, which is significantly higher than what families in the urban formal sector pay. Not only is the cost higher on a per-liter basis, but it also consumes a higher percentage of family household income.

The vended water in peri-urban areas is mostly of poor quality, and because of its high cost, families can buy only a limited amount of it. The limited availability of water leads to major sanitation problems when purchasers are forced to set priorities that may compromise public health; for example, peri-urban families are not apt to purchase water to flush a toilet.

Some peri-urban families have access either to a standpipe nearby or to water piped into the house. But, in either case, this water is usually limited in quantity and is erratic in flow. This leads to low levels of personal and domestic hygiene and thus favours the transmission of excreta-related infections.

High-Density Population

Demographic data are lacking for peri-urban areas. Because these communities are illegal and for the most part are not recognised by the formal sector, municipal tax, health, or other records do not exist for most of them. Typically, however, peri-urban settlements have a high population density often greater than 400 people per hectare. High population density without basic infrastructure entails greater health and environmental risks than those found in rural and formal urban areas. Moreover, a growing number of peri-urban areas (especially in the Middle East) have vertical construction, that is multi-family, multi-story housing that increases population density dramatically.

Organisation of Communities and Social Characteristics

Peri-urban settlements, in general, are not homogeneous with respect to ethnic background, income level, language, and social norms. Residents have migrated to these settlements from various parts of a region or country or, in many cases, from other countries. This heterogeneity often leads to misunderstandings and distrust among neighbours and may result in minimal contact between neighbours. Consequently, a broad-based sense of community often is lacking in peri-urban settlements. Nevertheless, community organisations can and do exist, often formed around an issue of universal interest to the settlement, such as school construction.

Among important forms of organisation, at least in the early stages after a peri-urban community is established, are the neighbourhood associations created in response to the problems connected with the establishment of the communities, that is, the need for security of land tenure and for basic urban services. These associations serve the dual functions of coordinating neighbourhood self-help activities and of providing the link between the communities and government authorities.

In cases of settlement by organised invasion, the makings of such organisations already exist before the communities themselves are formed. In cases of settlement by encroachment and purchase, individuals initially make what arrangements they can with respect to transportation, lighting, water supply, excreta disposal, and so on. Eventually, small groups and communities begin to form to address common concerns, as the settlers realise that without organisation they stand little chance of obtaining services from the government or any other outside agency. An important aspect of the socio-demographic composition of peri-urban population is the fact that a large number of households are headed by women. A disproportionate number of these female-headed households also fall in the lowest-income brackets. In addition, a significant percentage of peri-urban population is made up of children.

Legal Land Tenure and Lack of Government Recognition and Services

In most countries, a strict application of development regulations denies the legality of land and buildings developed in peri-urban communities. Laws governing property rights, land acquisitions, registration and transfer of titles, development regulations, taxation of real estate, and municipal institutions often were introduced by former colonial rulers. These laws and urbanisation standards were essentially adaptations of European models of urban planning that may no longer suit modern conditions in developing countries. In most developing countries, the existing legal, formal land development market is grid-locked by overregulation and its corresponding costs. This has been a major contributing factor to the creation of an illegal informal land market that is unencumbered by controls.

Because prohibitive costs lock them out of formally developed areas, in most peri-urban communities, occupants are in violation of tenure laws and/or development regulations. Residents of peri-urban areas often do not have legal land tenure, and, in most cases, the site itself has not been legally urbanised. Therefore, governments generally do not recognise the legality of these settlements.

Low Income Levels and Reliance on the Informal Economy

As noted above, families settle in peri-urban areas for rational reasons, primarily because land prices or rents are low. A significant percentage of the population of Third World cities cannot afford the formal sectors housing, even when costs are cut to a bare minimum. The economic crisis in many developing countries has reduced the purchasing power of low-income families and limited even further their ability to pay for formal sector housing or services. Many households in peri-urban areas do not enjoy a regular income, and large numbers of peri-urban households are headed by single women who in turn tend to have the lowest income levels of all workers.

Families in rural areas are for the most part not in the cash economy. Their life is more agricultural subsistence. In contrast, in formal urban areas, most families do operate in the cash economy as workers and have access to steady jobs, pay taxes, and so on. In peri-urban areas, families are also in the cash economy but their workers rely mainly on the informal economy (for example, carpenters working out of their backyards or women selling tortillas in the market). Though poor, they nonetheless make and spend money. Because cash in the informal economy is unsteady and unreliable, residents are not deemed creditworthy and cannot get conventional bank loans.

The Role of Informal Businesses

Informal businesses play a significant role in the construction and urbanisation of peri-urban settlements, whereas in rural areas, the community provides self-help (free or donated labour) for construction (for example, the digging of latrine pits). Sometimes a local non-governmental organisation (NGO) is hired to do the construction, or a local formal sector contractor is hired. In peri-urban areas, the existing practice is that most sanitation infrastructure is built by local private builders or manufacturers in the informal sectors. For example, a local manufacturer might produce toilet seats in the families backyard workshop, and local carpenters or masons might be hired to construct latrines.

Limited Political Influence

Because peri-urban settlements are not recognised as legal areas, their community leaders and residents have limited political influence. People living in peri-urban areas are not illegal their houses are, but even though the people living in these settlements are not illegal residents per se, they are mostly economically poor, marginalised, and uneducated, and historically have held limited political power. Residents in formal urban areas, on the other hand, enjoy the status of being recognised as constituents to whose needs politicians must respond in order to stay in office.

A political change is beginning to occur in peri-urban areas, however. Peri-urban residents can represent an enormous voting block and can have a major influence on elections. Yet, after elections, their political clout becomes limited because they do not know how to use the system by organising into political pressure groups. Furthermore, given the heterogeneous nature of most peri-urban settlements, the united strength and community organising around local issues that are visible in many rural and formal urban areas are not as apparent in peri-urban areas. Peri-urban residents in most places are less visible and vocal to municipal leaders.

In theory, decentralisation and democratisation should give informal settlements greater leverage and visibility. Also, in theory, once the urban poor have voting rights and representation, they will keep in office those politicians who manage resources wisely and respond to their needs. At present, however, those holding leadership positions in most peri-urban settlements do not necessarily represent the interests of the wide range of subgroups in these settlements.

Common Sanitation Practices

Peri-urban communities overwhelmingly lack adequate arrangements for waste disposal. Waste water from bathing and washing is typically spilled right outside shelters, where it may soak into the ground or form stagnant pools in poorly drained areas. Where sewers exist, they are virtually always open drainage canals. The ground by the side of the shelters or in alleyways serves as a frequent substitute for urinals. In general, residents have improvised sanitation systems in peri-urban areas to satisfy their perceived needs (privacy and convenience, for example), and as materials and labour become available. Some of the most common sanitation practices in peri-urban areas are described below.

1. *No system:* Defecation occurs in open areas within the settlement, on the perimeter of the settlement, or in drainage ditches. The lack of any planned waste

disposal system is characteristic of most peri-urban areas.

2. *Latrines:* Use of latrines is the second most common sanitation practice in peri-urban regions. A wide range of latrines can be found in peri-urban areas, including bucket latrines, pit latrines, and ventilated improved pit (VIP) latrines. In Asia, some systems for excreta removal from latrine pits exist, either through buckets or vacuum trucks, but in other areas excreta removal is not common. Latrines in peri-urban areas are often poorly designed and maintained and may not be used by all family members.
3. *Pour-flush toilets/septic tanks:* In peri-urban settlements experiencing regular or even irregular water supplies, pour-flush toilets with soak-away or septic tanks may exist, relying either on household or community septic tanks. However, the septic tanks often are poorly maintained or undersised.

Peri-Urban Sanitation Challenges

Why should peri-urban areas be distinguished from rural and urban areas for sanitation improvement activities? This section addresses this question and presents the unique challenges to sanitation improvement in peri-urban areas.

Demand-Driven Sanitation Interventions

A major difference between urban and peri-urban program design challenges is that the former are supply driven, and the latter are demand driven. Supply driven is used here to denote the traditional/conventional urbanisation process whereby a supply of housing stock is developed and then offered to the public for sale. This process can be summarised as follows:

1. Land use rights are legally transferred (usually sold).

2. The land use is changed (usually from agricultural to residential).
3. The land is subdivided into plots or parcels.
4. The land is registered in the new owners name.
5. The land is developed by installing basic urban services such as water, sewage and drainage, roads, and electricity.
6. A house is built on the land.
7. The house is put on the market and sold.
8. The house is occupied by a family.

In a supply-driven urbanisation process, the human factor does not enter into the equation until the end of the process.

Demand driven is used here to denote the more common urbanisation process that exists in peri-urban areas. This process can be generalised as follows:

1. Individual families or a large group of families need housing.
2. Unserviced but affordable land is ?acquired@ either through invasions or through informal purchases.
3. Individual houses are built, usually with rustic building materials (these initial houses usually do not meet building standards and usually have no provision for basic sanitation).
4. Families use their new home base to enter into the informal economy and start accumulating capital.
5. The houses are incrementally improved according to household priorities and available capital; this stage may include the construction of an improved latrine.
6. Communities get organised and start ?demanding@ that municipal authorities provide them with basic urban services such as electricity, roads, water, and sewage.

7. After infrastructure is installed, land is then legalised and registered by municipal authorities.

In this demand-driven process, people move in before the water supply, sanitation, and other infrastructure exist. Once they are on the land and have a house, their demand for infrastructure evolves.

In the peri-urban sector, a controlled supply-driven process is not possible; people reside in the areas before any formal development takes place and they live in overcrowded conditions. Sanitation improvements are more critical in crowded urban areas where population densities are very high, diseases are more common, and the assimilative capacity of the environment has been exceeded. These areas require a demand-oriented government response, which is quite different from the controlled and orderly process of most formal urban planning and development. The government action should be responsive to the demands and needs of families already living in peri-urban areas and be tailored to the conditions of the settlements.

It is important to keep in mind, however, that the demand by the community for sanitation improvements may be low compared with the demand for water, electricity, drainage, roads, or solid waste removal. Residents in peri-urban settlements often have higher priorities than excreta disposal to which to allot their scarce financial and other resources.

Political Motives

To address these features and the peculiar needs they elicit, the project designer and implementer must deal with engineers, legal specialists, financial analysts, social scientists, urban planners, and a wide range of institutions, such as the water and sanitation utility, the Ministry of Health, urban development authorities, and municipalities.

Because of the high visibility of these urban slum areas, and their higher numbers of people, the involvement of politicians is greater than it is in rural or formal urban sectors. The result can be a scenario involving a clash of values for example, the A.I.D. Development planner or NGO community organiser who favours assistance to peri-urban areas versus the politicians who prefer to help formal developments. Therefore, the choice of intervention sites can become politicised. In other words, political interest can become a criterion in site selection, rather than need or feasibility.

Conflict of Interest or Goals

Similar to motives that surface in political conflicts, the donors interest or goal may be to improve sanitation for peri-urban residents, whereas municipal authorities may see a sanitation intervention in an illegal settlement as counter to their interest. In most cases, this interest is *not* to formalise peri-urban settlements and thereby make them more permanent. The fundamental issue is this: Unless project designers can in the beginning of the process get a political commitment from the mayor or other key decision-maker to agree to sanitation interventions in illegal settlements, or to make illegal settlements legal, any further work on project design could prove to be fruitless.

Lack of Data

In contrast to rural and formal urban areas, statistics relating to residents of peri-urban areas (and their needs) are not gathered in many Latin American and African countries. Thus it becomes extremely difficult to analyse overall data about peri-urban settlements. Without bank mortgages or building permits, who can say how many houses are built each year? When people in these settlements do not show up on employers payrolls, how can one tell how many are employed or what incomes they earn? Without health records, who can detect their mortality or morbidity rates? When they pirate water from public aqueducts, buy it from vendors, or use home-made septic tanks or pits, how can their water consumption and level of sanitation be assessed?

A lack of real data makes it difficult to determine how many peri-urban houses lack access to sanitation systems and what kinds of systems would be most appropriate to introduce.

Cheap Land/Expensive Infrastructure

Ironically, for very rational reasons the urban poor settle on the cheapest land, which also requires the most expensive infrastructure. It is more costly to put low-cost systems on steep slopes or in flood plains than to put them on dry, flat ground. Even pit latrines, a very low-cost option, can be more expensive to construct in peri-urban settlements than in rural areas.

Limited Technologies Appropriate to Peri-Urban Areas

Because of the unique characteristics of peri-urban areas, the technological lessons learned from sanitation interventions in rural and formal urban areas are not always applicable to peri-urban sites. To date, construction of latrines has been the main sanitation intervention funded by external support agencies, including for projects in peri-urban areas. Latrines, however, have been shown to have serious limitations in the peri-urban sector. They usually are not feasible at population densities above 250 to 350 persons per hectare, and most peri-urban areas have population densities above 350 persons per hectare. For this reason, technologies appropriate to peri-urban areas are limited. In many high-density informal settlements, there will be little, if any, space available to dig a new pit after the existing one fills up. Often, not enough space exists for even the first pit. Pit latrines also are impractical for multi-story housing. In addition, soil conditions in most peri-urban settlements are often too rocky or too steep, contain too much clay, or have too high a water table to make latrines feasible.

HEALTH, ENVIRONMENTAL, AND SOCIAL CONSIDERATIONS

Improving community excreta sanitation in peri-urban areas is a complex endeavour. Choosing and building the right technology is only one of the areas that must be addressed in this process. Other concerns that must be considered include health, the environment, and social/community organisation.

Sanitation-Related Health Benefits

One of the more compelling justifications for improving community sanitation is improving health, yet the health benefits associated with improved sanitation are difficult to quantify. While this can be said about any location, it is particularly true in peri-urban areas. Part of the problem, is that baseline health information usually does not exist for peri-urban areas. Municipal governments usually do not keep records on peri-urban settlements, including information on current health status, environmental conditions, or existing sanitation coverage.

Another part of the problem is that certain environmental factors, such as intermittent water supply and poor drainage, interfere with accurate predictions of health effects of improved sanitation. The many environmental determinants that can have an impact on health in urban areas. The consequent lack of clear information and conclusions makes it difficult to rank the desirability of improving sanitation on the basis of health benefits. Therefore, if the justification for a peri-urban sanitation project is improved health, it will be complicated and expensive to measure health improvement resulting from a proposed peri-urban sanitation project.

Degree of Health Benefits as a Factor of Sanitation Level

Beyond the question of how improved sanitation improves health is the question of the relationship between the stages of improved sanitation and the degrees of improved health. Peri-urban sanitation improvements tend to evolve in rather large steps: from nothing to pit latrines to pour-flush toilets to full sewerage. Bateman and Smiths 1991 WASH study showed that the proportion of children stunted in Guatemalan urban areas was directly associated with the level of sanitation service . Stunting was lower in children who had access to a flush toilet when compared with those with access to latrines and to those without access to sanitary services.

The same WASH study showed that stunting was also associated with community levels of sanitation. Individual household sanitation improvements did not have a significant health impact if the surrounding households also did not improve their sanitation. The authors found that sanitation coverage of 75 percent or more of a densely populated community is needed before a health impact is apparent. Therefore, the project approach to sanitation improvement in peri-urban areas should focus on community-wide improvements, not on individual households. By contrast, in rural areas, where houses are further apart, the approach to sanitation improvement has largely been toward households.

The study found that children with access to flush toilets in their household but who lived in a community with a low level of sanitation coverage had 1.67 times the risk of stunting compared with those living in a community with high levels of sanitation coverage. More remarkable was the finding that children with no individual access to a toilet and living in a community with a high level of sanitation coverage have no increased risk of stunting compared with children with individual access to a toilet living in a community with a high level of sanitation coverage. These findings indicate that community measures of sanitation are better indicators of health risk than is individual access to improved sanitation.

From a program point of view, in a peri-urban water and sanitation program that expects to improve health, sanitation should receive the same degree of attention and resources as water supply. Further, to increase the health benefits of sanitation improvements, the most important goal and evaluation indicator is not improved individual level of service, but improved community sanitation to the point that at least 75 percent of the community has access to adequate sanitation services and uses them properly.

Transferring Excreta Off-Site

In examining the health effects of sanitation technologies, one must also evaluate threats posed by systems that transfer excreta off-site. Cortege systems and water-borne sewage, for example, result in the transfer of health risks off-site along with the excreta (if the waste is not treated, as it usually is not).

The health risks related to transferring excreta off-site can be reduced or increased depending on the situation. If sewage, for example, is treated and disposed of in a river away from people, health risks probably will be reduced. On the other hand, if untreated sewage is disposed of directly into a river that serves as an untreated drinking water supply, risks will likely be higher than if no sanitation improvements were made. Similarly, if sewage and night soil collected from latrines are discharged in the local environment or used untreated, the health risks are simply transferred and not necessarily reduced. That succeeded in providing improved sanitation to individual households but failed to dispose of the sullage. The result threatened the community with perhaps a more serious health problem than what existed before the project began.

Environmental Issues

The lack of adequate peri-urban sanitation provisions has grave environmental consequences that indirectly jeopardise human health. Peri-urban areas are the largest non-point source of focal contamination in a given city. The inadequate disposal of human waste contaminates surface and ground-water with organic compounds, nutrients, and solids. Organic compounds decompose in receiving waters, depleting oxygen and harming some aquatic life. Nutrients can be toxic to fish and humans and can cause eutrophication (the excessive growth of algae and aquatic plants utilising the nutrients which can lead to decreased oxygen concentrations when the algae and plants die and decay). Solids decay using up oxygen and can harm benthic organisms living at the bottom of water bodies.

Reducing such environmental contamination via improved sanitation technologies can be more compelling to development decision-makers than is improving general health, as can be seen in the following example from Kumasi, Ghana. A year study by the World Bank on sanitation in Kumasi estimated that 24,100 cubic meters of focal waste was generated by Kumasis 600,000 people every month. The types of sanitation technologies used by the Kumasi population included public latrines, bucket latrines, flush toilets (into septic tanks), pit latrines, and nothing (bushes). Independent of the type of sanitation technology or disposal system, the World Bank study showed that 21,600 cubic meters of the total focal waste (90%) eventually flowed untreated into the underground aquifers and streams. The environmental effects of such a quantity certainly would impress upon decision-makers the need to re-examine the sanitation system on hand.

Social Considerations

Community Organisation and Participation

Citizen involvement has been found to be a key ingredient in the success of peri-urban sanitation projects. Community participation can lead to cost reductions, increased cost recovery, and more effective operation and maintenance of systems. The Working Group on Urbanisation (WG/U) of the Water Supply and Sanitation Collaborative Council, an international organisation, recently reviewed 271 documents describing 67 peri-urban water supply and sanitation (WS&S) projects. Thirty-one of the 67 projects were reported to have been successful; 19 of these attributed a major role in their success to citizen participation.

The lack of a common social composition in peri-urban areas can make organising for community participation difficult, however. The major shared feature of peri-urban inhabitants is their place of residence. People in these areas are likely to come from different ethnic groups, speak different languages, have different religions, and earn a wide range of incomes. Nevertheless, it is imperative to include from the start the users in peri-urban areas because their heterogeneous nature increases the complexity of sanitation improvement approaches. That resulted from effective citizen participation in peri-urban settlements. One occurred in Zambia, the other in Kenya.

Community participation usually does not begin spontaneously and it rarely continues without enormous work and patience, which eventually must be rewarded financially. Often barriers exist that prevent organisation of local institutions in peri-urban communities. Residents may lack the free time to organise, or the knowledge and experience in how to organise n a sustainable way. Most community members cannot survive by working as full-time volunteers. However, communities can still be highly organised. For example, they may have carried out an invasion of the land to form the settlement in the first place.

To organise residents effectively, project planners need to explore opportunities for bridging cultural and other differences within peri-urban settlements early on in the planning of sanitation improvement activities. Residents of peri-urban settlements have shown they are willing to organise around specific issues. Identifying and working through an informal power structure, or through an NGO or other community group, can help overcome cultural or social differences within a settlement.

Organisations that have grown out of other development activities may turn their attention to sanitation projects. For example, community efforts to legalise land rights can lead to organising to get water into the community, followed by organising for a sanitation program. A related institutional issue is that economic rather than social project components often are seen as determining project viability or success. There is widespread belief that peri-urban sanitation projects are essentially technical in nature, with social aspects, including community participation, considered less important for a projects success. Consequently, the technical departments of the implementing agency have much more power and status than those dealing with social aspects, if the latter exist at all.

In most countries, engineers who control the technical departments are mainly senior men, while community development and social workers in the social division tend more to be junior women. Sexual inequalities reinforce the attitude among bureaucrats that the social components of projects are less important. A lack of recognition that community participation requires specialised training also hinders citizen involvement, as does the longer time frame required for implementation of projects based on participatory approaches. The latter implies higher initial up-front costs as well, further discouraging the process.

Behavioural Factors

Other major social considerations to focus on in planning improved peri-urban sanitation services centre around the recipients hygiene behaviour. Hygiene modifications are essentially the changes in peoples behaviour that, over time, improve health. One way behavioural change is demonstrated is by the ways people use improved infrastructure. Usage and sustainability are critical to the success of sanitation projects. Unless facilities are suitable for the people using them and unless the technologies are affordable and efficient, the facilities will remain unaccepted and under used. WASH studies have shown that health benefits associated with peri-urban sanitation projects require that changes in hygiene behaviour accompany infrastructure improvements.

Peri-urban sanitation planners have often given too little scrutiny to the types of technologies acceptable to a given community, or to hygiene education needed to support the chosen option. Behavioural components are often neglected. Because peri-urban areas often lack a common social make-up, however, such information about high-risk sanitation behaviour can be difficult to acquire.

High-risk behaviour can be defined as action by men, women, and children that allows exposure to human excreta. Two sets of information involving high-risk sanitation behaviour are required as a basis for determining the appropriate sanitation intervention: identifying existing high-risk sanitation behaviour and practices in a community, and specifying behavioural changes the community must undertake to improve health. In peri-urban communities, identifying and drawing conclusions about this information are difficult because of the cultural, ethnic, and religious mix typical of these settlements.

In all communities, barriers exist to changing high-risk behaviour. (A barrier as used here signifies a belief, norm, attitude, or condition that either reinforces the high-risk behaviour or limits the modified behaviour.) Barriers may be religious, cultural, social, economic, or technological in nature and may not be readily observable. For example, a crumbling slab or a dark latrine is a condition that may cause people to fear using the latrine, or religious beliefs may dictate that women and men cannot use the same latrine. Similarly, a community norm may allow a certain abandoned field or lot to be considered an acceptable place for children to defecate.

With the cultural, social, and economic diversity common to many peri-urban areas, high-risk sanitation behaviours and barriers to changing them will likely vary widely among inhabitants. This makes surveys and other approaches to information gathering complicated and very difficult, especially compared with a more homogeneous rural community. Because of the great variation in residents, a large sample size is needed for a survey of preferences or behaviours to be useful and truly indicative of a large, diverse community.

Institutional Considerations

In peri-urban areas, various socialite factors may limit the range of acceptable, appropriate sanitation interventions. Chief among these are individual citizens priorities, cost, institutional capabilities, and legal constraints. In addition, the appropriateness of on-site systems in peri-urban areas will be subject to the users perception of land availability, the maturity of the community, income levels, and other perceived priorities. (In peri-urban areas, where so much is needed, the perceived need for sanitation improvements may be low compared with the demand for water, electricity, dispensaries, schools, drainage, roads, or solid waste removal, for example.)

Costs of Improvements

The costs of peri-urban sanitation programs can vary significantly and include labour, material, management, operation, hygiene education, training, legalising land, and community organising. Location, site characteristics, and density also play a major role in cost. Bad soils and steep topography can double the cost of sewerage, for example, and high densities can preclude lower-cost options even where buildings are only one story high. Additionally, off-site connections can cloud estimates of project expenditures because their cost depends on their distance from existing trunk lines. Site variability also leads to difficulty in evaluating feasible options and monitoring project implementation. Ironically, because peri-urban families have settled on the cheapest land, they often require the most expensive sanitation infrastructure by the very nature of the terrains physical condition. As a result of the degree to which the above factors can vary, cost over-runs are common in upgrading programs and range from 50 to 200 percent. Many budgeting difficulties also arise involved in working within an existing social setting. Land tenure issues, rights-of-way problems, inaccurate reference maps, and inadequate soil investigations are common causes of delay and cost overrun.

Cost Recovery

Cost recovery schemes rely on two basic instruments to recover the capital costs of sanitation infrastructure improvements: direct charges to property owners benefiting from the improvements, and indirect charges to users through water or other utility rates.

In general, worldwide experience at full cost recovery for water supply and sanitation projects has not been very successful. In rural areas, recovery of capital costs mostly has not been tried, and even attempts at recovering simple operations and maintenance costs have had mixed results. Recent concern over spiralling public debt in developed and industrialised countries alike, coupled with growing awareness that water is a limited resource and that the majority of institutions responsible for providing water-related services cannot cover their costs, has led most governments and external support agencies (ESAs) to conclude that water and sanitation services should be recognised as an economic good for which it is appropriate to pay. Thus, the cost of WS&S services should be considered chargeable first and foremost to individual users, and not to the public at large. This means that service coverage should be extended on the basis of an assessment of effective demand; that is, the level of service for which potential users are willing to pay. Cost recovery has devoted great attention to the ability of beneficiaries to pay for the improvement provided. Too little attention has been given to willingness to pay and capacity to collect.

Willingness to Pay

To help determine the appropriate level of service for a given peri-urban community, a willingness-pay survey designed specifically for sanitation improvements in peri-urban areas must be devised. Willingness-to-pay surveys have been used successfully with water supply projects, but very few have been applied to peri-urban situations. Peri-urban residents may be less willing to pay for sanitation improvements than for water supply; a survey would reveal whether this is so.

Willingness-to-pay surveys also help identify technologies that are acceptable and affordable to a community. They also can help determine feasible methods of financing. Cost indexing of options, in fact, can be presented to users as questions in willingness-to-pay studies. The results of a willingness-to-pay survey in Kumasi, Ghana, and highlight the important components such a survey contains.

Credit Programs

In some peri-urban sanitation programs, access to credit should be considered as a mechanism for mobilising the economic resources of peri-urban inhabitants. Significant constraints to this access may exist, however, including high transaction costs, lengthy approval processes, high interest rates and loan security requirements, legal land registration, mortgage requirements, and an insufficient number of personnel allocated to serve customers in low-income brackets.

Uncertain Legal Status of Peri-Urban Areas

The underlying legal issue for peri-urban settlements is that they lack official recognition as legal residential areas because the land they occupy usually has not been zoned for housing or is considered dangerous or environmentally protected. Either the residents occupy the site without legal land tenure or they buy it from the landowner, who in turn has not legally urbanised the land (that is, legally registered the land or plots and installed or brought in municipal services such as electricity and water). In both cases, governments are reluctant to provide sanitation infrastructure to a settlement because that would imply that they recognise the settlements legality. In many developing countries, government officials hold biases against squatter areas and providing assistance to them.

In peri-urban settlements, households also may be reluctant to invest time and money in infrastructure improvements that may not benefit them in the long run. Because unstable land tenure means residents can eventually lose the land, they often are less willing make home improvements. Moreover, in these cases, lenders may decline to lend money for such improvements.

Politicians can hardly be blamed for their tough stand against peri-urban settlements. As elected or appointed officials, they are responsible for enforcing codes and laws. Unless project designers can get a political commitment from the mayor or other authorised key decision-maker to agree to sanitation interventions in illegal settlements, it makes little sense to go any further in the project design process.

The challenge to project designers and local authorities, who likely have different though equally legitimate interests, is to find a mutually acceptable resolution of their conflicts. Recognition of these inherent conflicts is important, and facilitated meetings often can help smooth the way for a continuation of the design and implementation process.

Specific legal issues that may need to be assessed when designing a sanitation improvement project include land tenure, plot registration with municipal authorities, and the applicability and appropriateness of building codes, design and construction standards, and environmental regulations. Describes a successful peri-urban infrastructure project that focused on legalisation as one of its first key stages. Indeed, sanitation improvement projects can help to accelerate the natural transformation of peri-urban areas into formally recognised communities. Conversely, when an area obtains legal land tenure, residents have more impetus to demand infrastructure.

Formal Institutions and Peri-Urban Settlements

An insufficient number of formal institutions government and private possess the motivation, mandate, experience, or capability to implement peri-urban sanitation programs. As noted above, governments do not want to condone the existence of informal communities for many reasons. Some municipalities cannot even provide services in more affluent areas; they are overwhelmed in general and do not want to recognise new areas and increase their responsibilities.

Demand-driven urbanisation infrastructure involves a different process than does formal, supply-driven urbanisation. Yet existing institutions have been et up for supply driven urbanisation infrastructure. They are not organisationally structured and prepared to carry out demand-driven urbanisation. These institutions have their own laws and regulations, institutional mission statements, goals, objectives, personnel, and methods. People hired by such institutions are trained at universities that are still supply-oriented in their approach to urban planning. As a result, when it comes to peri-urban areas, institutional staff are often confused about their institutional and personal responsibilities.

Another problem that can surface between formal institutions and the peri-urban community concerns the kind of skills needed to initiate sanitation interventions in peri-urban settlements. Standard technology and approaches as applied in developed countries and in planned urban neighbourhood of developing countries will not work in peri-urban areas because of the latter physical conditions, heterogeneous population, and population density. Consequently, formal institutions, in working with peri-urban settlements, must in the future be prepared to offer creative solutions and alternative technologies. They also must be willing to engage the community in the decision-making process from the beginning. Today, unfortunately, there exists in many places a professional bias among engineers and planners against alternative technologies and community participation. Strong local institutions thus are needed to implement and sustain projects in peri-urban areas, and engineers and planners in these institutions must be able and willing to identify and work with existing community leaders.

Formal institutions also must learn to cooperate with organisations from a variety of different sectors. For example, multiple ministries may require coordination, such as the Ministry of Health, the water and sewerage authority, and the Ministry of Planning. Regulations are needed for health and construction, and a tariff-setting authority is necessary to establish rates and collect fees. Project designers therefore should consult with each of these institutions. In most cases, the institutions have no clear mandates about their role in providing services to peri-urban settlements, given the latter illegal status. A key issue for project designers, then, is to assess whether the government staff members responsible for urban sanitation have the skills, experience, and institutional commitment necessary to change their approach to peri-urban communities.

Intermediary Organisations

NGOs can serve as useful bridges in overcoming the lack of recognition informal settlements suffer from government organisations. For example, it may be easier for NGOs to organise the community at first, followed by out reach to the formal institutions.

NGOs, in working with the community, usually can help find more economical solutions that are acceptable to all residents, ones that involve residents contributions in kind or in labour in building their own infrastructure. Although communities may be limited in resolving their own infrastructure problems, cases of locally built and managed aqueducts are known. With NGO assistance and community labour and pressure, the cost and red tape involved in acquiring infrastructure can generally be reduced, and government support and recognition can be fostered.

Technical Considerations

The decision of which technology or combination of technologies to use for peri-urban sanitation intervention will perhaps be one of the most challenging for project designers to make. Tried and true sanitation technologies for either rural areas or formal urban areas have, for the most part, been found to be inappropriate for peri-urban settlements. In recent years, new and more appropriate technologies for peri-urban sites have been developed by engineers working with social scientists, but actual experience with using these technologies is still relatively minimal.

Perhaps one of the most important points project planners must keep in mind is that the current range of sanitation technologies that might be considered for peri-urban areas is limited. In many peri-urban areas, the combination of harsh physical conditions, high population densities, extreme poverty, and the inability or unwillingness of governments to provide significant subsidies may lead to the conclusion that no existing technology is an appropriate solution. These impossible situations will likely become more common as the explosive rapid urbanisation process continues. Recognising that there very well may be no magic bullet technology will liberate project planners to explore alternative, non-technological approaches to addressing peri-urban sanitation.

Site Limitations

The physical limitations imposed by a peri-urban site can be the predominant constraint to upgrading the area. Cities and towns are often built on land that is unsuitable for productive use, such as farming. As discussed earlier, peri-urban settlements are almost always found on land with the cheapest value, which in turn usually indicates that the land has unattractive physical attributes such as extremely steep slopes or swampy conditions, or that it is subject to frequent flooding.

These types of physical site conditions can increase design and construction costs by 100 percent or more compared with what the same technology would cost on land more suitable for urbanisation. Operations and maintenance costs will also be more expensive on difficult terrain. Many peri-urban areas have soil that is either rocky, sandy, or clayey. Rocky soil makes even pit latrines difficult and expensive to build; sandy soil may require expensive lining of pits to prevent cave-ins or make contamination of underground aquifers very likely; clayey soils make infiltration difficult, resulting in the quick filling of pit latrines. These not uncommon conditions can make even the lowest-cost and simplest technologies either technically infeasible or unaffordable for many poor families living in peri-urban areas.

Institutional and Community Costs of Low-Cost Technologies

The term low-cost technologies usually refers to low capital costs especially the capital required for materials. From an institutional and community perspective, however, low-cost technologies can be far more labour intensive than conventional technologies. Project planners designing a peri-urban sanitation program need also to consider the additional costs of the corresponding labour when comparing technologies. For example, employees of the institutions implementing a peri-urban sanitation project usually must devote a significant number of days or even months to the soft side of appropriate technologies. Depending on the technology and community context, this process can be very labour intensive and may include activities in community organising, attending meetings, construction training, operations and maintenance training, hygiene education, monitoring and evaluation, managing credit programs, and so on. These labour costs can be significant for the implementing institution and need to be recovered if a program is to be sustainable. Nonetheless, they often are not factored into the comparison of costs corresponding to a given technology. Planners need to cost out the level of effort required to meet these tasks and consider these costs when comparing the technologies.

Lower-cost technologies also usually require more labour from community members than do other technologies. Many peri-urban sanitation project designs require communities to provide much of the construction labour, including digging pit latrines, digging trenches for sewage pipes, or building on-site latrine superstructures. Many low-cost technology sanitation schemes also require the community to play a significant role in the operation and maintenance of the systems, including cleaning out latrines, unplugging small-diameter sewer pipes, or emptying septic tanks. Despite this degree of community labour, project planners usually assign it no value or zero cost when comparing technologies.

In reality, labour provided by a community represents real and significant costs to the community and its members. In peri-urban areas, families are by and large in the cash economy and usually need to work very long hours in order to make enough money to meet their basic needs. The axiom time is money is very real to families living in peri-urban settlements. Contrary to the prevailing assumptions on the part of many project planners, labour provided for a peri-urban sanitation project by a community is not free. In many peri-urban sanitation projects, families that are required to contribute labour either lose an opportunity to be earning money or, more often than not, hire a lower-cost labourer to provide their labour contribution. As a result, many peri-urban sanitation projects that have used a low-cost appropriate technology have been stalled or have failed because the beneficiary families living in peri-urban settlements could not afford to donate their labour. Project planners must consider the real cost to a community of a given technology in deciding what is most affordable and appropriate.

They should also be prepared to conclude that even low-cost appropriate technologies may be unaffordable to a given community.

Design Standards and Engineers

In choosing a sanitation technology, project planners should use with caution existing selection and design guidelines. Although peri-urban sanitation needs typically are assessed using selection guidelines developed for rural or formal urban areas, these tools are not always appropriate for peri-urban areas. Rural and formal urban guidelines do not include new, alternative technologies such as con-dominial, shallow, and simplified collection systems, nor do they consider some of the constraints (such as lack of legal tenure) unique to peri-urban areas.

Local engineers, and often their expatriate advisors, prefer to use sanitation systems with which they are familiar. These systems are usually the most modern and are often based on the adoption of engineering design and construction standards for conventional sanitation technologies in developed countries, which in turn are based on the industrialised nations own health standards and institutional capabilities. These systems often turn out to be unsuitable for the difficult topography, soils, lack of water, and other conditions found in peri-urban settlements. In particular, such conditions can make installation of conventional sanitation infrastructure extremely costly.

Two factors that contribute to engineers over reliance on conventional sewage systems is the existing legal framework that has legally codified foreign engineering standards, and the traditional curricula and corresponding textbooks used in developing-country engineering schools that were often founded by expatriate engineering professors or local engineering professors who first received their training overseas. Even in urban areas where more than 50 percent of the city is considered peri-urban, it is very rare to find engineering students who take even one course dealing with peri-urban sanitation.

Another important constraint to servicing peri-urban areas, noted earlier, is that lower-cost technologies usually require a much higher level of user involvement than conventional technology to function properly. Yet engineers, who traditionally play a major role in the formulation of sanitation projects, often have little training or regard for the social mechanics of projects, such as mobilising communities and involving future users, and they have little patience for the sheer time it takes to address them.

Some instructive examples from around the world offer simple and ingenious solutions to providing sanitation under the adverse conditions found in most peri-urban areas. Of particular note are con-dominial or simplified sewers which are described . These options have also turned out to be much cheaper than conventional systems. Nevertheless, for the most part, the world engineering community (in both developed and developing countries) is either unaware of their existence or, because of a lack of hands-on experience, remains distrustful of and reluctant to consider these alternatives.

Finally, it should be pointed out that the conceptualisation, design, and construction of simplified sewerage systems that are appropriate for peri-urban areas pose extremely complicated engineering challenges that require skilled, experienced, innovative engineers working on interdisciplinary teams with social scientists, economists, and others.

Sanitation Technologies

Sanitation technologies can be divided into two general classes: on-site and off-site.

On-Site Technologies

On-site technologies rely on the disposal of excreta at the point of defecation. Material is not removed from the site, although liquids may leach into the ground and eventually be carried off-site. Latrines are an example of on-site systems. The pit of a pit latrine is covered when full, and the excreta stays in place. Composting latrines are emptied, but the composted material is used on-site or nearby.

Peri-urban situations present both advantages and disadvantages for on-site systems. The on-site systems lower cost and minimal institutional requirements match well with the lower incomes and weak institutional capabilities often found in informal settlements. However, peri-urban population densities frequently are too high to accommodate latrines, and site conditions often are inappropriate as well, leading to pit flooding or ground-water contamination.

Latrines

To date, construction of latrines has been the main sanitation intervention funded by external support agencies (ESAs), including for projects in peri-urban areas. Dry, non-flushed latrines can be built with a small initial investment, mainly labour, and require little operating skill. They are also inexpensive to maintain. They are suitable for use in areas where water is in short supply and where land is available to dig new pits when old ones fill up. If no land is available, provision for cartilage and treatment must be made. If piped water is provided to an area, provisions must be made for proper drainage away from the latrine, and care must be taken to prevent ground-water contamination from latrine leachate.

Experience to date has shown that latrines have serious limitations in peri-urban areas. For one, they usually are not technically feasible at population densities above 350 persons per hectare, and most peri-urban areas have population densities that significantly exceed that rate. In many high-density peri-urban settlements, little, if any, space exists to dig a new pit after the existing one fills up. Space may not even be available to build the first pit.

Additionally, latrines are impractical for multi-story housing. Settlements with many high buildings may have insufficient circulation of air streams normally required to blow over the tops of the vent pipes of ventilated improved pit (VIP) latrines. Finally, latrines used in high-density areas run a high risk of contaminating nearby wells and underground aquifers.

Double pit latrines may be an appropriate solution for many settlements until off-site technologies become feasible. Double pit latrines share many of the advantages of single pit latrines, but in addition, they last longer. These advantages, however, are countered by higher initial costs, the need for more user education, and more complex construction requirements.

Compost latrines: One current alternative that is currently in vogue as an appropriate technology for many ESAs is the dual vault composting (DVC) latrine. Unlike pit latrines, composting latrines have their contents composted and emptied. As with pit latrines, actual experience with the

DVC latrine in peri-urban areas has been generally unsatisfactory. The DVC only makes sense if there exists a market for the compost and a community tradition for human waste reuse.

Composting toilets require significant and conscientious user care and operation, which peri-urban inhabitants are unlikely to maintain unless the implementing agency provides significant and continuous extension work. The more typical scenario, in which implementing agencies do some up-front promotion of compost latrines, provide materials for their construction, and then move on to another site without providing ongoing education to reinforce proper maintenance of the latrines has consistently resulted in 50 to 80 percent of the latrines either being misused or not used at all.

Communal latrines: Communal sanitation facilities can be an appropriate interim solution for peri-urban areas. In general, communal latrines address the major constraints commonly found in peri-urban areas:

1. Low water availability
2. Site conditions inappropriate for latrines
3. Unwillingness to pay by users who have no legal land tenure or have very low incomes
4. Population densities too great for individual household latrines
5. Institutional capabilities insufficient to support off-site systems
6. Social factors that make the reuse of excreta implausible

Communal latrines address this combination of constraints by reducing the land area required for sanitation facilities, minimising cost, and requiring little water. However, project planners should use caution when considering this option because examples abound of such facilities that are not maintained because of ambiguity as to who owns the latrine (the community or the government) and who is responsible for its maintenance. In these situations, communal latrines fall into disrepair or become unsanitary and therefore are not used.

Pay-per-use communal latrines have been successful in some cases for those people who can afford it, but even when most users can pay, subsidies may still be necessary for those who cannot pay, to ensure more complete coverage of the entire population.

Septic Tanks

Septic tanks are another on-site sanitation system, although partially treated solids must be disposed of and further treated off-site. Septic tanks offer two particular advantages. They provide better treatment of waste than pit latrines and can be used to dispose of gray water, and they are simple enough to include the participation of the users, the community, and the local or regional governments.

The disadvantages of septic tanks versus latrines are the larger investment they require, their higher operating costs, the need to clean them, their land usage, and the higher level of water supply they require. In high-density areas, the same space constraints that affect pit latrines also affect technologies such as pour-flush toilets, which require soak pits or septic tanks. Water to flush the toilet may also be too costly, too cumbersome to carry from the public tap, or only intermittently available.

Dual soak-away pits, which are shared by several households, are a variation of the above. In this scheme, several households pour-flush toilets are connected to a common pair of soak-away pits. Cooperation must be assured among users to prevent blockage and ensure the cycling and the cleaning of the pits.

Off-Site Technologies

Off-site systems dispose of waste away from the user. A simple bucket latrine is one example of an off-site system. The more complex water-borne sewage collection system is another example.

Off-site sanitation interventions often solve sanitation-related health problems by isolating the excreta from the user, only to fail ultimately by contaminating ground-water or by exposing downstream population to disease. In the long term, cities must develop environmentally sustainable methods to treat and dispose of waste.

Conventional Sewage Collection Systems

Conventional sewage collection systems have a high initial construction cost (including a high foreign exchange requirement for certain materials and equipment) and require skilled labour for installation. These systems often include pump stations and screening equipment, which need trained maintenance personnel and moderate operation and maintenance expenditures. Maintenance of the sewer lines consists of the periodic cleaning and removal of obstructions. Rights of way are required for the initial construction of and maintenance access to conventional sewerage systems. They also require a significant water supply to minimise plugging of sewage lines. The overwhelming majority of peri-urban settlements around the world do not have the required amount and reliability of water supply for the proper operation of conventional sanitation systems. The most significant constraint, however, is the inability of the majority of peri-urban areas to afford conventional sewage systems.

Alternatives to Conventional Sewerage

Alternatives to conventional sewerage include simplified, con-dominial, and small bore systems.

Simplified sewerage: Design standards for conventional sewerage are altered; sewers can be built with smaller pipes, shallower trenches, and fewer appurtenances.

Con-dominial sewers: Simplified sewerage can be built and maintained by users and located between houses, rather than in streets or other rights of way.

Small bore sewers: Septic tanks can be connected to small-diameter pipes that carry the solids-free effluent.

All of these alternatives have significantly lower initial and operating costs and a lower requirement for amount and reliability of piped water supply than do conventional systems. However, project planners should recognise that even though these alternatives are much lower in cost, they may still be unaffordable to many peri-urban communities. Similarly, peri-urban areas may not have the required minimum piped water system to accommodate these technologies. In addition, project planners must realise that these alternative sewerage systems require more labour-intensive installation and increased maintenance. Unlike conventional sewerage, with its large pipes, the small pipes used in alternative systems frequently clog up. The increased maintenance needed to unclog the pipes is the responsibility of individual households and the community, and requires ongoing community organisation and extension work by the implementing agency.

A clogged pipe at a household in unconventional sewers affects a significant portion of the community, since these systems are more interdependent in their piping. Clogging at one household blocks up the pipe for everyone else using the system. As discussed earlier, these systems are not as common as conventional sewerage; therefore, there is relatively little operational data for engineers to use as a basis for rational design and planning.

Pit Latrines with Cartilage Systems

Under certain conditions, single pit latrines can work as a short-term intervention even in densely populated peri-urban areas to create a physical barrier between residents and excreta. As discussed above, in high-density areas, latrines must be emptied periodically because land is not available to dig another pit. Unfortunately, technologies for latrine emptying and excreta treatment that are appropriate for peri-urban areas are not yet widely known or available. However, presents one approach to overcoming the latrine emptying and collection problem that is proving successful in Nairobi.

Waste water Treatment

As discussed above, Con-dominial and small bore sewers offer significant initial cost savings over conventional sewage collection while still providing the advantages of water-borne sewage systems. These alternatives, however, must include waste water treatment to increase health and environmental benefits, and they require cartilage capabilities to empty septic or interceptor tanks, if used. Septic tanks have been used as a treatment receptacle for block sewers. However, innovative on-site treatment technologies, such as anaerobic filters, need to be tested on peri-urban applications. Decentralised treatment technologies have not yet been applied to peri-urban areas.

Conventional high-technology waste water treatment systems are usually too expensive to build and operate for peri-urban areas. Some of the small-scale, low-technology waste water alternatives worth considering are the following:

1. Stabilisation ponds
2. Constructed wet lands
3. Duckweed ponds
4. Up-flow anaerobic sludge blanket reactors

5. Communal septic tanks/anaerobic filters
6. Oxidation ditches

An important disadvantage of many of these alternatives is their requirement for a large area of land, which can be expensive, especially in urban areas.

Key Principles

This section summarises the key principles identified in this chapter, the key questions to ask and information to gather in planning and designing peri-urban sanitation projects, and the basic approaches that should be considered when devising project strategies for improving community excreta sanitation in peri-urban areas.

1. Improving the health of the rapidly growing number of families living in peri-urban areas and protecting the urban environment are urgent needs and compelling program objectives that host country governments, as well as external support agencies such as the Agency for International Development, must address. In reaching these objectives, improving community sanitation should be accorded the same (if not higher) priority as water supply.
2. To improve health in densely populated peri-urban areas, sanitation programs must target the community rather than individual households. Individual households with improved sanitation will not experience improved health if their neighbours are still disposing of focal matter in ways that contaminate the general environment of a peri-urban settlement. In addition, improved community excreta sanitation may not improve health if other environmental factors such as solid waste disposal and drainage are not also considered.

3. The current planning paradigm for formal urbanisation, which begins with the installation of basic urban services, does not coincide with the actual peri-urbanisation process, which begins with the informal and/or illegal settlement by poor urban families on land that has not been urbanised. The peri-urbanisation process is a reality for 50 to 80 percent of most cities in developing countries. Therefore, authorities must recognise that providing sanitation services to existing densely populated peri-urban settlements must follow a different paradigm than that of traditional urbanisation. Additionally, officials must acknowledge the need to reform existing service provision agencies to coincide with the particular needs of the peri-urban sector.
4. The economic, social, legal, and physical conditions generally found in peri-urban areas present unique challenges to WS&S sector specialists attempting to improve community sanitation. In large measure, conventional engineering approaches and standard technical solutions used for formal urban and rural sewerage systems must be significantly modified or even rejected for peri-urban areas.
5. Installing a sanitation technology can be done relatively rapidly. Setting up and implementing a long-term sustainable peri-urban sanitation program that successfully improves community health and protects the environment takes significantly more time.
6. To improve health, changing individual and community behaviours that cause focal-oral contamination is at least as important as constructing new sanitation facilities. For efforts to change behaviour to succeed, projects must be designed around a thorough and correct understanding of existing knowledge and hygiene practices in the community and a thorough knowledge of the social, cultural, and religious context

in which high-risk behaviour takes place. Moreover, efforts to change behaviour must be institutionalised and enjoy strong support from donors, governments, and other key actors.

7. Recognising that improving peri-urban community sanitation is a complex process, project planning should involve the many institutional actors that influence or have responsibility for peri-urban sanitation, including the respective agencies that handle sanitation, the agencies responsible for hygiene education, and non-health agencies such as municipalities, urban planning agencies, and credit institutions. The most effective way to ensure that cooperation is elicited from the widest possible range of agencies and institutions is to take an inclusive, participatory approach to the planning process.

8. Peri-urban sanitation projects should not be solely technology driven. Successful sanitation interventions should also consider health, economics, social, legal, and institutional factors.

9. The conceptualisation, design, and construction of peri-urban sanitation systems pose extremely complicated engineering challenges that require skilled, experienced, and innovative engineers working on interdisciplinary teams along with planners, social scientists, environmentalists, lawyers, economists, and others.

10. Citizen involvement and community participation are critical to successful peri-urban sanitation programs. Community participation can lead to initial cost reductions, increased acceptance of program interventions, increased cost recovery, and more effective operation and maintenance.

11. Institutions providing peri-urban sanitation services should seek to recover as much of their costs as

possible in order to reach some level of financial sustainability and be able to expand services to other peri-urban areas. Individual households should be expected to pay for the real value of the sanitation services. Providing access to credit can greatly facilitate peoples ability to pay for the services. If subsidies are necessary to reach the extremely poor, they should be clearly accounted for. Successful cost recovery results from providing services that families are able and willing to pay for and from developing effective institutional capacities to collect tariffs, loan payments, and other fees.

A comprehensive approach that recognises the interrelationships between various socialite sectors is needed to increase the effectiveness of a peri-urban sanitation project. Projects should be able to depend on cooperation between and among community, municipal, regional, or national organisations and involve both the formal and informal sectors. Complementary projects in water supply, solid waste collection, drainage, and health education may be needed to ensure the effectiveness of sanitation projects. Furthermore, implementation of a sanitation solution may be a multi-step process, starting with simple interventions to address the large problems and becoming more complex as finances and institutional capabilities allow. To promote a comprehensive approach, project design and implementation teams should be interdisciplinary. NGOs can also play an effective role because they can organise illegal/informal peri-urban settlements and serve as an intermediary with formal legal institutions such as banks, municipalities, and utilities.

Much was learned during the International Drinking Water Supply and Sanitation Decade (1981-90), especially about developing affordable, durable, and simple technologies, and about the equally important human elements of water and sanitation. Much of what was learned during the decade came from rural experiences, which may not be relevant to peri-urban situations. Similarly, the engineering sector in formal urban areas is strongly biased toward the use of conventional sewage technology that is clearly out of reach of the overwhelming majority of families living in peri-urban areas. This bias is reinforced by existing engineering and health regulations and standards. Consequently, the ?lessons learned from the rural WS&S experience, as well as the conventional wisdom of established engineering professions in urban areas, must be re-focused and altered dramatically to have meaning in a peri-urban context.

The greatest need is for action, comprising the following steps:

1. Making existing knowledge on peri-urban sanitation more accessible
2. Maintaining statistics that describe the residents of peri-urban areas and their needs
3. Sharing the practical implications of applied research within and among countries
4. Designing and implementing activities and projects that bring sanitation to the urban poor, and perhaps most importantly
5. Documenting and learning from the experiences of those carrying out sanitation activities in peri-urban areas of developing countries.

Everyone involved or interested in peri-urban upgrading projects must recognise the uniqueness of the sanitation challenges presented by peri-urban areas. Interested parties must also confront head-on the difficulties in providing appropriate excreta disposal systems in these areas and recognise that many impossible situations prevail for which no feasible technical solution exists. WS&S professionals must also challenge the status quo the reluctance of municipal and national governments to act and respond to the demands of peri-urban people who lack water and sanitation infrastructure. By necessity or choice, government institutions, bilateral and multilateral aid organisations, and NGOs in the foreseeable future will be compelled to shift more of their attention and resources to the sanitation needs of peri-urban population.

3

Challenges of Urban Sanitation

India is a nation of ancient and firmly entrenched tradition and culture. For thousands of years, religion, geography and the necessities of a rural agrarian society have sculpted a complex caste system based on status, hierarchy, and, above all, a strict division of labour. As India is becoming increasingly urbanised, and her people are leaving their traditional rural communities and entering into an environment marked by fluidity, change and drastically different technological and physical conditions, traditional divisions of labour and living habits forged in rural settings are increasingly out of step with contemporary conditions. Yet, Indians continue to cling to traditional cultural mores, often causing great problems, especially for the poor.

Bombay is India's largest and fastest growing city and exemplifies many of these problems as traditional, rural culture clashes with the reality of conditions in the modern mega city. Over half of Bombay's residents live in poorly serviced slums marked by overcrowding, pollution, poor sanitation and a host of other problems shared by the urban poor the world over. Of particular concern in Bombay is the problem of human waste. The lack of clean and adequate toilet facilities, the lingering rural custom of relieving oneself outdoors, and deeply entrenched attitudes and taboos preventing most slum dwellers from cleaning up human waste, have all resulted in slums littered with faces and reeking of urine. Despite the construction of public toilets by municipal agencies, the problem has persisted. The mere presence of toilets is not enough; they need to be maintained, kept clean, and widely used. This implies more than just the construction of new facilities, but a widespread change in the attitudes and traditions of all city residents, one that would promote sanitary practices, an appreciation of the importance of hygiene and the urban environment, and the reform of a cultural system that only allows a small minority to clean toilets or deal directly with human waste.

The Community of Resource Organisations (CORO), in response to a request from the Indian Department of Science and Technology (DST), has undertaken the management of several municipal pay-and-use toilet complexes in the slums of Bombay. CORO has reformed the toilets' management and maintenance structures, using local labour and introducing incentives which have resulted in cleaner toilets, less corruption and more community participation. By combining toilet maintenance and administration with their already existing work in literacy and book distribution, CORO has increased their reach into the slums, increased education about the importance of sanitation and the urban environment, and laid the groundwork for more effective community organisation around other issues. Through a two-pronged approach stressing literacy and hygiene, CORO has begun to create a whole new culture of urban sanitation, waste management and environmental education.

Over the last ninety years, India has seen phenomenal urban growth, concentrating more and more people in larger and larger towns. Between 1901 and 1991, the number of cities and large towns in India doubled, and their total population increased eight fold. In 1991 26% of Indians lived in cities and large towns, and the Registrar General projects that by 2001, 29.4% of the country, or 278 million people, will be urban dwellers. One of the most striking examples of this urban population explosion is Bombay, and as the largest and fastest growing city in India, it continues to struggle with many of the problems such drastic change entails.

Case of Bombay

Bombay was a group of seven swampy islands inhabited by fishermen when it caught the attention of European explorers and traders. As early as 1529 the Portuguese established a naval provisioning base there, and under the British East India Company, it became the most important port and trading centre in India, especially with the opening of the Suez Canal and the development of railroad in the Indian interior in the 19th century. Bombay continues to be the commercial and financial capital of India, as well as the centre of the largest film industry in the world, and an important transportation centre with an airport that handles 60% of the country's international flights and 40% of its domestic ones. Bombay provides 10% of the India's industrial jobs and pays one third of its income tax, one fifth of its excise tax, and 43% of its corporate tax.

Greater Bombay had a population of 9.9 million in 1991 and is one of the fastest growing cities in the world. An estimated 300 families, or about 1,500 people, move into the city every day, and the city is expected to grow to 15 million by the year 2000. With the expansion of industrial and commercial activities over the last few decades, land in the central island city has been converted to commercial use, and with no more space available in the core city, housing colonies and slums have developed in the eastern and western suburbs (Table 1). Most of Bombay's new residents live in slums far from the city centre and without many basic civic amenities; the city's recent growth has taken place far away from the traditional service networks and places of employment.

Table 1. Population of Bombay (in thousands)

Year	*City*	*Suburbs*	*Extended Suburbs*	*Percent Total Increase*
1951	510	155	2,924	—
1961	1,037	343	4,152	42
1971	2,167	733	5,970	43
1981	2,799	2,169	8,226	38
1991	3,986	2,762	9,907	20

Obviously, such a quickly growing population places extraordinary stresses on traditional service delivery systems and limited municipal resources. These stresses are exacerbated by economic and political factors. Despite higher revenues from an expanding tax base, Bombay has gotten little in return for its increased contributions to the state and national exchequer. Even more problematic has been the stagnation and recent decline of industrial growth and employment during the 1980s. From 1981 to 1988 only ninety additional factories were built in the Bombay Metropolitan Region, and actual industrial employment fell sharply from 604,000 to 474,000.

Because of the loss of industrial jobs many Bombay residents have had to look for work in an informal sector marked by low-skill, low paying jobs without any benefits or job security. This informal sector is accounting for a growing share of a stagnant labour market and is unable to fulfil the city's employment needs. Bombay's population growth has not been accompanied by an expanding job market, leaving many of Bombay's residents unable to pay for basic necessities and the city as a whole unable to provide for its ever-growing number of poor. Many of the city's basic services are inadequate, and the poor suffer especially. There is a lack of recreational space and educational opportunity. Although Bombay has more doctors and hospital beds per person than the national average, many of the medical services are inaccessible and unaffordable for the poor. There is an extensive public transportation system serving Bombay and its suburbs, but it is unable to alleviate the huge congestion caused by the large number of commuters to the city, and Bombay is plagued by traffic problems and air pollution from cars and buses.

Bombay produces 4,000 tons of rubbish a day and 1,500 tons of silt and debris. The city is hard-pressed to remove it all, though the department of solid waste management employs a work-force of 22,000 and has an annual budget of Rs. 12.6 million (US$ 400,000). Slums are especially cluttered with trash.

Bombay is unable to meet the high demand for water. The recommended daily use is 254 litres per capita per day (lpcd); yet in Greater Bombay, domestic supply of water on an average is not more than 130 lpcd. In the outer sections of the Bombay Metropolitan Region it is even less than 70 lpcd. In addition, most people have access to running water for just a few hours each day and must collect and store water for the day's use, often carrying it from public standpipes to their homes.

Despite the existence of a relatively modern sewage network installed in 1935, and even with a vast new system financed by the World Bank and scheduled to open in 2005, Bombay is simply unable to treat the vast amount of waste-water and human waste the city generates. Most of the city's sewage flows into local creeks and coastal waters inadequately treated.

Air pollution is also a major problem in Bombay, the result of factories, the vast numbers of motorised vehicles, cooking fires, and the nation's largest chemical industry (Bombay is home to about 50% of the nation's chemical production). 1,700 tons of pollutants, mostly sulfurdioxides, suspended particles, hydrocarbons, carbon monoxide, and oxides of nitrogen bensyprine, are discharged into the air every day. Not surprisingly, Bombay's residents suffer from unusually high and constantly rising rates of emphysema, asthma, bronchitis, coughs, colds and headaches. 25-30% of the city's children have emphysema or asthma as a result of sulphur and nitrogen oxide in the air.

The most obvious problem caused by exploding growth has been the incredible population density and an acute shortage of suitable and affordable housing. Government agencies and private developers are only able to build a third of the estimated 60,000 new housing units needed every year, and those that are built lie beyond the means of the vast majority of residents. By 1982, 82% of Bombay's households lived in one-room units and the city wide average of 3.99 persons per room made Bombay the mostly densely populated city in India.

Because of the great shortage of housing and the city's inability to expand infrastructure and services to its exploding population, an estimated 5 million people, or nearly one half of all Bombay, live in slums marked by overcrowding, poor living conditions, pollution and a lack of basic services and amenities.

Services in the slums vary, according to the slum's size, age, population, and residents' ability to establish links with municipal officers and elected officials. Nonetheless, conditions in the slums are generally awful. Lack of paved roads and improper drainage leads to widespread flooding and water logging in slums during the rainy season, and access to huts is often limited because of excessively muddy conditions. During the dry season, access is often blocked by accumulated garbage, as solid waste collection is often inadequate or simply nonexistent. The incredible overcrowding in the slums exacerbates all of these problems. With so many people living in such small areas without many basic services, life in the slums is marked by pollution, disease and squalor.

Obviously, the municipal government cannot begin to solve all of the problems of the slums on its own; however, it is widely seen as responsible for providing services and infrastructure and residents are extremely reluctant to assume the responsibility for conditions in their own neighbourhoods. In the absence of concerted community action and initiative, the government is left to itself to perform tasks way beyond its resources.

Lack of Toilet Facilities

The proper disposal of human waste is a huge problem in the slums of Bombay because of a great shortage of latrines and suitable sewage systems. Unfortunately, traditional technologies have been unable to solve Bombay's human waste problem and have proved impractical given Bombay's large slum population and scarce resources.

1. *Conventional Sewerage System.* Traditional sewer systems are very effective, but they require a large and continuous supply of water and sizable financial resources. Although they are convenient, their average per capita cost, including house connection, is more than Rs.5,000. Operation and maintenance costs, as well as necessary adjustments to house plumbing prior to connection, makes these systems even more expensive. The system often takes up to ten years to plan and install. They also require high levels of energy and a large quantity of water. At least 100 litters of water per capita per day is needed to maintain the minimum flow in the pipe without deposition. Lastly, although the number of microorganisms is substantially

reduced during treatment, the effluent from a conventional treatment plant is still highly charged with pathogens which are capable of polluting a river and spreading disease. This can hardly be considered an optimal solution for households in the slums.

2. *Septic Tank.* A septic tank with a soil absorption system is a method for excreta disposal in answered areas, but this is not an appropriate option in Bombay for a number of reasons. Septic tanks require extravagant use of water for flushing faces from the pan into the tank, and Bombay already suffers from inadequate supplies of water. Moreover, after partial treatment of sewage in the septic tank, the effluent has to be discharged in a drainage field having permeable soil. This, too, is impractical for Bombay, where the water table is very high and where there is a shortage of available land for drainage fields. Lastly, the capital cost is high, and it requires periodic dislodging necessitating expensive outside help.

In the face of these inadequate solutions, some alternatives have been designed to solve the problems of human waste in Bombay's slums.

1. *Mobile Toilets.* Mobile toilets have been introduced in Bombay to provide service for slum dwellers. Mobile toilets are made of easy-to-clean fibreglass and have a collecting tank at the bottom which can be emptied remotely by a valve at the site of disposal. Unfortunately, poor scheduling, inadequate maintenance and a lack of access to nearby sewer lines have undermined their effectiveness. However, if the operational problems were solved, this system could yield good results in urban slums.

2. *Sulabh Shauchalaya.* Sulabh Shauchalaya is a low cost pour flush water-seal sanitary latrine. It is an improved version of the designs already available in the country

based on research conducted by different organisations and institutions on pour flush water-seal latrines. The designers of Sulabh Shauchalaya sought to provide an appropriate, efficient, cost effective and affordable excreta disposal system and to free scavengers from having to collect night soil and carry it on their heads.

Sulabh Shauchayala is very popular in India because it has the following advantages:

1. It is odourless as it provides a water-seal between the pan and the pit.
2. It can be constructed inside the house. The cover slab of the pit may be used for various household uses like peeling vegetables, washing utensils, etc.
3. The excreta can be flushed with a small quantity (1-2 litters) of water per use.
4. It is a permanent structure requiring only a small space (1.80m x 1.20m).
5. It can be constructed in nearly all subsoil conditions.
6. After a period of 2 years, the digested sludge in the pit becomes odourless and free from pathogens, at which point it may be used as manure.
7. It is acceptable both from the aesthetic and health points of view, as the excreta is removed from sight and the smell is trapped under ground.
8. It is cost-effective and affordable for the majority of Indian households.
9. Its maintenance is very easy and hardly requires outside help.
10. It can be upgraded to the water-borne sewerage system without any alterations.

Even with the advent of such promising new technologies, people in the slums of Bombay suffer from a terrible lack of suitable latrines. Over 90% of slum dwellers depend on public latrines, and the Bombay Municipal Corporation has built 1,400 public toilets. However, there is widespread dissatisfaction with the city's public toilets, they cannot begin to meet the great demand and they are woefully overused. Long lines and inconvenience mark them.

In addition, existing latrines are very unhygienic and dirty. The municipal workers responsible for maintaining the toilets are often undependable, and there is rarely enough water to clean the latrines sufficiently. Indeed, they are often so filthy that they become a problem in and of themselves, breeding disease and discouraging the use of toilets, especially for small children who are too small to use toilets designed for adults.

As a result of all of these problems, many slum residents must relieve themselves in open spaces near their homes. This results in extremely dirty and unhealthy conditions, with streets and alleys dotted with human excrement.

Excreting in the open creates particular problems for women. In a culture which demands modesty for women, they suffer a humiliating lack of privacy when forced to use open spaces in lieu of a latrine. Most women feel forced to wait for darkness to maintain a minimum of privacy, and their effort to control themselves often has adverse effects on their health. Also, using open spaces in the dark can be unsafe for women, and there have been instances of women being molested while going to defecate at night or in the early morning. In addition to the present problems with Bombay's latrines, there are many substantial barriers to positive change.

1. *Cultural.* A vast majority of rural Indians still do not use confined space for toilets and generally relieve themselves in open spaces away from their homes. In Bombay, most slum dwellers belong to this rural

culture and are not yet fully urbanised in their habits. They do not understand that a toilet can be clean and hygienic, and do not attach toilets to their living spaces, perpetuating a dependence on public latrines. Furthermore, they often continue to use open spaces even when latrines are available, even though this practice is inappropriate and unhealthy in an urban setting.

2. *Spatial.* In a city like Bombay, as slums grow, people do not reserve space for toilets or baths, so there is often no place to put new public latrines. This lack of space contributes to the small number of toilets typically available to slum dwellers; a slum community of about 300 households may commonly have only about six to twelve common toilets. Also, as long as a community is not officially declared a slum, the Municipal Corporation of Greater Bombay does not provide toilet and water facilities. When it provides them, people are expected to pay for water while the corporation provides for toilet upkeep and maintenance. Unfortunately, there is often not enough water, either for individual use or for cleaning the toilets. Further, municipal maintenance is often unsatisfactory. Toilets are overused, filthy, and poorly maintained.

3. *Social and Historical.* In a city like Bombay it is also evident that an overwhelming majority of residents do not set high standards of cleanliness and sanitation for their toilets and urinals. Hence public toilets, including those in offices, hotels, restaurants, railway stations and streets, are filthy and unclean.

In India, over the last two thousand years, the caste system has dominated society, sharply separating intellectual work from physical work, productive work from services, and clean work from that associated with filth. Thus most people would be forbidden to clean up human waste, and there would always be a particular group who would be responsible for cleaning and removing it. Even today, most urban dwellers do not clean their own toilets. They usually engage someone else from the appropriate caste to do it, usually someone who is uneducated, culturally backward and without a sophisticated sense of sanitation. However, with growing urbanisation and industrialisation, even members of these castes have discontinued doing this particular work. Because of accelerating development, the caste system is beginning to break down, but Indian society has not found new ways to solve the problems of sanitation and related services.

Against this background, urban India needs not only clean toilets but also a whole new culture of urban sanitation and waste management. The construction of toilets must take place within the context of an overall effort to educate people about the need for sanitation and hygiene and to break down entrenched social attitudes which prevent urban dwellers from adopting healthier, more sanitary lifestyles.

Innovative Approach to Urban Sanitation

As an innovative approach to the problems of human waste disposal in the slums of Bombay, Community of Resource Organisations (CORO) combines literacy efforts with a new system of maintaining toilet complexes under a locally run pay for use plan. Using its experience with slum residents gained through its literacy program, CORO has set up a new administrative structure which uses local labour to clean and oversee public latrines. These administrative teams are able to provide residents with clean and effective toilets, encourage latrine use, and help create a new culture of cleanliness and responsibility among the poor of Bombay. With this well-run system, residents have proved willing to pay to use clean latrines with sufficient water, and have begun to move away from their traditional role as passive recipients of free government services which often proved to be inefficient or unusable.

Objectives

In combining its literacy campaign with efforts to run pay-for-use toilets CORO seeks to achieve the following objectives:

1. Promote literacy among uneducated slum dwellers and provide them with reading materials;
2. Provide clean, efficient and affordable toilet facilities for slum dwellers and promote their widespread use, especially among women and children;
3. Reduce defecation and urination in open, public spaces, providing a cleaner environment in the slums and reducing the health risks associated with large amounts of human waste;
4. Provide jobs for slum dwellers;
5. Make public toilets economically self-sufficient;
6. Use literacy and latrine use to educate slum dwellers about environmental issues and the importance of local sanitation;
7. Provide a structure for community activism;
8. Create a new culture of cleanliness and responsibility in which residents expect to pay for reliable service and in which they begin to take responsibility for conditions in their neighbourhood.

Moreover, through the toilet blocks, CORO hopes to promote reading habits among the users. For instance, it proposes to built libraries at D.N. Nagar, Chamber and Dharavi toilet complexes from where latrine users can borrow literacy kits and other reading material. The idea is to promote environmental education through literacy work and developing reading habits.

History of CORO

CORO began as a loosely formed group of different activists from several voluntary agencies in Bombay. These original members were concerned about increasing illiteracy levels among Bombay's slum residents. Despite a relative lack of experience in literacy training, they started a Mass Program of Functional Literacy in the Dharavi-BARC belt in Greater Bombay in 1989. At first, while visiting schools and trying to gain support for their efforts, the group was viewed with suspicion as outsiders from different backgrounds. It took some time for CORO to break down these barriers of mistrust. By establishing links with local community workers who were experienced political organisers, CORO was gradually able to generate community enthusiasm for literacy and reading.

Young community workers were especially helpful in this process of mobilising residents, and they became enthusiastic about the idea of promoting literacy. Contrary to their previous political experiences, which often involved frustrating encounters with passive residents or unresponsive bureaucracies, literacy training involved personal contact and visible, concrete, positive results.

Through CORO's initiatives, communities supported efforts to abolish illiteracy. With funding from the National Literacy Mission, teachers were trained, and materials were purchased and distributed. Famous celebrities were invited to distribute literacy kits in selected communities, creating interest and stimulating participation in the program.

In spite of their ability to mobilise slum residents, CORO had difficulties. The teachers were not highly qualified and the training programs were poorly designed.

CORO's survey indicated that 90 percent of the illiterates were women who were willing to learn but were often discouraged from learning to read by their husbands. The illiterate men were not willing to admit to illiteracy and were more difficult to contact since they had to commute long hours to work and often did not return until late in the evenings. Moreover, many men preferred to spend their free time drinking and gambling rather than learning to read. Lastly, CORO workers often found themselves over-extended, unable to take enough time away from their jobs to work on the literacy program. However, 12 CORO members were able to negotiate with their employers and voluntary organisations and began to work full-time for CORO. Gradually, the literacy program began to succeed.

Roving Libraries

The concept of libraries ('Savitri Vachanalaya') grew out of a need for a literacy network and in response to a lack of reading material in the slums. To form a library, a CORO activist consults with local contacts and recruits librarians, usually school children, adolescent school dropouts, or unemployed youths, but occasionally newly literate adults. First, the librarians count and number houses in the slum and organise the houses into clusters of four libraries, 100-150 households per library. Every librarian then goes house to house to enrol members. Membership is free, one member per household. There is no charge for torn or lost books since this is a part of learning to use books and happens very infrequently. Each librarian begins with about 25 books worth Rs.200 (US$ 6.67) and every month books worth Rs.100 (US$ 3.33) are added. Four libraries in a cluster receive different books and the stacks of books are rotated among the four libraries every week. Hence, members get to see new books all the time. The librarian gives books to about 25 households one day and collects them after one day to give them to the next 25. In this manner, 150 houses are served in a week. As the number of books grows, members can either keep a book for a longer period or can borrow more books.

The entire project costs about Rs.1.50 (US$ .05) per household per month. The cost has been kept deliberately low so that the members can run the libraries through monthly contributions after their first year. Most members who use the library free of cost are willing to pay membership fees after three months of operation, and about fifteen percent of the members are willing to participate in running the libraries.

Today, 80 libraries have became operational and provide at least one book every week to each one of the 10,000 households covered by them. A recent sample survey indicated that on average two to three people per household, especially girls and semi-educated women, read the books regularly and want more titles.

In addition to providing slum residents with reading materials, each library provides an organisational infrastructure for local slum people to come together free of so-called political or other petty rivalries.

Public Toilets

In 1984 the Government of India undertook several projects designed to apply science and technology in a manner more responsive to the needs of communities. One of these projects, over-seen by the secretary of the Department of Science and Technology (DST), was the Integrated Waste Management Pilot Project to be implemented in Bombay and then expanded to all major Indian cities. The pilot was to include a city wide project to provide clean, supervised, pay-and-use toilets for the entire city and to manufacture fuel pellets from 4,000 tons of daily municipal garbage.

The project began in late 1990 with the planning and construction of public toilets in several Bombay slums and the planning of a Refuse Derived Fuel (RDF) plant. By February, 1992, 12 toilet blocks had been constructed at Malwani, a large slum made up of displaced residents relocated from communities throughout Greater Bombay.

The toilet design has following features:

1. An attractive external appearance unlike a stereotypical Indian toilet facility;
2. Use of ferro-cement technology to produce pre-fabricated construction elements;
3. Excellent ventilation and lighting due to circular design with a central space open to sky;
4. Water storage tanks to store 20,000 litters of water;
5. Twenty-four to twenty-six toilets in two circles of a block.

While prefabricated materials were meant to facilitate on-site construction within one month or less, in reality, several problems related to drainage, sewerage, water, and electrical connections, all requiring interfacing with the municipal and other authorities, meant a minimum construction period of 3-4 months. Nonetheless, users have been happy with the design.

Until August, 1992, the toilets were managed and maintained on a pay-for-use basis by a small private contractor. The contractor was paid on a monthly basis to run, guard and maintain the toilet blocks. The toilets were to be open daily from 5 A.M. To 9 P.M. And continually manned by teams of one supervisor and two sweepers working in eight hour shifts. At night a watchman would guard the complex. Total expenditure was expected to be around Rs.5,800 (US$ 193) per block each month, with Rs.4,800 (US$160) going towards salaries and Rs.1000 (US

$33) for cleaning supplies and other maintenance costs. Thus to attain basic self-sufficiency, a block would have to collect Rs.200 (US$6.67) per day in fees.

The block-staff was to collect Rs.0.25 (25 praise) per use from the users above the age of eight and turn over these fees to CMC Ltd., a public sector undertaking entrusted with construction and maintenance of the toilet complexes. Water and electricity was provided free of cost.

By June, 1992 it was obvious that this maintenance system had some serious problems. The staff, especially the supervisors, were of questionable character. Their accounts and those of their employers could not be verified and considerable cheating was suspected. Assurance of monthly salaries regardless of how much was collected from latrine users eliminated any incentive to keep track of all the collected fees and to turn all of them over to CMC Ltd.

In addition, there was a resistance to the pay-and-use scheme. The Malwani toilets were constructed after demolishing existing public toilets that were filthy but free. Thus local people had no choice but to pay and use the new toilets. Daily payment of 0.25 praise per use was expensive, as the entire family would spend anywhere from Rs.30 to Rs.50 per month.

In comparison, monthly room rents in slums are generally Rs.15 and are hardly ever paid. Local elected representatives encouraged people to use the toilets without paying, even though these same officials had participated in the implementation of the scheme. The contractor who constructed the toilet blocks failed to complete planned improvements in areas surrounding the toilets, and construction faults interfered with the toilets' proper functioning. At 5 toilet blocks municipal corporation supply of water was insufficient. Finally, residents resented the profits made by the toilets' administrators. Residents felt forced to pay for a service that was inefficient in order to contribute to the profits of allegedly corrupt contractors.

In July of 1992 the private contractor was dismissed and CORO took over the management of the public toilets at Malwani. CORO had developed an interest in hygiene in the slums through their observation of conditions in the settlements where they were doing literacy work. In addition, the beginning of toilet construction in the Chamber, Govandi area, where CORO is promoting literacy further aroused their interest, and they went to Malwani to inspect the toilets being run under private management. Under CORO's direction, the management scheme was redesigned in response to the problems mentioned above. A family pass system for local users was instituted. At Rs. 10 a month, it represented an affordable alternative to the .25 praise charge for each use and encouraged families to use the latrine regularly. Non-pass holders continue to pay a .25 praise charge per use. CORO pays for a night watchman, cleaning materials and minor repairs as well as small stipend of Rs. 250 for substitute staff in case of illness or absence. The expenses incurred by CORO are reimbursed by the DST through CMC Ltd.

Staff members are in charge of keeping the latrines clean and collecting the fees, and their salary comes from an even division of the money collected. At Malwani, CORO hoped that community residents would take an active interest in managing and supervising the latrines. This has happened at two of the toilet blocks, and there is substantial community input and participation. However, the unsatisfactory initial experience with the pay-for-use toilets and Malwani's status as a relocated slum with little strong community feeling has limited community participation in the rest of the blocks to the presence of a community representative who monitors the work of the staff and keeps accounts of the daily records.

The improved model of management has resulted in the following:

a) The community has realised that this is not a commercial venture since their money goes towards salaries of those who serve.

b) The staff have less reason to cheat. If they cheat at all, it is at the expanse of their colleagues.

c) The blocks are staffed by only 3-4 persons who can be sustained by the block earnings.

d) The staff strives to keep the toilets clean since collection is also related to the standard of cleanliness.

As toilet blocks were completed in other slums, including Chamber, Govandi, where CORO had begun literacy work, CORO took over their management and operation. Having learned from mistakes made at Malwani, the new toilets were constructed in open space, and the old free toilets were left standing, giving residents a choice between free toilets that were dirty and poorly maintained, or pay toilets that were clean and well maintained.

With more time and experience, CORO was able to make improvements on its management scheme. As a first step, CORO created a cooperative comprised of its most active members, mostly literacy volunteers with experience working in the slums and community organisers from organisations like Stree Mukti Sanghatana, Granthali Readers' Movement, Yuvashakti Pratishthan and All India Women's Conference. As latrine maintenance staff were recruited from the communities themselves, they became cooperative members as well.

The cooperative (called the SUVIDHA cooperative) is committed to self-sufficiency; all salaries, materials and repairs would be paid for with money collected at the toilet block. DST continued to guarantee reimbursement for materials and repairs if necessary but the SUVIDHA units tried to avoid the use of any external funding. Finally, the entire cooperative general body meets once every month to discuss problems and progress. This reformed management structure has resulted in a more flexible, accountable and responsible staff and greater financial independence and allows for community input and democratic decision making as well as providing community residents with employment.

With introduction of this new concept, CORO started to tackle the main problem of sanitation faced by most of the slum dwellers in Greater Bombay. While implementing the scheme, CORO also tapped the need to promote reading habits among slum dwellers, which they thought would be useful in developing a new outlook towards sanitation and to create a clean and hygienic environment in Bombay.

Resource Utilisation

Ideally, public toilet blocks run by CORO would be clean and accessible for twenty-four hours a day; members of families that owned monthly passes would all use the toilets every day; and toilets would be affordable and completely self-sustaining. These goals have come to depend on two main factors – the availability of water and the ratio of users with passes to 25 p. Users. The relationship between these factors.

The factor which ultimately controls cleanliness and the number of users is water. Without enough water, the toilets cannot be cleaned, and users will not be willing to pay to use the latrines. Water has to be stored since it is supplied only for about 3-4 hours in the morning or evening. Toilet blocks that get their water in the mornings are better off than blocks that get their water in the evenings, since usage is heaviest in the morning. Where water is supplied in the evening, only the 15-20 thousand litters of available stored up water can be utilised. This often causes shortages, and water has to be used sparingly.

Demonstrates the balance that needs to be struck between users, self sufficiency and cleanliness. Obviously, larger numbers of users are needed to make the toilets self-sufficient, and the optimum number of users goes higher as the relative percentage of pass-holder users increases. This in turn puts pressure on available water. Also, although 3,600 pass-holder users can, in principle, make a block self-sufficient, it means each toilet will be used by more than 100 users, an unrealistic number.

At the moment, the toilets are managed with a large number of daily 25 p. Users. Now several systems are self-sufficient but they cannot be said to be fully successful because a 25 p. User often does not use the toilets every day. In spite of CORO's desire to give more family passes, to do so would cause a serious financial imbalance, since the toilets depend on 25 p. Users to be self sufficient; monthly passes will not pay for the toilets.

In order to achieve CORO's social goal of as extensive use of latrines as possible, the system must be based on family passes. This will mean that either the water storage capacity needs to be doubled to 40,000 litters or economic self sufficiency will have to be sacrificed and external financial sources sought. As the use of family passes rises, CORO will probably depend on a combination of these two strategies.

The self-sufficiency achieved in the CORO model is based on a monthly salary of Rs.1500/US $50 for the core Group members and the lower salary of Rs.600/US $20 for the sweeper. If people with much higher salaries are accommodated, self-sufficiency is lost. Furthermore, fees collected do not presently cover the cost of major repairs costing more than Rs. 2,000. It is estimated that every toilet block will need at least Rs.10,000 by way of external support per annum.

It is clear that ideal self-sufficiency coupled with high standards of cleanliness are unlikely with the present per use charges and limited water storage capacity. In the long run, with more and more community toilets being built, the percentage of 25 p. Users will come down and the system will not be self-sufficient unless salary requirements are reduced. In order for that to happen, users will have to be better educated about the environment, and the toilets will need to require less maintenance. Even so, CORO may need to depend on partial outside funding to keep public toilets running efficiently.

Through its literacy program, roving libraries and management of pay-and-use toilets, CORO has provided essential services to previously underserved communities and begun to lay the foundation for improved awareness of health and sanitation issues and a new culture of cleanliness and responsibility. By maintaining clean public toilets honestly and efficiently, CORO has provided a viable and affordable alternative to filthy, unhygienic free latrines or open spaces near homes. CORO-run toilets have been well received and are heavily used, demonstrating that slum residents are willing to pay for suitable service. Widely used latrines have also resulted in a noticeably cleaner and healthier environment in the slums, with less human waste in streets, fields and other open spaces.

Table 2. Characteristics of CORO-run toilets

Area	*Blocks*	*Toilets*	*Users*	*Self-sustaining*
Malwani	12 380	About	15,000	No
Jogeshwari	126	About	1,240	No
Andheri	126	About	1,800	Yes
Dharavi	126	About	1,400	Yes
Chembur	2 52	About	3,000	Yes
Govandi	4 120	About	6,000	Yes
TOTAL	21 600	About	28,440	No

For women, clean public latrines have provided a way to relieve themselves in privacy, avoiding the humiliation of using public, open spaces and the danger to their health and their personal safety resulting from waiting until dark to relieve themselves.

By enlisting local residents to serve as maintenance workers and SUVIDHA cooperative members, CORO provides employment and income in an area marked by unemployment and poverty. Maintenance workers and cooperative members gain valuable work and organisational experience. Use of local labour also ensures greater accountability and community participation; as community members, the maintenance workers are trusted, can raise community concerns during cooperative meetings and cater service to community needs.

Community workers also gain valuable experience in CORO's literacy campaign and working as librarians for the roving libraries. They have been able to enlist the support of slum residents and to recruit library members. There are now 80 functioning libraries providing over 10,000 households with reading materials in the slums of Bombay.

Taken together, CORO's literacy campaign and its management of pay-and-use municipal toilets have helped to lay the groundwork for more substantial changes in the attitude and culture of Bombay's poor. Through literacy classes, reading, and the efforts of local latrine workers, residents are learning about the importance of sanitation, hygiene, and the environment. Latrine workers have begun to provide an alternative to the increasingly unworkable system of cleaning and maintenance based on the caste system, and have begun to demonstrate that individuals and communities can take care of their own human waste problems. Maintenance workers, literacy advocates, and librarians have ceased to be passive recipients and are taking an active role in improving conditions in their neighbourhoods. Residents have shown a willingness to pay for service instead of demanding service for free and placing an even greater strain on an already over-extended municipal government. By combining libraries with latrines, CORO can serve communities, create a springboard for community efforts centered on other important issues, and extend their network's reach into more homes.

Obstacles

CORO has had to overcome several obstacles in order to achieve success in literacy training, distributing reading material, and running pay-and-use toilets. Attitudes take a long time to change, and there is still a considerable amount of resistance to the kind of change CORO envisions in Bombay's slums, as well as continuing problems of a more mundane and technical nature.

CORO has had difficulty getting children to use the public toilets, despite not charging them and even going into the neighbourhood in order to bring children accustomed to defecating outdoors to the toilets. A major problem lies in the toilet design, which is too large for small children. CORO is working on possible new designs to be used in new toilet complexes.

In spite of the generally cooperative nature of CORO's relationship with the municipal government, there have been problems. Toilet construction is often delayed because of difficulties with municipal agencies in charge of electricity, drainage, water and sewage. Despite prefabricated elements that should allow construction to be completed in one month, toilets usually take three to four months to be built. In addition, CMC Ltd. was initially skeptical of CORO's ability to run the toilets. A meeting had to be arranged with satisfied users to convince CMC that CORO was indeed able to manage toilets competently and efficiently.

There is continued resistance to pay-and-use toilets among many residents, especially at Malwani where the destruction of a free alternative, the actions of local politicians, and the initial experience with unsatisfactory service and inefficient, sometimes corrupt management created resentment among some residents. CORO's effective management and the cleanliness of the latrines themselves are gradually eroding this resistance, and residents are becoming more willing to pay in order to use clean toilets.

Initially, CORO had difficulties within the management units. Staff members felt that cleaning toilets was degrading work, beneath their station as educated citizens. Their ancestors had been discriminated against within the caste system for doing precisely this kind of work. After discussion and experience managing the toilets, workers began to feel that they were not engaged in demeaning work, but in cooperative self-development. They were beginning to make a difference in their communities and were fulfilling an essential role in a collective undertaking in which they had an important say.

Groups had problems with inefficient workers and dishonesty. They set up internal vigilance groups and even fired some workers who were cheating or not working. This was extremely difficult for the units to do, but it was essential in order to maintain standards. It represented a change in attitudes, one in which labour and honesty were rewarded and workers were held accountable for their behaviour.

Groups also had trouble with expensive repairs to the toilets, especially when they had to depend on outside repairmen. They were able to cut down on this expense by finding their own repair people from among CORO community literacy activists.

CORO also had troubles at the beginning of their literacy campaign. CORO activists had little experience with literacy training, and the program suffered from ineffective teachers and poor training courses. Men were especially difficult to teach, as they were unwilling to admit to illiteracy, and had little free time to learn because of long commutes to work. They also often discouraged their wives and daughters from learning how to read, further undermining CORO's efforts.

In all of CORO's efforts entrenched attitudes and cultural mores continue to cause problems. Most Indian slum dwellers retain rural customs and are unused to using toilets or reserving space for them when planning homes or communities. Such habits are difficult to change. Also, centuries of a rigid caste system has trained people to leave much essential work to others; they are forbidden by caste rules and custom to engage in a host of necessary activities. This has produced a culture of resignation and robbed many people of initiative; they do not see it as their responsibility to improve their lot, clean their toilet or any number of other things. CORO faces a constant challenge in motivating residents to fulfil roles and do jobs to which they are not accustomed and which they might find objectionable.

Diffusion

Because of the success of their programs CORO has been able to expand their management of public pay-and-use toilets as well as their roving libraries into new slums. DST has asked CORO to run new toilet blocks in five new slums since their successful administration of the Malwani toilet block in 1992. (The five slums are Jogeshwari, Andheri, Dharavi, Chembur and Govandi.) CORO is now forming new libraries, recruiting new librarians and signing up new library members.

In addition, the innovation has been documented and publicised in the press, on video-tape and on television.

Many voluntary agencies, community groups, and individuals within Bombay and throughout the country have learned about CORO in this way. Also, CORO workers have attended training programs, seminars, and workshops to make presentations and share their experiences.

Key Elements

When faced with the challenge of promoting literacy and managing public toilets in the slums of Bombay, CORO devised several strategies which were innovative and essential to the project's success.

Integrating Literacy and Sanitation

By combining the running of municipal toilets with pre-existing efforts to combat illiteracy, CORO was able to capitalise on community knowledge and contacts they already had.

As an organisation that was already working in the slums, CORO already had some understanding of the problems in the community and credibility with the residents. They were able to build on their pre-existing organisational strength and to call on the resources of their activists to motivate residents to utilise pay and use toilets and join roving libraries. As an organisation dedicated to promoting literacy and distributing reading material, CORO was already involved in education efforts. When CORO began to manage community toilets, they found themselves equipped to address the cultural and educational issues involved in promoting new norms of cleanliness and sanitation.

Using Local Volunteers and Labour

With local staff members running latrines, CORO was able to gain residents' trust and be responsive to community needs. CORO was able to provide jobs to slum residents, generate income for poor workers and give them organisational and job experience. As community-run enterprises, CORO managed toilets demonstrated that communities could work to solve their own problems, including problems of human waste. This is an important lesson for communities bound by habits of passive receivership and centuries of caste-determined labour and sanitary practices.

In their literacy work, the enthusiasm of local activists was essential in motivating residents to learn to read and to join the roving libraries. Local librarians distribute books, sign up families, and recruit other librarians. Such participation gives residents a stake in the project and a sense of being able to create positive change in their neighbourhoods.

Forming a Cooperative

By forming a cooperative and including local community members, CORO opened up the decision making process and involved the community in identifying problems, devising strategies and sharing responsibility. CORO became a community organisation run for and by the community.

Instituting Monthly Family Passes

By selling monthly family passes at a fixed price, CORO was able to encourage daily toilet use, while making it more affordable. With a pass, family members were more likely to use the toilets often, as each use did not cost any more.

Tying Salaries to Fees

By tying staff members' pay to the amount of fees collected, CORO devised a built-in incentive for workers to work efficiently and to encourage community members to use the toilets. Staff salaries are a result of staff efforts; the cleaner the toilets and the more effectively they can convince residents of the need to use latrines, the more people will use the toilets and the more money the staff will make. This system also minimises corruption. The staff monitor each other and are less likely to cheat since it would be depriving their co-workers, who often are also their neighbours, of money. The residents also appreciate this system and prefer that their fees go towards staff salaries rather than a corrupt private contractor.

Partnerships

CORO benefited from the efforts of the following important partners:

1. *Indian Government Department of Science and Technology (DST).* DST oversees the Integrated Waste Management Pilot Project, including the construction and maintenance of the public toilet blocks. DST was the agency which first approached CORO to take over the administration and maintenance of the toilet blocks and is the source of funds for construction, major maintenance projects and, when needed, materials.
2. *CMC Limited.* This is a public sector corporation which has been charged with the construction and maintenance of the public toilets in Bombay. CMC Ltd. distributes DST funds to CORO and works with them to construct and maintain toilet facilities.
3. *National Literacy Mission.* This organisation provided funding for teacher training and literacy materials.
4. *Famous celebrities.* Celebrities distributed literacy kits in the slums and helped raise interest and enthusiasm for CORO and literacy.
5. *Community organisers.* At the beginning of their literacy efforts and throughout the ensuing literacy

project and toilet maintenance scheme, community organisers lent enthusiastic and valuable support. They helped mobilise residents to participate in libraries, take literacy classes and use public pay-and-use latrines.

6. *Slum Residents.* Residents have shown a willingness to pay for clean latrines and to join local roving libraries. Without their participation, none of CORO's efforts would have been successful.

Despite its inexperience in sanitation and toilet management, CORO was able to maintain latrines, gain acceptance of a previously unpopular pay-for-use scheme, institute participatory management and increase latrine use in the slums of Bombay. The key to CORO's success was its fundamental redefinition of the basic problem; latrine maintenance and use was not a problem of service delivery, but one of organisation, education, and legitimacy in the eyes of the community. By creating a structure more open to community accountability and with built-in incentives for maintenance workers, and by combining toilet maintenance with education and literacy efforts, CORO was able to integrate latrine maintenance and promotion into an overall framework of community development and change.

The project itself is fairly specific, applicable only where people are forced to depend on public toilets for their sanitary needs and unaccustomed to using toilets in the first place. Given this, the following preconditions must be satisfied in order to implement a program based on CORO's New Culture of Urban Sanitation.

1. *Governmental Role.* When looking to solve toilet maintenance and usage problems, governments need to redefine the problem as one of organisation and awareness. They need to be open to the possibility of solving what seems like a straightforward service delivery problem by calling upon the services of

community organisations or NGO's with little experience in service delivery but organisational capacity, credibility and experience in the intended beneficiary community. Governments must also be willing to invest resources in sanitary improvements for the poor. The construction and maintenance of toilets is expensive, and CORO's experience shows that planning for them to be economically self-sustaining is unrealistic; an outside funding source will almost always be necessary.

2. *Implementing Agency.* There must be an organisation well-positioned to implement a new organisational structure for the maintenance of public toilets and able to integrate toilet maintenance into a broader program of community development and education. The implementing agency should have experience in the beneficiary community, be responsive to community concerns, and have effective mechanisms to ensure community input and participation in decision-making and action.

Beyond the issue of latrine use and maintenance, CORO's New Culture of Urban Sanitation has wider implications for municipal governments faced with what appear to be traditional service delivery problems. CORO has shown that those problems may be organisational or cultural ones, and the solution may be found by organisations with little experience in the specific problem area. Governments looking for solutions to such problems might find success in partnerships with community development organisations and NGO's.

4

Urban Ecological Problems

The science of ecology was born from the expansive curiosity of the biologists of the late 19th century, who wished to understand the distribution, abundance and interactions of the earth's organisms. Why do we have so many species, and why not more, they asked—and what causes them to be distributed as they are? What are the characteristics of a biological community that cause it to recover in a particular way after a disturbance?

Such questions took Charles Darwin and other naturalists on journeys far from human civilisation. And more than a century later, ecologists still tend to search for answers to these questions in "pristine" environments—the tropical rain forest, the coral reef. From the perspective of a field ecologist examining a natural ecosystem, people are an exogenous, perturbing force. Human beings—and especially their cities, seemingly so "artificial"—fail to fit neatly into ecological theory.

But people mobilise nutrients and pollutants, drive species extinct, promote the survival of others, change the composition of the atmosphere and alter landscapes. Thanks to advances in technology and to humanity's growing population and penchant for consumption, we are today a global ecological force capable of affecting every species and ecosystem on the planet. Over the past several decades, moreover, we have rushed to the cities. Soon more people worldwide will live in cities than in rural areas. In cities people mobilise some nutrients and deplete others, create habitats that never before existed, divert water, increase temperatures and, by intent or by accident, manipulate the communities of other species found within city boundaries and beyond. Cities are some of the most profoundly altered ecosystems on the planet; within their boundaries are also found some of the most diverse ecological conditions. If there is a laboratory where ecological change can be viewed at close hand, it is the city.

Ecologists, however, have hardly rushed to the city. A mere 0.4 percent—25 of 6,157—of the papers published in nine leading ecological journals in the past five years dealt with cities or urban species. Whatever the reasons for ecologists' persistent tendency to focus on pristine environments, human-dominated ecosystems represent a problem for the field.

Dependent Ecosystem

Urban-ecology research at this stage consists of vastly more questions than answers. If ecologists are to study urban ecosystems, for instance, they must decide two questions first: what an urban ecosystem is, and what measures appropriately describe its interactions with other ecosystems? In some respects these are the same question—and a good place to begin.

Among the traditional ways to look at an ecosystem is by examining how it balances primary production (photosynthesis, or solar-energy conversion by plants) with respiration, by which energy is converted to unusable form. Although the calculations that make up a system's internal energy budget are far more complicated than this simple ratio suggests, for most ecosystems the overall calculation is fairly well balanced between inputs and outputs. An urban ecosystem, a concentration of people and human activity, is an energy-intensive ecosystem, and viewed in traditional ecological terms it is more unbalanced than most other ecosystems. Its unique energy signature, then, is one way of distinguishing an urban ecosystem.

Howard T. Odum of the University of Florida noted that a typical city daily transforms into heat about 70 times more usable energy per square meter than a close non-human equivalent to a city—an oyster reef. A natural ecosystem is likely to be self-powered by photosynthesis or chemosynthesis. By contrast a city is a heterotrophic ecosystem, one that depends primarily on external sources of energy. Take Chicago's famed pizza: It may be made with wheat from Kansas, tomatoes from California, anchovies from the Mediterranean and cheese from a Wisconsin dairy farm. The pizza oven may be fired with fuel from the Middle East and made of steel forged in Pennsylvania or perhaps Japan. Pizza-making thus borrows, in one form or another, energy that originated with photosynthetic activity in other ecosystems. Heterotrophic ecosystems are rare on earth, including some marshes, the deep ocean and streams, but even among such systems cities are extreme.

There are a variety of ways of describing flows between urban areas and other ecosystems. One is an input-output model. People import to cities foodstuffs, fuels, building materials and other products that can be described in the energy currency of ecology. Land conversion or degradation, agricultural production and the harvesting of plant-derived building materials can be seen as ways in which the urban ecosystem appropriates the primary production of other ecosystems. In addition, we can consider how energy flows: Imports and exports are mediated by meteorologic, hydrologic and biologic vectors. A city along a river, for instance, imports energy via hydrologic vectors from an entire watershed and typically returns to the downstream environment water containing heat and nutrients such as phosphorus and nitrogen.

Urban energy budgets, dominated as they are by deliberate human energy imports and by losses via fossil-fuel burning, or "industrial respiration," do not resemble the energy budgets of any other ecosystem on earth, as the work of Eugene P. Odum of the University of Georgia has shown. Although calculating these budgets can be complex, energy use is a common currency that can be measured for all ecosystems, providing a basis for comparing systems that are human dominated with those that are not. Ecology has been called "nature's economy," and such calculations potentially afford a means for linking ecological theory with social-science theories using resource-economics concepts.

Urban Footprint

The different characteristics of urban ecosystems may call for some non-traditional ways of assessing how dependent they are on other ecosystems. Stuart Fisher and Gene Likens, both then at Dartmouth College, working in the Hubbard Brook Experimental Forest of New Hampshire, examined the heterotrophic ecosystem of Bear Brook. Primary production was negligible in the stream itself, and all of the ecosystem's respiration (2,935 kilocalories per square meter annually) was supported by material imported from the surrounding forest, which had an annual net primary production of 4,680 kilocalories per square meter. Yet the amount of material required could be supplied by an area of forest equivalent to a strip of vegetation about two feet wide (0.31 meters on each bank) along the stream's length, much narrower than the stream itself.

By contrast, William Rees of the University of British Columbia estimated that the city of Vancouver consumes an amount of material equivalent to that produced by a productive land area 180 times its size, assuming that area is not dominated by people.

Rees employs in his analysis an instructive measure of urban energy dependence called an "ecological footprint." The footprint of a city is the total area of productive land required to support its activities in a sustainable way. In other words, that land must produce an amount of resources equivalent to the sum of all resources consumed by the city—and assimilate an amount of waste equivalent to that produced by the city. Cities' footprints can be impressive—tens or hundreds of times larger than their actual area—because in addition to the plant, microbial and animal metabolisms that characterise all ecosystems, cities have an "industrial metabolism"—a metaphorical hunger whose satisfaction requires mining of non-renewable resources as well as exploitation of renewable ones.

The footprint concept is a new (and somewhat controversial) way of assessing ecosystem dependence. Matthew Luck and other LTER scientists at ASU are exploring, among other questions, how the concept of a footprint could be used to consider the impact of a city within its particular geology and climate. Many of the earth's fastest-growing cities are, like Phoenix, located in low-productivity arid or semi-arid lands. In terms of land area, these cities' footprints are huge, if this local context is taken into account.

Local conditions are just one of several independent variables that would be expected to influence the magnitude of an urban ecosystem's dependence on its surroundings. Others are the fertility of the surrounding land, the average income of the city's inhabitants, cultural variables, a city's size and age, and its political context. And this general dependence measure could be partitioned into separate measures for different ecological variables such as water, elements, food, waste assimilation and energy.

City In Space And Time

Since the characteristics of any ecosystem vary from one part to another, ecologists conceive of ecosystems as consisting of habitat "patches." A city—with its concrete-and-glass downtown, its golf courses, industrial parks and tree-lined residential streets—is quite a patchy ecosystem, and together with all its patches it is part of a larger landscape full of other patches. A landscape ecologist tackling an urban ecosystem would look at the pattern of patches within a city, and the variations in the way the land is used from one patch to the next, and ask how these patterns and this variability influence bio-geo-chemical processes and affect how organisms and resources are distributed, and how species interact.

As the pioneering ecologist C. C. Adams observed early in the 20th century, ecology will need to incorporate the social sciences to answer such questions when human beings are taken into account. Models to explain how people as a species affect the composition of habitat patches and their patterns will have to integrate historical, political, cultural and economic factors with traditional variables such as competition, predation and nutrient availability, which also control the distribution, abundance and relations of organisms.

But we can begin by looking for spatial patterns. Traditionally these include the species composition of patches and how the patches are arranged in space. These variables affect ecological processes by regulating competition among species and energy flows within the ecosystem. The scale of the pattern also affects the scale at which these processes operate. Such patterns have practical use: Once they are known, they can provide indicators for ecological monitoring.

The predictions one might make based on land-scapeecology concepts. If you consider a city in a semi-arid or arid region where water limits natural biotic productivity, you might predict that soil respiration would be more variable in the undisturbed natural ecosystem than in the fringes of an urban area, where water and nutrients are more uniformly supplied for agriculture and suburban residential development. As you move toward the urban core, the fine scale pattern of land use changes, and you would expect more variability in irrigation from one patch to the next. Therefore in the city's centre there is more point-to-point variation than in the natural ecosystem, although along the fringe there is less. Similarly, the natural temporal variation in hydrological conditions might be "smoothed out" by agricultural and horticultural activities along the fringe but might vary more in the centre because of extensive modification of hydrology.

One of the issues we face is defining what an urban ecosystem is. Having introduced the urban core, the urban fringe and the energy intensity and heterotrophic nature of the city, we can begin to sketch out an emerging view of what an urban ecosystem is. First, we have the advice of the U.S. Census Bureau, which defines an area with a population density over 620 individuals per square kilometre as "urban." These individuals exhibit a high per capita energy consumption and that their habitat is characterised by large-scale environmental modification. But these characteristics are variable. One useful paradigm for viewing them is that of the environmental gradient. Mark McDonnell (then at the Institute for Ecosystem Studies in New York) and colleagues in 1997 showed that urban-rural environmental gradients measuring change in these characteristics can be used to capture the indefinite boundaries of many urban ecosystems. But many other characteristics could be used to do so.

Strange Changes

Like any ecosystem, an urban ecosystem is dynamic and changing. Are the forces that drive change similar to those in a non-urban system? Some clearly are: Disturbances such as fire, flood and earthquake are inevitable in cities. Yet people constantly struggle to control and manage the frequency and magnitude of disturbance. Therefore—although we're not likely to be able to control earthquakes—disturbance regimes are often altered by human action. Separated from the Mississippi River by dikes, New Orleans is protected from much of the flooding that would be its natural disturbance regime.

Likewise, the way an urban ecosystem recovers from a disturbing event may be altered dramatically by human intervention. In non-urban ecosystems a fire or flood is typically followed by a gradual and somewhat predictable series of changes called ecological succession . Human intervention may suppress such patterns altogether. An abandoned home site may begin to fill with plant growth—vegetative succession, to an ecologist—but redevelopment typically truncates the process that might otherwise fill the patch with trees and animals. Such redevelopment is an example of the single most important force of landscape change in urban areas: land conversion, driven by institutional decisions, population growth and economic forces.

We generally think of climate change and biological evolution as occurring on much longer time scales than fire and flood—and far longer than the frame of reference for urban ecology. Yet evolutionary and climatic change are likely accelerated or enhanced in urban ecosystems. Recent studies have shown that fruit flies and egg-laying butterflies have rapidly adapted to prefer new human-introduced host plants. And in recent decades many organisms placed under strong selection pressure by human action have evolved resistance mechanisms—bacteria to antibiotics, rats to poison, weeds to herbicides. The extreme selective pressures exerted by human environmental changes suggest that evolution in urban ecosystems will likely be evolution under the non-equilibrium conditions of rapidly changing environments. Surviving species in urban ecosystems will be those, such as cockroaches, rats and cats, that cope with anthropogenic selection pressures by rapid evolution or phenotypes plasticity.

The possible effects of urban ecosystems on climate regimes have hardly been investigated, but a few observations suggest they should be. Consider the well-known "urban heat island" effect—the fact that temperatures within cities can exceed those in surrounding areas by several degrees on average. Current research in Phoenix shows that carbon dioxide concentrations within the city centre are elevated to several times the global average, a change that has likely taken place on a decade time scale. How such rapid change within an urban micro-climate affects plant, animal and microbial species has hardly been investigated.

In fact, there are findings that suggest that human activity may be capable of altering regional climate patterns in striking ways. In 1998 Randall S. Cerveny and Robert C. Balling, Jr. of Arizona State University demonstrated that the five-day work-week and accompanying commute affected precipitation patterns on the East Coast of the U.S. By making rainfall more likely on weekends than weekdays. In this case the patterns of human activity, unlike those of most animals, did not follow natural rhythms but seemed to alter them. In other cases human activity, of course, has tended to follow natural cycles: We are active by day and sleep by night; throughout human time our festivals have tracked harvests or grown out of the need to fill winter nights. Natural reliability in weather and climate can dictate temporal patterns in the organisation of society, but it is unclear whether people living in modern urban ecosystems are as likely to develop social rhythms responding to natural cycles as are rural human societies that depend vitally on a local resource hunter-gatherer societies or subsistence-agriculture villages, for example.

Can ecological theory be extended to study these new forms of change and disturbance? One way to do so is to analogise human disturbance regimes to known ecological regimes. Home construction may be viewed as an ecological disturbance, framing a new question: How does an urban ecosystem recover from such disturbance? Patricia Gober, an ASU geographer participating in the LTER study, and her colleagues viewed the zone of rapid land conversion at the Phoenix urban fringe as a wave of disturbance spreading outward from several urban nodes in the desert alluvial plain. They have calculated land consumption rates and are seeking indicators of incipient urban expansion at the fringe.

And the Cerveny and Balling result is provocative. In ecosystems not dominated by people, individual plants, dispersal distances and the scale of disturbance can define the spatial scales over which processes are influenced and patterns emerge. Both the temporal and spatial scales of patterns in human-dominated ecosystems are likely to emerge from social forces far removed from foraging and dispersal strategies. There are many clear examples of human-imposed spatial scales in our history. The opening of the American West and the Homestead Act enforced a pattern of 160-acre plots on the landscape. Urban ecosystems are usually developed within a grid of blocks each 100 or 200 meters long. Thus we should not be surprised to find new spatial scales emerging for ecological processes within urban systems. However unusual it seems to a landscape ecologist, we are likely to be studying processes on the scales determined by the human-built infrastructure: perhaps the individual home site, or a city block.

Toward Synthesis

Is there a possibility of simply stretching current ecological theory to encompass urban ecosystems? It can be argued that our understanding of dynamics and processes for population and soils can be extended to homeowners' associations and pavement. Perhaps the tools already developed for understanding the emergence of different life-history strategies can be extended, without conceptual changes, to people. Human beings, we might argue, are like other organisms. Selective pressures and evolved strategies lead to certain population dynamics and patterns, to certain impacts on surrounding regions and species and finally to certain changes in the allocation or flow of nutrients and resources. It could be that the differences in the ways in which people and other organisms evolve, interact with, and influence their surroundings are merely quantitative, not qualitative.

Or one can take the position that current ecological theory is insufficient to capture the key patterns and processes in these human-dominated or urban ecosystems. Human beings, that is to say, are qualitatively unlike other organisms. The emergence and influence of culture, the constraints and opportunities afforded by our institutions, and our ability to create strategies in response to anticipated (rather than realised) selection pressures mean that standard ecological and evolutionary theories and principles apply only imperfectly to human population. This view would obligate would-be urban ecologists to seek out a great deal of interaction with, or "borrowing from," the social sciences to advance ecology in general to a point where it can explain patterns and processes in human-dominated systems.

Either approach implies hard philosophical truths. If a person can be treated as any other organism, the distinction between "natural" and "unnatural" systems disappears, and with it the idea of a "pristine" ecosystem. The whole notion of environmental stewardship may suffer as well. If people act as other organisms do, guided by individual self-interest, there are no grounds for a moral or aesthetic call to stewardship. In the second case, we are forced to face the question of why people are not like other organisms: Is there, for instance, a spiritual or moral dimension that defies explanations offered by evolution or natural selection?

Philosophy aside, it is not clear that any ecologist has to make a hard choice. Standard ecological theories can be and have been applied to human systems; they can be used, for instance, to understand the "dispersal" or "successional dynamics" of urban systems. We can then determine which patterns or details, if any, are impervious to explanations emerging from these standard theories. At the same time, we should examine whether inter- or multi-disciplinary approaches between the biological and social sciences provide more elegant theories or explanatory power.

Consider some of the leading conceptual questions mentioned above. How do we study the change in the position or shape of the "urban fringe"—the dynamics of the edge of the city and its expansion? Borrowing tools strictly from ecology, we could begin by employing plant-dispersal and competition models. Thus expansion of the urban fringe could be understood in terms of the density of surrounding neighbourhoods, with residences "produced" from nearby "occupied" cells and dispersed to nearby empty cells. One can imagine density-dependent processes controlling neighbourhood changes. Another tool is the contact-process model, wherein the probability of a lot undergoing a transition from empty to occupied (with a house) could depend on the "state" of the neighbouring lots—whether they are devoted to residential, commercial, agricultural or recreational purposes. Empty cells could be assigned probabilities for colonisation based on their own properties, which could vary across the landscape: Is there good drainage, a good view, an adequate ground-water supply?

The processes of urban-fringe expansion also can be described in the ecologists' language of disturbance, as Patricia Gober has. Urbanisation at the outer edges of a sprawling metropolis involves both the spatial expansion of human disturbance and the alteration of ecological processes. For any given patch, we can assign a probability of transition (or new disturbance). We might hypothesise that this probability is low in the non-urban matrix, increases steeply at the urban fringe and returns to an intermediate level of disturbance in the centre of the city. As urbanisation of the surrounding matrix proceeds, the probability for patch transition increases in areas that were previously non-urban while decreasing in the former urban-fringe areas, now incorporated into the metropolis. A simple hypothesis derived from these patch-transition probabilities is that a wave of high disturbance radiates through time outward from the initial city edge.

These approaches could help us capture some of the patterns and dynamics of urban-fringe expansion. But what would they be missing? To start with, a dose of economics is surely necessary to explain year-to-year patterns in housing starts. What are the variations in interest rates? In unemployment? In inflation? Economic modelling might predict the number of new houses produced and sold each year, and we could return to ecological theory to examine their dispersal. But there are still more factors to consider. How are decisions for locating roads, establishing sewer lines, or extending emergency services made? How does the power and the approach of state or city institutions change as cities grow? Does the proximity of other municipal organisations affect decisions for developing city boundaries? To capture these effects, we would need to know much more about political theory and the evolution of government institutions.

At this point we would still lack insight into why people value certain spaces over others, or how those values vary by socioeconomic class, family situation and age. For this we may need to turn to sociology to improve our predictions about "dispersal" of houses, and how dispersal patterns might change with economic development, a changing age structure of inhabitants or with new cultural traditions introduced by new arrivals. A return to ecological theory would be required to understand how housing starts affect the landscape, including its bio-diversity, and thus potentially alter people's preferences for these sites.

We are still missing information, finally, on how individual and socialite preferences vary over time. To take an obvious example of changing preferences, consider the role of the city centre in medieval versus modern times. In medieval times, citizens returned to the city centre at night for protection. In modern times, we find many inhabitants avoiding the city centre at night, again for protection. Similarly, our desires for privacy or large yards or suburban/ rural surroundings have changed over the course of this century with changing socialite values. Both social sciences and evolutionary biology might provide tools for understanding this "evolution" of culture.

Evolutionary biology could be invoked to examine variations in selection pressures along urban to rural gradients. But social-science tools are required to explain the preferential cultivation or destruction of some species by the human inhabitants of the city, and how these preferences vary as a function of socioeconomic class, age or place of birth. The presence of exotic species and the increased opportunities for dispersal or invasion caused by habitat disruption and fragmentation would force us to return to the tools of ecology to understand the effects of introduced species on native population.

Ecological theory might benefit from the use of analogies to accelerate the development of new concepts that can be applied to urban human-ecological systems. Gregg Mitman has discussed how this approach was used in the 1920s and 1930s by University of Chicago sociologists Robert Park and Earnest Burgess and their colleagues and ecologists such as W. C. Allee, Alfred Emersion and Thomas Park to develop ideas of "human socialite." These were the early urban ecologists who attempted to understand human actions by analogy with ecological systems. Although we recognise the danger inherent in its indiscriminate use, comparison of succession and urbanisation reveals the heuristic utility of this kind of analogy. In a city with spreading growth, the perimeter or "urban fringe" can be viewed as an active disturbance area, and locations farther removed from the fringe (inward) as earlier in succession (space-for-time substitution).

William Cronon, an environmental historian, argued that the disciplines of ecology, history, geography, anthropology and others could "learn from one another if only we can scale the walls that separate us to start working together on the problems we all find fascinating." The challenge of understanding urban ecosystems will require disciplinary specialists, but it will also require at least some individuals willing to think in interdisciplinary and multi-disciplinary ways—a task that can be difficult to accomplish. These investigators will have to knock down the walls, rather than scale them, to integrate diverse disciplines into a synthetic research area and a novel perspective that will advance ecological theory.

5

Urban Population Dynamics

Rapid urbanisation in the poorest countries is straining the capacity of cities to provide basic amenities, degrading the quality of life, and impoverishing the environment. Although the same strains on quality of life, health, and the environment were evident in the earlier urban transition in the industrialised world, there are significant differences between the two transitions. Firstly, the sheer numbers of people taking part in it are of a dramatically different scale. Secondly, owing to complex changes in the global economy, the prospects for economic development among the poorest countries are not nearly as bright as the situation faced 150 years ago by today's industrialised countries. Lastly, the global environmental context has changed dramatically, and today there is real concern about the impacts of further industrial development in the face of climate change and the rapid loss of ecosystems. Unfortunately, instead of bringing economic dynamism, improved health, environmental standards, education and democratisation, urbanisation in many least developed countries is accompanied by economic stagnation, negligible health gains, lax environmental standards, low education levels, crime and social instability.

Urban Growth

At the present time, some 3.2 billion people already live in towns and cities; this is expected to rise to almost 5 billion by 2030. In comparison, the world's rural population is expected to decrease by some 28 million between 2005 and 2030. Ergo, at the global level, all population growth in the future will be in towns and cities. No less than 97 per cent of this huge absolute increase in urban population will accrue to developing regions. Asia will be, far and away, the primary site of all future growth, followed by Africa and then Latin America.

Urban growth is increasingly being recognised as one of the critical development issues of the 21st century. Yet discussions in the media and even among policy-makers persistently make three erroneous assumptions about ongoing trends. It is generally assumed that:

a) current trends are due to an unprecedented rapid rate of urban growth;

b) most urban growth is occurring in megacities;

c) most urban growth is due to migration from rural to urban areas.

All of these assertions are in fact misleading and can lead to erroneous policy decisions.

As observed in a seminal study by the US National Academy of Sciences, the main difference between the current urban transition in developing countries and the past experience of Europe and the United States lies in the *unprecedented scale of change*. The real story ere is no longer the rapid rates of city growth but *the absolute size of the increments* in the urban population of less developed regions. Between 2000 and 2030, according to the latest UN estimates, the urban population of the developed world is expected to grow only from 870 million to 1.01 billion. That of Latin America and the Caribbean will increase from 394 to 609 million, while Asia's will grow from 1.36 billion to 2.64 billion, and Africa's from 294 to 742 million. By 2030,

Africa, Asia and Latin America will include 8 out of every ten urban inhabitants in the world. And this unprecedented scale of urban growth is occurring despite a significant decline in actual *rates* of growth of the urban population.

As concerns the evolution of megacities, it is true that they have obviously grown in size and number in the last few decades. As countries urbanise, they inevitably develop one or more large agglomeration, often incorporating two or more large urban cores. In 1950, the world knew of only one behemoth (New York) having more than 10 million inhabitants: by 2005, there were 20 such megacities, 15 of which were located in less-developed regions and, by 2015, there will be 22 of them. However, the growth in the number and size of such cities has been much slower than predicted in earlier decades. Today, megacities account for 4 per cent of the world's population and 9 per cent of all urban inhabitants; this is undoubtedly an important slice, but not one that is expected to expand quickly in the foreseeable future as the growth of the major megacities has slowed down and will continue to do so, both in more and less developed regions.

A fact that has garnered much less attention but which is actually more important for the planning of our urban future is that small and intermediate cities are where most urbanities live. At the present time, 52 per cent of the urban population still lives in "small and intermediate cities". Moreover, contrary to popular opinion, this ascendancy of smaller cities will persist in the foreseeable future. Thus, it is expected that, in the future, most urban growth will actually take place in urban locations having less than 500,000 people. This observation concerning the prevalence of smaller towns and cities in the urban future of less developed regions is of the utmost significance in any effort aimed at improving the lives of urban dwellers in the future.

As regards the sources of urban growth, most people assume that rural to urban migration is the main demographic cause. Thus, policy-makers have increasingly tried to reduce urban problems by deviating migratory movements from cities to other rural destinations and/or dissuading migrants from coming to cities. The latest comprehensive effort to separate out the components of urban growth put the contribution of natural increase at about 60 per cent in the median country. The remainder is the result of a combination of migration and reclassification. The important point is that, over time, the ascendancy of natural increase in urban growth will inevitably grow as urbanisation (i.e. the rise in the proportion of the total population living in urban areas) progresses.

In short, urban administrators wishing to reduce urban growth thus need to give greater attention to the factors that affect fertility decline rather than to migration. At any rate, attempts to prevent rural-urban migration have generally met with failure.

Case Studies

Each of the five PRIPODE case study cities is experiencing rapid growth in excess of 3 percent per annum. Here we present the population and economic profiles of each city, with particular reference to their growth trends, starting with Ho Chi Minh City and then moving to Africa.

Ho Chi Minh City is the largest city in Vietnam and is located near the Mekong River delta. The city centre is situated on the banks of the Saigon River, 60 km from the South China Sea. It is the most important economic centre in Vietnam. Some 300,000 businesses, including many large enterprises, are involved in high-tech, electronic, processing and light industries, also in construction, building materials and agro-products. The economy is growing at an astounding 11% per annum.

In the study, the researchers found that the city grew from roughly 5 million people in 1997 to more than 6.2 million in 2005, or a 2.8% annual rate of growth. Recent rates are in excess of 3 percent. Natural increase was almost twice as important as migration in 1997, but between 2003 and 2005, this trend was reversed, with migration contributing roughly 63% of the total growth.

Moving over to Africa, where the remaining PRIPODE urban studies are located, four cities were studied (from east to west): Kampala, Brazzaville, Lagos, and Accra. Kampala is typical of many primate cities in Africa, insofar as it grew from the seat of a tribal kingdom (the Buganda) to become a colonial outpost of the British Empire, to eventually becoming the nation's capital, replacing Entebbe at independence. Since that time its population has grown at an annual rate of more than 5.5 percent, effectively doubling every 12 years. Kampala has grown in part by engulfing former satellite towns, which has yielded a metropolitan area spanning approximately 386 square kilometres. As a classic primate city, it houses 1.2 million people, which is 12 times larger than the next largest city, Jinja, and 40% of Uganda's urban population. What little industrial activity the country has is largely concentrated in the capital, and being the seat of national government, this is where most civil service jobs are also located.

Brazzaville is the capital and largest city of the Republic of the Congo and is located on the Congo River, across from Kinshasa, the capital of the Democratic Republic of Congo. More than a third of the population of the Republic of Congo lives in the capital, and it is home to 40% of the country's non-agricultural employment. Like Kampala, it serves as the financial and administrative capital, and many of the nation's small industries (e.g., drink and tobacco packaging, wood and metal working, food processing, construction, and chemical plants) are concentrated there. According to the PRIPODE study, based on 2005 census data, Brazzaville had a population of 1.2 million, having grown at a rate of 3.3% per year from 856,400 in 1996. Although the precise proportions attributed to natural growth and migration are not known, large population displacements from rural areas, owing to civil strive and the effects of structural adjustment programs, have contributed to the city's rapid growth.

At more than 12 million people, Lagos is the largest of the cities considered by the PRIPODE teams. The 2006 Census has reported national level results, but disaggregated results by city have yet to be released. The UN, however, projects a population of 20 million people by 2010, with an annual growth rate of more than 4 percent.

Unlike the other three African cities considered here, Lagos is not the capital, but it is the economic hub of the country, concentrating financial services, industry, and port facilities for the whole country. Rural-urban migration rates are assumed to be quite high due to "loss of prime rural land and weakening of traditional land management systems, lack of local multiplier effects needed to stimulate agro-industry and non-agricultural job creation in the region as well as disintegration of local cultural relations and institutions".

Finally, Accra has a population 1.97 million in 2005, playing host to one-fifth of Ghana's total population. The population growth rate is estimated at 3.4 % per annum in the city itself but up to 10% in its peri-urban districts. It is Ghana's largest city and its administrative, communications, and economic centre. Like Lagos, the primary economic activities are financial and government services, communications, construction, transportation and agriculture (including fishing). More than 70% of Ghana's manufacturing capacity is located within the capital area.

Economic Development

Population dynamics are intimately connected to economic development in developing country urban areas. On the one hand, the economically active population forms the labour pool for urban areas. Because of the shortage of formal employment opportunities in the public and private sectors (owing to the effects of structural adjustment programs and competition stemming from economic globalisation), many developing country cities have burgeoning informal sectors. On the other hand, economic development, and particularly changes in urban land markets, when coupled with population trends, has tended to lead to a process of urban spatial expansion into peri-urban areas.

Public and Private Sector

Inurah *et al.* point out that many medium sised cities find themselves unable to attract the external investment that would lead to job creation or that would provide the tax revenues necessary to create supportive infrastructures. According to their analysis, cities in low and medium-income countries suffer from two disadvantages. First, in terms of business opportunities, their markets are weak due to high levels of unemployment, low skill levels, low incomes and a weak infrastructure base. Second, weak governance, unstable political environments, the prevalence of corruption, high levels of crime and threats to property rights are viewed as major threats and risks to investment.

The results are high establishment and transaction costs that make these cities unattractive to global capital. This contributes to a vicious circle in which there is no or little economic growth, high unemployment and poverty, a weak revenue base, declining competitiveness and attractiveness, and thus further economic stagnation. That Inurah *et al.* find this dynamic operating in two reasonably prosperous African cities—Johannesburg, South Africa, and Gaberone, Botswana—bodes ill for the many less advantaged cities of that continent and elsewhere. Furthermore, lack of education and training for industry or service sector jobs means that many city dwellers or recent migrants do not stand a chance of employment in these sectors—in fact, even well-educated workers find a paucity of decent jobs.

In recent years there have been ominous predictions of the impacts of the "youth bulge" the large number of un and under-employed men under on social and political stability. Whether or not these dire predictions are borne out the presence of high fertility and continued in-migration, despite economic stagnation, paints a somewhat worrisome scenario in which far from being engines of growth, the cities may easily concentrate some of the worst socialite problems.

The problem of economic stagnation in the face of rapid population growth is characteristic of most African cities. By contrast, many cities in low income Asia–including many in India, China, and Vietnam–are experiencing unprecedented economic booms. As noted earlier, Ho Chi Minh City has experienced very rapid growth between 2002-2005. In the context of such an astounding growth rate, employment represents less of a problem than provision of services and infrastructure to new homes and enterprises. In fact, the unemployment rate has declined from 10.3 to 8.8% since 1997, despite a population growth rate in excess of 3%.

Urban Informal Sector

According to Hinrichson, most urban poverty does not result from a lack of jobs, but from a lack of well-paying, steady jobs. Unemployment rates are generally below 15% in most developing country cities, but wage rates are depressed in the formal sector, and many are self-employed in the informal sector. Although often maligned, the informal sector is not just a chaotic jumble of unproductive activities. On the contrary, it is an increasingly critical part of national and local productive structures. The very nature of poor countries' participation in globalised economic competition dictates the reduction of socially protected formal sector activities and increases their dependence on less stable but more flexible production structures.

The Kampala study which, as previously mentioned, is growing at more than 5% per year, found that migrants "cannot be absorbed by the narrow formal sector as most of them are untrained, un-trainable and illiterate." Owing to land shortages and economic stagnation, a return to the rural areas is inconceivable for most. So, migrants find jobs in the informal sector cottage industries (woodworking, auto repair, metal working, transport services) or are self-employed in street hawking and trade, urban agriculture, or waste recycling and reuse. Some fall into illegal activities such as drug trafficking, robbery, pick-pocketing, and prostitution.

The Accra study confirms the high rates of informal sector employment of 50% or more found by others in African cities. In one slum area, Nima, 54% were self-employed, and in another, Maamobi, the rate was 50%. Roughly 30% of the economically active adults in both neighbourhoods were employed by the public sector, but no one was employed by the private sector. In Accra as a whole, 65% of the population works in the informal sector.

One of the difficulties for city administrations is that many informal enterprises do not pay taxes and are difficult to regulate. Despite these concerns, it would be wrong to paint too bleak a picture of the informal sector. Studies reviewed by Montgomery et al. show that the boundary between the informal and formal sectors is fairly fluid, with many workers participating in both, and some formal workers using their savings to launch into self-employment. Indeed, were it not for the informal sector, there would be little if any economic vitality in most least developed country urban areas. Even rapidly developing economies such as that in Hô Chi Minh City, Vietnam, have significant levels of informal sector employment of around 12% of the work-force.

Peri-urban Development and Land Speculation

The growth of cities in the developing world is dynamic, diverse and disordered and increasingly space-intensive. A recent study commissioned by the World Bank shows that average urban densities (that is, the number of inhabitants per square kilometre of built-up area) have been declining at an annual rate of 1.7 per cent over the last decade in developing countries. This disordered and leapfrog process of urban expansion, which takes place largely in non-contiguous transitional zones between countryside and city, is increasingly being referred to as "peri-urbanisation". It defies easy characterisation or quantification.

Peri-urban areas put agricultural land to mixed economic uses. This ranges from farming and animal husbandry to the installation of globalised firms that are looking for large tracts of land in order to install production processes that benefit from economies of scale. Improved communications and transportation networks make these outlying areas increasingly accessible to such concerns. Cheaper infrastructure, land and labour also encourage the de-concentration of more traditional firms who can no longer find space in city centres.

Peri urban areas are also a critical site for settlement of the poor. Because of high rents in the centrally located urban core, the urban poor, low income residents and new migrants are by default pushed to the peripheries. For example, most newcomers to the city settle in peri-urban areas where land and jobs are more plentiful. Peri-urbanisation also transforms rural dwellers into urbanities without changing their place of residence. For example, villages on the fringes of Kampala have increasingly been incorporated into the urban agglomeration and integrated into the urban economy through provision of goods and services to the core. Such settlements generally lack infrastructure and services and their residents can be easily displaced by other economic or residential uses.

Peri-urban areas fulfil many other functions for cities, ranging from the supply of energy, water and building materials to the provision of ecological services such as wildlife corridors, micro-climates, buffer areas against flooding and sinks for waste disposal. Social and ecological systems are often incapable of the rapid and complex readjustment that this requires.

Population and the Environment

The relationship between population and the environment in developing country cities ranges from local environmental health concerns to issues of regional or global concern such as habitat loss, changes to the hydrological cycle, urban consumption "footprints" on distant areas, and greenhouse emissions from transportation and industry. Although the latter are undeniably important, we will focus only on health issues here, since they are a more frequent focus of the PRIPODE studies.

A worrying sign in recent years is that urban areas, which since the early 20th century have been characterised by improved public health relative to rural areas, increasingly have pockets of poverty so deep that the health metrics in those areas are sometimes worse than those in poor rural areas. The primary environmental challenges facing developing country urban areas are provision of adequate water and sanitation; adequate waste removal; slum and informal settlements in environmentally sensitive or risk-prone areas; and air pollution.

Water and Sanitation

Lack of access to adequate water and sanitation is, first and foremost, a public health concern. MDG 7, Target 10, aims to "halve by 2015 the proportion of people without sustainable access to safe drinking water and Sanitation." Infant mortality rates in urban areas are significantly lower in homes with piped water.

The PRIPODE studies confirm the severity of the situation. In a study of child (aged 0-5) diarrhoea prevalence in two medium-sized Cameroonian cities, Ebolowa in the south and Maroua in the north, researchers found prevalence rates of 13% in the former and 24% in the latter, compared to a national rate of 16%. In Maroua, only 6.5% of households had modern toilets, versus 18.4% in Ebolowa, though a slightly higher proportion had access to improved latrines (68.3% vs. 58.7%). The proportion of children with diarrhoea increased in direct relationship to the quality of toilet facilities. Perhaps reflecting source water quality, the semi-arid Maroua diarrhea had prevalence rates of 19% for internal tap water and 24-25% for public taps and wells, whereas in Ebolowa it was roughly half these levels. Treatment of water reduced prevalence by 62%. Demographic factors—such as the education level of the parents—are intimately associated with diarrhoea prevalence, presumably reflecting an income/amenity effect as well as a personal hygiene effect.

In the Brazzaville study, the researchers found that 85% of households report have access to tap water, but because of the unreliability of the public water supply, households also depend on rainwater, wells, water services, and the river (in descending order from 30 to 10%). The study found that 35% of respondents reported a case of typhoid in the household in the past 12 months. The researchers attribute this to the poor state of the public water service, which employs neither water testing nor treatment before delivering water to households. Malaria was the most widespread illness, with 96% of households reporting a case; this very high rate is attributable in part to poor drainage and environmental sanitation.

The study finds that industrial and agricultural wastes and runoff, especially heavy metals and agro-chemicals, are polluting streams and aquifers. Contamination is particularly acute near industrial facilities. Because of regular flooding (56% of households in the districts studied had experience flooding), contaminants mix with flood waters to produce severe environmental health problems. The study of Kampala finds that inadequate evacuation of solid wastes from disposal areas create lactates that are washed into water sources. As a result, 90% of protected springs have been declared unfit for human consumption, yet the population continues to drink the water for lack of alternatives.

Waste Disposal

Functioning solid waste disposal systems are generally lacking in low income country cities, which contributes to the spread of infectious diseases. The lack of adequate waste removal can be attributed to rapid growth of new settlements, reductions in public sector spending associated with SAPs, and budgetary constraints.

The Brazzaville study found that 38% of households reported some kind of trash collection (either public or private), whereas 36% threw their trash out in "natural areas" and 24% burned or buried their trash. The Cameroon PRIPODE study found a high proportion of residents disposed of waste by depositing them in pits outside their compounds or by burning. They found little relationship between the type of trash removal and diarrhea prevalence.

In a survey conducted for the Accra study, residents of the two slums, Nima and Maamobi, reported the lack of proper solid waste disposal as the biggest environmental risk. Poor drainage and clogged gutters ran a close second, which is also the result of improper waste disposal. A high percentage of residents in these slums favoured the provision of rubbish containers and regular trash collection.

In the Lagos study, a survey of residents in four Local Government Areas (LGAs) representing different income and population density levels found that about 8% of the respondents' claimed that the dump sites in their areas of abode were never evacuated, and almost 46% said that they made private arrangements to evacuate the dumps in their areas. Interviews with local government chairmen suggested that they understood that it was their responsibility to evacuate refuse, but that it required the assistance of the federal government and also local cooperation. Particularly they cited a need for behavioural changes by new migrants who, either because of poverty or practices brought with them from their places of origin, were used to dumping wastes at their backyards.

Slum and Informal Settlements

The increasing social segregation of housing in low-income countries has resulted in the dramatic growth of slums, the entrenchment of poverty, the concentration of violence and social problems, and growing environmental health problems . Given high rents in city centres and rapidly developing peri-urban areas, the resident poor and new migrants to the city have little alternative but to rent rooms in slum neighbourhoods or to construct shanties in hazard-prone areas: i.e., on steep slopes (such as in Rio de Janeiro and Caracas), flood prone areas (such as parts of Kampala and Lagos), in low elevation coastal zones (such as Mumbai), and in industrial zones handling hazardous materials (such as Bhopal).

The Accra study examined health levels across the city, with a focus on two poor neighbourhoods: Nima and Maamobi. Through a survey the researchers ascertained that 14% and 80% of respondents complained of flooding, and 88% and 91% complained of environmental health pollution. When it comes to city-wide assessment of slums, the results are somewhat ambiguous: according to the authors, many of the worst slums in Accra also have the poorest health levels, but some do not. Weeks *et al.* in related research, found that infant mortality rates vary significantly by ethnic group in Accra, with people of the Ga tribe having highest mortality rates because they tend to live in the most impoverished parts of the city, places where one-room dwellings and poor infrastructure predominate. As Utzinger and Keiser point out, such heterogeneity in urban contexts is quite common, and is illustrated by the prevalence of malaria.

The Kampala study found that informal settlements are rapidly encroaching on wet lands, which has significant public health consequences owing to flooding and reduces the overall capacity of the city to absorb and purify runoff from hill areas. Between 1991 and 2002, swamps were reduced from 20.6% to 1.9% of the land cover of the Kampala administrative area, and lowland forests also changed form 7.6% to 0.4%. This change implies loss of swamp forests to land uses including industrial and residential developments.

Air Pollution

Urban air pollution is a function of a number of factors, most notably transport-related emissions from the growing fleets of cars, trucks and buses, as well as industrial emissions and waste burning. In a 2003 PERN cyber seminar, 5 Cohen reported that considerable uncertainties exist in the estimates of the portion of the global burden of disease attributable to air pollution. Cohen estimates that outdoor air pollution (fine particulate matter smaller than 2.5

microns, PM2.5) is currently responsible for about 0.80 million (1.2% of world total) premature deaths and 6.4 million (0.5% of world total) years of life lost (YLL) in the population of the world's cities with more than 100,000 people. The estimates were subject to considerable uncertainty, due largely to the lack of air pollution measurements and information about the shape of concentration-response functions in developing countries.

Other health impacts include contamination of food, either due to lead uptake in urban agricultural plots or food preparation in polluted areas. The Lagos study found that street food prepared in the poorest slum areas had far higher contaminant levels of lead, cadmium, and zinc owing in part to air pollution contamination than street food prepared in more affluent neighbourhoods.

Air pollution can have regional impacts, especially through the transport of ground-level photochemical smog or ozone. This can reduce crop yields and affect forest growth. Air pollution may also be a factor in migration decisions. It was cited in a study of migrants who left Mexico City for secondary cities in Mexico as an important factor in their decisions to leave the capital.

Policy Implications

Here we look at policy implications of the research described in previous sections.

Population-environment linkages have received an enormous amount of attention from scholars, policy-makers and the general public over the last few decades. Most of this has focused on whether, and to what extent, population growth is responsible for the aggravation of environmental problems.The unprecedented scale of ongoing urbanisation is linked to large and rapidly growing population. Typically, such discussions have prompted out cries that the population bomb needs to be defused through aggressive fertility control. Such simplistic solutions overlook the inertia of demographic processes, overstate the ability of family planning programs to reduce fertility rapidly, and neglect the role of development in population environment interactions. Moreover, they detract attention from the other important ways in which population dynamics influence environmental change.

Population has grown rapidly in developing countries, especially over the last half century. But this is due to mortality decline, not to fertility conditions. Moreover, fertility has recently declined significantly in most regions of the world. The practical ability to "deal with the population problem" through population control and/or "family planning" programs is largely overestimated. Without some significant form of social transformation, modernisation or "development", it is highly unlikely that fertility can be forcefully reduced. Secondly, even with a drastic reduction in the current fertility rate, population size will continue to grow rapidly for some time in countries that have recently experienced high fertility levels. At the present time, almost 60% of all population growth at the world level is attributable to inertial factors (i.e. due to population composition stemming from patterns of growth in previous eras, rather than to current fertility and mortality patterns).

Both population and environmental outcomes are linked to development trajectories that need to be understood within their particular historical contexts. The critical framework which enfolds them all at this time is economic globalisation, wherein all countries are feverishly trying to emulate the production and consumption patterns of the world's main polluters. Ultimately, population control in the absence of some measure of development or social transformation is not likely to work from a demographic standpoint. Without drastic changes in the production and consumption patterns of both developed and developing countries–a sustainability transition–even rapid population stabilisation will not avert major environmental problems.

Sustainable Use of Space

As the focus on population growth per se diminishes in importance, spatial distribution, and within that, unprecedented urban spatial growth, assumes increasing significance in the environmental agenda of the 21st century. Indeed, it can be argued that, today, the most pertinent PDE relations are space specific. Where the resident population of a given territorial area actually lives, on what type of land, with what forms of occupation, in what ecological conditions, whether it is concentrated or dispersed, all this makes a great difference in terms of sustainability. Nevertheless, these aspects have received relatively little attention to this moment.

For much of the last century environmentalists took a dim view of urbanisation and city growth. But the recent turnaround among environmental scholars concerning the value of urban areas for global and local environmental outcomes is rather remarkable. It is increasingly recognised that urban localities actually offer better chances for long-term sustainability, starting with the fact that they concentrate half the Earth's population on less than three per cent of its land area.

The dispersion of population and economic activities would likely make the problems worse rather than better. Adopting the right approaches in anticipation of urban growth can also prevent many of the environmental problems linked to urbanisation. Density is potentially useful.

With world population at 6.6 billion people in 2007 and growing at over 75 million a year, demographic concentration gives sustainability a better chance. The protection of rural ecosystems ultimately requires that population be concentrated in non-primary sector activities and densely populated areas.

In this light, it has been suggested that instead of trying to figure out the theoretical carrying capacity of the Earth, we could profitably focus on a more practical issue, namely, how can an existing population make the most sustainable use of a given territory, in light of available resources, population, economic potential and the current development context? What is the best way that this concrete population can be distributed over its territory, currently and into the future, so that it will cause the least possible environmental damage and best promote sustainability, while also making the best possible use of its comparative advantages (and thus attaining the highest tolerable levels of economic growth and social development)? These arenot easy questions to answer, yet they open up an area that holds much promise and that is ripe for policy intervention.

Planning for the Needs of the Poor

A crucial fact that is often overlooked in discussions of the ongoing urban transformation is that the up coming massive growth of urban population will be largely composed of poor people. Urban growth stems largely from natural increase and rural to urban migration. In developing countries, the poor generally constitute the largest proportion of migrants. Poor people also tend to make the greatest contribution to natural increase in the cities because of the relative size of this population group and because they have higher fertility levels.

Hence, planning realistically for future urban growth means, first and foremost, planning for the needs of the poor. The current size of New York, Los Angeles, and Ottawa, may be comparable to that of Mumbai, Manila and Kampala, respectively. Yet, planning for the future of the latter three developing country cities requires a totally different paradigm, one that has an over arching concern with the needs of the poor at its core. It will also require more creative approaches, given the low level of resources available to local governments in most developing countries.

Improved governance—responding effectively to local needs in a participatory, transparent and accountable manner —will require an adequate understanding of the nature of the problems and good local information. The above discussion has highlighted some of the main problems and also some of the key misconceptions that have plagued planning efforts. Improved governance will also require that, while responding to current needs, those in charge turn a prospective eye to inevitable future growth. The trends towards massive increases in urban population, particularly in smaller and intermediate cities, will continue. The short-term mandate of most policy-makers favours attempts to resolve short-term problems without concern for the medium and longer-term future. Such an approach explains why so many master plans in developing country cities are outdated by the time their implementation begins.

The Millennium Project Slums Task Force lists a number of proposals to target the problem of urban poverty. They suggest community participation, including working with local communities to upgrade slum areas. They also describe processes that would decrease socioeconomic segregation by acknowledging poor people's "right to the city." A key issue is security of tenure and bringing an end to evictions, as well as providing adequate water and sanitation services, and access to public transportation. Although the task seems daunting, the financial resources required to provide basic services is surprisingly little–on the order of $294 billion by 2020.

Planning for Inevitable Urban Growth

Theoretically, urban areas present considerable advantages in economic, social, demographic and environmental terms. In a globalised economy, cities are better able to take advantage of emerging opportunities and thus better able than rural areas to improve the social or health situation for large numbers of people. Urbanisation may help to retard rural environmental degradation, by serving as an outlet for rural migration. Urbanisation also promotes the empowerment of women, while changing aspirations and lifestyles that accelerate fertility decline.

Despite these real advantages, poverty and environmental degradation are growing faster in urban areas and many least developed countries are struggling mightily to cope with rapid urban growth. The disparity between principle and practice can be attributed, to an important extent, to the difficulties being encountered by developing countries, and especially in Sub-Saharan Africa, to participate effectively in global markets. However, many of the difficulties faced by cities in developing countries can be traced to urban mismanagement.

A more effective approach would require, at the outset, a more pro-active and positive attitude towards urban growth. Urban policy-makers are increasingly set against urban growth and also fail to anticipate inevitable future growth. In this scenario, one can only expect a deterioration of existing conditions. Politicians and planners have to accept the reality of inevitable growth and learn to work with local community organisations and other Organisations of the Urban Poor (OUPs) to plan ahead for their social and environmental future.

Providing land and shelter for the poor ahead of the curve is critical; trying to help them after they have invaded inadequate lands is socially, economically and environmentally costly. Helping to orient future urban growth in directions that will be least harmful to the environment, and planning infrastructure needs ahead of time can save thousand of lives and billions of dollars.

Bringing together the different politico-administrative units that are affected by peri-urbanisation into some sort of regional entity and convoking the different social actors to participate in deliberations regarding the future of this area can help to head off some of its most negative outcomes. All this requires looking ahead.

6

Transportation Planning in Cities

Given the widely accepted and imminent peaking of world oil demand or the "big rollover", it is imperative that cities tackle the issue of transport energy use. Urban transport systems are the most dependent and vulnerable of all sectors to rises in the price of oil and potential shortages. This chapter examines a set of data on an international sample of 84 cities, 58 in developed countries and 26 in developing countries in order to better understand the range of urban transport and land use patterns that exist in the world today, the resulting energy consumption patterns in transport and some of the key factors that underpin these transport and energy use patterns.

Highlighting the critical importance of urban form, primarily the density factor, and the role of transport infrastructure provision and policies towards congestion in determining transport patterns and energy use, it suggests how to reconstruct an automobile dependent city around a set of centres bound together by high quality transit. Such centres would form a series of transit cities within the metropolitan region, each one with greatly enhanced opportunities for walking, cycling and transit, allowing more people to maintain there daily travel time budget or Marchetti Constant of 1 hour without resorting to excessive car use and significantly reducing their dependence on oil.

It is suggested that in order for cities to adapt to the post-petroleum age, relying purely on technological fixes will not provide the needed changes. Rather it is argued that a combination of changes are needed to provide the essential paradigm shift for cities to fundamentally reduce car use:

1. Curtailing or scrapping high capacity road construction;
2. Dumping congestion relief programmes and recognising that congestion can help cities move in a
3. Positive direction with respect to reducing car use and energy consumption;
4. Priorities the construction of speed competitive transit systems;
5. Integrating development around those transit systems, and;
6. Creating attractive conditions for walking and cycling through good urban design in and around centres, in effect making all centres small, contemporary "walking cities".

Technological changes in vehicles and fuels can occur in parallel with such broader urban systems changes and will be much more effective in the context of greatly reduced travel demand for private transport. It is argued that technological innovation is not a panacea to the energy problem in transport and that the time required to restructure cities for less car and energy use can be at least equal to or even less than the time required for significant technological changes in vehicles and fuels.

The data in this chapter are drawn from the *Millennium Cities Database for Sustainable Transport* compiled over three years by Kenworthy and Laube for the International Union (Association) of Public Transport (UITP) in Brussels. The database provides data on 100 cities on all continents, though 16 cities provide only partial data. Data summarised here represent averages from 84 of the fully completed cities in the USA, Australia and New Zealand, Canada, Western Europe, Asia (high and low income areas), Eastern Europe, the Middle East, Latin America, Africa and China.

The database contains data on 69 primary variables. The methodology of data collection for all variables was strictly controlled by agreed upon definitions contained in a technical booklet of over 100 pages and data were carefully checked and verified by three parties before being accepted into the database.

From these primary variables, some 230 standardised variables were calculated. Cities can thus be compared on urban form, private and public transport performance, overall mobility and modal split, private and public transport infrastructure, the economics of urban transport (operating and investment costs, revenues), passenger transport energy use and environmental factors. For this overview, which is focused on transport energy use in cities, only a selection of the most relevant features was chosen for comment.

Peaking of Global Oil Production

Urban automobile dependence, insights into which can be gained from the data, has large implications for energy use. In this new century, the world is going to have to face the reality that the assumption of cheap and easily available oil will no longer be valid. This change will affect every industry and aspect of life, e.g. food production and consumption, the automotive industries, land development patterns and how much private transport requirements are built into them, rising and unsustainable household expenses for transport and even perhaps the very survival of highly auto dependent cities or parts of cities. World oil production is predicted to peak by 2010 ("the big rollover") and then to enter a phase of irreversible decline, leading to shortage and supply interruptions, rapidly rising prices and a greater concentration of oil power in the Middle East. Some senior commentators in the field believe that world oil production may have already peaked, but this will probably not be known for sure for another 5 years, as was the case when US oil production peaked in 1970.

The peak in world oil production will have profound implications for transport, which is utterly dependent upon conventional oil and cannot restructure or alter its technologies overnight. The relative certainty of peaking oil can be seen historically in the accuracy of M. King Hubbert's original prediction of the US oil production peak in 1970 (Hubbert's bubble). He predicted in the 1950s and 60s that world oil production would peak shortly after the year 2000, which is now being confirmed by many people, based on much more comprehensive data, though there is still some dispute over the seriousness or immediacy of the problem.

Comparative Urban Transport Patterns

Car Usage

The critical factor that underpins transport energy use is car use. US cities 'require' over 18,000 car passenger kms per capita to meet the access needs and discretionary travel of their inhabitants. By contrast, their high-income counterparts in Europe and Asia have only between 20% and 63% of that level of use. In the lower income regions, car passenger kms per capita range from a mere 814 (4% of the US figure) in Chinese cities, up to 3,300 in Middle Eastern cities (18% of the US figure).

In order to gain some insight into the degree of motorisation in cities around the world relative to their wealth or "capacity to pay", we can express the above car use figures as per dollar of their GDP. Average metropolitan

GDP figures are shown for the respective regions. Amongst the wealthier cities, the US and ANZ cities are the leaders in car use relative to wealth with 578 and 576 car passenger kms per $1000 of GDP, with Canadian cities some way behind at 415. The Western European and prosperous Asian cities distinguish themselves in their significantly lower levels of private car mobility.

In lower income cities the rates of private car mobility per unit of wealth are comparatively high. African cities have some 940 car passenger kms per $1000 of GDP, which is close to double the US and ANZ level. This effect seems to come from the South African cities where two clearly distinct transport systems exist side-by-side (the sizeable automobile-based system for prosperous people and the informal, public transport and walking-based systems for the vast majority of poorer residents). Latin American and Middle Eastern cities are virtually identical to the US and ANZ cities in this factor (580 and 595 respectively). In 1995, low-income Asian cities and Chinese cities (494 and 344 car passenger km per $1000) had already far exceeded their wealthy Asian neighbours (193) and even Western European cities in this factor (114).

It is clear that less wealthy cities, although far lower in their per capita car use than most higher income cities (except those in Asia), are experiencing comparatively high levels of car use in relation to their modest wealth as motorisation proceeds, in most cases, unrestrained.

Motor Cycle Usage

Usage of motor cycles is comparatively small in high-income cities. Motor cycle use, as a percentage of total private passenger kms, ranges from 0.25% in the US cities up to 9% in the high-income Asian cities. By contrast, in low income Asian cities and Chinese cities, motor cycle mobility represents 26% of private passenger kilometres, while in the other lower income regions it again is small, at between 0.7% and 3.8%. Again, if we normalise this by wealth, the huge commitment to motor cycles in low income Asian cities and Chinese cities is apparent (averaging 152 motor cycle passenger km per $1000 of GDP, while all the other regions average a meagre 10).

Why motor cycles have burgeoned to this extent in most Asian cities and in no other parts of the world (nor in Manila where motor cycle ownership is actually about half the US level), is an interesting policy question. The low penetration of motor cycles in Manila is possibly a result of the extensive and effective jeepney system and paratransit-like motorised tricycles.

The role of motor cycles in urban transport, their potential to facilitate urban sprawl by providing low cost private transport to large numbers of people, and their environmental and human impacts, are important issues to understand. This is especially so in cities like Taipei where ownership is some 200 per 1000 people and usage represents 35% of private mobility. Notwithstanding this, they are the most energy-efficient form of private motorised mobility available.

Private Motorised Transport Modal Split

The final variable that provides insight into private transport patterns is the percentage of all daily trips (all purposes) that are catered for by private transport . Not surprisingly, US (89%), ANZ (79%) and Canadian cities (81%) head the list. By contrast, their wealthier counterparts in Europe and Asia have only 50% and 42% respectively of all trips by private transport. In the lower income cities private transport caters for only between 16% (Chinese cities) and 36% (Asian cities) of all trips. The exception is the Middle Eastern cities where the proportion rises to 56%.

Despite the overwhelming visual and sensory impacts of traffic and its capacity to rapidly saturate the public space of a city, private transport is a minority player, relative to public transport and non-motorised modes, in 7 out of the 11 areas in the study. Because of their size, cars and other private transport vehicles have a huge impact, even at relatively low ownership levels, in urban environments not designed for them. This is true in most dense, rapidly developing cities in the world and, of course, it has enormous social justice and equity implications. If urban transport priorities are primarily directed towards facilitating car and motor cycle travel through new freeways, parking facilities and so on, then this can threaten public and non-motorised mobility, which operate at high energy efficiency and provide effective transport services to a high proportion of people.

Public Transport Usage Levels

There are two clear extremes in public transport use. The US cities stand out globally with only 3% of daily trips, while Eastern European city residents use transit for 47% of all trips. The other high public transport modal split cities are high and low income Asian cities and Latin American cities. ANZ, Canadian and Middle Eastern cities are comparatively low public transport modal share cities. Western European cities have only 19% of daily trips on average by public transport, which is neither very low nor very high in this sample of cities.

Although some low-income cities enjoy comparatively healthy public transport use for their very low level of service (e.g. in China), this will not last. The crowded, unreliable and poor safety of public transport is something that people in such cities will try to escape at their first opportunity, given access to a car or motor cycle. Many low income cities may be unable to resist further rapid motorisation unless they improve the quality and speed-competitiveness of their public transport systems. This will generally mean developing more extensive rail systems, or fully segregated bus ways. If not, transport energy use is likely to rise rapidly.

Non-motorised Modal Split

The most egalitarian and sustainable modes of urban transport are foot and bicycle. These modes have few fossil fuel implications outside of the embodied energy in human food, bicycles and pedestrian and bicycle infrastructure. There is an extraordinary range in the use of these energy efficient modes. In US cities, only 8% of all trips are made by foot and bicycle.

Other auto cities are a little higher. Eastern and Western European, high and low income Asian, Middle Eastern and Latin American cities, all have very similar levels of non-motorised mode use, ranging from 26% to 32% of all trips. The African cities have 41% walking and cycling, due to the majority low-income population who rely heavily on walking, while the world leader in 1995 was still the Chinese city with 65%.

It would appear very sensible for social, environmental and economic reasons, and certainly from an energy perspective, to priorities the use of non-motorised modes by ensuring that facilities for them are actively promoted and not eroded by motorisation. This is especially urgent in rapidly developing cities, especially in China where their pedestrian and cycling advantage appears to be under increasing threat from policies against bicycles and the sheer scale of motorisation.

Private Passenger Transport Energy Use

What are the transport energy use implications of these broad transport patterns in cities? A very large range in transport energy consumption, with US cities leading the world at over 60,000 MJ per person per year of energy used for cars and motor cycles. This is twice as high as their nearest rivals, the Canadian and Australian cities, and four to six times more than their biggest competitors in the global economy, the western European and wealthy Asian cities, such as in Japan. Even cities in the oil-rich Middle East only use 10,600 MJ per person, despite some relatively conspicuous consumption in cities such as Riyadh. The three Chinese cities consume an average 2,500 MJ per person in private passenger transport, which means that an average US city of 400,000 people consumes in one year, the same amount as a Chinese mega-city of 10 million people.

Three groups of cities stand out as being the most intensive in passenger transport energy use relative to their wealth. These are the US and the Middle Eastern cities, and the African cities, again highlighting the high consumption and private transport orientation of a wealthy minority against a backdrop of widespread poverty in African cities. The outstanding cities are again the Western European cities and wealthy Asian cities who consume only 489 and 303 MJ/$1,000 respectively, showing comparatively modest demand for transport energy relative to their level of economic development and their economic capacity to sustain considerably higher private transport orientation. All the other regions fall between these extremes with an average of 1,364 MJ/$1,000.

As countries stake out their claims on ever diminishing and more costly conventional oil, especially those who so far have not yet significantly shared the benefits that flow from this valuable non-renewable resource, oil is likely to become a major destabilising geopolitical and economic issue. Oil is also likely to become a significant force in shaping urban development patterns, as it will no longer be economically or socially sustainable to create land use patterns that build in automobile dependence.

Public Transport Energy Use

The use of energy in urban public transport systems is small compared to private transport, regardless of the significance of the transport task undertaken by public transport, which varies widely, as already discussed. In the US, ANZ, Canadian, Western European and Middle Eastern cities, public transport energy use per capita does not exceed 7% of the combined private and public passenger transport energy use (average of 4%). The biggest contribution is in Latin American cities (23%), with the other five regions averaging 17%. Also, it should be noted that where rail is extensively used, electricity is a major energy source for public transport, which is often generated without oil (gas, hydroelectric, nuclear), and of course can also come from renewable sources. Public transport operations can thus more easily weather the coming peak in oil production because their demand for energy is numerically very much lower and also in many cities, not as reliant on petroleum-based fuels.

Modal Energy Consumption Differences Between Private and Public Transport. Relatively energy-inefficient private transport is compared to public transport. Energy consumed per passenger km in public transport in all cities is between one-fifth and one-third that of private transport, the only exception being in the US cities where large buses dominate public transport and attempt to pick up thinly spread passengers in suburbs designed principally around the car. In US cities, public transport energy use per passenger kilometre stands at 65% that of cars. Part of the reason for this is that in US cities the public transport vehicles have the highest use of energy per vehicle kilometre of all cities (26 MJ/km, with most other regions under about 16 to 17 MJ/km, or as low as 10 MJ/km in African cities).

Examining the overall modal energy consumption of motorised transport in cities (private and public transport combined), Canadian cities are the least efficient at 3.5 MJ per passenger km, followed closely by US cities at 3.2 MJ per passenger km. This reflects the large vehicles in use in North American cities, especially 4WD sports utility vehicles, their low use of motor cycles and their high levels of private versus public mobility. The private vehicles in US and Canadian cities consume about 5 MJ/km, whereas most other regions are under 4 or even 3 MJ/km, despite generally worse levels of congestion in these latter areas. By contrast to North America, ANZ cities average 2.4 MJ per passenger km for their total motorised passenger transport system, while all the lower income regions range between 0.9 (China) and 2.0 MJ per passenger km. All these lower income cities have a more significant role for energy-efficient public transport, some have high use of energy-efficient motor cycles and many operate fleets of minibuses, which are relatively energy-efficient (especially with high lodgings).

Energy Consumption by Different Public Transport Modes Modal energy use can be examined on a per vehicle km or per passenger km basis. The former is an indication of the inherent energy use of the particular vehicle, the technology it exploits and the environment in which it operates (congestion etc.). In the case of rail modes, the data are reported on a per wagon km basis, not train km. Energy use per passenger km is an indication of the mode's efficiency in carrying people, based on the kind of lodgings that the mode achieves in different cities.

Transport Energy Use Patterns in Cities

The first and most important is the urban density data, which are very important in explaining transport patterns, especially car use. If we correlate urban density data for the

58 wealthier cities with passenger car passenger kms per capita from Kenworthy and Laube, urban density explains 84% of the variance (Figure 1) and in the more heterogeneous low income sample it explains 47%.

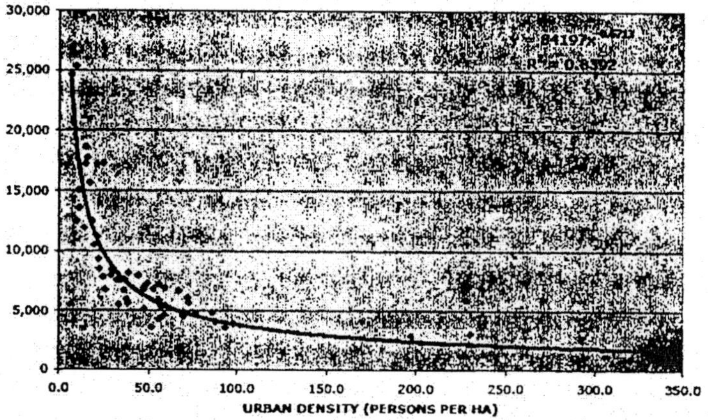

Figure 1. Urban density versus per capita car use in 58 higher income cities, 1995.

Similar correlations occur with private transport energy use per capita, all showing that as density increases, car use and energy use decline very significantly. The auto cities in North America and Australia/New Zealand are clearly the lowest density in the world and have the highest car use and energy use. Globally, the lower income cities are clearly denser than their wealthier counterparts (the clusters average 109 per ha, compared to the wealthier five clusters averaging 52 per ha). They contain the densest cities in the global sample, although Hong Kong at 320 per ha, which in the high income Asian group, is also exceptional. Cities throughout Asia, whether wealthy or not, are universally high density.

Transport Infrastructure

Urban freeways: It has been understood since the 1970s, how urban freeway provision is directly associated with higher car and energy use in cities. The mechanism for this, in terms of longer travel distances rather than savings in time, has been explained elsewhere. US cities, without any surprise, have the highest availability of freeway per person in the world, followed by ANZ and Canadian cities with 83% and 78% as much respectively. Outside of these three regions freeway provision falls away rapidly, especially in Latin American and Chinese cities (only 2% of the US level). The other 8 regions altogether average only 0.028 metres of freeway per capita, compared to 0.156 in US cities (18% of the US level).

It is not surprising that cities with the highest freeway provision also have the highest average speed of general traffic. The other cities with considerably lower freeway provision achieve only 29 km/h average road system speed. Lower income cities have marginally higher provision of freeways per $1000 of GDP than highincome cities (4.5 km compared to 4.1 km). In fact, Eastern European, Middle Eastern and African cities exceed the US figure in kilometres of freeway per $1000 of GDP. Poorer cities appear to be giving priority to freeway construction and are reaching higher levels of motorisation than one would expect based purely on wealth.

Public transport infrastructure: Western European, high income Asian and Eastern European cities, and to a lesser extent the ANZ cities, are the only regions that have significant reserved alignments for public transport. This consists mainly of railways, but also a few physically segregated bus ways. All of the lower income city groups, apart from Eastern Europe, have comparatively scarce reserved public transport right-of-way. Chinese cities stand out as being particularly low in this factor and in the wealthier auto-dependent groups, US cities are clearly the lowest in segregated public transport right-of-way, though Canadian cities are not far behind.

Congestion: Freeways and congestion issues are often linked together in discussions, especially in relation to efforts to save energy. Increasing urban traffic congestion is frequently cited as being responsible for huge wastage of energy in cities. The results in the study run directly counter to this assertion. They suggest that as congestion increases, there is less car use, more motor cycle use, more public transport use and more use of non-motorised modes. Conversely, lower congestion reflected in higher average speed of traffic, is associated with the direct opposite of this. Figures 2 and 3 demonstrate these points showing how car use per capita in cities around the world increases as the average speed of traffic increases (i.e. as congestion is reduced) and how public transport use is higher the more congested is the city.

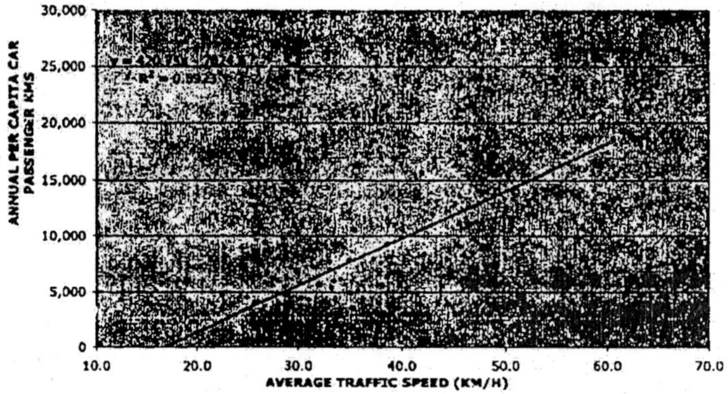

Figure 2. Average road traffic speed versus per capita car use in 58 higher income cities, 1995.

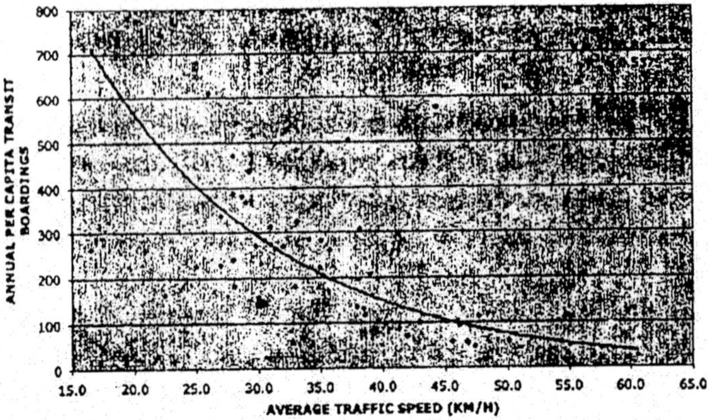

Figure 3. Average road traffic speed versus per capita public transport use in 58 higher income cities, 1995.

The results suggest that congestion acts as a brake on car use. Congestion encourages greater motorcycle use, and works in favour of public transport, but only where these options offer speed advantages over cars in congested conditions, and where parking is limited. This is often the case in more congested high-income cities, since they commonly have urban rail systems, or less frequently, bus ways. Such speed advantages to public transport occur on specific corridors and especially with urban rail systems where in every group except African cities, suburban rail system speed exceeds that of road traffic, often by a big margin (some metro systems also exceed traffic speed). However, it is only in the high income Asian cities that system-wide public transport speed exceeds that of road traffic. In all other groups of cities overall public transport system speed is significantly below that of general road traffic. This highlights in particular the need to improve operating speeds of buses, which are all always well below general road traffic speed. This means developing more dedicated rights-of-way for this mode and giving less priority to major new road construction.

Overall, the results suggest that rather than saving energy, reduced congestion, reflected in higher traffic speeds, increases energy use. Higher traffic speeds favour cars, increase urban sprawl and travel distances, and reduce the viability of other modes. Speed is not used to save time, it is used to travel further. Cities should not be in any rush to reduce congestion in order to decrease energy use. Rather they should be strategically improving the public transport and non-motorised mode alternatives to help travellers avoid congestion.

Importance of rail and comparative modal speeds: Not only are they the most energy-efficient modes, but they are the most effective at capturing modal share from private transport. In the high income cities, only the European and Asian cities have public transport systems that capture a healthy share of the overall transport market and these are the cities where urban rail systems are most developed, especially in relation to their private transport equivalent, the urban freeway. The ratio of fully segregated public transport right-of-way to urban freeways in these rail-oriented cities is over 3 compared, to 0.4 and 0.5 in US and Canadian cities and 2 in ANZ cities. In the lower income sample, by far the healthiest public transport use is in the Eastern European cities where segregated public transport right-of-way is some 9 times greater than urban freeways.

Whilst there are cities in Latin America, Africa and China that achieve significant public transport use with little or no rail systems, they rely mostly on poor 'captive' riders. As already suggested, as incomes rise and car ownership levels grow, the public transport systems of these low-income, bus based cities will tend to lose market share, because they cannot compete in speed or comfort with private transport. Motor cycles in particular tend to compete heavily with bus systems that are engulfed in traffic.This is seen in the comparative modal operating speeds. There are no regions where the average speed of bus systems exceeds 26 km/h and the overall average across the 11 regions is only 19 km/h. In Chinese cities buses operate at an average 12.5 km/h, or about the same speed as cycling. On the other hand, metro systems operate between 30 and 37 km/h (average 34 km/h). Suburban rail systems across the regions average 42.9 km/h. When these speeds are compared to general road traffic speed, which averages 34 km/h across all regions, it can be seen that only rail systems can compete.

Cities wishing to protect, rebuild and grow their public transport base, save energy (and reduce CO_2 emissions) as incomes rise and competition from motor cycles and automobiles escalates, need to seriously consider some form of segregated rail system. At the very least, cities need effective bus ways or Bus Rapid Transit (BRT) systems as demonstrated in Curitiba and São Paulo, and more recently, the Transmilenio BRT system in Bogota.

Parking: Parking in the central business districts (CBD) of cities is another indicator of private transport infrastructure, which varies dramatically across regions. Parking supply in the CBD is an important factor in determining modal split for trips to these space-constrained areas of cities. The availability of parking, much more than price, tends to determine the attractiveness of car commuting to the central city. High levels of parking will encourage the most energy consuming trips to work, while well-loaded, radial rail systems will use the least energy.

The highest providers of parking are the US, ANZ and, perhaps surprisingly, the Middle Eastern cities, all having over 1 parking space for every 2 jobs in the CBD. By contrast, Chinese, Eastern European and Latin American cities average 17, 75 and 90 spaces per 1000 jobs respectively, with Canadian cities at 390.

Reconstructing City for Post-petroleum Age

The previous discussion has highlighted, amongst other things, the importance of urban density and transport infrastructure in influencing private transport use and energy consumption in transport. In particular, the role of urban density and the provision of speed-competitive public transport systems as opposed to freeways, have been highlighted. The link between urban intensity and automobile dependence has been confirmed both between cities and it has also been demonstrated within cities. The vertical axis can be car use or it can be transport energy use and the horizontal axis can be population per urban hectare or jobs per urban hectare or both together – called activity intensity.

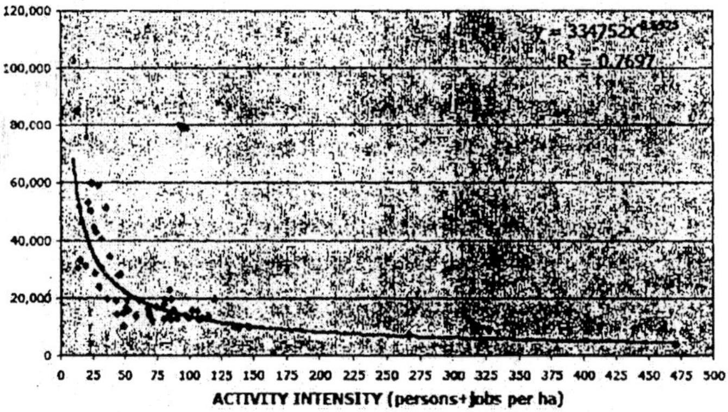

Figure 4. Activity intensity versus private passenger transport energy use in 58 higher income cities, 1995

The point on the graph where rapid acceleration in car usage appears to occur seems to be around 35 people and jobs per hectare; the error band is around 30 to 40 per ha.1 This same critical density figure, below which automobile dependence increases dramatically, has been noted in many studies.

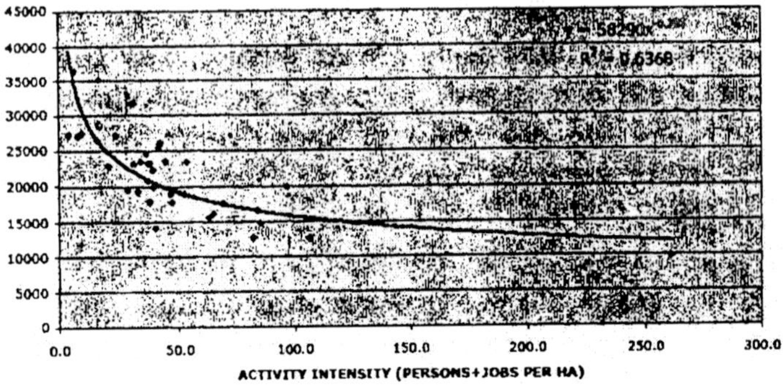

Figure 5. Per capita passenger transport energy use versus activity intensity in Sydney Local Government Areas in 1981.

Cities across North America and Australia that built in car dependence over the past 50 years are now trying to transform their urban environments into places where more transport options are available for the future. This usually involves developing new or refurbished transit systems, generally rail, and a set of centres to focus urban activity. However, one new rail line and a few centres are unlikely to significantly change a city because they lack sufficient coverage. However, based on the Marchetti idea, it is possible to restructure the expanses of an automobile city into a series of transit cities that are linked together with high quality speed-competitive rail transit. Transit cities are 20 to 30 kilometres across (based on typical overall transit operating speeds of 20 to 30 km/h), with a rail and bus service that feeds into a Town Centre lying at their heart. Along the lines feeding in to the Town Centre, which might be buses running on dedicated rights-of-way or LRT, would be a series of Local Centres. The whole region would be made up of a series of these transit cities joined together and linked by a fast rail service. Most people in the city could then live within the framework of local services in their Local Centre, or have easy access to an adjoining local centre. Main services, including work, would generally be located in the Town Centre. Some higher level services will always be in other Town Centres, especially the historic Central Business District, and these would typically be easily accessible by rail. However, the key to sustainability is to generate these Local Centres and Town Centres as genuinely viable, attractive and more people oriented places in each of the transit city sections comprising the majority of the city-region. Walking and cycling within such centres would be priority modes and the urban design of centres would be to maximise their use.

This has recently been applied to the development of the Metropolitan Plan for the Sydney Region where it is possible to see six distinct transit cities, each around 20 to 30 kilometres across and each having a major Town Centre and a series of Local Centres. By focusing the plan on these six areas and knowing the kind of intensity of activity that could make them viable, it becomes feasible to determine where to direct growth and where new transit infrastructure will assist the development of a more sustainable, energy-efficient city.

In many ways, the evolution of the city into the kind of polycentric structure described here is a natural urban systems response to the need to maintain the Marchetti Constant and is happening in many cities such as Vancouver, Sydney, Portland and even Perth. In this sense it is a response to the problem of traffic congestion where most cities find it simply impossible or downright self destructive to be trying to maintain this constant by building more and more high capacity roads to keep acceptable access time to work and other urban amenities. Rather, the city tends to "morph" into a new form to ensure that it remains functional and liveable.

Solving The Energy Problem

There are very large differences in the energy consumption levels between private and public transport, with public transport systems and especially urban rail systems offering dramatically greater energy efficiency than any private transport fleet in any city today. Clearly, the substitution of private transport passenger kilometres for public transport passenger kilometres has very large potential to save energy. This is enhanced by the fact that it has also been shown that there is a "transit leverage" effect at work in cities whereby one 1 kilometre of travel by public transport replaces between 9 and 12 kilometres of car travel in US cities. Globally "this appears to be more like between 5 and 7 to 1, based on the relative decline in vehicle kilometres travelled per capita for every passenger kilometre travelled per capita on transit.". Of course, the substitution of car travel for walking and cycling has enormous energy conservation potential as well. More compact, mixed use urban form that creates much shorter travel distances would make such substitution more feasible.

Of course, there is a view that the energy problem in transport can be solved primarily by technological means. This can involve the development of smaller, more fuel-efficient conventional internal combustion engine cars, new fuels to substitute for conventional oil, new energy systems for cars such as electric, hybrid or fuel cell vehicles or the development of radical new car designs such as Amory Lovins' "Hypercar". Such a single-sighted approach is not supported for a number of reasons:

1. From a more holistic urban viewpoint, the less car use in a city, the more manageable and liveable is the city,

regardless of the type of car or how it is fuelled. This is because energy and emissions are only two of the car's many problems. The most intractable problem is its space demands for movement and storage and the resulting impacts on the public realm of cities, especially the quality of the environment for pedestrians and cyclists. Car-based cities are not on a human scale and cannot deliver the quality public environments characteristic of, for example, many European cities.

2. More efficient cars or ones that run on new sources of potentially cheaper energy can actually encourage extra car use. As stated by Newman and Kenworthy, "The problem with technological solutions is that they invariably forget the Jevons Principle. This principle was first enunciated in 1865 by the economist Jevons, who predicted that making coal burning more efficient would lead to more coal use as the efficiency would lead to more economic uses of coal." Extra car ownership and use can exacerbate a whole range of other problems such as safety, sprawl-related social isolation and lack of community, the proliferation of non-human scale environments unsuitable for non-motorised modes, further marginalisaton of public transport systems and of course destruction of natural areas and productive food growing land. The energy problem must be tackled in a way that recognises and helps to address the many other problems of the car in cities.

3. Technological change is by no means instantaneous. The infrastructure systems that cities have built around internal combustion engine cars running on conventional oil are immense, as are the fleets of vehicles that need to be replaced. The penetration rate of new technologies is invariably slow and requires

multiple hundreds of billions of dollars to achieve the changes to factories producing the new cars, fuel distribution systems, support industries, retraining programmes etc. So far such changes have been very minimal.

4. One of the arguments used against land use change as a way of mitigating dependence on cars and tackling the energy problem is that the time required to effect significant change is very long, because urban systems change very slowly, whereas technological change can be introduced more rapidly. However, the time required for significant land use change and development of extensive new public transport systems can, in reality, be even less than that of technological change.

For example, in the space of 20 years the Vancouver metropolitan region has constructed a large new automated rail system that has led to very substantial high density, mixed use sub-centre development, which in turn has helped it to begin to change the region into a more sustainable form. Massive redevelopment of central and inner city land uses such as at False Creek and Coal Harbour have occurred over a slightly longer period allowing tens of thousands of people to lead a less car-dependent existence. During the same period from 1986 to 2006, the changes in vehicle technology and fuels has had a virtually negligible effect on fleet fuel consumption, notwithstanding the fact that much larger vehicles today are achieving similar rates of fuel use as much smaller vehicles decades ago.

From the initial vision in the mid-1970s Portland, Oregon scrapped a major planned freeway and instead has progressively constructed an extensive LRT system and separate inner city tram system. It has at the same time radically transformed its central area into a highly livable, people-oriented place, pulling down an elevated freeway, transforming car parks into public squares and focusing the majority of new development in the last 20 years around urban rail, thus helping to contain sprawl. The technologies for cars and fuels over the same period, although having improved, have not been able to have any real effect on fuel use because people are driving further, thus overriding any enhanced technological efficiency.

Perth, Australia since 1988 has electrified its entire train system, constructed a new 36 km line to the northern suburbs and will open a 74 km southern extension in July 2007. Urban rail use has more than quadrupled and is set to more than double again. Many examples of new transit-oriented developments have taken shape over the same period and many more are planned, These are helping to contain urban sprawl and beginning to create a more transit-oriented urban form for the city, allowing more and more people, even in distant outer areas to be less dependent on cars. Though the major policy response in Australia over the last 30 years to the need to save fuel in transport has been to improve the technology of vehicles, the average fleet fuel consumption of cars in Perth and Australia-wide has remained virtually unchanged from what it was in the 1960s. In 1963 it was 11.4 litres per 100 km and in 1995 it was 11.5 litres per 100 km. Relative gains in fuel efficiency through better technology have been eaten up by more power consuming items such as power steering and air conditioning and increased weight.

There are many other examples of significant and rapid trends in land use change, such as the revitalisation of downtown areas across the United States and Canada bringing hundreds of thousands of people closer to work and other destinations available as short walking trips. At the same time it is difficult to find any significant progress in the overall fuel-efficiency of vehicle fleets, notwithstanding improved technologies in cars and the gradual appearance of small numbers of electric and hybrid vehicles in cities.

Reconstructing cities to be more sustainable from a transport and energy perspective is clearly a long term project but can proceed at a significant rate when priority is given to it. Technological changes to improve vehicles and fuels should proceed in parallel with such changes but should not be seen as a panacea to the transport energy problem or as a soft option that avoids the need to address the structure of the city and the modes of transport available to people.

Cities around the world vary enormously in their transport patterns, energy use, infrastructure systems and urban form. Low density land use patterns, priority to freeway provision over speed competitive transit systems and policies that treat congestion always as a negative to be removed, are significant factors in understanding transport and energy use patterns. Many cities today are responding to the imperative to reduce automobile dependence through changes in transport policies that are generating attractive and well-utilised public transport systems and significant changes in land use and urban form in the form of central and inner area revitalisation and TOD around transit stations.

Such large scale changes to the structure of cities occur and have been occurring over relatively short time periods (10 to 20 years), allowing cities to reduce the growth in automobile dependence and energy use, whereas the long term policy in many cities to save energy or expand fuel options through technological fixes has produced almost no tangible changes to date. If cities are to achieve paradigm shifts to confront the post-petroleum era they are going to need to recognise that technology is not a panacea but only one factor in the bigger venture of fundamentally restructuring cities to reduce automobile dependence and creating overall more sustainable and liveable cities.

7

Regulatory Design of Basic Services

In the past, regulatory advisers often focused on the need to introduce international best practice— generally in the form of an independent regulatory organisation—to solve a wide range of performance problems. However, this approach was seldom straightforward, nor was it always successful. There is no one-size-fits-all regulatory design that can be reliably applied to resolve performance problems. Rather, regulation is best developed on a country-by-country basis through answering questions such as the following:

1. What are the real sector problems, and which of these can regulation solve?
2. What specific objectives is regulation aiming to achieve?
3. What combination of organisations and instruments is most suitable and would work best for achieving these regulatory objectives?

By carefully delimiting what the regulatory system is to achieve, and objectively determining how it can be structured to achieve these objectives, governments can design a system that is coherent, predictable, and legitimate. Identifying the key decisions to be made is just one element of design. The hard part can be actually making these decisions.

Water and Sanitation Services

Good water and sanitation services are essential for health, well-being, and economic development. However, in many developing countries the way these services are delivered can be less than ideal. Service quality may be low, service providers' financial capacity to deliver may be under threat, and large segments of the population may not receive service at all.

To improve urban water and sanitation services, a government first needs to identify the sector's underlying problems. Such problems become especially clear when the water services that people actually get are compared with the services people would like to get, and the conditions under which most stockholders would like the services to be provided. As the table shows, the gap between the actual and the ideal is often considerable.

Having identified the principal sector problems, the government then needs to define a path of reform that can move the sector from the actual (the services people get) toward the ideal (the services people want). This reform path needs to be well planned. It will involve a number of important decisions, including who should make policy decisions, who should own and manage the entities providing water services, who should invest and finance the investments, and how services should be paid for.

Regulation of Private and Public Providers

Water and sanitation is an essential service, and its provision—in particular, through piped supply and collection—has strong (natural) monopoly characteristics. This makes it important to control providers and make them accountable in some way, *regardless* of whether the provider is publicly or privately owned and operated. Private providers are generally regulated by autonomous agencies contracts, or both. Regulation is often considered necessary, because without it private providers might make unreasonable profits by overcharging and under-delivering.

Whether publicly owned providers can or should be regulated by an autonomous regulator is less clear. Among the questions to be considered are the following:

1. Whether certainty and predictability in the regulatory environment can strongly and positively influence the performance of government-owned water operators.
2. Whether transparency in political and policy interventions is also important for good policy making, and for stronger government and service provider accountability when the service provider is government-owned.
3. Whether potential benefits are outweighed by the costs and resource constraints—especially for small municipal service providers.

Public providers can be controlled and made accountable through ownership and governance. However, the line separating ownership and governance from regulation is not a bright one. Some analysts recommend making the separation between these forms of control more formal by turning the publicly owned and operated utility into a corporatised, regulated entity that mimics a privately owned company. This highlights the range of operating models that exist for government-owned water service providers.

A variety of regulatory approaches can be used across the range of operating models. In some cases, "autonomous" regulators try to control publicly owned providers as if they were privately owned. In other cases, mayors or ministers approve prices through informal, non-transparent processes. At present, there is little quantitative information on the linkage between regulation, governance structures, and performance outcomes. Some analysts highlight the success of some governments—such as national governments in Botswana and Burkina Faso, and municipalities in the Netherlands, New Zealand, and Scandinavia—in owning, operating, and controlling public utilities successfully without separate regulatory agencies. In other jurisdictions with public utilities—such as in Scotland and New South Wales (Australia)—regulatory agencies have been established to provide greater transparency and facilitate performance improvements and price reform, with some apparent success.

Approach to Regulatory Design

Governments embarking on water and sanitation sector reforms need to decide how providers will be given better incentives to deliver the services that people want at a reasonable price. This is where regulatory design becomes important. The regulatory system (a combination of rules and organisations) needs to be able to help solve the country's key regulatory problems, and to work well with existing sector institutions.

These may seem like simple objectives, but regulatory systems have often failed to resolve problems effectively. Many newly minted regulators have fit poorly with other sector institutions. Governments can reduce the risk of failures and poor fit by thinking carefully about regulatory design and by following a logical decision making process.

The process of regulatory design needs to assess where and how regulation is needed, before setting out to put regulatory systems in place. A good way to design effective regulation involves four basic steps:

1. Defining the underlying problems and objectives in the sector.
2. Assessing whether existing regulatory systems are well suited to achieving the objectives.

3. Identifying the specific regulatory functions needed to achieve those objectives.
4. Deciding, in light of existing institutions, which legal instruments are best suited to embody the regulatory rules, and which organisations are best suited to perform the regulatory functions.

These steps are illustrated in figure 1.

Defining the Problems and Sector Objectives

The provision of water supply and sanitation services in developing countries often faces a number of performance problems. On one level, these problems can easily be identified: leaking pipes, inadequate water pressure, poor water quality, and low service coverage. A one-off cash injection could feasibly solve many of these issues in the short term, but sector reform needs to focus on realising improvements that can be sustained in the long term. To achieve such improvements, the *underlying* causes of poor performance need to be identified and remedied. For many countries, the underlying causes of poor sector performance include the following:

1. Inadequate investment in, and maintenance of, system assets. This may be caused by
    a) Inadequate cash flow, due to tariffs being set below cost-recovery level, or costs being inefficiently high.
    b) Poor planning or disagreement between the government and provider over investment plans.
    c) Lack of confidence in the regulatory arrangements or, more generally, broad political risk.
2. Poor maintenance and operating practices.
3. Poorly defined or enforced service standards.

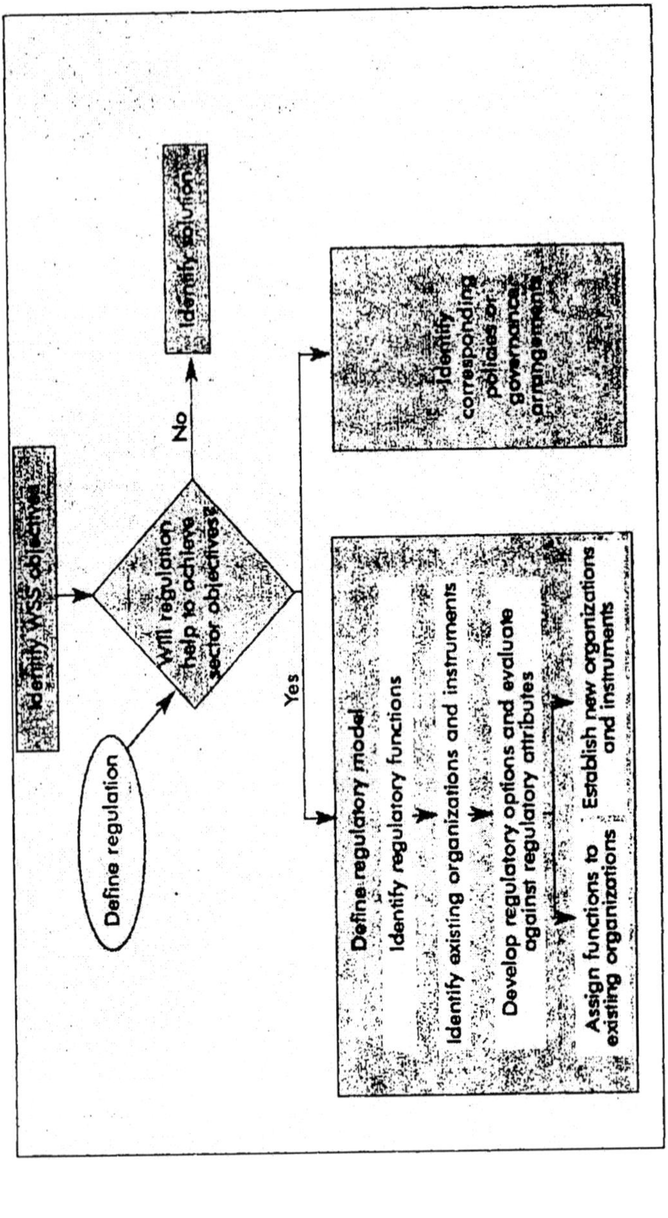

Figure 1. Framework for Thinking about Regulation

4. Lack of clear policies on service coverage expansion.
5. Barriers to entry for small private providers.

By examining existing sector policies and consulting with providers, consumers, and other sector participants, governments can build a clear picture of what the real problems are and thus what the reform objectives should be.

Assessing Whether Regulation Can Solve the Problems

Some of the underlying problems identified in the first stage can be effectively solved by a good regulatory system; other problems need a policy or structural solution. It is important to clearly identify which problems regulation can solve. This requires understanding what economic regulation is and does, and what it cannot do.

Defining Economic Regulation and the Problems It Can Solve

Economic regulation is best thought of as the legal controls placed on water and sanitation providers in order to overcome the problems inherent in an essential, monopoly service. This points to a core definition of economic regulation as the rules and organisations that set, change, monitor, and enforce allowed tariffs and allowed service standards for water providers.

Water is an essential service, and is generally worth a lot more to people than it costs to supply. Private providers could take advantage of this by overcharging and making high profits at the expense of consumers. In some cases, this opportunity for profiteering may be limited by competition. In the case of large-scale piped provision, however, competition is not feasible. Economic regulation can usefully be thought of as mimicking the pressures that competition provides in other markets. In other words, it can help to stop tariffs from increasing above the level required to recover reasonable costs and make the service provider bear costs that are considered excessive.

Regulation can also set and enforce service standards to ensure that utilities are providing the services that people want. However, tariffs and service standards are inevitably related—if tariffs are too low to recover costs, the provider may not be able to meet the required service standards, or the government may bear the fiscal burden of providing (implicit or explicit) subsides. Thus, regulation also has a role to play in ensuring that tariffs are not "too low."

Beyond this narrow role of setting, monitoring, and enforcing rules on tariffs and service quality, economic regulation begins to overlap with other areas of regulation and policy. This overlap is illustrated in figure 2. The darkest area in the middle represents the core of economic regulation—addressing the monopoly problem. In the "gray area" around the core, a choice is needed as to whether a particular regulatory function should be considered part of economic regulation or dealt with in another way.

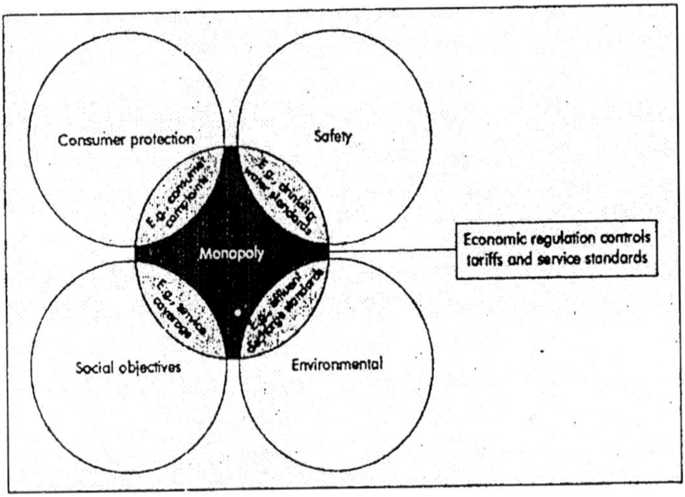

Figure 2. Economic Regulation—Addressing the Monopoly Problem

For example, setting drinking water standards may be considered part of economic regulation, or it may be dealt with as an aspect of health or food safety regulation. Service coverage may be governed by regulatory requirements on the provider to connect more customers, or by subsidies for service expansion, or both. Another way could mean a different form of regulation— governments can use the power of the law to instruct providers to do certain things, and to enforce these instructions through penalties and other forms of compulsion (such as providing incentives or withdrawing privileges). Another way could mean a different form of control altogether. Governments have a range of tools they can use to achieve social, environmental, safety, and consumer protection objectives. For example, governments may aim to achieve social objectives by influencing providers through subsidies and tax incentives.

There are also problems that economic regulation cannot solve—or at least cannot solve alone. For example, integrated policy approaches are often necessary for the following:

1. Ensuring that services remain affordable to low-income households.
2. Increasing provider efficiency.
3. Improving capital expenditure planning.
4. Improving poor payment records by government departments and agencies.

Thus, even when governments choose to expand the role of regulation beyond simply setting, monitoring, and enforcing rules on tariffs and service quality, supporting regulation with other policy initiatives is generally necessary.

There are vital government roles in water supply and sanitation services that support regulation, but which are distinct from it:

1. Policy making. Policy defines sector objectives and principles and sets out who should do what to achieve those objectives. The extent to which consumers or taxpayers should pay for water services and infrastructure is a policy decision, as is the ownership of the providers and the general strategy for controlling tariffs and service standards.
2. Ownership, service provision, and governance. Provider performance is greatly influenced by who owns the water assets, who is responsible for service provision, and how the owner exercises control over the utility's management (governance). The government needs to ensure that these factors and regulatory design are aligned with each other.
3. Coordination. Governments must coordinate water supply and sanitation services by ensuring that policy decisions and implementation plans are consistent, managing input from the various bodies involved in water sector activities, and coordinating public expenditure priorities.

Defining Specific Regulatory Functions

In developed countries with private providers, the core regulatory goals may be to keep tariffs down and to keep service standards up. In developing countries, it cannot be assumed that the regulatory functions are the same. Before putting a regulatory system in place, governments should be clear on the following issues:

1. Will the regulatory system be designed with the aim of keeping tariffs "down" and service standards "up," through regular and in-depth scrutiny of the provider's financial and technical performance?
2. Or is it more important to move tariffs up through rules that require cost-recovery tariffs?

3. Is there a need for neutral, fair adjudication between the government and a private provider ?
4. Or is the provider owned and managed by the government in a way that makes third-party adjudication less necessary or acceptable?

Clarity on sector objectives and priorities is essential for choosing effective regulatory instruments and organisations.

Choosing Legal Instruments and Organisations

Regulatory systems can take a number of forms. In the past, some regulatory advisors have advocated that some of these forms are better at achieving good regulation. In particular, advisors have viewed an "independent regulator" as the best-practice model. This view was based on the model's perceived success in other infrastructure sectors, and in such countries as the United States, the United Kingdom, and Australia. In practice, which models work best depends on a country's objectives and circumstances. Regulatory systems that seem structurally different may carry out the same regulatory functions to solve similar problems. As figure 3 illustrates, a number of different legal instruments and organisations can be combined to create a variety of regulatory architecture. For example, regulation in Florida is based on a combination of statute, a regulatory office, and a government ministry or department. The Public Services Commission (PSC) was established by statute, and it has broad discretion to set, change, monitor, and enforce limits on tariffs. However, the regulatory function of setting standards for water pressure is the job of the Department for Environmental Protection. This department also controls drinking water quality and effluent discharge standards.

A different regulatory architecture can be seen in Colombia. The Regulatory Commission for Water and Basic Sanitation Services (CRA) establishes the tariff-setting methodology. Providers set their own tariffs in accordance with this methodology (or apply to the CRA to set the tariffs a different way). Service standards are set by the Ministry of Economic Development. The Public Services Superintendent (SSP) monitors the providers to verify that they are following the tariff-setting rules and complying with the service standards. However, where private providers operate under concession contracts with a municipality, the general practice is for the contract to set service standards and tariffs, which are to be monitored and enforced by the municipality.

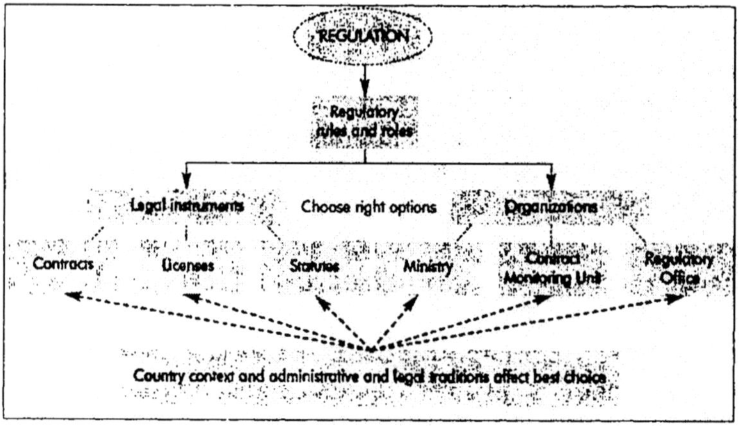

Figure 3. Selecting Legal Instruments and Organisations for Good Regulation

In Cote devoir, an affermage contract is the regulatory instrument. The Ministry of Economic Infrastructure designed, negotiated, and signed the affermage contract with the private provider. One of its departments, the Water Directorate, is the owner of the supply network and is responsible for monitoring the provider's compliance with the contract. The Directorate also leads negotiations on tariff adjustments and is responsible for granting approval for some construction projects. A separate government department monitors the costs incurred by the provider when it undertakes network renewal and extension activities.

Each of these designs represents a different regulatory architecture, but each is functionally equivalent in terms of the roles for setting tariffs and service standards that are performed.

Attributes of Good Regulation

Given that a range of functionally equivalent designs are possible, clear criteria for selecting the right legal instruments and organisations (for a specific country environment) are needed. These criteria can be thought of as attributes—the qualities that a good regulatory system should have.

The goal of regulation is to achieve good service for consumers at a price that enables providers to operate efficiently and sustainably, consistent with a clear and reasonable trade-off between service levels and tariffs. To achieve these goals, a regulatory system should have the following attributes:

1. *Coherence*. If a provider needs to meet higher service standards or to focus on system expansion, it is likely to incur higher costs, which will need to be compensated through higher tariffs or a combination of tariffs and subsidies. In contrast, if tariffs need to be lower (because the government believes the poor cannot afford water and sanitation services), but subsidies are not an option for achieving this, it makes sense that the required service standards are lower, too. The regulatory system should be able to select, and settle on the right combination of tariffs and subsidies, and service standards and coverage, such that providers are able to recover their costs, and people receive the services they are willing to pay for.

In Bogota, Colombia, a lack of coherence in regulatory decision making triggered friction and political intervention that undermined the regulator's independence and autonomy. The tariff setting methodology of the CRA (the regulator) focused on achieving full cost recovery through tariffs, partly on the assumption that municipalities were seeking political support by suppressing water rates. However, when the methodology was applied in Bogota, average tariffs increased by more than 100 percent. The municipality had included a large provision for capital works in the tariff calculation. Considerable debate ensued over whether the calculation was reasonable, with the President eventually intervening to direct the CRA's decision.

In contrast, in Senegal such tariff shocks for consumers were carefully avoided, and coherence between tariffs and services was maintained through the combination of a planned, gradual increase in consumer tariffs and guaranteed cost-recovery payments from the government to the provider. The government, having made a policy decision on the gradual tariff path, bore the risk of service costs and tariffs diverging. This risk was limited for the government as the service levels, the capital investments, and the performance of the operator were linked.

2. *Predictability and credibility*. Regulatory decisions should be time-consistent, and made on clear precedents and rules. This is essential for minimising risk to providers and, in turn, encouraging good service provision and adequate asset maintenance and capital investment.

   Many systems fail because of a lack of credible protection against regulatory expropriation. In Buenos Aires the water concessionaries suffered regulatory expropriation. Many other proposed reforms have failed because the regulatory system was not credible in assuring providers that they would be able to recover their costs. In contrast, in Vanuatu and Senegal, credibility was provided through the contract, which prevented short-term political intervention and created a predictable regulatory framework for providers. In Senegal, regulatory rules and processes that minimised the risk of steep tariffs increases also contributed to predictability and credibility.

3. *Legitimacy, transparency, and accountability.* Regulatory decisions need to be clear, widely accepted, and publicly accessible. Political and social stability is not only essential for a regulatory system's predictability; it also creates the conditions for the public to view regulation as legitimate. Moreover, beyond public scrutiny, regulatory institutions need reasons and incentives to make decisions in the long-term interests of consumers—strong, logical lines of accountability help. Accountability to the public, in turn, is essential for preventing corruption and improving legitimacy in the public eye.

   In Cochabamba, Bolivia, the lack of legitimacy and transparency in the way tariff decisions were made was a key contributing factor in the failure of the concession. The public rioted against tariff increases, largely because they lacked information on the contract and its monitoring organisations, and doubted the role of regulation in protecting their interests. As a result of intense public pressure, the government cancelled the contract.

   In contrast, in the United States, a highly transparent and participatory form of regulation is used in most states. Utilities submit applications (for example, for a rate increase) to the regulator, and any citizen or group

> has a right to contest the application in open hearings adjudicated by the regulator. All relevant technical and financial information is publicly available. The application of strong democratic principles helps regulation to achieve legitimacy, transparency, and accountability.

These attributes can be used as criteria for assessing the likely effectiveness of different regulatory architecture—that is, the combination of legal instruments and regulatory organisations.

Applying the Attributes to Build the Right Architecture

Each country's unique context and legal traditions should inform the way that regulatory roles are distributed amongst instruments and organisations, in order to achieve the desired attributes of regulation discussed above.

In many developed countries, an independent regulator model has worked well to achieve these attributes. For example, Of at, the water regulatory body for England and Wales, is viewed internationally as a model of successful, independent regulation. In the English political, economic, and social context—in which the government, administrators, regulators, and the general public share strong values on sector policy, and only modest changes in prices have been needed—a regulatory office like Of at has been able to regulate effectively, without direct political intervention. As this example shows, politicians are less prone to intervene where there is broad-based support for the regulatory mandate.

However, when this model is transposed to developing and transitional countries, regulatory independence is often undermined by frequent political intervention (in Manila, for example, the president intervened on tariff decisions a number of times). In an environment where there is a high risk that politicians will make decisions that focus on short-term interests and lack coherency (between tariffs and service standards), a contract can be a good legal instrument for locking in regulatory rules and achieving coherence and predictability. Many developing and transition nations have relatively effective contract law and dispute resolution mechanisms, so regulation by contract can be a credible and legitimate form of regulation. In some countries, predictability may be increased if regulation is embodied directly in statute. It is a question of finding the most appropriate instrument in a particular country context.

Contract-Based Regulation

Countries such as Senegal and Vanuatu have used contracts as an effective regulatory instrument for setting tariff rules and service standards. The legal systems in these countries were developed under influences from France, where a contract model of water regulation is widely and successfully used. As a result, in both Vanuatu and Senegal this model was well understood and respected by the government and sector participants.

For regulation by contract to work successfully, the rules must be monitored and enforced. Existing government organisations may lack the capacity or incentive to monitor performance effectively. Poor monitoring undermines customer protection, reducing the legitimacy of the regulatory system as a whole. This "legitimacy deficit" was evident, for example, in Vanuatu. Although the provider provides good services, the paucity of government monitoring has resulted in widespread concern over the lack of transparency, accountability, and legitimacy in the way the provider is controlled.

New organisational arrangements may be introduced to help increase government's capacity to enforce the rules and overcome the legitimacy deficit. This was done effectively in Senegal—where a combination of dedicated contract monitoring units, ongoing performance monitoring by the government-owned asset holding company, and timely, independent mediation on disputed issues by an outside conciliator provided the necessary support for regulation by contract to operate successfully. The combination of the rules set out in the contract, and the roles performed by monitoring organisations and government ministries created a regulatory system that was generally coherent, predictable, legitimate, and accountable to the public.

The choice of regulatory organisation must be made carefully to ensure an appropriate fit with existing institutions and with the legal instrument used for regulation. For example, a regulatory agency with broad powers and a contract may not be a sound combination, as the experience of Manila highlights. Because the concession contracts in Manila explicitly set out the tariff-setting and service standard rules for the providers, the role of the Regulatory Office was often unclear. Even Office staff became confused at times over the degree of discretion that the Office should exercise in setting and interpreting rules, or the extent to which it should focus solely on contract monitoring and enforcement. A better organisational choice may have been a contract monitoring unit with a clear mandate to monitor and enforce compliance with the regulatory rules already established in the contracts.

As the examples discussed above illustrate, a variety of regulatory architecture are possible. Although these architecture may be functionally equivalent, they are not equally successful in different country environments. Regulatory designers should choose legal instruments and organisations that form a sound overall design. The design should also be cognizant of the specific sector problems regulation needs to solve, and the particular country environment in which regulation will be seated.

Improving Regulatory Design

Since good regulatory design needs to reflect the country context, it is hard to provide singular guidelines. However, observations from regulatory successes and failures internationally, including experience from recently completed in-depth country case studies, reveal several lessons on what makes for effective regulation. These lessons point to several aspects of good regulatory design: designing-in political and context-specific features to a purpose-built regulatory model, rather than adopting a best-practice model that does not fit the country context and attempts to operate outside existing institutions.

From these lessons we have identified a number of design approaches that can help improve a regulatory regime's performance concerning the key attributes of coherence, predictability, and legitimacy.

These approaches include the following:

1. Working with the existing organisational framework.
2. Designing in the politics.
3. Limiting discretion in decision making.
4. Trading off sophistication in favour of simplicity.

These approaches are discussed in the sections that follow.

Working with the Existing Organisational Framework

Regulatory design never actually starts with a blank slate. Regulation is generally introduced in an environment where some sector organisations already exist; legal and political systems are well developed; some measures for consumer protection have already been introduced; and relationships between politicians, providers, and the public have been established. The resulting complexity of structures and incentives is not a backdrop that regulation should seek to overcome or be imposed on top of. Rather, it provides a framework for regulation to work *within*.

The choice of legal instruments and regulatory organisations should reflect the existing country conditions, but regulatory designers should also realise that these conditions may change. For example, as a country's institutional capacity and credibility improve over time, it may be appropriate for regulatory organisations to take on a stronger or more extensive role.

Sometimes such evolution is planned—initial legislation may limit the role and discretion of a new regulatory body for a limited period, but these limits may be relaxed over time (as in Victoria, Australia). Sometimes the need to modify a regulatory regime becomes apparent over time, as government policies change or weaknesses in the existing arrangements become obvious. For example, Vanuatu is currently developing a new agency to assist the government in monitoring and enforcing Port Vila's water concession contract.

In general, however, the choice of instruments (and related organisations) is a long-term one. For a regulatory system to be credible, the public and investors must perceive that it requires long term commitments and lasting structures.

Choice of Legal Instruments

A variety of legal instruments can be used to support regulation. Past approaches to regulatory design have often ignored or down-played the role of contracts in regulation. More emphasis has been placed on developing strong regulatory agencies with broad discretionary powers. However, contracts are often a good starting point for establishing clear and enforceable regulatory rules. In civil-law countries (including countries with French heritage—

such as Vanuatu and Senegal—and many countries in Latin America), contracts are seen as a familiar and legitimate tool for controlling service provision. For such countries, including service standard and rules for operator remuneration within a contract, rather than having an independent regulator set such rules, is more contextually consistent.

In some circumstances, a contract (or a contract alone) may not be the best choice. For example, if a given jurisdiction has several regulated water service providers, there may be some advantage in creating a single legal instrument, such as a statute or uniform license, that sets basic rules for all of them. Another potential attraction of setting rules in a statute is that it is generally difficult to change primary legislation. Investors may perceive regulatory risk as being lower if contractual provisions entered into with local governments are backed up by consistent laws at the national level.

Choice of Organisation

Some form of organisation will be needed to ensure that the rules are followed even where rules are set in a contract. The degree of organisational support that a contract requires will depend on the strength of existing administrative and judicial systems.

Vanuatu provides an example of a regulatory design that did not adequately consider the country's existing institutional context. The Vanuatu government had entered into a concession contract with a private provider, UNELCO. The contracting ministry was notionally responsible for monitoring the concessionaries's performance under the contract. In reality, little monitoring has been undertaken, and the government and public do not feel in control.

In retrospect, the government might have done better to give contract-monitoring responsibilities to stronger organisations. Candidates would have included the Ministry of Finance, a specially created contract monitoring unit, or a consulting firm hired for the purpose. Better contract monitoring could have increased the legitimacy of the regulatory system.

Senegal's regulatory system had a better organisational design. Regulation in Senegal worked better than in Vanuatu, largely for the following reasons:

1. The contracting party to the utility's performance contract, SONES (the state-owned, asset holding company, which had considerable technical expertise) undertook regular and thorough monitoring.
2. Dedicated contract monitoring units were established.
3. The government was active in its relationship with the utility.

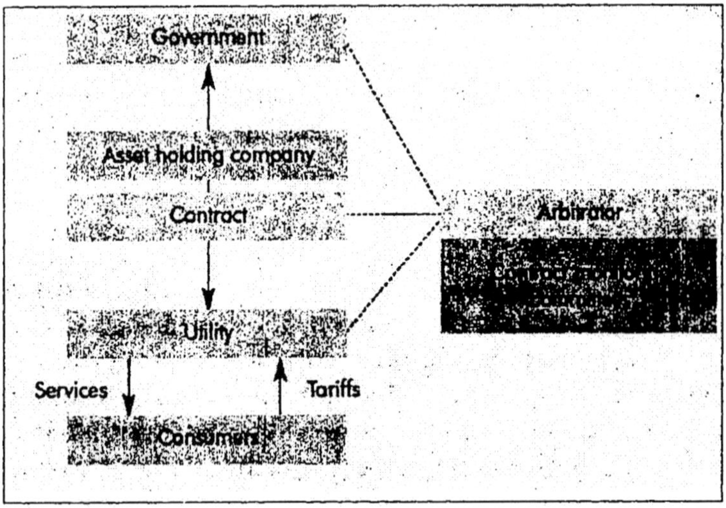

Figure 4. Regulatory Organisations Supported the Contract in Senegal

Conciliators (arbitrators) were brought in to help resolve disputes emerging between SONES and the utility (either because of contract imprecision or because of one of the parties failing on its commitments). Donors also played an ongoing and important mediating role. In summary, organisations were brought in at the potential weak points of the regulatory structure in Senegal. Regulation was more successful because the need for these organisations was identified during the design stage. A contract-based model of regulation was thus adapted to suit Senegal's existing institutional context better.

Consistency with Parallel Processes

In addition to considering the institutions that are *already* in place when regulation is designed, regulatory designers need to be fully cognizant of the institutions that are being introduced through parallel reforms. In particular, regulation is often introduced at the same time as private sector participation, which clearly influence which functions the regulatory system will need to fulfil.

Designing a package of economic regulation and contract-based private participation is more difficult than is sometimes realised. Common regulatory models were designed to work with utilities that are fully privately owned. However, private participation for WSS services is generally based on contracts between government and private companies, not outright sale of the utility. Lack of logical interface between the contract and regulatory design processes can create a mismatch between economic regulation and the private participation arrangements it was intended to support.

For example, in Manila, the Regulatory Office was not clear whether it should simply apply the rules in the concession contract, or whether it could change the rules when circumstances changed. This uncertainty contributed to a messy and confused response when a currency crisis created financial distress for one of the concessionaries. Similarly in Colombia, the relationship between rules set by the CRA (the regulator) and rules in municipal concession and lease contracts is not quite clear. This lack of clarity creates unnecessary risk for both the provider and the local government.

Create an Appropriate Role for Politics

Past approaches to regulation strove for regulatory independence with the objective of keeping politics out of regulatory decision making. Political intervention, however, may be inevitable. Moreover, politics can sometimes play a positive role. The key is to ensure that the regulatory and policy framework encourages or at least constrains politicians to make coherent decisions and honour long-term commitments. This means that the role of politics should be well defined and limited.

Governments can be made to commit to their decisions if key service and tariff provisions are locked into contracts. However, they can still be given a political safety valve to influence tariffs. For example, regulatory designers can de-couple consumer tariffs and operator revenue, or provide for government-funded, output-based subsidies that can help keep consumer tariffs down.

Political Decisions

Many advisors believe that regulation should adequately balance provider cost recovery and consumer protection, and that politics can interfere by tipping the scales or by undermining the entire balancing system. One of the principal problems with politicians playing a directive role in regulation is that their decisions tend to lack long-term commitment to coherent tariff and service combinations. Politicians are often tempted to make decisions that are based on short-term interests. They may push for tariffs that only recover short-run operating costs, meaning that the provider has insufficient funds to maintain long-lived assets or make new investments. This may win favour from consumers in the short term (lower tariffs are generally popular), but in the long term it will be detrimental as services begin to deteriorate.

Alternatively, politicians may demand that services be improved or coverage increased without allowing a corresponding increase in tariffs. The lack of coherence between services and tariffs harms both the provider and consumers in the long term.

With these negative consequences of political intervention in mind, many designs have focused on reducing political involvement in regulation. Nonetheless, politics seems to rather consistently intervene, especially when it comes to setting tariffs. For example, in the Philippines and Colombia, the presidents became directly involved in tariff decisions on several occasions, even though the regulatory bodies in both countries were ostensibly autonomous. This type of intervention damaged not only the regulators' independence, but also their credibility.

Politics is especially hard to exclude if independence is combined with wide discretion to make socially and politically sensitive decisions on prices for basic community infrastructure services. This can create excessive risks for all stockholders (investors, service providers, governments, and users)—especially where the current prices are far from levels that are sustainable in the medium to long term. In response, discretion may be reduced or a transparent, accountable role for government policy provided, or both.

The threat of damaging political intervention is not the only reason that regulatory designers should, from the outset, consider a role for political decision making in regulation. There are three important arguments for giving politicians a well-defined role in regulation:

1. Politicians can make decisions that represent a collective choice on trade-offs, such as having limited services for lower tariffs, or having better quality or more widely available services for higher tariffs. People will have different preferences on these choices; a democratically accountable government could be the best organisation to make a choice that best reflects the needs of the community.
2. Politicians may have accountability to the public through the voting system. Although accountability through a democratic political system may be imperfect or diffuse, it at least provides a channel for public involvement. In the case of basic infrastructure services, this channel may be stronger for municipal or local governments than for governments at the national level. The government can exercise its accountability indirectly, by appointing independent regulators to make regulatory decisions, or directly, by choosing a coherent tariff and service standard combination on behalf of consumers.
3. If extreme events—such as a sharp increase in tariffs—occur, the public will demand that the government *does something*. A well-defined regulatory role will provide the government with a safety valve, allowing it to act in a way that minimises damage to the regulatory system while responding to the public.

These arguments point to a positive, if limited, role for politics in regulation. However, regulatory designers still need to ensure that political decision makers will take into account relevant information and advice, act transparently, and make credible, coherent, and time-consistent decisions.

Long-Term Regulatory Coherence

A well-defined role for politics should be one that commits the government to coherent, long-term decisions on tariffs and service standards. The independent regulator model attempted to achieve such commitment by limiting government involvement to setting legislation that established the regulatory body, or appointing some of the regulators. In other words, under this approach the government commits to devolve all tariff and service standard decisions to the independent regulator.

However, the independent regulator approach has frequently failed to achieve political commitment to long-term regulatory coherence. Policy makers and politicians often feel uncomfortable with relinquishing decision-making powers, and face strong pressures to intervene on tariff issues anyway. An alternative way to achieve commitment and consistency is through a contract. The government and provider could decide on coherent rules on tariffs and service standards, which would be locked into the contract, and adjusted only through well-defined periodic reviews. For example, in both Vanuatu and Monteria, the governments were involved in deciding on appropriate service standards and acceptable tariff rules when the service contract was negotiated.

Once the contract is signed, government involvement should be limited to monitoring the contract, and ensuring that the legitimacy of regulation through the contract is maintained (for example, by providing sufficient information for the public, remaining active as a contracting partner, and participating in the renegotiation of the contract if it is desired by, and in the interest of, both parties).

The government may also take part in tariff reviews, which should occur on a pre-agreed periodic basis, or be triggered by pre-agreed changes in economic or social conditions. Such reviews can create another well-defined role for political decision making, and also provide the government with a safety valve to act if shocks (the triggers specified in the contract) occur.

There may be further ways in which regulatory designers can provide a safety valve for political decision making that minimises damage to regulatory credibility. These could enable the government to influence consumer tariffs, if necessary, without influencing operator revenues. For example, in Senegal, politicians take responsibility for public welfare decisions, such as the trade-off between high service levels and high tariffs. The Senegalese government pays the provider a contractually guaranteed fee, sets consumer tariffs, and is responsible for investing in the system assets. These arrangements let the government bear the political and fiscal risks involved in setting tariffs and in influencing long-term service levels (by choosing the level of investment), while ensuring that the provider can cover its costs.

Under an alternative arrangement, the government could set consumer rates at a "socially acceptable" (but below cost-recovery) level, and make a firm commitment to grant an output based subsidy for services provided at this reduced consumer rate. This approach has been used successfully for electricity services in the Philippines, where a kilowatt-per-hour consumption subsidy is provided for poor consumers in remote areas. This subsidy is financed by a levy on all electricity consumption.

A slightly different output-based aid (OBA) approach would involve the government agreeing with the provider on service extensions to new communities, and committing to providing a connection subsidy for each new household connection made by the provider. This type of OBA scheme is currently being implemented for water service expansion in countries such as Brazil and Indonesia.

Limiting the Discretion Given to Regulatory Decision Makers

The quality of the decisions made by a regulatory organisation will depend on both the people involved in making the decisions and the rules by which the decisions are made. By *quality* we mean whether the decision helps achieve regulatory predictability, coherence, and transparency. Good decisions require competent individuals whose incentives are aligned with regulatory goals, and well-defined rules that are easy to implement.

The relative importance of the individuals and the written rules depends on how much *discretion* individual decision makers are provided—either unintentionally, through poorly formulated rules, or intentionally, through the use of regulatory principles in place of precise rules, or through organisational design.

In the spectrum from low to high discretion, a "pure" regulation by contract model is sometimes identified with low discretion, and a "pure" independent regulator (regulation by agency) model is sometimes identified with high discretion. In practice, the relationship between discretion and the regulatory instrument is more complex.

Many contracts fail to specify price reset provisions in detail. Although the process for negotiation and arbitration of price resets may be well specified, the basis for negotiating tariffs, and the various factors to be taken into account, may be quite broadly specified—creating a high degree of discretion. By the same token, it is possible to establish an independent regulatory agency with clearly limited discretion. Legislation or subsidiary instruments can specify the initial price path and key parameters or approaches to be used by the regulator during price resets.

In practice, the reset provisions under regulation by contract or agency are often vague and poorly defined, and are a source of considerable risk and uncertainty for the investor. However, a key distinction is that under regulation by contract, the new price paths are to be agreed with the operator, with recourse to arbitration in the event that agreement cannot be reached. In contrast, under regulation by agency, a new price path may be imposed upon the utility, subject to possible recourse to appeal mechanisms. In either case, it is often preferable to define clear and binding rules for price resets, which will limit regulatory discretion and reduce uncertainty for investors and other stockholders.

Levels of Discretion in Regulatory Rules

High-discretion rules—that is, price-setting provisions in contracts or legislation that are effectively principles and that include concepts that need to be defined by the decision maker—have three key advantages:

1. Precise, low-discretion rules may result in the wrong decision in some circumstances (such as if unforeseen financial shocks occur, or if base conditions change over time).
2. High-discretion rules allow a competent decision maker to consider basic policy objectives when making a decision.
3. High-discretion rules may involve lower setup costs—more precise rules will take longer to develop and gain consensus on.

In the context of a competent, independent regulatory organisation or established legal precedents that provide clear guidance on the exercise of this discretion, these advantages may make higher-discretion rules the right choice. However, if such precedents are lacking, if the regulatory organisation lacks the competence or capacity to exercise a high degree of discretion, or if the impartiality of decision is likely to be threatened by political (or provider) intervention, low-discretion rules are likely to lead to better

Low-discretion rules are likely to be a better choice for countries with limited institutional capacity and regulatory traditions, because they:

a) Make the outcomes of regulatory decisions more certain and predictable.

b) Reduce the potential for decisions to be inconsistent, biased, or arbitrary.

c) Enable each regulatory decision to be made more quickly, and with fewer resources.

The advantages listed above suggest that low-discretion rules may be a good starting point for regulatory systems that involve a large degree of decision making by an organisation (in contrast to systems that set rules in contracts, and only call for decision making by an independent organisation in special circumstances).

As time passes and experience with the regulatory system grows, institutional strength—in particular, the competence of regulatory organisations—may improve; the legitimacy of the regulatory system may be enhanced; and sector participants may discover that certain regulatory rules have not been effective or useful in all situations. If these conditions hold, the government may decide that the regulatory organisation should have a greater degree of discretion. However, the purpose of increasing discretion should be to improve the quality of important regulatory decisions by permitting more flexibility in adjusting prices to changing circumstances and incorporating lessons learned from regulatory practice elsewhere, rather than to widen the scope of regulation.

Trading Off Sophistication in Favour of Simplicity

Once decisions are made on the general regulatory framework—which organisations and legal instruments work best given the country context—attention turns to filling in the regulatory details (for example, tariff formulas and rules for calculating costs). International experience has shown that a lack of detail in regulatory rules can lead to important decisions being disputed or can reduce the effectiveness of key processes. For example, in Manila an ongoing debate arose over the role of the financial models that the concessionaries had used when submitting their bids (it was not clear from the contract whether the assumptions in the models should be binding). In Vanuatu, the contract does not clearly specify how a tariff review should be undertaken, which may have discouraged the government from entering into this process. Such examples highlight the importance of ensuring adequate details in the rules.

Conversely, the drive to provide detail should not come at the cost of simplicity and usability. Tradition and professional instinct may urge those designing regulatory systems to aim for economic optimisation. For example, an ideal set of regulatory rules would achieve full cost recovery for the provider, at the most efficient tariff, and for the most appropriate level of service, given the community's needs and willingness to pay. This, however, is a demanding ideal. Regulatory designers should not let the perfect be the enemy of the good. By creating sophisticated rules, which require large amounts of information or considerable technical expertise, designers may inadvertently reduce the effectiveness of regulation.

Predictability and credibility if adequate information is not available to effectively apply rules, or if the rules are not well understood, regulatory decisions will not be made in a predictable way, and the regulator's credibility may be undermined.

Transparency is achieved when rules are simple and clear. Overly sophisticated rules may be hard to understand and implement.

A clear example of sophistication being successfully put aside in favour of simplicity occurred in Colombia. The CRA, the Colombian water regulator, had brought in a well-known international regulatory theoretician to advise on how it could improve its regulatory methodology. The advisor's recommendations were to regulate service quality, apply penalties for noncompliance (which were to be automatically paid by utilities to customers), and open the water sector to competition by regulating bulk water prices, cross-subsidy levels, and access to distribution networks.

These ideas, which were innovative even for the water sector in developed nations, were revolutionary and unprecedented in an emerging market, such as Colombia's. Government and industry believed that the water sector was not ready for these reforms, but the CRA's leadership tried to push them through. The World Bank and other international experts explained that the proposed changes were impractical, costly, would create high regulatory risk, and would not easily solve the key water sector problems (coverage and service quality) in Colombia. Eventually, the sophisticated reforms were abandoned. A conceptually simpler, cost-based methodology was retained for setting tariffs, allowing utilities a more reliable revenue flow, and enabling them to invest in improvements to service quality and coverage.

The provision of urban water and sanitation services in many countries is poor. The services people actually get generally fall short of the services people want and would be willing to pay for. In response, governments often engage in sector wide reform to help improve services. These reforms may involve introducing economic regulation—that is, rules and organisations that set, monitor, enforce, and change allowed tariffs and service standards for water and sanitation service providers.

Economic regulation helps to ensure that utilities with natural monopoly power in water supply and sanitation services provide the services people want at reasonable prices. The government can achieve other sector objectives, such as extending service to poor consumers, or managing environmental impacts, through tools other than economic regulation (for example, subsidies or environmental regulation). Early in the reform process, the decision makers in government should set out a clear, but limited, role for economic regulation in the context of other interventions.

Having defined the role of regulation, a regulatory structure needs to be designed with an appropriate combination of legal instruments and organisations. When building this structure, designers need to consider a range of country-specific factors: the existing organisational framework, legal and political systems, and culture and traditions. In other words, there is no international best practice for regulatory design—one standard model will not fit well with, or be successful in, every country context.

Although no best-practice design guarantees these attributes, they can be enhanced by focusing on particular design features. One such design feature is an appropriate avenue for political decision making. Politics can intervene in unpredictable ways, even when attempts are made to shut it out. Such ad hoc interventions can undermine the credibility and legitimacy of the regulatory system. Political decision making, however, can be channelled into the limited areas where the government is best placed to make decisions that require collective accountability. These areas include decisions on policy-related issues, such as whether and how to provide subsidies, or which of a range of consistent tariff and service standard combinations would best serve the public's needs. Contracts can be used to enshrine government commitments to decisions it has made. With careful design, a limited, well-defined decision-making role can provide a safety valve for government involvement in exceptional circumstances (such as tariff shocks caused by a sudden change in supply costs).

Other features of good regulatory design include limiting discretion for regulatory decision makers, and using clear and simple regulatory rules. When organisations lack strength and experience, more precise rules and well-defined roles will improve the predictability and transparency of regulation. However, rules must also be easy to understand and implement. This may mean trading off sophistication in favour of rules that are easier to use in practice.

8

Analysing the Impacts of Urbanisation

Traditional measures of urbanisation based on administrative and political geographic units are inadequate to address many questions related to population settlement patterns and ecological issues that arise in recent comparative studies. National differences in the definition of urbanisation and the dependence of those definitions on administrative designations of political subunits have always made cross national comparisons difficult. In studies of the relationship between population and the environment, these differences are heightened by the ecological emphasis on the natural environment. Urbanisation is usually conceptualised as a characteristic of the population or society, but in ecological studies there is equal interest in defining urbanisation in terms of land use and land cover characteristics. While measurement differences are difficult enough to deal with when comparing the percentage of the population that is urbanised, they are much more likely to cause variation in the percentage of the land area in urban designated areas. The choice of geographic unit of analysis and definitions criteria and methodology can result in varying degrees of "over bounding" or "under bounding," sometimes within the same area . The differences in over bounding and under bounding that are annoyances in the measurement of population size become major problems for measuring the extent of urban land use.

Because ecologists often are interested in how landscapes and the environment have changed over time,. changing definitions of urbanisation within a given nation also pose difficulties for analysis. In the U.S., demographic data from past censuses are presented only for administrative and political geographic units. Identifying degrees of urbanisation in the past is made more difficult by the paucity of population and land use data for small geographic areas comparable to the "patches," or small study areas, that feature in ecological research.

The lack of detailed population and spatial information often requires use of cartographic methods for defining urbanisation; that is, reliance on mapped portrayals of urban extent. Lack of census geographic area boundary information also poses problems when linking historical demographic data for urban population with information relating to environmental processes. Portrayal of population using point data and depicting urban growth and extent through various modelling procedures can overcome problems relating to lack of boundary information.

Defining levels of urbanisation is made more difficult by the fact that it is both a discrete *phenomenon* that can be observed and measured in place at a specific time, and a *process* that occurs across space and time. The difference between urbanisation as a phenomenon and urbanisation as a process creates challenges for researchers and policy makers who base conclusions and decisions on observation and measurement of something that has happened in order to affect changes and develop policies in advance of something that will happen.

There is no easy solution to the tension created by this dichotomy—we must define and measure the thing in order to understand the process and its ecological effects.

Population and Land Area

The countries in the study, China, India, and the United States of America, are the world's three most populous countries. In the year 2000, China had an estimated population of 1.261 billion; India had 1.014 billion people; and as of April 1 the population of the United States had reached 281,421,906. While the combined population of these three countries accounts for approximately 42 percent of the world's population, the countries occupy only 15 percent of the world's land area. How these countries handle their land and population relationships will have a major impact on how all nations cope with population pressures on environmental resources.

The crudest measure of that relationship is a simple population density measure, that is total land area divided by total population. The three countries differ substantially on their level of population density. In 1998, the world's population density was almost 40 persons per sq. Km. The U. S. Population density was only 28 persons per sq. Km., a level substantially below the world average. The population density in China at 130 people per sq. Km. Is more than three times the world average, even though vast arid areas in the western part of China are sparsely populated. India is one of the more densely populated countries of the world. Its density of 307 people per square km. Puts it at almost eight times the average world population density.

Simple population density can be modified by accounting for low density land set aside for nonresidential urban uses, such as industrial, commercial, and retail uses as well as park lands. Calculation of net residential densities yields a more accurate depiction of population densities, but does not present an overall depiction of the extent of urbanisation. In addition to accounting for different kinds of land uses and land covers in the definition of urbanisation and calculation of population densities, we should also consider that patterns of urbanisation differ from one location to another depending on local topography, land use regulations, cultural preferences, and so forth. To be truly useful for ecological researchers, definitions and measurements of urbanisation should be multi-dimensional, taking into account patterns of urban development from one place to another resulting in differences in levels of population density, concentration of residential or commercial uses within specific areas, mixing of residential and commercial land uses, amount of intervening land devoted to non-urban uses, and so forth.

More important than the density of each country as a whole is the spatial variation within the country. To illustrate differences between population density calculated for administrative units and small statistical geographic areas, we have chosen one site in each country that is at or above the average population density of the nation in which it is located. The Pearl River Delta area including the major districts of Guangdong province surrounding Hong Kong, Macau, and the Pearl River has a density of 893 persons per square kilometre and an official urban population of 70 percent. South Florida is 96 percent urban but much of the population is clustered along the coast while much of the inland area reserved for national parks and conservation areas. As a result, the average density is only 172 persons per sq. Kilometre. At the other extreme, Kerala with an urban percentage of only 26 percent has a dense system of village settlement that leads to a high average population density of 749 persons per sq. Kilometre.

Administratively-based Measures of Urbanisation

Most urban definitions take as a starting point the population living in "urban places." These urban places are primarily administratively defined areas generally with recognised municipal governments. These municipal entities can vary markedly in character as well as in size between nations, within nations, and over time. For example, in the United States, laws pertaining to incorporation and annexation vary from state-to-state. In states with relatively liberal annexation laws, municipalities can annex lands with relatively low population densities, lands that otherwise would be considered rural. Such situations tend to result in over-bounding of urban population and land area. On the other hand, in states with restrictive annexation policies, state laws make it difficult for municipalities to annex adjacent densely populated territory. As a result, when this occurs outside of Census Bureau-defined urbanised areas, the extent of urbanisation often is under bounded in census publications.

The dependence on administratively defined geography to define urban population makes comparisons of levels of urbanisation difficult across the three sites. Additional problems are posed by changing definitions over time. In China the municipal definition has been changed repeatedly—the most recent change resulting in the inclusion of a large number of municipal districts with boundaries that extend well into the countryside. In India, urban population includes the population of all "towns" defined as places with a municipal corporation, municipal area committee, town committee, notified area committee, or cantonment board.

Statistically-based Measures of Urbanisation

Statistical agencies have dealt with the limitations imposed by administrative units by modifying urban definitions in various ways. In India, there has been a definition attempt to include other areas outside of "towns" that met the following qualifications: places having 5,000 or more inhabitants, a density of not less than 1,000 persons per square mile, pronounced urban characteristics, and at least three fourths of the adult male population employed in pursuits other than agriculture. In the United States, the Census Bureau expanded its urban definition in 1950 to include the population in unincorporated places of 2,500 or more and in "urbanised areas" consisting of a central place and the adjacent continuously built-up area.

In the United States and other countries there have been attempts to account for decentralisation of settlement and economic activity by defining "metropolitan areas" that include not only urbanised areas and outlying urban places but also surrounding counties that are integrated with these urban centres as measured by substantial amounts of daily commuting, even if many of these areas have densities far too low to be classified as urban. In the U.S., the metropolitan area concept does not represent an alternative urban area definition, but rather identifies a functional area influenced by an urban centre of significant population size.

Density as a Comparative Measure

These different administrative and statistical definitions make international and temporal comparisons of urban population difficult. The measures of urbanisation, average density, and land use give very different pictures of the three case study areas. In fact, given our interest in the relationship between land and population, the traditional measures of urbanisation are not sufficient to represent the spatial distribution issues. The concepts of urbanisation differ between the countries, over time within each country, and between researchers.

Urbanisation can be viewed as a characteristic of the population, as a characteristic of particular kinds of land uses and land covers, as well as a characteristic of social and economic processes and interactions affecting both population and land. Social scientists—demographers generally, but also urban policy analysts, geographers, and others—generally define levels of urbanisation in terms of population densities. Physical scientists—ecologists especially—generally approach definitions of urbanisation from the standpoint of the built environment. To these researchers, density of buildings and impervious surfaces is just as important, if not more important, as population—indeed, urban ecologists often are concerned with changes to the environment as a result of human alteration of the landscape. McIntyre *et al.* note, however, that among ecologists a wide variety of urban definitions have been used in research, ranging from any human alteration of the landscape to more precise definitions based on density and specified land use characteristics.

Alternatively, regional economists, labour analysts, and related researchers might define urban in terms of the functional area integrated with an urban centre. For these researchers, urban becomes more of a sociological and functional definition than a structural (density-based) phenomenon. Reconciling these different perceptions of what constitutes urbanisation within a single definition poses challenges for any researcher or statistical agency.

Although the authors do not have the access to the detailed level of census tabulations necessary to refine this method for all sites, an example using South Florida can serve as an exposition of how the method might function. In the U. S. Decennial censuses, population are tabulated by small-area geographical units known as census tracts as well as by administrative boundaries such as counties and towns. Census tracts are drawn so as to include approximately 4000 inhabitants and are thus smaller in densely settled areas than in less densely populated areas. The census results by tract include information on both the population and the land area of each tract. Consequently, it is possible to tabulate density distributions of both the population and the land area.

To illustrate such a method, we arranged the 800 census tracts for the seven counties of South Florida (Dade, Broward, Palm Beach, Monroe, Hendry, Collier, and Lee) by their 1990 population density. In table 1 we compare the urban and rural population that are above various density levels to see which level would give a reasonable proxy for the urban population in terms of density. At 300 persons per sq km., 5.8 per cent of the urban population and 12.4 per cent of the rural population would be mis-classified by this simple density cutoff. At 400 persons per sq. Km., 8.7 per cent of the urban population and 4.4 per cent of the rural population would be mis-classified. In fact, for this particular case, a cutoff of about 360 persons per sq. Km. Gives a result in which the percentage of the rural and urban population mis-classified is equal at roughly 7.5 per cent each.

Table 1. Distribution of Census Tracts for Counties of South Florida by Density

Population density per sq. Km	*Percent of urban population above this*	*Percent of rural population above this density*	*Percent of total population above this density*	*Percent of total land area above this density*
100	98.4	42.6	96.1	17.4
200	96.2	25.9	93.2	13.7
300	94.2	12.4	90.8	11.9
400	91.3	4.4	87.6	10.4
500	87.9	3.6	84.3	9.1
600	85.6	2.4	82.1	8.38
700	82.4	2.1	79.0	7.5
800	80.8	1.7	77.4	7.2
900	77.3	1.5	74.1	6.5
1000	73.	1.3	0.1	5.7

To compare across areas, however, a higher density level might be preferable to reduce the likelihood that high density agricultural areas might be included in the high density category. Unfortunately, data with which to assess settlement patterns at similar levels of geographic detail in India and China are limited. However, a very crude idea of how this method might work is across countries can be obtained by using the method for the larger levels of geography (districts) that are published for all three countries. Table 2 shows that a population density of 500 people per sq. Mile applied to the large scale district geography would yield 89.9 percent of the population and 74.8 percent of the land area in high density areas.

Table 2. Distribution of Districts (14) by Density for Kerala, India: 1991

Population density per sq. Km.	*Percent of total population Above this density*	*Percent of total land area above this density*
100	100.0	100.0
200	100.0	100.0
300	96.3	87.1
400	94.0	81.6
500	89.9	74.8
600	78.0	58.2
700	78.0	58.2
800	70.3	50.5
900	53.4	35.7
1000	35.7	21.5

Table 3 shows similar results for the Pearl River Delta with 84.2 percent of the population and 62.2 percent of the land area in high density areas. Given the availability of data for smaller levels of geography for the India and China sites, this measure of high density areas could be useful in making comparative studies that are less influenced by administrative and statistical differences between the countries located in high density areas that are usually thought of as "urban"—and could provide useful information on the percentage of the land area as well as the percentage of the population.

Table 3. Distribution of Districts (13) by Density for Pearl River Delta, China, 1990

Population density per sq. Km.	*Percent of total population Above this density*	*Percent of total land area above this density*
100	100	100
200	100	100
300	95.4	84.3
400	84.2	62.2
500	84.2	62.2
600	73.8	48.0
700	73.8	30.6
800	58.8	30.6
900	51.4	24.0
1000	35.6	24.0

This greater detail on the spatial complexity of each area measured at similar levels of spatial disaggregation could begin to supply the comparative data needed for ecological and other studies across many different societies and landscapes.

Analysis of Urban Population Distributions

Human adaptation to the physical environment has resulted in habitation of almost every boom on Earth yet the current rate of urbanisation represents a significant transition of the human habitat. Within the past 40,000 years the human habitat has expanded over almost all of Earth's ice-free land area. Within the past 4000 years humans have intensified settlement in areas conducive to agriculture and begun to localise in cities. Within the past 40 years the growth rate of large cities has accelerated to the point where the majority of humans will soon live in urban environments. This represents a significant recent change in the human habitat.

Physical environments favourable to hunter-gatherers are fundamentally different from those favourable to pasteurellosis and agriculturists. Similarly, urban settlements often exist in areas unfavourable for agriculture. Throughout most of recorded history the majority of humans have engaged in agriculture so the recent large scale migration to urban centres represents an significant evolutionary transition for the human species. The purpose of this analysis is to quantify the extent to which modern human settlement patterns, specifically large urban areas, occupy different physical environments and to consider the implications of this migration for the sustainability of urban centres.

The environment of a large city is fundamentally different from the environment of smaller settlements in rural settings. The environments differ in terms of physical, biological, social and cultural factors. The focus of this discussion is on the physical factors. The other factors are at least as important as the physical factors but the physical factors are probably the most amenable to simple analysis at global scales. One significant difference between the urban environment and traditional human habitats is related to the energy balance. Solar energy flux is, by far, the largest and most persistent form of energetic exchange that most humans are exposed to on a daily basis. Interestingly, most of this energy is not exploited and an increasing number of humans expend significant amounts of resources in attempts to counteract the effects of solar energy flux. In most rural environments, humans live amidst moderately abundant vegetation but in most urban environments, vegetation is relatively sparse. Vegetation cover has a profound influence on solar energy flux. Vegetation absorbs radiation in the most energetic part of the solar spectrum to conduct photosynthesis. The unused fraction of the incoming solar energy is either transpired with water or reflected at Near

Infrared wavelengths. Most building materials used in the urban mosaic absorb a significant fraction of this incoming solar energy and re-radiate it as sensible heat resulting in the Urban Heat Island phenomenon. An increasing percentage of the human population lives in urban areas where this heat induces physical stress and even loss of life during heat waves. While the average temperature difference between urban and rural environments is small compared to the range of temperatures humans have adapted to, the nature of the physical space in urban areas tends to compound the effect of the heat island. The combination of higher temperature, restricted airflow and increased ozone and particulate concentrations creates a distinct physical environment associated with urban settlements at local scales. On a regional scale, there is also evidence that really extensive urban land cover may influence albedo and transpiration enough to influence local weather patterns near large cities.

Both deliberate and inadvertent human modification of the physical environment occur at different spatial scales. For the purposes of this discussion, micro refers to scales ranging from the individual to hundreds of meters while local scale covers the range from hundreds to tens of thousands of meters and regional refers to scales between tens and hundreds of kilometres. Although humans seem to be influencing the physical environment at all of these scales, deliberate manipulation of the physical environment is limited to micro and local scales. When available, significant resources are expended on "climate control" at the scale of residences and work-spaces. Cities represent extensive habitat modification on scales of tens of kilometres but this modification rarely encompasses deliberate manipulation of physical conditions at these scales. Light levels and water flow are often controlled at local scales but human influence on air temperature and quality is largely inadvertent. At regional and global scales, human influence on these components of the physical environment is not well understood but it could not be considered direct intentional manipulation. Questions related to human modification the physical environment at regional and global scales have been the subject of extensive research within the global change research community for several years now, but the study of local scale urban environments is still a comparatively new field. A complementary, and equally important, form of global change is occurring with the expansion of these urban environments where much of the world's population now resides.

The current demographic shift from sparsely populated rural to densely populated urban environments is a distinct form of global change. It is distinct from other types of global change in the sense that a rapidly increasing number of people are experiencing environmental change, not only as result of the environment of a particular location changing, but also as a result of growth centres shifting to different physical environments.

The regional physical environment of urban areas is often different from the physical environments of its catchment areas in the rural hinter-lands so the localisation of population in cities can result in the exposure of large numbers of people to different regional scale physical environments. On a smaller scale, locations where cities evolve are generally physio-graphically distinct from those of the nearby agricultural production regions.

In some cases, this localisation may result in dense habitation of hazard-prone sites. This is often a consequence of the physiography and climate of the city's location. The following analysis will quantify the extent of this localisation and the relationship of the densely populated areas to physio-graphic and climatic characteristics of the physical environment.

In this global analysis, population distribution and density are determined from the latest Gridded Population of the World (GPW2) population dataset produced by CIESIN in 1999. This compilation of 127,105 census estimates provides a median spatial resolution of 31 km, and allows 90% of the 1990 global population to be located to within 88 km. For the purposes of a global analysis, this dataset provides more than adequate spatial resolution relative to the regional environmental variables that will be considered. Each of the 127105 census estimates links a population count to an administrative area. Dividing the population count by.the area provides an average population density for that area and allows the population to be distributed evenly over the area of the administrative unit.

The spatial resolution of the population data supports inference at scales of tens of kilometres. For the purposes of this analysis, urban areas and population within the GPW2 dataset will be considered as those with a population density greater than 1000 people/sq.km. Justification for using this threshold density is provided by *Pozzi and Small.*

In addition to dense population, we will also consider the urban population living in large cities. In this case, large cities will be considered those with population greater than 1,000,000 people. The United Nations provides an enumeration of 290 cities with population greater than 1 million in 1990. The total population of these 290 cities is 795,009,000 people. By considering both administratively defined large urban areas and dense population two complementary measures of global urban population can be evaluated relative to different physical environmental factors.

Continental Physiography, Climate and Cities

Population are not uniformly distributed on Earth's landmass and neither are physical environments. Quantifying the spatial coincidence of population and environments can give some indication of the factors that may influence human settlement patterns. The spatial relationship between population and the physical environment can be quantified by calculating the distribution of people with respect to a particular parameter that characterises the environment. Environments are often described in terms of climatic parameters related to temperature and precipitation. Both of these parameters vary appreciably at different temporal and spatial scales so averages are often used to summarise the climate of specific locations. Environments are also characterised by landscape or continental physiography. Physio-graphic parameters that might be expected to influence human habitation include elevation and proximity to coastlines and rivers. All of these quantities can be measured or estimated to different degrees of accuracy and resolution and used as a basis on which to calculate global distributions of land area and population.

The distributions of global population, dense population and large cities have implications for the comparative influence of Physio-graphic and climatic components of the physical environment. This simple analysis does not account for micro-climate or the temporal components of climatic environment and, as such, should not be over interpreted. The point is to demonstrate how strongly population and cities are localised relative to Physio-graphic parameters on a global scale. Climate is obviously a very important influence on human settlement but it is presumably less of a constraint on dense urban settlements than on sparse agrarian population. This analysis quantifies the extent to which urban population are environmentally localised compared to the overall global population. The implication is that adaptation to climate change allows the expansion of the human habitat while the physical characteristics of the landscape drive a simultaneous spatial concentration of population within the expanding habitat. This impacts the sustainability of urban settlements because the Physio-graphic environments discussed here are often associated with natural hazards. Low elevation river basins and coastal zones are especially susceptible to the extreme weather events that some climate change scenarios show increases for. The tendency for cities to evolve in hazard prone Physio-graphic environments combined with the increasing shift of population from rural to urban environments implies that more people will be exposed to natural hazards as this transition progresses. Dense settlements in hazard prone locations expose large numbers of people to risk but at the same time the financial and organisational resources of some cities may allow for more effective hazard mitigation than would be possible for dispersed population. In any case, the current growth rate of urban population suggests that the impact of natural hazards on the global population may change.

9

Urban Growth and Human Development

The basic challenge facing post-industrial societies is not rural-urban co-development but sustainable development. In this perspective sustainability is the aim and rural-urban co-development one of the necessary ways. Thus, the point of departure for this note will be the connection between ecology and sustainability, followed by an introduction of society into that connection.

The World Commission emphasised the concept of sustainability in 1987. The term *sustainable development* was reshaped to describe a solution to current threats to the global society: unequal distribution of resources in time and space implying overuse of non-renewable resources besides pollution that damage natural mechanisms. Both overuse and pollution represent a fatal threat upon the future prospects of the human species and imply the need of radical changes. Sustainable development was then introduced as the headline of the necessary radical changes. In the meantime sustainability has been interpreted and used in a widespread range of contexts that infer the necessity to state the basics.

Natural Life Support Systems

In relation to natural life support systems sustainability

presumes two crucial points. One, actions that involve hazardous damage to the basic cyclical mechanisms must be avoided. Two, balance between the number of organisms - i.e., number of rabbits and amount of lettuce - must be ensured. So, we have to consider both function and capacity.

In nature, food is nothing but a biological input and the system is outbalanced by its own means. Problems do arise when one of the species (i.e., mankind) evolves and applicates skills (i.e., technology) to offset or modify the function, or to go beyond the bounds of the system's carrying capacity for instance due to overuse of resources. When so, mankind incurs responsibility in relation to *sine qua non* for fellow men in both time and space.

When human beings have entered the picture, it is also necessary to consider sustainability and natural life support systems from a social point of view and then ask: Does present social organisation support or counteract damage according to function and balance according to capacity?

Related to the latter questions complex difficulties emerge, as food in the modern world is not only a biological input but a commodity too. Then supplementary food is a source of revenue to farmers, industries, distributors, scientists, bureaucrats, etc. Besides, these actors are gathered in social institutions and are parts of societal structures. These complex structures and institutions - producing and reproducing social experience and knowledge -can support or counteract sustainability. From a social scientific point of view structures and institutions in which technology is adapted and evolved are then important analytical concepts when sustainability is studied. Structures are the material and institutions the immaterial framings of society.

Role of Technology

Now focus is turned to human production and a couple of statements about technology are needed. It is a basic function of any society to provide and ensure means by which the members can comply their reproductive needs. These imply productive activities; technology then becomes a crucial affair from a social point of view and a sphere by which a society might be characterised.

'Technology' is in everyday comprehension most often interpreted as similarly to technical devices and matters. This implies an inadequate limitation of the conceptual meaning where crucial social dimensions are cut off. In the Greek origin the concept consist of two parts, *techne* and *logos*. *Techne* is art and craft while *logos* is knowledge.

Combining *techne* and *logos* we face productive and reproductive activities, the tools, the labour with certain skills and knowledge, and the way in which the activities are organised. Tools are technical devices as machinery, hand tools, buildings, etc.—equipment that in economics are labelled as real capital. The labour is not only the physical power of human beings but particularly their skills and knowledge provided by their individual and social experience and by research and development. Skills and knowledge pertain to the ways in which the tools are effectively used in correspondence with material and labour. Organisation of the activities, however, pertain to the social framings in which the productive activities are carried out besides the relations between the elements included in the productive activities. Putting this into an actual approach seen from a social point of view implies the necessity to understand technology as consisting of three elements:

i) Technical devices,

ii) Skills/knowledge, and

ii) Social organisation.

So, technology is related to technical matters considered in the social context; the latter being the social framings in which techniques and tools are applied and organised. In this sense technology is dealing with social organisation of productive activities and the inclusion of nature in these. In this sphere it is also determined whether the productive activities are sustainable. That is so because it is in the social organisation that the interplay between human activities and natural life support systems is determined. Just one step further is needed in the investigation of technology to underline that point.

The material structure in which the productive activities are carried out consists of two main parts: those made by nature and those moderated by man. Both are necessary conditions to carry out social production; for that reason social production must be based on two kinds of productive forces, i.e., the ecological and the social. The ecological productive forces should here cover natural capital and natural mechanisms that in unity provides the fundamental basis for human life—so ecological productive forces are the forces embedded in natural life support systems. The social productive forces—embedded in societies—should here cover the human performance by means of labour and real capital. It is important to underline that the working capacities involve a physical dimension (the labour of hands) and a mental dimension (the labour of mind)—the latter for instance the ability to co-operate and learn, cognisance, etc.

The latter dimension could also be labelled as human resources. Among the two productive forces, the ecological is claimed to take precedence over the social due to the obvious fact that the ecological forces can exist (i.e., produce and be reproduced) independent of the social forces while the opposite situation is impossible. The ability of the social productive forces to produce and reproduce is fatally depending upon the ecological forces regarding both natural capital and natural mechanisms. The human reproduction (for the individual as well as for the species) is for instance only possibly by means of biological mechanisms;

simultaneously construction of real capital is only possible by means of natural resources converted by means of human labour. As individuals, society, and species we therefore bear a fatal interest in and responsibility for maintaining the natural capital and avoiding damaging intervention in natural mechanisms when we carry out productive activities. Although the social productive forces rest upon the ecological, we have of course to be careful and bear forethought in our use of social productive forces too.

Agriculture and the Environment

From the comments above follow that technology (and then human interplay and exchange with natural life support systems) both affect and depend upon social environs. To introduce fundamentally new technologies it is necessary to alter the institutional and structural design of society. When the social design is altered rigidity occur in a new epoch and tend to keep technological evolution locked in the new direction and evaluated against the new rationality.

The peasant production system went through changes when conversion into livestock production took place in several countries around the year 1900. However, the applied technology was still founded so that the farm constituted an ecological unit part of a local and transparent cycle including livestock and grain production using very limited external inputs. This system implied a high degree of farm self supply in relation to energy and raw materials. It implied a certain consciousness too. The transparent reliance and dependence upon natural life support systems did provide the foundation for a cyclical common notion of nature as well as of society. This notion was often explicitly stated as a comprehension concerning property rights of future generations: the soil should at least be passed on to the next generation as fertile as received from the past. Basis for this comprehension was experience and knowledge; if the farmer managed his livestock or soil contrary to the biological logic of ecological cycles he would experience negative productive reactions from both livestock and soil. These negative reactions would further result in negative economic performance and then economic pressure on the family. Shortage of material opportunities could of course force the families to act as short-sighted and then to ignore long term considerations. However, without romanticising the past, one can conclude that in those times farming technology was ecological; and a functional integrity was maintained between labour (often the farmer and his family) and the local natural life support system.

The surplus from the ecological cycle—produced by means of photosynthesis, labour and natural capital (primarily soil)—could be exchanged with the external economy. However, this exchange took for a major part place at the local level implying a relatively close relationship between the producer and the consumer—in other words, the social cycle too was transparent and rather horizontal. This implied that the consumer could personally experience the ecological cycles, while the farmer simultaneously could face the consumer and receive reactions from the latter concerning the food supplied. This user-producer relationship was basis for a mutual understanding and for directly sharing of the responsibilities attached. Similarly the farmer could in general experience how the potential spill over would affect the environs and how the input to his farm was provided.

Industrialisation of Farming

After World War II industrialisation of farming was speeded up which in turn implied a rather rapid technological transformation. However, the scientific basis was for a great part already established in the mid-19th century primarily attributed to the German chemist, Justus von Liebig. He laid down the theoretical foundation for applying chemicals in agriculture stating that the plants should only be supplied with water-soluble nutrients produced in an artificial/ industrial way. In his alternative statement Liebig simultaneously and explicitly rejected the common conception of that time which stated that efficiency of the living microbes in soil was the key to adequate and efficient farming. By means of Liebig's alternative approach the dynamic comprehension of natural life support systems—as farming was understood hitherto—could be substituted by a more clinical and industrial notion of an input-output production system. This system was to a high degree designed as decoupled from local natural life support systems and potentially also decoupled from local community.

In the mid-20th century the theoretical basis as well as an affiliated notion of decoupled relations between man and natural life support systems had thus already been offered for about 100 years. So the agricultural innovation in the mid-20th century did not reflect a new scientific but rather a new social invention. The structural and institutional framework of agriculture became transformed to enable implementation of this alternative technology quite in line with the view upon technology and in line with the current social experience of that time: the evolution of fordistic industries had prepared a general heavy increase in wealth. A structural and institutional transformation was necessary why industrialisation of agriculture implied increasing amounts produced per farm besides provision of equipment and industrial intermediates. Production and distribution of knowledge had to be altered too in accordance with the alternative technology and its alternative notions.

Introducing industrial technology in farming then involved a distinct break with the up to then practised relation between man and the natural life support systems besides a similar break with attached notions. According to industrial practices and notions the peasant was transformed into a specialised producer organising his production relatively detached from the ecological cycles looking upon soil.

Direct interrelation and interaction with natural capital and biological mechanisms were to a still wider degree substituted by technical approaches enabling an endless reiteration of similar processes on similar objects. This reiteration on similar objects implied a need to adjust the objects—fields and animals—to similarity. Simultaneously the main part of the necessary inputs was reached outside the local ecological cycle and then outside the local natural life support system; for instance energy and industrial raw material. Besides, the application of various chemical inputs, such as pesticides and antibiotics, implied that biological indications of mistreatment were missed. Indications such as crop rotation and livestock diseases were no longer interpreted as symptoms of the farmer's inadequate knowledge and experience but as inevitable parts of production.

According to the new approach such symptoms should just be cured through appliance of systematic—most often chemical treatment. Finally, the detachment involved a new demarcation between crop and livestock production by which manure tended to be interpreted as troublesome waste and not as a valuable and integrated element in an efficient symbiosis between livestock and soil.

Thus, the cyclic ecological relation between man and nature was substituted by a linear relation where agriculture to a certain extent became detached from living biology and interpreted and organised as an iterative production process; input at one end and output at the other. Nature then became an outdistanced object and the functional integrity between man and nature tended to disappear. The conversion also implied new fields of experience whereafter human learning about agriculture and natural life support systems changed. Where the peasant of the past experienced that actions adverse to basic ecology (knowledge about fundamental principles of cycles in nature) would give a negative pay off, the modern farmer experienced that actions adverse to industrial logic would give a negative pay off—for instance if he avoided pesticides. Certainly, not because the nature or the logic of its fundamental mechanisms was transformed but because the social institutions and structures around agriculture were so.

Supplementary the industrialisation caused a decoupling from the local level, whereafter inputs were provided from industries around the world and the farmer lost the breath of view of the interrelated connections his farm became part of.

Thus he lost insight into the production of his inputs and the subsequent dependence on natural life support systems in various parts of the world. Farmers' horizontal integration was then substituted by vertical, international integration where the individual farmer became a tiny part in an international system hard or impossible to take in. This internationalisation also implied that farmers tended to be separated from consumers who became spread all over the world and then became rather invisible. Governmental institutions took over responsibility for the veterinary quality and thus should secure that consumers did not catch diseases from eating the food—the personal user-producer relationship then disappeared. Similarly spill over—for instance pesticides—from farming seemingly disappeared out in nowhere whether these occurred at the farms providing food to the processing enterprises or at the farms in other parts of the world producing produce as input to the former farm.

POST-INDUSTRIAL SOCIETY AND SUSTAINABILITY

Over the past decades an increasing awareness has been dawning in the so-called developed world that sustainable development is necessary to alleviate local, national and global problems afflicting the natural environment. It is suggested that this acknowledgement can be understood on the background of changes in values (related to mass belief systems) that can be attributed to the transition from an industrial to a post-industrial and post-material epoch in our rich part of the world. It is further suggested to be seen as a consequence of experiences with the irreversible and fatal environmental effects that modern technologies can result in.

The post-industrial responses to the awareness about human misuse of natural life support systems have so far been of three kinds:

1) Several local, national, and global meetings supplemented by an endless stream of documents.

2) A marginal number of green consumers and producers trying to do something in delimited sectors like renewable energy and organic food.

3) Governmental regulations *after* natural life support systems have been damaged.

To put it polemical the comments on the reactions could be:

1) Words do not make a sustainable technology. It is not by means of words but by means of actions we poison our drinking water and damage the ozone layer.

2) We do not turn society into a sustainable trajectory by eating an organic roast on Sundays and junk food the rest of the week.

3) We do not reach sustainability if we keep on fighting symptoms and leave the fundamental causes unaffected.

This is of course an unfair and derogatory judgement. The efforts made by grass root activists and well-meaning politicians and bureaucrats ought not to be underestimated -

they represent essential social actors. However, the polemic characteristic brings forward the crucial point: a more comprehensive and fundamental modification of behaviour towards sustainability has yet to be attained. This is the case although most of us presumably know—and many of us obviously know—that a good deal of our actions are not sustainable; but with the current institutional framework and the social structures within which we act, we can only hardly do otherwise.

The comprehensive modifications of behaviour have fundamental changes in social structures and institutions as a prerequisite. One of these changes is re-establishment of rural-urban co-development founded on a conscious recognition of the basics of natural life support systems; under here it is necessary to recognise that urban areas have evolved as heterotroph without adequate linkages to recipient technologies in rural areas. From a social point of view such points call for a new design of social structures and institutions where regard for function and capacity in natural life support systems is couched in the basis for the social rationale just as is the case with democracy and human rights. By the way, who would for instance seriously calculate whether the monetary benefits in current prices would exceed the monetary costs if we abandon freedom of speech?

It is asserted above that a new institutional and structural design of post-industrial society is an urgent task if serious threats to human prospects should be avoided. To gain such sustainability, respect for the ecological forces of production is a prerequisite. On the other hand it is also necessary to recognise that the purpose of society's productive efforts is to meet human needs *and* in fulfilling that task, the social forces of production are a prerequisite too. Thus we must consider two productive forces and two allocation systems related to human production and then to technology. An allocation system exists within natural life support systems that is independent of man. Due to technology and the ensuing production, humanity has introduced its own supplementary system of allocation (economy within politically established frames). The human allocation system has implications for the ecological forces of production. Ecology concerns the allocation and circulation of matter in the environment, while economy concern society's allocation and circulation of exchange value between citizens. Both ecology and economy are realities that are necessary for human production and reproduction. So, we cannot abolish ecology nor economy. Conversely we can change the institutional and structural framings for the economy and so politically determine society's trajectory.

Hence, the challenge is to design social institutions and structures so that they escape the current mismatch between the two necessary allocative systems: ecology and economy. This is as far as we can get by now, because we are only equipped with a vague sense of what that design actually should entail when carried out in practice. So it is claimed that no one—for the time being—has a final recipe. Thus, the necessary knowledge and experience must be produced. We can use inspiration from the past—for instance acknowledge lessons from the peasant system as introduced above and as included in the *principles* of organic farming. But we can not turn the clock backwards and return to previous trajectories and if we could why then abandon progress that humanity after all has endeavoured in the time between now and then?

The proper and adequate solution is to carry out social experiments to produce the necessary knowledge and experience concerning institutional and structural design of sustainable technology in a post-industrial society. In this connection it must again be remembered that technology both consists of technique and society's organisation, and that sustainability involves the relationship of technology to the ecological forces of production. Sustainability is therefore not necessarily synonymous with substitution of existing techniques—we do not necessarily have to wait for new inventions and innovations on the technical level. Evolving *organisation* of society, which is the other dimension of technology, can advance more sustainable utilisation of the ecological forces of production, even in the short-term and with the continuing adaptation of existing error-friendly[2] techniques. Here it should also be remembered that organisation of society includes the relation between rural and urban activities.

In Denmark Ecological Experimental Areas (EEA's) are suggested as means to carry out the necessary experiments. EEA are geographically specified areas where communities can conduct experiments concerning the means by which not only delimited sub-sectors but an entirely sustainable society can evolve. It is pointed out that the EEA's must be founded in existing communities because the aim is to explore how present society can evolve institutions and structures supporting sustainable technology as an entire and consistent system able to produce and reproduce. Furthermore, basis in existing communities implies experiments concerning both the process and the substance. The *process* because the findings will indicate how to evolve society from the present stage to a sustainable stage. The *substance* because the findings will indicate how to design social framings that enable a sustainable interplay between the ecological and economic allocative systems.

If such experiments are to be meaningful then they must naturally have a high degree of freedom to gain experiences via trial and error. Indeed, they must be empowered to extricate from the current social framings that are the cause of present mismatch and social traps. But it must nevertheless be maintained that there is an indispensable objective for the experiments that they must seek a suitable design of society that promotes sustainable technology in a post-industrial society. In the design of institutional and structural framings for zones as EEA it is then of fundamental importance that the ecological forces of production are consciously reintegrated, and that one is deliberate about procuring the necessary empowerment to avoid social traps.

Delimited sub-technologies such as organic agriculture and renewable energy are developed with matching partial conceptions and stand together with historical inspiration available for the experiments. The challenge is to connect these delimited sub-technologies in interaction with, and with the utilisation of, other relevant technological conquests for entire systems of human production and reproduction. In this connection it is also necessary to carry out adaptations, changes, and the further development of these conquests.

Trends in Human Development

Human beings are distinguished among all living species by their capacity to develop and think. Though development is often measured in terms of so many miles of roads, number of tall buildings, airports, cars, TVs, computers etc., it is not things and places alone that define development. Development must be people centric. Twenty years hence, the people of India will be more numerous, better educated, healthier and more prosperous than at any other time in our long history. Having eradicated the scourge of famine that plagued the country for centuries, we still confront the challenging tasks of providing a nutritious diet to all our children, educating our teeming masses, abolishing epidemic diseases and creating employment opportunities for all our citizens.

Today India is the second most populous country in the world, with about 1.04 billion people, home to a-sixth of humanity. Although it is difficult to accurately predict population growth rates 20 years to the future, we expect this number to rise by another 300-350 million, in spite of continuous efforts to reduce fertility rates. This would raise the total population to about 1330 million by 2020.

India is in the process of a demographic transition from high fertility, high mortality and stable population to low fertility, low mortality and stable population. This transition is a global phenomenon generated by the improved availability and access to modern health care that sharply reduced mortality rates and increased life expectancy. The Crude death rate has declined to one-third of its level in 1941 and the expectation of life at birth has nearly doubled during this period. Falling mortality rates have been followed by a steady decline in birth rates, but this decline has not been as steep as the fall in death rate; even after reaching the replacement fertility rates, the population will continue to grow because of large numbers of young persons entering reproductive age.

While assessing future prospects, it is necessary to take into account the vast regional differences in demographic parameters. Population growth has recently decelerated below 2 per cent for the first time in four decades, but not uniformly across the length and breadth of the country. Several States in south India have already reached, or are about to attain, the replacement level of fertility that would ensure a zero growth rate of population in the long run. On the other hand, in many states in north India, characterised by high fertility rates, it may take several decades to reach the replacement level of fertility. There are also similar differentials in levels of mortality, especially in infant and child mortality.

At the national level, two alternate scenarios for achieving population stabilisation have been considered. In the optimistic scenario, which is based on achieving the demographic goals of the National Population Policy 2000, life expectancy is assumed to rise to 71 for males and 74 for females by 2020. Under the realistic scenario, life expectancy is assumed to reach 65 for males and 69 for females by 2020. Under either scenario India's population would exceed 1.3 billion in the year 2020.

In both cases the sex ratio of population (females per 1000 males) would marginally increase from 932 in 2000 to 950 in 2020; reversing the historical trend of falling sex ratio is expected in the 21st Century. We can be more certain of the changes in the age structure of the population as given in Table 1.

Table 1. Population Projections (millions)

Year	2000	2005	2010	2015	2020
Total	1010	1093	1175	1256	1331
Under 15	361	368	370	372	373
15-64	604	673	747	819	882
65+	45	51	58	65	76

Actually, the population under-15 years is expected to increase only marginally over the next 20 years. This means that pressure for expansion of the educational system will come only from increasing enrolment and efforts to reduce drop-out rates.

The largest growth of population will be in the 15-64 year age group, which will expand by about 46 per cent by 2020 (i.e, annually by 1.9 per cent as against the population growth of much lower, at 1.4 per cent). As shown in Table 1, it is expected to rise from 604 million in 2000 to 883 million in 2020, i.e., from 60 to 66 per cent of the total population. This rise will accentuate the need for challenge of reducing fertility and increasing employment opportunities, so that the family size comes down and incomes rise.

The elderly population is also expected to rise sharply from 45 to 76 million, (i.e., by 2.6 per cent per annum) and their share in the total population would rise from 4.5 to 5.7 per cent. As a consequence of these age structural changes, the age-dependency ratio (ratio of non-working age population to working age population) is expected to fall from 67 per cent in 2000 to 46 per cent in 2020, although the percentage of elderly people to population will increase.

Food Security

The single most important implication of India's rapid population growth during the second half of the twentieth century was the threat it posed to national food security. That threat reached dangerous proportions in the mid-1960s, leading to the launching of the Green Revolution, achievement of food self-sufficiency, and subsequently, a growing stock of surplus food grains by the mid-1970s. Happily, such a threat no longer exists for the country. Growth of food production has exceeded population growth for each of the past three decades.

Statistics present a confusing picture of India's progress on food security. Both per capita food grain consumption and total calorific intake have declined slightly in recent years among all levels of the population. At the same time, grain surpluses have reached peak levels and real per capita expenditure on food is rising among all income groups. The factors influencing this trend are numerous and complex, however, it can be primarily attributed to:

i) Reduction in calorie requirement due to a more sedentary life style among both the rural and urban population. Bicycle and bus travel, mechanised pumps and equipments, access to telephones and newspapers have reduced the physical work to a greater or lesser extent for most Indians.

ii) Diversification of the Indian diet to include a larger intake of fruits, vegetables, dairy products, sugar, oil and pulses, eggs, fish and meat products, thereby reducing the required intake of calories from cereals.

However, the challenge of achieving food security for all our people remains a real one even today, and will continue to demand our attention in the coming decades. Food security depends on both availability of food and access to it. Long-term food security requires not only producing sufficient food to meet the market demand, but also ensuring that all citizens have the required purchasing power to obtain the food they need for a nutritious and healthy life. India has won the first battle, but the second still looms large. By best estimates, nearly half of the population still suffers from chronic under-nutrition. The most vulnerable are children, women and the elderly, specially among the lower income groups. While the number of children suffering from severe malnutrition declined significantly in the 1990s, the prevalence of mild and moderate under-nutrition, especially among those in the lower 30 per cent income group, is still high. Prevalence of micro nutrient deficiencies such as anemia is also very high.

The problem of chronic macro and micro nutrient under-nutrition cannot be addressed simply by increases in food production or the accumulation of larger food buffer stocks. Nor has the public distribution system been able to effectively target the most needy in an effective manner. Targeted food for work programmes and targeted nutrition programmes can alleviate the problem temporarily. But in the long run, the solution is to ensure employment opportunities for all citizens so that they acquire the purchasing power to meet their nutritional requirements. Thus, employment or livelihood security becomes an essential and inseparable component of a comprehensive strategy for national food security and must be considered as one of the nation's highest priorities. Increasing food consumption alone is not a sufficient condition for overcoming malnutrition in India. It is also necessary to address the factors responsible for the high incidence of gastrointestinal and respiratory infections as well as cultural factors responsible for faulty child feeding and weaning practices. Assured provision of safe drinking water, improved health care and education for all women are necessary elements of a comprehensive strategy to eliminate malnutrition and achieve the goal of Food for All before 2020.

India's population is still rapidly expanding. Living standards are rising and slated to rise faster than in the past. As they rise, both calorific intake and diversification of diet will increase significantly. Although a portion of this increase can and will be obtained from abroad, a fulfilling vision of India 2020 depicts this nation—with its conducive and varied climate, the largest irrigated area in the world and a vast farming population—as a major food exporter. Both as a challenge and as an opportunity, India can and must do much more to modernise and diversify its agriculture to meet the increased domestic and international demand for a wide variety of food products.

Continued growth of the agriculture sector is particularly important because it plays such a vital role in generating purchasing power among the rural population. Therefore, it is essential that agricultural development strategies for the 21st Century focus on generating both higher incomes and greater on-farm and off-farm employment opportunities.

India is now entering the fourth stage of agricultural transformation. The Green Revolution phase spread in the north-western and southern states from the mid-1960s to the mid-1980s. From the early 1980s, it spread rapidly in the central and to a lesser extent the eastern states. This, coupled with a further growth of productivity in the north-western and southern states, enabled India to achieve a 3.77 per cent annual growth rate in agricultural production during the 1980s. The overall growth slowed to 2.72 per cent in the 1990s, which was associated with a reduction in public investment in both agriculture and agricultural research, slower growth of fertilizer consumption and the area under high yielding varieties, and degradation of soils.

There is enormous scope for accelerating growth in agriculture, through improved soil nutrition and pest management, diversification into higher value-added crops, expansion and more efficient use of irrigation potential, rainwater harvesting, and infrastructure development for agro-processing industries. India's productivity on major crops ranks far below the world average. This low productivity contributes to low farm incomes and wages, lower on-farm employment generation, and relatively high food prices for all Indians. Average yields from tomato cultivation, for example, are 76 per cent higher in Mexico and more than four times higher in the USA, while average yields on seed cotton are more than four times higher in Mexico and three times higher in USA.

Even within India, some progressive farmers have achieved yields comparable to their foreign counterparts till recently; but these high achievers are a rare exception. Progressive farming must become the rule and the standard. Raising the productivity of our soil and water resources is an effective way to increase the profit margins of farmers, while at the same time reducing the cost of farm produce, so that it is more affordable to the masses. A minimum target should be to double or triple the average yields of major commercial crops. This will reduce pressure on scarce land and water resources as well as enable the country to utilise less fertile areas for other purposes.

Tapping the full potential of Indian agriculture to meet the rising domestic demand and to take advantage of the liberalisation of international trade will require, first and foremost, the recognition of the vital role that agriculture can continue to play in national development. The other necessary conditions are: greater public investment in research; expansion and development of rural infrastructure including roads, storage capacity and organised markets; improved farmer education; effective involvement of the private sector to provide technology, investment and organisational expertise for commercialisation; and modification of land regulations to achieve greater production efficiency.

A suitable land use pattern will also need to be implemented, based on the principle that each region would focus on crops best suited to their agro-climatic characteristics, soil types and water resources. Strong measures will also be needed to address the problem of land degradation that affects an estimated 45 per cent of total land area. India's objective for 2020 must not only be to produce the food its population requires but also to fully exploit the comparative advantages it possesses—agro-climatic variety, irrigation, scientific capabilities and low labour cost— to become a low cost, high profit producer for the world market.

Business-as-usual (BAU) assumes that growth of production continues at the same rates as during the 1990s. The Best-case scenario (BCS) assumes that production grows at the higher rates achieved during the 1980s. Even under the BAU, India will be able to meet the projected demand in all five food categories. This indicates that more emphasis can be placed on diversifying production to other value added agricultural products.

India needs to sustain an agricultural growth rate of 4.0 to 4.5 per cent in order to reduce food insecurity and poverty, while increasing rural purchasing power. At this growth rate, agricultural development could more rapidly diversify into horticulture, fishery, dairying, animal husbandry and other areas. It would also spur the growth of agro-processing industries in rural areas. Such an achievement is well within reach, provided there is the requisite commitment to raising crop productivity through dissemination of advanced technologies; increasing investment in irrigation, research and training; water harvesting and improved access to credit.

While food production should be able to comfortably meet the total domestic demand, there will still be sections of the population that require assistance in order to meet their nutritional requirements. In view of the high cost and inefficiency of the public food distribution system, reform should directly target the most vulnerable sections, which can be more effectively accomplished through programmes such as food vouchers or food stamps. For the vast majority of the population, food security can best be achieved by ensuring creation of gainful employment opportunities for all job seekers.

Employment

Population, food security, education and remunerative employment opportunities are closely interconnected. Rising levels of education and rising living standards are powerful levers for reducing birth and mortality rates. As population growth slows to replacement levels over the next two decades, India's greatest challenge will be to expand the opportunities for the growing labour force, to enrich their knowledge and skills through education, raise their living standards through gainful employment and make provisions for ensuring a good life for the aged. India has met the challenge of producing sufficient food to feed everyone, but it has yet to meet the challenge of generating sufficient employment opportunities to ensure that all its people have the purchasing power to obtain the food they require. Gainful employment is one of the most essential conditions for food security and economic security. Conversely, food security is an essential requirement for raising the productivity of India's workforce to international levels.

India's labour force has reached 375 million approximately in 2002, and it will continue to expand over the next two decades. The actual rate of that expansion will depend on several factors including population growth, growth of the working age population, labour force participation rates, educational enrolment at higher levels and school drop-out rates. Projections based on these parameters indicate that India's labour force will expand by 7 to 8.5 million per year during the first decade of this century, and will increase by a total of about 160-170 million by 2020, i.e., 2.0 percent per annum.

Total unemployment in India has been estimated to be about 35 million persons in 2002. This figure takes into account the significant level of underemployment and seasonal variations in the availability of work. It also reflects wide variations in the rate of unemployment among different age groups and regions of the country. Approximately three-fourth of the unemployed are in rural areas and three-fifth among them are educated. The recent trends towards shedding excess labour to improve competitiveness and increasing capital intensity have further aggravated the situation. A clear consensus is now emerging that major changes in economic policy and strategy will be needed to meet the country's employment needs.

Future rates of unemployment will depend on a range of factors, including the growth rate of the labour force and changes in the structure of employment between different sectors, as well as the growth rate of the economy. Adopting the higher number takes us closer to understanding the full magnitude of the challenge the country faces for providing employment opportunities for all its people. India needs to generate on the order of 200 million additional employment opportunities over the next 20 years.

The first question that inevitably arises is whether generating nine or ten million jobs a year is feasible, and that naturally begets the question of what rates of economic growth would be required for achieving this. However logical and inevitable it may sound, we believe this is the wrong way to approach the problem. The right question to ask is: How important is it to us as a nation to create employment opportunities for all? The answer here is simple. It is extremely important. It is as important to create job opportunities for all citizens in a market economy as it is to provide universal suffrage to all adults in a democracy. Access to employment is an essential component of freedom of economic choice. Absence of such opportunity means depriving our young not only of economic freedom but of hope as well. India's vision for 2020 must be founded on the premise of gainful Jobs for All. Access to employment should not only be a top priority of the government but a constitutionally guaranteed fundamental human right.

But can we possibly achieve such an ambitious goal and that too within the framework of a non-subsidised market economy? In order to answer this question, first of all we need to recognise that the economy we build over the next two decades and the jobs we create will be products of the decisions we make, not some irreversible logic of economic science. It is we, the nation, that have to decide what we want to accomplish and how serious we are about doing it, how willing we are to change our attitudes and to alter our policies to achieve this desirable goal. We conclude that if the will and determination are present, the goal is achievable.

Achieving full employment will require a reorientation of national priorities, technology policy and government action. Until now, planning to achieve national goals has been largely done on a sector-wise basis by respective ministries assigned with the responsibility. These parallel lines of planning need to be integrated around a central vision and set of goals, of which full employment must be one. As we have incorporated an environmental analysis into all our planning, every plan initiative needs also to be re-evaluated to consider its impact on employment.

Despite a persistent tendency to associate employment with large industry in the organised sector, an in-depth examination of employment potentials makes it evident that the largest share of new jobs will come from the unorganised sector. In evaluating the importance of developing each sector, we must include an assessment of its potential contribution to employment. Such an assessment will have to be made for the unorganised sector, which currently contributes 92 per cent of the country's employment and generates seven times greater labour intensity per unit of production, as compared to the organised sector. The public organised sector has been and will continue to shed jobs. Although the private organised sector will contribute significantly to the growth of the economy, its contribution to the overall employment generation will be quite modest, since total employment in this sector currently represents only 2.5 per cent of all jobs. Even if this sector grows by 30 per cent per annum, over five years it will contribute less than one per cent to the growth of the workforce.

International comparisons reveal that small and medium enterprises (SMEs) create the majority of jobs. In the USA, nearly half of the private workforce is employed in small firms, of which three-fifth have less than five employees. In Japan, 78 per cent of jobs are generated by small and medium enterprises. The small and medium manufacturing enterprises in Korea account for 99 per cent of all manufacturing enterprises and 69 per cent of employment in this sector. Therefore, the unorganised sector, including small and medium enterprises, must play a central role in the country's employment strategy. This will require modification of policies and programmes to level the playing field, improve availability of credit, increase productivity, raise quality consciousness and competitiveness, and enhance job quality.

Recent experiences of different countries in the context of globalisation also demonstrate that SMEs are better insulated from the pressures generated by the volatility of world trade and capital markets. They are more resistant to the stresses, and more responsive to the demands of the fast-changing technologies and entrepreneurial responses. Indeed, they are observed to be a very important vehicle for new technology adoption and entrepreneurial development. What is true of the most developed countries today will be true for India in 2020. SMEs will play a crucial role in ensuring India's international competitiveness and its rapid assimilation of new technologies.

An assessment of the different sectors reveals a vast untapped employment potential in a wide range of fields for unskilled, semi-skilled, skilled and professionally educated workers. Table 2 provides a list of specific sectors with the largest gross employment potential per unit of output.

The growth of food grain production may not lead to a significant growth in on-farm employment opportunities. However, there is substantial scope for creating new jobs through watershed development programmes, expansion of the area under irrigated cultivation, raising crop yields which increases labour intensity, and diversification of cropping patterns into cash crops—especially vegetables and horticultural crops. Together, these could generate upwards of 20 to 30 million new on-farm employment opportunities during the next decade.

Table 2. High Employment Potential Sectors

- Commercial agriculture
- Agro-industry & agri-business
- Afforestation for pulp, fuel & power
- Retail and wholesale trade
- Tourism
- Housing
- Construction
- Garment industry
- Other small scale & medium industries
- IT & IT enabled services
- Education
- Health
- Financial services
- Transport
- Communications
- Community services

India processes less than 2 per cent of its fruit and vegetable products, as compared with 70 to 80 per cent in countries such as Brazil, Malaysia and Philippines. The development of downstream processing, packaging and distribution activities can generate millions of additional off-farm jobs. Policies are needed to attract greater private sector participation in terms of land development, production and processing technologies, investment, management and marketing. A concerted effort to fully develop the potentials of agri-business could generate millions of additional jobs.

The recorded forest area constitutes about 23 per cent of the geographical area (about 71 million hectares) of the country, but half of this area is degraded. Hence, it is unable to play an important role in environmental sustainability and in meeting the forest produce needs of the people, the industry and other sectors. India has more than 50 million hectares of degraded wasteland that lie outside the national forests, in addition to 30 million hectares within protected areas. In spite of this huge expanse, the country is a net importer of forest products to the extent of $2.5 billion annually. Afforestation of India's vast expanse of wastelands and depleted forest areas for production of wood pulp, timber, fuel, fodder, biomass power, edible and ·fuel soil, fuel, herbs and medicinal plants for exports can create millions of jobs, while reversing environmental degradation and supporting industrial development. Every two hectares of additional area placed under plantation of forest crop such as bamboo, casuarina, eucalyptus or oil-bearing plants can generate year-round employment for one person. Development of forests can generate 10 to 15 million additional employment opportunities over the next five year plan period and increase the livelihood opportunities of low income families during the transition period, while educational levels are rising and other sectors of the economy are developing.

The contribution of primary sector employment to the total workforce has been coming down very slowly, to 56-57 per cent in 1999-2000, and should decrease to about 51 per cent by 2006-2007. This slow rate of decline is likely to continue for at least a decade, because of the hidden under-employment in the agriculture sector, partly compensated for by the vast potential for additional job creation by crop diversification and afforestation. Increasing prosperity in agriculture will naturally lead to the growth of non-farm jobs in agri-industries, agro-business and other occupations required to meet the needs of an increasingly prosperous farming community. During the second decade of the 21st Century, increasing domestic demand for manufactured products and services, coupled with more rapid mechanisation of agriculture will draw in more and more people to non-farm occupations. By 2020, total employment in agriculture may fall to less than 45 per cent, while the share of the services sector increases proportionately.

The small scale industries (SSI) sector accounts for 95 per cent of industrial units, 40 per cent of value addition, 35 per cent of exports, and 80 per cent of manufacturing employment. Registered SSI units provide nearly 18 million jobs in the country at this time. Among manufacturing sectors, the single largest employment potential is in textiles, which is slated to generate 7 million jobs over the next five years alone. More than 40 per cent of these jobs are in garment production units in the SSI sector. A healthy and rapidly expanding small sector is essential for a vibrant growth of the Indian economy as a whole. This sector serves as the field for entrepreneurship to flourish, as an entry point for new entrepreneurs who can start small and then grow, as a vehicle for extending the regional spread of industry, as a laboratory for development of innovative products and services, and as an essential support to attract large manufacturing assembling industries from overseas. Since SSIs are generally more employment intensive per unit of capital than large scale industry, they are also a source of much needed employment. Employment in the registered SSI sector has nearly tripled over the past 20 years. A repetition of this performance would generate an additional 36 million jobs over the next 20 years. A comprehensive package of venture capital, credit, liberalisation of controls, technical training, marketing and management measures is needed to ensure the continuous expansion of this sector.

By far, the largest number of new jobs will be in the services sector. Over the past 100 years, the US economy has more than quadrupled the total number of those employed, yet the percentage of the US workforce engaged in manufacturing is now back to the same level as it was in 1850, while agricultural employment has shrunk to less than 3 per cent of the US workforce. Today, the fastest growing job categories in the USA are in services industries such as financial services, insurance, education, health, construction and real estate. Rapid growth is slated for a wide range of services in India, including professional, computer-related research and development, real estate, leasing, advertising, printing and packaging, marketing, telecommunications, postal and courier, audiovisual, engineering and construction, wholesale and retail distribution, all levels and types of education, environment, banking, insurance, health, travel, sports and recreation, and all categories of transport services. By the year 2020 more than 120 million jobs will come from the services sector alone.

Tourism-related occupations, including hotels and restaurants, employ 10.8 per cent of workers globally, compared to only 5.6 per cent in India. Domestic tourism will rise rapidly as living standards increase. India's domestic tourist sector is the fastest growing in the world, but with the lowest level of investment. The potential for international tourism too has not yet been exploited properly. China currently attracts more than five times as many foreign tourists, excluding visitors from Hong Kong. Thailand, Malaysia, and Turkey attract three to four times as many. By one estimate, development of India's tourism infrastructure such as roads, airports and medium priced hotels, combined with modifications in air and hotel pricing and tax policies, could generate more than 20 million additional employment opportunities in tourist related businesses within a decade.

Numerous studies have been undertaken to assess the potentials of the IT industry and to identify specific strategies needed to accelerate development of this sector. The NASSCOM-McKinsey study in 1999 projected creation of a $70 billion IT industry, employing more than two million persons within 10 years. The worldwide market for IT services is expected to exceed $900 billion by 2010.

The recent growth of IT-enabled service businesses in India—call centres, medical transcription, technical support and back office processing, engineering and design, geographic information services, payroll and other human resource services, insurance claim processing, legal databases—is powerful evidence that the potential of IT technology and knowledge based industries extends far beyond the development of software and hardware. The US experience shows that, as the application of information technology spreads and encompasses traditional industries, it can generate new employment opportunities ten times greater in number than those directly involved in core IT industries.

IT is also a stimulant to the growth of home-based employment opportunities, especially suitable for women. The trend towards tele-working, which is growing rapidly in USA and some other countries, is just beginning in India. The lower cost and greater convenience of home-based employment is bound to open up greater job opportunities for educated women with children.

IT services will be a powerful engine of job growth, but the term 'Knowledge-based industries' includes a much wider range of commercial opportunities. It encompasses all fields in which the application of mind, judgment and skill, rather than the application of mechanised production technology is the core resource. Education, health services, biotechnology, pharmaceuticals, insurance and financial services are among the leading industries in this category. They are also among the fastest growing industries in the world. Added to these, there is enormous scope for other knowledge intensive activities such as clinical drug trials and many other types of scientific research.

The management of all types of information is emerging as a major growth industry worldwide and India is well poised to become a global leader in this field. Increasing demand for education within the country and worldwide will create tremendous demand for qualified teachers with adequate language skills. An estimated two million additional teachers will be needed in India to support 100 per cent primary school enrolment and to reduce the teacher-student ratio for improved quality of teaching. Another two million or more will be required to support higher rates of upper primary and secondary school education and to reduce teacher-student ratios at those levels. Teaching staff for vocational training and higher education need to be expanded as well.

Demand for health services is increasing worldwide. Already nurses and medical technicians are in short supply. The USA has a doctor-nurse ratio of about twice that of India. Yet the US currently faces a shortfall of nurses, that is more than three times India's total annual production of new nurses. Physicians, nurses, medical technicians and other scientific occupations will become growth industries to rival the IT sector within the next decade. Creation of new jobs in existing industries can and should be supplemented by creation of new services industries that will in turn stimulate increased employment opportunities.

It is extremely difficult to project unemployment rates 20 years into the future, when so much doubt exists even about current levels of unemployment and underemployment. However, it is clear that rising levels of education and growth of the 60 plus age group will mitigate to some extent the growth of the labour force. Combined with the enormous opportunities for creation of new employment opportunities, the incidence of unemployment should be almost eliminated during the second decade of the century.

Education

Successful population policy is directly linked to successful education policy. Success in raising literacy rates and school enrolment rates while reducing drop-out rates, especially for women, are closely correlated with the delayed onset of marriage and child birth, improved mortality for both mothers and children, and reduction in family size. In fact, a successful education policy forms the bedrock of all fields of national development—political, economic, technical, scientific, social, and environmental. Education is the foundation for a vibrant democracy in which informed citizens exercise their franchise to support the internal growth of the nation and its constructive role in the world community. It is the foundation for growth in productivity, incomes and employment opportunities and for the development, application and adaptation of science and technology to enhance the quality of life. Education is the foundation for access to the benefits of the information revolution that is opening up vistas on the whole world. Education is also the foundation for improved health care and nutrition.

Literacy, the basis of all education, is as essential to survival and development in modern society as food is to survival and development of the human body. Literacy rates in India have arisen dramatically from 18 per cent in 1951 to 65 per cent in 2001, but these rates are still far from the UMI reference level of 95 per cent. Literacy must be considered the minimum right and requirement of every Indian citizen. Vast differences also remain among different sections of the population. Literacy among males is nearly 50 per cent higher than females, and it is about 50 per cent higher in urban areas as compared to the rural areas. Literacy rates range from as high as 96 per cent in some districts of Kerala to below 30 per cent in some parts of Madhya Pradesh. Rates are also significantly lower among scheduled castes and tribes than among other communities.

These differential rates of progress leave approximately 300 million illiterate adults in the country, the largest number of illiterates in the world. For these people, the traditional avenues of knowledge dissemination through education and printed information are ruled out. These are the people who are most vulnerable to the challenges of development, because they are least equipped to rapidly expand their knowledge base. Since many of them are relatively young adults who will still be active in 2020, the country cannot afford to ignore them or leave them behind. The Government has already set a goal to achieve 75 per cent literacy by the end of the Tenth Five Year Plan. A 100 per cent literate India is of paramount importance for realising the vision for the country in 2020. Even when this goal is achieved, innovative approaches will be needed to increase knowledge dissemination through TV and other means, to literate adults with little or no formal education.

Literacy is an indispensable minimum condition for development, but it is not sufficient. In this increasingly complex and technologically sophisticated world, ten years of school education must also be considered as an essential prerequisite for citizens to adapt and succeed economically, avail of the social opportunities and develop their individual potentials. Education is the primary and most effective means so far evolved for transmitting practically useful knowledge from one generation to another.

India's education system has expanded exponentially over the past five decades, but its current achievements are grossly inadequate for the nation to realise its potential greatness. The net enrolment rate in primary schools is around 77 per cent and in secondary schools it is around 60 per cent. These compare with the 99.9 per cent primary and 69 per cent secondary enrolment for the UMI reference level. The drop out rate was 40 per cent at the primary level and 55 per cent at the upper primary level in 1999-2000. These high drop out rates from both primary and secondary school, combined with low enrolment rates at the higher levels deprive tens of millions of children of their full rights as citizens. Out of approximately 200 million children in the age group 6-14 years, only 120 million are in schools and net attendance in the primary level is only 66 per cent of the enrolment. Further, less than 7 per cent of the children ever pass the 10th standard public examination.

Apart from addressing the needs of a large illiterate population, India's knowledge strategy must also develop innovative approaches to enhance knowledge acquisition among the large community of school drop-outs. Unless something is done to drastically reduce drop-out rates, by the year 2016 there will be approximately 500 million people in the country with less than five years of schooling, and another 300 million that will not have completed high school. In other words, about two-thirds of the population will lack the minimum level of education needed to keep pace with and take advantage of the social changes occurring within the country and worldwide.

Extending the primary school system to over 500,000 villages in India has brought education to the masses. Unfortunately, this huge quantitative expansion has been accompanied by a tremendous dilution in the quality of schooling. High drop out rates in rural areas is one result of single room schools, with few teaching aids and inadequate instruction both in terms of quantity and quality. Qualitative improvement in the system can be accomplished by promoting centralised schools serving clusters of 10 or more villages, wherever distances and transportation links make that feasible. This will permit greater investment in educational infrastructure, including introduction of computers.

Achieving 100 per cent enrolment of all children in the 6 to 14 year age group is an ambitious but achievable goal for 2020. This must be coupled with efforts to increase the quality and relevance of school curriculum to equip students not only with academic knowledge but also with the values and practical knowledge needed for success in life.

A tremendous expansion of schools and classrooms will be required to support a quantitative and qualitative improvement in the country's school system.

An enormous increase in the number of teachers will also be required to achieve the alternative scenario, i.e., eliminating primary school drop outs and reducing the teacher-pupil ratio from the present high level of 1:42 down to around 1:20, which is the UMI reference level. Together, this will require an additional three million primary school teachers, more than twice the number currently employed. Similar increases will be required at middle and secondary school levels. The training of such large number of teachers will require the establishment of additional teacher training colleges and much larger budget allocations for teachers' salaries.

Qualitative improvements in education should reflect a change in pedagogical methods and lay emphasis on several dimensions, including:

i) A shift from methods that emphasize passive learning to those that foster the active interest and ability of children to learn on their own.

ii) A shift from rote memorisation to development of children's capacity for critical thinking.

iii) A shift from traditional academic to practically relevant curriculum.

iv) A shift from imparting information to imparting life values such as independent thinking, self-reliance and individual initiative that are essential for success in any field of endeavour.

An important role of education is to foster in each child the attributes and values of a responsible, capable, active and healthy member of the family and society. The rigidity of curriculum, testing and teaching methods need to be relaxed so that innovative methods and new models of education can be evolved, tested and perfected. Vocational streams have to be developed and expanded to equip larger numbers of high school students with occupation-related knowledge and skills.

Experimentation is needed with new methods for knowledge delivery. Television can be a very effective means for educating both school going and non-school going children and adults. It can deliver teaching materials in a more dynamic, entertaining, and interesting manner, utilising the nation's best teachers and multimedia teaching materials on each subject. A TV based curriculum can help slow learners to supplement classroom teaching, fast learners to learn at much faster rates than the rest of the class, drop outs to acquire knowledge they missed out in school, and adults to expand their level of education without returning to school.

New methods of delivery will be particularly necessary to augment access and improve delivery at higher levels of education. Although India's college and university network has expanded dramatically, it is able to accommodate only a tiny fraction of the college-age population. In addition, the quality of facilities, teaching and course materials leaves much to be desired. Recruitment and promotion are highly politicised; seniority rule precludes merit advancement; and the cost of delivery is beyond the means of the vast majority of young Indians.

India in 2020 must be a nation in which all those who aspire for higher education have access to college and university level courses. A national network of community colleges, similar to the highly successful American system, is needed to provide knowledge and job-oriented skills to millions of young people who lack interest in or capacity for more stringent academic studies.

The advent of computer and the Internet-based educational methods offer an exciting new learning medium that can literally transform our concept of school and classroom from physical into virtual realities. Studies in the USA project a radical reshaping of higher education over the next two decades as a result of the digital revolution. Many traditional colleges will close as more course works are delivered at a distance through alternative channels. The traditional boundaries between education and other sectors will fade, as publishers, for-profit and non-profit organisations, offer accredited, multimedia-enhanced courses directly to students, by-passing the university. The traditional classroom type of education, which is most useful for students that require personal attention and assistance and for subjects that involve hands-on experimentation, will no longer be the predominant model of education. For all other purposes, it is very costly and not very efficient in the way it uses the time of both teachers and students.

Experience shows that computer-based educational methods can lead to much faster rates and higher quality of learning, which is more inter-active and motivating for students at all levels of education from pre-school to post-graduation. It is extremely effective for enhancing reading and language skills and general knowledge among the very young and even for some sophisticated professional courses such as medicine and engineering.

Given the huge number of young students that will quest for all levels of higher education in the coming decades and the severe shortage of qualified instructors, and in the light of India's outstanding expertise in the IT industry, the country needs to embark on a massive programme to convert the entire higher educational curriculum into a multi-media, web-based format and to establish accreditation standards for recognition of the distance education so imparted.

Our vision of India in 2020 is predicated on the belief that human resources are the most important determinants of overall development. As India's IT revolution has been fuelled by the availability of a very large reservoir of well-trained engineers, its future development in many different spheres will depend on commensurate development of sufficient and surplus capabilities.

Full development of India's enormous human potential will require a shift in national priorities, to commit a greater portion of the country's financial resources to the education sector. India currently invests 3.2 - 4.4 per cent of GNP on education. This compares unfavourably with the UMI reference level of 4.9 per cent, especially with countries such as South Africa, which invests 7.9 per cent of GNP on education. A near doubling of investments in education is the soundest policy for quadrupling the country's GDP per capita.

S&T Capabilities

Literacy and general education form the base of the knowledge pyramid that is essential for rapid and sustained development in the 21st century. The continuous advancement of science and application of improved technology form the middle rung; and social ideals and spiritual values form the apex.

Technical education, both vocational and professional, constitutes the foundation for development of science and technology. India is rightly proud of the international standing of its IITs, but a handful of world class technical institutions is not sufficient. A large number of the country's approximately 500 engineering colleges need to be upgraded to quality standards nearer to those of the IITs, and given similar autonomy. Private sector initiative and investment, whether from Indian corporates or NRIs or reputed foreign universities, need to be fully encouraged. Close links need to be fostered between technical institutions and industry.

India's enormous manpower base of scientists and engineers is often coveted. President Kalam observed that

India's human resource base is one of its greatest core competencies. This is true in absolute terms, but as a percentage of the total population, we are at 1/100th of the US levels and 1/50th of the Korean level. Even China's manpower base of scientists and engineers as a percentage of its population exceeds ours by more than three times.

Absolute numbers do count, but manpower alone is not sufficient to excel in the development and application of science and technology. In terms of total investment in R&D, India's expenditure is 1/60th of that of Korea, 1/250th of that of the USA, and 1/340th of that of Japan. More significantly, atomic energy, space and defence research account for 71 per cent of all central spending on science and technology, which means that relatively little is left for investment in agriculture, energy, telecommunications and other crucial sectors within the sphere of science and technology. R&D expenditure even in India's fast-growing IT sector has been averaging around 3 per cent of sales turnover (STO), which is much lower as compared to the 14-19 per cent expended by internationally reputed software firms.

These low figures reflect on our R&D performance. India's share of global scientific output in 1998 was only 1.58 per cent of the world's total. Out of 500,000 new patent applications filed globally each year, China accounts for 96,000 and Korea accounts for 72,000, while India accounts for only 8,000. Of greater concern has been the country's inability to capitalise on our huge pool of manpower and extensive network of scientific research organisations for transferring proven technologies from the lab to the land and to the factory. Despite possessing the world's largest cadre of agricultural scientists, we have not been able to extend the momentum of Green Revolution to other regions and crops and to update the scientific practices of our farmers to levels comparable with most other nations. Crop productivity remains far below and production costs far above world averages. A similar gap exists in the application of science and technology for food processing and many other industries. High technology exports account for only 6 per cent of total manufacturing exports for India, compared to over 20 per cent for the UMI reference level.

India has a number of premier universities for scientific and technical education which produce world class scientists and engineers, but the national research system rarely produces world class results. One reason is the missing link between scientists in universities and research institutes and practitioners in agriculture and industry. Another is that non-teaching research institutes lack the continuous inflow of young talented researchers required to challenge assumptions and infiltrate new ideas and approaches. Bureaucracy, tenure and lack of accountability minimise the pressure for practical application of scientific knowledge. Other countries have done a much better job of providing optimum incentives to their scientific community and creating close linkages between science and industry. The management of technology and the administration of government require different sets of skills and a different culture. Management of technology demands innovation, global competitiveness, and wide latitude for individual freedom, characteristics that are difficult to foster under an administrative regime.

The objectives of many institutes and the mechanisms for achieving them need a radical reorientation to bring them in tune with the changing environment brought about by liberalisation of imports, technology tie-ups with foreign agencies and foreign direct investment in key sectors. If the national R&D bodies do not reorganise themselves to face globalisation and global competition, nor take into consideration the nature of the factor endowment of the country along with many existing indigenous technologies so far neglected, then they risk becoming irrelevant to the mainstream activities of industrial development. The nature of service offered by these institutions has to undergo a sea change. Grass-root consultancy and turnkey project consultancy, including project implementation and monitoring are increasingly in demand.

Another essential step is to improve the linkages between technology development and technology application by fostering close ties between basic research and business. In the USA, a large proportion of scientific research at the university level is financed by business, and most leading universities operate technology incubators designed to promote commercialisation of new products and processes. India's recent experiment with the Science and Technology Entrepreneur Parks (STEPs) has been successful in promoting application of technologies, new business start-ups, and employment. The STEPs in combination with technology incubators need to be rapidly multiplied around the country. Effective R&D management backed by suitable incentives for commercialisation are essential for bridging the gap between the lab and the land or factory.

R&D is not only essential for propelling growth in industrial fields. It can also become a growth industry on its own. Much of the work done by Indian software companies for overseas clients and parent companies rightly fall under the category of new product development. Vast potential exists for complementing India's strengths in IT with corresponding strengthening of fields such as biotechnology, pharmaceuticals, designer-made materials, and others.

India's investment in the biotechnology sector is expected to increase five-fold by the end of the current decade, from US $2 billion to $10 billion, largely as a result of growing collaboration between multinational corporations and indigenous research efforts. Huge opportunities also exist for R&D in the field of genomics, bioinformatics, DNA technologies, clinical studies and genetically modified crops. Rationalisation of procedure, backed by effective bio-safety regulations are needed to govern testing and approval of biotech products. India has the potential of converting its strong R&D infrastructure into a global research, design and development platform.

Vocational Training

The knowledge and skill of our workforce will be a major determinant of India's future rate of economic growth as well as the type and number of jobs we create. The greater that knowledge and skill, the higher will be the productivity, the better the quality, and the lower the cost of the products and services we generate. Similarly, the better the quality and lower the cost, greater will be the comparative advantage and market potential. Currently only 5 per cent of the country's labour force in the 20-24 age category have undergone formal vocational training, compared with 28 per cent in Mexico, 60 to 80 per cent in most industrialised nations, and as much as 96 per cent in Korea. A strategy to achieve full employment must include as an important component, a strategy to ensure that all new entrants to the workforce are equipped with the knowledge and skill needed for high productivity and high quality.

India has over 4,200 industrial training institutes (ITI) imparting education and training in 43 engineering and 24 non-engineering trades. Of these, 1,654 are government run ITIs, while 2,620 are private. The total seating capacity in these ITIs is 6.28 lakh. Most of this training is conducted in classroom style in the form of one to two year diploma courses. In addition, about 1.65 lakh persons undergo apprenticeship vocational training every year in state-run enterprises. If a wider definition of applied courses is taken that includes agriculture, engineering and other professional subjects, the total number receiving job related training is about 17 lakh per annum, which still represents only 14 per cent of new entrants to the workforce.

The nature of vocational skills makes it impossible for vocational schools to fully address the nation's needs. The variety of skills needed by the workforce is far too great. The changes in technology and work processes are too rapid for training courses and their instructors to stay up-to-date. The cost of training is also relatively high as it often demands full time enrolment for a prolonged period. Some vocational fields do not lend themselves to classroom or laboratory study at all. A comprehensive strategy is thus needed to enhance the nation's employable skills. It must begin by preparing a catalogue of the entire range of vocational skills needed to support the development of the country. The network of vocational training institutes and the range of vocational skills taught needs to be expanded substantially to impart those skills for which institutional training is most suitable. The private sector, which promoted the rapid proliferation of computer training institutes throughout the country, should be encouraged to recognise the commercial potential of vocational training in many other fields. In addition, it is essential to fashion more effective and efficient mechanisms for disseminating useful knowledge and skills, especially through the TV media and through computerised vocational training. The importance of computer has been widely recognised as a means to improve efficiency in business, government and formal education, but its application in vocational training is not fully appreciated.

Use of Computers in Vocational Training

i) Rates of learning on computer for both academic as well as vocational or skill-based subjects are four to ten times faster than they are in a classroom setting, and learning retention is likely to be much higher.

ii) Computers can provide multimedia, interactive, customised and individually-paced learning with instantaneous feedback and testing.

iii) It eliminates the need for producing and deputing a large number of highly skilled instructors. Course contents can be rapidly modified to reflect changing needs.

iv) For many types of vocational skills, computerised training also offers specific advantages over the live delivery of skills in a classroom.

v) Training can be delivered wherever computers are available. A nationwide network of 50,000 computerised vocational centres, run as private self-employed businesses similar to the STD booths and Internet cafes, can deliver low-cost, high-quality training to 10 million workers every year—more than five times the total number covered by existing programmes.

Although 58 per cent of Indians are engaged in agriculture, vocational training for farmers is one of the weakest links in the Indian educational system. Agricultural universities cater to the nation's need for agricultural scientists and extension officers. An extensive network of more than 300 Krishi Vignan Kendras (KVK) offers short and medium term courses for farmers on specialised subjects. The KVK network provides training to several hundred thousand farmers each year, but it can cater to the needs of only a miniscule percentage of all farmers. Agricultural education can be moved from the campus into the village by establishing a national network of farm schools, offering practical demonstration and training on lands leased from farmers in the local community. The prime objective of the schools would be to impart knowledge and skills designed to double yields on important commercial crops. Educated farmers can be trained as self-employed instructors to operate the farm schools as private enterprises on a commercial basis.

HEALTH FOR ALL

The health of a nation is difficult to define in terms of a single set of measures. At best, we can assess the health of the population by taking into account indicators like infant mortality and maternal mortality rates, life expectancy and nutrition, along with the incidence of communicable and non-communicable diseases.

According to these measures, the health of the Indian population has improved dramatically over the past fifty years. Life expectancy has risen from 33 years to 64 years. The infant mortality rate (IMR) has fallen from 148 to 71 per 1000. The crude birth rate (CBR) has declined from 41 to 25 and the crude death rate (CDR) has fallen from 25 to under 9. The couple protection rate (CPR) and total fertility rate (TFR) have also improved substantially.

Despite these achievements, wide disparities persist between different income groups, between rural and urban communities, and between different states and even districts within states. The infant mortality rate among the poorest quintet of the population is 2.5 times higher than that among the richest. Maternal mortality remains very high. More than one lakh women die each year due to pregnancy-related complications.

Like population growth and economic growth, the health of a nation is a product of many factors and forces that combine and interact with each other. Economic growth, per capita income, employment, levels of literacy and education—especially among females—age of marriage, birth rates, availability of information regarding health care and nutrition, access to safe drinking water, public and private health care infrastructure, access to preventive health care and medical care, health insurance, public hygiene, road safety, and environmental pollution are among the factors that contribute directly to the health of the nation.

Communicable diseases such as malaria, kalaazar, tuberculosis and HIV infection remain the major causes of illness in India. During the next five to ten years, existing programmes are likely to eliminate polio and leprosy and substantially reduce the prevalence of kalaazar and filariasis. However, TB, malaria and AIDS will continue to remain major public health problems. India has about 1.5 million identified cases of TB that are responsible for more than 3,00,000 deaths annually. Improved diagnostic services and treatment can reduce the prevalence and incidence of TB by 2020. About 2 million cases of malaria are reported in India each year. Restructuring the "malaria workforce" and strengthening health infrastructure can reduce the incidence of this disease by up to 50 per cent within a decade. Assessing the impact of HIV epidemic is more difficult; according to an estimate, there are about 4 million persons infected with HIV. The National Health Policy aims at achieving a plateau in the prevalence of HIV infection by 2007.

Childhood diarrhoea, another major cause of illness, is largely preventable through simple community action and public education, and deaths due to diarrhoea can be eliminated by 2010. Childhood under-nutrition, the other major area of concern, can be addressed by targeting children of low birth weights and employing low-cost screening procedures to detect under-nutrition at an early age. Given the projected improvement in living standards, food security, educational levels and access to health care among all levels of the general population, substantial progress can be made in reducing the prevalence of severe under-nutrition in children by 2020. China's remarkable success in combating disease over the past two decades is proof that a determined commitment to improving public health can dramatically reduce the incidence of infectious diseases within one or two decades.

With the demographic and epidemiological transition taking place in the coming years, non-communicable diseases are also likely to emerge as major public health problems. Modernisation of life styles will further aggravate health problems. The rapid proliferation of two and four wheel motor vehicles, increasing congestion on city roads and intercity highways have all contributed to an increasing number of deaths and serious injuries from traffic related accidents. Greater emphasis on education and enforcement of road safety rules by both drivers and pedestrians is an urgent need of the hour.

As already noted, there will be a massive increase in population in the 15-64 age group. Reproductive and Child Health care programmes must meet the needs of this rapidly growing clientele. The population in this age group will be more literate and have greater access to information. They will have greater awareness and expectations about access to quality services for maternal and child health, contraceptive care, management of gynaecological problems, etc. A major focus of vision 2020 must be on improving access to health services to meet the health care needs of women and children.

India's significant achievements in the field of health have been made possible by the establishment of a huge rural health infrastructure, along with the formation of a massive health care manpower consisting of over five lakh trained doctors working under plural systems of medicine, and a vast frontline of over seven lakh nurses and other health care workers; 25,000 primary and community health care centres; and 1.6 lakh sub-centres, complemented by 22,000 dispensaries and 2,800 hospitals practicing Indian systems of medicine and homeopathy. This infrastructure remains under-equipped, under-manned and under-financed to cope with the challenge of eradicating major threats to human life.

The inadequacy of the current health care system is starkly illustrated by the fact that only 35 per cent of the population have access to essential drugs, while the UMI reference level is above 82 per cent. Infant immunisation against measles and DPT for children under 12 years is only 60 per cent and 78 per cent compared to the UMI level of over 90 per cent for both diseases.

As a larger proportion of the population reaches middle class standards of living, an increasing number of people will turn to private health care providers. This development is welcome, because it will permit the public health care system to concentrate more resources on meeting the needs of the poorer sections. But at the same time, the level of public expenditure on health care needs to rise about four-fold from the current level of 0.8 per cent of GDP to reach the UMI reference level of 3.4 per cent. Rapid growth of the private health care system, however, requires the formulation of competence and quality standards to check and balance the increasing emphasis on health care as a business.

Criteria for a More Equitable and Effective Health Care System

i) Universal access and access to an adequate level of health care without financial burden.

ii) Fair distribution of financial costs for access and fair distribution of burden in rational care and capacity.

iii) Ensuring that providers have the competence, empathy and accountability for delivering quality care and for effective use of relevant research.

iv) Special attention to vulnerable groups such as women, children, the disabled and the aged.

Development plans for India's health care systems need to place greater emphasis on public health education and prevention. The wide dissemination of health and nutrition related information through traditional channels should be supplemented by an ambitious and persistent programme of public health education through the print, television, radio and electronic media.

Health insurance can play an invaluable role in improving the overall health care system. The insurable population in India has been assessed at 250 million and this number will increase rapidly in the coming two decades. This should be supplemented by innovative insurance products and programmes by panchayats with reinsurance backup by companies and government to extend coverage to much larger sections of the population.

The life expectancy of the Indian population is expected to reach above 65 years in 2020, which compares favourably with the UMI reference level of 69 years. Mortality rates for infants is expected to decline to about 20 per 1000 in 2020, which compares favourably with the UMI reference level of 22.5.

VULNERABILITY

Economic growth, rising levels of education among the young, expansion of employment opportunities for the working age population, slower population growth, and declining infant mortality, however, will not eliminate and may even aggravate, inequalities between different age groups, the sexes, income groups, communities and regions, unless specific corrective steps are taken for levelling the different degrees of capacity and opportunity. The Vision 2020 must have special focus on bridging the existing gaps in the various levels of development and endeavour its best to fulfil the Constitutional commitment of raising the status of the vulnerable groups vis-à-vis the rest of the society.

During the next 20 years, the aged population in India will nearly double, placing much greater demand on the infrastructure of hospitals and nursing homes, while at the same time shifting the profile of health disorders from problems of the young to those of the aged. The population above 65 years of age will increase from 45 to 76 million persons by 2020. Reference has already been made to the very high incidence of malnutrition among this group and the growing incidence of diseases associated with aging, such as cancer and cardiovascular diseases. A disproportionate number of the aged population are illiterate and living below the poverty line. While majority of these people live in rural areas where the extended family system remains prevalent, increasing urbanisation and mobility will destabilise their situation in future. The problem of coping with a larger aged population will be partially solved by a big surge in the size of the working age labour force and a reduction in the dependency ratio, meaning that there will be a larger proportion of workers to support the aged. Specific strategies will be needed to provide targeted assistance for the most vulnerable members of this group, including research on the disabilities of the aged, greater development of geriatric medicine, training of minders for the aged, and establishment of innovative support systems such as the highly successful Japanese model.

Like the aged, the disabled persons also form another subgroup that is particularly vulnerable and unlikely to benefit directly from the general advance of society, unless specific provisions are made to address their particular needs, including a special system of schools, clinics and home-based learning programmes, combined with therapeutic and institutional care.

Increasing gender equity is an important challenge of the coming years. Literacy rates for females are 40 per cent lower than for males. Females represent only 43 per cent of all students at primary level, 37 per cent at higher secondary level, and 35 per cent of those in higher education. Drop out rates are also higher for girls. The UNDP's gender development index ranks India 108th among 174 countries in terms of gender equity. It is no coincidence therefore that countries ranking highest on this index are among the most prosperous in the world. Gender equity and social development are inseparably interlinked. Reducing the disparity in nutritional, literacy and educational levels between the sexes is essential for realisation of the country's full potentials.

Children being the supreme assets of the country, the 'Rights' based approach will continue to play an important role in ensuring their 'survival', 'protection' and 'development', with special attention to the girl child. Our vision for 2020 in this regard is to see a nation free from all forms of child labour. However, complete elimination of child labour through legal means is not only difficult to implement but may also prove to be counter productive in protecting the interest of these very children. While legal enforcement can contain the demand for child labour, it may leave the poor households supplying child labour more vulnerable rather than addressing the underlying socio-economic compulsions generating the supply of such labour. Indeed, poverty eradication combined with educational reforms to provide free (or affordable) access to quality education with an interesting, innovative and job-oriented curriculum for all can effectively eliminate child labour once and for all.

The other categories of the vulnerable groups include the scheduled castes (SC), scheduled tribes (ST), other backward classes (OBC) and minorities, constituting nearly three-fourths of the country's total population. They require special attention in order to narrow down the disparities between them and the more privileged section of the population. Literacy rates for SCs and STs are 25 per cent lower than for other communities. Education enrolment rates among this group, especially for females, lag significantly behind that of other communities. Low levels of education lead to lower paying employment opportunities and lower incomes. Thus, it becomes exceedingly difficult for these communities to come out of the vicious circle. Large number of people in other communities also suffer from similar disparities.

Regional disparities in rates of development are of similar concern. Regardless of the community or the region, the overall progress of the nation will depend to a large extent on its ability to provide increasing opportunities for the disadvantaged to take initiative for their self-development. Otherwise, these disadvantaged will exact an increasing toll on the stability, well-being and development of the country as a whole. It is notable that rising levels of violence and crime in society are not so much associated with overall low levels of development, as they are with wide disparities between levels of development, which create frustration and resentment. The progress of the whole will ultimately depend on the progress of its weakest links. India's Vision of 2020 must be one in which all levels and sections of the population and all parts of the country march forward together into a more secure and prosperous future.

Bibliography

Abu-Lughod, Janet L. *Changing Cities: Urban Sociology.* Harper Collins, 1991.

Anderson, Elijah. *A Place on the Corner.* Chicago: University of Chicago Press, 1978.

Beauregard, Robert and Sophie Body-Gendrot. *The Urban Moment: Cosmopolitan Essays on the Late 20th Century City.* Russell Sage, 1999.

Borden, Ian, et al. *The Unknown City: Contesting Architecture and Social Space.* Cambridge, Mass.: MIT Press, 2000.

Bouthillette, Anne-Marie, Gordon Brent Ingram and Yolanda Retter, eds. *Queers in Space: Communities/Public Places/Sites of Resistance.* Seattle, WA: Bay Press, 1997.

Boyer, Paul. *Urban Masses and Moral Order in America, 1820-1920.* Cambridge: Harvard University Press, 1978.

Castells, Manuel. *"Theory and Ideology in Urban Sociology."* Urban Sociology: Critical Essays. (New York: St Martin's, 1976).

Clark, Terry Nichols, ed. *Urban Innovation: Creative Strategies for Turbulent Times.* Sage Publications, 1994.

Cronon, William. *Nature's Metropolis: Chicago and the Great West.* Norton, 1991.

Cuff, Dana. *The Provisional City: Los Angeles Stories of Architecture and Urbanism.* Cambridge, Mass.: MIT Press, 2000.

Denton, Nancy and Douglas Massey. *American Apartheid: Segregation and the Making of the Underclass.*

Fischer, Claude. *"The Subcultural Theory of Urbanism: A Twentieth-Year Assessment."* American Journal of Sociology 101-3 (1995): 543-577.

Flanagan, William. *Contemporary Urban Sociology.* Cambridge: Cambridge University Press, 1993.

Gottdiener, Mark and Ray Hutchison. *The New Urban Sociology.* McGraw-Hill, 2000.

Hannerz, Ulf. *Exploring the City.* New York, Columbia University Press, 1984.

Jargowsky, Paul. *Poverty and Place: Ghettos, Barrios, and the American City.* Russell Sage, 1997.

Kasinitz, Philip. ed. *Metropolis: Center and Symbol of Our Times.* New York: New York University Press, 1995.

Leeds, A. *Cities, Classes, and the Social Order.* Ithaca: Cornell University Press, 1994.

LeGates, Richard T. and Frederic Stout, eds. *The City Reader.* New York: Routledge, 1996.

Logan, John and Harvey Molotch. *Urban Fortunes.* University of California Press, 1986.

Low, Setha M. *On the Plaza: The Politics of Public Space and Culture.* Austin: University of Texas Press, 2000.

Macionis, J. J. and V.N. Parrillo. *Cities and Urban Life.* Upper Saddle River, New Jersey: Prentice Hall, 1998.

Mitchell, Clyde. *Social Networks in Urban Situations.* Manchester: Manchester University Press, 1969.

Mollenkopf, John. *The Contested City.* Princeton University Press, 1983.

Mumford, Lewis. *The Culture of Cities.* New York: Harcourt Brace Jovanovich, 1970.

Popenoe, David. *Private Pleasure, Public Plight: American Metropolitan Community Life in Comparative Perspective.*

Saunders, Peter. *Social Theory and the Urban Question.* New York: Holmes & Meyer, 1981.

Sennet, Richard, ed. *Classic Essays in the Culture of Cities.* New York: 1969.

Simmel, Georg *"The Metropolis and Mental Life."* In *The Sociology of Georg Simmel.* (New York: Free Press, 1950).

Smith, Michael. *The City and Social Theory.* New York: 1979.

Sorio y Puig, Arturo. *Cerda: The Five Bases of the General Theory of Urbanization.* Corte Madera, CA: Ginko Press, 2000.

Sugrue, Thomas. *Origins of the Urban Crisis: Detroit, 1940-1960.* Princeton University Press, 1996.

Tönnies, Ferdinand. *Community and Society.* C. P. Loomis, trans. and ed. New York: Harper and Row, 1963.

Wadsworth, Nancy Kleniewski. *Cities, Change, and Conflict: A Political Economy of Urban Life.* 1997.

Whyte, William Foote. *Street Corner Society.* Chicago: University of Chicago Press, 1943.

Wirth, Louis. *On Cities and Social Life.* Chicago. The University of Chicago Press, 1964

Index

ENCYCLOPAEDIA OF SOCIOLOGY

Industrial Sociology

Volume -9

Satish Mittal
Sushil Kumar Saxena

Commonwealth

Encyclopaedia of Sociology

Edition : 2026

ISBN 978-81-311-0377-7 (set)

Published by :
COMMONWEALTH PUBLISHERS (P) LTD.
4831/24, Govind Lane,
Ansari Road, Darya Ganj,
New Delhi - 110002
Ph. : 23242541, 23272541
e-mail : commonwealthpublishers2016@gmail.com

Distributed by :
ARJUN PUBLISHING HOUSE
4831/24, Govind Lane,
Ansari Road, Darya Ganj,
New Delhi - 110002
Ph. : 23242541, 23272541
e-mail : arjunbooks2001@gmail.com
arjunpubhouse@gmail.com

Laser Typesetting by :
Dimple Computers
Delhi

Printed at :
Milan Enterprises
Delhi

Preface

Industrial sociology, or the sociology of work, examines the direction and implications of trends in technological change, globalisation, labour markets, work organisation, managerial practices and employment relations to the extent to which these trends are intimately related to changing patterns of inequality in modern societies and to the changing experiences of individuals and families the ways in which workers challenge, resist and make their own contributions to the patterning of work and shaping of work institutions.

The present book provides an indispensable introduction to industrial sociology. It not only includes clear explanations of theories and evidence, but also covers the most cutting-edge research, data, and debates. It examines different sociological approaches to work, emphasising the links between social processes, the institutions of employment, and their social and domestic contexts. Use of an international range of empirical evidence helps to make this book especially accessible to undergraduate readers.

Written in a lively and accessible style, the book has been specially designed to support students' understanding, and to develop their critical responses to the literature. It will be essential reading for students of the sociology of work, industrial sociology, organisational behaviour and industrial relations. Students studying business and management courses with a sociological component will also find the book of utmoist use.

Authors

Contents

1

Introduction to Industrial Sociology

Industrial sociology is a field of applied sociology, and has grown mainly out of interests in such issues as productivity, motivation, and unionisation. In many cases, however, the theoretical relevance of the studies is evident, and often it is explicitly discussed by those who conducted the research. "Overcoming Resistance to Change," a frequently quoted study, is a case in point: while the problem studied is how to introduce frequent changes into the system of production in a pajama factory without reducing productivity, it is discussed from the point of view of its contributions to Kurt Lewin's field theory. The studies of Mayo, Roethlisberger, Whyte, Warner, and many others have a theoretical perspective, and are not predominantly focused on practical problems. The applied nature of industrial sociology is revealed not so much in a lack of theoretical implications of the various studies as in a lack of conceptual codification and of systematic delimitation of the field. The accumulation of studies in this area seems now to have reached the stage at which one may attempt to offer such a systematic delimitation and to spell out the main dimensions of the field.

An important justification for this effort is that a successful conceptual delimitation of industrial sociology will make research in the field more economical. When it can be shown that an applied field is congruent with a theoretical area, and to determine its systematic boundaries, it becomes possible to see its relations to other fields of study and to make use of their hypotheses and concepts. Thus industrial sociologists have had a better understanding of the process of supervision and the role of the foreman since the concept of leadership, taken from other areas, has been introduced. Military sociology, on the other hand, has benefited from the idea of informal organisation, first used by industrial sociologists. Such "translations" of concepts are not possible unless it becomes clear that soldiers and officers on the one hand, and workers and foremen on the other, are phenomena that have some elements in common. This is where theory enters into applied fields. It will be attempted below to point out some general parallelisms between industrial sociology and other areas of study, in order that sets of concepts and hypotheses can be translated. And another reason for attempting to spell out the theoretical dimensions of a field is that this effort may fulfil the function that Mendeleev's table fulfilled in chemistry: it may help to point out the missing elements, the uncovered, neglected areas.

Such an attempt as here described should not be either too inclusive or too exclusive of the work already performed in the field. Thus if we should define industrial sociology as the study of the relationship between rational and non-rational elements, we would be too inclusive, since this definition would include many major research areas that industrial sociologists have never studied and are not in their realm, as for instance the sociology of science and the study of administrative behaviour (in all organisational structures, not only in industry). On the other hand, if we should define industrial sociology as the study of the social relationships in industry, the definition would be too exclusive, for it would leave out many relevant and significant studies in the field which have taken into account the industry's social environment and its influence on the relationships within the industry.

What is usually regarded as industrial sociology can be fruitfully conceived of as a branch of organisational sociology. Industrial sociology has an implicit delimitation which, when made explicit and somewhat rearranged, fits neatly into the model of organisational sociology.

The latter is concerned with roles, and with processes of inter-action, communication, and authority, that are specialised in serving specific social goals. Thus it studies civil service as pursuing the goals set by the government; and industry as creating goods and services, or as making profit. It has a relatively well developed theoretical model based on Max Weber's theory of bureaucracy, which has been significantly remodelled and improved by supplementing the study of rational aspects with the study of non-rational and irrational aspects of organisations.

Organisational sociology is potentially able to develop sound bases for a generic as well as a comparative study of organisations, and it has greatly benefited from the interchange of concepts and hypotheses among its various sub-fields. Thus, while there are many significant differences between a church, an army, a university, a factory, and a trade union, sociologists have found it helpful to treat all these organisations as having common problems that may serve as a basis for a generalised discussion of organisations and also for differentiating die various organisational structures. The various types of organisations seem to have common functional problems, but different structural solutions, though fortunately the number of alternative solutions seems to be limited, and this makes a fruitful study of the field possible. Considering the present state of knowledge in this area, the following discussion of some of die common problems and alternative solutions must be very tentative.

All organisational structures, for example, have to face the problem of recruiting, training or socialising, and motivating their personnel, diet it may function in accordance with the organisation's regulations and norms. All organisations have to create and maintain among their personnel a motivation adequate to the role expectations of the organisational structure. Many of the studies on leadership, informal organisation, small groups in organisational structures, morale, and other phenomena deal with this set of problems. Another element common to all organisational structures is the dynamic relationship among the organisation's goals, inner needs, and need to adapt to a changing environment.

These common problems, as well as many odiers, can serve also as a basis for differentiation, that is, for classification and comparison of the various organisations. Thus one of the common functional problems of all organisations is the need to obtain resources from the outside, through exchange, taxation, or private endowments. For the analysis of certain organisational processes (such as efficiency, social control, services to the clientele) it is of interest to compare organisations according to the ways they obtain their resources. Again, all organisations have some goals they serve or pretend to serve, and therefore are confronted with the problem of creating and maintaining some personal commitment to these goals in at least part of their personnel. These commitments may be established and reinforced by coercion, material sanctions, or social and symbolic rewards or deprivations. Which type of sanction is mainly applied is an important characterising factor in the comparative study of organisations.

Presumably the subject matter of industrial sociology is industry. But "industry" seems to be a concept with no direct sociological meaning, and it is difficult to specify a theoretical orientation along its lines. The term "industry" has been taken over from commonsense language, economics, and the census of occupations, without sociological scrutiny. It has been used mainly in two ways: as synonymous with factory; and as covering any large-scale employment of labour and capital.

In the first use industry is seen as the manufacturing unit. Sociologists who have used the term in this manner have called industrial sociology "plant sociology." This seems to be a too exclusive delimitation. There are many studies that fruitfully apply the ideas and concepts of industrial sociology to the study of offices, transportation, restaurants, and grocery stores, and to exclude these organisations from industrial sociology seems a rather arbitrary decision.

The second use of the term is widespread. Industry, according to Webster, is "any department or branch of art, occupation, or business; especially, one which employs much labour and capital and is a distinct branch of trade," or, in economics, "systematic labour or habitual employment." The census follows the same lines and classifies every field of full-time work as industry, including public administration, professional services, education, and private household work. All these demarcations of the field are obviously much too inclusive.

The proposed delimitation has an additional advantage: it classifies organisations according to a systematic conceptual scheme. Were we to classify study areas according to their subject matter, we would end up with an endless and unsystematic list: a sociology of industry, of financial institutions, of offices, services, mining, agriculture, and what not. For the purpose of systematising an applied field we have to find an analytical base for delimiting it, which means in the present case an analytical basis on which organisational sociology can be subdivided.

That basis is provided by the functions that an organisation fulfils for society, or for the social unit in which it is embedded. In line with Talcott Parsons' analytical scheme of four functional problems (or phases), organisations may be roughly differentiated in the following way: adaptive organisations (industries, financial institutions); political organisations (government agencies, political parties, trade unions); integrative organisations (clubs, some voluntary associations); and "cultural" organisations (churches, schools, universities). While most organisations serve more than one function, one function usually dominates, and thus it is possible to classify organisations according to their primary function.

The typology can be further refined by classifying organisations according to their primary and secondary functions. For instance, though most trade unions can be seen as political organisations, because of their power element, it would perhaps be more accurate to regard American trade unions, at least until recently, as having an economic-political orientation, and many European trade unions as political-ideological ("cultural") organisations. Similarly, industries can be meaningfully classified as having two functional orientations. Some, such as the small industries in the United States at the beginning of the century, are relatively close to the classical model of pure economic organisations. Others are economic-political, as for instance most monopolies and some industries in newly developed countries. Some will have to be classified as political-economic organisations, as for example public industries in countries and during periods in which the spoils system and other non-economic political considerations prevail and predominate over considerations of production and profit.

If this functional typology of organisations is adopted, the category closest to what is known as industrial sociology is that of adaptive (economic) organisations. This raises two questions: first, how to distinguish between economic and non-economic organisations; second, how to determine what is an organisation's primary or dominant orientation and what is its secondary one.

Economic organisations are those whose primary aim is to produce goods and services, to exchange them, or to organise and manipulate monetary processes. The profit motive as an institutionalised primary goal may often serve as a helpful empirical indicator, but it is not reliable because, on the one hand, some schools, hospitals, and social clubs are geared mainly to the maximising of profit, while on the other hand, publicly owned or managed industries may not be profit oriented.

The dominant orientation can be determined in several ways. What is considered to be the legitimate primary orientation can be established by communicating with the appropriate group of people. What the dominant functions actually are may be deter-mined by studying the goals that receive the preponderance of efforts, funds, and time. It would be even better to study critical decisions and the incidence of conflicts between two or more sets of considerations: if economic considerations are usually decisive, this may be considered an indicator of the dominant orientation. From this point of view the study of top management decisions is very significant, because secondary or even tertiary orientations may dominate on the lower levels.

Another clue may be gained from the structure of the hierarchy. In most economic organisations, technological considerations are usually subordinated to economic criteria and there is no room for the domination of expert perfectionism and pure technological achievement that cannot be geared to production under the existing economic conditions, or those predicted for the near future. This is reflected in the fact that those who make economic decisions are usually in higher positions of authority than the experts. In universities, on the other hand, where serving the goals of knowledge and following such "unproductive" interests as basic research are considered one of the main aims, and where economic considerations (such as decisions concerning the allocation of funds) are subordinated to these "expert" considerations, it is legitimate, and according to this analysis also functional, to subordinate the administration to the "experts," for instance to the academic senate or other faculty bodies. Thus by studying the distribution of activities, critical decisions and incidence, conflict situations and organisational hierarchies, we can determine which orientation is primary, which secondary, and so on.

If it is agreed that industrial sociology be defined as a part of organisational sociology, dealing specifically with those organisations whose primary function is economic, it remains to consider how the generic concerns of organisational sociology apply to the study of economic organisations in particular. It will be seen that industrial sociologists have already studied some of the areas that legitimately belong to the field, but have neglected others.

Organisational sociology focuses on the study of organisations from four levels or points of view. On the first level, organisations are studied as social units, and interest here is divided between the study of the formal and the informal structure. The formal dimension, often studied by administrators, is in itself of little inter-est to the sociologist of organisations. The latter usually focuses on the informal relations and their connection to the formal system. He is interested in the formal only as it impinges on the social process and sets a stage for the more "real" processes of interaction.

On the second level the study of organisations deals with the relation of an organisational structure as a unit to other organisational structures and to non-organisational social units (collectivises), such as families, communities, ethnic groups, social classes, and the society.

On the third level organisations are studied from the point of view of their relations to what would be called, in Parsons' frame of reference, personality and culture. The organisation-personality studies are concerned with the interrelationships between the needs of the organisational structure and the needs of the personalities of the actors; problems of motivation and involvement, mentioned above, are cases in point. The study of the relations of organisations to cultural systems focuses on two main concerns. Some scholars are interested in value orientations, and inquire into the sources of the legitimation of authority and into the dynamic relations between the ideals and goals of the organisation and the needs of the organisational structure itself. Others are more interested in the ways in which knowledge (mainly scientific knowledge) is recruited and institutionalised within the organisation. Other aspects of culture, such as myth, are also studied in relation to organisational behaviour.

The fourth level, the relations between organisations and their environment, has thus far received relatively little attention, but theoretically there is place for this focus of interest. It would include the study of relationships between organisational behaviour and the biological and physiological capacities and needs of the actors, and the study of the respective adaptations between the organisation and its geographical-physical environment.

Not all of these levels are of equal interest to sociologists, and not all of them have been equally explored. As regards the actual study of organisations, it can be said—and this is applicable also to the sociology of economic organisations—that most studies tend to focus on the organisational unit and the interrelations among its elements, and tend to neglect its relations to other social units, even such significant ones as other organisations and collectivises. The emphasis is often on the generic characteristics and processes of organisational units, rather than on the specific structures and processes of the various organisational subtypes. These points will be extensively illustrated in the following discussion of how the four levels of interest apply specifically to the study of economic organisations.

Organisations as Social Units

Study of the formal structure of economic organisations—the division of labour and the lines of communication and authority— is conducted mainly as part of the study of administration. Although this type of investigation is relatively well developed in regard to some kinds of organisations, such as hospitals, its application to economic organisations leaves much to be done. Often it is assumed that because the latter are close to the generic model of organisation, there is little need to study the specific nature of their administrative structure. Therefore the sociologist, though interested mainly in the relationship between the formal and the informal aspects, is quite often compelled to spell out the nature of the formal structure he is dealing with.

Analysis of the informal structure of economic organisations is one of the most important contributions of industrial sociology to the study of organisation in general. The findings of Mayo, Roethlisberger, Dixon, Whyte, Homans, K. Lewin, and many others are too well known to be repeated here. It seems more fruitful to point out the directions in which these findings have to be further elaborated, since there is a strong tendency to repeat the work already done and to ignore other areas.

One such area is very similar to that neglected by the administrative studies: the specific nature of the informal aspects of economic organisations. We know by now that informal organisation exists and influences the functioning of industries as well as armies, schools, and churches. But we know little about the significant differences in the amount of informal organisation, or about the different ways in which informal factors function in various organisational contexts. We can make guesses. We may presume, for instance, that informal organisation in the army is much more developed than in a bridge club, because army life is more encompassing (includes more spheres of life)—that, other things being equal, the more encompassing an organisation, the more involving and powerful its informal organisation. It may well be that different economic organisations have different types of informal organisations; thus in a small industry the informal organisation of the workers may be more strongly related to that of the foremen, and even to that of the management, than in a larger industry, and similar differences may exist between a unionised and a non-unionised plant. But all such possibilities are necessarily speculations, as so few comparative studies exist.

Even such a basic question as the conditions under which in-formal organisation of workers supports, withholds support from, or is hostile to management, striving to undermine the formal structure, has not been satisfactorily answered. Whereas we know something about "human relations" factors, such as two-way communication, leadership by the supervisor, participation, it seems that the study of other factors, such as distribution of rewards, the cultural background of workers, the social structure of the community, and many further structural factors that affect workers' attitudes to work and management, is relatively neglected.

The same holds true for the study of informal relations and groups on various levels in the hierarchy of economic organisations. A great deal of repetition research is conducted on groups of workers, but relatively little is known about informal relations in middle and top management. The difficulties of studying primary relations on these levels are obvious, but the extra effort may be rewarded by an extra premium in terms of significant findings, for these elates occupy crucial positions in the organisational structures and the decision-making processes.

Examination of the relations between the two aspects of organisation, the formal and the informal, constitutes a source of many interesting insights into the functioning of organisations, and has become an integral part of the approach of industrial sociologists to economic organisations.

Most industrial sociologists regard the factory as a social system; some even go so far as to see it as a "small society." But it is not enough to state that an industry is a social system, because the same is true of a family, a community, and a nation. What has to be explored is the specific nature of those social systems that are economic organisations, the characteristics that distinguish them from other social systems. It may well be that the differentiating line is to be found in the nature of the integration of rational and non-rational (or instrumental and expressive) elements. Moreover, some industries seem to be not a "small society," but a part of other systems—for example, part of the social system of a community. In these cases some basic functions, which every social system or subsystem has to fulfil in order to exist, are carried on for the industry by the community.

Organisations and Other Social Units

The significance of studying inter-organisational relationships, especially those between economic and non-economic organisations, has lately been emphasised by economists as well as by students of administration. But the examination of inter-organisational relationships from a sociological point of view leaves much to be desired. Even the relations between two organisations that are often studied—corporations and trade unions—are frequently seen from a legal or economic point of view, only rarely from a sociological perspective; also, many of the studies on this subject are merely descriptive and suffer from a lack of theoretical sophistication. Relations between corporations and other organisations are rarely studied.

Thus as regards specifically economic organisations, we know very little about the sociological meaning of their relations with one another—for example, the relations between financing and manufacturing institutions; the role of inter-organisational mobility; the functions of social contacts among the economic elates in maintaining informal monopolistic price regulations and "price leadership." And we know even less about the relations between economic and non-economic organisations. After centuries of abstract arguments concerning the influence of governmental control on economic organisations, there are only a handful of socio-logical studies on the subject, many of which are predominantly concerned with the sociology of law and not with the study of inter-administrative relations. When one turns from the Western world and studies industries and other economic organisations in newly developed countries or in countries of the Soviet orbit, one can make little progress, however, without taking into account at the very least the relations among economic organisations, governmental agencies, and political parties.

In turning now to the relations between economic organisations and collectivised, it should be repeated that by the latter term is meant social groups that have strong elements of solidarity, such as families, communities, ethnic groups, social classes, and society as a whole. All economic organisations are partial systems, in the sense that they do not regulate all the basic needs of the actors. Therefore they are always embedded in collectivised, which serve certain social and symbolic requirements. Economic organisations differ according to the degree and ways in which they are related to these collectivises.

The collectivised provide at least elementary socialisation and exercise a considerable degree of social control over the behaviour of their members, also in their role as organisational personnel. Thus the meaning of the pay check depends on the attitude of the worker's family and neighbours, his status in the community, and so on. Some industrial sociologists, following certain of Durkheim's and Mayo's ideas on the disintegration of collectivised, have expected the industry to take over the social functions of the collectivises, by becoming a community and a family to the worker. In recent years, however, industrial sociologists seem to agree that workers' peer groups are supplementing rather than substituting for collectivises. There are not enough studies that focus on this subject, or on the relationship between work groups and other collectivises. We have a number of studies on the relationship between industrial organisations and families, ethnic groups, or communities, but while most of these contribute a great deal to our understanding of workers and of the functioning of economic organisations, they stimulate our interest in this field more than they satisfy it.

Organisations are not only related to collectivises; they are also in collectivises, in the sense that a factory is in a community and the NAM and AFL-CIO are in the American society. It is not easy to spell out exactly what this "being in" means. From the legal point of view it means that the laws and regulations of the political organs of the collectivise apply to the organisation that is in it. But this is only a formal aspect of the more basic phenomenon: economic organisations are integrated with other organisations, and into the society, through collectivises.

Warner demonstrated this when he showed that the relations between the upper and lower classes in a community have an integrative effect on the work relations among managers and workers recruited from these classes. The power structure and the net of instrumental relations in the industry are embedded in the net of solidarity relations of the community. The managers, who are also the leaders of the community, display more than mere economic "exploitative" interests in the workers, and the latter have ways and means, other than grievances and strikes, of conveying their feelings and needs to management and of exerting pressure on it. When this balance is disturbed by a transference of the centre of power outside the community's solidarity framework, first a "pure" power relation emerges (the strike occurs), and then a new balance on the national level between a trade-union centre and an employer is established, with the directing aid of a government agency (the State Board of Arbitration and Conciliation). Gouldner reports a similar case in which relations in the community impinge on the labour-foremen relations in the industry, and describes the disturbance caused by the interference of an external centre of power.

A full multi-factor analysis, which would take into account all of the major organisational structures and all the significant collectivises to which organisations are related and in which they are embedded, may be far beyond the reach of industrial sociology at its present state. But a study of the interrelations of three or more organisations and collectivises, instead of the traditional examination of the relationship between corporations and trade unions, does not seem to be an exaggerated demand.

As for the relations between economic organisations and society as a whole, this is one of the most significant as well as best covered fields of sociology. It was one of the main interests of Marx and Weber, to name only two. Modern society is often said to be characterised by the supremacy of economic units, institutions, and values. Since the term industry is loosely applied, it is only one step further to speak of modern society as "industrial society" and to call its study "industrial sociology." The historical and psycho-logical reasons for this use of the term are of no interest here, as they cannot justify this doubtful extension. It obscures the fact that its subject matter is a major type of society and hence involves a general theory of societies and not a theory of social units or organisations within society. It obscures also the fact that modern society is characterised by many traits, and the supremacy of eco-nomic institutions is only one of them; modern society would be better described as characterised by the supremacy of rational values and institutions. The term "modern," since it is associated with the supremacy of science, technology, and secular ideology, no less than with the supremacy of the market system and industry as a mode of production, is preferable to the term "industrial," which brings up mainly economic associations.

Similarly, in order to avoid identifying the study of society (sociology) with the study of economic organisations (industrial sociology), the study of "industrial societies" as such should be conceived of not as part of industrial sociology but as a study in itself, the study of modern societies. Industrial sociology has a direct interest in the study of society only in the following cases: first, when the problem is the relations of economic organisations to other organisations and to collectivises, and the extent to which society regulates or directs these relations; and second, when there is direct interaction between economic organisations and integrative structures of the society itself, as in the political organs of modern society.

ORGANISATIONS, PERSONALITY, AND CULTURE

We turn now from the study of economic organisations on the social level to the study of such organisations as related to two other systems, those of personality and culture in Parsons' sense of the terms. The industrial sociologist is not expected to be an expert in the study of these systems in themselves; he is interested in them to the degree that they impinge directly on the functioning of economic organisations.

First, as to personality, the role is the smallest unit for organisational analysis; it is also the unit that links psychological to structural-functional analysis. Role analysis takes into account not only the needs of the personality but also the place of the actor in the system, that is, his social position and what it means for him in terms of role expectations. Thus, for instance, if we were to ask what it would mean for an economic organisation if a large number of its personnel had "authoritarian personalities," we would have to consider the roles assigned to such people. The answer would differ considerably according to whether they were assigned to unskilled jobs or foremen roles, to top management positions or to staff or line positions.

Certain types of roles seem better fitted to certain personality types than to others. In other words, different persons will gain different rewards and suffer different deprivations from the same role. Therefore, with a given group of people and a given cluster of roles, the allocation of people can be made in alternative ways, some of which would cause more personal or structural tensions than others. As economic structures are relatively rational, the possibility of controlling these tensions, as well as the effort to do so, is relatively great. Hence the analysis of these processes is a major challenge to industrial sociology, and many significant insights have been gained through comparative role analysis.

But this type of analysis, which regards roles as units, is only the first step. The next is studying the relationship of roles to one another, analysing their mutual influence and interaction and, finally, their integration into role clusters. The focus of interest can be on a certain role—such as how the relationship between staff and line influences the role of the foreman, or how the role of the steward reflects on that of the foreman—or it can be on the pattern of interrelation of different roles, such as the division of labour and authority, nets of communication, and the like. This seems to be one of the most promising areas of organisational sociology.

As for the relations between economic organisations and culture, the studies that belong in this category may be roughly divided into two groups: studies on the relationship between industrialisation and value systems, such as religions and ideologies (this was one of the major foci of Weber's interest, and has never since been abandoned by sociologists); and studies focusing on the dynamic relationship between goals and organisational processes. In the latter group Michel, for example, was interested in the degree to which an established organisation fails to realise its original goals. In his "Theory of Opportunism" Barnard dealt with the same problems, demonstrating the need to compromise ideals and goals in order to maintain the organisation and enable it to adapt to changes in the environment. Selsnick, who studied these problems perhaps more intensely and directly than any other sociologist, analysed in his most recent work the function of ideals, "mission and role," of the organisation, and the processes of organisational adaptation and their repercussion on the organisation's goals, especially when they are what he called "precarious values." This is clearly one of the most provocative areas of study, and a significant source for the understanding organisational processes.

Organisations and Their Environment

Environment as understood here consists of non-social and non psychological entities: the biological-physiological processes of the human body and the geographical-physical surroundings in which it lives. In this area of analysis there exist, for example, a considerable number of studies in industrial medicine, concerning the medical implication of certain occupational roles. But so far these studies have been of very little interest to the industrial sociologist, and in general the ecology of organisations is a field that has yet to be established. There may be good reasons for this relative lack of interest, for organisations may be relatively less bound to ecological factors than other social units, such as communities and neighbourhoods. On the other hand, in the few existing studies dealing with ecological placement of the workers in the factory, interesting findings have been reported, even though these studies are concerned mainly with the ecology of small groups in organisations rather than with that of organisations as a whole.

The ecology of economic organisations may develop as a field of high interest, for these are more influenced by their need to adapt to the environment than are most organisations. Gouldner has shown very interesting differences in social and power structures between work groups inside a mine and those working on the surface, where there was no danger factor. Environment often influences the time cycle of work, which in turn has many repercussions on the nature of the organisation, the rewards and deprivations caused by the work, and even the nature of unionisation and strikes. Thus we would like to have studies in which such industries as construction, which is sporadic, and farming, which still depends partially on "nature," are compared with industries where work is continuous (as in most industries) or where its fluctuations depend more on human regulation.

The differentiation of work according to the time cycle it requires is important from the point of view of possibilities for breaking the work process. Some jobs, such as steel casting, re-quire continuous action, while others allow breaks; some require a high degree of punctuality, such as certain railroad jobs. All such factors seem to have important repercussions—still to a large degree unknown—on the workers and on the structure of eco-nomic organisations. The ecological nature of work impinges also on the proportions of unskilled, semiskilled, and skilled workers that the industry can employ, as well as on the ratio of white-collar to blue-collar workers, and of administrative to professional personnel. The study of the interrelations between environment and economic organisations has remained almost untouched since the determinist theories of ecology were refuted.

In brief, organisational sociology studies the generic characteristics of organisations as well as the differentiating features of various sub-types of organisations, classified according to their functional nature. Industrial sociology can be fruitfully conceived of as the study of economic organisations, and thus fitted into the general theoretical model of the study of organisations. It seems useful to codify the findings of organisational studies on four levels: the organisation as a social unit; its relations to other social units; its relations to personality and to culture; and (less extensively studied so far) the ecology of organisations. Whether this somewhat abstract classification of organisations and of levels and dimensions of study will be of help to industrial sociology, or even, as would be preferable, to the sociology of economic organisations, will be determined only by further research.

2

Organisational Leadership

A new paradigm for business and society is emerging in which business is being asked, and in some cases pushed by social forces, to assume greater responsibility for social dimensions: the well being of the communities in which it operates, the impact of operations on the local and global environment, and even the relationship between consumer and producer. This new social framework includes business as a partner in the process of problem solving and drives innovation throughout society. Business is no longer only a source of economic production but also a participant in the development of socially just and ecologically sustainable social systems. Accounting for business impact across the three complementary dimensions of social, environmental and economic impact, known as the "triple bottom-line", provides a basis for a new business and socialite paradigm.

Businesses assuming responsibility for this triple bottom line commit themselves to an evolutionary process that requires change, learning, and a new world-view, that is, a new way of thinking and perceiving our world. Change toward sustainability is a process that presents a leadership challenge. In order for organisations to navigate this evolutionary journey, they need a new kind of leadership that:

1. Is educated in perceiving and understanding complex systems
2. Understands the scientific principles of sustainability, and
3. Is capable of envisioning and actualising the sustainable future of the organisation or the community.

We can call a leader that combines these characteristics an "Evolutionary Leader".

This type of leadership does not come easy for leaders in today's businesses and organisations. In fact, CEO's or senior managers may have committed to become a responsible or sustainable business without having the competencies and the processes to lead the organisation toward this goal.

Leadership Competencies

Leaders who commit to lead social responsibility in organisations or build sustainability in communities also commit themselves to a journey of personal transformation. This change begins with fundamental assumptions that we inherit from socialisation and education processes. The dominant modern world-view, based on the Cartesian legacy of linear and materialistic thinking, is one such example. From the Cartesian cognitive framework, the world is a metaphoric machine and human beings are separate from nature. The world-view of the Evolutionary Leader, on the other hand, is based on a systems view of life, whereby we perceive and respect the interconnections of living systems, human beings, and the biosphere. This is a world-view that sees whole systems and interdependent cycles of which we are a part.

Leadership is a way of being, a way of perceiving the world, as well as an "Activity" in which skills or competencies are used to mobilise people to take actions that bring about a desired future. Evolutionary Leaders, besides developing an appropriate world-view, are also educated in a set of competencies or disciplines that support them in managing and creating the socially responsible and ecologically sustainable business and communities. To lead an organisation through its adaptive changes, leaders need a new set of powerful competencies that can complement their more traditional leadership competencies. We propose the following five competencies as the basics for leading an organisation toward a sustainable future:

1. Vision and back-casting.
2. Language and conversations.
3. Systems thinking.
4. Scientific understanding of sustainability.
5. Culture and Organisational learning.

Vision and Back-casting

The most common trait among successful leaders is the ability to develop and communicate a vibrant and compelling vision of the future. Evolutionary Leaders have the capacity to envision not only the details of traditional business concerns, such as the development of new products and growth in market penetration, but also include issues of social and environmental context. Evolutionary Leaders create and sustain an intention in the design and development of the enterprise in order to work for continuous improvement in the triple bottom line of economics, society, and environment.

Visionary leaders need not be heroic leaders; rather they need the ability to see eye to eye with others and engage the rest of the organisation in creating a shared vision. They have the capacity to use language, conversations, and daily actions to involve others in the growth, development, and achievement of that vision.

The essence of a shared vision lies in bringing personal visions into harmony with a larger organisational vision. Personal vision cannot be dictated, and implicit in a shared vision is differences in perspectives regarding the same goal. If the vision is truly shared, responsibility for success does not rest on any one individual's shoulders. Instead, shared vision gives people a genuine sense of responsibility for their actions, and every member of the organisation shares responsibility for the collective result. When the shared vision includes social and environmental aspects, individuals in the organisation will be motivated and encouraged to achieve those goals.

Once there is commitment to a shared vision, the journey requires that leaders at all levels of the organisation mobilise the people and the systems toward achieving a sustainable future. The process of organisational change demands the collective intelligence of the whole organisation, and cannot be accomplished through mandate from the top of the organisational hierarchy. Back-casting is a participatory tool for re-orienting internal business processes toward the new goals of sustainability.

Back-Casting

Back-casting involves "looking back from the future" in order to link a vision of a future desired state to the current situation, and to develop a strategic plan of action that defines the path to the desired future. When sustainability is part of the vision, the enormous gap between current reality and a sustainable future can make the vision appear hopelessly unattainable. Often organisations and institutions, without a shared vision for a sustainable future, pursue solutions that only address symptoms rather than systemic causes. This can create stumbling blocks and foster a dependence on quick-fixes. Real solutions create flexible platforms for progressively more sustainable practices, which serve as a springboard for future measures and innovation rather than a quick-fix to a current problem that leads to dead-end or costly future options.

The key to back-casting is the development of the flexible platform. The platform is a place of dynamic stability between current reality and the vision. The platform may be an improvement in a production process, a substitution for more sustainable materials, or a more effective and productive means of communication with stockholders. Creating a platform for innovation should stretch the capacity and creativity of the organisation, and in the process, bring it closer to sustainability. Interdependent and attainable goals constitute a platform. A set of clear goals is important in the generation and maintenance of creative tension in the face of the seemingly insurmountable technical and systemic challenges to achieving real sustainability.

The advantages of back-casting become are apparent when contrasted with the traditional forecasting approach of many companies. In forecasting, a company may review its current impacts and set targets that incrementally reduce its impacts year after year. The process never challenges the current mindsets and patterns that are part of the problem and encourages a piecemeal approach to complex problems. Forecasting rarely produces more than incremental changes, whereas back-casting produces innovative leaps. By starting from a place of future success, back-casting promotes radical solutions that may not have been considered possible in the current reality and draws on the entire organisation's resources to create the desired reality.

Language and Conversations

Perhaps the most powerful tool available to leaders is language. Effective leaders are directors of language communities. Leaders live in a rhetorical world where their selection and use of language is what makes them more or less effective. The power for inventing a new vision takes place within language, in the act of declaration, and is manifested through the types of conversations that a leader chooses. Leaders choose not only the conversations that they have with themselves, but also influence the nature of the conversations in the organisation. Those conversations can support or prevent the organisation in moving toward its vision.

Managers live in a rhetorical universe where language and conversation is constantly used to get things done, to set the direction for the company, to coordinate actions toward the goals, to influence others, to build teams, to create and manage important relationships, and to envision new products and innovations. Rhetoric is used well when it mobilises actions of individuals in a way that contributes both to the individual aspirations and to the performance of organisations as a whole. Evolutionary Leaders recognise the power of language and conversations, and are competent in using specific types of conversations to achieve their vision.

Keen observers of management and its relationship to language, like Fernando Flores and Robert Eccles, believe that language is the core competency that all managers and leaders should be skilled at. Language allows us to create visions and reality, persuade others to collaborate, and evoke from others promises to take action and achieve results. When an Evolutionary Leader uses the power of language to invent a vision of sustainability and to mobilise people to make that vision the new reality, a vocabulary of sustainability will begin to emerge in the organisation: new words like ecological footprint, living systems, zero waste, and the vocabulary of the science of sustainability will become part of the culture of the organisation. In their role as leaders of language communities, leaders influence the networks of conversations that give life to the organisation.

By hosting participated, strategic conversations to involve the collective intelligence of the organisation in dealing with the challenges facing the organisation or community, Evolutionary Leaders leverage their conversations in making their vision a reality.

Systems Thinking

"Systems thinking is a framework for seeing interrelationships rather than things, for seeing patterns of change rather than static "snapshots". It is a set of general principles from science, ecology, and social sciences". Systems thinking is a competency for understanding the behaviour and dynamics of complex systems like organisations, ecosystems, and economies. Evolutionary Leaders, concerned with the performance of organisations as well as with society and the environment, must have a firm grasp of the fundamentals of systems thinking.

A systems perspective involves a shift in thinking that goes from seeing parts to seeing whole. It involves recognising our own role in manifesting our desired future. As Peter Senge says, it is to go "from seeing people as helpless reactors to seeing them as active participants in shaping their reality, from reacting to the present to creating the future". When we go beyond a focus on the individual parts of a problem, we can begin to understand the dynamics of the parts, their interrelationships, and the behaviour of the whole system.

Systems thinking is also a language, and one's language shapes perception. What we see depends on the kind of observer that we are, the world-view and distinctions that we hold, and what we are prepared to see. As a language, systems thinking allows for communicating about the relationship between the parts of the organisation and its overall performance, the dynamics of the whole system, and complexities in the socialite context.

Leaders who learn this language and develop a systemic world-view become systems thinkers, observers, and designers of their organisations and of their world. They become pro-active and more effective in shaping the behaviour, patterns, structures, and events of organisational systems, leading to performance that is in better alignment with the vision and purpose of the organisation.

At whatever level of power and influence they happen to be in the community, department, organisation, or society, systems thinking capacities will strengthen the effectiveness of Evolutionary Leaders. Systems thinking will enable a more complete understanding of the context within which organisations operate, and thus inform the development of sustainable organisations.

Scientific Understanding of Sustainability

In order to bring the direction of the organisation's development in line with sustainability, leaders needs a scientific understanding of the conditions that define sustainability. The systems conditions promoted by Karl-Hendrick Robert, founder of The Natural Step, are the result of broad scientific consensus. These basic principles derive from laws of physics and nature and provide boundaries for creating sustainable systems.

The Natural Step defines the first order principles of sustainability as follows:

> In a sustainable society,
>
> The biosphere (nature) is not subject to systematically increasing concentrations of substances extracted from the earth's crust, and
>
> The biosphere is not subject to systematically increasing concentrations of substances produced by society;
>
> Nature's functions should not be systematically impoverished by physical displacement, over harvesting, or other forms of

ecosystems manipulation that destroy the ecosystem's ability to renew itself.

In society resources are used fairly, efficiently, and responsibly in order to meet human needs worldwide.

The Natural Step systems conditions are rooted in the Laws of Thermodynamics and the history of the planetary evolution. A leader with a solid understanding of these systems conditions or "the rules of the game" can develop strategies, evolve processes, and take specific actions that contribute to achieving sustainability. In addition, by evaluating the impacts of the activities and goals of a business against each of the four systems conditions, a scientific understanding of its impacts on social and ecological systems is developed.

The Natural Step also gives a business or a community a common language to draw on when discussing sustainability. This enables scientists, engineers, management, and strategist to learn together effectively. Having a common language facilitates the development of shared vision and the communication of changes and innovation in manufacturing processes, business processes, and goals.

The Washington city of Whistler has chosen to adopt The Natural Step framework as a common language to support the implementation of the Whistler Environmental Strategy. The "learning community" has used the TNS framework to develop a common mental model of sustainability and to create common training programs and toolkits. All residents, second home owners and business have been invited to start their own journey toward sustainability through an integrated program known as "Whistler. It's Our Nature". Already numerous improvements have been made in environmental management at the ski resorts and industries throughout. Perhaps most importantly, the municipality understand that it has embarked on a journey of social and cultural change that will happen over time and in many different ways.

Culture and Organisational Learning

The culture of an organisation contributes to individual creativity and productivity and often determines the values, the behaviours, the understanding that people maintain and act on. In order to function well, an organisation must have a culture that supports its purpose, vision, strategic objectives, and the well being of the people working in that organisation. Culture, when consciously designed by management, is a powerful element in the performance of the organisation.

Most organisational cultures emerge over time, without attention to their design or strategic role. The result is that the culture is taken for granted and is not perceived as a key element in the success of the business. Thus, a major role of leadership is to be the architects and caretakers of the corporate culture. In mobilising an organisation around sustainability initiatives, the leadership has to be aware of how the culture works in relation to other key structural components and processes in the organisation.

Leaders in the design of organisational cultures will face challenges along the way. First of all is the challenge to be authentic in declarations of values and the kind of culture that they espoused. In addition, a continuous challenge is in being perceived as "walking the talk" of the values and vision in everyday practice.

A corporate culture that supports sustainable development promotes values such as corporate citizenship, quality, innovation, recycling, and sustainability and fosters a climate of learning, communication, team work and creativity. In such a culture, people can bring the best of themselves to their tasks and roles. They can utilise their intelligence and potential in the service of a vision of a company that renews the systems of society and rewards their efforts.

The organisation pursuing sustainability is a training ground for Evolutionary Leaders at all levels. These leaders can take their experiences, learning, and sustainable practices into other areas of their lives, such as communities, schools, and homes. The organisation becomes a learning organisation for human development and product innovation based on sustainable principles.

To create the new paradigm of sustainability, requires changing the unsustainable mind that we have inherited from our culture and the industrial revolution of the last two centuries. The work of evolutionary leaders is multidimensional, it requires leadership development as well as organisational learning and evolution. By developmental, we mean that the leaders engage in a process of self transformation, or personal learning of a new world-view, they become new observers of the world, and declare a purpose or vision that contributes toward sustainability. This leadership development also requires learning new competencies, or languages. This dual process of personal transformation and learning new languages has the benefit of producing a whole new type of leader, that can achieve personal satisfaction by engaging in this evolutionary journey, but also the satisfaction, of inventing new products and services that are good for people, the business, and the planet.

3

Systems Thinking

Although the field of systems thinking had not yet hatched at the time of this quote, it is clear that Einstein already knew about systems thinking, even if he didn't call it that. He was able to recognise that if we continually approached problems in the same way, we would continue to get the same outcomes. We humans are creatures of habit, and we often find it difficult to recognise patterns of behaviour that are counterproductive. Systems thinking offers tools and processes that enable organisations to see patterns and connections, leading to greater productivity.

Defining a System

According to *Merriam Webster's Collegiate Dictionary, Tenth Edition*, a system is "a regularly interacting or interdependent group of items forming a unified whole." The key words in this definition are "interdependent" and "unified whole." A pile of rocks is not a system because they do not interact with each other, and you do not really change anything by adding to it or taking away from it. However, if you take that pile of rocks and create a stone wall, you now have a system. Adding or removing a stone can create havoc. This stone wall system is more than just the sum of its parts; these stones work together to create something much greater than a pile of rocks.

Systems can range from very simple (filling a glass of water) to extremely complex (climate change) and are constantly working to maintain a level of stability. They do so by creating feedback loops using inputs and outputs. To understand systems in greater depth, let's take a look at a simple system: driving a car. Inputs into this system are the desired destination, actions of the driver, and the driving conditions. The output is the car moving in the desired direction.

Organisational systems are more complex than this. There are two distinct sections of an organisational system, the internal system and the external system. The internal system consists of a variety of parts, including the products or services produced, personnel, the materials and tools used to create products or services, the relationships that people have with each other – this list could be endless. The external system is everything outside the organisation that influences it: competitors, the economy, the condition of the financial industry, the environment, regulations, the political landscape, and the community, to name a few. Both the internal and external systems are not only interacting within themselves but are also interacting with each other. Observing and understanding these interactions is the crux of systems thinking.

What is Systems Thinking?

The discipline of systems thinking evolved from the field of systems dynamics and is both a set of tools and a new way of thinking involving new language. In systems thinking, we look at the whole system rather than trying to break it down into its individual parts; that is, we become expansive in our thinking rather than reductive. By looking at the whole, we are more capable of seeing interrelationships and patterns over time. We also begin to understand that the presenting problem may be symptomatic of deeper issues within the system, and so we start looking for the root causes. In doing so, we move away from assigning blame and focus on the desired outcomes.

Systems thinking is pro-active and circular in nature, as opposed to linear thinking, which tends to be reactive. There are three key concepts of systems thinking: reinforcing feedback, balancing feedback, and delays. Reinforcing or amplifying feedback loops are what fuel growth or create decline in systems. They either spiral up or down, although they rarely occur in isolation. There are limits both to growth and decline. A simple example of a reinforcing loop is how an organisation's productivity can influence growth which, in turn, influences financial rewards which comes full circle to influence productivity. This loop can move in either a positive direction or a negative direction but ultimately stops at an outer limit.

Balancing or stabilising feedback loops are those that attempt to maintain equilibrium. These systems are goal oriented and will do whatever is necessary to reach or maintain that goal. The previous example of driving a car is a balancing loop because the goal is to reach the desired destination. The driver will do what it takes to reach that destination in a safe and efficient manner. In organisations we are bumping up against a balancing loop when our attempts to make change only bring us back to where we started. We are encountering resistance to change because the existing system is attempting to maintain a particular goal. That goal, however, may not be obvious; we may find we need to uncover the mental models that are keeping that system in place before we have any hope of changing it.

Delays are inevitable in any system but are often not recognised. Delays cause instability in systems, and aggressive action to compensate for delays will likely cause organisations to overshoot or undershoot. To illustrate, let's use the example of a thermostat. These days with energy prices heading through the roof, many of us have developed the habit of setting the thermostat back at night to conserve energy. On those particularly frosty mornings, it is tempting to turn the heat up higher than necessary in the morning, but unlike a stove burner, turning the temperature up higher will not produce more heat. There is a delay from when the heat is turned up to when the room reaches its target temperature. If the heat is set higher than necessary, then the room will become overheated. In reaction to that, we set the heat back to cool the room off, but then the temperature drops too low and we once again set the heat up again. This might go on forever if we weren't capable of learning from our actions. In systems thinking, it is crucial to develop the patience to weather delays and not to react too quickly to changes in the system.

Characteristics of Systems Thinkers

According to *The Systems Thinking Play book*, a systems thinker is one who:

1. Sees the whole picture.
2. Changes perspectives to see new leverage points in complex systems.
3. Looks for inter-dependencies.
4. Considers how mental models create our futures.
5. Pays attention and gives voice to the long-term.
6. "Goes wide" (uses peripheral vision) to see complex cause and effect relationships.
7. Finds where unanticipated consequences emerge.
8. Lowers the "water line" to focus on structure, not blame.
9. Holds the tension of paradox and controversy without trying to resolve it quickly.

Systems thinkers are those who think outside the box. They understand that there are no right answers, only different paths to the same outcomes. They realise that quick fixes will most likely lead right back to where they started from and thus develop patience with the idea that cause and effect are not closely related in time and space. They understand that things may get worse before they get better, but they have learned to take the long view. In doing so, they are able to tap the creative asynergy that exists in organisations.

Applying Systems Thinking

As with the previous four disciplines, there are a variety of ways to implement systems thinking within an organisation, and each organisation must find what fits well within the organisational culture. However, there are key aspects of systems thinking to consider. Below is one possible approach that includes these key aspects:

> *Events*: Begin the practice of systems thinking by telling the story of the current situation. It is important to hear as many perspectives as possible. However, don't jump to solutions immediately. It may be necessary to provide a quick fix but do so with the understanding that it is a stopgap measure that is not designed for long-term solutions. Meanwhile, explore the nature of the event or problem in greater detail.
>
> *Patterns of behaviour*: Track the situation over a period of time. Look for patterns and trends that go below the surface. Go back in history, if you've got the data. Those patterns are key indictors for the system.
>
> *Systemic structure*: Look for interrelationships in the patterns and trends you've discovered. Look for balancing and reinforcing feedback and identify delays in the system. Uncover the mental models that are driving these patterns.
>
> *Mental models*: Create new mental models to introduce change into the system. Be patient – there will be delays, and things may get worse before they get better. Track and evaluate the effects of the changes. Determine if there are unintended consequences and decide what needs tweaking.

Although this might sound like a relatively straightforward process, it is far from it. There are many challenges to implementing systems thinking, the biggest of which is traditions and/or habits. Patterns of behaviour are hard to recognise and even harder to change, and we often feel pressure to act quickly with little or no systemic information. Finding the balance between attending to the present and creating the future is never easy.

Benefits of Systems Thinking

Systems thinking is the thread that ties the other four disciplines of organisational learning together. Organisations engaging in systems thinking are able to:

1. Develop new ways of looking at old problems.
2. Integrate new information more easily.
3. See interrelationships and cause and effect more clearly.
4. Develop patience with implementing change and tolerating delays.
5. Step away from the blame game toward shared responsibility.
6. See the whole rather than the parts.

Although each of the above benefits can take an inordinate amount of time to master, the investment in developing systems thinkers is worth the time and effort. Ultimately, organisations practising systems thinking will be able to step up to that next level of thinking in order to solve problems and create their desired futures. They will have greater control over their destiny and be more nimble in responding to environmental changes.

4

Employment Relationship

The employment relationship is a legal notion widely used in countries around the world to refer to the relationship between a person called an "employee" (frequently referred to as "a worker") and an "employer" for whom the "employee" performs work under certain conditions in return for remuneration. It is through the employment relationship, however defined, that reciprocal rights and obligations are created between the employee and the employer. The employment relationship has been, and continues to be, the main vehicle through which workers gain access to the rights and benefits associated with employment in the areas of labour law and social security. It is the key point of reference for determining the nature and extent of employers' rights and obligations towards their workers.

The profound changes occurring in the world of work, and particularly in the labour market, have given rise to new forms of relationship which do not always fit within the parameters of the employment relationship. While this has increased flexibility in the labour market, it has also led to a growing number of workers whose employment status is unclear and who are consequently outside the scope of the protection normally associated with an employment relationship. In 2004, the Director-General of the

International Labour Office described the challenge as follows:

> The State has a key role to play in creating an enabling institutional framework to balance the need for flexibility for enterprises and security for workers in meeting the changing demands of a global economy ... At the heart of national policies to meet the social challenges of globalisation is a dynamic strategy for managing labour market change.

The legal framework governing the employment relationship is an important component of national policy for managing labour market change taking account of the need for flexibility and security.

The International Labour Organisation (ILO) ILO has taken the employment relationship as the reference point for examining various types of work relationships. In recent years, the Conference has held discussions on self-employed workers, migrant workers, home-workers, private employment agency workers, child workers, in cooperatives, and workers in the informal economy and in the fishing sector. It has also addressed work relationships in the course of discussions on social security and maternity protection.

In 1997 and 1998, the Conference examined an item on "contract labour". The original intention of the Conference discussion on "contract labour" was to protect certain categories of unprotected workers through the adoption of a Convention and a Recommendation, but the proposal to adopt a Convention and Recommendation failed. However, at the end of the second discussion in 1998, the Conference adopted a resolution in which it invited the Governing Body of the ILO to place these issues on the agenda of a future session of the Conference with a view to the possible adoption of a Convention supplemented by a Recommendation if such adoption was, according to the normal procedures, considered necessary by that Conference. The Governing Body was also invited to instruct the Director-General:

(a) to hold meetings of experts to examine at least the following issues arising out of the deliberations of the Committee on Contract Labour:

(i) which workers, in the situations that have begun to be identified in the Committee, are in need of protection;

(ii) appropriate ways in which such workers can be protected, and the possibility of dealing separately with the various situations;

(iii) how such workers would be defined, bearing in mind the different legal systems that exist and language differences.

It is noteworthy that in the various debates mentioned above, delegates from all regions repeatedly alluded to the employment relationship, in its various forms and with different meanings, as a concept familiar to all.

In accordance with the 1998 resolution, a tripartite Meeting of Experts on Workers in Situations Needing Protection was held in Geneva in May 2000. The common statement adopted by the Meeting noted that the global phenomenon of transformation in the nature of work had resulted in situations in which the legal scope of the employment relationship (which determines whether or not workers are entitled to be protected by labour legislation) did not accord with the realities of working relationships. This had resulted in a tendency whereby workers who should be protected by labour and employment law were not receiving that protection in fact or in law. The scope of regulation of the employment relationship did not accord with the reality, which varied from country to country and, within countries, from sector to sector. It was also evident that while some countries had responded by adjusting the scope of the legal regulation of the employment relationship, this had not occurred in all countries.

The common statement also noted that various country studies had greatly increased the pool of available information concerning the employment relationship and the extent to which dependent workers had ceased to be protected by labour and employment legislation. The Meeting agreed that countries should adopt or continue a national policy in terms of which they would, at appropriate intervals review and, if appropriate, clarify or adapt the scope of the regulation of the employment relationship in the country's legislation in line with current employment realities. The review should be conducted in a transparent manner with participation by the social partners. The experts further agreed that the ILO could play a major role in assisting countries to develop policies to ensure that laws regulating the employment relationship cover workers needing protection.

Further to the resolution adopted by the Conference in 1998, the Office undertook a series of national studies. The objective of the national studies was to help identify and describe the principal situations in which workers lacked adequate protection, as well as the problems caused by the absence or inadequacy of protection, and to suggest measures to remedy such situations.

The research undertaken confirmed the universal importance of the idea of the employment relationship, on which labour protection systems are largely based, while highlighting the deficiencies affecting the scope, in terms of persons covered, of the regulations governing this relationship. It also confirmed the extent and repercussions of the problems of lack of workers' protection.

At the 91st Session of the Conference in June 2003, a general discussion was held on the scope of the employment relationship. During the discussion, many delegates emphasised that the concept of the employment relationship is common to all legal systems and traditions. There are rights and entitlements which exist under labour laws, regulations and collective agreements and which are specific to or linked to workers who work within the framework of an employment relationship. One of the consequences associated with changes in the structure of the labour market, the organisation of work and the deficient application of the law is the growing phenomenon of workers who are in fact employees but find themselves without the protection of an employment relationship. There was a shared concern among governments, employers and workers to ensure that labour laws and regulations are applied to those who are in employment relationships and that the wide variety of arrangements under which work is performed by a worker can be put within an appropriate legal framework.

The Conference also recognised that the protection of workers is at the heart of the ILO's mandate. Within the framework of the ILO's Decent Work Agenda, all workers, regardless of employment status, should work in conditions of decency and dignity.

The Conference noted that the ILO should envisage the adoption of an international response on this topic. A Recommendation was considered as an appropriate response. The Recommendation should focus on disguised employment relationships and on the need for mechanisms to ensure that persons with an employment relationship have access to the protection they are due at the national level. Such a Recommendation should provide guidance to member States without defining universally the substance of the employment relationship. The Recommendation should be flexible enough to take account of different economic, social, legal and industrial relations traditions and address the gender dimension. Such a Recommendation should not interfere with genuine commercial and independent contracting arrangements. It should promote collective bargaining and social dialogue as a means of finding solutions to the problem at national level and should take into account recent developments in employment relationships.

Employment Relationship and Law

The *employment relationship* is a legal concept which underpins the operation of the labour market in many countries. This was confirmed particularly in the discussions on "contract labour" at the International Labour Conference in 1997 and 1998, the Conference discussion leading to the adoption of the Private Employment Agencies Convention, 1997 (No. 181), the national studies undertaken by the ILO, the Meeting of Experts on Workers in Situations Needing Protection, and the 2003 Conference general discussion on the scope of the employment relationship. It is also reflected in a significant number of international labour standards: some ILO Conventions and Recommendations cover all workers without distinction, while others refer specifically to independent workers or self-employed persons, and others apply only to persons in an employment relationship.

The employment relationship continues to be the predominant framework for work in many countries. Moreover, a study published in 2000 found that in the industrialised countries, in particular, the employment relationship is not just predominant but is proving durable, contrary to persistent reports that major changes in employment relationships have led to less stability and greater numerical flexibility. Another study published in 2001 found similar results in six transition countries.

Of course, the situation with regard to the employment relationship is not the same in every country. Where the formal economy absorbs only a very small part of the population and where high unemployment swells the ranks of the self-employed, the reality tends to be different. Even in these cases, however, wage earners may represent a significant proportion of the working population in quantitative terms.

The widespread emergence of new forms of employment is frequently referred to in the context of changes in the organisation of work and flexible work arrangements. However, new forms of employment may be understood in different ways and mean different things, especially with respect to the legal implications, and for this reason an important distinction needs to be made at this point.

People may provide their labour either within the employment relationship under the authority of an employer and for remuneration or within a civil/commercial relationship independently and for a fee. Each of these relationships has certain characteristics which vary from one country to another and determine to what extent the performance of work falls within an employment relationship or a civil/commercial relationship.

In some countries and in some sectors more than others, employment relationships have become more diversified. They have become much more versatile and, alongside traditional full-time employees, employers are increasingly employing workers in other ways which allow them to use their labour as efficiently as possible. Many people accept short-term employment, or agree to work certain days of the week, for want of better opportunities. But in other cases, these options are an appropriate solution, both for the worker and for the enterprise. Recourse to various types of employment is in itself a legitimate response to the challenges faced by enterprises, as well as meeting the needs of some employees for more flexible work arrangements. These various types of work arrangements lie *within* the framework of the employment relationship.

At the same time, there are civil or commercial contractual relationships under which the services of self-employed workers may be procured, but on terms and conditions which differ from those within an employment relationship. Frequent recourse to such contractual arrangements has become increasingly widespread in recent years. From a legal standpoint, these arrangements lie *outside* the framework of the employment relationship.

The determination of the existence of an employment relationship should be guided by the *facts*, and not by the name or form given to it by the parties. That is why the existence of an employment relationship depends on certain objective conditions being met and not on how either or both of the parties describe the relationship. This is known in law as the principle of the *primacy of fact*, which is explicitly enshrined in some national legal systems. This principle is also frequently applied by judges in the absence of an express rule.

Various *factors* are used in many countries to determine the existence of an employment relationship. While these factors vary, some of the more common factors include the level of subordination to the employer, work for the benefit of another person, and work under instruction. In some cases, the law goes one step further, and classifies certain workers as employees whose situation could be ambiguous, or provides for a presumption in their case that there is an employment relationship. Conversely, legislation may specify that certain contractual arrangements are not employment relationships.

In some legal systems, certain *indicators* are relied on to identify whether or not the relevant *factors* are present to determine the existence of an employment relationship. These *indicators* include the extent of integration in an organisation, who controls the conditions of work, the provision of tools, materials or machinery, the provision of training and whether the remuneration is paid periodically and constitutes a significant proportion of the income of the worker. In common law countries, judges base their rulings on certain *tests* developed by case law, for example the tests of control, integration in the enterprise, economic reality, who bears the financial risk, and mutuality of obligation. In all systems, the judge must normally decide on the basis of the facts, irrespective of how the parties construe or describe a given contractual relationship.

The existence of a legal framework regulating the provision of labour does not, of course, preclude disagreement when it comes to the examination of specific cases to determine whether an employment relationship exists. Indeed, this is a frequent occurrence, given the proliferation and great diversity of situations in which the worker's status is unclear.

Employment Relationship and Workers' Protection

The Meeting of Experts in May 2000 highlighted the lack of protection of workers in certain situations in which the legal scope of the employment relationship did not accord with the realities of working relationships. The context in which this lack of protection has arisen varies considerably from one region to another and from one country to another, but in all cases it is linked to significant changes in the structure of employment. Some of these changes are associated with globalisation, technological change and transformations in the organisation and functioning of enterprises, often combined with restructuring in a highly competitive environment. In the words of the World Commission on the Social Dimension of Globalisation, has set in motion a process of far-reaching change that is affecting everyone". The impact of these changes is very uneven in terms of the degree to which they benefit countries, industries and enterprises.

Changes in workers' status and mass redundancies, especially in developing countries or those in transition, are frequently related to major financial crises, external debt, structural adjustment programmes and privatisation. These realities have been reflected in a drastic reduction in countries' financial capacity and a deterioration in conditions of employment and work. In this context, the growth of the informal economy and undeclared employment has been especially significant.

Associated with these developments, changes in the structure of the work force have been accentuated by migration from one country to another or from one sector of the economy to another. Other factors include a strong shift to services, greater participation of women, higher skill levels of young people in certain countries and deskilling of workers in others. Changing lifestyles, education levels and expectations also lead to workers demanding more flexibility. These changes inevitably influence workers' attitudes and the way in which they cope with finding and keeping a job.

Many enterprises, for their part, have organised their activities so as to utilise labour in increasingly diversified and selective ways, including various kinds of contracts, the decentralisation of activities to subcontractors or self-employed workers, or the use of temporary employment agencies. These arrangements are encouraged by rapid developments in technology and new management systems in response to the growing demands of competition. This kind of flexibility has frequently been preceded or accompanied by legislative and institutional reforms to enhance the supply and demand for labour or to promote self-employment with the aim of stimulating job creation.

Repercussions of the Lack of Protection

Above all, of course, the lack of labour protection has

adverse consequences for workers and their families. At the same time, however, the absence of workers' rights or guarantees can be counterproductive to the interests of the enterprise itself and have a negative impact on society generally. Moreover, there is some evidence indicating that these changes affect women more than men. Workers in these situations not only lose their rights under labour law, but also have difficulty securing the protection of the competent inspection services or seeking redress through the labour courts. In many countries, they are completely excluded from or on the fringe of social security protection and receive less favourable benefits than those workers recognised as employees.

The lack of labour protection of workers can also affect employers, to the extent that it undermines productivity and distorts competition between enterprises, both at national and sectorial or international level, often to the detriment of those who comply with the law. The lack of legal certainty can also result in judicial decisions reclassifying "self-employed" workers as employees, with considerable unforeseen economic consequences for enterprises. At the same time, the reality of work without any prospect of stability or promotion can ultimately make workers lose their commitment to the enterprise and contribute to an increasing and costly labour turnover.

Another dimension of the lack of labour protection is the neglect of training, including training for work in environments where there are inherent risks. Enterprises can be reluctant to invest in training workers who will probably not be with them for long. The user enterprise is unlikely to train the workers supplied by another firm, except for very specific purposes. Untrained workers are more vulnerable to accidents in the work place and can hamper the competitiveness of the enterprise. Furthermore, a lack of investment in training can undermine national competitiveness. In addition, in some sectors which have large numbers of unprotected workers, the negative image can create serious problems of recruitment and retention of workers. The construction industry is one example of such a sector.

The lack of labour protection can also impact on the health and safety of third parties and society in general. Some accidents, such as those caused by heavy vehicles or major accidents in industrial plants, have caused damage to the environment, as well as injuries and fatalities to third parties. The link between accident risks and the lack of workers' protection has also been observed in situations where there is extensive use of subcontracting. The issue is not subcontracting itself but its improper use, which can create or aggravate risks.

Lack of protection can also have a considerable financial impact, in terms of unpaid social security contributions and taxes. For example, in the United States, according to Treasury Department estimates, misclassification of dependent workers (employees) as independent workers results in a loss of some US$2.6 billion each year in unpaid contributions to social security, the health care system (Medicare) and the federal unemployment insurance scheme, as well as US$1.6 billion in income tax. In short, protection is necessary not just for the sake of workers and enterprises, but also because there are public goods at stake.

Uncertainty with Regard to the Law

Disputes concerning the legal nature of a relationship for the provision of labour are increasingly frequent. The employment relationship may be *objectively ambiguous* or *disguised.* Both situations create uncertainty as to the scope of the law and can nullify its protection.

The problems faced by workers involved in "triangular" employment relationships pose different legal questions. These are workers employed by an enterprise (the "provider") who perform work for a third party (the "user") to whom their employer provides labour or services. For these employees, their employment status is not in doubt, but they frequently face difficulties in establishing who their employer is, what their rights are and who is responsible for them.

Changes in the legal status of workers, whether real or apparent, seem to be a sign of the times and are commonly observed not only in traditional sectors such as transport (truck drivers, taxi drivers), construction and clothing, but in new areas as well, such as sales staff in department stores, or certain jobs in wholesale distribution or in private security agencies, although there are considerable differences from one country to another and from region to region.

Objectively Ambiguous Employment Relationships

In a standard employment relationship, the worker's status is not normally open to doubt. In some cases, however, a worker may have a wide margin of autonomy and this factor alone may give rise to doubt as to his or her employment status. There are situations where the main factors that characterise the employment relationship are not apparent. It is not a case of a deliberate attempt to disguise it, but rather one of genuine doubt as to the existence of an employment relationship. This may occur as a result of the specific, complex form of the relationship between workers and the persons to whom they provide their labour, or the evolution of that relationship over time. Such situations may occur with persons who are normally self-employed, such as electricians, plumbers and computer programmers, and who gradually enter into a permanent arrangement with a single client.

In other cases, especially in work environments affected by major changes, it is possible and sometimes necessary to resort to a range of flexible and dynamic employment arrangements which can be difficult to fit into the traditional framework of the employment relationship. A person may be recruited and work at a distance without fixed hours or days of work, with special payment arrangements and full autonomy as to how to organise the work. Some workers may never even have set foot in the enterprise if, for example, they have been recruited and work via the Internet and are paid through a bank. However, perhaps because they use equipment supplied by the enterprise, follow its instructions and are subject to subtle but firm control, it may be that the enterprise quite naturally considers them as employees. The emergence of "e-lancers" (electronically connected freelancers) is another phenomenon which is challenging the traditional employment framework.

Midway between the employment relationship and self-employment, there are "economically dependent workers" who are formally self-employed but depend on one or a few "clients" for their income. They are not easy to describe, let alone quantify, because of the heterogeneous nature of the situations involved and the lack of a definition or statistical tool.

In cases where the contract is clearly intended to procure the services of a self-employed worker, it is in employers' interest to make sure that they have not misclassified the worker, as they can be held financially liable if the authorities find that the worker is in fact an employee.

Disguised Employment Relationships

A disguised employment relationship is one which is lent an appearance that is different from the underlying reality, with the intention of nullifying or attenuating the protection afforded by the law or evading tax and social security obligations. It is thus an attempt to conceal or distort the employment relationship, either by cloaking it in another legal guise or by giving it another form. Disguised employment relationships may also involve masking the *identity of the employer*, when the person designated as an employer is an intermediary, with the intention of releasing the real employer from any involvement in the employment relationship and above all from any responsibility to the workers.

The most radical way to disguise the employment relationship consists of giving it the appearance of a relationship of a different *legal nature*, whether civil, commercial, cooperative, family-related or other. Some of the contractual arrangements most frequently used to disguise the employment relationship include a wide variety of civil and commercial contracts which give it the semblance of self-employment.

"Triangular" Employment Relationships

As already mentioned, "triangular" employment relationships occur when employees of a person (the "provider") work for another person (the "user"). A wide variety of contracts can be used to formalise an agreement for the provision of work. Such contracts can have beneficial effects for the provider's employees in terms of employment opportunities, experience and professional challenges. From a legal standpoint, however, such contracts may present a technical difficulty as the employees concerned may find themselves interacting with two (or more) interlocutors, each of whom assumes certain functions of a traditional employer.

There are also, of course, cases of *objectively ambiguous* or *disguised "triangular" employment relationships.* A "triangular" employment relationship normally presupposes a civil or commercial contract between a user and a provider. It is possible, however, that no such contract exists and that the provider is not a proper enterprise, but an *intermediary* of the supposed user, intended to conceal the user's identity as the real employer.

"Triangular" employment relationships have always existed, but this phenomenon is now on the increase. The national studies identified a growing tendency among enterprises in many countries to operate through other enterprises or with their collaboration. In these situations, workers provided by different enterprises can be found working on the user's own premises or outside, even in a different country.

"Triangular" employment relationships can take various forms. The best known is the use of contractors and private employment agencies. Another very common arrangement is franchises. In this case, an enterprise allows another enterprise or a person to use its trademark or product, in principle on an independent basis. However, the franchise has financial obligations towards the franchiser, which normally exercises control over the franchised business, including its staff.

In an employment relationship, there is usually no doubt about the identity of the employer where workers deal with only one person. This person is the one who hires the worker or who performs the normal functions of an employer: assigning tasks, providing the means to perform them, giving instructions and supervising their performance, paying wages, assuming risks, making profits and terminating the employment relationship. The situation may be different, however, in a "triangular" employment relationship, when these roles are assumed separately or jointly by more than one person and any one or a number of them may be perceived as the employer, in which case the employee may reasonably wonder. In particular, workers may not know, for example, from whom exactly to claim payment of remuneration or compensation for an accident at work, and whether they can file a claim against the user when the direct employer disappears or becomes insolvent. Doubt as to the identity of the employer, or the involvement of the user in the employment relationship, leads to the following key questions in the case of "triangular" relationships: what are the worker's rights – are they the rights agreed by the employee with his or her employer (the provider), or those of the employees employed by the user, or a combination of the two?

Workers may wonder who is responsible for their rights. The logical answer, which is normally consistent with the law, is that employers are primarily responsible for the rights of their employees, whether they are a contractor, an employment agency, a cooperative or any other employing enterprise or entity. However, the role of the user can be crucial with respect to ensuring respect of these rights (such as limits on working hours, rest breaks, paid leave, etc.). There are laws which in some circumstances also assign a measure of responsibility to the user, as the person who benefits directly from the labour of the worker and who often appears to be an employer or someone similar to an employer. Depending on the circumstances and national law, the employer (or provider) and the user may bear joint and several liability, so that the worker can claim against both or either of them without distinction. In other circumstances, the user bears subsidiary liability, in the sense that a claim may only be brought against the user in the event of noncompliance by the provider. A number of ILO instruments also address this.

The determination of the identity of the employer and other possible parties to "triangular" employment relationships, of the workers' rights and of the persons responsible for ensuring those rights raises legal issues which are not easy to resolve. However, the major challenge lies in ensuring that employees in such a relationship enjoy the same level of protection traditionally provided by the law for employees in a bilateral employment relationship, without impeding legitimate private and public business initiatives.

In summary, in cases of "triangular" employment relationships, employees are frequently faced with multiple interlocutors. In such circumstances, it is essential that such employees know who the employer is, what their rights are and who is responsible for them. It is equally important to determine the position of the user with respect to the employees of the provider enterprise. A balanced and constructive approach to the question should take into account the legal difficulties involved, and the legitimate interests concerned.

Closing the Gap

In response to the growing divergence between the law and the reality of the employment relationship, measures need to be taken to close this gap. The objective should be to update and clarify the law governing the employment relationship so as to facilitate recognition of the existence of an employment relationship, and deter attempts to disguise it. Given the proliferation of objectively ambiguous and disguised situations and the growth of "triangular" relationships, member States, with the involvement of the social partners, could examine their legislation so as to identify any deficits in the light of their own specific problems and comparative law. This would enable them to determine the nature and extent of the measures needed. The outcome of this exercise should be to enable the laws on the employment relationship to be regularly updated as part of an ongoing and dynamic process.

Clarifying the Scope of the Law

The first part of the strategy would be aimed at clarifying, supplementing and stating as precisely as possible the scope of the law. At this stage, it could be useful to examine the most common forms of disguised employment relationships and cases in which it is most difficult to determine whether there is an employment relationship or a civil or commercial relationship. The task would consist of remedying the technical deficiencies in the legislation in order to address objectively ambiguous cases and to tackle the phenomenon of disguised employment relationships. In relation to "triangular" relationships, the objective would be to clarify the law so that the employees know who the employer is, what their rights are and who is responsible for them.

Comparative law contains a wealth of notions and legal constructs as to what is meant by an employment relationship and the factors and indicators used for recognising it. In addition, there are mechanisms and institutions to enforce the law and guarantee workers' rights. These generally enable the regulation of the employment relationship to operate smoothly so that the status of the worker can usually be determined. However, the law does not cover all of these aspects equally or with the same degree of precision and effectiveness in all countries.

Adjusting the Limits of the Legislation

Clarification alone, however, may not be enough to regulate cases which do not fall within the current scope of the legislation. These call for certain adjustments to the limits of the legislation. This can be done in a number of ways. First, in the case of objectively ambiguous relationships, where some or all of the features of the employment relationship are blurred or absent, the law needs to be adjusted so as to enable a clearer identification of the employment relationship, where it exists. Second, the legislation can be extended to include categories of employees or sectors that are explicitly or implicitly excluded from the scope of the law. These exclusions frequently apply to employees in small and micro-enterprises and in some export processing zones (EPZs). Furthermore, in some countries, labour laws do not have general coverage, but apply only to certain employees. In such circumstances, progressive steps could be taken towards a more general application of the legislation concerned. Third, the scope of the law may be adequate, but it may be narrowly interpreted by the courts. The development of factors and indicators for determining the existence of an employment relationship can promote consistency and predictability in court decisions.

Balancing Equity and Adaptability

The lack of labour protection raises questions of equity, on the one hand, and flexibility or adaptability, on the other. A balance between the two must be sought through social dialogue aimed at building a broad consensus. Employers are constantly faced with the challenge of survival in a competitive global environment and legitimately seek viable solutions among the range of options offered by different forms of employment. However, it is difficult for enterprises to improve their productivity with a poorly trained, demotivated and rapidly changing work force.

Balancing equity and adaptability is at the very heart of the ILO's Decent Work Agenda, which offers a framework for reconciling the different interests and reaching a consensus through social dialogue. Countries have found different institutional and policy responses to reconcile these diverging interests. For instance, a number of European countries have moved away from a situation where flexibility creates insecurity to one in which security promotes flexibility.

Ensuring Compliance

The problem of objectively ambiguous, disguised or "triangular" employment relationships cannot, however, be entirely attributed to lack of clarity and the problems relating to the scope of the law. Another contributing factor, which is particularly serious in some countries, is failure to comply with the law, accompanied by poor enforcement.

The problem of noncompliance is particularly widespread in developing countries, although it also occurs in industrialised countries. The studies carried out confirm a commonly expressed view that traditional mechanisms to enforce labour laws are not used as they should be. In particular, mechanisms and procedures for determining the existence of an employment relationship and establishing the identity of the persons involved are generally insufficient to prevent infringements of labour law or to safeguard workers' rights. Problems of compliance and enforcement are particularly acute in the informal economy.

Enforcement of labour law by the administrative and judicial authorities is affected by financial constraints in most countries. Moreover, the limited powers of these authorities and their enforcement mechanisms, such as they are, often mean that they are unable to discharge their obligations.

Labour inspectorate frequently face considerable difficulties in carrying out their tasks. In some countries, the probability that an inspector will visit a particular enterprise, detect shortcomings, impose corrective measures and enforce them is very low or nonexistent. Particular difficulties arise where the premises are extensive or located in remote places and, for different reasons, in small and micro-enterprises. The situation is even more uncertain as regards the possibility of action by labour inspectors concerning workers in objectively ambiguous or disguised employment relationships, even in countries where inspectors are empowered to identify such cases and remedy them.

In principle, all workers have access to the courts. In practice, however, there are countries where restrictions on access to the courts are considerable and few workers can afford to enter into long, costly and inevitably uncertain judicial proceedings. Rarer still, of course, are those workers who, while still working, resort to the courts for a ruling on their employment status.

Improving protection for workers within the employment relationship requires that the mechanisms and institutions established to enforce compliance with labour law function effectively. Each country, depending on the deficits in its legal system and in the organisation and functioning of its labour institutions, should consider streamlining the task of labour inspection and making it more efficient, with advisory and enforcement powers appropriate to present-day circumstances.

Trends and Problems in Regulation

Many national labour laws contain provisions on the employment relationship, particularly with regard to scope. Despite certain similarities, however, not all national labour laws provide exhaustive or equal coverage of the subject. Some provisions deal with the regulation of the employment contract as a specific contract, its definition, the parties and their respective obligations. Other provisions are intended to facilitate recognition of the existence of an employment relationship and prescribe administrative and judicial mechanisms for monitoring compliance and enforcing these laws.

In general terms, the employment relationship creates a legal link between a person who performs work and the person for whose benefit the work is performed in return for remuneration, under certain conditions established by national law and practice.

Some laws define the employment contract as the framework for this relationship, and also provide a definition of an employee and an employer. A contractor or an employment agency may be included within the definition of employer, and the law may impose certain obligations on the user of the contractor's or the agency's services.

In many countries, the legislation contains a substantive definition of the employment contract, worded in such a way as to establish what *factors* constitute such a contract and hence what distinguishes it from other similar contracts. In other countries, however, the legislation is less detailed and the task of determining the existence of an employment contract is largely left to case law.

Substantive Definitions

Laws containing substantive definitions basically provide that the employment contract is an agreement under which a person undertakes to carry out work for another person in exchange for payment of remuneration, under specified conditions. Certain *factors* are used to determine whether or not a contract is an employment contract; the description of these *factors* varies in wording and level of detail from one country to another.

In Argentina and El Salvador, for example, the law stipulates that the work is performed in conditions of *dependency* on the employer; in Chile, the terms used are *dependency and subordination*; in Panama, *subordination or dependency*; in Colombia, *continuing dependency or subordination*; in Costa Rica, *permanent dependency and direct or delegated direction*; in Nicaragua, *subordination* to an employer; in Mexico and Peru, *subordinate work*; and in

Venezuela, *work for another person in conditions of dependency on that person.* In France, case law has found that there is an employment contract where the work is performed in *conditions of subordination to* an employer. Other laws refer to work according to internal regulations or under the employer's guidance.

The laws of Benin, Burkina Faso, Democratic Republic of the Congo, Gabon, Niger and Rwanda, among other countries, as well as the Labour Code of Portugal, provide that work done under an employment contract is performed under the employer's *direction* and/or *authority*. Further variations on these *factors* are found in Finland, where the law refers to work done under the employer's *direction and supervision*; in Bahrain and Qatar, under the employer's *direction or supervision*; in Tunisia, under the employer's *direction and control*; and in Morocco, under the employer's *direction*. In Angola and Botswana, there is deemed to be a contract of employment if the worker performs work under the employer's *orders*; in Slovenia the words *according to the instructions and under the control of the employer* are used.

Thus, the most commonly used *factors* for determining whether work is being performed under an employment contract are *dependency* and *subordination*, or work done under the *direction, authority, supervision* or *control* of the employer, or on the latter's *orders* or *instructions* or for the *employer's account*. Some legal systems use the terms *dependency* and *subordination* as alternatives or together, either with different meanings or as synonyms.

In Panama, for instance, the law assigns a different meaning to each word, and each is accompanied by a different qualifier: *legal subordination* and *economic dependency*. *Legal subordination* is understood to mean that the employer or his or her representatives direct or are likely to direct the performance of the work. There is deemed to be *economic dependency* where the sums received by the worker constitute his or her only or main source of income, where such sums are paid by a person or enterprise as a result of the worker's activity, and where the worker does not enjoy economic autonomy and is economically linked to the sphere of activity in which the person or enterprise that may be considered as the employer operates. It is interesting to note that in case of doubt, *economic dependency* may be used as a *factor* for determining whether there is an employment relationship.

In Costa Rica and Panama the law allows for degrees of subordination, since it recognises that there can be an employment relationship even in cases of "minimal" or "attenuated" subordination.

The labour codes in some countries define not only the employment contract but also the employment relationship, understood to mean the fact of performing a service, irrespective of the nature of the agreement under which it is perfr ned. In one country's legislation, the employment contract is placed in the broader context of the employment relationship. The Labour Code of Panama stipulates that an employment relationship has the same effect as an employment contract.

Descriptive Definitions

In other, mainly common-law countries, the employment contract is simply described, without referring to the *factors* characterising it as an employment contract. In Kenya, it is defined as a contract under which a person agrees to serve as an employee; in Nigeria, as an agreement to serve an employer as a worker; in Lesotho and Indonesia, as a contract between an employer and an employee; in Ireland and New Zealand, as a contract of service; and in the Republic of Korea, as a contract under which a person undertakes to work for remuneration. It has been defined in

Cambodia and China as a contract between a worker and an employer through which an employment relationship is established. In Malaysia a contract of service is defined as an agreement whereby one person agrees to employ another as an employee and that other agrees to serve his.

However, even countries whose legislation does not contain a substantive definition of the employment relationship or contract may have provisions giving a clear idea of the conditions in which a worker who is bound by such a relationship or contract works. For example, provisions governing a worker's duties often include the obligation to respect the employer's orders and instructions – which is characteristic of wage employment – and this provides an important indicator for determining the existence of an employment contract.

Parties to the Employment Relationship

The laws of many States also define the parties to the employment relationship or contract, and in some cases this definition serves to reiterate or specify the conditions under which the work is performed in the employment relationship.

Employee or Worker

The term "worker" is often used to refer to a person who performs services in an employment relationship, although strictly speaking this generic term can also cover self-employed workers. A "worker" is defined in Chile as a person who works in conditions of *dependency or subordination*; in Mexico, as someone performing *personal, subordinate work*; and in Nicaragua, as a person working under the employer's *direction and in direct or delegated subordination to the employer*.

By contrast, in countries where descriptive definitions are the rule, the legislation merely states that an employee is a person working for an employer. For example, in Lesotho, employee means any person who works in any capacity under a contract with an employer; in Thailand, a person who agrees to do work for an employer in return for a wage, regardless of the name given to describe that person's status; in Australia, any person whose usual occupation is that of employee, but does not include a person who is undertaking a vocational placement; in Pakistan, any and all persons not falling within the definition of employer who is employed in an establishment or industry for remuneration or reward either directly or through a contractor, whether the terms of employment be express or implied; and in the United Kingdom, an individual who has entered into or works under (or where the employment has ceased, worked under) a contract of employment. In this case one definition refers to another, and neither of them defines the term precisely. Hence, it is even more important in these countries for case law to establish the *factors* and *indicators* distinguishing an employment contract or relationship and identifying its parties. What is surprising is the amount of convergence between the legal systems of different countries in the way they deal with this and other aspects of the employment relationship, even between countries with different legal traditions or those in different parts of the world.

In any case, irrespective of the definition used, the concept of a worker in an employment relationship has to be seen in contrast to that of a self-employed or non-dependent worker; in Chile, for example, a self-employed worker is defined as a person who, in the exercise of his or her activity, does not depend on an employer or have workers dependent on him or her.

The Employer

Some laws merely define the employer as the person who employs the worker, or uses the latter's services, possibly under an employment contract. In Venezuela, an employer is a person responsible for an enterprise or work site where workers carry out their work. In Brazil, the employer is defined in more detail as the person who bears the business risk, hires and pays remuneration, and directs the performance of services. In Viet-Nam, the employer is defined in terms of three functions: recruiting, employing and paying wages to an employee.

In Spain, the law also refers expressly to employers lawfully engaged in supplying labour. An employer or entrepreneur means any legal or natural person, or joint-ownership arrangement, receiving services performed by workers employed by another person and integrated in the organisation and under their/its direction, as well as persons hired in order to be provided to user enterprises by legally established temporary work enterprises.

The law in the United Kingdom contains the following definition: employer, in relation to an employee or a worker, means the person by whom the employee or worker is (or, where the employment has ceased, was) employed.

The legislation of the Philippines defines an employer of home-workers in terms of specific aspects pertaining to the situation of the employer, and in terms of the employer's relationship with the worker. Employer, in this context, means any natural or artificial person who, for his own account or benefit, or on behalf of any person residing outside the Philippines, directly or indirectly, or through any employee, agent, contractor, subcontractor, or any other person, delivers or causes to be delivered, or sells, any goods or articles to be processed in or about a home and thereafter to be returned or to be disposed of or distributed in accordance with his direction, and then re buys them himself or through another after such processing.

Some definitions of employer refer to the person signing the contract with the worker, and in this case may also include a person representing the employer. In Botswana, for instance, the employer is defined as any person who has entered into a contract of employment to hire the labour of any person, including the Government or a public authority, or the person who owns or is carrying on for the time being or is responsible for the management of the undertaking, business or enterprise of whatever kind in which the employee is engaged.

In other countries, the law refers specifically to representatives of the employer and draws a distinction between them and employers.

Determining the Existence of Relationship

Even where the law contains clear provisions regulating the employment relationship, it may be difficult, or even impossible, to determine whether there is in fact an employment relationship in a given case. In many cases, a worker will not refer the matter to the courts as long as the employment contract is in force for fear of losing his or her job; and once the contract expires it may be even more difficult to collect and present evidence.

A comparison of the legislation reveals various alternative means of easing the burden of proof on the worker and facilitating the judge's task of determining the existence of an employment relationship. Perhaps the most important of these is the universal application of what is known as the principle of the *primacy of fact*.

The Principle of the Primacy of Fact

The determination of the existence of an employment relationship should be guided by the *facts* of what was actually agreed and performed by the parties, and not on how either or both of the parties describe the relationship. This is known in law as the principle of the *primacy of fact*.

In general, the judge must decide on the basis of the facts. For example, the law in many countries provides that the employment contract may be explicit or implicit. Allowing for the possibility of an implicit contract means giving weight to the facts surrounding the agreement reached between employer and worker when such agreement is not in writing and probably also in cases where the facts reflect a different reality from that which might be in a written contract. The idea of an implied contract is growing in importance in case law.

Other laws define the worker as a person who undertakes to place his or her professional activity, in exchange for remuneration, under the direction and authority of an employer, and go on to specify that neither the legal status of the employer nor that of the worker shall be taken into account in determining whether a person is a worker. Similarly, another labour code provides that in cases when it has been judicially determined that a civil contract actually regulates labour relations between an employee and an employer, the provisions of labour legislation shall be applied to such relations.

As regards remuneration – one of the key elements of the employment contract – the law in Finland applies regardless of the absence of any agreement on remuneration, if the *facts* indicate that the work was not intended to be performed without

To establish the facts, some legal systems rely on certain *indicators* to determine whether or not there is an employment relationship. These include, among others, compliance with the employer's instructions, being at the employer's disposal, and socioeconomic inequality between the parties.

In common-law countries, judges base their rulings on certain tests developed by case law, for example the tests of control, integration in the enterprise, economic reality (who bears the financial risk?) And mutuality of obligation.

Some legal systems even go so far as to lay down provisions to combat concealment or fraud in order to ensure that the principle of the *primacy of fact* prevails in the interests of the worker and/or the tax or social security institutions. In Panama, for example, the Labour Code provides that in determining whether there is an employment relationship, or identifying the subjects of such a relationship, account shall not be taken of fictitious contracts, the participation of intermediaries as alleged employers, or the establishment or fictitious operation of a legal entity as employer. It provides further that where a legal entity attempts to evade compliance with its obligations under labour law through fraudulent or false documents or through the establishment or operation of the legal entity, a worker employed by that entity may also assert his or her employment-related claims against its shareholders, partners or members. The law also stipulates that the simulated participation of a legal entity in the performance of the service or the work shall not prevent the natural person concerned being considered as a worker. In Argentina, a contract is void if it was concluded on the basis of fraud or fraudulent evasion of labour legislation, whether by simulating contractual terms that do not pertain to an employment contract, through the use of intermediaries or by any other means; in such cases the relationship is still governed by the Employment Contracts Act. Also in Argentina, the law refers specifically to fraudulent use of the cooperative system to evade the application of labour legislation and encourages the regularisation of the employment relationship while discouraging evasion through the imposition of fines and exemptions from contributions and fines in the event of voluntary compliance. In Chile, in addition to joint liability, the law provides for the imposition of fines on an employer who simulates the recruitment of workers through third parties or anyone using any subterfuge, concealing, disguising or altering his or her description or assets with the effect of evading compliance with labour and social security obligations. In these cases, subterfuge means any alteration through establishing different company names or legal identities, dividing the enterprise, or any other act which results in the impairment or loss of the workers' individual or collective labour rights. Moreover, the time limit for bringing actions and claiming rights in this regard has been extended to five years. Lastly, some laws protect home workers even where the relationship with the employer consists of the worker buying materials from the latter and selling him or her the products made from such materials as if it were a commercial sales-purchase operation.

Determination by Law

Some legal systems go a step further and describe certain potentially ambiguous or controversial situations as employment relationships, either in general or under certain conditions, or at least presume they are employment relationships.

In Spain, for example, professional sports-persons are deemed by law to have a special employment relationship where they devote themselves voluntarily on a regular basis to practising a sport on behalf of and under the organisation and direction of a sports body or club, in return for remuneration. Conversely, persons who devote themselves to practising a sport in a club and only receive compensation for the expenses incurred in their practice of the sport are not covered by the law. The same applies to artists engaged in public performances who enter into a relationship with an organiser of public performances or a manager, on behalf of and under the organisation and direction of the latter.

In France, the following categories are presumed to have an employment relationship under certain conditions: performing artists (as in Spain), models, professional journalists, sales representatives or travelling salespersons. Mexican law contains similar provisions on sales representatives, insurance salespersons, travelling salespersons, sales promoters and similar categories. In Mexico and Panama, the law refers to various public transport workers (drivers, operators, conductors, etc.).

The French Labour Code goes even further by protecting certain workers irrespective of whether or not they have an employment contract, provided certain conditions are met with regard to their activity.

In some cases, the legislation specifies whether a given type of work is excluded from its scope or whether or not it gives rise to a contract of employment, depending on the conditions under which it is performed. In Chile, for example, home work is deemed to be employment if it is neither discontinuous nor sporadic; on the other hand, work done by persons performing work or services directly for the public, or home work that is performed discontinuously or sporadically, is not deemed to give rise to an employment contract, and neither is work done by a student or graduate of higher education or secondary vocational and technical education for a specified period to fulfil a practical work requirement, even if the enterprise where this work is done provides food, transportation or an allowance in lieu of such benefits. Mexican legislation contains similar provisions concerning home workers. The Employment Contracts Act in Finland stipulates that the application of the Act is not prevented merely by the fact that the work is performed in the employee's home or a place chosen by the latter, or that it is performed using the employee's implements or machinery.

In Colombia, vendors of insurance policies, savings bonds and betting slips may or may not be employees, depending on whether they have agreed to an employment contract or rely on their own means, are not dependent on a company and have a commercial contract.

Conversely, legislation may specify that certain forms of employment are not employment relationships, or exclude certain categories of workers from their scope, while other laws authorise the Government to make such exclusions. The most common is the total or partial exclusion of public servants and similar workers; less frequently, that of public sector workers. Some laws also refer to compulsory labour or services, or work performed during imprisonment; ordinary non-vocational activities; domestic workers and persons regarded as such, and members of cooperatives. In Spain, the legislation also excludes business consultants, work done on an amicable, voluntary or goodwill basis, commercial activity and work done by family members, unless there is proof that they are employees. Some countries have excluded enterprises with fewer than a certain number of workers from the scope of legislation on the employment relationship, or from certain of its provisions. Other countries have adopted special regulations on the employment relationship of certain categories of workers; in the case of Morocco, for example, such regulations cannot provide inferior rights.

In other countries, however, the legislation authorises the Government to adapt the coverage of the legislation on the employment relationship; this may be done by including certain categories of workers, for example, in the United Kingdom, an order may provide that individuals are to be treated as parties to workers' contracts or contracts of employment. In South Africa, "the Minister may, on the advice of the (Employment Conditions) Commission and by notice in the *Gazette*, deem any category of persons specified in the notice to be... employees for purposes of the whole or any part of this Act, any other employment law other than the Unemployment Insurance Act, 1966 (Act No. 30 of 1966), or any sectorial determination". In Botswana, the partial or total exclusion of a specific occupation by ministerial order is possible.

Easing the Burden of Proof

In order to ease the burden of proof on workers seeking to prove the existence of an employment contract, the law may provide that such contracts are consensual, i.e. formed merely by the consent of the parties without further formalities. However, the law may require that the contract be in writing for various reasons relating to compliance or to evidence; or it may proceed from the assumption that the employment relationship exists based on the fact that services are provided. In this respect, the Labour Code of the Russian Federation provides that a contract of employment that is not drawn up in due form is considered to have been concluded if the employee starts working with the knowledge or on the instructions of the employer or the employer's representative. Once the employee starts to work, the employer is obliged to draw up a written contract of employment with the employee no later than three days from the day on which the employee started to work.

An important element of certainty, which also makes it easier to prove the existence of an employment contract, is the obligation on the employer to inform employees of the conditions applicable to the contract by providing a written contract, a letter of engagement or other documents indicating the essential aspects of the employment contract or relationship. This obligation is explicitly laid down in the European Union and further developed in national legislation. Noncompliance with this obligation may cause the worker to question his or her employee status.

Conversely, having the written information in question makes it easier for the worker to prove that status.

With the same aim of easing the burden of proof, some laws provide for a presumption of the existence of an employment relationship or contract.

The law may provide, for example, with some variations, that an employment relationship or contract is presumed to exist between a person providing a personal service and the person who receives it; or if it is proven that the worker performed services for more than two consecutive days or there is evidence of subordination. In the Netherlands, the law provides that any person who for the benefit of another person performs work for remuneration for three consecutive months on a weekly basis, or for no fewer than 20 hours per month, is presumed to perform such work on the basis of a contract of employment. In Portugal, an employment relationship is presumed to exist if all of the following indicators are present: (a) the worker is part of the organisational structure of the beneficiary of his or her activity and performs a service under the latter's guidance; (b) the work is performed in the beneficiary's enterprise or a place under its control, according to a previously defined timetable; (c) the worker is remunerated for the time spent on carrying out the activity or is economically dependent on the beneficiary of the activity; (d) the work tools are essentially supplied by the beneficiary; and (e) the services are performed for a continuous period of over 90 days. In Slovenia, in the event of a dispute as to the existence of an employment relationship between the worker and the employer, it shall be presumed that an employment relationship exists if certain *indicators* are present; in Estonia, the parties are deemed to have entered into an employment contract unless the alleged employer proves otherwise or unless it is evident that the parties entered into a different kind of contract. In

Malaysia, the employment, engagement or contracting of any person or class of persons to carry out work other than under a contract of service may be prohibited; in that case, the person or class of persons employed, engaged or contracted shall be deemed to be an employee or employees and the person or institution employing, engaging or contracting him/them shall be deemed to be the employer. The contravention of these provisions is an offence.

The law may also require that the contract be in writing and render the employer liable to court proceedings if the contract was purely verbal. The labour code of one country provides that, in the absence of a written contract, the facts or circumstances alleged by the worker which should have been in the contract are presumed true unless proved otherwise beyond reasonable doubt.

In addition to presuming the existence of an employment contract, the law may also provide for a presumption as to its terms, for example by deeming in certain conditions that a contract is for an unspecified duration, even if a duration is stipulated, if the nature of the work assigned to the worker is permanent in the enterprise.

THE SCOPE OF EMPLOYMENT RELATIONSHIP

Legislation adopted in some countries since the end of the twentieth century contains provisions re-focusing the employment relationship to extend the scope of the law and hence its protection to new categories of workers; to combat disguised or fraudulent employment relationships and improve compliance with the law; and to ease the burden of proof on the worker, in particular when seeking to prove the existence of an employment relationship in a given case. Parallel to this regulatory response to the growing concern at the lack of protection for workers who are in fact in an employment relationship which might be ambiguous or disguised, there has also been a continuing tendency in case law to apply the traditional approach on the employment relationship to new and complex situations.

The concern to clarify the scope of the employment relationship has been expressed in a variety of ways. One response has been to try to redefine more precisely the scope of the employment relationship, irrespective of the form of the contract, or to establish mechanisms to adjust the scope of the law in line with changing needs. Another approach to the problem has been to delineate more clearly the boundary between dependent and independent work. A third option combines both these elements. Provisions have also been introduced in legislation to deal with certain types of work which had hitherto been inadequately defined in some countries. Lastly, in one labour code the protection concerning the employment contract is extended to equivalent contracts. These five approaches are described in the following paragraphs, and illustrated by referring to relevant case law developments.

New Zealand has addressed the issue of protection of workers in the Employment Relations Act, which gives a broad definition of which workers are covered by the new legislation and empowers independent bodies (the Employment Court or the Employment Relations Authority) to investigate the real nature of the link between the person doing the work and the entity commanding that work. Such powers play a key role in eliminating fraudulent or disguised employment relationships. Section 6 of the Act provides as follows:

(1) In this Act, unless the context otherwise requires, employee:

    (a) means any person of any age employed by an employer to do any work for hire or reward under a contract of service; and

    (b) includes:

(i) a home worker; or

(ii) a person intending to work; but

(c) excludes a volunteer who:

(i) does not expect to be rewarded for work to be performed as a volunteer; and

(ii) receives no reward for work performed as a volunteer.

(2) In deciding for the purposes of subsection (1)(a) whether a person is employed by another person under a contract of service, the court or the authority (as the case may be) must determine the real nature of the relationship between them.

In Finland, the Employment Contracts Act applies to employment contracts entered into by an employee or employees, under which they agree to perform work personally for an employer under the latter's direction and supervision in return for payment or other remuneration. It reaffirms the prohibition on discrimination, the requirement for equal treatment and the broad scope of the employment relationship and, as mentioned above, it stipulates that its provisions do not cease to apply because of the fact that employees use their own tools or equipment. Finnish law already provided that the employment contract could take any form. The new Act specifies that the contract may be in oral, written or electronic form; the latter makes it easier to identify the employment relationship, even if it is between people located in different countries who do not know each other.

Like other older legislation, the new Act favours the open-ended contract over the fixed-term contract: it only allows the latter type of contract to be concluded for a justified reason. It also guarantees that workers retain their acquired rights in a continued relationship or even in the case of brief interruptions. In this way, the gap is narrowed between workers with fixed-term contracts and those with open-ended contracts. Fixed-term contracts that are concluded or consecutively renewed without a justified reason are considered open-ended. The provisions reaffirming the preference for the open-ended contract are particularly significant, since one of the main recent developments in the employment relationship in Finland has been the increase in fixed-term contracts. This trend has affected women and men differently: according to 1999 data, 21 per cent of women and 15 per cent of men worked under fixed-term contracts.

In a similar vein, the law in New Zealand specifies that, in agreeing to a fixed-term employment contract that will end on a specified date, on the occurrence of a specified event or at the conclusion of a specified project, the employer must have "genuine reasons based on reasonable grounds" for specifying that the employment of the employee is to end in that way. The law states that the following are not "genuine reasons": "(a) to exclude or limit the rights of the employee under this Act; (b) to establish the suitability of the employee for permanent employment."

In the United Kingdom, the law itself authorises the Government to adjust its scope – a novel power in response to the growing problem of disguised and objectively ambiguous employment relationships. Under section 23 of the Employment Relations Act 1999, the Government may confer employment rights on certain individuals vis-a-vis an employer (however defined), and may provide that such individuals are to be treated as parties to employment contracts and make provision as to who are to be regarded as their employers.

In India, the National Commission on Labour was created in October 1999. Its terms of reference were to suggest rationalisation of existing laws relating to labour in the "organised sectors", and to suggest "umbrella legislation" for ensuring a minimum level of protection for workers in the "unorganised sector".

Boundary Between Dependent and Independent Work

In Ireland, the difficulty of distinguishing between dependent and independent workers has prompted an approach based on consensus between the Government and the employers' and workers' organisations. The Irish system of industrial relations is based on broad social partnership reflected in a national agreement which fixes wage increases and other aspects of policy.

In the context of the negotiations on the agreement for 2000 to 2002, called the Programme for Prosperity and Fairness (PPF), it was agreed to establish an Employment Status Group with the task of devising a uniform definition of "employee". In the absence of a statutory definition of "employed" or "self-employed", there was growing concern that the number of people classified as "self-employed" was increasing, despite evidence that in their case the status of "employee" would be more appropriate.

The issue has far-reaching implications, since aspects such as the way in which taxes and social security contributions are payable, entitlement to unemployment, disability or sickness benefits, a number of rights under labour legislation and responsibility for the work performed all depend on whether or not the worker is classified as an employee. Incorrect classification of a worker can also entail serious consequences for the employer, including penalties. Finally, tax authorities have a special interest in the appropriate classification of workers and are very active in their efforts to identify who is an employee and who is self-employed, in order to prevent tax evasion. The Employment Status Group formulated a set of *indicators* for determining which workers were employees and which were self-employed. With these *indicators* in mind (even though not all of them may apply in every case) and taking into consideration the person's work as a whole, including the conditions of work and the real nature of the relationship, it should be easier to determine the employment status of the individual.

In addition to establishing the *indicators* for distinguishing between employees and the self-employed, the Employment Status Group also considered how these *indicators* should be expressed. The Group rejected the idea of embodying them in a law and preferred to introduce them in a code of practice, the application of which would be purely voluntary. The code had the legitimacy of having been approved by consensus by the employers' and workers' representative bodies, as well as by the competent authorities. Although it does not have binding effect, it was expected that it would be taken into account by the bodies responsible for handling disputes about employment status. The application of the code of practice would be monitored by the Employment Status Group itself to assess its effectiveness.

In Germany, there has been a legal definition of employee for the purposes of social security since January, 1999, when the revised Social Security Code came into force. A presumption has been introduced whereby a person is deemed to be an employee if he or she meets at least two of the following *indicators*: the person does not have employees subject to social security obligations; usually works for one contractor; performs the same work as regular employees; has performed the same work as an employee before; and does not show signs of engaging in entrepreneurial activities. The underlying idea was to achieve a sufficiently precise and practical definition to reduce the opportunity to disguise the employment relationship and to make it easier to deal with situations midway between a genuine and a disguised employment relationship.

Combined Approach

The 2002 legislative reform adopted in South Africa combines a number of the above elements. This reform, which amends labour legislation adopted in 1995 and 1997, is important not only for its content, but also for the process of intense, effective and constructive social dialogue leading up to it, in which all of the stockholders participated. Among other aspects, the reform addresses the scope of the employment relationship, a particularly difficult task in a country where ambiguous bilateral and "triangular" employment relationships have proliferated over the last decade and even more since the adoption of the 1995 legislation.

Two elements were introduced to clarify and adjust the scope of the law. The first, which is reminiscent of the German approach and the Irish code of practice, is a broad presumption in favour of employee status, which appears both in the Basic Conditions of Employment Amendment Act, 2002, and the Labour Relations Amendment Act, 2002. According to this presumption, a person is deemed to be an employee if one or more of seven *indicators* set out in the Act exist.

The presumption in favour of employee status does not apply, however, in the case of workers with a certain level of income. When the Basic Conditions of Employment Act (BCEA) was enacted in 2002, the income threshold was set at 89,445 rand (US$10,000) per year.

As a complementary measure, the Labour Relations Amendment Act required the National Economic Development and Labour Council (NEDLAC) to prepare and issue a code of good practice containing guidelines for determining whether persons, including those with incomes over the limit mentioned in the previous paragraph, are employees. Another innovation, as mentioned above, is the very special power granted to the minister to deem any category of persons to be employees for the purposes of employment legislation. It is not just a matter of clarifying the scope of the law but also of amending it by ministerial order.

In Peru, the General Labour Bill of July 2002 contains an explicit and broad definition of its scope. The Bill is intended to regulate the personal provision of services, on a subordinate and paid basis, based on an oral or written contract, irrespective of its name or form. A worker does not lose his or her status even if personal services are concealed in the guise of a legal entity. Thus, the provision of services is subordinate when a worker performs the service within the organisation and under the direction of the employer or a third party when the law so permits. The Bill contains a presumption that any provision of personal services for remuneration is subordinate and that an employment relationship exists when there is a provision of services in a work place. Furthermore, it indicates elements which are not essential to classifying a relationship as an employment relationship, but which can serve as indicators for that purpose or to determine entitlement to certain rights. Likewise, the Bill defines the parties to the employment contract (employer and worker) and presumes that such contracts are for an indefinite term.

Another initiative to re-focus the employment relationship was the appointment in 2002 of a committee of experts in Quebec, Canada, which produced a report on the social protection needs of people in non-traditional work situations. This was in response to the changes in work relationships arising out of new operating methods of some enterprises and the provision of certain public services, as well as the emergence of new categories of self-employed persons – some of them only apparently independent and others who are genuinely independent.

Categorising Certain Types of Work

Together with the general provisions on the scope of the employment relationship, there are also provisions specifically relating to certain workers or certain types of employment, intended to determine the existence of an employment relationship. This is the case of home work, tele-work, private employment agency workers and workers' cooperatives.

Since the 2001 reform of the Labour Code in Chile, home work which is neither discontinuous nor sporadic is presumed to be employment. In Finland, the Employment Contracts Act states expressly that its application is not prevented by the fact that the work is performed at the employee's home.

In New Zealand, in setting out the framework of the employment relationship, the Employment Relations Act lays particular emphasis on home workers. This Act deems as an employee anyone who is bound by a contract of service. However, it also expressly includes home workers in this category, even if they are engaged, employed or contracted under a form of contract whereby the parties are technically a vendor and a purchaser. With respect to buying and selling in home work, the Labour Act of Venezuela, as amended in 1997, provides that when a person habitually or with a degree of regularity sells materials to another to be processed or made up by the latter at his or her home and then purchases the product for a determined price, the former is deemed to be an employer *(patrono)* and the latter a home worker.

The Peruvian General Labour Bill mentioned above provides that the service is regarded as personal in the case of home work, even when it is performed with the assistance of the worker's immediate family members who are economically dependent.

As to tele-working, which is in some respects a modern kind of home work, a 2002 framework agreement at European Union level provided regulations emanating from the social partners themselves. The framework agreement covers different forms of tele-working, but is confined to regular tele-working, i.e. that which takes place in the context of an employment contract or relationship, and is based on the recognition that tele-workers have the same rights as workers who render services in the employer's premises. The agreement contains the following provision to prevent ambiguities concerning the worker's status and possible "conversion" to self-employment: "the passage to tele-work as such, because it only modifies the way in which work is performed, does not affect the tele-worker's employment status".

The Peruvian General Labour Bill defines tele-working and suggests indicators which can help to identify subordination in this kind of work. Under the Chilean Labour Code, tele-working (described as services rendered outside the premises of the enterprise, using computers or telecommunications) is exempted from the limits on working hours.

With respect to cooperatives, the ILO Promotion of Cooperatives Recommendation, 2002 (No. 193), provides that national policies should notably promote the ILO fundamental labour standards and the ILO Declaration on Fundamental Principles and Rights at Work, for all workers in cooperatives without distinction whatsoever.

Extending the Scope of Legislation to Equivalent Workers

The Labour Code of Portugal provides for partial extension of its scope beyond the limits of the employment contract, which, as pointed out above, concerns workers performing services under the authority and direction of another person or other persons. In this respect, it provides as follows: "Contracts for the performance of work without legal subordination shall be subject to the principles laid down in this Code, especially as regards the rights of the person, equality, nondiscrimination, and safety and health at work, without prejudice to any provisions in special legislation, provided that the worker is considered to be in a situation of economic dependence on the beneficiary of his or her activity." The Code refers to these as contracts "treated as" *("contratos equiparados")* an employment contract and makes them subject to the principles laid down in the Code.

Developments in Case Law

In considering developments on the employment relationship, it is always interesting and useful to keep an eye on case law. Courts and other judicial bodies play a crucial role in classifying the employment status of workers based on the facts. It is worth mentioning some decisions from different countries.

The Denny case in Ireland sets an important legal precedent in this area. A worker signed a contract of employment as a shop demonstrator with Denny, a food processing company, and was entered on a panel of demonstrators offering free samples of various products to customers. When a store requested a demonstrator, a member of the panel was contacted by the company and asked to carry out the demonstration. The demonstrator then submitted an invoice, which was signed by the store manager. The demonstrator was paid at a daily rate and was given a mileage allowance, but was not eligible for the pension scheme or to join a trade union. The annual contract was renewed several times. However, the contract for 1993 stated that the worker was an independent worker and as such was responsible for her own tax affairs. At that time, she worked an average of 28 hours a week for 48 to 50 weeks a year, during which she gave some 50 demonstrations. She did so without supervision from the company, but she complied with any reasonable instructions of the owner of the store and written instructions from the company, which provided her with the materials for the demonstration and gave its consent to carry it out. The question in the case was whether she was actually self-employed or an employee who should be insured by the company. Based on the particular facts of the case and the general principles developed by the courts, the Supreme Court held that she was an employee, bound as such by a contract of service, because she had performed services for another person and not for herself.

In another case in Ireland, the Labour Court considered the situation of a part-time temporary veterinary inspector who had worked for the Department of Agriculture since 1966, to determine whether or not he was an employee. As stated by the Court, the distinction between a contract *of* service and a contract *for* service is a fine one and surrounded by legal complexity, making it difficult to apply in borderline cases. The Court examined the provisions contained in the code of practice for determining employment or self-employment status of individuals, issued by the Employment Status Group. In the light of this code of practice and various other tests, the Court concluded that, given the right to refuse work and the degree of control exercised by the veterinary inspector over the performance of his duties, he was a free agent, economically independent from the person engaging his service. The Court found, therefore, that he was employed under a contract *for* service and was not an "employee".

In South Africa, a contractor specialising in the manufacture and installation of built-in cupboards persuaded the vast majority of its workers to resign and to continue rendering their services as independent workers. The Labour Court considered whether the contracts with the workers were genuine and bona fide, based on the case of one of the workers. The Court found that the worker in question merely helped to load cupboards on to a vehicle and then clean and touch them up once they were installed, and this work was an integral part of the service performed by the contractor. The Court held that the contractor had perpetrated a "cruel hoax" on the worker by inducing him to believe that he was a self-employed entrepreneur, which left him without any of the protections accorded to an employee under the law. The Court held that the contract was a sham and remained a sham even though the worker had consented to it.

In the Netherlands, in 2004 the District Court of Apeldoorn, in line with the case law of the Supreme Court, decided that "the existence of subordination does not require that the employer is actually giving instructions to the employee: it includes the *authority* to do so". Also in line with former case law, the Court of Appeal of Middelburg ruled that the content of a written agreement is not conclusive as to the existence of an employment contract; the purpose of the contract and the way it is carried out should also be taken into consideration. In the case of a medical advisor, the Court determined that there was an employment contract on the basis of the following facts: (a) the "employee" did not work for principals other than the "employer"; (b) he had to adjust to the working method and organisation of the "employer"; (c) he received instructions with regard to the content of his work; (d) he worked at the office of the "employer" on fixed days and at fixed hours; (e) he could not take leave without the consent of the "employer"; (f) his salary was fixed on the basis of a directive of the Association of Doctors in Employment; (g) taxes and contributions were withheld by the "employer"; and (h) the "employee" had to perform the work personally.

In France, the Supreme Court *(Cour de Cassation)* examined the case of a person who drove a taxi under a monthly contract which was automatically renewable, called a "contract for the lease of a vehicle equipped as a taxi", and paid a sum described in the contract as "rent". The Court held that this contract concealed a contract of employment, since the taxi driver was bound by numerous strict obligations concerning the use and maintenance of the vehicle and was in a situation of subordination. Also in France, the Supreme Court examined the case of workers engaged in the delivery and collection of parcels under a franchise agreement. The "franchises" collected the parcels from premises rented by the "franchiser" and delivered them according to a schedule and route determined by the latter. In addition, the charges were set by the enterprise, which collected payment directly from the customers. The Supreme Court examined the situation of three "franchises" in three separate cases and handed down three rulings on the same day. The Court held that the provisions of the Labour Code were also applicable to persons whose occupation consisted essentially of collecting orders or receiving items for handling, storage or transport, on behalf of a single industrial or commercial enterprise, when those persons performed their work in premises supplied or approved by that enterprise, under conditions and at prices imposed by that enterprise, without the need to establish a subordinate relationship. This is understood to amount to an extension of the scope of the Labour Code to certain "franchised" workers.

A case in Venezuela involved distributors of beer and other products who had each formed a limited company for the purpose of that activity. The distributors purchased products at a price fixed by the enterprise and sold them to retailers within a specified area covered by their trucks, painted with the logos of the brewery company, for another price, also set by the enterprise. Their income was the difference between the two prices. They could not sell the products outside the designated area, or sell products other than those of the enterprise in that area. In one case, the Supreme Court of Justice held that the distributors were in reality wage workers, since it had been shown that they provided personal services, despite being registered as businesses, and their work being structured around commercial contracts for sale and purchase. However, 80 other cases were referred for mediation and conciliation by the same tribunal and the parties admitted that the relationships were of a commercial nature.

Similarly, a cabin crew member with three years' service with a Venezuelan airline was withdrawn because of pregnancy from the flight programme and a training course with a view to promotion, without being assigned new functions. She was thus deprived of remuneration, since she only received a monthly commission based on flights and had not been declared for the purposes of social security. The company denied that it was bound by an employment relationship and claimed, on the contrary, that it had signed a commercial contract with her in her capacity as representative of a limited company. Nevertheless, since she had indeed provided her services to the airline, the Court of First Instance held that an employment relationship between the parties had been shown to exist and ruled in favour of the worker.

Since 1987, a major United States electronics firm employed "temporary agency employees" and "freelancers". The "freelancers" had agreed in writing that they would not enjoy certain employee benefits, including access to the stock purchase plan. It was held by the Court, however, that both the "agency workers" and the "freelancers" were common-law employees of the enterprise. After several years of negotiations, a settlement was reached whereby the company agreed to pay some US$97 million to compensate the workers in question. Furthermore, the company changed its practices for hiring and classifying personnel, which meant that some 3,000 workers in the category concerned were converted to employee status and as such were eligible to participate in employee benefit plans and programmes.

In the context of case law there is the problem of lengthy court proceedings, and even after such long delays often the outcome benefits only one or a few plaintiffs. In two of the three cases before the French courts mentioned above relating to franchises, the proceedings lasted approximately four years, while the relationships of each of the parties lasted for just over three years. The proceedings against the United States electronics company lasted more than eight years and only ended with an out-of-court settlement between the parties. Even so, the impact of that case affected an initially undefined category of persons, which proved to consist of several thousand, while the French rulings only directly benefited the plaintiffs.

Regulation of Triangular Relationships

Legislative provisions to address "triangular" employment relationships are considerably less extensive and less common than those on the traditional bilateral relationship between an employer and a worker, especially in certain regions. There is a marked contrast between, on the one hand, legal systems which provide for cases of "triangular" employment relationships and, on the other hand, systems which do not refer to "triangular" employment relationships or only mention them briefly. In particular, laws which cover "triangular" employment relationships contain provisions on the identity of the employers and the possible respective liabilities of the employer and user, as well as the rights of the workers.

The following paragraphs give some examples of legal provisions which address certain key aspects of "triangular" employment relationships.

Laws tend to focus on the two main types of "triangular" relationship: the performance of work and services, on the one hand, and the supply of labour under commercial contracts, on the other. In both cases, national legislation contains provisions identifying the employer, referring to working conditions and workers' rights and laying down the obligations and liability of the provider and the user.

Who is the Employer

Both recent and less recent legislation identify the employer (the provider) as the person or enterprise employing the worker and the user as the person using the labour services provided – although there are variations on this in some countries.

Contracting for Work or Services

Most of the provisions on "triangular" employment relationships refer to the performance of work or services under contract. A comparison of laws shows that this kind of "triangular" relationship is regulated from three different perspectives: that of the employer, the user and the worker.

Some laws classify as an employer a natural or legal person which, using its own equipment and personnel, undertakes to carry out work or perform a service for the benefit of a third party. The traditional concept of the contractor *(contratista)* is defined in Chile in the context of commercial or agro-industrial enterprises engaged in agriculture, forestry and similar activities, as a natural or legal person who hires workers on his or her own account to provide services to third parties. The Workers' Charter in Spain also refers to the contractor, in a provision concerning user enterprises that contract with others for the performance of work or services relating to their own

In other legislation, the term "contractor" is also used to refer to those who supply labour to a principal; in Mauritius, the term used is "job contractor", while still other laws refer to contractors without defining the term, but may specify their obligations or liabilities, or both.

Similarly, in some African countries, the law recognises the *"tâcheron"* or *"mature ouvrier"*, an independent subcontractor who contracts with an enterprise or a project manager to perform work or services for an agreed price.

In France, the Labour Code approaches this question from a different angle. It refers to an arrangement in which an industrial or commercial enterprise enters into a contract for the performance of certain work or the provision of certain services with a person who recruits the necessary workers but who does not own a business or is not an independent artisan. If the person who recruits the workers fails in his/her obligations to the workers, the liability transfers to the industrial or commercial enterprise in certain circumstances. The Tunisian Labour Code contains similar provisions. Similarly, the Moroccan Labour Code defines subcontracting *("contract de sous-enterprise")* as a written contract whereby an enterprise contracts with a subcontractor for the performance of a certain job or services.

A provider bears the usual obligations incumbent on any employer, but may have others in addition. In Spain, for example, providers are bound to inform both their workers and the social security institution in writing of the identity of the user enterprise to which they are providing services.

Supply of Labour Under Commercial Contracts

Unlike contracting for work or services, contracts dealing with the supply of labour are usually much more circumscribed in that they can only be carried out by certain enterprises in certain conditions. The supply of labour in conditions other than those provided for under legislation may be expressly prohibited and even constitute an offence.

The supply of labour by private employment agencies is the subject of the ILO Private Employment Agencies Convention, 1997 (No. 181), and its accompanying Recommendation (No. 188). Convention No. 181 attributes to the agency the function of employing workers with a view to making them available to a third party, expressly referred to as the "user enterprise". The workers have as interlocutors the agency that employs them and the clients of the agency to whom it provides services.

Some national legal systems contain provisions regulating private employment agencies, often along the lines set forth in the above ILO instruments. Problems concerning the protection of workers in these agencies tend to arise mainly in countries where there is no appropriate legislation, or where the law is not effectively applied.

While private employment agencies in many countries are normally the employer, this is not always the case. For example, a recent decision in the United Kingdom signals a shift in the legal relationship of temporary agency workers and those who use them. A person was registered with an employment agency, under a "temporary worker agreement", which made it clear that its provisions "shall not give rise to a contract of employment" between the agency and the worker, or the worker and the client. For a number of years, that person had been assigned by the agency to work as a cleaner exclusively at a council-run hostel for the long-term care of people with mental health problems. The council, through the hostel management, exercised day-to-day control over her and supplied her with cleaning materials, equipment and protective clothing. She worked prescribed hours five days a week. The agency paid her wages out of the price of its services to the council. In April 2001, following an incident at the hostel, the council asked that she be withdrawn from the agreement and the agency informed her that it would no longer be finding work for her. The worker lodged a complaint for unfair dismissal. A first-instance decision found that, in the absence of a contract of employment, she had not been employed by the agency or by the council. On appeal, the Employment Appeal Tribunal held that she had been employed by the agency, because of its considerable control over her and the mutuality of obligation between the agency and the worker. However, on hearing the further appeal of this case, the Court of Appeal decided that a contract of service could be implied between the council and the worker, as a necessary inference from the conduct of the parties and the work done, if the "irreducible minimum of mutual obligation necessary for a contract of service" existed. "This contractual relationship can be implied regardless of whether there is an express contract of employment and, indeed, regardless of whether the contract between the worker and the agency, as here, expressly stipulates that there is no contract of employment with the end-user (or with the agency)." The Court of Appeal held that the Employment Tribunal had erred in holding that the applicant was not an employee of the council to which she had been assigned by the agency to work as cleaner for a number of years because there was no express contract between the applicant and the council. In reaching that decision, the tribunal had failed to address the possibility that there was an implied contract of service between the applicant and the council.

Several countries have seen the emergence of "workers' cooperatives" as a system for supplying labour. In Colombia, for example, workers join workers' cooperatives to produce goods or perform work or services. The work should preferably be carried out by the worker members, who are not subject to the labour legislation applicable to dependent workers, unlike the workers employed by the cooperative, and may even contribute their work out of solidarity when the cooperative is in the start-up phase or at times of crisis, either free of charge or for an agreed remuneration.

A private employment agency that has concluded a contract with a user enterprise bears the normal obligations of any employer, but may have other obligations in addition. For example, it may have to inform the workers and their representatives of the identity of the user enterprise and the terms of the contract concluded, its purpose, duration, place of execution, number of workers involved, and measures to coordinate occupational risk prevention activities.

Position of the User

Providers are normally employers; they are linked in turn by a commercial contract with a user enterprise, to which they provide services. Some laws designate the user as the "principal entrepreneur". In Finland, the Employment Contracts Act refers to the "user enterprise" in cases where an enterprise assigns an employee to another enterprise.

The legislation in some countries lays down the obligations and responsibilities of the user with regard to the provider's workers. The user's obligations may cover aspects such as the selection and control of the provider, notification of its own employees of the terms of the agreement reached with the provider, compliance with labour and social security provisions and the payment of minimum wages and other remuneration by the provider, the inclusion of labour clauses in the contract concluded with the latter and keeping a copy of the agreements entered into with the provider.

The user's responsibility in the selection and control of the provider which it contracts is usually based on the obligation to ensure that the provider is appropriately registered, if applicable. In Spain, the user, designated by the law as the principal enterprise, is also required:

(a) to satisfy itself that the contractor is up to date with its social security payments;

(b) to inform the legal representatives of its own workers of the terms of each contract concluded with a contractor or subcontractor; and

(c) to inform the works committee of the conditions in which the subcontracting is to take place.

Where labour is supplied by an employment agency, the user enterprise is normally responsible for the statutory and agreed conditions of work as regards hours of work, night work, weekly rest and holidays, health and safety, and employment of women, children and young persons. The user also bears the obligations pertaining to occupational health and, in principle, has to provide personal protection equipment.

Cost-cutting by the user enterprise was a factor in one case, in which the responsibility of the user enterprise was highlighted by a ruling handed down by a court in the United States. In a case taken by the Department of Labour under the Fair Labour Standards Act, the Court prohibited a clothing manufacturer from selling goods made by contractors in breach of regulations on minimum wages and overtime. Apart from the harm done to the workers, the judgement held that the low-cost production gave a competitive advantage to those who broke the law and a comparative disadvantage to law-abiding manufacturers and distributors. The Court went further, however, and ordered the company, prior to entering into any agreement with a contractor, to examine whether the price that it proposed to pay to the contractor was sufficient to enable the contractor to comply with the regulations on minimum wages and overtime. In addition, the company was ordered to examine the contractor's willingness and ability to comply with such regulations and to require the contractor to inform it immediately if it were unable to do so. In addition, each contractor was required to allow the user enterprise to inspect its records and the enterprise was to review them when it suspected noncompliance by the contractor. Contractors also had to give a written assurance to the enterprise that they complied with the law. In turn, the enterprise in the case was obliged to maintain and keep full records of transactions with each contractor and to respond promptly to any request by the Department of Labour concerning such information. Finally, if any contractor violated the regulations on minimum wages and overtime, the enterprise had to notify the Department of Labour and refrain from marketing goods manufactured in breach of the law.

In Botswana, the Employment Act 1982, along the lines of the Labour Clauses (Public Contracts) Convention, 1949 (No. 94), provides for the inclusion of a declaratory clause in certain public contracts in relation to contracts of employment, to the effect that every contract of employment entered into pursuant to the contract shall be subject to the Employment Act.

There are also provisions of legislation making the user legally liable for the provider's noncompliance. While this principle has long-standing precedents in the legislation of many countries, it continues to be established or reiterated in new laws. The user may bear subsidiary liability for certain obligations in the event of noncompliance by the provider, or joint liability concerning transfers and the contracting or subcontracting of work or services. In Venezuela, the law provides for such liability if the provider's activity is inherent to or related to that of the user. The Labour Code of Panama provides that the user will be considered as the employer of all the provider's workers when the latter is exclusively or chiefly working for the user, but that both shall be jointly liable for all the benefits and compensation due to the workers.

In Mauritius, the law stipulates that, for purposes of securing payment of remuneration, workers employed by a job contractor shall have the same privileges in respect of the property of the user as they would have had if they had been directly employed by the user without the intervention of the provider. In Chile, the user does not bear subsidiary liability in cases where construction work is undertaken at a pre-agreed price, when the person ordering the work is a natural person.

On the issue of limits on the user's responsibility, the Supreme Court of Argentina has ruled that the user's joint responsibility does not extend to covering the payment of arrears in wages and dismissal compensation to the employees of enterprises which held a concession to run a bar and restaurant on the user's premises. In India, the Supreme Court issued a judgement on the abolition of labour engaged by or through a labour contractor which ruled that the user enterprise is under no obligation to absorb as its own employees the workers employed by or through a provider.

In Australia, the Federal Court has set limits on the transfer of activities and workers to another person or enterprise. The Court dealt with the dismissal of workers responsible for home and community care of elderly, disabled or disadvantaged persons by the Greater Dandenong City Council, in the State of Victoria. The provision of these services had been opened up to competitive tendering, although it was known beforehand that the staff already employed by the council would not be able to compete unless they accepted a reduction in their entitlements acquired through collective bargaining and that most of them would have to be dismissed. They did in fact lose the bid to a company offering the services at a cheaper rate with lower conditions of employment, and most of them were dismissed, some of them subsequently being employed by the lower-bidding company but with lower terms and conditions. The Court held that the dismissal had taken place for a "prohibited reason" in breach of the Work place Relations Act of 1996 – i.e. because of their entitlements under the collective agreement – and was thus in violation of freedom of association.

Worker's Rights

The third key question for workers in a "triangular" employment relationship concerns their rights.

In principle, employees' rights are the minimum rights laid down by law and collective agreements, and those set out in the employment contract. However, when the work is performed on behalf of a provider for the benefit of a third party who also has employees, there is often a demand to equalise conditions of employment. This urge may be more pressing if work takes place in the user's premises or work sites, alongside the user's employees, and if both perform work of equal value. This is what often happens when an agency employee is assigned to a team of employees in the user enterprise to carry out the same activity. Furthermore, the issue of breach of the law may arise where a provider enterprise is used to evade legal or contractual obligations. This occurred as regards wages and conditions of employment in the above mentioned case before the United States District Court for the Southern District of New York, and as regards the exercise of collective rights in the case before the Federal Court of Australia, also mentioned above.

Some legal systems provide for rights with regard to collective bargaining, freedom of association and certain conditions of work vis-a-vis the user enterprise, or comparable rights to those recognised by the user for its own employees.

The Employment Contracts Act of Argentina stipulates that a worker hired through a temporary work agency shall be covered by the collective agreement, be represented by the trade union and benefit from the social institution for the activity or category in which the user enterprise actually operates.

The Finnish Employment Contracts Act clearly promotes collective bargaining for workers assigned to an enterprise. The Act states that every employer must at least comply with a national collective agreement. If a provider enterprise is not bound by any collective agreement, then at least the terms of the collective agreement applicable to the user enterprise shall be applied to its employees.

The right of agency employees to bargain collectively was the subject of a decision by the National Labour Relations Board (NLRB) in the United States, of great importance not only because of the legal issue involved and the fact that the NLRB overturned its previous position, but because it situated the issue in the broader perspective of the "contingent work force" and the need to re-focus the protection contained in the National Labour Relations Act. In the specific case, the NLRB examined whether or not workers supplied by an employment agency were in the same bargaining unit as the employees of the manufacturer (the user enterprise). The manufacturing enterprise had given its consent, but there was no evidence that the agency had done so. For the Board, it was evident that the manufacturing enterprise and the employment agency were joint employers (or co-employers) of the agency workers in question, since both decided matters concerning the employment relationship, such as hiring, firing, discipline, supervision and direction, so that they co-determined essential aspects of those relationships. The agency workers worked side by side with the employees of the manufacturing enterprise, performed the same work and were subject to the same supervision. The Board came to the conclusion that the workers employed jointly by a "user employer" and a "supplier employer", in this case an employment agency, could be in the same collective bargaining unit without the need for the "supplier employer's" consent. On the issue of the consent of the employer, the Board overturned its previous position. Now, in this new approach, the principle of "community of interest" prevailed: in other words, it was shown that the temporary workers shared with the permanent employees common supervision, working conditions and interest in wages, hours and conditions of employment.

Under the Employment Act of Slovenia, the employment contract of a person assigned by the employer to provide services for a user shall stipulate that the level of the wage and of the compensation shall depend on the work actually performed with the user, taking into account the collective agreements and general acts binding on individual users. Moreover, during the period for which the worker works with the user, the user and the worker shall take into account the provisions of that Act, of collective agreements binding on the user, or of the user's general acts, with regard to those rights and obligations which are directly related to the performance of work.

Referring both to service enterprises and workers' cooperatives, Peruvian legislation provides that their workers and members shall enjoy the rights and benefits applicable to the other workers in the private sector, and that during their assignment to a user enterprise they shall be entitled to the remuneration and working conditions afforded by the enterprise to its own employees.

In the same vein, in Niger, the wages paid to temporary workers of an employment agency during each assignment cannot fall below what they would have received had they been employed by the user enterprise.

In Mauritius, the law contains detailed provisions expressly prohibiting discrimination and sexual harassment against contract workers by contractors, employment agencies and principals. In France, workers employed under a temporary employment contract have access, in the user enterprise, under the same conditions as the employees of that enterprise, to the collective transport and collective facilities (in particular catering facilities) available to such employees.

In the Netherlands, a new collective agreement for temporary employment, 2004-09, provides for the progressive protection of workers depending on their length of service in three phases as follows: (i) phase A: up to 78 weeks working for the same temporary employment agency; (ii) phase B: up to two years or eight contracts with the agency; and (iii) phase C: after three-and-a-half years with the same agency the worker obtains an open-ended contract with the employment agency. After 26 weeks in the same user enterprise, the temporary employee will receive the same wages as comparable employees of the user enterprise. In phase B, if the temporary work finishes during one of the contracts, the employment agency is obliged to pay wages until the end of the foreseen period.

Compliance and Enforcement

Provisions on enforcement and compliance are very important, especially in complex cases where the individual worker is not able to assert his or her rights effectively.

Certain recent initiatives have focused on problems of compliance with and enforcement of labour law, and seek to provide a suitable response. As regards voluntary compliance with the law, there is an emerging trend reflected in a number of declarations, codes of practice and framework agreements between international employers' and workers' organisations to promote compliance. These initiatives have proved to be crucial in a globalised economy, where corporate behaviour is closely watched by shareholders, consumers, the media and workers' organisations alike. Concerning the State's role in securing compliance, apart from the general re-focusing of legislation already discussed, some provisions and mechanisms have been specifically designed to prevent situations of uncertainty or fraud as to a worker's status, or to provide an effective remedy, although limitations on access to the courts continue to be a major problem.

The Employment Contracts Act in Finland sets out in detail the employer's obligation to inform the employee about the terms of his or her contract. While this provision in fact protects only the employee, at the same time it means that the employer has to decide at the outset whether he or she regards the worker as an employee or self-employed, since only in the former case will the employer have to provide the information required by law. Workers who do not receive such information but believe themselves to be employees may file a complaint with the competent authority.

The Labour Relations Amendment Act in South Africa is more explicit in this respect, since it creates an institutional advisory mechanism for workers who are uncertain of their status. Except in the case of persons earning in excess of the prescribed income limit, any of the contracting parties may apply to the Commission for Conciliation, Mediation and Arbitration (CCMA) for an advisory award on whether the persons involved are employees.

In Quebec, Canada, new legislation provides for a similar preventive mechanism, not just to determine whether or not a worker is an employee, but whether the employee will be converted into an independent worker without employee status as a result of changes that may be introduced in the enterprise by the employer. The employer must notify the relevant employees' association of the changes it proposes to introduce. If the association does not agree with the employer's view as to the consequences of the change on the employee's status, it may seek a determination by the *Commission des relations du travail*. If the association applies to the Commission, the employer may not implement the announced changes until the Commission has ruled or the two parties have reached an agreement.

The amendments introduced in the Labour Code in Chile contain important measures of a different kind, designed to prevent fraud in the employment relationship and improve enforcement of the law. The reform imposes a heavy fine on employers who simulate the recruitment of workers through third parties, or use any subterfuge to disguise or alter their identity or capital for the purpose of evading labour or social security obligations. The amending Act also authorised the creation of 300 labour inspectors' posts and the adoption of provisions to improve enforcement of labour legislation.

The General Labour Bill in Peru contains a number of important provisions in this regard: it reiterates the principle of the *primacy of fact*; it requires the employer to maintain a register of home-workers and to provide a copy to the worker; it requires registration of service suppliers; and it expressly extends the application of the law to members of cooperatives.

The legislation of some countries also contains specific provisions aimed at enforcement of the rights of workers involved in "triangular" employment relationships. Such provisions essentially cover the activity itself of the provider, the supervision to be carried out by the user, the employment contract, administrative supervision and access to the labour courts.

As regards the activity of the provider, there are provisions requiring licensing or registration, in order to operate as a provider, an employment agency or to establish a workers' cooperative. Guarantees may also be required in respect of solvency.

Under the legislation of Niger and Peru, labour supply must be the sole activity of an enterprise. Under Peruvian law, provider enterprises and workers' cooperatives are required to post a bond guaranteeing the discharge of their labour and social security obligations with regard to the workers assigned to a user enterprise.

In the African countries where the *tâcheron* system is practised, the principal entrepreneur is required to keep a list of all the *tacherons* with whom it has signed a contract.

In the United States, the State of California requires certain contractors to obtain a licence to operate from the Labour Commissioner.

In France, in order to operate as an employment agency the law requires that a declaration be made to the administrative authority, indicating the legal characteristics of the enterprise, the names of its directors and the geographical and occupational area in which it intends to operate; a sufficient financial guarantee must also be provided. A similar situation is found in Peru in the case of employment agencies and cooperatives. Once the agency or cooperative is in operation, it is required to sign contracts with its clients on the supply of the workers assigned to work for it, in which it shall state the reasons and characteristics of the assignment. It is also required to inform the competent authority of the employment contracts signed.

5

Labour Markets Trends

The current wave of globalisation starting around 1999-2000 (with the fall of the Berlin wall, with changes in the concepts of development and with the ensuing capital market liberalisation following earlier undertaken trade liberalisation) has profound effects on the labour market and on the employment situation of workers all over the world. These effects are in many cases accentuated by the current financial and economic crisis.

A major question is of course whether ongoing analyses on employment, inequality, and globalisation remain relevant in the current context of the large financial and economic crisis. Such analyses remain highly relevant for at least two reasons:

Firstly, several elements of the ongoing process of globalisation, especially the unfettered markets, (including the labour market) and the growing inequality (resulting for many households to in debt themselves in order keep up spending on basic needs) have given cause to the current crisis; therefore, the analysis of the structure and nature of current globalisation and its impact on employment and inequality as well as policy recommendations to alter current globalisation processes are even more relevant in times of the current crisis.

Secondly, there is growing evidence that the employment, human and social effects of the financial and economic crisis will last for a while, especially if no corrective action is taken. Reinhardt and Rogoff for example foresee that the deceleration or decline in GDP growth will lead to rising unemployment with a much longer duration than the deceleration or decline in GDP itself. Based on a sample of past crises, in the North and the South, they observe an average slump in employment lasting 4.8 years, compared to a deceleration or decline in output growth of only 1.9 years. There is also evidence that indicators for human development exhibit a similar ratchet effect. Arabic and Page for example show that in Africa child mortality increases during growth deceleration, but hardly falls during growth acceleration. Further, primary school completion rates and life expectancy are and remain substantially lower in countries experiencing growth deceleration.

There are thus are strong reasons to include policies for employment, income inequality and human development as priority issues in designing short term and longer policies to deal with the crisis. But, might there be trade-off between these policies for employment, income inequality and human development? A recent study on explanations for growing inequality over the last decade concludes that high employment levels reduce inequality and, especially for developing nations, high employment levels in the industrial sector reduce inequality. Targeting for employment and for reduction of income inequality can thus be combined objectives in policy making. In a similar vein Stewart and Ranis argued that human development and economic growth can be joint and reinforcing targets for policy making. It seems thus more than appropriate to argue for greater attention to employment, income inequality and human development in time of crises.

Stiglitz argues that the dominant view during the current process of globalisation was that unfettered markets were judged sufficient to ensure economic efficiency. The best role for government was a limited one, and somehow the benefits of the growth that this would engender would trickle down to everybody in society. Added to that was the view of a dominant strand of economists arguing that the problem in the market economy was rigid wages, and that if it were not for wage rigidities, the economy would work in the way that classical economics predicted. According to Stiglitz, the implication of the Keynesian rigid-wage theory was very invidious but very pervasive: Get rid of the rigid wages, and let labour markets be more "flexible". That has been the basis of a whole set of doctrines undermining job protections and labour rights. But as he rightly observes, wages are not rigid: in the Great Depression wages fell by about one-third; the problem that Keynes recognised was that wages can be too flexible. Stiglitz observes that lack of aggregate demand was the problem with the Great Depression, just as lack of aggregate demand is the problem today. Accordingly, imposing more wage flexibility can result in exacerbating the underlying problem of lack of aggregate demand. He puts the nature of the problem that we face today as follows:

> *The people in the global economy have the same skills as before the crisis, and the machines and real resources are the same as before the crisis. The problem is that there is an organisational failure, a coordination failure, and a macroeconomic failure.*

Modern Labour Market

Before we discuss in more detail the consequences of financial globalisation on employment we give first a longer term picture of the development of the labour markets in developing regions. We can distinguish a number of general labour market trends over the last two decades.

First we notice a decline in the employment to population rate for most regions in the world.. For the world as a whole the employment to population rate seems to remain rather constant, but there are important regional differences. All three Asian regions, having together with sub-Saharan Africa he highest ratio at the beginning of the 1990's show declines of several percentage points.

In contrast the ratio increases slightly from much lower levels in the middle East, North Africa and Latin America. The lower level in these regions can be explained by very low labour force participation of females at the beginning of the 1990's When de-constructing these global figures we notice two opposite trends namely an increased ratio for female labour force participants and a decline of male participation.

A second trend is the changing pattern in production. For the world as a whole the percentage of employment in service industry has risen from 33.6 per cent in 1991 to 43.8 per cent in 2008. High percentages prevailed already in developed countries the Middle East and North Africa where we consequently see small increases of around 9.5, 2.5 percent and 2 percentage points ; However massive in the percentage employment in the service sector took place in east Asia where it almost doubled from 19.5 per cent to 35.7 per cent and South Asia where it increased from 23.6 per cent to 30.1 per cent.

Some analysts interpret the increase of the employment in the service industry as an indication of post industrial society and an important indicator of progress in development. But this fails to recognise that the service industry encompasses wide range of activities this can range from sophisticated it support to hawking and peddling in the street. Therefore a better indication of broad development for developing countries is the size of manufacturing sector. Here we notice different trend over the last 2 decades. At world level the share of employment in industry has hardly changed from 1991 to 2008 at 21.5 per cent. But there are again important regional differences. The most dramatic increase is in South East Asia and the pacific where the share increased from 12.7 per cent in 1991 to 19.4 per cent and in south Asia where it increased from 15.4 to 22.4 almost reaching the share in East Asia which has remained more or less constant over the period. Noticeable are the very low and stagnant share in sub Saharan Africa at around 8.5 per cent and a decline share in North Africa.

It should be noted however that share of employment in industry can even underestimate the level of progress in industry. As Rada and Tailor, 2006, notice industry often has high productivity (or a low employment Value added elasticity). An important issue is therefore not only the size of employment in industry but also how the surplus generated in the industrial sector is used for reinvestment and how it is distributed in the rest of the economy.

A third noticeable trend over the last 20 year is the precarisation of labour or the increase of non standard forms of employment. Contrary to what has been argued by some this is not only the case for workers in developing countries but equally for workers in developed countries. Precarisation of workers in developed countries is manifested by changes in employment status, replacing traditional labour contracts by out sourcing contracts, more flexible work arrangements, part-time work etc. In developing countries the precariousness is most clearly manifested by the existence of a pervasive informal sector or economy. This phenomenon is not restricted to poorer developing countries.

The existence of the informal economy is partly related to the changes in the structure of employment: Especially for the poorer regions the increase of employment in the service sector reflects also an increase in the share of workers engaged in informal activities.There is evidence of a clear link between the increased non standard work and income inequality, mainly due to widening wage differentials between standard and non standard jobs. Some would explain this by the low education level of those engaged in the informal sector. As statistics show. But it is most likely the type of job rather than the educational attainment which drives inequality. An increase in education levels will result in better educated workers in the informal economy without a major decline in wage inequality in the absence of new created formal jobs.

A fourth trend which is partly related to the changing sectorial patterns of employment and the large informational is the declining wage share and the growing wage inequality which one notices in several regions in the world.

ILO 2008 reports that the wage share declined over the period 1995-2007 in two thirds of the developing countries, including the major countries. The only exception was the Latin American region which also has some countries with an increasing wage share. The ILO report attributes the declining wage share to increasing trade and globalisation and confirms earlier research findings that contrary to the conventional wisdom that sees the labour share in GDP as relatively constant, research by Diwan and Harrison shows that the proportion of GDP that goes into wages and other labour income is variable over time. Using a data set from 1960 to 1997, Harrison splits her sample of over 100 countries into two even groups. Her data show that, in the group of poorer countries, labour's share in national income fell on average by 0.1 percentage points per year from 1960 to 1993. The decline in the labour share accelerated after 1993, to an average decline of 0.3 percentage points per year. In the richer subgroup, the labour share grew by 0.2 percentage points prior to 1993, but then fell by 0.4 percentage points per year. These means indicate a trend reversal for the richer countries post-1993, and an acceleration of an already downward trend for the poorer subgroup.

Harrison tested for factors that could explain changes in labour shares, combining detailed national accounts data from the United Nations with measures of trade openness, capital account restrictions and capital flows. Overall, the results suggest that changes in factor shares are primarily linked to changes in capital/labour ratios. However, measures of globalisation (such as capital controls or direct investment flows) also play a role. Harrison found that exchange rate crises lead to declining labour shares, suggesting that labour pays a disproportionately high price when there are large swings in exchange rates (i.e., wages are more severely affected than GDP). Capital controls are associated with an increase in the labour share, an effect that Harrison attributes to the weaker bargaining position of capital vis-a-vis labour if the cost of relocating production increases with capital controls. Foreign investment inflows are also associated with a fall in the labour share. The weak bargaining position of labour under open capital accounts is also a causal mechanism explored by Lee and Jayadev. They find that financial openness exerts a downward pressure on the labour share both in developed and developing countries for the period from 1973-1995. Harrison also finds that increasing trade is associated with a fall in the labour share. This result is robust across specifications. These results point to a systematic negative relationship between various measures of globalisation and the labour share.

Diwan reports, based on a large sample of countries, an average drop in the labour share of GDP per crisis of 5.0 percentage points, and a modest catch-up thereafter. In the three years after the crisis, labour shares were still 2.6 percentage points below their pre-crisis average. Given the fact that most countries have undergone more than one crisis, the cumulative drop in the wage share over the last 30 years is estimated at 4.1 percent of GDP, and is especially large for Latin America, where the figure reached 6.7 percent of GDP over the period from the 1970s to the 1990s. The overall decline in the labour share is partly explained by what some call the ratchet effect: After an economic shock or a financial crisis the labour share in gross national income decreases.

However not only the inequality between wages and other components of gross domestic product has increased but also the distribution among wage earners (as measured by the ratio of the average wage of the top percent earners in relation to the bottom 10 per cent) shows in seventy percent of the countries an increase. Here one notice the same regional differences, an almost uniform pattern for most regions, but a mixed pattern for Latin America.

A fifth noticeable trend of the last two decades has been the internationalisation of the production process. Today there are some 82000 trans-national Corporations with 81000 affiliates in the world. These companies play a major role in the world economy. For instance exports form foreign affiliates of TNC's are estimated to have grown from about a quarter of total world exports of goods and services in 1982 to one third in 2007. And the number of people employed by these corporations has increased fourfold since 1982 amounted to about 77 million in 2008. A rate much faster that then the rate of growth of the labour force. These TNC are dominated by a number of large firms. The largest 100 TNCs account for 11 percent of all employment in TNC and to about 4 percent of world GDP. Over the last 15 years the largest TNC's have undergone a rapid process of internationalisation. There has also been a progressive increase in the proportion of companies operating in the service sector and of firms based in developing countries.

A sixth noticeable trend is the international migration. Global figures of migration does do not show a substantial change: In 1960 the stock of total migrants in the world population 2.7 per cent and in 2005 this percentage had not changed. This has lead some commentators argue that globalisation is characterised by increased capital flows and increased trade and services flows but not increased labour flows. However, this characterisation is over charged. If looks at more disaggregated regional figures one clearly sees a growing trend in some regions. In Europe the stock of migrants as part of the population increased from 3.0 % in 1960 to 8.8% in 2005, in Northern America from 6.7% to 13.6%, in Oceania from 13.5 % to 16.4% and the Gulf states from 4.9% to 37.1%. Migration ratios declined in Africa, Asia and Latin America as a whole. The increase in migration rates in the high income countries is substantive, despite the severe restriction most countries have put on inward migration (exceptions are the Gulf states and Oceania). This increased level of migration is leading to tensions in the country of destination but is providing a increasing source of foreign revenue of the sending countries.

Using a broad definition, the World Bank estimates that remittances to developing countries amounted to 166.9 billion US$ in 2005, compared to 85.6 billion US$ in 2000 and 31.2 billion US$ in 1990. Remittances are not only a rapidly growing source of external finance, but they are generally continuous over the years and not prone to sudden reversals of direction. They tend to be counter-cyclical for crises in developing countries (i.e. migrants send more money home to support their families) and hence help to smoothing consumption volatility. However, the current financial and economic crisis engendered by the sub-prime mortgage crisis in the United States is leading to greater job loses than ever, in particular in industries such as construction that have a disproportionate share of migrant workers, will have a negative impact on remittances.

The six labour market trends which we have ascribed above: declining employment population ratio, the increase in service employment, the continuing high share of workers in the informal economy, the declining wage share and greater income inequality, growing importance of multinational enterprises and the growing number of migrant workers in Industrialised countries give a general a picture of increased precarisation of many workers and their families, which can be partly ascribed to the ongoing process of globalisation, including financial globalisation. Freeman 2004 has even argued that financial globalisation affects employment and incomes of workers in developing countries more than trade liberalisation.

Financial globalisation and Labour

The current wave of globalisation is characterised by widespread adoption of policies for financial openness. Over the past two decades, many countries have liberalised their capital accounts and almost all policy measures related to foreign direct investment favoured a more open regime. These measures have been adopted autonomously by some countries, and also as conditions of adjustment loans. The major expected result from financial openness was that it would allow developing countries to better utilise resources and to increase capital formation by stimulating foreign direct investment (FDI) and other international capital flows such as private portfolios investment. A more open national financial system was seen as a necessary complement to the lifting of impediments to international capital flows.

Capital has become more globally mobile as a result of these policy changes, especially since the mid-1990s. Worldwide gross private capital flows (the sum of the absolute values of foreign direct, port-folio, and other investment in- and outflows) have exceeded 20 percent of world GDP every year since 1998 and reached a new record of 32.3 percent of GDP in 2005 – compared to less than 10 percent of world GDP before 1990. Worldwide FDI flows, a sub-category of private capital flows, also rose substantially during the 1990s. They peaked at 4.9 percent of world GDP in 2000 and declined when with the downturn of the early 2000s, but strongly rebound before the current global financial and economic crisis. On average, global FDI flows doubled between the 1980s and the 1990s, and again in the years from 2000 to 2007.

In spite of this substantial increase in capital flows, the expected benefits have not materialised for many countries. During the surge in foreign capital flows since the mid-1990s, actual investment into new infrastructure and productive capacity stagnated. This can in part be attributed to the fact that much FDI was spent on mergers and acquisitions, rather than on investment into new factories or equipment that would have added productive capacity. Gross fixed capital formation averaged 21.6 per cent of GDP in the 1990s and 21.0 percent in the years from 2000 to 2006.

Moreover, despite much excitement about the promise of 'emerging markets', cross-border capital flows are still largely a phenomenon of developed countries. In 2005, gross private capital flows equalled 37.2 percent of GDP in high-income countries, but only 12.7 percent of GDP in low- and middle-income countries. While there was a positive balance between in- and outflows for developing countries as a group, these flows by-and-large bypassed the poorest countries since the early 1990s as middle income countries accounted for more than 90 percent of the total. FDI, as well, is highly concentrated among industrialised countries and a small group of middle-income countries.

Low-income countries, to a large extent, still draw their foreign resources from remittances and official development assistance which decreased over the 1990s and only rebound in the past few years.

Meanwhile, international capital movements and their sometimes sharp reversals have led to greater economic volatility, a trend that has been well documented. That volatility has lead to more frequent financial and economic crises, predominantly in developing countries. While the current financial crisis had its origins in the industrialised world, the initial hope that developing countries had effectively 'de-coupled' proved to be an illusion when the upheaval in capital markets and the economic downturn spread around the globe within months. Such crises have negative effects on growth, investment and incomes, not only in the short term, but also in the long run.

How does financial openness affect labour? There are several potential channels of influence. First is the potential effect of openness on growth. In addition to the potential direct positive effect of capital flows on growth (as countries gain additional resources that can be invested), there can also be an indirect negative effect on growth when financial liberalisation forces countries to hold a larger foreign reserves, which reduces consumption and/or investment and hence growth potential. If financial flows have, on balance, a positive impact on growth, this would be generally beneficial for labour, while slow growth is usually disadvantageous for labour. However, even in the case of fast or steady growth, the distributional impact of financial openness on different categories of labour needs to be taken into account. Labour might benefit less than necessary for long term institutional and human capital development and for growth of domestic consumption.

Financial Globalisation, Growth and Employment

It has proven difficult to establish a robust causal relationship between financial globalisation and growth. A recent study by IMF researchers has confirmed the main findings of earlier studies, such as those undertaken in

UNCTAD, that find that growth depends more on the quality of domestic institutions and careful macroeconomic management than on financial liberalisation. Edison and others argue in the same direction and demonstrate that the findings of previous research (that found a positive association between capital account openness and growth) crucially depended on the country coverage, the choice of time periods and the indicator for capital account openness. They also find evidence for a suggestion that was first made by Rodrik, namely that conventional indicators for capital account openness closely proxy the reputation of a country's government. If governance is controlled for, capital account openness has no significant effect on economic performance.

Indirect Growth Effects Through Increased Reserve Holdings

The repeated financial crises of recent years have led many developing countries to build up foreign reserves. For some countries these reserves were created by surplus on the current account, while others built up reserves through capital inflows which were not spent on foreign goods. Rodrik estimates the cost of increased reserve holdings to be 1 percent of GDP on average for developing countries. While imposing costs on developing countries, increased reserve holdings are an indirect subsidy to the countries in whose currencies the reserves are held.

The trend has accelerated in recent years to a somewhat alarming level. Overall, reserves held by low- and middle-income countries were equal to 27.1 percent of their GNI in 2007, compared to 6.8 percent in the first half of the 1990s – a fourfold increase. The increase took place in low- and middle-income developing countries alike, and across regions. Even a poor region like sub-Saharan Africa now holds foreign reserves equal to 17.9 percent of its GNI, more than three times the ratio in the early 1990s. The trend is particularly strong in South Asia, East Asia and the Pacific.

Even when China (the developing country with the largest foreign reserves) is excluded, there remains a substantial increase from an already high 15.0 percent of GNI to 27.6 percent in 2007 for the rest of the region.

Financial Globalisation, Volatility, Crises and Employment

Financial liberalisation in developing countries is associated with increased GDP volatility and higher consumption volatility. Kaminsky, Reinhart and Vegh pointed out that the absence of sound financial regulation, both at the national and international levels, makes developing countries much more vulnerable to negative impacts of capital flows. When institutions with the ability to manage greater volatility are absent or not fully effective, the generally pro-cyclical nature of international capital flows ("when it rains it pours" syndrome) adds to the effects of fiscal policies, and, to a certain extent, also macroeconomic police, that tend to be pro-cyclical in most developing countries. Such behaviour deepens and prolongs a crisis.

Financial crises typically have a large impact on the real economy. In the five countries most affected by the East Asian crisis of 1997/98, GDP per capita fell between 2.6 percent (Philippines) and 14.8 percent (Indonesia). In Latin America, the Mexican crisis of 1994/95 led to a decline in incomes of 7.9 percent, and the Argentinean crisis of 2001/02 reduced the country's per capita incomes by 16.5 percent. A recent study by Hutchison and Noy documents that so-called "sudden stop" crises (a reversal in capital flows and a simultaneous currency crisis) have a particularly harmful effect on output–over and above that of 'normal' currency crises. On average, they cause a cumulative output loss of 13 to 15 percent of GDP over a three-year period.

The view that crises pose only a temporary setback is challenged by Cerra and Saxena, who de-construct what they call the 'myth of recovery' by using panel data for broad datasets of countries. They document that recessions are typically not followed by high-growth recovery phases, either immediately following the trough, over several years of the subsequent expansion, or even over the complete subsequent expansion that follows a recession. When output drops, it tends to remain well below its previous trend. Cerra and Saxena also find that frequent crises and instabilities interfere with convergence between rich and poor countries:

> "Countries that experience many negative shocks to output tend to get left behind and their long-term growth suffers. Thus, while standard growth theory may work well in explaining expansion, a fruitful direction for future research would be to explain the proclivity to wars, crises, and other negative shocks."

Financial crises generally provoke both economic decline and social costs. These are most prominently felt in terms of rising open unemployment, falling employment to population ratios, falling real wages, or a combination of the above. Moreover, the social costs are usually felt longer than the economic impact: Even when GDP per capita has recovered to pre-crisis level, the other indicators usually lack behind. This pattern can be observed in a majority of countries that were most affected by the financial crises of the past decade.

Impact of Financial Crises on Employment in Latin America

Latin American countries experienced several periods of financial turbulence in recent years. The most prominent examples are the Mexican "Tequila crisis" during 1994/95 and the currency crisis in several South American countries in the aftermath of the East Asian and Russian crises. Following extensive liberalisation policies in Mexico, financial inflows expanded rapidly in the early 1990s, but reversed in 1994. The peso devaluation of December 1994 brought the recently privatised, already fragile banking system into considerable difficulty as the peso value of foreign denominated debt soared. Similarly, the balance sheet positions of companies which had accumulated debt in US dollars deteriorated rapidly, which in turn led to a sharp fall in investment. Taken together, this can explain how a currency crisis rapidly turned into a crisis of the real economy and provoked a recession with an eight percent drop in per capita income in 1995. Unemployment, relatively stable at around three percent before the crisis, started to increase during 1994 and reached 5.8 percent in 1995, almost twice the pre-crisis rate. However, these figures mask the actual loss of jobs, since the share of informal employment rose from 30 percent in 1993 to 35 percent in 1995. By 1997 Mexico had achieved its pre-crisis income level, with the unemployment rate lagging the economic recovery by one year. However the share of informal employment remained above the pre-crisis level.

Brazil experienced large foreign capital inflows from 1994 onwards, when the Real Plan had introduced a new stable currency. When investor sentiment swung suddenly after the Russian debt default of August 1998, Brazil responded by tightening its monetary policy in an effort to defend the exchange rate. Even though interest rates reached 40 percent in late 1998, the capital outflows from Brazil were massive and the Central Bank allowed the Real to devalue. The currency crisis, in combination with the recessional impact of high real interest rates, led to a relatively modest decline of per capita incomes that was accompanied by an increase in unemployment from 7.7 percent in 1997 to 9.6 percent in 1999. Despite the subsequent economic recovery, unemployment rates have hardly recovered and remained close to nine percent in 2004

Like other emerging economies, Chile received large international capital inflows in the beginning of the 1990s. But unlike most other countries, Chile imposed controls on capital inflows in the form of an unremunerated reserve requirement (URR). Although it is uncertain whether this affected the overall amount of inflows, it reduced speculative capital inflows: the share of short-term debt in total external debt fell from an already low level of 19.4 percent in 1990 to 4.8 percent in 1997 at a time when other countries increasingly relied on short-term financing. At the onset of the Asian crisis, Chile was thus considerably less exposed to international volatility. The peso was also at the lower (appreciated) end of the exchange rate band at the time, leaving room for a relatively large devaluation within the band. However, the Central Bank feared that a depreciation could endanger the inflation target. Therefore, it defended the peso against growing pressure with a mix of monetary tightening and interventions on the foreign exchange market, before finally allowing the peso to float in September 1999.

Solimano and Larraín argue that the Central Bank effectively priorities "lower inflation over higher growth and employment". The high interest rates had a recessional impact, and unemployment increased from 5.3 percent in 1997 to 8.9 percent in 1999. While GDP per capita regained its 1998 level in 2000, unemployment only fell slowly and reached 6.0 percent only in 2006. Solimano and Larraín discuss several hypotheses that could explain the sluggish employment performance, among them firm-restructuring, continued job losses in small and medium enterprises (SMEs) and the noticeably slower rate of GDP growth after the crisis. They warn that unemployment could become a structural problem in Chile unless capital formation accelerates.

The case of Argentina stands out, for the country went through two financial crises, in 1995 (when investors withdrew capital following the Tequila crisis in Mexico) and again in 2001/02, leading to the collapse of a fixed exchange rate system. The first crisis caused only a relatively mild downturn, and, with considerable foreign support, pre-crisis income levels were again reached in 1996. As in other countries, the unemployment rate (that covers only urban areas in the case of Argentina) was still far above the pre-crisis level at this point, but it was approaching its 1994 level by 1998. A recession that year sent unemployment up again. Argentina therefore went into the 2001/02 crisis with an already high level of (urban) unemployment, that rose to almost 20 percent by 2002. More recent data indicate that a partial recovery had occurred by 2006, when unemployment fell below 10 percent for the first time. Economic turbulence and the cumulative effects of two financial crises have thus caused a substantial unemployment problem in a country where unemployment rates had fluctuated around five percent for most of the 1980s.

In Turkey, the frequency of crises was even higher than in Argentina. The country had liberalised its economy throughout the 1980s, but embarked on full capital account liberalisation only in August 1989. Since then, capital flows have been highly volatile and have contributed to the repeated crises that affected the country in 1994, 1998/99 and 2001. As Demir argues, the country went into a vicious cycle of crises, where the loss in output reduced public revenues and increased public borrowing through short-term treasury bills that were bought by domestic banks, which refinanced themselves through short-term loans from abroad – building up currency risks and setting the stage for the next crisis. Resulting high real interest rates reduced investment and prospects for long-term growth. Whereas recovery from the first crisis in 1994 was relatively smooth-both in terms of GDP and employment, the second and especially the third crisis proved to be more severe. Their combined effect meant that per capita incomes were still at their 1997/98 level in 2003. Unemployment peaked briefly during 1999 and was back at its previous level of around 6.5

percent in 2000 before the next crisis set in. The third crisis led to a dramatic rise in unemployment to 10.4 percent in 2002 and has remained close to ten percent since. While employment had recovered largely in line with GDP during the first crises, unemployment has not fallen significantly after the last, most severe crisis – despite a strong rebound in GDP.

Employment Impact of the East Asian Crisis

That financial crises typically translate into crises of the real economy is also clearly evident from the experience of East Asia. Here, both output and capacity utilisation fell sharply during the 1997/98 crisis. In a survey of firms in Korea, Thailand, Indonesia and Malaysia, entrepreneurs list the drop in domestic demand, rising costs for imported inputs, and the high interest rates as the most important reasons. The declining capacity utilisation had adverse impacts on the average profitability and liquidity of firms, and many companies abandoned or scaled down planned investments (ibid.: passim). Interest rate and currency shocks also forced many companies into bankruptcy as they found themselves unable to service their debt, much of which was denominated in foreign currency. Data from the five countries worst affected by the East Asian crisis show that many of the surviving firms reduced their work-force in 1998, while only a small fraction hired more staff. Unemployment increased throughout the region, and incomes fell – in some cases dramatically, pushing many people below the poverty line. According to ILO estimates, the number of working poor in South East Asia (using the threshold of 1 US$ per day) rose from its pre-crisis level of 33.7 million in 1996 to 50.6 million at the height of the financial crisis in 1998 – an increase of almost 17 million.

A more detailed look at the country level shows that in 1996, the year before the East Asian financial crisis, some countries had virtually achieved full employment with unemployment rates of 1.1 percent in Thailand, 2.0 percent in Korea and 2.5 percent in Malaysia. By 1998, the combination of production cutbacks and layoff through bankruptcies had brought unemployment to 3.4 percent in Thailand, or 1.1 million (up from 0.3 million). In addition, about 0:2 million workers left the labour force despite strong growth of the working age population. Many workers had to find a new source of income in the informal economy which grew significantly during the crisis. This development is mirrored by a rise in the number of self-employed by 0.8 million. Hidden unemployment in the form of underemployment also increased almost twofold (from 2.3 million to 4.4 million). A further effect of the crisis was a decline in real wages by 4 per cent within a year.

The Korean labour market suffered severely from the wave of redundancies that accompanied the bankruptcies of thirteen large conglomerates during 1997, and the reduction in the work force of surviving companies. Delays in payments by the large corporations dragged many small and medium enterprises (SMEs) into the crisis; 8,200 of them failed in 1997 and a further 10,500 in 1998. Open unemployment rose to 7.0 percent or 1.5 million (up from 0.6 million), a level not seen in decades. Among the hardest-hit groups were manual production workers and those in clerical grades. By the first quarter of 1999, total employment had fallen to 19 million, down by 2.1 million from the fourth quarter of 1997. The disparity between the growth in unemployment and the far larger decline in employment can be attributed to the fact that around 350,000 workers (in particular women) left the labour force altogether, resulting in a decline of the labour force participation rate by almost two percentage points.

The increase in unemployment was less dramatic in **Malaysia,** where the rate rose by less than a percentage point. Nonetheless, around 250,000 formal sector jobs were lost in 1998. Many of the retrenched workers were foreign migrant workers, which cushioned the effect on the domestic labour market but dispersed some of the negative impact to other countries. ILO data also show that agricultural employment expanded by 135,000 in 1998. The absorption of labour by the primary sector helped to contain the rise in open un-employment, but contributed to falling labour productivity in agriculture

Indonesia and the Philippines (7.4 percent) went into the financial crisis with considerably higher unemployment. From that higher base, about 2.5 million workers lost their jobs in Indonesia in 1997/1998, among them 1 million in manufacturing alone. The fall in industry and services employment was offset by an expansion of agriculture employment, so that open unemployment grew only modestly during 1998 despite strong labour force growth. However, unemployment continued to rise in subsequent years and reached 11.2 percent in 2005. Real earnings also fell by about 40 percent during the crisis and were still about 10 percent below their pre-crisis level in 2000. In the Philippines, where the crisis had a comparatively mild economic impact, unemployment rose to 9.4 percent in 1998 and has, much like in Indonesia, continued on an upward path during the early 2000s.

The East Asian experience shows that progress in returning to pre-crisis unemployment is generally far slower than the pace of economic recovery. Although all five countries returned to positive growth in 1999 or 2000, unemployment rates continued to increase in Indonesia, Korea, Malaysia and the Philippines and peaked only four or five years after the return to positive growth. This explains while the recovery of the labour market lagged far behind the economic recovery. Although all five countries have regained their pre-crisis GDP level – Korea as early as 1999,

Indonesia only in 2005, only Thailand had returned to pre-crisis levels of unemployment in 2007, a decade after the East Asian Crisis. Thus, while countries have largely managed to recover from the economic impact of the crisis, the devastating labour market effect seems to be much more long-lived.

On balance, the capital account liberalisation that many developing countries embarked upon in the 1990s has delivered disappointing results.

The preceding discussion has shown that capital account liberalisation fell not only far short of expectations, but did serious harm to some countries and had a disproportionately negative effect on labour. Six main conclusions emerge:

1. In the absence of adequate institutions, capital account liberalisation has little direct benefit for growth. This is especially true for poor countries where the institutional gap is greatest, but also for middle-income countries where capital inflows were not used to fill unmet investment needs.
2. Even if capital account liberalisation is managed prudently, it has cost to developing countries. In order to cushion the effects of sudden outflows, developing countries have sterilised inflows and built up large reserves. Since these are mainly held in low-yield treasury bonds issued by industrialised countries, the opportunity cost is large.
3. Capital account liberalisation has left developing countries vulnerable to crisis. These are often not triggered by a deterioration of a country's fundamental economic status, but by forces in the international financial system. The output losses associated with such crises are large, and even a subsequent recovery is usually insufficient to bring a country back onto its old growth path.

4. The negative effects of financial crises on the labour market can be detected in a number of indicators. Open unemployment typically rises substantially during a crisis, real wages often fall, underemployment rises, and workers shift from the formal sector to the informal economy and agriculture.
5. Labour markets typically flag the economic recovery by several years. Even when GDP per capita has reached its pre-crisis level, the consequences of the crisis are normally still evident in higher unemployment compared to pre-crisis levels. This flag means that labour pays a disproportionate cost.
6. Tracking the evolution of the labour share in national income also shows that financial openness and financial crises diminish labour's share. Financial openness is associated with stronger bargaining power for capital vis-a-vis labour. Financial crises have a negative and persistent effect on the share of labour compensation in GDP.

Crisis on Labour and Possible Policy Responses.

The above analysis on the effects on labour in previous crises, provides a useful indicator for an analysis of the current crises, where information on employment and labour issues is only to surface now.

The recent World Bank's Global Economic Prospects for 2010 argues that the severity of this recession is far larger than of earlier recessions. These observations are at variance with earlier assessments on the effects of the current recession on developing countries. The IMF 2008 World Economic Outlook, for example, argued that greater de-linking was taken place between industrialised and developing economies and that developing countries would be less affected by a crisis which had started in the developed world. However the decline in trade volumes and values, the substantial shrinking of foreign direct investment as well as a reversal in fast growing trend of increasing remittances, which some have labelled as de-globalisation, have all had in various ways, substantial consequences for developing countries and especially on the poorer segment of the population. One could argue that such de-globalisation might be beneficial for developing countries as it reversed the trend of increasing globalisation. Furthermore the decline in trade, FDI and remittance was not the consequence of any agreed change in internationally policy attitudes towards globalisation, but the outcome of serious downturn in GDP in industrialised countries, with rising tendencies of protectionism and a deterioration of attitudes to foreign workers.

The position of labour in the current crisis is actually extremely worrying: the trends over the last two decades indicate that the economic bubble, as a consequence of financial globalisation, in the second half of the first decade of the 21st century did not favour most participants in the labour-market. Only a small minority has really been profiting from this. Most workers did not profit from the bubble (as a.o. The low employment elasticity, the growing inequality and the persistent informations attest to), but after the bubble many workers suffer from consequence of the bursting of the bubble. And while business as usual, including the highly stewed remuneration packages, seems to be on the cards for financial institutions, this is not the case for many in the labour market.

To state briefly: current globalisation has made labour more precarious, a trend which has been magnified by the current crisis. This picture is consistent with the policy reaction in many countries to the crisis, to the effect that the governments have (rightly) acted as a banker of last resort to avoid the collapse of the financial system, but that governments, despite stimulus plans a monetary easing and some labour market policies, have not really acted as an employer of last resort.It seems thus important to frame policies favouring labour in the current context on two essential elements.

First by introducing or by strengthening those national and international policies, which try to undo the trends of precariousness and increasing inequality as a consequence of (financial) globalisation. Examples of such policies can be found in van der Heaven and Luebker 2007, UN DESA 2007 and World Commission on the Social Dimension of Globalisation 2004.

Secondly, in addition to the policies above, by applying special policies to deal with the out fall of the current crisis, such as employment policy schemes, special labour-market policies, cash transfers etc. The costs of these policies are often a fraction of the support the financial institutions and large industries have received recently. They can be in first instance financed as part of the current stimulus packages and, once the economy has picked up, from increased tax revenues or from reimbursements to the governments by bailed out financial institutions.

It is important to base policy interventions simultaneously on policies dealing with the structural problems, which financial globalisation has caused, and on policies assisting those who fall into poverty or experience poor working conditions as a consequence of the crisis; the current crisis is clearly the outcome of a longer trend of financial globalisation, which, if not arrested in its current form, may lead well to a new crisis.

6

Industrial Revolution

The world community needs a powerful new economic narrative that will push the discussion and the agenda around climate change and peak oil from fear to hope and from economic constraints to economic possibilities. That narrative is just now emerging as industries begin to lay the groundwork for a post-carbon Third Industrial Revolution.

The need for a new economic vision takes on an even greater urgency in light of the just released report issued by the leading U.S. Climatologist James Hansen, head of the NASA Goddard Institute for Space Studies, and coauthored with eight other leading scientists. Hansen and his colleagues say that the EU CO_2 target, the most rigorous of any government, needs to be slashed to 350 ppm if "humanity wishes to preserve a planet similar to that on which civilisation developed" and to which life on earth has adapted. According to Hansen, "what we have found is that the target we have all been aiming for is a disaster- a guaranteed disaster". The new findings, extrapolated from core samples taken from the bottom of the ocean, suggests that if CO_2 levels were to rise to 550 ppm, the planet's temperature would rise to 6° Celsius – previous estimate suggests a 3° Celsius rise in the temperature on earth by the end the of the century- with catastrophic results to life on earth.

As the nations of the world prepare for the Copenhagen Climate Summit in 2009, it is critical that we re-frame the global discussion on climate change and energy security to the mission of making the transition from the second industrial revolution to a Third Industrial Revolution. If we do not succeed in re-orienting the climate change and energy agenda from burden-sharing to commercial opportunities, it is likely that the Copenhagen Climate Summit will not achieve its full potential, with untold consequences to civilisation.

The key, for every nation, is to lay out a compelling "social vision" to accompany the new economic vision. The Third Industrial Revolution provides the framework for the birth of a new "Distributed Social Vision" in the first half of the 21st Century. Just as the distributed IT and internet communication revolutions dramatically changed the economic parameters of doing business, as well as the social context, a distributed renewable energy revolution will have a similar impact on the world. A new Distributed Social Vision flows directly from the coming together of distributed communication and information technology and distributed renewable energies. We are on the cusp of a new energy era and a new economic paradigm that will literally "empower" hundreds of millions of human beings to create their own energy and share their surpluses with neighbours across regions, nations and continents. The democratisation of energy gives rise to a new Distributed Social Vision in the 21st century that will change our economic, cultural and political institutions as dramatically as the Enlightenment vision that accompanied the first industrial revolution two centuries ago.

Towards the Third Industrial Revolution

While oil, coal, and natural gas will continue to provide a substantial portion of the world's and the European Union's energy well into the 21st century, there is a growing consensus that we are entering a twilight period where the full costs of our fossil fuel addiction is beginning to act as a drag on the world economy. During this twilight era, nations are making efforts to ensure that the remaining stock of fossil fuels is used more efficiently and are experimenting with clean energy technologies to limit carbon dioxide emissions in the burning of conventional fuels. The EU, in particular, is mandating that the member states increase energy efficiency 20 percent by 2020 and reduce their global warming emissions 20 percent (based on 1990 levels), again by 2020. But, greater efficiency in the use of fossil fuels and mandated global warming gas reductions, by themselves, are not enough to adequately address the unprecedented crisis of global warming and global peak oil and gas production. Looking to the future, every government will need to explore new energy paths and establish new economic models with the goal of achieving as close to zero carbon emissions as possible.

Convergence of Energy and Communication Regimes

The great pivotal economic changes in world history have occurred when new energy regimes converge with new communication regimes. When that convergence happens, society is restructured in wholly new ways. For example, the first hydraulic agricultural societies— Mesopotamia, Egypt, China, India—invented writing to manage the cultivation, storage, and distribution of grain. Surpluses of stored grain allowed for an expansion of population and the feeding of a slave labour force which, in turn, provided the "man power" to run the economy. The convergence of written communication and stored energy in the form of surplus grain, ushered in the agricultural revolution, and gave rise to civilisation itself.

In the early modern era, the coming together of coal powered steam technology and the print press gave birth to the first industrial revolution. It would have been impossible to organise the dramatic increase in the pace, speed, flow, density, and connectivity of economic activity made possible by the coal fired steam engine using the older codex and oral forms of communication. In the late nineteenth century and throughout the first two thirds of the twentieth century, first generation electrical forms of communication—the telegraph, telephone, radio, television, electric typewriters, calculators, etc.—converged with the introduction of oil and the internal combustion engine, becoming the communications command and control mechanism for organising and marketing the second industrial revolution.

Similarly, today, the same design principles and smart technologies that made possible the internet, and vast "distributed" global communication networks, are just beginning to be used to re-configure the world's power grids so that people can produce renewable energy and share it peer-to-peer, just like they now produce and share information, creating a new, decentralised form of energy use. We need to envision a future in which millions of individuals can collect and produce locally generated renewable energy in their homes, offices, factories, and vehicles, store that energy in the form of hydrogen, and share their power generation with each other across a continent-wide intelligent intergrade.

The question is often asked as to whether renewable energy, in the long run, can provide enough power to run a national or global economy. Just as second generation information systems grid technologies allow businesses to connect thousands of desktop computers, creating far more distributed computing power than even the most powerful centralised computers that exist, millions of local producers of renewable energy, with access to intelligent utility networks, can potentially produce and share far more distributed power than the older centralised forms of energy – oil, coal, natural gas and nuclear – that we currently rely on.

Pillars of the Third Industrial Revolution

The creation of a renewable energy regime, loaded by buildings, partially stored in the form of hydrogen, and distributed via smart intergrade, opens the door to a Third Industrial Revolution and should have as powerful an economic multiplier effect in the 21st century as the convergence of mass print technology with coal and steam power technology in the 19th century, and the coming together of electrical forms of communication with oil and the internal combustion engine in the 20th century.

Renewable Energy

Renewable forms of energy—solar, wind, hydro, geo-thermal, ocean waves, and bio-mass —make up the first of the four pillars of the Third Industrial Revolution. While these sunrise energies still account for a small percentage of the global energy mix, they are growing rapidly as governments mandate targets and benchmarks for their widespread introduction into the market and their falling costs make them increasingly competitive. Billions of dollars of public and private capital are pouring into research, development and market penetration, as businesses and homeowners seek to reduce their carbon footprint and become more energy efficient and independent. Global investment in renewable energies topped $148 billion in 2007, a 60 percent increase from 2006. Global investments in renewable energies are expected to leap to €250 billion by 2020 and €460 billion by 2030. Today, renewable energy manufacturing, operations, and maintenance provide approximately two million jobs worldwide. A recent study found that the number of jobs created per euro-invested (and per kilowatt-hour produced) from clean renewable energy technologies is 3 to 5 times the number of jobs created from fossil fuel based generation.

By becoming the first superpower to establish a mandatory target of 20 percent renewable energy by 2020, the EU has set in motion the process of vastly enlarging the renewable energy portion of its energy mix. Reflecting the new commitment to higher renewable energy targets, the European Investment Bank has retouched up its renewable energy investments and is slated to finance loans totalling more than €800 million per year. In Germany, alone, the renewable energy industry boasted an annual turnover of €21.6 billion and 214,000 workers in 2006, and the industry projects to grow to between 244,000 and 263,000 jobs by 2010, 307,000 to 354,000 jobs by 2020, and 333,000 to 415,000 jobs by 2030.

The 26 other EU member states are also creating new jobs as they bring renewable energy sources online to meet their objective of achieving a near zero carbon emission policy. Renewable energy in the EU generated €8.9 billion in earnings in 2005, and is expected to leap to 14.5 billion euros by 2010. More than 700,000 jobs are expected to be created in the EU by 2010 in the field of electricity generation from renewable energy sources. By 2050, renewable energy is projected to provide nearly half the primary energy, and 70 percent of the electricity produced within the EU, and account for several million new jobs.

Buildings as Positive Power Plants

While renewable energy is found everywhere and new technologies are allowing us to harness it more cheaply and efficiently, we need infrastructure to load it. This is where the building industry steps to the fore, to lay down the second pillar of the Third Industrial Revolution.

The construction industry is the largest industrial employer in many countries. In the EU, in 2003, construction represented 10 percent of the GDP, and 7 percent of the employment in the EU-15. Buildings are the major contributor to human induced global warming. Worldwide, buildings consume 30 to 40 percent of all the energy produced and are responsible for equal percentages of all CO2 emissions. Now, new technological breakthroughs make it possible, for the first time, to design and construct buildings that create all of their own energy from locally available renewable energy sources, allowing us to reconceptualise the future of buildings as "power plants". The commercial and economic implications are vast and far reaching for the real estate industry and, for that matter, the world.

In 25 years from now, millions of buildings – homes, offices, shopping malls, industrial and technology parks – will be renovated or constructed to serve as both "power plants" and habitats. These buildings will collect and generate energy locally from the sun, wind, garbage, agricultural and forestry waste, ocean waves and tides, hydro and geo-thermal– enough energy to provide for their own power needs as well as surplus energy that can be shared.

A new generation of commercial and residential buildings as power plants is going up now. In the United States, Frito-Lay is re-tooling its Case Grande plant, running it primarily on renewable energy and recycled water. The concept is called "net-zero". The factory will generate all of its energy on-site by installing solar roofs and by recycling the waste from its production processes and converting it into energy. In France, Bouygues, the giant French construction company is taking the process a step further, putting up a state-of-the-art commercial office complex this year in the Paris suburbs that collects enough solar energy to provide not only for all of its own needs, but even generates surplus energy as well.The Walqa Technology Park in Huesca, Spain is nestled in a valley in the Pyrenees and is among a new genre of technology parks that produce their own renewable energy on-site to power their operations. There are currently a dozen office buildings in operations at the Walqa Park, and 40 more already slated for construction. The facility is run entirely by renewable forms of energy, including wind power, hydro, and solar. The park houses leading high tech companies, including Microsoft and other IT companies, renewable energy companies, etc.

Hydrogen Storage

The introduction of the first two pillars of the Third Industrial Revolution- renewable energy and "buildings as power plants"- requires the simultaneous introduction of the third pillar of the Third Industrial Revolution. To maximise renewable energy and to minimise cost it will be necessary to develop storage methods that facilitate the conversion of intermittent supplies of these energy sources into reliable assets. Batteries, differentiated water pumping, and other media, can provide limited storage capacity. There is, however, one storage medium that is widely available and can be relatively efficient. Hydrogen is the universal medium that "stores" all forms of renewable energy to assure that a stable and reliable supply is available for power generation and, equally important, for transport.

Hydrogen is the lightest and most abundant element in the universe and when used as an energy source, the only by-products are pure water and heat. Our spaceships have been powered by high-tech hydrogen fuel cells for more than 30 years. Here is how hydrogen works. Renewable sources of energy—solar cells, wind, hydro, geo-thermal, ocean waves—are used to produce electricity. That electricity, in turn, can be used, in a process called electrolysis, to split water into hydrogen and oxygen.

Hydrogen can also be extracted directly from energy crops, animal and forestry waste, and organic garbage—so called bio-mass—without going through the electrolysis process.

The important point to emphasise is that a renewable energy society becomes viable to the extent that part of that energy can be stored in the form of hydrogen. That's because renewable energy is intermittent. The sun isn't always shining, the wind isn't always blowing, water isn't always flowing when there's a drought, and agricultural yields vary. When renewable energy isn't available, electricity can't be generated and economic activity grinds to a halt. But, if some of the electricity being generated, when renewable energy is abundant, can be used to extract hydrogen from water, which can then be stored for later use, society will have a continuous supply of power. Hydrogen can also be extracted from bio-mass and similarly stored.

The European Commission recognises that increasing reliance on renewable forms of energy would be greatly facilitated by the development of hydrogen fuel cell storage capacity and, in 2003, established the Hydrogen Technology Platform, a massive research and development effort to move Europe to the forefront of the race to a hydrogen future. Regions and national governments across Europe have already begun to establish hydrogen research and development programs and are in the early stages of introducing hydrogen technologies into the marketplace.

In 2006, the Federal Republic of Germany committed €500 million to hydrogen research and development and began readying plans to create a nationwide hydrogen road-map, with the stated goal of leading Europe and the world into the hydrogen era by 2020. Chancellor Angela Merkel and members of her cabinet called for a Third Industrial Revolution in public addresses in 2007.

In 2008, the European Commission announced a Joint Technology Initiative (JTI), an ambitious public/private partnership, to speed the commercial introduction of a hydrogen economy in the 27 member states of the EU, with the primary focus on producing hydrogen from renewable sources of energy.

Smartgrids and Plug-in Vehicles

By benchmarks a shift to renewable energy, advancing the notion of buildings as power plants, and funding an aggressive hydrogen fuel cell technology R&D program, the EU has erected the first three pillars of the Third Industrial Revolution. The fourth pillar, the re-configuration of the European power grid, along the lines of the internet, allowing businesses and homeowners to produce their own energy and share it with each other, is just now being tested by power companies in Europe.

The smart intergrade is made up of three critical components. Minigrids allow homeowners, small and medium size enterprises (SMEs), and large scale economic enterprises to produce renewable energy locally—through solar cells, wind, small hydro, animal and agricultural waste, garbage, etc.—and use it off-grid for their own electricity needs. Smart metering technology allows local producers to more effectively sell their energy back to the main power grid, as well as accept electricity from the grid, making the flow of electricity bi-directional.

The next phase in smart grid technology is embedding sensing devices and chips throughout the grid system, connecting every electrical appliance. Software allows the entire power grid to know how much energy is being used, at any time, anywhere on the grid. This interconnections can be used to redirect energy uses and flows during peaks and lulls, and even to adjust to the price changes of electricity from moment to moment.

In the future, intelligent utility networks will also be increasingly connected to moment to moment weather changes—recording wind changes, solar flux, ambient temperature, etc.-giving the power network the ability to adjust electricity flow continuously, to both external weather conditions as well as consumer demand. For example, if the power grid is experiencing peak energy use and possible overload because of too much demand, the software can direct a homeowner's washing machine to go down by one cycle per load or reduce the air conditioning by one degree. Consumers who agree to slight adjustments in their electricity use receive credits on their bills. Since the true price of electricity on the grid varies during any 24 hour period, moment to moment energy information opens the door to "dynamic pricing", allowing consumers to increase or drop their energy use automatically, depending upon the price of electricity on the grid. Up to the moment pricing also allows local minigrid producers of energy to either automatically sell energy back to the grid or go off the grid altogether. The smart intergrade will not only give end users more power over their energy choices, but also create significant new energy efficiency in the distribution of electricity.

The intergrade makes possible a broad redistribution of power. Today's centralised, top-down flow of energy becomes increasingly obsolete. In the new era, businesses, municipalities and homeowners become the producers as well as the consumers of their own energy—so-called "distributed generation."

Even electric plug in and hydrogen- powered fuel cell vehicles are "power stations on wheels" with a generating capacity of twenty or more kilowatts. Since the average car, bus and truck is parked much of the time, they can be plugged in, during non-use hours, to the home, office, or the main interactive electricity network, providing premium electricity back to the grid. Electric and fuel cell plug in vehicles thus become a way to store massive amounts of renewable energy that can be sent back in the form of electricity to the main power grid.

In 2008, Daimler and RWE, Germany's second largest power and utility company, launched a project in Berlin to establish recharging points for electric Smart and Mercedes cars around the German capital. Renault-Nissan is readying a similar plan to provide a network of hundreds of thousands of battery charging points in Israel, Denmark and Portugal. The distributed electric power charging stations will be used to service Renault's all electric Mégane car. Toyota has joined with EDF, France's largest power and utility company, to build charging points in France and other countries, for its plug-in electric cars. By 2030, charging points for plug-in electric vehicles and hydrogen fuel cell vehicles will be installed virtually everywhere— along roads, in homes, commercial buildings, factories, parking lots and garages, providing a seamless distributed infrastructure for sending electricity both from and to the main electricity grid. If just 25 percent of drivers used their vehicles as power plants to sell energy back to the intergride, all of the power plants in the US and the EU could be eliminated.

IBM and other global IT companies are just now entering the smart power market, working with utility companies to transform the power grid to intergrade, so that building owners can produce their own energy and share it with each other. Centre-point Utility in Houston, Texas, Xcel Utility in Boulder, Colorado, and Sempra and Southern Condition in California are laying down parts of the Smart Grid this year, connecting thousands of residential and commercial buildings.

The new EU energy plan is preparing the way for the intergrid, with the demand that the power grid be unbundled, or at least made increasingly independent of the power companies that also produce the power, so that new players—especially small and medium size enterprises and homeowners—have the opportunity to produce and sell power back to the grid with the same ease and transparency as they now enjoy in producing and sharing information on the internet. The European Commission has also established a European Smart Grid Technology Platform and prepared a long-term vision and strategy document in 2006 for reconfiguring the European power grid to make it intelligent, distributed, and interactive.

The central question that every nation needs to ask is where they want their country to be in twenty five years from now: In the sunset energies and industries of the second industrial revolution or the sunrise energies and industries of the Third Industrial Revolution. The Third Industrial Revolution is the endgame that takes the world out of the old carbon and uranium-based energies and into a non-polluting, sustainable future for the human race.

Distributed Social Vision in the 21st Century

The Third Industrial Revolution makes possible a new Distributed Social Vision in the 21st century. Most citizens of the world, when asked what they most hope for, say they envision a good "quality of life". The dream of quality of life emphasises individual opportunity, social and human rights, balancing the social and market models, and building bridges of cooperation and peace. Underlying this expansive new 21st century social vision is the commitment that millions of people share to create a just and sustainable society for their children and future generations.

The dream of a good quality of life is now endangered by the dramatic rise of oil and gas prices on the world market, and the real time impacts of climate change on communities and ecosystems across the continent.

Without a well-thought-out plan to usher in a Third Industrial Revolution, the hope of a new Distributed Social

Vision will begin to fade. The Third Industrial Revolution, therefore, is the beginning point for a new Distributed Social Vision. Indeed, a new Distributed Social Vision flows inexorably from the Third Industrial Revolution narrative and is impossible to achieve without it. Together, the Third Industrial Revolution and a new Distributed Social Vision offer a compelling game-plan for the next 50 years of global development.

What is needed now is a strong political vision capable of joining the two together. By articulating a clear political agenda to advance the Third Industrial Revolution and the accompanying programs for a new Distributed Social Vision, today's political leaders will set the stage for the next phase of human development, and, in the process, bequeath a powerful legacy for future generations. The new politics will also serve as a beacon of hope for the rest of the world in the 21st Century.

The new Distributed Social Vision is made up of 10 key building blocks, each erected on top of a Third Industrial Revolution framework:

1) *A Sustainable Standard of Living*: The long term rise in the price of oil on world markets and the increasing real time effects of climate change on commercial sectors ranging from agriculture to tourism are already having a dramatic impact on the standard of living of millions of people. Food prices are sky rocketing as well as the price of consumer products and services and home heating and petrol cost, threatening the economic well being of families around the world. These conditions are only going to worsen in the years ahead, imperilling the dream of advancing a quality of life society. Government, the business community and civil society need to join together in an unprecedented mobilisation to turn the corner on the sunset energies and industries of the second industrial revolution and

usher in a renewable energy regime if the human race is to enjoy a sustainable standard of living in the 21st century.

2) *The Economic Multiplier Effect:* The transition to the Third Industrial Revolution will require a wholesale re-configuration of the entire economic infrastructure of each country, creating millions of jobs, and countless new goods and services, with an economic multiplier effect that will stretch to the second half of the 21st century. We will need to invest in renewable energy technology on a massive scale; redesign millions of buildings, transforming them into positive power plants, embed hydrogen and other storage technology throughout the national infrastructures, transform the automobile from the internal combustion engine to the fuel cell car, and lay down an intelligent utility network across every nation.

3) *New Jobs and Business Models for the 21st Century:* The wholesale remaking of each nation's infrastructure and the re-tooling of industries is going to require a massive retraining of workers on a scale matching the vocational and professional training at the onset of the first and second industrial revolutions. The new high-tech work force of the Third Industrial Revolution will need to be skilled in renewable energy technologies, green construction, IT and embedded computing, nano-technology, sustainable chemistry, fuel cell development, digital power grid management, hybrid electric and hydrogen powered transport, and hundreds of other technical fields. Entrepreneurs and managers will need to be educated to take advantage of cutting edge businesses models, including open-source and networked commerce, distributed and collaborative research and development strategies, and sustainable low carbon logistics and supply chain management.

The skill levels and managerial styles of the Third Industrial Revolution work force will be qualitatively different from that of the work force of the second industrial revolution.

4) In the next 50 years, every nation will need to create a self-sufficient, distributed renewable energy regime to ensure energy independence and the ushering in of a post carbon future. A fully integrated intelligent intergrid allows each country to both produce its own energy and share any surpluses with neighbouring countries in a "Network" approach to assuring global energy security. When any given region enjoys a temporary surge or surplus in its renewable energy, that energy can be shared with regions that are facing a temporary lull or deficit.

5) *Empowering the People:* The Third Industrial Revolution leads to a new Distributed Social Vision where power, itself, is broadly distributed, encouraging unprecedented new levels of collaboration among peoples and nations. In the new era, businesses, municipalities and homeowners become the producers as well as the consumers of their own energy—so-called "distributed generation." Just as the distributed communication revolution of the last decade spawned network ways of thinking, open source sharing, and the democratisation of communications, the Third Industrial Revolution follows suit with the democratisation of energy. We began to envision a world where hundreds of millions of people are "empowered", both literally and figuratively, with far reaching implications for social and political life. The democratisation of energy becomes a rallying point of a new Distributed Social Vision. Access to power becomes an inalienable social right in the Third Industrial Revolution era. The 20th century saw the

extension of the political franchise and the broadening of educational and economic opportunities to millions of people around the world. In the 21st century, individual access to energy also becomes a social and human right. Every human being should have the right and the opportunity to create their own energy locally and share it with others across regional, national and continental intergrade. For a younger generation that is growing up in a less hierarchical and more networked world, the ability to share and produce their own energy in an open-access intergrid, like they produce and share their own information on the internet, will seem natural and commonplace.

6) *Education for the 21st Century:* The first and second Industrial Revolutions were accompanied by vast changes in the educational system. The Third Industrial Revolution will require equally innovative educational reforms if we are to prepare future generations to work and live in a post-carbon world. The new curriculum will focus increasingly on advanced information, bio and nano technologies, the earth sciences, ecology, systems theory, collaborative and distributive education, open-source learning models, and social capital. We will need to educate our children to think as global citizens and prepare them for the historic transition from 20th century conventional geopolitics to 21st century global Biosphere politics. Education will increasingly focus on both global responsibility to preserve the health of the planet's Biosphere and local responsibility to steward regional ecosystems. Living sustainable will become the anchor of 21st century learning environments.

7) *A Quality of life society:* In the new Distributed Social Vision of the 21st century, individual economic opportunity becomes part of a more expansive social

vision of creating a quality of life society. The conventional 20th century economic indicators that emphasise gross domestic product and per capita income are now being accompanied by equally important quality of life indicators that measure a good economy in terms of a commitment to social and human rights, an educated citizens, a healthy population, safe communities, a proper balance of work and leisure, and a clean and sustainable environment. A quality of life economy promotes both the social and market models simultaneously by emphasising personal economic opportunity along with a sense of social commitment to create a sustainable society for every citizen. In the Third Industrial Revolution, distributive power and sustainable communities provide the essential framework for creating a quality of life society.

8) *Rethinking Globalisation from the Bottom-up:* The half century transition from the second to the Third Industrial Revolution is going to dramatically change the globalisation process. The most significant impact is likely to be on developing nations. Incredibly, over half of the human population has never made a telephone call and a third of the human race has no access to electricity. Lack of access to electricity is a key factor in perpetuating poverty around the world. Conversely, access to energy means more economic opportunity. If millions of individuals and communities around the world were to become producers of their own energy, the result would be a profound shift in the configuration of power. Local peoples would be less subject to the will of far-off centres of power. Communities would be able to produce goods and services locally and sell them globally. This is the essence of the politics of sustainable development and

> re-globalisation from the bottom up. The developed nations, working with industries and civil-society organisations, can help facilitate the next phase of sustainable globalisation by re-orienting development aid, promoting clean development mechanism projects under the Emissions Trading system, leveraging macro and micro-financing and credit, and providing favoured-nation trade status in order to help developing nations establish a Third Industrial Revolution.

European industry has the scientific, technological, and financial know-how to spearhead the shift to renewable energies, positive power buildings, a hydrogen economy, and an intelligent power grid and, by so doing, lead the world into a new economic era. The EU's world class automotive industry, chemical industry, engineering industry, construction industry, software, computer and communication industries, and banking and insurance industries, give it a leg up in the race to the Third Industrial Revolution.

The EU also boasts one of the world's largest solar markets and is the world's leading producer of wind energy. The next stage of European integration is establishing a distributed energy regime that will allow Europe to complete the creation of a unified single market. While the EU is potentially the largest internal commercial market in the world, with 500 million consumers and an additional 500 million consumers in its associated regions stretching into the Mediterranean and North Africa, it has not yet created a seamless logistical infrastructure, with a common transport grid, communication grid, and power grid. Integrating the logistical infrastructure so that the billion plus people in the EU region can engage in commerce and trade with efficiency and ease, and with a low carbon dioxide footprint, is the critical unfinished business of the EU.

TOWARDS A SUSTAINABLE PLANET

In 1960, President Kennedy challenged the baby-boom generation in the United States to join him in putting a man on the moon within the decade and exploring the far reaches of outer space. The sequel, in the 21st century, is for the millennial generation to lead the world in saving the Biosphere of the earth.

The shift from elite fossil fuels and uranium based energies to distributed renewable energies, takes the world out of the "Geopolitics" that characterised the 20th century, and into the "Biosphere politics" of the 21st century. Much of the geopolitical struggles of the last century centered on gaining military and political access to coal, oil, natural gas, and uranium deposits. Wars were fought and countless lives lost, as nations vied with each other in the pursuit of fossil fuels and uranium security. The ushering in of the Third Industrial Revolution will go a long way toward diffusing the growing tensions over access to ever more limited supplies of fossil fuels and uranium and help facilitate Biosphere politics based on a collective sense of responsibility for safeguarding the earth's ecosystems.

Political parties and governments need to turn their attention to stewarding the Biosphere. At the same time, they need to communicate this mission across the world with the goal of unleashing the vast creative potential of the millennial generation to the task of preserving and renewing the planet.

The shift from the Second Industrial Revolution to the Third Industrial Revolution is going to require a carefully constructed long term transition plan. The EU understands this, and has committed itself to pursuing a two-track process: Track one, increasing the energy efficiency and reducing the carbon footprint by 20 percent, respectively, by the year 2020, in order to clean up the mature fossil fuel energies of the Second Industrial Revolution; track two, aggressively pursuing a 20 percent renewable energy target and laying down the foundation for a Third Industrial Revolution during the first half of the 21st century. Every nation needs to aggressively pursue both tracks simultaneously if we are to ease the transition to a post-carbon era.

In 2007, the EU Parliament became the first legislature in the world to pass a written declaration in support of the two-track approach to making the transition into a Third Industrial Revolution and a post-carbon energy era.

The story of a Third Industrial Revolution and a new Distributed Social Vision is powerful and provides the narrative we so desperately need at this critical point in history if we are to address climate change and peak oil and reheal the Biosphere of the planet.

7

Employment Laws

Why do governments intervene in the labour market? The rationale underlying such interventions is that free labour markets are imperfect, that as a consequence there are rents in the employment relationship, and that employers abuse workers to extract these rents, leading to both unfairness and inefficiency. For example, employers discriminate against disadvantaged groups, underpay workers who are immobile or invest in firm-specific capital, fire workers who then need to be supported by the state, force employees to work more than they wish under the threat of dismissal, fail to insure workers against the risk of death, illness or disability, and so on. In response to the perceived unfairness and inefficiency of the free market, every state intervenes in the employment relationship.

Countries have established a system of laws intended to protect the interests of workers and assure a minimum standard of living for the population at large. In addition to some basic civil rights protections, this system encompasses three bodies of law: employment law, collective relations law, and social security law. Employment laws govern the individual employment contract. Collective or industrial relations laws regulate the bargaining, adoption, and enforcement of collective agreements, the organisation of trade unions, and the industrial action by workers and employers. Social security laws govern the social response to needs and conditions that have a significant impact on the quality of life, such as old age, disability, death, sickness, and unemployment.

Studies on India

Basely and Burgess is the first study that isolates the effect of labour reforms (across Indian states) from macroeconomic variables and changes in policies that are common across states. Between 1958 and 1992 manufacturing grew by 3.3 percent in India as a whole. However, in West Bengal output per capita was falling at an average rate of 1.5 percent per annum. (West Bengal was also a state that had the greatest body of pro-worker labour regulation passed in the state legislature.) Its performance contrasts with Andhra Pradesh which grew at nearly 6 percent per year over the same period. Andra Pradesh also experienced reforms that made labour regulation more flexible.

The Basely-Burgess data on labour regulation code state amendments to the Industrial Disputes Act of 1947. While the act was passed at the national level, state governments were given the right, under the Indian Constitution, to amend it. The authors read the text of each amendment (121 in all) and classified each as pro-rigidity, pro-flexibility or neutral. This gave a sense of whether workers or employers benefited or whether the legislation had no appreciable impact on either group.

The main finding is that the pro-rigidity amendments to the Industrial Disputes Act are associated with lowered investment, employment, productivity and output in registered manufacturing. To illustrate this, consider Andhra Pradesh, which grew at 6 percent per annum between 1958 and 1992. The Basely-Burgess estimate predicts that it would have grown at 4.1 percent had it not passed flexible labour reforms. West Bengal, whose registered manufacturing output per capita declined at 1.5 percent per annum over the data period would have grown at 2.2 percent had it not legislated in a pro-worker direction. On average, labour reforms can explain more than two thirds of the difference in growth rates across states.

Regulating in a more-rigid direction is also associated with increases in urban poverty. West Bengal, for example, would have had 10 percent less poverty in 1990 had it not passed more rigid labour regulations. This amounts to 1.8 million less urban poor in West Bengal.

The study has inspired a series of papers that look at particular aspects of labour regulation and their effect of economic and social outcomes. The first such study is Dutta Roy, which examines the effects of a 1982 amendment to the Industrial Disputes Act. This amendment extended the prohibition to retrench workers without government authorisation to firms that employed hundred or more workers (previously the cutoff was 300 workers). Dutta Roy finds evidence of small adjustment costs in employment. These adjustments took place with significant time lags.

A second paper, Aghion et al, studies the 1991 elimination of the system of industrial regulations on entry and production, on registered manufacturing output, employment, entry and investment across Indian states with different labour market regulations. Aghion et al use the data on state-level labour regulations from Basely and Burgess and interact them with data on industry licenses and import tariffs. The main finding is that industries located in states with flexible labour regulation grew more quickly than those in states with rigid labour regulation. For example, the largest positive effects of delicensing on state output are found in Andhra Pradesh and Tamil Nadu (and to a lower extent Karnataka, Kerala and Rajahstan), the states with the most flexible labour regulations. The largest negative effects are found in West Bengal and Maharashtra, the states with most rigid labour regulations. In Andhra Pradesh and Tamil Nadu output in the manufacturing sector was 15% higher in 1997 than if there had been no reform. In West Bengal, to the opposite, output was 20% lower in 1997 than if there had been no reform.

Another study, Hasan, Mitra and Ramaswamy, looks specifically at the interaction of rigid labour regulation and trade policy and corroborates Aghion et al. It indicates that, at the state level in India, employment rises faster due to liberalisation where labour regulations are more flexible.

Bhattacharjea looks in detail at the Basely-Burgess coding and argues that there is some miscoding of individual amendments, as well as misleading aggregation procedures. Bhattacharjea shows that some econometric results do not appear to be robust. However, the overall result that rigid labour regulation results in net job losses remains.

Two recent papers extend the Basely-Burgess methodology to larger datasets of firms and more detailed treatment of laws. Ashan and Pages find that laws that increase job security or increase the cost of labour disputes substantially reduce registered employment and output, with larger effects on output for amendments that increase the cost of labour disputes. Workers do not gain either, as such interventions do not increase the labour share or the wage bill. Labour-intensive industries, such as textiles, are most affected by higher labour dispute resolution costs.

Another paper, Amin, studies the effect of rigid labour regulation on 2,000 retail stores in large Indian cities. In his dataset, 27% of the stores find labour regulations is a problem for their business. The author concludes that stricter labour regulation has a strong negative effect on employment. Labour reforms are likely to increase employment by 22 percent for the average store. This is a large effect when one takes into account the fact that the retail sector in India is the second largest employer, providing jobs to 9.4% of all workers. Rigid regulation is also shown to increase the size of the informal sector. In particular, labour reforms could reduce the level of informality by as much as 33% of the existing level.

Saha compares labour regulation in China and India. China's labour reforms were necessary for the creation of a free labour market, which then allowed fast industrial growth and rapid employment. In contrast, India's reluctance to reform its rigid labour laws has significantly lessened the favourable effects of industrial deregulation in the formal sector.

Sanyal and Menon study firms' locational choices and investment decisions in India. They consider rigid labour laws and their enforcement by labour courts and investigate whether these have detrimental effects on firm location and investment decisions. The study finds strong evidence that this is indeed the case: for a 1% increase in the number of labour courts within the state, the probability that a project will be located in this state decreases by approximately 0.3%.

This set of studies has had a significant impact on questioning the benefits of rigid labour regulation. A recent Ministry of Finance survey states: "Various studies indicate that Indian labour laws are highly protective of labour, and labour markets are relatively inflexible. Consequently, these laws have restricted labour mobility, have led to capital-intensive methods in the organised sector and adversely affected the sector's long-run demand for labour. Labour being a subject in the concurrent list, State-level labour regulations are also an important determinant of industrial performance. Evidence suggests that States, which have enacted more pro-worker regulations, have lost out on industrial production in general".

Studies on Latin America

Heckman and Pages is a collection of 11 studies on the effect of labour regulation on employment and growth in Latin America.

The timing of Heckman and Pages is propitious: in the 1980s and 1990s many Latin American countries restored democracy after long periods of military rule. These political changes brought about labour reforms. For example, in 1988 Brazil adopted a new Constitution that revised labour regulations that had been in place since the 1940s. It reduced the maximum working hours per week from 48 to 44 hours; reduced the maximum number of hours for a continuous work shift from 8 to 6 hours; increased the minimum overtime premium from 20 percent to 50 percent; and increased maternity leave from 3 to 4 months.

The new Constitution also modified the mandatory individual saving accounts system created in 1966. Prior to the reforms, the law required employers to deposit 8 percent of employees' wages in a worker-owned account. In case of separation, workers could withdraw the accumulated funds (plus the interest rate). In addition, if a firm initiated a separation it had to pay a penalty equivalent to 10 percent of the amount accumulated in the account. As part of the 1988 reform, this penalty was increased to 40 percent, considerably raising the cost of dismissing a worker. Similar reforms took place in Chile, the Dominican Republic and Nicaragua. In contrast, Colombia and Peru made labour regulation more flexible.

Mondino and Montoya and Saavedra and Torero study the effect of rigid labour regulation or the rate of employment in Argentina and Peru, respectively. Both find a significant adverse effect. Kugler analyses the impact of reduced job security costs in Colombia after 1990. She finds a declining duration in unemployment, mostly explained by increased use of fixed-term contracts. In particular, she estimates that the reform brought about a 1.3 to 1.7 percentage points decline in unemployment. Montenegro and Pages use a long series of repeated data spanning 40 years to study the effect of rigid labour regulation in Chile. They find that rigid regulation reduces the employment rates of youth and the unskilled, while increasing the employment rates of older and skilled workers. The most striking result is that women's employment declines with rigid regulation. Maloney and Nunez-Mendez study the effect of minimum wages on wages and employment across Latin America. They conclude that minimum wage regulation impacts the size of the informal sector as well as the wage levels in both the formal and informal sectors.

In contrast, Pages de Barros and Corseuil do not find significant effects of Brazil's 1988 reform, which increased the costs of dismissing redundant workers. Similarly, Downes et al find no significant effects of labour reform in three Caribbean states.

Outside of the research in Heckman and Pages, several other papers use data from Latin America to study the effect of labour regulation. Almeida and Carneiro do an in-depth analysis on Brazil. They find that stricter enforcement of labour regulation constrains firm size, and also leads to reduced employment. In particular, a one percent increase in the number of labour inspections is associated with approximately a half-percent decline in employment and sales.

Eslava et al use a 1982-1998 plant level dataset for Colombia to show an increased productivity after reductions in labour regulation rigidities. In particular, temporary and part-time contracts were allowed with Law 50 in 1990. There is also increased redundancy of unproductive workers who were previously retained due to high dismissal costs.

Pages and Montenegro develops and tests a model by which job security affects the age composition of employment. This model is based on the relative costs of dismissing young versus older workers resulting from job security provisions that are related to tenure. Using 39 consecutive annual household-surveys from Chile, they find that job security is associated with a substantial decline in the wage employment-to-population rate of young workers. In contrast, they do not find such a decline in young self-employment rates or in the wage employment rates of older workers. Comparing results for men and women and using measures of relative dismissal costs, Pages and Montenegro find that the adverse effect of job security on youth employment is driven by the link between severance pay and tenure.

Finally, Kaplan studies the effects of labour-regulation reform using data for 10,396 firms in 14 Latin American countries. The data come from the World Bank Enterprise Surveys, where firms are asked both how many permanent workers they would have hired and how many they would have terminated if labour regulations were made more flexible. Kaplan finds that making labour regulations more flexible would lead to an average net increase of 2.08% in total employment. Firms with fewer than 20 employees benefit the most, with average gains in net employment of 4.27%. Countries with more regulated labour markets, such as Argentina, would experience larger gains in total employment. These larger gains in total employment, however, would be achieved through higher rates of hiring and higher rates of termination. The results may explain why there is substantial opposition to labour reforms despite the predicted gains in efficiency and total employment.

Cross-country Studies

Botero et al is the first cross-country study on labour

regulation that covers developing countries. It investigates the regulation of labour markets through employment, collective relations, and social security laws in 85 countries. The main finding is that heavier regulation of labour is associated with lower labour force participation and higher unemployment, especially of the young. In particular, rigid collective relations laws are associated with a larger unofficial economy; rigid employment, collective relations, and social security laws lead to lower male (but not female) participation in the labour force; rigid employment laws lead to higher unemployment, especially of the young. Finally, there is weak evidence that more generous social security systems are associated with higher relative wages of privileged workers. The evidence on the unemployment of the young is consistent with the view that the privileged and older incumbents support more stringent labour laws, a finding echoed in the literature on developed countries.

Several studies followed, using the Botero et al dataset. Caballero and others use a sectorial panel for 60 countries to find that job security regulation hampers the creative-destruction process, especially in countries where regulations are likely to be enforced. The authors conclude that moving from the 20th to the 80th percentile in job security, in countries with strong rule of law, cuts the annual speed of adjustment to shocks by a third while shaving off about one percent from annual productivity growth. However, rigid labour regulation has no effect in countries with weak rule of law.

Two other studies - Pierre and Scarpetta and Micco and Pages-analyse the effect of rigid labour regulation on employment. Pierre and Scarpetta look at employers' perceptions on the rigidity of labour regulation in 80 developing countries. They find that employers' concerns about labour regulations are closely matched by the relative stringency of labour laws. But not all firms are affected in the same way by onerous labour regulations. Medium sized firms are those whose business and prospects for growth are most negatively affected. Similarly, innovating firms are disproportionately affected by rigid labour regulations. Micco and Pages use suctorial data for 69 countries to find that employment protection reduces turnover, employment, and value added by reducing the growth of highly volatile sectors, such as leather products and apparel. The decline in employment is mostly accounted by a decline in net entry of firms, with insignificant changes in average employment and output per firm.

Feldmann, using data on 74 countries for 2000-2003, finds that if Indonesia - a country with rigid regulations-had enjoyed the same flexibility in business regulation as Finland, Indonesia's unemployment rate would have been 2.1 percentage points lower among the total labour force and 5.8 percentage points lower among young people. The data on business regulation come from the Economic Freedom of the World index, developed by the Fraser Institute, whose labour regulation component is based on data from Botero et al. Feldmann uses an alternative dataset– by the World Economic Forum – to find similar results: rigid regulation reduces employment.

Several articles use the Botero et al dataset to study the interaction between labour regulation and trade policy. Freund and Bolaky, Chang and others (forthcoming), Cunat and Melitz and Helpman and Itskhoki show that in the absence of flexible labour regulation, economies do not benefit from trade openness and can forego large employment opportunities.

Finally, two studies look at the effect of labour regulation on entrepreneurship. Ardagna and Lusardi study the effect of rigid labour regulation on entrepreneurship. They use a sample of 37 rich and developing countries to show that with flexible regulation the probability of starting a new entrepreneurial activity increases for people below the age of 44. More importantly, the interaction term between labour regulation and the fear of starting a new business is statistically significant for every measure of entrepreneurship. In countries with heavy labour regulations, workers are less willing to become entrepreneurs.

Van Stel, Storey, and Thurik use data for 39 countries to find strong negative effects on business entry rates of the labour market regulation measures 'rigidity of employment' and 'rigidity of hours,' both taken from Botero et al. In countries where the flexibility of employers to hire and fire employees is higher, the various rates of entrepreneurship also tend to be higher. The authors offer two explanations. For employees, the safety of their paid job is less which may make them more likely to decide to start their own business (push effect). For entrepreneurs, they have more flexibility in running their business which makes business ownership more attractive (pull effect). Both effects imply higher entrepreneurship rates.

Correlations with Labour Market Outcomes

In this section we present partial correlations between labour regulation and labour market outcomes. The data do not allow a causal interpretation of the evidence: the analysis is purely suggestive. The reason for showing these correlations is to demonstrate the significant differences in the level of regulation across countries, and how regulation differs across types of countries.

Labour Market Rigidity Variables

Labour market rigidity is measured using the rigidity of employment index published by Doing Business. These data were originally developed by Botero et al. Labour lawyers and experts were contacted in 178 countries to answer specific questions about the applicable labour legislation.

The rigidity of labour regulations is assessed by scoring those answers and establishing indices. The rigidity of employment index varies from 0 to 100, where higher numbers imply more labour market rigidity.

The sample covers 24 countries in OECD high income countries, 46 in Sub-Saharan Africa, 28 in Eastern Europe and Central Asia, 24 in East Asia and Pacific, 8 in South Asia, 17 in Middle East and North Africa, and 31 in Latin America and Caribbean.

There are 5 countries that score zero, having the most flexible labour regulation as measured by this index: Singapore, Hong Kong, United States, the Maldives and the Marshall Islands. No country scores 100. The highest score in practice is 79 attributed to Venezuela and Bolivia. The other countries with the highest labour market rigidity are Democratic Republic of Congo, scoring 74, Niger at 70, Panama, the Republic of Congo, and Angola, all at 69.

On average low income countries have higher labour market rigidity than high income countries. This difference is statistically significant at the 5% level, at 40.4 for the poorest countries vs. 31.1 for the richest.

Size of the Informal Sector Variables

The size of the informal sector is measured as percentage of GDP. The data are based on the opinion of experts, who are asked to assess the size of the informal sector by choosing brackets with a size of 5 to10 percentage points.

The informal sector represents on average around 28% of the economy across the world. In poor countries this average jumps up to 36%. The sample covers 24 countries in OECD high income countries, 24 in Sub-Saharan Africa, 25 in Eastern Europe and Central Asia, 12 in East Asia and Pacific, 5 in South Asia, 8 in Middle East and North Africa, and 22 in Latin America and Caribbean. The country with the smallest informal sector is Singapore at 9%, followed by Switzerland, Iceland and Finland at 11% and Luxembourg and New Zealand at 12.5%. Zambia is the country with the largest informal sector (45%), followed by Bolivia (43%), the Kyrgyz Republic (42%), Benin (42%), and Venezuela (41%).

Directions for Future Research

The findings on the effect of labour regulation on employment and informality in developing countries are consistent with the new comparative economics literature started by Djankov. Studies in this literature show that economic outcomes are significantly affected by, for example, regulation of entry, enforcement of creditor rights, enforcement of labour laws, the presence of creditor rights and credit information, and the protection of minority shareholders.

Developing countries present an exciting venue for studying the impact of regulatory reforms, including of labour reforms. A number of countries, especially in Eastern Europe, have recently undergone significant reforms to make labour regulation more flexible. Examples include Albania, Azerbaijan, Georgia, and Macedonia FYR. In West Africa, Burkina Faso and Senegal passed significant amendments to their labour codes in 2007. In contrast, several Latin American countries, most notably Bolivia and Venezuela, have made labour regulation more rigid. These reforms are larger in magnitude than any reforms in developed countries. Their effect on labour market outcomes can inform research on the relative importance of labour reforms as opposed to other types of reform.

Second, the link between labour regulation and productivity is best studied in the context of developing economies which display larger productivity gaps across firms in the same sector than can be found in developed countries. Cumbersome regulation makes it difficult for workers to move across firms and across industries. The absence of free inter-firm and intersectoral movement impedes productivity increases, and likely contributes to higher job losses due to external economic shocks.

Third, reforms can be used to study job and wage dynamics: what happens to workers who are dismissed, who gets hired, and how do wages adjust when the labour market becomes more flexible. In Georgia, for example, aggregate employment statistics reveal that the share of single proprietorship (essentially, self-employed people) grew from 23,000 to half a million in the three years following the passing of the new labour law. In the same period, aggregate unemployment fell just 0.4%, as large gains in the private sector were accompanies by shrinking public employment.

Fourth, the link between labour regulation reforms and other reforms can be further investigated. A robust literature is emerging on the effect of labour regulation on trade liberalisation, as in Freund and Bolaky. This work can be extended to study entrepreneurship and innovation.

Finally, scholars can turn attention to the question why countries regulate their labour markets differently. A common hypothesis in the institutions literature is that culture determines the level of regulation, at least in countries where regulations have not been imposed forcefully through colonisation. A recent study investigates this direction of causality: that culture influences regulation, but also the demand for regulation. Using the World Values Survey, they show both in a cross-section of 45 countries, and in a sample of individuals from around the world, that culture (measured by distrust) fuels support for government control over the economy. Even more interesting, distrust generates demand for regulation even when people realise that the government is corrupt and ineffective. Essentially, they prefer state control to unbridled production by "uncivil" firms.

8

Migration for Labour

Studies on migration have been very few in India because, historically speaking; migration has never been considered an important demographic issue due to the small volume of internal migration relative to the total size of the population. However, these small-scale internal migrations within the subcontinent were replaced by large-scale external migration when the partition in 1947 created India and Pakistan. Withdrawal of the British from India and the partition were associated with a massive transfer of population estimated at 14.5 million between the short span of 1947-51. Immediately after the partition, about 5 million Hindus and Sikhs left Pakistan for India and about 6 million Muslims moved into Pakistan from India. As this politically-triggered exchange created very serious and long-term problems of refugee settlement and integration, the prospects of intra-south Asian migration to and from India gradually became more and more limited after independence.

In contrast, voluntary migration, attributed mainly to economic and social factors, although modest compared to that related to political cause, continues and seems to be on the rise. The principal flows have been the following:

a) Immigration to Britain, which was a traditionally favoured destination for temporary migration and, later attracted permanent settlers representing various social strata.

b) The three traditional settlement countries, Australia, Canada, and the USA became more attractive destinations once their highly selective immigration policies were modified. These developed countries, later joined by the UK and other EU countries attracted the highly skilled workers from India.

c) A new destination, that rapidly gained popularity has been the Middle East. The oil-rich countries mainly attracted semiskilled and unskilled labour on a temporary circulating basis. Some southeast countries like Malaysia became such destination later on.

The Second World War marks a crucial watershed in the history of the genesis of Indian disappear formation through emigration to the developed world. It was the beginning of the transformation of Indians' presence in the developed countries from one that was minuscules, transitory and peripheral, to one that became more substantial, permanent and central. The largest number of migrants in this period went to the UK, some because of old colonial links and others because of wartime experiences as soldiers and seamen. Subsequently, many more arrived after the 1947 partition of India that preceded its Independence. This was subsequently strengthened by the nexus of kinship and friend-ship, mainly originating from the state of Punjab, which enabled others to tap the economic opportunities in the broader labour markets abroad.

In Canada, anti-Asian sentiment was the characteristic of immigration policy prior to the Second World War. However, after the war, the changing composition of the Commonwealth exerted its influence on the Canadian government. After the Indian Prime Minister Jawaharlal Nehru visited Canada in 1949, Indo-Canadians were granted the right to vote, and the explicitly racist provisions in the Immigration Act were changed.

In the developed countries today, the focus on the Indian skilled migration remains in the United States, with up to 80 per cent of Indian skilled migration to all developed countries. It was in the 1970s that the US overtook both the UK and Canada as the prime developed country of their destination. Indian immigration in the US, which constituted a minuscule of less than 1 percent of global immigration from all countries during the 1950s and 1960s, crossed a mark of 7 per cent in 2004. Even in 2003, when security concerns in the post 9/11 phase had brought in a restrictive immigration regime in this country, Indian share amongst global immigrants thus continued to increase. In the two top categories of skilled immigrants in 2001, viz., "professional and technical", and "executive, administrative and managerial occupations", Indians occupied very high proportions of 24 per cent and 11 per cent respectively. In 2003 and 2004, one in every four global immigrants "with an occupation" has been an Indian.

The 1965 amendments to the US Immigration and Nationality Act, which formed the basis of all these, remained the principal determinant of Indian skilled immigration into the US for one quarter of a century between 1968 and 1992. Within the overall kinship–emphasis in family–reunification clause of the 1965 amendments, the new legislation gave priority to highly trained and educated professionals, at least for the first seven to ten years explicitly. As a result, urban, educated, and "English speaking" masses of Indian population became distinctly visible in the US, carrying a large share of India's human capital to the U.S., and causing "brain drain" for India because, as Jensen recorded, "almost a hundred thousand engineers, physicians, scientists, professors, teachers, and their dependents had entered the U.S. By

1975". However, since the mid–1970s until 1982, the annual number of Indians entering the US had levelled off to an average annual figure of 20,000 mainly because of the per country limit of quota in the US immigration law. Thereafter, it was the number of those exempt from this limit which added to the total – the "immediate relatives" of the increasing number of Indian–born naturalised U.S. Citizens, on an average one–third of the immigrants over time. Thus, migration of highly qualified Indians to the US actually did not come down; whatever decline registered since the mid–1970s was mainly a statistical and legalistic illusion of sorts which also proved to be temporary in retrospect. India's brain drain to the US had become less "visible" rather than really declining after the mid–1970s.

After 1992, it was the relatively less noticeable route of temporary migration that started to become predominant. The 1990 Amendments, brought into effect in 1992, explicitly favoured the building up of the human capital capabilities of America by fulfilling its current and future requirements of highly skilled knowledge workers, finally bringing to relevance the immigration of Indians to the American labour market needs. Whatever few restrictive clauses these amendments had, like the introduction of a new definition for the highly skilled temporary workers, viz., the well-known non-immigrant H1–B visa category, with an annual cap of 65,000 visas per year worldwide, the US Senate had to clear a bill for a limited expansion of these visas to 337,500 for the three-year period from 1999 to 2001. This was because the US had faced a decline in key undergraduate science degrees, an acute shortage of staff in high technology industries like soft-ware development, and exhaustion of the worldwide annual quota of H-1B visas too quickly in 1998, with 42 per cent (or two out of every five visas) being issued to Indian IT software professionals. After 2001, when the number of H-1B visas issued to Indians went down because the American immigration scenario came to be determined more by the post-9/11 security concern in the U.S. And the subsequent recession that burst the IT bubble than by its actual labour market needs, the U.S. Government has been under continuous pressure of different lobby groups, including the American industry and business to increase the H1–B visa limit once again.

The highly skilled Indians have migrated to the developed countries not only through the "employment gate"; another stream of skilled migration has been taking place through the "academic gate" as growing pools of revolving students formed a distinct set of actor amongst the Indian migrants - the "semi-finished human capital" of Indian professionals abroad. Data collated by the US Institute of International Education's *Open Doors 2005* survey revealed that in 2004-05 India retained its No. 1 position in the US university enrolment (followed by China, Korea, Japan, Canada, and Taiwan) for the fourth year in a row. In 2005-06, the numbers of applications from Indian students have been reported to have registered a 23 per cent increase over the previous year, the highest amongst all countries. To serve the dual purpose of sustaining an expensive higher education system, and meeting *short-term* labour shortages, both the UK and the US, with other developed countries following suit, have adopted a policy of allowing foreign students in their universities respectively, to stay on and work, rather than return to their countries of origin on completion of their degrees. In addition, the destination countries gain political mileage in the form of a bonus: The foreign students become their long-term ambassadors in the international political arena. India has thus become a "must destination for internationally renowned educational institutions shop- ping for knowledge capital – i.e., to woo the Indian student". In October 2000, four countries had mounted education "fairs" in Delhi and other Indian cities, and since then it has become a regular feature of bilateral relations in India. The growing competition among countries like the US, UK, Canada, Australia, New Zealand, Ireland, and Singapore, as well as non-English speaking countries like France, Germany, and the Netherlands, has brought even the Ivy league institutions to India, and to other South Asian countries, to look for the cream of students.

The Socioeconomic and political profile of the skilled Indian disappear in the developed countries reflects the empowerment of the Indian migrants in the developed countries over time. Within the European Union (EU) - the largest economic entity in the world today two-thirds of the entire Indian migrant community still resides in the UK. The Indian community is one of the highest-earning and best-educated groups, achieving eminence in business, information technology the health sector, media, cuisine, and entertainment industries. In Canada, with just 3 per cent share in a population of 30 million, Indo-Canadians have recorded high achievements in the fields of medicine, academic, management, and engineering. The Indian immigrants' average annual income in Canada is nearly 20 per cent higher than the national average, and their educational levels are higher too. In the east, there are 30,000 Indian citizens in Australia; and New Zealand has also witnessed a rise in the entry of Indian professional immigrants, those engaged in domestic retail trade, medical, hospitality, engineering, and Information Technology sectors, and countries like Japan, Korea, and Singapore are also trying to attract Indian talent.

The strong profile of Indian immigrants in general supports a proposition that the human capital content in the migration of Indians to the US has been the backbone of Indian scientific disappear formation there. No other disappear preceding the Indian numerical rank acquired its position predominantly because of an American demand for its labour skills, which has been the main factor for admitting the Indian skilled workers on a large scale. It is hardly surprising therefore if in terms of the place in the US economy indexed by employment, occupation, education and income of the immigrants, the Indian disappear had continued to rank amongst the top all through the 1970s till the present. There are over 1000 US-based organisations of Indians in North America, with branches in Canada. These represent various interest groups in India, ranging from regions to states to languages, etc. Religion, caste, cultural and linguistic identities find significant space in these associations and networks. However, some professional groups are involved in grass-root development activities in India as well as in the welfare of their members abroad in the professions. A sample of associations can be categorised by the main characteristics of their members.

Although Indians manned the clerical and technical positions of the oil companies in the Gulf after oil was discovered in the region during the 1930s, the over-all numbers were still small. Between 1948 and the early 1970s, these numbers gradually increased from about 1,400 to 40,000. When large scale development activities started following the 1973 spurt in oil prices in the six Gulf Cooperation Council (GCC) countries of Saudi Arabia, Bahrain, Kuwait, Oman, Qatar, and the UAE, an upsurge in the flow of workers and labourers began from India to the Gulf. India and Pakistan supplied most of such unskilled labour, registering almost 200 percent growth between 1970 and 1975. In 1975, Indian expatriates constituted 39.1 percent, Pakistanis 58.1 percent, and other Asians 2.8 percent of the total non-Arab expatriates in the Gulf. Since then, Indian migration has overtaken that of Pakistan and other Asian countries of origin. Further, since the Kuwait war of 1990-91, Indians has replaced even the non-national

Arabs in the Gulf, viz., the Jordanians, yemenis, Palestinians and Egyptians. From less than 258,000 in 1975, migrant Indian population in the Gulf went up to 3.318 million in 2001 which is now estimated to have crossed 3.5 million.

Admission to the GCC countries was not as difficult prior to the mid-1970s, but thereafter restrictions have been imposed by the host countries due to the fear of rapid growth of non-national population. Thus it has been difficult for families to accompany the non-nationals workers to these countries, particularly the unskilled contract workers. Foreigners are not allowed to own businesses or immovable property in the Gulf countries; for running business enterprises they are required to have local citizens or agencies as major partners in their ventures, whether active or as "sleeping" partner. When it comes to human resources, short-age of labour has been endemic in all the countries of the Gulf, for the entire range of work—from professionals like doctors and nurses, engineers, architects, accountants and managers, to semiskilled workers like craftsmen, drivers, artisans, and other technical workers, to unskilled labourers in construction sites, farm-lands, livestock ranches, shops and stores and households

However, a large majority of 70 per cent of the Indian migrants in the Gulf has comprised the semiskilled and unskilled workers, the rest being white-collar workers and professionals. Their occupational distribution till after the outbreak of the Gulf War in August 1990. The fall in numbers in 1991-92 is directly related to the control by Government of India in issuing emigration clearance in the year following the Gulf War in 1990-91 when large numbers of Indians were evacuated from the Gulf by the Government of India. However, the classification more or less resumed although some changes might have taken place due to the demand tilting more towards skilled professionals as infrastructure development progressed in the Gulf. On the supply side, Indian government's monitoring and control of labour migration has been to streamline the process of emigration to some extent, increasingly in the last couple of years.

The demand for low category of workers like housemaids, cooks, bearers, gardeners, etc. has been large, though systematic all-India data are not easily available, except for the state of Kerala where an exclusive state-level ministry for overseas Correlate affairs exists for many years. Some data are now in the process of being collected and compiled by the newly formed Union Ministry of Overseas Indians Affairs. The workers in these vocations however do not enjoy the protection of any local labour laws. Women, working as housemaids or governesses face ill treatment in some Gulf countries, sometimes being subjected to even sexual abuse. Unskilled and semiskilled workers working in infrastructure and development projects generally live in miserable conditions and are accommodated in small cramped rooms in the labour camps. Often toilet and kitchen facilities are inadequate, and working conditions are harsh. Thus, adverse working condition, unfriendly weather, inability to participate in social and cultural activities, and long periods of separation from families and relatives leading to emotional deprivation are known to have wrecked the lives of low skilled Indian workers in the Gulf.

The unskilled and semiskilled workers have a high rate of turnover as their contracts are for short periods of employment and work, usually not more than two years at a time. Those completing their contracts must return home, although a large proportion of them manage to come back with new contracts which are not available before a gap of one year. This has facilitated the proliferation of recruitment and placement agencies, sometimes colluding with the prospective employers and exploiting illiterate job seekers. The various forms of exploitation range from withholding of the passports; refusal of promised employment, wages, and overtime wages; undue deduction of permit fee from wages; unsuitable transport; inadequate medical facilities; denial of legal rights for re-dressal of complaints; use of migrants as carriers of smuggled goods; victimisation and harassment of women recruits in household jobs like maids, cooks, governesses etc.

Generally speaking, the Indian migrant communities in the Gulf maintain close contacts with their kith and kin in India, involving frequent home visits. They also keep track of political developments and socioeconomic changes taking place in India through newspapers, radio and television. At times of natural disasters like earthquake in India, they have also come forward with donations, and deposits in India Development Bonds. Most of the remittances have accrued from the unskilled workers whose consumption expenses in the Gulf are mini-mal because their families are not living with them.

The overseas Indian workers (OIWs) come mainly from the three states of Kerala, Tamil Nadu, and Andhra Pradesh, though Karnataka overtook Andhra Pradesh by a big margin in 2005. However, most of them have originated from Kerala. This had led to the establishment of a separate ministry for non-resident Keralites, and an international airport at Thiruvananthapuram. Some of the other states having sizeable number of total labour emigrants to Gulf are Karnataka, Maharashtra, Punjab and Rajasthan. The emigration clearance data gives an underestimate of Correlate worker migration to the Gulf because a person holding a graduate degree is exempt from emigration clearance, and the number of such graduates is very high among the Kerala migrants to the Gulf.

Compared to all India, Kerala contributed an average of 25 per cent of emigrants in 21st century, down from an average of 35 percent in the twentieth century. In other words, one out of every three or four Indians living in Gulf has been a Correlate. A preceding study conducted in 1998–99 had concluded, Migration has provided the single most dynamic factor in the otherwise dismal scenario of Kerala in the last quarter of the twentieth century... Kerala is approaching the end of the millennium with a little cheer in many of its homes, thanks to migration and the economic return that it brings.

In Kerala, migration must have contributed more to poverty alleviation than any other factor including agrarian reforms, trade union activities and social welfare legislation". But, another study conducted five years later says, "In the early stages of Kerala emigration, the beneficial effects overshadowed the adverse effects. Now that Kerala emigration has come of age, secondary effects, which are not so beneficial, are beginning to appear. One important negative effect has been the rise in unemployment rate due to education and replacement migration" into Kerala from other Indian states.

Emigration had a role in increasing the population with higher levels of education by boosting the willingness and the ability of the Correlate youth to acquire more education. Due to demonstration effect, a common aspiration is to emigrate to the Gulf, earn a lot of money, get married, and live happily ever after". In recent years, many countries in the Gulf have made it mandatory to have secondary level education for migrants to enter. This has led to considerable increase in the demand for secondary level education in Kerala. An important aspect of Indian labour migration to the Gulf has been its lion's share in the remittances sent home to India by the workers. Beginning in the mid–1970s, there was rapid increase in remittances coming from the developed countries, but as migrants to these countries were gradually joined by their kith and kin, these were gradually overtaken by larger proportions coming from the Gulf.

Remittances sent by expatriate Indians have supposedly contributed positively to the Indian economy. In the middle of 1991, India faced a serious balance of payments crisis. Foreign exchange reserves had fallen to a level hardly adequate to meet essential imports for just a few weeks. The Indian migrants in the developed countries withdrew their dollar deposits from Indian banks at an alarming rate. These problems warranted immediate action for India to avoid defaulting on its international obligations or a collapse of its economy for want of critical imports. It was the slowly but steadily growing remittances from the Indian workers in the Gulf which saved the situation for India. Today India is at the top of the list of countries receiving remittances from its migrants abroad, close to ten percent of the worldwide remittances sent home by 191 million migrants.

Kerala's share in attracting remittances from overseas Indian workers has not been insignificant. Zachariah *et al.* Have estimated the total remittances to Kerala households based on their survey carried out in 1998 in each of the districts. According to their estimates, total remittances to Kerala stood at Rs. 35,304 million, representing an average remittance of Rs 25,000 per emigrant, and a per capital receipt of Rs. 1,105 by the state population. As a rough proportion of Kerala's State Domestic product, this was close to 10 percent. They also constituted about 10 percent of the country's aggregate remittances of US$12,000 million in 1998 at an exchange rate of approximately Rs. 33 to a dollar.

India had a moderate number of universities at the time of independence but it lacked highly trained scientific and technical human resources and an institutional base in science and technology (S&T) to embark upon the industrialisation and modernisation planned under the Nehruvian leadership of the early decades. The first Indian Institute of Technology was established nine years after

India's independence, at Kharagpur in 1956. The five IITs, modelled on the Mas-sachusetts Institute of Technology (MIT), were created to train the best engineers who would play an important role in assimilating technological change and revolutionising India's industrialisation programme. The IITs not only created space for hundreds of faculty members, but also attracted a good number of them back from abroad. As all the IITs in the beginning had intellectual and material support from various advanced donor countries such as the USA, USSR, Germany, and the UK, they introduced the guest faculty system from the respective countries. The exchange put Indian scientists in touch with the cutting-edge of technological research and advanced training. The Council for Scientific and Industrial Research (CSIR) which instituted a National Register of Scientific and Technical Personnel in the late 1940s, created a special section the "Indians Abroad" section of the National Register in 1957 towards this end, which of course did not succeed.

The migration of the highly skilled from India to the developed countries was first seen as brain drain when the Nobel Prize of 1968 in medicine brought global recognition to gifted Indian scientists Har Gobind Khorana who had mi-grated to the United States and naturalised as an American citizen around that time. The onus, however, was put on the migrants as deserters of the motherland India", either openly or subtly From time to time various restrictive measures to contain the problem were conceived, but there has never been a consensus except in the case of the medical sector - where some restrictions were introduced, but with too many escape clauses to be effective.

The most striking feature of the period has still been the relative lack of policy attention to the problem of brain drain. Education policy documents of the time did not provide for any mechanism to check the problem of brain drain. The Kothari Commission had observed, "Not all who go out of India are necessarily first-rate scientists, nor are they of critical importance to the country's requirements. Gradually, the failure of India's industrialisation programme to absorb the increasing numbers of highly qualified personnel from educational institutes coupled with the shrinking of employment space in the science agencies led to a serious problem of supply and demand and aggravated this.

The policy discourse during this period thus did not pay attention the problem deserved in the face of stark realities of oversupply unemployment and the exodus of trained human resources to foreign countries. As a result, many Indian immigrants who fuelled the Silicon Valley were those educated in the US at the postgraduate level after they had emigrated with a first engineering degree of B.Tech, from the Indian Institutes of Technology. Similarly, many doctors who earned laurels in their respective fields in the US had emigrated with the first MBBS degree from the All India Institute of Medical Sciences.

In fact, it was the Gulf war of 1990-91 that had woken up the Indian policy makers about the vulnerability of its workers in the Gulf, and the importance of their remittances to the economy. However, with shifts in the paradigm of migration, it was the perception of high-skill emigration to developed countries which had changed much more dramatically than that on labour migration to the Gulf. Thus, in the mid 1980s, the political perception of "brain drain" had suddenly given way to the perception of brain bank abroad, a concept dear to Rajiv Gandhi when he took over as the prime-minister of the country in1984, after Indira Gandhi was assassinated. Through the 1990s, the gradual success and achievements of the Indian migrants in the US - particularly led by body shopping of the software professionals to the US from Bangalore, India's Silicon Valley, and working towards averting the looming global crisis of y2K drew real attention of the developed countries in the West and the East alike. The paradigm shift in the perception about professional migrants leaving India, thus took place in phases from the "brain drain" of the 1960s and 1970s to the "brain bank" of the 1980s and 1990s, and subsequently to brain gain in the twenty-first century.

However, the IT bubble burst in the wake of the American recession and hordes of teaches were sent back to India, having lost their H-1B visa contracts. Western European countries in the EU, including the UK looked as a more sustainable destination, and East/South East Asia looked at as an emerging destination. However, Germany's Chancellor Gerhard Schroeder's scheme of issuing 20,000 "Green Cards" to computer specialist from non-EU countries, mainly India and Eastern Europe launched in August, 2000 was met with street protests and the wave of xenophobia of *"kinder stat inder* sweeping Germany eventually, opportunities of employment multiplied within India under the emergence of business process out sourcing (BPO) MNCs moving their capital to India rather than labour moving out of India triggering return migration of Indians as a boon to the economy of India.

In fact, the latest NASSCOM Strategic Review and the NASS-COM-McKinsey Report, apprehends huge shortage of IT-related as well as BPO-related skills in India. The report said that currently only about 25 per cent of the technical graduates and 10-15 per cent of general college students were suitable for employment in the offshore IT and BPO industries respectively and estimated that by 2010 the two industries would have to employ an additional work-force of about one million workers near five Tier-I cities, viz., New Delhi, Bangalore, Hyderabad, Chennai and Mumbai, and about 600,000 workers across other towns in India. On talent supply, it said India would need a 2.3 million strong IT and BPO work-force by 2010 to maintain its current market share. The report projected a potential shortfall of nearly 0.5 million qualified employees nearly 70 per cent of which would be concentrated in the BPO industry. In fact, the BPO industry has also started attracting foreigners to India in search of employment.

This roller-coaster of perception in moving from one model of the Indian disappear-identity formation through migration to the other between "work-seeking" by workers and worker-seeking by employers- gets reflected in the current official and public response in India over the changing immigration quotas of the developed host countries. India's pro-active stance towards its population over-seas, incorporating a substantial scientific disappear, is reflective of this paradigm shift only. Not merely economic, but political mileage that the NRIs and PIOs can command for India in their countries of abode has also become a focus of pride in recent years, particularly with liberalisation, globalisation and world competitiveness becoming the agenda of the nations whether developed or developing.

Whereas provision regarding entry, regulation and prevention of "foreigners" into India and Indian citizenship are found in the Constitution, the Citizenship Act 1955, the Passport Act 1967, the Criminal Procedure Code and other regulations, there has been no systematic legal policy framework to deal with emigration out of the country. Despite the debates, discourses, and perspective, the Government of India does not have any comprehensive policy on labour migration or overseas employment, whether for skilled or unskilled workers. However, the paradigm of policy stance in India could be said to have moved over time from one of restrictive regime, to compensatory to restorative, to developmental. The Emigration Act, 1983, which replaced the earlier 1922 Emigration Act, has been designed mainly to ensure protection to vulnerable categories of unskilled, and semiskilled workers, and women going abroad to work as housemaids and domestic workers. Under the Act, it is mandatory for registration of all "Recruiting Agents" with the ministry. The government's role has been perceived as that of a facilitator in finding gainful employment to maximum number of persons, again a major development concern since India's independence, whether within or outside the country.

The newly formed Ministry of Overseas Indian Affairs, constituted in 2004, has taken the initiative to amend the Emigration Act, 1983, and introduce a number of measures. In addition, there are various other pro-active programmes that are in the pipeline of the MOIA, including benchmarks of the best practises of other progressive sending countries like the Philippines and Sri lanka. *Overseas Indian,* the house journal of the Ministry has been launched in five languages with an eversion also being made accessible. Of all the government measures and programmes in India, the Over-seas Citizenship of India (OCI) the dual citizenship is an important landmark in redefining the contours of a *migration policy* in the new millennium. This mea-sure seems to be relevant mainly to the highly skilled migrants to the developed countries. A second measure, that Indian citizens abroad would have the right to exercise their votes from abroad, is primarily meant for the Indian workers in the Gulf those who send large remittances back home but can never hope to become naturalised citizens of those countries because of restrictive regimes there. However, it is still too early to gauge the impact of these two measures as they are in their infancy.

How does one assess whether migration has changed society in India, and whether it has adequately contributed to social and economic development in India? In other words, what have been the socioeconomic gains and losses arising from migration? These questions have traditionally been raised in suggesting cost-benefit analysis at the micro-level for the individual migrant and the household, and at macro level for society and the economy as a whole.

Even if it is assumed that the micro-level assessment of benefits and losses to the households left behind in India can more accurately identify and mea-sure the benefits, there has not been many satisfactory surveys of the psychic losses that separation of family member brings, except for a few studies carried out in the state of Kerala. For example, emigration of married men who left behind the responsibility of the management of the household to women in the family, transformed about one million women into efficient home managers, but eventually also created the social and psychological problems of the "Gulf Wives" and the loneliness of the "Gulf Parents", who unlike the relatives of the skilled migrants to the developed countries were not accompanying the workers to their destination countries. Another related but unattended facet of Indian migration has been the gender issue. No comprehensive data are available on women migrants as dependents or workers, not to consider in-depth analyses of the trend and impacts. Some receiving-country data are available, like the US Census, or the UK work-force data indicating the proportion of women amongst Asian Indian ethnic group population which comprises migrants, or particular professional groups like Indian nurses respectively, and Singapore data on Indian maids. Beyond this, analyses of the gender dimension of Indian migration have remained, by and large, either stereotypical or case-study based.

Of course, there has been concern followed by diplomatic action at the plight of the migrant workers of Indian origin employed abroad whenever a crisis has erupted, be it the Gulf war, or the Iraq war, or the random abductions of Indian truck drivers, the recent beheading of an Indian engineer by the terrorists in Afghanistan, or the sudden arrests of Indian IT professionals in Malaysia or the

Netherlands and so on. However, India virtually exerts no control over migration flows of highly skilled categories. Even unskilled migration flows are controlled only to the ex-tent they fall under the purview of the Emigration Clearance Required (ECR) category of passports, with limitations mentioned earlier. As a result, what has not been looked into is how the possibility of migration itself has created a sense of desperation amongst the low-income Indian populace to emigrate for the sake of upward socioeconomic mobility of the family left behind in India, even at the risks that accompany migration overseas. Similarly there have been no studies on the impact of skilled migration on career choices and educational choices in India, where there have been a lot of choice distortion and inter-generational or even inter-community conflict over educational choices that have taken place but remained un-analysed if not unnoticed.

At the macro level, the attempts have not progressed beyond identification of the indicators, viz., remittances, transfer of technology, and human capital embodied in returning migrants. Even in the case of macroeconomic assessment of much talked about remittances, there has been a "silent backwash flow" from the south countries of origin like India to north countries of destination like the UK, Australia, and the US in the form of "overseas student" fees. This has remained unestimated and un-analysed so far. The rises in disposable income of the Kerala households arising from remittances have had its effect on the consumption pattern in the state, including on enhanced family investment in education for migration. But, consumerism and house building activities have drained the state of the development potential of its remittance receipts, leading many families to financial bankruptcy, even to suicides. Apart from this, the increasing economic and political clout of the "new rich" in Kerala is reported to have created a climate of resentment against them among the other communities.

Notwithstanding this, whereas the volume of remittances from Indian labour migrants in the Gulf have drawn a lot of attention, the other two areas, viz., transfer of technology and return migration that have been thought of as the positive outcome of skilled migration to the developed countries, even quantitative assessment have not been adequate. Most studies have not gone beyond talking about the need to assess the quantitative outcomes in terms of volumes of flows of technology collaborations and the numbers of returnees. Collection and availability of data have been the main constrains of researchers in going beyond this in these two areas, although sporadic information on transfer of technology has revealed not necessarily rosy pictures arising from the contribution in the field of transfer of technology; rather, the "reverse transfer of technology" - a term used by the UNCTAD studies carried out in the 1970s - from countries of the south to north still seems to be continuing in the form of brain drain of IT professionals and so on. Return migration has become topical in the context of "out sourcing" of business processes to India picking up after the IT bubble burst in the US, but here too there have been no systematic assessment of the numbers and quality of the returnees, although some studies emphasise the return to India as unsustainable because the returnees tend to go back after a short stay in India. Some involvement of circulating returnees have of course been noted in NGO activities for socioeconomic development at the grassroots level in India but these have remained largely anecdotal.

What would be useful as a policy tool is adversary analysis whereby the contribution to social and economic development in countries of origin would be assessed from the point of view of the stockholders in countries of destination. To do this in a multilateral international-relations framework at fora like the GATS under WTO, the benefits of remittances, technology, and return migration to south countries of origin can be weighed and even pitted against three advantages of "Age, Wage, and Vintage" that accrue to the destination countries of the north. These are the advantages derived through higher migrant turnover inbuilt in temporary and circulatory immigration, and operationalised by *(a)* bringing in of younger migrants to balance an ageing population, *(b)* keeping the wage and pension commitments low by replacing older and long-term mi-grants with younger and short-term migrants, and *(c)* stockpiling latest vintage of knowledge embodied in younger cohorts of skilled workers respectively. It remains to be judged and explored what are the cost aspects of these benefits.

The changed perceptions of the destination countries, in which the Indian professional migrants have settled to form a diaspora, might play a catalyst's role in this exercise. The changed values are now attributed to the Indian diaspora itself that has defied the anticipated doom by rising to unforeseeable economic success in the destinatioh countries of the north, leading to a paradigm shift in the societies and regions where Indians have settled. The reason lies in the realisation of the host countries that, given the appropriate help, resources, and local support, one type of migrants - the suspected "social parasite" can become the other, the social boon, or as someone has phrased it, the white West's great *off-white* hope.

This has led to a major paradigm shift in India too to look at migration as a process leading to formation of the "Indian Diaspora", an option for turning the challenge of migration into an opportunity, and therefore *gainfull.* What remain for India as well as these host countries in the emerging international relations paradigm is to judge where the loyalty of the Indian diaspora would lie? Whether Indian migrants would no longer be treated by India as the deserters of the motherland, or as social parasites by the host countries?

The diaspora option, because it is holistic in identity, would also foster the emphasis that the GCIM report has made in stating, the traditional distinction between skilled and unskilled workers is in certain respects an un-helpful one, as it fails to do justice to the complexity of international migration... While they may have different levels of educational achievement, all of them could be legitimately described as *essential workers* (emphasis added). While the dichotomy between skilled and unskilled migrant workers is unwarranted, lately India has drawn disproportionately high worldwide attention to the success stories of its highly skilled human resources doing remarkably well in the world labour markets abroad - the IT professionals, the nurses, the bio-technologists, the financial managers, the scientists, the architects, the lawyers, the teachers and so on - there being almost a fray for them amongst the developed countries - the German Green Card, the American H1–B visa, the British work permit, the Canadian investment visa, the Australian student visa, the New Zealand citizen-ship, all mushrooming to acquire Indian talent embodied in workers as well as students. In contrast, the Indian labour migrants in the Gulf have been considered more of a responsibility than pride for India. To neutralise this imbalance and empower the Indian labour migrants, the interest of the stockholders in the Gulf (and Southeast Asia too) are gradually being looked into, and innovative programmes are being introduced. The developments following the institution of the "Pravasi Bhartiya Divas" *(Expatriate Indians Day)* and constitution of a separate ministry of the government of India reflect a break from the past - a confidence emanating from a paradigm shift towards India taking pride in its diaspora, and vice-versa.

What is required, however, is a long-term policy that is aimed at establishing India's links with the Indian diaspora for sustainable socioeconomic development in the country. To arrive though at a proverbial win-win situation in international relations for all the three stockholders - India as a south country of origin, the Indian migrants as part of its diaspora, and the host destination countries of the north, two specific conditions must be met: A necessary condition of dominant or significant global geo-economic presence of the Indian workers; and a sufficient condition of India deriving *sustainable* benefits from that global geo-economic presence. In terms of the large demand for Indian skilled as well as unskilled workers abroad, and the migrants establishing excellent records of accomplishment in the labour markets of the destination countries, the first condition has more or less been met.

To satisfy the sufficient condition of India deriving significant gains from the global geo-economic presence of the Indian migrants, the flows of remittances, transfer of technology, and return migration must all be directed not "top down" but bottom up not towards trade and business but towards the removal of two kinds of poverty in India - the poverty of education and the poverty of health - areas where migration has so far failed to change the society in this country of origin by contributing to its economic and social development.

Large masses of the illiterate and uneducated population, incapacitated further by their poor health status are the root causes of India having one of the lowest levels of average productivity of labour, and therefore lowest average wages in the world a paradox when Indian diaspora members, on the average, figure amongst the largest contributing ethnic communities in their countries of destination. For example, it is indeed paradoxical that the average per-hour contribution of each employed worker within India to the production of India's gross domestic product (GDP) has been amongst the lowest in the world a mere 37 cents as compared to the United States' 37 dollars, i.e., one-hundredth of the latter. This is naturally ironical, because the same average Indian employed abroad contributes very high average share to the GDP of the country where one settles and works. The Indian diaspora networks and associations abroad could, therefore, play the catalyst's role be it economically, politically or culturally in raising the average productivity of mass Indian workers at home by thinking health and education in India as areas of diaspora engagement, rather than focusing on immediate "profit-making" ventures in industry and business.

This sets a double challenge of public policy for a sending country like India: First, to convince its own diaspora community to rethink the development process in India as a bottom up creation and enhancement of sustainable productivities of labour through development of education and health rather than a "top down" development through participation in business and industry one comprehensive, the other dispersed; one long-term, the other immediate. It is not just a matter of willingness; in many instances, it would entail long periods of struggle in creating those decision-making and priority-setting discerning capabilities amongst the leaders of the migrant community. Secondly, India must be able to convince the countries of destination (and the other countries of origin in the south as well) to distinguish between most painful and most "gainful" socioeconomic impacts of migration of its workers both skilled and unskilled.

The "adversary analysis" in multilateral fora would help a country like India press for international norms in the GATS negotiations around the issue of movement of natural persons as service providers under trade, which is just another description for promoting the temporary entry of migrants. At multilateral dialogues, the vulnerability of the migrants and the instability of trends underlying the "open-and-shut policy" of the destination countries in the north could be the two key aspects that the south countries of origin ought to negotiate out of international migration as the most hurting ones.

9

Working Parents and Child-care

For parents who work for income or would like to work, Child-care is a concern that is almost universal. One way that workers have been receiving various kinds of assistance with Child-care is through support that they can access through their Work-place. Work-place programmes are not the only, nor even the primary, means of accessing assistance with Child-care. However, they are nevertheless helping many working parents and are attracting increasing interest as a way of meeting the overall socialite challenge of finding mechanisms for making Child-care more accessible and available to working parents.

At any particular time, a child can be in the care of (i) a family member, (ii) someone from outside the family or (iii) no one. This simple schema is represented. Families are the main providers of care for their children. At birth, usually the round-the-clock care needed is provided by the family and a baby is not normally left with no one responsible. Someone has to ensure their basic needs are met (fed, washed, clothed, housed and so on) as well as to provide a loving and stimulating environment that will foster their social and psychological development. Much of this is done by the parents themselves. Many countries facilitate parental care by providing paid entitlements for working parents to temporarily leave their jobs to care for young children. Most countries have legislated maternity leave for working mothers and some also provide for a short paternity leave for fathers and/ or more extended parental leaves for either father or mother after maternity leave. From the end of maternity leave (the ILO norm is 14 weeks) until the age at which a child can go to school, working parents need someone to look after their child during the time they are working. In virtually all countries, some working parents receive help from grandparents or other family members who may be able to cover at least part of their Child-care needs. T is solution usually has the advantage of being without financial cost. Depending on the circumstances (such as where the grandparents reside, their health) this may or may not be a good solution. When the family member is a young child removed from school to look after a baby, this is clearly not the ideal solution from the point of view of society.

Once children attend school, working parents still have to make care arrangements for before or after school, lunch breaks and the school holidays. Family members may be able to cover at least a portion of this time. Also, as children get older, there may be less need for a care arrangement and they can belief to look after themselves with no one responsible for their care. Local contexts and norms influence perceptions of the age at which children do not need out-of-school care. However, leaving them in "no care", as "latchkey" children without supervision, may be problematic even for adolescents.

Non-family care is needed to look after children during the working hours of parents when there is no family member available. Evidence suggests that traditional family supports are weakening, particularly with the rise of nuclear and single-parent households, and with migration to cities and overseas such that many working parents in both industrialised and developing countries need non-family care for both preschool and school-age children.

In most countries, looking after children was traditionally considered to be a responsibility of families alone – mainly the women. It was not an issue of concern to trade unions or employers. As for governments, Child-care was of en regarded as mainly a matter of providing welfare assistance for poor families. The assumption was that most families can look after their children, which was perceived as "their responsibility anyhow".

Apart from a few welfare cases, Child-care usually has to be paid for by the parents, so that it is mainly well-of parents who can find arrangements for ensuring that their children are well looked after while they work. Paying a reliable nanny or child minder or putting a toddler into quality day-care can be quite expensive and of en out of the reach of low-income and even middle-income parents. So they are faced with a no-win choice. They can use parental time to fill in the Child-care gap by, for example, working at different times in the case of dual-parent households or reducing their work activity (typically that of the mother) and consequently their income. Or they can leave the child with poor-quality care or no care at all. Whatever their choice, the child will probably suffer, as will the parents. The consequences of lack of access to affordable, good-quality Child-care go beyond the welfare of individual children and their families and affect the social and economic development of the whole society. For society, benefits of Child-care include the following.

Child-care and Gender Inequality

Child-care can be a major factor in gender inequality, undermining women's ability to work and their opportunities for employment. In the European Union, Child-care is recognised as a critical factor in meeting its goal of full employment and a concrete way of eliminating barriers to women's participation in the labour market. As a result, at the Barcelona summit in 2002, EU governments set Child-care targets for the year 2010: 33 per cent coverage for children under 3 and 90 per cent coverage for children between 3 years and compulsory school age.

Evidence from Europe suggests that where governments support the costs of widely available Child-care, these countries tend to have higher rates of women's labour force participation and fertility and lower gender inequality, as is particularly the case in Nordic countries.

Child-care can help parents, particularly mothers, ensure continuity in their careers. If they are compelled to resign for lack of affordable, quality Child-care and do not work at all for a long period, they tend to have difficulty re-entering work, particularly at the same level as they were when they left. In countries where girls continue to be removed from school to look after younger siblings, lack of Child-care can be a factor in the lower educational level of girls.

Promoting the Rights and Development of Children

The UN Convention on the Rights of the Child explicitly recognises the need for parents to receive assistance in their Child-care responsibilities as well as the rights of children to benefit from Child-care facilities. Stories of harm coming to young children who have been left on their own while parents work have made headlines in a number of countries. In the Republic of Korea, for example, the grassroots movement for Child-care was reinforced by an incident in 1990 when two children died in a fire, locked in the house while their parents worked.

Improving the access of vulnerable and disadvantaged groups to quality care for pre-scholars can provide opportunities for these children to begin primary education on a more equal footing with more privileged children. In the United Kingdom, for example, disadvantaged children already flag behind their middle-class contemporaries in terms of cognitive development at the age of 3, so the provision of high-quality early years education is clearly one very important way to counter this. In developing countries, it is likely that a similar or even deflect might be found for disadvantaged children.

Contributing to the National Economy

Well-structured Child-care support policies can pay for themselves, according to a report from the Organisation for Economic Co-operation and Development (OECD): without support, parents can face a more difficult time participating in the labour force, which can lead to "higher welfare expenditure, lost tax revenues, inhibited growth and wasted human capital". Child-care not only increases women's access to employment, but also increases employment opportunities in Child-care, and contributes to job creation in the service sector to replace some of the unpaid household work such as cleaning and food preparation. One estimate of the job creation effects of women's employment is that ten jobs are created for every hundred additional women in work. Indeed, in most industrialised countries, there has been an increase in employment in Child-care. In the Netherlands, for example, the child-care sector has evolved since 1990 from a small sector with 8,000 employees into a mature sector employing over 60,000 employees in 2003.9 Similarly in France, the number of child mindersmore than tripled during the 1990s.

Breaking the Vicious Circle of Inter-Generational Poverty

For disadvantaged families, access to Child-care can help prevent the perpetuation of social disadvantage by:

1. Increasing the family income, of en through women's labour force participation; and

2. Fostering the physical, social and cognitive development of children, and improving their life chances.

Of en as a result of research and political pressure from civil society, governments are increasingly realising that many families are having difficulties ensuring that their children are well looked after while the parents work, and that lack of Child-care is leading to the inefficient functioning of labour markets, under-utilisation of public investments in human resources and insufficient care of the next generation.

Conventions and Labour Standards

A number of international conventions recognise the fact that working parents need outside support in coping with Child-care and call for the provision of child-care facilities.

The Convention on the Elimination of All Forms of Discrimination against Women (CEDAW), adopted in 1979 by the UN General Assembly, sets out an agenda for national action to end discrimination against women. Among the measures foreseen to prevent discrimination and ensure women's effective right to work is Article 11 2(c):

> States Parties shall take appropriate measures to encourage the provision of the necessary supporting social services to enable parents to combine family obligations with work responsibilities and participation in public life, *in particular through promoting the establishment and development of a network of child-care facilities.* (Authors ' it alics)

Similarly, with a view to creating effective equality of opportunity and treatment for men and women workers, the ILO Convention on Workers with Family Responsibilities, 1981 (No. 156), also calls for Child-care measures:

> All measures compatible with national conditions and possibilities shall further be taken to develop or promote community services, public or private, such as child-care and family services and facilities. (Article 5(b).

Both these Conventions indicate that the public authorities should "promote" Child-care facilities, but there is no compulsion for the government itself to pro-vide. The ILO Convention No. 156 specifically mentions the possibility of public or private provision. Nevertheless both conventions recognise the key role of government in promoting and encouraging the development of family or social services and specifically mention the need for Child-care for working parents.

It is important to note that both these instruments call for Child-care for working *parents* and not just working *mothers*, implicitly recognising the family responsibilities of men as well as women.

As discussed above, the issue of Child-care concerns not only the well-being of working parents but also of their children and how they are cared for. The UN Convention on the Rights of the Child (CRC), which has been ratified by 191 countries, specifies:

For the purpose of guaranteeing and promoting the rights set forth in the present Convention, States Parties shall render appropriate assistance to parents and legal guardians in the performance of their child-rearing responsibilities and shall *ensure the development of institutions, facilities and services for the care of children.*

States Parties shall take all appropriate measures to ensure that children of working parents have the right to benefit from child-care services and facilities for which they are eligible.

The CRC thus also recognises the need for parents to receive assistance in their Child-care responsibilities and specifically asserts the rights of the children of working parents to benefit from Child-care facilities. The responsibility lies with "States Parties" to ensure the development of services; however, this does not mean they necessarily provide these services themselves.

WORK-PLACE SOLUTIONS

Work-place solutions may be contrasted with the more common source of Child-care support–community services–which have no link to any particular Work-place. Municipalities may run Child-care centres or have a service providing information on existing private and public centres and approved child minders in the locality. Religious organisations may run after-school clubs. Private day-care centres and child minders who look after children in their homes exist in many communities. In these cases, the access to Child-care support is provided, irrespective of where the parent works, or indeed, in some cases, irrespective of whether one or both parents work for income at all.

The many workers who do not work in formal work-places, particularly in developing countries, where the majority are of en found in informal employment, are thus not covered. The Child-care problems of workers in informal settings, who are usually among the poorest, are even more acute and the Child-care solutions found in these types of work-places have been examined elsewhere.

Types of Measures

At the level of the Work-place, there are basically two types of measures which can help employed parents cope with their Child-care responsibilities:

1. Measures which concern the working conditions of parents so that they can themselves look after their children when they need attention; and
2. Measures which help parents access care by others.

Child-care Needs and Types of Solutions

The care services needed by workers depend on the ages of their children and also on the ages covered by the school system as well as school hours and holidays in the country or region concerned. The Child-care needs of parents also depend on their working conditions. For parents who work nights, on shifts or at unusual times, the difficulties in finding Child-care can be even greater. Parents who work long hours and have little vacation have more time away from the family that needs to be covered by Child-care.

The first is care for young children until the start of formal schooling, which is probably the most obvious need. Work-place assistance for this age group is the most common. Nevertheless, the second need—out-of-school care for children of school age—can be a major problem for parents, and some work-places provide help for this age group.

The need for emergency, backup care can occur for children of all ages, as even the best arrangements can go wrong when a career doesn't show up, a grand-mother is sick or there is a special school holiday. Help at the Work-place so parents can access emergency "backup" care is becoming increasingly common.

Various types of arrangements can help workers find affordable Child-care at the times they need and of the quality they want. Work-place solutions may be categorised into four main types:

1. A Child-care centre of the company (companies) or on-site;
2. A facility in the community which is linked to the Work-place (through arrangements such as negotiated discounts, reserved places, subsidised places);
3. Some form of financial support (Child-care vouchers, funds or subsidies); and
4. Advice and referral services.

Each type of solution can, in principle, be used for any of the three basic Child-care needs, namely care for preschool children, out-of-school care for schoolchildren and backup care. Advice and referral services, for example, can help parents to find care for babies, for children after school or for a child whose usual career is sick. Similarly, Work-place arrangements with community facilities can help workers access day-care for babies, holiday camps for schoolchildren or baby-sitters for backup care.

Role of Partnerships

In most situations, ways are being found to share the costs and responsibilities among various partners such as workers' organisations, employers' organisations, local and national governments, organisations specialising in providing Child-care, religious organisations and other NGOs as well as, of course, the parents themselves. Parents are typically major partners since they of en pay a high proportion of the costs, in some cases receiving some financial help from governments and their employers. Diverse systems for sharing the costs, including, in some cases, government grants or tax exemptions, mean that the actual costs of Child-care to parents and employers are highly variable. In order to obtain details on how partnerships for Child-care have developed and worked in different work-places and countries, the case studies have been designed to collect information on the partnerships involved: who provides what resources and who is responsible for organising or operating the different programmes.

In the few industrialised countries where there is extensive public provision of Child-care for children of all ages, there is little need for Work-place involvement and indeed it is practically nonexistent in countries like Sweden or Denmark. Such countries were not considered for inclusion in the current study.

Countries were chosen in an effort to show a variety of public approaches to Child-care and to the role of the Work-place in Child-care. They were also chosen to ensure some representation from the major regions.

The industrialised countries chosen are France, Hungary, the United Kingdom and the United States. Each of these countries has very different histories and approaches to Child-care. Two countries, France and Hungary, have relatively long histories of public concern with Child-care provision, although for different reasons and with different types of measures. The United Kingdom is interesting since the Government's efforts to improve access to Child-care are relatively recent – starting in 1999 and including a role for the Work-place. The case of the United States, where a low level of government involvement has left Child-care to a large extent to the private sector, provides examples of the active roles played by trade unions, employers' groups, individual companies, academics, research organisations, Child-care NGOs and the Child-care business.

The developing countries selected tend to be larger countries with a relatively high proportion of their population in urban areas and a significant number of workers in formal employment – Brazil and Chile from Latin America, India and Thailand from Asia and Kenya and South Africa from Africa. Urbanisation is important, since-for work-place programmes to exist, there must be some sort of Work-place with a certain concentration of workers, which is most likely in urban areas–although plantations are a major exception in rural areas. For most of these countries, preliminary investigations suggested that interesting innovations were taking place at some work-places which could provide ideas for others in similar circumstances.

National Contexts of Work-place Solutions

Work-place programmes for Child-care are situated in and adapted to the national and local contexts in which they are located. In an ideal world, there would be free public Child-care of quality for all children needing it and so little need for Work-place programmes. However, this ideal is far from reality in many countries. To some extent, Work-place programmes for Child-care are helping to fill in the gaps not covered by public programmes.

Ages of Children and Issues

The needs of children at different ages are to some extent similar in all countries, but perceptions of Child-care needs are affected by local norms and conditions. Children's needs are very different from one age to another and raise different concerns about the types of care that are most appropriate.

The need for care facilities for children under age 3 depends to some extent on the duration of maternity leave and other parental leaves (particularly those which are paid). In the European countries, paid maternity leave is much longer (in France 16 weeks for first child and 26 for others, in Hungary 24 weeks and in the United Kingdom 26 weeks) compared to many developing countries or the United States (12 weeks, unpaid). Where maternity and parental leaves are more generous, the need for non-parental care during the baby's first year or two would be less frequent.

In some European countries, policy has been to facilitate parental (mainly maternal) care through long parental leaves after maternity leave. In Hungary, for example, concerns about low fertility coupled with traditional views regarding women's roles as mothers 1 have led to leaves which can last until the child is 3 years old, while the Child-care services of the socialist era for children under age 3 have rapidly diminished. Similarly in Austria and Germany, the ideal of mother-care for young children has also resulted in policies for lengthy leaves and little development of Child-care services for young children. Such policies have been criticised as a trap for women, whose work-force participation is disrupted and who finder-entry after leave very difficult. In some countries, there has been considerable debate about whether very young children are best cared for by their mothers and whether putting children in child-care at an early age is harmful. For children age 2 or more, most evidence suggests that good-quality Child-care can contribute to child development. However, for very young children, the effects of non-parental care are less clear and depend on many intervening factors related to the cultural context, the quality of the substitute care, the duration of the care, the nature of the mother's work and her control over the use of the income earned. There is some evidence from industrialised countries that maternal *full-time* employment during the *first year* after birth is harmful to children's health, thus pointing to the need for more flexible schedules and longer maternity leaves.

As concerns physical growth and nutrition, studies in developing countries have tended to find that, for children over 2 years, those with working mothers have a better nutritional status than similar children whose mothers do not work. But for children under one year, their nutritional status may be less good. The negative effect of mothers' work on the growth of children under 1 year may be related to the challenges that many women, in developing and developed countries, face in continuing to breast-feed after returning to work in view of a lack of support and facilities. In contrast, for children aged 2 to 5 years, purchased foods (and parental income to buy them) would be relatively more important to nutritional status.

Much also depends on the quality of the substitute care. Evidence from developing countries consistently shows, for example, that when children are used as substitute care-givers, the association of maternal work and child nutrition is either negative or less favourable than when the care is provided by another adult. A study in the United States which followed children over a long period found that children who received higher-quality Child-care before kindergarten scored better on vocabulary tests in the fifth grade than children who received poor-quality care.

The results of the same US study underlined the importance of the quality of parenting, which was found to be a much more important predictor of child development than was the type, quantity or quality, of Child-care. So the results on the effects of non-parental care of young children are complex, but the key issue is the quality of the care, whether it be by parents or by someone else.

Given the importance of the quality of the care, there is also some concern that Child-care for under-3s may be seen mainly as a service for looking after children while parents work, and thus the overriding priority is to keep them safe and clean, while the needs of the child for stimulation and affection may be overlooked. The OECD notes, "Services for children under have of en been seen as an adjunct to labour market policies, with infants and toddlers assigned to services with weak developmental agendas." Ensuring that children have the necessary interaction and stimulation needed for their development is an important aspect of these services which depends greatly on the availability of trained and motivated staff

There is some consensus among those who have studied the effects of care arrangements on very young children that, for the period immediately following birth, the most effective policies are those that provide flexibility and choice offering a combination of maternity/paternity leaves and part-time jobs/flexible work arrangements and Child-care facilities for the following years. Such a combination is actually provided in Denmark, France, Norway and Sweden. However, most countries would be unable or unwillinig to finance such extensive provisions.

Role of Pre-primary Education

For children from age years until the start of compulsory primary schooling (usually at age 5/6 years), both parents and governments are increasingly aware of the benefits of preschool education. Early childhood is well known to be a critical period for physical, cognitive and socio-emotional development. Numerous studies have assessed the effects of early childhood education (ECE) interventions from about age 3 years on the development and future outcomes of children. Results show that such interventions have positive results on school readiness, retention and success in primary school. Effective programmes enhance children's physical well-being, cognitive and language skills, and social and emotional development. Even parents who do not need Child-care of en put their children into pre-primary education, given the benefits for the child.

For children from disadvantaged backgrounds, attending preschool education is particularly significant. Early education programmes are important for providing young children, especially those from low-income and second-language groups, with a strong foundation for their growth and development.

The evidence of the significant benefits to children of early childhood education, as well as pressures from citizens, have led many governments to expand access to pre-primary education. The World Bank and UNICEF both have extensive programmes to support this process in a number of developing countries.

For working parents with children of this age group, the situation can be rather complicated, as in many countries the opening hours of public pre-primary schools are limited, such as half a day in the United States or 12.5 hours per week in the United Kingdom. UNESCO notes that, in many countries, preschool programmes run for even less than 10 hours per week. When public programmes cover very few hours, working parents must find additional ways of caring for children in order to cover their working hours, or may alter their working arrangements, working part time or in flexible or informal economy jobs. For poorer workers, taking advantage of public preschool programmes which run for few hours may be difficult (even though they are free or relatively low cost), given the logistical problems of dropping of and picking up children and arranging additional care to cover their working hours.

School-age Children

Public concern about Child-care tends to focus on preschool children, of en over-looking the major problems which working parents may have in finding care for school-age children before and after school, during lunch breaks and during school holidays. Normal school hours can be more-or-less problematic for working parents. For example, in France, there is no school on Wednesdays. In Brazil, primary school operates on half-day shifts.

In the EU, Child-care policy was initially developed for children of preschool age. However, over the past decade, Member States have been addressing the need for Child-care for school-age children through the development of a range of strategies and programmes. Nevertheless, a report in 2006 notes that only a few Member States are addressing the need for Child-care services for school-age children.

Government initiatives for out-of-school programmes are of en driven by concerns about children in disadvantaged areas who are more likely to belief to their own devices than those of better-of families. The long hours of unsupervised time for children between the end of school hours and the time parents get home from work has been linked to antisocial youth behaviour, and out-of-school programmes can be effective ways of addressing the needs of working parents, the needs of youths and public safety concerns.

The age at which children can be left on their own after school or during summer holidays is highly debatable and parents are of en worried even about adolescent children who are left on their own. Recognising that Child-care problems persist even when children are teenagers, some government supports for Child-care expenses can be used for this age group. For example, in the United Kingdom, tax-free Child-care vouchers can be used for children up to age 15 years. There has been a growing trend in the United Kingdom towards providing out-of-school care to older children aged 12 and above, recognising that their needs and aspirations are different and that care needs to be provided in a different format (and with a different name).

In theory, the cost of providing out-of-school care is much lower for older children than for younger children as child-to-staff ratios for this older age group are relatively high and no new capital investment is necessary if existing school buildings can be used.

Concerns of Working Parents

The Child-care solutions available within their locality can facilitate parents' (mainly mothers) employment or act as a barrier to employment. For parents, the critical aspects of Child-care which influence whether they use it are:

1. Affordability in relation to their earnings.
2. Convenience in terms of opening hours and location.
3. The quality of care the child will receive.

Even when Child-care is available in theory, its cost to parents can be a major barrier to paid work for many families, leaving little option but parental care. As one new mother working in the UK National Health Service put it:

"What's the point in going back to work when you're paying out more for your Child-care than what you're actually earning?"

Similarly, a study in Kenya found that high costs of Child-care discourage households from using formal Child-care and have a negative effect on the level of mothers' participation in market work. A study by the OECD suggests that Child-care costs particularly affect the employment rates of low-skilled women or low-income families, mothers of younger children and lone parents. The cost problem for parents is particularly acute in countries where most Child-care is provided privately, as in the United States.

In some countries, publicly subsidised Child-care centres do exist for low-income families but the number of places is insufficient. In Rio de Janeiro, for example, long waiting lists for public day-care centres in slum areas testify to the insufficient number of places compared to the needs of parents. As a result, for-profit centres, whose quality cannot be guaranteed, have sprung up.

Convenience is another factor affecting whether parents use Child-care. Parents need Child-care which is not too far from either their work or their home and which is available to cover the hours during which they are working. In a study of 30 European countries, a problem identified by the majority of countries was the incompatibility of the Child-care services on offer with the working hours of parents. Even those that provide care over the course of a day from 9 a.m. Until 5 p.m. No longer fit the flexibility forms are requiring from working parents. Similarly in Thailand, the Women Workers Unity Group feels that the opening hours of existing Child-care centres do not cater to the needs of workers and it has been advocating for child-care centres to be set up in industrial communities. When parents need to juggle a multiplicity of care arrangements for children in order to be able to cover their working hours, this can discourage the use of Child-care.

For working parents who may have unexpected meetings or need to work overtime, the flexibility of Child-care arrangements is an important aspect of convenience. The rigid hours of Child-care centres can be problematic when parents' working times are variable.

Apart from cost and convenience, a major Child-care concern of parents is that their child is being well cared for while they work. The poor quality of avail-able non-parental care is of en cited as a major reason why women with young children who would like to work are not able to do so. For example, a report by the European Commission found that parents will be less likely to use Child-care if they feel that there are problems with its quality – as is the case with Child-care in the United Kingdom, where staff recruitment and retention are issues. In Thailand, a report suggests that the low quality of a number of day-care centres and newspaper reports of accidents or mistreatment of children discourage the use of day-care by parents.

There is an inherent conflict between the affordability and quality of child-care. Parents are looking for affordable Child-care of quality, but quality has a cost. When there is little public financial support for Child-care, finding a child-care arrangement that is affordable of en means sacrificing on the quality by, for example, using an overcrowded Child-care centre or hiring a young, inexperienced girl as a nanny, as many workers did on the Red Lands Roses plantation in Kenya, prior to the establishment of the Work-place centre.

Work-place programmes have been helping employed parents by addressing these key aspects of Child-care: mitigating the costs; making it more convenient; and/or helping ensure that Child-care arrangements are providing adequate care for workers' children. In some cases, particularly in rural areas where there are no Child-care facilities, Work-place programmes have established a much-needed service.

Child-care Options

As noted in the Introduction, there are basically three main categories of child-care which parents can use: care in the child's home (a nanny); care in a child-minder's home; and centre-based care. Child-care centres tend to cater for specific age groups whereas nannies and child minders can be used for children of any age. This section looks at the use of these three types of arrangements.

Employing Nannies

Employing a nanny has been a popular Child-care solution in both developed and developing countries for those families that can afford the cost. The actual numbers involved are difficult to determine since nannies are usually assimilated to domestic workers whose duties may involve more or less Child-care. In countries where income disparities are great and there are large pools of unemployed or underemployed women, the employment of domestic workers is frequent. In other countries, migrant workers have been a major source of domestic workers, as in the cases of Singapore and Spain.

Children of all ages can be looked after by a nanny and this solution can be advantageous when there are a number of children to be cared for. Government policies concerning nannies usually relate to their conditions of work under the labour laws that apply to them, often being classified as domestic workers. Legislation concerning child labour may also be relevant when there is a tendency to hire very young girls as nannies, as can be seen in the case examples from Kenya. Immigration policies may also affect the availability of migrant women for this kind of work.

An ILO review of legislation related to domestic workers in 60 countries found that they are often afforded lower protection than other workers and tend by law to have longer hours and sometimes fewer holidays. A major issue is the registration of domestic workers so they can benefit from social security. In some developing countries, legislative efforts have been made to improve the legal rights of domestic workers. In South Africa, for example, since 2002, domestic workers have had the right to minimum wages, paid leave, overtime payments and severance pay and employers are required to register them with the Unemployment Insurance Fund and pay contributions, thus making them eligible for unemployment and maternity benefits.

While in some countries salaries of domestic workers are subject to minimum wages, the isolation of domestic workers in households makes it difficult to ensure that legislation related to wages and also working hours is respected. Wages depend basically on supply and demand and what the worker can negotiate with the employing household.

Using a Child-minder

Paying a person, almost always a woman (variously called Child-minder, family day-care, day mother), to look after a child in her home is often an informal arrangement that parents make with neighbours, in which case it is impossible to know the numbers involved. In the United States, where there is more specific information on Child-care workers, the total number of jobs was estimated at about 1.4 million in 2006, of which about 35 per cent were self-employed; mostly as family Child-care providers.

Increasingly governments are seeking to formalise this type of care by registering child-minders and setting standards. In a number of countries (such as France,

Singapore and the United Kingdom), there is a system for their registration and some minimum of training required, as well as local (of en municipal) information services which can help parents to find local child-minders. In Hungary, there is now the possibility for licensed family day-care services but they have been slow to develop, perhaps because they are less subsidised than nurseries and thus much more expensive for parents.

For children under the age of 3 who require Child-care, there seems to be a preference in some countries for care that is in homes rather than centres. In France, for example, 18 per cent of this age group were cared for by child-minders ("assistant maternelles") while 8 per cent attended creches. Research results suggest that working parents appreciate the convenience of a Child-minder whose hours are of en more flexible than those of a centre.

In Singapore, family day-care has been promoted by government as being particularly suitable for children from 2 to 18 months since they need more individual care and there is felt to be less risk of catching infectious diseases than in a centre with many children.

In some countries of Latin America, government programmes for the care of poor children have also used an approach which is home based. In Colombia, the Government set up the *Hogares Comunitarios* programme in the mid-1980s for poor children from birth to age 6 years. The programme now serves more than one million children. Households eligible for the programme form parent associations that elect a "community mother", who must meet minimal requirements set by the authorities. The community mother opens her home (*huger*) to as many as 15 children. She gives them three meals a day..

A major disadvantage of using child-minders is that they of en have little training and may not provide the stimulation and educational opportunities that children are more likely to receive in centre-based care.

The earnings of child-minders depend on the number of children in their care and the hours worked. In France, for example, a collective agreement fixes the minimum hourly salary to be paid by parents. In 2005, it was estimated that a full-time Child-minder earned 815 euro per month, which amounts to only 56 per cent of the average salary of full-time women workers in the private sector. The OECD estimates that unless family day careers operate in a market with weak supply and high demand, compensation in this field is considerably less than an average family wage and tends to be considered by the woman as a supplement to the main salary earned by a working spouse.

Using a Child-care Centre

Children under age 3 UNESCO estimates suggest that government programmes for the care of babies and toddlers are not available in many countries; just 53 per cent of countries have at least one formal early childhood programme before pre-primary education, accepting very young children (from birth or age 1). These programmes typically provide organised custodial care and, in some cases, health services and educational activities. They of en have limited coverage, targeting a small proportion of very poor families, with most families left to pay for whatever private facilities they can find and afford. In countries with no government programmes, any available services would be private.

The proportion of children under age 3 that use a Child-care facility do not seem to be available for a number of the developing countries, the exceptions being Brazil (15.5 per cent) and Chile (4 per cent). In Chile, about two-thirds of the children attending centres are in free public centres. The Chilean Government is currently working aggressively to expand the number of Child-care places for children under 3.

Among the industrialised countries, the proportion is particularly low (7 per cent) in Hungary where maternity leave combined with parental leave can last until the child turns 3. Estimates for France, the United Kingdom and the United States are much higher (27 per cent, 26 per cent and 30 per cent respectively), although it should be noted that these figures include child-minders as well as Child-care centres.

Child-care centres for children under age 3 are expensive to provide since this age group needs much more attention and each career can look after fewer children at a time than is the case with older children. Fees of en reflect the higher cost for younger children as seen in the Work-place case studies. In countries where there is little government support for day-care centres, the costs for working parents can be particularly high between the end of maternity leave and the start of pre-primary school. In the United Kingdom, for example, a full-time private nursery school costs over £8,000 a year, more than double the fees for university.

Staff in Child-care centres tend to include a few professionals (of en trained nurses) managing the majority of auxiliary staff who care for and interact with the children. The hiring of a high proportion of unskilled, low-paid women is common in Child-care perhaps because the work is seen as being primarily a question of physical care which can be carried out by women without training.

Children from age 3 to primary school According to UNESCO, all countries have one or more programmes at pre-primary level (from age 3 to the age of primary school enrolment) to prepare children for primary school.

If one considers the coverage of 3–5-year-olds, the champion in our group of countries is France with 100 per cent of each age group. For other countries, enrolment rates in preschool increase with age, with more than 90 per cent of 5-year- old children enrolled in preschool in Chile, Hungary and the United Kingdom. In the other industrialised country, the United States, coverage is much lower: 42 per cent of 3-year-olds and 77 per cent of 5-year-olds are in preschool.

It is interesting to note that in countries with a higher government commitment to Child-care (such as France, Hungary and Thailand), pre-primary schooling tends to have longer hours covering the full day, and thus is more useful to working parents. In Kenya, programmes run a full nine hours a day, although they are closed for three months of the year, posing problems for working parents in arranging care during the break.

Pre-primary education is much more likely to receive some public support than care for younger children. In France, Hungary and the United Kingdom, more than 90 per cent of all funding comes from public sources. In Brazil, 71.5 per cent of children in pre-primary are in free public schools. In Chile, private sources account for one-third of expenditures on pre-primary education, almost all of which comes from households. Reliance on private funds is much greater in the United States, where two-thirds of expenditure on pre-primary school for children aged 3 to 6 comes from private sources, half of which comes from households. When considering Child-care (rather than early childhood education), public expenditure tends to be much lower, with parents assuming a much greater share of the costs.

Governments may provide classes directly through the Ministry of Education or through local authorities or by voluntary or private organisations that receive some funding from government and have agreed to run services according to government regulations or specific contractual obligations. In most countries, some government provision exists alongside private pre-primary schools, which may have the advantage of longer opening hours.

In countries such as the United States and India, public provision of pre-primary education is not general but rather targeted at disadvantaged groups, in the States through the Head Start programme (although there is free pre-kindergarten for 4-year-olds in some localities) and, in India, through the Integrated Child Development Services (ICDS) programme, which targets children in rural and tribal areas and urban slums.

Staff in pre-primary schools, particularly when they are government employees, are more likely to be qualified as teachers and earning higher salaries than those in Child-care for younger children. Earnings for teachers in pre-primary and primary education are usually not high but are more than those of Child-care workers, who are of en near minimum wages. In the United Kingdom, for example, the full-time weekly income of workers in Child-care services and nurseries in 2004 was about 378 euro, less than half of the 842 euro of professionals working in primary and nursery education. In Kenya, although the ECD centres are public, many teachers are actually employed by the Parent–Teacher Association using funds from parental fees, which results in low and sometimes irregular pay.

Out-of-school care for schoolchildren Out-of-school care or supervision can be needed for school-age children before and after school, during the holidays and during lunch breaks. Out-of-school programmes can take a variety of forms and involve various types of activities including education, play, sports or physical supervision.

After-school care is a traditional public service in both France and Hungary, usually provided at the same school that the child attends. In Hungary, the after school day-care service is open from the end of the teaching hours to 5.30 p.m. With no charge except for snacks. About 42 per cent of the primary school population attends after-school care. In Portugal, there has been a dramatic increase in after-school care due to new legislation passed in 2006, making it compulsory for all primary schools to deliver after-school activities between the hours of 3.00 p.m. And 5.30 p.m.

In the United Kingdom and the United States, the need for after-school care is well recognised but services are relatively rare and of en at the cost of parents. In the United Kingdom, evidence shows that only 16 per cent of children in primary schools and 6 per cent of 12–14-year-olds use after-school clubs. In the United States, a survey of parents with children of primary school age found that 13 per cent were in "self care" after school. In South Africa, where primary school finishes at 2.30 p.m., there have been some recent efforts by government to extend extracurricular activities for children without adult supervision but these appear to be limited.

Canteens for children who cannot return home during lunch breaks also offer important supports for working parents. In France, care facilities and meals are provided at lunchtime for primary school students, and more than half of primary school students use this service, for which fees are means-tested. Even if the child has to bring a meal from home, a service for supervision during the lunch break can greatly help working parents.

Summer camps offering activities for children during school holidays also receive some public support in certain industrialised countries. Daily activities during school holidays are typically organised at primary schools or municipal centres. In Hungary, for example, day-care summer camps are of en offered by public schools and local municipalities, at much lower rates than private camps. In the United Kingdom, "holiday clubs" are organised in sports centres, youth clubs and churches but some can be quite expensive. The cost may be reduced somewhat in countries where expenses on holiday camps can be tax exempt as in the United Kingdom and United States.

In developing countries, out-of-school programmes tend to be rare and are mainly NGO activities for disadvantaged youth or private facilities unaffordable for most. Little information is available on how the vast majority of working parents are coping with the care needs of school-age children. In Thailand, Petrat suggests that, for school holidays, most children stay at home or are sent back to rural areas. One interesting type of service provider for workers is found in Brazil, where industries are legally bound to contribute 1.5 per cent of payroll to the Service Social a Industry (SESI) which has a wide variety of programmes for workers, including activities for their children after school and during school holidays.

Government Approaches to Child-care

Government policies and involvement in Child-care tend to reflect the prevailing ideologies in society about who is responsible for Child-care and about the labour force participation of women. This section looks at differences in the extent to which Child-care is seen as a public responsibility and at the reasons motivating government programmes for Child-care.

Perceptions of Government Responsibility

There are big differences among countries in how much governments and their citizens consider that supporting Child-care for working parents is a public responsibility. At one extreme, Child-care may be considered to be the responsibility of families, in which case government involvement should be minimal and laissez-faire, leaving it to parents to pay for non-family care bought on the market from a private provider if they need it.

At the other extreme are countries that view Child-care as a public entitlement and a responsibility of government. Most countries are in between, with very different approaches to the questions of whether and how to finance Child-care and how to provide it. National policies can, of course, change depending on the political party which is in power, as witnessed by the cases of Chile and the United Kingdom, where Child-care has recently moved up the political agenda. Child-care and other work–family policies have moved higher on the policy agendas of many countries in response to major social changes, such as the increasing entry of women into the labour force and changes in family structure, resulting in a lack of family support for Child-care. Economic concerns to increase the labour force participation of women are also driving governments to improve access to Child-care, as in the EU.

Among the countries in the current study, France and Hungary are the closest to considering Child-care as a public entitlement and both provide considerable public services. In such countries, the child-care "gaps" left by public services and the resulting problems for working parents and their employers tend to be less than in countries where there is less government intervention. In France and Hungary, estimated public expenditure on early childhood care and education constitutes a much larger proportion of GDP (1.0 per cent and 0.8 per cent respectively) than in the United Kingdom and the United States (0.5 and 0.48 per cent).

Government Objectives

In many countries, government does not have "a" Child-care policy but a multitude of policies with each involved ministry having its own objectives, plans and pro-grammes related to children or Child-care. In the country reviews, the number of different ministries mentioned as having some responsibility in relation to child-care is impressive: for example, Ministries of Education for the development of preschool education, Ministries of Social Welfare for support to NGOs providing Child-care to the disadvantaged, or Ministries of Youth and Sports for after-school activities for children.

The various government services involved in Child-care often tend to be focusing on the well-being of children in terms of health, nutrition, education and safety and may overlook the needs of working parents. In some countries, early childhood education programmes have grown dramatically in recent years, but the primary preoccupation is to prepare children for primary school, with little consideration for the needs of working parents in terms of the hours and duration of programmes. In other countries such as France, Hungary, Kenya and Thailand, full-day programmes at pre-primary level are more helpful to working parents. Where public policy stems from concerns regarding employment growth, women's labour force participation and gender equality, public supports for Child-care tend to be more closely aligned to the needs of working parents.

Ministries of Labour in some countries recognise the problems of working parents but of en have many other priorities that take precedence. Moreover, they do not usually have any expertise or mandate concerning Child-care, the exception being where creches are required by labour law (as in Brazil, Chilè or India) and can be subject to labour inspections. Nevertheless, these ministries can and some-times do play decisive roles in inserting the care needs of working parents into the policy agenda for Child-care and education.

The case of **Brazil is interesting** since there is an ongoing effort to pro-vide integrated services and coordinate efforts for Child-care. But in recent consultations, there was no participation of the labour sector (Ministry of Labour, employers or trade unions) in discussions despite legislation requiring Work-place 6). Therefore the needs of working parents and of employers concerning Child-care provision would not seem to be represented in decisions about Child-care reform.

Government Funding Strategies

Basically, there are two main strategies for government funding of Child-care:

1. Funding the supply of Child-care by giving subsidies to facilities or supplying services directly; and
2. Funding the demand for Child-care by providing subsidies to parents.

These strategies are not mutually exclusive and can be combined. For example, the UK Government does both. On the demand side, it supports parents through tax exemptions and the Child-care element of the Working Tax Credit for low-income parents. On the supply side, it has a system of grants to providers, as well as directly setting up children's centres in poor areas.

Financing Facilities

By financing Child-care facilities, government helps to ensure that there is a supply of Child-care available. Direct government funding and provision of facilities is most common for early childhood education for children over age 3, although hours may be short and the coverage far from complete. Providing or subsidising Child-care for children under age 3 is more rare.

Responsibility for Child-care provision is often decentralised, with funds going to local governments, which have the major task of ensuring Child-care provision (which sometimes but not always includes pre-primary education) within a framework of government standards, regulations and oversight. Thus municipal-ties can have a major role in organising Child-care and may also contribute some of the funding.

Decentralising the funding and provision of Child-care to the local level has the potential advantage of making services more responsive to local needs – including those of local work-places.

Apart from direct public provision of services, government funding to facilities may be in the form of subcontracts to Child-care service organisations or grants. These contracts or grants may be the responsibility of municipalities or of a line ministry. Grants to providers can sometimes be used for capital expenditure to encourage start-ups, and at other times may apply to recurrent expenditures such as staff salaries, rent or meals.

In some countries (such as Hungary, Singapore or Thailand), Work-place Child-care centres can benefit from public grants to providers. In Thailand, the creches organised by the trade unions were receiving some sup-port from the municipalities in terms of milk subsidies which, given their limited budgets, was a welcome assistance. Singapore provides grants to licensed centres for children of working mothers.

To conserve resources and target those most in need, governments may concentrate on creating or subsidising facilities in specific disadvantaged regions, so that the poor in that area may benefit. However, such programmes may fail to benefit the equally poor in other regions that have no facility. T is has been a criticism of the children's centres in the United Kingdom, where fully one-half of at-risk children live outside the disadvantaged areas designated for setting up these centres. Another problem of targeted facilities is the potential segregation of low-income children.

Funding Parents

In countries with a more market-based approach to Child-care, governments tend to prefer to give funding support for Child-care to parents, who can then decide what facility they want to use. Financing demand for Child-care rather than providing public facilities or public support to facilities has been viewed as a means to rapidly stimulate the creation of Child-care services (mainly private), allowing greater sensitivity to parents' needs, bringing innovation and efficiency to the sector, and reducing government expenditures. An additional advantage of programmes providing subsidies to parents is that they can offer governments a way of targeting support to those most in need and can make support contingent on certain factors such as income, ages of children, employment and number of hours worked, like the Child-care element of the Working Tax Credit in the United Kingdom.

A common form of government subsidy to parents is through tax systems whereby working parents can claim reductions based on Child-care expenses. In the United States, this is one of the main ways the federal government provides support to working parents for Child-care (as well as elder care). However, the poor who do not pay tax do not benefit and those in higher tax brackets would benefit more than those in lower ones. Other governments have systems for financial transfers to parents using registered Child-care – the amount being greater for lower-income parents.

However, parental subsidies also have their shortcomings. The amount of the subsidies is of en low compared to the cost of good-quality care and so recipients may tend to choose cheaper, poorer-quality care options. In the United States, where some states provide vouchers for poor families, programmes have been criticised because the value of the vouchers is so small that receiving families cannot pay for high-quality care. The OECD suggests that funding Child-care through parental subsidies weakens the steering capacity of government services and tends to lead to the proliferation of family day-care, characterised by lower standards and quality than professional Child-care centres.

A further problem with providing subsidies to parents is that they may have difficulty in judging the quality of the services proposed, particularly in countries where there is a weak or nonexistence official system for registering or licensing child-minders. In addition, when low-income parents must cope with bureaucratic difficulties to make their claim for the subsidy, many who are eligible may not actually profit. In the United Kingdom the recent experience with the Working Tax Credit shows that low-income families of en have difficulty claiming their due and take-up has, so far, been low.

Whether through support to parents or to facilities, there seems to be general agreement that substantial government funding and interventions are needed in order for parents – particularly less affluent ones – to have access to Child-care they can afford that is of a reasonable quality. The OECD has concluded from a review of experience in 20 countries that sustained public investment is needed in Child-care (either directly to services or indirectly through parent subsidies) in order to ensure both affordability to parents and quality of services. But even among OECD countries, it is considered that investment by many governments is inadequate.

Balancing Quality and Cost

Those who pay for Child-care, whether they be parents, national governments, municipalities, NGOs, employers, private providers or some other entity, are caught in the inherent conflict between ensuring the quality of the care as well as its affordability. Cutting costs tends to mean reducing the quality while ensuring quality increases the cost. T is dilemma raises important policy questions about the setting of quality standards and the conditions of work of Child-care workers.

Setting Quality Standards

In order to ensure that Child-care environments are safe and healthy and that practices promote children's development and learning, most governments have regulations or standards that relate to Child-care centres (including those that are employer sponsored). In some countries, regulations or standards relating to child-minders also exist. Child-care quality is usually assessed by indicators such as:

1. Staff -to-child ratios;
2. Group size;
3. Premises and space;
4. Age-appropriate curricula and settings;
5. Hygiene and safety standards;
6. Staff qualifications and training; and
7. Staff salaries and turnover.

Each indicator has major implications for the cost of providing Child-care which will be greater when there are fewer children per staff member, smaller groups, more spacious and better equipped facilities, and highly qualified and well-paid staff.

Concern about quality raises major issues for poorer countries and locations where resources are scarce. What are the key elements of "high-quality" care? As an Indian writer remarks: "If high quality is defined as the use of highly trained and motivated teachers or care-givers, a scientifically tested curriculum, a rich variety of educational and other stimulation materials and a stress on staffing ratios and good physical structures, then what does this imply for poor countries?"

Importing standards from developed countries may be unrealistic for many developing country settings where facilities that do not meet standards of "high quality" may nevertheless improve the situation for children at risk.

Conditions of Work of Child-care Workers

In efforts to provide Child-care which is affordable and also of high quality, it is of en the Child-care workers who are "squeezed" by low salaries or high numbers of children per worker, or both. As noted by the UK trade union UNISON, "It is important that affordable Child-care is not provided at the expense of Child-care workers."

An interesting finding about the quality of Child-care is that the well-being of the children is particularly related to the nature of the interaction between the staff and the children. One of the key aspects of quality is a consistent and warm Child-care. UNESCO notes that the importance of the relationship between the adult care giver and the child is encouraging for those working in resource-poor situations where physical features are hard to address. But this finding also underlines the importance of careful selection of Child-care workers, adequate levels of staffing (staff -to-child ratios), and working conditions that permit this kind of interaction and promote continuity of their employment.

In virtually all countries, turnover of Child-care staff is high. In Kenya, the annual turnover rate of 40 per cent of trained ECD teachers is attributed to the poor remuneration and lack of supports. A 2004 survey of the Child-care work-force in Australia reported a turnover rate of 32 per cent and suggested that priorities for retention should be better pay, status, paid in-service training and more time for preparation. As the US Department of Labour notes in its career guide concerning future opportunities in child day-care services:

Job openings should be numerous because dissatisfaction with benefits, pay, and stressful working conditions causes many to leave the industry. Replacement needs are substantial, reflecting the low wages and relatively meagre benefits provided to most workers.

Since most workers in Child-care for preschool children are women, it is not really seen as a profession and the skills involved tend to be undervalued. Looking after children is perceived as a capacity possessed by all women and training is not really necessary – 'any woman can watch children' is the assumption. The OECD notes the need for a new vision recognising the requirements for well-trained professionals who can support the language and social development of young children and the child-rearing skills of parents. If parents and society in general were more aware of the skills needed, they might be more willing to pay better wages for the service.

10

The Global Jobs Crisis

The economic crisis which befell the global economy in 2009 the worst since the Great Depression of the 1930s – has had a profound impact on the world of work. The global policy response to stabilise financial markets and revive global growth has been unprecedented and there are encouraging signs of a rebound in economic growth. Recovery, however, will not be achieved until the employment situation improves in a sustainable manner.

Experience from past crises shows that the labour market tends to recover long after economic growth resumes. The impact of the crisis on the quality of employment is often more profound. In the aftermath of previous crises, wages were depressed over a sustained period, the incidence of informality increased and many small enterprises went out of business. These trends suggest that the career prospects of many workers will be hit, in some cases on a permanent basis. In addition, post-crises labour markets are often characterised by a high incidence of long-term unemployment and labour market detachment. These trends will not only affect the well-being of many workers and their families but will also depress long-term growth prospects. Immediate action to mitigate these pervasive labour market and social effects is therefore crucial.

Immediate Labour and Social Impacts

This section analyses the depth and intensity of the current economic crisis in the world of work. It examines changes in the labour market since the onset of the crisis in terms of job losses, changing employment patterns and labour market attachment.

In 2007, the rapid employment growth that preceded the crisis began to slow and, by 2008, all regions of the world experienced a deceleration of employment growth. Eventually, the situation worsened and translated into significant employment losses. In high GDP per-capital countries, over 10 million jobs have been lost since the fourth quarter of 2008. Job losses began even earlier in a number of countries including the United Kingdom and the United States (with financial sector jobs being the first casualty).

Emerging and developing economies (medium and low GDP per-capita) are facing many of the same challenges, but the nature of the country-level impacts also varies considerably. In the countries for which information is available, employment losses are estimated to total more than 10 million to date–nearly 9 million in the first quarter of 2009 (of which Brazil, China, the Russian Federation and South Africa accounted for over half). But Turkey, where employment declined by more than 2 million between the third quarter of 2008 and the first quarter of 2009 has also been dramatically affected as the reduction of private capital inflows had a substantial effect on countries with large current account deficits and limited ability to borrow from abroad. For the second quarter of 2009, employment losses are slowing for this group with some countries showing a return to positive employment growth while others continue to experience jobs losses.

Job losses, however, provide only a partial and incomplete picture of the global jobs crisis. To a certain degree, job losses have been mitigated by working-time reductions and other employment retention practices. Such practices reduce the social costs typically associated with job losses but also allow firms to avoid the excessive costs involved in firing and rehiring.

Indeed, most developed countries (for which data are available) have experienced significant falls in working hours since the start of the crisis. Per cent on average (fgure 1.2). All 37 countries analysed (except one) have experienced declines over this period. This is in stark contrast to the increases (25 of 36 countries) experienced in hours worked between 2007 and 2008.

This has translated into an increased incidence of part-time employment in many countries since the onset of the crisis. For example, in Estonia, part-time employment rose over 5 percentage points to reach 12 per cent in 2009. The increasing incidence of part-time employment has helped, to varying degrees, of set job losses and, therefore, to provide a stimulus to aggregate demand. In Canada, for example, 43 thousand part-time jobs were created in the first and second quarters of 2009 (compared to more than 105 thousand full-time jobs lost). Yet it is important to note that working hour reductions may not have necessarily translated into increases in part-time employment, e.g. workers could be working 33 hours instead of 37 or 23 hours instead of 25 with no change, necessarily, in employment status.

In some countries, working-time reductions have been supported by governments through subsidising partial unemployment policies. This policy has been adopted, for example, in France, Germany and the Netherlands to protect against additional job destruction in the short run with the expectation that the economy will resume growth in the near future. Others include wage moderation, e.g. in the case in the Republic of Kŏrea. Of course, another important consideration is the capacity of existing labour market institutions to absorb economic shocks and to mitigate immediate negative labour market impacts, e.g. a steep rise in unemployment.

In many countries, both advanced and developing, the extent of the employment losses due to the current crisis is (for the time being) dramatically lower compared to reductions in output. In fact, in examining GDP and employment changes during past crises, a number of important observations emerge in comparison to the present situation:

1. The gap between declines in output and employment was smaller during the previous crises (with the exception of Argentina, Mexico and the United States).
2. There were cases in which deterioration in employment exceeded those of output (such as in Brazil, Canada and Italy).

Labour Retention

While employment falling less than GDP has helped cushion the current jobs crisis, the issue arises of whether job retention can continue for much longer. With a weak economic recovery expected, there is a risk that currently retained workers will join the ranks of the unemployed and, thus, the global jobs crisis may worsen in the short term. In fact, if employment were to exhibit a similar relationship to GDP as was the case during earlier crises (as demonstrated above), the number of jobs currently at risk is in the order of 5 million. The risk is high as firms' and government budgets are increasingly constrained and the policy of partial benefits and similar measures are phased out or retracted. This could prolong what is already expected to be a slower labour market recovery compared to previous downturns.

The above analysis also suggests that labour market recovery depends critically on the speed with which firms will begin their hiring processes. If firms tap into existing resources first, i.e. increase the working hours of existing employees, and thus delay the hiring process, this would worsen employment prospects of disadvantaged groups, including new entrants and the unemployed.

Even as employment opportunities decline, some individuals have little choice but to continue their job search. Consequently, as the crisis prolongs, there is an increased risk of long-term unemployment. This was the case in previous recessions where the share of unemployed workers still looking for a job after a year or more continued to rise – and in most cases never returned to pre-crisis levels. In the EU-15, during the early 1990s, the incidence of long-term un-employment among prime-age workers (25-54) rose over 8 percentage points to reach over 50 per cent. During the recession of 2001, the rate had not yet fallen back to its 1991 level before it began to increase again, although less dramatically and for a shorter period. For older workers (55 and over) in the EU-15, similar trends are apparent except the increases were more dramatic, persisted for a longer period of time and at much higher rates. For the rest of the OECD similar trends emerge, i.e. increases were more dramatic in the 1990s compared to 2001, the impact was more severe for older workers in terms of intensity and duration, and for both age groups the incidence of long-term unemployment has yet to recover to the levels of the early 1990s.

As job-seekers experience increasing difficulties in finding employment, the likelihood that they leave the labour market entirely increases. In some countries, there are already signs of declining overall labour force participation rates. Available data suggests that since the beginning of 2009, labour force participation rates have decreased in most OECD countries, with the exception of Australia, France, Italy, Japan, and Luxembourg. In other countries such as Canada, Ireland, Sweden and the United States, overall participation rates began to decline even earlier, i.e. in early to mid-2008. If participation rates fall as little as 0.4 per-centage points among high GDP per-capita counties over the period 2009-2012, the number of inactive persons could rise by over 12 million.

Such trends often have pervasive effects on vulnerable groups such as older workers and youth. For youth, there are already early signs of declining labour market activity in the United Kingdom and the United States, where participation rates for youth workers have declined over 2008 and 2009 by around 2 and 4 percentage points respectively. Unless these drops in participation rates are matched by increased school enrolment, a sustained period out of the labour force can permanently compromise future employment prospects for youth workers and risk a mismatch between labour demand and supply once economic activity picks up.

In many cases, the desire to work is still there but many have become discouraged. In the United States where the trend in job losses began as early as December 2007, there are clear signs of discouragement: in October 2009, 800 thousand US workers were considered to be discouraged. This is nearly double the level found a year earlier and approximately one-quarter of a million more discouraged workers than during the peak after the most recent recession at the end of 2000. The concern is that the level of discouraged workers will continue to rise, as it did for four consecutive years in the United States following the 2001 slow-down. Other countries, with similar available data (e.g. Mexico, Hungary, South Africa and the United Kingdom) exhibit similar upward trends.

For developing countries, current data on participation rates is rather limited but similar trends occurred in countries affected by the Asian crisis. For working-age (15-64) men the trend decline in participation rates lasted between two years (Indonesia) and, in some cases, has yet to recover. Looking forward, for medium and low GDP per-capita countries, if participation rates among men fall by only 0.7 percentage points, the number of men exiting the labour market could rise by over 24 million by 2012. Taken together, almost 43 million persons over the period 2009-2012 could enter inactivity or long-term unemployment.

In many developing countries, when formal jobs are scarce, rather than long-term unemployment or discouragement the concern is that jobless workers tend to move into the informal sector due to the lack of social security provisions. Although data on informality are scarce and definitions vary, analyses of previous crises seem to support these predictions. In addition, evidence from previous crises illustrates that, once individuals move to the informal sector, it is difficult for them to return to regular employment. 10 Indeed, looking at six recent financial crises for which data are available, the following observations emerge:

1. Informality tends to increase immediately post-crisis, though the extent of the increase varies; and,
2. In some countries, informality returns to pre-crisis levels after two to three years, while others experience increased informality levels persisting even after five years.

These risks (including rising long-term unemployment, more prevalent inactivity, and increases in informality) are particularly unwelcome developments and as past experiences show, they are very difficult to reverse and can have profound impacts on recovery potential in a number of ways.

First, the stigma associated with an extended period out of the labour force can hinder efforts to find a new job once a recovery is under way, often giving rise to a permanent mismatch of skills between those offered and those demanded. Indeed, workers who remain without a job for a long period of time experience a loss of skills and deterioration of their general human capital. In this respect, if labour demand recovers, measures aimed at encouraging a return to the labour market could prove quite expensive.

Second, increased recourse to informal employment may increase the vulnerability of a country to shocks. Estimates show that countries with above average sized informal economies are more than three times as likely to suffer adverse effects of a crisis (higher cyclical volatility) than those with lower rates of informality. In addition, previous crises have shown that, as the informal economy expands it may generate substantial further downward pressure on informal-economy wages – which, before the current crisis were already declining. Also, to the extent that most informal employees are underemployed, a fall in hourly wages may push informal employees to take up two or more informal jobs or to extend their working hours (if they are self-employed). This will affect their future re-employment chances in the formal economy.

Finally, there is the risk that perceptions of unfairness and mistrust linked to the crisis will rise and potentially lead to social unrest. Already, in spring of 2009 the Edelman Trust Barometer reported that 60 per cent of respondents felt that their level of trust in corporations has dropped since 2007.12 And only 28 per cent of respondents in the United States believe that, even after a US$800 billion stimulus package, the Government has made real progress in fixing the issues caused by the crisis.

Consequently, even though the International Monetary Fund (IMF) now predicts that global economic growth will return to positive territory (3.1 per cent) in 2010, the recovery is rather fragile especially as regards the labour market. In fact, the crisis in the labour market is far from over. Indeed, the negative employment effects of crises, especially financial crises, tend to persist long after the start of an economic recovery.

LongOterm Under-Employment and Limited Social Protection

The purpose of this section is to gauge the extent of the expected negative effects of the current crisis on the labour market. This is important given the likelihood that the global jobs crisis is prolonged. It is also important to remember that a labour market recession (with profound implications for individual welfare) is also likely to dampen economic recovery (through lower wage growth and reduced potential output) and, in turn, potentially jeopardise efforts to restore fiscal sustainability.

As new employment opportunities become scarce, the immediate challenge for workers will be to continue to seek ways of replacing lost income to reduce the likelihood of a social crisis. But many workers, both formal and informal, do not have access to appropriate support mechanisms.

In some countries, the first order response to mitigating income loss is via temporary support in the form of unemployment benefits or assistance. Un-employment benefit systems – if well-designed – can play a critical role in alleviating the initial impacts of income loss by providing income support and other measures of assistance (e.g. job search assistance and training).

However, the coverage (amount and extent) of benefits and support measures available to individuals varies significantly across countries and regions. Two-thirds of countries for which data are currently available do not have unemployment insurance schemes in place to help job-seekers bridge the income gap. Of equal concern is the fact that even within countries with support systems in place, their effective reach is often very limited, which means that, on a global scale, there is a significant gap in income support coverage for unemployed workers. The variation between regions in terms of the share of the unemployed who are not receiving unemployment benefits. For example, in Advanced Economies, the share of unemployed persons not receiving benefits is just under 50 per cent. This rises to over 70 per cent in Asia and Central and Eastern European countries, and over 80 per cent in other emerging and developing regions.

In light of the crisis, some countries have extended their unemployment benefit systems, by increasing entitlement amounts, making eligibility criteria less strict or extending the length of time over which unemployed workers can receive benefits.

In most developing countries, the provision of social security measures, including unemployment benefits, is confined to a small section of formal sector workers (i.e. coverage and eligibility are typically limited to those who participate in the labour market within legally recognised employment relationships). However, in developing countries between 40 and 93 per cent of the work-force are in the informal sector and as section A illustrated increased recourse to informality is likely. And although, in some countries, social security provisions also apply to informal wage and self-employed workers, such coverage is rather limited.

Informal sector workers: with respect to health provisions (i.e. disability, work injury or sickness and maternity), less than 10 per cent of Middle Eastern countries have measures in place to cover informal wage workers (fgure 1.12, panel A). In Asian and Latin American countries, less than 40 per cent of countries have provisions in place for these workers. Similarly, few countries have old-age and widow/survivor pension schemes in place for informal wage workers; the totals range from 18 per cent of countries in the Middle East to 37 per cent in Africa. Even fewer countries have provisions for unemployment benefits or family allowances for informal wage workers. *Self-employed workers*: for these workers, there appears to be a greater number of schemes in place, especially with regard to disability and pensions, where one-third or more of countries have provisions of this nature. This is particularly the case in Latin America, where the incidence rises to two-thirds of countries or more. However, there remain important gaps: Latin America aside, less than 25 per cent of countries have provisions for work injury, unemployment or family allowances for self-employed workers. Similarly, more than half of the countries do not have pension provisions for self-employed workers (the exception, once again, is Latin America).

It is important to emphasise that, even in countries where social security schemes exist there is often a significant gap between the *provision* of social protection and the numbers of individuals who are *effectively* covered – as was the case above with respect to unemployment benefit systems. Data for a selection of countries in Africa, Asia and Latin America indicate such gaps between provision and coverage.

In this respect, the gap between formal and informal sector workers widens when examining the case of urban wage workers. For example, even in countries where social security coverage is relatively high for formal wage workers (e.g. more than 80 per cent in Chile, Costa Rica and Uruguay), it is less than half for informal wage workers. In most other Latin American countries, coverage is typically lower–ranging from 38.5 per cent to 78 per cent for formal wage workers – compared to less than 20 per cent for informal wage earners.

Consequently, given that so many workers lack adequate protection, the severe employment losses precipitated by the current crisis give rise to even greater concern in terms of their social impacts. The reality is that the majority of workers do not have a safety net to rely on in times of need. So, the schism is twofold– not just between employed and unemployed, but dividing those who have access to social protection and those who do not. Given the time it will take for the labour market to recover, this disparity may widen unless appropriate action is taken.

To date, significant efforts have been made to rescue the financial sector and restore confidence in financial markets - though, very little has been done to address the key failures of the financial system that lie behind the crisis. Fiscal and monetary policies have also been successful in stimulating an economic revival. However, the recent rebound in world output and equity markets should not mask the fact that, as shown in the previous two sections, the crisis which erupted in October 2008 still grips the world of work and is expected to do so for some time. According to some, however, governments can no longer afford further fiscal stimulus measures and they should therefore consider exit strategies.

In addition to financial rescue packages and monetary measures, most countries have intervened to tackle the crisis by introducing fiscal stimulus packages – the sizes of which vary considerably across countries. Globally, the IMF has reported that the average size of discretionary fiscal measures in 2009 is 1.9 per cent of GDP in advanced G20 countries and 2.2 per cent of GDP in emerging and developing G20 countries.

Given the magnitude of these expenditures, many countries (advanced and major emerging) are expected to incur significant fiscal deficits in 2010. Reflecting budget deficits and measures to bail out some financial institutions, almost all countries are likely see increases in their gross public debt as a percentage of GDP. Policy-makers are now concerned about how to scale down and limit further interventions in order to re-balance budgets and stabilise public debt. To shed light on the possible trade-offs between fiscal and employment goals, a macroeconomic model has been used. The potential scenarios for public intervention and spending include:

1. No intervention: public spending is kept constant. This case is used as a bench-mark to compare the relative performances of alternative fiscal policies;
2. Reduction in public spending with a view to debt stabilisation;
3. Public spending in response to changes in employment: fiscal authorities use employment losses (or gains) to determine increases (or decreases) in public spending.

Against the backdrop of the expected continued weakening in the labour market, the main finding illustrates that when fiscal authorities deploy spending in response to the level of employment, employment losses would be 7.2 per cent lower compared with no intervention. Whereas reducing public spending in an attempt to stabilise the level of public indebtedness could further increase employment losses by 6.9 per cent, prolonging the jobs crisis and potentially dampening recovery prospects. Moreover, while introducing employment-related measures would require expenditure outlays and thus raise public deficits in the short term, the potential gains to employment and output means that the increase in public debt is temporary and in the medium-term returns to its pre-crisis level.

Governments must carefully weigh concerns about levels of public debt, while considering that an overly hasty retraction of fiscal measures could generate even greater job losses, delay recovery and put even more pressure on public finances at a later date. Therefore, the challenge for policy-makers is to design short-term policies that address immediate labour market weaknesses and at the same time are consistent with efforts to address underlying issues. Achieving this balance can provide a solid basis for enduring recovery while maintaining reasonable levels of public debt. The ILO, through its Global Jobs Pact has proposed a range of crisis response measures to address the global jobs crisis while supporting the recovery process more broadly. Even in countries with shrinking fiscal space, elements of the Global Jobs Pact could prove beneficial in aiding a quicker and more sustainable recovery process – through such avenues as public infrastructure development, social protection, support for vulnerable groups and labour market skills and training programmes. Such policies would go a long way towards addressing labour market imbalances and helping to avoid the re-emergence of another global crisis in the future.

Global Jobs Pact

Some countries have devised policies in the spirit of the Global Jobs Pact and have not only shown resilient economic growth but are also witnessing early signs of a labour market recovery. The cases of Australia and Brazil—both large commodity exporters with adequate fiscal space—are interesting in this regard:

1. Economic growth in Australia was similarly supported by public infrastructure investment but aided by maintenance of household expenditures - of which increased social assistance to targeted groups was a significant catalyst. Labour market retention also helped to prop up employment until economic activity rebounded.

2. In Brazil, job creation and a rebound in economic activity were the result of steps taken to increase household income, which boosted domestic private consumption, and improvements in social assistance programmes, such as unemployment benefit and conditional cash transfers.

In countries where the recovery is more muted, specific labour market and social policies have aided the recovery process and provided critical support to those most in need:

1. In Germany, while declines in GDP growth at 3.8 per cent in the first quarter of 2008 have been the steepest in 40 years, job losses were limited by enhancements to existing schemes that support reduced working hours, work-sharing and partial unemployment benefits.
2. Cases such as Jordan show that, even with limited fiscal space, countries have been able to design Global Jobs Pact-friendly policies that have had positive impacts. Jordan has successfully increased provisions and support for poor families and vulnerable unemployed, while maintaining its commitment to universal social security.
3. The Republic of Korea's economic and labour market recovery has been more tepid but policy has been successful in reducing unemployment through job-sharing and negotiated wage restraint and providing targeted social assistance to the most vulnerable groups, particularly youth and the recently unemployed;

Of course, each country has a different level of policy space, resources and capacity to respond to the crisis. There is no "one size fits all" policy. Each country has been affected by the crisis in different ways prompting varying policy responses. Some of these measures, however, highlight ways in addressing labour market and social challenges that have helped support a broader recovery.

Making Finance Work for the Real Economy

Considerable support has been provided to the financial sector in developed countries as part of the response to the crisis.

Indeed, the crisis has highlighted the perverse effects of "financialisation"–an increasingly important role of financial markets in the operation of the non-financial sector. First, financialisation has reduced the scope for development of the real economy. Financial sector's share of total corporate profit reached 42 per cent before the crisis, up from about 25 per cent in the early 1980s. Furthermore, financial sector's profit as a share of total wages and salaries of all private sector workers increased from 24 per cent to 40 per cent in the period from 1990 to 2005. The sector has attracted many of the best qualified personnel, employing over 40 per cent of graduates from the most prestigious business schools. While real wages in the non-financial sector stagnated over the past 15 years or so, they grew significantly in the financial sector–driven by growing real compensation for the executives, traders and other qualified financial personnel.

Second, within the non-financial sector, incentives are increasingly driven by capital markets and the imperative for quick and better financial returns:

1 During the 2000s, less than 40 per cent of profits of non-financial firms in developed countries were used to invest in physical capacity, which is 8 percentage points lower than during the early 1980s. By contrast, dividend payout have increased in all advanced economies and, in some cases, most of the new profits have been used to finance these dividends.

2 Ever-growing pressures for quick and better financial returns have had a disproportionate effect on wages and job stability in the non-financial sector, where most

workers are employed. Among the advanced economies, wage shares fell by over 9 percentage points during the period 1980–2005.

3 Leverage buy-outs (LBOs) – a manifestation of finance's growing role in the real economy – saw significant growth across the globe. Nearly 70 per cent of all LBOs (or US$2.7 trillion) occurred after 2001. LBOs have a direct impact on employment and wages – they can result in renegotiation of contracts and wages with employees, reduce employment in a firm as part of its restructuring deal and may have an adverse impact on pension schemes and retirement benefits for workers.

The financial and economic crisis has underscored a structural transformation that has taken place in terms of the financial sector's role in the global economy. In particular, financial markets and institutions have an increasing influence in the operation of the real economy (i.e. workers, entrepreneurs and businesses).

More generally, while there are several systemic problems that collectively led to the financial crisis, there is a broad consensus that the two major contributing factors were: (i) inadequate financial regulation, which led to excessive risk taking, growth in shadow banking, such as private equities and hedge funds, and the compensation practices that were aligned with risk taking; and (ii) failures of corporate governance, which led to an obsessive focus among non-financial enterprises on quarterly reporting obligations and the quest for quicker and better financial returns, not necessarily in the interest of the long-term needs of the enterprises in question.

In order to look beyond the crisis, and create a financial system which is sustainable and which serves the real economy more effectively, it is imperative to understand the imbalances that financial developments have created in terms of enterprises, jobs and incomes.

Financial Sector Growth vis-a-vis the Non-financial Sector

This section examines the impact of growth in this sector on the sustainable development of the real economy.

In the last 30 years, finance's share of GDP among advanced economies has increased tremendously. For example, in the United States, the sector's share increased from 13 per cent in 1970 to 20 per cent in 2007. Similarly, in the case of the European Union, finance's share of GDP doubled from 15 per cent in 1970 to 30 per cent in 2007.2 In the case of emerging economies, finance's share of GDP is around 10 per cent, while for most developing economies, it is 5 per cent or less.

Profits accrue primarily through financial channels rather than through trade and commodity production. For advanced economies, finance's share of corporate profit almost doubled from 25 per cent in the early 1980s to 42 percent in 2007. For example, in Australia, Italy and Japan, finance's share of profit doubled in the period from 1970 to 2005. In Spain and France, finance's share of profit increased by a factor of 1.5 while, for Germany, the share of profits since the 1990s has hovered around 44 per cent. The United Kingdom saw the most spectacular increase in finance's share of corporate profit from the 1980s to the 2000s – it increased by a factor of three.

Financial sector's profit in 2005 was two thirds of the wages and salaries of all private sector workers. It increased from 25 per cent in 1990 to 40 per cent in 2005 – a spectacular rise in a period of a mere 15 years. These trends point to structural transformations of the global economy where finance has become the driver of the real economy rather than an enabler or a supporter of the real economy.

Meanwhile, in the case of developing and emerging economies, finance's share of corporate profits has increased modestly and in some cases, there has been virtually no increase.

Permitting Higher Compensation vis-a-vis Wages

As the financial sector grew, the wage gap between financial and non-financial firms widened. For example, the real wage gap between financial and non-financial firms in the United States widened from US$11,000 in 1987 to US$40,000 in 2007. Meanwhile, in the European Union, the wage gap between financial and non-financial firms doubled from 1985 to 2005. These past trends in compensation in the financial sector have continued throughout 2008 and 2009. For example, some recipients of government bailout money through the Troubled Asset Relief Program (TARP) in the United States paid handsome bonuses to their employees in 2008. City group, Merrill Lynch (which does not exist anymore) and Wells Fargo paid bonuses, even while enduring massive losses. In the case of Goldman Sacks, JP Morgan Chase and Morgan Stanley, bonus payments per employee exceeded earnings per employee.

Studies have shown that, compared to the non-financial sector in the United States, wages in the financial sector increased considerably from the 1980s to 2000s and, in the case of executives, was not linked to firm performance. Before the 2008 crisis and the Great Depression, "the compensation of employees in the financial industry appeared too high to be consistent with a sustainable labour market equilibrium".

For example, controlling for education level and other observable characteristics, employees in the financial sector earned 3 to 4 per cent more than employees in the rest of the private sector during the 1970s. However, in the post-1980s world of deregulation and innovation, the wage premium in the financial sector rose to 20 per cent. Furthermore, a more recent study by Philippine and Reshef finds a robust and economically positive effect of deregulation on wages in the financial sector. It shows that financiers in the United States have been "overpaid by 30 to 50 percent since the late 1990s".

As the financial sector grew in size, it often attracted the best and the brightest. For example, among the Master of Business Administration graduates from the top ten business schools in the world (which includes universities in China, France, the United Kingdom and the United States), 40 per cent of the graduates took jobs in the financial sector, while 60 per cent took jobs in the non-financial sector. For some years, for example 2002/03, the breakdown was 50:50.

Even after adjusting for the self-selection bias of students going into business schools, it is evident that the financial sector has been receiving a disproportionate share of the best and the brightest graduates. Longer time series data, available for a few business schools, show that, in the 1990s and 2000s, the share of graduates taking jobs in the financial sector is significantly higher than during the 1970s and 1980s. The general trend mimics the increasing size and influence of the financial sector in the real economy.

Growth was Fuelled by Securitisation Practices

Securitisation of credit (the practice of parcelling and selling of loans to investors), has grown in prominence since the early 1980s, with particularly strong growth between 2003 and 2007. Securitisation performs two very useful functions, namely providing greater liquidity for investors and reducing risks for individual banks by distributing credit risk more widely. However, securitisation can also lead to a concentration of risks within the banking system itself when banks buy each other's securities with borrowed money, which is what happened in the lead up to the crisis of 2008–

09. Securitisation of mortgages reflected two new developments within the global financial system: (i) financial globalisation, where securitisation creates financial paper that is freed from national boundaries (hence, foreign investors with no direct access to America's homeowners could buy Mortgage Backed Securities originating from the US real estate market); and (ii) the relative decline of the importance of banks, where the lines between commercial and investment banks were blurred. As highlighted by recent developments, these two features (while not necessarily detrimental) have proven to be powerful multipliers of the crisis.

Growth in securitisation was enabled by an increasing reliance on debt – among advanced economies, debt to GDP ratio for financial institutions took off in the mid-1990s. Leverage (debt to equity ratio) increased among major banks (investment and traditional), in both the United States and Europe. In June 2008, the average leverage ratio for Europe's 12 largest banks was 35 to 1 and, in some of the largest banks, the ratio was 50 to 1. This is significantly in excess of the 10–15 to 1 ratio that is typical of a more conservative bank. Meanwhile, the largest American banks had a leverage ratio of 30 to 1, and 50 to 1 in some cases.

Financialisation of the Non-financial Economy

Not only has the financial sector absorbed a disproportionate and growing share of valuable resources but, in addition, its practices and values have penetrated the non-financial economy. This is because firms have increasingly been managed according to the reporting rules and short-term goals of capital markets. Corporate managers have adopted the behaviour of the financial markets and, as a result, their interests are more closely aligned with those of financiers than with the real economy.

Growing Share of Profits

An important indicator of the capital markets' growing influence in the real economy is the evolution of dividend practices. In the past several decades, the distribution of profits between interest payments, dividends and retained earnings has been drastically modified. The reduction of debt by firms during the 1980s and 1990s has led to a decreasing share of interest payments into profits net of taxes from 70 per cent in 1980 to 50 per cent in 2007. However, the decline in interest payments has not produced an increase in retained earnings, as dividends have increased. Retained earnings stayed constant at around 18 per cent of profits after taxes, while the share of dividends has increased from 20 per cent in 1990 to 40 per cent in 2007. Dividends as a percentage of total profits in the United States doubled from 22.8 per cent in 1946–1979 to 46.3 per cent in 1980–2008.

This trend cannot be explained by a changing pattern in financing investment, as new stocks represent scarcely 3.8 per cent of new security issues. On the contrary, a possible explanation might be the deep institutional transformations that have taken place at the firm level since the 1970s. These transformations have led to the increasing power of shareholders. The share of profits distributed to shareholders has therefore increased from 30 per cent of corporate profits before tax in 1990 to 48 per cent in 2002.

Elsewhere, average dividend pay-outs (i.e., the share of profits distributed to shareholders) show similar patterns. For example, dividend pay-outs between 1995 and 2000 were above 50 per cent for Germany, Italy and the United Kingdom.

It was above 40 per cent for Austria and France. The marginal payout between 2001–05, exceeded 70 per cent for France, Italy and Netherlands. It was above 40 per cent for

Finland and Spain and around 30 per cent for Australia, Austria, Denmark and Japan. Changes in the composition of pay, especially at the executive level, have further strengthened the influence of capital markets over non-financial firms.

As discussed in *World of Work Report 2008*, although annual salaries have been increasing, the proportion of total pay that they represent has decreased in the past 20 years, while compensation through stock options has become the most important component, increasing from 35 per cent to 77 per cent. Leverage in compensation – where incentives pay outweighs salary–has increased tremendously over the years, which in turn has increased risk taking. For example, in 1987, a short-term incentive award was 60 per cent of an average executive's salary but, in 2008, short-term incentive awards comprised 200 per cent of the salary. While it is true that tying executive pay to stock options tends to lead to increased sensitivity of pay to performance, it also tends to encourage short-termism that is, a singular focus on quarterly earnings.

These changes have affected real investment in these companies: first, the "crowding out" of operational investment, because non-financial corporations earn higher returns from financial investments than non-financial investments; second, due to the increased pressure on firms to pay higher dividends, firms find themselves having to distribute a higher share of profits to shareholders. The direct consequence of this is that the share of profits directed into financing internal growth is reduced.

Empirical evidence shows that the share of investment as a percentage of operating surplus between the 1980s and the 2000s declined in almost all the advanced economies. For example, for the EU, investment as a percentage of operating surplus declined from 47 per cent to 40 per cent, while for the United States it declined from 44 per cent to

39 per cent – a 5 percentage point decline in both cases. Some of the countries in Europe that have registered the sharpest declines are Austria (from 50 to 44 per cent), Finland (from 57 to 36 per cent), Germany.

Meanwhile, investment as a percentage of GDP has declined in the majority of advanced economies since the 1980s. For example, for high-income OECD countries, investment as a percentage of GDP declined by 3.1 percentage points from 1980 to 2006. Furthermore, in the same period it declined by 3.1 percentage points in the Euro Area, by 6.3 percentage points in Germany, by 8.7 percentage points in Japan and by a little over a percentage point in the United Kingdom and the United States.

The transformations in the financial sphere have altered the bargaining power within firms. Although shareholders support the risk *ex ante*, they have been able to reduce the risk they support *ex post*. Part of the risk has been transferred to employees and managers through flexible labour contracts and flexible wage income. For the five most financialised countries, wage share declined by 3.6 per cent over the period 1989 to 2005, while for the five least financialised countries, wage share declined by 2 per cent. More generally, the decline in the wage share documented in *World of Work Report 2008* can be partly ascribed to the growing pressures from capital markets for quicker and better returns.

To some extent, social dialogue may mollify the pressures arising from financialisation. For the five least unionised advanced economies, the percentage change in finance's share of corporate profit was the highest, while for the five least unionised, the percentage change in finance's share of corporate profit was the lowest. In other words, countries with the highest union densities saw the lowest increase in financialisation while countries with the lowest union densities saw the greatest increase in financialisation.

Leverage buy outs (LBOs)

Leverage buy outs (LBOs), which involve acquisition of a firm or division of a firm by private equity firms or other investors, provide a vivid illustration of the growing role of finance within the real economy. LBOs are typically sponsored by private equity funds, which have a limited life and a limited investment horizon, after which they have to exit their investments. A typical funding of a buy out involves two-thirds of debt and, therefore, access to a highly liquid capital market is essential for buy outs and the environment during the boom years of the 2000s was conducive to their growth. The firm that is taken over is known as the "target firm", and the investor funding the takeover is known as the "buy out sponsor" (which is usually a private equity). Private equity advocates argue that buy outs occur in old and declining industries but, in fact, buy outs occur in all sectors and industries, among both failing and growing firms. This section examines the growth in LBOs and their impact on the non-financial sector in terms of employment, wages and pensions.

LBOs have undergone a period of explosive growth in the past few years: 68 per cent of all LBOs around the world – US$2.7 trillion out of US$3.6 trillion occurred after 2001. The main features of LBOs are: (i) transfer of assets to a new company; (ii) increase in equity ownership of managers; (iii) increase in debt secured against the "target firm's" assets and/or future cash flows; and (iv) involvement of "buy out sponsor" in the monitoring of the firm.

The United States is the primary market for LBOs. From 2003 to 2007, the number of buy outs in the United States increased eightfold. But the LBO market is no longer primarily a US phenomenon – in the past few years, non-US buy out activity has grown more rapidly than that of the United States.

Outside North America and Western Europe, buy outs account for 7 per cent of all LBOs in value, but this number masks the true growth of buy outs in developing and emerging economies. For example, in Africa and the Middle East, buy outs have more than quadrupled over the past seven years compared to the previous 30 years. In the same period, the number of buy outs has more than doubled in Asia and increased by more than five times in Eastern Europe. Moreover, buy outs in developing and emerging economies tend to be large in relation to the GDP of those economies.

There is a general tendency for "quick flips" – re-listing or exiting companies within a year after taking them private – that is, taking the "target firm" public (stock exchange listing) or selling it to another investor (new "buy out sponsor"). Of all the private equity buy outs, 42 per cent exited within the first five years of the initial transaction. Furthermore, the holding period for LBOs has declined steadily over the years– "although LBOs sponsored by private equity funds are more likely to experience a successful exit, they are also somewhat more likely to have their investments end up in financial distress, controlling for other factors".

In the past few years, hedge funds have grown increasingly interested in private equity due to the solid returns such investments can offer. Due to the entry of hedge funds into the market, competition among lenders to provide funds to the leverage finance industry has increased leverage ratios, driven down borrowing costs, and loosened terms. Hedge funds traditionally have a more short-term perspective, and that changes the dynamics of operational overhaul that follows a typical buy out. Since this a relatively new phenomenon, this area has not been explored by academics (at least not by those without explicit corporate connections).

In 2009, more than half of the approximately 220 companies in the United States that have defaulted on their debt were either owned at one time or are still controlled by private equity firms. So it should come as no surprise that buy outs have a direct impact on employment and wages at "target firms". LBOs can renegotiate contracts and wages with employees, reduce staff levels in a firm as part of the restructuring deal and, in general, provide strong incentives for managers to make employment changes.

A study of 1,350 LBOs in the United Kingdom reveals that the employment impact of LBOs depends on the type of buy out. It is important to separate management buy outs (MBOs – where managers become significant owners) and management buyins (MBIs – which involve acquisition by external management and investors) because insiders and outsiders play different roles and the consequences in terms of employment and wages may be markedly different. Disaggregation the LBOs, Amess and Wright find (i) that wage growth is 0.31 percentage points lower for MBOs and 0.97 percentage points lower for MBIs, and (ii) employment growth is 0.51 percentage points higher for MBOs and 0.81 percentage points lower for MBIs. Even though the overall employment impact becomes positive in the case of MBOs, more than one-third actually report a reduction in employment. Meanwhile, in the case of MBIs, the overall employment impact remains negative, even after six years. Overall, the employment impact of LBOs is negative in more than one-third of all cases.

The majority of recent studies of LBOs in the United States show that they have a negative impact on employment. A study of 5,000 US firms (with about 300,000 establishments) acquired in private equity transactions between 1980 and 2005 shows that employment shrinks more rapidly in "target firms" than in "control firms" and that the average difference after two years is about 7 per cent in favour of control firms. Furthermore, employment grows more slowly in "target firms" than in "control firms". This is primarily as a result of job destruction in "target firms" because, in terms of job creation, both target and control firms fare equally well. Moreover, following a buy out by a private equity company, firms tend to engage in more acquisitions and disinvestment than control firms. Furthermore, the employment impact of buy outs also stems from the fact that some of the firms subsequently fail and go out of business – 6 per cent of all LBO transactions eventually fail and end up in financial distress – this is a higher failure rate in comparison to bankruptcy rates among the publicly traded firms in the United States.

Meanwhile, a study of buy outs in France during the 1980s and 1990s reveals that "target firms" post-buy out do not perform well. The study shows that the return on equity falls for the "target firms" after the buy out when compared to their industry counterparts. Furthermore, the same is true with regard to return on investment and margin ratios and also, post-buy out, their risk grows because of the increase in debt level and decrease in liquidity ratio. Contrary to the popular conception that buy outs occur in declining firms, management buy outs in France are carried out on firms whose financial situation is better than that of other firms in the same sector of activity.

Besides the adverse impact on employment and wages, buy outs could adversely impact pension schemes. As part of the buy out deal, the sponsor (usually private equity firms) may stop contributing to the pension schemes, resulting in employees' retirement plans being jeopardised. For example, this happens in a case where the "buy out sponsor" cashes out by selling the firm to the firm's employee stock ownership plan (which is meant to pay for the employees' retirements).

There are several research papers, commissioned by the private equity industry, which have a general tendency to show significant positive effects of buy outs on employment. However, most of the studies suffer from a number of flaws, both in sampling and data quality, "rendering their estimates of employment impact effectively worthless". One of the main reasons why it is difficult to have any confidence in evidence and statistics provided by the private equity industry is due to "information opacity" – unlike publicly listed companies, private equity companies are not required by law to disclose information. Moreover, they control the information that comes out of firms, making it difficult to trust survey results from this source.

11

Globalisation and Labour Provisions

Numerous approaches have sought to reconcile the objective to promote free trade with the provision of decent working conditions. Part of the discussion has concerned the insertion of a labour provision into the multilateral framework of trade regulation, which has proven to be difficult to achieve. Instead, this process has continued to unfold through different channels. At the international level, an important step was taken with agreement on the four Core Labour Standards (CLS), as defined in the ILO Declaration of 1998, which are further specified in the ILO's Fundamental Conventions. The CLS have been a point of reference for many labour provisions elaborated within trade agreements. More recently, the adoption of the ILO Declaration of 2008 has further elaborated the implications of such labour standards.

Labour provisions have been included in numerous trade arrangements, which can be characterised as unilateral trade arrangements, or trade agreements concluded by two or more parties. While many trade agreements only cover trade-related aspects, other so called integration agreements also deal with non-trade issues, such as infrastructure programmes. Labour provisions may be included into the trade instrument itself, or in accessory documents, such as side agreements or memoranda of understanding, the latter of which are usually not legally binding.

Labour provisions differ considerably with regard to their normative content and the legal implications they entail. These provisions may contain legally binding normative standards or have the nature of a political commitment. With regard to the normative content, some of these provisions commit countries to adhere to certain labour standards, which may refer to CLS, as embodied in the ILO Declaration of 1998 or to ILO Conventions. In other cases, labour provisions may commit countries to enforce labour standards under their own national labour law. In addition, some labour provisions commit the state parties to raise the level of protection of their labour laws progressively, or at least not to downgrade them with a view to promoting exports or investment. Labour provisions may also require or allow for cooperation and technical assistance on labour issues, in the form of exchange of information or technical or financial assistance.

The scope of the application of labour provisions in trade agreements also differs. The provisions may apply to labour issues concerning trade relations between the parties, or to any trade relations of either of the parties. They may, however, apply more broadly to labour issues, regardless of their links to trade relations.

Labour provisions may also be categorised according to their legal implications in the event of a breach of the respective obligations. Some trade arrangements provide for additional trade concessions if a country takes specific steps to comply with specific labour standards. In other cases, a breach of the labour provisions may allow the states concerned to withhold certain trade advantages provided for by the arrangements (such as tariff preferences). Disincentives may also be non-trade-related, such as monetary fines or a suspension of cooperative activities. Finally, some labour provisions do not provide for specific economic consequences in the case of a breach of the commitment but rather allow the parties to address the issue by regular monitoring by expert bodies, diplomatic consultations and/or cooperation activities (such as exchange of information or technical and financial assistance).

Labour Provisions in Trade Arrangements

Labour provisions were first introduced into the United States' Generalised System of Preferences (GSP) in 1984. This trade arrangement includes, as one of the conditions for eligibility for the trade preferences, that the country concerned "must have taken or is taking steps to afford internationally recognised worker rights". Submissions alleging a breach of this provision may be filed by the social partners and relevant civil society organisations. However, the US administration has a margin of discretion regarding the application of this provision. The United States has inserted similar labour provisions into its more far-reaching preferential trade arrangements, such as the Caribbean Basin Recovery Act, the Andean Opportunity Act and the African Growth and Opportunity Act.

Particularly noteworthy in terms of this development is the shift from a merely sanction-based approach to a twofold "carrot and stick" approach, involving both sanctions in the event of "systematic and serious violations" of the labour provisions and additional preferences in the event of full implementation of these rights. It should be emphasised that, rather than developing its own criteria for labour standards, the EU has consistently referred to the relevant ILO conventions. A significant development concerns the fact that, initially, the EU GSP only referred to some of the ILO Fundamental Conventions but, following the 1998 Declaration, the EU has successively increased the scope of its two labour provisions and has covered all ILO Fundamental Conventions since 2002.

The first agreement linking labour provisions to economic consequences is the North American Agreement on Labour Cooperation (NAALC) of 1994, a side agreement to the North American Free Trade agreement (NAFTA). The United States has developed this approach further in later trade agreements, an overview of which is provided.

While striving for a high level of protection, the earlier US trade agreements focus on the obligation to enforce national labour law in the area detailed by the respective agreements. Also, all agreements concluded after 1998 refer to the ILO 1998 Declaration, although the scope of the labour provisions does not necessarily fully incorporate those of the Declaration. However, this approach has changed recently. The most recent US trade agreements with Peru, Colombia, and the Republic of Korea, the latter two of which have yet to enter into force, require the parties to comply with the ILO's CLS, in addition to enforcing their national labour laws.

All of the agreements provide for a follow-up mechanism related to differences about the labour provisions, which may, as a last resort, lead to economic consequences for the party in breach of the labour provisions. The NAALC allows fines up to US$ 20 million. However, these only applied to three out of the eleven areas of labour law mentioned in the agreement. With the notable exception of the United States–Jordan Trade Agreement, all the later agreements with Australia, Bahrain, the Central-American countries and the Dominican Republic (CAFTA), Chile, Morocco and Singapore, opted for fines. These fines are intended to be paid into a fund designed to address the labour rights violations concerned, capacity building and other measures. This approach has been reversed again in the most recent generation of US trade agreements, which makes breaches of labour provisions subject to the regular dispute settlement mechanism, which applies to trade disputes under these trade agreements. It should be noted, however, that all of these dispute-settlement mechanisms emphasise the amicable resolution of disputes and usually include numerous stages of consultation and reviews through a panel and/ or other neutral bodies before any economic disincentives may be applied.

A unique approach has been undertaken with the United States–Cambodia Textile Agreement, which employed positive incentives rather than disincentives. Under this agreement, enhanced market access was offered in exchange for compliance with certain labour standards. For this purpose, a number of goals in terms of compliance with labour standards were defined at the inception of the Textile Agreement; for example, the quota for market access would be increased if the companies within the apparel sector–which account for 90 per cent of all Cambodia's exports – met the criteria.

Labour provisions in the context of Canada's trade agreements have undergone a development comparable to that in the United States, from focusing on mere enforcement of national labour law to requiring compliance with minimum labour standards. Labour provisions have not been included in the text of a Canadian trade agreement proper but, similar to the case of NAFTA, in special side agreements. Each of Canada's labour provisions, except that with Costa Rica, provides for fines in the case of noncompliance. The fines are to be gathered into a fund for the remediation of labour rights problems. They range from a maximum of US$ 10 million in the older trade agreements, to a maximum of US$ 15 million in the more recent trade agreements, and are without any limits in the case of the Trade Agreement between Canada and Jordan, which was signed in 2009 but not yet entered into force at the time of writing. All of these agreements provide for dialogue between the parties and include technical assistance. These activities are handled by a ministerial council for each agreement; assisted by national offices for each country. With regard to the enforcement mechanism, the emphasis is again on the amicable resolution of the dispute through consultation, rather than on the imposition of sanctions.

Aside from conditional provisions which link the compliance with labour standards to tangible economic consequences, a number of promotional labour provisions can be identified. Three African regional trade agreements contain a labour dimension. These labour provisions do not contain commitments to specific labour standards or specific levels of protection, but instead focus upon cooperation in labour matters. Trade agreements concluded by Asian countries and areas also increasingly involve a labour dimension, often in the form of side arrangements.

Most of these labour provisions emphasise cooperation in labour matters, mainly through exchange of information and joint projects. Almost half of these have created specific institutions in this respect. Also, almost all of these arrangements provide for some sort of additional commitments. Among these commitments, the requirement not to lower the level of protection of their national labour law in order to encourage trade and investment is the most widespread. Four of these labour provisions are contained in side arrangements or memoranda of understanding. These arrangements are typically not legally binding, although three of them provide for amicable consultations for the resolution of differences.

In the case of the Taiwan, China–Nicaragua Trade Agreement, the Japan- Philippines Trade Agreement, and the Japan-Switzerland Trade Agreement, labour provisions were incorporated into the trade agreement itself. While the Taiwan, China-Nicaragua Trade Agreement contains a commitment to comply with certain labour rights and to implement national law in these areas, the Japan-Philippines Trade Agreement and the Japan-Switzerland Trade Agreement only preclude the state parties from lowering the level of their labour laws with the intention of encouraging investment. Disputes regarding interpretation and application under all three agreements may be submitted to the regular dispute settlement body, although the agreements emphasise prior consultation in order to avoid such a dispute arising.

A special case is the Association of Southeast Asian Nations (ASEAN), established 1992. While not including labour provisions in the text of the agreement or a side arrangement, the ASEAN countries adopted an action plan on occupational safety and health in 2007. This action plan commits ASEAN member states to develop a checklist based on ILO's international labour standards and best practices, which aims to enable member states to align their policies. The action plan encourages the exchange of experiences and the involvement of the ILO through capacity building.

Also the labour provisions of the trade agreements concluded by the EU and other states have undergone a considerable evolution. Labour provisions in the EU's trade agreements priorities technical assistance and development cooperation. The main patterns in the EU's approach to the labour dimension in trade are presented.

Certain agreements provide for cooperation and dialogue in a number of different areas. Since the late 1990s, the EU has increasingly made reference to ILO CLS in its bilateral agreements and has emphasised the role of the ILO in this regard. The recent EC–Cariforum Trade Agreement of 2008 goes one step further. Referring to the ILO Declaration of 1998 and the concept of decent work, it submits the parties to a number of concrete commitments. Parties may request consultations in the event of differences over the labour provisions' interpretation and implementation which may involve the consultation of an expert committee and the ILO. If no dispute resolution is achieved within nine months, either party may bring the case before the regular dispute settlement mechanism. If no agreement is reached, temporary measures can be taken. However, these measures may not affect trade concessions but only deal with other issues covered by the agreement, such as cooperation activities. This agreement also includes a cooperative framework, which may provide a tool for capacity building in problematic labour areas in the Cariforum States.

Labour provisions in Latin American and Caribbean trade agreements first emerged in the context of regional integration during the 1990s. While the three trade agreements (i.e. the agreements on the Andean Community, the Caribbean Community and MERCOSUR) differ in terms of their integration approaches, they all include a social dimension, albeit added as a complement to the respective agreements in the form of a declaration or another instrument. The state parties of all three trade agreements commit to various labour provisions although, in the case of the Andean Community, this is limited to occupational safety and health. Each of these labour provisions provides for some follow-up, be it through technical cooperation or monitoring by a specific body or committee.

Latin American countries and areas have also included labour provisions in more recent bilateral trade agreements or related side arrangements. In particular, the gradual evolution of the labour provisions in Chile's trade agreements is noteworthy. This development started with labour cooperation (in the context of the Trade Agreement with China) and, successively, included a reference to the ILO Declaration (in its Trade Agreement with Australia) and comprehensive commitments to labour standards (in its most recent Trade Agreement with Colombia, which, however, does not provide for recourse to the Trade Agreement's regular dispute settlement mechanism, which may entail trade sanctions).

Practical Implications of Labour Provisions

Due to their decentralised character and their high proliferation, it is difficult to quantify trade arrangements, in particular trade agreements. The following calculations are based on the WTO Regional Trade Agreements Information System, which lists trade agreements notified to the WTO, and the UNCTAD web site, which lists GSPs currently in force. Two of the eleven existing GSPs include conditional labour provisions. Out of the 186 trade agreements that are in force and have been notified to the WTO, 37 include either conditional or promotional labour provisions.

The number of trade agreements with conditional labour provisions, as well as those with promotional labour provisions, have increased considerably during the past 20 years. While no agreement containing labour provisions had entered into force in 1990, the number had risen to 14 promotional and seven conditional provisions, respectively, by 2005.28 By 2009, a total of 20 promotional and 17 conditional labour provisions had entered into force. Particularly noteworthy, the share of trade agreements which include labour provisions has risen in recent years.

There has been an increase in the number of agreements to which only developing and emerging economies are parties. From zero in 1990, nine trade agreements including labour provisions have been signed to date between developing and emerging economies. An analysis of these provisions indicates that, with one exception, only promotional labour provisions have been involved in these cases. The US GSP and the EU GSP cover less than one-fifth and less than one-tenth, respectively, of the imports from the beneficiary countries concerned. Under the African Growth and Opportunity Act (AGOA), 69 percent of the imports from beneficiary countries are covered and the figure is about 60 percent in the case of Andean Trade Preference Act (ATPA). The special incentive arrangement of the EU GSP and the US Caribbean Basin Economic Recovery Act (CBERA) cover about one-quarter of the imports of the beneficiary countries concerned.

The economic scope of regional trade agreements is not easy to measure, due to the difficulty of determining the precise trade volume covered by trade agreements. Kawai Dean and Wignaraja recognise that it is challenging to establish the volume of a country's trade covered by trade agreements due to the numerous exceptions for specific goods provided within those agreements. The overall trade volume is often quite significant. The final relevance for the countries concerned will, however, depend on a number of specific factors (such as the importance of trade covered by the labour provision versus trade with other trading partners, or the extent to which social provisions are, or are not, implemented). On a more general note, the application of sanctions through a labour provision may also affect the reputation of the country, which may lead to disadvantages in economic and political relations with other countries. Depending on the specific situation, this may provide political leverage beyond the economic scope of the agreement.

The growing number of bilateral and regional trade agreements concluded in recent years, and the variation in the character and specific content of these agreements as noted above, also raises a coordination issue. Countries which have concluded agreements with several trading partners may find themselves subject to different labour provisions, depending on the trade agreement in question. This may result in a situation where a country may be bound to comply with diverging types of labour provisions.

In relation to the US GSP, provides details concerning the 57 cases examined by the US Trade Representative (USTR), from 1985 to 2007, 13 of which have led to the withdrawal of preferences. In five cases, the preferential treatment was later reinstated. In 2008, the USTR accepted two new complaints, which are still under examination.

In the case of the EU GSP, two investigations have led to the withdrawal of trade preferences since the introduction of the labour provisions into this trade arrangement in 1995, relating to Myanmar and Belarus, respectively. Another complaint was filed with the Commission concerning bonded child labour in Pakistan. Here, the EU opted for a different approach, refraining from initiating an investigation and focusing instead on political dialogue. In this context, the EU also increased its support to the activities of the ILO's Programme on the Eradication of Child Labour in Pakistan.

As concerns the unilateral labour provisions of the US GSP, some scholars have argued that the threat of withdrawal of tariff preferences has led in certain cases to improvement in the situation of workers. In general, the effect of these labour provisions on the situation of workers depends to a large extent on the presence of domestic social partners. In addition, other factors, including the economic dependence of the beneficiary country on market access and its own technical capacity to re-mediate the problem, seem to co-determine the impact of the US GSP's labour provision.

Scholars generally agree that the impact of the NAFTA labour provisions has been rather limited and that only a few of these cases resulted in direct substantial improvement of workers' situations. In the absence of sanctions, the main enforcement tool has been public censure, the results of which are difficult to measure. Factors such as difficulty of implementation and lengthy or cumbersome procedures have been tied as possible reasons for the reduced interest of trade unions and NGOs in the NAALC. However, scholars increasingly point to indirect and long-term advantages that have been gained through NAALC; these include increased knowledge and understanding about the respective parties' labour law systems and the formation of a number of trans-national alliances between unions and NGOs.

In the light of the limited practical relevance of the sanction mechanisms, it has been argued that, in practice, the US trade agreements' main pillar is the element of cooperation. Extensive cooperation activities have been conducted under NAALC, which consisted mainly of conferences, workshops and research activities. However, the number of these activities has declined in recent years. Furthermore, a number of objections regarding their design have been raised. Others defend cooperative activities as a necessary condition for the creation of a favourable environment for sustained functioning of the NAALC.

With the United States–Chile Trade Agreement, a more practical approach to cooperation has been taken, involving activities to enhance Chile's institutional capacities by improving staff skills and enhancing institutional procedures for the application of labour law. This approach has been reinforced in the context of CAFTA, where the US Government has provided US$ 20 million per year since 2006 for capacity building in the area of labour standards in the CAFTA-DR countries. Action plans have been developed by the US administration and the individual CAFTA states in consultation with the national social partners. Cooperation activities have focused mainly on five areas, namely strengthening of labour ministries, improving the labour justice system and legal advice for workers, reducing discrimination in the *maquilas,* combating child labour and strengthening the culture of compliance regarding labour issues. While the US Department of Labour considers that a number of improvements have been made, in particular regarding the fight against child labour, NGOs and trade unions argued that the effect of these activities has been limited, citing the reluctance of employers to respect labour rights, insufficient involvement of the social partners and relevant civil society organisations in implementation, as well as the lack of evaluation and accountability of the projects or financial assistance.

In the context of the Canada–Chile Agreement on Labour Cooperation, a number of workshops and conferences were held, involving mainly information sharing and research into the implementation of labour standards. A three-year review of the agreement conducted in 2002 proposed, among other things, to render the activities more practical and to link them more strongly with the ILO.

The Canada–Costa Rica Labour Side Agreement has involved the provision of technical assistance with a view to strengthening the labour inspection and alternative dispute settlement in labour matters and promoting social dialogue in the legislative process.

So far, incentive-based labour provisions have been rather scarce, but first evidence on implementation points to relatively positive outcomes. As for the EU GSP, Orbie and Tortell (forthcoming) show that several countries have ratified ILO Fundamental Conventions in order to be eligible for the additional tariff preferences under the EU GSP incentive-based labour provision. However, the impact of these arrangements on the actual improvement of labour standards in the countries concerned is less clear. The US–Cambodia Textile Agreement has received rather positive evaluations regarding its impact.

Few comprehensive evaluations have been conducted of the impact of promotional labour provisions. An interesting test case is MERCOSUR. Being of a promotional character, the implementation mechanism utilised in MERCOSUR involves tripartite commissions at the national level and the MERCOSUR Social-Labour Commission at the regional level, which sits at least once a year. Its key tasks are the development of programmes and action plans for the promotion of the Social-Labour Declaration, as well as monitoring its implementation. Central to its activities are the annual reports that the MERCOSUR member States are required to submit, first to national tripartite commissions and, subsequently, to the regional Social-Labour Commission for comments. While progress has so far been rather slow, some authors expect the Social-Labour Declaration to influence the interpretation of national laws by the courts and, in this way, to impact indirectly the national laws of the MERCOSUR countries. The Social-Labour Declaration has also been used as a platform for social dialogue, at both a national and a regional level. This has, among other things, led to the conclusion of an international framework agreement between the Germany-based trans-national company Volkswagen and local trade unions.

International Development Finance

The following section discusses the use of labour provisions in the investment policies of DFIs. The analysis in this section refers to 17 DFIs about which information has been obtained to date. These DFIs comprise those listed in as well as the World Bank. Labour provisions in DFI policies refer to normative standards which are adopted by these institutions in relation to their investment operations and procedures.

The purpose of DFIs is to provide financial resources to economic actors in regions and sectors where access to capital is limited. There exist global, regional and bilateral DFIs. At the global level, the World Bank Group comprises five financial institutions, three of which operate in the field of development finance. The main DFIs at the regional level are the Asian Development Bank, the African Development Bank, the European Bank for Reconstruction and Development, the EU's European Investment Bank and the Inter-American Development Bank. Finally, numerous States have put in place bilateral DFIs.

While multilateral and regional DFIs are owned by their member States, some bilateral DFIs also have private owners, although the main shares usually remain with the national government. The World Bank Group covers both investment in the public sector (IBRD and IDA) and the private sector (International Finance Corporation (IFC)). The same is true for regional banks although the majority of them tend to priorities the public sector. Bilateral DFIs typically focus on the private sector. The main DFIs disbursed in total US$ 45 billion in loans, equity and guarantees during 2005, of which just less than half (US$ 21.3 billion) was directed into the private sector.

Increasingly, international bodies have called for DFIs to take into account, or at least not hamper, the realisation of decent working conditions in their investment operations. Hence, a context has been created for the introduction of labour concerns into the investment operations of DFIs. In recent years, labour issues have been progressively taken into account in DFI operations. In 2002, the World Bank publicly announced its support for all four CLS. Similar approaches have been adopted by regional DFIs49 and bilateral DFIs.

Unlike the case of labour provisions in trade arrangements, which refer primarily to states, labour provisions in DFI policies mainly apply to private-sector partners.

There are some exceptions, however:

1. The World Bank Group's public arms (IBRD and IDA) include ILO CLS as an aspect of the Country Assistance Strategies, which the Bank prepares in cooperation with the borrowing country concerned. Country Assistance Strategies do not make compliance with the CLS of the borrowing State an eligibility criterion for loans. However, the World Bank seeks to address CLS issues in dialogue with the country concerned, "in cases where non-implementation of one or more core standards negatively impacts the country's prospects for development".
2. A similar policy was recently adopted by the European Bank for Reconstruction and Development (EBRD).
3. Since 1985, the US Overseas Private Investment Corporation (OPIC) policies include labour provisions which are linked to those of the US GSP. This means that investment activities in countries which have lost trade preferences due to a breach of the US GSP's labour provisions are also excluded from OPIC's operations. For countries that do not benefit from the US GSP, an individual assessment is carried out.

Apart from these exceptions, DFI policies focus mainly on the compliance of companies involved in the respective DFI operations, although these may sometimes, as in the case of EBRD, also cover public enterprises owned by the state.

To date, many of the major DFIs have included labour provisions in their policies for their client companies. In this regard a leading role has been played by the IFC. By 1998, the IFC had already adopted a safeguard policy dealing with labour issues. Following an assessment by the IFC's Ombudsman in 2003 and consultations with a wide array of stockholders, including the ILO, the "IFC Policy and Performance Standards on Social and Environmental Sustainability" were adopted. Performance Standard 2 contains requirements specifically related to labour issues.

The Performance Standards have been applied to all IFC-financed projects since May 2006. The IFC policy contains a comprehensive set of good governance standards, which are systematically incorporated into contracts with its clients.

In general, the IFC Performance Standards have become a reference for other DFIs in developing integrated labour provisions within their own policies. For example, the EBRD's "Performance Requirements", adopted in May 2008, seem to have been inspired by the IFC's Performance Standards. The policies of other financial actors also have been influenced by these Standards. The Multilateral Investment Guarantee Agency (MIGA), which is the investment guarantee arm of the World Bank Group, adopted the Performance Standards in 2007. In 2003, the leading international private sector banks (known as the "Equator Banks") adopted provisions known as the "Equator Principles". Since their revision in 2006, the Equator Principles contain the social and environmental safeguards of the IFC Performance Standards. Banks that adopt the Equator Principles commit themselves to apply the principles to any project with a minimum value of US$ 10 million. Adherence to the Equator Principles rose from ten compliant banks in 2003 to more than 60 compliant banks in 2008.50 The IFC estimates that the Equator Principles are now applied to 80 per cent of project finance provided by private banks in developing countries.

A number of DFIs have included labour provisions in their policies before or in parallel to the IFC. An early example is the US OPIC, which started using such provisions in its investment activities in 1989, requiring clients to respect certain labour standards. From the late 1990s, European DFIs, in particular Denmark's Industrialisation Fund for Developing Countries (IFU), the Netherlands Development Finance Company (FMO) and the German Investment and Development Corporation (DEG), have integrated labour provisions into their investment policies. Numerous regional DFIs and more recent bilateral DFIs, including the Development Bank of Austria (OeEB), established in 2008, have followed suit.

These DFI policies typically incorporate a wide variety of labour issues. The scope of the labour provisions varies considerably. Some DFI policies, including those of EBRD and DEG, go beyond the IFC's Performance Standards. Many of these DFIs, including IFC, IDB and most of the European DFIs, also have an exclusion list in place that precludes DFIs from investing in clients that use child labour and forced labour.

Interestingly, twelve of the DFI policies containing labour provisions refer directly to at least some of the ILO Fundamental Conventions. This may be due in part to consultation with the ILO in the design of these policies, as in the case of the IFC and EBRD. That said, the DFI policies do not necessarily embrace all the specific requirements of the relevant ILO Conventions. Usually, the main reference point for labour provisions in DFI policies is, in the first instance, national law; although, a minimum standard is generally maintained on a number of issues, in particular related to CLS.

Labour concerns have also made inroads into the public procurement policies of various DFIs. Since 2007, the World Bank (IBRD and the IDA) require bidders to comply with the ILO CLS as well as a number of other labour standards. This policy applies to all contracts exceeding a value of US$ 10 million dollars. ADB joined the harmonised standard bidding practices in 2005. Also, the AfDB and EBRD have harmonised their public tender practices with that of the World Bank's public arm. In this case, contractors must sign a declaration that they will respect the CLS when carrying out these projects. Some commentators expect other DFIs and development agencies to adopt, at some point, conditions similar to the Standard Bidding Practices of the World Bank's IBRD and IDA.

While the details of the DFI policies differ with regard to their implementation, they are typically based on an initial social assessment of the proposed investment. If problems in relation to labour practices are identified, they may be addressed through an action plan.

One of the most comprehensive procedural frameworks for DFI policies has been developed by the IFC.54 First, an initial environmental and social assessment must be conducted by the client company. If potential risks of problems regarding compliance are identified, the client company will develop an action plan designed to avoid, or at least mitigate, the impact on labour conditions. The IFC will take this action plan into account when conducting its own social assessment, which includes consultations with NGOs and unions. Finally, in the event of compliance difficulties, the IFC will (in extreme cases) reject the project or require the company to address these issues, often in combination with technical assistance for the company. Similar procedures are also followed by the other DFIs, which have integrated labour concerns into their investment policies.

Given that projects often receive finance from more than one DFI, some DFIs have started to coordinate their policies, including the social requirements to be met by the client. Often, DFIs that co-finance a given project agree on joint environmental and social (E&S) requirements. A response to the need for coordination can be seen in the creation, in 1992, of the Association of the European Development Finance Institutions (EDFI), to which 16 bilateral DFIs subscribe at present. In May 2009, EDFI members signed a declaration on "Principles for Responsible Financing", which commits members to working with client companies in order to progressively realise the standards contained in a number of international instruments, including ILO Fundamental Conventions. Since 2007, the EDFI has also adopted "Harmonised Environmental, Social, and Governance Standards". While not harmonising the content of the labour provisions in DFI policies, these Standards do contain Social Category Definitions, and certain technical standards for social due diligence, social contractual requirements as well as an exclusion list for joint investment projects. Often, DFIs which co-finance a project also coordinate their responses if problems arise regarding the labour provisions. These arrangements can be seen as an important step towards providing some coordination between DFI police on labour and other social concerns.

A number of DFIs have also put in place specific review mechanisms to protect third parties from potentially harmful consequences of their operations, often in the context of specific safeguard policies. These policies typically allow the affected parties to bring their concerns before a committee that is formally independent from the operational part of the DFI and reports directly to the DFI's highest body. The review body usually works with both parties to resolve the dispute and may recommend amendments to the DFI's policy or offer redress if problems are identified. Most bodies not only provide a forum for addressing complaints, but may also independently examine whether a DFI has complied with its internal policies and may promote dialogue between the DFI and the affected group.

The first DFI to put a safeguard policy into place was the World Bank in 1994. Other DFIs, such as IFC, the EBRD and the EIB, have developed this approach further by also applying safeguards to their labour policies. The AfDB allows for review of gender issues. The EIB Complaints Mechanism is particularly comprehensive. Here, individuals may make a submission to the EIB's internal complaints office, but may also have recourse to the European Ombudsman (an independent EU institution) if they consider the reply from the complaints office to be unsatisfactory.

Very little is known about the practical application of labour provisions in the policies of DFIs, as much of the information is confidential and the recent nature of such policies makes it premature to conduct a comprehensive assessment. Among the DFIs, documentation on the application of labour provisions is most advanced in relation to the IFC Performance Standards. Some preliminary insights can, for example, be drawn from the IFC's report on their first three years of implementation of the Performance Standards, as well as a trade union assessment of the IFC Performance Standards.

Since the IFC Performance Standards entered into force, 21 submissions have been filed by trade unions, involving two requests for information and 19 reports of alleged breaches of IFC Performance Standards. The Performance Standards between July 2006 and August 2009. The IFC has reacted with enhanced monitoring and capacity building activities for finance recipients and has, in some cases, achieved positive changes through direct interventions. In a few cases, a project was suspended after the circumstances of the complaint were investigated.

In a case concerning a Brazilian airline, the IFC helped to end anti-union activities. In a similar case involving a Ugandan construction union, the IFC's intervention was instrumental in making the company apply a collective agreement.

Based on a review of existing cases, a case study in Turkey and one in Uganda, respectively, Bakvis and McCoy, Agtas and Murie respectively see potential in the Performance Standard 2 to positively influence the situation of workers. However, the consideration that the IFC relies to a large extent on the borrowers' self-assessment and consultants has led some to argue that the IFC Performance Standards are effective mainly in cases where local unions are present and are able to monitor the workers' situation. Moreover, when these local unions are linked to global unions, they can further inform the IFC and provide more detailed information regarding implementation. It should be mentioned, however, that trade unions are less involved in the implementation of other DFI policies.

The IFC has hired staff to implement its environmental and social policy, including a number of labour specialists, totalling 62 staff members in 2009, and has established a Labour Advisory Group. Also, strong emphasis was put on familiarising the IFC's own staff with the Performance Requirements. More than 1,600 staff members received face-to-face training on the IFC's Performance Standards, while 192 participated in an online training course on the IFC's E&S management. Furthermore, beyond the initial assessment, 17 projects were subject to a comprehensive labour audit. The IFC also has a number of tools for internal review in place, which seek to assess and gradually improve the IFC's E&S performance, such as an Environmental and Social Review Procedure and a Quality Assurance and Control System. These observations reinforce the view that capacity building is an important component in enabling staff to ensure that internal compliance with labour provisions is truly effective and sustainable.

Aside from the impact of DFI labour policies on workers, the question of their effect on client companies also arises. In an IFC survey, it was found that the Performance Standards are largely acceptable to IFC's clients. According to this survey, while 60 per cent of the respondents believe that costs under the Performance Standards are higher than in the average sector, only 21 per cent of the respondents consider that the Performance

Standards might negatively affect their decision to collaborate with the IFC.

The preliminary evidence regarding the business impact of the Equator Principles indicate that they have not negatively influenced the business relations of the banks adhering to the Principles. As Sims notes, the number of banks adhering to the Equator Principles continued to grow after the Equator Principles were revised so as to align with the IFC's enhanced Performance Standards in 2006. Further, Scholtens and Dam find that the adoption of the Equator Principles has not led to negative reactions by the banks' shareholders. However, Sims observes a drop in the percentage of the proceeds of the DFI project advisers (mandated arrangers) covered by the Equator Principles since 2006. This suggests that adopting the Equator Principles entails certain additional costs, which are, however, for a number of banks outweighed by the expected enhanced reputation.

The potential of labour provisions in trade arrangements and development finance policies to contribute to the social re-balancing of the global economy relies upon how these mechanisms are applied in practice. As yet, relatively limited information is available regarding the implementation of these labour provisions. In general, it would appear that both elements of conditionality and "soft" persuasion and capacity building, have a role to play, depending on the extent to which compliance problems are due mainly to lack of political will or lack of capacity. In the case of trade arrangements, incentive-based clauses in particular offer considerable potential. As regards labour provisions in DFI policies, the cases examined thus far indicate the importance of providing staff, loan recipients and other clients with training, technical guidance and support.

Bibliography

Aby, Stephen H. (2005). *Sociology: A Guide to Reference and Information Sources*, Littleton, Colorado, Libraries Unlimited Inc.

Autor, David, Adriana Kugler and William Kerr. (2007). "Do Employment Protections Reduce Productivity? Evidence from U.S. States, *Economic Journal*, 117, 2.

Besley, Timothy and Robin Burgess. (2004). "Can Labor Regulation Hinder Economic Performance? Evidence from India," *Quarterly Journal of Economics*, 119, 1: 91–134.

Bhattacharjea, Aditya. (2006) "Labour Market Regulation and Industrial Performance in India: A Critical Review of the Empirical Evidence," *Indian Journal of Labour Economics*, 49, 2: 211-232.

Dahrendorf, Ralf. (1959). *Class and Class Conflict in Industrial Society*. Stanford: Stanford University Press.

Dreze, J. and Sen, Amartya. (1996), *India: Economic Development and Social Oppor-tunity*, Oxford University Press, Delhi.

Durkheim, Émile. (1895). *The Rules of the Sociological Method.* Cited in Wacquant (1992).

Gary S. Becker and Kevin M. Murphy. (2001). *Social Economics: Market Behavior in a Social Environment*, Harvard University Press.

Giddens, A (1996). *The Constitution of Society*. California: University of California Press. pp. 14–19.

Landis, Judson R (1989). *Sociology: Concepts and Characteristics* (7th ed.). Belmont, California: Wadsworth.

Nisbet, Robert A. (1967). *The Sociological Tradition*, London, Heinemann Educational Books.

Nocera, J. (2009). "Risk mismanagement", *New York Times Magazine* (Working Paper, NYU), pp. 24–33, 46, 50–51.

Olsen, J. (2006). *Note on leveraged buyouts* (Foster Center for Private Equity).

Onaran, Ö.; Stockhammer, E.; Grafl, L. (2009). *The finance-dominated growth regime, distribution, and aggregate demand in the US* (Austria, Vienna University of Economics), Working Paper No. 126.

Palley, T. (2009). *Financialization: What it is and why it matters*, IMK Working Paper.

Philippon, T. (2007). *Why has the U.S. financial sector grown so much? The role of corporate finance*, NBER Working Paper No. 13405, revised Jan. 2008.

Renneboog, L.; Simons, T. (2005). *Public-to-private transactions: LBOs, MBOs, MBIs, and IBOs*, European Corporate Governance Institute, Finance Working Paper No. 94/2005.

Richard Swedberg. (1990). *Economics and Sociology: Redefining Their Boundaries: Conversations with Economists and Sociologists*. Princeton University Press.

Ritzer, George and Douglas J. Goodman. (2004). *Sociological Theory, Sixth Edition.* McGraw Hill.

Saunders, Peter (1990). *Social Class and Stratification.* Routledge.

Service Employees International Union. (2007). *Behind the buyouts: Inside the world of private equity*, p. 20.

Slattery, Martin. (1993). *Key Ideas in Sociology*. Cheltenham: Nelson Thornes, Ltd.

Smith, A.J. (1990). "Corporate ownership structure and performance: The case of management buyouts", in *Journal of Financial Economics*, Vol. 27, pp. 143–164.

Stiglitz, J. (2009). *Testimony before the congressional oversight panel: Regulatory reform hearing*, available at: cop.senate.gov/documents/testimony-011409-stiglitz.pdf

Stockhammer, E. (2007). *Some stylized facts on the finance-dominated accumulation regime*, PERI Working Paper, 142.

Taylor, J.B. (2009). *The financial crisis and the policy responses: an empirical analysis of what went wrong*, NBER Working Paper No. 14631.

Turner, P. (2008). *Financial globalisation and emerging market capital flows* (Basel, Switzerland, Bank for International Settlements).

Wallace, Ruth A. & Alison Wolf. (1995). *Contemporary Sociological Theory: Continuing the Classical Tradition*, 4th ed., Prentice-Hall.

Watson, Tony J. (2008). *Sociology, Work, and Industry*. Routledge

William, M.; VanBever, S. (2006). "Challenges for private equity: The shifting winds of risk", in *Chicago Fed Letter*, No. 232a, pp. 1–4.

Wright, M.; Wilson, N.; Robbie, K. (1997). "The longer term performance of management buy-outs", in *Frontiers of Entrepreneurship Research*, pp. 555–569.

Index

ENCYCLOPAEDIA OF SOCIOLOGY

Political Sociology

Volume –10

Satish Mittal
Sushil Kumar Saxena

Commonwealth

Encyclopaedia of Sociology

Edition : 2026

ISBN 978-81-311-0377-7 (set)

Published by :
COMMONWEALTH PUBLISHERS (P) LTD.
4831/24, Govind Lane,
Ansari Road, Darya Ganj,
New Delhi - 110002
Ph. : 23242541, 23272541
e-mail : commonwealthpublishers2016@gmail.com

Distributed by :
ARJUN PUBLISHING HOUSE
4831/24, Govind Lane,
Ansari Road, Darya Ganj,
New Delhi - 110002
Ph. : 23242541, 23272541
e-mail : arjunbooks2001@gmail.com
arjunpubhouse@gmail.com

Laser Typesetting by :
Dimple Computers
Delhi

Printed at :
Milan Enterprises
Delhi

Preface

Political sociology is the study of the relations between state and society. The discipline draws on comparative history to analyse sociopolitical trends. Political sociology looks at how major social trends can affect the political process, as well as exploring how various social forces work together to change political policies. Political sociologists apply several theories to substantive issues. Three major theoretical frameworks are pluralism, elite or managerial theory and class analysis which overlaps with Marxist analysis.

This book introduces the key conceptual debates and approaches in contemporary political sociology, including the power relationship between the state and civil society and the impact of recent social changes on this relationship. Important and topical issues including globalisation, rise of new social movements, neo-liberalism, citizenship, political culture and political participation are also explored.

The book is the definitive introduction to the key processes that are changing the nature of politics and society in the modern world. The focus is on clarity, accessibility, and the needs of the student. An extremely well-written and engaging book, it takes an upbeat and argumentative style that brings the subject matter to life. It strikes the right balance between covering the core theoretical and conceptual issues associated with the subject while also adopting a central thesis that gives structure to the field and stimulates further enquiry.

Authors

Contents

1

Political Sociology in Modern Society

The contemporary global society is marked by a skewed distribution of resources and capabilities accorded to different groups in the world and therefore a skewed distribution of power and capacity. The contemporary global society is also a society in transition, in the sense that some fundamentals changes to the structure of world economy—namely, globalisation—are leading to new developments that have not been the purview of political sociology as conceived at the time of bounded nation-state units, the hallmark of the times when political sociology came of age. It is important to remember that the field of political sociology as conceived in those times was also a product of a certain social and cultural milieu— which shows up in the importance accorded to topics that flow from the heart of European philosophy and history.

The contemporary global society is marked by a skewed distribution of economic resources. It is true that as compared to any other time in human history many more people are living on earth. It is also true that as compared to any other time in human history many more people are living longer and healthier lives. Yet it is also true that the level of economic inequality among different population groups is also bigger than any other time in human history. The question of skewed distribution of economic and cultural resources in the language of political sociology is a question of who has power and how this power is exercised. Three different perspectives try to answer this question. The first perspective, the pluralist perspective, finds its origin in classical liberal ideas of Hobbes, J.S. Mills and Jeremy Bentham and in work of French aristocrat DeTocqueville. The liberal thought of Hobbes and Mills were concerned with protecting the rights of individuals in the context of English society of 17th and 18th century. For them it was individual liberty—defined in a narrow economic and individualistic basis—that was of foundation importance. Hobbes conceptualised the world in terms of a jungle where the only reason we do not cheat or hurt each other is because of the presence of the institution of state— the Leviathan. But then the problem becomes how to stop the state from taking over the whole sphere of existence.

The economic activities in particular were held by the thinkers like Mills and Bentham—whose ideas Marx ridiculed as the view of the bourgeois of the market street— to be sacrosanct and therefore outside the purview of state. The truth is that liberalism in its own time was a revolutionary idea. The ending of royal privileges and the need for individual social dignity—although this for J.S. Mills did not include non-property owners and colonised people—was the goal. The goal was to dethrone the clerical authority. For Mills and Bentham the reason for the existence of human beings and the state was to maximise pleasure and minimise pain, the idea that is known as utilitarianism.

In the modern world, this notion of liberal idea of power came to be encapsulated in the form of pluralist perspective. With the royal privilege destroyed and the clerics in retreat, the freedom to undertake commerce became dominant and the pluralist perspective echoes the individualist, liberal ideas. For pluralists, the society is not dominated by any one particular interest, but rather different people with similar interest come together and they play a part in the electoral process via which the ideas with most appeal to the populace gets into the government and therefore become applied to the society. For pluralists the process of elections as conceived in the present fashion is sufficient; power for them is not concentrated and is in fact dispersed throughout the society. DeTocqueville's construction of the local level of democracy among Americans in 1830s—as described in *Democracy in America*—who self-organised at local level and took initiative without any direction from government or any other centralising authority, forms the basis of this model of power. The most famous statement of modern pluralist thought is found in Robert Dahl's work, *Who Governs? Democracy and Power in an American City*, in which he studies the distribution of power in local politics in New Haven and argues that there had occurred in New Haven a historical shift from "a system of cumulative inequalities in political resources to a system of non cumulative or dispersed inequalities in political resources". Pluralists extend this model to the polity at large and argue that there is no concentration of power.

They also down play the role of state; for them the state in the shape a minority (*homo politics* as Dahl had it) does not play an important role. Dahl terms most of the people in the society as *homo civics*, people who do not have much interest in the political affairs. The people who have an active interest in politics are characterises as *homo politics*. The population therefore is divided into two strata: apolitical statrum and political stratum. It is the second stratum—which does not require any special qualification for entrance such as wealth and education, except for an interest in politics—that people in government are selected from. The state then is a democratic state in the sense that it is elected by electoral process in which anyone can contend. People make the decisions and the words of Abraham Lincoln—"government of the people, by the people and for the people"—reflects the true nature of government. Democracy in this perception is defined as polyarchy, a system of limited democratic representation. For Dahl the idea of polyarchy is an improvement over the closed hegemonies of the authoritarian societies. William I. Robinson characterises this notion as "low intensity democracy" since it is associated with democracy in a formal rather than substantive sense. The notion of civil society in this perspective is the font from where the ideas that find representation in state arise. The state is not partial to any interest; it floats over all interest and its actions and policies are reflective of what the people at large want. Class and social movements do not exist in this language, because if they were real issues they will find a voice in the electoral process.

To begin with, this model is an idealised model of American society. This model does not even attempt to give a prescription to the world outside the United States. There are those who argue that American society is an exceptional society and that there is no existence of the notion of class in the American society because it does not requite the language of old world. It is a known fact that United States never had a strong socialist party and nor a strong socialist tradition. This for Seamier Martin Lipset had to with American exceptiones in the sense that America never had a feudal background so Americans were born conservatives and as well the limitations put on government from the beginning made Americans gravitate towards libertarianism and anarchism ideas than socialism. There are things that are truly different about America, but pluralism as a model does not even do justice to capturing how power is exercised, let along power on the global scale. The pluralist perspective applied to a global society will dictate that polyarchy is the answer for different parts of the world. Anywhere there is electoral process, which is nominally free, we have a polyarchy—which is all fine and well with the American government and as well as with capitalists who want to consolidate the present distribution of power in the world: in favour of those with money and power and against those lacking either capital and power. William I. Robinson in his perceptive work, *Promoting Polyarchy*, argues that polyarchy as a political program has been adopted by American foreign policy on the behalf of promoting interest of global capitalist fraction of the capitalist class.

Pluralist's notion of power, that they say exists in the world, is not complete. This conception of power—defined by Dahl as "the ability of A to make B do what otherwise B will not do"—is a relational one, that is visible in real world transactions. This model of power, as defined in this way, is focused on observable power—what Stiffen Lukes refers as one-dimensional notion of power. Lukes also points out that the one-dimensional power is about behaviour of making policy decisions about conflict of (subjective) observable interests. This kind of focus on what would be a model of behaviourism—which neglects the black box of consciousness—is a reflection of the electoral process that is central to Dahl's model.

As the United States preaches polyarchy to Middle East countries at this instance in global political situation—via its Greater Middle East Project—it is clear that they it does not want to let real substantive democracy come into play. Take, for example, of Egypt where supposedly American political pressure is bringing changes in the political structure. The supposed change that United States wants is the ability of different groups to be able to take part in elections and be able to get selected into government. So the visible conflict in the society is between Islamists and secularists (read American favoured)—but even when America is calling for changes in the political restructuring of Egypt, it is not asking for an open elections that will have the real conflicts of interests between the Mubarak regime and the Muslim brotherhood to come to the fore. While Mubarak has declared that he will allow other candidates to run against himself or the nominee of the ruling Nation Democratic Party nominee in the up coming presidential elections this year, in fact the desire of the Mubarak regime and the American side is very clear in actions of the ground: Mubarak has accepted that other people will run against him in the elections but he has attached an onerous and insuperable condition. Any candidate who would want to run the elections will have to get the signature of 50 members of the parliament (All but 10-15 of whom happen to be from another party); this then blocks out any chance for a real possibility that someone from Muslim brotherhood will run in the elections.

The state-civil society relations implied by pluralism are also partial in truth. For this perspective the state is but the clear representative of the democratic interests of the populace. And civil society therefore is truly represented in the state, which implies that there should not be antagonistic relation between the government and the civil society. It therefore makes no space for the social movements to in this equation. The only legitimate way of making one's voice heard is via organised lobby and pressure groups. In their reading, if people are not satisfied they can form a lobby or pressure group and influence the government. But for them there is no difference of a lobby group such as National Association of Manufacturers (NAM) and the Sierra club because each has an equal chance to be heard in the system. This, however, is patently false because the economic resources that a group such as NAM can bring to play are widely substantial from the resources that a group such as Sierra club can bring to play. Lastly, in relation to the differential economic resources, there is no sense of class differentials present in this perspective, which will be necessary to understand the contemporary global political and social situation. This then is a perspective that is very local to American society and it is even flawed when applied to that society.

The second perspective in political sociology that tries to answer the question of political power is the elite perspective. This perspective is based upon the work of Gaetano Mosca and Villfredo Pare to. Both these theorists held that societies are divided between elates and masses. This division comes from the differential abilities present in human beings. Those who end up elite have superior ability and those who remain in masses have lower abilities. These theorists point to the existence of a ruling group all through the human history as a factor supporting their theory. Pare to was so sure of his theory that he drew a curve that showed the distribution of elates and masses that parallel the curve of distribution of income among the population. Human nature, for these theorists, explains the persistence of elates and masses all through the history. Human nature for Pare to is an unchanging entity and therefore we have a universal presence of elates and masses throughout human history. Pare to explained the persistence of this division in terms of irrational behaviour of human psyche—in terms of "deep resides". He divided the population into two groups: those with "instinct for combination" and those with "instinct for aggregates". Those in the first group possess ability to make combinations and are cunning in their reason and they end up as elates. Those in second group are borne to resist change and have devotionals to stability. The combination of these two factors—the Machiavellian foxes and lions—keep society in stability. While the elite theorists are known for their critique of both liberal democracy and Marxism, one of them at least sees a limited role for liberal democracy. Mosca sees a limited liberal democracy as a mechanism for the circulation of elates since the elections will move those born in masses that have the ability of elite. This 'circulation of elates' will give the system an appearance of stability.

The second idea that is at the heart of elite perspective is that complex organisation need leadership to insure effective functioning. In this context of work of Robert Michaels in *Political Parties* put forward the "iron law of oligarchy". For Michaels, one "who says organisation, says oligarchy". Michaels studied the German Social Democratic Party to see how he can explain the concentration of power in the hand of a few people. His intention was critical, but he came to the conclusion that any organisation turns into an oligarchy because of the requirement of concentration of power in the hands of a small number of people—the elite—for effective running of any organisation. This kind of idea is also entertained by Marxism, as can be seen from the Lenin's idea of "dictatorship of proletariat" in *State and Revolution*, in which the working class is to be lead through the transition from capitalism to communism via the dictatorship of proletariat, which will wither away as people become prepared for communism.

As from the case of Soviet Union, this did not work as the dictatorship of proletariat become another kind of elite rule. Max Weber also drew attention to the process of bureau-cratisation that gets in the way of real democratic rule. For Weber, the only break out the "iron cage of bureaucracy" was to be provided by charismatic personality. In *Capitalism, Socialism and Democracy*, Schumpeter also talks about democracy as a system that inevitably leads towards elite rule because it bureaucratises the process of selection of leaders. The democratic process then become only a way for selecting as to who will rule them. The modern variant of the elite theory are found in the work of C. Wright Mills who in *Power Elite* argues that American society is ruled by elates from three different fields: military, corporate and political. Further work in Domhaff's Who *Rules America? Power and Politics* continues Mills tradition of democratic elite theory but with an increasing focus on class.

The notion of notion of power in the elite perspective is identified with the second-dimension of power in Steven Lukes' work, which assumes that there is a hierarchical relationship between groups in which the group in power is able to further its interest in not only the sense of the one dimension of power—that is by making an actor do something that the actor would not do otherwise—but also in the sense of being able to exercise political power by keeping certain issues off agenda. This perspective is identified with managerialism by Afford and Fried land in *Powers of Theory*, because it the power is concerned with the way structures of organisation allow the exercise of power by elite. The power flows from the organisation of structure via which decisions are made. In this sense the centralisation and the institution of bureaucracy becomes a central point of exercise of power.

The state then in this perspective is something that stands above the society to exercise in a non-partial manner that is for the good of the system. The bureaucrats in this model have independence from the economic elates. Echoing Weber, there is not only one basis for the socialite power. Class, which is understood in a different fashion than the Marxist notion of class, while an important factor is not the sole source of social power, and in addition to class, status and political party are other basis of power. The state in this system reflects two views: the sectional interest and structure of the interests of the dominant group—the elates—in the society and the functional interests of keeping the system going by making decisions that are important for the working of the system. Therefore the centralisation and rationalisation of the state are accompanied by the increasing coercive power of the elates against rebellious population.

The nature of democracy in this perspective is limited to an understanding of democracy in which is understood as a result of elite competition. Further democracy is understood to keep the circulation of elates going and in some more generous version of this perspective—namely, Mosca—democracy is a way by which individuals born among the masses can rise to become part of elates. Democracy here works to co-opt the populace. The political imperative that marks this system is one of reform and reaction. It is no accident that most of the major figures of this perspective found attraction in fascism. Pare to was sympathetic to fascism and Michaels left socialism for the fascist work under Benetino Mussolini. The state and civil society relationship in this perspective are organised around inter-organisational authority and conflict. The conflict is managed and resolved in this perspective and politics—which allows for the management of conflict—plays a central role in the world-view of this perspective. Given that the state is an autonomous entity in this perspective, the civil society and social movements do not get any importance, because the state can resolve the questions of importance without partiality to any one side.

This is an interesting perspective that works very well in some aspects on the global political situation today. The understanding of the growing role of state in surveillance and the control of human bodies can be understood via this perspective. This perspective also could be used to explain the persistence of inequality and evil in the world. It exists, because it is in human instincts to be unequal—and therefore those with ability can move up and become part of the elite and others will have to be content with being part of masses who will be looked after yet dictated to by state. There is a fundamental level of justification of inequality built into this system. At the national level, the absence of whole groups of peoples from the elite structures points to the problem with this perspective. For example, the lack of representation of minorities in the political power structure can be construed as if the whole of the population lacks in some of the capabilities that are needed in the elates. The elite perspective though if applied to the selection of ruling elates in the United States is not able to answer the question of whether it is possible for someone to be able to rise to a power of political prominence or even within the prominent political structure without a level of economic affluence? It seems as if anyone who runs in the elections has deep pockets. Another related question is whether the bureaucrats making decisions that are autonomous of the interests of the capitalists in their work? On this point, there are a number of instances where it could be argued that a managerial state makes decisions that seem to go against elite interests in the first instance. If elite perspective was the ruling paradigm in the world, the power hierarchy of the world would be made up of bureaucrats who made decisions about what the best way for maintaining the system—and this would have meant that there was more stability in the system.

The third approach to global political situation is the Marxist perspective in political sociology. The Marxist political sociology is based upon the work of Karl Marx who stressed that throughout the human history—except in the prehistoric times—there have always existed two classes of people, the oppressors and the oppressed. The oppressed are the ones who sell their capital to make a living and oppressors are the ones who own the means of production. Men make their own history but not the conditions of their own choosing—this sums up how Marx views the relationship of work to the making of history. The social conditions and relationships, according to this perspective, prevailing in a given society reflects its organisation of the mode of production. Different modes of production represent different relationships: the feudal mode of production has the master-slave relationship and the capitalist mode of production has capitalist-workers relationship. In works such as *Capital* Marx worked out the centrality of labour to the production of profit under capitalism. For Marx, the organisation of political life is to be understood in relation to the class relationship between its population. Whenever the mode of production becomes more productive than the social organisation that is present in the society, a revolution takes place and brings into being a new mode of society. For both Marx and Engels, as they argue in *The Communist Manifesto*, the history of all societies hitherto has been a history of class struggle and therefore under capitalism the struggle is between the bourgeoisie and the proletariat. The bourgeoisie's power over the proletariat is because of the formers control over the means of production.

The notion of power in Marxist approach flows from the control of economic resources. For Marx the economic differences within the civil society are manifest in the structure of state and the dominance in the realm of economic field implies dominance in the power in terms of state. Those who control capital in the society therefore also control the institution. In *The Communist Manifesto* Marx identities the state as the "executive committee of the bourgeois"—that is, it serves the interests of capitalists in a very straightforward way. Anything that benefits capitalists gets done by the state and anything that benefits the working class is not done by the state of its own volition but is rather forced by the working class if they are strong enough. But it has also to be said that this is not the only way Marx understands state. There are other times in which he gives more leeway to the way state acts.

The notion of power—a structural one—implied by the Marxist theory is captured in the three-dimensional model of power as captured by Steven Lukes in *Power: A Radical View*. The third degree of power is concerned not solely with what is on the agenda as is the case with pluralist perspectives or as to what is kept of the agenda as is the case of elite theory, but it deals with the latent issues along with observable issues and also with how some potential issues are kept out of politics by sectional interests. In Grammes's work on hegemony in *Selections from the Prison Notebooks* he is concerned with how the working class—even though it is suffering from exploitation at the hands of the capitalists—does not revolt in keeping with Marx's prediction of revolution. The answer for this for Gramsci is to be found in the way the civil society becomes the place where sectional interests are able to change the cultural modes of thinking via their deployment of hegemony eliciting mechanisms.

According to Gramsci, hegemony—the consent to leadership by the capitalist class—is established not in the narrow repressive way but also in ideological way. So the state was not only involved in the establishment of hegemony in repressive terms but more importantly in the ideological sense. Therefore for the resistance to this the real stagy will involve a war of position in the civil society, whose importance between state and economy was established by Gramsci within Marxists, and this will be a slow and long process, one that would need the involvement of organic intellectuals in creating alternative hegemony via cultural work. Gramsci is refreshing because he is saying that a society cannot be just changed by taking over the institution of state, as was the Lenin's program in Soviet Union. In so doing, Gramsci lays the foundation for an alternative understanding of why the revolution did not happen in the advanced industrial revolution, which was Marx's idea of how the transition from capitalism to communism will unfold. It is also important to realise here that this kind of work was later extended by the Frankfurt school scholars who centred culture in their analysis of capitalist societies. In recent times, the ideas of Robert Cox in *Production, Power and World Order: Social Forces in the Making of History*—who builds upon Gramsci's work—are interesting because he argues for understanding power at the global level by examining the "state-civil society" complexes not only in a given nation, but in an international field of power in which some states have maximum degree of external autonomy, and others are dominated by these states with maximum external autonomy.

The Marxist debates around the institution of state are perhaps the most important debates over the institution of state in any of these three approaches. Classical Marx's position—although he gave different stresses to it—was that state acted as the executive committee of the bourgeois. Therefore what was in the favour of the bourgeois was also in the favour of the state. But the debates between Ralph Miliband and Nicos Poulants as were the modern markers in increasing the understanding the nature of state. For Miliband who follows the instrumentalist approach in *The State in Capitalist Society*—that is, the state is an instrument of capitalist power pure and simple—and therefore argues that all the actions taken by the state are in favour of the ruling class. But Nicos Poulants as faults Miliband for thinking of the state as an 'empty space' and not as a social relationship. He argues that state has "relative autonomy" from the capitalist class and even though it the state might in the short term take act against what might be the interest of capitalist class in the last instance it will take the side of capitalist class. Fred Block in his article, "The Ruling Class

Does Not Rule" argues that the state is not concerned with working for each single capitalist but that in fact the role of the state is to maximise the accumulation of profit and therefore not each single action in case of individual capitalist should be seen as a signification of state's intent.

The idea of democracy favoured by this approach is also different from the other conceptions. The democracy here is not limited to the procedural and formal one or as something that is to be managed by the elates within a liberal democracy. The democracy in this approach is a real measure of economic as well as cultural equality for all the population. Democracy thus takes on the sphere of economy, state and the civil society. Marxists argue that for a democratic system we need to ensure that there is equal opportunity for the development of capacities of each individual from day one. There should be select few who can afford nice cars and schools from day one and others who cannot even afford to go to school. If only does the state provide free education for the children of the poor on par with the rich, argued Marxists, then only can we have a chance at a the establishment of a real democracy. But as studies such as Bourdieu's in *Distinction: A Social Critique of Value of Judgment* show, the markers of class are embedded within the family background so deep that the first institution of socialisation—the family itself—cancels out the impact of equalisation of education upon the possible establishment of a democratic education. The social movements that arouse out of the Marxist approach were class based and therefore they demanded actions to improve the economic and social position of workers. But since the defeat of the Soviet experiment, the labour movement the world over has suffered a strong blow.

The truth is the contemporary political situation in the world is marked by the shadows of 1989. The death of Soviet experiment in the graveyard of authoritarianism and the victory of capitalism marked the end of an era and the beginning of another. While Fukuyama wrote paeans to the victory of liberal democracy at the end of history, new ramblings were rising inside the very developments that were responsible for the fall of the Soviet Union. The world of today marked at it is by globalisation is not the same which was analysed by the classical perspectives of political sociology—pluralism, elite theory of class perspective. The rise of international trade and the corresponding need for a political structure that facilitates the process of trade and as well the movement of capital and goods across nation-state boundaries has impacted the world political dynamics. The increasing importance of trans-national institutions—such as the International Monetary Fund (IMF), World Bank (WB), World Trade Organisation (WTO), Group of Eight (G-8), Organisation for Economic Cooperation and Development (OECD) and Asia Pacific Economic Cooperation (APEC)—for political coordination of this system of increasing global trade has led to a focus on issues that cannot just be explained by reference to the notions of power and politics conceived in the political sociology literature. There is a need for a rethink in the basis concepts of political sociology. Since most of the concepts of political sociology come from the time when the world economy was divided into neat and bounded boxes of nation-states, the present conjuncture in the world political situation cannot be completely grasped by the concepts of political sociology.

Take, for instance, the concept of globalisation and its impact upon the institution of state. There three four basic positions that can identified in the impact of globalisation in the state. First, there are those who argue that the role of state is weakening under globalisation and the importance of trans-national institutions is increasing. This position has been called the hyper-globalism position, because it sees the role of nation-state as weakened and therefore it focuses on the trans-national. As part of global capitalism school, William I. Robinson's work, A Theory of Global Capitalism: Production, Classes and State in a Trans-national World, can be seen as a representation of this perspective. HE argues that "the apparent declining ability if national state to intervene in the process of capital accumulation and to determine economic policies reflects the new found power that capital acquired over the nation-state and popular classes..." and that "real power in the global system is shifting to a Trans-national space that is not subject a 'national control". Others of view that the nation-state as being weakened by this perspective include Kenichi Ohmae, who argues that the "global civilisation" will be the product of the changes brought about by globalisation and that nation-state is history. Second, there are those who argue that the world has seen a higher level of globalisation in the previous epoch and therefore the institution of nation-state is not weakening and in fact the process of globalisation is being controlled and shaped by nation-state This group is known as the skeptics. Third, the last group is made of those who are known as trans-formationalists who argue that the world is undergoing complex changes and although the role of nation-state is changing it is not yet okay to argue that its role has weakened.

In terms of democracy, the political situation in the contemporary times is marked by the absence of any real representation by majority of population in their own political systems. In most of the western democracies, there is certainly a much higher level of formal democracy today than in the past. The level of political participation in formal elections is also healthy, with the sole exception of the United States where political participation at the national level are very low and political culture is heavily dominated by irrational elements. Outside the western world, formal democracy has spread via the third wave of democracy . The biggest mark of this was the fall of Soviet Union and the conversion of the Eastern Europe to formal democracies in 1989. This then is the victory of capitalism that has made it possible for the capitalists to dominate the world political, economic and cultural scene like never before. The discourse of formal democracy has serviced the designs of the powerful countries and by extension the forces that stand behind these nations—the capitalist class.

The United States' discourse of support for democracy is about extension of the market and its logic into all parts of the globe and into all facets of human life, without regard for popular democratic ideals. William I. Robinson's path breaking *Promoting Polyarchy: Globalisation, US Interventionism and Hegemony* is the best work to capture the deployment of low intensity democracy for controlling the popular forces around the world. The low intensity is being used to make consumers of the people the world over, thereby superseding other more organic identities that people have. The invasion of Iraq and the gunboat democracy that we are seeing today shows the desperate nature of capitalist rule and its interest in consolidating formal democracy, which is integral to the capitalist system in our epoch. If one juxtaposes Venezuela next to the case of Iraq, one can really see the sordid nature of how capitalist power works. Despite coups and repeated attempts of overthrown Chives, the capitalist interests represented by the United States government cannot bring them to accept that Chives has the popular support of a solid majority of Venezuelans.

The resistance to exploitation that is part and parcel of capitalism, nonetheless, continues. The fall of the Soviet Union in 1989 was blow to the social movements and class movements that opposed capitalism. The nature of protest and rebellion has changed in the world over. But there is no end of history yet, as protest, rebellion and politics has come back on agenda again. In terms of social movements, there has been a differentiation in the number and types of social movements active in the world. The social movements that held sway in the past, such as the class based movements have suffered a loss of strength in the aftermath of the Soviet demise. The rise of the new social movements in Europe in 1980s has centred the issue of culture. Whereas the social movements before 1980s were based mostly around the issues of class, the NSMs stressed the quality of life issues. In this way, a number of questions that were limited to the class dimension were reconsidered to become questions of quality of life questions and a number of other agendas that were not represented in the class movements were brought forth.

Ronaldo Ingelhart has suggested that the rise of movement like the NSMs (New Social Movements) signify the movement of societies to a set of post-material values, in that the ideas beyond material ideas—which guided the class based opposition to large number of people—have become central to populace' life. This then shows up in their desire to think of politics in terms of quality of life issues rather than in material terms. This has meant proliferation of movements that range from identity-based movements to peace movements and the environmental movement.

But the NSMs are movements that are more present in the advanced industrial countries than in the global south. There is still space in the global south for the kinds of actions that are still concerned with the issues of material well being and economic justice. The rise of an energised global civil society has also made its mark on the global scene. The work of Kick and Sikkink in *Activists beyond Borders* and Jackie Smith in *Trans-national Social Movements and Global Politics: Solidarity Beyond State* shows the increasing engagement of global civil society with social justice issues beyond nation-state boundaries.

2

Elite Theory in Political Sociology

The origins of Elite theory lie most clearly in the writings of Gaetano Mosca, Vilfredo Pareto and Robert Michels. Mosca emphasised the ways in which tiny minorities out-organise and outwit large majorities, adding that "political classes" – Mosca term for political elates – usually have "a certain material, intellectual, or even moral superiority" over those they govern. Pareto postulated that in a society with truly unrestricted social mobility, elates would consist of the most talented and deserving individuals; but in actual societies elates are those most adept at using the two modes of political rule, force and persuasion, and who usually enjoy important advantages such as inherited wealth and family connections. Pareto sketched alternating types of governing elates, which he likened, following Machiavelli, to lions and foxes. Michels rooted elates ("oligarchies") in the need of large organisations for leaders and experts in order to operate efficiently; as these individuals gain control of funds, information flows, promotions, and other aspects of organisational functioning power becomes concentrated in their hands. Emphasising the in escapability and also the relative autonomy of elates, all three men characterised aspirations to fully democratic and egalitarian societies as futile.

Many democrats and social radicals have rejected this "futility thesis". They have sought to demonstrate that particular elates are not those with superior endowments or organisational capacities, but merely persons who are socially advantaged in power competitions. Adherents of this view have argued that the existence of elates can be terminated either by removing the social advantages that some people enjoy or by abolishing the power concentrations that spur competitions among them – remedies that often go hand-in-hand. There are no historical instances, however, where these remedies have been successfully applied in a large population for any significant length of time.

The writings of Mosca, Pareto, and Michels constitute a paradigm from which a general theory of elates and politics might be derived. But efforts to produce such a theory have not been conspicuously successful. Linking elates causally to major regularities in politics remains elusive; there is no accepted typology of elates and no accepted specification of the circumstances and ways in which one elite type replaces another; political interactions between elates and non-elite population are captured only piecemeal. Nevertheless, political scientists and sociologists pay much attention to elates and their key roles in democratic transitions and breakdowns, revolutions, political regimes of all kinds, mass movements, democratic politics, globalisation, and many other political phenomena.

ELITES

Elites derive from a fundamental and universal fact of social life, namely, the absence in any large collectivise of a robust common interest. While it is true that most large collectivised rest on a base of social and cultural understanding, these tend to be ambiguous and rough. The satisfaction some of their members seek are only partly compatible with the satisfaction sought by other members. Members constantly claim statuses and other valued goods for themselves, their kin, friends, and allies that other members do not accept as fully legitimate. Acceding to these claims is often more a matter of judging that it is dangerous or inexpedient to resist them than of recognising that the persons and groups making the claims have some right to do so. In large collectivised common interest is fairly minimal and must always be supplemented by authoritative decisions that dissenters and opponents dare not or find it inexpedient to resist.

Common interest is even more limited as regards the detailed features of any large collectivise functioning. Its operations involve day-to-day decisions and, thus, allocations and re-allocations of tasks and statuses. Merely for a large collectivise to survive, „intelligent and „objective decisions that transcend individual interests must regularly be taken. But there can seldom be any firm consensus among a collectivise members about the rightness of these decisions. This is partly because only a few are in positions that afford a relatively comprehensive view of the collective effort and its present location in time and space relative to its goals. Yet such a view is usually necessary for knowing if a particular decision is "right". Moreover, the need for constant decision-making deprives members of the time they would need to reach agreement about how their interests apply to current problems and needs. Even a relatively unimportant decision changes the line-up of influence for the next decision so that the details of a collectivity structure and needs are always different today from what they were yesterday. This means that any incipient consensus among its members necessarily focuses on yesterday's structure and needs.

These aspects of collectivities give to elites their importance in political and social theory. Collectivities of any size and complexity require decisions by persons who happen to be strategically located in them. Because such collectivities are concentrations of power in the wider society, their top decision-makers have disproportionate socialite power and influence, and they nearly always enjoy disproportionate privileges and protections. If we call these persons elites we casay that large and complex collectivities necessarily create elites. In this sense only are elites an inherent feature of societies; all other reasons for the existence of elites are less persuasive and more debatable. Recognising this is not, however, merely to echo Michels dictum that "Who says organisation says oligarchy." For oligarchy, aristocracy, and other euphemisms for elites imply or impute specific structural and behavioural features. Whether elites are cohesive, conspiratorial, self-conscious, and so on is answerable only through empirical investigation. While elites are the inescapable consequence of conflicting interests in all large and complex collectivities, their configurations vary according to political and social circumstance.

Elites may be defined as *persons who, by virtue of their strategic locations in large or otherwise pivotal organisations and movements, are able to affect political outcomes regularly and substantially*. Put differently, elites are persons with the *organised capacity* to make real political trouble without being promptly repressed. They consist not only of prestigious and "established" leaders – top politicians, important businessmen, high-level civil servants, senior military officers – but also, in varying degrees in different societies, relatively transitory and less individually known leaders of mass organisations such as trade unions, important voluntary associations, and politically consequential mass movements. "Counter-elites" are subsumed by this definition because they clearly have the organised capacity, although perhaps mainly through negation, to affect political outcomes regularly and substantially.

It is important to stress that this is a limited and specifically political definition of elites. It is restricted to persons who are at the top of the pyramid or pyramids of political, economic, and social power. It does not consider all those in a society who enjoy high occupational, educational, or cultural statuses to be elites in a political sense. As defined, national political elites are not large in number. Geraint Parry has observed that the entire British elite could be seated with ease in a soccer stadium. Using strict organisational and positions criteria, as well as data about sizes of elite networks, some researchers have estimated that the national political elite in the United States numbers perhaps ten thousand persons, maybe half this number in medium-sized countries like France, Australia or Germany and about fifteen hundred in small countries like Denmark and Norway. This last estimate of fewer than two thousand persons is probably the most plausible for all countries during the early modern historical period and all but the most populous developing countries today.

Elites and Political Stability

The presence or absence of stable political institutions is one of the major differences between political systems that can be explained on the basis of differences between elites. It is unusual for political power to be institutionalised effectively, as it has been for many years in Great Britain, the United States, the Netherlands, Sweden, Switzerland, and a few other Western countries. Stable political institutions are marked by the *absence* of irregular seizures of government executive power or obvious military influence in policymaking through threats of military intervention. Every four years since 1789 a president has taken office in the United States on the basis of election and has served out a term, unless dying in office, as the more or less effective head of the American political system. In Britain over an even longer time span prime ministers and cabinets have regularly succeeded each other as the chief political authority in accordance with principles and rules that, in spite of being largely informal, are well known.

The personalised manipulation of political institutions through individual and direct control of military and police forces has been, and is, much more common. Typically, there is a distinct elite group that effectively commands organised coercive forces and is prepared to arbitrate political decisions no matter what existing institutions prescribe. It is of little consequence analytically whether this group centres on a traditional monarch, a civilian coalition tied closely to professional military commanders, or it is an overt military junta. What is consequential analytically is that elites, no matter what their partisan inclinations may be, see power as personalised and directly dependent on the support of organised coercive forces. Elites critical of current social organisation, for whatever reason, necessarily view political change in terms of removing or altering the group that effectively commands those forces. In their eyes and the eyes of their opponents, power flows from gaining at least temporary control over the principal means of coercion. Attempts to seize government executive power by force are seen by all as plausible, even probable, eventualities.

This is the basic aspect of a *disunited elite*. For long periods, as in Spain, Portugal, and Latin America during the nineteenth and most of the twentieth centuries, governance oscillates between "dictatorial" and "democratic" poles. These oscillations are transitory and circumstantial manifestations of the political system inherent instability so long as most elite persons believe that the hold on government power is subject to sharp and sudden changes. The historical record shows overwhelmingly that politics in most countries normally approximate an unrestrained struggle among mutually distrustful elites to defend and advance their interests with little regard for cost or propriety.

Of supreme interest in political analysis, therefore, are the relatively few countries in which political instability is not the order of the day. For, as noted, a few countries have displayed patterns of institutionalised authority and procedure that have been respected and perpetuated over long periods. In them, irregular seizures of government power by force are unknown and informed observers consider such seizures highly unlikely. Elite theory holds that these deviant cases are explicable *only* in terms of elite behaviour. More specifically, the historically normal situation of political instability has been abrogated in countries only when a *united elite* has formed.

There are, however, two markedly different types of united elites and, consequently, two quite different forms of political stability. One type is an *ideologically united elite*, which is marked by the uniform profession of a single and defined ideology by all or nearly all elite persons. These persons consistently avoid taking conflicting positions in public about current policies and political beliefs; they foster the image of a single and homogeneous leadership group. But given the conflicting interests that exist in any society, this image is more apparent than real. To some extent it arises from the determination of uppermost leaders imbued with a specific ideology to afford no opening for the intrusion of "unsound" outsiders into policymaking. But even for elite insiders the ideological uniformity is in part coerced. Behind the public profession of more or less complete agreement about current policies and goals – behind the expression of a single and defined ideology – there exists an apparatus of power sufficient to force all or most current and aspiring elite persons to harmonise their public statements with the views that are currently orthodox. Defining what is orthodox is the task of a few individuals in the highest elite positions, and adhering to this orthodoxy obviously blocks the expression of divergent interests.

The content of the single ideology that marks an ideologically united elite is of little analytical importance. It must probably be sufficiently diffuse and removed from present conditions to permit flexibility in interpreting always changing realities. It must probably be focused on some future, imaginary social condition toward which society is allegedly moving. It must, in short, be substantially utopian. But analytically speaking, whether the ideology describes a future classless society or one in which eternal salvation or pastoral contentment for all will be realised is of little consequence for the enforced unity that prevails among elite persons. Because the only permissible public position for organising endeavours is defined and monopolised by those in power, political institutions can be centralised to a degree unknown elsewhere. Individuals and groups who want to alter those institutions can be identified easily, and they possess few means with which to appeal for public support. Evidence indicates that, once established, institutions operated by an ideologically united elite are stable for long periods.

The other type of united elite, a *consensually united elite*, does not depend on all elite persons taking essentially the same political position in public. There is no single and defined ideology to which all must adhere. Instead, persons with power and influence take clearly divergent positions on public matters. These positions often accord with opposing ideologies, as in the long conflict between conservatives and liberals within British and Swedish elites during the nineteenth century, and the subsequent conflict between liberals and socialists within the same elites during the first half of the twentieth century. The striking aspect of these conflicts is that they occur under a set of rules that is nowhere comprehensively codified but is tacitly and widely understood to remove serious personal danger from elite contests and competitions. These informal rules emanate from a structuring of power that gives all or most elite persons and groups sufficient access to decision-making so that it is in their collective interest to avoid seriously disruptive actions and keep the political situation manageable. Although elite members disagree and oppose each other in limited struggles for ascendancy, power is distributed so that all or most can have influence on political decisions sufficient to deter them from translating their oppositions into attempts to seize government power by force. Political institutions are, accordingly, stable for long periods.

Origins of Elite Types

Ideologically united elites originate in revolutionary circumstances that enable a movement dogmatically expressing a specific ideology or creed to suppress and supplant previously existing elites. Examples are Russia 1917-1921, Italy 1922-1925, Germany 1933-1934, North Korea 1946-1948, China after 1949, Cuba 1959-1961, and Iran 1979-1981. Ideologically united elites may also originate when an external power possessing such an elite imposes its clone on a conquered or otherwise subordinated country, as in East Germany and Eastern Europe following World War II. By contrast, consensually united elites sometimes originate through dramatic changes in the situations and attitudes of the key groups that have constituted a disunited elite. This involves an *elite settlement* in which warring elite camps manage to bring their major disputes to a close and establish a basis for mutual trust. The first historical instance of an elite settlement occurred in England „Glorious Revolution of 1688-1689, and it is worth recalling its basic features.

English elites had been bitterly and deeply disunited, as evidenced by the Civil Wars and Interregnum between 1642-1660. In 1660 the monarchical system was restored, albeit with some shifting of positions and blurring of lines between the previously warring elites. Thereafter one main elite camp, the Tories, sought to exploit their association with the monarchy, while the other main camp, the Whigs, maintained its anti-monarchical stance. The Tories were thoroughly identified with the religious doctrine and institutions connected to the Church of England. But when in 1685 the birth of a son to James II, who professed both Roman Catholicism and an absolutist version of monarchical power, made an indefinite Catholic succession to the throne likely, the Tories were as discomfited as their Whig rivals. Fearing a resumption of civil war, key leaders of the two elite camps conspired to invite the successful military intervention of the Dutch *stadtholder*, William of Orange, and the elite camps subsequently agreed, in early 1689, to establish William as king under terms that effectively guaranteed them joint political influence. Occurring in a predominantly agrarian society where the elite stratum was necessarily small and exclusive, these events marked the beginning of the limited and restrained political contests with understood informal rules that have characterised the British polity ever since.

Consensually united elites have also originated in the attainment of independence by former colonies in which local or "native" elites have been able to practice a restrained home-rule politics while waging long, in some cases violent, struggles for independence. As illustrated by elites in Britain North American colonies, both American and Canadian, local elites in partially self-governing colonies may develop a high enough level of mutual trust when resisting the colonial power interventions and seeking independence that they are consensually united from the date of independence or the grant of full home rule. In addition to the U.S. And Canada, this was the experience of elites in Australia and New Zealand during the latter part of the nineteenth century, and of white South African, Indian, and Malayan elites during the twentieth century first half. It is worth noting that Dutch elites became united in this manner before and during their successful struggle for independence from Spain late in the sixteenth century, although full integration of the seven Dutch provinces did not occur until after the Napoleonic Wars.

In cases where consensually united elites formed as an outgrowth of colonialism, colonial governments had active representative institutions that afforded elites a considerable practice of limited and restrained politics. But this was not the situation in the Latin American colonies of Portugal and Spain, where, moreover, there was little clear understanding of territorial boundaries when independence was gained. Consequently, military leaders and local political bosses (*caudillos*) tended to predominate in Latin America at independence and for long periods thereafter. Nor were the political experiences of elites under colonial rule and when struggling for independence propitious for the formation of consensually united elites in more than a few of the scores of ex-colonies that achieved independence during the decades following World War II. Except in India, Malaya (later Malaysia), Senegal, and no more than a handful of other ex-colonies, such as Jamaica and Barbados, independence brought with it disunited elites and long-lasting political instability.

To summarise, there have been two ways in which disunited elite became consensually united historically: (1) through basic and sudden elite settlements in societies at relatively low levels of socioeconomic development; (2) through colonial home rule and struggles for independence where local elites had already received, or received in the course of those struggles, experience in political bargaining and restrained competitions. Neither origin appears relevant to the situation of most disunited elites in today world. A necessary condition for an elite settlement appears to be a level of socioeconomic development lower than that of most developing countries with disunited elites today. At higher development levels elites are probably too numerous and closely tied to particular non-elite interests to be able to fashion a settlement. Colonial dependency is obviously a condition necessary for creating a consensually united elite through home rule and independence struggles, but it is a condition that is no longer seriously present. These observations raise the question of whether there may be a third way in which consensually united elites form.

In countries that have transited to democratic elections, the opposing camps and factions making up a disunited elite may begin to converge if some of the opposing elites form a broad political coalition that mobilises enough voters to win the elections repeatedly. This enables the coalesced elites to dominate government executive power and obtain the greater security that derives from this domination. An elite convergence may continue if factions hostile to the winning coalition conclude that seizing power by irregular means is not a realistic possibility and they must beat the winning coalition in election contests if they are to escape permanent political subordination. This means acknowledging the value of elections and promising to accept their results. An elite convergence may be considered complete when the formerly hostile and losing factions gain government executive power in an election and then govern in a way that is respectful of established institutions and tacit live-and-let-live reciprocities with the previously dominant elite coalition. As happens more clearly and quickly in elite settlements, through convergences elites gradually reach an underlying consensus about the norms of restrained political competition so that political institutions become stable.

Elite convergences occurred in several European countries and in Japan during the twentieth century second half. All were at a relatively high level of socioeconomic development and general prosperity when the convergences took place. The four clearest cases were France once General de Gaulle associates formed a winning electoral coalition after his return to power in 1958; Italy once the "organic" Christian Democrat - Socialist winning coalition took clear shape in 1963; West Germany after several victories by the Christian Democrat – Christian Socialist – Free Democrat winning coalition formed in 1953; Japan once the Liberal Democrats and centrist parties constituted a winning coalition starting in 1964. In each of these countries, dissident and hostile elite camps eventually came to see that they had no real political alternative to moderating their stances in order to compete effectively in elections, and in each what had previously been a disunited elite gradually became consensually united – by 1981 in France when the previously dissident Socialists won power and governed with moderation, during 1979 in Italy when the "revolutionary" Communist Party cooperated with the dominant Christian Democrats to repress extra-parliamentary terrorist groups; in West Germany when the dissident Social Democrats entered into a "grand" governing coalition with their previous nemesis, the CDU-CSU coalition; and in Japan once the Socialist Party jettisoned its Marxist baggage during the mid-1980s.

Elite Theory and Democracy

Although an elite theorist's personal preference may be for democratic politics, he or she does not believe that in most countries and circumstances a practical and stable form of democratic politics can be achieved. Meaningfully democratic institutions and practices depend upon the type of elite that a society has. No type of elite is compatible with the full democratic ideal, and only one of the three types is reasonably compatible with the stable democratic politics that are practised in Western countries and a few others today. However, none of the three elite types is *reliably* conducive to even this limited form of democracy.

The most common political situation, that of disunited elites, has the basic feature of institutional instability. While institutions operated by some part of a disunited elite may at times have a formally democratic facade, the institutions are hardly worth much promotion or defence because they are unlikely to survive a serious political crisis. Commonly, any substantial increase in normal political tensions leads, with or without a military coup, to a more authoritarian and repressive government. Although such a government may eventually mellow or even be replaced by a more democratic one that has the tacit consent of the elite veto group associated with the military, this improvement is likely to be merely an interval in a succession of more or less repressive governments. As noted, historical evidence is overwhelming that disunited elites and the unstable institutions they create persist through most vicissitudes and that each government is in practice one permitted by those who happen to control military and police forces.

The circumstances in which disunited elites become ideologically or consensually united are unlikely to appeal to people with democratic sentiments. An ideologically united elite does not allow competitive politics, and where it exists meaningful actions motivated by democratic sentiments are nearly impossible. The basic settlements in which a few consensually united elites originated historically had as their principal features substantial elite autonomy from mass pressures together with the sacrifice of deeply held political principles for which opposing elites and their supporters had long stood. The colonial origins of consensually united elites involved empires that are odious to convinced democrats and are, in any case, no longer feasible politically and economically. Where opposing camps in a disunited elite have gradually converged, those who have most liked to consider themselves genuine democrats have found themselves consistently in the minority, while more conservative and traditional persons who are part of the majority to which the winning coalition appeals are inclined to merely pretend that they are democrats. Moreover, although a consensually united elite may emerge via an elite convergence and open the way to a more widely accepted and stable democratic regime, the process depends on socially radical groups becoming disillusioned with their democratic ideals.

It is also the case that the regime created and operated by a consensually united elite may not, in fact, be very democratic. It can be based, as in most historical cases, on a highly restricted suffrage. Even temporary dictatorship or the long dominance of a high-handed chief executive is possible so long as the elite remains internally trusting and is prepared to cooperate in removing the dictator or chief executive if he or she becomes seriously incapacitated or incompetent. Fundamentally, practical democracy depends on the ability of a consensually united elite to keep political tensions moderate. Where such an elite exists the problem for people imbued with democratic ideals is deciding how much public attention they should try to centre on issues that they consider morally right but that are also potentially explosive. The champions of such morally charged issues are likely to find that members of a consensually united elite distort, partially suppress, or simply confuse the issues if doing so seems necessary to maintain institutional stability. Morally charged issues will be subject to "benign neglect" if elites conclude that the issues have reached a threshold of articulation and antagonism beyond which political stability is endangered.

Should those who cannot get the hearings that they believe their moral causes deserve acquiesce in such elite actions? If it is correct that consensually united elites are ordinarily quite capable of managing political tensions, the question is without significance. Yet, suppose that the elite cannot quite do this in the face of embittered demands and vehement mass demonstrations. On the assumptions of the approach to elites outlined here, this would break up the elite and in all probability create a disunited elite with the usual consequence of covert or overt military rule and the suppression of political dissent. Would it be right for staunch democrats to help bring this outcome about on behalf of a high moral cause? The answer is obvious.

Elite theory teaches, in other words, that a mature and experienced advocate of democracy must always settle for a political order that is considerably less than ideal. An elite that is consensually united, or one that approaches this condition, is necessary for practical democracy. Only such an elite will effectively manage conflicting interests whose open and dogmatic expression would create disastrous internal conflict. Where an elite does this over the course of many years, representative political institutions guided by reasonably competitive and influential elections are possible, although not inevitable. But where groups within the elite fully and openly reflect and express and conflicting non-elite interests, then at some point political freedom for considerable numbers of elite and non-elite persons alike will be suppressed or the polity will not survive. Elite theory rejects the fashionable but fatuous notion that the most desirable political system is one in which the divergent interests of a population are clearly represented and forcefully articulated at the elite level. Posing "a real choice, not an echo" in practical democratic politics threatens to weaken a consensually united elite and concomitant institutional stability. Recognising this, proponents of elite theory cannot properly feel compelled to pursue the democratic ideal in all circumstances and at all costs.

Elites and Revolution

There is no agreed definition of revolution that attaches the term to a clearly specified political event or process. It is sometimes used to mean almost any irregular and forcible seizure of power, thereby covering the many coups and sporadic uprisings that occur where elites are disunited. "Revolution" is also often used to label civil wars and wars of liberation that centre on dynastic, ethnic, regional, or religious divisions. This definition vagueness makes it a matter of subjective judgment whether to call a regime, movement, or violent conflict "revolutionary" – a judgment that is, indeed, frequently made after the fact, as happened with the so-called Cuban Revolution that established the Castro regime. When they were fighting the Batista dictatorship, Castro insurgents portrayed themselves as, and were widely believed to be, liberal and populist, not revolutionary. It was only after a year or two in power that Castro and his associates proclaimed themselves "revolutionaries" and a Cuban Revolution was widely perceived. By not distinguishing between many kinds of violent upheavals, "revolution" has lacked the precision required of a concept that can be utilised seriously in an elite theory of politics.

There is, however, one special kind of upheaval with features that are objectively different from those of coups, civil wars, secession, and popular outbursts. This is an upheaval that begins when normal government authority, most manifest in disciplined military and police forces, suddenly and dramatically collapses. During the shorter or longer interval that follows, maintaining order against riot or pillage becomes highly problematic until government authority and military and police discipline are either restored or built anew by some victorious group. One cannot say that an elite of any of the three types exists during this interval. Power resides, as radicals like to say, "in the people" or, more precisely, in persons who assemble fairly spontaneously, usually under arms, and respond to immediate propaganda and oratory with mass actions. Such assemblages typically include bodies of rank-and-file troops who have either liquidated their officers or are simply ignoring officers orders.

An upheaval of this kind eventually brings a substantially different body of persons to elite status, and it changes political and especially economic institutions in fundamental ways. But before such sweeping alterations become apparent, whoever attempts to restore or construct a semblance of organised power in the area where government authority has collapsed usually comes under attack from areas to which the government collapse did not extend. To survive this attack, the new power organisers must quickly create some degree of bureaucratic centralisation accompanied by disciplined military and police units. Sooner than later, the popular assemblages that have held forth are policed and suppressed. When this happens, the observer can again speak of a regime operated by one or another type of elite. In the English and French upheavals of 1642-1645 and 1789-1794, respectively, the new elite was again disunited. But after the upheaval in Russia, 1917-1921, the elite was ideologically united as a consequence of the victorious Bolsheviks tight organisation and doctrinal coherence during the upheaval.

If for purposes of conceptual order and terminological consistency "revolution" refers only to an upheaval involving the collapse of government authority and an ensuing interval when coercive power is located in more or less spontaneous popular assemblages, it is a rare and unlikely event. A revolution in this sense can probably occur only in societies at low levels of socioeconomic development, that is, largely agrarian or peasant societies. In more bureaucratic societies at higher development levels the widespread collapse of government authority and disciplined military and police forces seems even more implausible today than it did when proponents of revolution counted, for the most part mistakenly, on large numbers of citizen-soldiers turning on governments after hardships and defeats in large-scale warfare. Moreover, advances in military technology, especially nuclear weaponry, suggest that wars fought by mass armies may now be relics of history.

Whether or not they are any longer likely, do revolutions in the present sense of the term bring political improvements? From the standpoint of democratic and liberal criteria, the answer is an emphatic No. Because of the searing enmities and political scars they create, revolutions never eventuate in consensually united elites. Their consequences are either disunited or ideologically united elites, neither of which is congenial to reliable democratic practices. Although much has been heard from persons outraged by what they regard as fundamental moral deficiencies of contemporary political regimes, not least Western democracies, the sweeping "revolutionary" changes that these persons have demanded lie well beyond what elite theory depicts as possible; they are just dreams and wishful thoughts that are from a liberal and democratic standpoint deeply imprudent.

Elites and Non-Elites

How does elite theory treat non-elite population and link them to elites? The bulk of Pareto million-word *Treatise* was an attempt to answer this question and it is self-evident that no satisfactory answer to it can be offered here. The question requires conceptualising a dynamic relationship between elites and non-elites in which, under specifically conditions, elites override non-elites, but under different and equally specifically conditions non-elites override elites. Where elites prevail, a theory must be content to specify the *outer limits* of possible elite behavioural and, thus, of political outcomes. Where non-elites prevail, political outcomes can be forecast with greater certainty. Specifying the changing predominance of elites and non-elites theoretically is, therefore, the crucial task.

To illustrate how this might be tackled, consider the proposition that at low levels of socioeconomic development a leftist or levelling propensity is potentially widespread among non-elites. In extreme political circumstances, this propensity may eventuate in a revolutionary collapse of government authority and military discipline of the kind just discussed. But such levelling revolutions appear possible *only* in an early phase of development, and even then they are exceedingly rare: the English, French, and Russian revolutions are the classic instances and all three occurred in pre-industrial conditions. Much more normally in pre-industrial societies, bodies of peasants and artisans are not greatly aggravated by the encroachments of elites, and their fundamentally leftist or levelling propensity is not strongly activated. Non-elite propensities become more inflamed, however, when societies reach the industrial stage of development. In this stage, manual industrial workers, who are numerous, hold consistently to egalitarian sentiments and a hostile view of elites, clearly articulated by the powerful trade unions and leftist parties that mobilise them. Bureaucratic and service workers, who are also numerous, tend to accept the presence of elites even if they do not condone all of their actions and features. Diminished and now more or less comparable numbers of artisans and ex-peasants, who in industrial conditions typically own small farm properties, are ambivalent about elites and elite actions: they resent elite interferences in their farming and artisan endeavour but are inclined to support those elites who seek to check levelling forces. In extreme political circumstances, an anti-egalitarian and possibly "fascist" upheaval aimed at crushing levelling forces is possible: northern Italy in the 1920s; Weimar Germany in the late 1920s and early 1930s; Spain in the late 1930s; strong fascist movements in Austria, Belgium, France, and most other European countries during the interwar period. Normally in industrial societies, however, the large numbers and political influence of non-manual bureaucratic and service workers, augmented by ambivalent artisans and ex-peasants, are sufficient to prevent strongly egalitarian mobilisations of manual industrial workers from gaining government power. If elections are held, the latter are simply outvoted. Finally, the pervasiveness of non-manual bureaucratic and service workers in socioeconomic development post-industrial stage rules out the dramatic levelling and anti-levelling political changes that are possible in earlier stages of development.

There is an important caveat. In societies that are latecomers to socioeconomic development and in a handful of mostly small societies with large petroleum reserves it is clear that today production and communication technologies greatly accelerate the conversion of work-forces from an overwhelmingly peasant and artisan composition to one that consists predominantly of bureaucratic and service workers. In these accelerated and technologically more sophisticated circumstances, manual industrial workers are at once fewer in relative numbers and, perhaps because of their smaller numbers and more sophisticated work tasks, their outlooks appear to be less intransigently egalitarian and hostile toward elites. The main political problem in societies coming late to socioeconomic development may, consequently, reside less in the composition of their rapidly changing work forces than in the inability of these work forces to provide employment for large parts of swollen and mostly young non-elite population.

The illustrative point, in any case, is that non-elite configurations, sketched here as distinct work force compositions and concomitant mixes of orientation toward elites, rule out certain elite actions and political outcomes at different stages in socioeconomic development, but they do not determine what elites will do and what political outcomes they will produce. Thus, early in socioeconomic development non-elites tend toward a hostile view of power exercises by elites, and their impoverished situations give non-elites little reason to fear a general levelling of existing hierarchies. If elites are exceptionally incompetent or unlucky, a collapse of government authority that triggers a levelling revolution is possible.

But elites may circumvent this by couching effective appeals for non-elite support in terms of religious and other traditional beliefs. In socioeconomic development industrial stage, a shift to fascist rule is possible, although entrenched elites may circumvent it by holding elections in which levelling forces simply lack sufficient numbers to prevail. What is not possible in industrial societies – in other words, what is precluded by the non-elite configuration – is a successful levelling revolution, and, *pace* Marx, none has occurred. Meanwhile, industrial societies appear to prevent sudden and deliberate settlements of basic elite disputes because their relative complexity makes the elite stratum large and not sufficiently autonomous from non-elites. Elite actors are numerous and many give their primary allegiance to the partisan interests of the mass organisations and movements they head. Negotiating behind the political stage to compromise principled interest positions that elite factions have repeatedly taken when mobilising non-elite support and then getting followers to accept such compromises is unlikely. Forming a winning political coalition that successfully defends existing hierarchies is the more plausible option for elites in industrial societies.

Elites in Post-industrial Conditions

How do elites and non-elites affect each other in Post-industrial conditions? By the 1970s all of the Western countries that were experiencing these conditions – the Anglo-American, Scandinavian, and Benelux countries, plus West Germany and perhaps Austria - had consensually united elites and stable political institutions. Disunited elites in several countries that were just then reaching the Post-industrial stage of development were becoming more consensually united – French, Italian, Japanese, Greek, and Portuguese elites via convergences; Spanish elites via a dramatic elite settlement in the wake of the *Franquist* regime.

Initially, Postindustrial conditions seemed to accentuate the political stability that consensually united elites produce. This was because the preponderance of bureaucratic and service workers blurred class lines and weakened customary partisan alignments among non-elites. Consequently, elites needed less recourse to ideologies, such as socialism and liberalism, in order to justify their statuses, policy positions, and governing actions.

Elite political discourse shifted to discussing affluence and the welfare state as solvents of historic discontent and problems. Observers avidly discussed the „end of ideology, a thesis that is probably best seen in hindsight as rationalising blandly optimistic views of the Postindustrial landscape, especially as viewed by sub-elite commentators. With high productivity and nearly full employment, the absence of serious economic downturns, a shrunken working class acquiring middle-class life styles, and no other large and obviously discontented collectivities in sight, there was the appearance of considerable harmony among non-elite population. Elites, accordingly, adopted a more blatantly managerial posture and they voiced a complacent belief that mere „fair treatment of individuals and groups would ensure social progress and tranquility.

With the passage of time, however, the greater non-elite harmony and elite complacency that appeared to be the principal political effects of Postindustrial conditions diminished. Increased crime, narcotics use, and other deteriorating social conditions became apparent in many cities; a seemingly intractable form of poverty spread in urban slums and rural backwaters; and many young people with essentially privileged family backgrounds displayed considerable alienation and discontent. These trends suggested that Postindustrial conditions could be more difficult politically than they first seemed.

Postindustrial conditions are in important respects the terminus of socioeconomic development. They complete the conversion of work forces that consisted overwhelmingly of peasants and artisans at development outset into work forces pervaded by bureaucratic and service personnel. It is quite unlikely that some further stage of development, conceived in terms of new basic kinds of work and new work force components, lies beyond Postindustrial conditions. If this is so, it must be asked whether Postindustrial societies can over the longer haul remain viable politically without the sense of progress and spread of hope that development engendered historically. Crudely put, can Postindustrial societies "stagnate" indefinitely in their non-elite configuration without suffering major political upheavals?

One concern is the increased empathy between elites and non-elites that occurs in Postindustrial conditions. The preponderance of bureaucratic and service work intermingles previously distinct social strata. Persons more frequently and routinely ascend to elite positions from non-elite origins and locations than happens in more rigidly stratified societies at earlier development levels. As a consequence, not a few persons holding elite positions in Postindustrial conditions see themselves as one of a kind with non-elites, among whom they frequently have intimate personal associates and for whom they have considerable empathy. These close and empathetic ties to non-elites help ensure that elite persons are better able to determine measures that at least partially assuage non-elite discontent and aspirations. But what may happen if it is not possible to assuage non-elites? Presumably, actions and measures ranging from deception to discouragement to outright repression will be more reviled by non-elites and harder for elites to take.

A still wider difficulty confronts elites in Postindustrial conditions. In all earlier stages of socioeconomic development political action was not generally required to keep most persons steadily engaged in the performance of necessary work. For the most part, internalised attitudes and customary social controls supplied by neighbours and work mates sufficed. In Postindustrial conditions, however, such close social controls, along with most religious and other traditional belief systems, attenuate greatly. In earlier stages of socioeconomic development, moreover, most persons worked diligently in order to stave off dreadful personal circumstances – dismissal, eviction, hunger, etc. – and a significant proportion worked without surcease because they could plausibly believe that by doing so their strong personal ambitions could be realised. In these earlier societies only a small number of specially favoured persons – mainly the offspring or friends of the rich and powerful – were un motivated to work in disciplined ways and were inclined toward a self-indulgent, if perhaps aesthetically satisfying, leisure.

It is easy to see that the proportion of people who are un motivated for steady work increases markedly in materiall affluent and empathetically indulgent

Postindustrial conditions. It is useless to ignore this by holding that modern technology greatly reduces the need for human labour. Responsible work is not readily parcelled out in little pieces in any society. Some tasks must still – and presumably must always – be performed with care, diligence, and forethought, and those who perform them will not allow a large body of essentially idle people, however decorative they may be, to receive substantial rewards for their idleness. This disjunction between the diligent and the idle signals a growing clash between segments of non-elite population in Postindustrial societies, although it is uncertain if this clash will have a magnitude that consensually united elites are unable to manage.

Limits of Elite Theory

Elite theory's predictive pretensions are necessarily modest. Elite behavioural cannot be inferred, let alone projected, from knowledge of non-elite configurations and propensities. For instance, neither the creation nor persistence of a consensually or an ideologically united elite is discernibly linked with non-elite propensities. The probability of a united elite of either kind forming and creating stable political institutions can only be guessed at from knowledge of recent elite history. Does this history display long and costly, but essentially inconclusive, warfare between disunited elite factions who, in consequence, may be disposed toward a basic settlement of their disputes? Have elites recently suffered a defeat so grave that the way may be open for a well-organised but previously peripheral group to seize and consolidate power in revolutionary circumstances? The difficulty is not merely that elite behavioural is poorly understood; it always contains enough elements of arbitrariness, capriciousness, or simple lack of obvious explanation to defy deterministic explanation. Thus, while societies have displayed similar non-elite configurations during socioeconomic development, no such regularities in the behaviours and configurations of their elites can be identified. Any theory that recognises this disjunction between elites and non-elites must allow considerable leeway for political accident and unpredictable political choice, so that its explicative claims must be quite modest.

It must also be recognised that elite theory is distasteful to many because it rules out the more ideal aims and outcomes that are regularly voiced by intellectuals, mass movement leaders, and even loosely predicted by social scientists. Elite theory has no place for idealised visions of democracy or social revolution, nor does it have a place for the spread of new values that dispose human beings toward a consistent and thorough altruism. Human conflicts inevitably dilute social cohesion and constitute political problems that elites must manage as best they can. However well or poorly they accomplish this task, elites are the central actors in politics, but the theory that centres on them is unlikely to have many enthusiastic adherents.

3

Sociology of State Formation

The idea of the modern state is variously institutionalised, ideological, philosophical, and scientific. In the context of these wider discourses, the modern state-idea is articulated with respect to at least six key centres of gravity: discourses of legitimacy (e.g., Hume's concept of "natural liberty"); discourses of political representation (who should be represented and by what mechanism); discourses of nation (the "nation-state" idea); discourses regarding the proper scope of government authority (e.g., with respect to the economy, political liberties, etc.); discourses of security (including generalised health and safety); and discourses of design (schemes for governing land, the built environment, and the population). The focus of this study is on discourses of design, for it is there that ideas in science and government most clearly intersect. But it should be noted that a focus on design necessarily provides a route to discussions of the other five centres of gravity, for most matters concerning the modern state-idea ultimately become matters of design and craft, social and political engineering, and security.

DESIGNING STATES

The French revolutionaries of the late eighteenth century were among the first to suppose that one could wipe the political slate clean and engineer a state from the bottom up on the basis of an entirely new and abstract design. Their attempt, like that of the Bolsheviks in the early twentieth century, stumbled and failed, partly because the inertia of the existing conditions called forth the application of brute force, a strategy that from the outset betrayed and corrupted the very values the revolutionaries claimed their designs sought to realise. The English took a somewhat different approach, in which a strong tradition of localism, an ideology of self-government, a peculiarly modern worship of indigenous antiquities, and a more empirically oriented idea of science than one finds in Cartesian France shaped an engineering culture that sought to build into what already existed rather than erase older forms in the name of an overly abstract rational plan.

When Ireland was completely mapped in the second quarter of the nineteenth century, enormous effort was made to research the oldest and most "authentic" civic boundaries and place-names, and their inscription on the new map affirmed continuity with antiquity. The English and French cases demonstrate how the business of engineering the modern state in different contexts drew upon divergent designing ideas, sometimes highly abstract and "rational," other times resembling those of the *bricoleur*. These ideas about the state were, one might say, "internal" to its construction. There were others who sought to understand the state from the "outside," from the perspective, in particular, of the social, political, and economic sciences. The distinction, once again, involves a centre of gravity rather than an absolute or categorical separation, but the point of the distinction is to make possible a reflexive stance, one that places social-scientific conceptualistic of the state on the same level as those articulated by the state engineers. The interests of social scientists are generally quite different from those of state engineers, but that is not sufficient reason to treat the two asymmetrically. Indeed, as discursive formations, academic constructions of meaning often times exhibit an easily identifiable traffic with the ideas of state engineers. In this context an important effect of a critical reflexive stance is to question the idea of the state as an *actor*, an idea first fully elaborated by Hobbies and still central to discourses of state that emerge from both within and without the offices and chambers of government.

Limits of The Actor-State Idea

While it makes sense to speak of the state as an actor in some contexts, the idiom has its limitations, because, states are complex and historically changing configurations of meanings and institutions, agencies, technologies and practices, and land, built environment, and people. While sovereign governments act in the name of states, they are not co-terminous with states. Indeed, to conflate "the state" with the "government" or its bureaucratic agencies is in effect to rob a people of a body politic that is importantly constituted through that people's very corporeal being, bestowing on a particular government or regime, at a particular moment in time, the image of the universally representative state-as-actor, philosophically conceived by Hobbes as the sovereign. When social scientists uncritical adopt the idiom *the actor-state,* they do not so much describe a political reality as become agents in the construction and institutionalisation of the Hobbesian state-idea, the idea that when the head of state acts, the state itself acts. John Mayor has noted the problem, acknowledging that states "are by no means really actors," despite the deeply institutionalised idea that they are.

Questioning the idea of the actor-state is not an idle academic exercise. Philip Abrams, one of the founders of historical sociology in Britain, has suggested that one of the crucial ways through which organised political subjection is effected in modern societies is by a particular and interested government presenting itself as the universal and disinterested organisation of the society as a whole. A particular political organisation thus presents itself as a unitary entity, speaking and acting in a unitary manner and in a highly personified form. Abrams alerted sociologists to this state-supporting discursive strategy in order to warn about the ease with which social-scientific discourses might unwittingly serve it. Yet his remedy, that sociologists reject the notion of the state as a "real" object and instead focus on the ways the state-idea is constructed and legitimised, directs analysis toward ideology rather than material forms. Problematising the personified actor state-idea need not, however, lead analysis in this idealist direction. While accepting that such a state-idea is central to the ideological project of legitimising organised political subjection, one need not be diverted from the ways the material environment is itself constituted as a force of moral and political governance. Like Abrams's analysis, Mayor's analysis of the state does not get us there, because he reduces the state to its "tendentious" culture, suggesting that its real foundation is a series of discursive "myths."

If treating the state-idea as *the* centre of gravity of *the state* leads us into idealism, an exclusive focus on the state-system is also problematic. Treating the state-system as though it is coextensive with the state as a whole circumvents analysis of the material forms of state power that do not reside in the apparatus of governing bureaucratic agencies. Faculty rejected such an analysis precisely because it implied the existence of another domain, that of civil society, which was set in opposition to the state, and this is one of the reasons he was "led to raise the question of power by grasping it where it is exercised and manifested,... Without considering, for example, the presence of a state which would exercise its sovereignty upon a civil society which itself would not be the depository of analogous processes of power." Faculty suggested that we should cut off the king's head in political theory, and work inspired by Facuity has seriously questioned the value of talking about the state as an actor. Such work has not generally done so, however, on the basis of an analysis of ideology. Rejecting the idea that power and ideology stop at the water's edge of knowledge, the work focuses on discourses of knowledge-power and the discursive rationalists of governance. Though centrally concerned with issues of science and power, "governmental studies" largely remain at the level of discursive "mentalities." This is true even though governmental studies emphasise the importance of science and technology in politics. As Mitchell Dean acknowledges, "thought" rather than practice is the centre of gravity of governmental studies.

Discourse, Practice, and Ideology

Without an analysis of the ideological aspects of discourse, maintaining an efficacious analytic distinction between discourse and practice is difficult. For instance, by presenting "medical police" as an essentially German or Continental phenomenon inherently at odds with English political discourse, Thomas Osborne dispatches it as irrelevant to English history. "Britain," he declares, "was a country without a tradition of police." Osborne arrives at this conclusion because his theoretical orientation takes discursive formations at face value. Accepting the central premise of English liberal discourse, that is, the idea of self-government, as a sufficient measure of social reality, he precludes empirical analysis of the role of government through police in eighteenth-century England. Yet as Karl Polanyi has demonstrated, the discourse of classical liberalism was crucially ideological, because there was "nothing natural about lassies fair." On the contrary, the "road to the free market was opened and kept open by an enormous increase in continuous, centrally organised and controlled interventionism."

This mismatch between discourse and practice is difficult to grasp without acknowledging the ideological aspects of discourse. Polanyi's insight is readily applicable to the history of the relationship between police and public health in England. Though the liberal discourse of nonintervention and self-regulation with respect to markets was extended into the domain of public health, that domain was, in fact, secured (to the extent that it was) by the expansion of the police power of government. This is an important point, because it counters the claim that medical police was a feature of English colonial government but not of English domestic government. Such arguments tend to down play the role of police in modern liberal state formation. Thus, while governmental studies provide a rich resource for understanding the development of liberal rationalities of government, much greater attention needs to be paid to actual practices of government. This is beginning to happen. Patriot Joyce, in his remarkable book *The Rule of Freedom,* navigates the discontinuity across discourses and practices with respect to liberalism and the modern English city, noting that liberal ideas of self-government have never fully displaced practices of police government.

Science, technology and State Formation

The effort to integrate the theoretical and methodological strategies of historical sociology with those of science and technology studies (STS) has, however, great potential for advancing explanation in both areas. The scientific, engineering, and technological culture that facilitated the Western takeover of the world is now being recognised for the power that it has been. Jack Gold stone, for instance, explains why the technological "effervescence" of modern Europe did not give way, as in other regions and at other historical moments, to a period of technological stagnation. Gold stone's emphasis on the significance of the steam engine, and the science and engineering culture that fostered its invention and development, provides a more specific explanation of the rise of the West. than more general theories of rationalisation, bureau-cratisation, institutionalisation, capitalisation, or modernisation. Indeed, Gold stone demonstrates that much of what is cited as unique to the West can be found in many regions of the world at different points in history. The steam engine, however, was the first really powerful technology in that it transducer fire into mechanical motion, a dream pursued by a number of engine scientists in the seventeenth century, including William Petty. Though the steam engine represented a departure from previous technologies, its invention is not surprising when viewed in the context of over a century of experimental engine science, the engineering culture it fostered, and the material technologies it spawned.

Three crucial dimensions of the modern science idea can be distinguished:

— mechanical philosophy (the grand unifying concept),

— ingenuity (a cognitive culture of intellectual and technological inventiveness), and

— experimentation (the concept of how to practice natural philosophy).

Experimentation implies an overarching engine science that places material technologies at the heart of natural scientific inquiry. Engine science requires the integration of natural philosophy, engineering, and mathematics *in practice*. The result is a culture of inquiry in which the conceptualisations of theory are tied to the manipulations of engineering and the operations of mathematics.

This new culture of inquiry is importantly defined by the role of material engines in the key epistemic practices of measuring, scoping, graphing, and manipulating. The four forms of material engine that correlate with these practices are meters (barometer, hydrometer, etc.), scopes (telescopes, stethoscopes, etc.), graphing technologies (cartographic instruments), and chambers (e.g., hydraulic and pneumatic technologies). These are *epistemic engines,* because they generate objects of inquiry, institutionalise and structure practices of inquiry, and drive the research agenda.

In doing so, they become what Labour calls "obligatory passage points" in scientific inquiry Attention to these technologies facilitates a comprehensive and naturalistic understanding of science as a very specific cultural complex of discourses, practices, and material culture. And though the specific technologies employed in statecraft may differ from those in natural inquiry, analogous practices of scoping, metering, graphing, and manipulating can be identified. Geological surveys and censuses, for instance, can be understood as terra-scopes and socio-meters. The point is to view the specific technologies in terms of the wider practices of engineering culture that straddle science and government in the modern period. Practices are the linchpin between discourses and materiality, because they participate in both.

Science-State Relationship

The understanding of the state in international politics has its roots in Max Weber's classical definition of modern statehood. With reference to the violent history of European state-building, Weber defined the central feature of modern statehood as 'the monopoly of the legitimate use of physical force within a given territory'. In Weber's words, the war-prone formation of state monopolies of physical force was a long-lasting process of 'political expropriation' in which all political communities other than the state had gradually been deprived of the means of coercion. However, the establishment of state monopolies of physical force should not be conceptualised merely in terms of power relations through which power-holders carry out their will despite any resistance from the subordinated. In order to establish consolidated states, the factual monopoly of the use of physical force has to be considered legitimate by both rulers and ruled. Stable systems of political authority do not rest on a monopoly of coercion alone: this state monopoly also has to be anchored in the cultural order of society. A political order needs legitimacy.

Long-lasting political institutions require a stable set of rules, which, in normative and cognitive ways, regulate the social conduct of rulers and ruled. In referring to the inner justification of systems of domination, Weber precisely distinguished political authority from mere power relations by resort to the notion of legitimacy. His concept of legitimacy is intended to give an answer to the question of when and why people obey. According to Weber, modern statehood rests on legal or rational authority, i.e. belief 'in the legality of enacted rules and the right of those elevated to authority under such rule to issue commands'. He sharply distinguished this modern authority based on formal legal procedures from pre-modern or traditional forms of authority, which rest on personal ties and the 'established belief in the sanctity of immemorial traditions and the legitimacy of those exercising authority under them'.

In the 1930s, Norbert Elias critically took up Weber's core definition and conceptualised European state formation as a 'civilising process.' In doing so, he applied a double perspective: The civilising process, seen from the aspects of standards of conduct and drive control, is the same trend which, when seen from the point of view of human relationships, appears as the process of advancing integration, increased differentiation of social functions and interdependence, and the formation of ever-larger units of integration on whose fortunes and movements the individual depends, whether he knows it or not.

In his theory of the civilising process, Elias put together the macro-sociological aspects of state formation and the micro-sociological consequences of this process, that is, the ways in which the evolution of the modern state has shaped social practices. Combining Weber with Freud, he defined the immanent link between the macro- and micro-levels as the conversion of outer constraints into self-restraints, and concluded that the formation of modern states has been reflected in increasingly differentiated patterns of self-control on the part of the individual. The pacifying institutional setting of modern statehood was accomplished by a particular normative restriction of the public behaviour of individuals. In this sense, state structures and social practices are inseparably knitted together, and the maintenance of public order relies on both functioning state institutions and forms of social action that are able to transform legal authority into daily practices.

In historical terms, however, this civilising process has not been 'civilised' at all. On the contrary, Elias traced the origin of both the internal pacification of society and the autonomy of the modern individual back to an unrestricted and violent process of elimination in which any individual or small group struggled among many others for resources that had not yet become monopolised. In mainly abstracting from the history of France, Elias differentiated between two distinct phases in the emergence of the modern state monopoly of physical force:

1) In the first phase, a factual monopoly of physical force is established. An increasing number of people lose direct access to the means of force, which progressively become centralised in the hands of a few and thus placed outside open competition.

2) In the second phase, this relatively private control over the monopoly of physical force tends to become public, i.e. it moves from the hands of state-makers into a political setting of legal institutions and appointed rulers under the control of the public.

While the first phase of the monopoly process is associated with absolutist and authoritarian forms of rule, the second phase deposes coercive state-makers and establishes structures of legal political authority. The two phases conceptualise the transition from traditional to rational authority in the emergence of the modern state. Consequently, state formation comprises not only the establishment of the monopoly of physical force, but also the transition of the normative and institutional order on which this monopoly rests from personal rule towards democratic governance.

From the perspective of 'state-builders', however, this transition of forms of authority was never intended. On the contrary, sociology conceptualised the formation of the modern democratic state as the non-intended outcome of the intended actions of European state-builders. In his article 'War Making and State Making as Organised Crime', Charles Tilly compared the early European state-builders with 'criminal' racketeers. Their interest was not in building states, but in acquiring material resources through coercive action. Accordingly, Elias' first phase of the monopoly mechanism could be understood as a system of protection and extraction, leading to the accumulation and monopolisation of the means of physical force in the hand of state-makers. The second phase Tilly described as a long-lasting process of negotiation between state-makers and the emerging capitalist bourgeoisie in which 'the pursuit of war and military capacity, after having created national states as a sort of by-product, led to a civilisation of government and domestic politics.'

In terms of global state formation, this long-lasting negotiation process can be traced in the legalisation of state-society relations, which was accompanied by a gradual increase in the state's capacities. The modern state and democratic social practices developed through the expansion and growing density of written formal law, framing the specific social space within which civil society could emerge. In this context, Jürgen Habermas identified four particular steps of juridification:

1) The establishment and consolidation of the monopolies of physical force and of taxation in the absolutist state.
2) The break with the personal monopoly of power in the absolutist state in constitutional monarchies by legally anchoring state power in political institutions and civil law.
3) The bourgeois revolutions initiated the nationalisation of the state monopolies, eventually bringing about the democratic nation state, with its separation of juridical, legislative and executive powers.
4) The formation of the welfare state tamed the autonomous dynamics that spring from the accumulative logic of the economic system and incorporated a variety of social functions into the domain of modern statehood.

Modern State—Image and Social Practice

Political scientists summarised this legacy of historical sociology and European state formation in an ideal type of the modern state. In institutional terms, statehood is defined as a centralised form of representative government based on electoral procedures and a set of administrative, policing and military organisations. The modern state claims the legitimate monopoly of physical force which state agencies exert over a certain territory and a relatively cohesive population that forms a community of citizens with political, social and economic rights.

In the academic field, this ideal type of state is primarily an analytical instrument to measure empirical statehood: it does not directly portray the 'real world' but represents an instrument of academic research. The definition, therefore, disregards both the historical length and the social and developmental steps which eventually resulted in this form of modern social contract between state-builders and society. Yet this image of the state has travelled from the social sciences into the conceptual world of political actors and societies at large. It has acquired a normative quality, telling us what a state ought to be. It is a globally relevant ideal of political order according to which we imagine the modern state as a transcendental and neutral power, a democratically controlled arbitrator standing above social conflicts. With this image of the state in mind, we judge political action in accordance with distinctions such as legal/illegal, formal/informal or public/private in order to measure and judge social action.

In reality the modern state is both an abstract and coercive macrostructure and a network of interdependent social actions in everyday life. Modern statehood consists of two dimensions: historically developed and relatively stable institutional structures, and culturally defined social processes. The institutional structure gives societies politically isomorphic forms. In this sense, the sociological definition of the national state developed into a formal blueprint for the political organisation of societies. Modern statehood is a central feature of world culture, and its ideal image has been formalised in most state constitutions. Ye t the second perspective, the state as social practice, characterises the actual social content of statehood as forms of permanent interaction and ephemeral social groupings. On this level, we can observe a complex and often amorphous tangle of social actions of which we make sense in reference to the ideal image of the state. Apparently, the rules of statehood as an organisational pattern and the logic of social practices do not necessarily correspond. In particular, the post-colonial state is characterised by competing and conflicting organising principles and social practices. This contradictory interface between the state as institution, image and social practice becomes particularly transparent when we soon in on individual political leaders.

Franchise Madder, for instance, analysed African statesmen as 'political entrepreneurs', a reference to both the symbolic and material sides of legitimate rule. In accumulating economic, political and social resources, the political 'big men' act through a system of personalised power in the name of the abstract institution of the state. In this way, these statesmen represent both the patriarchal chief of an extended network of personal ties (traditional authority) and the head of a formally institutionalised system of rule (legal authority). The contradictions in their position are apparent in three strategies of social action that are necessary for their political survival. In order to extract resources from international and trans-national donors, they have to pretend that they are acting according to the standards of modern statehood, that is, following the rules of good governance which emanate from the normative image of the state. As political entrepreneurs, however, they apply strategies of personal enrichment in accumulating external and internal resources within their networks of personal ties. Finally, they must meet the normative expectations of 'traditional' African societies for a redistribution of their resources within a system of clients. Caught in this pattern of often contradictory organisational and social constraints, the 'big man entrepreneur' must act according to a hybrid normative setting, containing elements of both the universal image of the state and the particularised values of local social practices.In labelling African states as weak, fragile or even failed, we are applying the socio-logical definition of the state in a normative way. Social practices which are based on traditional reciprocity turn into corruption and nepotism, and the informal distribution of social resources appears as an illegal strategy. In particular, states with strongly donor-dependent economies have to please the expectations of two different audiences. The big man entrepreneur must take into consideration both the formal norms of the supply side and the social norms of his local constituencies. The dynamics of contemporary state-formation have to be sought in these structural contradictions, which provide a framework in which current state-builders act. What does this mean for the field of applied policies?

State-Building and International Intervention

In a recent article, Francis Fukuyama argued for ''Stateness' First'. He discerned in contemporary interventionist policies a contradiction between state-building and the promotion of democracy, between, on the one hand, the monopolisation of physical force in the hands of the state and, on the other hand, the building of public and legal institutions which can constrain the state's power monopoly. Indeed, applying the categories of historical sociology, contemporary state formation is characterised by a confusion of the (chrono-) logic of the two phases of the monopoly mechanism. In cases such as Afghanistan and Iraq, institutional features of the second phase – constitutions, elections, representative bodies – were implemented before achievement of the first phase, the establishment of a legitimate state monopoly of physical force. Oriented toward the normative image of the modern state, current state-building processes tend to invert the social logic of European state formation, in which the coercive formation of state monopolies preceded both the juridification of political authority and the enhancement of state capacities.

Contrary to European state formation, post-colonial state-builders achieved a form of 'negative sovereignty', a formal legal entitlement which actually hides the lack of empirical statehood, that is, the social content related to the definition of the mod-ern state. The de-colonisation process established statehood only as a form of external representation, as a formal territorial and legal framework of international politics guaranteed by the world state system and by international law. Behind the facade of modern state institutions, however, social practices of a quite different nature have continued. The synchronisation of the state as an institution and as daily social practices, as in Elias' model of the civilising process, is still under way. From this perspective, 'fragile states' are not a new phenomenon at all. On the contrary, measured by the standard of the ideal image of modern statehood, most post-colonial states have been defective states from the beginning. In many of them a legitimate monopoly of physical force has not yet been achieved, and the so-called new wars of our times are therefore less an expression of state decay than an indication that the 'classical' European path to modern statehood has been derailed.

If at all, the term 'state decay' applies to some states of the former socialist world. There, relatively firm monopolies of physical force had been established, yet in some cases the second phase of Elias' monopoly mechanism ended in the at least temporary dissolution of the first. In these cases, the simultaneous introduction of grand schemes of political and economic liberalisation eroded the core institutions of the state rather than brought about the blessings commonly associated with the democratic state. Contemporary state formation does not seem to be following the state-building logics which historical sociology abstracted from the European experience.

Looking at current state-building in Afghanistan, Iraq or the territories of the former Yugoslavia. In these territories, a multiplicity of actors are involved in taking over a broad range of tasks, from combating and disarming militias to the building of political, social and economic institutions. Although oriented towards the image of the state, these 'new protectorates' only dimly remind us of forms of legal political authority which we can call a state. Rather, we are confronted with a kind of 'controlled anarchy', with fragmented political arrangements in which various international, trans-national, regional, national and local interests and competence overlap. For all these actors, the image of the state serves as a central normative reference while they follow their own goals on the ground. Whether these complex social arrangements will ever lead to viable states nobody knows.

The lesson we can learn from historical sociology is to understand state formation as an ongoing and open-ended process. State formation is characterised by both successful state-building and state decay, and in European history too, more states may have disappeared than became established according to our modern image of the democratic state. Both phases of the monopoly mechanism are extremely fragile and war-prone periods of institution-building and social transformation. What decides success or failure is contextual and cannot be derived from the abstract concepts of sociology. In Afghanistan, for instance, the Taliban were the first political force ever to come close to establishing a factual state monopoly of force over Afghan territory. From the perspective of historical sociology, that is, they successfully built up the core institutions of modern statehood. Their fall was not due to contradictions in the inner logics of state-building, but a result of the historical political context in which they acted. Due to political interests and normative demands on the international level, state-building in Afghanistan had to start again from scratch, involving a new coalition of old and new actors. Given this general contingency of the historical context, contemporary state-builders are facing the same general uncertainty as their European predecessors, namely that even their intended actions will have unintended outcomes. This applies also to policies of international interventions whose political rationale and public justification cannot be found in sociological reasoning or long-term state-building strategies guided by scholarship. The decision-makers in both state agencies and non-governmental organisations are not driven by sociological grand schemes, but by their own organisational interests and the dominant issues of everyday politics.

4

Political Culture and Democratisation

The notion of political culture came from German sociology, where it had a long and diverse lineage by the early 20th century. The German tradition did not coalesce into a single coherent definition of culture; rather, different authors emphasised different characteristics of culture: as the sum total of all socialite norms and practices, a legacy of history, norms or accepted ways of thinking and acting, a set of psychological orientation, a system that organises society, or something that humans create and pass along to the next generation. This holistic understanding of political culture resonated well with the national/ethnic stereotypes and racism that were widespread in the West in the first decades. Cultural theories have fallen out of favour more than once since the Second World War—partly because of their dalliances with racism and ethnocentrism—but reformulated versions have been proposed periodically.

Today a variety of cultural approaches can be found in political science. The dominant version of political culture since the 1960s has been a behavioural approach that borrows from psychology and uses survey research and experiments. Nevertheless, other kinds of cultural theories survive that owe more to anthropology and the earlier German tradition. The anthropological view, most famously described by Clifford Geertz, holds that culture is a property of a whole society, or subgroups within society, but in any case not of individuals.

Culture consists of both attitudes and behaviours, especially those that have become stable and routine and unquestioned. Culture is therefore is relatively static, in this view. Culture is also rich and complex: there are many attitudes and behaviours. Furthermore, these cultural elements cohere, united by their own internal logic. In this view, individuals may deviate from cultural norms, but the culture exerts pressure on them to conform. For this reason, individuals cannot be fully understood apart from the culture in which they live. This approach calls for *verstehen*, which in German simply means "understanding," but in English-language academic circles has come to mean an empathic, deep understanding of the culture by a perceptive scholar who knows it intimately enough to see it through the eyes of its members.

This approach emphasises the *meaning* of words and actions to the actors themselves. Several authors have claimed to describe cultures that are distinctively favourable or unfavourable for democracy. For example, Howard Wiarda has repeatedly argued that Latin American societies have a "corporatism" culture influenced by the teachings of St. Thomas Aquinas and the hierarchical organisation of the Catholic Church. This corporatism culture carries values antithetical to individualism, pluralism, and capitalism, all of which have been associated with political democracy. Another example is Lucian Pye's *Asian Political Culture*, which derives various orientation to political authority – some compatible with democracy, others not – from thick descriptions of family structure and child-rearing practices in seventeen Asian countries.

One common criticism of this anthropological approach, or at least of its extreme stereotype, is that it exaggerates the homogeneity of a society. Societies, especially large ones on the scale of nations, always contain subgroups with their own subcultures, and these often contain individual dissenters. Another common criticism is that while a static version of culture may be very useful for explaining political stability, it provides no leverage for explaining political change. A third weakness is that this approach forces the social-scientific community to trust the subjective judgment of self-appointed expert interpreters of a culture, as it would be difficult or impossible for other researchers to replicate the expert's field experience, even if they had access to extensive documentation. Nevertheless, it is probably true that this approach yields more detailed, accurate, and insightful portraits of a culture than a battery of survey questions can. A recent reformulation, inspired by later work in critical anthropology, rectifies some of the drawbacks. The "semiotic practices" approach does not assume that cultures are uniform or static or internally coherent. Rather, culture is the ongoing process in which individuals "make meaning" by engaging in political activity. In this view, culture becomes a hive of constantly evolving activity that is means different things to different participants. This approach strives for even more fine-grained and exhaustive descriptions of a culture, which demand even more skill and effort to collect and analyse texts, conversations, and practices.

At the opposite extreme lies the behavioural approach to culture, inspired by psychology. In this approach, culture is merely the aggregation of individuals' attitudes and (in some applications) behaviours. Culture does not exist except in the minds of individuals, although for some purposes it may be useful to describe the culture of a group, society, or nation by referring to the collective distribution of attitudes or an average attitude. This approach takes as little as possible for granted concerning the uniformity, stability, and coherence of attitudes. It may be that certain attitudes are dominant, that various attitudes go together because they are constrained by underlying value orientation, and that these patterns are stable or slowly changing; but in this approach, these are hypotheses to be tested, not features that can be safely assumed or asserted, even after extensive "soaking and poking" by an insightful expert. The best way to understand culture, according this approach, is to conduct rigorous survey research. Sometimes researchers also conduct psychological experiments. One early example of this approach with relevance for democratisation was *The Authoritarian Personality*, a project that began as a study of anti-Semitism in 1943 but eventually led to a scale measuring a "right-wing authoritarian" personality presumed to be supportive of fascist regimes. On the democratic side, the landmark study was *The Civic Culture*, which used public opinion surveys in five countries to identify a cluster of attitudes that the authors believed to be most propitious for stable democracy. Both studies suffered fierce criticism on methodological grounds, much of which was justified. However, because their mistakes inspired others to do better, they founded what is now a vast body of survey research on political culture and democratisation.

Whether an anthropological or a psychological approach is better depends on one's purpose. If the goal is to provide a rich, "thick" description of a small, relatively homogeneous community, then the prolonged immersion that anthropological approaches require is likely to lead to better insights. But if one's goal is to develop and test fairly general ideas about the impact of political culture on democratisation, then survey research and statistical analysis are indispensable. Beyond the study of small, homogeneous communities, the psychological approach is superior overall to any anthropological approach. By making questionnaires more comprehensive and more in tune with how people really think, survey research can approach thick description;

but survey research has valuable advantages that anthropological approaches can never equal. Only survey research takes samples that are demonstrably representative of a population, eliminating the need to rely on the authority of one observer. Only survey research can reveal how a population is distributed among different attitudes—a great improvement over asserting that the culture is homogeneous or admitting that it is heterogeneous without revealing the sizes of the subgroups. Only survey research can rigorously test a claim that certain attitudes cohere in a more fundamental structure. Only survey research can tell us whether certain attitudes or patterns really are stable. And only survey research, in combination with probability theory and statistics, can estimate how confident we can be that a sample is representative, that a subgroup is of a certain size, that an underlying cultural dimension exists, or that attitudes are changing or stable.

The fundamental difference between the anthropological and psychological or statistical approaches to political culture is that the latter holds that the attributes of a culture should not be asserted by an authority or merely assumed; rather they should be demonstrated with evidence. This principle applies to descriptions of individual attitudes, claims about the structuring of attitudes, relationships between attitudes and behaviour, and claims that any aspect of a culture is dynamic or static. Before the 1990s, lack of data made it practically impossible to demonstrate trends or stability in political culture beyond a handful of countries and topics. However, repeated waves of surveys—especially the U.S. National Election Studies, the Euro Barometer, and the World Values Surveys—have begun to make such generalisations possible. Unfortunately for the anthropological approach, these studies cast doubt on the alleged stasis of political culture. In fact, much of this research has been devoted to explaining patterns of change such as the decline of institutional trust and the emergence of post-materialist values.

Macro-Macro Studies

The kind of political culture research that is most obviously relevant for democratisation examines associations between national averages of individual-level attitudes and levels of democracy, the duration of democratic regimes, or the probability of regime transitions. Almond and Verba's *The Civic Culture* inaugurated this line of research. This study of the United States, Britain, Germany, Italy, and Mexico argued that democracy was most likely to thrive and survive where citizens possess a "civic" culture. Such a culture is a balance of "participant" traits, which incline citizens to take an interest in politics and participate in elections and other activities that make democracy work, and "subject" traits, which incline citizens to respect the law and the authority of the state and the government. Because this was the first cross-national survey project, it was path-breaking for its time but amateurish by today's standards. Critics pounced on it for using unrepresentative samples, asking invalid questions, overestimating the stability of attitudes and underestimating the impact of short-term political events, and drawing unwarranted connections between cultural patterns and regimes; in general, for reaching conclusions not justified by the evidence. But it hinted at what would be possible if such research were done more rigorously, and therefore inspired innumerable other studies.

In subsequent decades, comparative survey research became much more rigorous and abundant. Consequently, social scientists gained the ability to describe attitudes, trends, and relationships with much greater confidence. And as knowledge of political culture improved and trends became evident, theories about the impact of culture on democratisation evolved considerably. In *The Crisis of*

Democracy, Crozier, Huntington, and Watanuki argued that slow economic growth and high inflation were eroding the capacity of governments in the U.S., Western Europe, and Japan at the same time that citizen demands on government were increasing. They predicted that the growing gap between expectations and performance would eventually undermine confidence in leaders, institutions, and democracy itself. Some scholars predicted that many advanced democracies would fail within a few decade. One of these predictions did come true: confidence in institutions did decline, even outside wealthy Western countries. In most countries, confidence or trust in "government," legislatures, courts, politicians, civil service, armed services, police, and especially political parties fell from the 1970s to the 1990s. There were signs of widespread deterioration in other symptoms of civic culture as well: electoral turnout, party membership, generalised social trust, and face-to-face participation in voluntary associations.

Nevertheless, Western democracies did not fail, and support for democracy is strong, if not stronger than before. It has been suggested that this paradox can be explained by the moderation of inflation and by the conservatism of the 1980s, which lowered expectations of government. But these reasons are incompatible with declining trust in institutions. Two other arguments are more convincing. First, Rose, Mishler, and Haerpfer's comparisons of post-Soviet countries suggest that no matter how unpopular politicians, parties, and democratic institutions become, democracy will not break down unless some alternative regime has *greater* legitimacy. If true, this means that in the West, support for democracy remains strong partly because the collapse of Communism left it without a rival. Second – and contrary to Almond and Verba's embrace of some degree of the "subject" orientation and the *Crisis of Democracy* school's fear of disorder – there is a growing consensus that a certain amount of distrust in government is actually healthy for democracy. The growing numbers of "critical citizens" who question elite authority, shun traditional forms of participation, and invent new ways to associate, act collectively, and make their demands heard may be improving the quality of democracy by making representatives more responsive and accountable to the public. This explanation is also consistent with the fact that many formal democracies in the Third World are "illiberal" or "hollow" because, being less economically developed, they have fewer critical citizens.

The culmination of research in this vein is Inglehart and Welzel's *Modernisation, Cultural Change, and Democracy: The Human Development Sequence* (2005). This ambitious book proposes a sweeping theory of cultural change and democratisation, based on a quarter-million survey interviews in up to 81 countries from 1981 to 2001. Using factor analysis, Inglehart and Welzel identify two fundamental dimensions that structure national-average attitudes across countries. The first is the preference for traditional authority vs. Secular-rational authority. The second is an "emancipative values" dimension ranging from concern with basic economic or physical survival to an emphasis on elite-challenging self-expression. The authors also confirm the existence of various civilisations, defined by religion and colonial heritage, which tend to occupy distinct positions on these two dimensions.

For example, Confucian national cultures tend to be relatively secular and survival-oriented, Islamic national cultures tend to be traditional and survival-oriented, English-speaking national cultures tend to be relatively traditional and oriented to self-expression, and Protestant European national cultures tend to be secular and oriented to self-expression. Socialite values shift along both dimensions in response to economic transformations, in two phases. First, industrialisation shifts the source of authority from religion and tradition to secular states, science, and technology. But often before this cultural shift is complete, postindustrial transformations (particularly the growth of the service sector) halt secularisation and promote the questioning of authority of any type. Any country's average position today in this two-dimensional cultural space is a function of which civilisation it started from and how far industrial and postindustrial transformations have shifted its values toward secular-rational authority and self-expression values.

Contrary to the modernisation theory of the 1960s, Inglehart and Welzel argue that secularisation has nothing to do with democratisation: secular culture is as compatible with Communism and fascism as it is with liberal democracy. Instead, the cultural tendency that really matters is the level of self-expression values. There is a logical connection between having a large proportion of citizens who value self-expression—who feel economically secure, independent from elite domination, and claim "the ability to make decisions and actions based on autonomous choices"—and the probability of a country having a democratic regime in which representatives respect citizens' demands. Inglehart and Welzel argue explicitly that the Linz-O'Donnell-Schmitter elite-bargaining frameworks for understanding regime change underestimated the impact of political culture:

> Democracy is not simply the result of clever elite bargaining and constitutional engineering. It depends on deep-rooted orientation among the people themselves. These orientation motivate them to press for freedom, effective civil and political rights, and genuinely responsive government – and to exert continual vigilance to ensure that the governing elites remain responsive to them.

Inglehart and Welzel present massive evidence and sophisticated analyses to support most of their key arguments. Their two fundamental dimensions are robust, i.e., they appear even when different sets of countries and different sets of variables are used. They show that the traditional–secular/rational dimension is associated more strongly with the degree of industrialisation, and the survival–self-expression dimension more with the degree of postindustrial transformation. They show that cultural zones cannot be reduced to economics or regime experience. They show that wealthier countries have tended to experience value shifts in the same direction and that these shifts are associated with increases in elite-challenging political activity. They distinguish between formal democracy and "effective" democracy, which incorporates information about elite integrity. They go to great lengths to show that self-expression values cause stable democracy but stable democracy does not cause self-expression values, while controlling for a variety of competing causes.

Nevertheless, the analysis is not airtight. Macro-macro comparisons generally are vulnerable to several criticisms. Inglehart and Welzel's book partially overcomes some of them, but not all, so it is still useful to evaluate their contribution while discussing five problems frequently encountered in other macro-macro analyses.

One of the biggest challenges in cross-national survey research is achieving conceptual validity. When surveys must be administered in different languages and different cultural contexts, where the meaning of words and symbols can vary in subtle ways, designing questionnaires that can measure what is demonstrably the same concept across many countries requires care, experience, and trial and error. *The Civic Culture* was harshly criticised for its failure to do this, for example, in its mishandling of the difficult-to-translate standard U.S. Question, "Do you think that quite a few of the people running the government are a little crooked, not very many are, or do you think hardly any of them are crooked at all?" One common tactic for dealing with this problem is simply to keep trying a variety of questions until a consensus develops that it validly measures what it purports to measure. A question is more likely to be valid to the extent that it elicits the answers that were expected from respondents, it is strongly correlated with questions designed to measure the same concept, and it is strongly correlated with factors that were expected to cause it and with phenomena that it was expected to cause. Another tactic, which has become very common in survey research, is to use factor analysis to create an index that measures a fundamental dimension captured imperfectly by multiple survey questions. Each question can be thought of as a reflection of both the concept that one wishes to measure and one or more contaminating ideas. The more questions one has that capture the concept of interest, even if each one is quite contaminated, the more feasible it is to isolate the variation in each one that reflects the concept from the contaminants. Factor analysis (or a common variant of it, principal-component analysis) is simply a statistical technique that reveals whether it is useful to reduce multiple questions or variables to a simpler set of underlying dimensions. The factor analyst still must use subjective judgment to interpret what the underlying dimensions are, but factor analysis is extremely useful for identifying how many dimensions there are and which variables reflect which ones.

Inglehart and Welzel's two dimensions are indices constructed from just this kind of factor analysis. Because interpreting dimensions requires as much art as science, they remain subject to challenge, especially when an analyst claims to have identified universal values that have the same meaning in all countries. For example, it is not obvious that all of the variables included in the index of self-expression values really belong there. Is rejection of science really part of self-expression? Toleration of homosexuality? A preference for female leaders? Describing one's own health as good? More generally, is "self-expression" the best label for the commonality in all these attitudes? Are "elite-challenging values," "individual autonomy," and "human development," different labels Inglehart and Welzel often attach to this same dimension, really interchangeable? Are all of these the same as "post-materialism," the label that Inglehart favoured for over 20 years before revising and reinterpreting his index? If not, why did the interpretation change? The dimensions Inglehart and Welzel identify are robust enough that there is little doubt that they are real, but there is some fussiness around the edges of the interpretation that has been imposed on them.

A second common problem in macro-macro comparisons is that it is hard to disentangle the impact of culture from that of other static or slowly changing country characteristics, such as institutions, geography, level of economic development (within a short time-frame), world-system position, or particular historical legacies. This problem is strictly insuperable when the data are cross-sectional: a "snapshot" of many countries at one instant in time. Unfortunately, for many years all comparative survey research was cross-sectional because there were no repeat surveys for large numbers of countries.

But even though public-opinion time series are now available for many countries, it is still difficult to distinguish the impact of cultural characteristics that change slowly from the impact of fixed effects or gradual trends that tend to move in a consistent direction. If many countries are simultaneously becoming more democratic, more prosperous, and shifting toward self-expression, then it is very hard to say with confidence whether it is the economy or culture that is driving democratisation. One of the great strengths of Inglehart and Welzel's study is that it is the first to take advantage of the three waves of World Values

Survey data from 1981 to 2001. This span of time is long enough to contain some dramatic cultural shifts and to contain changes in democracy and economic performance that do not necessarily parallel changes in culture. This makes it possible for the first time to estimate the relative impacts of culture and economic development on democratisation. By the standards of more advanced time-series research—for example, analyses of presidential approval ratings month by month over many years, which makes strong causal inferences possible—Inglehart and Welzel's research design is still primitive. It does not go beyond examining the impact of a change in culture (and control variables) in one period on changes in democracy in one subsequent period, across anywhere from 19 to 81 countries. It is still much more a cross-sectional analysis than a dynamic analysis. Nevertheless, it is a clear advance over other cross-national cultural research on democratisation in this respect.

A third weakness of cross-sectional research designs is that they say nothing about the direction of causation. Even if culture and regimes are strongly associated, cross-sectional analyses leave open the possibility that regimes shape culture, rather than culture shaping regimes. Indeed, this was a contentious issue in cultural research on democratisation as long as studies were cross-sectional, and some of the most rigorous analyses persuaded many political scientists that a democratic culture was a by-product, not a cause, of democracy. However, Inglehart and Welzel report a fairly sophisticated series of tests to show that the causal order is as they claim: economic transformations cause shifts in values, which then make countries become more democratic and remain so. More specifically, they rely on the notion (standard in quantitative analysis) of "Granger causality," which holds that one can infer causation when 1) the cause temporally precedes the effect, 2) one controls for any factor that might affect both the cause and the effect, and 3) one also controls for past values of the effect. In their most rigorous test, Inglehart and Welzel demonstrate that self-expression in the early 1990s has a significant impact on average levels of democracy in 1997-2002, controlling for socioeconomic resources and average levels of democracy in 1981-1986; but average levels of democracy in 1981-1986 have no significant impact on self-expression in the early 1990s, controlling for socioeconomic resources and self-expression values in 1981.

Studies that associate regimes with highly aggregated indicators of attitudes often suffer from a fourth problem. It is usually called the ecological fallacy, meaning the error of assuming that a relationship between variables at a higher level of analysis also holds at a lower level of analysis. The classic example is the positive association between the size of the Black population in Southern U.S. Congressional districts in the 1950s and the share of the vote won by segregationist candidates: the positive association at the district level does not mean that Blacks were voting for segregationists. One may also commit the opposite, individualistic fallacy of believing that a relationship among individuals must hold when aggregated to districts, states, nations, or any higher level of analysis. For example, the fact that observant Muslim citizens of countries on periphery of the Middle East tend to support democracy more than non-observant Muslims should not lead us to predict that Islamic countries tend to be democratic. The simple fact is that a relationship at the national level says nothing about the relationship at the individual level, and vice versa.

Davis and Davenport claim that the post-materialism dimension does not exist at the individual level (because some of its components do not covary), and that it cannot be valid at the cross-national level if it is invalid at the individual level. Seligson similarly argues that the apparent cross-national relationship between mean national self-expression values and democracy is spurious because there is no corresponding relationship between self-expression and support for democracy at the individual level. Inglehart mounts two somewhat contradictory defences against these charges

. On the one hand, he insists that political culture is a system-level (national) phenomenon whose relationship with democracy is appropriately studied at the system level. Critics who demand confirmation of the relationship at the individual level are committing the individualistic fallacy, he contends. On the other hand, he goes out of his way to report that some of the relationships he identifies at the system level also exist at the individual level, although much less strongly. If the relationship were purely a system-level phenomenon, this evidence would be irrelevant. Furthermore, his expositions of the theory behind these relationships frequently refer to the motives and behaviour of individuals.

In summary, Inglehart and Welzel present strong empirical evidence that countries with a high percentage of the population with self-expression values are very likely to be democracies, but the evidence prohibits them from claiming that there is a powerful dimension of survival vs. Self-expression values at the individual level within many countries, or that individuals who value self-expression do more, on average, to produce or sustain democracy than their fellow-citizens who care more about mere survival.

Finally, there is a related but more subtle problem in these macro-macro comparisons that has attracted little notice. Cross-national comparisons of means sacrifice information about variability within each case. In effect, they ask us to believe that all respondents hold the national mean attitude or that there is a purely random relationship at the individual level. To deal with this problem and the previous one, it would be advisable for scholars to use hierarchical linear modelling (also known as random-coefficients models), which takes intra-country variability into account when estimating cross-national relationships. Such models can also allow the relationship between two variables to be different (positive, negative, or anywhere in between) within countries than it is across countries. If researchers were to develop a good theory to resolve the ecological paradox, such models would allow them to test it.

Comprehensive Framework

This critique of macro-macro comparisons suggests that a fundamental problem with cultural theories of democratisation is that the alleged cause and the effect are on different levels of analysis. Culture (understood as individual attitudes) is a micro-level phenomenon, but democratisation is necessarily a macro-level phenomenon. Attempts to bring the two together in an explanation casually shift the level of analysis of either the cause or the effect. Micro-micro studies translate regime change or survival into individual level actions or attitudes, such as protest, voting, strikes, tolerance, trust, or regime support. The macro-macro studies aggregate individual attitudes into a national mean attitude. The latter is a defensible move, but it is certainly not the only way, and probably not the best way, to shift levels. It is the best way only if theory says that a) the impact of culture is a matter of degree: the larger the proportion of the population that has the attitude in question, the greater the impact on democratisation; and b) it does not matter which citizens have the relevant attitude: generals and beggars are interchangeable. Even if a theory made these assumptions explicit and justified them, it would be incomplete because it would not tell us how clusters of attitudes translate into behaviour by certain actors to bring about the regime outcome.

In order to avoid shifting levels, or even to know how best to shift levels, it is essential to develop theories that specify the causal mechanism linking culture to regime survival and regime change. At present we do not have such a theory, but we can describe several of its elements. First, a cultural theory of democratisation would have to connect attitudes to behaviour. Which attitudes produce which kinds of actions? How reliably? Under what conditions? Without an understanding of this linkage, we are left to imagine a population magically willing a regime into existence or oblivion. Second, a theory must identify which citizens are in a position to have a significant impact on the regime. The attitudes and actions of military officers, politicians, judges, police, guerrillas, and union leaders are clearly more consequential than those of ordinary citizens, especially if the latter are not politically active. Therefore, an adequate theory should focus attention on the actors whose subculture really matters. But the set of actors who are influential depends on the institutional context. So, third, a cultural theory of democratisation should be conditioned on the initial regime and the direction of the regime transition. More actors, especially mass actors, are relevant for the survival or breakdown of democracy than for the survival or breakdown of non-democratic regimes.

For the study of transitions to democracy, one would want to pay more attention to the official party if the initial regime is totalitarian, to the military if it is a military authoritarian regime, to the ruling family in a traditional monarchy, to parties and the legislature if it is an electoral authoritarian regime, and to the dictator's cronies if it is a sultanates regime. Each context requires a distinct variant of the theory, depending on who the most directly relevant actor is. Fourth, there are various pathways to regime change (or consolidation) within each context. A democracy can break down by military coup, presidential coup, civil war, revolution, or a more subtle slide into human rights violations, party proscription, manipulated elections, or other illiberal practices.

Different actors and behaviours are relevant for each one. Sixth, a theory should also distinguish among phases of a transition. Mass actors can play a leading role in a regime breakdown and their pacific behaviour is essential for its survival, but only elites can create the institutions of a new regime. A theory of the impact of culture on regimes should therefore be highly conditional. Each kind of transition requires a different variant of the theory for different contexts that focuses attention on different actors, behaviours, and attitudes.

Specifying the conditions under which culture could matter for regime change would be a substantial improvement, but an adequate theory should also tell us more about the dynamics of culture. The most common criticism of theories of political culture has been that culture is too static to explain political change. This criticism is directed more against the anthropological understanding of culture than against the individualistic behavioural view that prevails today.

But a behavioural understanding of culture is entirely compatible with a more dynamic and powerful causal role for attitudes. Breakdowns should be associated with declines in support for democracy among key actors, transitions to democracy should be associated with increasing support for democracy at least among some actors, and democratic consolidation requires, by definition, the spread and strengthening of regime support. An adequate cultural theory of regime change should incorporate and explain these attitudinal changes.

Such a theory would ideally show how the attitudes of the most directly relevant actor are influenced by the attitudes of other, indirectly relevant, actors. In some cases, for example, the most directly relevant actor is the military. Why do some top military officers sometimes reject democracy and carry out a coup? They are not completely isolated from the rest of society, so it would be good to know to what extent they are responding to, or anticipating, a rejection of the democratic regime by business elites, foreign powers, the middle class, or the Church. Or if the armed forces decide not to initiate a coup in spite of difficult structural conditions, it may be that they are constrained by the attitudes of these other groups in society. Theories of regime change that focus exclusively on elites may give culture too little credit if they ignore the broader cultural environment that influences elite actions. Influence can flow in both directions, however. The phenomenon known as leadership can be understood as elite influence on mass attitudes. For democratisation, therefore, it would be useful to know to what extent the positions of elites (executive, party leaders, business leaders, the military, leaders of ethnic or religious groups) move mass opinion for or against democracy.

It is also important to understand how different kinds of attitudes are interrelated. Certain attitudes seem to be closely connected to behaviours that would affect regime change and stability, such as support for the incumbent regime and government or the rejection of violence. But other attitudes, such as moderation, political trust, social trust, tolerance, and evaluations of government performance, may affect these attitudes and gradually move them toward a threshold of regime change. A good cultural theory should make these connections explicit. It should also identify non-attitudinal factors that directly affect attitudes that are relevant for regime change. These could include generation-defining events such as the Great Depression, wars, Waterage, and the 9/11 attacks; learning; crime; and corruption scandals. Whose attitudes are affected? Which attitudes are affected? How quickly? How long do these effects last? All of these questions are relevant for a cultural theory of democratisation.

No one has ever surveyed enough actors at sufficiently frequent intervals to test such a complete theory. However, a simulation can reveal the kinds of patterns that we should be looking for. Suppose that we have four elite actors – the executive, the legislature, the courts, and the military. Suppose further that each one has an orientation toward the regime that ranges from 1 (pro-democracy) to 0 (anti-democracy). Let us also assume that there is a mass public that has a variety of attitudes, also ranging from 0 to 1. Some are political support attitudes, from the very general and abstract to the very specific. These include support for democracy as an abstract principle, for the actual democratic regime, for the government, for government leaders, and for government policies (which could be further broken down, if necessary). The mass public also has other attitudes that may be related to democracy, such as trust, tolerance, and moderation.

Finally, the simulation lumps together all the non-attitudinal factors as a single variable that we will call "performance." It stands for economic performance, maintenance of public order, war, corruption scandals, and every other event that might influence elite or mass attitudes. Again, this variable could be broken up into a variety of variables to make the simulation more realistic, but this is not necessary in order to identify the fundamental patterns that interest us here.

The patterns of convergence reveal which actors, and which attitudes, are most important in each scenario. If one specifies purely top-down influence (elite positions shape mass attitudes, but elites are not constrained by mass attitudes) and if performance is neutral, then mass attitudes eventually converge on the average position of the elite actors. If one specifies purely bottom-up influence (the mass public constrains elites, who exercise no leadership over the mass public), then elite positions converge on the average mass position. If influence flows in both directions, then the simulation reveals vicious or virtuous circles that spiral toward the positions of the most influential actors. Such scenarios are completely endogenous: every element is both a cause and an effect.

If elites have more influence over the mass public than the mass public has over elites, then positions converge toward elite positions faster than they do toward the mass public's positions. If the patterns of influence are more bottom-up than top-down, then convergence is faster toward the mass public's positions. However, if any element is exogenous – a cause but not an effect – then all the endogenous elements converge toward its position. For example, if performance has a prolonged and consistently positive impact (without being influenced itself by mass attitudes or elite positions) and is the only exogenous element, then eventually the elite and the mass public converge toward pro-democratic attitudes. In the same way, negative performance leads to anti-democratic attitudes.

In practice, performance (or whatever the relevant exogenous forces are) is rarely so consistently and uniformly positive or negative in the long term; it is variable, so attitudes may never converge. Nevertheless, this simulation suggests an agenda for research on political culture and democratisation. First, the most important question is whether any elements in the system are exogenous, because they will drive the whole process in the long run. Second, we must specify which elements are endogenous, because they will tend to vary together. Third, it would be very interesting to know whether the patterns of influence are more bottom-up or more top-down. The answer has obvious implications for democratic theory, as well as for understanding democratic breakdown and consolidation.Cross-national survey research has been growing explosively, but it is still not adequate for answering these questions. This framework would require surveying not only the mass public, but also any elite groups whose behaviour may be relevant for regime change or consolidation. Furthermore, all these surveys would have to be repeated frequently, at intervals of weeks or months, to be able to detect patterns of convergence. It may be impossible to carry out such research, especially in non-democratic regimes where elites refuse to grant interviews.

Political Culture and Mass-Led Regime Change

The best place to begin taking stock of the literature is with the pathways to regime change or survival in which the mass public takes the leading role. These are only a minority of the pathways because usually elite involvement is necessary and the mass public plays only the indirect role of pushing or constraining elite attitudes and actions.

Many scholars reject the notion of democratic "consolidation" because it presupposes a situation in which it is no longer possible for a democratic regime to break down. However, "consolidation" can be interpreted in a less categorical way, to mean that a breakdown is very unlikely in the near future, while recognising that in the distant future all bets are off. In this sense, democratic consolidation is not a regime attribute that can be observed; rather, it is a prediction that can be made if one has a sound understanding of the warning signs of imminent regime breakdown.

Linz and Stepan propose a conception of democratic consolidation based on this kind of understanding. They propose that there are three dimensions of consolidation – behavioural, attitudinal, and constitutional – and that consolidation is achieved when civil society, political society, economic society, the state, and the rule of law all reinforce one another.

Violent mass disturbances such as rioting and civil war can initiate a transition *from* either democracy or non-democracy. Although such disturbances cannot complete a transition *to* a new regime without elites taking a leading role, they can be sufficient first steps and they should be examined here because mass attitudes presumably help cause them. Peaceful demonstrations can similarly start but not finish a transition, although they involve different attitudes and actions.

One would expect that if any attitude is closely associated with democracy, it would be support for democracy as the best form of government. This is not the case, however: an index of four democracy-support variables is correlated at only .351 with Freedom House scores for 1995 and at .506 with average Freedom House scores for 1981-2000.

Clearly, there are many countries that are not democratic despite strong popular support for it, and many countries that are democratic despite weaker support. Democracy does not come about simply because many people want it, or fail whenever they become disillusioned with it. There are several reasons for the weak correlation. First, there is surprisingly little variation in support for "democracy" in principle.

Questions that ask whether respondents support something called "democracy" tend to find high and stable support almost everywhere. In the World Values Surveys in 38 countries in the mid-1990s, for example, the percentages of people who agreed relatively strongly with the statements, "Democracy may have many problems but it's better than any other form of government" and "Having a democratic system" is very good or fairly good "way of governing this country" averaged 90 percent in Western Europe and 81 to 86 percent in the six other regions, falling below 71 percent in no country except Russia, where it was 51 percent. Using a different question, the regional Barometers found lower, but still majority, support: an average of 80 percent in Western Europe, 70 percent in twelve relatively democratic African countries, 59. Furthermore, there does not seem to be a trend in any direction since the 1970s, when systematic cross-national survey research began. A second reason for the weak correlations is that simply asking people whether they support democracy probably does not tell us what we want to know about culture and democratisation. For one thing, it is important to gauge the levels of *relative* support for democracy compared to alternative regimes. Rose, Mishler, and Haerpfer argue that the "Churchillian" hypothesis applies well to Eastern Europe and Russia: we should expect democracy to survive despite low support when citizens believe it is the worst form of government except for all the rest.

Mattes and Bratton confirm this argument in Africa. It is also reasonable to suppose that high support for democracy could coexist with non-democracy if the non-democratic regime had even higher support. For another thing, correlations between support for democracy and indicators of democracy such as the Freedom House index or Polity may underestimate the association because the democracy indicators were not designed to capture differences in the quality of democracy. If we had more sensitive indicators at the high end of democracy, we might find that societies with a very high level of support for democracy are in fact more democratic than societies with only a moderately high level of support. Many of the new democracies are not very democratic, and there is some evidence that their citizens tend to be less supportive of democracy. As long as we use indicators that make all democracies appear equally democratic, the observed relationship appears weak.

But the most important reason for the weak correlation is that "democracy" means different things to different people. For example, summarising survey research in three Latin American countries in 1999, Roderic Camp reports that "First, among Latin Americans there is no consensus on what democracy means. Second, only Costa Ricans see democracy in largely political terms, very similar in content to the view professed by North Americans. Third, the Mexicans and Chileans... view democracy in social and economic, not political, terms."

Because of these divergent interpretations, asking people whether they support "democracy" is, in effect, asking them whether they support whatever democracy means to them. Because democracy has become practically synonymous with "good government," it is not surprising that support is so high virtually everywhere. The best example of this is Venezuela. The 2005 Latin Barometer reported that support for democracy was higher in Venezuela than in any other Latin American country except Uruguay, at a time when Freedom House and many international observers were lamenting the rise of the illiberal, less democratic, regime of Hugo Chives. In reality, Venezuelans were bitterly divided about their regime. Chives's supporters believed that their leader had replaced a corrupt, elitist regime with the country's first true democracy, while his opponents believed that Chives was destroying a fairly successful liberal political democracy. They all agreed that "democracy" was good, but they had entirely incompatible understanding of the word. For this reason, Mitchell Seligson has said that "if you want to measure support for democracy, the one thing you should never do is use the word "democracy" in the question."

There is some debate about whether this is good advice, as there has long been a divide between idealists, for whom "meaning for the analyst has taken priority over meaning for the participants" and a phenomenology approach, which respects subjective meaning more Several research projects have sought to describe what "democracy" means to the citizens themselves. This can be fascinating work that furthers the goal of thick understanding. However, it must not tempt political scientists into concept stretching.

Because respondents cannot help but interpret the word "democracy" in their own ways, it is more useful to examine survey questions that refer to institutions and practices that we mean by democracy rather than to some undefined version of democracy. Some surveys ask whether it would be preferable to let the army rule or to have "a strong leader who does not have to bother with parliament and elections." The most common questions of this sort ask how much confidence or trust respondents have in various institutions, some of which are inseparable from liberal democracy, such as elections, political parties, and the legislature. Although confidence tends to be high in the political community and the principle of democracy, confidence in specific democratic institutions tended to decline from the 1960s to the 1990s in older democracies and was very low in most of the newer democracies

Engagement with parties declined in 17 out of 19 wealthy democracies, confidence in parliament declined in 11 out of 14 countries, and in 12 out of 13 countries, growing numbers of citizens agreed that "politicians are only interested in votes," "MPs are out of touch," politicians and government "don't care about people like me," "politicians are untrustworthy," and "there are many dishonest politicians". In Latin America by 2005, confidence had sunk to an average of 31 percent in the courts, 28 percent in congress, and 19 percent in political parties.

The fear that this trend presaged the breakdown of even established democracies was not fulfilled by the first decade of the 21st Century, and some came to believe that it is healthy for citizens to distrust their representatives. This optimistic view makes sense in the wealthy, older democracies, at least in the medium term. Individuals who distrust democratic institutions tend to be if anything more, not less, supportive of democratic principles. But it is hard to discount the possibility that distrust of institutions will eventually metastasis into a rejection of democracy in principle. As Putnam, Phoria, and Dalton note, "If the decline in public confidence is justified (because of growing corruption, for example), then we might applaud citizens' ire but not its cause, just as we would be glad to have discovered a child's fever without being glad that her temperature was high".

Other Mass Attitudes

But it may be that attitudes that are not explicitly about democracy or democratic institutions may have a greater impact on the birth and survival of democracy. The related attitude that has been most studied is generalised interpersonal trust, sometimes called simply "social trust," to distinguish it from "political trust" in politicians and political institutions. Interpersonal trust was one of the components (along with political efficacy and pride in institutions) of Almond and Verba's civic culture, which they believed to favour stable democracy in the U.S. And Britain, compared to West Germany, Italy, and Mexico . Other scholars flashed out the reasons for this hypothetical connection. Inglehart was best known for emphasising the cultural shift to post-materialism, but he also argued that interpersonal trust lowers the stakes in politics, which favours democratic legitimacy and stability. Putnam et al. added that social trust—a natural by-product of face-to-face participation in secondary associations—is self-reinforcing, because if society is generally trusting, it becomes rational for individuals to be trusting as well, and unwise to be distrustful. This virtuous circle encourages public officials to be responsive, which improves the quality of democracy, and presumably high-quality democracies tend to be more stable.

Generalised trust has declined in some democracies, but not in others. The evidence for a causal relationship has been mixed. For example, one study using World Values Survey data for 17 countries reports that there is an association between social trust and trust in the police, civil service, and parliament at the aggregate, cross-national level, but not at the individual level. This is probably because there tends to be much less cultural variation within countries than between them, which may make it impossible to detect this kind of weak relationship except in cross-national samples, where the variation on both variables is wider. This interpretation is consistent with a study of three Latin American countries in which social trust at the individual level is weakly related to support for democracy only when the model includes no country dummies, which capture more general cross-national differences. When actual democracy, rather than support for democracy, is the dependent variable, the most extensive and rigorous study finds that interpersonal trust explains only 15 percent of effective democracy and has no significant impact on formal democracy, even in a simple cross-sectional model with only one control variable. As Inglehart and Welzel conclude, the cultural variable that has the most direct and important impact on democracy is probably not interpersonal trust.

Over the years, various scholars have pointed to tolerance, moderation or consensus, and subjective well-being. But again, the most extensive and rigorous study – Inglehart and Welzel's – concludes that all other attitudes take a back seat to self-expression values. In a comparison of approximately 60 countries, the level of self-expression in the early 1990s explains 32 percent of formal democracy and 55 percent of effective democracy, averaged for 2000-2002. Political trust, overt preference for democracy, obedience, and other values are significantly related to democracy only to the extent that they are correlated with self-expression, for their coefficients fail to reach conventional significance levels when models control for self-expression.

There are many reasons to reserve some skepticism about their finding: the available samples limit the analysis of change to just the impact of values in the early 1990s on average levels of democracy in 2000-2002, their models fail to control for anything except prior democratic experience, the causal pathways and relevant actors are undefined, and there is still some doubt about how to interpret "self-expression values" which in the section in question are confusingly re-dubbed "liberty aspirations". But the best evidence available at this point suggests that the aspect of culture that is most closely associated with democracy cross-nationally and over time is self-expression.

Culture and Behaviour

Inglehart and Welzel spin an elaborate and plausible theory about the causal pathway that links self-expression values to democratic transitions. They argue that transitions happen when and where self-expression values increase the numbers of civil rights activists and dissidents. As these changes swell the ranks of civil rights movements and back them up with greater mass support, it becomes more likely that liberal elites will endorse regime change. When pro-democracy activists eventually take the initiative, these elites are less likely to attempt to repress them.

These are excellent hypotheses that suggest possible causal connections in several stages, and Inglehart and Welzel produce empirical evidence in support of two links in their chain. They demonstrate that elites (those with education) almost always value self-expression more than society in general does They also show that self-expression in the early 1990s is strongly associated with Anheier et al.'s Civil Society Index for 2000 in 31 countries. They also refer to several confirming case studies. Unfortunately, this evidence tells us nothing about several of the other links in the hypothesised chain. Are the individuals who value self-expression the same individuals who are politically active? Do societies that value self-expression more also consider civil rights and other movements more legitimate? Does the growth of self-expression increase the probability that elites will support democracy and refrain from repressing pro-democracy activists? Is this true for the elites who can actually make a difference? We must look elsewhere to find out whether all the elements of this plausible theory are empirically true.

Thorough testing is essential because there are compelling competing arguments suggesting that mass culture does *not* have an important impact on transitions to democracy. One strain of theorising holds that attitudes and behaviours that we usually think of as antithetical to democracy may actually help spur transitions, or at least not harm them. Nancy Bermeo argues that moderation is not required for transitions to democracy. She points out that Portuguese democracy emerged from a Socialist revolution and Spanish democracy has coexisted with Basque terrorism. She also calls attention to successful transitions in Brazil, Chile, Ecuador, South Korea, Peru, and the Philippines despite high strike rates. Echoing Barrington Moore, who argued that violence was necessary to break the power of conservative anti-democratic classes, Elizabeth Wood makes the case that armed insurgencies in South Africa and El Salvador brought authoritarian elites to the bargaining table. In these cases, the economic costs of violence were necessary to persuade business, political, and military leaders that it was time to share power.

These arguments do not contradict Inglehart and Welzel's finding of an association between culture and transitions to democracy as much as it might appear at first glance, for two reasons. First, Bermeo's brief is with moderation, which is not one of Inglehart and Welzel's self-expression values. In fact, extremism and perhaps even violence may have more in common with the qualities that Inglehart and Welzel emphasise: challenging elite authority and being critical rather than passive citizens. Second, extremism and violence are usually characteristics of a minority, not the majority culture. It is perfectly possible for the majority to be moderate and peaceful even where there is an extreme or violent minority, and the existence of such a minority may in fact make authoritarians more eager to transfer power to moderates. Such a situation would resemble formal theories that focus on pacts or alliances between soft liners and moderates: in effect, a "good cop, bad cop" routine acted out on an immense stage. A synthesis of these two theories would suggest that a good combination for transitions to democracy may be two subcultures: one radical, violent, but minority; the other moderate, peaceful, and the majority. But at this point this is mostly speculation, tested in only a handful of cases studies.

It is also possible that mass culture has *no* impact on transitions. One of the most prominent students of culture and democracy, Larry Diamond, has stated that "democratic culture is certainly not a precondition for the initiation of democracy. . ." because elites and activists usually have decisive influence at this stage, as opposed to during consolidation. It could also be that a democratic mass culture has only indirect influence. Mass support for democracy (or moderation, tolerance, or trust) may percolate up through society, either inducing elites to change their minds or replacing authoritarian elites with new leaders who are more in sync with attitudes of the majority culture.

There are opposing points of view about the impact of political culture on the *survival* of democracy. On the one hand, Linz and Stepan argue that belief in democracy as "the only game in town," the only legitimate means for resolving conflict, is one of the defining aspects of democratic consolidation; and democratic consolidation, in turn, means a low probability of breakdown.

To complete the syllogism, the more people believe in democracy, the less likely democracy is to break down and the more likely it is to survive. In Linz and Stepan's definition of "consolidation," supportive mass attitudes and behaviour are absolutely required: citizens who want political change must shun violent means in favour of peaceful, constitutional activity. They accept fundamental democratic rules and comply with the law; if they protest, they do so peacefully. Ideally, they vote, and they do not vote for anti-system parties or leaders. Inglehart and Welzel argue that the rise of self-expression values similarly helps existing democracies survive. The more citizens value self-expression, the more social movement activists there are, the more legitimate non-activists consider them to be, and the more likely elites are to be responsive to mass demands. Such democracies are more effective and therefore more likely to survive.

On the other hand, there are many reasons to question any tight linkage of democratic survival and mass culture. First, now that public opinion surveys have become common in new democracies, we know that democratic regimes can often survive for years even when the public has little confidence in political parties, legislatures, courts, elections, and other democratic institutions. Rose, Mishler, and Haerpfer have pointed out that we should not expect disillusionment to turn citizens against democracy unless they believe that some alternative regime is preferable. In the absence of a more legitimate alternative, democratic regimes can hobble on without enthusiastic support for a long time. Second, Putnam's thesis has come in for heavy criticism. It is not clear that participation in voluntary associations promotes trust and cooperation; at the very least, such effects depend on the type of association. One would not expect salutary consequences unless citizens have face-to-face contact, the group is more horizontal than hierarchical, and it reaches out into the community rather than bonding members into a united front against outsiders. Weimar Germany was full of associations, which did not stop, and may have aided, the rise of Nazism. Third, it is anything but clear how participation in clubs, social movements, and other secondary associations affects major outcomes such as regime change. There has been considerable research on social movements, but it has mostly focused on their causes rather than their consequences. It seems clear, for example, that democracy favours the formation of social movements, but whether social movements favour democracy remains an open question.

Fourth, much of what we do know suggests that elite opinion matters much more than mass culture. Democracies can fail despite a broad popular preference for democracy. In *Ordinary People in Extraordinary Times*, Nancy Bermeo advances the provocative argument that mass public opinion almost never favours authoritarianism.

Rather, elites—the executive, party leaders, parts of the armed forces—mistakenly interpret the demands of anti-democratic minorities as representative of the majority, and overreact. Sometimes elites install a right- or left-wing non-democratic regime in the mistaken belief that the majority wants it, and sometimes they lead a coup to prevent what they falsely perceive as a revolution from taking place. Bermeo's thesis may contradict the naive assumption of political culture theorists that regimes express mass preferences, but it is quite plausible from a lay person's understanding of politics: the squeaky wheel gets the grease and silent majorities tend to be ignored. Her brief cases studies of the failed democracies of interwar Europe lack the public opinion evidence necessary to make her case convincingly; it is always possible that elites judged, and responded to, mass *opinion* correctly, even if it was not fully expressed by votes, membership, or the other available indicators of *behaviour*. However, her more detailed analysis of four more recent South American cases—Brazil 1964, Uruguay 1973, Chile 1973, and Argentina 1976— have the benefit of public opinion data, which does establish that these right-wing military authoritarian regimes were not a fulfilment of the wishes of the majority.

In Brazil, although there was majority support for land reform, which conservatives and the military considered threatening, the majority never wavered in its preference for democracy. In Uruguay, majorities wanted the military to remove President Bordaberry but only in order to restore democracy; the military assumed power in spite of massive popular opposition and resistance. In Chile there was polarisation that was dangerous for democracy, but only among party elites, not among the mass of voters. Most Argentine in 1976 may have been exhausted by violence and strikes and grateful for the military removal of Isabel Person, but there is little evidence that they preferred prolonged military rule. Bermeo's argument is convincing for these cases in the narrow sense that popular majorities appear not to have turned against democracy *per se* or to have been polarised to the point of having more people at the extremes than in the centre.

However, while making her case, Bermeo also demonstrates that there is sometimes majority support for military coups and does not exclude the possibility that non-majority levels of polarisation may sometimes lead to disruptions of political order that make it difficult for democracy to survive, even if relatively few desire that outcome. Her evidence is therefore compatible with the possibility that mass, though not necessarily majority, attitudes make an indirect contribution to the breakdown of democracy. Overall, however, her analysis reinforces the conclusion that the search for cultural explanations of regime change should not focus on the mean or modal attitudes of the undifferentiated mass of ordinary people, but on the attitudes of groups in society who are in a position to effect change, whether they are extremist social movements, political party leaders, or military officers.

A fifth counter argument is that elite leadership shapes culture rather than culture constraining elite attitudes and actions . Most of the research on this question has examined the relationship between US members of Congress and their constituents, regarding policy, not regime choice, so the implications of this relationship for regime change are virtually unexplored, although they remain worth exploring rigorously. The one exception to this is the attention paid to ethnic violence. In this line of research, few scholars believe that violence (which obviously can undermine democracy) is an automatic expression of deep, primordial hatreds. Rather, contemporary emphasis is on "political entrepreneurs" (leaders), who reinforce latent religious, ethnic, racial, linguistic, and national identities and exploit them to maximise their own political power. It has also been shown that leaders sometimes have the ability to prevent violence where it otherwise would be expected to break out.

Sixth, it has often been argued that culture is epiphenomenal: it has little direct, independent impact once one controls for the forces and events that shape both culture and the outcomes that it supposedly causes. Welch cause this the phenomenon of the "retreating cause": the closer one comes to understanding when, where, and why culture matters, the more it appears that "culture" is only a mask for the forces that really matter.

There two other ways that it is commonly thought that mass culture might affect the survival of democracy. First, democracy may die not with a bang, but a whimper: apathy, withdrawal from participation, abstention, delegitimation of institutions and leaders. Perhaps democracy dies not because citizens care too much, but because they care too. This seems to be the motivating assumption behind the large literature on political culture and turnout, party membership, group membership, and voting behaviour.

5

Modern Democracies and Governance

At the most basic level, it can be argued that modern liberal democracies suffer from a number of structural characteristics that prevent them from tackling global collective action problems in general. These are:

— *Short-termism.* The electoral cycle tends to focus policy debate on short-term political gains and satisfying the median voter. The short duration of electoral cycles ensures that politicians are concerned with their own re-election, which may compromise hard policy decisions that require a great deal of political capital. It is extremely difficult for governments to impose large-scale changes on an electorate whose votes they depend on, in order to tackle a problem whose impact will only be felt by future generations.

— *Self-referring Decision-making.* Democratic theory and politics builds on a notion of accountability linked to home based constituencies. It assumes a symmetry and congruence between decision-makers and decision-takers within the boundaries of the nation-state. Any breakdown of equivalence between these parties, i.e. between decision-makers and stockholders, or between the inputs and outputs of the decision-making process, tends not to be heavily weighed. Democratic "princes" and "princesses" owe their support to that most virtuous source of power: their people. The externalities or border spill-over effects of decisions they take are not their primary concern.

— *Interest group concentration.* In democracies, greater interest group pluralism reduces the provision of public goods because politicians are forced to adopt polices that cater to the narrow interests of small groups. The democratic process rewards small, well organised interest groups and results in their proliferation. Also, strong competition among such groups leads to gridlock in public decision-making, delaying both the implementation and effectiveness of public goods provision.

— *Weak multilateralism.* Governments accountable to democratic publics often seek to avoid compliance with binding multilateral decisions if this weakens their relationship to their electorate. There is a notable exception; it occurs when strong democratic governments can control the multilateral game. Concerns such as these have generated scepticism about the compatibility of democratic forms of governance with the need for the drastic and urgent changes in policy required to combat climate change. The implication is that they are unable to meet the scale of the challenge posed by climate change, and that more coercive forms of government may be necessary. Such thinking finds its historical precedent in the work of the "eco-authoritarians" of the 1970s, who argued that it might be difficult in democracies to constrain economic activity and population growth that results in pressures on the environment. They suggested that some aspects of democratic rule would have to be sacrificed to achieve sustainable future outcomes, since authoritarian regimes are not required to pay as much attention to citizens' rights in order to establish effective policy in key areas.

Democracy Versus Autocracy

This type of argument has, however, been undermined by a body of theory arguing that there are a number of reasons why democracies are more likely than authoritarian regimes to protect environmental quality. Democracies have better access to information, with fewer restrictions on media and sources of information, and greater transparency in decision-making procedures. They encourage the advance of science, which is responsible for our awareness about climate change and other forms of environmental threat in the first place. Scientists and other experts are free to engage in research, exchange new evidence and travel to and obtain information from other countries. These factors make it more likely that environmental issues will be identified and placed on the political agenda, and tackled according to appropriate measures of risk. Moreover, concerned citizens can influences political outcomes not only through the ballot box, but through pressure groups, social movements and the free media – channels that are closed in autocracies. The presence of civil society also serves to inform the public, act as a watchdog on public agencies, and directly lobby government. There are many examples of cases where environmental interest groups have been able to overwhelm business interests pursuing environmentally damaging practices and of cases where they have changed the public agenda.

At the same time, authoritarian regimes have fewer incentives to adopt or stick to sustainable policies. Environmental concerns are often trumped by economic development plans and external security, as was the case with the Soviet regime. Leaders are unaccountable to the public, and have less ground to enact long-term policy . And in authoritarian regimes, those in power control a substantial fraction of society's resources, encouraging pay-offs to a relatively small elite, resulting in less public goods provision.

It does not seem unreasonable, then, to expect a strong correlation between democracy and environmental quality. Indeed, among the 40 highest carbon emitters internationally (cumulatively responsible for 91% of total world emissions), the countries that have the best records are all democracies. However, upon closer examination, the record is less compelling, and detailed empirical evidence is inconclusive. Environmental quality is not just measured by a broad based commitment to addressing emissions of carbon and other greenhouse gases (GHGs). While some studies have shown that authoritarian regimes have worse records than democracies on environmental protection, others find no evidence to suggest that this is the case. Indeed across a range of measures and geographical areas numerous studies prove that outcomes are varied.

On balance, while evidence on the link between political institutions and environmental sustainability does seem to suggest that democracies are preferable to authoritarian regimes, we might expect the effect to be far greater than it actually is. Why is this the case? Part of the reason might be attributed to the different types of transmission mechanisms that translate policy commitment into policy outcomes. Battig & Bernauer, for example, find that while the effect of democracy on political commitment to climate change is positive, the effect on policy outcomes, measured in terms of emissions and trends, is ambiguous. They observe that the causal chain from environmental risks to public perceptions of such risks, to public demand for risk mitigation, and to policy output is shorter than the one leading from risk via policy output to policy outcome. Because of that, outcomes are infuenced by a range of other factors, such as the properties of the resource in question, mitigation costs, and the efficiency of implementing agencies. Politicians might easily declare a set of public policy commitments to climate change mitigation, but the outcome of such efforts is affected by factors that are often outside of their control. The result is that policymakers respond quite well to public demands for more environmental protection, but tend to discount implementation problems, hoping that voters will not be able to identify these within a short enough time period to use their votes as a punishment for any failure to deliver.

Commitment Deliberative Democracy Approach

An additional concern is that political commitment to tackling climate change is critical, yet may require political leaders to adhere to a particular course of action that is potentially unpopular, and hence contrary to structural democratic pressures. The actual implementation of policies that reduce global warming may infringe on the democratic preferences of citizens. In such a context, political leaders can be caught between a desire for recognition and esteem in the international community—recognition that comes from peer admiration for leadership—and the need to ensure accountability to domestic electorates. However, good democratic leadership is not confined to policymaking alone —it also involves educating constituents about pressing issues that may not be obvious to them. In this sense, the fact that democratic publics do not always have fully formed preferences is an advantage as well as a risk. Citizens can significant shift their preferences, faced with new information and evidence about pressing issues. The democratic citizen that is capable of being "fact-regarding, future-regarding and other-regarding," is not simply a myth.

Such an approach to democratic "will formation" can be found within the tradition of what is known as deliberative democracy, broadly defned as "any one of a family of views according to which the public deliberation of free and equal citizens is the core of legitimate political decision-making and self-governance"

Deliberative democrats advocate that democracy moves away from any notion of fixed and given preferences, to be replaced with a view that democracy should become a learning process in and through which people come to terms with the range of issues they need to understand in order to hold defensible positions. They argue that no set of values or particular perspectives can lay claim to being correct and valid by themselves, but rather are valid only in so far as they are capable of public justification. Individual points of view need to be tested in and through social encounters which take into account the point of view of others. Ultimately, the key objective is the transformation of private preferences via a process of deliberation into positions that can withstand public scrutiny and test. Empirical findings show that citizens can and do alter their preferences when they engage with new information, fresh evidence and debate. These can lead to new and innovative ideas about public policy and about how democracy might function and work.

Deliberative democracy can, in principle, increase the quality, legitimacy and therefore the sustainability of environmental policy decisions. This is partly due to the uncertainty associated with environmental issues, which demands a wide range of experience, expertise and consultation. The complexity of climate change problems also require integrated solutions that have been vetted by multiple actors and that cut across the narrow confines of expert knowledge and the responsibilities of established institutions and organisations. And the concerns of environmental justice require the political process to be as inclusive as possible, giving voice to the under represented, including future generations. Effective and just action on climate change depends upon the continuing involvement of citizens in the making and delivery of policy; conventional representative democracy is a poor way to achieve this alone. To remodel environmental politics around deliberative democracy is thus to create an opening for a change in the way democracies address environmental management in general, and climate change in particular.

In shifting from policy commitments to real and binding action, democracies have all too often been unable to override the problems of short-termism, collective action and other factors that cut against emission reductions efforts. This is not to say that democracies are incapable of tackling climate change. Rather, certain aspects of them typically fall short. The question now is whether democratic systems can be evolved to handle the problem better, and how this may be achieved.

In shifting from policy commitments to real and binding action, democracies have all too often been unable to override the problems of short-termism, collective action and other factors that cut against emission reductions efforts. This is not to say that democracies are

Democracy, Governance and Climate Change

Complex global processes, from the ecological to the financial, connect the fate of communities to each other across the world, yet the problem solving capacity of the global system is in many areas not effective, accountable, or fast enough to resolve current global challenges. What has been called the paradox of our times refers to the fact that the collective issues we must grapple with are of growing cross-border extensive and intensity, but the means for addressing these are state-based, weak and incomplete. While there are a variety of reasons for the existence of these problems, at the most basic level the persistence of the paradox remains a problem of governance. The abilities of states to address critical issues at the regional and global level are handicapped by a number of structural difficulties, domestic and international, which compound the problems of generating and implementing urgent policies with respect to global goods and bads.

One significant problem is that a growing number of issues span both the domestic and the international domains. The institutional fragmentation and competition between states can lead to these issues being addressed in an ad hoc and dissonant manner. A second problem is that even when the global dimension of a problem is acknowledged, there is often no clear division of labour among the myriad of international institutions that seek to address it: their functions frequently overlap, their mandates conflict and their objectives often become blurred. A third problem is that the existing system of global governance suffers from significant deficits of accountability and inclusion, which can result in less economically powerful states and, hence, their entire population being marginalised or excluded from decision making.

Today, there is a new found recognition that global problems cannot be solved by any one nation-state acting alone, nor by states just fighting their corner in regional blocs. What is required is collective and collaborative action – something that the nations of the world have not been good at, and which they need to be much better at if the most pressing issues are to be adequately tackled. The failure to generate a sound and effective framework for managing global climate change is one of the most serious indications of the challenges facing the multilateral order. The former British chief scientist Sir David King has warned that the threat posed by climate change is more serious than that of terrorism, and Sir Nicholas Stern has referred to it as "the greatest market failure the world has ever seen" In the broad view of the scientific community climate change has the capacity to wreak havoc on the world's diverse species, bio-systems and socioeconomic fabric, and the process has clearly begun.

Anarchic Inefficiency

The number of actors and variety of organisations involved in both agenda setting and policymaking at the level of global environmental governance has increased substantially over the past decade. In addition to private, public and civil society actors, new types of actors have emerged such as Trans-national activist networks, private rule-making organisations, government agencies and public-private partnerships. Moreover, established organisations have adopted new roles and responsibilities. For example, many intergovernmental organisations have acquired a higher degree of autonomy from the governments that have established them, and many NGOs now engage in agenda setting, policy formulation and the establishment of rules and regulations. However, the increased engagement of diverse actors does not necessarily guarantee either effectiveness or equal access of diverse voice. In fact, it often leads to double representation of the west and north through both powerful states and NGOs.

At the institutional level, while many international environmental agreements exist, and possess some admirable characteristics, they are often both poorly coordinated and weakly enforced. Furthermore, they are supported by a plethora of different international organisations fulfllling various functions. The current constellation of over 200 international environmental agreements suffers from a problem of what might be called "anarchic inefficiency," featuring a diverse set of players whose roles are largely uncoordinated among each other. The most prominent

The UN system, including the United Nations Framework Convention on Climate Change (UNFCCC), the Environmental Management Group (EMG) and the Centre for Sustainable Development (CSD)

While international action on climate change relies overwhelmingly on the evidence presented by the UNFCCC (including the Kyoto Protocol), the UN system overall has so far been ineffective in reducing GHG emissions, and is hampered by major divisions between north and south. The internal UN system is also still arguably uncoordinated on climate change, although there are plans to change this. The EMG, chaired by United Nations Environmental Program (UNEP), is a key vehicle for this cooperation, but it remains too early to judge its progress. The CSD has engaged with NGOs in a constructive manner, and has an important agenda-setting role, but is also relatively ineffective.

Global Environment Facility (GEF)

The GEF has a climate change remit, including serving as the main financial mechanism for UNFCCC. However, it has suffered legitimacy problems: developing countries have opposed GEF control of the Kyoto Adaptation Fund, perceiving a voting bias in favour of richer countries and the control of the World Bank. The current governance structure of the Adaptation Fund is regarded as an interim solution until this can be resolved. Elsewhere, the GEF has delivered important grants for climate change mitigation and adaptation, but has a tendency to support smaller technical or pilot projects that are not mainstream in countries or economic sectors.

The OECD Environmental Directorate

While this division of the OECD is technically proficient (having conducted agenda-setting work, for example, on environmental indicators and economic modelling of carbon markets) it is globally unrepresentative. It also regards climate change as amenable to technical, pro-growth economic solutions, contrary to the views held by many of the key actors in the debate.

The World Trade Organisation (WTO) Committee on Trade and Environment

Collaboration between the UNEP and the WTO was proposed in 2006, yet the Committee has not even been able to agree to a limited environmental package within the Doha Round. There is little appetite to recognise climate change damage as grounds for unilateral member state exceptions (GATT/WTO Article XX) to world trade rules. Collaboration is, therefore, largely symbolic—the WTO is seeking more environmental legitimacy, while the UNEP wants access to WTO deliberations.

Environmental Chamber of the International Court for Justice (ICJ)

The ICJ has thus far played an insignificant role, with no cases since its formation in 1993. It has been hampered by limited rules of standing and divided opinion over the need for a separate International Court for the Environment.

Representation and the Responsibility of the Wealthy

Problems with representation at the level of global governance are high on the list of obstacles to addressing climate change. Multilateral bodies need to be inclusive; unless both developed and less developed states come on board, the net reduction of GHG emissions becomes a much harder task, if it can be achieved at all. Ensuring effective representation is not a question of just providing a seat at the negotiating table in a major IGO or at a major conference. For even if there is parity of formal representation (a condition typically lacking), it is generally the case that developed countries have large delegations equipped with extensive negotiating and technical expertise, while poorer developing countries frequently depend on one person delegations, or have even to rely on the sharing of a delegate, and lack the negotiating strength to participate fully in discussions. This is indicative not only of the problem of unequal access to decision-making, but of inequality of all types of resource. Many developing countries do not readily command the public funds, capacity or technology to come into compliance with agreed regulations designed to reduce emissions. As a result any future agreement cannot simply build on the traditional burden sharing approach of dealing with a problem inherent in the global commons; given the scale of transformation that is required for a sustainable future, wealthy industrialised states will have to bear a signifcant part of the cost of the transformation in developing countries.

Policy Debate

The greatest differences in the debate about the politics of climate change tend be revealed in issues of how to square the circle of participation, effectiveness and compliance. Or, to put the point more broadly—is it possible to combine coherently democracy, markets and universal standards?The answer is far from straightforward; if international rules become stricter, we can expect reluctant states to become even more reluctant to be bound by them, while if participation increases, agreement may only become possible via lax rules.

A critical component of a global deal will be the way in which market incentives are structured. In terms of targeting GHG emissions, two principal market-based instruments exist: cap and trade and taxation. Supporters of the former include Stern who points out a number of disadvantages with taxes. They do not allow certainty over how big future GHG reductions will be, since estimates are imprecise and there is a long flag time between policy output and actual outcomes. They are hard to coordinate internationally, and developing countries are unlikely to agree such arrangements, which impose economic burdens on industries without offering the of setting gain of being able to sell emissions permits. Moreover, electorates in general are mistrustful of governments' use of tax resources, potentially opposing them in the belief they provide an excuse for "stealth taxation". A better approach is to set targets, and then seek out the cheapest method (via the price mechanism) of reaching those.

Cap and Trade System

According to its supporters, cap and trade makes the most sense of the options available, because it allows for greater certainty about eventual emissions levels and produces better incentives for producers. At this point, it also appears to be the approach most likely to be adopted at the global level, with a European Union Emission Trading System (EU ETS) already in place, and a successful precedent in the form of markets for sulphur in the United States. However, global markets in carbon and other GHGs are likely to be far larger and more complex than any previous emissions trading schemes, with a commensurate increase in levels of risk, opportunity for leakage and distributional consequences. Negotiating a comprehensive global accord and meshing national systems so that they operate coherently will be a highly fraught and difficult process, if it can be achieved at all.

Indeed, while cap-and-trade seems to be an ideal solution on the surface, it is in fact an odd way to do business. Politicians like it because it is market-based, does not require the imposition of unpopular taxes, and can be worked out with special interest groups in back room negotiations. Indeed, with regular auctions to sell of emitting rights, and the lack of a long term or stable price, cap and trade is a lobbyist and trader's dream. Yet, putting the dangers of rent seeking aside, it is not even clear that cap and trade will lead to required emissions reductions. As Sachs observes, "a cap-and-trade system can be more easily manipulated to allow additional emissions; if the permits become too pricey, regulators would likely sell or distribute more permits to keep the price 'reasonable.' Since the long-term signals from cap-and-trade are less powerful than a multi-year carbon tax, the behavioural changes (e.g. choice of the type of power plant) brought about by cap-and-trade could well turn out to be far fewer, as well." Such concerns are borne out by the existing record on carbon emissions trading. The global market grew to £126 billion last year, up from £63 billion in 2007 and nearly 12 times the value in 2005. This represented the value of a total of 4.8 billion tonnes of carbon dioxide, up 61% from the 3 billion tonnes traded in 2007. However, the actual emissions cuts made and sold by United Nations-registered clean energy projects in developing countries fell by 30 % in 2008 to 389 million tonnes.

Tax on Carbon

Contrary to the claims of cap and trade advocates, it can thus be countered that taxes are less likely to result in policy failure. Economic efficiency demands that those who create emissions should pay the costs, and taxes are the simplest way of forcing them to do so. Their advantages are many. They offer a broader scope for emissions reductions, as opposed to trading systems which can only be implemented among private firms or countries, and not among households and individual consumers. In this sense, they are the more democratic option, since they create greater coverage and are less susceptible to strategic lobbying for exceptions by firms or non-governmental organisations. Their universal guiding principle is distributive, since they simultaneously discriminate against polluters while allocating priority to the most vital cases of environmental need. They involve less administrative costs, are less complicated and more familiar to policymakers, and provide new avenues of generating revenue to tackle climate change for governments that are increasingly unwilling to incur political costs by expanding general taxation. Finally, they place a clear price on emissions for many years ahead, allowing for better long term policy planning. Of course, there remains the substantial challenge of shifting taxation structures away from their primary focus on work and production toward a greater emphasis on pollution, externalities and consumption. It goes without saying that this will require a great effort, marked by short-term and long term objectives, which could be weakened by new election results, changing coalitions and so on.

New Policy Mix

In reality, the policy mix is likely to contain multiple policy instruments. The prospect of large revenues from permit auctions has established signifcant political and economic interests in the creation and maintenance of markets for GHGs. Cap and trade also offers the potential for far greater levels of private sector funding than is the case for government financed funds and schemes, and will create signifcant private sector flows from developed to developing countries, an absolute necessity for reaching a global deal. However, if policymakers are serious about putting a true price on carbon and other GHGs – essential if markets are to sort out efficient supply and demand side responses – then taxation will have to form a key element of policy as well, in order to ensure predictability of outcome, and the generation of new resources for the provision of urgent environmental goods.

Unfortunately, putting a price on all GHG emissions (whether through tradable permits or taxes) is not enough on its own to deliver the needed reductions. Existing market-based schemes, such as the EU ETS, or carbon taxation by individual European countries and US states, have so far failed to generate large scale research into the development of breakthrough technologies. Such schemes might eventually result in a levelling of or even a slight reduction of emissions, but will only stimulate a marginal diversification into alternative forms of energy such as solar and wind power. This is because private sector firms under invest in research and development if they fear they will not be able to earn a decent profit on resulting product development. What is ultimately required is a fundamental overhaul of energy systems through transformation technologies that require a combination of factors to succeed – not only market incentives, but also applied scientific research, early high-cost investments, regulatory changes (e.g. building codes and practices), infrastructure development, information instruments (e.g. eco-labelling of energy appliances) and public acceptance.

To ensure flexibility and encourage innovation, regulations should be based on achieving particular results, rather than simply specifying the methods or technologies to be used to achieve those outcomes. Care needs to be taken in choosing instruments in a policy mix to ensure that they are complementary and avoid unnecessary overlap, and that they are cost-effective. By setting too high a price or too tight a cap, policy will result in excess costs, while choosing policies that are too lenient will forego the potential benefits of added, cost-effective mitigation measures and risk the failure of meeting required targets.

Elements of a Democratic Global Deal

Climate change is a problem with global causes and

consequences. A coordinated international effort is therefore required to achieve cost effective and successful mitigation policies. However, the nature of the problem also means that international agreements will be difficult to reach. Countries and regions have very different interests in achieving a solution, implying a highly contested distribution of costs and benefits. In addition, developing countries, given their relatively small contribution to historical emissions, object to having their development impeded by restrictions. Finally, the challenges associated with enforcing a global solution may make some nations reluctant to participate, adding a source of uncertainty about how cost-effective the policies will be. However, despite the vigorous debate surrounding the type of policies required to combat climate change and how they should or should not be implemented, there is considerable overlap on what the political elements of a global deal might look like. At the most general level, most commentators agree that it should be broadly inclusive, multifaceted, state-centric and sustainable.

Participation

The key requirement is participation from all countries, and most importantly, participation by the most powerful democracy in the world. The world has been waiting for the United States to join the collective effort against climate change; there is now reason to believe that it is ready to act. The integration of less developed states is also crucial, as already noted. Even if the developed states of the world were to cut their emissions to zero by 2050, without signifcant cuts in the rest of the world the overall goal of keeping a global rise in temperatures to under 20C would be missed. Developing countries need to be convinced that they can simultaneously reduce their emissions and increase their growth rate by increasing their energy efficiency. They need, for instance, to eliminate distortions in their energy markets, such as large oil subsidies. But for most developing countries, the cheapest form of energy is coal (or other high-emission energy sources), and in those cases, there is a real trade-of. Money spent to reduce GHG emissions is money that could be spent to provide education, better health and clean water, or to grow faster. In such cases, developed countries, it can be argued, should pay for the incremental costs. However, as Victor et. Al. have pointed out, this is unlikely to happen – it is simply unrealistic to expect industrialised nations to contribute the tens or hundreds of billions of dollars needed for such a compensation scheme when official development assistance (including for wars in Iraq and Afghanistan) currently stands at around $100 billion for all purposes. Moreover, the countries that would get the most compensation, such as China, are now west's most potent economic competitors.

Offset Schemes and Financial Incentives

The alternative is some form of offset scheme that allows industrialised nations to fund emissions reductions in developing nations, and counting those reductions towards their own legal commitments. The idea is that this would require industrialised nations to pay a majority of the costs while also laying a foundation for the creation of a global emissions trading market. This was the aim behind the creation of the Clean Development Mechanism (CDM). However, although the CDM has, after a difficult start, been successful in creating a global market for GHGs, its design is fundamentally fawed, and it has done very little to actually cut emissions or to assist host countries in achieving sustainable development.

Another important requirement will be the prevention of deforestation, which contributes 17% of current carbon emissions, almost twice as much as transport. Developing countries' tropical forests are an important source of carbon sequestration, yet they are not provided with any compensation for these environmental services. Providing them with financial incentives will help to reduce emissions from frosted lands and invest in low-carbon paths to sustainable development. In this regard, encouraging steps have been made in the implementation of the United Nations Fund for Reducing Emissions from Deforestation and Forest Degradation. However, the establishment of a final framework for the transfer of funds is still some years away, with a final agreement only likely to come into effect after 2012. Moreover, there are serious concerns about the appropriate geographical scale of accounting and incentive mechanisms, monitoring, land tenure, elite capture of funds and the potential for fraud

Participation and deliberation on a global scale are necessary, yet in their current forms, existing instruments of global environmental governance are ill-equipped to achieve results. What is needed are representative institutions armed with the capacity and legitimacy required to translate policy commitments into real world outcomes. If a global deal is going to work it must have an answer to the problem of governance, and embody an institutional structure that shapes and determines decisions which reflect the whole world in an evenhanded way. Recourse to inclusive and broadly representative global decision-making channels is the most appropriate and effective way of doing this, and strengthening mechanisms of global governance will be key to constructing a global democratic response to the issue.

Democracy and the Policy Menu

The challenge of tackling climate change will require the development of considerable additional institutional capacity and policy innovation. The goal of achieving this capacity, and the means to get there, will be undermined if countries of all stages of development are not directly involved in the shaping of solutions. Current policy development demonstrates this concern. The short term path to effective environmental governance is to integrate a broader set of interests into existing multilateral governance capacity. The existing mandate of the GEF could be broadened in order to help coordinate and fund international environmental agreements and reflect developing country priorities. Complementary to this, the UNEP could increase its status and responsibilities by becoming a specialised UN agency, with all the compulsory UN funding that this entails. The central challenge in the years ahead of compliance monitoring and enforcement could be facilitated through a formal international mechanism for settling environmental disputes through mediation and arbitration, potentially similar to the World Bank's investment dispute body. Enhancing the capacities and responsibilities of the GEF and the UNEP in this way would be a step toward the more consolidated and formal institutional capacity of a World Environmental Organisation as a longer term goal, driven perhaps by the G2 + 1, but accountable to the G195.

Key Role of the State

In all of these challenges, states remain the key actors, as they hold the key to both domestic and international policymaking. The implementation of international agreements will be up to individual states, emissions trading and carbon pricing will require domestic legislation, and technological advance will need state support to get of the ground. However, state strategies at the domestic level should involve the creation of incentives, not overly tight regulation. Governments have an important role in "editing" choice, but not in a way that precludes it altogether. This approach is represented in the form of what Giddens calls "the ensuring state," whose primary role is help energise a diversity of groups to reach solutions to collective action problems. The state, so conceived, acts as a facilitator and an enabler, rather than as a top-down agency. An ensuring state is one that has the capacity to produce definite outcomes. The principle goes even further; it also means a state that is responsible for monitoring public goals and for trying to make sure they are realised in a visible and legitimate fashion.

This will require a return to planning – not in the old sense of top down hierarchies of control, but in a new sense of flexible regulation. This will require finding ways to introduce regulation without undermining the entrepreneurialism and innovation upon which successful responses will depend. It will not be a straightforward process, because planning must be reconciled with democratic freedom. There will be push and pull between the political centre, regions and localities, which can only be resolved through deliberation and consultation. Most importantly, states will require a long term vision that transcends the normal push and pull of partisan politics. This will not be easy to achieve.

All this takes place in the context of a changing world order. The power structure on which the 1945 multilateral settlement was based is no longer intact, and the relative decline of the west and the rise of Asia raises fundamental questions about the premises of the 1945 multilateral order. Democracy and the international community now face a critical test. However, addressing the issue of climate change successfully holds out the prospect of reverting a rule-based politics, from the nation-state to the global level.

Civic Learning in Changing Democracies

The times, they are a changing in long established European and North American democracies. Alarming numbers of young citizens seem to have turned their backs on government and conventional politics. It appears that contemporary politics in most societies increasingly fail to capture the interest and attention of young citizens, who are generally skeptical of politicians and party affiliation, and increasingly unlikely to vote. A study of voting turnout by age in 15 European democracies conducted by the Institute for Democracy and Electoral Assistance in Sweden concluded that youth voting decline is a serious and widespread problem for contemporary democracies looking to the new generation of citizens for participation, legitimacy and support.

To many observers, the civic deficit problem appears to run far deeper than voting. For example, Rahn finds a strong correlation between national integration in the global economy and diminished citizen identification with a range of civic activities and indicators of national citizenship. Some scholars have concluded that there is a distinctive Millennial Generation (roughly composed of those turning 21 around the turn of the century), and that this cohort is profoundly apolitical, as highlighted by a rejection of traditional citizen roles centred around civic duties such as voting. For example, 71 percent of British *Millennials* believe that voting makes no difference. The numbers of British youth who aspire to enter public service are dwarfed by nearly a fifty-to-one preference for entrepreneurial business careers. A follow-up survey in Britain in 1999 compared the *Millennials* to the general population and found that 40 percent of 18-24 year old in Britain were not even registered to vote, compared with just 8 percent of the general population. O'Toole observes that a media stereotype of the youth engagement crisis in Britain has evolved around the factoid that more young people voted on the reality TV show *Big Brother* than in the 2001 general election. (In a personal communication, Stephen Coleman avers that the possibility of multiple voting on Big Brother may cloud this claim).

Young Citizens and Politics

A general survey on the status of young people in Europe revealed a remarkable convergence of trends reported by researchers in 15 European Union member states and three nations outside the EU. A bulletin on the report posted by one of the participating research institutes sounded this alarm: "Young people's and young adults' limited political participation—voting, membership in political parties, youth organisations, and representation in decision-making bodies—is considered a major problem in most Western European countries. Young people's declining political engagement and participation in society are perceived as a challenge for the future of representative democracy.

A survey of the "civic and political health of the nation" in the United States concluded that the American Millennials might be better termed the "Dot Nets," both out of their strong self identification as a generation and their preferences for communicating through various digital interactive media, factors that seem important for thinking about civic education initiatives. Like their European counterparts, the American Dot Nets are turned off to conventional politics and government, but highly involved in issue activism, political consumerism, and protest activities.

Some observers contextually such trends in less alarmist terms based on theories of social change, arguing that recent generations have entered a time of more personalised, less institutionally (e.g., party, union, church) organised politics in which citizens participate by other means through "self actualising" or "self reflexive" involvement in personally meaningful causes guided by their own lifestyles and shifting social networks.

If we apply such perspectives on social change and political identity to the question of what defines the Millennials as a generation with similar cross-national political tendencies, we might consider first that they entered society at the height of the current wave of economic globalisation. Among other things, this period has been defined by high levels of labour market dislocation (more frequent career changes, less employment security, periods of unemployment and underemployment) and an overriding sense of generalised risk. Unlike earlier periods of modern era change, the contemporary experiences of risk and dislocation are negotiated by individuals largely through independent identity management strategies. The Millennials are less guided by encompassing ideologies, mass movements, party and governmental support structures, and other factors that might help individuals focus on government and politics in times of strain.

Living in these disrupted social contexts, young citizens find greater satisfaction in defining their own political paths, including: local volunteerism, consumer activism, support for issues and causes (environment, human rights), participation in various Trans-national protest activities, and efforts to form a global civil society by organising world and regional social forums. Bang has called this a generation of "everyday makers" who define their own sense of politics according to networks of personal relationships aimed at adding value to their lived experiences. Observers like O'Toole and Bang argue that new generations of citizens are simply redefining what they mean by politics, and that social scientists should embrace this shift. Others counter that citizens greatly diminish their political capacity when they replace familiar public action repertoires centred on government and collective identities with narrower discourses fashioned from highly personalised and localised concerns.

When politics becomes so personal, public policies that try to embrace the Millennials may fail because governments tend to deliver collective solutions, and collective solutions do not fit personalised problems. Consider, for example, the reaction of a 19 year old black woman (one of O'Toole's respondents) to an effort by the British Labour Party to address economic and social dislocation among young people:

> ......this New Deal thing that Tony Blair has come up with, it's not for everybody, it does not suit everybody's needs. It basically puts everybody in a little box and expects them to go either this way or that way. It doesn't work for everybody... You have to treat people as individuals, not just a little group so that everybody does have the opportunity to do something.

Some observers contend that changing definitions of citizenship are a natural feature of democratic life. This is surely true. However, the compelling issue remains that the turn away from such defining democratic activities as voting may also represent a serious threat to the core of democratic civic culture. In addition, the redefinition of politics in highly personal and localised terms raises questions about whether procrustean governments can appeal to their new generation citizens on the terms those governments were primarily designed for: delivering collective solutions to broadly defined social problems. These concerns present clear challenges for thinking about and designing effective civic education programs that may appeal to the young citizens who go through them, and at the same time serve the interests of democracy in changing societies. Since there appear to be very different brands of citizenship in play within the same societies, how can civic education address and reconcile these differences without forcing unappealing, one-size-fits-all models of political consciousness and behaviour on entire cohorts of young citizens?

Challenge for Civic Education

The challenges to civic education in this picture are obvious. Most policy makers define and fund civic education programs (which are run primarily in the schools) based on highly conventional citizen models which centre around the idea of the "Dutiful Citizen" (DC). At a minimum, the DC is expected to learn about the basic workings of government and related political institutions, to understand the values of the national civic culture, to become informed about issues and make responsible voting choices. The challenge for civic education, simply put, is how to integrate and adapt these conventional DC virtues to the changing civic orientation of the new "self- Actualising Citizen" (AC) who may see her political activities and commitments in highly personal terms that contribute more to enhancing the quality of personal life, social recognition, self esteem, or friendship relations, than to understanding, support, and involvement in government.

Civic identifications and practices, if they are to be adopted, must have some anchors and inducements in the lived experiences of individuals both inside and outside of the education and socialisation settings in which they are introduced. The Dutiful Citizen continues to have obvious appeal, particularly to educational policy makers, based on the reasonable perception that citizen activities centered on voting and informed opinion are necessary to instill in new generations in order to ensure the viability of democratic polities. At the same time, recognising that young citizens today may have substantially different social and political experiences than their elders did at comparable stages of life also seems important to incorporate into models of civic education. In short, effective civic education models need to address substantive changes in citizen roles, while finding ways to motivate young people to find ways to engage meaningfully and effectively in civic life.

Case Study of Australia

Australia offers an interesting national case both because of the awareness in the policy community of generation changes among young citizens, and because of the difficulty of incorporating this awareness into the classroom curriculum. Part of the policy innovation and implementation problem no doubt stems from the fact that there are so many sites of civics curriculum coordination and breakdown—as is the case in many nations. For example, the Civics Education Research Group at Canberra University lists 45 distinct sites of input and coordination—from international organisations such as the International Association for the Evaluation of Educational Achievement (IEA), to national governmental policy agencies involved with citizenship, education and immigration, to numerous state education boards and private councils. At the same time, the issues confronting the Australian civics project have been fairly well defined by The Australian Council of Education Research (ACER) following participation in the landmark IEA study of 90,000 fourteen year old in 28 nations.

Australian students scored around the middle of the international distribution in terms of overall civics skills scores. The authors of the ACER report conclude that despite this passing performance on the skills and knowledge tests, the data revealed a deeper problem. The adequate performance of Australian students on basic civic knowledge and skills measures did not translate into a desire to engage in the corresponding activities of civic life defined by the IEA study as "conventional citizenship". This is a form of what Rahn describes as the disconnection between identification and engagement, or the "being and doing" aspects of citizenship. Among the disturbing findings: 83% felt that joining a political party was not important in order to be considered a good citizen; only 55% felt that knowing about the nation's history was important; only 50% regarded following issues in the media important; and 66% regarded engaging in political discussion as unimportant. The relatively strong commitment to voting was down played in the report as merely echoing the compulsory status of voting in Australia. Yet what seemed equally clear in the IEA study is that the AC side of civic life is far more attractive to young Australians: 80% said it was important to engage in activities that benefit others, 74% wanted to protect the political environment, and 68% were concerned about human rights. The authors conclude that Australian students were inclined to look outside government for solutions to political problems.

What were the implications of this increasingly familiar young citizen profile for Australian civic education? The results of the IEA study became the basis of a report from the Australian Council of Educational Research on the goals for civic education in Australia. The recommendations of the ACER report included a sensible blend of the AC and DC sides of contemporary citizenship. Their recommendations below, taking the liberty of noting what seem to be the DC goals above the dotted line and the AC goals below it.

1. Knowledge of Australian political institutions and structures
2. Values concerning democracy, the rule of law, social justice, equity and fairness
3. Commitment to including all Australians in the political process
4. An obligation to see citizenship in an international perspective
5. Understanding the everyday lived experiences of young people and their apparent alienation
6. Recognising schools and classrooms as democratic institutions
7. Accepting that citizens are constructed by multiple identities rather than a single identity.

Where is Australia in crossing the AC/DC divide? The Ministerial Council on Education, Employment, Training and Youth of Australia surveyed national civic education policy, and analysed all available documents from agencies promoting or conducting civics education programs. The first conclusion was that civics is not even among the 8 key learning areas established for all schools in Australia. Indeed, there is concern that civics has slipped from the required curriculum in many nations, reflecting the educational turn toward basic academic skills and, perhaps, reflecting underlying struggles to de-politicise the schools. The second conclusion of this national survey was that only three content areas were widespread throughout Australian civics curriculum documents: 1) Australian democratic heritage and operation of government and law; 2) Australian national identity and cultural diversity; and 3) the set of skills and values necessary for informed and active participation in civic life. These goals are very similar to the three DC goals identified in the recommendations from the IEA study. Still missing from the general civics learning picture in Australia were the goals that might engage the AC citizen.

Communication-Based Model of Civics Education

The case of Australia suggests that even when the challenges of addressing complex citizenship are recognised, the solutions are elusive. In part, this may be due to generation differences in the perceptions of citizenship that favour policies and curriculum designed by older citizens who do not experience public life from the standpoint of younger generations. This may be compounded by the false, but commonly heard, impression that approaches to civic education that include AC perspectives necessarily sacrifice DC virtues. The overriding problem may be the absence of a model for integrating both AC and DC elements of citizenship in a coherent curriculum.

Using Standpoint Issues to Communicate Identity

A starting point for engaging AC learners who experience a distant and often disagreeable DC world is to allow them to define their own political standpoints—and avoid immediately requiring them to locate those standpoints in terms of conventional politics. This may be easier than it initially appears. Political standpoints for the AC emerge fairly easily around issues that matter in their daily lives. Moreover, exploring shared experiences with those issues enables shifting the framing of those experiences from private to common concerns.

There is evidence that the Dot Nets are concerned about issues and problem-solving, and even more inclined toward collective identification with their peers than predecessor generations. For example, the U.S. Civic health of the nation survey found higher levels of generation identification (69%) among the Dot Nets (those born between 1977 and 1987) than among GenX (42%), the Baby Boomers (50%), or the Matures (51%). However, in keeping with their AC citizenship bias, the Dot Nets were by far the least likely (38%, 48%, 60%, 59%) to say that good citizenship entails responsibility. At the same time, the Dot Nets are as likely as any generation to have engaged directly in political consumerism in support of environmental and other causes, and they are nearly twice as likely as other citizens to have participated in protest politics. What can be done to channel these clear indications of political interest and potential for common identification in more conventional political directions?

A simple proposition about civic learning consistent with these trends is that conventional skills such as engagement and information-seeking begin with motivation—generally powered by interest in specific issues or problems. A promising beginning to any civic learning experience is to empower the learners to find issues in their immediate communities that seem important to the people with whom they live and associate. One model for this is the Student Voices project, a national civic learning program developed by the Annenberg Public Policy Centre in the United States. Student Voices begins by training students to take simple surveys of their communities and bring the results (community concerns) back into the learning environment (usually a classroom) to explore through deliberations under the guidance of the learning facilitator (usually a teacher). The Student Voices model is interesting because learners introduce issues with which they identify personally, and they contribute through group deliberations to the development of a class issue agenda that results in a collectively constructed issue or problem that becomes the focus for subsequent civic learning. A similar model is offered by the Project Citizen curriculum developed by the Centre for Civic Education in the U.S.

Once learners have identified with a personal issue and participated in constructing a collective framing for a common issue (which may or not end up resembling their initial issue), they have taken the first step in understanding how to construct a public discourse and negotiate interests in common with others with whom they identify. These elements of the civic learning process can be enhanced through a combination of conventional and technology-driven communication processes. For example, the results of deliberations can be posted on discussion boards for follow-up reactions from those involved in the deliberations, and for sharing with others engaged in similar experiences in the same school, across the city, or around the world.

The mixture of face-to-face deliberation and subsequent individual-level input through online messages and chats can create a sense of personal ownership in the issue adopted by the learning community. The issues may cover a wide variety of topics, from crime, drugs, education, and teen recreation issues, to local or global environmental concerns. The actual issue is less important than its origins in individual and collective definition and mutual recognition processes, aided by the willingness of the facilitator not to impose too much definition from on high.

Navigating the Political Information Environment

Young citizens are immersed in what may be the richest, yet most fragmented information environment in human history. The channels that young citizens use to gather information and to communicate about their political issues are important considerations in creating engaged citizens. Tuning out is surely as useful a skill as knowing what and when to tune in. Media literacy training can create awareness of the dilemmas of incorporating DC information skills into the often discouraging real world media experiences of young citizens. This entails lessons aimed at more critical de-construction and use of available information channels, and at finding channels that address the issue at the centre of the learning experience. These aims can be advanced by introducing civic learners to several different slices of the media environment in which they live. Some obvious candidates for attention include: *election communication*, *conventional news and entertainment*, and *the digital information sphere*.

Electoral communication is important to highlight in order to demystify the process through which campaigns seek votes, a process that often excludes substantial voter blocs such as young people. Painting today's democratic process with a broad brush finds parties and politicians scrambling for electoral support by placing their appeals in the hands of professional communication consultants who target narrow voter blocs to gain tactical electoral advantage. The near universal consensus among these consultants is that spending precious campaign budgets on messages aimed at young voters is a waste of time and money. Young people are deemed hard to reach through conventional media strategies, and even harder to convince that politicians are not all alike. The idea that campaign messages and candidate images are marketed to voters much the same way that commercial products are sold may help young citizens to see that, in communication terms, they represent demographic market segments—highly prized for selling fashion and entertainment products, but less valued in electoral marketing strategies. A simple proposition about youth disengagement is that since they are not asked in meaningful terms to participate in the electoral process, they don't.

This introduction to political communication offers learners an honest appraisal of their place in the political scheme of things in most countries, and may help them see why many of their peers reject a political system that implicitly ignores them. At the same time, it is important to show that electoral results do have consequences for various social groups, including young people. It is also important at this point to introduce citizen engagement options—both electoral and non-electoral that provide both information and pathways to effective action concerning the issue defined in the last learning module. The general goal here is to begin moving away from the idea of the citizen as a passive spectator in the electoral arena, or more generally, in relation to government, and toward a model of active citizenship.

Understanding the political influence of news and entertainment media offers a next step for helping young citizen's think about their political views. A major obstacle to active citizenship is the relationship that many young citizens establish with the mass (particularly commercial) media. The absence of citizens —particularly young citizens—playing central roles in conventional news and public affairs programming reinforces impressions that issues are too confusing or that there is nothing that ordinary people can do about them. In addition, the portrayal of scandal and unpleasant images of politics may further reinforce negativity toward politics, politicians and government. Whether these media trends actively produce or merely echo a late modern culture of anti-politics, the evidence is clear that most mass media content, particularly on commercial television, ranges from apolitical, at best, to overtly negative toward politics. And, what may be just as civically isolating, most youth programming aims at full immersion in a commercialised environment selling fashion, entertainment, and other consumer products as the core elements of social identities anchored in lifestyles. Examining that media environment seems an appropriate next step in understanding the broad rejection of politics and the common experience of being lost when thinking about the problems and issues that do matter.

Case materials suitable for a politically focused media literacy curriculum abound in nearly every national context. Consider, for example, the market research materials produced by the Gérman public service broadcaster ARD. The monthly reports called *Media Perspectives* often publicise the network's market research with a focus on audience demographics and content comparisons between public service and commercial television outlets. These studies demonstrate common, cross national audience trends such as the greying of the public service news audience, and the disproportionate appeal of infotainment news on commercial channels to younger viewers. The implications of these trends for politics and citizenship are dramatic. For example, people who exclusively watch news on German public service channels consistently demonstrate two to three times the levels of interest in political affairs, depending on what is happening during the periods when polls are taken.

The explanation for this political interest gap is most likely a combination of what these audiences are offered by different media sources, and what interests they bring to their viewing in the first place. For example, an analysis of news content on the public and private channels shows that political content fills 66% and 63% of news programming on the two leading German public channels, ARD and ZDF, compared to just 29% and 28% on the leading private channels RTL and Sat. Audience political tastes are considerably at odds as well, with public service audiences preferring information about national politics, state politics, social issues and international affairs, and private channel audiences ranking natural disasters, crime, and accidents as their favourite news fare.

The moral of this media literacy story is that media choices matter. While it may be difficult to convince young learners to tune in public service news, there are other high quality and personalised news sources that may appeal to them. In learning environments with school or home access to the internet, the most obvious direction for Dot Nets who have issues that they want to understand is the rich sphere of discourse and information on the Web.

The digital information sphere offers a rich menu of interactive information options for individuals seeking information about issues that motivate learning and action. For example, the BBC has launched a prototype experiment called *can*, which enables citizens to define and post their own issues, link to broad networks of similarly concerned individuals, find information about public actions and government responses, and, ultimately, push for BBC coverage of their concerns. There are also many dubious sites that merit another round of communication literacy training in the digital sphere. In general, however, the information habits of *netizens* suggest two promising trends (based on research in the U.S.): 1) young people increasingly prefer their information in online, interactive environments, and 2) veteran internet users are among the most informed citizens.

A policy problem facing the incorporation of information technologies in civic education is that nations vary greatly in the development and distribution of internet access. For example, the United States leads in the category of computer-based online access, while Germany and France have been slower to introduce the levels of service competition and infrastructure necessary to democratise this important communication medium. However, increasing numbers of schools are wired, and next generation mobile phones will have search and information features that may enable young people to do more than down load the latest hit songs as ring tones.

Where access is available, young people follow. In the United States, the internet now rivals regular news programming and comedy shows as the leading sources of information about politics for young people. More importantly, those who use the internet are far better informed than those who rely on other sources of information, and these *netizens* are far more interested in politics. The universal attraction of young people to digital communication technologies can be important for motivating engagement with their chosen issues, and, as outlined in the next set of recommendations, for helping to establish collective identifications with those issues as well.

Citizenship as Communication Practice

Personalising the information process in the ways that many ICTs make possible may risk fragmenting publics and isolating individual citizens. Developing a highly individualised sense of politics may not be regarded as a problem in the AC world, but it is often seen as antithetical to the DC view of the democratic polity. In order to counter the perils of isolation through overly personalised digital media experiences, the learning environment for next generation citizens must be designed to appeal to the affinity for networks and communities of interest. Interactive communication technologies should be aimed at creating echoing online environments that enable others to engage with and contribute to emerging understanding of the public issues at the centre of the learning experience. This sense of common engagement with one's own and with others' issues introduces the experience of being part of a public as a core element of the learning process.

Research on the learning environments preferred by Dot Nets suggests that there are a number of fundamental changes that can be introduced productively into the traditional learning environment. As part of a Microsoft effort to design educational technology, Peden has summarised an effort in the United States to create national classroom technology standards for teachers. According to this perspective, the key to the successful introduction of technology in the learning environment is not just delivering hardware or software applications, but reorganising the social and psychological contexts in which they are used. Peden contrasts the new learning preferences with the traditional classroom learning environment as outlined below:

merging Learning Preferences that May Be Enabled by ICTs

New Learning Preferences	*Traditional learning Environment*
Student/group Centered	Teacher centered
Multimedia	Single media
Collaborative work	Isolated work
Critical thinking/informed decision-making	Fact/knowledge-based learning

These norms for introducing technology into the learning environment are also happily aligned with a more democratic experience for the AC learners. Current DC approaches to civic education often seem lamentably at odds with the ideal AC experience of peer-to-peer, non-hierarchical, network participation. For example, conventional civics education often treats the subject matter as: a) another academic subject, b) with right and wrong responses arbitrated by the teacher as central authority, and c) students competing in isolation for academic favour. For example, the results of the IEA survey of high school students in the U.S. Suggests that the dominant learning experience in civics classrooms was the traditional learning model of isolated learners, receiving fact-based material from teachers. For example 89 percent of 9th graders reported reading from textbooks, and 88 percent reported filling out work sheets, compared to only 45 percent reporting debating and discussing ideas, 40 percent engaging in role play or mock trials, 31 percent receiving visits from leaders, and 27 percent writing letters to express their opinions.

Further analysis of the U.S. IEA data by Campbell indicates that favourable attitudes toward a whole range of political activities were associated with the degree to which classrooms were more open, interactive, and focused on participation. However, the dilemma in his findings is that these open participation conditions seemed less likely to occur in mixed race classrooms, suggesting that young people are less likely to engage with each other across racial lines. The potential for ICTs to promote less racially cued communication might is worth exploring in this context.

In general, research indicates that not only do students prefer interactive learning environments, but that these environments matter for the translation of civics skills into civic practice. For example the U.S. "Civic health of the nation" study found that those who participated in high school debate were far more active politically after they entered public life than those who had no debate experience. The debaters were nearly twice as likely to attend community meetings and sign petitions, and three times as likely as those who did not debate to participate in boycotts. Joining groups in high school also significantly boosted a range of adult civic activities including regular voting.

The lesson seems clear: learning environments that emphasise old style, fact based, teacher-centered pedagogy may succeed in imparting abstract facts and skills of the sort that can be tested, but, to return to the findings from the Australian case, they do not help young citizens translate that knowledge into later civic practice. Perhaps the message here is that providing learners with tools to experience actual civic practice in the learning environment makes more sense. Communication environments that offer collective experiences and provide public displays of group projects may create a first semblance of public life. The Student Voices projects described earlier illustrate these principles, as learners are introduced to an interactive digital web environment that enables them to tailor information and communication to their group issue projects. In addition to having access to external media input for information purposes, this interactive web environment also enables learners to communicate among themselves about emerging understanding of issues, and about the ways in which government and larger publics might become engaged with their causes.

Translating Communication Skills into Participation

It is important for this issue-driven civic learning process to link ultimately to the entry points of public life such as press, government, issue organisations and community networks. For nearly every problem or issue identified by young citizens-in-training, there is abundant public information available about it, and much of that information shows how citizen interest and advocacy networks are trying to win the attention of government. In addition, citizens in nations that have embraced e-government initiatives have increasing access to relevant government activities through online record archives, and through televised coverage of government proceedings that are often archived digitally and streamed on demand. Perhaps most importantly, civic activists and public officials are often available to address the concerns of young citizens, whether through personal visits or participation in computer chats. Using these and other channels, the interactive learning situation can ultimately connect citizen-learners to sources of information about their political concerns, and to networks of citizens and officials involved in making policy about them.

One model that illustrates this linkage to the larger political world is Student Voices in the United States. The website for the project introduces a set of information resources, along with linkages to government and civic organisations. Once there is an active connection between a group's issue project and relevant spheres of politics and government, it is important to facilitate real contact with the various actors those spheres. It turns out that representatives of civic groups and public institutions are generally willing to meet with young people, and to have remarkably open exchanges about their political concerns. Various formats can be developed for bridging the learning environment and the policy arena. For example, Student Voices links into local elections by inviting candidates to talk with students in schools and preparing students to interrogate candidates in a press-debate format held in an open public forum that is televised on local public access television. In addition, class issue projects are often presented as public policy recommendations, and judged in a civics fair by community leaders. Students have even produced series of public affairs programs from their own perspectives that were aired on local public television and then archived and streamed on demand over the web. Linking the classroom and the surrounding political environment is also a major goal of Project Citizen.

Building bridges between the citizenship learning environment, the public sphere, and the policy process not only results in learning a set of civic skills, but, more generally, developing a higher regard for participating in the political world of civic activism, government and elections. In some cases, students have become actively involved in the policy process they developed as part of their issue projects. The overall result of this integration of the civics learning environment with the real political world is a bridge between the AC and DC models of citizenship that offers next generation citizens a broader repertoire of civic action than they might acquire in conventional approaches that; no matter how well-intentioned, risk reproducing the same aversion to the DC model of citizenship that many young citizens bring to the learning situation in the first place.

6

Sociological Issues in Indian Democracy

Democracies fall into two basic categories, direct and representative. In a direct democracy, all citizens, without the intermediary of elected or appointed officials, can participate in making public decisions. Such a system is clearly only practical with relatively small numbers of people – in a community organisation or tribal council, for example, or the local unit of a trade union, where members can meet in a single room to discuss issues and arrive at decisions by consensus or majority vote.

Modern society, with its size and complexity, offers few opportunities for direct democracy. Today, the most common form of democracy, whether for a town of 50,000 or nations of 1 billion, is representative democracy, in which citizens elect officials to make political decisions, formulate laws, and administer programmes for the public good. Ours is a representative democracy. Every citizen has the important right to vote her/his representative. People elect their representatives to all levels from Panchayats, Municipal Boards, State Assemblies and Parliament. There has increasingly been a feeling that democracy ought to involve people more regularly and should not just mean casting a vote every five years. Both the concepts of *participatory democracy* and *decentralised governance* have thus become popular. Participatory democracy is a system of democracy in which the members of a group or community participate collectively in the taking of major decisions.

Values of Indian Democracy

Like so many other features of modern India we need to begin the story about modern Indian democracy from the colonial period. You have just read about the many structural and cultural changes that British colonialism brought about deliberately. Some of the changes that came about happened in an unintended fashion. The British did not intend to introduce them. For instance, they sought to introduce western education to create a western educated Indian middle class that would help the colonial rulers to continue their rule. A western educated section of Indians did emerge. But, instead of aiding British rule, they used western liberal ideas of democracy, social justice and nationalism to challenge colonial rule.

Social change in modern India is not just about Indian or western ideas. It is a combination as well as reinterpretation of western and Indian ideas. We saw that in the case of the social reformers. We saw the use of both modern ideas of equality and traditional ideas of justice. Democracy is no exception. In colonial India the undemocratic and discriminatory administrative practice of British colonialism contrasted sharply with the vision of freedom which western theories of democracy espoused and which the western educated Indians read about. The scale of poverty and intensity of social discrimination within India also led to deeper *questioning of the meaning of democracy*. Is democracy just about political freedom? Or is it also about economic freedom and social justice? Is it also about equal rights to all irrespective of caste, creed, race and gender? And if that is so how can such equality be realised in an unequal society?

Many of these issues were thought of much before India became free. Even as India fought for its independence from British colonialism a vision of what Indian democracy ought to look like emerged. As far back as in 1928, Motilal Nehru and eight other Congress leaders drafted a constitution for India. In 1931, the resolution at the Karachi session of the Indian National Congress dwelt on how independent India's constitution should look like. The Karachi Resolution reflects a vision of democracy that meant not just formal holding of elections but a substantive reworking of the Indian social structure in order to have a genuine democratic society.

The Karachi Resolution clearly spells out the vision of democracy that the nationalist movement in India had. It articulates the values that were further given full expression in the Indian Constitution. You will notice how the Preamble of the Indian Constitution seeks to ensure not just political justice but also social and economic justice. You will likewise notice that equality is not just about equal political rights but also of status and opportunity.

CONSTITUENT ASSEMBLY DEBATES

In 1939, Gandhiji wrote an article in the 'Harijan' called 'The Only Way' in which he said "... the Constituent Assembly alone can produce a constitution indigenous to the country and truly and fully representing the will of the people" one based on "unadulterated adult franchise for both men and women". The popular demand in 1939 for a Constituent Assembly was, after several ups and downs conceded by Imperialist Britain in 1945. In July 1946, the elections were held. In August 1946, The Indian National Congress' Expert Committee moved a resolution in the Constituent Assembly. This contained the declaration that India shall be a Republic where the declared social, economic and political justice will be guaranteed to all the people of India. On matters of social justice, there were lively debates on whether government functions should be prescribed and the state should be bound down to them. Issues debated ranged from right to employment, to social security, land reforms to property rights, to the organisation of panchayats. Here are some snippets from the debates:

Constitution and Social Change

India exists at so many levels. The multi-religious and multi-cultural composition of the population with distinct streams of tribal culture is one aspect of the plurality. Many divides classify the Indian people. The impact that culture, religion, and caste have on the urban–rural divide, rich-poor divide and the literate-illiterate divide is varied. Deeply stratified by caste and poverty, there are groupings and sub-groupings among the rural poor. The urban working class comprises a very wide range. Then, there is the well-organised domestic business class as also the professional and commercial class. The urban professional class is highly vocal. Competing interests operate on the Indian social scene and clamour for control of the State's resources.

However, there are some basic objectives laid down in the Constitution and which are generally agreed in the Indian political world as being obviously just. These would be empowerment of the poor and marginalised, poverty alleviation, ending of caste and positive steps to treat all groups equally.

Competing interests do not always reflect a clear class divide. Take the issue of the close down of a factory because it emits toxic waste and affects the health of those around. This is a matter of life, which the Constitution protects. The flip-side is that the closure will render people jobless. Livelihood again, is a matter of life that the Constitution protects. It is interesting that at the time of drawing up the Constitution, the Constituent Assembly was fully aware of this complexity and plurality but was intent on securing social justice as a guarantee.

Constitutional Norms and Social Justice

It is useful to understand that there is a difference between law and justice. The essence of law is its force. Law is law because it carries the means to coerce or force obedience. The power of the state is behind it. The essence of justice is fairness. Any system of laws functions through a hierarchy of authorities. The basic norm from which all other rules and authorities flow is called the Constitution. It is the document that constitutes a nation's tenets. The Indian Constitution is India's basic norm. All other laws are made as per the procedures the Constitution prescribes. These laws are made and implemented by the authorities specified by the Constitution. A hierarchy of courts (which too are authorities created by the Constitution) interpret the laws when there is a dispute. The Supreme Court is the highest court and the ultimate interpreter of the Constitution.

The Supreme Court has enhanced the substance of Fundamental Rights in the Constitution in many important ways. The Constitution is not just a ready reference of do's and don'ts for social justice. It has the potential for the meaning of social justice to be extended. Social movements have also aided the Courts and authorities to interpret the contents of rights and principles in keeping with the contemporary understanding on social justice. Law and Courts are sites where competing views are debated. The Constitution remains a means to channels and civilise political power towards social welfare.

Rural Social Transformation

Panchayati Raj translates literally to 'Governance by five individuals'. The idea is to ensure at the village or grass root level a functioning and vibrant democracy. While the idea of grassroots democracy is not an alien import to our country, in a society where there are sharp inequalities democratic participation is hindered on grounds of gender, caste and class. Furthermore, traditionally there have been caste panchayats in villages. But they have usually represented dominant groups. Furthermore, they often held conservative views and often have, and continue to take decisions that go against both democratic norms and procedures.

When the constitution was being drafted panchayats did not find a mention in it. At this juncture, a number of members expressed their sorrow, anger and disappointment over this issue. At the same time, drawing on his own rural experience Dr. Ambedkar argued that local elites and upper castes were so well entrenched in society that local self-government only meant a continuing exploitation of the downtrodden masses of Indian society. The upper castes would no doubt silence this segment of the population further. The concept of local government was dear to Gandhiji too. He envisaged each village as a self-sufficient unit conducting its own affairs and saw *gram-swarajya* to be an ideal model to be continued after independence.

It was, however, only in 1992 that grassroots democracy or decentralised governance was ushered in by the 73rd Constitutional Amendment. This act provided constitutional status to the Panchayati Raj Institutions (PRIs). It is compulsory now for local self-government bodies in rural and municipal areas to be elected every five years. More importantly, control of local resources is given to the elected local bodies.

The 73rd and 74th amendments to the Constitution ensured the reservation of one third of the total seats for women in all elected offices of local bodies in both the rural and urban areas. Out of this, 17 per cent seats are reserved for women belonging to the scheduled castes and tribes.

This amendment is significant as for the first time it brought women into elected bodies which also bestowed on them decision making powers. One third of the seats in local bodies, gram panchayats, village panchayats, municipalities, city corporations and district boards are reserved for women. The 1993-94 elections, soon after the 73rd amendment brought in 800,000 women into the political processes in a single election. That was a big step indeed in enfranchising women. A constitutional amendment prescribed a three-tier system of local self-governance for the entire country, effective since 1992-93.

Powers and Responsibilities of Panchayats

According to the Constitution, Panchayats should be given powers and authority to function as institutions of self-government. It, thus, requires all state governments to revitalise local representative institutions.

The following powers and responsibility were delegated to the Panchayats:

1. To prepare plans and schemes for economic development
2. To promote schemes that will enhance social justice
3. To levy, collect and appropriate taxes, duties, tolls and fees
4. Help in the devolution of governmental responsibilities, especially that of finances to local authorities

Social welfare responsibilities of the Panchayats include the maintenance of burning and burial grounds, recording statistics of births and deaths, establishment of child welfare and maternity centres, control of cattle pounds, propagation of family planning and promotion of agricultural activities. The development activities include the construction of roads, public buildings, wells, tanks and schools. They also promote small cottage industries and take care of minor irrigation works. Many government schemes like the Integrated Rural Development Programme (IRDP) and Integrated Child Development Scheme (ICDS) are monitored by members of the panchayat.

The main income of the Panchayats is from tax levied on property, profession, animals, vehicles, cess on land revenue and rental. The resources are further increased by the grants received through the Zilla Panchayat. It is also considered compulsory for Panchayat offices to put up boards outside their offices, listing the break up of funds received, and utilisation of the financial aid received. This exercise was taken up to ensure that people at the grassroots level should have the 'right to information' – opening all functioning to the public eye. People had the right to scrutinise allocation of money. And ask reasons for decisions that were taken for the welfare and development activities of the village.

Nyaya Panchayats have been constituted in some states. They possess the authority to hear some petty, civil and criminal cases. They can impose fines but cannot award a sentence. These village courts have often been successful in bringing about an agreement amongst contending parties. They have been particularly effective in punishing men who harass women for dowry and perpetrate violence against them.

Panchayati Raj in Tribal Areas

Many tribal areas have had a rich tradition of grassroots democratic functioning. We give an illustrative example from Meghalaya. All the three major ethnic tribal groups, namely, the Khasis, Jaintias and the Garos have their own traditional political institutions that have existed for hundreds of years. These political institutions were fairly well-developed and functioned at various tiers, such as the village level, clan level and state level. For instance, in the traditional political system of the Khasis each clan had its own council known as the 'Durbar Kur' which was presided over by the clan headman. Though there is a long tradition of grassroots political institutions in Meghalaya, a large chunk of tribal areas lie outside the provisions of the 73rd Amendment. This may be because the concerned policy makers did not wish to interfere with the traditional tribal institutions.

However, as sociologist Tiplut Nongbri remarks that tribal institutions in themselves need not necessarily be democratic in its structure and functioning. Commenting on the Bhuria Committee Report that went into this issue Nongbri remarks that while the Committee's concern for the traditional tribal institutions is appreciable, it fails to take stock of the complexity of the situation. For notwithstanding the strong egalitarian ethos that characterised tribal societies the element of stratification is not altogether absent. Tribal political institutions are not only marked by open intolerance to women but the process of social change has also introduced sharp distortions in the system, making it difficult to identify which is traditional and which is not.

Political Parties, Pressure Groups and Democratic Politics

In a democratic form of government political parties are key actors. A political party may be defined as an organisation oriented towards achieving legitimate control of government through an electoral process. Political Party is an organisation established with the aim of achieving governmental power and using that power to pursue a specific programme. Political parties are based on certain understanding of society and how it ought to be. In a democratic system the interests of different groups are also represented by political parties, who take up their case. Different interest groups will work towards influencing political parties. When certain groups feel that their interests are not being taken up, they may move to form an alternative party. Or they form pressure groups who lobby with the government. Interest Groups are organised to pursue specific interests in the political arena, operating primarily by lobbying the members of legislative bodies. In some situations, there may be political organisations which seek to achieve power but are denied the opportunity to do so through standard means. These organisations are best regarded as movements until they achieve recognition.

It is obvious that all groups will not have the same access or the same ability to pressurise the government. Some, therefore, argue that the concept of pressure groups underestimate the power that dominant social groups such as class or caste or gender have in society. They feel that it would be more accurate to suggest that dominant class or classes control the state. This does not negate the fact that social movements and pressure groups also continue to play a very important role in a democracy.

Caste Politics

'Region' as a factor has only assumed significance in the nineties. Since after the disintegration of the 'Congress framework' of politics, observers have noted the 'regionalisation' of politics. Rise of regional and State-based parties to prominence is an expression of this regionalisation. But apart from the dramatic proliferation and rise of regional parties, less noticed and more interesting aspect of regionalisation has been related to 'all-India' parties. The Congress, Bharatiya Janata Party (BJP), Communist Party of India (Marxist) (CPI-M), have themselves become regionalised in terms of their strategies and practices.

Regionalisation refers to five factors. (i) *Issues* are/have become region specific. Although the press may continue to project issues in 'all-India' terms, these make sense only when translated into regional contexts. This applies equally to 'secular-communal' divide or to 'globalisation.' (ii) Secondly, *leadership* is structured regional and ratified regional. Parties may still project towering 'national' leaders but State level leadership is more relevant and only through this kind of leadership people relate to 'national' politics. (iii) Regionalisation further means that *social forces* are constituted at the regional level. Therefore, the support base of parties can be identified only at State level. Whether one can describe the base of parties at the all-India level by adding up its base at state level is somewhat doubtful. (iv) Fourthly, in electoral and mobilisation context, the *set of choices* exists at the State level. People, as voters and as groups, have to choose from among the State level choices only. (v) Following from the above factors, political *competition* takes place at the level of region. Consequently, the outcome makes sense only at the regional level. It is in this sense that the 'theatre' of politics has shifted to States — away from the 'all India' theatre.

Before turning to the question how does this regionalisation link up with caste, let us briefly explore the elements conveyed by the term 'region.' Territoriality is the most obviously conveyed element. However, the territoriality expressed by the term 'region' often has a flexibility and indeterminacy with regards to its physical boundary. In this sense, region refers to a wide range of territorial configurations: locality, sub region, State, supra-State region etc.We shall be invoking these various territorial units. Secondly, 'region' can bypass territoriality and convey a broader and perhaps more fluid element of 'space'. Thus understood, region would refer to a non-territorial, non-physical 'sphere' just as it would refer to a physical territory. We bring this element of 'region' into the discussion because caste can be seen both as interacting with territory and as providing space for following certain kind of politics. It needs to be seen how caste as social space interacts with region as territorial space.

One more point may be raised at this introductory stage. How does 'region' as territory become politically sustainable? It is possible to think of many factors, which prop up region as a relevant factor in politics. But the point is that territoriality needs to be translated as a political factor. Language, culture, economy, etc. provide a base to territoriality in order to sustain in politics. It may be argued that caste is not only yet another base, but one, which potentially combines other factors—particularly economy—in providing a base to region to operate as a factor in politics. Thus, we can imagine a complex relationship between caste and region—a relationship of interdependence: caste expresses through region (as territoriality), region becomes politically sustainable on the basis of caste; is bound up by territoriality and in constituting the social space, caste takes the form of a region.

We hope to understand the politics in post-congress phase by exploring the tension and relation between caste and region. The post-congress politics is often characterised by coalitions. However, an alliance of regional parties does not seem to be a possibility. On the other hand, caste emerged in the 1990s as a possible framework within which politics would be organised. However, it now appears that politics of backward castes—or OBC politics as it is popularly known—seems to be stagnating. Thirdly, expressions of regionalism are vocal in some part but muted in others. Fourthly, apart from region and caste, another contending framework of politics has emerged—that of Hindutva.

Cast as a system of vertical division, sustains on the basis of localisation. Caste hierarchy may invoke the ideologies of *chaturvarnya* and of purity-pollution. But the hierarchy makes sense operationally, only when it is concretes in a local situation. Studies concentrating on *Jati* by sociologists and social anthropologists, have always pointed out how hierarchical ranking of *Jati* makes sense in the context of village or small localities. Similarly, cultural, ritual life of members of *Jati* is organised around village or locality. It is only in comparison to some other caste within a locality that the higher or lower status of caste can be experienced. Anthropological studies, thus, look at the extent of intermixing among castes and the finer ethic followed in the course of such intermixing within a locality to assess the extent of separation and communalist among castes. A statement that 'carpenters dine with iron smiths' does not carry any meaning unless it is specified as to where this interdining took place. In other words, *Jati* as a unit of social relations, ritual status and cultural universe is firmly based within the framework of well-defined territorial boundaries. As much as vertical, horizontal separateness of a caste, too, has a locality as a point of reference.

Often, we find distinct 'pockets' of various castes. Most castes are not only specific to a certain State but also specific to a particular area. This means that a caste, which has a concentrated existence in one area, may also constitute numerically large or significant group in that area. In a study of north India, Schwartzeberg has shown how caste concentration takes place at village and district level. He shows that more than fifty percent of Ludhiana's population is Jat, and Chamars and Majahabis have separate pockets in Punjab. The same applies to UP, Bihar, Orissa, etc. He argues that both in the case of peasant castes and Dalits, exclusivity seems to be the rule. This means that if in one village, Jats are the largest group; other peasant castes would almost be non-existent. Similarly, in districts where Majahabis are numerous (e.g. Amritsar), other Dalit castes are rarely seen.

This section gives an indication of the strong link between caste and localities or sub-regions. In the case of peasant castes, the regional base is considerably expansive while non-peasant castes are often confined to smaller pockets. This pattern is evident in State after State: In Tamil Nadu (TN), Vanniyars belong to North and South Arcot, Salem and Chingleput Thevars in Ramnad; Nadars earlier belonged to Tirunelveli. Similarly, Izhava sub castes belonged to different parts of Kerala – Tiyyars to North, Izhavas to central parts and Tandans to south. The Vokkaligas of Karnataka are concentrated in the Mysore region, Constituting around 29 percent of the population of Mysore State). In Maharashtra Agris are concentrated in one district of Konkan-Raigad, Levy Patils in Jalgaon district of North Maharashtra, Vanjaris in Nasik, Ahmednagar and Bead district. Iravati Carve and Dandekar have given a detailed sketch of the residential pockets of different castes of Maharashtra. The Malis of Rajasthan belong to Jodhpur region, and most smaller castes are concentrated in specific areas. The case of Jats of Western UP is too famous to require a mention. In Bihar, Bhumihars have a concentrated strength in the south while Rajputs have in the western parts. Kammas belong to Andhra region and Reddis to Royalism. One can keep multiplying this list of examples. M.N. Srinivas observed in 1957 "this kind of relationship between a caste and a region is widespread in India...". More specifically, as Wash brook observes in the context of TN, most endogamous Jatis extended over no more than a few adjacent villages.

This association of many castes with specific territorial 'pockets' has produced two political results. One is the rise of 'locally dominant' castes. Srinivas' early use of the term 'dominant caste' was specifically with reference to a small locality or village or group of villages: In his 1955 essay 'The social system of a Mysore Village' Srinivas mentions that "The concept of the dominant caste is important for understanding inter-caste relations in any local area.". Elaborating on the concept in 1957, he uses the phrase 'locally' dominant and then adds, "Occasionally a caste is dominant in a group of neighbouring villages if not over a district or two, and in such cases, local dominance is linked with regional dominance.". As far as 'local dominance'' is concerned, there seems to be a direct link between domination and numerical preponderance. Large size of population, though, has one other implication. Often, a caste has numerical advantage when it also has a high degree of control over resources - at the village level, land. Thus, economic power and size combine to produce patterns of local domination. If one carefully follows Srinivas' account of locally dominant caste in Mysore, two things can be drawn from it: a) this political effect of caste-region interface is an outcome of local hierarchy based on caste and b) Just as dominance of one caste the subordination of other castes is a result of 'localisation'. Castes, which are 'trapped' by circumstances into that locality, face subordination. For some castes, localisation produced opportunities and experience of domination whereas, for others, localisation portends the fate of subordination.

The other, more commonly noted political result of caste pockets relates to electoral politics. Localised pockets of castes have come to mean that candidates of a particular caste will always get elected from certain areas. Our study of Maharashtra gives ample evidence of this: The Maratha-Kunbi caste cluster, which is spread almost over the State, manages to send largest number of MLAs to State legislature irrespective of political upheavals. In 51 constituencies, the elected candidate has always been a Maratha, consecutively for six elections since 1978. In other 19 constituencies also, a candidate of the same caste has been elected since 1978 (these exclude SC constituencies).

Thus, in one-fourth constituencies, the caste of the MLA has been the same since 1978. More specifically, Agris always get elected from Raigad district, Leva Patils from Jalgaon district, Telis from Wardha and Bhandara districts, Lingayats from Solapur and Kolhapur districts, Malis from Amravati district, etc. It is clear that there exists a tendency among parties to match caste by caste in selection of candidates. But the case of Maharashtra suggests that local pockets of castes have an important implication for the phenomenon of regional dominant castes. It is only through such localised pockets that smaller and non-dominant castes get an opportunity to stake their claims to power. If smaller, non-dominant castes are not concentrated in one area, they are not likely to get any representation on their own strength. In other words, localised concentration facilitates a space for contesting the domination of State-level dominant caste. In Uttar Pradesh (UP), the Kurmis and Binds have formed their separate parties, Apna Dal and Pragati-sheel Manavsamaj Party respectively and it has been observed that in 1999 Apna Dal did get large number of votes in five Lok Sabha (LS) constituencies although no candidate of the party was elected. The Binds, one of the more backward castes, rallied behind their caste candidates and made their presence felt in seven LS constituencies. This clearly shows that the Kurmis and Binds can draw upon their localised demographic 'resource' to at least protest against the domination of Yadavs; just as Maratha domination in Maharashtra can be contested through localised pockets of other non-Maratha castes.

Construction of Regional Dominant Castes

Localised concentration leads to localised domination and possibilities of some representation. One the other hand, throughout the twentieth century, certain Jatis evolved into castes spread over a large territory. This gave rise to the regional dominant castes. From mid-fifties onwards, politics in most states centred around one (or two) regional dominant caste(s). In most cases, middle level (often peasant) castes sought to contest the ritual superiority, material ascendance and political domination of 'upper' castes - mostly Brahmans, and in the north, Kayasthas and Thakurs. In the first half of twentieth century, the middle-caste protests took the form of non-Brahman movements in Maharashtra and in the south. In the second half of twentieth century, the middle castes extended their claims to state power at the regional level. In both these phases, the middle castes sought to transcend the localised nature and assume a 'regional' identity.

The non-Brahman movements in Maharashtra and south were concerned with creating 'regional' non-Brahman identities. In Maharashtra, the invocation of Shivaji and Maratha rule by the non-Brahman movement was crucial in bringing various peasant castes together. The movement also facilitated the emergence of Maratha politics on a larger scale geographically. In Tamil Nadu, the non-Brahman movement was built upon the collapse of caste and region. The Brahmans were excluded from Dravid identity. In Karnataka, the Vokkaliga 'Caste' came into being by the fusion of various peasant Jatis such as Morasui, Hallikar, Halu, Nonboard, and so on. In Gujarat, Kanabis of different areas came together in 1931 to constitute themselves as 'Patidars', although, Saurashtra Kanabis are still looked down upon by Gujarat Patidars. Also, the Leva and Kadvi divisions of Patidars are supposed to refer to sub-regional differences. Yet, from 1931 onwards, the 'Patidar' identity has evolved as a regional or State level identity. Similarly, despite internal tensions, Kshatriyas of Gujarat have been organising themselves as one group. Rajputs, who are in the forefront of the Kshatriya mobilisation, are regional differentiated. Gujarat Rajputs being mostly tenants or landless, sought to align with Kolis and Bariyas as Kshatriyas. Saurashtra Rajputs being landowners resisted the claims of non-Rajputs to Kshatriya status. However, over the years, the Kshatriya group of castes in Gujarat as a whole has provided a counterpoint to Patidar politics. The Kshatriya Sabha took an initiative in bringing together Rajputs and Kolis and shaping their politics. The Jats are probably the most regional structured caste. Various Khaps of Jats span specified villages and a meeting of all Khaps, the Sarvakhap meets to discuss common matters. But alongside Khaps, Jats of western UP as well as adjoining Haryana are also organised through the all India Jat Mahasabha, which always extended support to Charan Singh.

It can be argued that both the rise of non-Brahman movement and rise of middle caste as dominant caste in many States follow a similar pattern. A protest against castes ranking high in the hierarchy gives an impetus to these processes. But these processes gain momentum when small, localised, endogamous Jatis overcome their localisation by seeking either in mythology or history a link with a larger territorial unit. They ignore or under play the details about ritual separation and instead amalgamate large groups into their new boundaries, often expanding traditional identities. This development is accompanied by formation of territorial or even 'all-India' associations -Mahasabhas or Mahasanghas-of the newly evolved caste group. A moderately reformist posture follows vis-a-vis intra-caste practices, particularly marriage practices. Since the process is ideologically rooted in opposition to upper castes, the claims of such 'castes' relate to share in power, opportunities for material uplift and amelioration of tradition-inflicted disabilities. Central to this whole process is the journey from locality to region (mostly State). Once a caste crosses the threshold of locality, the possibilities of realising political claims become very real. A geographical expanse allows the concerned caste to make claims on representational basis besides the basis of caste injustice. Besides, association with a larger region allows access to other strategies like regional ideology, cultural-historical claims, etc. In fact, most dominant castes, as also proponents of non-Brahman movement, claim that the heritage of that region belongs to them; they are the true and authentic bearers of symbols associated with the particular region; they represent the culture of that region; the non-Brahmans are true Dravids, the Marathas are bearers of the symbol of Shivaji, Patidars exemplify the essence of Gujarati culture or Jats represent the true Kisans.

Linguistic States

If a caste claims that it represents the regional culture better than others, if follows that there will be a strong connection between such dominant castes and regionalist movements. Today we can talk about dominant castes in the context of States because in most cases, States have been linguistic States. These States constitute a region not only in just a geographical-administrative sense, but in sociocultural and political sense also. Hence the link between dominant castes and States.

One can come across many examples of different patterns of relations between caste and regional identity. These include assertions by upper castes, convenient collaboration between upper and middle castes, the rise of contending middle castes, exclusion of upper castes, etc. Probably the latest example would be Uttaranchal where caste played an indirect role. When the union government decided to implement the policy of reservations for OBCs, stiff opposition came from upper castes of Uttaranchal. It was argued that this region did not have OBCs–at least not in large numbers. From the point of anti-reservation movement, the issues of separate identity of hill people distinct from plains people, came to the forefront. Without much exaggeration, it could be said that formation of Uttaranchal is an instance of upper caste assertion where 'regional' distinctiveness was indirectly claimed on the basis of different caste composition of the population. Historically, such upper caste assertion may be detected in the regional nationalism of Orissa. When the Oriya speaking territory was part of Bengal, Brahmans and Karans came together to shape Oriya opposition to Bengali domination. In 1912, this same social force invoked Oriya nationalism to protest against Orissa's annexation to Bihar. Since the creation of Orissa State, the upper castes have generally retained their hold over the State's politics, culture and economy.

As far as collaboration between upper and middle castes is concerned, Maharashtra can serve as a very good example. Although the non-Brahman movement had considerably villainised Brahmans, the Samyukta Maharashtra Movement (SMM, Movement for united Maharashtra State) saw the Brahmans and sections of Marathas collaborating and mobilising the masses on the basis of regionalist sentiments. This collaboration had a major long-term effect. While formation of Maharashtra State ushered the Marathas into position of power, the sharpness of non-Brahmanism was almost lost. The Brahmans, of course, were not in a position to make a comeback to politics, but nor were they hounded out of politics in particular or the public domain in general. On the contrary, Brahmans continued to dominate culture, education, media, under the benign auspices of 'Maharashtra Dharma. More tangentially, the regional assertion led by Brahmans and Marathas displaced the main focus of non-Brahman movement, considerably weakening anti-caste discourse. Instead, Maratha domination became legitimised in the name of non-Maratha lower castes, identified in the sixties as Bahujan Samaj (majority of masses)–the contemporary OBCs. Caste-Region nexus in Maharashtra, thus, exemplifies the process of one caste legitimating its claims by usurping the claims of other smaller castes of that linguistic region.

Just as the Gujarati-Marwari baniya was the cause of Marathi Brahmans and Marathas coming together, the prominence of Tamil Brahmans resulted into the unity of Telugu Brahmans and non-Brahman castes of Andhra. Although initially the non-Brahman Telugus joined Justice Party, they were not enamoured by the anti-Brahman rhetoric. Instead, their anti-Brahman sentiment got directed against Tamil Brahmans, allowing cooperation among Telugu speaking people on regional-linguistic basis. This weakened the non-Brahman movement in Andhra. It has also been argued that co-option of elite Reddys into the congress facilitated a less acrimonious relationship between Brahmans and Reddys. The examples of Maharashtra and Andhra show that regionalism can intervene in the competition between upper castes and middle castes. Secondly, these examples suggest that regionalism can help a smooth transfer of State level political apparatus to middle castes. Often, in this 'smooth' transfer, radicalism as a basis of political claims is lost and claims of lower castes get a short shrift through symbolic gestures and tokenism.

Starting off from limited collaboration between upper and middle castes, Maharashtra and Andhra Pradesh witnessed the rise and assertion of middle castes. A similar assertion was witnessed in UP once the Jats of western UP became politically organised.The Jat assertion took the form of a demand for 'backward' status. From this, Charan Singh also attempted to project himself as representative of backwards. However, following Jats' association with land, their leaders, Charan Singh earlier and Tikait later, harped on a farmer identity as the identity of Jats in particular but of Gujjars as well. Interestingly, during Takait's farmers' agitation, at one stage, activists of Bharatiya Kisan Union proposed that they should ask for a separate state for western UP. Thus, the caste of Jats is an example of middle caste assertion at the regional level. Politics of Haryana is another instance of Jat assertion at State level while in Rajasthan; the Jat assertion took the form of a concerted effort to claim backward status. The Jats of Rajasthan deviated from pro-congress politics to vote for BJP in 1999 for the sole purpose of getting their backward status recognised. The Jat Mahasabha decided to vole for BJP once Vajpayee promised to concede their demand.

Many States have witnessed keen competition between two castes or caste clusters. In instances of such competition, the contending castes usually belong to a middle status. In Rajasthan, the competition between the Jats and Rajputs has been rather neatly transformed into a bipolar party situation. Gujarat and Karnataka are the other two examples of contending middle castes but politics there is not organised so neatly. The Patidars of Gujarat rose to prominence in the course of nationalist movement. The Patidar caste also gained control over resources and sought to displace the Brahmans and baniyas from political power. However, Gujarat politics is characterised by congress efforts to attract Kshatriyas, Swatantra Party's efforts to forge an alliance of Patidars and kshatriyas, Patidar alliance with Brahmans and Banias in opposition to reservation and growing affection among Kshatriyas towards the congress. These developments have led to the emergence of BJP as a Patidar force in the nineties. Karnataka witnessed a tussle between Vokkaligas and Lingayats right from the time of creation of a Kannada speaking State. Vokkaligas dominated Mysore area but they felt that if the other Kannada speaking areas were brought together, Lingayats would get an upper edge. Therefore, two Kannada speaking States were demanded. This has been recorded by the State Reorganisation commission Thus, here is an example of a large caste cluster opposing a unified linguistic State for fear of loosing its numerical advantage. Vokkaligas dominated Mysore politics between 1947 and 1956 (when one Kannada speaking State come into being). Since 1956, although Lingayats did get an upper hand, political dominance was shared by these two contending caste clusters till 1972. It was noted by Ambedkar that linguistic States would only lead to consolidation of the 'upper' castes, jeopardising the interests of scheduled castes. In Punjab, for instance, the scheduled castes were not very supportive of the demand for a separate State of Punjab by reorganising the State on linguistic communal lines. Even Sikh untouchable kept away from that demand fearing that a reorganised Punjab would facilitate domination of Jat Sikhs.

Tamil Nadu manifests a pattern of caste region relationship, which is distinct from other States in many respects. It did not throw up any single dominant caste although Vellalas and Nadars benefited the most from the Dravid non-Brahman movement. Secondly, the non-Brahman movement dealt with the issue of regional identity right from the beginning in the second decade of twentieth century. Non-Brahmanism was identified with Dravidianism. While attempting to unite all non-Brahman castes on the Dravid platform, the Dravid movement refused to recognise Brahmans as part of Dravid society. Just as this movement sought to effect a fusion of many non-Brahman castes, it also aspired to build a 'Southern' identity opposed to 'north'. In 1937 the movement led by Periyar waged an anti-Hindi agitation. The logical culmination of anti-Hindi, anti-north Dravidian non-Brahmanism was reached in 1939 when Justice Party demanded 'independent' Dravidsthan. Thus, caste-region interaction in Tamil Nadu strengthened an exclusionary regional nationalism. Further, it also sought to delegitimise Brahmans not only from their superior caste position but also from the scope of regional identity. However, this exclusion did not last long. Once the regional claims were realised through formation of Madras State and non-Brahman claims were translated into an extensive policy of reservations, Brahmans were incorporated as members into the Tamil society. Brahmans are accommodated as ideologies and legitimises of the regional legacy of Dravid movement. It is indeed ironical that a strong non-Brahman movement, through its regionalism allowed a re-entry of the Brahman caste both into the elite and into the political arena in general.

In the nineties, the political assertion of the Vanniyars marked the political scene in Tamil Nadu. However, Vanniyars have a long history of separate political organisation. In spite of the efforts of non-Brahman movement to bring together all non-Brahman castes, Vanniyars were organised through Tamilnad Toilers' Party and Common-weal party. Although DMK supported the latter in 1952 with a view to defeating Congress, Kamraj was successful in bringing both Vanniyar parties into congress fold. Another backward caste, the Thevars, backed the forward bloc for a long time. These details suggest that in spite of very vocal non-Brahman movement, Tamil politics did not throw up any single middle caste around which State politics could be organised. Even the large and dominant castes in a given district, do not account for more than one fourth of the population of that district. Probably, this peculiar situation led to sustained recourse to militant regional nationalism, particularly by the Dravid parties. However, as Wash brook observes, this Dravidianism 'neutralised many of the caste based issues of conflict that dominated Tamil Nadu politics in the first half of the twentieth century'. Perhaps, those contradictions, which Dravidianism sought to push under the carpet of regionalism, have resurfaced in Tamil Nadu with Dalit – OBC conflicts and Hinduisation of some backward castes. In the absence of any particular caste group as central to politics, Tamil politics took on an exclusionary character: exclusion of Brahmans, Aryans, North Indians and less explicitly, exclusion of even Adi Dravids.

Ruptures

Demography, agrarian relations, political economy of post-independence period combined to produce the strong linkages between region and caste. In particular, the different patterns of caste relations gave substance to region as a political category in States like Andhra Pradesh, Tamil Nadu and Karnataka. These developments established the feature of region specific dominant castes in most parts of India. This feature came under stress at two stages when certain types of caste politics attempted to cross the regional boundaries. Both these ruptures in the established pattern of caste-region equation came as opposition to upper as well as newly dominant castes in various regions. In the interplay of caste and region, Dalits and OBCs were/are often excluded or marginalised. Therefore these sections attempted to breach the happy coincidence of caste and region by pursuing the project of all-India 'Dalit politics' and all India 'OBC politics'.

At the intellectual level, Ambedkar was the first to grasp the implications of 'linguistic States' in terms of the consequent marginalisation of Dalits. But even before the issue of linguistic States came up, Ambedkar had realised the need to mobilise Dalits at an all-India level if they were to stake claims to political power. Thus, in the 1940s, abandoning the Independent labour party, he formed the Scheduled Castes Federation (SCF). On the one hand, through SCF, he sought to intervene in the negotiations for India's freedom and wrest minimum share in power. On the other hand, the SCF was also visualised as a major opposition (of SCs) to the upper caste dominated Congress in the period immediately after independence. The failure of the SCF notwithstanding, it is important to note that Ambedkar saw the unfolding of a process of conflict between SCs and upper castes and also believed that a united all-India instrument of SCs can alone take on the task of contesting upper caste claims. Although he once again veered to a more broad based party in the form of Republican party of India (RPI), this party came to be identified as Dalit party and could not sustain the all-India claims which Ambedkar had always insisted upon. In the mid-eighties, Kanshi Ram formed the Bahujan Samaj Party. This party is seen primarily as the party of Dalits. The BSP has made its presence felt outside of UP, in Punjab, Rajasthan, Madhya Pradesh, etc. And hopes to spread to Maharashtra and Karnataka also. In this sense, BSP manifests an all-India ambition and an awareness that upper caste domination has to be fought at the all-India level. Thus, initial lead by Ambedkar and more contemporarily the formation of BSP, challenge the caste-region nexus. They seek to problematic the caste question at the national level and force a solution through intervention in national politics. The approach of BSP is more instrumentalist than Ambedkar's approach. The former believes that only in a period of instability can Dalits force their entry into the network that controls national state apparatus. Therefore, unity of Dalits at all-India level and unity between Dalits and other disadvantaged castes are seen as strategies for shifting power away from Brahmanical (Manuvadi) sections of society towards the Bahujan Samaj (the masses).

In the mid-sixties, Lohia argued that 'backward castes' constitute a majority and they should be given a fair share in power. This was reminiscent of the arguments of non-Brahman movement in the south and in Maharashtra.

Although backward caste politics gradually emerged in UP and Bihar, it was only in the nineties that it became an issue at an all-India level. After the agitation against reservations in Gujarat and Bihar in the late seventies and early eighties, the agitation in many north Indian States on the issue of reservations for backward castes underlined the simmering conflict between what Lohia had described as forwards and backwards. Since the controversy over recommendations of the Mandal commission, sections of backward castes showed awareness about reservations and share in power. This resulted into large-scale mobilisation of backward castes dramatically catapulting protagonists of backward castes into positions of power.

These developments had two effects. Firstly, the political discourse in the country as a whole, changed considerably. 'Social justice' became the central term around which this discourse was constructed. Such a construction facilitated the entry of caste question onto the all-India political scene rather than remaining State-specific. Backwardness of certain castes and consequent political disadvantage was no more seen in State-specific contexts; instead it was conceived as a phenomenon following from Brahmanical Hindutva and domination of national politics by upper castes. As such, taking over power at Delhi was seen as the remedy. Secondly, 'OBC' (as the backward castes came to be known) claims were quickly recognised by the various political parties. In particular, the BJP exhibited remarkable adaptability by introducing changes in the social composition of its key workers in Maharashtra, Madhya Pradesh and UP. Most other parties, too, underwent the process of 'Mandalisation', the Congress probably being the slowest and most reluctant, However, even the Congress manifested awareness of this factor in Rajasthan, Gujarat, Madhya Pradesh, etc. In other words, OBC politics did not throw up any all-India instrument—any party claiming to be representative of OBC interests - instead; it forced certain changes in political parties and in politics in general. Social composition of many legislatures changed during the decade of 1990 to 2000. Reservations for OBCs became less controversial and also became part of the policies adopted by various parties. At least at the formal level, parties conceded the claims of OBCs in terms of share in power. Politics of backward castes became an all-India phenomenon.

In the case of Dalit politics, one can witness a steady fragmentation in the post-Ambedkar period. This fragmentation takes place at three levels: party factionalism, State-specific distinction and intra-Dalit fragmentation. The RPI could never project itself as a united party of Dalits. Various rival RPI parties emerged competing with each other. The absence of a single effective political instrument resulted into the fragmentation of Dalit votes also. On the other hand, concrete political issues faced by Dalits took a State specific turn. In Maharashtra, for instance, the issue of 'renaming' a university after Dr. Ambedkar remained an emotive issue for Dalits for over a decade.

In States like Bihar, atrocities by various middle castes became the main concern of Dalits. In Tamil Nadu, frustration with Dravid politics, non-accommodation in the regional identity and conflicts with lower OBC (Thevars and Vanniyars) has been shaping Dalit politics at State level. The long history of Marxist-Leninism agrarian struggles in Andhra Pradesh has produced Dalit radicalism in that State. Such State-specific situations are inevitable because of differences of levels of Dalit consciousness and differences in the political economy at State level. This means that the arena of conflict and the response by Dalits varies from State to State. The main adversaries of Dalits are also not necessarily common across States. The voting preferences of Dalits are also likewise shaped at State level. Dalits of

Rajasthan, Gujarat, MP, Maharashtra tend to vote in favour of Congress Dalits of W. Bengal and Kerala prefer the left fronts in those States. In UP, the BSP has established itself as the main party of Dalits. In Bihar the BJP led alliance gets more Dalit votes than RJD of Laloo Yadav, probably because of the JD faction led by Ramvilas Paswan who allied with BJP. Similarly, in Karnataka also, the BJP alliance gets more Dalit votes than the Congress.

A further complication regarding the Dalit situation needs to be noted. While ideologise of Dalit politics prefer to project 'Dalit' as one social force, even at State level, Dalits do not constitute a unified social force. For various reasons, the State-specific reasons not the least, internal stratification among Dalits of different States in a reality. In Maharashtra, the (ex) Mahar Dalits are seen as politically advanced, the Matang and Chamar Dalits resist the 'Mahar domination'. The Mala-Madiga dispute in Andhra Pradesh reached such a proportion that the State government decided to divide reservation between these two communities.

The Dalits of Bihar other than the Paswans do not look upon Ramvilas Paswan as their leader. In Karnataka, the large group of Madigas demand that the reservations for Dalits should be split; giving a fixed quota to Holey as and other Dalits which will allow Madigas to enjoy 90 percent of the reservations. In UP, Jatavs are seen as politically powerful and getting all advantages. The Balmikis and Passes feel deprived, In West Bengal, the Namsudras and Rajbanshis have their 'pockets' in Faridpur, Khulna, Jessore and in north Bengal districts of Cooch Behar, Jalpaiguri, Dinajpur, respectively. These two communities are seen as taking advantage of the reservations. All these details suggest the difficulty in organising an all India Dalit politics, Only by intervening in the State level political process; Dalits stand any chance of affecting politics.

The case of OBCs is not very different. To begin with, the 'OBC' category, though a convenient short hand for a large mass, is not very definitive. It includes, formally, castes included by governments in the State lists of other backward classes. As such, the question, 'Who are the OBCs?' Is itself a controversial one. Inclusion or exclusion in the OBC list is often a matter of politics for those castes who have attained enough political skills. It is a common experience that castes would press for inclusion in the list of OBCs–Jats in Rajasthan, Vokkaligas and Lingayats in Karnataka are two famous examples. This gives the mass called OBCs an amorphous character but moreover, produces tensions within the OBCs between more backward and less backward sections. Needless to say, all these factors develop in the backdrop of State specific situations. Except on general issue of reservations, all OBCs cannot be mobilised on an all-India level. Therefore, in the nineties, on the heels of Mandal controversy, many OBC organisations rallied round the issues of reservations. However, when it came to organising the nuts and bolts of OBC politics, the State specific situations asserted themselves. Thus, Janata Dal, which sought to bask in the glory of its pro-Mandal stand, witnessed internal bickering: the Orissa unit under Biju Patnaik distanced itself from the Mandal platform while the Karnataka unit under Hegde made its displeasure about 'Mandalisation' known to national leadership. Both State units felt it unnecessary to have V.P. Singh as a campaigner.

Much mobilisation on the Mandal platform took place in UP and Bihar. The politics of backward castes did not articulate in a substantial manner in Orissa and Andhra Pradesh. It did not have much relevance to Tamil Nadu since that State has had a long history of non-Brahman politics. In Karnataka, Congress under Devraj Urs had earlier mobilised the OBCs. Therefore, in the nineties, the Mandal platform did not evoke much enthusiasm there. In

Maharashtra, the small OBC castes cannot match the strength of the Maratha-Kunbi caste cluster. This leaves the States of Uttar Pradesh and Bihar as the main theatre of OBC politics. In a sense, the so-called all-India claims on behalf of OBC politics are based on politics in north India where the caste issue has emerged onto the political scene rather late. Thus the phenomenon of OBC politics is much more relevant to UP and Bihar than to other States.

The internal stratification among 'OBCs' is another matter where State specific issues come to the forefront. As noted above, identification of certain castes as OBCs, is itself State specific. This is borne out by the case of Jats and more effectively, by the case of Lingayats of Karnataka. The State government went on appointing commission after commission in order to resolve the issue of whether Lingayats are backward or not. Even when the issue of identification is resolved, the question of share of different castes/caste groups continues to pose a challenge. In the field of reservations, most States seem to be veering to the strategy of classifying OBCs into two or three groups and assuring them separate 'quotas' of reserved seats. This classification, again, takes place in the context of State politics as has been exemplified by the decision of BJP-led UP government.

Besides reservations, the question of 'share' involves claims over power. Various backward castes not only want to be 'included' in the apparatus of power, they hope to use power to their advantage and if possible, gain controlling share in power. Negatively put, backward castes push for exclusion of the upper castes so that complexion and content of power would change substantively. These claims bring a double conflict into focus. On the one hand there is a conflict between the already established dominant caste and the aspiring caste/caste group. The constellations of these conflicts are again State specific because the ideological battle line of upper vs. Backward translates differently in each state. In Maharashtra, for example, when Maratha domination is sought to be challenged, Kunbis, who are included in the list of OBCs, would pose a problem. The 'Maratha' caste cluster includes Kunbis. Thus, the battle is between the dominant caste and a section of OBCs vs. Other OBCs. In Karnataka, the OBCs compete with Lingayats who themselves have been claiming inclusion in the list of OBCs. Political economy of each State produces patterns of dominance in accordance to which these battle lines get defined. The other conflict involves the aspiring castes themselves. When the Brahmanical castes were displaced, on the whole, only one caste (or mega-caste bloc) sought to replace them at the State level. With democratisation penetrating larger sections in the contemporary period, a peculiar development has taken place. Just as the established dominant caste is about to be displaced, more than one claimants emerge to stake claims over power. This does not allow any single caste to stabilise in power. The recent history of UP and Bihar shows that among the OBCs, when one caste surges ahead 'on behalf' of OBCs, its representational claims are delegitimised by competitors from within the OBC fold. The Yadavs of UP and Bihar, who claimed in the nineties that they were leading the OBC revolution, have been challenged by non-Yadavs in both the States. Both these conflicts are reflected in the party preferences of OBCs. Backward castes in different States vote differently and within a State, they are often divided among different parties.

These claims and counterclaims have, in fact, further regionalised politics during the nineties. The unprecedented rise of regional parties in the nineties has been singularly unassociated with 'regionalism.' Caste occupied the centre stage of political discourse and regional parties became the vehicle of this often incoherent and fractured discourse.

The discussion so far suggests that the two 'ruptures' have been in fact, ideological formulations, which seek to challenge upper and middle caste domination by unifying all lower castes. This formulation has not been able to assert itself as a concrete principle around which politics is organised. The objective caste situation varies from the presupposition that all 'lower' castes have same experience of political exclusion/marginalisation. Also, the subjective identification of various castes with politics of 'lower' castes varies both caste wise and State wise. As a result, instead of being able to rupture caste-region nexus, both Dalit politics and OBC politics have themselves yielded to this nexus and become regionalised.

State as a sociolinguistic region is a very convenient unit for caste to operate. Although many instances can be shown where small castes intervene in local political process, effective role of caste can be detected at the State level only. At the same time, castes cannot assume all-India identities and caste alliances cannot be easily forged at the all-India level. The political salience of caste increased only after castes transcended the 'local' identities and by forging new 'mega' caste identities became significant players at 'regional' level. However, this process probably stops at the regional level. Efforts of Kurmis to forge an alliance with Kanbis and Kunbis did not succeed. The Yadavs of UP and Bihar follow separate politics from each other. Even in the case of Jats, though the Jat Mahasabha exists, Jat politics in Punjab, Rajasthan, Haryana and western UP cannot be clubbed together. Thus, patterns of caste politics cannot be replicated in different regions nor can they become all-India in their reach or spread. In this sense, caste as a factor in modern politics, has become well entrenched or rooted at the regional/State level. It retains its existence and relevance at local level while as the preceding section argued, existence of caste at all-India level or across States is more ideological than concrete.

The relevance of caste at the regional level flows from the following four factors: a) Social relations of hierarchy are identifiable at the regional level, some times even sub-regional level. The fact that somebody is a Brahman simply places that person in an ambiguous position of superiority outside the region where that person belongs; but in the region where S/he belongs, a fine tuning will be made depending upon whether that person is a Chitpavan or not. To take a concrete example, being a 'Maratha' carries meaning only in the context of Maharashtrian society. The Marathas will be simultaneously seen as farmers, warriors, ex-land lords, etc. Rather than their ritual status either as Kshatriyas or shudras, the historically constructed and materially experienced identity as 'powerful' will be quickly brought into focus. Regional associations also allow myths and prejudices / stereotypes operate as markers of ranking. These do not make sense outside of that region. Therefore for most castes, a hierarchical ranking is relevant only in specific region. Social relations based on these assumptions of hierarchy shape social attitudes about claims of power by different castes, giving way to competition or caste conflict. Thus, when non-Brahmans of Maharashtra were claiming separate representation in early twentieth century, the Brahmans derided them by asking what business ordinary agriculturists had in the legislature. All the same, Brahmans accepted -though unwillingly - Maratha entry into the political arena. In contrast, the claims of Dalits are not so silently accepted. Conflicts at the village level take place when Dalits in a village try to capture the village panchayat.

Historically, many middle castes and some times even lower castes seek upward mobility in their ritual / social status. Studies of caste point out that this happens when a caste achieves material strength. It must be noted that the process of gaining upward mobility is strictly region-based. It is not so merely because one particular caste in one region attains material strength. It is also because, the claims are made regional and accepted / legitimised regional. Such 'mobile' castes even change their caste names and this is accepted in the given region. Transformations from Kunbi to Maratha or Kanabi to Patidar are of course famous. Similarly, the mobility of Nadars (erstwhile shanars) of Tamil Nadu has been well documented (Hardgrave, 1969). Other examples include the awadhias, mahatos, jhanuks taking up Kurmi identity, gwalas, gopes, becoming Yadavs, Padayachis of Tamil Nadu becoming Vanniyar Kshatriyas, etc. Such mobility facilitates horizontal unity among castes. These developments are 'internal' matter of the concerned regions and often indicate the emergence of regional powerful caste groups. Thus, changing 'definitions' of caste status give rise to patterns of competition in each region.

In the course of competition among castes, regionalism or sub-regionalism can be very easily invoked. Regionalism servers either of the two purposes. It can project one caste/ group as inheritor, protector or representative of regional identity and pride. This way, an assault on that caste or caste group is easily seen / shown as assault on regional pride and self-respect. Implicitly, this also means that advancement of the interests of that caste constitutes regional advancement and therefore, the demands of the caste group can be transformed into demands for regional development. To be sure, regionalist politics is shaped by many factors. Once caste and region are identified, the interests of caste can be projected as regional interests. Alternately, regionalism can be invoked to construct a broad social alliance of different castes. In this second formulation, distinct caste identities are supersede by the ideology of regionalism. This often helps the already dominant castes.

Apart from the ideology of Regionalism, region can provide yet another advantage to the 'dominant' castes. Every dominant caste seeks to legitimise its dominant position on the basis of some ideological argument. Region as the social unit having a common cultural-linguistic context automatically forms a basis from which justification of domination can be adduced. Alternatively, arguments by the dominant caste make sense within the region. Thus, Jats' claim of being Kisans or Haryana Jats' claims for a martial tradition appeal the people in those respective regions rather than outside the regions. Similarly, Lingayats' claims of reformisms in the orthodox Brahmanical Hinduism become relevant only in the Kannada speaking region. The ideology of 'Maharashtra Dharma' justifying the Brahman-Maratha leadership or the Bhadralok ideology of elite domination also has similar region-specific appeals. Thus, region is the unit at which caste domination is sought to be legitimated. In the 'dominant caste thesis', the emphasis on numerical strength has deflected attention from both the contents of domination and the ways of attaining domination. Mere numerical strength would not lead to domination; claims of 'high' status usually accompany numerical strength. But a high ritual status is not the only 'ideological' component. 'Dominant' castes employ a more complex set of ideological arguments in order to win the 'dominant' position and we argue that region provides a helpful playground for working out these arguments.

It follows from this that any counter hegemonic assaults on the dominant caste would emanate from a similarly regional situated arguments. In Tamil Nadu, the non-Brahman movement sought to delegitimise the Brahmans by suggesting that Brahmans are not true Dravids. In Maharashtra, too, Phuley's argument turns to this point when he argues that Brahmans-Aryabhats-came from outside-Iran. But more forcefully, Phuley brings in the imagery of non-Brahmans as 'natives' by virtue of their association with agricultural activity. If both, the claims of domination and challenges to them, are regional situated, region becomes a theatre of caste conflicts and configuration caste with political and economic dimensions.

Given the mutually reinforcing relationship of caste and region in contemporary Indian politics, it is argued here that challenges to concrete instances of caste domination (as distinct from notions of caste superiority) can meaningfully rise at the regional level. This would further strengthen the links between caste and region. These links produce region/State-specific configurations of caste, which fit the region's political economy. In the light of this argument certain trends may be noticed. These trends indicate the possible ways in which caste is likely to be constructed in Indian politics. In a way the following discussion engages caste itself as a 'region' or sphere.

In many parts of the country, instead of neat polarisation, 'more complicated and fragmented constellations of power' emerged. Thus, in the arena of caste politics, on the one hand new 'dominant castes' have emerged on the scene; at least many new 'ascendant' castes have come to the forefront. On the other hand new equations have emerged. The most noted one is the BJP led equation of upper castes and lower OBCs in Uttar Pradesh. In Maharashtra, the Charmakars and Matangs have been veering away from Congress and RPI, preferring the Shiv Sena and BJP. The Bahujan Mahasangh in Maharashtra has been trying to forge an alliance of Dalits and OBCs. These new equations do not necessarily follow a similar pattern across the States. But one common factor needs to be noted. In the emerging alliances traditional boundaries of ritual status are seldom followed. Alliances would be formed depending upon the perceptions about which caste/caste group monopolises resources (including reservations). Beside, the choice of allies is often ad hoc, contingent upon who are perceived as adversaries. Underneath this contingent nature of alliances, there seems to be a consideration of two factors. One is consideration of material factors. Castes/caste groups tend to ally when their material interests do not clash —or in fact compliment—each other. The other consideration is share in power. When an alliance is likely to obtain some power for the caste, such an alliance becomes acceptable. Both these considerations go beyond simple alliances based on ritual status—alliances are not made simply because castes occupy a common status as Shudras or Dalits.

Secondly, and partly following from the above, there is a disintegration of caste 'blocs' of Dalits and OBCs. The trend seems to be moving in the direction of 'ethnicisation' of caste. One factor contributing to this process seems to be the pressure of modern reformist discourse delegitimising vertical structure of caste hierarchy. In this background, caste survives, if not as upper-lower then, as 'different' groups having different culture, ritual, 'histories', etc. Thus, caste becomes a 'community'. But ethnicisation of caste has other reasons as well. One is that small castes still find no place in calculations for electoral purposes. They may be relevant in constructing caste 'blocs' but do not receive the benefits either politically or materially. In such situation, organising a single caste as one community becomes useful for gaining some access to power and resources. It is not necessary for us here to accept this logic but that seems to be a factor influencing the process of formation of single caste organisations.

Such organisations function simultaneously as sociocultural associations, pressure groups pursuing immediate material concerns of the caste and vehicles of caste elites for riding into the power structure. Although it is tempting to look at such caste organisations as a political resource, they imply localisation of caste. Such localised ethnicisation is bound to entrap castes both into local boundaries and issues of culture, identity, history rather than of material advance

Thirdly, after reaching a high point through 'Mandlisation', caste appears to be reaching a dead end in terms of its mobilisation potential. At one stage (in the fifties) caste interests were advanced through regional mobilisation. In the next phase, (late seventies onwards) mobilisation took place on the issues of reservations for OBCs (in Bihar, Gujarat) followed up by the Mandal issues and claims of the leaders of OBCs for power sharing. The nineties have witnessed acceptance of OBC reservations as State policy. During the same period, various parties incorporated OBCs resulting in the changed composition of representatives. These developments have meant that the space to be occupied by caste issue is bound to shrink except for further competition among OBCs for greater share in power. At the local level, provision enabling reservations to SCs, STs and OBCs in local government bodies, has ensured that no effective mobilisation can take place and no party will take interest in such mobilisation. This does not imply that caste has lost relevance but that as an organising principle of politics, caste may have reached its limits. Like region earlier, caste may have to search for catalysts that will revitalise the emotive and mobilisation capacity of caste as a sphere of politics. In other words, the capacity of caste to construct new social forces and make politics revolve around them has become rather suspect.This obviously raises doubt about the democratising potential of caste as a sphere. The caste-region nexus meant that just as domination of a caste or caste group would get established, it will be challenged by rival groups or by newly emerging lower sections. However, if our assessment that caste alliances are ad hoc and less mobilisation is correct, then the arena of caste politics is likely to lose the potential to democratise Indian polity.

7

Political Sociology of Poverty

Any attempt to comprehend the Indian experience of poverty eradication through construction of welfare state and political mobilisation in the last five decades needs to recognise that India is a post-colonial society where a) the colonial heritage in the statecraft, and b) the legacy of anti-imperialist national movement in the political community and political culture, play critical roles. This relationship between the 'colonial past' and the 'democratic present' is very significant for understanding the changing nature and orientation of the state and society in the context of poverty in India since independence in 1947.

It is also necessary to remember the differences between the rise of democratic polity in Europe and the emergence of welfare state in India. To quote Jawaharlal Nehru, a pioneer of democratic socialism during the anti-colonial movement between 1920s and 1940s and the first Prime Minister of free India from 1947 to 1964, "In Western countries, full blooded democracy with adult suffrage came to the people very late, in the Twentieth Century". They had in the meantime profited from the Industrial Revolution. They got the resources before they gained democracy so that when the demands came for better living conditions they had the resources to fulfil them.

The results of the Indian endeavour of poverty eradication are not satisfactory in international terms. But the specific and comparative aspects of India help us in contextualising the Indian project of nation building through planning for a poverty free welfare state and a socialistic society between 1950 and the end of the millennium. They also provide insights about the international standing of India in the community of nation-states, where the largest democracy of the world is found to be lagging behind Sri Lanka, China and Indonesia. The Indian political process is being shaped by continuous interaction between the imperatives of interest group dynamics, democratisation, decolonisation and nation-building. These four factors provide the basis for legitimacy of the post-colonial state. They also give content to the concepts of 'public welfare' and 'national interest'.

As a consequence, there were several changes in the state and society relationship in India during this period, which have caused i) decline of politics and rise of economics, ii) rise of dominant caste coalitions and decline of upper caste hegemony, iii) erosion of national constitutional consensus and rise of centrifugal movements, iv) stress on decentralisation along with weakening of the process of centre-formation including planning, v) rise of movements of erstwhile marginalised categories of people e.g. women, depressed classes like Dalits and Scheduled Tribes, ethnic groups, etc., vi) rise of 'region' instead of 'nation' as the operational category of the party system, vii) weakening of the middle class political culture as well as rise of crime-politics nexus with patronage from the neo-rich classes, and viii) rolling back of the welfare state under the pressure of global forces of liberalisation.

The relationship between poverty, politics and state has continued to play a significant role in the political sociology of independent India as it did during the colonial era. The issue of poverty came onto the State's Agenda through different processes after the end of colonial period. First there was a constitutional process which was a consequence of the nationalist discourse where "Community Development" and decolonisation were presented as two sides of the same coin. It created an appropriate focus in the making of the constitution of independent India.

Secondly, there came a developmentalist phase which gained importance during the drive for promoting capacity building among the rural cultivators through "Land Reform" in the 1950s. The idea of 'poor peasant' became unacceptable in the discourse of development under the Congress Raj. Of course, it failed to include the landless labourers in its conceptualisation of recasting the rural power structure through 'land reforms'.

Then came the phase of nation wide rural agitations in the 1960s. The newly created propertied peasants started asking for increase in state's patronage and, the popularised peasants urged for radical transformations to ensure jobs, wages, dignity and justice. The states' responses were crystallised as the "Green Revolution".

Finally, India became market oriented in the 1980s as state-centric initiatives became counter productive at worst and ineffective at best. There was a new faith in market mediated system management among the propertied sections of Indian peasantry as well as the urban propertied classes. It was termed "the era of liberalisation". Rolling back of the state did show some results in the first few years. But the bifurcation of the propertied and the popularised was reinforced by the end of the 1990's. Thus there are new indications of pressures about continuity of chronic poverty and creation of 'new poor' in the context of liberalisation. In fact, it may be appropriate to suggest that after the 'first generation reforms' or 'structural adjustments' and the consequential rolling back of the state, there is resurfacing of poverty in rural and urban sectors resulting in unrest and conflicts. This rediscovery of poverty is accompanied by re-focusing of the political agenda of the India political sectors including political parties, trade unions, peasant bodies and other major components of the power pyramid in India.

In short, the link between active political mobilisation (of varying intensity) and rural transformation has played a vital role in shaping the destiny of the poor. The state and its legislative and bureaucratic apparatus have been a secondary factor. Hence the change in the national economic scenario with reference to peasants in general, and poor rural masses in particular has been primarily a political phenomenon.

Constitutional Content

The conceptualisation of poverty free welfare state in India has been accomplished in two phases: i) the period of national movement for freedom from foreign rule, and ii) the making of Indian Constitution through a constituent assembly. The Indian national movement was able to focus the attention of the masses on growing poverty and the recurrence of famine which was due to defective policies of the colonial government. It was the view of leading public men like Dadabhai Naoroji (1825-1917), M. G. Ranade (1842-1901) and R. C. Dutt (1848-1909) that the solution to the social and economic backwardness of India could not be found through the British Government's policy of laissez-faire, but that only a national government which actively promoted development by direct government action could bring about improvement in living standards. The resolutions of the Indian National Congress from 1929 onwards emphasised the need "to make revolutionary changes in the present economic structure of the society and to remove grave inequalities in order to remove poverty and ameliorate the condition of the masses". The resolution of 1931 underlined that "political freedom must include real economic freedom of the starving millions" and elaborated the fundamental rights which should be included in the Constitution of free India to provide a basis for it. It was followed by the formation of a National Planning Committee with Jawaharlal Nehru as Chairman in 1937 on the initiative of Subhash Chandra Bose as the President of Indian National Congress.

A complementary process of conceptualisation was contributed by the constant debate about the nature and priorities of the state in post-colonial India among the Gandhians, socialists, communists, radical humanists and other ideological groups in the national movement. The charter of demands and agitations by various class organisations of peasants and industrial workers provided the guidelines for the approach of the national movement to poverty and its eradication from villages and towns of India. In fact the decisive push to the colonial rule came with large scale peasant mobilisation in the last decades of the freedom movement.

The concept of welfare state became the lodestar of the Constituent Assembly of India. It made its impact on the thinking of the leading lights of the Assembly who wanted to secure 'justice – social, economic and political' for all citizens of the Republic. They were clear that without social and economic democracy, political democracy had no meaning in a poor country like India. The Preamble, Fundamental Rights (Articles 12 to 35), Directive Principles of State Policy (Articles 36 to 51), and the special provisions for Scheduled Castes and Tribes and Backward Classes (Articles 330 to 342) are significant dimensions of the Indian constitution from this perspective. They have created the imperatives for progress from political democracy to social and economic democracy which means "working for a certain measure of well-being for all".

The Preamble of the Constitution commits the state to the development of a free society based on the dignity of the individual in which there would be equality of status, opportunity and justice. The state has to endeavour towards harmonisation of interests between individuals, groups, and between individuals and groups on one hand and interests of the community on the other. The Preamble places justice above the other principles of liberty, equality and fraternity.

The values embedded in the Preamble are elaborated in the Fundamental Rights and the Directive Principles. The Fundamental Rights have covered all the traditional civil and political rights included in the Universal Declaration of Human Rights. There are six broad categories of the fundamental rights:

1. The right to equality (Articles 1, 15,16,17, and 18)
2. The right to freedom (Articles 19 and 21)
3. The right against exploitation (Articles 23 and 24);
4. The right to freedom of conscience and free profession, practice and propagation of religion (Articles 25 to 28);
5. The right to minorities to conserve their culture, (Articles 29 and 30); and
6. The right to constitutional remedies for the enforcement of all these Fundamental Rights (Article 32).

The Directive Principles of State Policy are basically inspired by the concept of a welfare state. Article 37 declares that the Directive Principles are "fundamental in the governance of the country" and that "it shall be the duty of the State to apply these principles in making laws". However these are non-justiciable. Article 38 defined the aim as follows; "The State shall strive to promote the welfare of the people by securing and protecting as effectively as it may a social order in which justice – social, economic and political, shall inform all the institutions of the national life". In Article 39, stress was laid on the right to adequate means of livelihood, equally for men and women; equal pay for equal work for both men and women; conditions of work ensuring health and strength, protection of children and youth against exploitation and against moral and material abandonment. It is also laid down that the state should ensure that 'the ownership and control of the material resources of the community are so distributed as best to subserve the common good'; and that the 'operation of the economic system does not result in the concentration of wealth and means of production to the common detriment'.

Furthermore, the duty is enjoined on the State that 'it should, within the limits of its economic capacity and development, make effective provision for securing the right to work, to education and to public assistance in cases of unemployment, old age, sickness and disablement, and in other cases of undeserved want' (Article 41). The state should also provide for 'securing just and human conditions of work and for maternity relief '; and 'security to all workers - agricultural, industrial and otherwise - a living wage, conditions of work ensuring a decent standard of life and full enjoyment of leisure and social and cultural opportunities' (Articles 42 and 43).

Particular stress is laid on special assistance to the weaker sections of the people, including the Scheduled Castes and the Scheduled Tribes and the other weaker sections with a view to promoting their educational and economic interests and to protecting them from social injustice and exploitation. With regard to rural economy, Articles 40 and 48 enjoin the application of modern scientific methods to agriculture and animal husbandry and the implementation of programmes and improvements through self-governing Panchayats. Promotion of cottage industries on an individual and cooperative basis is mentioned in Article 43.

Article 45 fixed a definite time limit during which the State would endeavour to provide free and compulsory education for all children until the age of fourteen years from the commencement of this Constitution.

The above principles were given a more precise direction when Parliament accepted the socialist pattern of society as the objective of social and economic policy in December 1954. In 1976, the 42nd Amendment Act added certain new directives to the Constitution of India:

a) that children are given opportunities and facilities to develop in a healthy manner and in conditions of freedom and dignity;

b) that the operation of the legal system promoted justice on a basis of equal opportunity, and in particular the State provided free legal aid in cases of economic and other disabilities;

c) that the participation of workers in management of industries is secured; and

d) that the environment is protected and improved and the forests and wild life are safeguarded.

Anti–Poverty Mobilisations

The direction of post-colonial polity in India was evolved during the three Five Year Plans between 1951 and 1965 in the context of peasant mobilisation and other protest movements. Self-reliance was the basic goal of the Nehruvian agenda under the hegemony of the Congress Party. It is important to recognise that the response to the peasant movements in the Fifties by the nascent post-colonial state and the hegemonic ruling party, Congress, was:

a) to eliminate intermediaries for creating a broad based proprietary class in the village who took interest in promoting agricultural production;

b) to facilitate infrastructure facilities through a variety of inputs and concessions;

c) to ensure minimum price support through purchase of agricultural products by public sector corporations.

The impact of these reforms created two opposite results .

1. It promoted the expansion of owner-cultivator class which came from upper and upper-middle strata of the caste system; and

2. It created insecurity among tenants, agrarian workers, and semi-bonded tillers due to increased pressure of market forces upon the agricultural sector.

Agriculture was changing into a 'market oriented, cash based, and profit claiming occupation, causing deterioration of the situation of the poorer strata in rural India. In short, there was emergence of commercialisation, pneumatisation and market/profit oriented production due to the state's plans and programmes between 1950 and 1965. The number of agricultural proletariat grew at an exponential rate. But the strategy of "incremental democratic modernisation" encountered a series of problems from 1963 onwards, which made the Nehruvian approach obsolete in many spheres of State policies. A new set of national issues regarding food scarcity, increase in prices, national defence, foreign dependence, economic stagnation, and regional inequalities generated a cumulative stress between 1963 and 1967. As a consequence a new agenda called Ten Point Programme came into being.

The dilemma of dependent accumulation and declining dominance of the Congress Party created a shift in India's direction of development. The slogan of "Jai Jawan - Jai Kisan" (victory to the soldiers - victory to the peasants) symbolised the new thrusts of the State. The 'sixties saw a wave of disenchantment with the entire planning process'. There was visible growth of discontent in the late sixties.

Between anti-Congressism and Naxalism, there was a great range of activism and mobilisation all over rural and urban India. This coincided with the 4th Five Year Plan and the 5th Lok Sabha elections. Despite the intelligence and experience, Indian planning had gotten into a rut. The results were disappointing. It was time, therefore, for the planners to ask themselves whether the things they had been trying to do were really correct. Thus the period of the 4th Five Year Plan was marked by political weakness and economic anxieties. The poorer sections of the society and the pro-poor political formations were making impressive moves for collective action. It was the era of second wave of land conflicts after the late nineteen forties and early fifties.

The second wave of rural mobilisation in the sixties contained two distinct groups of rural masses. There was a movement launched by the newly emerged proprietary classes constituted by rich farmers and middle peasant proprietors. The communists called them 'Kulaks' which was an exaggeration of their economic capacity. They were also named 'Bullock Capitalists'. Their mobilisation was aimed at securing increased patronage from the state. They did not come into conflict with the interests of the industrial and commercial urban proprietary classes. It was led by peasant based regional political formations which came into existence in 1960s in several provinces of India. Many of them got amalgamated into a national political party, Bharatiya Lok Dal, led by Charan Singh in 1974.

Another movement was launched by the agrarian poor with increasing prominence of the agricultural workers. The movements of the rural poor in the 1960s and 70s were centred around a combination of economic, social and political issues. Economically, they were in need of security of employment, minimum wages, rights over a certain share of the produce, distribution of surplus lands, and reduction and liquidation of debts. Socially, they were agitated about violation of legally acquired rights, gender discrimination, violence and humiliation by upper caste/class men and public officials. Politically, they were attempting to resist repression and terror of the upper and middle castes who had recently turned into land owning classes in rural India. They found a nexus of the newly emerging proprietors and the nascent post-colonial state. They also felt that the state was paying more attention to the proprietary classes as it considered them as the agents of development. They were led by the left wing parties like Communist Party, Communist Party (Marxist), Socialist Party and Communist Party (Marxist-Leninist).

The rural poor in the 1960s comprised o a) popularised peasants, b) agrarian workers belonging mostly to the depressed castes and tribes and other marginal groups, and c) a large section of women. Their struggles gave rise to uncomfortable questions regarding the usefulness of the socioeconomic framework of developmental planning adopted after independence. They exposed the limits of the development policies as they had failed to improve the condition of the poor even after three Five Year Plans, and a generation long political stability in the form of Congress rule. They brought the nation 'face to face' with the continuity of unimaginable forms of exploitation and oppression of the rural poor. It was an indictment of the post-colonial state and its patronage to newly propertied castes and communities in the name of development and nation building since 1950s.

Politics of Poverty Eradication

The issue of poverty became a central question during 1964-71. It was triggered by the Lohia-Nehru-Nanda debates in

Lok Sabha in 1964 about the nature of poverty and its extent. It became recognised as a political imperative of democratic governance as a large number of people were still trapped in economic settings which forced them to live below the levels of subsistence. It was legitimised by the slogan of Garibi Hatao (eliminate poverty) by the Congress Party under the leadership of Indira Gandhi who routed most of the anti-Congress political parties in the general elections of 1971-72. It appeared that after a long wait, the moment had arrived for fulfilling the dreams of Swaraj by creating an egalitarian social order based upon economic self-reliance and democratic social transformations.

It is another matter that the electoral mandate was not translated into effective socioeconomic steps due to a variety of reasons – domestic as well as international. Low savings, limited investment, sluggish industry, a steep rise in the money supply and a sharp decline in agricultural production were the prominent features of economic administration. The problems were further complicated by international 'price revolution' and a phase of 'stagflation' in the world economy. In 1973-74, inflation had turned everything topsy-turvy. It was coupled with the crisis of leadership within the Congress Party at the Central and the provincial levels. The situation gave rise to multiple political pressures, student-youth movements and working class protests which culminated in a national movement against the failures of the government in terms of checking corruption, controlling price rise, creating employment, and providing relief to the poor. It was led by Jayaprakash Narayan, one of the founders of democratic socialism in India and was supported by socialists and others. After a phase of indifference and tolerance, the ruling party declared the State of Emergency due to the intensity of internal protests. At the same time, it had to adopt a 20-Point programme of welfare measures to show that even in a situation of crisis, the government is committed to continue the process of relief and welfare.

Inspite of these adversities, the change in the orientation of the political community and the policy makers in the early 1970s, was remarkable. According to C.T. Kurien (1979), "When a small group in the Planning Commission proposed in 1962 that the central concern of our planning has to be the removal of poverty as early as possible, it was a novel and consequently very suspicious idea. But within a decade it had become not only the accepted economic dogma, but also a highly articulated political programme". The new mood was reflected in the Fifth Five Year Plan. For example, Towards An Approach to the Fifth Plan (1974-79) proclaimed "there would seem to be a conspicuous element of historic inevitability in a direct approach to reducing poverty becoming the main thrust of the Fifth Five Year Plan. The Plan is being formulated by a government that has massive mandate from the people, both in the Parliamentary elections of 1971 and the state elections of 1972, on the basis of a programme whose centre piece is Garibi Hatao. The homogeneity of the Governments at the Centre and most of the states during the formulation and early years of the Fifth Plan is guaranteed. This should enable bold and imaginative proposals being put through on the basis of an enlightened national consensus."

Thus, the Fifth Five Year Plan was a landmark due to its special thrust on creating the maximum possible dent on the low end poverty while ensuring that the country moves one more step in the direction of economic independence. It was also remarkable due to its recognition that the Indian economy had reached a stage where larger availability of resources makes it possible to launch a direct attack on – a) unemployment, b) underemployment, and c) poverty. It clearly admitted that the twin causes of poverty are i) underdevelopment, and ii) inequality and it is inadmissible to ignore or underplay either factor. Therefore, it pointed out that the problem of poverty couldn't be overcome within the foreseeable future by efforts in one direction only.

India entered the phase of liberalisation in 1980s under Prime Minister Rajiv Gandhi and the process continued inspite of change in leadership at the level of the Prime Minister. The year 1991 was the beginning of an explicit phase of rolling back of the state due to the imperatives of liberalisation. Relatively higher growth was recorded during 1980-2000 and particularly during 1990s which was a decade of structural economic reforms. It also showed decline in poverty and improvement in health and literacy levels of the people of India. But India continues to suffer from high levels of illiteracy, high rate of infant mortality, high incidence of disease, disability, and malnutrition even after half a century of freedom and democracy. Allocations for health and education have been only 4.1 per cent of the GDP (1996-97) which was lower than several developing post-colonial countries like Malaysia and Sri Lanka.

The sociological consequences of the liberalisation-globalisation drive have been summarised by Yogendra Singh (2002) as state versus market dilemma. He argues that the extent to which the power of market increases and expands, the significance of the state as a supreme political institution, undergoes major alterations. Idealistically, some protagonists of the market even anticipate the end of the notion of sovereignty. For societies such as India, where nation-building has still not reached the level of integrative maturity, such fears of the end of sovereignty or a threat to it due to unhindered play of the global market force cause not only acute anxiety but also pose a challenge.

Poverty and Conflict Lines

Analysis of poverty-politics relationship needs understanding of power dynamics and conflict patterns because inequality of access to resources generates processes of conflict in the context of interests between the included, the marginal and the excluded sections of any society. The conflicts make reform and strategies and processes of poverty elimination imperative. This requires a multi-dimensional understanding of the interconnections of the spheres of state, market and community and the interrelatedness of the local, regional/ national, and global domains. All these need special attention in exploring the challenges of chronic poverty.

Poverty and the poor are always associated with (a) resourcelessness, (b) choicelessness, (c) insecurity and (d) deprivation which creates incapacities in the pursuit of dignified life in a given society for a person, household, group or community. Furthermore, those suffering chronic poverty also suffer several simultaneous disadvantages including gender, age, caste, ethnicity, location, etc. According to A.R. Desai a new class configuration has emerged as a direct consequence of the conjunction of peasant mobilisation and government measures over the last few decades. It contains the following categories of rural population:

a) *Rich Farmers and Land lords* owning 15 acres and more, possessing 50 per cent of the total land and constituting 7 per cent of the population,

b) *Middle Farmers* with 5 to 15 acres of land, possessing 30 per cent of the total land and constituting 19 per cent of the population,

c) *Poor Farmers* owning between 1 and 5 acres, possessing 17 per cent of the total land and constituting 30 per cent of rural population, and

d) *Agricultural Labour* without land or owning less than 1 acre of land, possessing about 2 per cent of the total land and constituting 44 per cent of the population. The national picture also suggested presence of five categories on the basis of household income with 10, 19, 12, 192 and 420 million persons in them

The population below poverty line (1993-94) has two major features: i) Overwhelming presence of the Scheduled Castes and Scheduled Tribes population, ii) Assam, Bihar, Madhya Pradesh, Maharashtra, Orissa and Uttar Pradesh were found to be above the national figures of population below poverty line where as West Bengal, Tamil Nadu and Karnataka were within the proximity of national figure.

The relation between the resourcelessness of the chronic poor and settings of conflict is rooted in the quest for security and dignity through ending of choicelessness of the chronic poor in a variety of ways. Such households, loaded with a complex set of disadvantages and assetlessness, are usually involved in subsistence type of activities which get them poor returns. Since their earnings are meager, they survive on small amounts of borrowed money or they are forced to suffer from hunger. They are mostly unable to change the power relationships and there are no mechanisms of grievance redressal. The powerful local forces, in conjunction with the corruptible sections of the state apparatus, manipulate and misappropriate the common resources and pubic funds which create further helplessness and frustration. It has been termed as 'web of poverty' with centrality of continuous alienation of the people trapped in it and occasional confrontation in the society. This could lead to social tension, despair or a combination of both.

The increasing visibility of a "fault line of deprivation and conflict" is a consequence of such a setting in India today. It is visible in a number of districts of Uttar Pradesh, Bihar, Orissa, Jharkhand, Chattisgarh, Madhya Pradesh, Andhra Pradesh, Assam, Tripura and Arunachal Pradesh . In the terminology of bureaucracy and media, these states have a number of districts which are conflict prone due to the effective presence of "Naxalites", "Senas" (private armies), externally aided "extremists", and separatists. Despite the variation of labels, all of them indicate presence of deepening social conflicts around issues of deprivation and poverty. It is another matter that the pattern, form and objectives of mobilisation of discontent are defined by: a) social cleavages, and b) the political conditions of the states.

At the same time, the growth of economic, social and cultural disequilibria, rooted in chronic poverty and resourcelessness is a cause of national concern. It affects governability as well as social and economic development. It also promotes increasing togetherness between poverty and political violence, which causes legitimisation of crises and invites use of police force to control its proliferation. If the state gets tough, it creates "martyrs" and myths. If the state remains tolerant and mild it faces escalation of violence and disruption of law and order. The feeling of political and economic exclusion invites entrepreneurs of violence. Therefore, the advocates of violence enjoy such settings where a large number of persons are found to be living on the margins of the economy and society.

The issue of chronic poverty and conflict is associated with the persistence of insecurity in the life setting of a person, household, group, or community. Human security suggests that people can exercise their choices in pursuit of secure and dignified existence in society safely and freely. It has two main aspects; a) safety from chronic threats such as hunger, disease and repression, and b) protection from sudden and hurtful disruptions in the patterns of daily life whether in homes, in jobs or in communities. According to the United Nations approach, the many threats to human security, differing for individuals at different times, fall into seven categories:

1. Economic insecurity,
2. Food insecurity,
3. Health insecurity,

4. Personal insecurity,
5. Environmental insecurity,
6. Community and cultural insecurity,
7. Political insecurity

These insecurities and threats can affect people everywhere. Famines, ethnic conflicts, social disintegration, terrorism, pollution and drug and human trafficking can no longer be confined within national borders. Some global challenges to human security arise because threats within countries rapidly spill beyond national frontiers, such as greenhouse gases and trade in drugs. Other threats take on a global character because of the disparities between countries -disparities that encourage millions of people to leave their homes in search of a better life, whether the receiving country wants them or not. And frustrations over inequalities in incomes and political power often build up into serious civil conflicts between groups, whether ethnic, religious or social.

Those suffering chronic poverty are caught in the midst of a set of basic conflicts which perpetuate their insecurity through 'capability poverty', resourcelessness and choicelessness. Some of these conflicts are silent and invisible e.g. the crisis due to ecological factors. Several others are visible as demonstrated by the sufferers of class, caste, ethnic gender, religious (communal) and racial discrimination. Together they contribute towards the continuity of chronic poverty in a cumulative manner by sustaining the logic of power relations and marginality of the chronic poor in the discourse of power. They envelop the institutions and processes of state, market and community.

The most visible and loud conflicts in the context of chronic poverty are found to exist around a) class, b) caste, and c) tribes (ethno-regional issues).

Class-based Conflicts

The class based conflicts have industrial and rural spheres. Both kinds of conflicts are sinking into marginality in terms of their impact. In the industrial arena, economic liberalism has led to flexible labour market policies like subcontracting, outsourcing and the engagement of temporary and part-time workers in core activities of the labour process. India's integration into the global economy and far reaching structural adjustment for it in the 1990s has weakened the strategic position of the trade unions. According to the Labour Bureau figures of the Government of India, there has been a decline in the number of man-days lost due to strikes and lockouts in 2000 compared to the figures for 1992. Furthermore, more man-days are lost due to lockouts than strikes.

In the rural arena, 298 million persons constitute the labour force engaged in agricultural and allied activities which is 79 per cent of the total work force. A majority of the work force engaged in agriculture consists of small and marginal farmers and agricultural labourers. About 80 per cent of total rural labour households (over 30 per cent of total rural households) are agricultural labour households. Of them, the Scheduled Castes and the Scheduled Tribes constitute nearly 50 per cent. In general agricultural labourers suffer from seasonal unemployment, job insecurity, poverty, indebtedness, and lack of access to productive assets. They suffer from lack of social security and inability to form their own organisations. The economic reform measures have worsened their condition due to recent hike in the prices of food grains. There is also decline in their position in comparison to their counterparts in other activities in both rural and urban areas inspite of absolute rise in their wages. The hope of 'land to the tillers' generated before independence has receded beyond the realm of realisation.

Situations of direct and indirect conflict between the poor in rural and urban spheres of the economy and the propertied sections and the state are spreading in various parts of the country. A cycle of conflicts, control and suppression and re-emergence with added strength appears to occur in significant number of rural areas in most of the poor states. The issues causing conflict in rural areas are security of employment, minimum wages, share in the produce, securing of surplus lands, reduction and liquidation of debts and violence by the land owning classes. There are also tensions and clashes in the context of sexual and cultural oppression and political denial. In fact the year 2000-01 has been a difficult one for rural economy. Income has declined. Agricultural production has been sluggish; food production has declined by almost 5 per cent. Suicides persist. The rural development programmes have recorded declining growth. A combined view of the situation of the rural labourers, marginal farmers, and the rural sector's contribution to the national economy gives a depressing picture. It is marked by limited growth of high and upper middle-income households, increased regional disparity, and the general tenor of the National Agricultural Policy which ignores the agricultural labour and marginal farmers and may accentuate the preexisting inequities with possibilities of social strife and disenchantment .

Table 1. Suicides of Farmers in Karnataka (from 1-4-2003 to 8-09-2003)

Districts	*No. Of Suicides*	*Districts*	*No. Of Suicides*
Bagalkot	7	Belgaum	13
Bangalore (Rural)	8	Davangere	30
Bangalore (Urban)	1	Bellary	9
Bidar	4	Chitradurga	6
Hassan	15	Gulbarga	3
Chamarajnagar	3	Bijapur	1
Haveri	14	Dakshina Kannada	–
Uttara Kannada	–	Gadag	6

Dharwad	8	Koppal	7
Mandya	22	Chickmagalur	6
Raichur	2	Tumkur	9
Shimoga	18	Kolar	6
Mysore	8	Kodagu	2
		Udupi	–
		Total	208

The situation in the urban settings is diffused. But there is growing discontent due to the increasing belief that the current development policies do not have the capability to create the framework within which the conditions of the poor might improve. In urban India slums are growing at the rate of 5 per cent. 24 per cent to 28 per cent of the urban population in Karnataka, Maharashtra and Delhi lives in slums as a fall out of poverty and deprivation. This provides a setting of recurring conflict between the urban poor and the Government Machinery as they are created out of 'illegal encroachment of government land'. There is high frequency of inter-community strife and conflicts. In fact violence is forced upon them as a way of living. The slum dwellers work mostly in the unorganised sector (in jobs requiring less skill and training). Their incomes are quite insufficient to enable them to lead a dignified life and enjoy basic rights.

Paradoxically, the condition of the working class in the organised sector is found to be drifting from resistance to hopelessness and less conflict in the context of the new economic policies. The new labour laws have diminished the space for class conflict in the organised sector of industrial India. There are three major events which have contributed towards the decline of the 'class power' of the organised workers in the last decade – i) disinvestment in the public sector, ii) retrenchment and contractualisation of the private industrial establishments, and iii) global recession in the industrial sector. An overview of the changing labour relations scenario may be presented by comparing the figures of industrial disputes in India in 1992 and 2002. It is seen that the figure has declined from 1714 to 413. There was also phenomenal decline in the number of workers involved in disputes and man days lost in the last decade. It needs further enquiry to be able to understand the implications of declining number of trade union strikes in an era of economic transition in favour of entrepreneurs.

On Caste Oriented Conflicts

Caste based conflicts are increasing in the context of enlargement of the capacity of two blocks - the political power of the dominant castes and political mobilisation of the Dalit castes or the Scheduled castes. It is causing conflict in the electoral arena, labour market, and civil society.

Table 2. Industrial Disputes in India since 1992

Years	*Disputes*	*Workers Involved*	*Man days Lost*
1992	1714	1252225	31259000
1993	1393	953867	20301000
1994	1201	846429	20983000
1995	1066	989695	16290000
1996	1166	939304	20285000
1997	1305	981267	16971000
1998	1097	1288923	22062000
1999	927	1310695	26787000
2000	771	1418299	28763000
2001	674	687778	23767000
2002	413	523594	15697000

The quest for political power among the Scheduled Castes around the provisions of 'Reserved seats' in legislature has been a major feature of Indian Democracy. They achieved a significant breakthrough with the growth of coalition politics in 1969-71. The making of OBC and Dalit Vote Banks was a singular contribution of socialist politics which contributed towards a 'Silent Revolution' in the era of "Green Revolution" At the same time there is marginal increase in the percentage of Dalits below the poverty line during the privatisation-globalisation regime from 44.7 per cent in 1987-88 to above 48 per cent in 1993-94, which is significantly higher than estimates for the general population (39 per cent). The literacy gap between the SCs and rest of the population has also remained more than 17 per cent between 1961 and 1991. According to the Census of 1991 more than 80 per cent rural Dalit women were found to be illiterate. They were also sufferers at the hands of the dominant castes in different parts of India. Between 1995 and 1997, a total of 90,925 cases were registered between with the police under different categories of crimes and atrocities against the Dalits. Nearly 70 per cent of all the offences were reported from the BIMARU states - Bihar, Madhya Pradesh, Rajasthan and Uttar Pradesh.

Mass murders of the Dalits by dominant castes in Andhra Pradesh and Bihar has underlined the depth of conflict between the castes in rural India over the last several years. According to an estimate, the period between 1990 and 1999 witnessed 35 instances of caste-based massacres, the total number of victims being about 400. More than 350 of those killed were from among the lower castes. In short the issue of caste-class convergence in the context of chronic poverty in an era of dominant caste democracy and liberalisation-globalisation is promoting anti-Dalit caste violence in rural areas and decline in the opportunities for the Dalits in the urban-industrial economy.

According to the Sixth Report of the National Commission for Scheduled Castes and Scheduled Tribes (1999-2001), the extent of crimes and atrocities on persons belonging to Scheduled Castes is much higher than those on Scheduled Tribe. The cases of atrocities on Scheduled Castes are about 6-7 times more than STs, though the population of SCs is only twice that of STs. Uttar Pradesh (6122), Rajasthan (5623), and Madhya Pradesh (4667) have reported highest incidence of crime against Scheduled Castes. These three states account for 65.4 per cent of the total cases of atrocities on SCs in the country during 1999.

One of the most obvious reasons for so many attacks on SC men and women is related to the refusal of the SCs to work without dignity and appropriate wages. The assertiveness of these castes for higher wages, freedom of choice of work and endeavour to achieve mobility as cultivators are among the most frequent reasons for atrocities against SCs.

Tribes and Conflicts

The Tribal dimension of chronic poverty is most pronounced in the context of conflicts and movements. They constitute 8 per cent of the population. 83 per cent of them live in the area between West-Bengal and Gujarat, 12 per cent in the North eastern region, 4 per cent in Nilgiri Hills and 1per cent in J&K and Himachal Pradesh. It is believed that confrontation has been the quintessence of the situation in the tribal areas after the rise of 'state' as a formal system of political and administrative authority. The ever-increasing exploitation of the tribals and elimination of their lands led to revolts and rebellion in many parts of India. 'Leave them alone' (or 'exclusion') as in the hills of North-East and 'light' administration (or 'partial exclusion') elsewhere was the response of the Imperial Regime in the face of determined resistance to their advancement and consolidation. The dawn of independence ushered in a new era of high hopes and soaring aspirations with an ebullient nation committed to the ideals of democracy, equity and social justice. The cause of weaker sections, particularly the tribal people, was accepted as a national task with clear premises and constitutional commitments. But the hopes were belied. The tribal people in fact faced regression as the personalised administration gave way to an amorphous faceless system. Influx of immigrants, alienation of their lands and underdevelopment are three major problems of the Tribal communities.

According to the Report of MPs and Experts (Bhuria Committee Report, 1995), "Notwithstanding the rhetoric of the past four decades, on account of absence of effective democratic decentralisation at even district levels, demands and agitations for separate states in the country have taken root in Jharkhand, Bodoland, Uttarakhand, etc. Iniquitous policies and actions and economic imbalance have led to resentment among the deprived regions. Assertions on the basis of region, ethnicity, languages, etc. Have been made. They have come to feel that without the political power of a state, they are not able to claim their rightful due".

In economic terms, the Scheduled Tribes (ST) have been found to receive a total household income of Rs. 19,556 and a per capita income of Rs. 3,504, which are 76 and 78 per cent respectively, of the national average. Both incidence and intensity of poverty are higher among the Scheduled Tribes in comparison with the national average. They have recorded a literacy level of about 40 per cent in comparison to an all India average of 54 per cent. Only about one-fourth of ST women are literate. Literacy levels are extremely low for STs in Bihar, Rajasthan, Uttar Pradesh, Madhya Pradesh and Orissa.

More than 87 per cent of the total population has been depending on agriculture for their livelihood, supplemented by collection and sale of minor forest products. However the percentage of cultivators has declined from 68 per cent to 54.5 per cent in 1991 and the proportion of agricultural labour is increasing correspondingly. Vast areas of tribal lands have been acquired under the Land Acquisition Act and still are being acquired for industrial and infrastructural development. Out of the total 213 lakh displaced persons (1951– 1990), 85.4 lakhs are Scheduled Tribes. They constitute about 40 per cent of the total number of displaced persons. From the total 83.8 lakh rehabilitated persons, 21.2 lakhs i.e. 39.4 per cent belong to STs. Dams (41 lakhs), mining (6.5 lakhs) and industries (3.8 lakhs) are the major causes of tribal displacements. A land mark judgement of Supreme Court in the case of Samatha vs. The State of Andhra Pradesh and others (11th July, 1997) has placed a check on this. The Supreme Court has ordered that government lands, forest lands and tribal lands in the Scheduled Areas cannot be leased out to non-tribals or to private companies for mining and industrial operations.

Social insecurity among the Scheduled Tribes, particularly the ST women, is also a cause of concern. Out of nearly 4000 cases of atrocities committed against Scheduled Tribes in 2000, there were 391 cases (9.8per cent) of rape. The incidents of atrocities on Scheduled Tribes were highest in Madhya Pradesh (1756), followed by Rajasthan (1221), Gujarat (367), Orissa (335), Andhra Pradesh (178), Maharashtra (171), Tamil Nadu (105) and Kerala (81). The direct and indirect relationships between the efforts of STs to move out of exploitative dependencies and the acts of atrocities is a relevant question for further systematic enquiry. At the same time, it may be concluded that the extreme forms of exploitation and violation of civil rights that exist in areas such as Chattishgarh and Jharkhand have turned them into places of long standing insurgency. Another reason for the rising violence in forest areas is encroachment by migrants who are taking over the land of the local people. This causes conflict over resource use.

Such a profile of tribal India makes it obvious that the tribals are the worst sufferers of resourcelessness and choicelessness as well as the most disenchanted section of the Indian population in post-colonial India. They are leading components in a variety of mobilisations in the last two decades including movements for environmental protection (Narmada Bachao), states reorganisation (Jharkhand, Uttarakhand, and Chattisgarh), political separation (the separatist movements of the North-Eastern Tribals), and resistance to globalisation (Kashipur). Such conflictual mobilisations have brought the issue of chronic poverty of tribal India to the attention of national media and policy analysts in recent years thereby prompting the governments to come forward with a variety of anti-poverty measures and development packages. Creation of three new provinces Jharkhand (out of Bihar), Chattisgarh (out of Madhya Pradesh) and Uttaranchal (out of Uttar Pradesh) is a major effort to address the challenge of tribal alienation and unrest. It also marks the beginning of assertiveness for tribal autonomy and dignity in the Hindi belt of India.

Trajectories of Poverty, Politics And Conflicts

India is a vast economic, cultural and political area with diversities. But the policy of the elimination of rural intermediaries and land reforms adopted after independence caused "reshuffling" of class relations in the countryside. The transformation initiative was a response to long peasant mobilisations during the freedom movement for addressing poverty. However, it performed a dual function: i) elevating the richer section of the tenants into owner class which broadened the base of the proprietary classes who take active interest in agricultural development for maximising profit, and ii) growth of marginal farmers, 'back door' tenants and proletarianised labour due to new tenurial system. The change has promoted intense competition among the newly emerging proprietary classes. They are also contending with the demands and struggles of the rural masses which are being steadily pauperised and marginalised.

On the other hand, evolution of democracy has contributed to the metamorphosis of major caste groups including the Dalits into competing associations beyond the ascriptive principles of the caste system. There has been eruption of caste organisations with intense activities in nearly all sectors of the emerging economy and in the political processes which is a response to the imperatives of the democratic political system. The changes in the caste system have the following characteristics: i) There is simultaneous weakening of the upper castes and strengthening of intermediary agrarian caste promoting a dominant caste coalitional complex in the political space, and ii) The lower caste who are also major occupants of the lowest economic labels, are getting regrouped to counteract the adverse effect of new economic and political processes. This section has been offered preferential facilities ('reservations') and opportunities in elections, education and government services. It has contributed to making the lower castes vocal.

The impact of new constitutional projects for the abolition of the caste system and restructuring the class system through affirmative action in response to the modern India has been uneven and complex. It has contained and resolved some of the most prominent issues causing conflict in the society. But it has also given rise to new competition and conflicts due to realignment of political, social and economic groups. Therefore it is relevant to provide a glimpse of the paradoxical relationship between economic, social and political structures and processes in the context of poverty and social conflict by presenting the cases of West Bengal and Bihar.

West Bengal

West Bengal and Bihar are neighbouring states which belonged to the Bengal Presidency in the colonial era. Their political economy was organised through zamindari system. Both had strong peasant movements, trade union activities and anti-poverty political formations. Both were sites of intense rural conflicts and urban movements in the post colonial decades. Both were ruled by the Congress Party between 1952 and 1967 and both got their first non-Congress governments in 1967. But they followed different trajectories in the last four decades since 1967 that resulted in major reforms in favour of poorer sections in West Bengal. Today, there is no major industrial or agrarian conflict in West Bengal.

First, we look at the politics and social change in West Bengal which along with Bihar and Orissa had the highest proportion of population below the poverty line. West Bengal has been plagued by high population density, industrial stagnation, rural conflict and economic decline in the 1980s. But these conditions were changed through reorientation of the government policies via social mobilisation and political alliances which was steered by a left front coalition in office since 1977.

High levels of unrest in rural areas for effective implementation of agrarian reforms, radical trade union movements for better wages, cheaper food items, education, health and transport facilities and emergence of a leftist political front were the outstanding features of West Bengal since late 1960s. The movement of the small and marginal farmers accelerated after the foundation of first United Front Government in 1967. It culminated into the famous Naxalbari revolt and the birth of Naxalism (or Maoism and Marxist-Leninist Communist Party). The United Front Government was removed by the centre and the peasant protests and 'Naxalite' activists were ruthlessly suppressed under President's Rule. But within a decade, there was Left Front Government in Kolkata after sweeping out the Congress regime at the centre and the state in 1977.

Agrarian reforms and organisation of local governance system were given top priority by the Left Front Government. This resulted in a sustained period of conflict containment and political stability for decades after 1977. For example, the number of riots came down from 11,702 (1977) to 3,899 (2000) whereas there was no substantial change in the scene of Bihar or All-India.

How was this accomplished? There was redistribution of more than 9,13,000 acres of land amongst 19,93,660 households which covered a large proportion of the rural population of the landless and land-poor households. Decades old demands of tenants-farmers organisations for higher crop shares, security of tenures and legal status of tenancy agreements were accepted through "Operation Barga". It gave relief and strength to the vulnerable and exploited sections of rural Bengal, which accounted for 1.44 million share croppers in the state.

West Bengal is an example of generating conducive setting for poverty eradication and conflict resolution through a combination of reforming production relations and instruments of local governance. It has been achieved on the basis of political mobilisation and electoral strength around 'peasant unity'. Now West Bengal is engaged in negotiating the path beyond the agrarian agenda for satisfactory progress in universalisation of health care and basic education. In other words the record of West Bengal shows positive correlation between poverty and conflict on one hand, and conflict, political change and economic reforms on the other.

Bihar

The history of rural unrest and agrarian movement in Bihar goes back to the Kol and Bhumiji insurrections of 1831-33 against the newly established colonial administration in Chota Nagpur and adjoining areas. The peasant movements in the regions to the north and south of the Ganges, from mid 19th century to the present day, have been regularly studied due to their significance for the peasants and agricultural workers of India. It proved to be the nucleus of All India Kisan Sabha as well as the Indian National Congress, Socialist movements and Communist movements in the twentieth century. But Bihar failed to institutionalise any change in the exploitative agrarian structure after independence. While the introduction of democracy with universal adult franchise, raised the expectations of poor peasantry, changeless agrarian system of Bihar soon became a victim of the dual failures – continuity of extremely exploitative relations and growing stagnation in the agrarian economy.

The stagnation in agricultural production around 5 per cent annual compound rate of growth between 1969–70 and 1983–84; which was lowest in India, not only caused depeasantisation but also led to declining fortunes of the rich and middle peasants. It had widened the scope of conflict between the rich and middle peasants and the rural proletariat. The inability (as well as resistance) to pay minimum wages to the agricultural workers (most of whom belong to the Scheduled Castes) had turned them towards the new revolutionary leadership for their fight for wages. As a consequence violent clashes had become a general phenomenon in Central Bihar. According to official sources, there were 463 and 590 violent clashes in 1998 and 1999 respectively. It seems that the state machinery had become marginalised as most of these killings were carried out by armed groups belonging to peasant communities and the marginal and landless poor. These Senawars had become more prominent than the electoral and other institutional forms of conflicts and competition.

In short, Bihar is a case where politics has failed and there is absence of effective local governance apparatus, like Panchayats, Police Station and Block Development Offices.

The larger political system has been affected by corruption at high places. It has led to criminalisation of politics and politicisation of crime as a cumulative consequence which is indicated in the increasing number of kidnappings in Bihar. The incidents of kidnapping have increased from 580 in 1972 to 2711 in 2000 – a five-fold increase in the state of Bihar whereas it was 769 and 926 in 1972 and 2000 in West Bengal.

Bihar is also the state with the largest proportion of persons below the poverty line as 26 out of 37 districts are among the most backward districts in the country. Therefore, it should not be a surprise if Bihar is affected by increasingly violent settings of economy, polity and society as the state system has consistently failed to respond to poverty affected groups and social conflicts around poverty problems despite major changes in the governments between 1967 and 2002 at the provincial and central levels.

Limits of Planning and Reservation

It may be useful to have an overview of the relationship between poverty and politics, as articulated through the two processes of planning and reservation during the last five decades of post-colonial India. Poverty in India, whether it is measured in terms of income or nutritional levels, is concentrated among certain occupational classes and social categories in both the rural and urban sectors. Most of the rural poor are found among (i) peasant cultivators with very small holdings, and (ii) agricultural workers from the Scheduled Castes and the Scheduled Tribes. The causes of poverty in urban settings are mostly underemployment in various occupations with low productivity occupations such as porterage, insecure employment and low real wages in some industries. Migrant workers are prominent amongst the urban poor. Furthermore, as none of the urban poor are producers of food and have to buy a part of their total requirements in the open market, they are extremely susceptible to rising food prices. In addition, the urban poor suffer from extremely bad conditions of housing, water supply and sanitation.

There has been a steady decline in the proportion of people below poverty line from about 55 per cent in the mid-1970s to 36 per cent in 1993-94 and to around 30 per cent in 2001, but their actual numbers have been rising. At the same time it is true that food insecurity and income poverty have been brought on the state's agenda through series of mobilisations, as well as natural calamities, in the last five decades. It also shows that poverty continues to create severe adversities in the lives of the rural people, particularly the small and marginal farmers, agricultural labourers and artisans and has a high incidence among the Scheduled Castes and Scheduled Tribes in rural as well as urban areas. It is regional concentrated in seven states – Assam, Bihar, Orissa, Uttar Pradesh, Madhya Pradesh, Maharashtra, and West Bengal. But there are extremely poor districts in several other states as well.

As a consequence, food security and poverty eradication have been the key objectives of the Indian planning strategy. A number of direct poverty alleviation programmes were introduced from 1971-72 after the massive electoral success of the Congress led by Indira Gandhi in 1971-72. Integrated Rural Development Programme (IRDP) and Training for the Rural Youth for Self Employment (TRYSEM) were two key components of the poverty related programmes in this period.

Poverty was a major theme in politics and planning since 1971-72. But the crisis of implementation, non-viability of projects and slow economic growth created several weaknesses in it by the mid 1980s. It caused a shift from income generation to human development oriented schemes. It also exerted pressure for de-bureaucratisation of the poverty related programmes through peoples' participation via Panchayat Raj institutions and NGOs.

With a paradigm shift in the late 1980s to the early 1990s, the issue of poverty lost its significance in the political discourse of India. This decline in importance was reflected in the Election Manifestos of major Indian political parties where the idea of growth and governance found more prominence than poverty alleviation and expenditure on employment generation. Expectations from private sector activities were a new component of the planning strategy in the era of liberalisation.

Rise in the frequency of violent conflicts in the regions suffering from poverty is becoming a significant feature of the political landscape of India since the shift of political attention away from the challenge of poverty. Land reforms, removal of illiteracy and malnutrition, encouragement of shelter construction for the homeless, and social mobilisation for breaking down the caste barriers which have trapped the SC and ST population in rural areas are some of the neglected themes in the national politics of India since the inauguration of the phase of rolling back of the state from the economic sphere.

At the same time it may also be highlighted that the engagement with poverty alleviation through planning has experienced four kinds of limits- economic, administrative, political and international constraints. The Anti-Poverty Programme of today's India involves 1 percent of GDP or 6 per cent of the Central Budget, 55 per cent of which is allocated for food subsidy or Public Distribution System (PDS), 35 per cent is allocated for Rural Works Programme, and around 5 per cent is provided for Self Employment Programmes. But there are severe resource problems due to the compulsions of allocating 50 per cent of the available national resources for debt servicing and 25 per cent for defence needs. The challenge is compounded by the continuing mal-functioning of local self-governance mechanisms and bureaucratic inefficiencies in the poverty affected areas. Politically, the situation has worsened due to the rise of crime politics nexus and more importance being accorded to politics of identity over politics of 'common interests'. Internationally there are growing pressures upon the Indian state for 'rolling back'. It is further complicated by the presence of hostile neighbours who are not keen on promoting regionalisation in South Asia Economic Zone.

Reservation was the second most important political intervention in meeting the challenges of poverty and deprivation. But this has remained more symbolic than substantive. Let us first have a look at the constitutional provisions for safeguarding the interests of the SCs and STs. Article 17 (abolition of untouchability), Article 23 (prohibition of forced labour), Article 45 (universalisation of primary education), Article 46 (promotion of educational and economic interests of SCs and STs), Article 330 and 332 (proportionate reservation of seats in the Lok Sabha and the State assemblies) and Article 335 (appointment to services and posts in Union and State services), are the most important provisions of the constitution of India in the context of protective measures for the amelioration of the conditions of the weaker sections of Indian society.

In the case of the Other Backward Classes (OBCs), there has been the use of Article 16(4) of the Constitution of India to address the problem of inadequate access to representation in the services under the state. It was activated in 1990 on the basis of the recommendations of a Second National Commission on Backward Classes (also known as Mandal Commission) with the caution of the Supreme Court that the benefit of reservations will not be extended to persons/sections falling under the category of 'creamy layer'.

This system of special treatment to underprivileged sections involves three types of preferences.

1. Reservations, which provide easier access to valued positions within important social institutions like legislature, government services and academic institutions. It is also used in land allotments, housing and other scarce resources.
2. There are expenditures of government resources on behalf of the beneficiaries like scholarships, grants, loans, legal aids etc.
3. There are special protections, such as measures to protect "untouchables" from discriminatory treatment.

Given such an institutional approach, the policies of reservations have created a symbolic power for all those who belong to the SCs (16.7 percent of the population), STs (8 per cent) and OBCs (52 per cent). It has also given recognition to the need for national reorientation for such sections of the population who are found to be trapped in a 'web of poverty' due to conjunction of social, economic and political deprivations and discrimination over a period of time.

The reservation policy regime has promoted a progressive outlook in the society because it legitimises integrative representation and re-distributive mobilisation. Besides, it has to be recognised that the exclusive emphasis upon 'timeless' system of reservation in jobs and legislature has bypassed the poor of these categories. There has been evolution of blocks of vested interests in such category of the beneficiaries of reservation in the past five decades.

The majority of the Scheduled Castes and Scheduled Tribes are agricultural labourers. Because of economic compulsions, their children have to go to work when they should be in schools. Children who labour, lose education and therefore employment opportunities when they are adults. Without the means of income for want of education, they in turn may continue to send their children to work. It strengthens the vicious circle of poverty and this has not been addressed by 'job reservation'.

Similarly the question of number has played a crucial role in determining the chances of receiving attention of the state and gain of vote power. It has created cleavages between the large, medium and small groups of SCs, STs and OBCs. For example, the SCs are 21 per cent of the population in Uttar Pradesh. But chamars constitute 12.7 per cent and Pasis are 3 per cent. They have created a sub-category of empowered and mobile SCs. But there are 6.5 per cent other SCs, with a total share of only 2.8 per cent in population, who remain most depressed due to numerical marginality. The rise of dominant castes among the OBCs like Jats, Yadavas, Kurmis, Lodhis, Reddys, Kammars, Vokkaliggas, Lingayats, etc. Has led to marginalisation of the other OBCs who are recognised as Most Backward Castes (MBCs) in the discourse of power.

In short, the impact of reservation policies is visible in the political culture where the SCs the STs and the OBCs have emerged as new corporate identities with constitutional protection for representation and empowerment. But it has not contributed towards any qualitative shift in the lives of the poorer sections of these communities, where poverty is getting perpetuated in overwhelming numbers despite decades of freedom and democracy, planning and reservations.

Liberalisation, Poverty Alleviation and Conflicts

Opening the market of India to global companies and reducing the role of public sector have been two major components of the new economic policies. They are also associated with globalisation of capital mobility and ethnicisation of political mobilisation. It was found that there was i) a boom in the private sector, ii) stable growth in agricultural sector (3.6 per cent per annum), iii) declining rate of population growth (1.6 per cent per annum), and iv) improvement in social indicators (like literacy rate, infant mortality rate, gender related indicators etc.). In the early 1990's, poverty worsened following structural adjustments, a poor harvest and a decline in food availability. There was some decline in poverty and by 1993-94 it fell below the 1987 level. States in the north and east, that have 40 per cent of India's population have lagged in reducing poverty since the late 1970's. According to economic analysts, expenditure on social sector schemes as part of the welfare oriented programs of the Indian state has been increasing in real terms in the era of liberalisation. At the same time it has also been pointed out that it is mainly through increased expenditures of the Central government. The state governments are easing out of their constitutional commitment to sustain programmes in social sectors and it is a matter of concern. Here the social sector expenditure is defined as the total expenditure on social services and rural development. The social services include education, health and family welfare, water supply and sanitation. The rural development expenditure relates mostly to anti-poverty programmes and is presented as 'economic services' in the budget documents.

The realities of 'reforms' have created new challenges for India since: a) So far mostly the better off sections are able to respond to market signals and the rural population has benefited less. b) India is suffering marginalisation in a globalised world and loss of domestic market due to unfettered entry of the foreign companies under the WTO provisions. c) The role of government in economic and social matters is shrinking which has caused apprehensions about 'the future of the protective discrimination' for the weaker sections.

These challenges are being listed as tasks during the Second Generation Reforms. It is recognised by the policy makers that "Freedom from ignorance, diseases and fear, along with freedom from want, are the best guarantors of human development. But education, health care, water and sanitation services, which can ensure these freedom, are not accessible to all. To ensure easy accessibility, we need public action in these areas if human development has to gather momentum. Together, these facilities comprise a nation's social infrastructure that is as critical as physical infrastructure for a widely shared and inclusive development". These challenges have been integral in the making of the new approach to poverty.

A set of new goals has been adopted in the field of education, health, and safety nets. Ensuring 100 per cent literacy in the next five, if not three years; aim for 75 per cent enrolment in higher secondary schools of good quality with encouragement to private sector to provide good schools in every Taluka; raising college enrollment to 20 per cent in the age group 20-24 years; and revitalising the university system are the major goals in education. Healthcare policy goals include reducing the all-India infant and child mortality rate; expanding health care infrastructure to rural areas; ensuring access to clean drinking water; and encouragement to NGOs and private sector to engage in the health sector. The construction of social safety nets will be based on a) a model employment programme covering the whole country, b) Integrated child development services to reduce child mortality and poverty and c) group-based micro-credit schemes to cover the entire country. Thus, there are new tasks before India, in the context of Global Goals for moving further in the direction of construction of the welfare state after five decades of successful democratisation of the political culture and decolonisation of national economy.

The social sector expenditures have resulted in the decline of illiteracy from above 80 per cent in 1951 to less than 35 per cent in 2001. The longivity of the people of India has increased from less than 39 years in 1951 to above 65 years in 2001. Even the incidence of poverty has declined from over 50 per cent in 1950s to less than 30 per cent in 2001. But the new challenges are demanding a new interface between the nation-state and the modern world system at the global level and between the state and the market in Indian political economy. So far the shift of paradigm has been carefully utilised by dominant elite caste, the coastal zones of south and west, major industrial groups, and global financial firms. It has promoted consumerism among the middle classes and scans among the elite in power. At the same time a new wave of people's movements by political parties and non-party organisations has been created to demand freedom from illiteracy, hunger, diseases, environmental degradation, and unemployment.

The pressure groups for social justice and political empowerment are also becoming increasingly visible and assertive. The Dalit movement, the women's movement, the movement of local people (tribes) for control over land, forest, and water resources are some examples of it The movement for Right to Information and pressure for Electoral Reforms are becoming significant as the citizens are getting increasingly anguished about criminalistic of politics and increasing marginalisation of common people's concerns. It seems that the need of the hour is to drive India towards a system of participatory democracy through planning for decentralisation of power and empowerment of the marginal sections of the masses like women, the Scheduled Castes and the Scheduled Tribes, based upon the twin goals of rapid growth and elimination of poverty for the construction of a just and prosperous social order. It is likely that the heritage of Indian National Movement, the basic values of the Constitution of India and the continuous widening of the social base of democracy in India in the last five decades may provide the required support in the era of liberalisation and global market mediation.

It is important to take note of the roots of sluggishness in poverty reduction in the era of liberalisation and address the same. The World Bank approach attempts to argue that there are five interrelated compartments of problems which are contributing to the continuity of poverty:

1. Characteristics of agricultural growth in the 1990s,
2. The slow down of growth in the poorer states,
3. The problems of infrastructure, social services and poverty programmes (especially in the poorer states),
4. Poor incentive framework, and
5. Weakness in governance.

The World Bank analysis has also given content to the eradication of poverty in India in the new century:

a) up liftment of 300 million people concentrated in poorer states,
b) raising literacy rate from 62 per cent (50 per cent for females) by enrolling over 300 million children (mostly poor) who are out of school,
c) addressing the gender based inequalities faced by women in the political, legal and economic systems,
d) reversing the decline in infrastructure spending to meet urban needs and to increase the rate and spread of urbanisation.

It is arguing in favour of implementing "second phase of reforms" which involves – i) cuts in explicit and implicit subsidies together with privatisation of power, ii) government rolling back from infrastructure activities in favour of private sector, iii) more spending on health and elementary education, iv) improvement in government and governance, v) completion of deregulation of goods and factor markets, and vi) provision of high quality infrastructure services.

The critics of liberalisation are arguing that liberalisation has made the economy systematically "demand constrained". They indicate that the demand constrained nature of the Indian economy is manifested today as the combination of industrial recession and surplus stocks of foodgrains and foreign exchange. They argue that "withdrawal" by the state is the primary reason for the emergence of the demand constraint as it has created deflationary effects which are not offset by private investments. It has contributed negatively to the fields of employment and poverty. First of all employment in the organised sector has been virtually stagnant for some time; of late even rural employment expansion has begun to stagnate. According to the economic survey of 2003, there was a net 3 percent decline in rural employment in the preceding year which was a serious indicator of the crisis of employment. Secondly, the headcount ratio of rural poverty which had declined significantly during the eighties has ceased to decline over the nineties, and might have marginally increased.

This perspective points out that it is ironical that the government is claiming the existence of large foreign exchange reserves, massive food grain stocks and markedly low inflation, as achievements, while their simultaneous presence is indicative, on the contrary, of an unprecedented crisis in the Indian economy, a crisis of shrinking demand whose other manifestations are retrenchments, closures, and lay off in organised sector industrial units, a decimation of textile weavers leading to suicides, growing rural unemployment, and aggravation of rural poverty. The situation is more likely to deteriorate progressively.

8

Sociological Causes of Terrorism

The intellectual-political divide in defining terrorism as an analytical tool or policy-formation-abstract makes it a futile exercise to attempt a definition of terrorism in this chapter. The terrorist act, however, can be identified by the violent perpetrators and the organisation or social group (states, religious, ethane, sub-national groups or ideologies) behind them, the violent acts, the victims, the message the actors want to convey and the locus of authority where the message is intended. Terrorist acts are not much different from crime and suicide: they are the resultant of a sense of estrangement from the social milieu. These acts are intended to convey the existence of problems through spectacular violence, as other methods to broadcast the message are deemed ineffective. Blood and gore are presumed repulsive enough to public sensitivities to extend the resonance of the message to a wider audience.

Terrorist acts are committed against citizens (because of their vulnerability) in the country of the terrorist, in a neighbouring country or in the wider world, depending upon the audience. The assassination of leaders, politicians, decision-makers, opinion-formers and other high profile personalities, explosions (car bombs, IEDs, belt-bombers), massacres, hijackings, hostage taking, disruption of economic infrastructure, the destruction of high-value economic targets and attacks on a civilian populace are other examples of terrorism. The instruments of mega terror, with the diffusion of science and technology, are also accessible to terrorists. The danger of recourse to biological, chemical, radiological and nuclear weapons has made terrorism a threat to be dealt with swiftly in a coordinated manner.

Terrorism—A Sociological Perspective

Terrorist acts are not committed in a social vacuum. Terrorists are emergent of the social processes. A contextual, intuitive approach employing what was termed as 'the sociological imagination' by the redoubtable C. Wright Mills has been employed for this study. The level of abstraction has been extended from the individual to the interaction of two or more individuals, to larger social groups and ultimately to groups of nations.

Society is, in its simplest description, overlapping social groups composed of individuals with social roles, privileges and obligations implicit in their own cultural values and norms. Each social group undergoes the process of social integration and disintegration simultaneously. Social disintegration is the aggregate of personal disintegration. Disintegration causes three basic types of reactions: aggression, acquiescence or retreat. These reactions are not discrete and can combine in varying degrees in any covert or overt act. Terrorist acts are one such composite combination, as brought out in the following pages. Several factors, enumerated below, contribute to social disintegration

Social Structures, Change and Reaction

Social groups either adapt to environmental changes or perish. Adaptation leads to social change, which is a tension-ridden process. Change can be absorbed to the extent that management mechanisms and the elasticity of the group are developed. Members who perceive that the burden of adjustment is disproportionate to advantages either take to acquiescence, withdrawal or rebellion, depending upon their genetics and socialisation. Some such social processes are given below:

1. *Socialisation:* Social structures evolve over time. The stabilised structures, jolted by newer values, can upset the pattern of social ranking. Incumbent members perceiving slippage in their prestige take to either role-defence or acquiescence. Achievement, where the actor does not fit into the milieu and has either to move up the social scale or is pushed up, is elating, but is also depersonalising. The social traits of one class position may not.be functional in another, causing social stress. This depersonalisation, consequent to mismatch of orientation, position in the social hierarchy, and extant expectations in the new setting, causes social anomia – the pervasive feeling to both internalise and rebel from the norm. This less than optimal participation in society can lead to the quest for some supra-mundane activity, fulfilling some deeper psychological need of recognition, security and relationship

2. *Hiatus Between Social Provisions and Individual Needs:* Frustration is a natural product of mismatch of individual needs and social provisions. Those who are most deprived of need-satisfaction are also those most deprived of valued relationships that induce socially conforming behaviour. Deviance and violence is a plaintive call for deliberate action by authoritative roles for fulfilling these needs. Burton brings out this dilemma saying "If an attempt is made to subordinate individual values to social values, then, because it is not possible to enforce social values that are inconsistent with individual values, there will be

responses that are damaging both to the individual and through him, to the social system." Individuals either singly or in groups act deviant, sometimes despite themselves, to register their disaffection with the social group. Recourse to terrorism may appear to some to be a way to vent this 'structural conflict'–the gap between needs and provisions-possibility.

3. *Manifest and Latent Functions of the Social Structure:* Most social structures have both manifest functions and latent functions as brought out by Merton. Uprooting of such structures without social safety nets causes havoc (e.g. nuclear family efficient for social mobility displacing a joint family in rural India). This induces ambivalence towards both the new and old structures. Members displaced or dispossessed by this gap in fulfilment subconsciously take to social deviance.

4. *Mismatch Between Ideal and Reality:* The social ideal is an emergent of the social dynamic. Authority positions are expected to lead in attaining that ideal. If the elite, who are supposed to uphold the ideal, instead debase it, the lower echelons find themselves looking for either redefining the ideal or reviewing the prestige that they proffer on the elite. At the extreme stage of this skepticism comes the demand for removal of the elite or revolutionising of the structure so that the power wheel is turned upside down. The distancing of reality and the ideal is a cause of frustration. Deviance and disorganisation are its natural consequences.

5. *Ideal of Success:* Taking a cue from industrial societies, most developing societies now emphasise the ideal of success, forsaking the time-tested achievement of group goals. The pressures of modern production and consumption, underwritten by the rule of winner-take-all, create serious disequilibrium within societies, adjusting to the new industrial culture. The more

intense the pressures of success, the greater number of demoralised individuals it creates.

6. *Marginalisation:* Societies in flux tend to produce greater proportion of marginal individuals than stabilised societies. Marginalisation can be the resultant of diverse factors either by itself or in combination-genetic, environmental, faulty socialisation, lack of positions commensurate with the socialisation, intensity of competition for positions, etc. The flux in valued positions - due to changes in technology, levels of knowledge or rigours of training - leaves many newer entrants in each generation on the margins, unless newer opportunities open up, matching with the available social training. The modern labour-displacement technologies leave many seekers bereft of opportunities. The uprooting of some people, consequent to unsuitability for the new roles demanded by the milieu, throws them on the margins of acceptable behavioural patterns. This pool of marginalised people, under stress from the social group, but unable to adapt to newer structures, makes a fertile ground for the emergence of esoteric subgroups. Terrorism fills this need for conspicuous action and recognition. The greater the numbers of marginal people in society, the greater the danger of such deviant acts.

7. *No Safety Valves:* Each nation or social group has built-in safety valves for letting off stress. Religion, entertainment, expressive media, sports contests, gambling and prostitution are some of them. Authorities may have, at times, foreclosed these safety valves for some ulterior motive without taking into consideration the morale, habits and impulses of the people or without recognising their latent functions. Since the recourse to illegitimate wealth and

instruments of terrorism are necessarily a part of such operators of safety valves, terrorism becomes a proximate option.

Social Relationships as Integrative Mechanisms

(a) *Breakdown of Traditional Relationships:* Inter-generation social relationships have been continually changing. The latter day rapid pace of change and social flux upsets stabilised relationships, whether patriarchal, feudal or kinship, in most developing societies. Role models change rapidly. The most energetic elements in this dialectic seek emancipation from the internalised obligations, resulting in inter-generation friction. They cut themselves off from their groups of orientation or are thrown out by the milieu, for they cannot adapt to the greater flux of urban anonymity, ruthlessness, and open arena of intense competition. Such individuals and groups form a rich cache for future terrorists.

(b) *Transitory relationships:* By nature, the urban flux is depersonalising and transitory vocations cannot substitute for organic kinship. Life for the social animal that man is, in its metaphysical sense, is relationships. This floating is very disintegrated in the short run; there is a quest for the new and there is pining for the old with the present be fogged by both the future and the past. Some actors experience isolation for being far too above or below par of success in the given milieu. It is these individuals who gravitate towards delinquent gangs with their capability or inferiority pushing them to deviance. Most executors of terror acts come from this category offer of journalist Daniel Pearl in Karachi studied in London before taking to religiosity and terrorism.

Power Relations

Power relations in a society are the result of past power struggles and social accommodations. However, the tendency of the incumbents at authoritative roles to freeze social negotiation and perpetuate their legitimacy is a consistent cause of social mal-integration. The absence of mechanisms to de-freeze such a tendency forces recourse to deviance.

1. *Social Differentiation:* All societies have to move from the primitive mechanical solidarity, as in pre-literate societies, to organic solidarity with differentiation of functions, division of labour and prestige gradations in the modern world. Social differentiation is functional in case checks and balances are in place. In case accountability institutions are not available, authoritative roles can indulge in self-perpetuation causing social discontent, expressed in withdrawal of respect, privilege and subsequently aggressive acts to physically eliminate the depraved, devalued roles and the individuals holding them. Terrorism is one avenue to express this discontent.

2. *Relative Deprivation:* Deprivation and poverty *per se* do not cause disintegration. It is only when some individuals and subgroups perceive that the costs of change are being differentially apportioned and the allocation of resources are being inefficiently distributed that they experience relative deprivation even though they may be better-off from the *ex ante* position. Relative deprivation gradually coagulates into social resentment and loss of morale. It takes the form of regression, acquiescence or aggression, depending upon the strength of invidious experience.

3. *Creation of Power Positions:* Developing societies generally create far too few positions goods than could

assuage any significant number of entrants to the dynamic. Fewer power positions necessarily mean pride of ascension and its discretionary dispensation to favourites. The vicious circle of lack of empowerment leading to lack of morale and involvement, irresponsibility, malfeasance and sabotage, further concentrates power in fewer hands and operates with a vengeance in developing societies. Sabotage and malfeasance is social deviance.

4. *Legitimacy vs. External Support:* The breakdown of colonial rule has given rise to structures which hold and exercise power but which are not seen as legitimate by the various subgroups within the larger group - the nation. The lack of legitimacy is a potent source of dissent-suppression, frauds, opaque structures, nepotism and mis-governance. Depending upon the state of openness and tolerance for opposition and dissent, such subgroups either take to acquiescence, silent protests, strikes, demonstrations and even insurgencies. The lack of legitimacy is further exacerbated by wider power politics. Support to regimes patently illegitimate, partly representative or moving towards legitimacy evokes a sense of antipathy and resignation amongst the most vital of actors. The demoralisation amongst such individuals or subgroups leaves them flotsam in the power mart and they gravitate towards secretive, deviant organisations.

5. *Opposition and Religious Institutions:* The ambivalence of secular institutions (towards political participation by certain groups) hinders growth of functional opposition. This ambivalence opens a window for opposition groups that lack opportunities for expression, to channel their activities through the refuge of religion (e.g. Muslim Brotherhood, Islamic Jihad, etc). These groups lack available channels to disseminate their

ideas and thus, in order to gain acceptance from the wider mass, consolidate through public, religious charities, playing on the vulnerability of the state. The impulse to push forward an alternative then coagulates into reactionary activities, completing the vicious circle. The connection of terrorists with religious outfits, which in their nature cannot be democratic, allows the rise of religious autocracies - without dissent, discussions, compromise or consensus. Fundamentalism is a natural source of and only a step behind terrorism.

6. *Coercion as Major Form of Social Control:* Dissent is a natural concomitant of a living society. Progressive societies encourage it, but regressive regimes take to regulatory deterrence as the major and sometimes only means of social control. This is expensive, with large collateral damage on the morale of both sides, resulting in more acute deviance in new ways. This circularity of skepticism, its intolerance, coercion to suppress, loss of morale, overt defiance, and further suppression can culminate in leagues and networks, both overt and covert, to defy authority and garner adherents – the malcontents of the social group. Alternatively, the progressively waning social morale could lead to cynicism towards life. Withdrawal and suicide are symptoms of this process. Suicide *perse*, as a moral statement, is terrorism.

Management of Economy

1) *Alienation:* Social alienation is a typical reaction of the mass production-consumption social matrix. Alienated individuals seek means of adaptation and social stabilisation and to reach some equilibrium, though at a great emotional cost. But some individuals invariably slip outside the margins of sociability.

Similarly, modern education is a cause of typical alienation amongst the young. Most of them somehow adapt to mixed gender classes, new curricula, and new infrastructure. Some, however, cannot find their bearings until they drop out. Education dropouts, in almost all cases, have to settle for lower prestige, marginalisation and alienation, feeding the deviant networks.

Brutalisation and training in deviant activities (e.g. dropouts, returnees from jails convicted on minor offences) can lead to deviant networks. Ordinary criminality by such networks is sometimes transmuted into glorified deviance. Groups that start as criminals can transmute into social benefactors in case the milieu is willing to afford them legitimacy (Robin Hood type of gangs where the state has faltered). Such subgroups equipped with resources, training, and ideologies are a potent source of challenges to authority positions.

2. *Developmental Pressures:* Economic development, if not managed, causes social disruption. Development causes a strain on the physical environment, resulting in unforeseen sicknesses and disruptive absenteeism. Developmental pressures invariably give rise to centripetal forces. Sabotage, crime, rebellions, insurgencies are some common concomitants of developmental stress, especially if it is rapid and intense.

3. *Sectoral Grievances:* Social homogeneity is a matter of degree. Since the diverse actors vie for scarce resources, positions and need-filling mechanisms, there is competition amongst the contending subgroups. Sectoral grievances are expressed in the language of exploitation and can lead to noncooperation, withholding of consent, strikes, mobilisation, rebellion and insurgencies.

Culture

a) *Delinquency Subculture*: Most societies harbor a spectrum of social sanctions to outwit deviance. The allowance given to ideas (and their cultural manifestations - songs, dance, films, dress, body care, and general style of life) from the West in traditional societies wreaks havoc with the social morale there. This allows the growth of a delinquent subculture where the social signposts become blurred and ideals crumble to the warm, pink winds.

Successful individuals become the target of the masses (Foreign/American returned people in the local milieu in developing societies face derision if they vaunt the liberating values of the West and remain ever on the defensive; the expectation that people educated/ employed in the West would be bridges is misplaced). They either give-in, remaining maladapted and halfhearted social discontent, or openly defy the old order and perforce take to alien arenas. In either case it is a loss for the native milieu. The resultant anomia is a great source of deviance, often culminating into acceptance of questionable ideologies and ideal-constructs.

b) *Intensity of Communication:* The new technology ingress amidst traditional production, consumption and power relations, gives rise to the amorphous ubiquity of communication. Events, episodes, persons, ideals – totally alien in form and content, come to be internalised by distant and near actors. Symbols, whether suicide bombs or crashing planes, get embedded in the social ether. The communication mechanisms which are legitimately heralded as liberating influences can also become means of control, disinformation and coagulation of malcontents. Such mass dissemination, being impersonal, is generally out of the local context, and most of the times alienating. The skewed distribution of communications makes it a one-way affair, representing 'techniques of moral brokerage and encouragement to journalists to work on behalf of the established order.' As Erection says "it is the organisation of news, not events in the world that creates news." Terrorism is one way of communicating the reverse.

c) *Simplification of Reality:* In a society where anomie is pervasive, where relations and positions are in flux, intellectual leaders and opinion makers are atrophied with constricted imagination and intellectual sclerosis and the stage is set for the emergence of some normative patterns, intelligible to the atomic populace. Surrogates arise and propose simplification of reality into a series of pictures, images, and symbols, striking a chord amongst lethargic society -fatigued by the incessant flux of ideas and ideologies. These surrogates are essentially simple, impressionable people like children who lie and thereafter believe in the lies. They offer flimsy anchorage when the waters are choppy. Formation of cults is a logical progression in this simplification which gives meaning and content to lives made hollow otherwise. The failure of the intellectual leadership to adopt and channel the popular impulses into creative, productive and stabilising institutions is the sure sign of some messiah to emerge, some Moses bringing manna and the quest of the promised land. This is but the penultimate stage of social disintegration.

d) *Subculture of Violence:* Cultural traditions control behaviour patterns of individual members. Some subgroups emphasise violence (e.g. hunter groups) while others give acquiescence (e.g. agricultural societies) more weight in socialisation. The cultural traits of the subgroups, if not utilised in constructive ways, lead to anomie and less than optimal utilisation of their potential. Failure to recognise the potential of each subgroup can cause deviance and social dislocation resulting in violent protests.

e) *Non-rational Factors:* Non-rational factors play a great role in socialisation. Totems, myths, legends, however, can become a focus of rallying against the extant authorities if case avenues for expression of pent up frustrations are not available. Myths and totems become theatrical, raising the vision of an unrealised promised land, of the supposed 'grandeur' and 'justice' of the past. Apocalyptic groups which are but social failures can procure adherents by reverting to such episodes, symbols and myths which can neither be proved by empirical testing nor disproved because they are present in the social subconscious.

External Environment

The pervasive availability of ideas and cultures, artifacts and technologies, goods and wares is intense in a globalised world and has unintended, consequences. Technology can be imported but its appropriation calls for sustained social effort, which may not be forthcoming.

Similarly, the integration mechanisms such as entertainment and media make insidious ingress in social groups not ready for absorption and assimilation. The superstructure makes local culture inefficacious by what Gramsci called cultural hegemony. This subconscious hegemony is but a precursor of ideas coagulating towards repulsion and closing in. The skewed nature of ownership allows only a few to dictate what should be heard and seen, imbibed and referenced, rejected and consigned. These vulnerability are sustainable rallying points for terrorists – those who see that their life is being weaned away from its mooring. Material, intellectual and ideological aid, even if given with unadulterated benevolence, which is hardly the case with foreign aid anyway, can be a cause of demoralisation and disintegration unless reassuring mechanisms and social confidence have developed enough to counter the social demoralisation.

Terrorism in South Asia

South Asia, home to a fourth of the global population, is beset with serious problems of insurgencies, rebellions, militancy and movements giving occasion to several terrorist incidents, not allowing legitimate authorities time for consolidation and appropriate political dynamic to evolve. Terrorists of various hues—leftists, rightists, ethnic, religious, sub-national are active in the region, symbolising that the sociopolitical structures evolved during the past decades have not been able to satisfy major chunks of population.

Jihadi Terrorism

Jihad is a tenuous, perhaps expedient concept in Islamic theology. Muslim political ascendance during the seventh century called for *jihad* (righteous effort) and *fatah* (literally *opening* for the victory of the righteous). The cult of martyrs as the *shaheed* (witness, perhaps of God as he became the dearest of God) was for mass mobilisation in the essentially trading society. Jihad as a tenet of Islam, is defined, reviewed and redefined as per the predilection of the beholder. In the post-colonial, post-cold war period, with rampant demoralisation, Jihad transmuted from a guiding post to one of the pillars to the central pillar of Islam, and for some to be the basic of Islam, equal to the belief in Allah and his Prophet, with each Muslim obliged to do his duty to the religion and its dictates as interpreted by the pure and the learned (*ulema*). People in the sub-continent claim that though the Quoran descended in Arabia, it was interpreted in the sub-continent, decrying the Arabs as *jahils* (ignorant) and hailing the Deobandis as the rightful interpreters of Islam. This is hotly contested by the Arabs. Jihad came upon the subcontinent with a vengeance, with a combination of several sociopolitical factors. It is, however, a sociological puzzle that Indian Muslims did not find it expedient or even a teleological necessity to join the Jihadi movement, or even express solidarity with it.

1. *Similarities—Cultural Continuity:* The decadal census states that over 138 million citizens profess Muslim faith in India. Their growth rate of 2.93 percent over the decade 1991-2001 is comparable to growth rate in other parts of the Muslim world. Similarly the socioeconomic data on Pakistan, Bangladesh and India also reveals no wide diversity or difference in income levels. The per capita in dollar terms and PPP of the three countries, the HDI indexes and trends on economic growth and demographic profiles are roughly approximate. In addition, there are kinship ties among the Muslims across the borders in the subcontinent. The history of Islamic ingress and the adoption of Islam by the people at a certain socioeconomic level are common to all three peoples. All three countries share a common political background in terms of Arab-Turk-Mughal and colonial history. They also have commonality of languages and culture. Similarly the climate and topography, with regional variations, are similar. All three countries swear by democracy and tried to develop Westminster style of government.

2. *Differences in Political Evolution*: Muslims in India remain a significant minority, even if their relative percentage to the overall population is rather low—12.8 percent (a solid unitary group with a distinct identity, as opposed to the diffuse majority of Hindus

as a residual category without any cohesive identity). Over 150 million Muslims today form the second biggest Muslim population in one single country after Indonesia. This bulk and influence can give Indian Muslims a significant say in the Islamic dynamic. But this has somehow not come about. Muslims in Bangladesh and Pakistan, in contrast, are the overwhelming majority and compose both the elite as well as masses.

This obvious difference, however, does not explain the indifference to the *Ummah* and the *Jihad.* If anything, the contrary effect is plausible with the minority (Muslims) seeking their inspiration from their land of orientation, the Arab world. This inspiration is evident in cultural manifestations like names, religious festivals, marriage rites or civil laws. Minorities have complexes bordering on paranoia - threats of assimilation, overt discrimination and social prejudice, even if not explicit in the political discourse, can be prefigured. Such complexes lead them to seek support and inspiration elsewhere. Hence, the endorsement of the supervening Ummah should be their first refuge in the expectation of political and moral aid and reassurance. The pressures of development, resource allocations and the invidious social and economic ascent could also be a source of frustration, forcing the minority to look beyond the immediate governance of the state.

Is it expedient acquiescence, what Turkish secularists deride as *takkiye*, from which most of the present Muslims trace their descent, or is it something deeper, a wider process? Social processes and social structures in India, their evolution and consolidation could possibly throw some light on the question under examination.

Pakistan, India and Bangladesh have a republican form of government with their constitutions swearing by democracy. But they all have taken different trajectories in their interpretation and ascent to democratic governance. This has given a peculiar hue to their form of State and the informing institutions. The plurality of institutions, their power, influence, independence and autonomy are a matter of degree. Some of them approximate the institutions established in developed countries while others are still in their infancy in the countries. Similarly, the reach and depth of the State vary.

Role of Political Institutions to Comabt Terrorism

The Indian State has progressively reached all corners of the land and has accomplished depth not visible in other countries – by way of accommodations, legitimisation, representation and co-option. Contra-movements have been dealt with politically rather than as law and order problems. Successive governments have engaged various insurgent groups, in attrition, in dialogue and in resolution. Similarly, the constitutional obligation to hold elections for installing popular, constitutional governments obtained legitimacy for the State. This accommodative depth has allowed India to focus on the developmental needs of its vast and ever-growing population. Democracy, even with all its imperfections, is seeped in the individual consciousness and there is a characteristic allergy to order, discipline, and diktat from outside of India. Chaos is preferred to discipline from without.

Institution Building

Institution building, even if inexpedient and causing tremendous strain on the paltry resources of time and material, is *sui generis* in India. The legislature, judiciary and the media being afforded unrestricted freedom to evolve their traditions, culture and functional ethics, expanded their space, even at the cost of the Executive. Any encroachment or transgressions has built-in resistance.

Pluralism

As institutions consolidate, newer institutions representing civil society emerge. The increasing civil society intervention in spheres affecting both public life and private interests is firmly embedded in social governance. Several institutions developed along the way: in economic management, cultural organisations, environmental groups, rights protection societies, clubs, fraternities, professional organisations and trade unions. The public space expanded to incorporate several overlooked individuals and groups, marginal outfits and peripheral constituencies. This expansion increased integration for the State and achieved strategic depth to contain all centripetal tendencies and forces. Pluralism was firmly established. Religion receded into the background with other mechanisms that have a lead role in frustration venting. Religion was progressively confined into the personal rather than the public domain. *iv) Military under Civilian Rule in India:* The military is only one of the several pillars of self-defence in India. The clear delineation of the privileges, role expectations, powers and chain of command is traceable directly to the President, who is advised by the Prime Minister. The military has a clear sphere of activity. It has never attempted to advice on governance, unlike in other countries where the military has actually assumed power. The strain of governance and defence duties generally contorts the military in these countries, insulating the institution from the currents of national life, and making it bureaucratic, bent on preserving itself and its privileges rather than serving the purpose it was established for or the responsibilities it took upon itself. People demoralised by military action take recourse to non-rational and sometimes irrational means and ends whereby - God and God's-Just-World become social aspirations with the individual self becomes an ephemeral, transitory reality. India has been spared of this anathema.

Channels of Communication

Communication is a *sine quinone* of development and empowerment. Representative institutions in India draw out the essence from the masses for national consideration. Violence is a reaction to indifference and maladaptation. Communication is a safe way to pre-empt it. Indian democracy has mature communicating channels. Dissent smothered by power instruments could hardly cover the social malaise. One of the best known Pakistani poets expressed it in a couplet. Aspirations and dissent never got channelled into the pulpits and mosques in India. Secular institutions, even in their bumbling way, fulfilled this role.

Political Parties

Political parties in India are omnibus organisations without explicit polarisation on religious lines. All parties solicit Muslim support since they have a swing-potential in elections. To give representation to this constituency is a prime electoral necessity for all parties. The structural necessity of omnibus coalitions of various religions, castes, and interests groups pre-empts polarisation. Compromises and negotiations in coalition building have given a stable equilibrium to the linguistic, religious, and ethnic minorities in addition to peripheral geographical groups. There is no disconnect between the polity and the state, no void of proscribed parties to be filled by unrepresentative interests.

Social Control Mechanisms

Social control in India is mostly endogenous through family, kinship, school, neighbourhood and community. Various mechanisms have pre-empted social frustrations from reaching their boiling point. Some of them are given below:

Secularism in India: India rejected the theory that a people following one religion constitute a nation, as is propagated in Pakistan. The ideal of a uniform civil code for all citizens, given a prominent place in the Directive Principles of the India Constitution though implementation of this article is suspended due to the sensitivities and vulnerability of the minority religions. Unless the minority community is ready for such a uniform code and willingly disposes itself to such change, it will not be brought into effect. The accommodation shown has tempered the fear psychosis in the minds of minorities. The freedom of practising and propagating religion has been guaranteed by the (stitution. It has successfully pre-empted a potential source of discontent and violence. In addition to foreclosing dissent and perpetual friction, this has given the Muslims a sense of reassurance about their future within the Indian nation – irrespective of the denomination to which they belong - Sunni, Shia, Ahmedi, Sufi or Bohri. This freedom has also been emphasised for Christians and Parsis. Freedom guaranteed by the constitution and enforced both by social dictates and law and order mechanisms has resulted in the withdrawal of religion into the personal domain, prevented polarisation on religious lines and split the monolithic religious traditions into several localised sects. Religion, confined to the personal domain, has become an effective tool for socialisation and social control. This cannot be said of other countries in the region, where religion occupies public-political space.

Counter-ideologies: Indian culture is catholic and eclecticism is the predominant reality in matters of faith - no book is considered definitive to guide social conduct or explain cosmology. All creeds are fused in this 'melting pot': from atheism to pantheism and strict monotheism. In such a diverse and pluralistic cultural flux, no particular ideology can reach an overarching position. The dialectic is not only tolerated but also encouraged. Puritanism is considered a public nuisance. It is this spirit of eclecticism which gives rise to innumerable practices and within which fundamentalism is scoffed at, derided, and ostracised. Indian society recognises the impossibility of converting terrorist impulses into productive and creative channels (e.g. into fighting elections and defeating the war of ideas) making it difficult to sustain terrorism within the state. Developing institutions in India have the obligation of co-opting diverse values and opinions into their functioning, thus blunting the edge of deviance. This has not been, unfortunately the case in other countries, where heterodox traditions, have been proscribed, with accompanying state or group violence.

Open Channels for Dissent: The right to freedom of expression and association has been vigorously exercised for organising groups and venting frustrations. Even if the disruptive potential of active dissent and protest movements borders on violent, the sinister nature of it brewing towards a dangerous eruption is pre-empted. Lack of channels for expression of dissent in other countries has fomented pressures, without curing any of the problems, and resulted in social dislocation and the retardation of desirable social structures.

Jihadism Usurped by Criminal Underworld: Judicium was pre-empted in its works by constitutional guarantees. The desideratum of fundamentalist elements, who continued with the pan-Islamic identity and proclivity to align themselves to the wider Islamic currents, did not find fertile ground in India. Social friction over material resources such as land, water, resource allocation and regional prejudice continue however, taking at times the communal colour. Clashes continue sporadically between Muslim and Hindu communities at the local level. This dialectic, however, is not oriented by Arabic influences. The Muslim leadership is already well entrenched in the Indian political system with privileged positions. The fallout of the Babri Mosque demolition was catastrophic and communal riots were ubiquitous. However, the drift towards the Ummah was not seen even during the height of these clashes. Frustrated elements, which saw some "ethnological defeat" in this apathy, transmuted their rage, with the help of criminals and mafia dons in Bombay, into high blown bomb blasts in 1993. This criminalistics of what could have been an ideological rallying point was taken care of by law and order agencies (e.g. Dawood Ibrahim, Chota Shaqeel, etc and were given refuge in Pakistan). Criminals-on-the-run who take up the mantle of ideological purity enshrined in the ***Ummah or*** *Jihad* made it repulsive for ordinarily religious Muslims to follow suit.

Islamist terrorist events in India, even if occurring with regularity, invariably have the footprints of external support, instigation or execution, even if there is voluble denial. It follows from the ideological basis of a low-cost, covert war to 'complete the unfinished agenda' of partition. The native Muslims find it repulsive to identify and align themselves with Pakistan and its actions. Support to Kashmiri nationalism by Pakistan is considered an excuse to divert the Jihad-turned-upon-itself after finding no outlet following the Afghan war. This insurgency suits the oligarchy in Pakistan to both vindicate its *raison deter* as well as to deflect the Jihadi energy from challenging the position and privileges of the establishment. The partition of the country is considered in India to be a manipulation of historical currents for personal ambition and a sense of failure of leadership is pervasive amidst the Muslims in India, in hindsight.

Effect of External Influences: India has been the recipient of aid for some decades but its social and economic depth, its inward-looking orientation and its emphasis on self-sufficiency has never allowed external factors to play any major, determining role. Its political process was determined by its genius and neither the dictates of cold war nor the 'clash of civilisations' had any perceptible influence. What emerged in India was a broad moral consensus within which all processes and ideas had the space to play, consolidate, and eliminate the dysfunctional. Foreign influences always remained peripheral. Jihad, which is a foreign ideology, did not strike a chord within the Muslim community. This cannot be said of other countries where aid penetrated deeper into the popular psyche – through midtarsal schools, civic projects or religious fraternities. Demoralisation by external aid-effort is less apparent in India and Muslims remained insulated from the external, fundamentalist currents.

INTERNATIONAL COOPERATION IN COUNTERING TERRORISM

Terrorism is causing tremendous strain on the developmental process in the sub-continent, and elsewhere, resulting in the curbing of freedom otherwise taken for granted. Since terrorism transcends boundaries, international cooperation is an imperative. Terrorism has to be countered simultaneously at four levels: global, regional, national, and local. In the short run, terrorism should be tackled through a convergent approach using instruments of power, diplomacy, pre-emptive intelligence and covert action to pre-empt terrorist acts. This approach, however, cannot eliminate terrorism. A terrorist cannot be defeated but only made irrelevant. A divergent, holistic approach is therefore necessary to relegate terrorism to redundancy. Intensive cooperation between India and the United States in the following ways could help in addressing this problem.

At the international level, India and US could work closely to secure final agreement on a Comprehensive Convention on International Terrorism, which endeavours to close gaps in international laws to counter terrorism. Similarly, the tightening of controls on financial operations, without dislocating legitimate financial transfers, is an imperative where functional cooperation is possible and desirable. Cooperation in controlling narcotics and arms running, which together finance much of terrorism, may be prove decisive in curbing terrorism in the short run.

At the regional level, where US and Indian interests coalesce, cooperation could be intensified (e.g. stability and development of the region). The ambivalence displayed towards Judicium earlier has paroled the region. The US can, with its influence, steer the regional dynamics away from terrorism. Ambivalence towards terrorism, in the name of 'moral support' to 'freedom fighters,' should be progressively nailed by diplomatic pressure. Military/Police cooperation could be tried to overreach the 'minimum satisfied' type of actions in Afghanistan. Similarly, the emerging fundamentalist nurseries in Bangladesh need to be eliminated through moral and diplomatic pressures and cooperative action.

The Indian State has depth to counter its national and local terrorism with both accommodation and pre-emption by political and policing means respectively. Interference by foreign powers would heighten national sensitivity. However, cooperation in capacity building like training, equipment, etc. Could be helpful.

Indo-US cooperation to combat terrorism, crime and trafficking is covered under the Indo-U.S. Joint Working Group on Terrorism, the Extradition Treaty and the Mutual Legal Assistance Treaty. The Defence Framework Agreement, *inter alia* sets out cooperation in "areas of common interest of both countries in maintaining security and stability, defeating terrorism and violent religious extremism, protecting the free flow of commerce via land, air and sea lanes and preventing the spread of weapons of mass destruction and associated materials, data and technologies." Other legal instruments to combat new challenges like proliferation of nuclear and chemical weapons, delivery vehicles to non-state actors, digital and bio-piracy, maritime piracy, cyber crime, money laundering, etc. Could be negotiated to counter emerging terrorist threats.

Functional co-operation of the intelligence agencies is an imperative. All ways should be explored to intensify cooperation and exchange in information sharing and identification of: trends in terrorism, terrorist infrastructure, cadres, nurseries, new recruits, and returnees from areas affected by insurgencies to prevent their rejoining terrorist nets. Joint development of anti- terrorist equipment such as devices for intrusion-detection, x-ray screening, alarms, non-lethal weapons, body-armour, explosive detection portals and developing software and hardware for integrating data on terrorism and forensic facilities may be some areas to focus on. Joint training on tactical combat skills for urban warfare, post-terrorist-attack disaster management, etc. Could also be fruitful areas for cooperation. US technological intelligence could be combined with Indian human intelligence for optimal results.

A divergent, all-inclusive, heuristic approach, focused on problem solving, in addition to the convergent approach of the intelligence agencies, is indispensable to eliminate this threat in the long run. As Singer says: 'some systematic research which can simultaneously think big and think small and which embraces in a rigorous synthesis both the lone individual and all of mankind,' is necessary. The problem needs to be addressed by the civil society – academics, social scientists, bureaucrats, development planners, writers, journalists, politicians and public personalities. Exchanges at various levels, both structured and unstructured, can fill the gap and should be encouraged. The disintegrating factors need to be examined with all thoroughness and dexterity available in the non-ideological, secular and intellectual universe. Extensive, inter-disciplinary work needs to be carried out for chalking out relevant strategies. It is necessary to examine socialisation, social control, and social morale and tension management subsystems in the region. Comparative analysis on the causes of democratic attenuation or expansion in countries of the same region, ambivalence of states towards religious fanaticism, and ways and means to delegitimise 'non-state actors' in popular perceptions could also be helpful. The negative rôle of media and information technology in facilitating terrorism needs extensive examination. Broadening the mechanisms for dialogue between governments, academics and think tanks should be encouraged. There is a necessity to create more social space for various tiers of society. It is not impossible to create this space with accommodations, adjustments and negotiations. At the same time, it is necessary that geographic space (state sponsors of terrorism, failing states, ungoverned areas where terrorists can train and organise) and cyber space (internet-based means for communication, planning, resource transfer and intelligence collection) available to the terrorists is constricted and eliminated.

The United States as the oldest democracy and India as the largest democracy, both with their peculiarities, can work towards creation of an irreversible broad framework of democratisation, not only as a principle but also as an expedient. The South Asian region is on the cusp and needs very mature consideration. It has to be steered towards a course that guarantees security, development and recognition of the native genius. The US could, with its unlimited power and influence in the region, adopt policy initiatives similar to the EU's policies towards Turkey. India, with its civilisations linkage, political insight and as a social-intellectual repository of the region, can be of great help in this endeavour. This coalescence of interests could be built upon.

US power in the global context and Indian power in the regional context plays on the negative psychology of peoples. They derive vicarious sense of empowerment in opposition. US and Indian soft-power, films, media spread, academic, and digital depth, could be cooperatively utilised to create reassurance for the region in an inclusive manner, working in tandem with the comfort levels acceptable to the various countries. Joint projects in some high visible areas like film and print media, with the active involvement of local genius could be tried.

Regional economic consolidation is desirable and almost imperative in co-opting the forces which give rise to terrorism. India as a regional economic engine and the US as a global engine can help steer the region to greater exchange, towards the building of linkages and the development of cooperative constituencies. India cannot afford to move ahead with weak states surrounding it, for it will cause an unavoidable demographic strain on her development. It needs to develop all of its neighbours along the way and this endeavour requires assistance. India's intellectual and political depth has generated the capability to absorb help from external sources without dentine morale. Exploitation of regional asynergy could help in the development of organic linkages within the region. The United States, as the largest market for products from the region, could assist India. Increased regional economic interaction through institutional arrangements with SAFTA could be attempted. Business constituencies, having a vested interest in stability, could reduce dislocation by engendering maximum employment opportunities.

The development of Jihadist ideologies and their accompanying movements can only be countered by coherent alternative ideologies. Unorthodox but tried ideologies in the region—Pacifist, Gandhian Non-Violence, Buddhist Tempering, etc.—though outdated could be encouraged to revive and update their relevance to present conditions. Paucity of intellectual efforts should not be allowed to give space to simplifies of reality. This will reduce the ideological space of terrorists.

Terrorism is a global problem that transcends national boundaries, but does not emerge from a social vacuum. It is influenced, encouraged, and caused by interaction between the individual, society, and the state. Social disintegration can alienate individuals and groups to such an extent that terrorism is seen as an available and expedient recourse to address their grievances. For this reason, terrorism cannot be addressed exclusively as a military or political problem, but rather must be confronted on a socialite level as well. Indian society, shaped by India's unique history and commitment to democracy, has succeeded in deterring its Muslim population from turning towards the Islamic jihadist movement, unlike many of its regional neighbours. This success, while tenuous, should be seized upon as a lesson for other states combating terrorism. India and the United States, in particular, can enhance their already blossoming relationship by capitalising on India's success and cooperating with one another to combat terrorism.

9

Sociology of Women in Local Politics

India is a federal system of government with 25 states and 7 union territories. It has a population of about 1 billion out of which 26 percent live in urban areas. The per capita GDP of India is about US$ 370. Agriculture accounts for 31.1 percent of the economy, while industry and services account for 23 percent and 45.9 percent respectively, of the economy. The sex ratio of the population is 48.1 percent and is rather skewed in favour of males. The most favourable sex ratio in the country is in the state of Kerala at 50.9 percent, while the Union Territory of Lakshadweep has the worst sex ratio at 40 percent. Life expectancy at birth for women is 58.7 years and for men it is 57.7 per cent. The overall literacy rate is 52.2 percent. Literacy among men is 64.1 percent and among women it is 39.3 percent. Women make up about 28 percent of the labour force.

The political and administrative structure of the country is largely inherited from the British. The British introduced local democracy in India by constituting municipal councils and the municipal corporations in the last quarter of the nineteenth century. They also provided a federal structure to the country with the Government of India Act, 1935.

The country today has a quasi-federal structure. Apart from the Government of India in New Delhi, there are twenty-five States with their own state governments. The

Seventh Schedule to the Constitution of India divides the subjects of State activity between the Union and state governments. The Union (Centre) as well as State governments in India both have a parliamentary form of government based on the Westminster pattern. The executive powers of the central government are vested in the Council of Ministers with the Prime Minister at its head. Similarly, the executive powers in the State governments are vested in its Council of Ministers with the Chief Minister at its head. However, following the Westminster pattern, the Head of the State is not the Prime Minister but an indirectly elected President, who broadly performs the role as the Head of State. India has a bicameral parliament, with the Lower House directly elected by the people on the lines of the House of Commons in the U.K. or the House of Representatives in the U.S.A. The Upper House is more like the U.S. Senate. It is a permanent house with one-third members retiring every two years. Like in the U.S.A. The Vice President of the country presides on the Upper House.

Although local government in India is a subject of the State governments, the seventy-third and the seventy-fourth amendments to the Constitution of India now make it obligatory for the State governments to organise local bodies, to hold regular elections to them and to give them appropriate finances.

The urban local bodies are of three grades; municipal corporations for cities with a population of more than (0.3 million), municipal councils for towns smaller than this population limit and nagar panchayats for villages in transition to becoming towns. These bodies are elected on a universal suffrage basis, with all citizens above the age of eighteen years of age having a right to vote.

The rural local bodies are organised in three tiers, the village panchayat at the village level, the block panchayat samiti for about 100 villages and a district council for a district comprising about 1000 villages. The rural local bodies do not have many resources of their own. They actually spend the state government funds as implementing agencies.

The civil service in India is a closed system, with a very limited scope for lateral entry at senior level. Most permanent officials join the service as a lifetime career through an entrance examination/ interview conducted by the Public Service Commission. The age of entry is usually 21 to 30 years and the age of retirement either 58 or 60 years of age.

The subject matter of the Government of India is divided between the Union Government and the State Governments. The respective governments recruit most of their employees independently. However, a unique feature of the Indian system is the existence of three All India Services, the Indian Administrative Service, the Indian Police Service and the Indian Forest Service. The Government of India recruits the members of these services although they work with the States where they are allotted (their cadres) for most of their career. However, the Government of India obtains the services of these officers at higher and middle management levels through deputation for a period of about five years. This enables a regular exchange of officers between the field and the central levels. Senior Indian Administrative Service Officers who have had their initial grounding in different States of India thus man the top secretariat posts in most ministries of the Government of India.

India is a democratic republic and full freedom of speech and religion is allowed to all its citizens. The Constitution of India guarantees the following Fundamental Rights to the citizens of India.

Right to Equality: This includes equality before law (Article 14), prohibition of discrimination on grounds of religion, race, caste, sex or place of birth (Article 15) and equality of opportunity in matters of employment (Article 16).

Right to Freedom: This includes protection of certain rights regarding freedom of speech etc. (Article 19), protection of life and personal liberty (Article 21) and protection against arrest and detention in certain cases (Article 22).

Right against Exploitation: This includes prohibition of traffic in human beings and forced labour (Article 23) and prohibition of employment of children in factories etc.

Right to Freedom of Religion: This includes freedom of conscience and free profession, practice and propagation of religion (Article 25), freedom to manage religious affairs (Article 26), freedom as to payment of taxes for promotion of any particular religion (Article 27) and freedom as to attendance at religious instruction or religious worship in certain educational institutions (Article 28).

Cultural and Educational Rights: These include protection of interests of minorities (Article 29) and the right of minorities to establish and administer educational institutions (Article 30).

The Constitution of India further guarantees the right to move to the Supreme Court for enforcement of the above rights.

India has a multitude of political parties; some organised on economic ideology, some on religious ideology while some on local and linguistic aspirations. However, only three or four parties really have a presence at the National level; the Congress Party that was the ruling party for more than forty years, the Bharatiya Janata Party (the present ruling party with its allies), the Janata Dal and the Communists. There are many religion-based parties like the Akali Dal (Sikhs in Punjab), the Muslim League etc. The regional parties like the DMK and AIADMK (Tamil Nadu), Shiv Sena (Maharashtra), Telugu Desam (Andhra Pradesh) and some parties in the smaller North-Eastern States have been contenders of powers in the State governments of their respective states. However, at the National level, only three parties have been able to provide the Prime Minister i.e. the Congress, the BJP and the Janata Party/Janata Dal i n alliance with smaller parties.

An independent body called the Election Commission of India conducts elections to the parliament and the state legislatures in India. The elections are based on a universal adult suffrage with voting rights to all citizens above eighteen years of age. The lower houses of the national and the state legislatures have a five-year term although elections are regularly held before this term expires.

The elections to the local bodies have been brought under the purview of a similarly constituted body called the State Election Commission. These bodies also usually have a five-year term. It is statutory not possible to supersede the local bodies for long periods or to keep them under Government-appointed Administrators.

An age of more than twenty-one years is usually an eligibility condition for getting elected to an elective post in a local body. The eligibility for being a member of the Lower House of the National or state legislatures similarly prescribes the minimum age of twenty-five years. A minimum age-limit of thirty years is similarly a qualification for membership of the Upper Houses of the National and State legislatures. A minimum age-limit of thirty-five years is prescribed as a qualification for holding the post of the President or Vice-President of the Indian Republic.

The elections to both the urban and rural local bodies in India are ward based. The local area is divided into wards of more or less equal population. Each ward sends one representative to the concerned local body. After the

Seventy-third and Seventy-fourth Amendments to the Constitution of India, one-third of the wards are reserved for women candidates and only women candidates can contest elections from these wards. Apart from the reservation for women candidates, some other wards are reserved for candidates from socially underprivileged sections.

Political parties are allowed to take part in elections to all local bodies except the village panchayats in India. It is, however, not uncommon for locally influential politicians to form local fronts to contest and win elections to municipal councils and the smaller municipal corporations in the country.

India became independent in the year 1947. In all the elections held since independence, women had the voting rights. The pattern of participation by women in the national elections.

The percentage of seats won against the seats contested is showing a declining trend only because the number of women contesting elections has increased sharply. However, it may be seen that voting for women in all tiers of Government has always been a feature of the Indian polity since 1947.

Representation of Women in Politics

Women play a dual role in politics—as voters and political representatives. On the voting front, though adult franchise was granted in 1937, it was the progressive spirit that pervaded the making of the constitution that made it a reality. The Constitution of India guarantees equal rights to men and women as voters and citizens. Generally, in India, registration and participation of women as contestants is less than that of men. In recent past, records show that there has been an increase in the percentage of women who vote. Such participation is also contingent on the mobilisation efforts made by political parties, NGOs, Action Groups and the general awareness among the community of the importance of women exercising their franchise. Again, a note of caution is required, lest it be assumed that political participation always indicates political awareness on the part of the woman voter. Usually, however, countries that do hold regular elections show an improved recognition of women as a political constituency and parties and candidates tend to adopt pro-women stances and appeal specifically to women's votes, especially at the time of elections.

Since Independence, due to exercise of their franchise, Indian women have been exposed to the political processes and are showing increasing awareness about not only lack of rights but also their utility. A majority of illiterate rural women are also politically sensitive and aware of the various issues confronting them. Women get easily mobilised in the political processes by the political parties who approach women very often for party issues and for short-term goals by winning elections, but not for long-term goals of bringing about social changes and gender equality in political power-sharing.

In all the elections held since independence, women had the voting rights. The percentage of seats won against the seats contested is showing a declining trend only because the number of women contesting elections has increased sharply. However, it may be seen that voting by women in all tiers of Government has always been a feature of the Indian Polity since 1947. Due to the parternalistic family and male dominated political structures which do not provide space for women in decision-making bodies, women constituted 3.1% of the total contestants in 1996 election and did not occupy more than 6.10% of the total seats in the state legislative assemblies and Parliament.

The number of women contestants in Parliamentary elections has not increased significantly over the years.

Political parties are still reluctant to field women candidates at national level.

In the early days of the Indian republic, the number of women representatives was a mere 22, which was a lowly 4.4% of the total seats in the Lok Sabha. The sixth Loksabha in the year 1977 saw an all time low of just 19 woman representatives. The twelfth Lok Sabha had 44 women i.e. 8.8% of the total.

Even as early as the 19th century Indian women had begun to appear on the national scene in public and political activity. Women were not only being accepted in public activity but were organising themselves to fight for their rights in different walks of life.

Though women constitute nearly half of the population of the country, it was only after Independence that efforts were made to promote women's participation in public life. Though the Constitution of India provides for the Government to make special provisions to safeguard the interests of women as detailed in Article 15 (3) and Article 39, it has not made any provision for reservation for women in respect of jobs and political offices. However the 73rd and 74th Constitional Amendment Act mandated reservation of one-third seats in the village, block, districts, municipal elected bodies in India. As a consequence, women had not advanced much politically and economically. From the records available of the past 50 years, since the independence, it is seen that the strength of women in the political field as reflected in State legislatures remained at an average of 3 % to 5% of those elected. At the level of Parlaiment, the position of women members has varied between 5 to 7%.

It is seen that women in large numbers have come out against atrocities on women, in defence of their traditional control over crucial resources, water, forests, and land, mass literacy drives and other issues. They are also coming out in large numbers over ecological degradation, price rise or protests against police repression, etc. While there is the increased participation in grass root political movements, it is not getting translated into a growing share of women in the formal political structure of the country.

Amongst the several reasons for such a situation is the growing money power and muscle power required to contest even the smallest of elections in India, the intimidation, violence and slander that a woman candidate has to face combined with the traditional male domination that seeks to keep her indoors. Narrow electoral arthmetic and the necessity of fielding a winning candidate makes most political parties shy away from fielding more than a token number of women candidates. And if they are fielded at all, kinship and affinity factors play a major role. It is very common to observe that the relatives of politicians are promoted and supported to emerge as politicians.

Increasingly, women have stood for elections and got elected as members of State Legislative Assemblies and the Parliament. However, at the national level there is only one woman Cabinet Minister and 8 Ministers of State in a Cabinet of 70. There is only one woman Governor and one woman Chief Minister.

Some studies of Parliamentary participation indicate that women members participate more actively in 'women's issues' – health, welfare, atrocities against women, crimes like dowry and violations of human rights. This participation is confined to the more articulate women. In issues such as defence, finance, politics, etc. Their participation is relatively limited. Analysis of trends of women' participation to contest elections to the State Legislatures indicate that there is a gender discrimination which is responsible for poor representation of women in India.

Women's role in decision making is one of the most important questions for consideration in the movement for their empowerment. The 73rd and 74th Amendments(1992) to the Indian Constitution have served as a major break through towards ensuring women's equal access and increased participation in political power structures. This Amendment provided for reservation of one third of seats for women at level of local governance in urban areas. There is also a one-third reservation for women for posts of chairpersons of these local bodies. This amendment has initiated a powerful strategy of affirmative action for providing the structural framework for women's participation in political decision-making and provided an opportunity to bring women to be forefront and centre of city development and develop new grass-root level leadership. There are about 1 million elected women representatives in Panchayats and Municipal Bodies in India.

After 1993, women's participation in local governments increased quite radically, with the enactment of the legislation providing 33 percent reservation of seats for women in local bodies. The legislation and its implementation has added another level in political participation. The previous table indicates the total number of urban local bodies as well as elected representatives in India.

In Governments too, there has been limited representatives of women. A few eminent women have no doubt, occupied important administrative positions, such as Secretaries of Departments in the National Government as well as in State Governments. It is only 5.71% of the total number of persons in administrative services are women. It is noteworthy that within the premier civil services of India, the representation of women is not that encouraging.

Since relatively few women enter the civil services, several efforts have been made to improve the situation. The

Department of Personnel and Administrative Reforms of the Government of India has also provided, wherever possible, women officers on the selection boards for posts and services.

WOMEN'S PARTICIPATION IN LOCAL GOVERNANCE

The 74th Amendment to the Indian Constitution, 1992 has served as a major breakthrough towards ensuring women's equal access and increased participation in local government. The Constitution (74th Amendment) Act, 1992 aims at Constitutional guarantees to safeguard the interests of urban local self government to enable them to function as effective democratic and self governing institutions at the grass root level. This Amendment provides for reservation of 33 1/3 percent of elected seats for women at local government level in urban and rural areas. There is also a one-third reservation for women of posts of chairpersons of these local bodies. A very active role for women in local governance is envisaged as compared to governance at the state and national levels in India. These provisions have provided great opportunities and challenges to women in India, particularly in the local government field. This is of great significance, since this grass-root level participation has considerably broadened the base of women's participation in politics at city level.

Limits and Constraints

Involvement of women in the political arena and in decision-making roles is an important tool for empowerment as well as monitoring standards of political performance at local level. However, in the present political process of entry into decision making political institutions, there is growing influence of money and muscle power, backroom dealings, communalisation and criminalisation. In many respects women and men elected representatives face similar problems on election to office. Above all there is a need to understand just how to be a good local politician. The role of political representatives at local level is demanding and all new 'recruits' need time to gain experience and to understand the rules, regulations and procedures governing the administrative bureaucracy with which they now have to work – often quite closely in the urban service delivery system.

Some of the major constraints that prevent women from effective participation at local level are as follows:

1. Lack of orientation / training in urban development issues and municipal administration.
2. No proper knowledge / orientation about municipal acts and rules and regulations.
3. No prior experience about dealing with multidimensional urban development issues / civic issues and its complexities.
4. Lack of knowledge about technical inputs related to urban service delivery system.
5. Lack of support from senior male / female colleagues in the party / municipal body.
6. Less co-operation from municipal officials understanding about various facets of the budget, such as allocation of budget at ward level (at central / ward level).
7. Lack of party support and poor organisational structure.
8. Lack of money and resources to sustain the electoral campaigns (inspite of code of conduct by election commission).
9. Discrimination in decision making at party level.
10. Specific notions towards politics and political atmosphere.

11. Fear and insecurity.
12. Lack of confidence in public speaking.
13. Criminalisation of politics and use of money power.
14. Family responsibilities.

Civil Society Initiatives

Political system in India works through political parties who contend for power by invoking popular support. Therefore it is necessary that if women want to share power they have to make a place for themselves within the political parties through which the Indian democratic system operates. The experience of the last 52 years show an inability to create 'this space' and recent studies show that there has been no significant change in either the nature of women's functioning or in the political parties' approach to women and women's issues. If we examine women's participation (prior to 1993) it is seen that the political parties have given less importance to women's issues in terms of ideology, either in priority in their party manifesto or in terms of the number and importance of the position that women occupied in individual political parties. Women are not seen as a vote bank to be approached, and once the men are mobilised, women will merely endorse their choice of party and candidate. Male candidates rarely have access to the female electorate and there are not enough women involved in political campaigns to be able to reach out to a large section of women even in big cities. As a result, the exposure of women to political debates and issues has always remained indirect. According to women from all parties the political environment was not conducive to women's participation in politics. The analysis made by Kumari and Kidwai stated that political parties have dominated the conservative 'cultural' perspective and no conscious attempt has been made to increase active participation of women.

Women in India today are agitating at the doors of Parliament, demanding reservation for 33 per cent of the seats. The issue at stake here is more complex than it may seem. It is not only a question of a few more or a few less women in the corridors of Parliament and legislatures but also a response to the fact that a large section of society has historically been denied its legitimate share in the exercise of political power, that ultimately determines its destiny. In this demand for reservation, women are also raising their voice against a system, which has consistently denied them space by harnessing the forces of tradition in order to marginalise and travails their role. Reservation of seats for women in Panchayats/Municipal bodies have shown that it has tremendous implications, not merely in terms of the number of women entering the public arena and holding public office, but also in terms of the social, economic and political impact that these reservations have had for the total system.

It is for these reasons that women are increasingly demanding political roles for themselves. They recognise that constitutional guarantees do not ensure effective participation and that these cannot ensure political equality. Hence the need to gain entry into political institutions and in the functioning of the state, and to share control over the power the state exercises. This alone would lead to a situation where women are able to reverse the existing situation, which has consistently been against their interests, and bring about the necessary changes in policy and the social structure so as to ensure a more equitable and humane order.

The role of women's participation in elected bodies should not be undervalued. Elections are after all a forum for self government and democracy, they are significant in drawing the attention of the nation to the problems and needs of disadvantaged sections; the manifestos, campaigns, promises made by individual candidates, track record and future course of action of political parties are indicative of national concerns as well as mandates for action. Proper selection of candidates in an election is vital if this representative democracy is to function in the interests of a majority of the population that is depressed and disadvantaged. Hence, opportunities for participation at this level are significant for the adoption of politics and measures for women's development.

Strong and dynamic women who would not dream of appropriating privilege are today talking of reservation because they have come to recognise that they will not give "easy entry" in the corridors of power without reservation. This hierarchy is so rigid that the natural processes of democracy and constitutional guarantees have not been able to make a dent in these fortresses of power. The demand for reservation should not therefore be seen as either a gift or a privilege that women are seeking. For most women it is the last straw and a desperate measure to ensure their coming into the political mainstream. Their participation becomes vital in the context of the adoption of development strategies that are negative and harmful to women. Today most of the political parties in India have initiated some initiatives to activate political participation of women and develop their capacities. However, most of the political parties have not yet developed any special programmes to meet the special requirements of women in urban or rural areas, despite the fact that most of the women activists felt that if planned efforts were made, they could be easily mobilised. Different debates concerning struggles of women as well as various actions by women's groups and NGOs on local as well as national problems have forced the mainstream political parties to accept women's concerns in their political programmes. The political parties started changing their attitude towards women which is reflected in their election manifestos, their attitudes towards women candidates, speeches and slogans.

Statistics on women's participation in the electoral process are not very encouraging. It is important not only to pressurise the political parties but also to make the leaders understand the significance of organising systematic training of women's possessing leadership qualities, of carefully selecting women candidates and ensuring financial, technical and human resources for affirmative action.

The need to strengthen womens's participation and leadership is constantly emphasised by various institutions viz, All India Institute of Local Self Government, NIUA, HSMI, Rambhau Mhalaji Prabhodini, etc and several NGOs and Women's groups like SEWA, Working Women' Forum, YUVA, Disha, Prayas, Astha, Winavani, SNDT University, Aalochana, Agni, FASDSP (Forum Against Sex-determination and Sex Preselection), Stree Mukti Sanghathana, etc.

Many NGOs / CBOs, Women' groups have provided some training, however systematic training of women possessing leadership qualities is not enough and more concentrated efforts are required to facilitate the process of women's ascent to key positions in political field. It is essential that the women's groups and movement recognise the importance of women as a constitutency and ensure their participation and representation in policy formulation. The movement must provide a support system for women who enter political processes to win elections. As stated by Nath Kamale 'The women's movement has been a powerful agent of empowerment and has provided an alternative perspective for fundamental structural changes. The movement has created organisational strength of women, has focussed on women's issues and mobilised them around these issues. The women in the movement, however, have shied away from active participation in politics.

The women's groups and women activists thus aim to bring about a change in the women's perceptions, but not necessarily in the structures which subordinate women. If we want to bring about change in the lives of women and transform mainstream politics, there is no other way than to get involved in politics and transform it.

The women's movement and groups have to recognise the importance of women as a constituency and ensure their participation and representation in policy formulation. This can be achieved through reorienting existing structures for entry into decision-making including the political party system and introduce quotas or reservation as a temporary means of women's representation. The movement should also provide a support system (women's groups) for women who enter political processes to win elections.

The women's groups working at the grassroots level are small and scattered and have diverse ways of empowering women. There are no infrastructure facilities of networking available that could bring them together and strengthen them while allowing autonomy in their functioning. It is important to create unity in diversity between women's groups, organisations and individuals involved with women's empowerment. They need to adopt a common strategy, informed by a common vision, to be able to bring about changes in the policies and structures that perpetuate their subordinate status.

Encouraging Women to Participate in Local Governance

Reservation for women in local government is not just a question of getting a certain number 'in'; it also develops their capacities to play their rightful roles in the development process and makes an important difference as the local governments deals mostly with the quality of life for citizens. Municipal responsibilities relate both to women's practical needs and their strategic needs. The better we meet women's strategic needs, the better they are able to contribute to good city governance. Good Local Governance, in turn, enables a better response to women's practical needs.

Most local governments have initiated orientation / training programmes to encourage women to participate in local governance by organising city-specific induction or theme-based training programmes, wherein intensive training is given in various subject areas, such as, municipal acts and its implementation, laws of meetings, municipal budgeting, budgeting at ward level, municipal taxation, mobilisation of resources, urban service delivery systems (solid waste management, water supply, sewerage, health care services, traffic and transportation), poverty alleviation schemes, community management, environment management, shelter programmes, new reforms in municipal administration, functioning of ward committees, motivation techniques, communication skills, women and development, handling the media etc.

The Ministry of Urban Development, Government of India and Urban Development Department of State Governments organise a number of training programmes, workshops, seminars for women elected representatives at local level through various training institutions. Many municipal bodies have initiated a series of in-house training in m unicipal administration and urban development, in collaboration with premier training institutions in India. State governments through their State Training Centres organise capacity building programmes for women elected members from municipal bodies in their States. Special training / orientation programmes are organised by Ministry of Urban Development and Poverty Alleviation, Government of India under the UNICEF assistance and government's funds in the area of poverty alleviation schemes and its implementation in urban areas (e.g. SJSRY, NSDP, etc.)

Gender Sensitising of Local Government

Local governments are using sex-desegregated data for policy and programme formulation. It is an obligatory duty of municipal governments in India to collect, compile and maintain vital statistics in their city limits. Sex-disaggregated data is in use in many cities of the States in India for policy programme formulation and implementation of some special programmes and projects at local city level.

The Government of India regularly collects, analyses and disseminates quantitative and qualitative data on the number of women and men employed at various levels in government on an annual basis and many mechanisms have been set up within governmental structures for monitoring progress in this field.

The Department of Women and Child Development, Government of India is collecting and using gender-disaggregated data to evaluate development from a gender perspective. The Department is also developing a Gender Development Index (GDI) for the construction of EDI and Gender Empowerment Measure (GEM).

Bringing women to positions of political power in local government is just the first step in social transformation. Gender sensitisation of those in power, be they men or women, is of critical importance. Influencing the choices of those at decision – making levels and bringing gender issues to the political agenda are important factors. Over the years, this perspective has gained acceptance within organisations, action groups and political parties.

Government departments, other institutions, non-governmental organisations, and women's organisations have undertaken several programmes to sensitise local governments about the issues and needs of women in their cities.

It is recognised that law enforcement is a critical factor for bringing about enduring changes in gender perceptions. Several initiatives have been taken by the Government of India and the voluntary sector to sensitise law enforcement personnel and policy makers. Gender sensitisation of police personnel and urban administrators in the National and State level training centres is now a regular programme. A National Centre for Gender Training and Research has set up in the National Academy of Administration in Mussourie with the objective of sensitising young administrators and policy makers on gender issues.

The Election Commission of India maintains updated information on women representatives in each Parliament, including categorised information on the number of scheduled castes women representatives. With the recent revolution in information technology, the entire information is available not only in print but also on the Internet in the Parliament and Election Commission websites. This increases out-reach and access of this information to the general public.

The Ministry of Rural Development, Government of India maintains updated information on the representation of women in local self-government or Panchayati Raj. The Department of Women and Child Development, Government of India also has come out with publications like 'Women in India – A Statistical Profile' in 1997, which compiled information on all aspects related to women in India. The Planning Commission, which is mooting the process of collection of gender desegregated data by all concerned departments in various Ministers, has included information on women's representation in power and decision-making in its Ninth Five Year Plan Document.

Besides these, several independent organisations are carrying out their own research and surveys that provide updated information on the same. These are also widely used and are quoted in different public documents. Sensitising the leadership of people's movements in the country to gender issues need to be prioritised.

WOMEN'S REPRESENTATION IN LOCAL GOVERNMENT

Legal and Political Initiatives

The number of women in politics at the local level had been very small, and their influence negligible. As stated by Kumari and Kidwai, "Prior to 1990, the women in local politics were generally either politicians who had lost membership of higher institutions, and those who were given such an opportunity to serve the purpose of publicity. In many cases, the motive was partially also to satisfy the aspirations of these few women, since they could be kept under virtual control and denied higher aspirations. The insignificant presence of women at these levels was an important indicator of two basic facts: one that women who are planted at the top often lacked the kind of training required for effective participation, secondly, the society was unable to accept women in politics, particularly at the grass-root level.

If we examine the reasons for low participation, as stated by Nath, Kamle 'down the ages women have always been treated as subordinate to men in every aspect of life. Their place of work was confined to the domain of the household with household chores and rearing of children. Her identity was attached to that of her father, husband or son, i.e. she was given a status in accordance with that of her male partner. It is not that women in the past have not contributed substantially in politics, but because of their secondary status and low esteem, most of them were denied entry in political decision-making.

The 74th Amendment of the Indian Constitution in 1992 ushered in a new era in the democratic process of the country as it not only provided constitutional status to the municipal bodies but also provided an enabling environment for women to a direct part in the local self government and brought women to the forefront and centre of local development. Sharing power and responsibilities with immense control over resources for development and social change will be an empowering instrument for women.

Article 243 T (I) of Constitution Amendment (1992) states as follows: "Reservation of Seats:

1. Seats shall be reserved for the Scheduled Castes and the Scheduled Tribes in every Municipality and the number of seats so reserved shall bear, as nearly as may be, the same proportion to the total number of seats to be filled by direct election in that Municipality as the population of the Scheduled Castes in the Municipal area or of the Scheduled Tribes in the Municipal area bears to the total population of that area and such seats may be allotted by rotation to different constitutions in a Municipality.
2. Not less than one-third of the total number of seats reserved under clause (1) shall be reserved for women belonging to the Scheduled Castes or, as the case may be, the Scheduled Tribes.
3. Not less than one-third (including the number of seats reserved for women belonging to the Scheduled Castes and the Scheduled Tribes) of the total number of seats to be filled by direct election in every Municipality shall be reserved for women and such seats may be allotted by rotation to different constituencies in a Municipality.
4. The office of Chairpersons in the Municipalities shall be reserved for the Scheduled Castes, the Scheduled Tribes and common in such manner as the Legislature of a State may by law, provide.

5. The reservation of seats under clauses (1) and (2) and the reservation of office of Chairpersons (other than the reservation for women) under clause (4) shall cease to have effect on the expiration of the period specified in article 334.
6. Nothing in this Part shall prevent the Legislature of a State from making any provision for reservation of seats in any Municipality or office of Chairpersons in the Municipalities in favour of backward class of citizens."

Different political parties in India have shown great reluctance to field women candidates. Reservation of seats at Municipal level has put pressure on political parties to identify and field more women candidates.

Training and Support Mechanisms

Attention is being given to the training and capacity developing skills and capacities of all elected representatives in local government, including women. They are trained to acquire skills, knowledge and orientation needed to carry out the onerous responsibilities given to them. A time bound, systematic and comprehensive training programme has been drawn up which will be funded by the Central Government. The Indira Gandhi National Open University has been associated with the preparation of a syllabus on women and development. The Government of India is also committed to capacity building efforts by organising and funding training programmes for women elected to municipal bodies in India. A large number of such kind of training programmes for elected members are handled by All India Institute of Local Self Government which is a premier training institution in local government field in India. Ministry of Urban Development (MUD) supports several such kind of training programmes through Regional Centre for Urban and Environmental Studies (RCUES) which are functioning in all the regions of India. Apart from this, some of the theme-based training programmes are organised by State Training Institutions in several States for women elected members in municipal bodies.

Support Groups and Forums

Women elected to local governments have not formed any formal associations, groups and forums. However, all women mayors meet during meetings organised by All India Council of Mayors (AICM), which is an association of mayors representing all cities in India. These meetings give women mayors an opportunity to interact with each other and with other male Mayors and exchange ideas, information about effective urban service delivery, good governance and also provide issue based support. Similarly, various seminars, workshops, training programmes organised by Government of India, State Governments and National and Regional institutions provide wide opportunities for women elected members to meet and interact with elected women members from different municipal bodies in India. Similarly, events organised by political parties, women's groups, non-governmental organisations also provide an opportunity for women elected members for experience sharing, networking and sometimes lobbying for some specific purpose in urban development and good governance.It is also observed that in many cities women elected members have close links with local NGOs, CBOs or Residents' Associations or action groups and through such networking women members support each other and initiate networking among themselves about governance at local level or any issues related to women and development.

Training of Women in Local Government and Civil Service

The following institutions undertake training of appointed officials:

1. Urban Development Department, Government of India and Urban Development Departments of various State Governments in India have initiated several capacity building or training initiatives to train women working at various levels of municipal administration.
2. National Academy of Administration in Missouri is actively involved in training senior government officers from Indian Administrative Services in India. The Academy has set up a National Centre for Gender Training and Research to further issues related to women and development. Apart from this, several State Training Centres in various states organise training-cum -orientation and workshops for women appointed in local government.

It is observed that women officers from the Indian Administrative Service (IAS), Police (IPS), and Foreign Services (IFS) have their associations in all the States of India. These associations organise periodic meetings and 'get together' which provide an opportunity for the women officials to interact with each other. The City Managers' Association of Gujarat State also provides opportunities for women officials in local government in Gujarat State. 'Metro Forum' an association of Municipal Commissioners of Metro Cities will also provide an opportunity for women municipal commissioners to meet and interact on issues related to civic governance and any other issues related to women and development. Similar efforts are underway to establish an association of women officials in all municipal bodies in India.

All India Institute of Local Self Government, through its various Centres in India imparts training in the field of municipal administration. Besides short-term specialised programmes, it also organises full time diploma courses on various aspects of municipal administration for junior and middle level municipal personnel. These courses are attended by large number of women employed at junior and middle and senior levels in municipal bodies in India. The following main institutions also offer several need-based or tailor-made specialised programmes for women working at different levels of municipal administration in India.

The main purpose of urban management training is to develop capacities of officials to deal with the complex urban problems in a holistic manner to achieve efficiently the aim of municipal bodies and of the urban sector as a whole. These institutions cover the main areas for orientation / training or capacity building in urban development and municipal administration field.

Special Measures to Recruit Women in the Civil Service

One of the variables that go into the Gender Empowerment Measure, as depicted in the Human Development Report, is the proportion of men and women at senior levels of government. In this context the study initiated in 1996 by the Department of Personnel and Training (DoPT), as part of a project 'Capacity Building for Civil Services', was a significant step. In order to crystallise the problems faced by women in Civil Services as well as to isolate areas which needed to be addressed through policy guidelines, a survey was carried out across a cross section of the services, among men and women officers, to ascertain the issues on which guidelines would have to focus. The survey questionnarie was formulated keeping in mind different areas of concern for women officers like Gender Image in workplace and in the family to stress factors.

Various government studies have been undertaken in the past on problems and issues related to the various individual services that constitute the Indian Administration. But this survey broke new ground in terms of coverage of services and levels of both women and men, as well as the range of related issues. Many issues, such as stress and motivation and sexual harassment, that persist across the services were touched upon for the first time. A national level Project Steering Committee was set up for carrying out the Capacity Building project, and a Focal Point was identified in the DoPT for examining the sphere of "Women's Issues in the Civil Service".

The Lal Bahadur Shastri National Academy of Administration (LBSNAA) was appointed as consultant for developing a curriculum for Gender Sensitisation Programmes and ten Regional Seminars were conducted at nine State Administrative Training Institutes.

The Focal Point identified in the DoPT will begin work towards framing guidelines on women's issues by reviewing existing rules / regulations of various services. The task that has emerged for the Focal Point is as follows :

> Review of existing rules and regulations for possible gender bias and discrimination against women and suggest corrective action.

Co-ordinate output flowing from various activities of the project related to the issues requiring policy formulation.

In the Civil Services, the overall percentage of women in 1997 was 7.5%, the highest being 12.3% in the Indian Foreign Service. Women are increasing their presence in other sectors such as the Revenue Services, the Railway Management Cadres, Telecommunication etc. On the whole, women in 1997 represented 13.8% of the employee strength in the public sector, as against only 8.6% in 1971.

Women's Organisation or other civil society organisation have taken some initiatives in some states of India to encourage women to stand in local government elections, however, these groups or organisations are small and scattered and have diverse ways of empowering women. There are no infrastructure facilities of networking that could bring them together and strengthen them while allowing autonomy in their functioning. It is important to create unity in diversity between women's groups and civil society organisations involved with women's empowerment.

Political participation would make a significant different if it came from those who are at the helm of affairs of political parties, and if women are there wielding power, the situation can improve to a great extent and political participation would give every woman a sense of dignity as a individual.

The women's movement and groups have to recognise the importance of women as a constituency and ensure their participation and representation in policy formulation. This can be achieved through reorienting existing structures for entry into decision-making including the political party system and introduce quotas or reservation as a temporary means of women's representation. The movement should also provide a support system (women's groups) for women who enter political processes to win elections.

The women's groups working at the grassroots level are small and scattered and have diverse ways of empowering women. There are no infrastructure facilities of networking available that could bring them together and strengthen them while allowing autonomy in their functioning. It is important to create unity in diversity between women's groups, organisations and individuals involved with women's empowerment. They need to adopt a common strategy, informed by a common vision, to be able to bring about changes in the policies and structures that perpetuate their subordinate status.

Non-partisan women's groups should provide necessary moral and advisory support to women candidates to increase their chances of being elected to political offices. They should work towards enhancing the capacity of women candidates to win the elections by providing them with a forum whereby they could exchange ideas and experiences and learn from experts on electoral laws and politics and evolve issues and strategies to win elections.

Special Civil Society Initiatives

The 33 per cent for women in municipal bodies has brought into focus the fact that there is a need to bring more and more women into the party. But the problem is that many women are often not equipped to become members of the political parties, as the party expects a certain level of consciousness for membership – not everybody can become a member. Also, women have difficulty in attending party meetings, study circles or demonstrations because of their timings and the pressure of housework. Most of the parties have not yet developed any special tailor – made programme to meet the special requirements of women in urban areas, despite the fact that most women activists felt that if such an effort was made, they could easily be mobilised.

The party's ideology itself may be discriminatory, on the other hand its ambiguity in a traditional society may leave adequate space for discrimination. Party workers at times exhibit a sense of lack of gender equality because they carry with them their traditional value systems which are often feudal and patriarchal, into the party. Much of the discrimination against women in the party is because of the attitudes of these individuals. But at the same time women assert that the party does not try to change the attitude of both men and women who come to the party or make them more gender sensitive.

The nature of electoral politics in India also marginalises women and women's issues from the political agenda. Many women feel that electoral politics, at times limits the kind of support women politicians would like to extend to members of their own sex, since they realise that they cannot win elections on women's issues alone. Most of them are still assistant to identify themselves with women's issues, claiming that women form only one section of their constituency and till recently not the determining section. Also, elections are largely conducted by men and with men's support. Electoral expediency requires women participants to compromise to survive in the man's world of politics. All parties recognise the need to win women's votes, but often seem unsure of the best way to gain support among women.

The type of leadership required is of transformational type. Women's entry into processes of governance should create change in the very institutions of governance. In order to effect such change, leaders have to emerge which can occur only through participatory processes. The participation allows empowerment, which then generates leadership. It is only through their leadership, and their implied changes in the hierarchy of party and power that they may provide that they can justifiably participate in governance as representing something 'different'. This leadership can emerge only through active participation. Therein lies the role of the political parties in creating an enabling environment for active leadership generating participation. Prior to 1992, political parties have not been initiating any special initiatives or programmes to encourage women to stand in local government elections. The number of women in politics at the local level has been very small, and their influence negligible. After 1993, women's participation in local governments increased quite radically with the enactment of the legislation providing one-third reservation of seats for women in local bodies. The effective implementation of this legislation has added another level in political participation. According to women from all parties the one third reservation for women in local governments has brought into focus the fact that there is a need to bring more and more women into the local government field and develop their capacities.

This particular 74th Amendment of the Indian Constitution ushered in a new era in the democratic process in India as it not only provided constitutional status to the municipal bodies but also provided an enabling environment for women to take direct part in the process of local self government and brought women to the forefront of city development.

The 74th Amendment mandated reservation of one – third seats in municipal bodies for women. There is also one third reservations for women in position of chairpersons of these local bodies in India.

A very active role for women in local governance is envisaged as compared to governance at the state and national levels in India. These provisions have provided great opportunities and challenges to women in India.

The challenge now is to transfer this large presence of women at local government level supported by the real delegation of power and responsibilities.

Women's role in decision making is one of the most important questions for consideration in the movement for their empowerment. Reservation of seats for women in local bodies has shown that it has tremendous implications, not merely in terms of the number of women entering the public arena and holding public office, but also in terms of the social, economic and political impact that these reservations have had for the total system.

Recognising various constraints such as present day politics, elements of criminalistics, corruption, muscle power, violence, lack of awareness of political participation, preparation to fulfil the role and responsibilities as elected representative, etc, the Government, NGOs, Women Groups and activist's have been actively involved in providing necessary inputs to women. Women have been mobilised to participate in elections as candidates and voters, and to be vigilant citizens where elections are held. Communities have received gender sensitisation to facilitate acceptance of the new roles assigned to women. Leadership and organisational training of women has been conducted to enable them to be dynamic change agents. Networks have been interacting, to influence mass based political structures to prove more space to women.

Bibliography

Alford, Robert and Roger Friedland. 1985. *Powers of Theory: Capitalism, the State, and Democracy*. Cambridge: Cambridge University Press.

Block, Fred L. 1977. "The Ruling Class Does Not Rule: Notes on the Marxist Theory of the State" in *Socialist Review* 33:6-27.

Bourdieu, Pierre. 1984a. *Distinction: a Social Critique of the Judgement of Taste*. Cambridge, MA: Harvard University Press.

Burton, M., & Higley, J. 1998. "Political Crises and Elite Settlements." In M. Dogan & J. Higley (Eds.), *Elites, crises, and the origins of regimes* (pp. 47-70). Lanham MD: Rowman & Littlefield.

Chadha, G.K. and Sharma, Alakh (eds.) 1997. *Growth, Employment and Poverty: Change and Continuity in Rural India*. Delhi: Vikas Publishing House.

Cox, Robert. 1987. *Production, Power, and World Order: Social Forces in the Making of History*. New York: Columbia University Press.

Dahl, Robert. 1961. *Who Governs? Democracy and Power in an American City*. New Haven: Yale University Press.

De Tocqueville, Alexis. *Democracy in America*. Anchor Books edition, 1969.

Domhoff, William G. 1998. *Who Rules America? Power and Politics in the Year 2000, Third Edition*. Mountain View: Mayfield Publishing Company.

Fukuyama, Francis. 1989. "The End of History?" in *The National Interest* (Summer): 3-18. Gramsci, Antonio 1971. *Selections From the Prison Notebooks*. London: New Left Books.

Hegel, Georg Wilhelm Friedrich. 1830/1956. *The Philosophy of History*. New York: Dover Publications.

Held, D., A. McGrew, D. Goldblatt, and J. Perraton. (1999). *Global Transformations: Politics, Economics and Culture*. Polity and Stanford University Press.

Higley, J., & Burton, M. 2006. *Elite foundations of liberal democracy*. Lanham MD: Rowman & Littlefield.

Hirst, P and G. Thompson, 1996, "Globalization: A Necessary Myth?" in Hirst and Thompson, *Globalization in Question*, Cambridge: Polity Press, 1-17.

Huntington, Samuel. 1993. *The Third Wave: Democratization in the Later Twentieth Century*. Oklahoma: University of Oklahoma Press.

Inglehart, Ronald. 1977. *The Silent Revolution: Changing Values and Political Styles Among Western Publics*. Princeton: Princeton University Press

Jessop, Bob. 1990. *State Theory: Putting the Capitalist State in Its Place*, Cambridge: Polity Press.

Jessop, Bob. 2002. Globalization and the National State, in S. Aaronwitz and P. Bratsis, ed., *Rethinking the State: Miliband, Poulantzas and State Theory*, Minneapolis: *Alternatives: Turkish Journal of International Relations, Vol. 5, No.1&2, Spring & Summer 2006* 19 University of Minnesota Press, pp. 185-220.

Lenin, Vladimir. 1932. *State and Revolution*. New York: International Publishers

Lukes, Steven. 1974. *Power: A Radical View*. London: Macmillan.

Marx, Karl. 1848. "The Communist Manifesto" in *Karl Marx: Selected Writings* (ed.) David McLellan (1977). New York: Oxford University Press.

Michels, Robert. 1915. *Political Parties: A Sociological Study of the Oligarchical Tendencies of Modern Democracy*. New York: Hearst's International Library.

Mills, C. Wright. 1956. *The Power Elite*. New York: Oxford University Press.

Mosca, Gaetano. 1896/1939. *The Ruling Class*. New York: McGraw-Hill.

Pareto, Vilfredo. 1901/1968. *The Rise and Fall of Elites*. New Jersey: Bedminister Press.

Polanyi, Karl. 1944. *The Great Transformation*. Boston: Beacon Press.

Poulantzas, Nicos. 1969. "The Problem of the Capitalist State." New Left Review 58: 67-78.

Reich, Robert. 1991. *The Work of Nations: Preparing Ourselves for 21st Century Capitalism*. New York: Alfred A. Knopf.

Robinson, William I. 1996. *Promoting Polyarchy: Globalization, US Intervention, and Hegemony*. Cambridge: Cambridge University Press.

Robinson, William I. 2004. *A Theory of Global Capitalism: Production, Class and State in a Transnational World*. Baltimore: Johns Hopkins University Press.

Smith, J, Chatfied, C, and Pagnucco, R. 1997. *Transnational Social Movements and Politics and World Politics: Solidarity Beyond State*. Syracuse: Syracuse University Press.

Index